Vascular Surgery

Vascular Surgery

SIXTH EDITION

Robert B. Rutherford, MD, FACS, FRCS (Glasg.)

Emeritus Professor of Surgery
University of Colorado School of Medicine
Denver, Colorado

ELSEVIER
SAUNDERS

ELSEVIER
SAUNDERS

1600 John F. Kennedy Blvd., Ste 1800
Philadelphia, Pennsylvania 19103

VASCULAR SURGERY   ISBN 0-7216-0299-1
Copyright 2005, 2000, 1995, 1989, 1976 by Elsevier, Inc.

Notice

Knowledge and best practice in this field are constantly changing. As new research and experience broaden our knowledge, changes in practice, treatment and drug therapy may become necessary or appropriate. Readers are advised to check the most current information provided (i) on procedures featured or (ii) by the manufacturer of each product to be administered, to verify the recommended dose or formula, the method and duration of administration, and contraindications. It is the responsibility of the practitioner, relying on their own experience and knowledge of the patient, to make diagnoses, to determine dosages and the best treatment for each individual patient, and to take all appropriate safety precautions. To the fullest extent of the law, neither the Publisher nor the Editors assume any liability for any injury and/or damage to persons or property arising out of or related to any use of the material contained in this book.

Library of Congress Cataloging-in-Publication Data

Vascular surgery / [edited by] Robert B. Rutherford.— 6th ed.
    p. ; cm.
  Includes bibliographical references and index.
  ISBN 0-7216-0299-1 (set)
   1. Blood-vessels—Surgery.   I. Rutherford, Robert B.
  [DNLM: 1. Vascular Surgical Procedures. WG 170 V3311 2005]
  RD598.5.V37 2005
  616.4'13—dc22   2004056630

Publishing Director: Anne Lenehan
Publisher: Natasha Andjelkovic
Developmental Editor: Donna Morrissey
Senior Project Manager: Linda Lewis Grigg
Design Director: Ellen Zanolle
Senior Marketing Manager: Ethel Cathers
Updates Manager: Bob Browne

Printed in the United States of America.

Last digit is the print number: 9 8 7 6 5 4 3 2 1

To vascular surgeons everywhere

who strive for excellence in patient care.

Editors

Associate Editors

JACK L. CRONENWETT, MD
Professor of Surgery, Dartmouth Medical School, Hanover.
Chief, Section of Vascular Surgery, Dartmouth-Hitchcock
Medical Center, Lebanon, New Hampshire.

PETER GLOVICZKI, MD
Professor of Surgery, Mayo Clinic College of Medicine.
Chair, Division of Vascular Surgery and Director, Gonda
Vascular Center, Mayo Clinic, Rochester, Minnesota.

K. WAYNE JOHNSTON, MD, FRCSC
Professor and R. Fraser Elliott Chair in Vascular Surgery,
Department of Surgery, University of Toronto, Faculty of
Medicine.
Vascular Surgeon, Toronto General Hospital, Toronto,
Ontario, Canada.

WILLIAM C. KRUPSKI, MD*
Formerly Clinical Professor of Surgery, University of
California, San Francisco School of Medicine.
Attending Vascular Surgeon, The Kaiser Permanente Medical
Group, San Francisco, California.

KENNETH OURIEL, MD, FACS, FACC
Professor of Surgery, Cleveland Clinic Lerner College of
Medicine of Case Western Reserve University.
Chairman, Division of Surgery, Cleveland Clinic Foundation,
Cleveland, Ohio.

ANTON N. SIDAWY, MD, MPH
Professor of Surgery, George Washington University School
of Medicine.
Chief of Surgery, VA Medical Center, Washington, D.C.

*Deceased.

Assistant Editors

HUGH G. BEEBE, MD
Director Emeritus, Jobst Vascular Center, The Toledo Hospital,
Toledo, Ohio.

KIMBERLEY J. HANSEN, MD, FACS
Professor of Surgery and Head, Section on Vascular Surgery,
Division of Surgical Sciences, Wake Forest University School
of Medicine, Winston-Salem, North Carolina.

GREGORY L. MONETA, MD
Professor of Surgery, Oregon Health and Sciences University
School of Medicine.
Chief, Division of Vascular Surgery, Portland, Oregon.

MARK R. NEHLER, MD
Associate Professor of Surgery, University of Colorado Health
Sciences Center School of Medicine.
Program Director, Surgical Residency Program, University
of Colorado Health Sciences Center, Denver, Colorado.

WILLIAM H. PEARCE, MD
Violet R. and Charles A. Baldwin Professor of Vascular Surgery,
Northwestern University Feinberg School of Medicine.
Chief, Vascular Surgery Division, Northwestern Memorial
Hospital, Chicago, Illinois.

BRUCE A. PERLER, MD, MBA
Julius H. Jacobson II Professor of Surgery, Johns Hopkins
University School of Medicine.
Chief, Division of Vascular Surgery, Johns Hopkins Hospital,
Baltimore, Maryland.

JOHN J. RICOTTA, MD, FACS
Professor and Chair, Department of Surgery, State University
of New York at Stony Brook School of Medicine.
Surgeon in Chief, University Hospital at Stony Brook,
Stony Brook, New York.

RUSSELL H. SAMSON, MD, FACS, RVT
Former Associate Professor of Surgery, Albert Einstein
College of Medicine of Yeshiva University, New York,
New York.
Staff, Sarasota Memorial Hospital.
President, Mote Vascular Foundation, Inc., Sarasota, Florida.

JAMES M. SEEGER, MD
Professor of Surgery, University of Florida College of Medicine.
Chief, Division of Vascular Surgery and Endoscopic Therapy,
Shands at University of Florida, Gainesville, Florida.

R. James Valentine, MD
Frank H. Kidd Jr. Distinguished Professor and Vice-Chairman, Department of Surgery, University of Texas Southwestern Medical Center, Dallas, Texas.

Thomas William Wakefield, MD
S. Martin Lindenauer Collegiate Professor of Surgery, University of Michigan Medical School.
Staff Surgeon, Section of Vascular Surgery, Department of Surgery, University of Michigan Hospital and Ann Arbor Veterans Administration Medical Center, Ann Arbor, Michigan.

Fred A. Weaver, MD
Professor of Surgery, University of Southern California Keck School of Medicine.
Chief of Vascular Surgery, University of Southern California Hospital.
Attending Surgeon, Vascular Surgery, Los Angeles County–University of Southern California Medical Center, Los Angeles, California.

Contributors

AHMED M. ABOU-ZAMZAM, JR., MD
Associate Professor, Division of Vascular Surgery, Loma Linda University School of Medicine, Loma Linda, California.
Lower Extremity Amputation: Indications, Patient Evaluation, and Level Determination

ALI F. ABURAHMA, MD
Professor, Department of Surgery, West Virginia University School of Medicine; Chief, Vascular Section, Robert C. Byrd Health Sciences Center; Co-Director, Vascular Center of Excellence, Charleston Area Medical Center, Charleston, West Virginia.
Causalgia and Post-traumatic Pain Syndromes; Lumbar Sympathectomy: Indications and Technique

ERIC D. ADAMS, MD
Adjunct Assistant Professor of Surgery, Uniformed Services University of the Health Sciences, Bethesda, Maryland; Fellow, Vascular Surgery, Washington Hospital Center and Georgetown University, Washington, D.C.
Nonthrombotic Complications of Arteriovenous Access for Hemodialysis

SAMUEL S. AHN, MD
Professor of Surgery, David Geffen School of Medicine at UCLA; Attending Surgeon, UCLA Center for the Health Sciences, Los Angeles, California.
Upper Extremity Sympathectomy

JAMES C. ANDREWS, MD
Gonda Vascular Center, Mayo Clinic, Rochester, Minnesota.
Surgical Treatment of Superior Vena Cava Syndrome

ENRICO ASCHER, MD
Professor of Surgery, Division of Vascular Surgery, Maimonides Medical Center, Brooklyn, New York.
Secondary Arterial Reconstructions in the Lower Extremity

ZAKARIA I. ASSI, MD
Diagnostic Radiologist, Department of Interventional Radiology, The Toledo Hospital; Director, Interventional Radiology, Flower Hospital, Toledo, Ohio.
Catheter-Based Interventions for Acute Deep Venous Thrombosis

JUAN AYERDI, MD
Assistant Professor of Surgery, Department of General Surgery, Division of Surgical Sciences, Wake Forest University School of Medicine, Winston-Salem, North Carolina.
Principles of Arteriography; Fundamental Techniques in Endovascular Surgery; Open Surgical Repair of Renovascular Disease

MARTIN R. BACK, MD, FACS
Associate Professor of Surgery, University of South Florida College of Medicine, Tampa, Florida.
Infection in Prosthetic Vascular Grafts

J. DENNIS BAKER, MD
Professor of Surgery, David Geffen School of Medicine at UCLA; Chief, Vascular Surgery Section, West Los Angeles VA Medical Center, Los Angeles, California.
The Vascular Laboratory

WILLIAM H. BAKER, MD, FACS
Emeritus Professor of Surgery, Loyola University–Chicago Stritch School of Medicine, Maywood, Illinois.
Arteriovenous Fistulae of the Aorta and Its Major Branches

JEFFREY L. BALLARD, MD
Clinical Professor of Surgery, University of California, Irvine, School of Medicine; Staff Vascular Surgeon, St. Joseph Hospital of Orange, Orange, California.
Carotid and Vertebral Artery Injuries

DENNIS F. BANDYK, MD, FACS
Professor of Surgery, University of South Florida College of Medicine, Tampa, Florida.
Infection in Prosthetic Vascular Grafts

JOHN BARTHOLOMEW, MD
Head, Section of Vascular Medicine, Department of Cardiovascular Medicine, Cleveland Clinic, Cleveland, Ohio.
Atheromatous Embolization

MICHEL A. BARTOLI, MD
Fellow, Department of Vascular Surgery, Hospital La Timone, Marseille, France.
Neurogenic Thoracic Outlet Syndrome

HISHAM S. BASSIOUNY, MD
Professor of Surgery, The University of Chicago Pritzker School of Medicine; Attending Surgeon, The University of Chicago Hospitals and Clinics and Louis A. Weiss Memorial Hospital, Chicago, Illinois.
Diagnosis and Treatment of Nonocclusive Mesenteric Ischemia

B. TIMOTHY BAXTER, MD
Professor of Surgery, Cell Biology, and Anatomy, University of Nebraska College of Medicine, Omaha, Nebraska.
Arterial Aneurysms: Etiologic Considerations

HUGH G. BEEBE, MD
Director Emeritus, Jobst Vascular Center, The Toledo Hospital, Toledo, Ohio.
3D Image Processing

MARSHALL E. BENJAMIN, MD
Medical Director, Vascular Laboratory, Maryland Vascular Center, University of Maryland Medical Center, Baltimore, Maryland.
Endovascular Treatment of Renovascular Disease

JOHN J. BERGAN, MD, FACS, FRCS Hon. (Eng.)
Professor of Surgery, UCSD School of Medicine, San Diego; Attending Surgeon, Scripps Memorial Hospital, La Jolla, California.
Varicose Veins: Treatment by Intervention Including Sclerotherapy

RAMON BERGUER, MD, PHD
Frankel Professor of Vascular Surgery and Professor of Engineering, School of Medicine and Cullen College of Engineering, University of Michigan, Ann Arbor, Michigan; Vascular Surgeon, University of Michigan Health System.
Brachiocephalic Vessel Reconstruction; Vertebrobasilar Ischemia: Indications, Techniques, and Results of Surgical Repair

JOSHUA W. BERNHEIM, MD
Vascular Surgery Fellow, New York Presbyterian Hospital, New York.
Renal Artery Imaging and Physiologic Testing

KERSTIN BETTERMANN, MD, PHD
Assistant Professor, Department of Neurology, Wake Forest University School of Medicine; Neurologist, North Carolina Baptist Hospital of Wake Forest University, Winston-Salem, North Carolina.
Diagnostic Evaluation and Medical Management of Patients with Ischemic Cerebrovascular Disease

RODGER L. BICK, MD, PHD, FACP
Clinical Professor of Pathology, University of Texas Southwestern Medical Center; Director, Dallas Thrombosis Hemostasis and Difficult Hematology Clinical Center, Dallas, Texas.
Normal and Abnormal Coagulation

JAMES H. BLACK III, MD
Assistant Professor of Surgery, Johns Hopkins University School of Medicine; Vascular Surgeon, Division of Vascular and Endovascular Surgery, Johns Hopkins Hospital, Baltimore, Maryland.
Aortic Dissection: Perspectives for the Vascular/Endovascular Surgeon

W. TODD BOHANNON, MD
Assistant Professor of Surgery, Texas A & M University Health Science Center; Scott & White Memorial Hospital and Clinic, Temple, Texas.
Venous Transpositions in the Creation of Arteriovenous Access

THOMAS C. BOWER, MD
Professor of Surgery, Mayo Clinic College of Medicine; Consultant, Division of Vascular Surgery, Mayo Clinic, Rochester, Minnesota.
Evaluation and Management of Malignant Tumors of the Inferior Vena Cava

JOHN G. BRAWLEY, MD
Fellow, Vascular Surgery, University of Texas Southwestern Medical Center, Dallas, Texas.
Traumatic Arteriovenous Fistulae

DAVID C. BREWSTER, MD
Clinical Professor of Surgery, Harvard Medical School; Vascular Surgeon, Division of Vascular Surgery, Massachusetts General Hospital, Boston, Massachusetts.
Direct Reconstruction for Aortoiliac Occlusive Disease

PATRICIA E. BURROWS, MD
Professor of Radiology, Harvard Medical School; Staff Radiologist, Children's Hospital, Boston, Massachusetts.
Endovascular Treatment of Vascular Anomalies

RUTH L. BUSH, MD
Assistant Professor, Division of Vascular Surgery and Endovascular Therapy, Michael E. DeBakey Department of Surgery, Baylor College of Medicine, Houston, Texas.
Complications of Endovascular Procedures; Management of Thrombosed Dialysis Access

JACOB BUTH, MD, PHD
Consultant Vascular Surgeon, Department of Surgery, Catharina Hospital, Eindhoven, The Netherlands.
Endovascular Treatment of Aortic Aneurysms

KEITH D. CALLIGARO, MD
Chief, Section of Vascular Surgery, Department of Surgery, Pennsylvania Hospital, Philadelphia, Pennsylvania.
Renal Artery Aneurysms and Arteriovenous Fistulae

RICHARD P. CAMBRIA, MD
Professor of Surgery, Harvard Medical School; Chief, Division of Vascular and Endovascular Surgery, and Co-Director, Thoracic Aortic Center, Massachusetts General Hospital, Boston, Massachusetts.
Aortic Dissection: Perspectives for the Vascular/Endovascular Surgeon

TERESA L. CARMAN, MD
Attending, Vascular Medicine, Jobst Vascular Center, The Toledo Hospital, Toledo, Ohio.
Thrombolytic Agents and Their Actions

JEFFREY P. CARPENTER, MD
Professor, Department of Surgery; Director, Vascular Laboratory, Hospital of the University of Pennsylvania, Philadelphia, Pennsylvania.
Magnetic Resonance Imaging and Angiography

PATRICK J. CASEY, MD
Vascular Surgery Fellow, Division of Vascular and Endovascular Surgery, Massachusetts General Hospital, Boston, Massachusetts.
Anastomotic Aneurysms

JOAQUIN J. CERVEIRA, MD
Assistant Professor of Surgery and Chief, Endovascular Surgery, Kaiser Permanente Medical Center, Panorama City, California.
The Pathophysiology of Chronic Venous Disorders

JAE-SUNG CHO, MD
Assistant Professor, Department of Surgery, University of Pittsburgh Medical Center, Pittsburgh, Pennsylvania.
Surgical Treatment of Chronic Occlusions of the Iliac Veins and the Inferior Vena Cava

G. PATRICK CLAGETT, MD
Professor, Division of Vascular Surgery, University of Texas Southwestern Medical Center, Dallas, Texas.
Upper Extremity Aneurysms

HARRY CLOFT, MD, PHD
Associate Professor, Radiology, Mayo Medical School; Senior Associate Consultant, Department of Radiology, Mayo Clinic, Rochester, Minnesota.
Carotid Angioplasty and Stenting

RAUL COIMBRA, MD, PHD
Associate Professor, Department of Surgery, Division of Trauma Medicine, University of California, San Diego, School of Medicine; Associate Director of Trauma, Department of Surgery, Division of Trauma, UCSD Medical Center, San Diego, California.
Epidemiology and Natural History of Vascular Trauma

ANTHONY J. COMEROTA, MD, FACS
Clinical Professor of Surgery, University of Michigan Medical School; Director, Jobst Vascular Center, The Toledo Hospital, Toledo, Ohio.
Thrombolytic Agents and Their Actions; Intra-arterial Catheter–Directed Thrombolysis; Catheter-Based Interventions for Acute Deep Venous Thrombosis

JOHN P. CONNORS III, MD
Resident, Department of Plastic and Reconstructive Surgery, Brigham and Women's Hospital, Boston, Massachusetts.
Vascular Tumors and Malformations in Childhood

MICHAEL S. CONTE, MD
Associate Professor of Surgery, Harvard Medical School; Associate Surgeon (Vascular), Brigham and Women's Hospital, Boston, Massachusetts.
Molecular Biology and Gene Therapy in Vascular Disease

JUDITH W. COOK, MD
Fellow, Division of Vascular Surgery, Department of Surgery, University of Washington School of Medicine, Seattle, Washington.
Clinical and Diagnostic Evaluation of the Patient with Deep Venous Thrombosis

MICHAEL J. COSTANZA, MD
Clinical Associate Professor, Division of Vascular Surgery, Department of Surgery, SUNY Upstate Medical Center, Syracuse, New York.
Endovascular Treatment of Renovascular Disease

JACK L. CRONENWETT, MD
Professor of Surgery, Dartmouth Medical School, Hanover; Chief, Section of Vascular Surgery, Dartmouth-Hitchcock Medical Center, Lebanon, New Hampshire.
Overview [Arterial Aneurysms]; Abdominal Aortic and Iliac Aneurysms

JOHN A. CURCI, MD
Assistant Professor of Surgery, Washington University School of Medicine, St. Louis, Missouri.
Arterial Aneurysms: Etiologic Considerations

JACOB CYNAMON, MD
Professor of Clinical Radiology, Albert Einstein College of Medicine of Yeshiva University; Director, Vascular and Interventional Radiology, Montefiore Medical Center, Bronx, New York.
Techniques for Thromboembolectomy of Native Arteries and Bypass Grafts

MICHAEL D. DAKE, MD
Professor of Radiology, Medicine, and Surgery, University of Virginia; Professor and Chairman, Department of Radiology, University of Virginia Health System, Charlottesville, Virginia.
Endovascular Treatment of Vena Caval Occlusions

MICHAEL DALSING, MD
Professor of Surgery, Indiana University School of Medicine; Director of Vascular Surgery, Clarian Health, Indianapolis, Indiana.
The Surgical Treatment of Deep Venous Valvular Incompetence

R. CLEMENT DARLING III, MD
Professor of Surgery, Albany Medical College; Chief, Division of Vascular Surgery, Albany Medical Center Hospital, Albany, New York.
Arterial Thromboembolism

MARK G. DAVIES, MD, PHD
Associate Professor, Department of Vascular and Endovascular Surgery, University of Rochester School of Medicine and Dentistry; Medical Director, Vascular Diagnostic Laboratory, Vascular Biology and Therapeutics Program and Endovascular Therapy Program; Division of Vascular Surgery, Strong Heart and Vascular Center; Attending Physician, Strong Memorial Hospital, Rochester, New York.
Intimal Hyperplasia: Basic Response to Arterial and Vein Graft Injury and Reconstruction

RAJEEV DAYAL, MD
Clinical Instructor in Surgery, Weill Medical College of Cornell University; Fellow, Vascular Surgery, New York–Presbyterian Hospital, New York, New York.
Standardized Reporting Practices

RICHARD H. DEAN, MD
Professor of Surgery, Wake Forest University School of
Medicine; President and CEO, Wake Forest University Health
Sciences, Winston-Salem, North Carolina.
*Atherosclerotic Renovascular Disease and Ischemic
Nephropathy*

DEMETRIOS DEMETRIADES, MD, PhD, FACS
Professor of Surgery, University of Southern California
School of Medicine; Director, Division of Trauma and
SICU, Los Angeles County–University of Southern California
Medical Center, Los Angeles, California.
Abdominal Vascular Injuries

RALPH G. DE PALMA, MD, FACS
National Director of Surgery, Department of Veterans Affairs,
Medical-Surgical Group; Professor of Surgery, Uniformed
Services University of the Health Sciences F. Edward Hébert
School of Medicine; Staff Surgeon, Veterans Affairs Medical
Center, Washington, D.C.
*Atherosclerosis: Plaque Characteristics and Concepts of
Evolution; Postoperative Sexual Dysfunction after Aortoiliac
Interventions; Vasculogenic Erectile Dysfunction; Superficial
Thrombophlebitis: Diagnosis and Management*

TINA R. DESAI, MD
Assistant Professor of Surgery, The University of Chicago
Pritzker School of Medicine; Attending Surgeon, The Univer-
sity of Chicago Hospitals and Clinics, Chicago, Illinois.
*Diagnosis and Treatment of Nonocclusive Mesenteric
Ischemia; Acute Renovascular Occlusive Events*

**LARRY-STUART DEUTSCH, MD, CM,
FRCPC, FACR**
Chief-of-Service, Vascular and Interventional Radiology
Section, Good Samaritan Regional Medical Center and
St. Joseph's Hospital and Medical Center, and Chair, Depart-
ment of Medical Imaging, Clinical Diagnostic Radiology
Inc., Phoenix, Arizona.
*Anatomy and Angiographic Diagnosis of Extracranial and
Intracranial Vascular Disease*

MATTHEW J. DOUGHERTY, MD
Attending Surgeon, Department of Surgery, Pennsylvania
Hospital, Philadelphia, Pennsylvania.
Renal Artery Aneurysms and Arteriovenous Fistulae

WALTER N. DURAN, PhD
Professor of Physiology and Surgery, UMDNJ–New Jersey
Medical School, Newark, New Jersey.
The Pathophysiology of Chronic Venous Disorders

MATTHEW J. EAGLETON, MD
Assistant Professor of Surgery, Section of Vascular Sur-
gery, University of Michigan Medical School, Ann Arbor,
Michigan.
Perioperative Considerations: Coagulopathy and Hemorrhage

JAMES M. EDWARDS, MD
Associate Professor, Division of Vascular Surgery, Depart-
ment of Surgery, Oregon Health and Science University
School of Medicine; Chief of Surgery, Portland Veterans
Affairs Medical Center, Portland, Oregon.
Upper Extremity Revascularization

MATTHEW S. EDWARDS, MD
Assistant Professor of Surgery, Section on Vascular Surgery,
Wake Forest University School of Medicine, Winston-Salem,
North Carolina.
*Endovascular Treatment of Renovascular Disease; Open
Surgical Repair of Renovascular Disease*

BO EKLOF, MD, PhD
Emeritus Professor of Surgery, University of Hawaii John A.
Burns School of Medicine, Honolulu, Hawaii.
Surgical Thrombectomy for Acute Deep Venous Thrombosis

ERIC D. ENDEAN, MD, FACS
Gordon L. Hyde Professor of Surgery, Department of Surgery,
University of Kentucky College of Medicine; Chief, Division
of General and Vascular Surgery, University of Kentucky
Chandler Medical Center; Attending Surgeon, Lexington
Veterans Affairs Medical Center, Lexington, Kentucky.
*Treatment of Acute Intestinal Ischemia Caused by Arterial
Occlusions*

MARK S. ESKANDARI, MD
Assistant Professor of Surgery, Division of Vascular Sur-
gery, Northwestern University Feinberg School of Medicine;
Attending Surgeon, Division of Vascular Surgery, North-
western Memorial Hospital, Chicago, Illinois.
Occupational Vascular Problems

ANTHONY L. ESTRERA, MD
Assistant Professor, Department of Cardiothoracic and
Vascular Surgery, University of Texas at Houston Medical
School; Attending, Hermann Memorial City Hospital,
Houston, Texas.
Thoracoabdominal Aortic Aneurysms

JAWED FAREED, PhD
Professor, Department of Pathology and Pharmacology;
Director, Special Coagulation Laboratory and the Hemostasis
and Thrombosis Research Program, Loyola University
Medical Center, Maywood, Illinois.
Normal and Abnormal Coagulation

SCOTT R. FECTEAU, MD
Fellow in Training (Vascular Surgery), Albany Medical
Center Hospital, Albany, New York.
Arterial Thromboembolism

MARK F. FILLINGER, MD
Associate Professor of Surgery, Dartmouth Medical School,
Hanover; Faculty (Section of Vascular Surgery), Dartmouth-
Hitchcock Medical Center, Lebanon, New Hampshire.
*Computed Tomography, CT Angiography, and 3D Reconstruc-
tion for the Evaluation of Vascular Disease*

MICHELLE FLORIAN-KUJAWSKI, BS
Department of Pharmacology, Loyola University Medical Center, Maywood, Illinois.
Normal and Abnormal Coagulation

VIVIAN GAHTAN, MD
Chief, Section of Vascular Surgery, Department of Surgery, SUNY Upstate Medical University College of Medicine; Vascular Surgeon, Surgery Service, Syracuse Veterans Affairs Medical Center, Syracuse, New York.
Molecular Biology and Gene Therapy in Vascular Disease

GAIL L. GAMBLE, MD
Assistant Professor of Physical Medicine and Rehabilitation, Mayo Clinic College of Medicine, Rochester, Minnesota.
Nonoperative Management of Chronic Lymphedema

NICHOLAS J. GARGIULO, MD
Assistant Professor of Surgery, Albert Einstein College of Medicine of Yeshiva University; Attending Surgeon, Weiler Hospital, Bronx, New York.
Techniques for Thromboembolectomy of Native Arteries and Bypass Grafts; Secondary Arterial Reconstructions in the Lower Extremity

BRUCE L. GEWERTZ, MD, FACS
Dallas B. Phemister Professor and Chairman, Department of Surgery, The University of Chicago Pritzker School of Medicine; Attending Surgeon, The University of Chicago Hospitals and Clinics, Chicago, Illinois.
Acute Renovascular Occlusive Events

JOSEPH GIORDANO, MD
Professor and Chairman, Department of Surgery, George Washington University School of Medicine; Chief of Surgery, George Washington University Hospital, Washington, D.C.
Embryology of the Vascular System

MARY E. GISWOLD, MD
Resident, Department of Surgery, Oregon Health and Sciences University School of Medicine, Portland, Oregon.
Nonoperative Treatment of Chronic Venous Insufficiency

SEYMOUR GLAGOV, MD
Professor Emeritus, Department of Pathology, The University of Chicago Pritzker School of Medicine; Pathologist, University of Chicago Hospitals and Clinics, Chicago, Illinois.
Artery Wall Pathology in Atherosclerosis

PETER GLOVICZKI, MD
Professor of Surgery, Mayo Clinic College of Medicine; Chair, Division of Vascular Surgery and Director, Gonda Vascular Center, Mayo Clinic, Rochester, Minnesota.
Principles of Venography; Lymphatic Complications of Vascular Surgery; Introduction and General Considerations [The Management of Venous Disorders]; Management of Perforator Vein Incompetence; Surgical Treatment of Chronic Occlusions of the Iliac Veins and the Inferior Vena Cava; Surgical Treatment of Superior Vena Cava Syndrome; Lymphedema: An Overview; Clinical Diagnosis and Evaluation of Lymphedema; Nonoperative Management of Chronic Lymphedema; Surgical Treatment of Chronic Lymphedema and Primary Chylous Disorders

JERRY GOLDSTONE, MD, FACS, FRCS
Professor of Surgery, Case School of Medicine, Case Western Reserve University; Chief, Division of Vascular Surgery, University Hospitals of Cleveland, Cleveland, Ohio.
Aneurysms of the Extracranial Carotid Artery

MICHAEL J. V. GORDON, MD
Director, The Hand Center, Division of Plastic Surgery; Assistant Professor, Department of Surgery, University of Colorado Health Sciences Center, Denver, Colorado.
Upper Extremity Amputation

RICHARD M. GREEN, MD
Chairman, Department of Surgery, Lenox Hill Hospital, New York, New York.
Training in Endovascular Surgery; Subclavian-Axillary Vein Thrombosis

LAZAR J. GREENFIELD, MD
Professor of Surgery and Chair Emeritus, Department of Surgery, University of Michigan, Ann Arbor, Michigan.
Vena Caval Interruption Procedures

HOWARD P. GREISLER, MD
Professor of Surgery and Professor of Cell Biology, Neurobiology, and Anatomy, Loyola University Chicago Stritch School of Medicine, Maywood; Attending Surgeon, Loyola University Medical Center, Maywood; Staff Surgeon, Edward Hines Jr. VA Hospital, Hines, Illinois.
Prosthetic Grafts

NAVYASH GUPTA, MD, FACS
Assistant Professor, Department of Surgery, University of Pittsburgh School of Medicine; Attending Surgeon, University of Pittsburgh Hospitals and Clinics, Pittsburgh, Pennsylvania.
Acute Renovascular Occlusive Events

ALLEN D. HAMDAN, MD
Assistant Professor of Surgery, Harvard Medical School; Attending Vascular Surgeon and Director of Clinical Research, Department of Vascular Surgery, Beth Israel Deaconess Medical Center, Boston, Massachusetts.
Management of Foot Ulcers in Diabetes Mellitus

JAAP F. HAMMING, MD, PhD
Department of Surgery, Leiden University Medical Center, Leiden, The Netherlands.
Lower Extremity Aneurysms

KIMBERLEY J. HANSEN, MD, FACS
Professor of Surgery and Head, Section on Vascular Surgery, Division of Surgical Sciences, Wake Forest University School of Medicine, Winston-Salem, North Carolina.
Renal Complications; Renovascular Disease: An Overview; Atherosclerotic Renovascular Disease and Ischemic Nephropathy; Open Surgical Repair of Renovascular Disease

LINDA M. HARRIS, MD
Assistant Professor of Surgery, University of Buffalo School of Medicine and Biomedical Sciences; Program Director, Vascular Surgery Residency, and Interim Division Chief, Vascular Surgery, Millard Fillmore Hospital, Buffalo, New York.
The Modified Biograft; Endovascular Treatment of Aortic Aneurysms

PETER L. HARRIS, MD, FRCS
Director, Vascular and Transplant Services, Regional Vascular Unit, Royal Liverpool University Hospital, England, United Kingdom.
Endovascular Treatment of Aortic Aneurysms

PETER K. HENKE, MD
Assistant Professor, Section of Vascular Surgery, Department of Surgery, University of Michigan Medical School; Chief, Vascular Surgery, Ann Arbor Veterans Affairs Hospital, Ann Arbor, Michigan.
Vascular Thrombosis Due to Hypercoagulable States; Vena Caval Interruption Procedures

WILLIAM R. HIATT, MD
Professor of Medicine, Division of Vascular Medicine, University of Colorado Health Sciences Center School of Medicine, Denver, Colorado.
Atherogenesis and the Medical Management of Atherosclerosis

KIM J. HODGSON, MD
Professor and Chairman, Division of Vascular Surgery, Department of Surgery, Southern Illinois University School of Medicine, Springfield, Illinois.
Principles of Arteriography; Fundamental Techniques in Endovascular Surgery

DEBRA A. HOPPENSTEADT, PhD
Assistant Professor, Department of Pathology; Technical Director, Hemostasis and Thrombosis Research Program, Loyola University Medical Center, Maywood, Illinois.
Normal and Abnormal Coagulation

DAVID B. HOYT, MD, FACS
Professor, Department of Surgery, Division of Trauma, Burns, and Critical Care, University of California, San Diego, School of Medicine; Attending Surgeon, Trauma Center, UCSD Medical Center–Hillcrest, San Diego, California.
Epidemiology and Natural History of Vascular Trauma

THOMAS S. HUBER, MD, PhD
Associate Professor of Surgery, University of Florida College of Medicine, Gainesville, Florida.
Chronic Mesenteric Ischemia

JOSEPH HUH, MD
Assistant Professor, Department of Cardiothoracic Surgery, Baylor College of Medicine; Attending Surgeon, Veterans Affairs Medical Center Houston, Houston, Texas.
Thoracic Vascular Trauma

RUSSELL D. HULL, MBBS, MSc
Professor of Medicine, University of Calgary Faculty of Medicine; Director, Thrombosis Research Unit, Foothills Hospital, Calgary, Alberta, Canada.
Prevention and Medical Treatment of Acute Deep Venous Thrombosis

TAM T. HUYNH, MD
Assistant Professor, Department of Cardiothoracic and Vascular Surgery, University of Texas at Houston Medical School; Attending, Hermann Memorial City Hospital, Houston, Texas.
Thoracoabdominal Aortic Aneurysms

ERIK K. INSKO, MD, PhD
Adjunct Assistant Professor of Radiology, University of Pennsylvania School of Medicine; Attending, Hospital of the University of Pennsylvania, Philadelphia, Pennsylvania; Director of Cardiovascular Imaging, Mecklenburg Radiology Associates, Presbyterian Hospital, Charlotte, North Carolina.
Magnetic Resonance Imaging and Angiography

OMER IQBAL, MD
Assistant Professor, Department of Pathology, Hemostasis and Thrombosis Research Program, Loyola University Medical Center, Maywood, Illinois.
Normal and Abnormal Coagulation

GLENN R. JACOBOWITZ, MD
Associate Professor of Surgery, New York University School of Medicine; Attending Physician, New York University Medical Center, Bellevue Hospital, and New York Harbor VA Medical Center, New York, New York.
Surgical Management of Congenital Vascular Malformations

WALTER P. JESKE, PhD
Associate Professor, Departments of Pathology and Thoracic and Cardiovascular Surgery, Hemostasis and Thrombosis Research Laboratories, Loyola University Medical Center, Maywood, Illinois.
Normal and Abnormal Coagulation

KAJ JOHANSEN, MD, PhD
Clinical Professor of Surgery, University of Washington School of Medicine; Director of Surgical Education, Swedish Medical Center, Providence Campus, Seattle, Washington.
Vascular Pain; Compartment Syndrome: Pathophysiology, Recognition, and Management; Portal Hypertension: Surgical Management of Its Complications

K. WAYNE JOHNSTON, MD, FRCSC
Professor and R. Fraser Elliott Chair in Vascular Surgery, Department of Surgery, University of Toronto Faculty of Medicine; Vascular Surgeon, Toronto General Hospital, Toronto, Ontario, Canada.
Ischemic Neuropathy; The Chronically Ischemic Leg: An Overview

PETER G. KALMAN, MD, FRCSC, FACS
Professor, Departments of Surgery and Radiology, Loyola University Chicago Stritch School of Medicine; Chief, Division of Vascular Surgery, Loyola University Medical Center, Maywood, Illinois.
Profundaplasty: Isolated and Adjunctive Applications

MANJU KALRA, MBBS
Assistant Professor of Surgery, Mayo Clinic College of Medicine; Consultant, Division of Vascular Surgery, Mayo Clinic, Rochester, Minnesota.
Management of Perforator Vein Incompetence; Surgical Treatment of Superior Vena Cava Syndrome

VIKRAM S. KASHYAP, MD
Associate Professor of Surgery, Cleveland Clinic Lerner College of Medicine of Case Western Reserve University; Staff, Department of Vascular Surgery, Cleveland Clinic Foundation, Cleveland, Ohio.
Aortoenteric Fistulae

KARTHIKESHWAR KASIRAJAN, MD, FACS
Assistant Professor of Surgery, Emory University School of Medicine; Attending Surgeon, Emory University Hospital, Atlanta, Georgia.
Acute Limb Ischemia

K. CRAIG KENT, MD
Professor and Vice Chairman, Department of Surgery, Weill Medical College of Cornell University; Professor of Surgery, Columbia University College of Physicians and Surgeons; Director, Vascular Center, and Chief, Combined Columbia and Cornell Division of Vascular Surgery, New York–Presbyterian Hospital, New York, New York.
Standardized Reporting Practices; Renal Artery Imaging and Physiologic Testing

GEORGE E. KOPCHOK, BS (Biomed.Eng.)
Research Associate, Harbor-UCLA Medical Center, Torrance, California.
Intravascular Ultrasound

TIMOTHY F. KRESOWIK, MD
Professor of Surgery, University of Iowa Carver College of Medicine; Attending Surgeon, University of Iowa Hospitals and Clinics, Iowa City, Iowa.
Complications Following Carotid Endarterectomy and Perioperative Management

WILLIAM C. KRUPSKI, MD*
Formerly Clinical Professor of Surgery, University of California, San Francisco, School of Medicine; Attending Vascular Surgeon, The Kaiser Permanente Medical Group, San Francisco, California.
Endarterectomy; Cardiac Complications: Screening and Prevention; Indications, Surgical Technique, and Results for Repair of Extracranial Occlusive Lesions; Uncommon Disorders Affecting the Carotid Arteries

BRAJESH K. LAL, MD
Assistant Professor of Surgery; Assistant Professor of Vascular Surgery; Assistant Professor of Pharmacology/Physiology, UMDNJ–New Jersey Medical School, Newark, New Jersey.
The Pathophysiology of Chronic Venous Disorders

GLENN M. LAMURAGLIA, MD
Associate Professor of Surgery, Harvard Medical School; Attending Surgeon, Division of Vascular and Endovascular Surgery, Massachusetts General Hospital, Boston, Massachusetts.
Anastomotic Aneurysms

W. ANTHONY LEE, MD
Assistant Professor of Surgery, University of Florida College of Medicine, Gainesville, Florida.
Chronic Mesenteric Ischemia

LEWIS J. LEVIEN, MBBCh, PhD, FCSSA
Consultant Vascular Surgeon, Department of Surgery, Milpark Hospital, Johannesburg, South Africa.
Nonatheromatous Causes of Popliteal Artery Disease

PETER H. LIN, MD
Associate Professor, Division of Vascular Surgery and Endovascular Therapy, Michael E. DeBakey Department of Surgery, Baylor College of Medicine, Houston, Texas.
Complications of Endovascular Procedures; Management of Thrombosed Dialysis Access

THOMAS F. LINDSAY, MD, MDCM, FRCS, FACS
Associate Professor, Division of Vascular Surgery, University of Toronto Faculty of Medicine; Staff Surgeon, Division of Vascular Surgery, Toronto General Hospital, University Health Network, Toronto, Ontario, Canada.
Ruptured Abdominal Aortic Aneurysms

PAMELA A. LIPSETT, MD, FACS, FCCM
Professor of Surgery, ACCM, and Nursing; Surgical Critical Care Fellowship Director, Johns Hopkins University School of Medicine, Baltimore, Maryland.
Respiratory Complications in Vascular Surgery

EVAN C. LIPSITZ, MD
Assistant Professor of Surgery, Albert Einstein College of Medicine of Yeshiva University; Attending Surgeon, Montefiore Medical Center, Bronx, New York.
Techniques for Thromboembolectomy of Native Arteries and Bypass Grafts; Secondary Arterial Reconstructions in the Lower Extremity

JAYME E. LOCKE, MD
Department of Surgery, Johns Hopkins University School of Medicine, Baltimore, Maryland.
Respiratory Complications in Vascular Surgery

*Deceased.

FRANK W. LoGERFO, MD
William V. McDermott Professor of Surgery, Harvard Medical School; Chief, Division of Vascular Surgery, Beth Israel Deaconess Medical Center, Boston, Massachusetts.
The Autogenous Vein; Management of Foot Ulcers in Diabetes Mellitus

G. MATTHEW LONGO, MD
Instructor, Department of Surgery, Northwestern University Feinberg School of Medicine; Vascular Surgery Fellow, Northwestern Memorial Hospital, Chicago, Illinois.
Evaluation of Upper Extremity Ischemia

ROBERT C. LOWELL, MD, FACS, RVT
Horizon Vascular Surgery, PC, Gainseville, Georgia.
Lymphatic Complications of Vascular Surgery

ALAN B. LUMSDEN, MD, FACS
Professor and Chief, Division of Vascular Surgery and Endovascular Therapy, Michael E. DeBakey Department of Surgery, Baylor College of Medicine, Houston, Texas.
Complications of Endovascular Procedures; Management of Thrombosed Dialysis Access

M. ASHRAF MANSOUR, MD, FACS
Associate Professor of Surgery, Michigan State University College of Human Medicine, East Lansing; Vascular Surgery Program Director, Grand Rapids Medical Education and Research Center, Grand Rapids, Michigan.
Arteriovenous Fistulae of the Aorta and Its Major Branches

WILLIAM A. MARSTON, MD
Associate Professor, Division of Vascular Surgery, University of North Carolina at Chapel Hill School of Medicine, Chapel Hill, North Carolina.
Physiologic Assessment of the Venous System

JON S. MATSUMURA, MD
Associate Professor of Surgery, Division of Vascular Surgery, Northwestern University Feinberg School of Medicine; Staff Physician, Division of Vascular Surgery, Northwestern Memorial Hospital, Chicago, Illinois.
Arterial Complications of Thoracic Outlet Compression

KENNETH L. MATTOX, MD
Professor and Vice Chair, Department of Surgery, Baylor College of Medicine; Chief of Staff and Chief of Surgery, Ben Taub General Hospital, Houston, Texas.
Thoracic Vascular Trauma

JAMES MAY, MD, MS, FRACS, FACS
Bosch Professor of Surgery, University of Sydney Faculty of Medicine; Vascular Surgeon, Royal Prince Alfred Hospital, Sydney, New South Wales, Australia.
Basic Techniques of Endovascular Aneurysm Repair

MICHAEL A. McKUSICK, MD
Assistant Professor of Radiology, Mayo Clinic College of Medicine, Rochester, Minnesota.
Principles of Venography

ROBERT B. McLAFFERTY, MD
Associate Professor of Surgery, Division of Vascular Surgery, Southern Illinois University School of Medicine; Memorial Medical Center; St. John's Hospital, Springfield, Illinois.
Revascularization versus Amputation

MARK H. MEISSNER, MD
Associate Professor, Division of Vascular Surgery, University of Washington School of Medicine, Seattle, Washington.
Venous Duplex Scanning; Antithrombotic Therapy; Pathophysiology and Natural History of Acute Deep Venous Thrombosis; Clinical and Diagnostic Evaluation of the Patient with Deep Venous Thrombosis

ROBERT R. MENDES, MD
Division of Vascular Surgery, University of North Carolina at Chapel Hill School of Medicine, Chapel Hill, North Carolina.
Physiologic Assessment of the Venous System

LOUIS M. MESSINA, MD
Professor of Surgery, and Chief, Division of Vascular Surgery, University of California San Francisco; Director, UCSF Heart and Vascular Center, UCSF Medical Center, San Francisco, California.
Endarterectomy; Renal Artery Fibrodysplasia and Renovascular Hypertension

CHARLES C. MILLER III, PhD
Associate Professor, Department of Cardiothoracic and Vascular Surgery, University of Texas at Houston Medical School, Houston, Texas.
Thoracoabdominal Aortic Aneurysms

JOSEPH L. MILLS, SR., MD
Professor of Surgery, University of Arizona College of Medicine; Chief, Division of Vascular and Endovascular Surgery, University Medical Center, Tucson, Arizona.
Infrainguinal Bypass

MARC E. MITCHELL, MD
Assistant Professor of Surgery, University of Pennsylvania School of Medicine; Chief of Surgery, Philadelphia VA Medical Center, Philadelphia, Pennsylvania.
Basic Considerations of the Arterial Wall in Health and Disease

J. GREGORY MODRALL, MD
Associate Professor, Department of Surgery, University of Texas Southwestern Medical Center at Dallas Southwestern Medical School; Chief, Section of Vascular Surgery, Dallas Veterans Affairs Medical Center, Dallas, Texas.
Traumatic Arteriovenous Fistulae

GREGORY L. MONETA, MD
Professor of Surgery, Oregon Health and Sciences University School of Medicine; Chief, Division of Vascular Surgery, OHSU Hospitals and Clinics, Portland, Oregon.
Nonoperative Treatment of Chronic Venous Insufficiency

SAMUEL R. MONEY, MD, MBA, FACS
Clinical Associate Professor of Surgery, Tulane University School of Medicine; Chief, Vascular Surgery, Ochsner Clinic Foundation, New Orleans, Louisiana.
Medical Treatment of Intermittent Claudication

ERIN MARC MOORE, MD
Clinical Instructor in Surgery, University of Kentucky College of Medicine; Staff, Department of Surgery, Section of Vascular Surgery, University of Kentucky Chandler Medical Center and Veterans Affairs Hospital Lexington, Lexington, Kentucky.
Treatment of Acute Intestinal Ischemia Caused by Arterial Occlusions

WESLEY S. MOORE, MD
Professor of Surgery, Division of Vascular Surgery, David Geffen School of Medicine at UCLA; Vascular Surgeon, Division of Vascular Surgery, UCLA Medical Center, Los Angeles, California.
Fundamental Considerations in Cerebrovascular Disease; Indications, Surgical Technique, and Results for Repair of Extracranial Occlusive Lesions

MARK D. MORASCH, MD
Assistant Professor of Surgery, Division of Vascular Surgery, Northwestern University Feinberg School of Medicine; Attending Surgeon, Division of Vascular Surgery, Northwestern Memorial Hospital, Chicago, Illinois.
Brachiocephalic Vessel Reconstruction; Intestinal Ischemia Caused by Venous Thrombosis; Vertebrobasilar Ischemia: Indications, Techniques, and Results of Surgical Repair

JOHN B. MULLIKEN, MD
Professor of Surgery, Division of Plastic Surgery, Harvard Medical School; Director, Craniofacial Centre, and Co-Director, Vascular Anomalies Center, Children's Hospital Boston, Boston, Massachusetts.
Vascular Tumors and Malformations in Childhood

PETER NEGLÉN, MD, PhD
Vascular Surgeon, River Oaks Hospital, Jackson, Mississippi.
Endovascular Treatment of Chronic Occlusions of the Iliac Veins and the Inferior Vena Cava

MARK R. NEHLER, MD
Associate Professor of Surgery, University of Colorado Health Sciences Center School of Medicine; Program Director, Surgical Residency Program, University of Colorado Health Sciences Center, Denver, Colorado.
Selection of Patients for Vascular Interventions; Natural History and nonoperative Treatment of Chronic Lower Extremity Ischemia; Amputation: An Overview; Revascularization versus Amputation

AUDRA NOEL, MD
Assistant Professor of Surgery, Mayo Clinic College of Medicine; Consultant, Division of Vascular Surgery, Mayo Clinic, Rochester, Minnesota.
Surgical Treatment of Chronic Lymphedema and Primary Chylous Disorders

PATRICK J. O'HARA, MD
Professor of Surgery, Cleveland Clinic Lerner College of Medicine; Staff, Department of Vascular Surgery, Cleveland Clinic Foundation, Cleveland, Ohio.
Aortoenteric Fistulae

W. ANDREW OLDENBURG, MD, FACS
Associate Professor of Surgery, Mayo Medical School, Rochester, Minnesota; Head, Section of Vascular Surgery, Mayo Clinic, Jacksonville, Florida.
Primary Tumors of Major Blood Vessels: Diagnosis and Management

JEFFREY W. OLIN, DO
Professor of Medicine, Mount Sinai School of Medicine; Director, Vascular Medicine, Zena and Michael A. Wiener Cardiovascular Institute, Mount Sinai Medical Center, New York, New York.
Thromboangiitis Obliterans (Buerger's Disease); Atheromatous Embolization

KENNETH OURIEL, MD, FACS, FACC
Professor of Surgery, Cleveland Clinic Lerner College of Medicine of Case Western Reserve University; Chairman, Division of Surgery, Cleveland Clinic Foundation, Cleveland, Ohio.
Perioperative Considerations: Coagulopathy and Hemorrhage; Training in Endovascular Surgery; Acute Limb Ischemia

FRANK T. PADBERG, JR., MD, FACS
Professor of Surgery, Division of Vascular Surgery, UMDNJ–New Jersey Medical School, Newark; Chief, Section of Vascular Surgery, VA New Jersey Health Care System, East Orange, New Jersey.
Classification and Clinical and Diagnostic Evaluation of Patients with Chronic Venous Disorders

PETER J. PAPPAS, MD
Professor of Surgery, UMDNJ–New Jersey Medical School; Director, Division of Vascular Surgery; Director, General Surgery Residency Program; Director, Vascular Surgery Residency Program, UMDNJ–Newark, New Jersey.
The Pathophysiology of Chronic Venous Disorders

JEFFREY D. PEARCE, MD
Research Fellow in Vascular Surgery, Department of General Surgery, Division of Surgical Sciences, Wake Forest University School of Medicine, Winston-Salem, North Carolina.
Renal Complications

WILLIAM H. PEARCE, MD
Violet R. and Charles A. Baldwin Professor of Vascular Surgery, Northwestern University Feinberg School of Medicine; Chief, Vascular Surgery Division, Northwestern Memorial Hospital, Chicago, Illinois.
Overview [Neurovascular Conditions Involving the Upper Extremity]; Evaluation of Upper Extremity Ischemia

DEBORAH PEATE, RVT
Senior Technologist, David B. Pilcher Vascular Diagnostic Laboratory, Division of Vascular Surgery, Fletcher Allen Health Care, Burlington, Vermont.
The Role of Noninvasive Studies in the Diagnosis and Management of Cerebrovascular Disease

ERIC K. PEDEN, MD
Assistant Professor, Division of Vascular Surgery and Endovascular Therapy, Michael E. DeBakey Department of Surgery, Baylor College of Medicine, Houston, Texas.
Complications of Endovascular Procedures; Management of Thrombosed Dialysis Access

BRUCE A. PERLER, MD, MBA
Julius H. Jacobson II Professor of Surgery, Johns Hopkins University School of Medicine; Chief, Division of Vascular Surgery, Johns Hopkins Hospital, Baltimore, Maryland.
Overview [Complications of Vascular Surgery and Ischemia: Prevention and Management]

DAPHNE M. PIERRE-PAUL, MD
Clinical Assistant Instructor, Department of Surgery, Section of Vascular Surgery, SUNY Upstate Medical University College of Medicine, Syracuse, New York.
Molecular Biology and Gene Therapy in Vascular Disease

GRAHAM F. PINEO, MD
Professor of Medicine, University of Calgary Faculty of Medicine; Director, Thrombosis Research Unit, Foothills Hospital, Calgary, Alberta, Canada.
Prevention and Medical Treatment of Acute Deep Venous Thrombosis

FRANK B. POMPOSELLI, JR., BS, MD
Associate Professor of Surgery, Harvard Medical School; Clinical Chief of Vascular Surgery, Beth Israel Deaconess Medical Center, Boston, Massachusetts.
The Autogenous Vein

MARY C. PROCTOR, MD
Senior Research Associate, Department of Surgery, University of Michigan School of Medicine, Ann Arbor, Michigan.
Vena Caval Interruption Procedures

WILLIAM J. QUINONES-BALDRICH, MD
Professor of Surgery, Division of Vascular Surgery, University of California Los Angeles, Los Angeles, California.
Takayasu's Disease: Nonspecific Aortoarteritis

JOYESH K. RAJ, MD
Attending Surgeon, Fairview Hospital, Cleveland Clinic Health System, Westlake, Ohio.
Upper Extremity Amputation

SESHADRI RAJU, MD
Emeritus Professor of Surgery, University of Mississippi School of Medicine; Honorary Surgeon, University Hospital, Jackson, Mississippi.
Endovascular Treatment of Chronic Occlusions of the Iliac Veins and the Inferior Vena Cava

JOHN E. RECTENWALD, MD
Clinical Assistant Professor of Surgery and Radiology, University of Michigan, Department of Surgery, University of Michigan, Ann Arbor, Michigan.
Vena Caval Interruption Procedures

DANIEL J. REDDY, MD, FACS
D. Emerick and Eve Szilagyi Chair in Vascular Surgery, Henry Ford Health System, Detroit, Michigan.
Infected Aneurysms

MICHAEL A. RICCI, MD
Roger H. Allbee Professor of Surgery, Division of Vascular Surgery, University of Vermont College of Medicine, Burlington, Vermont.
The Role of Noninvasive Studies in the Diagnosis and Management of Cerebrovascular Disease

JOHN J. RICOTTA, MD, FACS
Professor and Chair, Department of Surgery, State University of New York at Stony Brook School of Medicine; Surgeon in Chief, University Hospital at Stony Brook, Stony Brook, New York.
General Strategies: Choice of Procedure and Technique [Open Vascular Surgery: Basic Considerations]; Vascular Conduits: An Overview

DAVID A. RIGBERG, MD
Assistant Professor of Surgery, Division of Vascular Surgery, David Geffen School of Medicine at UCLA, Los Angeles, California.
Takayasu's Disease: Nonspecific Aortoarteritis

THOMAS S. RILES, MD
George David Stewart Professor and Chair, Department of Surgery, New York University School of Medicine, New York, New York.
Surgical Management of Congenital Vascular Malformations

KYUNG M. RO, MD
Resident, Department of Radiology, UCDavis Medical Center, Sacramento, California.
Upper Extremity Sympathectomy

SEAN P. RODDY, MD
Associate Professor of Surgery, Albany Medical College; Attending Vascular Surgeon, Albany Medical Center Hospital, Albany, New York.
Arterial Thromboembolism

THOM ROOKE, MD
Krehbiel Professor of Vascular Medicine, Mayo Clinic College of Medicine; Head, Section of Vascular Medicine, Mayo Clinic, Rochester, Minnesota.
Uncommon Arteriopathies; Nonoperative Management of Chronic Lymphedema

RANDI ROSE, MD
Clinical Instructor, Department of Surgery, Mount Sinai School of Medicine; Staff, Zena and Michael A. Wiener Cardiovascular Institute, Mount Sinai Medical Center, New York, New York.
Atheromatous Embolization

VINCENT L. ROWE, MD
Assistant Professor of Surgery, University of Southern California Keck School of Medicine; Attending Surgeon, Los Angeles County–University of Southern California Medical Center, Los Angeles, California.
Vascular Injuries of the Extremities

C. VAUGHAN RUCKLEY, MB, ChM, FRCSE
Emeritus Professor of Vascular Surgery, University of Edinburgh; Former Consultant Surgeon, Royal Infirmary, Edinburgh, Lothian, Scotland, United Kingdom.
Lower Extremity Amputation: Technique and Perioperative Care

ROBERT B. RUTHERFORD, MD, FACS, FRCS (Glasg.)
Emeritus Professor of Surgery, University of Colorado School of Medicine, Denver, Colorado.
Essentials of Clinical Evaluation; Selection of Patients for Vascular Interventions; Essential Considerations in Evaluating the Results of Treatment; Basic Vascular Surgical Techniques; Causalgia and Post-traumatic Pain Syndromes; Lumbar Sympathectomy: Indications and Technique; Overview [Arteriovenous Fistulas, Congenital Vascular Malformations, and Vascular Tumors]; Diagnostic Evaluation of Arteriovenous Fistulas and Vascular Anomalies; Surgical Thombectomy for Acute Deep Venous Thrombosis

EVA M. RZUCIDLO, MD
Assistant Professor, Department of Vascular Surgery, Dartmouth Medical School; Vascular Surgeon, Dartmouth Hitchcock Medical Center, Lebanon, New Hampshire.
Arterial Duplex Scanning

HAZIM J. SAFI, MD
Professor and Chairman, Department of Cardiothoracic and Vascular Surgery, University of Texas at Houston Medical School; Vascular Surgeon, Hermann Memorial City Hospital, Houston, Texas.
Thoracoabdominal Aortic Aneurysms

RUSSELL H. SAMSON, MD, FACS, RVT
Former Associate Professor of Surgery, Albert Einstein College of Medicine of Yeshiva University, New York, New York; Staff, Sarasota Memorial Hospital; President, Mote Vascular Foundation, Inc., Sarasota, Florida.
Maintaining a Computerized Vascular Registry; Overview: Medical Management in a Vascular Surgery Practice; Hypertension and Patients with Vascular Disorders

MARC L. SCHERMERHORN, MD
Assistant Professor of Surgery, Harvard Medical School; Chief, Section of Interventional and Endovascular Surgery, Beth Israel Deaconess Medical Center, Boston, Massachusetts.
Abdominal Aortic and Iliac Aneurysms

ALVIN SCHMAIER, MD
Professor of Internal Medicine and Pathology; Course Director, M2 Hematology Sequence, University of Michigan Medical School; Director, Coagulation Laboratory, University of Michigan Hospitals and Health Centers, Ann Arbor, Michigan.
Vascular Thromboses Due to Hypercoagulable States

DARREN B. SCHNEIDER, MD
Assistant Professor of Surgery and Radiology, University of California San Francisco; Attending Surgeon, Division of Vascular Surgery, UCSF Medical Center, San Francisco, California.
Renal Artery Fibrodysplasia and Renovascular Hypertension

JOSEPH R. SCHNEIDER, MD, PhD
Professor of Surgery, Division of Vascular Surgery, Northwestern University Feinberg School of Medicine, Chicago; Senior Attending, Evanston Northwestern Health Care, Evanston, Illinois.
Extra-anatomic Bypass

PETER A. SCHNEIDER, MD
Vascular and Endovascular Surgeon, Division of Vascular Therapy, Hawaii Permanente Medical Group, Honolulu, Hawaii.
Endovascular Surgery in the Management of Chronic Lower Extremity Ischemia; Endovascular and Surgical Management of Extracranial Carotid Fibromuscular Arterial Dysplasia

JAMES M. SEEGER, MD
Professor of Surgery, University of Florida College of Medicine; Chief, Division of Vascular Surgery and Endovascular Therapy, Shands at UF, Gainesville, Florida.
Chronic Mesenteric Ischemia

TAQDEES SHEIKH, MD
Associate Professor, Department of Anesthesiology, Loyola University Health System, Maywood, Illinois.
Normal and Abnormal Coagulation

ROGER F. J. SHEPHERD, MB, BCH
Assistant Professor of Medicine, Mayo College of Medicine; Staff, Gonda Vascular Center, Mayo Clinic, Rochester, Minnesota.
Uncommon Arteriopathies; Raynaud's Syndrome: Vasospastic and Occlusive Arterial Disease Involving the Distal Upper Extremity

KEVIN M. SHERIDAN, MD
Resident (General Surgery), Department of Surgery, Indiana University Hospital; Division of Vascular Surgery, Clarian Health Hospitals, Indianapolis, Indiana.
The Surgical Treatment of Deep Venous Valvular Incompetence

ANTON N. SIDAWY, MD, MPH
Professor of Surgery, George Washington University School of Medicine; Chief of Surgery, VA Medical Center, Washington, D.C.
Basic Considerations of the Arterial Wall in Health and Disease; Hyperglycemia, Diabetes, and Syndrome X; Strategies of Arteriovenous Dialysis Access; Nonthrombotic Complications of Arteriovenous Access for Hemodialysis

MICHAEL B. SILVA, JR., MD
Professor of Surgery, Texas Tech University Health Sciences Center; Vice-Chairman, Department of Surgery; Chief, Vascular Surgery and Vascular Interventional Radiology, University Medical Center, Lubbock, Texas.
Venous Transpositions in the Creation of Arteriovenous Access

JAMES C. STANLEY, MD
Professor and Associate Chair, Department of Surgery, University of Michigan Medical School; Co-Director, University of Michigan Cardiovascular Center, and Head, Section of Vascular Surgery, University Hospital, Ann Arbor, Michigan.
Arterial Fibrodysplasia; Splanchnic Artery Aneurysms; Renal Artery Fibrodysplasia and Renovascular Hypertension

W. CHARLES STERNBERGH III, MD
Clinical Assistant Professor of Surgery, Tulane University School of Medicine; Program Director, Vascular Surgery, Ochsner Clinic Foundation, New Orleans, Louisiana.
Medical Treatment of Intermittent Claudication

RONALD J. STONEY, MD
Professor Emeritus, Division of Vascular Surgery, University of California-San Francisco School of Medicine, San Francisco, California.
Endarterectomy

EUGENE STRANDNESS, JR., MD*
Formerly Professor of Surgery and Chief, Vascular Surgery, University of Washington School of Medicine, Seattle, Washington.
Pathophysiology and Natural History of Acute Deep Venous Thrombosis

*Deceased.

RICHARD J. STRILKA, MD, PhD
Division of Vascular Surgery, Department of Surgery, University of Maryland, Baltimore, Maryland.
Endovascular Treatment of Renovascular Disease

TIMOTHY M. SULLIVAN, MD, FACS
Associate Professor of Surgery, Division of Vascular Surgery, Mayo Clinic, Rochester, Minnesota.
Carotid Angioplasty and Stenting

DAVID S. SUMNER, MD
Distinguished Professor of Surgery Emeritus, Department of Surgery, Division of Peripheral Vascular Surgery, Southern Illinois University School of Medicine, Springfield, Illinois.
Vascular Physiology: Essential Hemodynamic Principles; Physiologic Assessment of Peripheral Arterial Occlusive Disease; Evaluation of Upper Extremity Ischemia

PETER R. TAYLOR, MA, MChir, FRCS
Consultant Vascular and Endovascular Surgeon, Guy's and St. Thomas' NHS Foundation Trust, London, United Kingdom.
Functional Outcome and Natural History of Major Lower Extremity Amputation

THEODORE H. TERUYA, MD
Clinical Assistant Professor of Surgery, University of Hawaii John A. Burns School of Medicine, Honolulu, Hawaii.
Carotid and Vertebral Artery Injuries

ROBERT W. THOMPSON, MD
Professor of Surgery, Radiology, and Cell Biology and Physiology, Washington University School of Medicine; Attending Surgeon, Barnes–Jewish Hospital, St. Louis, Missouri.
Arterial Aneurysms: Etiologic Considerations; Neurogenic Thoracic Outlet Syndrome

MAHMUT TOBU, MD
Department of Pathology, Loyola University Medical Center, Maywood, Illinois.
Normal and Abnormal Coagulation

JAMES F. TOOLE, MD
The Walter C. Teagle Professor of Neurology and Professor of Public Health Sciences, Wake Forest University School of Medicine; Past President of the International Stroke Society and the World Federation of Neurology, Winston-Salem, North Carolina.
Diagnostic Evaluation and Medical Management of Patients with Ischemic Cerebrovascular Disease

J. JEAN E. TURLEY, MD, FRCPC
Associate Professor, Department of Medicine (Neurology), University of Toronto Faculty of Medicine; Staff, St. Michael's Hospital, Toronto, Ontario, Canada.
Ischemic Neuropathy

GILBERT R. UPCHURCH, JR., MD
Associate Professor of Surgery and Leland Ira Doan Research Professor of Vascular Surgery, University of Michigan Medical School, Ann Arbor, Michigan.
Splanchnic Artery Aneurysms

R. JAMES VALENTINE, MD
Frank H. Kidd Jr. Distinguished Professor and Vice-Chairman, Department of Surgery, University of Texas Southwestern Medical Center, Dallas, Texas.
Anatomy of Commonly Exposed Arteries

J. HAJO VAN BOCKEL, MD, PhD
Professor, Department of Surgery, Leiden University Medical Center, Leiden, The Netherlands.
Lower Extremity Aneurysms

FRANK J. VEITH, MD
Professor and Vice Chairman, Department of Surgery, Albert Einstein College of Medicine of Yeshiva University; William J. von Liebig Chair in Vascular Surgery, Montefiore Medical Center, Bronx, New York.
Techniques for Thromboembolectomy of Native Arteries and Bypass Grafts; Secondary Arterial Reconstructions in the Lower Extremity

HEINZ W. WAHNER, MD
Professor Emeritus of Radiology, Mayo Clinic, Rochester, Minnesota.
Clinical Diagnosis and Evaluation of Lymphedema

THOMAS WILLIAM WAKEFIELD, MD
S. Martin Lindenauer Collegiate Professor of Surgery, University of Michigan Medical School; Staff Surgeon, Section of Vascular Surgery, Department of Surgery, University of Michigan Hospital and Ann Arbor Veterans Administration Medical Center, Ann Arbor, Michigan.
Arterial Fibrodysplasia; Vascular Thromboses Due to Hypercoagulable States; Vena Caval Interruption Procedures

MATTHEW J. WALL, JR., MD
Associate Professor, Michael E. DeBakey Department of Surgery, Baylor College of Medicine; Deputy Chief of Surgery and Chief of Cardiothoracic Surgery, Ben Taub General Hospital, Houston, Texas.
Thoracic Vascular Trauma

DANIEL WALSH, MD
Professor of Surgery (Vascular), Dartmouth Medical School, Hanover; Vice-Chair, Department of Surgery, Dartmouth-Hitchcock Medical Center, Lebanon, New Hampshire.
Postoperative Graft Thrombosis: Prevention and Management

MARYANNE WATERS, RN, RVT
Instructor in Surgery, Department of Surgery, Division of Vascular Surgery, University of Vermont College of Medicine, Burlington, Vermont.
The Role of Noninvasive Studies in the Diagnosis and Management of Cerebrovascular Disease

JAMES C. WATSON, MS, MD
Clinical Instructor in Surgery, University of Washington School of Medicine, Seattle, Washington.
Compartment Syndromes: Pathophysiology, Recognition, and Management

FRED A. WEAVER, MD
Professor of Surgery, University of Southern California Keck School of Medicine; Chief of Vascular Surgery, University of Southern California University Hospital; Attending Surgeon, Vascular Surgery, Los Angeles County–University of Southern California Medical Center, Los Angeles, California.
Vascular Injuries of the Extremities

MITCHELL R. WEAVER, MD
Vascular Surgery Fellow, Henry Ford Health System, Detroit, Michigan.
Infected Aneurysms

JONATHAN M. WEISWASSER, MD
Assistant Professor of Surgery, George Washington University School of Medicine; Chief, Vascular Surgery, Washington VA Medical Center, Washington, D.C.
Hyperglycemia, Diabetes, and Syndrome X; Strategies of Arteriovenous Dialysis Access

GEOFFREY H. WHITE, MD, FRACS
Associate Professor of Surgery, University of Sydney Faculty of Medicine; Head, Department of Vascular Surgery, Royal Prince Alfred Hospital, Sydney, New South Wales, Australia.
Basic Techniques of Endovascular Aneurysm Repair

JOHN V. WHITE, MD
Clinical Professor of Surgery, University of Illinois School of Medicine, Chicago; Chairman, Department of Surgery, Advocate-Lutheran General Hospital, Park Ridge, Illinois.
Proper Outcomes Assessment: Patient-Based and Economic Vascular Interventions; Evaluation of the Patient with Chronic Lower Extremity Ischemia

RODNEY A. WHITE, MD
Professor of Surgery, David Geffen School of Medicine at UCLA, Los Angeles; Associate Chair, Department of Surgery, Harbor-UCLA Medical Center, Torrance, California.
Intravascular Ultrasound

DAVID R. WHITTAKER, MD
Fellow, Section of Vascular Surgery, Dartmouth-Hitchcock Medical Center, Lebanon, New Hampshire.
Computed Tomography, CT Angiography, and 3D Reconstruction for the Evaluation of Vascular Disease

DAVID B. WILSON, MD
Vascular Surgery Fellow, Section of Vascular Surgery, Department of General Surgery, Wake Forest University School of Medicine, Winston-Salem, North Carolina.
Atherosclerotic Renovascular Disease and Ischemic Nephropathy

GARY G. WIND, MD, FACS
Professor of Surgery, Uniformed Services University of the Health Sciences F. Edward Hébert School of Medicine; Staff Surgeon, Bethesda Naval Hospital, Bethesda, Maryland.
Anatomy of Commonly Exposed Arteries

CHARLES L. WITTE, MD*
Former Professor of Surgery, University of Arizona College of Medicine; Former Attending Surgeon, General Surgery/ Trauma, University Medical Center, Tucson, Arizona.
Lymph Circulatory Dynamics, Lymphangiogenesis, and Pathophysiology of the Lymphovascular System

MARLYS H. WITTE, MD
Professor of Surgery; Director, Student Research Programs, University of Arizona College of Medicine; Attending in Surgery (Lymphology), University Medical Center; Secretary-General, International Society of Lymphology, Department of Surgery, University of Arizona, Tucson, Arizona.
Lymph Circulatory Dynamics, Lymphangiogenesis, and Pathophysiology of the Lymphovascular System

HEATHER WOLFORD, MD
Chief Resident, Department of Surgery, University of Colorado Health Sciences Center, Denver, Colorado.
Natural History and Nonoperative Treatment of Chronic Lower Extremity Ischemia; Amputation: An Overview; Revascularization versus Amputation

KENNETH R. WOODBURN, MD, FRCSG (Gen.)
Honorary Clinical Lecturer, Peninsula Medical School, Devon and Cornwall; Consultant Vascular Surgeon, Royal Cornwall Hospital, Truro, Cornwall, United Kingdom.
Lower Extremity Amputation: Technique and Perioperative Care

MARK C. WYERS, MD
Assistant Professor, Dartmouth Medical School, Hanover; Assistant Professor of Surgery, Vascular, Dartmouth-Hitchcock Medical Center, Lebanon, New Hampshire.
Physiology and Diagnosis of Splanchnic Arterial Occlusion

CHENGPEI XU, MD, PhD
Senior Research Scientist, Department of Surgery, Division of Vascular Surgery, Stanford University School of Medicine, Stanford, California.
Artery Wall Pathology in Atherosclerosis

LIAN XUE, MD, PhD
Research Assistant Professor, Loyola University Medical Center, Chicago, Illinois.
Prosthetic Grafts

JAMES S. T. YAO, MD, PhD
Magerstadt Professor of Surgery, Division of Vascular Surgery, Northwestern University Feinberg School of Medicine; Attending Surgeon, Division of Vascular Surgery, Northwestern Memorial Hospital, Chicago, Illinois.
Occupational Vascular Problems

RICHARD A. YEAGER, MD
Professor of Surgery, Oregon Health and Sciences University; Vascular Chief, Portland VA Medical Center, Portland, Oregon.
Lower Extremity Amputation: Perioperative Complications

ALBERT E. YELLIN, MD, FACS
Professor of Surgery, Division of Vascular Surgery, University of Southern California Keck School of Medicine; Associate Chief of Staff and Medical Director, Surgical Services, Los Angeles County–University of Southern California Medical Center, Los Angeles, California.
Vascular Injuries of the Extremities

CHRISTOPHER K. ZARINS, MD
Professor of Surgery, Stanford University School of Medicine; Chief, Division of Vascular Surgery, Stanford University Medical Center, Stanford, California.
Artery Wall Pathology in Atherosclerosis

GERALD B. ZELENOCK, MD
Chair, Department of Surgery, and Chief of Surgical Services, William Beaumont Hospital, Royal Oak, Michigan.
Splanchnic Artery Aneurysms

R. EUGENE ZIERLER, MD
Professor of Surgery, University of Washington School of Medicine; Medical Director, Vascular Diagnostic Service, University of Washington Medical Center, Seattle, Washington.
Vascular Physiology: Essential Hemodynamic Principles; Physiologic Assessment of Peripheral Arterial Occlusive Disease

ROBERT M. ZWOLAK, MD, PhD
Professor of Surgery, Dartmouth Medical School; Attending Surgeon, Section of Vascular Surgery, Dartmouth-Hitchcock Medical Center, Lebanon, New Hampshire; Chief, Section of Vascular Surgery, White River Junction Veterans Affairs Medical Center, White River Junction, Vermont.
Arterial Duplex Scanning; Physiology and Diagnosis of Splanchnic Arterial Occlusion

*Deceased.

Preface

Since the publication of the last edition of *Vascular Surgery* 5 years ago, the changes that have occurred in the practice of vascular surgery have been extraordinary, and their impact on this new edition has been major.

The trend of more vascular surgery being done by fewer but better-trained surgeons, those committed to this field as their primary or sole activity, has continued. We will need to train more vascular surgeons to meet the rapidly increasing elderly population, as the "baby boomer" population peak carries on into the "Medicare population," although this may not be as easy to achieve as it once seemed when first predicted by the Stanley and Ernst manpower surveys more than a decade ago. All surgical training programs, vascular surgery included, have encountered a significant decrease in the numbers of applicants and are having difficulty filling the existing fellowships positions, let alone creating more. Length of training has become an issue with applicants, yet this comes at an exciting time when the scope and breadth of vascular surgery is rapidly expanding to the point where additional time to train surgeons in this field is being called for.

The development of stent grafts for endovascular repair of aortic aneurysms opened the doors to new horizons in vascular surgery. Having re-acquired and expanded their angiographic skills and techniques of catheter manipulation under fluoroscopic monitoring, with these procedures vascular surgeons soon embraced many other endovascular procedures. Thus, today's vascular surgeon not only needs experience in the traditional core of our specialty, open vascular reconstructions and repairs (and now how to perform some of them using laparoscopic or mini-incision approaches), but also experience in endovascular aneurysm repair, balloon angioplasty, and stenting of occlusive disease in major arteries (extremity, carotid, and visceral), and an array of other percutaneous procedures. Noninvasive vascular testing (NIT) and vascular imaging, angiography, duplex and computer tomographic (CT) scans, and magnetic resonance imaging and angiography (MRI/MRA) are expanding in versatility and importance in diagnosing vascular disease. Today's vascular surgeon needs expertise not only in interpreting them but also in personally performing some of them (e.g., NITs, duplex scanning, angiography). Traditionally, vascular surgeons have played a major role in the nonoperative management of many vascular conditions (e.g., venous ulcers, deep venous thrombosis [DVT], and claudication). Many also feel a responsibility for risk factor control in their atherosclerotic and venous thromboembolism patients, administering anticoagulant therapy, as indicated.

Clearly, then, training the "complete vascular surgeon" of today is a time-consuming and challenging process. To enable this without lengthening overall surgical training, the Society of Vascular Surgery and the Vascular Surgery Board of the American Board of Surgery have obtained approval to formally pursue different training stratagems. In addition to retaining the current, traditional 5 years of general surgery

residency followed by 2 years of vascular surgery fellowship, two shorter plans are proposed: 4 rather than 5 years of general surgery training before vascular surgery fellowship (with a common year devoted largely to vascular surgery) and 3 years of general surgery plus a 3-year vascular surgery fellowship. Should future vascular surgeons be trained in every aspect of managing vascular disease: open surgery, endoluminal techniques, vascular imaging and noninvasive vascular laboratory methods, and vascular medicine, or is a certain degree of specialization within vascular surgery inevitable? Time will tell, but this book continues to be geared toward the "complete" vascular surgeon and, as a result, has undergone major changes with this edition.

This very major change in the makeup of the clinical practice of many if not most vascular surgeons is reflected in the increase in chapters on endovascular surgical procedures in this edition and the fact that vascular surgeons now are the authors, for the most part, of these chapters. Successful endovascular surgery, particularly endovascular AAA repair (EVAR), demands precise imaging, and the applicable vascular imaging techniques have also developed at a rapid rate. This edition's coverage reflects recognition of the importance of modern imaging techniques in vascular surgery.

Arteriovenous hemodialysis access continues to play a major role in the practice of many vascular surgeons, often the most common procedure category in many practices. The DOQI guidelines have had a major impact on the practice of access surgery. The percentage of autogenous accesses will continue to increase; preoperative duplex evaluation has increased vein availability and led to increasing use of vein transposition. Postoperative surveillance is being used increasingly to predict failing access—in time for rescuing interventions. The importance of employing a sound strategy in selecting access site and configuration cannot be overstated; a chapter dedicated to this subject is included. The emergence of thrombolysis and stenting in the management of failing or failed access is also addressed in detail.

In dealing with vascular malformations and tumors, the role of surgery has become even more circumspect, limited, for the most part, to clearly resectable lesions. Attempts at hemodynamic control of unresectable lesions by inflow ligation have been condemned and mostly abandoned, because it cannot achieve control and precludes embolotherapy. Angiography is reserved for cases in which intervention is clearly indicated and imminent. In its place, duplex scan, MRI, and radionuclide AV shunt study provide more appropriate initial evaluation and follow-up. Embolotherapy/sclerotherapy continues to improve in technique, available agents, and "cure rate." Endovascular techniques will provide adequate control and occasional cure for most high-flow lesions and can and should be used more often as an adjunct to enable resection of lesions previously beyond the limits of safe surgical resection. On the other hand, low flow lesions (venous malformations, microfistulous AVMs) can be treated more conservatively, with intervention restricted mainly to localized, superficial "mass lesions" causing symptoms, unacceptable appearance, or significantly interfering with function. This section has been completely revised to reflect these changes.

Carotid endarterectomy (CEA) has survived its challenge from randomized prospective trials versus the best medical therapy, but now has been challenged by carotid artery stenting (CAS). Recent management changes, that is, the use of duplex scanning instead of arteriography as the preoperative imaging method in the majority of patients, same-day admission for surgery, selective avoidance of monitoring in intensive care units, and discharging a sizable portion of patients from the hospital on the day after surgery, although instigated by competitive pressures related to increased managed care, have *not* reduced the safety of carotid endarterectomy while reducing its cost. All of this has improved CEA's chances of withstanding the new challenge of CAS. The popularity of CAS has been spurred by a series of industry-driven trials with carefully selected inclusion and exclusion criteria and participating centers, while still waiting for the results of a prospective, randomized trial, like the current CREST trial.

The management of aneurysms has undergone rapid changes with the availability of EVAR and covered stent grafts elsewhere in the arterial tree. Improving technology may ultimately justify EVAR being applied to older "fit" patients and those with more difficult anatomy using fenestrated or branched endografts. It remains only for the demonstration of a long-term mortality advantage and structural durability. EVAR results are steadily improving, and the results of two recent randomized trials are encouraging in that regard. EVAR will be increasingly applied to ruptured AAAs and thoracic AAs where there is potentially a much greater mortality advantage. Retroperitoneal and mini-incision approaches have increased in popularity, with the aim of decreasing the length of hospital stay and morbidity.

In the area of lower extremity ischemia, a number of trends continue. Bypass for claudication is being more strictly limited. Control of arteriosclerotic risk factors, which has been an appallingly low 30%, needs to become routine. Proximal bypass, both direct and extra-anatomic, has yielded further to PTA/stent, which is now being applied for most TASC C lesions. Prosthetic infrainguinal bypass is being increasingly limited to selected AK fem-pop bypasses, while there has been a further relative increase in crural and pedal artery bypasses with autogenous vein. In those patients with ischemic ulcers or gangrene and renal failure, the results of infrainguinal bypass are known to be poor. It is now becoming apparent that the results of operations for recurrent bypass failure, especially when a single length of adequate vein is not available, are also poor, with higher mortality, recurrent failure, and limb loss rates; this, after many years of advocating bypass over amputation. As a result, there may be a shift away from limb salvage and back to amputation in subgroups like these two, where outcomes are particularly disappointing.

In acute limb ischemia, it is likely that thrombolytic therapy will ultimately prevail over thrombectomy *for restoring patency,* whereas arterial reconstruction will prevail over stenting for correcting most underlying lesions. Angioplasty and stenting will continue to be used for discrete lesions, including anastomotic and valvular stenoses (using newer cutting balloons), but, rather than the previously common practice of persisting with the initial mode of therapy, crossover from percutaneous to open revascularization should become the more common scenario, with vascular surgeons increasingly performing both.

The management of deep venous thrombosis has changed. The use of D-dimer techniques and patient risk profiling will decrease the workload of vascular diagnostic laboratories, inundated by knee-jerk "rule out DVT" requests. Catheter-directed thrombolysis, aided by debulking thrombus using better percutaneous mechanical thrombectomy (PMT) devices, seems likely to supplant anticoagulant therapy for iliofemoral venous thrombosis *in active patients with good longevity outlook,* and primary subclavian venous thrombosis is being increasingly treated—*in young healthy patients with a need for active arm use*—with thrombolysis, stenting, and first rib removal performed during the same hospital admission. Low-molecular-weight heparin has finally pushed unfractionated heparin aside, but the ambulatory outpatient treatment of DVT, which it allows, seems better restricted to more distal DVTs. On the other hand, we can expect a new breed of thrombin inhibitors (e.g., Ximelagatran) to compete strongly with warfarin-like drugs for long-term anticoagulant treatment. Venous thromboembolism is being more aggressively managed, in terms of preventing DVT, not only by antithrombotic therapy in high-risk patients but in IVC filter placement; that is, not only in those in whom anticoagulants are contraindicated, have caused bleeding, or have failed to prevent PE, but also those at high risk of PE, including trauma patients and others. The categorical indications for prophylactic use have grown, and this use has outgrown therapeutic indications. They include major trauma, paralyzed or bed-ridden patients, advanced malignancy/chemotherapy, gastric bypass for morbid obesity, protection during venous interventions, and several other situations. Clearly, the duration of risk differs and needs to be better defined for each category. For those with prophylactic indications, the trend toward greater use of temporary or retrievable filters is likely to continue, particularly in young patients in whom leaving in permanent filters exposes them to unnecessary risks, such as a higher risk of DVT. Further improvements in filter design allowing longer implantation time before safe removal are needed to support this trend.

In the endoluminal management of varicose veins, the original challenger to high ligation and stripping, radiofrequency ablation, is being given a run for its money by endoluminal laser treatment. Increasingly, varicose vein surgery is being displaced to "vein clinics." High ligation may make a comeback if collateral development around the saphenofemoral junction and late recurrence rates prove to be high with the endoluminal techniques. Control of superficial incompetence, by either technique, is being increasingly applied as initial treatment for varicose veins, with subcutaneous perforator interruption (SEPS) being withheld even if perforator incompetence is demonstrated. Thus, SEPS will most likely be limited to treating those with ulceration. Reconstructions for valvular incompetence are likely to become even more limited (i.e., for recurrent ulceration, only after failure of procedures to control superficial and perforator incompetence and a proper trial of compression therapy).

This review is intended to show some of the changes and trends in the 5 years since the last edition of the book. But it has always been a frustration of my colleagues and myself, having worked so hard to produce an up-to-date comprehensive textbook, only to see fast developing areas of it gradually become out of date as the years pass. Well, finally, the need to lament out-of-date passages will have passed for this textbook, for there will be a Web version with this edition, one that will be systematically updated throughout its life, giving subscribers an updated version, with new passages and references identifiably highlighted. Despite that new option, the print version of the Sixth Edition has been greatly revised and reorganized to keep up with the changes alluded to above, and more.

The number of chapters in this edition totals 176, up from 166, but there are more new chapters than the numerical difference would suggest. Some chapters have actually been consolidated, but more than 20 chapters are topically new. There is, as one would expect, a much greater emphasis on endovascular procedures, and, in addition to a heavier endovascular coverage in many chapters dealing with specific vascular disorders, there are 13 chapters devoted entirely or primarily to endovascular interventions, including a new section on basic endovascular techniques. There is also a new section on the medical management of patients with vascular disease, 4 of the 6 chapters of which are entirely new. A new section editor has treated even the seemingly stable subject of amputations to a complete overhaul. In fact, although 4 sections can be identified as being new, there are new section editors for 19 of the 23 sections, which is partly responsible for over 90 chapters being written by new authors or a new primary author. Many other primary authors have enlisted new coauthors in bringing about major revisions. Thus, more than two thirds of the chapters are new or have been extensively revised, and the remainder have been appropriately updated.

I owe my deep appreciation to the associate and assistant editors who have shared the hard work of putting together yet another comprehensive and thoroughly updated edition. With each new edition, we resist the temptation to cut back and make it a more comfortable size, for knowledge is increasing and we believe that there should be one text in this field that endeavors to be almost encyclopedic, one in which the reader can expect essentially every aspect of vascular surgery to be covered. As this work is not meant to be read from cover to cover, there is deliberate repetition in addition to thorough cross-referencing, which saves the reader from having to skip all over to get full coverage of the desired topic.

For those who reserve this book mainly for specific topical reference, yet wish to strengthen their knowledge, there will again be a companion review book, *Review of Vascular Surgery*, coming out with this edition. It contains close to 600 questions, approximately three per each chapter topic. Each question has five possible answers, only one of which is correct, with the correct answer and a point-by-point discussion of all the answers appearing separately. It should serve as an excellent teaching vehicle and study guide, pinpointing topics in which the reader is deficient in knowledge or understanding, and allowing the reader to identify chapters that deserve further study.

The associate and assistant editors join me in thanking each and every author and coauthor of the many chapters. Writing chapters is a difficult and sometimes thankless task, with little reward other than being recognized for one's expertise and the satisfaction of contributing to and perpetuating a textbook that has become, and will continue to be, by their efforts and the efforts of past contributors, a valuable resource in one's chosen field. It is my hope that they all will share my pride in a job well done and that their unselfish efforts will continue to sustain *Vascular Surgery* in the role into which it has grown—that of vascular surgery's leading textbook. We also wish to acknowledge the support of dedicated staff at Elsevier—publishers Natasha Andjelkovic and formerly Richard Lampert, developmental editor Donna Morrissey, senior project manager Linda Grigg, senior book designer Ellen Zanolle, updates manager Bob Browne, and senior marketing manager Ethel Cathers.

In the final words of the last edition's preface I implied that the Fifth Edition might be my last, yet here I am again. Maybe the Sixth Edition will be my last, but at least I am assured that this book will live on and some of the associate and assistant editors will see to it that it goes forth to future editions, with the aid of continual updating via the online version, a process that should pave the way for the next print version.

ROBERT B. RUTHERFORD

Contents

Color Figures appear in the sections in which they are referred to in the text.

Section **XIII**

MANAGEMENT OF CHRONIC ISCHEMIA OF THE LOWER EXTREMITIES

K. Wayne Johnston, MD

Section **XIV**

NEUROVASCULAR CONDITIONS INVOLVING THE UPPER EXTREMITY

William H. Pearce, MD

Section XVII

ARTERIOVENOUS HEMODIALYSIS ACCESS

Anton N. Sidawy, MD, MPH

Section XVIII

THE MANAGEMENT OF SPLANCHNIC VASCULAR LESIONS AND DISORDERS

James M. Seeger, MD

Section XIX

THE MANAGEMENT OF RENOVASCULAR DISORDERS

Kimberley J. Hansen, MD

Section **XX**

MANAGEMENT OF EXTRACRANIAL CEREBROVASCULAR DISEASE
William C. Krupski, MD

Section **XXI**

THE MANAGEMENT OF VENOUS DISORDERS
Peter Gloviczki, MD

Section XXII

THE MANAGEMENT OF LYMPHATIC DISORDERS

Peter Gloviczki, MD

Vascular
Surgery

NEUROVASCULAR CONDITIONS INVOLVING THE UPPER EXTREMITY

WILLIAM H. PEARCE, MD

Chapter

89

Overview

WILLIAM H. PEARCE, MD

Upper extremity vascular disease is uncommon and accounts for less than 10% of all cases in most vascular surgical practices. The incidence and spectrum of disease are widely different between the upper and lower extremities. Atherosclerosis is the most common arterial disease that affects the lower extremity. Atherosclerosis is rare in the upper extremity, however, and most commonly affects the left subclavian artery. Similarly, deep venous thrombosis in the lower extremity is much more common than in the upper extremity. Lower extremity deep venous thrombosis is associated with hypercoagulable conditions and stasis, whereas in the upper extremity, deep venous thrombosis is occasionally associated with a hypercoagulable state, but is most commonly associated with trauma (thoracic outlet or central venous catheterization). In some instances, the explanation for the differences in the distribution of the diseases is obvious—mechanical trauma, mediastinal radiation, central catheterization. In others, the differences are unknown. Takayasu's disease preferentially involves the supra-aortic branches, coronaries, and mid-aorta. These differences in pattern of disease highlight the regional difference of the circulatory system and heterogeneity of the vascular biology.

With the unique distribution of diseases that affect the upper extremity, it is important to have a logical and separate diagnostic algorithm. Arterial diseases of the upper extremity have been categorized in a variety of ways. Table 89-1 lists all the possible diseases based on etiology and provides a broad framework for making clinical decisions. Another and perhaps more specific approach is to determine the affected artery (Table 89-2). Atherosclerosis, giant cell arteritis, and Takayasu's disease affect the large proximal vessels (subclavian and axillary arteries). Medium and small arteries are more likely to be affected by diabetes mellitus and connective tissue diseases. Digital vessel damage may reflect more proximal lesions, embolic lesions, connective tissue diseases, diabetes mellitus, and localized trauma.

For unexplained reasons, the upper extremity contains more precapillary vasoconstrictors than the lower extremity. As a result, vasomotor problems are more common in the hand. The categorization of these vasomotor changes in the hand into either *Raynaud's syndrome* or *Raynaud's phenomenon* is confusing because the terms are not descriptive of the underlying mechanism. Porter and his group in Oregon suggested more descriptive terminology that has been widely accepted by the vascular surgical community. Vasospastic disease of the hand may be associated with either obstructed or nonobstructed digital arteries (Fig. 89-1). If a patient presents with Raynaud's and the underlying arteries are obstructed, the possible diagnoses are limited to those listed in Table 89-2. In some patients, diagnostic arteriography is avoided if the noninvasive test is positive for digital artery occlusion and the serology is positive. For patients with nonobstructive Raynaud's, the underlying arteries are normal and suggest a pure vasomotor disorder. The topic of vasomotor problems in the upper extremity is covered extensively in Chapter 93. This comprehensive review emphasizes the need for management of Raynaud's.

■ CLINICAL AND DIAGNOSTIC EVALUATION

In determining the diagnosis, it is important to obtain an accurate history and physical examination supplemented with noninvasive blood flow studies. Systemic symptoms, such as fever, chills, and joint pain, and history of diabetes mellitus and renal failure provide specific insights into the disease process. In addition, social and occupational histories are important with digital gangrene. Chapter 98

Table 89-1	Causes of Severe Hand Ischemia

Arterial Vasospasm

Ergotism
Idiopathic vasospastic Raynaud's syndrome
Vinyl chloride exposure

Arterial Obstruction

Large artery causes
   Atherosclerosis
   Thoracic outlet compression
   Arteritis
      Takayasu's
      Giant cell
   Fibromuscular disease
Small artery causes
   Connective tissue diseases
      Scleroderma
      Rheumatoid arthritis
      Sjögren's syndrome
      Systemic lupus erythematosus
   Myeloproliferative disorders
      Thrombocytosis
      Leukemia
      Polycythemia
      Buerger's disease
      Hypersensitivity angiitis
      Cold injury
      Henoch-Schönlein purpura
      Cytotoxic drugs
      Hypercoagulable states
      Arterial drug injection

Proximal Large Artery Sources of Embolism to Distal Small Arteries

Ulcerated or stenotic atherosclerotic plaques
   Aortic arch
   Innominate artery
   Subclavian artery
Aneurysms
   Innominate artery
   Subclavian artery
   Axillary or brachial artery
   Ulnar artery

From Landry GL, Moneta GL, Taylor LM: Severe hand ischemia. In Pearce WH, Matsumura JS, Yao JST (eds): Trends in Vascular Surgery 2003. Chicago, Precept Press, 2004, p 280.

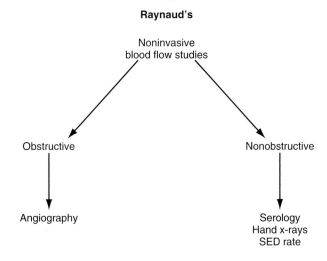

FIGURE 89-1 Vasospastic disease of the hand. SED, sedimentation.

describes a detailed physical examination of the arm. Many clues to the disease can be found, ranging from splinter hemorrhages of the nail beds to bruits and bony neck masses. Sumner's classic and noninvasive evaluation has been retained for readers studying for the vascular boards.

■ SUPRA-AORTIC BRANCHES

The management of supra-aortic trunk lesions is challenging for some surgeons. In Chapter 91, Morasch and Berguer bring together a wealth of experience of old and new techniques. Extra-anatomic and extra-cavity procedures are durable and obviate the need for median sternotomy and direct revascularization of the carotid and subclavian arteries. New endovascular procedures alone or in combination with open procedures have changed many operative approaches to these lesions. Antegrade or retrograde balloon angioplasties of brachiocephalic vessels should be part of a vascular surgeon's skill set. When needed, standard open procedures remain a safe and effective treatment for supra-aortic branch lesions.

■ THORACIC OUTLET SYNDROME

The thoracic outlet syndrome is a complex, multifaceted problem associated with much confusion and skepticism. The anatomic thoracic outlet is actually the diaphragm and

reviews the anatomy, physical examination, and diagnostic evaluation of a patient with upper extremity vascular disease. This chapter describes the important anatomy and anatomic variations. In particular, the variability of the palmar arches and digital blood supply is discussed. A section

Table 89-2	Arterial Diseases and Artery Affected				
	SUBCLAVIAN	**AXILLARY**	**BRACHIAL**	**FOREARM**	**HAND**
Atherosclerosis	●				
Giant cell arteritis	●				
Takayasu's disease	●	●			
Fibromuscular dysplasia		●			●
Embolic		●	●		●
Connective tissue disease				●	●
Diabetes mellitus				●	●
Repetitive trauma					
Hypercoagulation					●
Cryoglobulins					●
Pressors/polyvinyl chloride					●

not the upper extremity. For historical reasons, the incorrect nomenclature of the thoracic outlet has never been changed to be anatomically correct. Clinically the thoracic outlet includes all of the structures from the second portion of the subclavian artery to the third portion of the axillary artery. This area also includes the scalene muscles, first rib, neurovascular bundle, subclavian muscles, major and minor pectoralis muscles, clavicle, humeral head, and shoulder girdle muscles.

The shoulder girdle is a remarkable structure. The scapulae and clavicle provide a mobile platform for the glenohumeral joint. The system functions well when opposing muscles are balanced. Overuse, hypertrophy of muscles, and posture may damage any part of the neurovascular bundle. In addition, the neurovascular bundle is entrapped in many locations by muscles, bony structures (normal or abnormal), and fibrous bands. This complex region and symptoms are divided according to the structure most affected—venous, arterial, or neurogenic thoracic outlet syndrome. The pathologic mechanisms, diagnostics, and treatment strategies are explored in detail in Chapters 94, 95, and 96. The dynamic characteristics of this area are highlighted in Chapter 95. Positional computed tomography scanning has added a great deal to understanding about bone structures of the thoracic outlet. Abduction and external rotation pushes the clavicle up an inclined plane of the first rib. In this process, the neurovascular structures are being tethered by the scalene muscles and are compressed and distorted. In addition, hypertrophy of the muscles from overuse narrow the structures of the thoracic outlet, leading to further problems.

Neurogenic thoracic outlet syndrome is discussed in detail in Chapter 94. This chapter describes the latest reports and personal experience with patients. Chapter 96 examines venous thrombosis in the upper extremity not only from the perspective of thoracic outlet compression, but also in patients with central lines and hypercoagulable conditions. Deep venous thrombosis in the upper extremity is a common clinical problem in the hospital. The use of heparin is an important adjunct in these patients. In addition, for patients with venous thoracic outlet syndrome, controversy surrounds whether the patient should undergo aggressive therapy or should be treated conservatively. Green provides his perspective in Chapter 96.

■ UPPER EXTREMITY BYPASSES

The treatment of upper extremity ischemia is similar to the treatment for the lower extremity. Inflow vessels and outflow vessels must be identified before the surgical procedure. In general, most upper extremity bypasses use autogenous saphenous vein or arm veins for reconstruction. What is unique about the upper extremity is the hypothenar hammer syndrome, in which distal bypasses are performed to palmar vessels. Chapter 92 reviews the various surgical procedures available for the treatment of upper extremity ischemia and digital gangrene. Important among these is the treatment of patients with arterial complications of arteriovenous fistulae and iatrogenic trauma.

■ HAND PROBLEMS

The hand is the first manifestation of a variety of diseases (see Tables 89-1 and 89-2). Among these are neurosympathetic problems, including hyperhidrosis and Raynaud's. Hyperhidrosis is a serious problem producing disabling sweating of the hands. This embarrassing and sometimes job-limiting disease can be treated simply by interruption of the sympathetic outflow. Before the early 1990s, dorsal sympathectomy was performed by a small thoracotomy. The stellate ganglion and several distal ganglia were taken in this proceess. A clearer understanding of the sympathetic outflow and the development of new technology has created a minimally invasive operation, however, with excellent results and few complications. Chapter 97 reviews hyperhidrosis and details thoracoscopic-assisted dorsal sympathectomy.

Digital and hand ischemia is updated in Chapter 98. The traditional hypothenar hammer syndrome has been revisited in Chapter 92. Histologic examination of operative specimens shows fibromuscular dysplasia. Commonly when performing bilateral arteriography for patients with hypothenar hammer syndrome, fibromuscular dysplasia is found in the asymptomatic hand. This finding leads to a new perspective on this disease process. Chapter 92 reviews all of the occupational and recreational activities that lead to digital and hand ischemia.

■ COMMENT

Diseases of the upper extremity are challenging for the vascular surgeon. Standard operative surgical techniques that have been applied to the lower extremity can be used in the upper extremity. In addition, new endovascular procedures, such as angioplasty and covered stenting, can be used in the upper extremity, although only preliminary data are available on long-term patency. The most interesting aspect of upper extremity arterial disease is the unusual differential diagnosis and the concomitant hyperactivity of neurogenic control of precapillary vasoconstrictors. With a logical approach and a basic understanding of the differences between the upper and lower extremity, however, a successful outcome may be achieved.

Evaluation of Upper Extremity Ischemia

G. MATTHEW LONGO, MD

WILLIAM H. PEARCE, MD

DAVID S. SUMNER, MD

The clinical evaluation of upper extremity ischemia is more complex than that of the lower extremity. Atherosclerosis and complications of diabetes mellitus are the most common causes of lower extremity ischemia. However, the etiology of upper extremity ischemia includes not only atherosclerosis but arteritis, blood dyscrasias, drug-induced occlusions, occupational trauma, thoracic outlet syndrome, trauma, aneurysms, and complications of renal dialysis fistulae as well. In order to accurately diagnose the disorder, one must identify both the location of the obstruction and its nature (fixed or vasospastic). It is important to document whether the process is proximal or distal to the brachial artery. Once the location of the lesion is identified, the differential diagnosis can be narrowed. The vasospastic component of the process can be defined as either primary or secondary. A careful history and physical examination constitute essential first steps in identifying the problem. However, a combination of physiologic and imaging tests is needed to refine the diagnosis and develop a plan of treatment.

■ ANATOMY

Subclavian Artery

The right subclavian artery arises from the innominate artery behind the right sternoclavicular joint (Fig. 90-1). The right subclavian passes upward and lateral to the medial margin of the scalenus anterior muscle. The left subclavian artery arises from the aortic arch at the level of the fourth thoracic vertebrae, ascending in the mediastinum to the root of the neck, then arching lateral toward the medial border of the scalenus anterior muscle. The second portion of the subclavian artery passes behind and lateral to the lateral margin of the scalenus anterior to the outer border of the first rib, where it becomes the axillary artery (Fig. 90-2).

The branches of the subclavian artery are the vertebral, thyrocervical, and internal mammary arteries, and the costocervical trunk. On the left side, all four branches generally arise from the first portion of the vessel. Because the left internal mammary artery is frequently used to revascularize the heart, proximal subclavian stenosis may lead to recurrent angina pectoris. On the right side, the costocervical trunk usually originates from the second portion of the vessel.

Axillary Artery

The axillary artery begins at the outer border of the first rib and ends at the lower border of the tendon of the teres major muscle, where it becomes the brachial artery. The vessel is divided into three portions; the first part lies above the pectoralis minor muscle, the second behind it, and the third below it. The first part of the vessel along with the axillary vein and brachial plexus is enclosed with the axillary sheath, a fibrous sheath continuous with the deep cervical fascia. The branches of the axillary artery are (1) the highest

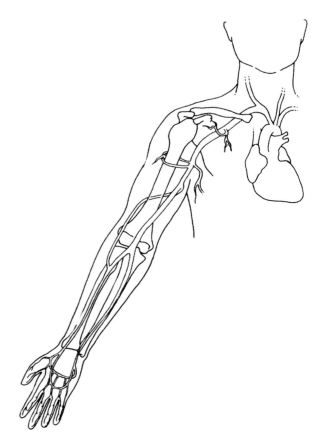

FIGURE 90-1 Diagram depicting the "textbook" normal arterial patterns of the upper extremity.

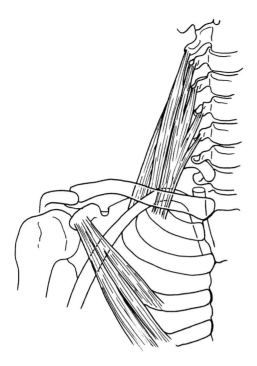

FIGURE 90-2 The classic course of the right subclavian and axillary artery, demonstrating its position in relation to the scalenus anterior muscle, first rib, and pectoralis minor muscle.

thoracic (first part), (2) the thoracoacromial and the lateral thoracic (second part), and (3) the subscapular, posterior humeral circumflex, and anterior humeral circumflex (third part). The highest thoracic is usually encountered during the axillary dissection for axillofemoral bypasses. The posterior humeral circumflex may become aneurysmal in professional athletes.

Brachial Artery

The brachial artery begins at the lower margin of the tendon of teres major and ends about a centimeter below the elbow, where it divides into the radial and ulnar arteries. Initially, the brachial artery lies medial to the humerus. However, as it proceeds down the arm, it moves anterior, to lie midway between the two epicondyles of the humerus. The artery is superficial throughout its extent, being covered by integument and the superficial and deep fasciae. The branches of the brachial artery are the profunda brachii, superior ulnar collateral, inferior ulnar collateral, nutrient, and muscular arteries.

Forearm Vessels

The radial artery originates at the bifurcation of the brachial artery and passes along the radial side of the forearm to the wrist. It then winds around the lateral side of the carpus beneath the palmar tendons of the hand, moving to the space between the metacarpal bones of the thumb and the index finger. Finally, it passes between the heads of the first dorsal interosseous muscle into the palm of the hand, where it crosses the metacarpal bones and unites with the deep volar

branch of the ulnar artery to form the deep volar arch (see Fig. 90-5). The branches of the radial artery may be divided into three groups according to where the vessel is situated: the forearm, the wrist, and the hand. In the forearm, the branches are the radial recurrent, muscular, volar carpal, and superficial volar arteries. At the wrist are the dorsal carpal and first dorsal metacarpal arteries. In the hand are the princeps pollicis, volaris indicis radialis, volar metacarpal, perforating, and recurrent branches.

The ulnar artery is the larger of the two terminal branches of the brachial artery. It begins below the elbow and passes obliquely downward, reaching the ulnar side of the forearm roughly midway between the elbow and the wrist. Throughout its course in the forearm, the ulnar artery is deeply seated until it reaches the wrist. The ulnar artery runs along the ulnar border to the wrist, where it crosses the transverse carpal on the radial side of the pisiform bone. In the hand, the ulnar artery is in close proximity to the hamate and pisiform bones, where it has little protection. It divides into two branches that enter into the superficial and deep volar arches. The branches of the ulnar artery can also be grouped according to the vessel's location. In the forearm are the anterior recurrent, posterior recurrent, common interosseous, and muscular branches. At the wrist are the volar carpal and dorsal carpal branches. The branches in the hand consist of the deep volar artery and the superficial volar arch.

Interosseous Artery

The common interosseous artery is a branch of the ulnar that may be used as a target vessel. The common interosseous divides into the palmar and dorsal interosseous arteries on either side of the interosseous membrane. The two arteries join to form the dorsal interosseous artery, which also gives rise to digital arteries. During planning of bypasses to the interosseous artery, a lateral forearm angiogram is needed to determine whether the interosseous artery to be used is either the dorsal or the palmar branch.

Congenital Variations

Variations of the arterial patterns in the upper limb occur with a relatively high frequency, and therefore, the vascular surgeon should be familiar with the most common variations. The right subclavian artery may arise as a separate trunk from the arch of the aorta. In rare instances, it arises from the thoracic aorta, as low as the fourth thoracic vertebra (Fig. 90-3). The left subclavian is occasionally joined at its origin with the left carotid. Both vessels are known to vary in their course and in how high they rise to in the neck.

Other than the variation in subclavian arteries, there are 12 major arterial variations of the upper limb (Table 90-1). Abnormal origins of the radial and ulnar arteries are not uncommon and can be inadvertently injured during surgical procedures (Fig. 90-4). In addition, arteriography performed through a brachial puncture may mistakenly be misinterpreted as an occlusion of the abnormal vessel, because the contrast agent was injected below the origin of the abnormal vessel.

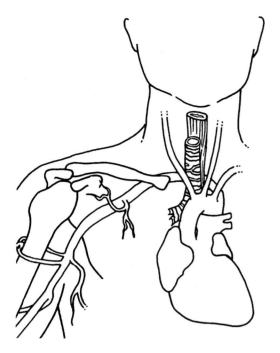

Table 90-1	Twelve Categories of Variant Patterns of Arm and Forearm Arteries

Superficial brachial artery
Accessory brachial artery
Superficial brachioulnar artery
Brachioulnar artery
Brachioradial artery
Superficial brachioradial artery
Brachiointerosseous artery
Superficial brachiomedian artery
Superficial brachioulnoradial artery
Superficial radial artery
Absence of the radial artery
Absence of the ulnar artery

Adapted from Rodriguez-Niedenfuhr M, Vazquez T, Nearn L, et al: Variations of the arterial patterns in the upper limb revisited: A morphological and statistical study, with a review of the literature. J Anat 199:547, 2001.

FIGURE 90-3 Diagram showing the right subclavian artery arising as a separate trunk.

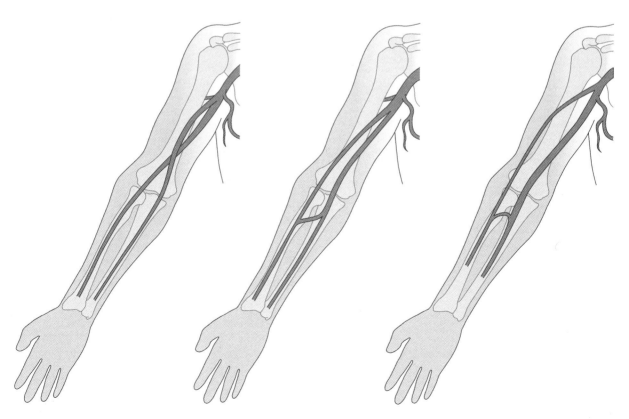

FIGURE 90-4 Three of the more common arterial variations of the upper extremity demonstrating abnormal origins of the radial and ulnar arteries.

Hand

Beneath the aponeurosis palmaris muscle lies the superficial volar arch. It is formed primarily by the ulnar artery, which usually unites with the superficial volar ramus of the radial artery. The superficial volar arch provides the digital arteries for fingers two through five. The superficial volar arch can be classified as a complete arch (80% of patients) or an incomplete arch (20%). The group of patients with a complete superficial volar arch can be divided into five subgroups based on anastomotic patterns with the ulnar artery, and the group with an incomplete arch into subgroups determined by the vessels contributing to the arch (Fig. 90-5).

The deep volar arch lies upon the ends of the metacarpal bones and is covered by all the flexor tendons. It is formed primarily by the radial artery, which goes on to anastomose with the deep volar ramus of the ulnar artery. Having less variability than the superficial volar arch, the deep volar arch gives off the branches to the rete carpi volare and four volar metacarpal arteries. The deep volar arch can also be classified as either complete (97%) or incomplete (3%). The complete volar arch has four variations based on differences in ulnar supply to the radial artery, and the incomplete arch has two variations.

■ PATHOPHYSIOLOGY

Some knowledge of the pathophysiology of upper extremity ischemia is necessary to an understanding of the results of noninvasive testing. As in the lower extremities, the system responsible for delivering blood to the tissues of the arms and hands consists of (1) *inflow arteries* (innominate and subclavian), (2) *intrinsic arteries* (axillary, brachial, antecubital, radial, ulnar, palmar, and digital), and (3) *arterioles*, which terminate in sphincters that control flow into the capillaries. The collateral circulation around the shoulder, axilla, and elbow is particularly well developed; also, within the forearm, hand, and fingers, the radial and ulnar arteries, the deep and superficial palmar arches, and the paired proper digital arteries provide parallel systems in which either one of the pair can usually sustain circulation independent of the other. Arteriovenous anastomoses, which are situated proximal to the capillary bed and divert blood away from the capillaries, are more common in the upper than in the lower extremities and are especially numerous in the tips of the fingers. They are also found in the volar surfaces of the fingers and hands but are essentially absent in the forearm.

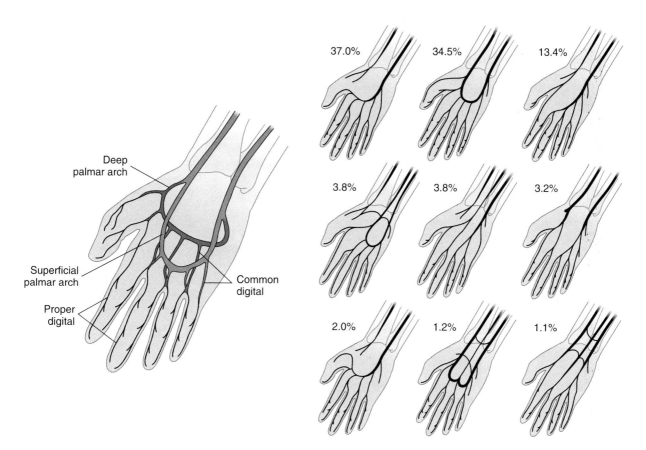

FIGURE 90-5 Variations of the superficial volar arterial arch are shown, with the relative frequency of each variation represented as the percentage next to its diagram. The classic normal superficial volar arch is shown with the 9 variants. The variants include both complete and incomplete arches.

Fixed Arterial Obstruction

The term *fixed* is used to designate obstructions that are due to well-defined anatomic changes involving the wall or lumen of the artery. Lesions seldom produce recognizable hemodynamic changes unless the cross-sectional area of the arterial lumen is diminished by more than 75%. Disturbances of pressure and flow are less severe when the process is localized and when collaterals are well developed. Impairment is more severe when the disease is extensive or multisegmental, when entry or exit of collaterals is blocked, or when terminal arteries or vessels without efficient collateral beds are involved. Lesions that are asymptomatic under normal resting conditions may become symptomatic during exercise or when stimuli that produce vasospasm are superimposed.

Chronic stenoses or occlusions isolated to the subclavian, axillary, or brachial arteries are usually well tolerated because of the abundant collateral circulation. Although peripheral blood pressures are reduced, blood flow at rest remains normal. Exercise, however, may produce symptoms. In the forearm, hand, and fingers, chronic (and even some acute) occlusions limited to either one of the paired arteries may cause few or no hemodynamic changes. Multiple occlusions, on the other hand, may be so extensive or so critically located that they overwhelm the compensatory mechanisms, resulting in ischemia. Chronic obstruction of an end artery (such as the common digital) or of both proper digital arteries commonly causes ischemia of the involved finger.

As a rule, acute occlusions, especially those involving unpaired or terminal arteries, prove to be more devastating. Owing to the instantaneous nature of the obstruction, blood flow distal to the site of trauma or an embolic occlusion must be maintained by preexisting collaterals, which may not be adequate to sustain tissue viability. Moreover, emboli tend to lodge at bifurcations, where they obstruct both the main arterial channel and the collateral input. Consequently, peripheral arterial pressure is usually severely reduced and may not be measurable.

Intermittent Obstruction

The two major causes of intermittent episodes of arm or hand ischemia are (1) extrinsic compression of the large inflow arteries and (2) vasospasm of the digital arteries. Although the two sometimes occur together, their clinical manifestations and pathophysiology are radically different. Both may also occur in conjunction with fixed arterial obstruction.

Extrinsic Compression

The structures responsible for extrinsic arterial compression are the bones, muscles, tendons, and ligaments. In the upper extremity, compression is most likely to occur at the thoracic outlet, where the subclavian artery must traverse a narrow triangular opening bounded by the first rib, the scalenus anticus and scalenus medius muscles, and their associated ligaments (see Fig. 90-12). Compression may also occur around the pectoralis minor muscle and humeral head. In these areas, obstruction is related to the position of the arm. Unless emboli arising from a post-stenotic dilatation of the subclavian artery have lodged in the more peripheral arteries of the arm, hemodynamic changes are evident only while the artery is actually being compressed.

Vasospasm

The peripheral arterioles of the upper extremity, especially those in the fingers, are normally quite sensitive to sympathetic or α-adrenergic stimuli. Emotional factors, pain, respiratory reflexes, local cold exposure, and total body cooling all cause arteriolar constriction. Release of arteriolar constriction by local or total body heating, administration of sympatholytic agents or vasodilating drugs, and surgical or pharmacologic sympathectomy ordinarily all cause a great increase in blood flow. Much of this increase is due to the opening of arteriovenous shunts, which are abundant in the fingertips. Flow through the capillaries is less affected. Fingertip blood flow is therefore quite variable; in normal subjects at room temperature, blood flow has been reported to range from 60 mL per 100 mL of tissue per minute to 400 mL per 100 mL of tissue/minute.[1]

Ischemia caused by vasospasm is much more common in the upper extremities than in the lower extremities. The episodic color changes in the fingers and toes of patients with cold sensitivity are known as *Raynaud's phenomenon*, for the French physician who initially described the condition in 1862. Classically, in response to cold exposure, the fingers initially become pallid, then cyanotic, and finally red, as the vasospasm subsides. Variations are common, and many patients never experience the typical triphasic color changes. The causes of Raynaud's phenomenon are multifactorial and, despite intensive investigation, remain incompletely understood. Although many classifications have been proposed, none is entirely satisfactory.

For the purpose of discussing the hemodynamics of vasospastic disease, this chapter employs the term *secondary Raynaud's phenomenon* to designate conditions in which a fixed anatomic obstruction has been identified (or is strongly suspected) and the term *primary Raynaud's disease* to identify conditions in which the cause remains obscure.[2-5]

Secondary Raynaud's Phenomenon (Obstructive)

Arteriolar constriction is usually tolerated well, but when it is superimposed on a substrate of fixed arterial obstruction, the previously adequately perfused fingers may become ischemic (Fig. 90-6).[5-7] This is the mechanism principally responsible for the appearance of Raynaud's phenomenon in patients with autoimmune diseases (e.g., scleroderma), Buerger's disease, or traumatic arteritis. Although the fingers typically display hemodynamic alterations even when they are warm, the changes become more marked with cold exposure.

Primary Raynaud's Disease (Vasospastic)

Although the digital arteries in patients with this form of episodic ischemia may be histologically normal, they are hypersensitive to cold and to α-adrenergic stimuli.[8-13]

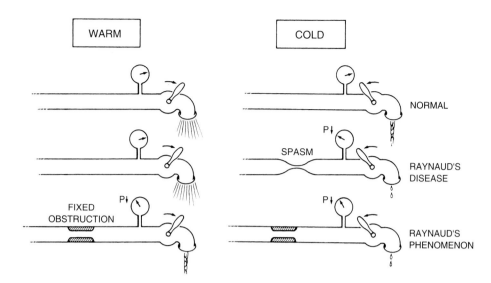

FIGURE 90-6 Effect of cold exposure on normal fingers, fingers with primary Raynaud's disease, and fingers with Raynaud's phenomenon secondary to fixed arterial obstruction. Faucets represent arteriolar sphincters. When a faucet handle is turned to the right, the arterioles are dilated; when it is turned to the left, the arterioles are constricted. Gauges represent digital arterial pressure, with increasing pressure indicated by clockwise rotation of the hand. Digital blood flow is represented by the output of the faucets.

Unlike the digital arteries of normal individuals, which are relatively unresponsive to cold, those of patients with primary Raynaud's disease display a remarkable ability to constrict, with complete closure occurring when the skin temperature falls below a threshold level.[14] This, together with cold-induced arteriolar constriction, produces profound but temporary digital ischemia.[15-17] Even when the hands are warm, enhanced sympathetic activity is evident. Although the digital arterial pressure is normal, blood flow in the fingers is moderately reduced.[16,18] The arterioles are sensitive both to local and to remote cold exposure, but the digital arteries respond almost exclusively to local cold.[16]

■ PHYSICAL EXAMINATION

The physical examination is performed in a warm room to avoid peripheral vasospasm. A systematic physical examination is performed from the fingertips to the thoracic cavity. The nail beds offer many clues as to the diagnosis, including splinter hemorrhages, digital gangrene, acrocyanosis, clubbing, and syndactyly. A simple continuous wave handheld Doppler probe can be used to identify common digital artery, proper digital arteries, palmar arches, and radial, ulnar, and brachial arteries. In the office or at the patient's bedside, forearm and brachial pressures are measured bilaterally. Discrepancies in pressures between segments or between arms are characteristic of an arterial occlusion. In patients with digital steal from a proximal arterial venous fistula, compression of the fistula may augment Doppler tones.

Inspection of the hand may also reveal coolness, pallor, and pain associated with Raynaud's phenomenon. In patients with reflex sympathetic dystrophy (RSD), the hand is cold with bluish discoloration. The hand is also moist and very painful to light touch. Patients with hyperhidrosis have a normally colored hand with excessive perspiration.

Physical examination of the hand should also include a neurologic examination, which may identify potential problems associated with arterial injury or neurologic compression. As in the lower extremities, motor function is important to document acute arterial ischemia. The brachial plexus and the major peripheral nerves parallel the arterial anatomy, so localized trauma is likely to cause an associated neurologic injury. Therefore, it is important to document any neurologic deficit prior to surgery. Neuromotor function of the peripheral nerves (ulnar, median, and radial) can be readily tested in the hand. Apposition of the thumb and little finger is a test of median nerve motor function, whereas pinching paper between two fingers is a test of ulnar nerve function (Figs. 90-7 and 90-8). The radial nerve function can be tested by dorsiflexing the wrist. Sensory aspects of the upper extremity nerves follow standard dermatome distribution (Fig. 90-9).

Palpation of all peripheral pulses—the radial, ulnar, brachial, axillary, and supraclavicular subclavian—is important. In addition, the radial pulse should be assessed with the arm abducted and externally rotated if thoracic outlet compression is suspected. The infraclavicular space should be auscultated to search for bruits associated with

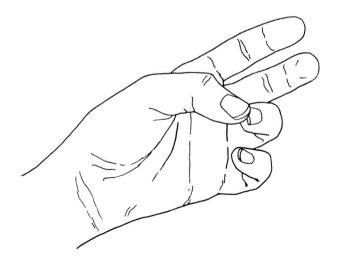

FIGURE 90-7 Apposition of the thumb and little finger is a test of median nerve function.

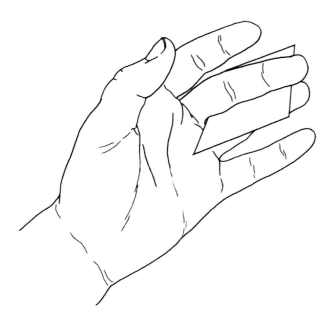

FIGURE 90-8 Pinching paper between two fingers can be used to demonstrate ulnar nerve function.

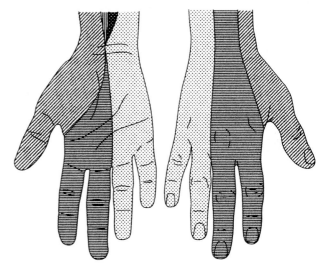

FIGURE 90-9 A depiction of the standard dermatome distribution. The *diagonal lines* represent the area supplied by C6, with its fibers forming the median nerve. The *horizontal lines* indicate C7 innervation, with its fibers forming the medial and radial nerves. C8 distribution is denoted by the *dotted* regions. C8 fibers contribute to the median, ulnar, and radial nerves.

position change. All peripheral pulses as well as the supra-clavicular subclavian pulse may be palpated for aneurysms. However, it is easy to mistake a tortuous subclavian artery for an aneurysm.

■ NONINVASIVE STUDIES

Segmental Pressure Measurements

The examination of any patient with complaints suggestive of upper extremity ischemia should begin with the measurement of segmental arterial pressures. Pneumatic cuffs are placed around the brachial area, the upper forearm, and the wrist; each cuff in turn is inflated above the systolic pressure and then slowly deflated while the return of flow, signifying the pressure at each level, is detected by a Doppler probe placed over the radial or ulnar artery or the palmar arch.

At each of the three anatomic levels, the pressure in one arm is compared with that in the other.[19] Normally, the difference in pressure between the two arms at any given site seldom exceeds 15 to 20 mm Hg and is usually considerably less (≈5 to 8 mm Hg). Indices obtained by dividing the lower of the two pressures by the higher average about 0.95 and are rarely less than 0.85. Pressure gradients between adjacent levels of the same arm are usually less than 15 mm Hg, with a mean in the range of 5 to 7 mm Hg (Table 90-2). Because the relationship between cuff width and arm diameter varies at the different levels, and perhaps because peripheral augmentation of systolic pressure may occur, the gradients are occasionally reversed, with pressures at the more distal sites exceeding those measured farther up the arm. Indices obtained by dividing the pressure at the forearm or wrist by the ipsilateral brachial pressure fluctuate around 1.0 and almost always exceed 0.85 (see Table 90-2).

A reduction in the brachial pressure indicates occlusive disease of the ipsilateral innominate, subclavian, axillary, or upper brachial artery.[20,21] In a series of patients with lesions

in one or more of these arteries, Sumner and colleagues[19] observed that the brachial pressures in the involved arms were 20 to 124 mm Hg less than those in the control arms, with a mean difference of 50 ± 33 mm Hg. The average ipsilateral-contralateral pressure index was 0.65 ± 0.15, with a range of 0.38 to 0.81. Because bilateral subclavian artery obstruction is not uncommon, both brachial pressures may be reduced. Bilateral disease is suggested by the presence of bruits over both subclavian arteries and may be confirmed by the detection of abnormal Doppler signals from the subclavian arteries. In such cases, the ankle pressure can be used as a reference value, provided that there is no evidence of arterial obstruction in the lower limbs.

An abnormally large pressure gradient between any two adjacent levels in the arm implies significant obstructive disease of the arteries in the intervening segment.[22] As with similar studies in the leg, segmental pressure measurements lack sensitivity and specificity. Gradients, for example, may be reduced when the ipsilateral brachial pressure is also low. In a series of arms with occlusions of the distal brachial,

Table 90-2	Pressure Data: Normal Arms*	
	GRADIENT (mm Hg)	
Brachial-forearm	5.0 ± 4.8	−6 to +15
Forearm-wrist	6.6 ± 4.6	−19 to +14
	INDEX	
Forearm-brachial	0.97 ± 0.06	0.87 to 1.06
Wrist-brachial	0.99 ± 0.06	0.89 to 1.15

*Pressures at different levels in the same arm.

Data from Sumner DS, Lambeth A, Russell JB: Diagnosis of upper extremity obstructive and vasospastic syndromes by Doppler ultrasound, plethysmography, and temperature profiles. In Puel P, Boccalon H, Enjalbert A (eds): Hemodynamics of the Limbs 1. Toulouse, France, GEPESC, 1979, pp 365-373.

antecubital, radial, and ulnar arteries, the gradients were 42 ± 30 mm Hg.[19] The range, however, was large (12 to 114 mm Hg). Forearm-brachial and wrist-brachial indices in these patients ranged from 0.37 to 0.86, with a mean of 0.68 ± 0.16. A marked difference between the pressure measured at the wrist with the Doppler probe over the radial artery and that obtained with the probe over the ulnar artery indicates which of these two vessels is more severely diseased.

Finger Pressure Measurements

The technique for measuring systolic blood pressures in the fingers is analogous to that employed in the arms.[23-26] To avoid vasoconstriction, one should perform all measurements in a warm (≈25° C), draft-free room. The patient should be relaxed, and efforts should be made to allay apprehension. A pneumatic cuff with a width of at least 1.2 times the diameter of the finger is wrapped around the proximal phalanx. A Doppler probe applied to a volar digital artery at the distal interphalangeal joint may be used to detect the return of blood flow as the cuff is deflated. Alternatively, a mercury strain-gauge or a photoplethysmograph placed over the distal phalanx can be used. The values obtained with the cuff at the proximal phalangeal level reflect pressures in the common and proximal proper digital arteries.

Nielsen and colleagues,[26] using a 2.4-cm cuff, found that finger pressures exceeded brachial pressures by 9 ± 7 mm Hg in subjects 17 to 31 years of age. The range was from 3 mm Hg lower to 21 mm Hg higher. In normal older subjects (43 to 57 years of age), the average pressure difference was approximately zero, with a standard deviation of ±7 mm Hg. Using a somewhat larger cuff (3.8 cm), Downs and associates[23] observed that simultaneously measured pressures in corresponding fingers of the two hands differed by only 3.5 ± 3.2 mm Hg. In only 3% of subjects was the difference greater than 9 mm Hg. In their study, finger pressures averaged 9.5 ± 6.8 mm Hg less than wrist pressures, which in turn were 9.6 ± 7.0 mm Hg lower than those at the brachial level. These investigators considered a pressure difference exceeding 15 mm Hg between corresponding fingers, a wrist-digital gradient greater than 30 mm Hg, and an absolute finger pressure of less than 70 mm Hg to be abnormal. Hirai,[25] whose results were similar to those of Nielsen and colleagues,[26] considers any arm-finger pressure gradient greater than 19 mm Hg in subjects younger than 50 years or greater than 25 mm Hg in older subjects to be abnormal.

In a series of normal subjects, the mean finger-ipsilateral brachial index was 0.97 ± 0.09. Values ranged from 0.78 to 1.27 (Fig. 90-10).[19] Finger-ipsilateral brachial indices in patients thought to have primary Raynaud's disease on the basis of clinical and laboratory findings were similar to those in normal persons (mean, 0.96 ± 0.11; range, 0.60 to 1.23). In patients with evidence of proximal digital or palmar arterial obstruction in limbs with no inflow disease, however, the finger-ipsilateral brachial indices were markedly decreased, averaging 0.56 ± 0.27 and ranging from 0 to 0.95. Low pressures were found in the fingers of both hands in 57% of the patients. Only one finger was affected in 17% of the hands, two fingers were affected in

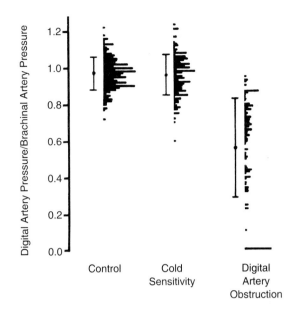

FIGURE 90-10 Finger pressure indices (mean ± 1 standard deviation). Data for cold sensitivity are derived from patients with primary Raynaud's disease. Those in the digital artery obstruction category are from patients who may or may not have secondary Raynaud's phenomenon. (From Sumner DS, Lambeth A, Russell JB: Diagnosis of upper extremity obstructive and vasospastic syndromes by Doppler ultrasound, plethysmography, and temperature profiles. In Puel P, Boccalon H, Enjalbert A [eds]: Hemodynamics of the Limbs 1. Toulouse, France, GEPESC, 1979, pp 365-373.)

11%, three or four in 39%, and all five in 33%. As shown in Figure 90-11, finger pressures accurately predict arteriographic findings.

According to one report of finger pressures in patients with connective tissue disease, mean digital pressure indices were 0.62 in patients with rheumatoid arthritis, 0.53 in patients with systemic lupus erythematosus (SLE), and 0.38 in patients with scleroderma.[27] Indices of 0 were observed only in patients with scleroderma.

Interpretation

Pressures in all fingers are reduced in proportion to any reduction in the ipsilateral brachial, forearm, or wrist pressure. When the disease is confined to the arm arteries and the palmar or digital arteries are spared, pressures in all fingers are approximately equal and the wrist-finger gradients are within normal limits. When the pressure in one or more fingers is distinctly lower than that in the others, however, obstruction of the palmar or digital arteries must also be present.

When arm pressures are normal at all levels, a reduction in finger pressure indicates disease in the palmar or digital arteries. If pressures in all fingers are equally decreased, the lesion must involve the palmar arch or the terminal portions of both the radial and the ulnar arteries. A reduction in pressure limited to the fingers on one side of the hand suggests that the palmar arch is incomplete or occluded at some point. Isolated obstruction of a common digital artery is implied when the pressure reduction is confined to a single finger and pressures in adjacent fingers remain normal.

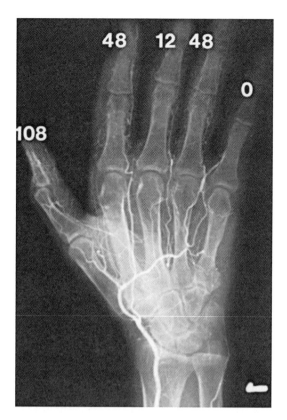

FIGURE 90-11 Digital artery pressures from the proximal phalanges of a 49-year-old man with an ischemic ulcer on the tip of the middle finger. The ipsilateral brachial pressure was 108 mm Hg. The arteriogram shows major obstruction of the proper digital arteries to all fingers except the thumb, which has a normal pressure. Pressures in all the other fingers are markedly reduced.

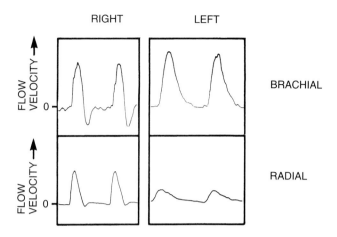

FIGURE 90-12 Analogue recordings of Doppler flow signals from the right and left brachial and radial arteries of an 89-year-old woman with occlusion of the left subclavian artery. Brachial pressure: right, 164 mm Hg; left, 101 mm Hg. Wrist pressure: right, 154 mm Hg; left, 77 mm Hg. (From Sumner DS: Vascular laboratory diagnosis and assessment of upper extremity vascular disorders. In Machleder HI [ed]: Vascular Disorders of the Upper Extremity, 2nd ed. Mount Kisco, NY, Futura Publishing, 1989, pp 9-57.)

Occlusion of only one of the paired proper digital arteries may have no perceptible effect on finger pressure.[23,25] Not infrequently, the disease process is confined to arteries in the middle or distal phalanx, in which case the pressure measured at the base of the finger is likely to be normal.[23] In such cases, one can obtain pressures representing the true perfusion potential by moving the cuff to the middle or terminal phalanx.[25,28,29]

Doppler Flow Studies

The contour of the Doppler blood flow signal in the upper extremity is similar to that in the leg. Normally, the velocity rises rapidly to a peak in early systole. It then falls abruptly to the baseline value, frequently reversing in early diastole. In late diastole, a final, low-level forward-flow phase may be present. This gives rise to the typical biphasic or triphasic audible signal that is easily recognized by the experienced observer. Beyond or distal to an obstruction or a high-grade stenosis, the signals become attenuated and have a slower upslope, a more rounded peak, and a downslope that continues throughout diastole. Flow reversal no longer occurs (Fig. 90-12). Audible signals have a low frequency and are monophasic. When the probe is placed over or just distal to a stenosis, noisy, high-frequency signals are obtained,

reflecting the presence of disturbed high-velocity flow. No signals are obtained over a totally occluded artery.

Because of the extensive collateral network in the forearm and hand, signals obtained from the radial and ulnar arteries at the wrist may sound normal, even though one of the pair may be occluded proximally. Clues to the true condition of either one of the two arteries can be obtained by observing the direction of flow and the effect of compression of the other major artery. For example, if flow in the radial artery at the wrist is reversed or compression of the ulnar artery obliterates the signal, an obstruction of the proximal radial artery is present. We can ascertain the patency of the distal radial and ulnar arteries and the palmar arch by noting the effect of sequential compression of the radial and ulnar arteries on the midpalmar signal.[30] Normally, there should be no interruption of flow when either one of the arteries is compressed. When both arteries are compressed simultaneously, flow in the palm should disappear or should be markedly decreased, unless a well-developed interosseous arterial communication exists. Flow should resume with release of the compression, provided that the artery being compressed was patent and communicated with the palmar arch. With the probe placed over a digital artery, similar compression maneuvers can be used to determine the primary source of the blood supply to any one of the fingers.

The hands must be warm when the digital arteries are being studied in order to avoid vasoconstriction, which may lead to a false-positive interpretation of results.[31] A complete examination requires evaluation of the volar proper digital arteries on both sides of each finger at the proximal and distal interphalangeal joints. Signals from each finger should be compared with those obtained from other fingers on both hands. It is not unusual to detect a signal at the distal interphalangeal joint in the absence of a signal at the proximal interphalangeal joint or at the base of the finger.[19,31] Examination of the signal over the volar surface of the fingertip is also often informative. A loud signal in this area signifies good perfusion and is typical of the hyperemic phase of primary Raynaud's disease. Poor signal or absence of signal implies vasospasm or fixed arterial obstruction.

Duplex and Color-Flow Doppler Ultrasonography

As in all other areas of the peripheral circulation, duplex scanning has had a significant effect on the evaluation of upper extremity arterial disease.[32-35] Unlike other noninvasive methods, duplex scanning provides precise anatomic information, locates stenotic or occlusive lesions as well as evaluates their extent and severity, identifies collateral pathways, and defines the patency of arteries distal to an occlusion. Arteriographic verification is infrequently required. In addition, arteriovenous malformations and aneurysms of the upper extremity arteries are easily recognized and differentiated from other masses with this modality.[36,37] Now that the sophisticated and versatile duplex scanners are widely available and technologists have become skilled in their operation, duplex scanning is rapidly replacing many of the more cumbersome and less specific noninvasive tests, especially when the information required is largely anatomic. All major arteries of the arm, forearm, wrist, and hand are readily identified, and even those of the digits can be studied with this method. Absence of color in an artery clearly visualized by B-mode imaging is diagnostic of total occlusion, and a color shift from red to white (or to yellow or green for some instruments) identifies stenotic sites, where flow velocities are increased. This feature reduces the need for serial Doppler investigations of flow patterns.

The subclavian artery is less easily visualized with duplex scanning than the other major arteries of the upper extremity, owing to its origin in the thorax and to the "blind spot" where it passes under the clavicle. Lesions in these areas can be detected and their severity evaluated, albeit indirectly, by examining Doppler flow patterns in accessible portions of the subclavian artery above or below the clavicle.

Because of their small size, finger arteries are the most challenging of the upper extremity vessels to study.[35] Encouraging results, however, have been reported by Langholz and coworkers.[38] In their study, color duplex scans of 450 digital arteries in 45 hands of 41 symptomatic patients were compared with conventional hand arteriograms. Of 160 occluded arteries, 138 (86%) were correctly identified by color duplex scanning. Of 290 arteriographically patent arteries, 270 (93%) were correctly identified. The positive predictive value of the color duplex scan interpretations was 87%, and the negative predictive value was 93%. In terms of the whole hand, 39 (95%) of the diagnoses were accurate. Most false-positive results were due to incomplete visualization of the entire length of the digital arteries. False-negative results were attributed to segmental occlusions that were overlooked by the ultrasonography scan and to mistaking collateral vessels for the native artery.

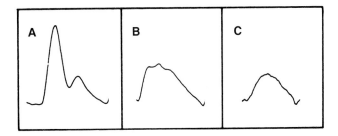

FIGURE 90-13 Plethysmographic pulse contours. **A,** Normal. **B,** Peaked. **C,** Obstructed. (From Sumner DS: Noninvasive assessment of upper extremity ischemia. In Bergan JJ, Yao JST [eds]: Evaluation and Treatment of Upper and Lower Extremity Circulatory Disorders. Orlando, FL, Grune & Stratton, 1984, pp 75-95.)

Plethysmographic Studies

Volume pulses can be recorded from the tips of the fingers with a variety of plethysmographs. For most clinical studies, the photoplethysmograph is entirely satisfactory and is somewhat easier to use than the mercury strain-gauge. Quantification, however, requires a strain-gauge.[19] Although venous occlusion plethysmography can be used to measure digit volume flow, these measurements are cumbersome and are reserved for research purposes.[10,16,39,40] For diagnostic evaluations, recording the pulse volume and contour is sufficient.

Pulse Contour

The normal fingertip pulse has a rapid upslope, a sharp systolic peak, and a downslope that bows toward the baseline. A dicrotic notch or wave is usually present on the downslope (Fig. 90-13A). The pulse recorded distal to a hemodynamically significant stenosis or occlusion has a delayed upslope, a rounded peak, and a downslope that bows away from the baseline (Fig. 90-13C). No dicrotic wave is present on the downslope. An intermediate form, characterized by a rapidly ascending limb, an anacrotic notch or an abrupt bend terminating in a systolic peak, and a dicrotic notch high on the downslope, has been called a *peaked pulse* (Fig. 90-13B).[41] Another variant resembles the normal pulse but has a dicrotic notch high on the downslope just after the systolic peak.[42,43]

Initial studies should be conducted with the fingers warm to eliminate the effects of vasoconstriction. Not only must the room temperature be warm, but it may also be necessary to warm the hands by immersing them in warm water. Although mild vasoconstriction merely decreases the pulse amplitude, more severe vasoconstriction may alter the contour of the pulse or result in its disappearance.[44]

Absence of a fingertip pulse or an obstructed pulse recorded under conditions conducive to vasodilatation suggests fixed arterial obstruction somewhere in the vascular pathway supplying the terminal phalanx.[45] The obstruction may be confined to the digital arteries or the palmar arch, or it may involve the forearm, brachial, axillary, or subclavian arteries. Multilevel disease may be present. Obstructions limited to one of the paired digital arteries or one of the forearm arteries may not produce an obstructed pulse if collateral channels are well developed. This finding, of course, is not unexpected; to affect the contour of the plethysmographic pulse adversely, a stenosis must be hemodynamically significant and all vessels feeding the fingertip must be involved. As a rule, plethysmographic pulses tend to be less sensitive than pressure measurements to the presence of disease. Normal pulses, however, are highly specific for the absence of fixed arterial disease.

Owing to the lack of sensitivity, some patients with secondary Raynaud's phenomenon may have relatively normal pulse contours in one or more fingers or, occasionally, in all.[46] Thus, the negative predictive value of a normal pulse may not be great, particularly if the patient belongs to a population with a high prevalence of obstructive disease. Nonetheless, in our experience, the finding of a normal pulse in all fingers of both hands in a patient complaining of cold sensitivity is highly suggestive of primary Raynaud's disease.

Although the significance of peaked pulses remains uncertain, they have been observed frequently in patients with autoimmune (collagen) disorders who do not have major arterial obstruction proximal to the terminal phalanges.[5,41,47,48] Peaked pulses may also be present in a significant number of patients thought, on the basis of other criteria, to have primary Raynaud's disease. Ohgi and associates[42] showed that normal pulses can become peaked with both direct and indirect exposure to cold, even in subjects with no history of cold sensitivity.[42] Peaked pulses, therefore, at least in some cases, appear to be associated with vasospasm of the digital arteries and arterioles.[47]

Additional diagnostic information can be obtained if one observes the effects of cold exposure and spontaneous rewarming on the amplitude of the finger pulse.[49] Cooling of normal fingers to 20° C or below markedly reduces the pulse amplitude, which on rewarming rapidly and steadily returns to pre-exposure levels. Similarly, in patients with secondary Raynaud's phenomenon, exposure to cold causes the pulse either to disappear or to become barely detectable; recovery to pre-exposure levels is gradual and takes longer than in normal subjects. Reflecting the critical closure phenomenon that characterizes the vasospastic response in patients with primary Raynaud's disease, plethysmographic pulses in patients with this condition disappear entirely on cold

exposure and remain undetectable until the finger temperature rises above 24° to 26° C; a normal waveform then suddenly reappears. Other investigators have found this test to be more useful for assessing vasospasm in the foot than in the hand.[50,51]

McLafferty and coworkers[52] have proposed a "plethysmographic digital obstruction index" for evaluating patients with hand ischemia. For each finger, a score of 8 points is assigned if the digital waveform is normal, 4 points if the upstroke time is longer than 0.2 seconds and the dicrotic notch is lost, 2 points if minimal waveform activity is detected, and no points if there is no digital waveform. The scores of all five fingers of each hand are added, and the result is divided by 40 (a perfect or normal score). The investigators observed that the plethysmographic index corresponded well with a similar index based on arteriography and that it was significantly higher in hands with moderate ischemia (0.75 ± 0.15) than in hands with severe ischemia (0.51 ± 0.20). An index less than 0.65 in patients with connective tissue disorders predicted digital ulceration with a sensitivity of 77%, a specificity of 100%, a positive predictive value of 100%, and a negative predictive value of 73%. These observations led McLafferty and coworkers[52] to conclude that digital photoplethysmography is the test of choice for evaluating patients with hand ischemia. Arteriography is required only for ruling out a source of emboli and for investigating patients who have no evidence of systemic illness that would explain the hand ischemia.

Responses to Sympathetic Stimuli

In normal limbs, both the amplitude of the digital pulse and the volume of the fingertip vary with respiration. Respiratory waves are superimposed on larger, but less frequent, α-, β-, and γ-waves.[5,53,54] For these responses to occur, the sympathetic innervation must be intact. Absence of these waves is therefore abnormal, suggesting a lack of sympathetic activity. One can also monitor sympathetic activity by recording the response of the pulse amplitude and fingertip volume to taking a deep breath, performing mental arithmetic, or placing ice on the chest or forehead (Fig. 90-14, *left*).[11,41,55,56] Normally, these maneuvers cause significant vasoconstriction. Reduction of the pulse amplitude

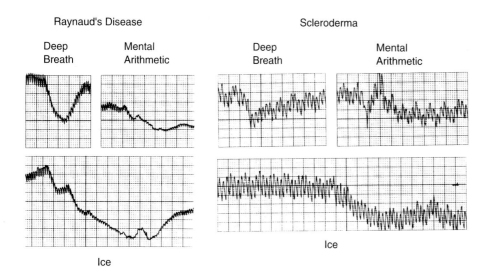

Raynaud's Disease

Deep Breath   Mental Arithmetic

Ice

Scleroderma

Deep Breath   Mental Arithmetic

Ice

FIGURE 90-14 Effect of sympathetic stimuli on digit volume and digital pulse amplitude in a patient with primary Raynaud's disease and in a patient with scleroderma. Recordings in the *right-hand panels* were made at a higher sensitivity than those in the *left*. The patient with scleroderma shows little or no response. (From Sumner DS, Lambeth A, Russell JB: Diagnosis of upper extremity obstructive and vasospastic syndromes by Doppler ultrasound, plethysmography, and temperature profiles. In Puel P, Boccalon H, Enjalbert A [eds]: Hemodynamics of the Limbs 1. Toulouse, France, GEPESC, 1979, pp 365-373.)

reflects a comparable decrease in digital blood flow, and a reduction in fingertip volume reflects both a decrease in arterial inflow and constriction of the terminal arteries and veins. A diminished response or no response (commonly seen in patients with collagen diseases) indicates impaired sympathetic activity (Fig. 90-14, *right*). Sympathectomy is unlikely to be effective in limbs that display little evidence of sympathetic activity. To record the larger, slower changes in fingertip volume, it is necessary to employ direct current (DC) coupling; the more rapid changes in digital pulse amplitude are more conveniently recorded with an alternating current (AC)–coupled plethysmograph.[57]

Reactive Hyperemia

The capacity of the digital arterioles to dilate can be determined by monitoring the response of the pulse amplitude to a short period of ischemia (reactive hyperemia test).[57] A pneumatic cuff is placed around the arm, inflated for 5 minutes to a suprasystolic pressure, and then rapidly deflated. In normal limbs and in limbs with purely vasospastic disease, the finger pulse returns promptly and its amplitude increases rapidly (within 30 seconds) to double that of the control pulse (Fig. 90-15).[41] In contrast, in a limb in which the peripheral arterioles have dilated maximally to compensate for increased proximal resistance imposed by a fixed arterial lesion, little or no increase in pulse amplitude is observed. A similarly poor response is also commonly observed in the limbs of patients whose microvasculature has been stiffened by autoimmune disease.[41] Although sympathectomized limbs may continue to display reactive hyperemia, lack of vasodilatation after a period of ischemia is usually associated with a similarly poor response to a surgical sympathectomy or to administration of vasodilator drugs. Vasodilatation can also be induced by warming the patient with an electric blanket, by oral administration of alcohol, or by immersing the hands in warm water.

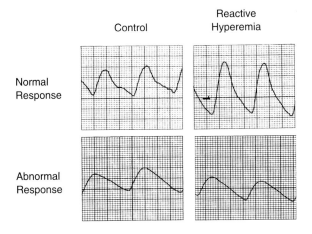

FIGURE 90-15 Normal and abnormal reactive hyperemia responses in a patient with primary Raynaud's disease (*upper panels*) and a patient with scleroderma (*lower panels*). Both patients had normal digital pressures at the level of the proximal phalanges. (From Sumner DS, Lambeth A, Russell JB: Diagnosis of upper extremity obstructive and vasospastic syndromes by Doppler ultrasound, plethysmography, and temperature profiles. In Puel P, Boccalon H, Enjalbert A [eds]: Hemodynamics of the Limbs 1. Toulouse, France, GEPESC, 1979, pp 365-373.)

Cold Tolerance Tests

The simple cold tolerance test described by Porter and associates[58] has proved reasonably reliable. Thermistors are taped to the fingertips, and pre-exposure temperatures are noted. The hands are immersed in iced water for 20 seconds and then removed and dried; post-exposure temperatures are monitored for 20 minutes or until temperatures return to pre-exposure levels. Because the relationship between skin temperature and digital blood flow is so markedly curvilinear, temperature measurements do not accurately reflect blood flow.[16] Recovery times after cold exposure are, however, roughly comparable, signifying the end of vasoconstriction.

Under the same environmental conditions, fingertip temperatures in normal subjects tend to be several degrees higher than those in patients with cold sensitivity (Fig. 90-16). Immersion in iced water cools the fingertips of both groups to similar levels; however, within 10 minutes after exposure, most normal fingers recover to pre-exposure temperatures, whereas relatively few cold-sensitive fingers do.[19] Recovery in cold-sensitive fingers is often delayed 20 minutes or longer.[50]

This test has been found to be 87% sensitive and 79% specific for detecting or ruling out cold-induced vasospasm (after a 20-second cold exposure, a 10-minute recovery time was used to divide normal from abnormal responses).[19] Using a modification of their original protocol (in which cold exposure was limited to 5 to 10 seconds and a 5-minute recovery time was taken as the upper limit of normal), Edwards and Porter[50] reported a specificity of 95% but a disappointingly low sensitivity of 50% to 60%.[50]

Nielsen and Lassen and others have devised a more elegant test that measures the decrease in digital blood pressure as the finger is cooled.[15,59,60] A cuff with a double inlet, placed around the middle phalanx, is used first to cool the finger and the underlying arteries to the desired temperature and then to measure blood pressure at that level. To ensure rapid and complete cooling, the finger is made ischemic by inflating a cuff placed around the proximal phalanx to suprasystolic pressure while a cooling solution is circulated through the more distal cuff. When the desired temperature has been attained, the distal cuff is inflated, the proximal occluding cuff is deflated, and finger pressure is measured by noting the return of blood flow with a mercury strain-gauge or photoplethysmograph placed around the fingertip as the distal cuff is gradually deflated. The process is repeated at progressively lower temperatures until 10° C is reached.

Whereas the digital artery pressure in normal subjects decreases only 16 ± 3% at a skin temperature of 10° C, the pressure in patients with primary Raynaud's disease falls rapidly with decreasing temperature and then precipitously to undetectable levels as a "trigger point" is reached. The trigger point at which zero pressures are reached varies from 10° to 20° C, depending on the individual patient, but it is reproducible in any given patient. In a study reported by Alexander and colleagues, the Nielsen test had sensitivity of 100%, specificity of 79%, positive predictive value of 95%, and negative predictive value of 100% for identifying the presence or absence of digital artery vasospasm in patients with primary Raynaud's disease and secondary Raynaud's phenomenon.[47] According to Carter and associates,[8] the test is most sensitive during total body cooling and is more

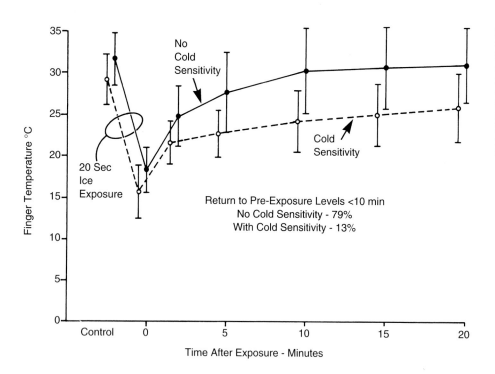

FIGURE 90-16 Fingertip temperatures (mean ± SD) before, during, and after 20-second immersion of the hands in iced water. (From Sumner DS, Lambeth A, Russell JB: Diagnosis of upper extremity obstructive and vasospastic syndromes by Doppler ultrasound, plethysmography, and temperature profiles. In Puel P, Boccalon H, Enjalbert A [eds]: Hemodynamics of the Limbs 1. Toulouse, France, GEPESC, 1979, pp 365-373.)

accurate in patients with secondary Raynaud's phenomenon than in patients with primary disease. Corbin and coworkers[61] also noted low sensitivity in patients with primary Raynaud's disease.

Using a modification of Nielsen's method, Maricq and associates[62] found that digital-brachial pressure ratios in patients with scleroderma approached 0 at a finger temperature of 10° to 15° C. Mean ratios in patients with primary Raynaud's disease were significantly higher (30%), and both were much lower than ratios in normal patients (75% to 80%) and in patients with cold sensitivity who did meet the clinical criteria for Raynaud's phenomenon (60% to 70%). From their observations, these researchers concluded that the Nielsen test may be helpful for differentiating between primary Raynaud's disease and Raynaud's phenomenon associated with scleroderma.

Unfortunately, the Nielsen test is time-consuming, requires special equipment not available in most vascular laboratories, and is somewhat artificial in that ischemia is necessary to ensure local cooling.[16] In fact, the lower pressure measured in the cooled finger may be in part the result of prolonged digital artery contraction or delayed relaxation caused by the combined effects of suprasystolic cuff pressure and increased stiffness of the cooled digital artery. For this reason, the measurements are more appropriately termed *apparent systolic pressures*.[16]

Another, and perhaps more physiologic, method of studying the effect of cold on finger pressures is to make the measurements while the entire hand is immersed in a water bath at progressively lower temperatures. Arterial occlusion is not used. In normal fingers, there is little change in pressure at 10° C, but in cold-sensitive fingers, blood pressure drops precipitously, reaching 0 in about half the subjects. In a study by DiGiacomo and associates,[39] finger pressures in patients with primary Raynaud's disease

averaged 105 ± 24 mm Hg in 40° C water and 13 ± 38 mm Hg in 10° C water.

Naidu and colleagues[63] have described a more direct test for detecting digital artery spasm. Their method uses a 20-MHz ultrasonic probe to measure the diameters of finger arteries at room temperature (25° C) and then again after the hand has been immersed in cold water (10° C) for 5 minutes. At room temperature, the average diameter of normal arteries (1.18 ± 0.17 mm) was only slightly greater than that of cold-sensitive arteries (1.06 ± 0.26 mm). After cold exposure, the diameters of normal arteries decreased by only 8.7 ± 11.5%, to 1.07 ± 0.15 mm, whereas those of cold-sensitive arteries decreased by 92.4 ± 16.4%, to 0.09 ± 0.21 mm. When a cold-induced decrease in diameter of 45% was used as a cutoff point, vasospastic arteries were identified with sensitivity of 97% and normal arteries with specificity of 100%. Although this method is of interest to clinical scientists investigating cold sensitivity, it is too technically demanding to be used routinely to evaluate patients with Raynaud's phenomenon.

■ APPLICATION OF NONINVASIVE TESTS

A careful history and physical examination often suggest a diagnosis or at least eliminate a number of disease categories. This information enables the examiner to select the noninvasive tests that are apt to be most productive. In most cases, only a few tests are required. The diagnostic approach should be modified according to the suspected site of obstruction, the duration of symptoms, the presence or absence of cold sensitivity or vasospasm, and the constant or intermittent character of the complaints. Simple algorithms, such as those in Figure 90-17, serve as rough guidelines for the efficient use of noninvasive diagnostic tests.[64]

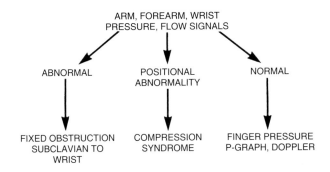

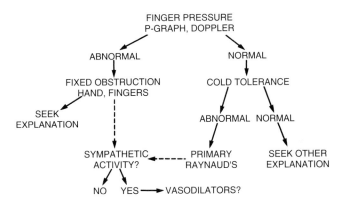

FIGURE 90-17 Approach to noninvasive diagnosis of upper extremity ischemia. P-graph, plethysmograph. (From Sumner DS: Noninvasive assessment of upper extremity and hand ischemia. J Vasc Surg 3:560, 1986.)

Obstruction of Arm and Forearm Arteries

When symptoms suggest ischemia of the arm or forearm, one usually can easily establish the diagnosis of obstruction involving the subclavian, axillary, brachial, radial, or ulnar arteries by measuring and comparing the segmental pressures in the two arms. Pressure levels also serve to define the severity of the circulatory impairment. A rapid survey with a Doppler flow detector often localizes the obstruction to one or more of these arteries and may indicate the approximate site of obstruction. A more precise definition of the problems is obtained with a duplex scanner or with a real-time, color-coded Doppler flow-mapping device. Unless intermittent obstruction or hand involvement is suspected, additional noninvasive tests are not required (see Fig. 90-16).

Acute Obstruction

Acute ischemia of the arm may be caused by emboli originating from the heart or ipsilateral subclavian artery or by penetrating, blunt, or iatrogenic trauma. When symptoms are compatible with an embolus, especially in patients with atrial fibrillation or a recent myocardial infarction, noninvasive tests confirm the diagnosis and help the surgeon choose the appropriate incision. Duplex scanning is especially helpful for locating the obstruction. Preoperative arteriography is seldom necessary, but intraoperative arterio-

graphy should be employed to confirm the patency of the distal vessels after the embolus has been extracted.

Although a decreased pressure or an abnormal Doppler signal distal to the site of penetrating trauma establishes the diagnosis of arterial injury, normal distal pressure does not necessarily rule out the diagnosis. In all cases of external bleeding or extensive hematoma formation, an arterial injury must be excluded (or identified) by duplex scanning, arteriography, or surgical exploration.

Arterial obstruction caused by blunt trauma, fractured bones, joint dislocations (especially at the elbow), or prolonged extrinsic pressure (e.g., crutch injuries) can be recognized from a reduction in arterial pressure distal to the site of the injury. It must be emphasized that the presence of an audible Doppler signal or even a palpable pulse does not exclude an injury, because collateral development may continue to supply some blood flow to the peripheral tissues. Careful pressure measurements are necessary to avoid overlooking a potentially disastrous injury. Duplex scanning should be performed whenever there is any question. Depending on the clinical presentation, the nature of the trauma, and the certainty of the noninvasive diagnosis, arteriography may or may not be required.

Cardiac catheterization, diagnostic venous or arterial puncture, and radial artery pressure monitoring still occasionally cause iatrogenic injuries.[65-67] Many of these mishaps may initially be attributed to spasm. True vasospasm, however, usually causes relatively little reduction in distal arterial pressure even though the radial or ulnar pulses may be difficult to palpate. A distinct reduction in pressure implies mechanical obstruction. If the pressure is only moderately reduced, it is safe to delay further investigation for a few hours. In the event that vasospasm was indeed the culprit, the pressure will have returned to normal levels. Some transient obstructions attributed to vasospasm are in reality due to thrombi that undergo lysis or fragmentation, the fragments then being dispersed to "silent" areas of the forearm or hand.

Although prompt operative intervention is the recommended approach in most cases of acute obstruction of the arteries of the upper extremity, it is possible to temporize when the patient's condition makes immediate surgery hazardous or otherwise inadvisable and the noninvasive findings are compatible with continued viability of the arm and hand. As long as distal pressures exceed 40 mm Hg, digital plethysmographic pulses are present, and Doppler signals can be detected in the hand and fingers, the potential for tissue survival is good. Because the condition can deteriorate at any time, however, these parameters must be monitored frequently until it is certain that the limb is out of danger.

Chronic Obstruction

Segmental pressure measurements will establish the diagnosis, determine the severity of the circulatory compromise, and usually provide some clue to the site of obstruction. More information regarding the location of the obstructive process can be obtained with the Doppler flow detector or with duplex scanning. Digital plethysmography and finger pressure measurements are necessary only when

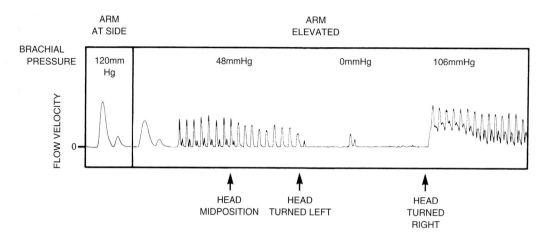

FIGURE 90-18 Doppler flow signals from the right radial artery of a 34-year-old man with thoracic outlet syndrome. Signals decrease with arm elevation and disappear when the head is turned to the left. Hyperemia appears when the head is turned to the right. The brachial blood pressure shows similar changes. (From Sumner DS: Vascular laboratory diagnosis and assessment of upper extremity vascular disorders. In Machleder HI [ed]: Vascular Disorders of the Upper Extremity, 2nd ed. Mount Kisco, NY, Futura Publishing, 1989, pp 9-57.)

involvement of the hand arteries is also suspected. Arteriography is required only when operative intervention is being considered.

As with similar diseases of the lower extremity, the decision for surgical intervention should be based primarily on symptoms and on the degree to which the patient is incapacitated; however, regardless of the symptoms, finding a distal pressure within the ischemic range (<40 mm Hg) provides a strong impetus.

Subclavian Artery Occlusion

An occasional patient with symptoms compatible with arm claudication may have essentially normal segmental pressures at rest. In such cases, a distinct drop in arm pressure after exercise of sufficient intensity to duplicate the symptoms provides confirmation of the diagnosis.[20,21] Comparing the effect of reactive hyperemia on the blood pressure in the two arms is another technique for demonstrating subtle degrees of arterial obstruction. If the pressure drop in the symptomatic arm is significantly greater (≥20 mm Hg) than that in the asymptomatic arm, arterial obstruction is the likely explanation for the patient's complaints. Most patients, however, tolerate chronic upper extremity arterial obstruction quite well, especially if the lesion is confined to the proximal subclavian artery. In fact, pressure differences between the arms in excess of 20 mm Hg are frequently observed in completely asymptomatic patients.

Although a normal brachial artery pressure essentially eliminates the diagnosis of subclavian steal, a decreased pressure does not establish the diagnosis, because the obstruction responsible for the pressure drop may be distal to the origin of the vertebral artery. If a normal Doppler signal is obtained from the axillary artery or the infra-clavicular subclavian artery, the obstruction responsible for the pressure drop must lie farther distally in the arm, thus ruling out the diagnosis of subclavian steal. Finding an abnormal Doppler signal in the supraclavicular subclavian artery raises the likelihood that subclavian steal is present. For confirmation of the diagnosis, reversed flow must be demonstrated in the vertebral artery. This is best accomplished with duplex scanning or with arteriography.[68-70]

The first rib, the scalene muscles, the pectoralis minor muscle, and associated ligaments may cause intermittent compression of the subclavian and axillary arteries. When the arm is subjected to the various thoracic outlet maneuvers, a reduction in arterial cross-section of 75% or more can be detected noninvasively through monitoring of changes in the radial artery flow pattern, the brachial blood pressure, and the digital plethysmographic pulse (Fig. 90-18).[21,71] Because compression of a lesser degree goes undetected and because pressure on the brachial plexus is responsible for most of the arm symptoms, negative test findings do not exclude the diagnosis of thoracic outlet syndrome. However, positive test results do not confirm the diagnosis, because some arterial compression is often present during these maneuvers, even in normal subjects. In our opinion, noninvasive tests add little to a carefully performed physical examination during which the radial pulses are palpated and the infraclavicular area is auscultated for bruits as the arm is manipulated. Objective tests are valuable, however, for detecting emboli originating from post-stenotic subclavian dilatation that obstruct arteries farther distally in the arm or hand.

Repeated trauma to the vessels of the shoulder girdle resulting from strenuous athletic activities, such as pitching a baseball or passing a football, may also cause local thrombosis and emboli to the distal arm arteries. Because highly motivated athletes tend to minimize their symptoms or attribute them to muscle strain, the diagnosis may be overlooked. Noninvasive tests provide an easy way of making the diagnosis and avoiding a result that may prove disastrous to these patients' careers.[72]

Obstruction of Hand and Finger Arteries

Conditions responsible for obstruction of the arteries of the hand and fingers include emboli, vibratory trauma (in chain saw or jackhammer operators), repetitive percussive trauma (hypothenar hammer syndrome, baseball catching), frostbite, autoimmune diseases (scleroderma or rheumatoid arthritis),

Buerger's disease, intra-arterial administration of drugs, and exposure to various toxins. Patients with end-stage renal disease may have heavily calcified obstructed digital arteries. Atherosclerotic involvement does occur but is relatively rare. In many cases, the cause remains unclear despite extensive investigation. Fixed obstruction of the arteries of the hand or fingers may be entirely asymptomatic; may be symptomatic only during cold exposure (secondary Raynaud's phenomenon); or may cause continued pain, fingertip ulcers, or gangrene.

Noninvasive detection of arterial obstruction is usually not difficult.[22] Even when symptoms are confined to the hand or fingers, the first step is to ascertain whether disease is present in the more proximal arteries (see Fig. 90-17). If lesions are demonstrated in the subclavian, brachial, or forearm arteries, it is likely that any additional obstructions in the hand are part of the same pathologic process. When the proximal findings are normal, the next step is to determine whether the hand symptoms are indeed due to arterial obstruction or whether they represent an exclusively vasospastic process. This distinction is important because vasospasm generally has a benign prognosis, whereas that of arterial obstruction is more ominous.

The patency of the palmar arch should be investigated in all cases, and the relative contributions of the radial, ulnar, and interosseous arteries should be determined. Blood pressure at the proximal phalangeal level should be measured in all ten fingers, especially when symptoms are bilateral.[19,25] If measurements are restricted to the symptomatic finger or fingers, more generalized involvement may be overlooked. Similarly, digital pulse waveforms should be recorded from the tips of all fingers. When proximal finger pressures are normal, this step is particularly important to avoid missing disease of the intervening arteries. A pressure measurement at the middle or distal phalangeal level may be revealing in fingers with normal proximal digital pressures and abnormal plethysmographic pulses. Because extensive Doppler surveys and duplex scanning of the digital arteries are time-consuming and may not be rewarding, these tests ordinarily need not be performed on all fingers; however, selective studies of individual fingers may be informative. As emphasized earlier, to avoid vasospasm and arteriolar constriction, studies designed to detect fixed arterial obstruction should be undertaken only when the hands are warm.

The distribution of the lesions identified by noninvasive testing may suggest a cause. An incomplete palmar arch may represent a common congenital variant, in which case the digital pressures and plethysmographic waveforms in all fingers are normal, or it may be due to any of a host of pathologic entities, including trauma, atherosclerosis, emboli, and collagen diseases. If pressures are decreased and pulses are abnormal in the fourth and fifth fingers and the patient gives a history of repetitive percussive trauma to the palm of the hand, the hypothenar hammer syndrome is a strong possibility.[22,33,73,74] In this event, compression of the radial artery at the wrist obliterates Doppler signals and reduces pressures in the involved fingers, whereas compression of the ulnar artery has no effect.[75]

Patients often present with symptoms and signs confined to one finger. Noninvasive tests, however, may disclose widespread subclinical lesions in both hands, confirming the presence of a generalized process such as scleroderma or another autoimmune disease. At some point, more fingers inevitably become symptomatic.[46] If the obstructions are diffuse but are confined to one hand, a traumatic or embolic cause should be considered. Possible causes include use of a jackhammer or chain saw or an unrecognized proximal lesion that is a source of emboli. When, after all fingers have been carefully studied, the obstruction appears to be localized to a single finger, it is reasonable to postulate that isolated trauma or a single small embolus might be responsible. Nonetheless, the clinician should never discount the possibility that the disease process is generalized and that other lesions may eventually appear.

Abnormalities of the plethysmographic pulses may be the only objective evidence of arterial disease. When all other study results are negative, obstructive or peaked pulses imply disease localized to the terminal vasculature. Autoimmune diseases can manifest in this fashion.[41,76]

Arteriography is necessary only when an occult embolic focus is suspected or in the relatively rare situation when microsurgical arterial reconstruction is contemplated. Revascularization may be feasible when noninvasive tests reveal patent digital arteries lying distal to an occluded palmar arch (as in the hypothenar hammer syndrome). Doppler surveys and duplex scanning are especially useful for mapping out the extent of arterial involvement. When hand ischemia is due to diffuse arterial involvement, extensive blood tests are required to identify the cause.

Although unrelenting pain, digital ulceration, and gangrene suggest severe ischemia, objective methods may be necessary to define the severity of circulatory impairment in other, less obvious situations. During the acute phase of the disease, digital pressures may lie in the ischemic range and plethysmographic pulses may be absent. Over a period of a few days or weeks, digital pressures often rise and plethysmographic pulses become more nearly normal. Not infrequently, improvement in the circulation of one finger parallels deterioration in the circulation of another. Once the dynamic phase of the disease runs its course, noninvasive findings may remain remarkably stable for long periods. For this reason, the surgeon should avoid precipitous action and adopt a wait-and-see attitude. Because the natural history of digital arterial disease is ordinarily one of fluctuating degrees of ischemia, the clinician must be cautious in attributing improvement to vasodilating drugs, surgical sympathectomy, or other therapeutic measures.[77]

Vasospasm: Intermittent Digital Ischemia

Episodic ischemia of the fingers in response to cold exposure or emotional stimuli (Raynaud's phenomenon) is a common complaint of patients referred for vascular evaluation. Estimates of the prevalence of this condition in the general population vary widely, from less than 1.0% to as much as 20%. Of 1752 randomly selected subjects from South Carolina in one study, 10% complained of cold sensitivity.[62] About 5% reported color changes, and 3% sought medical attention. Although the apparent prevalence may be considerably higher in regions of the world where the climate is colder and damper, this difference may reflect more frequent exposure to the triggering stimulus rather than a difference in the prevalence of the underlying disorder.

An attempt to classify the patient's disease process is made in order to formulate a treatment plan and to offer a short-term prognosis. If, in addition to cold sensitivity, the patient has symptoms or signs of fixed arterial obstruction (e.g., trophic skin changes, ulcers, severe pain), or if results of noninvasive tests are positive for arterial obstruction, the process is classified as secondary Raynaud's phenomenon.[6,19] In most such patients, cold sensitivity is overshadowed by other complaints. One or both hands may be symptomatic, but digital involvement is seldom symmetrical.

If digital pressures, pulses, and Doppler study results are normal when the hands are warm, a diagnosis of primary Raynaud's disease or vasospastic Raynaud's syndrome can be made, provided that the existence of cold sensitivity can be documented by history, direct observation, or cold tolerance tests.[6,41,78] Patients with primary Raynaud's disease are usually young, and the majority are female. Although these patients may complain of discomfort during the attacks, severe pain is rare. Symptoms are bilateral and symmetrical, and there are no skin changes. Responses to sympathetic stimuli are active, and reactive hyperemia studies demonstrate a normal capacity for vasodilatation.[19] In our experience, blood test results in all patients with this constellation of symptoms and signs but with normal noninvasive test findings have consistently been normal.

Between these two extremes is a group of patients whose history and physical findings are consistent with primary Raynaud's disease but whose noninvasive test results suggest an underlying disorder.[3,41,46,76] In some or all of the fingers, digital artery pressures may be moderately decreased and plethysmographic pulses may be peaked or may have a high dicrotic notch. The Doppler survey may show isolated abnormalities. Laboratory tests may disclose abnormalities in the sedimentation rate, antinuclear antibody (ANA) titers, or serum immunoelectrophoretic patterns; however, in the majority of patients, the results are normal. Although it is likely that some of these patients will ultimately be shown to have scleroderma or another connective tissue disease, currently available data are insufficient to substantiate this prediction.

Among the criteria proposed in the early 1930s by Allen and Brown[2] for primary Raynaud's disease was the stipulation that episodic cold sensitivity must be present for 2 years without the appearance of any associated disease. Subsequently, many investigations have shown that this period is too short and that Raynaud's syndrome may be present for as long as 30 years before an associated disease becomes apparent. Indeed, there seems to be no clearly defined upper limit.

Although it is impossible to predict which patients will ultimately have a connective tissue disease, the likelihood that such diseases will become manifest during follow-up appears to be related to the initial clinical and laboratory findings. Cumulative results of those articles published after 1980 extracted from the literature review by Edwards and Porter[9] show that only 12 of 408 patients (2.9%) classified on the basis of serologic and clinical evaluations as having primary Raynaud's disease demonstrated a connective tissue disease over a follow-up period averaging 3.7 years.[9] In contrast, 60 of 184 patients (32.6%) with one or more clinical or serologic abnormalities but without all the necessary criteria for a definitive diagnosis of connective tissue disease as set forth by the American Rheumatism Association[79] were diagnosed with a connective tissue disease over an average follow-up period of 4.0 years. The term *suspected secondary Raynaud's phenomenon* has been proposed to differentiate this high-risk group from the group without evident abnormalities.[80,81]

Among the clinical features that suggest the diagnosis of connective tissue disease in patients with Raynaud's syndrome are sclerodactyly, digital pitting scars, puffy fingers, telangiectasias, pulmonary fibrosis, and esophageal motility problems. Although elevated ANA titers often correlate with the subsequent appearance of an associated disease, positive ANA findings have been reported in 12% of otherwise normal women who manifested no connective tissue disease over a period of 5 years.[9,82] Perhaps the test with the greatest prognostic value is capillary microscopy.[4,81,83] It seems reasonable to speculate that many, if not most, patients classified as having suspected secondary Raynaud's phenomenon would also demonstrate some changes in digital pulse waveforms, Doppler signals, or digital pressures.

■ UPPER EXTREMITY ARTERIOGRAPHY

Upper extremity arteriography should visualize the entire upper extremity beginning with the subclavian artery and ending with the digital tuft arteries. The proximal portion of the upper extremity is generally cannulated via a femoral access site using the Seldinger technique. The proximal subclavian axillary arteries are visualized beginning at the arch. In patients with thoracic outlet compression, the arm is placed in the neutral position as well as in the position of function. In baseball pitchers, the arm must often be positioned in abduction and marked external rotation. In order to visualize the hand, catheters are placed into the brachial artery via the femoral artery or through direct puncture of the brachial artery. Direct puncture may be associated with significant distal vasospasm and embolization. In either case, distal vasospasm is a significant problem associated with arterial catheterization. To properly visualize the digital vessels, one may use intra-arterial nitroglycerin, papaverine, or reactive hyperemia. Actual puncture should be avoided because of associated nerve compression, which could produce flail arm. Minute amounts of blood within either the brachial or axillary sheath may compress the adjacent nerves. Any neurologic symptoms after either a brachial or axillary injection should be treated with immediate decompression of the neurovascular compartment (see earlier discussion of neurologic evaluation).

■ COMPUTED TOMOGRAPHY, MAGNETIC RESONANCE STUDIES

Other noninvasive imaging may be used to delineate arterial and bony structures of the upper extremity. The computed tomography (CT) scan is very useful in identifying the bony structures of the thoracic outlet (see Chapter 95). In such scans, the arm may be placed in neutral position or in the position of function. CT scans are also useful in identifying aneurysms of the subclavian and brachial vessels as well as aortic dissections, which involve the branch and cephalic vessels. Magnetic resonance imaging (including MR angiography) has not been particularly useful in the upper extremity. For proper imaging, the arms must be placed above the head with coils. The images, however, lack sufficient detail for making the diagnosis. Perhaps new technology will allow better delineation of the arteries with MRA. This modality is very useful, however, in visualizing problems with the aortic arch and brachial cephalic vessels. In patients with Takayasu's disease and other forms of arteritis, MRA is helpful in following disease progression and can be used to narrow the appropriate diagnosis.

■ THERAPY

Noninvasive tests are helpful in identifying the lesions that compromise the circulation sufficiently to require direct therapy. After treatment, these tests are valuable not only for assessing the extent of immediate physiologic improvement but also for following the results over the long term (Table 90-3).[37,72] Restoration of flow to completely or partially severed arms, hands, and fingers is now being performed routinely in many centers. Although continued viability of the severed part confirms the patency of the vascular anastomoses, noninvasive measurement of digital pulses, blood flow, and digital pressures provides objective data about the adequacy of the blood supply. Manke and associates[29] showed that perfusion of tissues that survive reimplantation is usually within normal limits but often lower than that in normal tissues in the same person (Fig. 90-19).

Many patients, however, have lesions that are situated too far distally or are too extensive to be amenable to vascular reconstruction, such as autoimmune and connective tissue diseases, vibratory trauma, frostbite, Buerger's disease, and a host of other problems. To increase blood flow, the physician may turn to vasodilating drugs, calcium channel blockers, prostaglandins, hemorheologic agents, fish oil supplements, or surgical sympathectomy.[39,40,77,84-87] All of

these methods have been reported to be successful by some investigators and unsuccessful by others, but few controlled studies have been performed. Given sufficient time, the circulation of most ischemic fingers improves spontaneously, although the improvement may be temporary and may be concurrent with a decrease in circulation to another finger.[68] Noninvasive tests, therefore, provide an objective method of assessing the effect of a specific therapy and of documenting the natural history of the disease.[39,77,84,85,88-90] Although alleviation of symptoms is the principal goal, subjective evaluations are notoriously unreliable.

Vasodilating drugs and sympathectomy are likely to be beneficial only when the terminal vasculature is capable of vasodilatation. Noninvasive tests designed to evaluate sympathetic activity should be performed when these forms of therapy are contemplated (see Fig. 90-17). If, in response to a reactive hyperemia test, the digital pulse volume does not increase appreciably, it is doubtful that vasodilating drug therapy will be successful (see Fig. 90-15). Even when reactive hyperemia develops, sympathectomy or sympatholytic drugs would not be expected to increase blood flow in the absence of a positive response to a deep-breath test (see Fig. 90-14). Before the patient is subjected to sympathectomy, plethysmographic pulses should be monitored, both before and after sympathetic block, to confirm that vasodilatation is possible.

Patients with primary Raynaud's disease almost invariably demonstrate reactive hyperemia and an active response to taking a deep breath (see Figs. 90-14 and 90-15). Although sympathectomy usually increases blood flow (at least temporarily), it is seldom if ever indicated in these patients because their symptoms are rarely severe and their disease does not jeopardize tissue survival. Vasodilators may, however, be helpful. Unfortunately, sympathectomy and sympatholytic drugs are least efficacious in patients

Table 90-3	Blood Pressure (mm Hg) Before and After Revascularization in Patients with Brachial, Radial, and Ulnar Artery Obstruction					
	BRACHIAL ARTERY		RADIAL (FOREARM) ARCH ARTERY		ULNAR PALMAR ARTERY	
SITE OF OBSTRUCTION	Before	After*	Before	After†	Before	After‡
Brachial	100	110	90	100	132	130
Forearm	88	102	70	104	—	—
Wrist	86	94	—	—	—	—
Finger (1)	0	106	22	98	126	128
Finger (2)	46	100	25	82	130	136
Finger (3)	30	102	—	—	130	128
Finger (4)	55	87	—	—	100	124
Finger (5)	25	103	—	—	60	118

*Proximal brachial–antecubital bypass graft.
†Distal brachial–distal radial bypass graft.
‡Distal ulnar–common digital bypass graft.

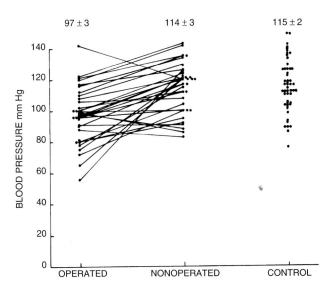

FIGURE 90-19 Blood pressures in the distal phalanges of 32 replanted fingers (Operated) compared with those of the comparable fingers of the other hand (Nonoperated). Control pressures are from 52 normal fingers. (From Manke DA, Sumner DS, Van Beek AL, et al: Hemodynamic studies of digital and extremity replants or revascularizations. Surgery 88:445, 1980.)

with secondary Raynaud's phenomenon, who most need increased perfusion, because the arterioles are often maximally dilated to compensate for a proximal obstruction and the compliance of the terminal vessels is impaired by the disease process that is producing the ischemia.[77] A few drugs—particularly calcium channel blockers—do seem to afford some relief, but noninvasive tests show little objective evidence of increased perfusion.[40,77,84-86,90,91]

■ SUMMARY

Evaluation of acute or chronic ischemia of the upper extremity requires a thorough knowledge of both conditions affecting the vasculature of the upper extremity and the vascular anatomy of the upper extremity. The physical examination combined with the noninvasive tests available in the vascular laboratory can help locate sites of obstructive lesions, assess the severity of circulatory impairment, and distinguish between primarily obstructive and vasospastic disease. At this point, the need for further laboratory tests, arteriography, or another imaging modality is clarified. Furthermore, the physical examination combined with noninvasive vascular laboratory tests provides objective methods for evaluating the results of therapeutic interventions as well as a means to define the natural history of the disease.

■ REFERENCES

1. Mead J, Schoenfeld RC: Character of blood flow in the vasodilated fingers. J Appl Physiol 2:680, 1950.
2. Allen E, Brown G: Raynaud's disease: A critical review of minimal requisites for diagnosis. Am J Med Sci 183:187, 1932.
2. Balas P, Tripolitis AJ, Kaklamanis P, et al: Raynaud's phenomenon: Primary and secondary causes. Arch Surg 114:1174, 1979.
4. Jacobs MJHM, Breslau PJ, Slaaf DW, et al: Nomenclature of Raynaud's phenomenon: A capillary microscopic and hemorheologic study. Surgery 101:136, 1987.
5. Strandness DE Jr, Sumner DS: Raynaud's disease and Raynaud's phenomenon. In: Hemodynamics for Surgeons. New York, Grune & Stratton, 1975, pp 543-581.
6. Hirai M: Cold sensitivity of the hand in arterial occlusive disease. Surgery 85:140, 1979.
7. Mendlowitz M, Naftchi N: The digital circulation in Raynaud's disease. Am J Cardiol 4:580, 1959.
8. Carter SA, Dean E, Kroeger EA: Apparent finger systolic pressures during cooling in patients with Raynaud's syndrome. Circulation 77:988, 1988.
9. Edwards JM, Porter JM: Long-term outcome of Raynaud's syndrome. In Yao JST, Pearce WH (eds): Long-Term Results in Vascular Surgery. Norwalk, CT, Appleton & Lange, 1993, pp 345-352.
10. Freedman RR, Mayes MD, Sabharwal SC: Induction of vasospastic attacks despite digital nerve blood in Raynaud's disease and phenomenon. Circulation 80:859, 1989.
11. Jamieson GG, Ludbrook J, Wilson A: Cold hypersensitivity in Raynaud's phenomenon. Circulation 44:254, 1971.
12. Lewis T: Experiments relating to the peripheral mechanism involved in spasmodic arrest of circulation in fingers: A variety of Raynaud's disease. Heart 15:7, 1929.
13. Lynn RB, Steiner RE, Van Wyk FAK: The digital arteries of the hands in Raynaud's disease. Lancet 1(6862):471, 1955.
14. Singh S, de Trafford JC, Baskerville PA, et al: Digital artery calibre measurement: A new technique of assessing Raynaud's phenomenon. Eur J Vasc Surg 5:199, 1991.
15. Krähenbühl B, Nielsen SL, Lassen NA: Closure of digital arteries in high vascular tone states as demonstrated by measurement of systolic blood pressure in the fingers. Scand J Clin Lab Invest 37:71, 1977.

16. Ohgi S, Moore DJ, Miles RD, et al: The effect of cold on circulation in normal and cold-sensitive fingers. Bruit 9:9, 1985.
17. Rösch J, Porter JM, Gralino BJ: Cryodynamic hand angiography in the diagnosis and management of Raynaud's syndrome. Circulation 55:807, 1977.
18. Pyykkö I, Kolari P, Fäkkilä M, et al: Finger peripheral resistance during local cold provocation in vasospastic disease. Scand J Work Environ Health 12:395, 1986.
19. Sumner DS, Lambeth A, Russell JB: Diagnosis of upper extremity obstructive and vasospastic syndromes by Doppler ultrasound, plethysmography, and temperature profiles. In Puel P, Boccalon H, Enjalbert A (eds): Hemodynamics of the Limbs 1. Toulouse, France, GEPESC, 1979, pp 365-373.
20. Gross WS, Flanigan P, Kraft RO, et al: Chronic upper extremity arterial insufficiency. Arch Surg 113:419, 1978.
21. Yao JST, Gourmos C, Pathanasiou K, et al: A method for assessing ischemia of the hands and fingers. Surg Gynecol Obstet 135:373, 1972.
22. Bartel P, Blackburn D, Peterson L, et al: The value of non-invasive tests in occupational trauma of the hands and fingers. Bruit 8:15, 1984.
23. Downs AR, Gaskell P, Morrow I, et al: Assessment of arterial obstruction in vessels supplying the fingers by measurement of local blood pressures and the skin temperature response test: Correlation with angiographic evidence. Surgery 77:530, 1975.
24. Gundersen J: Segmental measurements of systolic blood pressure in the extremities including the thumb and the great toe. Acta Chir Scand 426(Suppl):1, 1972.
25. Hirai M: Arterial insufficiency of the hand evaluated by digital blood pressure and arteriographic findings. Circulation 58:902, 1978.
26. Nielsen PE, Bell G, Lassen NA: The measurement of digital systolic blood pressure by strain gauge technique. Scand J Clin Lab Invest 29:371, 1972.
27. Salem ME-S, El-Girby AH, El-Moneim NAA, et al: Value of finger arterial blood pressure in diagnosis of vascular changes in some connective tissue diseases. Angiology 44:183, 1993.
28. Hirai M, Ohta T, Shionoya S: Development of a bladder-free cuff for measuring the blood pressure of the fingers and toes. Circulation 61:704, 1980.
29. Manke DA, Sumner DS, Van Beek AL, et al: Hemodynamic studies of digital and extremity replants or revascularizations. Surgery 88:445, 1980.
30. Mozersky DJ, Buckley CJ, Hagood Co Jr, et al: Ultrasonic evaluation of the palmar circulation: A useful adjunct to radial artery cannulation, Am J Surg 126:810, 1973.
31. Balas P, Katsogiannis A, Katsiotis P, et al: Comparative study of evaluation of digital arterial circulation by Doppler ultrasonic tracing and hand arteriography. J Cardiovasc Surg 21:455, 1980.
32. Hutchison DT: Color duplex imaging: Applications to upper extremity and microvascular surgery. Hand Clin 9:47, 1993.
33. Koman LA, Bond MG, Carter RE, et al: Evaluation of upper extremity vasculature with high resolution ultrasound. J Hand Surg 10:249, 1985.
34. Payne MP, Blackburn DR, Peterson LK, et al: B-mode imaging of the hand and upper extremity. Bruit 10:168, 1986.
35. Trager S, Pignatoro M, Anderson J, et al: Color flow Doppler: Imaging the upper extremity. J Hand Surg 18:621, 1993.
36. Jones CE, Anderson FA Jr, Cardullo PA: Duplex ultrasound evaluation of radial artery diameter and hemodynamics before and after placement of a radial artery cannula. J Vasc Technol 15:181, 1991.
37. Nehler MR, Dalman RL, Harris EJ, et al: Upper extremity arterial bypass distal to the wrist. J Vasc Surg 16:633, 1992.
38. Langholz J, Ladleif M, Blank B, et al: Colour coded duplex sonography in ischemic finger artery disease: A comparison with hand arteriography. Vasa 26:85, 1997.
39. DiGiacomo RA, Kremer JM, Shah DM: Fish-oil dietary supplementation in patients with Raynaud's phenomenon: A double-blind, controlled, prospective study. Am J Med 86:158, 1989.
40. Rademaker M, Cooke ED, Almond NE, et al: Comparison of intravenous infusions of iloprost and oral nifedipine in treatment of Raynaud's phenomenon in patients with systemic sclerosis: A double blind randomized study. Br Med J 298:561, 1989.

41. Sumner DS, Strandness DE Jr: An abnormal finger pulse associated with cold sensitivity. Ann Surg 175:294, 1972.

42. Ohgi S, Moore DJ, Miles RD, et al: Physiology of the peaked finger pulse in normal and cold-sensitive subjects. J Vasc Surg 3:516, 1986.

43. Thulesius O: Methods for the evaluation of peripheral vascular function in the upper extremities. Acta Chir Scand 465(Suppl):53, 1975.

44. Hertzman AB, Roth LW: The reactions of the digital artery and minute pad arteries to local cold. Am J Physiol 136:680, 1942.

45. Peller JS, Gabor GT, Porter JM, et al: Angiographic findings in mixed connective tissue disease: Correlation with fingernail capillary photomicroscopy and digital photoplethysmography findings. Arthritis Rheum 28:768, 1985.

46. Zweifler AJ, Trinkaus P: Occlusive digital artery disease in patients with Raynaud's phenomenon. Am J Med 77:995, 1984.

47. Alexander S, Cummings C, Figg-Hoblyn L, et at: Usefulness of digital peaked pulse for diagnosis of Raynaud's syndrome. J Vasc Technol 12:71, 1988.

48. Huff SE: Observations on peripheral circulation in various dermatoses. Arch Dermatol 71:575, 1955.

49. Holmgren K, Bauer GM, Porter JM: Vascular laboratory evaluation of Raynaud's syndrome. Bruit 5:19, 1981.

50. Edwards JM, Porter JM: Diagnosis of upper extremity vasospastic disease. In Ernst CB, Stanley JC (eds): Current Therapy in Vascular Surgery, 2nd ed. Philadelphia, BC Decker, 1991, pp 186-190.

51. Janoff KA, Phinney ES, Porter JM: Lumbar sympathectomy for lower extremity vasospasm. Am J Surg 150:147, 1985.

52. McLafferty RB, Edwards JM, Taylor LM Jr, et al: Diagnosis and long-term clinical outcome in patients diagnosed with hand ischemia. J Vasc Surg 22:361, 1995.

53. Burch GE: Digital Plethysmography. New York, Grune & Stratton, 1954.

54. Honda N: The periodicity in volume fluctuations and blood flow in the human finger. Angiology 21:442, 1970.

55. Browse NL, Hardwick PJ: The deep breath-venoconstriction reflex. Clin Sci 37:125, 1969.

56. Delius W, Kellerova E: Reactions of arterial and venous vessels in the human forearm and hand to deep breath or mental strain. Clin Sci 40:271, 1971.

57. Sumner DS: Mercury strain-gauge plethysmography. In Bernstein EF (ed): Noninvasive Diagnostic Techniques in Vascular Disease, 3rd ed. St. Louis, CV Mosby, 1985, pp 133-150.

58. Porter JM, Snider RL, Bardana EJ, et al: The diagnosis and treatment of Raynaud's phenomenon. Surgery 77:11, 1975.

59. Hoare M, Miles C, Girvan R, et al: The effect of local cooling on digital systolic pressure in patients with Raynaud's syndrome. Br J Surg 69(Suppl):527, 1982.

60. Nielsen SL, Lassen NA: Measurement of digital blood pressure after local cooling. J Appl Physiol 43:907, 1977.

61. Corbin DOC, Wood DA, Housley E: An evaluation of finger systolic pressure response to local cooling in the diagnosis of primary Raynaud's phenomenon. Clin Physiol 5:383, 1985.

62. Maricq HR, Spencer-Green G, LeRoy EC: Skin capillary abnormalities as indicators of organ involvement in scleroderma (systemic sclerosis), Raynaud's syndrome and dermatomyositis. Am J Med 61:862, 1976.

63. Naidu S, Baskerville PA, Goss DE, et al: Raynaud's phenomenon and cold stress testing: A new approach. Eur J Vasc Surg 8:567, 1994.

64. Sumner DS: Noninvasive assessment of upper extremity and hand ischemia. J Vasc Surg 3:560, 1986.

65. Barnes RW, Peterson JL, Krugmire RB, et al: Complications of brachial artery catheterization: Prospective evaluation with the Doppler velocity detector. Chest 66:363, 1974.

66. Jones CE, Anderson FA Jr, Cardullo PA: Duplex ultrasound evaluation of radial artery diameter and hemodynamics before and after placement of a radial artery cannula. J Vasc Technol 15:181, 1991.

67. Machleder HI, Sweeney JP, Barker WF: Pulseless arm after brachial artery catheterization. Lancet 1(7747):407, 1972.

68. Berguer R, Higgins R, Nelson R: Noninvasive diagnosis of reversal of vertebral-artery blood flow. N Engl J Med 302:1349, 1980.

69. Corson JD, Menzoian JO, LoGerfo FW: Reversal of vertebral artery blood flow demonstrated by Doppler ultrasound. Arch Surg 112:715, 1977.

70. Mozersky DJ, Barnes RW, Sumner DS, et al: Hemodynamics of innominate artery occlusion. Ann Surg 178:123, 1973.

71. Gelabert HA, Machleder HI: Diagnosis and management of arterial compression at the thoracic outlet. Ann Vasc Surg 11:359, 1997.

72. McCarthy WJ, Yao JST, Schafer MF, et al: Upper extremity arterial injury in athletes. J Vasc Surg 9:317, 1989.

73. Abshire J, Fruscha JD, Jones TR, Schellack JV: Demonstration of hypothenar hammer syndrome by duplex ultrasound. J Vasc Technol 16:39, 1992.

74. McNamara MF, Takaki HS, Yao JST, et al: A systematic approach to severe hand ischemia. Surgery 83:1, 1978.

75. Hirai M: Digital blood pressure and arteriographic findings under selective compression of the radial and ulnar arteries. Angiology 31:21, 1980.

76. Dabich L, Bookstein JJ, Zweifler A, et al: Digital arteries in patients with scleroderma: Arteriographic and plethysmographic study. Arch Intern Med 130:708, 1972.

77. Mills JL, Friedman EI, Taylor LM Jr, et al: Upper extremity ischemia caused by small artery disease. Ann Surg 206:521, 1987.

78. Tordoir JHM, Haeck LB, Winterkamp H, et al: Multifinger photo-plethysmography and digital blood pressure measurement in patients with Raynaud's phenomenon of the hand. J Vasc Surg 3:456, 1986.

79. Preliminary criteria for the classification of systemic sclerosis (scleroderma). Subcommittee for Scleroderma Criteria of the American Rheumatism Association Diagnostic and Therapeutic Criteria Committee. Arthritis Rheum 23:581, 1980.

80. Kallenberg CGM, Pastoor GW, Wouda AA, et al: Antinuclear antibodies in patients with Raynaud's phenomenon: Clinical significance of anticentromere antibodies. Ann Rheum Dis 41:382, 1982.

81. Priollet P, Vayssairat M, Housset E: How to classify Raynaud's phenomenon: Long-term follow-up study of 73 cases. Am J Med 83:494, 1987.

82. Yadin O, Sarov B, Naggan L, et al: Natural autoantibodies in the serum of healthy women: A five-year follow-up. Clin Exp Immunol 75:402, 1989.

83. Fitzgerald O, O'Connor GT, Spencer-Green G: Prospective study of the evolution of Raynaud's phenomenon. Am J Med 84:718, 1988.

84. Pardy BJ, Hoare MC, Eastcott HHG, et al: Prostaglandin El in severe Raynaud's phenomenon. Surgery 92:953, 1982.

85. Roald OK, Seem E: Treatment of Raynaud's phenomenon with ketanserin in patients with connective tissue disorders. Br Med J 289:577, 1984.

86. Rodeheffer RJ, Rommer JA, Wigley F, et al: Controlled double-blind trial of nifedipine in the treatment of Raynaud's phenomenon. N Engl J Med 308:880, 1983.

87. Welling RE, Cranley JJ, Krause RJ, et al: Obliterative arterial disease of the upper extremity. Arch Surg 116:1593, 1981.

88. Graafsma SJ, Wollersheim H, Droste HT, et al: Adrenoceptors on blood cells from patients with primary Raynaud's phenomenon. Clin Sci 80:325, 1991.

89. Nobin BA, Nielsen SL, Eklov B, et al: Reserpine treatment of Raynaud's disease. Ann Surg 87:12, 1978.

90. Mohrland JS, Porter JM, Kahaleh MB, et al: A multiclinic, placebo-controlled, double-blind study of prostaglandin E1 in Raynaud's syndrome. Ann Rheum Dis 44:754, 1985.

91. Creager MA, Pariser KM, Winston EM, et al: Nifedipine-induced fingertip vasodilation in patients with Raynaud's phenomenon. Am Heart J 108:370, 1984.

Brachiocephalic Vessel Reconstruction

MARK D. MORASCH, MD
RAMON BERGUER, MD, PhD

Atherosclerotic occlusive disease involving the branches of the aortic arch is common in patients older than 65 years. The Joint Study of Arterial Occlusions reported that one third of patients undergoing arteriography are found to have significant lesions involving one or more of the vessels supplying blood to the head and arms.[1] Occlusive diseases affecting the supra-aortic trunks (SATs) make up a relatively small fraction of these lesions, however. Nonetheless, a number of well-recognized and well-documented ischemic manifestations of occlusive and aneurysmal diseases affect the SAT in the cerebral hemispheric, ocular, vertebrobasilar, upper extremity, and cardiac vascular territories.

Surgical SAT revascularization for both cerebrovascular and noncerebrovascular indications, including upper extremity ischemia, is performed relatively rarely. Repair of occlusive lesions of the SATs accounts for less than 10% of the operations performed on the extracranial cerebral vasculature. Reconstruction for aneurysms involving the SAT is even more uncommon. Nevertheless, and despite the fact that these vessels are relatively difficult to image noninvasively, substantive data have accumulated about the natural history of these diseases, and significant experience with surgical SAT reconstruction has accrued over the past four decades. In addition, after two decades of experience with endoluminal therapy for treatment of SAT disease, some useful data have become available.

■ HISTORY OF REPAIR

Savory was the first to describe a patient with signs and symptoms suggesting occlusive disease involving the SATs.[2] Twenty years later, in 1875, Broadbent[3] chronicled a patient who, while living, had no radial pulses and at postmortem examination was found to have brachiocephalic and left subclavian artery occlusion. In 1908, Takayasu[4] reported a patient with an ischemic retinopathy on ophthalmologic examination who later was found to have occlusive lesions in all three SATs from a chronic inflammatory process that Shimizu and Sano[5] later called "pulseless disease." The inflammatory arteritis involving the arch branches now bears Takayasu's name. In 1960, Contorni[6] was the first to describe the anatomy of subclavian artery steal.

The first surgical procedures used to treat diseases of the SAT were performed for aneurysmal changes in these vessels, most of which were syphilitic subclavian lesions. The first attempt at surgical correction of a proximal sub-

clavian aneurysm, by innominate ligation, was carried out by Valentine Mott in 1818[7]; unfortunately, the patient did not survive long. A.W. Smyth has been credited with the first successful proximal ligation for a subclavian artery aneurysm in 1864.[8] Halsted[9] combined arterial ligation with subclavian aneurysm resection in 1892, and the first successful subclavian aneurysm resection was performed by Braithwaite in 1920.[10] Subclavian aneurysm resection followed by replacement bypass grafting was first reported by Bjork[11] in 1965.

Henry T. Bahnson[12] was the first to perform a bypass from the ascending aortic arch to the innominate artery (IA) using an aortic homograft in a patient with occlusive lesions from syphilitic arteritis.[12] One year later, in 1954, Davis and colleagues[13] described endarterectomy of an IA through a right anterior thoracotomy for a symptomatic atherosclerotic occlusive lesion. Endarterectomy to reestablish flow through obliterated subclavian vessels was described by Cate and Scott[14] in 1957. In 1956, Lyons and Galbraith[15] first reported a series of four subclavian–carotid artery bypasses from a cervical approach, and, in 1964, Parrott[16] described two subclavian–carotid transpositions performed through a similar exposure. In 1994, Berguer and colleagues[17] described transcervical extra-anatomic revascularization of the SAT via a retropharyngeal route.

The first reports of subclavian artery angioplasty were published by Bachman and Kim[18] and Mathias and coworkers[19] in 1980, and retrograde endoluminal techniques for stenting innominate and common carotid occlusive lesions were reported by Queral and Criado[20] in 1996. The first successful usage of stent-graft technology in a human was completed by Becker and associates[21] for the treatment of a post-traumatic subclavian artery pseudoaneurysm in 1991, and a single-center series reporting successful treatment of SAT aneurysms using endografts was published by Hilfiker and colleagues[22] in 2000.

■ ANATOMY

The SAT normally develops as three separate trunks, taking origin from the arch of the aorta within the superior mediastinum. The conventional definition of the SAT includes the innominate artery, the subclavian arteries to involve the origins of the vertebral arteries, and the common carotid arteries proximal to their bifurcations. The innominate artery and the left common carotid artery originate in close proximity to each other and ascend in the neck on either side of the trachea. The brachiocephalic venous trunk crosses the mediastinum anterior to the origins of these vessels. The left subclavian artery, the third of three trunks, originates posterior to and to the left of the left common carotid. The vagus and right recurrent laryngeal nerves cross the anterior aspect of the right subclavian artery adjacent to the innominate bifurcation (Fig. 91-1). On the

left, the vagus and phrenic nerves cross each other between the left common carotid and left subclavian arteries under the cover of the pleura.

Anatomic variations are common, seen in 20% to 30% of patients (Fig. 91-2). Bergman and associates[23] observed that there may be as few as one great vessel or as many as six trunks arising from the transverse aorta. The most common variation is the bovine-type aortic arch, in which the first and second branches (innominate and left carotid) arise from a common ostium (16%) or as a single trunk (8%). The vertebral artery can also be found to take origin as a separate branch arising from the aortic arch. This configuration usually involves the left vertebral artery alone; this vessel takes origin between the left common carotid and left subclavian arteries in 6% of the population.

Developmental anomalies of the trunk vessels are less common. The arch configuration with an aberrant right subclavian artery that arises as the fourth of four vessels occurs in approximately 0.5% to 1.0% of individuals.[24] A so-called truncus bicarotidus, in which the two carotid arteries take origin together and the two subclavian vessels arise as one in a two-trunk configuration, occurs even less commonly. Retroesophageal subclavian arteries (RSAs), which are always found in association with these two configurations, occur with the same incidence, approximately 0.5% to 0.7% (Fig. 91-3).[25,26] In most cases, the aberrant vessel passes behind the esophagus, although it can course between the esophagus and the trachea or even anterior to the trachea.[27] In rare cases, certain symptom complexes, including dysphagia (dysphagia lusoria) and chronic cough (from tracheal compression), can develop in patients with developmental errors and aberrant right subclavian artery anatomy. Adjacent to the origin of an aberrant right subclavian artery, there may be congenital dilatation of the wall, called a *diverticulum of Kommerell*. This aortic wall outpouching is a remnant of the developmental right fourth aortic arch. The right inferior laryngeal nerve is not "recurrent" in patients with an aberrant right subclavian artery; instead the nerve exits the vagus higher in

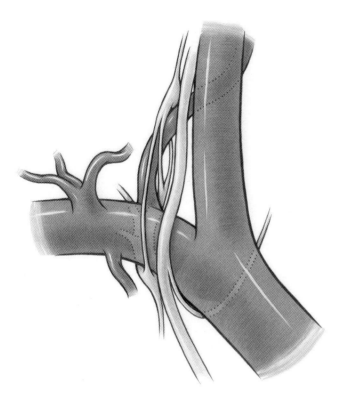

FIGURE 91-1 Course of the normal right recurrent laryngeal nerve. (From Berguer R, Kieffer E: Surgery of the Arteries to the Head. New York, Springer-Verlag, 1992.)

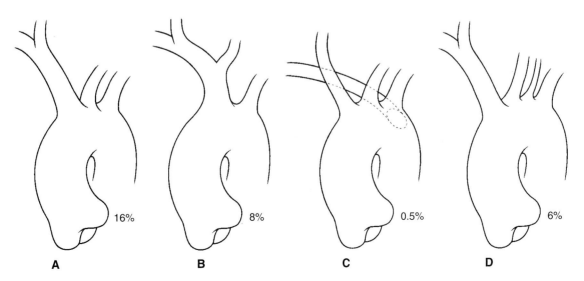

FIGURE 91-2 Common anomalies of the supra-aortic trunk, with percentage distribution. **A** and **B,** Bovine configuration. **C,** Aberrant right subclavian artery. **D,** Aortic origin on left vertebral artery. (From Berguer R, Kieffer E: Surgery of the Arteries to the Head. New York, Springer-Verlag, 1992.)

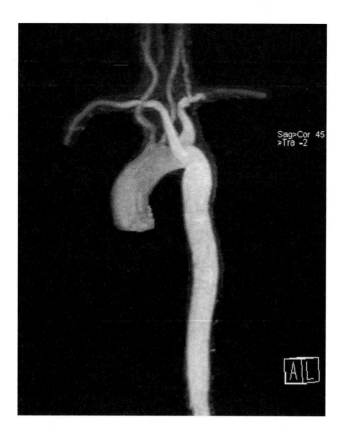

FIGURE 91-3 Magnetic resonance angiograph demonstrating an aberrant right subclavian artery as the fourth of four trunks.

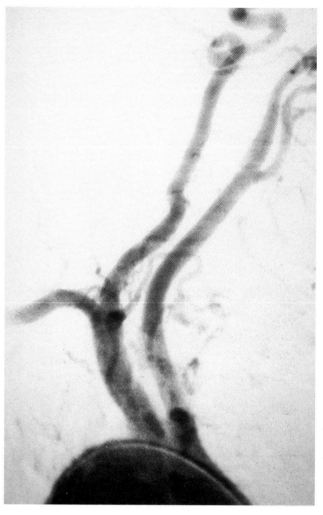

FIGURE 91-4 Aplasia of the innominate artery in a patient with a right-sided arch.

the neck and takes a more direct route to the larynx, resting on the wall of the common carotid artery. A thoracic duct that empties into the right jugulosubclavian confluence should also be expected.

Developmental anomalies can also be found in conjunction with a right-sided or a double aortic arch. A right-sided aortic arch is a rare congenital defect, occurring in 0.05% to 0.1% of individuals in radiologic and autopsy series.[28,29] A mirror image of the left arch configuration occurs in most individuals with a right-sided arch, but a right-sided arch with an aberrant left subclavian vessel can also occur. Right-sided arch anomalies are usually associated with congenital cardiac abnormalities, but they can develop in isolation as well.[30,31] Individuals with a right-sided aortic arch can have involution of the remainder of the left-sided aortic arch, resulting in hypoplasia or absence of the IA (Fig. 91-4). The latter vessel is embryologically part of the left aortic arch (between ascending aorta and left subclavian artery). Another rare anomaly is isolation of the left subclavian artery, in which the subclavian vessel is not in continuity with the aorta at all but, instead, exits through collateral flow and is tethered to the pulmonary artery by the ligamentum arteriosum (Fig. 91-5).

■ DISEASES OF THE SUPRA-AORTIC TRUNK

Atherosclerosis is, by far, the most common disease affecting the SAT vessels. Occlusive lesions less commonly result from inflammatory diseases such as Takayasu's

arteritis or exposure to therapeutic irradiation. The SAT vessels also can dissect or become aneurysmal. More distally, the subclavian arteries can be damaged from the long-term effects of thoracic outlet syndrome.

Symptoms from nonatherosclerotic diseases such as Takayasu's or radiation-induced arteritis, dissections, aneurysm, and congenital lesions account for less than 20% of the disease that requires intervention.[32-35,83] The more common atherosclerotic lesions tend to cause occlusive and embolic symptoms equally, whereas vessel obliteration from arteritis generally causes symptoms related to hemodynamic insufficiency.

Occlusive lesions involving the SATs develop in a younger age group than atherosclerotic occlusive lesions elsewhere in the extracranial cerebrovascular circulation. Mean and median ages are commonly reported to range from 50 to 61 years. Single-vessel atherosclerotic occlusive disease involving the SAT is often seen in younger adults (fifth decade), but patients with extensive or multiple trunk involvement tend to be older. The usual male preponderance noted with other atherosclerotic vascular conditions may not be found with disease of the SAT. Berguer and colleagues[32,33] reported that women were treated in 53% of

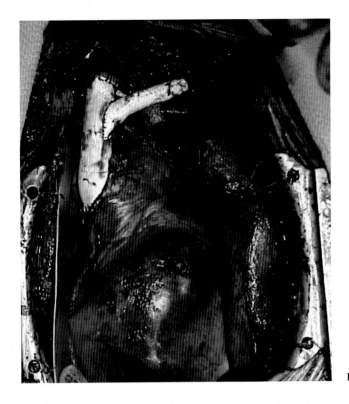

FIGURE 91-18   Aorto-innominate artery–left carotid artery bypass.

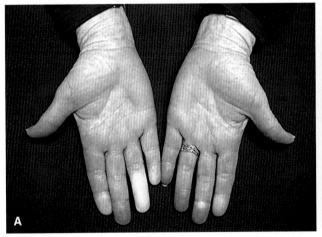

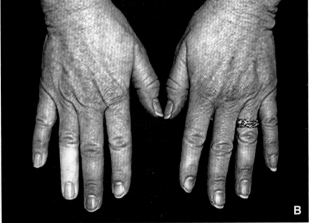

FIGURE 93-1   Top (**A**) and palms (**B**) of hands of patient with a textbook example of Raynaud's syndrome. Note that attacks of digital vasospasm cause well-demarcated pallor or cyanosis affecting one or more fingers brought on by cold exposure or emotional stress.

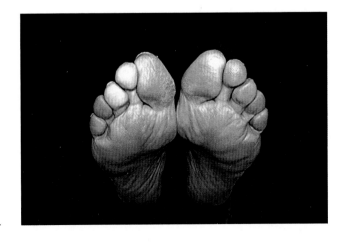

FIGURE 93-3   Digital vasospasm can affect the toes as well as the fingers.

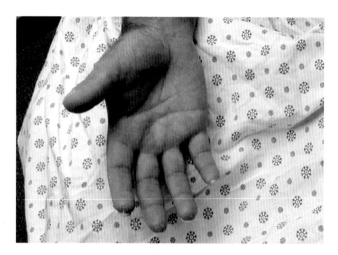

FIGURE 93-5 Systemic sclerosis. Raynaud's syndrome secondary to limited systemic sclerosis in a young male patient. There is cyanotic discoloration of the right third and fourth fingers. The diagnosis of scleroderma can be made by physical examination. There is resorption of the end of the distal right index finger with healed ulcerations of several fingertips.

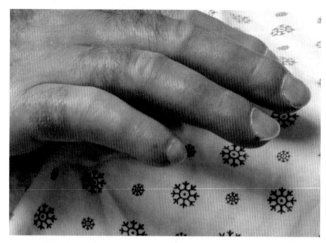

FIGURE 93-9 CREST (*c*alcinosis, *R*aynaud's, *e*sophageal dysmotility, *s*clerodactyly, *t*elangiectasia) syndrome. A pathognomonic finding in systemic sclerosis is sclerodactyly and telangiectasia of the finger.

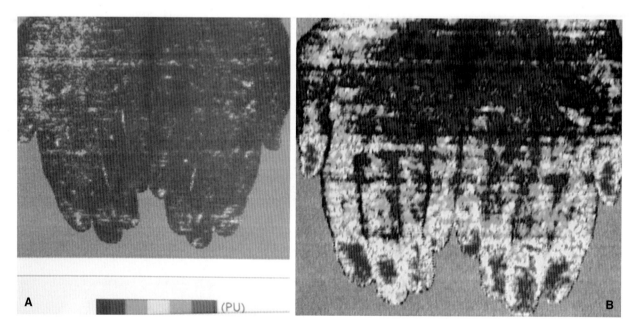

FIGURE 93-19 Scanning laser Doppler imaging shows low laser Doppler flow due to vasospasm (**A**). After warming the hands (**B**), a marked increase in digital blood flow is seen. On examination, the fingers were cool, with resting digital temperatures of 28° C. Physical examination was normal, and there was no evidence of occlusive arterial disease. Blood tests, including complete blood count, sedimentation rate, cryoglobulin, antinuclear antibody, and extractable nuclear antigens all were negative. This patient was diagnosed with primary Raynaud's syndrome and treated with a long-acting nifedipine medication.

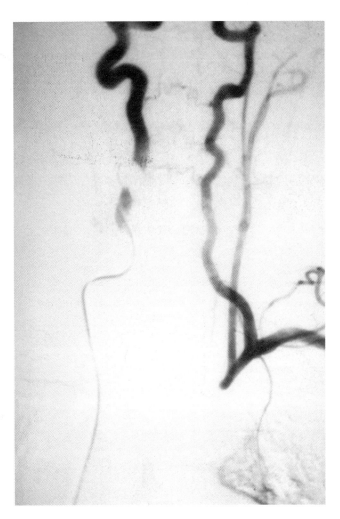

FIGURE 91-5 Isolation of the left subclavian artery.

cases in their series. In contrast, Kieffer and associates[34] noted that only 18% of patients in their large surgical series were women.

Cigarette smoking is certainly a significant risk factor for the development of atherosclerotic occlusive disease involving these vessels. Smoking is identified as a risk factor in 82% of all patients who require intervention for SAT atherosclerosis.[33] Concomitant coronary artery disease (CAD) is present in one fourth to two thirds of patients who present for SAT reconstruction. In one report, 63% of patients had significant CAD, and 15% of patients had undergone a previous myocardial revascularization.[33] In the same report, 47% of patients undergoing transthoracic reconstruction were hypertensive, and a smaller proportion (15%) were diabetic.

Atherosclerotic occlusive disease involving the SAT can be either unifocal or multifocal, involving just one or more than one trunk vessel. In addition, the distribution of atherosclerosis within a single vessel can often be segmental in nature. Severe disease is defined as stenosis of more than 75% of vessel diameter. In addition, in symptomatic patients, a deep ulcerated plaque or a thrombus within the arterial lumen is also considered a severe lesion even though the defect may be less than 75% of the diameter. Severe

lesions can be seen developing focally within and isolated to a single vessel. Alternatively, when the disease is seen in multiple trunks, the occlusive process is likely an extension of disease originating within the aortic arch that has "spilled over" into the vessel ostia. In the series of 282 transthoracic and cervical revascularizations of the SAT reported by Berguer and colleagues,[32,33] significant disease was present in more than a single vessel in 40% of cases. All three of the trunks were critically diseased in 13%. Revascularization of unifocal disease was necessary in 60% of cases. When disease was limited to one trunk, the left subclavian artery was the vessel most commonly found to be involved with disease.

When multiple trunks are involved, patients usually experience symptoms of vertebrobasilar ischemia from low flow. Single-trunk disease manifests more commonly as symptoms from hemispheric or upper extremity emboli. Isolated proximal disease within the subclavian artery can lead to symptomatic subclavian-vertebral steal, whereas innominate occlusion can result in steal from the anterior cerebral circulation (carotid-subclavian steal). Complete obliteration of the common carotid lumen can occur in a retrograde fashion after occlusion of the carotid bifurcation and internal carotid artery. Alternatively, an occlusion originating in a lesion in the proximal common carotid artery propagates distally up to the bifurcation. The internal carotid artery, not uncommonly, remains patent in this situation. Duplex ultrasonographic scans or delayed arteriographic images may show that the internal carotid artery is perfused anterograde via retrograde external carotid flow.

The traditional description of aneurysms of the SATs refers to those of syphilitic etiology. Nowadays, aneurysms of syphilitic origin have virtually disappeared. Most of the aneurysms of the innominate or left common carotid arteries encountered today are associated with concomitant dilatation of either the proximal ascending aorta or the thoracoabdominal aorta. An aneurysm of the innominate or proximal common carotid artery that does not involve the ostium is exceedingly rare but, because of the lack of association with aneurysmal disease of the ascending aorta, is the easiest to repair. An occasional aneurysm involving the innominate or common carotid arteries can be seen in association with Takayasu's disease.

Subclavian artery aneurysms, on the other hand, do occur with some frequency. It has been estimated that true subclavian aneurysms account for more than 0.1% of all aneurysms[36] and for 2% of all peripheral aneurysms with most subclavian dilatation involving the middle or distal third of the vessel.[37] Subclavian aneurysms can develop proximally (intrathoracic aneurysms) or distally (extrathoracic aneurysms). Extrathoracic subclavian aneurysms usually develop distal to the vertebral artery origin and manifest in the form of a post-stenotic dilatation or as the result of repetitive trauma to the artery in patients with arterial thoracic outlet syndrome (Fig. 91-6).[38] Aneurysms that involve the proximal third of the subclavian artery when they develop in a normally configured SAT are usually related to atherosclerosis. Other causes of proximal subclavian aneurysm formation are infection (including those that are the result of syphilis or tuberculosis), cystic medial necrosis, Marfan's syndrome, and a few other, rare genetic disorders. Aneurysms found anywhere in the SAT

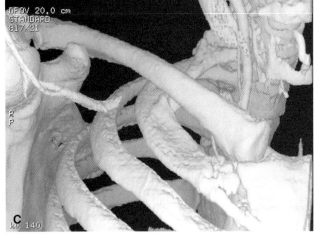
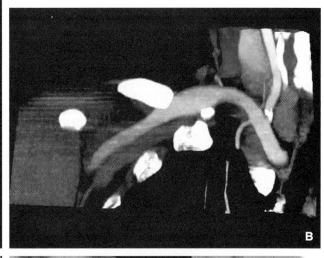
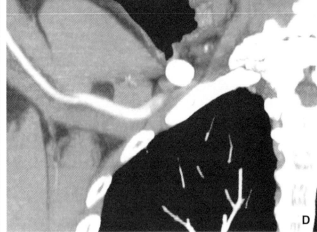

FIGURE 91-6 Reconstructed three-dimensional computed tomography. Shaded-surface display projection (**A**) and maximum intensity projection (**B**) demonstrate subclavian aneurysm with arm in a neutral position. **C** and **D,** Same imaging techniques used to show aneurysm compression and subclavian artery obliteration between the clavicle and first rib in a patient with arterial thoracic outlet syndrome.

have the potential to thrombose, embolize, and cause symptoms from local compression or rupture.

Post-traumatic false aneurysms or short-segment dissections of the SAT are uncommon and are usually the result of rupture of the intima-media complex during deceleration in motor vehicle accidents (Fig. 91-7). Blunt traumatic pseudoaneurysms usually involve the origin of the IA. Penetrating traumatic pseudoaneurysms often involve the mid-subclavian artery and follow iatrogenic attempts at subclavian vein puncture.

Approximately 5% of retroesophageal subclavian arteries produce symptoms.[39] The most common symptoms are dysphagia. The most frequent type of disease found in an aberrant RSA is atherosclerosis although traumatic, dysplastic, and infectious lesions have also been reported. The most serious problems in patients with congenitally anomalous anatomy such as RSA are related to development of aneurysmal disease. These lesions usually involve the diverticulum at the origin of this artery (Kommerell's diverticulum). Aneurysms that involve only the middle or

distal segment of an RSA are fairly rare and are usually atherosclerotic in nature. As with other aneurysms involving the normal SAT, RSA aneurysms can lead to serious complications as a result of thromboembolism, compressive syndromes, or rupture.

Takayasu's arteritis frequently involves all three SAT vessels proximally. The true etiology of this nonspecific inflammatory disease has not been elucidated, but the disorder is known to predominantly affect women in their second or third decades of life. The hypertrophic occlusive lesions of Takayasu's disease usually have smooth surfaces with low embolic potential, and most symptoms relate to low flow as the disease progresses to multivessel occlusion (Fig. 91-8). The histopathologic appearance of the lesions depends on the phase of the disease. They appear intensely inflammatory during the acute phase and more sclerotic when the disease is "burned out." The inflammatory process is characterized by fibrosis and thickening of the arterial wall, with pathologic changes usually most noticeable in the adventitial and medial layers of the involved vessels.

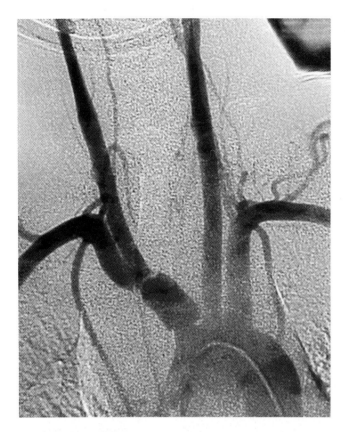

FIGURE 91-7 Traumatic innominate injury.

Aneurysmal changes with embolic potential can develop during the chronic phase of the disease. The incidence of Takayasu's disease has been estimated at 2.6 cases per million per year in North America,[40] approximately one tenth that of giant cell disease.

Giant cell arteritis rarely affects the proximal SAT. Occasionally it does involve the more distal subclavian arteries and can be differentiated from Takayasu's on the basis of both its location and the fact that it affects a much older patient population.

The SAT can develop an accelerated form of atherosclerosis as a result of radiation injury to the vessels (Fig. 91-9). The rate at which the process develops depends on the radiation dose range. The SAT may be involved after radiotherapy for, among other diseases, breast cancer, intrathoracic tumors, or Hodgkin's lymphoma.

Nontraumatic isolated SAT dissection is rare but can occur and can cause symptoms.[41-48] More commonly, type A aortic arch dissections occur and may disrupt or extend into the trunk vessels, impinging upon cerebrovascular or upper extremity flow or prompting local thrombus, which can embolize. As with dissections elsewhere, chronic aneurysmal changes can develop later as a result, but rarely.

■ DIAGNOSIS

Physical examination remains the most important screening modality. Bilateral brachial artery cuff pressure measurement, palpation of upper extremity, carotid, and superficial temporal pulses, and auscultation for subclavian or carotid bruits should be performed at every initial patient

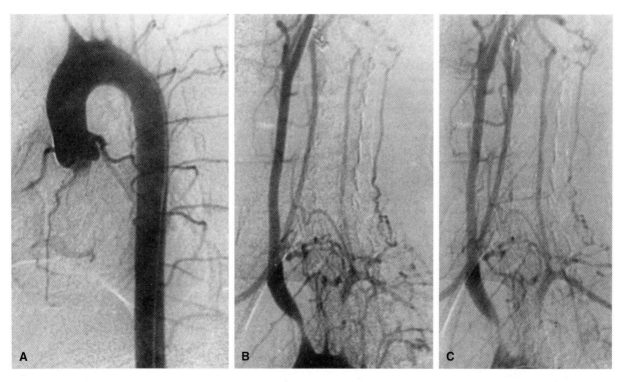

FIGURE 91-8 Young woman with severe, symptomatic Takayasu's arteritis. (From Berguer R, Kieffer E: Surgery of the Arteries to the Head. New York, Springer-Verlag, 1992.)

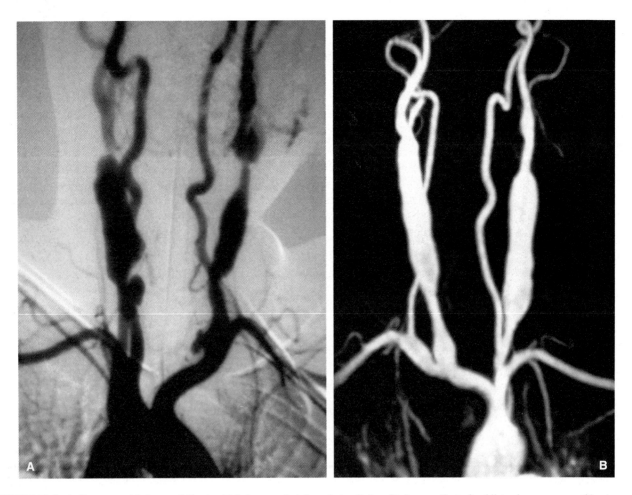

FIGURE 91-9 A, Severe arterial damage following high-dose cervical thoracic irradiation. **B,** Same patient after bilateral common carotid vein graft replacement of vessels damaged by radiation.

encounter. Duplex scanning of the aortic arch is utilized in some centers as a screening tool for SAT disease, but ultrasound findings can be difficult to interpret because insonation through the bony structures of the mediastinum requires the skills of an experienced technologist. Once a diagnosis has been established, multiplanar views of the aortic arch utilizing digital subtraction angiography are still considered by many authorities to be a necessary tool for planning SAT revascularization. A complete arch and four-vessel study should be performed with specific emphasis on the vessel's origins and late views to demonstrate patent vascular anatomy through reconstitution from steal. Magnetic resonance (MR) (Fig. 91-10) and CT angiography are newer, noninvasive modalities with imaging capabilities that may soon overcome those of invasive angiography. These newer modalities provide multiplanar images that rival those of biplanar digital subtraction angiography. In our institution, gadolinium-enhanced MR angiography has already replaced digital subtraction angiography as the imaging modality of choice for SAT disease. In addition, CT provides excellent images of the SAT vessels within the chest and can also supply information about the extent of calcification in the aortic arch itself, which is important to know before placement of an aortic arch clamp.

A CT scan or MR image of the brain should also be

performed before SAT revascularization. Surgery should be delayed in patients with recent brain infarcts (symptomatic or silent), especially if multiple trunk revascularization is considered, to decrease the risk of reperfusion injury. It may also be useful to obtain transesophageal echocardiography (TEE) to assess myocardial function and to rule out a cardioembolic source. Also, like CT, TEE allows for the identification of significant calcific lesions or atheromas within the arch that would preclude aortic clamping or contraindicate passage of wires and catheters for antegrade endoluminal therapy.

Kieffer and associates[34] advocate routine coronary angiography in these patients because the incidence of coronary atherosclerosis approaches 40% and these researchers believe that, if transthoracic SAT reconstruction is indicated, concomitant coronary disease should be corrected at the same operation. However, Berguer and colleagues[32] reported a high incidence of complication in patients who underwent combined SAT and myocardial revascularization. If a cervical approach to trunk revascularization is planned, preoperative cardiac evaluation should follow guidelines similar to those for carotid bifurcation surgery. Cardiac evaluation prior to nonsurgical endovascular reconstruction is probably not necessary.

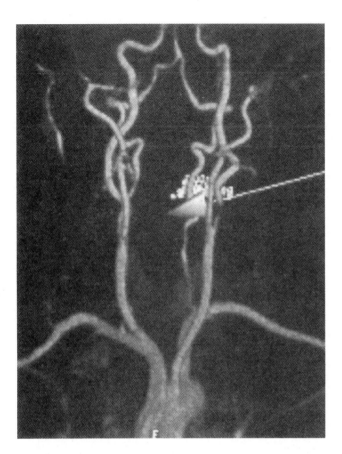

FIGURE 91-10 Gadolinium-enhanced arch and four-vessel magnetic resonance angiograph. (From Yao JST, Pearce WH [eds]: Modern Vascular Surgery. New York, McGraw-Hill, 2000.)

■ INDICATIONS FOR RECONSTRUCTION

Indications for revascularization of occlusive SAT disease are multiple. Symptomatic atherosclerotic disease may manifest as ocular, hemispheric, or vertebrobasilar transient ischemic attacks (TIAs), or stroke. Commonly, patients present with a combination of both anterior and posterior cerebrovascular ischemic symptoms. Cerebrovascular symptoms can be the result of emboli or low flow. In addition, patients can present with symptoms of isolated upper extremity ischemia. Patients may experience varying degrees of arm ischemia, ranging from the claudication observed in patients with subclavian steal to limb-threatening ischemia resulting from extensive arterial occlusion or emboli. Patients with subclavian steal syndrome, which results when blockage in the first portion of the subclavian artery causes distal pressure to drop below that at the vertebrobasilar junction, present with posterior cerebrovascular symptoms as blood is siphoned away from the basilar artery (Fig. 91-11). A similar but less common steal phenomenon can occur when the IA is occluded and flow in the common carotid and ipsilateral vertebral arteries is reversed to supply the right arm. Myocardial ischemia from the phenomenon of coronary steal is another indication for SAT repair. Coronary steal can develop in patients with innominate or subclavian disease proximal to an internal mammary revascularization of the coronary arteries.

Asymptomatic severe (>75% diameter) atherosclerotic lesions of the innominate or common carotid arteries should be repaired in patients in whom surgery presents a reasonable risk (including those with common carotid occlusion and a patent bifurcation) for the same reasons we repair asymptomatic severe carotid bifurcation stenoses.

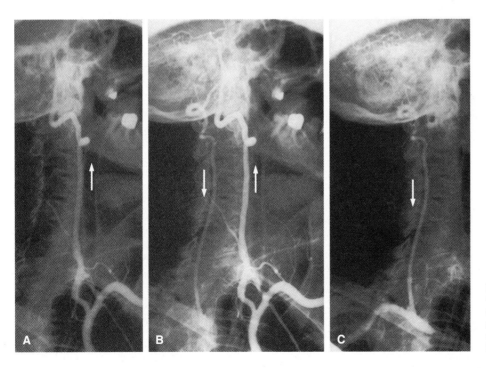

FIGURE 91-11 Proximal right subclavian artery occlusion accounts for radiographic evidence of subclavian vertebral steal. (From Berguer R, Kieffer E: Surgery of the Arteries to the Head. New York, Springer-Verlag, 1992.)

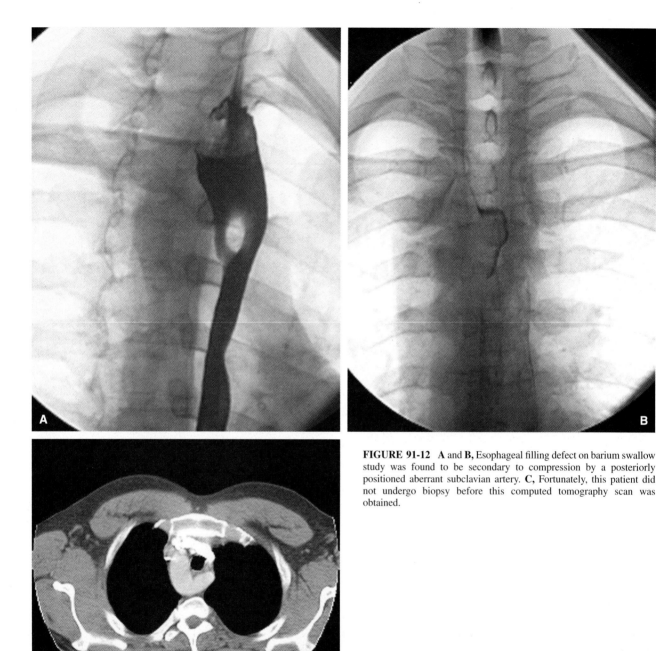

FIGURE 91-12 **A** and **B,** Esophageal filling defect on barium swallow study was found to be secondary to compression by a posteriorly positioned aberrant subclavian artery. **C,** Fortunately, this patient did not undergo biopsy before this computed tomography scan was obtained.

Asymptomatic lesions in the proximal subclavian artery should also be repaired in patients contemplating myocardial revascularization via an internal mammary artery and in patients with bilateral subclavian artery disease in order to permit and facilitate management of hypertension.

True asymptomatic degenerative aneurysms involving the normally configured SATs are very rare but, when found, should be repaired in patients for whom the risks of surgery are good to prevent emboli to the arm and brain or, less likely, vessel rupture.

In general, no operation should be undertaken in patients with Takayasu's arteritis whose disease is active. An active state is usually signaled by the presence of the constitutional symptoms associated with acute inflammation and an elevated erythrocyte sedimentation rate. Steroid therapy usually treats the acute inflammatory process and may make attempts at surgical reconstruction much safer. The indications for vascular reconstruction in patients with Takayasu's disease are the same as those for treating patients with atherosclerosis.

Rarely, patients with developmental anomalies involving the arch vessels require surgery to treat symptoms arising from esophageal (Fig. 91-12) or tracheal compression by a normal or aneurysmal RSA. Symptoms of dysphagia can

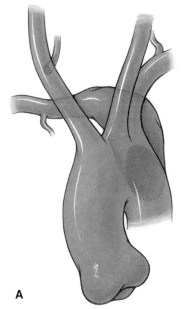

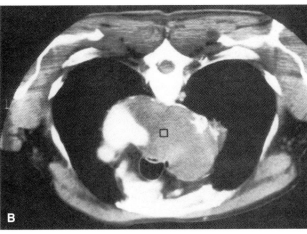

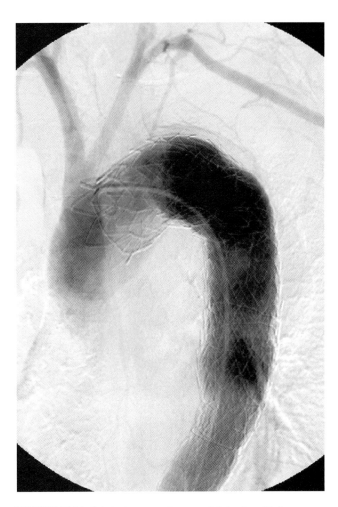

FIGURE 91-14 Subclavian artery transposed into site of left common carotid artery in a patient with bovine anatomy followed by thoracic aneurysm repair with an endograft.

FIGURE 91-13 A, Anatomy of aneurysmal aberrant subclavian artery. **B,** Aberrant vessel as seen on computed tomography scan. (From Berguer R, Kieffer E: Surgery of the Arteries to the Head. New York, Springer-Verlag, 1992.)

result from compression of the esophagus between the aortic arch anteriorly and the posteriorly positioned RSA. In children, compression by the RSA is exerted on the soft trachea and can result in upper respiratory obstruction. In most adults who present with dysphagia associated with RSA, the vessel has aneurysmal dilatation (Fig. 91-13). The mere presence of RSA is not an indication for surgical repair. Only RSAs that are symptomatic or have undergone significant aneurysmal degeneration should be considered for repair. It is accepted that asymptomatic aneurysms of RSA less than 4 cm in diameter should be observed.

Of particular note, in our institution over the last 5 years, the most common indication for surgical manipulation of the SAT has been to prepare patients with thoracic and thoracoabdominal aortic aneurysms, dissections, or traumatic tears for an endovascular stent-graft repair. Subclavian artery and even left common carotid artery transposi-

tions are not infrequently performed in order to preserve vertebral and left upper extremity flow while extending the proximal neck "landing zone" before endograft deployment (Fig. 91-14).

■ DISEASE TREATMENT

Three broad-based approaches have been developed for the treatment of SAT lesions, each with distinct advantages and disadvantages; they are direct transthoracic reconstruction, remote cervical reconstruction, and endovascular recanalization. Transthoracic revascularization may be chosen in patients who are good candidates for surgery and have isolated innominate artery stenosis or occlusion and in patients with disease that involves multiple trunks. Remote cervical and endovascular techniques are alternatives to direct reconstruction and should be considered in patients with single-vessel disease that involves the carotid or subclavian arteries and in patients who have previously undergone a median sternotomy or who have prohibitive medical co-morbidity.

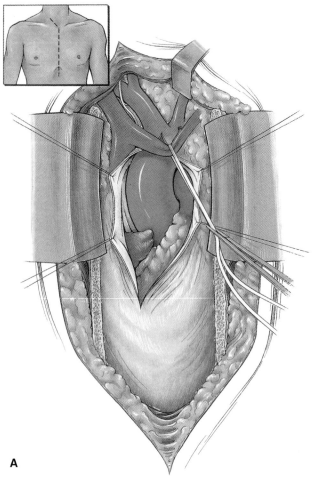

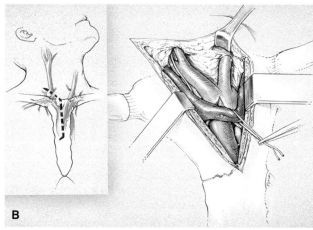

FIGURE 91-15 A, Exposure of the supra-aortic trunk through full median sternotomy. **B,** Upper partial sternotomy. (From Berguer R, Kieffer E: Surgery of the Arteries to the Head. New York, Springer-Verlag, 1992.)

Unfortunately, most researchers who report on the surgical treatment of SAT disease combine the many indications for reconstruction and data from both cervical and transthoracic approaches together, making accurate assessment difficult.[49-54] Furthermore, papers that discuss endovascular options are heavily weighted toward the treatment of subclavian disease. Often, fair comparisons cannot be made because the characteristics of the lesions (multiple vs. single, hemodynamic vs. embolizing) mandate one approach or the other. Single lesions of the subclavian or common carotid artery are well suited for a cervical operation or can be considered for endovascular therapy, whereas definitive treatment of combined innominate and carotid artery disease often requires a transthoracic approach. Likewise, embolizing lesions of the IA usually require transthoracic repair because this approach provides for the most effective reconstruction to exclude the embolic source. The patient's cardiopulmonary risk, previous operations, and history of irradiation or infection may also dictate the most appropriate course.

Direct Reconstruction

Direct reconstruction of the SAT is approached through a complete or partial median sternotomy. In the past, the most common approach for a transthoracic repair has been through a full sternotomy (Fig. 91-15A). Nowadays, we usually use an upper (partial) sternotomy to perform direct SAT reconstruction (Fig. 91-15B). With this approach, the upper three sternal segments are divided in the midline, and the sternum is fractured subperiosteally to the right. Although access is a bit more restricted, it is adequate if the standard site for clamping of the ascending aorta is to be used. This exposure should not be utilized when a substantial perimeter of the ascending aorta needs to be explored to find an area free of calcification for clamping or when there are plans to revascularize the left subclavian artery. Patients with a partial sternotomy have less postoperative pain and fewer disturbances of respiratory mechanics because the lower thoracic cage is left intact. The cervical target vessels are easily exposed through this same full or partial sternotomy via an extension of the incision onto the neck as necessary.

Endarterectomy remains an option for reconstruction, particularly for isolated middle or distal innominate stenoses, but tends to be utilized less frequently than bypass. Lesions that involve the more proximal portion of the vessel are more difficult to manage with endarterectomy. The majority of atherosclerotic lesions of the IA do involve the proximal portion of the vessel; these lesions are contiguous with the atherosclerotic plaque that extends over the dome of the aortic arch and insinuates, as well, into the origin of the left carotid and subclavian arteries. In this common

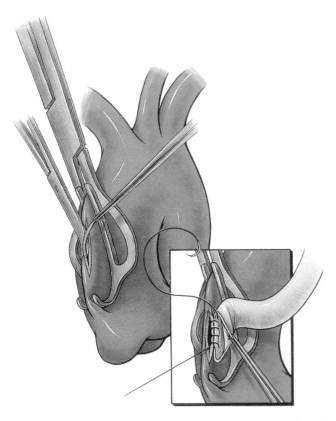

FIGURE 91-16 Partial-occluding clamp facilitates proximal graft anastomosis. (From Berguer R, Kieffer E: Surgery of the Arteries to the Head. New York, Springer-Verlag, 1992.)

situation, endarterectomy of the IA requires division, under direct view, of plaque as it blends with the aortic arch atheroma. This divided intima-media can easily separate and become the origin of a dissection if it is not properly tacked. Furthermore, in order to perform an adequate endarterectomy of these often calcified innominate lesions, the plane from which the plaque must be removed mandates leaving an extremely thin wall through which sutures often tear or cause leaks. Another disadvantage of innominate endarterectomy follows from the fact that, in 24% of patients, the origin of the IA and left common carotid artery are shared in a bovine configuration. In this circumstance, clamping the origin of the IA also impinges on left common carotid artery flow and results in unacceptable brain ischemia. Innominate endarterectomy should be reserved for the rare circumstance of a lesion involving just the middle or distal IA, in which the surgeon does not wish to dissect the ascending aorta or open the pericardium.

Bypasses that take origin from the ascending aorta tend to be safer and less technically demanding than endarterectomy. With few exceptions, the aorta 4 to 6 cm above the aortic valve is spared of disease, even if the rest of the aortic arch is involved. After the pericardium is open and a sufficient length and width of the ascending aortic arch has been exposed, a partial-occlusion Lemole-Strong clamp can be placed on the anterior wall of the ascending aorta and a bypass conduit (usually a 9-mm or 10-mm prosthesis) is anastomosed to it (Fig. 91-16). The proximal anastomosis is easier and less likely to leak if the systolic blood pres-

sure can be kept below 110 mm Hg during clamping and unclamping. Also, heparin therapy should be delayed until after the proximal end of the graft is sewn in place and the aortic clamp has been removed. Because much of the morbidity of the transthoracic approach is related to embolization from the clamp site in the ascending aorta, it is important that the proximal anastomotic site be well flushed to prevent particle embolization. In addition, the patient must be placed in the Trendelenburg position when the clamp is removed in order to prevent air embolization. Heparin is administered when the proximal suture line is hemostatic.

The bypass conduit is positioned anterior to the brachiocephalic vein and cut to length to reach the target artery (Fig. 91-17). When bypasses to more than one trunk vessel are planned, it is better to use sequential bypass grafting with hand-sewn limbs rather than commonly manufactured bifurcated grafts. We use this approach because this type of limb arrangement (Fig. 91-18) has a smaller diameter than a commercially available bifurcated graft. The side arms of sequential bypasses can be oriented in such a fashion so as not to crowd the thoracic inlet. These side branches can then be routed to any of the proximal trunks or up to a carotid bifurcation if need be. Once the reconstruction is complete, the thymus, which has been divided through the midline or flipped laterally, is interposed between the sternum and the prosthetic graft.

Anterior approach to the proximal left subclavian artery, a posterior mediastinal structure, can be difficult. To dissect the proximal left subclavian artery through a median sternotomy usually requires ligation and division of the innominate vein in order to separate the sternal edges enough to permit dissection of the posterior mediastinum. Dividing the innominate vein should be avoided whenever possible because significant arm swelling has been noted after this maneuver in some patients.[33] An alternative is to approach the proximal subclavian artery through a high posterolateral thoracotomy (although a cervical approach usually has as much utility).

The mortality rates for transthoracic SAT reconstruction vary in the reported literature from 0% to 14%. With present-day techniques, the combined stroke and death rate for direct reconstruction of the SAT should be less than 10%. In the report by Berguer and colleagues,[33] which spanned the 1980s and 1990s, the operative mortality for SAT reconstruction alone was 6%. Kieffer and associates[34] reported a similar perioperative mortality rate of 5%.

The long-term durability of transthoracic repair is excellent. In the Berguer report, the 5- and 10-year patency rates were 94% and 88%, respectively, and the patients who survived the operation had a median stroke-free life expectancy of 10 years, 7 months.[33] In the report by Kieffer and associates,[34] 5- and 10-year primary graft patencies were, respectively, 98% and 96%, and the probability of freedom from stroke was 80% at 10 years.

Direct reconstruction of aneurysms involving both normal and aberrant SAT vessels is carried out through a transsternal or transthoracic approach. Aneurysms involving the innominate or left common carotid artery can safely be bypassed and resected using transmediastinal techniques similar to those used to treat occlusive lesions. Aneurysms involving the left subclavian can be approached through

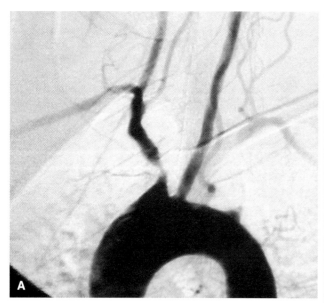

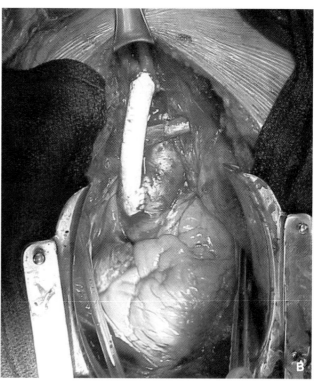

FIGURE 91-17 A, Embolizing innominate lesion. **B,** Expanded polytetrafluoroethylene graft used to bypass the lesion.

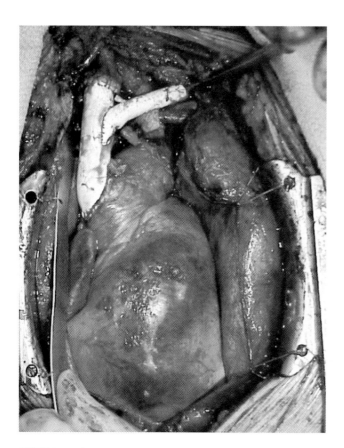

FIGURE 91-18 Aorto-innominate artery–left carotid artery bypass. (See color figure in this section.)

either transthoracic or cervical exposure, depending upon the position and the extent. Symptomatic or aneurysmal aberrant subclavian vessels have been resected and replaced through transsternal exposure or, more commonly, by transposing the more distal subclavian into the adjacent common carotid and then ligating the subclavian origin through the left chest or left neck.[25,55]

Cervical Reconstruction

Cervical reconstruction is the surgical technique of choice for single lesions involving the common carotid or subclavian arteries. Multiple remote cervical bypasses should also be considered for patients with multiple trunk involvement in whom there are contraindications to a transthoracic or endovascular approach. When there is a usable ipsilateral "source vessel," an arterial transposition should be the first choice (Fig. 91-19).

The subclavian artery may be transposed to the adjacent carotid artery, or vice versa. Not only is preservation of the vertebral artery critical; it is equally important to mobilize and preserve the valuable internal mammary artery when a subclavian transposition is performed. In the reverse, a common carotid–subclavian artery transposition, an adequate length of proximally narrowed common carotid artery can easily be mobilized for reimplantation into the adjacent subclavian artery.

Arterial transpositions are completed through a short, transverse cervical incision above the clavicle. For a transposition, the surgical dissection is carried out between

A

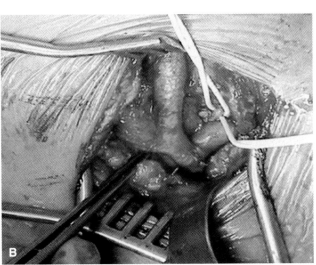

B

FIGURE 91-19 A to C, Subclavian artery–common carotid artery transposition. (**A** from Berguer R, Kieffer E: Surgery of the Arteries to the Head. New York, Springer-Verlag, 1992.)

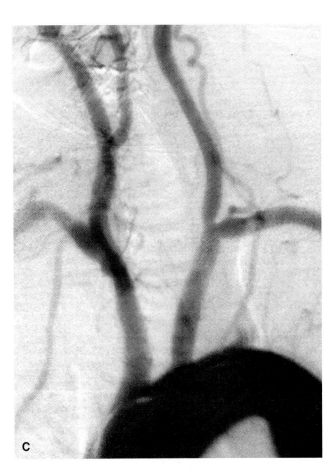

C

the two heads of the sternocleidomastoid muscle. After the omohyoid muscle is divided, the jugular vein and the vagus nerve are reflected laterally, and the common carotid artery is mobilized circumferentially and reflected medially. On the left side, the thoracic duct is identified, ligated, and divided. On the right, multiple cervical lymphatic channels must also be tied. After the vertebral vein is divided, the subclavian artery and its proximal branches can be controlled. The surgeon must take care when isolating and controlling the vertebral artery as it takes origin from an awkward position on the posterior aspect of the subclavian. Once heparin has been administered, the subclavian or common carotid artery can be transected, depending on

which vessel is to be reimplanted. It is important to secure the proximal stump immediately after the diseased artery has been divided; if control of the transected stump is lost in the chest or mediastinum, the consequences clearly can be devastating. A punch arteriotomy is created in the side of the donor vessel, and the end-to-side anastomosis completed without tension.

Occasionally, it is not feasible to perform a straightforward arterial transposition, so the use of a bypass conduit becomes necessary (Fig. 91-20). Arterial transposition is not possible when the vertebral artery takes off early from the subclavian artery. Another indication for carotid-subclavian bypass is proximal subclavian disease in a patient with

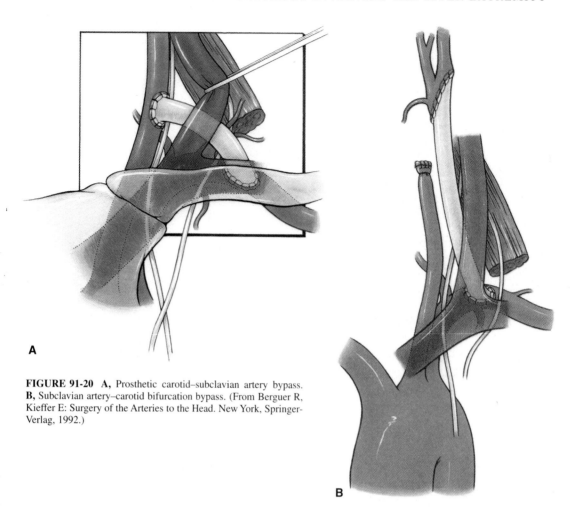

FIGURE 91-20 A, Prosthetic carotid–subclavian artery bypass. **B,** Subclavian artery–carotid bifurcation bypass. (From Berguer R, Kieffer E: Surgery of the Arteries to the Head. New York, Springer-Verlag, 1992.)

symptomatic coronary steal from a patent internal mammary artery graft. With the use of a cervical bypass, the arterial clamps can be placed beyond the internal mammary artery to avoid myocardial ischemia. Bypasses are performed, most expediently, through dissection just lateral to the clavicular head of the sternocleidomastoid muscle. The jugular vein is reflected medially to expose the common carotid artery. The subclavian artery is identified more distally than during transposition through division of the anterior scalene muscle. The bypass is completed to or from the retroscalene portion of the subclavian artery, usually with prosthetic conduit rather than vein, through sequential clamping and serial anastomoses. Prosthetic conduits clearly outperform autogenous vein with regard to long-term patency.[56,57]

If an extra-anatomic approach is considered and the only source vessel is on the other side of the neck, the midline should be crossed with a retropharyngeal rather than a presternal or pretracheal path.[58] The retropharyngeal route is shorter and more direct (Fig. 91-21). Furthermore, pretracheal or presternal routing of a bypass graft can result in erosion of overlying skin and will be found obtrusive if the patient ever needs a sternotomy or a tracheotomy. Because of significantly poor patency rates, long subclavian-subclavian, axillary-axillary, and femoroaxillary bypasses should also be avoided unless there is no other alternative.

Short-term outcome of cervical SAT reconstruction is different in two distinct subgroups of patients. The first are those patients with complex or extensive extracranial disease in whom reconstruction is performed preferentially through the neck because of a variety of relative contra-indications to a transthoracic or endovascular approach. The second consists of patients with a single lesion of the subclavian or common carotid artery who are choice candidates for a straightforward, limited cervical operation. The researchers in one review were surprised to find that the two groups faired equally well with regard to long-term patency and survival.[33] The more complex group did, however, experience a significantly greater perioperative stroke and death rate. The combined stroke and death rate for the entire group of 182 patients was 4%, with a single patient dying (from stroke). Among the 103 patients who were considered straightforward, choice candidates for cervical repair, the perioperative mortality rate was 0 and a single patient (1%) had a stroke. In this series, virtually all patients were rendered asymptomatic by the procedure. The primary 10-year patency rates compared favorably with those of other published series at 82%.[33,52,59] Stroke-free survival was 84% at 10 years.[33] It is important to note that there were no late failures in the group who underwent arterial transposition. The long-term patency rate for arterial transposition, when performed by surgeons with experience, is virtually 100%.[33,60,61]

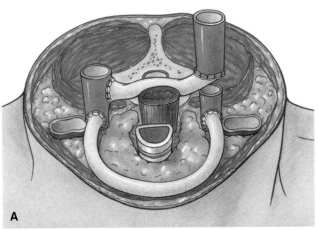

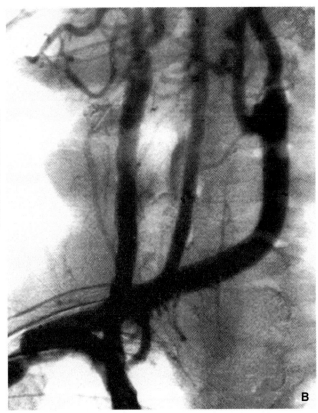

FIGURE 91-21   **A,** The retropharyngeal route is the shortest and most direct route for a transcervical bypass. **B,** Retropharyngeal right subclavian artery–left carotid bifurcation bypass. (**A** from Berguer R, Kieffer E: Surgery of the Arteries to the Head. New York, Springer-Verlag, 1992.)

Endovascular Repair

Balloon angioplasty and stenting of isolated innominate, common carotid, or subclavian artery disease is becoming more commonplace. Patients with atherosclerotic occlusive disease as well as patients with inflammatory arteriopathies have been treated with endovascular therapy. Endoluminal SAT therapies can be undertaken in antegrade fashion from the femoral artery or, in the case of innominate or subclavian lesions, percutaneously and in a retrograde fashion from the brachial artery. Perhaps equally common would be retrograde treatment of common carotid or innominate lesions via cervical cutdown as a lone procedure or during exposure of the carotid bifurcation for carotid endarterectomy (Fig. 91-22).

Endovascular recanalization of the SAT, introduced during the early 1980s, is performed under fluoroscopic control via remote arterial access with wires, catheters, and angioplasty balloons that are directed to the target SAT. As an alternative, in order to prevent embolization, Queral and Criado[20] advocate an open retrograde approach whereby the common carotid arteries are exposed in the neck and surgically controlled. Significantly more experience has been accumulated in the treatment of subclavian lesions than in the treatment of carotid or innominate disease, but this difference is likely due to the higher incidence of left subclavian lesions. Despite conflicting evidence for the routine use of metallic intravascular stents, their deployment has become a routine adjuvant to balloon angioplasty in the proximal segments of these vessels. Covered stent-grafts may soon have a role as well.[62] Stents should not be placed in the postvertebral subclavian artery because it is possible for the metallic framework to be crushed in the thoracic outlet.

Uniformly, luminal stenoses are treated endovascularly with more success than complete vessel occlusions (the incidence for rethrombosis of an occluded subclavian artery that has been recanalized by angioplasty and stent is as high as 50% at 8 months).[63-65] Calcified lesions, long stenoses, and embolizing lesions may also be problematic. It should also be noted that once re-stenosis develops in a subclavian artery that has undergone endovascular treatment, a second and earlier re-stenosis is likely. Endoluminal treatment of arteritis, despite marginal success in some small case series,[66] should be condemned.

Despite more than 20 years of experience, reports have been sporadic and patient series have been reported with small numbers only. The largest series published in the literature often combine immediate and mid-term results of innominate, subclavian, and common carotid interventions together, making it difficult to interpret the results.[20,59,67] Some investigators enthusiastically suggest that patient morbidity is markedly lower than that for open surgical reconstruction. Close scrutiny suggests, however, that overall complication rates are actually very similar to those of open reconstruction and that long-term durability of endoluminal therapy is probably inferior. This conclusion is hard to come by because reporting standards do not yet exist, few papers on endoluminal therapy were published with intent-to-treat reporting, and long-term patient follow-up and well-documented patency data for angioplasty and stent placement are lacking.

Primary success rates range from 73% to 100%, and complication rates from 0 to 10%.[67-76] Death after endovascular treatment is rare. Henry and coworkers[67] reported

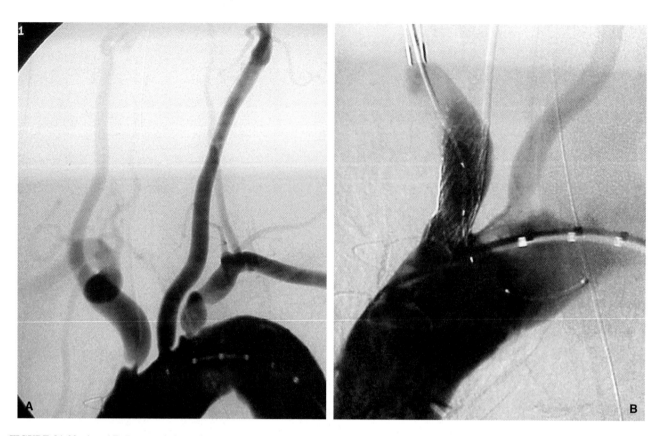

FIGURE 91-22   A and **B,** Retrograde innominate artery angioplasty in a patient with a prior sternotomy.

percutaneous endoluminal treatment of 113 subclavian lesions from a percutaneous femoral or brachial approach. The initial technical success rate was 91% for stenotic lesions and 47% in occlusions. As with most interventional techniques, success was defined as a residual narrowing of 30% of the diameter or less. The complication rate was 5.3%. The clinically significant recurrence rate was 16% after a mean of 4.3 years. Tyagi and colleagues[66] dilated 61 prevertebral and postvertebral subclavian lesions, reporting a 90% initial success rate and a 5.4% complication rate. Schillinger and associates[77] retrospectively identified 115 patients who were treated for atherosclerotic subclavian disease (patients with arteritis were excluded) over 15 years. Initial success was achieved in 85%. Complete occlusion and long lesions correlated with low success rate. Four-year patency rates were 59% in arteries with stents and 68% in arteries without stents.[77] Sullivan and colleagues[78] achieved initial success in 94% of patients with subclavian (n = 66), carotid (n = 14), or innominate (n = 7) lesions, and a broad range of complications occurred in 21% of the patients. This group concluded that the short-term and long-term results of treatment favor surgical therapy, especially when the lesions are complete occlusions.[78]

Our experience with endovascular repair has been limited and the results are not particularly bright. Anecdotally, we have noted dissections (with and without thrombosis) during angioplasty of the left common carotid artery, and we have also seen disastrous vertebrobasilar embolization after subclavian angioplasty. We would recommend avoiding

endoluminal techniques in patients who harbor embolizing lesions of the SAT, heavily calcified stenoses, or complete vessel occlusion. Atherosclerotic subclavian lesions that extend into the origin of the vertebral artery and disease that develops as the result of arteritis are better treated surgically. These procedures should certainly be considered, however, in patients with short-segment, unifocal atherosclerotic lesions of the SAT in whom the indications are clear, especially when there is no good surgical option. Atherosclerotic or hyperplastic lesions that develop after SAT bypass and disease that develops after therapeutic irradiation, like those at the carotid bifurcation, may more safely be treated endoluminally. As techniques become more refined, standard materials improve (including cerebral protection devices), and experience accumulates (especially for carotid and innominate lesions), angioplasty and stent placement will likely assume a complementary role with surgery for treating SAT disease.

The concept of endovascular stent-graft repair for select traumatic injuries, arteriovenous fistulae, and aneurysms involving the SAT has certain appeal (Fig. 91-23). Endoluminal repair obviates thoracotomy or sternotomy and avoids the technically challenging dissection associated with chronic disease and the risk of significant hemorrhage that can occur during treatment of acute vascular injury. Risk to surrounding venous and nervous structures is virtually eliminated by the choice of an endovascular approach. Experience with these endoluminal devices is limited, however. To date, the literature contains only case reports or

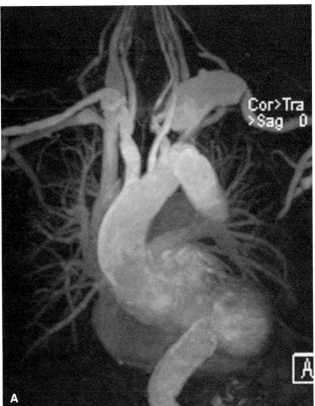

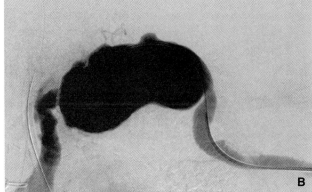

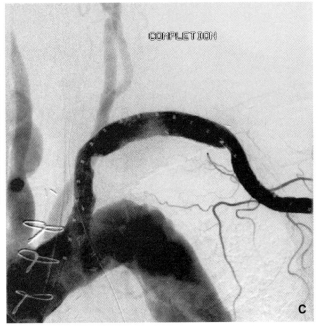

FIGURE 91-23 **A,** Magnetic resonance angiograph showing symptomatic true left subclavian aneurysm. **B,** Same subclavian aneurysm before stent-graft repair but after surgical vertebral artery–carotid artery transposition. **C,** Successful endovascular repair (note vertebral artery anastomosed to the common carotid artery).

small series of 12 or fewer patients.[22,79-82] Most devices have been placed in the subclavian artery from a brachial access site, but a few have also been deployed from a femoral approach. As with open repair, obliteration of important branch flow must be avoided. Early success rates are promising, and complication rates compare favorably with those of standard techniques. The durability of these devices, however, remains in question, and further study is clearly needed. As with stents used for occlusive disease, stent-grafts placed under the clavicle are at risk of compression and device fracture.

■ CONCLUSION

As in the group of patients who undergo carotid bifurcation endarterectomy, long-term outcome data suggest that about half of patients who undergo surgical reconstruction of the SAT are still alive after 10 years.[32-34] On the basis of these data, patients who are good surgical candidates with proper indications for intervention should undergo standard revas-

cularization by competent surgeons utilizing techniques with proven long-term patency. Endovascular repair and remote bypass should be considered in patients with higher cardiopulmonary risk or limited life expectancy. It is important to base the approach on the individual patient's anatomy and operative risk.

■ REFERENCES

1. Blaisdell WF, Clauss RH, Galbraith JG, et al: Joint study of extracranial arterial occlusion. IV: A review of surgical considerations. JAMA 209:1889, 1969.
2. Savory WS: Case of a young woman in whom the main arteries of both upper extremities, and of the left side of the neck, were through-out completely obliterated. Med Chir Trans 39:205, 1856.
3. Broadbent WH: Absence of pulsation in both radial arteries, the vessels being full of blood. Read 165, 1875.
4. Takayasu M: Case of queer changes in central blood vessels of retina. Acta Soc Ophthalmol Jpn 12:554, 1908.
5. Shimizu K, Sano K: Pulseless disease. J Neurol Clin Neurol 145:1095, 1951.

6. Contorni L: Il circolo collaterale vertebro-vertebrale nella obliterazione dell'arteria succlavia alla sua origine. Minerva Chir 15:268, 1960.

7. Rutkow IM: Valentine Mott and the beginnings of vascular surgery. Arch Surg 136:1441, 2001.

8. Temple LJ: Aneurysm of the first part of the left subclavian artery: Review of the literature and case history. J Thorac Surg 19:412, 1950.

9. Halsted WS: Ligature of the left subclavian artery in its first portion. J Hopkins H Bull 24:93, 1892.

10. Stahl RD, Lawrence PF, Bhirangi K: Left subclavian artery aneurysm: Two cases of rare congenital etiology. J Vasc Surg 29:715, 1999.

11. Bjork VO: Aneurysm and occlusion of the right subclavian artery. Acta Chir Scand Suppl 356:103, 1965.

12. Bahnson HT, Spencer FC, Quattlebaum JK: Surgical treatment of occlusive disease of the carotid artery. Ann Surg 149:711, 1959.

13. Davis JB, Grove WJ, Julian OC: Thrombic occlusion of the branches of the aortic arch, Martorell's syndrome: Report of a case treated surgically. Ann Surg 144:124, 1956.

14. Cate WR, Scott HW: Cerebral ischemia of central origin: Relief by subclavian vertebral artery thromboendarterectomy. Surgery 45:19, 1959.

15. Lyons C, Galbraith G: Surgical treatment of atherosclerotic occlusion of the internal carotid artery. Ann Surg 146:487, 1956.

16. Parrott JC: The subclavian steal syndrome. Arch Surg 88:661, 1964.

17. Berguer R, Gonzalez JA: Revascularization by the retropharyngeal route for extensive disease of the extracranial arteries. J Vasc Surg 19:217, 1994.

18. Bachman DM, Kim RM: Transluminal dilatation for subclavian syndrome. AJR Am J Roentgenol 135:995, 1980.

19. Mathias K, Schlosser V, Reimke M: Catheterization of subclavian occlusions [in German]. ROFO Fortschr Geb Rontgenstr Nuklearmed 132:346, 1980.

20. Queral LA, Criado FJ: The treatment of focal aortic arch branch lesions with Palmaz stents. J Vasc Surg 23:368, 1996.

21. Becker GJ, Benenati JF, Zemel G, et al: Percutaneous placement of a balloon-expandable intraluminal graft for life-threatening subclavian arterial hemorrhage. J Vasc Interv Radiol 2:225, 1991.

22. Hilfiker PR, Razavi MK, Kee ST, et al: Stent-graft therapy for subclavian artery aneurysms and fistulas: Single-center mid-term results. J Vasc Interv Radiol 11:578, 2000.

23. Bergman RA, Thompson SA, Afifi AK, et al: Compendium of Human Anatomic Variation: Text, Atlas and World Literature. Baltimore, Urban and Schwarzenberg, 1988.

24. Freed K, Low V: The aberrant subclavian artery. AJR Am J Roentgenol 168:481, 1997.

25. Berguer R, Kieffer E: Surgery of the Arteries to the Head. New York, Springer-Verlag, 1992.

26. Molz G, Burri B: Aberrant subclavian artery (arteria lusoria): Sex differences in the prevalence of various forms of the malformation: Evaluation of 1378 observations. Virchows Arch Pathol Anat Histopathol 380:303, 1978.

27. Bayford D: An account of a singular case of obstructed deglutition. Memoirs Med Soc London 2:275, 1794.

28. Shuford WH, Sybers RG, Gordon IJ, et al: Circumflex retroesophageal right aortic arch simulating mediastinal tumor or dissecting aneurysm. AJR Am J Roentgenol 146:491, 1986.

29. Hastreiter AR, D'Cruz IA, Cantez T: Right-sided aorta. Part 1: Occurring of right aortic arch in various types of congenital heart disease. Br Heart J 28:722, 1966.

30. Cina CS, Althank H, Pasenau J, Abouzahr L: Kommerell's diverticulum and right-sided aortic arch: A cohort study and review of the literature. J Vasc Surg 39:131, 2004.

31. Williams GD, Edmonds HW: Variations in the arrangements of the branches arising from the aortic arch. Anat Rec 62:139, 1935.

32. Berguer R, Morasch MD, Kline RA: Transthoracic repair of innominate and common carotid artery disease: Immediate and long-term outcome for 100 consecutive surgical reconstructions. J Vasc Surg 27:34, 1998.

33. Berguer R, Morasch MD, Kline RA, et al: Cervical reconstruction of the supra-aortic trunks: A 16-year experience. J Vasc Surg 29:239, 1999.

34. Kieffer E, Sabatier J, Koskas F, et al: Atherosclerotic innominate artery occlusive disease: Early and long-term results of surgical reconstruction. J Vasc Surg 21:326, 1995.

35. Rhodes JM, Cherry KJ Jr, Clark RC, et al: Aortic-origin reconstruction of the great vessels: Risk factors of early and late complications. J Vasc Surg 31:260, 2000.

36. Dent TL, Lindenauer SM, Ernest CB, Fry W: Multiple arteriosclerotic arterial aneurysms. Arch Surg 105:388, 1972.

37. McCann RL: Basic data related to peripheral artery aneurysms. Ann Vasc Surg 4:411, 1990.

38. Bower TC, Pairolero PC, Hallett JW Jr, et al: Brachiocephalic aneurysm: The case for early recognition and repair. Ann Vasc Surg 5:125, 1991.

39. Beabout JW, Steward JR, Kincaid OW: Aberrant right subclavian artery: Dispute of commonly accepted concepts. AJR Am J Roentgenol 92:855, 1964.

40. Hall S, Barr W, Lie JT, et al: Takayasu arteritis: A study of 32 North American patients. Medicine 64:89, 1985.

41. Burkland C: Spontaneous dissecting aneurysm of the cervical carotid artery: A report of surgical treatment in two patients. Johns Hopkins Med J 126:154, 1970.

42. O'Dwyer J, Moscow N, Trevor R, et al: Spontaneous dissection of the carotid artery. Radiology 136:379, 1980.

43. Graham JM, Miller T, Stinentt D: Spontaneous dissection of the common carotid artery: Case report and review of the literature. J Vasc Surg 7:811, 1988.

44. Early T, Gregory R, Wheeler J, et al: Spontaneous carotid dissection: Duplex scanning in diagnosis and management. J Vasc Surg 14:391, 1991.

45. Humphrey P, Keller M, Spadone D, Silver D: Spontaneous common carotid artery dissection. J Vasc Surg 18:95, 1993.

46. Kawajiri K, Kiyama M, Hayazaki K: Spontaneous dissection in the common carotid artery—case report. Neurol Med Chir 35:373, 1995.

47. Lubin J, Capparella J, Vecchione M: Acute monocular blindness associated with spontaneous common carotid dissection. Ann Emerg Med 38:332, 2001.

48. Lee C, Kim G, Crupi R: A common carotid artery dissection. J Emerg Med 23:291, 2002.

49. Reul GJ, Jacobs MJHM, Gregoric ID, et al: Innominate artery occlusive disease: Surgical approach and long-term results. J Vasc Surg 14:405, 1991.

50. Melliere D, Becquemin JP, Benyahia E, et al: Atherosclerotic disease of the innominate artery: Current management and results. J Cardiovasc Surg (Torino) 33:319, 1992.

51. Crawford ES, Stowe CL, Powers RW: Occlusion of the innominate, common carotid, and subclavian arteries: Long-term results of surgical treatment. Surgery 11:781, 1983.

52. Vogt DP, Hertzer NR, O'Hara PJ, Beven EG: Brachiocephalic arterial reconstruction. Ann Surg 11:541, 1982.

53. Cherry KJ Jr, McCullough JL, Hallett JW Jr, et al: Technical principles of direct innominate artery revascularization: A comparison of endarterectomy and bypass grafts. J Vasc Surg 9:718, 1989.

54. Schroeder T, Hansen HJ: Arterial reconstruction of the brachiocephalic trunk and the subclavian arteries: 10 years' experience with a follow-up study. Acta Chir Scand Suppl 502:122, 1980.

55. Valentine RJ, Carter DJ, Clagett GP: A modified extrathoracic approach to the treatment of dysphagia lusoria. J Vasc Surg 5:498, 1987.

56. Ziomek S, Quinones-Baldrich WJ, Busuttil RW, et al: The superiority of synthetic arterial grafts over autologous veins in carotid-subclavian bypass. J Vasc Surg 3:140, 1986.

57. Morasch MD, Berguer R: Supra-aortic trunk revascularization. In Yao JST, Pearce WH (eds): Modern Vascular Surgery. New York, McGraw-Hill, 2000, p 137.

58. Berguer R: Revascularization across the neck using the retropharyngeal route. In Veith FJ (ed): Current Critical Problems in Vascular Surgery. St. Louis, Quality Medical Publishing, 1996.

59. Moore WS, Malone JM, Goldstone J: Extrathoracic repair of branch occlusions of the aortic arch. Am J Surg 132:249, 1976.

60. Schardey HM, Meyer G, Rau HG, et al: Subclavian-carotid transposition: An analysis of a clinical series and a review of the literature. Eur J Vasc Endovasc Surg 12:431, 1996.

61. Cina CS, Safar HA, Lagana A, et al: Subclavian carotid transposition and bypass grafting: Consecutive cohort study and systematic review. J Vasc Surg 35:422, 2002.

62. Montarjeme A: Percutaneous transluminal angioplasty of supra-aortic vessels. J Endovasc Surg 3:171, 1996.

63. Kachel R, Basche St, Heerklotz I, et al: Percutaneous transluminal angioplasty (PTA) of supra-aortic arteries especially the internal carotid artery. AJNR Am J Neuroradiol 33:191, 1991.

64. Duber C, Klose JK, Kopp H, Schmiedt W: Percutaneous transluminal angioplasty for occlusion of the subclavian artery: Short- and long-term results. Cardiovasc Intervent Radiol 15:205, 1992.

65. Martinez R, Rodriguez-Lopez J, Rorruella L, et al: Stenting for occlusion of the subclavian arteries. Tex Heart Inst J 24:23, 1997.

66. Tyagi S, Verma PK, Gambhir DS, et al: Early and long-term results of subclavian angioplasty in aortoarteritis (Takayasu disease): Comparison with atherosclerosis. Cardiovasc Intervent Radiol 21:219, 1998.

67. Henry M, Amor M, Henry I, et al: Percutaneous transluminal angioplasty of the subclavian arteries. J Endovasc Surg 6:33, 1999.

68. Montarjeme A, Keifer JW, Zuska AJ, Nabawi MD: Percutaneous transluminal angioplasty for treatment of subclavian steal. Radiology 155:611, 1985.

69. Erbstein RA, Wholey MH, Smoot S: Subclavian artery steal syndrome: Treatment by percutaneous transluminal angioplasty. AJR Am J Roentgenol 155:291, 1988.

70. Becker CJ, Katzen BT, Date MD: Noncoronary angioplasty. Radiology 170:921, 1989.

71. Millaire A, Trinca M, Marache P, et al: Subclavian angioplasty: Immediate and late results in 50 patients. Cathet Cardiovasc Diagn 29:8, 1993.

72. Bogey WM, Demasi RJ, Tripp MD, et al: Percutaneous transluminal angioplasty for subclavian artery stenosis. Ann Surg 60:103, 1994.

73. Rodriguez-Lopez JA, Werner A, Martinez R, et al: Stenting for atherosclerotic occlusive disease of the subclavian artery. Ann Vasc Surg 13:254, 1999.

74. Hadjipetrou P, Cox S, Piemonte T, et al: Percutaneous revascularization of atherosclerotic obstruction of aortic arch vessels. J Am Coll Cardiol 33:1238, 1999.

75. Crowe KE, Iannone LA: Percutaneous transluminal angioplasty for subclavian artery stenosis in patients with subclavian steal syndrome and coronary subclavian steal syndrome. Am Heart J 126:229, 1993.

76. Mathias KD, Luth I, Haarmann P: Percutaneous transluminal angioplasty of proximal subclavian artery occlusions. Cardiovasc Intervent Radiol 16:214, 1993.

77. Schillinger M, Haumer M, Schillinger S, et al: Risk stratification for subclavian artery angioplasty: Is there an increased rate of restenosis after stent implantation? J Endovasc Ther 8:550, 2001.

78. Sullivan TM, Gray GH, Bacharach JM, et al: Angioplasty and primary stenting of the subclavian, innominate, and common carotid arteries in 83 patients. J Vasc Surg 28:1059, 1998.

79. Babatasi G, Massetti M, LePage O, et al: Endovascular treatment of a traumatic subclavian artery aneurysm. J Trauma 44:545, 1998.

80. May J, White G, Waugh R, et al: Transluminal placement of a prosthetic graft-stent device for treatment of subclavian artery aneurysm. J Vasc Surg 18:1056, 1993.

81. Davidian M, Kee ST, Kato N, et al: Aneurysm of an aberrant right subclavian artery: Treatment with PTFE covered stent graft. J Vasc Surg 28:335, 1998.

82. Schoder M, Cejna M, Holzenbein T, et al: Elective and emergent endovascular treatment of subclavian artery aneurysms and injuries. J Endovasc Ther 10:58, 2003.

83. Kieffer E, Sabatier J, Koskas F: Brachiocephalic arterial reconstruction. In Yao JST, Pearce WH (eds): Arterial Surgery. Stamford, CT, Appleton and Lange, 1996, p 141.

Chapter

Upper Extremity Revascularization

92

JAMES M. EDWARDS, MD

Symptomatic upper extremity arterial ischemia is present in less than 5% of patients presenting for medical treatment of extremity ischemia.[1] Most of these patients have a primary vasospastic condition (Raynaud's syndrome), and there is no indication for operative intervention. Of the remaining patients, many have small artery occlusive disease, often from an associated autoimmune disease that is not amenable to revascularization.[2,3] The few patients who may benefit from arterial revascularization have a wide variety of pathologic conditions that may be seen elsewhere in the body, such as the lower extremities. Because of differences in collateral circulation, muscle mass, and typical use between the upper and lower extremities, there are differences in how ischemia is tolerated and how patients present with ischemia. This chapter discusses the surgical treatment of occlusive disease of the axillary, brachial, radial, ulnar, and palmar arch arteries. Surgery of the brachiocephalic arteries and of digital artery occlusive disease is discussed in Chapters 91 and 93.

■ CLINICAL PRESENTATION

As in the lower extremity, patients may present with acute or chronic ischemia. Acute ischemia of the upper extremity results in pain, pallor, pulselessness, paresthesias, and later paralysis. Chronic upper extremity ischemia may present with the upper extremity equivalent of claudication, with hand pain or forearm and upper arm muscular pain with repetitive use. This pain typically occurs in the dominant hand, even if the severity of ischemia is equivalent in both upper extremities.[4] More severe symptoms, including rest pain and gangrene, may result from either proximal disease or multilevel disease. Patients with digital gangrene have either significant multilevel disease or extensive distal palmar/digital arterial disease. Because of the rich collateral network, acute occlusion of upper extremity arteries rarely results in tissue loss. It has been estimated that axillary artery ligation results in limb loss in only about 10% of cases and that ligation of the brachial artery distal to the deep brachial artery results in gangrene in only 3% to 5% of cases.

■ ETIOLOGY

As in the lower extremity, upper extremity arterial ischemia may be due to myriad conditions. For the purpose of this chapter, these conditions are divided into the following groups:

1. Intrinsic arterial disease
2. Trauma
   a. Iatrogenic
   b. Non-iatrogenic
3. Emboli

Additionally, as in the lower extremity, patients may present with acute or chronic ischemia.

Intrinsic Arterial Disease

Although the most common cause of arterial disease in the lower extremity is atherosclerosis, typical atherosclerosis is rare in the arteries of the upper extremity.[5] Patients with end-stage renal disease develop an advanced diffuse and primarily distal atherosclerosis, which rarely is amenable to arterial revascularization and is not discussed further in this chapter.[6] More typical-appearing atherosclerosis is seen occasionally in axillary, brachial, radial, and ulnar arteries. Fibromuscular disease of the upper extremity has been reported in all arteries from the axillary artery to the distal ulnar artery in the palm. The syndrome of distal ulnar artery occlusion associated with using the hand as a hammer (hypothenar hammer syndrome) is likely the result of preexisting fibromuscular disease.[7,8] In these patients, the diseased ulnar artery apparently thromboses with the added injury of local trauma. Giant cell arteritis and radiation arteritis may result in axillary and brachial artery stenosis or occlusion.[9] Giant cell arteritis often responds acutely to medical therapy, but in the chronic stages may lead to clinically significant upper extremity ischemia.[10]

Thromboangiitis obliterans and connective tissue diseases rarely affect the larger arteries of the upper extremity.[11] These diseases typically affect the most distal arteries. Bypass is rarely possible because of the lack of distal targets.

Trauma

Trauma, either iatrogenic or non-iatrogenenic, is a common cause of upper extremity arterial occlusion. Injury as a result of brachial artery catheterization is the most common cause of iatrogenic trauma. The incidence of significant brachial artery complications after catheterization is reported to range from 0.9% to 4%.[12-15] This percentage is higher than the 0.4% thrombotic complication rate reported with transfemoral catheterization.[16,17]

The factors associated with brachial artery complications during or after transbrachial catheterization include the experience of the cardiologist, preexisting brachial atherosclerosis, number of catheter changes, degree of anticoagulation during the procedure, duration of the procedure, and female gender. The incidence of complications after brachial artery catheterization may be higher because acute and chronic thrombotic complications involving the brachial artery may be asymptomatic or result in minimal symptoms. Currently, most interventional cardiologists use the transfemoral approach, and as a result it is rare to see complications of the brachial artery approach.

Although the diagnosis of acute brachial artery occlusion after transbrachial cardiac catheterization is made by physical examination with the findings of hand ischemia and the absence of a distal brachial, radial, or ulnar pulse after completion of the procedure, these findings may not be present if there is an intimal injury or a short segment arterial occlusion. In these cases, patients may not notice symptomatic hand ischemia until they return to their home and use their extremity.

Transaxillary catheterization is a valuable approach, particularly in patients with aortic occlusion. The reported incidence of thrombotic complications after transaxillary catheterization is 0.8%, but most complications after transaxillary catheterization are nerve compression as a result of bleeding into the axillary sheath.[18] Either complication of transaxillary catheterization typically results in acute symptoms, which if recognized lead to prompt treatment.

Radial artery catheterization may result in radial artery occlusion in 5% to 40% of cases, particularly if the catheter is left in for a prolonged time.[19,20] Other factors associated with radial artery occlusion are large catheter size, hypotension or hypoperfusion, treatment with vasoconstrictors, and preexisting arterial disease. Although the performance of an Allen test is recommended before placement of a radial arterial line, significant hand ischemia as a result of radial artery thrombosis is rare, on the order of 0.3% to 0.5%.

Intra-arterial chemotherapy rarely may be administered via catheterization of the brachial or axillary artery. Thrombotic complications have been reported and are associated with prolonged catheter placement and the degree of anticoagulation.

Non-iatrogenic trauma may be the result of blunt, penetrating, or traction injuries. Intimal disruption is seen with blunt upper extremity trauma.[21] This injury may produce immediate or delayed arterial occlusion and symptoms. Mild traction injuries also produce intimal injuries, whereas arterial disruption is seen with more significant injuries. Penetrating trauma may cause direct arterial injury or arterial injury secondary to a blast effect.[22] Acute arterial disruption may present as hemorrhage or pseudoaneurysm. The symptoms of an upper extremity pseudoaneurysm depend on the size and location of the pseudoaneurysm. Small pseudoaneurysms adjacent to nerves may cause significant and early symptoms, whereas pseudoaneurysms located in muscles may grow with minimal symptoms. Non-iatrogenic trauma also may be seen in athletes, particularly baseball pitchers.[23,24] Injuries in these patients are due to injury of the axillary artery and its branches by the humeral head.

Emboli

The upper extremity is the recipient of approximately 25% of arterial emboli.[25] The source of the emboli may be external to the upper extremity (cardiac, aortic arch, subclavian artery pathology—stenosis or aneurysm) or intrinsic to the upper extremity (intimal flaps, stenoses, injections of foreign substances).[26,27] Most emboli are cardiac in origin, typically from atrial fibrillation. Cardiac emboli to the upper extremity lodge in the brachial artery 60% of the time, but also may lodge in the axillary and more distal arteries of the forearm and hand. In the brachial artery, emboli lodge just proximal to branch point, such as the deep brachial artery and the brachial bifurcation.

Although the clinical presentation of large arterial emboli is usually dramatic, symptoms often improve rapidly as the emboli break up and travel distally. The degree of ischemia seen on physical examination also improves, but rarely returns to normal. The diagnosis of emboli to the upper extremity also may be delayed if the degree of ischemia is such that only repetitive use of the upper extremity is sufficient to produce clinical symptoms. Emboli from noncardiac sources are often smaller than emboli from the heart and lodge in the small arteries of the hand and fingers; this is also seen with emboli from septic endocarditis.

■ EVALUATION

The primary diagnostic modality in the diagnosis of acute upper extremity ischemia is the physical examination. Because of the limited size of the upper extremity and the fact that the arteries in the upper extremity are superficial, palpation is a reliable diagnostic modality assuming normal hemodynamics. Localization of the level of occlusion is based on the presence or absence of pulses at each arterial level. Pulse status is not entirely reliable for the evaluation of chronic arterial ischemia because of the rich collateral network.

Other diagnostic modalities used in the upper extremity include segmental pressures including measurement of digital pressures and waveforms; duplex ultrasound visualization; and angiography via direct injection, intravenous digital subtraction, computed tomography, and magnetic resonance imaging. Noninvasive vascular laboratory studies are as accurate as angiography in determining the presence or absence of arterial occlusion, and angiography should be reserved for diagnostic purposes when there is uncertainty about the cause of the ischemia and for when intervention is being planned.[28,29] Angiography also is indicated for situations in which there is a high index of suspicion of arterial injury (traumatic injury of adjacent structures without physical examination findings of arterial injury), although some authors believe that duplex ultrasound, if available, is the preferred diagnostic imaging modality (see Chapter 90).

■ TREATMENT

The treatment of upper extremity ischemia depends on the severity of ischemia and the location of the lesion. The treatment of each arterial section is described in turn without particular reference to the type of injury. Acute injuries resulting in severe upper extremity ischemia should be treated with the urgency of treatment based on the severity of symptoms and comorbidities. Expectant therapy of severe symptomatic acute upper extremity ischemia is rarely successful. The treatment of chronic upper extremity ischemia is based on the clinical picture. In the absence of rest pain, ischemic ulcers, or gangrene, the need for revascularization depends on the patient's perception of disability, which may vary markedly from patient to patient.

The treatment of nonocclusive intimal injuries is controversial. There is evidence in the literature that smaller injuries with less than 50% luminal compromise have a benign outcome. Nonintervention for these injuries is an acceptable treatment if the patient is carefully observed.[30]

Axillary Artery

There are many approaches to the axillary artery, and the approach chosen depends on the type, location of the injury, urgency of the repair, and body habitus of the patient. The most proximal axillary artery is approached through a transverse incision on the chest located in the deltopectoral groove (Figs. 92-1 and 92-2). After dissection down through the pectoralis major fascia, the pectoralis major muscle is divided along its fibers. There are usually several venous branches crossing the axillary artery that need to be divided. After division of the veins, dissection and control of the artery is possible. Division of the pectoralis major or minor muscles may enhance visualization of the artery. Care should be taken to avoid injuring adjacent veins and nerves.

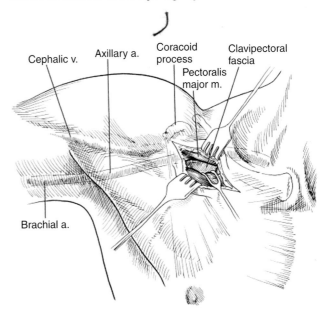

FIGURE 92-1 Approach to the right axillary artery. A transverse incision is made as indicated. The axillary artery is beneath the pectoralis major fascia, and typically numerous crossing veins need to be ligated during the approach. (From Valentine RJ, Wind CG: Anatomic Exposures in Vascular Surgery, 2nd ed. Philadelphia, Lippincott Williams & Wilkins, 2003.)

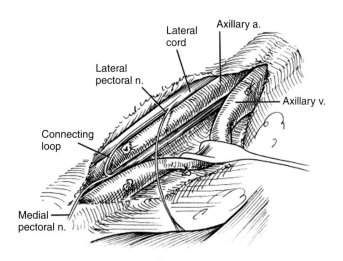

FIGURE 92-2 After the fascia is entered and the crossing veins are ligated, the vein is mobilized off the artery, and the axillary artery can be mobilized. (From Valentine RJ, Wind CG: Anatomic Exposures in Vascular Surgery, 2nd ed. Philadelphia, Lippincott Williams & Wilkins, 2003.)

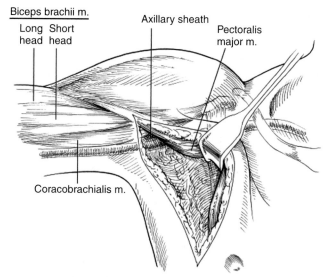

FIGURE 92-3 The approach to the second portion of the axillary artery. A vertical incision along the lateral border of the pectoralis major muscle allows medial retraction of the muscle and exposure of the artery. (From Valentine RJ, Wind CG: Anatomic Exposures in Vascular Surgery, 2nd ed. Philadelphia, Lippincott Williams & Wilkins, 2003.)

For embolectomy, a transverse incision should be made. Proximal embolectomy is performed with a size 4 or 5 embolectomy catheter, and distal embolectomy is performed with a size 4 embolectomy catheter. On the right side care must be taken with proximal passage of the embolectomy catheter because it will pass the right vertebral and common carotid arteries with the possibility of embolization to the cerebral circulation.

Proximal control of the subclavian artery is necessary if the injury to the axillary artery is in this area, requiring a thoracotomy in most instances. Division of the clavicle may be necessary in certain cases, but often a combination supra-clavicular and infraclavicular incision gives satisfactory exposure to the proximal axillary artery.

The more distal axillary artery can be exposed through an axillary or upper arm incision (Fig. 92-3). Although the incision shown in Figure 92-3 is vertical, the more distal axillary and proximal brachial arteries are found using a transverse incision. Division of the pectoralis minor muscle is necessary for approaching the more proximal portion of the axillary artery. Repair of the artery from iatrogenic trauma can be performed through either a transverse or a longitudinal incision. The artery is surrounded by nerve roots in the arm, and care must be taken to prevent injury.

Repair of the axillary artery can be accomplished by the usual techniques. The axillary artery rarely can be mobilized enough to allow débridement of a significant injury and an end-to-end anastomosis. Although the axillary artery may be of an acceptable size to place a prosthetic graft, saphenous vein bypass should be used when possible. Carotid-to-brachial or axillary-to-brachial vein bypass is a useful alternative for chronic occlusive disease of the axillary artery when direct repair is not required (Fig. 92-4). Patency of carotid-to-brachial artery vein bypass is excellent and is our treatment of choice for occlusive disease of the axillary artery.

Embolectomy of the axillary artery can be performed from either the brachial artery in the antecubital fossa or the distal axillary artery. A transverse arteriotomy is recom-

mended. Interventional radiologic treatment of axillary artery injuries has been reported.[31] Because of the small number of cases, the long-term outcome is not well defined.

Brachial Artery

For the brachial artery, embolectomy is usually performed through an incision just below the antecubital fossa (Fig. 91-5). This incision allows embolectomy of the proximal brachial artery and the distal radial and ulnar arteries

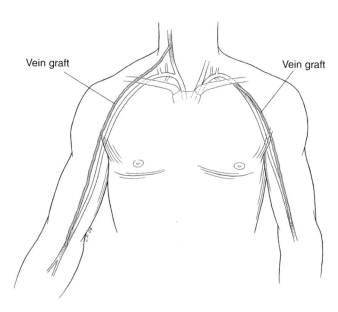

FIGURE 92-4 Carotid-to-brachial and axillary-to-brachial artery bypass are shown. The vein graft is tunneled subcutaneously and in the case of the carotid-to-brachial bypass over the clavicle.

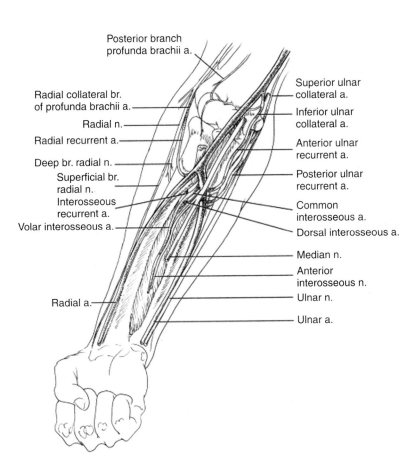

Posterior branch
profunda brachii a.

Radial collateral br.
of profunda brachii a.

Radial n.

Radial recurrent a.

Deep br. radial n.

Superficial br.
radial n.

Interosseous
recurrent a.

Volar interosseous a.

Radial a.

Superior ulnar
collateral a.

Inferior ulnar
collateral a.

Anterior ulnar
recurrent a.

Posterior ulnar
recurrent a.

Common
interosseous a.

Dorsal interosseous a.

Median n.

Anterior
interosseous n.

Ulnar n.

Ulnar a.

FIGURE 92-5 The brachial artery typically bifurcates just below the elbow. This approach allows retrograde embolectomy of the brachial artery and antegrade embolectomy of the radial and ulnar arteries. (From Valentine RJ, Wind CG: Anatomic Exposures in Vascular Surgery, 2nd ed. Philadelphia, Lippincott Williams & Wilkins, 2003.)

individually. For iatrogenic injury or intrinsic disease, the brachial artery is approached directly over the area of stenosis or occlusion. The more proximal brachial artery is surrounded by a set of paired veins and the median and ulnar nerves, which mandates careful dissection (Fig. 92-6). Saphenous vein bypass or interposition graft is necessary for long segment occlusions or injuries, but mobilization and end-to-end anastomosis may be possible for more discrete injuries. Carotid-to-brachial or axillary-to-brachial artery bypass with vein is used for bypass of long segment brachial artery occlusions (see Fig. 92-4).

Radial and Ulnar Arteries

Repair of radial and ulnar artery injuries is rarely necessary because of the rich collateral network. Despite this fact and the small size of these arteries, repair for acute traumatic injury is recommended, particularly if exploration for bleeding is required, and if there are no contraindications in terms of overall patient condition. Repair can be accomplished by either end-to-end anastomosis or vein bypass. Occluded radial and ulnar arteries that are asymptomatic should be left alone. A combination of radial or ulnar artery and palmar and digital artery occlusive disease may be seen particularly with embolic disease. Little can be done about the palmar and digital artery occlusive disease, but bypass to the palmar arches of occlusive lesions in the radial and ulnar arteries at the wrist may be helpful in this situation. Figure 92-7 is an example of a patient with significant hand ischemia secondary to occlusion of the radial and the ulnar

arteries treated with saphenous vein bypass from the distal radial artery to the plantar arch.

Embolectomy of the radial and ulnar arteries may be accomplished either via an antecubital brachial artery, which is the preferred approach because of the small size of the arteries, or by a direct approach either proximally or distally. Arteriovenous reversal, performed by connecting the distal cephalic vein to the radial artery at the wrist, has been suggested as a possible alternative for revascularization, but in my limited experience, it has not given any long-term benefits, and the short-term results seem limited.[32]

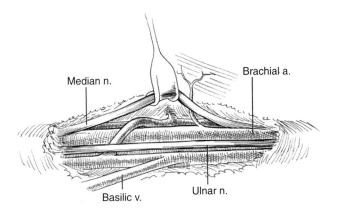

Median n.

Brachial a.

Basilic v.

Ulnar n.

FIGURE 92-6 The proximal brachial artery is surrounded by the median and ulnar nerves and typically paired veins. (From Valentine RJ, Wind CG: Anatomic Exposures in Vascular Surgery, 2nd ed. Philadelphia, Lippincott Williams & Wilkins, 2003.)

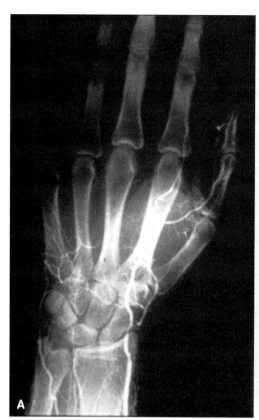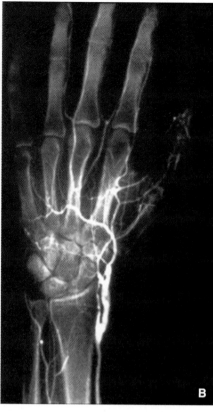

FIGURE 92-7 Angiogram shows radial and ulnar artery occlusion (**A**) and patent distal radial-to-palmar arch bypass (**B**).

■ CONCLUSION

As with the lower extremity, numerous disease conditions may result in occlusive disease in the upper extremity. Although the collateral network in the upper extremity is rich, occlusive disease of the upper extremity may result in life-limiting and limb-threatening ischemia. With the exception of the occlusive disease of the distal arterial vessels of the digits, revascularization or embolectomy of the upper extremity or both may be readily performed. In contrast to the lower extremity, long-term outcome data are not readily available because the number of upper extremity revascularizations is minuscule compared with revascularizations in the lower extremity. As in the lower extremity, proximal bypasses have excellent patency, whereas distal bypasses have intermediate results.

■ REFERENCES

1. Casey RG, Richards S, O'Donohoe M: Vascular surgery of the upper limb: The first year of a new vascular service. Ir Med J 95:104, 2002.
2. Edwards JM, Porter JM: Associated diseases with Raynaud's syndrome. Vasc Med Rev 1:51, 1990.
3. Edwards JM, Porter JM: Upper extremity arterial disease: Etiologic considerations and differential diagnosis. Semin Vasc Surg 11:60, 1998.
4. Greenfield LJ, Rajagopalan S, Olin JW: Upper extremity arterial disease. Cardiol Clin 20:623, 2002.
5. Roddy SP, Darling RC 3rd, Chang BB, et al: Brachial artery reconstruction for occlusive disease: A 12-year experience. J Vasc Surg 33:802, 2001.
6. Yeager RA, Moneta GL, Edwards JM, et al: Relationship of hemodialysis access to finger gangrene in patients with end-stage renal disease. J Vasc Surg 36:245, 2002.
7. Ferris BL, Taylor LM Jr, Oyama K, et al: Hypothenar hammer syndrome: Proposed etiology. J Vasc Surg 31:104, 2000.
8. Edwards JM, Antonius J, Porter JM: Critical hand ischemia caused by forearm fibromuscular dysplasia. J Vasc Surg 2:459, 1985.
9. Kretschmer G, Niederle B, Polterauer P, et al: Irradiation-induced changes in the subclavian and axillary arteries after radiotherapy for carcinoma of the breast. Surgery 99:658, 1986.
10. Rivers SP, Baur GM, Inahara T, et al: Arm ischemia secondary to giant cell arteritis. Am J Surg 143:554, 1982.
11. Mills JL Sr: Buerger's disease in the 21st century: Diagnosis, clinical features, and therapy. Semin Vasc Surg 16:179, 2003.
12. Brener BJ, Couch NP: Peripheral arterial complications of left heart catheterization and their management. Am J Surg 125:521, 1973.
13. Kitzmiller JW, Hertzer NR, Beven EG: Routine surgical management of brachial artery occlusion after cardiac catheterization. Arch Surg 117:1066, 1982.
14. Chatziioannou A, Ladopoulos C, Mourikis D, et al: Complications of lower-extremity outpatient arteriography via low brachial artery. Cardiovasc Interv Radiol 27:31-34, 2004.
15. Criado FJ, Wilson EP, Abul-Khoudoud O, et al: Brachial artery catheterization to facilitate endovascular grafting of abdominal aortic aneurysm: Safety and rationale. Vasc Surg 32:1137, 2000.
16. Davis K, Kennedy JW, Kemp HG Jr: Complications of coronary arteriography from the collaborative study of coronary artery surgery. Circulation 59:1105, 1979.
17. Eggebrecht H, Naber C, Woertgen U, et al: Catheter percutaneous suture-mediated closure of femoral access sites deployed through the procedure sheath: Initial clinical experience with a novel vascular closure device. Cardiovasc Interv 58:313-321, 2003.
18. AbuRahma AF, Robinson PA, Boland JP, et al: Complications of arteriography in a recent series of 707 cases: Factors affecting outcome. Ann Vasc Surg 7:122, 1993.

19. Stella PR, Kiemeneij F, Laarman GJ, et al: Incidence and outcome of radial artery occlusion following transradial artery coronary angioplasty. Cathet Cardiovasc Diagn 40:156, 1997.

20. Scheer B, Perel A, Pfeiffer UJ: Clinical review: Complications and risk factors of peripheral arterial catheters used for haemodynamic monitoring in anaesthesia and intensive care medicine. Crit Care 6:199, 2002.

21. Katras T, Baltazar U, Rush DS, et al: Subclavian arterial injury associated with blunt trauma. Vasc Surg 35:43, 2001.

22. Hunt CA, Kingsley JR: Vascular injuries of the upper extremity. South Med J 93:466, 2000.

23. Jackson MR: Upper extremity arterial injuries in athletes. Semin Vasc Surg 16:232, 2003.

24. Yao JS: Upper extremity ischemia in athletes. Semin Vasc Surg 11:96, 1998.

25. Hernandez-Richter T, Angele MK, Helmberger T, et al: Acute ischemia of the upper extremity: Long-term results following thrombembolectomy with the Fogarty catheter. Arch Surg 386:261, 2001.

26. Nehler MR, Taylor LM Jr, Moneta GL, Porter JM: Upper extremity ischemia from subclavian artery aneurysm caused by bony abnormalities of the thoracic outlet. Arch Surg 132:527, 1997.

27. Pentti J, Salenius JP, Kuukasjarvi P, Tarkka M: Outcome of surgical treatment in acute upper limb ischaemia. Ann Chir Gynaecol 84:25, 1995.

28. Edwards JM, Zierler RE: Duplex ultrasound assessment of upper extremity arteries. In Zwiebel WJ (ed): Introduction to Vascular Ultrasonography, 4th ed. Philadelphia, WB Saunders, 2001, pp 249-261.

29. Mclafferty RB, Edwards JM, Taylor LM Jr, Porter JM: Diagnosis and long-term clinical outcome in patients presenting with hand ischemia. J Vasc Surg 22:361, 1995.

30. Schwartz M, Weaver F, Yellin A, Ralls P: The utility of color flow Doppler examination in penetrating extremity arterial trauma. Am Surg 59:375, 1993.

31. Xenos ES, Freeman M, Stevens S, et al: Covered stents for injuries of subclavian and axillary arteries. J Vasc Surg 38:451, 2003.

32. King TA, Marks J, Berrettoni BA, Seitz WH: Arteriovenous reversal for limb salvage in unreconstructible upper extremity arterial occlusive disease. J Vasc Surg 17:924, 1993.

Chapter

Raynaud's Syndrome:
Vasospastic and Occlusive Arterial Disease Involving the Distal Upper Extremity

93

ROGER F. J. SHEPHERD, MB, BCH

Upper extremity arterial disease is often considered to be one of the most challenging areas of vascular practice. Not only is it less commonly encountered than lower extremity arterial disease but it is more complex, with a wide range of clinical manifestations and pathologic causes.

Ischemic symptoms of the hand and fingers often invoke a sense of concern and apprehension not only for the patient but also for the consulting physician. The patient is concerned about potential major disability from impaired hand function, and the consulting physician is concerned with finding the correct diagnosis to ensure proper management and the best outcome. If it is determined that the patient has a primary vasospastic disorder, all that may be necessary is education and reassurance; however, if a more serious underlying disease is present, the evaluation and management become significantly more complex.

Impaired arterial perfusion to the hands and fingers can result from obstruction of large proximal arteries, smaller distal arteries, or the microvasculature. Digital ischemia may be episodic or constant and can result from reversible vasospasm or be due to fixed obstructive arterial disease.[1] Symptoms may range from cold hands and pallor of the fingers to severe, irreversible tissue loss with digital ulcers, skin necrosis, and gangrene.

The vascular clinician who sees patients with Raynaud's syndrome needs to be familiar with a large number of diverse disorders. These include thromboangiitis obliterans, connective tissue diseases (CTDs), vasculitis, and hematologic disorders as well as conditions unique to the upper extremity including thoracic outlet syndrome and vibratory and traumatic occlusive arterial disease of occupational origin. A multidisciplinary approach is often necessary to ensure optimal management of these complex patients.

The focus of this chapter is vasospastic and occlusive disorders causing Raynaud's syndrome. The chapter begins with the terminology and classification of Raynaud's syndrome, followed by a review of the anatomy and physiology of blood flow in the upper extremities, factors regulating the microcirculation in the fingers, and possible alterations of normal vascular function that may be responsible for primary vasospasm. Secondary causes of Raynaud's syndrome are discussed and outlined in table format. Clinical presentations, physical examination, non-invasive vascular laboratory testing, and angiographic features are reviewed with discussion of current treatment modalities for both primary vasospasm and secondary obstructive disease causing Raynaud's syndrome.

■ RAYNAUD'S DISEASE AND RAYNAUD'S PHENOMENON

In 1882, Maurice Raynaud, a French physician, entitled his thesis for the Academy of Medicine "On Local Asphyxia and Symmetrical Gangrene of the Extremities."[2] In this paper he described 25 patients with intermittent digital ischemia and recognized the relationship of local cold and emotional stress in the causation of these episodes. He attributed the attacks of digital ischemia to excessive sympathetic activity producing vasoconstriction of digital arteries. He also described the classic tricolor skin changes of digital pallor, cyanosis, and rubor that are now associated with his name. These patients with intermittent vasospastic episodes of digital ischemia were hence diagnosed as having "Raynaud's disease."[3]

Raynaud's original series included a mixture of patients; some did have a primary vasospastic disease, but others with gangrene of the fingers likely had significant arterial obstruction. In 1901, Hutchinson recognized that there can be multiple causes of Raynaud's observations and coined the term *Raynaud's phenomenon* to indicate the presence of an underlying abnormality causing this disorder. Over the past 100 years, by tradition, we have therefore classified all patients with digital vasospasm into the following two groups based on the presence or absence of associated disease:

- *Raynaud's disease* refers to a primary vasospastic disorder where there is no identifiable underlying cause.
- *Raynaud's phenomenon* refers to individuals where vasospasm is secondary to an underlying condition or disease.

In clinical practice, use of the term *Raynaud's disease* or *Raynaud's phenomenon* has not been intuitive. These terms are commonly misunderstood and are often mistakenly interchanged; as a result, they have lost much of their original meaning. Review of the Raynaud's literature is complicated by the lack of a standard accepted diagnostic classification.

For more than 20 years John Porter and others have advocated replacing the old terms of *disease* and *phenomenon* with Raynaud's *syndrome*.[4]

Patients with *Raynaud's syndrome* can be subdivided into two groups: (1) primary Raynaud's syndrome, indicating those with idiopathic vasospasm, and (2) secondary Raynaud's syndrome, indicating those who have an underlying disease causing vasospastic episodes.

It has also been helpful to classify those with Raynaud's syndrome as having either vasospastic or obstructive disease. This has important clinical utility because it under-scores the different pathologic mechanisms, treatment options, and outcomes of these two groups.

When vasospasm is due to another disorder such as Buerger's disease, the diagnostic label should reflect the underlying causative disease (e.g., Buerger's disease with secondary Raynaud's syndrome).

If the patient has significant occlusive arterial disease, without features of vasospasm, this should not be referred to as Raynaud's syndrome but instead should be identified by the underlying disease such as atherosclerosis. It is recognized that patients with atherosclerosis may indeed have secondary Raynaud's, but the main abnormality is occlusive disease. The mistaken use of the term *Raynaud's syndrome* for all patients with fixed arterial occlusive disease has led to much of the current confusion and per-ceived difficulty in evaluating and treating upper extremity arterial disease. There are many examples of severe, nonreversible, limb-threatening hand ischemia misdiag-nosed as vasospastic Raynaud's disease with resultant delayed or inappropriate treatment.

This chapter is entitled "Raynaud's Syndrome" but may at times use the older terms of *Raynaud's disease* and *Raynaud's phenomenon* solely to reflect historical literature. It is strongly recommended that *Raynaud's syndrome* replace the older terminology.

Raynaud's Syndrome: Definition

Raynaud's syndrome is defined as episodic pallor or cyanosis of the fingers due to vasoconstriction of small arteries or arterioles in the fingers occurring in response to cold or emotional stress.

The hallmark of primary Raynaud's syndrome is the change in skin temperature and color, brought on by cold exposure. A typical vasospastic attack is characterized by the sudden onset of waxy pallor of part or all of one or more digits. Cyanosis follows as static blood in the capillaries becomes desaturated. The attack subsides with return of arterial inflow, and postischemic vasodilation results in hyperemia and rubor of the skin (Figs. 93-1 and 93-2).

Vasospastic attacks most commonly involve the fingers but can affect both the fingers and toes in up to one third of patients (Fig. 93-3). Vasospasm of the nose and ear and nipple[5] has been reported but is unusual.

Other vascular beds prone to vasospasm include the coronary and cerebral vessels. Patients with Prinzmetal's angina are more likely to have Raynaud's phenomenon and migraine headaches. In one study of 62 patients with variant angina, 15 had Raynaud's phenomenon and 16 had migraine headaches.[6] This suggests a common factor causing generalized vasospasm.

Raynaud's syndrome predominantly affects young women, but it can affect both sexes and occur in any age group, including children. Older studies have noted that Raynaud's syndrome affects women four times more often than men. More recent surveys indicate men are commonly affected, with a male-to-female ratio closer to 1:1.6.[7,8] The age of onset for primary Raynaud's ranges from 11 to 45 years. A study by Allen and Brown of 474 patients with Raynaud's syndrome reported an average age of 31 years.[9] Older patients with Raynaud's syndrome are more likely to have a contributing underlying arterial disease.

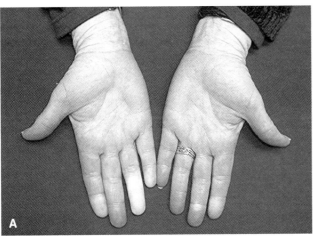
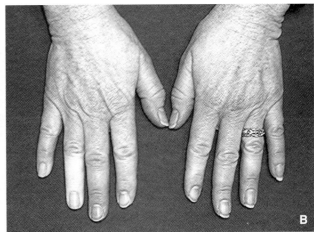

FIGURE 93-1 Palmar (**A**) and dorsal (**B**) views of hands of patient with a textbook example of Raynaud's syndrome. Note that attacks of digital vasospasm cause well-demarcated pallor or cyanosis affecting one or more fingers brought on by cold exposure or emotional stress. (See color figure in this section.)

Prevalence of Raynaud's Syndrome

Raynaud's syndrome is a common disorder. In one large survey conducted in South Carolina, 4.6% of 1752 randomly selected individuals indicated they had experienced symptoms of white or blue color changes of the fingers.[10] In a further study by Weinrich and associates in 1990 using a health survey of 5246 adults with selective interviews, the prevalence of Raynaud's syndrome was found to be 3.5%.[7]

The prevalence is higher in cooler climates, especially in European countries including England, Denmark, and France. A study from England found 8% of men and 17% of women have attacks of cold, numb, and white fingers.[11] In a general practice setting in the United Kingdom, Raynaud's phenomenon was found to affect 26 (11%) of 231 men and 34 (19%) of 182 women as determined by a postal questionnaire.[12] In Denmark, a study found that 22% of healthy physical therapists aged 21 to 50 years reported episodic white fingers for more than 2 years.[13]

Cold fingers are common and, in the absence of any other symptoms, may be a normal finding. Not surprisingly, complaints of cold fingers are more common in cooler and damper climates. For example, in one study in France, 31% of people surveyed reported they had unusual coolness of the fingers.[14]

Diagnosis of Raynaud's Syndrome

The diagnosis of Raynaud's syndrome is based on the patient's personal description of a typical vasospastic attack involving one or more fingers related to cold exposure.[15,16]

Coffman suggested the following criteria for the diagnosis of Raynaud's syndrome: "Episodic attacks of well demarcated blanching or cyanosis of one or more digits brought on by cold exposure or emotion."[16]

Episodic means the attacks are reversible as opposed to persistent ischemia. A well-demarcated change occurs with local vasospasm, and this avoids the problem of overdiag-

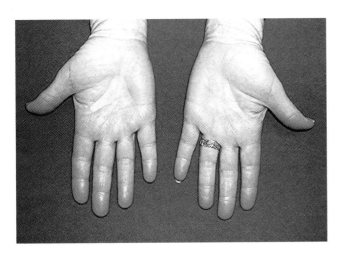

FIGURE 93-2 Resolution of vasospasm with postischemic hyperemia (same patient as in Fig. 93-1).

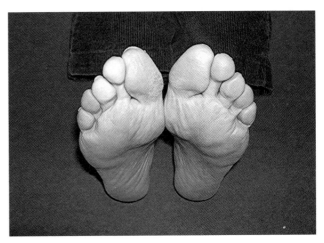

FIGURE 93-3 Digital vasospasm can affect the toes as well as the fingers. (See color figure in this section.)

nosis in normal individuals who simply have pale fingers. By definition, episodes of vasospasm must be provoked by cold or emotional stress.

All three color changes do not have to be present to make the diagnosis of Raynaud's syndrome. Gifford and Heins reported in 1957 that 65% of 133 patients had classic white to blue to red changes; however, many patients describe only episodic pallor or cyanosis of the fingers.[17] A study of 78 patients by Maricq found that white (38%) or blue (44%) was the most common color change reported by patients.[10] Maricq and colleagues used color charts to assist patients with description of their symptoms.[18] Rarely does the patient have a spontaneous episode of vasospasm at the physician's office, and it is surprisingly difficult to provoke a typical vasospastic episode in the vascular laboratory.

Although clinical presentations may be variable, the typical patient is a young woman who describes attacks of "dead" pallor involving part or all of one or many fingers brought on by cold exposure with full and rapid recovery on rewarming of the digits. The episodes are self-limiting and may last from less than a minute to generally not more than 10 to 20 minutes. Local warming of the hands is usually successful in terminating attacks. Pallor may involve part of the digit or the entire finger. In most patients with primary disease, arterial vasospasm involves all the fingers of both hands but may spare the thumb.

Attacks may occur several times a day to several times a week. Episodes of vasospasm are more common in the cooler winter months, and some patients have few or no attacks during the summer.

Pain is usually not a feature during the pallor or cyanotic phase in primary Raynaud's syndrome. The absence of pain and lack of tissue damage during arterial vasospasm may be because during cooling of the fingers, as well as vasoconstriction, there is also cold-induced intermittent vasodilation, and this allows just enough blood flow to protect the fingers from severe ischemia or freezing. Minor finger discomfort, but not pain, may occur during the hyperemic recovery phase.

In contrast, patients with underlying occlusive disease have little or no reserve and cannot increase digital blood flow with the result that ischemic damage can occur during cold exposure. These patients with secondary Raynaud's phenomenon are more likely to complain of digital pain on rewarming of cold fingers because the blood flow cannot increase to match the increased metabolic activity of the fingers.

Regulation of Blood Flow in the Fingers

Blood flow in the fingers is highly variable and can range from less than 1 mL/min per 100 mL of tissue to 180 mL/min.[19]

Only a very small portion of digital blood flow (<10%) is needed to provide nutrients and oxygen to the tissues.[20] Most blood flow in the fingers serves an important role in thermoregulation to control body temperature. Blood vessels that are superficially located in the skin dilate to radiate off excess heat to the environment, and this reduces body core temperature. In response to cold, these arteries constrict to decrease blood flow and conserve body heat. Fifty years ago, Greenfield and Shepherd showed that one hand can lose 800 calories of heat per minute, causing a fall in esophageal temperature of 0.6° C in 9 minutes.[21]

Changes in blood flow in the fingers occur due to environmental temperature, and this is effected in part by the central nervous system with input from the cerebral cortex, hypothalamus, and medullary vasomotor centers. The hypothalamus changes body temperature by altering the sympathetic outflow to the digital vessels via the medulla, spinal cord, sympathetic ganglion, and local nerves. The sympathetic nerves innervate vascular smooth muscle in the digital arteries and regulate vessel diameter and blood flow. Activation of sympathetic nerves on vascular smooth muscle causes vasoconstriction, and decreased sympathetic activity allows for vasodilation.

The fingers and the palms of the hands contain many arteriovenous (AV) anastomoses (connecting the arterial and venous circulation), and blood can return to the venous circulation before reaching the distal small capillaries. Studies by Coffman and others have shown that reflex sympathetic vasoconstriction produced by total body cooling causes a marked decrease in total finger blood flow; however, capillary blood flow is not affected.[20,22] This is due to constriction of AV shunts while maintaining nutritional blood flow to the fingers. During vasodilation, 80% to 90% of finger blood flow is shunted through AV anastomoses.

In warm environments the fingers are able to dramatically increase blood flow by shunting more blood through these AV fistulae. The AV shunts are also under the control of the sympathetic nervous system.[23] In response to cold exposure or body cooling, increased sympathetic tone causes the digital AV shunts to close; hence less blood flows through the fingers and the core body temperature is maintained.

As the fingers are cooled, maximum vasoconstriction to cold occurs at 10° C to 20° C. At lower temperatures, cold-induced vasodilation results in slight reopening of arteries to allow a trickle of blood to the fingertips. Lewis in 1930 measured blood flow in the finger with a thermoelectric junction and found during immersion in cold water there was initial vasoconstriction followed by alternating periods of vasodilation.[24]

This cold-induced vasodilation, which protects the fingers from freezing in a cold environment, is impaired in those with Raynaud's syndrome secondary to occlusive arterial disease. With cold exposure, there is a regular rhythmic fluctuation of finger flow due to periods of vasoconstriction and vasodilation in the fingers every 30 seconds to 2 minutes.[25] Other investigators have found similar rhythmic fluctuations of finger flow with a frequency of 5 to 10 per minute.[26] Since the time of Lewis, these alternating periods of vasoconstriction and dilation have been called the *hunting response*.[27]

Mechanisms of Primary Vasospasm

The exact cause of vasospastic attacks in primary Raynaud's disease is unknown. There is no demonstrable structural abnormality of the digital arteries. Whether primary Raynaud's disease represents an exaggeration of normal thermoregulatory mechanisms causing constriction of digital vessels in response to cooling or is due to a specific local or systemic fault remains an area of controversy.

Raynaud in 1888 hypothesized that overactivity of the sympathetic nervous system was the sole cause of vasospasm.[3] For example, the autonomic nervous system is responsible for maintaining arteriolar tone and blood pressure, and emotional stimuli can bring on vasospastic attacks.

Lewis in 1929 thought that there must be a local fault in the digital arteries causing increased sensitivity of the blood vessel to cold.[28] In a series of studies, he found that local cooling produced ischemic attacks in a single finger and nerve blocks or surgical sympathectomy could not prevent cold-induced attacks. He also found that cooling of the proximal finger, but keeping the distal finger warm, would still cause distal vasospasm. He concluded that this must be due to local factors causing constriction of the more proximal digital artery by cold.[29]

Although the actual cause of primary Raynaud's disease remains unknown, there are likely a number of different factors affecting the normal regulation of blood flow to the fingers including local, humoral, and nervous mechanisms. Derangement of any of these may predispose to vasospastic attacks in primary Raynaud's syndrome.[30]

Postulated abnormalities in primary Raynaud's include lower systolic blood pressure, variation in neurotransmitters released from sympathetic nerves, increased sensitivity of α_2-adrenoreceptors on the nerve endings, endothelial dysfunction with a change in the balance from endothelium-derived relaxing to contracting factors, increased platelet serotonin, and neurohumoral transmitters released from local nerves (Fig. 93-4).[30]

Primary Raynaud's Disease: potential mechanisms

- Increased sensitivity of α_2 receptors to norepinephrine
- Insufficient nitric oxide
- Increased endothelin-1
- Decreased distending pressure
- Platelets release increased 5-HT and TX_{a2}

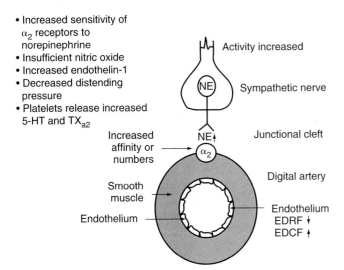

Activity increased

Sympathetic nerve

Junctional cleft

Increased affinity or numbers

Smooth muscle

Endothelium

Digital artery

Endothelium
EDRF ↓
EDCF ↑

FIGURE 93-4 There are many potential causes of vasospastic attacks in primary Raynaud's syndrome. Norepinephrine released from the sympathetic nerve ending acts on the postjunctional α_2-receptor located on vascular smooth muscle. Local cooling enhances the response of the α_2-receptor, causing increased arterial contraction. Endothelial dysfunction may lead to insufficient nitric oxide or increased endothelin-1, changing the balance toward arterial constriction. Activated platelets release the thromboxane A_2 (TX_{a2}) and serotonin, which may aggravate arterial vasospasm. A decrease in intraluminal distending pressure may decrease the "critical closing pressure" threshold and result in a vasospastic attack. 5-HT, 5-hydroxytryptamine; NE, norepinephrine; EDCF, endothelium-derived contracting factor; EDRF, endothelium-derived relaxing factor.

Transluminal Distending Pressure and the Critical Closing Pressure

Transmural arterial distending forces are decreased with lower systolic blood pressure. Any stimulus that causes further contracture of smooth muscle in the wall of the artery may cause abrupt vessel closure. Women have been shown to have a lower basal hand blood flow compared to men of similar age, which may reflect higher sympathetic activity.[31] This may account for the increased incidence of Raynaud's disease in women.

Norepinephrine and the α_2 Receptor

Sympathetic nerves can respond to cold and emotional stress by releasing neurotransmitters such as norepinephrine that acts on the postsynaptic α_2 receptor causing vascular smooth muscle contraction. Although cooling slows the rate of nerve transmission and weakens the force of muscle contraction, cold also causes increased affinity of the α_2 receptor for norepinephrine, resulting in enhanced smooth muscle contraction in the cold.[32-34]

The Endothelium

Since the initial discoveries by Furchgott and Zawadzki[35] and Moncada,[36] Vane,[37] and their associates elucidating the role of the endothelium in producing vasoactive substances, it is now known that vascular endothelial cells synthesize a number of vasodilating and vasoconstricting substances.[38-40] Endothelial-derived relaxing factors include nitric oxide (NO), prostacyclin, adenosine triphosphate (ATP), and bradykinin. NO is a potent vasodilator synthesized from the amino acid, L-arginine, by the activity of the enzyme NO synthetase. NO diffuses from the endothelium into the smooth muscle where it activates guanylate cyclase to increase intracellular cyclic guanine monophosphate, leading to vascular relaxation.

The endothelial cell also produces factors that cause vessel contraction, such as endothelin (ET)-1, which is a potent vasoconstrictor as well as a promoter of fibroblast and smooth muscle proliferation. Other endothelium-derived contracting factors include angiotensin II, thromboxane A_2, and superoxide anion, which is an oxygen-derived free radical. Patients with primary Raynaud's disease have been found to have increased circulating and intraplatelet serotonin.[41] Thromboxane A_2 and serotonin produced by platelets can induce vasospasm.

Normally the endothelial cells continually form and release enough NO to keep the vascular smooth muscle relaxed. If the endothelium is damaged, NO production is decreased and vasoconstrictor substances such as ET may predominate.[42] Increased levels of ET-1 would potentiate arterial contraction by other agents such as norepinephrine and serotinin.[43]

A number of studies have suggested endothelial dysfunction as an important cause of Raynaud's syndrome. In one study, patients underwent a sequential series of infusions with acetylcholine, prostacyclin, glyceryl trinitrate, and L-arginine. Patients with a history of Raynaud's syndrome had a greater digital artery vasodilator response to intra-arterial glyceryl trinitrate (an endothelium-independent vasodilator) than to acetylcholine (an endothelium-dependent vasodilator) compared to control patients.[44]

The potential role of ET in primary Raynaud's disease has also been studied. Plasma ET-1 levels become elevated in response to the cold pressor test, which may suggest an association between the rise in ET-1 levels and cold-induced vasoconstriction.[45] Whole-body cooling also increases ET-1 levels in women with primary Raynaud's syndrome.[46]

A threefold rise in ET-1 concentration has been reported in subjects with primary Raynaud's phenomenon.[47] Although a recent study did not find a relationship between ET levels in those with Raynaud's phenomenon compared with normal subjects,[48] a larger study did document elevated ET-1 and elevated asymmetrical dimethyl-arginine in secondary Raynaud's syndrome.[49]

Increased ET-1 levels may cause vascular structural changes with adverse consequences on vascular reactivity.[42] ET levels are also elevated in secondary Raynaud's disease associated with CTDs.

Neurohumoral Substances

Sympathetic nerves also release neuropeptide Y and ATP, which are vasoconstrictor agents.[50] The vasoconstrictor effect of ATP is also augmented in response to the cold.

Substance P and calcitonin gene-related peptides are vasodilators released by sensory-motor nerves. Both induce the synthesis of NO in the endothelial cell causing smooth muscle relaxation. A relative deficiency may occur in some CTDs, aggravating vasoconstriction.

The parasympathetic nerves release acetylcholine and vasoactive intestinal peptide, which are both vasodilators. Acetylcholine acts in an endothelial-dependent fashion, and vasoactive intestinal peptide is endothelial independent. With endothelial damage, as in atherosclerosis or small vessel fibrosis in scleroderma, acetylcholine-induced vasodilation is impaired.

Secondary Vasospastic Disorders: Occlusive Arterial Disease

Secondary causes of Raynaud's disease all have one thing in common: They all cause some degree of fixed vascular obstruction to blood flow, which decreases the threshold for cold-induced vasospasm to occur. When the artery is narrowed due to preexisting large- or small-vessel disease, there is a lower "critical closing pressure" and a relatively normal vasoconstrictor response to cold or other stimuli will result in temporary vessel closure. Any disease that narrows the vessel lumen or increases blood viscosity may cause Raynaud's syndrome. Raynaud's syndrome is common in CTDs such as scleroderma where intimal hyperplasia, thrombosis, and fibrosis result in arterial narrowing. Abnormal plasma proteins in myeloma and other hematologic cancers cause hyperviscosity and decreased blood flow.

Anatomy of Upper Extremity Blood Flow

An understanding of anatomy of blood flow in the upper extremity is important to all physicians and surgeons who see patients with Raynaud's syndrome. Arterial disorders that are associated with Raynaud's syndrome may affect the circulation at any level from the aortic arch to the distal fingers.

The arterial circulation of the hands and fingers is complex with many anatomic variations. The innominate artery branches off the ascending aortic arch and divides into the right subclavian artery and common carotid artery. Rarely an aberrant right subclavian artery originates from the left side of the aortic arch coursing in back of the esophagus and leading to symptomatic compression of both the native artery and local structures (see Fig. 93-1). The left carotid usually arises separately from the aortic arch but sometimes can arise from the innominate artery (an anatomic variant called a *bovine arch*). The left subclavian generally arises directly off the distal aortic arch. At the level of the clavicle, the left and right subclavian artery exits the thoracic cavity and runs over the first rib and under the proximal to mid one third of the clavicle. A thoracic outlet syndrome results from extrinsic arterial compression owing to a number of muscles and fibrous bands between the first rib and clavicle. Repetitive trauma to the subclavian artery from a thoracic outlet syndrome can result in intimal damage and localized aneurysm formation with potential for distal embolization. Atheroembolism from a friable plaque in the upper extremity often travels to the most distal part of the circulation, the fingertips.

Occlusive disease at any level from the arch of the aorta to the palmar and digital arteries can result in ischemic symptoms to the hands and fingers. Atherosclerosis frequently involves proximal large vessels but is uncommon distal to the subclavian artery.[51]

Radiation-induced arterial disease may involve the subclavian and axillary arteries because these vessels may be in the field of therapeutic radiation for breast cancer, lymphoma, or other head and neck malignancies.[52]

The brachial artery runs along the medial aspect of the upper arm where it can be damaged by local trauma, for example resulting from improper use of a crutch. Takayasu's arteritis generally involves aortic branch arteries; however, in older individuals with temporal (giant cell arteritis), 10% of individuals may have extracranial involvement that most commonly involves the distal subclavian, axillary, and brachial arteries but almost never involves the forearm or hand arteries.

At the level of the elbow, the brachial artery divides into the ulnar and radial arteries, producing a dual arterial supply to the hands and fingers. Either the ulnar or the radial artery may provide the predominant blood supply to the hand as branches from both unite from the palmar arches that supply the digits.

Circulation in the hand is more complex with frequent anatomic variants. The deep and superficial arches are most important to the blood flow to the hand, supplying the metacarpal arteries and in turn the proper digital arteries. In most patients, branches of both the deep and superficial arches provide blood flow to all five fingers and the two palmar arches provide important collateral flow between the radial and ulnar system.[53] This dual blood supply provides important flow reserve in the hand. The radial artery can be harvested for coronary artery bypass; loss of the radial artery does not cause hand ischemia as long as the ulnar artery and superficial arch in the hand are patent.

The superficial arch is incomplete in 21.5% of people.[54] Occupational trauma to the hand is a common cause of damage to the hand arteries, in particular affecting the ulnar artery and the superficial arch in the palm. Severe consequences of digital ischemia can occur with occlusion of the ulnar artery and an incomplete superficial arch.

Metacarpal arteries in the palm originate from the superficial arch and provide blood flow to the digits. At the web space the common digital (metacarpal) arteries branch to supply the proper digital arteries that run the length of each finger. In at least 86% of extremities, all five digits are supplied by arteries from both the deep and superficial arches.[53] Each finger has two digital arteries, which is important because this prevents critical ischemia if one digital artery becomes occluded. The end of the finger is highly vascular with a dense network of blood vessels in the pulp space of the fingers.

Disorders Associated with Secondary Raynaud's Syndrome

In most series, at least one third of patients presenting for initial evaluation of Raynaud's syndrome are found to have primary vasospasm with no identifiable secondary cause. In a large series of 615 patients with Raynaud's syndrome referred to Oregon Health Sciences University from 1970 to 1987, more than one half had primary vasospasm with no identifiable disease. In those with associated abnormalities, CTD was the most common underlying disorder, accounting for 27% with Raynaud's syndrome. Scleroderma was the most likely CTD, followed by undifferentiated and mixed CTD. Atherosclerosis was less common followed by "hypersensitivity angiitis," Buerger's disease, cancer, and vibration white finger.[55]

Our experience at the Mayo Clinic is similar. In a group of 125 patients referred to the noninvasive vascular laboratory for evaluation of possible Raynaud's syndrome, we found 38% had primary Raynaud's syndrome and 42% had secondary Raynaud's syndrome. Twenty percent did not fulfill the criteria for Raynaud's syndrome. Of the secondary causes of Raynaud's syndrome, one third had an underlying CTD and another one third was found to have atherosclerotic occlusive arterial disease. Less commonly associated diseases included thoracic outlet syndrome, reflex sympathetic dystrophy, and acrocyanosis. Most of those with CTDs were diagnosed with scleroderma or mixed CTD.

In clinical practice, the differentiation between primary and secondary Raynaud's syndrome has always been challenging. In 1932 Allen and Brown[9] established clinical criteria for the diagnosis of primary Raynaud's disease, which are summarized as follows by Coffman[16]:

1. Vasospastic attacks precipitated by exposure to cold or emotional stimuli
2. Symmetrical or bilateral involvement of the extremities
3. Absence of gangrene
4. Symptom present for a minimum of 2 years
5. Absence of any other underlying disease

These clinical features continue to be useful today. In addition to these criteria, Coffman added the requirement

Table 93-1	Clinical Features to Distinguish Primary from Secondary Raynaud's Syndrome	
TYPE	**GENDER**	**OTHER FEATURES**
Primary	Usually female	Age < 45 years Vasospasm of multiple or all digits Normal vascular examination No skin abnormalities Normal laboratory studies
Secondary	Male or female	Any age Single digit involved Abnormal pulse examination Vascular laboratory abnormalities Positive autoantibodies

for a normal physical examination and normal blood tests including at least a complete blood count and sedimentation rate. Many clinicians would suggest a normal antinuclear antibody and in selected cases further blood tests to ensure the absence of other autoantibodies to exclude unsuspected CTD. Noninvasive vascular laboratory testing complements the history and physical examination. Table 93-1 outlines the clinical features to differentiate primary from secondary Raynaud's syndrome.

There is an extensive list of secondary causes of Raynaud's syndrome (Table 93-2). These conditions may be classified into CTDs (in particular, scleroderma), atherosclerotic large-vessel disease and diabetic small-vessel disease, thromboangiitis obliterans, vasculitis, arterial emboli, and atheroemboli. Diseases unique to the upper extremity include arterial entrapment—the thoracic outlet syndrome, occupational arterial disease, including the hypothenar hammer syndrome, vibration white finger, and thermal damage to the fingers. Drug- and toxin-induced vasospasm are common. Lastly, systemic disorders leading to increased viscosity cause vasospasm including cryoglobulinemia and hepatitis antigenemia.

Connective Tissue Disease

Raynaud's syndrome occurs in more than 90% of patients with scleroderma and can be the initial presenting symptom in one third of patients.[56] Other CTDs associated with Raynaud's syndrome include systemic lupus erythematosus, mixed CTD, dermatomyositis, rheumatoid arthritis, and small-vessel vasculitis.[16] A basic knowledge of CTDs is necessary for anyone who deals with patients with Raynaud's syndrome.

Systemic Sclerosis

Systemic sclerosis is the most common CTD associated with Raynaud's syndrome, and it is therefore important that salient clinical features are recognized. There is a wealth of rheumatology literature dealing with Raynaud's and scleroderma.[34,57-59]

Systemic sclerosis is also called *scleroderma,* which is derived from the words "skleros" (hard) and "derma" (skin). This is a rare multisystem disease of unknown etiology affecting an estimated 40,000 to 165,000 people in the United States with an incidence of 20 to 75 cases per 100,000.[60]

Table 93-2	Conditions Associated with Secondary Raynaud's Syndrome

GENERAL CATEGORY	SPECIFIC DISORDERS
Connective tissue disease	Scleroderma, CREST Systemic lupus erythematosus Rheumatoid arthritis Mixed connective tissue disease Overlap connective tissue disease Dermatomyositis and polymyositis Vasculitis (small, medium-sized vessel)
Occlusive arterial disease	Atherosclerosis Thromboangiitis obliterans (Buerger's disease) Giant cell arteritis Arterial emboli (cardiac and peripheral) Thoracic outlet syndrome
Occupational arterial disease	Hypothenar hammer syndrome Vibration induced
Drug-induced vasospasm	β-Adrenergic blocking drugs Vasopressors Ergot Cocaine Amphetamines Vinblastine/bleomycin
Myeloproliferative and hematologic disease	Polycythemia rubra vera Thrombocytosis Cold agglutinins Cryoglobulinemia Paraproteinemia
Malignancy	Multiple myeloma Leukemia Adenocarcinoma Astrocytoma
Infection	Hepatitis B and C antigenemia Parvovirus Purpura fulminans

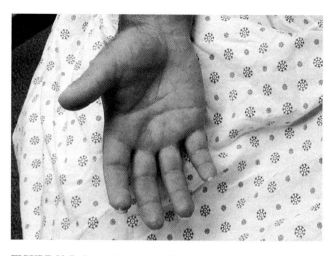

FIGURE 93-5 Systemic sclerosis. Raynaud's syndrome secondary to limited systemic sclerosis in a young male patient. There is cyanotic discoloration of the right third and fourth fingers. The diagnosis of scleroderma can be made by physical examination. There is resorption of the end of the distal right index finger with healed ulcerations of several fingertips. (See color figure in this section.)

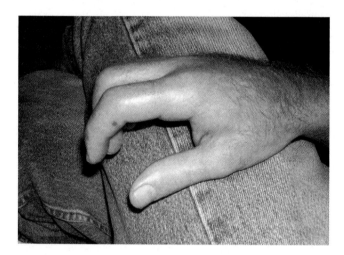

FIGURE 93-6 Systemic sclerosis. Note the tight, shiny, fibrotic skin encasing the fingers.

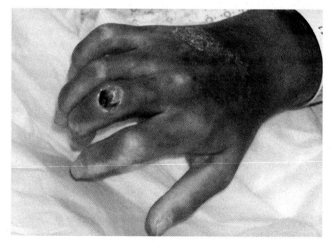

FIGURE 93-7 Advanced scleroderma with flexion contraction of the fingers and ulceration over joints. Even with the best wound care, these ulcers can be quite difficult to heal.

Scleroderma is characterized by fibrosis of skin and internal organs and causes widespread small-vessel vasculopathy and fibrosis. Small arteries, arterioles, and capillaries are affected by obliterative and proliferative structural changes in the vessel wall causing tissue ischemia.

Although autoantibodies are present in 95% of patients, systemic sclerosis is not an inflammatory vasculitis. The pathogenesis of arterial disease is not well understood; however, it is likely initiated by proliferation of smooth muscle cells in blood vessel intima causing luminal narrowing. Activated platelets release platelet-derived growth factors and thromboxane A_2, which can induce vasoconstriction and stimulate growth of endothelial cells and fibroblasts. Fibrin is deposited within and around vessels, causing vessel obstruction.[60]

The most characteristic feature of scleroderma is tightening or thickening of the skin initially noted as puffiness of fingers and hands. In advanced scleroderma, the skin becomes tight and shiny. Joint contraction leads to a claw-hand deformity. Ulcers typically form at the fingertips and over joints. These ulcers may be refractory to therapy and are slow to heal, causing significant ischemic digital pain (Figs. 93-5 through 93-7).

Systemic sclerosis is divided into the following two subsets depending on degree of skin involvement[61]:

- *Limited scleroderma* is by definition limited to the distal limbs without truncal involvement. Patients with limited scleroderma may have features of the CREST syndrome: *c*alcinosis, *R*aynaud's phenomenon, *e*sophageal dysmotility, *s*clerodactyly, and *t*elangiectasia. *Calcinosis* refers to subcutaneous calcification found in the fingers, forearms, and pressure points (Fig. 93-8). These calcium deposits may cause local tenderness and can ulcerate, exuding a white, hard material. Telangiectasias are prominent on the fingers and hands as well as on the face and mucus membranes. The finding of multiple small telangiectasias is a pathognomonic finding in scleroderma (Fig. 93-9). Esophageal dysmotility leads to dysphagia, regurgitation, and aspiration. Despite these complications, limited scleroderma is thought of as the more benign disease with a long, often stable course and a low incidence of heart, lung, or kidney complications. Raynaud's syndrome may be present for a number of years before other signs of scleroderma become evident.

- *Diffuse systemic sclerosis* causes skin thickening of proximal limbs and the trunk. Diffuse systemic sclerosis is often rapidly progressive with a short interval between the onset of Raynaud's syndrome and severe multiorgan disease. The diffuse form has a much worse prognosis with a 10-year survival of 40% to 60% compared to survival of more than 70% in the limited form of scleroderma. Scleroderma renal involvement results in severe hypertension and renal failure. Angiotensin-converting enzyme (ACE) inhibitors may decrease intraglomerular pressure and should be considered for all patients with scleroderma renal disease. Dyspnea, hypoxia, and resulting pulmonary hypertension occur in scleroderma lung disease. Digital involvement is disabling, but death results from the cardiac and pulmonary complications of scleroderma. Once hypoxia or right heart failure develops, mean survival is less than 2 years.[59]

Serologic studies may help to confirm the diagnosis of scleroderma and are also useful in screening for occult underlying CTD. Antinuclear antibodies are present in 95% of systemic sclerosis patients.[60] Antinuclear antibodies are not specific for scleroderma and can be present in a number of other CTDs—in particular, lupus erythematosus. A positive antinuclear antibody raises suspicion but on its own does not make a diagnosis of a CTD. Several autoantibodies are specific for systemic sclerosis, including topoisomerase 1, centromere, scl-70, RNA polymerase 1, and U3 RNP. The anticentromere antibody is associated with limited CREST syndrome. As opposed to vasculitis, the erythrocyte sedimentation rate is usually normal in systemic sclerosis.

Mixed and Undifferentiated Connective Tissue Disease

Mixed CTD is an overlap syndrome with features of at least two CTDs: usually scleroderma and systemic lupus erythematosus with elevated antinuclear antibody. Undifferentiated CTD may have a mixture of clinical findings including polyarthritis, Raynaud's syndrome, and lupus-type symptoms. Many patients who do not fit into a specific CTD category end up with a diagnosis of overlap syndrome or mixed CTD.

Systemic Lupus Erythematosus   Lupus can affect all age groups but most frequently occurs in young females. Arthralgias, skin rash, pericarditis, pleuritis, and glomerulonephritis are some of the frequent features, usually with a positive antinuclear antibody. Raynaud's syndrome is a frequent manifestation of systemic lupus erythematosus, occurring in up to 80% of patients.

Small-Vessel Vasculitis   Rheumatoid arthritis and Sjögren's syndrome can be complicated by a small-vessel vasculitis with obliterative fibrosis causing digital ischemia, sometimes

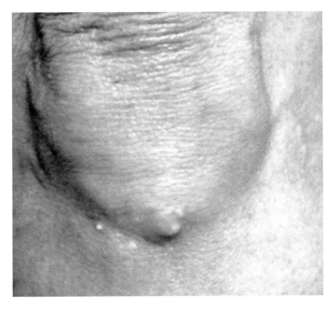

FIGURE 93-8 Calcinosis. Multiple areas of subcutaneous calcification in a patient with scleroderma.

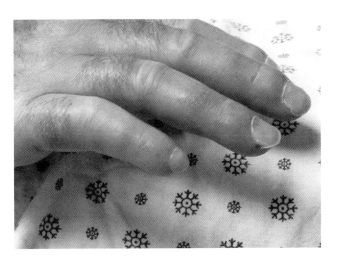

FIGURE 93-9 CREST (*c*alcinosis, *R*aynaud's, *e*sophageal dysmotility, *s*clerodactyly, *t*elangiectasia) syndrome. A pathognomonic finding in systemic sclerosis is sclerodactyly and telangiectasia of the finger. (See color figure in this section.)

with skin necrosis or digital gangrene. Other small-vessel vasculitis includes Wegener's granulomatosis, microscopic polyarteritis nodosum, and cutaneous livedo vasculitis. Malignancy can be associated with vasculitis with a similar presentation.

Future Risk of Developing a Connective Tissue Disease

The onset of Raynaud's may precede the clinical onset of a CTD by up to several years. A number of studies have looked at the future risk of developing a CTD in patients initially diagnosed with primary Raynaud's syndrome. In one study, 4 (5%) of 87 patients followed for an average of 5.1 years developed a CTD. All 4 were ultimately found to have scleroderma.[62] In another study, Harper found 3 (8%) of 39 patients initially diagnosed with primary Raynaud's syndrome subsequently developed a CTD after an average of 2 years' follow-up.[62a] Porter and Edwards combined data from 11 studies and concluded that if there are no signs or symptoms at initial presentation, the average risk of developing a CTD is only 6.6% at 3.3 years.[63] Patients with apparent primary Raynaud's syndrome should be told that the risk of developing a CTD is low but that follow-up evaluation is recommended.

Some patients at the time of their evaluation are found to have subtle abnormalities by history, examination, or blood tests, which may be suspicious but not diagnostic of CTD (such as a low positive antinuclear antibody or abnormal nailfold microscopy). These patients are at higher risk of future development of a CTD.

In one study, 73 patients with a history of vasospastic attacks but no clinical, laboratory, or serologic abnormality were followed for an average of 4.7 years and then re-evaluated. None of the 49 patients initially classified as having primary disease developed evidence of a secondary etiology during this follow-up period. In contrast, 14 of 24 who were suspected but not proven to have secondary cause were later found to have an underlying disease. Thirteen of the 14 of these patients developed a CTD. The author concluded that some patients should be followed for more than 2 years before confirming primary Raynaud's syndrome.[64]

Angiography in Connective Tissue Disease

Angiography in patients with scleroderma (and other CTDs) shows distal occlusive arterial disease in the hand and fingers. Intimal hyperplasia with fibrosis and inflammatory thrombosis causes diffuse small-vessel obstruction with obliteration of hand and finger arteries. The digital arteries are the most severely involved, with segmental or total occlusion of one or both digital arteries. Sometimes there is a striking lack of digital vessels and a lack of new or collateral vessels. In more severe cases there is disease of common digital and palmar arch vessels. Distal ulnar artery involvement can occur in up to 50% of patients but usually the radial artery is spared.[65] A nonspecific vasculitic appearance with alternating occlusive disease and artery dilation can be seen in many diseases, including Buerger's disease, trauma, small-vessel vasculitis and CTDs. All can can have similar angiographic findings (Fig. 93-10).

Angiography is generally not indicated in most patients with CTD but may be helpful when searching for another cause of hand ischemia such as atheroembolism or arterial thrombosis. Surgical or endovascular revascularization is usually not an option for digital ischemia related to CTDs because the disease involves distal small vessels.

Most patients who develop severe obliterative vasculopathy and digital ulcers due to an underlying CTD have a history of Raynaud's syndrome. It is unusual for critical ischemia with ulcers or gangrene to appear before other systemic manifestations of underlying disease.

Arterial Occlusive Disease

Arterial occlusive disease of the upper extremity can result from atherosclerosis, a variety of systemic disorders, emboli from the heart or more proximal arteries, and local trauma causing artery thrombosis.[66] Occlusive arterial disease at any level causes decreased transluminal distending pressure in the distal artery and can precipitate Raynaud's syndrome.

Atherosclerosis is a common cause of Raynaud's phenomenon. Arterial occlusive disease involving the arch or proximal vessels decreases distal perfusion pressure to the hand. Atherosclerosis affects larger proximal arteries but is unusual distal to the subclavian level. Digital ischemia due to atherosclerosis is more often caused by atheroembolism from an ulcerated plaque in the innominate or subclavian artery traveling distally and obstructing digital arteries than occurring as a result of decreased arm blood pressure.[66] In general, a proximal arterial stenosis in the upper extremity is unlikely to cause critical ischemia. More distal arterial disease as can occur in diabetic atherosclerosis does increase the risk of digital loss and gangrene (Fig. 93-11).

Thromboangiitis obliterans (Buerger's disease) is a non-atherosclerotic, inflammatory disorder involving distal, small-, and medium-sized arteries in the fingers and toes and progresses proximally.[67] Although Buerger's disease can present with distal extremity vasospasm, often it causes chronic ischemia with very painful fingertip ulcerations and necrosis. Typically Buerger's disease occurs in young male smokers who are younger than 45 years of age. Up to one half of patients develop a migratory superficial thrombophlebitis. Arteriography can be diagnostic of vascular obstruction with chronic vessel thrombosis and inflammatory changes with alternating segmental occlusions and artery dilation often with the pathognomonic finding of corkscrew collaterals. The proximal arteries are normal with no evidence of atherosclerosis. The only way to prevent progression of thromboangiitis obliterans is absolute cessation of all tobacco products (Fig. 93-12).[68]

Thromboembolism

Cardiac thromboembolism may arise from the ventricle after a myocardial infarction or more frequently from the left atrium as a common complication of atrial fibrillation. Cardiac emboli are relatively large and tend to lodge at bifurcation points in the forearm (i.e., brachial bifurcation). Most upper extremity thromboemboli (>70%) are of cardiac origin. The second most likely embolic source is from the subclavian artery.[66] Not all patients with thromboembolism have acute arterial occlusion, and not all present with the

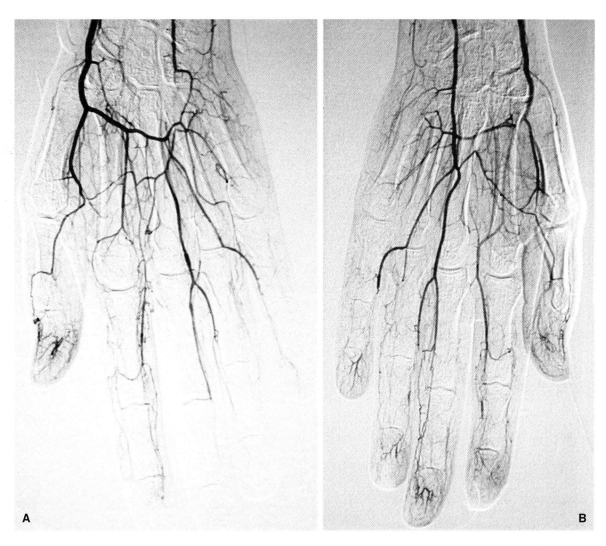

FIGURE 93-10 Bilateral upper extremity arteriogram of left (**A**) and right (**B**) hands in a patient with mixed connective tissue disease. There were features of scleroderma and CREST syndrome with strongly positive antinuclear antibody. The patient presented with an ischemic right index fingertip that did not respond to topical nitroglycerin (see also Fig. 93-24).

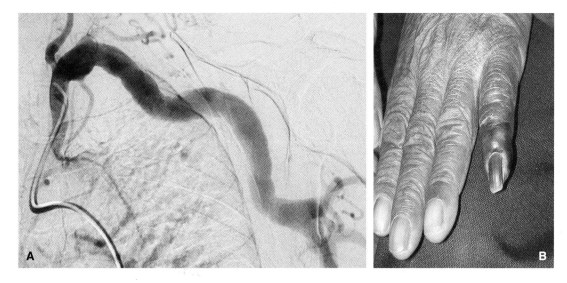

FIGURE 93-11 Angiogram (**A**) of an elderly man with ischemic gangrene of the left little finger (**B**). The angiogram shows diffuse atheromatous disease and a localized subclavian aneurysm, which was the likely source of atheroemboli to the hand. The patient underwent surgical repair of the aneurysm with a subclavian-to-brachial bypass with saphenous vein.

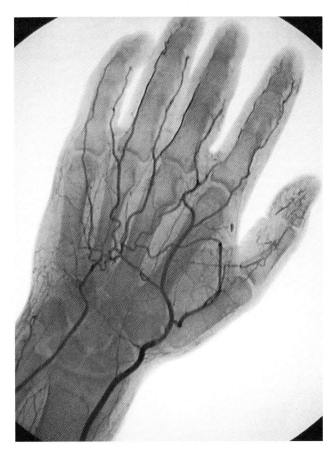

FIGURE 93-12 A young male patient with thromboangiitis obliterans presenting with digital vasospastic attacks. An upper extremity angiogram documents occlusive arterial disease involving several digits. Angiographic findings in thromboangiitis obliterans may show palmar and digital artery occlusions and irregularity, sometimes with corkscrew collaterals. The angiographic findings, however, often are not specific for Buerger's disease and can be seen in vasculitis and repetitive hand trauma.

"five Ps" (*p*ain, *p*aresthesias, *p*allor, *p*aralysis, and absent *p*ulses). More subtle presentations have included intermittent ischemia symptoms of the hands and fingers aggravated by cold exposure. This diagnosis should be considered in any patient with paroxysmal atrial fibrillation or history of cardiac disease.

Upper extremity arterial disease localized to the brachial artery suggests the possibility of local trauma, in particular cardiac catheterization,[69] or extracranial giant cell arteritis.

Occupational Arterial Injury

Occupational arterial disease can result from the use of vibratory tools such as pneumatic hammers and chain saws or from repetitive pounding to the palm of the hand in those people who use their hand as a hammer (hammer-hand syndrome). Traumatic ulnar artery occlusion is common in carpenters and mechanics but can occur in any occupation that uses instruments or hand tools, including secretaries pounding a stapler and obstetricians using forceps. Palmar and digital occlusive disease has been seen in baseball, handball, and even volleyball players.[70] Thoracic outlet compression occurs in swimmers and weight lifters.

Specific diseases include vibration-induced Raynaud's syndrome and hypothenar hammer syndrome.

Vibration-induced Raynaud's syndrome was first recognized in 1918 by Hamilton, who described a group of stonecutters from Indiana with "spastic anemia of the hands."[71] It has been estimated that as many as 1.2 million American workers are now at risk.[50] Terms that have been used to describe Raynaud's syndrome caused by chronic vibration include *hand-arm vibration syndrome* and *vibration white finger.*

Vibration-induced Raynaud's syndrome occurs in many different occupations in which workers who use chain saws, grinders, sanders, riveters, jack hammers, and pneumatic hammers. A report from Sweden found the prevalence of vibration white finger in car mechanics to be 25% for those who had worked 20 years.[72]

The risk of vibration-induced Raynaud's syndrome is proportional to the duration of exposure.[73] In a study of workers who used compressed air drills to clean castings, 4% had Raynaud's syndrome by 2 years, 48% by 3 years, and 55% by 10 years.[74]

Porter's group studied 16 autoglass workers who used a pneumatic air knife for removal of automobile windshields. The mean onset of Raynaud's syndrome was 3 years, and workers had used the vibrating knife for an average time of 2450 hours. Screening tests for underlying CTD were negative; however, most were smokers, and some may have had underlying occlusive disease. None of the workers improved after they stopped using the air knife, and one third worsened.[75]

Chronic vibration appears to cause structural damage to the artery wall with hypertrophy of the intima and media. Vibration is believed to cause sympathetic overactivity, endothelial damage, and smooth muscle hypertrophy leading to vibration-induced vasospasm.[76,77] In addition, formation of microthrombi can lead to fixed digital ischemia and fingertip necrosis.

The prognosis may be poor due to the development of digital artery obstruction after prolonged exposure to vibration. It is unknown if vibration-induced Raynaud's syndrome is reversible in earlier stages. Early symptoms may include tingling and numbness from peripheral nerve damage. Preventive measures may minimize damage, including wearing gloves, providing a cushioned surface on handles, and avoiding prolonged exposure.[78]

Hypothenar hammer syndrome is an important cause of Raynaud's syndrome and digital ischemia. Repetitive trauma to the palmar surface of the hand (from using the hand as a hammer) results in damage to the underlying palmar branch of the ulnar artery. The ulnar artery has a superficial course in the palm as it passes laterally to the hook of the hamate and this makes it especially vulnerable to localized trauma. Endothelial injury results in intraluminal thrombosis, aneurysm formation, and subsequent embolization to the fingers. The diagnosis of occlusive disease is suggested by eliciting a history of repetitive occupational hand trauma in a patient with digital ischemia and demonstrating a positive Allen test (Fig. 93-13).

Hypothenar hammer syndrome occurs in mechanics, farmers, plumbers, and especially carpenters, who use hand-held tools such as wrenches and hammers that exert pressure over the hypothenar eminence of the hand.[70,79-82] Arterial

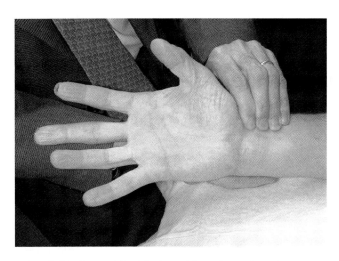

FIGURE 93-13 A positive Allen's test. The patient makes a fist to exsanguinate blood from the hand and then opens the hand while the examiner compresses both the radial and ulnar artery. After release of the ulnar artery, the hand remains pale, indicating occlusion of the ulnar artery distal to the wrist level.

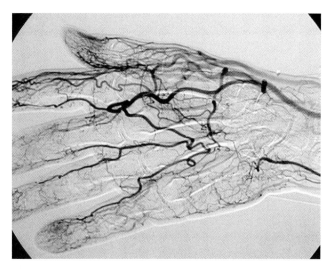

FIGURE 93-14 Hypothenar hammer syndrome. Right hand angiogram demonstrating ulnar artery occlusion in a 44-year-old laborer at a manufacturing company presenting with ulcers and gangrene of the fingertips. The patient had been using the palm of the hand as a hammer to strike machinery at work. Ulnar artery reconstruction using reversed saphenous vein bypass graft resulted in dramatic improvement in hand symptoms and healing of all ulcers.

obstruction in the hand has also been reported in professional and recreational sports, including golf and tennis, resulting from local pressure from the handle of the golf club or racket impacting on palmar arteries in the hand.[83,84] Ultrasound may document an aneurysm or thrombosis of the ulnar artery in the palm.[85] Magnetic resonance angiography has adequate resolution to be used to identify ulnar artery occlusion,[86] but usually contrast angiography is necessary to confirm the diagnosis. Surgery to excise an aneurysm may stop further episodes of embolization to the digits. Segmental ulnar artery excision in the palm with vein bypass has been successful in selected patients (Fig. 93-14).[82, 87-89]

Thoracic outlet syndrome is caused by dynamic compression of the subclavian artery at the thoracic outlet level. When an anomalous cervical rib is present, this often crowds the thoracic outlet space leading to compression of structures, including the subclavian artery. Cervical ribs are present in 0.5% to 1% of the population. They can vary on length and be bony or fibrous and not always be obvious by chest radiograph.[16] Thoracic outlet syndrome can be complicated by local subclavian aneurysm formation with mural thrombus and embolization downstream causing secondary Raynaud's with intermittent digital ischemia.[90,91]

Drugs and Medications

β-Adrenoreceptor blocking drugs are well-established medications for arterial hypertension and cardiac disease. β blockers, however, are a common cause of cool fingers and arterial vasospasm due to inhibition of β_2-mediated arterial vasodilation.

The incidence of Raynaud's phenomenon among hypertensive patients taking β blockers was 40% in a Scandinavian study where patients responded to a questionnaire. It is doubtful that all symptoms were drug related because half of these patients had symptoms before starting antihypertensive therapy and 18% on diuretics also complained of Raynaud's symptoms.[92] Approximately 5% of patients treated with β-blocker medications for hypertension

require discontinuation of the medication or dose reduction due to Raynaud's phenomenon.[16,93]

Vasospasm occurs with both selective and nonselective β blockers. Drugs with combined α- and β-adrenoceptor blocking activity such as labetalol would be expected to cause less symptomatic vasospasm.[94] In one study, no differences in finger temperature or symptoms were found in a double-blind, crossover trial of propranolol and labetalol.[95]

Despite these concerns, most patients, including many with Raynaud's syndrome, do tolerate β blockers, and many studies show no adverse effects on digital blood flow. In a double-blind, crossover trial in 16 patients with Raynaud's syndrome, Coffman and Rasmussen[97] compared the hemodynamic effects of 80 mg/day of propranolol or 100 mg/day of metoprolol compared with placebo. There was no significant difference in finger systolic pressure or fingertip capillary flow measured at 28° C and 20° C in warm or cold environment as compared with placebo. In addition, there was no significant change in the number of vasospastic attacks when patients were treated with β-blocker drug. Another study also found no adverse effects of intravenous β blockers on finger skin temperature and laser Doppler blood flow in the fingers compared with placebo.[96] Both of these studies would indicate that the use of β blockers is not contraindicated in every patient with Raynaud's syndrome.[97]

Chemotherapy Agents

There are a number of case reports suggesting increased incidence of Raynaud's in chemotherapy patients.[98] Vinblastine and bleomycin are used for the treatment of testicular cancer and lymphoma and can induce Raynaud's syndrome in 2.6% of patients on chemotherapy.[99] Digital gangrene has also been reported in small series or single case reports. For example, treatment of lung cancer with

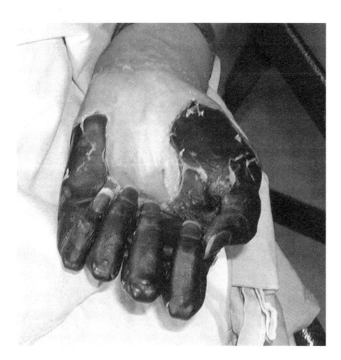

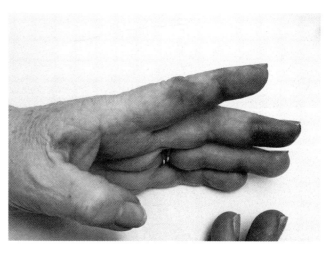

FIGURE 93-16 Cryoglobulinemia. A 70-year-old woman with cryoglobulinemia type 1 associated with low-grade lymphoma. Cryoglobulins cause small-vessel occlusive arterial disease with cutaneous necrosis involving the extremities. Treatment with apheresis, chemotherapy, and prednisone resolved the digital ischemia, and 4 years later the patient had no tissue loss.

FIGURE 93-15 Purpura fulminans. Previously healthy woman with disseminated intravascular coagulation due to sepsis from a dog bite resulting in gangrene of all digits of both hands and feet.

carboplatin and gemcitabine was associated with the development of ischemic ulcers in a patient with scleroderma.[100]

Other Drugs and Toxins

Ergot preparations used for migraine headaches are well known to cause severe extremity vasospasm and ischemia with absent pulses.[101] Amphetamine abuse can also cause arterial vasoconstriction.[102] Other drugs that have been reported associated with Raynaud's syndrome have included oral contraceptives and cyclosporine. Bromocriptine as an ergot derivative and dopamine agonist used to treat Parkinson's disease may cause mild Raynaud's phenomenon, but discontinuation of the medication is usually not required.[16]

Accidental intra-arterial injection of drugs meant for intravenous use can cause severe vasospasm and digital ischemia with gangrene and digital loss.[103]

Cocaine abuse has been reported to cause ischemic finger necrosis. The mechanism of vascular damage from cocaine is multifactorial but likely involves initial vasospasm from elevated noradrenaline levels, with subsequent arterial thrombosis. In one report involving a 36-year-old patient who had developed digital necrosis attributed to snorting crack cocaine, resolution of ischemia was achieved with intravenous infusion of a prostacyclin analogue, iloprost.[104]

Alpha interferon is used in the treatment of leukemia and melanoma, and there are rare cases of Raynaud's symptoms with digital ulceration reported occurring after several months to 3 years of therapy. In one case report, complete resolution of symptoms occurred with immunosuppression therapy and discontinuation of interferon.[105]

Infections   Purpura fulminans can result in severe digital ischemia often requiring amputation (Fig. 93-15). Parvovirus has been reported to be associated with severe digital ischemia and secondary Raynaud's syndrome.[106] Intravenous epoprostenol has been reported to improve ischemic symptoms in single case reports.[107]

Endocrine Disorders   Endocrine diseases that have been associated with Raynaud's syndrome include hypothyroidism, Graves' disease, Addison's disease and Cushing's disease. These all are unusual causes of vasospasm.

Increased Blood Viscosity   Blood flow varies indirectly with blood viscosity, and any abnormality that increases blood viscosity results in decreased blood flow. Disorders that affect blood viscosity include cryoglobulinemia, paraproteinemia in myeloma, and polycythemia. Cold-induced precipitation of proteins increases the viscosity of blood. Cryoglobulins occur with malignancies such as lymphomas and some viral infections and can cause skin necrosis and gangrene of fingers, toes, and ears. Hepatitis C in particular is associated with secondary cryoglobulinemia.[108] The treatment of cryoglobulinemia is plasmapheresis to remove the cryoglobulin, steroids, and chemotherapy to treat the underlying malignancy (Fig. 93-16).[109]

Malignancy

A wide range of cancers has been associated with secondary Raynaud's syndrome. Digital ischemia is an uncommon but well-recognized paraneoplastic manifestation of malignancy. The most common malignancies associated with Raynaud's syndrome are adenocarcinoma of the lung, stomach, colon, pancreas, ovaries, testes, and kidney and hematologic malignancies including myeloma, leukemias, lymphomas, and melanoma. Raynaud's syndrome has also been seen in astrocytomas.[16,110-113] Possible mechanisms

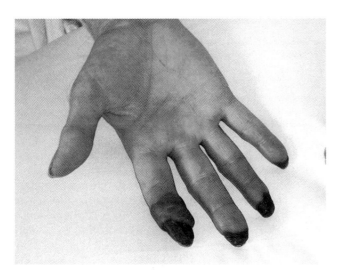

FIGURE 93-17 Paraneoplastic vasculitis with gangrene of several digits in a patient recently diagnosed with small cell lung cancer. Digital ischemia improved with chemotherapy.

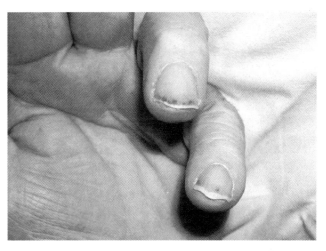

FIGURE 93-18 Splinter hemorrhages under the nails may be a normal finding due to local trauma but can also be an important indicator of distal atheroembolism as seen in this 45-year-old carpenter with hypothenar hammer syndrome. Note the splinter hemorrhages under the fourth and fifth fingernails.

of arterial disease caused by malignancy may include coagulopathy, cryoglobulinemia, or a small-vessel vasculitis (Fig. 93-17).

Treatment of the cancer may result in remission of the Raynaud's symptoms and digital ischemia.[114] Raynaud's syndrome associated with malignancy has a sudden onset at an older age, with severe symptoms and asymmetrical digital involvement. Many patients (80%) progress to digital infarcts and gangrene.[110]

Some patients who present with unexplained digital occlusive disease later in follow-up have been found to have an occult cancer as a cause of the digital ischemia.[115]

■ PHYSICAL EXAMINATION

The diagnosis of Raynaud's syndrome is made on the basis of historical features. The determination of primary or secondary disease is aided by a focused physical examination. The vascular examination should determine the presence of large-, medium-, or small-vessel occlusive disease and should detect signs of a CTD.

The vascular examination should start with the heart. Heart rate and rhythm should be confirmed by cardiac auscultation because atrial fibrillation can be missed by radial pulse palpation. Cardiac auscultation may detect an increased P_2 pulmonary valve closure sound indicating pulmonary hypertension as can occur in scleroderma. Significant valvular heart disease such as mitral stenosis may be apparent on cardiac auscultation.

Pulse examination should include palpation of subclavian, brachial, radial, and ulnar arteries. Palpation above the clavicle can determine the presence of a cervical rib and/or aneurysm of the subclavian artery. A palpable thrill indicates high-grade arterial stenosis. Auscultation over large arteries for a bruit, in particular over the sternoclavicular joint and above the clavicle, may identify an arterial stenosis.

In the hand, pulse examination should include palpation over the hypothenar eminence to identify the ulnar artery and palpation in the palm to identify the superficial arch. In some patients, a digital artery pulse can be appreciated in the medial and lateral aspect of the proximal finger.

A palpable ulnar pulse at the wrist does not mean the ulnar artery is open into the hand. The most common site of blockage of the ulnar artery is at the hypothenar eminence where it crosses the hook of the hamate. The Allen test should be performed in every patient with suspected Raynaud's syndrome to detect the presence of ulnar artery occlusion. A positive reverse Allen test may signify occlusion of the radial artery.

Detailed inspection of the skin may discover telangiectasias of the fingers or hands or sclerodactyly with thickening of the skin. Splinter hemorrhages under the nails may be a normal finding in manual workers with hand trauma but is also a sensitive indicator of distal cholesterol emboli (Fig. 93-18).

Thoracic outlet maneuvers can be done in the office to assess for entrapment of the subclavian artery between structures of the first rib and clavicle. Standardized provocative arm maneuvers include hyperabduction, costoclavicular, and the "exercise abduction stress test." Dynamic arterial compression is suggested by positional loss of the radial pulse and an intermittent subclavian artery bruit at the proximal to mid-clavicle level. Up to 15% of normal subjects experience obliteration of the pulse with this maneuver, and a positive thoracic outlet maneuver on its own does not make the diagnosis of thoracic outlet syndrome.

Abnormal findings on physical examination suggesting a secondary cause of Raynaud's syndrome include pulse abnormality (subclavian, axillary, brachial, radial, ulnar arteries), a positive Allen test, and positive thoracic outlet maneuvers. Concerning skin abnormalities include telangiectasias, digital ulcerations, pits, mottling, cyanosis, nailfold infarcts, and tight, shiny skin that may be suggestive of a CTD.

■ NONINVASIVE VASCULAR LABORATORY EVALUATION OF RAYNAUD'S SYNDROME AND OCCLUSIVE DISEASE

The noninvasive vascular laboratory is an important adjunct to the office-based clinical assessment of patients with Raynaud's syndrome.[116] It provides objectivity to the clinical evaluation and assists in decision making for medical and surgical treatment. Noninvasive vascular laboratory testing can assist in differentiating between fixed arterial obstruction and pure vasospasm and can provide assessment of the location and severity of the circulatory impairment.

The diagnosis of Raynaud's syndrome should not be made on the basis of any laboratory test,[16] and the vascular laboratory should not take the place of a good history and physical examination.[53] Even though attacks of Raynaud's are classically brought on by cold exposure, it is surprisingly difficult to reproduce an attack of vasospasm in the vascular laboratory, even with digital cooling. The quantitative evaluation of vasospasm has also been difficult,[51] and symptoms do not always correlate to finger skin blood flow measurements.[117]

Resting blood flow in the finger is highly variable. Patients with primary vasospasm are likely to have cooler fingers with decreased baseline digital temperatures and baseline laser Doppler flow. Dynamic thermal stress testing is necessary for the evaluation of vasospasm. Patients with Raynaud's syndrome have significantly greater reduction in finger systolic pressure than normal subjects during cooling of the fingers and may show decreased finger systolic pressure or actual digital arterial closure.[53,51]

The most useful noninvasive laboratory tests for Raynaud's syndrome include measurement of digital temperatures, systolic blood pressures, and laser Doppler flow of the fingers before and after local digital cooling

Segmental Pressure Measurements

To evaluate for large vessel occlusive arterial disease, segmental blood pressure measurements in the upper extremity can be obtained. Pneumatic cuffs are wrapped around the brachial, upper elbow, and wrist, and systolic blood pressures are measured at these levels. Pressures are compared to adjacent levels and a pressure differential exceeding 10 mm Hg may be significant, indicating proximal occlusive arterial disease.[1] Wrist-brachial ratio can be calculated, but there may be a wide range of normal values (as low as 0.8) due to variation in cuff size and arm diameter.[51]

Finger Systolic Blood Pressures

Measurement of finger systolic pressures is possible by using small digital cuffs applied to the proximal finger. The cuff is inflated above systolic blood pressure to occlude the digital artery. As the cuff is slowly deflated, the pulse returns to the distal finger and assessment of systolic blood pressure can be made by pulse-volume recording, strain-gauge plethysmography, or photoplethysmography.[118,119]

A decreased systolic pressure usually indicates fixed arterial occlusive disease in that finger; however, the range of normal digital pressure is quite variable and is influenced by temperature.

The normal finger-brachial index may range from 0.8 to 1.27. The fingers are especially temperature sensitive, and cool fingers can result in falsely low indices. When fingers are very cold, digital indices may be unobtainable until the fingers are warmed up. Conversely when the fingers are warm, finger systolic blood pressure may be lower than arm pressure by 10 mm Hg. Noncompressible vessels (similar to those in the lower extremity) can result in supranormal digital pressures.

A difference of more than 15 mm Hg between fingers, or an absolute finger systolic blood pressure of less than 70 mm Hg may indicate occlusive disease.[151] Because the digits have dual arteries, early disease with occlusion of one of the digital arteries cannot be detected by finger pressure measurement if the contralateral artery is open.

The effect of temperature on digital blood pressure can be studied by applying a second cuff on the same finger used to heat or cool the finger. Nielsen and Lassen devised a double-inlet plastic cuff for local digital cooling.[120] They found a mild, progressive decrease in finger systolic pressure with local cooling in normal young women (≤15% digital systolic pressure drop at 10° C). During further cooling, 60% of females with primary Raynaud's showed digital artery occlusion.[121]

Thulesius and coworkers[122] used the Nielsen method to study the effect of local cooling in a group of patients with primary and secondary Raynaud's syndrome compared to normal controls. They also found a successive reduction in systolic pressure by cooling in normal subjects, but a much greater reduction was found in those with Raynaud's syndrome. In half of patients, at a critical temperature there was an abrupt closure of digital arteries with no recordable pulsation. This is called the *critical closing temperature*. Anatomic change of the vessel wall, such as fibrosis or hypertrophy or partial obstruction, could increase susceptibility to cold-induced vasospasm and artery closure. Based on a positive history of vasospasm, the diagnostic accuracy of this study was only 50% to 77% depending on degree of cooling. This test did not separate out obstructive from vasospastic disease.[122] The Nielsen method has been used to study the effects of drug therapy.

Finger Tip Thermography

Skin surface temperature can be used as an indirect index of capillary blood flow in the skin. At temperatures lower than 30° C, blood flow is proportional to skin surface temperature. At temperatures higher than 30° C, due to minimal increase in skin temperature, larger increases in flow may not be appreciated. Patients with vasospasm have increased vascular tone leading to decreased blood flow and decreased surface skin temperature. Measurement of skin temperature can be combined with cold immersion.

Cold Recovery Time

Cold recovery time is a time-honored test used to measure the vasoconstrictor and vasodilator response of the fingers to cold exposure. It is based on the principle that patients with Raynaud's syndrome have greater vasoconstriction in response to cooling of the fingers compared with normal subjects. After cold exposure, Raynaud's syndrome patients also take longer for blood flow to increase and, consequently, a longer time for the fingers to rewarm back to baseline temperature.

The change in blood flow induced by temperature change can be indirectly assessed by measuring fingertip skin temperatures or by recording laser Doppler flux of the fingertips. There are many variations of the cold immersion test with various immersion times and temperatures. A standard protocol is to record baseline digital temperatures using a temperature probe at the end of the finger pulp. The hands are then immersed in cold water of 4° C for 20 seconds. The hands are dried, and digital skin temperature is recorded for each finger as the hands and fingers gradually warm up to ambient room temperature. The length of time it takes for the hands to rewarm to baseline is noted by recording finger temperatures or laser Doppler flux at 5-minute intervals until recovery of preimmersion temperatures. A delay in rewarming suggests a vasospasm tendency. Raynaud's patients typically may take more than 10 minutes and sometimes 30 minutes or longer to recover resting finger temperatures compared with less than 10 minutes for normal subjects.

Reproducibility of finger skin temperatures has been good in some studies but not in others and may limit the value of this test.[123,124] In our personal experience, we find that a number of patients, especially those with Raynaud's syndrome, have very cold hands when they present for testing at the vascular laboratory. If resting baseline digital temperatures are less than 30° C, the fingers never rewarm in less than 10 minutes following ice water immersion, and no further information is gained from this cold challenge test in these patients. The test cannot differentiate between primary and secondary Raynaud's syndrome, and some have questioned the ability to diagnose Raynaud's syndrome owing to larger overlap of normal subjects and those with Raynaud's phenomenon.

Laser Doppler Flux

Laser Doppler is a noninvasive test that measures microvascular skin perfusion in the fingers. A laser Doppler probe transmits a low-powered helium-neon light via a quartz glass fiberoptic system. The light is scattered by both static and moving tissue. Most moving structures are red blood cells. Laser light scattered by moving red blood cells undergoes a frequency shift according to the Doppler effect. The scattered light is detected by a photodetector in the probe and produces an output signal proportional to the flux (number and velocity) of red blood cells in the volume of tissue illuminated.

Baseline measurements are highly variable and are affected by emotion, sympathetic tone (anxious patient), and environmental temperature. Cold stress testing can be combined with laser Doppler by cooling the fingers with a laser Doppler probe.[125] When finger temperatures are decreased, vasoconstriction results in decreased skin blood flow and reduced laser Doppler flux. With slow rewarming there is an increase in laser Doppler flux. Normal response to cooling is a decrease in skin temperature and symmetrical decrease in laser Doppler flow.[126,127]

Laser Doppler with Thermal Challenge

Laser Doppler can be used to measure increased blood flow in the digits with ambient warming of the hand and fingers.[128] In most individuals who present to the noninvasive vascular laboratory with cold hands, we have found that measurement of digital laser Doppler flow at rest and after gentle warming of the hands in a hot-air box provides a better indication of primary vasospasm. This test can also assist in distinguishing between obstructive and vasospastic disease. After baseline laser Doppler values are obtained from each digit, the hands are placed in a warming box (at 45° C) for up to 25 minutes or until a finger temperature of 37° C is reached. Laser Doppler flows are again determined from each digit. In general, patients with a history of vasospasm who present with cold fingers have low resting laser Doppler blood flow due to vasoconstricted vessels. After ambient warming there may be a marked increase (4-to 50-fold) in laser Doppler flow in these digits. Failure of Doppler flow to increase after warming of the hands is indicative of significant arterial occlusive disease. In our laboratory, the response of laser Doppler flow to warming correlates well with clinical and angiographic findings.

The scanning laser Doppler has been used in our laboratory and has a number of potential advantages over the single-site laser Doppler. Because the Doppler probe does not come in contact with the patient, the scanning laser Doppler can be used to assess blood flow at the base of ulcers or other wounds, and it is able to scan the entire hand. Unfortunately there is a great deal of variability limiting interpretation, and the scanning laser Doppler has not found the same applicability as the single-digit Doppler probes (Fig. 93-19).

Imaging Studies

Duplex ultrasound can examine the large vessels of the upper extremity but can also image the palmar arch and digital arteries for patency. It may provide further information on disease process in addition to confirming flow or obstruction.[129] Doppler ultrasound can help to determine completeness of the superficial palmar arch. If there is no change in Doppler flow over the superficial arch during occlusion of the radial or ulnar artery, the arch is likely to be complete.[16]

Magnetic resonance angiography is excellent for imaging of upper extremity arteries and can provide accurate imaging of hand and wrist vessels. Magnetic resonance angiography can accurately diagnose ulnar artery occlusion in the hypothenar hammer syndrome.[86] The resolution is not as good as contrast angiography, which remains the gold standard for arterial imaging (Fig. 93-20).[130]

Contrast Angiography

Contrast angiography remains the best imaging modality when a detailed examination is necessary to look for the cause of digital ischemia such as microembolism from an ulcerated plaque, thrombus in an ulnar artery, the tapered narrowing of vasculitis, or the corkscrew collaterals of thromboangiitis obliterans. As an invasive test, angiography is reserved for those with severe disease or those who may be candidates for intervention with thrombolytic agents, angioplasty, or surgical revascularization.

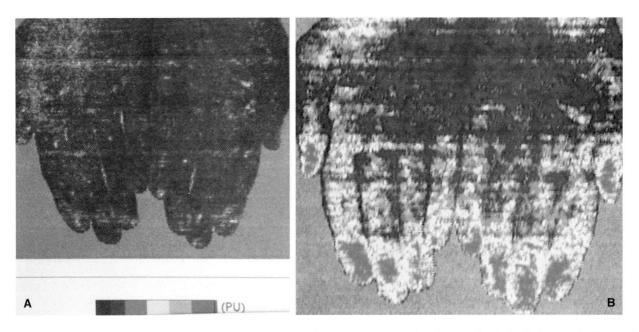

FIGURE 93-19   Scanning laser Doppler imaging shows low laser Doppler flow due to vasospasm (**A**). After warming the hands (**B**), a marked increase in digital blood flow is seen. On examination, the fingers were cool, with resting digital temperatures of 28° C. Physical examination was normal, and there was no evidence of occlusive arterial disease. Blood tests, including complete blood count, sedimentation rate, cryoglobulin, antinuclear antibody, and extractable nuclear antigens all were negative. This patient was diagnosed with primary Raynaud's syndrome and treated with a long-acting nifedipine medication. (See color figure in this section.)

Nailfold Capillary Microscopy

The superficial capillaries in the nailfold can be visualized applying a drop of immersion oil over the cuticle of the finger to make it translucent and imaging with a low-powered microscope (×10 or ×20) or an ophthalmoscope at 40 diopters.

Normal capillaries are seen as regularly spaced hairpin loops comprising a venous and arterial limb. The arterial limb has a more narrow diameter (7 to 12 μm) with more rapid flow, and the venous limb has a larger diameter with slower capillary flow.[53]

Structural changes in capillary morphology can be seen. Abnormal capillaries are seen in scleroderma and mixed CTD as enlarged, tortuous, and deformed or loop dropout causing avascular areas.[131-134]

■ TREATMENT OF RAYNAUD'S SYNDROME

The approach to therapy for Raynaud's syndrome should be individualized, depending on the patient's symptoms, frequency of vasospastic attacks, underlying disease, and risk of development of ischemic ulcerations, gangrene, or digital loss. For most patients with primary Raynaud's syndrome there is no cure; however, a number of simple measures can be effective in reducing the frequency and duration of attacks. Preventive measures with education and reassurance with avoidance of cold exposure constitute the basis of therapy for most patients.

Management principles can be considered in three groups including nonpharmacologic behavioral therapies, pharmacologic treatment, and interventional-surgical proce-

dures. Potential therapies in the future could be specifically targeted at one of the many underlying abnormalities responsible for Raynaud's syndrome, including the endothelium, autonomic nervous system, or specific neurohumoral and hematologic factors (Fig. 93-21).

Nonpharmacologic Therapies

Preventive Measures

Most patients with primary Raynaud's syndrome have only mild symptoms that do not require the use of vasodilatory medications. These patients are best managed with a conservative program stressing the concepts of heat conservation and avoiding factors that cause arterial vasoconstriction. Education and reassurance are the mainstay of therapy. Patients with primary disease should be reassured that they have a benign disorder with little risk of progression, finger ulcers, or digital loss. The risk of developing a collagen vascular disorder should be less than 10%.

The patient should be educated about the nature and prognosis of primary Raynaud's syndrome, in particular emphasizing that the underlying arterial circulation is normal and that episodes of pallor and cyanosis are an exaggeration of the normal response of the finger arteries to cold exposure and emotional stress.

Simple measures to maintain warmth and avoid cold are quite effective. Protection from the cold involves the use of mittens rather than gloves to keep the fingers warm in cold weather. The concept of "total-body warmth" should be emphasized. If the patient feels warm, the hands will be warmer. Conversely, if the patient feels chilly, the natural response of the body is to constrict flow to the extremities to conserve body heat. The thermostat in the room should be

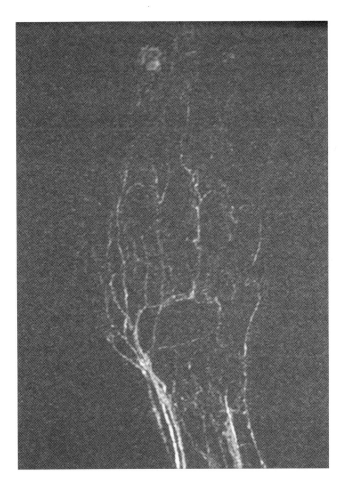

FIGURE 93-20 Magnetic resonance angiography of the hand shows distal ulnar artery occlusion, incomplete deep palmar arch, and severe disease of digital arteries with only faintly visualized arteries to the index, middle, and ring fingers. This patient presented with a 3-year history of Raynaud's symptoms and recent onset of ischemic pain involving the right index finger. Digital ischemia was refractory to vasodilator medication, and the patient was treated with an upper extremity pneumatic pump to improve arterial perfusion to the fingers.

increased to a comfortable temperature in excess of 70° F. The patient should dress appropriately with long-sleeved garments so as to stay warm. Chemical or electrical hand warmers can be obtained at sporting goods stores.[135] Situations likely to cause vasospasm should be avoided or minimized. Gloves should be worn when handling frozen food or taking cold food out of the refrigerator. Putting the hands in cold water should be avoided. Warming up the car before trips avoids vasospasm from grabbing onto a cold steering wheel. Patients realize that they have more frequent attacks of vasospasm in the winter than in the summer, and some may elect to spend more time in warmer climates.

Avoidance of Factors that Cause Vasoconstriction

Nicotine is a potent vasoconstrictor, and every effort should be made to encourage the patient to abstain from all nicotine products. Some over-the-counter medications have constrictor substances, including weight loss pills that contain stimulants such as ephedrine. β Blockers are a common cause of Raynaud's syndrome. If used to treat hypertension, it may be possible to change to an alternative antihypertensive medication such as a calcium-channel blocker or α blocker that may have benefit for Raynaud's syndrome. Other medications with potent vasoconstrictor properties include ergotamine preparations used in the treatment of migraine headaches. These can sometimes cause ergotism with severe and intense vasospasm. Drugs of abuse such as cocaine and amphetamines may cause severe arterial constriction that may not be reversible, with permanent arterial damage.

Behavioral Therapies and Maneuvers

Arm Rotation Swinging the arms in a circular motion increases centrifugal force and blood pressure to the hand and is often successful in breaking an attack of vasospasm.

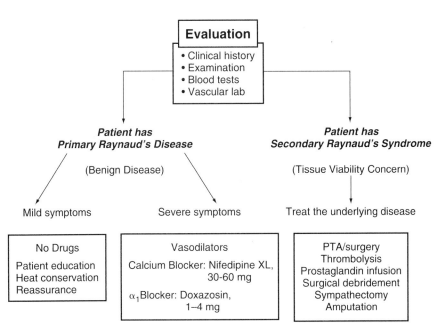

FIGURE 93-21 Algorithm for management of primary and secondary Raynaud's syndrome. PTA, percutaneous transluminal angioplasty.

Temperature Biofeedback Control of autonomic functions such as temperature control can be learned. Patients imagine themselves in a warm environment such as lying on warm sand and become able to increase skin temperature at will; with training, they can learn to reverse vasospastic attacks. Freedman reported a benefit in 66% to 92% of primary Raynaud's patients with biofeedback in those who can master the technique. Significant time must be invested—it may take 12 sessions of 45 minutes each of biofeedback training to learn the techniques of relaxation and meditation.[136]

Temperature biofeedback has been studied in randomized trials with variable results. Some studies show that a small but significant increase in skin temperature and blood flow with biofeedback; however, in one randomized, multicenter trial, biofeedback was no better than control.[137] There is a learning curve with biofeedback, and the results may depend on the training. Behavioral therapy can help some, but not all can learn temperature control techniques.

Pharmacologic Therapy

Pharmacologic therapy is indicated for patients with severe symptoms whose activities of daily life are affected and who do not respond to simple conservative measures. Most patients with mild or moderate symptoms respond well to conservative measures and do not need vasodilator medications. Some patients have symptoms and require medications only during cold winter months and not during the warmer summer months.

Physicians and patients share a great deal of frustration in the drug treatment of Raynaud's syndrome. Patients should understand that medications might decrease the intensity or the frequency of vasospastic episodes but do not cure the underlying cause of vasospasm. The patient should be informed that only 50% to 75% of people respond to any one medication. Potential side effects and adverse consequences of medications should be balanced against expected benefit. Vasodilator medications are more effective in patients with primary Raynaud's disease. Individuals with secondary Raynaud's often have fixed obstructive arterial disease, and vasodilators are less effective or at times have no benefit at all.

A number of medications are routinely used for vasospasm; however, there are no currently available drugs that are specifically approved by the U.S. Food and Drug Administration for the treatment of Raynaud's syndrome. Choosing the one best medication has been difficult owing to a lack of large prospective, randomized, double-blind studies comparing the efficacy of different medications in Raynaud's syndrome. Most clinical trials rely on the patient's self-assessment of frequency and severity of Raynaud's episodes, and laboratory confirmation of benefit has been difficult to discern. There is a striking dissociation between clinical and physiologic laboratory measurements of outcome. For example, Raynaud's attack of vasospasm is notoriously difficult to reproduce in the vascular laboratory setting.

Calcium-Channel Blockers

Calcium-channel blockers are the most commonly prescribed medications for vasospasm associated with Raynaud's syndrome. These drugs share a common mode of action and inhibit the influx of extracellular calcium ions into the smooth muscle cell by blocking specific ion channels in the cell membrane. The contractile process of the smooth muscle in the artery wall is dependent on extracellular calcium, and a reduction in calcium influx causes vascular smooth muscle relaxation and arterial dilation. Because they do not act on a receptor, they are considered direct-acting vasodilator drugs.

The three main classes of calcium-channel blockers differ in their mode of action on the slow calcium channels and vary in their selectivity for vascular or cardiac tissue. The dihydropyridines such as nifedipine are the most potent in relaxing vascular smooth muscle and are better vasodilators than diltiazem or verapamil. However, as a consequence of this vasodilatory property, dihydropyridines are also more likely than other calcium-channel blockers to cause well-known adverse effects of flushing and peripheral edema that may require discontinuation of the medication. Diltiazem is less potent and consequently has less adverse effects. Verapamil has more cardiac than peripheral vascular selectivity and is not a good peripheral vasodilator.

Dihydropyridines Dihydropyridine calcium-channel blockers are the best studied of all calcium-channel blockers and have been shown in multiple studies to be effective therapy for the treatment of Raynaud's syndrome. There are more than 10 drugs in this class, but they all share similar properties. Nifedipine has been, and continues to be, the gold standard, but most of the newer dihydropyridines (including amlodipine, nicardipine, felodipine, isradipine, and nisoldipine) all appear to be equally efficacious. Short-acting calcium-channel blockers were previously used but are no longer recommended. Only long-acting or sustained-release preparations of calcium-channel blockers are currently approved for other disorders such as arterial hypertension, and the same logic applies to the treatment of Raynaud's syndrome.

Nifedipine is considered by many to be the drug of first choice if drug treatment of symptoms is required. In many clinical studies nifedipine is the standard by which other medications are compared. There are many studies of nifedipine used for Raynaud's syndrome. A 66% reduction in attacks has been reported in a recent multicenter, randomized, controlled trial of 313 patients with primary Raynaud's syndrome treated with a sustained-release form of nifedipine compared with placebo. Nifedipine dosage ranged from 30 to 60 mg daily for 1 year, and the primary endpoint was self-reported vasospastic attacks occurring during a winter month, after taking the medication for a full year. Of note, adverse side effects were common, necessitating discontinuation of nifedipine in 15% of patients. Only half the patients tolerated the 60-mg dose. Peripheral edema was reported in 24%, headache in 18%, facial flushing in 8%, and tachycardia in 3%.[137]

The incidence of nifedipine side effects is dose dependent and increases at larger doses of 60 or 90 mg daily. Patients intolerant to nifedipine may try changing to a different dihydropyridine (although side effects are similar in all drugs in this class) or a different class of medication such as diltiazem. If intolerant to all calcium-channel blockers, a change to another group of medications such as an α blocker may be necessary.[138]

An unusual erythromelalgia-like syndrome can result from dihydropyridine medications. We have noted several presentations of red, swollen, painful feet simulating erythromelalgia, which resolved after discontinuation of the nifedipine. Sunahara and colleagues[139] described a similar condition in a patient who experienced acute erythema and a burning sensation in the feet 1 hour after taking short-acting nifedipine. Symptoms in this patient also resolved within 24 hours after discontinuation of the medication.[139]

Laboratory studies have been inconsistent in documenting improved blood flow or less susceptibility to vasospastic attacks with nifedipine therapy. In some studies, nifedipine has been shown to improve the temperature recovery time after cold immersion of the hands and fingers.[127] In other studies, using cold provocation, nifedipine-treated patients were found to have less decrease in finger systolic pressure in the cooled finger compared with placebo.[140]

Similar findings were reported in a recent study of 158 patients with primary Raynaud's phenomenon who were randomized to sustained-release nifedipine. Digital blood pressure response to local finger cooling at 30° C to 10° C was measured. Patients treated with nifedipine had a higher relative mean digital systolic blood pressure during finger cooling than those treated with placebo.[141]

Amlodipine is similar to nifedipine but has a longer half-life. In a 3-week Italian trial, amlodipine 10 mg once daily was found to reduce the frequency of vasospastic attacks by 27% (from a baseline of 11.4 attacks to 8.6 attacks per week). Amlodipine has a theoretical advantage of fewer adverse effects due to its long half-life of more than 24 hours; however, adverse reaction in this study were common and included ankle edema in 55%, flushing in 10%, and headache in 20%.[142]

Nicardipine in most studies has been shown to be effective in the treatment of vasospasm and can be administered by oral or intravenous route. Only a few studies have been able to document improvement based on any laboratory test. Patients with primary Raynaud's syndrome have the greatest response, and those with secondary Raynaud's syndrome may have less or no benefit from these medications.

Oral slow-release nicardipine (20 mg two times daily) was better than placebo in a randomized, double-blind, crossover, and placebo-controlled trial. The number of Raynaud's episodes decreased and the severity of discomfort and hand disability scores improved in 21 patients (18 women and 3 men) with Raynaud's phenomenon who had no underlying disease. Two discontinued the trial due to headache. The time to peak flow after postischemic reactive hyperemia was significantly reduced after nicardipine.[143]

Some investigators have found nicardipine to be of no benefit in either primary or secondary Raynaud's patients. No statistically significant differences were found between nicardipine and placebo for the number, duration, or severity of vasospastic attacks in a double-blind, placebo-controlled, crossover study of oral nicardipine (30 mg three times a day) in 25 patients (16 primary and 9 secondary Raynaud's phenomenon). Microcirculatory assessment with finger skin temperature and laser Doppler flux measured during a finger cooling test also showed no differences for nicardipine-treated patients or placebo.[144]

Intravenous nicardipine has been shown to raise resting skin temperature in those with primary Raynaud's syndrome and improve recovery after cold-induced vasospasm, but again these effects were not seen in patients with secondary Raynaud's syndrome.[145]

Other dihydropyridines have also been used in Raynaud's syndrome. *Felodipine* was found to be equally efficacious as nifedipine in a double-blind, crossover trial of 16 patients.[146] *Nisoldipine* reduced the number but not the severity of attacks in 19 patients with primary Raynaud's syndrome in a European controlled, double-blind trial of 19 patients.[147] *Isradipine* has also been studied in Raynaud's syndrome with documented benefit.

Diltiazem   Diltiazem has less potent vasodilator properties but less common adverse effects. Patients intolerant of nifedipine could be switched to diltiazem.[138]

Verapamil   Verapamil has more cardiac than vascular effects and is not as effective as other calcium-channel blockers in Raynaud's syndrome.

α₁-Adrenergic Blockers

There are two major types of α blockers. The nonselective α blockers include phenoxybenzamine and phentolamine, which today are primarily used to control hypertensive emergencies in patients with pheochromocytoma, and are rarely used for any other purposes due to the high incidence of adverse side effects including orthostatic hypotension and reflex tachycardia.

The selective α_1-adrenergic receptor blocking agents include *prazosin* and longer-acting *terazosin* (Hytrin) and *doxazosin* (Cardura) (Table 93-3). When the sympathetic nerve is stimulated, norepinephrine is released from the nerve terminal and crosses the synapse to act on the α_1 receptor located on vascular smooth muscle. Drugs such as prazosin cause competitive inhibition of the postsynaptic α_1 receptor, thus blocking the vasoconstrictor action of norepinephrine. At the same time, the presynaptic α_2 receptor located on the nerve terminal remains intact. Released norepinephrine feeds back on the α_2 receptor, limiting further release of catecholamines and preventing the tachycardia seen in nonselective α blockers.[148]

Prazosin is a selective α_1-adrenergic antagonist that significantly reduces the number of attacks in both primary and secondary Raynaud's. Side effects are unusual but can include postural hypotension (first-dose phenomenon), usually resolving within several days as tolerance develops. In one study, 3 of 24 patients on a maximal dose of prazosin withdrew due to intolerable side effects of orthostatic hypotension.[149] Dizziness and presyncope can be minimized

Table 93-3	Selective α₁-Adrenergic Receptor Blocking Agents		
DRUG	DURATION OF ACTION, hr	THERAPEUTIC DOSE, mg	FREQUENCY OF ADMINISTRATION
Prazosin	4-6	1-5 mg	2 or 3 times per day
Terazosin	>18	1-10 mg	Once daily
Doxazosin	18-36	1-8 mg	Once daily

by starting with a lower dose (1 mg of terazosin) and administering the first dose at bedtime.

In a double-blind, placebo-controlled, crossover study of 24 patients, prazosin was reported superior to placebo in the treatment of Raynaud's phenomenon. Subjective benefit with significant reduction in number and duration of attacks was noted in two thirds of those patients treated with prazosin (1 mg three times a day) compared with placebo with improvement in finger blood flow assessed during a finger cooling test. Complete relief was observed in only 2 patients (8%).[150]

Long-acting forms of prazosin include doxazosin and terazosin, which allows once-daily dosing. These drugs have also been shown to be effective therapy for treatment for Raynaud's syndrome by decreasing the number, intensity, and duration of attacks.[151] Adverse side effects may be less.

Nitrates have been used in the treatment of Raynaud's syndrome as oral, topical, or intravenous preparations but in general are not first-line therapy. Topical nitrates in the form of nitroglycerine ointment 2% can be applied locally to an ischemic finger but can cause paradoxical worsening of ischemia if there is fixed obstructive disease. Oral nitrates generally are limited by symptoms of nitrate-induced headaches and poor dose-response characteristics.[50] Intravenous nitroglycerine produces predominantly systemic vasodilation but may not improve digital perfusion.

ACE inhibitors block angiotensin II and ET novel transforming growth factor-β_1 and have an antifibrotic effect. ACE inhibitors and angiotensin II receptor inhibitors may be of benefit in both primary and secondary Raynaud's syndrome. The use of ACE inhibitors should be considered in all patients with systemic sclerosis and hypertension to prevent scleroderma renal crisis.

Losartan is an angiotensin II receptor type 1 antagonist. In a recent study, losartan 50 mg daily was found to be more effective than nifedipine 40 mg daily in reducing the frequency of vasospastic episodes in patients with primary Raynaud's syndrome and those with secondary Raynaud's syndrome due to systemic sclerosis.[152]

Antiplatelet Therapy

There is no evidence that antiplatelet therapy is of benefit in primary Raynaud's syndrome, but therapy with aspirin or clopidogrel should be considered for most patients with secondary Raynaud's syndrome due to atherosclerosis obliterans.

Anticoagulation

Anticoagulation with intravenous or subcutaneous heparin may prevent further thrombosis in acute ischemia. Chronic anticoagulation is generally not indicated for most patients with small-vessel occlusive disease because the underlying process is an obliterative and not a thrombotic vasculopathy.

Thrombolysis

Thrombolysis with urokinase or tissue plasminogen activators in standard vascular practice lyses acute thrombus and acute arterial emboli. Rarely have thrombolytics been attempted in distal small-vessel occlusions.

Novel Drug Therapies

There are a number of novel drug therapies that may have potential benefit for Raynaud's syndrome, including the following[58]:

- *Fluoxetine* is a selective serotonin reuptake inhibitor. A significant reduction in attack frequency and severity was found in both primary and secondary Raynaud's syndrome treated with fluoxetine 20 mg daily but not in those treated with nifedipine 40 mg daily in a crossover trial. Laboratory testing showed improvement in recovery after a cold challenge test, with the greatest improvement seen in women with primary Raynaud's syndrome.[153]
- *Piracetam* inhibits thromboxane A_2 and may be of modest benefit in Raynaud's syndrome. Piracetam is not available in the United States.
- *Phosphodiesterase inhibitors* (cilostazol and sildenafil) are potent vasodilators with potential but unproven benefit in Raynaud's syndrome. Sildenafil has marked vasodilator properties of benefit for erectile dysfunction but has not been studied in Raynaud's syndrome.[154] Cilostazol may have additional antiplatelet properties but also has not been studied in patients with Raynaud's syndrome.

Endothelin Inhibitors

ET is a potent vasoconstrictor and also causes cell proliferation. Bosentan may block vasoconstriction and has potential benefit in vasospastic disorders.

Estrogen therapy has been suggested as a potential treatment of Raynaud's syndrome; however, studies have not shown any benefit of estrogen or progesterone on digital blood flow.[155]

Food Supplements

Fish oil may decrease thromboxane A_2 production and increase prostacyclin synthesis; however, this requires a large number of fish oil capsules daily.[50,156]

L-Arginine is a substrate for NO synthesis and has a theoretical benefit of improving endothelial dysfunction in patients with both primary and secondary Raynaud's syndrome, but relatively few studies have been able to show any benefit.[42]

In one study, brachial artery infusion of L-arginine or sodium nitroprusside (a direct donor of NO) both decreased vasospastic attacks in 15 patients with scleroderma. Attacks were induced by holding a beaker of iced water for 2 minutes and reducing the room temperature to 4° C. Attacks were fewer in hands infused with L-arginine.[157]

In another study of 20 patients with primary Raynaud's syndrome, there was no improvement in endothelium-dependent vasodilation in a double-blind, crossover trial of oral L-arginine (8 g daily for 28 days).[158] Patients with systemic sclerosis have reduced vasodilation to acetylcholine and nitroglycerine due to fixed occlusive disease. Another study by Khan and Belch found that administration of L-arginine did not improve vasodilation.[159]

Acupuncture may be of benefit in some patients. In a small, randomized trial, acupuncture was found to be effective in reducing the frequency and severity of attacks in patients with primary Raynaud's syndrome. The mechanism of action is believed to be stimulation of sensory nerves causing release of vasodilators such as substance P and calcitonin gene-related peptide.[160,161]

Nerve Stimulation

Transcutaneous nerve stimulation has also been used in some patients to induce vasodilation with varying results.[162]

Spinal Cord Stimulator   A spinal cord stimulator may reduce pain and promote ulcer healing in severe cases of secondary Raynaud's syndrome with trophic lesions. In one small study of 10 patients with Raynaud's syndrome or reflex sympathetic dystrophy, 90% had significant relief of chronic pain; thermographic and plethysmographic changes were also observed.[163]

Management of Critical Digital Ischemia

General measures for critical ischemia includes keeping the extremity at body temperature with the use of a vascular mitten, providing local therapy of digital ulcers with wound care products to prevent infection, and protecting the finger from trauma (Fig. 93-22). Local débridement of dead tissue or removal of the fingernail is sometimes necessary, but local amputation of the end of a digit may be necessary in 10% to 20% of patients.[164] Whenever possible, amputation should be avoided because the amputation site may take longer to heal (if ever) than the original ulcer, and this can result in further skin necrosis at the amputation stump, necessitating a more proximal amputation.

Pumping Therapy

Intermittent pneumatic compression is established therapy in atherosclerotic limb ischemia after exhausting all surgical and medical options. Currently several pumps are on the market similar to venous pumps used for thromboembolic prophylaxis but with more rapid and higher compression

FIGURE 93-22 A vascular mitten protects and maintains warmth of the hands. Patients with critical hand and finger ischemia can have further compromise in distal perfusion as a result of cool ambient room temperature causing vasoconstriction. A vascular mitten keeps the hands at body temperature and maximizes distal finger blood flow by avoiding cold-induced vasoconstriction.

cycles. An increase in digital laser Doppler flow during the pump phase may indicate improved distal perfusion during pneumatic pumping of the upper extremity (Fig. 93-23).

Hyperbaric oxygen is useful in healing ischemic ulceration, but availability of hyperbaric oxygen chambers is limited.

Vasodilator Therapy in Critical Ischemia

Topical Nitroglycerine Ointment   A vasodilator medication that can be applied to the affected finger sounds like a reasonable therapeutic option; however, it is rarely effective for distal finger ischemia. Critical digital ischemia almost always denotes severe fixed occlusive disease. Vasodilators are not of much benefit for fixed disease. Sometimes drug-induced vasodilation of normal proximal vessels can cause a steal phenomenon by dilating proximal arteries at the expense of distal finger blood flow resulting in worsening ischemia (Fig. 93-24). Headache and flushing are often limiting side effects of nitroglycerine ointment.

Minoxidil is a potent vasodilator and medication for arterial hypertension but not of much use in Raynaud's syndrome. Topical minoxidil 5% was applied to the fingers in a randomized, double-blind, placebo-controlled, cross-over trial of 10 subjects with primary Raynaud's phenomenon. No improvement was found in digital temperature, systolic blood pressure, and laser Doppler flow before and after cold challenge compared to placebo.[165]

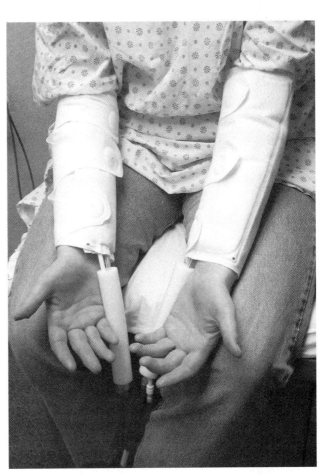

FIGURE 93-23 Pneumatic pumping of both upper extremities in a patient with digital ischemia due to scleroderma.

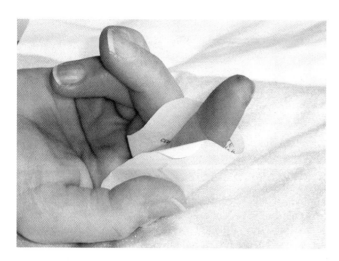

FIGURE 93-24 This patient presented with acute ischemia of the right fingertip. She was found to have a positive antinuclear antibody and anti-centromere antibody. An angiogram showed severe digital artery occlusive disease consistent with a connective tissue disease (see Fig. 93-10). Topical nitroglycerine ointment often fails to improve blood flow in the setting of critical ischemia due to severe underlying fixed small-vessel occlusive disease. The patient was treated with multiple agents, including oral, topical, and intravenous vasodilators, antiplatelet therapy, doxazosin, and nifedipine.

Intravenous vasodilators such as nitroprusside, phentolamine, and hydralazine have been used in the past with minimal benefit in patients with fixed occlusive disease due to collagen vascular disorders or atherosclerosis.

Prostaglandins and Analogues

Prostacyclins are vasodilators that have been used for patients with critical digital ischemia secondary to fixed occlusive disease. Much of the early experience has been in Europe using iloprost (a prostacyclin analogue not available in the United States).

Epoprostenol is a naturally occurring prostaglandin with potent vasodilatory and antiplatelet actions and can be given through a peripheral line as a continuous intravenous infusion. Epoprostenol (Flolan) is now available in the United States and has been approved for the treatment of primary pulmonary hypertension and pulmonary hypertension associated with scleroderma. For patients with pulmonary hypertension, it is administered as a continuous ambulatory infusion by an indwelling catheter using a small infusion pump. Major side effects are flushing, headache, nausea, vomiting, and hypotension.

Patients with severe Raynaud's syndrome and digital ischemia have been treated with epoprostenol, administered as a continuous intravenous infusion (0.5 to 2 ng/kg/min), for 1 to 3 days. In one study, 12 patients with severe Raynaud's syndrome received intravenous epoprostenol in a double-blind, placebo-controlled trial. A significant increase in fingertip skin temperature and laser Doppler flow was documented before and after a finger cooling test, but improved blood flow was not sustained and beneficial effects were gone after 1 week.[166]

Iloprost is a prostacyclin analogue that has been reported to reduce the severity, frequency, and duration of Raynaud's attacks and promote healing of ischemic ulcers.[167] Iloprost (ciloprost) is investigational in the United States. In systemic sclerosis, complete healing of ulcers was observed 10 weeks after treatment in 6 of 7 patients receiving intravenous infusion of iloprost (0.5 to 2 ng/kg/min) administered as a 6-hour infusion over 5 consecutive days compared to no healing of ulcers in those treated with saline placebo. In this study improvement was sustained over the 9-week follow-up period.[168]

Intravenous iloprost was more effective than oral nifedipine in a 12-month prospective, single-blind trial. Forty-six patients with systemic sclerosis were randomized to receive intravenous iloprost (at a rate of up to 2 ng/kg/min) over 8 hours for 5 consecutive days, then once every 6 weeks. Raynaud's severity score was decreased and skin thickening was reduced. The study was limited by adverse effects of headache, nausea, and vomiting during iloprost infusion.[169]

Another smaller study also found benefit with iloprost in patients with systemic sclerosis and Raynaud's phenomenon. Over the 16-week study, 12 patients with systemic sclerosis were treated with iloprost administered by intravenous infusion on 3 consecutive days for 8 hours or randomized to nifedipine orally. Both agents produced reductions in the mean number, duration, and severity of attacks of Raynaud's phenomenon. Hand temperature and blood flow increased with iloprost but not nifedipine; however, there was healing of digital ulcers in both groups.[170]

Most studies have failed to show any significant improvement for Raynaud's syndrome or digital ischemia with oral formulations of iloprost. A multicenter trial of 143 patients with Raynaud's phenomenon secondary to systemic sclerosis randomized to oral iloprost (50 μg twice daily for 6 weeks) or placebo found no significant difference in the number or duration of Raynaud's attacks.[171] Another trial of 103 patients with scleroderma and Raynaud's phenomenon showed only minimal benefit with oral iloprost, but adverse side effects required discontinuation of the medication in a number of patients.[172]

Prostaglandin E₁

Prostaglandin E₁ (prostin) is also a potent vasodilator that may provide temporary relief of ischemic pain and reverse severe acute ischemic attacks when administered as an intravenous or intra-arterial infusion (5 to 10 ng/kg/min intravenously for 72 hours). The hyperemia and increased perfusion unfortunately are gone shortly after discontinuation of the infusion.[50]

Misoprostol is an oral form of prostaglandin E₁. Efficacy is unknown with oral prostaglandin. A recent study was unable to document any improvement in any fingertip temperature, systolic pressure, blood flow determined by laser Doppler, or rewarming response to cold challenge after a single dose of 400 μg of misoprostol.

Sympathectomy for Raynaud's Syndrome

Surgical treatment for Raynaud's can include reconstruction of occluded vessels, cervical or digital sympathectomy, and thoracic outlet syndrome correction.[87]

Cervicothoracic sympathectomy was previously used as a surgical treatment for Raynaud's syndrome but rarely is used now.[173] Sympathectomy is rarely if ever indicated for those with primary Raynaud's syndrome but may be effective in some patients who have critical ischemia of the digits, in particular to alleviate pain. The benefit may be short lived.

The first reported use of cervicothoracic sympathectomy to treat Raynaud's phenomenon was in 1929 by Adson and Brown.[174] Proximal sympathectomy can now be done by a thoracoscopic procedure that limits complications such as pneumothorax, phrenic nerve injury, or Horner's syndrome.

Hand and digital sympathectomy has been successful in healing ulcers and improving ischemic pain.[65,87,175,176]

Currently, the main indication for sympathectomy in Raynaud's syndrome is for nonhealing digital ulceration refractory to intensive medical therapy. In one study, 26 (92%) of 28 patients had initial resolution or improvement of symptoms, but there was a high rate of symptom recurrence in 82% within 16 months after surgery. Despite this, a number of patients believed that they had some long-term symptomatic improvement, and digital ulcers healed in all 7 patients.[177] Unfortunately, sympathectomy does not provide long-lasting benefit.[178] Initial improvement is followed by a high relapse rate due to regeneration of nerve fibers or hypersensitivity to catecholamines or progression of underlying disease.

■ REFERENCES

1. Sumner DS: Evaluation of acute and chronic ischemia of the upper extremity. In Rutherford R (ed): Vascular Surgery, 4th ed. Philadelphia, WB Saunders, 1995, pp 918-935.
2. Raynaud M: De L'asphyxie locale et de la gangrene symetrique des extremities [Selected Monographs 121, London Translation]. London, Sydenham Society, 1862, pp 1-199.
3. Raynaud, M: On Local Asphyxia and Symmetrical Gangrene of the Extremities: L. Selected Monographs [Translated by T. Barlow]. London, New Sydenham Society, 1888, pp 98-108.
4. Blunt RJ, Porter JM: Raynaud syndrome. Semin Arthritis Rheum 10:282-308, 1981.
5. Garrison CP: Nipple vasospasms, Raynaud's syndrome, and nifedipine. J Hum Lactat 18:382-385, 2002.
6. Miller D, Waters DD, Warnica W, et al: Is variant angina the coronary manifestation of a generalized vasospastic disorder? N Engl J Med 304:763-766, 1981.
7. Weinrich MC, Maricq HR, Keil JE, et al: Prevalence of Raynaud phenomenon in the adult population of South Carolina. J Clin Epidemiol 43:1343-1349, 1990.
8. Valter I, Maricq HR: Prevalence of Raynaud phenomenon in Tartu and Tartumaa, southern Estonia. Scand J Rheumatol 26:117-124, 1997.
9. Allen E, Brown G: Raynaud's disease: A critical review of minor requisites for diagnosis. Am J Med Sci 183:187, 1932.
10. Maricq HR, Weinrich MC, Keil JC, et al: Prevalence of Raynaud phenomenon in the general population: A preliminary study by questionnaire. J Chron Dis 39:423-427, 1986.
11. Heslop J, Coggon D, Acheson ED: The prevalence of intermittent digital ischaemia (Raynaud's phenomenon) in a general practice. J R Coll Gen Pract 33:85-89, 1983.
12. Silman A, Holligan S, Brennan P, et al: Prevalence of symptoms of Raynaud's phenomenon in general practice. BMJ 301:590-592, 1990.
13. Olsen N, Nielsen SL: Prevalence of primary Raynaud phenomena in young females. Scand J Clin Lab Invest 38:761-764, 1978.
14. Maricq HR, Carpentier PH, Weinrich MC, et al: Geographic variation in the prevalence of Raynaud's phenomenon: Charleston, SC, USA, versus Tarentaise, Savoie, France. J Rheumatol 20:70-76, 1993.
15. Maricq HR, Valter I, Maricq JG: An objective method to estimate the severity of Raynaud phenomenon: Digital blood pressure response to cooling. Vasc Med 3:109-113, 1998.
16. Coffman J: Raynaud's Phenomenon. New York, Oxford University Press, 1989.
17. Gifford R, Heins E: Raynaud's disease among women and girls. Circulation 16:1012, 1957.
18. Maricq HR, Weinrich MC: Diagnosis of Raynaud's phenomenon assisted by color charts. J Rheumatol 15:454-459, 1988.
19. Greenfield A, Shepherd J: A quantitative study of the response to cold of the circulation through the fingers of normal subjects. Clin Sci 9:323, 1950.
20. Coffman JD: Total and nutritional blood flow in the finger. Clin Sci 42:243-250, 1972.
21. Greenfield A, Shepherd J: The loss of heat from the hands and from the fingers immersed in cold water. J Physiol (Lond) 112:459, 1950.
22. Coffman JD, Cohen AS: Total and capillary fingertip blood flow in Raynaud's phenomenon. N Engl J Med 285:259-263, 1971.
23. Coffman JD, Cohen RA: Alpha-adrenergic and serotonergic mechanisms in the human digit. J Cardiovasc Pharmacol 11(Suppl 1):S49-S53, 1988.
24. Nuzzaci G, Evangelisti A, Righi D, et al: Is there any relationship between cold-induced vasodilatation and vasomotion? Microvasc Res 57:1-7, 1999.
25. Burton A, Taylor R: A study of the adjustment of peripheral vascular tone to the requirements of the regulation of body temperature. Am J Physiol 129:565, 1940.
26. Engelhart M, Kristensen JK: Raynaud's phenomenon: Blood supply to fingers during indirect cooling, evaluated by laser Doppler flowmetry. Clin Physiol 6:481-488, 1986.
27. Marshall R, Shepherd J, Thompson I: Vascular responses in patients with high serum titres of cold agglutinins. Clin Sci 12:155, 1953.
28. Lewis T: Observations upon reactions of vessels of human skin to cold. Heart 15:177, 1930.
29. Lewis T: Experiments relating to the peripheral mechanism involved in spasmodic arrest of the circulation in the fingers, a variety of Raynaud's disease. Heart 15:7: 1929.
30. Shepherd RF, Shepherd JT: Raynaud's phenomenon. Int Angiol 11:41-45, 1992.
31. Cooke JP, Creager MR, Osmundson PJ, et al: Sex differences in control of cutaneous blood flow. Circulation 82:1607-1615, 1990.
32. Flavahan NA, Lindblad LE, Verbeuren TJ, et al: Cooling and α_1- and α_2-adrenergic responses in cutaneous veins: Role of receptor reserve. Am J Physiol 249:H950-H955, 1985.
33. Flavahan NA, Cooke JP, Shepherd JT, et al: Human postjunctional α_1- and α_2-adrenoceptors: Differential distribution in arteries of the limbs. J Pharmacol Exp Therap 241:361-365, 1987.
34. Flavahan NA, Flavahan S, Mitra S, et al: The vasculopathy of Raynaud's phenomenon and scleroderma. Rheum Dis Clin North Am 29:275-291, 2003.
35. Furchgott RF, Zawadzki JV: The obligatory role of endothelial cells in the relaxation of arterial smooth muscle by acetylcholine. Nature 288:373-376, 1980.
36. Moncada S, Palmer RM, Higgs EA: Biosynthesis of nitric oxide from L-arginine: A pathway for the regulation of cell function and communication. Biochem Pharmacol 38:1709-1715, 1989.
37. Vane JR, Anggard EE, Botting RM: Regulatory functions of the vascular endothelium. N Engl J Med 323:27-36, 1990.
38. Furchgott R, Vanhoutte PM: Endothelium-derived relaxing and contracting factors. FASEB J 3:2007-2018, 1989.
39. Luscher T, Vanhoutte PM: The Endothelium: Modulator of Cardiovascular Function. Boca Raton, CRC Press, 1990.
40. Shepherd JT, Vanhoutte PM: Endothelium-derived relaxing (EDRF) and contracting factors (EDCF) in the control of cardiovascular homeostasis: The pioneering observations. In Rubanyi GM (ed): Cardiovascular Significance of Endothelium-Derived Vasoactive Factors. Mount Kisco, NY, Futura, 1991, pp 39-64.

41. Biondi ML, Marasini B, Bianchi E, et al: Plasma free and intraplatelet serotonin in patients with Raynaud's phenomenon. Int J Cardiol 19:335-339, 1988.

42. Cohen RA: The role of nitric oxide and other endothelium-derived vasoactive substances in vascular disease. Progr Cardiovasc Dis 38:105-128, 1995.

43. Yang ZH, Richard V, von Segesser L, et al: Threshold concentrations of endothelin-1 potentiate contractions to norepinephrine and serotonin in human arteries: A new mechanism of vasospasm? Circulation 82:188-195, 1990.

44. Singh S, De Trafford JC, Baskerville PA, et al: Response of digital arteries to endothelium-dependent and -independent vasodilators in patients with Raynaud's phenomenon. Eur J Clin Invest 25:182-185, 1995.

45. Fyhrquist F: Raised plasma endothelin-1 concentration following cold pressor test. Biochem Biophys Res Commun 169:217-221, 1990.

46. Leppert J, Ringqvist A, Karlberg BE, et al: Whole-body cooling increases plasma endothelin-1 levels in women with primary Raynaud's phenomenon. Clin Physiol 18:420-425, 1998.

47. Zamora MR, O'Brien RF, Rutherford RB, et al: Serum endothelin-1 concentrations and cold provocation in primary Raynaud's phenomenon [see comment]. Lancet 336:1144-1147, 1990.

48. Smyth AE, Bell AL, Bruce IN, et al: Digital vascular responses and serum endothelin-1 concentrations in primary and secondary Raynaud's phenomenon. Ann Rheum Dis 59:870-874, 2000.

49. Rajagopalan S, Pfenninger D, Kehrer C, et al: Increased asymmetric dimethyl-arginine and endothelin 1 levels in secondary Raynaud's phenomenon: Implications for vascular dysfunction and progression of disease. Arthritis Rheum 48:1992-2000, 2003.

50. Merritt WH: Comprehensive management of Raynaud's syndrome. Clin Plast Surg 24:133-159, 1997.

51. Greenfield LJ, Rajagopalan S, Olin JW: Upper extremity arterial disease. Cardiol Clin 20: 623-631, 2002.

52. Rubin DI, Schomberg PJ, Shepherd RF, et al: Arteritis and brachial plexus neuropathy as delayed complications of radiation therapy. Mayo Clin Proc 76:849-852, 2001.

53. Koman LA, Smith BP, Smith TL: Stress testing in the evaluation of upper-extremity perfusion. Hand Clin 9:59-83, 1993.

54. Coleman S, Anson B: Arterial patterns in the hand based upon a study of 650 specimens. Surg Gynecol Obstet 113:409, 1961.

55. Edwards JM, Porter JM: Raynaud's syndrome and small vessel arteriopathy. Semin Vasc Surg 6:56-65, 1993.

56. Tuffanelli DL, Winkelmann RK: Systemic scleroderma: A clinical study of 727 cases. Arch Dermatol 84:359, 1961.

57. Anonymous: Raynaud's phenomenon, scleroderma, overlap syndromes, and other fibrosing syndromes. Curr Opin Rheumatol 14:737-746, 2002.

58. Hummers LK, Wigley FM: Management of Raynaud's phenomenon and digital ischemic lesions in scleroderma. Rheum Dis Clin North Am 29:293-313, 2003.

59. Medsger TA Jr: Natural history of systemic sclerosis and the assessment of disease activity, severity, functional status, and psychologic well-being. Rheum Dis Clin North Am 29:255-273, 2003.

60. White B: Systemic sclerosis and related syndromes: A. Epidemiology, pathology, and pathogenesis. In Klippel JH (ed): Primer on the Rheumatic Diseases. Atlanta, Arthritis Foundation, 2001, pp 353-357.

61. Wigley FM: Systemic sclerosis and related syndromes: B. Clinical features. In Klippel JH (ed): Primer on the Rheumatic Diseases. Atlanta, Arthritis Foundation, 2001, pp 357-364.

62. Gerbracht DD, Steen VD, Ziegler GL, et al: Evolution of primary Raynaud's phenomenon (Raynaud's disease) to connective tissue disease. Arthritis Rheum 28:87-92, 1985.

62a. Harper FE, Marica HR, Turner RE, et al: A prospective study of Raynaud phenomenon and early connective tissue disease; A five-year report. Am J Med 72:883-888, 1982.

63. Porter JM, Edwards JM: Occlusive and vasospastic diseases involving distal upper extremity arteries: Raynaud's syndrome. In Rutherford R (ed): Vascular Surgery, 4th ed. Philadelphia, WB Saunders, 1995, pp 961-976.

64. Priollet P, Vayssairat M, Housset E: How to classify Raynaud's phenomenon: Long-term follow-up study of 73 cases [erratum appears in Am J Med 83:A11, 1987]. Am J Med 83:494-498, 1987.

65. Miller LM, Morgan RF: Vasospastic disorders: Etiology, recognition, and treatment. Hand Clin 9:171-187, 1993.

66. Zimmerman NB: Occlusive vascular disorders of the upper extremity. Hand Clin 9:139-150, 1993.

67. Olin JW: Thromboangiitis obliterans (Buerger's disease). N Engl J Med 343:864-869, 2000.

68. Joyce JW: Buerger's disease (thromboangiitis obliterans). Rheum Dis Clin North Am 16:463-470, 1990.

69. McCollum CH, Mavor E: Brachial artery injury after cardiac catheterization. J Vasc Surg 4:355-359, 1986.

70. Spittell PC, Spittell JA: Occlusive arterial disease of the hand due to repetitive blunt trauma: A review with illustrative cases. Int J Cardiol 38:281-292, 1993.

71. Hamilton G: Effect of the air hammer on the hands of the stonecutters. U.S. Bureau Labor Stat Bull 236:53-66, 1918.

72. Barregard L, Ehrenstrom L, Marcus K: Hand-arm vibration syndrome in Swedish car mechanics. Occup Environ Med 60:287-294, 2003.

73. Griffin MJ, Bovenzi M, Nelson CM: Dose-response patterns for vibration-induced white finger. Occup Environ Med 60:16-26, 2003.

74. Seyring M: Maladies from work with compressed air drills. Bull Hyg 6:25, 1931.

75. McLafferty RB, Edwards JM, Ferris BL, et al: Raynaud's syndrome in workers who use vibrating pneumatic air knives. J Vasc Surg 30:1-7, 1999.

76. Liapina M, Tzvetkov D, Vodenitcharov E: Pathophysiology of vibration-induced white fingers—current opinion: A review. Centr Eur J Public Health 10:16-20, 2002.

77. Stoyneva Z, Lyapina M, Tzvetkov D, et al: Current pathophysiological views on vibration-induced Raynaud's phenomenon. Cardiovasc Res 57:615-624, 2003.

78. Nilsson T, Burstrom L, Hagberg M: Risk assessment of vibration exposure and white fingers among platers. Int Arch Occup Environ Health 61:473-481, 1989.

79. Birrer M, Baumgartner I: Images in clinical medicine: Work-related vascular injuries of the hand—hypothenar hammer syndrome. N Engl J Med 347:339, 2002.

80. Cooke RA: Hypothenar hammer syndrome: A discrete syndrome to be distinguished from hand-arm vibration syndrome. Occup Med (Oxford) 53:320-324, 2003.

81. Lorelli DR, Shepard AD: Hypothenar hammer syndrome: An uncommon and correctable cause of digital ischemia. J Cardiovasc Surg 43:83-85, 2002.

82. Taylor LM Jr: Hypothenar hammer syndrome. J Vasc Surg 37:697, 2003.

83. Noel B, Hayoz D: A tennis player with hand claudication. Vasa 29:151-153, 2000.

84. Mueller LP, Mueller LA, Degreif J, et al: Hypothenar hammer syndrome in a golf player: A case report. Am J Sports Med 28:741-745, 2000.

85. Velling TE, Brennan FJ, Hall LD, et al: Sonographic diagnosis of ulnar artery aneurysm in hypothenar hammer syndrome: Report of two cases. J Ultrasound Med 20:921-924, 2001.

86. Winterer JT, Ghanem N, Roth M, et al: Diagnosis of the hypothenar hammer syndrome by high-resolution contrast-enhanced MR angiography. Eur Radiol 12:2457-2462, 2002.

87. Troum SJ, Smith TL, Koman LA, et al: Management of vasospastic disorders of the hand. Clin Plast Surg 24:121-132, 1997.

88. Ferris BL, Taylor LM Jr, Oyama K, et al: Hypothenar hammer syndrome: Proposed etiology. J Vasc Surg 31:104-113, 2000.

89. Brodmann M, Stark G, Aschauer M, et al: Hypothenar hammer syndrome caused by posttraumatic aneurysm of the ulnar artery. Wien Klin Wochenschr 113:698-700, 2001.

90. Cormier JM, Amrane M, Ward A, et al: Arterial complications of the thoracic outlet syndrome: Fifty-five operative cases. J Vasc Surg 9:778-787, 1989.

91. Dorazio RA, Ezzet F: Arterial complications of the thoracic outlet syndrome. Am J Surg 138:246-250, 1979.

92. Feleke E, Lyngstam O, Rastam L, et al: Complaints of cold extremities among patients on antihypertensive treatment. Acta Med Scand 213:381-385, 1983.

93. Anonymous: Adverse reactions to bendrofluazide and propranolol for the treatment of mild hypertension. Report of Medical Research Council Working Party on Mild to Moderate Hypertension. Lancet 2:539-543, 1981.

94. van der Veur E, ten Berge BS, Wouda AA, et al: Effects of atenolol, labetalol, and propranolol on the peripheral circulation in hypertensive patients without obstructive vascular disease. Eur J Clin Pharmacol 28:131-134, 1985.

95. Steiner JA, Cooper R, Gear JS, et al: Vascular symptoms in patients with primary Raynaud's phenomenon are not exacerbated by propranolol or labetalol. Br J Clin Pharmacol 7:401-403, 1979.

96. Franssen C, Wollersheim H, de Haan A, et al: The influence of different beta-blocking drugs on the peripheral circulation in Raynaud's phenomenon and in hypertension. J Clin Pharmacol 32:652-659, 1992.

97. Coffman JD, Rasmussen HM: Effects of beta-adrenoreceptor-blocking drugs in patients with Raynaud's phenomenon. Circulation 72:466-470, 1985.

98. Grau JJ, Grau M, Milla A, et al: Cancer chemotherapy and Raynaud's phenomenon. Ann Intern Med 98:258, 1983.

99. Scheulen ME, Schmidt CG: Raynaud's phenomenon and cancer chemotherapy. Ann Intern Med 96:256-257, 1982.

100. Clowse ME, Wigley FM: Digital necrosis related to carboplatin and gemcitabine therapy in systemic sclerosis. J Rheumatol 30:1341-1343, 2003.

101. Shepherd RFJ: Ergotism. In White R, Hollier L (eds): Vascular Surgery. Philadelphia, Lippincott, 1994, pp 177-191.

102. Bowen JS, Davis GB, Kearney TE, et al: Diffuse vascular spasm associated with 4-bromo-2,5-dimethoxyamphetamine ingestion. JAMA 249:1477-1479, 1983.

103. Hager DL, Wilson JN: Gangrene of the hand following intra-arterial injection. Anesth Analg 47:423-427, 1968.

104. Balbir-Gurman A, Braun-Moscovici Y, Nahir AM: Cocaine-induced Raynaud's phenomenon and ischaemic finger necrosis. Clin Rheumatol 20:376-378, 2001.

105. Al-Zahrani H, Gupta V, Minden MD, et al: Vascular events associated with alpha interferon therapy. Leuk Lymph 44:471-475, 2003.

106. Kern P: Digital arterial occlusive disease and parvovirus B19 infection. Vasa 31:274-275, 2002.

107. Dingli D, Pfizenmaier DH, Arromdee E, et al: Severe digital arterial occlusive disease and acute parvovirus B19 infection [see comment]. Lancet 356:312-314, 2000.

108. Nadir A, Smith JW, Matter B, et al: Type 2 cryoglobulinemia and hepatitis C virus: Its recognition and treatment. J Okla State Med Assoc 87:449-453, 1994.

109. McLeod BC, Sassetti RJ: Plasmapheresis with return of cryoglobulin-depleted autologous plasma (cryoglobulinpheresis) in cryoglobulinemia. Blood 55:866-870, 1980.

110. Wong AS, Hon Yoon K: Paraneoplastic Raynaud phenomenon and idiopathic thrombocytopenic purpura in non-small-cell lung cancer. Am J Clin Oncol 26:26-29, 2003.

111. Fam AG: Paraneoplastic rheumatic syndromes. Best Pract Res Clin Rheumatol 14:515-533, 2000.

112. Taillan B, Castanet J, Garnier G, et al: Paraneoplastic Raynaud's phenomenon. Clin Rheumatol 12:281-282, 1993.

113. DeCross AJ, Sahasrabudhe DM: Paraneoplastic Raynaud's phenomenon. Am J Med 92:571-572, 1992.

114. Kohli M, Bennett RM: Raynaud's phenomenon as a presenting sign of ovarian adenocarcinoma [see comment]. J Rheumatol 22:1393-1394, 1995.

115. Zweifler AJ, Trinkaus P: Occlusive digital artery disease in patients with Raynaud's phenomenon. Am J Med 77:995-1001, 1984.

116. Ouriel K: Noninvasive diagnosis of upper extremity vascular disease. Semin Vasc Surg 11:54-59, 1998.

117. Leesmans E, Bartelink ML, Wollersheim H, et al: The relationship between subjective vasospastic complaints and finger blood flow measurements in Raynaud's phenomenon. Neth J Med 43:13-17, 1993.

118. Hirai M, Nielsen SL, Lassen NA: Blood pressure measurement of all five fingers by strain gauge plethysmography. Scand J Clin Lab Invest 36:627-632, 1976.

119. Krahenbuhl B, Nielsen SL, Lassen NA: Closure of digital arteries in high vascular tone states as demonstrated by measurement of systolic blood pressure in the fingers. Scand J Clin Lab Invest 37:71-76, 1977.

120. Nielsen SL, Lassen NA: Measurement of digital blood pressure after local cooling. J Appl Physiol 43:907-910, 1977.

121. Nielsen SL: Raynaud phenomena and finger systolic pressure during cooling. Scand J Clin Lab Invest 38:765-770, 1978.

122. Thulesius O, Brubakk A, Berlin E: Response of digital blood pressure to cold provocation in cases with Raynaud phenomena. Angiology 32:113-118, 1981.

123. Bartelink ML, Wollersheim H, Jansen RW, et al: Reproducibility of the finger cooling test. Microvasc Res 45:65-73, 1993.

124. Bartelink ML, Wollersheim H, Leesmans E, et al: A standardized finger cooling test for Raynaud's phenomenon: Diagnostic value and sex differences. Eur Heart J 14:614-622, 1993.

125. Del Bianco E, Magini B, Muscarella G, et al: Raynaud's phenomenon (primary or secondary to systemic sclerosis): The usefulness of laser-Doppler flowmetry in the diagnosis. Int Angiol 20:307-313, 2001.

126. Engelhart M, Nielsen HV, Kristensen JK: The blood supply to fingers during Raynaud's attack: A comparison of laser-Doppler flowmetry with other techniques. Clin Physiol 5:447-453, 1985.

127. Cesarone MR, Laurora G, Smith SR, et al: Laser-Doppler flowmetry in the assessment of "mild" Raynaud's phenomenon and its treatment. Panminerva Med 32:151-154, 1990.

128. Wollersheim H, Reyenga J, Thien T: Laser Doppler velocimetry of fingertips during heat provocation in normals and in patients with Raynaud's phenomenon. Scand J Clin Lab Invest 48:91-95, 1988.

129. Chikui T, Izumi M, Eguchi K, et al: Doppler spectral waveform analysis of arteries of the hand in patients with Raynaud's phenomenon as compared with healthy subjects. AJR Am J Roentgenol 172:1605-1609, 1999.

130. Rofsky NM: MR angiography of the hand and wrist. Magn Reson Imaging Clin North Am 3:345-359, 1995.

131. Maricq HR, Weinberger AB, LeRoy EC: Early detection of scleroderma-spectrum disorders by in vivo capillary microscopy: A prospective study of patients with Raynaud's phenomenon. J Rheumatol 9:289-291, 1982.

132. Maricq HR, Maize JC: Nailfold capillary abnormalities. Clin Rheum Dis 8:455-478, 1982.

133. Maricq HR: Capillary abnormalities, Raynaud's phenomenon, and systemic sclerosis in patients with localized scleroderma. Arch Dermatol 128:630-632, 1992.

134. Dolezalova P, Young SP, Bacon PA, et al: Nailfold capillary microscopy in healthy children and in childhood rheumatic diseases: A prospective single blind observational study. Ann Rheum Dis 62:444-449, 2003.

135. Kempson GE, Coggon D, Acheson ED: Electrically heated gloves for intermittent digital ischaemia. BMJ 286:268, 1983.

136. Freedman RR: Physiological mechanisms of temperature biofeedback. Biofeedback Self-Regulat 16:95-115, 1991.

137. Anonymous: Comparison of sustained-release nifedipine and temperature biofeedback for treatment of primary Raynaud phenomenon: Results from a randomized clinical trial with 1-year follow-up. Arch Intern Med 160:1101-1108, 2000.

138. Belch JJ, Ho M: Pharmacotherapy of Raynaud's phenomenon. Drugs 52:682-695, 1996.

139. Sunahara JF, Gora-Harper ML, Nash KS: Possible erythromelalgia-like syndrome associated with nifedipine in a patient with Raynaud's phenomenon. Ann Pharmacother 30:484-486, 1996.

140. Weber A, Bounameaux H: Effects of low-dose nifedipine on a cold provocation test in patients with Raynaud's disease. J Cardiovasc Pharmacol 15:853-855, 1990.

141. Maricq HR, Jennings JR, Valter I, et al: Evaluation of treatment efficacy of Raynaud phenomenon by digital blood pressure response to cooling. Raynaud's Treatment Study Investigators. Vasc Med 5:135-140, 2000.

142. La Civita L, Pitaro N, Rossi M, et al: Amlodipine in the treatment of Raynaud's phenomenon. Br J Rheumatol 32:524-525, 1993.

143. Ferri C, Cecchetti R, Cini G, et al: Slow-releasing nicardipine in the treatment of Raynaud's phenomena without underlying diseases. Clin Rheumatol 11:76-80, 1992.

144. Wollersheim H, Thien T: Double-blind placebo-controlled crossover study of oral nicardipine in the treatment of Raynaud's phenomenon. J Cardiovasc Pharmacol 18:813-818, 1991.

145. van Heereveld H, Wollersheim H, Gough K, et al: Intravenous nicardipine in Raynaud's phenomenon: A controlled trial. J Cardiovasc Pharmacol 11:68-74, 1988.

146. Schmidt JF, Valentin N, Nielsen SL: The clinical effect of felodipine and nifedipine in Raynaud's phenomenon. Eur J Clin Pharmacol 37:191-192, 1989.

147. Gjorup T, Hartling OJ, Kelbaek H, et al: Controlled double-blind trial of nisoldipine in the treatment of idiopathic Raynaud's phenomenon. Eur J Clin Pharmacol 31:387-389, 1986.

148. Kaplan MJ: Clinical Hypertension. Baltimore, Williams & Wilkins, 1994.

149. Wollersheim H, Thien T: Dose-response study of prazosin in Raynaud's phenomenon: Clinical effectiveness versus side effects. J Clin Pharmacol 28:1089-1093, 1988.

150. Wollersheim H, Thien T, Fennis J, et al: Double-blind, placebo-controlled study of prazosin in Raynaud's phenomenon. Clin Pharmacol Ther 40:219-225, 1986.

151. Paterna S, Pinto A, Arrostuto A, et al: [Raynaud's phenomenon: Effects of terazosin.] Minerva Cardioangiol 45:215-221, 1997.

152. Dziadzio M, Denton CP, Smith R, et al: Losartan therapy for Raynaud's phenomenon and scleroderma: Clinical and biochemical findings in a fifteen-week, randomized, parallel-group, controlled trial. Arthritis Rheum 42:2646-2655, 1999.

153. Coleiro B, Marshall SE, Denton CP, et al: Treatment of Raynaud's phenomenon with the selective serotonin reuptake inhibitor fluoxetine [comment]. Rheumatology 40:1038-1043, 2001.

154. Cremers B, Bohm M: Nonerectile dysfunction application of sildenafil. Herz 28:325-333, 2003.

155. Bartelink ML, Wollersheim H, Vemer H, et al: The effects of single oral doses of 17 beta-oestradiol and progesterone on finger skin circulation in healthy women and in women with primary Raynaud's phenomenon. Eur J Clin Pharmac 46:557-560, 1994.

156. Digiacomo R, Kremer J, Shaw D: Fish-oil dietary supplementation in patients with Raynaud's phenomenon: A double-blind, controlled, prospective study. Am J Med 86:158-164, 1989.

157. Freedman RR, Girgis R, Mayes MD: Acute effect of nitric oxide on Raynaud's phenomenon in scleroderma. Lancet 354:739, 1999.

158. Khan F, Litchfield SJ, McLaren M, et al: Oral L-arginine supplementation and cutaneous vascular responses in patients with primary Raynaud's phenomenon. Arthritis Rheum 40:352-357, 1997.

159. Khan F, Belch JJ: Skin blood flow in patients with systemic sclerosis and Raynaud's phenomenon: Effects of oral L-arginine supplementation. J Rheumatol 26:2389-2394, 1999.

160. Kashiba H, Ueda Y: Acupuncture to the skin induces release of substance P and calcitonin gene-related peptide from peripheral terminals of primary sensory neurons in the rat. Am J Chin Med 19:189-197, 1991.

161. Appiah R, Hiller S, Caspary L, et al: Treatment of primary Raynaud's syndrome with traditional Chinese acupuncture. J Intern Med 241:119-124, 1997.

162. Kaada B: Vasodilation induced by transcutaneous nerve stimulation in peripheral ischemia (Raynaud's phenomenon and diabetic polyneuropathy). Eur Heart J 3:303-314, 1982.

163. Robaina FJ, Dominguez M, Diaz M, et al: Spinal cord stimulation for relief of chronic pain in vasospastic disorders of the upper limbs. Neurosurgery 24:63-67, 1989.

164. Landry GJ, Edwards JM, McLafferty RB, et al: Long-term outcome of Raynaud's syndrome in a prospectively analyzed patient cohort. J Vasc Surg 23:76-85, 1996.

165. Whitmore SE, Wigley FM, Wise RA: Acute effect of topical minoxidil on digital blood flow in patients with Raynaud's phenomenon. J Rheumatol 22:50-54, 1995.

166. Kingma K, Wollersheim H, Thien T: Double-blind, placebo-controlled study of intravenous prostacyclin on hemodynamics in severe Raynaud's phenomenon: The acute vasodilatory effect is not sustained. J Cardiovasc Pharmacol 26:388-393, 1995.

167. Torley HI, Madhok R, Capell HA, et al: A double-blind, randomised, multicentre comparison of two doses of intravenous iloprost in the treatment of Raynaud's phenomenon secondary to connective tissue diseases. Ann Rheum Dis 50:800-804, 1991.

168. Wigley FM, Siebold JR, Wise RA, et al: Intravenous iloprost treatment of Raynaud's phenomenon and ischemic ulcers secondary to systemic sclerosis. J Rheumatol 19:1407-1414, 1992.

169. Scorza R, Caronni M, Mascagni B, et al: Effects of long-term cyclic iloprost therapy in systemic sclerosis with Raynaud's phenomenon: A randomized, controlled study. Clin Exp Rheumatol 19:503-508, 2001.

170. Rademaker M, Cooke ED, Almond NE, et al: Comparison of intravenous infusions of iloprost and oral nifedipine in treatment of Raynaud's phenomenon in patients with systemic sclerosis: A double-blind randomised study. BMJ 298:561-564, 1989.

171. Wigley FM, Korn JH, Csuka ME, et al: Oral iloprost treatment in patients with Raynaud's phenomenon secondary to systemic sclerosis: A multicenter, placebo-controlled, double-blind study. Arthritis Rheum 41:670-677, 1998.

172. Black CM, Halkier-Sorensen L, Belch JJ, et al: Oral iloprost in Raynaud's phenomenon secondary to systemic sclerosis: A multicentre, placebo-controlled, dose-comparison study. Br J Rheumatol 37:952-960, 1998.

173. Lowell RC, Gloviczki P, Cherry KJ Jr, et al: Cervicothoracic sympathectomy for Raynaud's syndrome. Int Angiol 12:168-172, 1993.

174. Adson AW, Brown GE: The treatment of Raynaud's disease by resection of the upper thoracic and lumbar sympathetic ganglia and trunks. Surg Gynecol Obstet 48:577-603, 1929.

175. McCall TE, Petersen DP, Wong LB: The use of digital artery sympathectomy as a salvage procedure for severe ischemia of Raynaud's disease and phenomenon. J Hand Surg Am 24:173-177, 1999.

176. Balogh B, Mayer W, Vesely M, et al: [Periarterial sympathectomy of the radial and ulnar arteries in Raynaud's phenomenon—a preliminary study.] Handchir Mikrochir Plast Chir 34:374-380, 2002.

177. Matsumoto Y, Ueyama T, Endo M, et al: Endoscopic thoracic sympathicotomy for Raynaud's phenomenon. J Vasc Surg 36:57-61, 2002.

178. Sayers RD, Jenner RE, Barrie WW: Transthoracic endoscopic sympathectomy for hyperhidrosis and Raynaud's phenomenon [see comment]. Eur J Vasc Surg 8:627-631, 1994.

Neurogenic Thoracic Outlet Syndrome

ROBERT W. THOMPSON, MD
MICHEL A. BARTOLI, MD

The thoracic outlet represents a unique anatomic region dominated by the anterior and middle scalene muscles, the first rib, and their associated structures. The neurovascular structures that pass through this relatively confined space—the subclavian artery, the subclavian vein, and the five nerve roots of the brachial plexus—are all potentially subject to extrinsic compression. Clinical problems that develop as a result of neurovascular compression in this area are collectively known as *thoracic outlet syndrome* (TOS).

The three distinct clinical types of TOS are classified according to the primary structure subject to compression as follows: (1) *arterial TOS* (subclavian artery), (2) *venous TOS* (subclavian vein), and (3) *neurogenic TOS* (brachial plexus nerve roots). All of these conditions are uncommon, and their true incidence is unknown. Arterial TOS and venous TOS account for approximately 1% and 5% of all patients with TOS, respectively, whereas neurogenic TOS is far more common. Vascular lesions associated with thoracic outlet compression typically give rise to easily recognized syndromes, such as effort thrombosis of the subclavian vein or post-stenotic aneurysms of the subclavian artery complicated by thromboembolism. In contrast, the diagnosis of neurogenic TOS often remains difficult, confusing, and elusive.

A growing body of experience demonstrates that excellent outcomes can be achieved by a comprehensive, multidisciplinary approach to neurogenic TOS, including a prominent role for surgical treatment in well-selected cases.[1-3] Nonetheless, uncertainties in diagnosis and disappointing results of treatment have led some authorities to question the need for surgical management of neurogenic TOS and even to challenge whether the condition actually exists.[4-6] The purpose of this chapter is to review current understanding of the diagnosis, optimal management, and surgical techniques for neurogenic TOS. Because the vascular (arterial and venous) forms of TOS give rise to distinct clinical syndromes and require variations in management, these conditions are covered in Chapters 95 and 96.

■ ANATOMY

As shown in Figure 94-1,[38] the anatomy of the thoracic outlet region comprises several bony and soft tissue structures as well as the nerves and blood vessels that pass through this area. A number of important variations in these structures may be associated with neurogenic TOS,

including changes extending from gross anatomy to the microscopic structure of the scalene muscles.

Boundary Structures

The central feature of the thoracic outlet is the anatomic space known as the *scalene triangle*. The scalene triangle is covered anteriorly by the *scalene fat pad*, a discrete structure that contains abundant adipose tissue and lymph nodes and is crossed by the distal portion of the omohyoid muscle. These structures must therefore be reflected, resected, or traversed for the surgeon to obtain initial exposure of the thoracic outlet. The sides of the scalene triangle are composed of the anterior and middle scalene muscles, and the base of the triangle is formed by the first rib. The *anterior scalene muscle* originates on the transverse processes of the lower cervical vertebrae (C4 to C6) and inserts on the superior aspect of the first rib at the site of a small bony protuberance known as the *scalene tubercle*. Although the belly of the anterior scalene muscle is usually soft, its posterior aspect is often firm and tendinous near its attachment to the rib. The *middle scalene muscle* also arises from the transverse processes of the C4 to C6 cervical vertebrae and inserts on the superolateral surface of the first rib. Its origin is incompletely separated from the origin of the posterior scalene muscle, which otherwise passes to insert on the second rib and is not a boundary of the scalene triangle. The *first rib* forms a small, tight semicircle, arising from the transverse process of the T1 vertebra and attaching anteriorly to the sternum just below and behind the sternoclavicular joint.

Nerves and Vessels

The space formed by the scalene triangle is traversed by the five nerve roots that make up the *brachial plexus*, arising from cervical spine levels C5 through T1. Although each of these nerves can be identified as an individual structure upon entering the scalene triangle, they begin to fuse into the initial trunks of the brachial plexus within this space and as they pass over the first rib. The three trunks of the brachial plexus are the *upper trunk* (formed by fusion of the C5 and C6 nerve roots), the *middle trunk* (composed of the C7 nerve root), and the *lower trunk* (formed by fusion of the C8 and T1 nerve roots). Further merging and branching of these trunks outside the thoracic outlet result in formation of

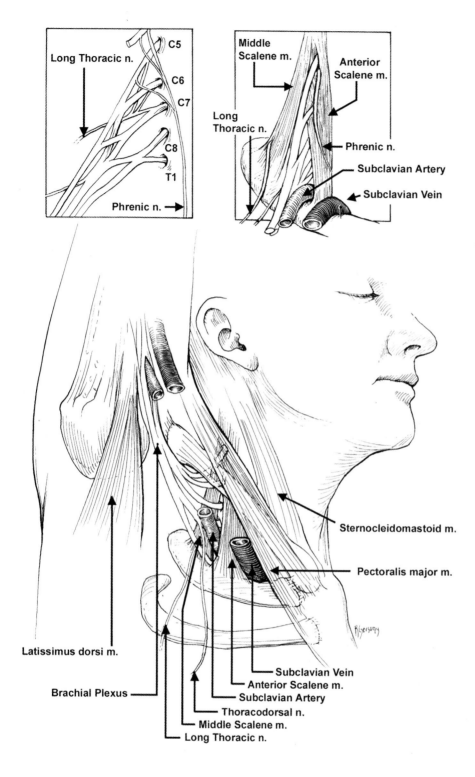

FIGURE 94-1 Anatomy of the thoracic outlet. The surgical anatomy of the thoracic outlet is centered on spinal nerve roots C5 through T1, which interdigitate to form the brachial plexus as they cross under the clavicle and over the first rib. The long thoracic and phrenic nerves also arise within the thoracic outlet region. The brachial plexus nerve roots pass through the scalene triangle, bordered by the anterior and middle scalene muscles on each side and the first rib at the base. The subclavian artery also courses through the scalene triangle in direct relation to the brachial plexus nerve roots. The subclavian vein crosses over the first rib immediately in front of the anterior scalene muscle, before joining with the internal jugular vein to form the innominate vein. Symptoms of TOS are often exacerbated by arm elevation, in which greater strain is placed on the neurovascular structures passing through the scalene triangle. (Adapted from Thompson RW, Petrinec D: Surgical treatment of thoracic outlet compression syndromes. I: Diagnostic considerations and transaxillary first rib resection. Ann Vasc Surg 11:315-323, 1997.)

the divisions, cords, and terminal nerves of the brachial plexus.

Additional nerves of surgical importance pass through the thoracic outlet, including the phrenic nerve, the long thoracic nerve, and the cervical sympathetic chain. The *phrenic nerve* forms from the C4 nerve root at the lateral border of the anterior scalene muscle, where it also receives contributions from the C3 and C5 nerve roots. It passes from lateral to medial along the anterior surface of the scalene muscle, then descends behind the subclavian vein into the mediastinum, where it subsequently innervates the diaphragm. Unilateral phrenic nerve palsy is thereby characterized by paralysis of the ipsilateral hemidiaphragm. The *long thoracic nerve* arises as three branches from the C5, C6, and C7 nerve roots. It passes through the belly of the middle scalene muscle, where its three components typically fuse to form a single nerve. It then descends to supply the serratus anterior muscle. Interruption of the long thoracic nerve results in the defect described as a "winged scapula." The *cervicodorsal sympathetic chain* consists of a series of interconnected ganglia passing from the chest to the neck, lying along the posterior inner aspect of the ribs. At the level of the first rib, a fusion of several ganglia results in formation of the large stellate ganglion, which supplies part of the face and upper extremity. Interruption of the sympathetic chain is occasionally indicated in some patients with neurogenic TOS, in whom neurogenic symptoms have become amplified by concomitant reflex sympathetic dystrophy. Horner's syndrome occurs when sympathetic fibers passing through the upper half of the stellate ganglion are interrupted, resulting in ptosis, ipsilateral pupillary constriction, and vasodilatation with absence of facial sweating.

The *subclavian artery* ascends from the superior mediastinum to enter the supraclavicular space, where it gives rise to the vertebral artery, the internal thoracic artery, and the thyrocervical trunk. The subclavian artery then passes behind the anterior scalene muscle to enter the scalene triangle, where it lies immediately in front of the brachial plexus nerve roots. Within this region, the subclavian artery may also give origin to additional branches, such as the costocervical trunk and the dorsal scapular artery. The subclavian artery becomes surrounded by the trunks of the brachial plexus just after it passes over the first rib, where it then becomes the axillary artery as it passes behind the pectoralis minor muscle.

The *subclavian vein* does not pass through the scalene triangle; rather, it passes over the first rib and through the thoracic outlet immediately in front of the anterior scalene muscle. It then joins the internal jugular vein to form the brachiocephalic (innominate) vein. The central portion of the subclavian vein is subject to compression between the anterior scalene muscle, the anteromedial first rib, the subclavius muscle, and the clavicle, thereby producing the venous form of TOS. Additional venous branches are also commonly encountered near the scalene triangle, including the anterior and external jugular veins, the cephalic vein, and unnamed collateral vessels that may enlarge with central obstruction of the subclavian vein.

The *thoracic duct* is the principal route of lymphatic drainage from the chest and abdomen. It is usually found on the left side, where it passes from the anterior mediastinum to enter the venous system at the junction of the internal jugular and subclavian veins. Right-sided and accessory thoracic ducts are also commonly encountered.

Musculofascial Variations

The "textbook" description of scalene triangle anatomy probably occurs in no more than one third of individuals, variations in the soft tissue structure of this region being very common.[7,8] Because many of these variations occur too frequently to be termed true anomalies, it is unclear whether they add significantly to the potential for anatomic compression of neurovascular structures or they simply represent anatomic variants with little relationship to symptoms. For example, the posterior aspect of the anterior scalene muscle is commonly quite firm and tendinous in nature, potentially exerting pressure on adjacent nerve roots. It may also give origin to fascial bands that extend from the posterior surface of the muscle to the thickened extrapleural fascia over the dome of the pleura (Sibson's fascia) or that circumscribe the subclavian artery. The most common muscular variation in this region is known as the *scalene minimus muscle*, a structure that originates within the plane of the middle scalene muscle. This muscle passes between various nerve roots of the brachial plexus and inserts on the first rib in conjunction with the anterior scalene muscle; thus, the scalene minimus muscle may contribute to nerve root compression when present. Additional soft tissue variations include fascial bands that pass across or between individual nerve roots, subsequently attaching to either the first rib or the extrapleural fascia. During operations for TOS, it is particularly common for the surgeon to encounter a dense fascial band crossing over the origin of the T1 nerve root where it passes from underneath the first rib to contribute to the brachial plexus. Although the surgical significance of these structures is not entirely clear, a spectrum of other muscular and fascial variations in this region have been described and classified by several investigators (Table 94-1).

Table 94-1	Classification of Congenital Bands and Ligaments Within the Scalene Triangle
Type 1	Extending from anterior tip of an incomplete cervical rib to the middle of the first thoracic rib; inserts just posterior to the scalene tubercle on the upper rib surface.
Type 2	Arises from an elongated C7 transverse process in the absence of a cervical rib and attaches to the first rib just behind the scalene tubercle; associated with extension of the transverse process of C7 beyond the transverse process of T1 on anteroposterior spine radiographs.
Type 3	Both originates and inserts on the first rib; starts posteriorly near the neck of the rib and inserts anteriorly just behind the scalene tubercle.
Type 4	Originates from a transverse process along with the middle scalene muscle and runs on the anterior edge of the middle scalene muscle to insert on the first rib; the lower nerve roots of the brachial plexus lie against this band.
Type 5	The scalene minimus muscle arises with the lower fibers of the anterior scalene muscle, runs parallel to this muscle but passes deep to the muscle to cross behind the subclavian artery and in front of or between the nerve roots, and inserts on the first rib; any fibers passing anterior to or between the plexus but posterior to the artery.
Type 6	Scalene minimus muscle inserts onto Sibson's fascia over the cupula of the pleura instead of onto the first rib; labeled separately to distinguish its point of insertion.
Type 7	Fibrous cord runs on the anterior surface of the anterior scalene muscle down to the first rib, attaching to the costochondral junction or sternum; lies immediately behind the subclavian vein where it may be a cause of partial venous obstruction.
Type 8	Arises from the middle scalene muscle and runs under the subclavian artery and vein to attach to the costochondral junction.
Type 9	Web of muscle and fascia fills the inside posterior curve of the first rib, compressing the origin of the T1 nerve root.

Adapted from Roos DB: Congenital anomalies associated with thoracic outlet syndrome. Am J Surg 132:771-778, 1976.

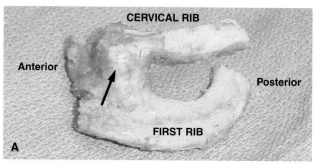

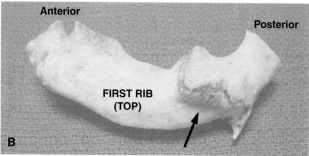

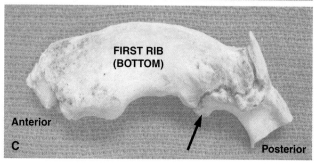

FIGURE 94-2 First rib anomalies. Operating room photographs depicting bony abnormalities associated with neurogenic thoracic outlet syndrome. **A,** Resected specimen including a congenital cervical rib removed along with its attachment to the first rib, which consisted of a complete joint (*arrow*). **B,** Top view of the resected specimen of a first rib that contained a healed fracture site from previous trauma (*arrow*). **C,** Bottom view of the same rib shown in **B,** showing healed fracture site (*arrow*).

Bony Anomalies

Cervical ribs occur in approximately 0.45% to 1.5% of the population and in up to 5% of patients with TOS. They arise in the plane of the middle scalene muscle and typically attach to the midlateral portion of the first rib; the anomalous rib may join the first rib as an immobile bony fusion or as a fully developed joint (Fig. 94-2A). *Incomplete cervical ribs* may also occur, arising as bony or cartilaginous extensions from the C7 cervical vertebra without extension to join the first rib, and in some cases are attached to the first rib only by a band of cartilage or tendinous tissue. *Rudimentary first ribs* are not as commonly recognized as cervical rib anomalies, and their actual incidence is unknown. These structures consist of a first rib that tends to lie higher in the neck than normal and often inserts into the second rib rather than the sternum. Abnormalities of the first rib may also occur as a result of previous trauma, such as fractures with formation of thickened callus at the site of bony healing (Fig. 94-2B and C).

Histopathology

Microscopic studies of the scalene muscles from patients with neurogenic TOS have consistently revealed two major abnormalities: (1) predominance of type I muscle fibers and (2) endomysial fibrosis (Fig. 94-3).[9,10] Although the anterior scalene muscle normally exhibits an equal distribution of type I ("slow-twitch") and type II ("fast-twitch") muscle fibers, type I fibers compose up to 78% of the scalene muscle fibers in patients with neurogenic TOS associated with atrophy and pleomorphism of type II fibers. Alongside these changes there is marked thickening of the connective tissue matrix that surrounds individual muscle fibers, with double the connective tissue content of normal scalene muscles, and in some cases, there are mitochondrial abnormalities resembling those seen in muscular dystrophy. Biopsy of unaffected muscles in patients with neurogenic TOS fails to reveal similar abnormalities; thus, these

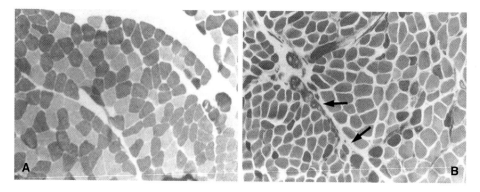

FIGURE 94-3 Scalene muscle histopathologic sections showing changes consistently observed in neurogenic thoracic outlet syndrome (TOS). Sections of the anterior scalene muscle were stained with myosin ATPase (pH 9.4) to visualize fiber types, with type I fibers staining lightly and type II fibers staining dark (original magnification ×100). **A,** Normal muscle has an equal distribution of type I and type II fibers. **B,** The muscle from a patient with TOS exhibits predominance of type I fibers, atrophy of type II fibers, and a significant increase in the connective tissue matrix between fibers (*arrows*). (Adapted from Sanders RJ: Thoracic Outlet Syndrome: A Common Sequela of Neck Injuries. Philadelphia, JB Lippincott, 1991.)

changes represent not a general myopathy but only a local abnormality. These findings are therefore thought to reflect the histopathologic changes occurring after long-standing muscle injury, sustained muscle spasm, and abnormal tissue remodeling, most likely resulting from previous trauma to the scalene muscles. These observations are therefore consistent with the common history of neck trauma in patients with neurogenic TOS.

■ ETIOLOGY

Predisposing Anatomic Factors

Current concepts hold that neurogenic TOS is caused by a combination of predisposing anatomic factors and previous neck trauma. Indeed, the normal anatomy of the thoracic outlet serves as a predisposing factor in the development of neurogenic TOS, in that the neurovascular structures that traverse this region are prone to compression even during the course of regular daily activity. Activities involving sustained or repeated elevation of the arm or vigorous turning of the neck may place additional tension on the scalene muscles, thereby potentiating any positional compression of the underlying nerve roots. This anatomic predisposition may be further increased by congenital structural variants, such as scalene muscle variations, abnormal tendinous bands, or cervical rib anomalies. However, because many individuals harbor such variations in the absence of neurogenic symptoms, anatomic factors are considered only a predisposing factor for neurogenic TOS rather than a distinct and separate cause, and they appear merely to lower the threshold for development of symptoms after injury.

Neck Trauma

Most patients with neurogenic TOS describe some form of previous trauma to the head, neck, or upper extremity, followed by a variable interval before the onset of progressive upper extremity symptoms. The interval between injury and the onset of symptoms may range from days and weeks to several years. This frequent delay in symptoms, which is thought to reflect the variable time frame for scalene muscle injury to result in sustained compression and irritation of the brachial plexus nerve roots, may therefore obscure the relationship between a specific injury and development of neurogenic TOS. In some patients, the inciting injury has been long forgotten, and a history of trauma may be overlooked if not specifically sought by the examining physician. Persistent use of the upper extremity in activities that promote brachial plexus compression may further exacerbate progression of symptoms over time, leading to progressive disability, and many patients do not seek medical attention until symptoms are well advanced. Thus, it is important to recognize that low-grade repetitive trauma can also contribute to this disorder. Conversely, it is evident that not all cases of neurogenic TOS are brought on by a specific traumatic event. In these cases, it is likely that age-related changes in posture, superimposed upon congenital variations of scalene musculature, may be a significant factor leading to extrinsic neural compression.

Pathophysiology

The development of neurogenic TOS is thought to arise as a result of scalene muscle trauma, the pathophysiologic response to muscle injury, and anatomic factors predisposing to compression of the brachial plexus nerve roots as they pass through the scalene triangle. Hyperextension injury of the anterior scalene muscle likely leads to acute and chronic inflammation and a reparative process that involves fibrosis and persistent muscle spasm. Chronic changes in the scalene musculature also include fibrotic contracture and stiffening as well as histopathologic alterations reflecting persistent muscle injury. The resulting changes in the scalene muscles likely potentiate nerve root compression and irritation, which may be exacerbated by positional effects, resulting in a progression of symptoms over time. Intermittent exacerbations of neurogenic symptoms may occur as a result of additional scalene muscle injury, producing local inflammation and spasm, interspersed with periods in which symptoms are quiescent. Unfortunately, knowledge of the specific pathophysiologic mechanisms leading to neurogenic TOS is limited, and there remain many gaps in our understanding of this complicated disorder.

■ CLINICAL PRESENTATION

The diagnosis of neurogenic TOS rests largely on clinical pattern recognition, with diagnostic suspicion being raised by the patient's history and typical symptoms. The provisional diagnosis of neurogenic TOS is supplemented by physical examination and may be supported by a limited number of diagnostic studies. Although no single diagnostic test is specific for TOS, the studies generally serve to exclude other important diagnostic considerations.

Symptoms

Demographics

Neurogenic TOS most commonly occurs in individuals between 20 and 40 years old, and approximately 70% of affected patients are women. Neurogenic TOS may arise in individuals engaged in a variety of occupational or recreational activities, most often those involving repeated use of the arm or arms in elevated positions, or after a spectrum of injuries to the head, neck, or upper extremity. Patients with no apparent predisposition, either due to anatomic variations or a history of trauma, may also have neurogenic TOS.

Pain and Paresthesia

The primary symptoms of neurogenic TOS are pain, dysesthesias, numbness, and weakness. These symptoms usually occur throughout the affected hand or arm without any localization to a specific peripheral nerve distribution, and they often involve different areas of the entire upper extremity. Extension of symptoms from the hand to the shoulder, neck, and upper back is not uncommon, and in many patients, the symptoms in the neck or upper back may be perceived as the most functionally disabling. Although most patients with neurogenic TOS have symptoms affecting just one upper extremity, bilateral symptoms are not uncommon; in such cases the dominant extremity is often more symptomatic at first presentation, but the other arm may become involved over time, perhaps as a result of compensatory overuse. The lack of distribution of symptoms into patterns referable to a single peripheral nerve and the common extension of symptoms to the shoulder, neck, and back allow distinction of neurogenic TOS from compressive conditions that affect the ulnar nerve at the elbow (cubital compression syndrome), the median nerve at the wrist (carpal tunnel syndrome), and other related disorders.

Different symptomatic presentations of TOS may be observed, depending on the brachial plexus nerve roots principally involved. Upper plexus disorders (nerve roots C5, C6, and C7) are dominated by symptoms in the distribution of the radial and musculocutaneous nerves, whereas lower plexus disorders (nerve roots C7, C8, and T1) most commonly involve the median and ulnar nerves. In many cases, however, it is not possible to draw these distinctions because of a wider distribution of symptoms.

Positional Effects

In almost all patients affected by neurogenic TOS, symptoms are reproducibly exacerbated by activity that requires elevation or sustained use of the arms or hands. These activities include simply reaching for objects overhead, lifting, prolonged typing or work at computer consoles, driving, speaking on the telephone, shaving, and combing or brushing the hair. Positional symptoms may also be brought on by lying supine, especially when the arms are positioned overhead, resulting in pain and difficulty sleeping at night.

Headache

Headaches are a common complaint associated with neurogenic TOS.[11] It is most likely the result of referred pain to the occiput from secondary spasm within the trapezius and paraspinous muscles. Headaches associated with neurogenic TOS are therefore typically occipital in nature, whereas frontal headaches are not specifically associated with TOS. Although neurogenic TOS and migraine headaches are often seen together, there is currently no evidence for a specific link between the two conditions.

Weakness and Muscle Atrophy

Prolonged, severe, extrinsic compression of peripheral nerves can result in muscle weakness and atrophy, but such findings are actually rare in patients with neurogenic TOS. This is probably due to the intermittent nature of nerve compression in TOS, which produces pain and other neural symptoms but prevents permanent motor nerve dysfunction. Most commonly, hand or arm pain with use of the affected extremity may lead to the perception of weakness, leading the patient to avoid use of the arm or positions that exacerbate symptoms; this distinction should be sought

during evaluation to help identify other conditions that may be responsible for symptoms of muscle weakness. The presence of authentic muscle weakness may therefore indicate particularly severe and long-standing compression of the brachial plexus nerve roots due to TOS or to another condition.

Disability

The majority of individuals with positional complaints related to neurogenic TOS are affected to only a mild and tolerable degree. These symptoms are usually due to transient irritation of the brachial plexus in certain positions of the arm or during certain activities, and to some extent, such symptoms are common in the normal population. There is little risk of progressive injury in these situations, and no specific intervention is warranted.

A smaller subset of patients with clinically significant neurogenic TOS, however, exhibit progressively disabling symptoms that effectively prevent them from working or carrying out simple daily activities. These patients often describe progressive disability and a long history of physician consultations and partial or ineffective treatments. Such patients may have been prevented from working for a long period prior to consultation or may have attempted to persist in work-related activities despite ongoing neurogenic symptoms. Part of the initial assessment of the patient with neurogenic TOS is therefore concerned with assessing the extent of the disability and the patient's expectations for the potential to continue working or return to work. It is particularly helpful in this regard to obtain a detailed description from the patient of activities that exacerbate symptoms associated with neurogenic TOS as well as those activities normally required in the workplace. Documentation of this assessment is often a valuable adjunct if relief from work is necessary in the management of the patient and in guiding decisions about the role of surgical treatment.

Vascular Symptoms and Reflex Sympathetic Dystrophy

Vascular symptoms should be specifically sought in the history of patients with suspected TOS, particularly discoloration or coldness in the hands and fingers. It is important to note that ischemia is actually very unusual in such patients, whereas symptoms of vasomotor disturbance are not uncommon in those with long-standing or severe neurogenic TOS. Indeed, in some, the symptoms of TOS may have progressed to resemble those of causalgia (i.e., reflex sympathetic dystrophy), with persistent vasospasm, disuse edema, and extreme hypersensitivity. The acuity of these symptoms often leads to avoidance of and withdrawal from even light touch of the affected extremity. The diagnosis of reflex sympathetic dystrophy can be supported by vascular laboratory studies showing abnormal vasoconstrictive responses (cold-pressor tests) or imaging studies of the hand microcirculation, but in most cases, the diagnosis is made on clinical grounds. The identification of this condition in patients with neurogenic TOS is quite important, because it may lead to an earlier recommendation for operative treatment and consideration of concomitant cervical sympathectomy.

For the patient with a history suggesting arterial insufficiency or thromboembolism, vascular laboratory studies and contrast-enhanced arteriographic imaging are necessary to exclude the possibility of subclavian artery aneurysm or occlusive disease. Conversely, a history of arm swelling, cyanotic discoloration, and distended subcutaneous collaterals may indicate venous TOS due to obstruction of the subclavian vein, which requires contrast venography for full evaluation. Identification of these conditions in patients with neurogenic TOS is vital, because the coexistence of neurogenic and vascular types of TOS affects the decisions and plans for surgical treatment.

Physical Examination

Physical examination is initially directed to eliciting the extent of neurogenic disability and identifying particular factors that exacerbate painful hand and arm complaints. The range of motion of the upper extremity and lateral motion of the neck are assessed, under both passive and active conditions. Pain and tenderness over the shoulder joint are evaluated as potentially related to rotator cuff tendinitis, and tenderness over the trapezius muscle may indicate fibromyalgia. A thorough peripheral nerve examination is performed to exclude ulnar nerve entrapment or carpal tunnel syndrome, two conditions that may mimic the symptoms of neurogenic TOS. The base of the neck is examined (1) to identify the extent of any local muscle spasm over the scalene triangle itself as well as over the trapezius, pectoralis, and parascapular muscles and (2) to localize specific areas that reproduce the individual patient's symptom pattern upon focal digital compression. The presence of "trigger points" is sought to identify specific sites where palpation recreates the patient's typical symptoms of upper extremity pain and paresthesia. Localization of trigger points over the scalene triangle serves to reinforce the diagnosis of neurogenic TOS.

Perhaps the most useful component of physical examination is the elevated arm stress test (EAST), in which the patient is positioned with the arms elevated in a "surrender" position and is asked to repetitively open and close the fists. Most patients with neurogenic TOS report the rapid onset of their typical upper extremity symptoms with the EAST, often being unable to continue the exercise beyond 30 to 60 seconds. In a patient who has no difficulty performing EAST for several minutes, the diagnosis of TOS is suspect and an alternative explanation for the symptoms should be sought more vigorously.

Vascular Examination

The Adson maneuver is commonly used to identify positional compression of the subclavian artery; a positive result is detection of ablation of the radial pulse when the patient inspires deeply and turns the neck away from the affected extremity. Although this maneuver does not specifically reveal nerve root compression, a positive result may be associated with neurogenic TOS. It is important to recognize that presence of Adson's sign is also quite common in the asymptomatic general population. This maneuver may therefore serve to support, but not confirm, the diagnosis of TOS. It is equally important to recognize that absence of arterial compression does not exclude a diagnosis of neurogenic TOS. Many physicians experienced with TOS therefore find the Adson maneuver of little value.

Patients presenting with symptoms of neurogenic TOS may on occasion have vascular findings related to either arterial or venous TOS. It is important that these conditions be identified early in the evaluation, as their presence may lead to specific tests and modification of treatment recommendations. During physical examination, the surgeon should seek evidence of arterial compromise to the upper extremity, such as sympathetic overactivity with vasospasm, digital or hand ischemia, cutaneous ulceration or emboli, forearm claudication, and the pulsatile supraclavicular mass or bruit characteristic of a subclavian artery aneurysm. Venous TOS, in contrast, may be associated with hand and arm edema, cyanosis, enlarged subcutaneous collateral veins, and early forearm fatigue in the absence of arterial compromise.

Diagnostic Tests

A wide variety of diagnostic tests and imaging studies are used in the evaluation of patients with neurogenic TOS, and most patients have had a number of such studies prior to consultation with the vascular surgeon. It is important to emphasize that the results of specific diagnostic tests are negative or equivocal in most cases of neurogenic TOS and that no specific diagnostic test or imaging study can replace the clinical diagnosis of this condition. Thus, the principal value of the studies described here is to exclude other conditions, thereby helping to strengthen the diagnosis of neurogenic TOS.

Radiography

Plain radiographs of the neck are helpful in determining presence of an osseous cervical rib or abnormally wide transverse processes of the cervical vertebrae. Although each of these findings may solidify the diagnostic impression of TOS, neither of them is essential.

Cross-Sectional Imaging

The findings of computed tomography, magnetic resonance imaging, and other imaging examinations are usually normal in neurogenic TOS, because the anatomic factors leading to intermittent or positional nerve compression are usually beyond the resolution of these studies. Even in situations in which an apparent imaging abnormality exists in the region of the scalene triangle, it is usually impossible to prove the functional importance of the abnormality with respect to the patient's upper extremity complaints. Imaging studies are nonetheless important to exclude other conditions that could be responsible for upper extremity symptoms, such as degenerative cervical disk or spine disease, shoulder joint disease, and various forms of intracranial disease.

Neurophysiologic Testing

Nerve conduction (NC) and electromyography (EMG) studies are often utilized early in the evaluation of patients in whom neurogenic TOS is suspected, particularly when symptoms are suggestive of a specific radiculopathy, a peripheral nerve syndrome, or a general myopathy. Positive results of neurophysiologic testing are therefore quite useful, as they point to specific conditions that must be evaluated further. Unfortunately, the results of NC and EMG studies are usually negative in neurogenic TOS, because nerve root compression in TOS (1) occurs in an extremely proximal location and (2) is intermittent and not usually associated with permanent changes in motor nerve function.[12] Negative results of these studies are nonetheless valuable in the diagnostic evaluation of some patients, in that they help exclude other conditions from further consideration. Positive NC or EMG results in patients with neurogenic TOS are a poor prognostic finding in the absence of an alternative explanation, in that they indicate an advanced stage of neural damage that is unlikely to resolve despite adequate decompression.

Scalene Muscle Block

Injection of local anesthetic into the belly of the anterior scalene muscle may be used as an adjunct to the clinical diagnosis of neurogenic TOS, particularly in predicting the potential response to surgical decompression. Successful scalene muscle block is indicated by relief of symptoms in the hand or arm, along with a reduction in local tenderness over the anterior scalene muscle. Injection of anesthetic to the level of the brachial plexus precludes accurate interpretation of this test, because it causes temporary numbness and weakness in the arm, making assessment of pain relief unreliable. Although scalene muscle block is not necessary in patients with clear-cut symptoms, for whom the diagnosis of TOS is not questioned, it is most useful in patients with an equivocal diagnosis of neurogenic TOS. Thus, a number of investigators have reported a strong correlation between the relief of symptoms after scalene muscle block and the success of surgical decompression.[13-15] Although a variation of scalene muscle block using locally injected botulinum toxin has been described as a treatment for TOS, this approach cannot yet be generally recommended.[16]

Angiography and Vascular Laboratory Studies

Patients with features suggesting an arterial component to the disorder should undergo positional noninvasive vascular laboratory studies (segmental arterial pressures and waveform analysis with duplex imaging), but contrast arteriography may be necessary to completely exclude or prove the existence of a fixed arterial lesion. Those in whom venous TOS is suspected should be studied by contrast venography, if the procedure has not previously performed in the context of an "effort thrombosis" event. In each case, the vascular surgeon must specifically alert the vascular radiologist of the need to perform positional maneuvers during radiologic examination and also must consider bilateral studies if there is any suggestion of contralateral symptoms. Indeed, in patients with proven arterial or venous TOS, contrast studies of the asymptomatic arm are often recommended.

Making the Diagnosis

Most patients with suspected neurogenic TOS who consult with a vascular surgeon are referred to help resolve a diagnostic dilemma, especially when previous tests and consultations have resulted in uncertainty and a long list of conditions has already been considered in the diagnostic evaluation (Table 94-2). Although some of these entities can be distinguished by specific findings or tests, one is often

Table 94-2 Differential Diagnosis of Neurogenic Thoracic Outlet Syndrome (TOS)

CONDITION	DIFFERENTIATING FEATURES
Carpal tunnel syndrome	Hand pain and paresthesia in median nerve distribution; positive findings of nerve conduction studies.
Ulnar nerve compression	Hand pain and paresthesia in ulnar nerve distribution; positive findings of nerve conduction studies.
Rotator cuff tendinitis	Localized pain and tenderness over biceps tendon and shoulder pain on abduction; positive findings on MRI; relief from NSAIDs, local steroid injections, or arthroscopic surgery.
Cervical spine strain/sprain	Post-traumatic neck pain and stiffness localized posteriorly along cervical spine; paraspinal tenderness; relief with conservative measures over weeks to months.
Fibromyositis	Post-traumatic inflammation of trapezius and parascapular muscles; tenderness, spasm and palpable nodules over affected muscles; may coexist with TOS and persist after surgery.
Cervical disk disease	Neck pain and stiffness, arm weakness, and paresthesia involving thumb and index finger (C5-C6 disk); symptom improvement with arm elevation; positive findings on CT or MRI.
Cervical arthritis	Neck pain and stiffness; arm or hand paresthesia infrequent; degenerative rather than post-traumatic; positive findings of spine radiographs.
Brachial plexus injury	Caused by direct injury or stretch; arm pain and weakness, hand paresthesias; symptoms constant, not intermittent or positional; positive findings on neurophysiologic studies.

CT, computed tomography; MRI, magnetic resonance imaging; NSAIDs, nonsteroidal anti-inflammatory drugs.

left with a diagnosis of exclusion. The surgeon recognizing neurogenic TOS should not be dissuaded by the impression that these problems are frequently associated with psychiatric overtones, dependency on pain medications, and ongoing litigation. Many patients with TOS have suffered a progressively disabling condition at a relatively young age without the satisfaction of diagnostic certainty or a reliable sense of prognosis. The evaluating surgeon must therefore be willing to expend considerable time and energy to provide such patients with a thorough evaluation, detailed information, lengthy discussion, and ongoing support. The surgeon should explain the suspected nature of the condition, discuss the diagnostic and therapeutic uncertainties that surround neurogenic TOS, and present an honest but reassuring outline of treatment expectations. Surgeons making this effort are typically rewarded by grateful patients with renewed hope for long-awaited improvement.

■ TREATMENT

Conservative Treatment

Physical therapy serves as the initial treatment for almost all patients with neurogenic TOS.[17] It is important that the patient be referred to a therapist with experience, expertise, and interest in TOS, because the management of this condition is different from that of other disorders affecting the neck, shoulder, and upper extremity. Many physical therapists do not have great experience with neurogenic TOS, and incorrect approaches to therapy can result in worsening of symptoms and premature failure of conservative management.[18]

The therapist treating the patient outlines a specific plan for initial treatment over 4 to 6 weeks, after which progress is reassessed. The initial goals of physical therapy are to maintain and improve the range of motion of the neck and affected upper extremity through a combination of passive and assisted exercises.[19-21] In particular, exercises designed to relax and stretch the scalene muscle are used, combined with hydrotherapy, massage, and other techniques. These efforts may be accompanied by use of nonsteroidal anti-inflammatory agents, muscle relaxants, and non-narcotic pain medications as needed. Once initial improvement has been achieved, subsequent efforts can be focused on strengthening the muscles of posture and increasing achievable levels of activity.

After the initial course of therapy the physician reassesses the progress made and outlines plans for future treatment. Most patients with mild symptoms of neurogenic TOS, and those in whom therapy has been started early after the onset of symptoms, exhibit significant improvement. Therapy is then continued with the expectation that continued benefits will preclude the need to consider surgical treatment. Although in our experience this outcome is obtained in only 20% to 30% of patients referred for management of neurogenic TOS, the proportion of patients responding to conservative treatment is much higher in a more general population.[22]

When progress with the initial course of conservative management has been unsatisfactory, the basis for the diagnosis of neurogenic TOS is reviewed and any further testing thought to be appropriate is carried out. If the patient has not responded sufficiently to conservative management and the physician is confident of the diagnosis of neurogenic TOS, surgical treatment is considered.[23] Even when this decision appears predictable at the time of the initial visit, helping to form an established relationship between patient and physical therapist is a valuable first step in treatment, because physical therapy and rehabilitation remain an important part of patient care after the operation.

Surgical Treatment

Selection of Operative Approach

The first operations for thoracic outlet compression were focused on treatment of subclavian artery aneurysms in patients with a cervical rib, as described by Coote[24] in 1861. By the turn of the century, the "cervical rib syndrome" was widely recognized, and in 1927, Adson and Coffey[25] described the use of anterior scalenotomy in treatment of this condition, including symptomatic patients without a cervical rib anomaly. The term "thoracic outlet syndrome" was introduced by Peet and colleagues[26] in 1956, and several new operative approaches to TOS were described in the 1960s, including posterior thoracotomy (Clagett[27]) and transaxillary first rib resection (Roos[28]).

Although transaxillary first rib resection became popular and widely used during the 1970s, disenchantment arose when results were found to be no better than those of scalenectomy and a national survey indicated a significant incidence of permanent nerve injuries after this operation.[14,29] Surgeons also began to understand that symptomatic recurrences after transaxillary first rib resection often involved reattachment of the unresected scalene muscles to the remaining end of the first rib or adjacent tissues, leading to diminished enthusiasm for first rib resection and a reemphasis on alternative operative approaches to include more complete resection of the scalene muscle.[30] Combined use of supraclavicular and transaxillary approaches was reported in 1984 by Qvarfordt and associates,[31] followed by further description of the supraclavicular approach by Sanders and Raymer[32] and by Reilly and Stoney.[33] During the past decade, the supraclavicular approach appears to have become the most commonly employed approach in current practice. Although a number of other operative techniques for thoracic outlet decompression have also been described, this section focuses on the transaxillary and supraclavicular approaches.

With regard to the selection of operative approach, it is now generally accepted that neurogenic TOS may arise from compression of the brachial plexus nerve roots at several different levels through different etiologic factors, not solely as a consequence of bony deformation by the first rib. Numerous soft tissue anomalies within the thoracic outlet have been described and classified, each of which can give rise to symptomatic neural compression. Significant factors playing a role in this process include scalene muscle injury with spasm, scarring, and fibrotic inflammatory reactions surrounding the brachial plexus nerve roots, which may also be associated with pathologic changes in the scalene musculature. Current approaches to surgical treatment must take each of these potential contributing factors into account in the selection of the optimal treatment for the individual patient.

The primary advantages of *transaxillary first rib resection* are a relatively limited field of operative dissection, a cosmetically placed skin incision, and sufficient exposure to reliably accomplish resection of the anterolateral first rib. This approach also makes it possible to achieve at least partial resection of the anterior scalene muscle as well as identification and removal of most anomalous ligaments and fibrous bands that may be associated with TOS. The disadvantages of the transaxillary approach include incomplete exposure of the structures composing the scalene triangle, difficulty achieving complete anterior and middle scalenectomy or brachial plexus neurolysis, and the necessity for first rib resection in all cases. This approach is also limited when vascular reconstruction is needed, requiring the addition of a separate incision or repositioning of the patient.

The *supraclavicular approach* carries the advantages of wider exposure of all anatomic structures associated with thoracic outlet compression. It allows complete resection of the anterior and middle scalene muscles as well as brachial plexus neurolysis with direct visualization of all five nerve roots. In many cases, symptomatic relief of neurogenic TOS can be achieved by extended scalenectomy without first rib resection, an option permitted by the supraclavicular approach. This approach also allows for resection of cervical ribs, anomalous first ribs, or the normal first rib. A further advantage is that all forms of vascular reconstruction can also be accomplished through supraclavicular exposure; although removal of the anteromedial portion of the first rib and distal control of the vessels may require addition of a second infraclavicular incision, this incision is performed without the need for repositioning the patient.

The balance of advantages and disadvantages between these two operative approaches has now led many groups to prefer the supraclavicular approach to TOS. Some surgeons adopt a highly selective approach in which resection of the first rib is reserved solely for patients with vascular complications.[34]

Transaxillary Approach

After induction of general anesthesia, the patient is positioned supine with the back of the table raised about 30 degrees. A small towel pack is placed behind the shoulder to elevate the affected side. The arm is prepared circumferentially and wrapped in stockinette, with the sterile field comprising the neck, upper chest, and posterior shoulder to the scapula. The arm is not placed on a table or crossbar; rather, it is held and positioned by a reliable, flexible, and sturdy assistant (Fig. 94-4).

A transverse skin incision is made at the lower border of the axillary hairline, extending from the anterior border of the latissimus dorsi muscle to the lateral edge of the pectoralis major muscle (see Fig. 94-4). This incision is carried through the subcutaneous tissues directly to the chest wall, with blunt dissection used to establish a plane extending to the apex of the axilla. The long thoracic,

thoracodorsal, and second intercostobrachial nerves are identified near the chest wall to avoid direct injury. Excessive elevation of the arm (unique to transaxillary exposure) is a potential mechanism of injury to the second intercostobrachial cutaneous nerve, resulting in postoperative pain and numbness along the medial aspect of the upper arm. The first rib is typically palpable at the upper reaches of the areolar tissue plane along the chest wall. With use of a Deaver retractor to gently lift the subcutaneous tissues and axillary contents away from the chest wall, the first rib is more clearly exposed in the upper aspect of the wound. It is necessary to carefully lift the arm to facilitate this exposure, both at this stage and throughout the remainder of the procedure, and the operating surgeon should use a fiberoptic headlight to properly illuminate the operative field.

Exposure obtained during the transaxillary approach is generally limited to the operating surgeon. It is therefore important that the surgeon be constantly aware of how the assistants are positioned and how the retractors are positioned with respect to the nerve roots and blood vessels. In order to avoid serious injury, the blades of the retractors must not apply excess traction to the neurovascular structures visible above the first rib. In addition to the nerve roots of the brachial plexus, proper attention must be given to avoid traction on the long thoracic nerve, which exits the plane between the middle and posterior scalene muscles

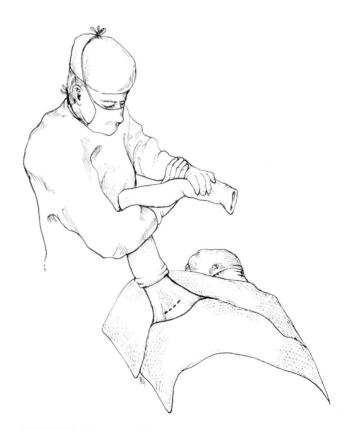

FIGURE 94-4 Patient positioning for transaxillary first rib resection. While the arm is carefully elevated by a reliable assistant, the initial skin incision is made at the lower edge of the axillary hair line. (Adapted from Thompson RW, Petrinec D: Surgical treatment of thoracic outlet compression syndromes. I: Diagnostic considerations and transaxillary first rib resection. Ann Vasc Surg 11:315-323, 1997.)

before coursing over the first rib to the serratus anterior muscle. Periodic inspection of the retractors and relief for the assistants are recommended, through the use of a staged approach to the operation as described by Machleder.[35]

Once the first rib is sufficiently exposed, the subclavian vein and subclavian artery are identified along with the intervening anterior scalene muscle (Fig. 94-5A). These structures are carefully dissected such that the anterior scalene tendon can be encircled with a right-angle clamp just above its insertion onto the scalene tubercle of the first rib, which is typically palpable as a slight bony prominence. The anterior scalene muscle is exposed over several centimeters superior to the first rib, and with care taken to avoid the phrenic nerve, the muscle is divided with a scissors at the highest level feasible. The importance of resecting a portion of the scalene muscle, rather than simply dividing it at the level of the first rib itself, has been underscored by analysis of the factors causing recurrent TOS.

The soft tissues attaching to the inferior and medial borders of the first rib are progressively divided with scissors, beginning with the attachments medial to the subclavian vein (the subclavius muscle tendon and the costosternal and costoclavicular ligaments). A periosteal elevator is used to scrape the inferior border of the rib, extending underneath the rib from the vantage point of the exposure used. The intercostal muscle is fully divided, and the parietal pleura is pushed away from the deep aspect of the rib with blunt dissection. The middle scalene muscle is detached from the superior surface of the rib, posterior to the brachial plexus nerve roots (Fig. 94-5B). Although the proximal aspect of the long thoracic nerve is not directly visualized during this maneuver, injury to this nerve must be prevented to avoid postoperative weakness of the serratus anterior muscle. Prevention is best accomplished by keeping the periosteal elevator directly upon the rib during scalene muscle detachment, avoiding any tendency to allow it to stray laterally where the long thoracic nerve can be easily injured. The long thoracic nerve is thereby gently pushed away from the rib indirectly as the middle scalene muscle is detached, effectively protecting it despite the lack of direct visualization.

Once the posterior surface of the first rib is exposed and the T1 nerve root is in full view to protect it from injury, a bone-cutting instrument is carefully applied across the neck of the rib. The lateral portion of the divided rib is pulled downward, and its anterior aspect is cut in a similar fashion, just medial to the subclavian vein at the costochondral junction. The first rib is then fully detached and removed from the operative field (Fig. 94-5C). A bone rongeur is used to trim the remaining ends of the bone to a smooth surface well beyond the neurovascular structures. With an additional amount of extrapleural dissection, the same exposure can be used to perform adjunctive cervical sympathectomy for patients with neurogenic TOS complicated by reflex sympathetic dystrophy.

Any additional soft tissue bands found to be crossing the brachial plexus nerve roots are sought and carefully divided, particularly those that may insert upon Sibson's fascia, the thickened aspect of the apical pleural surface. After hemostasis is achieved, the wound is irrigated, and the lung is inflated to detect any breaks in the pleural lining. If small air bubbles are observed during positive-pressure ventilation

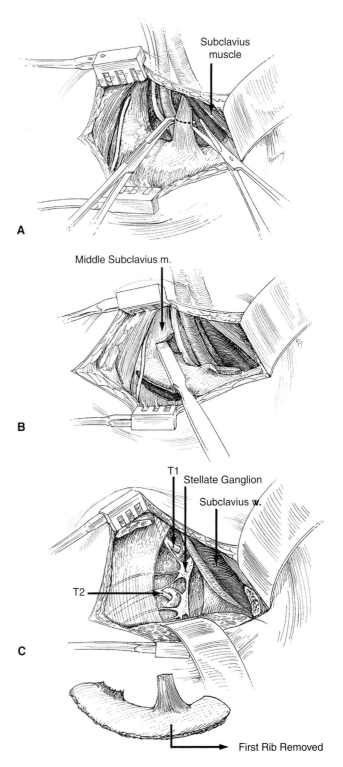

FIGURE 94-5 Transaxillary resection of the first rib. **A,** Transaxillary division of the anterior scalene muscle. The tendinous insertion of the anterior scalene muscle onto the first rib is elevated with a right-angle clamp and divided with a scissors. **B,** Detachment of the middle scalene muscle. After the intercostal attachments to the first rib are divided, a periosteal elevator is used to detach the middle and posterior scalene muscles. Injury to the proximal portion of the long thoracic nerve is prevented by keeping the dissection directly on the rib. **C,** Removal of the first rib. The anterior and posterior aspects of the first rib are divided, with the surgical specimen including the resected portion of the anterior scalene muscle and the site of attachment of the middle scalene muscle. (Adapted from Thompson RW, Petrinec D: Surgical treatment of thoracic outlet compression syndromes. I: Diagnostic considerations and transaxillary first rib resection. Ann Vasc Surg 11:315-323, 1997.)

or if the irrigation fluid appears to be lost into the pleural space, a small chest tube may be placed through a separate wound. The incisional wound is closed in two layers after placement of a small closed-suction drain in the operative field.

Supraclavicular Approach

After induction of general anesthesia, the patient is positioned supine with the head of the bed elevated 30 degrees. The hips and knees are flexed, and the neck is extended and turned to the opposite side. The neck, upper chest, and upper extremity are prepared into the field with the arm wrapped in a stockinette, then held comfortably across the abdomen. This positioning allows for arm movement through an extended range of motion during the operation, when it may be necessary to assess any residual neurovascular compression after scalenectomy. A transverse skin incision is made two fingerbreadths above the clavicle, beginning at the lateral border of the sternocleidomastoid muscle (Fig. 94-6A).[39] This incision is carried through the platysma muscle layer to expose the scalene fat pad. Several supraclavicular cutaneous nerves cross the operative field in this region. Division of these sensory nerves results in postoperative numbness and dysesthesia below the clavicle, but division of these small cutaneous branches, when necessary, does not appear to produce significant problems.

The scalene fat pad is mobilized beginning at the lateral edge of the internal jugular vein. As this tissue plane is entered, the fat pad is progressively dissected off the anterior surface of the anterior scalene muscle and reflected laterally (Fig. 94-6B). The phrenic nerve is identified within the investing fascia of the muscle, coursing in a superolateral to inferomedial direction. The inferior and superior attachments of the scalene fat pad are divided between ligatures to allow full exposure of the anterior scalene muscle. Lateral retraction of the scalene fat pad then permits exposure of the underlying roots of the brachial plexus.

The anterior scalene muscle is dissected, with special effort made to avoid excessive traction on the phrenic nerve (Fig. 94-7A). The C5 and C6 roots of the brachial plexus and the subclavian artery are observed at the lateral edge of the anterior scalene, with care taken to avoid injury to these structures during mobilization of the anterior scalene muscle. The proximal subclavian artery must also be well visualized and protected at the medial edge of the muscle. After circumferential mobilization of the anterior scalene muscle to its site of attachment to the first rib, a finger or right-angled clamp is passed behind the muscle, and the muscle tendon is sharply divided from the edge of its insertion (Fig. 94-7B). This division is made under direct vision and with a curved scissors rather than the cautery. Additional slips of muscle or tendon must be divided more posteriorly, including direct attachments of the muscle to the thickened pleural lining behind the rib itself.

Once the insertion of the anterior scalene muscle has been divided, the muscle is lifted superiorly to detach it from the additional structures underneath, including the pleural apex, the subclavian artery, and the brachial plexus nerve roots (Fig. 94-7C). This dissection is carried superiorly to the level of the scalene muscle origin on the

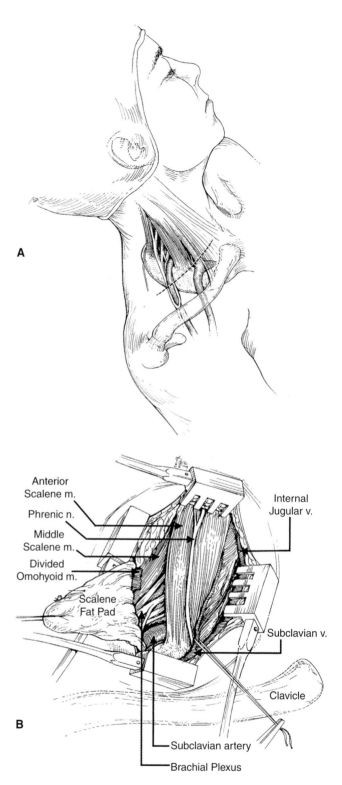

FIGURE 94-6 Patient positioning for supraclavicular decompression of the thoracic outlet. **A,** A transverse skin incision is made two fingerbreadths above the clavicle to obtain full exposure of the structures associated with the scalene triangle. **B,** The scalene fat pad is mobilized laterally to expose the underlying anterior scalene muscle, with identification and protection of the phrenic nerve. The omohyoid muscle is divided. The subclavian artery and the upper roots of the brachial plexus are identified behind the lateral edge of the anterior scalene muscle. (Adapted from Thompson RW: Treatment of thoracic outlet syndromes and cervical sympathectomy. In Lumley JSP, Siewert JR, Hoballah JJ [eds]: Springer Surgery Atlas Series: Vascular Surgery. London, Springer-Verlag, 2004.)

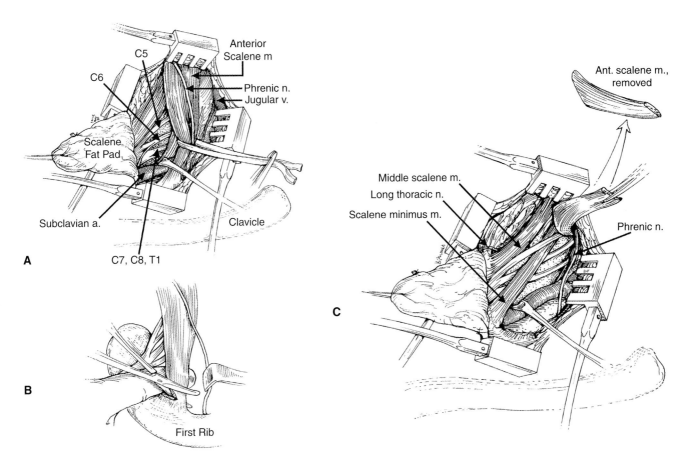

FIGURE 94-7 Supraclavicular anterior scalenectomy. **A,** The anterior scalene muscle is circumferentially mobilized from the underlying subclavian artery and the roots of the brachial plexus. **B,** The insertion of the anterior scalene muscle upon the first rib is sharply divided with scissors, with the surgeon's finger protecting the subclavian artery and the roots of the brachial plexus. **C,** The anterior scalene muscle is reflected superiorly and dissected free of underlying structures to the level of its origin. Any muscle fibers passing between the upper nerve roots of the brachial plexus are also removed, including the scalene minimus muscle if it is present. (Adapted from Thompson RW: Treatment of thoracic outlet syndromes and cervical sympathectomy. In Lumley JSP, Siewert JR, Hoballah JJ [eds]: Springer Surgery Atlas Series: Vascular Surgery. London, Springer-Verlag, 2004.)

transverse process of the sixth cervical vertebra. Great care must be taken to avoid irretrievable neural injury during removal of muscle fibers interdigitating with the proximal roots of the upper brachial plexus. The entire anterior scalene muscle is then removed and sent to the neuromuscular pathology laboratory.

After anterior scalenectomy and removal of any scalene minimus muscle fibers, each of the nerve roots contributing to the brachial plexus is identified and meticulously dissected free of inflammatory scar tissue. Moderately dense fibrotic tissue encasing the nerve roots is not uncommon in patients with neurogenic TOS; because this scar tissue may contribute to nerve root compression, irritation, and neurogenic symptoms, failure to perform an adequate neurolysis may be one cause of persistent symptoms. During the course of this dissection, it is also important to ensure full mobility of the upper aspect of roots C5 and C6, which might remain entrapped by any residual scalene muscle or other fibrous tissue at the apex of the scalene triangle. Similarly, the origin of the T1 nerve root may be compressed by the posterior neck of the first rib. Relief of this source of nerve compression requires adequate visualization of the proximal first rib to effect complete nerve root mobility.

This aspect of the operation is not complete until each nerve root from C5 to T1 is completely dissected throughout its course in the operative field.

Osseous cervical ribs or their soft tissue counterparts occur within the same plane as the middle scalene muscle. Although the middle scalene muscle lies posterior to the roots of the brachial plexus, in some cases its insertion upon the first rib may occur as far anteriorly as the scalene tubercle (the site of attachment of the anterior scalene muscle). The composition of the middle scalene muscle may also be firm and tendinous in this region, thereby serving as another potential source of nerve root compression or irritation. The attachment of the middle scalene muscle is divided from the first rib with a periosteal elevator or curved Mayo scissors, with the division extending to a point posterior to the brachial plexus nerve roots. If a cervical rib is present in the plane of the middle scalene muscle, it may also be detached from the first rib at this time. It is important to note the separation between the middle scalene and posterior scalene muscles, as defined by the oblique course of the long thoracic nerve. Muscle tissue anterior to this nerve is detached along the plane delineated by the nerve, which is left intact. In order to avoid motor dysfunction of scapular apposition to the chest wall, it is also important to recognize that the long thoracic nerve may be represented by two or three branches at this level, rather than a single nerve as often described.

After resection of the anterior and middle scalene muscles and completion of a thorough brachial plexus neurolysis, an intraoperative decision is made regarding the potential role of the first rib in neurovascular compression. The surgeon's finger is placed alongside the subclavian artery and brachial plexus nerve roots while the arm is elevated through a normal range of motion at the shoulder, allowing the surgeon to readily detect any residual compression during arm elevation. In many patients with neurogenic TOS, there is little residual compression by the first rib after adequate scalenectomy, and in these cases, retention of the first rib may be considered. In contrast, the first rib should be removed when there is any question that it might contribute to residual neurovascular compression as well as in all patients with arterial or venous TOS.

First rib resection is readily accomplished through the supraclavicular approach, given the exposure already achieved at this stage of the operation. With use of a periosteal elevator, any remaining muscle fibers of the middle scalene muscle are detached from their insertion on the top of the posterior first rib. This dissection is always performed under direct vision to protect the C8 and T1 nerve roots. Using a fingertip covered with gauze, the surgeon bluntly dissects the pleural membrane away from the inferior aspect of the first rib. Intercostal muscle attachments to the first rib are divided with a periosteal elevator, to relieve the posterior and lateral aspects of the first rib of all soft tissue attachments, and any remaining intercostal attachments are divided along the anterolateral aspect of the rib up to the scalene tubercle. The brachial plexus nerve roots are displaced anteriorly to expose the posterior neck of the rib.

While the assistant protects the nerve roots with a fingertip, the surgeon inserts a rib cutter over the neck of the isolated first rib and applies it. A Kerrison bone rongeur is used to resect additional amounts of bone as needed to ensure that the end of the rib will not impinge upon the lower nerve roots and to create a smooth surface on the posterior stump of the first rib. The proximal portion of the rib is displaced inferiorly to open the anterior costoclavicular space, and a bone cutter is inserted at a level immediately medial to the scalene tubercle to divide the proximal rib. The first rib is then extracted from the operative field and discarded, and the proximal end of the rib is remodeled to a smooth surface with a bone rongeur. In rare situations in which the first rib is particularly enlarged and cannot be removed through the supraclavicular exposure alone, a second transaxillary incision may be employed to accomplish this step in the procedure.

Upon completion of the operation, several sheets of a bioresorbable hyaluronidate membrane (Seprafilm, Genzyme Biosurgery, Cambridge, MA) are placed within the wound to limit the potential for postoperative scarring. One sheet is placed posterior to the brachial plexus nerve roots, a second is used to wrap individual nerve roots, and a third is placed anteriorly, between the surface of the brachial plexus and the scalene fat pad. A closed-suction drain is placed into the supraclavicular field, and the scalene fat pad is reapproximated over the brachial plexus before the wound is closed.

Cervical Sympathectomy

Patients with disabling neurogenic TOS may at times present with sympathetic overactivity resulting in painful vasospasm, delayed healing of digital skin lesions, and reflex sympathetic dystrophy. In these situations the primary procedure done for thoracic outlet decompression can be accompanied by cervical sympathectomy. This step adds little to the procedure itself and may be of substantial benefit with respect to alleviating vasospastic complaints or facilitating the healing of digital lesions. The surgeon first identifies the cervical sympathetic chain through the supraclavicular wound by palpation, finding a rubber band-like structure passing vertically over the neck of the first or second rib. The sympathetic chain is elevated with a vagotomy nerve hook and mobilized to the level of the third rib through sharp division of its lateral rami. The stellate ganglion is also identified just above the level of the first rib. After placement of metal clips at each end of the sympathetic chain, it is divided sharply and removed; in order to reduce the incidence of Horner's syndrome, the proximal extent of sympathetic resection is marked by the lower half of the stellate ganglion.

Postoperative Management

An upright chest x-ray is performed in the recovery room to detect residual pneumothorax or pleural fluid, which may be present in up to 10% of patients. These small air or fluid collections are carefully observed with the expectation of spontaneous resolution; although transthoracic aspiration may be necessary for a large or expanding pneumothorax, we have not found it necessary in our experience. Postoperative pain medication is provided by intravenous opioids until adequate control can be achieved by oral medications, and we routinely prescribe oral narcotics, muscle relaxants, and nonsteroidal anti-inflammatory agents for at least the first 2 weeks after surgery. The closed-suction drain is removed 3 days after surgery unless there is persistent lymphatic fluid present, in which case the patient is discharged with the drain in place, and the drain is removed in the outpatient office once the leak has subsided. In several hundred operations for TOS, we have had to perform only one secondary procedure to control a persistent lymph leak.

There are no strict restrictions with respect to use of the arm after operation, but patients are advised to avoid excessive reaching overhead and heavy lifting. Physical therapy is resumed as soon as feasible, usually upon discharge from the hospital or in the first postoperative week. Patients are cautioned against activities that can result in muscle strain, spasm, and significant pain in the trapezius and other neck muscles, and a gradual return to use of the upper extremity is encouraged. The majority of patients resume fairly regular activity within several weeks after operation, and most are permitted a cautious return to light-duty work by 4 to 6 weeks. Work restrictions are recommended to prevent heavy activity during the early stages of return to work, particularly to avoid excessive use of the upper extremity by lifting or repetitive activities that may contribute to postoperative complaints. It is important to recognize that patients with long-standing neurogenic TOS often display residual symptoms such as dysesthesias, numbness, and other complaints that may not be eliminated by thoracic outlet decompression; although these symptoms may be tolerable, the surgeon must provide continuing support and reassurance during the period of recovery and rehabilitation. Physical therapy is continued for as long as necessary to allow the patient to return to an optimal level of function. The patient is then seen at least yearly to assess the long-term results of operative intervention.

Surgical Complications

Nerve Injuries

The most serious complications associated with thoracic outlet decompression are injuries to the brachial plexus nerve roots. Although nerve injuries are uncommon, the rate of nerve injuries reported to occur after transaxillary first rib resection was one of the factors leading many surgeons to diminish their enthusiasm for this procedure in the 1980s.[14,29] Such injuries can occur through both direct and indirect mechanisms; limited exposure during transaxillary exposure can leave the upper nerve roots susceptible, and traction on the brachial plexus during retraction can also injure the nerve roots in a manner not recognized until after operation. These factors are reduced in procedures performed through the supraclavicular route because of the improved exposure of the nerve roots, but brachial plexus palsies can still occur secondary to retraction. In the absence of direct injury, however, these complications are temporary and will resolve within weeks to months of the operation.

Phrenic nerve dysfunction is relatively common after supraclavicular thoracic outlet decompression, occurring in approximately 10% of patients. This complication is most often associated with retraction of the nerve necessary to accomplish anterior scalenectomy and results in temporary diaphragmatic paralysis. This finding is often not perceived by the patient given adequate compensation by the contralateral diaphragm, and diagnosis may require chest fluoroscopy. Although most patients with phrenic nerve palsy are asymptomatic and exhibit respiratory difficulty only with extremes of exertion, patients with underlying lung disease before surgery may have more significant symptoms. These symptoms typically resolve with recovery of phrenic nerve and diaphragmatic function within weeks to months of operation, but in some cases, full recovery may take up to 10 months.

In patients with bilateral TOS requiring operation on the contralateral side, it is essential to ensure that any phrenic nerve paresis has completely resolved before the second operation is performed. Although unilateral paralysis of the diaphragm is generally innocuous and asymptomatic in most patients, the surgeon must keep in mind that however carefully performed, contralateral operation in this setting may lead to complete diaphragmatic paralysis and severe ventilatory incapacity. We therefore routinely perform fluoroscopic visualization of diaphragmatic function to ensure complete return of innervation before planning any form of contralateral operation.

Lymph Leakage

It is not uncommon to observe minor postoperative lymphatic fluid collections in the area of the wound or emanating from the closed-suction drain, at least within the first week of operation. It is notable that such fluid may be seen despite ligation of the thoracic duct on the left side, usually because of lymph fluid leakage from small tributaries subjected to higher fluid pressures than normal. In the majority of cases, these lymph leaks resolve spontaneously with time, usually several weeks. In an experience of several hundred supraclavicular operations for TOS, we have encountered only one patient in whom a secondary procedure was necessary for persistent lymph drainage.

Results of Surgery

Outcome Measures

Thoracic outlet decompression for the treatment of neurogenic TOS is intended to provide functional relief of preoperative upper extremity symptoms that have been refractory to conservative management. Assessment of results therefore depends on functional evaluation of symptoms and the patient's somewhat subjective perception of the degree of disability. Because this evaluation depends in large part on the extent of disability existing prior to operation, reported results may vary considerably for patients with differing degrees or duration of disabling symptoms before surgical treatment. Unfortunately, there are no well-defined classification schemes in common use by which to stratify cases before surgical treatment.

Published reports on surgical treatment for neurogenic TOS also vary widely in how outcomes for different operations are defined. Thus, a second difficulty in assessing the results of surgery remains the absence of well-established outcome measures or reporting standards for TOS. Most investigators describe results as divided into separate categories: (1) *excellent*, or complete relief of all symptoms, (2) *good*, or relief of major symptoms but some persistent symptoms, (3) *fair*, or partial relief with persistence of some major symptoms, and (4) *poor*, or no improvement. In general, patients whose results fit into the excellent, good, or fair categories believe that the operation was worthwhile, whereas those with poor results believe that the operation was a failure.

Another variable complicating the interpretation of outcomes for surgical treatment is the type of operation performed. As is evident from the earlier discussion, several different operations are currently in use for neurogenic TOS, each with its own advantages and disadvantages. No single operation has been adopted by all who perform operations for neurogenic TOS, and the operations performed by some may have changed over time. Each operative approach has its advocates and detractors, but it has been difficult to demonstrate a significant difference in outcome between the different procedures in common use. Further complicating

Table 94-3 Collected Results for Anterior Scalenotomy

STUDY*	YEAR	NO. OPERATIONS	OUTCOMES REPORTED (%)		
			Good	Fair	Failed
Annersten[40]	1947	19	89	0	11
Holden et al[41]	1951	28	79	14	7
Raaf[42]	1955	17	47	0	53
Shenkin & Somach[43]	1963	28	50	0	50
deBruin[44]	1966	106	52	18	30
Urschel et al[45]	1971	23	26	39	35
Narakas et al[46]	1986	10	40	0	60
Takagi et al[47]	1987	10	80	0	20
Totals		241	58	9	33

*Superscript numbers indicate chapter references.

Adapted from Sanders RJ: Thoracic Outlet Syndrome: A Common Sequela of Neck Injuries. Philadelphia, JB Lippincott, 1991.

Table 94-4 Collected Results for Anterior Scalenectomy

STUDY*	YEAR	NO. OPERATIONS	OUTCOMES REPORTED (%)		
			Good	Fair	Failed
Adson[48]	1947	53	84	6	13
Stowell[49]	1956	154	84	9	7
Woods[50]	1978	90	75	11	14
Gu et al[51]	1988	12	58	17	25
Loh et al[52]	1989	14	59	21	0
Cikrit et al[53]	1989	15	93	0	7
Totals		338	76	11	11

*Superscript numbers indicate chapter references.

Adapted from Sanders RJ: Thoracic Outlet Syndrome: A Common Sequela of Neck Injuries. Philadelphia, JB Lippincott, 1991.

these assessments is the fact that some reports do not distinguish between operations performed for neurogenic TOS and those performed for arterial or venous TOS, making it impossible to separate the results for treatment of neurogenic TOS alone.

It is recognized that the overall success of operations for neurogenic TOS can be considered only in the context of long-term outcomes. Most of these operations are performed in relatively young and active individuals, with the aim of improving function for many years. Because the level of improvement obtained in the first few months after surgery may diminish with time, the durability of successful outcomes becomes another important measure of results. Unfortunately, many reports in the literature do not include follow-up or assessment of results beyond several months to a few years, making it difficult to assess possible differences between different operations over longer periods.

Finally, it is uncertain whether the results reported by surgeons regularly performing operations for neurogenic TOS can be extended to those who perform thoracic outlet decompression only occasionally, since these procedures are technically demanding operations not often performed by the majority of vascular surgeons. Thus, varying experience with different operations for TOS may also be a confounding factor in interpreting the results reported in various series.

Operative Results

Anterior scalenotomy was initially described by Adson and Coffey[25] and was widely applied until the 1960s. Table 94-3 summarizes eight reports published between 1947 and 1987 that describe results in a total of 241 patients undergoing anterior scalenotomy. The overall outcomes for this operation were good in 26% to 89% (mean 58%), fair in 0 to 39% (mean 9%), and failed in 7% to 60% (mean 33%). *Anterior scalenectomy* was also popularized by Adson and Coffey[25] as a means to avoid potential injury to the brachial plexus in patients with cervical ribs. Table 94-4 summarizes six reports of this procedure published up to 1989 (a total of

338 patients), with good results in 26% to 89% (mean 56%), fair results in 0 to 39% (mean 13%), and poor results in 7% to 60% (mean 31%). At present neither of these operations is performed frequently for neurogenic TOS, in part because the long-term results do not appear as good as those achieved with approaches involving resection of the first rib.

Transaxillary first rib resection has been one of the most frequently performed operations for neurogenic TOS since its introduction by Roos[28] in 1966. By 1989, more than 3000 of these operations had been reported in 21 separate publications. The largest of these series involved 1315 patients, with a successful outcome in 92% and a failure rate of 8%. As summarized in Table 94-5, the overall rate of good outcomes for transaxillary first rib resection has ranged from 37% to 100% (mean 80%), with fair outcomes in 0 to 14% (mean 6%) and failure of operation in 0 to 41% (mean 15%).

Supraclavicular first rib resection with anterior and middle scalenectomy has become one of the more commonly performed operations for neurogenic TOS over the past two decades. Table 94-6 summarizes results of operation from seven different publications involving a total of 1222 patients, the largest being the series reported by Hempel and colleagues[3] (770 operations). Overall, the results for supraclavicular decompression were good in 59% to 91% of cases (mean 77%), fair in 5% to 33% (mean 15%), and poor in 3% to 18% (mean 8%).

The most comprehensive analysis of results for neurogenic TOS has been presented by Sanders and colleagues,[1,14,36,37] who used the life-table method to compare outcomes for different operative procedures. In a comparison of patients undergoing transaxillary first rib resection (n = 112), anterior and middle scalenectomy (n = 286), or supraclavicular scalenectomy with first rib resection (n = 249), there was no difference in the initial success rate among the three procedures (91%, 93% and 93%, respectively). The percentage of patients with successful outcomes also declined over time with all three procedures. Although the long-term success of supraclavicular scalenectomy and first rib resection appeared somewhat better at 10 to 15 years (71%) than the results of either anterior scalenectomy (66%) or transaxillary first rib resection (64%), there was no

Table 94-5	Collected Results for Transaxillary First Rib Resection

STUDY*	YEAR	NO. OPERATIONS	OUTCOMES REPORTED (%) Good	Fair	Failed
Sanders et al[54]	1968	69	90	0	10
Roeder et al[55]	1973	26	92	4	4
Hoofer & Burnett[56]	1973	135	100	0	0
Dale[57]	1975	49	94	0	6
Kremer & Ahlquist[58]	1975	48	86	0	14
McGough et al[59]	1979	113	80	13	7
Youmans & Smiley[60]	1980	258	75	16	9
Roos[61]	1982	1315	92	0	8
Batt et al[62]	1983	94	80	0	20
Sallstrom & Gjores[63]	1983	72	81	12	7
Heughan[64]	1984	44	75	0	25
Quarfordt et al[31]	1984	97	79	0	21
Narakas et al[46]	1986	43	77	0	23
Tagaki et al[47]	1987	48	79	0	21
Davies & Messerschmidt[65]	1988	115	89	0	11
Selke & Kelly[66]	1988	460	79	14	7
Stanton et al[67]	1988	87	85	4	11
Wood et al[68]	1988	54	89	9	2
Cikrit et al[53]	1989	30	63	0	37
Lindgren et al[69]	1989	175	59	0	41
Lepantalo et al[70]	1989	112	52	25	23
Jamieson & Chimick[71]	1996	380	53	25	22
Totals		3824	80	6	15

*Superscript numbers indicate chapter references.

Adapted from Sanders RJ: Thoracic Outlet Syndrome: A Common Sequela of Neck Injuries. Philadelphia, JB Lippincott, 1991.

Table 94-6	Collected Results for Supraclavicular Scalenectomy with First Rib Resection

STUDY*	YEAR	NO. OPERATIONS	OUTCOMES REPORTED (%) Good	Fair	Failed
Adson[48]	1947	53	84	6	13
Graham & Lincoln[72]	1973	78	91	5	4
Thompson & Henandez[73]	1979	15	87	0	13
Thomas et al[74]	1983	128	83	13	4
Reilly & Stoney[33]	1988	39	59	33	8
Loh et al[52]	1989	22	68	23	9
Hempel et al[3]	1996	770	86	13	1
Axelrod et al[75]	2001	170	65	17	18
Totals		1222	77	15	8

*Superscript numbers indicate chapter references.

Adapted from Sanders RJ: Thoracic Outlet Syndrome: A Common Sequela of Neck Injuries. Philadelphia, JB Lippincott, 1991.

statistically significant difference between these operations. It must therefore be concluded that at present, there is no demonstrable difference in either short-term or long-term outcomes among these three operative approaches as applied to neurogenic TOS.

Persistent and Recurrent Thoracic Outlet Syndrome

Patients with neurogenic symptoms after thoracic outlet decompression are characterized as having either persistent or recurrent symptoms. *Persistent symptoms* are those that were not relieved even for a short time by the initial operation. In most cases, persistent symptoms are due to another condition, and the diagnosis should be completely reevaluated. If the symptoms cannot be attributed to another condition and they resist conservative management for at least several months, the possibility of persistent TOS is then considered. If the initial operation was a transaxillary first rib resection, symptoms may persist if there was inadequate relief of compression of the upper nerve roots,

because scalenectomy was not performed. In these cases, a supraclavicular scalenectomy should be considered. Although it is unusual to observe persistent TOS after supraclavicular scalenectomy, this possibility may be considered if the procedure did not include first rib resection. In such cases, it may be reasonable to consider reoperation to remove the first rib by either the transaxillary or the supraclavicular route.

Recurrent symptoms of neurogenic TOS are considered to be present when the patient had good initial results from operation but later experiences symptoms of neurogenic TOS. The majority of such recurrences are observed within the first 2 years of the primary operation. The symptoms are often the same as those present before the initial operation, and the diagnosis is made in the same manner as described earlier. If reoperation is considered, the choice of procedure again depends on the type of operation performed initially. If a transaxillary first rib resection was performed, reoperation should occur through supraclavicular exposure to include scalenectomy, brachial plexus neurolysis, and resection of any remaining portion of the first rib. Experience with such operations shows that the stump of the residual anterior scalene muscle has often become attached to the extrapleural fascia or the brachial plexus nerve roots; it is also common to find a segment of the posterior rib still present, because this portion cannot be resected easily through the transaxillary approach. If the initial operation was a supraclavicular scalenectomy, a second operation should include first rib resection. The cause of recurrent TOS after supraclavicular scalenectomy and first rib resection is usually formation of perineural adhesions, so reoperation through the supraclavicular route may still be of value because it permits a complete brachial plexus neurolysis to be achieved. Because reoperations are associated with a higher risk of nerve and vascular injury than primary procedures, the decision to reoperate should not be taken lightly, and the procedure should be performed by an individual with considerable experience in these operations.

■ REFERENCES

1. Sanders RJ: Thoracic Outlet Syndrome: A Common Sequela of Neck Injuries. Philadelphia, JB Lippincott, 1991.

2. Lindgren KA, Oksala I. Long-term outcome of surgery for thoracic outlet syndrome. Am J Surg 169:358-360, 1995.

3. Hempel GK, Shutze WP, Anderson JF, Bukhari HI: 770 consecutive supraclavicular first rib resections for thoracic outlet syndrome. Ann Vasc Surg 10:456-463, 1996.

4. Wilbourn AJ: The thoracic outlet syndrome is overdiagnosed. Arch Neurol 47:328-330, 1990.

5. Wilbourn AJ: Thoracic outlet syndromes: A plea for conservatism. Neurosurg Clin North Am 2:235-245, 1991.

6. Lindgren KA: Thoracic outlet syndrome with special reference to the first rib. Ann Chir Gynaecol 82:218-230, 1993.

7. Roos DB: Congenital anomalies associated with thoracic outlet syndrome. Am J Surg 132:771-778, 1976.

8. Juvonen T, Satta J, Laitala P, et al: Anomalies at the thoracic outlet are frequent in the general population. Am J Surg 170:33-37, 1995.

9. Machleder HI, Moll F, Verity MA: The anterior scalene muscle in thoracic outlet compression syndrome: Histochemical and morphometric studies. Arch Surg 121:1141-1144, 1986.

10. Sanders RJ, Jackson CG, Banchero N, Pearce WH: Scalene muscle abnormalities in traumatic thoracic outlet syndrome. Am J Surg 159:231-236, 1990.

11. Raskin NH, Howard MW, Ehrenfeld WK: Headache as the leading symptom of the thoracic outlet syndrome. Headache 25:208-210, 1985.

12. Komanetsky RM, Novak CB, Mackinnon SE, et al: Somatosensory evoked potentials fail to diagnose thoracic outlet syndrome. J Hand Surg [Am] 21:662-666, 1996.

13. Gage M: Scalenus anticus syndrome: A diagnostic and confirmatory test. Surgery 5:599-601, 1939.

14. Sanders RJ, Monsour JW, Gerber FG, et al: Scalenectomy versus first rib resection for treatment of the thoracic outlet syndrome. Surgery 85:109-121, 1979.

15. Jordan SE, Machleder HI: Diagnosis of thoracic outlet syndrome using electrophysiologically guided anterior scalene blocks. Ann Vasc Surg 12:260-264, 1998.

16. Jordan SE, Ahn SS, Freischlag JA, et al: Selective botulinum chemodenervation of the scalene muscles for treatment of neurogenic thoracic outlet syndrome. Ann Vasc Surg 14:365-369, 2000.

17. Wilbourn AJ, Porter JM: Neurogenic thoracic outlet syndrome: Surgical versus conservative therapy. J Vasc Surg 15:880-882, 1992.

18. Lindgren KA: Conservative treatment of thoracic outlet syndrome: A 2-year follow-up. Arch Phys Med Rehabil 78:373-378, 1997.

19. Aligne C, Barral X: Rehabilitation of patients with thoracic outlet syndrome. Ann Vasc Surg 6:381-389, 1992.

20. Walsh MT: Therapist management of thoracic outlet syndrome. J Hand Ther 7:131-144, 1994.

21. Novak CB: Conservative management of thoracic outlet syndrome. Semin Thorac Cardiovasc Surg 8:201-207, 1996.

22. Novak CB: Thoracic outlet syndrome. Clin Plast Surg 30:175-188, 2003.

23. Mackinnon SE, Novak CB: Thoracic outlet syndrome. Curr Probl Surg 39:1070-1145, 2002.

24. Coote H: Exostosis of the left transverse process of the seventh cervical vertebra, surrounded by blood vessels and nerves; successful removal. Lancet 1:360-361, 1861.

25. Adson AW, Coffey JR: Cervical rib: A method of anterior approach for relief of symptoms by division of the scalenus anticus. Ann Surg 85:839-857, 1927.

26. Peet RM, Hendriksen JD, Anderson TP, Martin GM: Thoracic outlet syndrome: Evaluation of a therapeutic exercise program. Proc Mayo Clin 31:281-287, 1956.

27. Clagett OT: Presidential address: Research and proresearch. J Thorac Cardiovasc Surg 44:153-166, 1962.

28. Roos DB: Transaxillary approach for first rib resection to relieve thoracic outlet syndrome. Ann Surg 163:354-358, 1966.

29. Dale A: Thoracic outlet compression syndrome: Critique in 1982. Arch Surg 117:1437-1445, 1982.

30. Sanders RJ, Monsour JW, Gerber WJ: Recurrent thoracic outlet syndrome following first rib resection. Vasc Surg 13:325-330, 1979.

31. Qvarfordt PG, Ehrenfeld WK, Stoney RJ: Supraclavicular radical scalenectomy and transaxillary first rib resection for the thoracic outlet syndrome: A combined approach. Am J Surg 148:111-116, 1984.

32. Sanders RJ, Raymer S: The supraclavicular approach to scalenectomy and first rib resection: Description of technique. J Vasc Surg 2:751-756, 1985.

33. Reilly LM, Stoney RJ: Supraclavicular approach for thoracic outlet decompression. J Vasc Surg 8:329-334, 1988.

34. Fantini GA: Reserving supraclavicular first rib resection for vascular complications of thoracic outlet syndrome. Am J Surg 172:200-204, 1996.

35. Machleder HI: Transaxillary operative management of thoracic outlet syndrome. In Ernst CB, Stanley JC (eds): Current Therapy in Vascular Surgery, 2nd ed. Philadelphia, BC Decker, 1991, pp 227-230.

36. Sanders RJ, Pearce WH: The treatment of thoracic outlet syndrome: A comparison of different operations. J Vasc Surg 10:626-634, 1989.

37. Sanders RJ: Results of the surgical treatment for thoracic outlet syndrome. Semin Thorac Cardiovasc Surg 8:221-228, 1996.

38. Thompson RW, Petrinec D: Surgical treatment of thoracic outlet compression syndromes. I: Diagnostic considerations and transaxillary first rib resection. Ann Vasc Surg 11:315-323, 1997.

39. Thompson RW: Treatment of thoracic outlet syndromes and cervical sympathectomy. In Lumley JSP, Siewert JR, Hoballah JJ (eds): Springer Surgery Atlas Series: Vascular Surgery. London, Springer-Verlag, 2004.

40. Annersten S: Studies on the scalenus anticus syndrome. Acta Surg Scand 95:419-439, 1947.

41. Holden WD, Murphy JA, Portmann AF: Scalene anticus syndrome: Unusual diagnostic and therapeutic aspects. Am J Surg 81:411-416, 1951.

42. Raaf J: Surgery for cervical rib and scalenus anticus syndrome. JAMA 157:219-223, 1955.

43. Shenkin HA, Somach FM: Scalenotomy in patients with and without cervical ribs. Arch Surg 87:30-34, 1963.

44. deBruin TR: Costoclavicular space enlargement: Eight methods for relief of neurovascular compression. Int Surg 46:340-360, 1966.

45. Urschel HC, Razzuk MA, Wood RE, et al: Objective diagnosis (ulnar nerve conduction velocity) and current therapy of the thoracic outlet syndrome. Ann Thorac Surg 12:608-620, 1971.

46. Narakas A, Bonnard C, Egloff DV: The cervico-thoracic outlet syndrome. Ann Chir Main 5:185-207, 1986.

47. Takagi K, Yamaga M, Morisawa K, Kitagawa T: Management of thoracic outlet syndrome. Arch Orthop Trauma Surg 106:78-81, 1987.

48. Adson AW: Surgical treatment for symptoms produced by cervical ribs and the scalenus anticus muscle. Surg Gynecol Obstet 85:687-700, 1947.

49. Stowell A: The scalenus anticus syndrome. J Int Coll Surg 26:711-717, 1956.

50. Woods WW: Thoracic outlet syndrome. West J Med 128:9-12, 1978.

51. Gu YD, Wu M, Zheng Y, et al: Combined supra-infraclavicular approach for excision of the first rib in the treatment of the thoracic outlet syndrome. Chung Hua Wai Ko Tsa Chih 22:692-693, 1984.

52. Loh CS, Wu AVO, Stevenson IM: Surgical decompression for thoracic outlet syndrome. J R Coll Surg Edin 34:66-68, 1989.

53. Cikrit DF, Haefner R, Nichols WK, Silver D: Transaxillary or supraclavicular decompression for the thoracic outlet syndrome: A comparison of the risks and benefits. Amer Surgeon 55:347-352, 1989.

54. Sanders RJ, Monsour JW, Baer SB: Transaxillary first rib resection for the thoracic outlet syndrome. Arch Surg 97:1014-1023, 1968.

55. Roeder DK, Mills M, McHale JJ, et al: First rib resection in the treatment of thoracic outlet syndrome: Transaxillary and posterior thoracoplasty approaches. Ann Surg 178:49-52, 1973.

56. Hoofer WD, Burnett AD: Thoracic outlet relief. J Kansas Med Soc 74:329-331, 1973.

57. Dale WA: Management of thoracic outlet syndrome. Ann Surg 181:575-585, 1975.

58. Kremer RM, Ahlquist REJ: Thoracic outlet compression syndrome. Am J Surg 130:612-616, 1975.

59. McGough EC, Pearce MB, Byrne JP: Management of thoracic outlet syndrome. J Ther Card Med 77:169-174, 1979.

60. Youmans CRJ, Smiley RH: Thoracic outlet syndrome with negative Adson's and hyperabduction maneuvers. Vasc Surg 14:318-329, 1980.

61. Roos DB: The place for scalenectomy and first-rib resection in thoracic outlet syndrome. Surgery 92:1077-1085, 1982.

62. Batt M, Griffet J, Scotti L, LeBas P: Le syndrome de la transversée cervico-brachiale: à propos de 112 cas: vers une attitude tactique plus nuancée. J Chir Paris 120:687-691, 1983.

63. Sallstrom J, Gjores JE: Surgical treatment of the thoracic outlet syndrome. Acta Chir Scand 149:555-560, 1983.

64. Heughan C: Thoracic outlet syndrome. Can J Surg 27:35-36, 1984.

65. Davies AL, Messerschmidt W: Thoracic outlet syndrome: A therapeutic approach based on 115 consecutive cases. Del Med J 60:307, 1988.

66. Selke FW, Kelly TR: Thoracic outlet syndrome. Am J Surg 154:56, 1988.

67. Stanton PEJ, Vo NM, Haley T, et al: Thoracic outlet syndrome: A comprehensive evaluation. Am Surg 54:129-133, 1988.

68. Wood VE, Twito R, Verska JM: Thoracic outlet syndrome: The results of first rib resection in 100 patients. Orthop Clin North Amer 19:131-146, 1988.

69. Lindgren SHS, Ribbe EB, Norgren LEH: Two year follow-up of patients operated on for thoracic outlet syndrome: Effects on sick-leave incidence. Eur J Vasc Surg 3:411-415, 1989.

70. Lepantalo M, Lindgren KA, Leino E, et al: Long term outcome after resection of the first rib for thoracic outlet syndrome. Br J Surg 76:1255-1256, 1989.

71. Jamieson WG, Chinnick B: Thoracic outlet syndrome: Fact or fancy? A review of 409 consecutive patients who underwent operation. Can J Surg 39:321-326, 1996.

72. Graham GG, Lincoln BM: Anterior resection of the first rib for thoracic outlet syndrome. Am J Surg 126:803-806, 1973.

73. Thompson JB, Hernandez IA: The thoracic outlet syndrome: a second look. Am J Surg 138:251-253, 1979.

74. Thomas GI, Jones TW, Stavney LS, Manhas DR: The middle scalene muscle and its contribution to the TOS. Am J Surg 145:589-592, 1983.

75. Axelrod DA, Proctor MC, Geisser ME, et al: Outcomes after surgery for thoracic outlet syndrome. J Vasc Surg 33:1220-1225, 2001.

Chapter

Arterial Complications of Thoracic Outlet Compression

95

JON S. MATSUMURA, MD

Patients with symptoms of arterial complications are a small fraction (<5%) of the patients presenting with thoracic outlet compression.[1-3] This chapter reviews the history, pathophysiology, diagnosis, and management of arterial compression with emphasis on several features that are unique from neurologic and venous compression, which are addressed in Chapters 94 and 96. Usual features distinct to arterial compression syndrome are presence of a bony abnormality, frequent indication for operative treatment, need to address a primary arterial injury and secondary emboli, and complete resolution of presenting symptoms.[4]

■ HISTORY

The history of arterial thoracic outlet syndrome dates back to the 2nd century, when Galenus and Vesalius described compression due to cervical rib.[5] In 1815, Hodgson recognized the association of bony anomalies and arterial symptoms when he reported in the modern literature a man with a cervical rib, absent pulses, and finger ischemia.[1] In 1831, Mayo diagnosed a first rib abnormality and a diseased subclavian artery. In 1861, Coote[6] performed the first decompressive operation, in which a cervical rib was removed from a young woman with improvement in the wrist pulse. In 1905, Murphy[7,8] reported a case of subclavian aneurysm associated with a cervical rib, which is the typical presenting pair of bony anomaly and arterial damage. In 1945, Wright[9] recognized axillary artery occlusion in the "hyperabduction syndrome." In 1956, Schein replaced a thrombosed subclavian artery associated with a cervical rib with an arterial homograft. In 1958, Lord and Rosati[10] identified arterial compression by the humeral head. More recent decades have witnessed greater understanding of normal and pathologic arterial anatomy, improvement in diagnostic imaging, and introduction of therapeutic endovascular options. Vascular reconstructive techniques have continued to improve (see Chapter 92), and direct arterial repair is a durable procedure.

■ PATHOPHYSIOLOGY

Arterial compression symptoms are commonly due to emboli from a proximal arterial injury that is associated with a combination of bony anomaly and overuse.

Bony Anomaly

A key feature of arterial compression in the thoracic outlet is the frequent presence of a bony abnormality, usually a complete cervical rib. Among arterial thoracic outlet patients, 88%

XIV

section

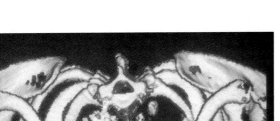

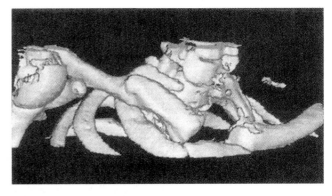

FIGURE 95-1 The complete cervical rib is the most common cause of thoracic outlet arterial compression, as seen in this computed tomography (CT) reconstruction.

FIGURE 95-2 Shaded-surface rendering by spiral CT shows a large clavicular callus after previous fracture. With the arm in abduction, the subclavian artery is compressed.

had an osseous abnormality.[2] In striking contrast, these anomalies are rarely found in asymptomatic individuals. In chest radiographs of 40,000 military recruits, abnormalities of the first rib or cervical ribs occurred in 263 (1.3%) recruits.[11] In a radiographic survey of 2000 college students, 2.8% were found to have bony deformities.[12] Likewise, bony anomalies are uncommon in venous compression syndromes.[4,13]

Although arterial injury may occur at the scalene triangle, pectoralis minor tendon, humeral head, or quadrilateral space, the most common site is the costoclavicular space. Complete cervical ribs articulate with the upper surface of the first rib lateral to the insertion of the anterior scalene muscle and cause injury to the subclavian artery as it crosses over these bones (Fig. 95-1). Frequently an aneurysm develops lateral to the arterial pinch caused by the osseous narrowing. Other bony anomalies that can produce arterial compression are long seventh cervical transverse processes, partial cervical ribs, and first rib abnormalities that produce protuberances, pronounced widening or arching that narrows the costoclavicular space. The clavicle also may narrow the costoclavicular space when it heals after a fracture with a hypertrophic callus or is otherwise abnormally deformed (Fig. 95-2).

Although not classically considered part of the thoracic outlet syndrome, patients with arterial compression at the shoulder present with identical symptoms, and the general principles of treatment are similar. This syndrome is addressed in detail in Chapter 98. Throwing athletes may develop humeral head enlargement with overuse, and a lax shoulder capsule can permit anterior subluxation, producing arterial thrombosis.[14] Tethering of the axillary artery between the chest and the loop of circumflex humeral arteries across the humeral head also may produce a traction injury with repetitive exaggerated motion.[10]

Overuse

Several observations suggest that repetitive motion is a significant, although not essential, contributor for arterial injury. First, in publications that report hand dominance, symptoms are more frequent in the dominant arm of patients with bilateral cervical ribs.[15] Second, in studies in which hand dominance was not specified, arterial symptoms

occurred more often on the right side, although cervical ribs were usually bilateral or slightly more frequent on the left.[11,16-18] Third, duplex ultrasound has shown arterial compression in equal distributions of dominant and nondominant arms in 46 subjects.[14] Fourth, in a study of 100 healthy adult volunteers, of whom 84 were right-handed and 2 were ambidextrous, there were 235 vascular responses to the hyperabduction, Adson, and costoclavicular maneuvers. Of these responses, 115 (49%) were in the dominant extremity, suggesting that the normal left and right thoracic outlets have similar frequency of anatomic impingement regardless of dominance.[19] Taken together, these observations strongly suggest that repetitive motion, reflected in hand dominance, is necessary to progress from asymptomatic positional compression to arterial injury.

Overuse leads to injury via multiple mechanisms. A simplistic hypothesis is that the repetition of normal motion results in injury, but this is not consistent with the young age of arterial patients. A more plausible theory is that soft tissue hypertrophy occurs with overuse and results in cramped space in the bony outlet. Another mechanism may be due to subclinical ligamentous injury leading to improper anatomic relationships and increased compression with shoulder movement. The severity of arm deceleration forces may contribute to intimal trauma, dissection, or aneurysmal degeneration in some athletes.[16] Shear injury of the axillary artery from acute trauma has been described with proximal anchoring of the artery by previous clavicle fracture.[20]

Arterial Injury

The most common presenting arterial pathology is a focal aneurysm with secondary embolization (Fig. 95-3). Earlier in the pathogenesis, stenosis may be noted with mild post-stenotic dilatation (Fig. 95-4). Often there may be subtle angiographic findings and no extrinsic visual evidence of arterial injury, yet inspection of the inside of the subclavian artery reveals an embolizing lesion (Fig. 95-5). Progression may result in complete occlusion and retrograde thrombosis with embolization into the cerebral circulation. Sometimes, side branches of the axial artery may develop aneurysms that are sources of hand emboli when positional distal occlusion causes reflux into the axial artery.[16,21-24]

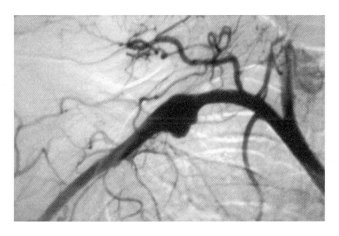

FIGURE 95-3 Arteriogram of right subclavian artery shows large subclavian aneurysm.

■ DIAGNOSIS

Signs and Symptoms

Patients and physicians often ignore symptoms of arterial thoracic outlet compression because the usual clinical markers of atherosclerotic occlusive disease are absent, and it is an uncommon disease. Symptoms may include cold intolerance, Raynaud's phenomenon, forearm exertional pain, rest pain, ulceration, and gangrene. Although uncommon, stroke may be the presenting complaint owing to retrograde propagation or reflux of clot from a thrombosed subclavian artery.[25] Aneurysm rupture with intrapleural rupture is rare but can be fatal.[18] Many mild symptoms may overlap with neurologic compression syndromes. Arterial compression is a frequent finding in normal asymptomatic individuals (Fig. 95-6) and may be noted incidentally during imaging of a neck mass or contralateral symptomatic lesion.[19]

Several findings are helpful to identify patients with arterial thoracic outlet syndrome. These patients often present with unilateral symptoms. There may be occupational or recreational history of arm overuse, such as in painters, mechanics, weightlifters, rowers, and throwing athletes.[24] Physical examination of the supraclavicular area may reveal a bruit or mass, or there may be a diminished arm pulse or blood pressure compared with the contralateral side. The fingers and nail beds are inspected for ischemic signs, and neurologic function is assessed. Positional maneuvers may be helpful, but are not definitive for diagnosis. A positional bruit or pulse loss increases clinical suspicion, but many normal persons have these findings.[19] Conversely, there can be a normal pulse examination despite a nonocclusive arterial lesion and microembolization.

Other causes of upper extremity ischemia may be suspected from the history and physical examination. A family history of venous thrombosis suggests a coagulation disorder, or a history of atrial fibrillation supports a cardio-embolic etiology. Other considerations include atherosclerosis, aortic dissection, vasculitis, radiation injury, and iatrogenic trauma.[26]

Noninvasive Testing

Vascular laboratory testing can help discriminate the diagnosis in some patients with equivocal clinical findings and possibly avoid arteriography. Digital occlusion pressures may identify bilateral digital ischemia, which suggests systemic diseases, such as vasculitis.[27] Photoplethysmography and duplex ultrasound can measure arterial patency in a range of provocative positions compared with the limited positions in contrast arteriography. Noninvasive testing is an excellent choice for postoperative assessment when there is concern over the patency of the reconstruction.

Cervical spine or chest radiographs can show most bony abnormalities of the neck, thorax, and shoulder, but some subtle bony deformities may be missed. Computed tomography (CT) with three-dimensional reconstruction is more sensitive for defining the cause of compression in the thoracic outlet. Subtle findings include anterior deviation of the seventh cervical transverse processes, which has been associated with thoracic outlet syndrome (Fig. 95-7). CT scans are acquired with the symptomatic arm in the neutral and provocative positions. The artery is enhanced by infusing full-strength contrast material into the contralateral arm. Reconstruction requires hours of skilled attention, but provides excellent three-dimensional images and multiplanar

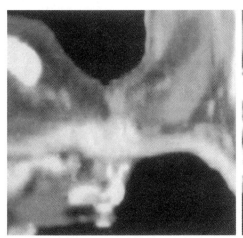
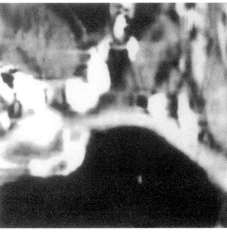

FIGURE 95-4 CT "snake" reconstructions show subclavian aneurysm immediately lateral to costoclavicular pinch. (From Matsumura JS, Pearce WH: Mechanisms and treatment of arterial abnormalities in the thoracic outlet: The role of bony abnormalities. In Veith FJ [ed]: Current Critical Problems in Vascular Surgery, vol 8. St Louis, Quality Medical Publishers, 1998, pp 292-299.)

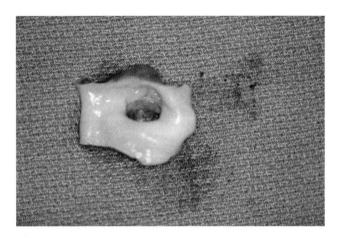

FIGURE 95-5 Operative specimen of excised subclavian aneurysm that was the source of distal emboli.

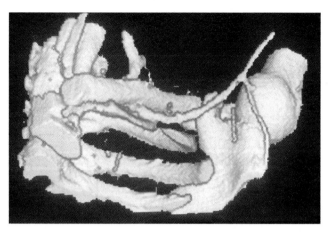

FIGURE 95-6 Shaded-surface rendering of a normal volunteer shows arterial compression with arm abducted.

views.[28] An exuberant clavicular callus is seen in a shaded-surface CT reconstruction (see Fig. 95-2), and arterial compression is shown with abduction of the arm.

Magnetic resonance imaging also can be useful for assessment of the thoracic outlet, but requires experience with technique and interpretation.[29] Cross-sectional imaging is helpful in the rare cases when an abnormal soft tissue mass is identified. Although noninvasive tests identify arterial compression and the elements causing that compression, clinical assessment is still important to differentiate asymptomatic compression from arterial thoracic outlet syndrome.

Arteriography

Arteriography for evaluation of arm ischemia may be performed with several variations depending on what clinical information is desired. Objectives of testing are localization of the arterial damage, evaluation of arterial runoff, and assessment for operative planning. The thoracic

arch and selective injections of the ipsilateral vessel in neutral and positional views are common (Fig. 95-8). Runoff images identify normal anatomic variants in addition to acquired abnormalities. Similar to the lower extremity, multiple projections are sometimes necessary to visualize overlapping branch artery origins. Magnified views of the hand with vasodilators can implicate embolization based on a pattern of involvement derived from the source artery. Rarely, small distal aneurysms or ulcerated lesions may be discovered. Selective views of the contralateral arm may suggest an alternative diagnosis if bilateral disease involving multiple small branches is identified. Operative revascularization requires specific identification of a target vessel location, such as discrimination of the interosseous arteries with oblique imaging.

■ MANAGEMENT

General

Treatment of arterial thoracic outlet syndrome is indicated for most patients with ischemia and asymptomatic patients with arterial damage. The general therapeutic approach has

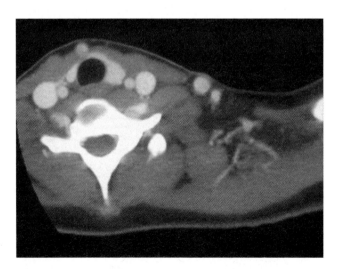

FIGURE 95-7 Transverse CT scan shows anterior deviation of the seventh cervical transverse process that is associated with thoracic outlet abnormalities.

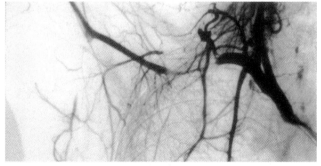

FIGURE 95-8 Arteriogram with arms in position of use shows compression of the subclavian artery and branches, including circumflex humeral arteries. (From Matsumura JS, Pearce WH: Mechanisms and treatment of arterial abnormalities in the thoracic outlet: The role of bony abnormalities. In Veith FJ [ed]: Current Critical Problems in Vascular Surgery, vol 8. St Louis, Quality Medical Publishers, 1998, pp 292-299.)

three goals: (1) decompression of the structures compressing the artery, (2) removal of the source of emboli, and (3) restoration of distal perfusion. Preoperative identification of the bony abnormality and arterial source enables ideal operative positioning and incisions. Anterior supraclavicular and infraclavicular incisions provide adequate exposure for most patients who require arterial repair.[30] If decompression only is required, an isolated supraclavicular, axillary, or posterior approach may be suitable. Occasionally a claviculectomy, second rib resection, or even thoracotomy may be necessary to provide adequate decompression or emergency exposure for vascular control. Catastrophic vascular and nerve injuries may occur even with experienced surgeons.[31] Removal of the clavicle in throwing athletes is avoided because of potential shoulder instability, unless the primary compressive lesion is a clavicular abnormality.

Regardless of approach, preparing the entire upper extremity into the field allows for arm movements that may facilitate exposure. Placing a finger in the planned arterial tunnel during provocative positioning of the arm permits ongoing assessment of the adequacy of decompression. During dissection in this region, neurologic and vascular injuries are obvious concerns, and use of cautery is minimized. In patients with abnormal ribs, developmental abnormalities of the brachial plexus may be present, which increases risk of nerve damage. When vascular reconstruction is planned, vein harvest sites also are prepared.

Decompression

For the typical patient with a cervical rib, the supraclavicular approach yields excellent access. The skin, subcutaneous tissue, and platysma are incised transversely about 1 cm above the clavicle. The scalene fat pad is reflected medially with meticulous ligation of the small vessels and lymphatics. After the phrenic nerve is gently dissected off the anterior scalene muscle, the pliable muscle fibers may be selectively divided with a scraping motion of the open scissors; this technique reduces the chance of inadvertent division of other structures. Resection of the muscle prevents reattachment and may reduce the risk of recurrent compression. The subclavian artery and brachial plexus are identified before resection of the cervical rib. If replacement of the subclavian artery is planned, this can be resected first to decompress the outlet, facilitate exposure of the bony elements, and reduce risk of intraoperative embolization. The middle scalene may be divided to expose the posterior first rib for resection. Blunt dissection separates the pleura from the underside of the rib. With specific attention to avoiding injury to the peripheral nerves, rib resection is done through a piecemeal technique using a Raney rongeur.[32]

If the anterior portion of the first rib is to be removed or axillary artery access is needed for arterial reconstruction, a second infraclavicular incision is made transversely below the clavicle, and the pectoralis major is split along its fibers. A hypertrophied subclavius muscle may be resected to improve exposure of the anterior first rib, and the subclavian vein is mobilized. If necessary for lateral exposure, the pectoralis minor is divided, and distal dissection is performed.

Arterial Repair

Removing an embolic source usually is done by resection and interposition graft replacement, although segmental resection with reanastomosis or patch closure of a partial resection may be possible with small focal lesions. Often the artery appears normal externally, but after opening it, an ulcerated intimal lesion is identified.

Distal Revascularization

In the setting of acute ischemia, endovascular techniques for revascularization may be attempted and include regional thrombolytic therapy, mechanical thromboembolectomy, and balloon thromboembolectomy. When symptoms are more chronic, distal bypass is often required because these young patients may experience more disability from exercise-induced ischemia. Standard bypass techniques use subclavian or common carotid artery inflow, saphenous vein as the preferred conduit, and tunneling that minimizes traction and compression during arm movement.

The distal target artery is selected by size, runoff to the palmar arches, and access through a familiar dissection. When there is occlusion of the radial and ulnar arteries, an interosseous artery anastomosis is chosen. This uncommon exposure requires determination of the dominant patent anterior or posterior branch on an oblique arteriogram. The anterior interosseous artery is accessed between the flexor digitorum profundus and flexor pollicis longus muscles, and the posterior branch is exposed through incision on the dorsum of the forearm.[30]

Upper extremity arteries are often more fragile and prone to spasm, which may be treated with topical papaverine.[26] Completion arteriography or Doppler evaluation is performed frequently before closing. Long-term outcomes are excellent after distal vein bypass for thoracic outlet syndrome. In the Northwestern experience with 34 patients, 4 patients have had reoperation: two graft thrombectomies, one revision for aneurysmal degeneration, and one for incomplete initial decompression. The secondary patency is 100% at mean follow-up of 31 months.[16]

For cases of chronic digital vessel occlusion, when a distal bypass is not indicated or when it is not possible, alternative therapies are considered. These include long-term anticoagulation, protection from cold, prostaglandin infusion, and sympathectomy. The long-term prognosis of hand ischemia not due to connective tissue disease is good; in a report from the Oregon Health Sciences University hand clinic, with mean follow-up of 15 years in 18 patients, 22% had ulceration, and only 6% required any amputation.[27]

Asymptomatic Lesions

Patients who have bony or soft tissue anomalies that compress the subclavian artery but are free of arterial damage, embolization, and symptoms can be managed with abstinence from strenuous and repetitive arm movement. If an athlete desires to continue the provocative activity, modification of arm motion and surveillance for arterial injury may be offered. Anticoagulation also has been reported as effective, and although invasive, decompression before arterial injury occurs is successful.[14,24]

■ SUMMARY

Arterial injury is the least common type of thoracic outlet syndrome. It usually presents with ischemic symptoms, and nearly all patients have a bony abnormality that can be identified with radiographic testing. Most patients present with a classic profile of a complete cervical rib and subclavian artery aneurysm with distal embolization in the dominant arm. Arteriographic evaluation and identification of the bony compressing structure are helpful in operative planning. Operative management frequently is indicated for symptomatic patients and focuses on three goals: (1) relief of arterial compression, (2) resection of the diseased artery, and (3) restoration of distal perfusion. Familiarity with the diagnostic aspects and therapeutic options in arterial thoracic outlet syndrome usually leads to excellent results.

■ REFERENCES

1. Kieffer E: Arterial complications of thoracic outlet syndrome. In Bergan JJ, Yao JST (eds): Evaluation and Treatment of Upper and Lower Extremity Circulatory Disorders. Orlando, Grune & Stratton, 1984, pp 249-275.

2. Sanders RJ, Haug C: Review of arterial thoracic outlet syndrome with a report of five new instances. Surg Gynecol Obstet 173:415-425, 1991.

3. Makhoul RG, Machleder HI: Developmental anomalies at the thoracic outlet: An analysis of 200 consecutive cases. J Vasc Surg 16:534-545, 1992.

4. Davidovic LB, Kostic DM, Jakovljevic NS, et al: Vascular thoracic outlet syndrome. World J Surg 27:545-550, 2003.

5. Adson AW, Coffey JR: Cervical rib. Ann Surg 85:839, 1927.

6. Coote H: Exostosis of the left transverse process in the 7th cervical vertebra surrounded by blood vessels and nerves: Successful removal. Lancet 1:360-361, 1861.

7. Murphy JB: A case of cervical rib with symptoms resembling subclavian aneurysm. Ann Surg 41:399-406, 1905.

8. Murphy JB: The clinical significance of cervical rib. Surg Gynecol Obstet 3:514-520, 1906.

9. Wright IS: The neurovascular syndrome produced by hyperabduction of the arm. Am Heart J 29:1-19, 1945.

10. Lord JW, Rosati LM: Neurovascular compression syndromes of the upper extremity. Clin Symp 10:35-62, 1958.

11. Etter LE: Osseous abnormalities of the thoracic cage seen in forty thousand consecutive chest photoroentgenograms. Am J Roentgenol Rad Ther 51:359-363, 1944.

12. Sycamore LK: Common congenital anomalies of the bony thorax. Am J Roentgenol Rad Ther 51:593-599, 1944.

13. Hood DB, Kuehne J: Vascular complications of thoracic outlet syndrome. Am Surg 63:913, 1997.

14. Rohrer MJ, Cardullo PA, Pappas AM: Axillary artery compression and thrombosis in throwing athletes. J Vasc Surg 11:761-769, 1990.

15. Short DW: The subclavian artery in 16 patients with complete cervical ribs. J Cardiovasc Surg 16:135-141, 1975.

16. Durham JR, Yao JST, Pearce WH, et al: Arterial injuries in the thoracic outlet syndrome. J Vasc Surg 21:57-70, 1995.

17. Scher LA, Veith FJ, Haimovici H: Staging of arterial complications of cervical rib: Guidelines for surgical management. Surgery 95:644-649, 1984.

18. Pairolero PC, Walls JT, Payne WS, et al: Subclavian-axillary artery aneurysms. Surgery 90:757-763, 1981.

19. Rayan GM, Jensen C: Thoracic outlet syndrome: Provocative examination maneuvers in a typical population. J Shoulder Elbow Surg 4:113-117, 1995.

20. Erez I, Amdor B, Witz M, et al: Unusual blunt trauma causing complete disruption of the axillary artery. Eur J Vasc Surg 8:233-235, 1994.

21. Nijhuis HHAM, Muller-Wiefel H: Occlusion of the brachial artery by thrombus dislodged from a traumatic aneurysm of the anterior humeral circumflex artery. J Vasc Surg 13:408-411, 1991.

22. Reekers JA, den Hartog BMG, Kuyper CF, et al: Traumatic aneurysm of the posterior circumflex humeral artery: A volleyball player's disease? J Vasc Interv Radiol 4:405-408, 1993.

23. Kee ST, Dake MD, Wolfe-Johnson B, et al: Ischemia of the throwing hand in major league baseball pitchers: Embolic occlusion from aneurysms of axillary artery branches. J Vasc Interv Radiol 6:979-982, 1995.

24. McCarthy WJ, Yao JST, Schafer MF, et al: Upper extremity arterial injury in athletes. J Vasc Surg 9:317-327, 1989.

25. Fields WS, Lemak NA, Ben-Menachem Y: Thoracic outlet syndrome: Review and reference to stroke in a major league pitcher. AJNR Am J Neuroradiol 7:73-78, 1986.

26. McCarthy WJ: Revascularization of upper extremity. In Ernst CB, Stanley JC (eds): Current Therapy in Vascular Surgery, 2nd ed. Philadelphia, BC Decker, 1991, pp 182-186.

27. McLafferty RB, Edwards JM, Taylor LM, et al: Diagnosis and long-term clinical outcome in patients diagnosed with hand ischemia. J Vasc Surg 22:361-369, 1995.

28. Matsumura JS, Pearce WH: Mechanisms and treatment of arterial abnormalities in the thoracic outlet: The role of bony abnormalities. In Veith FJ (ed): Current Critical Problems in Vascular Surgery, vol 8. St Louis, Quality Medical Publishers, 1998, pp 292-299.

29. Krinsky G, Rofsky NM: MR angiography of the aortic arch vessels and upper extremities. Magn Reson Imaging Clin N Am 6:269-292, 1998.

30. Yao JST, Pearce WH: Reconstructive surgery for chronic upper extremity ischemia. Semin Vasc Surg 3:258-266, 1990.

31. Melliere D, Becquemin JP, Etienne G, Le Cheviller B: Severe injuries resulting from operations for thoracic outlet syndrome: Can they be avoided? J Cardiovasc Surg 32:599-603, 1991.

32. Pearce WH, Tropea BI, Baxter BT, et al: Arterial complications in the thoracic outlet. Semin Vasc Surg 3:236-241, 1990.

Subclavian-Axillary Vein Thrombosis

RICHARD M. GREEN, MD

■ HISTORICAL PERSPECTIVE

Primary thrombosis of the subclavian-axillary vein was described by Paget[87] in 1875. He called the syndrome of acute swelling and pain of the upper extremity *gouty phlebitis* and attributed it to vasospasm. In 1884, Von Schroetter[109] postulated that thrombosis of the subclavian and axillary veins caused these symptoms. The term *Paget-Schroetter syndrome* first appeared in 1949 in Hughes'[56] comprehensive review of the world's literature. At that time, subclavian-axillary vein thrombosis was relatively rare; Hughes found only 320 cases of the disease.

By the 1960s, it had been established that primary subclavian-axillary vein thromboses were seen after exertion of the affected upper extremity, and the term *effort thrombosis* came into use. The condition has been reported in athletes, painters, beauticians, and many others who are highly functional.[65] In the early 1970s, a steady shift in the predominant cause began as more cases of subclavian-axillary vein thrombosis were encountered in patients with indwelling central venous catheters. Aubaniac[7] had described the first use of a subclavian vein catheter in 1952. These central venous lines were used for fluid resuscitation and were placed via a cutdown. In 1968, Dudrick and coworkers[35] described the first percutaneous placement of a subclavian vein catheter for total parenteral nutrition. Reports of catheter-associated subclavian-axillary vein thrombosis started appearing in the literature soon after the initial descriptions of placement of these catheters.[26,106] An autopsy study by McDonough and Altemeier[76] in 1971 confirmed the association.

The use of central venous catheters increased rapidly after 1973 with the introduction of a silicone-rubber (Silastic) catheter, which was more flexible and easier to handle than previous catheters.[20] Currently the subclavian vein is cannulated for a variety of reasons, including nutrition, cardiac monitoring, hemodialysis, chemotherapy, resuscitation, and pacemakers. As the indications for central venous access have increased, so has the incidence of catheter-related subclavian-axillary vein thrombosis.

The following conditions are associated with an increased risk of subclavian-axillary vein thrombosis: extrinsic compression syndromes (thoracic outlet syndrome, mediastinal malignancy, mediastinitis); venous scarring from central venous catheterizations or indwelling catheters; trauma, particularly of the clavicle and first rib; and hypercoagulable states. Some classifications consider thrombosis in association with thoracic outlet syndrome as primary and the other etiologies as secondary. There are acute and chronic consequences of subclavian-axillary vein thrombosis. Pulmonary embolism rates range from 7% to 20%.[48,52,83] Postphlebitic symptoms can lead to functional disability in 25% to 40% of affected patients.[41] Any long-term sequelae are determined by the extent of the thrombosis, the degree of recanalization and collateralization, and the functional needs of the patient.

■ INCIDENCE

Upper extremity deep venous thrombosis (DVT) occurs in 1% to 4% of all DVTs.[5,10,26,51,53,70,88] The introduction of percutaneous techniques and flexible, easily handled catheters brought about a large increase in the number of central venous cannulations and a subsequent increase in the number of catheter-related thromboses. Primary subclavian-axillary vein thrombosis is reported to constitute about 25% of all upper extremity DVTs, catheter-associated subclavian-axillary vein thrombosis constitutes 40%, and other forms of secondary subclavian-axillary vein thrombosis make up the remainder of upper extremity DVTs. Because primary and secondary subclavian-axillary vein thromboses have different etiologic patterns and treatment considerations, they are considered separately here.

■ PRIMARY SUBCLAVIAN-AXILLARY VEIN THROMBOSIS

Etiology

The underlying cause of primary subclavian-axillary vein thrombosis is compression of the subclavian vein at the costoclavicular space, the most medial aspect of the thoracic outlet (Fig. 96-1). This dynamic compression leads to fibrosis, stasis of blood flow, and subsequent thrombosis. Repetitive arm and shoulder activity predisposes to thrombosis in numerous ways. Lifting heavy objects leads to depression of the shoulder.[6] Adams and colleagues[4] showed compression of the subclavian vein in the costoclavicular space with hyperabduction of the arm, hyperextension of the neck, or downward and backward movement of the shoulder *in normal patients* without thrombosis of the subclavian vein. Microscopic intimal damage may occur, stimulating the coagulation process. Although patients usually present with acute swelling of the arm preceded by strenuous upper body exertion, the pathophysiologic process is a chronic one.[1,8,63,102]

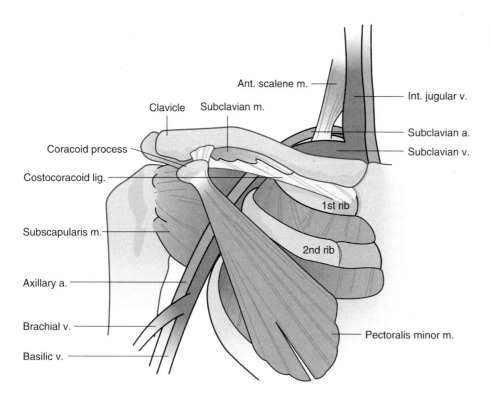

FIGURE 96-1 Anatomy of the thoracic outlet.

Occasionally, anatomic abnormalities or congenital defects increase the susceptibility to positional compression of the vein and can be incriminated in patients with subclavian-axillary vein thrombosis. Common anatomic anomalies are abnormalities of the anterior scalene, subclavius, pectoralis minor, and scalenus minimus muscles. Bony abnormalities of the clavicle and ribs also have been observed. Other authors have found congenital bands, an aberrant phrenic nerve, or an abnormal costocoracoid ligament at the time of thoracic outlet decompression.[1,3,4,27,30,31,44,66,90,100,101] It is unknown how many patients with these abnormalities would have a clinically significant upper extremity thrombosis, but in the studies that specifically looked for any anatomic defect, an overwhelming majority of patients had some anatomic abnormality at surgery. The most common abnormality was extrinsic compression at the costoclavicular space. Venographic studies evaluating the contralateral arm in patients with subclavian-axillary vein thrombosis found venous compression in 56% to 80% of these limbs. The incidence of bilateral thrombosis is only 2% to 15%.[6,11,39,62,70,95,104]

Clinical Presentation

There is a male-to-female predilection of 2:1, with an average age of 31 years.[53] Of patients, 75% report an antecedent event of strenuous or repetitive activity before onset of symptoms. The dominant arm is involved in 60% to 80% of cases.[1,3,5,23,24,70,102] Neurologic symptoms usually do not accompany the venous variant of thoracic outlet syndrome; this is not surprising, when one considers that the vein and nerves are at opposite ends of the thoracic outlet.[21,23,40,41,92]

The hallmarks of subclavian-axillary vein thrombosis are swelling and cyanosis of the involved extremity. Virtually every patient presents with some degree of upper extremity swelling. The edema usually involves the entire arm and hand and is characteristically nonpitting. In time, patients develop venous engorgement of the superficial collateral veins over the upper arm, base of the neck, and anterior chest as collateral drainage is established. Most patients eventually also complain of pain in the affected extremity. The pain is described as "aching," "stabbing," or a feeling of "tightness" referred to the arm or axilla and usually worsens with exertion.[3] The pathophysiology underlying the clinical characteristics of subclavian-axillary vein thrombosis is venous hypertension. The intensity of signs and symptoms is directly related to the length of the occlusion, the existence of prethrombotic venous collateral pathways, and the amount of activity of the involved extremity. Historically the treatment of this syndrome consisted of anticoagulation and elevation of the arm. After recovery from the acute event, some patients have residual symptoms from venous obstruction manifested by arm swelling, pain, and early fatigue. Before the advent of surgical or thrombolytic therapy, 80% of patients with primary subclavian-axillary vein thrombosis had persistent symptoms.[3,5,26,30,32,34,57,59,95] The persistent symptoms likely reflect an above-average activity level with an ongoing need for active use of the involved extremity. In contrast to lower extremity DVT symptoms, symptoms in the upper extremity are related to residual obstruction rather than reflux. Most patients complain of pain and swelling that are made worse by dependency and active use of the involved extremity. The increased arterial blood flow to the exercising upper extremity cannot be met by a proportional increase in venous outflow through the limited collateral vessels without significant venous hypertension.

In their series of primary subclavian-axillary vein thrombosis patients, Swinton and coauthors[102] found that only 9% had no symptoms, 52% had symptoms but were able to work, and 39% were completely disabled, and the use of oral anticoagulation after thrombosis made no difference in the degree of disability. Donayre and associates[33] reported a 78% incidence of persistent symptoms in patients taking warfarin (Coumadin). Tilney and colleagues[104] reported that 55% of patients in their series were unable to work, 18% were working but symptomatic, and 27% had no symptoms.

Most studies that reported pulmonary embolism rates grouped primary and secondary subclavian-axillary vein thrombosis together. It seems that primary and secondary subclavian-axillary vein thrombosis have a similar incidence of pulmonary embolism.[3,5,27,33,48,52,65,83,84,95,104] In a retrospective study, Hingorani and colleagues[52] found no difference in the rate of pulmonary embolism between primary or secondary subclavian-axillary vein thrombosis. The overall incidence in their study was 7%. As the methods of detecting pulmonary embolism have improved, the incidence has increased. Hughes[56] reported pulmonary embolism in only 3 of 302 patients in his review. Monreal and coauthors[83] prospectively examined 30 consecutive patients with ventilation-perfusion scanning who had upper extremity DVT. They discovered that 15% of patients had evidence of pulmonary emboli. Of these patients, only one was symptomatic. Overall, the symptomatic pulmonary embolism rate is about 12%.[48,52,65] Regardless of the underlying cause, pulmonary embolism can be a significant complication of subclavian-axillary vein thrombosis. Only the relatively small clot burden reduces its usual clinical impact.

Venous gangrene is an extremely rare complication of upper extremity DVT. It is estimated that upper extremity phlegmasia cerulea dolens constitutes 2% to 5% of all phlegmasia cases.[60] Only 15 cases of upper extremity phlegmasia were reported before 1993.[22] All of these cases were secondary to an underlying hypercoagulable state or malignancy. This same report documented a single patient with venous gangrene secondary to a spontaneous upper extremity DVT. Their extensive evaluation revealed no underlying cause of the thrombosis. There have been no reports of phlegmasia arising from effort-induced subclavian-axillary vein thrombosis.

Diagnosis

The diagnosis of primary subclavian-axillary vein thrombosis is based on the clinical presentation of upper extremity swelling, venous engorgement, and pain of relatively sudden onset. Of patients, 85% eventually have symptoms within the first 24 hours of the precipitating event.[5,59,95] Patients with progressive narrowing at the costoclavicular space and ample collateral vessels may not have many symptoms. This fact or the lack of a clear precipitating event can cause delays in making the diagnosis. When subclavian-axillary vein thrombosis is thought to be present, diagnostic studies are indicated to confirm the diagnosis and to determine the extent of the thrombus. Some of the comments that follow apply to primary and secondary subclavian-axillary vein thrombosis.

Duplex ultrasonography is helpful in the diagnosis of acute subclavian-axillary vein thrombosis. The area of acute thrombosis may be hidden under the clavicle, however, and the axillary and basilic veins may appear normal. The lack of appreciation of this entity may lead to a delay in diagnosis. Although Haire and coworkers[46] found no false-positive results in their prospective series comparing duplex with venography, sensitivity of duplex scanning was only 44% in their study. In a later study, Koksoy and colleagues[64] found that duplex scanning had a sensitivity of 94% and a specificity of 96% compared with venography. Advances in ultrasound technology (e.g., color-flow scan) and adjunctive use of indirect criteria for proximal occlusion (distended, incompressible vein with continuous flow and poor augmentation by compressive maneuvers) may improve sensitivity. A prospective study of color duplex ultrasonography compared with contrast venography in 126 patients suspected of having upper extremity deep venous thrombosis was conducted in the Netherlands.[50] The results indicate that the prevalence of DVT was 44% among patients clinically suspected of having DVT. The sensitivity and specificity of duplex ultrasonography were 82% (95% confidence interval, 70% to 93%) and 82% (95% confidence interval, 72% to 92%). Venous incompressibility correlated well with thrombosis, whereas only 50% of isolated flow abnormalities proved to be thrombus related. The analysis indicates that there is an 18% probability of a DVT with a "negative" color duplex examination. The utility of the test is limited, unless one is willing to withhold treatment when the probability of a potentially lethal condition is 18%. No study has evaluated the safety of withholding anticoagulant therapy without additional testing in patients with negative duplex studies.[85]

Although ultrasound is widely available, results are operator dependent, and newer noninvasive imaging modalities may be used with the expectation of higher sensitivity and specificity. Magnetic resonance venography has become increasingly used to confirm the diagnosis noninvasively.[31,44] In addition to increased accuracy, magnetic resonance imaging allows the cross-sectional evaluation of the structures in the costoclavicular space.

Venography remains the "gold standard" in evaluating upper extremity vein thrombosis but is necessary only when an intervention is anticipated. Important planning information can be obtained, such as the nature and extent of the obstruction and whether it is extrinsic or intrinsic or both. The basilic vein should be accessed, and ultrasound guidance may be necessary in the presence of arm edema. The cephalic vein should not be used because it joins directly with the subclavian vein, and venography through this vein may miss an axillary vein thrombosis.

Positioning of the patient is important in upper extremity venography. The patient's arm must be abducted at least 30 degrees. The pectoralis major muscle may compress the axillary vein if the arm is at the patient's side and may mimic a complete occlusion. A positive venogram can show various degrees of occlusion or stenosis of the subclavian-axillary vein (Fig. 96-2). It also shows the presence and extent of the collateral circulation. The extent of the collateral circulation can help determine the chronicity of the occlusion and the hemodynamic significance of the occlusion or stenosis.

Patients with a normal venogram with the arm in the neutral position still may have intermittent compression of

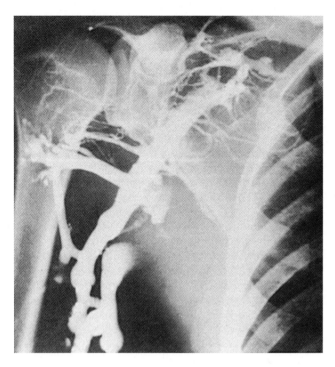

FIGURE 96-2 Venogram of an acute primary subclavian-axillary vein thrombosis.

the subclavian vein (Fig. 96-3).[4] Patients with symptoms without an occluding thrombus or patients with normal venograms after clot removal by thrombolysis or thrombectomy should undergo provocative maneuvers under fluoroscopy to show the compression. These maneuvers recreate the most likely positions for compressing the subclavian vein. The abduction and externally rotated position is commonly recommended, but holding the arm overhead or pulling it down by the side, as if carrying a weight, also may show extrinsic compression. If one maneuver fails to show compression, others should be tried.

Contrast venography is not without pitfalls. False-positive results are possible from inadequate positioning of the patient or by the inflow of nonopacified blood, as in the confluence of the internal jugular vein and the subclavian vein. The contrast material itself can precipitate venous thrombosis.[89] Injection of contrast media into the subcutaneous tissues can cause blistering and tissue necrosis. Intravenous contrast media also can induce an anaphylactic reaction or nephrotoxicity.

Treatment

Historically the treatment of acute primary axillary-subclavian vein thrombosis relied on rest and elevation of the affected extremity along with systemic anticoagulation therapy. The incidence of long-term morbidity associated with conservative therapy was high because most of the patients are highly functional.[1,5,27,95] The management has become staged and multimodal.[74,90]

It is now accepted that optimal treatment of primary subclavian-axillary vein thrombosis requires restoration of luminal patency and removal of any extrinsic compression. Absent any contraindications, patients with acute primary subclavian-axillary vein thrombosis should undergo catheter-directed thrombolysis without delay. Patients treated within a few days of onset have a better response rate than patients treated within a few weeks.[74] The likelihood of success is a function of the time from thrombosis to the initiation of treatment. Zimmermann and colleagues[114] found residual lesions in 100% of patients given systemic urokinase if therapy was initiated more than 10 days from the onset of thrombosis. Wilson and associates,[112] using systemic streptokinase, had noted a marked increase in the incidence of incomplete thrombolysis if the clot was more than 7 days old. Adelman and colleagues[6] found that catheter-directed thrombolysis was not as successful if the thrombus was more than 8 days old. For primary subclavian-axillary vein thrombosis, opinions vary as regards the age of the thrombus that can be treated successfully, but according to the available data, beyond 10 to 14 days the chances of success diminish markedly.

If catheter-directed thrombolysis is successful, an underlying abnormality often is identified in or around the vein at the level of the costoclavicular space. If extrinsic (i.e., the venous abnormality is produced only with

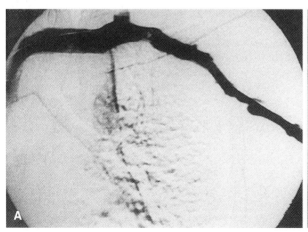

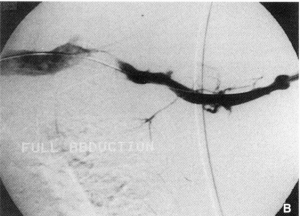

FIGURE 96-3 **A,** Post-thrombolysis venogram with the arm to the side. **B,** Post-thrombolysis venogram with the arm in full abduction.

abduction of the shoulder), a first rib resection done through the axillary or anterior cervical approach with external venolysis as needed is sufficient treatment and can be performed in the same hospital setting or at a later date. When the lesion is intrinsic (i.e., the abnormality is within the vein itself), the treatment and the timing are controversial. Options include anticoagulation and delayed outlet decompression depending on the level of symptoms, outlet decompression with external venolysis, outlet decompression followed by angioplasty and stenting, and outlet decompression with venous reconstruction.

Thrombectomy

Initially, subclavian vein patency was restored by operative thrombectomy. Short-term results were good in small series, but re-thrombosis was common,[66] unless thoracic outlet decompression followed. DeWeese and colleagues[3,32] reported a series of six patients who underwent operative thrombectomy along with thoracic outlet decompression via a first rib resection. There were no symptomatic limbs after 0 to 12 years of follow-up. Although the numbers were small, these authors established the effectiveness of this combined therapy. Some of the veins reoccluded in this small series, but despite that, the patients remained improved. It may be that bony decompression is often sufficient treatment even when the subclavian vein is thrombosed.

Operative thrombectomy is attractive in concept because vein recanalization and thoracic outlet decompression can be accomplished in the same setting. Exposure of the vein can be achieved after a medial claviculectomy or first rib resection from the anterior approach. Aziz and coworkers[8] reported excellent results in their series of four patients treated with combined thrombectomy and first rib resection. Green and associates[43] showed that medial claviculectomy with direct venous repair is well tolerated with excellent long-term results. Venous thrombectomy is now reserved for patients with a contraindication to, or failure of, thrombolytic therapy. In this setting, venous reconstruction is usually necessary either by excision of venous scarring and patch venoplasty or by a bypass using the ipsilateral jugular vein.

Thrombolytic Therapy

Catheter-directed thrombolysis is less morbid than operative thrombectomy, but is associated with a poor outcome if not combined with thoracic outlet decompression. In an early study, Zimmermann and coauthors[114] gave systemic urokinase to 13 primary patients with subclavian-axillary vein thrombosis. More than half of these patients were still symptomatic after treatment and had residual stenoses, as shown by venography. In a study by Sheeran and others,[113] nine patients underwent catheter-directed thrombolysis with urokinase but did not receive thoracic outlet decompression; 36% of patients had residual lesions, and 55% had symptomatic limbs. Recanalization of the vein without decompression of the thoracic outlet is not adequate for treatment of primary subclavian-axillary vein thrombosis.[1,65,90,92,95,108]

Although catheter-directed thrombolysis has proved effective in treating subclavian-axillary DVT, there are several disadvantages, including bleeding complications and cost. For these reasons, various approaches have been proposed to minimize the dose and duration of thrombolytic therapy, including (1) new pharmacologic agents with greater thrombolytic efficiency, (2) pulse-spray daily dosing rather than continuous infusion, and (3) adjunctive endovascular techniques including balloon maceration and mechanical thrombectomy.

Technique of Thrombolysis The ipsilateral basilic vein is accessed, and the thrombosed vein is crossed with a wire and pulse-spray catheter (2-cm infusion length; Angiodynamics, Queensbury, NY). The current recommendations for thrombolytic treatment emphasize short treatment times and adjunctive use of mechanical clot extraction devices. Currently available agents include urokinase (Abbott Laboratories, North Chicago, Ill), with initial doses of 120,000 to 250,000 U/hr; tissue plasminogen activator (Genentech, South San Francisco, Calif), with initial doses of 1.4 to 3.3 mg; and reteplase (Centocor, Malvern, Pa), with doses of 0.5 to 1 U/hr. The duration of therapy should be limited to 24 to 30 hours if possible. Mechanical thrombectomy devices are approved for use in hemodialysis grafts and can be used in an off-label fashion during venous thrombolysis. The devices available are the Amplatz Thrombectomy Device (Microvena, White Bear Lake, Minn), Angiojet (Possis, Minneapolis, Minn), Trerotola Percutaneous Thrombectomy Device (Arrow International, Reading, Pa), and Oasis (Boston Scientific/Medi-tech, Natick, Mass). These devices are advanced into the venous system through a 7F to 9F sheath. In most cases, two back-and-forth passes through the thrombosed venous segment are sufficient. Similar to balloon maceration, mechanical thrombectomy increases the surface area of residual thrombus and creates a central flow channel within an occluded vein, improving the efficiency of thrombolysis.

Management after Thrombolysis The management of a patient after thrombolysis is determined by the clinical result and the functionality of the patient. Patients can be separated into four groups: (1) successful thrombolysis and no residual lesion, (2) unsuccessful thrombolysis, (3) successful thrombolysis resulting in a normal axillosubclavian vein in the neutral position and a stenosis/occlusion at the costoclavicular space with shoulder abduction, and (4) incomplete thrombolysis that uncovers a residual intrinsic venous occlusion or severe stenosis at the level of the costoclavicular space with persistent clinical venous obstruction.

A small group of patients has no residual lesions after thrombolysis, and extrinsic compression cannot be shown by positional venography. One explanation is that the appropriate position was not mimicked properly during the study. The other possibility is that the thrombosis may have been caused by conditions specific to the precipitating event, not by repetitive trauma to the vein. A hypercoagulable condition must be aggressively pursued. If no evidence exists, 3 months of anticoagulation therapy and avoidance of vigorous arm use or extremes of position rather

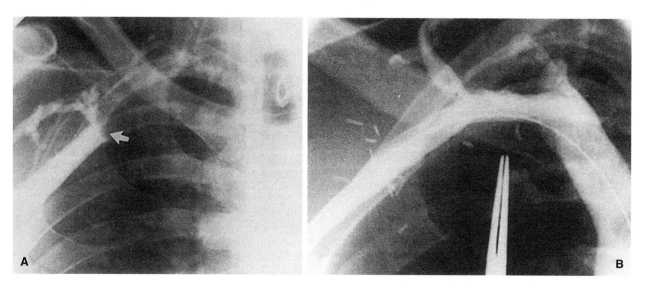

FIGURE 96-4 A, Venogram of acute primary subclavian-axillary vein thrombosis before therapy. *Arrow* shows site of occlusion. **B,** Venogram after successful thrombolysis and first rib resection. (From Molina JE: Need for emergency treatment in subclavian vein effort thrombosis. J Am Coll Surg 181:414-420, 1995.)

than empirical first rib resection is recommended.[95] If the patient has recurrent symptoms or thrombosis, re-evaluation is indicated. There are no data on the long-term outcome with this approach, but many authors do not perform thoracic outlet decompression if the positional venogram results are negative.[2,6,41,53,65,74]

Patients with unsuccessful thrombolysis should be anticoagulated with warfarin and discharged with appropriate follow-up with subsequent treatment depending on the level of upper extremity dysfunction present. Patients with significant symptoms should be considered for intervention. Some authors suggest that a period of 1 month is sufficient to distinguish between patients who do and do not require operative intervention. It is not inevitable that patients require intervention in this situation. Figure 96-4 is a venogram that shows the final result after thrombolysis and mechanical maceration. This patient was employed as a house painter and did not want any surgical procedures done. He continues to work with minimal obstructive symptoms 8 years after his event. A venogram (Fig. 96-5) shows the vein stenosed but with abundant collaterals.

Patients with demonstrable extrinsic compression should undergo first rib resection and external venolysis after successful thrombolysis during the same hospitalization.[6,65,108] Historical recommendations suggest that the patient receive oral anticoagulation agents and that 3 months elapse from thrombolysis to surgery.[74] This interval was to allow for healing of the endothelium and to avoid thrombosis of the vein at the time of operation. The delay also provided time to evaluate the significance of the obstruction after return of full use of the arm.[65] The disadvantages to waiting so long are the definite risk of re-thrombosis, the delay in returning to a normal lifestyle, and the need for a second hospitalization. Re-thrombosis rates in the literature range from 6% to 18%.[6,57,74] Molina[80,81] has advocated immediate first rib resection after thrombolysis to prevent chronic fibrous narrowing of the vein and to decrease the formation of collateral vessels,

which may adversely affect the patency of a subsequent stent or operative angioplasty. He reported no episodes of re-thrombosis in eight patients who presented with acute, first-time subclavian-axillary vein thrombosis. Urschel and Razzuk[108] performed thoracic outlet decompression 4 hours after stopping lytic therapy in 35 patients and noted no re-thromboses or excessive bleeding. Lee and colleagues[68] performed thoracic outlet decompression in 11 patients within 4 days of thrombolysis in 4, venolysis in 7, patch angioplasty in 3, and bypass in 2, with good results in 9 of 11. Chang and coauthors[23] performed thoracic outlet decompression followed by venography with stenting as needed, all within 24 hours of thrombolysis, with uniformly good results.

Patients in the third group should undergo bony decompression and venous repair by endovascular or open techniques. Patients with mild symptoms can be treated by

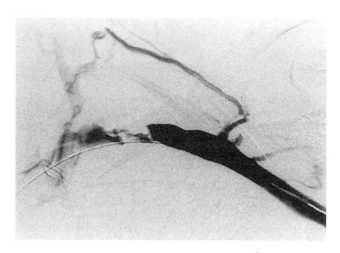

FIGURE 96-5 Venogram after thrombolysis but with a residual intrinsic stenosis.

transaxillary first rib resection with or without external venolysis.[6,14,52,74,90,92,98,101] The pivotal questions that must be addressed on an individual basis are whether and how the subclavian vein needs to be repaired when there is a severe intrinsic abnormality present on the postlysis venogram and symptoms of venous obstruction. Although it is clear that stents should not be placed before bony decompression, there are conflicting reports regarding their efficacy after decompression. Glanz and coworkers[38,39] performed balloon angioplasty in 19 primary subclavian-axillary vein thrombosis patients with persistent stenoses after thrombolysis. The initial success rate was 76% with a 1-year primary patency of 35% and a 2-year patency rate of only 6%. None of these patients underwent thoracic outlet decompression. Machleder[73] reported immediate re-thrombosis in 7 of 12 balloon angioplasties performed before first rib resection. In nine patients who had thoracic outlet decompression before angioplasty, seven underwent successful dilatation of venous stenoses. Two patients had lesions that could not be crossed with a guide wire. Other authors have confirmed the high rate of rethrombosis or restenosis in venous stenoses dilated without thoracic outlet decompression.[6,13,95] This high rate is not only because balloon angioplasty does nothing to address the underlying problem of extrinsic compression seen in effort thrombosis, for even after thoracic outlet decompression, some patients have stenoses resistant to balloon dilatation. Venous stenoses are composed of large amounts of collagen and elastin and may not fracture and remodel like atherosclerotic lesions.[95] Instead, these lesions tend to spring back to their original shape after dilatation. Figure 96-6 is a venogram of a subclavian vein in a patient who underwent thrombolysis, first rib resection, and venoplasty. Her arm is asymptomatic, and she remains fully functional. The residual venous fibrosis is evident, however. In the absence of obstructive symptoms, no further therapy is indicated.

Various types of stents have been used to counteract this intrinsic elastic recoil. If the underlying pathophysiology has not been addressed, primarily stenting venous stenoses (i.e., without thoracic outlet decompression) leads to poor outcomes because of stent deformation or fracture, which has occurred with balloon-expanded[16] and self-expanding stents.[78] After problems were reported with the Palmaz stent (Cordis Endovascular, Warren, NJ), it was recognized that when deployed, these stents, having no recoil properties, would be permanently deformed after external compression in the thoracic outlet.[16] It was thought that self-expanding stents, because they have an inherent memory and resume their shape after external compression, should fare better in this location. Meier and associates[78] placed self-expanding Wallstents in four patients without prior first rib resection. Two of these stents fractured, and the other two stents thrombosed. Four different patients underwent stent placement and thoracic outlet decompression with an acceptable clinical outcome. For this reason, most authors now suggest that the decision to use a stent to deal with a residual intrinsic stenosis requires a commitment also to perform a thoracic outlet decompression. Figure 96-7 shows a crushed Wallstent (Boston Scientific, Natick, Mass) placed before bony decompression in a patient successfully treated with thrombolytic therapy. This patient underwent a first rib resection with re-dilatation of the stent.

The proper timing and sequence of balloon angioplasty and stenting is still not defined. Most authors perform thoracic outlet decompression during the same hospital admission if the lesion is stented at the time of its discovery after thrombolysis. Most studies are small, however, and follow-up is limited. There are no direct comparisons of endovascular and surgical therapies. The relative rarity of primary subclavian-axillary vein thrombosis makes such direct comparisons unlikely. Chang and associates[23] evaluated 23 patients with primary axillary subclavian venous thrombosis treated with thrombolysis and immediate first rib resection and percutaneous transluminal angioplasty. Fourteen patients with residual venous stenoses underwent stenting. All patients were followed for a mean of 4 years (range 1 to 6 years). Nine of the 14 veins with stents remained patent. Two of these occluded within 2 days of the procedure, and both subsequently were found to have the factor V Leiden mutation.

Currently, direct operative repair of the subclavian vein is limited to cases in which (1) an endovascular solution

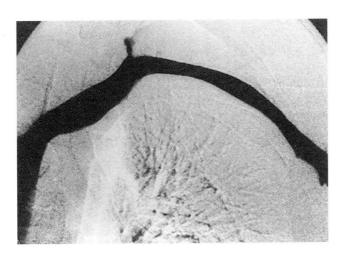

FIGURE 96-6 Venogram after percutaneous transluminal angioplasty and stenting of the subclavian vein with a Wallstent.

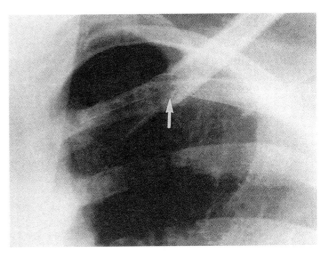

FIGURE 96-7 Fractured Wallstent (*arrow*) in the subclavian vein.

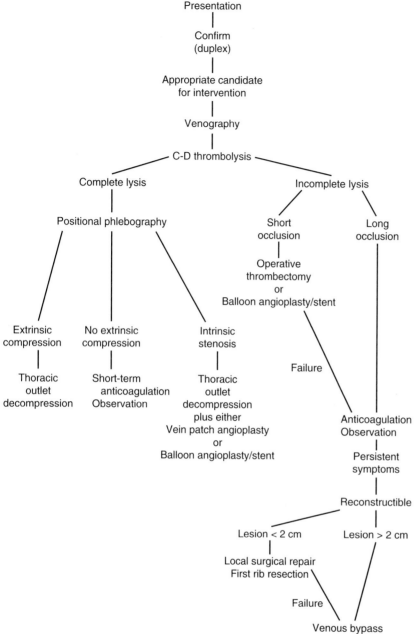

FIGURE 96-8 Algorithm for the treatment of primary subclavian-axillary vein thrombosis. C-D, catheter-directed.

has failed to restore luminal patency, and (2) the patient is severely symptomatic from venous obstruction (Fig. 96-8). The experience with short venous bypass for upper extremity venous occlusions is favorable but largely anecdotal. If the patient has the proper anatomy (i.e., a short occlusion extending not much distal to the entrance of the cephalic vein), internal jugular vein transposition or turndown is a good option. Green and colleagues,[43] Malcynski and associates,[75] and Sanders and Cooper[92] documented excellent results with this procedure. Molina[82] reported success in only 37% of patients with lesions longer than 2 cm. Longer occlusions require venous bypass. The saphenous vein is usually a poor size match for the larger subclavian vein, and use of the superficial femoral vein or the spiraled saphenous vein provides a better size match.

Patients with no accessible patent major veins proximally or with only distal, below-elbow veins patent (i.e., patients who are generally most symptomatic) cannot be candidates for any bypass. The use of prosthetic materials for the treatment of primary axillary subclavian thrombosis is not recommended. Table 96-1 summarizes the results of multiple series of venous reconstructions.

Direct repair of the subclavian vein and thoracic outlet decompression can be approached anteriorly with either a first rib resection or medial claviculectomy. Molina[82] advocates removal of the first rib and the scalene muscles through an anterior subclavicular approach and extension of the incision into the sternum and upward into the sternal notch. The mediastinal tissues are dissected away, and the innominate and subclavian veins are easily exposed. This

Table 96-1 Results of Short Upper Extremity Venous Bypass for Subclavian-Axillary Vein Occlusion

AUTHOR	NO. PATIENTS	BYPASS	PATENCY (%)	FOLLOW-UP
Inahara[69]	1	GSV axillojugular bypass	100	11 mo
Hashmonai et al[59]	1	Cephalic vein crossover	100	5.5 mo
Hansen et al[57]	1	IJ	100	1 yr
Currier et al[34]	6	PTFE axillojugular bypass	50	1-3 yr
Malcynski et al[88]	2	IJ	100	5 yr
Molina[94]	4	GSV axillojugular bypass	50	4 yr
Sanders and Cooper[109]	5	IJ	100	2-4 yr
Sanders and Cooper[109]	1	PTFE axillojugular bypass	100	9 mo
Green et al[52]	11	IJ/GSV	100	11 yr

GSV, greater saphenous vein; IJ, internal jugular vein; PTFE, polytetrafluoroethylene.

approach is useful when venous reconstruction of the innominate vein is required but does not provide sufficient access to the jugular vein for a transposition.[43,82] DeWeese and coworkers[32] recognized that exposure of the subclavian vein for operative thrombectomy was facilitated when medial claviculectomy was performed. Medial claviculectomy is an effective treatment for many entities affecting the sternoclavicular joint, such as osteomyelitis, tumors, arthritis, fractures, and subluxations/dislocations. In these settings, patients undergoing excision of the medial clavicle can expect full range of motion, acceptable cosmesis, and relief of symptoms. Regeneration of the excised portion occurs frequently, especially in younger patients, probably because the medial clavicular epiphysis is the last of the long bones to ossify and the last to fuse. Excision of the medial clavicle offers a particular advantage over first rib resection in the effort thrombosis syndrome when a significant intrinsic abnormality persists after thrombolysis because it allows for easy access to the involved venous structures. For properly selected patients (patients with significant arm swelling, patients with significant aching after modest arm use, highly active patients) with significant subclavian venous obstruction after thrombolysis, the claviculectomy and venous reconstruction approach seems to provide excellent long-term patency with relatively few side effects.

■ SECONDARY SUBCLAVIAN-AXILLARY VEIN THROMBOSIS

Secondary subclavian-axillary vein thrombosis can be caused by a variety of factors. Where possible, the treatment is directed at the underlying cause and the occlusion itself. Many patients have one or more risk factors for DVT. The common denominator in most patients with secondary subclavian-axillary vein thrombosis is a central venous catheter. There are currently more than 5 million central venous catheters inserted per year in the United States.[95] It is a relatively rare patient who has severe congestive heart failure, sepsis, an underlying malignancy, or other systemic risk factors for thrombosis without a concurrent central venous line. Because of the widespread and increasing use of these catheters and the related increase in upper extremity DVT, this section focuses primarily on catheter-related thrombosis.

Incidence

The overall incidence of catheter-associated thrombosis has been difficult to determine. The literature has not shown consistency in the degree of aggressiveness or in the methods of detecting the presence of subclavian-axillary vein thrombosis. Estimates of the overall incidence range from 2% to 26% of all central lines placed.[76,77] Overall, approximately one third of patients with central lines eventually have DVT, but only 10% to 15% of these are symptomatic. The risk of thrombosis after internal jugular vein insertion is four times greater than after subclavian vein insertion.[105]

Etiology

Virchow's triad (stasis, hypercoagulability, and intimal trauma) plays a major role in secondary subclavian-axillary vein thrombosis. From the time a central venous catheter is placed, there is ongoing injury to the vein. The method of insertion, composition, size, and duration of use of the catheter all are important in the development of a thrombus. Difficulty in gaining percutaneous access to a central vein increases the risk of thrombosis.[52,61,99,103] Strategies to reduce the incidence of thrombotic complications are listed in Table 96-2. These strategies include recognizing risk factors for difficult catheterizations, getting help from an experienced operator, using ultrasound guidance for internal jugular cannulation, and avoiding routine catheter changes.[77]

When central venous catheters were first developed, they were composed of relatively inflexible polyvinyl chloride and polyethylene. Newer catheters composed of Silastic and polyurethane are softer and more flexible and cause less injury to the venous intima. A reduced rate of thrombosis has been found with less rigid catheters. Larger diameter catheters (e.g., sheath introducers and catheters used for hemodialysis) also are relatively inflexible and result in a higher incidence of subclavian vein thrombosis. Besides intimal injury, larger catheters also may cause stasis within the vein owing to their size in relation to the diameter of the blood vessel.[17,54,69,86,110]

Thrombosis rates are high with short-term and long-term catheterizations.[10,42,45,50,69,105,110] Catheter-related thrombosis is most common in hemodialysis and oncology patients and patients requiring long-term parenteral nutrition. Parenteral

Table 96-2	Catheter-Associated Thrombosis: Strategies to Reduce Thrombotic Complications
STRATEGY	**RATIONALE**
Recognition of risk factors for difficult cannulation	History of failed attempts, skeletal anomalies, prior surgical sites[107]
Seek assistance	Insertion by a physician with >50 cannulations is 50% less likely to result in complication than insertion by physician with <50 cannulations[107]
Use ultrasound for IJ cannulations	Reduces time and incidence of unsuccessful cannulation and carotid artery puncture and hematoma[116]
Do not schedule routine catheter changes	Increases risk of complications[31]

IJ, internal jugular vein.

Data from Ryan JA, et al: N Engl J Med 290:757-761, 1974; and Steed DL, et al: J Vasc Surg 4:28-32, 1986..

nutrition and many cancer chemotherapeutic agents are directly toxic to vascular endothelium because of hyperosmolarity and extremes of pH.[37] *Drug incompatibility* also may contribute to venous trauma.[71] Other risk factors related to the catheter include left-sided cannulation,[42] placement of the tip of the catheter in veins other than the superior vena cava,[18] the presence of bilateral catheters,[42] and the caliber of the catheter.[79]

Besides local trauma from the catheter, many patients have systemic factors that contribute to thrombosis. The presence of malignancy is probably the best-studied risk factor for thrombosis. The hypercoagulable state associated with malignancy has been well documented.[53,69] Patients with solid tumors seem to be at higher risk for thrombosis than patients with hematologic malignancies.[71,83,104] Other disease processes, such as inflammatory bowel disease, sepsis, and obesity, also may be associated with hypercoagulability.[111]

Stasis also plays a role in the development of secondary subclavian-axillary vein thrombosis. Many critically ill patients require central venous access for nutritional support and hemodynamic monitoring. Congestive heart failure, hypotension, dehydration, and prolonged bed rest all can lead to stasis in the venous system.[50,69]

One final issue in the etiology of catheter-associated thrombosis is the presence of a *fibrin sheath*, which invariably forms around an indwelling catheter. Venographic and autopsy studies have documented the presence of a fibrin sheath in almost all patients whose catheters have been in place for at least 1 week. The fibrin sheath is a result of the catheter surface's being exposed to circulating platelets. To date, there is no evidence to suggest that the fibrin sheath contributes to the formation of an occlusive thrombus.[9,18,25,55,72,105]

Clinical Presentation

The clinical presentation of catheter-associated thrombosis may be subtle. The onset of thrombosis is usually slower than in primary subclavian-axillary vein thrombosis, and the affected segment is shorter; this may allow time for adequate collateral vessels to form. Also, many patients with long-term indwelling catheters are critically ill or have other debilitating illnesses that limit the use of their upper extremity. These patients may be asymptomatic mainly because they are unable to use their arms enough to produce symptoms. These reasons may account for the low incidence of clinically evident thrombosis.[29,50,72,76] Symptomatic patients present similarly to patients with primary subclavian-axillary vein thrombosis. Most patients have edema of the affected extremity, with some experiencing pain over the vein and in the arm, and distended veins around the shoulder girdle. In a large epidemiologic study, the incidence of pain, distended veins, erythema, and acrocyanosis was lower in catheter-associated thrombosis than in primary subclavian-axillary vein thrombosis.[77]

The natural history of catheter-associated thrombosis is usually indolent. Donayre and colleagues[33] found that of 10 limbs that initially presented with symptomatic thrombosis, none were symptomatic in long-term follow-up. Most patients who are symptomatic initially become asymptomatic without further treatment other than removal of the catheter.[42] The isolated nature of these thromboses and the extensive venous collaterals of the shoulder girdle limit the long-term sequelae of catheter-associated thrombosis. As mentioned, pulmonary embolus is common, even in secondary subclavian-axillary vein thrombosis. In a prospective study, Monreal and colleagues[84] examined 79 patients, all of whom had indwelling central venous catheters, with ventilation-perfusion scans. Of these patients, 16% had evidence of pulmonary embolism; of these patients, however, only 31% were symptomatic. Although many patients with subclavian-axillary vein thromboses are clinically asymptomatic, there is still a risk of pulmonary embolism. Venous gangrene is a rare complication of catheter-related thrombosis and is usually a preterminal event.[21,60]

Treatment

Because there are no controlled studies on treatment, therapy guidelines are based on observational reports. The treatment of catheter-associated thrombosis depends primarily on the patient's symptoms and the need for further central venous access. The catheter does not need to be removed unless access is no longer required. In symptomatic patients who no longer need lines, catheter removal is usually adequate treatment for the thrombosis itself.[19,29,42] Patients may remain asymptomatic even without oral anticoagulation, but short-term therapy is indicated to prevent clot extension, recurrence, or pulmonary embolus.[69] If the patient still requires central venous access and if the catheter is functioning, anticoagulation agents are given until the catheter is no longer needed. The thrombus may resolve without removal of the catheter.[19,42]

Symptomatic patients should be anticoagulated. Symptoms usually resolve after a couple of days of heparin therapy.[19,29,42,65] If the need for central venous access persists, anticoagulation should be continued until the catheter can be removed.[42] When thrombosis occurs with a poorly positioned catheter, the catheter should be removed. If thrombolysis is used in the setting of a more proximal occlusion, the catheter should be left in place to decrease the likelihood of bleeding from the puncture site. When angioplasty is performed and relief of the stenosis is achieved, the catheter can be removed.

Because the course of catheter-associated thrombosis is usually benign, thrombolytic therapy has only a limited role. The direct instillation of thrombolytic agents into a catheter has been successful, at least temporarily, in reopening thrombosed catheters.[19] This procedure can be done expeditiously on an outpatient basis. Thrombolytic therapy also has been employed to salvage catheters in completely occluded veins.

Beygui and colleagues[14] successfully treated six of six veins with catheter-related thrombosis with thrombolysis. Seigel and coworkers[94] treated 38 secondary subclavian-axillary vein thrombosis patients with catheter-directed thrombolysis and were able to salvage catheter access in 87%. Because these patients required 1 to 5 days of thrombolytic therapy to lyse the clot and because this study was uncontrolled, it is unknown how many patients could have had access restored with transcatheter infusion of lytic agents and anticoagulation with less morbidity and cost. Until more data are forthcoming, it seems reasonable to institute thrombolytic therapy only for significantly symptomatic patients when conventional therapy fails or when the patient has an extended need for catheter access and is in danger of running out of available venous sites.

Endovascular therapies are more successful in treating secondary axillary-subclavian vein thrombosis than they are in treating the primary form. Symptomatic patients should be treated with thrombolytic and mechanical clot removal. Residual disease in symptomatic patients can be treated with self-expanding stents. Stents are particularly effective in the treatment of superior vena cava lesions.[93,95,97] The patency rates after stenting of subclavian and axillary venous stenoses in hemodialysis patients are not as favorable, and repeated angioplasty or surgical bypass is indicated. Seigel and colleagues[94] reported a 64% early success rate for angioplasty in patients with residual stenoses after thrombolysis. Stents should be used only in situations in which satisfactory flow cannot be achieved with the use of oversized angioplasty balloons and high-pressure prolonged inflation.[107] Nitinol self-expanding stents oversized by 2 mm with 1 to 2 cm axial coverage on each side of the stenosis are a good choice in this location. Careful follow-up is necessary because repeated dilatations are often required.

Surgical bypass with polytetrafluoroethylene and greater saphenous vein have shown mixed results, but generally the longer the bypass, particularly with the use of a prosthetic conduit, the worse the outcome.[47,49,92] In constructing these bypasses, most authors recommend placing an arteriovenous fistula distal to the bypass for 6 weeks to 3 months. With longer or prosthetic bypasses, closure of a well-tolerated arteriovenous fistula is not advised.[28,67,75,90]

With the increasing recognition of catheter-associated thrombosis, prevention of thrombus formation has been emphasized. Fabri's group[36] administered 3000 U of heparin per liter of total parenteral nutrition in 24 patients with central venous catheters. There was a significant decrease in the incidence of subclavian-axillary vein thrombosis compared with the control group. Other authors have confirmed that the addition of heparin to total parenteral nutrition formula decreases the incidence of catheter-associated thrombosis.[19,58]

There is not a clear role for prophylactic anticoagulation in high-risk patient populations. Bern and coworkers[12] randomized 82 patients with long-term central venous catheters for cancer chemotherapy to receive 1 mg/day of warfarin or none. At the end of 90 days, there was a significantly lower incidence of thrombosis in the patients taking warfarin. There were no adverse bleeding complications in the group receiving oral anticoagulation. Bisset and associates[15] found that anticoagulation to an international normalized ratio of 2.0 to 3.0 in an oncology patient population was effective in the management of catheter-related thrombosis, but that prophylactic administration of 1 to 3 mg of warfarin per day was not effective in preventing catheter-related thrombosis. Although there may be some benefit to prophylactic anticoagulation in high-risk cancer patients, the data are not conclusive.

■ REFERENCES

1. AbuRahma AF, Sadler D, Stuart P, et al: Conventional versus thrombolytic therapy in spontaneous (effort) axillary-subclavian vein thrombosis. Am J Surg 161:459-465, 1991.
2. AbuRahma AF, Short YS, White JF, et al: Treatment alternatives for axillary-subclavian thrombosis: Long-term follow-up. Cardiovasc Surg 4:783-787, 1996.
3. Adams JT, DeWeese JA: "Effort" thrombosis of the axillary and subclavian veins. J Trauma 11:923-930, 1971.
4. Adams JT, DeWeese JA, Mahoney EB, et al: Intermittent subclavian vein obstruction without thrombosis. Surgery 63:147-165, 1968.
5. Adams JT, McEvoy RK, DeWeese JA: Primary deep venous thrombosis of upper extremity. Arch Surg 91:29-42, 1965.
6. Adelman MA, Stone DH, Riles TS, et al: A multidisciplinary approach to the treatment of Paget-Schroetter syndrome. Ann Vasc Surg 11:149-154, 1997.
7. Aubaniac R: L'injection intraveineuse sousclaviculaire: Avantage et technique. Presse Med 60:1456, 1952.
8. Aziz S, Straehley CJ, Whelan TJ: Effort-related axillosubclavian vein thrombosis. Am J Surg 152:57-61, 1986.
9. Balestreri L, DeCicco M, Matovic M, et al: Central venous catheter-related thrombosis in clinically asymptomatic oncologic patients: A phlebographic study. Eur J Radiol 20:108-111, 1995.
10. Barker NW, Nygaard KK, Watters W, et al: Statistical study of postoperative venous thrombosis and pulmonary embolism: Location of thrombosis: Relation of thrombosis and embolism. Proc Mayo Clin 16:33-37, 1941.
11. Becker GJ, Holden RW, Rabe FE, et al: Local thrombolytic therapy for subclavian and axillary vein thrombosis. Radiology 149:419-423, 1983.
12. Bern MM, Lokich JJ, Wallach SR, et al: Very low doses of warfarin can prevent thrombosis in central venous catheters. Ann Intern Med 112:423-428, 1990.
13. Benenati J, Shlansky-Goldberg R, Meglin A, et al: Thrombolytic and Antiplatelet Therapy in Peripheral Vascular Disease with Use of Reteplase and/or Abciximab: The SCVIR Consultants' Conference; May 22, 2000; Orlando, FL. J Vasc Interv Radiol 12:795-805, 2001.

14. Beygui RE, Olcott C, Dalman RL: Subclavian vein thrombosis: Outcome analysis based on etiology and modality of treatment. Ann Vasc Surg 11:247-255, 1997.

15. Bisset D, Kaye SB, Baxter G, et al: Successful thrombolysis of SVC thrombosis associated with Hickman lines and continuous infusion chemotherapy. Clin Oncol 8:247-249, 1996.

16. Bjarnason H, Hunter DW, Crain MR, et al: Collapse of a Palmaz stent in the subclavian vein. AJR Am J Roentgenol 160:1123-1124, 1993.

17. Bottino J, McCreadie KB, Groschel DHM, et al: Long-term intravenous therapy with peripherally inserted silicone elastomer central venous catheters in patients with malignant diseases. Cancer 43:1937-1943, 1979.

18. Bozzetti F, Scarpa D, Terno G, et al: Subclavian vein thrombosis due to indwelling catheters: A prospective study on 52 patients. J Parenter Enteral Nutr 7:560-562, 1983.

19. Brismar B, Hardstedt C, Jacobson S, et al: Reduction of catheter-associated thrombosis in parenteral nutrition by intravenous heparin therapy. Arch Surg 117:1196-1199, 1982.

20. Broviac JW, Cole JJ, Scribner BH: A silicone rubber atrial catheter for prolonged parenteral alimentation. Surg Gynecol Obstet 136:603-606, 1973.

21. Campbell CB, Chandler JG, Tegtmeyer CJ, et al: Axillary, subclavian, and brachiocephalic vein obstruction. Surgery 82:816-826, 1977.

22. Chandrasekar R, Nott DM, Enabi L, et al: Upper limb venous gangrene, a lethal condition. Eur J Vasc Surg 7:475-477, 1993.

23. Chang BB, Kreienberg PB, Darling RC III, et al: Long-term results in patients treated with thrombolysis, thoracic inlet decompression, and subclavian vein stenting for Paget-Schroetter syndrome. J Vasc Surg 33S:100-105, 2001.

24. Chang R, Cannon O, Chen C, et al: Daily catheter-directed single dosing of t-PA in treatment of acute deep venous thrombosis of the lower extremity. J Vasc Interv Radiol 12:247-252, 2001.

25. Cook D, Randolph A, Kernerman P, et al: Central venous catheter replacement strategies: A systematic review of the literature. Crit Care Med 25:1417-1424, 1997.

26. Coon WW, Willis PW: Thrombosis of axillary and subclavian veins. Arch Surg 94:657-663, 1967.

27. Crowell DL: Effort thrombosis of the subclavian and axillary veins: Review of the literature and case report with two-year follow-up with venography. Ann Intern Med 52:1337-1343, 1960.

28. Currier CB, Widder S, Ali A, et al: Surgical management of subclavian and axillary vein thrombosis in patients with a functioning arteriovenous fistula. Surgery 104:561-567, 1986.

29. Damascelli B, Patelli G, Frigerio L, et al: Placement of long-term central venous catheters in outpatients. AJR Am J Roentgenol 168:1235-1239, 1997.

30. Daskalakis E, Bouhoutsos J: Subclavian and axillary vein compression of musculoskeletal origin. Br J Surg 67:573-576, 1980.

31. Demondion X, Boutry N, Drizenko A, et al: Thoracic outlet: Anatomic correlation with MR imaging. AJR Am J Roentgenol 175:417-422, 2000.

32. DeWeese JA, Adams JT, Gaiser DL: Subclavian venous thrombectomy. Circulation 42(Suppl):158-163, 1970.

33. Donayre CE, White RW, Mehringer SM, et al: Pathogenesis determines late morbidity of axillosubclavian vein thrombosis. Am J Surg 152:179-184, 1986.

34. Drapanas T, Curran WL: Thrombectomy in the treatment of "effort" thrombosis of the axillary and subclavian veins. J Trauma 6:107-119, 1966.

35. Dudrick JJ, Wilmore DW, Vans HM, et al: Long-term total parenteral nutrition with growth, development, and positive nitrogen balance. Surgery 64:134-142, 1968.

36. Fabri PJ, Mirtallo JM, Ebbert ML, et al: Clinical effect of non-thrombotic total nutrition catheters. J Parenter Enteral Nutr 8:705-707, 1984.

37. Fonkalsrud EW: The effect of pH in glucose infusions on development of thrombophlebitis. J Surg Res 8:539, 1968.

38. Glanz S, Gordon DH, Butt KMH, et al: The role of percutaneous angioplasty in the management of chronic hemodialysis fistulas. Ann Surg 206:777-781, 1987.

39. Glanz S, Gordon DH, Lipkowitz GS, et al: Axillary and subclavian vein stenosis: Percutaneous angioplasty. Radiology 168:371-373, 1988.

40. Glass BA: The relationship of axillary venous thrombosis to the thoracic outlet compression syndrome. Ann Thorac Surg 19:613-621, 1975.

41. Gloviczki P, Kazmier FS, Hollier LH: Axillary-subclavian venous occlusion: The morbidity of a non-lethal disease. J Vasc Surg 4:333-337, 1986.

42. Gould JR, Carloss HW, Skinner WL: Groshong catheter-associated subclavian venous thrombosis. Am J Med 95:419-423, 1993.

43. Green RM, Waldman D, Ouriel K, et al: Claviculectomy for subclavian venous repair: Long-term functional results. J Vasc Surg 32:315-321, 2000.

44. Hagspiel KD, Spinosa DJ, Angle JF, et al: Diagnosis of vascular compression at the thoracic outlet using gadolinium-enhanced high-resolution ultrafast MR angiography in abduction and adduction. Cardiovasc Interv Radiol 23:152-154, 2000.

45. Haire WD, Lieberman RP, Edney J, et al: Hickman catheter-induced thoracic vein thrombosis. Cancer 66:900-908, 1990.

46. Haire WD, Lynch TG, Lund GB, et al: Limitations of magnetic resonance imaging and ultrasound-directed (duplex) scanning in the diagnosis of subclavian vein thrombosis. J Vasc Surg 13:391-397, 1991.

47. Hansen B, Feins RS, Detmer DE: Simple extra-anatomic jugular vein bypass for subclavian vein thrombosis. J Vasc Surg 2:921-923, 1985.

48. Harley DP, White RA, Nelson RJ, et al: Pulmonary embolism secondary to venous thrombosis of the arm. Am J Surg 147:221-224, 1984.

49. Hashmonai M, Schramek A, Farbstein J: Cephalic vein cross-over bypass for subclavian vein thrombosis: A case report. Surgery 80:563-564, 1976.

50. Henk-Jan Baarslag, van Beek EJR, Koopman MMW, et al: Prospective study of color duplex ultrasonography in patients suspected of having deep venous thrombosis of the upper extremities. Ann Intern Med 136:865-872, 2002.

51. Hill SL, Berry RE: Subclavian vein thrombosis: A continuing challenge. Surgery 108:1-9, 1990.

52. Hingorani A, Ascher E, Lorenson E, et al: Upper extremity deep venous thrombosis and its impact on morbidity and mortality rates in a hospital-based population. J Vasc Surg 26:853-860, 1997.

53. Horattas MC, Wright DJ, Fenton AH, et al: Changing concepts of deep venous thrombosis of the upper extremity: Report of a series and review of the literature. Surgery 104:561-567, 1988.

54. Horne MK, May DJ, Alexander HR, et al: Venographic surveillance of tunneled venous access devices in adult oncology patients. Ann Surg Oncol 2:174-178, 1995.

55. Hoshal VC, Ause RG, Hoskins PA, et al: Fibrin sleeve formation on indwelling central venous catheters. Arch Surg 102:353-358, 1971.

56. Hughes ESR: Venous obstruction in the upper extremity. Int Abstr Surg 88:89-127, 1949.

57. Hurlbert SN, Rutherford RB: Primary subclavian-axillary vein thrombosis. Ann Vasc Surg 9:217-223, 1995.

58. Imperial J, Bistrian BR, Bothe A Jr, et al: Limitation of central vein thrombosis in total parenteral nutrition by continuous infusion of low-dose heparin. J Am Coll Nutr 2:63-73, 1982.

59. Inahara T: Surgical treatment of "effort" thrombosis of the axillary and subclavian veins. Am Surg 34:479-483, 1968.

60. Kammen BF, Soulen MC: Phlegmasia cerulea dolens of the upper extremity. J Vasc Interv Radiol 6:283-286, 1995.

61. Kearns RJ, Coleman S, Wehner JG: Complications of long-arm catheters: A randomized trial of central vs. peripheral tip location. J Parenter Enteral Nutr 20:20-24, 1996.

62. Kerr TM, Lutter KS, Moeller DM, et al: Upper extremity venous thrombosis diagnosed by duplex scanning. Am J Surg 160:202-206, 1990.

63. Kleinsasser LJ: "Effort" thrombosis of the axillary and subclavian veins. Arch Surg 59:258-274, 1949.

64. Koksoy C, Kuzu A, Kutlay J, et al: The diagnostic value of colour Doppler ultrasound in central venous catheter related thrombosis. Clin Radiol 50:687-689, 1995.

65. Kommareddy A, Zaroukain MH, Hossounia HI: Upper extremity deep venous thrombosis. Semin Thromb Hemost 28:89-99, 2002.

66. Kunkel JM, Machleder HI: Treatment of Paget-Schroetter syndrome. Arch Surg 124:1153-1158, 1989.

67. Lee MC, Grassi CJ, Belkin M, et al: Early operative intervention after thrombolytic therapy for primary subclavian vein thrombosis: An effective treatment approach. J Vasc Surg 27:1101-1108, 1998.

68. Lee WA, Hill BB, Harris JJ, et al: Surgical intervention is not required for all patients with subclavian vein thrombosis. J Vasc Surg 32:57-67, 2000.

69. Lindblad B: Thromboembolic complications and central venous catheters. Lancet 2:936, 1982.

70. Lindblad B, Tengborn L, Bergqvist D: Deep vein thrombosis of the axillary-subclavian veins. Eur J Vasc Surg 2:161-165, 1988.

71. Lokich JJ, Becker B: Subclavian vein thrombosis in patients treated with infusion chemotherapy for advanced malignancy. Cancer 52:1586-1589, 1983.

72. Lokich JJ, Bothe A Jr, Benotte P, et al: Complications and management of implanted venous access catheters. J Clin Oncol 3:710-717, 1985.

73. Machleder HI: Upper extremity venous thrombosis. Semin Vasc Surg 3:219-226, 1990.

74. Machleder HI: Evaluation of a new treatment strategy for Paget-Schroetter syndrome: Spontaneous thrombosis of the axillary-subclavian vein. J Vasc Surg 17:305-317, 1993.

75. Malcynski J, O'Donnell TF, Mackey WC, et al: Long-term results of treatment for axillary subclavian vein thrombosis. Can J Surg 4:365-371, 1993.

76. McDonough JJ, Altemeier WA: Subclavian venous thrombosis secondary to indwelling catheters. Surg Gynecol Obstet 133:397-400, 1971.

77. McGee DC, Gould MK: Preventing complications of central venous catheterization. N Engl J Med 348:1123-1133, 2003.

78. Meier GH, Pollak JS, Rosenblatt M, et al: Initial experience with venous stents in exertional axillary-subclavian vein thrombosis. J Vasc Surg 24:974-983, 1996.

79. Merrer J, De Jonghe B, Golliot F, et al: Complications of femoral and subclavian venous catheterization in critically ill patients: A randomized controlled trial. JAMA 286:700-707, 2001.

80. Molina JE: Surgery for effort thrombosis of the subclavian vein. J Thorac Cardiovasc Surg 103:341-346, 1992.

81. Molina JE: Need for emergency treatment in subclavian vein effort thrombosis. J Am Coll Surg 181:414-420, 1995.

82. Molina JE: A new surgical approach to the innominate and subclavian vein. J Vasc Surg 27:576-581, 1998.

83. Monreal M, Lafoz E, Ruiz J, et al: Upper-extremity deep venous thrombosis and pulmonary embolism. Chest 99:280-283, 1991.

84. Monreal M, Raventos A, Lerma R, et al: Pulmonary embolism in patients with upper extremity DVT associated with venous central lines—a prospective study. Thromb Haemost 72:548-550, 1994.

85. Mustafa BO, Rathbun SW, Whitsett TL: Sensitivity and specificity of ultrasonography in the diagnosis of upper extremity deep vein thrombosis: A systemic review. Arch Intern Med 162:401-404, 2002.

86. Openshaw KL, Picus D, Hicks ME, et al: Interventional radiologic placement of Hohn central venous catheters: results and complications in 100 consecutive patients. J Vasc Interv Radiol 5:111-115, 1994.

87. Paget J: Clinical Lectures and Essays. London, Longmans Green & Co, 1875.

88. Prescott SM, Tikoff G: Deep venous thrombosis of the upper extremity: A reappraisal. Circulation 59:350-355, 1979.

89. Raad I: Intravascular-catheter-related infections. Lancet 351:893-898, 1998.

90. Rutherford RB, Hurlbert SN: Primary subclavian-axillary vein thrombosis: Consensus and commentary. Cardiovasc Surg 4:420-423, 1996.

91. Ryan JA, Abel RM, Abbott WM, et al: Catheter complications in total parenteral nutrition: A prospective study of 200 consecutive patients. N Engl J Med 290:757-761, 1974.

92. Sanders RJ, Cooper MA: Surgical management of subclavian vein obstruction, including six cases of subclavian vein bypass. Surgery 118:856-863, 1995.

93. Schlindler N, Vogelzang RL: Superior vena cava syndrome: Experience with endovascular stents and surgical therapy. Surg Clin North Am 79:683-694, 1999.

94. Seigel EL, Jew AC, Delcore R, et al: Thrombolytic therapy for catheter-related thrombosis. Am J Surg 166:716-719, 1993.

95. Sharafuddin MJ, Sun S, Hoballah JJ: Endovascular management of venous thrombotic diseases of the upper torso and extremities. J Vasc Interv Radiol 13:975-990, 2002.

96. Sheeran SR, Hallisey MJ, Murphy TP, et al: Local thrombolytic therapy as part of a multidisciplinary approach to acute axillosubclavian vein thrombosis (Paget-Schroetter syndrome). J Vasc Interv Radiol 8:253-260, 1997.

97. Shoenfeld R, Hermans H, Novick A, et al: Stenting of proximal venous obstruction to maintain hemodialysis access. J Vasc Surg 19:532-539, 1994.

98. Smith-Behn J, Althar R, Katz W: Primary thrombosis of the axillary/subclavian vein. South Med J 79:1176-1178, 1986.

99. Sznajder JI, Zveibil FR, Bitterman H, et al: Central vein catheterization: Failure and complication rates by three percutaneous approaches. Arch Intern Med 146:259-261, 1986.

100. Stevenson IM, Parry EW: Radiological study of the aetiological factors in venous obstruction of the upper limb. J Cardiovasc Surg 16:581-585, 1975.

101. Strange-Vognsen HH, Hauch O, Andersen J, et al: Resection of the first rib, following deep arm vein thrombolysis in patients with thoracic outlet syndrome. J Cardiovasc Surg 30:430-433, 1989.

102. Swinton NW, Edgett JW, Hall RJ: Primary subclavian-axillary vein thrombosis. Circulation 38:737-745, 1968.

103. Teichgraber UK, Benter T, Gebel M, et al: A sonographically guided technique for central venous access. AJR Am J Roentgenol 169:731-733, 1997.

104. Tilney NL, Griffiths HJG, Edwards EA: Natural history of major venous thrombosis of the upper extremity. Arch Surg 101:792-796, 1970.

105. Timsit JF, Farkas JC, Boyer JM, et al: Central vein catheter-related thrombosis in intensive care patients: Incidence, risk factors, and relationship with catheter-related sepsis. Chest 114:207-213, 1998.

106. Torosian MH, Meranze S, Mullen JL, et al: Central venous access with occlusive superior central venous thrombosis. Ann Surg 203:30-33, 1986.

107. Turmel-Rodrigues L, Bourquelot P, Raynaud A, et al: Primary stent placement in hemodialysis-related central venous stenoses: The dangers of a potential "radiologic dictatorsip." Radiology 217:600-602, 2000.

108. Urschel HC, Razzuk MA: Improved management of the Paget-Schroetter syndrome secondary to thoracic outlet compression. Ann Thorac Surg 52:1217-1221, 1991.

109. Von Schroetter L: Erkrankungen der gefasse. In: Nathnagel Handbuch der Pathologie und Therapie. Vienna, Holder, 1884.

110. Wanscher M, Prifelt JJ, Smith-Sivertsen C, et al: Thrombosis caused by polyurethane double-lumen subclavian superior vena cava catheter and hemodialysis. Crit Care Med 16:624-628, 1988.

111. Warden GD, Wilmore DW, Pruitt BA: Central venous thrombosis: A hazard of medical progress. J Trauma 13:620-625, 1973.

112. Wilson JJ, Zahn CA, Newman H: Fibrinolytic therapy for idiopathic subclavian-axillary vein thrombosis. Am J Surg 159:208-211, 1990.

113. Yim CD, Sane SS, Bjarnason H: Superior vena cava stenting. Radiol Clin North Am 38:409-424, 2000.

114. Zimmerman R, Mor IH, Harenberg J, et al: Urokinase therapy of subclavian-axillary vein thrombosis. Klin Wochenschr 59:851-856, 1981.

■ SELECTED READING

Beathard GA: Gianturco self-expanding stent in the treatment of stenosis in dialysis access grafts. Kidney Int 43:872-877, 1993.

Beathard GA: Percutaneous transvenous angioplasty in the treatment of vascular access stenosis. Kidney Int 42:1390-1397, 1992.

Brismar B, Hardstedt C, Jacobson S: Diagnosis of thrombosis by catheter phlebography after prolonged central venous catheterization. Ann Surg 194:779-783, 1981.

Brothers TE, Von Moll LK, Niederhuber JE, et al: Experience with subcutaneous infusion ports in three hundred patients. Surg Gynecol Obstet 166:295-301, 1988.

Burt ME, Dunnick MR, Krudy AG, et al: Prospective evaluation of subclavian vein thrombosis during total parenteral nutrition by contrast venography. Clin Res 29:264A, 1981.

Cohen GS, Braunstein L, Ball DS, et al: Effort thrombosis: Effective treatment with vascular stent after unrelieved venous stenosis following a surgical release procedure. Cardiovasc Interv Radiol 19:37-39, 1996.

Druy EM, Trout HH, Giordano JM, et al: Lytic therapy in the treatment of axillary and subclavian vein thrombosis. J Vasc Surg 2:821-827, 1985.

Gmelin E, Winterhoff R, Rinast E: Insufficient hemodialysis access fistulas: Late results of treatment with percutaneous balloon angioplasty. Radiology 171:657-660, 1989.

Gray RJ, Horton KM, Dolmatch BL, et al: Use of Wallstents for hemodialysis access-related venous stenosis and occlusions untreatable with balloon angioplasty. Radiology 195:479-484, 1995.

Hall LD, Murray JD, Boswell GE: Venous stent placement as an adjunct to the staged, multimodal treatment of Paget-Schroetter syndrome. J Vasc Interv Radiol 6:565-570, 1995.

Kovalik EC, Newman GE, Suhocki P, et al: Correction of central venous stenoses: Use of angioplasty and vascular Wallstents. Kidney Int 45:1177-1181, 1994.

Landercasper J, Gall W, Fischer M, et al: Thrombolytic therapy of axillary-subclavian venous thrombosis. Arch Surg 122:1072-1075, 1987.

Lumsden AB, MacDonald MJ, Kikeri DK, et al: Hemodialysis access graft stenosis: Percutaneous transluminal angioplasty. J Surg Res 68:181-185, 1997.

Painter TD, Karpf M: Deep venous thrombosis of the upper extremity: Five years' experience at a university hospital. Angiology 35:743-749, 1984.

Pottecher T, Forrler M, Picardat P, et al: Thrombogenicity of central venous catheters: Prospective study of polyethylene, silicone, and polyurethane catheters with phlebography or post-mortem examination. Eur J Anaesthesiol 1:361-365, 1984.

Ray S, Stacey R, Imrie M, et al: A review of 560 Hickman catheter insertions. Anaesthesia 51:981-985, 1996.

Saeed M, Newman GE, McCann RL, et al: Stenosis in dialysis fistulas: Treatment with percutaneous angioplasty. Radiology 164:693-697, 1987.

Steed DL, Teodori MF, Peitzman AB, et al: Streptokinase in the treatment of subclavian vein thrombosis. J Vasc Surg 4:28-32, 1986.

Stoney WS, Addlestone RB, Alford WC, et al: The incidence of venous thrombosis following long-term transvenous pacing. Ann Thorac Surg 22:166-170, 1976.

Sundqvist SB, Hedner U, Kullenberg HKE, et al: Deep venous thrombosis of the arm: A study of coagulation and fibrinolysis. BMJ 283:265-267, 1981.

Swedberg SH, Brown BG, Sigley R, et al: Intimal fibromuscular hyperplasia at the venous anastomosis of PTFE grafts in hemodialysis patients. Circulation 80:1726-1736, 1989.

Taylor LM, McAllister WR, Dennis DL, et al: Thrombolytic therapy followed by first rib resection for spontaneous ("effort") subclavian vein thrombosis. Am J Surg 149:644-647, 1985.

Thompson RW, Schneider PA, Nelken NA, et al: Circumferential venolysis and paraclavicular thoracic outlet decompression for "effort thrombosis" of the subclavian vein. J Vasc Surg 16:723-732, 1992.

Trerotola SO, Fair GH, Davidson D, et al: Comparison of Gianturco Z-stents and Wallstents in a hemodialysis access graft animal model. J Vasc Interv Radiol 6:387-396, 1995.

Turmel-Rodrigues L, Pengloan J, Blanchier D, et al: Insufficient dialysis shunts: Improved long-term patency rates with close hemodynamic monitoring, repeated percutaneous balloon angioplasty, and stent placement. Radiology 187:273-278, 1993.

Valerio D, Hussey JK, Smith FW: Central vein thrombosis associated with intravenous feeding. J Parenter Enteral Nutr 5:240-242, 1981.

Vanherweghem JL, Yassine T, Goldman M, et al: Subclavian vein thrombosis: A frequent complication of subclavian vein cannulation for hemodialysis. Clin Nephrol 26:235-238, 1986.

Vorwerk D, Guenther RW, Mann H, et al: Venous stenosis and occlusion in hemodialysis shunts: Follow-up results of stent placement in 65 patients. Radiology 195:140-146, 1995.

Williams EC: Catheter-related thrombosis. Clin Cardiol 13(Suppl IV): IV-34-IV-36, 1990.

Upper Extremity Sympathectomy

SAMUEL S. AHN, MD
KYUNG M. RO, MD

The use of cervicothoracic sympathectomy for the treatment of upper extremity disorders dates back to 1889, when Alexander performed the first cervical sympathectomy to treat epilepsy. Over the past century, this procedure has been used as therapy for a variety of conditions, ranging from treatment of angioma of the external carotid artery in 1917 to the current treatment of hyperhidrosis (Table 97-1). Various open surgical approaches have been described, including Telford's[1] supraclavicular approach, Atkins'[2] axillary transthoracic approach, Adson and Brown's[3] dorsal paravertebral approach, Cloward's[4] dorsal midline approach, and Goetz and Marr's[5] anterior transthoracic approach. Because of the morbidity and technical difficulties associated with these operations, however, minimally invasive endoscopic surgical techniques have largely replaced open approaches to sympathectomy.

In 1942, Hughes[6] was the first to perform thoracoscopic sympathectomy, and in 1954, Kux[7] published his experience with thoracoscopic sympathectomy using electrocautery in more than 1400 cases. This technique was largely ignored until 1994, when Ahn and colleagues[8] described their preliminary results of successful thoracoscopic sympathetomy in 19 consecutive patients. In 1995, Drott and associates[9] reported their results from 850 bilateral endoscopic transthoracic sympathectomies using electrocautery to destroy the T2-3 ganglia. Many other reports followed thereafter.

Although most studies have reported the use of thoracoscopic sympathectomy for the treatment of essential hyperhidrosis, several investigators have extended this technique for the treatment of sympathetically mediated

Table 97-1	Conditions That Have Been Treated by Sympathectomy
Raynaud's phenomenon	Causalgia
Erythrocyanosis	Hyperhidrosis
Frostbite	Deep venous thrombosis
Migraine	Perniosis
Constipation	Pancreatitis
Renal pain	Arteriosclerosis
Vasospasm	Exophthalmic goiter
Dysmenorrhea	Hirschsprung's disease
Poliomyelitis	Chronic arthritis
Paget's disease of bone	Retinitis pigmentosa
Obliterative endarteritis	Venous ulceration
Epilepsy	Angioma
Erythromelalgia	

From Gordon A, Zechmeister K, Collin J: The role of sympathectomy in current surgical practice. Eur J Vasc Surg 8:129-137, 1994.

pain, vasospastic disorders, and long Q-T syndrome. The primary indication continues to be essential hyperhidrosis, however, because of its favorable long-term results and high patient satisfaction rates compared with other treatments.

■ HYPERHIDROSIS

General Considerations

Primary or *idiopathic hyperhidrosis* refers to a condition in which the eccrine glands produce sweat beyond that required for physiologic needs.[10] Typical stimuli include anxiety, heat, and taste; however, hyperhidrosis often occurs without triggers. This sweating is localized to specific parts of the body, particularly the hands, axilla, and feet, and often results in sweat literally dripping off the patient.[11] Although no physiologic harm comes from this excessive sweating, the emotional, social, and occupational impact cannot be understated.

Indications

The diagnosis of hyperhidrosis is often straightforward and can be made by the patient's history alone. Nevertheless, the clinician should attempt to witness an episode of sweating to document the severity. The hand is often cool, clammy, erythematous, and scaling from repeated episodes of drying the hands. Hyperhidrosis should not be confused with diaphoresis, exercise-induced sweating, or night sweats, all of which cause diffuse rather than focal sweating. A complete preoperative medical examination is mandatory to evaluate for any hypermetabolic states that could be responsible for the symptoms and any underlying diseases of the lung and thorax that could prohibit successful surgical intervention. Patients often present to the surgeon after years of failed medical or allopathic therapy. Noninvasive medical therapy should be attempted before surgery is considered. Topical drying agents, iontophoresis, biofeedback, phenol blocks, and botulinum toxin A injections have had varying success rates.[12-18] Generally, long-term results of these treatments have been inferior to the results reported with surgical intervention.

Results

Thoracoscopic sympathectomy has been well established in the literature as an effective treatment for primary palmar hyperhidrosis. In most studies of thoracoscopic sympathectomy for the treatment of patients with hyperhidrosis, the overall success rates range from 93% to 100%, with recurrence rates of 0 to 13%.[8,9,19-24] Zacherl and coworkers[20] conducted a retrospective review of 630 thoracoscopic sympathectomies performed in 352 patients, with a mean follow-up duration of 16 years. They reported a 93% long-term technical success rate and found that 68% of patients were fully satisfied with their results, and 26% were partially satisfied but would undergo the procedure again. The patients who were dissatisfied with results of the procedure cited compensatory hyperhidrosis as the cause.

Claes and colleagues,[21] using the electrocautery ablation technique, reported a 98% technical success rate in 130 patients undergoing thoracoscopic sympathectomy for palmar hyperhidrosis; however, their recurrence rate was 13% at a mean follow-up of 6.5 months. Chen and coworkers[25] conducted a retrospective study of 180 patients during a 2-year period, with a follow-up of 2 to 12 months. They found that only five patients complained of recurrence of palmar hyperhidrosis 2 to 3 months postoperatively, and the symptoms were still milder than the preoperative symptoms. In addition, these authors found that 95% of patients were satisfied with the results. In a survey of nearly 10,000 patients who were treated with endoscopic sympathectomy for hyperhidrosis over a 5-year period, Kao and others[26] reported impressive intermediate and long-term results, with recurrence rates of 1% and 3% at 1 and 3 years of follow-up, respectively. In addition, complications, including Horner's syndrome and pneumothorax/hemothorax, were rare, with reported rates of 0.5% and 0.2%.

■ SYMPATHETICALLY MAINTAINED PAIN

General Considerations

Complex regional pain syndrome (CRPS) is a term introduced in 1995 to describe a constellation of symptoms previously categorized as *causalgia* and *reflex sympathetic dystrophy (RSD)*. Patients present with pain conditions that often follow injury, occur regionally, have findings that are disproportionate to their inciting event, and often result in motor function impairment.

The International Association for the Study of Pain categorizes CRPS into two distinct subtypes.[27] CRPS type I (formerly RSD) is defined by four diagnostic criteria, as follows:

1. Presence of an initiating noxious event or a cause of immobilization
2. Continuous pain that is disproportionate to an inciting event, with allodynia or hyperalgesia
3. Edema, change in skin blood flow, or sudomotor activity in the region of pain
4. Exclusion of other conditions that otherwise would account for the degree of pain

CRPS type II (formerly causalgia) is defined by three diagnostic criteria, as follows:

1. Evidence of peripheral nerve injury as the initiating factor
2. Continuous pain that is disproportionate to an inciting event, with allodynia or hyperalgesia

3. Exclusion of other conditions that otherwise would account for the degree of pain

In addition to these broad diagnostic subtypes of CRPS, it has been postulated that CRPS, if left untreated, progresses through three sequential stages, each with its distinct constellation of symptoms, as follows[28]:

- *Stage I:* characterized by hyperalgesia, allodynia, signs of vasomotor dysfunction, and edema
- *Stage II:* dystrophic stage, which often occurs 3 to 6 months after onset and is characterized by increased pain and sensory dysfunction and the development of motor or trophic changes or both
- *Stage III:* atrophic stage, characterized by decreased pain and sensory disturbances

Categorizing CRPS into different subtypes allows for distinct definition of disease state. Surgical intervention generally is limited to patients with stage II disease. The surgeon should focus on selecting patients with significant sympathetically driven pain that is refractory to medical treatment.

Indications

To determine whether a patient has sympathetic mediated pain (SMP) and may be a candidate for a sympathectomy, the clinician must pay close attention to the constellation of symptoms. SMP is a characteristically severe, continuous burning pain in an extremity that does not fit a pattern of nerve root or peripheral nerve injury. In addition, the pain is often associated with vasomotor and trophic changes and may be triggered by strong emotional stimuli, a weather change, or severe auditory stimuli. On physical examination, the patient may exhibit hyperalgesia, allodynia, or hyperpathia, which may lead to excessive guarding of the affected limb. Often, patients with SMP are exquisitely sensitive to mild cold stimuli and may respond to application of acetone or ethyl chloride as opposed to saline. Invasive laboratory evaluation also can assist the clinician; paravertebral sympathetic blocks are the most widely used. Successful blocks are diagnostic of SMP, are often therapeutic, and may predict the outcome of permanent cervicothoracic sympathectomy.

There are numerous medical approaches to SMP, and these should be exhausted before surgical intervention. It has been reported that 50% to 70% of patients respond to conservative treatment.[29] Medical therapy consists of corticosteroids, sympatholytics including phenoxybenzamine and clonidine, tricyclic antidepressants, calcium channel blockers, neuroleptics, and nonsteroidal anti-inflammatory drugs. These pharmacologic approaches are not intended to be first-line therapy or the sole method of therapy, but rather serve as an adjunct to augment an intensive rehabilitation effort, which is the mainstay of therapy. Other reported therapies include transcutaneous electrical nerve stimulation, biofeedback, and psychological support. Sympathetic blocks are therapeutic and diagnostic. For SMP, surgical sympathectomy is considered only after non-surgical steps have been attempted and failed.

Results

The outcome of cervicothoracic sympathectomy for the treatment of SMP is difficult to evaluate because of varying anatomic targets, different patient selection criteria, and subjective outcome measures. Nevertheless, long-term successful outcome is obtained in approximately 75% to 80% of thoracic sympathectomies. Samuelsson and colleagues[30] examined seven patients who underwent transthoracic electrocautery of the sympathetic chain for causalgia. They reported a 79% postoperative reduction in pain but had follow-up limited to only 1 year on only two patients, who had no recurrence. Singh and others[31] reported on 42 patients with CRPS type II who were referred for sympathectomy over a 9-year period. Initial management was pharmacologic; for patients whose pain persisted beyond 6 weeks, a stellate ganglion block was performed to determine if the pain was sympathetically mediated. The authors reported excellent results of sympathectomy in 80.9% of group I and 23.5% of group II and satisfactory clinical outcome in 100% of group I and 64.7% of group II. Group I consisted of patients with symptoms of less than 3 months' duration, and group II consisted of patients with symptoms of greater than 3 months' duration, which suggests that surgical sympathectomy should be considered early in the natural history of SMP. Bandyk and colleagues,[32] in their report of sympathectomy for CRPS type I (RSD), also argued that staging for RSD is a dying concept due to the unpredictable course of the disease. They found that two thirds of their patients who underwent sympathectomy had stage I or II disease and one third had stage III disease; moreover, the incidence rate of sympathectomy failure was similar in patients with stage II and III RSD syndromes, 22% and 26%. Other investigators also reported that the interval between the inciting injury and surgical intervention affects long-term outcome and found good results in patients operated on within 12 months of injury.[33] Factors such as age, gender, and site and type of injury did not affect outcome. The effects of these variables, especially timing of intervention, are controversial.

■ VASOSPASTIC DISORDERS

General Considerations

The surgeon's approach to patients with vasospastic disorders is similar to that of SMP. Careful diagnosis and preoperative evaluation are crucial to determine the appropriateness of intervention. The review of the literature is difficult to interpret because of poor patient definition. Although the use of sympathectomy for upper extremity vasospastic disorders is controversial and is limited by the mediocre long-term results, its utility in treatment for these disorders cannot be fully abandoned, given some favorable results in select patients.

Indications

In the treatment of these disorders, it is important to consider underlying collagen vascular or autoimmune diseases as the underlying cause; 20% of patients initially diagnosed with Raynaud's disease are found eventually to have collagen vascular disease. After a rheumatologic cause has been ruled out, the patient should undergo medical therapy, which may include vasodilators and calcium channel blockers to increase blood flow. Additional therapies may include steroids and methotrexate. A patient who has upper extremity ulcers is not an automatic candidate for surgical interventions and should undergo a trial of local wound care and vasodilators first. If a patient with a vasospastic disorder fails the preceding therapeutic algorithm or cannot tolerate it, he or she should be considered for surgical sympathectomy. Also, sympathectomy should remain an option for patients with severe arterial disease of the hands who are not candidates for arterial bypass surgery

Results

Johnston and associates,[34] using the open technique, reported that none of the patients in their study were completely relieved of their symptoms after surgery, but all had some relative improvement. Several other investigators also reported poor long-term results of sympathectomy for the treatment of Raynaud's syndrome, with high 12-month recurrence rates.[35-37]

■ LONG QT SYNDROME

General Considerations

Idiopathic or congenital long QT syndrome (LQTS) is a rare cardiac condition, which carries high morbidity and mortality with risk of life-threatening ventricular arrhythmia and sudden cardiac death. The mechanism of LQTS is still not fully understood, but it is believed to involve the sympathetic nervous system as a trigger of an already abnormal cardiac transmembrane channel or as the primary defect.[38,39] T-wave alternans is characteristic of this disorder and can be reproduced by stimulating the left stellate ganglion.[38] Studies suggest that the ablation of the left stellate ganglion has the effect of shortening the Q-T interval and increases ventricular fibrillation threshold, whereas ablating the right stellate ganglion has the opposite effect.[40]

Indications

Nonsurgical therapeutic options for the treatment of LQTS include beta blockers, implantable cardioverters-defibrillators, and permanent pacing.[39] Oral beta blockers have been the mainstay of therapy. Although beta blockers have been proven valuable, many patients fail to respond to this therapy. As a result, left cervicothoracic sympathectomy has been used by a few centers as an alternative method of therapy for patients who remain refractory to pharmacologic treatment.

Results

Left cervicothoracic sympathectomy for LQTS was first reported in 1970 by Moss and McDonald,[41] who successfully performed this procedure in a patient with LQTS that was refractory to medical therapy. In 1984, Bhandari and coworkers[42] performed left cervicothoracic sympathectomy in 10 patients and reported that the mean Q-T$_c$ interval was shortened after sympathectomy and continued to remain abnormal in 9 of 10 patients. They concluded that left cervicothoracic sympathectomy was inadequate for long-term control of symptoms in most patients with LQTS. The rationale behind this technique was to normalize the Q-T interval by removing the abnormal sympathetic stimulation. In practice, sympathectomy failed to normalize the Q-T interval in these patients in the long term, and as a consequence, the surgical approach to therapy began to fall out of favor. However, In 1991, Schwartz and colleagues[43] identified 85 patients (mean age 20) worldwide who were treated with left cardiac sympathetic denervation for LQTS. They found that sympathectomy resulted in a large reduction in the number of patients with cardiac events, from 99% to 45%, with a 5-year survival rate of 94%.

As with vasospastic disorders, cervicothoracic sympathectomy for the treatment of LQTS is controversial and limited by poor long-term results. The role of sympathectomy in the treatment of LQTS has not been widely accepted because of variable results, reports that indicate that most patients do not have complete reversal of the long Q-T interval, and a lack of clear predictive clinical outcomes.

■ INTRACTABLE ANGINA PECTORIS

The first reported sympathectomy for angina was by Jonnescu in 1921.[44] In subsequent years, reports of open sympathectomy were encouraging. Studies conducted in the latter half of the 20th century showed, however, that sympathectomy for the treatment of angina was generally effective in alleviating the symptoms of angina, but provided no treatment of the underlying coronary artery disease. Instead the resultant loss of the "warning signal" of angina placed patients at a greater risk of overexertion and death from myocardial infarction.[45,46] Now with the advent of modern myocardial revascularization and percutaneous intervention, sympathectomy, even thoracoscopically, is not recommended.

■ OPERATIVE APPROACHES

Open Sympathectomy

As with many procedures, numerous approaches are available to perform an effective upper extremity sympathectomy. The methods deployed by various surgeons are likely influenced more by anatomic and technical familiarity than other factors. Neurosurgeons historically have favored the open paravertebral route, whereas most vascular surgeons have preferred the open transaxillary approach. The various methods have their own inherent advantages and disadvantages. The supraclavicular approach is limited because of the increased incidence of Horner's syndrome and frequency of brachial plexus injury. The paravertebral approach, although offering good visualization, involves extensive dissection, including back muscle division. As a result, this operation is associated with long hospitalization and extensive rehabilitation. Finally, the transaxillary

approach is associated with increased pain and resultant increased recovery time. All of these shortcomings can be eliminated or minimized through the transthoracic approach.

Adar and associates[47] performed 198 bilateral upper dorsal sympathectomies in 100 patients with hyperhidrosis using the supraclavicular approach. The reported follow-up involved 93% of patients and ranged from 4 to 50 months. Dry hands were achieved in 98% of these patients, and 58% had recurrence of "moisture" that was distinctly milder than their presurgical hyperhidrotic state; however, some degree of compensatory sweating was found in many patients. Subjectively, 89% of the patients reported excellent results; there was one technical failure, and that patient reported a dissatisfactory outcome. The issue of temporary sweating and compensatory hyperhidrosis was not unique to the report by Adar and associates.[47] Greenhalgh and others[48] also found that after sympathectomy using the supraclavicular approach, temporary sweating occurred on postoperative day 3 or 4, and compensatory sweating in the axilla was common.

Endoscopic Sympathectomy

Endoscopic thoracodorsal sympathectomy has essentially replaced the open surgical approach, with the open procedure being limited to unique circumstances in which an endoscopic approach is contraindicated. Since the 1980s, numerous investigators have reported their experience using a broad range of surgical techniques, including en bloc electrocautery of T2-4, sharp excision, radiofrequency ablation, clipping, limited resection of the sympathetic trunk, and selective division of the rami communicantes—all in an effort to decrease postoperative complications. The currently available techniques also differ in the use of various port sizes, number of ports, and video assistance.

Presently, resection of the second and third thoracic ganglion is likely the most efficient method of sympathetic denervation of the upper extremities. A meta-analysis conducted by Hashmonai and colleagues[19] examined all thoracoscopic sympathectomies performed from 1974 to 1999 and compared the efficacy of complete resection versus electrocautery ablation. Although the ablation method is simpler, faster, and requires less surgical skill than resection, the resection method is associated with a greater immediate success rate compared with ablation (99.8% versus 95.2%). In 1998, Ahn and Ro[49] described a refined technique of thoracoscopic sympathectomy, which is outlined subsequently. The use of three separate 5- to 7-mm ports, complete sharp resection of the T2-3 ganglia, and no clips or electrocautery reduced the incidence of Horner's syndrome and compensatory hyperhidrosis and increased the long-term success rate.

Other approaches to thoracoscopic sympathectomy include the use of a single endoscopic port[50,51] and selective T2 sympathetic block by clipping.[52,53] The single port technique is associated with decreased scarring and impressive immediate success rates; however, the data suggest that these techniques are associated with slightly higher postoperative pneumothorax or hemothorax rates and late recurrence. T. S. Lin and colleagues[53] and C. C. Lin and

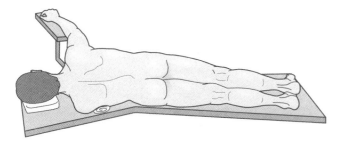

FIGURE 97-1 Patient in lateral decubitus position with ipsilateral arm abducted. The table is flexed to open the rib spaces.

colleagues[53] reported their experience with selective T2 block by clipping, leaving open the possibility for reversal of the procedure for patients with severe compensatory hyperhidrosis. C. C. Lin and colleagues[53] performed reversal procedures in 5 of 326 patients with improvement to some extent in 4 out of 5 patients, whereas T. S. Lin and colleagues[52] performed reversal procedures in 2 of 52 patients with improvement of compensatory hyperhidrosis in both patients. These authors[53] postulated that the efferent fibers that control the eccrine sweat glands in the hand are more susceptible to injury so that adjusting the force of the endoclips to block only the efferent fibers while maintaining the integrity of the myelin sheath allows for reversal of the procedure if performed in a timely manner after the initial procedure. T. S. Lin and colleagues[52] had a recurrence rate of 2% at 3 years, however, whereas C. C. Lin and colleagues[53] reported a mean follow-up of less than 1 year.

Surgical Technique

Thoracoscopic sympathectomy is performed under general endotracheal anesthesia using a double-lumen endotracheal tube with the ipsilateral lung deflated and nonventilated. The patient is placed in the lateral decubitus position with the ipsilateral arm abducted (Fig. 97-1). The operating table should be flexed, the arm abducted and placed at a 90-degree elbow flex in a arm holder, and the torso hyperextended in the lateral position for maximal expansion of the intercostal spaces. An endoscopic video monitor, three soft flexible 7-mm-diameter plastic thoracoports, and a 5-mm-diameter rigid laparoscope allow for good endoscopic visualization of the sympathetic chain. The three ports are ideally placed: One port is placed in the posterior chest line along the sixth or seventh intercostal space, a second is placed in the same sixth or seventh intercostal space near the tip of the scapula, and a third is placed in the third intercostal space along the anterior chest line (Fig. 97-2). Any adhesions of the lung to the parietal pleura should be lysed with endoshear connected to electrocautery to allow proper deflations and retraction of the lung.

After mechanical collapse and deflation of the lung, the first through fourth ribs and the vertebral bodies can be identified. Opacification of the pleura often impedes clear visualization of the sympathetic chain, especially in older patients with pleural scarring. The superior aspect of the sympathetic chain and the upper extent of surgical

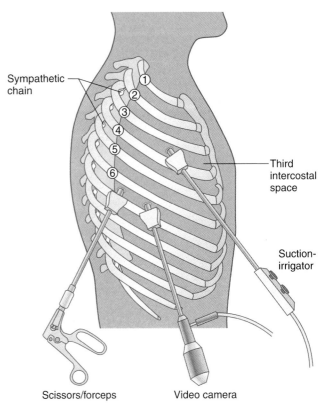

FIGURE 97-2 Port placement: one in the third intercostal space along the anterior chest line (the chest line is not the same as the axillary line), a second port in the mid-chest line in the sixth (or seventh) intercostal space, and a third port along the posterior chest line near the scapula in the sixth (or seventh) intercostal space. These last two ports should be in the same intercostal space to optimize mobility of the instruments.

dissection are identified by visualization of the subclavian artery. The azygos and subclavian vein along with the phrenic and vagus nerves should be identified early in the procedure to ensure their preservation. The phrenic and vagus nerves run ventral to the vertebral bodies, whereas the sympathetic chain runs dorsal to the spine (Fig. 97-3).

The parietal pleura is incised longitudinally to unroof the sympathetic chain from the top of the fourth rib to the top of the second rib. The chain is dissected and mobilized from its bed by using sharp dissection. The rami communicantes of the sympathetic ganglia T3 and T4 are cut using sharp scissors without electrocautery or clips to prevent injury to the adjacent intercostal nerves or vessels (Fig. 97-4). The dissection is carried in a rostral fashion to the lower portion of the stellate ganglion, where the nerve of Kuntz, a large branch of the T1 ramus that runs parallel and lateral to the trunk of the sympathetic chain at the inferior aspect of the superior stellate ganglion, is located. The lower portion of the stellate ganglion is below a yellowish fat pad at the top of the pleural cavity and envelops the subclavian artery. The dissection is carried to just below the inferior aspect of the stellate ganglion, which corresponds to the rostral margin of the second rib. It is important to maintain the integrity of the stellate ganglion and any rami coursing in the rostral direction because injury or traction to the upper portion

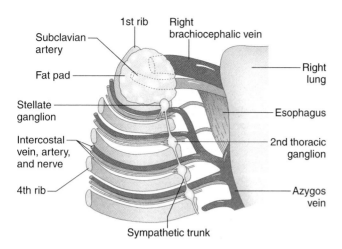

FIGURE 97-3 Sympathetic chain coursing over the posterior neck of ribs. The stellate ganglion ends at the superior rostral rim of the second rib, the T2 ganglion is between the second and third ribs, and the T3 ganglion is between the third and fourth ribs. Note the relationship of the various anatomic landmarks.

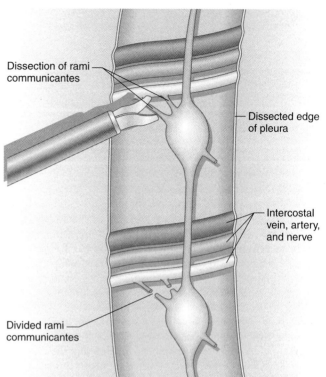

FIGURE 97-4 Dissection of rami communicantes away from the underlying intercostal vein, artery, and nerve, which normally course deep or posterior to the rami. Care must be taken not to injure the neurovascular bundle.

of the stellate ganglion can increase the risk of developing Horner's syndrome. The sympathetic chain is divided sharply just below the T1 ganglion at the rostral margin of the second rib and just below the T3 ganglion, which corresponds to the rostral margin of the fourth rib.

Bilateral thoracoscopic sympathectomy can be performed safely in one session. Surgery time is 2 hours for bilateral procedures, and total anesthesia time is approximately 3 hours; the operating time depends on the surgeon's experience and anatomic complexity of the patient.

Contraindications

The contraindications to sympathectomy are the same as for any surgical intervention in which general endotracheal anesthesia is used. In addition, cervicothoracic sympathectomy should not be performed in patients who have had previous thoracic operations or pulmonary infections or who may have dense adhesions that can impede visualization of the sympathetic chain.

Complications

Potential complications from thoracoscopic sympathectomy are listed in Table 97-2. The most distressing and common complication of thoracoscopic sympathectomy in the treatment of hyperhidrosis is compensatory hyperhidrosis. Most investigators use subjective measures as reported by the patient to determine severity. Although it has been suggested that the incidence of disabling compensatory hyperhidrosis is decreased with the ablation method,[23] the evidence is inconclusive and highly variable. This is also true of the claim that the degree of compensatory hyperhidrosis is associated with the extent of sympathectomy.[23,24,54,55] Lesiche and associates[56] used a "limited sympathectomy" approach with resection at varying levels of the sympathetic chain and found that no significant difference was seen in the incidence of compensatory

hyperhidrosis with respect to the extent of resection. The mechanism of compensatory hyperhidrosis is more complex than previously believed and may involve numerous factors, including genetic factors, climate, and individual changes in the thermoregulatory process. Although gustatory and phantom hyperhidrosis also are possible sequelae of sympathectomy, these side effects have been inadequately reported with either technique, and no conclusion can be drawn at this time.

Postoperative pneumothorax from a thoracoscopic procedure usually is due to inadequate reinflation of the collapsed lung. This complication is usually self-limited and treated conservatively. Intercostal neuralgia from injury to the intercostal nerves can occur during port placement, from direct pressure by the instruments, or from cauterization of

Table 97-2	Complications Associated with Thoracoscopic Sympathectomy	
COMMON	**RARE**
Compensatory sweating	Postsympathectomy neuralgia
Horner's syndrome	Hemothorax
Pneumothorax	Pleural effusions
Intercostal neuralgia	Injury to vagus nerve
Segmental atelectasis	Injury to phrenic nerve
	Injury to subclavian artery
	Injury to subclavian vein

the intercostal nerves during the procedure. The incidence of this complication can be minimized by the use and careful placement of small, 7-mm, soft flexible ports rather than the rigid plastic ports. Also, the preferential use of sharp dissection and minimal use of electrocautery limit inadvertent damage to the intercostal nerves and help prevent postoperative neuralgia.

Complete excision of the T2-3 ganglia with transthoracic thoracodorsal sympathectomy is the optimal technique to achieve permanent resolution of primary hyperhidrosis in the upper extremity, particularly in palmar hyperhidrosis. In the study reported by Drott and others,[9] complications included intercostal drainage secondary to hemothorax or pneumothorax (1%), treatment failure (2%), and recurrence of symptoms (2%); there was no mortality or life-threatening complications. At the end of follow-up (median 31 months), 98% of the patients reported satisfactory results.[9] Although multiple late adverse effects may occur, they are generally acceptable to the patient. The above-described surgical techniques correlate with reduced incidence of compensatory hyperhidrosis and Horner's syndrome. Overall, patients are satisfied with the long-term results.

In the meta-anaylsis conducted by Hashmonai and co-workers,[19] reported rate of ptosis (the term *Horner's syndrome* was not used to avoid confusion and to be more precise, as most authors report the incidence of ptosis alone as Horner's without the complete triad of miosis, anhidrosis, and ptosis) was 0.9% and 1.72% in the ablation and resection groups and was noted to be statistically significant ($P = .017$). Although the explanation for this difference is unclear, it was postulated that the higher rate of ptosis may be due to the traction exerted on the sympathetic chain during resection. Ahn and colleagues, in a review of 232 transthoracic thoracodorsal sympathectomies performed over 10 years (unpublished data), found that the incidence of Horner's syndrome was only 2.2% (2 patients) after changes were made in the surgical technique; it was transient with complete resolution in both patients. The higher rate of permanent and transient Horner's syndrome in this series before 1998 can be attributed to the fact that the lower portion of the T1 ganglion was resected in the initial series.[8]

■ SUMMARY

Advances in minimally invasive techniques have made the thoracoscopic approach the standard and preferable method to perform cervicothoracic sympathectomy. Hyperhidrosis has become the most common indication for this procedure. Long-term results and patient satisfaction have been favorable, leading to the widespread application of this technique. The results of this procedure for CRPS, vasospastic disorders, and LQTS are less favorable with less predictable outcomes. Sympathectomy is contraindicated for angina.

■ REFERENCES

1. Telford ED: The technique of sympathectomy. Br J Surg 21:113-130, 1935.
2. Atkins HJB: Sympathectomy of the axillary approach. Lancet 1:538-539, 1954.
3. Adson AW, Brown GE: Raynaud's disease of the upper extremities: Successful treatment by resection of the sympathetic cervicothoracic and thoracic ganglions and the intervening trunk. JAMA 92:444-449, 1925.
4. Cloward RB: Hyperhidrosis. J Neurosurg 30:545-551, 1969.
5. Goetz RH, Marr JAS: The importance of the second thoracic ganglion for the sympathetic supply of the upper extremities with a description of two new approaches for its removal. Clin Proc 3:102-114, 1944.
6. Hughes J: Endothoracic sympathectomy. Proc R Soc Med 35:585-586, 1942.
7. Kux E: The endoscopic approach to the vegetative nervous systems and its therapeutic possibilities. Dis Chest 20:139-147, 1951.
8. Ahn S, Machleder H, Concepcion B, et al: Thoracoscopic cervicodorsal sympathectomy: Preliminary results. J Vasc Surg 20:511-517, 1994.
9. Drott C, Gothberg C, Claes G: Endoscopic transthoracic sympathectomy: An efficient and safe method for the treatment of hyperhidrosis. J Am Acad Dermatol 33:78-81, 1995.
10. Sato K, Kang WH, Saga K, et al: Biology of sweat glands and their disorders II. J Am Acad Dermatol 20:713-725, 1989.
11. Quinton PM: Sweating and its disorders. Ann Rev Med 34:429-452, 1983.
12. Tabet J, Bay JW, Magdines M: Essential hyperhidrosis: Current therapy. Cleve Clin Q 53:83-88, 1986.
13. Holzle E, Braun-Falco O: Structural changes in axillary eccrine glands following long-term treatment with aluminum chloride hexahydrate solution. Br J Dermatol 110:399-403, 1984.
14. Sato K: Hyperhidrosis. JAMA 265:651, 1991.
15. Stolman LP: Treatment of excess sweating of palms by iontophoresis. Arch Dermatol 123:893-896, 1987.
16. Midtgaard K: A new device for treatment of hyperhidrosis by iontophoresis. Br J Dermatol 114:485-488, 1986.
17. Adler OB, Engel A, Saranga D: Palmar hyperhidrosis treatment by percutaneous transthoracic chemical sympathicolysis. Eur J Radiol 4:57-62, 1994.
18. Schneider P, Binder M, Auff E, et al: Double-blind trial of botulinum toxin-A for treatment of focal hyperhidrosis of the palms. Br J Dermatol 136:548-552, 1997.
19. Hashmonai M, Assalia A, Kopelman D: Thoracoscopic sympathectomy for palmar hyperhidrosis—ablate or resect? Surg Endosc 15:435-441, 2001.
20. Zacherl J, Huber ER, Imhof M, et al: Long-term results of 630 thoracoscopic sympathectomies for primary hyperhidrosis: The Vienna experience. Eur J Surg 58(Suppl):43-46, 1998.
21. Claes G, Drott G, Gothberg G: Endoscopic electrocautery of the thoracic sympathetic chain: A minimally invasive way to treat palmar hyperhidrosis. Scand J Past Reconstr Hand Surg 27:29-33, 1993.
22. Noppen M, Herregoots P, D'Heaese J, et al: A simplified T2-T3 thoracoscopic sympathicolysis technique for treatment of essential hyperhidrosis: Short-term results in 100 patients. J Laparoendosc Surg 6:151-159, 1996.
23. Gossot D, Toledo L, Fritsch S, et al: Thoracoscopic sympathectomy for the upper limb hyperhidrosis: Looking for the right operation. Ann Thorac Surg 64:975-978, 1997.
24. Hsia JY, Chen G, Hsu C, et al: Outpatient thoracoscopic limited sympathectomy for hyperhidrosis palmaris. Ann Thorac Surg 67:258-259, 1999.
25. Chen HJ, Shih DY, Fung ST: Transthoracic endoscopic sympathectomy in the treatment of palmar hyperhidrosis. Arch Surg 129:630-633, 1994.
26. Kao MC, Lin JY, Chen YL, et al: Minimally invasive surgery: Video endoscopic thoracic sympathectomy for palmar hyperhidrosis. Ann Acad Med Singapore 25:673-678, 1996.
27. Merskey H, Bogduk N: Classification of Chronic Pain: Descriptions of Chronic Pain and Definitions of Pain Terms/Prepared by Task Force on Taxonomy of the International Association for the Study of Pain. Seattle, IASP Press, 1994.
28. Bonica JJ: Causalgia and other reflex sympathetic dystrophies. In Bonica JJ (ed): Management of Pain, 2nd ed. Philadelphia, Lea & Feibger, 1990, pp 220-243.

29. Olcott C, Eltherington LG, Wilcosky BR, et al: Reflex sympathetic dystrophy—the surgeon's role in management. J Vasc Surg 14:485-495, 1991.

30. Samuelsson H, Claes G, Drott C: Endoscopic electrocautery of the upper thoracic sympathetic chain: A safe and simple technique for the treatment of sympathetically maintained pain. Eur J Surg S572:55-57, 1994.

31. Singh B, Moodley J, Shaik AS, et al: Sympathectomy for complex regional pain syndrome. J Vasc Surg 37:508-511, 2003.

32. Bandyk DF, Johnson BL, Kirkpatrick AF: Surgical sympathectomy for reflex sympathetic dystrophy syndromes. J Vasc Surg 352:269-277, 2002.

33. AbuRahma AF, Robinson PA, Powell M: Sympathectomy for reflex sympathetic dystrophy: Factors affecting outcome. Ann Vasc Surg 8:372-379, 1994.

34. Johnston EN, Summerly R, Birnstingi M: Prognosis in Raynaud's phenomenon after sympathectomy. BMJ (5440):962-964, 1965.

35. Peacock JH: The treatment of primary Raynaud's disease of the upper limb. Lancet 2:65-69, 1960.

36. Campbell WB, Cooper MJ, Sponsel WE, et al: Transaxillary sympathectomy—is a one stage bilateral procedure safe? Br J Surg 69:S29-31, 1982.

37. Millewski PJ, Hodgson SP, Higham A: Transthoracic endoscopic sympathectomy. J R Coll Surg Edinb 30:221-223, 1985.

38. Schwartz PJ, Priori SG, Napolitano C: The long QT syndrome. In Zipes DP, Jalife J (eds): Cardiac Electrophysiology: From Cell to Bedside. Philadelphia, WB Saunders, 1990, pp 589-605.

39. Moss AJ: Prolonged QT syndrome. JAMA 256:2985-2987, 1986.

40. Kashima T, Tanaka H, Minagoe S, et al: Electrocardiographic changes induced by stellate ganglion block in normal subjects. J Electrocardiol 14:169-174, 1981.

41. Moss AJ, McDonald J: Unilateral cervicothoracic sympathetic ganglionectomy for the treatment of long QT syndrome. N Engl J Med 285:903-904, 1970.

42. Bhandari AK, Scheinman HM, Morady F, et al: Efficacy of left cardiac sympathectomy in the treatment of patients with long QT syndrome. Circulation 70:1018-1023, 1983.

43. Schwartz PJ, Locat EH, Moss AJ, et al: Left cardiac sympathetic denervation in the therapy of congenital long QT syndrome: A worldwide report. Circulation 84:503-511, 1991.

44. Jonnescu T: Traitment chirurgical de pangine de poietrine par la resection du sympathetique cervico-thoracique. Presse Med 29:193-195, 1921.

45. Kadowski MH, Levett JM: Sympathectomy in the treatment of angina and arrhythmias. Ann Thorac Surg 41:572-578, 1986.

46. Noppen M, Pendale P, Hagers Y: Thoracoscopic sympathectomy. Lancet 345:803-804, 1995.

47. Adar R, Kurchin A, Zweig A, et al: Palmar hyerhidrosis and its surgical treatment: A report of 100 cases. Ann Surg 186:34-41, 1977.

48. Greenhalgh R, Rosengarten D, Martin P: Role of sympathectomy for hyperhidrosis. BMJ 1:332-334, 1971.

49. Ahn S, Ro K: Thoracoscopic sympathectomy. Ann Vasc Surg 12:509-514, 1998.

50. Vanaclocha V, Saiz-Sapena N, Panta F: Uniportal endoscopic superior thoracic sympathectomy. Neurosurgery 46:924-928, 2000.

51. Lardinois D, Ris HB: Minimally invasive video-endoscopic sympathectomy by use of transaxillary single port approach. Eur J Cardiothorac Surg 21:67-70, 2002.

52. Lin TS, Huang LC, Wang NP: Video-assisted thoracoscopic T2 sympathetic block by clipping for palmar hyperhidrosis: Analysis of 52 cases. J Laparosc Adv Surg Tech 11:59-62, 2001.

53. Lin CC, Mo LR, Lee LS: Thoracoscopic T2-sympathetic block by clipping—a better and reversible operation for the treatment of hyperhidrosis palmaris: Experience with 326 cases. Eur J Surg 580(Suppl): 13-16, 1998.

54. Andrews BT, Rennie JA: Predicting changes in the distribution of sweating following thoracoscopic sympathectomy. Br J Surg 84:1702-1704, 1997.

55. Zacherl J, Imhof M, Huber E, et al: Video assistance reduces complication rate of thoracoscopic sympathectomy for hyperhidrosis. Ann Surg 68:1177-1181, 1999.

56. Lesiche G, Castier Y, Thabut G, et al: Endoscopic transthoracic sympathectomy for upper limb hyperhidrosis: Limited sympathectomy does not reduce postoperative compensatory sweating. J Vasc Surg 37:124-128, 2003.

Occupational Vascular Problems

98

MARK K. ESKANDARI, MD
JAMES S. T. YAO, MD, PhD

Upper extremity work-related injuries are a major societal problem in regards to disability, cost, and loss of workdays. Occupational injuries affecting the shoulders, arms, and hands have been recognized for nearly 300 years and generally are categorized into injuries caused by accidents at work and injuries resulting from long-standing repetitive tasks.[1] Injuries in the latter category result from small but additive amounts of tissue damage sustained from repetitive motions; they are known collectively as *cumulative trauma disorders*. According to data released by the U.S. Bureau of Labor Statistics, cumulative trauma disorders account for more than 50% of all occupational illnesses in the United States today.[2] Although most of these injuries affect the musculoskeletal system, injuries to arteries and veins are known to occur.[3] Work-related vascular injuries develop because of excessive or exaggerated job-related physical activity involving the shoulders, arms, or hands. Arterial occupational trauma includes vibration-induced white finger syndrome, hypothenar hammer syndrome, acro-osteolysis, electrical burns, extreme thermal exposures, and athletic injuries.

■ VIBRATION-INDUCED WHITE FINGER

The term *vibration-induced white finger* was favored by the Industrial Injuries Advisory Council in 1970 to describe symptoms similar to those of Raynaud's disease that were caused by exposure to vibration.[4] Other investigators have used the term *Raynaud's phenomenon of occupational origin* or *traumatic vasospastic disease*. Regardless of the designation, the common and presenting symptoms are those of Raynaud's phenomenon secondary to prolonged use of vibrating mechanical tools.

In the early stages, vibration injury may be manifested as slight tingling and numbness. Later, the tips of one or more fingers exposed to vibration experience attacks of blanching, usually precipitated by cold. With continued exposure to vibration, the affected area increases in size, and the blanching extends to the entire finger exposed to vibration. Attacks of white finger typically last about 1 hour and terminate with reactive hyperemia (red flush) and often considerable pain. Prolonged exposure to vibration may induce a blue-black cyanosis in the affected fingers. Only about 1% of cases progress to ulceration or gangrene.[5] Hand-held tools (e.g., pneumatic hammers and drills, grinders, and chain saws) are associated with vibration-induced white finger. Such injury potential is not restricted to a few types of tools but is present in a variety of situations in which workers' hands are subjected to significant vibration exposure.[4] Table 98-1 lists the types of tools that commonly cause vibration-induced white finger.

The first cases of this type of injury were reported in Rome in 1911 by Loriga.[6] Blanching and numbness of the hands after using pneumatic drills was noted by Cottingham in 1918,[7] and subsequent reports by Taylor and Pelmear[8] and Ashe and associates[9] firmly established vibration-induced white finger as a discrete clinical entity associated with hand ischemia. According to Taylor and Pelmear,[8] the disease can be divided into five categories (Table 98-2); this classification has been accepted as a standard by workers in this field. This classification is particularly useful in determining workers' compensation.

The exact mechanism of injury is unknown. Repetitive trauma from the vibration of the tool is the main cause of the problem. The frequency of the vibration and the intensity of the trauma it produces affect the extent of damage to the endothelium.[10] Local platelet adhesion seems to be an important factor in arterial occlusion. It has been shown that sympathetic hyperactivity, in combination with local factors such as vibration-induced hyperresponsiveness of the digital vessels to cold, may be responsible for finger-blanching attacks.[11]

Diagnosis is made from a history of using vibrating tools and from the classic Raynaud's symptoms. For a vasospastic condition, the most promising single objective test is cold provocation and recording of the recovery time of digital temperature. Digital artery occlusion is best detected by recording the systolic pressure of the affected fingers with transcutaneous Doppler ultrasound,[12,13] although more recently B-mode scanning has been adopted.[14] In advanced disease, arteriography is helpful. Barker and Hines[15] first documented arterial occlusion by brachial arteriography in a group of workers who complained of hand blanching and attacks of numbness. Other authors have reported on the use of arteriography in investigating this injury.[16-18]

Table 98-1	Tools Associated with Vibration-Induced White Finger	
Pneumatic tools	Chain saws	
Riveting	Grinders	
Caulking	Pedestal	
Drilling	Hand-held	
Clinching and flanging	Chipping hammers	
Rotary bur tools	Concrete vibrothickener	
Pneumatic hammers	Concrete-leveling vibrotables	

Table 98-2 Stages of Vibration-Induced White Finger

STAGE	CONDITION OF DIGITS	WORK AND SOCIAL INTERFERENCE
0	Vibration exposure but no signs or symptoms	No complaints
0_T	Intermittent tingling	No interference with activities
0_N	Intermittent numbness	No interference with activities
1	Blanching of ≥1 fingertips, with or without tingling and numbness	No interference with activities
2	Blanching of ≥1 fingers with numbness, usually in winter	Slight interference with home and social activities; no interference with work
3	Extensive blanching; frequent episodes in summer and winter	Definite interference at work, at home, and with social activities; restriction of hobbies
4	Same as stage 3: extensive blanching, most fingers involved, frequent episodes in summer and winter	Same as stage 3, but occupation changed to avoid further vibration exposure because of the severity of signs and symptoms

Updated from Taylor W, Pelmear PL (eds): Vibration White Finger in Industry. New York, Academic Press, 1975.

Arteriographic changes in vibration tool injury are confined largely to the hands. Multiple segmental occlusions of the digits and sometimes a corkscrew configuration are seen.[18] The intensity of symptoms and extent of digital artery occlusion depend on vibration magnitude, frequency of vibration, and lifetime exposure duration.[19] In advanced cases, occlusion of digital arteries is common. Of 80 workers (chippers) with vibration-induced white finger investigated at the Blood Flow Laboratory at Northwestern University, 25 (28%) exhibited significant reduction in systolic pressure in one or more digits.[20] In 6 of the 25 workers, arteriography showed occlusion of digital arteries (Fig. 98-1). Incompleteness of the palmar arch was seen not only in the symptomatic hand, but also in the contralateral, asymptomatic one. Symptoms of Raynaud's phenomenon were present in 73 of 80 workers (91%). Abnormal cold response was observed in 53% of the workers (Fig. 98-2).

Treatment of vibration-induced white finger consists of symptomatic relief of Raynaud's symptoms. Surgical treatment, such as cervical sympathectomy or digital sympathectomy, is rarely indicated or needed. The most important step is to discontinue use of vibrating tools by changing jobs or rotating on and off that particular task. In most instances, prevention is more effective than cure. Factory standards should conform to standards suggested by the American Conference of Governmental Industrial Hygienists in 1984,[21] and perhaps more operations should be automated to eliminate human exposure to vibratory insults. In advanced cases, a calcium channel blocker, such as nifedipine (30 to 80 mg daily), may be useful. Calcium antagonists inhibit the response of arterial smooth muscle to norepinephrine and have been reported to be effective.[22]

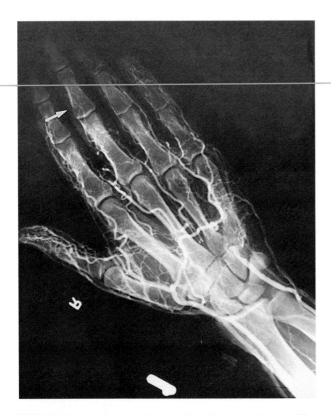

FIGURE 98-1 Arteriogram of the hand in a vibratory tool worker. There is occlusion of the digital arteries *(arrow)*.

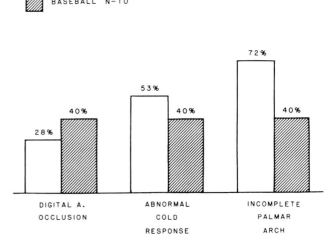

□ VIBRATION N=80

▨ BASEBALL N=10

FIGURE 98-2 Incidence of abnormal cold response, digital artery occlusion, and incomplete palmar arch by Doppler examination in vibratory tool workers and baseball players. (From Bartel P, Blackburn D, Peterson L, et al: The value of non-invasive tests in occupational trauma of the hands and fingers. Bruit 8:15, 1984.)

Intravenous infusion of a prostanoid (prostaglandin E_1, prostacyclin, or iloprost) usually is reserved for patients with digital gangrene.[23]

■ HYPOTHENAR HAMMER SYNDROME

The predisposing factor in the development of hypothenar hammer syndrome is repetitive use of the palm of the hand in activities that involve pushing, pounding, or twisting. The anatomic site of the ulnar artery in the area of the hypothenar eminence makes it vulnerable. The terminal branches of the ulnar artery (deep palmar branch and superficial arch) arise in a groove named *Guyon's tunnel*, which is bounded medially by the pisiform and the hook of the hamate and dorsally by the transverse carpal ligament. Over a distance of 2 cm, the ulnar artery lies quite "superficially" in the palm, being covered only by skin, subcutaneous tissue, and the palmaris brevis muscle (Fig. 98-3). When this area is repeatedly traumatized, ulnar or digital arterial spasm, aneurysms, occlusion, or a combination of these lesions can result. Embolization from an aneurysm may cause multiple digital artery occlusions distally. The type of arterial abnormality observed often depends on the nature of the vessel damage.

Intimal damage often results in thrombotic occlusion, whereas injury to media causes palmar aneurysms (Fig. 98-4).[24] This type of occupational injury has been called the *hypothenar hammer syndrome*.[25] In 1934, Von Rosen provided the first descriptive report of this condition,[26] and subsequently it was recognized as an occupational disease.[27] Table 98-3 lists the types of workers who developed this syndrome in reported series.[28] Among 79 workers who habitually used their hands as a hammer, Little and Ferguson[29] found that 11 (14%) showed evidence of ulnar artery occlusion in one or both hands. The traditional dogma regarding the etiology of hypothenar hammer syndrome has been challenged by Ferris and colleagues.[30] These investigators reviewed the arteriographic and histologic findings of 21 patients treated for hypothenar hammer syndrome. Similar radiographic findings of "corkscrew" elongation of the ulnar artery in the dominant and nondominant hand were identified in 12 of 13 patients with bilateral angiograms. Additionally, in patients undergoing surgical resection and bypass grafting of symptomatic aneurysms, histologic findings were consistent with fibromuscular dysplasia with superimposed trauma. Based on this evidence, they proposed that the etiology of hypothenar hammer syndrome depends on the presence of underlying ulnar artery fibromuscular dysplasia in the face of repetitive palmar trauma.

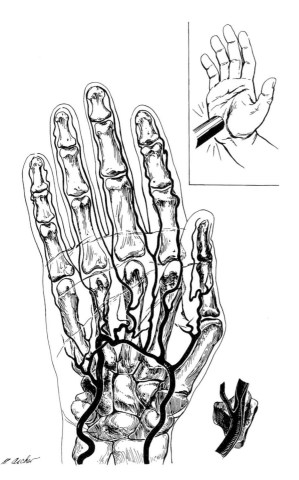

FIGURE 98-3 Mechanism of ulnar artery injury in a patient with hypothenar hammer syndrome. The terminal branch of the ulnar artery is vulnerable to injury because of its close proximity to the hamate bone *(inset)*.

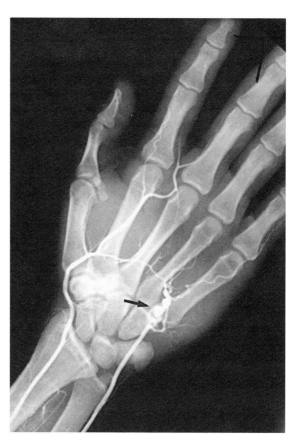

FIGURE 98-4 Arteriogram of the hand in a carpenter. Note the aneurysm of the ulnar artery *(arrow)* because of repetitive trauma from using the hand as a hammer.

Table 98-3	Occupations of 33 Patients with Hypothenar Hammer Syndrome	
	Mechanic/automobile repair	15
	Lathe operator	3
	Fitter and turner	2
	Tire braider	2
	Carpenter	2
	Engineer	2
	Machinist	2
	Painter	1
	Butcher	1
	Gardener	1
	Tool and die worker	1
	Bus conductor	1

Modified from Pineda CJ, Weisman MH, Bookstein JJ, et al: Hypothenar hammer syndrome: Form of reversible Raynaud's phenomenon. Am J Med 79:561, 1985. With permission of Excerpta Medica, Inc.

Clinically the patient reports symptoms of Raynaud's phenomenon—numbness, paresthesias, stiffness, coldness, and blanching of one or more digits of the dominant hand. In the series of patients described by Conn and colleagues,[25] the ring finger was most often involved. The traditional triphasic color changes (white-blue-red) and thumb involvement are uncommon.[28] Physical examination may disclose a prominent callus over the hypothenar eminence, coldness or mottling of the involved fingertip, and atrophic ulceration. A positive Allen's test result, which indicates ulnar artery occlusion, is common. Occasionally an aneurysm is observed as a pulsatile mass in the hypothenar eminence.

The diagnosis is suggested by a history of repetitive trauma to the dominant hand and physical finding of a pulsatile mass in the palm. B-mode ultrasound scanning is particularly useful in confirming the presence of an ulnar artery aneurysm. Traditional arteriography is helpful in diagnosis of hypothenar hammer syndrome and in treatment planning. Arteriography defines the type of vascular lesion (spasm, aneurysm, occlusion), shows its site and extent, and identifies the presence of significant collateral vessels. Frequently, these patients have an incomplete superficial palmar arch, even in the asymptomatic hand. More recently, high-resolution contrast-enhanced magnetic resonance angiography has been used as a noninvasive modality in place of standard angiography.[31]

Treatment of ulnar artery occlusion is often supportive, and surgical intervention is seldom needed or possible. Catheter-directed intra-arterial thrombolytic therapy may be beneficial if ischemic symptoms occur within 2 weeks. Occasionally an ulnar aneurysm is uncovered by thrombolysis. Aneurysms of the ulnar artery should be resected to eliminate the source of emboli and can be treated by resection with end-to-end anastomosis or by an interposed vein graft. Satisfactory long-term results have been reported with this approach by Vayssairat and coworkers.[32]

■ OCCUPATIONAL ACRO-OSTEOLYSIS

Occupational acro-osteolysis was first described by Wilson and colleagues[33] in workers exposed to polyvinyl chloride. Many of these workers present with ischemic symptoms in

the hand. Resorption of the distal phalangeal tufts develops, similar to that seen with scleroderma. The dominant presenting symptoms are those of Raynaud's phenomenon. Few reports of angiography in this syndrome have been published to document damage to the digital arteries.[34-36] The findings include multiple arterial stenoses and occlusions of the digital arteries along with nonspecific hypervascularity adjacent to the areas of bony resorption. The reason for the hypervascularity is not clear, but it may be related to stasis of contrast medium in digital pulp arteries secondary to shortening and retraction of the fingers. Some of these digits were clubbed, a finding that also has been associated with hypervascularity in the fingertips.

■ ELECTRICAL BURNS

Electrical burns inflict tissue destruction in relation to the voltage applied. Currents of less than 1000 V cause injuries limited to the immediate underlying skin and soft tissues. High voltage (>1000 V) usually causes extensive damage as the current travels from the point of entry to the point of exit. No tissue is immune to the devastating effects of high-voltage injury, and arterial injury may occur. The upper extremity, especially the hand, is more often involved than other parts of the body because of its grasping function. The arterial injury is often manifested by arterial necrosis with thrombus or bleeding, occasionally producing gangrenous digits.

Bookstein[34] described the angiographic changes in the upper extremity after electrical injury. The findings include extensive occlusion of the ulnar and digital arteries and thrombosis of the radial artery. Arterial spasm also may be present. Later on, damage of the media may cause aneurysm formation. Figure 98-5 shows a brachial artery aneurysm in a patient who had sustained electrical burns 9 months earlier. Treatment depends on the associated soft tissue and bone injuries. Major artery occlusion documented by arteriography requires bypass grafting, and good results have been reported.[37]

■ EXTREME THERMAL INJURIES

Vasomotor disturbances in the hands of individuals exposed to extreme chronic thermal trauma typically present with Raynaud's phenomenon. Workers at highest risk for thermal injuries are those in a profession that subjects their hands to chronic cold exposure, such as slaughterhouses, canning factories, and fisheries.[38,39] Epidemiologic studies examining this dilemma are limited. The action of alternating ice cold and hot exposure, use of plastic gloves in cold exposure, and long-term cold exposure seem to be identifiable risk factors.

■ ATHLETIC INJURIES

Athletes, particularly professionals who engage in strenuous or exaggerated hand or shoulder activity, may develop hand or upper extremity ischemia as a result of arterial injury. Hand ischemia often is manifested by Raynaud's phenomenon, symptoms of sudden arterial occlusion, or embolization to digits. Three types of arterial injuries are common: hand ischemia, quadrilateral space syndrome, and thoracic

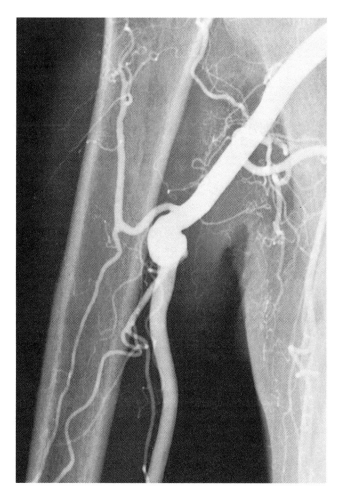

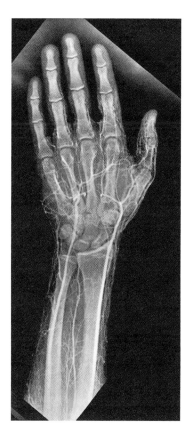

FIGURE 98-6 Occlusion of the palmar arch in a Frisbee player. Because of the injury, there is poor filling of the contrast media in the second, third, fourth, and fifth fingers.

FIGURE 98-5 Aneurysm of the brachial artery in an electrician who had sustained a high-voltage electrical burn 9 months previously.

outlet compression of the subclavian-axillary artery. The exact incidences are unknown; however, vascular injury has been reported in professional or competitive players of baseball, karate, volleyball, handball, Frisbee, and lacrosse and in weightlifters and butterfly swimmers.[20,28,40-44]

Hand Ischemia

Repetitive trauma is the principal cause of hand ischemia. Mechanisms of ischemia fall into two main categories: (1) direct digital artery injury or (2) embolization from a source more proximal in the upper extremity. Nearly all hand activity involved in any sport can cause blunt force injury to the arteries.[45] Although infrequent, hand ischemia due to direct digital arterial trauma is encountered more often in handball players, baseball catchers, and practitioners of karate. Among baseball players, hand ischemia is more common in pitchers, catchers, and first-basemen owing to frequent contact with the baseball. Figure 98-6 illustrates an occlusion of the palmar arch in a Frisbee player; ischemia of all fingers occurred suddenly after he caught the Frisbee. It has been suggested that handball players with more than 200 hours of accumulated playing time are at greater risk for symptomatic alterations in perfusion.[46,47]

Professional baseball players, particularly catchers, are likely to develop chronic hand ischemia. Many catchers have symptoms of Raynaud's phenomenon, especially in the off-season when they engage in outdoor activity in cool autumn or winter weather. Lowrey[48] reported decreased digital perfusion to the index finger of the glove hand in 13 of 22 baseball catchers examined by Doppler flow detector and Allen's test. Of 10 professional catchers studied in the author's laboratory, 40% had evidence of digital artery occlusion (see Fig. 98-2).[20] Considering the speed of the baseball and the impact of the force on the hands, perhaps arterial injury in professional baseball catchers occurs more often than would be expected.

Another form of hand ischemia occasionally observed in baseball pitchers is compression of the digital artery by Cleland's ligament. These ligamentous structures are found on the palmar surface of the digits and span from the phalanx to the subcutaneous tissue (Fig. 98-7). The proposed mechanism is compression of the digital vessels on hyperextension of the proximal interphalangeal joints.

Treating hand ischemia depends on the mode of presentation. With acute injury, a conservative approach using dextran 40 infusion and pain control is in order. Surgical intervention is rarely needed; however, attempts at digital sympathectomy or release of Cleland's ligaments have met with some short-term successes.[49] Preventing injury is important and can be accomplished by the use of gloves with padding and other protective devices.[48]

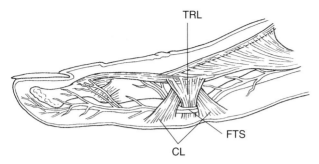

FIGURE 98-7 With the proximal interphalangeal joint in hyperextension, Cleland's ligaments may compress and occlude the vascular supply to the fingertip. CL, Cleland's ligaments; FTS, flexor tendon sheath; TRL, transverse retinacular ligament.

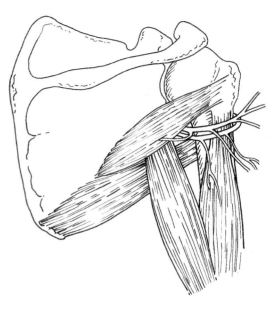

FIGURE 98-8 The posterior humeral circumflex artery and axillary nerve traverse the interval of the quadrilateral space.

Quadrilateral Space Syndrome

Quadrilateral space syndrome was first described in 1983 by Cahill and Palmer,[50] who reported on the diagnosis and surgical treatment of 18 patients presenting with this entity. The quadrilateral space is defined as the area bordered by the teres minor superiorly, humeral shaft laterally, teres major inferiorly, and long head of the triceps muscle medially (Fig. 98-8). Found within this space are the posterior humeral circumflex artery and the axillary nerve. Compression of the posterior humeral circumflex artery within this space has been shown to occur with the arm in the "cocked" position (abduction and external rotation). Chronic compression and trauma to this artery among throwing athletes, particularly pitchers, can lead to aneurysmal dilation or occlusion. Aneurysms in this location are prone to distal embolization in the hand. Surgical treatment of aneurysms in this location involves ligation of the posterior humeral circumflex artery. The anterior and posterior humeral circumflex arteries provide blood supply to the humeral head, and at least one of the two vessels must be preserved or repaired to prevent avascular necrosis.

Thoracic Outlet Compression

Athletes who engage in overextended shoulder motion, such as baseball pitchers, butterfly swimmers, weightlifters, and oarsmen, are potential candidates for thoracic outlet compression. Injuries to the subclavian artery or vein have been reported in these athletes. In professional baseball pitchers, the injury is most likely due to the violent throwing motion. The act of pitching has five phases: (1) wind-up, (2) cocking, (3) acceleration, (4) release and deceleration, and (5) follow-through. Most injuries occur during the acceleration and deceleration phases.[51] It has been estimated that the fast ball creates 600 inch-lb of forward momentum at release of the ball. It is understandable that soft tissue injury may occur because of the force absorbed by the shoulder and the elbow.[52]

Symptoms are more common in pitchers whose throwing motion is overhand rather than sidearm. Symptoms are pain in the region of the elbow associated with easy fatigue and loss of pitch velocity after several innings. Raynaud's phenomenon also has been observed in these pitchers. Diagnosis is often difficult, and a complete evaluation by an orthopedic surgeon to rule out musculoskeletal abnormalities is mandatory. Duplex scanning and transcutaneous Doppler flow detection with the athlete in pitching position help to detect compression of the subclavian or axillary artery. Finally, definitive diagnosis is established by arteriography with positional exposure (Figs. 98-9 and 98-10).

Arterial injury in the pitching arm affects the subclavian artery,[41] the axillary artery,[40] and the humeral circumflex arteries.[50] Compression to the subclavian or axillary artery is often due to hypertrophy of the anterior scalene or the pectoralis minor muscle; however, arterial injury can occur at the costoclavicular space, humeral head, or quadrilateral space. In 1964, Tullos and colleagues[40] were the first to report an axillary artery thrombus secondary to pectoralis minor compression in a major league pitcher. In 1978, Strukel and Garrick[53] reported on three competitive baseball pitchers who had thoracic outlet compression. Until Fields'[54] report on athletic injury in the thoracic outlet, the injury had received little attention. The report by Fields and associates[41] on a major league pitcher who suffered a catastrophic stroke resulting from subclavian artery thrombosis with proximal clot propagation is of great interest. The humeral head and the pectoralis minor muscle and other shoulder muscles have been shown to be hypertrophied in pitchers; these structures are more prone to cause local trauma to the nearby vessels in this group of athletic individuals.[55,56]

It is now recognized that aneurysm formation in the anterior and, more commonly, the posterior circumflex arteries resulting from repetitive athletic activities is responsible for severe hand ischemia secondary to distal embolization.[57] Tethering of the axillary artery between the chest and the loop of circumflex arteries, around the humeral neck, can produce a traction injury resulting in intimal damage with subsequent thrombosis or aneurysm formation. Distal embolization occurs because of retrograde

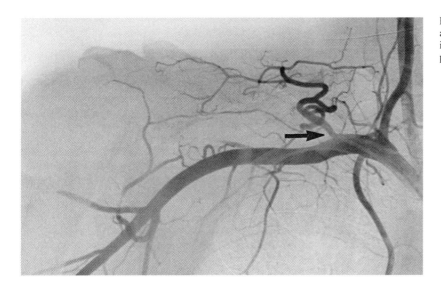

FIGURE 98-9 Arteriogram of the right subclavian artery *(arrow)* in a professional baseball pitcher. No injury is seen when the arm is placed in neutral position.

clot extrusion from the side branch aneurysm with persistent excessive activity of the upper extremity. Such injury has been observed in baseball pitchers and volleyball players (Fig. 98-11).[55,58,59] Reekers and coworkers[59] believe that the downward pull of the humeral head during the "smash" in volleyball is a mechanism of axillary artery trauma akin to pitching. In both instances, the circumflex artery is not the only one affected; aneurysm formation in the suprascapular and subscapular arteries also has been reported.[60] Additionally, direct trauma from the head of the humerus can cause compression to the axillary artery with similar sequelae.[55,58,61]

In addition to arterial injury, thrombosis of the subclavian-axillary vein, so-called effort thrombosis or Paget-Schroetter syndrome, has been reported in baseball pitchers,[62] weight-lifters,[63] and competitive swimmers.[64] The presumed mechanism of injury is similar to that of the arterial system, and treatment options are similar.

Treatment depends on the extent of injury. Compression only is best treated by division of the offending muscle and tendon. Occlusion of a major artery requires bypass grafting together with decompression of the thoracic outlet. Traditional reconstruction is advocated; however, some authors have reported on the successful use of an extra-anatomic bypass over the pectoralis muscle after arterial injury in pitchers.[65] Aneurysms of the circumflex artery and thrombosis in the axillary artery are best treated via a transaxillary approach with resection of the aneurysm or vein grafting or both if indicated.[61] Management of acute venous thrombosis is controversial, varying from anti-coagulation alone to decompressive surgery to venoplasty and stenting.[66-69] In athletes, some form of decompression is needed to return to competitive activity. To return a professional athlete to full activity, close consultation with a trainer or sports medicine specialist and carefully supervised rehabilitation are necessary.

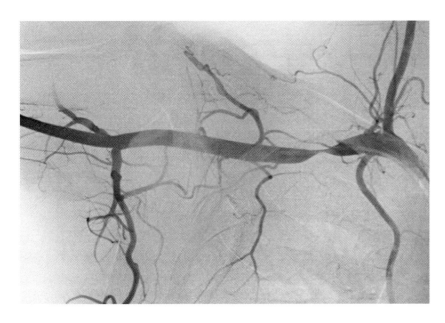

FIGURE 98-10 In the same patient shown in Figure 98-9, there is compression of the subclavian artery when the arm is placed in the pitching position (hyperabduction).

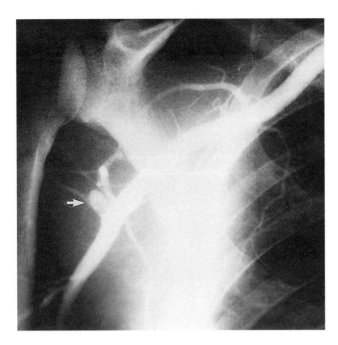

FIGURE 98-11 Artery of a major league baseball pitcher. Note the emboli of the posterior circumflex artery *(arrow)*. (From Yao JST: Upper extremity ischemia in athletes. Semin Vasc Surg 11:96, 1998.)

■ REFERENCES

1. Buckle PW: Fortnightly review: Work factors and upper limb disorders. BMJ 315:1360, 1997.
2. Bureau of Labor Statistics Reports on Survey of Occupational Injuries and Illness in 1977-1989. Washington, D.C., Bureau of Labor Statistics, U.S. Department of Labor, 1990.
3. Rempel DM, Harrison RJ, Barnhart S: Work-related cumulative trauma disorders of the upper extremity. JAMA 267:838, 1992.
4. Griffin MJ: Vibration injuries of the hand and arm: Their occurrence and the evolution of standards and limits. London, Her Majesty's Stationery Office, 1980.
5. Yodaiken RE, Jones E, Kunicki R: The Raynaud phenomenon of occupational origin. In Altura BM, Davis E (eds): Advances in Microcirculation, vol. 12. Basel, Karger, 1985, p 6.
6. Loriga G: Ill lavoro con i martelli pneumatic boll. Ispett Lavoro 2:35, 1911.
7. Cottingham CE: Effects of use of air hammer on hands of Indiana stone cutters. U.S. Bureau of Labor Statistics 19:125, 1918.
8. Taylor W, Pelmear PL (eds): Vibration White Finger in Industry. New York, Academic Press, 1975.
9. Ashe WF, Cook WT, Old JW: Raynaud's phenomenon of occupational origin. Arch Environ Health 5:63, 1962.
10. Newem RM: Vibration-induced arterial shear stress: The relationship to Raynaud's phenomenon of occupational origin. Arch Environ Health 26:105, 1973.
11. Bovenzi M: Some pathophysiological aspects of vibration-induced white finger. Eur J Appl Physiol 55:381, 1986.
12. Pearce WH, Yao JST, Bergan JJ: Noninvasive vascular diagnostic testing. In Ravitch MM (ed): Current Problems in Surgery, vol. 20. Chicago, Year Book Medical Publishers, 1983.
13. Sumner DS: Vascular laboratory diagnosis and assessment of upper extremity vascular disorders. In Machleder HI (ed): Vascular Disorders of the Upper Extremity. Mt. Kisco, NY, Futura Publishing Company, 1983, p 1.
14. Payne KM, Blackburn DR, Peterson LK, et al: B-Mode imaging of the arteries of the hand and upper extremity. Bruit 10:168, 1986.
15. Barker NW, Hines EA Jr: Arterial occlusion in the hands and fingers associated with repeated occupational trauma. Mayo Clin Proc 19:345, 1944.
16. Shatz IJ: Occlusive arterial disease in the hand due to occupational trauma. N Engl J Med 268:281, 1963.
17. Ashe WF, Williams N: Occupational Raynaud's: II. Further studies of this disorder in uranium mine workers. Arch Environ Health 9:425, 1964.
18. Wegelius U: Angiography of the hand: Clinical and postmortem investigations. Acta Radiol Suppl (Stockh) 315:1, 1972.
19. Griffin MJ, Bovenzi M, Nelson CM: Dose-response patterns for vibration-induced white finger. Occup Environ Med 60:16, 2003.
20. Bartel P, Blackburn D, Peterson L, et al: The value of noninvasive tests in occupational trauma of the hands and fingers. Bruit 8:15, 1984.
21. Threshold limit values approved by ACGIH for hand-arm vibration. Noise Reg Reporter 11:3, 1984.
22. Kahan A, Amor B, Menkes CJ: Nifedipine and allied substances in the treatment of Raynaud's phenomenon. In Altura BM, Davis E (eds): Advances in Microcirculation, vol. 12. Basel, Karger, 1985, p 95.
23. Chetter IC, Kent PJ, Kester RC: The hand arm vibration syndrome: A review. Cardiovasc Surg 6:1, 1998.
24. Kleinert HE, Burget GC, Morgan JA, et al: Aneurysms of the hand. Arch Surg 106:554, 1973.
25. Conn J, Bergan JJ, Bell JL: Hypothenar hammer syndrome: Post-traumatic digital ischemia. Surgery 68:1122, 1970.
26. Von Rosen S: Ein Fall von Thrombose in der Arteria ulnaris nach Einwirkung von stumpfer Gewalt. Acta Chir Scand 73:500, 1934.
27. Short DW: Occupational aneurysm of the palmar arch. Lancet 2:217, 1948.
28. Pineda CJ, Weisman MH, Bookstein JJ, et al: Hypothenar hammer syndrome: Form of reversible Raynaud's phenomenon. Am J Med 79:561, 1985.
29. Little JM, Ferguson DA: The incidence of the hypothenar hammer syndrome. Arch Surg 105:684, 1972.
30. Ferris BL, Taylor LM Jr, Oyama K, et al: Hypothenar hammer syndrome: Proposed etiology. J Vasc Surg 31:104, 2000.
31. Winterer JT, Ghanem N, Roth M, et al: Diagnosis of the hypothenar hammer syndrome by high-resolution contrast-enhanced MR angiography. Eur Radiol 12:2457, 2002.
32. Vayssairat M, Debure C, Cormier J, et al: Hypothenar hammer syndrome: Seventeen cases with long-term follow-up. J Vasc Surg 5:838, 1987.
33. Wilson R, McCormick W, Tattum C, et al: Occupational acro-osteolysis. JAMA 201:577, 1967.
34. Bookstein JJ: Arteriography. In Poznanski AK (ed): The Hand in Radiologic Diagnosis with Gamuts and Pattern Profiles, vol. 1, 2nd ed. Philadelphia, WB Saunders, 1984, p 97.
35. Veltman G: Raynaud's syndrome in vinylchloride disease. In Heidrich H (ed): Raynaud's Phenomenon. Berlin, TM-Verlag, 1979, p 211.
36. Falappa P, Magnavita N, Bergamaschi A, et al: Angiographic study of digital arteries in workers exposed to vinyl chloride. Br J Ind Med 39:169, 1982.
37. Wang X, Roberts BB, Zapata-Sirvent RL, et al: Early vascular grafting to prevent upper extremity necrosis after electrical burns: Commentary on indications for surgery. Burns 11:359, 1985.
38. Kaminski M, Bourgine M, Zins M, et al: Risk factors for Raynaud's phenomenon among workers in poultry slaughterhouses and canning factories. Int J Epidemiol 26:371, 1997.
39. Mackiewicz Z, Piskorz A: Raynaud's phenomenon following long-term repeated action or great differences of temperature. J Cardiovasc Surg (Torino) 18:151, 1977.
40. Tullos HS, Erwin WD, Woods GW, et al: Unusual lesions of the pitching arm. Clin Orthop 88:169, 1972.
41. Fields WS, Lemak NA, Ben-Menachem Y: Thoracic outlet syndrome: Review and reference to stroke in a major league pitcher. AJNR Am J Neuroradiol 7:73, 1986.
42. Green DP: True and false traumatic aneurysms in the hand: Report of two cases and review of the literature. J Bone Joint Surg Am 55:120, 1973.

43. Ho PK, Dellon AL, Wilgis EFS: True aneurysms of the hand resulting from athletic injury: Report of two cases. Am J Sports Med 13:136, 1985.

44. Arko FR, Harris EJ, Zarins CK, Olcott C IV: Vascular complications in high-performance athletes. J Vasc Surg 33:935, 2001.

45. Noel B, Hayoz D: A tennis player with hand claudication. Vasa 29:151, 2000.

46. Buckhout BC, Warner MA: Digital perfusion of handball players: Effects of repeated ball impact on structures of the hand. Am J Sports Med 8:206, 1980.

47. McCue FC III, Miller GA: Soft-tissue injuries to the hand. In Pettrone FA (ed): Upper Extremity Injuries in Athletes. St Louis, CV Mosby, 1986, p 85.

48. Lowrey CW: Digital vessel trauma from repetitive impacts in baseball catchers. J Hand Surg 1:236, 1976.

49. Itoh Y, Wakano K, Takeda T, Murakami T: Circulatory disturbances in the throwing hand of baseball pitchers. Am J Sports Med 15:264, 1987.

50. Cahill B, Palmer R: Quadrilateral space syndrome. J Hand Surg 8:65, 1983.

51. McLeod WD: The pitching mechanism. In Zarins B, Andrews JR, Carson WG Jr (eds): Injuries to the Throwing Arm. Philadelphia, WB Saunders, 1985, p 22.

52. Sain J, Andrews JR: Proper pitching techniques. In Zarins B, Andrews JR, Carson WG Jr (eds): Injuries to the Throwing Arm. Philadelphia, WB Saunders, 1985, p 34.

53. Strukel RJ, Garrick JG: Thoracic outlet compression in athletes: A report of four cases. Am J Sports Med 6:35, 1978.

54. Fields WS: Neurovascular syndromes of the neck and shoulders. Semin Neurol 1:301, 1981.

55. McCarthy WJ, Yao JST, Schafer MF, et al: Upper extremity arterial injury in athletes. J Vasc Surg 9:317, 1989.

56. Jones HH, Priest JD, Hayes WC, et al: Humeral hypertrophy in response to exercise. J Bone Joint Surg Am 59:204, 1977.

57. Nijhuis HHAM, Muller-Wiefel H: Occlusion of the brachial artery by thrombus dislodged from a traumatic aneurysm of the anterior humeral circumflex artery. J Vasc Surg 13:408, 1991.

58. Rohrer MJ, Cardullo PA, Pappas AM, et al: Axillary artery compression and thrombosis in throwing athletes. J Vasc Surg 11:761, 1990.

59. Reekers JA, den Hartog BMG, Kuyper CF, et al: Traumatic aneurysm of the posterior circumflex humeral artery: A volleyball player's disease? J Vasc Interv Radiol 4:405, 1993.

60. Kee ST, Dake MD, Wolfe-Johnson B, et al: Ischemia of the throwing hand in major league baseball pitchers: Embolic occlusion from aneurysms of axillary artery branches. J Vasc Interv Radiol 6:979, 1995.

61. Durham JR, Yao JST, Pearce WH, et al: Arterial injuries in the thoracic outlet syndrome. J Vasc Surg 21:57, 1995.

62. Dale WA: Thoracic outlet compression syndrome. In Dale WA (ed): Management of Vascular Surgical Problems. New York, McGraw-Hill, 1985, p 562.

63. Baker CL, Thornberry R: Neurovascular syndromes. In Zarins B, Andrews JR, Carson WG Jr (eds): Injuries to the Throwing Arm. Philadelphia, WB Saunders, 1985, p 176.

64. Vogel CM, Jensen JE: "Effort" thrombosis of the subclavian vein in a competitive swimmer. Am J Sports Med 13:269, 1985.

65. Ishitobi K, Moteki K, Nara S, et al: Extra-anatomic bypass graft for management of axillary artery occlusion in pitchers. J Vasc Surg 33:797, 2001.

66. Lee WA, Hill B, Harris EJ Jr, et al: Surgical intervention is not required for all patients with subclavian vein thrombosis. J Vasc Surg 32:57, 2000.

67. Azakie A, McElhinney DB, Thompson RW, et al: Surgical management of subclavian-vein effort thrombosis as a result of thoracic outlet compression. J Vasc Surg 28:777, 1998.

68. Kreienberg PB, Chang BB, Darling RC III, et al: Long-term results in patients treated with thrombolysis, thoracic inlet decompression, and subclavian vein stenting for Paget-Schroetter syndrome. J Vasc Surg 33:S100, 2001.

69. AbuRahma AF, Robinson PA: Effort subclavian vein thrombosis: Evolution of management. J Endovasc Ther 7:302, 2000.

ARTERIAL ANEURYSMS

JACK L. CRONENWETT, MD

Chapter

Overview

99

JACK L. CRONENWETT, MD

The term *aneurysm* is derived from the Greek word *aneurysma,* meaning "a widening." By current reporting standards, an aneurysm is defined as a permanent localized dilatation of an artery, having at least a 50% increase in diameter compared with the expected normal diameter.[1] Arterial dilatation less than 50% of normal is termed *ectasia*. Normal arterial diameter depends on age, gender, body size, and other factors. By practical convention, an aneurysm is defined as a localized dilatation at least 50% larger than an adjacent normal portion of the same artery.[1] If there is no adjacent normal artery segment, this definition must rely on an estimate of the expected normal diameter (Table 99-1). Diffuse arterial enlargement involving several arterial segments with an increase in diameter greater than 50% of normal is termed *arteriomegaly*. This condition is distinct from multiple aneurysms that are separated by normal-diameter arterial segments (sometimes termed *aneurysmosis*), although arteriomegaly often is associated with multiple aneurysms.

■ HISTORICAL PERSPECTIVE

Arterial aneurysms have been recognized since ancient times. One of the earliest texts known, the Ebers Papyrus (2000 B.C.), contains a description of traumatic aneurysms of the peripheral arteries.[2] Galen (A.D. 131-200) defined an aneurysm as a localized pulsatile swelling that disappeared on pressure.[3] The first elective operation for treatment of an aneurysm was reported by Antyllus in the 2nd century A.D. He recommended ligating the artery above and below the aneurysm, then incising the sac and evacuating its contents.[4] This recommendation for aneurysm repair remained the basis of direct arterial operations for the next 1500 years. In the 7th century, Aetius of Amida recognized the difference between true degenerative aneurysms and traumatic false aneurysms.[5] In medieval times, brachial artery false aneurysms were frequent iatrogenic complications of blood letting during attempted puncture of the median cubital vein. Paré (1510-1590) applied his principles of proper wound care to these brachial aneurysms.[6] Paré's contemporary, Vesalius, wrote one of the first descriptions of an abdominal aortic aneurysm (AAA).[2] A century later, Wiseman (1625-1686), known as "the father of English surgery," successfully ligated a brachial artery false aneurysm, despite its rupture after exposure for repair.[5]

Hunter (1728-1793) performed perhaps the most famous operation for an arterial aneurysm.[5] Hunter had observed variation in blood vessel content in the horns of deer that were grown and shed and inferred that "reserve vessels"—now termed *collaterals*—might develop in humans if obstruction occurred in their arteries. In 1785, he treated a coachman with a pulsatile mass in the popliteal fossa, possibly secondary to repetitive trauma against the coach seat while driving on rough streets. The patient also had claudication, presumably from arterial occlusion distal to the aneurysm, and Hunter concluded that collateral arteries must have developed around the occlusion. Standard treatment at that time entailed above-knee amputation, as strongly advocated by another renowned London surgeon, Pott (1714-1788).[7] Hunter incised above the knee at a location now called *Hunter's canal* and ligated the artery with four sutures to avoid sawing through the vessel. After a bout of local infection, the patient survived and was discharged. Later, Hunter performed four similar operations, and three were successful.

Cooper (1768-1841) was Hunter's most acclaimed disciple. Although he is best remembered for his contributions to inguinal hernia repair and breast anatomy, his most celebrated operation was performed for a leaking iliac artery aneurysm in 1817.[8] His attempt to ligate the abdominal aorta

Table 99-1   Reported Diameter of Normal Adult Arteries

ARTERY	DIAMETER (cm)	GENDER
Aorta, thoracic		
Root	3.50-3.72	Female
	3.63-3.91	Male
Ascending	2.86	Female/male
Descending, mid	2.45-2.64	Female
	2.39-2.98	Male
At diaphragm	2.40-2.44	Female
	2.43-2.69	Male
Aorta, abdominal		
Supraceliac	2.10-2.31	Female
	2.50-2.72	Male
Suprarenal	1.86-1.88	Female
	1.98-2.27	Male
Infrarenal	1.19-2.16	Female
	1.41-2.39	Male
Celiac	0.53	Female/male
Superior mesenteric	0.63	Female/male
Iliac		
Common	0.97-1.02	Female
	1.17-1.23	Male
Internal	0.54	Female/male
Common femoral	0.78-0.85	Female
	0.78-1.12	Male
Popliteal	0.9	Male
	0.3	Male
Carotid		
Common	0.77	Female
	0.63-0.84	Male
Bulb	0.92	Female
	0.99	Male
Internal	0.49	Female
	0.55	Male
Brachial	0.39	Female
	0.42-0.44	Male

From Johnston KW, Rutherford RB, Tilson MD, et al: Suggested standards for reporting on arterial aneurysms. J Vasc Surg 13:452, 1991.

initially seemed successful, but the patient died suddenly after 40 hours. Cooper also reported the first documented case of a spontaneous aortoenteric fistula resulting from aneurysmal disease and cautioned that patients who present with one aneurysm should be evaluated for the coexistence of others.[8] The 18th century can be characterized as the era of arterial ligation for treatment of aneurysms with surgeons such as Anel, Brasdor, and Wardrop defending the merits of different sites of ligation in relation to the aneurysm. Subsequent studies showed the ongoing risk of rupture in patients treated with nonresective methods.[9]

In 1804, Scarpa (1747-1832) wrote a definitive treatise on the forms and diagnosis of arterial aneurysms. About this time, several ingenious treatments were introduced. Monteggia (1762-1815) unwisely attempted to cure an aneurysm by injecting a sclerosant into it, which predictably failed because of rapid blood flow. Attempts to thrombose aneurysms by passing an electric current between needles stuck into the vessel were begun in 1832 and were still going on in the 1930s. Moore (1821-1870), at Middlesex Hospital in London, introduced obliteration of aneurysms by inserting steel wires in 1864, once using 26 yards of the material.[5] One of the most prominent Americans known to have aneurysmal disease in the 19th century was Kit Carson, who died of a ruptured AAA in rural Colorado in 1868.[10] Albert Einstein also died of a ruptured AAA.[11] In contrast to

Carson, Einstein had been treated for his disorder by means of wrapping the aneurysm in cellophane, a technique introduced by Rea in 1948.[12]

A better method of treatment of peripheral aneurysms had been developed in 1888 by the legendary New Orleans surgeon, Matas (1860-1957). His technique of endoaneurysmorrhaphy involved clamping above and below the aneurysm, opening it, ligating branches from within, and buttressing the wall with imbricating sutures. By 1906, he had performed 22 obliterative operations and 7 restorative operations (preserving the arterial lumen) with no recurrences. Matas[13] performed the first successful proximal ligation of an aortic aneurysm in 1923, approximately 106 years after Cooper's innovative operation. Matas' endoaneurysmorrhaphy presaged the current prevailing method of "internal" or intrasaccular reconstruction conceived by Creech[14] and DeBakey. Another notable achievement at the turn of the 20th century is attributed to Goyanes of Madrid.[15] In 1906, Goyanes excluded a popliteal aneurysm by proximal and distal ligation. In addition, he mobilized the adjacent popliteal vein and used it as an in-situ interposition graft between the proximal femoral artery and the distal popliteal artery by means of end-to-end anastomoses. This important contribution, which had a good outcome, remained largely ignored until many years later.

Modern techniques of aneurysm repair were made possible by Carrel (1873-1944), who showed in animals that a segment of aorta could be replaced with a piece from another artery or vein by successfully anastomosing these blood vessels. Carrel won the Nobel Prize for this work in 1912. It was not until March 29, 1951, however, that his countryman DuBost performed the first successful replacement of an aortic aneurysm with a freeze-dried homograft.[16] He was inspired by a similar operation for an occluded abdominal aorta by Oudot in 1950.[17] The second and third aortic aneurysm repairs in which patients survived were performed on October 25, 1952, one by Julian's group[18] in Chicago and the other by Brock and associates[19] in London. DeBakey and Cooley[20] in Houston soon reported survival of five of six patients operated on for replacement of AAAs. In a series of 17 aortic aneurysm operations, Bahnson[21] from Johns Hopkins described the first successful repair of a ruptured aortic aneurysm. In 1953, Voorhees and colleagues[22] introduced a major innovation by substituting Vinyon-N cloth for the unreliable homograft. The modern era of aneurysm repair had truly begun. The first successful repair of a thoracoabdominal aortic aneurysm was reported by Etheredge and colleagues in 1955.[23] Crawford[24] became the authority on this formidable procedure beginning with his 1974 report delineating good results with 28 consecutive operations for thoracoabdominal aortic aneurysms. Crawford's contributions to the repair of complex aortic aneurysms were extraordinary and have greatly reduced the risks of surgery. Throughout the late 1950s and early 1960s, aortic aneurysm repair became a common and safe surgical procedure throughout the world.

■ ANEURYSM CLASSIFICATION

Aneurysms are classified according to their location, size, shape, and etiology. By definition, (true) aneurysms represent a dilatation of all layers of the arterial wall. Confusion

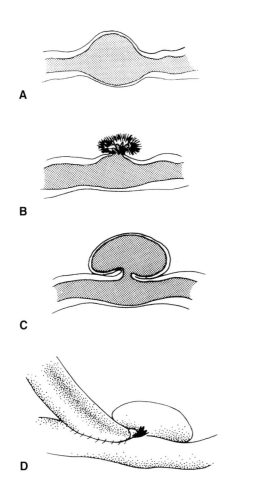

FIGURE 99-1 True arterial aneurysm (**A**) showing localized dilatation of all layers of the arterial wall with marked thinning of the media. Arterial injury causes hemorrhage (**B**), which, if contained by surrounding connective tissue, can result in a false aneurysm (**C**) consisting of the contained hematoma in communication with the artery. False aneurysms also commonly arise if an arterial graft anastomosis is partially disrupted (**D**), owing to infection or degeneration of the native arterial tissue.

Table 99-2	Aneurysm Classification by Etiology
TYPE	**EXAMPLE**
Congenital	Idiopathic Tuberous sclerosis Turner's syndrome Menkes' syndrome Persistent sciatic artery
Connective tissue disorder	Marfan's syndrome Ehlers-Danlos syndrome Cystic medial necrosis Berry (cerebral)
Degenerative	Nonspecific ("atherosclerotic") Fibromuscular dysplasia
Infectious	Bacterial Fungal Syphilis
Inflammatory arteritis	Takayasu's disease Behçet's disease Kawasaki's disease Polyarteritis nodosa Giant cell arteritis Periarterial (e.g., pancreatitis)
Post-dissection	Idiopathic Cystic medial necrosis Trauma
Post-stenotic	Thoracic outlet syndrome Coarctation
Pseudoaneurysm	Trauma Anastomotic disruption
Miscellaneous	Pregnancy-associated Inflammatory abdominal aortic

exists concerning the definition of false aneurysms (or pseudoaneurysms) because these often have been described as aneurysms that do not involve all layers of the arterial wall. In reality, false aneurysms are just that; they are not arterial aneurysms. Rather, they represent contained hematomas that result from localized arterial disruption, with a persistent channel to the arterial lumen so that they are pulsatile and have the appearance of a true aneurysm on examination (Fig. 99-1). False aneurysms do not contain *any* layers of the arterial wall, but rather represent a disruption of the arterial wall with extravasation of blood that is contained by surrounding layers of connective tissue. When chronic, the fibrotic reaction around such hematomas can become well organized, and it resembles a true aneurysm wall even when exposed at surgery. Historically, false aneurysms most frequently resulted from penetrating trauma. Today, they more frequently result from iatrogenic injury during arterial catheterization or arterial graft anastomotic disruption. False aneurysms are discussed in detail in Chapter 60.

Aneurysm shape is commonly described as saccular versus fusiform (spindle-shaped), although these represent a continuum rather than discrete entities. In general, saccular or eccentric aneurysms are believed to have a higher rupture risk,[25] but new analyses of calculated wall stress based on shape show that this is a complex relationship (see Chapter 100).[26,27] Aneurysm size is described by diameter and length, with diameter being the important risk factor for rupture. Aneurysm etiology is the most clinically relevant classification system because it directly influences not only natural history, but also treatment. Although the specific etiology of some aneurysms is well-known (Table 99-2), most aneurysms are nonspecific in etiology. Such aneurysms formerly were termed *atherosclerotic* because they are universally associated with atherosclerotic changes in the arteries of elderly patients. It is now apparent, however, that the etiology of these degenerative aneurysms is much more complex (see Chapter 29). For lack of a better descriptor, they are termed *degenerative* or *nonspecific* and constitute most aneurysms. Congenital aneurysms and aneurysms associated with arteritis and connective tissue abnormalities are rare. Infected aneurysms are more common. Aneurysms that result from wall weakness after arterial dissection represent the most common specific etiology of aneurysms. Considerable confusion also exists concerning the term *dissecting aneurysm.* As discussed in Chapter 104, arterial dissection is a distinct pathologic entity that does not result in aneurysm formation. Chronic arterial dissections frequently are associated with aneurysmal degeneration, however, leading to the confusion in terminology.

■ ANEURYSM LOCATION

The most common site for degenerative aneurysms is the infrarenal abdominal aorta. In a large autopsy series of patients with aortoiliac aneurysms, the relative frequency by location was abdominal aorta alone, 65%; thoracic aorta alone, 19%; abdominal aorta plus iliac, 13%; thoraco-abdominal, 2%; and isolated iliac, 1%.[28] Population-based studies estimate the incidence of clinically apparent AAAs to be 21 per 100,000 person-years[29] compared with 6 per 100,000 person-years for thoracic aortic aneurysms.[30] Although nearly all AAAs are degenerative in etiology, thoracic aortic aneurysms are much more diverse in etiology, with approximately half resulting from prior aortic dissection.[30] AAAs also cause the largest number of deaths from aneurysm rupture. In a Swedish study with a high autopsy rate, ruptured AAAs caused 0.6% of all annual deaths in men, a rate of 648 per 100,000 deaths.[31] This rate was seven times higher than death caused by ruptured thoracic aneurysms; death from ruptured AAA was twice as likely as death from aortic dissection. In women, the mortality rate from ruptured AAAs was only 285 per 100,000 deaths, which was three times higher than deaths caused by ruptured thoracic aneurysms, but less common than death from aortic dissection, which is relatively more frequent in women (343 per 100,000 deaths in this study).[31]

Nonaortic aneurysms are much less common. The incidence of AAAs in hospitalized patients in the United States is approximately 50 per 100,000[32] compared with only 3 per 100,000 for iliac aneurysms and 4 per 100,000 for femoropopliteal aneurysms.[33] Popliteal aneurysms account for 70% of all peripheral aneurysms, whereas carotid aneurysms constitute less than 4%.[34,35] Visceral and renal artery aneurysms are rare. The common femoral artery is the most common site for false aneurysms because arterial grafts commonly begin or end there, and it is the preferred entry site for radiologic and interventional procedures. The femoral artery also is the most common location of infected aneurysms because of the frequency of vascular intervention there and its preferred location for intravenous drug abuse.

■ CLINICAL PRESENTATION

The clinical presentation of an aneurysm depends on the type, size, location, and any confounding factors in the patient, such as connective tissue disorders, hypertension, or intravenous drug abuse. In general, aneurysms can rupture, thrombose, embolize contained thrombus, cause symptoms from local compression of adjacent structures, or be detected in an asymptomatic state. Occasionally, systemic signs, such as sepsis, may be the first manifestation. The relative frequency of these presentations varies significantly among different aneurysm types and locations. Among degenerative aneurysms, those involving the aorta, iliac, and visceral arteries are most prone to rupture, whereas femoral, popliteal, renal, and brachiocephalic aneurysms are more likely to thrombose or embolize. Aneurysms of specific etiology, including congenital, infectious, and dissecting and aneurysms associated with arteritis are usually complicated by rupture. Details of the clinical presentation

of different aneurysms are discussed in the chapters of this Section. Because renal and carotid artery aneurysms are treated with methods similar to methods used for other disorders of these arteries, they are discussed separately in Chapters 133 and 143.

■ ARTERIOMEGALY AND MULTIPLE ANEURYSMS

Arteriomegaly originally was described by Leriche[36] in 1943 as diffuse ectasia of the aorta and iliofemoral arteries without discrete aneurysm formation, which he termed *dolicho et mega-artere* (which means elongated and enlarged arteries). The term *arteriomegaly* was first proposed by Lea Thomas[37] in 1971 to describe diffusely enlarged arteries. In nearly 6000 patients who underwent aortofemoral arteriography, Hollier and coworkers[38] identified arteriomegaly in 5%, of whom one third also had discrete aneurysms in at least three different arterial segments. Arteriomegaly and multiple aneurysms often are associated. Hollier and coworkers[38] recognized three distinct patterns of involvement: type I, with aneurysms of the aorta to common femoral segments with more distal arteriomegaly; type II, with aneurysm of the femoropopliteal segments and more proximal arteriomegaly; and type III, with aneurysms of the aorta to popliteal segments and arteriomegaly of intervening nonaneurysmal segments. All of these patients with arteriomegaly and multiple aneurysms were men who were approximately 5 years younger than the average-age patient with a solitary aneurysm. Arteriomegaly associated with femoral and popliteal aneurysms seemed to increase the risk of thrombosis in this segment. The recommended surgical reconstruction varied according to the exact location of aneurysms, but generally encompassed the intervening ectatic segments.[38] Arteriomegaly also is associated with a familial risk of AAA because 36% of patients with arteriomegaly had a first-degree relative with an aneurysm, all of which were aortic.[39]

Although the term *arteriomegaly* generally is applied to the infrarenal aorta, iliac, femoral, and popliteal segments, the more proximal aorta often is involved with diffuse aneurysmal changes. In a review of more than 1500 patients treated for aortic aneurysms in a specialized referral practice, Crawford and Cohen[40] found that 13% had multiple aortic aneurysms. Most of these patients (72%) presented with multiple aneurysms synchronously, whereas 28% developed later metachronous aortic aneurysms. The etiology of most aneurysms was degenerative (62%), followed by post-dissection (23%) and other specific etiologies (e.g., Marfan's syndrome). The most common location of the primary aneurysm in these patients was the abdominal aorta (63%), followed by the thoracoabdominal (14%), descending (13%), arch (5%), and ascending (5%) aorta. The most common pattern for multiple aneurysms was an infrarenal aortic aneurysm associated with a discrete descending thoracic aortic aneurysm. Although 12% of patients with abdominal aneurysms had thoracic aneurysms, 68% of patients with thoracic aneurysms had other aortic aneurysms, most commonly an infrarenal AAA. In a more recent review of patients with multiple aortic aneurysms,

Gloviczki and associates[41] reported similar findings, although multiple aneurysms were found in only 3.4% of all patients with aortic aneurysms, of whom 75% were men. These studies indicate the need for evaluation of the entire aorta in patients with a known aortic aneurysm; this is especially true for patients with a thoracic aortic aneurysm because of the high likelihood of finding of AAA. Patients who present with thoracic or thoracoabdominal aneurysms should have an initial imaging study of their infrarenal aorta, with subsequent follow-up dictated by patient age and other risk factors. Conversely, for a patient with an AAA, initial computed tomography to exclude a thoracic aneurysm is appropriate if the chest radiograph suggests an aneurysm, if there is evidence of previous dissection or suprarenal aneurysmal involvement, or if the patient is young at presentation, when multiple aneurysms are more likely.[41]

In addition to multiple aortic aneurysms, patients with AAAs have a proclivity for lower extremity aneurysms. In a review of nearly 1500 patients with degenerative aortoiliac aneurysms, 3.5% had other aneurysms, of which 3% were femoral or popliteal, and 0.5% were visceral.[42] All of these patients with aortoiliac and peripheral aneurysms were men. The likelihood of detecting an AAA was high in men with peripheral aneurysms, 92% for men with a common femoral artery aneurysm and 64% for men with a popliteal aneurysm. Although other reviews have found lower probabilities for this association, it is generally agreed that at least one third of patients with femoral or popliteal aneurysms have an associated AAA (see Chapter 105); this emphasizes the necessity for abdominal aortic imaging to exclude an AAA in such patients. Although it is likely that other aneurysms, such as renal, visceral, or carotid aneurysms, also are more likely in patients with aortic aneurysms, these are so rare that screening generally is not recommended. Details concerning the specific aneurysms discussed in this overview are presented in subsequent chapters in this Section.

■ REFERENCES

1. Johnston KW, Rutherford RB, Tilson MD, et al: Suggested standards for reporting on arterial aneurysms. Subcommittee on Reporting Standards for Arterial Aneurysms, Ad Hoc Committee on Reporting Standards, Society for Vascular Surgery and North American Chapter, International Society for Cardiovascular Surgery. J Vasc Surg 13:452, 1991.
2. Osler W: Aneurysm of the abdominal aorta. Lancet 2:1089, 1905.
3. Erichsen J: Observations on Aneurism. London, C&J Allard, 1844.
4. Osler W: Remarks on arterio-venous aneurysm. Lancet 2:949, 1915.
5. Haeger K: The Illustrated History of Surgery. New York, Bell Publishing, 1988.
6. Johnson T: The Workes of That Famous Chirurgeon Ambrose Pare. London, Coates & Dugard, 1649.
7. Pott P: Remarks of the Necessity and Propriety of the Operation of Amputation in Certain Cases. London, J Johnson, 1779.
8. Cooper AP: Lectures on the Principles and Practice of Surgery, 2nd ed. London, FC Westley, 1830.
9. Cho SI, Johnson WC, Bush HL, et al: Lethal complications associated with nonresective treatment of abdominal aortic aneurysms. Arch Surg 117:1214, 1982.
10. Abernathy CM, Baumgartner R, Butler HG, et al: The management of ruptured abdominal aortic aneurysms in rural Colorado: With a historical note on Kit Carson's death. JAMA 256:587, 1986.
11. Cohen JR, Graver LM: The ruptured abdominal aortic aneurysm of Albert Einstein. Surg Obstet Gynecol 170:455, 1990.
12. Rea CE: The surgical treatment of aneurysm of the abdominal aorta. Minn Med 31:153, 1948.
13. Matas R: Ligation of the abdominal aorta: Report of the ultimate result, one year, five months and nine days after the ligation of the abdominal aorta for aneurysm of the bifurcation. Ann Surg 81:457, 1925.
14. Creech O Jr: Endo-aneurysmorrhaphy and treatment of aortic aneurysm. Ann Surg 164:935, 1966.
15. Goyanes J: The Arteries, Part I. Austin, Tex, Silvergirl, 1988.
16. DuBost C, Allary M, Oeconomos N: Resection of an aneurysm of the abdominal aorta: Reestablishment of the continuity by a preserved arterial graft, with result after five months. Arch Surg 64:405, 1952.
17. Oudot J: La greffe vasculaire dans les thromboses du carrefour aortique. Presse Med 59:234, 1951.
18. Julian OC, Grove WJ, Dye WS, et al: Direct surgery of atherosclerosis: Resection of abdominal aorta with homologous aortic graft replacement. Ann Surg 138:387, 1953.
19. Brock RC, Rob CG, Forty F: Reconstructive arterial surgery. Proc R Soc Med 46:115, 1953.
20. DeBakey ME, Cooley DA: Surgical treatment of aneurysm of abdominal aorta by resection of continuity with homograft. Surg Gynecol Obstet 97:257, 1953.
21. Bahnson HT: Considerations in the excision of aortic aneurysms. Ann Surg 97:257, 1953.
22. Voorhees A, Jaretzki A, Blakemore AH: The use of tubes constructed from Vinyon "N" cloth in bridging arterial defects. Am Surg 135:332, 1952.
23. Etheredge SN, Yee J, Smith JV, et al: Successful resection of a large aneurysm of the upper abdominal aorta and replacement with homograft. Surgery 38:1071, 1955.
24. Crawford ES: Thoraco-abdominal and abdominal aortic aneurysms involving renal, superior mesenteric and celiac arteries. Ann Surg 179:763, 1974.
25. Vorp DA, Raghavan ML, Webster MW: Mechanical wall stress in abdominal aortic aneurysm: Influence of diameter and asymmetry. J Vasc Surg 27:632, 1998.
26. Fillinger MF, Raghavan ML, Marra SP, et al: In vivo analysis of mechanical wall stress and abdominal aortic aneurysm rupture risk. J Vasc Surg 36:589, 2002.
27. Fillinger MF, Marra SP, Raghavan ML, Kennedy FE: Prediction of rupture risk in abdominal aortic aneurysm during observation: Wall stress versus diameter. J Vasc Surg 37:724, 2003.
28. Brunkwall J, Hauksson H, Bengtsson H, et al: Solitary aneurysms of the iliac arterial system: An estimate of their frequency of occurrence. J Vasc Surg 10:381, 1989.
29. Bickerstaff LK, Hollier LH, Van Peenen HJ, et al: Abdominal aortic aneurysms: The changing natural history. J Vasc Surg 1:6, 1984.
30. Bickerstaff LK, Pairolero PC, Hollier LH, et al: Thoracic aortic aneurysms: A population-based study. Surgery 92:1103, 1982.
31. Svensjo S, Bengtsson H, Bergqvist D: Thoracic and thoracoabdominal aortic aneurysm and dissection: An investigation based on autopsy. Br J Surg 83:68, 1996.
32. Gillum RF: Epidemiology of aortic aneurysm in the United States. J Clin Epidemiol 48:1289, 1995.
33. Lawrence PF, Lorenzo-Rivero S, Lyon JL: The incidence of iliac, femoral and popliteal artery aneurysms in hospitalized patients. J Vasc Surg 22:409, 1995.
34. Gaylis H: Popliteal arterial aneurysms: A review and analysis of fifty-five cases. S Afr Med J 48:75, 1974.
35. Welling RE, Taha JA, Goel T, et al: Extracranial carotid artery aneurysms. Surgery 93:319, 1983.
36. Leriche R: Dolicho et mega-artere dolicho et mega-veine. Presse Med 51:554, 1943.
37. Lea Thomas M: Arteriomegaly. Br J Surg 58:690, 1971.
38. Hollier LH, Spittell JA, Gloviczki P, et al: Arteriomegaly: Classification and morbid implications of diffuse aneurysmal disease. Surgery 93:700, 1983.

39. Lawrence PF, Wallis C, Dobrin PB, et al: Peripheral aneurysms and arteriomegaly: Is there a familial pattern? J Vasc Surg 28:599, 1998.

40. Crawford ES, Cohen ES: Aortic aneurysm: A multifocal disease. Presidential address. Arch Surg 117:1393, 1982.

41. Gloviczki P, Pairolero P, Welch T, et al: Multiple aortic aneurysms: The results of surgical management. J Vasc Surg 11:19, 1990.

42. Dent TL, Lindenauer SM, Ernst CB, Fry WJ: Multiple arteriosclerotic arterial aneurysms. Arch Surg 105:338, 1972.

43. Johnston KW, Rutherford RB, Tilson MD, et al: Suggested standards for reporting on arterial aneurysms. J Vasc Surg 13:452, 1991.

Chapter

Abdominal Aortic and Iliac Aneurysms

100

MARC L. SCHERMERHORN, MD

JACK L. CRONENWETT, MD

Since the first description of abdominal aortic aneurysms (AAAs) by the 16th century anatomist Vesalius,[1] the history of this disease has reflected the remarkable progress of vascular surgery. Before the development of modern surgical techniques, successful management was rare. Initial attempts at ligation of the aorta failed. In 1923, Matas[2] performed the first successful aortic ligation in a patient with an AAA. Others attempted to induce thrombosis of AAAs by inserting intraluminal wires.[3] In 1948, Rea[4] wrapped reactive cellophane around the neck and over the anterolateral surfaces of an aneurysm to induce a fibrotic reaction and limit expansion. In 1949, Nissen used this technique to treat the symptomatic AAA of Albert Einstein, who survived 6 years before dying as a result of eventual rupture.[5] Durable and successful management of AAAs was not achieved, however, until resection and graft replacement was first performed in 1951. Although Dubost and coworkers[6] published the first account of successful replacement of an AAA, a case subsequently reported by Schaffer and colleagues[7] preceded that of Dubost. The current standard procedure, endoaneurysmorrhaphy with intraluminal graft placement, was popularized by Creech[8] and others.

AAAs are the most common type of true aneurysm and have a high propensity to rupture, which makes them a significant health care problem. In the United States, ruptured AAAs are the 15th leading cause of death overall and the 10th leading cause of death in men older than age 55.[9] In 1991, AAAs caused more than 8500 hospital deaths in the United States,[10] which underestimates their true number because 30% to 50% of all patients with ruptured AAAs die before they reach a hospital.[11] In addition, 30% to 40% of patients with ruptured AAAs die after reaching a hospital but without operation.[11] When combined with an operative mortality rate of 40% to 50%,[12-16] this results in an overall mortality of 80% to 90% for AAA rupture.[11,13,17,18] This high mortality rate has not changed since the 1980s, despite improvements in operative technique and perioperative

management that have reduced elective surgical mortality to less than 5% in most series.[12] The effectiveness of elective AAA repair means that most deaths from AAAs are theoretically preventable. Elective AAA repair is one of the most frequent vascular surgery procedures, with a relatively constant volume of 40,000 operations performed annually in the United States since the 1990s.[10] Despite the frequency of elective repair, however, death from AAA rupture has remained relatively constant because many AAAs are undetected or untreated. In a review of ruptured AAAs that were easily palpable, more than 50% either were not detected or were not referred for treatment despite recent medical examination.[19] Ruptured aneurysms also impose a substantial financial burden on overall health care costs. One report estimated that $50 million and 2000 lives could have been saved if AAAs had been repaired before they ruptured.[20] Another study showed that emergency operations for AAAs resulted in a mean financial loss to the hospital of $24,655 per patient.[21] For all of these reasons, AAAs remain a central focus for vascular surgeons and a common health care problem for all physicians.

Nearly all AAAs involve the infrarenal aorta, but only about 5% of AAAs undergoing surgical repair also involve the suprarenal aorta.[22] By definition, suprarenal AAAs extend above the renal arteries so that they require reimplantation of at least one renal artery during AAA repair. The term *juxtarenal* is used to describe AAAs that do not involve the renal arteries, but because of proximity require clamping above the renal arteries to complete the proximal aortic anastomosis. Although 25% of AAAs also involve the iliac arteries,[22] isolated iliac artery aneurysms are rare (<1%).[23] Isolated aneurysms of the suprarenal aorta are extremely rare, unless they have an associated thoracic or infrarenal component. Concomitant thoracic aneurysms have been found in 12% of patients with AAAs, but this is likely a high estimate based on a selected referral practice.[24] Peripheral aneurysms of the femoral or popliteal artery are present in approximately 3.5% of patients with AAAs.[25] As aneurysmal dilatation of the aorta occurs, elongation also results, leading to a tortuous configuration of the aneurysmal aorta and iliac arteries.

Aneurysms are defined as a focal dilatation at least 50% larger than the expected normal arterial diameter.[26] A practical working definition of an AAA is a transverse diameter 3 cm or greater and for a common iliac aneurysm a transverse diameter 1.8 cm or greater. As shown by Pearce and associates,[27] normal aortic diameter gradually decreases from the thorax (28 mm in men) to the infrarenal location (20 mm in men). At all levels, normal aortic diameter is approximately 2 mm larger in men than in women and increases with age and increased body surface area.[27] A large ultrasound screening study by Lederle and colleagues[28] found that increasing age; male gender; black race; and increasing height, weight, body mass index, and body surface area all were independently associated with increased infrarenal aortic diameter, but that the effect of all these variables was small. Because the average infrarenal aortic diameter was 2 cm for these patients, using a 3-cm definition for an infrarenal AAA was recommended, without the need to consider a more complicated definition based on factors such as gender or body surface area. Although such definitions are useful for large patient groups, in clinical practice with individual patients, it is more common to define an aneurysm based on a 50% or greater enlargement compared with the diameter of the adjacent, nonaneurysmal artery diameter.[26] This is particularly true for patients with unusually small arteries, in whom even a 2.5-cm local dilatation of the infrarenal aorta might be aneurysmal if the adjacent aorta was only 1.5 cm in diameter.

Most AAAs are spindle-shaped, beginning below the renal arteries and ending at the aortic bifurcation. Considerable variation exists, however, with saccular aneurysms and other eccentric geometry being common. Computer modeling of AAA wall stress suggests that asymmetry may influence rupture risk significantly.[29,30] It seems that 10% to 20% of AAAs have focal outpouchings or "blebs" that also may increase the risk of rupture.[31,32] As AAAs enlarge, thrombus is laminated along the aneurysm wall, often preserving a relatively normal arterial lumen despite considerable aneurysmal dilatation (Fig. 100-1).

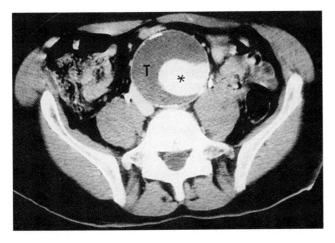

FIGURE 100-1 CT scan of abdominal aortic aneurysm shows contrast-filled lumen (*) surrounded by thrombus (T) within the aneurysm sac.

■ PATHOGENESIS

AAAs represent a degenerative process that has often been attributed to atherosclerosis because of the advanced age of affected patients and the universal atherosclerotic changes found in AAAs. An atherosclerotic etiology of AAAs fails to explain the alternative development of occlusive rather than aneurysmal changes in the aorta of similar patients, however, which implies a more complex cause of AAAs. Rather than being termed *atherosclerotic*, AAAs more accurately are referred to as *degenerative* or *nonspecific* in etiology. Extensive research is being conducted to understand the etiology of aneurysms better (see Chapter 29 and several reviews[33-40]). This section briefly considers issues particularly relevant to AAAs.

The aortic wall contains not only vascular smooth muscle cells, but also the important matrix proteins elastin and collagen, which are arranged in organized, concentric layers to withstand arterial pressure.[41] In the normal aorta, there is a gradual but marked reduction in the number of medial elastin layers from the proximal thoracic aorta (60 to 80 layers) to the infrarenal aorta (28 to 32 layers), accompanied by medial thinning and intimal thickening in the more distal aorta.[41,42] Associated with this structural change is a reduction in collagen and elastin content from the proximal to distal aorta, as reported by Halloran and colleagues.[41] These investigators also found a marked 58% decrease in elastin content between the suprarenal and the infrarenal aorta and noted that this was the only location within the aorta where the proportion of elastin decreases relative to collagen. Because elastin fragmentation and degeneration is observed histologically in aneurysm walls, these observations help explain the predilection for aneurysm formation in the infrarenal aorta.[38] Elastin is the principal load-bearing element in the aorta that resists aneurysm formation, whereas collagen acts as a strong "safety net" to prevent rupture after an aneurysm occurs.[43] Elastin is not synthesized in the adult aorta, but has a half-life of 40 to 70 years, accounting for its reduction with age and the occurrence of AAAs primarily in elderly patients.[44]

In addition to reduced elastin content in the infrarenal aorta, increased susceptibility to aneurysm formation has been attributed to hemodynamic, structural, and autoimmune factors unique to this location. Reflected waves from the aortic bifurcation increase pulsatility and wall tension in the distal, less compliant atherosclerotic aorta.[45] Increased prevalence of AAAs many years after above-knee amputation has been attributed to increased aortic pulsatility resulting from increased peripheral resistance,[46] although this was not found in another study.[47] Absence of vasa vasorum in the infrarenal aorta has been suggested to reduce nutrient supply and potentiate degeneration.[34] More recently, Xia and coworkers[48] proposed an autoimmune mechanism for aneurysm formation and found that immunoreactive protein is more conspicuously expressed in the abdominal compared with the thoracic aorta, which also may explain the increased frequency of aneurysms in this location.

Degradation of proteolytic aortic media in aneurysmal disease implies an increase in proteolytic enzymes relative to their inhibitors. Numerous reports have documented increased expression and activity of matrix metalloproteinases (MMPs) in the wall of aortic aneurysms.[33,34,38,49]

McMillan and associates[49] found threefold higher activity of MMP-9 (the primary elastolytic enzyme) in 5- to 7-cm diameter AAAs compared with AAAs less than 5 cm, consistent with the increased expansion rates observed for larger AAAs. This group also found increased levels of MMP-9 in aortic tissue and serum of patients with AAA compared with patients with aortoiliac occlusive disease.[50] Ailawadi and colleagues[51] showed increased expression of MMP-9 in the abdominal aorta relative to the aortic arch and descending thoracic aorta. Other MMPs, serine proteinases such as plasmin, and neutrophil elastase have been shown to be increased in AAAs compared with normal aortic tissue, whereas their inhibitors appear unchanged, leading to a net increase in matrix-degrading activity in AAAs.[33,39] Animal studies have shown that elastase infusion recruits an inflammatory reaction that results in aneurysm formation, which can be prevented by inhibiting inflammatory cell recruitment or blocking MMP activity with an inhibitor such as doxycycline.[52-55] Reactive oxygen species such as superoxide (O_2^-) also have been shown to be increased in human AAAs.[56] Elastase infusion in animal models has been shown to increase inducible nitric oxide synthase gene expression and decrease expression of the antioxidant superoxide dismutase.[57] These studies emphasize the importance of proteinase activity in the development of AAAs and the likely inflammatory source or stimulation of these enymes.

Histologic studies of AAAs show not only fragmentation of elastin fibers and decreased elastin content, but also a chronic adventitial and medial inflammatory infiltrate, which is different from aortic occlusive disease, in which the inflammatory reaction is found primarily in the intimal plaque.[37] This transmural inflammatory response in AAAs seems to be central to their development, but its cause is not clearly understood. The finding of *Chlamydia pneumoniae* in the wall of AAAs has suggested that infection with this common pathogen could be a possible stimulus.[58,59] Tambiah and Powell[60] showed that *Chlamydia* can induce AAA in a rabbit model. Characteristics of the inflammatory infiltrate in human AAAs, including the presence of B lymphocytes, plasma cells, and large amounts of immunoglobulin (including Russell bodies), suggests an autoimmune component, however.[36,38,61] Tilson and coworkers[36] identified a 40-kD matrix protein, which is immunoreactive with IgG isolated from the aneurysm wall.[62] This putative autoantigen seems to be a collagen-associated microfibril, which they termed *aortic aneurysm antigenic protein* (AAAP-40) and found to be most conspicuous in the abdominal aorta.[48] Microfibrillar integrity is known to be important for preventing aneurysms because defective fibrillin in Marfan's syndrome leads to aneurysm formation.[63] AAAP-40 shares amino acid sequence homologies with *Treponema pallidum* and cytomegalovirus, microorganisms known to be associated with aneurysmal disease.[64] This association raises the possibility that aneurysms in these infections might result by an immune response against the pathogen, which also attacks a similar self-protein in the aneurysm wall, a concept known as *molecular mimicry*.[64]

Numerous studies have noted familial clustering of AAAs, which is observed in 15% to 25% of patients undergoing AAA repair.[65-68] Inheritance patterns of autosomal dominant, autosomal recessive, and autosomal dominant with incomplete penetrance all have been shown.[69] Although the genetic cause for AAA remains elusive, there seems to be a multifactorial combination of genetic and environmental factors.[69] A potential genetic basis for the autoimmune manifestations of AAAs has been reported in a study by Tilson and colleagues.[36] These investigators identified potential susceptibility alleles for AAAs involving the DR-B1 major histocompatibility locus. The alleles they have identified occur rarely in North American blacks, but were found in all five black patients with AAAs.[36] These DR-B1 alleles were found in 75% to 100% of white patients with AAAs, depending on the degree of similarity required. This research points to a specific DR-B1 genetic basis for AAA development, which could lead to genetic testing for susceptibility. The DR-B1 major histocompatibility locus also has been identified as a likely genetic basis for inflammatory AAAs.[70] A wide array of genetic alterations has been detected in patients with AAAs.[71] Genetic screening for AAA susceptibility is likely to be available in the future.[39]

Degenerative aneurysms account for more than 90% of all infrarenal AAAs. Less frequent causes include infection, cystic medial necrosis, arteritis, trauma, inherited connective tissue disorders, and pseudoaneurysm from anastomotic disruption. Aortic aneurysms are rare in children and are of diverse etiologies,[72] with infection from umbilical artery catheters being most common.[73]

■ EPIDEMIOLOGY

AAAs are largely a disease of elderly white men. They increase steadily in frequency after age 50, are two to six times more common in men than in women, and are two to three times more common in white men than in black men.[10,74-76] The reported incidence, or likelihood of developing an AAA, has varied from 3 to 117 per 100,000 person-years.[77] These estimates were based on rates of repair or incidental discovery, however. More recent screening studies that have performed sequential scans have provided new information on incidence rates of AAA formation. In the Huntingdon, United Kingdom, screening program for men older than age 50, the incidence of new AAA was much higher, at 3.5 per 1000 person-years.[78] New AAAs were discovered in 2% of patients screened a second time at a mean of 5.5 years after an initial negative study. In a screening study of U.S. male veterans, Lederle and colleagues[79] found new AAAs in 2.6% of patients 4 years after an initial normal aortic ultrasound study, an incidence of 6.5 per 1000 person-years. In men, AAAs begin to occur at about age 50 and reach a peak incidence near age 80.[80-82] In women, AAA onset is delayed, beginning around age 60, with incidence continuing to increase thereafter (Fig. 100-2).[80-82] Overall, the age-adjusted incidence is twofold to sixfold higher in men than in women for asymptomatic and ruptured AAAs.

A significant increase in the incidence of asymptomatic AAAs has been noted in recent years,[76,77,80] in part because of increased case finding as a result of more frequent use of ultrasonography and other abdominal imaging modalities. In addition to increased case finding, however, there seems to have been a real increase in the incidence of aortic aneurysmal disease. The finding of a 2.4% per year increase in the age-adjusted incidence of death from AAA rupture

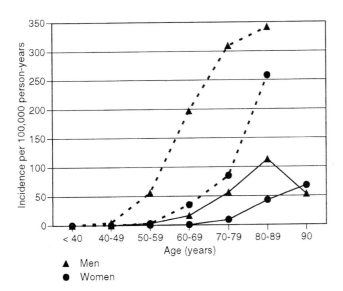

FIGURE 100-2 Incidence of clinically apparent[27] and ruptured abdominal aortic aneurysms (AAAs)[21] from population-based studies. *Dashed lines* = incidence of all AAAs; *solid lines* = incidence of ruptured AAAs.

from 1952 to 1988 supports this assumption,[77] as this statistic is less influenced by more frequent abdominal imaging. An analysis of hospital deaths in the United States indicates that AAA rupture rates stabilized from 1979 to 1990, with 4 deaths per 100,000 in white men.[10] The reported incidence of ruptured AAA varies from 1 to 21 per 100,000 person-years.[77] For patients older than age 50, the incidence of AAA rupture is much higher because this increases dramatically with age (see Fig. 100-2).[11] A population-based study by Chosky and associates[83] of ruptured AAAs in England noted an incidence of 76 per 100,000 person-years for men and 11 per 100,000 person-years for women older than 50, for a male-to-female ratio of 4.8:1.[83] The median age at rupture was 76 in men and 81 in women. The median AAA size at rupture was 8 cm, but 4.5% of the ruptured AAAs were less than 5 cm in diameter (measured at autopsy or operation). The overall mortality of rupture was 78%, and three fourths of these deaths occurred outside the hospital. Most deaths from ruptured AAAs occur in winter months, similar to deaths from coronary artery disease (CAD).[84,85] Noting that atmospheric pressure is lower in winter, Bown and colleagues[86] showed that mean atmospheric pressure is lower in calendar months preceding the months with high numbers of ruptured AAAs.

Prevalence estimates for asymptomatic AAAs (likelihood of having an AAA) are more accurate than incidence estimates (likelihood of developing an AAA) now that large ultrasound screening surveys have been performed. Ultrasound screening and autopsy series indicate that the prevalence of AAAs (≥3 cm) is 3% to 10% for patients older than age 50 in the Western world.[77] Necropsy studies from Sweden and the United States have shown increases in the detection of AAA over the past several decades. In Sweden, the age-standardized prevalence of AAA at necropsy increased by 4.7% per year for men and 3% per year for women between 1958 and 1986.[81] In Kansas City, the prevalence of necropsy-detected AAA increased 1.5-fold for

men and 2.5-fold for women between 1950 through 1959 and 1970 through 1984.[82] In a Veterans Administration (VA) screening study of more than 73,000 patients 50 to 79 years old, the prevalence of AAAs 3 cm or greater was 4.6% and AAAs 4 cm or greater was 1.4%.[87] Prevalence of AAAs in a given population depends on risk factors that are associated with AAAs, including older age, male gender, white race, positive family history, smoking, hypertension, hypercholesterolemia, peripheral vascular occlusive disease, and CAD.[88] Although these risk factors are associated with increased AAA prevalence, they may not be independent predictors and may be markers rather than causes of AAA disease. Of these risk factors, age, gender, and smoking have the largest impact on AAA prevalence.[76,77,89]

In the VA study, smoking was the risk factor most strongly associated with AAA.[90] The relative risk of an AAA 4 cm or greater (compared with <3 cm) was fivefold higher in smokers compared with nonsmokers, and the risk increased significantly with the number of years of smoking. The excess prevalence associated with smoking accounted for 75% of all AAAs that were 4 cm or greater in this study. Other relatively important risk factors that increased AAA prevalence in this study were male gender (5.6-fold risk), age (1.7-fold risk per 7-year increase), white race (2-fold risk), and positive family history (2-fold risk); diabetes decreased risk (0.5-fold risk). Less important independent risk factors for increased AAA prevalence were height, CAD, any atherosclerosis, high cholesterol level, and hypertension. Associations for AAAs 3 to 3.9 cm (most AAAs found) were similar but weaker (odds ratios for smoking = 3, male gender = 2.1, age = 1.6 per 7 years, family history = 1.9, white race = 1.6, diabetes = 0.7).[90] Other investigators have confirmed the association of smoking, gender, and age with AAA.[75,91-101] Among smokers, AAA prevalence in one study was increased not only by the number of cigarettes smoked and increasing depth of inhalation, but also by elevated mean arterial or diastolic blood pressure.[103] In another study of male smokers, AAA prevalence increased with increasing age, years of smoking, systolic and diastolic blood pressure, and cholesterol.[102] Although there is less agreement that hypertension increases AAA prevalence, it does increase rupture risk in patients with established AAAs (see later).[92,93,95,103-106] Larger screening studies employing multivariate analysis and including patients whose hypertension has been controlled with medications have found hypertension to be an independent predictor of AAA.[87,95,104] An analysis of patients enrolled in screening studies in the United Kingdom showed that after adjustment for other risk factors, use of calcium channel blockers was associated with an increased risk of AAA (odds ratio 2.6, 95% confidence interval [CI] 1.5 to 4.3). Use of beta blockers showed a trend toward protection, but this did not reach statistical significance (odds ratio 0.6, 96% CI 0.4 to 1.1).[107] The estimated impact of various risk factors on AAA prevalence is summarized in Table 100-1.

Familial clustering of patients with AAAs has been well described in the literature. Of patients undergoing AAA repair, 15% to 25% have a first-degree relative with a clinically apparent AAA compared with only 2% to 3% of age-matched control patients without AAAs.[65-68,108-110] Conversely and more clinically relevant, approximately 7% of siblings of patients with AAAs have a clinically apparent

Table 100-1	Independent Risk Factors for Detecting an Unknown 4 cm or Larger Diameter Abdominal Aortic Aneurysm During Ultrasound Screening		
RISK FACTOR	ODDS RATIO*	95% CI	
Increased Risk			
Smoking history	5.1	4.1-6.2	
Family history of AAA	1.9	1.6-2.3	
Older age (per 7-yr interval)	1.7	1.6-1.8	
Coronary artery disease	1.5	1.4-1.7	
High cholesterol	1.4	1.3-1.6	
COPD	1.2	1.1-1.4	
Height (per 7-cm interval)	1.2	1.1-1.3	
Decreased Risk			
Abdominal imaging within 5 yr	0.8	0.7-0.9	
Deep vein thrombosis	0.7	0.5-0.8	
Diabetes mellitus	0.5	0.5-0.6	
Black race	0.5	0.4-0.7	
Female gender	0.2	0.1-0.5	

*Odds ratio indicates relative risk compared with patients without that risk factor. AAA, abdominal aortic aneurysm; CI, confidence interval; COPD, chronic obstructive pulmonary disease.

From Lederle FA, Johnson GR, Wilson SE, et al: The aneurysm detection and management study screening program: Validation cohort and final results. Aneurysm Detection and Management Veterans Affairs Cooperative Study Investigators. Arch Intern Med 160:1425, 2000.

AAA.[111] This prevalence increases if ultrasound screening of relatives is performed. Webster and coworkers[68] showed that ultrasound screening of siblings of a patient with an AAA yielded AAAs 3 cm or larger in 25% of the male and 7% of the female siblings older than 55 year old. The likelihood that relatives will have an AAA increases if the proband (patient with the AAA) is a woman. If the proband is a man, 7% of relatives have a clinically apparent AAA, but if the proband is a woman, 12% of these relatives have an AAA.[111] It is estimated that first-degree relatives of a patient with an AAA have a 12-fold increased risk for aneurysm development themselves.[66] Brothers of a patient with an AAA have an 18-fold increased risk for AAA development—highest in the 50- to 60-year-old range and decreasing thereafter.[67] Analysis of patients with familial aneurysms indicates that on average these patients are 5 to 7 years younger and are more frequently women.[65,67] In the surgical series by Darling and associates[65] of patients undergoing AAA repair, women accounted for 35% of patients with a positive family history of AAAs, but for only 14% of patients without familial AAAs. Although AAAs in women are much less common than in men, women with AAAs are more likely to have affected relatives. For a given patient with an AAA (male or female), however, brothers are still twice as likely to have an AAA as sisters.

■ CLINICAL PRESENTATION AND DIAGNOSIS

Most AAAs are asymptomatic, which leads to difficulty in their detection. Occasionally, patients may describe a "pulse" in their abdomen or may palpate a pulsatile mass. Although most clinically significant AAAs are potentially palpable during routine physical examination, the sensitivity of this technique depends on the AAA size, the obesity of the patient, the skill of the examiner, and the focus of the examination.[112] A pooled analysis of the literature showed that with physical examination alone, the diagnosis is made in 29% of AAAs 3 to 3.9 cm, 50% of AAAs 4 to 4.9 cm, and 75% of AAAs 5 cm or larger.[113] Although a focused physical examination detected 50% of 3.5- to 6-cm diameter AAAs, these all had been missed on a recent, nonfocused examination.[112] Conversely, AAAs may be falsely suspected in thin patients with a prominent, but normal-sized aorta or in patients with a mass overlying the aorta that transmits a prominent pulse. Patients with hypertension, a wide pulse pressure, or a tortuous aorta also can have a prominent aortic pulsation that may be mistaken for an AAA. The positive predictive value of physical examination for identifying AAAs greater than 3.5 cm diameter is only 15%.[114] The accuracy of physical examination for measuring size of a known AAA also is poor, usually resulting in an overestimate of size secondary to intervening intestine and abdominal wall tissue. As a result of these factors, most AAAs are detected by incidental abdominal imaging studies done for other reasons. In a review of 243 patients who underwent elective AAA repair, Chervu and colleagues[115] found that 38% initially were detected by physical examination, whereas 62% were detected by incidental radiologic studies, even though 43% of these were palpable on subsequent examination. Of these clinically significant AAAs, 23% were not palpable even when the diagnosis was known, and in obese patients, two thirds were not palpable. These findings emphasize the potential role for ultrasound screening in high-risk patients, as discussed subsequently.

Several imaging modalities are available to confirm the diagnosis of AAA. Abdominal B-mode ultrasonography is the least expensive, least invasive, and most frequently used examination, particularly for initial confirmation of a suspected AAA or for follow-up of small AAAs. Diameter measurements using ultrasound have an interobserver variability less than 5 mm in 84% of studies and are more accurate in the anteroposterior than the lateral dimension.[116] Visualization of the suprarenal aorta and iliac arteries may be obscured by bowel gas or be difficult in obese patients. Ultrasonography cannot accurately determine the presence of rupture[117] and often cannot accurately determine the upper extent of an AAA.[118] Computed tomography (CT) is more expensive than ultrasound and involves radiation and intravenous contrast exposure, but provides more accurate diameter measurement, with 91% of studies showing interobserver variability less than 5 mm.[116] Accuracy can be increased by using standardized techniques, electronic calipers, and magnification.[119] CT precisely defines the proximal and distal extent of an AAA, more accurately images the iliac arteries, and provides other important information for operative planning (see later and Chapters 20 and 21). CT is particularly useful for excluding AAA rupture in a stable but symptomatic patient, for defining the proximal extent of an AAA, and for detecting other unsuspected pathology, such as an inflammatory aneurysm or other intra-abdominal pathology in the absence of AAA. Ultrasonography and CT can overestimate AAA diameter if an oblique rather than a perpendicular section is obtained in a tortuous aneurysm. This results in an elliptical rather than a circular cross section, and the larger diameter of the ellipse overestimates the true AAA diameter (see Chapter 21). Compared with CT, ultrasound seems to underestimate the diameter of AAAs systematically by 2 to 4 mm in the anteroposterior direction.[116,119-121] Spiral CT is a new, more rapid method of CT that provides excellent resolution of even visceral aortic branches when thin "slices" are obtained. Refinements of spiral CT include three-dimensional reconstruction, which provides more user-friendly images and facilitates accurate measurement for endovascular graft sizing (see Chapter 21).

Magnetic resonance imaging (MRI) is comparable in accuracy to CT for AAA measurement and evaluation and avoids radiation exposure (see Chapter 20). This technique is more expensive, less readily available, and less well tolerated by claustrophobic patients than CT, however. MRI is particularly valuable when intravenous contrast administration is contraindicated, such as in patients with renal failure. Improvements in the spatial resolution of spiral CT, combined with its more rapid, less expensive technique, have largely relegated MRI, however, to a secondary role in the evaluation of AAAs. Spiral CT with arterial phase contrast (CT angiography) or magnetic resonance angiography (MRA) may be valuable in the preoperative evaluation of AAAs when information about occlusive disease in adjacent arteries is required (see later). Arteriography is not an accurate technique to confirm the diagnosis of AAA or to measure diameter accurately because thrombus within an AAA usually diminishes the size of the contrast-filled lumen. Rather, arteriography is used in the preoperative evaluation of some patients with AAAs to define pathology in adjacent arteries that might affect the AAA repair (see the section on preoperative evaluation).

Most AAAs that become symptomatic do so because of rupture or acute expansion. Patients with a ruptured AAA experience abrupt onset of abdominal or back pain that can radiate into the flank or groin. Most ruptured AAAs are palpable, if this is not prevented by obesity or abdominal distention, and are usually tender. When rupture occurs, extravasation of blood occurs through the disrupted aortic wall. The extent of hemorrhage and cardiovascular compensation determines the severity of hypotension and shock associated with rupture; this usually depends on the specific location of rupture, which in 20% occurs anteriorly into the peritoneal cavity.[122] In this location, little tamponade can be expected so that massive hemorrhage ensues. Eighty percent of ruptures occur posteriorly into the retroperitoneal space, where the hematoma is usually initially contained, increasing the possibility of survival. Most patients with ruptured AAAs present with at least transient hypotension, which develops into frank shock over a period of hours. Occasionally, rupture is so effectively contained within the retroperitoneum that symptoms can persist for days or weeks without hypotension. These patients with chronic "contained rupture" can be difficult to diagnose because their symptoms often mimic an acute inflammatory condition. Although the classic presentation of ruptured AAA includes abdominal or back pain, hypotension, and a pulsatile abdominal mass, all three findings are evident in only 26% of patients with proven AAA rupture.[123] Temporary loss of consciousness is a potentially important symptom of ruptured AAA because it occurs in combination with pain in

50% of patients and as the only initial symptom in 17% of patients with AAA rupture.[11] Ruptured AAAs are discussed in detail in Chapter 102.

Early diagnosis of patients with ruptured AAAs who do not have hypotension or other signs of bleeding can be difficult, particularly in obese patients if an AAA is not palpable. A high index of suspicion for ruptured AAA must exist in patients who present with back or abdominal pain, especially if they are older men in whom the prevalence is higher. If an AAA is not palpable, such patients should have an abdominal imaging study to exclude an AAA, unless the abdomen is so thin that physical examination is completely reliable. If such patients have a palpable or known AAA, CT is useful to diagnose or exclude rupture and may provide useful information concerning alternate diagnoses. The accuracy of CT for determining AAA rupture in this setting is approximately 90%.[124,125] In a review of stable but symptomatic patients with a suspected ruptured AAA, CT showed aneurysm rupture in 30%, a nonruptured AAA in 50%, and other pathology to explain the symptoms in 20% of patients.[124] This is valuable information because patients with symptomatic but nonruptured aneurysms (termed *acutely expanding*) have a substantially higher operative mortality rate than that associated with the elective AAA repair (average 23%).[126,144] This higher mortality likely results from a combination of factors, including suboptimal preoperative evaluation and management of comorbid disease and fatigue or inexperience of the emergency surgical and anesthesia teams. Because acute expansion is considered an immediate precursor of rupture, however, such patients must undergo expeditious AAA repair. In-hospital evaluation and preoperative preparation of patients with symptomatic but nonruptured AAAs is recommended to reduce perioperative morbidity and mortality, but allow emergent operation if rupture occurs.[126]

Much less frequently, AAAs may present with symptoms unrelated to rupture. Rarely, large AAAs cause symptoms from local compression, such as early satiety, nausea, or vomiting from duodenal compression; urinary symptoms secondary to hydronephrosis from ureteral compression; or venous thrombosis from ileocaval venous compression. Posterior erosion of AAAs into adjacent vertebrae can lead to back pain. Even without bony involvement, AAAs can cause chronic back pain or abdominal pain that is vague and ill-defined. Acute ischemic symptoms can result from distal embolization of thrombotic debris contained within an AAA. This seems to be more common in smaller AAAs, especially if the intraluminal thrombus is irregular or fissured.[127] Acute thrombosis of an AAA occurs rarely, but causes catastrophic ischemia comparable to any acute aortic occlusion. Embolism is much more common than acute AAA thrombosis, but both combined occur in less than 2% to 5% of patients with AAAs.[127] Nonetheless, an aortic aneurysm source for distal emboli always must be considered, especially in patients without overt atherosclerotic occlusive disease. Such symptoms are nearly always an indication for AAA repair.

Although AAAs are primarily a disease of the elderly, they can present in patients younger than age 50. As reported by Muluk and coworkers,[128] AAAs in younger patients are more often symptomatic and on average are 1 cm larger at presentation than in older patients. This presentation may relate to fewer incidental abdominal imaging studies performed in younger patients, such that AAAs escape detection until they are larger or symptomatic. Younger patients tend to have more proximally located AAAs, with 46% being juxtarenal or higher compared with 18% at this level in older patients. Smoking is nearly universal in young patients with AAAs, whereas only 23% have a defined etiology, such as Marfan's syndrome.[128]

■ SCREENING

Because asymptomatic AAAs are often not discovered until they rupture, the potential benefit of ultrasound screening programs has been suggested. Although not yet reimbursed by most payers in the United States, numerous screening programs have been introduced in other countries.[129-138] Screening is generally considered appropriate when a disease has a long latency period; when the disease can be detected by the screening study at an early stage; when intervention at this early stage would improve outcome relative to intervention at a later stage; when the screening study is inexpensive, is accurate, has minimal associated risk, and causes little or no pain; and when the screening study is cost-effective. An important caveat is that steps should be taken to ensure a high attendance rate for screening to avoid the "healthy volunteer effect." People who are most likely to attend screening tend to be more health conscious than people who refuse. They stand to benefit less. The healthy volunteer effect is particularly important for a disease associated with smoking and uncontrolled hypertension. Targeted ultrasound screening for AAAs is recommended to focus efforts on people most at risk (e.g., older age, male gender, smoking, or a positive family history). In the absence of an effective medical therapy, it seems reasonable to withhold screening from people who would not be offered intervention if the disease were discovered (patients unfit for even endovascular repair). Two nonrandomized studies and four randomized controlled trials have been completed that address these issues and are summarized in a review by Lederle.[139]

In the Gloucestershire Aneurysm Screening Programme, all men age 65 to 73 were offered ultrasound screening.[133] No prescreening evaluation of potential fitness for AAA repair by a general practitioner was made. The attendance rate was 84%. AAAs greater than 4 cm were detected in 2.2% of volunteers scanned, and during subsequent follow-up there was a 66% reduction in overall AAA-related mortality (including deaths resulting from elective repair and rupture), which was statistically significant. In Huntingdon, United Kingdom, general practitioners reviewed their lists of male patients older than age 50.[140] They excluded patients considered unfit for potential AAA repair. The remaining patients were invited for ultrasound screening with an attendance rate of 74%. A significant (49%) reduction in future ruptured AAAs was noted in patients who were invited. Even though only 74% to 84% of patients were screened in these two studies, detection of small AAAs and subsequent management reduced rupture risk by half in the entire group of patients invited for AAA screening.

The first randomized trial of AAA screening enrolled 6058 unselected men in Chichester, United Kingdom, age 65 to 80, of whom 74% attended screening.[141] AAAs (≥3 cm) were detected in 7.6%. AAA-related death subsequently was reduced by 41% at 5 years and 21% at 10 years, but this difference was not significant (relative risk 0.79, 95% CI 0.53 to 1.40; P = not significant).[134] The investigators also enrolled 9342 unselected women age 65 to 80, of whom 65% attended screening.[135] The prevalence of AAA in women was only 1.3%. Women did not seem to benefit from screening because there was no difference in elective AAA repair, ruptured AAA, or AAA-related mortality at 5 or 10 years in women offered screening. The average age of women with ruptured AAA was 6 years older than men. The Chichester group noted that a substantial number of ruptured AAAs occurred in patients invited for screening who refused screening, did not adhere to follow-up, or were considered unfit for surgery after AAA was diagnosed. This study highlights the importance of preselecting for screening only individuals who may benefit. In the second randomized trial of AAA screening, all 12,658 65- to 73-year-old men in Viborg County, Denmark, were randomized.[136] The attendance rate was 76%. AAA (≥3 cm) was diagnosed in 4%. In-hospital AAA-related mortality was reduced by 68% in men invited for screening (odds ratio 0.31, 95% CI 0.11 to 0.90; P < .01). Outpatient deaths were not recorded, however. Additionally, studies reporting simply a reduction in AAA-related deaths fail to account for the timing of death. Patients who die as a result of elective surgery of screening-detected AAAs tend to die sooner than patients who die as a result of rupture of an undiagnosed AAA, resulting in a greater loss of life-years per death in the screened group.

The Multicentre Aneurysm Screening Study (MASS) was a well-designed, carefully conducted, and thoughtfully analyzed randomized trial that involved 70,495 men age 65 to 74 and excluded 4% who were considered unfit for possible surgical repair.[137] Of the 33,839 patients randomized to ultrasound screening (versus no screening), 80% accepted and were scanned. The aorta was not visualized in 1.2%, and AAAs greater than 3 cm were detected in 5%. The 33,961 control patients were not contacted. After a mean follow-up of 4 years, there were 113 AAA-related deaths in controls and 65 in the invited group. To account for timing of death, the investigators calculated the rate of AAA-related death per 1000 person-years of follow-up. This was 0.85 in the control group and 0.49 in the invited group with a hazard ratio of 0.58 (95% CI 0.42 to 0.78; P = .0002). Nonfatal ruptured AAAs were similarly reduced in the invited group (hazard ratio 0.59, 95% CI 0.45 to 0.77; P = .00006). Although there were more deaths as a result of elective AAA repair in the screened group (15 versus 9), this was more than offset by the reduction in deaths from ruptured AAA (37 versus 91). AAA-related death was similar in the two groups over the first year, but after 1 year the curves continued to separate over the remainder of the trial period, suggesting that the benefit still may increase over time. AAA-related death accounted for only 3% of all deaths in control patients and 2% of patients invited for screening. It is not likely that any trial would be able to show a significant reduction in all-cause mortality. The 32% reduction in AAA-related mortality rate was significant, however.

Quality of life also was assessed carefully in the MASS trial.[137] At all times and in all groups, anxiety, depression, and health-status measures were within the age-matched and gender-matched population norms. Patients who screened positive for AAA had slightly lower scores, however, on some physical and mental health scales and self-rated health immediately after screening. Patients undergoing surgery compared with surveillance had lower scores in mental health at 3 months, but scores were similar by 12 months. Surgery also was associated with better self-rated health at 3 and 12 months compared with surveillance and similar to ratings by patients screening negative. These results are similar to prior studies and indicate that AAA screening does not have a negative impact on quality of life.[142-146]

In a parallel publication, the MASS group showed that screening men age 65 to 74 for AAA is cost-effective with an incremental cost-effectiveness ratio of $30,000 per life-year saved when analyzed after only 4 years (the duration of the trial) and a projected cost-effectiveness ratio of $8500 per life-year saved after 10 years.[147] Adjusting for the quality-of-life changes described earlier, the cost-effectiveness ratio at 4 years is increased slightly to about $38,000 per quality-adjusted life-year saved.

All randomized trials have shown at least a trend toward reduced AAA-related mortality with ultrasound screening. This benefit was shown best in the largest trial, which, in addition to large numbers, also had a high attendance rate. If attendance rate is low, it becomes more likely that patients at greatest risk will not undergo screening, and the overall benefit may be reduced or lost. Targeting patients at greatest risk for AAA is likely to increase the benefit. Screening seems reasonable for men older than age 60 who would be candidates for at least an endovascular repair. Screening may be beneficial for women if they have other risk factors for AAA, such as a smoking history or a family history of AAA. Because familial AAAs tend to occur at younger ages, screening for patients with a family history should be performed earlier, such as age 50 to 55.

If an initial screening study is negative, there is little additional value of an additional future ultrasound scan.[78,79,148,149] In all studies, additional small AAAs were detected in 2% to 4% at 4 to 12 years of follow-up, but almost all were less than 4 cm, and none were considered likely to require repair during the life of the patient. It is unlikely that repeat screening would be helpful for most patients. Repeat screening may be reasonable, however, in patients with a positive family history who undergo an initial scan at a young age.

■ DECISION MAKING FOR ELECTIVE ABDOMINAL AORTIC ANEURYSM REPAIR

The choice between observation and prophylactic surgical repair of an AAA for an individual patient at any given time should take into account (1) the rupture risk under observation, (2) the operative risk of repair, (3) the patient's life expectancy, and (4) the personal preferences of the patient.[150,151] Two randomized trials have provided substantial information to assist with this decision-making process.

The UK Small Aneurysm Trial was the first randomized trial to compare early surgery with surveillance for AAAs 4 to 5.5 cm in 1090 patients age 60 to 76 who were enrolled.[152] AAAs were characterized using the maximal anteroposterior diameter with ultrasound. Patients undergoing surveillance underwent repeat ultrasound every 6 months for AAAs 4 to 4.9 cm and every 3 months for AAAs 5 to 5.5 cm. If AAA diameter exceeded 5.5 cm, the expansion rate was more than 1 cm per year, the AAA became tender, or repair of an iliac or thoracic aneurysm was needed, elective surgical repair was recommended. At the initial report in 1998, after a mean 4.6 years of follow-up, there was no difference in survival between the two groups (Fig. 100-3). Survival was initially worse in the early surgery group because of operative mortality. After 3 years, patients who had undergone early surgery had better late survival, but the difference was not significant. Greater than 60% of patients randomized to surveillance eventually underwent surgery at a median time of 2.9 years (Fig. 100-4). The rupture risk among patients undergoing careful

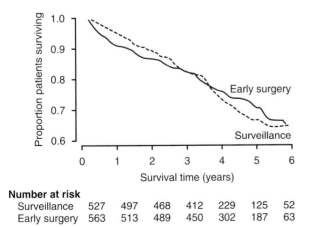

FIGURE 100-3 Survival for early surgery and surveillance groups in the UK Small Aneurysm Trial. (From mortality results for randomised controlled trial of early elective surgery or ultrasonographic surveillance for small abdominal aortic aneurysms. The UK Small Aneurysm Trial Participants. Lancet 352:1649, 1998.)

Number at risk							
Surveillance	527	497	468	412	229	125	52
Early surgery	563	513	489	450	302	187	63

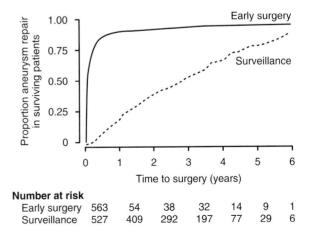

FIGURE 100-4 Proportion of patients undergoing abdominal aortic aneurysm repair in early surgery and surveillance groups in the UK Small Aneurysm Trial. (From mortality results for randomised controlled trial of early elective surgery or ultrasonographic surveillance for small abdominal aortic aneurysms. The UK Small Aneurysm Trial Participants. Lancet 352:1649, 1998.)

Number at risk							
Early surgery	563	54	38	32	14	9	1
Surveillance	527	409	292	197	77	29	6

surveillance was 1% per year. Operative mortality was 5.8% in the early surgery group and 7.2% in the surveillance group (this included more emergent and urgent repairs than the early surgery group). The operative mortality was more than twice the rate used in the power calculations for the design of the trial, causing some to question the generalizability of these results.

The Aneurysm Detection And Management (ADAM) study conducted at U.S. VA hospitals was published in 2002.[153] In this trial, 1163 veterans (99% male) age 50 to 79 with AAAs 4 to 5.4 cm were randomized to early surgery versus surveillance. Surveillance entailed ultrasound or CT every 6 months with elective surgery for expansion to 5.5 cm, expansion of greater than 0.7 cm in 6 months or greater than 1 cm in 1 year, or development of symptoms attributable to the AAA. CT was used for the initial study, with the AAA diameter defined as the maximal cross-sectional measurement in any plane that was perpendicular to the aorta. Ultrasound was used for most surveillance visits, but CT was used when the diameter reached 5.3 cm. Patients with severe heart or lung disease were excluded, as were patients who were not thought to be likely to comply with surveillance. As in the UK Small Aneurysm Trial, there was no survival difference after a mean follow-up of 4.9 years (Fig. 100-5). Similarly, more than 60% of patients in the surveillance arm underwent repair (Fig. 100-6). Initial AAA diameter predicted subsequent surgical repair in the surveillance group because 27% of patients with AAAs initially 4 to 4.4 cm underwent repair during follow-up compared with 53% of patients with AAAs 4.5 to 4.9 cm and 81% of patients with AAAs 5 to 5.4 cm. Operative mortality was 2.7% in the early surgery group and 2.1% in the surveillance group. Rupture risk in patients undergoing surveillance was 0.6% per year. The ADAM study confirmed the results of the UK Small Aneurysm Trial showing the lack of benefit of early surgery for AAAs 4 to 5.5 cm even if operative mortality is low. Compliance with surveillance was high in both trials.

In 2002, the UK Small Aneurysm Trial Participants published results of long-term follow-up.[154] At 8 years, there was a small survival advantage in the early surgery group (7.2% improved survival; $P = .03$). The proportion of deaths caused by rupture of an unrepaired AAA was low (6%), however. The early surgery group had a higher rate of smoking cessation, which may have contributed to a reduction in overall mortality. An additional 12% of surveillance patients underwent surgical repair during extended follow-up to bring the total to 74%. Fatal rupture occurred in only 5% of men but 14% of women. Risk of rupture was more than four times as high for women as for men. This finding prompted the UK Small Aneurysm Trial Participants to recommend a lower diameter threshold for elective AAA repair in women. A separate analysis of the UK Small Aneurysm Trial showed that a strategy of early surgery for small AAAs is more costly but associated with small gains in health-related quality of life.

Taken together, these two randomized trials indicate that in general it is safe to wait for AAA diameter to reach 5.5 cm before performing surgery in selected men who would be compliant with surveillance, even if their operative mortality is predicted to be low. Compliance in these carefully monitored trials of selected patients was high, however. In another VA population, Valentine and associates[155] reported that 32 of 101 patients undergoing AAA surveillance were not compliant despite several appointment reminders, and 3 or 4 of these 32 patients experienced rupture. Additionally the increased rupture risk for women seen in the UK Small Aneurysm Trial highlights the need to individualize treatment based on a careful assessment of individual patient characteristics (rupture risk, operative risk, life expectancy, and patient preferences).

Rupture Risk

Estimates of AAA rupture risk are imprecise because large numbers of patients with AAAs have not been followed

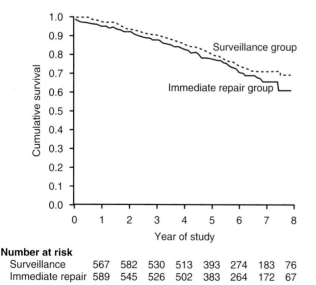

Number at risk

Surveillance	567	582	530	513	393	274	183	76
Immediate repair	589	545	526	502	383	264	172	67

FIGURE 100-5 Survival for early surgery and surveillance groups in the UK Aneurysm Detection and Management Trial. (From Lederle FA, Wilson SE, Johnson GR, et al: Immediate repair compared with surveillance of small abdominal aortic aneurysms. N Engl J Med 346:1437, 2002.)

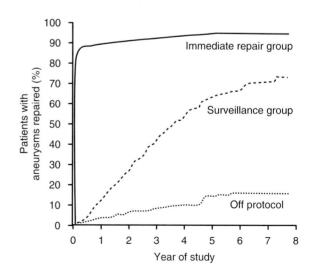

FIGURE 100-6 Proportion of patients undergoing abdominal aortic aneurysm repair in early surgery and surveillance groups in the UK Aneurysm Detection and Management Trial. (From Lederle FA, Wilson SE, Johnson GR, et al: Immediate repair compared with surveillance of small abdominal aortic aneurysms. N Engl J Med 346:1437, 2002.)

without intervention. Studies conducted before the widespread application of surgical repair documented the likelihood of large AAAs to rupture, although many of these AAAs not only were large, but also symptomatic.[156,157] Contemporary reports have focused on the natural history of small AAAs because larger ones are nearly always repaired when detected. Data are insufficient to develop an accurate prediction rule for AAA rupture in individual patients, which makes surgical decision making difficult. Knowledge of available natural history data can assist these decisions, however.

From a hemodynamic perspective, AAA rupture occurs when the forces within an AAA exceed the wall-bursting strength. Laplace's law indicates that the wall tension of an ideal cylinder is directly proportional to its radius and intraluminal pressure and inversely proportional to wall thickness. Real AAAs are not ideal cylinders and have wall thickness of variable strength. Theoretically, however, Laplace's formula predicts that larger AAA diameter and hypertension should increase wall tension and rupture risk. Decreasing wall thickness (or strength), although difficult to measure clinically, also theoretically should increase the probability of rupture.

The paramount importance of diameter in determining AAA rupture risk is universally accepted, based initially on a pivotal study reported by Szilagyi and colleagues[158] in 1966. These authors compared the outcome of patients with large (>6 cm by physical examination) and small (<6 cm) AAAs who were managed nonoperatively, even though at least half were considered fit for surgery in that era. During follow-up, 43% of the larger AAAs ruptured compared with only 20% of the small AAAs, although the actual size at the time of rupture is unknown. This difference in rupture rate contributed to a 5-year survival of only 6% for patients with large AAAs compared with 48% for patients with small AAAs. Foster and coworkers[159] confirmed these results in 1969, reporting rupture in 16% of AAAs less than 6 cm diameter compared with 51% for AAAs greater than 6 cm in patients managed nonoperatively. Because modern imaging techniques were not available to measure these aneurysms accurately, it is likely that diameter was overestimated by physical examination, such that the "large" 6-cm AAAs in these studies were closer to 5 cm by today's standards. Nonetheless, the influence of size on AAA rupture risk was firmly established and has provided a sound basis for recommending elective repair for large AAAs, especially because both of these studies showed a marked improvement in survival after operative repair.[158,159]

Autopsy studies also have shown that larger AAAs are more prone to rupture. In an influential study from 1977, Darling and associates[122] analyzed 473 consecutive patients who had an AAA at autopsy, of which 25% had ruptured. Probability of rupture increased with diameter: less than 4 cm, 10%; 4 to 7 cm, 25%; 7 to 10 cm, 46%; and greater than 10 cm, 61%. These results were confirmed by Sterpetti and colleagues[160] in a more recent autopsy series of 297 patients with AAAs in which rupture had occurred in 5% of AAAs 5 cm or smaller, in 39% of AAAs 5 to 7 cm, and in 65% of AAAs 7 cm or larger. Although these autopsy studies have shown the impact of relative AAA size on rupture rate, absolute diameter measurements at autopsy likely underestimate actual size because the aorta is no longer pres-

surized. After rupture, size measurement is more difficult because the AAA is not intact. Autopsy series are biased toward patients with larger AAAs that rupture and more likely lead to autopsy than smaller AAAs in asymptomatic patients who die of other causes. The rupture rates assigned to specific aneurysm diameters by autopsy studies almost certainly overestimate true rupture risk.

Despite the inability to relate precisely rupture risk with size, there is widespread agreement that rupture risk depends primarily on AAA diameter and increases substantially in extremely large AAAs. There seems to be a transition point between 5 and 6 cm diameter, below which rupture risk is low and above which rupture risk is high.[161] A survey of members of the Society for Vascular Surgery yielded median estimates for annual rupture risk of 20% per year for a 6.5-cm diameter AAA and 30% per year for a 7.5-cm diameter AAA, but there was large variability in these responses, reflecting the lack of precise data.[162] Because more than 90% of vascular surgeons agreed that the annual rupture risk of a 6-cm or larger AAA is at least 10% per year, however, elective repair is recommended for nearly all patients with AAAs 6 cm or larger, unless the predicted operative mortality is very high. A precise definition of rupture risk for large AAAs is relevant only for patients with high operative risk or poor life expectancy. For this reason, current attention is focused on the natural history of smaller AAAs (4- to 6-cm diameter), where lower rupture risk makes decision making more difficult even for patients with low operative risk.

Data from the more recent randomized trials suggest a low rupture risk for AAAs of 4 to 5.5 cm diameter. Rupture risk for 4- to 5.5-cm AAAs under surveillance was 0.6% and 1% per year for the ADAM study and UK Small Aneurysm Trial.[152,153] This likely reflects a reasonable estimate for an average (male) patient undergoing careful surveillance with prompt surgical repair not only for expansion greater than 5.5 cm, but also if expansion is rapid (>0.7 cm in 6 months or >1 cm in 1 year) or if symptoms develop. When examined according to the most recent AAA diameter in the United Kingdom study, the annual rupture risk was 0.3% for AAA 3.9 cm or smaller, 1.5% for AAA 4 to 4.9 cm, and 6.5% for AAA 5 to 5.9 cm.[163] These numbers do not accurately represent the rupture risk for women, who composed 17% and 1% of the United Kingdom and ADAM trials. In the UK Small Aneurysm Trial, the risk of rupture was 4.5-fold higher for women than for men. It is also likely that these numbers underestimate the actual annual rupture risk for small AAAs because some patients who underwent repair for rapid expansion or the development of symptoms were likely the patients at greatest risk within a given diameter range. Highlighting the fact that small AAAs can rupture, Nicholls and colleagues[164] published a review of 161 consecutive patients with ruptured AAAs who had an ultrasound (or rarely CT scan) of the aorta before surgery. They noted that 10% of these patients had AAA diameters equal to or less than 5 cm.

In a population-based study from Minnesota, Nevitt and associates[161] reported the outcome of 176 patients initially selected for nonoperative management and noted no rupture during 5-year follow-up for AAAs less than 5 cm in diameter, but a 5% annual rupture risk for AAAs larger than 5 cm at initial presentation. In a subsequent analysis of the same patients, these authors examined rupture risk as a function of the most recent ultrasound diameter measurement, rather than AAA size at entry.[165] They estimated annual rupture risk to be 0 for AAAs less than 4 cm, 1% per year for 4- to 4.9-cm AAAs, but 11% per year for 5- to 5.9-cm AAAs. These rates also likely underestimate rupture risk, however, because 45% of AAAs underwent elective repair during follow-up, presumably the AAAs at greatest risk for rupture within any size category.[165] In another study of 114 patients with small AAAs initially selected for nonoperative management, Limet and coworkers[166] observed rupture in 12% during 2-year follow-up, despite elective repair because of rapid expansion in 38%. This yielded an annual rupture rate of 0 for AAAs less than 4 cm, 5.4% per year for AAAs 4 to 5 cm, and 16% per year for AAAs greater than 5 cm. Because this was a referral-based study, it probably overestimated rupture risk of the entire population, but may portray accurately the group of patients referred for surgical consultation. In another referral-based study of 300 patients with AAAs initially managed nonoperatively, the observed annual rupture risk during 4-year follow-up was only 0.25% per year for AAAs less than 4 cm, 0.5% per year for AAAs 4 to 4.9 cm, and 4.3% per year for AAAs greater than 5 cm, even though only 8% of patients underwent elective repair.[167] These differences highlight the difficulty of predicting AAA rupture risk in individual patients.

In series of selective AAA management with surveillance until a threshold diameter is reached, patients typically are offered repair below the threshold diameter if there is rapid expansion or development of symptoms. The effect of these repairs is likely to lower the apparent rupture risk. To address this issue, Scott and coworkers[168] reviewed the results of 166 patients from the Chichester screening program with AAAs less than 6 cm. The patients were followed until diameter reached 6 cm, expansion was greater than 1 cm per year, or symptoms developed. They determined the annual rupture rate and the annual operation rate, and these were summed to yield the maximal potential rupture rate, assuming all AAAs that were repaired would have ruptured. For AAAs 3 to 4.4 cm, the maximal potential rupture rate was 2.1% per year, whereas for AAAs 4.5 to 5.9 cm, it was 10.2% per year (Table 100-2).

Studies of patients considered unfit for or refusing surgery provide additional information about rupture risk, particularly for larger diameter AAAs. These studies likely are affected by an increased incidence of comorbid conditions that may predispose to rupture, such as chronic pulmonary disease and hypertension, increasing the apparent rupture risk. These patients also are at increased

risk of death from these comorbid conditions, however, which would potentially decrease the apparent rupture risk. Cronenwett and associates[169] reported the outcome of 67 patients with 4- to 6-cm diameter AAAs, only 3% of whom underwent elective repair during 3-year follow-up. In this series, the annual rupture rate was 6% per year, causing a 5% annual mortality from AAA rupture. Most AAAs expanded during follow-up to a larger size before rupture, however, so that the rupture rate for AAAs that remained less than 5 cm in diameter was only 3% per year.[150] For large AAAs, Lederle and colleagues[170] reported on 198 veterans with AAAs 5.5 cm or larger unfit for or refusing surgery. The 1-year rupture risk was 9% for AAAs 5.5 to 5.9 cm, 10% for AAAs 6 to 6.9 cm, and 33% for AAAs 7 cm or larger, based on the initial diameter. The subgroup of patients with initial AAA diameter 6.5 to 6.9 cm had an annual rupture risk of 19%. Jones and coworkers[171] analyzed 57 patients unfit for surgery and found annual rupture rates of 8% for AAAs 5 to 5.9 cm and 16% for AAAs 6 cm or larger. There is general agreement that the rupture risk in AAAs larger than 6 cm is substantially higher than for smaller AAAs.

The simple observation that not all AAAs rupture at a specific diameter indicates that other patient-specific and aneurysm-specific variables also must influence rupture. Several studies have employed multivariate analysis to examine the predictive value of various clinical parameters on AAA rupture risk. The UK Small Aneurysm Trialists followed 2257 patients over the 7-year period of the trial, including 1090 randomized patients and an additional 1167 patients who were ineligible for randomization.[163] There were 103 documented ruptures. Predictors of rupture using proportional hazards modeling (adjusted hazard ratio in parentheses) were female gender (3), initial AAA diameter (2.9 per cm), smoking status (never-smokers 0.65, former smokers 0.59—both versus current smokers), mean blood pressure (1.02 per mm Hg), and forced expiratory volume in 1 second (FEV_1) (0.62 per L). The mean diameter for ruptures was 1 cm lower for women (5 cm) compared with men (6 cm). This analysis confirmed early work by Cronenwett and associates,[169] who determined that larger initial AAA diameter, hypertension, and chronic obstructive pulmonary disease (COPD) were independent predictors of rupture.

By comparing patients with ruptured and intact AAAs at autopsy, Sterpetti and colleagues[160] also concluded that larger initial AAA size, hypertension, and bronchiectasis were independently associated with AAA rupture. Patients with ruptured AAAs had significantly larger aneurysms (8 versus 5.1 cm), more frequently had hypertension (54% versus 28%), and more frequently had emphysema (67% versus 42%) and bronchiectasis (29% versus 15%). In a review of 75 patients with AAAs managed nonoperatively, Foster and coworkers[159] noted that death from rupture occurred in 72% of patients with diastolic hypertension, but in only 30% of the entire group. Among 156 patients with AAAs managed nonoperatively, Szilagyi and colleagues[172] found that hypertension (>150 mm Hg) was present in 67% of patients who experienced rupture, but in only 23% of patients without rupture. In addition to AAA size, these reports strongly implicate hypertension, COPD, female gender, and current smoking status as important risk factors for AAA rupture. The explanation for a causative role of

| Table 100-2 | Annual Rupture, Operation, and Maximal Potential Rupture Rates, According to Initial Diameter |

AAA DIAMETER (cm)	RUPTURE RATE (per yr)	OPERATION RATE (per yr)	MPRR (per yr)
3-4.4	0.7%	1.4%	2.1%
4.5-5.9	1.7%	8.5%	10.2%

AAA, abdominal aortic aneurysm; MPRR, maximal potential rupture rate.

hypertension is straightforward, based on Laplace's law. The UK Small Aneurysm Trial was the first to show that smoking status predicts rupture in addition to chronic pulmonary disease.[163] This study prospectively measured pulmonary disease with FEV_1 and documented smoking status with self-reported status and serum cotinine (a nicotine breakdown product with a plasma half-life of 16 hours). This study suggests that smoking has a two-tiered effect in that FEV_1, which is likely a measure of duration and quantity of smoking, is related to rupture, but also current smokers were more likely to rupture than former smokers, even after adjusting for the FEV_1. The UK Small Aneurysm Trialists found that serum cotinine was a better predictor of rupture than self-reported smoking status. Many clinicians consider the ratio of the aneurysm diameter to the adjacent normal aorta to be important in determining rupture risk. Women are known to have smaller aortas than men.[173] A 4-cm AAA in a small woman with a 1.5-cm diameter native aorta would be at greater rupture risk than a comparable 4-cm AAA in a large man with a native aortic diameter of 2.5 cm. The validity of this concept has not been proved, however. Ouriel and associates[174] have suggested that a relative comparison between aortic diameter and the diameter of the third lumbar vertebra may increase the accuracy for predicting rupture risk, by adjusting for differences in body size. The improvement in prediction potential was minimal, however, compared with absolute AAA diameter and the relative risk of gender.

Although a positive family history of AAA is known to increase the prevalence of AAAs in other first-degree relatives, it also seems that familial AAAs have a higher rupture risk. Darling and colleagues[65] reported that the frequency of ruptured AAAs increased with the number of first-degree relatives who have AAAs: 15% with two first-degree relatives, 29% with three first-degree relatives, and 36% with four or more first-degree relatives. Women with familial aneurysms were more likely (30%) to present with rupture than men with familial AAAs (17%). Verloes and associates[67] found that the rupture rate was 32% in patients with familial AAAs versus 9% in patients with sporadic aneurysms and that familial AAAs ruptured 10 years earlier (65 years old versus 75 years old). These observations suggest that patients with a strong family history of AAA may have an individually higher risk of rupture, especially if they are female. These studies did not consider other potentially confounding factors, however, such as AAA size, which might have been different in the familial group. Further epidemiologic research is required to determine whether a positive family history is an independent risk factor for AAA rupture in addition to a risk factor for increased AAA prevalence.

Although rapid AAA expansion is presumed to increase rupture risk, it is difficult to separate this effect from the influence of expansion rate on absolute diameter, which alone could increase rupture risk. Two studies have reported that expansion rate was larger in ruptured than intact AAAs, but these ruptured AAAs were also larger.[166,175] Other studies have found that absolute AAA diameter, rather than expansion rate, predicted rupture.[161,169] One study of patients with thoracoabdominal aneurysms showed that not only initial diameter, but, more importantly, subsequent expansion rate were independent predictors of rupture.[176]

One study with seven ruptures in 39 patients examined with serial three-dimensional CT scans found expansion rate to be a predictor of rupture.[177] Sharp and Collin[178] reported 32 patients with AAA diameter expansion of 0.5 cm or more in 6 months, but still with maximal diameter less than 5.5 cm, who did not undergo surgery. No ruptures occurred in these patients. The authors noted that many patients had apparent negative expansion directly before or after the episode of rapid expansion, which suggests that one or more of the measured diameters (all measured with ultrasound) may have been erroneous. They also noted that rapid expansion was sustained in only 11% of their patients and that most had expansion rates that regressed toward the population average. Although far from being proved, rapid AAA expansion frequently is regarded as a risk factor for rupture and often is used as a criterion for elective repair of small AAAs. It would seem prudent to confirm rapid expansion with CT or MRI before recommending surgery for this indication alone.

Clinical opinion also holds that eccentric or saccular aneurysms represent greater rupture risk than more diffuse, cylindrical aneurysms. Vorp and associates[29] used computer modeling to show that wall stress is substantially increased by an asymmetric bulge in AAAs. The influence of asymmetry was as important as diameter over the clinically relevant range tested. Fillinger and coworkers[30] compared wall stress measured using finite element analysis of three-dimensional CT scans in ruptured AAAs, emergent intact AAA repairs, and elective repairs. They found peak wall stress to be significantly higher in ruptured and emergent AAAs than in electively repaired AAAs. They subsequently performed wall stress analysis on CT scans of patients who did not undergo surgery or rupture for at least 6 months to determine whether the increase in wall stress happens acutely at the time of symptoms or rupture or if it can be predicted in advance.[179] Using multivariate analysis with proportional hazards modeling, these investigators found that peak wall stress was the greatest predictor of rupture (hazard ratio 25) followed by gender (hazard ratio 3), and that after accounting for wall stress and gender, diameter did not predict rupture. This study raises the possibility that estimates of AAA rupture risk might be improved by using biomechanical modeling of individual AAAs. In addition to a large bulge over the entire AAA, localized outpouchings or "blebs," ranging from 5 to 30 mm in size, can be observed on AAAs intraoperatively or on CT scans.[32] These areas of focal wall weakness show marked thinning of the tunica media elastin and have been suggested to increase rupture risk, although this is not firmly established.[31] The effect of intraluminal thrombus on rupture risk also is debated. One study has reported thinner thrombus in AAAs that ruptured,[180] and thrombus has been suggested to reduce aneurysm wall tension.[181] The practical impact of these variables on AAA rupture risk requires further study. Further analysis of the predictive ability of wall stress analysis is under way.

AAA rupture risk requires more precise definition. Currently, available data suggest the following estimates for rupture risk as a function of diameter: AAAs less than 4 cm, 0% per year; AAAs 4 to 5 cm, 0.5% to 5% per year; AAAs 5 to 6 cm, 3% to 15% per year; AAAs 6 to 7 cm, 10% to 20% per year; AAAs 7 to 8 cm, 20% to 40% per year; and

AAAs greater than 8 cm, 30% to 50% per year. For a given sized AAA, gender, hypertension, COPD, current smoking status, and wall stress seem to be independent risk factors for rupture. Family history and rapid expansion are probably risk factors for rupture, whereas the influence of thrombus content and diameter ratio are less certain.

Expansion Rate

Estimating expected AAA expansion rate is important to predict the likely time when a given AAA will reach the individual threshold diameter for elective repair. Numerous studies have established that aneurysms expand more rapidly as they increase in size.[166,182-185] Expansion rate is represented most accurately as an exponential rather than a linear function of initial AAA size. Limet and colleagues[166] calculated the median expansion rate of small AAAs to be $e^{0.106t}$, where t = years. For a 1-year interval, this formula predicts an 11% increase in diameter per year, nearly identical to the 10% per year calculation reported by Cronenwett and colleagues[183] in 1990. Several more recent studies have confirmed this estimate of approximately 10% per year for clinically relevant AAAs in the size range of 4 to 6 cm in diameter.[14,185-187] In particular, a literature review by Hallin and coworkers[14] found mean expansion rates of 0.33 cm/yr for AAAs 3 to 3.9 cm, 0.41cm/yr for AAAs 4 to 5 cm, and 0.51 cm/yr for AAAs greater than 5 cm. Studies that have identified very small AAAs, usually through screening, suggest that expansion rate may be less than 10% per year for AAAs smaller than 4 cm.[14,167,188,189] Santilli and colleagues[189] point out that the median expansion rate is lower than the mean and may be more appropriate given the skewed nature of the data. The median expansion rate may be more useful for predicting expansion for an individual patient and should be reported in future studies.

Although average AAA expansion rate can be estimated for a large population, individual AAAs behave in a more erratic fashion. Periods of rapid expansion may be interspersed with periods of slower expansion.[190,191] Episodes of sudden, rapid expansion do not seem predictable.[191] Chang and associates[190] found that in addition to large initial AAA diameter, rapid expansion is independently associated with advanced age, smoking, severe cardiac disease, and stroke. The influence of smoking has been confirmed by others.[192-194] The UK Small Aneurysm Trialists showed that current smoking is predictive of more rapid expansion, whereas former smoking is not.[193] This distinction may explain why some investigators failed to find smoking as a predictor of expansion. In addition to these factors, hypertension and pulse pressure have been identified as independent predictors of more rapid expansion rate.[175,183,184,189] Finally, Krupski and associates[195] and Wolf and colleagues[196] have shown that increased thrombus content within an AAA and the extent of the aneurysm wall in contact with thrombus are associated with more rapid expansion.

Beta blockade has been postulated to decrease the rate of AAA expansion. This was first shown in animal models.[197-201] Subsequent retrospective analyses in humans seemed to corroborate this.[187,202,203] Two subsequent randomized trials failed to show any reduction in growth rate with beta blockade.[204,205] The randomized trial from Toronto showed that patients taking beta blockers had worse quality of life and did not tolerate the drug well.[204] Even when the study analyzed only patients who tolerated the medication, there was no effect of propranolol on AAA expansion rate.

Doxycycline, 150 mg daily, was shown to slow the rate of AAA expansion in one small randomized trial, whereas roxithromycin, 30 mg daily, was shown to reduce expansion rate in another.[206,207] These antibiotics have activity against *C. pneumoniae,* which has been shown to be present in many AAAs.[58,59] Vammen and associates[208] showed that antibodies to *Chlamydia* predicted expansion in small AAAs and suggested that antibody-positive patients may benefit from anti-*Chlamydia* treatment. Doxycycline also has been shown to suppress MMP expression in human AAAs and to reduce aneurysm formation in animal models.[54,209,210] Further research in this exciting area is needed before routine treatment with these antibiotics can be recommended, but the low incidence of side effects has stimulated some clinicians to use doxycycline treatment for patients with small AAAs under surveillance.

Elective Operative Risk

Reported operative mortality associated with elective AAA repair varies widely. Blankensteijn and colleagues[211] reviewed the literature to examine differences based on whether the report was population-based or hospital-based and prospective or retrospective. The authors found that mean operative mortality was 8% in population-based prospective studies and 7.4% in population-based retrospective studies. These rates were significantly higher than the rates of individual hospital-based prospective and retrospective studies (both 3.8%). In a separate literature review by Hallin and colleagues,[14] the weighted mean operative mortality for elective AAA repair was 5%. This is similar to the rate reported in the UK Small Aneurysm Trial (5.6% elective operative mortality),[212] 1996 U.S. Medicare data (5.5%),[213] and a review of U.S. hospital discharge data with approximately 360,000 elective AAA repairs (5.6%).[12] This elective operative mortality does not seem to have improved since the 1980s.[12,14,214] Other, more recent statewide, national, and international reviews have shown similar results.[215-226] Many referral-based series from vascular centers of excellence report operative mortality less than 5% for elective AAA repair, showing that well-trained surgeons in experienced centers using careful patient selection are capable of performing elective AAA repair with mortality rates substantially lower than population averages.[153,227-229]

As expected, considerable variation in operative risk occurs among individual patients and depends on specific risk factors. A meta-analysis by Steyerberg and coworkers[230] identified seven prognostic factors that were independently predictive of operative mortality after elective AAA repair and calculated the relative risk for these factors (Table 100-3). The most important risk factors for increased operative mortality were renal dysfunction (creatinine >1.8 mg/dL), congestive heart failure (CHF) (cardiogenic pulmonary edema, jugular vein distention, or the presence of a gallop rhythm), and ischemic changes on resting electrocardiogram (ECG) (ST-segment depression >2 mm). Age had a limited effect on mortality when corrected for the highly associated

| Table 100-3 | Independent Risk Factors for Operative Mortality After Elective Abdominal Aortic Aneurysm Repair |

RISK FACTOR	ODDS RATIO*	95% CI
Creatinine >1.8 mg/dL	3.3	1.5-7.5
Congestive heart failure	2.3	1.1-5.2
ECG ischemia	2.2	1-5.1
Pulmonary dysfunction	1.9	1-3.8
Older age (per decade)	1.5	1.2-1.8
Female gender	1.5	0.7-3

*Odds ratio indicates relative risk compared with patients without that risk factor. CI, confidence interval.

From Steyerberg EW, Kievit J, Alexander de Mol Van Otterloo JC, et al: Perioperative mortality of elective abdominal aortic aneurysm surgery: A clinical prediction rule based on literature and individual patient data. Arch Intern Med 155:1998, 1995.

comorbidities of cardiac, renal, and pulmonary dysfunction (mortality increased only 1.5-fold per decade). This limited effect explains the excellent results reported in multiple series in which selected octogenarians have undergone elective AAA repair with mortality comparable to younger patients.[223] Based on their analysis, Steyerberg and colleagues[230] developed a clinical prediction rule to estimate the operative mortality for individual patients undergoing elective AAA repair (Table 100-4). This scoring system takes into account the seven independent risk factors plus the average overall elective mortality for a specific center. To show the impact of the above-mentioned risk factors on a hypothetical patient, the predicted operative mortality for a 70-year-old man in a center with an average operative mortality of 5% could range from 2% if no risk factors were present to greater than 40% if cardiac, renal, and pulmonary comorbidities all were present. This range would have a substantial impact on the decision to perform elective AAA repair. A similar Bayesian model for perioperative cardiac risk assessment in vascular patients has been reported by L'Italien and associates,[231] which showed the added predictive value of dipyridamole-thallium studies in patients with intermediate risk for cardiac death. This study also showed the protective effect of coronary artery bypass graft surgery within the previous 5 years, which reduced the risk of myocardial infarction (MI) or death after AAA repair by 2.2-fold. Although this type of statistical modeling cannot substitute for experienced clinical judgment, it helps identify high-risk patients who might benefit from further evaluation, risk factor reduction, or medical management instead of surgery if AAA rupture risk is not high.

The review of Hallin and colleagues[14] supports the findings of Steyerberg and colleagues[230] that renal failure is the strongest predictor of mortality with a 4-fold to 9-fold increased mortality risk. Cardiac disease (a history of CAD, CHF, or prior MI) was associated with a 2.6-fold to 5.3-fold greater operative mortality risk. Older age and female gender seemed to be associated with increased risk, but the evidence was not as strong. Valuable data regarding predictors of operative risk have been generated by prospective trials. In the Canadian Aneurysm Study, overall operative mortality was 4.8%.[232] Preoperative predictors of death were ECG evidence of ischemia, chronic pulmonary disease, and

| Table 100-4 | Predicting Operative Mortality After Elective Abdominal Aortic Aneurysm Repair* |

Surgeon-Specific Average Operative Mortality

Mortality (%):	3	4	5	6	8	12	
Score:	−5	−2	0	+2	+5	+10	_____

Individual Patient Risk Factors

Age (yr):	60	70	80	
Score:	−4	0	+4	_____

Gender:	Female	Male	
Score:	+4	0	_____

Cardiac comorbidity:	MI	CHF	ECG ischemia	
Score:	+3	+8	+8	_____

Renal comorbidity:	Creatinine >1.8 mg/dL	
Score:	+12	_____

Pulmonary comorbidity:	COPD, dyspnea	
Score:	+7	_____

Estimated Individual Surgical Mortality, Total Score   _____

Total score:	−5	0	5	10	15	20	25	30	35	40
Mortality (%):	1	2	3	5	8	12	19	28	39	51

*Based on total score from sum of scores for each risk factor, including surgeon-specific average mortality for elective abdominal aortic aneurysm repair, estimated patient-specific mortality.
CHF, congestive heart failure; COPD, chronic obstructive pulmonary disease; ECG, electrocardiogram; MI, myocardial infarction.

From Steyerberg EW, Kievit J, Alexander de Mol Van Otterloo JC, et al: Perioperative mortality of elective abdominal aortic aneurysm surgery: A clinical prediction rule based on literature and individual patient data. Arch Intern Med 155:1998, 1995.

renal insufficiency. The randomized UK Small Aneurysm Trial found older age, lower FEV_1, and higher creatinine to be associated with mortality on univariate analysis.[212] With multivariate analysis, the effect of age was diminished, whereas renal disease and pulmonary disease remained strong predictors of operative mortality. The predicted mortality ranged from 2.7% for younger patients with below-average creatinine and above-average FEV_1 to 7.8% in older patients with above-average creatinine and below-average FEV_1. The UK Small Aneurysm Trial Participants noted that the Steyerberg prediction rule did not work well for their patients. The randomized UK Small Aneurysm Trial did not gather information on a history of CHF (one of the strongest predictors in Steyerberg's analysis), however. Female gender also has been found to be associated with higher operative risk in several population-based studies using administrative data.[12,74,230,233] These databases may suffer from inaccurate coding of comorbidities, however, and lack of ability to adjust fully for comorbid conditions.[234] Gender has not been found to be associated with operative mortality in prospective trials.[212,232]

Center-specific mortality is an important consideration because results vary among centers and individual surgeons, independent of patient-specific risk factors. In part, this variation is due to volume and experience because low-volume hospitals and surgeons have demonstrably worse outcome for AAA repair than higher volume centers. Cronenwett and Birkmeyer[213] reviewed Medicare data from

1996 in the Dartmouth Atlas of Vascular Healthcare. This analysis showed that high-volume surgeons (>10 AAA repairs per year) had an elective AAA 30-day mortality rate of 4%, whereas low-volume surgeons (<4 AAA repairs per year) had a mortality rate of 8%. In a review of AAA repairs from an administrative database, Dimick and coworkers[235] found that high-volume hospitals (>35 AAA repairs per year) had a 30-day operative mortality of 3%, whereas low-volume hospitals (<35 AAA repairs per year) had a mortality of 5.5%. Surgeon specialty training also has been shown to affect operative mortality.[213,225,235,236] In the Dartmouth Atlas of Vascular Healthcare, operative mortality with elective AAA repair was 4.4% for vascular surgeons, 5.4% for cardiac surgeons, and 7.3% for general surgeons.[213] High-volume surgeons tend to operate in high-volume hospitals. To account for this, Dimick and coworkers[235] used multilevel analysis to evaluate the relative impact of hospital and surgeon volume and surgeon specialty. They showed that high-volume surgeon, vascular surgery specialization, and high-volume hospital all were independently associated with lower mortality after elective AAA repair. The effects of hospital volume[74,218,220,222,224,237-241] and surgeon volume[225,238,242,243] on operative mortality after elective AAA repair have been shown by others as well.

Life Expectancy

Assessment of life expectancy is crucial to determine if an individual patient would benefit from prophylactic repair of an AAA. Because most patients with AAAs have been long-term smokers, it is not surprising to learn that most AAA patients have extensive comorbid disease, particularly CAD, COPD, hypertension, hyperlipidemia, cerebrovascular disease, and cancer.[77,90,96,101,102,152,244] Many of these chronic conditions increase operative risk, as noted earlier. In addition, these factors shorten life expectancy. Patients who survive elective AAA repair have a reduced life expectancy compared with the age-matched and gender-matched population.[245-247] In 2001, Norman and coworkers[138] reviewed 32 publications over 20 years that described long-term survival after AAA repair. They found that the mean 5-year survival after AAA repair was 70% compared with 80% in the age-matched and gender-matched population without AAAs. Predictors of late death after successful AAA repair include age, cardiac disease, chronic pulmonary disease, renal insufficiency, and continued smoking.[228,246,248] The UK Small Aneurysm Trial Participants found (after adjustment for age, gender, and AAA diameter, but not cardiac disease) that FEV_1 and current smoking status (plasma cotinine) predicted late death.[248] Table 100-5 shows U.S. census data from 1998 that have been adjusted to reflect the life expectancy of an average patient surviving elective AAA repair. These numbers should be adjusted according to the relative severity of comorbid disease, but may be used to guide clinical decision making.

■ SURGICAL DECISION MAKING

In patients with symptomatic AAAs, operative repair is nearly always appropriate because of the high mortality associated with rupture or thrombosis, and the high likelihood of limb loss associated with peripheral embolism. Occasionally, patients with very high risk or patients with short life expectancy may choose to forego emergency repair of symptomatic AAAs, but in general, surgical decision making for symptomatic AAAs is straightforward.

For patients with asymptomatic AAAs, more recent randomized trials have provided assurance that the typical male patient generally can be monitored safely with careful ultrasound surveillance until the AAA reaches 5.5 cm, at which time elective repair can be performed. Decision analyses and cost-effectiveness modeling have previously shown, however, that individual patient rupture risk, operative risk, and life expectancy need to be considered to determine the optimal threshold for intervention.[150,151,249,250] The UK Small Aneurysm Trial and ADAM trial excluded patients who were considered "unfit" for repair, highlighting the fact that patients with high operative risk and short life expectancy should have a threshold diameter greater than 5.5 cm. In the UK Small Aneurysm Trial, the rupture risk for women was 4.5-fold higher than for men, prompting the authors to recommend a lower threshold for women than men. It seems logical also to consider other factors that may make rupture more likely during surveillance. In both randomized trials, 60% to 75% of patients undergoing surveillance eventually underwent AAA repair.[153,154] In the UK Small Aneurysm Trial, 81% of patients with initial diameters 5 to 5.4 cm eventually underwent repair. For many patients with this size AAA, the question is not whether to perform AAA repair but when. Patients with AAA diameters approaching 5.5 cm whose life expectancy is expected to be more than 5 years and whose operative risk is estimated to be low should be informed that they are likely to require AAA repair within the next few years. This subgroup of patients could be offered surgery at a time when it is convenient for them, with the understanding that waiting for expansion to 5.5 cm has little risk. In these cases, patient preference should weigh heavily in the decision-making process. For patients with multiple risk factors for rupture, long life expectancy, and low operative risk, it would seem prudent to recommend AAA repair at less than 5.5 cm diameter. Additionally, the ability of the patient to comply with careful surveillance should be considered. Although more recent randomized trials have provided a great deal of information to guide decision making, clinicians should not adopt a "one size fits all" policy for treating patients with AAA.

Table 100-5	Life Expectancy in Years for Patients with Abdominal Aortic Aneurysm by Age, Gender, and Race				
		MALE		FEMALE	
AGE (yr)	TOTAL	White	Black	White	Black
60	13	12	11	14	13
65	11	11	10	12	11
70	10	9	8	10	10
75	8	8	7	9	8
80	6	6	6	7	6
≥85	5	4	4	5	5

■ PREOPERATIVE ASSESSMENT

Patient Evaluation

A careful history, physical examination, and basic laboratory data are the most important factors for estimating perioperative risk and subsequent life expectancy. These factors not only may influence the decision to perform elective AAA repair, but they may focus preoperative management to reduce modifiable risk. Because CAD is the largest single cause of early and late mortality after AAA repair,[251] it is discussed in detail in Chapter 56 and summarized briefly here. The first issue to consider in preoperative evaluation is whether a patient's current quality of life is sufficient in his or her opinion to justify a surgical procedure potentially to prolong life. In some debilitated elderly patients or patients with mental deterioration, this decision is difficult and must be made in conjunction with the extended family. When this decision is made, attention must be directed toward identifying risk factors that would increase operative risk or decrease otherwise expected survival such that prophylactic repair might not be warranted. Assessment of activity level, stamina, and stability of health is important in this regard and can be translated into metabolic equivalents to help assess cardiac and pulmonary risk.[252] Because COPD is an independent predictor of operative mortality,[212,232] it should be assessed by pulmonary function studies with or without room air arterial blood gas measurement in patients who have apparent pulmonary disease. In some cases, preoperative treatment with bronchodilators and pulmonary toilet can reduce operative risk.[253] In more extreme cases, pulmonary risk may reduce life expectancy substantially, and in these cases, formal pulmonary consultation may be helpful to estimate survival. Serum creatinine is one of the most important predictors of operative mortality[232] and must be assessed. The impact of other diseases, such as malignancy, on expected survival also should be considered carefully.

It is well established that patients with AAAs have a high prevalence of CAD. Hertzer and colleagues[254] in 1979 performed routine preoperative coronary arteriography at the Cleveland Clinic and reported that only 6% of patients with AAAs had normal arteries; 29% had mild to moderate CAD; 29% had advanced compensated CAD; 31% had severe correctable CAD; and 5% had severe uncorrectable CAD. This study established that clinical prediction of the severity of CAD was imperfect because 18% of patients without clinically apparent CAD had severe correctable CAD on arteriography compared with 44% of patients whose CAD was clinically apparent. This pivotal study has led to intense efforts to identify risk factors and algorithms that more accurately predict the presence of severe CAD that would justify its correction before AAA repair or would lead to avoiding AAA repair. Many clinical parameters, including angina, history of MI, Q wave on ECG, ventricular arrhythmia, CHF, diabetes, and increasing age, have been reported to increase the risk of postoperative cardiac events.[255] Various combinations of these risk factors have been used to generate prediction algorithms for perioperative cardiac morbidity.[252] In general, these algorithms identify low-risk, high-risk, or intermediate-risk patients. For high-risk patients, such as patients with unstable angina, more sophisticated

cardiac evaluation is required; low-risk patients may undergo elective AAA repair without further testing. For intermediate-risk patients, who constitute most patients with AAAs, decision making is more difficult and may be facilitated by additional cardiac testing.[255] Radionuclide stress scanning (either exercised-induced or dipyridamole-induced) or stress echocardiography (dobutamine-induced) is used most frequently for this purpose and has a high negative predictive value; that is, patients with a normal stress response have a low probability of perioperative myocardial complications.[256-258] For patients with abnormal stress response, however, the positive predictive value of these tests is low because many such patients can undergo elective AAA repair safely. Although many initial studies showed a high predictive value for dipyridamole-thallium scanning in patients undergoing AAA repair,[259-261] subsequent studies have not found that routine screening is cost-effective.[262-264] It seems that increasing age and clinical indicators of CAD are better predictors of adverse cardiac outcome after AAA repair.[265] There has been considerable debate about the appropriateness of extensive cardiac evaluation and potential treatment of patients before elective AAA repair.

If significant CAD or other cardiac risk factors, such as valvular disease or CHF, are identified preoperatively in a patient with an AAA, four options are possible: (1) perform endovascular AAA repair ; (2) delay or avoid AAA repair; (3) perform AAA repair with more intensive cardiac monitoring and management, particularly with perioperative beta blockade (see section on perioperative management); or (4) reduce cardiac risk before AAA surgery with coronary artery bypass graft, coronary angioplasty, or coronary stenting. Option 1 is discussed in detail in Chapter 101. Although most surgeons consider this a lower risk option, this has not yet been proved by randomized trials. Option 2 is most applicable to patients with small, low-risk AAAs or to elderly patients in whom the added benefit of AAA repair is marginal. Proponents of option 3 cite the low mortality of AAA repair without preoperative cardiac surgery, especially in patients treated with beta blockers, and the added mortality from cardiac intervention that must be considered.[266] In contrast, proponents of option 4 point out the need to ensure long-term survival to gain the benefit of AAA repair and the survival benefit of coronary artery bypass graft in appropriately selected patients.[267,268] Because no randomized trial has been conducted to address the benefit of prophylactic coronary revascularization before elective AAA repair, this question remains an issue for individualized decision making, based on local outcomes. In general, however, with improved techniques for perioperative management of AAA patients, such as the routine use of perioperative beta blockade, there is a trend toward less extensive preoperative cardiac evaluation. In this regard, the American Heart Association has developed consensus recommendations regarding the preoperative cardiac evaluation of patients with peripheral vascular disease.[252]

The impact of cardiac risk assessment is particularly relevant for AAA repair (or any prophylactic operation) because it can change the decision of whether to repair a given aneurysm. For patients without clinically apparent heart disease, sophisticated cardiac testing has little impact on decision making for large, high-risk AAAs, but is more relevant for lower risk, small AAAs, in which operative mortality must be especially low to justify elective repair.[264] For the rare patient with unstable CAD and a large (or symptomatic) AAA, coronary revascularization combined with AAA repair may be indicated.[269,270] Alternatively, perioperative intra-aortic balloon counterpulsation has been used successfully in high-risk cardiac patients who require AAA repair.[271] In these cases, the intra-aortic balloon can be introduced via the femoral artery and advanced through the graft after completing the proximal aortic anastomosis. The distal aortic or iliac anastomosis is constructed with the device in place, maintaining hemostasis with a Rumel tourniquet around the proximal graft. These techniques are seldom required, however, because elective AAA repair is not likely to prolong life in patients with such severe cardiac disease, unless this can be corrected. Lower risk endovascular AAA repair seems particularly well suited for such patients (see Chapter 101).

Aneurysm Evaluation

Most surgeons recommend a preoperative imaging study using CT, MRI, MRA, or arteriography. Contrast-enhanced CT seems to be the most useful study for preoperative AAA evaluation when considering information obtained, invasiveness, and cost. This is particularly true for spiral CT, with thin slices in the region of interest. Spiral CT allows not only accurate size measurements, but also accurate definition of the relationship of an AAA to visceral and renal arteries. CT detects iliac artery aneurysms easily, and even occlusive disease of intra-abdominal vessels is often apparent. CT aids in the identification of venous anomalies, such as a retroaortic left renal vein or a duplicated vena cava, or renal abnormalities, such as horseshoe or pelvic kidney, which would influence operative techniques and approach. CT is the technique of choice to identify suspected inflammatory aneurysms and may reveal unsuspected abdominal pathology, such as associated malignancy or gallbladder disease. For juxtarenal or suprarenal aneurysms, CT can define the most appropriate location for suprarenal cross-clamping, based on the detailed relationship of the visceral arteries, and can identify potentially associated aortic wall calcification. The ability of CT with arterial phase contrast and thin slices to show stenotic lesions of the iliac, renal, and visceral arteries has improved and now rivals that of MRA. In centers with experience with these techniques, CT angiography has made percutaneous intra-arterial angiography unnecessary in most AAA patients, even patients with suprarenal AAAs and occlusive disease of the aortic branch vessels (see Chapter 103).

MRI is comparable to CT in terms of AAA measurement accuracy and other preoperative planning issues. MRI avoids intravenous contrast administration, which may represent an advantage over CT for selected patients. Because it is more expensive and time-consuming, MRI is not as widely used as CT scanning. When MRA is included with this technique, however, it can increase significantly the value in patients where arteriography otherwise would be required. In centers with sufficient experience using this technique, MRA also has been shown to be accurate for determining the presence of occlusive disease in intra-abdominal arteries (see Chapter 22).

Historically, arteriography was nearly always used for the preoperative evaluation of AAAs and adjacent arteries. Arteriography has substantially more risk than the other imaging techniques because of its invasive nature, is associated with contrast and radiation exposure, and is expensive. As a result, CT has been relied on more for routine preoperative AAA evaluation, especially because CT scanning can detect associated pathology that cannot be detected with arteriography. Arteriography is now reserved for the preoperative evaluation of AAAs in patients who have suspected disease of adjacent arteries where detailed evaluation of the arterial lumen would affect the conduct of the AAA repair, in whom sufficient information cannot be gained from CT.[272] Usually these are patients with associated renal or mesenteric disease or iliofemoral occlusive disease or patients with anomalies such as horseshoe or pelvic kidney. The development of endovascular AAA repair initially renewed the need for arteriography for precise preoperative device measurement, but even for this indication three-dimensional CT seems to have comparable value (see Chapter 21).[273]

■ MEDICAL MANAGEMENT

For patients with low-risk AAAs (small diameter without other risk factors for rupture) being followed with periodic size measurements, attempts should be made to reduce expansion rate and rupture risk. Smoking cessation is crucial, and hypertension should be aggressively controlled. As noted earlier, despite initial promising results from retrospective analyses, beta blockers have not been shown to slow the rate of growth of AAA in subsequent randomized trials, but doxycycline seems more promising.[204,206]

Because diameter measurement by CT is more accurate than ultrasound, it has been suggested that AAAs should be followed by CT, rather than ultrasound size measurements. Because ultrasound is much less expensive and less invasive, however, most physicians continue to use this technique. Comparing sequential ultrasound scans should provide increased accuracy in terms of relative change, if current and previous images are compared. The question remains as to whether CT should be used as the final determinant for recommending repair of "borderline"-sized AAAs. Because essentially all patients undergo a CT scan for preoperative planning, however, this is usually a moot point. It also can be argued that the accuracy of ultrasound is as precise as present knowledge of AAA rupture risk based on size. Nonetheless, because ultrasound seems systematically to underestimate AAA diameter by 2 to 4 mm compared with CT,[116,119,120] it seems reasonable to recommend a CT size measurement for AAAs, followed by ultrasound if they approach the threshold for elective repair.

■ SURGICAL TREATMENT

Since the 1960s, AAAs have been repaired using the technique of endoaneurysmorrhaphy with intraluminal graft placement, as described by Creech.[8] This procedure is described subsequently (transperitoneal approach). The development of this technique was based in part on the failure of previous "nonresective" operations, including aneurysm ligation, wrapping, and attempts at inducing

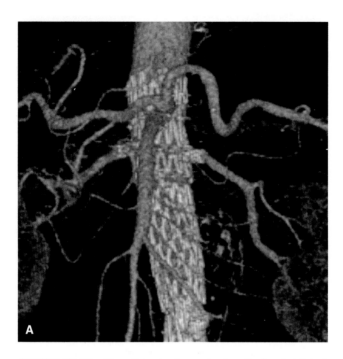

FIGURE 101-3A. Three-dimensional reconstruction after fenestrated stent-graft with bare stents in the renal arteries. (Courtesy Dr. E. L. Verhoeven.)

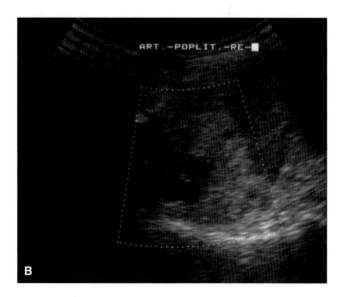

FIGURE 105-17B. During follow-up, the diameter of the aneurysm increased, and duplex ultrasonography showed flow in the aneurysm.

aneurysm thrombosis, that yielded uniformly dismal results. AAA thrombosis by iliac ligation combined with axillobifemoral bypass enjoyed a brief resurgence in popularity for extremely high risk patients, but showed a high complication rate, including late aneurysm rupture, and an operative mortality rate comparable to conventional repair in similar patients.[274-278] This technique was similarly abandoned. As an alternative to standard open AAA repair, Shah and colleagues[279] proposed exclusion of an AAA with bypass to reduce operative blood loss. This group has since published long-term follow-up results and no longer recommends this procedure because of persistent flow in the excluded AAA sac and rupture in rare cases.[280] In another attempt to reduce the invasiveness of AAA repair, the use of laparoscopy has been suggested to assist AAA repair. This approach uses laparoscopic techniques to dissect the aneurysm neck and iliac arteries followed by a standard endoaneurysmorrhaphy through a minilaparotomy. Kline and colleagues[281] reported their results in 20 patients to show the feasibility of this approach, but a clear benefit has not been shown because the intraoperative, intensive care unit, and total hospital durations seem comparable to conventional AAA repair. Further experience with this technique may identify a subgroup of patients for which a laparoscopic-assisted AAA repair is advantageous.

Endovascular AAA repair was introduced by Parodi and coworkers[282] in 1991 and has gained rapidly in popularity in the United States after reports of clinical trials and subsequent Food and Drug Administration approval. Endovascular AAA repair has been shown to reduce operative morbidity, mortality, length of stay, and disability after surgery.[283-285,285a] Recovery time is shorter after endovascular repair than after open repair.[285,286] Endovascular repair may not be as durable as open repair, however.[287-292] Frequent and lifelong surveillance is required after endovascular repair along with a second intervention or conversion to open repair in some cases. There seems to be a small ongoing risk of rupture after endografting as well. Decision analysis suggests that there is little difference between open and endovascular repair for most patients.[292] Endovascular AAA repair may be preferred, however, for patients who are at high operative risk for open surgery. Open surgery may be preferred for younger, healthier patients in whom there is little difference in operative risk between the two strategies and for whom long-term durability is a concern. For most patients, patient preference should weigh heavily in the decision-making process. Randomized trials comparing open with endovascular surgery are currently under way in Europe and in the VA system in the United States. An additional trial is under way in Europe comparing endovascular repair with observation in high-risk patients. These trials will provide much more information for planning AAA repair in individual patients. Rapid advances continue to be made, however, in stent-graft technology that will need to be considered. Endovascular AAA repair is discussed in detail in Chapter 101.

Perioperative Management

Preoperative intravenous antibiotics (usually a cephalosporin) are administered to reduce the risk of prosthetic graft infection.[293] Ample intravenous access, intra-arterial pressure recording, and Foley catheter monitoring of urine output are routine. For patients with significant cardiac disease, pulmonary artery catheters are used frequently to guide volume replacement and vasodilator or inotrope therapy intraoperatively and in the early postoperative period. Mixed venous oxygen tension measurement, available with these catheters, can provide an additional estimate of global circulatory function. Transesophageal echocardiography can be useful in selected patients to monitor ventricular volume and cardiac wall motion abnormalities and to guide fluid administration and the use of vasoactive drugs. Despite their frequent usage, studies examining the use of pulmonary artery catheters during AAA surgery have been unable to show added value easily.[294,295] These studies usually have excluded very high risk patients, however, who are most likely to benefit from such monitoring. Because these techniques are not risk-free, selective use is probably more appropriate than routine application.

Because the volume of blood lost during AAA repair often requires blood replacement, intraoperative autotransfusion and preoperative autologous blood donation have become popular, primarily to avoid the infection risk associated with allogeneic transfusion. Studies of the cost-effectiveness of such procedures question their routine use, however.[296-298] Autologous blood donation is less important for elderly patients, in whom life expectancy is shorter than the usual time for development of transfusion-associated viral illness. Because the allogeneic blood pool has become safer and the transfusion requirement for elective AAA repair lower, autologous blood donation does not seem to be cost-effective in elderly cardiovascular patients.[296] Intraoperative autotransfusion during AAA repair is widely used because of the documented safety of this technique.[299] Systems that use cell separation and return only red blood cells cause fewer coagulation disturbances than systems that return whole blood.[300] Because of the fixed costs associated with autotransfusion equipment, however, studies have shown that this technique is not cost-effective, unless a blood loss of approximately 1000 mL occurs.[297,298,301] Because it is usually difficult to predict the volume of blood loss during AAA repair, most surgeons employ autotransfusion in case blood loss becomes extensive. An intermediate solution is to employ only the reservoir component of an autotransfusion system and process the collected blood (using the more expensive components of these systems) only if blood loss is sufficient to justify this.[298] Optimizing oxygen delivery to patients with reduced cardiac output by maintaining an adequate hematocrit seems beneficial in patients undergoing AAA repair. One study showed that a postoperative hematocrit less than 28% was associated with significant cardiac morbidity in vascular surgery patients.[302]

Maintenance of normal body temperature during aortic surgery is important to prevent coagulopathy, allow extubation, and maintain normal metabolic function. In a review of patients undergoing elective AAA repair, Bush and colleagues[303] noted significantly more organ dysfunction (53% versus 29%) and higher mortality (12% versus 1.5%) in hypothermic patients (temperature <34.5°C) compared with normothermic patients. The only predictor of intraoperative hypothermia was female gender; prolonged hypothermia was related to initial hypothermia, indicating the difficulty in rewarming cold patients. A randomized trial found significantly reduced cardiac morbidity (1.4% versus 6.3%) in patients who were normothermic (36.7°C) versus hypothermic (35.4°C) intraoperatively.[304] To prevent hypothermia, a recirculating warm forced-air blanket should be placed in contact with the patient, and intravenous fluids, including any blood returned from an autotransfusion device, should be warmed before administration.

Anesthesia

Nearly all patients undergo general anesthesia for AAA repair. The supplemental use of continuous epidural anesthesia, begun immediately preoperatively and continued for postoperative pain control, is increasing in popularity.[305] This technique allows a lighter level of general anesthesia to be maintained, while controlling pain through the epidural blockade. Additional benefits may include a reduction in the sympathetic catecholamine stress response, which might decrease cardiac complications. One randomized trial comparing general anesthesia with combined general-epidural anesthesia showed decreased deaths, cardiac events, infections, and overall complications.[306] These benefits were not observed in another randomized trial,[307] however, suggesting that the details of perioperative management and patient selection may determine the impact of epidural anesthesia. It is possible that the major benefit of epidural anesthesia accrues in the postoperative period, rather than intraoperatively.[308] Although concern has been raised about possible complications of epidural hematoma in patients who are anticoagulated, this has proved to be extremely rare when the epidural catheter is inserted before and removed after anticoagulation.[309]

Preoperative β-adrenergic blockade is an important adjunct to reduce left ventricular work by decreasing heart rate, blood pressure, and cardiac contractility; this decreases myocardial oxygen demand to reduce or prevent ischemia. Pasternack and colleagues[310] showed that patients who underwent vascular surgery and received metoprolol immediately before operation had significantly lower heart rate and less intraoperative myocardial ischemia than untreated controls. Mangano and associates[311] performed the first randomized, placebo-controlled trial to assess the effect of atenolol (given intravenously immediately before and after surgery and orally during hospitalization) in patients at risk for CAD who underwent noncardiac surgery. A significant reduction in mortality extending 2 years after discharge was observed in the atenolol-treated patients (3% versus 14% 1-year mortality) as a result of a reduction in death from cardiac causes. In a separate analysis, the investigators noted that atenolol-treated patients had a 50% lower incidence of myocardial ischemia during the first 48 hours after surgery and a 40% lower incidence during postoperative days 0 through 7.[312] Patients with perioperative myocardial ischemia were significantly more likely to die within 2 years after surgery. Poldermans and co-workers[313] performed a randomized trial of perioperative beta blockade with bisoprolol in patients with abnormal dobutamine echocardiograms undergoing aortic or lower extremity arterial reconstruction and found that perioperative cardiac death was significantly reduced from 17% (placebo) to 3% (bisoprolol). Additionally, nonfatal MI

occurred in 17% of patients given placebo versus none of the patients given bisoprolol. A subsequent publication from the same authors showed that during a mean follow-up of 22 months, cardiac events were significantly lower in patients who had received perioperative beta blockade (12% versus 32%).[314] Given this knowledge, it has been suggested that beta blockers are underused, likely because of fears about use in patients with COPD or prior heart failure. Heart failure is now a major indication for beta blockade, however.[315,316] Additionally, Gottlieb and colleagues[316] showed that COPD should not be considered a contraindication for beta blockade. They found a 40% reduction in risk of death after MI in patients with COPD who were taking beta blockers compared with patients who were not. In Mangano's trial, the only exclusion criteria were preexisting ECG abnormalities that would preclude detection of new ischemic events. Beta blockers were withheld during the trial only for heart rate less than 55 beats/min, systolic blood pressure less than 100 mm Hg, acute bronchospasm, current evidence of CHF, or third-degree heart block. The weight of evidence supports the routine use of beta blockers for nearly all patients undergoing AAA repair.

Choice of Incision

AAA repair can be accomplished through an anterior transperitoneal incision (midline or transverse) or through a retroperitoneal approach (left or right side). Midline, transperitoneal incisions can be performed rapidly and provide wide access to the abdomen, but may be associated with more pulmonary complications secondary to postoperative splinting from upper abdominal pain. Transverse abdominal incisions, just above or below the umbilicus, require more time to open and close, but may be associated with fewer pulmonary complications and late incisional hernias, although this has not yet been proved. Retroperitoneal incisions, from the lateral rectus margin extending into the 10th or 11th intercostal space, afford good exposure of the infrarenal and the suprarenal aorta, but limit exposure of the contralateral renal and iliac arteries. In addition, this exposure does not allow access to intra-abdominal organs, unless the peritoneum is purposely opened; therefore associated abdominal disease can remain undetected. The left retroperitoneal approach usually is favored over the right for exposure of the upper abdominal aorta because the spleen is easier to mobilize and retract than the liver. The right retroperitoneal approach is used when specific abdominal problems, such as a stoma, preclude the left-sided approach.[317] In recent years, the left retroperitoneal approach has enjoyed a resurgence in popularity because of suggestions that pulmonary morbidity, ileus, and intravenous fluid requirements are decreased postoperatively.

Randomized trials have reached different conclusions about the potential advantages of retroperitoneal over transabdominal incisions. Sicard and associates[318] reported more prolonged ileus, small bowel obstruction, and overall complications after transabdominal compared with retroperitoneal aortic surgery, although pulmonary complications were similar. Cambria and colleagues[319] found no difference in these incisions in terms of pulmonary complications, fluid or blood requirements, or other postoperative complications except slightly prolonged return to oral intake after the transperitoneal approach. In a more recent randomized trial, Sieunarine and coworkers[320] found no difference in operating time, cross-clamp time, blood loss, fluid requirement, analgesia requirement, gastrointestinal function, intensive care unit stay, or hospital stay for transperitoneal versus retroperitoneal approaches for aortic surgery. In long-term follow-up, however, there were significantly more wound problems (hernias, bulging, and pain) in the retroperitoneal group.

These results suggest that in most cases, the choice of incision for AAA repair is a matter of personal preference. The transperitoneal and retroperitoneal approaches have advantages in certain patients, however. Relative indications for retroperitoneal exposure include a "hostile" abdomen secondary to multiple previous transperitoneal operations, an abdominal wall stoma, a horseshoe kidney, an inflammatory aneurysm, or anticipated need for suprarenal endarterectomy or anastomosis. Relative indications for a transperitoneal approach include a ruptured AAA, coexistent intra-abdominal pathology, uncertain diagnosis, left-sided vena cava, large bilateral iliac aneurysms, or need for access to both renal arteries. Exposure of sufficient normal aorta proximal to a juxtarenal AAA may be difficult via a transperitoneal approach. Ligation and division of the left renal vein is an alternative, but can lead to renal dysfunction.[321,322] Left retroperitoneal exposure, with displacement of the left kidney anteriorly, avoids this problem and facilitates suprarenal exposure.[323] Need for concomitant renal or mesenteric revascularization may dictate specific operative approaches. The left retroperitoneal approach is optimal for left renal, celiac, and superior mesenteric artery (SMA) revascularization and transaortic endarterectomy of these vessels. Bypass grafting (and endarterectomy) of the right renal artery is more easily accomplished by a transperitoneal exposure (or a right retroperitoneal approach if other visceral arteries need not be exposed). The advantages of each approach in the situations described make it advisable for surgeons to become proficient with both techniques.

Transperitoneal Approach

After entering the abdomen through a transperitoneal incision, the abdomen is explored thoroughly to exclude other pathology and to assess the extent of the aneurysm. The transverse colon is retracted superiorly, and the ligament of Treitz is divided to allow retraction of the small bowel to the right. Exposure is greatly facilitated using a fixed, self-retaining retractor. A longitudinal incision is made in the peritoneum just to the left of the base of the small bowel mesentery to expose the aneurysm. This incision extends from the inferior border of the pancreas proximally to the level of normal iliac arteries distally. Care must be taken to avoid the ureters, especially if exposure includes the iliac bifurcation, where the ureters normally cross. Autonomic nerves to the pelvis course anterior to the proximal left common iliac artery and should be retracted with associated retroperitoneal tissue rather than incised, to prevent sexual dysfunction in men. The left renal vein should be identified and retracted superiorly if necessary to expose the neck of the aneurysm fully. Care must be taken not to avulse renal vein tributaries, particularly a descending

lumbar vein, frequently encountered to the left of the aorta, which must be divided before the left renal vein is mobile enough to allow upward retraction. Rarely, proximal exposure cannot be obtained without division of the left renal vein. In such cases, this should be done at its junction with the vena cava to maintain patency of collateral drainage via adrenal and gonadal branches. In most cases, reanastomosis is not required, but can be performed if renal vein engorgement suggests inadequate collateral drainage.

After obtaining adequate aortoiliac exposure, the normal aorta and iliac arteries are dissected sufficiently to place a vascular clamp proximal and distal to the aneurysm. Regardless of the proximal extent of an infrarenal AAA, it is desirable to construct the proximal aortic anastomosis near the renal arteries to avoid subsequent aneurysmal degeneration of residual infrarenal aorta. When an AAA approaches or involves the renal arteries, it can be safer to apply the cross-clamp proximal to the celiac artery, rather than between the renal arteries and the SMA. Chervu and colleagues[115] showed much higher operative mortality (32% versus 3%) and renal failure requiring dialysis (23% versus 3%) after infrarenal AAA repair when clamping was performed between the SMA and renal arteries versus proximal to the celiac artery. They attributed this increased mortality to the greater likelihood of dislodging atherosclerotic debris in the pararenal aorta as opposed to the supraceliac aorta, which is usually less diseased. Complications resulted from atheroembolization to the kidneys, legs, and intestine or injury to the aorta or renal arteries. Others also have noted the relative safety of clamping the supraceliac aorta, which can be accessed easily by dividing the gastrohepatic ligament and the diaphragmatic crus.[324] Aortic clamping between the renal arteries and the SMA also is safe, however, when performed in properly selected patients without extensive plaque in this region.[325] Occasionally, it is possible to obtain distal control of an AAA on the aorta, but usually aneurysmal changes or calcification in this location make iliac clamping preferred. A disease-free area of proximal aorta and iliac arteries should be identified for clamping, to minimize the possibility of clamp injury or embolization of arterial debris. Some iliac arteries may be so diffusely calcified that clamping without injury is impossible. In such cases, internal occlusion with a balloon catheter or extension of the graft to the femoral arteries is required. In most cases, it is unnecessary to encircle the aorta and iliac arteries completely because vascular clamps can be placed in the anteroposterior direction, leaving the back wall undissected. This minimizes the likelihood of injury to lumbar and iliac veins. Sometimes posterior arterial plaque necessitates placement of a vascular clamp transversely on either the aorta or the iliac arteries, which then require careful posterior dissection precisely on the plane of the artery to avoid venous injury.

AAA repair can be accomplished with a straight ("tube") graft in 40% to 50% of patients, without extension onto the iliac arteries.[22,227] Although concern has been raised about the potential for future aneurysm development in the iliac arteries after tube graft repair of AAAs, late follow-up has shown that this is not clinically significant if the iliac arteries were not aneurysmal at the time of AAA repair.[326] Extension to the iliac arteries with a bifurcated graft for AAA repair is necessary in the remaining 50% to 60% of patients because of aneurysmal involvement of the iliac arteries or severe calcification of the aortic bifurcation. Extension of the graft to the femoral level is indicated for severe concomitant iliac occlusive disease or rarely because of technical difficulties associated with a deep pelvic anastomosis. Iliac anastomoses are preferred, however, owing to decreased infection and pseudoaneurysm complications compared with femoral anastomoses. Prosthetic grafts available for AAA repair include knitted Dacron, knitted Dacron impregnated with collagen or gelatin to decrease porosity, woven Dacron, and polytetrafluoroethylene (PTFE). These and other graft choices are discussed in detail in Chapter 49. There is no clear evidence that any of these graft types provides a superior outcome. In a prospective randomized comparison of PTFE and Dacron, long-term patency was equivalent, but PTFE had a higher incidence of early graft failure and graft sepsis.[327] In contrast, in a smaller trial with shorter follow-up, PTFE was found to be superior.[328] Most surgeons prefer an impervious graft to avoid the need for preclotting and select impregnated knitted Dacron, PTFE, or woven Dacron.[329] This type of graft not only saves time and more reliably prevents bleeding through the graft, but also allows graft selection to be delayed until the aneurysm is opened so that a graft diameter corresponding to the inner diameter of the normal proximal aorta can be selected. It also allows delayed selection of a straight versus bifurcated graft that may not always be obvious before the aneurysm is open and the distal aorta can be carefully inspected.

Most surgeons use heparin anticoagulation during aortic cross-clamping to reduce lower extremity thrombotic complications. Heparin dosage varies from 50 to 150 U/kg, based on personal preference. Activated clotting time measurement is useful to determine the need for supplemental heparin in prolonged cases and the appropriate dose of protamine sulfate to reverse anticoagulation after declamping.[330] The sequence for applying proximal and distal vascular clamps is selected to apply the initial clamp in the area of least atherosclerotic disease to reduce the risk of distal embolization. The aneurysm is opened longitudinally along its anterior surface, away from the inferior mesenteric artery (IMA) in case this requires later reimplantation. The proximal aorta is incised horizontally at the level selected for proximal anastomosis (Fig. 100-7). To avoid potential injury to posterior veins, this incision does not need to extend through the back wall of the aorta, although some surgeons prefer complete transection for better exposure. Intraluminal thrombotic material and atherosclerotic debris are extracted from the aneurysm, which usually discloses several backbleeding lumbar artery orifices, which require suture ligation. If the IMA is patent, it should be controlled temporarily with a small vascular clamp (see Fig. 100-7) so that its need for reimplantation can be assessed after the revascularization is completed. IMA revascularization may be advised if the hypogastric arteries are diseased or if one requires ligation for technical reasons.

When hemostasis within the opened aneurysm sac has been achieved, the proximal anastomosis is performed. There is often a distinct ring at the aneurysm neck that defines the appropriate level for this anastomosis. Usually polypropylene suture is used, taking large aortic "bites" and

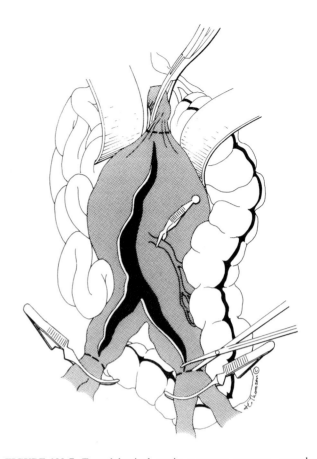

FIGURE 100-7 Transabdominal aortic aneurysm exposure, vascular clamps in place, incising the aneurysm.

incorporating a double thickness of posterior aortic wall for added strength. If the aortic wall is friable, pledgets of PTFE or Dacron can be incorporated into the suture line. After completing the proximal anastomosis, the graft is clamped, and the proximal aortic clamp is released briefly to check for and correct any suture line bleeding. If the distal anastomosis is to the aorta, a similar technique is used just above its bifurcation, suturing from within the lumen and encompassing both iliac artery orifices within the suture line. If iliac artery aneurysms exist, these are incised anteriorly so that the limbs of a bifurcated graft can be sutured to the normal iliac artery beyond these aneurysms (Fig. 100-8). Often this requires graft extension to the common iliac bifurcation, including the orifices of the internal and the external iliac arteries within the distal anastomosis. In rare instances, aneurysmal involvement of the distal common iliac artery may preclude anastomosis to the internal and the external iliac artery orifices because these are widely separated. In such cases, an external iliac artery anastomosis can be constructed, but care must be taken to preserve adequate pelvic blood flow, which may mean direct revascularization of at least one internal iliac artery. The need for internal iliac revascularization usually is assessed by the extent of backbleeding, as discussed later. For large aneurysms of the left iliac artery, medial reflection of the sigmoid mesocolon facilitates a retroperitoneal approach to the distal common iliac artery and prevents unnecessary

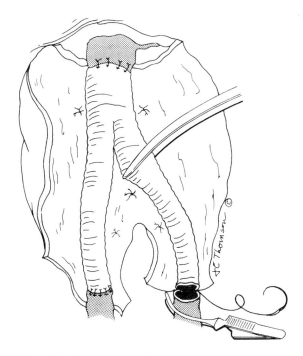

FIGURE 100-8 Completing the iliac anastomosis of an abdominal aortic aneurysm repair. Lumbar artery orifices have been suture ligated. Flow already has been established through the right graft limb.

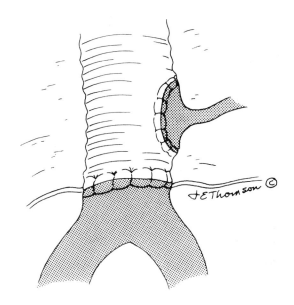

FIGURE 100-9 Reimplanting the inferior mesenteric artery with Carrel patch technique after abdominal aortic aneurysm repair with tube graft.

dissection of autonomic nerves crossing the proximal left common iliac artery. Before completing the distal anastomoses, arterial clamps are carefully removed, and vigorous irrigation is used to flush out any thrombus or debris.

When the first iliac (or distal aortic) anastomosis is completed, flow into that extremity should be restored, releasing the clamp slowly to minimize "declamping" hypotension. Declamping shock is rare if adequate intravenous fluid replacement has been administered. Sudden restoration of blood flow into a dilated distal vascular bed and the associated venous return of vasoactive substances that have accumulated in the ischemic limbs usually cause some hypotension, however. Declamping should be gradual and coordinated carefully with the anesthesia team because additional volume administration can be required. In some cases, the clamp must be reapplied intermittently to allow adequate volume resuscitation and to prevent hypotension. After restoration of lower extremity and pelvic blood flow, the IMA and sigmoid colon are inspected. The IMA can be ligated with a transfixing suture applied to its internal orifice if it is small and not associated with known SMA occlusive disease, if it has good backflow on release of its vascular clamp, if the sigmoid colon and arterial pulsations are good, and if at least one internal iliac artery is patent. In questionable cases, Doppler signals from the sigmoid colon or an assessment of IMA stump pressure[331] may be necessary to determine the need for IMA reimplantation (see complications later). In the rare circumstances when sigmoid colon perfusion appears marginal, a circular cuff of the aortic wall around the IMA orifice is excised (Carrel patch) and anastomosed to the left side of the graft (Fig. 100-9).

Next, the adequacy of lower extremity blood flow is determined by visual inspection of the feet, palpation of distal pulses, or more sophisticated Doppler or pulse volume recording. If reduced blood flow is detected, intraoperative arteriography can differentiate thrombosis or embolism from peripheral vasoconstriction, which is relatively common if the procedure is prolonged and the patient is cold. Embolism or thrombosis requires prompt surgical correction, whereas vasoconstriction requires correction of any volume deficit and rewarming. After ensuring adequate intestinal and lower extremity circulation, heparin is reversed with protamine sulfate if sufficient heparin has been given to justify reversal, and hemostasis is achieved. The aneurysm wall and retroperitoneum are closed over the graft to provide a tissue barrier between the prosthesis and the adjacent intestine (Fig. 100-10). The aortic prosthesis and upper anastomosis must be isolated from the overlying duodenum during closure; if necessary, a pedicle of greater omentum can be interposed to achieve this purpose. The small bowel should be inspected carefully and replaced in its normal position before abdominal closure.

Retroperitoneal Approach

Proper patient positioning is essential to achieve optimal exposure using the retroperitoneal approach. For most infrarenal AAAs, a left retroperitoneal incision centered on the 11th or 12th rib is employed. The patient's left shoulder is elevated at a 45- to 60-degree angle relative to the table, while the pelvis is positioned relatively flat. The table is flexed with the break positioned at a level midway between the iliac crest and the costal margin (Fig. 100-11). An air-evacuating "bean bag" is helpful to maintain proper positioning. Beginning at the lateral border of the left rectus muscle midway between the pubis and the umbilicus, the skin incision is carried superiorly then curved laterally up to the tip of the 11th or 12th rib. If extensive exposure of the right iliac artery is required, the incision can be extended inferolaterally into the right lower quadrant, or a separate

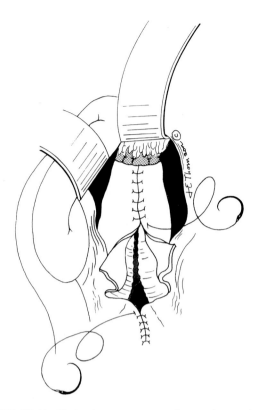

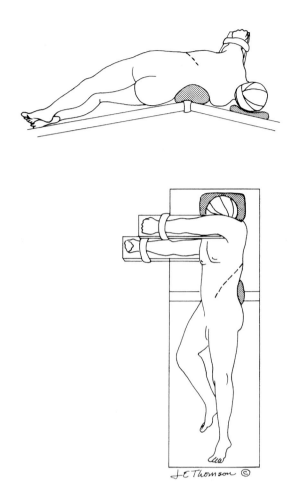

FIGURE 100-10 Closing the aneurysm sac and retroperitoneum between the graft and duodenum.

FIGURE 100-11 Positioning and skin incision for retroperitoneal approach for abdominal aortic aneurysm repair.

right lower quadrant retroperitoneal incision can be used. The underlying lateral abdominal wall muscles are divided, exposing the underlying peritoneum and the anterior edge of the properitoneal fat layer at the lateral aspect of this exposure. Dissection in the retroperitoneal plane is then developed, either anterior or posterior to the left kidney, until the aorta is encountered.

For infrarenal aneurysm exposure, it is often sufficient to proceed anteriorly and leave the left kidney in its normal position. For juxtarenal or suprarenal aneurysms, which require more cephalad exposure, the kidney is mobilized anteriorly to approach the aorta from behind the left renal artery (Fig. 100-12). If the need for higher exposure is anticipated, the incision should be directed more cephalad over the 9th or 10th rib, and the shoulders are positioned as near perpendicular to the table as possible. In this case, more table flexion is required to open the space between the pelvis and ribs, and the trunk is twisted so that the angle between the pelvis and the table is about 30 degrees. When approaching the aorta from behind the left renal artery, it is necessary to divide a large lumbar branch of the left renal vein to mobilize the kidney and renal vein anteriorly. The ureter must be identified and retracted medially with the kidney, taking care to separate it from the iliac bifurcation distally. Medial mobilization of the peritoneal contents exposes the IMA, which usually is divided for more complete exposure of the aortic bifurcation and right renal artery, depending on the size of the AAA. Exposure is greatly facilitated by using a fixed, self-retaining retractor. If necessary, exposure of the right iliac artery and right renal

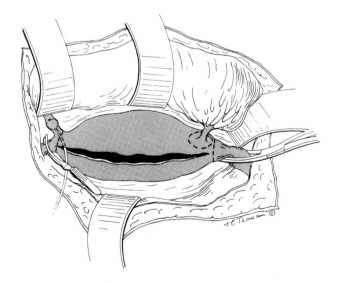

FIGURE 100-12 Retroperitoneal aortic exposure with left kidney retracted anteriorly for repair of suprarenal abdominal aortic aneurysm. The left renal artery is to be reimplanted as a Carrel patch. The right iliac artery is controlled with a balloon catheter.

artery is easier after opening and decompressing the AAA. Right iliac artery control is often best accomplished by using a balloon occlusion catheter after entering the aneurysm (see Fig. 100-12). After achieving adequate exposure, repair of the AAA is usually carried out as described earlier for the transperitoneal approach. The retroperitoneal technique does not normally afford an opportunity to inspect colonic and intestinal viability, but the peritoneum can be opened to accomplish this if any concern exists.

Associated Arterial Disease

Indications for concomitant mesenteric or renal artery revascularization during elective AAA repair are comparable to the indications for isolated disease in these arteries. Occasionally, patients with asymptomatic, high-grade stenoses of these arteries warrant "prophylactic" concomitant reconstruction, if the patient is at low operative risk, and the AAA repair proceeds uneventfully. Although the natural history of asymptomatic mesenteric artery stenosis is not well characterized, it seems that patients with critical disease of all three mesenteric arteries are at sufficiently high risk for future complications of mesenteric ischemia that concomitant revascularization is justified.[332] Progression of renal artery stenosis has been better documented,[333,334] but the ultimate clinical impact of such progression seems minimal in nonhypertensive patients with normal renal function.[335] The adjacency of the renal arteries to the operative field for AAA repair has led some authors to recommend prophylactic repair of critical, but asymptomatic renal artery stenoses.[336] Although this repair may be appropriate in younger, good-risk patients, it adds morbidity and mortality to the AAA repair, leading other authors to recommend the combined procedure only for standard indications of hypertension or ischemic nephropathy.[337,338]

■ COMPLICATIONS OF ABDOMINAL AORTIC ANEURYSM REPAIR

Despite major improvements in the outcome of elective AAA repair, major complications occur and must be managed correctly or avoided to maintain the low mortality necessary to justify prophylactic AAA repair. MI is the leading single-organ cause of early and late mortality in patients undergoing AAA repair[232] and must be assessed and managed carefully to reduce mortality. In a review of patients undergoing elective AAA repair, Huber and associates[298] found that multisystem organ failure (MSOF) caused more deaths (57%) than cardiac events (25%). Visceral organ dysfunction was the most common cause of MSOF, followed by postoperative pneumonia. Most patients with MSOF had associated cardiac dysfunction, however, which may have aggravated visceral ischemic injury. Several factors may be responsible for the emergence of MSOF as a more prominent cause of death after elective AAA repair. First, with modern techniques of intensive care, it is uncommon for patients to die with single-system failure (even cardiac) after AAA repair. Second, strict attention to cardiac risk in these patients may have reduced the relative impact of cardiac complications. Finally, older patients with more associated visceral and renal artery disease underwent

Table 100-6	Early (30-day) Complications After Elective Abdominal Aortic Aneurysm Repair Estimated from Surgical Series
COMPLICATION	**FREQUENCY (%)**
Death	<5
All cardiac	15
Myocardial infarction	2-8
All pulmonary	8-12
Pneumonia	5
Renal insufficiency	5-12
Dialysis dependent	1-6
Deep venous thrombosis	8
Bleeding	2-5
Ureteral injury	<1
Stroke	1
Leg ischemia	1-4
Colon ischemia	1-2
Spinal cord ischemia	<1
Wound infection	<5
Graft infection	<1
Graft thrombosis	<1

Data from references 22, 227, 232, and 469-471.

AAA repair in this series and had the highest likelihood of MSOF postoperatively. The relative frequency of single-system complications after elective AAA repair is presented in Table 100-6.

Cardiac Complications

Most cardiac ischemic events occur within the first 2 days after surgery, during which time intensive care monitoring is appropriate for high-risk patients. Maximizing myocardial function with adequate preload, controlling oxygen consumption by the reduced heart rate and blood pressure product, ensuring adequate oxygenation, and establishing effective analgesia are important techniques for preventing myocardial ischemia postoperatively. Patients with cardiac dysfunction have a greater risk of MI when the postoperative hematocrit is less than 28%, even though this is well tolerated by normal individuals.[339] Postoperative epidural analgesia, in addition to providing excellent pain control, may reduce myocardial complications by decreasing the catecholamine stress response.[306]

Hemorrhage

Intraoperative or postoperative hemorrhage usually results from difficulties with the proximal aortic anastomosis or from iatrogenic venous injury. Proximal suture line bleeding, particularly when posterior, can be difficult to control, especially if the proximal anastomosis is juxtarenal. In this event, temporary supraceliac aortic compression facilitates anastomotic repair, without excessive additional blood loss. Interrupted pledgeted sutures can be helpful if the aortic wall is friable. Venous bleeding usually results from injury to the iliac or left renal veins during initial exposure. Often the distal aortic aneurysm or common iliac aneurysm is densely adherent to the associated iliac vein, making circumferential arterial dissection hazardous. In such cases, vascular clamps usually can be applied successfully without complete dissection of the posterior wall of the iliac artery, or vascular control can be obtained with balloon occlusion catheters. A posterior left renal vein or a large lumbar vein may pose similar hazards during the proximal dissection. If undetected by preoperative CT, such anomalies pose a high risk for venous injury. Careful suture repair of venous injuries is required and occasionally is facilitated by temporary division of the overlying artery. Diffuse bleeding after substantial intraoperative blood loss is usually due to exhausted coagulation factors and platelets, combined with hypothermia. Aggressive rewarming with platelet and coagulation factor replacement is required to overcome this complication.

Hemodynamic Complications

Aortic clamping (especially supraceliac) results in a sudden increase in cardiac afterload, evidenced by hypertension, which can precipitate myocardial ischemia. Gradual clamp application, carefully coordinated with anesthetic and vasoactive drug administration, is required to avoid this problem. In contrast, sudden aortic declamping often is associated with significant hypotension. This hypotension is due to a combination of reduced cardiac afterload, "washout" of potassium, acidic metabolites, myocardial depressant factors from reperfusion of ischemic legs, and preload reduction secondary to increased venous capacitance in the legs. Gradual declamping combined with adequate fluid and blood replacement is crucial to avoid this complication. Careful intraoperative monitoring, including pulmonary capillary wedge pressure recording and transesophageal echocardiography, may facilitate fluid, anesthetic, and vasoactive drug administration in patients at known cardiac risk.

Iatrogenic Injuries

Injury to an adjacent organ is possible during AAA repair. Ureteral injury is rare during elective surgery, unless the course of the ureter has been distorted by a large AAA, fibrosis, or inflammation. If injury occurs, it should be repaired immediately. A double-J stent is inserted through the injury site to traverse the ureter from the renal pelvis to the urinary bladder. The ureter is closed using fine, interrupted absorbable sutures. Omentum can be mobilized on a vascular pedicle and wrapped around the site of injury. After copious irrigation, repair of the aneurysm can proceed, assuming the urine is not infected. After repair, an early postoperative CT scan is advised to detect possible urinoma formation. Urinoma is unlikely to occur if the stent is working properly, but if present, percutaneous closed drainage should be instituted using CT or ultrasound guidance. If ureteral injury is unrecognized, hydronephrosis or urinoma may develop, requiring re-exploration and more complex repair. Careful identification of the ureter, especially during pelvic dissection, successfully prevents this complication. Splenic injury resulting from excessive retraction may result in hemorrhage that should be controlled by splenectomy because late hemorrhage is poorly tolerated if attempted splenic repair fails. Inadvertent enterotomy before graft placement should prompt termination of the procedure with subsequent elective AAA repair to avoid

graft infection. Pancreatitis is an unusual complication of AAA repair that has been attributed to a retractor injury at the base of the transverse mesocolon. It should be suspected as a cause for prolonged postoperative ileus, particularly when proximal aortic exposure has been difficult.

Renal Failure

Although previously common after infrarenal AAA repair, renal failure is now rare, owing to adequate volume replacement and maintenance of normal cardiac output and renal blood flow. Precautions still are required, however, to reduce the risk of this complication. Because of the renal toxicity of intravenous contrast material, it is prudent to delay AAA repair after arteriography or contrast-enhanced CT, to be certain that renal dysfunction has not been induced. A more likely cause of renal failure after infrarenal AAA repair is embolization of aortic atheromatous debris into the renal arteries during proximal aortic cross-clamping. Preoperative CT may reveal pararenal atheromatous debris or thrombus, which should prompt temporary supraceliac cross-clamping until the infrarenal aorta is open. At this point, such material can be removed and the clamp moved to the normal infrarenal location. During such manipulation, the renal arteries should be temporarily clamped and the orifices carefully irrigated before restoring blood flow. Because preoperative renal insufficiency is the best predictor of postoperative renal failure,[232,340] special precautions are appropriate in such patients. There is some evidence to support a beneficial effect of intravenous mannitol when given before aortic cross-clamping (approximately 25 g).[340] Although some authors have advocated maintenance of higher urine volume using furosemide, the efficacy of this approach has not been proved, and it may hinder the assessment of fluid balance by artificially increasing urine output. Because renal failure is more likely in patients who require prolonged suprarenal clamping,[232,341] special measures such as renal cooling are recommended, as discussed subsequently.

Gastrointestinal Complications

Some degree of bowel dysfunction occurs after any major abdominal procedure. The paralytic ileus that follows evisceration and dissection of the base of the mesentery during transperitoneal AAA repair often lasts longer, however, than that occurring after other procedures. Consequently, one must use caution in reinstituting oral feeding postoperatively. Anorexia, periodic constipation, or diarrhea is commonly seen in the first few weeks after aneurysm surgery.

Colon Ischemia

Colon ischemia is an infrequent but often lethal complication that can result from disruption of sigmoid colon blood flow during AAA repair. To prevent this complication, it is important to understand the blood supply to the sigmoid colon and pelvis. As shown in Figure 100-13, a network of collaterals from the SMA, IMA, internal iliac artery, and profunda femoris artery supplies this circulation.[342] The meandering mesenteric artery is the most

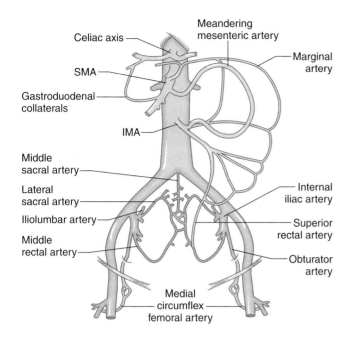

FIGURE 100-13 Important collateral pathways for the sigmoid colon and pelvis. IMA, inferior mesenteric artery; SMA, superior mesenteric artery. (From Bergman RT, Gloviczki P, Welch TJ, et al: The role of intravenous fluorescein in the detection of colon ischemia during aortic reconstruction. Ann Vasc Surg 6:74, 1992.)

collateral branches. Because of the richness of this collateral pathway, however, bowel infarction is infrequent. In the Finnish national vascular registry of 1752 patients who underwent aortoiliac operations during 1991 through 1993, bowel infarction occurred in 3.1% after ruptured AAA repair, 1% after nonruptured AAA repair, and 0.6% after reconstruction of occlusive disease.[345] These all were clinically significant infarctions, treated at a median of 8 days postoperatively, with a 30-day mortality of 67%. Generally, the incidence of clinically apparent colon ischemia has been reported to be 1% to 2% after elective AAA repair and 3% to 30% after ruptured AAA repair, with an associated mortality of 40% to 100%.[342,346-351] Less significant colon ischemia occurs more frequently, as judged by studies employing routine colonoscopy after AAA repair. In a prospective study of 100 patients undergoing AAA repair, colonoscopy showed some degree of ischemia in 4.5% after elective repair and 17.6% after ruptured repair.[352] A similar prospective study of 105 patients undergoing flexible sigmoidoscopy found colon ischemia in 11.4%,[353] whereas another study found biopsy evidence of colon ischemia in fully 30% of 53 patients, of whom 50% had a normal macroscopic appearance.[354] Most patients with colon ischemia detected by colonoscopy alone do not progress to transmural necrosis, and the colon ischemia resolves with conservative treatment. Endovascular AAA repair also can cause colonic ischemia. In a study of 278 patients undergoing endovascular repair, colon ischemia occurred in 2.9%.[355] It was unrelated to internal iliac artery interruption, but rather seemed to be caused by micro-embolization in most cases.

Recognition of colon ischemia after AAA repair can be difficult. The classic presentation of bloody diarrhea early after surgery occurs in only one third of patients with documented ischemic colitis.[346,348] When it occurs, diarrhea usually begins within 24 to 48 hours of operation, but may be more delayed and should always prompt flexible sigmoidoscopy. Other signs, such as abdominal pain, distention, fever, oliguria, thrombocytopenia, and leukocytosis, are less specific and frequently associated with recovery, especially from ruptured AAA repair.[343] A high index of suspicion is necessary to detect this complication before transmural necrosis, perforation, and sepsis occur. Flexible sigmoidoscopy is a sensitive and effective technique because 95% of ischemic colitis after aortic surgery is within the rectosigmoid colon.[346] The severity of symptoms and clinical outcome of colon ischemia depends on the pathologic extent (Table 100-7).[356] Patients with mild

important connection between the SMA and IMA, connecting the left branch of the middle colic artery to the left colic artery or the IMA. The antimesenteric marginal artery of Drummond is of less hemodynamic importance, but can provide important collateral if the meandering mesenteric artery is injured or absent.[343] The sigmoid colon also can receive important collateral circulation from the internal iliac artery via the superior rectal artery and even from the circumflex femoral branches of the profunda femoris artery if the internal iliac artery is occluded. Ipsilateral collateral circulation from the external iliac and femoral arteries is more important than contralateral pelvic collateral flow in the presence of an internal iliac artery occlusion.[344]

AAA repair (or aortoiliac reconstruction for occlusive disease) can jeopardize sigmoid blood flow by ligation of a patent IMA or internal iliac artery; embolization of debris into these arteries; prolonged hypotension, especially during ruptured AAA repair; and retractor injury of important

Table 100-7	Classification and Clinical Course		
TYPE	**PATHOLOGIC FINDINGS**	**CLINICAL FINDINGS**	**CLINICAL OUTCOME**
I	Mucosal ischemia, submucosal edema, or hemorrhage; mucosal slough ulceration may follow	Diarrhea with or without blood; presence or absence of fever; onset usually in 24-48 hr	Reversible; no sequelae; near-zero mortality
II	As above, with penetration of muscularis	Symptoms vary between type I and type II	Reversible; residual ischemic stricture possible
III	Transmural bowel involvement	Profound physiologic changes; sepsis, acidosis, cardiovascular collapse; may develop feculent peritonitis or late fecal fistula	Irreversible; mortality 70% ± 10%

(mucosal) and moderate (muscularis but not transmural) ischemia can be managed nonoperatively, with antibiotics and bowel rest, with good results, although strictures may develop after moderate ischemia resolves.[348] Transmural colitis shows deep ulcerations and pseudomembranes on colonoscopy, mandates bowel resection, and is associated with a 40% to 100% mortality rate.[348] Although colonoscopy can detect ischemic colitis easily, it is more difficult to differentiate transmural infarction, such that clinical correlation and experience are required to determine optimal management.[357]

Given the high mortality of postoperative colonic ischemia that requires bowel resection, prediction and prevention are most important. The etiologic factor that has received the most attention is ligation of a patent IMA in the presence of inadequate collateral blood flow. Collateral flow could be insufficient in patients with underlying celiac/SMA disease, patients in whom previous bowel resection has eliminated collateral pathways, patients with extensive pelvic occlusive disease or previous radiation, and patients with prolonged hypotension complicating AAA repair.[343] Celiac/SMA disease may be recognized preoperatively by imaging studies or intraoperatively by a large IMA supplying a large meandering mesenteric artery collateral to the SMA circulation. Such cases require IMA revascularization. Hypotension, low pH, low temperature, low cardiac output, high fluid/transfusion requirement, and the use of α-adrenergic vasoconstrictor agents have been associated specifically with ischemic colitis after ruptured AAA repair.[345,351,358] Factors that have been identified to increase the risk of colon ischemia after elective AAA repair include increased age, increased cross-clamp time, ligation of one or both internal iliac arteries, and ligation of the IMA, although none of these has been identified in all studies.[347,352,359] Retractor injury to collateral vessels and embolization during aneurysm manipulation also are potential etiologic factors that must be avoided.

Prevention of colonic ischemia requires attention to the above-mentioned risk factors, plus intraoperative assessment of colonic blood flow and revascularization if required. In patients undergoing AAA repair, approximately 50% have a patent IMA,[360] which could be reimplanted or revascularized with a short bypass graft (Fig. 100-14). Most surgeons judge the adequacy of collateral circulation by temporarily clamping a patent IMA during aneurysm reconstruction, then subjectively judging IMA backbleeding after restoring aortic flow. Pulsatile backbleeding through the IMA orifice, combined with normal inspection of the sigmoid colon, generally allows safe IMA ligation. (IMA ligation should be done close to its origin to preserve collateral flow through more distal branches.) A more sophisticated method is to measure IMA stump pressure, as advocated by Ernst and colleagues,[331] who showed that ischemic colitis did not develop after IMA ligation if the IMA/systolic blood pressure ratio was greater than 0.4. Other techniques have been recommended to assess the adequacy of colonic blood flow, including Doppler ultrasound,[361] photoplethysmography,[362] pulse oximetry,[363] laser Doppler,[364,365] intravenous fluorescein,[342] and intraluminal pH,[366] but none of these has achieved widespread clinical application. Intraluminal pH seems most promising

because low colonic mucosal pH after AAA repair has been associated with ischemia, especially in the emergent setting.[367,368] In one study of 34 patients, mucosal pH less than 6.86 predicted severe ischemic colitis, whereas mild colitis developed in patients whose minimum pH was 6.99, and no colitis developed in patients whose minimum pH was 7.21.[369]

Given the potential inaccuracy or cumbersome nature of determining adequate colonic blood flow, some authors have recommended routine reimplantation of a patent IMA after AAA repair.[370,371] These studies have reported a low incidence of colonic ischemia compared with historic controls, but have not proved the advantage of routine IMA reimplantation. Several studies have shown that IMA reimplantation or internal iliac preservation or both did not influence postoperative colonic ischemia.[349,350,369,372] At present, there is insufficient evidence to recommend routine IMA reimplantation, but this technique seems to be associated with minimal risk and is advantageous in any borderline situation.

Distal Embolization

Lower extremity ischemia may occur after AAA repair, usually from embolization of aneurysmal debris that occurs during aneurysm mobilization or aortoiliac clamping. Usually such emboli are small (termed *microemboli*); are not amenable to surgical removal; and result in transient, patchy areas of dusky skin or "blue toes." This condition can result in persistent pain or skin loss, occasionally necessitating amputation. Some authors have recommended treatment with low-molecular-weight dextran or even sympathectomy for such microembolic lesions, but their management is largely expectant. Occasionally, larger emboli or distal intimal flaps, particularly in diseased iliac

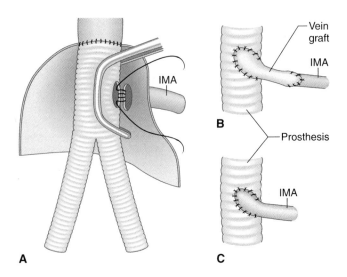

FIGURE 100-14 Reconstruction of the inferior mesenteric artery (IMA). **A,** Anastomosis of the rim of the aneurysmal sac, including the arterial orifice to the prosthesis (suture of hole-to-hole technique). **B,** Reconstruction with autogenous saphenous vein graft. **C,** Implantation of the large artery into the prosthesis. A button of prosthesis must be excised to ensure a patulous anastomosis.

arteries, may require operative intervention. For this reason, the legs should be carefully inspected intraoperatively for ischemia after AAA repair, while the incision is still open and arterial access can be obtained easily if necessary.

Paraplegia

Paraplegia, resulting from spinal cord ischemia, is rare after infrarenal AAA repair. It can result when important spinal artery collateral flow via the internal iliac arteries or an abnormally low origin of the accessory spinal artery (arteria magna radicularis or artery of Adamkiewicz) is obliterated or embolized during AAA repair.[373] Because the accessory spinal artery normally originates from the descending thoracic or upper abdominal aorta, this complication is much more common after thoracoabdominal aneurysm repair. Reports have emphasized the importance of preserving normal internal iliac artery perfusion of important spinal artery collateral vessels to avoid this complication.[374,375] Occlusive disease of the spinal collateral arteries, combined with severe hypotension, also may result in paraplegia, accounting for the higher frequency of this complication during ruptured AAA repair.[373] Paraplegia has been reported as the presenting symptom of infrarenal AAAs, suggesting that important spinal artery collateral blood flow originating from the distal aorta can be occluded by mural thrombus within the aneurysm or actual aneurysm thrombosis.[376]

Impaired Sexual Function

Impotence or retrograde ejaculation may result after AAA repair as a result of injury of autonomic nerves during para-aortic dissection.[377] The incidence of this complication is difficult to determine because of the multiple causes of impotence in this age group and frequent underreporting. In the ADAM trial in U.S. VA Hospitals, 40% of men had impotence before AAA repair.[378] Contrary to most other reports that asked patients retrospectively if they had impotence before AAA repair, in the ADAM trial, fewer than 10% developed new impotence in the first year after repair. The proportion reporting new impotence increased over time, however, such that by 4 years after AAA repair, more than 60% reported having impotence, which underscores the multifactorial etiology of impotence in this age group. Careful preservation of nerves, particularly as they course along the left side of the infrarenal aorta, course around the IMA, and cross the proximal left common iliac artery, has been shown to reduce this complication substantially, which has been reported to occur in 25% of patients.[379,380] Other possible causes of postoperative impotence include reduction in pelvic blood flow secondary to internal iliac occlusion or embolization.

Venous Thromboembolism

Pulmonary embolism and deep venous thrombosis are less common after AAA repair than after other abdominal operations, perhaps owing to intraoperative anticoagulation. Unrecognized deep venous thrombosis can occur, however, in 18% of untreated patients.[381] Perioperative prophylaxis with intermittent pneumatic compression stockings or subcutaneous heparin is appropriate.

Functional Outcome

Williamson and colleagues[382] reviewed their experience with open AAA repair with regard to functional outcome. They found that two thirds of patients experienced complete recovery at an average time of 4 months, whereas one third had not fully recovered at an average time of nearly 3 years. Additionally, 18% of patients said they would not undergo AAA repair again after knowing the recovery process, despite seeming to understand the implications of AAA rupture. Eleven percent of patients initially were discharged to a skilled nursing facility with an average stay of 3.7 months. This is similar to a 9% rate of discharge to a facility other than home found in a review of national administrative data by Huber and coworkers.[222] Although all patients in Williamson's review[382] were ambulatory preoperatively, at a mean of 25 months follow-up, only 64% were fully ambulatory, 22% required assistance, and 14% were nonambulatory. Although it is difficult to determine the extent of this disability that is due to the AAA repair, this report highlights the high rate of disability after open AAA repair. More research into long-term functional outcomes is needed.

Late Complications

Late complications after successful AAA or iliac aneurysm repair are infrequent.[246,383-386] In a population-based study, only 7% of patients experienced such complications within 5 years after AAA repair.[387] Anastomotic disruption, usually secondary to arterial degeneration, can result in a pseudoaneurysm (a hematoma locally contained by surrounding connective tissue). After 3-year follow-up, the incidence of anastomotic pseudoaneurysm is only 0.2% for aortic anastomoses, 1.2% for iliac anastomoses, and 3% for femoral anastomosis.[388] Aortic pseudoaneurysms seem to increase progressively with time, however, and in young patients who survive many years after AAA repair, follow-up imaging studies may be appropriate to detect late asymptomatic pseudoaneurysms. One study reported an incidence of aortic pseudoaneurysms of only 1% after 8 years, but 20% after 15 years.[389] The population-based study of Hallett and associates[387] reported a 4% likelihood of anastomotic pseudoaneurysm after 10 years. In the Canadian Aneurysm Study, proximal pseudoaneurysms were detected in 10% of patients who underwent a CT scan at 8 to 9 years after AAA repair.[390] When identified, aortic and iliac pseudoaneurysms warrant repair because of the high likelihood of mortality if rupture occurs.[391] Pseudoaneurysms are discussed in detail in Chapter 60.

Graft infection after AAA repair is also rare, unless a femoral anastomosis is required.[392] For aortoiliac grafts, the likelihood of infection is 0.5%, usually presenting 3 to 4 years after implantation.[393] Early presentation is possible and more likely if a femoral anastomosis is present.[394] The development of a secondary aortoenteric fistula after AAA repair also is unusual (0.9%), but much more frequent than a primary aortoenteric fistula associated with an AAA.[395] Aortoenteric fistulae usually develop approximately 5 years after AAA repair, nearly always involve the duodenum at the proximal suture line, and usually present with gastrointestinal hemorrhage. Less commonly, aortoenteric fistulae may involve the central portion of the graft and lead to infection rather than hemorrhage. The combined likelihood of graft infection and graft-enteric fistula seems to be 5% after 10 years.[387] Aortic graft infection and aortoenteric fistula usually require graft resection and extra-anatomic bypass. Both of these complications have a high associated mortality rate and are discussed in Chapters 59 and 61.

Thrombosis of an aortoiliac graft after AAA repair is unusual, unless extensive iliac occlusive disease coexists, which can lead to early graft thrombosis if unrecognized. Hallett and associates[387] estimated the likelihood of graft thrombosis to be only 3% after 10 years. In long-term follow-up after AAA repair, approximately 5% of patients develop complications secondary to other aneurysms, at a mean interval of 5 years postoperatively.[396] Kalman and colleagues[390] reported late results from the Canadian Aneurysm Study in 1999. They performed CT 8 to 9 years after AAA repair and noted aneurysms (of a diameter at which surgery would be considered) of the abdominal or thoracic aorta in 14% (most of which were proximal pseudoaneurysms) and of the iliac arteries (in patients who had undergone tube graft repair) in 15% of these late survivors. These authors recommend routine CT follow-up at 5 years after AAA repair. If these secondary aneurysms rupture, less than 5% of patients survive.[397] It is important to detect these aneurysms before rupture occurs. Hypertension significantly increases the risk of secondary aneurysm development.[397] Less than 10% of patients experience late complications of AAA repair during their lifetime. Most of these are severe, however, and often fatal.[383]

■ LONG-TERM SURVIVAL

As noted previously, the early (30-day) mortality after elective AAA repair in properly selected patients is 5% or less, whereas the early mortality after ruptured AAA repair averages 54% (not including patients who died from rupture before repair).[14,150] Five-year survival after successful AAA repair in modern series is approximately 70% compared with approximately 80% in the age-matched and gender-matched general population.[22,138,228,268,386,398-401] Ten-year survival after AAA repair is approximately 40%. Although survival is similar in men and women, women without AAA have longer survival than men. Survival relative to gender-specific norms is lower in women after AAA repair than in men.[401] Survival after successful ruptured AAA repair versus successful elective repair was similar in one report,[402] but reduced in others.[403,404] In a population-based analysis from Western Australia, survival after ruptured or elective AAA repair was similar for men but significantly reduced for women with ruptured AAA.[401] Overall, survival after AAA repair is reduced compared with an age-matched and sex-matched population because of greater associated comorbidity in patients with aneurysms.[244,268]

Systemic complications of atherosclerosis cause most late deaths after AAA repair in this predominately elderly, male population. The cause of late deaths after AAA repair are cardiac disease (44%), cancer (15%), rupture of another aneurysm (11%), stroke (9%), and pulmonary disease (6%).[268,386,405] Combining cardiac causes, aneurysmal disease, and stroke indicates that vascular complications account for two thirds of the late deaths after AAA repair. When outcome is stratified according to these risk factors, the 5-year survival rate improves to 84% in patients without heart disease, which is substantially better than the 54% survival rate observed in patients with known heart disease.[386] Hypertension also reduces 5-year survival after AAA repair, from 84% to 59%.[386] In patients without hypertension or heart disease, late survival after AAA repair is identical to normal, age-matched controls.[268] Multivariate analysis indicates that uncorrected CAD is the most significant variable associated with late mortality after AAA repair, but that age, renal dysfunction, COPD, and peripheral occlusive disease also contribute.[22,138,228,406] An analysis of coronary artery bypass graft surgery performed in preparation for AAA repair indicates that improved long-term survival is likely in patients younger than age 70 with severe CAD, but that older patients do not benefit from this aggressive approach.[406] A prospective, multicentered study identified not only age and cardiac, carotid, and renal disease as independent predictors of late mortality after elective AAA repair, but also aneurysm extent, as judged by size, suprarenal extension, and external iliac involvement, which has not been previously reported.[398]

■ SPECIAL CONSIDERATIONS

Suprarenal Aneurysms

By definition, AAAs that extend above at least one renal artery but end below the diaphragm are termed *suprarenal* and constitute approximately 5% of AAAs. If these aneurysms extend above the celiac artery and above the crus of the diaphragm, they are classified as *thoracoabdominal aneurysms* (see Chapter 103). CT or MRI is required to define the proximal extent of an AAA and is especially important for discerning the detailed anatomy of a suprarenal aneurysm. Arteriography usually detects suprarenal extension (although it may underestimate this owing to intraluminal thrombus), but is more useful to delineate associated renal or mesenteric occlusive disease. It is rare for an AAA to be isolated to the suprarenal segment, unless an infrarenal AAA has been repaired previously. The natural history of suprarenal AAAs is even less well defined than that of infrarenal AAAs because they are encountered less frequently. Lacking other data, rupture risk of suprarenal AAAs should be considered comparable to infrarenal AAAs for comparably sized aneurysms.[407] Surgical risk is higher, however, because of the necessity for renal and mesenteric artery revascularization and potential ischemic injury during suprarenal cross-clamping.[325,408] Most surgeons use a threshold size for elective repair of a suprarenal AAA that is approximately 1 cm larger than would be used for an infrarenal AAA in the same patient. Surgical treatment of ruptured suprarenal AAAs is even more complicated and associated with nearly 100% mortality.

Suprarenal AAAs are best approached surgically with a left retroperitoneal incision that can be extended into the chest if more proximal exposure is required. If an unsuspected suprarenal aneurysm is discovered during transperitoneal exposure, medial visceral rotation (reflecting the left colon, spleen, pancreas, and stomach medially to gain proximal retroperitoneal exposure) can be used.[409] Optimal placement of the aortic cross-clamp in these cases depends on the proximal extent of the AAA and the proximity of the renal arteries to the SMA and associated aortic atherosclerosis and calcified plaque.[325] If the AAA does not extend above the renal arteries and sufficient length of undiseased aorta exists above the AAA but below the SMA, clamping in this location avoids visceral ischemia. Often the aorta is less diseased above the celiac artery, however, in which case clamping in this location is safer and well tolerated, despite the associated temporary visceral ischemia.[410] This clamping must be individualized and can be facilitated by preoperative CT, especially with three-dimensional reconstruction to visualize the location of calcified plaque in relation to visceral and renal orifices (see Chapter 21). In many cases, the proximal aortic anastomosis for a low suprarenal AAA can be constructed on an angle that allows incorporation of the right renal artery orifice and requires only reimplantation of the left renal artery as an onlay patch.

If a suprarenal AAA extends to involve the SMA and celiac arteries, repair is accomplished using the inclusion technique popularized by Crawford and colleagues,[411] in which the orifices of the mesenteric and renal arteries are attached to the bypass graft as a patch. Usually the celiac, SMA, and right renal artery can be incorporated as one large patch, with the left renal artery reimplanted separately. The proximal aortic anastomosis for a suprarenal (but not thoracoabdominal) aneurysm often can incorporate the visceral and right renal artery origins using a beveled technique that excludes the entire aneurysm except for the small portion of the wall where these arteries originate. Ischemic injury to the liver, intestines, and kidneys is unlikely if proximal aortic clamp time can be kept at less than 30 minutes. After the visceral and renal arteries are revascularized, the aortic clamp is moved onto the graft, distal to these vessels, before completing the distal aortic or iliac anastomosis. Intraoperative cooling by iced saline perfusion of the renal or mesenteric arteries is useful if more than 30 minutes of ischemia is anticipated, which is usually the case for the left renal artery when this must be reimplanted separately.[408] Wahlberg and coworkers[341] from the University of California at San Francisco showed that the risk of renal dysfunction is increased 2-fold with supra-renal or supraceliac cross-clamp time of 26 to 50 minutes compared with 25 minutes or less and increased 10-fold with ischemic time greater than 50 minutes. Predictors of a postoperative increase in creatinine (>20%) were preoperative renal insufficiency and ischemic time. Significantly greater hemodynamic changes occur with aortic clamping and declamping above the celiac artery, necessitating careful coordination of anesthesia, fluid administration, and vaso-active drug use. Long-term outcome after successful repair is comparable to infrarenal AAAs, although operative mortality is higher on average (4% to 10%).[325,408,412,413] Compared with infrarenal AAA repair, increased postoperative renal failure is more likely after suprarenal aneurysm repair.[324] Although many of these issues are discussed in more detail for thoracoabdominal aneurysms in Chapter 103, they also apply to the management of suprarenal aneurysms that are entirely within the abdomen.

Inflammatory Abdominal Aortic Aneurysms

Inflammatory AAAs are a distinct clinical entity characterized by marked thickening of the aneurysm wall, especially in the anterior and lateral aspects, with extensive perianeurysmal and retroperitoneal fibrosis and dense adhesions to adjacent abdominal organs.[414-416] The thickened aneurysm wall consists of an intense fibrotic, inflammatory response in the adventitial and periadventitial layers with a lymphocytic (primarily T cells) and monocytic infiltrate.[70] Although these changes suggest an immune mechanism, the exact etiology is unclear. Because mild chronic inflammation is often present in the walls of typical degenerative aneurysms, it has been suggested that inflammatory aneurysms simply reflect an accentuation of this reaction.[70] The inflammatory process may be a response to the aneurysm rather than a cause because AAA repair is accompanied by resolution of the inflammation and fibrosis in more than half of the patients.[417] This process also may be related to more diffuse retroperitoneal fibrosis, but is unique because of its predominance in the aneurysm wall. Inflammatory changes of this magnitude occur in approximately 5% of infrarenal AAAs.[70,416]

Patients with inflammatory AAAs nearly always complain of abdominal or back pain, which frequently leads to urgent exploration for suspected AAA rupture. They also may present with a febrile illness, elevated sedimentation rate, and systemic symptoms (including weight loss) that confuse the diagnosis. Patients with inflammatory aneurysms are more likely have a positive family history of AAA and are more likely to be current smokers.[418] Patients with these AAAs usually present 5 to 10 years sooner than patients with noninflammatory aneurysms, and on average these AAAs are 1 cm larger. Most studies have found that the diagnosis of inflammatory AAA can be made accurately by CT, which reveals a "halo" of soft tissue around the anterior AAA that is enhanced by intravenous contrast (Fig. 100-15). A more recent study questions the accuracy of CT, however, and suggests that MRI is more accurate, showing characteristic arrays of concentric alternating layers of high and

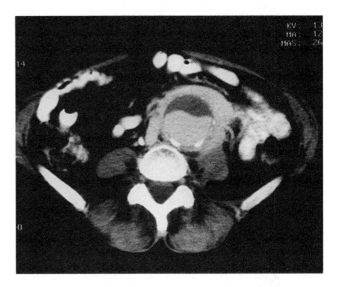

FIGURE 100-15 CT scan of an inflammatory aneurysm shows contrast-enhanced, thickened aortic wall along anterolateral aspects of the abdominal aortic aneurysm.

low signal intensity on T1-weighted images.[419] Preoperative recognition of an inflammatory aneurysm may facilitate management with a retroperitoneal approach, to avoid the most thickened and inflamed portion of the anterior wall.

Although the dense fibrotic reaction around inflammatory AAAs might suggest protection from rupture, this is not the case, probably because rupture may occur through the less thickened posterior wall. Current indications for repair of inflammatory AAAs are identical to indications for noninflammatory aneurysms. When approached transabdominally, the fibrosis around these aneurysms has a characteristic shiny, pearly gray appearance and extends to involve the duodenum in greater than 90%, the vena cava and left renal vein in greater than 50%, and the ureters in greater than 25% of cases.[419] To avoid injuring these structures during operative repair, supraceliac control, direct AAA incision without duodenal dissection, and endoaneurysmal repair (analogous to a ruptured AAA) are recommended if a transperitoneal approach is used. By avoiding anterior fibrosis, the left retroperitoneal approach reduces the risk to adjacent structures and is recommended when inflammatory AAAs are recognized preoperatively. Complications associated with injury to adjacent structures should be minimal if these techniques are used. Preoperative ureteral stenting can facilitate the identification of ureters and treats hydronephrosis if present. Reports suggest that ureters may remain entrapped in one third of patients, but less than 5% require dialysis.[417,418] Prophylactic ureterolysis is generally not recommended because injury is common.

Ureteral obstruction can be managed with a stent placed preoperatively and left in place until the inflammation resolves after AAA repair. In a comparison of patients treated with ureterolysis versus temporary stent decompression, no difference in renal function was noted.[420] If associated retroperitoneal fibrosis does not resolve, and the ureter remains obstructed, steroid therapy has been used successfully,[421] and later surgical decompression or drainage can be undertaken if necessary. Results of inflammatory AAA repair indicate that elective operative mortality is similar to that for noninflammatory aneurysms, with a greater risk of operative complications.[416,418,422] Steroid treatment of inflammatory AAAs has been reported to reduce the fibrotic reaction and AAA wall thickness.[423] The benefit of reducing aneurysm wall thickness is controversial, however, because reduced strength might precipitate rupture, which has been reported during steroid treatment.[423] Appropriately sized or symptomatic inflammatory AAAs should be repaired surgically; steroid treatment might be useful for postsurgical treatment of associated retroperitoneal fibrosis, especially if ureteral compression persists.

Infected Abdominal Aortic Aneurysms

An infected AAA can result from degenerative changes caused by primary infection of a previously normal aorta or from a secondary infection of an already established aneurysm.[424-427] If sufficiently severe, primary aortic infection can lead to aortic degeneration, localized wall disruption, and aneurysm formation, usually in a localized, asymmetric fashion. The source of aneurysm infection can be septic embolization from a distant site, bacteremia, or contiguous spread from local infection. Primary aortoiliac

infection leading to aneurysm formation is rare, accounting for less than 1% of aneurysms in this location. Before the antibiotic era, systemic syphilis and septic emboli from bacterial endocarditis were common causes of AAAs. Although any bacterial or fungal infection can lead to an infected aneurysm, the most common pathogens are *Salmonella* species and *Staphylococcus aureus*.

Clinically significant secondary infection of an already established AAA is also rare. Inapparent infection, more appropriately described as bacterial colonization, is frequent; 37% of AAAs show positive intraoperative cultures.[393] In these cases, the most frequent organisms cultured are consistent with normal skin flora (coagulase-negative *Staphylococcus, Corynebacterium,* and *Streptococcus faecalis*). The significance of this bacterial colonization seems minimal because the finding of a positive intraoperative culture has not increased the rate of subsequent prosthetic graft infection. This must be differentiated from more severe infections that often result from contiguous spread of an established infection and lead to marked inflammatory changes of the AAA wall or even purulence.

Because infected AAAs are rare and the symptoms are nonspecific, diagnosis can be delayed or unsuspected until surgery. Abdominal pain, fever, bacteremia, and a pulsatile abdominal mass should suggest an infected AAA, but these findings may not all be present, and the AAA may be small enough to escape detection. For this reason, an infected AAA should be considered in the differential diagnosis of fever of unknown origin, particularly if *Salmonella* is cultured from the blood of a patient older than age 50. In the absence of systemic signs of infection, a localized, noncalcified, asymmetric AAA in an otherwise normal-appearing aorta should suggest a primary infected AAA. Traditionally the treatment for an infected infrarenal AAA has been aortic excision with proximal and distal closure, débridement of surrounding infected tissue, and extra-anatomic (axillobifemoral) bypass.[426] Complications of proximal aortic stump "blowout" after this procedure have led some to recommend in-situ graft replacement after débridement of all infected tissue.[427] Experience suggests that aortic excision with extra-anatomic bypass is optimal for patients with overtly purulent infection, especially infections caused by *Salmonella, Pseudomonas,* or other gram-negative organisms. In-situ replacement is more applicable to less purulent infections, especially from gram-positive organisms or infections involving the suprarenal aorta where visceral reconstruction requires in-situ replacement. Infected iliac aneurysms are more easily treated by local excision and femorofemoral bypass because the risk of aortic blowout is not present. Experimental evidence suggests that PTFE grafts may be more resistant to infection than Dacron, although this has not been proved clinically.[428] Aortic replacement with autogenous tissue should resist infection more than prosthetic replacement, but size mismatch with peripheral veins is unsatisfactory. Good results have been described using larger, deep veins harvested from the leg for aortoiliac replacement in infected circumstances.[429] Similarly, aortic homografts have been used effectively in this setting.[430] Infected AAAs are rare so that most experience with aortic replacement for infection arises from previously placed infected aortofemoral prosthetic grafts. Concomitant antibiotic treatment is important for these patients, with the duration sometimes extended indefinitely for more virulent organisms.[425] Infected aneurysms are discussed in detail in Chapter 108.

Primary Aortocaval Fistulae

Rarely, large AAAs may erode into the adjacent vena cava or proximal left iliac vein leading to a direct aortovenous fistula.[431-433] Usually these patients experience symptoms of pain associated with AAA rupture, but sometimes a chronic, stable arteriovenous fistula may result.[434] Sudden AAA rupture into the vena cava also may be associated with more typical retroperitoneal hemorrhage, in which case the aortocaval fistula may not be recognized until emergent surgery is performed. The extent of hemodynamic compromise caused by the aortocaval fistula depends on its size. A typical machinery bruit is present in more than two thirds of cases, whereas venous hypertension leads to leg swelling in one third of cases.[433,435] Renal vein hypertension may lead to microscopic or gross hematuria in 25% of patients.[433,436] Acute CHF results in 25% of patients when the fistula is large or if baseline cardiac function is poor.[432,433] In the rare case of a stable, chronic aortocaval fistula, sustained increased venous pressure can result in lower extremity swelling, venous thrombosis, perineal and hemorrhoidal varices, scrotal edema, and hematuria.[437] In these cases, an abdominal bruit and high-output CHF may aid an otherwise confusing diagnosis, which is best confirmed by arteriography.

Surgical treatment of an aortocaval fistula consists of conventional repair of the AAA, with closure of the fistula from within the aneurysm. Dissection of the vena cava or iliac vein away from the aneurysm is extremely hazardous. Control of the vena cava adjacent to the fistula with direct pressure from within the aneurysm allows the fistula to be closed without excessive bleeding or air embolization. Mortality from an aortocaval fistula is high (20% to 50%).[432,433] This condition is discussed in detail in Chapter 111.

Primary Aortoenteric Fistulae

It is possible for an AAA to erode into adjacent intestine, usually the fourth portion of the duodenum.[438-440] This rare but dramatic complication usually is associated with large AAAs. Much more common is the "secondary" aortoenteric fistula that arises as a late anastomotic complication of a prosthetic aortic graft (see Chapter 61). Initially, gastrointestinal bleeding may be limited, leading to melena or anemia. Eventually, and often abruptly, severe hemorrhage leads to hematemesis and shock. Classically, patients with aortoenteric fistulae present with a small "herald" hemorrhage secondary to bowel mucosal bleeding, before sudden brisk hemorrhage and collapse. A primary aortoduodenal fistula should be suspected in a patient with gastrointestinal hemorrhage, abdominal pain, and a pulsatile abdominal mass. Because of the rarity of this complication, however, it is much more frequent for patients with AAAs to develop upper gastrointestinal hemorrhage from the more common etiologies of peptic ulcer disease, gastritis, or esophageal varices. The first diagnostic step in these patients should be upper gastrointestinal endoscopy, which often localizes the source of bleeding. An aortoenteric fistula should be suspected when no obvious source of bleeding is found. Rarely a mucosal defect may be seen in the third or fourth portion of the duodenum. Because severe hemorrhage can occur suddenly, evaluation must proceed rapidly in a patient with a known or suspected AAA and gastrointestinal hemorrhage. A CT scan can confirm the diagnosis of AAA, but usually does not show local inflammatory changes diagnostic of an aortoduodenal fistula. Similarly, arteriography usually is not beneficial, unless it localizes an alternative source of gastrointestinal hemorrhage. Often the diagnosis of primary aortoduodenal fistula cannot be definitively established. When other, more common sources of gastrointestinal bleeding have been excluded, exploratory laparotomy is indicated because of the universal mortality of an untreated aortoduodenal fistula. Closure of the duodenum, aortic ligation with aneurysm exclusion, and extra-anatomic bypass usually are required, although in-situ AAA repair has been accomplished successfully if contamination is minimal. This problem is discussed in detail in Chapter 61.

Associated Developmental Anomalies

Renal developmental anomalies may complicate AAA repair.[441] Multiple renal arteries are relatively frequent (15% to 30%), whereas pelvic kidney, horseshoe kidney, and multiple ureters are quite rare.[442] These anomalies may be detected by preoperative arteriography, spiral CT, or MRA. Accessory renal arteries also can be found during careful dissection of the aorta, usually arising more anteriorly than the normal lateral renal artery orifices. Arteries that are sufficiently large to supply distinct areas of renal parenchyma should be reimplanted onto the aortic graft if they arise from the AAA; this is facilitated by excising a surrounding collar (Carrel patch) of associated aortic wall along with the orifice. Pelvic kidneys usually have a single renal artery, but their origin may be displaced to the distal aorta or even iliac arteries and require reimplantation. Distal origins of a renal artery require special consideration to avoid prolonged ischemic injury when clamping the more proximal aorta. This may be accomplished by perfusing the renal artery with cold saline or with blood by using a shunt from the aortic graft after the proximal aortic anastomosis is constructed.[443] Horseshoe kidneys pose more technical difficulty because they limit access to the distal aorta and because they usually are supplied by multiple renal arteries arising from the aorta, the AAA itself, or the iliac arteries.[444] The isthmus of the horseshoe kidney should not be divided unless it is extremely thin and atrophic. Rather, the aortic graft usually can be tunneled beneath the kidney if the aorta is approached anteriorly. Care must be taken, however, to revascularize the major, multiple arteries by reimplantation, using cold perfusion for renal preservation during temporary ischemia.[445] Preoperative arteriography facilitates identification of these branches, but careful intraoperative dissection and inspection is required to avoid injury. A retroperitoneal approach offers significant advantages because the graft can be placed easily behind the horseshoe kidney and the renal arteries reimplanted similar to the inclusion technique used for suprarenal aneurysms.

Major venous anomalies, although rare, also can pose technical difficulties during AAA repair. Failure to recognize these anomalies can lead to venous injury and significant hemorrhage. A retroaortic left renal vein (2% to 3% incidence) and a circumaortic anterior and posterior left renal vein (7% incidence) are the most common anomalies encountered.[446-448] These should be suspected if the left renal vein is not encountered anteriorly during the proximal aortic dissection or if it appears small.[34] Preoperative CT discloses these anomalies and less frequently encountered left-sided or duplicated inferior vena cava.[449] Except in cases of situs inversus, a left-sided vena cava usually crosses anteriorly to the right side of the aorta at the level of the renal veins.[450] If this is not the case, the right renal vein crosses the aorta to join the left-sided vena cava. These venous anomalies complicate aortic exposure and must be approached with care. Duplicated veins often may be ligated to facilitate exposure, but the details of venous anatomy must be fully appreciated to avoid inadvertent ligation of a nonduplicated system.

Associated Abdominal Disease

Frequently an AAA is detected during the evaluation of another disease process, such as prostate cancer, lumbar disk disease, cholelithiasis, or colon or renal cancer. If such an AAA warrants surgical repair, a decision must be made concerning the prioritization of treatment of the two disease processes. The general guidelines are to treat the most life-threatening process first and to avoid simultaneous operations that increase the risk of prosthetic graft infection. Usually the AAA takes priority, such as in patients with lumbar disk disease or prostate cancer, when the other procedure can be secondarily staged without increased risk. More difficult decisions arise with cholelithiasis or abdominal malignancies, in which simultaneous surgical treatment is attractive, but may increase the risk of prosthetic graft contamination. This is especially true for colon operations so that AAA repair and colon resection should be staged except in extraordinary circumstances. The larger the AAA, the more likely that it should be treated first. Alternatively, colon cancers that are obstructing and potentially liable to perforate or cause total obstruction (particularly cancers on the left side) usually should be treated before AAA repair.[451] In contrast, nephrectomy for renal malignancy does not seem to increase the risk of prosthetic graft infection and usually can be performed during the same operation as AAA repair.[452-454] The same consideration would apply to other "clean" procedures, such as oophorectomy if required in patients undergoing AAA repair. When performed, such additional procedures should be done after the AAA is repaired and the retroperitoneal closure is complete, provided that the patient's condition remains stable. Although there have been anecdotal reports of AAA rupture after unrelated abdominal surgery,[455] a cause-and-effect relationship has not been proved[456]; this should not affect decision making in patients with large AAAs who require urgent surgical treatment of an unrelated problem. For patients with large AAAs, repair should be offered soon after the preceding operation, optimally during the same hospitalization.

There is controversy concerning the advisability of cholecystectomy at the time of AAA repair. Because positive bile cultures may be present in 33% of cases,[457] many surgeons have avoided concomitant cholecystectomy for asymptomatic cholelithiasis because of the fear of prosthetic graft infection. This complication has been reported,[458] but concomitant cholecystectomy has been performed in many patients during AAA repair without an apparent increase in graft infection.[457,458] The incidence of graft infection is sufficiently low in general and the onset so delayed that these optimistic results must be viewed cautiously. The likelihood of acute cholecystitis after AAA repair is also low, even if cholelithiasis is present.[459] Half of these patients develop symptoms that require cholecystectomy during the next 5 years.[457] For this reason, adjunctive cholecystectomy has been recommended by some authors when cholelithiasis is present during AAA repair.[457,458] If performed, cholecystectomy should follow AAA repair and careful closure of the retroperitoneum to minimize the possibility of graft contamination. The possible advantages of this combined procedure have been reduced by laparoscopic techniques, which allow later cholecystectomy with low morbidity. In general, when an unsuspected intra-abdominal problem is discovered during AAA repair, the AAA reconstruction should proceed, and the other (probably asymptomatic) condition should be dealt with secondarily, if concomitant treatment would lead to an increased risk of prosthetic graft infection. Rarely an unexpected intra-abdominal process, such as widespread metastatic disease or abscess, would warrant abandoning the planned AAA repair.

■ ISOLATED ILIAC ARTERY ANEURYSMS

Isolated iliac aneurysms, without an associated AAA, are rare (Fig. 100-16). A population-based study estimates their prevalence to be 0.03% based on autopsy findings.[460] Of all aortoiliac aneurysms, only 0.6% were isolated to the iliac arteries.[460] Based on hospital admissions in the United States, the incidence of known, isolated iliac aneurysms in men age 65 to 75 is 70 per 100,000 person-years; in women, the incidence is only 2 per 100,000 person-years, emphasizing the predominance of these aneurysms in men.[461] Similar to AAAs, these aneurysms increase in frequency with age and are rare before age 60. Their deep location in the pelvis makes detection by physical examination nearly impossible, although large iliac aneurysms sometimes are discovered by rectal examination. Because of the increased performance of abdominal imaging studies for other reasons, more small iliac aneurysms are now being detected. The common iliac artery is most frequently involved (70% to 90%), followed by the internal iliac artery (10% to 30%), with the external iliac usually spared, for reasons not understood.[462,463] There is a clear male predominance (male-to-female ratios of 5:1 to 16:1), with most patients being 65 to 75 years old in surgical series.[462-464] Approximately 50% are bilateral.[464] Although iliac artery aneurysms are usually asymptomatic until rupture, they may present with unique signs secondary to local compression of adjacent pelvic structures. Ureteral obstruction, hematuria, iliac vein thrombosis, large bowel

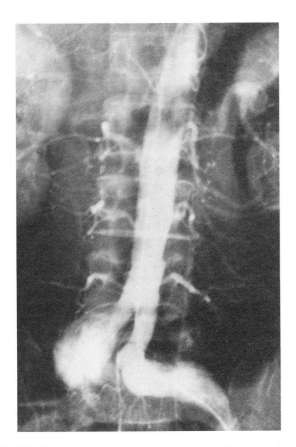

FIGURE 100-16 Arteriogram of an isolated common iliac aneurysm associated with a normal-caliber aorta (confirmed by CT scan).

obstruction, and lower extremity neurologic deficit may be present, but are much more frequently caused by other entities, frequently confusing the initial diagnosis of an iliac aneurysm.

Before the era of widespread use of CT and MRI, most isolated iliac aneurysms presented with rupture, with a resulting high mortality rate. The natural history of small iliac aneurysms is not well defined, however, because iliac aneurysms are uncommon and usually have not been followed with sequential imaging. In most surgical series, the average size of these aneurysms is 4 to 5 cm, whereas the average size of ruptured iliac aneurysms has been estimated to be 6 cm.[465] During follow-up of iliac aneurysms, varying rates of rupture have been reported ranging from 10% to 70% after 5 years.[463,466] Follow-up of large iliac aneurysms from 4 to 12 cm in diameter indicates that there is not a clear relationship between rupture and size in this range.[466] Santilli and coworkers[467] reported on 189 patients with iliac aneurysms in whom no ruptures occurred at diameters less than 4 cm. Mortality from rupture is high (25% to 57%), whereas mortality from elective repair is less than 5%.[462-464] Most surgeons now recommend elective repair of isolated iliac aneurysms at a threshold diameter of approximately 3 to 4 cm in good-risk patients. All of the issues concerning decision making for patients with AAAs apply here, primarily a comparison of rupture risk versus operative risk.

Iliac aneurysms can be approached through a lower abdominal retroperitoneal incision, but when bilateral or potentially requiring aortic repair, a transabdominal approach is more versatile. Unilateral common iliac aneurysms can be repaired with a simple interposition graft, but bilateral aneurysms are treated more easily with aortoiliac reconstruction. If preclinical aneurysmal changes are present in the infrarenal aorta, even though this is not excessively enlarged, aortoiliac reconstruction should be employed to prevent later aneurysmal degeneration of the aorta. Proximal ligation of an internal iliac aneurysm without distal ligation or endoaneurysmorrhaphy may lead to persistent aneurysm expansion and rupture.[468] Internal iliac artery aneurysms should be repaired with an interposition graft or more often should be excluded by distal ligation, with endoaneurysmal ligation of branches because these are usually large, deep, and difficult to reconstruct. When internal iliac aneurysms are bilateral, or the contralateral artery is occluded, pelvic blood flow must be assessed carefully. In these cases, one internal iliac artery may require direct revascularization. Although back pressure recording from the distal internal iliac artery is possible, the adequacy of pelvic circulation usually is assessed by clinical grading of backbleeding and visual and Doppler assessment of the sigmoid colon blood flow after temporary iliac clamping. Rare complications of iliac aneurysm rupture into adjacent rectum, bladder, or small intestine may require ligation with reconstruction outside the surgical field if contamination is significant.

Endovascular repair of isolated iliac aneurysms using commercially available covered stents or using iliac limbs of stent-graft systems designed for aortic aneurysm repair is possible if a sufficient length of normal iliac artery exists above and below the aneurysm to allow graft sealing. In cases in which there is insufficient normal proximal common iliac artery, an aortoiliac stent-graft system may be employed, even though the aorta may be of normal diameter. Internal iliac aneurysms also frequently are treated with endovascular coil occlusion. For these cases, it is important to coil the outflow branches of the hypogastric artery, similar to endoaneurysmal ligation, to avoid progressive expansion and rupture, which may occur if coils are simply placed in the aneurysmal artery. Endovascular treatment of iliac aneurysms is discussed in detail in Chapter 101.

■ REFERENCES

1. Leonardo R: History of Surgery. New York, Froben Press, 1943.
2. Matas R: Ligation of the abdominal aorta: Report of the ultimate result, one year, five months and nine days after the ligation of the abdominal aorta for aneurysm of the bifurcation. Ann Surg 81:457, 1925.
3. Power DA: The palliative treatment of aneurysms by "wiring" with Colt's apparatus. Br J Surg 9:27, 1921.
4. Rea CE: The surgical treatment of aneurysm of the abdominal aorta. Minn Med 31:153, 1948.
5. Cohen JR, Graver LM: The ruptured abdominal aortic aneurysm of Albert Einstein. Surg Obstet Gynecol 170:455, 1990.
6. Dubost C, Allary M, Oeconomos N: Resection of an aneurysm of the abdominal aorta: Reestablishment of the continuity by a preserved arterial graft, with result after five months. Arch Surg 64:405, 1952.
7. Schaffer PW, Hardin CW: The use of temporary and polythene shunts to permit occlusion, resection and frozen homologous artery graft replacement of vital vessel segments. Surgery 31:186, 1952.

8. Creech O Jr: Endo-aneurysmorrhaphy and treatment of aortic aneurysm. Ann Surg 164:935, 1966.

9. Silverberg E, Boring CC, Squires TS: Cancer statistics, 1990. Cancer 40:9, 1990.

10. Gillum RF: Epidemiology of aortic aneurysm in the United States. J Clin Epidemiol 48:1289, 1995.

11. Bengtsson H, Bergqvist D: Ruptured abdominal aortic aneurysm: A population-based study. J Vasc Surg 18:74, 1993.

12. Heller J, Weinberg A, Arons R, et al: Two decades of abdominal aortic aneurysm repair: Have we made any progress? J Vasc Surg 32:1091, 2000.

13. Adam DJ, Mohan IV, Stuart WP, et al: Community and hospital outcome from ruptured abdominal aortic aneurysm within the catchment area of a regional vascular surgical service. J Vasc Surg 30:922, 1999.

14. Hallin A, Bergqvist D, Holmberg L: Literature review of surgical management of abdominal aortic aneurysm. Eur J Vasc Endovasc Surg 22:197, 2001.

15. Bown MJ, Sutton AJ, Bell PR, Sayers RD: A meta-analysis of 50 years of ruptured abdominal aortic aneurysm repair. Br J Surg 89:714, 2002.

16. Ernst CB: Abdominal aortic aneurysm. N Engl J Med 328:1167, 1993.

17. Heikkinen M, Salenius JP, Auvinen O: Ruptured abdominal aortic aneurysm in a well-defined geographic area. J Vasc Surg 36:291, 2002.

18. Kantonen I, Lepantalo M, Brommels M, et al: Mortality in ruptured abdominal aortic aneurysms. The Finnvasc Study Group. Eur J Vasc Endovasc Surg 17:208, 1999.

19. Craig SR, Wilson RG, Walker AJ, et al: Abdominal aortic aneurysm: Still missing the message. Br J Surg 80:450, 1993.

20. Pasch AR, Ricotta JJ, May AG, et al: Abdominal aortic aneurysm: The case for elective resection. Circulation 70(Suppl I):I-1, 1984.

21. Breckwoldt WL, Mackey WC, O'Donnell T Jr: The economic implications of high-risk abdominal aortic aneurysms. J Vasc Surg 13:798, 1991.

22. Olsen PS, Schroeder T, Agerskov K, et al: Surgery for abdominal aortic aneurysms: A survey of 656 patients. J Cardiovasc Surg (Torino) 32:636, 1991.

23. Brunkwall J, Hauksson H, Bengtsson H, et al: Solitary aneurysms of the iliac arterial system: An estimate of their frequency of occurrence. J Vasc Surg 10:381, 1989.

24. Crawford ES, Cohen ES: Aortic aneurysm: A multifocal disease. Presidential address. Arch Surg 117:1393, 1982.

25. Dent TL, Lindenauer SM, Ernst CB, Fry WJ: Multiple arteriosclerotic arterial aneurysms. Arch Surg 105:338, 1972.

26. Johnston KW, Rutherford RB, Tilson MD, et al: Suggested standards for reporting on arterial aneurysms. Subcommittee on Reporting Standards for Arterial Aneurysms, Ad Hoc Committee on Reporting Standards, Society for Vascular Surgery and North American Chapter, International Society for Cardiovascular Surgery. J Vasc Surg 13:452, 1991.

27. Pearce WH, Slaughter MS, LeMaire S, et al: Aortic diameter as a function of age, gender, and body surface area. Surgery 114:691, 1993.

28. Lederle FA, Johnson GR, Wilson SE, et al: Relationship of age, gender, race and body size to infrarenal aortic diameter. J Vasc Surg 26:595, 1997.

29. Vorp DA, Raghavan ML, Webster MW: Mechanical wall stress in abdominal aortic aneurysm: Influence of diameter and asymmetry. J Vasc Surg 27:632, 1998.

30. Fillinger MF, Raghavan ML, Marra SP, et al: In vivo analysis of mechanical wall stress and abdominal aortic aneurysm rupture risk. J Vasc Surg 36:589, 2002.

31. Faggioli GL, Stella A, Gargiulo M, et al: Morphology of small aneurysms: Definition and impact on risk of rupture. Am J Surg 168:131, 1994.

32. Hunter GC, Smyth SH, Aguirre ML, et al: Incidence and histologic characteristics of blebs in patients with abdominal aortic aneurysms. J Vasc Surg 24:93, 1996.

33. Grange JJ, Davis V, Baxter BT: Pathogenesis of abdominal aortic aneurysm: An update and look toward the future. Cardiovasc Surg 5:256, 1997.

34. Patel MI, Hardman DT, Fisher CM, Appleberg M: Current views on the pathogenesis of abdominal aortic aneurysms. J Am Coll Surg 181:371, 1995.

35. Thompson RW: Basic science of abdominal aortic aneurysms: Emerging therapeutic strategies for an unresolved clinical problem. Curr Opin Cardiol 11:504, 1996.

36. Tilson MD, Ozsvath KJ, Hirose H, Xia S: A genetic basis for autoimmune manifestations in the abdominal aortic aneurysm resides in the MHC class II locus DR-beta-1.   Ann N Y Acad Sci 800:208, 1996.

37. van der Vliet JA, Boll AP: Abdominal aortic aneurysm. Lancet 349:863, 1997.

38. Wills A, Thompson MM, Crowther M, et al: Pathogenesis of abdominal aortic aneurysms—cellular and biochemical mechanisms. Eur J Vasc Endovasc Surg 12:391, 1996.

39. Ailawadi G, Eliason JL, Upchurch GR Jr: Current concepts in the pathogenesis of abdominal aortic aneurysm. J Vasc Surg 38:584, 2003.

40. Davies MJ: Aortic aneurysm formation: Lessons from human studies and experimental models. Circulation 98:193, 1998.

41. Halloran BG, Davis VA, McManus BM, et al: Localization of aortic disease is associated with intrinsic differences in aortic structure. J Surg Res 59:17, 1995.

42. Wolinsky H, Glagov S: Comparison of abdominal and thoracic aortic medial structure in mammals: Deviation of man from the usual pattern. Circ Res 25:677, 1969.

43. Dobrin PB, Mrkvicka R: Failure of elastin or collagen as possible critical connective tissue alterations underlying aneurysmal dilatation. Cardiovasc Surg 2:484, 1994.

44. Shah PK: Inflammation, metalloproteinases, and increased proteolysis: An emerging pathophysiological paradigm in aortic aneurysm. Circulation 96:2115, 1997.

45. Moulder PV: Physiology and biomechanics of aneurysms. In Webb WR (ed): Aneurysms. Baltimore, Williams & Wilkins, 1983, p 19.

46. Vollmar JF, Paes E, Pauschinger P, et al: Aortic aneurysms as late sequelae of above-knee amputation. Lancet 2:834, 1989.

47. Lorenz M, Panitz K, Grosse-Furtner C, et al: Lower-limb amputation, prevalence of abdominal aortic aneurysm and atherosclerotic risk factors. Br J Surg 81:839, 1994.

48. Xia S, Ozsvath K, Hirose H, Tilson MD: Partial amino acid sequence of a novel 40-kDa human aortic protein, with vitronectin-like, fibrinogen-like, and calcium binding domains: Aortic aneurysm-associated protein-40 (AAAP-40) [human MAGP-3, proposed]. Biochem Biophys Res Commun 219:36, 1996.

49. McMillan WD, Tamarina NA, Cipollone M, et al: Size matters: The relationship between MMP-9 expression and aortic diameter. Circulation 96:2228, 1997.

50. McMillan WD, Pearce WH: Increased plasma levels of metalloproteinase-9 are associated with abdominal aortic aneurysms. J Vasc Surg 29:122, 1999.

51. Ailawadi G, Knipp BS, Lu G, et al: A nonintrinsic regional basis for increased infrarenal aortic MMP-9 expression and activity. J Vasc Surg 37:1059, 2003.

52. Anidjar S, Dobrin PB, Eichorst M, et al: Correlation of inflammatory infiltrate with the enlargement of experimental aortic aneurysms. J Vasc Surg 16:139, 1992.

53. Boyle JR, McDermott E, Crowther M, et al: Doxycycline inhibits elastin degradation and reduces metalloproteinase activity in a model of aneurysmal disease. J Vasc Surg 27:354, 1998.

54. Petrinec D, Liao S, Holmes DR, et al: Doxycycline inhibition of aneurysmal degeneration in an elastase-induced rat model of

abdominal aortic aneurysm: Preservation of aortic elastin associated with suppressed production of 92 kD gelatinase. J Vasc Surg 23:336, 1996.

55. Ricci MA, Strindberg G, Slaiby JM, et al: Anti-CD 18 monoclonal antibody slows experimental aortic aneurysm expansion. J Vasc Surg 23:301, 1996.

56. Miller FJ Jr, Sharp WJ, Fang X, et al: Oxidative stress in human abdominal aortic aneurysms: A potential mediator of aneurysmal remodeling. Arterioscler Thromb Vasc Biol 22:560, 2002.

57. Yajima N, Masuda M, Miyazaki M, et al: Oxidative stress is involved in the development of experimental abdominal aortic aneurysm: A study of the transcription profile with complementary DNA microarray. J Vasc Surg 36:379, 2002.

58. Juvonen J, Juvonen T, Laurila A, et al: Demonstration of *Chlamydia pneumoniae* in the walls of abdominal aortic aneurysms. J Vasc Surg 25:499, 1997.

59. Petersen E, Boman J, Persson K, et al: *Chlamydia pneumoniae* in human abdominal aortic aneurysms. Eur J Vasc Endovasc Surg 15:138, 1998.

60. Tambiah J, Powell JT: *Chlamydia pneumoniae* antigens facilitate experimental aortic dilatation: Prevention with azithromycin. J Vasc Surg 36:1011, 2002.

61. Brophy CM, Reilly JM, Smith GJ, Tilson MD: The role of inflammation in nonspecific abdominal aortic aneurysm disease. Ann Vasc Surg 5:229, 1991.

62. Gregory AK, Yin NX, Capella J, et al: Features of autoimmunity in the abdominal aortic aneurysm. Arch Surg 131:85, 1996.

63. Dietz HC, Cutting GR, Pyeritz RE, et al: Marfan syndrome caused by a recurrent de novo missense mutation in the fibrillin gene. Nature 352:337, 1991.

64. Ozsvath KJ, Hirose H, Xia S, Tilson MD: Molecular mimicry in human aortic aneurysmal diseases. Ann N Y Acad Sci 800:288, 1996.

65. Darling RCD, Brewster DC, Darling RC, et al: Are familial abdominal aortic aneurysms different? J Vasc Surg 10:39, 1989.

66. Johansen K, Koepsell T: Familial tendency for abdominal aortic aneurysms. JAMA 256:1934, 1986.

67. Verloes A, Sakalihasan N, Koulischer L, Limet R: Aneurysms of the abdominal aorta: Familial and genetic aspects in three hundred thirteen pedigrees. J Vasc Surg 21:646, 1995.

68. Webster MW, Ferrell RE, St Jean PL, et al: Ultrasound screening of first-degree relatives of patients with an abdominal aortic aneurysm. J Vasc Surg 13:9, 1991.

69. Kuivaniemi H, Shibamura H, Arthur C, et al: Familial abdominal aortic aneurysms: Collection of 233 multiplex families. J Vasc Surg 37:340, 2003.

70. Rasmussen TE, Hallett JW Jr: Inflammatory aortic aneurysms: A clinical review with new perspectives in pathogenesis. Ann Surg 225:155, 1997.

71. Tung WS, Lee JK, Thompson RW: Simultaneous analysis of 1176 gene products in normal human aorta and abdominal aortic aneurysms using a membrane-based complementary DNA expression array. J Vasc Surg 34:143, 2001.

72. Sarkar R, Coran AG, Cilley RE, et al: Arterial aneurysms in children: Clinicopathologic classification. J Vasc Surg 13:47, 1991.

73. Sterpetti AV, Hunter WJ, Schultz RD: Congenital abdominal aortic aneurysms in the young: Case report and review of the literature. J Vasc Surg 7:763, 1988.

74. Katz, DJ, Stanley JC, Zelenock GB: Operative mortality rates for intact and ruptured abdominal aortic aneurysms in Michigan: An eleven-year statewide experience. J Vasc Surg 19:804, 1994.

75. LaMorte WW, Scott TE, Menzoian JO: Racial differences in the incidence of femoral bypass and abdominal aortic aneurysmectomy in Massachusetts: Relationship to cardiovascular risk factors. J Vasc Surg 21:422, 1995.

76. Blanchard JF: Epidemiology of abdominal aortic aneurysms. Epidemiol Rev 21:207, 1999.

77. Wilmink AB, Quick CR: Epidemiology and potential for prevention of abdominal aortic aneurysm. Br J Surg 85:155, 1998.

78. Wilmink AB, Hubbard CS, Day NE, Quick CR: The incidence of small abdominal aortic aneurysms and the change in normal infrarenal aortic diameter: Implications for screening. Eur J Vasc Endovasc Surg 21:165, 2001.

79. Lederle FA, Johnson GR, Wilson SE, et al: Yield of repeated screening for abdominal aortic aneurysm after a 4-year interval. Aneurysm Detection and Management Veterans Affairs Cooperative Study Investigators. Arch Intern Med 160:1117, 2000.

80. Melton LJ 3rd, Bickerstaff LK, Hollier LH, et al: Changing incidence of abdominal aortic aneurysms: A population-based study. Am J Epidemiol 120:379, 1984.

81. Bengtsson H, Bergqvist D, Sternby NH: Increasing prevalence of abdominal aortic aneurysms: A necropsy study. Eur J Surg 158:19, 1992.

82. McFarlane MJ: The epidemiologic necropsy for abdominal aortic aneurysm. JAMA 265:2085, 1991.

83. Chosky SA, Wilmink AB, Quick CR: Ruptured abdominal aortic aneurysm in the Huntingdon district: A 10-year experience. Ann R Coll Surg Engl 81:27, 1999.

84. Castleden WM, Mercer JC: Abdominal aortic aneurysms in Western Australia: Descriptive epidemiology and patterns of rupture. Br J Surg 72:109, 1985.

85. Ballaro A, Cortina-Borja M, Collin J: A seasonal variation in the incidence of ruptured abdominal aortic aneurysms. Eur J Vasc Endovasc Surg 15:429, 1998.

86. Bown MJ, McCarthy MJ, Bell PR, Sayers RD: Low atmospheric pressure is associated with rupture of abdominal aortic aneurysms. Eur J Vasc Endovasc Surg 25:68, 2003.

87. Lederle FA, Johnson GR, Wilson SE, et al: Prevalence and associations of abdominal aortic aneurysm detected through screening. Aneurysm Detection and Management (ADAM) Veterans Affairs Cooperative Study Group. Ann Intern Med 126:441, 1997.

88. Alcorn HG, Wolfson SK Jr, Sutton-Tyrrell K, et al: Risk factors for abdominal aortic aneurysms in older adults enrolled in the Cardiovascular Health Study. Arterioscler Thromb Vasc Biol 16:963, 1996.

89. Lee AJ, Fowkes FGR, Carson MN, et al: Smoking, atherosclerosis and risk of abdominal aortic aneurysm. Eur Heart J 18:671, 1997.

90. Lederle FA, Johnson GR, Wilson SE, et al: The aneurysm detection and management study screening program: Validation cohort and final results. Aneurysm Detection and Management Veterans Affairs Cooperative Study Investigators. Arch Intern Med 160:1425, 2000.

91. O'Kelly TJ, Heather BP: General practice-based population screening for abdominal aortic aneurysms: A pilot study. Br J Surg 76:479, 1989.

92. Alcorn HG, Wolfson SK Jr, Sutton-Tyrrell K, et al: Risk factors for abdominal aortic aneurysms in older adults enrolled in the Cardiovascular Health Study. Arterioscler Thromb Vasc Biol 16:963, 1996.

93. Pleumeekers H, Hoes A, van der Does E, et al: Aneurysms of the abdominal aorta in older adults. Am J Epidemiol 142:1291, 1995.

94. Smith FCT, Grimshaw GM, Paterson IS, et al: Ultrasonographic screening for abdominal aortic aneurysm in an urban community. Br J Surg 80:1406, 1993.

95. Vardulaki K, Walker N, Day N, et al: Quantifying the risks of hypertension, age, sex, and smoking in patients with abdominal aortic aneurysm. Br J Surg 87:195, 2000.

96. Singh K, Bonaa KH, Jacobsen BK, et al: Prevalence of and risk factors for abdominal aortic aneurysms in a population-based study: The Tromso Study. Am J Epidemiol 154:236, 2001.

97. Strachan DP: Predictors of death from aortic aneurysm among middle-aged men: The Whitehall study. Br J Surg 78:401, 1991.

98. Reed D, Reed C, Stemmermann G, Hayashi T: Are aortic aneurysms caused by atherosclerosis? Circulation 85:205, 1992.

99. Wilmink TB, Quick CR, Day NE: The association between cigarette smoking and abdominal aortic aneurysms. J Vasc Surg 30:1099, 1999.

100. Franks PJ, Edwards RJ, Greenhalgh RM, et al: Risk factors for abdominal aortic aneurysms in smokers. Eur J Vasc Endovasc Surg 11:487, 1996.

101. Rodin MB, Daviglus ML, Wong GC, et al: Middle age cardiovascular risk factors and abdominal aortic aneurysm in older age. Hypertension 42:61, 2003.

102. Tornwall ME, Virtamo J, Haukka JK, et al: Life-style factors and risk for abdominal aortic aneurysm in a cohort of Finnish male smokers. Epidemiology 12:94, 2001.

103. Smith FCT, Grimshaw GM, Paterson IS, Shearman CP: Ultrasonographic screening for abdominal aortic aneurysm in an urban community. Br J Surg 80:1406, 1993.

104. Lederle F, Johnson G, Wilson S, et al: The aneurysm detection and management study screening program validation cohort and final results. Arch Intern Med 160:1425, 2000.

105. Grimshaw G, Thompson J, Hamer J: Prevalence of abdominal aortic aneurysm associated with hypertension in an urban population. J Med Screen 1:226, 1994.

106. Lindholt JS, Henneberg EW, Fasting H, Juul S: Mass or high-risk screening for abdominal aortic aneurysm. Br J Surg 84:40, 1997.

107. Wilmink AB, Vardulaki KA, Hubbard CS, et al: Are antihypertensive drugs associated with abdominal aortic aneurysms? J Vasc Surg 36:751, 2002.

108. Baird PA, Sadovnick AD, Yee IM, et al: Sibling risks of abdominal aortic aneurysm. Lancet 346:601, 1995.

109. Salo JA, Soisalon-Soininen S, Bondestam S, Mattila PS: Familial occurrence of abdominal aortic aneurysm. Ann Intern Med 130:637, 1999.

110. Frydman G, Walker PJ, Summers K, et al: The value of screening in siblings of patients with abdominal aortic aneurysm. Eur J Vasc Endovasc Surg 26:396, 2003.

111. Powell JT, Greenhalgh RM: Multifactorial inheritance of abdominal aortic aneurysm. Eur J Vasc Surg 1:29, 1987.

112. Lederle FA, Walker JM, Reinke DB: Selective screening for abdominal aortic aneurysms with physical examination and ultrasound. Arch Intern Med 148:1753, 1988.

113. Lederle FA, Simel DL: The rational clinical examination: Does this patient have abdominal aortic aneurysm? JAMA 281:77, 1999.

114. Beede SD, Ballard DJ, James EM, et al: Positive predictive value of clinical suspicion of abdominal aortic aneurysm: Implications for efficient use of abdominal ultrasonography. Arch Intern Med 150:549, 1990.

115. Chervu A, Clagett GP, Valentine RJ, et al: Role of physical examination in detection of abdominal aortic aneurysms. Surgery 117:454, 1995.

116. Jaakkola P, Hippelainen M, Farin P, et al: Interobserver variability in measuring the dimensions of the abdominal aorta: Comparison of ultrasound and computed tomography. Eur J Vasc Endovasc Surg 12:230, 1996.

117. Shuman WP, Hastrup WJ, Kohler TR, et al: Suspected leaking abdominal aortic aneurysm: Use of sonography in the emergency room. Radiology 168:117, 1988.

118. Pavone P, Di Cesare E, Di Renzi P, et al: Abdominal aortic aneurysm evaluation: Comparison of US, CT, MRI, and angiography. Magn Reson Imaging 8:199, 1990.

119. Lederle FA, Wilson SE, Johnson GR, et al: Variability in measurement of abdominal aortic aneurysms. Abdominal Aortic Aneurysm Detection and Management Veterans Administration Cooperative Study Group. J Vasc Surg 21:945, 1995.

120. Thomas PR, Shaw JC, Ashton HA, et al: Accuracy of ultrasound in a screening programme for abdominal aortic aneurysms. J Med Screen 1:3, 1994.

121. Sprouse LR 2nd, Meier GH 3rd, Lesar CJ, et al: Comparison of abdominal aortic aneurysm diameter measurements obtained with ultrasound and computed tomography: Is there a difference? J Vasc Surg 38:466, 2003.

122. Darling RC, Messina CR, Brewster DC, Ottinger LW: Autopsy study of unoperated abdominal aortic aneurysms: The case for early resection. Circulation 56(3 Suppl):II-161, 1977.

123. Marston WA, Ahlquist R, Johnson G Jr, Meyer AA: Misdiagnosis of ruptured abdominal aortic aneurysms. J Vasc Surg 16:17, 1992.

124. Kvilekval KH, Best IM, Mason RA, et al: The value of computed tomography in the management of symptomatic abdominal aortic aneurysms. J Vasc Surg 12:28, 1990.

125. Seeger JM, Kieffer RW: Preoperative CT in symptomatic abdominal aortic aneurysms: Accuracy and efficacy. Am Surg 52:87, 1986.

126. Sullivan CA, Rohrer MJ, Cutler BS: Clinical management of the symptomatic but unruptured abdominal aortic aneurysm. J Vasc Surg 11:799, 1990.

127. Baxter BT, McGee GS, Flinn WR, et al: Distal embolization as a presenting symptom of aortic aneurysms. Am J Surg 160:197, 1990.

128. Muluk SC, Gertler JP, Brewster DC, et al: Presentation and patterns of aortic aneurysms in young patients. J Vasc Surg 20:880, 1994.

129. Bengtsson H, Bergqvist D, Ekberg O, et al: A population based screening of abdominal aortic aneurysms (AAA). Eur J Vasc Surg 5:53, 1991.

130. Lindholt JS, Henneberg EW, Fasting H, et al: Mass or high-risk screening for abdominal aortic aneurysm. Br J Surg 84:40, 1997.

131. Morris GE, Hubbard CS, Quick CRG: An abdominal aortic aneurysm screening programme for all males over the age of 50 years. Eur J Vasc Surg 8:156, 1994.

132. Scott RA, Ashton HA, Kay DN: Abdominal aortic aneurysm in 4237 screened patients: Prevalence, development and management over 6 years. Br J Surg 78:1122, 1991.

133. Heather BP, Poskitt KR, Earnshaw JJ, et al: Population screening reduces mortality rate from aortic aneurysm in men. Br J Surg 87:750, 2000.

134. Vardulaki KA, Walker NM, Couto E, et al: Late results concerning feasibility and compliance from a randomized trial of ultrasonographic screening for abdominal aortic aneurysm. Br J Surg 89:861, 2002.

135. Scott RA, Bridgewater SG, Ashton HA: Randomized clinical trial of screening for abdominal aortic aneurysm in women. Br J Surg 89:283, 2002.

136. Lindholt JS, Juul S, Fasting H, Henneberg EW: Hospital costs and benefits of screening for abdominal aortic aneurysms: Results from a randomised population screening trial. Eur J Vasc Endovasc Surg 23:55, 2002.

137. Ashton HA, Buxton MJ, Day NE, et al: The Multicentre Aneurysm Screening Study (MASS) into the effect of abdominal aortic aneurysm screening on mortality in men: A randomised controlled trial. Lancet 360:1531, 2002.

138. Norman PE, Semmens JB, Lawrence-Brown MM: Long-term relative survival following surgery for abdominal aortic aneurysm: A review. Cardiovasc Surg 9:219, 2001.

139. Lederle FA: Ultrasonographic screening for abdominal aortic aneurysms. Ann Intern Med 139:516, 2003.

140. Wilmink TB, Quick CR, Hubbard CS, Day NE: The influence of screening on the incidence of ruptured abdominal aortic aneurysms. J Vasc Surg 30:203, 1999.

141. Scott RAP, Wilson NM, Ashton HA, Kay DN: Influence of screening on the incidence of ruptured abdominal aortic aneurysm: 5-year results of a randomized controlled study. Br J Surg 82:1066, 1995.

142. Lindholt JS, Vammen S, Fasting H, Henneberg EW: Psychological consequences of screening for abdominal aortic aneurysm and conservative treatment of small abdominal aortic aneurysms. Eur J Vasc Endovasc Surg 20:79, 2000.

143. Health service costs and quality of life for early elective surgery or ultrasonographic surveillance for small abdominal aortic aneurysms. UK Small Aneurysm Trial Participants. Lancet 352:1656, 1998.

144. Lucarotti ME, Heather BP, Shaw E, Poskitt KR: Psychological morbidity associated with abdominal aortic aneurysm screening. Eur J Vasc Endovasc Surg 14:499, 1997.

145. Khaira HS, Herbert LM, Crowson MC: Screening for abdominal aortic aneurysms does not increase psychological morbidity. Ann R Coll Surg Engl 80:341, 1998.

146. Shaw C, Abrams K, Marteau TM: Psychological impact of predicting individuals' risks of illness: A systematic review. Soc Sci Med 49:1571, 1999.

147. Multicentre Aneurysm Screening Study (MASS): Cost effectiveness analysis of screening for abdominal aortic aneurysms based on four year results from randomised controlled trial. BMJ 325:1135, 2002.
148. Scott RA, Vardulaki KA, Walker NM, et al: The long-term benefits of a single scan for abdominal aortic aneurysm (AAA) at age 65. Eur J Vasc Endovasc Surg 21:535, 2001.
149. Crow P, Shaw E, Earnshaw JJ, et al: A single normal ultrasonographic scan at age 65 years rules out significant aneurysm disease for life in men. Br J Surg 88:941, 2001.
150. Katz DA, Littenberg B, Cronenwett JL: Management of small abdominal aortic aneurysms: Early surgery vs watchful waiting. JAMA 268:2678, 1992.
151. Brewster DC, Cronenwett JL, Hallett JW Jr, et al: Guidelines for the treatment of abdominal aortic aneurysms. Report of a subcommittee of the Joint Council of the American Association for Vascular Surgery and Society for Vascular Surgery. J Vasc Surg 37:1106, 2003.
152. Mortality results for randomised controlled trial of early elective surgery or ultrasonographic surveillance for small abdominal aortic aneurysms. The UK Small Aneurysm Trial Participants. Lancet 352:1649, 1998.
153. Lederle FA, Wilson SE, Johnson GR, et al: Immediate repair compared with surveillance of small abdominal aortic aneurysms. N Engl J Med 346:1437, 2002.
154. Long-term outcomes of immediate repair compared with surveillance of small abdominal aortic aneurysms. N Engl J Med 346:1445, 2002.
155. Valentine RJ, Decaprio JD, Castillo JM, et al: Watchful waiting in cases of small abdominal aortic aneurysms—appropriate for all patients? J Vasc Surg 32:441, 2000.
156. Schatz IJ, Fairbairn JF 2nd, Juergens JL: Abdominal aortic aneurysms: A reappraisal. Circulation 26:200, 1962.
157. Estes E: Abdominal aortic aneurysm: A study of one hundred and two cases. Circulation 2:258, 1950.
158. Szilagyi DE, Smith RF, DeRusso FJ, et al: Contribution of abdominal aortic aneurysmectomy to prolongation of life. Ann Surg 164:678, 1966.
159. Foster JH, Bolasny BL, Gobbel WG Jr, Scott HW Jr: Comparative study of elective resection and expectant treatment of abdominal aortic aneurysm. Surg Gynecol Obstet 129:1, 1969.
160. Sterpetti AV, Cavallaro A, Cavallari N, et al: Factors influencing the rupture of abdominal aortic aneurysms. Surg Gynecol Obstet 173:175, 1991.
161. Nevitt MP, Ballard DJ, Hallett JW Jr: Prognosis of abdominal aortic aneurysms: A population-based study. N Engl J Med 321:1009, 1989.
162. Lederle FA: Risk of rupture of large abdominal aortic aneurysms: Disagreement among vascular surgeons. Arch Intern Med 156:1007, 1996.
163. Brown LC, Powell JT: Risk factors for aneurysm rupture in patients kept under ultrasound surveillance. UK Small Aneurysm Trial Participants. Ann Surg 230:289, 1999.
164. Nicholls SC, Gardner JB, Meissner MH, Johansen HK: Rupture in small abdominal aortic aneurysms. J Vasc Surg 28:884, 1998.
165. Reed WL, Hallett JW Jr, Damiano MA, et al: Learning from the last ultrasound: A population-based study of patients with abdominal aortic aneurysm. Arch Intern Med 157:2064, 1997.
166. Limet R, Sakalihassan N, Albert A: Determination of the expansion rate and incidence of rupture of abdominal aortic aneurysms. J Vasc Surg 14:540, 1991.
167. Guirguis EM, Barber GG: The natural history of abdominal aortic aneurysms. Am J Surg 162:481, 1991.
168. Scott RA, Tisi PV, Ashton HA, Allen DR: Abdominal aortic aneurysm rupture rates: A 7-year follow-up of the entire abdominal aortic aneurysm population detected by screening. J Vasc Surg 28:124, 1998.
169. Cronenwett JL, Murphy TF, Zelenock GB, et al: Actuarial analysis of variables associated with rupture of small abdominal aortic aneurysms. Surgery 98:472, 1985.
170. Lederle FA, Johnson GR, Wilson SE, et al: Rupture rate of large abdominal aortic aneurysms in patients refusing or unfit for elective repair. JAMA 287:2968, 2002.
171. Jones A, Cahill D, Gardham R: Outcome in patients with a large abdominal aortic aneurysm considered unfit for surgery. Br J Surg 85:1382, 1998.
172. Szilagyi DE, Elliott JP, Smith RF: Clinical fate of the patient with asymptomatic abdominal aortic aneurysm and unfit for surgical treatment. Arch Surg 104:600, 1972.
173. Sonesson B, Lanne T, Hansen F, Sandgren T: Infrarenal aortic diameter in the healthy person. Eur J Vasc Surg 8:89, 1994.
174. Ouriel K, Green RM, Donayre C, et al: An evaluation of new methods of expressing aortic aneurysm size: Relationship to rupture. J Vasc Surg 15:12, 1992.
175. Schewe CK, Schweikart HP, Hammel G, et al: Influence of selective management on the prognosis and the risk of rupture of abdominal aortic aneurysms. Clin Invest 72:585, 1994.
176. Lobato, A, Puech-Leao P: Predictive factors for rupture of thoracoabdominal aortic aneurysm. J Vasc Surg 27:446, 1998.
177. Hatakeyama T, Shigematsu H, Muto T: Risk factors for rupture of abdominal aortic aneurysm based on three-dimensional study. J Vasc Surg 33:453, 2001.
178. Sharp MA, Collin J: A myth exposed: Fast growth in diameter does not justify precocious abdominal aortic aneurysm repair. Eur J Vasc Endovasc Surg 25:408, 2003.
179. Fillinger MF, Marra SP, Raghavan ML, Kennedy FE: Prediction of rupture risk in abdominal aortic aneurysm during observation: Wall stress versus diameter. J Vasc Surg 37:724, 2003.
180. Kushihashi T, Munechika H, Matsui S, et al: [CT of abdominal aortic aneurysms—aneurysmal size and thickness of intra-aneurysmal thrombus as risk factors of rupture]. Nippon Igaku Hoshasen Gakkai Zasshi 51:219, 1991.
181. Mower WR, Quinones WJ, Gambhir SS: Effect of intraluminal thrombus on abdominal aortic aneurysm wall stress. J Vasc Surg 26:602, 1997.
182. Bengtsson H, Nilsson P, Bergqvist D: Natural history of abdominal aortic aneurysm detected by screening. Br J Surg 80:718, 1993.
183. Cronenwett JL, Sargent SK, Wall MH, et al: Variables that affect the expansion rate and outcome of small abdominal aortic aneurysms. J Vasc Surg 11:260, 1990.
184. Grimshaw GM, Thompson JM: The abdominal aorta: A statistical definition and strategy for monitoring change. Eur J Vasc Endovasc Surg 10:95, 1995.
185. Hirose Y, Hamada S, Takamiya M: Predicting the growth of aortic aneurysms: A comparison of linear vs exponential models. Angiology 46:413, 1995.
186. Bengtsson H, Ekberg O, Aspelin P, et al: Ultrasound screening of the abdominal aorta in patients with intermittent claudication. Eur J Vasc Surg 3:497, 1989.
187. Englund R, Hudson P, Hanel K, Stanton A: Expansion rates of small abdominal aortic aneurysms. Aust N Z J Surg 68:21, 1998.
188. Vardulaki KA, Prevost TC, Walker NM, et al: Growth rates and risk of rupture of abdominal aortic aneurysms. Br J Surg 85:1674, 1998.
189. Santilli SM, Littooy FN, Cambria RA, et al: Expansion rates and outcomes for the 3.0-cm to the 3.9-cm infrarenal abdominal aortic aneurysm. J Vasc Surg 35:666, 2002.
190. Chang JB, Stein TA, Liu JP, et al: Risk factors associated with rapid growth of small abdominal aortic aneurysms. Surgery 121:117, 1997.
191. Sterpetti AV, Schultz RD, Feldhaus RJ, et al: Factors influencing enlargement rate of small abdominal aortic aneurysms. J Surg Res 43:211, 1987.
192. MacSweeney ST, Ellis M, Worrell PC, et al: Smoking and growth rate of small abdominal aortic aneurysms. Lancet 344:651, 1994.
193. Brady AR, Thompson RW, Greenhalgh RM, Powell JT: Cardiovascular risk factors and abdominal aortic aneurysm expansion: Only smoking counts [abstract]. Br J Surg 90:492, 2003.
194. Lindholt JS, Heegaard NH, Vammen S, et al: Smoking, but not lipids, lipoprotein(a) and antibodies against oxidised LDL, is correlated to the expansion of abdominal aortic aneurysms. Eur J Vasc Endovasc Surg 21:51, 2001.

195. Krupski WC, Bass A, Thurston DW, et al: Utility of computed tomography for surveillance of small abdominal aortic aneurysms: Preliminary report. Arch Surg 125:1345, 1990.

196. Wolf YG, Thomas WS, Brennan FJ, et al: Computed tomography scanning findings associated with rapid expansion of abdominal aortic aneurysms. J Vasc Surg 20:529, 1994.

197. Simpson CF: Sotalol for the protection of turkeys from the development of β-aminopropionitrile-induced aortic ruptures. Br J Pharmacol 45:385, 1972.

198. Simpson CF, Boucek RJ: The B-aminopropionitrile-fed turkey: A model for detecting potential drug action on arterial tissue. Cardiovasc Res 17:26, 1983.

199. Simpson CF, Boucek RJ, Noble NL: Influence of d-, l-, and dl-propranolol, and practolol on beta-amino-propionitrile-induced aortic ruptures of turkeys. Toxicol Appl Pharmacol 38:169, 1976.

200. Brophy CM, Tilson JE, Tilson MD: Propranolol stimulates the crosslinking of matrix components in skin from the aneurysm-prone blotchy mouse. J Surg Res 46:330, 1989.

201. Ricci MA, Slaiby JM, Gadowski GR, et al: Effects of hypertension and propranolol upon aneurysm expansion in the Anidjar/Dobrin aneurysm model. Ann N Y Acad Sci 800:89, 1996.

202. Leach SD, Toole AL, Stern H, et al: Effect of beta-adrenergic blockade on the growth rate of abdominal aortic aneurysms. Arch Surg 123:606, 1988.

203. Gadowski GR, Pilcher DB, Ricci MA: Abdominal aortic aneurysm expansion rate: Effect of size and beta-adrenergic blockade. J Vasc Surg 19:727, 1994.

204. Propranolol Aneurysm Trial Investigators: Propranolol for small abdominal aortic aneurysms: Results of a randomized trial. J Vasc Surg 35:72, 2002.

205. Wilmink AB, Hubbard CS, Day NE, Quick CR: Effect of propranolol on the expansion of abdominal aortic aneurysms: A randomized study. Br J Surg 87:499, 2000.

206. Mosorin M, Juvonen J, Biancari F, et al: Use of doxycycline to decrease the growth rate of abdominal aortic aneurysms: A randomized, double-blind, placebo-controlled pilot study. J Vasc Surg 34:606, 2001.

207. Vammen S, Lindholt JS, Ostergaard L, et al: Randomized double-blind controlled trial of roxithromycin for prevention of abdominal aortic aneurysm expansion. Br J Surg 88:1066, 2001.

208. Vammen S, Lindholt JS, Andersen PL, et al: Antibodies against *Chlamydia pneumoniae* predict the need for elective surgical intervention on small abdominal aortic aneurysms. Eur J Vasc Endovasc Surg 22:165, 2001.

209. Curci JA, Petrinec D, Liao S, et al: Pharmacologic suppression of experimental abdominal aortic aneurysms: A comparison of doxycycline and four chemically modified tetracyclines. J Vasc Surg 28:1082, 1998.

210. Curci JA, Mao D, Bohner DG, et al: Preoperative treatment with doxycycline reduces aortic wall expression and activation of matrix metalloproteinases in patients with abdominal aortic aneurysms. J Vasc Surg 31:325, 2000.

211. Blankensteijn JD, Lindenburg FP, Van der Graaf Y, Eikelboom BC: Influence of study design on reported mortality and morbidity rates after abdominal aortic aneurysm repair. Br J Surg 85:1624, 1998.

212. Brady AR, Fowkes FG, Greenhalgh RM, et al: Risk factors for postoperative death following elective surgical repair of abdominal aortic aneurysm: Results from the UK Small Aneurysm Trial. On behalf of the UK Small Aneurysm Trial Participants. Br J Surg 87:742, 2000.

213. Cronenwett JL, Birkmeyer JD: The Dartmouth Atlas of Vascular Healthcare. Chicago, AHA Press, 2000.

214. Bradbury AW, Adam DJ, Makhdoomi KR, et al: A 21-year experience of abdominal aortic aneurysm operations in Edinburgh. Br J Surg 85:645, 1998.

215. Bayly PJ, Matthews JN, Dobson PM, et al: In-hospital mortality from abdominal aortic surgery in Great Britain and Ireland: Vascular Anaesthesia Society audit. Br J Surg 88:687, 2001.

216. Becquemin JP, Chemla E, Chatellier G, et al: Peroperative factors influencing the outcome of elective abdominal aorta aneurysm repair. Eur J Vasc Endovasc Surg 20:84, 2000.

217. Collins TC, Johnson M, Daley J, et al: Preoperative risk factors for 30-day mortality after elective surgery for vascular disease in Department of Veterans Affairs hospitals: Is race important? J Vasc Surg 34:634, 2001.

218. Dardik A, Lin JW, Gordon TA, et al: Results of elective abdominal aortic aneurysm repair in the 1990s: A population-based analysis of 2335 cases. J Vasc Surg 30:985, 1999.

219. Dimick JB, Stanley JC, Axelrod DA, et al: Variation in death rate after abdominal aortic aneurysmectomy in the United States: Impact of hospital volume, gender, and age. Ann Surg 235:579, 2002.

220. Birkmeyer JD, Siewers AE, Finlayson EV, et al: Hospital volume and surgical mortality in the United States. N Engl J Med 346:1128, 2002.

221. Galland RB: Mortality following elective infrarenal aortic reconstruction. A Joint Vascular Research Group study. Br J Surg 85:633, 1998.

222. Huber TS, Wang JG, Derrow AE, et al: Experience in the United States with intact abdominal aortic aneurysm repair. J Vasc Surg 33:304, 2001.

223. Kazmers A, Perkins AJ, Jacobs LA: Outcomes after abdominal aortic aneurysm repair in those > or =80 years of age: Recent Veterans Affairs experience. Ann Vasc Surg 12:106, 1998.

224. Manheim LM, Sohn MW, Feinglass J, et al: Hospital vascular surgery volume and procedure mortality rates in California, 1982-1994. J Vasc Surg 28:45, 1998.

225. Pearce WH, Parker MA, Feinglass J, et al: The importance of surgeon volume and training in outcomes for vascular surgical procedures. J Vasc Surg 29:768, 1999.

226. Semmens JB, Norman PE, Lawrence-Brown MM, et al: Population-based record linkage study of the incidence of abdominal aortic aneurysm in Western Australia in 1985-1994. Br J Surg 85:648, 1998.

227. Johnston KW, Scobie TK: Multicenter prospective study of nonruptured abdominal aortic aneurysms: I. Population and operative management. J Vasc Surg 7:69, 1988.

228. Hertzer NR, Mascha EJ, Karafa MT, et al: Open infrarenal abdominal aortic aneurysm repair: The Cleveland Clinic experience from 1989 to 1998. J Vasc Surg 35:1145, 2002.

229. Zarins CK, Harris EJ Jr: Operative repair for aortic aneurysms: The gold standard. J Endovasc Surg 4:232, 1997.

230. Steyerberg EW, Kievit J, Alexander de Mol Van Otterloo JC, et al: Perioperative mortality of elective abdominal aortic aneurysm surgery: A clinical prediction rule based on literature and individual patient data. Arch Intern Med 155:1998, 1995.

231. L'Italien GJ, Paul SD, Hendel RC, et al: Development and validation of a Bayesian model for perioperative cardiac risk assessment in a cohort of 1,081 vascular surgical candidates. J Am Coll Cardiol 27:779, 1996.

232. Johnston KW: Multicenter prospective study of nonruptured abdominal aortic aneurysm: Part II. Variables predicting morbidity and mortality. J Vasc Surg 9:437, 1989.

233. Katz DJ, Stanley JC, Zelenock GB: Gender differences in abdominal aortic aneurysm prevalence, treatment and outcome. J Vasc Surg 25:561, 1997.

234. Iezzoni LI: Assessing quality using administrative data. Ann Intern Med 127(8 Pt 2):666, 1997.

235. Dimick JB Cowan JA Jr, Stanley JC, et al: Surgeon specialty and provider volumes are related to outcome of intact abdominal aortic aneurysm repair in the United States. J Vasc Surg 38:739, 2003.

236. Tu JV, Austin PC, Johnston KW: The influence of surgical specialty training on the outcomes of elective abdominal aortic aneurysm surgery. J Vasc Surg 33:447, 2001.

237. Amundsen S, Skjaerven R, Trippestad A, et al: Abdominal aortic aneurysms: Is there an association between surgical volume, surgical experience, hospital type and operative mortality? Acta Chir Scand 156:323, 1990.

238. Veith FJ, Goldsmith J, Leather RP, et al: The need for quality assurance in vascular surgery. J Vasc Surg 13:523, 1991.

239. Hannan EL, Kilburn H Jr, O'Donnell JF, et al: A longitudinal analysis of the relationship between in-hospital mortality in New York State and the volume of abdominal aortic aneurysm surgeries performed. Health Serv Res 27:517, 1992.

240. Wen SW, Simunovic M, Williams JI, et al: Hospital volume, calendar age, and short term outcomes in patients undergoing repair of abdominal aortic aneurysms: The Ontario experience, 1988-92. J Epidemiol Community Health 50:207, 1996.

241. Dimick JB, Pronovost PJ, Cowan JA, et al: The volume-outcome effect for abdominal aortic surgery: Differences in case-mix or complications? Arch Surg 137:828, 2002.

242. Hannan EL, O'Donnell JF, Kilburn H Jr, et al: Investigation of the relationship between volume and mortality for surgical procedures performed in New York State hospitals. JAMA 262:503, 1989.

243. Kantonen I, Lepantalo M, Salenius JP, et al: Mortality in abdominal aortic aneurysm surgery—the effect of hospital volume, patient mix and surgeon's case load. Eur J Vasc Endovasc Surg 14:375, 1997.

244. Newman AB, Arnold AM, Burke GL, et al: Cardiovascular disease and mortality in older adults with small abdominal aortic aneurysms detected by ultrasonography: The Cardiovascular Health Study. Ann Intern Med 134:182, 2001.

245. Batt M, Staccini P, Pittaluga P, et al: Late survival after abdominal aortic aneurysm repair. Eur J Vasc Endovasc Surg 17:338, 1999.

246. Johnston KW: Nonruptured abdominal aortic aneurysm: Six-year follow-up results from the multicenter prospective Canadian aneurysm study. J Vasc Surg 20:163, 1994.

247. Aune S, Amundsen SR, Evjensvold J, Trippestad A: Operative mortality and long-term relative survival of patients operated on for asymptomatic abdominal aortic aneurysm. Eur J Vasc Endovasc Surg 9:293, 1995.

248. Smoking, lung function and the prognosis of abdominal aortic aneurysm. The UK Small Aneurysm Trial Participants. Eur J Vasc Endovasc Surg 19:636, 2000.

249. Michaels JA: The management of small abdominal aortic aneurysms: A computer simulation using Monte Carlo methods. Eur J Vasc Surg 6:551, 1992.

250. Schermerhorn M, Birkmeyer J, Gould D, Cronenwett J: Cost-effectiveness of surgery for small abdominal aortic aneurysms on the basis of data from the United Kingdom small aneurysm trial. J Vasc Surg 31:217, 2000.

251. Roger VL, Ballard DJ, Hallett JW Jr, et al: Influence of coronary artery disease on morbidity and mortality after abdominal aortic aneurysmectomy: A population-based study, 1971-1987. J Am Coll Cardiol 14:1245, 1989.

252. Eagle KA, Berger PB, Calkins H, et al: ACC/AHA guideline update for perioperative cardiovascular evaluation for noncardiac surgery—executive summary: A report of the American College of Cardiology/American Heart Association Task Force on Practice Guidelines (Committee to Update the 1996 Guidelines on Perioperative Cardiovascular Evaluation for Noncardiac Surgery). Circulation 105:1257, 2002.

253. Fagevik Olsen M, Hahn I, Nordgren S, et al: Randomized controlled trial of prophylactic chest physiotherapy in major abdominal surgery. Br J Surg 84:1535, 1997.

254. Hertzer NR, Young JR, Kramer JR, et al: Routine coronary angiography prior to elective aortic reconstruction: Results of selective myocardial revascularization in patients with peripheral vascular disease. Arch Surg 114:1336, 1979.

255. Eagle KA, Coley CM, Newell JB, et al: Combining clinical and thallium data optimizes preoperative assessment of cardiac risk before major vascular surgery. Ann Intern Med 110:859, 1989.

256. Cutler BS, Hendel RC, Leppo JA: Dipyridamole-thallium scintigraphy predicts perioperative and long-term survival after major vascular surgery. J Vasc Surg 15:972, 1992.

257. Lalka SG, Sawada SG, Dalsing MC, et al: Dobutamine stress echocardiography as a predictor of cardiac events associated with aortic surgery. J Vasc Surg 15:831, 1992.

258. Boersma E, Poldermans D, Bax JJ, et al: Predictors of cardiac events after major vascular surgery: Role of clinical characteristics, dobutamine echocardiography, and beta-blocker therapy. JAMA 285:1865, 2001.

259. Boucher CA, Brewster DC, Darling RC, et al: Determination of cardiac risk by dipyridamole-thallium imaging before peripheral vascular surgery. N Engl J Med 312:389, 1985.

260. Lette J, Waters D, Lassonde J, et al: Multivariate clinical models and quantitative dipyridamole-thallium imaging to predict cardiac morbidity and death after vascular reconstruction. J Vasc Surg 14:160, 1991.

261. Levinson JR, Boucher CA, Coley CM, et al: Usefulness of semiquantitative analysis of dipyridamole-thallium-201 redistribution for improving risk stratification before vascular surgery. Am J Cardiol 66:406, 1990.

262. Bry JD, Belkin M, O'Donnell TF Jr, et al: An assessment of the positive predictive value and cost-effectiveness of dipyridamole myocardial scintigraphy in patients undergoing vascular surgery. J Vasc Surg 19:112, 1994.

263. D'Angelo AJ, Puppala D, Farber A, et al: Is preoperative cardiac evaluation for abdominal aortic aneurysm repair necessary? J Vasc Surg 25:152, 1997.

264. Schueppert MT, Kresowik TF, Corry DC, et al: Selection of patients for cardiac evaluation before peripheral vascular operations. J Vasc Surg 23:802, 1996.

265. Baron JF, Mundler O, Bertrand M, et al: Dipyridamole-thallium scintigraphy and gated radionuclide angiography to assess cardiac risk before abdominal aortic surgery. N Engl J Med 330:663, 1994.

266. Taylor LM Jr, Yeager RA, Moneta GL, et al: The incidence of perioperative myocardial infarction in general vascular surgery. J Vasc Surg 15:52, 1992.

267. Hertzer NR, Young JR, Beven EG, et al: Late results of coronary bypass in patients with infrarenal aortic aneurysms. The Cleveland Clinic Study. Ann Surg 205:360, 1987.

268. Hollier LH, Plate G, O'Brien PC, et al: Late survival after abdominal aortic aneurysm repair: Influence of coronary artery disease. J Vasc Surg 1:290, 1984.

269. Hinkamp TJ, Pifarre R, Bakhos M, Blakeman B: Combined myocardial revascularization and abdominal aortic aneurysm repair. Ann Thorac Surg 51:470, 1991.

270. Ruby ST, Whittemore AD, Couch NP, et al: Coronary artery disease in patients requiring abdominal aortic aneurysm repair: Selective use of a combined operation. Ann Surg 201:758, 1985.

271. Hollier LH, Spittell JA Jr, Puga FJ: Intra-aortic balloon counter-pulsation as adjunct to aneurysmectomy in high-risk patients. Mayo Clin Proc 56:565, 1981.

272. Campbell JJ, Bell DD, Gaspar MR: Selective use of arteriography in the assessment of aortic aneurysm repair. Ann Vasc Surg 4:419, 1990.

273. Wyers MC, Fillinger MF, Schermerhorn ML, et al: Endovascular repair of abdominal aortic aneurysm without preoperative arteriography. J Vasc Surg 38:730, 2003.

274. Hollier LH, Reigel MM, Kazmier FJ, et al: Conventional repair of abdominal aortic aneurysm in the high-risk patient: A plea for abandonment of nonresective treatment. J Vasc Surg 3:712, 1986.

275. Inahara T, Geary GL, Mukherjee D, Egan JM: The contrary position to the nonresective treatment for abdominal aortic aneurysm. J Vasc Surg 2:42, 1985.

276. Karmody AM, Leather RP, Goldman M, et al: The current position of nonresective treatment for abdominal aortic aneurysm. Surgery 94:591, 1983.

277. Lynch K, Kohler T, Johansen K: Nonresective therapy for aortic aneurysm: Results of a survey. J Vasc Surg 4:469, 1986.

278. Schwartz RA, Nichols WK, Silver D: Is thrombosis of the infrarenal abdominal aortic aneurysm an acceptable alternative? J Vasc Surg 3:448, 1986.

279. Shah DM, Chang BB, Paty PS, et al: Treatment of abdominal aortic aneurysm by exclusion and bypass: An analysis of outcome. J Vasc Surg 13:15, 1991.

280. Darling RC 3rd, Ozsvath K, Chang BB, et al: The incidence, natural history, and outcome of secondary intervention for persistent collateral flow in the excluded abdominal aortic aneurysm. J Vasc Surg 30:968, 1999.

281. Kline RG, D'Angelo AJ, Chen MH, et al: Laparoscopically assisted abdominal aortic aneurysm repair: First 20 cases. J Vasc Surg 27:81, 1998.

282. Parodi JC, Palmaz JC, Barone HD: Transfemoral intraluminal graft implantation for abdominal aortic aneurysms. Ann Vasc Surg 5:491, 1991.

283. Zarins CK, White RA, Schwarten D, et al: AneuRx stent graft versus open surgical repair of abdominal aortic aneurysms: Multicenter prospective clinical trial. J Vasc Surg 29:292, 1999.

284. Moore WS, Brewster DC, Bernhard VM: Aorto-uni-iliac endograft for complex aortoiliac aneurysms compared with tube/bifurcation endografts: Results of the EVT/Guidant trials. J Vasc Surg 33(2 Suppl):S11, 2001.

285. Matsumura JS, Brewster DC, Makaroun MS, Naftel DC: A multicenter controlled clinical trial of open versus endovascular treatment of abdominal aortic aneurysm. J Vasc Surg 37:262, 2003.

285a. Lee WA, Carter JW, Upchurch G, et al: Perioperative outcomes of open and endovascular repair of intact abdominal aortic aneurysms in the United States during 2001. J Vasc Surg 39:491, 2004.

286. Aquino RV, Jones MA, Zullo TG, et al: Quality of life assessment in patients undergoing endovascular or conventional AAA repair. J Endovasc Ther 8:521, 2001.

287. Harris P, Vallabhaneni S, Desgranges P, et al: Incidence and risk factors of late rupture, conversion, and death after endovascular repair of infrarenal aortic aneurysms: The EUROSTAR experience. J Vasc Surg 32:739, 2000.

288. Holzenbein TJ, Kretschmer G, Thurnher S, et al: Midterm durability of abdominal aortic aneurysm endograft repair: A word of caution. J Vasc Surg 33(2 Suppl):S46, 2001.

289. Zarins CK, White RA, Fogarty TJ: Aneurysm rupture after endovascular repair using the AneuRx stent graft. J Vasc Surg 31:960, 2000.

290. Ohki T, Veith FJ, Shaw P, et al: Increasing incidence of midterm and long-term complications after endovascular graft repair of abdominal aortic aneurysms: A note of caution based on a 9-year experience. Ann Surg 234:323, 2001.

291. Bernhard VM, Mitchell RS, Matsumura JS, et al: Ruptured abdominal aortic aneurysm after endovascular repair. J Vasc Surg 35:1155, 2002.

292. Schermerhorn ML, Finlayson SR, Fillinger MF, et al: Life expectancy after endovascular versus open abdominal aortic aneurysm repair: Results of a decision analysis model on the basis of data from EUROSTAR. J Vasc Surg 36:1112, 2002.

293. Kaiser AB, Clayson KR, Mulherin JL Jr, et al: Antibiotic prophylaxis in vascular surgery. Ann Surg 188:283, 1978.

294. Bender JS, Smith-Meek MA, Jones CE: Routine pulmonary artery catheterization does not reduce morbidity and mortality of elective vascular surgery: Results of a prospective, randomized trial. Ann Surg 226:229, 1997.

295. Ziegler DW, Wright JG, Choban PS, Flancbaum L: A prospective randomized trial of preoperative "optimization" of cardiac function in patients undergoing elective peripheral vascular surgery. Surgery 122:584, 1997.

296. Birkmeyer JD, AuBuchon JP, Littenberg B, et al: Cost-effectiveness of preoperative autologous donation in coronary artery bypass grafting. Ann Thorac Surg 57:161, 1994.

297. Goodnough LT, Monk TG, Sicard G, et al: Intraoperative salvage in patients undergoing elective abdominal aortic aneurysm repair: An analysis of cost and benefit. J Vasc Surg 24:213, 1996.

298. Huber TS, McGorray SP, Carlton LC, et al: Intraoperative autologous transfusion during elective infrarenal aortic reconstruction: A decision analysis model. J Vasc Surg 25:984, 1997.

299. Ouriel K, Shortell CK, Green RM, DeWeese JA: Intraoperative autotransfusion in aortic surgery. J Vasc Surg 18:16, 1993.

300. Bartels C, Bechtel JV, Winkler C, Horsch S: Intraoperative autotransfusion in aortic surgery: Comparison of whole blood autotransfusion versus cell separation. J Vasc Surg 24:102, 1996.

301. Clagett GP, Valentine RJ, Jackson MR, et al: A randomized trial of intraoperative autotransfusion during aortic surgery. J Vasc Surg 29:22, 1999.

302. Nelson AH, Fleisher LA, Rosenbaum SH: Relationship between postoperative anemia and cardiac morbidity in high-risk vascular patients in the intensive care unit. Crit Care Med 21:860, 1993.

303. Bush HL Jr, Hydo LJ, Fischer E, et al: Hypothermia during elective abdominal aortic aneurysm repair: The high price of avoidable morbidity. J Vasc Surg 21:392, 1995.

304. Frank SM, Fleisher LA, Breslow MJ, et al: Perioperative maintenance of normothermia reduces the incidence of morbid cardiac events: A randomized clinical trial. JAMA 277:1127, 1997.

305. Mason RA, Newton GB, Cassel W, et al: Combined epidural and general anesthesia in aortic surgery. J Cardiovasc Surg (Torino) 31:442, 1990.

306. Yeager MP, Glass DD, Neff RK, Brinck-Johnsen T: Epidural anesthesia and analgesia in high-risk surgical patients. Anesthesiology 66:729, 1987.

307. Baron JF, Bertrand M, Barre E, et al: Combined epidural and general anesthesia versus general anesthesia for abdominal aortic surgery. Anesthesiology 75:611, 1991.

308. Raggi R, Dardik H, Mauro AL: Continuous epidural anesthesia and postoperative epidural narcotics in vascular surgery. Am J Surg 154:192, 1987.

309. Baron HC, LaRaja RD, Rossi G, Atkinson D: Continuous epidural analgesia in the heparinized vascular surgical patient: A retrospective review of 912 patients. J Vasc Surg 6:144, 1987.

310. Pasternack PF, Grossi EA, Baumann FG, et al: Beta blockade to decrease silent myocardial ischemia during peripheral vascular surgery. Am J Surg 158:113, 1989.

311. Mangano DT, Layug EL, Wallace A, Tateo I: Effect of atenolol on mortality and cardiovascular morbidity after noncardiac surgery. Multicenter Study of Perioperative Ischemia Research Group. N Engl J Med 335:1713, 1996.

312. Wallace A, Layug B, Tateo I, et al: Prophylactic atenolol reduces postoperative myocardial ischemia. McSPI Research Group. Anesthesiology 88:7, 1998.

313. Poldermans D, Boersma E, Bax JJ, et al: The effect of bisoprolol on perioperative mortality and myocardial infarction in high-risk patients undergoing vascular surgery. Dutch Echocardiographic Cardiac Risk Evaluation Applying Stress Echocardiography Study Group. N Engl J Med 341:1789, 1999.

314. Poldermans D, Boersma E, Bax JJ, et al: Bisoprolol reduces cardiac death and myocardial infarction in high-risk patients as long as 2 years after successful major vascular surgery. Eur Heart J 22:1353, 2001.

315. Cleland JG, McGowan J, Clark A, Freemantle N: The evidence for beta blockers in heart failure. BMJ 318:824, 1999.

316. Gottlieb SS, McCarter RJ, Vogel RA: Effect of beta-blockade on mortality among high-risk and low-risk patients after myocardial infarction. N Engl J Med 339:489, 1998.

317. Chang BB, Paty PS, Shah DM, et al: The right retroperitoneal approach for abdominal aortic surgery. Am J Surg 158:156, 1989.

318. Sicard GA, Reilly JM, Rubin BG, et al: Transabdominal versus retroperitoneal incision for abdominal aortic surgery: Report of a prospective randomized trial. J Vasc Surg 21:174, 1995.

319. Cambria RP, Brewster DC, Abbott WM, et al: Transperitoneal versus retroperitoneal approach for aortic reconstruction: A randomized prospective study. J Vasc Surg 11:314, 1990.

320. Sieunarine K, Lawrence-Brown MM, Goodman MA: Comparison of transperitoneal and retroperitoneal approaches for infrarenal aortic surgery: Early and late results. Cardiovasc Surg 5:71, 1997.

321. AbuRahma AF, Robinson PA, Boland JP, Lucente FC: The risk of ligation of the left renal vein in resection of the abdominal aortic aneurysm. Surg Gynecol Obstet 173:33, 1991.

322. Calligaro KD, Savarese RP, McCombs PR, DeLaurentis DA: Division of the left renal vein during aortic surgery. Am J Surg 160:192, 1990.

323. Shepard AD, Tollefson DF, Reddy DJ, et al: Left flank retroperitoneal exposure: A technical aid to complex aortic reconstruction. J Vasc Surg 14:283, 1991.

324. Breckwoldt WL, Mackey WC, Belkin M, O'Donnell TF Jr: The effect of suprarenal cross-clamping on abdominal aortic aneurysm repair. Arch Surg 127:520, 1992.

325. Nypaver TJ, Shepard AD, Reddy DJ, et al: Repair of pararenal abdominal aortic aneurysms: An analysis of operative management. Arch Surg 128:803, 1993.

326. Provan JL, Fialkov J, Ameli FM, St Louis EL: Is tube repair of aortic aneurysm followed by aneurysmal change in the common iliac arteries? Can J Surg 33:394, 1990.

327. Polterauer P, Prager M, Holzenbein T, et al: Dacron versus polytetrafluoroethylene for Y-aortic bifurcation grafts: A six-year prospective, randomized trial. Surgery 111:626, 1992.

328. Lord RS, Nash PA, Raj BT, et al: Prospective randomized trial of polytetrafluoroethylene and Dacron aortic prosthesis: I. Perioperative results. Ann Vasc Surg 2:248, 1988.

329. Piotrowski JJ, McCroskey BL, Rutherford RB: Selection of grafts currently available for repair of abdominal aortic aneurysms. Surg Clin North Am 69:827, 1989.

330. Mabry CD, Thompson BW, Read RC: Activated clotting time (ACT) monitoring of intraoperative heparinization in peripheral vascular surgery. Am J Surg 138:894, 1979.

331. Ernst CB, Hagihara PF, Daugherty ME, Griffen WO Jr: Inferior mesenteric artery stump pressure: A reliable index for safe IMA ligation during abdominal aortic aneurysmectomy. Ann Surg 187:641, 1978.

332. Thomas J, Blake K, Pierce G, et al: The clinical course of asymptomatic mesenteric arterial stenosis. J Vasc Surg 27:840, 1998.

333. Tollefson DF, Ernst CB: Natural history of atherosclerotic renal artery stenosis associated with aortic disease. J Vasc Surg 14:327, 1991.

334. Zierler RE, Bergelin RO, Davidson RC, et al: A prospective study of disease progression in patients with atherosclerotic renal artery stenosis. Am J Hypertens 9:1055, 1996.

335. Dean RH, Benjamin ME, Hansen KJ: Surgical management of renovascular hypertension. Curr Probl Surg 34:209, 1997.

336. Cambria RP, Brewster DC, L'Italien G, et al: Simultaneous aortic and renal artery reconstruction: Evolution of an eighteen-year experience. J Vasc Surg 21:916, 1995.

337. Benjamin ME, Hansen KJ, Craven TE, et al: Combined aortic and renal artery surgery: A contemporary experience. Ann Surg 223:555, 1996.

338. Williamson WK, Abou-Zamzam AM Jr, Moneta GL, et al: Prophylactic repair of renal artery stenosis is not justified in patients who require infrarenal aortic reconstruction. J Vasc Surg 28:14, 1998.

339. Nenhaus HP, Javid H: The distinct syndrome of spontaneous aortic-caval fistula. Am J Med 44:464, 1968.

340. Miller DC, Myers BD: Pathophysiology and prevention of acute renal failure associated with thoracoabdominal or abdominal aortic surgery. J Vasc Surg 5:518, 1987.

341. Wahlberg E, Dimuzio PJ, Stoney RJ: Aortic clamping during elective operations for infrarenal disease: The influence of clamping time on renal function. J Vasc Surg 36:13, 2002.

342. Bergman RT, Gloviczki P, Welch TJ, et al: The role of intravenous fluorescein in the detection of colon ischemia during aortic reconstruction. Ann Vasc Surg 6:74, 1992.

343. Welborn MB 3rd, Seeger JM: Prevention and management of sigmoid and pelvic ischemia associated with aortic surgery. Semin Vasc Surg 14:255, 2001.

344. Iliopoulos JI, Hermreck AS, Thomas JH, Pierce GE: Hemodynamics of the hypogastric arterial circulation. J Vasc Surg 9:637, 1989.

345. Jarvinen O, Laurikka J, Salenius JP, Lepantalo M: Mesenteric infarction after aortoiliac surgery on the basis of 1752 operations from the National Vascular Registry. World J Surg 23:243, 1999.

346. Bjorck M, Bergqvist D, Troeng T: Incidence and clinical presentation of bowel ischaemia after aortoiliac surgery—2930 operations from a population-based registry in Sweden. Eur J Vasc Endovasc Surg 12:139, 1996.

347. Brewster DC, Franklin DP, Cambria RP, et al: Intestinal ischemia complicating abdominal aortic surgery. Surgery 109:447, 1991.

348. Longo WE, Lee TC, Barnett MG, et al: Ischemic colitis complicating abdominal aortic aneurysm surgery in the U.S. veteran. J Surg Res 60:351, 1996.

349. Pittaluga P, Batt M, Hassen-Khodja R, et al: Revascularization of internal iliac arteries during aortoiliac surgery: A multicenter study. Ann Vasc Surg 12:537, 1998.

350. Van Damme H, Creemers E, Limet R: Ischaemic colitis following aortoiliac surgery. Acta Chir Belg 100:21, 2000.

351. Levison JA, Halpern VJ, Kline RG, et al: Perioperative predictors of colonic ischemia after ruptured abdominal aortic aneurysm. J Vasc Surg 29:40, 1999.

352. Bast TJ, van der Biezen JJ, Scherpenisse J, Eikelboom BC: Ischaemic disease of the colon and rectum after surgery for abdominal aortic aneurysm: A prospective study of the incidence and risk factors. Eur J Vasc Surg 4:253, 1990.

353. Fanti L, Masci E, Mariani A, et al: Is endoscopy useful for early diagnosis of ischaemic colitis after aortic surgery? Results of a prospective trial. Ital J Gastroenterol Hepatol 29:357, 1997.

354. Welch M, Baguneid MS, McMahon RF, et al: Histological study of colonic ischaemia after aortic surgery. Br J Surg 85:1095, 1998.

355. Dadian N, Ohki T, Veith FJ, et al: Overt colon ischemia after endovascular aneurysm repair: The importance of microembolization as an etiology. J Vasc Surg 34:986, 2001.

356. Tollefson DF, Ernst CB: Colon ischemia following aortic reconstruction. Ann Vasc Surg 5:485, 1991.

357. Houe T, Thorboll JE, Sigild U, et al: Can colonoscopy diagnose transmural ischaemic colitis after abdominal aortic surgery? An evidence-based approach. Eur J Vasc Endovasc Surg 19:304, 2000.

358. Meissner MH, Johansen KH: Colon infarction after ruptured abdominal aortic aneurysm. Arch Surg 127:979, 1992.

359. Bjorck M, Troeng T, Bergqvist D: Risk factors for intestinal ischaemia after aortoiliac surgery: A combined cohort and case-control study of 2824 operations. Eur J Vasc Endovasc Surg 13:531, 1997.

360. Batt M, Ricco JB, Staccini P: Do internal iliac arteries contribute to vascularization of the descending colon during abdominal aortic aneurysm surgery? An intraoperative hemodynamic study. Ann Vasc Surg 15:171, 2001.

361. Hobson RW 2nd, Wright CB, Rich NM, Collins GJ Jr: Assessment of colonic ischemia during aortic surgery by Doppler ultrasound. J Surg Res 20:231, 1976.

362. Ouriel K, Fiore WM, Geary JE: Detection of occult colonic ischemia during aortic procedures: Use of an intraoperative photoplethysmographic technique. J Vasc Surg 7:5, 1988.

363. Yilmaz EN, Vahl AC, van Rij G, et al: Endoluminal pulse oximetry of the sigmoid colon and the monitoring of the colonic circulation. Cardiovasc Surg 7:704, 1999.

364. Krohg-Sorensen K, Kvernebo K: Laser Doppler flowmetry in evaluation of colonic blood flow during aortic reconstruction. Eur J Vasc Surg 3:37, 1989.

365. Sakakibara Y, Jikuya T, Saito EM, et al: Does laser Doppler flowmetry aid the prevention of ischemic colitis in abdominal aortic aneurysm surgery? Thorac Cardiovasc Surg 45:32, 1997.

366. Fiddian-Green RG, Amelin PM, Herrmann JB, et al: Prediction of the development of sigmoid ischemia on the day of aortic operations: Indirect measurements of intramural pH in the colon. Arch Surg 121:654, 1986.

367. Bjorck M, Lindberg F, Broman G, Bergqvist D: pHi monitoring of the sigmoid colon after aortoiliac surgery: A five-year prospective study. Eur J Vasc Endovasc Surg 20:273, 2000.

368. Lebuffe G, Decoene C, Raingeval X, et al: Pilot study with air-automated sigmoid capnometry in abdominal aortic aneurysm surgery. Eur J Anaesthesiol 18:585, 2001.

369. Schiedler MG, Cutler BS, Fiddian-Green RG: Sigmoid intramural pH for prediction of ischemic colitis during aortic surgery: A comparison with risk factors and inferior mesenteric artery stump pressures. Arch Surg 122:881, 1987.

370. Seeger JM, Coe DA, Kaelin LD, Flynn TC: Routine reimplantation of patent inferior mesenteric arteries limits colon infarction after aortic reconstruction. J Vasc Surg 15:635, 1992.

371. Zelenock GB, Strodel WE, Knol JA, et al: A prospective study of clinically and endoscopically documented colonic ischemia in 100 patients undergoing aortic reconstructive surgery with aggressive colonic and direct pelvic revascularization, compared with historic controls. Surgery 106:771, 1989.

372. Kuttila K, Perttila J, Vanttinen E, Niinikoski J: Tonometric assessment of sigmoid perfusion during aortobifemoral reconstruction for arteriosclerosis. Eur J Surg 160:491, 1994.

373. Szilagyi DE, Hageman JH, Smith RF, Elliott JP: Spinal cord damage in surgery of the abdominal aorta. Surgery 83:38, 1978.

374. Picone AL, Green RM, Ricotta JR, et al: Spinal cord ischemia following operations on the abdominal aorta. J Vasc Surg 3:94, 1986.

375. Gloviczki P, Cross SA, Stanson AW, et al: Ischemic injury to the spinal cord or lumbosacral plexus after aorto- iliac reconstruction. Am J Surg 162:131, 1991.

376. Meagher AP, Lord RS, Graham AR, Hill DA: Acute aortic occlusion presenting with lower limb paralysis. J Cardiovasc Surg (Torino) 32:643, 1991.

377. DePalma RG, Levine SB, Feldman S: Preservation of erectile function after aortoiliac reconstruction. Arch Surg 113:958, 1978.

378. Lederle FA, Johnson GR, Wilson SE, et al: Quality of life, impotence, and activity level in a randomized trial of immediate repair versus surveillance of small abdominal aortic aneurysm. J Vasc Surg 38:745, 2003.

379. Flanigan DP, Schuler JJ, Keifer T, et al: Elimination of iatrogenic impotence and improvement of sexual function after aortoiliac revascularization. Arch Surg 117:544, 1982.

380. Weinstein MH, Machleder HI: Sexual function after aorto-Iliac surgery. Ann Surg 181:787, 1975.

381. Olin JW, Graor RA, O'Hara P, Young JR: The incidence of deep venous thrombosis in patients undergoing abdominal aortic aneurysm resection. J Vasc Surg 18:1037, 1993.

382. Williamson WK, Nicoloff AD, Taylor LM Jr, et al: Functional outcome after open repair of abdominal aortic aneurysm. J Vasc Surg 33:913, 2001.

383. Cronenwett JL: Factors influencing the long-term results of aortic aneurysm surgery. In Pearce W (ed): Vascular Surgery: Long Term Results. East Norwalk, Conn, Appleton & Lange, 1993, p 171.

384. Hallett JW Jr, Marshall DM, Petterson TM, et al: Graft-related complications after abdominal aortic aneurysm repair: Reassurance from a 36-year population-based experience. J Vasc Surg 25:277, 1997.

385. Plate G, Hollier LA, O'Brien PO, et al: Recurrent aneurysms and late vascular complications following repair of abdominal aortic aneurysms. Arch Surg 120:590, 1985.

386. Crawford ES, Saleh SA, Babb JWD, et al: Infrarenal abdominal aortic aneurysm: Factors influencing survival after operation performed over a 25-year period. Ann Surg 193:699, 1981.

387. Hallett JW Jr, Marshall DM, Petterson TM, et al: Graft-related complications after abdominal aortic aneurysm repair: Reassurance

from a 36-year population-based experience. J Vasc Surg 25:277, 1997.

388. Szilagyi DE, Smith RF, Elliott JP, et al: Anastomotic aneurysms after vascular reconstruction: Problems of incidence, etiology, and treatment. Surgery 78:800, 1975.

389. Edwards JM, Teefey SA, Zierler RE, Kohler TR: Intraabdominal paraanastomotic aneurysms after aortic bypass grafting. J Vasc Surg 15:344, 1992.

390. Kalman PG, Rappaport DC, Merchant N, et al: The value of late computed tomographic scanning in identification of vascular abnormalities after abdominal aortic aneurysm repair. J Vasc Surg 29:442, 1999.

391. Treiman RL, Hartunian SL, Cossman DV, et al: Late results of small untreated abdominal aortic aneurysms. Ann Vasc Surg 5:359, 1991.

392. Bunt TJ: Synthetic vascular graft infections: I. Graft infections. Surgery 93:733, 1983.

393. Farkas JC, Fichelle JM, Laurian C, et al: Long-term follow-up of positive cultures in 500 abdominal aortic aneurysms. Arch Surg 128:284, 1993.

394. Szilagyi DE, Smith RF, Elliott JP, Vrandecic MP: Infection in arterial reconstruction with synthetic grafts. Ann Surg 176:321, 1972.

395. Bunt TJ: Synthetic vascular graft infections: II. Graft-enteric erosions and graft-enteric fistulas. Surgery 94:1, 1983.

396. Calcagno D, Hallett JW Jr, Ballard DJ, et al: Late iliac artery aneurysms and occlusive disease after aortic tube grafts for abdominal aortic aneurysm repair: A 35-year experience. Ann Surg 214:733, 1991.

397. Plate G, Hollier LA, O'Brien P, et al: Recurrent aneurysms and late vascular complications following repair of abdominal aortic aneurysms. Arch Surg 120:590, 1985.

398. Koskas F, Kieffer E: Long-term survival after elective repair of infrarenal abdominal aortic aneurysm: Results of a prospective multicentric study. Association for Academic Research in Vascular Surgery (AURC). Ann Vasc Surg 11:473, 1997.

399. Soreide O, Lillestol J, Christensen O, et al: Abdominal aortic aneurysms: Survival analysis of four hundred thirty-four patients. Surgery 91:188, 1982.

400. Vohra R, Reid D, Groome J, et al: Long-term survival in patients undergoing resection of abdominal aortic aneurysm. Ann Vasc Surg 4:460, 1990.

401. Norman PE, Semmens JB, Lawrence-Brown MM, Holman CD: Long term relative survival after surgery for abdominal aortic aneurysm in western Australia: Population based study. BMJ 317:852, 1998.

402. Stonebridge PA, Callam MJ, Bradbury AW, et al: Comparison of long-term survival after successful repair of ruptured and non-ruptured abdominal aortic aneurysm. Br J Surg 80:585, 1993.

403. Cho JS, Gloviczki P, Martelli E, et al: Long-term survival and late complications after repair of ruptured abdominal aortic aneurysms. J Vasc Surg 27:813, 1998.

404. Kazmers A, Perkins AJ, Jacobs LA: Aneurysm rupture is independently associated with increased late mortality in those surviving abdominal aortic aneurysm repair. J Surg Res 95:50, 2001.

405. Hertzer NR: Fatal myocardial infarction following abdominal aortic aneurysm resection: Three hundred forty-three patients followed 6-11 years postoperatively. Ann Surg 192:667, 1980.

406. Reigel MM, Hollier LH, Kazmier FJ, et al: Late survival in abdominal aortic aneurysm patients: The role of selective myocardial revascularization on the basis of clinical symptoms. J Vasc Surg 5:222, 1987.

407. Crawford ES, Hess KR, Cohen ES, et al: Ruptured aneurysm of the descending thoracic and thoracoabdominal aorta: Analysis according to size and treatment. Ann Surg 213:417, 1991.

408. Allen BT, Anderson CB, Rubin BG, et al: Preservation of renal function in juxtarenal and suprarenal abdominal aortic aneurysm repair. J Vasc Surg 17:948, 1993.

409. Reilly LM, Ramos TK, Murray SP, et al: Optimal exposure of the proximal abdominal aorta: A critical appraisal of transabdominal medial visceral rotation. J Vasc Surg 19:375, 1994.

410. Green RM, Ricotta JJ, Ouriel K, DeWeese JA: Results of supraceliac aortic clamping in the difficult elective resection of infrarenal abdominal aortic aneurysm. J Vasc Surg 9:124, 1989.

411. Crawford ES, Snyder DM, Cho GC, Roehm JO Jr: Progress in treatment of thoracoabdominal and abdominal aortic aneurysms involving celiac, superior mesenteric, and renal arteries. Ann Surg 188:404, 1978.

412. Qvarfordt PG, Stoney RJ, Reilly LM, et al: Management of pararenal aneurysms of the abdominal aorta. J Vasc Surg 3:84, 1986.

413. Jean-Claude JM, Reilly LM, Stoney RJ, Messina LM: Pararenal aortic aneurysms: The future of open aortic aneurysm repair. J Vasc Surg 29:902, 1999.

414. Crawford JL, Stowe CL, Safi HJ, et al: Inflammatory aneurysms of the aorta. J Vasc Surg 2:113, 1985.

415. Pennell RC, Hollier LH, Lie JT, et al: Inflammatory abdominal aortic aneurysms: A thirty-year review. J Vasc Surg 2:859, 1985.

416. Sterpetti AV, Hunter WJ, Feldhaus RJ, et al: Inflammatory aneurysms of the abdominal aorta: Incidence, pathologic, and etiologic considerations. J Vasc Surg 9:643, 1989.

417. Stella A, Gargiulo M, Faggioli GL, et al: Postoperative course of inflammatory abdominal aortic aneurysms. Ann Vasc Surg 7:229, 1993.

418. Nitecki SS, Hallett JW Jr, Stanson AW, et al: Inflammatory abdominal aortic aneurysms: A case-control study. J Vasc Surg 23:860, 1996.

419. Tennant WG, Hartnell GG, Baird RN, Horrocks M: Radiologic investigation of abdominal aortic aneurysm disease: Comparison of three modalities in staging and the detection of inflammatory change. J Vasc Surg 17:703, 1993.

420. Lindblad B, Almgren B, Bergqvist D, et al: Abdominal aortic aneurysm with perianeurysmal fibrosis: Experience from 11 Swedish vascular centers. J Vasc Surg 13:231, 1991.

421. Stotter AT, Grigg MJ, Mansfield AO: The response of perianeurysmal fibrosis—the "inflammatory" aneurysm—to surgery and steroid therapy. Eur J Vasc Surg 4:201, 1990.

422. Lacquet JP, Lacroix H, Nevelsteen A, Suy R: Inflammatory abdominal aortic aneurysms: A retrospective study of 110 cases. Acta Chir Belg 97:286, 1997.

423. Baskerville PA, Blakeney CG, Young AE, Browse NL: The diagnosis and treatment of peri-aortic fibrosis ('inflammatory' aneurysms). Br J Surg 70:381, 1983.

424. Ewart JM, Burke ML, Bunt TJ: Spontaneous abdominal aortic infections: Essentials of diagnosis and management. Am Surg 49:37, 1983.

425. Gomes MN, Choyke PL, Wallace RB: Infected aortic aneurysms: A changing entity. Ann Surg 215:435, 1992.

426. Reddy DJ, Shepard AD, Evans JR, et al: Management of infected aortoiliac aneurysms. Arch Surg 126:873, 1991.

427. Oderich GS, Panneton JM, Bower TC, et al: Infected aortic aneurysms: Aggressive presentation, complicated early outcome, but durable results. J Vasc Surg 34:900, 2001.

428. Zdanowski Z, Ribbe E, Schalen C: Bacterial adherence to synthetic vascular prostheses and influence of human plasma: An in vitro study. Eur J Vasc Surg 7:277, 1993.

429. Clagett GP, Bowers BL, Lopez-Viego MA, et al: Creation of a neoaortoiliac system from lower extremity deep and superficial veins. Ann Surg 218:239, 1993.

430. Kieffer E, Bahnini A, Koskas F, et al: In situ allograft replacement of infected infrarenal aortic prosthetic grafts: Results in forty-three patients. J Vasc Surg 17:349, 1993.

431. Brewster DC, Cambria RP, Moncure AC, et al: Aortocaval and iliac arteriovenous fistulas: Recognition and treatment. J Vasc Surg 13:253, 1991.

432. Gilling-Smith GL, Mansfield AO: Spontaneous abdominal arteriovenous fistulae: Report of eight cases and review of the literature. Br J Surg 78:421, 1991.

433. Duong C, Atkinson N: Review of aortoiliac aneurysms with spontaneous large vein fistula. Aust N Z J Surg 71:52, 2001.

434. Houben PF, Bollen EC, Nuyens CM: "Asymptomatic" ruptured aneurysm: A report of two cases of aortocaval fistula presenting with cardiac failure. Eur J Vasc Surg 7:352, 1993.

435. Ghilardi G, Scorza R, Bortolani E, et al: Rupture of abdominal aortic aneurysms into the major abdominal veins. J Cardiovasc Surg (Torino) 34:39, 1993.

436. Salo JA, Verkkala KA, Ala-Kulju KV, et al: Hematuria is an indication of rupture of an abdominal aortic aneurysm into the vena cava. J Vasc Surg 12:41, 1990.

437. Saxon SR, Glover WM, Youkey JR: Aortocaval fistula and contained rupture of an abdominal aortic aneurysm presenting with pelvic venous congestion. Ann Vasc Surg 4:381, 1990.

438. Calligaro KD, Bergen WS, Savarese RP, et al: Primary aortoduodenal fistula due to septic aortitis. J Cardiovasc Surg (Torino) 33:192, 1992.

439. Sweeney MS, Gadacz TR: Primary aortoduodenal fistula: Manifestation, diagnosis, and treatment. Surgery 96:492, 1984.

440. Wheeler WE, Hanks J, Raman VK: Primary aortoenteric fistulas. Am Surg 58:53, 1992.

441. Crawford ES, Coselli JS, Safi HJ, et al: The impact of renal fusion and ectopia on aortic surgery. J Vasc Surg 8:375, 1988.

442. Bauer S, Perlmutter A, Retik A: Anomalies of the upper urinary tract. In Walsh PC, Retik AB, Stamey TA (eds): Campbell's Urology, 6th ed. Philadelphia, WB Saunders, 1992, p 1357.

443. Schneider JR, Cronenwett JL: Temporary perfusion of a congenital pelvic kidney during abdominal aortic aneurysm repair. J Vasc Surg 17:613, 1993.

444. Starr DS, Foster WJ, Morris GC Jr: Resection of abdominal aortic aneurysm in the presence of horseshoe kidney. Surgery 89:387, 1981.

445. Hollis HW, Rutherford RB: Abdominal aortic aneurysms associated with horseshoe or ectopic kidneys: Techniques of renal preservation. Semin Vasc Surg 1:148, 1988.

446. Baldridge ED Jr, Canos AJ: Venous anomalies encountered in aortoiliac surgery. Arch Surg 122:1184, 1987.

447. Beckman CF, Abrams HL: Circumaortic venous ring: Incidence and significance. Am J Radiol 132:561, 1979.

448. Giordano JM, Trout HH 3rd: Anomalies of the inferior vena cava. J Vasc Surg 3:924, 1986.

449. Bartle EJ, Pearce WH, Sun JH, Rutherford RB: Infrarenal venous anomalies and aortic surgery: Avoiding vascular injury. J Vasc Surg 6:590, 1987.

450. Dupont JR: Isolated left-sided vena cava and abdominal aortic aneurysm. Arch Surg 102:211, 1971.

451. Nora JD, Pairolero PC, Nivatvongs S, et al: Concomitant abdominal aortic aneurysm and colorectal carcinoma: Priority of resection. J Vasc Surg 9:630, 1989.

452. Hafez KS, El Fettouh HA, Novick AC, Ouriel K: Management of synchronous renal neoplasm and abdominal aortic aneurysm. J Vasc Surg 32:1102, 2000.

453. Baskin LS, McClure RD, Rapp JH, et al: Simultaneous resection of renal carcinoma and abdominal aortic aneurysm. Ann Vasc Surg 5:363, 1991.

454. Ginsberg DA, Modrall JG, Esrig D, et al: Concurrent abdominal aortic aneurysm and urologic neoplasm: An argument for simultaneous intervention. Ann Vasc Surg 9:428, 1995.

455. Swanson RJ, Littooy FN, Hunt TK, Stoney RJ: Laparotomy as a precipitating factor in the rupture of intra-abdominal aneurysms. Arch Surg 115:299, 1980.

456. Durham SJ, Steed DL, Moosa HH, et al: Probability of rupture of an abdominal aortic aneurysm after an unrelated operative procedure: A prospective study. J Vasc Surg 13:248, 1991.

457. String ST: Cholelithiasis and aortic reconstruction. J Vasc Surg 1:664, 1984.

458. Ouriel K, Ricotta JJ, Adams JT, DeWeese JA: Management of cholelithiasis in patients with abdominal aortic aneurysm. Ann Surg 198:717, 1983.

459. Fry RE, Fry WJ: Cholelithiasis and aortic reconstruction: The problem of simultaneous surgical therapy: Conclusions from a personal series. J Vasc Surg 4:345, 1986.

460. Brunkwall J, Hauksson H, Bengtsson H, et al: Solitary aneurysms of the iliac arterial system: An estimate of their frequency of occurrence. J Vasc Surg 10:381, 1989.

461. Lawrence PF, Lorenzo-Rivero S, Lyon JL: The incidence of iliac, femoral, and popliteal artery aneurysms in hospitalized patients. J Vasc Surg 22:409, 1995.

462. McCready RA, Pairolero PC, Gilmore JC, et al: Isolated iliac artery aneurysms. Surgery 93:688, 1983.

463. Richardson JW, Greenfield LJ: Natural history and management of iliac aneurysms. J Vasc Surg 8:165, 1988.

464. Krupski WC, Selzman CH, Floridia R, et al: Contemporary management of isolated iliac aneurysms. J Vasc Surg 28:1, 1998.

465. Bolin T, Lund K, Skau T: Isolated aneurysms of the iliac artery: What are the chances of rupture? Eur J Vasc Surg 2:214, 1988.

466. Brin BJ, Busuttil RW: Isolated hypogastric artery aneurysms. Arch Surg 117:1329, 1982.

467. Santilli SM, Wensing SE, Lee ES: Expansion rates and outcomes for iliac artery aneurysms. J Vasc Surg 31(1 Pt 1):114, 2000.

468. Deb B, Benjamin M, Comerota AJ: Delayed rupture of an internal iliac artery aneurysm following proximal ligation for abdominal aortic aneurysm repair. Ann Vasc Surg 6:537, 1992.

469. AbuRahma AF, Robinson PA, Boland JP, et al: Elective resection of 332 abdominal aortic aneurysms in a southern West Virginia community during a recent five-year period. Surgery 109(3 Pt 1):244, 1991.

470. Diehl JT, Cali RF, Hertzer NR, Beven EG: Complications of abdominal aortic reconstruction: An analysis of perioperative risk factors in 557 patients. Ann Surg 197:49, 1983.

471. Richardson JD, Main KA: Repair of abdominal aortic aneurysms: A statewide experience. Arch Surg 126:614, 1991.

472. Bickerstaff LK, Hollier LH, Van Peenen HJ, et al: Abdominal aortic aneurysms: The changing natural history. J Vasc Surg 1:6, 1984.

Chapter

Endovascular Treatment of Aortic Aneurysms

101

JACOB BUTH, MD

PETER HARRIS, MD, FRCS

Treatment of an asymptomatic aortic aneurysm is indicated when the risk of rupture outweighs the risk of operation. Thus, the indication for elective repair depends substantially on the risks of the procedure. But the long-term efficacy of the repair is an important factor also. Conventional open aneurysm surgery is associated with considerable operative mortality because the operation is extensive and the patients often have serious co-morbidities. In published series, the 30-day or in-hospital mortality has ranged from 3.8% to 8.2% in patients undergoing elective open repair of abdominal aortic aneurysms (AAAs), depending on whether the study was reported from a single institution, often specializing in the care of patients with aneurysms, or from regional or national databases.[1] Severe postoperative complications are common, and intensive care unit and hospital admission stays are considerable. Moreover, the time taken for recovery to the preoperative state of well-being is usually prolonged.[2] In the case of descending thoracic aneurysm repair, the early mortality of elective surgery in centers with excellent services ranges from 3% to 12%.[3]

The advent of minimally invasive endovascular stent-graft techniques as an alternative treatment has radically extended the management options for patients with aortic aneurysms. The physical insult of the operative trauma is minimal and the patient's recovery is rapid.[4-7] The issue that remains incompletely resolved is the durability of stent-graft repair. There is a possibility that the need for secondary interventions in the longer term could outweigh the early advantages of this minimally invasive method.[8,9] But the likelihood of this being the case is diminishing with continuing refinements of stent-graft design and technology.

■ INDICATIONS FOR ENDOVASCULAR REPAIR

Aneurysm diameter is the principal criterion upon which decisions to treat aneurysms are based. Recently reported randomized trials assessing the outcome of conventional surgical treatment of small abdominal aortic aneurysms clearly demonstrated that a lower risk is associated with initial conservative management in patients with AAAs less than 5.5 cm in diameter.[10,11] Open surgery should generally be reserved for patients demonstrating aneurysm expansion to this diameter (see Chapter 100). Although lower operative mortality and morbidity rates associated with endovascular aneurysm repair (EVAR) may change the risk-benefit ratio for elective interventional treatment of AAAs, no randomized controlled trials have been undertaken to compare the efficacy of this approach with that of noninterventional management of small aneurysms. Therefore, as a general rule, it seems advisable to adhere to the same criteria for elective intervention by endovascular repair as for open surgery with respect to aneurysm size.[12] The size threshold for operative repair of thoracic aortic aneurysm (TAA) is less well defined. However, most institutions consider that operation is not justified in asymptomatic aneurysms less than 6 cm in diameter.[3]

■ DEVELOPMENT OF STENT-GRAFT SYSTEMS

Early Stent-Graft Systems

The first animal studies on EVAR by stent-graft combinations date from the mid-1980s.[13,14] Unpublished clinical experience with stent-grafts in Russia dates from 1985.[15] Parodi and colleagues,[16] from Buenos Aires, Argentina, were the first to publish experience with a balloon-expandable stent attached to a polyester tubular prosthesis to treat AAAs in patients who were unfit for open surgery. Their homemade stent-graft combination was packaged in a delivery catheter and introduced into the aneurysm from the femoral artery. The group's first patients received an endograft with one proximal stent for infrarenal fixation only. A second stent for distal fixation to obtain effective exclusion of the aneurysm from the blood flow was added later. These early patients had an aorto-aortic tube graft. However, an aorto-uni-iliac stent-graft was also used early in the Parodi series, resolving the problem of an inadequate distal aortic cuff for securing "fixation" and "seal."

Commercially Manufactured Systems

Over the next decade, a succession of industry-manufactured endoprostheses was introduced into the market for treatment of a broad spectrum of patients with AAA and TAA. A variety of endografts from different manufacturers are currently available. The primary objective of all of these devices is to exclude the aneurysm sac from systemic arterial pressure. The ideal endograft should provide lifelong protection from rupture of the aneurysm without any risk of migration or displacement from the attachment sites. Components should be sufficiently robust and at the same time small enough to fit into a delivery system that can be negotiated easily through the access vessels. Most of the current endografts can be judged on the following criteria: (1) caliber and flexibility of introducer system, (2) user-friendliness, and (3) mechanism of the attachment system. The common femoral artery is the vessel used most commonly for introduction of the delivery sheath. Access to the aorta may be hampered by severe atherosclerotic stenoses in the iliac arteries, excessive tortuosity especially with heavy calcification, or small-diameter native iliac arteries. Delivery catheters of aortic endografts from most manufacturers have an outer diameter ranging from 18 to 26 French (Fr), and easily traverse iliac segments as narrow as 5.5 to 7.5 mm in diameter (Table 101-1). An optimal profile includes a long tapered tip to facilitate passage of the device through stenotic arterial segments. Sometimes predilatation with a balloon catheter is required. Flexibility of the introducer system is important for negotiating tortuous iliac arteries.

Existing Configurations of Stent-Graft

Bifurcated endoprostheses that allow sealing and attachment in both iliac arteries are used most frequently today. Aorto-aortic straight tubes and aorto-uni-iliac devices are reserved for specific indications (see discussion on planning the procedure). Different designs of bifurcated stent-grafts include modular or unipiece systems, entirely stent-supported or largely unsupported structures, and the availability of suprarenal fixation by a bare stent at the proximal extremity of the prosthesis. In modular stent-grafts, the iliac limbs are connected with the aortic component of the endograft in situ (Fig. 101-1). Some modular endografts consist of two components, the aortic component with a fixed ipsilateral limb and a contralateral iliac limb, whereas others have separate ipsilateral and contralateral iliac limbs. Modular endografts tend to be relatively user-friendly, although the junctions between the components carry an intrinsic risk of late disconnection.[17,18] Unipiece endografts have a cross-femoral wire to bring the "second limb" to the contralateral iliac artery. The introduction and deployment of unipiece devices is more complex, with a propensity for the "pull wire" to wrap around the introducer system or guidewires.

Materials Used for the Construction of Stent-Grafts

The fabric consists of polyester (Dacron) or expanded polytetrafluoroethylene (ePTFE) (see Table 101-1). Most commercial endoprostheses are fully supported by stents covering their entire length. Partly unsupported devices, which have stents only at the attachment sites, commonly require secondary deployment of bare stents within the device to prevent kinking of their iliac limbs.[19] Endografts constructed with full support come with the stent wires on the outside or the inside of the fabric, in other words, an exoskeleton or endoskeleton. The stents are usually constructed from two types of metal alloy, stainless steel and nitinol. Nitinol is a thermal memory alloy of nickel and titanium that increases in strength at body temperature. Elgiloy, which is used in some systems, is a modified version of stainless steel. The stent configuration may consist of separate or continuous Z-shaped rings. Separate rings allow greater flexibility in short unsupported zones. One endoprosthesis comes with a helical stent along the entire length (see Fig. 101-1). Motion between fabric and stent materials has resulted in a high incidence of erosion of the fabric in some device brands.[20] Thus, a firm connection between the two components made of different materials is essential.

Fixation and Adaptation of Stent-Grafts

For optimal long-term performance, the ability to adapt to morphologic changes—increased tortuosity or shortening of the aneurysm because of shrinking of the sac—is advantageous. Stiff grafts may be prone to late dislocation of the iliac limb from the intermodular connection or migration from the arterial attachment sites. Discontinuous stent rings or a helical stent may allow better adaptation to angulation of the neck (Fig. 101-2) and to changes of aneurysm shape during the years after stent-graft implantation.

Table 101-1   Characteristics of Available Stent-Graft Systems for Abdominal Aortic Aneurysm Repair

COMPANY	DEVICE	GRAFT POSITIONING & MATERIAL	DEPLOYMENT METHOD	FRENCH SIZE AORTIC DELIVERY SYSTEM (OD)	FIXATION METHOD	SUPRARENAL STENT	MAXIMUM AVAILABLE SIZE OF AORTIC DEVICE COMPONENT (mm)	MAXIMUM RECOMMENDED IN A INFRARENAL DIAMETER THAT CAN BE TREATED	RECOMMENDED OVERSIZING AT AORTIC LEVEL (%)
Cook	Zenith	Internal Polyester	Self-expanding/ stainless steel	24	Compression-fit barbs	Yes	36*	30	15-20
Cordis	Fortron	External Polyester	Self-expanding/ Nitinol	20	Compression-fit barbs	Yes	34	30	15-20
Edwards-Lifesciences	Lifepath	Interwoven Full-thickness	Balloon-expandable/ Elgiloy	25-26	Friction & crimps	No	31	28	10
Endologix	Powerlink	External ePTFE	Self-expanding/ Elgiloy	20	Compression-fit	Optional	28	25	15
Gore	Excluder	Internal ePTFE	Self-expanding/ Nitinol	18	Compression-fit and anchors	No	31	28	Maximum 20
Guidant	Ancure	External (mostly unsupported proximal and distal stent only) Polyester	Balloon-expandable & self-expanding	23.5	Hooks	No	26	25	5-10
Lombard	Anson-Aortofix	Internal Polyester	Self-expanding/ Nitinol	22	Compression-fit barbs	No	No data	No data	No data
Medtronic	AneuRx	Internal Polyester	Self-expanding/ Nitinol	21.5	Compression-fit	No	28	29	15-20
Medtronic	Talent	External Polyester	Self-expanding/ Nitinol	22-24	Compression-fit	Yes	36*	32	15-20

*Custom-made devices in larger size available.
ePTFE, expanded polytetrafluoroethylene; OD, outer diameter.

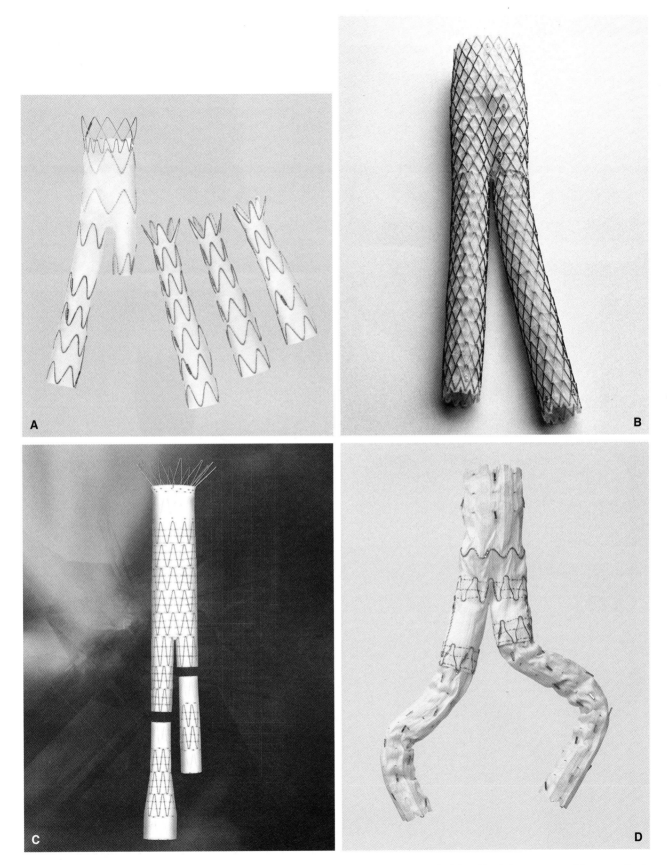

FIGURE 101-1 Various commercially available stent-grafts for abdominal aortic aneurysm repair. **A,** Talent. Exoskeleton, suprarenal bare stent fixation. Modular design. **B,** AneuRx. Exoskeleton, no suprarenal stent. Early version had "stiff" body, and later version discontinuous stent rings for improved adaptability. Modular design. **C,** Zenith. Exoskeleton and bare suprarenal stent. Long body. Modular design. **D,** Lifepath. Balloon expandable configuration, full-thickness polyester, discontinuous stent rings. Modular design.

Continued

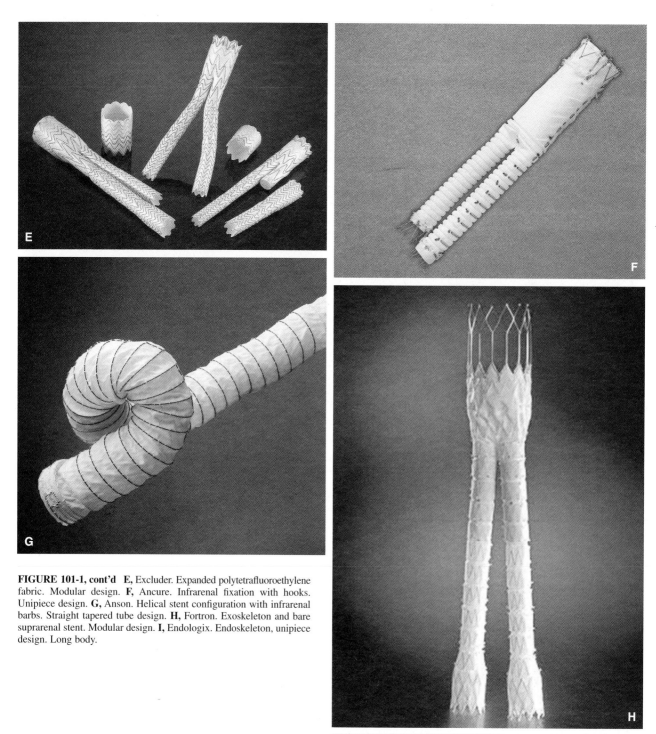

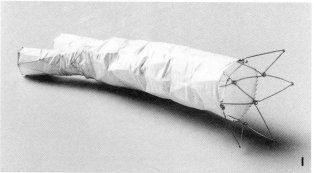

FIGURE 101-1, cont'd E, Excluder. Expanded polytetrafluoroethylene fabric. Modular design. **F,** Ancure. Infrarenal fixation with hooks. Unipiece design. **G,** Anson. Helical stent configuration with infrarenal barbs. Straight tapered tube design. **H,** Fortron. Exoskeleton and bare suprarenal stent. Modular design. **I,** Endologix. Endoskeleton, unipiece design. Long body.

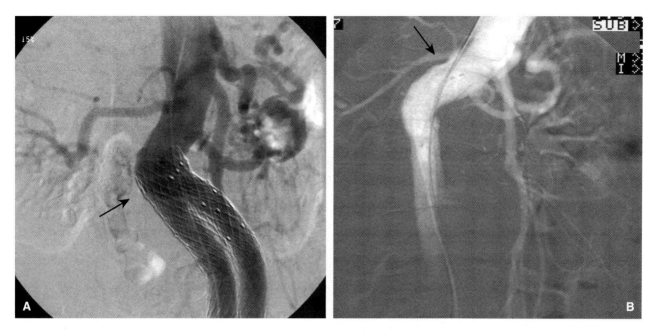

FIGURE 101-2   Different adaptability to angulated aortic neck. **A,** Poor adaptability of early version of a stiff endograft. **B,** Good adaptability of later-generation stent-graft with discontinuous stent rings. *Arrows* in **A** and **B** indicate proximal extremity of stent-grafts.

For proximal fixation several mechanisms are used, including "compression fit" or radial force exerted by self-expanding stents, hooks, and barbs. Concern about instability of the infrarenal necks resulted in the development of suprarenal fixation by a bare stent ring connected to the proximal covered portion of the endoprosthesis. This feature has become a key component of many of the current stent-graft systems. Initial concerns about renal artery occlusion or embolic infarction of the kidney because of stent struts crossing the renal orifices have not materialized, and renal flow disturbances seem to be minimal.[21-24] Landing the fabric-covered body of the stent-graft close to but not overlapping the level of the lower renal arteries is essential. This requirement places great demands on both the accuracy of the delivery system and the resolution of the radiologic equipment used for stent-graft procedures.

Finally, stent-graft systems are available in a range of lengths and diameters for proximal and distal fixation. Optimal fixation and sealing to exclude the aneurysm from systemic flow are obtained by oversizing of the device (usually in the order of 20%) in relation to the arterial diameter. However, excessive oversizing should be avoided because it may result in pleating of the fabric with failure to seal.

Stent-Graft Configurations and Auxiliary Devices Under Development

The latest developments in stent-graft technology address previous limitations of the technique for the treatment of juxtarenal, suprarenal, and other complex aneurysms. Two approaches are being investigated. "Fenestrated devices" allow the covered portion of the stent-graft to be extended above the visceral arteries or, in the case of TAA, proximal to the supra-aortic branches. An aperture in the fabric allows blood flow into the branch artery, and in some circumstances, a stent may be deployed within the orifice to protect its patency and prevent movement of the stent-graft. These

stents may be "flared" by use of appropriate balloons to resemble metal "rivets."[25,26] With this technology, a short sealing zone below the renal arteries is still needed. The initial clinical experience documented procedural success in all 45 patients reported in two publications combined.[26,27] Short-term follow-up demonstrated no endoleaks in the first and 6.2% endoleaks in the second series. Of the total of 115 visceral arteries incorporated, only 2 demonstrated late stenoses, and 1 an occlusion. The other approach involves the use of "branched endografts." Clinical experience is limited to date, although animal experiments appear exciting and promising.[28-30] Figure 101-3 is a representation of the concepts of fenestrated and branched endografts.

An auxiliary device under development is the vascular Endostaple.[31] This system consists of a laser fiber and overlying Endostaple, which can pass through a 13 Fr sheath that is inserted through the femoral artery and introduced in an inserted endograft. The laser system is used to penetrate the endograft and aortic wall from the lumen at the level of the neck. The Endostaple, which consists of a coil made of shape memory metal, secures the position and improves the attachment of the endograft. Possible applications include (1) sealing or preventing endoleak and (2) preventing migration of the endograft. It is speculated that Endostaples may expand the application of endograft repair to aneurysms with necks that are "unfavorable," such as angulated, short, or wide in diameter.

■ PATIENT SELECTION FOR ENDOVASCULAR ANEURYSM REPAIR

Preoperative Imaging Studies

Suitability for EVAR is primarily determined through an analysis of the vascular morphology as represented by

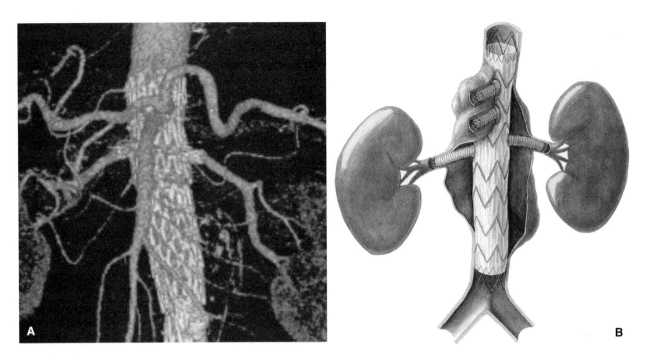

FIGURE 101-3   A, Three-dimensional reconstruction after fenestrated stent-graft with bare stents in the renal arteries. (See color figure in this section.) (Courtesy Dr. E. L. Verhoeven.) **B,** Artist's impression of branched endograft currently validated in experiment. (Courtesy Dr. W. Wisselink.)

imaging studies. EVAR requires precise measurement of aortoiliac lengths and diameters so that an endograft of appropriate size is selected. Previously, conventional computed tomography (CT) and contrast arteriography, applied in combination, were used most commonly for the assessment of abdominal aortic aneurysms prior to EVAR.[32] Both of these diagnostic modalities have shortcomings with regard to the accuracy of the measurements that can be made of the aorta and iliac arteries. Standard CT produces axial slice images, allowing accurate measurement of anatomic structures only in the axial plane. Length measurements of the aorta and iliac arteries made along the craniocaudal axis tend to underestimate the distance to be followed by the endograft. Figure 101-4A illustrates the method of measuring aneurysm dimensions.

Calibrated aortography is a more accurate method than standard CT for determining the optimal length of the endograft. A catheter calibrated with radiopaque markers positioned within the lumen avoids magnification artifacts (Fig. 101-4B). Arteriograms also allow excellent assessment of angulations of the neck, aneurysm, and iliac arteries and provide the surgeon with a road map. However, arteriography does not identify thrombus or atheromatous plaques within the aneurysm neck or the iliac arteries, knowledge of which may be critical to the decision whether or not to proceed with endograft repair. Currently, optimal preoperative evaluation of patients considered for EVAR relies on spiral CT angiography (CTA), with image processing for graft sizing. This technique represents a single diagnostic test upon which accurate planning can be made. Three-dimensional reconstruction is a function of CTA, which is useful but not essential for all EVAR cases. Central lumen line constructions are time consuming and require

skilled radiology staff to generate them, but they can provide valuable information to aid selection of a device of optimum length. The central lumen line can be delineated automatically by computer, but the product still must be checked by specialized staff. At present, CTA with curved-linear reformatting (CRF) is the most commonly used preoperative imaging method. Occasionally it is supplemented by angiography when sizing for length or further assessment of the infrarenal neck appears critical.

Significant advances have been made in the use of CTA, magnetic resonance arteriography, and intravascular ultrasonography in the assessment of aneurysms. Chapters on these techniques can be found in Section IV.

Anatomic Criteria

Anatomic inclusion criteria for endovascular AAA repair relate to the following issues: (1) suitability of the proximal and distal attachment sites, (2) adequacy of the access arteries, and (3) the presence of side-branches of the aortoiliac segment to be excluded from the systemic circulation.

With regard to the attachment sites, it is generally considered that at least 15 mm of nonaneurysmal vessel proximal and distal to the aneurysm is needed for secure graft fixation. Most interventionalists would agree that the diameter of the infrarenal neck should be less than 3 cm, although this guidance has been challenged in a report in which the incidence of late proximal endoleak and the frequency of migration associated with neck diameters larger than 3 cm were comparable to those found after EVAR in patients with aneurysm necks of smaller diameter.[33] Excessive calcification and a thick layer of thrombus may interfere with secure endograft fixation. However, the

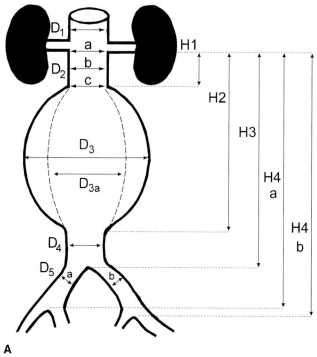

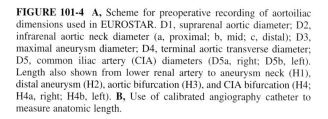

A

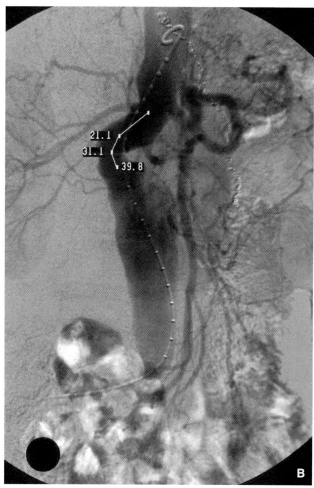

FIGURE 101-4 A, Scheme for preoperative recording of aortoiliac dimensions used in EUROSTAR. D1, suprarenal aortic diameter; D2, infrarenal aortic neck diameter (a, proximal; b, mid; c, distal); D3, maximal aneurysm diameter; D4, terminal aortic transverse diameter; D5, common iliac artery (CIA) diameters (D5a, right; D5b, left). Length also shown from lower renal artery to aneurysm neck (H1), distal aneurysm (H2), aortic bifurcation (H3), and CIA bifurcation (H4; H4a, right; H4b, left). **B,** Use of calibrated angiography catheter to measure anatomic length.

relevance of thrombus in the infrarenal neck has been questioned in another publication that reported no increase in the incidence of early or late endoleak in a small group of patients with filling defects in the aortic neck.[34] Despite these few reports of satisfactory outcomes after EVAR undertaken in breach of the usual selection criteria, adherence to accepted guidelines is strongly recommended at least until the long-term efficacy of endograft procedures has become properly established (Fig. 101-5).[35-37] Permissible exceptions to this rule may be some patients who have large aneurysms and for whom surgery presents a high risk.

The most common reason (>50%) for patients with AAA to be considered ineligible for endovascular repair is unsuitable anatomy at the proximal aortic neck, which may be too short, too wide, or too tortuous.[36,38,39] In the presence of a short distal landing zone in the common iliac artery, usually due to aneurysmal dilatation of this vessel, a number of options are available to secure adequate sealing.[40] Extension of the repair to the external iliac artery, which is rarely aneurysmal, is permissible, although coil occlusion of the hypogastric artery should be performed to prevent type II endoleak (see later) from this source. Antegrade inflow into one of the hypogastric arteries should be preserved, if possible, to maintain pelvic perfusion; however, the risks

associated with bilateral hypogastric artery occlusion may have been overestimated in the past because several later studies have demonstrated that the effects are usually limited to buttock claudication.[41,42] A number of other options exist for dealing with the situation of inadequate sealing zones in both common iliac arteries. First, one or both of the hypogastric arteries may be revascularized by transposition or bypass grafting to the distal external iliac artery.[43] Second, "bell-bottomed" or flared iliac limbs may be employed that are capable of sealing in ectatic or mildly aneurysmal common iliac arteries.[44] Other techniques under evaluation include the use of iliac bifurcation or branched endografts.

Assessment of Access Arteries

The technique of EVAR is described in detail in Chapter 52, but some additional information is provided here. Access to the aneurysm may impeded by small diameter, tortuosity, angulation, and severe calcification of the iliac arteries. Tortuosity and angulation can be often be corrected with the use of super-stiff guidewires, whereas localized stenoses will usually be resolved by high-pressure balloon dilatation. But neither of these techniques is likely to be effective in the

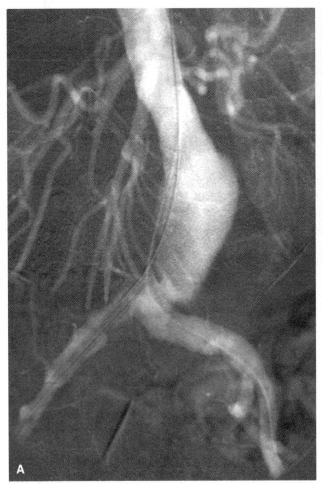

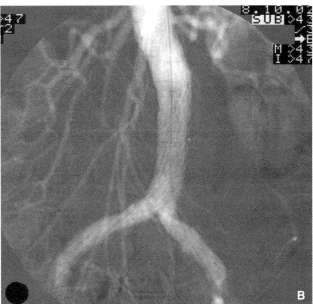

FIGURE 101-5   A, Abdominal aortic aneurysm with uncomplicated morphology. **B,** Postoperative angiogram.

presence of severe vascular calcification. Stenotic disease in the external iliac artery that remains a problem despite balloon angioplasty may be managed by construction of an iliac conduit, that is, a prosthetic graft attached to the common iliac artery via a retroperitoneal incision for delivery of the device. This graft may then be anastomosed to the common femoral artery after the endoprosthesis is deployed in order to bypass the external iliac occlusive disease.[45] Alternatively, if one of the iliac arteries will accept the introducer sheath, an aorto-uni-iliac endograft can be deployed in combination with a crossover femorofemoral bypass and an occluder cuff to close the contralateral common iliac artery.

Issues Relating to Aortic Side-Branches

Obliteration of side-branches arising from the excluded aortoiliac segment may be associated with two potential problems. The first comprises the consequences of ischemia in the area supplied by the side-branch. The presence of a large meandering arch of Riolan may indicate occlusion of the superior mesenteric artery; under these circumstances, sacrifice of the inferior mesenteric artery (IMA) risks ischemia of the left colon. Confirmation of the patency of the IMA by preoperative imaging is as important in EVAR as it is in open aneurysm surgery. The second issue is that

patent aortic side-branches may be a source of retrograde flow into the aortic sac after EVAR, thereby compromising the objective of excluding the aneurysm from the systemic circulation totally (type II endoleak). This phenomenon is relatively uncommon, but its consequences should not be exaggerated (see later).

Eligibility for Endovascular Repair

The proportion of patients with AAAs for whom treatment by EVAR is considered suitable has risen from a reported 20% in the early experience of this technique[46] to 45% to 80%.[37,39,47] Factors relevant to this increase include improved clinical experience with the procedure, technical developments in the design and construction of endoprostheses, and an increasing number of referrals of patients with appropriate anatomy who are considered unsuitable candidates for open surgery because of serious comorbidity.[39] As mentioned previously, adverse anatomy of the infrarenal neck of the aneurysm is the predominant reason for exclusion from EVAR candidacy, followed by the presence of bilateral common iliac artery disease. Other factors that adversely affect the eligibility rate are female gender and patients for whom open surgical repair poses a high risk.[48,49] Females tend to have smaller iliac arteries, possibly precluding transfemoral access to the aorta.

However, unsuitable neck morphology remains the most common cause for exclusion of women from undergoing EVAR.[37] It is ironic that the vascular anatomy of patients who are unfit for open repair and who have the most to gain from EVAR is less often amenable to this technique than that of lower-risk patients. Finally, in addition to patient-related factors, the ability to offer treatment by EVAR depends on the availability of devices of appropriate configuration and size. The introduction of aorto-uni-iliac endoprostheses for patients with unilateral iliac artery obstructions or a narrow distal aorta increased the proportion of patients treatable by endovascular repair by 19% to 50%.[37,47]

■ PLANNING THE PROCEDURE

Having determined that EVAR is technically feasible for a particular patient and having reached agreement with the patient to proceed, after fully informing him or her of the relative risks and benefits in comparison with the alternative treatment strategies available, the surgeon must turn attention to planning of the procedure itself.

First, it is necessary to select the most suitable endograft. There are three basic configurations to choose from, as indicated previously—straight aorto-aortic tube graft, bifurcated aortoiliac, and aorto-uni-iliac graft with iliac occlusion and crossover bypass. Straight tube grafts are used rarely at present. Early experience demonstrated that the distal aortic cuff above the iliac bifurcation is rarely of adequate length to secure a durable seal in fusiform AAAs. Furthermore, even when exclusion of the aneurysm is initially successful, the aorto-aortic reconstruction is extremely vulnerable to late failure.[50,51] Saccular aneurysms or false suture line aneurysms occurring after previous conventional aortic prosthesis may be the only justifiable indications for tube endografts within the abdominal aorta. Aorto-uni-iliac endografts are indicated when one of the iliac arteries cannot be traversed because of occlusive disease and in the AAA with a narrow distal aorta that may not accommodate two iliac device limbs.[52] It may also be the configuration of choice for emergency AAA repair (see repair). A bifurcated aortoiliac endograft is the most appropriate device configuration for the majority of patients undergoing elective EVAR. Basic techniques of EVAR are described in Chapter 52.

■ EARLY OUTCOME OF ENDOVASCULAR ANEURYSM REPAIR

Operative Aspects

Well-documented short-term benefits of EVAR compared with conventional open surgery include reduced blood loss at operation and shorter stay in the intensive care unit and hospital.[53-60] Factors that adversely affect early outcome are procedural failure, perioperative mortality, systemic morbidity, and vascular or local complications. Primary technical success requires, in the first place, successful introduction and deployment of the device. In the initial experience, early conversion to open surgery was necessary in as many as 7% to 18% of cases for a variety of technical mishaps, including inability to reach the aneurysm through the available access channels, arterial injury, and failure to deploy the device at the intended location.[61-63] This high rate of primary conversion was related to a combination of poor operator experience, inappropriate patient selection, and large-caliber, rigid introducer systems.[64-67] Of patients enrolled between 1994 and 1999 in the EUROSTAR (EUROpean collaborators on Stent-graft Techniques for abdominal aortic Aneurysm Repair) series, primary conversion to open surgery was performed in 1.7%. However, with greater experience and better devices, the rate of early conversion has fallen to 0.7%.[68] Other variables determining primary success of endovascular aortic aneurysm repair, as defined by the Society for Vascular Surgery/American Association for Vascular Surgery's Ad Hoc Committee on Standardized Reporting Practices in Vascular Surgery, include secure fixation of the endovascular graft, absence of type I and type III endoleak, and an unobstructed graft.[69]

Perioperative Mortality

A mean 30-day mortality of 2.4% (range 0 to 6.1%) was reported from a meta-analysis of nine published series of EVAR procedures,[70] which is in close agreement with the rate of 2.6% observed in the EUROSTAR Registry program.[71] Preexisting co-morbidity is the major determinant of perioperative mortality. Patients considered fit for open surgery had a procedure-related 30-day mortality of 0.4% to 2.0%, compared with 4.8% to 8.0% in patients with significant associated risk factors of varying severity.[49,72] Although the prevailing view of most investigators in the field is that the perioperative mortality of EVAR may be lower than that of conventional surgery, no data are currently available from randomized trials to support this contention.

Postoperative Morbidity

Nonrandomized comparison of the outcomes from EVAR and open repair suggest that the incidence of most systemic complications is lower with EVAR. A meta-analysis found a mean incidence of systemic complications of 9% for EVAR, compared with 22% in the combined studies on open surgery.[70] When observations of another meta-analysis on open surgery[1] were compared with the outcome of EVAR in two contemporary studies,[53,54] the reduced rate of systemic complications was attributable primarily to lower incidences of adverse events affecting the cardiac and pulmonary systems, with reductions from 11% to 5% and 5% to 3%, respectively. These reductions were observed despite the fact that the incidence of preexisting cardiac and other risk factors was significantly higher in the patients treated by EVAR.

Contrast nephropathy occurred relatively frequently in the early years of EVAR.[54] With greater endovascular experience and the development of more user-friendly introducer systems, however, smaller volumes of contrast media are now used during the performance of EVAR, and this complication is now uncommon.[53] As a result of the lesser operative trauma and a lower incidence of perioperative complications, the recovery time after EVAR is considerably shorter than that associated with the conventional open operation. In nonrandomized studies assessing quality of life by means of standardized questionnaires, patients treated with EVAR returned to their preoperative state of well-being within 1 month, but recovery to this level was delayed until the third postoperative month for patients undergoing open surgery.[73,74]

Local or vascular complications occur in 9% to 16% of patients with EVAR, a range that is probably comparable to the incidence of these complications after open surgical aneurysm repair.[70,75] Intraoperative embolization, which was once seen more often, has become rare with the low-profile introducer systems currently used. Unsupported endografts have a tendency to kink, leading to thrombotic occlusion of the limbs. However, this problem can be prevented by deployment of a bare stent within the device at the time of the initial procedure.[76] Modern endovascular grafts are designed to resist kinking. The incidence of local or vascular complications is related inversely to the experience of the operating team. Several studies have demonstrated a relatively high incidence of these complications in the first 30 procedures performed in an institution compared with the subsequent experience.[65,77,78]

Endoleaks and Intra-aneurysm Pressure

One of the factors that threaten the durability of endovascular repair is persistent blood flow and pressure within the aneurysm sac, which is termed an *endoleak*. A generally accepted classification of endoleaks is indicated in Table 101-2. The different types are discriminated according to the site and origin of blood flow into the aneurysm sac.[79-81] The incidence of early endoleaks, as observed on postoperative arteriography, varies from 12% to 44%.[7,62,72,82,83] Endoleaks, regardless of size or type, can transmit some proportion of systemic pressure to the aneurysm sac.[84-86] Even a thrombosed endoleak may result in systemic pressure in the aneurysm sac (*endotension*) and a higher risk of delayed rupture of the aneurysm.[87]

At present, the majority of physicians rely upon indirect methods to detect evidence of continued pressurization of the aneurysm after EVAR—for instance, evidence of expansion of the sac on sequential contrast-enhanced spiral CT. Noninvasive systems for direct measurement of pressure within the excluded aneurysm sac are being developed, but currently there is no information about their value in clinical practice. Pressure distribution within an aneurysm is heterogeneous, and there are concerns that pressure measurements made at one point may not be representative.[88] Invasive pressure measurements within the sac have been obtained in conjunction with stent-graft placement, at follow-up during embolization of persistent type II endoleaks via endoluminal catheters, and by percutaneous translumbar needle puncture.[86,89-91] Complete exclusion of the sac by an endograft results consistently in an intrasac pressure of less than 50 mm Hg with little or no pulsatility.

Approximately 70% of all early endoleaks disappear within the first postoperative month.[55,62,71] Most are type II endoleaks, and it is these that tend to close spontaneously. Additional interventions are not required for type II endoleaks when they are identified with angiography on completion of the procedure. In contrast, type I and type III endoleaks tend to persist and are dangerous, in that they continue to threaten rupture of the aneurysm. Every effort must be made, therefore, to resolve these endoleaks before termination of the initial procedure. Proximal type I endoleak is associated with a high risk of early postoperative rupture. If it persists despite additional balloon expansion, it can usually be resolved either by placement of an aortic extension cuff closer to the lowest renal artery (Fig. 101-6) or by application of a balloon-expandable "giant" Palmaz stent within the endograft at the level of the neck. When the initial patient selection has been appropriate, complete exclusion of the aneurysm sac can be achieved with these additional procedures in most cases. However, if a type I endoleak cannot be resolved by these means, consideration must be given to conversion to open repair. Occasionally,

Table 101-2   Classification of Endoleak

CLASSIFICATION	ALTERNATIVE TERMS	FORMS	THERAPEUTIC
Type I endoleak	Attachment endoleak Perigraft channel Perigraft leak Graft-related endoleak	Proximal graft attachment zone Distal attachment zone	Proximal or distal extension or cuff Embolization Secondary endograft Open repair (conversion)
Type II endoleak	Retrograde endoleak Collateral flow Branch endoleak	Patent lumbar artery Patent inferior mesenteric artery Patent intercostal artery Others (accessory renal artery, internal iliac, subclavian, etc.)	Conservative Coil embolization Laparoscopic clip application
Type III endoleak	Fabric tear Modular disconnection	Midgraft fabric tear Contralateral stump disconnection	Secondary endograft
Type IV endoleak	Porosity	Graft wall fabric porosity Suture holes	Conservative
Endoleak of undefined origin Endotension	Endopressure Pressure-leak Pseudo-endoleak	High pressure in sac, but no endoleak shown Thrombotic seal	Secondary endograft Open repair Others?

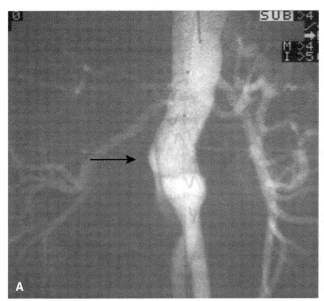

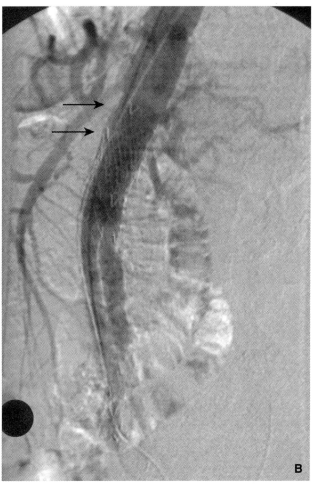

FIGURE 101-6 **A,** Proximal endoleak after stent-graft treatment (*arrow*). **B,** Secondary sealing with use of an extension cuff (*arrows*).

application of a ligature around the neck of the aneurysm, or "external banding," may seal the endoleak without the necessity for explantation of the endograft.[92] In most cases, however, the endograft must be replaced with a conventionally sutured graft.

Use of Endovascular Aneurysm Repair in High-Risk Patients

A substantial number of patients with AAA are excluded from treatment by open operation because they are not fit for major surgery.[93,94] The proportion of patients rejected for open surgical treatment may be as high as 30%,[95] and this figure reflects, primarily, the high incidence of cardiorespiratory co-morbidity associated with AAA. EVAR is an attractive option for many of these patients, and several series have reported high rates of clinical success with an acceptably low incidence of perioperative complications and death.[49,54,82,83,96] The 30-day mortality rates in these high-risk patients have varied from 4.9% to 8%; in the same studies, the 30-day mortality rates for low-risk patients ranged from 0.4% to 2%.[49,72,97]

Using a decision analysis model, Schermerhorn and colleagues[98] demonstrated that the greatest potential benefit of EVAR over open aneurysm treatment (expressed in quality-adjusted life years) may be in older patients for whom surgery poses a higher risk, whereas in younger and "good-risk" patients, open surgery may be the better option.[98] However, the differences in outcome between the two treatment modalities were small in this analysis. A study reported by the EUROSTAR investigators concluded that EVAR improves the survival of high-risk patients, provided that they do not die from the effects of their co-morbid conditions within the first year after treatment. This conclusion depended on a number of assumptions about the rupture rate of untreated aneurysms.[72] A randomized controlled trial comparing noninterventional management with EVAR in high-risk patients (the EVAR 2 Trial) is currently being performed in the United Kingdom and is anticipated to provide more reliable evidence of efficacy in due course.

■ INTERMEDIATE AND LATE RESULTS

Postoperative Follow-up

It is now understood that the configuration of the vascular anatomy, especially the diameter and length of the aneurysm sac, the diameter of the proximal neck, and the diameter and tortuosity of the iliac arteries, may change significantly

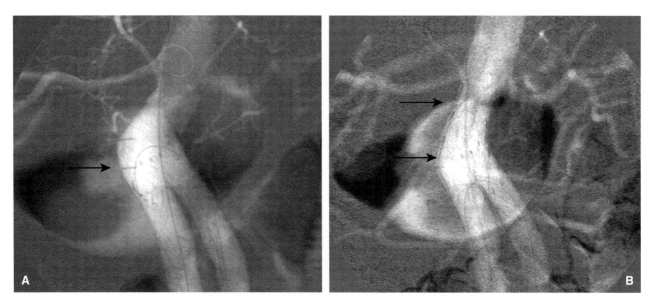

FIGURE 101-7 A, Proximal device migration (*arrow*). **B,** Proximal attachment secured by using extension cuff (*arrows*).

after EVAR. These morphologic changes may occur in response to (1) successful exclusion and, therefore, depressurization with shrinkage of the aneurysm sac, (2) incomplete exclusion with continued pressurization and expansion of the sac, (3) continued aneurysmal degeneration of adjacent segments, or (4) the internal radial force exerted by the fixation stent on the proximal neck. The position and configuration of the implanted endograft may be subject to changes also, either in response to the changes in the vascular anatomy or independently of them. These evolutions may have a significant effect on the late performance of the device and the durability of the repair.

A growing number of investigators have reported aneurysm rupture after treatment with the endovascular technique.[18,99-101] These have mostly involved earlier devices, but not exclusively. Therefore, vigilant postoperative surveillance with clinical examination, ultrasonography, plain abdominal radiographic studies, and CT is mandatory, with the object of identifying the aneurysm at continued risk.[69,102] An expanding sac is the main indicator of high risk, whereas shrinking of the sac is reassuring evidence that complete exclusion has been achieved successfully. Sequential recordings, at intervals, of the maximum aneurysm diameter on CT are the method most commonly used for follow-up. A diameter change of 5 mm is considered significant.[69] Computation of the volume of the sac is a more sensitive indicator of expansion or shrinkage, but because it takes considerably longer and requires special skills and facilities, this method is generally reserved for cases in which accurate knowledge of the evolution of aneurysm morphology is critical.[69,103] There is a good correlation between diameter and volume measurements, and the former is generally accepted as adequate for routine surveillance.

Stent-Graft Migration

Stent-graft migration is an important complication of EVAR that is recognized to be associated with late aneurysm

rupture, proximal endoleak, graft kinking, and graft limb thrombosis.[104,105] Movement of the endograft occurs when the displacement forces on the endograft exceed the strength of fixation at the proximal and distal attachment zones. With early generations of endografts, migration was a frequent event, the incidence of which increased progressively with time. The cumulative rate of migration in these older series was as high as 75% after 7 years of follow-up.[66,106] Displacement of the device from the proximal neck is the most worrisome type of migration with the greatest potential for sac rupture (Fig. 101-7). Improvements in graft design and technology have addressed this issue in a number of ways, including stronger columnar support, increased radial force exerted by self-expanding stents, hooks, barbs, and suprarenal fixation. Another factor with favorable impact on this issue is the tendency of clinicians to oversize the stent-graft relative to the proximal neck by 20% or more rather than the 5% to 10% originally advocated. When commercial devices first became available, the incidence of clinically significant migration of the proximal stent (> 5 mm distal movement) decreased to 3.0%, and in one study relating to a second-generation endograft, evidence of clinically significant migration was observed in just 1.0% of cases at 2 years after operation.[60,107]

Opinions about the mechanisms of late migration vary. Some investigators have reported progressive enlargement of the aneurysm neck and claim that this process may destabilize fixation. Patients with larger aneurysms appear to be at significantly higher risk from neck dilatation.[108,109] Conversely, May and associates[110] have presented evidence to suggest that endografts positioned correctly immediately below the renal arteries may protect the infrarenal aortic segment from further dilatation in a manner that does not occur after open repair of AAA. There is agreement, however, that careful patient selection, exclusion of aneurysms with necks that are excessively angulated or too short, and accurate placement of the graft adjacent to the renal arteries help to minimize the risk of distal migration.[109,111] As a general principle, maximal overlapping of all potentially diseased arterial segments within the acknowledged anatomic boundaries—renal arteries proximally and common iliac bifurcations distally—should be the aim.

There are reasons to suspect that stent-graft migration can lead to sudden loss of "seal" with immediately disastrous consequences. Therefore, secondary intervention, usually by placement of an extension cuff, should be undertaken sooner rather than later when migration has been identified. Plain abdominal radiography, undertaken according to a standardized protocol, is an excellent method to detect migration. Lateral projections are most valuable, with the bone landmarks of the spine used as reference points.[112] CT also is able to depict migration, especially with orthogonal reformatting of images (see Chapter 20).

Late Endoleaks and Endotension

One of the unresolved concerns about EVAR is uncertainty about the long-term effects of persisting blood flow within the aneurysm sac from type II endoleaks. The purpose of EVAR is to prevent rupture of the aneurysm, and early identification of endoleaks is intended to help achieve this goal. Protocols for managing the different types of endoleak have been suggested (see Table 101-2),[113] and treatment of this complication represents the most common reason for readmission of patients after EVAR.

Positive preoperative predictive factors for endoleak include wide neck diameter, large aneurysm size, severe angulation of the infrarenal neck, patency of the IMA, and either no thrombus or a small volume of thrombus in the aneurysm sac. Approximately 20% of patients experience an endoleak at some time during follow-up. Of these endoleaks, 7% are present at the time of the first CT examination 1 month after operation, and the remaining 13% develop later.[111,114-116]

There is good evidence that graft-related endoleaks (types I and III) and collateral endoleaks (type II) behave differently, with significantly different consequences for the outcome of the primary treatment.[115] In one study, the incidence of expansion of the aneurysm at 2 years after surgery was significantly higher in patients with type I and type III endoleaks than in those with type II endoleaks and those with no endoleak. Furthermore, the rate of late rupture during follow-up was significantly higher, at 3.4% after follow-up of 1 to 72 months (mean 15.4 months), in patients in whom graft-related endoleaks had been detected at some stage after operation, even if treated, than in those with type II collateral endoleaks, in whom the incidence of rupture was just 0.5%. The cumulative rates of freedom from rupture in patients with different endoleaks are presented in Figure 101-8. Secondary interventions were more often required in patients with types I and III endoleaks and the secondary clinical success rate was, therefore, lower.[115]

There is general agreement about the need for secondary intervention in patients in whom graft-related endoleaks are identified, but controversy remains about the most appropriate management of type II endoleaks. Coil embolization of the feeding branch, by catheter techniques, or direct puncture of the aneurysm sac, have been used.[117,118,122] Alternative techniques include laparoscopic clipping of

feeding branches, injection of thrombin-polymer, and placement of a thrombogenic sponge within the sac to induce aneurysm thrombosis. However, because very few clinical consequences of type II endoleak have been described to date, most physicians adopt a policy of observation and intervene only if the aneurysm is expanding.[119-122]

Endotension is persistent or recurrent pressurization of the aneurysm sac after EVAR. The term is usually applied to describe continued expansion of the aneurysm in absence of a discernible endoleak.[69] However, according to another definition, endotension is pressurization of the sac with or without a detectable endoleak, the point being that it is pressure rather than blood flow within the sac that leads to rupture and that pressure is therefore the dominant factor.[81] Endotension in the absence of detectable endoleak has been attributed to missed endoleak, thrombosed endoleak, and diffusion of fluid or blood through the fabric of the endograft. The absence of a detectable cause poses considerable therapeutic problems. If further in-depth investigation, including arteriography, fails to identify any endoleak, the physician must decide whether or not to offer the patient open surgical repair of the aneurysm. Direct translumbar measurement of sac pressure may assist this decision. A finding of a mean pressure close to systemic arterial pressure with a pulsatile waveform is a strong indication for intervention; conversely, low pressure and no pulsation are supportive of continued observation. In a report from the EUROSTAR registry on 2463 patients, endotension was identified in 97 patients (3.7%), of whom only 3 (3.3%) underwent open repair.[123]

Time-Related Alterations in Stent-Grafts

Although a shrinking aneurysm sac is considered to be evidence of depressurization of the sac and therefore a good sign, this phenomenon can also cause late adverse problems affecting the endograft. Kinking or buckling of the limbs leading to occlusion or migration and disconnection of

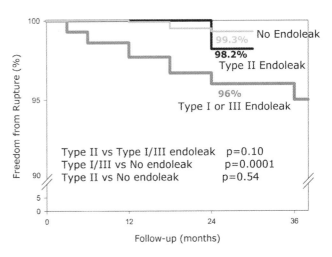

FIGURE 101-8 Freedom from aneurysm rupture after endovascular aneurysm repair in patients categorized according to endoleak: with isolated type II endoleak, with type I or type III endoleak, and without endoleak. (From Van Marrewijk C, Buth J, Harris PL, et al: Significance of endoleaks after endovascular repair of abdominal aortic aneurysms: The EUROSTAR experience. J Vasc Surg 35:461-473, 2002.)

the modular parts of the device have been attributed to shrinking of the sac, notably in its longitudinal axis.[124,125] Devices with relatively long limbs and short bodies are particularly vulnerable to these complications, which are therefore seen much less frequently with modern "long-bodied" endografts.

Another important cause of delayed failure of EVAR is structural failure of the endovascular device itself. Material fatigue, leading to breakdown of the mechanical components of the endograft, has unfortunately been a common feature of the earliest commercial endografts. Reports of structural deterioration of early devices appeared in increasing numbers during the late 1990s, and in a number of cases, this finding led to temporary or permanent withdrawal of a device.[126-128] Stent fractures are caused by stress fatigue, whereas fabric tears and erosions result from friction between the metallic stent and the fabric. Not infrequently, stent fractures are followed by breach of the fabric. They can also result in separation of rows of stents and partial migration of the device.

Angulation or kinking of the stent, either during difficult deployment or due to the shrinking process of the excluded aneurysm (as described previously), may raise the risk of stent fracture.[124,129] Fractures were first identified in devices that had been explanted after evidence of endoleak or aneurysm growth.[129,130] There are no associated symptoms until the integrity of the device is breached, at which point rupture may be imminent. Therefore, meticulous postoperative surveillance involving appropriate imaging is essential. Stent fractures and other types of disruption of the metal frame are best seen on plain abdominal radiographs.[102,131] Fabric tears or erosions result in type III endoleaks, which are apparent on contrast-enhanced CT scans.

Manufacturers have recognized and responded to many of the mechanisms of device failure. Improvement in corrosion resistance was achieved by a number of processes, including electropolishing and chemical etching of the metal surface.[132] Stronger fabrics are also being used, and mechanisms have been found to eliminate or reduce friction between components constructed from different materials. Therefore, there is optimism that this type of problem will be much less common in the second- and third-generation devices.[133]

Secondary Interventions Including Late Conversion to Open Repair

Despite the considerable progress that has been made with respect to the technologic and clinical aspects of EVAR, patients treated by this method today remain exposed to a small risk of rupture of the aneurysm. The risk for patients treated previously with earlier generations of endografts is considerably higher. For this reason, lifelong surveillance is mandatory to identify those at risk with a view to secondary intervention. Risk factors for rupture include endoleak, stent-graft migration, and expansion of the aneurysm. Other indications for secondary intervention are kinking, stenosis, and thrombosis of the limbs of the endograft.

In a EUROSTAR study, the cumulative overall rate of reintervention was almost 10% per year.[8] This constitutes a significant additional burden for the patient as well as for health care resources. Thus, the need for secondary inter-

ventions is an important indicator of intermediate and long-term success after EVAR. These interventions can be classified according to their extent as transabdominal surgery with or without preservation of the endograft, femorofemoral bypass, and transfemoral endovascular interventions. There were considerable differences in the frequency with which these different categories of reintervention were undertaken in the EUROSTAR series.

Of late transabdominal procedures, the majority consisted of conversion, with open banding of the neck or iliofemoral bypass being performed only sporadically. Late conversion was most often undertaken for endoleak, migration of the device, or rupture. Other reasons for conversion were device failures in the form of fabric damage and disruption of the metal frame with or without stent fractures. Structural disintegration was usually an independent finding on the CT or plain abdominal radiograph without any clinically relevant events. Secondary femorofemoral crossover bypass was invariably undertaken for unilateral iliac limb occlusion.

Transfemoral procedures constituted the most frequently performed secondary interventions. These procedures consisted of aortic or iliac limb extensions and stent-graft interposition for migration, modular dislocation, or endoleak. Angioplasty with or without stent placement and thrombolysis were performed for thrombosis or stenosis and kinking of the endograft. Coil embolization was performed for side-branch endoleak.[19,134,135]

Rupture after Endovascular Aneurysm Repair

Rupture of the aneurysm, the ultimate, unequivocal failure of EVAR, has been reported anecdotally and in a small number of series of patients, including the EUROSTAR registry. The incidence of rupture after endograft placement varies from 0.2% to 1% annually, depending on whether the studies were conducted in single or multiple institutions.[105,136-140] Frequently identified causes of rupture include migration, modular disconnection, endoleak, and fabric erosion, all previously described. Modular disconnection was identified as the mechanism responsible for 5 out of 47 ruptures reported in the literature and analyzed by Bernhard and colleagues.[138] Post-EVAR rupture is most commonly managed by emergency open conversion, but successful secondary endovascular grafting has been reported. It has been suggested that post-EVAR rupture of the AAA may be associated with a lower mortality than primary aneurysm rupture, because the presence of an endograft would offer some protection against rapid hemorrhage.[141] This assumption was not confirmed by other studies, in which secondary surgical repair for rupture resulted in a mortality rate of 50%.[138,142]

Conditions Associated with Increased Complication Rate After Endovascular Aneurysm Repair

Although complex anatomy at the attachment sites remains the principal cause of complications after EVAR, certain other conditions relating to the patient, the device, and the size of the aneurysm have been recognized as important determinants of outcome.

Female gender has an adverse influence on outcomes. A higher rejection rate of women for EVAR on the grounds of adverse anatomy has been described. Despite this, EVAR in women is associated with a relatively high incidence of technical problems at the time of the procedure. In addition, the frequency of late adverse events, including limb thrombosis and type I endoleak, is higher.[71,143-145] The higher complication rate in women has been attributed to a less favorable anatomy of the aortic neck, including angulation and a shorter and wider neck, as well as to smaller-diameter iliac arteries.

Specific device designs may influence the incidence of some clinical adverse events. Device limb occlusions are significantly more common in endografts in which the body and limbs are unsupported by stents. Type I endoleak was observed more frequently with PTFE-lined devices without suprarenal bare stent fixation.[146] In one EUROSTAR study, a lower rate of aneurysm-related death was observed in patients treated with modern devices than in those in whom earlier generations of devices were used.[147] The difference was attributable to a lower incidence of late complications and a smaller requirement for secondary intervention.

Finally, the initial size of the AAA affects EVAR in various ways. Larger-diameter aneurysms are less likely to have favorable anatomy at the neck. Therefore, they can be treated by EVAR less often. The necks tend to be wider, shorter, and more angulated than those of smaller aneurysms.[37,108,111,148] In addition, there is a positive correlation between the size of an aneurysm and the incidence of preoperative co-morbidities.[97,147] In the EUROSTAR series, the results after 4 years were significantly less favorable in patients with large and medium-sized aneurysms with respect to death, both related and unrelated to the aneurysm, in comparison with results in patients with smaller

aneurysms.[147] The risk of late rupture was also significantly higher in patients with large aneurysms (Fig. 101-9). From these observations, which are in agreement with those of other studies,[149] it can be concluded that the outcome after endovascular repair of AAA is influenced strongly by the preoperative size of the aneurysm. The results appear superior in patients with small aneurysms and less favorable in patients with larger aneurysms. However, the relative benefit of EVAR for patients with large aneurysms is likely to be just as great as that for those with smaller aneurysms.

Meta-Analyses Comparing the Outcome of Endovascular Aneurysm Repair and Open Surgery; Aneurysm-Related Death

Currently available information from comparative but nonrandomized studies suffers from selection bias. Patients deemed to be at high risk from open operation tend to be selected for EVAR, and patients with anatomic contraindications to EVAR are offered open surgery. One should bear this issue of selection bias in mind when reviewing the results of two meta-analyses comparing the outcome of open and endovascular repair.[70,75] In these studies, a significant difference in outcome in favor of EVAR was found with respect to operative blood loss, intensive care unit and hospital stay, the total number of complications, the incidence of systemic or remote complications, and 30-day mortality. Relatively inferior outcomes in patients treated by endovascular technique were noted with respect to graft failure and the need for secondary interventions. No difference was found between the groups with respect to 2-year survival.

The concept of aneurysm-related death as an important outcome event was introduced by Arko and colleagues.[150] In series from their own institution, these investigators documented 3-year cumulative aneurysm-related death rates of 1% for EVAR and 6% for open repair. This difference did not reach statistical significance ($P = .06$). The conclusions of both the meta-analysis and the single-center series were that endovascular repair mandated long-term surveillance and that prospective randomized trials were required to establish the value of this approach in comparison with the conventional operation.

■ EMERGENCY ENDOVASCULAR REPAIR OF ACUTE OR RUPTURED ABDOMINAL AORTIC ANEURYSMS

Emergency endovascular repair of acute symptomatic or ruptured AAA has received little attention compared with the immense interest in EVAR for elective AAA. This is surprising, because the gain in overall survival and reduction of costs might be relatively larger with EVAR than with open surgery After the first reported emergency case in 1994,[151] it was some time before several small series involving selected patients were reported.[152-155] In these studies, aorto-uni-iliac endografts were used. Some groups described the use of intra-aortic occlusion balloons introduced from the axillary artery to assist the management of hemodynamically unstable patients. The early mortality

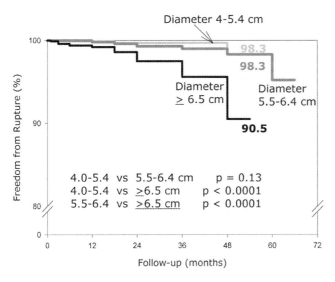

FIGURE 101-9 Cumulative freedom from rupture after endovascular aneurysm repair in patients with aneurysms measuring 4 to 5.4 cm, 5.5 to 6.4 cm, and more than 6.5 cm. (From Ouriel K, Clair DG, Greenberg RK, et al: Endovascular repair of abdominal aortic aneurysms: Device-specific outcome. J Vasc Surg 37:991-998, 2003.)

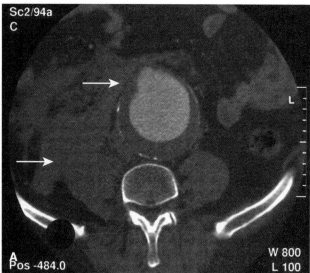

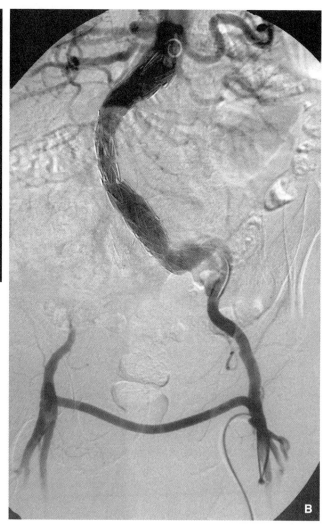

FIGURE 101-10 A, CT of ruptured AAA subsequently treated with endovascular aneurysm repair. *Small arrow* indicates site of rupture, and *bold arrow* indicates retroperitoneal hematoma. **B,** Postoperative angiogram after aorto-uni-iliac endografting and femorofemoral bypass.

rates were 6% and 24% in two of the reports.[152,155] In the two other reports, patient numbers were too small for meaningful reporting of mortality rates. Subsequently, other groups reported the use of bifurcated stent-grafts for treatment of acute aneurysms with low mortality rates.[156-158] However, a common feature of these studies was that only selected patients were treated with emergency EVAR. Many patients presenting during the study period were treated with conventional open surgery.

Preoperative CT is useful for ascertaining whether emergency EVAR is feasible and for measuring anatomic dimensions (Fig. 101-10). Obtaining such an evaluation, however, may involve potentially unacceptable treatment delay in critically ill patients. Prompt availability of CT facilities for emergency cases is an important requirement for an institution that intends to perform emergency EVAR. Other important logistical issues relate to the availability of both the necessary multidisciplinary team out of hours and at short notice and of a stock of appropriately sized devices.

At this point, it can certainly be concluded that EVAR is a feasible option for patients with ruptured or acutely symptomatic AAA. However, questions remain as to whether wide application of this treatment will reduce the currently very high overall mortality from ruptured AAAs. Estimates of the applicability of EVAR based on the anatomy of the aortoiliac segment, vary from 50% to 62% in patients with true rupture of an aneurysm.[159,160] Although it is likely that comparatively low early mortality can be achieved with endovascular management, it is possible that because their vascular anatomy is unsuitable, the mortality rate for patients treated by conventional emergency operation will be proportionally higher and there may be no improvement of overall mortality. Large-scale multicenter studies are needed to answer this question.

■ THORACIC AORTIC STENT-GRAFT REPAIR

Elective endovascular treatment repair of thoracic aortic disease has been applied to a variety of conditions, including degenerative aneurysm, pseudoaneurysm, chronic dissection, and infected or mycotic aneurysms. Emergency indications for stent-graft treatment have included ruptured

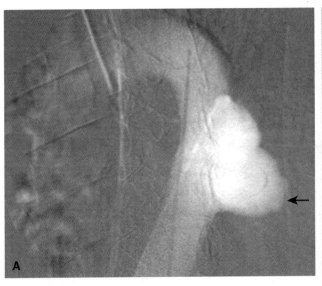

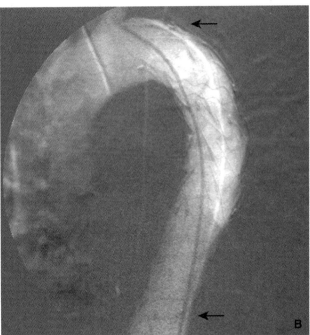

FIGURE 101-11 A, Ruptured aneurysm of the descending thoracic aorta (*arrow*). **B,** Angiogram after stent-graft repair; *arrows* indicate proximal and distal extensions of stent-grafted segment.

aneurysm, traumatic aortic tear from blunt chest trauma, and acute manifestations of type B aortic dissection or its precursors, intramural hematoma and penetrating aortic ulcer. This review considers degenerative aneurysms only, because the role of endovascular management in the treatment of aortic dissections is discussed in Chapter 104.

Elective Repair of Thoracic Aortic Aneurysm

The lower incidence of TAA in comparison with AAA has resulted in slower development and less widespread experience with endovascular procedures to treat TAA. The minimally invasive EVAR of thoracic aneurysms, especially those affecting the descending aorta, is a particularly attractive option because it avoids the dangerous sequelae of thoracotomy, aortic cross-clamping, and left heart bypass associated with open repair (Fig. 101-11). The application rate of stent-graft repair in a series of diverse pathologic conditions of the descending thoracic aorta was as high as 57% in one series.[161] The possibility of using this technique in older patients who are poor candidates for surgery and therefore would not be considered for open repair may increase its applicability significantly. Given the higher prevalence of poor-risk patients in endovascular series, the perioperative mortality associated with endovascular repair of descending aortic aneurysms, which ranges from 3.5% to 12.5%,[161-164] cannot simply be compared with the results of open surgery, in which mortality rates of approximately 10% are reported.

Patient selection is based primarily on spiral CT angiography findings. Suitability for endografting depends on the presence or absence of adequate anchoring and sealing zones proximal and distal to the aortic lesions. The availability of an access route for introducing the thoracic stent-graft to the TAA via the femoral artery, iliac artery, or

abdominal aorta should be ascertained. Often, angiography catheters are introduced via an axillary artery for injection of contrast agent or to serve as a marker for the origin of the left subclavian artery. Details of the endograft procedure are discussed in Chapter 52.

Postoperative Complications

The incidence of spinal cord ischemia and paraplegia after endovascular repair of TAAs has been consistently low, even in patients in whom long aortic segments and the "danger zone" (T9 to L1) that usually gives origin to the anterior spinal artery have been covered by the endograft. The risk of spinal complications has ranged from 0 to 6%.[161,163-168] Avoidance of both clamping of the proximal thoracic aorta and prolonged episodes of hypotension may account for the low incidence of spinal problems. One group has observed that simultaneous open infrarenal aortic replacement and endovascular thoracic repair is associated with a higher incidence of paraplegia,[165] so this combination of procedures should be avoided if possible. This finding indicates that the abdominal aorta is an important source of collateral blood supply to the spinal cord after occlusion of the artery of Adamkiewicz. Other investigators have observed that the incidence of neurologic deficit rises linearly with the length of thoracic aorta covered by the stent-graft.[164]

Endoleak after stent-graft treatment of descending TAAs is relatively infrequent and is usually related to graft fixation (type I endoleak). Type II endoleaks are relatively uncommon.[164] Late migration of the endoprosthesis occurs with an incidence of 0 to 30%, the higher rates associated with the use of early designs of thoracic endografts and multiple overlapping or "tromboned slide" endografts.[163,164,169] However, migration occurs also with modern endografts, and this complication is attributed to the high force of blood flow within the thoracic aorta. There is a tendency for thoracic stent-grafts to kink in the center of the aneurysm, where such devices have no lateral support. As a result, the proximal part of the endograft may be pulled downward into the aneurysm, especially if the proximal attachment zone is short. Most researchers recommend a sealing zone of at least 2 cm in the thoracic aorta, which is rather more than the minimum considered necessary for AAA endograft repair.[161,163,170]

Adjunctive Procedures

When stent-graft attachment is required in proximity to the left subclavian artery, it is acceptable to cover the origin of this vessel to extend the length of neck available for fixation and seal in endovascular repair of TAAs. However, opinions differ about the need for extra-anatomic revascularization of the subclavian artery under these circumstances. There is potential for complications to develop in association with a possible retrograde endoleak via the subclavian artery and from ischemic symptoms of the left arm and hand. We are aware of two patients in whom stroke related to obstructed inflow into the vertebral artery developed after the left subclavian artery origin was covered with a thoracic stent-graft. In both cases the right vertebral artery was obstructed by preexisting disease. In recognition of this risk, some groups routinely perform transposition of the left subclavian artery to the common carotid artery (Fig. 101-12).[163,165,167,168] Other groups, however, simply cover the subclavian artery, provided that the right vertebral artery is patent, and reserve later extra-anatomic reconstruction for the few patients in whom symptoms develop.[171] Detailed preoperative imaging of the supra-aortic arteries is essential if this latter policy is to be followed.

Adjunctive reconstructions to revascularize the other supra-aortic arteries are needed when more extensive covering of the aortic arch is required during EVAR of TAAs. Although direct antegrade bypass to the left common carotid artery and the subclavian artery from the ascending thoracic aorta has been performed, extra-anatomic cervical procedures may be as effective and also avoid sternotomy.[172,173] Criado and associates[173] have described their experience with eight patients in whom disconnection and revascularization of different combinations of supra-aortic branches was performed via cervical approaches before placement of the stent-graft encroached into the aortic arch (Fig. 101-13).[173] Most of these patients had comorbidities that made open surgical reconstruction an unattractive option. In this small series, there were no instances of postoperative neurologic deficit.

Emergency Thoracic Endograft Repair

Endovascular repair offers a minimally invasive alternative to conventional surgery in patients with thoracic aortic rupture. With emergency thoracotomy as the only therapeutic option, the early mortality rate is approximately 50%.[174-176] Avoidance of open thoracotomy and aortic cross-clamping is of major benefit in these patients, who are often hemodynamically very unstable and, if the rupture was traumatic, may have multiple injuries. Semba and co-workers[177] were the first to report successful endovascular

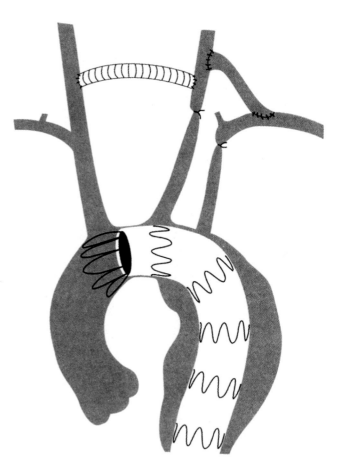

FIGURE 101-12 Diagram of revascularization of the left carotid artery to extend the sealing zone for the stent-graft in stent-graft repair of an aortic arch aneurysm. (From Criado FJ, Clarck NS, Barnatan MF: Stent-graft repair in the aortic arch and descending thoracic aorta: A 4-year experience. J Vasc Surg 36:1121-1128; 2002.)

management of acute thoracic aortic rupture; only 2 of their 11 patients died in association with the procedure. Others have reported similar rates of early mortality (9% to 20%) as well as paraplegia rates of 0 to 7.7%.[161,176,178] None of these reports differentiated between ruptured TAA and other emergency conditions. Data compiled from a number of separate reports show that emergency EVAR for traumatic rupture of the thoracic aorta is associated with mortality rates ranging from 0 to 9.1% and no paraplegia in a total of 34 patients.[179-182]

CONCLUSION

Accumulating experience with TAA stent-graft repair indicates that it presents an effective alternative to open repair in an emergency as well as in the elective setting. Although durability of stent-grafts in TAA repair must be assessed after longer follow-up, early survival and complication rates compare very favorably with those for open repair. Given the relatively high risks associated with thoracotomy for some patients, there may well prove to be a bigger advantage for EVAR over open surgery for TAA than for AAA in the future. At present, endograft repair may be considered the procedure of choice for emergency treatment

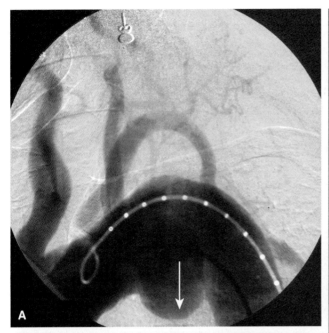

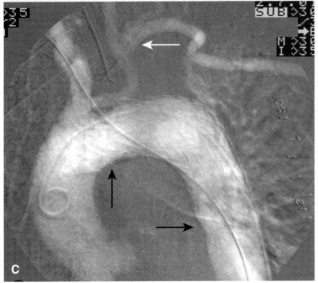

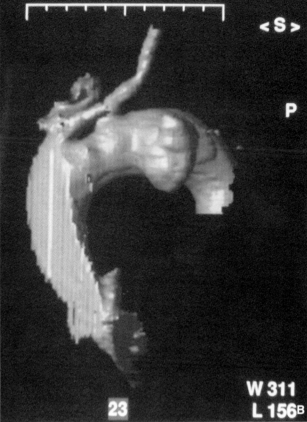

FIGURE 101-13 **A,** Saccular aneurysm (*arrow*) of the aortic arch in proximity to the left subclavian artery. A calibrated angiography catheter was used to assess the distance between the aneurysm and the left subclavian and left carotid arteries. **B,** Three-dimensional magnetic resonance angiographic reconstruction of a saccular aneurysm, left lateral view. **C,** Angiogram after subclavian–carotid transposition (*white arrow*) and stent-graft repair (*black arrows*).

of traumatic rupture of the thoracic aorta, especially in patients with multiple injuries.

■ REFERENCES

1. Blankensteijn JD, Lindenburg FP, Van der Graaf Y, Eikelboom BC: Influence of study design on reported mortality and morbidity rates after abdominal aortic aneurysm repair. Br J Surg 85:1624-1630, 1998.

2. Williamson W, Nicoloff A, Taylor L, et al: Functional outcome after open repair of abdominal aortic aneurysm. J Vasc Surg 33:913-920, 2001.

3. Kouchoukos NT, Dougenis D: Surgery of thoracic aorta. N Engl J Med 26:1876-1888, 1997.

4. May J, White GH, Yu W, et al: Endoluminal grafting of abdominal aortic aneurysms: Causes of failure and their prevention. J Endovasc Surg 1:44-52, 1994.

5. Moore WS, Vescera CL: Repair of abdominal aortic aneurysm by transfemoral endovascular graft placement. Ann Surg 220:331-341, 1994.

6. Yusuf SW, Baker DM, Chuter TA, et al: Transfemoral endoluminal repair of abdominal aortic aneurysm with bifurcated graft. Lancet 344:650-651, 1994.

7. Blum U, Voshage G, Lammer J, et al: Endoluminal stent-grafts for infrarenal abdominal aortic aneurysms. N Engl J Med 336:13-20, 1997.

8. Laheij RJ, Buth J, Harris PL, et al: Need for secondary interventions after endovascular repair of abdominal aortic aneurysm: Intermediate-term follow-up results of a European collaborative registry (EUROSTAR). Br J Surg 87:166-173, 2000.

9. Carpenter JP, Baum RA, Barker CF, et al: Durability of benefits of endovascular versus conventional abdominal aortic aneurysm repair. J Vasc Surg 35:222-228, 2002.

10. Mortality results from randomised controlled trial of early selective surgery or ultrasonographic surveillance for small abdominal aortic aneurysms. The UK Small Aneurysm Trial Participants. Lancet 352:1649-1655, 1998.

11. Lederle FA, Wilson SE, Johnson GR, et al: Immediate repair compared with surveillance of small abdominal aortic aneurysms. N Engl J Med 346:1437-1444, 2002.

12. Finlayson SR, Birkmeyer JD, Fillinger MF, Cronenwett JL: Should endovascular surgery lower the threshold for repair of abdominal aortic aneurysms? J Vasc Surg 29:973-985, 1999.

13. Balko A, Piasecki GJ, Shah DM, et al: Transfemoral placement of intraluminal polyurethane prosthesis for abdominal aortic aneurysm. J Surg Res 40:305-309, 1986.

14. Lawrence DD, Charnsangavey C, Wright KC, et al: Percutaneous endovascular graft: Experimental evaluation. Radiology 163:357-360, 1987.

15. Volodos NL, Shekhanin VE, Karpovitch IP: Distant endo replacement of the aorta and iliac arteries (abstract). All Union Conference, Irkutsk, 1985;11:163.

16. Parodi JC, Palmaz JC, Barone HD: Transfemoral intraluminal graft implantation for abdominal aortic aneurysm. Ann Vasc Surg 5:491-499, 1991.

17. Alimi YS, Chakfe N, Rivoal E, et al: Rupture of an abdominal aortic aneurysm after endovascular graft placement and aneurysm size reduction. J Vasc Surg 28:178-183, 1998.

18. Politz JK, Newman VS, Stewart MT: Late abdominal aortic aneurysm rupture after AneuRx repair: A report of three cases. J Vasc Surg 31:599-606, 2000.

19. Fairman RM, Baum RA, Carpenter JP, et al: Limb interventions in patients undergoing treatment with an unsupported bifurcated aortic endograft system: A review of the phase II EVT trial. J Vasc Surg 36:118-126, 2002.

20. Becquemin JP, Poussier B, Allaire E, et al: Endograft fabric disintegration simulating a type II endoleak. J Endovasc Ther 9:203-207, 2002.

21. Lobato AC, Quick RC, Vaughn PL, et al: Transrenal fixation of aortic endografts: Intermediate follow-up of a single-center experience. J Endovasc Ther 7:273-278, 2000.

22. Burks JA, Faries PL, Gravereaux EC, et al: Endovascular repair of abdominal aortic aneurysms: Stent-graft fixation across the visceral arteries. J Vasc Surg 35:109-113, 2002.

23. Bove PG, Long GW, Shanley CJ, et al: Transrenal fixation of endovascular stent-grafts for infrarenal aortic aneurysm repair: Mid-term results. J Vasc Surg 37:938-942, 2003.

24. Lau LL, Hakaim AG, Oldenburg WA, et al: Effect of suprarenal versus infrarenal aortic endograft fixation on renal function and renal artery patency: A comparative study with intermediate follow-up. J Vasc Surg 37:1162-1168, 2003.

25. Browne TF, Hartley D, Purchas S, et al: A fenestrated covered suprarenal aortic stent. Eur J Vasc Endovasc Surg 18:445-449, 1999.

26. Anderson JL, Berce M, Hartley DE: Endoluminal aortic grafting with renal and superior mesenteric artery incorporation by graft fenestration. J Endovasc Ther 8:3-15, 2001.

27. Greenberg R, Haulon S, Turc A, et al: Primary endovascular repair of juxtarenal aneurysms with fenestrated endovascular grafting. Eur J Vasc Endovasc Surg 27:484-491, 2004.

28. Wisselink W, Abruzzo FM, Shin CK, et al: Endoluminal repair of aneurysms containing ostia of essential branch arteries: An experimental model. J Endovasc Surg 6:171-179, 1999.

29. Hosakawa H, Iwase T, Sato M, et al: Successful endovascular repair of juxtarenal and suprarenal aortic aneurysms with a branched stent-graft. J Vasc Surg 33:1087-1092, 2001.

30. Chuter TAM, Gordon RL, Reilly LM, et al: An endovascular system for thoracoabdominal aortic aneurysm repair. J Endovasc Ther 8:25-33, 2001.

31. Trout HH 3rd, Tanner HM: A new vascular Endostaple: A technical description. J Vasc Surg 34:565-568, 2001.

32. Beebe HG, Jackson T, Pigott JP: Aortic aneurysm morphology for planning endovascular aortic grafts: Limitations of conventional imaging methods. J Endovasc Surg 2:139-148, 1995.

33. Ingle H, Fiskwick G, Thompson MM, Bell PRF: Endovascular repair of wide neck AAA—preliminary report on feasibility and complications. Eur J Vasc Endovasc Surg 24:123-127, 2002.

34. Gitlitz DB, Ramaswami G, Kaplan D, et al: Endovascular stent-grafting in the presence of aortic neck filling defects: Early clinical experience. J Vasc Surg 33:340-344, 2001.

35. Wolf YG, Hill BB, Lee WA, et al: Eccentric stent-graft compression: An indicator of insecure proximal fixation of aortic stent-graft. J Vasc Surg 33:481-487, 2001.

36. Stanley BM, Semmens JB, Mai Q, et al: Evaluation of patient selection guidelines for endoluminal AAA repair with the Zenith stent-graft: The Australasian experience. J Endovasc Ther 8:457-464, 2001.

37. Carpenter JP, Baum RA, Barker CF, et al: Impact of exclusion criteria on patient selection for endovascular abdominal aortic aneurysm repair. J Vasc Surg 34:1050-1054, 2001.

38. Wolf YG, Fogarty TJ, Olcott C IV, et al: Endovascular repair of abdominal aortic aneurysms: Eligibility rate and impact on the rate of open repair. J Vasc Surg 32:519-523, 2000.

39. Zarins CK, Wolf YG, Hill BB, et al: Will endovascular repair replace open surgery for abdominal aortic aneurysm repair? Ann Surg 232:501-507, 2000.

40. Parlani G, Zannetti S, Verzini F, et al: Does the presence of an iliac aneurysm affect outcome of endoluminal AAA repair? An analysis of 336 cases. Eur J Vasc Endovasc Surg 24:134-138, 2002.

41. Mehta M, Veith FJ, Ohki T, et al: Unilateral and bilateral hypogastric artery interruption during aortoiliac aneurysm repair in 154 patients: A relatively innocuous procedure. J Vasc Surg. 33(Suppl):S27-S32, 2001.

42. Morrissey NJ, Faries PL, Carrocio A, al: Intentional internal iliac artery occlusion in endovascular repair of abdominal aortic aneurysms. J Invasive Cardiol 14:760-763, 2002.

43. Parodi JC, Ferreira M: Relocation of the iliac artery bifurcation to facilitate endoluminal treatment of abdominal aortic aneurysms. J Endovasc Surg 6:342-347, 1999.

44. Kritpracha B, Pigott JP, Russell TE, et al: Bell-bottom aortoiliac endografts: An alternative that preserves pelvic blood flow. J Vasc Surg 35:874-881, 2002.

45. Abu-Ghaida AM, Clair DG, Greenberg RK, et al: Broadening the application of endovascular aneurysm repair: The use of iliac conduits. J Vasc Surg 36:111-117, 2002.

46. Treiman GS, Lawrence FP, Edwards WH Jr, et al: An assessment of the current applicability of the EVT endovascular graft for treatment of patients with an infrarenal abdominal aortic aneurysm. J Vasc Surg 30:68-75, 1999.

47. Armon MP, Yusuf SW, Latief K, et al: Anatomical suitability of abdominal aortic aneurysms for endovascular repair. Br J Surg 84:178-180, 1997.

48. Velazquez OC, Larson RA, Baum RA, et al: Gender-related differences in infrarenal aortic aneurysm morphologic features: Issues relevant to Ancure and Talent endografts. J Vasc Surg 33:S77-S84, 2001.

49. Zannetti S, De Rango P, Parlani G, et al: Endovascular abdominal aortic aneurysm repair in high-risk patients: A single-center experience. Eur J Vasc Endovasc Surg 21:334-338, 2001.

50. May J, White GH, Yu W, et al: Importance of graft configuration in outcome of endoluminal aortic aneurysm repair: A 5-year analysis by the life table method. Eur J Vasc Endovasc Surg 15:406-411, 1998.

51. Faries PL, Biggs VL, Rhee JY, et al: Failure of endovascular aortoaortic tube grafts: A plea for preferential use of bifurcated grafts. J Vasc Surg 35:868-873, 2002.

52. Heijmen RH, Tutein Nolthenius RP, van den Berg JC, et al: A narrow-waisted abdominal aortic aneurysm complicating endovascular repair. J Endovasc Ther 7:198-202, 2000.

53. Brewster DC, Geller SC, Kaufman JA, et al: Initial experience with endovascular aneurysm repair: Comparison of early results with outcome of conventional open repair. J Vasc Surg 27:992-1003, 1998.

54. May J, White GH, Yu W, et al: Concurrent comparison of endoluminal versus open repair in treatment of abdominal aortic aneurysms: Analysis of 303 patients by life table method. J Vasc Surg 27:213-221, 1998.

55. Zarins CK, White RA, Schwarten D, et al: AneuRx stent-graft versus open surgical repair of abdominal aortic aneurysms: Multicenter prospective clinical trial. J Vasc Surg 29:292-308, 1999.

56. Moore WS, Kashyap VS, Vescera CL, Quinones-Baldrich WJ: Abdominal aortic aneurysm: Six-year comparison of endovascular versus transabdominal repair. Ann Surg 230:298-308, 1999.

57. Scharrer-Pamler R, Kapfer X, Orend KH, Sunder-Plassmann L: Endoluminal grafting of infrarenal aortic aneurysms. Thorac Cardiovasc Surg 47:119-121, 1999.

58. Becquemin JP, Bourriez A, D'Audiffret A, et al: Mid-term results of endovascular versus open repair for abdominal aortic aneurysm in patients anatomically suitable for endovascular repair. Eur J Vasc Endovasc Surg 19:656-661, 2000.

59. Cohnert TU, Oedert F, Wahlers T, et al: Matched-pair analysis of conventional versus endoluminal AAA treatment outcomes during the initial phase of an aortic endografting program. J Endovasc Ther 7:94-100, 2000.

60. Matsumura JS, Brewster DC, Makaroun MS, Naftel DC: A multicenter controlled clinical trial of open versus endovascular treatment of abdominal aortic aneurysm. J Vasc Surg 37:262-271, 2003.

61. Chuter TAM, Risberg B, Hopkinson BR, et al: Clinical experience with a bifurcated endovascular graft for abdominal aortic aneurysm repair. J Vasc Surg 24:655-666, 1996.

62. Moore WS, Rutherford RB: Transfemoral endovascular repair of abdominal aortic aneurysms: Results of the North-American EVT phase 1 trial. J Vasc Surg 23:543-553, 1996.

63. May J, White GH, Yu W, et al: Endovascular grafting for abdominal aortic aneurysms: Changing incidents and indications for conversion to open operation. Cardiovasc Surg 6:194-197, 1998.

64. Cuypers PW, Laheij RJ, Buth J: Which factors increase the risk of conversion to open surgery following endovascular abdominal aortic aneurysm repair? Eur J Vasc Endovasc Surg 20:183-189, 2000.

65. Laheij RJF, Van Marrewijk CJ, Buth J, Harris PL; EUROSTAR Collaborators: The influence of team experience on outcomes of endovascular stenting of abdominal aortic aneurysms. Eur J Vasc Endovasc Surg 24:128-133, 2002.

66. Alric P, Hinchcliffe RJ, Wenham PW, et al: Lessons learned from the long-term follow-up of a first-generation aortic stent graft. J Vasc Surg. 37:367-373, 2003.

67. Bockler D, Probst T, Weber H, Raithel D: Surgical conversion after endovascular grafting for abdominal aortic aneurysms. J Endovasc Ther 9:111-118, 2002.

68. Van Marrewijk CJ, Fransen G, Laheij RJF, et al; EUROSTAR Collaborators: Is type II endoleak after EVAR a harbinger of risk? Causes and outcome of open conversion and aneurysm rupture during follow-up. Eur J Vasc Endovasc Surg. In press.

69. Chaikof EL, Blankensteijn JD, Harris PL, et al: Reporting standards for endovascular aortic aneurysm repair. J Vascular Surg 35:1048-1060, 2002.

70. Adriaensen ME, Bosch JL, Halpem EF, et al: Elective endovascular versus open surgical repair of abdominal aortic aneurysms: Systematic review of short-term results. Radiology 224:739-747, 2002.

71. Buth J, Laheij RJ: Early complications and endoleaks after endovascular abdominal aortic aneurysm repair: Report of a multicenter study. J Vasc Surg. 31:134-146, 2000.

72. Buth J, van Marrewijk CJ, Harris PL, et al; EUROSTAR Collaborators: Outcome of endovascular abdominal aortic aneurysm repair in patients with conditions considered unfit for an open procedure: A report on the EUROSTAR experience. J Vasc Surg. 35:211-221, 2002.

73. Malina M, Nilsson M, Brunkwall J, et al: Quality of life before and after endovascular and open repair of asymptomatic AAAs: A prospective study. J Endovasc Ther 7:372-379, 2000.

74. Arko FR, Hill BB, Reeves TR, et al: Early and late functional outcome assessments following endovascular and open aneurysm repair. J Endovasc Ther 10:2-9, 2003.

75. Maher MM, McNamara AM, MacEneaney PM, et al: Abdominal aortic aneurysms: Elective endovascular repair versus conventional surgery—evaluation with evidence-based medicine techniques. Radiology. 228:647-658, 2003.

76. Makaroun MS: The Ancure endografting system: An update. J Vasc Surg 33(Suppl):S129-S134, 2001.

77. Lee WA, Wolf YG, Hill BW, et al: The first 150 endovascular AAA repairs at a single institution: How steep is the learning curve? J Endovasc Ther 9:269-276, 2002.

78. Lobato AC, Rodrigues-Lopez J, Diethrich EB: Learning curve for endovascular abdominal aortic aneurysm repair: Evaluation of a 277-patient single-center experience. J Endovasc Ther 9:262-268, 2002.

79. White GH, Yu W, May J, et al: Endoleak as a complication of endoluminal grafting of abdominal aortic aneurysms: Classification, incidence, diagnosis, and management. J Endovasc Surg 4:152-168, 1997.

80. White GH, May J, Waugh RC, et al: Type III and type IV endoleak: Toward a complete definition of blood flow in the sac after endoluminal AAA repair. J Endovasc Surg 5:305-309, 1998.

81. Gilling Smith G, Brennan J, Harris P, et al: Endotension after endovascular aneurysm repair: Definition, classification, and strategies for surveillance and intervention. J Endovasc Surg 6:305-307, 1999.

82. Mialhe C, Amicabile C, Becquemin JP: Endovascular treatment of infrarenal abdominal aneurysms by the Stentor system: Preliminary results of 79 cases. J Vasc Surg 26:199-209, 1997.

83. Stelter W, Umscheid TH, Ziegler P: Three-year experience with modular stent-graft devices for endovascular AAA treatment. J Endovasc Surg 4:362-369, 1997.

84. Schurink GW, Aarts NJ, Wilde J, et al: Endoleakage after stent-graft treatment of abdominal aneurysms: Implications on pressure imaging: An in vitro study. J Vasc Surg 28:234-241, 1998.

85. Mehta M, Ohki T, Veith FJ, Lipsitz EC: All sealed endoleaks are not the same: A treatment strategy based on an ex-vivo analysis. Eur J Vasc Endovasc Surg 21:541-544, 2001.

86. Baum RA, Carpenter JP, Cope C, et al: Aneurysm sac pressure measurements after endovascular repair of abdominal aortic aneurysms. J Vasc Surg 33:32-41, 2001.

87. Gilling Smith GL, Martin J, Sudhindran S, et al: Freedom from endoleak after endovascular aneurysm repair does not equal treatment success. Eur J Vasc Endovasc Surg 19:421-425, 2000.

88. Vallabhaneni SR, Gilling-Smith GL, Brennan J, et al: Can intrasac pressure monitoring reliably predict failure of endovascular aneurysm repair? J Endovasc Ther 10:524-530, 2003.

89. Chuter T, Ivancev K, Malina M, et al: Aneurysm pressure following endovascular exclusion. Eur J Vasc Endovasc Surg 13:85-87, 1997.

90. Treharne GD, Loftus IM, Thompson MM, et al: Quality control during endovascular aneurysm repair: Monitoring aneurysmal sac pressure superficial femoral artery flow velocity. J Endovasc Surg 6:239-245, 1999.

91. Mehta M, Veith FJ, Ohki T, et al: Significance of endotension, endoleak and aneurysm pulsatility after endovascular repair. J Vasc Surg 37:842-846, 2003.

92. Tzortzis E, Hinchliffe RJ, Hopkinson BR: Adjunctive procedures for the treatment of proximal type I endoleak: The role of peri-aortic ligatures and Palmaz stenting. J Endovasc Ther 10:233-239, 2003.

93. Szilagyi DE, Elliott JP, Smith RF: Clinical fate of the patient with asymptomatic abdominal aortic aneurysm and unfit for surgical treatment. Arch Surg 104:600-606, 1972.

94. Jones A, Cahill D, Gardham R: Outcome in patients with a large abdominal aortic aneurysm considered unfit for surgery. Br J Surg 85:1382-1384, 1998.

95. Magee TR, Galland RB, Collin J, et al: A prospective survey of patients presenting with abdominal aortic aneurysm. Eur J Vasc Endovasc Surg 13:403-406, 1997.

96. Chuter TAM, Reilly RM, Farqui RM, et al: Endovascular aneurysm repair in high-risk patients. J Vasc Surg 31:122-133, 2000.

97. Chaikof EL, Lin PH, Brinkman WT, et al: Endovascular repair of abdominal aortic aneurysms: Risk stratified outcomes. Ann Surg 235:833-841, 2002.

98. Schermerhorn ML, Finlayson SRG, Fillinger MF, et al: Life expectancy after endovascular versus open abdominal aortic aneurysm repair: Results of a decision analysis model on the basis of data from EUROSTAR. J Vasc Surg 36:1112-1120, 2002.

99. Torsello GB, Klenk E, Kaspizak B, Umscheid T: Rupture of abdominal aortic aneurysm previously treated by endovascular stent-graft. J Vasc Surg 28:184-187, 1998.

100. Darling RC, Ozsvath K, Chang BB, et al: The incidence, natural history and outcome of secondary intervention for persistent collateral flow in the excluded abdominal aortic aneurysm. J Vasc Surg 30:968-976, 1999.

101. Zarins CK, White RA, Fogarty TJ: Aneurysm rupture after endovascular repair using the AneuRx stent-graft. J Vasc Surg 31:960-970, 2000.

102. May J, White GH, Yu W, Sieunarine K: Importance of plain X-ray in endoluminal aortic graft surveillance. Eur J Vasc Endovasc Surg 13:202-206, 1997.

103. Prinssen M, Verhoeven ELG, Verhagen HJM, Blankensteijn JD: Decision-making in follow-up after endovascular aneurysm repair based on diameter and volume measurements: A blinded comparison. Eur J Vasc Endovasc Surg 26:184-187, 2003.

104. Resch T, Ivancev K, Brunkwall J, et al: Distal migration of stent-grafts after endovascular repair of abdominal aortic aneurysms. J Vasc Interv Radiol 10:257-264, 1999.

105. Harris PL, Vallabhaneni SR, Desgranges P: Incidence and risk factors of late rupture, conversion and death after endovascular repair of infrarenal aortic aneurysms: The EUROSTAR experience. J Vasc Surg 32:739-749, 2000.

106. Resch T, Malina M, Lindblad B, Ivancev K: The impact of stent-graft development on outcome of AAA repair: A 7-year experience. Eur J Vasc Endovasc Surg 22:57-61, 2001.

107. Mohan IV, Harris PL, van Marrewijk CJ, et al: Factors and forces influencing stent-graft migration after endovascular aortic aneurysm repair. J Endovasc Ther 9:748-755, 2002.

108. Cao P, Verzini F, Parlani G, et al: Predictive factors and clinical consequences of proximal aortic neck dilatation in 230 patients undergoing abdominal aorta aneurysm repair with self-expandable stent-graft. J Vasc Surg 37:1200-1205, 2003.

109. Conners MS, Sternbergh WC, Carter G, et al: Endograft migration 1 to 4 years after endovascular abdominal aortic aneurysm repair with the AneuRx device: A cautionary note. J Vasc Surg 36:476-484, 2002.

110. May J, White GH, Ly CN, et al: Endoluminal repair of abdominal aortic aneurysm prevents enlargement of the proximal neck: A 9-year life table and 5-year longitudinal study. J Vasc Surg 37:86-90, 2003.

111. Sternbergh WC, Carter G, York JW, et al: Aortic neck angulation predicts adverse outcome with endovascular abdominal aortic aneurysm repair. J Vasc Surg 35:482-486, 2002.

112. Murphy M, Hodgson R, Harris PL, et al: Plain radiographic surveillance of abdominal aortic stent-grafts: The Liverpool/Perth protocol. J Endovasc Ther 10:911-912, 2003.

113. Karch LA, Henretta JP, Hodgson KJ, et al: Algorithm for the diagnosis and treatment of endoleaks. Am J Surg 178:225-231, 1999.

114. Matsumura JS, Moore WS: Clinical consequences of periprosthetic leak after endovascular repair of abdominal aortic aneurysm. J Vasc Surg 27:606-613, 1998.

115. Van Marrewijk C, Buth J, Harris PL, et al: Significance of endoleaks after endovascular repair of abdominal aortic aneurysms: The EUROSTAR experience. J Vasc Surg 35:461-473, 2002.

116. Broeders IAMJ, Blankensteijn JD, Gvakharia A, et al: The efficacy of transfemoral endovascular aneurysm management: A study of size changes of the abdominal aorta during mid-term follow-up. Eur J Vasc Endovasc Surg 14:84-90, 1997.

117. Görich J, Rilinger N, Sokiranski R, et al: Embolisation of type II endoleaks fed by the inferior mesenteric artery: Using the superior mesenteric artery approach. J Endovasc Ther 7:297-301, 2000.

118. Baum RA, Carpenter JP, Golden MA, et al: Treatment of type II endoleaks after endovascular repair of abdominal aortic aneurysms: Comparison of transarterial and translumbar techniques. J Vasc Surg 35:23-29, 2002.

119. Resch T, Ivancev K, Lindh M, et al: Persistent collateral perfusion of abdominal aortic aneurysm after endovascular repair does not lead to progressive change in aneurysm diameter. J Vasc Surg 28:242-249 1998.

120. Chuter TA, Faruqi RM, Sawhney R, et al: Endoleak after endovascular repair of abdominal aortic aneurysm. J Vasc Surg 34:98-105, 2001.

121. Vallabhaneni SR, Gilling-Smith GL, How TV, et al: Aortic side-branch perfusion alone does not account for high intra-sac pressure after endovascular repair (EVAR) in the absence of graft-related endoleak. Eur J Vasc Endovasc Surg 25:354-359, 2003.

122. Faries PL, Cadot H, Agarwal G, et al: Management of endoleak after endovascular aneurysm repair: Cuffs, coils, and conversion. J Vasc Surg 37:1155-1161, 2003.

123. Buth J, Harris PL, van Marrewijk C, Fransen G: The significance and management of different types of endoleaks. Semin Vasc Surg 16:95-102, 2003.

124. Harris PL, Brennan J, Martin J, et al: Longitudinal aneurysm shrinkage following endovascular aortic aneurysm repair: A source of intermediate and late complications. J Endovasc Surg 6:11-16, 1999.

125. Umscheid T, Stelter WJ: Time-related alterations in shape, position, and structure of self-expanding, modular aortic stent-grafts: A 4-year single-center follow-up. J Endovasc Surg 6:17-32, 1999.

126. Moore WS, Rutherford RB: Transfemoral endovascular repair of abdominal aortic aneurysm: Results of the North-American EVT phase I trial. J Vasc Surg 23:543-553, 1996.

127. Norgren L, Jernby B, Engellau L: Aortoenteric fistula caused by a ruptured stent-graft: A case report. J Endovasc Surg 5:269-272, 1998.

128. Najibi S, Steinberg J, Katzen BT, et al: Detection of isolated hook fractures 36 months after implantation of the Ancure endograft: A cautionary note. J Vasc Surg 34:353-356, 2001.

129. Riepe G, Heilberger P, Umscheid T, et al: Frame dislocation of the body middle rings in endovascular stent tube grafts. Eur J Vasc Endovasc Surg 17:28-34, 1999.

130. Guidoin R, Marois Y, Douville Y, et al: First-generation aortic endo-grafts: Analysis of explanted Stentor devices from the EUROSTAR Registry. J Endovasc Ther 7:105-122, 2000.

131. Jacobs TS, Won J, Gravereaux EC, et al: Mechanical failure of prosthetic human implants: A 10-year experience with aortic stent-graft devices. J Vasc Surg 37:16-26, 2003.

132. Criado J, Clark NS, McKendrick C, et al: Update on the Talent LPS AAA stent-graft: Results with "enhanced Talent." Semin Vasc Surg 16:158-165, 2003.

133. May J, White GH, Waugh R, et al: Improved survival after endoluminal repair with second-generation prosthesis compared with open repair in the treatment of abdominal aortic aneurysms: A five-year concurrent comparison using life-table method. J Vasc Surg 33:S21-S26, 2001.

134. Conners MS, Sternbergh WC, Carter G, et al: Secondary procedures after endovascular aortic aneurysm repair. J Vasc Surg 36:992-996, 2002.

135. Sampram ESK, Karafa MT, Mascha EJ, et al: Nature, frequency, and predictors of secondary procedures after endovascular repair of abdominal aortic aneurysm. J Vasc Surg 37:930-937, 2003.

136. Zarins CK, White RA, Moll FL, et al: The AneuRx stent-graft: Four-year results and worldwide experience 2000. J Vasc Surg 33:S135-S145, 2001.

137. Ohki T, Veith FJ, Shaw P, et al: Increasing incidents of mid-term and long-term complications after endovascular graft repair of abdominal aortic aneurysms: A note of caution based on a 9-year experience. Ann Surg 234:323-335, 2001.

138. Bernhard VM, Mitchell RS, Matsumura JS, et al: Ruptured abdominal aortic aneurysm after endovascular repair. J Vasc Surg 35:1155-1162, 2002.

139. Datillo JB, Brewster DC, Fan C-M, et al: Clinical failures of endovascular abdominal aortic aneurysm repair: Incidence, causes and management. J Vasc Surg 35:1137-1144, 2002.

140. Makaroun MS, Chaikof EL, Naslund T, Matsumura JS: Efficacy of a bifurcated endograft versus open repair of abdominal aortic aneurysms: A reappraisal. J Vasc Surg 35:203-210, 2002.

141. May J, White GH, Waugh R, et al: Rupture of abdominal aortic aneurysms: A concurrent comparison of outcome of those occurring after endoluminal repair versus those occurring de novo. Eur J Vasc Endovasc Surg 18:344-348, 1999.

142. Cuypers PWM, Laheij RJF, Buth J: Which factors increase the risk of conversion to open surgery following endovascular abdominal aortic aneurysm repair? Eur J Vasc Endovasc Surg 20:183-189, 2000.

143. Wolf YG, Arko FR, Hill BR, et al: Gender differences in endovascular abdominal aortic aneurysm repair with the AneuRx stent-graft. J Vasc Surg 35:882-886, 2002.

144. Shames ML, Sanchez LA, Rubin BG, et al: Delayed complications after endovascular AAA repair in women. J Endovasc Ther 10:10-15, 2003.

145. Parlani G, Verzini F, Zannetti S, et al: Does gender influence outcome of AAA endoluminal repair? Eur J Vasc Endovasc Surg 26:69-73, 2003.

146. Ouriel K, Clair DG, Greenberg RK, et al: Endovascular repair of abdominal aortic aneurysms: Device-specific outcome. J Vasc Surg 37:991-998, 2003.

147. Peppelenbosch N, Buth J, Harris PL, et al; EUROSTAR Collaborators: Diameter of AAA and outcome of endovascular aneurysm repair. Does size matter? A report from the EUROSTAR. J Vasc Surg 39:288-297, 2004.

148. Armon MP, Yusuf SW, Whitaker SC, et al: Influence of abdominal aneurysm size on the feasibility of endovascular repair. J Endovasc Surg 4:279-283, 1997.

149. Ouriel K, Srivastava SD, Sarac TP, et al: Disparate outcome after endovascular treatment of small versus large abdominal aortic aneurysms. J Vasc Surg 37:1206-1212, 2003.

150. Arko FR, Lee WA, Hill BB, et al: Aneurysm-related death: Primary endpoint analysis for comparison of open and endovascular repair. J Vasc Surg 36:297-304, 2002.

151. Yusuf SW, Whitaker SC, Chuter TAM, et al: Emergency endovascular repair of leaking aortic aneurysm. Lancet 344:1645, 1994.

152. Ohki T, Veith FJ, Sanchez LA, et al: Endovascular graft repair of ruptured aortoiliac aneurysms. J Am Coll Surg 189:102-113, 1999.

153. Greenberg RK, Srivastava SD, Ouriel K, et al: An endoluminal method of hemorrhage control and repair of ruptured abdominal aortic aneurysms. J Endovasc Ther 7:1-7, 2000.

154. Hinchliffe RJ, Yusuf SW, Marcierewicz JA, et al: Endovascular repair of ruptured abdominal aortic aneurysm: Challenge to open repair? Results of a single-center experience in 20 patients. J Eur Vasc Endovasc Surg 22:528-534, 2001.

155. Yilmaz N, Peppelenbosch N, Cuypers PW, et al: Emergency treatment of symptomatic or ruptured abdominal aortic aneurysms: The role of endovascular repair. J Endovasc Ther 9:449-457, 2002.

156. Verhoeven EL, Prins TR, van den Dungen JJAM, et al: Endovascular repair of acute AAAs under local anesthesia with bifurcated endografts: A feasibility study. J Endovasc Ther 9:729-735, 2002.

157. Orend KH, Kotsis T, Scharrer-Pamler R, et al: Endovascular repair of aortic rupture due to trauma and aneurysm. Eur J Vasc Endovasc Surg 23:61-67, 2002.

158. Lachat ML, Peammatter TH, Witzke HJ, et al: Endovascular repair with bifurcated stent-grafts under local anesthesia to improve outcome of ruptured aortoiliac aneurysms. Eur J Vasc Endovasc Surg 23:528-536, 2002.

159. Peppelenbosch N, Yilmaz N, van Marrewijk C, et al: Emergency treatment of acute symptomatic or ruptured abdominal aortic aneurysm: Outcome of a prospective intent-to-treat by EVAR protocol. Eur J Vasc Endovasc Surg 26:303-310, 2003.

160. Hinchliffe RJ, Alric P, Rose D, et al: Comparison of morphologic features of intact and ruptured aneurysms of infrarenal abdominal aorta. J Vasc Surg 38:88-92, 2003.

161. Orend KH, Scharrer-Pamler R, Kapfer X, et al: Endovascular treatment in diseases of the descending thoracic aorta: 6-year results of a single-center. J Vasc Surg 37:91-99, 2003.

162. Dake MD, Miller DC, Semba CP, et al: Transluminal placement of endovascular stent-grafts for the treatment of descending thoracic aortic aneurysms. N Engl J Med 331:1729-1734, 1994.

163. Cambria PR, Brewster DC, Lauterbach SR, et al: Evolving experience with thoracic aortic stent-graft repair. J Vasc Surg 35:1129-1136, 2002.

164. Greenberg R, Resch T, Nyman U, et al: Endovascular repair of descending thoracic aortic aneurysms: An early experience with intermediate-term follow-up. J Vasc Surg 31:147-156, 2000.

165. Mitchell RS, Miller DC, Dake MD, et al: Thoracic aortic aneurysm repair with an endovascular stent-graft: The "first generation." Ann Thorac Surg 67:1971-1974, 1999.

166. Gravereaux E, Faries PL, Burks JA, et al: Risk of spinal cord ischemia after endograft repair of thoracic aortic aneurysms. J Vasc Surg 34:997-1003, 2001.

167. White R, Donayre CE, Walot I, et al: Endovascular exclusion of descending thoracic aortic aneurysm and chronic dissections: Initial clinical results with the AneuRx device. J Vasc Surg 33:927-934, 2001.

168. Grabenwoger M, Hutschala D, Ehrlich MP, et al: Thoracic aortic aneurysm: Treatment with endovascular self-expandable stent-grafts. Ann Thorac Surg 69:441-445, 2000.

169. Resch T, Koul B, Dias NV, et al: Changes in aneurysm morphology and stent-graft configuration after endovascular repair of aneurysms of the descending thoracic aorta. J Thorac Cardiovasc Surg 122:47-52, 2001.

170. Thompson CS, Gaxotte VD, Rodriguez JA, et al: Endoluminal stent-grafting of the thoracic aorta: Initial experience with the Gore Excluder. J Vasc Surg 35:1163-1170, 2002.

171. Görich J, Asquan Y, Seifarth H, et al: Initial experience with intentional stent-graft coverage of the subclavian artery during endovascular thoracic aortic repairs. J Endovasc Ther 9(Suppl):II39-II43, 2002.

172. Buth J, Penn O, Tielbeek A, Mersman M: Combined approach to stent-graft treatment of an aortic arch aneurysm. J Endovasc Surg 5:329-332, 1998.

173. Criado FJ, Clark NS, Barnatan MF: Stent-graft repair in the aortic arch and descending thoracic aorta: A 4-year experience. J Vasc Surg 36:1121-1128, 2002.

174. Velaquez OC, Bavaria JE, Pochettino A, Carpenter JP: Emergency repair of thoraco-abdominal aortic aneurysms with immediate presentation. J Vasc Surg 30:996-1003, 1999.

175. Lewis ME, Ranasingae AM, Revell MP, Bonser RS: Surgical repair of ruptured thoracic and thoracicoabdominal aortic aneurysms. Br J Surg 89:442-445, 2002.

176. Bell RE, Taylor PR, Aukett M, et al: Results of urgent and emergency thoracic procedures treated by endoluminal repair. Eur J Vasc Endovasc Surg 25:527-531, 2003.

177. Semba CP, Kato N, Kee ST, et al: Acute rupture of the descending thoracic aorta: Repair with use of endovascular stent-grafts. J Vasc Interv Radiol 8:337-342, 1997.

178. Alric P, Berthet J-P, Branchereau P, et al: Endovascular repair for acute rupture of the descending thoracic aorta. J Endovasc Ther 9(Suppl):II51-II59, 2002.

179. Nio D, Vos PM, de Mol BA, et al: Emergency endovascular treatment of thoracic aortic rupture in three accident victims with multiple injuries. J Endovasc Ther 9(Suppl):II60-II66, 2002.

180. Lachat M, Pfammatter T, Witzke H, et al: Acute traumatic aortic rupture: Early stent-graft repair. Eur J Cardiothorac Surg 21:959-963, 2002.

181. Orend KH, Pamler R, Kapfer X, et al: Endovascular repair of traumatic descending aortic transection. J Endovasc Ther 9:573-578, 2002.

182. Marty-Ané CH, Berthet JP, Branchereau P, et al: Endovascular repair for acute traumatic rupture of the thoracic aorta. Ann Thorac Surg 75:1803-1807, 2003.

Ruptured Abdominal Aortic Aneurysms

102

THOMAS F. LINDSAY, MDCM, MSc, FRSC, FASC

Aortic rupture is a lethal event. It is estimated that 80% of the mortality secondary to abdominal aortic aneurysm (AAA) is secondary to rupture. The mortality rate for patients who arrive at hospital alive ranges from 40% to 70%.[1-4] When autopsy data are taken into account, including patients who die before reaching the hospital, the mortality rate is 90%.[5] Over the more than 50 years since the first successful elective AAA repair, the mortality rate for ruptured repair has decreased only 3.5% per decade since the initial successful repairs were reported.[6] This conclusion is supported by a large English language meta-analysis and a statewide analysis; however, data from U.S. Veterans Administration (VA) hospitals and the U.S. National Hospital Discharge database (over the years 1979 through 1997) have not shown this decline.[1,6,7] Most deaths occur postoperatively, and progress to reduce these deaths has been slow. The cost of treating ruptured aneurysms is at least four times higher than elective cases and much higher for ruptured abdominal aortic aneurysm (RAAA) patients who have a complicated postoperative course.[8] Endovascular repair of RAAA has yet to be widely adopted, and although early reports of low mortality rates from selective centers are promising, it is too soon to determine the impact of endovascular repair on the mortality rates on a state or national level.[9] Future reductions in mortality for this condition will depend on implementation of population-based screening, endovascular repair of RAAA, and strategies to prevent postoperative organ injury.[10]

■ DEFINITION

AAA rupture is defined as disruption of a dilated aortic wall that leads to blood outside the aortic wall. RAAA can be subclassified further into retroperitoneal and free rupture. Free rupture is defined as direct rupture into the peritoneal cavity or secondary to the failure of the retroperitoneum to contain the hematoma. The prognosis of free rupture is significantly worse because of the larger amount of bleeding that can occur intraperitoneally.[11]

Differentiation between symptomatic and ruptured aneurysms is crucial. Patients with symptomatic aneurysms may have symptoms of variable severity (ranging from mild tenderness to pain indistinguishable from rupture); however, no blood is identified outside the aortic wall at laparotomy. The etiology of the pain is thought to be related to acute expansion of the wall, intramural hemorrhage, and wall degeneration or bleeding into the thrombus. These patients do not have hypotension; their prognosis is much better than the prognosis of patients with rupture (but worse than with elective repair), and they should be excluded from a discussion of aortic rupture.[12]

■ EPIDEMIOLOGY

Chapter 100 describes the incidence and prevalence of AAAs. Population statistics from the United States show that aortic aneurysm accounted for 15,810 deaths per year (2000 data), with 83.5% of these deaths occurring in patients older than age 65 years and 93% occurring in patients older than age 55.[13] RAAA is the tenth leading cause of death of men older than age 65. RAAA accounts for a similar number of deaths as prostate, gastric, and esophageal cancers.

The rates of AAA repair (elective and ruptured) in male Medicare enrollees remained stable between 1988 and 1997 at less than 2 per 1000 compared with 0.4 per 1000 women. The percentage of AAA repairs that were performed for rupture were similar in women and men. Areas of the United States that had high rates of elective repair did not seem to have reduced rates of RAAA repair.[14]

There is little evidence that elective repair has resulted in a reduction in the number of RAAAs over the years 1980 through 2000.[7] Rates of elective AAA repair are similar, and there has not been a decrease in the U.S. national incidence of RAAA repair. These statistics suggest that the ability to detect AAA and treat this condition has not improved dramatically. Data from England with a large screening program showed that aneurysm-related mortality was reduced by 53% despite a 6% perioperative mortality rate.[10] These data show conclusively that the incidence of RAAA and its attendant death rate can be reduced by screening the at-risk population.

The incidence of RAAA in the general population has been noted to be 6.3 per 100,000; in the population older than age 65, the rate is 35.5 per 100,000.[15] As the age of the post–World War II generation begins to exceed 65, the numbers of elective and ruptured repairs are expected to increase. Rupture risk as a function of size and other factors that predict rupture and expansion are discussed in Chapter 100.

■ CLINICAL PRESENTATION

The classic triad for RAAA presentation is severe abdominal or back pain, hypotension, and a pulsatile mass.[16,17] The pulsatile mass often is obscured in patients with large abdominal girth. Syncope may indicate an episode of hypotension. A clinical history that suggests this combination of symptoms mandates consideration of RAAA and steps to rule out this diagnosis. Other common symptoms include groin or flank pain, hematuria, and groin hernia (even incarceration) secondary to increased intra-abdominal pressure. Patients who have rupture into the vena cava may present in congestive heart failure with distended neck veins, an abdominal bruit, and microscopic or macroscopic hematuria; this is an infrequent clinical situation. Other possible communications between the aorta and venous structures include rupture into the iliac or renal vein. Rupture into the renal vein can lead to an acute left varicocele.[18]

A rapid and accurate history and physical examination of patients older than age 50 presenting with hypotension is crucial to the identification of RAAA. The differential diagnosis includes renal colic, diverticulitis, pancreatitis, gastrointestinal hemorrhage, inferior myocardial infarction, and perforated ulcer. Of these, RAAA has the worst prognosis. The presentation of RAAA frequently is clear-cut. In the early stages, the presentation may be nondescript, however. Studies have examined the clinical presentation of patients subsequently diagnosed with RAAA.[16] The rate of incorrect diagnosis ranged from 16% to 30%. Only 23% of patients were given a definitive and immediate diagnosis of RAAA by the first physician who examined the patient. The most common misdiagnoses assigned were renal colic, perforated viscus, diverticulitis, gastrointestinal hemorrhage, and ischemic bowel. The classic triad was present in only 9% of the misdiagnosed group compared with 34% of the correctly diagnosed group. The presence of a pulsatile mass was identified in 72% of patients correctly diagnosed, whereas it was identified in only 26% of misdiagnosed patients. The lack of a pulsatile mass frequently confuses the diagnosis. Mortality rates were 58% for correctly diagnosed patients compared with 44% who were misdiagnosed. This and other studies have noted that misdiagnosis is not associated with an increase in mortality.[19] This negative correlation may be attributed to patients with less severe rupture who have a more subtle presentation and can survive a more prolonged delay. Prompt recognition, referral, and treatment can only help to reduce the mortality rate.

Diagnostic Studies

Plain radiographs are performed frequently on patients with abdominal pain, and the identification of an enlarged outline of a calcified aortic wall suggests the presence of an aneurysm and can alter the investigations performed by the emergency physician. A retrospective review of plain films from patients with RAAAs noted evidence of the diagnosis on 90% of films.[20] Calcification of the aortic wall beyond normal limits was noted in 65%; loss of a psoas shadow was identified in 75%. Careful review of plain films by an expert radiologist at an early stage in presentation may be helpful.

Abdominal ultrasound has been used in the emergency department to identify AAA. It has been used in the

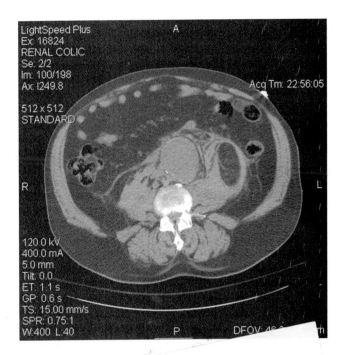

FIGURE 102-1 CT scan of ... the pattern of ... retrop... perfor...

#2

emerger...
patients...
sensitive...
in its ab...
shown tha...
identify A...
may iden...
aneurysm f...
reducing m...

Compute...
of diagnosin...
about associa... ... ig. 102-1).
Significant de... ...to the performance of these studies ... past. With the new rapid multislice detectors, CT scanning time is much shorter. In more recent series, patients have been evaluated in less time when endovascular RAAA repair was being considered.[23] Delays still may occur in obtaining the scan, so in unstable patients transfer to the operating room is a better choice.

The presence of retroperitoneal blood when used as the "gold standard" to diagnose RAAA on CT scan was found to be 77% sensitive and 100% specific.[24] The positive predictive value was 100%; however, the negative predictive value was 89% (see Fig. 102-1). The low rate of false-negative studies (no leak on CT scan but found to have RAAA at surgery) is comforting. Any patient with hypotension or another clinical symptom that is suspicious for RAAA should undergo operative management, however. Patients with an intact aneurysm but otherwise unexplained abdominal pain should be observed in the hospital, and semiurgent repair should be arranged.

Resuscitation and Transfer

When RAAA is being considered in any patient, crossmatch (minimum 6 U of packed red blood cells) and large-bore intravenous access should be established. When the diagnosis is confirmed, immediate transfer to the operating room is arranged. Trained anesthesia, nursing, and technical personnel can ready the patient for operative intervention. Large-bore access, arterial line insertion, and Foley catheter placement can be done simultaneously. Any deterioration in the patient's condition should prompt rapid surgical intervention. If the patient presents to a location where definitive management cannot be carried out, urgent transfer to a center with trained individuals is required. The patient is prepared and draped before anesthesia is induced with agents designed to have minimal effect on blood pressure. This practice allows the operation to be started immediately after induction, which is often associated with hypotension necessitating rapid aortic clamping or compression.

The optimal degree of preoperative resuscitation before operative intervention is controversial.[8,22,25-27] Aggressive resuscitation with crystalloid solution before arrival in the operating room can elevate blood pressure and lead to rupture of the temporary aortic seal that may occur after initial rupture. This second rupture may lead to further bleeding and hypotension before the patient arrives in a setting where definitive therapy can be carried out. In one study, aggressive fluid resuscitation, prehospital paramedic care, transport to a trauma center, and vascular surgical repair were associated with a 78% mortality after RAAA.[2] The excessive mortality in this series is close to the 90% mortality observed in the Malmö, Sweden, autopsy series and may reflect the rapid transport of patients who might not otherwise survive to arrive at the hospital for therapy in other parts of the country.[5] It also might reflect overly aggressive fluid resuscitation. The alternative strategy is to give the minimal resuscitation necessary to maintain consciousness with a systolic blood pressure of approximately 80 mm Hg. If possible, resuscitation with blood is recommended. Crawford[27] initially suggested minimal fluid resuscitation to maintain the systolic blood pressure at 50 to 70 mm Hg. More recent reports also have recommended algorithms that include hypotensive resuscitation.[25] There are no randomized trials of varying degrees of resuscitation in patients with RAAA. Among patients with penetrating trauma and hypotension (systolic blood pressure <90 mm Hg), improved survival was observed in patients who received minimal fluid resuscitation therapy until they arrived in the operating room.[26] The mortality difference was small (30% with delayed resuscitation group compared with 38% with immediate resuscitation), however, and these results may not apply to older patients with RAAA, who usually have significant comorbidities.

Animal studies document increased blood loss and reduced survival in animal models in which resuscitation occurs before control of hemorrhage.[28,29] A British consensus statement supports judicious small boluses of fluid titrated to maintain a radial pulse in patients with penetrating trauma.[28,30] The consensus statement notes, however, that elderly patients tolerate hypotension poorly. Moderate resuscitation to a blood pressure of 80 to 90 mm Hg is suggested for patients with RAAA.

■ OPERATIVE STRATEGY

Currently, open surgical repair is the standard treatment for RAAA, although there are different incisions and options for control. Endovascular repair is being increasingly reported, and small studies suggest a lower mortality rate (see Chapter 101). Currently, many centers do not have experienced personnel, equipment, and stock of grafts available to attempt RAAA repair. This situation may change rapidly in the future.

Open Repair

The crucial element in the repair of a RAAA is safe, rapid, and effective proximal aortic control. Most surgeons prefer a transperitoneal, midline incision because it affords wide exposure to the abdominal aorta and allows rapid supraceliac control if necessary.[2,27] In this approach, the supraceliac aorta is exposed at the diaphragm by retracting the left lobe of the liver to the right (Fig. 102-2). The gastrohepatic omentum is opened to allow entry into the lesser sac. The nasogastric tube is used to identify the esophagus and proximal stomach, which are retracted to the left. The aorta is identified between the crura of the diaphragm. The crura may need to be split with electrocautery to allow rapid and accurate clamp placement. After clamping the supraceliac aorta, the aneurysm is opened, and the clamp may be repositioned to the infrarenal neck if possible. Alternatively the proximal anastomosis is completed from within the aneurysm sac, and a clamp is placed on the graft, and the supraceliac clamp is removed to reperfuse the viscera and kidneys. Supraceliac clamping should be as brief as possible. Unclamping to the visceral and renal vessels may result in significant hypotension and requires careful coordination with anesthesia to ensure that the proper fluids are administered and that pressor agents and bicarbonate are prepared for use if required. Supraceliac control is beneficial in cases of severe hypotension or uncontrolled bleeding from intraperitoneal rupture. It also helps avoid renal and gonadal vein injury often associated with blind dissection to identify the infrarenal aortic neck if there is substantial hematoma in this area. Supraceliac clamping has the disadvantage, however, of ischemic injury to the liver, bowel, and kidneys, which in addition to the injury induced by hemorrhagic shock may contribute to the development of multisystem organ failure (see later).[31,32]

Rather than automatically proceeding to supraceliac control, we prefer to inspect the retroperitoneum after the bowel and duodenum are reflected, unless hypotension requires immediate clamping. If there is not an extensive hematoma in the pararenal area, careful dissection frequently is rewarded with infrarenal control. If during this dissection, uncontrolled bleeding develops, then supraceliac control is obtained.

Some authors have recommended the retroperitoneal approach for RAAA repair, using a 10th interspace incision. In one retrospective analysis, the retroperitoneal approach was associated with less intraoperative hypotension and a lower mortality than the transperitoneal approach, although some patients with unusual features were excluded.[33] This series shows that the retroperitoneal approach for RAAA repair is safe when performed by surgeons familiar with

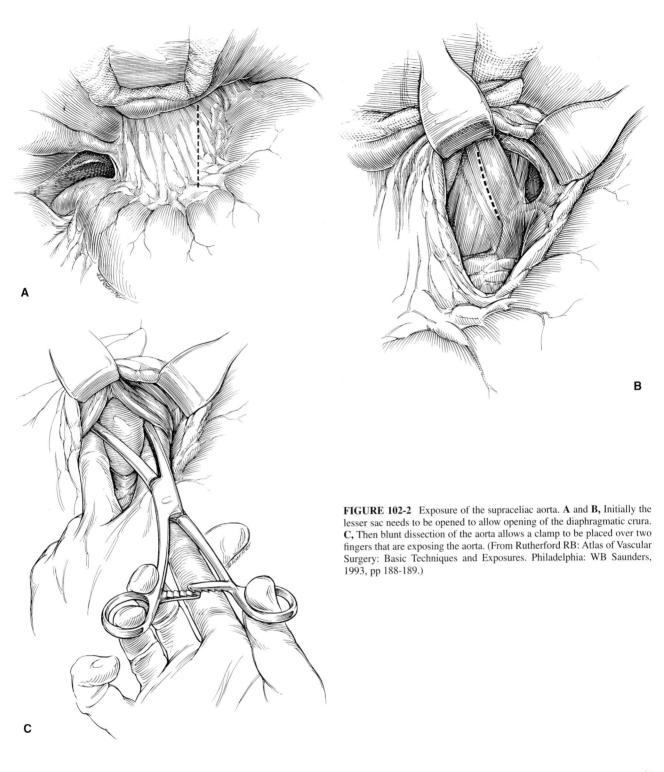

FIGURE 102-2 Exposure of the supraceliac aorta. **A** and **B,** Initially the lesser sac needs to be opened to allow opening of the diaphragmatic crura. **C,** Then blunt dissection of the aorta allows a clamp to be placed over two fingers that are exposing the aorta. (From Rutherford RB: Atlas of Vascular Surgery: Basic Techniques and Exposures. Philadelphia: WB Saunders, 1993, pp 188-189.)

its use during elective repair. It is particularly recommended for pararenal or suprarenal RAAA, if this is known from a preoperative CT scan, or for other hostile abdominal situations, in which this approach would be recommended for elective repair. If a suprarenal AAA is approached anteriorly, medial visceral rotation is required to expose the suprarenal aorta. In this technique, the left colon is mobilized to incise the lateral peritoneal attachments. The colon, pancreas, spleen, and kidney are elevated, allowing access to the diaphragmatic crura, which cover the aorta at this level. Division of the crura allows access to the entire intra-abdominal aorta and visceral and renal vessels.[34] Occasionally a thoracoabdominal incision is required, and in massively obese patients or other special circumstances (e.g., hostile abdomen), a separate thoracic incision has been recommended by some authors.[35]

Other options for proximal aortic control include a brachial or femoral puncture or cut-down to insert an occlusion balloon into the visceral aorta using fluoroscopic guidance.[36,37] Direct placement of an aortic balloon through the aneurysm sac also has been described, but this method can disrupt the aortic thrombus, leading to embolization, and is associated more frequently with balloon malposition or movement as the aneurysm sac is opened.[35,38] An aortic compressor (Fig. 102-3) sometimes is used over the supraceliac aorta to compress it against the lumbar spine if rapid control is required before exposure can be obtained for clamp control.[35] The compressor and balloon techniques are blind and may not provide complete control. A direct approach to the infrarenal or supraceliac aorta is recommended in most cases.

Distal control can be achieved with clamps on the iliac arteries or occasionally the distal aorta (Fig. 102-4). When substantial hematoma is present, however, distal dissection can be difficult and associated with iliac vein injury. In this circumstance, occlusion balloons can be placed in the iliac arteries after opening the aneurysm sac.

When proximal control is achieved, it is useful to allow the anesthesia team several minutes before opening the aneurysm for further resuscitation. During this period, blood replacement can occur to prepare for blood loss that occurs from lumbar arteries or unclamped iliac arteries on opening the aneurysm.

After opening the aneurysm, retrograde bleeding from the inferior mesenteric and lumbar arteries can be controlled with suture ligation. Bleeding from the proximal aorta needs to be controlled with suction if a supraceliac clamp is used. If bleeding occurs from a proximal infrarenal clamp that is not completely applied posteriorly, this usually can be remedied by posterior pressure on the clamp while the proximal anastomosis is completed.

Rarely, venous bleeding continues to fill the opened aneurysm, which can be secondary to an aortocaval fistula. Direct digital pressure or the use of proximal and distal sponge sticks is recommended for control of the vena cava above and below the fistula. Suture of the fistula from within the aneurysm is performed. It is important not to allow air embolism or to push thrombus or other aortic debris into the vena cava during this repair. Attempts to dissect the vena cava proximally and distally greatly increase the chance of a venous injury (see Chapter 111). Aortic repair should be accomplished rapidly with a tube graft if possible; this results in the shortest operation and the least overall systemic physiologic insult. Moderate (3 to 4 cm diameter) iliac aneurysms can be repaired at a later date, unless they are the site of rupture. If aortobi-iliac repair is required, the easiest limb is repaired first to reduce the lower torso ischemic time. Rarely aortobifemoral grafting may be required. With either of these approaches, it is important to ensure that at least one internal iliac artery is revascularized to reduce the risk of pelvic and colon ischemia.

Most surgeons avoid systemic heparinization because of bleeding complications, although heparinized saline can be given directly into the iliac arteries to try to reduce distal thrombosis. Retrograde iliac artery flushing is important to remove any soft clot before distal anastomotic completion, especially if no heparin is used.

The use of red blood cell salvage using a cell saver device has proven benefit in reducing mortality in RAAA patients. When red blood cell salvage was not used, the odds ratio of postoperative death at 1 month was 25 times higher than with autotransfusion.[39] One study suggested that the use of the cell saver increased respiratory complications. The device was used based on surgeon preference, however, and likely was biased toward more complicated cases.[40] In a study by Alric and colleagues,[25] red blood cell salvage was a part of a protocol designed to standardize and reduce mortality from RAAA. In that study, red blood cell salvage was considered an important element in improved survival.

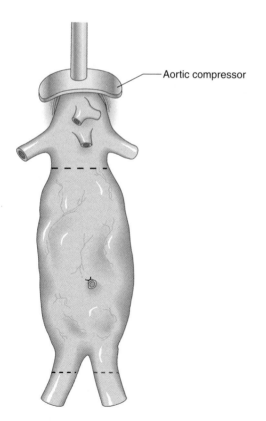

FIGURE 102-3 A compressor can be placed over the supraceliac aorta for rapid temporary aortic control while infrarenal control is being obtained. (From Nyhus LM, Baker RJ: Mastery of Surgery. Boston, Little, Brown, 1984, p 1370.)

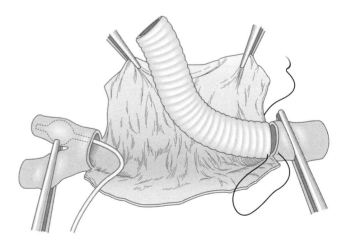

FIGURE 102-4 A combination of intraluminal balloon occlusion and direct aortic and iliac clamps can be used to gain rapid aortic control for ruptured abdominal aortic aneurysm repair. This combination can save time by minimizing dissection and avoiding injuries to surrounding structures that may be obscured by hematoma. (From Yao JST, Pearce WH: Aneurysms: New Findings and Treatments. Norwalk, Com: Appleton & Lange, 1994, p 261.)

Red blood cell salvage has been shown to reduce the need for transfusion in elective repair situations.[41] A decision analysis of elective AAA repair suggested that routine use is not cost-effective, but that its use can be justified when increased blood loss is anticipated.[42] When a red blood cell salvage device is used, the clinician must remember to replace coagulation factors because they are removed during processing.

Hypothermia is associated with an increased incidence of surgical bleeding, wound infection, and an increased incidence of morbid cardiac events.[43] Prevention of hypothermia (by 1.3°C) can reduce cardiac events in elective noncardiac surgery.[43] Although this has not been specifically studied in RAAA, prevention of hypothermia by the use of warmed anesthetic gases, warming of all intravenous fluids, and use of forced air warming devices should be beneficial in this patient population.

Anatomic Abnormalities

The discovery of variant anatomy can complicate repair of an RAAA greatly. Arterial and venous injuries increase the mortality rate in RAAA repairs. The most common venous abnormalities encountered include retroaortic renal vein (1% to 3%), circumaortic renal vein (0.5% to 1.5%), left-sided vena cava (0.15% to 0.5%), and duplicate inferior vena cava (0.4% to 3%).[44] Closure of the aortic clamp can tear a retroaortic renal vein, resulting in significant venous bleeding. The best approach is direct venous repair or ligation; however, this may require division of the aorta after moving the clamp to a more proximal location, retracting the aorta superiorly to accomplish ligation. In patients with left-sided vena cava or duplicate inferior vena cava, frequently these structures cross in front of the aorta at the level of the renal vein; this can prevent access to the proximal aorta and preclude repair. If elevation and mobilization fail to allow sufficient access to repair the aneurysm, the venous structure may need to be divided to allow adequate repair.

A horseshoe kidney discovered during RAAA repair presents a significant technical challenge. The position of the kidney (high or low) and the number of renal arteries are the key factors that require assessment before proceeding. A kidney at the neck of the aneurysm may prevent adequate exposure for aortic cross-clamping, and a supraceliac clamp site may be required. When control is achieved, assessment of the renal blood supply can be determined. If only a fibrous cord is joining the kidneys anteriorly, this can be divided, and the operation can proceed. The isthmus often contains substantial renal tissue, possibly the renal collecting system and blood vessels. If this is the case, identification of the renal blood supply is crucial. If the blood supply is from the iliac arteries, rapid aneurysm repair should be completed. If the blood supply is from the anterior aortic wall, a patch of aortic wall and separate Carrel patches may be required to reperfuse the kidney. If the diagnosis is made preoperatively, a retroperitoneal approach may be selected. Adjunctive measures for renal protection may include systemic mannitol (3 to 5 mL/kg) or N-acetylcysteine (600 mg intravenous bolus or 100 mg/kg based on animal studies)[45,46] and renal cooling. The identification of an inflammatory aneurysm may require supra-renal or supraceliac control. Then minimal dissection of the duodenum from the aorta and repair of the aneurysm from within is crucial to achieving success; this is described further for elective repair in Chapter 100.

Abdominal Closure After Ruptured Abdominal Aortic Aneurysm

At the conclusion of RAAA repair, most commonly the abdomen can be closed primarily. In 25% to 30% of patients, the abdomen cannot be closed without significant tension secondary to swollen bowel or massive retroperitoneal hematoma or both.[47,48] Abdominal compartment syndrome results from increased intraperitoneal pressure that results in hypoventilation, decreased venous return, hypoxemia, increased intracranial pressure, and renal failure. Organ and capillary bed perfusion is impaired, leading to mucosal ischemia, which may predispose these patients to the development of multiple organ dysfunction syndrome.[49] A bladder pressure greater than 30 cm H_2O or 25 mm Hg is diagnostic. Bladder pressure reflects intra-abdominal pressure when the bladder volume is 50 to 100 mL.[49] To measure this pressure, the bladder is drained and filled with 50 to 100 mL of sterile saline. The drainage tubing is clamped beyond the aspiration port, and a needle is inserted into the aspiration port and connected to a pressure transducer. The transducer is zeroed at the pubic symphysis. Intra-abdominal pressures have been shown to be higher at the conclusion of RAAA repair compared with elective open or endovascular repair. These early measurements were unable to predict organ failure accurately; however, patients with higher initial intra-abdominal pressure did have more physiologic abnormalities compared with the lower pressure group.[50]

Although delayed closure after RAAA has been reported since 1991, it has been suggested more recently to reduce the development of subsequent organ failure in trauma and RAAA patients.[48] Early mesh closure seems to reduce the incidence of multiple-organ failure (MOF) and may reduce mortality compared with patients who eventually returned to the operating room for a decompressive laparotomy and a delayed mesh closure. Patients who have severe preoperative anemia, prolonged shock, preoperative cardiac arrest, massive resuscitation, profound hypothermia, and severe acidosis may benefit from early mesh closure sewn to the fascia. Different types of mesh are available; however, nonabsorbable mesh covered with a polyurethane drape to prevent fluid loss is most commonly used.[51] When patients with early mesh closure were compared with patients with late mesh closure, the incidence of colon ischemia was 6% versus 40%.[47] Also, no aortic graft infections have been observed to date. The abdomen is closed after 2 to 5 days, and there is an increase in the wound complication rate. Although the data to date are retrospective, early mesh closure to prevent the development of abdominal compartment syndrome leading to MOF seems to be a useful adjunct in selected patients in the treatment of RAAA.

Endovascular Repair

Expertise in elective endovascular AAA repair has enabled several centers to treat RAAA with an endovascular

Table 102-1 | Reported Data on Ruptured Abdominal Aortic Aneurysms (RAAA) Treated by Endovascular Aneurysm Repair

FIRST AUTHOR	RAAA RE-EVALUATED (no.)	EVAR COMPLETED (%)	EVAR MORTALITY (%)	CONVERSION RATE (%)
Ohki, 2001[54]	25	100	10	20
Hinchliffe, 2001[9]	20	85	45	15
Lachat, 2002[55]	57	37	9.5	0
Orend, 2002[39]	21	71	14	29
Resch, 2003[94]	21	100	19	0
Scharrer-Pamler, 2003[95]	24	100	12.5	4
Peppelenbosch, 2003[52]	40	65	15	0
Reichart, 2003[23]	25	23	17	0
Totals	*219*	*71*	*18*	*8.5*

EVAR, endovascular aneurysm repair.

approach.[9] Although the reports describing this therapy are increasing in frequency, many of the centers that have reported their experience are centers that have been early adopters of endovascular AAA treatment. Their level of expertise, stock of grafts available, and resources has facilitated extension of this therapy to patients with RAAAs.

The preoperative investigations used to assess patients before endovascular aneurysm repair (EVAR) have varied among institutions. A barrier to the use of EVAR for RAAA repair has been the lack of detailed preoperative imaging before patient transfer to the operating room. The most recent reports describe the use of fine-cut spiral CT scanning with contrast enhancement on the way to the operating room, allowing assessment of the neck diameter, angulation, and iliac size.[52] Appropriate endovascular candidates then can be selected. Several authors have attempted to estimate the number of RAAA patients for whom EVAR may be a realistic option. Patients with RAAAs have been shown to have larger neck diameters but shorter neck length.[53] The number suggested to be suitable for endovascular repair varies from 20% to 46%.[53] The proportion of patients with RAAAs who are suitable for EVAR seems to be lower compared with patients with asymptomatic aneurysms (rates suitable for EVAR were 74% to 78% in the same studies).

Different strategies have been employed to treat RAAAs with endovascular therapy. The Montefiore group has used an in-house device that is an aorto-unifemoral graft that requires ipsilateral internal iliac exclusion and a femoro-femoral crossover graft.[54] Modular aorto-uni-iliac and aortobi-iliac configurations also have been used. Manufacturers are beginning to market rupture kits, which enable most aneurysms to be repaired with a minimal amount of stock.

Special considerations required to perform RAAAs using EVAR include rapid availability of CT scanning, a team of trained personnel, a stock of devices, and the proper suite in which to perform the procedure. Local anesthesia has been used by several groups; however, it can be difficult if the patient is unable to remain still.[9,55] The advantage of local anesthesia is that the sympathetic tone sustaining blood pressure is not negated. Several groups begin under local anesthesia and convert to general anesthesia for the positioning and release of the graft. Proximal control has been achieved using a balloon that is placed either via the

brachial or via the femoral approach. Endoleaks pose a unique problem in this setting because they may result in failure to control hemorrhage. Several persistent type I leaks have been reported, including one with a 4-month follow-up.[52] Type II leaks have been observed after resolution of the hematoma; however, these have not been reported to result in continued leakage of blood outside the aneurysm. It seems surprising that all the endoleaks reported to date after RAAA have had such a benign natural history. Despite the predictions that fewer RAAAs are suitable for EVAR, several European groups reported that on an intent-to-treat basis, they treated 58% to 80% of patients with RAAA with EVAR.[52,53] Few conversions have been reported. Blood loss, total fluid administration, intensive care unit days, and hospital stays are shorter.[39] Larger single-center or multicenter series are required to show conclusively that this therapy can be applied effectively outside of specialized centers.

The 30-day mortality rates range from 10% to 45%. Most series still have relatively limited numbers of patients included (20 to 35) compared with the open RAAA literature (Table 102-1). Deaths have been secondary to colon ischemia, MOF, and continued hemorrhage. Postoperative complications include renal failure, arterial ischemia, wound infections, and abdominal compartment syndrome related to the hematoma. Although hematoma is rarely opened at the time of surgery, hematoma that directly surrounds the aorta is removed during aneurysm repair. Drainage of retroperitoneal hematoma after EVAR has been reported.[39] Renal dysfunction or failure can be due to the combination of the insult induced by hemorrhage and the contrast material required for the CT scan and implantation procedure. The incidence of renal dysfunction has been reported in one series at 28% with only two patients requiring hemofiltration and none requiring permanent dialysis.[55]

Overall the reports of therapy of RAAA by EVAR seem encouraging. To date, no large multicenter study that reports on a group of consecutively treated patients is available that would suggest this therapy can be offered on a population-wide basis. As noted earlier, expertise, rapid access to thin-slice CT scanning, proper equipment, and a modest stock of devices are required around the clock to make this therapy feasible in a few specialized centers. As EVAR expertise becomes more widespread, this technology has the potential to reduce the mortality rate from RAAA—something that has been slow to be achieved over the last 50 years.

■ COMPLICATIONS OF RUPTURED ABDOMINAL AORTIC ANEURYSM REPAIR

Local Complications

Postoperative bleeding is noted to develop with a frequency of 12% to 14.4%.[12] The incidence is related to the prevalence of coagulopathy, which can develop secondary to the lack of coagulation factor replacement and hypothermia. Limb ischemia can be related to embolization of aortic debris resulting in trash foot, large clot emboli, or thrombosis of major vessels. Because many surgeons do not use systemic heparin administration, particular attention must be paid to retrograde iliac flushing before completion of the distal anastomosis. Colonic ischemia can range from patchy mucosal necrosis to full-thickness colon necrosis with perforation. The incidence of this complication ranges from 3% to 13%, but it is associated with a mortality of 73% to 100%.[12,56] Factors that are responsible for colonic ischemia include the degree and duration of hypotension, patency of the inferior mesenteric artery, collateral supply from the superior mesenteric and pelvic collaterals, and site of the hematoma. Care must be taken at the conclusion of the aortic repair to examine the colon, and Doppler examination is done of the colon blood supply if of concern. Reimplantation of the inferior mesenteric artery may be beneficial even if both internal iliac arteries have been preserved by the repair. If colonic ischemia is suspected during the postoperative period, sigmoidoscopy to visualize the area is diagnostic. Laparotomy to remove the injured colon is required; however, this still is associated with a mortality rate greater than 50%. Paraplegia and paraparesis are rare complications that have been reported after ruptured aneurysm repair. The incidence has been noted to be 2.3% with a mortality of 50%.[12] Interruption of pelvic blood supply, prolonged aortic cross-clamping, intraoperative hypotension, aortic embolization, and internal iliac interruption all have been suggested to cause spinal cord injury.[57] To date, spinal cord drainage has not been effective after symptoms were noted.

Systemic Complications

RAAA frequently is associated with the development of complications distant to the site of the aortic repair. Rupture results in blood loss and hypotension. Repair requires aortic clamping resulting in a second ischemic insult to the lower torso. Young patients who have penetrating arterial trauma with hypotension have survival rates between 62% and 70%. These patients have intraoperative blood loss between 2.5 and 3.1 L, yet the incidence of systemic complications, such as acute respiratory distress syndrome (1% to 4%), sepsis syndrome (5%), and renal failure (1% to 4%), is dramatically lower than after RAAA.[26] Evidence from basic research models and patient-derived data suggests that the combination of hypotension followed by resuscitation (an ischemia reperfusion event) primes the inflammatory response, and when a second insult occurs, this results in the development of a systemic inflammatory response leading to the development of systemic organ failure.[32,58]

The most common systemic complications are myocardial infarction, respiratory failure, renal failure, congestive heart failure, arrhythmias, hyperbilirubinemia, sepsis, and MOF. Other complications include deep venous thrombosis, stroke, wound dehiscence, elevated serum amylase, and pulmonary embolus.

Respiratory Failure

Respiratory failure develops in 26% to 47% of cases and is associated with a mortality of 34% to 68%.[11,59,60] It is characterized by high oxygen requirements, increased lung permeability, and a decrease in lung compliance. Large volumes of fluid and blood product predispose to the development of this respiratory failure. Patients with preexisting pulmonary dysfunction and long cross-clamp times are predisposed to develop this syndrome. The relative lower torso ischemia induced by aortic cross-clamping may cause the release of mediators that result in the development of respiratory failure.

Renal Dysfunction

Many studies have shown a relationship between renal dysfunction and mortality after RAAA repair. The incidence of renal dysfunction after aneurysm repair is low in elective cases but rises progressively in symptomatic patients and RAAA patients, in whom the rates vary between 26% and 42%. Renal failure requiring dialysis has been noted to develop in 11% to 40% of patients. Patients who require dialysis have mortality rates of 76% to 89%.[11,12,59] Renal dysfunction has been noted to be increased in patients who require suprarenal cross-clamping, longer duration of aortic cross-clamping, preexisting renal dysfunction, shock, and increasing age.[61] Although the etiology of renal dysfunction is multifactorial, patients who develop it often also have sustained a greater insult to other organs. Suprarenal clamping is used more commonly in patients with RAAA and is associated with an increased incidence of renal dysfunction and dialysis.[62] Development of renal dysfunction after RAAA repair with an infrarenal clamp, especially in patients with previously normal renal function, is a reflection of the severity of the systemic insult the patient has experienced.

Irreversible Shock

In the late stages of hemorrhagic shock, an irreversible state can develop in which aortic clamping, aggressive fluid resuscitation, and inotropic support can fail to reverse hypotension.[22] This condition also is observed in animal models of hemorrhage. These deaths usually occur in the operating room and frequently account for 10% to 15% of RAAA deaths.

Cardiac Complications

Myocardial infarction, arrhythmias, cardiac arrest, and congestive heart failure all represent life-threatening situations that increase mortality after RAAA.[12] Cardiac arrest is associated with a mortality of 81% to 100% and occurs in 20% of cases. Myocardial infarction develops in 14% to 24% and is associated with a mortality of 19% to 66%. The development of an arrhythmia that required therapy occurred in 23% with an associated mortality of 46%. Congestive heart failure developed in 20% and was associated with 41% mortality. If all patients with cardiac events are pooled, 42% of patients sustained a cardiac event, which was associated with a 44% early mortality. Myocardial infarction develops secondary to the increased demand placed on the heart to compensate for blood loss, resuscitation, aortic clamping, and declamping. These increased demands are placed on a heart that frequently has preexisting coronary disease. Rapid detection of postoperative myocardial infarction, arrhythmias, or congestive heart failure must lead to prompt measures to reduce and relieve the situation; otherwise, mortality is significant.

Liver Failure

Hepatic failure is a late event after RAAA. Early studies suggested that hepatic failure occurred after the development of pulmonary, cardiac, and gastrointestinal dysfunction.[63] Hermreck and associates[64] noted that jaundice did not become evident until postoperative day 6. The mortality was noted to be 83%. No hepatic necrosis was noted, and the dysfunction was ascribed to hypoxic hepatic injury. Maziak and colleagues[65] identified that hepatic function began to diverge between survivors and nonsurvivors on postoperative day 7 and became significantly different on postoperative day 10.

The liver can sustain a hypoxic injury after hemorrhagic shock but must cope with the reabsorption of the hematoma and the increased metabolism that this demands. At present, predictive factors for hepatic failure have not been identified, and the etiology of the dysfunction is poorly understood.

Multisystem Organ Failure

The preceding discussion has focused on individual organ dysfunction; however, many RAAA patients experience multiple-organ dysfunction. This condition first was reported in a 1973 review of renal failure after RAAA in which progressive organ failure was described.[63] Since that report, MOF has been reported with a postoperative incidence of 64%, and in several series, MOF is the most common cause of death after 48 hours, accounting for 93% of deaths.[66,67] The development of MOF or a systemic inflammatory syndrome has been described extensively in trauma patients, patients with pancreatitis, and patients with perforated viscus. Relatively few RAAA patients have positive blood cultures as an initiating event to MOF.[65,66] When elective, urgent, and ruptured AAA patients were compared for the evidence of systemic inflammation, organ failure, or MOF, the incidence of systemic inflammation was 89% to 100% in all three groups. Organ failure was similar in elective and urgent patients (46% to 54%); however, 100% of the ruptures had at least single-organ failure. The distinction between the three groups occurred when MOF was noted to be highest in the ruptured group (64%) and was only 4.5% in the elective group. The mortality in patients with RAAA with MOF was 69% versus 0% in patients who did not have MOF. RAAA is a potent stimulus to induce organ dysfunction.

The etiologic factors responsible for the induction of multiple organ dysfunction syndrome center on the magnitude, number, and timing of the inducing inflammatory insults. The evidence from the RAAA data suggests that suprarenal clamping and longer duration of aortic clamping are associated with higher rates of postoperative complications and death.[31]

A hypothesis that may account for the excessive complications and the persistently high mortality in this patient population is the "two-hit" hypothesis.[32,58] Rupture and repair of an aneurysm is a combination of two ischemia-reperfusion events. Hemorrhagic shock is the initial ischemic event, which primes the inflammatory response.[68] This response affects the entire body, although the insult to various tissues may be different.[69] Aneurysm repair requires a second ischemic event, aortic clamping, which causes relative lower torso ischemia.[70] Resuscitation initiates the first reperfusion event, and aortic unclamping is the second hit that occurs in the face of a system primed by hemorrhagic shock. This theory is supported by data from an animal model of RAAA and data collected from clinical cases.[58,71]

In an animal model of RAAA, the individual insults of hemorrhagic shock alone or aortic clamping alone were insufficient to result in the development of systemic organ injury.[32] When the events were combined, a synergistic effect occurred that resulted in rapid onset of systemic organ injury, which resembled the clinical situation but over a much shorter time course (Fig. 102-5). This model has implicated neutrophils and more recently the complement cascade as significant mediators of the systemic injury.[71,72] Further studies with this model suggest that cardiac contractile dysfunction may develop in the postoperative period, which may account for the high incidence of cardiac events in the postoperative phase of RAAA therapy.[73] Studies from human aneurysm patients have shown that elective AAA repair primes the neutrophils to respond to an ex vivo stimulus on the second through the fifth postoperative day.[74] In contrast, RAAA patients have neutrophils that are primed to respond to ex vivo stimulation on arrival to the emergency department and before any surgical therapy. There was a further elevation in neutrophil oxidative burst in the postoperative period suggesting that the operative repair further activated these cells.

Neutrophil-mediated injury has been implicated as a key mediator of tissue injury in many models of ischemia-reperfusion injury (myocardial infarction, intestinal ischemia, and hemorrhagic shock).[75-77] When markers of neutrophil lipid peroxidation injury were assessed in elective AAAs, no oxidative injury was noted.[58] In the RAAA group, there was evidence of significant oxidative injury on arrival in the emergency department, and further

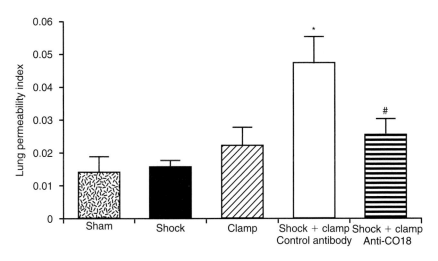

FIGURE 102-5 Lung permeability index as a measure of systemic lung injury in sham, shock, and clamp animals and shock plus clamp animals treated with control and CD18 monoclonal antibody (anti-CD18). The synergy of the two injuries results in systemic organ injury, which is reduced by neutralization of the CD18 neutrophil adhesion receptor. *$P < .05$ compared with sham, shock, and clamp. #$P < .05$ compared with shock plus clamp (control antibody). (Modified from Boyd AJ, Rubin BB, Walker PM, et al: A CD18 monoclonal antibody reduces multiple organ injury in a model of ruptured abdominal aortic aneurysm. Am J Physiol 277: H172-H182, 1999.)

significant elevations were noted by postoperative day 3. A significant relationship between the level of neutrophil oxidative burst and the level of these products of tissue oxidative injury was identified, suggesting a mechanistic link. These data provide evidence from a laboratory model and human subjects that RAAA is a two-hit model of ischemia reperfusion injury. These data may begin to explain why the mortality secondary to RAAA has failed to decrease dramatically despite all the advances in intraoperative and postoperative repair. The fact that endovascular repair of RAAAs seems to be associated with a significantly lower mortality is consistent with this two-hit theory. The lower torso ischemia is minimized resulting in a diminished second hit, resulting in a reduction in mortality. Further advances in therapy for this group of patients may come from the administration of inhibitors that restrict the activation of the inflammatory response.

■ PROGNOSIS AND SURVIVAL AFTER RUPTURED ABDOMINAL AORTIC ANEURYSM

The early survival of patients after RAAA repair often has been quoted at 50%. This estimate has been generated from statewide audits, community centers, and tertiary centers.[1,12,78,79] Other studies suggest that the mortality is closer to 70%.[22,80] A survey of the U.S. hospital discharge database for 1994 noted a 68% mortality rate for RAAA.[4] A further analysis that looked at the trend between 1979 and 1997 noted the overall mortality was 47.5% and appeared to be decreasing over the last several years of the study.[60] A statewide analysis of 527 cases in Maryland between 1990 and 1995 noted that there was a reduction in mortality from 59.3% to 43.2%.[1]

A meta-analysis of the 50 years of RAAA repair included 171 articles, which provided sufficient information so that mortality rates could be determined.[6] The overall operative mortality was 48%. The intraoperative mortality was 15%, and the postoperative mortality after successful surgery was 40%. The mortality declined 3.5% over each 10-year period of the study. Although this study suggests progress has been made over 50 years, the reduction in mortality is not dramatic. This result suggests that factors other than those easily controlled by the entire health care team are responsible for the excessive mortality observed in patients with this condition.[96]

■ PREDICTORS OF MORTALITY AFTER RUPTURED ABDOMINAL AORTIC ANEURYSM

Surgeons would like to be able to predict with certainty which patients will survive surgical repair and return to a functional life with a minimum of complications. Scoring systems have been devised and tested, but they do not predict with sufficient accuracy to deny repair to an individual patient in the emergency department. Important variables, however, have been evaluated that help the surgeon to determine the likelihood of survival, and to provide better counsel to elderly, high-risk patients who may elect not to undergo emergent RAAA repair.

Many studies have attempted to predict mortality after RAAA retrospectively. Variables that have been identified that are associated with a reduction in survival include loss of consciousness, preoperatively increased creatinine, preexisting congestive heart failure, low hemoglobin, chronic obstructive pulmonary disease, sex, race, size of the hospital, duration of hypotension, preoperative cardiac arrest, APACHE II score, base deficit, core temperature, and payer status.[1,3,7,11,12,22,45,46,59,81-86]

Prospective data from the Canadian aneurysm study identified individual variables that were predictors of early survival,[12] including preinduction blood pressure (≤ 70 mm Hg, 36% early survival; 70 to 119 mm Hg, 38%; ≥ 120 mm Hg, 75%), creatinine (≤ 1.3 mg/dL, 77% survival versus >1.3 mg/dL, 47%), intraoperative urine output (0 mL, 4%; 1 to 199 mL, 55%; ≥ 200 mL, 69%), site of cross-clamp (infrarenal, 56% versus 29%, suprarenal), and duration of cross-clamp (<60 minutes, 67% versus >60 minutes, 43%). Multiple logistic regression analyses identified that preinduction blood pressure and serum creatinine variables known in the emergency department could predict survival.

Table 102-2	Logistic Regression Model Showing the Interaction of Significant Preoperative and Intraoperative Variables That Predicted Early Survival After Ruptured Abdominal Aortic Aneurysm Repair

CREATININE (mg/dL)	CLAMP SITE	URINE OUTPUT (mL)	PROBABILITY OF SURVIVAL (%)
≤1.3	Infrarenal	≥200	90
≤1.3	Infrarenal	1-199	76
>1.3	Infrarenal	≥200	71
≤1.3	Suprarenal	≥200	65
≤1.3	Infrarenal	0	52
>1.3	Infrarenal	1-199	46
≤1.3	Suprarenal	1-199	39
>1.3	Suprarenal	≥200	33
>1.3	Infrarenal	0	23
≤1.3	Suprarenal	0	18
>1.3	Suprarenal	1-199	15
>1.3	Suprarenal	0	6

Modified from Johnston KW: Ruptured abdominal aortic aneurysm: Six-year follow-up results of a multicenter prospective study. Canadian Society for Vascular Surgery Aneurysm Study Group. J Vasc Surg 19:888-900, 1994.

Even with a blood pressure <70 mm Hg and a creatinine of >1.3 mg/dL, however, the survival was still 25%. The addition of intraoperative variables to the model further enhanced the ability to predict survival. The site of the aortic clamp, the volume of blood administered, and the intraoperative urine output also helped to predict early survival. An infrarenal clamp with less than 1800 mL of blood

administered and a urine output had 89% survival. In a patient who required a suprarenal clamp, had greater than 3500 mL of blood, and had no intraoperative urine output, survival was predicted to be 3%. When the preoperative and intraoperative variables were added to a single model, serum creatinine, clamp site, and intraoperative urine output were predictive of survival. When all preoperative, intraoperative, and postoperative variables were included, early survival was predicted by site of the aortic cross-clamp, occurrence of a myocardial infarction, respiratory failure, kidney damage, or coagulopathy.[12] At the conclusion of the operation, the surgeon can review these variables and begin to give the family an idea of the expected outcome. Table 102-2 combines the preoperative and intraoperative variables that were significant in the prospective analysis of early survival using a logistic regression model. Table 102-3 shows the postoperative variables that had a significant effect on early survival. Dialysis has a dramatic impact on survival even when no other complications are present. The development of two complications also has a dramatic impact on mortality, especially if one is an increase in creatinine or dialysis requirement.

Scoring systems have been used to predict mortality (POSSUM, P-POSSUM, MODS, and Hardman index).[87,88] The POSSUM and its modifications use 12 physiologic variables and 6 operative variables to give a calculated risk of morbidity and mortality. More recent publications suggest that POSSUM can predict RAAA mortality; however, the Hardman index, which is calculated preoperatively based on five variables (age, serum creatinine, hemoglobin, electrocardiogram evidence of ischemia,

Table 102-3	Logistic Regression Model Showing the Interaction of Significant Postoperative Complications That Predicted Early Survival After Ruptured Abdominal Aortic Aneurysm Repair

MYOCARDIAL INFARCTION	RESPIRATORY FAILURE	COAGULOPATHY	RENAL DYSFUNCTION	PROBABILITY OF SURVIVAL (%)
No	No	No	No	96
No	No	Yes	No	91
No	Yes	No	No	74
Yes	No	No	No	66
No	No	No	↑ Cr	66
No	Yes	Yes	No	58
Yes	No	Yes	No	49
No	No	Yes	↑ Cr	48
Yes	Yes	No	No	21
No	Yes	No	↑ Cr	20
Yes	No	No	↑ Cr	15
No	No	No	Dialysis	15
Yes	Yes	Yes	No	11
No	Yes	Yes	↑ Cr	11
Yes	No	Yes	↑ Cr	8
No	No	Yes	Dialysis	8
Yes	Yes	No	↑ Cr	2
No	Yes	No	Dialysis	2
Yes	No	No	Dialysis	2
Yes	Yes	Yes	↑ Cr	1
No	Yes	Yes	Dialysis	1
Yes	No	Yes	Dialysis	1
Yes	Yes	No	Dialysis	0
Yes	Yes	Yes	Dialysis	0

Cr, creatinine.

Modified from Johnston KW: Ruptured abdominal aortic aneurysm: Six-year follow-up results of a multicenter prospective study. Canadian Society for Vascular Surgery Aneurysm Study Group. J Vasc Surg 19:888, 1994.

history of loss of consciousness), also performed well. The data used in this study were retrospective; no prospective study of the Hardman index is available. These scoring systems do provide the surgeon with a rapid method to estimate mortality objectively, which helps determine the course of therapy.

Maziak and coworkers[65] calculated the multiple organ dysfunction score (MODS) to track alterations in the function of six key organ systems (respiratory, renal, hepatic, hematologic, neurologic, and cardiac) over time to determine the relationship between progressive organ dysfunction and mortality. Deaths occurred in a bimodal distribution before and after 48 hours. The survivors had little alteration in their MODS; however, patients who died after 48 hours had significantly larger increases in their MODS. The renal and hepatic components of the MODS were responsible for the progressive increase in MODS and were significantly higher in patients who died after 48 hours compared with survivors. Renal dysfunction became significantly different between survivors and nonsurvivors on postoperative day 3, whereas it took until postoperative day 10 for the hepatic dysfunction scores to become significantly different. The development of renal dysfunction followed by hepatic dysfunction indicates patients who are at the highest mortality risk.

Quality of Life After Ruptured Abdominal Aortic Aneurysm

The quality of life after RAAA has been assessed using the SF-36, an adapted Life Function Scale questionnaire and a Rosser index questionnaire.[89,90] Using the SF-36, it was noted that physical functioning was significantly reduced in patients who survived RAAA compared with age-adjusted and sex-adjusted population controls. There was no difference in the quality of life in RAAA patients who had major postoperative complications compared with patients who did not. The studies using the other questionnaires had fewer patients but compared quality of life after RAAA with quality of life in elective AAA patients. The Rosser index showed a significant reduction in the level of functional capacity in the RAAA group. The Life Functional Scale showed, however, that physical independence was similar between the two groups. The disability is greater in the ruptured group compared with elective patients, which confirms the benefit of elective repair.[91] The data from these three studies with different assessment tools suggest that overall the quality of life after RAAA is satisfactory; however, there seems to be a reduction in physical functioning.

Late Survival

After successful RAAA repair, the mortality rate of these patients is increased compared with patients who have undergone elective AAA repair and the general population. In the Canadian aneurysm study, the 5-year survival for patients alive at 30 days was 53% compared with 71% of patients who had undergone elective repair (Fig. 102-6).[12] These data are similar to the data from U.S. VA medical

centers. In the VA system, the 5-year survival was 54% for RAAA patients compared with 69% for the elective group.[92] In the long-term study centered at the Mayo Clinic, the survival was 64% and 74% for RAAAs and elective AAAs.[93] The survival of RAAA patients is significantly less than their elective counterparts. When survival of the elective AAA patients is compared with the age-matched and sex-matched population, there was no difference in survival.

The Canadian aneurysm study and the VA study looked at variables associated with late mortality. The Canadian aneurysm study identified preoperative, intraoperative, and postoperative variables that were associated with late survival. When all the variables were considered together using a Cox model, intraoperative urine output, respiratory failure, and myocardial infarction were predictors of late survival (Fig. 102-7). The VA study, using stepwise logistic regression, identified increasing age, illness severity, and patient complexity as independently associated with late mortality after hospital discharge.[92] Complications related to the aortic graft are higher in the RAAA group (5.6% VA, 17% Mayo) compared with the elective AAA group (1.9% VA, 8% Mayo).

The most frequent causes of late death were coronary artery disease, pulmonary disease, cancer, cerebrovascular disease, and renal failure. RAAA patients' early postoperative survival is dramatically lower compared with elective AAA patients. In addition, survival of RAAA patients over the long-term also is reduced compared with the elective AAA and general population.

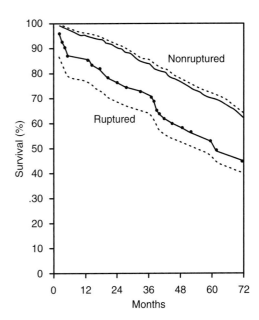

FIGURE 102-6 Long-term survival after elective or ruptured abdominal aortic aneurysm repair from the Canadian aneurysm study for patients who survived longer than 30 days. In the ruptured abdominal aortic aneurysm group, survival declines rapidly in the first several months, but subsequently begins to parallel the elective abdominal aortic aneurysm group. (Data from Johnston KW: Ruptured abdominal aortic aneurysm: Six-year follow-up results of a multicenter prospective study. Canadian Society for Vascular Surgery Aneurysm Study Group. J Vasc Surg 19:888-900, 1994.)

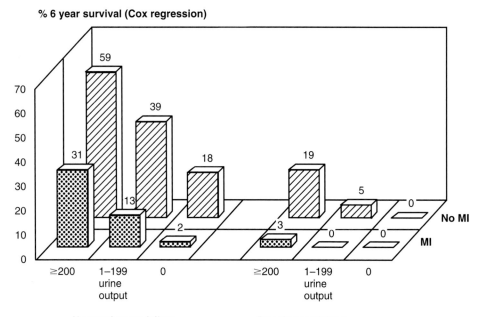

% 6 year survival (Cox regression)

FIGURE 102-7 Late postoperative survival. When all variables were considered together, intraoperative urine output, respiratory failure, and myocardial infarction (MI) were predictors of late survival. Cox proportional hazards model. (From Johnston KW: Ruptured abdominal aortic aneurysm: Six-year follow-up results of a multicenter prospective study. Canadian Society for Vascular Surgery Aneurysm Study Group. J Vasc Surg 19:888-900, 1994.)

■ REFERENCES

1. Dardik A, Burleyson GP, Bowman H, et al: Surgical repair of ruptured abdominal aortic aneurysms in the state of Maryland: Factors influencing outcome among 527 recent cases. J Vasc Surg 28:413-420, 1998.

2. Johansen K, Kohler TR, Nicholls SC, et al: Ruptured abdominal aortic aneurysm: The Harborview experience. J Vasc Surg 13:240-245, 1991.

3. Wakefield TW, Whitehouse WM Jr, Wu SC, et al: Abdominal aortic aneurysm rupture: Statistical analysis of factors affecting outcome of surgical treatment. Surgery 91:586-596, 1982.

4. Lawrence PF, Gazak C, Bhirangi L, et al: The epidemiology of surgically repaired aneurysms in the United States. J Vasc Surg 30:632-640, 1999.

5. Bengtsson H, Bergqvist D: Ruptured abdominal aortic aneurysm: A population-based study. J Vasc Surg 18:74-80, 1993.

6. Bown MJ, Sutton AJ, Bell PR, Sayers RD: A meta-analysis of 50 years of ruptured abdominal aortic aneurysm repair. Br J Surg 89:714-730, 2002.

7. Heller JA, Weinberg A, Arons R, et al: Two decades of abdominal aortic aneurysm repair: Have we made any progress? J Vasc Surg 32:1091-1100, 2000.

8. Tang T, Lindop M, Munday I, et al: A cost analysis of surgery for ruptured abdominal aortic aneurysm. Eur J Vasc Endovasc Surg 26:299-302, 2003.

9. Hinchliffe RJ, Yusuf SW, Macierewicz JA, et al: Endovascular repair of ruptured abdominal aortic aneurysm—a challenge to open repair? Results of a single centre experience in 20 patients. Eur J Vasc Endovasc Surg 22:528-534, 2001.

10. Ashton HA, Buxton MJ, Day NE, et al: The Multicentre Aneurysm Screening Study (MASS) into the effect of abdominal aortic aneurysm screening on mortality in men: A randomised controlled trial. Lancet 360:1531-1539, 2002.

11. Gloviczki P, Pairolero PC, Mucha P Jr, et al: Ruptured abdominal aortic aneurysms: Repair should not be denied. J Vasc Surg 15:851-859, 1992.

12. Johnston KW: Ruptured abdominal aortic aneurysm: Six-year follow-up results of a multicenter prospective study. Canadian Society for Vascular Surgery Aneurysm Study Group. J Vasc Surg 19:888-900, 1994.

13. http://www.cdc.gov/nchs/releases/02facts/final2000.htm. 2003.

14. Cronenwett JL, Birkmeyer JD: The Dartmouth Atlas of Vascular Health Care. Chicago, American Hospital Association Press, 2000.

15. Heikkinen M, Salenius JP, Auvinen O: Ruptured abdominal aortic aneurysm in a well-defined geographic area. J Vasc Surg 36:291-296, 2002.

16. Marston WA, Ahlquist R, Johnson G Jr, Meyer AA: Misdiagnosis of ruptured abdominal aortic aneurysms. J Vasc Surg 16:17-22, 1992.

17. Khaw H, Sottiurai VS, Craighead CC, Batson RC: Ruptured aortic aneurysm presenting as symptomatic inguinal mass: Report of six cases. J Vasc Surg 4:384-389, 1986.

18. Linsell JC, Rowe PH, Owen WJ: Rupture of an aortic aneurysm into the renal vein presenting as a left-sided varicocoele: Case report. Acta Chir Scand 153:477-478, 1987.

19. Akkersdijk GJ, van Bockel JH: Ruptured abdominal aortic aneurysm: Initial misdiagnosis and the effect on treatment. Eur J Surg 164:29-34, 1998.

20. Loughran CF: A review of the plain abdominal radiograph in acute rupture of abdominal aortic aneurysms. Clin Radiol 37:383-387, 1986.

21. Shuman WP, Hastrup WJ, Kohler TR, et al: Suspected leaking abdominal aortic aneurysm: Use of sonography in the emergency room. Radiology 168:117-119, 1988.

22. Johansen K, Kohler TR, Nicholls SC, et al: Ruptured abdominal aortic aneurysm: The Harborview experience. J Vasc Surg 13:240-247, 1991.

23. Reichart M, Geelkerken RH, Huisman AB, et al: Ruptured abdominal aortic aneurysm: Endovascular repair is feasible in 40% of patients. Eur J Vasc Endovasc Surg 26:479-486, 2003.

24. Weinbaum FI, Dubner S, Turner JW, Pardes JG: The accuracy of computed tomography in the diagnosis of retroperitoneal blood in the presence of abdominal aortic aneurysm. J Vasc Surg 6:11-16, 1987.

25. Alric P, Ryckwaert F, Picot MC, et al: Ruptured aneurysm of the infrarenal abdominal aorta: Impact of age and postoperative complications on mortality. Ann Vasc Surg 17:277-283, 2003.

26. Bickell WH, Wall MJ Jr, Pepe PE, et al: Immediate versus delayed fluid resuscitation for hypotensive patients with penetrating torso injuries. N Engl J Med 331:1105-1109, 1994.

27. Crawford ES: Ruptured abdominal aortic aneurysm [editorial]. J Vasc Surg 13:348-350, 1991.

28. Holmes JF, Sakles JC, Lewis G, Wisner DH: Effects of delaying fluid resuscitation on an injury to the systemic arterial vasculature. Acad Emerg Med 9:267-274, 2002.

29. Kim SH, Stezoski SW, Safar P, et al: Hypothermia and minimal fluid resuscitation increase survival after uncontrolled hemorrhagic shock in rats. J Trauma 42:213-222, 1997.

30. Revell M, Porter K, Greaves I: Fluid resuscitation in prehospital trauma care: A consensus view. Emerg Med J 19:494-498, 2002.

31. Bauer EP, Redaelli C, von Segesser LK, Turina MI: Ruptured abdominal aortic aneurysms: Predictors for early complications and death. Surgery 114:31-35, 1993.

32. Lindsay TF, Walker PM, Romaschin A: Acute pulmonary injury in a model of ruptured abdominal aortic aneurysm. J Vasc Surg 22:1-8, 1995.

33. Chang BB, Shah DM, Paty PS, et al: Can the retroperitoneal approach be used for ruptured abdominal aortic aneurysms? J Vasc Surg 11:326-330, 1990.

34. Green RM: When and how should pararenal aortic aneurysms be repaired: Critical dimensions and technical adjuncts. In Veith FJ (ed): Current Critical Problems in Vascular Surgery, vol 6. St. Louis, Quality Medical Publishing, 1994, pp 201-213.

35. Stephenson HE Jr: Ruptured abdominal aneurysms. In Nyhus LM, Baker RJ (eds): Mastery of Surgery, vol 2. Boston, Little, Brown, 1984, pp 1366-1371.

36. Veith FJ, Ohki T: Endovascular approaches to ruptured infrarenal aorto-iliac aneurysms. J Cardiovasc Surg (Torino) 43:369-378, 2002.

37. Wolf RK, Williams EL, Kistler PC: Transbrachial balloon catheter tamponade of ruptured abdominal aortic aneurysms without fluoroscopic control. Surg Gynecol Obstet 164:463-465, 1987.

38. Ohki T, Veith FJ: Endovascular grafts and other image-guided catheter-based adjuncts to improve the treatment of ruptured aortoiliac aneurysms. Ann Surg 232:466-479, 2000.

39. Orend KH, Kotsis T, Scharrer-Pamler R, et al: Endovascular repair of aortic rupture due to trauma and aneurysm. Eur J Vasc Endovasc Surg 23:61-67, 2002.

40. Posacioglu H, Apaydin AZ, Islamoglu F, et al: Adverse effects of cell saver in patients undergoing ruptured abdominal aortic aneurysm repair. Ann Vasc Surg 16:450-455, 2002.

41. Szalay D, Wong D, Lindsay T: Impact of red cell salvage on transfusion requirements during elective abdominal aortic aneurysm repair. Ann Vasc Surg 13:576-581, 1999.

42. Huber TS, McGorray SP, Carlton LC, et al: Intraoperative autologous transfusion during elective infrarenal aortic reconstruction: A decision analysis model. J Vasc Surg 25:984-993, 1997.

43. Frank SM, Fleisher LA, Breslow MJ, et al: Perioperative maintenance of normothermia reduces the incidence of morbid cardiac events: A randomized clinical trial. JAMA 277:1127-1134, 1997.

44. Aljabri B, MacDonald PS, Satin R, et al: Incidence of major venous and renal anomalies relevant to aortoiliac surgery as demonstrated by computed tomography. Ann Vasc Surg 15:615-618, 2001.

45. Briguori C, Manganelli F, Scarpato P, et al: Acetylcysteine and contrast agent-associated nephrotoxicity. J Am Coll Cardiol 40:298-303, 2002.

46. Sekhon CS, Sekhon BK, Singh I, et al: Attenuation of renal ischemia/reperfusion injury by a triple drug combination therapy. J Nephrol 16:63-74, 2003.

47. Rasmussen TE, Hallett JW Jr, Noel AA, et al: Early abdominal closure with mesh reduces multiple organ failure after ruptured abdominal aortic aneurysm repair: Guidelines from a 10-year case-control study. J Vasc Surg 35:246-253, 2002.

48. Akers DL Jr, Fowl RJ, Kempczinski RF, et al: Temporary closure of the abdominal wall by use of silicone rubber sheets after operative repair of ruptured abdominal aortic aneurysms. J Vasc Surg 14:48-52, 1991.

49. Loftus IM, Thompson MM: The abdominal compartment syndrome following aortic surgery. Eur J Vasc Endovasc Surg 25:97-109, 2003.

50. Papavassiliou V, Anderton M, Loftus IM, et al: The physiological effects of elevated intra-abdominal pressure following aneurysm repair. Eur J Vasc Endovasc Surg 26:293, 2003.

51. Foy HM, Nathens AB, Maser B, et al: Reinforced silicone elastomer sheeting, an improved method of temporary abdominal closure in damage control laparotomy. Am J Surg 185:498-501, 2003.

52. Peppelenbosch N, Yilmaz N, van Marrewijk C, et al: Emergency treatment of acute symptomatic or ruptured abdominal aortic aneurysm: Outcome of a prospective intent-to-treat by EVAR protocol. Eur J Vasc Endovasc Surg 26:303-310, 2003.

53. Hinchliffe RJ, Alric P, Rose D, et al: Comparison of morphologic features of intact and ruptured aneurysms of infrarenal abdominal aorta. J Vasc Surg 38:88-92, 2003.

54. Ohki T, Veith FJ: Endovascular therapy for ruptured abdominal aortic aneurysms. Adv Surg 35:131-151, 2001.

55. Lachat ML, Pfammatter T, Witzke HJ, et al: Endovascular repair with bifurcated stent-grafts under local anaesthesia to improve outcome of ruptured aortoiliac aneurysms. Eur J Vasc Endovasc Surg 23:528-536, 2002.

56. Harris LM, Faggioli GL, Fiedler R, et al: Ruptured abdominal aortic aneurysms: Factors affecting mortality rates. J Vasc Surg 14:812-818, 1991.

57. Rosenthal D: Spinal cord ischemia after abdominal aortic operation: Is it preventable? J Vasc Surg 30:391-397, 1999.

58. Lindsay TF, Luo XP, Lehotay DC, et al: Ruptured abdominal aortic aneurysm, a "two-hit" ischemia/reperfusion injury: Evidence from an analysis of oxidative products. J Vasc Surg 30:219-228, 1999.

59. Harris LM, Faggioli GL, Fiedler R, et al: Ruptured abdominal aortic aneurysms: Factors affecting mortality rates. J Vasc Surg 14:812-820, 1991.

60. Heller JA, Weinberg A, Arons R, et al: Two decades of abdominal aortic aneurysm repair: Have we made any progress? J Vasc Surg 32:1091-1100, 2000.

61. Bauer EP, Redaelli C, von Segesser LK, Turina MI: Ruptured abdominal aortic aneurysms: Predictors for early complications and death. Surgery 114:31-35, 1993.

62. El Sabrout RA, Reul GJ: Suprarenal or supraceliac aortic clamping during repair of infrarenal abdominal aortic aneurysms. Tex Heart Inst J 28:254-264, 2001.

63. Tilney NL, Bailey GL, Morgan AP: Sequential system failure after rupture of abdominal aortic aneurysms: An unsolved problem in postoperative care. Ann Surg 178:117-122, 1973.

64. Hermreck AS, Proberts KS, Thomas JH: Severe jaundice after rupture of abdominal aortic aneurysm. Am J Surg 134:745-748, 1977.

65. Maziak DE, Lindsay TF, Marshall JC, Walker PM: The impact of multiple organ dysfunction on mortality following ruptured abdominal aortic aneurysm repair. Ann Vasc Surg 12:93-100, 1998.

66. Bown MJ, Nicholson ML, Bell PR, Sayers RD: Cytokines and inflammatory pathways in the pathogenesis of multiple organ failure following abdominal aortic aneurysm repair. Eur J Vasc Endovasc Surg 22:485-495, 2001.

67. Kniemeyer HW, Kessler T, Reber PU, et al: Treatment of ruptured abdominal aortic aneurysm, a permanent challenge or a waste of resources? Prediction of outcome using a multi-organ-dysfunction score. Eur J Vasc Endovasc Surg 19:190-196, 2000.

68. Fan J, Marshall JC, Jimenez M, et al: Hemorrhagic shock primes for increased expression of cytokine-induced neutrophil chemoattractant in the lung: Role in pulmonary inflammation following lipopolysaccharide. J Immunol 161:440-447, 1998.

69. Vedder NB, Fouty BW, Winn RK, et al: Role of neutrophils in generalized reperfusion injury associated with resuscitation from shock. Surgery 106:509-516, 1989.

70. Forbes TL, Harris KA, Jamieson WG, et al: Leukocyte activity and tissue injury following ischemia-reperfusion in skeletal muscle. Microvasc Res 51:275-287, 1996.

71. Boyd AJ, Rubin BB, Walker PM, et al: A CD18 monoclonal antibody reduces multiple organ injury in a model of ruptured abdominal aortic aneurysm. Am J Physiol 277:H172-H182, 1999.

72. Harkin DW, Rubin BB, Romaschin AD, Lindsay TF: Complement C5a receptor antagonist attenuates multiple organ dysfunction following ruptured abdominal aortic aneurysm. J Vasc Surg 39:196-206, 2003.

73. Shahani R, Marshall JG, Rubin BB, et al: Role of TNF-alpha in myocardial dysfunction after hemorrhagic shock and lower-torso ischemia. Am J Physiol Heart Circ Physiol 278:H942-H950, 2000.

74. Lindsay TF, Memari N, Ghanekar A, et al: Rupture of an abdominal aortic aneurysm causes priming of phagocytic oxidative burst. J Vasc Surg 25:599-610, 1997.

75. Vedder NB, Winn RK, Rice CL, et al: A monoclonal antibody to the adherence-promoting leukocyte glycoprotein, CD18, reduces organ injury and improves survival from hemorrhagic shock and resuscitation in rabbits. J Clin Invest 81:939-944, 1988.

76. Simpson PJ, Todd RF 3rd, Fantone JC, et al: Reduction of experimental canine myocardial reperfusion injury by a monoclonal antibody (anti-Mo1, anti-CD11b) that inhibits leukocyte adhesion. J Clin Invest 81:624-629, 1988.

77. Hill J: A CD18 antibody prevents lung injury but not hypotension after intestinal ischemia-reperfusion. J Appl Physiol 74:659-664, 1993.

78. Katz DJ, Stanley JC, Zelenock GB: Operative mortality rates for intact and ruptured abdominal aortic aneurysms in Michigan: An eleven-year statewide experience. J Vasc Surg 19:804-817, 1994.

79. AbuRahma AF, Woodruff BA, Lucente FC, et al: Factors affecting survival of patients with ruptured abdominal aortic aneurysm in a West Virginia community. Surg Gynecol Obstet 172:377-382, 1991.

80. Bengtsson H, Bergqvist D: Ruptured abdominal aortic aneurysm: A population-based study. J Vasc Surg 18:74-80, 1993.

81. AbuRahma AF, Woodruff BA, Stuart SP, et al: Early diagnosis and survival of ruptured abdominal aortic aneurysms. Am J Emerg Med 9:118-121, 1991.

82. Halpern VJ, Kline RG, D'Angelo AJ, Cohen JR: Factors that affect the survival rate of patients with ruptured abdominal aortic aneurysms. J Vasc Surg 26:939-945, 1997.

83. Boxer LK, Dimick JB, Wainess RM, et al: Payer status is related to differences in access and outcomes of abdominal aortic aneurysm repair in the United States. Surgery 134:142-145, 2003.

84. Chen JC, Hildebrand HD, Salvian AJ, et al: Predictors of death in nonruptured and ruptured abdominal aortic aneurysms. J Vasc Surg 24:614-620, 1996.

85. Noel AA, Gloviczki P, Cherry KJ Jr, et al: Ruptured abdominal aortic aneurysms: The excessive mortality rate of conventional repair. J Vasc Surg 34:41-46, 2001.

86. Piper G, Patel NA, Chandela S, et al: Short-term predictors and long-term outcome after ruptured abdominal aortic aneurysm repair. Am Surg 69:703-709, 2003.

87. Lazarides MK, Arvanitis DP, Drista H, et al: POSSUM and APACHE II scores do not predict the outcome of ruptured infrarenal aortic aneurysms. Ann Vasc Surg 11:155-158, 1997.

88. Neary WD, Crow P, Foy C, et al: Comparison of POSSUM scoring and the Hardman Index in selection of patients for repair of ruptured abdominal aortic aneurysm. Br J Surg 90:421-425, 2003.

89. Korhonen SJ, Kantonen I, Pettila V, et al: Long-term survival and health-related quality of life of patients with ruptured abdominal aortic aneurysm. Eur J Vasc Endovasc Surg 25:350-353, 2003.

90. Joseph AY, Fisher JB, Toedter LJ, et al: Ruptured abdominal aortic aneurysm and quality of life. Vasc Endovasc Surg 36:65-70, 2002.

91. Korhonen SJ, Kantonen I, Pettila V, et al: Long-term survival and health-related quality of life of patients with ruptured abdominal aortic aneurysm. Eur J Vasc Endovasc Surg 25:350-353, 2003.

92. Kazmers A, Perkins AJ, Jacobs LA: Aneurysm rupture is independently associated with increased late mortality in those surviving abdominal aortic aneurysm repair. J Surg Res 95:50-53, 2001.

93. Cho JS, Gloviczki P, Martelli E, et al: Long-term survival and late complications after repair of ruptured abdominal aortic aneurysms. J Vasc Surg 27:813-819, 1998.

94. Resch T, Malina M, Lindblad B, et al: Endovascular repair of ruptured abdominal aortic aneurysms: Logistics and short-term results. J Endovasc Ther 10:440-446, 2003.

95. Scharrer-Pamler R, Kotsis T, Kapfer X, et al: Endovascular stent-graft repair of ruptured aortic aneurysms. J Endovasc Ther 10:447-452, 2003.

96. Ouriel K, Geary K, Green RM, et al: Factors determining survival after ruptured aortic aneurysm: The hospital, the surgeon, and the patient. J Vasc Surg 11:493-496, 1990.

Chapter

103

Thoracoabdominal Aortic Aneurysm

HAZIM J. SAFI, MD
TAM T. T. HUYNH, MD
ANTHONY L. ESTRERA, MD
CHARLES C. MILLER III, PhD

For a patient with a large thoracoabdominal aortic aneurysm (TAAA), the options are limited. If the aneurysm is left untreated, fatal rupture is a constant, albeit unpredictable, threat. Although emergency repair can save the life of a patient with a ruptured aneurysm, the associated morbidity and mortality remain extremely high. Elective surgical repair is the only effective treatment in eradicating the risk of aneurysm rupture and improving survival (Fig. 103-1). TAAA repair is a major undertaking, however, because all major organs, including the heart, lung, liver, kidneys, intestines, and spinal cord, are at risk during surgery.

Aortic graft replacement using the inclusion technique with reimplantation of intercostal and visceral arteries forms the basis of surgical repair of TAAAs. During the "clamp and sew" era, the expediency of surgery was key in determining patient outcome. Next in importance for predicting patient outcome was the extent and location of the aneurysm, and a classification system was devised (Fig. 103-2). This chapter reviews the etiology, pathogenesis, epidemiology, natural history, and clinical manifestations of TAAAs. Patient management is discussed in detail, including preoperative diagnostic imaging and evaluation, operative

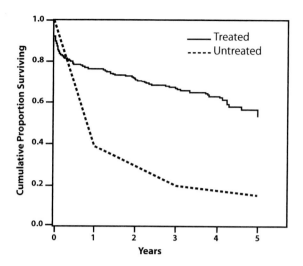

FIGURE 103-1 Thoracoabdominal aortic aneurysm. Comparison of survival rates in untreated versus surgically treated patients.[23,56]

techniques, and postoperative care. Finally, we report our surgical results and the advances in organ protection.

■ ETIOLOGY

Most TAAAs are degenerative, with an underlying pathology similar to the more frequently encountered infrarenal abdominal aortic aneurysm. These degenerative aneurysms are characterized by thinning of the media with destruction of smooth muscle cells and elastin, infiltration of inflammatory cells, neovascularization, and other characteristics (see Chapter 29).[1-3]

Familial clustering of aortic aneurysms is evident because 20% of patients with thoracic aortic aneurysms (TAAs) have one or more first-degree relatives with a TAA.[4-6] Marfan's syndrome, an inherited connective tissue disorder, is the most common syndrome related to aortic aneurysm and dissection. Marfan's syndrome occurs at a frequency of 1:5000 worldwide and is characterized by skeletal, ocular, and cardiovascular abnormalities.[7] Cardio-

vascular complications are the major cause of morbidity and mortality in Marfan's syndrome and include TAA, thoracic aortic dissection, aortic valve regurgitation, and mitral valve prolapse and regurgitation. Aortic dilatation observed in Marfan's syndrome patients has been linked to mutation in fibrillin-1 (FBN1). FBN1 is a large extracellular glycoprotein and major constituent of the microfibrils that together with elastin confers the biomechanical properties of the aortic wall. Marfan's syndrome is inherited in an autosomal dominant manner with high penetrance and clinical variability.

Approximately 25% of patients have Marfan's syndrome as the result of a new mutation, without a family history.[8] A total of 137 mutations have been entered in the international Marfan's syndrome database (http://www.umd.necker.fr). To add to the complexity of Marfan's syndrome, a distinct group of patients who do not fulfill the usual diagnostic criteria for Marfan's syndrome but nevertheless have FBN1 mutations also can develop TAA and dissection.[9,10] In addition, mutations in fibrillin-2 (FBN2) that cause congenital contractural arachnodactyly have been found; this is a rare condition, characterized by joint contractures, muscle hypoplasia, and crumpled ears.[11]

Other known genetic syndromes that predispose individuals to TAA and dissection include Turner's syndrome, Ehlers-Danlos syndrome, and polycystic kidney disease.[12-15] In addition, a familial syndrome in which multiple members have TAA and dissection, with yet to be identified genetic abnormalities, has been reported in the literature.[16] In most of these families, the phenotype for TAA and dissection is inherited in an autosomal dominant manner with marked variability in the age at onset of aortic disease and decreased penetrance.[16]

A small percentage of TAAAs are the result of infection or trauma. An infected aneurysm usually results from bacterial or septic emboli that seed an atherosclerotic aorta. Another mechanism is contiguous spread from empyema or adjacent infected lymph nodes. Although any organism can infect the aortic wall, commonly described organisms include *Salmonella, Haemophilus influenzae, Staphylococcus, Mycobacterium tuberculosis,* and *Treponema pallidum* (syphilis).[17,18] Infected aortic aneurysms are usually saccular

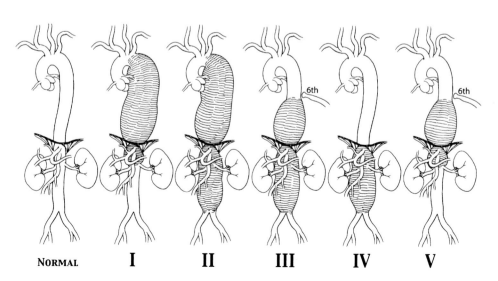

FIGURE 103-2 Normal thoracoabdominal aorta and aneurysm classification. Extent I, distal to the left subclavian artery to above the renal arteries. Extent II, distal to the left subclavian artery to below the renal arteries. Extent III, from the sixth intercostal space to below the renal arteries. Extent IV, from the 12th intercostal space to the iliac bifurcation (total abdominal aortic aneurysm). Extent V, below the sixth intercostal space to just above the renal arteries.

NORMAL   I   II   III   IV   V

and thought to be at greater risk for rupture. Traumatic aortic rupture is a common cause of death during blunt thoracic trauma. In more than 90% of cases, aortic rupture results in exsanguination and death at the accident site.[19] A few patients develop chronic traumatic false aneurysms related to previously unrecognized traumatic aortic transection. These false aneurysms are prone to rupture so that surgical repair is warranted at the time of diagnosis.

■ NATURAL HISTORY

Aortic aneurysms are among the top 15 causes of death in the United States.[20] The incidence of TAAs has increased gradually and is estimated to be 10.4 cases per 100,000 person-years.[21] The increasing prevalence may be attributable to improved imaging techniques, an aging population, or the heightened awareness of patients and general practitioners combined.[22] The mean age of patients with TAA is between 59 and 69 years with a male-to-female ratio of 2:1 to 4:1.[23] Reports estimate that less than 39% of patients with untreated large TAAs survive beyond 5 years, with most deaths resulting from rupture.[23-26] Crucial to understanding of the natural history of TAAs is the identification of the factors related to aneurysm expansion rates and rupture. Aneurysm size is the most important risk factor for rupture. Studies have confirmed that rupture is more likely to occur when TAAs exceed 5 cm and that the rate of rupture increases with increasing aneurysm size.[24,27-30] Aneurysms 8 cm or larger have an 80% risk of rupture within 1 year of diagnosis.[31] The lifetime probability of rupture for any untreated aortic aneurysm is 75% to 80%, but the size at which the aneurysm ruptures and how long it takes to reach that point cannot be calculated easily. The expansion rate of a TAA is significant, however, and has been shown to predict the risk of rupture. The average overall expansion rate for TAAs is 0.10 to 0.42 cm per year,[27,32-35] with an exponential expansion rate for aneurysms exceeding 5 cm in diameter.[29,30] Expansion by more than 1 cm per year may signal impending rupture.[32] The median size at which a TAAA is likely to rupture has been calculated to be around 7 cm.[33,36]

Systemic hypertension is widely recognized as a risk factor for aneurysm formation and rupture. In addition, multiple reports have noted an association between increased diastolic blood pressure (>100 mm Hg) and rupture of abdominal aortic aneurysms and TAAs.[31,37,38] In particular, Wheat and Palmer[39] showed that decreasing the force of myocardial contraction *(dp/dt)* may slow the progressive aortic dilatation of TAAAs and prevent possible rupture. Consequently, we recommend the inclusion of β-adrenergic blocking agents in the antihypertensive treatment for patients with known aortic aneurysms. Patients who smoke tobacco or who have chronic obstructive pulmonary disease (COPD) also are at risk for increased rates of aneurysm expansion and rupture.[30,31,40-42] This correlation may be related to the increased collagenase activity observed in these patients (see Chapter 29).[43] An indicator of susceptibility may be seen in patients with COPD whose connective tissue shows an intolerance to smoking-related toxicity.[44] Other factors affecting the risk of rupture are gender and age.[30,38,45,46] In general, women develop aortic aneurysms 10 to 15 years later than men,[47] but the risk of rupture is greater in women than in men. Patients who are 70 years old or older with large aortic aneurysms have a 50% risk of death resulting from rupture within 1.5 years if the aneurysms are not resected.[24] The relative risk of rupture may increase by a factor of 2.6 for every decade of age.[30] Significant alterations in the structure of the aortic wall occur with aging, distinct from the formation of aneurysms, including fragmentation of elastic fibers, atrophy of the smooth muscle cells, and increases in collagen and ground substance.[48]

Extensive Aortic Aneurysms

Aneurysmal disease occurs in more than one part of the aorta in approximately 20% of cases. The most extensive aortic aneurysm is the so-called mega-aorta, involving the ascending, transverse arch, and thoracoabdominal aorta. Although associated factors include Marfan's syndrome and chronic aortic dissection, the cause of extensive aortic aneurysm remains unknown. In approximately 20% to 40% of patients with chronic aortic dissection, the descending thoracic and thoracoabdominal aorta eventually become aneurysmal within 2 to 5 years.[38,49-54] Conversely, 25% of descending TAAs and TAAAs are associated with chronic aortic dissection.[55-57] Frequently, patients may present with acute dissection in a preexisting aortic aneurysm. Persistent patency of the false aortic lumen has been shown to be a significant predictor of aneurysm formation.[50,53] The presence of chronic aortic dissection or patent false lumen or both has not been linked to a higher risk of aortic rupture.[38] Aortic dissection and resulting aneurysms are discussed in detail in Chapter 104.

■ CLINICAL PRESENTATION

In our cumulative experience (1991 to 2003), 1004 patients underwent TAAA and descending TAA repair; 63% of patients were men. The median age was 65 years (range 8 to 89 years). More than 70% of our patients were treated for systemic hypertension, 26% had associated atherosclerotic occlusive coronary artery disease, and 10% had cerebrovascular disease. Most patients reported a history of tobacco smoking, and approximately 30% continued to smoke up to the time of surgery. COPD was present in 32% of patients undergoing aneurysm surgery. Approximately 6.8% of patients had emergency surgery for free or contained rupture of TAAA or descending TAA.

Most TAAAs are discovered incidentally in asymptomatic patients. As an aneurysm grows, however, it can put pressure on adjacent structures and cause discomfort or pain. The most frequent complaint is an ill-defined chronic back pain, although pain also can occur in the chest, flank, or epigastrium. Often, back pain that is musculoskeletal in origin is difficult to differentiate from pain related to the aneurysm. Acute changes in the characteristics and severity of pain can indicate sudden expansion or impending aortic rupture. Hoarseness, resulting from vocal cord paralysis secondary to compression of the left recurrent laryngeal or vagus nerves, usually is seen in patients with large aneurysms of the proximal descending thoracic aorta.

Patients also may experience dyspnea related to compression of the tracheobronchial tree. Rarely, pulmonary hypertension can result from aneurysm pressure on the pulmonary artery. Dysphagia is a common complaint reported by patients and may be due to extrinsic compression of the esophagus by the aneurysm. A large TAAA also can press against the duodenum and cause weight loss related to early satiety or obstruction. Direct erosion of the aneurysm into the adjacent tracheobronchial tree or esophagus or both can cause exsanguination, presenting as massive hemoptysis or hematemesis or, less frequently, slow intermittent blood loss. Paraplegia or paraparesis can occur in patients with TAAA secondary to acute occlusion of intercostals or spinal arteries or both, usually associated with acute aortic dissection, but also can result from thromboembolization. Although most TAAAs have a varying amount of mural thrombus, distal embolization causing acute mesenteric, renal, or lower extremity ischemia is a rare occurrence.

Rupture seems to be the first clinical manifestation of a TAAA in 10% to 20% of patients. The acute onset of severe chest, abdominal, or back pain associated with hypotension must raise the suspicion of a ruptured aneurysm. A pulsatile mass may be palpable in the abdomen; however, if the larger part of the TAAA is positioned deep in the thorax, the aneurysm may not be apparent on physical examination. Although most ruptured aneurysms are fatal unless treated emergently, the ruptured arterial wall may seal temporarily for several hours or days before free rupture. In patients who are brought to the hospital alive, rupture usually is contained within the pleura or retroperitoneum. Free rupture is accompanied by severe hypotension, and patients are more likely to die before reaching the hospital.

■ DIAGNOSTIC IMAGING

Spiral computed tomography (CT) has replaced conventional CT in most large medical centers. Spiral CT records data using 360-degree rotation of the x-ray beam source around the object being imaged, providing fast image acquisition with great resolution. This allows accurate measurement of the aortic diameter on axial images, from the outermost part of the aortic wall on one side to the outermost part of the opposite wall. Aortic diameters can be measured serially, from the ascending aorta, aortic arch, and thoracoabdominal aorta at specific levels, to determine the extent of the aneurysm. CT angiography (CTA) acquires images during the arterial phase after a bolus of intravenous contrast material. CTA can define the aortic lumen, such as the distinction between the false and true lumina in aortic dissection (Fig. 103-3A), and show the presence or absence of thrombus (Fig. 103-3B) or inflammatory changes or both in the aortic wall. The presence of free (or contained) fluid or blood may indicate free (or contained) rupture. Thin-slice CTA image acquisition also can identify patent intercostal arteries. Coronal reformatting or three-dimensional reconstruction of axial CT images may provide additional views of TAAA, but is usually not necessary (Fig. 103-3C). A general assessment of other intrathoracic, intra-abdominal, and intrapelvic solid organs can be obtained from CT scans. Associated pathology, such as lung or kidney disease, can be detected and evaluated accordingly. CTA is the imaging modality of choice in defining the extent of TAAA and for planning operative strategy. Intravenous iodinated contrast material is not essential to determine TAAA size and extent and can be omitted in patients with impaired renal function.

Historically, before CT became widely available, conventional aortography was performed in all TAAA patients (Fig. 103-4). Today aortography is limited to patients with suspected aortic branch occlusive disease, such as atherosclerotic occlusive disease of the mesenteric, renal, or iliac arteries. In general, owing to the magnification, aortography tends to overestimate aneurysm size; however, an aneurysm may appear angiographically small in the presence of a large intramural thrombus that occupies most of the lumen. Preoperative selective aortography has been reported as a means for identifying patent intercostal arteries and the artery of Adamkiewicz.[58,59] These results have not been duplicated in large clinical series, however. Because of the risks associated with the selective injection of iodinated contrast material, including paraplegia, and yet-to-be shown clinical benefits, we do not recommend preoperative selective catheterization of intercostal arteries.

Magnetic resonance imaging is a noninvasive modality that has become widely available.[60] Magnetic resonance angiography (MRA) with gadolinium is used frequently as a screening test to detect diseases of the aorta and its branches (Fig. 103-5). The principal advantage of MRA over CTA is that it does not require intravenous iodinated contrast administration and can be performed safely in patients with impaired renal function. Although MRA provides better contrast resolution, its spatial resolution is less compared with spiral CT. In addition, CT shows aortic calcification and intramural thrombus better than MRA. The time required to acquire images, claustrophobia, internal metallic hardware (e.g., pacemakers, orthopedic rods), and higher cost are other limiting factors of MRA. In general, patients with TAAA do not require MRA if good-quality CT scans of the aneurysm are available.

Transesophageal echocardiography (TEE) also can provide excellent imaging of the ascending and descending thoracic aorta. It can be performed at the bedside or in the operating room. We favor using TEE for patients with impaired renal function or patients who are too unstable to be transported to the CT scanner. In the operating room, TEE can show aortic wall disease and help locate the optimal area for aortic cross-clamping (Fig. 103-6) while providing excellent assessment of cardiac function. TEE is an invasive modality, however, and requires an experienced operator for optimal visualization and interpretation. Examination of the aorta by TEE is limited to the supradiaphragmatic aorta because the ultrasound probe loses contact with the aorta as it crosses the gastroesophageal junction.

■ PREOPERATIVE EVALUATION

The initial consultation with the TAAA patient focuses on a thorough history and physical examination. CT scans of the aneurysm are reviewed to determine the extent of the aneurysm. Preoperative screening tests include basic blood chemistry profile, complete blood cell count, coagulation profile, electrocardiogram, and chest radiograph (Fig. 103-7).

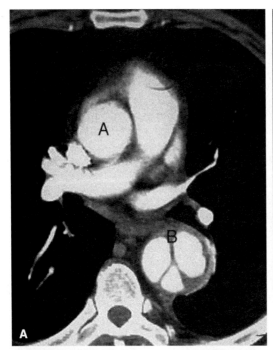

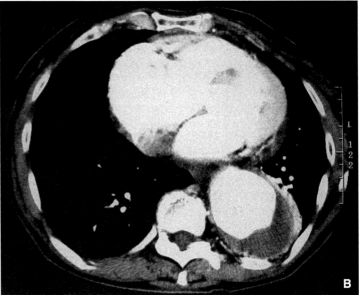

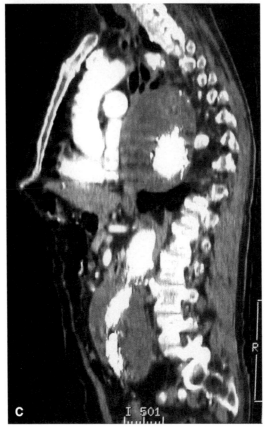

FIGURE 103-3 A, CT scan of type A and type B aortic dissections with true and false lumina shown in type B. **B,** CT scan of thoracoabdominal aortic aneurysm with thrombus in lower right hand corner of scan. **C,** Three-dimensional reconstruction of axial CT scan of extent II thoracoabdominal aortic aneurysm.

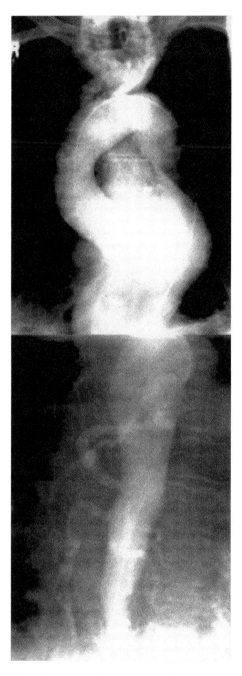

FIGURE 103-4 Aortogram of thoracoabdominal aortic aneurysm.

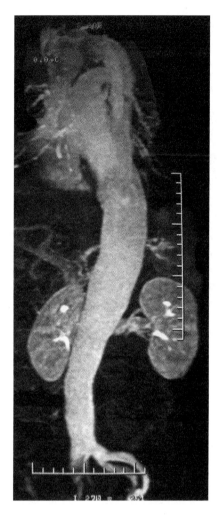

FIGURE 103-5 MRA of extent II thoracoabdominal aortic aneurysm.

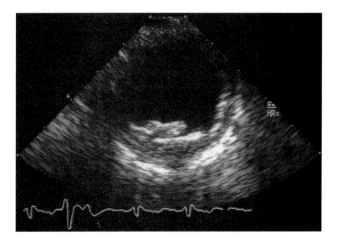

FIGURE 103-6 Transesophageal echocardiogram of aortic dissection.

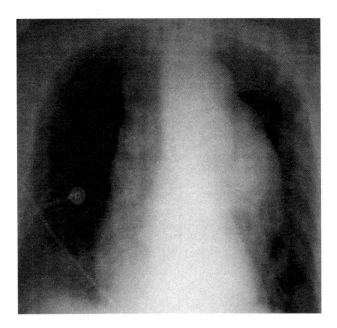

FIGURE 103-7 Chest radiograph of thoracoabdominal aortic aneurysm.

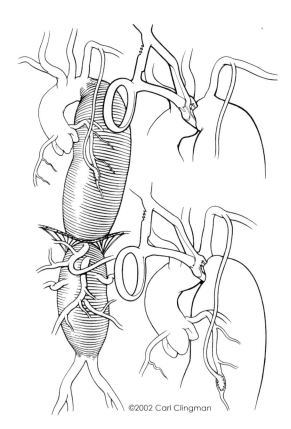

©2002 Carl Clingman

FIGURE 103-8 Saphenous vein graft bypass to the left anterior descending artery is preferable to internal mammary artery bypass if the patient has to undergo proximal clamping of the thoracic aorta as illustrated here.

To evaluate the patient's risk factors further, other organ-specific tests are obtained. Cardiac function is estimated by echocardiography. Pulmonary function tests are performed to evaluate for COPD. Initial appraisal of renal function is based on serum creatinine level. Consultations with cardiologists, pulmonologists, and nephrologists help to stratify preoperative risks. In our practice, duplex ultrasound studies of the carotid arteries also are obtained to screen for arteriosclerotic occlusive disease. Patients with severe carotid artery stenosis are advised to undergo endarterectomy before TAAA surgery to minimize the risk of perioperative stroke. Usually we wait 2 to 3 days after carotid endarterectomy before proceeding with TAAA repair.

Patients with known or suspected coronary artery disease may require cardiac catheterization for further evaluation. Coronary artery revascularization, using either percutaneous intervention or surgical bypass, may be indicated before TAAA repair. For patients who undergo coronary artery stenting, 3 to 4 weeks of platelet inhibition (clopidogrel and aspirin) is required to prevent acute stent thrombosis. Clopidogrel is stopped 7 days before TAAA repair. In patients who have to undergo coronary artery bypass before TAAA repair, we prefer to use a saphenous vein graft as the conduit of choice. Specifically, we avoid using the left internal mammary artery to obviate the possibility of cardiac ischemia should aortic cross-clamping proximal to the left subclavian artery be required during the TAAA repair (Fig. 103-8). The internal mammary artery may provide important collateral blood supply to the spinal cord. Patients who undergo coronary artery bypass usually require 4 to 6 weeks to recover before TAAA repair.

COPD is defined by a history of COPD or pulmonary function tests showing a forced expiratory volume in 1 second of less than 60% of predicted. The incidence of COPD has been reported in 30% to 40% of patients with TAAA and is associated with increased operative mortality.[61,62] Preoperative preparations to improve lung function include immediate cessation of tobacco smoking, chest physical therapy, bronchodilators, and antibiotics when indicated. Occasionally, perioperative steroids also are prescribed for acute exacerbation of reactive airway disease.

Careful evaluation of the patient's renal function is mandatory because preoperative renal insufficiency has been shown to be a predictor of postoperative renal failure. Postoperative renal dysfunction is a known risk factor for higher mortality rate and increased incidence of postoperative neurologic deficits. To minimize preoperative renal injury in patients with suspected chronic renal insufficiency, nephrotoxic agents, such as aminoglycosides, nonsteroidal anti-inflammatory drugs, and iodinated contrast agents, may have to be withheld. Preoperative renal function also can be optimized with good hydration.

■ OPERATIVE TECHNIQUES

The patient is brought to the operating room and placed in the supine position on the operating table and prepared for surgery. The right radial artery is cannulated for continuous arterial pressure monitoring. General anesthesia is induced. Endotracheal intubation is established using a double-lumen tube for selective one-lung ventilation during surgery. A sheath is inserted in the internal jugular vein, and a Swan-Ganz catheter is floated into the pulmonary artery for continuous monitoring of the central venous and pulmonary

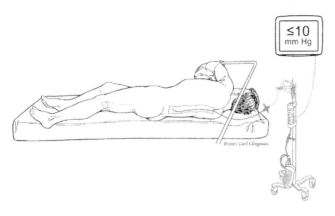

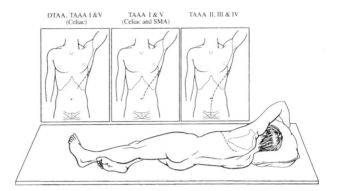

FIGURE 103-9 Placement of the lumbar catheter in the third or fourth lumbar space to provide cerebrospinal fluid drainage and pressure monitoring.

FIGURE 103-10 Thoracoabdominal incisions tailored for aneurysm extent.

artery pressures. Large-bore central and peripheral venous lines are established for fluid and blood replacement therapy. Temperature probes are placed in the patient's nasopharynx, rectum, and bladder. Electrodes are attached to the scalp for electroencephalogram and along the spinal cord for somatosensory evoked potential to assess the central nervous system and spinal cord function. The patient is positioned on his or her right side with the hips and knees flexed to open the intervertebral spaces. A lumbar catheter is placed in the third or fourth lumbar space to provide cerebrospinal fluid (CSF) drainage and pressure monitoring (Fig. 103-9). The CSF pressure is kept at 10 mm Hg or less by gravity drainage of CSF throughout the procedure.

The patient is repositioned in the right lateral decubitus position with the hips slightly turned to allow access to both groins. We tailor the incision to complement the extent of the aneurysm (Fig. 103-10). The full thoracoretroperitoneal incision begins posteriorly between the tip of the scapula and the spinous process, curving along the sixth intercostal space to the costal cartilage, then obliquely to the umbilicus, and finally in the midline to above the symphysis pubis. The latissimus dorsi muscle is divided, and the insertion of the serratus anterior muscle is mobilized. The left lung is deflated, and the left thoracic cavity is entered. Resection of the sixth rib facilitates exposure and is performed routinely for all TAAAs except extent IV. Usually a full thoracoretroperitoneal exploration is necessary for extent II and III TAAAs. Extent IV TAAAs sometimes can be approached only with a retroperitoneal incision and division of the diaphragmatic crus, but sometimes a full thoracoretroperitoneal exposure is preferred, depending on the details of the proximal extent. A modified thoracoretroperitoneal incision begins similar to the full thoracoretroperitoneal incision but ends at the costal cartilage or above the umbilicus. The modified thoracoretroperitoneal incision provides excellent exposure for surgery involving a descending TAA, extent I TAAA, and extent V TAAA, if the aneurysm ends above the superior mesenteric artery.

A self-retaining retractor maintains full thoracic and abdominal exposure during the procedure. The dissection begins at the level of the hilum of the lung cephalad to the proximal descending thoracic aorta. We identify the liga-

mentum arteriosum and transect it, taking care to avoid injury to the left recurrent laryngeal nerve. The extent of the distal abdominal aneurysm is assessed. For modified thoracoretroperitoneal exploration, the diaphragm is retracted downward to expose the infradiaphragmatic aorta. When the aortic aneurysm extends below the renal arteries, we use the full thoracoretroperitoneal exploration below the diaphragm. We no longer divide the diaphragm. Taking care to avoid injury to the left phrenic nerve, only the muscular portion of the diaphragm is cut (Fig. 103-11). A retroperitoneal plane is developed, mobilizing the spleen, bowel loops, and left kidney to the right side of the abdominal aorta (medial visceral rotation). To prepare for distal aortic perfusion, the patient is anticoagulated with 1 mg/kg of heparin. The pericardium is opened posterior to the left phrenic nerve to allow direct visualization of the pulmonary veins and left atrium. The left atrium is cannulated through the left inferior pulmonary vein or atrial

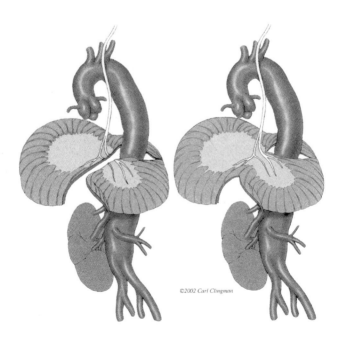

FIGURE 103-11 Previously the diaphragm was divided (*left*); currently only the muscular portion of the diaphragm is cut.

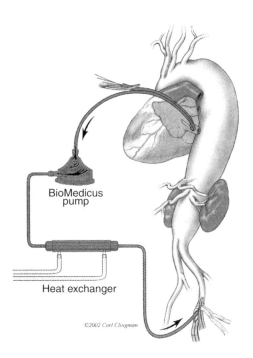

FIGURE 103-12 Distal aortic perfusion from the left pulmonary vein to the left femoral artery.

appendage (Fig. 103-12). Bleeding from the site of cannulation can cause postoperative cardiac tamponade if the pericardium is not adequately opened. A BioMedicus pump (Minneapolis, Minn) with an in-line heat exchanger is attached to the left atrial cannula, and the arterial inflow is established through the left common femoral artery or the descending thoracic aorta if the femoral artery is not accessible. Distal aortic perfusion is begun.

Clamps are applied to the proximal descending thoracic aorta just distal to the left subclavian artery and to the mid-thoracic aorta (Fig. 103-13A). When the proximal extent of the aneurysm is too close to the left subclavian artery, we clamp the aorta between the left common and left subclavian arteries and clamp the left subclavian artery separately. Because of the danger of esophageal fistula, we no longer use the inclusion technique[63] in the proximal anastomosis. Instead, we completely transect the aorta to separate it from the underlying esophagus (Fig. 103-13B). We prefer a woven Dacron graft impregnated with gelatin or collagen for replacement. We suture the graft in an end-to-end fashion to the descending thoracic aorta, using a running 3-0 or 2-0 monofilament polypropylene suture (Fig. 103-13C). We check the anastomosis for bleeding and use pledgeted polypropylene sutures for reinforcement, if necessary. We use sequential clamping for all TAAAs. After completion of the proximal anastomosis, the mid-descending aortic clamp is moved distally onto the aorta just above the celiac axis to accommodate intercostal reattachment. Reattachment of patent, lower intercostal arteries (T8-12) is performed routinely except in cases of occluded arteries, heavily calcified aorta, or acute aortic dissection (Fig. 103-13D). After completion of intercostal reattachment, the proximal clamp is released from the aorta and reapplied on the aortic graft beyond the intercostal patch, restoring pulsatile flow to the reattached intercostal arteries. The distal clamp is moved

onto the infrarenal aorta, the abdominal aorta is opened, and the graft is passed through the aortic hiatus (Fig. 103-13E). The celiac, superior mesenteric, and renal arteries are identified and cold perfused using No. 9 or No. 12 Pruitt catheters (Cryolife, St. Petersburg, Fla), depending on the size of the ostia (Fig. 103-13F).

The cold perfusate, most often cold blood (4° C), delivered to the viscera depends on the proximal aortic pressure and is maintained between 300 and 600 mL/min total to all four arteries. Renal temperature is monitored directly by inserting a temperature probe in the left renal cortex and is kept at approximately 15° C. Because renal cooling without prewarming or warming of the lower body could result in a precipitous drop in core temperature to less than 32° C leading to serious cardiac arrhythmias, core body temperature is kept between 32° C and 33° C by warming the lower body (i.e., lower extremities). If we cannot clamp the infrarenal abdominal aorta because of problems such as aortic calcification or an overly large aorta, we clamp the left common or external iliac artery instead. Alternatively, we temporarily stop the left femoral perfusion and sew a short second graft end-to-end to the aortic bifurcation. The distal graft is clamped, and femoral perfusion is restarted to permit warming of the lower body during active visceral cooling. One further option is to prewarm the patient to a safe systemic temperature (35° C), then renal cooling can be achieved.

The visceral vessels usually are reattached using the inclusion technique (Fig. 103-13G). On completion of this anastomosis, the perfusion catheters are removed, and attention is turned to the distal anastomosis. In most cases, an island patch accommodates reattachment of the celiac, superior mesenteric, and both renal arteries. Reattachment of the right or left renal artery located at too great a distance from other viscera usually requires a separate interposition bypass graft. We no longer use a visceral patch for patients with connective tissue disorders, such as Marfan's syndrome, because of the high incidence of recurrent patch aneurysms in these patients. Instead, we use a woven Dacron graft with side-arm grafts of 10 mm and 12 mm for separate attachment of the celiac, superior mesenteric, and left and right renal arteries. When the visceral and renal arteries are reimplanted, the proximal clamp is moved beyond the visceral patch, restoring pulsatile flow to the viscera and kidneys. The patient is given intravenous indigo carmine. The urinary dye clearance time is recorded and used to estimate immediate postoperative renal function. The distal anastomosis is fashioned to the aortic bifurcation (Fig. 103-13H) or occasionally to the iliac or femoral arteries, if there is associated aneurysmal or occlusive disease. Before completion of the distal anastomosis, the graft is flushed proximally, and the aorta is flushed distally.

We wean the patient from partial bypass when the core body or nasopharyngeal temperature reaches 36° C to 37° C. Protamine is administered (1 mg/1 mg heparin), and the atrial and femoral cannulae are removed. When hemostasis is achieved, two or sometimes three 36F chest tubes are placed in the pleural cavity for drainage. The diaphragm is reapproximated using running No. 1 polypropylene suture. The left lung is reinflated, and the incision is closed. The patient is placed in the supine position, and a single-lumen endotracheal tube is exchanged for the double-lumen tube.

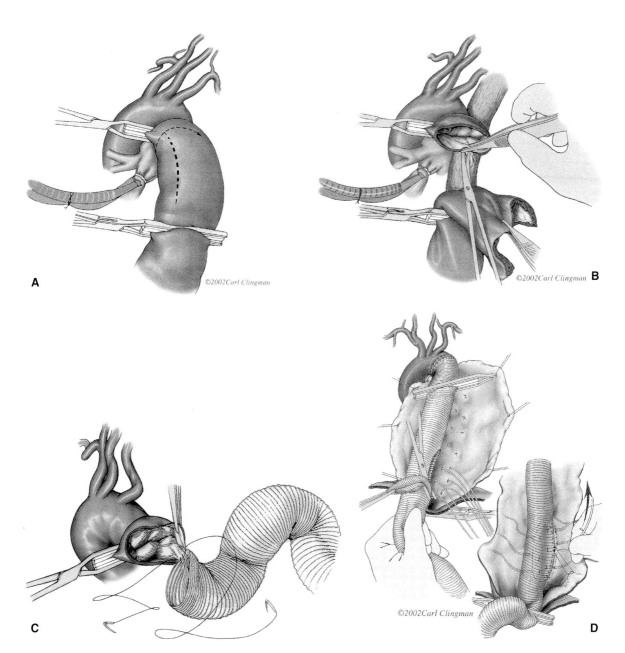

FIGURE 103-13 A, First application of proximal and distal clamps in sequential clamping, thoracoabdominal aortic aneurysm repair. **B,** The aorta is completely transected and separated from the esophagus. **C,** Thoracoabdominal aortic aneurysm proximal anastomosis. **D,** An elliptical hole is cut in the graft, and the lower intercostal arteries are reattached as a patch to the graft.   *Continued*

If the vocal cords are swollen, the double-lumen tube is kept in place until the swelling resolves. The patient is transferred to the intensive care unit (ICU). Figure 103-14 illustrates an extent II TAAA before and after surgery.

■ POSTOPERATIVE MANAGEMENT

In the ICU, we monitor the arterial pressure, pulmonary artery pressures, cardiac index, mixed venous saturation, and pulse oximetry continuously. We try to wake the patient as quickly as possible to check neurologic status. Most of our patients are kept on mechanical ventilation the first postoperative night. Chest tube drainage is monitored closely, and blood loss is liberally replaced using packed red

blood cells. The patient's mean arterial pressure is maintained between 90 and 100 mm Hg to ensure good organ perfusion, particularly to the spinal cord. Fresh frozen plasma and platelets are administered liberally for coagulopathy as needed. Patients are warmed using a warming blanket and blood warmer for transfusion therapy. Urinary output is recorded hourly. CSF pressure is monitored continuously. Approximately 10 to 15 mL of CSF is drained hourly to keep CSF pressure at 10 mm Hg or less. We start weaning the patient off the ventilator on the first postoperative day. Oral diet is resumed when the patient is extubated and has bowel sounds. If the patient requires longer mechanical ventilation, a nasoduodenal feeding tube is placed, and enteral feeding is begun on postoperative day

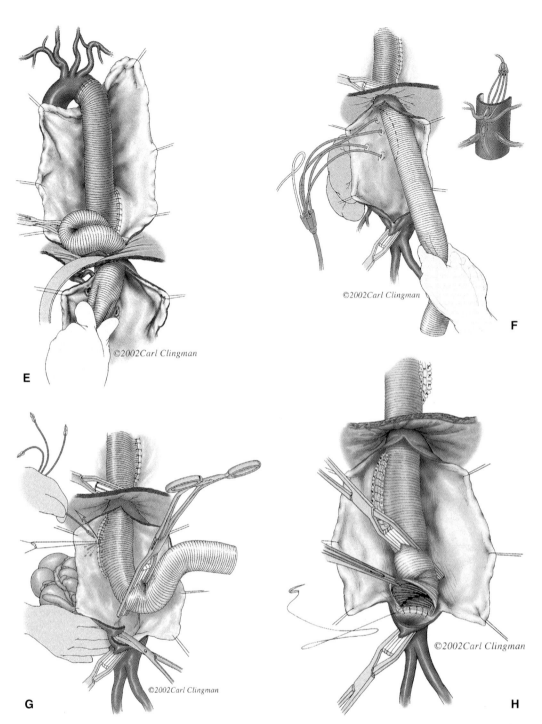

FIGURE 103-13, cont'd E, The graft is pulled down through the diaphragm. **F,** Perfusion of the celiac, superior mesenteric, and renal arteries. **G,** Reattachment of the visceral vessels to the graft. **H,** Thoracoabdominal aortic aneurysm, completion of the distal anastomosis.

2 or 3, when bowel activity returns. At times, patients can develop postoperative ileus and require total parenteral nutrition. After the patient recovers from anesthesia and is moving all extremities, physicians still have to be on the alert for delayed neurologic deficit. Factors associated with development of delayed neurologic deficit are unstable arterial blood pressure, hypoxemia, low hemoglobin, or increased CSF pressure.[64,65] CSF drainage is discontinued on postoperative day 3.

The length of stay in the ICU is about 3 or 4 days, depending on the neurologic and pulmonary status of the patient. The patient subsequently is transferred to the telemetry floor. Physical therapy is initiated in the ICU and continued throughout the patient's hospital stay. Patients are discharged home when they resume normal daily activities or transferred to a rehabilitative facility if they still require further physical assistance. The median length of stay for patients after TAAA repair is 15 days.[66] A subset of our

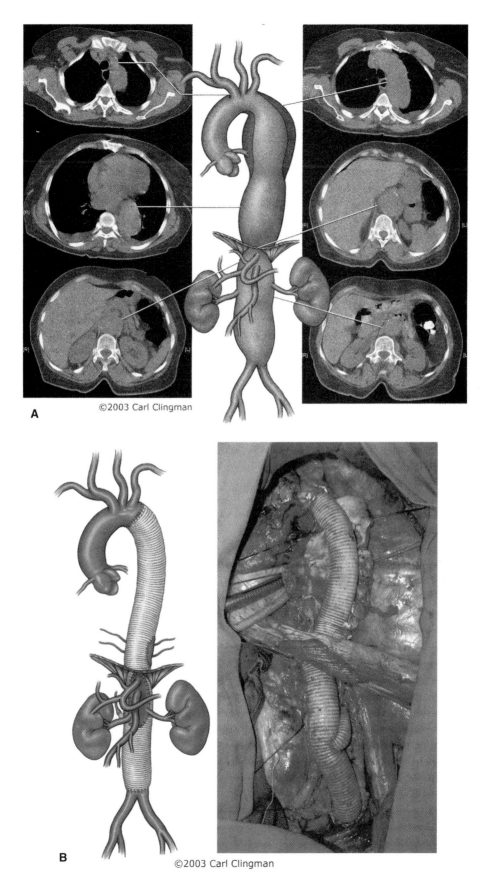

FIGURE 103-14 A, CT scans and illustration of extent II thoracoabdominal aortic aneurysm. **B,** Illustration and photograph of completed extent II thoracoabdominal aortic aneurysm repair.

patients develops postoperative complications that may lengthen hospital stay (see later). For patients who develop postoperative renal failure, we generally initiate early continuous venovenous hemodialysis or daily intermittent hemodialysis. We favor early tracheostomy for patients who remain ventilator-dependent.

After the patient is discharged, we recommend an annual follow-up with CT to screen for the development of new aneurysm or graft-related pseudoaneurysm formation as required. The frequency of follow-up visits or CT scans may vary based on TAAA etiology. Patients with remaining unoperated aortic dissection, connective tissue disorders (Marfan's syndrome or Ehlers-Danlos syndrome), a family history of aortic aneurysm, or concurrent aneurysms may need closer surveillance.

■ SURGICAL RESULTS

Patient Survival

Depending on the series, mortality rates for patients undergoing TAAA and descending TAA repair range from 4% to 21%.[28,62,67,68] The variable success rates are related partly to the heterogeneity of the patient population and to the expertise of the treating team. Currently, our 30-day mortality rate is around 14%. Using multivariable analysis, we have identified advanced age, renal failure, and paraplegia as important risk factors for mortality.[66,69,70] Patients age 79 or older with at least one of three factors—emergency presentation, a history of diabetes, or congestive heart failure—have been identified as a particularly high-risk group with 30-day mortality of 50%.[66] Overall, 70% of our patients recover from TAAA without significant postoperative complications.[71] The 5-year survival for our patients after TAAA is 60% to 70%, consistent with other

reports.[92-94] We found the negative predictors for long-term survival to include advanced age, extent II TAAA, renal failure, emergency surgery, cerebrovascular disease, and active tobacco smoking (Fig. 103-15).[56]

Spinal Cord Protection and Neurologic Deficits

Postoperative neurologic deficit is the most devastating complication after TAAA repair. Many strategies have been devised to protect the spinal cord during aortic surgery, including the sole use of active or passive distal aortic perfusion; total cardiopulmonary bypass; profound hypothermic circulatory arrest; direct spinal cord cooling; CSF drainage alone; monitoring of somatosensory and motor evoked potentials; and pharmacologic methods using papaverine, naloxone, or steroids.[72-77] These adjuncts have had varying degrees of success in preventing neurologic deficit.[72-77] When the descending thoracic aorta is cross-clamped, the spinal cord is quickly rendered ischemic because of the immediate interruption of perfusion to the spinal cord and consequent increased CSF pressure. In the cross-clamp-and-sew era, the most important predictor of neurologic deficit was the length of the clamp time. The rationale for our method of protection is to increase the spinal cord perfusion pressure directly by distal aortic perfusion and indirectly by reducing CSF pressure to 10 mm Hg or less (Fig. 103-16). Despite the negative results of an early clinical prospective randomized trial that examined the efficacy of intraoperative CSF drainage,[78] animal and human studies have since confirmed that CSF drainage reduces CSF pressure and can improve spinal cord perfusion during aortic cross-clamping.[79-81] The failure of the earlier clinical trial may have been due to study restrictions imposed by the institutional review board that limited CSF drainage to 50 mL.[78]

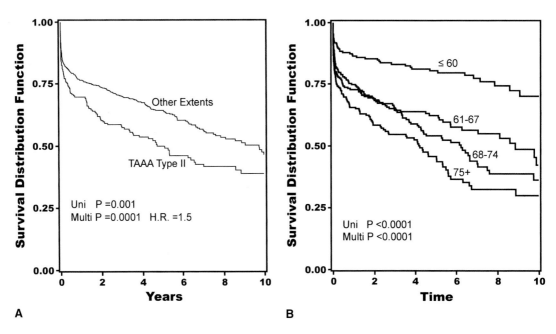

FIGURE 103-15 A, Ten-year actuarial survival, thoracoabdominal aortic aneurysm type II versus all other thoracoabdominal aortic aneurysms. **B,** Ten-year actuarial survival for patients at 60 years old or younger, 61 to 67 years old, 68 to 74 years old, and 75 years older or older.

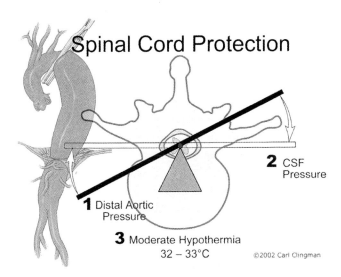

FIGURE 103-16 Illustration of rationale; cerebrospinal fluid drainage and distal aortic perfusion.

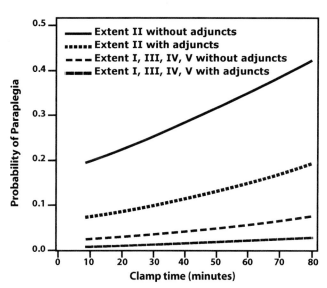

FIGURE 103-17 The probability of paraplegia increases with clamp time and is highest in extent II thoracoabdominal aortic aneurysm.

Distal Aortic Perfusion and Cerebrospinal Fluid Drainage

Since 1991, we have used the adjuncts distal aortic perfusion and CSF drainage for all patients undergoing elective repair of TAAA or descending TAA.[82] Overall, in a total of 1004 patients, immediate postoperative neurologic deficit (paraplegia or paraparesis that occurs as the patient awakens from anesthesia) occurred in 2.4% of patients operated with adjuncts and in 6.8% of patients without adjuncts (Fig. 103-17).[56] This combination of adjuncts has reduced our cumulative rate of neurologic deficits to 0.9% for descending TAA repair and to 3.3% for TAAA repair.[70] Repair of the most extensive TAAAs (extent II) has long been known to result in the highest incidence of neurologic deficits. In the cross-clamp-and-sew era, this incidence was 30% to 40%.[62] With the use of adjuncts, the rate of immediate neurologic deficits for extent II TAAA has been reduced to 6.6% in our series (Fig. 103-18).[56] In addition to the extent of the aneurysm, other perioperative risk factors for immediate neurologic deficits include age, emergency presentation, renal dysfunction, active smoking, and cerebrovascular disease.[56,66,70,83] Our current strategy, using the combination of intraoperative distal aortic perfusion and perioperative CSF drainage, prevents 1 neurologic deficit in 20 cases for all patients and 1 in 5 for extent II TAAAs.[56]

Other Adjunctive Measures

Also important in spinal cord protection is the reimplantation of intercostal arteries. During the cross-clamp-and-sew era, reimplantation of intercostal arteries was found to be a risk factor for postoperative neurologic deficit.[84] This link was explained by the longer cross-clamp time required to reattach the intercostal arteries. The level at which the anterior radicular artery (also called the artery of *Adamkiewicz* or *arteria radicularis magna*) originates is known to be variable (Fig. 103-19). Most commonly, it

originates from one of the lower intercostal arteries with or without additional collateral branches from nearby intercostal arteries. The anterior radicular artery is believed to be the major blood supply to the anterior spinal artery of the spinal cord. We studied the relationship of neurologic deficit to ligation, reimplantation, and preexisting occlusion of intercostal arteries in patients undergoing TAAA repair using adjuncts. We found that ligation of patent lower intercostal arteries (T9 to T12) increased the risk of paraplegia (Fig. 103-20).[85] We reattach all patent lower intercostal arteries from T9 to T12, either together as a patch to a side-hole made in the Dacron graft or, if the

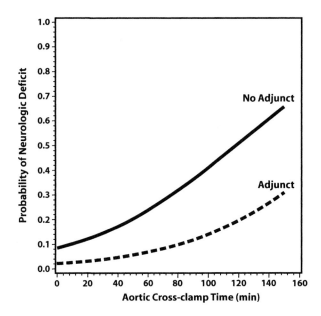

FIGURE 103-18 The probability of neurologic deficit increases with clamp time and is markedly higher in patients undergoing thoracoabdominal aortic aneurysm surgery without adjuncts.

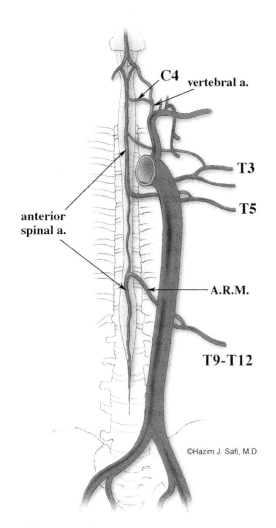

FIGURE 103-19 The arteria radicularis magna (A.R.M.) arises from the lower intercostal arteries.

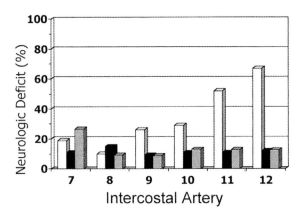

FIGURE 103-20 Ligation of patent lower intercostal arteries (T9 to T12) increases the risk of paraplegia. *White,* ligation; *gray,* reimplantation; *black,* occlusion.

Delayed Neurologic Deficits

Delayed neurologic deficit refers to the onset of paraplegia or paraparesis after a period of observed normal neurologic function. Delayed-onset neurologic deficit after TAAA repair was first reported in 1988, at which time the condition was considered irreversible and beyond the surgeon's control.[86] Two subsequent anecdotal reports in the literature showed reversal of delayed paraplegia with CSF drainage.[80,87] Since then, numerous reports have described improvements in patients' neurologic function by using CSF drainage for delayed neurologic deficits.[88-90] We have observed delayed neurologic deficit as early as 2 hours and as late as 2 weeks after surgery (median 3 days) in 2.7% of patients.[65] We have found no single risk factor responsible for delayed neurologic deficit. Using multivariate analysis, we identified acute dissection, extent II TAAA, and renal insufficiency as significant preoperative predictors for delayed neurologic deficit.[65] In a subsequent case-control study, postoperative mean arterial pressure of less than 60 mm Hg and CSF drain complications were found to be predictors in the development of delayed neurologic deficit, independent of preoperative predictors (Fig. 103-21).[91]

As improved spinal cord protection during TAAA surgery has reduced the incidence of neurologic complications, delayed neurologic deficit has emerged as an important clinical entity. The exact mechanisms involved in the development of delayed neurologic deficit are unknown. We speculate that delayed neurologic deficit after TAAA repair may result from a "second-hit" phenomenon. Adjuncts can protect the spinal cord intraoperatively and reduce the incidence of immediate neurologic deficit, but the spinal cord remains vulnerable during the early postoperative period. Additional ischemic insults caused by hemodynamic instability or malfunction of the CSF drainage catheter may constitute a second hit, causing delayed neurologic deficit. In the rigid unyielding spinal column, any increase in CSF pressure could lead to an increase in compartment pressure, with consequent decreased spinal cord perfusion. This is analogous to other clinical compartment syndromes, such as cerebral ischemia secondary to intracranial pressure or increased limb compartment pressure secondary to

intercostal arteries are too far apart, separately as buttons or using interposition bypass grafts. Backbleeding from patent intercostal arteries can be minimized with temporary placement and inflation of balloon catheters (size 3F) before reimplantation. In general, we ligate the upper (above T9) intercostal arteries. If the lower intercostal arteries are occluded, however, we reimplant the patent upper intercostal arteries because these are thought to assume a more important role in the collateral system to the anterior spinal artery.

Adequate spinal cord perfusion pressure should be maintained with avoidance of hypotension during and after surgery. Intravenous nitroprusside, in particular, can precipitate systemic hypotension, and has been shown to cause a paradoxical increase of CSF pressure.[64] To avoid the risk of neurologic deficit, we no longer use nitroprusside as an afterload-reducing agent. Although a detailed account of the essential anesthetic care during TAAA repair is beyond the scope of this chapter, the importance of adequate maintenance of systemic arterial pressure with judicious blood transfusion cannot be overemphasized because organ perfusion greatly depends on the systemic circulation.

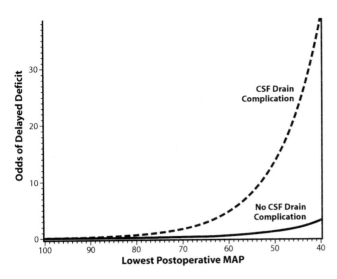

FIGURE 103-21 The odds of delayed neurologic deficit increase with complications in cerebrospinal fluid drainage.

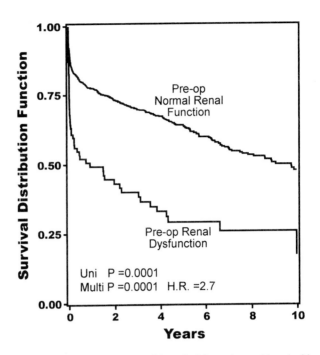

FIGURE 103-22 Ten-year actuarial survival for patients with and without preoperative renal dysfunction.

decreased limb perfusion. We drain CSF freely when delayed neurologic deficit develops to relieve the compartment pressure. Some authors have hypothesized, however, that delayed neurologic deficit may be due to apoptosis or "programmed cell death,"[64,90] in which case we would not expect to see improvements in neurologic outcome with the use of CSF drainage.

To optimize postoperative spinal cord perfusion and oxygen delivery, we keep the mean arterial pressure greater than 90 to 100 mm Hg, hemoglobin greater than 10 mg/dL, and cardiac index greater than 2.0 L/min. If delayed neurologic deficit occurs, measures to increase spinal cord perfusion are instituted immediately. The patient is placed flat in the supine position, and patency and function of the drain are ascertained immediately. If the drain has been removed, the CSF drainage catheter is reinserted immediately, and CSF is drained freely until the CSF pressure decreases to less than 10 mm Hg. The systemic arterial pressure is increased, blood transfusion is liberally infused, and oxygen saturation is increased, as indicated earlier. CSF drainage is continued for at least 72 hours for all patients with delayed neurologic deficit. Using this multifaceted approach to treating delayed neurologic deficit, we have seen improvement in neurologic function in 57% of our patients.[65] Of patients, 75% recovered function when the CSF drain was still in place at the onset of delayed neurologic deficit; 43% recovered neurologic function if the CSF drain had to be reinserted at the time of the delayed neurologic deficit. Patients who developed delayed neurologic deficit but did not have CSF drainage failed to recover function.

Renal Failure and Protection

The reported rate of acute renal failure from large series of patients undergoing TAAA repair ranges from 5% to 40% and is associated with mortality rates of 70%.[68,92,95-99] Patients who develop acute renal failure also more frequently sustain

nonrenal complications, such as respiratory failure, central nervous system dysfunction, sepsis, and gastrointestinal hemorrhage. Preoperative chronic renal insufficiency and ruptured aneurysms are known predictors of acute postoperative renal failure.[100] We define acute postoperative renal failure by an increase in serum creatinine of 1 mg/dL per day for 2 consecutive days or the need for hemodialysis. In 1004 patients, we found that the overall incidence of acute renal failure was 18%; the incidence was 7% in patients with descending TAA repair and 23% in patients with TAAA repair. Among our patients with acute renal failure, 30-day mortality was 30% compared with 10% mortality in all other patients. Approximately one third of our patients who develop acute renal failure remain on hemodialysis and, predictably, have a prolonged length of hospital stay.[66] Long-term survival for patients on hemodialysis is dismal (Fig. 103-22). Although we have theorized that patients with the most extensive extent II TAAA are at highest risk for the development of postoperative renal failure, multivariate analysis did not find the extent of TAAA to be a significant predictor in this study.

Renal Protection Methods

We have used several methods of renal protection, including different perfusion techniques and fenoldopam administration. Although our primary purpose for distal aortic perfusion was spinal cord protection, we had hoped that it also would provide renal protection. Distal aortic perfusion has emerged as protective, but only for aortic repair that does not directly involve the renal arteries or require renal artery reconstruction (descending thoracic aorta, extent I or V TAAA).[101] This finding is in contrast to a previously

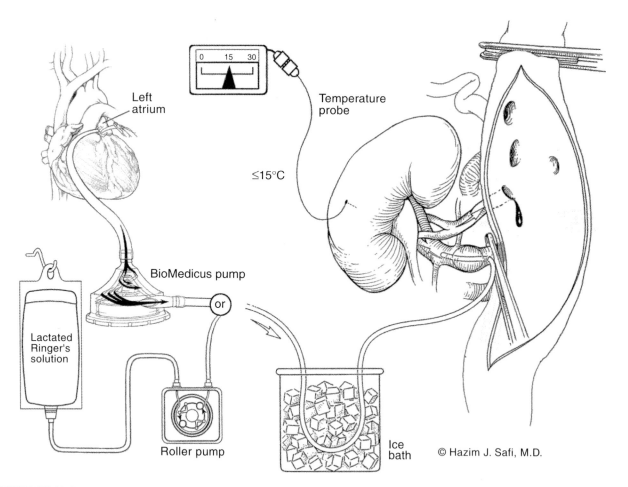

FIGURE 103-23   Retrograde renal perfusion via the left renal vein cools the left kidney to approximately 15° C.

reported series, in which the use of left heart bypass was found to be associated with a greater incidence of acute renal failure.[100]

During reattachment of the celiac axis, superior mesenteric, and renal arteries to the aortic graft in TAAA with renal artery involvement, distal aortic perfusion is necessarily interrupted. We consequently added selective visceral perfusion to provide additional ischemic protection during this period. We first used warm blood, but with poor results later switched to cold blood perfusion. The rate of flow depends on the proximal aortic pressure (decreased if hypotensive; increased if hypertensive) but is kept between 300 and 600 mL/min. Renal temperature for cold visceral perfusion is kept at less than 20° C, preferably around 15° C. Although there is some evidence that patients with cold visceral perfusion have superior survival and recovery rates, this strategy has not decreased the incidence of acute renal failure. Visceral perfusion techniques are described in detail in the section on operative technique.

We also have used retrograde renal perfusion via the left renal vein (Fig. 103-23). A No. 9 or No. 12 Pruitt balloon-tipped catheter is inserted into the left renal vein, and the distal balloon is inflated to prevent escape of the perfusate into the inferior vena cava. Cold blood from the BioMedicus pump via a roller pump through an ice bath is perfused into

the left renal vein, at a rate of 100 to 200 mL/min, or cold Ringer's lactate solution is perfused directly to the left renal vein to lower renal temperature to 15° C. The perfusate is washed out through the renal artery into the opened aneurysm. Cold retrograde renal vein perfusion is analogous to retrograde cerebral perfusion via the superior vena cava during aortic arch repair or retrograde cardiac protection via the coronary sinus, both of which have produced positive results in providing organ protection. Although cold retrograde venous perfusion has been reserved primarily for cases in which the renal artery cannot be accessed easily (owing to severe atherosclerotic occlusive disease), it can flush atherosclerotic debris and may provide better renal perfusion. This method of renal protection shows promise and will continue to be explored.

Currently we are evaluating a method of integrated cooling, in which the kidneys receive cold lactated Ringer's solution cooled to 4° C, while the celiac axis and superior mesenteric arteries are perfused with cold blood (Fig. 103-24). An initial bolus of 300 to 800 mL of cold lactated Ringer's solution is infused into the kidneys, followed by additional periodic 100-mL aliquots as needed, to maintain renal temperature around 15° C. The flow rate is approximately 200 mL/min and 150 mL/min for the renal and visceral arteries. The benefit of cold temperatures for

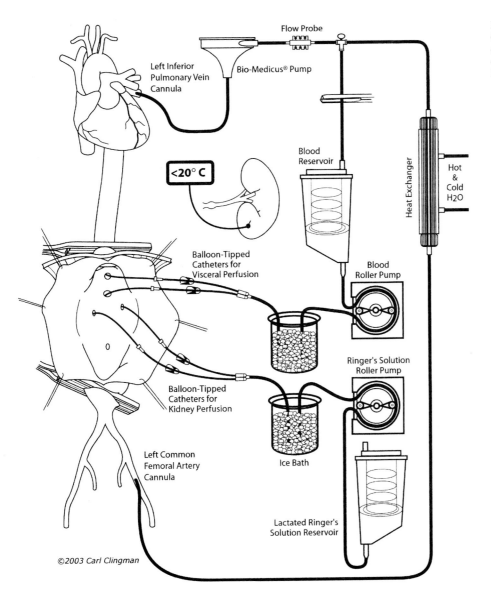

Left Inferior
Pulmonary Vein
Cannula

Flow Probe

Bio-Medicus® Pump

<20° C

Blood
Reservoir

Heat Exchanger

Hot
&
Cold
H2O

Balloon-Tipped
Catheters for
Visceral Perfusion

Blood
Roller Pump

Ringer's Solution
Roller Pump

0

Balloon-Tipped
Catheters for
Kidney Perfusion

Ice Bath

Left Common
Femoral Artery
Cannula

Lactated Ringer's
Solution Reservoir

©2003 Carl Clingman

FIGURE 103-24 Integrated cooling. Cold lactated Ringer's solution (4° C) cools the kidneys to less than 20° C, and cold blood cools the viscera, while the lower extremities continue to be warmed.

metabolic suppression in organ protection is well known. Local hypothermia has been shown to protect against renal ischemia and reperfusion injury in laboratory animals.[102] Whenever visceral cooling is employed, however, caution should be exercised to keep the core body temperature between 32° C and 33° C by warming the lower extremities to avoid systemic hypothermia and its consequent risks of cardiac arrhythmia and coagulopathy.

Although pharmacologic agents such as dopamine and prostaglandin inhibitors have not proved beneficial for renal protection, we have found some benefit in the use of fenoldopam. Fenoldopam is a dopaminergic agonist that increases the renal blood flow, sodium excretion, and water excretion and maintains the glomerular filtration rate.[103,104] As an antihypertensive, it causes systemic vasodilatation, increased mesenteric vasodilatation, and increased coronary vasodilatation. Based on animal experiments in which researchers reported an increase in renal blood flow and urine output with histologic confirmation of renal protec-

tion, we have used fenoldopam as a continuous perioperative infusion.[105] Our experience has been encouraging, but not definitive. In an unpublished randomized, placebo-controlled prospective study of 58 patients with elective repair of TAAA, we found that fenoldopam significantly decreased the urinary dye clearance time from 17 minutes to 8 minutes. The fenoldopam group also showed an inclination toward reduction in mortality, dialysis requirements, length of ICU stay, and total length of hospital stay, but none of these was statistically significant.

The goals of perioperative renal protection are to maintain adequate renal oxygen delivery, reduce renal oxygen use, and reduce direct renal tubular injury, but good strategies to protect renal function during surgical TAAA repair remain elusive. Our quest for a satisfactory method of renal protection has produced no definitive results. The incidence of postoperative renal failure remains troublesome, and the pursuit of the optimal method of renal protection continues to be one of our top priorities.

Visceral Protection

Direct visceral perfusion has been shown to provide protection to the liver.[106] Perfusing the celiac and the superior mesenteric arteries with either cold or warm blood has the greatest impact on extent II TAAA, which has been associated with the longest ischemic periods and the highest incidence of postoperative liver dysfunction. In an analysis of TAAA patients, we found that acute rupture and emergency presentation were risk factors for hepatic injury after repair.[106] Visceral perfusion during extent II aneurysm repair effectively negated the associated rise in postoperative laboratory values for extent II aneurysm repairs done with the simple cross-clamp technique. Intraoperative bleeding was reduced, and postoperative liver enzymes fell more frequently within normal range.[106]

Cardiac Complications

In TAAA repair, the association between atherosclerotic occlusive coronary artery disease and decreased rates of early and late survival is well known. In a large series of 1509 patients undergoing TAAA surgery, the incidence of coronary artery disease was 31% with a mortality rate of 12% compared with a mortality rate of 8% in patients without coronary artery disease.[73] The incidence of postoperative cardiac complications was 12% and was associated with increased early mortality (30% versus 5% without cardiac complications). We evaluated the effect of cardiovascular disease on early mortality in our own patients.[107] The overall incidence of coronary artery disease was approximately 34%, and the 30-day mortality rate was significantly higher in these patients (18%) compared with patients without coronary artery disease (13%). Almost half of our patients had a coronary artery bypass graft before surgery, and in these patients mortality was 22% compared with 14% in patients without prior coronary artery bypass. In univariate analysis, coronary artery disease and previous coronary artery bypass emerged as risk factors for early mortality. In multivariate analysis, the effects that coronary artery disease and previous coronary artery bypass had on mortality were negated, however, by consideration of low left ventricular ejection fraction (<50%). Twenty-six percent of patients with an ejection fraction less than 50% died within 30 days after TAAA or descending TAA surgery compared with 14% of patients with normal ejection fraction.

It is well established that aortic cross-clamping leads to proximal systemic hypertension and left ventricular distention. Left ventricular distention can lead to increased wall stress and decreased subendocardial perfusion. To reduce proximal hypertension and minimize cardiac ischemia, we routinely use left atrial-to-femoral bypass, or distal aortic perfusion, to "unload" the heart. Afterload-reducing pharmacologic agents, such as nitrates, are used frequently to protect the heart further. Occasionally, severe cardiac dysfunction may require mechanical support using intra-aortic balloon counterpulsation. Ventricular dysrhythmias also can be precipitated by severe hypothermia (when the body temperature falls to <32° C). We use passive moderate hypothermia (i.e., allow the body temperature to drift at the beginning of the case) and a perfusion circuit that includes a heat exchanger to permit active warming. Also,

we exercise caution when actively cooling the viscera and kidneys to ensure that the body temperature does not decrease to less than 32° C. Other cardiac dysrhythmias include postoperative atrial arrhythmias, which occur in approximately 10% of patients. Treatment for atrial arrhythmias usually involves one or more pharmacologic agents (amiodarone, beta blockers, and calcium channel blockers). Occasionally, electrical cardioversion may be required in refractory cases or when there is associated hypotension.

Pulmonary Complications

The incidence of pulmonary complications after TAAA repair ranges from 20% to 50%. Respiratory failure usually is described as days of required postoperative mechanical ventilatory support. Predictors of prolonged postoperative respiratory failure include advanced age, aortic cross-clamp time (>60 minutes), number of packed red blood cells transfused, and tobacco use.[83] More importantly, we have found that diaphragmatic preservation during TAAA repair results in an earlier weaning from mechanical ventilation and consequently a shorter length of hospital stay.[83] Since 1994, we cut only the muscular portion of the diaphragm, leaving the central tendinous portion intact and preserving the phrenic nerve (see Fig. 103-11). This technique allows for maintenance of pulmonary mechanics closer to normal and faster weaning from mechanical ventilatory assistance.

Endoluminal Technique

Since the first successful thoracic endograft procedure was reported in 1991,[108] endovascular therapy has evolved rapidly. The feasibility of deploying an endoluminal graft in the thoracic aorta is no longer in doubt. There have been numerous reports of series of patients receiving thoracic endograft for a variety of conditions, including acute and chronic type B aortic dissections, traumatic thoracic transections, and descending TAAs and TAAAs.[109-111] Although the short-term benefits of endovascular therapy are clear with less morbidity and shorter length of hospital stay compared with conventional surgery, the reported mortality rates appear to replicate those from conventional surgery in large centers. The long-term effectiveness of endoluminal exclusion of aneurysms remains to be seen, and several issues need to be resolved before endografts are widely accepted as an alternative to surgical repair of TAAs and TAAAs. How to deal with patent intercostal arteries in patients receiving endografts for TAAs and TAAAs remains problematic. Patent intercostal arteries are a major source of type II endoleak. Exclusion of the lower intercostal arteries also has been identified as a significant risk factor for postoperative paraplegia.[85] Several cases of immediate and delayed paraplegia have been reported in the literature after thoracic endograft placement.[112,113] Endografts with side-branches are being designed to allow reimplantation of patent intercostal arteries, visceral arteries, and renal arteries. In addition to the complications related to the deployment of the endograft, other reported serious problems related to thoracic endograft deployment include aortic dissection, aneurysmal degeneration, and graft-esophageal fistula.[114-116] Finally, our endovascular experience with abdominal aortic aneurysms has taught us that the rate of aneurysm rupture may be even higher in the patients with endografts compared with untreated patients. Other authors have voiced this opinion.[117]

■ SUMMARY

Remarkable progress has been made in the surgical treatment of TAAAs. The decline in morbidity and mortality rates can be attributed to improvements in surgical technique, particularly the adoption of perfusion adjuncts and CSF drainage. Neurologic deficit is no longer a major threat to patients because the use of adjuncts has brought the incidence down to 2.4% for all TAAAs and to 6.6% for extent II aneurysms. Despite best efforts to protect the kidneys, however, renal failure continues to be a major hindrance to patient survival. As we look to the future, we continue to pursue research to improve organ preservation, particularly for the most troublesome extent II TAAAs.

Acknowledgments Thanks to our editor, Amy Wirtz Newland, and to our illustrator, Carl Clingman.

■ REFERENCES

1. Ailawadi G, Eliason JL, Upchurch GR Jr: Current concepts in the pathogenesis of abdominal aortic aneurysm. J Vasc Surg 38:584, 2003.
2. Lopez-Candales A, Holmes DR, Liao S, et al: Decreased vascular smooth muscle cell density in medial degeneration of human abdominal aortic aneurysms. Am J Pathol 150:993, 1997.
3. Pan JH, Lindholt JS, Sukhova GK, et al: Macrophage migration inhibitory factor is associated with aneurysmal expansion. J Vasc Surg 37:628, 2003.
4. Biddinger A, Rocklin M, Coselli J, et al: Familial thoracic aortic dilatations and dissections: A case control study. J Vasc Surg 25:506, 1997.
5. Coady MA, Davies RR, Roberts M, et al: Familial patterns of thoracic aortic aneurysms. Arch Surg 134:361, 1999.
6. Hasham SN, Willing MC, Guo DC, et al: Mapping a locus for familial thoracic aortic aneurysms and dissections (TAAD2) to 3p24-25. Circulation 107:3184, 2003.
7. Dietz HC: New insights into the genetic basis of aortic aneurysms. Monogr Pathol 37:144, 1995.
8. Pyeritz RE, McKusick VA: The Marfan syndrome: Diagnosis and management. N Engl J Med 300:772, 1979.
9. Kainulainen K, Karttunen L, Puhakka L, et al: Mutations in the fibrillin gene responsible for dominant ectopia lentis and neonatal Marfan syndrome. Nat Genet 6:64, 1994.
10. Milewicz DM, Grossfield J, Cao SN, et al: A mutation in FBN1 disrupts profibrillin processing and results in isolated skeletal features of the Marfan syndrome. J Clin Invest 95:2373, 1995.
11. Gupta PA, Putnam EA, Carmical SG, et al: Ten novel FBN2 mutations in congenital contractural arachnodactyly: Delineation of the molecular pathogenesis and clinical phenotype. Hum Mutat 19:39, 2002.
12. Hossack KF, Leddy CL, Johnson AM, et al: Echocardiographic findings in autosomal dominant polycystic kidney disease. N Engl J Med 319:907, 1988.
13. Elsheikh M, Casadei B, Conway GS, et al: Hypertension is a major risk factor for aortic root dilatation in women with Turner's syndrome. Clin Endocrinol (Oxf) 54:69, 2001.
14. Pepin M, Schwarze U, Superti-Furga A, et al: Clinical and genetic features of Ehlers-Danlos syndrome type IV, the vascular type. N Engl J Med 342:673, 2000.
15. Wenstrup RJ, Meyer RA, Lyle JS, et al: Prevalence of aortic root dilation in the Ehlers-Danlos syndrome. Genet Med 4:112, 2002.
16. Milewicz DM, Chen H, Park ES, et al: Reduced penetrance and variable expressivity of familial thoracic aortic aneurysms/dissections. Am J Cardiol 82:474, 1998.
17. Jarrett F, Darling RC, Mundth ED, et al: Experience with infected aneurysms of the abdominal aorta. Arch Surg 110:1281, 1975.
18. Bakker-de Wekker P, Alfieri O, Vermeulen F, et al: Surgical treatment of infected pseudoaneurysms after replacement of the ascending aorta. J Thorac Cardiovasc Surg 88:447, 1984.
19. Kelley MJ, Bettmann MA, Boxt LM, et al: Blunt chest trauma—suspected aortic injury. American College of Radiology. ACR Appropriateness Criteria. Radiology 215(Suppl):35, 2000.
20. Kochanek KD, Smith BL, Anderson RN: Deaths: Preliminary data for 1999. National Vital Statistics Reports 49(3):1-48, 2001.
21. Clouse WD, Hallett JW Jr, Schaff HV, et al: Improved prognosis of thoracic aortic aneurysms: A population-based study. JAMA 280:1926, 1998.
22. LaRoy LL, Cormier PJ, Matalon TA, et al: Imaging of abdominal aortic aneurysms. AJR Am J Roentgenol 152:785, 1989.
23. Bickerstaff LK, Pairolero PC, Hollier LH, et al: Thoracic aortic aneurysms: A population-based study. Surgery 92:1103, 1982.
24. Perko MJ, Norgaard M, Herzog TM, et al: Unoperated aortic aneurysm: A survey of 170 patients. Ann Thorac Surg 59:1204, 1995.
25. Pressler V, McNamara JJ: Thoracic aortic aneurysm: Natural history and treatment. J Thorac Cardiovasc Surg 79:489, 1980.
26. Crawford ES, DeNatale RW: Thoracoabdominal aortic aneurysm: Observations regarding the natural course of the disease. J Vasc Surg 3:578, 1986.
27. Cambria RA, Gloviczki P, Stanson AW, et al: Outcome and expansion rate of 57 thoracoabdominal aortic aneurysms managed nonoperatively. Am J Surg 170:213, 1995.
28. Elefteriades JA, Hartleroad J, Gusberg RJ, et al: Long-term experience with descending aortic dissection: The complication-specific approach. Ann Thorac Surg 53:11, 1992.
29. Lobato AC, Puech-Leao P: Predictive factors for rupture of thoraco-abdominal aortic aneurysm. J Vasc Surg 27:446, 1998.
30. Juvonen T, Ergin MA, Galla JD, et al: Prospective study of the natural history of thoracic aortic aneurysms. Ann Thorac Surg 63:1533, 1997.
31. Dapunt OE, Galla JD, Sadeghi AM, et al: The natural history of thoracic aortic aneurysms. J Thorac Cardiovasc Surg 107:1323, 1994.
32. Coady MA, Rizzo JA, Hammond GL, et al: What is the appropriate size criterion for resection of thoracic aortic aneurysms? J Thorac Cardiovasc Surg 113:476, 1997.
33. Davies RR, Goldstein LJ, Coady MA, et al: Yearly rupture or dissection rates for thoracic aortic aneurysms: Simple prediction based on size. Ann Thorac Surg 73:17, 2002.
34. Masuda Y, Takanashi K, Takasu J, et al: Expansion rate of thoracic aortic aneurysms and influencing factors. Chest 102:461, 1992.
35. Rizzo JA, Coady MA, Elefteriades JA: Procedures for estimating growth rates in thoracic aortic aneurysms. J Clin Epidemiol 51:747, 1998.
36. Coady MA, Rizzo JA, Hammond GL, et al: Surgical intervention criteria for thoracic aortic aneurysms: A study of growth rates and complications. Ann Thorac Surg 67:1922, 1999.
37. Szilagyi DE, Smith RF, DeRusso FJ, et al: Contribution of abdominal aortic aneurysmectomy to prolongation of life. Ann Surg 164:678, 1966.
38. Juvonen T, Ergin MA, Galla JD, et al: Risk factors for rupture of chronic type B dissections. J Thorac Cardiovasc Surg 117:776, 1999.
39. Wheat MW Jr, Palmer RF: Dissecting aneurysms of the aorta: Present status of drug versus surgical therapy. Prog Cardiovasc Dis 11:198, 1968.
40. Cronenwett JL, Murphy TF, Zelenock GB, et al: Actuarial analysis of variables associated with rupture of small abdominal aortic aneurysms. Surgery 98:472, 1985.

41. Strachan DP: Predictors of death from aortic aneurysm among middle-aged men: The Whitehall study. Br J Surg 78:401, 1991.

42. Lindholt JS, Jorgensen B, Fasting H, et al: Plasma levels of plasmin-antiplasmin-complexes are predictive for small abdominal aortic aneurysms expanding to operation-recommendable sizes. J Vasc Surg 34:611, 2001.

43. Cannon DJ, Read RC: Blood elastolytic activity in patients with aortic aneurysm. Ann Thorac Surg 34:10, 1982.

44. Griepp RB, Ergin MA, Galla JD, et al: Natural history of descending thoracic and thoracoabdominal aneurysms. Ann Thorac Surg 67:1927, 1999.

45. Ergin MA, Spielvogel D, Apaydin A, et al: Surgical treatment of the dilated ascending aorta: When and how? Ann Thorac Surg 67:1834, 1999.

46. Johansson G, Markstrom U, Swedenborg J: Ruptured thoracic aortic aneurysms: A study of incidence and mortality rates. J Vasc Surg 21:985, 1995.

47. Pearce WH, Slaughter MS, LeMaire S, et al: Aortic diameter as a function of age, gender, and body surface area. Surgery 114:691, 1993.

48. Movat HZ, More RH, Haust MD: The diffuse intimal thickening of the human aorta with aging. Am J Pathol 34:1023, 1958.

49. Bachet JE, Termignon JL, Dreyfus G, et al: Aortic dissection: Prevalence, cause, and results of late reoperations. J Thorac Cardiovasc Surg 108:199, 1994.

50. Bernard Y, Zimmermann H, Chocron S, et al: False lumen patency as a predictor of late outcome in aortic dissection. Am J Cardiol 87:1378, 2001.

51. Elefteriades JA, Lovoulos CJ, Coady MA, et al: Management of descending aortic dissection. Ann Thorac Surg 67:2002, 1999.

52. Gysi J, Schaffner T, Mohacsi P, et al: Early and late outcome of operated and non-operated acute dissection of the descending aorta. Eur J Cardiothorac Surg 11:1163, 1997.

53. Marui A, Mochizuki T, Mitsui N, et al: Toward the best treatment for uncomplicated patients with type B acute aortic dissection: A consideration for sound surgical indication. Circulation 100(19 Suppl):II-275, 1999.

54. Schor JS, Yerlioglu ME, Galla JD, et al: Selective management of acute type B aortic dissection: Long-term follow-up. Ann Thorac Surg 61:1339, 1996.

55. Safi HJ, Miller CC, 3rd, Estrera AL, et al: Chronic aortic dissection not a risk factor for neurologic deficit in thoracoabdominal aortic aneurysm repair. Eur J Vasc Endovasc Surg 23:244, 2002.

56. Safi HJ, Miller CC, 3rd, Huynh TT, et al: Distal aortic perfusion and cerebrospinal fluid drainage for thoracoabdominal and descending thoracic aortic repair: Ten years of organ protection. Ann Surg 238:372, 2003.

57. Coselli JS, LeMaire SA, de Figueiredo LP, et al: Paraplegia after thoracoabdominal aortic aneurysm repair: Is dissection a risk factor? Ann Thorac Surg 63:28, 1997.

58. Kieffer E, Richard T, Chiras J, et al: Preoperative spinal cord arteriography in aneurysmal disease of the descending thoracic and thoracoabdominal aorta: Preliminary results in 45 patients. Ann Vasc Surg 3:34, 1989.

59. Williams GM, Perler BA, Burdick JF, et al: Angiographic localization of spinal cord blood supply and its relationship to postoperative paraplegia. J Vasc Surg 13:23, 1991.

60. Fillinger MF: Imaging of the thoracic and thoracoabdominal aorta. Semin Vasc Surg 13:247, 2000.

61. Estrera AL, Rubenstein FS, Miller CC, 3rd, et al: Descending thoracic aortic aneurysm: Surgical approach and treatment using the adjuncts cerebrospinal fluid drainage and distal aortic perfusion. Ann Thorac Surg 72:481, 2001.

62. Svensson LG, Crawford ES, Hess KR, et al: Experience with 1509 patients undergoing thoracoabdominal aortic operations. J Vasc Surg 17:357, 1993.

63. Crawford ES: Thoraco-abdominal and abdominal aortic aneurysms involving renal, superior mesenteric, celiac arteries. Ann Surg 179:763, 1974.

64. Huynh TT, Miller CC 3rd, Safi HJ: Delayed onset of neurologic deficit: Significance and management. Semin Vasc Surg 13:340, 2000.

65. Estrera AL, Miller CC 3rd, Huynh TT, et al: Preoperative and operative predictors of delayed neurologic deficit following repair of thoracoabdominal aortic aneurysm. J Thorac Cardiovasc Surg 126:1288, 2003.

66. Huynh TT, Miller CC 3rd, Estrera AL, et al: Determinants of hospital length of stay after thoracoabdominal aortic aneurysm repair. J Vasc Surg 35:648, 2002.

67. Kouchoukos NT, Daily BB, Rokkas CK, et al: Hypothermic bypass and circulatory arrest for operations on the descending thoracic and thoracoabdominal aorta. Ann Thorac Surg 60:67, 1995.

68. Cambria RP, Clouse WD, Davison JK, et al: Thoracoabdominal aneurysm repair: Results with 337 operations performed over a 15-year interval. Ann Surg 236:471, 2002.

69. Safi HJ, Campbell MP, Ferreira ML, et al: Spinal cord protection in descending thoracic and thoracoabdominal aortic aneurysm repair. Semin Thorac Cardiovasc Surg 10:41, 1998.

70. Estrera AL, Miller CC 3rd, Huynh TT, et al: Neurologic outcome after thoracic and thoracoabdominal aortic aneurysm repair. Ann Thorac Surg 72:1225, 2001.

71. Miller CC 3rd, Porat EE, Estrera AL, et al: Analysis of short-term multivariate competing risks data following thoracic and thoraco-abdominal aortic repair. Eur J Cardiothorac Surg 23:1023, 2003.

72. Acher CW, Wynn MM, Archibald J: Naloxone and spinal fluid drainage as adjuncts in the surgical treatment of thoracoabdominal and thoracic aneurysms. Surgery 108:755, 1990.

73. Cambria RP, Davison JK, Carter C, et al: Epidural cooling for spinal cord protection during thoracoabdominal aneurysm repair: A five-year experience. J Vasc Surg 31:1093, 2000.

74. de Haan P: Pharmacologic adjuncts to protect the spinal cord during transient ischemia. Semin Vasc Surg 13:264, 2000.

75. de Haan P, Kalkman CJ, de Mol BA, et al: Efficacy of transcranial motor-evoked myogenic potentials to detect spinal cord ischemia during operations for thoracoabdominal aneurysms. J Thorac Cardiovasc Surg 113:87, 1996.

76. Jacobs MJ, Meylaerts SA, de Haan P, et al: Assessment of spinal cord ischemia by means of evoked potential monitoring during thoracoabdominal aortic surgery. Semin Vasc Surg 13:299, 2000.

77. Kouchoukos NT, Masetti P, Rokkas CK, et al: Safety and efficacy of hypothermic cardiopulmonary bypass and circulatory arrest for operations on the descending thoracic and thoracoabdominal aorta. Ann Thorac Surg 72:699, 2001.

78. Crawford ES, Svensson LG, Hess KR, et al: A prospective randomized study of cerebrospinal fluid drainage to prevent para-plegia after high-risk surgery on the thoracoabdominal aorta. J Vasc Surg 13:36, 1991.

79. Jacobs MJ, de Mol BA, Elenbaas T, et al: Spinal cord blood supply in patients with thoracoabdominal aortic aneurysms. J Vasc Surg 35:30, 2002.

80. Hollier LH, Money SR, Naslund TC, et al: Risk of spinal cord dysfunction in patients undergoing thoracoabdominal aortic replacement. Am J Surg 164:210, 1992.

81. Coselli JS, Lemaire SA, Koksoy C, et al: Cerebrospinal fluid drainage reduces paraplegia after thoracoabdominal aortic aneurysm repair: Results of a randomized clinical trial. J Vasc Surg 35:631, 2002.

82. Safi HJ, Bartoli S, Hess KR, et al: Neurologic deficit in patients at high risk with thoracoabdominal aortic aneurysms: The role of cerebral spinal fluid drainage and distal aortic perfusion. J Vasc Surg 20:434, 1994.

83. Engle J, Safi HJ, Miller CC 3rd, et al: The impact of diaphragm management on prolonged ventilator support after thoracoabdominal aortic repair. J Vasc Surg 29:150, 1999.

84. Crawford ES, Crawford JL, Safi HJ, et al: Thoracoabdominal aortic aneurysms: Preoperative and intraoperative factors determining immediate and long-term results of operations in 605 patients. J Vasc Surg 3:389, 1986.

85. Safi H, Miller CC 3rd, Carr C, et al: The importance of intercostal artery reattachment during thoracoabdominal aortic aneurysm repair. J Vasc Surg 27:58, 1998.

86. Crawford ES, Mizrahi EM, Hess KR, et al: The impact of distal aortic perfusion and somatosensory evoked potential monitoring on prevention of paraplegia after aortic aneurysm operation [published erratum appears in J Thorac Cardiovasc Surg 1989 May;97(5):665]. J Thorac Cardiovasc Surg 95:357, 1988.

87. Hill AB, Kalman PG, Johnston KW, et al: Reversal of delayed onset paraplegia after thoracic aortic surgery with cerebrospinal fluid drainage. J Vasc Surg 20:315, 1994.

88. Widmann MD, DeLucia A, Sharp J, et al: Reversal of renal failure and paraplegia after thoracoabdominal aneurysm repair. Ann Thorac Surg 65:1153, 1998.

89. Azizzadeh A, Huynh TT, Miller CC 3rd, et al: Reversal of twice-delayed neurologic deficits with cerebrospinal fluid drainage after thoracoabdominal aneurysm repair: A case report and plea for a national database collection. J Vasc Surg 31:592, 2000.

90. Safi HJ, Miller CC 3rd, Azizzadeh A, et al: Observations on delayed neurologic deficit after thoracoabdominal aortic aneurysm repair. J Vasc Surg 26:616, 1997.

91. Azizzadeh A, Huynh TT, Miller CC, 3rd, et al: Postoperative risk factors for delayed neurologic deficit after thoracic and thoraco-abdominal aortic aneurysm repair: A case-control study. J Vasc Surg 37:750, 2003.

92. Cina CS, Lagana A, Bruin G, et al: Thoracoabdominal aortic aneurysm repair: A prospective cohort study of 121 cases. Ann Vasc Surg 16:631, 2002.

93. Dardik A, Krosnick T, Perler BA, et al: Durability of thoracoabdominal aortic aneurysm repair in patients with connective tissue disorders. J Vasc Surg 36:696, 2002.

94. Schepens M, Dossche K, Morshuis W, et al: Introduction of adjuncts and their influence on changing results in 402 consecutive thoraco-abdominal aortic aneurysm repairs. Eur J Cardiothorac Surg 25:701, 2004.

95. Coselli JS, Conklin LD, LeMaire SA: Thoracoabdominal aortic aneurysm repair: Review and update of current strategies. Ann Thorac Surg 74:S1881, 2002.

96. Gloviczki P: Surgical repair of thoracoabdominal aneurysms: Patient selection, techniques and results. Cardiovasc Surg 10:434, 2002.

97. Kashyap VS, Cambria RP, Davison JK, et al: Renal failure after thoracoabdominal aortic surgery. J Vasc Surg 26:949, 1997.

98. Kouchoukos NT, Masetti P, Rokkas CK, et al: Hypothermic cardiopulmonary bypass and circulatory arrest for operations on the descending thoracic and thoracoabdominal aorta. Ann Thorac Surg 74:S1885, 2002.

99. Singri N, Ahya SN, Levin ML: Acute renal failure. JAMA 289:747, 2003.

100. Svensson LG, Coselli JS, Safi HJ, et al: Appraisal of adjuncts to prevent acute renal failure after surgery on the thoracic or thoraco-abdominal aorta. J Vasc Surg 10:230, 1989.

101. Safi HJ, Huynh TTT, Hassoun HT, et al: Preventing renal failure in thoracoabdominal aortic aneurysm repair. Perspect Vasc Surg Endovasc Ther 16:3, 2004.

102. Carattino MD, Cueva F, Zuccollo A, et al: Renal ischemia-induced increase in vascular permeability is limited by hypothermia. Immunopharmacology 43:241, 1999.

103. Jorkasky DK, Audet P, Shusterman N, et al: Fenoldopam reverses cyclosporine-induced renal vasoconstriction in kidney transplant recipients. Am J Kidney Dis 19:567, 1992.

104. Brooks DP, Drutz DJ, Ruffolo RR Jr: Prevention and complete reversal of cyclosporine A-induced renal vasoconstriction and nephrotoxicity in the rat by fenoldopam. J Pharmacol Exp Ther 254:375, 1990.

105. Halpenny M, Markos F, Snow HM, et al: The effects of fenoldopam on renal blood flow and tubular function during aortic cross-clamping in anaesthetized dogs. Eur J Anaesthesiol 17:491, 2000.

106. Safi HJ, Miller CC 3rd, Yawn DH, et al: Impact of distal aortic and visceral perfusion on liver function during thoracoabdominal and descending thoracic aortic repair. J Vasc Surg 27:145, 1998.

107. Suzuki S, Davis CA 3rd, Miller CC 3rd, et al: Cardiac function predicts mortality following thoracoabdominal and descending thoracic aortic aneurysm repair. Eur J Cardiothorac Surg 24:119, 2003.

108. Volodos NL, Karpovich IP, Troyan VI, et al: Clinical experience of the use of self-fixing synthetic prostheses for remote endoprosthetics of the thoracic and the abdominal aorta and iliac arteries through the femoral artery and as intraoperative endoprosthesis for aorta reconstruction. Vasa 33(Suppl):93, 1991.

109. Buffolo E, da Fonseca JH, de Souza JA, et al: Revolutionary treatment of aneurysms and dissections of descending aorta: The endovascular approach. Ann Thorac Surg 74:S1815, 2002.

110. Dake MD, Miller DC, Mitchell RS, et al: The "first generation" of endovascular stent-grafts for patients with aneurysms of the descending thoracic aorta. J Thorac Cardiovasc Surg 116:689, 1998.

111. Greenberg R, Resch T, Nyman U, et al: Endovascular repair of descending thoracic aortic aneurysms: An early experience with intermediate-term follow-up. J Vasc Surg 31(1 Pt 1):147, 2000.

112. Kasirajan K, Dolmatch B, Ouriel K, et al: Delayed onset of ascending paralysis after thoracic aortic stent graft deployment. J Vasc Surg 31(1 Pt 1):196, 2000.

113. Gravereaux EC, Faries PL, Burks JA, et al: Risk of spinal cord ischemia after endograft repair of thoracic aortic aneurysms. J Vasc Surg 34:997, 2001.

114. Hance KA, Hsu J, Eskew T, et al: Secondary aortoesophageal fistula after endoluminal exclusion because of thoracic aortic transection. J Vasc Surg 37:886, 2003.

115. Pasic M, Bergs P, Knollmann F, et al: Delayed retrograde aortic dissection after endovascular stenting of the descending thoracic aorta. J Vasc Surg 36:184, 2002.

116. Kato N, Hirano T, Kawaguchi T, et al: Aneurysmal degeneration of the aorta after stent-graft repair of acute aortic dissection. J Vasc Surg 34:513, 2001.

117. Collin J, Murie JA: Endovascular treatment of abdominal aortic aneurysm: A failed experiment. Br J Surg 88:1281, 2001.

Aortic Dissection:
Perspectives for the Vascular/ Endovascular Surgeon

104

JAMES H. BLACK III, MD
RICHARD P. CAMBRIA, MD

■ OVERVIEW

The depiction of the lesion of aortic dissection and the premise of therapy can be traced back to the early 1800s, when Shekelton[1] reported obliteration of the false lumen in a healed dissection, and Laennac coined the term *dissecting aneurysm*. The term *dissecting aneurysm* is a misnomer in most cases; although acute dissection can occur in dilated or diseased aortas, it also occurs in normal-caliber aortas and in young, otherwise healthy individuals. The terms *acute dissection* and *aneurysm* should be used in an exclusive context, although dissection can occur in a preexistent degenerative aneurysm. It is well recognized that chronic dissection is the etiology in 20% of thoracoabdominal aneurysms. Finally, as detailed subsequently, other distinct thoracic aortic lesions, such as intramural hematoma (IMH) and penetrating aortic ulcer (PAU), have significant clinical and radiographic parity with acute dissection, such that diagnostic confusion commonly occurs.

Overall, acute aortic dissection is the most common catastrophe of the aorta, with an incidence of 5 to 30 cases per 1 million people per year.[2-5] Within a population, the actual incidence varies based on predisposing risk factors, including age, hypertension, and structural abnormalities of the aortic wall.[5,6] The process of aortic dissection is dynamic and can occur anywhere along the course of the aorta, resulting in a wide spectrum of clinical manifestations. The pathognomonic lesion is an intimal tear followed by blood surging typically antegrade and cleaving the intimal and medial layers of the aortic wall longitudinally for a variable distance; the degree of the aortic wall circumference involved also is variable.[6] Typically, one or more tears in the intimal septum allow communication between the true and false lumina.

Despite expected and documented improvements in treatment results over time, acute dissection remains a lethal disease. In a population-based longitudinal study by Meszaros and coworkers,[7] 21% of patients with aortic dissection died before hospital admission. This substantial mortality rate underscores the urgency for diagnosis and initiation of appropriate therapy; the mortality of acute dissection left untreated may exceed 22.7% within 6 hours, 50% within 24 hours, and 68% within the first week.[7] Mortality typically is quoted at 1% per hour in the acute phase of the disease; when the ascending aorta is involved, mortality is largely related to the central cardioaortic complications of aortic rupture into the pericardium, acute aortic regurgitation, and coronary ostia compromise.[8,9] Mortality in the acute phase of an acute distal dissection not involving the ascending aorta may occur in patients with visceral or extremity vessel obstruction or aortic rupture, although the incidence of aortic rupture has decreased over time.[10,11] When territories such as the central nervous system and the viscera are compromised, the mortality rate of aortic dissection increases dramatically.[10,11] A contemporary perspective on the ongoing lethality of aortic dissection is gained from the International Registry of Acute Aortic Dissection (IRAD) study.[5] This report, summarizing treatment results from 12 international referral centers of excellence, is notable because a large number (464) of aortic dissection patients treated in a contemporary interval (1996 through 1998) were prospectively studied. Given the institutions participating, treatment results can be considered a best-case scenario, yet overall mortality was 27.4% in the IRAD study. Mortality for patients treated with graft replacement of the ascending aorta was 26%. The highest mortality (58%) occurred in patients with ascending aortic dissection managed medically. The most common causes of death among patients with ascending dissections were aortic rupture (41.6%), followed by mesenteric ischemia (13.9%). When medical management could be used for patients with distal dissections, mortality was 10.7%. Alternatively, when invasive intervention was required for complicated distal dissections, mortality increased to 31.4%, emphasizing the need for improved diagnostic and treatment modalities in this subgroup.[5]

This chapter reviews the classification, pathologic anatomy, clinical presentation, and diagnostic and treatment modalities for acute aortic dissection with emphasis on the role of the vascular/endovascular surgeon. Although a thorough understanding of all components of acute dissection seems requisite for surgeons who propose to treat aortic dissection, the technical principles of graft replacement of the ascending aorta, being the province of cardiac surgeons, is not detailed. Because open graft replacement for treatment of descending aortic dissection is rarely indicated, it is anticipated that the vascular/endovascular surgeon will become the primary interventionalist in the care of patients with acute dissection of the descending aorta and complications of peripheral vascular compromise. Finally, treatment of the principal late complication of acute aortic dissection—the development of thoracoabdominal aneurysms—is considered in Chapter 103.

ANATOMIC CLASSIFICATION OF AORTIC DISSECTION

Aortic dissection is classified as acute or chronic depending on the duration of symptoms at presentation. *Acute dissection* refers to circumstances when the diagnosis is made within 2 weeks after the initial onset of symptoms, and *chronic dissection* is diagnosed when the symptoms are present for greater than 2 weeks. Although such designation is arbitrary and long-standing in the literature, it is reasonable to state that the immediate life-threatening complications usually manifest within this time frame in most patients. Anatomically, aortic dissection is classified in two schemes based on the location of the intimal tear and the extent of the dissection along the aorta. The classification scheme proposed by DeBakey and colleagues[12] in 1965 is most commonly used and specifically delineates the extent of the descending aortic dissection.[12] The scheme (Fig. 104-1) uses the following classification:

- Type I—dissection originates in the ascending aorta and extends through the aortic arch and into the descending aorta or abdominal aorta or both for a varying distance
- Type II—dissection originates in and is confined to the ascending aorta

- Type III—dissection originates in the descending aorta and is limited to same in type IIIa; type IIIb involves descending and variable extents of the abdominal aorta.

Dailey and colleagues[13] introduced the Stanford classification scheme in 1970 and simplified the anatomic classification. Stanford type A includes dissections that originate in the ascending aorta and includes DeBakey type I and type II dissections. In contrast, Stanford type B includes only dissections that originated in and are confined to the descending aorta (DeBakey type IIIa and IIIb). The immediate distinction of anatomic classification is a crucial step in clinical management because it directs initial therapy. Prompt graft replacement of the ascending aorta is the appropriate treatment for most patients with proximal aortic dissections (for exceptions, see later). This treatment is predicated on the high risk of lethal cardioaortic complications (principally aortic rupture) in the hours and days after symptom onset. Alternatively, patients with type B dissections generally are managed with medical therapy except for patients with specific anatomic or clinical complications, as reviewed subsequently.

EPIDEMIOLOGY

A 27-year, population-based evaluation calculated an incidence of 2.9 acute aortic dissections per 100,000 person-years.[7] In a population-based study from the Mayo Clinic, the incidence of acute aortic dissection was estimated to be 3.5 per 100,000 person-years.[14] Men are affected more

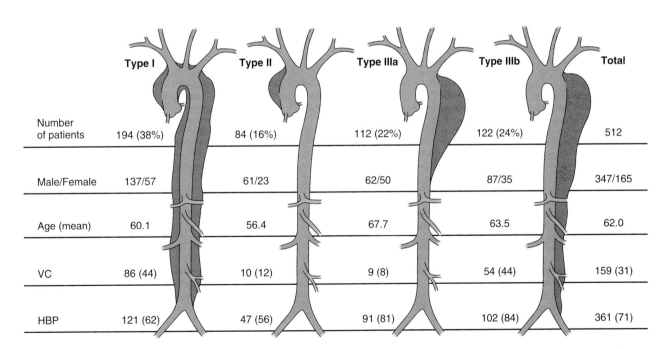

	Type I	Type II	Type IIIa	Type IIIb	Total
Number of patients	194 (38%)	84 (16%)	112 (22%)	122 (24%)	512
Male/Female	137/57	61/23	62/50	87/35	347/165
Age (mean)	60.1	56.4	67.7	63.5	62.0
VC	86 (44)	10 (12)	9 (8)	54 (44)	159 (31)
HBP	121 (62)	47 (56)	91 (81)	102 (84)	361 (71)

FIGURE 104-1 Demographic and clinical features of 512 patients with acute aortic dissection classified by the DeBakey system. The distribution of dissection extent, demographic features, and incidence of peripheral vascular complications were similar over the 35-year period (1965-1999) in which these patients were treated. Patients with type III dissections tend to be older and almost universally hypertensive. As anticipated, vascular complications tend to cluster among the more extensive type I and IIIb dissections. HBP, high blood pressure; VC, vascular complications. (Adapted from Lauterbach SR, Cambria RP, Brewster DC, et al: Contemporary management of aortic branch compromise resulting from acute aortic dissection. J Vasc Surg 33:1185-1192, 2001; and Cambria RP, Brewster DC, Gertler J, et al: Vascular complications associated with spontaneous aortic dissection. J Vasc Surg 7:199-209, 1988.)

frequently by acute aortic dissection, and a male-to-female ratio of 5:1 has been reported in many series.[15,16] The peak incidence of type A dissection is between 50 and 60 years of age and of type B dissection is between 60 and 70 years.[5] Hypertension is present in 70% to 80% cases,[4,5] and in our cumulative experience, type A dissections account for approximately 60% of cases (see Fig. 104-1). Acute aortic dissection displays a circadian and seasonal chronobiologic pattern.[17] Similar to acute myocardial infarction, sudden death, and cerebrovascular accidents, the onset of dissection occurs most frequently in the morning hours between 6 and 10 A.M. and more often in the colder seasons (fall, winter, and spring) than the summer.[18-20]

Regarding aortic diseases, bicuspid aortic valve with its accompanying aortic root dilatation is a well-established risk factor for ascending aortic dissections and has been documented in 7% to 14% of all aortic dissections.[4,5] Other aortic diseases, such as coarctation of the aorta, annuloaortic ectasia, chromosomal abnormalities (Turner syndrome and Noonan syndrome), aortic arch hypoplasia, aortic arteritis, and hereditary conditions (Marfan's syndrome and Ehlers-Danlos syndrome), are well-established risk factors for the development of acute aortic dissection.[21] Marfan's syndrome accounts for most cases of acute aortic dissection in patients younger than 40 years old.

In women younger than 40 years old, 50% of aortic dissections occur during pregnancy.[22] Overall, hypertension, as a part of preeclampsia, may complicate 25% to 50% of all pregnancies in which aortic dissection occurs. In some cases, the diagnosis of Marfan's syndrome is first made when such women present with a peripartum acute dissection. For women with a diagnosis of Marfan's syndrome, the presence of a dilated aortic root (>4 cm) places them at certain risk of acute dissection in the peripartum interval.[23] The most common site of pregnancy-associated aortic dissection is in the ascending aorta. The intimal tear occurs within 2 cm of the aortic valve in 75% of cases. Aortic rupture can occur without warning during the third trimester or during labor.[6]

Cocaine ingestion is a rare cause of acute aortic dissection in otherwise healthy individuals.[24] The prototypical patient is young and African American with a history of hypertension.[25] The presumed mechanism is thought to relate to an underlying defect in the aortic media from untreated hypertension and the severe shear forces generated from profound sympathetic activity caused by ingestion of cocaine, which creates a dramatic, acute increase in ventricular contraction force (dP/dT) on the aortic wall. The intimal tear occurs most often at the ligamentum arteriosum, where the aorta is relatively fixed and unable to tolerate the shear from the profound tachycardia and blood pressure elevation.[25]

■ PATHOLOGIC ANATOMY OF ACUTE AORTIC DISSECTION

Rupture of the intima and media is the initial event in most cases of aortic dissection. The violation of the intimal surface results in formation of a cleavage plane into the outer media and subsequent propagation for a varying distance in this plane, either antegrade or retrograde.[26] The blood-filled space created between the layers of the aortic wall becomes the false lumen. From the entry point, the column of blood may dissect proximally or distally as a consequence of the hydrodynamic gradient between the true and false lumina. In addition, the false lumen may enlarge by blood cleaving the layers of the aortic wall in a longitudinal or circumferential pattern. The continued hemodynamic stress may cause additional intimal tears, yielding points of entry for additional dissections or exit points for the column of blood within the false lumen. Such spontaneous windows or fenestrations often occur at aortic branch ostia, such as the left renal artery. The presence of an "intimal flap," representing the intimomedial septum between true and false lumina, is the most characteristic pathology in acute aortic dissection. The intimal flap/tear is located in the ascending aorta in 65% of patients, in the descending aorta in 25%, and in the arch and abdominal aorta in 5% to 10%.[5] The typical tear is transverse and does not involve the entire circumference of the aorta. In the descending aorta, the intimal tear typically originates within a few centimeters of the left subclavian artery.[27,28] In the usual pattern of a descending thoracic aortic dissection (DeBakey I or III, Stanford B), the cleavage plane progresses with characteristic topography as the false lumen progresses down the left posterolateral aspect of the aorta; the celiac, superior mesenteric, and right renal arteries typically emanate from the true lumen, and the left renal artery arises from the false lumen. Variations in this pattern are frequently encountered, however.

There is compelling evidence to suggest that intimal tears occur in the segments of the aorta that are subject to greatest dP/dt and pressure fluctuations.[29] In the cardiac cycle, the contractile function of the heart results in a flexion stress on the aortic wall that is greatest in the ascending aorta and in the first portion of the descending thoracic aorta.[6,29] In addition, the force of systolic flow is stored in the aortic wall as a form of potential energy (most dramatically in the elastic ascending aorta), which is used to encourage prograde flow during the diastolic phase of the cardiac cycle. The magnitude of the forces delivered into the aortic wall is related to the absolute blood pressure and the dP/dt, a surrogate measure of the steepness of the pulse wave.[7] A combination of these factors—elasticity and mobility of the aorta versus blood pressure and dP/dT—may culminate in the intimal tear and cleavage of the aortic wall and subsequent propagation of the acute dissection.

Aside from the repetitive hemodynamic stresses that may initiate aortic dissection in even healthy individuals, it has been suggested that medial degeneration of the aortic wall may predispose it to dissection by decreasing the structural integrity of the aortic layers.[29,30] The common denominator underlying the defect in the aortic wall seems to be loss of vascular smooth muscle cells and increased elastolysis of the media. The phenotypic similarity of human disease to the fibrillin q–deficient mouse lends credence to the concept that medial fragmentation starts the cycle of aortic dilatation that predisposes to dissection, as appreciated in Marfan's syndrome.[31] The central lesion seems to be the deterioration of medial collagen and elastin, and this is considered to be a factor in most cases of aortic dissection.[32] In particular, classic cystic medial degeneration seems to be an essential feature of several hereditary conditions, such as Ehlers-Danlos syndrome and Marfan's syndrome.[21] Specific connective tissue diseases account for only 10% to 15% of all acute aortic dissections, however.[5] Even in previously healthy individuals in whom dissections occur without any antecedent diagnosis of syndromic diseases, the degree of medial degeneration still tends to be greater than expected as part of normal aging. The exact cause of this medial degeneration is unclear, but advanced age and hypertension seem to be the most important factors.[20,32,33]

Atherosclerosis has not been considered to be an important etiologic feature of acute aortic dissection; however, Jex and associates[34] noted either gross or microscopic atheroma in 83% of patients in their series. Atherosclerotic plaque may be protective in serving to terminate the dissection process because the transmural inflammatory nature of atherosclerosis may serve to fuse the aortic layers.[35] The presence of an atherosclerotic aneurysm presenting with concurrent aortic dissection is uncommon, occurring in only 2% to 12% of dissections.[5,36] The unusual coexistence of an aortic dissection and a preexistent atherosclerotic aneurysm seems to change the natural history of each pathologic entity substantially.[35] In such a scenario, rupture of the preexistent aneurysm is the more likely scenario. In a review of 325 patients with aortic dissection, rupture in the abdomen occurred only in the setting of antecedent degenerative, atherosclerotic aneurysm.[11] In a separate series of 41 patients with infrarenal aortic dissection, rupture complicated the presentation in 14% of patients, and 67% of patients died after rupture.[36] These findings have important implications for therapy when medical therapy is touted as the preferred treatment for DeBakey type III dissections. In the setting of an associated aneurysm in any involved aortic segment, such dissections should be considered as "complicated" dissections and warrant an aggressive surgical posture. Because the risk of rupture is higher in aortic segments with coexisting aneurysm and dissection, initial surgical priority should be given to the aorta in which both entities are present (usually the infrarenal abdominal aorta).

■ PATHOGENESIS OF MALPERFUSION SYNDROMES

Aortic branch compromise may occur in aortic dissection through several mechanisms, and the resultant end-organ ischemia has been termed *malperfusion syndrome*. One or more vascular beds may be affected simultaneously, and an important clinical aspect is the recognition that such branch vessel obstruction is often subtotal and prone to intermittent and varying severity over the hours and even days to weeks after symptom onset. The diagnostic corollary is that imaging studies may add confusion because they are generally not capable of providing quantitative information (see later). Consistent over several series, malperfusion syndromes may complicate aortic dissection in 31% of patients.[11,37,38] We documented that such aortic branch compromise was a significant correlate of early mortality, particularly when patients with aortic rupture were excluded.[10] This effect has decreased over time, simultaneous with the percentage of patients with frank rupture (18% before 1986 versus 6% for 1990 through 1999).[10] These data indicate that more timely diagnosis and referral and the recognition of the importance of aortic branch compromise have been important factors

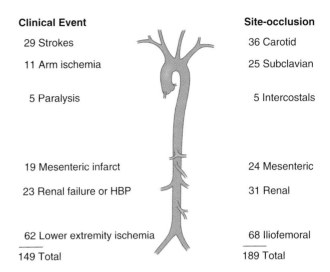

Clinical Event		Site-occlusion
29 Strokes		36 Carotid
11 Arm ischemia		25 Subclavian
5 Paralysis		5 Intercostals
19 Mesenteric infarct		24 Mesenteric
23 Renal failure or HBP		31 Renal
62 Lower extremity ischemia		68 Iliofemoral
149 Total		189 Total

FIGURE 104-2 Distribution of peripheral vascular complications in 512 patients over a 35-year period (1965-1999). Peripheral vascular complications are classified by aortic branch site. Differences between site occlusions and clinical events represent asymptomatic occlusions. HBP, high blood pressure.

in improving treatment results. As shown in Figure 104-2, virtually any aortic branch can be affected, and as intuitively suspected, the morbid clinical events vary as a function of the vascular territory involved. Carotid involvement is associated with significant stroke risk, whereas subclavian or lower extremity occlusive events are often well tolerated.

In the past, the extent of the dissection and its propagation into any branch vessel with resultant obstruction was considered to be the basic mechanism for ischemic complications, and this observation was based on cross-clamped aortae without flow, or necropsy studies.[39] More recently, real-time imaging studies have shown the dynamic interplay of pressure relationships within the lumina of the dissected aorta and the mobility of the aortic septum yielding intermittent, near-complete obstruction of ostia at the aortic level often with the vessel ostia left intact.[11,40,41] Williams and colleagues[42] have shown malperfusion in 20 of 24 patients with ongoing ischemia in the viscera or limb resulting from dynamic obstruction related to collapse of the true lumen. Identification of the mechanisms of branch compromise is crucial to formulate effective treatment modalities. The anatomic and physiologic variables underpinning any compromised vascular bed include (1) the percentage of aortic circumference dissected, (2) the presence of a distal reentrant focus in the false lumen or true lumen outflow, and (3) the topography of branch ostia to the true lumen versus the false lumen.[8]

In the minutes after an aortic dissection is initiated, the true lumen (representing the remnant of the original aortic lumen) collapses to a variable degree, and the false lumen becomes ectatic with an overall increase in aortic diameter.[41] The disparity in cross-sectional area available for the column of blood to enter and perfuse the true lumen is explained, in part, by the anatomy of the dissected aortic wall. In aortic dissection, the dissection flap consists of the intima and most of the media, whereas the outer wall of the false lumen contains remnants of the media and the entire adventitia.[28] In the normal aorta, the aortic circumference expands during systole to accommodate the wall tension generated by the systolic pulse wave in accordance with the law of LaPlace. In dissection, the structural components of the aortic wall predict false lumen dilatation. Being thinner and lacking elastin, the outer wall of the dissected aorta (and false lumen) must expand to a larger diameter to accommodate the same wall tension at any given blood pressure. In contrast, the true lumen, perhaps over a large percentage of its circumference, is released from the "load-bearing" adventitia. The true lumen, which contains most of the elastic components of the aortic wall, undergoes radial elastic collapse.[41] The degree to which the true lumen recoils and the false lumen expands (i.e., their respective cross-sectional area) depends on the percentage of the total aortic circumference involved with the dissection. As shown in Figure 104-3, the topographic relationship of the true lumen and false lumen and the extension of the dissection into the branch itself are the principal anatomic factors that determine malperfusion syndrome.

In acute dissection, the inner surface of the false lumen extends longitudinally and circumferentially down the aorta. Several common features warrant mention regarding the propagation of this false lumen. First, in acute dissection, the false lumen is highly thrombogenic as a result of the exposed adventitial and medial layers. In this phase, thrombus formation may occur in the false lumen secondary to stasis of the blood column in the blind end of the dissection.[43] If the blind end or the propagating end of the dissection column enters and constricts the ostia of a branch vessel, organ injury can occur by thrombosis or hypoperfusion of the involved vessel. This malperfusion syndrome has been termed *static obstruction*, to imply that relief of ongoing ischemia is unlikely to reverse unless the vasculature is reperfused from another conduit or reentry of the advancing column of the false lumen occurs so that it is decompressed.[42] Static obstruction of branch ostia can lead to two alternatives. In the first scenario, the dissecting process extends into the branch vessel proper, narrowing it to a variable degree—so-called static obstruction (see Fig. 104-3B). Alternatively the more common scenario occurs when the dissection process shears the aortic intimomedia around the vessel ostium, and the vessel anatomy itself remains intact with flow provided by the false lumen. As such, most false lumen branches rarely show evidence of ongoing malperfusion (see Fig. 104-3C).[43]

The phenomenon of true lumen collapse is an important causative factor when discussing the second mechanism of malperfusion syndromes. In *dynamic obstruction*, the compressed true lumen is unable to afford adequate flow volume, or the dissection flap prolapses into the branch ostia, which remains anatomically intact (see Fig. 104-3A) This is the more common mechanism of branch compromise, being responsible at least in part for approximately 80% of malperfusion syndromes.[42] The severity of the true lumen collapse with its attendant compromise of the ostia of any vessel is determined in part by the percentage of aortic circumference dissected locally, cardiac output, blood pressure, heart rate, and the peripheral resistance of the outflow.[40] Given the fluctuation of these physiologic and anatomic variables in the hours after onset, pulse deficits

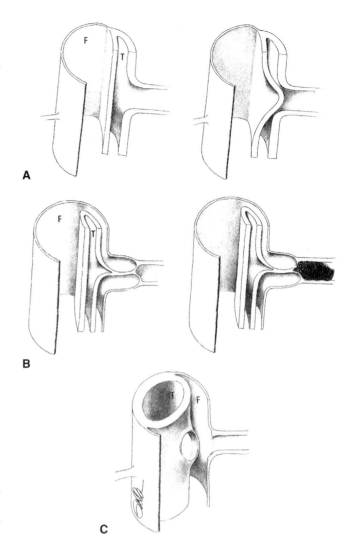

FIGURE 104-3 Mechanisms of aortic branch obstruction in acute dissection. **A,** In dynamic obstruction, the septum may prolapse into the vessel ostium during the cardiac cycle, and the compressed true lumen flow is inadequate to perfuse branch vessel ostia, which remain anatomically intact. **B,** Near-complete circumferential dissection with static obstruction—the cleavage plane of the dissection extends into the ostium and compromises inflow. Thrombosis beyond the compromised ostia may worsen perfusion further. **C,** Spontaneous perfusion of aortic branches perfused from the false lumen occurs if the dissecting process tears the ostia away from the true lumen. Such spontaneous "fenestrations" may account for persistent false lumen flow. F, false lumen, T, true lumen.

based on dynamic obstruction commonly may wax and wane over time.[8,44] Chung and colleagues[40] modeled the anatomy and physiologic conditions of a DeBakey type IIIB aortic dissection in vitro to study the hydrodynamic effects that worsen true lumen collapse. In conditions of equal outflow from each lumen in pulsatile flow, increasing the size of the aortic entry tear from 10 to 30 mm significantly aggravated the degree of true lumen collapse. On the basis of these observations, the investigators concluded that the movement of the dissection flap to produce dynamic obstruction of any branch vessel is related to the size of the entry tear, the limitation of false lumen outflow, and increased true lumen outflow produced by falling peripheral resistance.[40] In addition, the topography of aortic dissection, in particular the extent of the aortic circumference involved, contributes to dynamic obstruction of aortic branch vessels.

RELATED CONDITIONS OF THE THORACIC AORTA

In the spectrum of thoracic aortic pathology, IMH and PAU warrant mention because diagnostic confusion commonly occurs with the more classic acute aortic dissection. Such confusion is related to the fact that these entities share the feature of an intimal violation with the flowing blood gaining entry or propagating between the aortic wall layers, and IMH and PAU may present concurrently. The unifying feature of IMH and PAU is that they are secondary manifestations of degenerative aortic pathology. Extensive atherosclerotic changes, even remote from the focal aortic pathology, are common, and severe hypertension is nearly universal. IMH of the thoracic aorta is characterized by the absence of a definable (by radiographic means) entry tear and the crescentic column of clotted blood in the cleavage space that if not clotted would constitute the false lumen of a more typical dissection.[45-47] The extent of this IMH is variable in terms of length and circumference of the aorta involved and prograde versus antegrade propagation. The original etiologic concepts of IMH involved speculation that spontaneous rupture of vasa vasorum was responsible because a definable aortic ulcer or "entry tear" was often not radiographically demonstrable. More consistent with our own observations and a recent report, a penetrating atherosclerotic ulcer resulting in violation of the internal elastic lamina and allowing efflux of blood into the layers of the aortic wall is the more likely primary causative factor.[48-51]

The clinical presentation of an IMH is similar to that of acute aortic dissection, typically heralded by the abrupt onset of chest or back pain. The natural history of IMH has been reported to include progression to false aneurysm, rupture, or spontaneous regression.[52,53] In a study of 65 symptomatic patients with an IMH,[54] the authors observed that in patients with PAU and IMH, 90% were confined exclusively to the descending aorta, and the association of PAU and IMH was rare in the ascending aorta. IMH without PAU typically had a stable course, especially when limited to the descending thoracic aorta.[54] A report of 35 patients with IMH detailed a highly significant correlation of progression based on initial aortic diameter and the thickness of the hematoma. Patients with an initial aortic diameter greater than 40 mm had a 30-fold increased risk of progression to either aneurysm formation or rupture. Aortic wall thickness of greater than 1 cm also was associated with a nine-fold increased risk of progression.[50] Overall the treatment implications of these reports would support a posture of surgical or endovascular repair of an IMH when the diameter approaches the 6-cm range.[52]

PAUs of the thoracic aorta were first described by Shennan in 1934.[55] Full characterization and depiction of patients' pathology and natural history was outlined in 1986 by Stanson and coworkers.[48] Work by Coady and colleagues[56] has highlighted the worsened prognosis of patients with PAU, revealing a high incidence of rupture in the setting of preexistent aneurysms. Although in their series

the mean age for type A and type B dissection was 54 and 67, the mean age for patients with PAUs was much older (mean age 77; $P = .01$). In support of the postulate that PAU requires the milieu of extensive degenerative disease, 40% of patients diagnosed with a PAU of the thoracic aorta had been treated previously for an abdominal aortic aneurysm. Most worrisome was the 40% incidence of acute aortic rupture in patients with PAU (6 of 15 patients) as opposed to 7.3% for type A dissection and 4% for type B dissection; however, mean aortic diameter was significantly greater in patients with PAU versus dissections. For a given aortic diameter, the presence of a PAU may worsen overall prognosis, but intervention for PAU is still predicated on overall aortic diameter or clinical or radiographic signs of deterioration.

It seems logical that PAU and IMH represent different extents of a similar degenerative process. If the PAU gains intramural access of sufficient depth, a "dissecting" process can occur propagating antegrade or retrograde. Typically the propagating blood column does not gain egress or reentry to the aortic lumen, and the space is filled with clotted blood—giving the crescentic and rindlike appearance of the aortic wall characteristic of IMH.

CLINICAL PRESENTATION

The clinical manifestations of acute aortic dissection are diverse and often may be dominated by a specific malperfusion syndrome, such as stroke or mesenteric ischemia. The most common presenting symptom is pain in more than 93% of patients, with 85% noting the onset to be *abrupt*.[5,57] Although the pain typically is described as anterior in location in type A dissection, for type B dissection, the pain was experienced more often in the back (78% versus 64%).[5] In the series described by Spitell and associates,[4] the localization of pain to the interscapular region indicated involvement of the descending aorta (type B) in 90% of patients, whereas strictly anterior pain or pain radiating to the arm, neck, or jaw indicated involvement of the ascending aorta. The localization of pain to the abdomen was reported by 21% of patients in type A dissection and 43% of patients in type B dissection.[5] In such patients, a high index of suspicion for mesenteric vascular compromise is warranted. The character of the pain in aortic dissection is often described as sharp (68%), ripping or tearing (50%), and, less often, migratory (19%). The pain was described as being "the worst ever" by 90% of patients.[5] The control of pain by antihypertensive therapy is considered to be paramount in the early management of acute aortic dissection, and the recurrence of pain has been considered to imply failure of medical therapy.

Our group studied 53 patients who experienced pain after diagnosis of type B aortic dissection. Recurrent pain occurred in 34 of 53 patients (64%) at a median of 2.8 days (range 0 to 17) after presentation. The location of the pain was typically different from the initial complaint (85%). Overall, patients who had hypertension refractory to medical therapy were more likely to have recurrent pain ($P = 0.05$). Repeat imaging studies were performed in 31 of the 34 patients with no change in aortic diameter noted. Radiographic signs of dissection extension were absent in

30 of 31 patients (97%). Overall, only 2 of the 34 patients (2%) had a complicated hospital course. One patient developed abdominal pain owing to extension of the dissection into the abdomen as shown by axial tomography, required surgical intervention, and survived to discharge. The other patient died suddenly, presumably from aortic rupture, after reporting recurrent pain similar in quality to his initial complaint. On the basis of these observations, the authors concluded that among patients with early recurrent pain after type B aortic dissection, in the absence of clinical or radiographic signs of pathoanatomic changes, a conservative strategy of continued medical management was a reasonable approach.[58]

Syncope may complicate the presentation of acute aortic dissection in 5% to 10% of patients, and its presence often indicates the development of cardiac tamponade or involvement of the branchiocephalic vessels.[59] As an isolated symptom, without any complaint of chest or back pain, it occurred in less than 3% of all patients in the IRAD.[5] Overall, patients in the IRAD study presenting with syncope were more likely to have a type A dissection than type B dissection (19% versus 3%; $P < .001$) and more likely to have cardiac tamponade (28% versus 8%; $P < .001$).[60] Similarly, they were more likely to have a stroke (18% versus 4%; $P < .001$) and more likely to die in the hospital (34% versus 23%; $P = .01$). Although patients presenting with syncope had a higher rate of severe complications (tamponade, stroke, death), almost half had none of the aforementioned complications to explain their loss of consciousness. The mechanisms underlying this fact may be related to other pathophysiologic perturbations, such as vasovagal events or direct stretching of baroreceptors in the aortic wall.[61,62] Given the attendant morbidity and mortality that may accompany syncope, the rapid search to exclude serious complications in patients with acute aortic dissection is justified.

Spinal cord ischemia from the interruption of intercostal vessels is clearly more common with type B aortic dissections and may occur in 2% to 10% of all patients.[63] Direct compression of any peripheral nerve can occur rarely, resulting in paresthesia (lumbar plexopathy), hoarseness of voice (compression of recurrent laryngeal nerve), or Horner's syndrome (compression of sympathetic ganglion).[64-66]

On initial physical examination, hypertension is present in 70% of type B dissections, but only in 25% to 35% of type A dissections. The presence of hypotension complicating a type B dissection is rare (< 5% of patients). In contrast, hypotension may be present in 25% of dissections that involve the ascending aorta, potentially as a result of aortic regurgitation or intrapericardial rupture. The malperfusion of brachiocephalic vessels by the dissection may falsely depress brachial cuff pressures.[67] Refractory hypertension in the course of medical management of type B aortic dissections is common, occurring in 64% of patients with involvement of the descending aorta.[68] Such refractory hypertension is not associated with renal artery compromise or aortic dilatation, however, and continued medical therapy is indicated.

Pulse deficits are common and occur in 30% to 50% of patients in whom the aortic arch or the thoracoabdominal aorta or both are involved.[11,37,38] In examination of the IRAD population, the involvement of the brachiocephalic trunk was noted in 14.5% of patients; left common carotid artery in 6%; left subclavian artery in 14.5%; and femoral arteries in 13% to 14% (see Fig. 104-2).[69] Patients presenting with pulse deficits more often had neurologic deficits, coma, and hypotension. Carotid pulse deficits correlated strongly with fatal stroke, consistent with prior observations.[10] The number of pulse deficits was associated with increased mortality. Within 24 hours of presentation, 9.4% of patients with no deficits died, 15.8% of patients with one or two deficits died, and 35.3% of patients with three or more deficits died.[69] In regard to isolated lower extremity pulse deficits, mortality resulting from lower extremity ischemia or its sequelae is uncommon, occurring in only 4 of 38 patients with clinically evident lower extremity ischemia associated with acute dissection.[11] Nonetheless, leg ischemia caused by acute dissection was a marker of extensive dissection and may be accompanied by other compromised vascular territories. The clinical course of the peripheral ischemia is variable; one third of this group may show spontaneous resolution of pulse deficits.[11] Rapid bedside pulse examination can provide important information in the diagnosis of acute aortic dissection and patients at risk for complications.

Given the high morbidity of a missed diagnosis of aortic dissection, the history and physical findings can increase clinical accuracy. In one clinical predictive model, the presence of aortic-type pain alone (chest or interscapular of abrupt onset) was associated with a positive likelihood ratio of 2.6. The addition of pulse or blood pressure changes to the symptom of pain increased the positive likelihood ratio to 10.5. The addition of mediastinal or aortic widening on chest radiograph to the pain and pulse changes increased the likelihood ratio to 66. This diagnostic triad was found in only 27% of patients. Alternatively the absence of abrupt pain, pulse changes, and radiographic findings made the diagnosis of acute dissection exquisitely rare (4% of patients). Given the morbidity of a missed diagnosis of aortic dissection, even such a profound negative likelihood ratio may be insufficient to exclude aortic dissection if the diagnosis is otherwise clinically suspected.[70]

■ DIAGNOSIS

On a yearly basis, almost 4.6 million patients in the Untied States present to emergency departments with acute chest pain (8.2% of all visits).[71] Although multiple modalities can diagnose thoracic aortic dissection properly, it is inefficient, unrealistic, and costly to perform axial imaging for every patient complaining of chest pain. The indiscriminate application of thoracic imaging to patients with low pretest probability of having an aortic dissection has been predicted to yield an 85% false-positive rate.[72] Historically the diagnosis of acute aortic dissection has been inaccurate, and physicians correctly suspect the entity in only 15% to 43% of presentations.[7] When the diagnosis is made, it is often an incidental finding discovered during the evaluation of another intended pathology.[73] The rapid diagnosis of aortic dissection is essential given the dramatic benefits that appropriate medical, surgical, and endovascular therapy can provide. The modalities currently available for use in the diagnosis of acute aortic dissection include chest radiography, aortography, contrast computed tomography (CT), magnetic resonance imaging (MRI), and transthoracic or transesophageal echocardiography (TTE/TEE). Although the choice of diagnostic modality may be predicated on local availability and practice pattern, certain essentials exist. First, the diagnosis of acute aortic dissection must be confirmed or refuted. Second, the extent of the dissection, the potential involvement of branch vessels, and the presence of immediate life-threatening complications, such as tamponade, should be provided.

Plain Radiography

The findings of aortic dissection on chest radiography are nonspecific and rarely diagnostic. Often cited in discussion are the findings of widening of the cardiac or aortic silhouette, displacement of aortic calcifications, and effusions. The most common abnormality seen in aortic dissection is widening of the aortic silhouette, appearing in 60% to 90% of cases.[4,5] If calcification of the aortic knob is present, separation of the intimal calcification from the outer aortic soft tissue border by more than 1 cm—the "calcium sign"—is suggestive but not diagnostic of aortic dissection. The calcium sign was the only abnormality that reached a level of significance ($P = .05$) in distinguishing a type A versus a type B dissection.[4,5] The occurrence or worsening of a pleural effusion detected by chest radiograph in a patient with acute dissection has been suggested to be a relative indication for invasive therapies. The course of these effusions was reviewed by Hata and colleagues[74] in 48 patients diagnosed with acute aortic dissection. Pleural effusion was detected after admission in 42 of 48 patients (87.5%), of whom 18 patients were noted to have effusions at first radiograph. For the remaining 30 patients, the onset of effusion was noted to occur 4.5 ± 3.9 days (range 1 to 15 days) after the diagnosis of aortic dissection and resolved before discharge in 22 patients (42.2 ± 20.1 days). The effusion was bilateral in 31 patients (73.8%) and left-sided in 11 other patients (26.2%). The pleural effusions appeared most frequently in patients with type B dissections. On the basis of a higher white blood cell count, C-reactive protein, and fever noted in more patients with effusions than without, the authors concluded the pleural effusions seen in acute aortic dissection are largely associated with the inflammatory reaction of the mediastinal pleura.[74]

Aortography

Formerly the "gold standard" for the diagnosis of aortic dissection, aortography has largely been replaced by axial imaging studies in the initial diagnosis of aortic dissection. Aortography has a sensitivity of 86% to 88% and a specificity of 75% to 94% for the diagnosis of thoracic aortic dissection.[75-77] Overall the false lumen is visualized in 87% of cases, the intimal flap in 70%, and the site of the intimal tear in 56%.[78] False-negative aortograms may occur when thrombosis of the false lumen has occurred, in the presence of an IMH, or when equal flow into the true and false lumen obscures delineation.[79] The aortographic findings considered supportive of a diagnosis of aortic dissection include distortion of the normal contrast column, flow reversal or stasis into a false channel, failure of major branches to fill, and aortic valvular regurgitation.[77] Although

coronary angiography may be performed in conjunction with aortography, the imposed delay in treatment of an ascending dissection may be dangerous and lead to mortality.[80] Most contemporary diagnostic paradigms have de-emphasized the role of aortography. Pressurized contrast injections into either lumen in the presence of aortic dissection can lead to diagnostic confusion with respect to malperfusion syndromes. As reviewed earlier, branch ostia are anatomically normal in circumstances of dynamic obstruction; true lumen pressurized injection typically leads to an erroneous interpretation of "adequate perfusion." Given the need for rapid diagnosis, the limitation of aortography is clear—it is time-consuming, is invasive, incurs the risks of contrast nephropathy, and is expensive. In addition, Rizzo and colleagues[81] discovered at autopsy that in patients with ascending aortic dissection and unrecognized coronary artery disease, none died of coronary ischemia, but several died of aortic rupture. In contemporary practice, aortography is unnecessary before surgical repair of proximal dissection. In the management of distal dissection, it is used as a part of a treatment (see later) rather than diagnostic modality.

Transthoracic Echocardiography/ Transesophageal Echocardiography

The sensitivity and specificity of TTE range from 35% to 80% and 40% to 95%.[82,83] The chief technical limitations of TTE, whether performed in the suprasternal or subcostal views, are narrow intercostal spaces, obesity, and emphysema. In addition, false-positive results have been reported in TTE of the ascending aorta because of artifacts.[84] TEE overcomes the limitations of surface echocardiography by the anatomic proximity of the esophagus to the aorta. The sensitivity of TEE has been reported to be 98%, and the specifity ranges from 63% to 96%.[85-87] The advantages of TEE include wide availability, ease of use, and bedside capability. TEE also possesses the ability to detect entry tear sites, false lumen flow/thrombus, involvement of the arch or coronary arteries, degrees of aortic valvular regurgitation, and pericardial effusions. The addition of color-flow Doppler patterns may decrease false-positive results by recognizing differential flow velocities in the true and false lumina.[88] The chief limitations of TEE are the anatomic blind spot in the distal ascending aorta and arch secondary to the air-filled trachea and left main stem bronchus and inability to document dissection extension beyond the diaphragm.[89] Despite these shortcomings, TEE can be particularly useful in delineating dissection and relevant surgical pathology in the ascending aorta and is chiefly applied in this territory.[90] In an unstable patient with a suspected acute dissection in the ascending aorta, TEE may be performed in the operating room to expedite diagnosis and definitive therapy. In the IRAD study, TEE was employed second most frequently (after CT) in the diagnosis and workup of an acute aortic dissection.[91]

Magnetic Resonance Imaging

MRI has an overall sensitivity and specificity for diagnosis of aortic dissection ranging from 95% to 100%.[91-93] MRI can detect the site of the entry tear, the extent of the dissection, potential branch vessel involvement, and differential true lumen versus false lumen flow. The overall sensitivity and specificity for diagnosis of branch vessel involvement are 90% and 96%.[94] The chief limitations of MRI include lack of immediate availability, long examination times, and lack of monitoring for critically ill patients. In addition, patients who have had pacemakers, aneurysm clippings, or ocular implants are not candidates for MRI.

Computed Tomography

Contrast-enhanced CT was the most common diagnostic test used in patients in IRAD, being employed in 63% of patients.[91] CT is readily available, is less invasive, and has a reported sensitivity of 83% to 95% and specificity of 87% to 100% for the diagnosis of acute aortic dissection.[95-97] The chief limitation of imaging is the ascending aorta, where the sensitivity may decrease to less than 80%, but this is readily overcome by the addition of TEE.[67] A dedicated protocol to image the entire aorta is usually sufficient to provide the necessary diagnostic information. On a helical CT scanner, 2.5- to 5-mm section collimation and 1.5- to 2.5-mm section spacing used during 120- to 200-mL iodinated contrast administration at 3 to 4 mL/sec produce excellent aortic imaging of the true and false lumina and approximate entry tear sites and aid in planning intervention. In most cases, the true lumen may be localized by its continuity with an undissected segment of the aorta.[98] In circumferential dissection of the aortic root or when imaging of the aortic arch is omitted, this rule may be difficult to apply. The presence of intraluminal thrombus was a fairly good marker of the false lumen, but in patients with a concomitant degenerative aneurysm, thrombus may be present in the true lumen.[98] The finding of greatest significance was the observation in the descending thoracic aorta of the false lumen being larger than the true lumen in greater than 90% of cases ($P < .05$); this simple guideline is clinically quite useful.[98] As reviewed earlier in the pathogenesis of malperfusion syndromes, the orientation and mobility of the dissection flap represent vital information available from axial imaging studies. If the dissection flap was oriented concave toward the false lumen, this CT finding was 91% sensitive and 72% specific for a true lumen pressure deficit.[43] In CT scans of acute dissection, the dissection flap was more often noted to be in this curved orientation (63% of cases), whereas in chronic dissection, the flap was flat in 75% of cases.[98] As shown in Figures 104-4 and 104-5, a slitlike compressed true lumen is perhaps the key radiographic finding that should substantially raise the index of suspicion for renal/visceral/lower extremity malperfusion syndrome.

Regardless of whether or not an initial diagnosis has been made by some other modality (TEE or MRI), we believe that all patients with suspected acute aortic dissection should be evaluated thoroughly with chest and abdominal dynamic contrast-enhanced, fine-cut CT scanning. Three-dimensional CT scan reconstructions can aid in treatment planning, but axial imaging affords the best opportunity to detect topographic relationships of the true and false

lumina and potential aortic branch compromise. It may be appropriate if open surgical intervention is chosen as the revascularization procedure to proceed directly to surgery after CT alone in circumstances in which the clinical or laboratory signs dictate the need for urgent revascularization (see Fig. 104-5). Compared with other modalities, CT is the least operator dependent, provides useful anatomic correlates for surgical and endovascular therapy, and most reliably collects information for follow-up analysis and measurement.

■ PRINCIPLES OF TREATMENT

Optimal treatment of acute dissection depends on prompt diagnosis and an understanding of the anatomic extent of the pathologic process. Prompt institution of medical therapy to lower systemic blood pressure and dP/dT is a key element of initial therapy for all patients with the goal of stabilizing the extent of the dissection, reducing intimal flap mobility, relieving dynamic aortic branch obstruction, and decreasing the risk of rupture. Type A dissections are characterized by an intimal tear in the ascending aorta and occasionally are limited to the arch, but often can progress to involve the arch and considerable lengths of the thoracoabdominal aorta. Mortality in the acute phase of a proximal dissection may exceed 1% per hour related to the central cardioaortic complications of tamponade, acute aortic valvular insufficiency, and coronary obstruction. Prompt graft replacement with or without aortic valve repair/replacement is the treatment of choice for most patients with exceptions as detailed subsequently. For patients with type B dissections, the catastrophic complication of rupture is uncommon

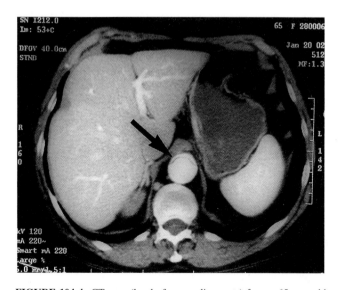

FIGURE 104-4 CT scan (level of supraceliac aorta) from a 65-year-old man with rapidly deteriorating renal function and mesenteric vascular insufficiency after acute distal dissection. CT scan shows crescentic compressed true lumen (*arrow*), associated with true lumen pressure deficit, and malperfusion of vessels arising from the same. In this case, the aortic circumference from the 2-o'clock to the 10-o'clock position is involved in the dissection, creating the milieu for true lumen collapse.

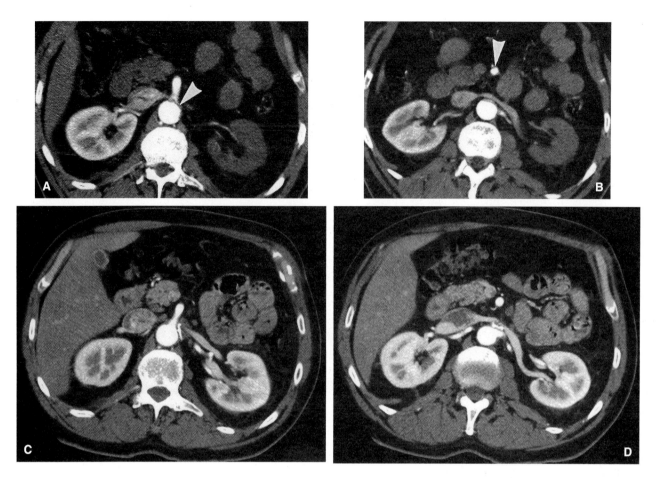

FIGURE 104-5 A 48-year-old man with acute DeBakey type I dissection with severe abdominal pain and progressive acidosis was treated by visceral segment surgical fenestration before ascending aortic replacement. **A,** Axial image at the superior mesenteric artery (SMA) suggests dynamic aortic obstruction with a barely discernible true lumen perfusing the SMA *(arrowhead)*. False lumen flow fills nearly the entire aortic circumference and cross-sectional area, yet flow in the SMA could be interpreted as "normal." **B,** Slitlike true lumen appreciated from 11-o'clock to 2-o'clock position with obstruction and malperfusion of the left renal artery. Note contrast visualized in more distal SMA *(arrowhead)*. At surgery, severe restriction of celiac/superior mesenteric/left renal artery flow was identified. **C,** Postsurgical fenestration result at SMA; Teflon felt noted on anterolateral visceral segment. **D,** Postsurgical fenestration result with good left renal artery perfusion.

except for patients who present with advanced false lumen dilatation or the equivalent of aneurysm formation at the aortic entry site.[8,99] In patients with uncomplicated type B dissections, surgical therapy has not shown superiority over medical or interventional therapy.[57] The application of stent-graft technology to these patients may alter this paradigm in the near future. Aortic branch compromise by the propagating false lumen and subsequent malperfusion syndrome may complicate the initial presentation of patients with extensive type B dissections. A "complication-specific" approach to these patients, involving open surgical and endovascular options to treat such malperfusion syndromes, is advocated and reviewed subsequently.

■ MEDICAL THERAPY

In the 1960s, Wheat and Palmer[100] first advocated medical treatment of aortic dissection as an alternative for patients too ill to withstand surgical therapy. Currently, medical management in a critical care setting is now the initial therapy for virtually all patients with the tentative diagnosis of aortic dissection. The immediate management of acute aortic dissection is directed toward reducing the hemo-dynamic forces that have initiated and propagated the intimal tear and cleavage of the aortic wall. By reducing dP/dT, the forces predisposing the dissected aorta to rupture or compromise branch vessels are lessened. Intravenous antihypertensive therapy should be started in all patients in whom acute aortic dissection is suspected, with the exception of patients with hypotension.[67] For patients with hypotension in the setting of acute dissection, an expeditious evaluation for tamponade is warranted, but percutaneous pericardiocentesis as a temporizing measure is not advised because it often accelerates bleeding or shock.[101] The immediate goal of medical therapy is to eliminate the pain of dissection and reduce systolic blood pressure and dP/dT.[67] In contemporary practice, a combination of a beta blocker and vasodilator is standard medical therapy. In addition, the beta blocker should be initiated before the direct vasodilator (i.e., sodium nitroprusside); otherwise the reflex sympathetic stimulation from direct vasodilatation would stimulate cathecholamine release and resultant increases in dP/dT—opposite of the desired effect.

The cornerstones of medical therapy are the reduction of dP/dT *and* arterial blood pressure. For the acute reduction of dP/dT, an intravenous beta blocker is infused in incremental doses until evidence of effective beta blockade is achieved, usually indicated by a heart rate of 60 to 80 beats/min. Propranolol was the first generally available beta blocker and is given in intravenous doses of 1 mg every 3 to 5 minutes until effect, not to exceed 0.15 mg/kg (approximately 10 mg). Propranolol may be given every 4 to 6 hours. Labetalol is an α- and β-adrenergic receptor blocker that may achieve dP/dT reduction in concert with blood pressure lowering. The initial dose is 20 mg, administered intravenously over 2 minutes, followed by additional doses of 40 to 80 mg every 10 to 15 minutes until the hemodynamic parameters are acceptable (to a maximum dose of 300 mg). Maintenance dosing can be achieved with continuous infusion of 2 mg/min titrating to 5 to 10 mg/min. Esmolol is a short-acting beta blocker with a half-life of only 9 minutes that may be administered as a 500 µg/kg intravenous bolus followed by a continuous infusion at 50 µg/kg/min up to 200 µg/kg/min; it may be particularly useful as a test of beta-blockade tolerance in patients at risk for bronchospasm or chronic obstructive pulmonary disease flare. In these patients, a cardioselective beta blocker, such as atenolol or metoprolol, may be desirable. For the acute reduction of arterial pressure, the direct vasodilator sodium nitroprusside is effective and should be used after beta blockade is achieved. The infusion is started at 20 µg/min and may be titrated to 800 µg/min. With increasing doses, cyanide toxicity from nitroprusside metabolism may manifest as worsening acid-base status, mental status changes, or hyperreflexia and is more common in patients with hepatic or renal dysfunction.

■ SURGICAL THERAPY

Graft Replacement of Ascending Aortic Dissection

A complete review of the surgical literature and state-of-the-art management of acute type A dissection is beyond the scope of this chapter. Urgent surgical repair of acute type A dissection is mandated because medical treatment is associated with a 60% in-hospital death rate.[5] Since the first report of a successful type A dissection repair in 1963 by Morris, substantial improvements have been made in the intraoperative management of these patients by inclusion of intraoperative TEE, cerebral protection by profound hypothermia, and advanced prosthetics for managing the dissected aorta and aortic valve.[102] The anatomic goal is resection of the aortic intimal tear to eliminate the threat of rupture and to reconstruct the aortic wall layers in the distal anastomosis so as to eliminate false lumen flow. Persistent false lumen flow continues in many patients after ascending aortic graft replacement despite liberal use of circulatory arrest and technical adjuncts, such as glue aortoplasty. Despite these advances in the treatment of type A dissection, operative mortality in contemporary series remains in the 10% to 25% range (Table 104-1).[103-105] One of the main determinants of poor outcome is neurologic status at the time of presentation. In a series of 104 consecutive patients who underwent repair of type A aortic dissection, mortality was universal in patients presenting neurologically unresponsive and intubated. In addition, a 45% death rate was reported when patients presented with a stroke and underwent an otherwise successful type A dissection repair. Controversy continues as to the optimal technique for neuroprotection, with no consensus among cardiac surgeons on the utility of hypothermic circulatory arrest alone versus selective arterial (via the right axillary artery) or retrograde venous cerebral perfusion.[102-106]

Table 104-1   Results of Graft Replacement of Acute Type A Aortic Dissection

FIRST AUTHOR	PERIOD	ADJUNCTS (% PATIENTS)	NO. PATIENTS	PREOPERATIVE SHOCK (%)	MORTALITY (%)
Fann[111]	1983-2002	NA	91	NA	26
Kazui[108]	1983-2001	HCA, 20 RCP, 20	138	NA	16
Pompilio[112]	1984-1999	HCA, 25 RCP, 25	110	21	20
Sinatra[113]	1992-1998	HCA, 100 RCP, 21 ACP, 27	85	25	25
Apaydin[103]	1993-2001	HCA, 99	108	12	25
Mehta[80]	1996-1999	HCA, 87 RCP, 56	437	28	26
Bavaria[102]	1994-2001	HCA, 100 RCP, 100 EEG, 66	104	10	9

ACP, antegrade cerebral perfusion; EEG, neurocerebral monitoring (electroencephalogram); HCA, hypothermic circulatory arrest; NA, not available; RCP, retrograde cerebral perfusion.

Deciding which patients require aortic valve replacement in concert with ascending aortic dissection is greatly facilitated by intraoperative TEE. The procedure may be avoided in 80% of patients.[107,108] Indications for aortic valve replacement include Marfan's syndrome, sinus of Valsalva aneurysm, bicuspid valve or other leaflet pathology, and extension of the tear and dissection into the annulus.[102] A secondary technical issue is related to the issue of extent of arch replacement because 20% to 30% of patients with type A dissections may have intimal tears in the aortic arch or descending aorta.[109] One of the largest published experiences with various surgical techniques to manage type A dissection was reported from the Stanford group,[110] and this series addresses the problem of treating or leaving unrecognized intimal tears in the aorta. Although arch involvement by the dissection was associated with an increased risk of future distal aortic reoperations, an aggressive posture in replacement of the aortic arch, including hypothermic circulatory arrest and selective head vessel perfusion, has not yet been associated with improved outcome.[108,110]

Graft Replacement of Descending Aortic Dissection

Threatened or actual rupture at the aortic intimal tear in the proximal descending aorta remains in our view the only indication for acute graft replacement in distal dissection. Unless an extensive aneurysm is present, resection should be confined to the proximal descending aorta because mortality and spinal cord ischemia risk increase dramatically with extensive aortic replacement in the setting of an acute dissection. Although an anatomic goal of central aortic replacement is reconstruction of the aortic wall layers in the distal anastomosis and obliteration of false lumen flow, 25% to 50% of patients who are treated surgically can be expected to have persistent false lumen flow.[114,115] In addition to a significant incidence of persistent false lumen flow, other reasons for the abandonment of central aortic repair in acute type B dissection include the substantial morbidity, the equivalent results of medical therapy, and the variable success in relieving distal malperfusion. We applied this approach in only 1 patient over a decade in a series of nearly 100 type B dissection patients.[10] Table 104-2 shows representative data of surgical morbidity in patients treated with

central aortic graft replacement for acute type B dissections. Although mortality averaged 39%, the small numbers and the remote treatment intervals in many of these reports should be noted. In addition, central aortic grafting may be unsuccessful in alleviating distal malperfusion syndromes depending on the mechanism of obstruction, the anatomic complexity of the dissection, and the successful obliteration of false lumen flow. Prior reports wherein 10% of endovascular procedures performed for distal vascular complications were performed in the setting of unresolved malperfusion after central aortic repair are noteworthy.[116]

Albeit seldom indicated, central aortic graft replacement for type B aortic dissection presents significant technical challenges. The traditional surgical approach to establishing anastomotic integrity has been the application of strips of polytetrafluoroethylene (Teflon) felt inside the true lumen and outside the aortic wall, which is tedious and time-consuming.[104] In contradistinction, the introduction of glue aortoplasty is an important contribution to modern-day aortic dissection surgery. With the aorta transected and a sponge inserted in the true lumen to protect its diameter, the glue is applied for a length of 2 cm between the dissected layers, at a thickness of 2 mm. After 2 minutes, the aortic layers are fused and strengthened to accept a collagen-impregnated woven Dacron graft with a running polypropylene suture. Since the 1970s, the use of glue aortoplasty has been reported to decrease the number of aortic valve replacements (for type A dissection), the amount of postoperative bleeding, the volume of intraoperative transfusion, and the severity of postoperative complications.[117-119] The friable, acutely dissected aorta may require prolonged cross-clamping times to achieve anastomotic integrity. The addition of distal aortic perfusion allows for maintenance of visceral and spinal blood supply. In a series of 22 patients undergoing graft replacement of the descending aorta for acute type B dissections, spinal cord ischemic complications were reported in 7 patients (32%). Safi and colleagues[120] reported acute dissection to be a significant predictor of postoperative neurologic deficit (odds ratio 10.59; 95% confidence interval 2.45 to 45.82; P = .002). These authors concluded that surgical repair of acute type B aortic dissection carries the same overall operative mortality as operations for degenerative aneurysms, yet by comparison, the neurologic morbidity was disproportionately high.[120]

Table 104-2 Results of Graft Replacement of Acute Type B Aortic Dissection

FIRST AUTHOR	PERIOD	ADJUNCTS (% PATIENTS)	NO. PATIENTS	MORTALITY (%)	PARAPLEGIA/ PARAPARESIS (%)
Jex[121]	1962-1983	PB, 66	29	45	24
Verdant[122]	1974-1994	NA	52	12	0
Glower[123]	1975-1988	PB, 44 GS, 39	19	18	NA
Miller[124]	1977-1982	PB, NA	26	13	25
Neya[125]	1979-1991	PB, NA	13	69	NA
Fann[111]	1983-1992	PB, 100	17	41	NA
Svensson[126]	1986-1989	PB, NA	67	6	25
Coselli[127]	1986-1994	PB, NA CSF, NA	28	14	7

CSF, cerebrospinal fluid drainage; GS, Gott shunt; NA, not available; PB, partial bypass.

Stent-Graft Repair of Aortic Dissection Entry Site

Stent-graft repair at the aortic entry tear ultimately may provide the means to accomplish the intuitively logical short-term and long-term goals of central aortic repair, while obviating the substantial morbidity of conventional surgical repair. In 1999, the endovascular treatment of acute type B dissections with stent-graft technology was described in two sentinel reports.[128,129] Such an approach may lessen the incidence and severity of malperfusion syndromes and reduce late aortic related complications by minimizing the incidence of aneurysmal degeneration of the outer wall of the false lumen. As appreciated in the natural history of medically managed type B dissections, continued patency of the false lumen is an independent risk factor for progression of chronic dissections to aneurysmal dilatation.[35,129-135] During the first 4 to 7 years after acute aortic dissection, an aneurysm of the false lumen in the thoracic aorta may develop in 14% to 40% of patients treated with medical therapy alone.[29,136] The concept of inducing false lumen thrombosis by sealing the aortic tear with an aortic endograft has the potential to reduce early and late complications of type B dissection. Clinical trials of this approach have been initiated.

Stent-graft repair for acute dissection has yet to be studied in any systematic way, largely related to the lack of suitable stent-graft constructs. Particular technical points of stent-graft repair for aortic dissection deserve emphasis. First, the placement of uncovered stents over the entry tear within the proximal true aortic lumen is ill advised. The ability of an uncovered stent to direct flow away from the false lumen relies on sheer radial force, and the tolerance of the acutely dissected intimal flap to accommodate aggressive oversizing in an effort to compress the false lumen is unknown. In addition, the eccentricity of the true and false lumen geometry may place demands on radial force distribution, resulting in overdistention of the true lumen in tortuous portions of the aorta. By these two mechanisms, deployment of such uncovered stents may cause aortic rupture. These observations on the poor performance of uncovered stents in the acutely dissected aorta have been confirmed in multiple animal studies.[137-139] Finally, the indiscriminate use of uncovered stents in the true or false lumen may compromise later interventions by limiting sheath access or device deployment.[140]

Overall, if a patient is to be considered a candidate for stent-graft treatment, the location of the entry tear and proper recognition of proximal and distal fixation zones are fundamental to the successful performance of the stent-graft repair. When selected, stent-graft repair of acute aortic dissection should be performed in an operating room with adequate fluoroscopic imaging. True lumen access should be obtained from either a brachial or a femoral approach; typically, because the tear in type B dissection is distal to the left subclavian artery, rapid true lumen access is obtained easily through a transbrachial approach. If device tracking is difficult as a result of tortuosity or associated occlusive aortic disease, "through-and-through" access from the brachial to femoral artery can be obtained with intravascular snares to facilitate device delivery. When definitive true and false lumen access is achieved, the specific location of the entry tear and any branch vessel compromise should be documented with a combination of intravascular ultrasound and angiography. The operator should have definitive knowledge of the three-dimensional aortic topography displayed on the preintervention CT scan. The induction of hypotension or bradycardia by pharmacologic means may increase the accuracy of entry tear sealing during deployment. The use of compliant, large-diameter (33 to 40 mm) aortic occlusion balloons may be needed to ensure adequate apposition of the device to the aortic wall.

The short-term outcomes of stent-graft therapy of acute type B dissection using custom-made devices initially were reported by Dake and colleagues[129] using first-generation homemade devices. These authors treated 19 patients in the acute phase of dissection by stent-graft coverage over the aortic entry tear in the descending thoracic aorta. Of the 19 patients, 4 had acute type A dissection (all with entry tear distal to the arch and retrograde extension to involve the ascending aorta), and 15 had acute type B dissection. The acute dissections involved aortic branch vessels in 14 of 19 patients (74%), with symptomatic malperfusion present in 7 patients (37%). The average length of the entry tear as discerned by arteriography or intravascular ultrasound was 1.9 cm (range 1.2 to 2.9 cm). The mean diameter of the implanted stent-graft was 29.7 ± 5.1 mm with an average length of 6.9 ± 1.5 cm. Two patients (11%) required deployment of more than one stent-graft to cover the tear completely secondary to residual false lumen flow from either a proximal or a distal communication. Early mortality was observed in three patients (16%); two patients died from false lumen rupture 8 hours and 9 days after stent-grafting, and one patient died from sepsis secondary to gut infarction 7 days after apparently successful stent-graft therapy of malperfusion syndrome. Stent-graft therapy was successful in achieving complete thrombosis of the false lumen in 15 of 19 patients (79%). In the four patients with acute type A dissections, the mean diameter of the ascending aorta decreased from 41 mm (range 35 to 46 mm) before therapy to 34 mm (range 32 to 36 mm) after stent-graft implantation. For the 15 patients with acute type B dissection, the diameter of the proximal descending aorta was significantly smaller after the procedure ($P = .04$). An increase in true lumen diameter and flow correlated with clinical and hemodynamic improvement in malperfusion syndromes in all 22 vascular territories compromised by dynamic aortic obstruction. Alternatively, for vascular territories compromised by a combination of static and dynamic aortic obstruction, only 6 of 15 beds (40%) were improved by stent-grafting alone, and additional stents were required to open the true lumen into the aortic branch vessel. With an average follow-up of 13 months, no patients were found to have enlargement of their aortic diameter, and no cases of aortic rupture were reported. The authors concluded that stent-graft therapy provides acceptable results for a highly selected group of patients with acute aortic dissection that includes an entry tear distal to the left subclavian artery.[129]

In a second report of endovascular therapy of acute type B aortic dissection published concurrently with the aforementioned series, Nienaber and colleagues[128] described their early experience of stent-graft therapy in 12 consecutive patients with acute type B dissection. Their stent-graft results were compared with 12 matched controls who underwent surgery for acute type B dissection. Using a commercially manufactured stent-graft with uncovered proximal stent fixation, these investigators described no mortality or morbidity in stent-graft deployment within 12 months of treatment. Conversely, surgery for acute type B dissection in their centers was associated with a 33% mortality and 42% morbidity ($P = .09$ and $P = .04$ versus stent-grafting). Ultrasonography detected thrombosis of the false lumen in 10 of 12 patients (83%) within minutes of stent-graft deployment. At 3 months, all remaining false lumina were noted to have thrombosed. True lumen diameter also was observed to increase by 8 to 19 mm (27% to 202% expansion of preimplantation width). In direct comparison of the two modalities, significantly less intensive care unit length of stay, less overall length of stay, less transfusion requirement, and better functional recovery were recorded in favor of stent-graft therapy versus surgery. The investigators found stent-graft therapy of acute type B dissection to be a promising endovascular strategy that may promote remodeling of the aortic wall by initiating false lumen thrombosis.[128] Other authors have reported that stent-graft repair is more likely to be effective when applied in the acute phase of the disease.[141] It seems logical that mobility of the septum and consequent ability of the aorta to remodel would be optimal in the acute phase of dissection, before fibrosis of the septum ensues.

The efficacy of stent-graft therapy in the treatment of acute distal dissections in the setting of ongoing visceral or extremity ischemia or aortic rupture was reviewed by Greenberg and coworkers.[142] Outcomes of stent-graft therapy in 31 patients were retrospectively reviewed to determine if luminal relationships, aortic diameters, and stent-graft therapy could predict clinical outcomes. The indication for treatment was malperfusion syndromes (77%) or aortic rupture (23%). Of the 31 patients, 29 patients were treated by stent-graft therapy alone, and 2 were treated by fenestrations when definitive true lumen access could not be established. When true lumen compression resulted in visceral vessel malperfusion, the authors established definitive true lumen access to a minimum of at least two visceral vessels (typically the superior mesenteric artery and a renal artery). Early mortality was 29% in these critically ill patients with a historically documented mortality in the 80% range.[11] Four of these deaths occurred immediately after stent-grafting owing to massive reperfusion injuries with hyperkalemic cardiac arrest. Hemodialysis was instituted in 14 patients (45%), with permanent dialysis requirement in 3 (9%). Overall, mesenteric infarction accounted for 44% of the early mortalities. The authors reported that a small true lumen (a true-to-false lumen ratio of ≤0.35) was 83% sensitive and 89% specific in predicting critical mesenteric ischemia. The authors concluded that the morbidity and mortality associated with a stent-graft approach to acute distal aortic dissection with end-organ ischemia may be lower than conventional surgical approaches but still carries a significant risk.[142] In the particular circumstance of mesenteric ischemia, a low threshold for laparotomy, regardless of the technical mode of revascularization (open versus endovascular), is appropriate.

The use of stent-graft repair in the treatment of acute dissections holds promise to reduce early complications and the progression over time to aneurysmal degeneration. The instantaneous and dramatic occurrence of false lumen thrombosis by coverage of the aortic entry tear seems to be a key determinant in the process; the significance of small distal fenestrations is unknown. Early treatment of acute type B dissection seems to be associated with improved technical outcomes consistent with the hypothesis that true lumen/septum malleability may diminish in the chronic phase of the disease. A prospective, randomized study of stent-graft repair versus medical therapy for acute type B dissections is needed.

Endovascular Approach to Malperfusion Syndrome

Malperfusion syndromes may complicate the initial presentation of acute aortic dissection in 25% to 40% of patients.[11,143,144] Even in patients treated for concomitant ascending and descending aortic dissection (DeBakey type I), ischemic complications may persist in 25% of patients after ascending aortic graft replacement.[143] In such cases, surgical management of aortic branch compromise has been associated with excessive morbidity and mortality often related to delayed diagnoses, particularly in the period after proximal cardioaortic repair when such treatment has failed to resolve distal malperfusion syndromes. In this setting, the application of endovascular techniques, such as fenestration of the aortic septum and branch orifice stenting, is gaining favor. The operative mortality rate for aortic dissection patients with renal ischemia is 50% to 80%, and in mesenteric ischemia the mortality rate is 87%.[11,69] In several series of surgical fenestration of dissected aortas to alleviate malperfusion syndromes, overall operative mortality has remained consistently greater than 20% for decades.[116,145] Endovascular therapy may occupy a niche indication for treatment of such complicated dissections, but definitive data on this treatment modality do not yet exist.[57] Current indications for aortic fenestration or branch vessel stenting rely on clinical suspicion, which in the absence of obvious clinical parameters, is largely driven by the anatomic considerations as revealed on CT.[144] Duplex ultrasonography of the renal or visceral vessels or both to check for decrements in velocities is a convenient way to investigate perfusion.

In the initial arteriographic evaluation of a patient with an acute aortic dissection complicated by malperfusion, true and false lumen access must be obtained. The confirmation of position within the true or false lumen is facilitated by intravascular ultrasound.[146,147] Angiography should be performed in the proximal, undissected aorta to appreciate fully intimal flap mobility and any dynamic aortic obstruction, and this may be verified by brachial artery cannulation in most cases. As noted earlier, power injection in the true lumen of the dissected aorta may give the false impression of adequate perfusion to branch vessels compromised by dynamic obstruction. Similarly, showing equal catheter-derived pressures in the true and false lumina does not ensure adequate perfusion in particular branches for the reasons reviewed earlier. Such pressure measurements have meaning only if obtained in the vessel of inquiry as opposed to the aortic lumen. All aortic branches should be visualized before intervention because changes in flap mobility secondary to relief of obstruction in any single vessel may alter perfusion in other aortic side branches. If compromise of any aortic branch vessel is identified by the dissection, wire access into the distal true lumen of the vessel should be secured. In general, placement of self-expanding stents in a potentially compromised aortic branch should precede aortic fenestration because fenestration may alter aortic flow unpredictably and make it extremely difficult to regain endovascular access to compromised vessels.[144]

Fenestration of the intimal flap may be performed by several techniques using the combination of ultrasound and fluoroscopy. Most commonly, fenestration is performed from the smaller (usually true lumen) to the larger (false) lumen. Using a Roesch-Uchida needle, Brockenbrough needle, or Colopinto needle, or the back end of a 0.014 wire, a fenestration is created close to the compromised aortic branch. After the needle and a stiff wire are advanced from the true to the false lumen, a 5F catheter is advanced into the alternate lumen. Confirmation of the position across the membrane is performed by contrast injection. Subsequently an angioplasty balloon of at least 12 to 15 mm in diameter and 20 to 40 mm in length is used to create a fenestration tear. In some instances, an angioplasty balloon may be needed into the target lumen so that the intimal flap can be stabilized.[148] At the same time, this balloon may act as a target for the needle or wire. An alternative technique of fenestration has been termed the *scissors technique*.[149] In this technique, stiff guide wires are placed in each lumen from a single femoral access. Then by advancing a single long sheath over the two wires, the membrane is divided over a long distance. Authors familiar with use of the scissors technique have reported clean longitudinal tears (the ideal result) and circumferential separation of the flap from the aortic wall with aortoaortic intussusception (not ideal).[150]

The use of a snare to deliver a wire from one femoral access through the flap and down the contralateral femoral access has been described. By pulling this "U" down the distal aorta, a fenestration defect may be created with the same potential risk of intimal dehiscence described previously. In light of these dramatic and unpredictable alterations in intimal flap anatomy and flow dynamics incurred by overaggressive fenestration in the visceral aorta, investigators with the largest series of patients currently recommend percutaneous fenestration be limited to the distal aorta.[116] The ideal hemodynamic result for fenestration of the dissected intima is realized when there is equalization of peak systolic pressures between the two lumina in the aorta, and the false lumen is decompressed.[39,40,144] Intravascular ultrasound is another useful modality to show alleviation of malperfusion generated by dynamic aortic obstruction.

The largest reported series of percutaneous balloon fenestration and endovascular stenting for peripheral ischemic complications in the setting of acute aortic dissection was reported by the Stanford group.[116] In their series of 40 patients with malperfusion syndromes, 14 patients underwent combined stenting and balloon fenestration, 24 underwent stenting alone, and 2 underwent fenestration alone. The location of the balloon fenestration was in the thoracic aorta in eight patients, in the upper abdominal aorta in three patients, and just above the aortic bifurcation in seven patients. Overall, flow was restored to the ischemic territories in 37 of 40 patients (93%). By 30 days postprocedure, an additional 7 patients had died, for an overall survival rate of 75% (30 of 40 patients). The variables found to be significant predictors of death on multivariate analysis were ischemia of three vascular beds (nearly fourfold increase in risk) and advanced age. In follow-up beyond 30 days postprocedure, five more patients died; one patient's death was related to false lumen rupture, and two other patients died suddenly without autopsy. Although the authors recognize that strict comparison of their endovascular approach to peripheral ischemic complications from acute aortic dissection cannot be made to the published surgical series, their 30-day death rate of 25% would seem to compare favorably with the historical surgical series, in which operative mortality was reported to be 64%.[111] Contemporary surgical series have shown substantially improved operative mortality, however, even for patients with mesenteric compromise,[10] and it is noteworthy that mortality in such patients is more often referable to delayed diagnosis than to morbidity of the intervention itself. Finally, endovascular and conventional surgical approaches should be viewed in a complementary, rather than competitive, fashion, particularly in the circumstances of mesenteric ischemia, in which our approach typically has been to proceed directly to surgery. This relates to the clinical trap of apparently adequate percutaneous mesenteric revascularization followed by the evolution of ischemic bowel to frank infarction. We have seen this sequence, which was responsible for several deaths in the endovascular fenestration series.[10,42,116,148]

The effect of fenestration on long-term outcome of false lumen expansion in patients with distal dissections remains in question because the false lumen remains pressurized and remains at risk for continued progression to aneurysm. Beregi and colleagues[151] reported a series of 46 patients treated by either stent-graft therapy ($n = 12$) or balloon fenestration ($n = 34$) for peripheral ischemic complications of acute aortic dissection. In examination of the diameter of the true and false lumina after intervention, decreases in aortic diameters were observed only in patients treated with stent-graft therapy. Alternatively, surviving patients in whom balloon fenestration was employed experienced worrisome increases in true lumen diameter, false lumen diameter, and overall aortic diameter.

Triaging of patients presenting with malperfusion syndromes as to the initial mode of intervention is straightforward for patients with type B dissections. Because morbid events related to the entry tear itself are uncommon, there is consensus that such patients should be managed with directed peripheral vascular intervention—a so-called complication-specific approach. Currently, this situation has involved the decision between endovascular revascularization or open surgical fenestration (see later). As reviewed previously, stent-graft repair at the aortic entry tear site has become an additional "revascularization" modality likely to be effective in most patients with dynamic aortic obstruction mechanisms. More complex is the treatment algorithm in patients with type A dissections complicated by malperfusion syndromes. Although the literature suggests that prompt ascending aortic repair may relieve distal malperfusion in most such patients,[81,111,152] there is also abundant documentation of excessive mortality with central aortic repair in this setting.[5,116,153] The reasons for this seem obvious and are related to the reperfusion phenomenon in compromised vascular territories, the evolution of mesenteric infarction, and the clinical milieu of the postoperative setting, which complicates recognition of unresolved malperfusion states.

As shown in Figure 104-6, malperfusion syndromes—particularly when the mesenteric circulation is involved—constitute one of the exceptions to prompt central aortic repair for type A dissection. Such an exception is essential to a treatment strategy that directs initial intervention toward the immediate life-threatening problem. Deeb and associates[153] examined the utility of a delayed approach (with respect to grafting of the ascending aorta) in acute type A dissection complicated by malperfusion syndromes. In patients with acute type A dissection, preoperative malperfusion syndromes were associated with the highest risk of death of all variables analyzed. Their strategy was to delay ascending aortic graft replacement so that distal malperfusion could be treated using percutaneous fenestration and stenting in a series of 20 patients. During the same study interval, nine patients with ongoing malperfusion underwent immediate ascending aortic graft replacement with a mortality rate of 89%. Of the 20 patients in whom operation was delayed, 3 (15%) died before operation (only 1 related to aortic rupture). The mean time to ascending aortic repair was 21 days (range 2 to 67 days),

and overall survival rate in the "delay" group was 75%. Delay of ascending aortic surgery was the only independent variable predictive of favorable outcome, showing that the likelihood of death in patients with an acute type A dissection complicated by malperfusion is 33 times greater if they undergo immediate central aortic surgical repair as opposed to the delay sequence with initial treatment of malperfusion syndrome.

Surgical Treatment of Malperfusion Syndromes

Because dynamic obstruction at the aortic level is the most common mechanism of malperfusion syndromes (see Fig. 104-3), surgical fenestration has been the most commonly applied procedure.[8] This operation at the abdominal aortic level was first described by Shaw[154] from the Massachusetts General Hospital in a 1955 case report. Later that year, Cooley and DeBakey[155] reported the initial graft replacement of the proximal thoracic aorta for acute dissection, and the fenestration procedure was rapidly eclipsed. As several series have documented the unpredictable relief of malperfusion syndromes and substantial morbidity and mortality of open graft replacement, however, surgical fenestration has regained favor.[152,156-158] The fundamental technique of surgical fenestration is wide resection of the dissected septum to relieve aortic obstruction by equalizing flow between the true and false lumina (Fig. 104-7).

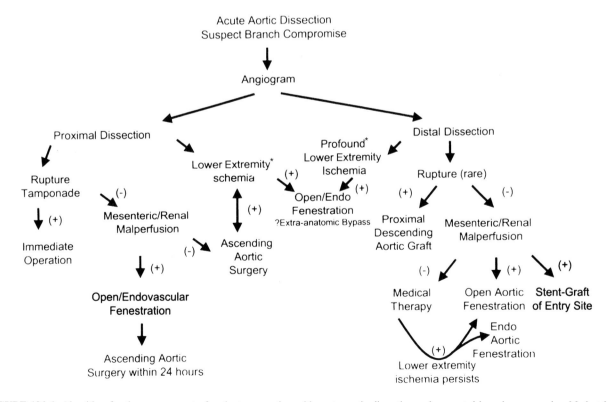

FIGURE 104-6 Algorithm for the management of patients presenting with acute aortic dissection and suspected branch compromise. Modest lower extremity ischemia (pulse deficit alone) does not have the same therapeutic implications as acute aortic level obstruction. Proximal descending aortic graft may be accomplished with stent-grafting if available. Similarly, the choice between open versus endovascular fenestration likely depends on local expertise.

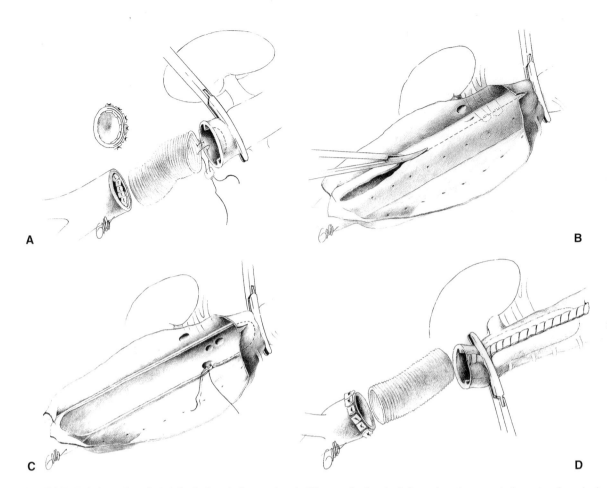

FIGURE 104-7   Technique of surgical abdominal aortic fenestration. **A,** When confined to the infrarenal aortic segment, the septum is excised up to the aortic cross-clamp. The proximal anastomosis is performed with pledgetted 4-0 sutures as the anastomosis is extended to the remaining adventitia over the dissected aortic circumference. The distal anastomosis is created by reconstituting the distal aortic layers with a felt composite. **B,** If static obstruction of the renal or visceral vessels is suspected based on axial imaging studies, the fenestration can be carried onto the visceral aortic segment. The left kidney has been swept anteriorly, and the left renal artery is perfused from the false lumen. The septum is incised to expose the origins of the celiac/superior mesenteric/right renal artery perfused via the true lumen. **C,** Direct suture repair of the vessel ostium may be required, herein shown at the right renal origin whose orifice abuts the circumferential terminus of the dissection. **D,** After septectomy in the visceral segment, the outer aortic wall is closed over Teflon felt, and the clamp is moved to the infrarenal aorta, which is most conveniently reconstructed with a tube graft as in **A.**

A fundamental consideration is whether aortic clamping and the fenestration are confined to the infrarenal aorta. It may be desirable to extend the septectomy into the visceral segment, permitting direct inspection and repair of the ostia of the mesenteric and renal vessels.[159] Experience has shown that the duration of supraceliac clamping can be limited to the 20-minute range, with repositioning of the clamp to an infrarenal location after closure of the visceral segment aortotomy. Interposition of a short-segment polyester graft in the infrarenal aorta facilitates reconstruction of the aortic layers at the distal anastomosis with the double-layer Teflon felt technique (see Fig. 104-7). Our approach relative to extending the fenestration/septectomy into the visceral aortic segment is dictated by the anatomic complexity displayed on the CT scan. Small aortic diameter, total absence of visceral artery flow, the dissected septum extending directly to or beyond a vital branch orifice, and radiographic evidence of intussuscepted septum into a renal/mesenteric vessel all are considerations that prompt extension of the aortotomy into the visceral segment. Such an approach also permits direct repair of a static obstruction (i.e., where

the branch vessel itself is dissected). This repair can be accomplished by circumferential suture of the vessel intima to the aortic wall at the ostia (see Fig. 104-7). Because continuous exposure of the visceral segment is desirable in surgical treatment of malperfusion syndrome, we prefer left flank approaches for this procedure. Depending on body habitus, a 9th or 10th interspace thoracoabdominal approach is used to allow for complete infradiaphragmatic aortic exposure and transperitoneal inspection of the viscera and palpation of the superior mesenteric artery pulse caudal to the mesocolon. At a median follow-up of 19 months, no significant aortic dilatation occurred with such aortic tailoring as a surgical technique.[159] Advocates of surgical fenestration for malperfusion syndromes have asserted that the "surgical" morbidity and mortality rates quoted to support endovascular therapies are outdated and strongly influenced by delays in diagnosis and treatment.[160]

In 1992, Elefteriades and colleagues[145] reported their experience using a "complication-specific" approach to acute aortic dissection. Overall survival for the total population was 65% at 1 year, 57% at 3 years, 50% at 5 years, and 28%

at 10 years. Of the 14 patients in the total experience treated by fenestration, the actuarial survival was 77%, 77%, and 53% at 1, 3, and 5 years. None of the surgically fenestrated patients were noted to have expansion of their aortic diameters on follow-up. Surgical fenestration was performed in the infrarenal aorta and resulted in relief of ischemia in 13 of 14 patients (93%). The authors concluded that the relative simplicity of surgical fenestration allows subsequent survival almost uniformly, unless the patient's preoperative overall status had been severely compromised.[145]

A report from the Mayo Clinic affords perspective on the infrequent need for and the durability of surgical fenestration.[161] From their database of 857 patients with a diagnosis of aortic dissection, only 321 patients underwent surgical intervention of any kind. Clinical or radiographic evidence of malperfusion was observed in 81 patients (25%). Fourteen patients underwent surgical fenestration during the study period, representing 1.6% of the total study population. Four patients had organ or limb malperfusion after proximal aortic replacement for aortic dissection, a similar finding to other reports. The mean interval between malperfusion onset and fenestration was 19 hours (range 3 to 48 hours). Surgical fenestration relieved the malperfusion syndrome for all 10 patients with organ or limb ischemia. Operative mortality was 43% (three of seven) in the acute dissection group; seven patients were treated in the chronic phase of the disease with no mortality. Follow-up at a mean of 5.1 years for the 11 survivors revealed no evidence of aneurysm formation at the site of fenestration. The authors noted that in comparison of surgical fenestration with series of endovascular fenestration, the likelihood of subsequent aortic complications related to expansion or rupture of the false lumen may be greater in patients treated by endovascular means. Although endovascular fenestration may offer more rapid restoration of perfusion, its durability would seem less than surgical fenestration techniques.[161]

Our cumulative experience affords a perspective over a 35-year period involving approximately 200 patients with acute aortic dissection treated during the 1990s and in part clarifies the role of open surgical fenestration and peripheral endovascular intervention in patients with malperfusion syndromes.[10] Nearly a third of the patients had evidence of branch occlusion; 17 (32%) of these 53 patients underwent peripheral vascular intervention to restore circulation. The overall mortality rate in the interval 1990 through 1999 was significantly lower compared with an earlier report from 1965 through 1986 (18% versus 37%, P < .006).[10] In discerning the factors associated with improved results over time, three variables were important: (1) Aortic rupture occurred in just 6% of patients versus 18% in the prior interval. Presumably, patients were being diagnosed and referred more promptly. (2) The impact of branch occlusion on mortality was no longer significant, implying that recognition and treatment of malperfusion syndromes had improved overall results. (3) Mortality in patients with mesenteric ischemia had improved to 37%, whereas an 87% mortality rate was observed in our earlier report. The IRAD data implicated mesenteric ischemia as responsible for 15% of all deaths related to acute dissection.[5] For patients with mesenteric or renal malperfusion syndromes, surgical fenestration was used in nine patients. Restoration of flow was successful in all patients, and all patients so treated

survived, whereas two deaths occurred in patients with mesenteric ischemia managed with percutaneous fenestration. Open aortic fenestration is an excellent method of restoring circulation to vascular territories affected by malperfusion syndromes, especially when mesenteric and renal beds are involved, and affords the opportunity to assess bowel viability and plan second-look procedures. Treatment priority should be assigned to the most life-threatening condition in patients with acute aortic dissection. The presence of mesenteric ischemia assumes such priority in virtually all patients and constitutes an exception to prompt central aortic repair in patients with type A dissections (see Fig. 104-6).

■ NATURAL HISTORY AND FOLLOW-UP

The principal late complication of aortic dissection is aneurysmal dilatation of the outer wall of the false lumen. Of patients surviving acute dissection, 25% to 40% progress to have aneurysmal dilatation of the dissected aorta despite medical management.[162-164] In most clinical series of thoracoabdominal aneurysms, approximately 20% of cases are the sequelae of chronic dissection.[158,165,166] Marui and associates[167] reported that 43% of patients who were able to be treated medically during the acute phase of type III dissection progressed to have aortic enlargement. Dilatation to 6 cm or greater occurred in nearly 30%. Factors that seem to have a significant impact on chronic aneurysm development after dissection include poorly controlled hypertension, maximal aortic diameter of at least 4 cm in the acute phase, and continued patency of the false lumen.[99,131,167] Approximately 10% to 20% of patients with dissection subsequently experience late rupture of the aneurysm.[99,125]

Aneurysms that are the sequelae of chronic dissection tend to be more extensive and occur in younger patients compared with degenerative aneurysms. Patients with true cystic medial necrosis, such as patients with Marfan's syndrome, have an increased risk of aneurysm formation after acute dissection. Although aortic disease traditionally led to early death in Marfan's syndrome, the surgical and diagnostic advances in aortic disease in the 1970s through 1990s have allowed the life expectancy to approach that of the population at large.[133,168,169] Ascending aortic and aortic valve disease is the most common lesion addressed, with 90% of initial operations occurring in this segment; however, 40% proceed to a second aortic procedure, which typically involves the thoracoabdominal aorta.[133]

Treatment with effective beta blockade is an essential feature of long-term therapy and follow-up. The rationale of such therapy is founded on the recognition that patients with aortic dissection have a systemic illness that places their entire aorta at risk for further dissection, aneurysm, or rupture. Guidelines recommend progressive upward titration of beta blockade to achieve a blood pressure less than 125/80 mm Hg in usual patients and less than 120 mm Hg in patients with Marfan's syndrome.[170,171] In addition, aggressive beta blockade has been shown to retard the growth of the aortic root in Marfan's syndrome patients and may have a similar effect on the thoracoabdominal aorta.[172,173] Serial imaging is a cornerstone of long-term follow-up. Axial imaging modalities should encompass the entire aorta. Because the clinical course of an acutely dissected aorta may be difficult to predict in the weeks or months after presentation, an aggressive surveillance program is mandatory.[132]

■ CONCLUSION

Perhaps this chapter could be subtitled (as in the IRAD study[5]) "new perspectives on an old disease." These new perspectives help to clarify the factors associated with the still substantial (27%) mortality in the acute phase of the disease. Central cardioaortic complications, such as rupture, continue as the dominant problem in patients with type A dissections. Despite considerable advances over time, ascending aortic graft replacement still is associated with significant risk. Operative mortality even in the hands of experts is in the 20% range. A paradigm shift has occurred in the management of acute type B dissections wherein open graft replacement of the descending aorta is seldom used because of significant morbidity and the uncertain efficacy of successfully treating distal malperfusion syndromes. Directed peripheral vascular intervention is currently the treatment of choice for malperfusion syndromes, although the potential for stent-graft repair at the aortic entry tear could change this scheme in the near future. As such, the vascular/endovascular surgeon will become the primary invasive therapist for patients with distal dissections, a role the cardiac surgeon currently serves in proximal dissection. A thorough understanding of the clinical and anatomic features of acute dissection as reviewed in this chapter is requisite for surgeons managing aortic dissection in its many presentations.

■ REFERENCES

1. Shekelton J: Healed dissecting aneurysm. Dublin Hosp Rep 3:231-232, 1922.
2. Kouchoukos NT, Dougenis D: Surgery of the thoracic aorta. N Engl J Med 336:1876-1888, 1997.
3. Pate JW, Richardson RL, Eastridge CE: Acute aortic dissections. Am Surg 42:395-404, 1976.
4. Spitell PC, Spitell J, Joyce JW: Clinical features and differential diagnosis of aortic dissection: Experience with 236 cases. Mayo Clin Proc 68:897-903, 1993.
5. Hagan PG, Nienaber CA, Isselbacher EM, et al: The International Registry of Acute Aortic Dissection (IRAD): New insights into an old disease. JAMA 283:897-903, 2000.
6. Khan IA, Nair CK: Clinical, diagnostic, and management perspectives of aortic dissection. Chest 122:311-328, 2002.
7. Meszaros I, Morocz J, Szlavi J, et al: Epidemiology and clinico-pathology of aortic dissection. Chest 117:1271-1278, 2000.
8. Cambria RP: Surgical treatment of complicated distal aortic dissection. Semin Vasc Surg 15:97-107, 2002.
9. Mehta RH, Suzuki T, Hagan PG, et al: Predicting death in patients with acute type a aortic dissection. Circulation 105:200-206, 2002.
10. Lauterbach SR, Cambria RP, Brewster DC, et al: Contemporary management of aortic branch compromise resulting from acute aortic dissection. J Vasc Surg 33:1185-1192, 2001.
11. Cambria RP, Brewster DC, Gertler J, et al: Vascular complications associated with spontaneous aortic dissection. J Vasc Surg 7:199-209, 1988.
12. DeBakey ME, Henly WS, Cooley DA: Surgical management of dissecting aneurysms of the aorta. J Thorac Cardiovasc Surg 49:130-148, 1965.
13. Dailey PO, Trueblood H, Stinson EB: Management of acute aortic dissection. Ann Thorac Surg 10:237-246, 1970.
14. Clouse WD, Hallett JW, Schaff H, et al: Acute aortic dissection: The most common aortic catastrophe? Mayo Clin Proc 79:176–180, 2003.
15. Auer J, Berent R: Aortic dissection: Incidence, natural history, and impact of surgery. J Clin Basic Cardiol 3:151-154, 2000.
16. Hirst AE, Johns V, Dougenis D: Dissecting aneurysm of the aorta: A review of 505 cases. Medicine 37:217-219, 1958.
17. Kobza R, Ritter M, Seifert B, Jenni R: Variable seasonal peaks for different types of aortic dissection? Heart 88:640, 2002.
18. Willich SN, Levy D, Rocco MB, et al: Circadian variation in the incidence of sudden cardiac death in the Framingham Heart Study population. Am J Cardiol 60:801-806, 1987.
19. Kono T, Mortia H, Nashina T, et al: Circadian variations in the onset of acute myocardial infarction and efficacy of thrombolytic therapy. J Am Coll Cardiol 27:774-778, 1996.
20. Mehta RH, Manfredini R, Hassan F, et al: Chronobiological patterns of acute aortic dissection. Circulation 106:1110-1115, 2002.
21. Larson EW, Edwards W: Risk factors for aortic dissection: A necropsy study of 161 patients. Am J Cardiol 53:849, 1984.
22. Williams GM, Gott VL, Brawley RK, et al: Aortic disease associated with pregnancy. J Vasc Surg 8:470-475, 1988.
23. Elkayam U, Ostrzega E, Shotan A, Mehra A: Cardiovascular problems in pregnant women with the Marfan syndrome. Ann Intern Med 123:117-122, 1995.
24. Eagle KA, Isselbacher EM, DeSanctis RW: Cocaine-related aortic dissection in perspective. Circulation 105:1529-1530, 2002.
25. Hsue PY, Salinas C, Bolger AF: Acute aortic dissection induced by crack cocaine. Circulation 105:1592-1595, 2002.
26. Wilson SK, Hutchins GM: Aortic dissecting aneurysms: Causative factors in 204 subjects. Arch Pathol Lab Med 106:175-180, 1982.
27. Hirst A, Johns VJ, Dougenis D: Dissecting aneurysm of the aorta: A review of 505 cases. Medicine 37:217-219, 1958.
28. Williams DM: Pathophysiology of aortic dissection. In Ernst CE (ed): Current Therapy in Vascular Surgery. St. Louis, Mosby, 1997, pp 211-215.
29. Wheat MW Jr: Acute dissection of the aorta. Cardiovasc Clin 17:241-262, 1987.
30. O'Gara PT, DeSanctis RW: Acute aortic dissection and its variants: Toward a common diagnostic and therapeutic approach. Circulation 92:1376-1378, 1995.
31. Lesauskaite V, Tanganelli P, Sassi C, et al: Smooth muscle cells of the media in the dilatative pathology of the ascending aorta: Morphology, immunoreactivity for osteopontin, matrix metalloproteinases, and their inhibitors. Hum Pathol 32:1003-1011, 2001.
32. Marsalese DL, Moodie DS, Lytle BW, et al: Cystic medial necrosis of the aorta in patients without Marfan's syndrome: Surgical outcome and long-term follow-up. J Am Coll Cardiol 16:68-73, 1990.
33. Reed D, Reed C, Stemmerman G, et al: Are aortic aneurysms caused by atherosclerosis? Circulation 85:205-211, 1992.
34. Jex RK, Schaff H, Piehler JM, Ilstrup D: Early and late results following repair of dissections of the descending thoracic aorta. J Vasc Surg 3:226-236, 1986.
35. Cambria RP, Brewster DC, Moncure AC, et al: Spontaneous aortic dissection in the presence of coexistent or previously repaired atherosclerotic aortic aneurysm. Ann Surg 208:619-624, 1988.
36. Mozes G, Gloviczki P, Park WM, Schultz HL: Spontaneous dissection of the infrarenal aorta. Semin Vasc Surg 15:128-136, 2002.
37. DeBakey ME, Henly WS, Cooley DA, et al: Dissection and dissecting aneurysms of the aorta: Twenty year follow-up of five hundred twenty seven patients treated surgically. Surgery 92:1118-1134, 1982.
38. Fann JI, Sarris G, Mitchell RS, et al: Surgical management of aortic dissection during a 30 year period. Circulation 92(Suppl II):113-121, 1995.
39. Chung JW, Elkins C, Sakai T, et al: True-lumen collapse in aortic dissection: Part I. Evaluation of causative factors in phantoms with pulsatile flow. Radiology 214:87-98, 2000.

40. Chung JW, Elkins C, Sakai T, et al: True-lumen collapse in aortic dissection: Part II. Evaluation of treatment methods in phantoms with pulsatile flow. Radiology 214:99-106, 2000.

41. Williams DM, LePage MA, Lee DY: The dissected aorta: Part I. Early anatomic changes in an in vitro model. Radiology 203:23-31, 1997.

42. Williams DM, Lee DY, Hamilton BH, et al: The dissected aorta: Percutaneous treatment of ischemic complications—principles and results. J Vasc Interv Radiol 8:605-625, 1997.

43. Williams DM, Lee DY, Hamilton BH, et al: The dissected aorta: Part III. Anatomy and radiologic diagnosis of branch-vessel compromise. Radiology 203:37-44, 1997.

44. Young JR, Humphries AW: The ischemic leg: A clue to dissecting aneurysm. Cardiovasc Clin 7:201-205, 1975.

45. von Kodolitsch Y, Csosz SK, Koschyk DH, et al: Intramural hematoma of the aorta: Predictors of progression to dissection and rupture. Circulation 107:1158-1163, 2003.

46. Nienaber CA, von Kodolitsch Y, Petersen B, et al: Intramural hemorrhage of the thoracic aorta: Diagnostic and therapeutic implications. Circulation 92:1465-1472, 1995.

47. Yamada T, Tada S, Harada J: Aortic dissection without intimal rupture: Diagnosis with MR imaging and CT. Radiology 168:347-352, 1988.

48. Stanson AW, Kazmier FJ, Hollier LH, et al: Penetrating atherosclerotic ulcers of the thoracic aorta: Natural history and clinicopathologic correlations. Ann Vasc Surg 1:15-23, 1986.

49. Mohr-Kahaly S, Erbel R, Kearney P, et al: Aortic intramural hemorrhage visualized by transesophageal echocardiography: Findings and prognostic implications. J Am Coll Cardiol 23:658-664, 1994.

50. Sueyoshi E, Imada T, Sakamoto I, et al: Analysis of predictive factors for progression of type B aortic intramural hematoma with computed tomography. J Vasc Surg 35:1179-1183, 2002.

51. Cambria RP: Regarding analysis of predictive factors for progression of type B aortic intramural hematoma with computed tomography. J Vasc Surg 35:1295-1296, 2002.

52. Muluk SC, Kaufman JA, Torchiana DF, et al: Diagnosis and treatment of thoracic aortic intramural hematoma. J Vasc Surg 24:1022-1029, 1996.

53. Ohmi M, Tabayashi K, Moizumi Y, et al: Extremely rapid regression of aortic intramural hematoma. J Thorac Cardiovasc Surg 118:968-969, 1999.

54. Ganacha F, Sugimoto K, Do SY: Prognosis of aortic intramural hematoma with and without penetrating atherosclerotic ulcer: A clinical and radiological analysis. Circulation 106:342-348, 2002.

55. Shennan T: Dissecting aneurysms. Medical Research Council, 1934.

56. Coady MA, Rizzo JA, Hammond GL, et al: Penetrating ulcer of the thoracic aorta: What is it? How do we recognize it? How do we manage it? J Vasc Surg 27:1006-1016, 1998.

57. Nienaber CA, Eagle KA: Aortic dissection: New frontiers in diagnosis and management: Part II. Therapeutic management and follow-up. Circulation 108:772-778, 2003.

58. Januzzi JL, Movsowitz HD, Choi J, et al: Significance of recurrent pain in acute type B aortic dissection. Am J Cardiol 87:930-933, 2001.

59. Nallamothu BK, Kolias TJ, Eagle KA: Of nicks and time. N Engl J Med 345:359-363, 2001.

60. Nallamothu BK, Mehta RH, Saint S, et al: Syncope in acute aortic dissection: Diagnostic, prognostic, and clinical implications. Am J Med 113:468-471, 2002.

61. Slater EE: Aortic dissection: Presentation and diagnosis. In Dorogahzi RM (ed): Aortic Dissection. New York, McGraw-Hill, 1983, pp 13-53.

62. Sanders JS, Ferguson DW, Mark AL: Arterial baroreflex control of sympathetic nerve activity during elevation of blood pressure in normal man: Dominance of aortic baroreflexes. Circulation 77:279-288, 1988.

63. Syed MA, Fiad TM: Transient paraplegia as a presenting feature of aortic dissection in a young man. Emerg Med J 19:174-175, 2002.

64. Khan I, Wattanasauwan N, Ansari AW: Painless aortic dissection presenting as hoarseness of voice: Cardiovocal syndrome, Ortner's syndrome. Am J Emerg Med 17:361-363, 1999.

65. Greenwood WR, Robinson M: Painless dissection of the thoracic aorta. Ann Emerg Med 4:330-333, 1986.

66. Lefebre V, Leduc J, Choteau PH: Painless ischemic lumbosacral plexopathy and aortic dissection. J Neurol Neurosurg Psychiatry 58:641, 1995.

67. Isselbacher EM: Diseases of the aorta. In Braunwald E (ed): Heart Disease. Philadelphia, WB Saunders, 2002, pp 1422-1455.

68. Januzzi JL, Sabatine MS, Choi JC, et al: Refractory systemic hypertension following type B aortic dissection. Am J Cardiol 88:686-688, 2001.

69. Bossone E, Rampoldi V, Nienaber CA, et al: Usefulness of pulse deficit to predict in-hospital complications and mortality in patients with acute type A aortic dissection. Am J Cardiol 89:851-855, 2002.

70. von Kodolitsch Y, Schwartz AG, Nienaber CA: Clinical prediction of acute aortic dissection. Arch Intern Med 160:2977-2982, 2000.

71. Burt C: Summary statistics for acute cardiac ischemia and chest pain visits to the United States EDs, 1995-1996. Am J Emerg Med 17:552-559, 1999.

72. Barbant S, Eisenberg MJ, Schiller NB: The diagnostic value of imaging techniques for aortic dissection. Am Heart J 124:541-543, 1992.

73. Rosman HS, Patel S, Borzak S, et al: Quality of history taking in patients with aortic dissection. Chest 114:793-795, 1998.

74. Hata N, Tanaka K, Imaizumi T, et al: Clinical significance of pleural effusion in acute aortic dissection. Chest 121:825-830, 2002.

75. Dinsmore RE, Wedeen VJ, Miller SW, et al: MRI of dissection of the aorta: Recognition of the intimal tear and differential flow velocities. AJR Am J Roentgenol 146:1286-1288, 1986.

76. Guthaner DF, Miller DC: Digital subtraction angiography of aortic dissection. AJR Am J Roentgenol 141:157-161, 1983.

77. Petasnick JP: Radiologic evaluation of aortic dissection. Radiology 180:297-305, 1991.

78. Earnest FT, Muhm JR, Sheedy PF 2nd: Roentgenographic findings in thoracic aortic dissection. Mayo Clin Proc 54:43-50, 1979.

79. Mugge A, Daniel WG, Laas J, et al: False-negative diagnosis of proximal aortic dissection by computed tomography or angiography and possible explanations based on transesophageal echocardiographic findings. Am J Cardiol 65:527-529, 1990.

80. Mehta RH, O'Gara PT, Bossone E, et al: Acute type A aortic dissection in the elderly: Clinical characteristics, management, and outcomes in the current era. J Am Coll Cardiol 40:685-692, 2002.

81. Rizzo RJ, Aranki SF, Aklog L, et al: Rapid noninvasive diagnosis and surgical repair of acute ascending aortic dissection: Improved survival with less angiography. J Thorac Cardiovasc Surg 108:567-575, 1994.

82. Erbel R, Engberding R, Daniel W, et al: Echocardiography in diagnosis of aortic dissection. Lancet 1:457-461, 1989.

83. Victor MF, Mintz GS, Kotler MN, et al: Two dimensional echocardiographic diagnosis of aortic dissection. Am J Cardiol 48:1155-1159, 1981.

84. Granato JE, Dee P, Gibson RS: Utility of two-dimensional echocardiography in suspected ascending aortic dissection. Am J Cardiol 56:123-129, 1985.

85. Adachi H, Omoto R, Kyo S, et al: [Diagnosis of acute aortic dissection with transesophageal echocardiography and results of surgical treatment]. Nippon Kyobu Geka Gakkai Zasshi 39:1987-1994, 1991.

86. Keren A, Kim CB, Hu BS, et al: Accuracy of biplane and multiplane transesophageal echocardiography in diagnosis of typical acute aortic dissection and intramural hematoma. J Am Coll Cardiol 28:627-636, 1996.

87. Vignon P, Spencer KT, Rambaud G, et al: Differential transesophageal echocardiographic diagnosis between linear artifacts and intraluminal flap of aortic dissection or disruption. Chest 119:1778-1790, 2001.

88. Erbel R: Role of transesophageal echocardiography in dissection of the aorta and evaluation of degenerative aortic disease. Cardiol Clin 11:461-473, 1993.

89. Erbel R, Bednarczyk I, Pop T, et al: Detection of dissection of the aortic intima and media after angioplasty of coarctation of the aorta: An angiographic, computed tomographic, and echocardiographic comparative study. Circulation 81:805-814, 1990.

90. Movsowitz HD, Levine RA, Hilgenberg AD, Isselbacher EM: Transesophageal echocardiographic description of the mechanisms of aortic regurgitation in acute type A aortic dissection: Implications for aortic valve repair. J Am Coll Cardiol 36:884-890, 2000.

91. Moore AG, Eagle KA, Bruckman D, et al: Choice of computed tomography, transesophageal echocardiography, magnetic resonance imaging, and aortography in acute aortic dissection: International Registry of Acute Aortic Dissection (IRAD). Am J Cardiol 89:1235-1238, 2002.

92. Fruehwald FX, Neuhold A, Fezoulidis J, et al: Cine-MR in dissection of the thoracic aorta. Eur J Radiol 9:37-41, 1989.

93. Tomiguchi S, Morishita S, Nakashima R, et al: Usefulness of turbo-FLASH dynamic MR imaging of dissecting aneurysms of the thoracic aorta. Cardiovasc Intervent Radiol 17:17-21, 1994.

94. Prince MR, Narasimham DL, Jacoby WT, et al: Three-dimensional gadolinium-enhanced MR angiography of the thoracic aorta. AJR Am J Roentgenol 166:1387-1397, 1996.

95. Fisher ER, Stern EJ, Godwin JD 2nd, et al: Acute aortic dissection: Typical and atypical imaging features. Radiographics 14:1263-1274, 1994.

96. Hartnell G, Costello P: The diagnosis of thoracic aortic dissection by noninvasive imaging procedures [letter and author reply]. N Engl J Med 328:1637-1638, 1993.

97. Clague J, Magee P, Mills P: Diagnostic techniques in suspected thoracic aortic dissection. Br Heart J 67:428-429, 1992.

98. LePage MA, Quint LE, Sonnad SS, et al: Aortic dissection: CT features that distinguish true lumen from false lumen. AJR Am J Roentgenol 177:207-211, 2001.

99. Juvonen T, Ergin M, Galla JD, et al: Risk factors for rupture of chronic type b dissections. J Thorac Cardiovasc Surg 117:776-786, 1999.

100. Wheat MW Jr, Palmer RF: Dissecting aneurysms of the aorta: Present status of drug versus surgical therapy. Prog Cardiovasc Dis 11:198-210, 1968.

101. Isselbacher EM, Cigarroa JE, Eagle KA: Cardiac tamponade complicating proximal aortic dissection: Is pericardiocentesis harmful? Circulation 90:2375-2379, 1994.

102. Bavaria J, Pochettino A, Brinster DR, et al: New paradigms and improved results for the surgical treatment of acute type a dissection. Ann Surg 234:236-242, 2001.

103. Apaydin AZ, Buket S, Posacioglu H, et al: Perioperative risk factors for mortality in patients with acute type A aortic dissection. Ann Thorac Surg 74:2034-2039, 2002.

104. Ahmed AA, Mahadevan VS, Webb SW, MacGowan SW: Glue aortoplasty repair of aortic dissection after coronary angioplasty. Ann Thorac Surg 72:922-924, 2001.

105. Estrera AL, Huynh TT, Porat EE, et al: Is acute type A aortic dissection a true surgical emergency? Semin Vasc Surg 15:75-82, 2002.

106. Ghariani S, Matta A, Dion R, Guerit JM: Intra- and postoperative factors determining neurological complications after surgery under deep hypothermic circulatory arrest: A retrospective somatosensory evoked potential study. Clin Neurophysiol 111:1082-1094, 2000.

107. Crawford ES, Kirklin JW, Naftel DC, et al: Surgery for acute dissection of ascending aorta: Should the arch be included? J Thorac Cardiovasc Surg 104:46-59, 1992.

108. Kazui T, Yamashita K, Washiyama N, et al: Impact of an aggressive surgical approach on surgical outcome in type A aortic dissection. Ann Thorac Surg 74(5):S1844-1863, 2002.

109. Schor JS, Yerlioglu ME, Galla JD, et al: Selective management of acute type B aortic dissection: Long-term follow-up. Ann Thorac Surg 61:1339-1341, 1996.

110. Lai DT, Robbins RC, Mitchell RS, et al: Does profound hypothermic circulatory arrest improve survival in patients with acute type a aortic dissection? Circulation 106(12 Suppl 1):I218-I228, 2002.

111. Fann JI, Smith JA, Miller DC, et al: Surgical management of aortic dissection during a 30-year period. Circulation 92(9 Suppl):II113-II121, 1995.

112. Pompilio G, Spirito R, Alamanni F, et al: Determinants of early and late outcome after surgery for type A aortic dissection. World J Surg 25:1500-1506, 2001.

113. Sinatra R, Melina G, Pulitani I, et al: Emergency operation for acute type A aortic dissection: Neurologic complications and early mortality. Ann Thorac Surg 71:33-38, 2001.

114. Sasaki S, Yasuda K, Kunihara T, et al: Surgical results of Stanford type B aortic dissection: Comparisons between partial and subtotal replacement of the dissected aorta. J Cardiovasc Surg (Torino) 41:227-232, 2000.

115. Lansman SL, Hagl C, Fink D, et al: Acute type B aortic dissection: Surgical therapy. Ann Thorac Surg 74:S1833-1863, 2002.

116. Slonim SM, Miller DC, Mitchell RS, et al: Percutaneous balloon fenestration and stenting for life-threatening ischemic complications in patients with acute aortic dissection. J Thorac Cardiovasc Surg 117:1118-1126, 1999.

117. Bachet J, Goudot B, Dreyfus G, et al: The proper use of glue: A 20-year experience with the GRF glue in acute aortic dissection. J Card Surg 12(2 Suppl):243-255, 1997.

118. Hata M, Shiono M, Orime Y, et al: The efficacy and mid-term results with use of gelatin resorcin formalin (GRF) glue for aortic surgery. Ann Thorac Cardiovasc Surg 5:321-325, 1999.

119. Hata M, Shiono M, Orime Y, et al: Pathological findings of tissue reactivity of gelatin resorcin formalin glue: An autopsy case report of the repair of ventricular septal perforation. Ann Thorac Cardiovasc Surg 6:127-129, 2000.

120. Safi HJ, Miller CC 3rd, Reardon MJ, et al: Operation for acute and chronic aortic dissection: Recent outcome with regard to neurologic deficit and early death. Ann Thorac Surg 66:402-411, 1998.

121. Jex R, Schaff HV, Piehler JM, Ilstrup D: Early and late results following repair of dissections of the descending thoracic aorta. J Vasc Surg 3:226-236, 1986.

122. Verdant A, Cossette R, Page A, et al: Aneurysms of the descending thoracic aorta: Three hundred sixty-six consecutive cases resected without paraplegia. J Vasc Surg 21:385-391, 1995.

123. Glower DD, Speier RH, White WD, et al: Management and long-term outcome of aortic dissection. Ann Surg 214:31-41, 1991.

124. Miller DC, Mitchell RS, Oyer PE, et al: Independent determinants of operative mortality for patients with aortic dissections. Circulation 70(3 Pt 2):I153-I164, 1984.

125. Neya K, Omoto R, Kyo S, et al: Outcome of Stanford type B acute aortic dissection. Circulation 86(5 Suppl):II1-II7, 1992.

126. Svensson LG, Crawford ES, Hess KR, et al: Dissection of the aorta and dissecting aortic aneurysms: Improving early and long-term surgical results. Circulation 82(5 Suppl):IV24-IV38, 1990.

127. Coselli JS: Thoracoabdominal aortic aneurysms: Experience with 372 patients. J Card Surg 9:638-647, 1994.

128. Nienaber CA, Fattori R, Lund G, et al: Nonsurgical reconstruction of thoracic aortic dissection by stent-graft placement. N Engl J Med 340:1539-1545, 1999.

129. Dake MD, Kato N, Mitchell RS, et al: Endovascular stent-graft placement for the treatment of acute aortic dissection. N Engl J Med 340:1546-1552, 1999.

130. Auer J, Berent R: Aortic dissection: Incidence, natural history, and impact of surgery. J Clin Basic Cardiol 3:151-154, 2002.

131. Bernard Y, Zimmermann H, Chocron S, et al: False lumen patency as a predictor of late outcome in aortic dissection. Am J Cardiol 87:1378-1382, 2001.

132. Erbel R, Alfonso F, Boileau C, et al: Diagnosis and management of aortic dissection. Eur Heart J 22:1642-1681, 2001.

133. Finkbohner R, Johnston D, Crawford ES, et al: Marfan syndrome: Long-term survival and complications after aortic aneurysm repair. Circulation 91:728-733, 1995.

134. Hausegger KA, Tiesenhausen K, Schedlbauer P, et al: Treatment of acute aortic type B dissection with stent-grafts. Cardiovasc Intervent Radiol 24:306-312, 2001.

135. Ergin MA, Phillips RA, Galla JD, et al: Significance of distal false lumen after type A dissection repair. Ann Thorac Surg 57:820-825, 1994.

136. Greenberg R: Treatment of aortic dissections with endovascular stent grafts. Semin Vasc Surg 15:122-127, 2002.

137. Kato N, Hirano T, Takeda K, et al: Treatment of aortic dissections with a percutaneous intravascular endoprosthesis: Comparison of covered and bare stents. J Vasc Interv Radiol 5:805-812, 1994.

138. Moon MR, Dake MD, Pelc LR, et al: Intravascular stenting of acute experimental type B dissections. J Surg Res 54:381-388, 1993.

139. Trent MS, Parsonnet V, Shoenfeld R, et al: A balloon-expandable intravascular stent for obliterating experimental aortic dissection. J Vasc Surg 11:707-717, 1990.

140. Greenberg RK, Haulon S, Khwaja J, et al: Contemporary management of acute aortic dissection. J Endovasc Ther 10:476-485, 2003.

141. Bortone AS, Schena S, D'Agostino D, et al: Immediate versus delayed endovascular treatment of post-traumatic aortic pseudo-aneurysms and type B dissections: Retrospective analysis and premises to the upcoming European trial. Circulation 106(12 Suppl 1):I234-I240, 2002.

142. Greenberg R, Khwaja J, Haulon S, et al: Endovascular grafting for aortic dissections with life-threatening complications: Early and mid-term results. Submitted for publication.

143. Elefteriades JA, Hammond GL, Gusberg RJ, et al: Fenestration revisited: A safe and effective procedure for descending aortic dissection. Arch Surg 125:786-790, 1990.

144. Clair DG: Aortic dissection with branch vessel occlusion: Percutaneous treatment with fenestration and stenting. Semin Vasc Surg 15:116-121, 2002.

145. Elefteriades JA, Hartleroad J, Gusberg RJ, et al: Long-term experience with descending aortic dissection: The complication-specific approach. Ann Thorac Surg 53(1):11-21, 1992.

146. Chavan AH, Dresler C, Jaeger K, et al: Intravascular ultrasound-guided percutaneous fenestration of the intimal flap in the dissected aorta. Circulation 96:2124-2127, 1997.

147. Bartel T, Eggebrecht H, Ebradlidze T, et al: Images in cardiovascular medicine: Optimal guidance for intimal flap fenestration in aortic dissection by transvenous two-dimensional and Doppler ultrasonography. Circulation 107:e17-e18, 2003.

148. Slonim SM, Nyman U, Semba CP, et al: Aortic dissection: Percutaneous management of ischemic complications with endovascular stents and balloon fenestration. J Vasc Surg 23:241-253, 1996.

149. Beregi JP, Prat A, Gaxotte V, et al: Endovascular treatment for dissection of the descending aorta. Lancet 356:482-483, 2000.

150. Lookstein RA, Mitty H, Falk A, et al: Aortic intimal dehiscence: A complication of percutaneous balloon fenestration for aortic dissection. J Vasc Interv Radiol 12:1347-1350, 2001.

151. Beregi JP, Haulon S, Otal P, et al: Endovascular treatment of acute complications associated with aortic dissection: Midterm results from a multicenter study. J Endovasc Ther 10:486-493, 2003.

152. Safi HJ, Bartoli S, Hess KR, et al: Neurologic deficit in patients at high risk with thoracoabdominal aortic aneurysms: The role of cerebral spinal fluid drainage and distal aortic perfusion. J Vasc Surg 20:434-444, 1994.

153. Deeb GM, Williams DM, Bolling SF, et al: Surgical delay for acute type A dissection with malperfusion. Ann Thorac Surg 64:1669-1677, 1997.

154. Shaw RS: Acute dissecting aortic aneurysm: Treatment by fenestration of the internal wall of the aneurysm. N Engl J Med 253:331-333, 1955.

155. Cooley DA, DeBakey ME: Resection of the thoracic aorta with replacement by homograft for aneurysms and constrictive lesions. J Thorac Surg 29:66-104, 1955.

156. DeBakey ME, Henly WS, Cooley DA, et al: Surgical management of dissecting aneurysms of the aorta. J Thorac Cardiovasc Surg 49:130-149, 1965.

157. Crawford ES, Crawford JL, Stowe CL, Safi HJ: Total aortic replacement for chronic aortic dissection occurring in patients with and without Marfan's syndrome. Ann Surg 199:358-362, 1984.

158. Coselli JS, LeMaire SA, de Figueiredo LP, Kirby RP: Paraplegia after thoracoabdominal aortic aneurysm repair: Is dissection a risk factor? Ann Thorac Surg 63:28-36, 1997.

159. Webb TH, Williams GM: Abdominal aortic tailoring for renal, visceral, and lower extremity malperfusion resulting from acute aortic dissection. J Vasc Surg 26:474-481, 1997.

160. Oderich GS, Panneton JM: Acute aortic dissection with side branch vessel occlusion: Open surgical options. Semin Vasc Surg 15:89-96, 2002.

161. Panneton JM, Teh SH, Cherry KJ Jr, et al: Aortic fenestration for acute or chronic aortic dissection: An uncommon but effective procedure. J Vasc Surg 32:711-721, 2000.

162. Panneton JM, Hollier LH: Dissecting descending thoracic and thoracoabdominal aortic aneurysms: Part II. Ann Vasc Surg 9:596-605, 1995.

163. Money SR, Hollier LH: The management of thoracoabdominal aneurysms. Adv Surg 27:285-294, 1994.

164. Hollier LH, Symmonds JB, Pairolero PC, et al: Thoracoabdominal aortic aneurysm repair: Analysis of postoperative morbidity. Arch Surg 123:871-875, 1988.

165. Cambria RP, Davison JK, Zannetti S, et al: Thoracoabdominal aneurysm repair: Perspectives over a decade with the clamp-and-sew technique. Ann Surg 226:294-305, 1997.

166. LeMaire SA, Miller CC 3rd, Conklin LD, et al: Estimating group mortality and paraplegia rates after thoracoabdominal aortic aneurysm repair. Ann Thorac Surg 75:508-513, 2003.

167. Marui A, Mochizuki T, Mitsui N, et al: Toward the best treatment for uncomplicated patients with type B acute aortic dissection: A consideration for sound surgical indication. Circulation 100(19 Suppl):II275-II280, 1999.

168. Silverman DI, Gray J, Roman MJ, et al: Family history of severe cardiovascular disease in Marfan syndrome is associated with increased aortic diameter and decreased survival. J Am Coll Cardiol 26:1062-1067, 1995.

169. Silverman DI, Burton KJ, Gray J, et al: Life expectancy in the Marfan syndrome. Am J Cardiol 75:157-160, 1995.

170. Nienaber CA, Von Kodolitsch Y: Therapeutic management of patients with Marfan syndrome: Focus on cardiovascular involvement. Cardiol Rev 7:332-341, 1999.

171. Ramirez F, Gayraud B, Pereira L: Marfan syndrome: New clues to genotype-phenotype correlations. Ann Med 31:202-207, 1999.

172. Shores J, Berger KR, Murphy EA, Pyeritz RE: Progression of aortic dilatation and the benefit of long-term beta-adrenergic blockade in Marfan's syndrome. N Engl J Med 330:1335-1341, 1994.

173. Genoni M, Paul M, Jenni R, et al: Chronic beta-blocker therapy improves outcome and reduces treatment costs in chronic type B aortic dissection. Eur J Cardiothorac Surg 19:606-610, 2001.

Lower Extremity Aneurysms

105

J. HAJO VAN BOCKEL, MD
JAAP F. HAMMING, MD

After the aorta, the arteries in the lower limb are most affected by dilatation and aneurysm formation. Femoral and popliteal aneurysms are much less common than abdominal aortic aneurysms (AAAs), but they are more frequent than isolated iliac aneurysms and are the most frequently encountered peripheral aneurysms.[1] No exact information on the incidence of true aneurysms in the femoropopliteal region is available. A few reports provide an estimate of the incidence in selected populations of hospitalized patients in Utah and the United States, but these data probably underestimate the true incidence of these aneurysms. The age-adjusted rates were 4.85 per 100,000 person-years for men in Utah and 7.39 per 100,000 person-years in the United States for femoropopliteal artery aneurysms, emphasizing regional variation and errors in estimates.[1] Aneurysms rarely are diagnosed before age 55 years, and the incidence at least doubles during each next decade. Also, femoropopliteal aneurysms occur five times as often in men compared with women.[1] Finally, there seems to be a clear relationship between arteriomegaly and the occurrence of popliteal aneurysm. Chan and Thomas[2] observed in an angiographic study that more than half of patients with arteriomegaly had an aneurysm of the popliteal artery.

The information in this chapter is based mainly on relatively small surveys and case series, owing to the infrequency of these aneurysms. These case series are biased by selection for the presence of certain characteristics, such as existence of an aneurysm elsewhere, symptoms, or a specific therapy. Many conclusions are based on common sense, personal and expert opinion, and accumulated experience.

■ FEMORAL ARTERY ANEURYSMS

Common Femoral Artery Aneurysms

True aneurysms of the femoral artery must be clearly distinguished from pseudoaneurysms, which are common in this location. Femoral anastomotic pseudoaneurysms are discussed in Chapter 60, and traumatic pseudoaneurysms are discussed in Chapter 73. The normal diameter of the common femoral artery varies between 0.78 cm and 0.85 cm in women and between 0.78 cm and 1.12 cm in men with a range of reported standard deviation of 0.09 to 0.30 cm in men.[3] Other authors have reported a normal diameter of 0.82 ± 0.11 cm[4] and of 0.98 cm in men and of 0.82 cm in women.[5] The diameter of the common femoral artery is correlated with weight, height, and sex and increases with age.[5] Nomograms of the normal diameter have been calculated.[5] These data imply that an aneurysm is present if the diameter of the femoral artery has increased to approximately 1.5 cm (50% increase in normal diameter), although a threshold of 2 cm is commonly used clinically.

Incidence

True aneurysms of the common femoral artery are relatively uncommon. They are the second most common peripheral artery aneurysm after popliteal aneurysms. Femoral aneurysms are predominantly found in elderly (>55 years old) men who smoke. The mean age at presentation is around 65 years. Femoral aneurysms are rarely seen in women, and the prevalence ratio between men and women is 28:1. In approximately half of the patients, the lesion is bilateral. More than half of the patients with a femoral aneurysm also have an AAA (weighted mean of seven series is 52%, with a range of 28% to 85% among the series).[6-12] The wide range in the association of femoral and aortic aneurysms reported is probably due to the fact that four of the seven series were published before 1980. At that time, the association between the two locations was not universally known, and simple diagnostic tools such as ultrasound to diagnose the presence or absence of an AAA were unavailable. The associated incidence of AAA in this group as estimated from the three more recent series probably would be around 75%.[9,10,12] There is an association of femoral with popliteal artery aneurysms. Approximately one third of the patients with a femoral aneurysm also have a popliteal aneurysm (weighted mean of six series is 32%, with a range of 11% to 44% among the series).[6-11]

Patients with an AAA are at risk for a femoral artery aneurysm. Diwan and colleagues[13] found a 7% prevalence of popliteal aneurysm in patients with AAAs (17 of 251 male patients), whereas Sandgren and coworkers[14] observed a prevalence of 5% (8 of 158 male patients). Cutler and Darling[8] found that the external iliac artery was rarely involved. Cutler and Darling[8] also classified femoral aneurysms as type I and type II according to their relationship to the common femoral bifurcation. This classification is relevant for the surgical treatment. Type I aneurysms are confined to the common femoral artery, whereas type II aneurysms arise in the common femoral artery but extend into the proximal part of the profunda femoris artery (Fig. 105-1). In the study by Cutler and Darling,[8] 44% of the true femoral aneurysms were limited to the common femoral artery, and 56% involved also the femoral bifurcation, in particular the profunda femoris artery. In one of the largest

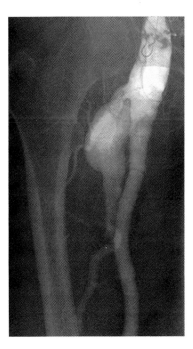

FIGURE 105-1 Angiogram of a type II femoral aneurysm including the common femoral and profunda femoris artery.

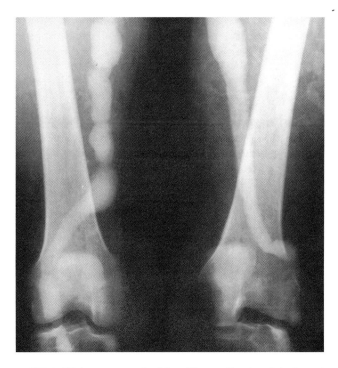

FIGURE 105-2 Aneurysmosis, diffuse bilateral dilatation of the femoral and popliteal arteries.

series, 85% had aneurysms restricted to the common femoral artery, whereas 15% had concomitant aneurysmal involvement of the superficial or profunda femoris vessels.[9]

Pathogenesis

The precise pathogenesis of femoral artery aneurysms is unknown. Traditionally, these aneurysms are described as "degenerative" or "atherosclerotic." More insight in the pathogenesis of AAA provides substantial evidence, however, of the contribution of proteolytic degradation of the vessel wall (see Chapter 29).[15-17] This also may explain the more generalized character of aneurysmal disease of the aortic, femoral, and popliteal arteries simultaneously. It is likely that the same mechanisms involved in aneurysms of the aorta also play a role in the pathogenesis of peripheral aneurysms, such as femoral aneurysms. This hypothesis is supported by Ward,[18] who showed that in individuals with aortic aneurysms, the diameters of femoral and popliteal arteries were significantly greater than in controls. This observation was not confirmed by Sandgren and associates,[14] however.

In occasional patients, femoral aneurysms are part of *arteriomegaly*, which is defined as diffuse enlargement involving several arterial segments, and diffuse aneurysmal disease below the level of the renal arteries (see Chapter 99). In a highly selected angiographic population of the Mayo Clinic, the prevalence of arteriomegaly was 91 out of 5771 patients (1.6%). In these 91 patients, 430 aneurysms were identified, including 145 aneurysms of the femoral arteries and 80 aneurysms of the popliteal arteries (Fig. 105-2).[19] Infection (e.g., with *Salmonella*) rarely may cause a true femoral aneurysm.[20] Multiple arterial aneurysms rarely

may occur at various locations in the lower limb. Possible etiologies include inflammatory arteritis, Behçet's syndrome, dysplasia, and idiopathic primary aneurysms.[21,22] Finally, arteriovenous malformations may be associated with aneurysmal changes of the femoral arteries (Fig. 105-3).

Clinical Manifestations

The clinical presentation of femoral artery aneurysms is usually asymptomatic. Large aneurysms, owing to restricted space at the level of the inguinal ligament, may be associated with symptoms of compression of the femoral vein (edema) or nerve (pain, paresthesia) or both. Potential complications include acute and chronic thrombosis of

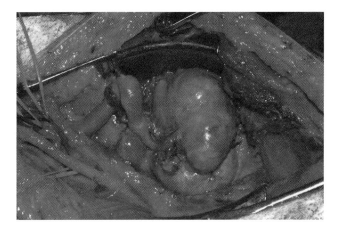

FIGURE 105-3 Femoral aneurysms in combination with an arteriovenous fistula caused by a large arteriovenous malformation.

the aneurysm and, occasionally, distal embolization and rupture. The occurrence of these complications seems to be related to the diameter of the aneurysms and the content of thrombus. Similar to aneurysms of the aorta, most femoral aneurysms are small, and the incidence of complications is low. Levi and Schroeder[10] reported that the risk of rupture was low for aneurysms with a diameter less than 5 cm, but the risk of thrombosis was not clearly related to the diameter of the aneurysm and occurred with relatively small aneurysms. Reports of complications are necessarily from selected patient series and consequently are relatively high. Acute thrombosis reportedly occurs in 15% of cases. Thrombosis may include occlusion of the superficial and profunda femoris artery and is associated with severe distal ischemia. Distal embolization may produce a "blue toe syndrome." Distal embolization is reported in 26% of the cases. Rupture is rare, varying between 0% and 24% with a higher incidence in earlier series.[6-12,23,24]

Diagnosis

A femoral aneurysm can be suspected by physical examination. Although this test seems simple and accurate, one third (53 of 172 aneurysms) were missed by physical examination alone.[9] A more recent prospective series confirms this observation; only 4 out of 20 femoral aneurysms were diagnosed by physical examination alone.[13] Duplex ultrasound accurately identifies the presence or absence of a femoral aneurysm. In addition, it provides information about the diameter, the presence or absence of intraluminal thrombus, and the location of the aneurysm in relation proximally to the iliac artery and distally to the femoral bifurcation.[25] If an aneurysm is diagnosed, ultrasound of the aorta and the popliteal arteries should be done to exclude the presence of aneurysmal disease. Computed tomography (CT) and magnetic resonance imaging (MRI)/magnetic resonance angiography also are accurate diagnostic imaging techniques that may be useful in the evaluation and precise localization of femoral aneurysms.

Natural History

The natural history of small aneurysms of the femoral artery is benign, and complications are rare. Most patients present with an asymptomatic swelling in the groin. Reports on the prevalence of complications are probably biased because of the inclusion of predominantly symptomatic cases. Graham and colleagues[9] reported a benign course in 58 of 105 patients with small aneurysms followed for 28 months. Limb-threatening complications occurred in only 3%. This was a selected group remaining after primary operation on 50 aneurysms. During follow-up, in only 2.9% of all aneurysms, serious limb-threatening complications occurred.[9] One would expect that complications occurred with greater frequency in the larger aneurysms. The size of the aneurysms in patients in whom complications developed (mean 2.8 cm) was not greater, however, than the size of aneurysms in patients in whom complications did not develop among the nonoperative group.[9] A clearly defined threshold diameter for surgical treatment cannot be defined precisely. Tolstedt and colleagues[26] reported a thrombosis

rate of 43% in 12 femoral aneurysms. Cutler and Darling[8] reported a 47% major complication rate in 45 femoral aneurysms.

This high prevalence of complications has not been reported in well-documented series since the 1970s, and it seems reasonable to assume that the natural history of these aneurysms is more benign. Life-threatening complications, such as rupture, are rare. It can be estimated from the literature that serious limb-threatening complications during conservative follow-up may occur in approximately 1% to 2% per year at most.

Indications for Intervention

The threshold diameter for surgical treatment of asymptomatic aneurysms is not evidence based. Not only larger, but also smaller aneurysms (from a diameter of 2 cm) may produce thrombotic or embolic complications.[10] Most surgeons recommend surgical intervention for asymptomatic femoral aneurysms greater than 2.5 to 3 cm in diameter. In older patients who are at risk for operation, however, observation may be indicated until further expansion has been shown. If watchful waiting is preferred, serial ultrasound examinations and physical examination of the pedal pulses should be performed. If the diameter increases or any evidence of distal embolization occurs, even if asymptomatic, as indicated by absence of previously present distal pulses, surgical reconstruction should be considered. For all symptomatic aneurysms, surgical repair is recommended. Even evidence of asymptomatic peripheral embolization is generally considered an indication for repair because embolization may progress with resultant symptoms of limb ischemia.

Surgical Technique

Surgical reconstruction should be individualized and is based primarily on symptoms, the presence of concomitant aneurysms, and the extent of the femoral aneurysm. In patients with asymptomatic aortic, femoral, and popliteal lesions, a staged approach is used, first repairing the aneurysm at greatest risk for complications. When an aortofemoral bypass is required in a patient with a femoral aneurysm, the femoral anastomosis should not be attached to the aneurysmal wall of a femoral aneurysm because of the high incidence of anastomotic aneurysm formation. The distal anastomosis can be performed beyond the aneurysm, but usually an interposition graft replacing the femoral aneurysm is inserted first.

The surgical treatment of an isolated femoral artery aneurysm is determined by aneurysmal involvement and patency of the superficial and profunda femoris arteries. The approach is usually through a vertical groin incision. If the aneurysm is large, and proximal control cannot be obtained via the standard groin incision, the distal external iliac artery can be controlled through a separated retroperitoneal approach or by extending the groin incision through the inguinal ligament. Alternatively, balloon occlusion of the external iliac artery can be achieved through a contralateral femoral artery approach. After heparinization followed by proximal and distal clamping, the aneurysm is opened,

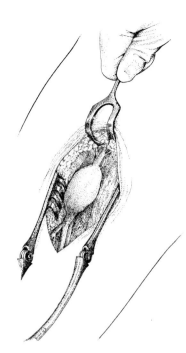

FIGURE 105-4 Reconstruction of a type I femoral aneurysm.

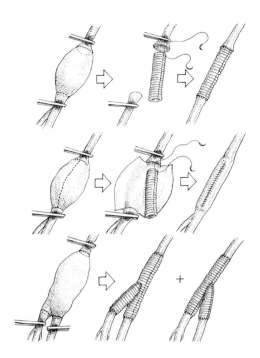

FIGURE 105-5 Various types of reconstruction of a type I and II femoral aneurysm (end-to-end to the profunda femoris artery with end-to-side anastomosis of the superficial femoral artery and end-to-end to the superficial femoral artery with end-to-side anastomosis of the profunda femoris artery).

and thrombus is removed. Small type I aneurysms can be excised completely and replaced by an interposition prosthetic graft using end-to-end anastomoses. Larger type I aneurysms can be repaired with a prosthetic graft inserted using the "inlay" technique, and the aneurysm can be closed over the graft. The prosthetic graft should match the diameter of the femoral artery (usually 8 or 10 mm). The choice of the material depends on the preference of the surgeon and can be either Dacron or polytetrafluoroethylene (PTFE) (Figs. 105-4 and 105-5).

The surgical treatment of an isolated femoral artery type II aneurysm, involving the femoral bifurcation, in particular the profunda femoris artery, is more complicated. As a principle, reconstruction of the profunda femoris artery always should be included. Usually a prosthetic graft is used to replace the common femoral artery and the proximal part of the superficial femoral artery (SFA) with two end-to-end anastomoses. Subsequently the profunda femoris origin can be sutured to this prosthesis using either an end-to-side anastomosis or a side-arm graft as an interposition prosthesis between the common femoral prosthesis and the profunda femoris artery (see Fig. 105-5).

Alternatively, in particular if the SFA is occluded, the common femoral aneurysm may be replaced by an interposition graft, which is sutured in an end-to-end fashion to the profunda femoris artery. With a prosthetic or venous side-arm, the SFA can be connected to this reconstruction with a proximal end-to-side and a distal end-to-end anastomosis (see Fig. 105-5). For short bypasses or interposition grafts (i.e., <5 to 10 cm), we also have used an arterial autograft taken from an occluded SFA. To accomplish this, a segment of the occluded SFA is excised through the same distally extended groin incision. Subsequently an eversion endarterectomy of the excised and occluded arterial segment is performed. These grafts usually

have the appropriate diameter (much larger than saphenous vein), are autologous with a durable patency, and have the advantage that the vein is left intact for later use. Graham and colleagues[9] reported excellent results without mortality of reconstruction of isolated femoral aneurysms. Sapienza and associates[12] reported a 5-year patency of 80% of interposition grafts for isolated femoral aneurysms.

Profunda Femoris Artery Aneurysms

Isolated aneurysms of the profunda femoris artery are rare, and they are estimated to account for 0.5% of all peripheral aneurysms (Fig. 105-6). Aneurysmal dilatation of the profunda femoris artery beyond a type II common femoral aneurysm is even rarer and occurs in only 1% to 2.6% of all femoral artery aneurysms.[27] Only 24 cases have been reported in the literature, mostly published because of associated complications (10 aneurysms presented with rupture and 4 with thrombosis). A high complication rate at presentation (58%) and the significant incidence of concomitant aneurysms elsewhere are emphasized.[28] The diagnosis is usually difficult because these aneurysms are hidden deep in the muscular compartment of the thigh. Ultrasound or CT angiography may be used to establish the diagnosis and develop a treatment plan. Because aneurysms of the profunda femoris artery are not easily detected in an asymptomatic stage, patients mostly present with a complication, which may explain the high complication rate as reported in the literature.

The literature consists mainly of case reports of true aneurysms and traumatic pseudoaneurysms (e.g., after

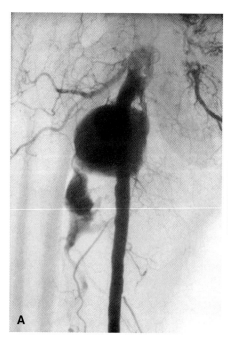

FIGURE 105-6 A, Angiogram of a large symptomatic aneurysm of the profunda femoris artery. **B,** Intraoperative view (same patient).

orthopedic operations).[29] In a review of the literature, 20 aneurysms of the profunda femoris artery were identified. Because nine of these aneurysms ruptured, it was suggested that profunda femoris artery aneurysms have a greater tendency to rupture than peripheral aneurysms,[30] an observation supported by other authors.[31] These conclusions are tentative, however, and probably based on a bias toward publication of complicated aneurysms because of the spectacular presentation of the condition. Accurate information about the natural history of profunda femoris artery aneurysms is not available. Because most of these are not detected until they are large, surgical intervention usually is indicated even if an aneurysm is asymptomatic.

Surgical Technique

Surgical repair consists of graft replacement, using vein or prosthetic material, with care to revascularize major branches if possible. The hip and knee are slightly flexed to relax the sartorius muscle and allow for external rotation. The profunda femoris artery is approached via a standard groin incision, which may extend inferiorly in the direction of the medial border of the patella.[32,33] The femoral bifurcation is dissected, and the origin of the profunda femoris artery, lateral and posterior to the common femoral artery, is controlled. The small vein located at the femoral bifurcation is ligated. The SFA can be retracted medially or, if occluded, can be transected for better exposure of the profunda femoris artery. The medial edges of the sartorius and rectus femoris muscles are mobilized and retracted laterally. It is usually necessary to dissect and transect multiple lateral branches of the deep femoral vein. These are usually short and broad and should be controlled by suturing rather than simple ligation because ligatures tend to slide off during further manipulation. Care also should be taken to prevent neurapraxia of branches of the femoral nerve caused by the self-retaining retractor. Now the profunda femoris artery can be dissected from the beginning to its

disappearance dorsal to the adductor longus muscle. The deep femoral vein and its tributaries are often adherent to the aneurysm. Care should be taken to avoid dissection resulting in venous hemorrhage, which is more bothersome than arterial bleeding. A pool of blood forms after laceration of a major vein, and usually standard vascular clamps are not adequate for control. Control with finger pressure and subsequently a wide-tipped Allis clamp may be applied to grasp the venous wall at the laceration, resulting in immediate temporary control because the venous blood is at a low pressure and allowing for subsequent suturing of the lesion.[34] If it is difficult to achieve arterial control by clamping the outflow and collateral perforating arteries, hemostasis with balloon catheters can be helpful. In an overview of 24 cases reported in the literature, 9 cases (38%) were treated by ligation, which may be necessary if the aneurysm is located at the distal part of the deep femoral artery. It has been suggested that in carefully selected patients with minimal atherosclerotic disease of the SFA, embolization of the profunda femoris artery aneurysms may offer a safe nonoperative alternative.

Superficial Femoral Artery Aneurysms

Isolated true degenerative aneurysms of the SFA, not associated with generalized dilatation of the common femoral or popliteal artery, are rare and probably represent only 1% of all femoral aneurysms (Fig. 105-7). Only 21 cases have been reported, mostly in men. Complications such as thrombosis, distal embolization, or rupture may occur but are less frequent than in patients with popliteal aneurysms.[35] A study by Jarrett and coworkers[36] reported 13 patients with SFA aneurysms, of whom 76% presented with either limb-threatening ischemia or with a painful thigh mass. In an overview of 14 studies with 38 aneurysms, the authors estimated the incidence of rupture to be 34%, thrombosis to be 26%, and other aneurysms to be present in 39%.[36]

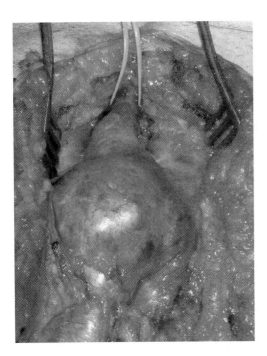

FIGURE 105-7 Aneurysm of the superficial femoral artery (intraoperative photo of vessel loop around the common femoral artery).

These aneurysms may present with either limb-threatening ischemia or rupture. Rigdon and Monajjem[37] reviewed 17 "atherosclerotic" SFA aneurysms in 14 patients whose cases were reported in the literature and found a complication at presentation in 65%, with rupture in 35%, thrombosis in 18%, and distal embolism in 12%. Limb salvage was 94%, and there were no perioperative deaths. AAAs were discovered in 40%. Male patients (75%) were more common than females, and the average age was 77 years (range 61 to 93 years). Another review of the literature stressed the high incidence of symptoms, including rupture (34%) and distal ischemia (26%).[36] SFA aneurysms may be detected when asymptomatic, but most are large or already have developed symptoms. Surgical repair of most SFA aneurysms is recommended, using a vein or prosthetic graft.

Surgical Technique

The patient lies supine on the operating table. The leg is completely prepared and fully exposed with the foot wrapped in a sterile plastic bag, which allows inspection of the foot during the operation. The skin and superficial fascia are incised longitudinally over the femoral pulsations, in the middle between the superior anterior iliac spine and the pubic bone, from approximately 2 cm above the inguinal ligament inferiorly to the distal end of the aneurysm. The femoral arterial sheath is opened, and the femoral bifurcation is dissected. Subsequently the proximal SFA and the artery just distal to the aneurysm are identified and dissected. If the aneurysm is located in the mid-portion or distal portion of the SFA, extension of the incision inferiorly is required in the direction of the medial border of the patella. The artery is covered by the sartorius muscle and is dissected at its medial border, while the muscle is retracted laterally. Resection of a SFA aneurysm is accomplished

easily, and reconstruction usually is performed with a synthetic prosthesis because the dilated superficial artery requires a reconstruction with a 6- to 8-mm graft.[36] Alternatively the aneurysm may be opened, the thrombus evacuated, a major part of the sac resected, and reconstruction with an interposition graft performed. If the distal anastomosis is performed with the distal popliteal artery below the knee, a venous graft is preferred. If a vein is not available, a venous cuff is recommended for the distal anastomosis.[38] Exact results of reconstructive surgery are not available. Rigdon and Monajjem[37] reported a limb salvage rate of 94% at short-term follow-up without mortality. In uncomplicated aneurysm repair, it can be expected that the patency would be on the order of reconstructive surgery of the SFA with a patency of venous bypasses of approximately 80% at 2 years compared with 65% for PTFE bypasses.[39]

Vein Graft Aneurysms

Vein grafts used to treat lower extremity aneurysm also may develop aneurysms. Loftus and colleagues[40] hypothesized that aneurysmal changes would occur more often in vein grafts used for reconstruction of aneurysmal disease compared with occlusive disease. This hypothesis was supported by the observation that spontaneous aneurysmal changes occurred in 42% of vein grafts used for reconstruction for popliteal aneurysms compared with only 2% in grafts applied for bypasses of occlusive disease.[40] Repair of the lesions is performed simply with a short interposition graft.

■ POPLITEAL ARTERY ANEURYSMS

The normal diameter of the popliteal artery is 0.90 ± 0.20 cm.[3,41] Other authors have reported a smaller mean diameter (0.52 ± 0.11 cm).[4] A popliteal aneurysm may be considered to be present if the diameter is more than 1.5 cm, although 2 cm also is a commonly used clinical threshold in this location.

Incidence

Aneurysms of the popliteal artery are uncommon. They are the most common peripheral artery aneurysm, however, accounting for more than 70% of all peripheral aneurysms. The prevalence and incidence of popliteal aneurysms are not precisely known. A report from an era when ultrasound was not routinely available observed that the incidence of popliteal aneurysms was increased in patients with aneurysms in the aorta and its peripheral branches (36 of 1488 patients [2.4%]).[42] The observation that the incidence of popliteal aneurysms is higher in patients with an AAA than in the normal population is confirmed by more recent reports. A total of 51 femoral and popliteal aneurysms were encountered in 313 consecutive patients with AAAs, all occurring in men. The prevalence of popliteal aneurysms in this series was 8% (24 of 313 patients).[13] This prevalence is similar to that observed in other series evaluating the same population: 10% (24 of 232 patients)[43] and 7.5% (4 of 54 patients).[44] Sandgren and colleagues[14] found, however, the prevalence of popliteal aneurysms to be only 3% (4 of 158) in patients with AAAs, indicating some variation in these populations.

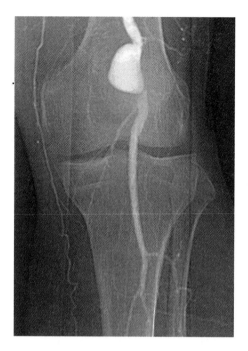

FIGURE 105-8 Angiogram of an aneurysm of the popliteal artery.

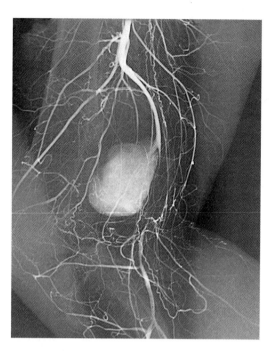

FIGURE 105-9 Angiogram of a pseudoaneurysm of the popliteal artery caused by a benign bone tumor. Note the displacement and compression of the popliteal artery.

Our review of the literature, including 29 series published in the English literature, indicated that, at most, only four or five patients are seen each year by any major vascular center. Of the patients with an AAA, 6% to 12% also had a popliteal aneurysm. Our review showed that 36% of the patients with a popliteal aneurysm also had an aortic aneurysm.[45] In the period from 1958 to 1990, 1453 patients underwent reconstruction for AAAs in Rochester, New York, but only 42 patients with a popliteal aneurysm were operated on.[46] If a popliteal aneurysm was found, however, there was a 43% chance that an abdominal aneurysm would be present and that there also was an aneurysm in the opposite popliteal artery. The mean age at presentation is around 65 years. Approximately 95% of the patients are men. In approximately half of the patients, the lesion is bilateral. About 55% of the patients present with symptoms.[47] Presence of a popliteal aneurysm is a marker of risk to limb and life because 33% to 43% are associated with an AAA.[23,48] During a 10-year follow-up, 50% of the patients who had a popliteal artery repair developed an aneurysm at a second location, a finding that justifies subsequent surveillance.[49]

Pathogenesis

Most popliteal aneurysms are degenerative (Fig. 105-8). As explained in Chapter 29, the cause is probably a combination of a genetic defect and inflammation with an increase in local production of enzymes that degrade elastin and collagen. This was confirmed by Jacob and associates,[50,51] who found an inflammatory infiltrate, including T lymphocytes, in the wall of popliteal artery aneurysms that was associated with increased apoptosis and degradation of extracellular matrix.

True popliteal aneurysms also can result from popliteal artery entrapment syndrome (see Chapter 86). The mechanism seems to be chronic repetitive trauma similar to subclavian

artery dilatation distal to a cervical rib. Gyftokostas and coworkers[52] found 10 cases of an aneurysm (13.5%) in a retrospective review of 74 cases of popliteal entrapment syndrome. This represented a substantial proportion (26%) of all popliteal aneurysms of any etiology seen during the same period.

False aneurysms of the popliteal artery can be caused by chronic trauma from benign bone tumors, such as osteochondromas, in the distal femoral metaphysis (Fig. 105-9).[53] Penetrating trauma also can be responsible for pseudoaneurysms of the popliteal artery.[54] Delayed presentation of these has been reported when trauma was caused by low-velocity gunshot or stab wounds; patients presented after a median interval of 1.5 months.[55] Catheterization occasionally may produce an iatrogenic pseudoaneurysm of the popliteal artery.[56] Iatrogenic trauma also can occur during knee surgery, either prosthetic replacement or arthroscopy.[57-59] Finally, pseudoaneurysm formation after blunt trauma has been reported[60] after previous femoropopliteal bypass operation, especially after using a prosthetic graft.

Clinical Manifestations

In a systematic review of the literature published between 1980 and 1995, including data from 2445 aneurysms, only 37.2% of popliteal aneurysms (range 5% to 58%) were asymptomatic, limb ischemia was the presenting symptom in 55% (range 38% to 90%), local compression was present in 6.5% (range 0% to 23%), and rupture occurred in 1.4% (range 0% to 7%).[45] The occurrence of symptoms is related to the diameter of the popliteal aneurysm and the presence or absence of pedal pulses. If the aneurysm is less than 2 cm diameter, the occurrence of symptoms is rare, but above this threshold symptoms are frequent because larger aneurysms

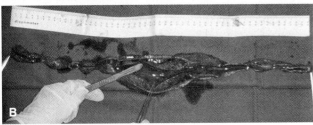
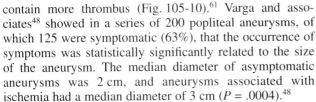

FIGURE 105-10 **A,** Large symptomatic aneurysm with compression of veins and nerves of the femoropopliteal artery after excision (intraoperative photo). **B,** Large symptomatic aneurysm of the femoropopliteal artery opened and showing thrombus and localization of thrombus (intraoperative photo).

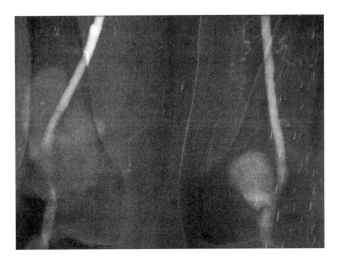

FIGURE 105-11 Angiogram of bilateral popliteal aneurysms with rupture on the right-hand side.

contain more thrombus (Fig. 105-10).[61] Varga and associates[48] showed in a series of 200 popliteal aneurysms, of which 125 were symptomatic (63%), that the occurrence of symptoms was statistically significantly related to the size of the aneurysm. The median diameter of asymptomatic aneurysms was 2 cm, and aneurysms associated with ischemia had a median diameter of 3 cm ($P = .0004$).[48]

Approximately one third of patients with popliteal aneurysms are asymptomatic at the time of initial diagnosis. In 43% of asymptomatic popliteal aneurysms, one or both pedal pulses were absent. Most likely, these aneurysms already had produced asymptomatic distal emboli, emphasizing the risk for progressive occlusion of the infrapopliteal arteries. These limbs experienced a high risk of developing complications. The risk of developing complications, including acute thrombosis, chronic thromboembolism, and pain caused by compression, was 36% at 3 years for patients with normal pedal pulses, which was significant compared with 86% at 3 years for patients with absent pulses ($P < .005$).[61]

In our experience with 124 true popliteal aneurysms, 45% were asymptomatic, 44% had thromboembolic complications, 7% had symptoms of local compression, and 4% had a rupture.[62] This is similar to the experience of others. Symptoms may include claudication, blue toe syndrome[63] caused by thromboembolism, and limb-threatening ischemia caused by acute thrombosis. Pain may occur secondary to local compression and a neurologic deficit peroneal nerve paresis, which may occur in approximately 7%. Venous congestion, including acute venous thrombosis, has been reported.[64] Rupture is a rare complication, occurring in 2.5% of 3046 popliteal aneurysms in 29 studies (Fig. 105-11). Symptoms of rupture included pain and swelling, distal edema, and acute venous thrombosis. Occasionally, rarer manifestations were observed, including hemorrhage with shock, hemarthrosis, and limb ischemia.[62]

Limb ischemia is the most common clinical presentation, which occurs in around two thirds of patients. The absence of pedal pulses may indicate silent distal embolization and is associated with a less favorable natural history. Symptoms are associated with increased aneurysm size. Rupture is rare.

Diagnosis

It is important to detect popliteal aneurysms in the asymptomatic stage before complications occur. This is particularly relevant in patients with aortic or femoral aneurysms. A high index of suspicion in these patients should result in physical examination and duplex ultrasonography of the aorta and femoral and popliteal arteries. During careful physical examination, a popliteal artery aneurysm should be suspected when prominent pulsations are felt in the popliteal space with slight flexion of the knee joint. When the aneurysm is thrombosed, a firm mass without pulsations may be palpated. If the presence of an aneurysm is suspected or if the examiner is inexperienced, confirmation of the diagnosis by ultrasound is mandatory. Physical examination is associated with false-positive[41] and false-negative results. Ultrasound has been shown to be superior to physical examination as a diagnostic tool, diagnosing twice as many aneurysms.[43] This finding has been confirmed in two other studies, showing that only 74% (50 of 689) and 19% (6 of 31) of popliteal aneurysms were found by physical examination.[13] Probably half of the popliteal aneurysms would not be detected by physical examination alone.

Duplex ultrasonography provides important information relevant for the diagnosis and decision regarding treatment, including the diameter of the artery, the flow velocity, the presence or absence of thrombus, and the patency of outflow arteries. If treatment is considered, additional evaluation usually is required to obtain more information to decide on the best strategy and technique for intervention. Additional information can be obtained with arteriography, CT, and MRI. Arteriography is traditionally best equipped to provide information on outflow. CT and MRI have demonstrated this as well, however, and may provide three-dimensional information not only on the arterial tree, but also on the popliteal space.

Physical examination alone is often not reliable and may produce false-positive and false-negative test results. Ultrasound is an accurate diagnostic tool. For planning treatment, angiography, three-dimensional CT, and MRI are helpful.

Natural History

The natural history of popliteal aneurysms is not precisely known. It is likely that many asymptomatic small aneurysms are never recognized and can be followed conservatively. The natural history of many untreated aneurysms is enlargement, however, and finally the development of symptoms and complications. For popliteal aneurysms, thromboembolic complications, often with irreversible ischemia, are feared. In a review of 13 studies published between 1953 and 1994, a selected group of 536 asymptomatic popliteal artery aneurysms was followed and not treated surgically for various reasons, including medical contraindications to surgery and patient refusal. After a mean follow-up of 45 months, 35% developed thromboembolic complications. These complications were associated with an amputation rate of 25%.[45] In our own experience, complications depended on the diameter of the popliteal aneurysm and occurred after a mean follow-up of only 18 months. Calculated by the life-table method, the complication rate was 24% at 1 year and increased to 74% after 5 years (Fig. 105-12). All complications resulted from aneurysms with a diameter greater than 2 cm. In addition, the risk of developing complications was 36% at 3 years in patients with palpable pedal pulses, whereas it was 86% for patients with absent pulses.[61] This unfavorable natural history with complications such as ischemia, increase in diameter, rupture, and compression within a median follow-up of 14 months also has been reported in other more recent series. Varga and coworkers[48] reported 58 patients followed by observation, mostly because of medical unfitness, during a median period of 22 months. They observed a high mortality rate with 18 deaths; 18 initially observed patients required a bypass. Mahmood and associates[65] reported the conservative treatment of seven asymptomatic aneurysms with a sac diameter of less than 2 cm. All seven patients required surgery at median follow-up because of acute ischemia (*n* = 3), pain (*n* = 1), rupture (*n* = 1), and increase in size (*n* = 2).

Special attention is required for the association of aortic aneurysm repair and thrombosis of a popliteal aneurysm. During follow-up for asymptomatic popliteal aneurysms, 16 patients underwent open repair of an aortic aneurysm. Three patients developed acute thrombosis of the popliteal aneurysm within 24 hours after the operation, suggesting that aneurysm repair is a risk factor for acute thrombosis of a popliteal aneurysm.[66]

Indications for Intervention

The decision for intervention depends on weighing the risks of conservative treatment and follow-up against the risks and results of treatment. Although Galland and Magee[67] suggested that asymptomatic popliteal aneurysms with a diameter of 3 cm also can be followed safely, we recommend repair of aneurysms greater than 2 cm in good-risk patients. Ascher and coworkers[68] studied the correlation between the popliteal artery aneurysm diameter with initial symptoms and presence of associated occlusive disease. They found no significant difference in the presence of thrombosis between smaller and larger aneurysms. Smaller popliteal artery aneurysms were associated with a higher incidence of the combination of the endpoints thrombosis, clinical symptoms, and distal occlusive disease.

If the risk of operation is high, selected patients with 2- to 3-cm diameter aneurysms can be carefully followed. The presence of distortion of the popliteal artery, either within or outside the aneurysm, seems to be an additional argument for repair.[69] Small aneurysms containing intraluminal thrombus and asymptomatic patients with absence of distal pulses (indicative of asymptomatic distal embolization) also should be considered for repair. In particular, the risk of follow-up is repeated "silent" distal embolization.[61,70]

The indications for early operation in an asymptomatic stage have been confirmed by many others.[69,71-75] Computerized modeling of the disease using a Markov decision analysis showed that early elective treatment is preferable to follow-up, unless the risk of developing complications of the asymptomatic aneurysm is less than 10% per year.[76] A few authors believe, however, that a more conservative approach in selected asymptomatic patients is justifiable.[67,77-79] The arguments for this policy are the low complication rate in small aneurysms, the higher complication rate after arterial surgery, and the introduction of effective thrombolysis for acute ischemia. Schellack and colleagues[77] showed that conservative management is justified in selected patients with a mean age of 70 years and small asymptomatic aneurysms and observed no complications in 24 aneurysms during a mean follow-up of 37 months. This policy has been supported by Varga and coworkers,[48] who defined "small" as less than 2 cm in diameter. A plea for a more conservative approach also has been proposed based on a low complication rate during follow-up in combination with the observation that patients with asymptomatic popliteal aneurysms may develop significant distal ischemia after vascular reconstruction because of the development of recurrent aneurysms, complications of the graft, or even expansion and rupture of the sac. Hands and Collin[79] observed a less favorable outcome in 3 of 11 limbs that underwent elective arterial reconstruction.

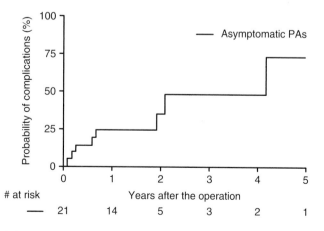

FIGURE 105-12 Probability of nonsurgically treated asymptomatic popliteal artery aneurysms (PAs) to develop complications during follow-up, shown by the life-table method. Numbers of limbs at risk are shown at each interval. (*From Dawson I, van Bockel JH, Brand R, Terpstra JL: Popliteal artery aneurysms: Long-term follow-up of aneurysmal disease and results of surgical treatment. J Vasc Surg 13:398-407, 1991.*)

Finally, a conservative approach is based on the concept that thromboembolic complications occurring during follow-up can be treated with thrombolysis and subsequent surgical reconstruction and that safe, effective thrombolysis is the initial management of choice for complications in these popliteal aneurysms.[78,80] Bowyer and associates[78] based their advice on the treatment of a small series of eight patients (seven with rest pain and one with claudication). The mean thrombolytic infusion time was more than 24 hours (range 14 to 48 hours), and successful lysis was achieved in six of the eight patients. Such protocols are based on small series, however, and are not generally accepted.[48] In a more recent series from another institution, Bowyer and associates[81] showed results that supported early elective repair in patients with aneurysms greater than 2 cm and intra-arterial thrombolysis in patients with aneurysm thrombosis. Although a conservative approach toward asymptomatic popliteal aneurysms has been suggested by some, most agree that the results of elective repair are excellent with a low morbidity and mortality and significantly better than treatment of thrombosed aneurysms presenting with ischemia.[65,75,81] Small aneurysms, defined as less than 2 cm in diameter, without symptoms may be followed without reconstructive surgery.

Treatment

Proximal ligation of the popliteal artery as performed by Hunter in 1785 has long since been replaced by ligation and bypass reconstruction, which remains the "gold standard" for treatment of popliteal aneurysms.[82] Before operation, information should be obtained concerning variables that are relevant for the long-term durability of the reconstruction: availability of saphenous vein, the quality of inflow and outflow arteries, and the planned location of possible proximal and distal anastomotic sites. This information can be obtained with duplex ultrasonography or standard digital subtraction angiography, but often magnetic resonance angiography and (spiral) CT angiography provide adequate information for planning an operation.

Elective Treatment

Surgical Technique The patient lies supine on the operating table. The leg is completely prepared and fully exposed with the foot wrapped in a sterile plastic bag, which allows inspection of the foot during the operation. The operation can be performed either through a standard medial approach,[83] with the patient supine, or through a posterior approach,[84] with the patient prone. In most cases, a medial approach, with the incision parallel to the sartorius muscle, is preferred. It provides wider access to the distal SFA and the distal outflow arteries, especially the tibial vessels when necessary. It also provides easier access to the greater saphenous vein and is the best approach when a longer segment of aneurysmal or occluded arteries must be bypassed. The greater saphenous vein is superior to bypasses of prosthetic materials. As with bypass grafting for femoropopliteal occlusive disease, it seems to make no difference whether the bypass is performed with reversed vein or in-situ vein with valve disruption.[85]

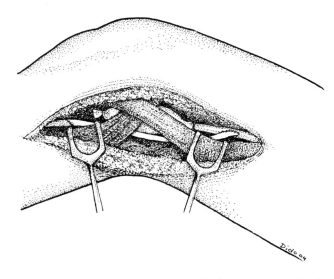

FIGURE 105-13 Reconstruction of a popliteal artery aneurysm by the medial approach.

The popliteal artery and the saphenous vein are approached through the same incision, which is usually continuous, and placed over the saphenous vein to prevent undermining of skin flaps and poor wound healing. The popliteal artery is proximally identified at the level of the adductor hiatus. The distal popliteal artery is identified at the posterior surface of the tibia. The popliteal vein is carefully separated from the artery with sharp dissection. If the aneurysm is small, the popliteal artery just proximal and distal to the aneurysm is ligated with a strong ligature. After performing the proximal anastomosis, either end-to-end or end-to side, the bypass is tunneled between the heads of the gastrocnemius through the apex of the popliteal space. Care must be taken to prevent entrapment, which may occur when the bypass is located medial of the medial gastrocnemius or between the medial gastrocnemius and other tendons. Unobstructed flow should be checked during flexion and extension of the knee joint. Subsequently an end-to-end or end-to side anastomosis with the distal popliteal artery is performed (Fig. 105-13).

For the posterior approach, the patient is in a prone position.[84] An S-shaped incision is used with the superior limb of the incision placed on the medial side of the thigh to expose the proximal popliteal artery and the greater saphenous vein (Fig. 105-14). Distally the exposure of the distal popliteal artery is limited, and care should be taken to avoid neurapraxia of the peroneal nerve by excess retraction. The superior neck of the aneurysm is exposed by separating the semimembranosus and semitendinosus muscle on the medial side from the long head of the biceps femoris on the lateral side. Transection of these tendons is not required. The distal neck is exposed by separating the medial and lateral heads of the gastrocnemius muscle. Decompression of the aneurysm via this approach is not difficult. This approach is best suited for treatment of localized popliteal aneurysms, although more distal exposure of tibial arteries has been described using this approach. Occasionally the lesser saphenous vein is large enough and accessible through this approach, but more often the greater

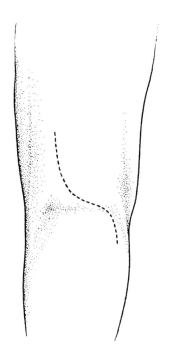

FIGURE 105-14 S-shaped incision used for the posterior approach to the popliteal artery.

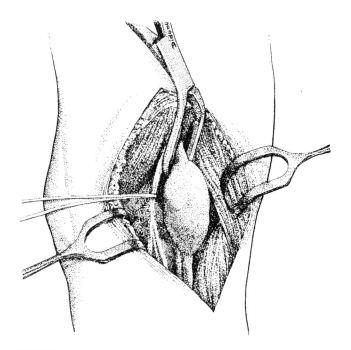

FIGURE 105-15 Reconstruction of a popliteal artery aneurysm by the posterior approach.

saphenous vein is used, often harvested though a separate distal incision (Fig. 105-15).

Popliteal aneurysms can be treated by excluding the aneurysm with a bypass graft or with an interposition graft. When a bypass graft is performed, the popliteal artery proximal and distal to the aneurysm is ligated, and continuity is restored by a bypass graft. In these cases, the aneurysm, which is usually small, is left intact. When an interposition graft is performed, the popliteal aneurysm, which is usually larger, is incised longitudinally, the thrombus is evacuated, and any collaterals are oversewn from within the aneurysm. The network of popliteal veins surrounding and closely adherent to the aneurysms is not dissected from the sac. Continuity is restored by an interposition graft, usually with a proximal and distal end-to-end anastomosis with the inlay technique as performed for the open repair of aortic aneurysms. This technique can be employed in the medial and the posterior approaches. At the end of the operation, the adequacy of the reconstruction is evaluated by duplex ultrasonography or completion angiography depending on the experience and preference of the surgeon.

The bypass technique is currently the most popular technique for treating popliteal aneurysms, especially from the medial approach. Operative trauma is reduced because the gastrocnemius muscle is left intact; the aneurysm is left intact; and injuries to structures adherent to the aneurysm, in particular, the popliteal veins to which the aneurysm often is intimately attached, are avoided. The disadvantage of this technique is that compression by the aneurysms is not relieved, which is a problem with symptoms related to compression (Fig. 105-16). In addition, the aneurysm may not thrombose if there is sufficient collateral circulation and still can expand and cause compression[86] and even rupture.[87]

This situation is similar to a type II endoleak in endovascular treatment of abdominal aneurysms (Fig. 105-17A).[88] For this reason, large aneurysms that already are causing any compression symptoms should be approached directly and evacuated, with repair by an interposition graft. The medial gastrocnemius muscle and tendons have to be transected and sutured afterward, although this can be done safely without too much discomfort.

Jones and colleagues[89] reviewed their experience over a 10-year period with the various methods of excluding popliteal artery aneurysms. In a retrospective study, three methods of exclusion of the aneurysm were evaluated: proximal and distal ligation with a short (type I) or with a

FIGURE 105-16 Large popliteal aneurysm, which is treated by opening and decompression and reconstruction by an interposition graft (intraoperative view, the gastrocnemius muscle has been transected).

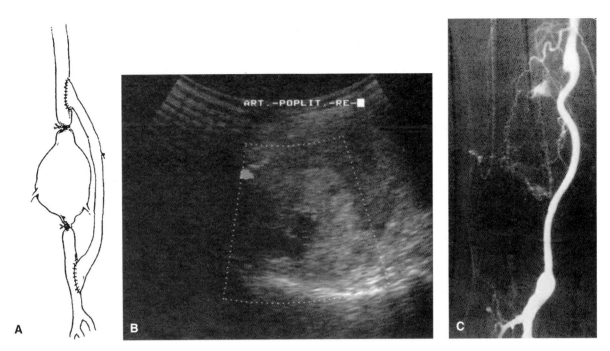

FIGURE 105-17 A, Technique for treatment of small popliteal aneurysms by exclusion and bypass. Popliteal aneurysm treated by proximal and distal ligation and a venous bypass. **B,** During follow-up, the diameter of the aneurysm increased, and duplex ultrasonography showed flow in the aneurysm. (See color figure in this section.) **C,** Angiography confirmed flow in the aneurysm (a type II endoleak of contrast material in the aneurysmal sac visualized during angiography) and mediodorsal displacement of the bypass. Four years after the initial operation, the aneurysm was decompressed via the dorsal route, the thrombus was removed, and a collateral was sutured. (**A** from Jones WT III, Hagino RT, Chiou AC, et al: Graft patency is not the only clinical predictor of success after exclusion and bypass of popliteal artery aneurysms. J Vasc Surg 37:392-398, 2003.)

long (type II) popliteal segment isolated or a single proximal ligature (type III). Duplex examination showed that 5.6% of the aneurysms remained patent. Twelve aneurysms enlarged after occlusion and bypass, however, and three of these developed new compressive symptoms, in particular, in patients with an increase of 25% to 50% in diameter. Type I (short segment of popliteal artery excluded between ligatures) was superior to type II or type III exclusions. In particular, type III exclusions resulted in increases in diameter. Visible arterial branches feeding the excluded sac on duplex scan also influenced aneurysm expansion after treatment (Fig. 105-17B and C).[89] We, among others, recommend decompression of the aneurysm whenever feasible.[90]

Endoprosthesis Endoluminal bypass with a percutaneously delivered stent-graft has been suggested as an alternative for treatment of popliteal aneurysms. Although stent-grafting is feasible, the results for femoropopliteal lesions are up to now clearly inferior to open reconstruction. One of the problems is that a stent-graft has to be placed crossing the knee joint with all the inherent problems associated with movement of the popliteal artery and the stent-graft during walking. Angiographic studies have shown that knee joint flexion increased tortuosity between two fixed points, one proximal (the adductor canal) and the other distal (the origin of the anterior tibial artery) (Fig. 105-18).[91]

The endovascular technique was first reported by Marin and colleagues.[92] Henry and associates[93] treated seven patients with lesions of the popliteal artery with a stent-graft, and although five stent-grafts remained patent, the primary patency of occlusive and stenotic lesions was only 59% at 6 months. Additional case reports of stent-grafts for popliteal aneurysms indicate that the endovascular technique is feasible.[94-97] More recently, experience with PTFE-lined nitinol stent-grafts has been published. Gerasimidis and coworkers[98] reported nine patients with a mean follow-up of 14 months and a primary patency rate of 47%. Tielliu and associates[99] reported on 23 popliteal aneurysms with a median diameter of 30 mm treated with a stent-graft. A mean of two stent-grafts was required to cover the entire length of the aneurysm. The median follow-up was 15 months, and the overall patency was 74% at 6 and 12 months. In both series, thrombosis was relatively frequent. Currently, results are still inferior compared with conventional open repair, and this technique is still considered experimental. So far, endovascular treatment cannot be recommended except in patients at high risk for standard surgical repair.

Emergency Treatment

Surgical Technique In severe acute limb ischemia, thromboembolectomy or intraoperative thrombolysis combined with popliteal or tibial bypass reconstruction is effective treatment for a thrombosed popliteal aneurysm (Fig. 105-19). Instrumentation with thrombectomy catheters should be performed with utmost care, however, to prevent irreparable damage of small-caliber tibial arteries. Thrombectomy is difficult to perform via the popliteal artery because blind selective catheterization of the anterior and posterior tibial artery is not possible, and the balloon catheter usually is introduced in the peroneal artery. Trifurcation

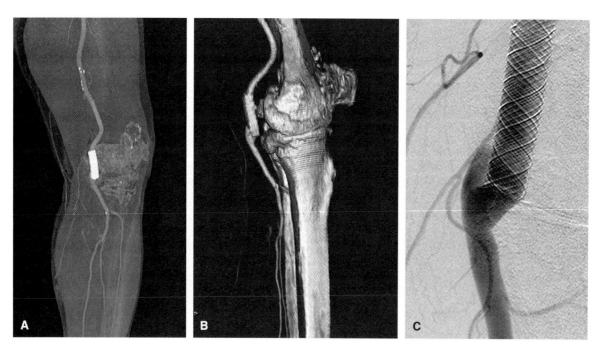

FIGURE 105-18 **A,** Failure to repair popliteal aneurysm by endovascular technique (covered stent-graft). **B** and **C,** Note stent dislocation (**B**) and endoleak (**C**).

embolectomy is a first alternative. Thrombectomy of the tibial and pedal vessels via arteriotomy with a No. 2 balloon catheter at the level of the ankle may be an alternative, more successful, approach, especially if substantial distal embolization has occurred. If necessary, this approach may be followed by intraoperative thrombolysis to dissolve residual thrombus.[100,101]

Thrombolysis In cases of acute thrombosis or substantial distal thromboembolism, surgical treatment has been less successful compared with elective repair because of failure to clear the outflow arteries effectively, resulting in a higher need for subsequent amputation. Mortality (0.4%) and limb loss (0.8%) with elective operation for asymptomatic, uncomplicated aneurysms was favorable compared with mortality (4.7%) and amputation (18.2%) for symptomatic aneurysms.[102] It has been shown, however, that in acute cases with outflow obstruction, the distal arteries often can be cleared partially or completely by preoperative[102] or intraoperative[103] thrombolysis. Thrombolysis is often incomplete, and the time to reperfusion usually is several hours, with complete thrombolysis requiring 25 to 32 hours.[74,78,104] If the limb is threatened, delay is usually not justifiable, and an emergent surgical reconstruction is required. If ischemia is too severe to allow preoperative lysis, but the outflow is completely obstructed, isolated limb perfusion using a thrombolytic agent has been attempted.[105] After exposure of the distal popliteal artery, an arteriogram is performed, and a catheter is introduced for intraoperative thrombolysis.[106]

The technique of catheter-directed intra-arterial thrombolysis has been described extensively,[102,107,108] and details are provided in Chapter 67. Even old thrombus may contain an adequate amount of plasminogen[109]; even older thrombus

can be dissolved, provided that the plasminogen activator comes in direct contact with the plasmin in the thrombus. This implies that it is essential to put the catheter into the thrombus and preferably saturate the complete thrombus with plasmin activator, rather than positioning the catheter directly above the thrombus. With this approach, the

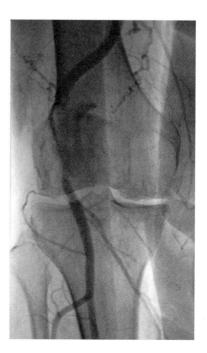

FIGURE 105-19 Acute thrombosis of a popliteal aneurysm with limb-threatening ischemia. This was successfully treated by thrombolytic therapy and subsequent operation.

duration of thrombolytic treatment is reduced, and systemic effects are limited. Adequate heparinization is required to prevent thrombus formation around the intra-arterial catheter if the catheter is left in place for several hours.

One of the complications of thrombolysis is acute deterioration of limb ischemia during thrombolysis caused by propagation of clot and thrombus fragments by the restoration of blood flow. Such severe and irreversible deterioration occurred in 2.3%, but mild deterioration occurred in 13% during thrombolysis for popliteal aneurysms, often caused by pericatheter thrombosis if heparinization is not adequate, rethrombosis, or distal embolization.[110] Mild deterioration is usually treatable by continuing the thrombolysis, whereas more severe deterioration may require acute surgical intervention. These complications occur significantly more often during the treatment of thrombosed popliteal aneurysm than during treatment of emboli or thrombosed atheromatous arteries or grafts. The amputation rate associated with complications of thrombolysis is high, and operative intervention seems to provide better results than continuation of thrombolysis.[110]

There is still some debate about the value of preoperative thrombolysis concerning the risk of acute deterioration of ischemia by distal embolization. Some authors believe that it is better to perform open surgery and clear the runoff by intraoperative thrombolysis and to reserve percutaneous thrombolysis for selective cases with few if any ischemic symptoms.[70] An overview of the results of thrombolysis for thrombosed popliteal aneurysms has been published by Dorigo and coworkers.[111] They reported a series of 109 elective operations and 24 emergency cases resulting from thrombosis. Of patients with acute limb ischemia 10 underwent surgery, and 14 were treated with thrombolysis. Reviewing the literature between 1990 and 2002, these authors found reports on 143 patients treated with thrombolysis resulting in a weighted primary patency of 86% and a limb salvage rate of 93%.[111]

Although a publication bias may be assumed, there is a place for thrombolysis in selected patients presenting with acute limb ischemia caused by a thrombosed popliteal aneurysm, in particular, if tibial outflow is severely obstructed and if a delay of several hours is permitted. In patients who present with acute thrombosis, but in whom there are adequately patent outflow arteries to maintain patency of a surgical bypass, thrombolysis is not required. This situation is usually established by arteriography, at which point a decision is made concerning immediate surgical bypass versus preoperative catheter-directed thrombolysis.

Results of Open Reconstruction

Overall results of treatment of asymptomatic popliteal aneurysms are superior to results with acute or chronic symptomatic aneurysms.[65,70,71,112,113] This observation is due to the quality of outflow. Lilly and colleagues[114] found a patency rate of 91% at 5 years for asymptomatic patients versus 54% for symptomatic patients. It also has been pointed out, however, that good results can be obtained despite occluded outflow arteries.[115] Evidence indicates that patency after 5 years is better after elective repair, and limb salvage is better than after bypass for a thrombosed popli-

teal aneurysm.[67] This finding was confirmed in other series (elective 100% patency versus emergency reconstruction 72% patency), although late occlusion of a bypass does not always result in severe ischemia.[70] Similar results were reported by Mahmood and associates.[65] Overall a high 7.7% mortality rate was observed attributable to emergency treatment; there were no deaths with elective operation, but acutely ischemic limbs had a 30-day mortality of 11.8% (2 of 1765). Reviewing the literature, Michaels and Galland[76] found that surgery for symptomatic aneurysms was associated with an average mortality of 4.7% (range 1% to 10%), limb loss of 18.2% (range 3% to 30%), and residual symptoms of 10.6% (range 0% to 28%), whereas treatment of asymptomatic cases was associated with an average mortality of 0.4% (range 0% to 1%), limb loss of 0.8% (range 0% to 2%), and residual symptoms of 1% (range 0% to 2%).

Data for long-term results from a systematic review of the literature also are available. The overall 5-year patency rates range from 29% to 100 %. Patients with an autologous vein graft had a superior patency compared with patients with a synthetic bypass (range 77% to 100% versus 29% to 74%). The 5-year limb salvage rate ranged from 75% to 98%. Patient survival at 5 years ranged from 60% to 85%. Acute ischemia was associated with an amputation rate of 25%. Most of the series reported better results with elective surgery than with emergency procedures.[47]

Follow-up After Reconstruction

After reconstruction of a popliteal aneurysm, follow-up should be focused on surveillance of the reconstruction, in particular, if an autologous vein graft has been inserted. This surveillance implies duplex scanning at regular intervals, in particular, during the first year after operation. Further aneurysmal degeneration just proximal and distal to a short bypass may occur in 5% after a follow-up period of 10 years, emphasizing the need for regular and lifelong follow-up.[116]

In addition, follow-up should be focused on surveillance for the development of new aneurysms because these patients exhibit a high incidence of aortic, femoral, and contralateral popliteal aneurysms. In our series, 23 new aneurysms developed in 16 of 50 patients (32%) during a mean follow-up of 5 years (Fig. 105-20).[117] Usually an annual ultrasound examination is sufficient to exclude or confirm dilatation of these vessels in most patients. The interval for screening is arbitrary, but in several series, an indication for arterial reconstruction occurred within 24 months, even in small asymptomatic aneurysms (see earlier).[48,65,66] Dilatation and aneurysm formation may occur in venous grafts used for reconstruction of popliteal aneurysms, which should be detected by duplex graft surveillance because these sometimes require repair.[40,89]

■ TIBIAL ARTERY ANEURYSMS

Aneurysms of the tibial arteries are infrequent and consist mainly of pseudoaneurysms of traumatic etiology. A major cause is catheterization (e.g., during thromboembolectomy with a balloon catheter). For this reason, completion arteriography is recommended after balloon

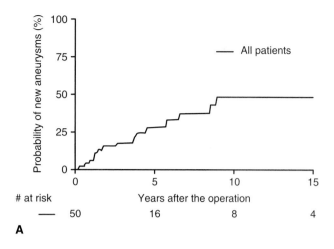

FIGURE 105-20 Cumulative risk for patients with popliteal artery aneurysms to develop new arteriosclerotic aneurysms during follow-up, shown by the life-table method, for all 50 patients (**A**) and according to advanced age (**B**). Numbers of patients at risk are shown at each interval. (From Dawson I, van Bockel JH, Brand R, Terpstra JL: Popliteal artery aneurysms: Long-term follow-up of aneurysmal disease and results of surgical treatment. J Vasc Surg 13:398-407, 1991.

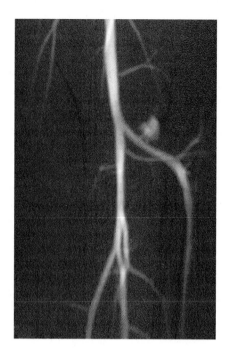

FIGURE 105-21 Aneurysm in tibial artery caused by benign bone tumor.

obliteration of pseudoaneurysms can be considered, if the neck of the aneurysm would allow thrombosis without distal propagation or if the artery can be sacrificed because of other patent tibial arteries.[120]

■ REFERENCES

1. Lawrence PF, Lorenzo-Rivero S, Lyon JL: The incidence of iliac, femoral, and popliteal artery aneurysms in hospitalized patients. J Vasc Surg 22:409-415, 1995.
2. Chan O, Thomas ML: The incidence of popliteal aneurysms in patients with arteriomegaly. Clin Radiol 41:185-189, 1990.
3. Johnston KW, Rutherford RB, Tilson MD, et al: Suggested standards for reporting on arterial aneurysms. Subcommittee on Reporting Standards for Arterial Aneurysms, Ad Hoc Committee on Reporting Standards, Society for Vascular Surgery and North American Chapter, International Society for Cardiovascular Surgery. J Vasc Surg 13:452-458, 1991.
4. Zierler RE, Zierler BK: Duplex sonography of lower extremity arteries. In Zwiebel WJ (ed): Introduction to Vascular Ultrasonography. Philadelphia, WB Saunders, 1983, pp 237-251.
5. Sandgren T, Sonesson B, Ahlgren R, Lanne T: The diameter of the common femoral artery in healthy human: Influence of sex, age, and body size. J Vasc Surg 29:503-510, 1999.
6. Adiseshiah M, Bailey DA: Aneurysms of the femoral artery. Br J Surg 64:174-176, 1977.
7. Baird RJ, Gurry JF, Kellam J, Plume SK: Arteriosclerotic femoral artery aneurysms. Can Med Assoc J 117:1306-1307, 1977.
8. Cutler BS, Darling RC: Surgical management of arteriosclerotic femoral aneurysms. Surgery 74:764-773, 1973.
9. Graham LM, Zelenock GB, Whitehouse WM Jr, et al: Clinical significance of arteriosclerotic femoral artery aneurysms. Arch Surg 115:502-507, 1980.
10. Levi N, Schroeder TV: True and anastomotic femoral artery aneurysms: Is the risk of rupture and thrombosis related to the size of the aneurysms? Eur J Vasc Endovasc Surg 18:111-113, 1999.

catheter embolectomy to detect possible complications of distal catheterization.[118-120] Occasionally, no apparent cause of tibial artery aneurysms can be identified.[121] Other traumatic causes of pseudoaneurysms include fractures, external fixation of fractures,[122] and gunshot wounds.[123] Tibial aneurysms may be associated with benign bone tumors (Fig. 105-21).

Usually symptoms are absent, especially when the aneurysm is small. Occasionally, swelling of the calf may be present.[121] The diagnosis is made by duplex ultrasonography. Digital subtraction arteriography is performed to confirm the diagnosis.

The usual management is surgical repair, usually by means of ligation or occasionally by reconstruction. Alternatively, coil embolization or thrombin injection for

11. Pappas G, Janes JM, Bernatz PE, Schirger A: Femoral aneurysms: Review of surgical management. JAMA 190:489-493, 1964.

12. Sapienza P, Mingoli A, Feldhaus RJ, et al: Femoral artery aneurysms: Long-term follow-up and results of surgical treatment. Cardiovasc Surg 4:181-184, 1996.

13. Diwan A, Sarkar R, Stanley JC, et al: Incidence of femoral and popliteal artery aneurysms in patients with abdominal aortic aneurysms. J Vasc Surg 31:863-869, 2000.

14. Sandgren T, Sonesson B, Ryden A, Lanne T: Arterial dimensions in the lower extremities of patients with abdominal aortic aneurysms—no indications of a generalized dilating diathesis. J Vasc Surg 34:1079-1084, 2001.

15. Wassef M, Baxter BT, Chisholm RL, et al: Pathogenesis of abdominal aortic aneurysms: A multidisciplinary research program supported by the National Heart, Lung, and Blood Institute. J Vasc Surg 34:730-738, 2001.

16. Thompson RW, Geraghty PJ, Lee JK: Abdominal aortic aneurysms: Basic mechanisms and clinical implications. Curr Probl Surg 39:110-230, 2002.

17. Ferrans VJ: New insights into the world of matrix metalloproteinases. Circulation 105:405-407, 2002.

18. Ward AS: Aortic aneurysmal disease: A generalized dilating diathesis. Arch Surg 127:990-991, 1992.

19. Hollier LA, Stanson AW, Gloviczki P, et al: Arteriomegaly: Classification and morbid implications of diffuse aneurysmal disease. Surgery 93:700-708, 1983.

20. Klicks RJ, van Aken PJ: False aneurysm formation of the right common femoral artery: A rare complication of a Salmonella infection. Eur J Vasc Surg 7:747-749, 1993.

21. Bordeaux J, Guys JM, Magnan PE: Multiple aneurysms in a seven-year-old child. Ann Vasc Surg 4:26-28, 1990.

22. Kasirajan K, Marek JM, Langsfeld M: Behcet's disease: Endovascular management of a ruptured peripheral arterial aneurysm. J Vasc Surg 34:1127-1129, 2001.

23. McCann RL: Basic data related to peripheral artery aneurysms. Ann Vasc Surg 4:411-414, 1990.

24. Levi N, Schroeder TV: Arteriosclerotic femoral artery aneurysms: A short review. J Cardiovasc Surg (Torino) 38:335-338, 1997.

25. Gooding GA, Effeney DJ: Ultrasound of femoral artery aneurysms. AJR Am J Roentgenol 134:477-480, 1980.

26. Tolstedt GE, Radke HM, Bell JW: Late sequela of arteriosclerotic femoral aneurysms. Angiology 12:601-602, 1961.

27. Levi N, Schroeder TV: Arteriosclerotic femoral artery aneurysms: A short review. J Cardiovasc Surg (Torino) 38:335-338, 1997.

28. Yahel J, Witz M: Isolated true atherosclerotic aneurysms of the deep femoral artery: Case report and literature review. J Cardiovasc Surg (Torino) 37:17-20, 1996.

29. Roseman JM, Wyche D: True aneurysm of the profunda femoris artery: Literature review, differential diagnosis, management. J Cardiovasc Surg (Torino) 28:701-705, 1987.

30. Tait WF, Vohra RK, Carr HM, et al: True profunda femoris aneurysms: Are they more dangerous than other atherosclerotic aneurysms of the femoropopliteal segment? Ann Vasc Surg 5:92-95, 1991.

31. Burchi C, Cavallaro G, Amato D, Cavallaro A: Isolated true atherosclerotic aneurysm of the profunda femoris artery: Case report. J Cardiovasc Surg (Torino) 40:577-581, 1999.

32. Henry AK: Extensile Exposure, 2nd ed. Edinburgh, E & S Livingstone, 1957.

33. Hershey FB, Auer AI: Extended surgical approach to the profunda femoris artery. Surg Gynecol Obstet 138:88-90, 1974.

34. Linton RR: Atlas of Vascular Surgery. Philadelphia, WB Saunders, 1973.

35. Atallah C, al Hassan HK, Neglen P: Superficial femoral artery aneurysm—an uncommon site of aneurysm formation. Eur J Vasc Endovasc Surg 10:502-504, 1995.

36. Jarrett F, Makaroun MS, Rhee RY, Bertges DJ: Superficial femoral artery aneurysms: An unusual entity? J Vasc Surg 36:571-574, 2002.

37. Rigdon EE, Monajjem N: Aneurysms of the superficial femoral artery: A report of two cases and review of the literature. J Vasc Surg 16:790-793, 1992.

38. Stonebridge PA, Prescott RJ, Ruckley CV: Randomized trial comparing infrainguinal polytetrafluoroethylene bypass grafting with and without vein interposition cuff at the distal anastomosis. The Joint Vascular Research Group. J Vasc Surg 26:543-550, 1997.

39. Klinkert P, Schepers A, Burger DH, et al: Vein versus polytetrafluoroethylene in above-knee femoropopliteal bypass grafting: Five-year results of a randomized controlled trial. J Vasc Surg 37:149-155, 2003.

40. Loftus IM, McCarthy MJ, Lloyd A, et al: Prevalence of true vein graft aneurysms: Implications for aneurysm pathogenesis. J Vasc Surg 29:403-408, 1999.

41. Davis RP, Neiman HL, Yao JS, Bergan JJ: Ultrasound scan in diagnosis of peripheral aneurysms. Arch Surg 112:55-58, 1977.

42. Dent TL, Lindenauer SM, Ernst CB, Fry WJ: Multiple arteriosclerotic arterial aneurysms. Arch Surg 105:338-344, 1972.

43. MacSweeney ST, Skidmore C, Turner RJ, et al: Unravelling the familial tendency to aneurysmal disease: Popliteal aneurysm, hypertension and fibrillin genotype. Eur J Vasc Endovasc Surg 12:162-166, 1996.

44. Ebaugh JL, Matsumura JS, Morasch MD, et al: Morphometric analysis of the popliteal artery for endovascular treatment. Vasc Endovasc Surg 37:23-26, 2003.

45. Dawson I, Sie RB, van Bockel JH: Atherosclerotic popliteal aneurysm. Br J Surg 84:293-299, 1997.

46. DeWeese JA, Shortell C, Green R, Ouriel K: Operative repair of popliteal aneurysm: Twenty-five years experience. In Yao JS, Pearce WH (eds): Long-Term Results in Vascular Surgery. Norwalk, Conn, Appleton & Lange, 1993, pp 287-293.

47. Dawson I, Sie RB, Van Bockel JH: Atherosclerotic popliteal aneurysm. Br J Surg 84:293-299, 1997.

48. Varga ZA, Locke-Edmunds JC, Baird RN: A multicenter study of popliteal aneurysms. Joint Vascular Research Group. J Vasc Surg 20:171-177, 1994.

49. Dawson I, van Bockel JH, Brand R, Terpstra JL: Popliteal artery aneurysms: Long-term follow-up of aneurysmal disease and results of surgical treatment. J Vasc Surg 13:398-407, 1991.

50. Jacob T, Hingorani A, Ascher E: Examination of the apoptotic pathway and proteolysis in the pathogenesis of popliteal artery aneurysms. Eur J Vasc Endovasc Surg 22:77-85, 2001.

51. Jacob T, Schutzer R, Hingorani A, Ascher E: Differential expression of YAMA/CPP-32 by T lymphocytes in popliteal artery aneurysm. J Surg Res 112:111-116, 2003.

52. Gyftokostas D, Koutsoumbelis C, Mattheou T, Bouhoutsos J: Post stenotic aneurysm in popliteal artery entrapment syndrome. J Cardiovasc Surg (Torino) 32:350-352, 1991.

53. Perez-Burkhardt JL, Gomez Castilla JC: Posttraumatic popliteal pseudoaneurysm from femoral osteochondroma: Case report and review of the literature. J Vasc Surg 37:669-671, 2003.

54. Holcomb GW III, Meacham PW, Dean RH: Penetrating popliteal artery injuries in children. J Pediatr Surg 23:859-861, 1988.

55. Woolgar JD, Reddy DS, Robbs JV: Delayed presentation of traumatic popliteal artery pseudoaneurysms: A review of seven cases. Eur J Vasc Endovasc Surg 23:255-259, 2002.

56. Nguyen HH, Chleboun JO: False popliteal aneurysm after femoral embolectomy. Aust N Z J Surg 65:362-364, 1995.

57. Karkos CD, Thomson GJ, D'Souza SP, Prasad V: False aneurysm of the popliteal artery: A rare complication of total knee replacement. Knee Surg Sports Traumatol Arthrosc 8:53, 2000.

58. Mullen DJ, Jabaji GJ: Popliteal pseudoaneurysm and arteriovenous fistula after arthroscopic meniscectomy. Arthroscopy 17:E1, 2001.

59. Langkamer VG: Local vascular complications after knee replacement: A review with illustrative case reports. Knee 8:259-264, 2001.

60. Mikulin T, Walker EW: False aneurysm following blunt trauma. Injury 15:309-310, 1984.

61. Dawson I, Sie R, Van Baalen JM, Van Bockel JH: Asymptomatic popliteal aneurysm: Elective operation versus conservative follow-up. Br J Surg 81:1504-1507, 1994.

62. Sie RB, Dawson I, van Baalen JM, et al: Ruptured popliteal artery aneurysm: An insidious complication. Eur J Vasc Endovasc Surg 13:432-438, 1997.

63. Rosenberg MW, Shah DM: Bilateral blue toe syndrome: A case report. JAMA 243:365-366, 1980.

64. Walsh JJ, Williams LR, Driscoll JL, Lee JF: Vein compression by arterial aneurysms. J Vasc Surg 8:465-469, 1988.

65. Mahmood A, Salaman R, Sintler M, et al: Surgery of popliteal artery aneurysms: A 12-year experience. J Vasc Surg 37:586-593, 2003.

66. Dawson I, Sie R, van Baalen JM, van Bockel JH: Asymptomatic popliteal aneurysm: Elective operation versus conservative follow-up. Br J Surg 81:1504-1507, 1994.

67. Galland RB, Magee TR: Management of popliteal aneurysm. Br J Surg 89:1382-1385, 2002.

68. Ascher E, Markevich N, Schutzer RW, et al: Small popliteal artery aneurysms: Are they clinically significant? J Vasc Surg 37:755-760, 2003.

69. Anton GE, Hertzer NR, Beven EG, et al: Surgical management of popliteal aneurysms: Trends in presentation, treatment, and results from 1952 to 1984. J Vasc Surg 3:125, 1986.

70. Gouny P, Bertrand P, Duedal V, et al: Limb salvage and popliteal aneurysms: Advantages of preventive surgery. Eur J Vasc Endovasc Surg 19:496-500, 2000.

71. Reilly MK, Abbott WM, Darling RC: Aggressive surgical management of popliteal artery aneurysms. Am J Surg 145:498-502, 1983.

72. Shortell CK, DeWeese JA, Ouriel K, Green RM: Popliteal artery aneurysms: A 25-year surgical experience. J Vasc Surg 14:771-776, 1991.

73. Roggo A, Brunner U, Ottinger LW, Largiader F: The continuing challenge of aneurysms of the popliteal artery. Surg Gynecol Obstet 177:565-572, 1993.

74. Carpenter JP, Barker CF, Roberts B, et al: Popliteal artery aneurysms: Current management and outcome. J Vasc Surg 19:65-72, 1994.

75. Berridge DC, Wolfe JH: Popliteal aneurysms—the case for elective surgery "don't wait too long ... Norman Hertzer, 1986." Eur J Vasc Endovasc Surg 9:127-128, 1995.

76. Michaels JA, Galland RB: Management of asymptomatic popliteal aneurysms: The use of a Markov decision tree to determine the criteria for a conservative approach. Eur J Vasc Surg 7:136-143, 1993.

77. Schellack J, Smith RB III, Perdue GD: Nonoperative management of selected popliteal aneurysms. Arch Surg 122:372-375, 1987.

78. Bowyer RC, Cawthorn SJ, Walker WJ, Giddings AE: Conservative management of asymptomatic popliteal aneurysm. Br J Surg 77:1132-1135, 1990.

79. Hands LJ, Collin J: Infra-inguinal aneurysms: Outcome for patient and limb. Br J Surg 78:996-998, 1991.

80. Quraishy MS, Giddings AE: Treatment of asymptomatic popliteal aneurysm: Protection at a price. Br J Surg 79:731-732, 1992.

81. Bowrey DJ, Osman H, Gibbons CP, Blackett RL: Atherosclerotic popliteal aneurysms: Management and outcome in forty-six patients. Eur J Vasc Endovasc Surg 25:79-81, 2003.

82. Edwards WS: Exclusion and saphenous vein bypass of popliteal aneurysms. Surg Gynecol Obstet 128:829-830, 1969.

83. Szilagyi DE, Whitcomb JG, Smith RF: Anteromedial approach to the popliteal artery for femoropopliteal arterial grafting. Arch Surg 78:647-651, 1959.

84. Lim RA, Scott SA, McKittrick JE: Surgical approach to the treatment of popliteal aneurysm. Ann Vasc Surg 3:1-4, 1989.

85. Porter JM: In situ versus reversed vein graft: Is one superior? J Vasc Surg 5:779-780, 1987.

86. Flynn JB, Nicholas GG: An unusual complication of bypassed popliteal aneurysms. Arch Surg 118:111-113, 1983.

87. Battey PM, Skardasis GM, McKinnon WM: Rupture of a previously bypassed popliteal aneurysm: A case report. J Vasc Surg 5:874-875, 1987.

88. Resnikoff M, Darling RC, Chang BB, et al: Fate of the excluded abdominal aortic aneurysm sac: Long-term follow-up of 831 patients. J Vasc Surg 24:851-855, 1996.

89. Jones WT III, Hagino RT, Chiou AC, et al: Graft patency is not the only clinical predictor of success after exclusion and bypass of popliteal artery aneurysms. J Vasc Surg 37:392-398, 2003.

90. Ebaugh JL, Morasch MD, Matsumura JS, et al: Fate of excluded popliteal artery aneurysms. J Vasc Surg 37:954-959, 2003.

91. Avisse C, Marcus C, Ouedraogo T, et al: Anatomo-radiological study of the popliteal artery during knee flexion. Surg Radiol Anat 17:255-262, 1995.

92. Marin ML, Veith FJ, Panetta TF, et al: Transfemoral endoluminal stented graft repair of a popliteal artery aneurysm. J Vasc Surg 19:754-757, 1994.

93. Henry M, Amor M, Cragg A, et al: Occlusive and aneurysmal peripheral arterial disease: Assessment of a stent-graft system. Radiology 201:717-724, 1996.

94. Manns RA, Duffield RG: Case report: Intravascular stenting across a false aneurysm of the popliteal artery. Clin Radiol 52:151-153, 1997.

95. Burger T, Meyer F, Tautenhahn J, et al: Initial experiences with percutaneous endovascular repair of popliteal artery lesions using a new PTFE stent-graft. J Endovasc Surg 5:365-372, 1998.

96. Muller-Hulsbeck S, Link J, Schwarzenberg H, et al: Percutaneous endoluminal stent and stent-graft placement for the treatment of femoropopliteal aneurysms: Early experience. Cardiovasc Intervent Radiol 22:96-102, 1999.

97. van Sambeek MR, Gussenhoven EJ, van der LA, et al: Endovascular stent-grafts for aneurysms of the femoral and popliteal arteries. Ann Vasc Surg 13:247-253, 1999.

98. Gerasimidis T, Sfyroeras G, Papazoglou K, et al: Endovascular treatment of popliteal artery aneurysms. Eur J Vasc Endovasc Surg 26:506-511, 2003.

99. Tielliu IF, Verhoeven EL, Prins TR, et al: Treatment of popliteal artery aneurysms with the Hemobahn stent-graft. J Endovasc Ther 10:111-116, 2003.

100. Wyffels PL, DeBord JR: Increased limb salvage: Distal tibial/peroneal artery thrombectomy/embolectomy in acute lower extremity ischemia. Am Surg 56:468-475, 1990.

101. Mahmood A, Hardy R, Garnham A, et al: Microtibial embolectomy. Eur J Vasc Endovasc Surg 25:35-39, 2003.

102. Giddings AEB: Influence of thrombolytic therapy in the management of popliteal aneurysms. In Yao JS, Pearce WH (eds): Aneurysms: New Findings and Treatments. Norwalk, Conn, Appleton & Lange, 1994, pp 493-508.

103. Thompson JF, Beard J, Scott DJ, Earnshaw JJ: Intraoperative thrombolysis in the management of thrombosed popliteal aneurysm. Br J Surg 80:858-859, 1993.

104. Marty B, Wicky S, Ris HB, et al: Success of thrombolysis as a predictor of outcome in acute thrombosis of popliteal aneurysms. J Vasc Surg 35:487-493, 2002.

105. Greenberg R, Wellander E, Nyman U, et al: Aggressive treatment of acute limb ischemia due to thrombosed popliteal aneurysms. Eur J Radiol 28:211-218, 1998.

106. Comerota AJ, Rao AK: Intraoperative intraarterial thrombolytic therapy. In Comerota AJ (ed): Thrombolytic Therapy. Philadelphia, JB Lippincott, 1995, pp 313-328.

107. McNamara TO, Bomberger RA, Merchant RF: Intra-arterial urokinase as the initial therapy for acutely ischemic lower limbs. Circulation 83(2 Suppl):I-106-I-119, 1991.

108. Comerota AJ, White JV: Overview of catheter-directed thrombolytic therapy for arterial and graft occlusion. In Comerota AJ (ed): Thrombolytic Therapy. Philadelphia, JB Lippincott, 1995, pp 225-252.

109. Brommer EJ, van Bockel JH: Composition and susceptibility to thrombolysis of human arterial thrombi and the influence of their age. Blood Coagul Fibrinolysis 3:717-725, 1992.

110. Galland RB, Earnshaw JJ, Baird RN, et al: Acute limb deterioration during intra-arterial thrombolysis. Br J Surg 80:1118-1120, 1993.

111. Dorigo W, Pulli R, Turini F, et al: Acute leg ischaemia from thrombosed popliteal artery aneurysms: Role of preoperative thrombolysis. Eur J Vasc Endovasc Surg 23:251-254, 2002.

112. Vermilion BD, Kimmins SA, Pace WG, Evans WE: A review of one hundred forty-seven popliteal aneurysms with long-term follow-up. Surgery 90:1009-1014, 1981.

113. Anton GE, Hertzer NR, Beven EG, et al: Surgical management of popliteal aneurysms: Trends in presentation, treatment, and results from 1952 to 1984. J Vasc Surg 3:125-134, 1986.

114. Lilly MP, Flinn WR, McCarthy WJ III, et al: The effect of distal arterial anatomy on the success of popliteal aneurysm repair. J Vasc Surg 7:653-660, 1988.

115. Hagino RT, Fujitani RM, Dawson DL, et al: Does infrapopliteal arterial runoff predict success for popliteal artery aneurysmorrhaphy? Am J Surg 168:652-656, 1994.

116. Towne JB, Thompson JE, Patman DD, Persson AV: Progression of popliteal aneurysmal disease following popliteal aneurysm resection with graft: A twenty year experience. Surgery 80:426-432, 1976.

117. Dawson I, Van Bockel JH, Brand R, Terpstra JL: Popliteal artery aneurysms: Long-term follow-up of aneurysmal disease and results of surgical treatment. J Vasc Surg 13:398-407, 1991.

118. Cronenwett JL, Walsh DB, Garrett HE: Tibial artery pseudo-aneurysms: Delayed complication of balloon catheter embolectomy. J Vasc Surg 8:483-488, 1988.

119. van Schil P, Vanmaele R, Moses F, et al: Pseudoaneurysm of the posterior tibial artery as an early complication after Fogarty catheter thrombectomy. Eur J Vasc Surg 4:197-199, 1990.

120. Neary WD, Tottle AJ, Earnshaw JJ: False aneurysm of the posterior tibial artery after femoral embolectomy. Eur J Vasc Endovasc Surg 23:460-461, 2002.

121. Rowe P, Taylor P, Franklin A, et al: Unusual causes of calf swelling: 1. Unusual presentation of a tibial artery false aneurysm. Postgrad Med J 63:649-652, 1987.

122. Paul MA, Patka P, van Heuzen EP, et al: Vascular injury from external fixation: Case reports. J Trauma 33:917-920, 1992.

123. Edwards H, Martin E, Nowygrod R: Nonoperative management of a traumatic peroneal artery false aneurysm. J Trauma 22:323-326, 1982.

Chapter

Upper Extremity Aneurysms

106

G. PATRICK CLAGETT, MD

Upper extremity aneurysms are relatively rare compared with other peripheral arterial aneurysms.[1] Their recognition and treatment are important, however, because these aneurysms can cause major disability; lead to limb and digit loss; and, in the case of proximal aneurysms of the subclavian artery, result in death from rupture and exsanguination. In addition to rupture, proximal aneurysms are complicated by thromboembolism with ischemic upper extremity signs and symptoms (including gangrene), neuromuscular and sensory dysfunction from brachial plexus compression, and central neurologic deficits secondary to retrograde thromboembolism in the vertebral and right carotid circulations. In contrast, more distally located upper extremity aneurysms are manifested almost exclusively by thromboembolic complications of the hand and digits.

Because of the relative rarity of upper extremity aneurysms, the natural history and the overall incidence of associated complications are unknown. In reviewing the reported cases in the literature, however, one is impressed by the serious morbidity encountered with the first manifestations of these aneurysms. Because of this, optimal surgical treatment should be carried out early, preferably before symptoms arise.

■ SUBCLAVIAN ARTERY ANEURYSMS

Subclavian artery aneurysms arise from degenerative disease, thoracic outlet obstruction, or trauma. Aneurysms involving the proximal and mid-subclavian artery are usually nonspecific; degenerative[2,10]; or, less commonly, associated with fibromuscular dysplasia,[3] syphilis,[4] cystic medial necrosis,[5] invasion of the wall by contiguous tuberculous lymphadenitis,[6] and idiopathic congenital causes.[7,8] Thirty percent to 50% of patients with nonspecific, degenerative subclavian aneurysms have aortoiliac or other peripheral aneurysms.[9,11] Patients presenting with subclavian aneurysms should be evaluated thoroughly for associated aneurysms. These aneurysms usually occur in patients older than 60 years of age of either sex, but they seem to be more common in men. Aneurysms of the distal subclavian artery, frequently with extension into the first portion of the axillary artery, are appropriately considered aneurysms of the subclavian-axillary arteries and are associated most commonly with a thoracic outlet obstruction, cervical rib, and other bony abnormalities that result in compression and post-stenotic dilatation.[9]

Iatrogenic injury from inadvertent cannulation of the subclavian artery with false aneurysm formation is uncommon but increasing in frequency because of the common requirements for invasive monitoring and hemodialysis via the subclavian vein. In most cases, simple removal of the misplaced catheter and careful compression is all that is necessary. Many patients with this problem are unstable and coagulopathic, however. This situation, along with the inability to compress the artery effectively when the injury is beneath the clavicle, may result in significant hemorrhage and false aneurysm formation.

Clinical Presentation

Presenting symptoms of subclavian aneurysms include (1) chest, neck, and shoulder pain from acute expansion or rupture; (2) upper extremity acute and chronic ischemic symptoms from thromboembolism; (3) upper extremity pain and neurologic dysfunction from brachial plexus compression; (4) hoarseness from compression of the right recurrent laryngeal nerve; (5) respiratory insufficiency from tracheal compression; (6) transient ischemic attacks and stroke from retrograde thromboembolism in the vertebral and right carotid circulations; and (7) hemoptysis from erosion into the apex of the lung. Patients without symptoms may note the presence of a supraclavicular pulsatile mass. Most asymptomatic pulsatile masses in this area represent tortuous common carotid and subclavian arteries, however (Fig. 106-1). These masses usually can be distinguished from true aneurysms by duplex ultrasonography. In addition to a supraclavicular mass, physical signs may include (1) a supraclavicular bruit, (2) absent or diminished pulses in the upper extremity, (3) normal pulses with signs of micro-embolization ("blue finger" syndrome), (4) sensory and motor signs of brachial plexus compression, (5) vocal cord paralysis, and (6) Horner's syndrome resulting from compression of the stellate ganglion and other contributions to the cervical sympathetic chain at the base of the neck.[12]

Plain films of the chest may reveal a superior mediastinal mass that can be confused with a neoplasm. Ultrasonography or computed tomography (CT) establishes the

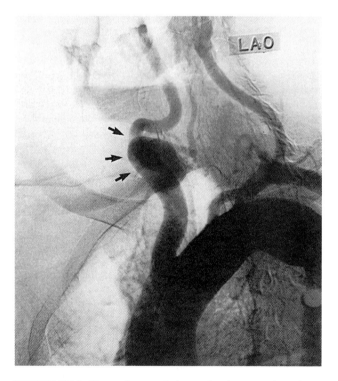

FIGURE 106-1 The confluence of elongated and tortuous innominate, subclavian, and common carotid arteries gives rise to a pulsatile mass in the right supraclavicular fossa and base of neck *(arrows)*. This common condition is harmless, but is frequently confused on physical examination with a subclavian or common carotid aneurysm. Ultrasonography usually can differentiate between these; however, arteriography is sometimes required. LAO, left anterior oblique view.

diagnosis. Complete arch and upper extremity angiography or CT angiography is important to delineate the extent of the aneurysm, to assess the sites of vascular occlusion in cases complicated by thromboembolism, and to note the competency of the contralateral vertebral circulation if the ipsilateral vertebral artery originates from an aneurysmal vessel. These points are essential in planning appropriate surgical reconstruction or endovascular repair.

Surgical Repair

The first attempted surgical correction of a proximal subclavian artery aneurysm was performed in 1818 by Mott in New York, who ligated the innominate artery.[4] The first successful treatment of a subclavian artery aneurysm was achieved in 1864 by Smyth in New Orleans, who ligated the right common carotid and the innominate artery.[4] The aneurysm recurred and ruptured 10 years later. Halsted was the first to combine ligation successfully with resection of a subclavian artery aneurysm in 1892 at the Johns Hopkins Hospital.[13] In 1913, Matas reported 225 cases of treatment of aneurysms by endoaneurysmorrhaphy, and 7 of these were subclavian aneurysms.[14]

Contemporary surgical repair of proximal and mid-subclavian artery aneurysms involves resection and re-establishment of arterial continuity with an end-to-end anastomosis (for very small aneurysms) or, more commonly, an interposition arterial prosthesis. Although proximal and distal ligation of subclavian aneurysms occasionally has been successful in the past, ligation without reconstruction generally should not be performed because ischemic symptoms develop in 25% of cases so treated.[9] For proximal right subclavian aneurysms, median sternotomy with extension into the supraclavicular fossa is usually necessary to gain adequate exposure for proximal control.[11] Resection of the clavicle also offers excellent exposure of the subclavian artery. In cases of proximal left subclavian aneurysms, a left thoracotomy combined with supraclavicular exposure may be necessary.

Extra-anatomic reconstruction combined with proximal and distal aneurysm ligation also has been described in unusual circumstances.[15] For aneurysms involving the mid-subclavian artery and the distal subclavian artery, a supraclavicular incision often gives adequate exposure and may be complemented by an infraclavicular incision for distal control. Division or resection of the mid-portion of the clavicle may be necessary to gain additional exposure,[10] and if so, the clavicle may be reconstructed at the completion of the operation. If the aneurysm involves the origin of the vertebral artery, reconstruction by reimplantation or other means is appropriate, particularly if the contralateral vertebral artery is hypoplastic or diseased.

Aneurysm resection with graft replacement is durable and yields excellent long-term results. In one of the largest reported series, normal upper extremity circulation was maintained, and there were no procedure-related complications during a mean follow-up of 9.2 years.[9]

There are many reports of endovascular stent-graft treatment of subclavian aneurysms.[16-33] This approach is attractive for unstable patients with multiple medical morbidities that make them unfit for open procedures. It also may be helpful in actively bleeding, coagulopathic patients with iatrogenic, catheter-induced, or other penetrating injury of the subclavian artery.[16,23,25-27,29,33] The proximal portion and mid-portion of the subclavian artery are most amenable to stent-graft treatment. The distal subclavian artery is between the clavicle and the first rib, and stent-grafts in this location are subject to compression, deformation, and fracture.[26,29-31] Another potential complication of stent-graft placement in the right subclavian artery is stroke from embolic debris dislodged into the right common carotid artery.[33] The vertebral artery origin is vulnerable on both sides and may be covered during stent-graft deployment. This usually is well tolerated when the contralateral vertebral artery is patent and of adequate size. Posterior circulation stroke may occur, however, when the contralateral vertebral artery is highly stenotic, hypoplastic, or occluded. In this circumstance, the ipsilateral vertebral artery should be revascularized by end-to-side anastomosis to the common carotid artery or other means.

The long-term durability of stent-grafts in the subclavian artery is unknown. Short-term patency ranges from 83% to 100% over a mean follow-up of 7 to 29 months.[18,26-29] Stent-graft compression, deformation, and fracture and stenosis from intimal hyperplasia have been reported and may limit the applicability of stent-graft placement in this location.[26,29-31] For these reasons, open surgical repair remains the preferred approach for good-risk patients with subclavian aneurysms.

Another innovative approach that is minimally invasive and avoids placement of a stent-graft combines coil embolization of the subclavian artery aneurysm and carotid-subclavian bypass.[34] Complete exclusion of the subclavian aneurysm is facilitated by ligation of the subclavian artery proximal to the distal anastomosis of the carotid-subclavian bypass. These procedures can be staged or combined in an operating room equipped with high-resolution imaging equipment. As with stent-graft placement, care must be taken to preserve flow in the vertebral artery if the contralateral vertebral artery is inadequate.

■ SUBCLAVIAN-AXILLARY ARTERY ANEURYSM: POST-STENOTIC DILATATION FROM THORACIC OUTLET COMPRESSION

Subclavian-axillary artery aneurysms are encountered most frequently in younger patients and seem to be more common in women. Although the first case of upper extremity ischemic complications associated with a cervical rib was reported by Hodgson in 1815, it is not clear that the presence of an underlying subclavian-axillary artery aneurysm was recognized.[35] Mayo,[36] in 1831, described a subclavian aneurysm in association with thoracic outlet syndrome caused by exostosis of the first rib. A cervical rib causing compression of the subclavian artery with resulting ischemia of the arm was reported in 1861 by Coote,[37] who successfully performed the first decompressive operation by removing the cervical rib.

In 1916, Halsted[38] reported 27 cases of cervical rib in association with subclavian artery aneurysm and, based on experimental observation in dogs, hypothesized the rheologic mechanisms leading to post-stenotic dilatation

and aneurysm formation. Symonds[39] showed thromboembolic complications emanating from cervical rib compression of the subclavian artery in 1927; he reported two cases of contralateral hemiplegia from retrograde embolization in the carotid territory. In 1934, Lewis and Pickering[40] described the much more frequent occurrence of upper extremity thromboembolic complications. The first case of arterial reconstruction for treatment of the thromboembolic complications from cervical rib was described by Schein and colleagues[41] in 1956, who replaced the subclavian artery with a homograft.

Aneurysms of the distal subclavian artery and proximal axillary artery almost always are associated with cervical ribs.[10,42] Rarely, anomalous first ribs, nonunion of the clavicle, and other anatomic abnormalities of the thoracic outlet have been associated with subclavian-axillary aneurysms (see Chapter 95).[43-46] Although cervical ribs are estimated to occur in 0.6% of the population,[47] most are asymptomatic, and arterial lesions are uncommon. In reviewing 716 patients with cervical ribs, Halsted[38] found 27 cases (3.8%) of associated subclavian aneurysms. Six of these patients (0.8%) had gangrene of the fingers. Because cervical ribs are bilateral in 50% to 80% of individuals with this anomaly,[47,48] subclavian-axillary aneurysms in association with cervical ribs also may be bilateral.[49]

Women may be more susceptible to arterial complications from cervical ribs (Fig. 106-2). A review of the literature shows a female predominance among reported cases.

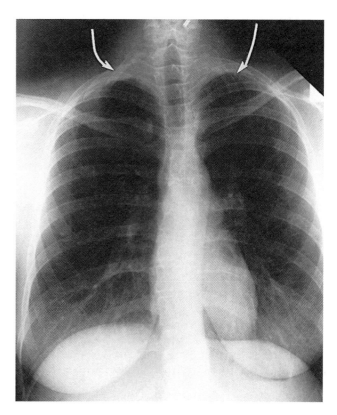

FIGURE 106-2 Bilateral, complete cervical ribs *(curved arrows)* in a young woman. Only the right cervical rib was associated with arterial dilatation and complications (complete thrombosis of the subclavian artery, as seen in the arteriogram of this patient, shown in Figure 106-5).

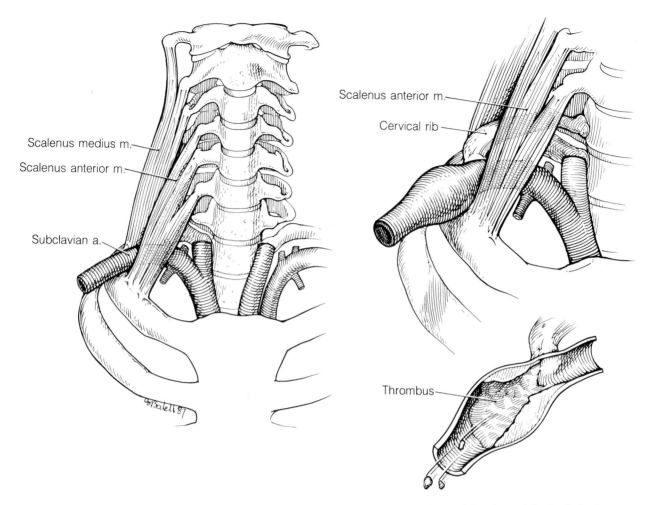

FIGURE 106-3 Pathologic anatomy of a cervical rib giving rise to subclavian-axillary aneurysm with mural thrombus and distal embolization.

This predominance may be because cervical ribs are more common in women.[47] The right-sided predominance of arterial complications is also evident, perhaps because more frequent muscular activity with the dominant upper extremity leads to earlier and more pronounced changes in the artery on that side.

Cervical ribs may compress the subclavian artery at the point where the vessel crosses the first rib (Fig. 106-3). This is most often the case with complete cervical ribs that join the first rib lateral to the subclavian artery.[44] In this region, the anterior end of the rib may unite with the first rib by a fibrous band, a diarthrodial joint, or a synostosis.[44,50] The resulting upward, medial, and anterior displacement of the subclavian artery against the tendinous portion of the scalenus anterior muscle causes trauma to the vessel by extrinsic compression and angulation. Post-stenotic dilatation leads to aneurysmal changes, which begin in the distal subclavian artery and extend into the proximal axillary artery. Intraluminal thrombus, engendered by aneurysm formation and intimal damage, may become dislodged and embolize distally (Fig. 106-4). In some cases, the aneurysm may completely thrombose, and retrograde propagation may result in emboli in the vertebral circulation and, on the right side, in the common carotid artery (Fig. 106-5).[44,51,52]

Central neurologic sequelae can result from vertebral or carotid artery involvement.

Patients with subclavian-axillary aneurysms associated with thoracic outlet syndrome may present with acute or chronic symptoms of upper extremity ischemia. Occasionally, Raynaud's phenomenon may occur.[46] In some cases, neurologic symptoms typical of thoracic outlet obstruction predominate. On physical examination, a cervical rib may be palpated in the supraclavicular fossa along with the prominent subclavian artery pulsation that results from the anterior and upward displacement of this vessel. A loud, harsh subclavian bruit is usually present, unless the artery is thrombosed, and a thrill is common. Patients with cervical ribs or other symptoms of thoracic outlet syndrome who present with any ischemic symptoms need expeditious and complete upper extremity angiography. The urgency of diagnosis is mandated by the imminent threat of limb or digit loss, a point emphasized by most authors.[46,53-59]

Surgical treatment of subclavian-axillary aneurysms associated with thoracic outlet syndrome depends on the size of the aneurysm, the symptomatic status of the patient, and the presence and extent of thromboembolic complications.[48] In asymptomatic individuals who are found to have a cervical rib with a prominent supraclavicular

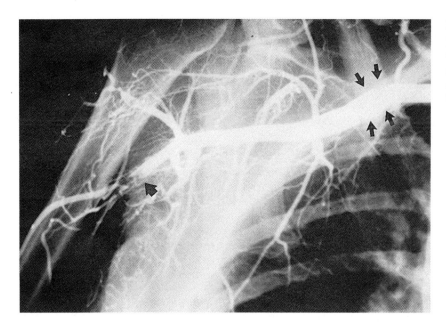

FIGURE 106-4 Embolic occlusion *(single arrow)* of the distal axillary and brachial arteries just proximal to the origin of the profunda brachii (deep brachial) artery. The source of the embolus was an unimpressive-appearing subclavian-axillary aneurysm *(arrows)* associated with a cervical rib. The operative specimen of this resected artery is shown in Figure 106-7, which reveals the mural thrombus.

pulse and bruit, arteriography, CT angiography, or magnetic resonance angiography is recommended to assess the degree of post-stenotic dilatation of the subclavian artery (Fig. 106-6). Duplex ultrasonography also may allow partial visualization of this portion of the subclavian artery and has been used to document dilatation.[60] If significant dilatation is present, and the patient has an acceptable surgical risk, thoracic outlet decompression with cervical rib removal is indicated. In the early stage, if only mild arterial dilatation is present, relief of compression by removal of the rib may result in return to normal arterial caliber.[48] It more often occurs that an aneurysm is already present at initial evaluation, and arterial repair also is indicated (see later).

Although it is unknown how many patients in the asymptomatic stage would go on to develop complications if untreated, the natural history of the disorder seems to be progressive with the eventual development of thromboembolic complications. Because the first manifestations may threaten limb or digit, an aggressive approach is warranted. In asymptomatic individuals with more extensive aneurysmal change (more than two times the normal artery diameter), repair of the subclavian aneurysm in addition to cervical rib removal usually should be performed. Scher and associates[42] observed that these aneurysms frequently contain thrombus, even in asymptomatic patients, and it is unlikely that regression to normal size would occur because of irreversible wall changes. Others have reported delayed embolic events occurring months to years after removal of a cervical rib without repair of the dilated subclavian artery.[46,59] Operative inspection of the artery to assess its size accurately and, in selected cases, its luminal aspect to look for mural irregularity and thrombus may be useful to determine the need for repair.[56,60] Evidence of thromboembolism mandates repair of the aneurysm.

In patients with thromboembolic complications associated with a cervical rib, the subclavian artery aneurysm

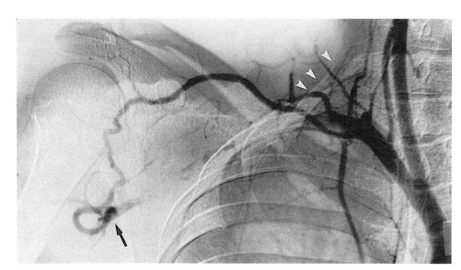

FIGURE 106-5 Arteriogram of the patient whose chest film is shown in Figure 106-2. There is complete occlusion of the subclavian artery with filling of the distal axillary artery *(arrow)* via the suprascapular branch of the subclavian artery to the circumflex scapular branch of the subscapular artery collateral pathway. The cervical rib is outlined by the *arrowheads*. Continued retrograde thrombosis of the subclavian artery would render the right vertebral and common carotid arteries susceptible to thromboembolism.

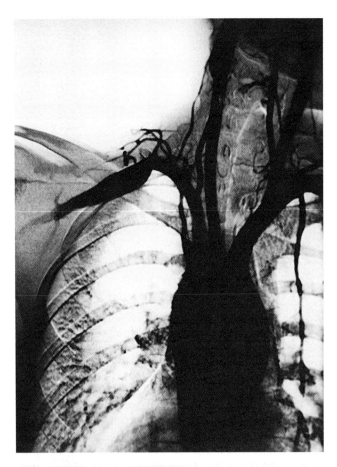

FIGURE 106-6 Large, asymptomatic subclavian-axillary aneurysm with a cervical rib in a young woman in whom a pulsatile right supraclavicular mass was found incidentally on physical examination. A harsh bruit and thrill also were present.

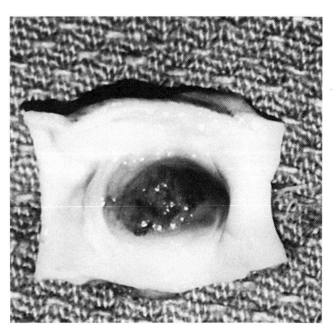

FIGURE 106-7 Mural thrombus within a minimally dilated segment of the subclavian artery distal to the cervical rib in a patient who presented with upper extremity rest pain and digital tip necrosis. The arteriogram of this patient is shown in Figure 106-4.

should be repaired regardless of its size. The extent of intimal damage and thrombus in the aneurysm frequently is underestimated by angiography (see Fig. 106-4); invariably, mural thrombus is found in the aneurysm, usually along the inferior wall (Fig. 106-7). Rarely, vascular reconstruction can be accomplished by proximal and distal mobilization of the ends of the artery and end-to-end anastomosis. Most cases require a short interposition vein or prosthetic graft, however. In most cases, small subclavian aneurysms are resected, and the graft is interposed. Occasionally, large or adherent aneurysms may be opened but left in place and treated with the graft inclusion technique. In view of the relatively young age of affected patients and the need for long-term graft function, a proximal saphenous vein of suitable size would seem to be the optimal conduit for this reconstruction.[46] Supraclavicular and infraclavicular incisions are used to mobilize the distal subclavian and proximal axillary arteries.[42] Resection of the clavicle is unnecessary. If present, the cervical rib is resected through the supraclavicular incision by standard techniques.[50]

Key points in effectively relieving arterial compression include (1) complete resection of bony, cartilaginous, and fibrous parts of the anterior portion of the cervical rib where it attaches to or articulates with the first rib and (2) complete resection of the scalenus anterior muscle at the scalene

tubercle on the first rib. Resection of most of the posterior portion of the cervical rib also should be performed so that it is free of the brachial plexus, which is usually draped over the rib. Most patients with arterial complications of cervical ribs do not have neurologic symptoms of the thoracic outlet syndrome, and complete resection of the cervical rib along with arterial reconstruction is all that is needed.[48] Although concomitant first rib resection has been advocated by some authors with either the transaxillary or the supraclavicular approach,[60,61] this rarely should be necessary. Adequate decompression of the artery and the brachial plexus almost always can be accomplished by near-complete resection of the cervical rib and scalenus anterior muscle. In the less common cases in which no cervical rib is present, however, first rib resection is advisable to decompress the thoracic outlet adequately.

Balloon catheter thromboembolectomy is necessary to restore patency to recently occluded distal arteries crucial to limb viability. This procedure may require separate exposure of the brachial and forearm arteries to effect complete thrombectomy. Many patients have experienced chronic repetitive embolic episodes, and the occluding thrombi may be partially organized and impossible to extract. In such cases, vein graft bypasses to arm and forearm arteries may be necessary to relieve critical ischemia and to promote healing of digital tip gangrene and ischemic ulcerations. Because of the inferior patency of prosthetic bypasses in this more distal region, vein grafts are required for optimal results.[46,62] Adjunctive cervicodorsal sympathectomy has been advocated in the past, but most experts believe that this is unnecessary and that the emphasis should be placed on adequate arterial reconstruction.[42,46,60] Sympathectomy might be considered for selected patients in whom vasospastic symptoms are prominent, and complete restoration of pulsatile flow at the level of the hand is not possible.

ANEURYSM OF ABERRANT SUBCLAVIAN ARTERY: KOMMERELL'S DIVERTICULUM

Aneurysms of an aberrant subclavian artery are encountered most frequently in adults of either sex older than age 50 years. An aberrant right subclavian artery arising from the proximal portion of the descending thoracic aorta is the most common congenital anomaly of the aortic arch.[63] Most patients with this anomaly are asymptomatic, and the aberrant subclavian artery is of no clinical consequence. Rarely the vessel compresses the esophagus against the posterior trachea and gives rise to difficulty in swallowing, a condition termed *dysphagia lusoria*.[64] Even more rarely, degenerative aneurysmal change occurs in the anomalous vessel. This condition has been termed *Kommerell's diverticulum* after Kommerell, who in 1936 described a diverticulum of the aorta at the origin of the anomalous subclavian artery.[63] McCallen and Schaff[65] first called attention to the clinical significance of aneurysmal change in an anomalous right subclavian artery in a report of 1956. The largest experience to date with this condition was reported by Kieffer and associates,[66] who surgically treated 33 adults with aberrant subclavian arteries, 17 of whom had a Kommerell's diverticulum or aneurysmal change of the thoracic aorta at the origin of the aberrant subclavian artery.

Patients with aneurysm of an aberrant right subclavian artery may present with dysphagia from esophageal compression, dyspnea and coughing from tracheal compression, chest pain from expansion or rupture, or symptoms of right upper extremity ischemia secondary to thromboembolism. Death from rupture has been reported and seems to be unrelated to the size of the aneurysm.[63] Many reported cases were in asymptomatic patients whose aneurysm was found on chest radiography and interpreted as a superior mediastinal mass. Chest CT can detect this condition noninvasively, but angiography is necessary to plan surgical treatment. Approximately one fifth of reported patients with this anomaly have an associated abdominal aortic aneurysm.[63]

Because of the propensity of these aneurysms to cause symptoms, and because of the possibility of lethal rupture, resection of the aneurysmal artery with vascular reconstruction of the subclavian artery is recommended. This repair may be accomplished via a right or left posterolateral thoracotomy[63,67,68] or a median sternotomy.[66] The subclavian artery is reconstructed by an interposition arterial prosthesis anastomosed proximally to the ascending arch of the aorta. Alternatively a left posterolateral thoracotomy for proximal resection of the aneurysm coupled with a right supraclavicular incision for reconstruction of the subclavian artery by end-to-side anastomosis to the right common carotid artery has been described.[69] A staged approach with right carotid-subclavian bypass or transposition (end-subclavian to side-carotid) preceding left thoracotomy and aneurysm resection with oversewing of the origin from the aortic arch is attractive because the risk of cerebral and right upper extremity embolization is minimized.[70] Extraanatomic reconstruction of the right subclavian artery also has been described.[71] Because it is necessary to resect the aneurysmal vessel near its origin from the aorta, the modified extrathoracic approach alone, described for treatment of dysphagia lusoria, would not be effective.[64]

AXILLARY ARTERY ANEURYSMS

Except for rare congenital causes,[7,72] axillary aneurysms are caused by blunt or penetrating trauma (Fig. 106-8).[73] They occur typically in young men. Crutch-induced blunt trauma producing aneurysmal dilatation of the axillary artery occurs in older patients and was first described by Rob and Standeven[74] in 1956, with subsequent cases reported by Brooks and Fowler[75] and Abbott and Darling.[76] Pathologic examination of these aneurysms reveals markedly thickened walls and wrinkled, roughened intima. Instead of the typical intimal changes of atherosclerosis, severe fragmentation of medial elastic fibers and marked periadventitial fibrosis are present, suggesting chronic trauma.[76] Thrombus, usually loosely adherent to the damaged intima, may become

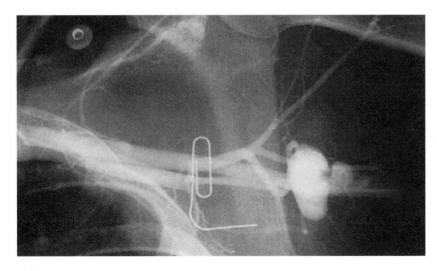

FIGURE 106-8 False aneurysm of the axillary artery as a result of a stab injury.

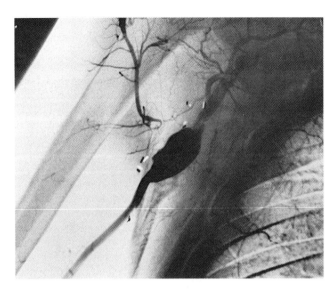

FIGURE 106-9 Aneurysmal dilatation of an interposition brachial vein graft used to reconstruct the axillary artery at the time of penetrating trauma 4 years previously.

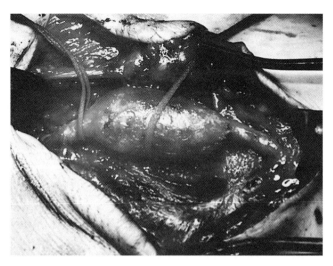

FIGURE 106-10 Operative dissection of the aneurysmal interposition brachial vein graft shown in Figure 106-9.

dislodged by further trauma from crutches and is the source of acute, chronic, or repetitive emboli. In many cases, the aneurysm thromboses completely when symptoms begin. The most common presenting complaints relate to upper extremity ischemia, and these aneurysms should be suspected when a patient who has been using crutches for a prolonged period presents with an absent brachial pulse.[76]

False aneurysms of the axillary artery usually occur with penetrating trauma, but also may occur with blunt trauma in the form of humeral fractures and anterior dislocation of the shoulder.[77-79] In the latter instance, the mechanism may be avulsion of the tethered thoracoacromial, subscapular, or circumflex humeral vessels at the time of dislocation. These aneurysms often present late as chronic false aneurysms because diagnosis is delayed. This is especially true after blunt trauma, when lack of recognition is fostered by the difficulty of obtaining an adequate examination of the axillary artery because of the surrounding bone and muscles of the shoulder and the considerable pain and muscle spasm that prevent arm abduction to allow examination of the axilla.[77] Because of the excellent collateral circulation in this area, distal perfusion may be adequate despite extensive axillary artery injury. These aneurysms can lead to serious and permanent neurologic disability, however, because of hemorrhage into the axillary sheath and compression of the brachial plexus.

Because of these possibilities, arteriography should be considered in all cases of significant penetrating trauma to the shoulder or arm, blunt trauma with abnormal pulse examination, and blunt trauma with normal pulse examination but brachial plexus palsy because the likelihood of concomitant vascular injury is high in these cases. Duplex ultrasonography also may allow accurate diagnosis. Arteriography, CT angiography, or magnetic resonance angiography should be performed in patients with blunt trauma to the shoulder or axilla with a normal neurovascular examination initially but with signs of brachial plexus

neuropathy on follow-up. The presence of an expanding chronic false aneurysm should be suspected in such cases.[77]

Surgical treatment of axillary artery aneurysms is straightforward and involves resection of the aneurysm and interposition of a vein graft. The surgeon must be careful to protect the brachial plexus and its major branches during dissection of the aneurysm. Prosthetic reconstruction of the axillary artery has been successful; however, because of the superior patency of vein grafts in upper extremity reconstructions,[62] these are preferred. Occasionally, an adjacent segment of the axillary or brachial vein has been used to reconstruct the artery (Fig. 106-9). This vein is extremely thin walled, however, and itself may become aneurysmal with time (Figs. 106-10 and 106-11). For this reason, a segment of saphenous vein is the conduit of choice.

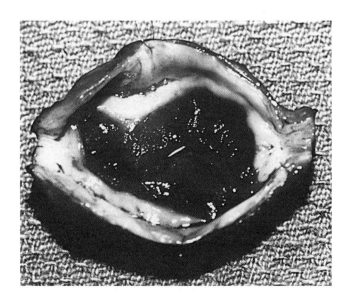

FIGURE 106-11 Mural thrombus lining the aneurysmal interposition brachial vein graft shown in Figures 106-9 and 106-10.

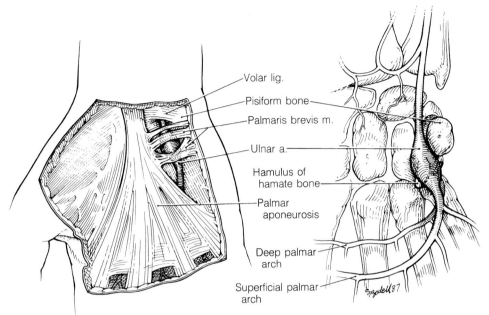

FIGURE 106-12 Pathologic anatomy of the hypothenar hammer syndrome. The distal ulnar artery is particularly vulnerable to external trauma in the 2-cm distance between its exit point from Guyon's canal (the roof of which is the volar carpal ligament) and the point where the artery dives under the tough palmar aponeurosis. In this short distance, the ulnar artery courses on top of the hook of the hamate bone and is covered incompletely by the thin palmaris brevis muscle and skin and subcutaneous tissue.

Endovascular stent-grafts also have been used successfully to treat these aneurysms.[80] Case series of endovascular treatment are small, however, with limited follow-up. Endovascular stent-grafting for axillary aneurysms may be an alternative to surgical treatment in patients with major comorbidities and high surgical risk.[80]

■ ULNAR ARTERY ANEURYSM: THE HYPOTHENAR HAMMER SYNDROME

Ulnar artery aneurysms are most commonly seen in men younger than age 50, but they can occur in older patients and in women. Although rare, ulnar artery aneurysms are one of the most common causes of ischemia limited solely to the digits.[81,82] It is important to recognize this disorder because ischemia arising from these aneurysms is frequently correctable and, if untreated, may lead to digital necrosis and severe disability. Diagnosis and treatment are all the more urgent when one considers that most individuals with the hypothenar hammer syndrome are middle-aged working men whose livelihood depends on using their dominant hand, which is invariably involved.

The first reported case occurred in a Roman coachman and was described by Guattani in 1771.[83] Middleton reported 16 cases in 1993,[84] Smith described 35 cases in 1962,[85] and Pineda and colleagues reviewed 53 cases in 1985.[86] All authors have identified trauma to the hand as the cause of this disorder, and in 1970 Conn and associates[87] coined the term *hypothenar hammer syndrome.*

The syndrome develops in people who use the palms of their hands for pushing, pounding, or twisting. The practice of repeatedly striking with the dominant hand is common in many industries. The hypothenar hammer syndrome has been described most often in mechanics, automobile repairmen, lathe operators, pipe fitters, tire braiders, carpenters, and machinists. The disorder also has been described in

individuals with hobbies (sculpting) and athletic pursuits (volleyball, skiing, and karate) that involve repetitive trauma to the hand.[88-94]

The incidence is probably much higher than one would suspect from the number of patients reported in the literature (<150 cases). Little and Ferguson[95] used noninvasive means to screen a population at risk. Among 79 automobile repairmen who habitually used their hands as a hammer, 11 (14%) showed some evidence of digital ischemia and were deemed to have the hypothenar hammer syndrome. Duration of employment was positively correlated with the syndrome, and there was no evidence of the syndrome in workers who did not use their hands as hammers.[95] Many authors have stressed the importance of accuracy of diagnosis and its relationship to work activities because of insurance and workers' compensation considerations.[87,95,96]

The pathophysiology is based on the unique vascular anatomy of the hand (Fig. 106-12).[85] The ulnar artery and nerve enter the hand by traversing Guyon's canal, bounded medially (ulnarly) by the pisiform bone, dorsally by the transverse carpal ligament, and superficially by the volar carpal ligament. Within this tunnel, the artery and the nerve each bifurcate into deep and superficial branches. The deep branch of the artery along with the motor branch of the ulnar nerve penetrates the hypothenar muscle mass, where the artery becomes the deep palmar arch. The superficial division of the ulnar artery remains superficial to the hypothenar musculature and penetrates the palmar aponeurosis to form the superficial palmar arch, the main blood supply to the fingers via the common palmar digital arteries. Over this short distance of approximately 2 cm between the distal margin of Guyon's canal and the palmar aponeurosis, the artery lies just anterior to the hook of the hamate bone and is covered only by the slight palmaris brevis muscle, overlying skin, and subcutaneous tissue.

With little protection above and the bony floor below, the artery is vulnerable to trauma. Fixation of the artery by the course of its deep branch allows little movement to escape blunt forces. In addition, the hook of the hamate may function as an anvil, accentuating the untoward results of repeated trauma. Similar vulnerable conditions exist for a short segment of the superficial branch of the radial artery at the base of the thenar eminence, a much less frequent site of vessel trauma.[85] In an extensive study of arterial patterns of the hand, Coleman and Anson[97] found that in 78% of dissections, the superficial palmar arch was complete. In approximately three fourths of these, the ulnar artery was the dominant component. In 22% of dissections, the arch was incomplete, and there were diverse contributions to digital blood supply from the radial, ulnar, and, rarely, a persistent median artery. These anatomic variations are responsible for the diverse distribution of digital ischemic signs and symptoms in patients with the hypothenar hammer syndrome.

Trauma to the ulnar artery in this vulnerable area causes mural degeneration.[98] Damage to the intima alone results in thrombosis, whereas injury of the media leads to a true arterial aneurysm. Thrombosis of the ulnar artery or aneurysm is associated with downstream embolization. Pathologic studies of ulnar artery aneurysms have documented organizing thrombus adherent to the intimal surface and absence or severe fragmentation of the internal elastic lamina.[99] Fibrosis and focal intramural hemorrhage also are present, along with variable amounts of acute and chronic inflammation.[86] Although most authors have described true aneurysms with no loss in continuity of the arterial wall, some have reported false aneurysms of the ulnar artery, usually in association with penetrating trauma.[100-102]

The traumatic etiology has been questioned in a report that hypothesizes that the hypothenar hammer syndrome stems from fibromuscular dysplasia of the ulnar arteries.[103] In this plausible scenario, preexisting abnormalities of the vessel make it vulnerable to traumatic injury. Many of the histopathologic findings, including intimal and medial hyperplasia and internal elastic lamina disruption, are characteristic of fibromuscular dysplasia. Angiographic findings of alternating areas of stenosis and dilatation (see Fig. 106-18A) also suggest fibromuscular dysplasia. The striking incidence of bilateral abnormalities (92% in one series of patients undergoing bilateral hand angiography)[103] in patients with unilateral symptoms in the dominant hand also suggests the presence of an underlying arteriopathy.

Although the syndrome most often follows chronic, repetitive trauma, it may result from a single, acute episode.[86] The syndrome usually has a slow, insidious onset.[82] At the time of injury, many patients report episodes of severe lacerating pain over the hypothenar eminence. Typically, dull aching pain and tenderness are present over the hypothenar area after these episodes, and ischemic symptoms develop weeks or months later. A variety of ischemic signs and symptoms may be present, including pain, cold sensation, paresthesias, cyanosis, and mottling of the digits. The fourth and fifth fingers are most frequently symptomatic, but any digit or any combination of digits may be involved with the exception of the thumb, which is invariably spared because of its radial blood supply. *Raynaud's phenomenon* may be the chief presenting symptom and is distinguished from "typical" Raynaud's phenomenon in that it is unilateral, the thumb is not involved, and there is an absence of the classic triphasic

color changes[86] because reactive hyperemia would not be expected to occur in the presence of fixed arterial obstruction.

On physical examination, in addition to the ischemic changes of the fingers, localized tenderness over the hypothenar eminence may be present with a pulsatile or nonpulsatile mass. A hypothenar callus also may be present. Atrophy and softening of the distal finger pads, ischemic fingertip ulcers, and subungual hemorrhages are sometimes evident. An abnormal Allen's test suggests occlusion or incomplete development of the superficial palmar arch or the distal ulnar artery and is present in most patients with the hypothenar hammer syndrome.[86] Some patients may have an ulnar sensory deficit due to compression of the superficial ulnar sensory branch by the aneurysm.[104]

Noninvasive studies helpful in diagnosis include digital plethysmography, Doppler-derived digital pressures, and duplex ultrasonography. Angiography is mandatory for patients thought to have this disorder, and the angiographic features are virtually pathognomonic (Fig. 106-13),[105-107] including irregularity, aneurysmal change, or occlusion of the ulnar artery segment overlying the hook of the hamate bone with occasional extension of these changes into the superficial palmar arch, embolic occlusion of the proper digital arteries in the distribution of the ulnar artery, and

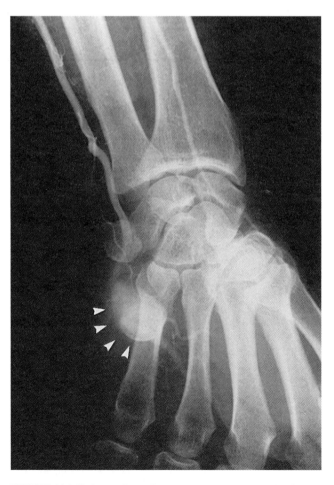

FIGURE 106-13 Large distal ulnar artery aneurysm *(arrowheads)* in a middle-aged man who frequently used his hand as a hammer in his work as an automobile repairman.

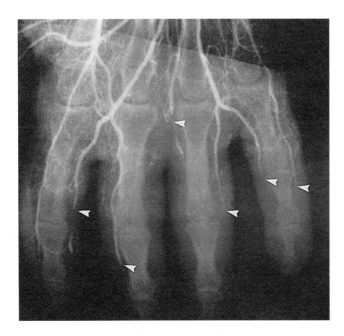

FIGURE 106-14 Delayed magnification views of the hand after papaverine injection, showing multiple embolic occlusions *(arrowheads)* of the digital arteries in the patient whose initial arteriogram (see Fig. 106-15) showed only occlusion of the ulnar artery.

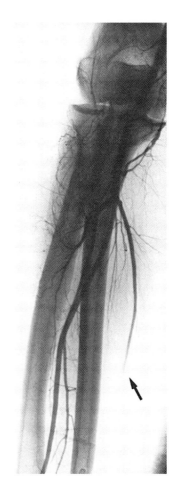

FIGURE 106-15 Initial arteriogram in a patient presenting with signs of small vessel embolism in the digits ("blue finger" syndrome). The arteriogram shows ulnar artery occlusion *(arrow)*.

normal proximal and contralateral arteries (Fig. 106-14). Magnification views and pharmacoangiography are helpful in defining these features.[107] Frequently, distal ulnar artery occlusion is the only finding on initial arteriography (Fig. 106-15). Proximal angiography of the innominate, subclavian, and axillary arteries is important to rule out potential embolic sources.

Surgical therapy for the hypothenar hammer syndrome has included cervicodorsal sympathectomy, excision of the ulnar artery aneurysm with ligation of the ulnar artery, and aneurysmectomy with microsurgical reconstruction of the ulnar artery by reanastomosis or interposition vein graft (Fig. 106-16).[86] Although it is not clear which of these approaches is superior, most authors recommend microsurgical vascular reconstruction because it eliminates the thromboembolic source, removes the painful aneurysmal mass that may cause ulnar nerve compression, adds the vasodilatory benefits of a local periarterial sympathectomy, and improves digital perfusion.[81,82,98,108-111] Resection of the aneurysm and placement of a vein interposition graft is the optimal treatment for either a patent ulnar aneurysm with clinical or radiographic evidence of distal embolization or a thrombosed ulnar aneurysm that has resulted in profound digital ischemia (Fig. 106-17).

Patients with minimal symptoms and no threat of digit loss after ulnar aneurysm thrombosis may not require revascularization.[70,112,113] Adjunctive preoperative thrombolytic therapy has been reported with excellent results (Fig. 106-18).[114,115] The principal benefit of thrombolytic therapy is the restoration of patency to digital arteries, reducing adverse sequelae and improving distal runoff, theoretically enhancing patency of the reconstruction. When the ulnar artery and superficial palmar arch are chronically thrombosed and thrombolytic therapy is unsuccessful in restoring

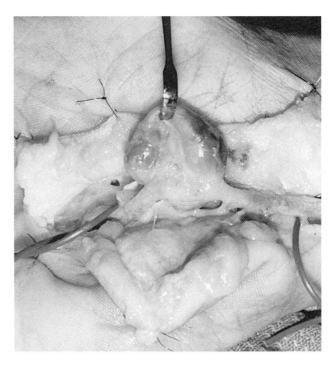

FIGURE 106-16 Operative exposure of an embolizing ulnar artery aneurysm in the right hand treated with resection and vein graft replacement.

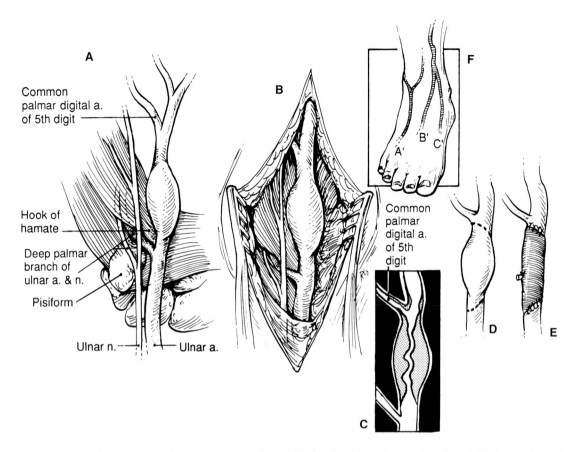

FIGURE 106-17 A, Detail of post-traumatic ulnar artery aneurysm, located distal to the pisiform bone at the wrist and distal to the deep palmar branch of the ulnar artery, but typically proximal to or just involving the common digital artery of the fifth digit. **B,** Operative exposure via longitudinal incision directly over the palpable ulnar artery pulse. **C,** Schematic of the arteriographic appearance of fusiform post-traumatic ulnar aneurysms. Frequently the artery appears irregular or serpiginous, characteristically described as having a "corkscrew" appearance. **D,** Repair usually involves excision of the aneurysm, with interposition repair with reversed autogenous vein. **E** and **F,** Ideally the dorsal foot vein provides the appropriate-sized match.

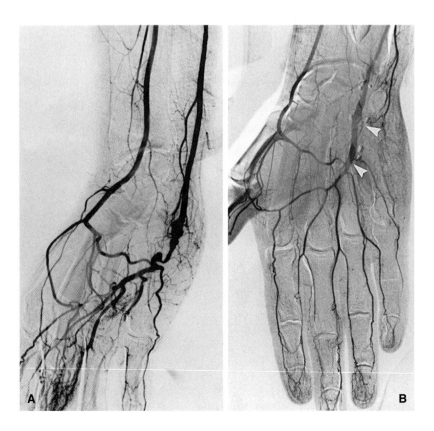

FIGURE 106-18 A, Urokinase was infused regionally for 24 hours in same patient whose initial arteriograms are shown in Figures 106-14 and 106-15. Near-complete lysis of thromboemboli restored patency to the distal ulnar artery, the superficial palmar arch, and some of the common digital arteries in addition to showing the underlying ulnar artery aneurysm. **B,** A repeated arteriogram in the same patient after microvascular resection of the ulnar artery aneurysm and reconstruction with an interposition vein graft *(arrowheads)* harvested from the forearm. Complete circulation to the digits has been restored, and all digital arteries have been cleared of thrombus by the adjunctive preoperative use of regional urokinase infusion.

flow, medical therapy with calcium channel blockers may be helpful if vasospastic symptoms are prominent.[86] All patients with this disorder should be counseled to stop smoking and to avoid further hand trauma.

■ REFERENCES

1. Dent TL, Ernst CB: Multiple arteriosclerotic arterial aneurysms. Arch Surg 105:338, 1972.
2. Hobson RW II, Sarkaria J, O'Donnell JA, et al: Atherosclerotic aneurysms of the subclavian artery. Surgery 85:368, 1979.
3. Bonardelli S, Vettoretto N, Tiberio GAM, et al: Right subclavian artery aneurysms of fibrodysplastic origin: Two case reports and review of literature. J Vasc Surg 33:174, 2001.
4. Bjork VO: Aneurysm and occlusion of the right subclavian artery. Acta Chir Scand 356(Suppl):103, 1965.
5. Persaud V: Subclavian artery aneurysm and idiopathic cystic medionecrosis. Br Heart J 30:436, 1968.
6. Hara M, Bransford RM: Aneurysm of the subclavian artery associated with contiguous pulmonary tuberculosis. J Thorac Cardiovasc Surg 46:256, 1963.
7. Applebaum RE, Caniano DA, Sun C-C, et al: Synchronous left subclavian and axillary artery aneurysms associated with melorheostosis. Surgery 99:249, 1986.
8. Dobbins WO: Bilateral calcified subclavian arterial aneurysms in a young adult male. N Engl J Med 265:537, 1961.
9. Pairolero PC, Walls JT, Payne WS, et al: Subclavian-axillary artery aneurysms. Surgery 90:757, 1981.
10. Hobson RW II, Israel MR, Lynch TG: Axillosubclavian arterial aneurysms. In Bergan JJ, Yao JST (eds): Aneurysms: Diagnosis and Treatment. New York, Grune & Stratton, 1982, p 435.
11. McCollum CH, Da Gama AD, Noon GP, et al: Aneurysm of the subclavian artery. J Cardiovasc Surg 20:159, 1979.
12. Temple LJ: Aneurysm of the first part of the left subclavian artery: A review of the literature and a case history. J Thorac Surg 19:412, 1950.
13. Halsted WS: Ligation of the first portion of the left subclavian artery and excision of a subclavio-axillary aneurysm. Johns Hopkins Hosp Bull 24:93, 1892.
14. Muller GP: Subclavian aneurysm with report of a case. Ann Surg 101:568, 1935.
15. Elefteriades JA, Kay HA, Stansel HC Jr, et al: Extra-anatomical reconstruction for bilateral intrathoracic subclavian artery aneurysms. Ann Thorac Surg 35:188, 1983.
16. Becker GJ, Benenati JF, Zemel G, et al: Percutaneous placement of a balloon-expandable intraluminal graft for life-threatening subclavian arterial hemorrhage. J Vasc Interv Radiol 2:225, 1991.
17. Criado E, Marston WA, Ligush J, et al: Endovascular repair of peripheral aneurysms, pseudoaneurysms, and arteriovenous fistulas. Ann Vasc Surg 11:256, 1997.
18. Marin ML, Veith FJ, Panetta TF, et al: Transluminally placed endovascular stented graft repair for arterial trauma. J Vasc Surg 20:466, 1994.
19. May J, White G, Waugh R, et al: Transluminal placement of a prosthetic graft-stent device for treatment of subclavian artery aneurysm. J Vasc Surg 18:1056, 1993.
20. Davidian M, Kee ST, Kato N, et al: Aneurysm of an aberrant right subclavian artery: Treatment with PTFE covered stent-graft. J Vasc Surg 28:335, 1998.
21. Bartorelli AL, Trabattoni D, Agrifoglio M, et al: Endovascular repair of iatrogenic subclavian artery perforations using the Hemobahn stent-graft. J Endovasc Ther 8:417, 2001.
22. Phipp LH, Scott DJA, Kessel D, et al: Subclavian stents and stent-grafts: Cause for concern? J Endovasc Surg 6:223, 1999.
23. Marston WA, Criado E, Mauro MA, et al: Transbrachial endovascular exclusion of the axillary artery pseudoaneurysms with PTFE-covered stents. J Endovasc Surg 2:172, 1995.
24. Szeimies U, Kueffer G, Stoeckelhuber B, et al: Successful exclusion of subclavian aneurysms with covered nitinol stents. Cardiovasc Intervent Radiol 21:246, 1998.
25. Marin ML, Veith FJ, Cynamon J, et al: Initial experience with transluminally placed endovascular grafts for the treatment of complex vascular lesions. Ann Surg 222:449, 1995.
26. Patel AV, Marin ML, Veith FJ, et al: Endovascular graft repair of penetrating subclavian artery injuries. J Endovasc Surg 3:382, 1996.
27. du Toit DF, Strauss DC, Blaszczyk M, et al: Endovascular treatment of penetrating thoracic outlet arterial injuries. Eur J Vasc Endovasc Surg 19:489, 2000.
28. Hilfiker PR, Razavi MK, Kee ST, et al: Stent-graft therapy for subclavian artery aneurysms and fistulas: Single-center midterm results. J Vasc Interv Radiol 11:578, 2000.
29. Ohki T, Veith FJ, Kraas C, et al: Endovascular therapy for upper extremity injury. Semin Vasc Surg 11:106, 1998.
30. Mathur A, Dorros G, Iyer SS, et al: Palmaz stent compression in patients following carotid artery stenting. Cathet Cardiovasc Diagn 41:137, 1997.
31. Rosenfield K, Schainfeld R, Pieczek A, et al: Restenosis of endovascular stents from stent compression. J Am Coll Cardiol 29:328, 1997.
32. Tepe G, Duda SH, Hanke H, et al: Covered stents for prevention of restenosis: Experimental and clinical results with different stent designs. Invest Radiol 31:223, 1996.
33. Schoder M, Cejna M, Holzenbein T, et al: Elective and emergent endovascular treatment of subclavian artery aneurysms and injuries. J Endovasc Ther 10:58, 2003.
34. Bush RL, Lin PH, Najibi S, et al: Coil embolization combined with carotid-subclavian bypass for treatment of subclavian artery aneurysm. J Endovasc Ther 9:308, 2002.
35. Hodgson J: Diseases of the Arteries and Veins. London, T Underwood, 1815, p 262.
36. Mayo H: Exostosis of the first rib with strong pulsations of the subclavian artery. Lond Med Phys J (NS) 11:40, 1831.
37. Coote H: Pressure on the axillary vessels and nerve by an exostosis from a cervical rib: Interference with the circulation of the arm: Removal of the rib in exostosis: Recovery. Med Times Gaz 2:108, 1861.
38. Halsted WS: An experimental study of circumscribed dilation of an artery immediately distal to a partially occluding band, and its bearing on the dilation of the subclavian artery observed in certain cases of cervical rib. J Exp Med 24:271, 1916.
39. Symonds CP: Two cases of thrombosis of subclavian artery, with contralateral hemiplegia of sudden onset, probably embolic. Brain 50:259, 1927.
40. Lewis T, Pickering GW: Observations upon maladies in which the blood supply to digits ceases intermittently or permanently, and upon bilateral gangrene of digits: Observations relevant to so-called "Raynaud's disease." Clin Sci 1:327, 1934.
41. Schein CJ, Haimovici H, Young H: Arterial thrombosis associated with cervical ribs: Surgical considerations. Surgery 40:428, 1956.
42. Scher LA, Veith FJ, Samson RH, et al: Vascular complications of thoracic outlet syndrome. J Vasc Surg 3:565, 1986.
43. Fidler MW, Helal B, Barwegen GMH, et al: Subclavian artery aneurysm due to costoclavicular compression. J Hand Surg 9B:282, 1984.
44. Matsumura JS, Yao JST: Thoracic outlet arterial compression: Clinical features and surgical management. Semin Vasc Surg 9:125, 1996.
45. Whelan TJ Jr: Management of vascular disease of the upper extremity. Surg Clin North Am 62:373, 1982.
46. Nehler MR, Taylor LM Jr, Moneta GL, et al: Upper extremity ischemia from subclavian artery aneurysm caused by bony abnormalities of the thoracic outlet. Arch Surg 132:527, 1997.
47. Adson AW: Cervical ribs: Symptoms, differential diagnosis and indications for section of the insertion of the scalenus anticus muscle. J Int Coll Surg 16:546, 1951.

48. Scher LA, Veith FJ, Haimovici H, et al: Staging of arterial complications of cervical rib: Guidelines for surgical management. Surgery 95:644, 1984.

49. Siu K, Ferguson I: Bilateral cervical rib and subclavian aneurysm. Aust N Z J Surg 42:245, 1973.

50. Schein CJ: A technic for cervical rib resection. Am J Surg 121:623, 1971.

51. Blank RH, Connar RG: Arterial complications associated with thoracic outlet compression syndrome. Ann Thorac Surg 17:315, 1974.

52. Fields WS, Lemak NA, Ben-Menachem Y: Thoracic outlet syndrome: Review and reference to stroke in a major league pitcher. AJR Am J Roentgenol 146:809, 1986.

53. Banis JC, Rich N, Whelan TJ Jr: Ischemia of the upper extremity due to noncardiac emboli. Am J Surg 134:131, 1977.

54. Bertelsen S, Mathiesen RR, Ohlenschlaeger HH: Vascular complications of cervical rib. Scand J Thorac Cardiovasc Surg 2:133, 1968.

55. Dorazio RA, Ezzet F: Arterial complications of the thoracic outlet syndrome. Am J Surg 138:246, 1979.

56. Judy KL, Heymann RL: Vascular complications of thoracic outlet syndrome. Am J Surg 123:521, 1972.

57. Martin J, Gaspard DJ, Johnston PW, et al: Vascular manifestations of the thoracic outlet syndrome: A surgical urgency. Arch Surg 111:779, 1976.

58. Mathes SJ, Salam AA: Subclavian artery aneurysm: Sequela of thoracic outlet syndrome. Surgery 76:506, 1974.

59. Desai Y, Robbs JV: Arterial complications of the thoracic outlet syndrome. Eur J Vasc Endovasc Surg 10:362, 1995.

60. Kieffer E: Arterial complications of thoracic outlet syndrome. In Bergan JJ, Yao JST (eds): Evaluation and Treatment of Upper and Lower Extremity Circulatory Disorders. Orlando, Fla, Grune & Stratton, 1984, p 249.

61. Fantini GA: Reserving supraclavicular first rib resection for vascular complications of thoracic outlet syndrome. Am J Surg 172:200, 1996.

62. McCarthy WJ, Flinn WR, Yao JST, et al: Result of bypass grafting for upper limb ischemia. J Vasc Surg 3:741, 1986.

63. Austin EH, Wolfe WG: Aneurysm of aberrant subclavian artery with a review of the literature. J Vasc Surg 2:571, 1985.

64. Valentine RJ, Carter DJ, Clagett GP: A modified extrathoracic approach to the treatment of dysphagia lusoria. J Vasc Surg 5:498, 1987.

65. McCallen AM, Schaff B: Aneurysm of an anomalous right subclavian artery. Radiology 66:561, 1956.

66. Kieffer E, Bahnini A, Koskas F: Aberrant subclavian artery: Surgical treatment in thirty-three adult patients. J Vasc Surg 19:100, 1994.

67. Campbell CF: Repair of an aneurysm of an aberrant retroesophageal right subclavian artery arising from Kommerell's diverticulum. J Thorac Cardiovasc Surg 62:330, 1971.

68. Hunter JA, Dye WS, Javid H, et al: Arteriosclerotic aneurysm of anomalous right subclavian artery. J Thorac Cardiovasc Surg 59:754, 1970.

69. Stoney WS, Alford WC Jr, Burrus GR, et al: Aberrant right subclavian artery aneurysm. Ann Thorac Surg 19:460, 1975.

70. Rothkopf DM, Bryan DJ, Cuadros CL, et al: Surgical management of ulnar artery aneurysms. J Hand Surg 15A:891, 1990.

71. Esquivel CO, Miller GE Jr: Aneurysm of anomalous right subclavian artery. Contemp Surg 24:81, 1984.

72. Perry SP, Massey CW: Bilateral aneurysms of the subclavian and axillary arteries. Radiology 61:53, 1953.

73. Ho PK, Weiland AJ, McClinton MA, et al: Aneurysms of the upper extremity. J Hand Surg 12A:39, 1978.

74. Rob CG, Standeven A: Closed traumatic lesions of the axillary and brachial arteries. Lancet 1:597, 1956.

75. Brooks A, Fowler B: Axillary artery thrombosis after prolonged use of crutches. J Bone Joint Surg 46A:863, 1964.

76. Abbott WM, Darling RC: Axillary artery aneurysms secondary to crutch trauma. Am J Surg 125:515, 1973.

77. Gallen J, Wiss DA, Cantelmo N, et al: Traumatic pseudoaneurysm of the axillary artery: Report of three cases and literature review. J Trauma 24:350, 1984.

78. Majeed L: Pulsatile haemarthrosis of the shoulder joint associated with false aneurysm of the axillary artery as a late complication of anterior dislocation of the shoulder. Injury 16:566, 1985.

79. Stein E: Case report 374. Skeletal Radiol 15:391, 1986.

80. Sullivan TM, Bacharach JM, Perl J, et al: Endovascular management of unusual aneurysms of the axillary and subclavian arteries. J Endovasc Surg 3:389, 1996.

81. Silcott GR, Polich VL: Palmar arch arterial reconstruction for the salvage of ischemic fingers. Am J Surg 142:219, 1981.

82. Dalman RL: Upper extremity arterial bypass distal to the wrist. Ann Vasc Surg 11:550, 1997.

83. Guattani C: De externis aneurysmaibus, manu chirurgica methodice perctrandis. Rome, 1771. [Translated by JE Erischsen.] London, London Sydenham Society, 1844, p 268.

84. Middleton DS: Occupational aneurysm of the palmar arteries. Br J Surg 21:215, 1933.

85. Smith JW: True aneurysms of traumatic origin in the palm. Am J Surg 104:7, 1962.

86. Pineda CJ, Weisman MH, Bookstein JJ, et al: Hypothenar hammer syndrome: Form of reversible Raynaud's phenomenon. Am J Med 79:561, 1985.

87. Conn J Jr, Bergan JJ, Bell JL: Hypothenar hammer syndrome: Post-traumatic digital ischemia. Surgery 68:1122, 1970.

88. Annetts DL, Graham AR: Traumatic aneurysm of the palmar arch: Lemon squeezer's hand. Aust N Z J Surg 52:584, 1982.

89. Aulicino PL, Hutton PMJ, Du Puy TE: True palmar aneurysms: A case report and literature review. J Hand Surg 7:613, 1982.

90. Bayle E, Tran K, Benslamia H, et al: Ulnar artery aneurysm of the hand. Int Surg 68:215, 1983.

91. Foster DR, Cameron DC: Hypothenar hammer syndrome. Br J Radiol 54:995, 1981.

92. Gaylis H, Kushlick AR: The hypothenar hammer syndrome. S Afr Med J 50:125, 1976.

93. Ho PK, Dellon AL, Wilgis EFS: True aneurysms of the hand resulting from athletic injury: Report of two cases. Am J Sports Med 13:136, 1985.

94. Little JM, Grant AF: Hypothenar hammer syndrome. Med J Aust 1:49, 1972.

95. Little JM, Ferguson DA: The incidence of the hypothenar hammer syndrome. Arch Surg 105:684, 1972.

96. Ettien JT, Allen JT, Vargas C: Hypothenar hammer syndrome. South Med J 74:491, 1981.

97. Coleman SS, Anson BJ: Arterial patterns in the hand based upon a study of 650 specimens. Surg Gynecol Obstet 113:409, 1961.

98. Vayssairat M, Debure C, Cormier J-M, et al: Hypothenar hammer syndrome: Seventeen cases with long-term follow-up. J Vasc Surg 5:838, 1987.

99. Von Kuster L, Abt AB: Traumatic aneurysms of the ulnar artery. Arch Pathol Lab Med 104:75, 1980.

100. Green DP: True and false traumatic aneurysms in the hand. J Bone Joint Surg 55A:120, 1973.

101. Sanchez A, Archer S, Levine NS, et al: Traumatic aneurysm of a common digital artery: A case report. J Hand Surg 7:619, 1982.

102. Walsh MJ, Conolly WB: False aneurysms due to trauma to the hand. Hand 14:177, 1982.

103. Ferris BL, Taylor LM, Oyama K, et al: Hypothenar hammer syndrome: Proposed etiology. J Vasc Surg 31:104, 2000.

104. Kalisman M, Laborde K, Wolff TW: Ulnar nerve compression secondary to ulnar artery false aneurysm at the Guyon's canal. J Hand Surg 7:137, 1982.

105. Benedict KT, Chang W, McCready FJ: The hypothenar hammer syndrome. Radiology 111:57, 1974.

106. Dubois P, Stephen D: Angiographic findings in the hypothenar hammer syndrome. Aust Radiol 19:370, 1975.

107. Maiman MH, Bookstein JJ, Bernstein EF: Digital ischemia: Angiographic differentiation of embolism from primary arterial disease. AJR Am J Roentgenol 137:1183, 1982.

108. Given KS, Puckett CL, Kleinert HE: Ulnar artery thrombosis. Plast Reconstr Surg 61:405, 1978.

109. Martin RD, Manktelow RT: Management of ulnar artery aneurysm in the hand: A case report. Can J Surg 25:97, 1982.

110. May JW Jr, Grossman JAI, Costas B: Cyanotic painful index and long fingers associated with an asymptomatic ulnar artery aneurysm: Case report. J Hand Surg 7:622, 1982.

111. Millender LH, Nalebuff EA, Kasdon E: Aneurysms and thromboses of the ulnar artery in the hand. Arch Surg 105:686, 1972.

112. Nehler MR, Dalman RL, Harris EJ, et al: Upper extremity arterial bypass distal to the wrist. J Vasc Surg 16:633, 1992.

113. Mehlhoff TL, Wood MB: Ulnar artery thrombosis and the role of interposition vein grafting: Patency with microsurgical technique. J Hand Surg 16A:274, 1991.

114. Lawhorne TW Jr, Sanders RA: Ulnar artery aneurysm complicated by distal embolization: Management with regional thrombolysis and resection. J Vasc Surg 3:663, 1986.

115. Kartchner MM, Wilcox WC: Thrombolysis of palmar and digital arterial thrombosis by intra-arterial thrombolysin. J Hand Surg 1:67, 1976.

Chapter

Splanchnic Artery Aneurysms

107

GILBERT R. UPCHURCH, JR., MD

GERALD B. ZELENOCK, MD

JAMES C. STANLEY, MD

Aneurysms of splanchnic arteries represent an uncommon but important vascular disease. Nearly 22% present as clinical emergencies, including 8.5% that result in death.[130] The pathogenesis and natural history of these aneurysms have been reassessed, and in most instances redefined, since the 1970s as advances in imaging technology and endovascular treatments have influenced diagnostic and management strategies. There has been an increased recognition of splanchnic aneurysms because of the greater availability of advanced imaging capabilities, such as high-resolution computed tomography (CT), magnetic resonance imaging (MRI), magnetic resonance angiography (MRA), sophisticated ultrasonography, and arteriography. Nevertheless, selective arteriography remains the most valuable examination in planning therapy.[63]

Surgery remains the mainstay of therapy for many splanchnic aneurysms, especially in the setting of rupture,[147] but certain aneurysms, particularly those involving solid organs, are being treated more often with catheter-based interventions. Select endovascular control of bleeding accompanying aneurysm rupture has been advocated, and prophylactic treatment of incidentally discovered intact aneurysms has become common,[117,154] particularly for aneurysms embedded in pancreatic or hepatic parenchyma with their extensive collateral vascular beds. Although long-term results of such interventional therapies are lacking, their performance accounts in part for the increasing reports of these aneurysms. Inconsistencies in outcome after endovascular interventions are exemplified by two reports: One noted successful early coil placement in 92% of cases, 4% mortality at 1 month, and only a single recurrence at 4 years. The second study reported early success in only 57% of cases, with open operative therapy needed in slightly more than 20%, and one patient dying before operation could be undertaken.[40,108] An absence of long-term follow-up after transcatheter interventions has not tempered the enthusiasm for this form of therapy.

More than 3000 splanchnic artery aneurysms have been documented in the literature. The increasing discovery of these lesions supports the contention that they are more common than previously claimed.[91] Distribution of aneurysms among splanchnic arteries has varied little since the 1970s (Fig. 107-1).[25,26,32,51,63,68,69,135] Vessels affected, in descending order of involvement, include the splenic (60%), hepatic (20%), superior mesenteric (5.5%), celiac (4%), gastric and gastroepiploic (4%), intestinal (jejunal, ileal, colic) (3%), pancreaticoduodenal and pancreatic (2%), gastroduodenal (1.5%), and inferior mesenteric arteries (rare). Anomalous arteries in the splanchnic circulation, such as a common celiacomesenteric trunk, may become aneurysmal, and there seems to be a predilection for this to occur.[10,123] Nearly one third of splanchnic artery aneurysms are associated with other nonvisceral aneurysms, involving, in decreasing frequency, the thoracic aorta, abdominal aorta, renal arteries, iliac arteries, lower extremity arteries, and intracranial arteries.[25] Cumulative experience with some aneurysms is so meager that discussion of them is anecdotal. In other instances, evidence is sufficient to develop a rational basis for treatment.[24] Specific biologic differences between individual aneurysms make it imperative to comment on them separately rather than collectively.

XV

Section

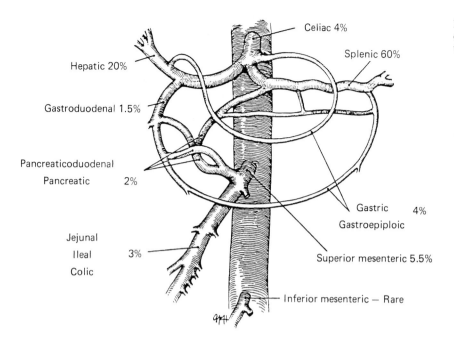

Hepatic 20%

Gastroduodenal 1.5%

Pancreaticoduodenal
Pancreatic   2%

Jejunal
Ileal   3%
Colic

Celiac 4%

Splenic 60%

Gastric   4%
Gastroepiploic

Superior mesenteric 5.5%

Inferior mesenteric — Rare

FIGURE 107-1 Relative incidence of aneurysms described in the literature affecting the arteries of the splanchnic circulation.

■ SPLENIC ARTERY ANEURYSMS

Incidence and Etiology

The most common abdominal visceral vessel affected by aneurysmal disease is the splenic artery. Aneurysms of this vessel constitute 60% of all splanchnic artery aneurysms. More than 1800 patients with splenic artery aneurysms have been described in previous publications, yet few clinical series of more than 20 patients from a single institution exist in the English literature.[39,90,95,133,141] The incidence of these lesions remains ill defined,[74] ranging from 0.098% among nearly 195,000 necropsies[94] to 10.4% in a careful autopsy study of the splenic vessels in elderly patients.[14] Incidental demonstration of splenic aneurysms in 0.78% of nearly 3600 abdominal arteriographic studies may be a relatively accurate approximation of the actual frequency of these lesions in the general population.[133] Macroaneurysms of the splenic artery usually are saccular. These lesions occur most often at bifurcations and are multiple in approximately 20% of patients.

In sharp contrast to aneurysms of the abdominal aorta and lower extremity arteries, splenic artery aneurysms exhibit an unusual sex predilection, with a female-to-male ratio of 4:1. The propensity for aneurysm development in the splenic artery rather than in other splanchnic arteries has been attributed to acquired derangements of the vessel wall, including elastic fiber fragmentation, loss of smooth muscle, and internal elastic lamina disruption. Three distinct phenomena may contribute to these changes.

The first contributing factor to splenic artery aneurysms is the presence of systemic arterial fibrodysplasia. The recognized disruption of arterial wall architecture by medial dysplastic processes[134] is a logical forerunner of aneurysms. Patients with medial fibrodysplasia of the renal artery exhibit splenic artery aneurysms with a frequency six times greater than that seen in the normal population.[133]

The second contributing factor to the development of splenic artery aneurysms is portal hypertension with splenomegaly.[15,37,42,71,88,120] Splenic artery aneurysms have been encountered in 10% to 30% of patients with portal hypertension and splenomegaly.[32,111,130] In these instances, aneurysms may have been sequelae of the apparent hyperkinetic process that causes increased splenic artery diameters in portal hypertension.[88,97,101] Whatever underlies dilatation of the artery, a similar process at vessel bifurcations would increase the likelihood of aneurysm formation. In this regard, aneurysm size in patients with portal hypertension has been directly correlated with splenic artery diameter.[111] Most of these aneurysms are multiple.[71] These particular splenic artery aneurysms are recognized often in patients who have undergone orthotopic liver transplantation.[8] Screening for splenic artery aneurysms has been recommended in all patients before undergoing liver transplantation.[76]

The third contributing factor relevant to the evolution of splenic artery aneurysms is the vascular effects of repeated pregnancy.[32,133,141] In one large series, 40% of female patients described with no obvious cause of their aneurysms had completed six or more pregnancies.[133] The importance of pregnancy in the genesis of these lesions receives further support from the fact that 45% of female patients with splenic artery aneurysms reported in the English literature from 1960 to 1970 in whom parity was stated were grand multiparous.[135] Gestational alterations in the vessel wall due to hormonal and local hemodynamic events may have a causal relation to medial defects and aneurysmal formation. Such effects may be similar to the effects underlying the vascular complications of pregnancy associated with Marfan's or Ehlers-Danlos syndromes. The predilection for aneurysms to occur in the splenic artery instead of in other similar-sized muscular vessels may reflect increased splenic arteriovenous shunting during pregnancy with

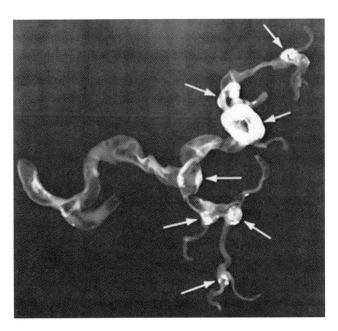

FIGURE 107-2 Splenic artery aneurysms (specimen radiograph). Marked calcific arteriosclerosis limited to splenic artery aneurysms occurring at vessel bifurcations *(arrows)*. Intervening arterial segments are unaffected by advanced arteriosclerotic changes.

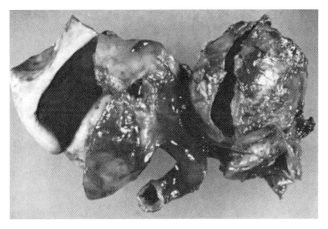

FIGURE 107-3 Splenic artery aneurysms. Multiple aneurysms involving a splenic artery with extensive arteriosclerosis and calcium deposition involving one aneurysm *(left)*, immediately adjacent to a thin nonatherosclerotic aneurysm *(right)*. Arteriosclerosis is considered a secondary event, not a primary factor in initiating splenic artery aneurysms.

excessive blood flow, or it may represent preexisting structural abnormalities inherent to the splenic artery.

Certain splenic artery aneurysms seem to have evolved with arteriosclerotic weakening of the vessel wall.[103] Frequent localization of calcific arteriosclerotic changes to aneurysms, without involvement of the adjacent artery (Fig. 107-2), supports the contention, however, that arteriosclerosis often occurs as a secondary process rather than a primary etiologic event. Calcific arteriosclerotic changes in some, but not all, aneurysms in which multiple lesions occur (Fig. 107-3) lend further credence to this hypothesis.

Inflammatory processes adjacent to the splenic artery, particularly chronic pancreatitis with associated pseudo-cysts, also are known to cause aneurysms. Peripancreatic false aneurysms occur in more than 10% of patients with chronic pancreatitis, and many of these involve the splenic artery.[62] Similarly, penetrating and blunt trauma may precipitate aneurysmal development. Infected (mycotic) lesions, often associated with subacute bacterial endocarditis in intravenous drug addicts, are being encountered more frequently. Microaneurysms of intrasplenic vessels are usually a manifestation of a connective tissue disease, such as periarteritis nodosa, and are of less surgical importance than macroaneurysms due to other causes.

Presentation and Diagnosis

The presence of a splenic artery aneurysm may be suspected with radiographic demonstration of curvilinear, signet ring–like calcifications in the left upper quadrant (Fig. 107-4). Such findings have been reported in 70% of cases.[113]

These aneurysms most often are diagnosed by conventional arteriography (Fig. 107-5), ultrasonography, CT, or MRI[70,89] in patients in whom there were no prior suspicions of the lesion's presence.[124,133]

Splenic artery aneurysms usually are asymptomatic, although 17% and 20% of patients in two large series allegedly had symptoms referable to these lesions.[109,113] Others have reported even higher incidences of symptomatic aneurysms. A common complaint among symptomatic patients is vague left upper quadrant or epigastric discomfort with occasional radiation to the left subscapular area. Acute expansion of splenic artery aneurysms intensifies

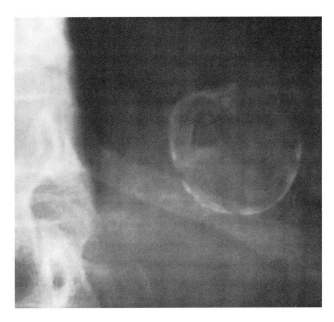

FIGURE 107-4 Splenic artery aneurysm. Curvilinear, signet ring–like calcifications in the left upper quadrant are characteristic of splenic artery aneurysms.

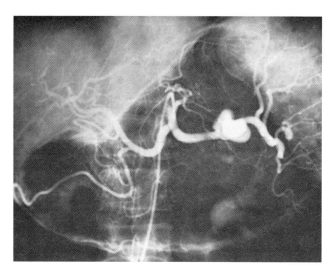

FIGURE 107-5 Splenic artery aneurysm. Arteriographic documentation of a pancreatitis-related aneurysm affecting the mid-splenic artery.

these symptoms. Abdominal tenderness is unlikely in an intact aneurysm. A bruit ascribed to these lesions is more likely to arise from turbulent blood flow through the aorta and its branches than from splenic aneurysmal disease. Most splenic artery aneurysms are smaller than 2 cm in diameter. Pulsatile abdominal masses associated with these lesions are palpated infrequently. A recent report raises the possibility that circulating matrix metalloproteinase–9 levels in patients with these aneurysms may serve as a marker to monitor disease progression.[34]

Aneurysmal rupture with intraperitoneal hemorrhage accounts for the most dramatic clinical presentation of a splenic artery aneurysm. In nonpregnant patients, rupture often presents as an acute intra-abdominal catastrophe with associated cardiovascular collapse. In most cases, bleeding initially occurs into the retrogastric area. Symptoms distant from the left upper quadrant and epigastrium may follow as blood escapes through the foramen of Winslow. Hemorrhage invariably proceeds to severe intraperitoneal bleeding as lesser sac containment is lost. Such a "double rupture phenomenon" occurs in nearly 25% of cases and often provides an opportunity for treatment before the onset of fatal hemorrhage. In pregnant patients, aneurysmal rupture may mimic other obstetric emergencies, such as placental abruption, amniotic fluid embolism, or uterine rupture.[3,12,22,80,100]

Occasionally, intermittent gastrointestinal bleeding may reflect a communication between a splenic artery aneurysm and the intestinal tract or pancreatic ductal system.[146] These latter lesions usually are products of an inflammatory process, and the communication most often occurs directly, as with penetrating gastric ulcers. In cases associated with pancreatitis, bleeding may occur through the pancreatic ducts.[57] Splenic arteriovenous fistulae are an even more uncommon complication of aneurysmal rupture, but when they do occur, they are often associated with secondary left-sided portal hypertension.[18]

Life-threatening rupture seems to affect fewer than 2% of bland splenic artery aneurysms.[133] Factors contributing to rupture of previously asymptomatic splenic artery aneurysms

remain poorly defined. There is no basis for the contention that rupture is less likely to occur in patients with calcified aneurysms, in normotensive as opposed to hypertensive patients, or in patients older than 60 years old. It has been suggested that the use of beta blockers may be associated with less risk of rupture.[2] Aneurysms in patients who have received orthotopic liver transplants may be at greater risk of rupture than other bland aneurysms.[8,17,42] The highest reported incidence of aneurysmal rupture occurs in young women during pregnancy. More than 95% of aneurysms reported during pregnancy have ruptured.[3,22,80,133] Despite this observation, it is logical to believe that many splenic artery aneurysms develop during pregnancy and that most of these do not rupture during the pregnancy.

Indications and Technique for Treatment

Indications for surgical therapy of splenic aneurysms have become better defined.[11,133,141] Symptomatic aneurysms warrant early surgical therapy. Operative intervention seems to be justified for splenic artery aneurysms encountered in pregnant patients or in women of childbearing age who subsequently may conceive. Maternal mortality of aneurysmal rupture during pregnancy is approximately 70%, and fetal mortality exceeds 75%.[3,12,22,100,133] Survival of the mother and the fetus after rupture of a splenic artery aneurysm, as of 1993, had been reported only 12 times.[3,22,78,119] In nonpregnant patients, operative mortality after surgical treatment for aneurysmal rupture is less than 25%.[135] The mortality after splenic artery aneurysm rupture in liver transplant patients is greater than 50%.[42]

Although rupture has been reported to occur in 3% to 9.6% of all patients with splenic artery aneurysms,[128,133,141] disruption of bland lesions probably occurs in no more than 2% of cases. Elective operation for bland splenic artery aneurysms is appropriate only when the predicted surgical mortality rate is no greater than 0.5%. This latter figure represents the product of the reported 2% incidence of rupture and the 25% mortality rate accompanying operative treatment of patients with ruptured aneurysms. In most instances, elective operation is recommended for good-risk patients with splenic artery aneurysms greater than 2 cm in diameter. In certain patients in whom operative therapy entails a prohibitively high risk, transcatheter embolization of the aneurysm may be the preferred treatment.[86,110] Several authors suggest that transcatheter embolization may be the procedure of choice for all splanchnic aneurysms, including splenic aneurysms. Temporizing enthusiasm for this approach is the 10% to 15% failure rate following embolization, and continued enlargement of the aneurysm with potential for subsequent rupture.

Surgical techniques for treating splenic artery aneurysms have become standardized. Aneurysms of the proximal vessel may be treated by aneurysmectomy or simple ligation-exclusion without arterial reconstruction. Restoration of splenic artery continuity when treating aneurysms of this vessel is rarely indicated. Proximal splenic artery aneurysms are easily exposed through the lesser sac after the gastrohepatic ligament has been incised. Entering and exiting vessels are ligated. These lesions usually are excised if they are not embedded within pancreatic tissue. Certain mid–splenic artery aneurysms, especially aneurysms occurring as a result of pancreatic inflammatory disease, may not be removed so easily. Such false aneurysms, which often occur as a consequence of pancreatic pseudocyst erosion into the splenic artery, may be treated by arterial ligation from within the aneurysmal sac. Monofilament suture, such as polypropylene, is used to ligate vessels in this situation to lessen the risk of chronic infection that might occur in the presence of bacterial contamination of pseudocyst contents. Proximal splenic artery ligation or clamping, if easily accomplished, is recommended to lessen bleeding encountered on opening the false aneurysm. Internal or external drainage of associated pseudocysts is often necessary after arterial ligation, and later extirpation of the diseased pancreas frequently is required. Distal pancreatectomy including the affected artery is preferred when treating inflammatory false aneurysms involving the distal body and tail regions of the pancreas.

In the past, surgical therapy of aneurysms within the hilus of the spleen usually entailed a conventional splenectomy. Given the importance of splenic preservation in maintaining host resistance, simple suture obliteration, aneurysmorrhaphy, or excision of distal aneurysms have become favored over traditional splenectomy. Mortality after surgical therapy for pancreatitis-related bleeding arterial aneurysms, most commonly affecting the splenic artery, approaches 30%.[128] Operative mortality after elective surgical treatment of bland noninflammatory splenic artery aneurysms, without concomitant vascular or gastrointestinal tract operations, has not been described among cases reported in the more recent literature.[133,135,141] Laparoscopic treatment of these aneurysms, often guided by intraoperative ultrasound, is likely to decrease the expected blood loss and morbidity and shorten the hospital length of stay accompanying conventional open procedures.[5,59]

Endovascular occlusion using coil embolization of splenic artery aneurysms provides an alternative to operative intervention,[81] but splenic infarction and the inability to ensure durable obliteration of the aneurysm mandate careful follow-up of patients treated in this fashion (Fig. 107-6). Migration of coils into the stomach after transcatheter coil embolization of a bleeding splenic artery aneurysm has been described.[138] The use of a stent-graft to preserve splenic artery flow may be justified in rare clinical situations.[6,19,155] One such situation was reported in a patient in whom continued splenic artery flow was required in anticipation of creating a mesocaval shunt as a means of treating portal hypertension with bleeding jejunal varices.[6]

■ HEPATIC ARTERY ANEURYSMS

Incidence and Etiology

Aneurysmal disease of the hepatic artery accounts for 20% of aneurysms affecting splanchnic vessels.[79] Infected aneurysms, previously considered the most common type of hepatic artery aneurysm,[52] accounted for 16% of lesions described in the literature from 1960 to 1970.[135] At present, they represent only 10% of known hepatic artery aneurysms, occurring most often as a complication of illicit intra-venous

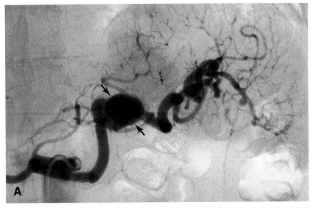
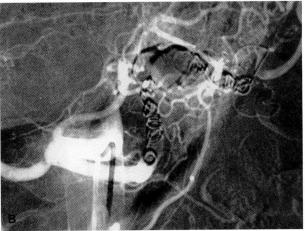

FIGURE 107-6 Splenic artery aneurysm. **A,** Arteriographic documentation of splenic artery aneurysm *(arrows)* treated by coil embolization proximal and distal to aneurysm (**B**).

drug use. Arteriosclerotic changes have been encountered in 32% of hepatic artery aneurysms. In most instances, however, arteriosclerosis is not considered an etiologic process, but rather a secondary phenomenon.

Medial degeneration, including alterations similar to those encountered in many splenic artery aneurysms, has been documented in 24% of these lesions. Medial defects seem to be acquired and are unrelated to congenital abnormalities. Specific events leading to the development of aneurysms in this latter setting are unknown. False aneurysms developing as a consequence of trauma represent an additional 22% of reported hepatic artery aneurysms, and the frequency of such lesions is increasing. Central hepatic rupture and deep parenchymal fractures subsequent to blunt abdominal injury or gunshot wounds are responsible for most traumatic false aneurysms (Fig. 107-7). Polyarteritis nodosa, cystic medial necrosis, and other more unusual arteriopathies have been associated with a few hepatic artery aneurysms. A possible association between excessive oral amphetamine use and multiple visceral aneurysms has also been reported.[149] Lastly, periarterial inflammation, such as occurs with cholecystitis or pancreatitis, is a recognized but uncommon cause of hepatic artery aneurysms.

Hepatic artery aneurysms reported in surgical series have averaged greater than 3.5 cm in diameter.[1] Aneurysms larger than 2 cm usually are saccular in character (Fig. 107-8).

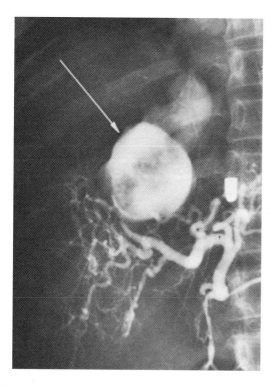

FIGURE 107-7 Traumatic hepatic artery aneurysm. Blunt abdominal injury and gunshot wounds cause most traumatic lesions. (From Whitehouse WM Jr, Graham LM, Stanley JC: Aneurysms of the celiac, hepatic, and splenic arteries. In Bergan JJ, Yao JST [eds]: Aneurysms: Diagnosis and Treatment. New York, Grune & Stratton, 1981, pp 405-415.)

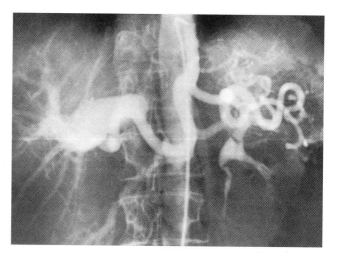

FIGURE 107-8 Hepatic artery aneurysms. Selective celiac arteriogram shows a large saccular aneurysm at the bifurcation of the proper hepatic artery. Of all hepatic artery aneurysms, 80% are extrahepatic.

Smaller aneurysms tend to be fusiform. Of these lesions, 80% involve the extrahepatic vessels; 20% occur within the substance of the liver, with traumatic aneurysms dominating this latter group. A review of 163 aneurysms in which the specific site of the lesion could be ascertained revealed the following locations: common hepatic, 63%; right hepatic, 28%; left hepatic, 5%; and right and left hepatic arteries, 4%.[135] Excluding multiple microaneurysms associated with inflammatory arteriopathies, such as polyarteritis nodosa,[104] most hepatic artery aneurysms are solitary. More than a third of aneurysms affecting the hepatic artery are associated with other visceral artery aneurysms, most commonly splenic artery aneurysms.[1]

Presentation and Diagnosis

Men with hepatic artery aneurysms outnumber women 2:1. Most of these lesions, excluding traumatic aneurysms, occur in patients in their 50s. Most aneurysms remain asymptomatic. Among symptomatic patients with intact aneurysms, the most common complaint is right upper quadrant or epigastric pain. Discomfort, although frequently vague, usually is persistent and is often attributed to cholecystitis. In most instances, this pain is not related to meals. Symptoms are most likely to evolve in patients with nonarteriosclerotic and multiple aneurysms. Expanding hepatic artery aneurysms usually cause severe upper abdominal discomfort, often with radiation to the back, similar to that accompanying pancreatitis. Exceedingly large

aneurysms may compress the biliary tree and result in clinical manifestations similar to other forms of extrinsic extrahepatic bile duct obstruction. Pulsatile masses and abdominal bruits are uncommon findings in the presence of intact aneurysms.

Rupture of hepatic artery aneurysms occurs into the hepatobiliary tract and the peritoneal cavity with equal frequency. Rupture into bile ducts often is responsible for the characteristic findings of hematobilia.[36,56,66] In such a setting, patients may complain of intermittent abdominal pain similar to that of biliary colic. Most patients exhibit massive gastrointestinal bleeding with periodic hematemesis.[113] More than half of patients become jaundiced when blood clots obstruct the biliary ducts.

Most patients with hematobilia are febrile at some time during their illness. Symptoms of chronic anemia associated with insidious bleeding and melena are less common manifestations of aneurysmal communication with the biliary tree. Hematobilia occurs most often in the presence of traumatic intrahepatic false aneurysms. Erosion of nontraumatic hepatic artery aneurysms into the stomach, duodenum, common bile duct, pancreatic duct, or portal vein is a recognized, but relatively rare, complication of these lesions. Intraperitoneal bleeding and exsanguinating hemorrhage, producing clinical signs of abdominal apoplexy, frequently accompany extrahepatic aneurysmal rupture.[113] In this regard, aneurysms associated with polyarteritis nodosa that rupture into the intraperitoneal cavity are most likely to arise from the hepatic artery.[96] Many patients destined to develop such catastrophes do not exhibit prior symptoms.

In the past, the diagnosis of hepatic artery aneurysms was made most often at autopsy or at the time of surgical exploration for major complications of these lesions. Vascular calcifications in the upper abdomen and displacement of contiguous structures evident on barium studies or cholecystography may suggest the presence of these aneurysms. More recently, arteriographic studies in patients with unknown causes of gastrointestinal hemorrhage and in patients with major abdominal trauma have led to an increased recognition of hepatic artery aneurysms. Ultrasonography and CT may be valuable in screening patients for suspected hepatic artery aneurysms and in maintaining noninvasive follow-up.[7]

Indications and Technique for Treatment

Excision or obliteration of all hepatic artery aneurysms seems justified, unless unusual risks preclude operation. Although not every aneurysm eventually ruptures, rupture occurred in 44% of the lesions described in the literature from 1960 to 1970.[135] In some isolated experiences, high incidences of rupture have been reported,[118] but the overall rupture rate is probably less than 20%. Mortality associated with rupture continues to be exceedingly high and is not less than the 35% previously reported.[21] An aggressive approach to managing these aneurysms seems appropriate.

Preoperative arteriographic delineation of the foregut and midgut arterial circulation is essential in planning optimal surgical therapy of these aneurysms.[148] Common hepatic artery aneurysms often may be treated by aneurysmectomy or aneurysmal exclusion without arterial reconstruction. Extensive foregut collateral circulation to the liver through the gastroduodenal and right gastric arteries frequently provides adequate hepatic blood flow despite common hepatic artery interruption. If blood flow to the liver seems compromised after a 5-minute trial of intraoperative hepatic artery occlusion, aneurysmorrhaphy or formal hepatic revascularization should be pursued. Failure to confirm the adequacy of existing collateral vessels may lead to hepatic necrosis.[115] Similarly, coexisting liver parenchymal disease makes ligation of the proximal hepatic artery less advisable and arterial reconstruction preferable.

Restoration of normal hepatic blood flow is important in the management of aneurysms involving the proper hepatic artery and its extrahepatic branches. Aneurysms of the hepatic artery usually are approached through an extended right subcostal or a vertical midline incision. Intact common hepatic artery aneurysms are easily isolated. Proximal proper hepatic artery aneurysms should be cautiously dissected, however, especially near the gastroduodenal artery and its pancreaticoduodenal artery branch, which often cross over the common bile duct inferiorly. Similarly, distal proper hepatic or hepatic artery branch aneurysms must be carefully dissected to avoid bile duct injuries. Expeditious vascular control of entering and exiting vessels from within an aneurysm may be safer than dissecting the adjacent arteries when treating large or inflammatory aneurysms.

Many therapeutic alternatives exist in repairing aneurysmal hepatic arteries.[79] Aneurysmorrhaphy, with or without a vein patch closure, may be appropriate in managing select traumatic aneurysms. Fusiform and large saccular aneurysms that involve greater arterial circumferences are best treated by resection and arterial reconstruction. The use of an autogenous saphenous vein, despite occasional failures,[116] is preferred over synthetic prostheses in most circumstances. Anastomoses are best undertaken by spatulation of the hepatic artery and vein graft to provide an ovoid anasto-mosis that would be less likely to become narrowed with healing. Interposition grafts within the hepatic arterial circulation are often possible, and when not, an aortohepatic bypass may be undertaken. An extended Kocher maneuver with medial visceral rotation allows exposure of the vena cava and aorta. A vein graft from the anterolateral aspect of the infrarenal aorta may be carried out behind the duodenum to the porta hepatis. After the aneurysmectomy has been performed, the spatulated vein can be anastomosed in an end-to-end fashion to either the common or the proper hepatic artery.

Resection of liver parenchyma for intrahepatic aneurysms that are not amenable to reconstruction is occasionally necessary. Control of bleeding intrahepatic aneurysms by means of simple ligation of the proximal vessel, despite the possibility of subsequent liver necrosis, may be preferable to undertaking a major liver resection in a critically ill patient. Similarly, percutaneous transcatheter balloon embolization with occlusion of hepatic artery aneurysms in high-risk cases may be an acceptable alternative to operative therapy (Fig. 107-9).[11,45,67,102] This procedure may be the preferred treatment for small intrahepatic false aneurysms. A reported 42% recanalization rate after hepatic artery embolization mandates careful follow-up. Stent-graft repair of a hepatic artery aneurysm has been described.[75] The potential for migration of embolic material or stent-graft occlusion with central lobular necrosis and abscess formation is also a recognized complication of transcatheter treatment of these aneurysms. Percutaneous thrombin injection of a false aneurysm of the hepatic artery may be considered in high-risk patients and has been reported in a liver transplant patient after repair of a perforated duodenum in the setting of bile peritonitis.[106]

■ SUPERIOR MESENTERIC ARTERY ANEURYSMS

Incidence and Etiology

The third most common splanchnic artery aneurysm, accounting for 5.5% of these lesions, involves the main trunk of the SMA. These lesions, affecting the proximal 5 cm of the SMA, have been reported to be most often infectious in etiology.[30,38,135] However, the SMA harbors more infectious aneurysms than any other muscular artery. Nonhemolytic streptococcus, related to left-sided bacterial endocarditis, has been the organism reported most often in these lesions. A variety of other pathogens, especially staphylococcal organisms, have been described in aneurysms associated with noncardiac septicemia. A recent report suggested that an infectious etiology accounted for less than 5% of these aneurysms.[137] Nevertheless, syphilitic aneurysms, frequently described in early reports, have not been observed in contemporary times. Dissecting aneurysms associated with medial defects are rare,[28] but affect this vessel more than any other splanchnic artery (Fig. 107-10).[53] Arteriosclerosis, most likely representing a secondary event, is evident in approximately 20% of reported SMA aneurysms. Trauma is a rare cause of these aneurysms.

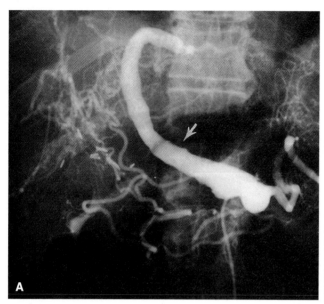
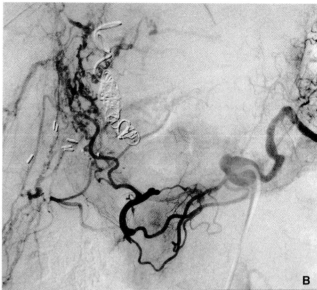

FIGURE 107-9 Hepatic artery aneurysm. **A,** Pre-embolization celiac arteriogram shows fusiform aneurysm of common hepatic artery *(arrow).* **B,** Postembolization celiac arteriogram documents occlusion of common and left hepatic arteries with coils and reconstitution of right and left lobe intrahepatic branches by biliary collateral vessels. (From Welling TH, Williams DM, Stanley JC: Excessive oral amphetamine use as a possible cause of renal and splanchnic arterial aneurysms: A report of two cases. J Vasc Surg 28:727, 1998.)

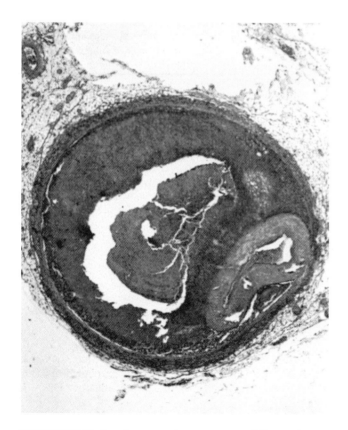

FIGURE 107-10 Superior mesenteric artery aneurysm. Microscopic cross section of a dissecting aneurysm affecting the proximal superior mesenteric artery. (H&E.)

Presentation and Diagnosis

Intermittent upper abdominal discomfort that progresses to persistent and severe epigastric pain often accompanies symptomatic SMA aneurysms. In certain cases, it may be difficult to distinguish symptoms that are due to mesenteric ischemia from symptoms due to aneurysmal expansion. A tender pulsatile abdominal mass that is not rigidly fixed has been discovered in nearly half of these patients.

Female patients were predominant in earlier series of SMA aneurysms. More recent experience has not confirmed such a sex predilection, and men and women are affected equally. Most infected aneurysms occur in patients younger than 50 years of age. Noninfected aneurysms of the SMA most often affect patients after age 60. This older subgroup of patients often experiences prodromes of intestinal angina before aneurysm rupture. SMA aneurysm rupture, although uncommon in earlier times, was recently reported in nearly 40% of patients in one series.[137]

Aneurysmal expansion with dissection or propagation of intraluminal thrombus beyond the vessel's inferior pancreaticoduodenal and middle colic branches effectively isolates the SMA from the collaterals of the celiac and inferior mesenteric artery circulations. In such circumstances, any compromise of blood flow through the SMA may cause intestinal angina. Because of the critical location of most SMA aneurysms, the existence of asymptomatic lesions is not as common as with many other splanchnic aneurysms. Antemortem diagnosis of uncomplicated SMA aneurysms is uncommon. Recognition of asymptomatic solitary dissecting SMA aneurysms has not been reported.[28] Radiographic evidence of calcified aneurysms and abdominal angiograms made during studies for unrelated disease have been responsible for most antemortem diagnoses.

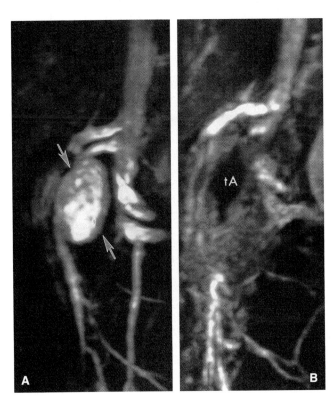

FIGURE 107-11 Superior mesenteric artery aneurysm. **A,** MRA documenting large saccular aneurysm in a patient with Ehlers-Danlos syndrome *(arrows)*. **B,** Postoperative MRA documents thrombosed aneurysm (tA) after proximal and distal ligation.

Indications and Technique for Treatment

Surgical treatment of most SMA aneurysms seems justified in light of the seemingly common occurrence of rupture or arterial occlusion. Nearly one third of reported SMA aneurysms have been treated successfully by operation.[83] This includes fewer than 20 infected aneurysms of this vessel.[38] Operative exposure for more distal lesions may be obtained by a transmesenteric route or for proximal lesions by a retroperitoneal approach after the lateral parietes are incised, allowing the colon, pancreas, and spleen to be reflected medially. Since the first successful surgical treatment of an aneurysm of the SMA was reported in the 1950s,[30,72] the most common procedures attempted have been aneurysmorrhaphy and simple ligation, the latter having been undertaken in more than a third of cases. Ligation of the vessels entering and exiting these aneurysms without arterial reconstruction has proved to be an acceptable, simple means of treatment (Fig. 107-11).[44,135,137] The existence of preformed collaterals involving the inferior pancreaticoduodenal and middle colic arteries allows this approach usually to be successful. Temporary occlusion of the SMA with intraoperative assessment of bowel viability offers a means of identifying cases in which mesenteric revascularization is necessary.

SMA aneurysmectomy may prove hazardous because of the close proximity of neighboring structures, such as the superior mesenteric vein and the pancreas. Endoaneurysmorrhaphy in selected patients with saccular aneurysms

may be possible. Arterial reconstruction, with an interposition graft or aortomesenteric bypass after exclusion or excision of the aneurysm, has been rarely accomplished.[83,145,153] Use of synthetic prostheses, taking origin from the anterior aorta or intact proximal SMA and carried to the normal vessel beyond the aneurysm, is acceptable in the absence of an infected aneurysm or infarcted bowel. In the presence of infection, an autogenous saphenous vein is a more appropriate conduit for reconstruction. In such cases, long-term antibiotic therapy also is recommended. Contemporary surgical intervention for all types of SMA aneurysms carries a mortality of less than 15%.[137]

Transcatheter occlusion of saccular aneurysms with discrete necks arising from the side of the SMA occasionally may be justified.[11] In theory, endovascular coil occlusion of SMA aneurysm may be an appropriate alternative to surgical ligation or repair, especially in the setting of a hostile abdomen, such as acute pancreatitis.[35,55] Percutaneous stent-graft treatment of a proximal SMA traumatic false aneurysm has been described.[4] This approach may avoid the excessive mortality associated with open surgical repair in high-risk patients. Stent-graft treatment of a false aneurysm of the SMA in the setting of infection, although described,[29] is not favored.

■ CELIAC ARTERY ANEURYSMS

Incidence and Etiology

Aneurysms of the celiac artery are unusual lesions that account for 4% of all splanchnic aneurysms. In 1985, only 108 celiac artery aneurysms had been described in the literature.[47] Arteriosclerosis and medial degeneration were the most common histologic changes observed in these aneurysms. The former, noted in 27% of patients, probably represents a secondary rather than a primary causative process. A preexisting paucity of elastic tissue and smooth muscle at major branchings seems to be a contributing factor in an additional 17% of patients in whom developmental aneurysms were suspected.

Traumatic false aneurysms caused by penetrating injuries are uncommon. Post-stenotic dilatation occasionally progresses to frank aneurysmal change, but is an uncommon cause of these lesions. Infected celiac artery aneurysms are rare,[150] and in recent times syphilitic and tuberculous lesions have not been encountered. Associated aortic aneurysms were noted in 18% of patients with celiac artery aneurysms, and other splanchnic artery aneurysms affected 38% of these patients.[49]

Presentation and Diagnosis

Most celiac artery aneurysms are asymptomatic. Although men outnumber women among all reported cases, there has been no sex predilection in patients reported since the 1960s. The average age of patients reported before 1950 was 40 years, in contrast to an average age of 52 years reported since then.[35]

Abdominal discomfort localized to the epigastrium accompanies more than 60% of symptomatic celiac artery

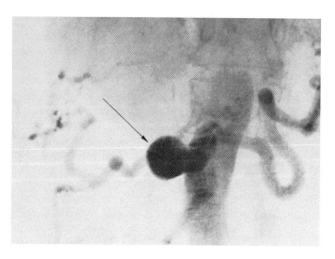

FIGURE 107-12 Celiac artery aneurysm *(arrow)*. Aortogram reveals saccular aneurysm that exhibited medial degenerative changes and secondary arteriosclerosis. (From Stanley JC, Whitehouse WM Jr: Aneurysms of splanchnic and renal arteries. In Bergan JJ, Yao JST (eds): Surgery of the Aorta and Its Body Branches. New York, Grune & Stratton, 1979, pp 497-519.)

aneurysms. Intense discomfort, often with radiation to the back, and nausea and vomiting have been attributed to aneurysmal expansion and may be confused with pancreatitis. Abdominal bruits are heard frequently in patients with celiac artery aneurysms. Nevertheless, such bruits are rarely due to the aneurysm. Celiac artery aneurysms are apparent as pulsatile abdominal masses in nearly 30% of cases.[35] Symptoms suggesting intestinal angina are a rare accompaniment of celiac artery aneurysms and, when present, are usually due to significant coexisting arteriosclerotic occlusive disease affecting the SMA and inferior mesenteric artery.

The most serious clinical complication of celiac artery aneurysmal disease is rupture. Although nearly 80% of all previously reported lesions had ruptured, clinical experience since 1980 has documented the risk of rupture as 13%.[35] The contemporary incidence of rupture may be even lower.[136] Aneurysmal disruption is most often associated with intraperitoneal hemorrhage, although communication with the gastrointestinal tract can occur.

Recognition of most celiac artery aneurysms encountered before 1950 occurred at the time of autopsy. Currently, unexpected discovery of aneurysms during angiography accounts for the diagnosis in nearly 65% of cases (Fig. 107-12).[49,54,135] Calcification of the aneurysm, which affects 20% of these lesions, and displacement of contiguous structures are occasional radiographic findings that suggest the diagnosis. Ultrasonography, CT, and MRA may be of diagnostic use in assessing certain lesions[54,60] and should be useful in longitudinal follow-up of nonoperative cases.

Indications and Technique for Treatment

Surgical treatment of celiac artery aneurysms is warranted except when operative risks contraindicate an abdominal operation.[54,136] Successful operations in more than 90% of

cases reported since the first successful surgical treatment in the 1960s support such a therapeutic approach.[126,136]

Most patients, especially patients with small bland aneurysms, can be treated by the abdominal route alone. This approach is particularly applicable if there is a broad costal margin. In these instances, a medial visceral rotation of the left colon, spleen, and pancreas allows exposure of the aorta at the diaphragmatic hiatus. Transection of the crus and median arcuate ligament provides access to the origin of the celiac artery and adjacent aorta. Exposure of celiac artery aneurysms for symptomatic or large lesions is more difficult and may require a thoracoabdominal approach with the incision extending from the mid-axillary line on the left, usually in the seventh intercostal space, across the costal margin into the abdomen.

Aneurysmorrhaphy has been advocated in select cases. It is favored only for discrete saccular aneurysms in which the integrity of the remaining arterial wall appears normal. Aneurysmectomy with arterial reconstruction accounts for 50% of reported operations.[49] Aneurysmectomy and primary reanastomosis of the celiac artery trunk are sometimes possible, but should be undertaken only in the presence of a relatively normal and lengthy proximal celiac artery. When reanastomosis is not feasible, an aortoceliac bypass with a synthetic prosthesis or autogenous vein graft should be performed, originating from the supraceliac aorta. The former conduit may be advantageous compared with vein grafts.[136]

Celiac axis ligation with interruption of antegrade blood flow through the common hepatic, left gastric, and splenic vessels has been undertaken in 35% of reported operations.[49] Ligation is preferred in certain settings, such as with Ehlers-Danlos syndrome, in which vessel wall fragility precludes safe arterial reconstructions.[105] Although celiac artery ligation rarely results in hepatic necrosis, it should be undertaken only when there is no preexisting liver disease, and intraoperative findings suggest that hepatic blood flow would not be severely compromised.[92] Mortality for open operative treatment of patients with ruptured celiac artery aneurysms is 40% compared with only 5% for patients with nonruptured celiac artery aneurysms.[49] Glue embolic occlusion of the celiac trunk through the gastroduodenal artery for a ruptured false aneurysm has been described.[121]

■ GASTRIC AND GASTROEPIPLOIC ARTERY ANEURYSMS

Aneurysms of gastric and gastroepiploic arteries account for approximately 4% of splanchnic aneurysms. These lesions seem to be acquired, although their exact cause often remains undefined.[143] Histologic evidence of arteriosclerosis in many aneurysms led to an earlier belief that this was an important etiologic factor.[93] It is more likely that medial degeneration of undetermined origin or degeneration resulting from periarterial inflammation precedes the arteriosclerotic changes, which are considered a secondary event. Most clinically important aneurysms involving vessels to the stomach are solitary. Aneurysms of gastric arteries are nearly 10 times more common than aneurysms of gastroepiploic arteries. They are considered together because their natural history and management are similar.

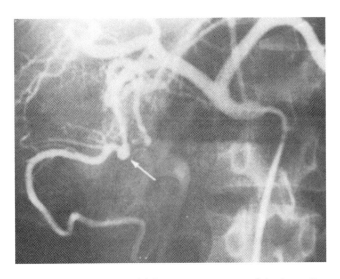

FIGURE 107-13 Gastroepiploic artery aneurysms. Selective celiac arteriogram. This saccular aneurysm *(arrow)* was responsible for massive gastrointestinal hemorrhage.

Asymptomatic aneurysms of the gastric and gastroepiploic arteries have not been commonly reported. Most aneurysms described in the literature have presented as vascular emergencies, with rupture at the time of diagnosis occurring in more than 90% of cases. Nearly 70% were associated with serious gastrointestinal bleeding. A few patients describe antecedent dyspeptic epigastric discomfort, but most have no abdominal pain before aneurysmal rupture. Intestinal bleeding in these cases usually manifests by acute massive hematemesis,[87] although a few patients experience chronic occult gastrointestinal bleeding. Rupture of gastric and gastroepiploic artery aneurysms causes life-threatening intraperitoneal bleeding in approximately 30% of cases.[65,140] As is the case with intestinal bleeding, most patients are asymptomatic before the occurrence of acute intraperitoneal aneurysmal disruption. Most cases affect individuals in their 50s and 60s. Men outnumber women approximately 3:1.

Antemortem diagnosis of gastric and gastroepiploic artery aneurysms most often occurs during urgent operation for gastrointestinal or intraperitoneal bleeding. Intraoperative search for gastric and gastroepiploic aneurysms requires careful palpation and transillumination of the entire stomach. Arteriographic studies for unexplained gastrointestinal bleeding result in occasional preoperative recognition of these lesions (Fig. 107-13). Mucosal alterations associated with these aneurysms are often minimal, and endoscopic recognition is difficult. Larger lesions may be mistaken for gastric ulcers or malignancies.

Treatment of gastric and gastroepiploic aneurysms is directed at controlling life-threatening hemorrhage. Approximately 70% of patients reported to have these lesions die after aneurysm rupture.[135] Early diagnosis and urgent operative intervention are necessary to improve survival. Ligation of aneurysmal vessels, with or without excision of the aneurysm, is appropriate treatment for extraintestinal lesions and for aneurysms associated with inflammatory processes adjacent to the stomach. Intramural aneurysms and aneurysms associated with bleeding into the gastrointestinal tract should be excised with portions of the involved gastric tissue.

■ JEJUNAL, ILEAL, AND COLIC ARTERY ANEURYSMS

Small intramural and intramesenteric aneurysms of jejunal, ileal, and colic arteries are uncommon, accounting for only 3% of reported splanchnic aneurysms.[20,61,84,98,114] Excluding aneurysms associated with connective tissue disorders, 90% of these intestinal branch aneurysms are solitary and range from a few millimeters to 1 cm in size. Occasionally, patients have two or three lesions, often in the same region of the intestinal circulation. The pathogenesis of these aneurysms is poorly understood. Most seem to be the result of congenital or acquired medial defects. Arteriosclerotic changes exist in approximately 20% of these lesions,[84] being most often a secondary process. Multiple lesions may represent late sequelae of an endarteritis associated with an immunologic injury or septic emboli from subacute bacterial endocarditis.[142] Necrotizing vasculitides, such as polyarteritis nodosa, are another recognized cause of multiple mesenteric branch microaneurysms.[122]

There does not seem to be any gender predilection in the development of mesenteric branch aneurysms. The peak age of involvement is during the 60s. Intact aneurysms are rarely symptomatic. Most aneurysms are recognized at operation for complications of rupture into the mesentery, intestinal lumen, or peritoneal cavity. Rupture of aneurysms affecting the jejunal arteries is relatively rare.[33] Rupture of colic artery aneurysms is more common.[139] Abdominal pain associated with aneurysmal rupture, the presence of a tender mass, and the development of uncontained hemorrhage have been the initial manifestations of these lesions in 70% of reported cases.[83] Mortality after rupture approaches 20%.[135] Contemporary recognition of intestinal artery aneurysms is increasingly the result of more frequent abdominal arteriographic studies for nonvascular disease (Fig. 107-14),[58,91] often during assessment of insidious gastrointestinal bleeding or massive rectal hemorrhage. Preoperative arteriographic localization of these small aneurysms is often essential for successful operative intervention.

Surgical therapy of mesenteric branch aneurysms necessitates arterial ligation, aneurysmectomy, and resection of the affected bowel if the intestinal blood supply is compromised. An intraoperative search should be undertaken for multiple aneurysms of the jejunal and ileal arteries. The risk of aneurysmal rupture is undefined in the case of uncomplicated intestinal aneurysms. The seriousness of rupture and the limited risks of operative intervention support the contention, however, that these lesions usually should be treated when their existence becomes known.

Aneurysms of the proximal inferior mesenteric artery or its branches are exceedingly rare (Fig. 107-15). Fewer than 30 of these lesions have been described in the literature. Aneurysms of this vessel have diverse causes and varied clinical manifestations.[48] Although their natural history remains poorly defined, operative intervention seems justified in most instances.

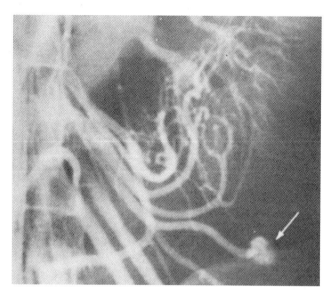

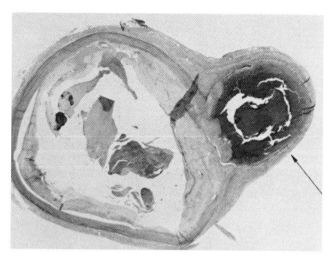

FIGURE 107-15 Inferior mesenteric artery aneurysm. Microscopic cross section of aorta and a thrombus containing aneurysm *(arrow)* of the inferior mesenteric artery trunk. (H&E.)

FIGURE 107-14 Ileal artery aneurysm. Mesenteric arteriogram documenting the presence of a saccular aneurysm *(arrow)* of a distal ileal artery.

■ GASTRODUODENAL, PANCREATICODUODENAL, AND PANCREATIC ARTERY ANEURYSMS

Periduodenal and peripancreatic aneurysmal disease of the communicating vessels between the celiac artery and SMA circulations is uncommon.[27,64] Gastroduodenal artery aneurysms account for 1.5% of all splanchnic artery aneurysms. These cases all have been reported since 1960.[125] Aneurysms of pancreaticoduodenal and pancreatic vessels account for an additional 2% of splanchnic artery aneurysms. Eighty-eight such aneurysms had been reported as of 1995, of which 53 presented with rupture carrying an attendant 49% mortality. The most common age of involvement is the 50s. Men are affected more often than women by nearly 4:1. This incidence reflects the increased incidence of alcoholic pancreatitis in men and the fact that most of these lesions evolve as complications of acute or chronic pancreatitis.[35,58,132,152]

Periarterial inflammation, actual vascular necrosis, and erosion by expanding pancreatic pseudocysts may produce true and false aneurysms, the latter of which are the most common type.[41,129,131] Pancreaticoduodenal artery false aneurysms have been noted after liver transplantation.[156] Noninflammatory pancreaticoduodenal artery aneurysms have no gender predilection.[50] Increased blood flow through these vessels, such as occurs with celiac artery entrapment by the median arcuate ligament or occlusion, seems to be an important etiologic factor.[31,46,107,112] Arteriosclerosis used to be considered the most common cause of these aneurysms,[135] but is now usually considered a secondary rather than a primary etiologic process.

Most patients with aneurysms involving the gastroduodenal, pancreaticoduodenal, or pancreatic arteries are symptomatic at the time of diagnosis. Epigastric pain, frequently with radiation to the back, is common. Silent inflammatory aneurysms are rare. In some cases, this discomfort is indistinguishable from that caused by underlying pancreatitis. This fact is particularly important because nearly 60% of all gastroduodenal artery aneurysms and 30% of all pancreaticoduodenal aneurysms are pancreatitis related.[35] Aneurysmal rupture is second only to abdominal pain as the most frequent manifestation of these lesions. Gastrointestinal hemorrhage affects nearly 75% of these inflammatory aneurysms. Bleeding in these circumstances occurs most often into the stomach or duodenum and less often into the biliary or pancreatic ductal system.[43,131] An occasional patient becomes jaundiced,[13] but a direct association with aneurysmal disease and bilirubin elevations is not always easily documented. Rupture affects approximately 50% of noninflammatory aneurysms, occurring into the intestinal tract and peritoneal cavity with equal frequency.

Arteriographic studies are essential in evaluating patients suspected of having symptomatic gastroduodenal, pancreaticoduodenal, or pancreatic arterial aneurysms, especially aneurysms associated with pancreatitis (Figs. 107-16 and 107-17).[16,35,132] Endoscopic examinations, barium contrast studies, and ultrasonography may show coexisting gastroduodenal or pancreatic disease, but their usefulness in directly identifying these aneurysms is limited. CT has greater value as a means of evaluating these aneurysms (Fig. 107-18).[35]

Reported mortality after rupture of gastroduodenal artery aneurysms approaches 50%. Mortality is less for ruptured pancreaticoduodenal artery aneurysms and is approximately 20% for rupture of non–pancreatitis-related lesions.[31,50] Surgical intervention for aneurysms of the gastroduodenal or pancreaticoduodenal arteries, especially aneurysms in hemodynamically unstable patients,[23] is justified in all but the poorest risk patients.[35,50,131,144]

In general, pancreaticoduodenal and pancreatic artery aneurysms are more difficult to manage operatively than gastroduodenal artery aneurysms.[35,151] The multiple vessels

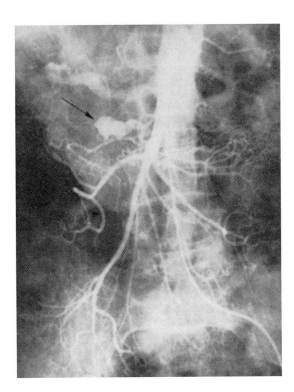

FIGURE 107-16   Inferior pancreaticoduodenal artery aneurysm. Aortogram shows false aneurysm *(arrow)* that evolved as a complication of pancreatitis. (From Stanley JC, Frey CF, Miller TA, et al: Major arterial hemorrhage: A complication of pancreatic pseudocysts and chronic pancreatitis. Arch Surg 111:435, 1976. Copyright 1976, American Medical Association.)

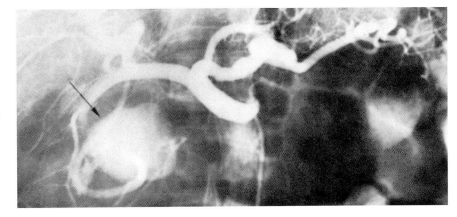

FIGURE 107-17   Gastroduodenal artery aneurysm *(arrow)*. Selective celiac arteriogram. (From Eckhauser FE, Stanley JC, Zelenock GB, et al: Gastroduodenal and pancreaticoduodenal artery aneurysms: A complication of pancreatitis causing spontaneous gastrointestinal hemorrhage. Surgery 88:335, 1980.)

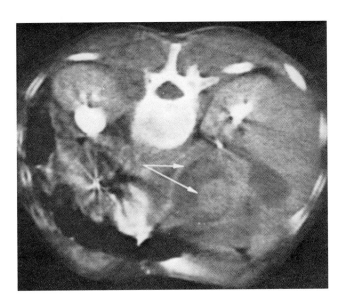

FIGURE 107-18   Gastroduodenal artery aneurysm. CT scan of a pancreatic pseudocyst *(short arrow)* containing an aneurysmal gastroduodenal artery *(long arrow)*. (From Eckhauser FE, Stanley JC, Zelenock GB, et al: Gastroduodenal and pancreaticoduodenal artery aneurysms: A complication of pancreatitis causing spontaneous gastrointestinal hemorrhage. Surgery 88:335, 1980.)

that communicate with these smaller aneurysms and the difficulty of identifying them within the substance of the pancreas limit the efficacy of aneurysmal exclusion by simple ligature alone. Intraoperative arteriography may prove useful when lesions involve the proximal pancreas or other critical structures.[127] Suture ligature of entering and exiting vessels from within the aneurysmal sac rather than extra-aneurysmal dissection and arterial ligation is a more appropriate means of treating most gastroduodenal or pancreaticoduodenal artery aneurysms embedded within the pancreas. When aneurysms involve pancreatic pseudocysts, some manner of cyst decompression should be undertaken. The choice between external or internal drainage usually is determined on the basis of intraoperative findings. Major resections of pancreatic tissue, including pancreatico-duodenectomy, may be necessary for adequate treatment of some patients exhibiting extensive aneurysmal involvement of the pancreatic arteries.[109]

Transcatheter embolization may be performed to ablate certain aneurysms.[23,86] Rebleeding and rupture may complicate this type of therapy.[77] Although embolization may prove a reasonable alternative to operation in hemo-dynamically unstable patients, it is perhaps better to view it as a temporizing intervention before definitive surgical therapy is undertaken. Stent-grafting of the SMA resulting in occlusion of the pancreaticoduodenal artery origin with complementary embolization of small feeding branches to exclude blood flow into an inferior posterior pancreatico-duodenal artery aneurysm has been reported as an alternative to surgery.[99] Percutaneous and ultrasound-guided intraoperative thrombin occlusions of gastroduodenal and pancreatic arterial aneurysms also have been described[82,85] and may be useful in the treatment of selected patients, including patients with acute pancreatitis.[82,85]

■ REFERENCES

1. Abbas MA, Fowl RJ, Stone WM, et al: Hepatic artery aneurysm: Factors that predict complications. J Vasc Surg 38:41, 2003.
2. Abbas MA, Stone WM, Fowl RJ, et al: Splenic artery aneurysms: Two decades' experience at Mayo Clinic. Ann Vasc Surg 16:442, 2002.
3. Angelakis EJ, Bair WE, Barone JE, Lincer RM: Splenic artery aneurysm rupture during pregnancy. Obstet Gynecol Surg 48:145, 1993.
4. Appel N, Duncan JR, Schuerer DJE: Percutaneous stent-graft treatment of superior mesenteric and internal iliac artery pseudoaneurysms. J Vasc Interv Radiol 14:917, 2003.
5. Arca MJ, Gagner M, Heniford BT, et al: Splenic artery aneurysms: Methods of laparoscopic repair. J Vasc Surg 30:184, 1999.
6. Arepally A, Dagli M, Hofmann LV, et al: Treatment of splenic artery aneurysm with use of stent-graft. J Vasc Interv Radiol 13:631, 2002.
7. Athey PA, Sax SL, Lamki N, Cadavid G: Sonography in the diagnosis of hepatic artery aneurysms. AJR Am J Roentgenol 147:725, 1986.
8. Ayalon A, Wiesner RH, Perkins JD, et al: Splenic artery aneurysms in liver transplant patients. Transplantation 45:386, 1988.
9. Deleted in revision.
10. Bailey RW, Riles TS, Rosen RJ, Sullivan LP: Celiacomesenteric anomaly and aneurysm: Clinical and etiologic features. J Vasc Surg 14:229, 1991.
11. Baker JS, Tisnado J, Cho SR, Beachley MC: Splanchnic artery aneurysms and pseudoaneurysms: Transcatheter embolization. Radiology 163:135, 1987.
12. Barrett JM, Caldwell BH: Association of portal hypertension and ruptured splenic artery aneurysm in pregnancy. Obstet Gynecol 57:255, 1981.
13. Bassaly I, Schwartz IR, Pinchuck A, Lerner R: Aneurysm of the gastroduodenal artery presenting as common duct obstruction with jaundice. Am J Gastroenterol 59:435, 1973.
14. Bedford PD, Lodge B: Aneurysm of the splenic artery. Gut 1:321, 1960.
15. Boijsen E, Efsing HO: Aneurysm of the splenic artery. Acta Radiol [Diagn] (Stockh) 8:29, 1969.
16. Boijsen E, Gothlin J, Hallbook T, Sandblom P: Preoperative angiographic diagnosis of bleeding aneurysms of abdominal visceral arteries. Radiology 93:781, 1969.
17. Bronsther O, Merhav H, Van Thiel D, Starzl TE: Splenic artery aneurysms occurring in liver transplant recipients. Transplantation 52:723, 1991.
18. Brothers TE, Stanley JC, Zelenock GB: Splenic arteriovenous fistula. Int Surg 80:189, 1995.
19. Brountozos EN, Vagenas K, Apostolopoulou SC, et al: Pancreatitis-associated splenic artery pseudoaneurysm: Endovascular treatment with self-expandable stent-grafts. Cardiovasc Intervent Radiol 26:88, 2003.
20. Buehler PK, Dailey TH, Lazarevic B: Spontaneous rupture of colic-artery aneurysms. Dis Colon Rectum 19:671, 1976.
21. Busuttil RW, Brin BJ: The diagnosis and management of visceral artery aneurysms. Surgery 88:619, 1980.
22. Caillouette JC, Merchant EB: Ruptured splenic artery aneurysm in pregnancy: Twelfth reported case with maternal and fetal survival. Am J Obstet Gynecol 168:1810, 1993.
23. Carr JA, Cho J-S, Shepard AD, et al: Visceral pseudoaneurysms due to pancreatic pseudocysts: Rare but lethal complications of pancreatitis. J Vasc Surg 32:722, 2000.
24. Carr SC, Pearce WH, Vogelzang RL, et al: Current management of visceral artery aneurysms. Surgery 120:627, 1996.
25. Carr SC, Mahvi DM, Hoch JR, et al: Visceral artery aneurysm rupture. J Vasc Surg 33:806, 2001.
26. Chen HZ, Chen F, Yang J, et al: Diagnosis and treatment of splanchnic artery aneurysms: A report of 57 cases. Chin Med J 112:29, 1999.
27. Chiou AC, Josephs LG, Menzoian JO: Inferior pancreaticoduodenal artery aneurysms: Report of a case and review of the literature. J Vasc Surg 17:784, 1993.
28. Cormier F, Ferry J, Artru B, et al: Dissecting aneurysms of the main trunk of the superior mesenteric artery. J Vasc Surg 15:424, 1992.
29. Cowan S, Kahn MB, Bonn J, et al: Superior mesenteric artery pseudoaneurysm successfully treated with polytetrafluoroethylene covered stent. J Vasc Surg 35:805, 2002.
30. DeBakey ME, Cooley DA: Successful resection of mycotic aneurysm of superior mesenteric artery: Case report and review of the literature. Am Surg 19:202, 1953.
31. DeParrot M, Berney T, Deleaval J, et al: Management of true aneurysms of the pancreaticoduodenal arteries. Ann Surg 229:416, 1999.
32. Deterling RA: Aneurysm of the visceral arteries. J Cardiovasc Surg (Torino) 12:309, 1971.
33. Diettrich NA, Cacioppo JC, Ying DPW: Massive gastrointestinal hemorrhage caused by rupture of a jejunal branch artery aneurysm. J Vasc Surg 8:187, 1988.
34. Ebaugh JL, Chiou AC, Morasch MD, Pearce WH: Staged embolization and operative treatment of multiple visceral aneurysms in a patient with fibromuscular dysplasia—a case report. Vasc Surg 35:145, 2001.
35. Eckhauser FE, Stanley JC, Zelenock GB, et al: Gastroduodenal and pancreaticoduodenal artery aneurysms: A complication of pancreatitis causing spontaneous gastrointestinal hemorrhage. Surgery 88:335, 1980.
36. Erskine JM: Hepatic artery aneurysms. Vasc Surg 7:106, 1973.
37. Feist JH, Gajarej A: Extra and intrasplenic artery aneurysms in portal hypertension. Radiology 125:331, 1977.
38. Friedman SG, Pogo GJ, Moccio CG: Mycotic aneurysm of the superior mesenteric artery. J Vasc Surg 6:87, 1987.

39. Fukunaga Y, Usui N, Hirohashi K, et al: Clinical courses and treatment of splenic artery aneurysms: Report of 3 cases and review of literature in Japan. Osaka City Med J 36:161, 1990.

40. Gabelmann A, Gorich J, Merkle EM: Endovascular treatment of visceral artery aneurysms. J Endovasc Ther 9:38, 2002.

41. Gadacz TR, Trunkey D, Kieffer RF: Visceral vessel erosion associated with pancreatitis: Case reports and a review of the literature. Arch Surg 113:1438, 1978.

42. Gaglio PJ, Regenstein F, Slakey D, et al: α-1-Antitrypsin deficiency and splenic artery aneurysm rupture: An association? Am J Gastroenterol 95:1531, 2000.

43. Gangaher DM, Carveth SW, Reese HE, et al: True aneurysm of the pancreaticoduodenal artery: A case report and review of the literature. J Vasc Surg 2:741, 1985.

44. Geelkerken RH, van Bockel JH, de Roos WK, Hermans J: Surgical treatment of intestinal artery aneurysms. Eur J Vasc Surg 4:563, 1990.

45. Goldblatt M, Goldin AR, Shaff MI: Percutaneous embolization for the management of hepatic artery aneurysms. Gastroenterology 73:1142, 1977.

46. Gouny P, Fukui S, Aymard A, et al: Aneurysm of the gastroduodenal artery associated with stenosis of the superior mesenteric artery. Ann Vasc Surg 8:281, 1994.

47. Graham JM, McCollum CH, DeBakey ME: Aneurysms of the splanchnic arteries. Am J Surg 140:797, 1980.

48. Graham LM, Hay MR, Cho KJ, Stanley JC: Inferior mesenteric artery aneurysms. Surgery 97:158, 1985.

49. Graham LM, Stanley JC, Whitehouse WM Jr, et al: Celiac artery aneurysms: Historic (1745-1949) versus contemporary (1950-1984) differences in etiology and clinical importance. J Vasc Surg 5:757, 1985.

50. Granke K, Hollier LH, Bowen JC: Pancreaticoduodenal artery aneurysms: Changing patterns. South Med J 83:918, 1990.

51. Grego FG, Lepidi S, Ragazzi R, et al: Visceral artery aneurysms: A single center experience. Cardiovasc Surg 11:19, 2003.

52. Guida PM, Moore SW: Aneurysm of the hepatic artery: Report of five cases with a brief review of the previously reported cases. Surgery 60:299, 1966.

53. Guthrie W, Maclean H: Dissecting aneurysms of arteries other than the aorta. J Pathol 108:219, 1972.

54. Haimovici H, Sprayregen S, Eckstein P, Veith FJ: Celiac artery aneurysmectomy: Case report with review of the literature. Surgery 79:592, 1976.

55. Hama Y, Iwasaki Y, Kaji T, et al: Coil compaction after embolization of the superior mesenteric artery pseudoaneurysm. Eur Radiol 12:S189, 2002.

56. Harlaftis NN, Akin JT: Hemobilia from ruptured hepatic artery aneurysm: Report of a case and review of the literature. Am J Surg 133:229, 1977.

57. Harper PC, Gamelli RL, Kaye MD: Recurrent hemorrhage into the pancreatic duct from a splenic artery aneurysm. Gastroenterology 87:417, 1984.

58. Harris RD, Anderson JE, Coel MN: Aneurysms of the small pancreatic arteries: A cause of upper abdominal pain and intestinal bleeding. Radiology 115:17, 1975.

59. Hashizume M, Ohta M, Ueno K, et al: Laparoscopic ligation of splenic artery aneurysm. Surgery 113:352, 1993.

60. Herzler GM, Silver TM, Graham LM, Stanley JC: Celiac artery aneurysm. J Clin Ultrasound 9:141, 1981.

61. Hoehn JG, Bartholomew LG, Osmundson PJ, Wallace RB: Aneurysms of the mesenteric artery. Am J Surg 115:832, 1968.

62. Hofer BO, Ryan JA Jr, Freeny PC: Surgical significance of vascular changes in chronic pancreatitis. Surg Gynecol Obstet 164:499, 1987.

63. Hong Z, Chen F, Yang J, et al: Diagnosis and treatment of splanchnic artery aneurysms: A report of 57 cases. Chin Med J 112:29, 1999.

64. Iyomasa S, Matsuzaki Y, Hiei K, et al: Pancreaticoduodenal artery aneurysm: A case report and review of the literature. J Vasc Surg 22:161, 1995.

65. Jacobs PPM, Croiset van Ughelen FAAM, Bruyninckx CMA, Hoefsloot F: Haemoperitoneum caused by a dissecting aneurysm of the gastroepiploic artery. Eur J Vasc Surg 8:236, 1994.

66. Jeans PL: Hepatic artery aneurysms and biliary surgery: Two cases and a literature review. Aust N Z J Surg 58:889, 1988.

67. Jonsson K, Bjernstad A, Eriksson B: Treatment of a hepatic artery aneurysm by coil occlusion of the hepatic artery. AJR Am J Roentgenol 134:1245, 1980.

68. Jorgensen BA: Visceral artery aneurysms: A review. Dan Med Bull 32:237, 1985.

69. Kanazawa S, Inada H, Murakami T, et al: The diagnosis and management of splanchnic artery aneurysms: Report of 8 cases. J Cardiovasc Surg 38:479, 1997.

70. Keehan MF, Kistner RL, Banis J: Angiography as an aid in extraenteric gastrointestinal bleeding due to visceral artery aneurysm. Ann Surg 187:357, 1978.

71. Kobori L, Van der Kolk MJ, DeJong KP, et al, the Liver transplant group. Splenic artery aneurysms in liver transplant patients. J Hepatol 27:890, 1997.

72. Kopatsis A, D'Anna JA, Sithian N, Sabido F: Superior mesenteric artery aneurysm: 45 years later. Am Surg 64:263, 1998.

73. Deleted in revision.

74. Kreel L: The recognition and incidence of splenic artery aneurysms: A historical review. Australas Radiol 16:126, 1972.

75. Larson RA, Solomon J, Carpenter JP: Stent graft repair of visceral artery aneurysms. J Vasc Surg 36:1260, 2002.

76. Lee PC, Rhee RY, Gordon RY, et al: Management of splenic artery aneurysms: The significance of portal and essential hypertension. J Am Coll Surg 189:483, 1999.

77. Lina JR, Jaques P, Mandell V: Aneurysm rupture secondary to transcatheter embolization. AJR Am J Roentgenol 132:553, 1979.

78. Lowry SM, O'Dea TP, Gallagher DI, Mozenter R: Splenic artery aneurysm rupture: The seventh instance of maternal and fetal survival. Obstet Gynecol 67:291, 1986.

79. Lumsden AB, Mattar SG, Allen RC, Bacha EA: Hepatic artery aneurysms: The management of 22 patients. J Surg Res 60:345, 1996.

80. MacFarlane JR, Thorbjarnason B: Rupture of splenic artery aneurysm during pregnancy. Am J Obstet Gynecol 95:1025, 1966.

81. McDermott VG, Shlansky-Goldberg R, Cope C: Endovascular management of splenic artery aneurysms and pseudoaneurysms. Cardiovasc Intervent Radiol 17:179, 1994.

82. McIntyre TP, Simone ST, Stahlfield KR: Intraoperative thrombin occlusion of a visceral artery aneurysm. J Vasc Surg 36:393, 2002.

83. McNamara MF, Bakshi KR: Mesenteric artery aneurysms. In Bergan JJ, Yao JST (eds): Aneurysms: Diagnosis and Treatment. New York, Grune & Stratton, 1981, p 285.

84. McNamara MF, Griska LB: Superior mesenteric artery branch aneurysms. Surgery 88:625, 1980.

85. Manazer JR, Monzon JR, Dietz PA, et al: Treatment of pancreatic pseudoaneurysm with percutaneous transabdominal thrombin injection. J Vasc Surg 38:600, 2003.

86. Mandel SR, Jaques PF, Mauro MA, Sanofsky S: Nonoperative management of peripancreatic arterial aneurysms: A 10-year experience. Ann Surg 205:126, 1987.

87. Mandelbaum I, Kaiser GD, Lemple RE: Gastric intramural aneurysm as a cause for massive gastrointestinal hemorrhage. Ann Surg 155:199, 1962.

88. Manenti F, Williams R: Injection studies of the splenic vasculature in portal hypertension. Gut 7:175, 1966.

89. Martin KW, Morian JP, Lee JKT, Scharp DW: Demonstration of a splenic artery pseudoaneurysm by MR imaging. J Comput Assist Tomogr 9:190, 1985.

90. Mattar S, Lumsden AB: The management of splenic artery aneurysms: Experience with 23 cases. Am J Surg 169:580, 1995.

91. Miani S, Arpesani A, Giorgetti PL, et al: Splanchnic artery aneurysms. J Cardiovasc Surg 34:221, 1993.

92. Michels NA: Collateral arterial pathways to the liver after ligation of the hepatic artery and removal of the celiac axis. Cancer 6:708, 1953.

93. Millard M: Fatal rupture of gastric aneurysm. Arch Pathol 59:363, 1955.

94. Moore SW, Guida PM, Schumacher HW: Splenic artery aneurysm. Bull Soc Int Chir 29:210, 1970.

95. Moore SW, Lewis RJ: Splenic artery aneurysm. Ann Surg 153:1033, 1961.

96. Naito A, Toyota N, Ito K: Embolization of a ruptured middle colic artery aneurysm. Cardiovasc Intervent Radiol 18:56, 1995.

97. Nishida O, Moriyasu F, Nakamura T, et al: Hemodynamics of splenic artery aneurysm. Gastroenterology 90:1042, 1986.

98. Nordenstoft EL, Larsen EA: Rupture of a jejunal intramural aneurysm causing massive intestinal bleeding. Acta Chir Scand 133:256, 1967.

99. Nyman U, Svendsen P, Jivegard L, et al: Multiple pancreaticoduodenal aneurysms: Treatment with superior mesenteric artery stent-graft placement and distal embolization. J Vasc Interv Radiol 11:1201, 2000.

100. O'Grady JP, Day EJ, Toole AL, Paust JC: Splenic artery aneurysm rupture in pregnancy: A review and case report. Obstet Gynecol 50:627, 1977.

101. Ohta M, Hashizume M, Ueno K, et al: Hemodynamic study of splenic artery aneurysm in portal hypertension. Hepatogastroenterology 41:181, 1994.

102. Okazaki M, Higashihara H, Ono H, et al: Percutaneous embolization of ruptured splanchnic artery pseudoaneurysms. Acta Radiol 32:349, 1991.

103. Owens JC, Coffey RJ: Aneurysm of the splenic artery including a report of six additional cases. Int Abstr Surg 97:313, 1953.

104. Parangi S, Oz MC, Blume RS, et al: Hepatobiliary complications of polyarteritis nodosa. Arch Surg 126:909, 1991.

105. Parfitt J, Chalmers RTA, Wolfe JHN: Visceral aneurysms in Ehlers-Danlos syndrome: Case report and review of the literature. J Vasc Surg 31:1248, 2000.

106. Patel JV, Weston MJ, Kessel DO, et al: Hepatic artery pseudo-aneurysm after liver transplantation: Treatment with percutaneous thrombin injection. Transplantation 75:1755, 2003.

107. Paty PSK, Cordero JA, Darling RC III, et al: Aneurysms of the pancreaticoduodenal artery. J Vasc Surg 23:710, 1996.

108. Pilleul F, Dugougeat F: Transcatheter embolization of splanchnic aneurysms/pseudoaneurysms: Early imaging allows detection of incomplete procedure. J Comput Assist Tomogr 26:107, 2002.

109. Pitkaranta P, Haapiainen R, Kivisaari L, Schroder T: Diagnostic evaluation and aggressive surgical approach in bleeding pseudo-aneurysms associated with pancreatic pseudocysts. Scand J Gastroenterol 26:58, 1991.

110. Probst P, Castaneda-Zuniga WR, Gomes AS, et al: Nonsurgical treatment of splenic-artery aneurysms. Radiology 128:619, 1978.

111. Puttini M, Aseni P, Brambilla G, Belli L: Splenic artery aneurysms in portal hypertension. J Cardiovasc Surg 23:490, 1982.

112. Quandalle P, Chambon JP, Marache P, et al: Pancreaticoduodenal artery aneurysms associated with celiac axis stenosis: Report of two cases and review of the literature. Ann Vasc Surg 4:540, 1990.

113. Reber PU, Baer HU, Patel AG, et al: Life-threatening upper gastrointestinal tract bleeding caused by ruptured extrahepatic pseudoaneurysm after pancreatoduodenectomy. Surgery 124:114, 1998.

114. Reuter SR, Fry WJ, Bookstein JJ: Mesenteric artery branch aneurysms. Arch Surg 97:497, 1968.

115. Rokke O, Sondenaa K, Amundsen SR, et al: Successful management of eleven splanchnic artery aneurysms. Eur J Surg 163:411, 1997.

116. Rutten APM, Sikkenk PJH: Aneurysm of the hepatic artery: Reconstruction with saphenous vein graft. Br J Surg 58:262, 1971.

117. Salam TA, Lumsden AB, Martin LG, Smith RB III: Nonoperative management of visceral aneurysms and pseudoaneurysms. Am J Surg 164:215, 1992.

118. Salo JA, Aarnio PT, Jarvinen AA, Kivilaakso EO: Aneurysms of the hepatic arteries. Am Surg 55:705, 1989.

119. Salo JA, Salmenkivi K, Tenhunen A, Kivilaakso EO: Rupture of splanchnic artery aneurysms. World J Surg 10:123, 1986.

120. Scheinin TM, Vanttinen E: Aneurysms of the splenic artery in portal hypertension. Ann Clin Res 1:165, 1969.

121. Schoder M, Cejna M, Langle F, et al: Glue embolization of a ruptured celiac trunk pseudoaneurysm via the gastroduodenal artery. Eur Radiol 10:1335, 2000.

122. Sellke FM, Williams GB, Donovan DL, Clarke RE: Management of intra-abdominal aneurysms associated with periarteritis nodosa. J Vasc Surg 4:294, 1986.

123. Settembrini PG, Jausseran J-M, Roveri S, et al: Aneurysms of anomalous splenomesenteric trunk: Clinical features and surgical management in two cases. J Vasc Surg 24:687, 1996.

124. Shanley CJ, Shah NL, Messina LM: Common splanchnic artery aneurysms: Splenic, hepatic and celiac. Ann Vasc Surg 10:315, 1996.

125. Shanley CJ, Shah NL, Messina LM: Uncommon splanchnic artery aneurysms: Pancreaticoduodenal, gastroduodenal, superior mesenteric, inferior mesenteric, and colic. Ann Vasc Surg 10:506, 1996.

126. Shumacker HB Jr, Siderys H: Excisional treatment of aneurysms of celiac artery. Ann Surg 148:885, 1958.

127. Spanos PK, Kloppedal EA, Murray CA: Aneurysms of the gastro-duodenal and pancreaticoduodenal arteries. Am J Surg 127:345, 1974.

128. Spittell JA, Fairbairn JF, Kincaid CW, ReMine WH: Aneurysm of the splenic artery. JAMA 175:452, 1961.

129. Stabile BE, Wilson SE, Debas HT: Reduced mortality from bleeding pseudocysts and pseudoaneurysms caused by pancreatitis. Arch Surg 118:45, 1983.

130. Stanley JC: Abdominal visceral aneurysms. In Haimovici H (ed): Vascular Emergencies. New York, Appleton-Century-Crofts, 1981, p 387.

131. Stanley JC, Eckhauser FE, Whitehouse WM Jr, Zelenock GB: Pancreatitis related splanchnic arterial microaneurysms and macroaneurysms. In Dent TL, Eckhauser FE, Vinik AI, Turcotte JG (eds): Pancreatic Disease. New York, Grune & Stratton, 1981, p 325.

132. Stanley JC, Frey CF, Miller TA, et al: Major arterial hemorrhage: A complication of pancreatic pseudocysts and chronic pancreatitis. Arch Surg 111:435, 1976.

133. Stanley JC, Fry WJ: Pathogenesis and clinical significance of splenic artery aneurysms. Surgery 76:898, 1974.

134. Stanley JC, Gewertz BL, Bove EL, et al: Arterial fibrodysplasia: Histopathologic character and current etiologic concepts. Arch Surg 110:561, 1975.

135. Stanley JC, Thompson NW, Fry WJ: Splanchnic artery aneurysms. Arch Surg 101:689, 1970.

136. Stone WM, Abbas MA, Gloviczki P, et al: Celiac arterial aneurysms. Arch Surg 137:670, 2002.

137. Stone WM, Abbas M, Cherry KJ, et al: Superior mesenteric artery aneurysms: Is presence an indication for intervention? J Vasc Surg 36:234, 2002.

138. Takahashi T, Shimada K, Kobayashi N, Kakita A: Migration of steel-wire coils into the stomach after transcatheter arterial embolization for a bleeding splenic artery pseudoaneurysm: Report of a case. Surg Today 31:458, 2001.

139. Tessier DJ, Abbas MA, Fowl RJ, et al: Management of rare mesenteric arterial branch aneurysms. Ann Vasc Surg 16:586, 2002.

140. Thomford NR, Yurko JE, Smith EJ: Aneurysm of gastric arteries as a cause of intraperitoneal hemorrhage: Review of literature. Ann Surg 168:294, 1968.

141. Trastek VF, Pairolero PC, Joyce JW, et al: Splenic artery aneurysms. Surgery 91:694, 1982.

142. Trevisani MF, Ricci MA, Michaels RM, Meyer KK: Multiple mesenteric aneurysms complicating subacute bacterial endocarditis. Arch Surg 122:823, 1987.

143. Varekamp AP, Minder WH, VanNoort G, Wassenaar HA: Rupture of a submucosal gastric aneurysm, a rare cause of gastric hemorrhage. Neth J Surg 35:100, 1983.

144. Verta MJ Jr, Dean RH, Yao JST, et al: Pancreaticoduodenal artery aneurysms. Ann Surg 186:111, 1977.

145. Violago FC, Downs AR: Ruptured atherosclerotic aneurysm of the superior mesenteric artery with celiac axis occlusion. Ann Surg 174:207, 1971.

146. Wagner WH, Cossman DV, Treiman RL, et al: Hemosuccus pancreaticus from intraductal rupture of a primary splenic artery aneurysm. J Vasc Surg 19:158, 1994.

147. Wagner WH, Allins AD, Treiman RL, et al: Ruptured visceral artery aneurysms. Ann Vasc Surg 11:342, 1997.

148. Weaver DH, Fleming RJ, Barnes WA: Aneurysm of the hepatic artery: The value of arteriography in surgical management. Surgery 64:891, 1968.

149. Welling TH, Williams DM, Stanley JC: Excessive oral amphetamine use as a possible cause of renal and splanchnic arterial aneurysms: A report of two cases. J Vasc Surg 28:727, 1998.

150. Werner K, Tarasoutchi F, Lunardi W, et al: Mycotic aneurysm of the celiac trunk and superior mesenteric artery in a case of infective endocarditis. J Cardiovasc Surg 32:380, 1991.

151. West JE, Bernhardt H, Bowers RF: Aneurysms of the pancreatico-duodenal artery. Am J Surg 115:835, 1968.

152. White AF, Baum S, Buranasiri S: Aneurysms secondary to pancreatitis. AJR Am J Roentgenol 127:393, 1976.

153. Wright CB, Schoepfle J, Kurtock SB, et al: Gastrointestinal bleeding and mycotic superior mesenteric aneurysm. Surgery 92:40, 1982.

154. Yamakado K, Nakatsuka A, Tanaka N, et al: Transcatheter arterial embolization of ruptured pseudoaneurysms with coils and n-butyl cyanoacrylate. J Vasc Intervent Radiol 11:66, 2000.

155. Yoon H-K, Lindh M, Uher P, et al: Stent-graft repair of a splenic artery aneurysm. Cardiovasc Intervent Radiol 24:200, 2001.

156. Zajko AB, Bron KM, Starzl TE, et al: Angiography of liver transplantation patients. Radiology 157:305, 1985.

Chapter

Infected Aneurysms

108

DANIEL J. REDDY, MD
MITCHELL R. WEAVER, MD

■ HISTORICAL BACKGROUND

Although aneurysmal disease was reported in Western literature in ancient times by Galen, 14 centuries passed until Paré,[117] writing in the mid-16th century, first noted the association between an aneurysm and infection. He described the fatal outcome and autopsy findings of a patient who had rupture of a syphilitic aneurysm of the descending thoracic aorta.

During the 19th century, Rokitansky[139] in Austria, Virkow[177] and Koch[78] in Germany, and Tufnell[173] in Ireland predated Osler's landmark work with case reports associating endocarditis, septic emboli, arterial abscesses, and ruptured infected aneurysms of the superior mesenteric and popliteal arteries. In 1885, Osler[113] presented the first comprehensive discussion of an infected aneurysm, remarking on the "anatomical characters ..., clinical features, and ... etiological and pathological relations." He used the term *mycotic aneurysm* to describe these infected aneurysms, which had developed as complications of bacterial endocarditis. Because there was no apparent association with fungal disease, Osler's choice of the term *mycotic* has been a source of discussion and confusion in the literature. Some authors have used this term when referring to an "infected" aneurysm regardless of pathogenesis.[3,5,10,22,27,39,52,109,119,124,170,185,187] Fungal infection is *not* implied when this designation is used. Strictly speaking, the term *mycotic aneurysm* should be used only to describe an infected aneurysm resulting from bacterial endocarditis complicated by septic arterial emboli or an infected aneurysm of the sinus of Valsalva resulting from contiguous spread from an infected aortic valve. Following Osler by 2 years, Eppinger[45] pro-

vided evidence supporting the embolic etiology of a mycotic aneurysm when he documented identical strains of bacteria in the peripheral embolus and the valvular vegetations of a patient with a mycotic aneurysm.

At the beginning of the 20th century, Lewis and Schrager[89] reviewed several cases of mycotic aneurysm occurring in young patients with endocarditis. They commented on a case reported by Ruge involving a streptococcal coronary artery aneurysm in a 12-year-old boy with streptococcal osteomyelitis and hypothesized that not all infected aneurysms were "embolomycotic" in origin.

In 1923, Stengel and Wolferth[164] described 4 patients and reviewed another 213 with a total of 382 bacterial aneurysms of intravascular origin. Multiple aneurysms were found in 49 patients. Although aortic, mesenteric, and intracranial mycotic aneurysms predominated, virtually every other named vessel in the arterial tree also was involved. Of greater significance in the evolving understanding of the pathogenesis of infected aneurysms was the finding that in 30 patients (14%), there was no evidence of bacterial endocarditis, showing that infected aneurysms occur in connection with a variety of other septic conditions.

In 1937, Crane[34] presented the clinical course and autopsy findings of a 35-year-old man with a primary multilocular infected aortic arch aneurysm in association with a hypoplastic aorta and an infected superior mesenteric arterial aneurysm. He postulated that in arteries predisposed by disease, blood-borne bacteria could settle and produce infected aneurysms. Six years later, this hypothesis—that bacteremia unassociated with endocarditis could cause an infected aneurysm—was confirmed by Revell.[137] Later authors reported that atherosclerotic vessels were susceptible to bacterial infection, particularly by various *Salmonella* species.[15,27,40,60,64,114,119,133,160,169,171,193] Such arterial infections are considered to be examples of microbial arteritis starting in nonaneurysmal arteries and producing infected aneurysms after the vessel wall has been destroyed by infection.

The classification of infected aneurysm was refined further by the 1959 report of Sommerville and colleagues[159] of more than 20,000 Mayo Clinic autopsies as they related to atherosclerotic abdominal aortic aneurysms (AAAs). In all, 178 aneurysms (0.8%) were found. Of these, 172 were bland (97%), and 6 were infected (3%); 4 of the 6 infected aneurysms had ruptured. This report established the existence of a third type of arterial infection: one occurring in a preexisting atherosclerotic aneurysm. Bennett and Cherry[13] in 1967, Mundth and associates[107] in 1969, and Jarrett and associates[71] in 1975 all reported series detailing the clinical course, bacteriology, treatment, and outcome for patients with this type of infected aneurysm. With the advent of antibiotic therapy, the overall incidence of arterial infection declined, paralleling the successful treatment of bacterial endocarditis.[171]

In more recent years, the incidence of arterial infections and infected aneurysms has increased in response to the increasing prevalence of immunosuppressed hosts,[60,72,84] invasive hemodynamic monitoring,[158] angiography,[8,47] and drug addiction.[3,74,115,123,130] This change in pathogenesis has been noted by other authors, who emphasize that a fourth type of infected aneurysm has emerged as a significant clinical entity—*post-traumatic infected false aneurysm (pseudoaneurysm)*.[190] Although the greatest number of such infected aneurysms has been associated with intravenous or intra-arterial drug injections, the trend away from parenteral drug use in favor of smoking "crack" has resulted in a decline in incidence in more recent years.[74] Owing to developing treatment modalities that employ catheter-based percutaneous approaches for a variety of occlusive or aneurysmal vascular lesions, iatrogenic infected false aneurysms seem to be increasing in frequency.[146] In contemporary practice, the option of in-line (in situ) arterial reconstruction after resection of an infected aneurysm has

become closer to an everyday reality owing to preserved homografts, innovative superficial vein conduits, early detection, and effective antimicrobial therapies.[110,181]

■ CLASSIFICATION

On the basis of the foregoing historical review and the classifications suggested by others,[96,190] this chapter considers four types of infected aneurysm:

- Mycotic aneurysms (i.e., from septic arterial emboli)
- Microbial arteritis with aneurysm
- Infected preexisting aneurysms
- Post-traumatic infected false aneurysms

Excluded are aneurysms resulting from contiguous infection, spontaneous aortoenteric fistulae, and infections of synthetic vascular prostheses (Table 108-1).

Mycotic Aneurysms

Incidence

Mycotic aneurysms develop when septic emboli of cardiac origin lodge in the lumen or the vasa vasorum of peripheral arteries. Mycotic aneurysms can occur in normal and abnormal arteries. In the preantibiotic era, approximately 90% of all infected aneurysms were mycotic aneurysms.[89,137,164] They occurred in virtually every named artery intracranially; the great vessels; the thoracoabdominal aorta; and the visceral, extremity, pulmonary, and coronary arteries. The century following Osler's initial description of this entity saw antibiotic therapy, the advancement of microbiologic techniques allowing identification and treatment of specific bacterial infections, and the development of open heart surgery to permit replacement of the infected cardiac valve. These advances have sharply lowered the incidence of mycotic aneurysms occurring as embolic complications of infective endocarditis.[92]

In 1951, Cates and Christie[24] reported the results of penicillin treatment of 442 patients with endocarditis; 145

Table 108-1	Clinical Characteristics of Infected Aneurysms			
	MYCOTIC ANEURYSM	**MICROBIAL ARTERITIS**	**INFECTION OF EXISTING ANEURYSM**	**POST-TRAUMATIC INFECTED FALSE ANEURYSM**
Etiology	Endocarditis	Bacteremia	Bacteremia	Narcotic addiction Trauma
Age	30-50	>50	>50	<30
Incidence	Rare	Common	Unusual	Very common
Location	Aorta Visceral Intracranial Peripheral	Atherosclerotic Aortoiliac Intimal defects	Infrarenal Aorta	Femoral Carotid
Bacteriology	Gram-positive cocci	*Salmonella* Others	*Staphylococcus* Others	*Staphylococcus aureus* Polymicrobial
Mortality	25%	75%	90%	5%

From Wilson SE, Van Wagenen P, Passaro E Jr: Arterial infection. Curr Probl Surg 15:5, 1978. Reproduced with permission of Year Book Medical Publishers, Inc.

patients (35%) had a major arterial embolization, and 20 (4.5%) died after hemorrhage from a mycotic aneurysm. These results were a marked improvement over previously quoted embolism rates of 80%.[113] In a comprehensive review of infected aneurysms, Brown and associates[18] found that endocarditis was implicated in the pathogenesis of only 16% of all reported infected aneurysms and in only 10% of cases since 1965.

The relationship between bacterial endocarditis and peripheral arterial embolization has been reported from the Henry Ford Hospital.[41,43,91,157] Patient admissions for peripheral (extracranial) embolization during the period 1950 to 1964 were 23.1 per 100,000 and during the period 1960 to 1979 were 50.4 per 100,000. During this interval (1950 to 1979), 225 patients were admitted for 337 individual emboli.[92] A mycotic aneurysm developed from these emboli in only two patients from this group,[42] and both patients were treated between 1957 and 1961, giving a hospital incidence of mycotic aneurysm of 1 per 35,000 during those 5 years. Since 1962, mycotic aneurysms occurring as an embolic complication of endocarditis have been encountered in only eight patients. Six of these eight aneurysms involved the intracranial arteries.[91]

From 1971 to 1983, Johansen and Devin[72] reported that nine patients with infective endocarditis were treated for 14 episodes of mycotic embolization resulting in 17 individual emboli. Six of these nine patients required cardiac valve replacement, but no mycotic aneurysm developed. From 1972 to 1984, 91 patients underwent cardiac valve replacement for endocarditis, and a mycotic cerebral aneurysm developed in 5 patients.[92] Other authors have noted this decreasing incidence of mycotic aneurysms in absolute terms and as a percentage of infected aneurysms.[3,71,89,92,159,190]

Location

Even though mycotic aneurysms may occur in multiple sites in a given patient, certain anatomic locations predominate[113]—the aorta and the intracranial, superior mesenteric, and femoral arteries (Table 108-2).[92,164] The predilection of mycotic aneurysms for certain anatomic sites relates to their pathogenesis. In larger arteries, such as the aorta, infected emboli may lodge in the relatively large vasa vasorum, causing vessel wall ischemia and infection. As the media is destroyed by this process, an aneurysm forms. In smaller arteries, the infected macroscopic emboli may lodge in the vessel lumen or wall and may initiate a similar pathologic process. Sites predisposed to the formation of mycotic aneurysms are bifurcations, arteriovenous fistulae, and coarctations.[89,135] Reports of mycotic aneurysms occurring in the tibioperoneal trunk, the common hepatic artery, the ascending aorta, the carotid artery, and the cerebral artery represent the variety of arterial segments in which mycotic aneurysms are found.[1,28,38,69,153,187]

Bacteriology

In 1923, Stengel and Wolferth[164] reported that the predominant organisms were nonhemolytic streptococci, pneumococci, and staphylococci. In 1986, Magilligan and Quinn[92] reported that the dominant infecting organisms in patients with no history of drug abuse ($n = 55$) with native valve

ARTERY	PREANTIBIOTIC ERA (1909-1943)	1968-1986
Pulmonary	11 (3%)	—
Coronary	8 (2%)	—
Aorta	87 (25%)	20 (12%)
Iliac	14 (4%)	9 (5%)
Gluteal	2 (<1%)	—
Upper extremity	35 (10%)	12 (13%)
Subclavian	3	3
Axillary	1	2
Brachial	8	3
Radial	1	4
Ulnar	2	—
Lower extremity	40 (12%)	69 (63%)
Femoral	10	69
Popliteal	2	—
Visceral	87 (25%)	3 (2%)
Celiac	1	—
Hepatic	15	—
Superior mesenteric	47	2
Splenic	18	—
Renal	5	1
Gastroepiploic	1	—
Extracranial cerebrovascular	3 (<1%)	2 (1%)
Innominate	1	—
Carotid	1	2
Vertebral	1	—
Intracranial cerebral	50 (15%)	6 (4%)
Other	7 (2%)	—
Total	344 (100%)	121 (100%)

Table 108-2 Frequency Distribution of Infected Aneurysms

Data from Anderson et al,[3] Johnson et al,[74] Lewis and Schrager,[89] Mundth et al,[107] Reddy et al,[130] and Stengel and Wolferth.[164]

endocarditis were *Streptococcus viridans* (22%), *Staphylococcus aureus* (20%), *Streptococcus faecalis* (14%), and *Staphylococcus epidermidis* (11%). Exotic bacteria, such as *Eikenella corrodens* and *Propionibacterium acnes,* and the fungus *Aspergillus* also were noted. In narcotic addicts ($n = 36$), the infecting organisms were *S. aureus* (36%), *Pseudomonas* (16%), polymicrobial species (15%), *S. faecalis* (13%), and *S. viridans* (11%). Exotic organisms, such as *Micrococcus, Corynebacterium,* and *Candida albicans,* also were isolated. The responsible organism in each of the six intracerebral mycotic aneurysms among these 91 patients was *S. faecalis* (three), *S. viridans* (one), *Pseudomonas* (one), and *C. albicans* (one).[92] In 1984, Brown and colleagues[18] reported that *S. aureus* and various streptococcal species accounted for 38% of infected aneurysms of all types (Table 108-3). In six large published series of aortoiliac aneurysms, *Staphylococcus* species and *Streptococcus* species accounted for 28% of infected aneurysms (Table 108-4).[68,101,111,154,161,166]

Microbial Arteritis with Aneurysm

Prevalence and Location

In the preantibiotic era, microbial arteritis with aneurysm occurred in approximately 14% of patients.[164] In modern times, as a result of the decline in rheumatic fever and bacterial endocarditis, microbial arteritis with aneurysm is becoming more prevalent than mycotic aneurysm.[18] This

Table 108-3 Organisms Cultured from Infected Aneurysms*

ORGANISMS	BEFORE 1965	1965-1984	TOTAL
Salmonella spp.	14 (38%)	15 (10%)	29 (15%)
Staphylococcus aureus	7 (19%)	47 (30%)	54 (28%)
Streptococcus spp.	5 (14%)	15 (10%)	20 (10%)
Pseudomonas spp.	1	6	7
Staphylococcus epidermidis	1	5	6
Escherichia coli	—	4	4
Proteus spp.	2	1	3
Serratia spp.	—	3	3
Enterobacter spp.	—	3	3
Neisseria spp.	—	3	3
Clostridium spp.	—	2	2
Enterococcus group	—	2	2
Bacteroides spp.	—	2	2
Candida spp.	—	2	2
Klebsiella spp.	—	2	2
Bacteroides fragilis	—	1	1
Peptostreptococcus spp.	—	1	1
Corynebacterium spp.	—	1	1
Arizona hinshawii	—	1	1
Citrobacter freundii	—	1	1
Culture negative	7 (19%)	41 (25%)	48 (25%)
Total	*37*	*158*	*195*

*Collected series from previous review of English-language literature up to 1984.

From Brown SL, Busutill RW, Baker JD, et al: Bacteriologic and surgical determinants of survival in patients with mycotic aneurysms. J Vasc Surg 1:541, 1984.

Table 108-4 Reported Organisms Recovered from Combined Series of 143 Aortoiliac Aneurysms, 1996-2002

	NO. ORGANISMS RECOVERED (%)
Salmonella spp.	45 (30)
Staphylococcus spp.	29 (19)
Streptococcus spp.	11 (9)
Escherichia coli	13 (9)
Bacteroides spp.	7 (5)
Clostridium spp.	4 (3)
Enterococcus group	4 (3)
Acinetobacter spp.	3 (2)
Enterobacter spp.	2 (1)
Listeria monocytogenes	2 (1)
Pseudomonas spp.	2 (1)
Campylobacter fetus	1 (<1)
Corynebacterium spp.	1 (<1)
Aspergillus	1 (<1)
Coccidioides immitis	1 (<1)
Candida spp.	1 (<1)
Mycobacterium avium complex	1 (<1)
Haemophilus influenzae	1 (<1)
Mycobacterium tuberculosis	1 (<1)
Culture negative	17 (11)

Data from Hsu et al,[68] Moneta et al,[101] Muller et al,[106] Oderich et al,[111] Sessa et al,[154] and Sriussadaporn.[161]

increase is due to the aging of the population and the corresponding increase in atherosclerosis, an important factor predisposing arteries to infection.

The prevalence in adults of infected aneurysms produced by microbial arteritis is estimated to be 0.06% to 0.65%.[15,133] Diseased intima, which when normal is highly resistant to infection, allows blood-borne bacteria to inoculate the arterial wall. When infection is established, suppuration, localized perforation, and false aneurysm formation follow (Fig. 108-1). Supporting atherosclerosis as the principal predisposing factor in the pathogenesis of microbial arteritis is the fact that the aorta, the most frequent site of atherosclerosis, is also the most frequent location of these lesions (by a 3:1 margin over peripheral sites).[13,27,107,109,124] In our series, microbial arteritis accounted for 77% of infected aortoiliac aneurysms (Table 108-5).[133]

It has been thought that patients with acquired immunodeficiency syndrome (AIDS) may be susceptible to infectious aortitis. AIDS patients might represent a large

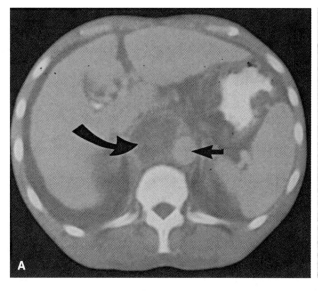
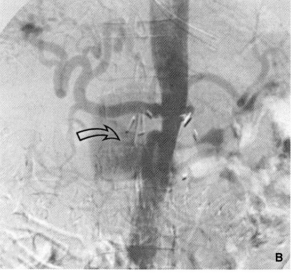

FIGURE 108-1 Diagnostic radiology studies of a patient with *Staphylococcus aureus* microbial aortitis with aneurysm. **A,** Contrast-enhanced CT scan shows contained rupture of infected aneurysm *(curved arrow)* and the adjacent aorta *(straight arrow)*. **B,** Digital subtraction aortogram shows saccular eccentric infected aneurysm of the infrarenal aorta *(arrow)*.

Table 108-5	Anatomic Location and Type of Infected Aneurysms			

TYPE OF ANEURYSMS	NO. ANEURYSMS (%)			TOTAL NO. (%) ANEURYSMS
	SRAA	IRAA	CIA	
Microbial arteritis	3	5	2	10 (77)
Mycotic aneurysm	0	0	1	1 (7.7)
Infection in preexisting aneurysms	0	1	0	1 (7.7)
Adjacent soft tissue infection	0	1	0	1 (7.7)
Total (%)	3 (23)	7 (54)	3 (23)	13 (100)

CIA, common iliac artery; IRAA, infrarenal abdominal aorta; SRAA, suprarenal abdominal aorta.

From Reddy DJ, Shepard AD, Evans JR, et al: Management of infected aortoiliac aneurysms. Arch Surg 126:873, 1991. Copyright 1991, American Medical Association.

cohort that would increase the incidence and alter the microbiology of this pathologic entity in the future.[40,60] Patients undergoing hemodialysis are thought to be particularly vulnerable to *Staphylococcus* bacteremia and resulting microbial arteritis.[150] Microbial arteritis of the subclavian artery after irradiation for breast cancer,[63] aortic infection after gastrointestinal endoscopy in an immunosuppressed patient, and appendicitis and lumbar osteomyelitis have been reported.[54,142,144]

Bacteriology

The predominant microorganisms associated with microbial arteritis leading to aneurysm are *Escherichia coli* and *Salmonella* and *Staphylococcus* species.[190] *Bacteroides fragilis* aneurysms of the suprarenal aorta also have been reported, highlighting the necessity of culturing for anaerobes in these cases.[133,165] The overall 25% culture-negative rate may indicate a deficiency in obtaining anaerobic cultures (see Table 108-3).

The importance of *Salmonella* species in microbial arteritis, particularly microbial aortitis, has been mentioned in many reports and confirmed in our own review at the Henry Ford Hospital.[133] The diseased aorta has a unique vulnerability to *Salmonella* (Fig. 108-2). The most virulent species are *S. choleraesuis* and *S. typhimurium*, which account for 62% of the reported cases of *Salmonella* arteritis.[190] Although *Salmonella* species are the predominant organisms reported worldwide,[26,50,93,112] other organisms (e.g., *Listeria monocytogenes*,[55,86] *Klebsiella pneumoniae*,[168] *Clostridium septicum*[103,108,145]) and fungal species (e.g., *Aspergillus niger*[156]) also have been reported.

Infected Preexisting Aneurysms

Prevalence and Location

The prevalence of infection in preexisting atherosclerotic aneurysms was estimated by Sommerville and associates to be 3.4%.[159] Bennett and Cherry[13] and Jarrett and coauthors[71] reported parallel findings, noting the relative rarity of this lesion and its propensity for rupture.

The related entity of aortic aneurysms colonized by bacteria has been identified in two nearly simultaneous reports by Ernst and colleagues[46] and Williams and Fisher.[188] Patients undergoing abdominal aortic aneurysmectomy were studied prospectively with operative bacterial cultures taken from the aneurysm wall and contents and from bowel bag fluid. Overall, 15% of cultures yielded positive results.[46] There was a higher prevalence of positive cultures among patients with ruptured aneurysms (38%) compared with patients with asymptomatic (9%) and symptomatic (13%) aneurysms.[46] Although the clinical significance of these findings is unknown, it seems that colonized aneurysms do not pose the same threat to patients as infected aneurysms. Steed and colleagues[163] concluded that significant contamination of intraluminal thrombus in aneurysms is rare. Other authors have confirmed this report and advise that routine culture of aneurysm contents or wall

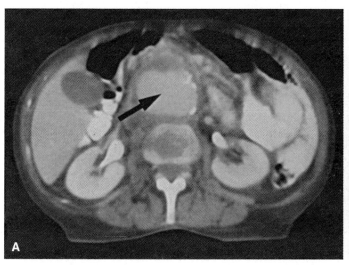
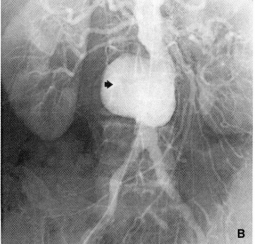

FIGURE 108-2 Diagnostic radiology studies of a patient with *Salmonella* infection of a preexisting small atherosclerotic aneurysm. **A,** Contrast-enhanced CT scan shows saccular aneurysm with calcification *(arrow).* **B,** Transfemoral aortogram shows saccular atherosclerotic infrarenal aneurysm *(arrow).*

is not necessary when the clinical picture does not suggest aneurysm infection.[51] The abdominal aorta is the predominant site reported for secondary infection of aneurysms. Lesions have been discovered in other locations, and in earlier times, bacterial overgrowth in luetic aneurysms of the thoracic aorta was encountered.[190]

Bacteriology

Some authors have noted that the index of suspicion for infected AAAs is generally low, and consequently these lesions may have been underreported.[188] The Jarrett study of infected preexisting AAAs documented a predominance of gram-positive organisms (59%) over gram-negative organisms (35%).[71] The most prevalent organism was *Staphylococcus* (41%). Although less common, gram-negative infections were more virulent than gram-positive infections from the standpoints of aneurysm rupture (84% versus 10%) and patient mortality (84% versus 50%).

In another study,[46] colonized aneurysms yielded 81% gram-positive and 19% gram-negative organisms. The most prevalent organism was *S. epidermidis*, accounting for 53% of positive cultures. Coliform sepsis in a preexisting AAA has been associated with an appendiceal abscess.[105]

As emerging technologies based on percutaneous or minimally invasive endovascular repairs gain popularity,[118] infection in a previously existing aneurysm and microbial arteritis may be associated with postimplantation infection, particularly when synthetic prostheses are employed. Unintentionally, grafts may be placed in a septic field that otherwise would have been subject to débridement in the course of a conventional open procedure.

Post-traumatic Infected False Aneurysms

Prevalence and Location

Post-traumatic infected false aneurysms have become the most prevalent type of infected aneurysm in recent decades (Table 108-6). The primary factor in this shifting emphasis in pathogenesis is drug addiction. In the 25 years following Huebl and Read's[69] initial report of two infected femoral

artery false aneurysms in narcotic addicts, an additional 195 such cases have been reported.[3,49,52,56,69,74,115,123,130,193]

The femoral artery, used by narcotic addicts for repeated groin injections, is the most common site in which these lesions occur (Fig. 108-3). Other locations, such as the external iliac and carotid arteries, also have been reported (Fig. 108-4).[74,89,102]

Another factor contributing to the increasing incidence of these lesions is the proliferation of various invasive testing and monitoring procedures. In susceptible individuals, percutaneous arterial puncture may result in an iatrogenic post-traumatic infected false aneurysm.[8,158] Along with the increase in percutaneous endovascular procedures has come the increased use of percutaneous femoral artery closure devices, which may be associated with the increased incidence of infected pseudoaneurysms.[126]

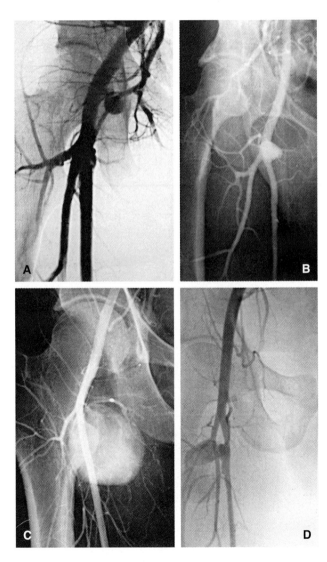

FIGURE 108-3 Arteriograms show the appearance of an infected femoral artery false aneurysm in each of four locations. **A,** Common femoral artery. **B,** Common femoral bifurcation. **C,** Deep femoral artery. **D,** Superficial femoral artery. (**A, B,** and **D** from Reddy DJ, Smith RF, Elliott JP Jr, et al: Infected femoral artery false aneurysms in drug addicts: Evolution of selective vascular reconstruction. J Vasc Surg 3:718, 1986.)

Table 108-6	Etiology of Infected Aneurysms*		
ETIOLOGY	**BEFORE 1965**	**AFTER 1965**	**TOTAL**
Arterial trauma	4 (10%)	71 (51%)	75 (42%)
Endocarditis	15 (37%)	14 (10%)	29 (16%)
Local infection	3 (7%)	6 (4%)	9 (5%)
Bacteremia	—	9 (6%)	9 (5%)
Retroperitoneal abscess	2 (5%)	2 (1%)	4 (2%)
Gastrointestinal tract	1 (2%)	3 (2%)	4 (2%)
Oropharynx	—	3 (2%)	3 (2%)
Pneumonia	1 (2%)	—	1 (<1%)
Carcinoma	—	1 (1%)	1 (<1%)
Unknown	15 (36%)	30 (22%)	45 (25%)
Total	*41*	*139*	*180*

*Collected series from a published review of English literature.

From Brown SL, Busutill RW, Baker JD, et al: Bacteriologic and surgical determinants of survival in patients with mycotic aneurysms. J Vasc Surg 1:541, 1984.

Malanoski and coworkers[93] reported that 55 of 102 patients (54%) with blood cultures positive for *S. aureus* at the New England Deaconess Hospital over 2 years had bacteremia attributable to an intravascular catheter. Five of these patients had *Staphylococcus* sepsis after percutaneous transluminal coronary angioplasty (PTCA). Two of the five patients also manifested a post-traumatic infected false aneurysm of the accessed femoral artery.

Samore and colleagues,[146] reporting on catheter-related bacteremia in 3473 PTCA patients from the Beth Israel Deaconess Medical Center, noted a low frequency (0.24%) of PTCA-related bacteremia. They reported significant morbidity, however, including post-traumatic infected false aneurysms of the punctured femoral artery. Independent risk factors for development of septic complications of PTCA were noted as follows:

- Duration of the procedure
- Number of catheterizations at the same site
- Difficult vascular access
- Arterial sheath in place more than 1 day
- Congestive heart failure

Bacteriology

Since 1965, when the most prevalent form of infected aneurysm has been post-traumatic infected false aneurysm, the predominant infecting organism has been *S. aureus* (30%).[18,58] In one report of infected femoral artery false aneurysms in drug addicts, 35 of 54 patients (65%) had pure cultures of *S. aureus* from the aneurysm. Seventeen of these 35 staphylococcal cultures (48%) were found to be

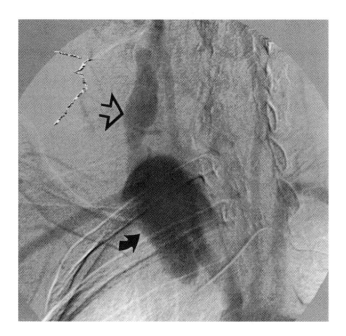

FIGURE 108-4 Digital subtraction angiogram of a patient with polymicrobial post-traumatic false aneurysm of the innominate artery *(closed arrow)* caused by repeated cervical injections of narcotics. There was an associated arteriovenous fistula to the internal jugular vein *(open arrow)* and a right recurrent laryngeal nerve paralysis.

methicillin resistant. An additional eight patients (33%) had mixed polymicrobial cultures, including *S. aureus, E. coli, S. faecalis, Pseudomonas aeruginosa,* and various *Enterobacter* organisms.[130] Johnson and coworkers,[74] reporting on drug-related infected false aneurysms in a variety of anatomic locations, isolated *S. aureus* from a high percentage of blood (71%) and wound (76%) cultures.

■ CLINICAL PRESENTATION

The clinical presentation of infected aneurysms depends on the etiologic mechanism and the anatomic site involved. Clinical characteristics of various aneurysm types are summarized in Table 108-1. Although infected aneurysms occur in all age groups, including neonates[22,170] and children,[99] when there is no antecedent history of arterial injury, the typical patient is older with atherosclerosis.[12,159] The principal signs and symptoms of an aneurysm and sepsis may be subtle (Table 108-7). Infection in an AAA may be difficult to detect. Patients with infected aortic aneurysms usually present with fever of unknown origin. Because of the insidious signs and symptoms of infected aneurysms, a high index of suspicion is needed in the following situations[22,27,71,178]:

- A positive blood specimen
- Erosion of lumbar vertebrae
- Female sex
- Presence of uncalcified aneurysms
- First presentation of an aneurysm after bacterial sepsis

Of infected AAAs, 40% may not be palpable and may go unrecognized until rupture.[107,174,191,196] Infected aneurysms of the femoral or carotid arteries or other superficial peripheral locations are readily appreciated, however, and 90% are palpable.[107] Infected femoral false aneurysms present with a tender groin mass, indicating contained rupture; with some other manifestation of sepsis; or with bleeding in almost every patient.[115,123,130]

Fungal arterial infections are rare but characteristically occur in patients with chronic immune suppression[84] or diabetes mellitus[97] or after treatment for a disseminated fungal disease.[100] The clinical presentation of these rare infections may be limited to fever or malaise or may be more apparent, with gangrene in an extremity after distal embolization.

Table 108-7	Infected Aneurysms: Clinical Presentation

CLINICAL MARKER	NO. (%) PATIENTS
Abdominal pain	12 (92)
Fever	10 (77)
Leukocytosis*	9 (69)
Positive blood cultures	9 (69)
Palpable abdominal mass	6 (46)
Rupture	4 (31)

*Leukocyte count >10 × 10⁹/L.

From Reddy DJ, Shepard AD, Evans JR, et al: Management of infected aortoiliac aneurysms. Arch Surg 126:873, 1991. Copyright 1991, American Medical Association.

Although infected aneurysms can occur in virtually any artery and may present with a variety of clinical signs and symptoms, they are similar in that they all eventually lead to sepsis or hemorrhage. Consequently, whenever the surgeon suspects this diagnosis, it must be assumed that the patient's life or limb is in jeopardy, and confirmation of the diagnosis and urgent surgical therapy are required.

■ DIAGNOSIS

Laboratory Studies

In most patients, leukocytosis is a sensitive but nonspecific indicator of an infected aneurysm.[15,71,130,133,169] The sensitivity of this finding may be limited, however, by intercurrent antimicrobial therapy that has suppressed but not cured the infection.[100] A lack of specificity also is underscored by reports of sealed ruptures of bland, uninfected, atherosclerotic aneurysms that may simulate sepsis and exhibit leukocytosis.[166] Likewise, an elevated erythrocyte sedimentation rate is often present but nonspecific. These limitations underscore the need for more specific and sensitive tests to confirm the presence of an infected aneurysm (see Table 108-7).

Positive blood specimens in a patient with an aneurysm are considered specific for an infected aneurysm until proved otherwise, although positive cultures lack sensitivity. Anderson and colleagues[3] found positive cultures in only 50% of such patients. It follows that negative blood cultures alone are not sufficiently sensitive to rule out the diagnosis of an infected aneurysm.

When the diagnosis of an infected aneurysm is first entertained during operation, samples of the aneurysm wall and contents should be obtained for culture with a search for aerobic and anaerobic bacteria and fungi. Additional information may be gained by Gram stains. These studies should not be considered sufficient, however, to ensure that the aneurysm is not infected because neither negative blood cultures nor intraoperative Gram stains are sufficiently sensitive to exclude the diagnosis of infected aneurysm.[18] Aneurysm wall and contents culture results are not available during the operation and can be used only to direct postoperative antimicrobial therapy; even final culture results may be misleading in patients treated with antibiotics. Some authors have advocated wider use of aneurysm content and wall cultures in routine operations for aortic aneurysm.[46,71] In our experience with infected aortoiliac aneurysms, 69% of patients had positive preoperative blood cultures, and 92% had positive aneurysm wall cultures. Operative Gram stains were positive in 50% of patients with ruptured infected aneurysms but in only 11% of patients with unruptured but infected aneurysms.[133]

Radiologic Studies

Aortic aneurysms associated with vertebral body erosion or aneurysms devoid of calcification should raise the suspicion of an infected aneurysm. Plain films are not sufficiently sensitive to confirm the diagnosis, and additional studies are needed. Of value are computed tomography (CT) and either conventional or digital subtraction angiography (DSA). Although ultrasonography of the abdominal aorta provides general information about aneurysm size and location, it is less reliable for detecting the presence or extent of arterial infection. Ultrasonography has proven utility in the diagnosis of femoral artery false aneurysm, but the ability of duplex scanning to detect infection is uncertain, and we do not employ it for this purpose.[130]

The utility of intravenous DSA in evaluating the femoral artery for infected aneurysm has been established.[155] DSA is particularly valuable for screening in drug addicts and for similar lesions in the great vessels and the arteries of the upper and lower extremities. DSA is of comparable diagnostic accuracy and may be less expensive and more easily accomplished than cut-film arteriography.[155]

Arteriography, either digital subtraction or conventional, is indispensable in the evaluation of patients with a suspected infected aneurysm. The arteriographic criteria for infection in an aneurysm are as follows (Fig. 108-5; see also Figs. 108-1 to 108-4):

■ Saccular aneurysm in an otherwise normal-appearing vessel
■ Multilobulated aneurysm
■ Eccentric aneurysm with a relatively narrow neck

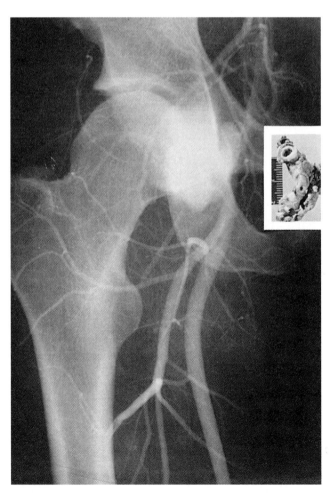

FIGURE 108-5 Femoral arteriogram of a patient with a post-traumatic infected false aneurysm of the common femoral artery shows a lobulated aneurysm. *Inset,* Resected femoral artery specimen shows the injured and infected artery.

An infected aneurysm may not exhibit any arteriographic characteristics indicative of infection, however.[185]

Contrast-enhanced CT is valuable in determining etiology and assessing the presence or absence of aneurysm rupture (see Figs. 108-1 and 108-2), but often fails to give specific information about the presence or absence of infection.[57,59,87,141] Case reports documenting the potential utility of CT performed early in the clinical course of infected aortic aneurysms suggest subtle diagnostic features and have documented the rapidly deteriorating clinical course often experienced by such patients.[23,59] Short-interval serial CT scans may be valuable in suspected cases when initial CT findings are nondiagnostic.[192]

Magnetic resonance imaging may prove helpful for screening certain anatomic sites or when radiography or contrast media are contraindicated. The use of magnetic resonance imaging is being reported with increasing frequency.[104,183] Although some investigators have found indium 111–labeled white blood cell scanning useful in diagnosing prosthetic graft infection, this modality has not always been accurate in confirming the diagnosis of an infected aneurysm.[19,29] Australian investigators have reported on the utility of bone and leukocyte scintigraphy to show the extent of adjacent soft tissue and lumbar osteomyelitis in a case of ruptured infected aneurysm of the abdominal aorta.[175]

■ MANAGEMENT

Preoperative Care

When an infected aneurysm is suspected, but efforts to identify the specific organisms are unsuccessful, broad-spectrum antibiotic therapy should be initiated. Chloramphenicol, ampicillin, a quinolone, or a third-generation cephalosporin should be included to combat *Salmonella* species. Drug therapy is begun before surgery and continued postoperatively and, in certain circumstances, for life.[27,35] Multidrug-resistant strains pose a serious risk and have been associated with clinical cases originating from livestock vectors.

Treatment of narcotic addicts should include active and passive tetanus prophylaxis. Although organism-specific antibiotic therapy is an essential element of successful surgical management of an infected aneurysm, patient survival depends on prompt diagnosis and operation.[71,133] Ruptures of infected aneurysms have been reported in patients undergoing antibiotic therapy while awaiting operation and in patients who have completed antibiotic therapy and are thought, erroneously, to have bland aneurysms, sterilized by antibiotics.[24,32,159] Undue delay in operative intervention must be avoided. Reported spontaneous cures of infected aneurysms are exceptions.[47] In cases of a ruptured or symptomatic aneurysm, surgery should be undertaken urgently.

Operation

General Principles

Six general principles apply in the operative management of infected aneurysms:

1. Control of hemorrhage

2. Confirmation of the diagnosis, including tissue smears for Gram stains and culture specimens for aerobic and anaerobic bacteria and fungi
3. Operative control of sepsis, including aneurysm resection and ligation of healthy artery followed by wide débridement of all surrounding infected tissue with antibiotic irrigation and placement of drains when needed
4. Thorough postoperative wound care, including frequent dressing changes and necessary débridement
5. Continuation of antibiotics for a prolonged period after operation
6. Arterial reconstruction of vital arteries through uninfected tissue planes with selected use of interposition grafting through the bed of the resected aneurysm and use of autologous tissue for reconstruction

The first five principles are established, uncontroversial surgical tenets. Controversy exists, however, about the selection of patients for arterial reconstruction and the timing and methods of reconstruction, particularly when the infected aneurysm involves the aorta, the femoral artery, or the carotid artery.[5,18,27,48,49,73,74,110,114,115,119,130,132,169,171,181] Cryopreserved homografts are being reported as reasonable alternatives for grafting.

Aorta

The classic approach to management of an infected aneurysm of the abdominal aorta is similar to the treatment of an infected aortic prosthesis. The entire aneurysm is resected, the infected tissues are thoroughly débrided, drainage is established, and arterial reconstruction is carried out through uninfected planes by an axillobifemoral bypass.[43,48,71,169] This conservative approach avoids the risks associated with the placement of a graft in the infected retroperitoneum, which is reported to be associated with an overall 23% reoperation rate that increases to 63% when the infecting organism is gram-negative.[48] Axillobifemoral bypass is a less durable reconstruction, however, than successful interposition aortic grafting.[129,133,171] Some surgeons advocate "in-situ" interposition aortic grafts after resection of an infected aortic aneurysm.[18,27,73,114,171]

The adjunctive use of antibiotic-releasing beads implanted in the perigraft tissue, omental coverage, and rifampin-bonded polyester (Dacron) grafts has been reported.[61,119,194] Others have speculated about the use of aortic homografts, but unfavorable previous experience with the late fate of homografts in noninfected sites argues against their use.[7,167]

Experimental data in a canine model suggest that in-situ arterial allografts are less vulnerable to infection than commonly available synthetic prostheses.[80] If this suggestion is true, this decreased infectability may make arterial allografts an appropriate choice when circumstances require re-establishment of aortic continuity in a contaminated field. Clinical reports from many centers in the United States and Europe have detailed the use of cryopreserved arterial homografts for in-situ replacement of infected aneurysms of various aortic segments.[2,79,83,110,116,121,179-182] Vogt and colleagues[181] reported a series of 72 patients with either mycotic aneurysms or graft infections of the thoracic or abdominal aorta comparing the group treated with prosthetic

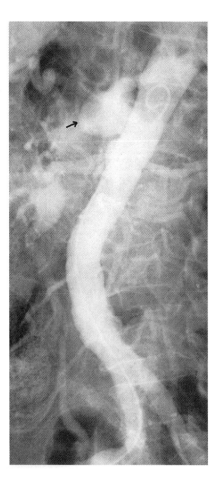

FIGURE 108-6 Aortogram of a 72-year-old man with a methicillin-resistant *Staphylococcus aureus*–infected aneurysm of the periceliac aorta *(arrow)* caused by microbial arteritis. The presumed cause of the antecedent bacteremia was a mediastinal infection with the same organism after sternotomy for coronary artery bypass graft months earlier. Repair through the bed of the débrided aorta was required.

graft (extra-anatomic or in-situ) versus in-situ cryopreserved allografts and showed superior disease-related survival free of reoperation in the allograft group. Noel and colleagues,[110] in a review of the U.S. cryopreserved aortic allograft registry concluded, however, that preliminary data failed to justify their preferential use. It seems that in-situ repair through the bed of the resected aneurysm may be justified in favorable lesions with no gross sepsis, but it should be avoided when the retroperitoneum is grossly purulent.[122,154] Even complex reconstruction of the suprarenal aorta may be accomplished with extra-anatomic techniques.[94,129]

Some reports have emphasized that recognition of organism virulence and the severity and extent of the aortic infection is more important than strict adherence to any single operative approach or method of arterial reconstruction.[30,138,161] Proper patient selection and surgical judgment are among the prime determinants of management success. In infected aneurysms of the aortic arch, thoracic aorta, thoracoabdominal aorta, and suprarenal abdominal aorta, interposition grafting may be the only feasible approach (Fig. 108-6).[5,27,33,66,120]

Clagett and colleagues[31] reported a prospective study suggesting the feasibility and durability of autogenous aortoiliac or aortofemoral vein grafts to treat prosthetic infections. This method may have application in the treatment of infected aneurysms and is gaining wider clinical acceptance and application.[11]

Femoral Artery

Management options in the treatment of infected femoral artery aneurysms are (1) arterial excision alone and (2) arterial excision followed by arterial reconstruction. The various operative techniques for arterial reconstruction are illustrated in Figure 108-7. If the cause of the infected aneurysm is other than drug injection, obturator bypass or interposition grafting usually seems to be the preferred treatment.[65,134] Drug addicts are unsuitable candidates for arterial reconstruction with synthetic arterial prostheses because continued drug use carries a high risk of graft infection (Table 108-8).[3,115,130] In this select group of patients, when reconstruction of the femoral artery is considered desirable, it is necessary to control groin sepsis and to use autogenous grafts. Greater saphenous vein from the mid-thigh usually is available even in patients with a long history of drug abuse (Fig. 108-8).[130]

Although selection criteria and methods of femoral arterial reconstruction in drug addicts are controversial, there is general agreement that most patients do not require reconstruction to avoid amputation.[49,74,115,119,130] Collateral circulation is usually sufficient to maintain limb viability even after the femoral artery bifurcation has been ligated (Fig. 108-9). Amputation is almost never necessary when femoral artery ligation-excision is limited to a single femoral artery segment—the common, superficial, or deep femoral artery (see Table 108-8).

Patients at risk for amputation are patients in whom the femoral artery bifurcation must be excised. Under these circumstances, autogenous vein interposition reconstruction may be considered when local wound conditions are favorable, although experience with this technique is limited.[130] When ligation of the femoral bifurcation is required but reconstruction is not feasible, we empirically instill a concentrated heparin-sodium solution antegrade into the ligated femoral artery in an effort to preserve all possible arterial collaterals. Unless there is a specific indication, however, anticoagulation therapy is not continued in the postoperative period.

The optimal management of these lesions is a matter of debate.[4,53,119,123,130-132,172,195] It is generally agreed that surgical therapy is required, and prolonged use of antibiotics is inappropriate.

Carotid Artery

Although ligation without arterial reconstruction is often safe in the treatment of infected aneurysms of the innominate, common carotid, or upper extremity vessels, there is a major risk of stroke or death after ligation of the cervical internal carotid artery. Although ligation-excision without reconstruction is controversial, many authors favor it, preferring to avoid the potential disastrous consequences of post–reconstruction graft sepsis and hemorrhage.[67,88] Other authors favor primary reconstruction of the carotid artery with autogenous vein[102,147] or progressive clamp

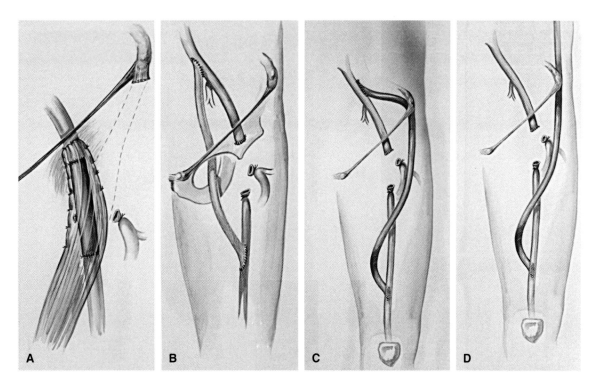

FIGURE 108-7 Methods of femoral artery reconstruction. **A,** Interposition vein autograft covered by rotated sartorius muscle. **B,** Obturator bypass. **C,** Lateral femoral bypass. **D,** Axillodistal femoral bypass. (**A, B,** and **D** from Reddy DJ, Smith RF, Elliott JP Jr, et al: Infected femoral artery false aneurysms in drug addicts: Evolution of selective vascular reconstruction. J Vasc Surg 3:718, 1986.)

occlusion of the internal carotid artery, while observing the awake patient for clinical signs of cerebral ischemia.[6]

Data providing a rational basis for selection of patients for carotid artery ligation versus reconstruction have been reported by Ehrenfeld and colleagues.[41] They found carotid ligation to be safe if carotid stump systolic pressure exceeded 70 mm Hg. This was a selected group of patients who had received anticoagulation therapy and in whom systemic blood pressures had been maintained at defined levels, but this may not be a representative group. The rarity of these lesions highlights the need for individualized patient management.[76,98,187] In the special circumstance of cerebral mycotic aneurysms, stereoscopic synthesized brain-surface imaging with magnetic resonance angiography for anatomic localization has emerged as a useful modality.[38,75]

Visceral Arteries

Although visceral arterial aneurysms are uncommon, a high percentage are infected.[162] Treatment must be individualized and directed by angiography. When feasible, aneurysm ligation-excision is desirable, but arterial reconstruction with saphenous autografts or other innovations may be required to preserve organ or bowel viability.[64,176,187]

Endovascular Approaches

As endovascular techniques have become more prevalent, the use of stent-grafts and antibiotic therapy in the successful treatment of mycotic aneurysms is being reported. Our review of endografts placed for infected aneurysms found six endografts placed in the aortic position,[14,77,125,152] three

Table 108-8	Treatment Method and Results for Infected Femoral Artery False Aneurysms Resulting from Drug Addiction			
	NO.	VIABLE LIMB	GRAFT SEPSIS	AMPUTATION
Common femoral artery: ligation-excision	14	14	—	0
Deep femoral artery: ligation-excision	11	11	—	0
Superficial femoral artery: ligation-excision	4	4	—	0
Common femoral bifurcation				
Ligation-excision	21	14	—	7 (33%)
Reconstruction with autogenous vein	6	6	1	0
Reconstruction with synthetic prosthesis	3	3	3 (100%)	0
Reconstruction by primary anastomosis	1	1	0	0
Total	*60*	*53*	*4*	*7 (12%)*

From Reddy DJ, Smith RF, Elliott JP Jr, et al: Infected femoral artery false aneurysms in drug addicts: Evolution of selective vascular reconstruction. J Vasc Surg 3:718, 1986.

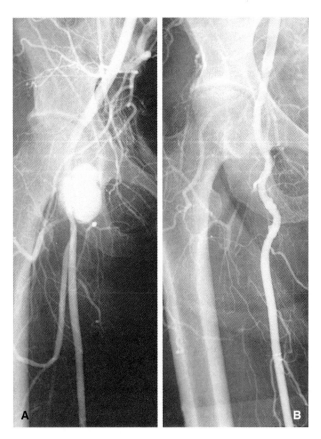

FIGURE 108-8 Angiographic sequence shows preoperative appearance of infected false aneurysm of femoral bifurcation (**A**) and postoperative appearance of patent interposition vein graft after arterial reconstruction (**B**). (**A** and **B** from Reddy DJ, Smith RF, Elliott JP Jr, et al: Infected femoral artery false aneurysms in drug addicts: Evolution of selective vascular reconstruction. J Vasc Surg 3:718, 1986.)

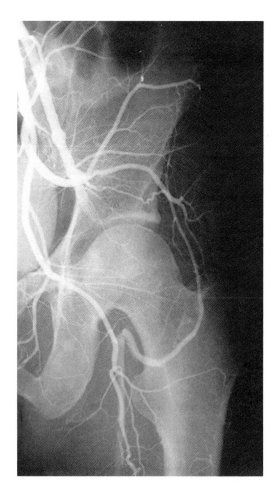

FIGURE 108-9 Arteriogram after ligation of femoral artery bifurcation shows reconstitution of superficial femoral artery beyond the occlusion by numerous collaterals.

endografts in the femoral position,[82,85,149] and one each in the brachial artery[81] and innominate artery positions.[21] This approach should be viewed with caution because it challenges the surgical tenet of aneurysm resection and wide débridement of the infected field without providing long-term follow-up. Review of the literature reports five single case studies of infected pseudoaneurysms after stent placement in a noninfected artery[17,20,25,128,184] and one case of failed stent-graft treatment of an infected thoracic aortic aneurysm.[70]

Results

Successful surgical management of an infected aneurysm depends on the following factors:

- Type of aneurysm
- Location of aneurysm
- Microorganism responsible
- Patient's general condition
- Patient's clinical presentation

In general, results after treatment of infected aneurysms have steadily improved because of prompt diagnosis, better surgical techniques, and modern antimicrobial

therapy. In 1967, Bennett and Cherry[13] reported that infected AAAs were invariably fatal. Since then, rates of 74% survival among 96 cases have been reported in 26 series from 1978 to 1992, although management remains challenging.[5,9,15,18,22,27,37,39,40,48,60,73,95-97,114,119,129,133,143,148,165,171,174,189,191] Although some reports have tended to emphasize the improved outlook for patient survival, most authors believe that infected aneurysms of all types, particularly aneurysms that do not respond to therapy, are underreported. To this end, Wilson and coworkers[190] estimated, from a literature review, that mycotic aneurysms in treated patients had a mortality rate of 25%; microbial arteritis with aneurysm, 75%; infected preexisting aneurysms, 75%; and post-traumatic infected false aneurysms, 10% (see Table 108-1).

A review of six large series published in the English language from 1996 to 2002 comprised 149 patients with infected aortoiliac aneurysms; 143 patients underwent operation, with 110 undergoing in-situ arterial reconstruction after aneurysm resection, whereas 32 patients required the more extensive and classic extra-anatomic reconstruction. The overall early postoperative mortality was 23%.[68,101,106,111,154,161] Oderich and colleagues[111] in the largest series of 43 patients reported postoperative survival rates of 82% and 50% at 1 and 5 years.

Lower extremity amputation rates after treatment for infected femoral artery false aneurysms have ranged from 11% to 25%.[3,49,74,115,119,130] The above-knee amputation rate after ligation-excision of the femoral artery bifurcation in drug addicts approximates 33%. When groin sepsis is not controlled, revascularization in an attempt to prevent amputation may pose an unnecessary and potentially lethal risk of graft sepsis and should be undertaken with caution. Amputation may be unavoidable among patients with infected femoral false aneurysms.

■ REFERENCES

1. Akers DL Jr, Fowl RJ, Kempczinski RF: Mycotic aneurysm of the tibioperoneal trunk: Case report and review of the literature. J Vasc Surg 16:71, 1992.
2. Alonso M, Caeiro S, Cachaldora J: Infected abdominal aortic aneurysm: In situ replacement with cryopreserved arterial homograft. J Cardiovasc Surg 38:371, 1997.
3. Anderson CB, Butcher HR Jr, Ballinger WF, et al: Mycotic aneurysms. Arch Surg 109:712, 1974.
4. Arora S, Weber MA, Fox CJ, et al: Common femoral artery ligation and local debridement: A safe treatment for infected femoral artery pseudoaneurysms. J Vasc Surg 33:990, 2001.
5. Atnip RG: Mycotic aneurysms of the suprarenal abdominal aorta: Prolonged survival after in situ aortic and visceral reconstruction. J Vasc Surg 10:635, 1989.
6. Avellone JC, Ahmad MY: Cervical internal carotid aneurysm from syphilis: An alternative to resection. JAMA 241:238, 1979.
7. Bahnini A, Ruoyolo C, Koskas F, Kieffer E: In situ fresh allograft replacement of an infected aortic prosthetic graft: Eighteen months' follow-up. J Vasc Surg 14:98, 1991.
8. Baker WH, Moran JM, Dormer DB: Infected aortic aneurysm following arteriography. J Cardiovasc Surg 20:313, 1979.
9. Bardin JA, Collins GM, Devin JB, et al: Nonaneurysmal suppurative aortitis. Arch Surg 116:954, 1981.
10. Barker WF: Mycotic aneurysms. Ann Surg 139:84, 1954.
11. Benjamin ME, Cohn EJ, Purtill WA, et al: Arterial reconstruction with deep leg veins for the treatment of mycotic aneurysms. J Vasc Surg 30:1004, 1999.
12. Bennett DE: Primary mycotic aneurysms of the aorta. Arch Surg 94:758, 1967.
13. Bennett DE, Cherry JK: Bacterial infection of aortic aneurysms: A clinicopathologic study. Am J Surg 113:321, 1967.
14. Berchtold C, Eibl C, Seelig MH, et al: Endovascular and complete regression for an infected abdominal aortic aneurysm. J Endovasc Ther 9:543, 2002.
15. Bitseff EL, Edwards WA, Mulherin JL Jr, Kaiser AB: Infected abdominal aortic aneurysms. South Med J 80:309, 1987.
16. Deleted in revision.
17. Blunt TJ, Gill HK, Smith DC, et al: Infection of a chronically implanted iliac artery stent. Ann Vasc Surg 11:529, 1997.
18. Brown SL, Busutill RW, Baker JD, et al: Bacteriologic and surgical determinants of survival in patients with mycotic aneurysms. J Vasc Surg 1:541, 1984.
19. Brunner MC, Mitchell RS, Baldwin JC, et al: Prosthetic graft infection: Limitations of indium white blood cell scanning. J Vasc Surg 3:42, 1986.
20. Bukhari RH, Muck PE, Schlucter FJ, et al: Bilateral renal artery stent infection and pseudoaneurysm formation. J Vasc Interv Radiol 11:337, 2000.
21. Bush RL, Hurt JE, Bianco CC: Endovascular management of a ruptured mycotic aneurysm of the innominate artery. Ann Thorac Surg 74:2184, 2002.
22. Byard RW, Leduc JR, Chambers J, Walley VM: The rapid evolution of a large mycotic aneurysm of the abdominal aorta. J Can Assoc Radiol 39:62, 1988.
23. Carreras M, Larena JA, Tabernero G, et al: Evolution of Salmonella aortitis towards the formation of abdominal aneurysm. Eur Radiol 1:54, 1997.
24. Cates JE, Christie RV: Subacute bacterial endocarditis. QJM 24:93, 1951.
25. Chalmers N, Eadington DW, Gandanhamo D, et al: Case report: Infected false aneurysm at the site of an iliac stent. Br J Radiol 66:946, 1993.
26. Chan P, Tsai CW, Huang JJ, et al: Salmonellosis and mycotic aneurysm of the aorta: A report of 10 cases. J Infect 30:129, 1995.
27. Chan YF, Crawford ES, Coselli JS, et al: In situ prosthetic graft replacement for mycotic aneurysms of the aorta. Ann Thorac Surg 47:193, 1989.
28. Chen YF, Lin PY, Yen HW, et al: Double mycotic aneurysm of the ascending aorta. Ann Thorac Surg 63:529, 1997.
29. Chen P, Lamski L, Raval B: Indium-111 leukocyte appearance of Salmonella mycotic aneurysm. Clin Nucl Med 19:646, 1994.
30. Chiba Y, Muraoka R, Ihaya A, et al: Surgical treatment of infected thoracic and abdominal aortic aneurysms. Cardiovasc Surg 4:476, 1996.
31. Clagett GP, Valentine RJ, Hagino RT: Autogenous aortoiliac/femoral reconstruction from superficial femoral-popliteal veins: Feasibility and durability. J Vasc Surg 25:255, 1997.
32. Cooke PA, Ehrenfeld WK: Successful management of mycotic aortic aneurysm: Report of a case. Surgery 75:132, 1974.
33. Cordero JA Jr, Darling RC 3rd, Chang BB, et al: In situ prosthetic graft replacement for mycotic thoracoabdominal aneurysms. Am Surg 62:35, 1996.
34. Crane AR: Primary multilocular mycotic aneurysm of the aorta. Arch Pathol 24:634, 1937.
35. Crawford ES, Crawford JL (eds): Diseases of the Aorta Including an Atlas of Angiographic Pathology and Surgical Techniques. Baltimore, Williams & Wilkins, 1984.
36. Deleted in revision.
37. Cull DL, Winter RP, Wheller JR, et al: Mycotic aneurysm of the suprarenal aorta. J Cardiovasc Surg 33:181, 1992.
38. D'Angelo V, Fiumara E, Gorgoglione L, et al: Surgical treatment of a cerebral mycotic aneurysm using the stereo-angiographic localizer. Surg Neurol 44:263, 1995.
39. Davies OG, Thorburn JD, Powell P: Cryptic mycotic abdominal aortic aneurysms. Am J Surg 136:96, 1978.
40. Dupont JR, Bonavita JA, DiGiovanni RJ, et al: Acquired immunodeficiency syndrome and mycotic abdominal aortic aneurysms: A new challenge? Report of a case. J Vasc Surg 10:254, 1989.
41. Ehrenfeld WR, Stoney RJ, Wylie EJ: Relation of carotid stump pressure to safety of carotid arterial ligation. Surgery 93:299, 1983.
42. Elliott JP, Hageman JH, Szilagyi DE, et al: Arterial embolization: Problems of source, multiplicity, recurrence, and delayed treatment. Surgery 88:833, 1980.
43. Elliott JP, Smith RF, Szilagyi DE: Aortoenteric and paraprosthetic-enteric fistulas. Arch Surg 114:1041, 1974.
44. Deleted in revision.
45. Eppinger H: Pathogenesis (histogenesis und aetiologie) der anerysmen eimschliesslich des aneurysma equi verminosum. Arch Klin Chir 35:404, 1887.
46. Ernst CB, Campbell C Jr, Daugherty ME, et al: Incidence and significance of intra-operative bacterial cultures during abdominal aortic aneurysmectomy. Ann Surg 185:626, 1977.
47. Eshaghy B, Scanlon RJ, Amirparviz F, et al: Mycotic aneurysm of brachial artery: A complication of retrograde catheterization. JAMA 228:1574, 1974.
48. Ewart JM, Burke ML, Bunt TJ: Spontaneous abdominal aortic infections: Essentials of diagnosis and management. Am Surg 49:37, 1983.

49. Feldman AJ, Berguer R: Management of an infected aneurysm of the groin secondary to drug abuse. Surg Gynecol Obstet 157:519, 1983.

50. Flamand F, Harris KA, DeRose G, et al: Arteritis due to *Salmonella* with aneurysm formation: Two cases. Can J Surg 35:248, 1992.

51. Fourneau I, Nevelsteen A, Lacroix H, et al: Microbiological monitoring of aortic aneurysm sac contents during abdominal aneurysmectomy: Results in 176 patients and review of the literature. Acta Chir Belg 96:119, 1996.

52. Fromm SH, Lucas CE: Obturator bypass for mycotic aneurysm of the drug addict. Arch Surg 100:82, 1970.

53. Gan JP, Leiberman DP, Pollock JG: Outcome after ligation of infected false femoral aneurysms in intravenous drug abusers. Eur J Vasc Endovasc Surg 19:158, 2000.

54. Garb M: Appendicitis: An unusual cause of infected abdominal aortic aneurysm. Australas Radiol 38:68, 1994.

55. Gauto AR, Cone LA, Woodard DR, et al: Arterial infections due to *Listeria monocytogenes*: Report of four cases and review of world literature. Clin Infect Dis 14:23, 1992.

56. Geelhoed GW, Joseph WL: Surgical sequelae of drug abuse. Surg Gynecol Obstet 139:749, 1974.

57. Gomes MN, Schellinger D, Hufnagel CA: Abdominal aortic aneurysms: Diagnostic review and new techniques. Ann Thorac Surg 27:479, 1979.

58. Gomes MN, Choyke PL, Wallace RB: Infected aortic aneurysms: A changing entity. Ann Surg 215:435, 1992.

59. Gomes MH, Choyke PL: Infected aortic aneurysms: CT diagnosis. J Cardiovasc Surg 33:684, 1992.

60. Gouny P, Valverde A, Vincent D: Human immunodeficiency virus and infected aneurysm of the abdominal aorta: Report of three cases. Ann Vasc Surg 6:239, 1992.

61. Gupta AK, Bandyk DF, Johnson BL: In situ repair of mycotic abdominal aortic aneurysms with rifampin-bonded gelatin impregnated Dacron grafts: A preliminary case report. J Vasc Surg 24:472, 1996.

62. Deleted in revision.

63. Har Shai Y, Schein M, Molek AD, et al: Ruptured mycotic aneurysm of the subclavian artery after irradiation: A case report. Eur J Surg 159:59, 1993.

64. Hashemi HA, Comerota AJ, Dempsey DT: Foregut revascularization via retrograde splenic artery perfusion after resection of a juxtaceliac mycotic aneurysm: Complicated by pancreatic infarction because of cholesterol emboli. J Vasc Surg 21:530, 1995.

65. Hegenscheid M, Alveizacos P, Hepp W: Autogene Rekonstruktion bei mykotischem inquinalem Aneurysma-Langzeitsergebnis. Vasa 23:159, 1994.

66. Hollier LH, Money SR, Creely B, et al: Direct repair of mycotic thoracoabdominal aneurysms. J Vasc Surg 18:477, 1993.

67. Howell HS, Barburao T, Graziano J: Mycotic cervical carotid aneurysm. Surgery 81:357, 1977.

68. Hsu RB, Tsay YG, Wang SS, Chu SH: Surgical treatment for primary infected aneurysm of the descending thoracic aorta, abdominal aorta and iliac arteries. J Vasc Surg 36:746, 2002.

69. Huebl HC, Read RC: Aneurysmal abscess. Minn Med 49:11, 1966.

70. Ishida M, Kato N, Hirano T, et al: Limitations for endovascular treatment with stent-grafts for active mycotic thoracic aortic aneurysm. Cardiovasc Intervent Radiol 25:216, 2002.

71. Jarrett F, Darling RC, Mundth ED, et al: Experience with infected aneurysms of the abdominal aorta. Arch Surg 10:1281, 1975.

72. Johansen K, Devin J: Spontaneous healing of mycotic aortic aneurysm. J Cardiovasc Surg 21:625, 1980.

73. Johansen K, Devin J: Mycotic aortic aneurysms: A reappraisal. Arch Surg 118:583, 1983.

74. Johnson JR, Ledgerwood AM, Lucas CE: Mycotic aneurysm: New concepts in surgery. Arch Surg 118:577, 1983.

75. Kato Y, Yamaguchi S, Sano H, et al: Stereoscopic synthesized brain surface imaging with MR angiography for localization of a peripheral mycotic aneurysm: Case report. Minim Invas Neurosurg 39:113, 1996.

76. Khalil I, Nawfal G: Mycotic aneurysms of the carotid artery: Ligation vs. reconstruction—case report and review of the literature. Eur J Vasc Surg 7:588, 1993.

77. Kinney EV, Kaebnick HW, Mitchell RA, et al: Repair of mycotic paravisceral aneurysm with a fenestrated stent-graft. J Endovasc Ther 7:192, 2000.

78. Koch R: Ueber aneurysma der arteria mesenterica superior [About an aneurysm of the superior mesenteric artery]. In Erlangen JJ (ed): Inaug Dural-Abhandlung. Barfus'schen Universitaets-Buchdruckerei, 1851.

79. Koskas F, Plissonnier D, Bahnini A, et al: In situ arterial allografting graft infection: A 6-year experience. Cardiovasc Surg 4:495, 1996.

80. Koskas F, Goeau-Brissoniere O, Nicolas MH, et al: Arteries from human beings are less infectible by *Staphylococcus aureus* than polytetrafluoroethylene in an aortic dog model. J Vasc Surg 23:472, 1996.

81. Kurimoto Y, Tsuchida Y, Saito J, et al: Emergency endovascular stent-grafting for infected pseudoaneurysm of brachial artery. Infection 31:186, 2003.

82. Kwon K, Choi D, Choi SH, et al: Percutaneous stent-graft repair of mycotic common femoral artery aneurysm. J Endovasc Ther 9:690, 2002.

83. Knosalla C, Weng Y, Yanakh AC, et al: Using aortic allograft material to treat mycotic aneurysms of the thoracic aorta. Ann Thorac Surg 61:1053, 1996.

84. Kyriakides GK, Simmons RL, Najarian JS: Mycotic aneurysms in transplant patients. Arch Surg 111:472, 1976.

85. Lagattolla NR, Baghai M, Biswas S, et al: Tuberculous false aneurysm of the femoral artery managed by endoluminal stent graft. Eur J Vasc Endovasc Surg 19:440, 2000.

86. Lamothe M, Simmons B, Gelfand M, et al: *Listeria monocytogenes* causing endovascular infection. South Med J 85:193, 1992.

87. Lee MH, Chan P, Chiou HJ, et al: Diagnostic imaging of *Salmonella*-related mycotic aneurysm of aorta by CT. Clin Imaging 20:26, 1996.

88. Ledgerwood AM, Lucas CE: Mycotic aneurysm of the carotid artery. Arch Surg 109:496, 1974.

89. Lewis D, Schrager J: Embolomycotic aneurysms. JAMA 63:1808, 1909.

90. Deleted in revision.

91. Magilligan DJ: Neurologic complications. In Magilligan DJ Jr, Quinn EL (eds): Endocarditis: Medical and Surgical Management. New York, Marcel Dekker, 1986, p 187.

92. Magilligan DJ, Quinn EL: Active infective endocarditis. In Magilligan DJ Jr, Quinn EL (eds): Endocarditis: Medical and Surgical Management. New York, Marcel Dekker, 1986, p 207.

93. Malanoski GJ, Samore MH, Pefanis A, et al: *Staphylococcus aureus* catheter-associated bacteremia: Minimal effective therapy and unusual infectious complications associated with arterial sheath catheters. Arch Intern Med 155:1161, 1995.

94. Marty Ane C, Alric P, Prudhoomme M, et al: Bilateral splenorenal bypass and axillofemoral graft for management of juxtarenal mycotic aneurysm. Cardiovasc Surg 4:331, 1996.

95. McIntyre KE, Malone JM, Richards E, et al: Mycotic aortic pseudo-aneurysm with aortoenteric fistula caused by *Arizona hinshawii*. Surgery 91:173, 1982.

96. McNamara MF, Roberts AB, Bakshi KR: Gram-negative bacterial infection of aortic aneurysms. J Cardiovasc Surg 28:453, 1987.

97. Mendelowitz DS, Ramstedt R, Yao JST, et al: Abdominal aortic salmonellosis. Surgery 85:514, 1979.

98. Michielsen D, Van Hee R, Discart H: Mycotic aneurysm of the carotid artery: A case report and review of the literature. Acta Chir Belg 97:44, 1997.

99. Millar AJ, Gilbert RD, Brown RA, et al: Abdominal aortic aneurysms in children. J Pediatr Surg 31:1624, 1996.

100. Miller BM, Waterhouse G, Alford RH, et al: *Histoplasma* infection of abdominal aortic aneurysms. Ann Surg 197:57, 1983.

101. Moneta GL, Taylor LM, Yeager RA, et al: Surgical treatment of infected aortic aneurysm. Am J Surg 175:396, 1998.

102. Monson RL, Alexander RH: Vein reconstruction of a mycotic internal carotid aneurysm. Ann Surg 191:47, 1980.

103. Montoya FJ, Weinstein-Moreno LF, Johnson CC: Mycotic thoracic aneurysm due to *Clostridium septicum* and occult adenocarcinoma of the cecum. Clin Infect Dis 24:785, 1997.

104. Moriarity JA, Edelman RR, Tumeh SS: CT and MRI mycotic aneurysms of the abdominal aorta. J Comput Assist Tomogr 16:941, 1992.

105. Mostovych M, Johnson L, Cambria RP: Aortic sepsis from an appendiceal abscess. Cardiovasc Surg 2:67, 1994.

106. Muller BT, Wegener OR, Grabitz K, et al: Mycotic aneurysms of the thoracic and abdominal aorta and iliac arteries: Experience with anatomic and extra-anatomic repair in 33 cases. J Vasc Surg 33:106, 2001.

107. Mundth ED, Darling RC, Alvarado RH, et al: Surgical management of mycotic aneurysms and the complications of infection in vascular reconstructive surgery. Am J Surg 117:460, 1969.

108. Murphy DP, Glazier DB, Krause TJ: Mycotic aneurysm of the thoracic aorta caused by *Clostridium septicum*. Ann Thorac Surg 62:1835, 1996.

109. Nabseth DC, Deterling RA: Surgical management of mycotic aneurysms. Surgery 50:347, 1961.

110. Noel AA, Gloviczki P, Cherry KJ Jr, et al: Abdominal aortic reconstruction in infected fields: Early results of the United States cryopreserved aortic allograft registry. J Vasc Surg 35:837, 2002.

111. Oderich GS, Panneton JM, Bower TC, et al: Infected aortic aneurysms: Aggressive presentation, complicated early outcome but durable results. J Vasc Surg 34:900, 2001.

112. Oskoui R, Davis WA, Gomes MN: *Salmonella* aortitis: A report of a successfully treated case with a comprehensive review of the literature. Arch Intern Med 153:517, 1993.

113. Osler W: The Gulstonian lectures on malignant endocarditis. BMJ 1:467, 1885.

114. Oz MC, Brener BJ, Buda JA, et al: A ten-year experience with bacterial aortitis. J Vasc Surg 10:439, 1989.

115. Padberg F, Hobson R II, Lee B, et al: Femoral pseudoaneurysm from drugs of abuse: Ligation or reconstruction? J Vasc Surg 15:642, 1992.

116. Pagano D, Guest P, Bonser RS: Homograft replacement of thoraco-abdominal segment of the aorta for leaking mycotic aneurysm. Eur J Cardiothorac Surg 10:383, 1996.

117. Paré A: Of aneurismas. In The Apologie and Treatise Containing the Voyages Made into Divers Places with Many of His Writings upon Surgery. Birmingham, Ala, The Classics of Surgery Library, 1984.

118. Parodi JC: Endovascular repair of abdominal aortic aneurysms and other arterial lesions. J Vasc Surg 21:549, 1995.

119. Pasic M, Segesser L, Turina M: Implantation of antibiotic-releasing carriers and in situ reconstruction for treatment of mycotic aneurysm. Arch Surg 127:745, 1992.

120. Pasic M, Carrel T, Vogt M, et al: Treatment of mycotic aneurysms of the aorta and its branches: The location determines the operative technique. Eur J Vasc Surg 6:419, 1992.

121. Pasic M, Carrel T, von Segesser L, et al: In situ repair of mycotic aneurysm of the ascending aorta. J Thorac Cardiovasc Surg 105:321, 1993.

122. Pasic M, Carrel T, Tonz M, et al: Mycotic aneurysm of the abdominal aorta: Extra-anatomic versus in situ reconstruction. Cardiovasc Surg 1:48, 1993.

123. Patel KR, Semel L, Clauss RH: Routine revascularization with resection of infected femoral pseudoaneurysms from substance abuse. J Vasc Surg 8:321, 1988.

124. Patel S, Johnson KW: Classification and management of mycotic aneurysms. Surg Gynecol Obstet 144:691, 1977.

125. Patetsios PP, Shutze W, Holden B, et al: Repair of a mycotic aneurysm of the infrarenal aorta in a patient with HIV, using a Palmaz stent and autologous femoral vein graft. Ann Vasc Surg 16:521, 2002.

126. Pipkin W, Brophy C, Nesbit R, Mondy JS III: Early experience with infectious complications of percutaneous femoral artery closure devices. J Vasc Surg 32:205, 2000.

127. Deleted in revision.

128. Pruitt A, Dodson TF, Najibi S: Distal septic emboli and fatal brachiocephalic artery mycotic pseudoaneurysm as a complication of stenting. J Vasc Surg 36:625, 2002.

129. Reddy DJ, Lee RE, Oh HK: Suprarenal mycotic aortic aneurysm: Surgical management and follow-up. J Vasc Surg 3:917, 1986.

130. Reddy DJ, Smith RF, Elliott JP Jr, et al: Infected femoral artery false aneurysms in drug addicts: Evolution of selective vascular reconstruction. J Vasc Surg 3:718, 1986.

131. Reddy DJ: Treatment of drug-related infected false aneurysms of the femoral artery: Is routine revascularization justified? J Vasc Surg 8:344, 1988.

132. Reddy DJ: Letter to editor. J Vasc Surg 10:358, 1989.

133. Reddy DJ, Shepard AD, Evans JR, et al: Management of infected aortoiliac aneurysms. Arch Surg 126:873, 1991.

134. Reddy DJ, Shin LH: Obturator bypass: Technical considerations. Semin Vasc Surg 13:49, 2000.

135. Reid MR: Studies on abnormal arteriovenous communications, acquired and congenital: I. Report of a series of cases. Arch Surg 10:601, 1925.

136. Deleted in revision.

137. Revell STR: Primary mycotic aneurysms. Ann Intern Med 22:431, 1943.

138. Robinson JA, Johansen K: Aortic sepsis: Is there a role for in situ graft reconstruction? J Vasc Surg 13:677, 1991.

139. Rokitansky CF: Handbuch der Pathologischen Anatomie, 2nd ed. Austria, 1844, p 55.

140. Rose HD, Stuart JL: Mycotic aneurysm of the thoracic aorta due to *Aspergillus fumigatus*. Chest 70:81, 1976.

141. Rozenblit A, Bennett J, Suggs W: Evolution of the infected abdominal aneurysm: CT observation of early aortitis. Abdom Imaging 21:512, 1996.

142. Rubery PT, Smith MD, Cammisa FP, et al: Mycotic aortic aneurysm in patients who have lumbar vertebral osteomyelitis: A report of two cases. J Bone Joint Surg Am 77:1729, 1995.

143. Rutherford EJ, Eakins JW, Maxwell JG, et al: Abdominal aortic aneurysm infected with *Campylobacter fetus* subspecies *fetus*. J Vasc Surg 10:193, 1989.

144. Sailors DM, Barone GW, Gagne PJ, et al: *Candida* arteritis: Are GI endoscopic procedures a source of vascular infections? Am Surg 62:472, 1996.

145. Sailors DM, Eidt JF, Gagne PJ, et al: Primary *Clostridium septicum* aortitis: A rare cause of necrotizing suprarenal aortic infection: A case report and review of the literature. J Vasc Surg 23:714, 1996.

146. Samore MH, Wessolossky MA, Lewis SM, et al: Frequency, risk factors, and outcome for bacteremia after percutaneous transluminal coronary angioplasty. Am J Cardiol 79:873, 1997.

147. Samson DS, Gewertz BL, Beyer CW Jr, et al: Saphenous vein interposition grafts in the microsurgical treatment of cerebral ischemia. Arch Surg 116:1578, 1981.

148. Scher A, Brener B, Goldendranz RJ, et al: Infected aneurysms of the abdominal aorta. Surgery 115:975, 1980.

149. Schneider PA, Abcarian PN, Leduc JR, et al: Stent-graft repair of mycotic superficial femoral artery aneurysm using a Palmaz stent and autologous saphenous vein. Ann Vasc Surg 12:282, 1998.

150. Schrander-van de Meer AM, Guit GL, van Bockel JH: Mycotic aneurysm of the suprarenal abdominal aorta. Neth J Med 44:23, 1994.

151. Deleted in revision.

152. Semba CP, Sakai T, Slonim SM, et al: Mycotic aneurysms of the thoracic aorta: Repair with the use of endovascular stent-grafts. J Vasc Interv Radiol 9(1 Pt 1):33, 1998.

153. Senocak F, Cekirge S, Senocak ME, et al: Hepatic artery aneurysm in a 10-year-old boy as a complication of infective endocarditis. J Pediatr Surg 31:1570, 1996.

154. Sessa C, Farah I, Voirin L, et al: Infected aneurysms of the infrarenal abdominal aorta: Diagnostic criteria and therapeutic strategy. Ann Vasc Surg 11:453, 1997.

155. Shetty PC, Krasicky GA, Sharma RP, et al: Mycotic aneurysms in intravenous drug abusers: The utility of intravenous digital subtraction angiography. Radiology 155:319, 1985.

156. Smith FC, Rees E, Elliott TS, et al: A hazard of immunosuppression: *Aspergillus niger* infection of abdominal aortic aneurysm. Eur J Vasc Surg 8:369, 1994.

157. Smith RF, Szilagyi DE, Colville JM: Surgical treatment of mycotic aneurysms. Arch Surg 85:663, 1967.

158. Soderstrom CA, Wasserman DJ, Ransom KJ, et al: Infected false femoral artery aneurysms secondary to monitoring catheters. J Cardiovasc Surg 24:63, 1983.

159. Sommerville RI, Allen EV, Edwards JE: Bland and infected arteriosclerotic abdominal aortic aneurysms: A clinicopathologic study. Medicine 38:207, 1959.

160. Sower ND, Whelan TJ: Suppurative arteritis due to *Salmonella*. Surgery 52:851, 1967.

161. Sriussadaporn S: Infected abdominal aortic aneurysms: Experience with 14 consecutive cases. Int Surg 81:395, 1996.

162. Stanley JC, Thompson NW, Fry WJ: Splanchnic artery aneurysms. Arch Surg 101:689, 1970.

163. Steed DL, Higgins RS, Pasculle A, et al: Culture of intraluminal thrombus during abdominal aortic aneurysm resection: Significant contamination is rare. Cardiovasc Surg 1:494, 1993.

164. Stengel A, Wolferth CC: Mycotic (bacterial) aneurysms of intravascular origin. Arch Intern Med 31:527, 1923.

165. Suddleson EA, Katz SG, Kohl RD: Mycotic suprarenal aortic aneurysm. Ann Vasc Surg 1:426, 1987.

166. Szilagyi DE, Elliott JP, Smith RF: Ruptured abdominal aneurysms simulating sepsis. Arch Surg 91:263, 1965.

167. Szilagyi DE, Rodriquez FT, Smith RF, Elliott JP: Late fate of arterial allografts: Observations 6 to 15 years after implantation. Arch Surg 101:721, 1970.

168. Tatebe S, Kanazawa H, Yamazaki Y, et al: Mycotic aneurysm of the internal iliac artery caused by *Klebsiella pneumoniae*. Vasa 25:184, 1996.

169. Taylor LM Jr, Deitz DM, McConnell DB, Porter JM: Treatment of infected abdominal aneurysms by extra-anatomic bypass, aneurysm excision, and drainage. Am J Surg 155:655, 1988.

170. Thompson TR, Tilleli J, Johnson DE, et al: Umbilical artery catheterization complicated by mycotic aortic aneurysm in neonates. Adv Pediatr 27:275, 1980.

171. Trairatvorakul P, Sriphojanart S, Sathapatayavongs B: Abdominal aortic aneurysms infected with *Salmonella*: Problems of treatment. J Vasc Surg 12:16, 1990.

172. Tsao JW, Marder SR, Goldstone J, et al: Presentation, diagnosis and management of arterial mycotic pseudoaneurysms in injection drug users. Ann Vasc Surg 16:652, 2002.

173. Tufnell J: On the influence of vegetation of the valves of the heart in the production of secondary arterial disease. Dublin Q J Med 15:371, 1885.

174. Van Damme H, Belachew M, Damas P, et al: Mycotic aneurysm of the upper abdominal aorta ruptured into the stomach. Arch Surg 127:478, 1992.

175. Van der Wall H, Palmer A, Thomas M, Chu J: Bone and leukocyte scintigraphy of a complicated case of ruptured mycotic aneurysm of the aorta: A case history. Angiology 45:315, 1994.

176. Viglione G, Younes GA, Coste P, et al: Mycotic aneurysm of the celiac trunk: Radical resection and reconstruction without prosthetic material. J Cardiovasc Surg 34:73, 1993.

177. Virkow R: Ueber die akute entzuendung der arterian. Virchows Arch Pathol 1:272, 1847.

178. Vogelzang RL, Sohaey R: Infected aortic aneurysms: CT appearance. J Comput Assist Tomogr 12:109, 1988.

179. Vogt PR, von Segesser LK, Goffin Y: Cryopreserved arterial homografts for in situ reconstruction of mycotic aneurysms and prosthetic graft infections. Eur J Cardiothorac Surg 9:502, 1995.

180. Vogt PR, von Segesser LK, Goffin Y: Eradication of aortic infections with the use of cryopreserved arterial homografts. Ann Thorac Surg 62:640, 1996.

181. Vogt PR, Brunner-LaRocca HP, Lachat M, et al: Technical details with the use of cryopreserved arterial allograft for aortic infection: Influence on early and mid term mortality. J Vasc Surg 35:80, 2002.

182. von Segesser LK, Vogt P, Genoni M, et al: The infected aorta. J Card Surg 12:256, 1997.

183. Walsh DW, Ho VB, Haggerty MF: Mycotic aneurysm of the aorta: MRI and MRA features. J Magn Reson Imaging 7:312, 1997.

184. Weinberg DJ, Cronin DW, Baker AG Jr: Infected iliac pseudoaneurysm after uncomplicated percutaneous balloon angioplasty and (Palmaz) stent insertion: A case report and literature review. J Vasc Surg 23:162, 1996.

185. Weintraub RA, Abrams HL: Mycotic aneurysm. AJR Am J Roentgenol 102:354, 1968.

186. Deleted in revision.

187. Willemsen P, De Roover D, Kockx M, et al: Mycotic common carotid artery aneurysm in an immunosuppressed pediatric patient: Case report. J Vasc Surg 25:784, 1997.

188. Williams RD, Fisher FW: Aneurysm contents as a source of graft infection. Arch Surg 112:415, 1977.

189. Wilson SE, Gordon E, Van Wagenen PB: *Salmonella* arteritis. Arch Surg 113:1163, 1978.

190. Wilson SE, Van Wagenen P, Passaro E Jr: Arterial infection. Curr Probl Surg 15:5, 1978.

191. Yao JST, McCarthy WJ: Contained rupture of a thoracoabdominal aneurysm. Contemp Surg 33:47, 1988.

192. Yasuhara, Muto T: Infected abdominal aortic aneurysm presenting with sudden appearance: Diagnostic importance of serial computed tomography. Ann Vasc Surg 15:582, 2001.

193. Yellin AE: Ruptured mycotic aneurysm. Arch Surg 112:981, 1977.

194. Yokoyama H, Maida K, Takahashi S, et al: Purulently infected abdominal aortic aneurysm: In situ reconstruction with transmesocolic omental transposition technique. Cardiovasc Surg 2:78, 1994.

195. Zainal AA, Yusha AW: A 3 year audit of infected pseudoaneurysms in intravenous drug users managed surgically in the Vascular Unit, Hospital Kuala Lumpur. Med J Malay 53:372, 1998.

196. Zak FG, Strauss L, Saphra I: Rupture of diseased large arteries in the course of enterobacterial (*Salmonella*) infection. N Engl J Med 258:824, 1958.

ARTERIOVENOUS FISTULAS, VASCULAR MALFORMATIONS, AND VASCULAR TUMORS

ROBERT B. RUTHERFORD, MD

Chapter

Overview

109

ROBERT B. RUTHERFORD, MD

The management of arteriovenous fistulas (AVFs); vascular anomalies (VAs) and vascular malformations (VMs), many of which contain AVFs; and vascular tumors, as addressed by the chapters in this section, represents some of the greatest challenges facing vascular surgeons and other specialists called on to deal with them. In contrast to atherosclerotic occlusive arterial disease, involving extremity or extracranial arteries and the aorta or its major branches; aneurysmal disease; and primary or secondary (post-thrombotic) venous disease, all of which tend to have recognized anatomic patterns of involvement and characteristic clinical presentations at different levels of clinical severity, the conditions discussed in the chapters in this section are much more varied and much rarer. As a result, few vascular specialists and relatively much fewer primary physicians can develop an approach to their management based on personal experience. The chapters in this section provide adequate background information, descriptive detail, and strategic advice regarding their management to aid the reader in dealing with these challenging conditions.

AVFs involving the aorta and its branches are a special category that lends itself to separate treatment, and these are discussed in Chapter 111. Their central position and high flow usually cause major hemodynamic consequences, frequently leading to forward heart failure, so they usually present early and with progressive symptoms requiring prompt diagnosis and operative intervention. Other *acquired* AVFs are almost always single and usually traumatic in origin, although other etiologic factors, such as infection, aneurysm, and neoplasm, occasionally may be involved, and, rarely, spontaneous fistulae can occur without an obvious underlying cause. One of the earliest and classic

descriptions of an acquired AVF was of one that resulted from blood-letting by a physician; it is a remarkable coincidence that iatrogenic trauma, in the form of arterial puncture, catheterization, or device access, has now increased to the point that it accounts for most traumatic fistulae. Traumatic fistulae are discussed in Chapter 112; the iatrogenic variety receive special consideration in that chapter and in Chapter 54 because their diagnosis and management are different from the classic traumatic AVF resulting from penetrating trauma outside of hospitals. Another form of iatrogenic or acquired AVF—fistulas deliberately created by surgeons for hemodialysis access—are discussed in Section XVII, which is entirely devoted to what has developed into a major area of clinical activity for vascular surgeons, nephrologists, and interventional radiologists. AVFs also are deliberately created by surgeons as adjuncts to limb salvage bypasses (see Chapter 81) and to increase flow temporarily after iliofemoral venous thrombectomy (see Chapter 151).

The diagnostic evaluation of AVFs and VMs containing them (arteriovenous malformations [AVMs]) is primarily concentrated in Chapter 110 because similar tests are involved, but the approaches that are unique for each type of AVF or VA, particularly VMs, are featured in their respective chapters. The treatment of VAs in this edition is addressed in three chapters, one with a special view to VAs (hemangiomas and malformations) of childhood (see Chapter 113) followed by the surgical and endovascular treatment of VAs, primarily VAs containing AVFs (see Chapters 114 and 115). Finally, the last chapter in this section addresses vascular tumors, but because malignant tumors involving the inferior vena cava are discussed in the venous section (see Chapter 163), and the vascular tumors of childhood are discussed in Chapter 113. Chapter 116 focuses primarily on tumors involving the aorta and major arteries, most of which present in adult life. Having summarized this section's organization, numerous basic considerations regarding VAs not fully discussed in the subsequent chapters deserve discussion here.

■ VASCULAR ANOMALIES OR MALFORMATIONS

First, a comment about nomenclature is warranted. For many years, I and many, if not most, other authors have used the term *congenital vascular malformation* to distinguish these lesions from the vascular tumors of childhood. Currently, by agreement of the International Society for Vascular Anomalies in 1996, these conditions are encompassed by the term *vascular anomalies,* but then are separated into tumors and malformations. The term *congenital* has been dropped because although most of the true hemangiomas of infancy are not readily apparent at birth, some are, and the others are represented at the cellular level at least; the designation *congenital* does not separate these two anomalies properly. The term *vascular malformation* is descriptive enough alone, without the word *congenital,* and is used here and in subsequent chapters.

The difficulties in managing VAs stem from many factors. Even more than the acquired conditions addressed elsewhere in this section, the relative rarity of vascular tumors and VMs creates difficulties in diagnosis and treatment because of the treating physician's lack of sufficient personal experience from which to develop or refine proper management strategies. This "neglect of the uncommon" also has resulted in the persistent use of eponyms and difficulties in developing a universally accepted classification system. This rarity also means there is a lack of sufficient numbers for definitive clinical studies or trials of different management approaches. As a result, the development, evaluation, and dissemination of new or better approaches to management have lagged, and there seems to be a lack of agreement regarding appropriate treatment for various lesions (conservative versus interventional, surgical versus endovascular).

These lesions generally have not been well managed in the past, but only partly because of their rarity and the associated lack of understanding. Clinical evaluation of many lesions is not reliably diagnostic, and even when the clinical diagnosis is correct, the anatomic extent and severity of the lesion require additional studies. There has been persistent overreliance on angiography and underuse of noninvasive tests and imaging. Proper (i.e., specific) indications for intervention are frequently not observed. Surgeons still are operating on unresectable lesions, frequently ligating inflow vessels "to control hemodynamic effects," and there has been an overenthusiastic application of embolotherapy by some, beyond the reasonable limits of its capabilities, although these admittedly are steadily improving (see Chapter 115).

The tendency to treat all treatable lesions needs to be restrained in favor of intervening for specific indications. The following are accepted indications: (1) distal steal with ischemic rest pain, (2) nonhealing ulcer, (3) bleeding lesions, (4) high-output heart failure (occurs infrequently,

primarily with major central AVMs), (5) mass lesion with either local pressure effects or obstructing orifice or intolerable appearance or deformity, (6) arterial or venous maturational stage axial lesions with obstruction or aneurysm formation, (7) disseminated intravascular coagulation, and (8) predictable significant leg-length discrepancy. In the last indication, the more common intervention now is premature epiphyseal closure on the affected side, based on study of bone age films. This is not to say that intervention should never be undertaken without one of the above-mentioned reasons, for these amount to mandatory indications, and experts in the field are experienced enough to predict the ultimate need for intervention before reaching some critical endpoint. Rather the point is that there should be some specific reason for intervention more than the existence of a lesion. Often the absence of a mandatory indication allows the treatment of infants to be delayed until they are older and larger, at a point where they can understand better and cooperate more with the proposed procedure. On the other hand, it is not necessary to allow a child to go through school sensitive about an unsightly lesion, when the lesion can be safely treated earlier. The prognosis of many intermediate lesions is difficult when first evaluated in infancy, but becomes apparent with follow-up.

There is much room for improvement in treatment and the indications for treatment. These improvements undoubtedly will occur with better endovascular techniques and technical experience with them. It is hoped that the chapters in this section will provide a clearer view of the proper modern management of this challenging group of vascular malformations. The additional comments are intended to provide background information and an overall perspective.

How Common Are Vascular Malformations?

VMs are not as rare as the relative infrequency of their clinical presentation would suggest. Most reports in the literature focus on patients presenting for evaluation and treatment. For this reason, good data are hard to obtain, but records from the Heim Pal Hospital for Children in Budapest, Hungary, a major district hospital in which all children are delivered and followed during childhood, indicated an incidence of 1.2%, greater than that for spina bifida, cleft lip, and congenital heart disease.[1] If one considered all VAs, including the true hemangiomas of infancy, many more children are involved because these are three to eight times more common than VMs (see Chapter 113). Only a small portion of children with VMs are likely to have needed or sought medical attention because many have capillary malformations (CMs) or VMs. VMs are an exceedingly rare cause for hospital admission and are underrepresented in hospital-based data.

What Are Vascular Malformations and How Do They Develop?

The plethora of names applied over time to VMs reflects their wide spectrum of clinical presentations, which vary from subtle, asymptomatic "birthmarks" or scattered varicosities to grotesquely deformed extremities and hemodynamic compromise. The designations applied by earlier physicians represent an attempt to reduce the protean clinical manifestations into distinct entities. These were descriptive terms, often with a Latin base, and included *hemangioma simplex, angioma telangiectaticum, hemangioma cavernosum, strawberry birthmark, nevus angiectoides, port-wine mark, angioma arteriale racemosum* or *plexiform, cirsoid aneurysm, serpentine aneurysm, congenital arteriovenous aneurysm,* and *congenital arteriovenous fistula.* Some lesion complexes acquired eponyms, such as *Klippel-Trenaunay syndrome*[2] (varicose veins, enlarged limb, and a birthmark, without apparent AVF) and *Parkes Weber syndrome*[3] (the same triad *with* AVF). This confusing diversity in nomenclature developed because early authors did not have the modern diagnostic tools by which to show which of these visibly similar lesions shared common vascular components. Reid[4] and Rienhoff[5] in the 1920s were the first to suggest that VMs result from an arrest or misdirection in development of the primitive vascular system. Pursuit of this concept, soon aided by the frequent use of angiography, eventually allowed this archaic descriptive nomenclature to be replaced by simpler terms that reflect the common developmental etiology of VMs and the stage and location of the responsible "errors" in embryonic development.

Embryologic Basis for Vascular Malformations

The vascular system first appears during the third gestational week as a network of interlacing blood spaces in the primitive mesenchyme.[6] The blood does not yet circulate in any organized fashion, and no separate arterial or venous channel can be identified yet. The vascular system gradually develops by processes of vascular coalescence and cellular differentiation, culminating in the appearance of separate arterial and venous conduits. Woollard[7] described this process in 1922 as a sequence that he divided into three stages. During the *undifferentiated* stage (I), primitive blood lakes coalesce into more organized capillary networks. No arterial or venous conduits can be recognized yet. During the *retiform* stage (II), the capillaries formed in stage I themselves coalesce into larger plexiform structures that are the progenitors of the arterial and venous conduits they are predestined to become. During the *maturation* stage (III), histologically mature vascular channels and principal arterial stems appear. The capillary network that persists beyond fetal life into adulthood may be thought of as a remnant from the original blood lakes in stage I. Translating this into what we see in patients, to give a few examples, the capillary malformations and the cystlike peripheral venous malformations represent arrested development in the syncytial stage; microfistulous AVMs and embryonal veins represent the retiform stage; and macrofistulous AVMs involving branches of named vessels, popliteal venous aneurysms, and persistent sciatic artery represent maturational stage anomalies.

What Types of Venous Anomalies Are There and How Common Is Each Type?

VAs and particularly VMs cover a spectrum of developmental abnormalities that may involve all components of the peripheral circulation—arteries, veins, capillaries, and lymphatics. Most clinically significant lesions contain

	Table 109-1	Hamburg Classification of Vascular Anomalies and Malformations

MAIN CLASS	SUBCLASS	SUBGROUP
Arterial	Truncular	Obstructive Dilating
	Extratruncular	Diffuse Limited (localized)
Venous	Truncular	Obstructive Dilating
	Extratruncular	Diffuse Limited/localized
Arteriovenous	Truncular	Deep Superficial
	Extratruncular	Diffuse/infiltrating Limited/localized
Combined, mixed	Truncular	Venous and arterial Hemolymphatic
	Extratruncular	Diffuse Limited/localized

primarily arteriovenous elements (i.e., AVFs). Predominantly venous defects are the most common, accounting for almost half of those discovered in children,[1] but because they produce less severe clinical manifestations, they do not predominate in reported series, particularly series related to interventional treatment (surgery or embolotherapy). The latter articles emphasize AVMs, which compose just over one third of all VMs.[1] Finally, most lymphatic malformations are combined with other malformations, particularly venous malformations, and have been dubbed *hemolymphatic lesions*; pure localized lymphatic lesions (e.g., lymphoceles) are seen relatively infrequently.

Numerous classification schemes have been suggested over the years, each with certain merit, but they have been too complicated or too incomplete (or not widely enough promulgated) to gain universal acceptance.[8-10] Currently the scheme with the widest worldwide acceptance is the so-called Hamburg classification scheme,[11] so named because it was developed by leaders in the field attending a meeting in Hamburg, Germany (Table 109-1). The Hamburg classification attempted to simplify classification by separating malformations by their predominant component—arterial, venous, arteriovenous, and combined or mixed. The last class may seem imprecise (i.e., a depository for lesions that do not fit elsewhere), but it recognizes the fact that a significant number of VMs have either mixed venous and arterial or mixed venous and lymphatic components, without either one being predominant. Logically, each of these four classes is divided according to whether the lesions involve central, axial vessels (truncular lesions) or peripheral rather than mainstream vessels (extratruncular lesions). Then each of the latter is divided into diffuse (infiltrating) or limited (localized) subgroups. The truncular lesions are not uniformly subgrouped, however. Although the arterial and venous truncular lesions are subgrouped into either obstructive (e.g., aplasia/hypoplasia) or dilating (e.g., aneurysmal) lesions, the arteriovenous truncular lesions are separated into either deep or superficial groups, and the combined/mixed truncular lesions are designated as either venous plus arterial or venous plus lymphatic (so-called hemolymphatic lesions).

One of the potential drawbacks of this scheme is that, logical though it is, the names of the final subgroups are not readily identifiable with their common clinical counterparts. Some clinical examples may indicate, however, that the logic of the scheme allows proper lesion classification. An example of a truncular arterial obstructive lesion would be an aplastic or hypoplastic artery, such as a coarctation or the aplastic arterial segments that result in a persistent sciatic artery. Examples of truncular venous obstructive lesions include aplasia or hypoplasia of the femoral vein and an obstructing web in the proximal subclavian vein. The former results in persistent primitive veins, the embryonal and the marginal veins, which present as varicose veins in atypical anatomic locations. Aneurysms are the obvious example of dilating arterial and venous truncular lesions, one of the best-known being a popliteal venous aneurysm. The typical extratruncular venous lesion consists of almost cystlike lesions, thin-walled venous lakes, with only tangential communication to small peripheral veins. These have been incorrectly called *cavernous hemangiomas* or *venous angiomas*. These may be diffuse and infiltrate throughout the muscles or may be limited to a localized vascular mass. AVFs can involve truncular (named *axial*) vessels (macrofistulous AVMs) or be diffuse and scattered throughout peripheral (extratruncular) arteries, as are so many difficult-to-visualize microfistulous AVMs.

Using this scheme, the relative distribution of lesions has been studied.[1] The most common lesions, by category, are venous malformations, constituting almost half of all (48%). Next are arteriovenous malformations, constituting a little more than one third of the total (36%). Mixed/combined anomalies constitute 15% of the total, but pure arterial defects constitute only 1% of all lesions.

■ OVERALL MANAGEMENT STRATEGY

An outline of a suggested approach to the diagnosis and management of VMs or VAs[12] is presented in Figure 109-1. The clinical evaluation of VMs can be difficult. Some present as a mass lesion, others with diffuse changes involving all or most of the extremity, and still others with no more obvious abnormality than a birthmark. Although none of these features is pathognomonic for a given type, the presence of one or more of these features should lead one at least to suspect a VA. Noting whether there is primarily a birthmark or colored skin lesion, atypical (onset or distribution) varicosities, a mass lesion, or changes in limb dimension can help direct the diagnostic evaluation.

In children presenting with birthmark lesions, the first step is to separate capillary malformations from true hemangiomas. The differentiation usually can be made on clinical grounds (see Chapter 113). With true hemangiomas ruled out, one can focus on what type of VM one is dealing with: Superficial skin lesions may be isolated capillary malformations or be associated with more complex deeper malformations (i.e., AVMs or VMs). The next step is to detect or rule out AVF. Segmental limb systolic pressures, segmental plethysmography or pulse volume recordings, and arterial velocity waveforms can detect most congenital AVF of the extremities (see Chapter 110), although they have been largely supplanted by duplex scanning for superficially accessible or reasonably well-localized lesions. A nuclear medicine arteriovenous shunt study may be used to quantitate arteriovenous shunting if necessary in questionable cases and to monitor interventional treatments. It is valuable in separating Klippel-Trenaunay syndrome from Parkes Weber, the latter containing AVF, often quite small though numerous (microfistulous AVM). These two

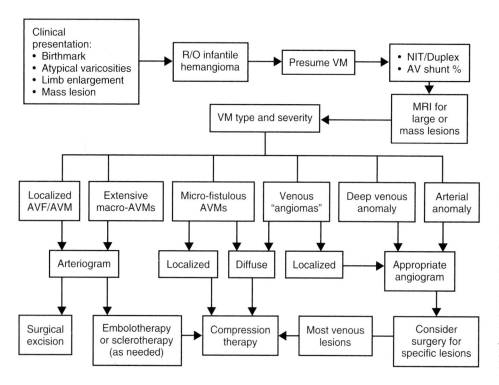

FIGURE 109-1 Algorithm outlining the diagnostic and therapeutic approach to vascular malformations as described in the text. *Note: Venous and arterial anomalies* in this algorithm refer to mature stage axial/truncal lesions. AV, arteriovenous; AVF, arteriovenous fistula; AVM, arteriovenous malformation; NIT, noninvasive test; VM, vascular malformation. (Modified from Rutherford RB: Congenital vascular malformation. In Cronenwett JL, Rutherford RB [eds]: Decision Making in Vascular Surgery. Philadelphia, WB Saunders, 2001.)

syndromes are eponyms for what are now officially called *capillary-lymphaticovenous malformation* and *capillary-arteriovenous malformation,* respectively, which commonly are associated with soft tissue/skeletal hypertrophy. The persistence of these eponyms may relate to their uniquely different-sounding names. For mass lesions, magnetic resonance imaging (MRI) offers sufficient advantages to be used in the initial diagnostic evaluation. MRI shows the lesion's flow characteristics (e.g., distinguishing venous malformations from AVMs) and its anatomic extent, particularly the involvement of surrounding muscle, bone, and subcutaneous tissues, which determines resectability. MRI has supplanted computed tomography because it provides better soft tissue definition and avoids intravenous contrast administration (see Chapter 110).

After using the above-mentioned diagnostic tests, *without the use of angiography,* one should be able to categorize the lesion as one of the following: a localized AVF, an extensive malformation with macrofistulous AVFs (an AVM) fed by specific named vessels, diffusely scattered microfistulous AVFs (which may or may not be associated with venous malformations), venous angiomas (an extratruncular VM consisting of multiple venous lakes), a malformation of the deep veins, or an arterial anomaly. In most cases, duplex scanning aids in sorting these out if the other screening tests are not completely definitive. Angiography is rarely used initially; it is saved to guide interventions when they have been deemed necessary. This approach would apply to AVFs, which occasionally may be localized enough for complete surgical excision; AVMs, with multiple high-flow macrofistulas best controlled by embolotherapy or sclerotherapy; and truncal venous or arterial anomalies, in which surgical treatment may be indicated. Microfistulous AVFs usually have so little hemodynamic effect that they can be treated conservatively for the secondary effects of venous hypertension, as can diffuse venous angiomas. When the latter present as mass lesions, however, they are often amenable to surgical resection or sclerotherapy, using ethanol or other agents (described in Chapter 115). Sclerotherapy has been disappointing for larger mass venous lesions because they require multiple sessions and often leave tender pigmented residua. Removing secondary varicosities and varicose marginal or embryonal veins associated with truncal VMs can be worthwhile in carefully selected cases, but not if the varicosities serve as collateral pathways to axial venous obstruction. Many venous lesions can be treated conservatively with elastic compressive stockings, which also may mitigate the venous hypertensive effects of underlying AVFs not amenable to or incompletely controlled by embolotherapy or surgery. The details of management of these various lesions are discussed thoroughly in the ensuing chapters.

■ REFERENCES

1. Tasnadi G: Epidemiology and etiology of congenital vascular malformations. Semin Vasc Surg 6:200-203, 1993.
2. Lindenauer SM: The Klippel-Trenaunay syndrome: Varicosity, hypertrophy and hemangioma with no arteriovenous fistula. Ann Surg 162:303-314, 1965.
3. Parkes Weber F: Angioma formation in connection with hypertrophy of limbs or hemihypertrophy. Br J Dermatol 19:231, 1907.
4. Reid MR: Studies on abnormal arteriovenous communications, acquired and congenital: 1. Report of a series of cases. Arch Surg 10:601-638, 1925.
5. Rienhoff WF: Congenital arteriovenous fistula: An embryologic study with the report of a case. Johns Hopkins Hosp Bull 35:271-284, 1924.
6. Moore KL: The cardiovascular system. In: The Developing Human: Clinically Oriented Embryology, 4th ed. Philadelphia, WB Saunders, 1988, pp 286-333.
7. Woollard HH: The development of the principal arterial stems in the forelimb of the pig. Contemp Embryol 14:139-154, 1922.
8. Malan E: Vascular Malformations. Milan, Carlo Erba Foundation, 1974, pp 41-43.
9. deTakats G: Vascular anomalies of the extremities. Surg Gynecol Obstet 55:227-237, 1931.
10. Mulliken J, Glovacki J: Hemangiomas and vascular malformation in infants and children: A classification based on endothelial characteristics. Plast Reconstr Surg 69:412-420, 1982.
11. Belov S: Anatomopathological classification of congenital vascular defects. Semin Vasc Surg 6:219-224, 1993.
12. Rutherford RB: Congenital vascular malformation. In Cronenwett JL, Rutherford RB (eds): Decision Making in Vascular Surgery. Philadelphia, WB Saunders, 2001.

Diagnostic Evaluation of Arteriovenous Fistulas and Vascular Anomalies

110

ROBERT B. RUTHERFORD, MD

■ HISTORY AND PHYSICAL EXAMINATION

Some arteriovenous fistulas (AVFs) and vascular anomalies (VAs), some of which contain AVFs, are clinically obvious, particularly to an experienced clinician, but many are not. Most physicians see these problems only occasionally with little opportunity to develop or sharpen their diagnostic acumen. Even experienced specialists usually need additional studies for clinical decision making. For these reasons, in most cases, one or more diagnostic tests are needed to confirm the diagnosis and to assess the anatomic extent or hemodynamic characteristics of the presenting lesion. This chapter focuses mainly on the available tests and their applications in terms of capabilities and limitations. The clinical features of AVFs and VAs are discussed in greater detail in subsequent chapters in this section, but some characteristic features are mentioned here. The basic overall approach to the diagnosis and treatment of vascular malformations (VMs) is discussed in Chapter 109, which includes a management algorithm.

Most clinically significant VAs present well before adult life because of a vascular "birthmark"; localized skin color change; varicose veins or other prominent blood vessels; or occasionally a distinct vascular mass, tumor, or enlargement of the limb (swelling, increase in length or girth) that has gained the attention of parent or child. Changes in limb dimension are unusual in the absence of significant AVFs, and minor differences may be overlooked. Characteristically, these changes occur in the presence of a long-standing arteriovenous malformation (AVM) or AVF, present during the growth period, but they also are reported to occur with pure *venous* anomalies, in the absence of AVF. Whether or not this presentation relates to failure to detect occult microfistulous AVFs in earlier clinical descriptions of such "pure" venous anomalies is debatable, but this should not be a problem in current and future reports if the diagnostic tests described subsequently are employed.

Most birthmarks represent either true hemangiomas or cutaneous capillary or superficial venous malformations, the latter also still being referred to as *cavernous malformations*. Differentiating between these lesions is extremely important in early childhood and usually can be done on clinical grounds given their time of appearance and their growth or lack of growth with time. These and other telltale clues are discussed in Chapter 113. The parents should be questioned as to whether the lesion was clearly present at birth or appeared subsequently and whether it has grown significantly or remained the same size relative to the child.

Localized warmth may be an important physical finding, as is compressibility of vascular masses, the presence of a thrill or bruit, and inequalities in the dimensions of the limb, which should always be measured. Hemangiomas of infancy during the infant's rapid growth phase are hypervascular or high-flow lesions, and this is reflected by their appearance and associated physical signs. The triad of birthmark, varicose veins, and limb enlargement is well known and usually sought, but the involved limb may or may not harbor congenital AVFs. This triad has been the basis for the traditional distinction between Parkes Weber syndrome and Klippel-Trenaunay syndrome, the former being associated with AVFs and the latter not, as discussed further subsequently. These physical findings are inconsistent even in the presence of AVFs. In Sziylagyi and colleagues'[1] classic study of 82 cases of congenital AVMs, the classic triad was present in only 57%.

Acquired AVFs are usually traumatic and often iatrogenic, being related either to some invasive procedure, such as catheterization, or deliberately created for the purpose of hemodialysis access. The latter are discussed in Section XVII, including the diagnostic tests employed before and after hemodialysis access procedures. Traumatic AVFs, which are discussed in detail in Chapter 113, are associated with a penetrating wound, possibly remote or overlooked, but, in contradistinction to AVMs, acquired AVFs are usually single, and when suspected and the wound is located, diagnosis usually is readily confirmed by the finding of a pulsatile lesion with a thrill or bruit, a machinery-like to-and-fro sound, the prominent diastolic component of which distinguishes it from other bruits. In long-standing AVFs, the feeding arteries and draining veins are enlarged, and there may be secondary signs of chronic venous hypertension.

Large, acquired AVFs may produce all the classic signs of forward heart failure. This is a major consideration in large central AVFs; this aspect of diagnostic evaluation is discussed in Chapter 111. Significant cardiac changes also can occur in association with *long-standing* traumatic AVFs, the larger and more centrally located ones at least, but are uncommonly (approximately 10%) associated with AVMs—primarily with AVMs that are large and centrally located. The evaluation of these central effects is only briefly discussed in this chapter.

■ DIAGNOSTIC STUDIES: BASIC STRATEGIES

The basic approach to the evaluation and treatment of VMs is presented in an algorithm in Chapter 109; a more focused and detailed discussion of diagnosis is offered here. Determining whether or not a vascular anomaly or malformation contains AVFs is the usual starting point, even in presumed venous lesions, and particularly in presumed Klippel-Trenaunay syndrome. The vascular diagnostic laboratory (VDL) can provide much useful information in this regard, using much of the same instrumentation and techniques employed in diagnosing peripheral arterial occlusive disease, including segmental limb pressures and plethysmography, velocity waveform analysis, and duplex scanning,[2] and vascular malformations containing AVFs can be evaluated with these basic VDL tests. A radionuclide labeled microsphere shunt study can be added, as needed, to quantify the arteriovenous shunting, and magnetic resonance imaging (MRI) is used to determine the anatomic extent of mass lesions. Truncal/axial venous malformations are best first evaluated by duplex scanning, whereas MRI is used in extratruncular (peripheral) mass lesions. Angiography now is reserved mainly for preinterventional evaluations.

Numerous considerations govern how these diagnostic methods can or should be applied to greatest advantage. First, one needs to understand the hemodynamic characteristics of AVFs to apply and interpret properly the various available tests. Second, the diagnostic capabilities and limitations of the various available tests differ, and this must be understood in applying them. Physiologic tests simply gauge the pressure, volume, or velocity changes associated with the AVFs; they do not visualize the AVFs, as ultrasound and MRI can do. Most of these tests are qualitative, not quantitative, and most can be applied only to peripheral or extremity AVF (see later). Third, acquired AVFs and AVMs differ from each other significantly in terms of multiplicity and anatomic localization. AVMs characteristically are much more diffuse with multiple-component AVFs and as a result usually cannot be as well localized by the so-called physiologic tests, and all but the more superficial ones cannot be completely visualized by Doppler ultrasonography. Fourth, the diagnostic goals may vary considerably in different clinical settings, and this significantly affects the application of the tests. The simplest diagnostic goal may be to determine the presence or absence of arteriovenous shunting, but often the presence of an AVF is obvious and it is the relative magnitude of its peripheral hemodynamic effects that needs to be gauged (e.g., the presence of a distal steal and the severity of the associated ischemia).

Diagnostic Studies for Congenital Arteriovenous Fistulas or Arteriovenous Malformations

AVMs are less common than venous malformations. Nevertheless, they constitute more than a third (versus one half) of all VMs and constitute most of VMs presenting clinically. Although much is made of the diagnostic triad of birthmark, varicose veins, and limb enlargement, it is not in itself diagnostic of congenital AVFs because a bare majority of patients presenting with congenital AVFs present with the complete triad and patients with purely venous malformations and no AVFs (e.g., Klippel-Trenaunay syndrome) may present with the same triad. The vascular diagnostic techniques described subsequently can be valuable in ruling in or out the presence of AVFs in this setting, in patients presenting with atypical (location, age of onset) varicose veins or a birthmark or both, with or without limb enlargement.[2] Depending on their location and localization, the same simple physiologic tests used in diagnosing peripheral arterial occlusive disease can be employed in diagnosing AVFs or AVMs and can diagnose quickly and inexpensively, avoiding the need for angiography, which is particularly important because many patients are young children. Although qualitative in nature, the degree of abnormality observed in these tests in association with congenital AVFs gives the clinician a rough impression of their relative magnitude. Increasingly the current workhorse of the VDL, the duplex scan, has found useful application in evaluating AVFs.

These noninvasive tests have been underused in the past in this clinical setting because many, if not most, physicians who encounter these patients have persisted with a primary reliance on angiography. This misguided "AGA" approach ("always get an angiogram") still prevails because many clinicians do not realize that angiography is required only if the need for therapeutic intervention for congenital AVFs has been determined *and* will be undertaken soon. Otherwise, the presence or absence of AVFs and their relative severity can be determined by noninvasive methods in most cases, allowing management decisions to be made without angiography and its attendant discomfort and associated risks, a major consideration in infants and young children.

Although this addiction to contrast angiography deserves opposition, there are a number of noninvasive or minimally invasive imaging approaches that have emerged in recent decades that deserve discussion in that they offer significant additional perspectives over that which can be achieved by VDL-based tests, particularly in the evaluation of congenital AVF. These diagnostic modalities (radionuclide quantification of arteriovenous shunting, computed tomography [CT], and MRI) also are discussed in detail in this chapter as additional diagnostic options that must be considered in this setting to provide the reader with knowledge of their capabilities and clinical applications. These new imaging methods are considerably more expensive and time-consuming than the VDL studies, so, if the information they add is not required for decision making, their use may be inappropriate despite the additional perspective they offer.

Diagnostic Studies for Acquired Arteriovenous Fistulas

The basic diagnostic methods described in this chapter also have application to acquired AVFs, whether due to iatrogenic or other penetrating trauma (see Chapter 112), in detecting and localizing them and assessing their hemodynamic significance. As one might expect of the treating physicians (often trauma surgeons), arteriography is commonly used. As will become apparent, noninvasive diagnostic tests have application here and have specialized applications in the management of acquired AVFs created by direct anastomosis or interposed shunts for hemodialysis access, but these are discussed separately in Chapter 120. Traditionally, most acquired AVFs have been traumatic in origin. Currently the most common traumatic form results as a complication of invasive catheter techniques, particularly techniques using a transfemoral artery approach. The standard Seldinger technique involves puncture of the posterior wall of the artery and, depending on the anatomic location, and particularly in the groin, may enter the vein as well. It is not surprising that AVFs inadvertently can be created iatrogenically, although pseudoaneurysms are more commonly the result of such puncture trauma. These AVFs can be readily visualized by duplex scanning, and duplex scanning can aid in monitoring attempts at closure by compression or injection of thrombogenic material or both. There is little need for using noninvasive physiologic testing directed toward assessing the peripheral hemodynamic changes associated with traumatic AVFs. Assessing the cardiac effects of a large central AVF may be important and is discussed subsequently.

■ LOCAL AND SYSTEMIC EFFECTS OF ARTERIOVENOUS FISTULAS: DIAGNOSTIC IMPLICATIONS

Local Hemodynamic Changes

From a hemodynamic perspective, AVF can be considered a "short-circuit" between the high-pressure arterial system and the low-pressure venous system. If the AVF, or in the case of congenital malformations, the AVMs, are significant enough hemodynamically, they result in an arterial pressure decrease, a significant diversion of flow into the venous system rather than through the microcirculation, and an increase in velocity, often with turbulence. These hemodynamic changes often increase progressively with time. The *mean* arterial blood pressure distal to an AVF is always reduced to some degree as a result of blood being shunted away from the peripheral vascular bed into the low-resistance pathway offered by the arteriovenous communication.[3] The reduction in pressure is particularly severe when the fistula is large and the arterial collaterals are small. Even when collaterals are well developed, reversal of flow in the artery distal to the AVFs further decreases peripheral arterial pressure because much of the collateral flow is diverted back into the fistulous circuit and never reaches the periphery. When the fistula is small and the collaterals are large, there may be little or no perceptible effect on the peripheral pressures. The magnitude of the pressure decrease across a fistula or the limb segment containing AVFs can provide the surgeon with a fair assessment of its hemodynamic consequences. If the pressure drop is severe enough, there may be distal ischemia. If fistula flow is great enough, there is associated venous hypertension. These two conditions are responsible for the major peripheral manifestation and symptoms.

A pattern of low flow and high resistance, which characterizes the *normal resting* extremity circulation, shifts to a high-flow and low-resistance pattern with exercise. The velocity pattern of a peripheral AVF is similar to that associated with exercise, and these different velocity patterns are

readily distinguished from patterns observed in a normal resting limb. These differences are key to the noninvasive diagnosis of AVFs. Other conditions can increase extremity flow, such as external heat, infection, certain vasodilating drugs, and sympathectomy. These conditions are rarely present in patients referred to a VDL, but one must be aware of them as an occasional source of error.

Systemic Effects of Arteriovenous Fistulas

Just as there can be a local or regional decrease in pressure and resistance beyond an AVF, so can larger AVFs produce a decrease in *total* peripheral resistance. The latter is responsible for all of the systemic or central effects attributable to AVFs. If no circulatory adjustments were made, this reduction in total peripheral resistance would result in a decrease in arterial pressure, an increase in venous pressure, and diversion of blood from the peripheral tissues. To compensate for this, rather than increasing the systemic resistance to maintain arterial pressure (but further reduce flow to the peripheral tissues), cardiac output is augmented by increasing heart rate and stroke volume. This change not only maintains arterial pressure and reduces venous pressure, but also it supports blood flow to the peripheral tissues. Secondarily, blood volume must increase to support venous return to the heart. Depending on the size of the fistula, there may be no perceptible increase in pressure, or there may be an increase, particularly in the diastolic pressure, but the heart rate is usually within normal limits. The opening and closing of *large* AVFs is associated with profound local and systemic hemodynamic changes, best described by Sumner.[4] These are associated with Nicoladoni-Branham sign, a significant (>4 beats/min) slowing of the pulse rate with compression of the fistula or the proximal artery. Cardiac enlargement is seen frequently in patients with a large chronic AVF, and this may be detected on a chest radiograph, although echocardiography is more sensitive in detecting earlier changes. With the passage of time, a gradual increase in cardiac output results, and ultimately cardiac failure may make a delayed appearance, even in patients who initially were able to tolerate the fistula without evident difficulties. In patients with large, longstanding AVFs, the above-mentioned signs of cardiac failure should be sought. The cardiac failure associated with acute fistulas originating in the aorta or its major branches may be florid and difficult to manage (see Chapter 111).

■ DIAGNOSTIC TESTS: DESCRIPTIONS AND APPLICATIONS

The first focus of this section is on diagnostic approaches that are available in most VDLs. The basic diagnostic methods and the instrumentation behind all but one of these diagnostic methods have been covered in earlier chapters (see Chapters 14 through 17 and 22) and are not described at length here, but their utility in this setting is discussed, as is their interpretation, appropriate clinical applications, and limitations.

The pressure, flow volume, and velocity changes associated with AVFs in an extremity can be readily detected and their relative magnitude roughly assessed by noninvasive physiologic tests, *particularly compared with the normal*

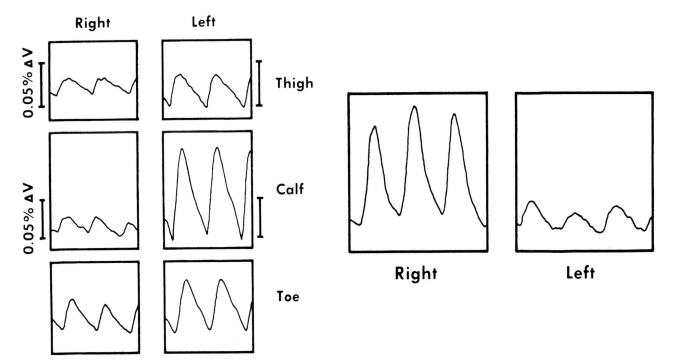

FIGURE 110-1 Plethysmographic (PVR) tracings at thigh, calf, and toe levels in a 4-year-old girl with multiple congenital AVFs involving the entire left leg. (From Rutherford RB (ed): Vascular Surgery, 5th ed. Philadelphia, WB Saunders, 2000.)

FIGURE 110-2 Toe plethysmographic (PVR) tracings from a patient with a congenital AVM involving the left calf. The reduced PVRs reflect a distal steal from this, but not to critical ischemic levels, for some pulsatility remains. The left ankle pressure was 55 mm Hg. (From Rutherford RB (ed): Vascular Surgery, 5th ed. Philadelphia, WB Saunders, 2000.)

contralateral extremity. The noninvasive "physiologic" tests that can be employed are the same as the tests used for many decades in the diagnosis of peripheral arterial occlusive disease and are described subsequently.

Segmental Limb Pressures

Segmental limb pressure measurement is a standard technique (see Chapter 14). Noninvasive methods of measuring systolic blood pressure are reasonably accurate and reproducible and are painless, rapid, and simple in application. A pneumatic cuff is placed around the limb segment at the required site and inflated to above systolic pressure. As the cuff is deflated, the systolic pressure at which blood flow returns distal to the cuff is noted on an aneroid or mercury manometer. Return of flow can be detected with a Doppler flowmeter, a mercury-in-Silastic strain gauge, a photoplethysmograph, or a pulse volume recorder. In the upper extremity, pressure measurements can be made at the upper arm, forearm, wrist, or finger levels; in the lower extremity, pressure measurements can be made at the thigh, calf, ankle, foot, or toe. Cuffs should be applied bilaterally to allow comparison with the normal contralateral limb, which is particularly important in assessing AVF.

A hemodynamically significant AVF reduces *mean* pressure in the limb or in the arterial tree close to the fistula. These cuffs measure *systolic* pressure, and even though mean pressure is reduced in the arterial tree as one approaches an AVF, the pressure swings between systolic and diastolic (i.e., the pulse pressure) may be *increased* so

that systolic pressure is likely to be elevated *proximal to a fistula.* The *systolic* pressure can be detected as being elevated by comparison with that of the opposite limb at the same level.[5] It also is found to be elevated if the pressure cuff has been placed directly over the site of the fistula or its afferent tributaries. In general, however, compared with the contralateral extremity, cuffs at or above a hemodynamically significant fistula or group of fistulas usually record a higher systolic pressure, whereas cuffs below the fistula record a normal or lower systolic pressure, depending on the magnitude of the fistula, with major fistulas being associated with a detectable degree of distal steal. A detectable pressure difference between limbs, greater than measurement variability, indicates a significant AVF.

Segmental Plethysmography

Segmental plethysmography is another standard technique (see Chapter 14); it employs cuffs of precise dimensions applied at various levels/locations along an extremity, similar to those used for measuring segmental limb pressures. Air-filled cuffs are normally used. The resulting tracing contour is generally assessed in terms of magnitude and shape. When the pulse-sensing device is placed over the fistula or just proximal to it, the pulse volume may be increased.[5,6] This increase is commonly seen in a limb with AVM, the increased pulsation being almost diagnostic in itself (Fig. 110-1). Although the pulse contour may be normal (or nearly so) in a limb *distal* to an AVF, it is frequently reduced, particularly in the presence of a steal (Fig. 110-2).[7] As in the case of segmental limb pressure measurements, the reduction in pulse volume depends on the size of the fistula and the adequacy of the collateral arteries. Similar to those described earlier for segmental limb pressures, plethysmography tracings are increased in magnitude above or at the level of an AVF or group of AVFs, and depending on the degree of distal steal, the tracings below the fistula are reduced or, at best, normal in magnitude. A study of the tracings compared with the contralateral extremity often allows the general location or level of a significant AVF to the identified.

Velocity Waveform Analysis

Velocity tracings can be recorded over any extremity artery by a Doppler probe connected to the DC recorder and strip chart or by the velocity readout of a duplex scan. In evaluating for AVFs, the velocity is recorded over the major proximal inflow artery (e.g., femoral or axillary). The reason for selecting this location, rather than directly over the suspected fistulae, will become apparent later. Finding a high-velocity flow pattern in an artery leading to a suspicious lesion is good evidence that the artery is serving as the inflow for AVFs.[7,8] For many, if not most, clinical purposes, a qualitative estimate of flow velocity and the contour of the analogue velocity tracings or waveforms obtained in this manner with a directional Doppler velocity detector provides sufficient information for clinical diagnosis, and the magnitude of the changes provides some indication of the size of the fistulas.

The velocity tracings of a *resting* normal extremity is characterized by end-systolic reversal at the end of peak systolic flow, followed by low flow in early diastole and negligible flow in late diastole. Such a low-flow, high-resistance pattern is most pronounced in the lower extremity. In the upper extremity, there may be little end-systolic reversal. In contrast, high-flow, low-resistance arterial velocity patterns are seen in many major organ artery beds (e.g., renal, carotid, celiac arteries). In the extremities, high-flow patterns are seen after exercise and, importantly, in association with AVFs. In these settings, peak systolic velocity may be quite high, but, more characteristically, there is *continuous flow throughout diastole, and the dip in the tracing between systole and diastole does not approach the zero-velocity baseline,* let alone show an end-systolic reversal as it does in the normal resting extremity. The characteristic arterial pattern associated with AVFs (Fig. 110-3) consists of an *elimination of end-systolic reversal and a marked increase in diastolic velocity, which "elevates" the entire tracing above the zero-velocity baseline.* The degree of elevation in end-diastolic velocity correlates directly with the flow increase caused by the AVFs.[5,6] By using these characteristic Doppler velocity signals as a guide, one can detect and localize congenital or traumatic AVFs that otherwise might escape detection.[10,11] Peripheral AVFs constituting 5% of extremity flow or more can be detected by this means. This test is more sensitive than segmental pressures and plethysmography.

Care must be taken to compare the signal from one limb with that from the other at the same anatomic location. Also, one must appreciate the fact that hyperemic tissues can produce similar signals. False-positive readings can occur in

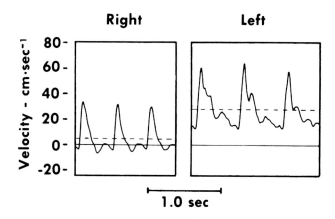

FIGURE 110-3 Velocity tracing from the femoral arteries in a 4-year-old girl with a large AVM involving the left thigh. Note that the tracing on the left, compared to the normal right tracing, has higher peak and mean (*dashed line*) systolic velocity, and there is no end-systolic reversal. Rather, there is high flow continuing throughout diastole, as a result of which the tracing does not drop back to the zero baseline at the end of diastole, but is elevated well above the zero baseline. (From Rutherford RB [ed]: Vascular Surgery, 5th ed. Philadelphia, WB Saunders, 2000.)

other hyperemic settings (e.g., inflammation associated with superficial thrombophlebitis, lymphangitis, bacterial infection, thermal or mechanical trauma). Inflammation of the limb is usually evident on clinical examination. Hyperdynamic flow associated with conditions such as beriberi or thyrotoxicosis is generalized and should cause no confusion because it is generalized and affects all extremities. Other causes of hyperemia isolated to an individual vessel or limb (e.g., exercise or reactive hyperemia after a period of ischemia) are transient. Externally applied heat, local infection (e.g., cellulitis or abscess), or sympathetic blockade also can increase flow. None of these should create any significant confusion in the usual patient referred to the VDL for evaluation of congenital or acquired AVF.

Evaluation for Arteriovenous Fistulas Using Three Physiologic Tests in Combination

Advantages

These three tests are inexpensive, quickly applied, and require only basic operator or interpretive skill. The instrumentation is simple and used on an everyday basis in most VDLs.

Limitations

These tests give qualitative rather than quantitative information and can be applied only to AVFs located in the extremity proper (at or below the highest cuff). They may not detect microfistulas or any fistulous flow constituting less than 5% of total extremity flow. Single-limb data are not as diagnostic when considered alone compared with a normal contralateral extremity.

Primary Clinical Applications

Primary clinical applications are (1) screening for congenital AVFs in the extremities of patients presenting with suggestive signs (e.g., a vascular birthmark, atypical varicose veins, limb enlargement) and (2) detecting, roughly localizing, and assessing the relative magnitude of congenital AVMs and traumatic AVF. With anatomically localized lesions, these tests, with or without duplex scanning (see later) suffice for most clinical decision making.

Duplex Scanning

The basic Duplex scanner combines an ultrasound image with a focused directional Doppler probe. In modern instruments, the velocity signal is color-coded so that red represents arterial flow and blue represents venous flow (going in opposite directions). The velocity signal also is displayed on the screen as needed for specific applications.

Because the duplex scanner provides velocity information, it can serve as a means of performing velocity waveform analysis, as described earlier, the pattern serving as a simple yet sensitive means of diagnosing an AVF. Because of the other information obtainable from duplex scanning, it has replaced using a simple Doppler probe connected to a DC recorder for this purpose in most VDLs. High peak mean velocity readings recorded over the main inflow artery of the involved extremity compared with readings at the same location of the contralateral normal extremity confirm the presence of an AVF or AVMs in that limb. The characteristic pattern of the velocity tracing, described earlier, distinguishes this high-velocity reading from the more focused high-velocity reading observed in association with a stenosis.

The software of some of today's duplex scanners also allows a rough estimation of volume flow, with diameter measurements being used to estimate cross-sectional area and the velocity signals and the angle of incidence of the probe allowing the Doppler equation to be applied: flow = velocity (frequency shift) × cosine θ (angle of incidence of the ultrasound beam) × cross-sectional area ÷ C (velocity of sound in tissue, a constant). A significant problem in using the duplex scan to obtain accurate velocity or flow measurements *directly over* an AVF is the presence of turbulence, multidirectional flows, and aliasing. Flashes of yellow representing turbulent fistula flow are seen, and higher than normal velocities are registered, so the diagnosis is readily made, but quantification is not accurate at the fistula site. Traumatic AVF, particularly the iatrogenic variety resulting from the percutaneous introduction of catheters via the femoral vessels, are readily seen as multicolored, orange-to-white "flashes" between the red and blue artery and vein. The nearby tissues transmitting the thrill appear to "light up" with each cardiac cycle because of a motion artifact. Congenital AVFs are more complex, but their high-flow patterns are readily recognized, and the nature and extent of the more localized superficial lesions can be well characterized. This in itself can be diagnostic and is particularly useful when applied to mass lesions, often presenting as a cluster of varicosities, which are but the superficial component of an underlying VM.

The diagnostic dilemma—that these varicosities may be part of a venous malformation or may be associated with an underlying AVM—can be resolved by this approach. The detection of high velocities or flashes of turbulence when viewed by a duplex scanner often quickly identifies the type of malformation one is dealing with. The Duplex scan can

be valuable in detecting and localizing an acquired fistula or a localized AVM and, although not able to measure fistula flow *directly*, can do so indirectly by velocity readings obtained proximally over the major inflow artery, comparing the involved limb with the contralateral normal extremity at the same level. The latter approach is recommended when quantitative measurements of fistula flow are desired. Subtracting the contralateral normal limb flow from that of the involved limb provides a fairly reliable estimate of arteriovenous shunt flow, if the interrogation sites and monitoring techniques are the same on both limbs.

Advantages

Duplex scanners are in everyday use in VDLs today, so the necessary instrumentation and the operator skills are there. The duplex scan is versatile in evaluating AVFs, and is used to interrogate a penetrating wound or groin hematoma after a catheterization procedure or a mass lesion suspected of harboring congenital AVFs in a young patient. It may visualize and interrogate an AVF directly and provide velocity evidence of its existence (e.g., high flow in the artery leading to a suspected fistula area).

Limitations

In the case of congenital AVMs, in which the AVFs may be multiple and spread out over a larger area, the duplex scanner may not be able to visualize (encompass) the fistulas directly and not be able to assess fully the anatomic extent, although it can supply indirect information by interrogating the velocity characteristics of the inflow artery. Similar to the previously described physiologic tests, it can be applied to extremity lesions but not to central lesions (e.g., in the trunk or pelvis). Much of its application is qualitative, not quantitative, although flow estimates are possible, by comparing flows between the involved and contralateral normal limb, as described.

Primary Clinical Applications

The primary clinical applications are detecting and localizing AVF and AVMs and guiding thrombotic or embolic therapy in traumatic and congenital AVFs, but only if they are superficially located and well localized.

Radionuclide Arteriovenous Shunt Quantification

Radionuclide labeled albumin microspheres can be used to diagnose and *quantitate* arteriovenous shunting. The basic principle behind the study is simple: Radionuclide labeled albumin microspheres too large to pass through capillaries are injected into the inflow artery proximal to the suspected AVF. The microspheres passing through arteriovenous communications are trapped in the next vascular bed, in the lung, and may be quantified by counting the radioactivity of the lungs with a discrete sample from a gamma camera, by maintaining a rectilinear scintillation scanner in a fixed position over a limited pulmonary field.[6,12]

The fraction of microspheres reaching the lungs is determined by comparing these counts with the lung counts after another injection of microspheres introduced into *any* peripheral vein, 100% of which should lodge in the lungs. The agent usually used consists of a suspension of 35-μ human albumin microspheres labeled with technetium-99m (similar to that commonly used in lung scans). To ensure similar counting efficiencies, the suspension injected into the vein contains only one fourth to one third of the activity of that injected into the artery, approximately 1 mCi versus 4 mCi. The relative radioactivity of the microsphere suspensions injected is measured by scintillation counting of the syringes before and after the microspheres have been administered.

The formula used to estimate the percentage of arteriovenous shunting is $Pa - Bg/Pv - Pa \times Ia_1 - Ia_2/Iv_1 - Iv_2 \times 100$, where Bg is background pulmonary counts per unit time, Pa is pulmonary counts per unit time after arterial injection, Pv is pulmonary counts per unit time after venous injection, Iv_1 is counts per unit time of venous syringe before injection, Iv_2 is residual counts per unit time of venous syringe after injection, Ia_1 is counts per unit time of arterial syringe before injection, and Ia_2 is residual counts per unit time of arterial syringe after injection.[11] For example, if the pulmonary radioactivity after the arterial injection $(Pa - Bg)$ is half that measured after the venous injection $(Pv - Pa)$, and the ratio of the activity of the venous injectate $(Iv_1 - Iv_2)$ to that of the arterial injectate $(Ia_1 - Ia_2)$ is one fourth, the estimated shunt volume would be 12.5% of the total flow to the extremity, or $(\frac{1}{2})(\frac{1}{4})(100) = 12.5\%$

Advantages

The study is minimally invasive, relatively simple to perform, causes little discomfort, and carries a negligible risk. It quantifies the degree of arteriovenous shunting, something none of the other tests do. Because shunt flow can be quantified, the results have prognostic value.[5,6] One can estimate the hemodynamic significance of an AVF or AVM and be better able to predict the need for intervention. Serial measurements also can be used to gauge the success of interventions designed to eliminate or control AVFs.

Limitations

Although naturally occurring "physiologic" arteriovenous shunts are present in normal human extremities, less than 3% of the total blood flow (and usually much less) is diverted through these communications, so they normally do not produce an interpretive error.[12] Measurements made during anesthesia are not accurate, however, because anesthesia, both general and regional, significantly increases shunting through these naturally occurring arteriovenous communications. The examiner also must be aware that the percentage of blood shunted through arteriovenous communications can be significant (range of 20% to 40%) in the limbs of patients soon after sympathetic denervation and in patients with cirrhosis or with hypertrophic pulmonary osteopathy.[13] Finally, this study shares the limitation of the physiologic studies previously described in that it does not ordinarily localize the lesion. Several injections can be made, however, at key locations at the time of arteriography and quantified against a later venous injection, to give localizing informa-

tion. If one recorded 50% shunting after injection into the common iliac artery, 70% shunting after injection into the external iliac artery, 100% shunting after injection into the profunda femoris, and 0% shunting in the superficial femoral artery, the AVM is entirely localized to the distribution of the profunda femoris artery (actual case of the author).

Clinical Applications

Radionuclide labeled microspheres are most useful for studying patients with suspected congenital AVFs.[2,6] Arteriography occasionally may fail to show the fistulas because they are too small or because the flow is too rapid. Almost 30% of congenital AVFs are missed by arteriography, and the diagnosis is made based on indirect signs.[1] Early venous filling or enlargement of feeding and draining vessels may be the only clues to the existence of AVFs. In such instances, injection of microspheres in conjunction with arteriography can be used to establish the diagnosis, with the patient being taken to the nuclear medicine laboratory later for pulmonary counting before and after a venous injection. In patients with diffuse or extensive congenital VMs presenting with a vascular birthmark, varicose veins, or limb overgrowth, it may be difficult to distinguish clinically between patients with multiple AVFs (Parkes Weber syndrome), some so small they cannot be visualized angiographically, and patients with the same triad but with predominantly venous malformations (Klippel-Trenaunay syndrome). The labeled microsphere study solves this dilemma. The success of surgical or endovascular interventions in eliminating or controlling AVFs can be adequately gauged by preintervention and postintervention studies. Finally, serial measurements indicate whether the AVM is following a stable or progressive course and whether previously dormant arteriovenous communications have begun to open up or "grow."

Magnetic Resonance Imaging and Computed Tomography

The previously described studies cannot properly assess the anatomic extent of large or deep VMs, and even angiographic studies tend to underestimate their full anatomic extent. CT usually shows the location and extent of the lesion and the involvement of specific muscle groups and bone.[14,15] Deep intramuscular lesions give a mottled appearance, and with the bolus administration of contrast material, there is enhancement that depends on the rate of arteriovenous shunting in and the degree of cellularity of the lesion. Offsetting these desirable features of CT are the need for contrast, the lack of an optimal protocol for its administration, and the practical limitation of having to use multiple transverse images to reconstruct the anatomy of the lesion. Three-dimensional reconstruction of CT angiography data overcomes some of these limitations, but subtracting away muscle, skin, and bone, as performed in most vascular applications prevents the true anatomic extent of congenital VMs from being accurately determined.

MRI possesses numerous distinct advantages over CT in evaluating VMs. There is no need for contrast, the anatomic extent is more clearly shown, longitudinal and transverse sections may be obtained, and the flow patterns in the VM can be characterized. As a result, *MRI has become the pivotal diagnostic study in the evaluation of most VMs presenting with mass lesions.*

The MRI signal intensity depends on the proton density, the magnetic relaxation times (T1 and T2), and the bulk proton flux (the last-named reflecting blood flow). If an image is obtained after the pulsed protons (in rapidly moving blood) have left the field, a (black) flow void appears on T2-weighted scans, identifying high-flow vascular spaces and their feeding arteries and draining veins. In contrast, a predominantly venous malformation with its slow flow would appear white. Cellularity can be appreciated because stromal tissues "relax" at different rates. Cellularity produces a higher intensity signal than blood-filled spaces.[16] Clinical examples of the value of MRI in the setting of VMs are illustrated in Figures 110-4, 110-5, and 110-6.

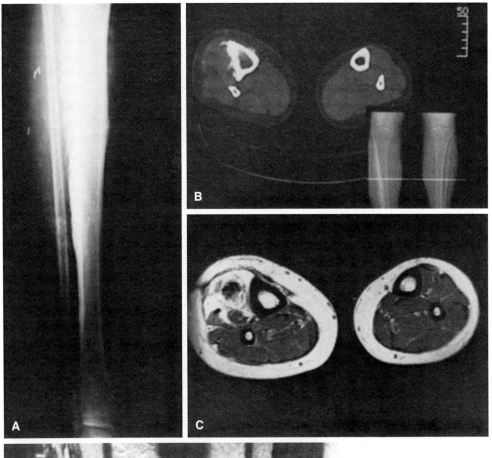

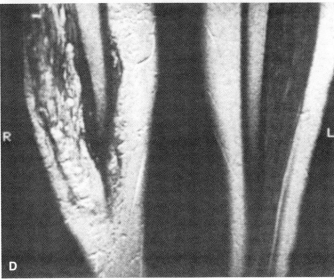

FIGURE 110-4 **A,** Radiograph of the lower leg of a 29-year-old woman with a right anterior tibial mass present since birth shows speckled calcifications, metal clips from multiple previous operations, and tibial cortical irregularities. An arteriogram (not shown) revealed "hypervascularity and one area of early venous filling." **B,** CT scan also suggests bone involvement. **C,** Transverse MRI shows lesion filling the anterior tibial compartment, but the margins of the tibia are clean. **D,** Longitudinal MRI also shows the lack of fast-flow voids. Total excision of the lesion was performed without difficulty or significant blood loss. Histologic study revealed a "highly cellular and fibrotic cavernous (venous) malformation." (**A-D** from Pearce WH, Rutherford RB, Whitehill TA, Davis K: Nuclear magnetic resonance imaging: Its diagnostic value in patients with congenital vascular malformations of the limbs. J Vasc Surg 8:64, 1988.)

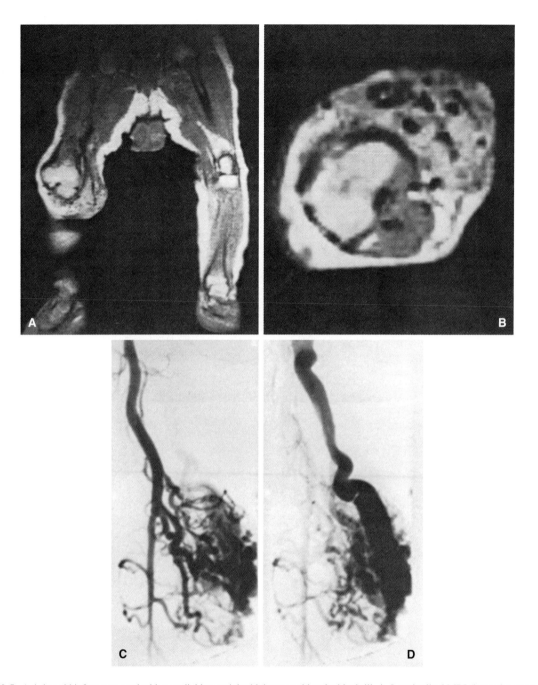

FIGURE 110-5   A 4-day-old infant presented with a medial lower right thigh mass with palpable thrill. **A,** Longitudinal MRI shows the mass with a large, high-flow draining vein. **B,** Transverse MRI shows multiple fast-flow voids with involvement of muscle and bone. **C,** After several months, this arteriogram was obtained because of the onset of high-output heart failure. **D,** Later phase view shows the same large draining vein seen on MRI. Therapeutic embolization was carried out, resulting in transient disseminated intravascular coagulation but with a diminution of the mass and control of heart failure. (**A-D** from Pearce WH, Rutherford RB, Whitehill TA, Davis K: Nuclear magnetic resonance imaging: Its diagnostic value in patients with congenital vascular malformations of the limbs. J Vasc Surg 8:64, 1988.)

■ VENOUS MALFORMATIONS: DIAGNOSTIC CONSIDERATIONS

Venous malformations are the most common VM and constitute a diverse variety of lesions. Truncular obstructive lesions include localized webs or stenoses or aplasia/hypoplasia of deep venous segments. Particularly in the latter circumstance, collateral veins often dilate, and the patient may present with varicose veins of atypical distribution, or,

if the anomaly develops early enough embryologically, primitive embryonal or marginal veins may persist. Venous aneurysms represent the most common dilating type, most often occurring in the popliteal segment. In a more diffuse dilating anomaly, patients may present with chronic venous insufficiency from widespread dilatation and valvular incompetence throughout the deep venous system.

Because all of these truncular lesions involve axial veins, they should be investigated first by duplex scanning,

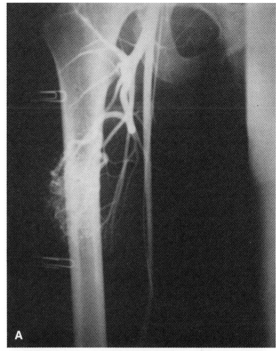

FIGURE 110-6 A 24-year-old man had been aware of a painless soft mass on his upper anterolateral thigh for many years. **A,** An arteriogram was obtained, which showed a localized arteriovenous malformation fed by the profunda femoris artery. The patient was referred for surgery. **B,** Sagittal MRI view shows high-flow voids and large draining veins. **C,** Transverse MRI shows not only the high-flow voids, but also diffuse involvement of the anterior thigh muscles. Operation was withheld in this asymptomatic man because excision would have produced immediate neuromuscular disability. There was no distal steal or cardiac embarrassment.

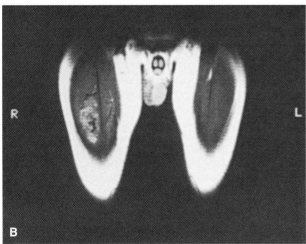

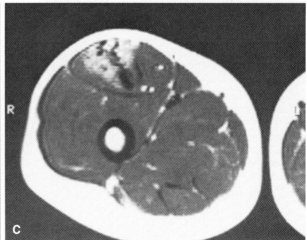

although major obstructive lesions should produce abnormal physiologic test findings (air plethysmography or venous occlusion plethysmography). In patients presenting with atypical varicose veins, it is important to eliminate the possibility of deep venous obstructive defects before making matters worse by removing secondary varicose veins or a persistent embryonal or marginal vein that has become varicose because these may be serving as crucial collaterals around the deep obstruction. Duplex scanning can provide this assurance. Similarly, universal valvular incompetence of the deep venous system is apparent on duplex scanning, and popliteal venous aneurysms should be discovered by duplex scanning when performed for deep venous thrombosis or pulmonary embolus of obscure origin. For *truncular* venous defects, duplex scanning represents the most useful diagnostic method. Venography has been relegated by duplex scanning to a secondary role and generally should be performed only when needed for planning and carrying out interventions, such as sclerotherapy, if indicated.

Extratruncular lesions may be diffuse or localized. The diffuse lesions are often scattered throughout the extremity and may infiltrate deeper tissues, such as muscle groups. They produce little, if any, functional disturbance and are for the most part not amenable to, and do not need, interventional treatments, so the considerable difficulty in defining their anatomic extent carries no therapeutic penalty. MRI is the only feasible method of investigation, but this should be used primarily for localized mass lesions, which may justify intervention. The latter are common and consist of grapelike clusters of venous lakes (commonly misnamed *venous angiomas*), which are tangential to the veins to which they are connected. For this reason, the usual technique of ascending venography often misses them. They can be partially visualized by direct puncture contrast injection, but MRI better appreciates their full extent. They can be more completely filled by distally injected contrast material if a tourniquet is first applied with an Esmarch bandage and the contrast is injected on release of the bandage. This technique is rarely justified, however, because MRI usually supplies the necessary decision-making data. Duplex scanning can visualize these extratruncular lesions but cannot usually fully delineate either the diffuse lesions or the larger mass lesions, so although it may be used preliminarily to confirm the presence of these peripherally located venous malformations and rule out associated AVFs, duplex scanning does not play the central role it does for truncular lesions.

■ CONCLUSION

Great progress has been made in the evaluation of AVFs and venous malformations in recent decades with the introduction of noninvasive VDL tests, minimally invasive arteriovenous shunt quantification using radionuclide labeled microspheres, and advanced imaging techniques, particularly MRI. Angiography, previously used routinely in all cases, is no longer the first-choice modality because it is no longer necessary to subject patients, particularly children, to its attendant risks and discomfort, unless absolutely needed to plan or guide interventions. As discussed in Chapter 115, this is commonly the case with embolotherapy and sclerotherapy, and good examples of the use of various imaging techniques are presented in that chapter. It is hoped that these changes in the evaluation of these complex vascular disorders and anomalies will become even more widely recognized.

■ REFERENCES

1. Szilagyi DE, Smith RF, Elliott JP, et al: Congenital arteriovenous anomalies of the limbs. Arch Surg 111:423, 1976.
2. Rutherford RB: Congenital vascular malformations of the extremities. In Moore WS (ed): Vascular Surgery: A Comprehensive Review, 5th ed. Philadelphia, WB Saunders, 1998.
3. Strandness DE Jr, Sumner DS: Arteriovenous fistula. In: Hemodynamics for Surgeons. New York, Grune & Stratton, 1975, p 621.
4. Sumner DS: Hemodynamics and pathophysiology of arteriovenous fistulae. In Rutherford RB (ed): Vascular Surgery, 5th ed. Philadelphia, WB Saunders, 2000.
5. Rutherford RB, Fleming PW, Mcleod FD: Vascular diagnostic methods for evaluating patients with arteriovenous fistulas. In Diethrich EB (ed): Noninvasive Cardiovascular Diagnosis: Current Concepts. Baltimore, University Park Press, 1978, pp 189-203.
6. Rutherford RB: Noninvasive testing in the diagnosis and assessment of arteriovenous fistula. In Bernstein EF (ed): Noninvasive Diagnostic Techniques in Vascular Disease. St. Louis, CV Mosby, 1982, p 430.
7. Brener BJ, Brief DK, Alpert J, et al: The effect of vascular access procedures on digital hemodynamics. In Diethrich EB (ed): Noninvasive Cardiovascular Diagnosis: Current Concepts. Baltimore, University Park Press, 1978.
8. Barnes RW: Noninvasive assessment of arteriovenous fistula. Angiology 29:691, 1978.
9. Stella A, Pedrini LD, Curti T: Use of ultrasound technique in diagnosis and therapy of congenital arteriovenous fistulas. Vasc Surg 15:77, 1981.
10. Bingham HG, Lichti EL: The Doppler as an aid in predicting the behavior of congenital cutaneous hemangioma. Plast Reconstr Surg 47:580, 1971.
11. Pisko-Dubienski ZA, Baird RJ, Bayliss CE, et al: Identification and successful treatment of congenital microfistulas with the aid of directional Doppler. Surgery 78:564, 1975.
12. Rhodes BA, Rutherford RB, Lopez-Majano V, et al: Arteriovenous shunt measurement in extremities. J Nucl Med 13:357, 1972.
13. Rutherford RB: Clinical applications of a method of quantitating arteriovenous shunting in extremities. In Vascular Surgery, 1st ed. Philadelphia, WB Saunders, 1977, p 781.
14. Rauch RF, Silverman PM, Korobkin M, et al: Computed tomography of benign angiomatous lesions of the extremities. J Comput Assist Tomogr 8:1143, 1984.
15. Pearce WH, Rutherford RB, Whitehill TA, Davis K: Nuclear magnetic resonance imaging: Its diagnostic value in patients with congenital vascular malformations of the limbs. J Vasc Surg 8:64, 1988.
16. Mills CM, Brant-Zawadzki M, Crooks LE: Nuclear magnetic resonance: Principles of blood flow imaging. AJR Am J Roentgenol 142:165, 1984.

Arteriovenous Fistulas of the Aorta and Its Major Branches

111

M. ASHRAF MANSOUR, MD, FACS

WILLIAM H. BAKER, MD, FACS

The diagnosis and management of arteriovenous fistulas (AVFs) of the aorta and its major branches present an unparalleled challenge in patient care. Because of their central location, blood flow through these fistulae may be massive; the associated complications are usually dramatic, resulting in severe refractory congestive heart failure, massive venous hypertension, or extensive hemorrhage during an ill-fated surgical repair. The average vascular surgeon does not have an extensive experience with this disorder owing to its relative rarity. It behooves the surgeon to become well acquainted with the problem to avoid complications and to ensure optimal patient care.

■ ETIOLOGY

AVFs of the aorta and its major branches may be congenital or acquired. Congenital AVFs are rare and considered only briefly here; they are discussed further in Chapters 114 and 115. Any disease that spontaneously weakens the wall of the aorta or one of its major branches might logically lead to the formation of an AVF. Rare causes are erosion of false aneurysms secondary to sepsis and specific aortitis. There has been one report of a mesenchymal tumor between the aorta and the inferior vena cava leading to an aorta–vena cava fistula, but AVFs secondary to tumors most often are reported with hypernephromas.[6,15] Rupture of an atherosclerotic aneurysm is a relatively common cause of acquired fistulas.

Trauma is the major cause of acquired AVFs. Low-velocity trauma from a knife or small-caliber missile leads to fistula formation, whereas higher velocity wounds made by large-caliber missiles tend to disrupt the major vessels, more likely leading to immediate exsanguination.

The surgeon unwittingly may be another source of trauma. If, during lumbar disk operations, the rongeur penetrates the anterior longitudinal ligament, the immobile major vessels beneath it may be injured. The aorta and inferior vena cava are injured opposite the L4-5 disk space, whereas the iliac vessels are injured opposite the L5-S1 space.[21] Lumbar arteries and veins can be injured at any level. The advent of microdiskectomy seems to have decreased the incidence of this complication. Closure of the mesentery following gastrectomy and small bowel resections has damaged adjacent arteries and veins and has led to arterioportal venous fistulas. Mass ligations of major arteries and veins, such as the renal and splenic pedicle, have produced fistulas. Finally, needle biopsy of the kidney has led to renal AVFs.

■ DIAGNOSIS

The diagnosis of a major AVF is not usually difficult for an alert physician, but may escape a casual examiner. The patient often complains of a noise or a thrill over the fistula. There may be a pulsating mass caused by a false aneurysm. If there is a large flow of blood through the fistula, congestive heart failure may be evident. There may be symptoms related to the "stealing" of blood from a variety of end organs, producing renal ischemia and hypertension, visceral ischemia and abdominal angina, cerebrovascular insufficiency, and intermittent claudication.

The classic signs of increased pulse pressure, a bruit over the fistula, pulsating veins, venous hypertension and edema, and diminished distal pulses may or may not be present. In addition, renal function may be impaired, either because of reduced arterial flow through the kidney or because of venous hypertension leading to lower glomerular filtration rates. Hematuria, microscopic or gross, is a common finding with aorta-to-left renal vein fistulas.[25] Hematuria is not commonly present with aortocaval fistulas, however, unless venous engorgement of the bladder occurs.[7,31]

Many of these AVF have an associated false aneurysm or are secondary to aneurysm rupture. These aneurysms notoriously are partially filled with thrombus. The thrombus may cover the fistula partially, completely, or intermittently, and symptoms may be intermittently present or totally absent.[1] The surgeon may be unaware of this until the clot is removed in the operating room, and the surgical field is flooded with venous blood.

The noninvasive tests described in Chapter 110 apply primarily to peripherally located AVF and so are not much help here, with the exception of color-flow duplex scanning, using "deep Doppler" probes and techniques popularized for diagnosing renal and mesenteric arterial occlusive disease. With color-flow duplex scanning, the presence and location of the fistula can be confirmed (Fig. 111-1). Doppler interrogation of the inferior vena cava shows the characteristic high-flow signals and turbulence typically associated with a fistula. Groin venous flow is pulsatile.

The precise site of any AVF is best identified by arteriography, although computed tomography (CT)[30,34,36] and ultrasonography[24] have been helpful in detecting this condition (Fig. 111-2). Spiral CT scans and CT angiography with thin cuts are most helpful in evaluating patients with aortic abdominal aneurysms (AAAs). With currently available software, accurate three-dimensional reconstructions can be done, providing the surgeon with detailed

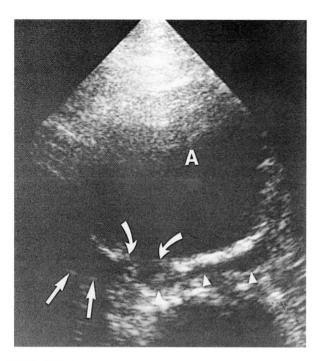

FIGURE 111-1 Duplex ultrasonography shows an abdominal aortic aneurysm (A), with a fistulous communication in the posterior wall *(curved arrows)* to a retroaortic left renal vein *(arrowheads)* and a normal vena cava *(straight arrows)*. (From Mansour MA, Russ PD, Subber SW, Pearce WH: Aorto-left renal vein fistula: Diagnosis by duplex sonography. AJR Am J Roentgenol 152:1107, 1989.)

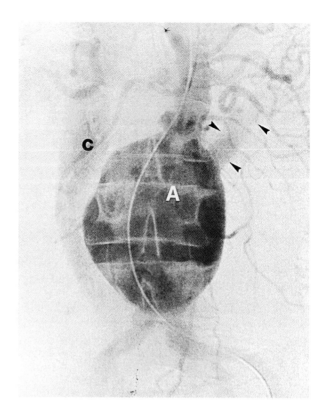

FIGURE 111-2 Angiogram shows a large abdominal aortic aneurysm (A) with early filling of the inferior vena cava (C) and the retroaortic left renal vein *(arrowheads)*. (From Mansour MA, Russ PD, Subber SW, Pearce WH: Aorto-left renal vein fistula: Diagnosis by duplex sonography. AJR Am J Roentgenol 152:1107, 1989.)

information. This modality has been used to identify aortacaval fistulas preoperatively.[28,30] Several case reports have described the use of magnetic resonance angiography for the same purpose.[13,32,39,41] In elective cases, comprehensive preoperative testing can be initiated. In unstable cases, expeditious CT angiography is probably the modality of choice.

Early and frequent films must be taken because of the increased velocity of flow through the fistula. In a patient who is bleeding actively from either trauma or ruptured aneurysm, there is not enough time to obtain arteriograms; the diagnosis of necessity must be made in the operating room. In elective cases, arteriography not only informs the surgeon of the exact arterial site (suprarenal or infrarenal aorta), but also yields information concerning venous drainage (left renal vein or inferior vena cava) (Fig. 111-3).

■ PRINCIPLES OF THERAPY

Preoperative recognition of an AVF of the aorta or its major branches is paramount. It is necessary that the surgeon spend the extra time needed to examine the patient completely, with the following questions kept in mind: Is there a "to-and-fro" bruit over the aneurysm? Does the patient with penetrating abdominal trauma have distended leg veins? If the diagnosis is delayed until the patient is going into congestive heart failure from overtransfusion or until the thrill of the fistula is first felt through an inadequate or misplaced incision, the patient ultimately suffers.

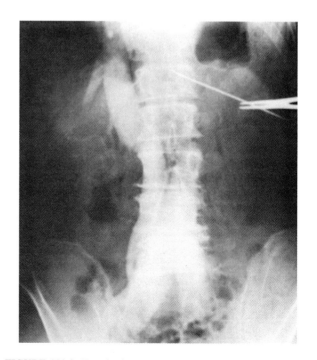

FIGURE 111-3 Translumbar aortogram reveals that this abdominal aortic aneurysm has eroded into the distal inferior vena cava. (From Baker WH, Sharzer LA, Ehrenhaft JL: Aortocaval fistula as a complication of abdominal aortic aneurysms. Surgery 72:933, 1972.)

Chapter 110 reviews the basic hemodynamics in patients with AVFs. Patients with acute fistulas may have associated blood loss and may be hypovolemic despite the presence of pulsating veins. Individuals with chronic fistulas are usually hypervolemic. In general, they do not need volume-for-volume blood replacement; the surgeon should beware of overtransfusion lest overloading occur when the fistula is closed.

The central venous pressure is abnormally elevated in a patient with a central AVF, so this measurement cannot be used to guide fluid administration. A pulmonary artery (Swan-Ganz) catheter facilitates fluid management, however, and allows the surgical team to measure the pulmonary wedge pressure and cardiac output and to assess the function of the left ventricle. The cardiac output may be elevated owing to the hyperdynamic circulation resulting from the fistula. The oxygen saturation of mixed venous blood is elevated secondary to direct infusion of arterial blood into the vena cava.[19] Functional renal impairment may be present as a result of renal venous hypertension; however, renal function returns to normal after successful repair.[4]

Transesophageal echocardiography also should be helpful in assessment of cardiac performance. In many centers, intraoperative transesophageal echocardiography is used to monitor cardiac function during major cardiovascular operations. In the case of aortocaval fistula repair, a noticeable change in cardiac filling and ventricular contraction is observed.

Although these principles are well known to the well-trained surgical team, when hypotension and hemorrhage occur during the hurried repair of these fistulas, fluid administration is difficult and critical. Whenever surgery is to be undertaken, enough blood must be available in case of hemorrhagic catastrophes. Acute fistulas are easily entered. Chronic fistulas have thinned, large arteries and bulging veins and are encased in a fibrotic or inflammatory mass. Their dissection may be extremely difficult and bloody. Autotransfusion is an ideal way to replace large amounts of blood lost by hemorrhage in a clean surgical field and has been used successfully in patients with aorta–vena cava fistulas.[9] Total circulatory arrest also has been used successfully in patients with large central AVFs.[16]

The goals of surgical therapy for a major AVF are to close the fistula, restoring normal hemodynamics, and to re-establish or maintain vascular continuity. There is little place in modern surgery for quadruple ligation of a major fistula involving the aorta or its major branches.

Before the patient is brought to the operating room, some care must be taken in planning the incision. It is always best to prepare an extensive area so that an adequate incision can be made to control major bleeding. If the wound is at the base of the neck, the thorax is always prepared so that a thoracotomy or sternotomy can be performed for control of the major vessels as they come off the aortic arch. For treating high abdominal fistulas, the thorax is prepared so that the descending thoracic aorta can be controlled if major bleeding is encountered. It is imperative that the surgeon obtain proximal and distal control of the artery involved. If arterial control is obtained at some distance from the fistula, the uncontrolled branches should also be individually controlled.

Occlusion of the aorta from the level of the aortic arch to the level of the renal arteries may cause significant hypertension. A young, vigorous heart usually can tolerate elevated blood pressure, but the increased afterload may cause cardiac failure with diminished cardiac output and hypoperfusion. In this situation, the pressure and peripheral resistance should be pharmacologically controlled until the afterload caused by the occluding clamp is removed. At the time of clamp removal, the administration of antihypertensive drugs must be carefully stopped lest profound hypotension ensue.

Ideally, proximal and distal venous control should be obtained, but often this is difficult to accomplish. The veins are distended from the increased pressure and the increased volume of blood. Blood under arterial pressure gushes forth from every small venous tributary that ordinarily retracts and bleeds only a few drops. If venous control is obtained, it is facilitated by intermittent clamping of the proximal and distal artery. This maneuver diminishes the flow through the fistula, reduces the venous hypertension, and makes dissection easier. Fogarty and Foley balloon catheters can be passed proximally and distally in the vein as an alternative to digital occlusion until the fistulous communication is repaired.[7,18]

When venous control is obtained, the surgeon must have careful communication with the anesthesiologist. Control of the inferior vena cava may seriously diminish the venous return to the heart, and this may cause dire cardiac effects in an already hypovolemic patient. In many cases, the patient can tolerate this hemodynamic insult for only a few seconds, and allowing intermittent flow through the vena cava may be necessary to maintain acceptable hemodynamics.[27,29]

More often, the vein is not encircled, but proximal and distal arterial control is obtained, and the artery is opened. The fistula can be controlled by a finger or thumb placed over the communication. Compression with sponge sticks caudad and cephalad to the fistula diminishes blood flow through the vein (Fig. 111-4; see Fig. 111-2). This maneuver ordinarily takes only a few seconds and disturbs the patient's venous return only temporarily. If the surgeon is careful in sewing under his or her finger, blood loss can be kept at a minimum. Repair of the fistula should be performed from within the aneurysm sac. Polytetrafluoroethylene (Teflon) pledgets may be helpful; rarely, a synthetic patch of polyester (Dacron) or polytetrafluoroethylene is used to close a large defect and avoid narrowing of the vein.[7]

After the vein is repaired, the preferred method for restoring arterial continuity is with a graft. Ordinarily a Dacron graft is used to bridge the deficit. If the surgical field is contaminated by concomitant injury to the adjacent viscera or by a wounding missile, however, the management becomes much more complicated. These patients should be managed in the same way as patients with arterial infections. That is, the area of sepsis should be débrided, the artery should be closed proximally and distally, and arterial continuity should be restored extra-anatomically. After the abdomen is closed, a subcutaneous bypass can be performed in a clean surgical field to maintain viability of the extremities.

An alternative approach is to place a prosthetic graft into the potentially contaminated field. The operative area is completely débrided and irrigated with saline or antibiotic

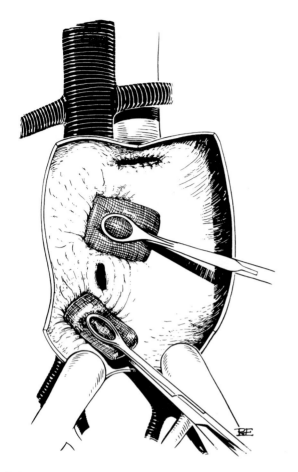

FIGURE 111-4 Sponge stick control of the inferior vena cava, as seen through the open aortic aneurysm. (From Baker WH, Sharzer LA, Ehrenhaft JL: Aortocaval fistula as a complication of abdominal aortic aneurysms. Surgery 72:933, 1972.)

solution. If antibiotic grafts are available, they should be used. After the prosthetic graft is sutured into place, it is isolated from the contaminated peritoneal cavity with an omental pedicle. Patients should be given ample doses of antibiotics, and they must be followed continuously for many months to ensure that graft infection, false aneurysm formation, and exsanguination do not result. Homografts and autogenous superficial femoral veins have been used in contaminated fields with reported success (see Chapter 59).

Endovascular repair of AVF and aneurysms is being performed successfully with commercially available endoluminal grafts (see Chapters 52 and 101). Several more recent reports have shown that successful management of aortocaval and ilioiliac fistulae is possible with minimal complications and blood loss.[2,10,14,17,22,33] Umscheid and Stelter[40] successfully treated a patient with a ruptured AAA into the inferior cava with a stent graft. In the treatment of aortovenous fistulas, complete exclusion of the fistulous connection must be accomplished to ensure proper repair, and the location of some fistulas may not leave enough of a "target zone" on either side to allow this. In deteriorating cases, even incomplete occlusion might allow a more deliberate surgical repair later, however. Careful follow-up of endograft repair is imperative because endoleaks can occur postoperatively in 10% to 20%.[5] In one case, a type II endoleak caused the aortocaval fistula to be re-established.[14] Ilioiliac fistulas also can be readily repaired easily with stent-grafts.[17,21,23] The long-term performance of these grafts is presently unknown. One patient was able to have a successful twin pregnancy after an iliac stent-graft, however.[12]

■ FISTULAS AT SPECIFIC SITES

Base of the Neck

It is rare to find an AVF that involves the thoracic aorta and superior vena cava or the great vessels as they come off the thoracic arch. Thoracic aortic aneurysms tend to dissect rather than form saccular aneurysms that erode into adjacent veins. Wounds of this area are usually explored immediately, before a fistula has had a chance to develop. Direct puncture of the carotid and vertebral arteries for arteriography is an uncommon cause of fistulas nowadays.

Subclavian artery and vein fistulas present with the symptoms that are discussed in Chapters 110 and 112 and with local symptoms of a palpable mass and thrill. They may be secondary to trauma (penetrating or blunt, causing fractures of the thoracic outlet). Associated brachial plexus symptoms may be present, depending on the size of the aneurysm or the extent of the trauma.

A fistula between the carotid artery and the internal jugular vein may divert enough blood from the carotid system to create symptoms of cerebrovascular insufficiency. In addition, thrombus from an associated false aneurysm may embolize cephalad to the eye or brain. The patient usually complains of a mass in the neck, which represents the false aneurysm. In addition, a thrill or bruit is present over the fistula.

If the fistula is located low in the base of the neck, the surgeon should plan to gain proximal control by thoracotomy or median sternotomy. The left common carotid artery and the innominate artery can be controlled through a full or limited median sternotomy, but the left subclavian artery is best controlled through a left anterior thoracotomy because of its posterior position on the arch. In most patients, the artery is opened, the fistula is closed from the arterial side, and the divided artery is repaired with an end-to-end anastomosis. If too much artery is resected to allow reanastomosis without undue tension, an interposition graft of vein or prosthetic material can be used with good results.

When the carotid circulation is interrupted during repair of a fistula involving the great vessels of the neck, an indwelling shunt may be used to ensure adequate cerebral circulation. The use of these shunts is a debatable topic. Ordinarily, at the base of the neck there is enough collateral circulation so that a shunt is unnecessary most, if not all, of the time.

There is no place for nonoperative therapy in the management of acquired AVF at the base of the neck. Their natural history is that they will continue to grow, and the patient will experience either rupture of the false aneurysm or symptoms of cerebrovascular insufficiency. The risk of repair is related to cerebral complications and blood loss. Because these risks can be kept to a minimum, surgical repair is the treatment of choice. A few case reports have described endovascular techniques to treat carotid injuries.

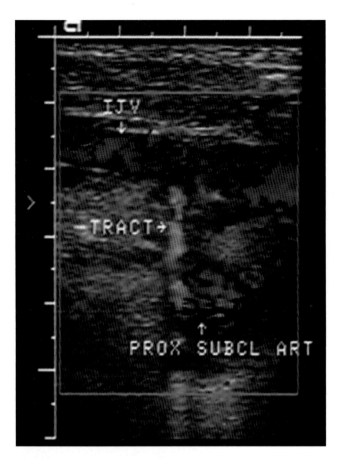

FIGURE 112-2 Duplex ultrasound image in cross section of fistulous connection between the proximal subclavian artery and the jugular vein.

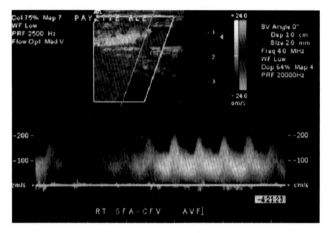

FIGURE 112-3 Characteristic Doppler waveforms of an iatrogenic arteriovenous fistula between the proximal superficial femoral artery and common femoral vein.

FIGURE 112-4 Completed repair of an iatrogenic arteriovenous fistula between the proximal subclavian artery and jugular vein, using an interposition graft of superficial femoral vein. The choice of conduit was influenced by the presence of infection (osteomyelitis of the clavicle) in the operative field.

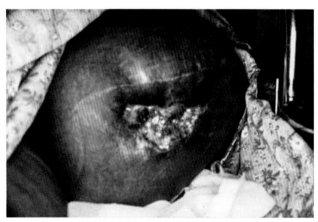

FIGURE 114-1 Nonhealing, ulcerated above-knee amputation stump in a patient with a pelvic and upper thigh arteriovenous malformation. Hip disarticulation was performed after transcatheter embolization of the nidus.

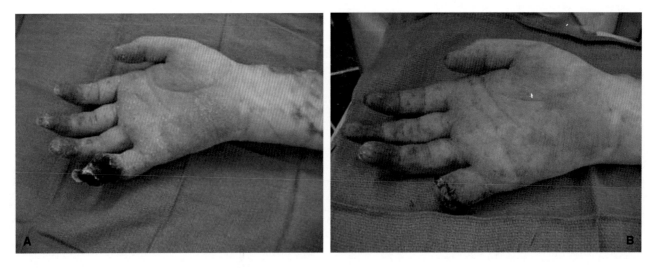

FIGURE 114-4 A, Gangrenous distal fifth digit after embolization of distal digit arteriovenous malformation. **B,** Subsequent distal digit amputation.

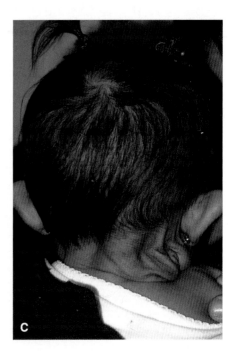

FIGURE 115-9B. Infant girl with right posterior neck mass consistent with lymphatic malformation. Radiograph taken after injection of opacified doxycycline.

Aorta and Vena Cava

Fistulas of the aorta and vena cava are most commonly due to rupture of AAAs into the vena cava. There have been more than 250 cases of aortocaval fistulas reported in the literature. The incidence is slightly higher in association with ruptured aortic aneurysms. In a series of six patients with aortocaval fistulas from the University of Iowa, classic symptoms (abdominal bruit, widened pulse pressure, venous hypertension, lower limb edema, arterial insufficiency, and congestive heart failure) were present in three, and a proper preoperative diagnosis was made in one.[1] Proximal and distal control of the aortic aneurysm was obtained in the usual manner. Venous control was not attempted, but the aneurysm was opened and the fistula controlled with compression, as mentioned earlier. The fistula was closed, and the aneurysm was replaced with a graft.

The development of aortocaval fistula is accompanied by significant pathophysiologic and biochemical changes that have been described in detail.[37] The decrease in peripheral vascular resistance is responsible for all the systemic effects observed in patients presenting with aortocaval fistulas. As a result of the diminished peripheral resistance, the mean arterial pressure decreases, and the central venous pressure increases. The cardiac output increases as a result of increased venous return, and there is commensurate enlargement of the atria and ventricles. A cascade of biochemical changes occurs. In the juxtarenal apparatus, the renin-angiotensin system is activated to raise the blood pressure via the direct vasoconstricting properties of angiotensin II and the indirect mechanism of salt and water retention through aldosterone secretion. More recent work suggests that there is increased expression of renin and angiotensin-converting enzyme in the cardiac ventricles in response to volume overload.[8] Atrial natriuretic peptide is secreted in response to atrial stretch. Closure of the AVF can result in profound changes, as reported by Eiseman and Hughes in a patient who lost 61 lb (41.5% of his body weight) in the first 12 days after repair of an aortocaval fistula.[11]

In a series from Boston of less urgent cases, 75% were correctly diagnosed preoperatively, and the mortality rate was reduced from 50% to 10%.[3] Another report from the Mayo Clinic identified 18 patients over a 27-year period (0.3% of all aortoiliac aneurysms performed in that institution). Although 94% of patients were symptomatic at presentation, only 17% had the classic triad of pain, pulsatile mass, and abdominal bruit.[7]

The surgeon should take special care to manipulate the aortic aneurysm as little as possible before closing the fistula. These aneurysms are notoriously filled with thrombus, and if this clot becomes dislodged, it embolizes through the fistula and returns via the inferior vena cava to the right side of the heart and the pulmonary artery (Fig. 111-5). This complication can be avoided by careful surgical technique with proximal and distal control before AAA manipulation.

Traumatic fistulas between the aorta and the inferior vena cava are less common. Direct trauma usually causes massive blood loss, and most patients do not survive to the operating room.

The formation of an AVF between the aorta and the vena cava or the iliac vein after a total diskectomy is uncommon. About 50% of these patients are not noted to have extreme blood loss during the operation, although many have un-

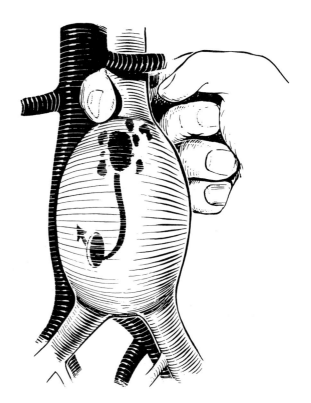

FIGURE 111-5 Dissection of the clot-containing aneurysm must be delicate lest the thrombus become dislodged, enter the inferior vena cava, and embolize to the pulmonary artery. (From Baker WH, Sharzer LA, Ehrenhaft JL: Aortocaval fistula as a complication of abdominal aortic aneurysms. Surgery 72:933, 1972.)

explained hypotension during the diskectomy. The blood loss is into the retroperitoneum, however, and may not be obvious to the surgeon operating posteriorly through the disk space. The treatment of these fistulas is surgical because they continue to grow. They are located relatively caudad in the abdominal aorta, and exposure is usually not difficult. It is safer to close the fistula through the artery because dissection at the confluence of the iliac veins and the inferior vena cava can be extremely hazardous in the presence of arterialized venous pressure. As covered stents and endoluminal grafts become more widely available, endovascular repair may become the preferred method of treatment.[2,10,14,22,42] Because these devices are relatively new, no long-term results have yet been reported (see Chapters 52 and 101).

Aorta and Renal Vein

AAAs can rupture anteriorly into the left renal vein as it crosses in its normal position over the aorta, but they most often rupture into a retroaortic left renal vein. Preoperative abdominal CT scans commonly are obtained before urgent and elective AAA repair. It is important to identify the position and location of the left renal vein relative to the aorta and the neck of the aneurysm so as not to be surprised intraoperatively at the time of placement of the proximal clamp. In the case of aorta-to-left renal vein fistula, the preoperative CT scan obtained with intravenous contrast can show a silent left kidney. Early opacification of the left renal vein or inferior cava is an important clue.[25] The triad of abdominal pain, hematuria, and silent left kidney is present in more than 75% of patients with an aorta-to-left renal vein fistula. Abdominal color-flow scanning shows the turbulent flow of the arteriovenous communication, and in at least one case, the exact location of the fistula was clearly shown (see Fig. 111-1).[24]

There have been 23 reports of aorta-to-left renal vein fistula in the English literature; all were men and in all but three, the left renal vein was retroaortic.[19,25,38] AAAs rupturing into the left renal vein should be treated as other aorta–inferior vena cava fistulas. The vein is closed from within the artery, and a graft is used to replace the AAA. Sacrifice of the vein is possible without sequelae if the adrenal or gonadal vein is left intact to provide collateral venous circulation. Endovascular repair of aorta-to-left renal vein fistula was attempted in one case; however, open conversion was necessary.

Renal Artery and Vein

Renal AVFs are discussed in detail separately in Chapter 133. Most are secondary to mass ligation of the renal hilum during nephrectomy.[26] Traumatic fistulas are caused by knife and missile wounds. The renal biopsy needle is a cause of intrarenal arteriovenous fistulization. Hypernephromas commonly grow caudad through the renal veins. Such a tumor has been reported to grow into the renal artery, producing a major AVF.[20] The indication for repair is usually the presence of a fistula. Rarely a fistula is small and fails to enlarge. Hypertension, if present, is usually poorly controlled until the fistula is repaired or until the kidney is removed.

Portal Vein and Systemic Artery

Systemic artery–portal vein fistulas are extremely rare.[35] They may occur after surgical procedures, sepsis that erodes adjacent arteries and veins, rupture of aneurysms, and trauma. Splenic AVFs occur when splenic artery aneurysms rupture into the splenic vein. Congenital fistulas are reported to occur most commonly between the hepatic artery and the portal vein and are associated with hemangiomas and telangiectasia. These fistulas characteristically do not cause symptoms of congestive heart failure, presumably because of the buffer of the hepatic venous circulation. Portal venous hypertension is produced, however, and esophageal, gastric, or small bowel varices may lead to gastrointestinal hemorrhage, ascites, or both.

The treatment of these fistulas depends on the vessels involved. Splenic fistulas may be excised by splenectomy. Peripheral mesenteric fistulas may be simply excised, but more centrally located fistulas should be excised, the arterial flow restored to maintain bowel viability, and the portal venous flow restored to correct the portal hypertension and to avoid venous infarction of the bowel. Peripheral hepatic aneurysms and fistulas may be treated by percutaneous embolization.

■ REFERENCES

1. Baker WH, Sharzer LA, Ehrenhaft JL: Aortocaval fistula as a complication of abdominal aortic aneurysms. Surgery 72:933, 1972.
2. Biasi GM: Aortocaval fistula: A challenge for endovascular management. J Endovasc Surg 6:378, 1999.
3. Brewster DC, Cambria RP, Moncure AC, et al: Aortocaval and iliac arteriovenous fistulas: Recognition and treatment. J Vasc Surg 13:253, 1991.
4. Brunkwall J, Lanne T, Bergentz SE: Acute renal impairment due to primary aortocaval fistula is normalized after a successful operation. Eur J Endovasc Surg 17:191, 1999.
5. Burke C, Mauro MA: SIR 2003 film panel case 8: Aortocaval fistula supplied by a type-II endoleak. J Vasc Interv Radiol 14:813, 2003.
6. Crawford ES, Turrell DJ, Alexander JK: Aorto-inferior vena caval fistula of neoplastic origin. Circulation 27:414, 1963.
7. Davis PM, Gloviczki P, Cherry KJ, et al: Aorto-caval and ilio-iliac arteriovenous fistulae: Rare and challenging problems. Am J Surg 176:115, 1998.
8. Dostal DE, Baker KM: The cardiac renin-angiotensin system: Conceptual or a regulator of cardiac function? Circ Res 85:643, 1999.
9. Doty DB, Wright CB, Lamberth WC, et al: Aortocaval fistula associated with aneurysm of the abdominal aorta: Current management using autotransfusion techniques. Surgery 84:250, 1978.
10. Duxbury MS, Wells IP, Roobottom C, et al: Endovascular repair of spontaneous non-aneurysmal aortocaval fistula. Eur J Vasc Endovasc Surg 24:276, 2002.
11. Eiseman B, Hughes RH: Repair of an abdominal aortic vena caval fistula caused by rupture of an arterisclerotic aneurysm. Surgery 39:498, 1956.
12. Frego M, Kontothanassis D, Miotto D, et al: Twin pregnancy following endoluminal exclusion of an iliac arteriovenous fistula. J Endovasc Ther 9:699, 2002.
13. Gaa J, Bohm C, Richter A, et al: Aortocaval fistula complicating abdominal aortic aneurysm: Diagnosis with gadolinium-enhanced three-dimensional MR angiography. Eur Radiol 9:1438, 1999.
14. Gandini R, Ippoliti A, Pampana E, et al: Emergency endograft placement for recurrent aortocaval fistula after conventional AAA repair. J Endovasc Ther 9:208, 2002.
15. Gomes MMR, Bernatz PE: Arteriovenous fistulas: A review and ten-year experience. Mayo Clin Proc 45:81, 1970.
16. Griffin LH Jr, Fishback ME, Galloway RF, et al: Traumatic aortorenal vein fistula: Repair using total circulatory arrest. Surgery 81:480, 1977.
17. Hart JP, Wallis F, Kenny B, et al: Endovascular exclusion of iliac artery to iliac vein fistula after lumbar disk surgery. J Vasc Surg 37:1091, 2003.
18. Ingoldby CJ, Case WG, Primrose JN: Aortocaval fistulas and the use of transvenous balloon tamponade. Ann R Coll Surg Engl 72:335, 1990.
19. Jabbour N, Radulescu OV, Flogiates T, Stahl W: Hemodynamics of an aorta-left renal vein fistula: A case report and a review of the literature. Crit Care Med 21:1092, 1993.
20. Jantet GH, Foot EC, Kenyon JR: Rupture of an intrarenal arteriovenous fistula secondary to carcinoma: A case report. Br J Surg 49:404, 1962.
21. Kwon TW, Sung KB, Cho YP, et al: Large vessel injury following operation for a herniated lumbar disc. Ann Vasc Surg 17:438, 2003.
22. Lau LL, O'Reilly MJG, Johnston LC, Lee B: Endovascular stent-graft repair of primary aortocaval fistula with an abdominal aortoiliac aneurysm. J Vasc Surg 33:425, 2001.
23. Lee KH, Park JH, Chung JW, et al: Vascular complications in lumbar spinal surgery: Percutaneous endovascular treatment. Cardiovasc Interv Radiol 22:439, 1999.
24. Mansour MA, Russ PD, Subber SW, Pearce WH: Aorto-left renal vein fistula: Diagnosis by duplex sonography. AJR Am J Roentgenol 152:1107, 1989.
25. Mansour MA, Rutherford RB, Metcalf RK, Pearce WH: Spontaneous aorto-left renal vein fistula: The "abdominal pain, hematuria, silent left kidney" syndrome. Surgery 109:101, 1991.
26. Matos A, Moreira A, Mendonca M: Renal arteriovenous fistula after nephrectomy. Ann Vasc Surg 6:378, 1992.
27. Neema PK, Ramkrishnan S, Sinha PK, Rathod RC: Anesthetic implications of surgical repair of an aortocaval fistula. J Cardiothorac Vasc Anesth 17:236, 2003.
28. Quiroga S, Alvarez-Castells A, Hidalgo A, et al: Spontaneous aortocaval fistula: CT findings with pathologic correlation. Abdom Imaging 20:466, 1995.

29. Ratnalikar V, Mangat PS, Earnshaw G: A case of aortocaval fistula: Biochemical and hemodynamic changes. Anaesthesia 57:831, 2002.

30. Rosenthal D, Atkins CP, Jerrius HS, et al: Diagnosis of aortocaval fistula by computed tomography. Ann Vasc Surg 12:86, 1998.

31. Salo JA, Verkkala KA, Ala-Kulju KV, et al: Hematuria is an indication of rupture of an abdominal aortic aneurysm into the vena cava. J Vasc Surg 12:41, 1990.

32. Schott EE 3rd, Fitzgerald SW, McCarthy WJ, et al: Aortocaval fistula: diagnosis with MR angiography. AJR Am J Roentgenol 169:59, 1997.

33. Sharma ML, George KA, Gamble JA: Anaesthetic implications of endovascular repair of aortocaval fistula. Anaesthesia 55:697, 2000.

34. Sheward SE, Spencer RR, Hinton RT, et al: Computed tomography of primary aortocaval fistula. Comput Med Imaging Graph 16:121, 1992.

35. Strodel WE, Eckhauser FE, Lemmer JH, et al: Presentation and perioperative management of arterioportal fistulas. Arch Surg 127:563, 1987.

36. Subber SW, Russ PD, Whitehill TA, Krysl J: Diagnosis and localization of spontaneous aortocaval fistula by computed tomography with angiographic confirmation: Case report. Can Assoc Radiol J 49:35, 1998.

37. Sumner DS: Hemodynamics and pathophysiology of arteriovenous fistulae. In Rutherford RB (ed): Vascular Surgery, 5th ed. Philadelphia, WB Saunders, 2000, p 1400.

38. Thompson RW, Yee LF, Natuzzi ES, Stoney RJ: Aorta-left renal vein fistula syndrome caused by rupture of a juxtarenal abdominal aortic aneurysm: Novel pathologic mechanism for a unique clinical entity. J Vasc Surg 18:310, 1993.

39. Torigian DA, Carpenter JP, Roberts DA: Mycotic aortocaval fistula: Efficient evaluation by bolus-chase MR angiography. J Magn Reson Imaging 15:195, 2002.

40. Umscheid T, Stelter WJ: Endovascular treatment of an aortic aneurysm ruptured into the inferior vena cava. J Endovasc Ther 7:31, 2000.

41. Walter F, Blum A, Quirin-Cosmidis I, et al: An aortocaval fistula diagnosed with 1.5-T magnetic resonance angiography. J Cardiovasc Magn Reson 2:213, 2000.

42. Zajko AB, Little AF, Steed DL, Curtiss EI: Endovascular stent-graft repair of common iliac artery to inferior vena cava fistula. J Vasc Interv Radiol 6:803, 1995.

Chapter

Traumatic Arteriovenous Fistulas

112

JOHN G. BRAWLEY, MD
J. GREGORY MODRALL, MD

Arteriovenous fistula (AVF) formation is an uncommon clinical manifestation of arterial trauma. AVFs have been reported after penetrating, blunt, and iatrogenic trauma.[1-5] Because the clinical presentation, diagnosis, and management of AVFs often differ for iatrogenic trauma compared with other traumatic AVFs, these entities are discussed separately in this chapter. AVFs resulting from blunt or penetrating (noniatrogenic) trauma are denoted as *traumatic AVFs* to distinguish these injuries from AVFs resulting from iatrogenic trauma.

■ ETIOLOGY

Traumatic Arteriovenous Fistulas

A large series of traumatic AVFs noted that stab wounds accounted for 63% of 202 traumatic AVFs, whereas gunshot wounds and blunt trauma accounted for 26% and 1% of AVFs, respectively.[2] Shotgun wounds are a notorious source of AVFs; one report noted that 7 of 15 patients with shotgun wounds had multiple AVFs.[2] AVFs secondary to blunt trauma are usually a consequence of long bone fractures with laceration of adjacent arteries by bony fragments.[3,5]

The most common anatomic site of a traumatic AVFs is the arteries of the neck and thoracic outlet (54%).[2] AVFs in the upper (22%) and lower limbs (20%) are less common.[2]

AVFs of the vessels of the abdomen and thorax constitute only 4% of fistulas.[2] Aortocaval fistulas and AVFs involving the iliac, renal, superior mesenteric, splenic, and hepatic arteries also have been reported, but are rare.[6,7] The most common individual vessels involved in AVF are the carotid artery and jugular vein.[2]

Iatrogenic Arteriovenous Fistulas

Most iatrogenic AVFs result from attempted percutaneous femoral artery cannulation for peripheral or coronary arteriography.[8] Attempted central venous cannulation can result in inadvertent arterial injury to the subclavian, carotid, and innominate arteries with AVF formation.[9] Rarely, orthopedic operations, such as total knee arthroplasty, intramedullary nailing, or lumbar disk surgery, may injure adjacent arteries to produce an AVF.[4,6,10,11]

■ CLINICAL PRESENTATION

Traumatic Arteriovenous Fistulas

Although two thirds (65%) of patients with traumatic AVFs are diagnosed within 1 week after the inciting injury, a significant subset of patients (35%) presents weeks to years later.[2] A delayed diagnosis of AVF of 15 years has been

XVI

Section

reported, underscoring the potential for missing these injuries.[2,12-16] During the acute period, most AVFs are asymptomatic and are identified by physical examination or arteriography.[2] A large series of patients with traumatic AVF found that the most common finding during the first week after injury was a machinery-like bruit overlying the fistula in 61% of patients.[2] Less common findings included a pulsatile mass (20%), palpable thrill (11%), distal pulse deficit (8%), active hemorrhage (7%), and nerve compression (1%).[2] AVFs rarely produce symptoms of congestive heart failure, venous hypertension, or distal ischemia in the acute period.[1,2] In contrast, 20% of patients who presented with an AVF greater than 1 week after injury manifest symptoms distant from the site of injury, including superficial venous dilatation (12%), congestive heart failure (4%), and pulsatile tinnitus (4%).[2] Other findings included a machinery-like bruit or murmur in 96% of patients, pulsatile mass in 52%, and palpable thrill in 14% of patients.[2] The significant incidence of delayed recognition of AVFs underscores the need for a cogent diagnostic algorithm that recognizes the potential for an AVF in the patient with a vascular injury.

Iatrogenic Arteriovenous Fistulas

Iatrogenic AVFs usually present with signs and symptoms at the site of arterial cannulation. The most common local symptoms include the presence of a large or expanding hematoma, pulsatile mass, atypical pain, or a new bruit.[8,17,18] The development of systemic symptoms from an AVF is rare,[8,17,18] which is probably related to early identification by clinicians treating the underlying condition that prompted the inciting procedure.

■ DIAGNOSIS

Traumatic Arteriovenous Fistulas

A high index of suspicion is tantamount to the diagnosis of any arterial injury, and the diagnosis of an AVF is no exception to this tenet. The clinical presentation of AVFs varies between acute (≤1 week postinjury) and delayed (weeks to years later).[2,12,16,19,20] During the acute period, AVFs are rarely symptomatic, whereas AVFs presenting weeks and years later more commonly produce symptoms and are more apparent on physical examination. The diagnostic evaluation for AVF varies according to the time of presentation relative to the injury.

During the acute period after injury, standard algorithms for the diagnosis of arterial trauma guide the workup. Patients with classic signs of arterial injury, including pulsatile hemorrhage or hematoma, absent distal pulses, or overt distal ischemia, require immediate operative exploration.[21-23] In this clinical setting, intraoperative arteriography may aid in localizing the injury when the site of injury is not apparent, such as a blunt injury or shotgun wound. Most arterial injuries are clinically occult, however. In the case of penetrating extremity trauma, patients presenting with "soft" signs of arterial injury (history of hemorrhage or hypotension, hematoma, bruit, delayed capillary refill, fracture, or neurologic deficit) merit further

evaluation to select patients at highest risk of arterial injury for further evaluation by arteriography.

Prospective studies by Schwartz and colleagues[21] and Johansen and colleagues[23] validated a diagnostic algorithm in which patients are selected for arteriography based on the presence of a pulse deficit or an abnormal ankle-brachial index (ABI). Any pulse deficit in an injured extremity prompted arteriography in those studies.[21,23] Schwartz and colleagues[21] used a threshold ABI of 1, whereas Johansen and colleagues[23] used an ABI 0.9 or less for recommending arteriography. These algorithms recommended observation alone for patients with a normal pulse examination and an ABI of 1.0 (or 0.9) in the injured extremity,[21,23] although more recent studies have advocated hospital discharge for such patients.[24] Routine arteriography is advisable for shotgun wounds to the extremity because of the relative insensitivity of pulse examination and ABIs for the detection of arterial injuries secondary to shotgun pellets.[21,22] With the exclusion of shotgun wounds, this diagnostic algorithm showed a sensitivity of 96% for "major" arterial injuries.[21] The algorithm advocated by Schwartz and colleagues[21] showed a slightly lower sensitivity (86%) for identifying "minor" arterial injuries, defined as injuries to branch and nonessential vessels. "Minor" arterial injuries included small, branch vessel injuries, including AVFs that may mature over time to produce clinical symptoms. Despite the risk of occasionally missing a minor injury, a policy of routine arteriography of all extremity wounds is not cost-effective when arterial injuries are documented in only 6% to 9% of patients undergoing evaluation.[22] Poor patient compliance with follow-up regimens among trauma patients has been cited as an additional pitfall of such algorithms.[15]

Prospective analyses for detection of arterial injuries after blunt trauma concluded that the only predictors of an arterial injury after blunt extremity trauma are an abnormal pulse examination or ABI of 1 or less.[25] Because malalignment of long bones may adversely affect arterial flow in an extremity, re-examination is warranted after reduction of fractures. Persistent pulse deficits warrant arteriography,[25] which may be performed in the operating room if operative reduction of fractures is contemplated. In a study of 53 patients with blunt extremity trauma, this approach yielded a sensitivity of 100%.[25]

In contrast to extremity injuries, traumatic injuries to the neck, chest, and abdomen may produce arterial injuries, including AVFs, which are difficult to detect on physical examination. The clinical presentation of these injuries usually dictates the extent of diagnostic evaluation. Overt arterial injuries in these anatomic regions usually present with signs of uncontrolled hemorrhage that mandate immediate exploration.[26] In the absence of hemorrhage, arterial injuries in the neck or trunk may be clinically silent early after injury,[26] presenting years later with systemic signs or symptoms of an AVF.[2] Minimizing the risk of a missed injury requires an aggressive use of diagnostic imaging. Most authors agree that penetrating injuries to zones I through III of the neck warrant routine arteriography, unless operative exploration is warranted based on other indications.[27] Some authors have suggested that any significant arterial injury of the carotid and vertebral arteries may be detected on careful history and physical examination,[28,29] but the implications of a missed injury to these vessels have tempered enthusiasm for such an approach.[2] In the absence of an intracranial injury, blunt trauma with neurologic deficits may herald the presence of a blunt carotid injury that warrants further evaluation by arteriography. Early after injury, subtle arterial injuries in the thorax and abdomen may be difficult to detect,[26] which may lead to a delay in diagnosis of these injuries. Because arterial injuries due to penetrating trauma at the thoracic outlet have a documented propensity of developing AVFs that present with systemic symptoms months and years later,[2] the liberal use of arteriography should be encouraged in this anatomic location.[2,26]

The diagnosis of an AVF often becomes clinically apparent months or years after the inciting trauma. The trauma may be so remote as to be forgotten by the patient, so careful interrogation of the patient is essential. As noted previously, approximately 20% of patients who present with chronic AVFs are symptomatic.[2] Patients with more central AVFs may present with symptoms of congestive heart failure,[2] including dyspnea at rest or with exertion, paroxysmal nocturnal dyspnea, and peripheral edema. On examination, there may be classic signs of heart failure, such as jugular venous distention, rales on pulmonary auscultation, and S_3 gallop on cardiac auscultation. Compression of the artery feeding the AVF may elicit the Nicoladoni-Branham sign, manifested by an increase in the systolic blood pressure and a slowing of the heart rate.[30] Chronic AVFs may induce venous hypertension in the affected extremity, producing edema, varicosities, stasis dermatitis, or venous ulceration.[2,16] Rarely, patients may develop arterial insufficiency due to arteriovenous shunting and distal steal, producing symptoms of claudication, ischemic rest pain, or ischemic ulceration.[12] In the absence of symptoms, many patients with a chronic AVF present with marked physical findings suggesting an AVF, including a machinery-like bruit or murmur, pulsatile mass, or palpable thrill.[1,2] Any of these symptom complexes or examination findings, coupled with a remote history of trauma, warrants imaging to identify the AVF or other arterial injury.

Noninvasive diagnostic methods for diagnosing peripheral AVFs, as detailed in Chapter 110, have application in the diagnosis of traumatic AVF but are rarely applied in this setting. Duplex ultrasonography represents the only noninvasive diagnostic method with some utility in the diagnosis of traumatic AVFs. Most patients present with signs or symptoms suggesting an AVF associated with a wound and a history of penetrating trauma. With a suspected AVF, the diagnosis is often readily confirmed by interrogation of the wound area with duplex scanning (see Chapter 110). For chronic AVFs, in which intervention is clearly indicated, definitive imaging with arteriography should be pursued.

Imaging for Arteriovenous Fistulas

Digital subtraction arteriography remains the "gold standard" for defining traumatic arterial injuries, including AVFs. The hallmark of an AVF on arteriography is early venous filling (Fig. 112-1). Associated signs of an AVF include failure to opacify the arterial tree below the AVF despite ample venous filling, which may be particularly evident in a proximal AVF. Any evidence of early venous filling should prompt more careful imaging of the area in question,

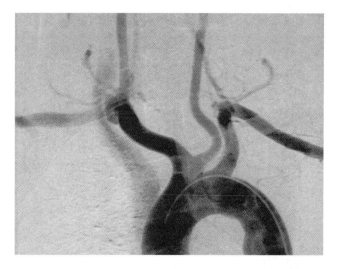

FIGURE 112-1 Arteriogram of an iatrogenic arteriovenous fistula between the proximal subclavian artery and jugular vein caused by attempted central venous line placement. Note the characteristic early filling of the jugular vein.

occasionally necessitating selective catheterization of the artery in question. Demonstration of a fistulous connection between an artery and vein is not necessary if abnormal venous filling is identified and localized to a specific arterial segment. Persistence usually is rewarded with identification of an area of concern for AVF. Occasionally the AVF itself is not visualized, but an associated pseudoaneurysm or intimal flap is identified. The latter findings are sufficient to prompt operative exploration in most cases. Reid and associates[31] reported the sensitivity of arteriography for the detection of arterial injuries in 507 patients as 100%. Because AVFs are relatively rare, the sensitivity for identifying this particular subset of arterial injuries is unknown.

Duplex scanning represents a second imaging option and may be particularly applicable to iatrogenic AVFs caused by arterial puncture or catheterization, as discussed subsequently. The characteristic findings of an AVF in the color images and spectral waveforms include a visible connection between the artery and vein (Fig. 112-2), high diastolic flow in the arterial waveform proximal to the fistula site, decreased flow in the artery distal to the fistula, and high-velocity turbulent flow (sometimes with a pulsatile component) in the vein near the fistula (Fig. 112-3).[32] Turbulent AVF flow may appear as yellow pulsatile flashes on duplex ultrasonography. Bynoe and colleagues[33] reported a study of 198 patients with 319 vascular injuries who underwent duplex ultrasonography for the diagnosis of arterial trauma of the neck or extremities. These authors reported the sensitivity of duplex ultrasonography in this setting to be 95%.[33] The two false-negative examinations in that report involved shotgun wounds, confirming the need for arteriography in that subset of injuries.[33] Other reports have confirmed a similar sensitivity of duplex ultrasonography for identifying arterial injuries in carefully selected patients.[34,35] Although the noninvasive nature of duplex ultrasonography makes it an attractive imaging option, its major limitation is that many anatomic areas, such as the thoracic outlet, are difficult to visualize with this modality.[26]

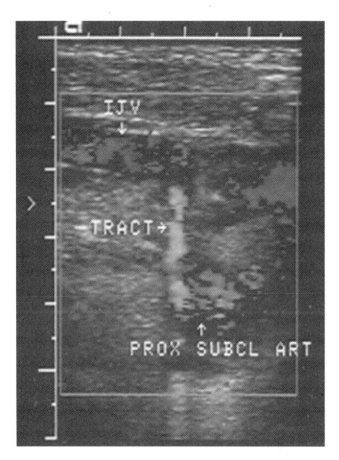

FIGURE 112-2 Duplex ultrasound image in cross section of fistulous connection between the proximal subclavian artery and the jugular vein. (See color figure in this section.)

Helical computed tomography angiography (CTA) is another imaging modality that offers potential advantages over standard catheter-based arteriography. CTA does not require arterial cannulation and can be performed by a radiology technician, making it well suited to rapid imaging of trauma patients. A comparative study of CTA with arteriography in 60 patients with penetrating neck trauma found that CTA correctly identified 9 of 10 injuries noted by arteriography, providing a sensitivity of 90% and a specificity of 100%.[36] Others have found CTA to be equally effective for identifying arterial injuries after penetrating neck trauma.[37] A sensitivity of 95.1% has been reported for the use of CTA in diagnosing "large artery" (proximal to the elbow and ankles) injuries after penetrating and blunt trauma.[38,39] The lack of large-scale comparative studies between CTA and arteriography for the entire spectrum of traumatic injuries indicates that experience with CTA is still evolving. It is likely that CTA will continue to find applications in the evaluation of arterial trauma, but digital subtraction arteriography remains the gold standard at this time.

Magnetic resonance angiography (MRA) has become a routine imaging modality in many centers for the evaluation of cerebrovascular, aortoiliac, and infrainguinal arterial occlusive disease. Its role in the evaluation of arterial trauma is less defined. Small series have reported an initial experience using MRA for evaluation of the cervical carotid and

vertebral arteries after blunt trauma and confirmed the feasibility of MRA for this application.[40,41] Case reports also have indicated that MRA is a useful diagnostic option to rule out thoracic aortic disruption after blunt trauma.[42] To date, however, MRA has not been extensively validated against the gold standard of arteriography for the evaluation of arterial trauma.

Iatrogenic Arteriovenous Fistulas

The presence of an iatrogenic AVF usually is heralded by the presence of local signs and symptoms at the site of arterial cannulation, including the presence of atypical pain, a large or expanding hematoma, pulsatile mass, or new bruit.[8,17,18] These signs and symptoms warrant further investigation. The ability of duplex ultrasonography to identify AVFs (and pseudoaneurysms) in anatomically accessible areas, such as the common femoral or superficial femoral arteries, makes it the imaging test of choice for presumed arterial injuries after arteriography or any diagnostic and therapeutic procedure using femoral artery access.[8,17,18] The characteristic findings of an AVF on duplex scanning (discussed earlier) include a visible connection between the artery and vein (see Fig. 112-2), high diastolic flow in the arterial waveform proximal to the fistula site, decreased flow in the artery distal to the fistula, and high-velocity turbulent flow (sometimes with a pulsatile component) in the vein near the fistula (see Fig. 112-3).[32] An additional benefit of using duplex ultrasonography is the potential for compressive therapy, as discussed subsequently. Rarely, arteriography will be necessary to diagnose an iatrogenic AVF in an anatomically inaccessible location.

■   TREATMENT

Traumatic Arteriovenous Fistulas

Spontaneous closure of AVFs has been described, particularly related to iatrogenic AVFs, prompting some authors to advocate conservative management as an option for AVFs.[8,17,18] This approach may be appropriate for certain iatrogenic AVFs, as discussed subsequently, but is not advisable for most AVFs caused by noniatrogenic trauma because of the undefined natural history of the traumatic AVFs and the notoriously unpredictable compliance of trauma patients. Compressive therapy is a reasonable therapeutic option that is discussed more extensively later.

Early repair remains the mainstay of treatment for traumatic AVFs. Robbs and coworkers[2] noted that the mortality of early repair (2%) was substantially less than delayed repair (12%), owing to the technical difficulties associated with the massive venous hypertension produced by the AVF. The goal of AVF repair is interruption of the fistulous connection and repair or exclusion of the injured arterial segment. Historically, AVF repair has entailed operative interruption of the fistula, but endovascular options now exist for many AVFs.

For AVFs involving small, nonessential vessels, ligation of the involved vessels may represent a reasonable surgical option. The preferred approach to small, peripheral AVFs is catheter-based embolization if the fistula is accessible by this approach.[44] Using this technique for the treatment of arterial injuries to axillary artery branches around the shoulder, one group reported success in eight of nine (88.9%) patients.[44] The only failed embolization occurred in a patient with an AVF that was embolized twice without success.[44] A recognized complication of embolization of AVFs is the potential for embolization into the venous circulation, including pulmonary embolism.[44] For most AVFs, sacrificing the feeding artery is not an option. For these AVFs, surgical repair is the mainstay of therapy.

Surgical Technique

The complexity of surgical repair of AVFs is often significantly greater than other types of arterial trauma and necessitates careful preoperative planning. Patients with congestive heart failure often need pulmonary artery catheterization for intraoperative management. Extensive blood loss may be encountered during operative repair. The use of red blood cell scavenging systems and autotransfusion may limit the dependence on banked blood products during repair of AVFs.[45] Large central AVFs may necessitate cardiopulmonary bypass to facilitate repair.[46]

The operative approach to AVF repair should permit proximal and distal arterial control remote from the fistula because the immediate vicinity of the AVF may be encased in reactive fibrosis. Because of venous hypertension, the dissection often is hindered by the presence of engorged veins that are prone to bleed with minimal provocation. Without prior vascular control, dissection near the fistula may disrupt the fistula prematurely and incite massive hemorrhage. For intra-abdominal fistulas, proximal arterial control may require supraceliac or thoracic aortic control. For AVFs involving arteries at the thoracic outlet, sternotomy or thoracotomy may be required. For large central AVFs, arterial control should be supplemented by proximal and distal venous control to minimize backbleeding from the fistula when the injured artery is opened. When venous control is not feasible, control may be obtained within the fistula using digital pressure, sponge sticks, or balloon catheters until the venous injury is repaired. Communication with the anesthesiologist is important because the reduction in venous return induced by venous occlusion may decrease cardiac output dramatically.

After the fistula is disconnected, the arterial reconstruction follows the basic principles of arterial repair. Arterial repair usually requires an interposition graft. The choice of conduit is based primarily on proper size match. Occasionally the presence of a contaminated or infected operative field may necessitate either an extra-anatomic bypass or in-situ repair with an autogenous conduit. Options for autogenous conduits include the superficial femoral vein and superficial femoral artery (Fig. 112-4), which have provided adequate patency and durability in small series.[47-49]

The venous injury at the site of the fistula is usually small and may be repaired by lateral venorrhaphy. In the event of more extensive venous injury, venous repair may be performed with a vein patch or interposition graft. With larger veins, this often leads to a tremendous size discrepancy. Prosthetic grafts and spiral grafts using greater saphenous vein and superficial femoral vein are options for venous

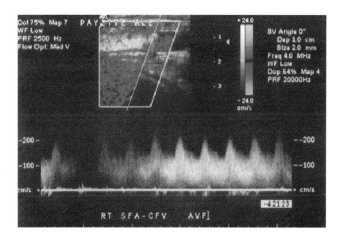

FIGURE 112-3 Characteristic Doppler waveforms of an iatrogenic arteriovenous fistula between the proximal superficial femoral artery and common femoral vein. (See color figure in this section.)

interposition grafting. Repair of major veins is important. Smaller veins, especially when collaterals exist, may be interrupted.

Iatrogenic Arteriovenous Fistulas

The management of iatrogenic AVFs is based on the presence of symptoms and the perceived natural history of the AVF. AVFs that present with significant symptoms, such as congestive heart failure, venous hypertension, or distal ischemia, warrant prompt repair.[2] Additional patient factors that warrant early AVF repair include severe local symptoms (pain, nerve compression), associated infection, enlarging hematoma or pseudoaneurysm, requirement for long-term anticoagulation, patient noncompliance or inability to follow up, and refusal of conservative therapy.[18] In the absence of significant symptoms or infection, the natural history of the AVF should be considered to determine if conservative management is a reasonable option.

The two clinical factors that most closely predict the natural history of an AVF are its anatomic location and the time interval since the inciting trauma. AVFs involving central vessels often fail to resolve spontaneously,[2] whereas only 19% of postcatheterization femoral artery AVFs failed to close with conservation management.[18] The time interval after injury also is predictive of the natural history because spontaneous closure of femoral artery AVFs required an average of 28 days, and 90% of AVFs closed by 4 months.[18] These data suggest that a trial of conservative therapy may be reasonable in carefully selected patients if the AVF is located in the upper or lower extremities. Patients who are followed expectantly should undergo surveillance imaging at regular intervals to determine whether the AVF has resolved spontaneously. In the absence of spontaneous closure, repair of the AVF should be contemplated at 4 months after injury.[18] In contrast, symptomatic or infected AVFs, AVFs in noncompliant patients, and AVFs involving vessels in the neck, chest, or abdomen are poor candidates for conservative management and should be evaluated for early repair.

A noninvasive therapeutic option for an iatrogenic AVF is ultrasound-guided compression. Although many clinicians are familiar with compressive therapy for obliteration of pseudoaneurysms, this approach also has been applied to iatrogenic AVFs of the femoral artery, with or without an associated pseudoaneurysm.[43] Successful obliteration of the AVF occurred in only 3 of 9 (33%) iatrogenic AVFs, which was substantially lower than the success rate for pseudoaneurysms in the same series.[43] An inherent prerequisite for this approach is accessibility for ultrasound-guided compression. Another option for treatment of some pseudoaneurysms is direct thrombin injection, but experience with this approach has not been described for AVFs. Although conservative therapy may be appropriate for certain iatrogenic AVFs, this approach may compromise the possibility of achieving AVF closure using other nonoperative approaches because the best chance of closure of an AVF with duplex ultrasonography–guided compression or thrombin injection is immediately after injury. Another mitigating factor in choosing a conservative approach is the potential need for long-term anticoagulation in patients with underlying cardiac conditions because anticoagulation has been associated with failure of conservative therapy.[8] These approaches to early closure are worth trying at an early stage if other considerations permit, keeping in mind these small fistulas are unlikely to have any significant hemodynamic effect early after injury and may close spontaneously. Their persistence would justify intervention at a later time.

Embolization may be an option for small AVFs, particularly if the arterial source is a nonessential branch vessel (see earlier). If alternative approaches fail, surgical repair remains a viable option. The operative approach to the repair of AVFs was outlined previously. Iatrogenic AVFs often pose less difficulty for operative repair than traumatic AVFs because of their relatively small size and anatomic accessibility in most cases.

■ RESULTS

Traumatic Arteriovenous Fistulas

The results for surgical repair of traumatic AVFs are related to their anatomic location and chronicity.[2] It is predictable that more central fistulas are associated with greater risk of mortality.[2,26] In addition, more chronic AVFs are associated with a higher risk of operative repair because of the difficulty of repair and propensity for bleeding.[2] There is also a small risk of recurrence. Recurrence is not usually a consequence of inadequate repair, but often reflects maturation of a missed AVF from the original injury. Missed AVFs are more common with shrapnel and shotgun injuries, which produce multiple AVFs.[2]

The complexity and potential morbidity associated with operative repair of some AVFs has generated interest in endovascular repair of AVFs. The most common endovascular approach to AVFs involves the use of a covered stent placed endoluminally within the artery to cover the fistulous connection between the artery and the vein. Marin and colleagues[50] reported the use of polytetrafluoroethylene grafts mounted on balloon-expandable stents to treat seven traumatic arterial injuries (one AVF and six pseudoaneurysms) of the superficial femoral artery, common iliac artery, and subclavian

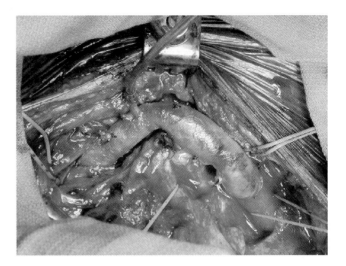

FIGURE 112-4 Completed repair of an iatrogenic arteriovenous fistula between the proximal subclavian artery and jugular vein, using an interposition graft of superficial femoral vein. The choice of conduit was influenced by the presence of infection (osteomyelitis of the clavicle) in the operative field. (See color figure in this section.)

artery.[50] Similar approaches have been reported for AVFs involving brachiocephalic, renal, and femoral arteries.[51-53] This approach does not guarantee AVF obliteration, however, because a delayed endoleak may develop via the fistula, allowing the AVF to reopen.[54] The use of detachable balloons for closure of the fistula also has been reported, but this approach does not permit repair of the injured segment of artery if there is an associated pseudoaneurysm.[55]

Iatrogenic Arteriovenous Fistulas

The anatomic accessibility and lack of chronicity of most iatrogenic AVF simplify operative repair and facilitate acceptable short-term outcomes. Long-term outcomes in this patient population are dictated by the underlying comorbidities.

■ SUMMARY

AVFs represent a complex subset of traumatic arterial injuries. AVFs that present early after injury are usually asymptomatic and are identified during standard workup for arterial trauma. Acute AVFs of extremity vessels may warrant consideration of conservative therapy in carefully selected patients, whereas AVFs of central vessels always warrant immediate repair. Chronic AVFs have a greater propensity for producing symptoms, such as congestive heart failure, venous hypertension, and distal ischemia. Because of their risk of producing systemic complications, chronic AVFs merit prompt repair. Long-standing venous hypertension in the vicinity of a chronic AVF complicates repair of chronic AVFs, but a safe repair is possible with careful operative planning. In some patients, endovascular placement of covered stents may permit a less invasive option for surgical repair.

■ REFERENCES

1. Rich NM, Hobson RW, Collins GJ: Traumatic arteriovenous fistulas and false aneurysms: A review of 558 lesions. Surgery 78:817, 1975.

2. Robbs JV, Carrim AA, Kadwa AM, Mars M: Traumatic arteriovenous fistula: Experience with 202 patients. Br J Surg 81:1296, 1994.

3. Snyder LL, Binet EF, Thompson BW: False aneurysm with arteriovenous fistula of the anterior tibial artery following fracture of the fibula. Radiology 143:405, 1982.

4. DeCasas R, Lazaro FJ, Garcia-Rayo MR, Arias J: Arteriovenous fistula after interlocking nailing of the femur: a case report. J Trauma 38:303, 1995.

5. Wolford H, Peterson SL, Ray C, Morgan SJ: Delayed arteriovenous fistula and psuedoaneurysm after an open tibial fracture successfully managed with selective angiographic embolization. J Trauma 51:781, 2001.

6. Brewster DC, Cambria RP, Moncure AC, et al: Aortocaval and iliac arteriovenous fistulas: Recognition and treatment. J Vasc Surg 13:253, 1991.

7. Saunders MS, Riberi A, Massullo EA: Delayed traumatic superior mesenteric arteriovenous fistula after a stab wound: Case report. J Trauma 32:101, 1992.

8. Kent KC, McArdle CR, Kennedy B, et al: A prospective study of the clinical outcome of femoral pseudoaneurysm and arteriovenous fistulas induced by arterial puncture. J Vasc Surg 17:131, 1993.

9. Finlay DJ, Sanchez LA, Sicard GA: Subclavian artery injury, vertebral artery dissection, and arteriovenous fistulae following attempt at central line placement. Ann Vasc Surg 16:774, 2002.

10. Smith DE, McGraw RW, Taylor DC, Masri BA: Arterial complications and total knee arthroplasty. J Am Acad Orthop Surg 9:253, 2001.

11. Salander JM, Youkey JR, Rich NM, et al: Vascular injury related to lumbar disk surgery. J Trauma 24:628, 1984.

12. Escobar GA, Escobar SC, Marquez L, et al: Vascular trauma: Late sequelae and treatment. J Cardiovasc Surg 21:35, 1980.

13. Linder F: Acquired arterio-venous fistulas: Report of 223 operated cases. Ann Chir Gynaecol 74:1, 1985.

14. Hegarty MM, Angorn IB, Gollogly J, Baker LW: Traumatic arteriovenous fistulae. Injury 7:20, 1975.

15. Perry MO: Complications of missed arterial injuries. J Vasc Surg 17:399, 1993.

16. Erdol C, Baykan M, Goyce M, et al: Congestive heart failure associated with chronic venous insufficiency and leg ulcers secondary to an arteriovenous fistula caused by a shotgun wound 15 years ago. Vasa 31:125, 2002.

17. Allen BT, Munn JS, Stevens SL, et al: Selective non-operative management of pseudoaneurysms and arteriovenous fistulae complicating femoral artery catheterization. J Cardiovasc Surg 33:440, 1992.

18. Toursarkissian B, Allen BT, Petrinec D, et al: Spontaneous closure of selected iatrogenic pseudoaneurysms and arteriovenous fistulae. J Vasc Surg 25:805, 1997.

19. de Andrade DR, Wood CA, Tedesco J: Aortocaval fistula due to remote gunshot wound. Am J Med 113:699, 2002.

20. Stigall KE, Dorsey SD: Late complications of traumatic arteriovenous fistula: Case report and overview. Am Surg 55:180, 1989.

21. Schwartz MR, Weaver FA, Bauer M, et al: Refining the indications for arteriography in penetrating extremity trauma: A prospective analysis. J Vasc Surg 17:116, 1993.

22. Weaver FA, Yellin AE, Bauer M, et al: Is arterial proximity a valid indication for arteriography in penetrating extremity trauma? A prospective analysis. Arch Surg 125:1256, 1990.

23. Johansen K, Lynch K, Paun M, Copass M: Noninvasive vascular tests reliably exclude occult arterial trauma in injured extremities. J Trauma 31:515, 1991.

24. Dennis JW, Frykberg ER, Veldenz HC, et al: Validation of nonoperative management of occult vascular injuries and accuracy of physical examination alone in penetrating extremity trauma: 5- to 10-year follow-up. J Trauma 44:242, 1998.

25. Applebaum R, Yellin AE, Weaver FA, et al: Role of routine arteriography in blunt lower-extremity trauma. Am J Surg 16:221, 1990.

26. Hyre CE, Cikrit DF, Lalka SG, et al: Aggressive management of vascular injuries of the thoracic outlet. J Vasc Surg 27:880, 1998.

27. Beitsch P, Weigelt JA, Flynn E, Easley S: Physical examination and arteriography in patients with penetrating zone II neck wounds. Arch Surg 129:577, 1994.

28. Sekharan J, Dennis JW, Veldenz HC, et al: Continued experience with physical examination alone for evaluation and management of penetrating zone 2 neck injuries: Results of 145 cases. J Vasc Surg 32:483, 2000.

29. Demetriades D, Theodorou D, Cornwell E, et al: Evaluation of penetrating injuries of the neck: Prospective study of 223 patients. World J Surg 21:41, 1997.

30. Longo T, Brusoni B, Merlo L, Marchetti GV: Haemodynamics at rest and under effort in chronic arteriovenous fistulae (AVFs). J Cardiovasc Surg 18:509, 1977.

31. Reid JDS, Redman HC, Weigelt JA, et al: Wounds of the extremities in proximity to major arteries: Value of angiography in the detection of arterial injury. Am J Radiol 151:1035, 1988.

32. Roubidoux MA, Hertzberg BS, Carroll BA, Hedgepeth CA: Color flow and image-directed Doppler ultrasound evaluation of iatrogenic arteriovenous fistulas in the groin. J Clin Ultrasound 18:463, 1990.

33. Bynoe RP, Miles WS, Bell RM, et al: Noninvasive diagnosis of vascular trauma by duplex ultrasonography. J Vasc Surg 14:346, 1991.

34. Fry WR, Dort JA, Smith RS, et al: Duplex scanning replaces arteriography and operative exploration in the diagnosis of potential cervical vascular injury. Am J Surg 168:693, 1994.

35. Ginzburg E, Montalvo B, LeBlang S, et al: The use of duplex ultrasonography in penetrating neck trauma. Arch Surg 131:691, 1996.

36. Munera F, Soto JA, Palacio D, et al: Diagnosis of arterial injuries cause by penetrating trauma to the neck: Comparison of helical CT angiography and conventional angiography. Radiology 216:356, 2000.

37. Ofer A, Nitecki SS, Braun J, et al: CT angiography of the carotid arteries in trauma to the neck. Eur J Vasc Endovasc Surg 21:401, 2001.

38. Soto JA, Munera F, Cardoso N, et al: Diagnostic performance of helical CT angiography in trauma to large arteries of the extremities. J Comput Assist Tomogr 23:188, 1999.

39. Soto JA, Munera F, Morales C, et al: Focal arterial injuries of the proximal extremities: Helical CT arteriography as the initial method of diagnosis. Radiology 218:188, 2001.

40. Weller SJ, Rossitch E, Malek AM: Detection of vertebral artery injury after cervical spine trauma using magnetic resonance angiography. J Trauma 46:660, 1999.

41. Bok AP, Peter JC: Carotid and vertebral artery occlusion after blunt cervical injury: the role of MR angiography in early diagnosis. J Trauma 40:968, 1996.

42. Mirvis SE, Shanmuganathan K: MR imaging of thoracic trauma. Magn Reson Imaging Clin N Am 8:91, 2000.

43. Schaub F, Theiss W, Heinz M, et al: New aspects in ultrasound-guided compression repair of postcatheterization femoral artery injuries. Circulation 90:1861, 1994.

44. Levey DS, Teitelbaum GP, Finck EJ, Pentecost M: Safety and efficacy of transcatheter embolization of axillary and shoulder arterial injuries. J Vasc Interv Radiol 2:99, 1991.

45. Doty CB, Wright CB, Lamberth WC, et al: Aortocaval fistula associated with aneurysm of the abdominal aorta: Current management using autotransfusion techniques. Surgery 84:250, 1978.

46. Fowl RJ, Kempczinski RF, Bailey WW, Dickhoner WH: Management of a complex, posttraumatic pelvic arteriovenous fistula with the use of cardiopulmonary bypass: Case report and review of the literature. J Vasc Surg 6:257, 1987.

47. Modrall JG, Joiner DR, Seidel SA, et al: Superficial femoral-popiteal vein (SFPV) as a conduit for brachiocephalic arterial reconstructions. Ann Vasc Surg 16:17, 2002.

48. Modrall JG, Sadjadi J, Joiner DR, et al: Comparison of superficial femoral vein and saphenous vein as conduits for mesenteric arterial bypass. J Vasc Surg 37:362, 2003.

49. Sessa CN, Morasch MD, Berguer R, et al: Carotid resection and replacement with autogenous arterial graft during operation for neck malignancy. Ann Vasc Surg 12:229, 1998.

50. Marin ML, Veith FJ, Panetta TF, et al: Transluminally placed endovascular stented graft repair for arterial trauma. J Vasc Surg 20:466, 1994.

51. Sprouse LR, Hamilton IN: The endovascular treatment of a renal arteriovenous fistula: Placement of a covered stent. J Vasc Surg 36:1066, 2002.

52. Amar AP, Teitelbaum GP, Gianotta SL, Larsen DW: Covered stent-graft repair of the brachiocephalic arteries: technical note. Neurosurgery 51:247, 2002.

53. Uflacker R, Elliot BM: Percutaneous endoluminal stent-graft repair of an old traumatic femoral arteriovenous fistula. Cardiovasc Interv Radiol 19:120, 1996.

54. Reber PU, Patel AG, Do DD, Kniemeyer HW: Sugical implications of failed endovascular therapy for postraumatic femoral arteriovenous fistula repair. J Trauma 46:352, 1999.

55. Deshmukh H, Prasad S, Patankar T: Balloon embolization of a postraumatic carotid-jugular fistula. Cardiovasc Interv Radiol 23:244, 2000.

Chapter

113

Vascular Tumors and Malformations in Childhood

JOHN P. CONNORS III, MD

JOHN B. MULLIKEN, MD

The field of vascular anomalies falls within the purview of several medical and surgical specialties and overlaps the traditional borders of the surgical subspecialties. Management of these lesions is truly interdisciplinary, but communication among specialists has been hampered by confusing and often contradictory nomenclature. Proper terminology, diagnostic techniques, and principles of management are not taught in vascular surgical training programs. This chapter is intended to be useful to surgeons whose primary focus is acquired vascular disease.

■ TERMINOLOGY

Vascular anomalies look similar, whether located in the skin, mucosa, or viscera. They are either flat or raised in various hues of blue, pink, or red. For centuries, laymen and physicians called vascular anomalies *birthmarks (naevi)*, using familiar words for food ("strawberry" and "cherry") and drink ("port-wine"). With the advent of histopathology in the middle of the 19th century, these anomalies became known as *angiomas*. Over the next 100 years, descriptive and histologic terms became confused, impeding the development of this field. Classification systems failed to discriminate between disparate vascular lesions. Words became the major obstacles to diagnosis, treatment, and basic research. The word *hemangioma* is the most egregious example. It has been applied generically to vascular lesions of differing etiology and clinical behavior.

A nosologic scheme initially proposed in 1982[1] subsequently was accepted by the International Society of Vascular Anomalies in 1996.[2] On the basis of cellular kinetics and clinical behavior, there are two major categories of vascular anomalies: *tumors* (lesions that arise by endothelial hyperplasia) and *malformations* (lesions that arise by dysmorphogenesis and exhibit normal endothelial turnover) (Table 113-1). This classification permits accurate diagnosis

and prognosis and guides therapy and basic research. This binary scheme has also improved communication among disciplines. Surgeons, pediatricians, radiologists, and other clinical specialists are now working together in vascular anomaly teams. These centers serve as a haven for these patients, who once wandered from physician to physician searching for someone who understood their condition.

■ VASCULAR TUMORS

Infantile Hemangioma

Pathogenesis

The hallmark of *infantile hemangioma* is rapid growth during the *proliferating phase,* lasting until 1 year of age, followed by slow regression in the *involuting phase* from 1 to 7 years and ending with the *involuted phase.*

Proliferating Phase   An early, rapidly growing hemangioma is composed of plump, rapidly dividing endothelial cells that form tightly packed sinusoidal channels. These endothelial cells express phenotypic markers of maturity, such as CD31, factor VIII–related antigen (von Willebrand

Table 113-1	Vascular Anomalies	
TUMORS	**MALFORMATIONS**
Infantile hemangioma	Arterial (AVM, AVF, coarctation, ectasia,
Hemangioendothelioma	aneurysm)
Angiosarcoma	Capillary
Miscellaneous	Lymphatic
	Venous
	Combined

AVF, arteriovenous fistula; AVM, arteriovenous malformation.

factor), *Ulex europaeus* lectin I, VE-cadherin (an interendothelial adhesion molecule), and E-selectin (a cell-specific leukocytic adhesion molecule).[3-7]

Involuting Phase By light microscopy, regression is characterized by dilatation of the vascular lumina, flattening of endothelial cells, and progressive deposition of perivascular fibrous tissue, which establishes a lobular architecture. Inhibition of matrix metalloproteinase, a protein that suppresses formation of new blood vessels, also occurs during the involuting phase.[8] Mitotic activity diminishes, and endothelial cells degenerate; apoptosis or programmed cell death begins, reaching an apogee at 2 years of age.

Involuted Phase After regression is complete, all that remains are a few tiny, capillary-like feeding vessels and draining veins, lined by flat, mature endothelium and surrounded by islands of loose fibrofatty tissue intermingled with dense collagen and reticular fibers.

Clinical Features

Infantile hemangioma is the most common tumor in the pediatric age group, appearing in 4% to 10% of full-term white neonates, more often in girls (ratio 3:1 to 5:1).[9] They are less common in infants of African or Asian descent. Hemangiomas typically are single tumors, but 20% grow in multiple cutaneous sites, including other organ systems, notably the liver, gastrointestinal tract, and brain. The median age of appearance for cutaneous infantile hemangioma is 2 weeks after birth. Approximately 30% to 50% of hemangiomas are nascent at birth, presenting as a barely visible pale spot, a telangiectatic/macular red stain, or a pseudoecchymotic patch. The term *congenital hemangioma* defines a tumor that is fully developed at birth and does not exhibit the usual postnatal rapid growth.[10,11]

Proliferating Phase If the tumor permeates the superficial dermis, the skin becomes raised and firm with a vivid crimson color ("strawberry hemangioma"). The tumor is a firm, tense, noncompressible mass. If the tumor spreads within the lower dermis, subcutis, or muscle, however, the overlying skin is only slightly raised, warm, and bluish in color. Draining veins are commonly seen radiating from the tumor. Spontaneous epithelial breakdown, crusting, ulceration, and necrosis complicate 5% of cutaneous hemangiomas (Fig. 113-1).[12] Ulceration can occur in any anatomic location, but it is more common with lesions located on the lips, anogenital region, and limbs. Ulcerations are painful, causing irritability, poor eating, and sleep deprivation. Few indicators herald the eventual volume or forecast accurately the onset or outcome of involution. Infantile hemangioma growth typically begins to stabilize by 10 to 12 months of age.

Involuting Phase After 1 year, hemangiomas seem to grow in proportion to the child, and the first telltale signs of clinical regression appear. The bright crimson color fades to a dull purplish hue, the skin begins to pale, typically beginning at the center of the lesion, and a patchy gray mantle forms. By palpation, the tumor feels less tense. Regression continues from 1 year until 5 to 7 years of age;

the rate is unrelated to gender or the appearance, cutaneous depth, site, or size of the original tumor.[13] Typically the last traces of color disappear by 5 to 7 years of age (see Fig. 113-1). Involution is complete in approximately 50% of children by 5 years of age and 70% of children by 7 years of age; gradual improvement continues through age 12.[14]

Involuted Phase Nearly normal skin is restored in approximately 50% of children. Stigmata of involuted infantile hemangioma include telangiectasias, crepe-like cutaneous laxity owing to destruction of elastic fibers, and yellowish discoloration or scarred patches. If the tumor was once large and protuberant, fibrofatty residuum and redundant skin often remain. Even extensive and bulky subcutaneous hemangiomas can regress completely, however, and conversely, a flat, superficial hemangioma can alter irreversibly the cutaneous texture, resulting in an atrophic patch of skin.

Differential Diagnosis

Two maxims are worth remembering in the differential diagnosis of a vascular lesion in infancy: *Not all hemangiomas look like strawberries,* and *not all strawberries are hemangiomas.*[15] Deep hemangioma, particularly a tumor located in the cervical region or trunk, can be confused with a *lymphatic malformation* (LM) or *venous malformation* (VM). Congenital hemangioma can be mistaken for a vascular malformation because both are present at birth.

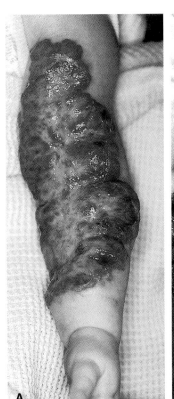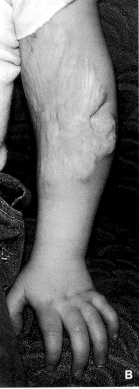

FIGURE 113-1 A, Proliferating phase: 3-month-old infant with large, ulcerated hemangioma of left forearm, treated with dressings and systemic corticosteroid. **B,** Involuting phase: age 3 years, healed with thick scar.

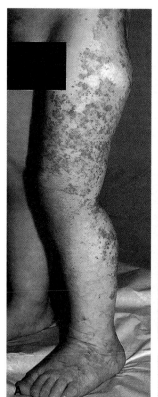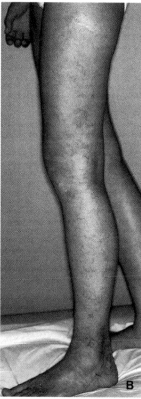

FIGURE 113-2 **A,** Infant with extensive reticular-type hemangioma of left lower limb. These are prone to ulceration (note scar on upper thigh) and can be associated with anogenital structural anomalies and congestive heart failure. Note dilated veins and puffy skin. **B,** Involuted phase: age 10 years. Note residual tiny draining veins.

Congenital hemangiomas have a characteristic red-violaceous color and coarse telangiectases, and often there is central pallor or a peripheral pale halo. Remarkably, most congenital hemangiomas regress rapidly.[10,11] A macular hemangioma can imitate a capillary malformation (CM) ("port-wine stain"), but its true nature is revealed by fine telangiectatic vessels, variegated color, and slight elevation of irregular margins. A reticular type of hemangioma can involve an entire extremity and present with a "fast flow" characteristic leading to confusion with *arteriovenous malformation* (AVM). Complications of reticular hemangioma in a limb include ulceration, high-output cardiac failure, and genitourinary anomalies (Fig. 113-2).

Pyogenic granuloma is an exophytic cutaneous vascular tumor that is often confused with infantile hemangioma. These common lesions can occur anywhere, but most typically arise in the central face in older infants and children and rarely appear before age 6 months (mean age 6.7 years). Usually there is no history of trauma or a pre-existing dermatologic condition. Pyogenic granuloma grows rapidly, is sessile at the outset, and erupts on a stalk or pedicle. These lesions generally remain small (average diameter 6.5 mm). The surface epithelium crusts and is followed by a slough of the distal tissue. The treatment is curettage, shave excision followed by laser phototherapy,[16] or full-thickness excision (definitive treatment).[17]

Other congenital tumors that can be confused with hemangioma of infancy include *kaposiform hemangioepithelioma* (KHE), *tufted angioma* (TA), *infantile myofibromatosis* (hemangiopericytoma), and *infantile fibrosarcoma*.[18-20] If there is any question about the diagnosis on clinical examination, radiologic evaluation is indicated. Biopsy is mandatory if there is any suspicion of malignancy by history, physical examination, or radiologic imaging.

Cutaneous and Visceral Hemangiomatosis

The occurrence of multiple infantile hemangiomas has been called *disseminated hemangiomatosis,* which suggests, but has not yet been proved to be, metastases from a primary tumor. In this setting, the cutaneous lesions are usually tiny (<5 mm in diameter) and domelike, although some lesions have the typical morphologic features of solitary hemangioma. An infant with several cutaneous hemangiomas (five or more) is a suspect for having visceral tumors, most commonly in the liver, followed by the brain, gastrointestinal tract, and lung. The infant should be screened by ultrasonography or magnetic resonance imaging (MRI) or both, as indicated.

Intrahepatic infantile hemangioma manifests variably, from tiny incidental asymptomatic tumors to large single or multiple tumors with or without associated cardiac sequelae (Fig. 113-3). Typically, these infants are seen at 1 to 16 weeks after birth with congestive heart failure, hepatomegaly, and anemia.[21] Hepatic hemangioma occurs more commonly in girls, similar to the frequency of cutaneous lesions. There is a subset of intrahepatic hemangioma with massive enlargement, with jaundice, and without evidence of significant shunting that can cause abdominal compartment syndrome. There also are reports of hepatic rupture in newborns with life-threatening intra-abdominal hemorrhage. Although minor thrombocytopenia can occur with hepatic hemangioma, this should not be confused with Kasabach-Merritt phenomenon (see later).

Duplex ultrasonography and MRI are needed to confirm the diagnosis of intrahepatic infantile hemangioma, but these studies can be inconclusive. Ultrasonography shows either a single lesion or multiple lesions with draining veins and dilated proximal abdominal aorta. There also may be signs of intrahepatic shunting. MRI best documents either a single tumor or multiple enhancing tumors with discrete intralesional and adjacent vessels and dilated hepatic veins. Angiographic features of intrahepatic hemangiomas are variable, ranging from discrete hypervascular tumors to diffuse tumors with macroscopic arteriovenous, arterioportal, and portosystemic shunting. Intrahepatic hemangioma and AVMs are often mistaken for one another because both are rheologically fast flow. Confusion in the terminology and diagnosis probably accounts in part for the high mortality rate (30% to 80%).[22,23] In our series of 43 children with hepatic vascular anomalies treated over 25 years, 90% were hemangiomas, and 10% were AVMs.[21]

Hepatoblastoma is also on the differential list of intrahepatic tumors in children. They can be quite vascular, but they do not show the same degree of arteriovenous shunting. Metastatic neuroblastoma also can simulate multiple hepatic hemangiomas. Imaging and clinical characteristics

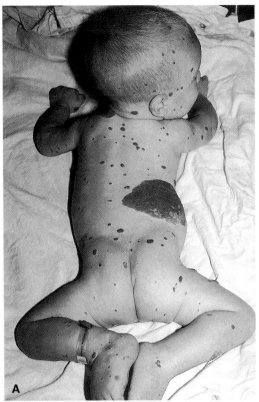
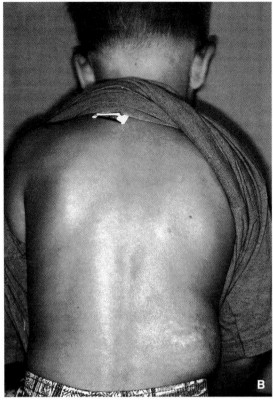

FIGURE 113-3 **A,** Infant with multiple hemangiomas. Ultrasonography and MRI revealed intrahepatic tumors. Treatment was interferon alfa-2a for 8 months. **B,** Appearance at age 6 years. Note fibrofatty residuum in right flank.

usually allow differentiation of hemangioma from intrahepatic malignancy without recourse to biopsy. Intrahepatic infantile hemangioma should not be confused with a venous anomaly of the liver in adults, referred to as "cavernous hemangioma."

Radiologic Features of Infantile Hemangioma

Ultrasonography   Ultrasonography is useful in differentiating deep hemangioma from VM. The sonographic hallmarks of proliferating-phase hemangioma are dense parenchyma and fast flow. Hemangioma shows decreased arterial resistance, increased venous velocity on duplex evaluation, and discrete soft tissue mass effect with conventional ultrasonography.[24,25] Sonography also is useful for frequent, noninvasive, cost-effective documentation of response to pharmacologic therapy, particularly for intrahepatic hemangiomas.

Magnetic Resonance Imaging   MRI is the "gold standard" for evaluation of a vascular anomaly; however, it generally requires sedation or general anesthesia if the child is younger than 6 years of age. Hemangioma appears as a parenchymatous (solid) tissue of intermediate intensity on T1-weighted, spin-echo images and moderate hyperintensity on T2-weighted, spin-echo images. Flow-voids, prominent around and within the tumor mass, are indicators of shunting between feeding arteries and dilated draining veins.[26,27] Gradient recalled echo sequences confirm the presence

of fast-flow vessels. Hemangioma in the involuting phase becomes progressively slower flow with decreasing size and number of feeding/draining vessels. Lobularity becomes more obvious, and fatty tissue can be a prominent feature. Involuted cutaneous hemangioma appears as an avascular fatty mass.

Intracranial hemangiomas are more commonly detected incidentally because of the more frequent use of MRI. These are usually located on the dura, but choroidal and intraparenchymal tumors also can occur. Hydrocephalus, Dandy-Walker malformation, and other posterior fossa cysts have been documented. Intracranial arterial anomalies can coexist with cervicofacial hemangiomas. Developmental anomalies (including agenesis, hypoplasia, and persistent embryonic vessels and aneurysmal changes) have been noted in a small subset of patients with large cervicofacial hemangioma.[28,29] Progressive, acquired occlusive changes of the cervical internal carotid artery and "moya-moya"–like findings, including occlusion of the intracranial vessels, have been associated with cerebral infarction.[30]

Treatment

Observation   Most hemangiomas of infancy are small tumors. These lesions should be allowed to undergo proliferation and involution under the watchful eye of a pediatrician because they leave normal or slightly blemished skin. An infant should be referred to a vascular anomalies specialist whenever the tumor involves vital structures (e.g., the airway, visual field or eye, or oral cavity) or grows rapidly to a large size and causes distortion. There are few indicators of prognosis, and the consultant must rely on clinical experience in managing these tumors.[30] The parents require repeated assurance about the expected outcome. Poor communication can cause parents to seek assistance elsewhere. Specialists may differ on the indications for intervention for such harmless hemangiomas.[31] Often, parents poignantly ask, "Doctor, what would you do if this were your child?"

Treatment for Ulceration or Bleeding   Ulcerated hemangioma is treated with daily cleansing, application of hydrated petrolatum, a topical antibiotic, or a hydrocolloid dressing and viscous lidocaine. Sharp débridement and wet-to-dry dressings are used if there is an eschar. Superficial ulceration usually heals within days to weeks; a deep ulceration can take longer. Flashlamp pulsed-dye laser (two applications, 4 to 6 weeks apart) is reported to aid healing and alleviate pain associated with ulcerated lesions.[32,33] Complete resection of a small ulcerated hemangioma may be the most expeditious treatment, usually indicated for a tumor located on the scalp, chest, or extremity, but rarely for a facial lesion. Punctate bleeding from a bosselated hemangioma is a rare complication and is frightening to parents. If bleeding occurs, parents should be instructed to compress the bleeding area with a clean pad, holding pressure for exactly 10 minutes by the clock. Local tamponade controls bleeding in most circumstances; occasionally a suture is needed to control a bleeding site.

Pharmacologic Therapy for Endangering Complications
Endangering and life-threatening complications have been estimated to occur in approximately 10% of infantile hemangiomas, primarily in the cervicofacial region.[34] A large hemangioma can cause a mass effect and expansion, compression, and distortion of tissue. Even a small hemangioma can obstruct a vital structure, such as the eye or subglottis. A periorbital hemangioma can block the visual axis and cause deprivation amblyopia or extend into the retrobulbar space causing ocular proptosis. Less well appreciated is the fact that even a small hemangioma in the upper eyelid or supraorbital area can insidiously deform the growing cornea, producing astigmatic amblyopia. Any infant with a periorbital hemangioma should be examined promptly by a pediatric ophthalmologist.

Subglottic hemangioma is a potentially life-threatening lesion. The initial symptoms are hoarseness progressing to biphasic stridor and manifesting at approximately 6 to 12 weeks of age. Approximately half of these infants have cutaneous cervical hemangioma, typically in the "beard distribution."[35] High-output congestive heart failure is another potentially life-threatening complication, usually in the presence of multiple intrahepatic hemangiomas, although a large cutaneous hemangioma also can shunt enough blood to cause failure. Gastrointestinal hemangiomas are rare; they can be isolated single, multifocal, or diffuse tumors, or they may carpet the bowel and adjacent mesentery. Single and multiple lesions can bleed, but these are generally controllable with pharmacologic treatment or locally invasive measures, either endoscopic or surgical.

Caution in diagnosis is necessary because vascular malformations of the gastrointestinal tract are more common than hemangioma, and these anomalies do not respond to drug treatment.

Intralesional Corticosteroid   Injection of corticosteroid into the tumor should be considered for a small, well-localized cutaneous hemangioma and typically for lesions located in the nasal tip, cheek, lip, or eyelid. Intralesional corticosteroid effectively stabilizes an ulcerated hemangioma and facilitates healing. The goal is to minimize the volume of the proliferating tumor. Triamcinolone (2 to 3 mg/kg) is injected slowly at low pressure with a 3-mL syringe and 25-gauge needle. When possible, the periphery of the lesion should be compressed (using the finger ring of an instrument) to minimize the chances of systemic embolization of colloidal particles. There are reported cases of blindness with intralesional steroid for periorbital hemangioma, presumed to be due to retrograde flow and embolic occlusion of the retinal artery. In the periorbital area, this method must be used with extreme caution.[36] Overdosage (>3 to 5 mg/kg per injection) can cause transient subcutaneous atrophy. On average, three sessions are needed at 6- to 8-week intervals. The response rate is similar to that for systemic corticosteroid therapy while avoiding its potential complications.[37]

Systemic Corticosteroid   Oral administration of corticosteroid is the first-line treatment for problematic, endangering, or life-threatening infantile hemangioma. Prednisolone is initially given at 2 to 3 mg/kg/day, in the morning. For an acute situation, such as upper airway obstruction, impaired visual field, intestinal bleeding, or high-output cardiac failure, an equivalent dose of intravenous corticosteroid can expedite shrinkage of a sensitive tumor. Signs of responsiveness occur within several days to 1 week of the initiation of the drug and include a diminished rate of growth, fading of color, and softening of the tumor. If there is a response, the dosage is tapered slowly, usually every 2 to 4 weeks, and the drug is discontinued when the child is 10 to 11 months old. Minor rebound growth can occur after stopping corticosteroid, and an additional 4 to 6 weeks of therapy may be administered, if necessary. Rebound growth also is likely to occur if the drug is tapered too rapidly or administered on alternate days. Live vaccines (e.g., polio, measles, mumps, rubella, and varicella) are withheld during corticosteroid therapy.

Using systemic corticosteroid therapy, 30% of hemangiomas show accelerated regression, 40% exhibit stabilization of growth, and 20% to 30% fail to respond.[38] Some investigators claim better results with higher dosages (5 mg/kg/day)[39]; however, there are no studies to show that mega-dose either alters tumor sensitivity or improves response. Cushingoid facies is expected and occurs in virtually all infants. Swelling usually subsides as the dose is tapered, toward the end of therapy. Based on a retrospective study, approximately 35% of infants exhibit a slowing in the rate of gain for height and 25% for weight while on corticosteroid therapy. All children return to their pretreatment curves for height and weight gain by 14 to 24 months of age. Approximately 15% of children gain weight faster while receiving corticosteroids. Using a dose of 2 to 3 mg/kg/day, there is no increased incidence of infection, documented hypertension, or bone resorption. The only major complications encountered—steroid myopathy and localized infectious—occurred in a few infants who were given a prolonged high dose (in the 5 mg/kg/day range).[40] Adrenal suppression can occur with repeated intralesional or prolonged systemic corticosteroid treatment.

Interferon alfa-2a or Interferon alfa-2b   Recombinant interferon (IFN) (interferon alfa-2a or interferon alfa-2b) should be considered the second-line drug for endangering or life-threatening hemangioma.[41-48] There is no evidence that IFN and corticosteroid are synergistic; they are not coadministered at therapeutic levels.[49] If corticosteroid fails to control the tumor, it should be tapered quickly and stopped within a few weeks after the initiation of IFN. Indications for IFN therapy include (1) failure of response to corticosteroid, (2) contraindications to prolonged systemic corticosteroid, (3) complications of corticosteroid, and (4) the rare instance of parental refusal to use corticosteroid.

The empirical dose of IFN is 2 to 3 million U/m², injected subcutaneously every day for 6 to 12 months. The response is generally less dramatic compared with corticosteroid therapy. The absolute dose of IFN must be titrated upward as the infant gains weight, particularly if there is evidence of rebound growth of the tumor. IFN therapy is successful in more than 80% of hemangiomas and is effective for tumors that fail to respond to corticosteroid.

Side effects of IFN include elevated hepatic enzymes (fivefold elevation of hepatic transaminases), transient neutropenia, and anemia.[42,50] Infants receiving IFN grow and gain weight normally. The most serious toxicity of IFN is spastic diplegia, which occurs in an estimated 5% of cases.[51] The mechanism for this serious neurologic disorder is unknown; symptoms improve and resolve after the termination of IFN. It is imperative that these infants are monitored monthly by a neurologist throughout the duration of therapy. Because of the risk of neurologic sequelae, there has been a shift toward using cytotoxic chemotherapy (vincristine) for infantile vascular tumors—hemangiomas and hemangioendotheliomas—that are unresponsive to corticosteroids.[52]

Embolic Therapy   Embolization is indicated for infantile hemangioma that causes severe congestive heart failure or does not respond rapidly to drug therapy; typically these are hepatic tumors. The effectiveness of embolization in controlling congestive heart failure depends on the ability of the interventionalist to occlude a large percentage of the shunts. Cardiac failure often recurs even after initial improvement, and it is best to continue antiangiogenic therapy after an apparently successful embolization.

Laser Therapy   Photocoagulation of infantile hemangioma has a popular appeal, but its role is debatable. Some investigators advocate prompt laser therapy of the nascent hemangioma in the belief that this prevents further growth of the tumor and potential complications. Flashlamp pulsed-dye laser penetrates only 0.75 to 1.2 mm (577 to 585 nm

wavelength) into the dermis; only the superficial portion of the hemangioma is affected, resulting in moderate lightening of the color. Lesions that are destined to remain small and flat can be treated effectively with one or two laser sessions. These superficial hemangiomas are the very tumors, however, that would be expected to regress in time, leaving nearly normal skin.[53] Most hemangiomas begin in the middle dermis or deeper. Infantile hemangiomas arise in a field, not as a tiny focus with centrifugal spread. As a result, most are beyond the reach of the laser beam, even at their earliest manifestation. There is no evidence that even repeated laser application diminishes the bulk or accelerates involution of the deep portion of a cutaneous hemangioma.[54] Finally, overzealous use of the laser can result in ulceration, partial-thickness skin loss, hypopigmentation, and consequent scarring. There is no controversy about the important role of pulsed-dye laser for telangiectasias that often persist in the involuting/involuted phases.

Another well-accepted indication for laser is the proliferative phase excision of unilateral subglottic hemangioma using the continuous-wave carbon dioxide laser.[55] Another laser strategy is intralesional photocoagulation with a bare fiber (neodymium:yttrium-aluminum-garnet) inserted through multiple needle passages into the tumor.[56] This technique carries an added risk, however, of cutaneous ulceration caused by thermal damage.[57]

Operative Therapy in Infancy   There are generally accepted indications for excision of infantile hemangioma during the proliferative phase, such as a well-localized or pedunculated lesion, particularly if there is ulceration or repeated bleeding. A problematic hemangioma in the upper eyelid that does not respond to pharmacologic therapy can be either excised or debulked. Focal or multifocal gastrointestinal hemangiomas, which bleed despite pharmacotherapy, can be excised by either a formal enterotomy or by endoscopic band ligation in selected patients.

Early Childhood   Staged or total excision of a large or protuberant involuting-phase hemangioma should be considered in the preschool period. At this age, children first become aware of their facial differences. The scar must be weighed against the child's, not the parents', emotional distress. Excision of hemangioma in early childhood is indicated if (1) it is obvious that resection is inevitable (e.g., there is postulceration scarring and expanded and inelastic skin or fibrofatty residuum), (2) the scar would be the same were excision postponed until the involuted phase, or (3) the scar is easily hidden.[58] Surgical expertise is necessary for correction of involuting hemangioma of the face, particularly tumors involving nasal tip, eyelids, lips, and ears.

Late Childhood   Often it is best to postpone the excision of hemangiomatous residuum until the involuted phase. A previously protrusive hemangioma usually leaves behind irrevocably expanded skin or fibrofatty tissue or both. Resection may be possible in one operation, but more often staged resection is needed to minimize distortion and scarring. Uncommonly, there is extensive scarring and loss of tissue so that reconstructive techniques are needed.

Kasabach-Merritt Phenomenon and Kaposiform Hemangioendothelioma

Since the case report in 1940, the term *Kasabach-Merritt syndrome* has been used for profound thrombocytopenia, petechiae, and bleeding in the presence of a "giant hemangioma."[59] This same eponym is often misapplied to localized or disseminated intravascular coagulopathy that can occur in adults with an extensive venous malformation. Platelet trapping does not occur with common infantile hemangioma. Kasabach-Merritt phenomenon is caused by a more invasive type of infantile vascular tumor, either KHE or TA.[60-62] These tumors have overlapping clinical and histologic features, suggesting they are on the same neoplastic spectrum. Usually these coagulopathic tumors are present at birth, although they can appear postnatally. In contrast to typical infantile hemangioma, KHE and TA affect both sexes equally. They are solitary and typically involve the trunk, shoulder, thigh, or retroperitoneum (Fig. 113-4). The overlying skin is deep red-purple in color, tense, and shiny or edematous. Ecchymosis appears over and around the tumor, along with generalized petechiae. Thrombocytopenia is profound (typically <10,000 mm³), fibrinogen is low, and fibrin-split products (D-dimer) are increased. The prothrombin time and activated partial thromboplastin time are variably, but minimally, elevated. An infant with Kasabach-Merritt thrombocytopenia is at risk for hemorrhage, including intracranial, pleuropulmonic, intraperitoneal, or gastrointestinal.

If there is any question about the diagnosis, MRI clearly differentiates KHE and TA from common hemangioma.[62] Histopathologic examination of KHE shows an aggressive pattern of infiltrating sheets or nodules of slender endothelial cells lining capillaries and slitlike vascular spaces filled with hemosiderin and fragments of red blood cells and coexistent dilated lymphatic spaces. Biopsy is almost never necessary, however.

TA can be congenital or acquired and is referred to as "angioblastoma of Nagakawa."[2,63] The anatomic location is similar to that of KHE, and the tumor manifests as an erythematous macule or plaque. The microscopic findings are distinctive, consisting of small tufts of capillaries (cannonballs) in the middle to lower dermis. Low-grade thrombocytopenia also has been reported with congenital multifocal hemangiopericytoma.[64,65] Until more is known about the hematologic mechanism for the platelet trapping, Kasabach-Merritt coagulopathy is best designated a *phenomenon*, not a *syndrome*, as it is likely to be pathogenically heterogeneous.[62]

Treatment

There are two caveats in managing thrombocytopenia associated with these tumors: (1) Platelet transfusion should be avoided, unless there is active bleeding or a surgical procedure is indicated, and (2) heparin should *not* be administered because it can stimulate the growth of the tumor, aggravate platelet trapping, and worsen bleeding. Although several pharmacologic therapies have been successful in controlling KHE and TA, no single drug has proved to be consistently effective. Corticosteroid is only 10% successful, IFN is about 50% effective, and vincristine is often given.[52] Mortality rates remain high (range 20% to 30%), particularly for retroperitoneal tumors. KHE and

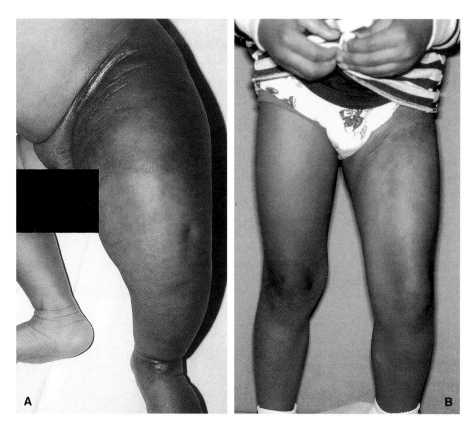

FIGURE 113-4 A, Infant with kaposiform hemangioendothelioma in left thigh. Note ecchymosis and swelling. Platelet levels less than 5000/mm³. Treated with interferon alfa-2a for 10 months. **B,** Appearance at age 4 years. Skin is slightly indurated. MRI showed residual subcutaneous tumor.

TA often continue to proliferate into early childhood and evidence some regression in mid-childhood. Even if drug therapy is successful in correcting the coagulopathy and shrinking the tumor, long-term follow-up evaluation often reveals persistent, although usually asymptomatic, tumor beneath the skin.[66]

■ VASCULAR MALFORMATIONS

Vascular malformations can be localized or diffuse errors of embryonic development. The classification of these anomalies is based on the type of abnormal vascular channels and flow characteristics. The abnormal channels resemble capillaries, lymphatics, veins, arteries, or any combination thereof (Table 113-2). The term *vasculogenesis* refers to the processes by which mesodermally derived endothelial precursors align to form primitive blood vessels. The differences between arteries and veins are imprinted early in embryogenesis. Arterial endothelial cells express the transmembrane ligand *ephrin-B2*, whereas veins express the receptor *Eph-B4*.[67] The term *angiogenesis* refers to the formation of new vessels from pre-existing vasculature. The various types of vascular malformations can be envisioned as faulty development at some stage of either vasculogenesis or angiogenesis.

Most vascular malformations are sporadic, but some are inheritable in a classic mendelian autosomal dominant pattern. The causative genes for several familial vascular disorders have been identified, opening the door to understanding of the basic mechanisms involved in their pathogenesis. Molecular studies suggest that vascular anomalies are caused by dysfunctional signaling processes that regulate proliferation, apoptosis, differentiation, maturation, and adhesion of vascular cells.[68]

Capillary Malformation

Pathogenesis

CMs are composed of dilated capillary-to-venular–sized vessels in the superficial dermis. Immunohistochemical studies show a paucity of normal surrounding nerve fibers.[69] CMs can be confused with the most common vascular birthmark, called *naevus flammeus neonatorum*. This fading pink stain occurs in 50% of white newborns and is popularly known as "angel's kiss" (when on the forehead, eyelids, nose, and upper lip) and "stork bite" (on the nuchal area).

Table 113-2	Combined Vascular Malformations	
SLOW-FLOW	**FAST-FLOW**
Klippel-Trenaunay (CVM, CLVM)	Parkes Weber (CAVM, CAVF, CLAVM)
Proteus (CM, LM, CVM, CLVM)	Bannayan-Riley-Ruvalcaba syndrome (AVM)
Maffucci (VM, enchondroma)	

AVM, arteriovenous malformation; CAVF, capillary arteriovenous fistula; CAVM, capillary arteriovenous malformation; CLAVM, capillary-lymphatic-arterivenous malformation; CLVM, capillary-lymphatic venous malformation; CM, capillary malformation; CVM, capillary-venous malformation; LM, lymphatic malformation; VM, venous malformation.

Clinical Features

The 19th century expression for CM is "port-wine stain." CMs can be localized or extensive and are rarely multiple; they can occur anywhere on the body. Facial CMs are the most obvious. In adults, typically these stains become a deeper hue and are prone to nodular fibrovascular overgrowth. Cutaneous CM often is associated with overgrowth of the soft tissue and underlying skeleton. In the face, there can be enlargement of the affected lip and gingiva, and usually the maxilla or the mandible. In the limb, CM is associated with hypertrophy in length and girth (Fig. 113-5).

CM can be a harbinger of an underlying structural abnormality. Midline occipital CMs can overlie an encephalocele or ectopic meninges. CMs over the cervical or lumbosacral spine can be a clue to occult spinal dysraphism.[29] *Sturge-Weber syndrome* is composed of a facial CM with ipsilateral ocular and leptomeningeal vascular anomalies. The capillary stain is in the ophthalmic (V1) division or extends into the maxillary (V2) division; sometimes all three trigeminal dermatomes are involved.[38] CMs also can be scattered, patchy lesions on the trunk and extremities in this disorder. Extensive leptomeningeal capillary and venous anomalies can cause seizures, contralateral hemiplegia, and variably delayed motor and cognitive skills. Early diagnosis by MRI shows pial vascular enhancement. Resection of the involved brain may be necessary if seizures cannot be controlled by medication. Funduscopic examination and tonometry are essential in the evaluation for Sturge-Weber syndrome because these children with increased choroidal vascularity are at risk for retinal detachment, glaucoma, and blindness.

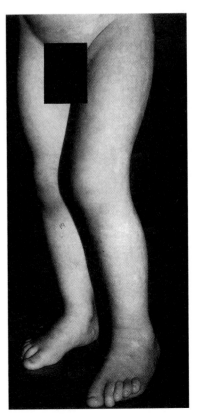

FIGURE 113-5 Circumferential capillary malformation of left lower limb with axial overgrowth (19 cm versus 20.5 cm).

Glaucoma must be detected early before irreversible ocular damage occurs. Ophthalmologic examination should be performed biannually until age 2 years and yearly thereafter for any child at risk. Diffuse, geographic capillary stains on a limb also are features of both Parkes Weber and Klippel-Trenaunay syndromes, although they differ in appearance (see section on Combined Vascular Malformations).

Treatment

CM is treated by tunable flashlamp pulsed-dye laser. There are reports that the results are better if treatment begins in infancy[70] or that age makes no difference.[71] In general, significant lightening occurs in approximately 70% of patients. The outcome is better for lesions on the face than on the trunk and the limbs. Often laser therapy must be repeated. Soft tissue and skeletal hypertrophy requires surgical procedures. Small fibrovascular nodules are easily excised. In rare instances, an area of hypertrophied facial stain is resected and resurfaced with a skin graft. Contour resection for labial ptosis and macrocheilia is effective. Orthognathic correction may be indicated for occlusal canting as the result of hemimaxillary vertical overgrowth or for mandibular prognathism.

Lymphatic Malformation

Pathogenesis

There was a controversy throughout the 20th century as to whether the lymphatics sprout from pre-existing veins (centrifugal theory) or arise separately and later connect to veins (centripetal theory). More recent investigations support Sabin's model of centrifugal-lymphatic vascular development.[72,73] Studies of normal lymphangiogenesis are beginning to reveal clues as to the causes of lymphatic malformations. Histologically, LMs are composed of vascular spaces filled with eosinophilic, protein-rich fluid. The walls are of variable thickness and are composed of abnormally formed smooth and skeletal muscular elements, along with lymphocytic aggregates. Vascular endothelial growth factor (VEGF) receptor 3 (VEGFR3) is specifically expressed in lymphatic endothelium. VEGF3 knock-out mice die at embryonic day 9 with major venous anomalies, just before lymphatics sprout.[74] Abnormally distended lymphatic channels occur in transgenic mice that overexpress the VEGFR3 ligand VEGF-C,[75] whereas lymphatic sprouting from veins fails to occur in mice genetically deficient in the ligand (VEGF-C).[76]

Midline cystic lymphatic anomalies, detected by prenatal ultrasonography, are usually lethal. They are associated with aneuploidy, the most common being 45XO (Turner syndrome)[77,79]; trisomy 13, 18, and 21; Roberts syndrome; and Noonan syndrome.[80] Mutations have been found for many of the known forms of lymphedema (a generalized or regional type of lymphatic anomaly): type I (Milroy syndrome), type II (Meige lymphedema), lymphedema-distichiasis syndrome, lymphedema and ptosis, and yellow nail syndrome (Table 113-3).[81-85] The gene mutation has not been identified for Meige syndrome, but is known for hypotrichosis (see Table 113-3).

Clinical Features

LMs are usually noted at birth; the remainder usually manifest before age 2 years. LMs can appear suddenly in childhood and occasionally in adolescence or adulthood. Prenatal ultrasonography can detect macrocystic LM in the late first trimester.[90] LMs occur in various forms, from a localized spongelike lesion to diffuse involvement of a particular region or in multiple organ systems. LMs are characterized as microcystic ("lymphangioma"), macrocystic ("cystic hygroma"), or combined. LMs occur in recognized locations with a variable combination of microcystic and macrocystic elements. The most common locations for LM are the axilla/chest, cervicofacial region, mediastinum, retroperitoneum, buttock, and anogenital areas (Fig. 113-6). Often the overlying skin is normal or a bluish hue. Dermal involvement manifests as puckering or deep cutaneous dimpling. LM in the subcutis or submucosa presents as tiny vesicles, and often there is intravesicular bleeding. LMs in the forehead and orbit cause proptosis, strabismus, amblyopia, and recurrent intralesional bleeding. Facial LM is the most common basis for macrocheilia, macroglossia, macrotia, and macromala (overgrown check or malar bone). Cervicofacial LM is associated with the overgrowth of the mandibular body, which typically results in open bite and underbite.[91] LMs in the floor of the mouth and tongue are characterized by mucosal vesicles, intermittent swelling, bleeding, and often oropharyngeal obstruction. Cervical LMs involving the supraglottic upper airway often necessitate early tracheostomy. Mediastinal LM is an extension of

Table 113-3	Lymphedema Genetic Mutations				
TYPE	**INHERITANCE**	**GENE MAP**	**GENE**	**MUTATION**	
Milroy syndrome (hereditary lymphedema type I)	Autosomal dominant	5q34-q35	*VEGFR3[84,86] (FLT4)*	Gly857Arg Arg1041Pro His1035Arg Leu1044Pro Pro1114Leu[87]	
Meige syndrome (lymphedema praecox, hereditary lymphedema type II)	Autosomal dominant	16q24.3	*FOXC2[85] (MPH1)*	? 1-BP INS, 589C	
Lymphedema-distichiasis syndrome (yellow-nail syndrome, lymphedema and ptosis)	Autosomal dominant	16q24.3	*FOXC2[88] (MPH1)*	297C→G	
Noonan syndrome	Autosomal dominant	12q24.1	*PTPN11[89]*	SHP2→SH2	
Hypertrichosis-lymphedema-telangiectasia	Autosomal dominant	—	*SOX18*	ALA104PRO	

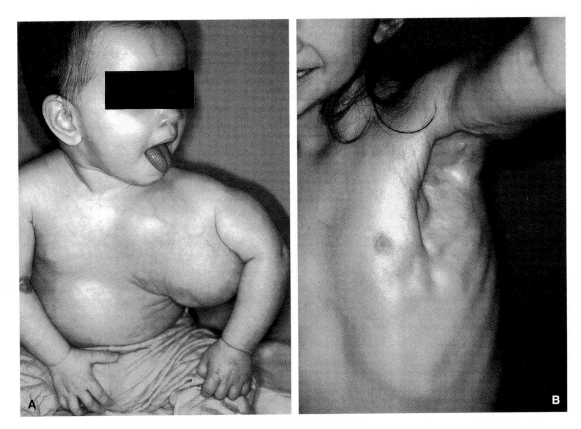

FIGURE 113-6   A, Macrocystic lymphatic malformation in the left chest. MRI showed involvement of brachial plexus and mediastinum. **B,** Appearance 8 years after subtotal resection.

cervical or axillary LM. Lymphatic anomalies of the thoracic duct or cisterna chyli present as recurrent pleural and pericardial chylous effusions or chylous ascites. Anomalous lymphatics in the gastrointestinal tract can cause hypoalbuminemia as the result of a chronic protein-losing enteropathy; often there is LM in other organ systems (*generalized lymphangiomatosis*). LMs in an extremity cause diffuse or localized swelling or gigantism with soft tissue and skeletal overgrowth. There is a rare type of spongiform LM in the lower extremity with a large proximal cystic lymphatic reservoir in the groin. Pelvic LMs may cause bladder outlet obstruction, constipation, and recurrent infection. Progressive osteolysis, caused by diffuse soft tissue and skeletal LMs, is called *Gorham-Stout syndrome,* also known as "disappearing bone disease" and "phantom bone disease."[92]

Imaging

MRI is the best imaging study; ultrasonography confirms the presence of macrocystic LM. Because of a high water content, LM is hyperintense on T2-weighted sequences. Macrocystic lesions often have fluid levels because of contained protein or blood. Contrast administration usually gives rim enhancement around large cysts or within septae, although the contents of the microcysts also can enhance, especially in patients with intralesional bleeding. Large or anomalous venous channels are part of LMs.[93] Teratoma and infantile fibrosarcoma can appear cystic on radiologic imaging and be confused with cystic LMs.[94] Magnetic reso-

nance lymphangiography shows the dilated or interrupted lymphatic channels, especially in the limbs.[95] Although conventional contrast lymphangiography is rarely performed, it is still used to determine the precise location of lymphatic or chylous leakage in a patient with a thoracic lymphatic anomaly.

Treatment

The two major complications of LMs are intralesional bleeding and infection. Bleeding is either spontaneous or secondary to trauma. The LM suddenly enlarges, turns bluish in color, and is exquisitely painful. Analgesic medication, rest, and time are all that are needed. If there is a large collection of intralesional blood, prophylactic antibiotics may be indicated. LM often swells coincident with a viral or bacterial infection anywhere in the body. This is a harmless event, presumably the result of changes in flow or stimulation of the lymphocytic component in the walls of the anomalous channels. Bacterial cellulitis in LM is more dangerous. Infection in a cervicofacial LM can cause obstruction of the upper airway and difficulty in swallowing. The incidence of cellulitis in cervicofacial LMs is reported to be 17%.[91,96] There is rapid onset of localized swelling, tenseness, erythema, pain, and systemic signs of toxicity. Parents become alert to these signs and symptoms and learn to administer antibiotics immediately. Often these infections cannot be controlled by oral antibiotics, and the child must be hospitalized for prolonged intravenous therapy. Blood cultures rarely isolate the responsible organism. The choice of antibiotic is based on the presumption that oral pathogens are the source of infection in the head and neck, and enteric organisms are responsible for infection in the trunk, perineum, or lower extremities. Aspiration of fluid from a macrocystic LM gives only temporary decompression and rarely provides a positive culture.

The two strategies for interventional treatment of lymphatic anomalies are sclerotherapy and resection. LMs must be macrocystic to permit injection of sclerosant. The commonly used sclerosing agents are pure ethanol, sodium tetradecyl sulfate, and doxycycline. OK-432 (a killed strain of group A *Streptococcus pyogenes*) is also used for macrocystic LMs.[97-100] Resection offers the only potential cure of LMs. Often staged excision is necessary, and total removal is rarely possible. For each resection, the surgeon should (1) concentrate on a defined anatomic region, (2) try to limit the blood loss to less than the patient's blood volume, (3) perform as thorough a dissection as possible (given anatomic restrictions and preserving vital structures), and (4) be prepared to operate for as long as necessary. Neural and vascular structures must be dissected painstakingly; otherwise, disappointing results are expected. Prolonged suction drainage is necessary after resection. Immediate postoperative complications include protracted serous drainage, hematoma, and cellulitis. Often a cystic area must be tapped repeatedly after the operation to remove serous fluid and to allow the cutaneous flaps to adhere.

The recurrence rate is 40% after incomplete excision and 17% after macroscopically complete excision.[101] The surgeon should not be surprised if postoperative imaging shows that the resection was less than estimated in the operating room. Regrowth and re-expansion from microcystic channels are responsible for postoperative recurrence. Regeneration also produces the typical warty vesicles in the surgical scar.

LM in particular areas demands specialized surgical expertise. Cutaneous LM (*lymphangioma circumscriptum*) must be resected widely, and the defect often requires closure with a split-thickness skin graft. Management of orbital LM necessitates craniofacial surgical techniques. Cervical and axillary lesions require experience in the dissection of the brachial plexus. Cervicofacial LM with associated maxillary and mandibular overgrowth necessitates orthognathic correction.[91] Mediastinal lymphatic anomalies must be teased from the cardiovascular structures and the vagus, phrenic, and recurrent laryngeal nerves. Intrapelvic and extrapelvic LMs require a thorough knowledge of the anatomy of the ischiorectal fossa and sciatic nerve.

Venous Malformation

Pathogenesis

Histologically, VM is composed of thin-walled, dilated, spongelike abnormal channels. Smooth muscle–actin staining reveals muscle in clumps instead of the normal spiral architecture. Presumably, this mural muscular abnormality is responsible for the tendency for expansion of anomalous channels. Microscopy often reveals evidence of clot formation, various stages of fibrovascular ingrowth, and pathognomonic phleboliths.

Although most VMs are sporadic, there are families wherein these anomalies are inherited in an autosomal dominant pattern. Multiple familial cutaneous-mucosal VMs are caused by a single amino acid alteration in the gene for the endothelial receptor *TIE*-2.[102] Another VM subtype called glomuvenous malformation (GVM) (*multiple glomangiomas*) is often familial and caused by the gene *glomulin* found on chromosome 1p.[103] Multiple cerebral "cavernous" VMs also are inheritable, caused by mutations in *KRIT*-1.[104]

Clinical Features

VM is the most common congenital vascular anomaly. Venous anomalies are present at birth, although they are not always clinically evident. These slow-flow anomalies manifest in many forms. Typically, they are bluish, soft, and compressible. They can be localized or extensive within an anatomic region. They are tiny or large enough to distort structures in the face, limbs, or trunk (Fig. 113-7). Although most VMs occur in the skin and subcutaneous tissues, they also can involve underlying muscle (see Fig. 113-7),[105] abdominal viscera, and central nervous system. Unfortunately, the archaic term *cavernous hemangioma* is still used, rather than VM, by specialists in these organ systems. Phleboliths can appear in patients by 2 years of age. Patients often complain of pain and stiffness in the area of the VM, especially on awakening in the morning. VM grows proportionately to the child, expands slowly, and often enlarges during puberty. VM is easily compressible and enlarges when the affected area is dependent or after a Valsalva maneuver in the case of a head and neck lesion.

Most VMs are solitary, but multiple cutaneous or visceral lesions also occur. Whenever there are multiple VMs, familial transmission should be considered. GVM is the most common inheritable form, presenting as tender, blue nodular cutaneous lesions. GVM lesions may be scattered, or there may be large clusters of nodules or protuberant lesions; the extremities are typically involved (Fig. 113-8). In contrast to the common VM, GVMs are tender on palpation, painless on morning awakening, and do not respond to elastic compression garments.[103]

Anatomic Differentiation

Head and Neck   VMs in the head and neck region are usually unilateral. Often a mass effect causes facial asymmetry and progressive distortion of the features. Intraorbital VM induces expansion of the orbital cavity. Oral VM can involve the tongue, palate, and oropharynx and typically cause dental malalignment leading to an open-bite deformity. Pharyngeal, laryngeal, and deep cervical-oropharyngeal VM can expand to compress and deviate the upper airway, often causing obstructive sleep apnea.

Extremities   VM in a limb can involve skin only or can extend into muscles, joints, and bone. Often there is growth disturbance manifested as leg-length discrepancy. Chronic pain and disuse can result in slight undergrowth of an affected limb. Intraosseous VM in an extremity can cause structural weakening of the shaft and pathologic fracture. VM in the synovial lining of the knee causes episodic joint pain because of repeated bloody effusion. Hemarthrosis is particularly troublesome in children with VM-associated

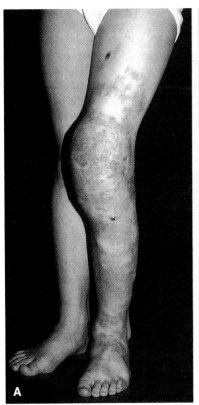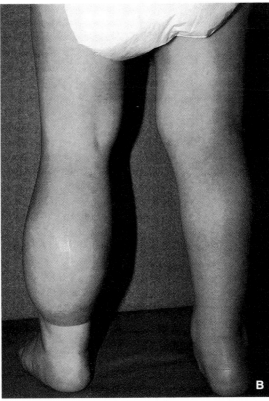

FIGURE 113-7 **A,** Extensive venous malformation of lower extremity with bleeding into knee joint. **B,** Venous malformation of gastrocnemius; scar indicates prior attempted resection.

intravascular coagulopathy. Hemosiderin-arthropathy leads to degenerative arthritis.

Bowel   VM in the gastrointestinal tract commonly manifests as chronic bleeding and anemia.[106] These anomalies are best visualized directly by endoscopy, but also can be detected by MRI, technetium-99m red blood cell radionuclide scanning, or arteriography. Lesions can be located anywhere from the esophagus to the anus. They can be polypoid, sessile, or nodular and can involve any or all layers of the bowel wall. They range in size from minute mucosal abnormalities to massive VMs that replace large sections of the gut. The most common distribution is VM encompassing the entire left colon and rectum and surrounding pelvic and retroperitoneal structures. Lesions that involve the foregut can be associated with central mesenteric and portal venous anomalies.

Blue Rubber Bleb Nevus Syndrome   *Blue rubber bleb nevus syndrome* is an uncommon, sporadic disorder composed of cutaneous and gastrointestinal VMs. Autosomal-dominant inheritance has been reported.[107] This is the most common vascular anomaly responsible for chronic gastrointestinal bleeding. The cutaneous lesions are soft, blue, and sometimes nodular, occurring anywhere on the body with a predilection for the trunk, palms, and soles of the feet (see Fig. 113-8).[108] The lesions enlarge and become more numerous with age. The gastrointestinal lesions arise throughout the gut, most commonly in the small bowel. In addition to bleeding, these lesions can cause intussusception and volvulus.[109] VMs also frequently are found in the liver, gallbladder, mesentery, and retroperitoneum.

Imaging

MRI is the most informative radiologic technique to diagnose and characterize VMs. They are hyperintense lesions on T2-weighted images and differ from LMs by contrast enhancement of the contents of the vascular spaces. Phleboliths or thrombi are seen as signal voids on all MRI sequences, but are emphasized on gradient or "susceptibility" sequences. Flow-sensitive sequences show no evidence of increased arterial flow. Magnetic resonance venography is useful for the evaluation of an extensive VM in an extremity. Direct phlebography may be needed for more detailed assessment.

Coagulopathy   A coagulative profile should be performed on any patient with an extensive VM (or VM combined with LM), particularly if there is a history of easy bruising or extensive bleeding during an operation. Stagnation within the VM causes a localized intravascular coagulopathy. The prothrombin time can be prolonged; activated partial thromboplastin time is usually normal; fibrinogen level is low (150 to 200 mg/dL); and there is increased insoluble cross-linked fibrin by D-dimer assay. The platelet count is minimally diminished, in the 30,000/mm^3 to 50,000/mm^3 range (not as low as in Kasabach-Merritt phenomenon).

Treatment

Sclerotherapy   Treatment of VM is indicated for appearance, pain, or functional problems. Elastic supporting stockings are indispensable for a patient with an extremity VM. Low-dose aspirin (81 mg every day or every other day) minimizes painful phlebothromboses. The therapeutic

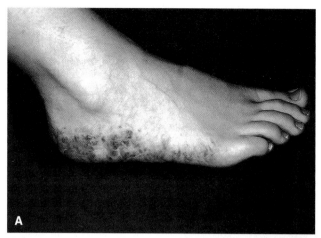

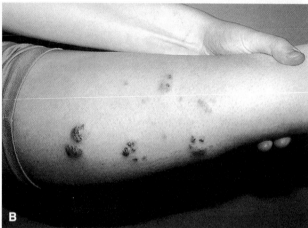

FIGURE 113-8 **A,** Glomuvenous malformation of foot. **B,** Blue rubber bleb nevus syndrome: typical dome-shaped venous lesions in calf. The patient was monitored for gastrointestinal bleeding.

mainstays are sclerotherapy and resection, in that order. A small cutaneous or oromucosal VM can be injected with a mild sclerosant, such as 1% sodium tetradecyl sulfate, just as for varicose veins. For large cutaneous or intramuscular VMs, more formal sclerotherapy involving general anesthesia and real-time fluoroscopic monitoring is necessary. Sclerotherapy is potentially dangerous and requires the skills of an experienced interventional radiologist. Absolute ethanol (100%) is commonly used in the United States. The use of tourniquets, compression, and other maneuvers minimizes the passage of sclerosing agent into the systemic circulation. Local complications include blistering, full-thickness cutaneous necrosis, or damage to local nerves. Systemic complications include hemolysis and a potential for renal toxicity and cardiac arrest. Multiple sclerotherapeutic sessions are often necessary, usually at bimonthly intervals. Venous anomalies have a perverse propensity for recanalization and recurrence.

Resection   Excision of a VM is usually successful if the lesion is small and well localized. In some locations (e.g., the hand), staged, subtotal removal can be accomplished without preoperative sclerotherapy. In general, it is preferable to shrink the VM with multiple sclerosant injections

before resection.[110] Preoperative control of intravascular coagulopathy with heparin should be considered before resecting a large VM. Tourniquet causes a temporary coagulopathy, which can cause a postoperative hematoma in the operative site.

Large or full-thickness focal gastrointestinal VMs usually require excision to control chronic bleeding. In contrast to cutaneous VMs, complete resection is necessary in the gastrointestinal tract; tamponade for massive hemorrhage is not possible in the peritoneal cavity. Multifocal gut lesions (as in blue rubber bleb nevus syndrome) are best treated by multiple excisions. Bowel resection should be conservative and done only for segments in which there is a high density of VMs. Multiple enterotomies are necessary so that bowel length is preserved. Multiple lesions often can be removed through a single enterotomy by the intussusception of segments.[106] Endoscopic therapy is a useful adjunct in the esophagus, stomach, duodenum, and colorectum.

Diffuse VMs of the colorectum and surrounding pelvic structures are left alone, unless bleeding necessitates multiple blood transfusions. Some VMs of the rectum can be controlled by sclerotherapy.[111] For severe bleeding from VM of the large bowel, the definitive surgical alternatives are to divert the fecal stream by colostomy or, preferably, a colectomy with endorectal mucosectomy and coloanal endorectal pull-through.[112] This procedure entails a risk of pulmonary embolism because of the manipulation of the abnormal pelvic vessels.

Arteriovenous Malformation

Pathogenesis

Hereditary hemorrhagic telangiectasia (HHT) (Rendu-Osler-Weber disease) is the first vascular anomaly to be understood at a molecular level. The disorder begins in the capillary beds as tiny capillary-venous shunts appear in the skin and mucous membranes, lungs, liver, and brain in the 20s or 30s.[109] Patients with HHT have mucocutaneous telangiectasias, cerebral arteriovenous shunts, pulmonary AVMs, and hepatic vascular anomalies. Two causative genes on chromosome 9q have been identified, both involving transforming growth factor-β binding and signaling resulting in the loss of function. HHT-1 is caused by a mutation in *endoglin,* a gene that encodes an endothelial glycoprotein, and HHT-2 is caused by a mutation in *activin* receptor-like kinase. *Capillary malformation–arteriovenous malformation* is another autosomal dominant condition that is caused by mutations in *RASA*-1.[114] Some affected family members have Parkes Weber syndrome (see later).

Clinical Features

Intracranial AVMs are far more common than extracranial lesions. Cutaneous AVM is usually noted at birth but given little attention because of its innocent appearance. In infancy, the blush of an AVM can be mistaken for hemangioma, or more often the birthmark is mislabeled as "port-wine stain." Fast flow typically becomes evident in childhood. Often hormonal changes during puberty or minor trauma triggers expansion. The cutaneous stain deepens in

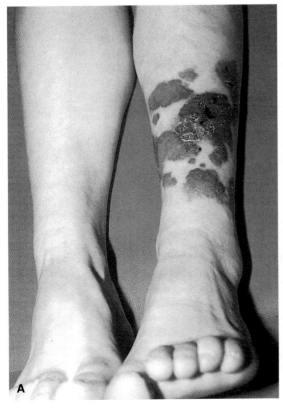
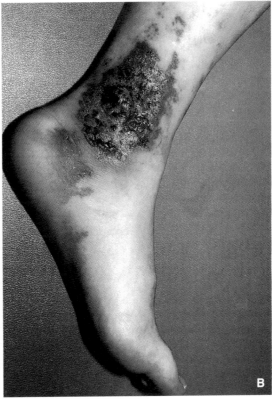

FIGURE 113-9 A, Arteriovenous malformation in lower limb with painful, chronic ulceration and bleeding: Schobinger stage III. **B,** Arteriovenous malformation in lower limb with pseudo-Kaposi plaques: Schobinger stage II.

color, or a mass appears beneath the stain. Characteristic physical findings include local hyperthermia, a palpable thrill, bruit, and prominent veins. Later cutaneous manifestations include ischemic changes, indolent ulceration, intractable pain, and intermittent bleeding. In the lower limb, curious dry, brown-violaceous plaques may appear, histologically termed *pseudo–Kaposi sarcoma* (Fig. 113-9). An extensive AVM, either in a limb or the pelvis, can cause major shunting, leading to increased cardiac output and congestive failure. The clinical staging system introduced by Schobinger is useful for documentation of AVM in any anatomic site (Table 113-4).[115]

Table 113-4	Schobinger Staging for Arteriovenous Malformations
I (quiescence)	Pink bluish stain, warmth, and arteriovascular shunting
II (expansion)	Same as stage I, plus enlargement, pulsations, thrill, bruit, and tortuous/tense veins
III (destruction)	Same as stage II, plus dystrophic skin changes, ulceration, bleeding, persistent pain, or tissue necrosis
IV (decompensation)	Same as stage III, plus cardiac failure

From Kohout MP, Hansen M, Pribaz JJ, Mulliken JB: Arteriovenous malformations of the head and neck: Natural history and management. Plast Reconstr Surg 102:643-654, 1998.

Imaging

The clinical diagnosis is confirmed by ultrasonography and color-flow Doppler examination. MRI and magnetic resonance angiography best document the extent of the AVM. Superselective angiography usually is not performed until therapeutic intervention is indicated.

Treatment

Prompt embolization may be necessary in the uncommon occurrence of postnatal congestive heart failure caused by shunting through an AVM. Otherwise treatment rarely is indicated during infancy or early childhood for a stage I AVM. When the diagnostic evaluation is complete, the child should be screened annually. In some instances and after careful deliberation, resection is indicated for a well-localized stage I AVM. In general, intervention is delayed until there are intractable symptoms or endangering signs (e.g., recalcitrant ulceration, ischemic pain, bleeding [Schobinger stage III], increased cardiac output [Schobinger stage IV]).

Ligation or proximal embolization of feeding vessels should never be performed. This causes the rapid recruitment of flow from nearby arteries to supply the *nidus* (the epicenter of the AVM composed of arterial feeders, microarteriovenous and macroarteriovenous fistulae, and enlarged veins). Proximal arterial blockage denies access for future embolization.

Angiography precedes interventional therapy or extirpation. Superselective arterial or retrograde venous embolization can be palliative (e.g., to control pain, bleeding, or congestive heart failure). This is indicated for patients in whom resection is not possible or would result in mutilation or disfigurement. Embolization of feeding arteries with particles or coils provides only transient improvement. Sclerotherapy also may be used, particularly if conventional inflow access is difficult because of a tortuous arterial tree or impossible if feeding vessels have been ligated. Sclerotherapy involves direct puncture of the nidus, in conjunction with local arterial and venous occlusion. There is a high risk of severe neurologic and soft tissue damage with this combined technique; it should be reserved for carefully selected patients and performed by an appropriately trained and experienced interventional radiologist. Most specialists in the field of vascular anomalies prefer not to use the term "cure" in referring to the management of AVM; "control" is a more realistic assessment.[116]

The usual strategy is arterial embolization for temporary occlusion of the nidus, followed 24 to 72 hours later by resection. The surgeon's goal is complete resection if possible. Preoperative embolization or sclerotherapy minimizes intraoperative bleeding but does not diminish the limits of resection. The nidus and usually the involved skin must be excised widely. If the overlying skin is normal, it can be saved. The surgeon must decide on the extent of resection. To answer this question before the operation, the surgeon should review the earliest angiograms (before embolization and other interventions) and the MRI studies. Intraoperative frozen sectioning of the resection margins can be helpful. The most accurate way to determine the completeness of resection is observing the pattern of bleeding from the wound edges. The defect should be primarily closed with either local tissue or distant tissue free transfer using microsurgical technique. If there is any question about the adequacy of resection, depending on the location of the defect, temporary coverage with a split-thickness skin graft is often the best strategy.

In the head and neck region, the success of combined embolization and surgical resection is better with stage I or II well-localized AVM.[115] These patients must be followed for years by clinical examination, ultrasonography, or MRI for signs of occult recurrence, which can occur despite a long asymptomatic period. Many AVMs are not well localized, and they often permeate throughout the deep craniofacial structures or the soft and skeletal tissues of an extremity.[116] In these instances, embolization is usually palliative, and major resection is rarely indicated. These patients await a pharmacologic alternative to ablative therapy.

■ COMBINED VASCULAR MALFORMATIONS

Combined (complex) vascular malformations are associated with overgrowth of adjacent soft tissue and skeleton. Many of these disorders are named after the physician who is credited with the most memorable description of the condition. These eponymous terms are often misused, they are misleading, and they tell us nothing of the pathogenesis. Until basic mechanisms are understood, a simple nosologic scheme, using anatomic terms to describe the anomalous channel architecture, best serves the care of the patient. Similar to pure or single channel–type vascular malforma-

tions, the combined anomalies can be categorized broadly as either slow flow or fast flow.

Slow-Flow Anomalies

Klippel-Trenaunay syndrome is the well-worn eponym for *capillary-lymphatic-venous malformation* (CLVM), which is associated with soft tissue/skeletal hypertrophy, usually of one or more limbs and sometimes the trunk.[115] CLVM is thought to be sporadic; it is obvious at birth. The CMs are multiple, sometimes contiguous, and disposed in a characteristic geographic pattern over the lateral side of the extremity, buttock, or thorax. The CM component is macular in a newborn, but in time, stained areas become studded with hemolymphatic vesicles. Anomalous lateral veins become increasingly prominent because of incompetent valves and deep venous anomalies. Lymphatic hypoplasia is present in more than 50% of patients, and there can be lymphedema or isolated lymphatic macrocysts.[117] Limb hypertrophy also is obvious at birth; axial overgrowth can be progressive in childhood (Fig. 113-10). In a few patients with classic CLVM, the involved limb is short or hypotrophic. Sometimes the opposite foot or hand is enlarged by fatty tissue, often in the absence of a capillary stain.

Pelvic involvement commonly is seen with CLVM in the lower extremity, although usually asymptomatic. Hematuria, hematochezia, constipation, bladder outlet obstruction, and recurrent infection with gut flora can occur, however. Upper extremity or truncal CLVM can extend into the posterior mediastinum and retropleural space, but rarely evokes symptoms. Thrombophlebitis occurs in 20% to 45% of patients with CLVM, and pulmonary embolism has been reported in 4% to 25% of patients.[117-120]

Imaging

Plain radiographs or scanograms are used to assess leg-length discrepancy. Further radiologic imaging is unnecessary in a child, unless symptoms are present. MRI and magnetic resonance venography document the specific type and distribution of vascular anomalies and delineate the anatomy of the venous drainage. The MRI findings are variable because of the wide range of severity. The LM component is typically macrocystic and located in the pelvis and upper thighs, whereas it tends to be microcystic in the abdominal wall, buttocks, and distal limbs, or it can be predominantly subcutaneous or diffusely infiltrate muscle. Increased fat often is seen in the areas of soft tissue overgrowth.

The VM component also is phenotypically variable in CLVM. In severe cases, the deep venous system is hypoplastic or interrupted, and venous drainage is mainly through dilated, often valveless, anomalous superficial veins. The pathognomonic "marginal vein of Servelle" is frequently identified in the subcutaneous fat of the lateral calf and thigh and communicates with the deep venous system at various levels. Contrast venography is useful in selected patients to depict the route of drainage and the feasibility of resecting or sclerosing varicosities. The procedure is difficult, however, because it usually requires multiple injections with various compressive maneuvers. Catheter angiography may reveal discrete microarteriovenous fistulae in the thighs, but these are not clinically important.

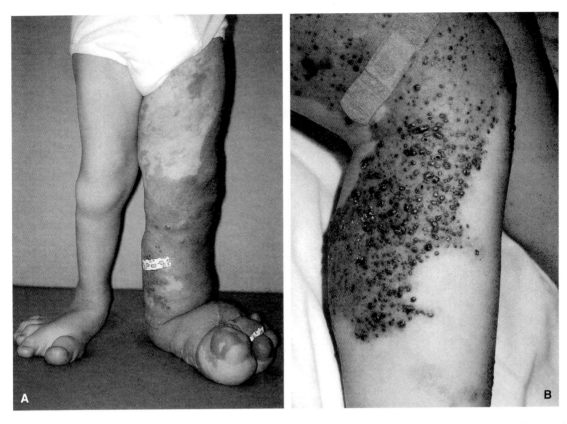

FIGURE 113-10   A, Klippel-Trenaunay syndrome (capillary-lymphatic-venous malformation) with extensive capillary stain and limb hypertrophy. Venous anomalies seen by MRI. Note curious overgrowth and dorsal fatty tissue in contralateral limb. **B,** Capillary-lymphatic-venous malformation: hyperkeratotic lymphatic vesicles in capillary stain. Band-aid controls bleeding.

Treatment

Grotesque enlargement of the foot requires selective ablative procedures, such as a ray/midfoot, or Syme amputation, to allow the infant to wear proper footwear. For many children, a slightly increased limb girth is not a problem, but they must be monitored annually for axial overgrowth. By 2 years of age, the leg length is measured radiologically. If the length discrepancy is more than 1.5 cm, a shoe-lift is prescribed to prevent limping and secondary scoliosis. If necessary, endoscopic epiphysiodesis at the distal femoral growth plate is performed around age 11 years. It is generally unnecessary to correct for length differential in the upper limb.

Otherwise, management of the venous component in CLVM is fundamentally conservative.[118,121] Magnetic resonance venography or phlebography documents the deep drainage system. An elastic compressive stocking is recommended if there is clinical evidence of venous insufficiency. Superficial varicose veins sometimes are removed if they are grossly incompetent (and deep system is functioning) and only if the patient complains of symptoms (e.g., leg fatigue, heaviness, or an inability to wear shoes because of enlarged dorsal veins in the foot). In some patients, reconstruction of the deep system, excision of a persistent sciatic vein, or subfascial (endoscopic) ligation of perforators is undertaken.[118]

In selected patients, sclerotherapy is used to obliterate incompetent superficial veins and to shrink focal VMs or lymphatic cysts. The superficial venous system should not be sclerosed, excised, or ligated during debulking procedures unless the deep system has been documented as present and functioning. These superficial varicosities can be "excluded" by embolization and sclerotherapy with tourniquets, microcoils, and sclerosants. Intermittent lymphatic oozing and bleeding from the hemolymphatic vesicles is an annoying problem (see Fig. 113-10). Compression with custom-made elastic stockings is helpful. Laser photocoagulation or injection with 1% sodium tetradecyl sulfate or 100% ethanol usually provides temporary control. If bleeding persists, other alternatives include stripping or ligation of the underlying veins or excision of the hypertrophic-stained patch and replacement with a split-thickness skin graft. Thoracic wall CLVM can be resected in stages. Postoperative healing is often problematic, and prolonged drainage should be expected. Resection of the intrathoracic component is usually unnecessary.

Proteus syndrome is a sporadic and progressive vascular, skeletal, and soft tissue condition; its only constant features are asymmetry and variable expression. Vascular anomalies in Proteus syndrome can be of the capillary, lymphatic or venous type,[118] and these patients are at risk for thromboembolism similar to patients with CLVM[123] The major diagnostic features include verrucous (linear) nevus, lipomas and lipomatosis, macrocephaly (calvarial hyperostoses), asymmetric limbs with partial gigantism of the hands and feet or both, and curious cerebriform plantar thickening ("moccasin" feet).[124]

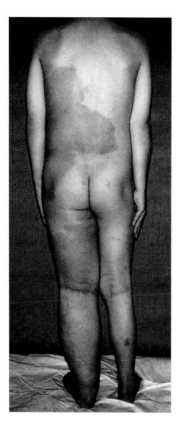

FIGURE 113-11 Parkes Weber syndrome (capillary-lymphatic-arteriovenous malformation). Capillary blush throughout limb, buttock, and thorax with generalized overgrowth and scoliosis.

Maffucci syndrome denotes the coexistence of exophytic vascular anomalies with bony exostoses and enchondromas. This rare condition is not thought to be inheritable and usually is not detected at birth. The osseous lesions appear in childhood, whereas the vascular lesions manifest later. These venous malformations occur in the subcutaneous tissue and bones, particularly in the limbs. The bony and vascular lesions can be unilateral or bilateral. These patients often develop spindle cell hemangioendotheliomas. Previously considered to be a low-grade tumor, these lesions now are recognized to be a reactive vascular proliferation within a pre-existing vascular malformation.[125] Malignant transformation, usually chondrosarcoma, occurs in 20% to 30% of patients, which suggests that the mutation for Maffucci syndrome may involve a tumor-suppressor gene.[126,127]

Fast-Flow Anomalies

Parkes Weber syndrome is designated as a capillary blush with underlying subcutaneous intramuscular microarteriovenous fistulae (capillary-arteriovenous fistula) or capillary-arteriovenous malformation (CAVM). Rarely, there are associated lymphatic anomalies, capillary-lymphatic-arteriovenous malformations. The lower limb is affected more often than the upper limb, and the vascular anomaly is obvious at birth. The involved limb is covered by a geographic pink, macular stain and is symmetrically enlarged

(Fig. 113-11). There is more cutaneous warmth than with a typical CM. Presence of a bruit or thrill on physical examination confirms the diagnosis. In contrast to CLVM, soft tissue overgrowth in the CAVM limb is shown by MRI to be muscular and bony. The enlarged muscles and bones exhibit an abnormal signal and enhancement. Magnetic resonance angiography and magnetic resonance venography show generalized arterial and venous dilatation. Catheter angiography often shows discrete arteriovenous shunts at the joints.

Treatment

Rarely, an infant with CAVM presents at birth with high-output congestive heart failure and anasarca. Emergent embolization, using permanent occlusive agents, is indicated. The child with Parkes Weber syndrome is followed annually. Ultrasonography and color Doppler evaluation of the arterial flow is indicated when the child is 3 to 4 years old. The treatment is predicated on symptoms. Superselective embolization is indicated for pain, ischemia, or cutaneous ulceration.

Bannayan-Riley-Ruvalcaba syndrome was integrated by Cohen.[128] This autosomal dominant disorder has been defined molecularly by germline mutations in *PTEN* (phosphatase-tensin homologue on chromosome 10), a tumor-suppressor gene on chromosome 10q. There is clinical and phenotypic overlap with Cowden's syndrome.[129,130] The major clinical features are macrocephaly, multiple lipomas (encapsulated or diffusely infiltrating), hamartomatous polyps of the distal ileum and colon, Hashimoto thyroiditis, pigmented macules on the penile glans, and vascular malformations. The latter are capillary, venous, or arteriovenous and are usually a minor component of the syndrome. There are extreme examples of Bannayan-Riley-Ruvalcaba syndrome with hemihypertrophy, lower limb asymmetry, lipomatosis, and extensive AVM.[131] These patients must be assessed long term because they are at risk for developing malignant tumors, especially breast carcinoma.

■ CONCLUSION

In the 1990s, the cloud of terminologic confusion that obscured the field of vascular anomalies lifted. Interested specialists currently are able to communicate effectively, not only with one another, but also with patients and families. Notwithstanding the information provided in this chapter, the field of vascular anomalies remains largely unexplored and is constantly evolving. Even experienced clinicians can make a wrong diagnosis, and they are always learning something new. Many of these patients are "too complicated" or "too complex" to be managed without interdisciplinary support. These patients deserve to be cared for by a team of physicians who are fascinated by and devoted to vascular anomalies. Teams are becoming established in major referral centers. Vascular surgeons need to familiarize themselves with the newer terminology and management of these conditions. Whether working as an individual or on a team, a vascular surgeon may be asked to play a major role in the care of a patient born with a vascular anomaly.

■ REFERENCES

1. Mulliken JB, Glowacki J: Hemangiomas and vascular malformations in infants and children: A classification based on endothelial characteristics. Plast Reconstr Surg 69:412, 1982.
2. Enjolras O, Mulliken JB: Vascular tumors and vascular malformations. Adv Dermatol 13:375, 1998.
3. Takahashi K, Mulliken JB, Kozakewich HPW, et al: Cellular markers that distinguish the phases of hemangioma during infancy and childhood. J Clin Invest 93:2357, 1994.
4. Gonzalez-Crussi F, Areyes-Mugica M: Cellular hemangiomas ("hemangioendotheliomas") in infants: Light microscopic, immunohistochemical, and ultrastructural observations. Am J Surg Pathol 15:769, 1991.
5. Martin-Padura I, de Castellarnau C, Uccini S, et al: Expression of VE (vascular endothelial)-cadherin and other endothelial-specific markers in haemangiomas. J Pathol 175:51, 1995.
6. Kräling BM, Razon MJ, Boon LM, et al: E-selectin is present in proliferating endothelial cells in human hemangiomas. Am J Pathol 148:1181, 1996.
7. Takahashi K, Mulliken JB, Kozakewich HPW, et al: Cellular markers that distinguish the phases of hemangioma during infancy and childhood. J Clin Invest 93:2357, 1994.
8. Dethlefsen SM, Mulliken JB, Glowacki J: An ultrastructural study of mast cell interactions in hemangiomas. Ultrastruct Pathol 10:175, 1986.
9. Mulliken JB, Fishman SJ, Burrows PE: Vascular anomalies. Curr Probl Surg 37:520, 2000.
10. Boon LM, Enjolras O, Mulliken JB: Congenital hemangioma: Evidence of accelerated involution. J Pediatr 128:329, 1996.
11. Enjolras O, Mulliken JB, Boon LM, et al: Noninvoluting congenital hemangioma: A rare cutaneous vascular anomaly. Plast Reconstr Surg 107:1647, 2001.
12. Margileth AM, Museles M: Cutaneous hemangiomas in children: Diagnosis and conservative management. JAMA 194:523, 1965.
13. Finn MC, Glowacki J, Mulliken JB: Congenital vascular lesions: Clinical application of a new classification. J Pediatr Surg 18:894, 1983.
14. Bowers RE, Graham EA, Tomlinson KM: The natural history of the strawberry nevus. Arch Dermatol 82:667, 1960.
15. Martinez-Perez D, Fein NA, Boon LM, Mulliken JB: Not all hemangiomas look like strawberries: Uncommon presentations of the most common tumor of infancy. Pediatr Dermatol 12:1, 1995.
16. Kirschner RE, Low DW: Treatment of pyogenic granuloma by shave excision and laser photocoagulation. Plast Reconstr Surg 104:1346, 1999.
17. Patrice SJ, Wiss K, Mulliken JB: Pyogenic granuloma (lobular capillary hemangioma): A clinicopathologic study of 178 cases. Pediatr Dermatol 8:267, 1991.
18. Jones EW, Orkin M: Tufted angioma (angioblastoma): A benign progressive angioma, not to be confused with Kaposi's sarcoma or low grade angiosarcoma. J Am Acad Dermatol 20:214, 1989.
19. Chung KC, Weiss SW, Kuzon WM Jr: Multifocal congenital hemangiopericytomas associated with Kasabach-Merritt syndrome. Br J Plast Surg 48:240, 1995.
20. Boon LM, Fishman SJ, Lund DP, Mulliken JB: Congenital fibrosarcoma masquerading as congenital hemangioma: Report of two cases. J Pediatr Surg 30:1378, 1995.
21. Boon LM, Burrows PE, Paltiel HJ, et al: Hepatic vascular anomalies in infancy: A twenty-seven-year experience. J Pediatr 129:346, 1996.
22. Berman B, Lim W-PH: Concurrent cutaneous and hepatic hemangiomata in infancy: Report of a case and review of the literature. J Dermatol Surg Oncol 4:869, 1978.
23. Selby DM, Stocker JT, Waclawiw MA, et al: Infantile hemangioendothelioma of the liver. Hepatology 20:39, 1994.
24. Dubois J, Patriquin HB, Garel L, et al: Soft tissue hemangiomas in infants and children: Diagnosis using Doppler sonography. AJR Am J Roentgenol 171:247, 1998.
25. Paltiel H, Burrows PE, Kozakewich HPW, et al: Soft-tissue vascular anomalies: Utility of US for diagnosis. Radiology 214:747, 2000.
26. Meyer JS, Hoffer FA, Barnes PD, Mulliken JB: Biological classification of soft-tissue vascular anomalies: MR correlation. AJR Am J Roentgenol 157:559, 1991.
27. Huston J III, Forbes GS, Ruefenacht DA, et al: Magnetic resonance imaging of facial vascular anomalies. Mayo Clin Proc 67:739, 1992.
28. Pasquale-Castroviejo I, Viano J, Moreno F, et al: Hemangiomas of the head, neck and chest with associated vascular brain anomalies: A complex neurocutaneous syndrome. AJNR Am J Neuroradiol 17:461, 1996.
29. Burrows PE, Robertson RL, Mulliken JB, et al: Cerebral vasculopathy and neurologic sequelae in infants with cervicofacial hemangioma: Report of eight patients. Radiology 207:601, 1998.
30. Enjolras O, Mulliken JB: The current management of vascular birthmarks. Pediatr Dermatol 10:311, 1993.
31. Frieden IJ (ed): Management of hemangiomas [special symposium]. Pediatr Dermatol 14:57, 1997.
32. Achauer BM, VanderKalm VM: Ulcerated anogenital hemangiomas of infancy. Plast Reconstr Surg 87:861, 1991.
33. Morelli JG, Tan QT, Yohn JJ, Weston WL: Treatment of ulcerated hemangiomas in infancy. Arch Pediatr Adolesc Med 148:1104, 1994.
34. Enjolras O, Gelbert F: Superficial hemangiomas: Associations and management. Pediatr Dermatol 14:174, 1997.
35. Orlow SJ, Isakoff MS, Blei F: Increased risk of symptomatic hemangiomas of the airway in association with cutaneous hemangiomas in a "beard" distribution. J Pediatr 131:643, 1997.
36. Ruttum MS, Abrams GW, Harris GJ, et al: Bilateral retinal embolization associated with intralesional steroid injection for capillary hemangioma of infancy. J Pediatr Ophthalmol Strabis 30:4, 1993.
37. Sloan GM, Renisch JF, Nichter LS, et al: Intralesional corticosteroid therapy for infantile hemangiomas. Plast Reconstr Surg 83:459, 1989.
38. Enjolras O, Riché MC, Merland JJ, Escande JP: Management of alarming hemangiomas in infancy: A review of 25 cases. Pediatrics 85:491, 1990.
39. Sadan N, Wolach B: Treatment of hemangiomas of infants with high doses of prednisone. J Pediatr 128:141, 1996.
40. Boon LM, MacDonald DM, Mulliken JB: Complications of systemic corticosteroid therapy for problematic hemangiomas. Plast Reconstr Surg 104:1616, 1999.
41. White CW, Wolf SJ, Korones DN, et al: Treatment of childhood angiomatous diseases with recombinant interferon-alpha-2a. J Pediatr 118:59, 1991.
42. Ezekowitz RAB, Mulliken JB, Folkman J: Interferon-alfa-2a therapy for life-threatening hemangiomas of infancy. N Engl J Med 326:1456, 1992.
43. Ricketts RR, Hatley RM, Corden BJ, et al: Interferon-alpha-2a for the treatment of complex hemangiomas of infancy and childhood. Ann Surg 219:605, 1994.
44. Soumekh B, Adams GL, Shapiro RS: Treatment of head and neck hemangiomas with recombinant interferon-alpha-2-b. Ann Otol Rhinol Laryngol 105:201, 1994.
45. Deb G, Donfrancesco A, DeSio L, Standoli L:. Treatment of hemangiomas of infants and babies with interferon-alfa-2a: Preliminary results. Int J Pediatr Hematol Oncol 3:109, 1996.
46. Chang E, Boyd A, Nelson CC, et al: Successful treatment of infantile hemangiomas with interferon-alpha-2b. J Pediatr Hematol Oncol 19:237, 1997.
47. Tamayo L, Ortiz DM, Orozco-Covarrubias L, et al: Therapeutic efficacy of interferon-alfa-2b in infants with life-threatening giant hemangiomas. Arch Dermatol 133:1567, 1997.
48. Grienwald JH, Burke DK, Bonthius DJ, et al: An update on the treatment of hemangiomas in children with interferon-alfa-2a. Arch Otolaryngol Head Neck Surg 125:21, 1999.
49. Mulliken JB, Boon LM, Takahashi K, et al: Pharmacologic therapy for endangering hemangiomas. Curr Opin Dermatol 2:109, 1995.

50. Dubois J, Hershon L, Carmant L, et al: Toxicity profile of interferon-alfa-2b in children: A prospective evaluation. J Pediatr 135:782, 1999.

51. Barlow CF, Priebe C, Mulliken JB, et al: Spastic diplegia as a complication of interferon-alfa-2a treatment of hemangiomas of infancy. J Pediatr 132:527, 1998.

52. Haisley-Royster C, Enjolras O, Frieden IJ, et al: Kasabach-Merritt phenomenon: A retrospective study of treatment with vincristine. J Pediatr Hematol Oncol 24:459, 2002.

53. Mulliken JB: A plea for a biologic approach to hemangiomas of infancy [editorial]. Arch Dermatol 127:243, 1991.

54. Scheepers JH, Quaba AA: Does the pulsed tunable dye laser have a role in the management of infantile hemangiomas: Observations based on 3 years' experience. Plast Reconstr Surg 95:305, 1995.

55. Sie KC, McGill T, Healy GB: Subglottic hemangioma: Ten years' experience with carbon dioxide laser. Ann Otol Rhinol Laryngol 103:167, 1994.

56. Berlien HP, Miller G, Waldschmidt J: Lasers in pediatric surgery. Prog Pediatr Surg 25:5, 1990.

57. Achauer BM, Celikoz B, VanderKam VM: Intralesional bare fiber laser treatment of hemangioma of infancy. Plast Reconstr Surg 101:1212, 1998.

58. Frieden IJ (ed): Management of hemangiomas. Pediatr Dermatol 14:57, 1997.

59. Kasabach HH, Merritt KK: Capillary hemangioma with extensive purpura: Report of a case. Am J Dis Child 59:1063, 1940.

60. Zuckerberg LR, Nikoloff BJ, Weiss SW: Kaposiform hemangioendothelioma of infancy and childhood: An aggressive neoplasm associated with Kasabach-Merritt syndrome and lymphangiomatosis. Am J Surg Pathol 17:321, 1993.

61. Enjolras O, Wassef M, Mazoyer E, et al: Infants with Kasabach-Merritt syndrome do not have "true" hemangiomas. J Pediatr 130:631, 1997.

62. Sarkar M, Mulliken JB, Kozakewich HP, et al: Thrombocytopenic coagulopathy (Kasabach-Merritt phenomenon) is associated with kaposiform hemangioendothelioma and not with common infantile hemangioma. Plast Reconstr Surg 100:1377, 1997.

63. Jones EW, Orkin M: Tufted angioma (angioblastoma): A benign progressive angioma, not to be confused with Kaposi's sarcoma or low grade angiosarcoma. J Am Acad Dermatol 20:214, 1989.

64. Chung KC, Weiss SW, Kuzon WM Jr: Multifocal congenital hemangiopericytomas associated with Kasabach-Merritt syndrome. Br J Plast Surg 48:240, 1995.

65. Resnick SD, Lacey S, Jones G: Hemorrhagic complications in a rapidly growing congenital hemangiopericytoma. Pediatr Dermatol 10:267, 1993.

66. Enjolras O, Mulliken JB, Wassef M, et al: Residual lesions after Kasabach-Merritt phenomenon in 41 patients. J Am Acad Dermatol 42:225, 2000.

67. Wang HU, Chen Z-F, Anderson DJ: Molecular distinction and angiogenic interaction between embryonic arteries and veins revealed by ephrin-B2 and its receptor Eph-B4. Cell 983:741, 1998.

68. Vikkula M, Boon LM, Mulliken JB, Olsen BR: Molecular basis of vascular anomalies. Trends Cardiovasc Med 8:281, 1998.

69. Smoller BR, Rosen S: Port-wine stains: A disease of altered neural modulation of blood vessels? Arch Dermatol 122:177, 1986.

70. Tan T, Sherwood K, Gilchrest BA: Treatment of children with port wine stains using the flashlamp pumped tunable dye laser. N Engl J Med 320:416, 1989.

71. van der Horst CMAM, Koster PHL, deBorgie CAJM, et al: Effect of the timing of treatment of port-wine stains with the flash-lamp-pumped pulsed-dye laser. N Engl J Med 338:1028, 1998.

72. Kaipainen A, Korhonen J, Mustonen T, et al: Expression of the fms-like tyrosine kinase 4 gene becomes restricted to lymphatic endothelium during development. Proc Natl Acad Sci U S A 92:3566, 1995.

73. Wigle JT, Oliver G: *Prox 1* function is required for the development of the murine lymphatic system. Cell 98:769, 1999.

74. Dumont DJ, Fong GH, Puri MC, et al: Vascularization of the mouse embryo: A study of flk-1, tek, tie, and vascular endothelial growth factor expression during development. Dev Dyn 203:80, 1995.

75. Jeltsch M, Kaipainen A, Joukov V, et al: Hyperplasia of lymphatic vessels in VEGF-C transgenic mice. Science 276:1423, 1997.

76. Karkkainen MJ, Haiko P, Sainio K, et al: Vascular endothelial growth factor C is required for sprouting of the first lymphatic vessels from embryonic veins. Nat Immunol 5:74, 2004.

77. Chervenak FA, Isaacson G, Blakemore KJ, et al: Fetal cystic hygroma: Cause and natural history. N Engl J Med 309:822, 1983.

79. Langer JC, Fitzgerald PG, Desa D, et al: Cervical cystic hygroma in the fetus: Clinical spectrum and outcome. J Pediatr Surg 25:58, 1990.

80. Gallagher PG, Mahoney MJ, Goshe JR: Cystic hygroma in the fetus and newborn. Semin Perinatal 23:341, 1999.

81. Ferrell RE, Levinson KL, Esman JM, et al: Hereditary lymphedema: Evidence for linkage and genetic heterogeneity. Hum Mol Genet 7:2073, 1998.

82. Evans AL, Brice G, Sotirova V, et al: Mapping of primary congenital lymphedema to the 5q35.3 region. Am J Hum Genet 64:547, 1999.

83. Mangion J, Rahman N, Manour S, et al: A gene for lymphedema: Distichiasis maps to 16q24.3. Am J Hum Genet 65:427, 1999.

84. Karkkainen MJ, Ferrell RE, Lawrence EC, et al: Missense mutations interfere with VEGFR-3 signalling in primary lymphedema. Nat Genet 25:153, 2000.

85. Finegold DN, Kimak MA, Lawrence EC, et al: Truncating mutations in *FOXC2* cause multiple lymphedema syndromes. Hum Mol Genet 10:1185, 2001.

86. Irrthum A, Karkkainen MJ, Devriendt K, et al: Congenital hereditary lymphedema caused by a mutation that inactivates *VEGFR3* tyrosine kinase. Am J Hum Genet 67:295, 2000.

87. Holberg CJ, Erickson RP, Bemas MJ, et al: Segregation analyses and a genome-wide linkage search confirm genetic heterogeneity and suggest oligogenic inheritance in some Milroy congenital primary lymphedema families. Am J Med Genet 98:303, 2001.

88. Fang J, Dagenais SL, Erickson RP, et al: Mutations in *FOXC2* (*MFH-1*), a Forkhead family transcription factor, are responsible for the hereditary lymphedema-distichiasis syndrome. Am J Hum Genet 67:1382, 2000.

89. Tartaglia M, Niemeyer CM, Fragale A, et al: Somatic mutations in PTPN11 in juvenile myelomonocytic leukemia, myelodysplastic syndromes and acute myeloid leukemia. Nat Genet 34:148, 2003.

90. Marler JJ, Fishman SJ, Upton J, et al: Prenatal diagnosis of vascular anomalies. J Pediatr Surg 37:318, 2002.

91. Padwa BL, Hayward PG, Ferraro NF, Mulliken JB: Cervicofacial lymphatic malformation: Clinical course, surgical intervention, and pathogenesis of skeletal hypertrophy. Plast Reconstr Surg 95:951, 1995.

92. Gorham LW, Stout AP: Massive osteolysis (acute spontaneous absorption of bone, phantom bone, disappearing bone): Its relations to hemangiomatosis. J Bone Joint Surg 37:986, 1955.

93. Burrows PE, Laor T, Paltiel H, Robertson RL: Diagnostic imaging in the evaluation of vascular birthmarks. Dermatol Clin 16:455, 1998.

94. Hayward PG, Orgill DP, Mulliken JB, Perez-Atayde AR: Congenital fibrosarcoma masquerading as lymphatic malformation: Report of two cases. J Pediatr Surg 30:84, 1995.

95. Laor T, Burrows PE, Hoffer F, Kozakewich HPW: MR lymphangiography in infants, children, and young adults. AJR Am J Roentgenol 171:1111, 1998.

96. Ninh TN, Ninh TX: Cystic hygroma in children: Report of 126 cases. J Pediatr Surg 9:191, 1974.

97. Ogita S, Tsuto T, Deguchi E, et al: OK-432 therapy for unresectable lymphangiomas in children. J Pediatr Surg 26:263, 1991.

98. Ogita S, Tsuto T, Nakamura K, et al: OK-432 therapy in 64 patients with lymphangioma. J Pediatr Surg 29:784, 1994.

99. Ogita S, Deguchi E, Tokiwa K, et al: Ongoing osteolysis in patients with lymphangioma. J Pediatr Surg 33:45, 1998.

100. Hall N, Ade-Ajayi N, Brewis C, et al: Is intralesional injection of OK-432 effective in the treatment of lymphangioma in children? Surgery 133:238, 2003.
101. Alqahtani A, Nguyen LT, Flageole H, et al: 25 years' experience with lymphangiomas in children. J Pediatr Surg 34:1164, 1999.
102. Vikkula M, Boon LM, Carraway KL III, et al: Vascular dysmorphogenesis caused by an activating mutation in the receptor tyrosine kinase TIE-2. Cell 87:1181, 1996.
103. Brouillard P, Boon LM, Mulliken JB, et al: Mutations in a novel factor, glomulin, are responsible for glomuvenous malformations ("glomangiomas"). Am J Hum Genet 70:866, 2002.
104. Laberge-le Couteulx S, Jung HH, Labauge P, et al: Truncating mutations in CCM1, encoding KRIT1, cause hereditary cavernous angiomas. Nat Genet 23:189, 1999.
105. Hein HD, Mulliken JB, Kozakewich HPW, et al: Venous malformations of the skeletal muscle. Plast Reconstr Surg 110:1625, 2002.
106. Fishman SJ, Burrows PE, Leichtner AM, Mulliken JB: Gastrointestinal manifestations of vascular anomalies in childhood: Varied etiologies require multiple therapeutic modalities. J Pediatr Surg 33:1163, 1998.
107. Gallione CJ, Pasyk KA, Boon LM, et al: A gene for familial venous malformations maps to chromosome 9p in a second large kindred. J Med Genet 32:197, 1995.
108. Oranje AP: Blue rubber bleb nevus syndrome. Pediatr Dermatol 3:304, 1986.
109. Tyrell RT, Baumgartner BR, Montemayor KA: Blue rubber bleb nevus syndrome: CT diagnosis of intussusception. Am J Radiol 154:105, 1990.
110. Berenguer B, Burrows PE, Zurakowski D, Mulliken JB: Sclerotherapy of craniofacial venous malformations: Complications and results. Plast Reconstr Surg 104:1, 1999.
111. Keljo DJ, Yakes WF, Anderson JM, Timmons CF: Recognition and treatment of venous malformations of the rectum. J Pediatr Gastroenterol 23:442, 1996.
112. Fishman SJ, Shamberger RC, Fox VL, Burrows PE: Endorectal pull-through abates gastrointestinal hemorrhage for colorectal venous malformations. J Pediatr Surg 35:982, 2000.
113. Guttmacher AE, Marchuk DA, White RI Jr: Hereditary hemorrhagic telangiectasia. N Engl J Med 333:918, 1995.
114. Eerola I, Boon LM, Mulliken JB, et al: Capillary malformation-arteriovenous malformation, a new clinical and genetic disorder caused by RASA1 mutations. Am J Hum Genet 73:1240, 2003.
115. Kohout MP, Hansen M, Pribaz JJ, Mulliken JB: Arteriovenous malformations of the head and neck: Natural history and management. Plast Reconstr Surg 102:643, 1998.
116. Upton J, Coombs CJ, Mulliken JB, et al: Vascular malformations of the upper limb: A review of 270 patients. J Hand Surg 24:1019, 1999.
117. Jacob AG, Driscoll DJ, Shaughnessy WI, et al: Klippel-Trenaunay syndrome: Spectrum and management. Mayo Clin Proc 73:28, 1998.
118. Gloviczki P, Stanson AW, Stickler GB, et al: Klippel-Trenaunay syndrome: The risks and benefits of vascular interventions. Surgery 110:469, 1991.
119. Samuel M, Spitz L: Klippel-Trenaunay syndrome: Clinical features, complications and management in children. Br J Surg 82:757, 1995.
120. Baskerville PA, Akroyd JS, Thomas ML, Browse NL: The Klippel-Trenaunay syndrome: Clinical, radiological, and hemodynamic features and management. Br J Surg 72:232, 1985.
121. Samuel M, Spitz L: Klippel-Trenaunay syndrome: Clinical features, complications and management in children. Br J Surg 82:757, 1995.
122. Biesecker LG, Happle R, Mulliken JB, et al: Proteus syndrome: Diagnostic criteria, differential diagnosis, and patient evaluation. Am J Med Genet 84:389, 1999.
123. Cohen MM Jr: Causes of premature death in Proteus syndrome. Am J Med Genet 101:1, 2001.
124. Cohen MM Jr, Neri G, Weksberg R, et al: Overgrowth Syndromes. New York, Oxford University Press, 2002, p 75.
125. Perkins P, Weiss SW: Spindle cell hemangioendothelioma: An analysis of 78 cases with reassessment of its pathogenesis and biologic behavior. Am J Surg Pathol 20:1196, 1996.
126. Sun T-C, Swee RG, Shives TC, Unni KK: Chondrosarcoma in Maffucci's syndrome. J Bone Joint Surg 67:1214, 1985.
127. Kaplan RP, Want JT, Arnron DM, Kaplan L: Maffucci's syndrome: Two case reports with a literature review. J Am Acad Dermatol 29:894, 1994.
128. Cohen MM Jr: Bannayan-Riley-Ruvalcava syndrome: Renaming three formerly recognized syndromes as one etiologic entity [letter]. Am J Med Genet 35:291, 1990.
129. Marsh DJ, Dahia PLM, Zheng Z, et al: Germline mutations in PTEN are present in Bannayan-Zonana syndrome. Nat Genet 16:333, 1997.
130. Marsh DJ, Kum JB, Lunetta KL, et al: PTEN mutation spectrum and genotype-phenotype correlations in Bannayan-Riley-Ruvalcaba syndrome suggest a single entity with Cowden syndrome. Hum Mol Genet 8:1461, 1999.
131. Zhou XP, Marsh DJ, Hampel H, et al: Germline and germline mosaic PTEN mutations associated with a Proteus-like syndrome of hemihypertrophy, lower limb asymmetry, arteriovenous malformations and lipomatosis. Hum Mol Genet 9:765, 2000.

Surgical Management of Vascular Malformations

114

THOMAS S. RILES, MD
GLENN R. JACOBOWITZ, MD

The management of vascular malformations (VMs) has been a challenging problem for many years. Surgical treatment alone historically has been inadequate or even disastrous, often leading to extensive damage to adjacent structures with high recurrence rates or major amputation.[1-3] As Szilagyi and associates[4] noted in 1965, "the most impressive lesson taught ... was the realization of the futility of any attempt to cure by surgical means any but the simplest and most sharply localized of these lesions." More recently, transcatheter treatment has been effective in controlling these lesions.[5,6] Transcatheter treatment is usually palliative in nature, however, and often requires multiple interventions over many years to treat recurrent symptoms. Complete eradication of VMs, when possible, can be achieved by initial transcatheter treatment and subsequent surgical ablation. Surgical resection must be performed in a carefully planned manner with appropriate preoperative imaging of a lesion, however, and it can be performed only in selected lesions. This chapter reviews the surgical treatment of vascular malformations.

■ TYPES OF VASCULAR MALFORMATIONS TREATED

Surgical management of VMs cannot be discussed without addressing the major different types, which include arteriovenous malformations (AVMs) and venous malformations. The major difference between these two lesions is the arteriovenous component of AVMs. There is often a nidus of an AVM, which is considered to be the most central area of the arteriovenous connections within a malformation. There is usually no such nidus in venous malformations, which tend to be more diffuse in nature. These lesions most commonly occur as isolated anomalies in otherwise healthy patients and can occur anywhere in the body. The most common anatomic locations are the pelvis, extremities, and intracranial circulation. They are often stable lesions requiring no specific treatment, and many of these malformations probably go undetected throughout life.

Natural History

Surgeons treating these lesions need to be aware of their natural history. The clinical behavior of VMs is not well

defined, but it can be extremely variable.[5,9] Several reports have shown that asymptomatic lesions may be safely observed with no intervention.[5,9-11] Evaluation of the size of the malformation and the location with respect to adjacent structures can be followed with computed tomography and magnetic resonance imaging (MRI). Advances in MRI technology have made this modality the noninvasive test of choice for imaging vascular malformations.[12-14]

The clinical presentation and application of diagnostic methods in evaluating these lesions are discussed in detail in Chapter 110. Treatment usually is reserved for symptomatic lesions, but larger mass lesions; visible, cosmetically unacceptable lesions; and lesions in critical locations (e.g., encroaching on orifices or key organ structures, including the mouth or eye) also may be considered for treatment even though the lesion itself is asymptomatic. Some lesions become apparent or increase in size after trauma or during periods of hormonal stimulation, such as pregnancy. Although measured cardiac output often may be increased in patients with AVMs, clinically significant cardiovascular consequences have been relatively rare in our experience.[5,15]

■ TRANSCATHETER THERAPY

The techniques of superselective catheterization of feeding vessels and the transcatheter administration of embolic agents have revolutionized the treatment of VMs. These techniques are discussed thoroughly in Chapter 115, but their effectiveness and limitations merit comment here to underscore why they have replaced surgery as primary treatment in most cases. Catheterization techniques can be used effectively in combination with surgery, to facilitate subsequent resection, by greatly decreasing lesion vascularity, and can be combined strategically with surgery to produce more effective control or even cure.

Catheter-based embolization has been shown to be effective in treating AVMs in several anatomic areas.[10,16-18] The development of currently available embolization materials, particularly the rapidly polymerizing agents, has greatly improved the ability to control or eradicate complex arteriovenous connections.[5,19] Regarding venous malformations, transcatheter or percutaneous treatment with sclerosing agents, such as absolute ethanol, has been shown to be effective treatment.[20] These lesions have no arterial component and are more amenable to direct injection. Percutaneous injection of sclerosing agents for venous malformations or transarterial embolization of AVMs can result in necrosis of adjacent organs or of overlying skin and soft tissue, however.[6,20,21] These complications and the lasting effects of discoloration and tenderness of thrombosed venous masses suggest the need for caution in applying these techniques to stable venous lesions, which pose no significant hemodynamic threat.

Although multiple treatments are often necessary, published results have shown good long-term outcomes with transcatheter therapy of VMs.[5,6,20,21] Transcatheter embolization currently plays a major role in the treatment of vascular malformations in all parts of the body.[18,23] It can be performed as the sole method of therapy or as a preoperative treatment to decrease vascularity before a planned surgical resection.

■ COMBINED TRANSCATHETER AND SURGICAL THERAPY

There are few large studies of transcatheter embolization used in conjunction with surgical resection in the treatment of AVMs. The existing reports can largely be divided into reports involving pelvic AVMs and reports involving the extremities. The largest series of pelvic AVMs to date is from our institution[5] and involved 35 patients. There was a mean age of 37 years, and 51% were male. Previous, unsuccessful attempted surgical resection had been attempted in 32% of patients. A mean of 2.4 embolization procedures (range 1 to 11) were performed over a mean period of 23 months. More than one embolization procedure was required in 57% of patients. These additional procedures were performed as planned, stage embolizations (20%) or because of residual or recurrent symptoms (37%). Adjunctive surgical procedures were performed in five patients (14%). Among these was a hip disarticulation after embolization of an AVM in the upper thigh, which had left the patient with a nonhealing, bleeding, ulcerated high-above knee amputation (Fig. 114-1). After the embolization, the AVM was resected in the hip disarticulation, and the patient

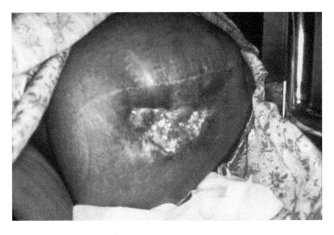

FIGURE 114-1 Nonhealing, ulcerated above-knee amputation stump in a patient with a pelvic and upper thigh arteriovenous malformation. Hip disarticulation was performed after transcatheter embolization of the nidus. (See color figure in this section.)

has been able to ambulate with a prosthesis for 20 years. The rapidly polymerizing cyanoacrylate adhesives were most commonly used for embolization, and the vessels most commonly embolized were branches of the internal iliac arteries (82%) and branches of the inferior mesenteric artery (11%). At a mean follow-up of 84 months, 83% of patients were asymptomatic or significantly improved.

Several more recent studies on extremity AVMs have revealed disappointing long-term outcomes. Dickey and associates[25] reported on four patients with large AVMs of the shoulder and upper extremity treated with transcatheter embolotherapy and found these lesions refractory to intravascular treatment. Mendel and Louis[9] reported on 17 cases of major vascular malformations of the upper extremity, but only three embolizations were performed; recurrence after surgery occurred in 12 patients, and there were four amputations. Carr and coworkers[26] reported on 12 cases of extremity vascular malformations; 8 recurred after treatment, which was either surgery or embolization. More recently, White and colleagues[22] reported an analysis of 20 patients with high-flow extremity AVMs treated with embolotherapy. Excellent long-term results (mean 7.4 years) were shown in upper extremity cases; five of nine patients with lower extremity malformations required major amputation. Among 11 upper extremity AVMs, 7 were treated with transcatheter embolization alone, and 4 had subsequent resection of the AVM. The poor outcome in five patients with lower extremity AVMs was attributed to the involvement of all three trifurcation vessels. Lee and Bergan[6] reported on a large series of 99 patients with VMs. Among these patients, 60% were venous malformations, and 22% were AVMs. Fourteen patients underwent surgical resection after embolotherapy, all with minimal complications reported. Follow-up was short at an average of 10.6 months, but the authors reported no recurrence of lesions in that time.

At New York University Medical Center, transcatheter embolization therapy was performed in 50 patients with extremity VMs, of which 95% were AVMs.[27] These were evenly divided among upper and lower extremity lesions. The mean age was 22 years, and 34% were male. The most commonly embolized vessels were branches of the profunda femoris and tibial arteries (83% of lower extremity lesions) and branches of the brachial and radial arteries (82% of upper extremity lesions). Patients required a mean of 1.6 embolization procedures (range 1 to 5) over a mean period of 57 months. Sixteen patients (32%) underwent more than one embolization procedure. Of these, 1 was a planned, staged procedure, and 15 were for residual or recurrent symptoms. Adjunctive surgery was performed after embolization in three cases (6%). These included local resections (Figs. 114-2 and 114-3) and distal amputation after embolization (Fig. 114-4). Of patients, 92% were asymptomatic or improved at a mean follow-up of 56 months. There was one case of limb loss (2%). The most common agents used for embolization were the cyanoacrylate adhesives.

Although numerous authors have shown the benefit of initial transcatheter embolization followed by surgical resection,[22,23,28-31] there has been little consensus on which lesions should have surgical resection. Calligaro and colleagues[32] reviewed the literature in 1992 for pelvic AVMs and recommended surgical intervention only for localized

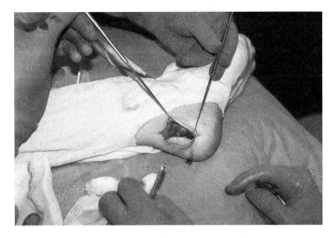

FIGURE 114-2 Complete excision of a localized arteriovenous malformation including all feeding vessels and nidus.

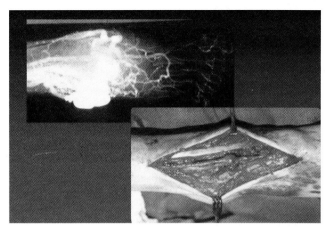

FIGURE 114-3 Angiography of arteriovenous malformation in dorsal leg and intraoperative view after surgical division of all arteriovenous connections.

AVMs that did not involve adjacent organs and only after optimal preoperative trancatheter embolization.

Surgical resection should be performed only after appropriate evaluation of a VM. Preoperative evaluation must include extensive imaging, which can determine the extent of involvement of adjacent tissues and organs and angiographic identification of feeding vessels. MRI has been shown to be useful in this regard.[12-14] MRI is effective for viewing the extent to which subcutaneous tissue, muscle, bone, and organs are involved. VMs often can best be treated with the combined expertise of vascular surgeons, plastic surgeons, interventional radiologists, and others. At our institution, the departments of vascular surgery and interventional radiology have been part of a multidisciplinary center (the New York University Medical Center Trunk and Extremity Vascular Anomaly Center) that has treated a large volume of patients with vascular malformations. Others also have shown excellent results with the multidisciplinary structure.[6]

Imaging via magnetic resonance angiography and MRI and possibly angiography allows the visualization of adjacent structures and feeding vessels. Transcatheter embolization should be the first treatment of choice except in well-circumscribed, surgically accessible lesions. For all other VMs, there should be further imaging with MRI after transcatheter treatment. If a *well-circumscribed* lesion remains, surgery may be performed with the goal of eradicating the lesion. Surgery should involve the ligation of all feeding vessels and the malformation in its entirety. Surgery should not be performed as a means of palliation. If the proposed surgery would not eradicate the lesion, additional palliative transcatheter treatment is preferred. Proximal ligation of feeding vessels in AVMs without resection of the nidus has been particularly troublesome, often resulting in continued enlargement of the AVM and increased recruitment of smaller feeding and draining vessels.[15] Of importance, such proximal ligation may make subsequent transcatheter therapy impossible by obstructing access.[9,15,22,26]

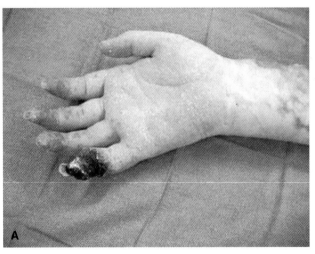
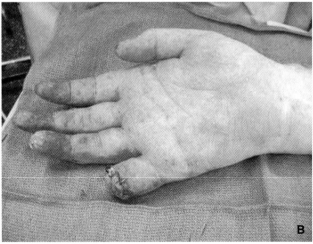

FIGURE 114-4 **A,** Gangrenous distal fifth digit after embolization of distal digit arteriovenous malformation. **B,** Subsequent distal digit amputation. (See color figures in this section.)

In some instances, surgical reconstruction of feeding arteries has been performed to re-establish access to an AVM for more effective embolization therapy.[33] Although it is preferable to allow 3 to 4 weeks before passing catheters through the reconstructed conduits, embolization may be performed immediately if necessary. The reconstruction of large feeding arteries may cause a temporary increase in pressure and size in an AVM, necessitating prompt embolization if symptoms acutely worsen. Surgical and interventional radiology teams should be prepared for this scenario of rapid decompensation when feeding artery reconstruction is performed.

■ SUMMARY

Trancatheter embolization should be considered the current mainstay of therapy for symptomatic AVMs. Until the 1990s, emphasis on treating these lesions centered largely around surgical extirpation. If a lesion is clearly resectable with respect to involvement of adjacent structures, surgical resection for cure should be considered. When performed, every effort should be made to control and ligate all feeding arteries and the nidus. Surgical resection also should be considered for distal extremity AVMs after preoperative embolization. This resection may involve digit or distal extremity amputation, particularly if gangrenous tissue is present after embolization. For more complex lesions, transcatheter embolization alone, although often necessary multiple times, is sufficient to eliminate or improve symptoms in a high percentage of patients. At present, cyanoacrylate adhesives seem to be the most effective agents for embolization, administered through the technique of superselective catheterization of arterial branches allowing access to the nidus of the AVM. Absolute alcohol seems to be an effective agent for sclerotherapy of lower flow venous malformations. The available agents and their choice in different VMs are discussed in Chapter 115.

If a lesion is symptomatically improved with embolization or sclerotherapy and is still difficult to access surgically or not well circumscribed, no further therapy is needed because return of symptoms is variable. As Szilagyi and colleagues[1] noted in 1976, it would be inaccurate to claim a "cure" for most vascular malformations, and treatment with transcatheter therapy must be considered largely palliative. To obtain a cure, VMs must be meticulously imaged to determine the extent of invasion and involvement of adjacent structures, and in most cases the first-line treatment should be transcatheter therapy. If subsequent complete surgical resection is possible, this should be performed. Only then can complete eradication be achieved. Eradication can be performed safely in about 15% of lesions, although each lesion must be evaluated individually and treated according to the specific functional and anatomic characteristics of that lesion. Patients may be reassured, however, that even when surgical resection is imprudent or impossible, VMs can be well controlled with transcatheter therapy, repeated as needed, over many years.

■ REFERENCES

1. Szilagyi DE, Smith RF, Elliott JP, Hageman JH: Congenital arteriovenous anomalies of the limbs. Arch Surg 111:423, 1976.

2. Coursely G, Ivins JC, Barker NW: Congenital arteriovenous fistulas in the extremities: An analysis of 69 cases. Angiology 7:201, 1956.

3. Gomes MM, Bernatz PE: Arteriovenous fistulas: A review and ten-year experience at the Mayo Clinic. Mayo Clin Proc 45:81, 1970.

4. Szilagyi DE, Elliot JP, DeRusso FJ, Smith RF: Peripheral congenital arteriovenous fistulas. Surgery 57:61, 1965.

5. Jacobowitz GR, Rosen RJ, Rockman CB, et al: Transcatheter embolization of complex pelvic malformations: Results and long-term follow-up. J Vasc Surg 33:51, 2001.

6. Lee BB, Bergan JJ: Advanced management of congenital vascular malformations: A multidisciplinary approach. Cardiovasc Surg 10:523, 2002.

7. Folkman J: Toward a new understanding of vascular proliferative disease in children. Pediatrics 74:850, 1984.

8. Mulliken JB, Zetter BR, Folkman J: In vivo characteristics of endothelium from hemangiomas and vascular malformations. Surgery 92:348, 1982.

9. Mendel T, Louis DS: Major vascular malformations of the upper extremity: Long-term observation. J Hand Surg 22A:302, 1997.

10. Natali J, Merland JJ: Superselective arteriography and therapeutic embolization for vascular malformations (angiodysplasias). J Cardiovasc Surg 17:465, 1976.

11. Kaufman SL, Kumar AA, Roland JA, et al: Transcatheter embolization in the management of congenital arteriovenous malformations. Radiology 137:21, 1980.

12. Pearce WH, Rutherford RB, Whitehill TA, Davis K: Nuclear magnetic resonance imaging in patients with congenital vascular malformations of the limbs. J Vasc Surg 8:64, 1988.

13. Dobson MJ, Hartley RW, Ashleigh R, et al: MR angiography and MR imaging of symptomatic peripheral vascular malformations. Clin Radiol 52:595, 1997.

14. Chen AC, Sheu MH, Hung JH, Yu KJ: Three-dimensional magnetic resonance angiography guidance for conservative surgical management of pelvic arteriovenous malformation. Acta Obstet Gynecol Scand 82:302, 2003.

15. Rosen RJ, Riles TS: Congenital vascular malformations. In Rutherford RB (ed): Vascular Surgery, 5th ed. Philadelphia, WB Saunders, 2000, p 1451.

16. Palmaz JC, Newton TH, Reuter SR, Bookstein JJ: Particulate intraarterial embolization in pelvic arteriovenous malformations. AJR Am J Roentgenol 137:117, 1981.

17. Flye MW, Jordan BP, Schwartz MZ: Management of congenital arteriovenous malformations. Surgery 94:740, 1983.

18. Olcott C IV, Newton TH, Stoney RJ, Ehrenfeld WK: Intra-arterial embolization in the management of arteriovenous malformations. Surgery 79:312, 1976.

19. Widlus DM, Murray RR, White RI Jr, et al: Congenital arteriovenous malformations: Tailored embolotherapy. Radiology 169:511, 1988.

20. Lee BB, Kim DI, Huh MD, et al: New experiences with absolute ethanol sclerotherapy in the management of a complex form of congenital venous malformation. J Vasc Surg 33:764, 2001.

21. Yakes WF, Luethke JM, Merland JJ, et al: Ethanol embolization of arteriovenous fistulas: A primary model of therapy. J Vasc Interv Radiol 1:89, 1990.

22. White RI Jr, Pollak J, Persin J, et al: Long-term outcome of embolotherapy and surgery for high-flow arteriovenous malformations. J Vasc Interv Radiol 11:1285, 2000.

23. Gomes AS, Busotti RW, Baker JD, et al: Congenital arteriovenous malformations. Arch Surg 118:817, 1983.

24. Zanetti PH: Cyanoacrylate/iophenylate mixtures: Modification and in vitro evaluation as embolic agents. J Interv Radiol 2:65, 1987.

25. Dickey KW, Pollak JS, Meier GH 3rd, et al: Management of large high-flow arteriovenous malformations of the shoulder and upper extremity with transcatheter embolotherapy. J Vasc Interv Radiol 6:765, 1995.

26. Carr MM, Mahoney JL, Bowen CV: Extremity arteriovenous malformations: Review of a series. Can J Surg 37:394, 1994.

27. Rockman CB, Rosen RJ, Jacobowitz GR, et al: Transcatheter embolization of peripheral vascular malformations: The long-term success of multiple interventions. Ann Vasc Surg 17:417, 2003.
28. Laurian C, Leclef Y, Gigou F, et al: Pelvic arteriovenous fistulas: Therapeutic strategy in five cases. Ann Vasc Surg 4:1, 1990.
29. Palmaz JC, Newton TH, Reuter SR, Bookstein JJ: Particulate intra-arterial embolization in pelvic arteriovenous malformations. AJR Am J Roentgenol 137:117, 1981.
30. Van Poppel H, Claes H, Suy R, et al: Intraarterial embolization in combination with surgery in the management of congenital arterio-venous malformation. Urol Radiol 10:89, 1988.
31. Osuga K, Hori S, Kitayoshi H, et al: Embolization of high flow arterio-venous malformations experience with use of sperabsorbent polymer microspheres. J Vasc Interv Radiol 13:1125, 2002.
32. Calligaro KD, Sedlacek TV, Savarese RP, et al: Congenital pelvic arteriovenous malformations: Long-term follow-up in two cases and a review of the literature. J Vasc Surg 16:100, 1992.
33. Riles TS, Berenstein A, Fisher FA, et al: Reconstruction of the ligated external carotid artery for embolization of cervicofacial arteriovenous malformations. J Vasc Surg 17:491, 1993.

Chapter

115

Endovascular Treatment of Vascular Anomalies

PATRICIA E. BURROWS, MD

■ CLASSIFICATION

Vascular anomalies are divided into two groups—tumors (e.g., hemangiomas) and vascular malformations. Malformations are categorized according to channel type (e.g., arterial, arteriovenous, venous, lymphatic) and flow characteristics.[1] High-flow vascular anomalies include hemangiomas, arteriovenous fistulas (AVFs), and arteriovenous malformations (AVMs); low-flow malformations include capillary malformations, venous malformations (VM), and lymphatic (LM) malformations. Some patients have combined channel anomalies (e.g., Klippel-Trenaunay syndrome [capillary-lymphatic-venous malformation]). AVMs have a characteristic evolution classified by Schobinger stages (Table 115-1).[2] This categorization has therapeutic implications in regard to endovascular therapy.

■ INDICATIONS

Indications for endovascular treatment of vascular anomalies are evolving. At Children's Hospital, Boston, most patients referred for treatment are presented to a multidisciplinary Vascular Anomalies team, and after review of all available data (clinical history and physical findings, imaging, and histology, if available), a consensus is reached regarding the appropriateness of treatment, then a treatment plan is recommended. Hemangiomas usually are managed pharmacologically except in the presence of refractory high-output cardiac failure. Angiography and embolization are carried out rarely in infants with hemangiomas and only after a trial of antiangiogenesis medication. In general, treatment, if available, is offered to patients with vascular malformations who have progressive symptoms not responding to simple measures, such as compression garments or antiplatelet medication. Presently, there is little to offer other than endovascular treatment and resection, but research is being directed toward future therapies based on inhibition of biologic abnormalities that distinguish malformed vessels from normal ones.

■ TECHNIQUES

Endovascular techniques used in the treatment of vascular malformations include *embolization,* which is administration of an occlusive agent or device into blood vessels through an angiographic catheter, and *sclerotherapy,* which is delivery of an ablative or irritant liquid directly into anomalous channels, usually via a percutaneously placed cannula.[3-5] Embolization is reserved for high-flow vascular anomalies, whereas sclerotherapy can be effective in high-flow and low-flow lesions.

Embolization Agents

Temporary occluding agents, including polyvinyl alcohol foam, acrylic/gelatin microspheres, and absorbable gelatin sponge (Gelfoam), generally are reserved for preoperative embolization of high-flow vascular malformations, to aid

Table 115-1	Schobinger Clinical Classification of Arteriovenous Malformations
Stage I (quiescent)	Erythema, warm to touch, increased flow on Doppler
Stage II (expansion)	Venous engorgement, swelling, pulsatile
Stage III (destruction)	Skin necrosis, pain, bleeding
Stage IV	Stage III, plus cardiac decompensation

surgery by reducing the vascularity of the lesion. These materials usually are suspended in radiopaque contrast medium and injected into the feeding arteries with fluoroscopic or "roadmap" (real-time digital subtraction) control. They require blood flow to deliver them to the nidus. Particles that are too small pass directly into the draining veins, whereas larger particles cause proximal occlusion of the feeding arteries.

In contrast to this preoperative *adjunctive treatment,* *primary treatment* of vascular malformations is accomplished using various liquid agents that cause a combination of vascular thrombosis and endothelial ablation resulting in fibrosis. Adhesive polymer, *n*-butyl-2-cyanoacrylate (NBCA), has been used for decades to treat AVMs. Adhesive polymer results in permanent occlusion because it polymerizes to form a solid mass conforming to the shape of the embolized vessel and because polymerization is an exothermic reaction that causes transmural vessel necrosis. Precise placement of this material is difficult, and arterial rather than nidal occlusion usually occurs. Larger occlusive devices, such as coils, are reserved for AVF and for venous occlusion.

Coils are preshaped fibered stainless steel or platinum wires that are advanced through standard angiographic catheters or microcatheters and packed into the vessel to be occluded. They are available in different lengths, diameters, and configurations, including straight, helical, or conical shapes, as "pushable" (deployed through the catheter with an introducer, guide wire, or saline flush) and "detachable" (released from an introducing wire after placement) forms in 0.018-inch, 0.035-inch, and 0.038-inch sizes. Nester coils are soft, long platinum fiber coils, which are excellent for packing a large varix or arteriovenous connection and are available in 0.035-inch and 0.018-inch diameters. In treating patients with vascular malformations, consideration should be given to the use of platinum rather than stainless steel coils because the former are compatible with future magnetic resonance imaging (MRI).

Sclerosing Agents

Ethanol

Ethanol preparations suitable for sclerotherapy include 95% or 98% dehydrated forms, generally available through hospital pharmacies for neurolysis. Ethanol rapidly denatures proteins in the endothelial lining of vessels and, *in stagnant channels,* results in immediate thrombosis. Having a low viscosity, ethanol passes readily through arteriovenous shunts, making it suitable for embolization of AVMs in conjunction with supraselective catheterization of the nidus itself. The latter is important; ethanol should never be injected into a proximal feeding artery. Penetration of the capillary bed results in severe tissue necrosis. Alcohol causes local neurolysis. Systemic effects include central nervous system depression, hypoglycemia, hypertension, hyperthermia, cardiac arrhythmias, pulmonary vasoconstriction and pulmonary hypertension, and electromechanical dissociation. Cardiovascular collapse, sometimes fatal, can result from the effects of ethanol on the pulmonary vasculature or myocardium.[4] Consideration should be given to monitoring

of pulmonary artery pressure. A total dose of 1 mL/kg or 60 mL per procedure should not be exceeded because blood ethanol levels are directly proportional to the dose injected, regardless of technique or type of lesion.[6,7] Ethanol is most effective when it is administered without dilution. If fluoroscopic monitoring of the injections is desired, it can be mixed with oily contrast material, in a ratio of 1 to 2 mL of ethiodized oil (Ethiodol) per 10 mL of ethanol.[8]

Detergent Sclerosants

This category includes sodium tetradecyl, the most commonly used sclerosant; ethanolamine; and polydocanol. Sodium tetradecyl is not commercially available in the United States. It can be prepared in some hospital pharmacies and is available in Canada and Europe. Similar to alcohol, detergent sclerosants damage the endothelial cells and cause local intravascular coagulation. They can be opacified with water-soluble contrast medium or with oily contrast medium, to allow fluoroscopic control of the injection. Addition of air combined with mixing the solution across a three-way stopcock can result in a foam, which is believed to be a more effective sclerosant than the simple solution itself.[9] Sodium tetradecyl should not be used intra-arterially because it causes excessive arterial spasm and reflux.

Other Sclerosants

Doxycycline is available as a powder that can be suspended in saline or contrast medium and is often used for sclerotherapy of LMs.[10] Injection is painful, but the drug is relatively nontoxic and effective.

Bleomycin has been used for decades in the sclerotherapy of LMs.[11] It has some systemic side effects, including pulmonary fibrosis, hair loss, and pigmentation. The quantity of this drug used in each session must be carefully limited.

OK432 is a "superantigen" made by suspending killed streptococcus A in a solution of penicillin.[12] This agent has been shown to be effective in treating macrocystic LMs. It is not commercially available in the United States.

Intravascular use of sclerosant results in thrombosis, swelling, and hemolysis. When large amounts of sclerosants are used, hemoglobinuria frequently occurs, and renal damage must be avoided by the use of aggressive hydration and urine alkalization.

Ethibloc is a mixture of zein protein, ethanol, and contrast medium. It is used for LMs in a few centers.[13,14]

■ EMBOLIZATION OF HIGH-FLOW VASCULAR ANOMALIES

MRI is usually the best imaging modality to determine the nature and extent of a vascular malformation. Angiography is performed at the time of the embolization, to delineate the arterial supply and venous drainage of the lesion. Proximal arterial injections are performed with a guiding catheter. The catheter is positioned selectively in the supplying arteries. In most cases, a microcatheter, introduced coaxially through the guiding catheter, is used to inject the embolic material.

Hemangiomas

Hemangiomas are true vascular tumors encountered in childhood (see Chapter 113). Although they often involute, they are high-flow lesions that can cause problems in certain locations. Embolization of hemangiomas is indicated occasionally to treat high-output cardiac failure refractory to antiangiogenesis pharmacotherapy or severe bleeding, most frequently in infantile hepatic hemangiomas and rapidly involuting congenital hemangiomas, both of which tend to contain direct vascular shunts.[15,16] In the former, complete angiographic assessment of the hepatic, collateral, and portal circulation is important. Extensive portovenous fistulae are often present, making hepatic artery embolization hazardous because of the lack of a dual blood supply to the liver. Embolization of the portovenous fistulas is feasible but technically difficult. Focal hepatic hemangiomas tend to have arteriovenous shunting, and these respond well to embolization. Generally, it is best to continue to treat an infant with angiogenesis inhibitors because embolization does not always result in accelerated involution.

Arteriovenous Malformation

An AVM consists of feeding arteries, fistula or nidus, and draining veins. Occlusion of the feeding arteries alone produces a temporary decrease in flow through the malformation, but if the nidus is still present, it is reperfused through collateral vessels quickly. Unpublished data from our Vascular Anomalies Center have shown that embolization results in release of basic fibroblast growth factor, which stimulates angiogenesis. Reperfusion of the shunt from collateral arteries results in a relative worsening of the "arterial steal" from the surrounding tissue and subsequent ischemia. Some AVMs seem to become more active (increased swelling and shunting) after this type of embolization. Arterial embolization with particles, coils, and acrylic polymer (NBCA) tends to produce occlusion proximal to the nidus and does not improve the natural history of the lesion significantly. To eliminate or reduce the shunt permanently, the actual nidus must be ablated (Fig. 115-1). Ablation can be accomplished through supraselective microcatheter placement by the arterial catheterization route or by direct percutaneous puncture and injection of the nidus. Intranidal embolization requires that the tip of the microcatheter be beyond any potential branches that supply normal tissue. In many instances, the arterial branches that supply an AVM are small and tortuous, preventing sufficiently distal catheter placement. In such circumstances, direct puncture of the nidus is safer and more effective.

Preoperative AVM embolization aims to occlude selectively the arterial supply to the lesion to reduce bleeding during operative resection (see also Chapter 114). The embolic material should be chosen to occlude the most distal feeding arteries, avoiding proximal occlusion, especially with permanent devices, and avoiding embolization of normal tissue with excessively small particles. Polyvinyl alcohol particles greater than 250 μ are relatively safe in terms of avoiding damage to adjacent skin or nerves. After the flow through the AVM is interrupted by particles, more proximal occlusion of the feeding arterial trunks with Gelfoam pledgets is useful in preventing early recanalization. Coils

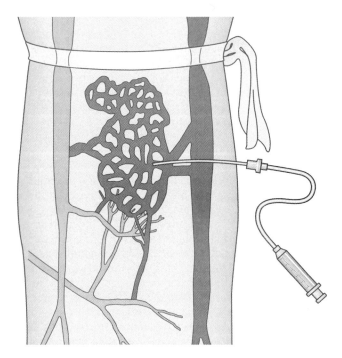

FIGURE 115-1 Diagram illustrating techniques for embolization of arteriovenous malformation. The dark lines on the left of the nidus represent results of transarterial embolization using particles or *n*-butyl-2-cyanoacrylate. The lighter channels indicate the part of the nidus that is generally not reached by these materials and must be reached by the injection of liquid agents.

should not be used for this purpose because they hinder future embolization if the patient has recurrence of the AVM. In general, surgery should be scheduled 24 to 48 hours after embolization. Control angiography to assess the completeness of embolization should be carried out in potential collateral arteries.

Primary AVM embolization usually involves a series of procedures using ablative agents, such as ethanol delivered directly into the nidus. NBCA is useful in controlling direct AVFs, but generally is less effective at penetrating the nidus than ethanol. A variety of techniques, including supraselective arterial catheterization, direct percutaneous nidal puncture, and transvenous approach, are used and often combined in the same patient. The procedures are long and tedious, and each one is limited in scope by the limited "safe" volume of alcohol and the resultant swelling. It is not unusual for a patient to undergo 20 or more of these procedures, spaced 1 or 2 months apart, each requiring general anesthesia and recovery. The cost of such treatment can be high. Each procedure carries a significant risk of complications, including skin necrosis, nerve injury, severe tissue loss, and cardiovascular collapse. Patients should be selected carefully before starting treatment.

Although no large series of long-term results of this approach has been published, I have formed some general conclusions, based on my own experience. The technique works well for AVMs with macrofistulas and a limited number of draining veins. Patients with diffuse AVMs of the limb often have a combination of macroshunts and microshunts (Fig. 115-2). Ablative embolization of the macroshunts often results in a marked improvement in pain.

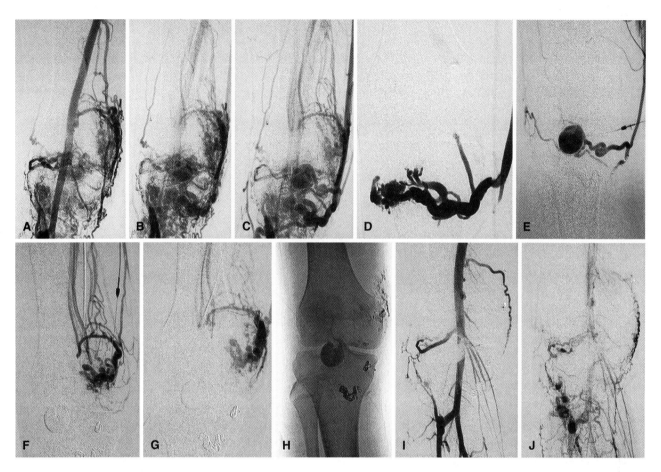

FIGURE 115-2 Schobinger stage III arteriovenous malformation (AVM) involving the right leg of a teenage boy. The steps for primary embolization using permanent liquid agents and adjunctive coils are shown. The patient had an excellent result after four embolizations carried out in two hospital visits and is now symptom-free. **A-C,** Right superficial femoral arteriogram, frontal projection, centered on the knee, shows an AVM supplied by geniculate and anterior tibial branches, draining into several large venous channels anterior to the knee and, subsequently, mainly into the saphenous system. **D,** Venogram after selective retrograde venous cannulation, using tourniquet control. This site was sclerosed with ethanol and embolized with platinum fiber microcoils. **E,** Direct injection into varix draining the anterior mid-part of the AVM. This varix, using tourniquet control, was injected with *n*-butyl-2-cyanoacrylate. **F,** Direct injection into the medial superior part of the nidus, showing venous drainage toward the femoral vein. This site was injected with ethanol. **G,** Superselective angiogram of a branch of the medial superior geniculate artery shows intranidal catheter placement, before embolization with absolute ethanol. **H,** Radiograph shows the adjunctive *n*-butyl-2-cyanoacrylate and coils in place in the main draining veins. **I** and **J,** Superficial femoral angiograms after embolization show only small amount of residual venous opacification at the inferolateral aspect of the AVM. The patient returned 1 year later and angiography was unchanged from the view shown in **J.** He remained asymptomatic.

Venous occlusion and sclerosis are effective in treating extensive AVMs with a single draining vein.[3,4,17] Pelvic AVMs often have this type of anatomy, and other authors and I have seen patients with apparent "cure" shown by 5-year angiographic follow-up (Fig. 115-3).[4] Schobinger stage I AVMs are not amenable to primary embolization because the shunts are too small for direct cannulation. Patients with Parkes Weber syndrome (diffuse high-flow vascular malformation of the limb with overgrowth) often have diffuse microshunts with cardiac volume overload. Particle embolization is ineffective in long-term control of this type of lesion. Occasionally, if the patient has focal pain related to an incompetent vein, sclerosis of the vein without arterial embolization can be effective palliation. After such procedures, patients should be given anticoagulation to prevent pulmonary embolism. Some infants with Parkes Weber syndrome present in high-output cardiac failure. Embolization of focal AVFs is helpful (Fig. 115-4).

Arteriovenous Fistulas

Direct arteriovenous communications are curable by embolotherapy if the actual shunt or the immediate draining vein is occluded with a permanent device. Congenital AVFs are uncommon and occur most frequently in the head and neck area, the spine, and the liver (Figs. 115-5 and 115-6). Some patients present with high-output cardiac failure in the newborn period, but most AVFs are detected by the presence of a pulsatile mass or bruit. Detachable balloons have been used in large AVFs but are difficult to obtain now and require large guiding catheters for deployment. Most AVFs can be occluded with either NBCA or coils. In occluding large AVFs, some type of flow control may be necessary to prevent migration of the first device. Upstream or downstream balloon catheters, venous snares, and tourniquets are examples.

Text continues on page 1658

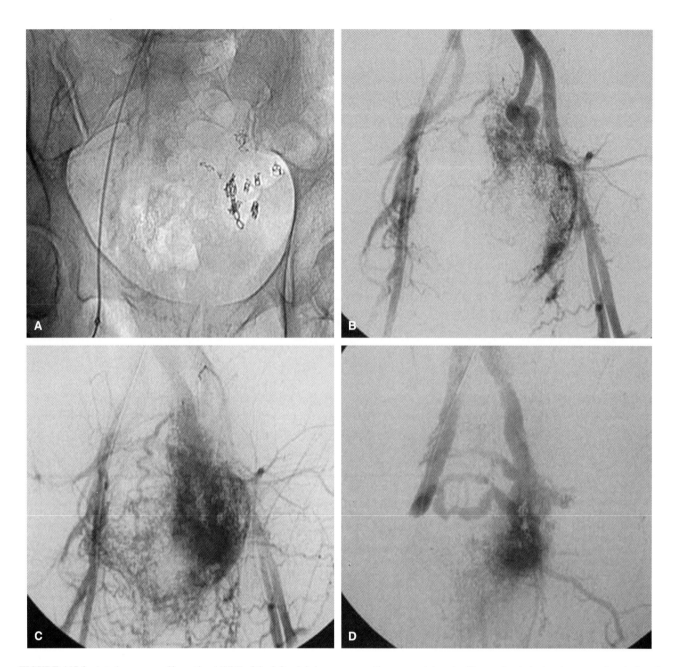

FIGURE 115-3 Arteriovenous malformation (AVM) of the left pelvis in a woman with severe pelvic pain. She previously had undergone coil and ethanol embolization of the proximal feeding arteries, resulting in severe complications, and hysterectomy to remove part of the AVM. **A,** Radiograph shows the previously placed steel coils in the proximal feeding arteries. **B-D,** Aortic bifurcation angiograms show the AVM supplied by numerous collaterals from both internal iliac arteries, but draining predominantly into the left internal iliac vein (obturator internus branch).

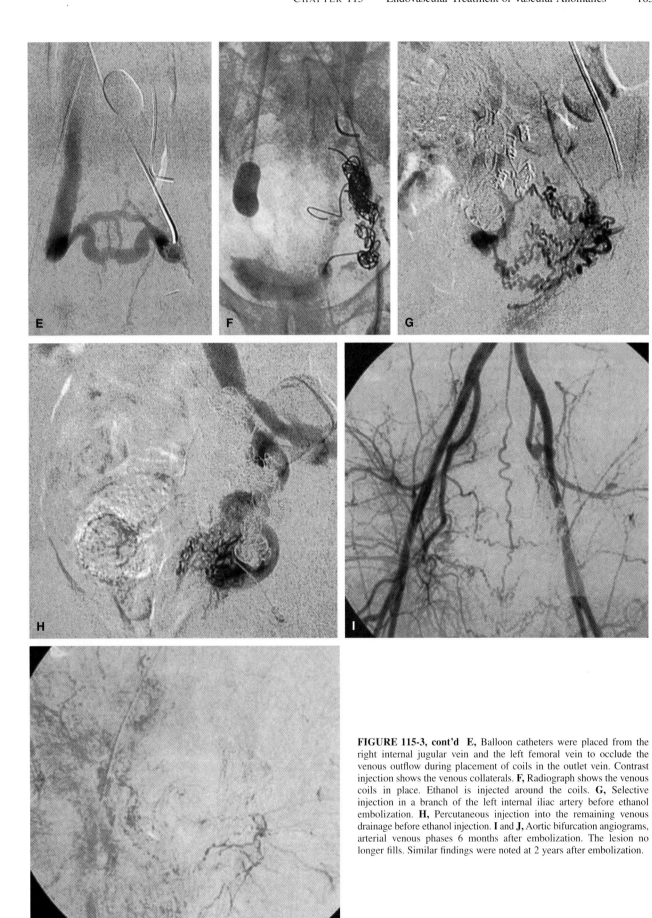

FIGURE 115-3, cont'd E, Balloon catheters were placed from the right internal jugular vein and the left femoral vein to occlude the venous outflow during placement of coils in the outlet vein. Contrast injection shows the venous collaterals. **F,** Radiograph shows the venous coils in place. Ethanol is injected around the coils. **G,** Selective injection in a branch of the left internal iliac artery before ethanol embolization. **H,** Percutaneous injection into the remaining venous drainage before ethanol injection. **I** and **J,** Aortic bifurcation angiograms, arterial venous phases 6 months after embolization. The lesion no longer fills. Similar findings were noted at 2 years after embolization.

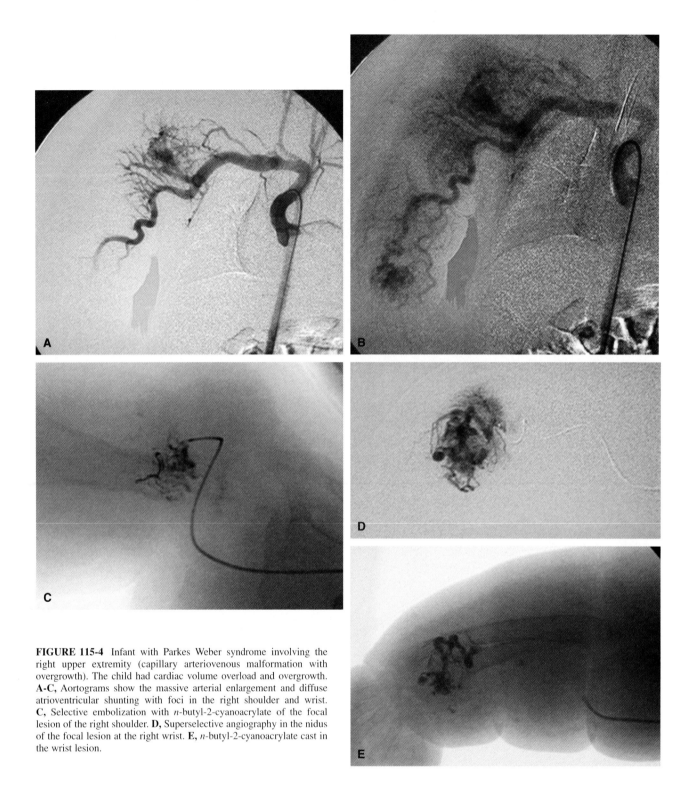

FIGURE 115-4 Infant with Parkes Weber syndrome involving the right upper extremity (capillary arteriovenous malformation with overgrowth). The child had cardiac volume overload and overgrowth. **A-C,** Aortograms show the massive arterial enlargement and diffuse atrioventricular shunting with foci in the right shoulder and wrist. **C,** Selective embolization with *n*-butyl-2-cyanoacrylate of the focal lesion of the right shoulder. **D,** Superselective angiography in the nidus of the focal lesion at the right wrist. **E,** *n*-butyl-2-cyanoacrylate cast in the wrist lesion.

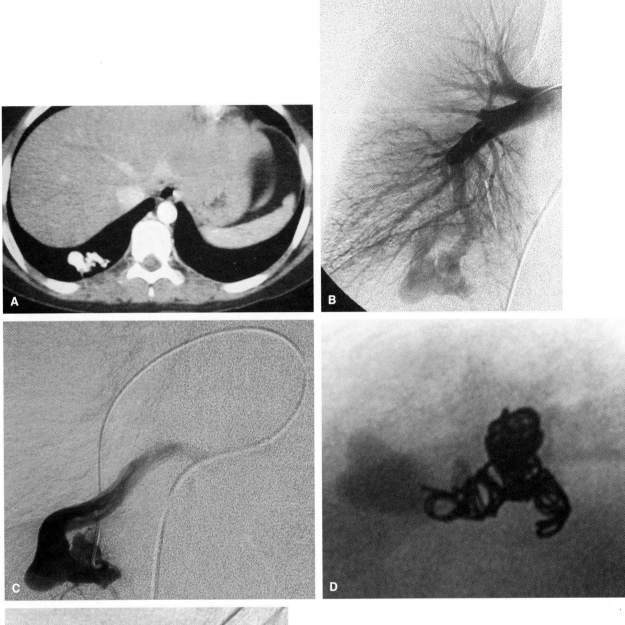

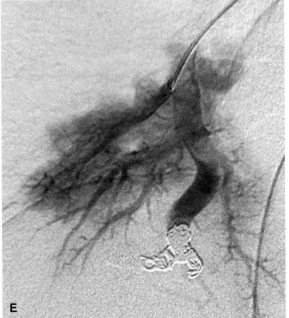

FIGURE 115-5 Pulmonary arteriovenous fistula (AVF) in a teenage boy with hereditary hemorrhagic telangiectasia. **A,** Computed tomography scan shows the AVF in the right lower lobe. **B,** Right pulmonary angiogram shows the focal AVF. **C,** Selective angiogram before coil placement shows a direct fistula with a varix of the right lower lobe pulmonary vein. **D,** Placement of nester coils in the immediate feeding arteries. **E,** Postembolization angiogram in the right lower lobe shows occlusion.

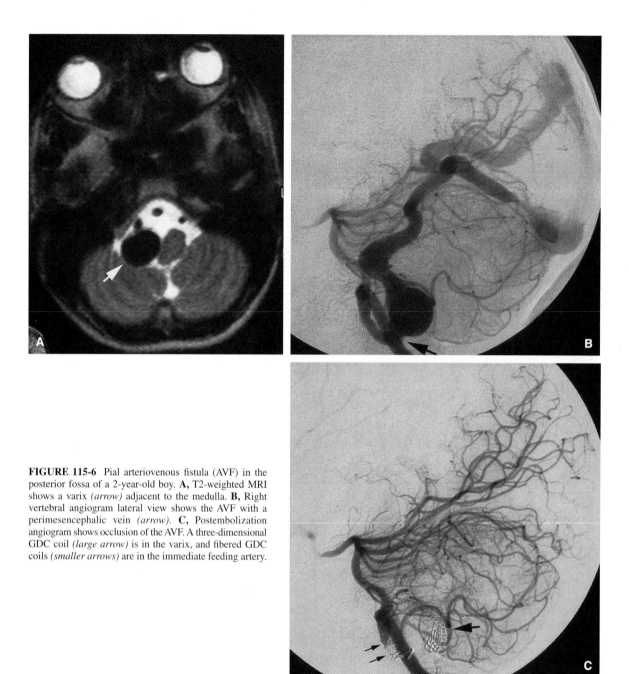

FIGURE 115-6 Pial arteriovenous fistula (AVF) in the posterior fossa of a 2-year-old boy. **A,** T2-weighted MRI shows a varix *(arrow)* adjacent to the medulla. **B,** Right vertebral angiogram lateral view shows the AVF with a perimesencephalic vein *(arrow)*. **C,** Postembolization angiogram shows occlusion of the AVF. A three-dimensional GDC coil *(large arrow)* is in the varix, and fibered GDC coils *(smaller arrows)* are in the immediate feeding artery.

■ ENDOVASCULAR TREATMENT OF LOW-FLOW VASCULAR MALFORMATIONS

Venous Malformations

VM is the most common symptomatic vascular malformation referred for treatment by interventional radiologists. The basic defect is maldevelopment of the vessel wall, especially the muscular media, resulting in abnormalities of shape and size of the affected vessels.[18] There are a large variety of morphologic types, and VMs can involve the skin, subcutaneous tissues, muscle, bone, and other tissues.[19-21] In general, VMs are focal, multifocal, or diffuse and, in terms of connection to the conducting veins, are sequestered or communicating. Clinically, VMs are soft and compressible and become distended when the affected area is dependent or when the venous outflow is obstructed. Most patients present for treatment because of progressive swelling and pain. Evaluation should include MRI, which shows the lesions as T2 hyperintense areas that enhance with contrast medium. Diffuse VMs of the lower extremity often involve the knee joint, causing repeated hemorrhage and cartilage destruction. In the latter situation, precautions must be taken to isolate the treated segments of veins, to retain the sclerosant and subsequent thrombus in the VM.

Most VMs are amenable to sclerotherapy (Figs. 115-7 and 115-8). Small, sequestered VMs are easiest to treat, but

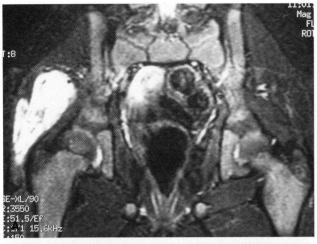

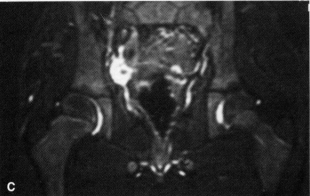

FIGURE 115-7 Focal intramuscular venous malformation of the right hip, treated by single-procedure ethanol sclerotherapy. The patient is symptom-free now. **A,** T2-weighted MRI before treatment shows a large focal venous malformation in the right gluteal muscle. **B,** Radiograph shows the opacified ethanol within the superior part of the lesion. The lower part was then treated. **C,** T2-weighted coronal MRI obtained 2 years after a single sclerotherapy procedure shows an excellent result.

diffuse lesions may benefit as well, as long as the goals of treatment are defined at the outset. Except for very focal lesions, the patient should be aware that the malformation is not curable, and the goal of treatment is to reduce the swelling, pain, and disfigurement caused by the lesion. Patients with diffuse VM and consumption coagulopathy do not respond well to sclerotherapy, unless the coagulopathy is corrected before injection. Pretreatment with low-molecular-weight heparin for 2 weeks usually results in normalization of fibrinogen and platelet levels. Infusions of cryoprecipitate may be provided during sclerotherapy, and the anticoagulation should be continued for a few days after sclerotherapy.

Sclerotherapy involves percutaneous cannulation of the vascular spaces, often using ultrasound guidance. Contrast injection is performed and recorded radiographically for several reasons: to confirm appropriate cannula placement, to rule out arterial injection, to show the venous drainage, and to estimate the volume of the lesion. In some lesions, an attempt is made to exsanguinate the VM, to reduce the volume of sclerosant needed and decrease the size of the resultant clot. The amount of sclerosant needed is estimated from the amount of contrast medium that can be injected before opacification of the draining veins. Outflow occlusion, to keep the sclerosant in the malformation, can be achieved in the limbs by using a proximal occluding tourniquet (sterile orthopedic automatic tourniquet) or by occluding the outflow veins with coils or NBCA. Variceal

masses draining to conducting veins can be sclerosed effectively with the combination of intraluminal fibered coils and sclerosant.[22] Sclerotherapy of VMs usually is performed with ethanol or sodium tetradecyl,[8,23-26] although polydocanol and ethanolamine also have been reported to be effective.[9,27,28] Sclerotherapy is associated with induration and swelling, which resolve slowly over about 6 to 8 weeks. A week-long tapered course of corticosteroids is helpful to minimize pain and swelling. Patients are advised to elevate the treated area as much as possible for a few weeks after the procedure, and patients with lesions involving the lower extremities are asked to avoid weight bearing as much as possible for 2 weeks.

Lymphatic Malformations

LMs generally are divided into macrocystic, microcystic, and mixed forms. Macrocystic forms (e.g., cystic hygroma or lymphocele) respond best or sclerotherapy, although if a cyst or channel is large enough to see by ultrasound, it can be injected, and some of these "microcystic" lesions respond nicely. In our Vascular Anomalies Center, sclerotherapy has become the preferred treatment for most macrocystic LMs (Fig. 115-9). A variety of methods exist for sclerosing LMs. The best results are achieved when the cysts are cannulated with ultrasound guidance, and intracystic fluid is aspirated before the injection of the sclerosant. Intralesional contrast

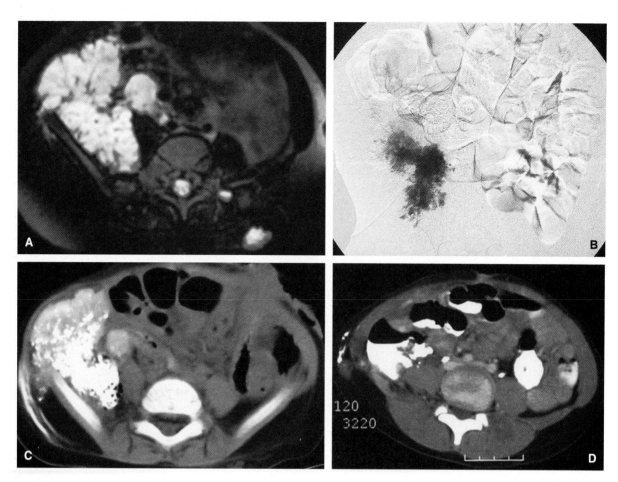

FIGURE 115-8 Infant with blue rubber bleb nevus syndrome presenting with a large abdominal mass, which recurred after resection. This mass is treated by serial injections of opacified ethanol with a good result. **A,** MRI before treatment shows a large multilocular venous malformation in the right flank and retroperitoneum. **B,** Subtracted image shows contrast injection in part of the lesion. **C,** Computed tomography scan after sclerotherapy shows opacified ethanol within the lesion. **D,** Computed tomography scan obtained 2 years after a series of sclerotherapy procedures shows obliteration of most of the malformation.

injection with fluoroscopic imaging confirms the intracystic location of the cannula, but also may result in the dilution of the sclerosant. It is preferable to aspirate the fluid and inject the sclerosant medication with continuous monitoring by ultrasound. Ultrasound monitoring is especially helpful in injecting microcysts, where fluid aspiration and contrast injection generally are not feasible or desirable. Vesicles usually are injected with sclerosant during the same procedure as treatment of a deep vascular malformation. The resulting scarring of the vesicles provides control of fluid leakage for about 1 year.

Sclerosants found to be useful in LMs include OK432, doxycycline, bleomycin, ethanol, and Ethibloc.[10-12,26,29] Extremely large lesions can be treated like lymphoceles, by placing a pigtail catheter and repeatedly injecting sclerosant until there is no further fluid drainage.

Combined Vascular Malformations

Patients with Klippel Trenaunay syndrome (capillary-lymphatic-venous malformation) often present with severe pain, orthostatic hypotension, or pulmonary emboli secondary to insufficiency of the anomalous subcutaneous veins. In the presence of pulmonary emboli, placement of an inferior vena caval filter and appropriate anticoagulation are important. The anomalous veins can be eliminated, if the patient has an adequate deep venous system. The advantage of doing this by an endovascular approach is that the extensive branches can be treated at the same time, and there is no problem with poor tissue healing, as is seen frequently after excision. Simple sclerosant injection into the channels is not effective because recanalization occurs. My technique has been to place a microcatheter into the vein and place platinum/fiber microcoils at the points of communication between the anomalous and deep veins, with sclerosant "sandwiched" between (Fig. 115-10). This technique results in permanent occlusion, and most patients have had excellent, long-lasting pain relief. Pulmonary embolization with microthrombi still can be a problem, and patients usually are given anticoagulation after the procedure. Endovascular laser ablation may prove to be a useful adjunctive procedure to miminize the amount of thrombus that results from the venous ablation. In the absence of

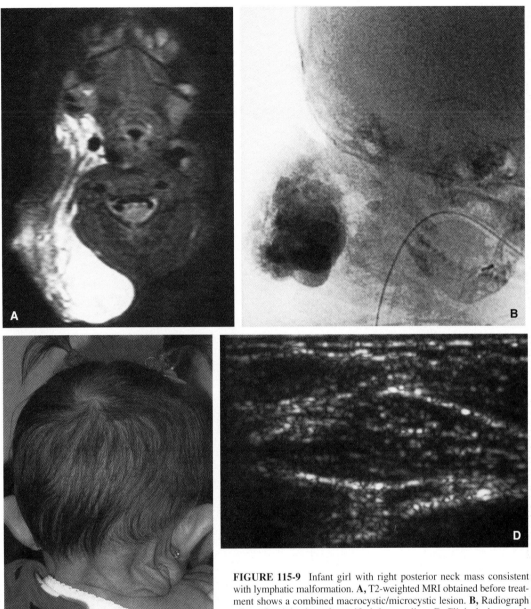

FIGURE 115-9 Infant girl with right posterior neck mass consistent with lymphatic malformation. **A,** T2-weighted MRI obtained before treatment shows a combined macrocystic/microcystic lesion. **B,** Radiograph taken after injection of opacified doxycycline. **C,** Clinical photograph taken 2 months after sclerotherapy shows complete obliteration of the mass, with residual loose skin. **D,** Ultrasound image of the neck shows no residual fluid. (See color figures in this section.)

adequate deep venous drainage, venous ablation is contraindicated or at least must be done in a selective fashion. These patients may benefit in the future by endovascular placement of valve prostheses.

■ RESULTS OF ENDOVASCULAR THERAPY

Arteriovenous Malformations

Few series of AVMs have been reported with sufficient follow-up to document a "cure" rate of *primary* endovas-

cular treatment.[4,5,17,30-32] AVMs are notorious for recurring after proximal embolization. Several reports documented initial palliation of stage III AVMs by embolization with particles and NBCA, but some patients ultimately required amputation for management of ischemic pain.[5,30] In some cases, embolization worsens the patients' symptoms, owing to the aggravation of adjacent tissue ischemia. It seems that long-term "cure" or control of some extensive AVM is possible, however.[4,31] In particular, the technique of dominant vein occlusion and sclerosis seems to be effective in obliterating AVMs. Diffuse AVMs composed of small shunts (Parkes Weber syndrome) generally do not respond well to primary embolization.

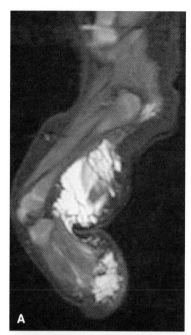

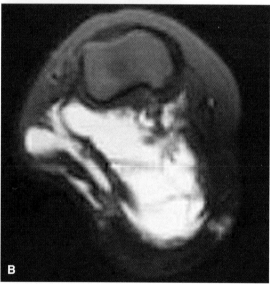

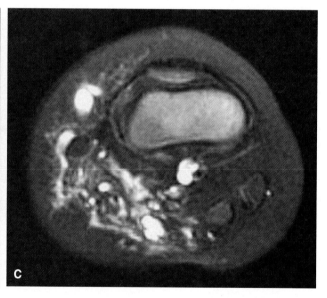

FIGURE 115-10 Infant boy with Klippel-Trenaunay syndrome (capillary-lymphatic-venous malformation), with recurring masslike swelling of the posterior thigh. He was treated with two sessions of sclerotherapy using doxycycline with an excellent result. **A,** Sagittal T2-weighted MRI shows the macrocystic lesion in the posterior thigh. **B,** Axial image shows the cysts before sclerotherapy. **C,** Axial image shows obliteration of the large cysts after two procedures.

Venous Malformations

Cure of VMs is rare because the defect involving the vein walls affects all of the veins of the affected anatomic area. Recanalization occurs after most sclerotherapy, so large lesions are treated by a series of procedures to minimize this effect. Approximately 75% to 85% of patients report excellent or good results, in terms of cosmetic improvement or relief of pain.[8,24,25,33]

Lymphatic Malformations

There are few published series reporting results of sclerotherapy for LMs except for the use of OK432, which is effective in about 80% of macrocystic lesions. It has been noted that LMs in the head and neck respond better to OK432 than LMs in the trunk or limbs. In our experience,

the results of sclerotherapy of LMs are similar to the results in VMs; most patients have good-to-excellent results. In general, large diffuse malformations require a series of endovascular procedures. Partial treatment is generally followed by recurrence.

■ COMPLICATIONS

Tissue Necrosis

Damage to skin or more extensive tissues is the most common complication of liquid embolization or sclerotherapy of vascular malformations. Approximately 10% of patients having sclerotherapy of VMs have some skin necrosis resulting in scarring. In many of these cases, such scarring is inevitable because the malformation involves the skin. Ulcers are treated with topical antibiotic ointment or polymer dressings, and most heal well, without need for surgical débridement or skin grafting. Some ulcerated lesions become infected, requiring systemic antibiotics and débridement or drainage. Ulceration is more common after AVM treatment, especially if the patient has ischemic changes before treatment. Tissue damage caused by reflux of sclerosant into nourishing arteries can be extensive, resulting in loss of digits or limbs or requiring débridement and skin grafting. Even injection into the venous component of AVM can be hazardous; sclerosant can enter the arterial circulation when the venous outflow is completely occluded, causing severe tissue damage.

Nerve Injuries

Neurologic injury can result from three mechanisms. Extravasation of ethanol around a nerve trunk can result in demyelinization and necrosis. Penetration of arteries supplying nerve trunks can result in ischemic necrosis. Severe swelling caused by intravascular sclerotherapy can cause compartment syndrome and subsequent nerve injury. Most peripheral nerve injuries recover. It is important to arrange for splinting or physical therapy or both and pain management (gabapentin [Neurontin]) during the healing phase.

Hematologic Effects

Endovascular treatment of large vascular malformations results in intravascular thrombosis and consumption of clotting factors.[34] In patients with extensive VMs, this may be significant. Although the coagulopathy usually is not symptomatic, patients should not undergo any open surgical procedures until the coagulation parameters return to normal. Patients with preexisting consumption coagulopathy can be pretreated with low-molecular-weight heparin to build up their fibrinogen stores, minimizing this complication.[35] Such patients also often require infusion of plasma or cryoprecipitate during the procedure because sclerotherapy in the presence of low fibrinogen levels is not effective.

Pulmonary Embolism

Massive pulmonary embolism is an infrequent but potentially fatal complication of embolization of malformations involving large conducting channels. Migration of microthrombi during sclerotherapy, particularly if there are multiple sessions, also can affect the pulmonary vascular reserve and result in cardiovascular collapse. In neonates, right-to-left shunting across a patent foramen ovale can cause systemic embolization, resulting in stroke or death due to myocardial infarction.

Hemoglobinuria

Hemoglobinuria is a common event secondary to hemolysis and generally is not significant if the patient is well hydrated and the urine is alkalinized. In the presence of poor hydration, hemoglobinuria can result in acute renal failure requiring hemodialysis.

■ VASCULAR BIOLOGY RESEARCH

Too little research is being done to study vascular malformations. Discoveries of genetic defects in familial vascular malformations and subsequent reproduction of the defects in transgenic animal experiments have contributed significantly to understanding of the biology of these lesions.[18,36-41] Although vascular malformations are not caused directly by abnormal angiogenesis, it seems from ongoing research in Folkman's laboratory that matrix metalloproteinases and vascular growth factors may play important roles in the evolution and symptoms of some of these lesions. It is hoped that future research will delineate methods of inhibition of these processes.

■ SUMMARY

Endovascular treatment is useful in controlling symptoms and improving appearance in patients with most types of vascular malformations, but most patients require multiple procedures, and the complication rate of such treatment is relatively high. Appropriate training, a multidisciplinary approach to patient assessment and care, and availability of general anesthesia and intensive care support are important prerequisites for treating these patients as effectively and safely as possible. As general understanding of the biology of vascular anomalies is gained, there is hope that future treatment will be gentler and more effective, aimed at vascular remodeling, rather than ablation.

■ REFERENCES

1. Mulliken JB, Glowacki J: Hemangiomas and vascular malformations in infants and children: A classification based on endothelial characteristics. Plast Reconstr Surg 69:412, 1982.
2. Kohout MP, Hansen M, Pribaz JJ, Mulliken JB: Arteriovenous malformations of the head and neck: Natural history and management. Plast Reconstr Surg 102:643, 1998.
3. Holt P, Burrows P: Interventional radiology in the treatment of vascular lesions. Fac Plast Surg Clin N Am 9:585, 2001.
4. Yakes WF, Rossi P, Odink H: Arteriovenous malformation management. Cardiovasc Interv Radiol 19:65, 1996.
5. Gomes AS: Embolization therapy of congenital arteriovenous malformations: Use of alternate approaches. Radiology 190:191, 1994.
6. Mason KP, Michna E, Zurakowski D, et al: Serum ethanol levels in children and adults after ethanol embolization or sclerotherapy for vascular anomalies. Radiology 217:127, 2000.
7. Hammer FD, Boon LM, Mathurin P, Vanwijck RR: Ethanol sclerotherapy of venous malformations: Evaluation of systemic ethanol contamination. J Vasc Interv Radiol 12:595, 2001.
8. Suh J, Shin K, Na J, et al: Venous malformations: Sclerotherapy with a mixture of ethanol and lipiodol. Cardiovasc Interv Radiol 20:268, 1997.
9. Cabrera J, Cabrera J Jr, Garcia-Olmedo MA, Redondo P: Treatment of venous malformations with sclerosant in microfoam form. Arch Dermatol 139:1409, 2003.
10. Molitch HI, Unger EC, Witte CL, van Sonnenberg E: Percutaneous sclerotherapy of lymphangiomas. Radiology 194:343, 1995.
11. Orford J, Barker A, Thonell S, et al: Bleomycin therapy for cystic hygroma. J Pediatr Surg 30:1282, 1995.
12. Giguere CM, Bauman NM, Sato Y, et al: Treatment of lymphangiomas with OK-432 (Picibanil) sclerotherapy: A prospective multi-institutional trial. Arch Otolaryngol Head Neck Surg 128:1137, 2002.

13. Dubois JM, Sebag GH, De Prost Y, et al: Soft-tissue venous malformations in children: Percutaneous sclerotherapy with ethibloc. Radiology 180:195, 1991.

14. Dubois J, Garel L, Abela A, et al: Lymphangiomas in children: Percutaneous sclerotherapy with an alcoholic solution of zein. Radiology 204:651, 1997.

15. Konez O, Burrows PE, Mulliken JB, et al: Angiographic features of rapidly involuting congenital hemangioma (RICH). Pediatr Radiol 33:15, 2003.

16. Burrows PE, Dubois J, Kassarjian A: Pediatric hepatic vascular anomalies. Pediatr Radiol 31:533, 2001.

17. Jackson JE, Mansfield AO, Allison DJ: Treatment of high-flow vascular malformations by venous embolization aided by flow occlusion techniques. Cardiovasc Interv Radiol 19:323, 1996.

18. Vikkula M, Boon LM, Mulliken JB: Molecular genetics of vascular malformations. Matrix Biol 20:327, 2001.

19. Claudon M, Upton J, Burrows PE: Diffuse venous malformations of the upper limb: Morphologic characterization by MRI and venography. Pediatr Radiol 31:507, 2001.

20. Enjolras O, Ciabrini D, Mazoyer E, et al: Extensive pure venous malformations in the upper or lower limb: A reveiw of 27 cases. J Am Acad Dermatol 36:219, 1997.

21. Burrows P, Laor T, Paltiel H, Robertson R: Diagnostic imaging in the evaluation of vascular birthmarks. Pediatr Dermatol 19:455, 1998.

22. Furst SR, Burrows PE, Holzman RS: General anesthesia in a child with a dynamic, vascular anterior mediastinal mass. Anesthesiology 84:976, 1996.

23. deLorimier A: Sclerotherapy for venous malformations. J Pediatr Surg 30:188, 1995.

24. Berenguer B, Burrows PE, Zurakowski D, Mulliken JB: Sclerotherapy of craniofacial venous malformations: Complications and results. Plast Reconstr Surg 104:1, 1999.

25. Donnelly LF, Bissett GS 3rd, Adams DM: Combined sonographic and fluoroscopic guidance: A modified technique for percutaneous sclerosis of low-flow vascular malformations. AJR Am J Roentgenol 173:655, 1999.

26. Lee BB, Bergan JJ: Advanced management of congenital vascular malformations: A multidisciplinary approach. Cardiovasc Surg 10:523, 2002.

27. Jain R, Bandhu S, Sawhney S, Mittal R: Sonographically guided percutaneous sclerosis using 1% polidocanol in the treatment of vascular malformations. J Clin Ultrasound 30:416, 2002.

28. Choi YH, Han MH, O-Ki K, et al: Craniofacial cavernous venous malformations: Percutaneous sclerotherapy with use of ethanolamine oleate. J Vasc Interv Radiol 13:475, 2002.

29. Burrows P, Fellows K: Techniques for management of pediatric vascular anomalies. In Cope C (ed): Current Techniques in Interventional Radiology, 2nd ed. Philadelphia, Current Science, 1995, p 11.

30. Dickey KW, Pollak JS, Meier GH III, et al: Management of large high-flow arteriovenous malformations of the shoulder and upper extremity with transcatheter embolotherapy. J Vasc Interv Radiol 6:765, 1995.

31. Yakes WF, Krauth L, Ecklund J, et al: Ethanol endovascular management of brain arteriovenous malformations: Initial results. Neurosurgery 40:1145, 1997.

32. Yakes WF, Luethke JM, Merland JJ, et al: Ethanol embolization of arteriovenous fistulas: A primary mode of therapy. J Vasc Interv Radiol 1:89, 1990.

33. Lee BB, Do YS, Byun HS, et al: Advanced management of venous malformation with ethanol sclerotherapy: Mid-term results. J Vasc Surg 37:533, 2003.

34. Mason KP, Neufeld EJ, Karian VE, et al: Coagulation abnormalities in pediatric and adult patients after sclerotherapy or embolization of vascular anomalies. AJR Am J Roentgenol 177:1359, 2001.

35. Mazoyer E, Enjolras O, Laurian C, et al: Coagulation abnormalities associated with extensive venous malformations of the limbs: Differentiation from Kasabach-Merritt syndrome. Clin Lab Haematol 24:243, 2002.

36. Abbruzzese TA, Guzman RJ, Martin RL, et al: Matrix metalloproteinase inhibition limits arterial enlargements in a rodent arteriovenous fistula model. Surgery 124:328, 1998.

37. Abdalla SA, Geisthoff UW, Bonneau D, et al: Visceral manifestations in hereditary haemorrhagic telangiectasia type 2. J Med Genet 40:494, 2003.

38. Adams RH, Wilkinson GA, Weiss C, et al: Roles of ephrinB ligands and EphB receptors in cardiovascular development: Demarcation of arterial/venous domains, vascular morphogenesis, and sprouting angiogenesis. Genes Dev 13:295, 1999.

39. Dolgilevich SM, Siri FM, Atlas SA, Eng C: Changes in collagenase and collagen gene expression after induction of aortocaval fistula in rats. Am J Physiol Heart Circ Physiol 281:H207, 2001.

40. Zhou XP, Marsh DJ, Hampel H, et al: Germline and germline mosaic PTEN mutations associated with a Proteus-like syndrome of hemihypertrophy, lower limb asymmetry, arteriovenous malformations and lipomatosis. Hum Mol Genet 9:765, 2000.

41. Li DY, Sorensen LK, Brooke BS, et al: Defective angiogenesis in mice lacking endoglin. Science 284:1534, 1999.

Primary Tumors of Major Blood Vessels:

Diagnosis and Management

116

W. ANDREW OLDENBURG, MD, FACS

Primary tumors originating in the wall of large arteries and veins are extremely rare. W. Brodowski[1] described the first case of a primary aortic tumor in 1873. By 2002, only 111 primary aortic tumors had been described in the world literature (Table 116-1). The most common artery involved has been the aorta, but primary arterial tumors have been reported to occur in the iliac,[2] subclavian,[3] carotid,[4,5] renal,[6] splenic,[7] and popliteal[8] arteries. These tumors begin insidiously, frequently mimicking other disease processes and resulting in delays in diagnosis and poor outcomes.

This chapter deals predominantly with primary tumors originating in the walls of large arteries. For information on primary tumors involving the large veins, especially the vena cava, see Chapter 163.

■ CLASSIFICATION OF PRIMARY ARTERIAL TUMORS

Theoretically, any cellular components of the artery wall can undergo malignant degeneration, although the majority of vascular tumors described in the literature have been mesenchymal in origin. Major arteries can be either pri-

marily or secondarily involved by tumor. More commonly, spread of other malignancies—gynecologic, head and neck, pulmonary, musculoskeletal, colon, and rectal cancers—affect arteries secondarily. Most primary tumors of large arteries have occurred de novo, although several cases have been noted to occur after polyester grafting.[9-13] Experimentally, polyester has been shown to induce tumor formation in animal models.[14,15] With so few cases being reported in humans, however, a coincidental rather than causal relationship is suggested.

Various classification schemes of aortic tumors have been described (Table 116-2). In 1972, Salm[16] described three distinct morphologic types of primary aortic tumors: intraluminal, intimal, and adventitial. Polypoid or intraluminal tumors, such as myxomas, have a focal attachment to the intimal surface, with most of the growth extending into the lumen of the vessel (Fig. 116-1). Because of their projections into the lumen of the artery, tumor embolization is common. Intimal tumors grow along the endothelial surface of the aorta with less pronounced projections into the lumen, leading to large branch vessel occlusion. As the name implies, *adventitial aortic tumors* originate in the media or adventitia and grow outward, invading surrounding

Table 116-1 Primary Aortic Tumors: Review of the Literature 1873 to 2002 (n = 111)

HISTOLOGY	NO. CASES	% MALE	THORACIC	ABDOMINAL	THORACOABDOMINAL	METASTASES (%)	% INTIMAL
Sarcoma	33	67	15	17	1	16 (49)	94
Malignant fibrous histiocytoma	17	59	11	5	1	11 (65)	41
Angiosarcoma	17	71	5	12	0	10 (59)	82
Leiomyosarcoma	13	39	6	5	2	11 (85)	39
Fibrosarcoma	9	67	4	5	0	6 (67)	67
Myxoma	4	50	3	0	1	2 (50)	75
Fibromyxosarcoma	3	67	1	1	1	1 (33)	100
Hemangiopericytoma	2	50	2	0	0	1 (50)	0
Hemangioendothelioma	3	67	2	1	0	3 (100)	67
Malignant endothelioma	2	100	2	0	0	2 (100)	100
Aortic intimal sarcoma	2	100	0	0	2	2 (100)	100
Myxoid chondrosarcoma	1	100	0	1	0	1 (100)	100
Myxosarcoma	1	100	0	0	1	0 (0)	100
Myxomatous endothelioma	1	100	0	1	0	0 (0)	100
Endotheliosarcoma	1	100	1	0	0	0 (0)	100
Fibromyxoma	1	0	0	0	1	1 (100)	100
Fibroxanthosarcoma	1	0	1	0	0	1 (100)	0
Totals	111	63	53	48	10	67 (60.3)	72

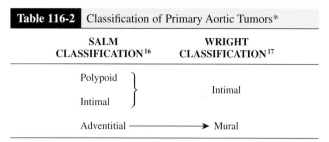

Table 116-2	Classification of Primary Aortic Tumors*

SALM CLASSIFICATION[16]	WRIGHT CLASSIFICATION[17]
Polypoid ⎫ ⎬	Intimal
Intimal ⎭	
Adventitial ⟶	Mural

*Superscript numbers indicate chapter references.

structures. Wright and colleagues[17] simplified this classification in 1985 by combining the polypoid and intimal groups into intimal tumors and labeling adventitial tumors as mural tumors. More than 70% of primary aortic tumors are of the intimal type, with roughly equal distribution throughout the aorta (see Table 116-1).

In the past, histopathologic diagnosis of primary arterial tumors was based on gross appearance as well as light and electron microscopic findings. Frequently, these tumors are so advanced and so poorly differentiated as to make the appropriate histopathologic diagnosis difficult. Historically, this fact has led to a confusing array of pathologic diagnoses, as seen in Table 116-1. Today, with the advent of immunohistochemistry, the pathologic classification of arterial tumors is more precise. Vascular endothelial antigenic stains to von Willebrand factor (vWF), clusters of differentiation CD31 and CD34, and *Ulex europeas* agglutinin 1(UEA-1), in association with an atypical spindle cell morphology would be suggestive of angiosarcoma and intimal sarcomas. Positive antigenic staining for desmin, smooth muscle actin, and vimentin would suggest leiomyosarcoma. Metastatic lesions can be ruled out by the absence of immunohisto-

chemical staining for S100 protein and HMB-45 (melanoma); chromogranin, synaptophysin, and neuron-specific enolase (neuroendocrine tumors); carcinoembryonic antigen and epithelial membrane antigen (epithelial tumors); and CD20, CD30, CD43, and CD99 (hematolymphoid tumors).

■ DIAGNOSIS

Because of the rarity of these tumors as well as the fact that the arteries involved are centrally located, the diagnosis is difficult and frequently delayed. Less than 5% of all primary aortic tumors have been diagnosed preoperatively. Metastatic disease is identified in 60% of patients at the time of initial diagnosis (see Table 116-1). Hence, the majority of patients complain of nonspecific symptoms such as malaise, fatigue, weight loss, and nausea. Patients with intimally based tumors commonly present with symptoms from tumor embolization, such as blue toe syndrome, acutely ischemic arm or leg, and acute renal or mesenteric ischemia. The diagnosis is commonly made after pathologic review of an embolectomy specimen, underscoring the need for routine histologic analysis of all embolectomy material. Despite this recommendation, fewer than 70 cases of nonmyxomatous arterial tumor emboli have been described in the literature.[18] Primary arterial tumors have also been mistaken or mistakenly diagnosed at the time of vascular reconstruction for what was thought to be an atherosclerotic process,[19] an aortic aneurysm,[20] an aortic psuedoaneurysm,[21] or an aortic dissection.[22,23]

Conventional arterial imaging such as ultrasonography, computed tomography, and arteriography can detect intraluminal filling defects but cannot characterize and differentiate between a degenerative or thrombotic process and a malignancy. Being invasive, arteriography also carries

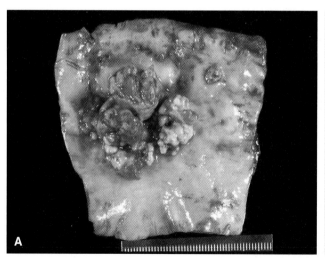

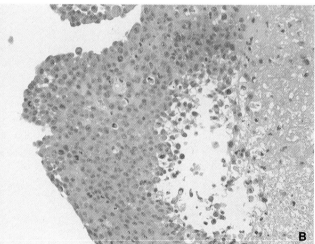

FIGURE 116-1 **A,** Macroscopic appearance of a polypoid intimally based sarcoma of the thoracic aorta. **B,** Histologic section demonstrating a high-grade pleomorphic epithelioid neoplasm with irregular nuclei consistent with an intimal sarcoma.

the risk of potentially precipitating tumor embolization, especially in patients with intimally based tumors. Primary intimal sarcoma of the aorta has been diagnosed on transesophageal echocardiography (TEE) on the basis of the identification of an inhomogeneous and echodense mass with an outer membrane that was atypical for thrombus.[24] Magnetic resonance imaging (MRI) may well be the most sensitive modality for detecting a primary aortic tumor. MRI has the advantage of providing multiplanar structure imaging, which can differentiate tumor from atheromatous material through enhancement of the tumor on T1-weighted and T2-weighted images without the risk of embolization (Fig. 116-2).[25]

Arterial tumors may manifest in two clinically relevant scenarios, as follows: (1) the patient presents with evidence of embolization, the etiology of which is unknown and (2) the patient has undergone an embolectomy and the pathologic examination shows tumor. In both scenarios, the source of embolization is unknown. For this reason, a systematic approach to identifying the culprit lesion should be carried out, starting with noninvasive imaging proximally in the arterial tree and moving distally. This would include TEE to exclude a cardiac source and to visualize the ascending and descending aorta, followed by MRI of the thoracic and abdominal aorta to visualize the areas not well seen by the TEE. If a source is not identified in the heart or thoracic or abdominal aorta, an arteriogram, preferably from the axillary-brachial approach, is performed to visualize the vessels below the iliac bifurcation and to avoid the risk of causing further embolization (Fig. 116-3).

■ TREATMENT

If a discrete lesion is found by the evaluation and the patient is a good surgical candidate, resection of the mass is the treatment of choice. This typical requires resection of the involved artery or aorta with interposition grafting. Endarterectomy of intimally based tumors has been described with free margins.[26] However, if the patient is known to have an arterial tumor, aortic or arterial resection is the appropriate treatment.

The patient who has a diffuse aortic process of unknown etiology presents a therapeutic dilemma. The treatment in such a patient, regardless of whether the process is atherosclerotic or neoplastic, is usually palliative. Unfortunately, because more than 70% of all aortic tumors are intimally based, tumor embolization has commonly occurred by the time the diagnosis has been made. In fact, metastatic disease is found in near 60% of patients, located primarily in the bone (29%), the kidneys (27%), the liver (24%), the adrenal glands (20%), or the lungs (15%).[26] Consequently, the prognosis for primary aortic tumors is poor. When the diagnosis is made before death, the mean survival is only 14 months.[26] The role of chemotherapy and radiation therapy in the treatment of these tumors is unknown, although as a general rule, sarcomas have not been very receptive to these treatment modalities. In light of the poor response to chemotherapy and radiation therapy, primary resection of the tumor is recommended in the absence of identifiable metastatic disease.

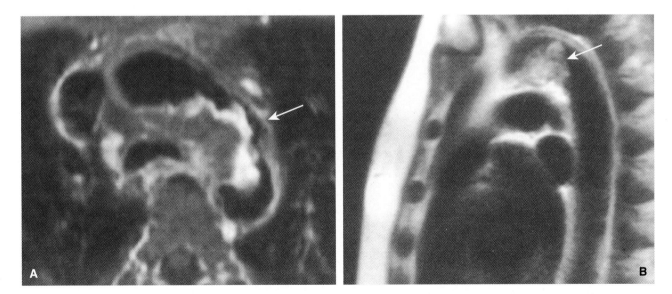

FIGURE 116-2 Magnetic resonance imaging (MRI) of an intimal sarcoma of the thoracic aorta. **A,** Axial gadolinium-enhanced, fat-saturated, T1-weighted spin-echo MR image demonstrating peripheral enhancement. **B,** Half-Fourier acquisition, single-shot, turbo spin-echo MR image showing high T2 signal within the mass. (Modified and reproduced with permission from Mohsen NA, Haber M, Urrutia VC, Nunes LW: Intimal sarcoma of the aorta. AJR Am J Roentgenol 175:1289-1290, 2000.)

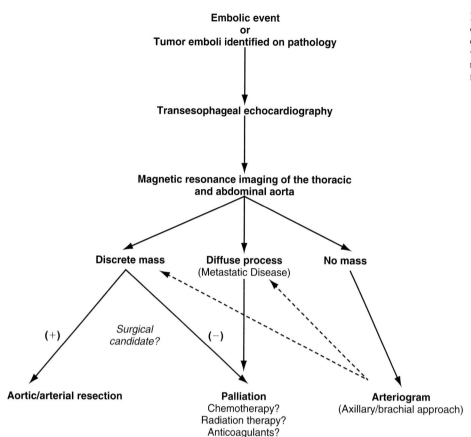

FIGURE 116-3 Algorithm for evaluation of a patient who presents with evidence of embolization of the thoracic aorta or in whom embolectomy and pathologic evaluation identify tumor emboli. (+), positive finding; (−), negative finding.

■ REFERENCES

1. Brodowski W: Primares sarkom der aorta thoracica mit verbreitung des neugebildes in der unteren Korperhalfte. Jahresb Leistung Fortschr ges Med 8:243-246, 1873.
2. Weickert U, Puschel W, Langenscheidt P, Remberger K: Intimal sarcoma of the left iliac artery. Histopathology 33:286-287, 1998.
3. Novak K, Hajek M, Pesek M, Chudacek Z: Successful surgical treatment of the brachial plexus paresis in leiomyosarcoma of the subclavian artery. Int Surg 84:78-80, 1999.
4. Mikami Y, Manabe T, Lie JT, et al: Intramural sarcoma of the carotid artery with adventitial inflammation and fibrosis resembling 'inflammatory aneurysm'. Pathol Int 47:569-574, 1997.
5. Whyte R, Joseph M, Bennett W, et al: Angiosarcoma of the carotid artery: A case report. Head Neck Surg 10:264-268, 1988.
6. Gill IS, Hobart MG, Kaouk JH, et al: Leiomyosarcoma of the main renal artery treated by laparoscopic radical nephrectomy. Urology 56:669, 2000.
7. Rohde H, Riesener K, Buttner R, Schumpelick V: Leiomyosarcoma of the splenic artery [German]. Chirurg 72:844-6, 2001.
8. Kogon B, Kabeer M, Sawchuk AP, et al: Angiosarcoma presenting as an occluded popliteal artery pseudoaneurysm. J Vasc Surg 27:970-973, 1998.
9. Burns A, Kanhoun S, Tillman L, et al: Fibrosarcoma occurring at the site of a plastic vascular graft. Cancer 29:66-72, 1972.
10. O'Connell T, Fee H, Golding A: Sarcoma associated with Dacron prosthetic material. J Thorac Cardiovasc Surg 72:94-96, 1976.
11. Fehrenbacher J, Bowers W, Strate R, Pittman J: Angiosarcoma of the aorta associated with a Dacron graft. Ann Thorac Surg 32:297-301, 1981.
12. Weinberg D, Maini B: Primary sarcoma of the aorta associated with a vascular prosthesis: A case report. Cancer 46:398-402, 1980.
13. Weiss W, Riles T, Gouge T, Mizrachi H: Angiosarcoma at the site of a Dacron vascular prosthesis: A case report and literature review. J Vasc Surg 14:87-91, 1991.

14. Oppenheimer B, Oppenheimer E, Stout A: Sarcomas induced in rats by implanting cellophane. Proc Soc Exp Biol Med 67:33-4, 1948.
15. Oppenheimer B, Oppenheimer E, Stout A, et al: The latent period in carcinogenesis by plastics in rats and its relation to the presarcomatous stage. Cancer 11:204-12, 1958.
16. Salm R: Primary fibrosarcoma of aorta. Cancer 29:73-83, 1972.
17. Wright E, Glick A, Virmani R, Page D: Aortic intimal sarcoma with embolic metastases. Am J Surg Pathol 9:890-897, 1985.
18. Morasch M, Shanik G: Tumor embolus: A case report and review of the literature. Ann Vasc Surg 17:210-213, 2003.
19. Ghanem N, Riede U, Uhrmeister P, et al: Epithelioid angiosarcoma of the aorta. Vasa 31:269-273, 2002.
20. Miracco C, Laurini L, Santopietro R, et al: Intimal-type primary sarcoma of the aorta: Report of a case with evidence of rhabdomyosarcomatous differentiation [comment]. Virchows Archiv 435:62-66, 1999.
21. Neri E, Miracco C, Luzi P, et al: Intimal-type primary sarcoma of the thoracic aorta presenting as a saccular false aneurysm: Report of a case with evidence of rhabdomyosarcomatous differentiation. J Thorac Cardiovasc Surg 118:371-372, 1999.
22. Szekely E, Kulka J, Miklos I, Kaliszky P: Leiomyosarcomas of great vessels. Pathol Oncol Res 6:233-236, 2000.
23. Yasuda T, Yamamoto S, Yamaguchi S, Ishida Y: Leiomyosarcoma of the thoracic aorta. Jpn J Thorac Cardiovasc Surg 47:510-513, 1999.
24. Rhee M, Myong N, Park Y: Primary intimal sarcoma of the aorta: Role of transesophageal echocardiography. Circulation 66:111-113, 2002.
25. Mohsen NA, Haber M, Urrutia VC, Nunes LW: Intimal sarcoma of the aorta. AJR Am J Roentgenol 175:1289-1290, 2000.
26. Seelig MH, Klingler PJ, Oldenburg WA, Blackshear JL: Angiosarcoma of the aorta: Report of a case and review of the literature. J Vasc Surg 28:732-737, 1998.

ARTERIOVENOUS HEMODIALYSIS ACCESS

ANTON N. SIDAWY, MD, MPH

Strategies of Arteriovenous Dialysis Access

JONATHAN M. WEISWASSER, MD
ANTON N. SIDAWY, MD, MPH

With the ever-increasing longevity of the population and physicians' improving ability to treat end-stage renal disease, insertion of vascular access is becoming one of the most common procedures performed by a typical vascular surgeon. Similar to many procedures in our specialty, the type, location, and longevity of long-term vascular access has been extensively studied and subjected to practice guidelines based on "evidence-based" outcomes and longevity studies. The Kidney Dialysis Outcomes Quality Initiative (DOQI),[1] as published by the National Kidney Foundation, set forth recommendations as part of a national consensus that practitioners avoid percutaneous catheter–based arteriovenous (AV) hemodialysis access in favor of autogenous access (AA), followed by prosthetic access (PA) as a second preference. With vascular access complications accounting for 15% of hospital admissions among hemodialysis patients[2,3] and Medicare costs approximating $182 million in 2000,[3] the population of patients requiring hemodialysis access is expected to increase by 10% per year from a group that exceeded 345,000 patients in 2000.[4]

The multidisciplinary approach to a patient who may require AV access affords the clinical team the ability to anticipate access need and allow for time for maturation of an AA. The current DOQI recommendations for practice patterns is the insertion of an AA in 50% of long-term access patients; however, some centers have had trouble achieving this goal as a result of vein mapping results or availability of forearm basilic vein.[5] The DOQI guidelines–recommended surgical referral pattern should begin when a patient exhibits a creatinine clearance of less than 25 mL/min or a serum creatinine of greater than 4 mg/dL or when AV access is anticipated within 1 year.[1] This interval allows for evalua-

tion, placement, maturation, and possible revision without the need for catheter insertion in the most ideal circumstance. Although this interval may be ideal, however, it is often not the case, and late presentation to a dialysis unit is associated with increased mortality and increased need for temporary vascular access.[6] Additionally the primary AA requires 3 months to "mature" before cannulation and is the primary access of choice.

■ STRATEGIES OF ACCESS LOCATION

The timing of hemodialysis dictates the type of initial access. This decision can be divided into acute, semiacute, and long-term access techniques. Often, as in a patient in whom initial access has failed and who is presently hemodialysis dependent, access is obtained by insertion of a catheter synchronous with a form of long-term access so that the patient may undergo hemodialysis while the access matures.

Acute Access Location and Strategy

For patients who require immediate dialysis access, which for the purposes of this discussion are patients who require hemodialysis of less than 3 weeks' duration, a double-lumen cuffed or noncuffed catheter should be inserted into the femoral, internal jugular, or subclavian vein.[7] The most common catheter for this purpose is the Quinton catheter, which can be placed at the bedside and must be able to support a flow rate of 250 mL/min.[8] When catheterization of the femoral vein is employed, the catheter should remain for no more than 5 days, given the high propensity for infection and dislodgment with ambulation.[9] Most importantly, the subclavian position should be avoided if the patient is to be considered for an ipsilateral arm access procedure because the incidence of subclavian stenosis or thrombosis or both increases steadily with the presence of a catheter in this position, rendering the extremity useless for insertion of a permanent access.[10-12]

Semiacute Access Location and Strategy

In a situation in which the patient would require hemodialysis for more than 3 weeks' duration, insertion of a cuffed, tunneled, double-lumen catheter should be considered. These catheters also may be employed in situations in which the patient has exhausted all other options for long-term access or in whom hemodialysis is required while an AA matures. Preference of location mirrors that of an acutely placed catheter: The internal jugular vein is preferred because of its proximity to the atrial-caval junction (allowing for better flow), but with the added emphasis of placing the catheter in the right internal jugular vein because this is associated with fewer complications compared with other insertion sites.[13,14] Insertion into the left internal jugular vein is associated with an increased rate of stenosis and thrombosis and inadequate flow rates.[15,16]

In contrast to a noncuffed temporary bedside catheter, a cuffed catheter must be inserted in a fluoroscopically capable operating room or interventional suite. Although noncuffed catheters can be inserted using Seldinger technique, cuffed catheters are constructed of a softer Silastic material and must be placed by means of a larger "breakaway" introducer catheter. Some surgeons prefer to insert these catheters using venous cutdown with insertion through a venotomy; however, this may sacrifice distal vasculature for use in a later autogenous or prosthetic access and is discouraged.

Aside from complications associated with insertion (hemothorax and pneumothorax), the tunneled cuffed catheter can be relied on to function for an average of 6 months, after which infection, fibrin sheath formation, or thrombosis may curtail usage.[17] Using endoluminal therapy or percutaneous mechanical techniques, Suchoki and colleagues[18] were able to prolong average catheter patency to 12.7 months. Local infection and sepsis[17] and infection elsewhere[19] are typical reasons for removal of the catheter.

Strategies of Location and Type of Access

Preoperative Evaluation

Before consideration of any long-term access procedure, a thorough history and physical examination should be performed. Aspects of prior history, other than typical items of interest to the surgeon, should include type and location of *any indwelling catheters,* even subsequent to removal, given the association with deep vein stenosis[10,20]; this includes any history of transvenous pacemaker or internal automatic cardiac defibrillator. The surgeon should also evaluate the patient for congestive heart failure or diabetes,

Table 117-1	Indications of Venous Imaging Before Access Insertion

Edema in the extremity in which an access is planned
Collateral vein development in any planned access site
Differential extremity size of the considered limb
Current or previous transvenous catheter, of any type, in the ipsilateral limb
Previous arm, neck, or chest trauma or surgery in venous drainage of planned access site
Multiple previous accesses in the ipsilateral extremity

Adapted from NKF-K/DOQI Clinical practice guidelines for vascular access: Update 2000. Am J Kidney Dis 37:S137-S181, 2001.

which can adversely affect autogenous or prosthetic access hemodynamics or can render distal AA a dismal patency rate. The surgeon should make note of the patient's dominant extremity and whether the extremity has endured penetrating trauma or recent catheter insertion.[21,22]

The assessment of the vasculature in the chosen limb should include palpation of pulses at all levels and an Allen test, which, if abnormal, may contraindicate a distal AA. The blood pressure of both upper extremities should be measured and compared for difference, indicating more proximal arterial disease. Special attention is given to the status and adequacy of the veins of the hand, wrist, forearm, elbow, and upper arm. A vein is considered adequate if it is visible through the skin with or without a tourniquet applied.[27] In instances in which a prior access has failed, imaging of the arterial or venous system may be necessary to plan a procedure adequately. Table 117-1 lists the indications for preoperative venography. The use of venous duplex examination may suffice as long as the surgeon recognizes the limitations of the study to detect proximal deep vein stenoses[23] and the technician dependency.[24,25] An added advantage of injection venography is the ability to correct underlying lesions that are amenable to such therapy before the access placement.[26] Lesions that cannot be corrected should disqualify the limb as a potential access site.

Site and Type Access Selection

Along with increased ability to manage patients with end-stage renal disease successfully comes longevity and the possibility of multiple access procedures. In a study of 466 access procedures (autogenous and prosthetic), Kalman and associates[27] showed a cumulative overall patency (including primary, assisted primary, and secondary success) rate of 66% at 2 years. The primary patency rate at 2 years was only 36% (Fig. 117-1). As such, the ability to preserve the limb for future access placement is paramount, while providing the patient with an access with a generous long-term patency. Preference is given to the *nondominant arm* over the dominant arm, followed by *distal location before proximal location.* A nondominant upper arm PA is preferred over a dominant arm AA. Because AA is ascribed a better long-term patency rate, it is strongly preferred over PA when possible. Some controversy exists in situations in which type of access conflicts with proximity, such as prosthetic brachial-antecubital forearm loop access versus an

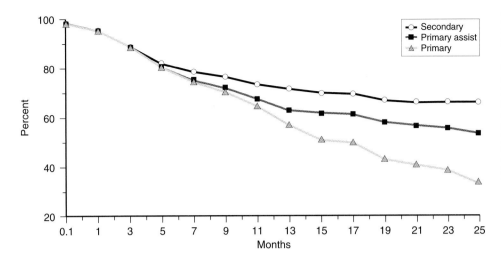

FIGURE 117-1 Cumulative primary (12 months, n = 162; 24 months, n = 53), primary-assisted (12 months, n = 162; 24 months, n = 55), and secondary success (patent and effective dialysis) (12 months, n = 162; 24 months, n = 72) for all 466 vascular access procedures combined (only data with a standard error <10% are shown). (From Kalman PG, Pope M, Bhola C, et al: A practical approach to vascular access for hemodialysis and predictors of success. J Vasc Surg 30:727-733, 1999.)

autogenous brachial-cephalic upper arm direct access in a patient who already has failed more distal accesses. In this situation, although the AA may entitle a better patency overall, its creation may eliminate the option of ipsilateral PA placement because of obliteration of venous runoff, whereas the converse may not be so.

■ STRATEGIES OF AUTOGENOUS ACCESS CREATION

The first autogenous access creation for the purposes of hemodialysis access was the Brescia-Cimino radiocephalic direct wrist access in 1966.[28] Overall, the AA affords a superior patency of 75% at 4 years, yet has a higher rate of early failure.[29] Although the AA carries a better patency rate when established, it must be allowed to mature for approximately 6 to 8 weeks, occasionally longer, and may require the patient to undergo insertion of a percutaneous catheter for hemodialysis if referral for creation of the fistula was not timely. In addition, results of AA creation have been associated with poor results in certain subsets of patients, such as diabetics or women who underwent forearm AA or in older patients.[30] The AA carries a much lower rate of complications compared with the PA,[31-33] however, and adequate flows are more easily attainable.

Autogenous Posterior Radial Branch–Cephalic Direct Access

The autogenous posterior radial branch–cephalic direct access (*snuffbox fistula*) is to date the most distal AA described. It consists of an end-to-side anastomosis between the distal cephalic vein and the thenar branch of the radial artery, the pulse of which is usually palpable through the floor of the anatomic snuffbox, created through one incision (Fig. 117-2). Although not as common as the autogenous radial-cephalic wrist access as a primary choice of AA, the snuffbox fistula has enjoyed popularity in Europe. Wolowczyk and coworkers[34] described their experience with 210 snuffbox fistulae over a 12-year period. Of their cohort,

11% thrombosed within 24 hours of creation, and 80% had matured for hemodialysis within 6 weeks. The 1- and 5-year patency rates were 65% and 45%. Of the fistulae that thrombosed, ipsilateral wrist AA was successfully constructed in 45%. Success was more likely in men who had access placed on the left side. Diabetes, advanced age, or need for hemodialysis did not affect outcome. Similar results were obtained by Horimi and associates,[35] who reported on 139 patients who underwent snuffbox fistula creation with and without diabetic nephropathy. After 57 months, 87% of patients without diabetic nephropathy had patent access, whereas 72% were patent among patients with diabetic nephropathy, and they concluded that patients with diabetic nephropathy may not arterialize their accesses as well as patients without diabetic nephropathy.

Autogenous Radial-Cephalic Direct Wrist Access

The autogenous radial-cephalic direct wrist access (*Brescia-Cimino fistula*) is perhaps the "gold standard" of AA creation. First described in 1966,[28] this access also has been called the *Cimino fistula* or the *wrist fistula*. Its construction consists of anastomosis between the cephalic vein at the

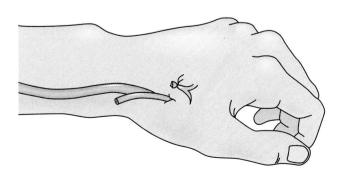

FIGURE 117-2 The autogenous posterior radial branch–cephalic direct access.

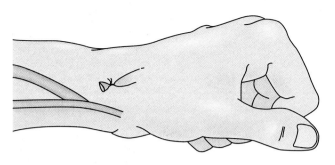

FIGURE 117-3 The autogenous radial-cephalic direct wrist access, depicted with typical end-to-side configuration.

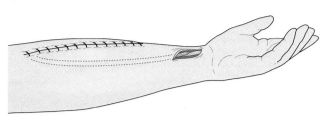

FIGURE 117-4 The autogenous ulnar-basilic forearm transposition. (From Silva MB, Hobson RW, Pappas PJ, et al: Vein transposition in the forearm for autogenous hemodialysis access. J Vasc Surg 26:981-988, 1997.)

wrist to the radial artery (Fig. 117-3). This anastomosis can be accomplished through either one or two separate incisions, although dual incisions afford the surgeon the ability to ligate adequately any collateral branches that may interfere with access maturation. Different configurations of anastomosis have been employed with varying results as far as development of a steal phenomenon or speed of maturation,[29] although the cephalic vein end-to-side configuration seems to be the most popular. Cephalic veins of less than 1.6 mm in diameter have been associated with early failure.[36]

Results of the Cimino fistula have been generally good. Similar to most experiences with AA, most failures occur within the first 12 months, beyond which the patency rates are excellent. Kherlakian and associates[33] described their results with the Cimino fistula in 100 patients studied retrospectively. At 6, 12, and 36 months, the patency rate was 80%, 71%, and 64%, which compared favorably with a similar cohort of patients undergoing PA insertion.[33] Alternatively, Palder and colleagues[21] described their results over a 4-year interval with PA and Cimino fistula among 154 autogenous accesses and 163 prosthetic accesses. PA fared better initially, with 24% of AA failing within the first month. At 48 months, the results of AA and PA patency were equivalent.[21]

Long-term patency of the Cimino fistula may be enhanced by additional procedures that encourage the maturation process or establish more reliable inflow or outflow. Golledge and colleagues[37] described a 56% patency of AA at 24 months, which improved to 63% with the addition of endovascular or surgical assist procedures. Manninen and associates[38] reported on the use of prograde brachial endovascular techniques in treating 53 Cimino fistulae, including the use of thrombolytic therapy and vascular brachytherapy. With a 92% clinical success rate, this group attained a 79% 3-year secondary patency rate. Finally, Weyde and coworkers[39] described the superficialization of deeper veins of the forearm as a means to enhance Cimino fistula maturation and use among 24 obese patients with success in 23.

Radial-Basilic Forearm Transposition

As an alternative before the use of a more proximal vein in a patient who has failed or is not a candidate for Cimino fistula, transposition of the basilic vein of the forearm to a

ventral position with end-to-side radial-basilic anastomosis is a viable option (Fig. 117-4). Described first by Silva and colleagues,[40] the results of radial/ulnar–basilic forearm transposition have been similar to that of other forearm AA. Of 89 procedures, 91% matured to be used for dialysis. At 1 year, 84% were patent, and 69% were patent at 30 months, with most failures occurring early. Other reports describe the basilic vein tunneled in a forearm loop fashion (autogenous brachial-cephalic forearm looped transposition) with anastomosis to the brachial or proximal radial or ulnar arteries as a means of avoiding the almost 70% nonmaturation rates of fistulae among diabetics with favorable results.[41]

Brachial-Cephalic Direct Elbow Access

Anastomosis of the antecubital veins with the brachial artery can be accomplished with good result. Termed *brachial-cephalic direct elbow access* (*cephalic turndown* or *brachial-cephalic fistula*), this type of AA, which involves anastomosis between the cephalic or basilic vein and the brachial artery, has been suggested in patients with diabetes for its superior flow and maturation rate (Fig. 117-5). Despite favorable results, the fistula has a higher incidence of steal, especially with long donor arteriotomies. It also eliminates the remainder of the forearm as a possible site of future access. Sparks and colleagues[42] described their results with 111 antecubital vein fistulae over a 10-year period at their institution. The antecubital vein fistula had a primary patency rate of 80% at a median follow-up of 36 months compared with 66% of brachial-cephalic fistulae at 24 months and 64% of PA at 7 months. Concluding that the brachial-cephalic fistula was a favorable alternative in elderly patients, women, and diabetics, Revanur and coworkers[43]

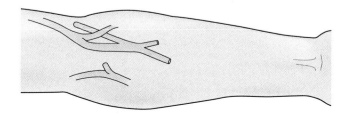

FIGURE 117-5 The autogenous brachial-cephalic upper arm direct access.

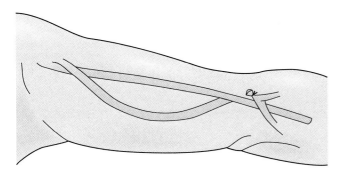

FIGURE 117-6 Autogenous brachial-basilic upper arm transposition.

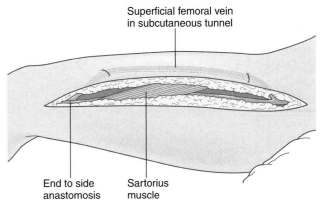

FIGURE 117-7 The autogenous femoral-popliteal indirect femoral vein transposition. (From Gradman WS, Cohen W, Massoud HA: Arteriovenous fistula construction in the thigh with transposed superficial femoral vein: Our initial experience. J Vasc Surg 33:968-975, 2001.)

described a 74% 1-year patency rate among 137 procedures. Lastly, Hakaim and colleagues[44] showed superior patency rates and maturation rates of primary brachial-basilic and transposed basilic AA compared with brachial-cephalic fistulae among 58 diabetic patients who required dialysis access. In their cohort, there was a 70% nonmaturation rate of brachial-cephalic fistula compared with 27% and 0% among patients with primary brachial-basilic and transposed brachial-basilic AA. At 18 months, cumulative patency was 33% among patients with brachial-cephalic fistulae compared with 78% and 79% for brachial-basilic and transposed brachial-basilic AA.

Autogenous Brachial-Basilic Upper Arm Transposition

Usually considered the last routine AA alternative of the upper limb, the autogenous brachial-basilic upper arm transposition (basilic transposition) was first described by Dagher and colleagues in 1976.[45] The procedure involves mobilization, distal division, and superficial tunneling and transposition of the basilic vein with distal end-to-side anastomosis with the brachial artery (Fig. 117-6). Other surgeons have modified the procedure by merely elevating the basilic vein rather than rerouting it[46] or superficializing the basilic vein as part of a staged procedure.[47] Others have expanded on the concept and shown the use of endoscopic techniques as a means of reducing incision length.[48]

The results of basilic transposition have been generally good, especially in patients who have compromised vasculature distally. In their study of a large cohort of patients who had undergone basilic transposition, Humphries and associates[49] examined long-term follow-up of 101 of 114 patients having undergone the procedure. Of these, actuarial patency was 84% at 1 year, 73% at 3 and 5 years, and 52% at 10 years. Less favorable results were reported by Murphy and coworkers[50] in their study of 74 basilic transpositions, of which 68% were successfully used for dialysis, and patency was 53% at 2 years and 43% at 3 years. Compared with the upper arm PA equivalent, basilic transposition fares well. In their study of 98 upper arm procedures (30 basilic transpositions and 68 PA), Matsuura and colleagues[51] showed patency of 70% in the autogenous group versus 46% in the polytetrafluoroethylene (PTFE) group at 24 months. Secondary patency remained favorable toward autogenous access (70% versus 51%).

Lower Extremity Autogenous Access

In the rare, yet particularly cumbersome, patient in whom all upper extremity dialysis access options have been exhausted, the surgeon may consider the use of the lower extremity for insertion of an AA. Use of a loop of saphenous vein and transposition of the superficial femoral vein has been described; results have been mixed. Lower extremity AA is more likely to fail to mature, to subject the patient to steal syndrome, and to experience thrombosis earlier than upper extremity AA and probably PA as well, in addition to the added morbidity of saphenous harvest and groin wound infection.[52]

Use of the superficial femoral vein for creation of an AA has been advocated in patients who have exhausted all other possible sites for an AA.[53] The technique involves dissection and mobilization of the entire superficial femoral vein, with transposition into a superficial position in the thigh and end-to-side anastomosis (Fig. 117-7). In Gradman and colleagues'[53] retrospective analysis of 25 patients over 2 years, cumulative patency was 78% and 73% for 6 and 12 months of follow-up. Steal syndrome necessitated further intervention in 40%, and of those, 80% required another procedure to treat steal. Major wound complications affected 28%, and one patient required above-knee amputation after developing a compartment syndrome. We advocate the construction of this AA only in good-risk patients who have no other possible sites for fistula creation.

■ STRATEGIES OF PROSTHETIC ACCESS INSERTION

With the advent of safe, reliable, and widely available vascular synthetic, the access options for patients needing hemodialysis grew enormously. A graft material that is resistant to thrombosis or infection and that promotes neoendothelialization has yet to be discovered, however. PTFE is currently preferred over other synthetics, such as Dacron, because of its lower rate of disintegration and better surgical handling. Although the PA may be expected to remain patent on average for approximately 3 to 5 years,[54]

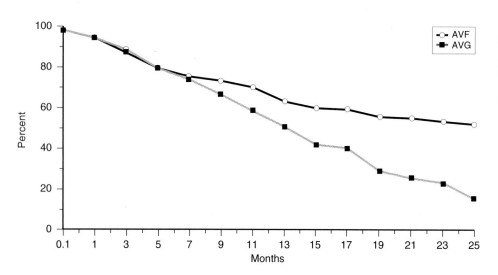

FIGURE 117-8 Cumulative success of autogenous versus prosthetic access. (Adapted from Kalman PG, Pope M, Bhola C, et al: A practical approach to vascular access for hemodialysis and predictors of success. J Vasc Surg 30:727-733, 1999.)

patency rates may be lower (Fig. 117-8). Advantages of the graft include the large surface area available for cannulation[55]; the ease in cannulation; and the dramatically shorter and more reliable time to maturity for use, an interval on the order of 10 to 14 days.[56]

Prosthetic Materials

Although expanded PTFE remains the prosthetic of choice in most practices, several alternatives and iterations of this material have been studied. Bacchini and colleagues[57] prospectively reported on the survival of 63 PTFE and 22 bovine vein grafts implanted over a 9-year period, each with 2-year follow-up. Their results showed a higher patency rate of bovine vein grafts versus PTFE (17.4% PTFE versus 23.9% bovine vein primary patency at 1 year). The disappointing results of Bacchini and colleagues[57] may be explained partly by their study cohort—patients had recently failed an autogenous access. There are currently two major manufacturers of expanded PTFE for use in hemodialysis access: Gore-Tex (W.L. Gore & Associates, Flagstaff, Ariz) and Impra (Impra, Inc, Tempe, Ariz). Although each has been advertised by the manufacturer as having distinct patency and cost advantages over the other, this has not been borne out by comparative investigation of either product.[58,59]

Stenosis of the venous outflow, generally as a result of neointimal hyperplasia, remains the sentinel cause of graft failure, accounting for approximately 80% of graft failure.[60] Measurements of the outflow tract have been correlated with graft patency: Lesions that account for less than 30% stenosis were associated with a less than 30% thrombosis rate at 6 months, whereas lesions that accounted for greater than 50% of the outflow were associated with an almost 100% failure rate at 6 months.[61] As a result of the association of turbulent flow at the anastomosis with the formation of neointimal hyperplasia,[62,63] investigators designed expanded PTFE grafts that incorporated a cuffed geometry of the venous anastomosis site, a design that had shown bench utility in minimizing shear stress.[64] This configuration was studied prospectively in 48 patients,

and although overall primary patency was not affected, secondary patency was increased from 32% to 64% at 12 months.[65]

Sites of Insertion

Sites for insertion are typically the forearm and the upper arm, in either a loop or a straight configuration. DOQI guidelines suggest the use of a site and configuration that provide the greatest surface area available for cannulation, while providing the highest flow rate.[1] Different configurations, as depicted in Figure 117-9, require skill in advanced planning because the surgeon should anticipate the need for future thrombectomy and possible revision and should construct the access in such a manner as to facilitate manipulation in the future. Sites available for obtaining inflow include the radial artery at the wrist, antecubital brachial artery, proximal brachial artery, axillary artery, and rarely the femoral artery. Of these, the arm remains the location of choice because of the ease of needle insertion and the presence of abundant collaterals, which provide adequate supply in the event of an access failure or complication. Outflow sites in the arm include the median antecubital vein, proximal and distal cephalic veins, and the basilic vein in the upper arm.

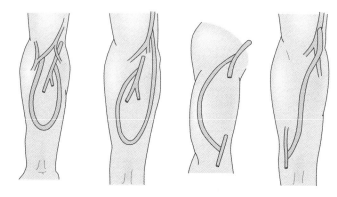

FIGURE 117-9 Variations of prosthetic access configuration.

When the upper extremity has been exhausted of possible access sites, more unusual sites for insertion may be considered. Among these sites are the axillary artery, with either contralateral axillary vein runoff or runoff into the ipsilateral or contralateral jugular vein. McCann[66] described the use of 26 axillary artery–based prosthetic accesses, which encompassed 8.6% of prosthetic access insertions over a 5-year period. Cumulative life-table analysis of these grafts shows a 60% patency at 2 years; in none of their patients did an arterial steal develop.

Because of the high incidence of complications, the groin and lower leg can be considered for prosthetic access insertion after exhaustion of all other available sites. The early experience with this location was particularly discouraging and was associated with a high incidence of infection, steal syndrome, and limb loss.[67,68] Tashjian and coworkers[69] reviewed their experience with lower extremity prosthetic access insertions in 73 patients, for which they reported primary and secondary patencies of 63% and 83% at 2 years. Infection developed in 22%, and one episode of steal led to amputation of the limb.

■ REFERENCES

1. NKF-K/DOQI Clinical practice guidelines for vascular access: Update 2000. Am J Kidney Dis 37:S137-S181, 2001.
2. Chazan JA, London MR, Pono LM: Long term survival of vascular accesses in a large chronic hemodialysis population. Nephron 69:228-233, 1995.
3. Feldman HI, Held PJ, Hutchinson JT, et al: Hemodialysis vascular access morbidity in the United States. Kidney Int 43:1091-1096, 1993.
4. United States Renal Data Service, 2002 ADR/Atlas, table k4, 532.
5. Fullerton JK, McLafferty RB, Ramsey DE, et al: Pitfalls in achieving the Dialysis Outcome Quality Initiative guidelines for hemodialysis access? Ann Vasc Surg 16:613-617, 2002.
6. Chesser AM, Baker LR: Temporary vascular access for first dialysis is common, undesirable and usually avoidable. Clin Nephrol 51:228-232, 1999.
7. Bander SJ, Schwab SJ: Central venous angioaccess for hemodialysis and its complications. Semin Dial 5:121-128, 1992.
8. Quinton W, Dillar D, Scribner B: Cannulation of blood vessels for prolonged hemodialysis. Trans Am Soc Artif Intern Organs 6:104-113, 1960.
9. Kelber J, Delmez JA, Windus DW: Factors affecting delivery of high-efficiency dialysis using temporary vascular access. Am J Kidney Dis 22:24-29, 1993.
10. Schwab SJ, Quarles LD, Middleton JP, et al: Hemodialysis-associated subclavian vein stenosis. Kidney Int 33:1156-1159, 1988.
11. Barrett N, Spencer S, McIvor J, Brown EA: Subclavian stenosis: A major complication of subclavian dialysis catheters. Nephrol Dial Transplant 3:423-425, 1988.
12. Spinowitz BS, Galler M, Golden RA, et al: Subclavian vein stenosis as a complication of subclavian catheterization for hemodialysis. Arch Intern Med 147:305-307, 1987.
13. Schillinger F, Schillinger D, Montagnac R, Milcent T: Post catheterisation vein stenosis in haemodialysis: Comparative angiographic study of 50 subclavian and 50 internal jugular accesses. Nephrol Dial Transplant 6:722-724, 1991.
14. Cimochowski GE, Worley E, Rutherford WE, et al: Superiority of the internal jugular over the subclavian access for temporary hemodialysis. Nephron 54:154-161, 1990.
15. Moss AH, Mclaughlin MM, Lempert KD, Holley JL: Use of a silicone catheter with a Dacron cuff for dialysis short-term vascular access. Am J Kidney Dis 12:492-498, 1988.
16. DeMeester J, Vanholder R, Ringole S: Factors affecting catheter and technique survival in permanent silicone single lumen dialysis catheters [abstract]. J Am Soc Nephrol 3:361A, 1992.
17. Schwab SJ, Buller GL, McCann RL, et al: Prospective evaluation of a Dacron cuffed hemodialysis catheter for prolonged use. Am J Kidney Dis 11:166-169, 1988.
18. Suchoki P, Conlon P, Knelson M, et al: Silastic cuffed catheters for hemodialysis vascular access: Thrombolytic and mechanical correction of HD catheters malfunction. Am J Kidney Dis 28:379-386, 1996.
19. Kovalik EC, Raymond JR, Albers FA, et al: A clustering of epidural abscesses in chronic hemodialysis patients: Risks of salvaging access catheters in cases of infection. J Am Soc Nephrol 7:2264-2267, 1996.
20. Trerotola SO: Interventional radiology in central venous stenosis and occlusion. Semin Interv Radiol 11:291-304, 1994.
21. Palder SB, Kirkman RL, Whittemore AD, et al: Vascular access for hemodialysis: Patency rates and results of revision. Ann Surg 202:235-239, 1985.
22. Raju S: PTFE grafts for hemodialysis access: Techniques for insertion and management of complications. Ann Surg 206:666-673, 1987.
23. Middleton WD, Picus DD, Marx MV, Melson GL: Color Doppler sonography of hemodialysis vascular access: Comparison with angiography. AJR Am J Roentgenol 152:633-639, 1989.
24. Tordoir JHM, Hoeneveld H, Eikelboom BC, Kitslaar PJEHM: The correlation between clinical and duplex ultrasound parameters and the development of complications in arterio-venous fistulae for hemodialysis. Eur J Vasc Surg 4:179-184, 1990.
25. Tordoir JHM, De Bruin HG, Hoeneveld H, et al: Duplex ultrasound scanning in the assessment of arteriovenous fistulas created for hemodialysis access: Comparison with digital subtraction angiography. J Vasc Surg 10:122-128, 1989.
26. Glanz S, Bashist B, Gordon DH, et al: Axillary and subclavian vein stenosis: Percutaneous angioplasty. Radiology 168:371-373, 1988.
27. Kalman PG, Pope M, Bhola C, et al: A practical approach to vascular access for hemodialysis and predictors of success. J Vasc Surg 30:727-733, 1999.
28. Brescia M, Cimino J, Appel K, et al: Chronic hemodialysis using venipuncture and a surgically created arteriovenous fistula. N Engl J Med 275:1089-1092, 1966.
29. Rutherford R (ed): Vascular Surgery, 5th ed. Philadelphia, WB Saunders, 2000.
30. Miller PE, Tolwani A, Luscy CP, et al: Predictors of adequacy of arteriovenous fistulas in hemodialysis patients. Kidney Int 56:275-280, 1999.
31. Palder SB, Kirkman RL, Whittemore AD, et al: Vascular access for hemodialysis: Patency rates and results of revision. Ann Surg 202:235-239, 1985.
32. Kinnaert P, Vereerstraeten P, Toussaint C, Van Geertruyden J: Nine years' experience with internal arteriovenous fistulas for hemodialysis: Study of some factors influencing results. Br J Surg 64:242-246, 1977.
33. Kherlakian GM, Roedersheimer LR, Arbaugh JJ, et al: Comparison of autogenous fistula versus expanded polytetrafluoroethylene graft fistula for angioaccess in hemodialysis. Am J Surg 152:238-243, 1986.
34. Wolowczyk L, Williams AJ, Donovan KL, et al: The snuffbox arteriovenous fistula for vascular access. Eur J Vasc Endovasc Surg 19:70-76, 2000.
35. Horimi H, Kusano E, Hasegawa T, et al: Clinical experience with an anatomic snuff box arteriovenous fistula in hemodialysis patients. ASAIO J 42:177-180, 1996.
36. Wong V, Ward R, Taylor J, et al: Factors associated with early failure of arteriovenous fistulae for hemodialysis access. Eur J Vasc Endovasc Surg 12:207-213, 1996.
37. Golledge J, Smith CJ, Emery J, et al: Outcome of primary radiocephalic fistula for hemodialysis. Br J Surg 86:211-216, 1999.
38. Manninen HI, Kaukanen ET, Ikaheimo R, et al: Brachial arterial access: Endovascular treatment of failing Brescia-Cimino hemodialysis fistulas—initial success and long term results. Radiology 218:711-718, 2001.

39. Weyde W, Krajewska M, Letachowicz W, et al: Superficialization of the wrist native arteriovenous fistula for effective hemodialysis vascular access construction. Kidney Int 61:1170-1173, 2002.

40. Silva MB, Hobson RW, Pappas PJ, et al: Vein transposition in the forearm for autogenous hemodialysis access. J Vasc Surg 26:981-988, 1997.

41. Gefen JY, Giangola G, Ewing DR, et al: The transposed forearm loop arteriovenous fistula: A valuable option for primary hemodialysis access in diabetic patients. Ann Vasc Surg 16:89-94, 2002.

42. Sparks SR, Vanderlinden JL, Gnanadev DA, et al: Superior patency of perforating antecubital vein arteriovenous fistulae for hemodialysis. Ann Vasc Surg 11:165-167, 1997.

43. Revanur VK, Jardine AG, Hamilton DH, et al: Outcome for arteriovenous fistula at the elbow for hemodialysis. Clin Transplant 14:318-322, 2000.

44. Hakaim AG, Nalbandian M, Scott T: Superior maturation and patency of primary brachiocephalic and transposed basilic vein arteriovenous fistulae in patients with diabetes. J Vasc Surg 27:154-157, 1998.

45. Dagher F, Gelber R, Ramos E, et al: The use of basilic vein and brachial artery as an A-V fistula for long term hemodialysis. J Surg Res 20:373-376, 1976.

46. Davis JN, Howell CG, Humphries AL: Hemodialysis access: Elevated basilic vein arteriovenous fistula. J Pediatr Surg 21:1182-1183, 1986.

47. Zielinski CM, Mittal SK, Anderson P, et al: Delayed superficialization of brachiobasilic fistula: Technique and initial experience. Arch Surg 136:929-932, 2001.

48. Hayakawa K, Tsuha M, Aoyagi T, et al: New method to create arteriovenous fistula in the arm with an endoscopic technique. J Vasc Surg 36:635-638, 2002.

49. Humphries AL, Colborn GL, Wynn JJ: Elevated basilic vein arteriovenous fistula. Am J Surg 177:489-491, 1999.

50. Murphy GJ, White SA, Knight AJ, et al: Long-term results of arteriovenous fistulas using transposed autologous basilic vein. Br J Surg 87:819-823, 2000.

51. Matsuura JH, Rosenthal D, Clark M, et al: Transposed basilic vein versus polytetrafluorethylene for brachial-axillary arteriovenous fistulas. Am J Surg 176:219-221, 1998.

52. Illig KA, Orloff M, Lyden SP, et al: Transposed saphenous vein arteriovenous fistula revisited: New technology for an old idea. Cardiovasc Surg 10:212-215, 2002.

53. Gradman WS, Cohen W, Massoud HA: Arteriovenous fistula construction in the thigh with transposed superficial femoral vein: Our initial experience. J Vasc Surg 33:968-975, 2001.

54. Albers F: Causes of hemodialysis access failure. Adv Ren Replace Ther 1:107-118, 1994.

55. Windus DW: Permanent vascular access: A nephrologist's view. Am J Kidney Dis 21:457-471, 1993.

56. Owens ML, Stabile BE, Gahr JA, Wilson SE: Vascular grafts for hemodialysis: Evaluation of sites and materials. Dial Transplant 8:521-530, 1979

57. Bacchini G, Del Vecchio L, Andrulli S, et al: Survival of prosthetic grafts of different materials after impairment of native arteriovenous fistula in hemodialysis patients. ASAIO J 47:30-33, 2001.

58. Hurlbert SN, Mattos MA, Henretta JP, et al: Long-term patency rates, complications and cost-effectiveness of polytetrafluoroethylene (PTFE) grafts for hemodialysis access: A propective study that compares Impra versus Gore-tex grafts. Cardiovasc Surg 6:652-656, 1998.

59. Kaufman JL, Garb JL, Berman JA, et al: A prospective comparison of two expanded polytetrafluoroethylene grafts for linear forearm hemodialysis access: Does the manufacturer matter? J Am Coll Surg 185:74-79, 1997.

60. Roberts A, Valji K, Bookstein J, et al: Pulse-spray pharmacomechanical thrombolysis for the treatment of thrombosed dialysis access grafts. Am J Surg 166:221-226, 1983.

61. Strauch B, O'Connell R, Geoly K, et al: Forecasting thrombosis of vascular access with Doppler color flow imaging. Am J Kidney Dis 19:554-557, 1992.

62. Stehbens W, Karmody A: Venous atherosclerosis associated with arteriovenous fistulas for hemodialysis. Arch Surg 110:176-180, 1975.

63. Scholz H, Zanow J, Petzold K, et al: Five years' experience with an arteriovenous patch prosthesis as access for hemodialysis. In Henry M (ed): Vascular Access for Hemodialysis IV. Chicago, Precept Press, 1999, pp 241-254.

64. Escobar FI, Schwartz S, Aboulijoud M, et al: A preliminary study comparing a new "hooded" vs. conventional ePTFE graft in hemodialysis patients. Proceedings of Vascular Access for Hemodialysis VI, Miami, Fla, 1998.

65. Sorom A, Hughes CB, McCarthy J, et al: Prospective, randomized evaluation of a cuffed expanded polytetrafluoroethylene graft for hemodialysis vascular access. Surgery 132:135-140, 2002.

66. McCann R: Axillary grafts for difficult hemodialysis access. J Vasc Surg 24:457-462, 1996.

67. Mandel ST, McDougal EG: Popliteal artery to saphenous vein vascular access for hemodialysis. Surg Gynecol Obstet 160:358-359, 1985.

68. Connolly JE, Brownell DA, Levine EF, et al: Complications of renal dialysis access procedures. Arch Surg 119:1325-1328, 1984.

69. Tashjian D, Lipkowitz G, Madden R, et al: Safety and efficacy of femoral-based hemodialysis access grafts. J Vasc Surg 35:691-696, 2002.

Venous Transpositions in the Creation of Arteriovenous Access

118

W. TODD BOHANNON, MD

MICHAEL B. SILVA, JR., MD

Autogenous arteriovenous fistulae are currently preferred over hemodialysis accesses constructed with prosthetic grafts. The National Kidney Foundation's Dialysis Outcome Quality Initiative (DOQI), in 1997, recommended guidelines to increase the utilization of autogenous arteriovenous fistulae.[1] In order to attain the goals recommended by DOQI, which have been updated in 2001, surgeons are expected to increase their rates of autogenous arteriovenous fistulae to at least 50% of all new permanent hemodialysis accesses constructed.[2] An important objective of DOQI is to have a prevalence of autogenous fistulae in 40% of all hemodialysis patients. Venous transposition procedures have aided in the greater utilization of autogenous fistulae as the nation strives to achieve the goals set forth by DOQI.

■ VENOUS TRANSPOSITIONS AND DIALYSIS OUTCOME QUALITY INITIATIVE GUIDELINES

Currently, autogenous fistulae are preferred to prosthetic grafts because of their higher primary patency rates and lower frequency of stenosis, thrombosis, and infection.[2,3] Before the DOQI guidelines were issued, prosthetic conduit was often used for the initial hemodialysis access. Justification for a preference for prosthetic grafts included technical ease of procedure, avoidance of prolonged maturation times, ease of cannulation, differences in reimbursement, and disbelief in the superiority of autogenous fistulae.[4] The reluctance to perform native fistulae was also fueled by the wide range of reported patency rates as well as the maturation to a functional access with traditional single-incision direct arteriovenous fistulae such as the wrist radial-cephalic fistula. Maturation rates of arteriovenous fistulae have ranged between 25% and 90%.[4-8]

As the dialysis population grows and includes older patients, the traditional radial-cephalic arteriovenous fistula, introduced in 1966 by Brescia and associates, is often not an option because of unsuitable venous or arterial anatomy. This is the case with the radial-cephalic arteriovenous fistula, in which the venous outflow depends on a cephalic vein that is of sufficient caliber and is without the sclerotic changes associated with repetitive trauma from previous intravenous access and phlebotomy. The inability to identify suitable veins and arteries and the use of marginal veins that were available through the single radial-cephalic wrist incision have contributed to the high early failure rates for arteriovenous fistulae.[7,9-12]

In order to maximize autogenous hemodialysis access options, many institutions incorporate venous transposition procedures such as the radial-basilic forearm transposition and the brachial-basilic upper arm transposition when traditional fistula options are not possible (i.e., radial-cephalic or brachial-cephalic fistulae).[4,8,13,14] Silva and associates[8] were able to increase the rate of native arteriovenous fistulae from 14% to 63% by utilizing a preoperative non-invasive imaging protocol in combination with venous transpositions.[8] Huber and colleagues[4] demonstrated that using an algorithm designed to increase autogenous fistula rates enabled them to give 71% of patients at their institution evaluated for hemodialysis access an arteriovenous fistula suitable for cannulation. Ascher and coworkers[13] demonstrated a dramatic increase in the autogenous fistula rates after the DOQI guidelines were published. Their fistula rate increased from 5% (pre-DOQI) to 68% (post-DOQI).[13]

■ NOMENCLATURE

In 2002, the Committee on Reporting Standards for Arterio-Venous Accesses of the Society for Vascular Surgery and the American Association for Vascular Surgery published standardized definitions related to arteriovenous access procedures and recommended reporting standards for patency and complications.[15] *Autogenous* refers to the native vein. An *autogenous AV access* is an access created by a connection between an artery and vein, and the vein serves as the access site for needle cannulation. A *transposition* is an access performed with a transposed vein. The peripheral portion of the vein is moved from its original position, usually through a superficial subcutaneous tunnel and connected to the artery. The more central venous segment in a transposed access is left in its anatomic position. In contrast, the term *translocated* is used to describe an access that is constructed from a segment of vein that has been completely mobilized, disconnected proximally and distally, and placed in a location remote from its origin. The recommended nomenclature for the autogenous transposition procedures can be found in Table 118-1.[15]

Configuration descriptors provide information about the anastomotic connection and the course of the conduit. An

Table 118-1 Recommended Nomenclature for Transposition Access Procedures	
RECOMMENDED NOMENCLATURE	**TRADITIONAL NOMENCLATURE**
Forearm	
Autogenous radial-basilic forearm transposition	Superficial venous transposition in the forearm, basilic vein to radial artery
Autogenous ulnar-basilic forearm transposition	Superficial venous transposition in the forearm, basilic vein to ulnar artery
Autogenous radial-cephalic forearm transposition	Superficial venous transposition in the forearm, cephalic vein to radial artery
Autogenous brachial-cephalic forearm transposition	Superficial venous transposition in the forearm, cephalic vein to brachial artery
Upper arm	
Autogenous brachial-basilic upper arm transposition	Basilic vein transposition
Lower extremity	
Autogenous femoral–greater saphenous looped access transposition	Greater saphenous vein end-to-side to femoral artery fistula

Adapted from the Committee on Reporting Standards for Arterio-Venous Accesses of the Society for Vascular Surgery and the American Association for Vascular Surgery. J Vasc Surg 35:603-610, 2002.

access has either a direct or indirect configuration.[15] A *direct access* describes the connection between native artery and vein and involves such configurations as the end-to-side, side-to-side, and end-to-end anastamoses.[15] In an *indirect access,* either autogenous or prosthetic graft is interposed between the native artery and vein.[15] Additional descriptors may be used, such as *transposed, translocated, straight,* and *looped.*[15]

Primary patency refers to the interval from the time of access placement to the intervention designed to maintain or re-establish patency, access thrombosis, or the time of measurement of patency. *Assisted primary patency* refers to the interval from the time of access placement until access thrombosis or the time of measurement or patency including interventions designed to maintain the function of a patent access. *Secondary patency* refers to the interval from the time of access placement until access abandonment, thrombosis, or the time of patency measurement, including interventions to re-establish function in thrombosed access.[15]

■ SUPERFICIAL VENOUS SYSTEM OF THE UPPER EXTREMITY

An understanding of the venous anatomy of the upper extremity is essential in the planning of permanent hemodialysis access. Figure 118-1 depicts the superficial venous

anatomy of the upper extremity. However, many anatomic variations may be identified by preoperative assessment.

Cephalic Vein

The cephalic vein arises from the radial aspect of the veins draining the dorsum of the hand and travels around the radial border of the forearm. On the proximal aspect of the volar forearm, the median cubital vein arises. This vein communicates with the deep veins in the forearm and then crosses the antecubital fossa to join the basilic vein. As it crosses the elbow, the cephalic vein is found in an anatomic groove between the brachioradialis and biceps muscles. The cephalic vein travels superficial to the musculocutaneous nerve and then ascends in the groove along the lateral border of the biceps muscle. In the upper third of the arm, the cephalic vein passes between the pectoralis major and deltoid muscles, crosses the axillary artery, and joins the axillary vein just below the clavicle. The accessory cephalic vein arises from the ulnar side of the dorsum of the hand or the posterior aspect of the forearm and usually joins the cephalic vein below the elbow.

Basilic Vein

The basilic vein originates on the ulnar aspect of the dorsum of the hand and travels in the subcutaneous space up the

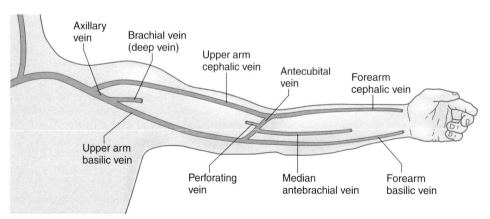

FIGURE 118-1 Superficial venous anatomy of the upper extremity.

ulnar side of the forearm, shifting from the posterior surface distally toward a more anterior orientation below the elbow. The median antecubital vein joins the basilic vein in the antecubital fossa and then travels in the groove between the biceps and pronator teres muscles to cross the brachial artery. In this region, the vein is crossed anteriorly and posteriorly by branches of the median cutaneous nerve. As it courses proximately along the medial border of the biceps muscle, the basilic vein descends below the deep fascia to travel parallel to the brachial artery and vein. The union of the basilic and brachial veins in the axilla forms the axillary vein.

Median Antebrachial Vein

The median antebrachial vein drains the palmar surface of the hand and is located on the ulnar side of the anterior forearm. In the proximal forearm, it joins either the basilic vein or the median antecubital vein.

■ TYPES OF VENOUS TRANSPOSITIONS

Upper Arm Venous Transposition (Brachial-Basilic Transposition)

The basilic vein in the upper arm is often a good conduit for dialysis access because of its relatively large size and location in the deeper tissue planes. The traumatic consequences of repeated venipunctures observed in more superficial veins are not seen in the basilic vein because of its deeper position. Classically, the brachial-basilic transposition was regarded as a secondary option after failed forearm fistula or graft.[16] The creation of an access using the proximal basilic vein was devised on the basis of the theoretical benefits of using a superficial vein spared repeated venipunctures and with a relatively large diameter and long length. As with all venous transpositions, only one anastomosis is required, and anatomic continuity with the axillary vein is maintained. The transposition of the basilic vein to the brachial artery was described by Dagher and colleagues[17] in 1976. Four years after their original description of 24 brachial-basilic fistulae, Dagher and colleagues[18] reported their 5-year follow-up of a series of 90 fistulae with a 73.5% patency rate. The long-term patency remained good, as this group reported a 70% functional patency rate at 8 years in 176 fistulae.[19]

Long-term patency with translocated brachial-basilic fistulae that have matured has been good, with reported primary patency rates as high as 90% at 1 year and 86% at 2 years.[20] In 2000, a series of 74 arteriovenous fistulae constructed using transposed basilic vein was reported by Murphy and associates.[21] Successful needle cannulation for hemodialysis was accomplished in 50 fistulae (68%), and the cumulative secondary patency rate was 73% at 1 year, 53% at 2 years, and 43% at 3 years.[21] In 2003, Taghizadeh and coworkers[22] reported a series of 75 brachial-basilic transpositions performed over 5 years with a mean follow-up of 14 months. In this series, 92% of fistulae matured to allow hemodialysis access.[22] The cumulative patency was

66% at 1 year, 52% at 2 years, and 43% at 3 years. Overall, complications developed in 55% of fistulae. The complications included thrombosis (33%), stenosis (11%), local infection (6%), arm edema (5%), hemorrhage (3%), aneurysm (1%), and steal syndrome (1%).[22]

The overall patency rate for autogenous brachial-basilic transpositions is superior to that of polytetrafluoroethylene (PTFE) upper arm dialysis grafts.[20,23] A review of all basilic vein transpositions and brachial PTFE arteriovenous fistulae created over a 5-year period demonstrated a statistically significant difference in primary patency rate at one (90% vs. 70%; $P <.01$) and 2 years (86% vs. 49%; $P < .001$).[20] In this study, complications occurred approximately 2½ times more frequently with the PTFE grafts than with the venous transpositions.[20] Another comparison between brachial-basilic transpositions and PTFE upper arm grafts showed significant better patency rate at 2 years with venous transpositions (70%, vs. 46% for PTFE grafts).[23]

In certain patient subgroups, such as those with small cephalic veins, peripheral vascular disease, and diabetes, the maturation rate of the radial-cephalic fistula has been poor. The brachial-basilic transposition has been a good second option in these patients.

Hakaim and colleagues[5] reported on the superior fistula maturation in brachial-basilic transpositions (73%) compared with primary radial-cephalic arteriovenous fistulae (30%). When the forearm cephalic vein is not suitable for access creation, the basilic vein in both the forearm and upper arm are excellent secondary options.[24] Ascher and coworkers[25] reviewed their experience using arm veins to create brachial-cephalic and brachial-basilic arteriovenous fistulae. They found no significant difference between primary patency rates at 1 year (72% for brachial-cephalic vs. 70% for brachial-basilic).[25] Because of excellent patency with these fistulae, this group proposed an algorithm for the placement of arteriovenous fistulae. If a radial-cephalic fistula is not feasible, brachial-cephalic fistula should first be attempted. If the brachial-cephalic fistula fails or is not possible, a brachial-basilic fistula should be placed before an arteriovenous graft.[25] In an attempt to maximize the autogenous fistula rate, we favor a similar algorithm, with the addition of the superficial venous transposition of the forearm before performance of the brachial artery–based fistulae—that is, radial-cephalic fistula, followed by forearm venous transposition, followed by brachial-cephalic fistula, followed by brachial-basilic fistula.

Forearm Venous Transpositions

The radial-cephalic fistula, performed through a single incision, was initially described in 1966 by Brescia and associates.[26] This primary arteriovenous fistula was a dramatic improvement over the other, less durable modes of hemodialysis access available at the time and soon became the preferred approach to long-term dialysis access. The hemodialysis population has changed, and the dialysis patient who has a suitable vein in close proximity to the radial artery is becoming uncommon. Therefore, venous transposition procedures in the forearm have become important in enabling such patients to have a primary arteriovenous fistula.

Physical examination and visual inspection alone poorly identify suitable arteries and veins in the upper extremity. Duplex ultrasound examination has allowed a more thorough evaluation of the superficial venous system, increasing the number of patients who may have a forearm fistula.[27] The duplex scan can identify veins in the forearm that may have been spared repeated venipunctures because of their deeper subcutaneous location. The size of such veins may be suitable for arteriovenous creation, but if they are left in situ, their position in the deeper subcutaneous tissues and their anatomic position on the forearm make needle cannulation for hemodialysis technically more difficult. These usable veins on the posterior aspect of the forearm, such as the basilic vein, if not transposed, require uncomfortable and awkward positioning of the arm for dialysis. Therefore, once identified by duplex scanning, these veins are mobilized and transposed to a more favorable location on the forearm through a superficial subcutaneous plane.[27]

In order to increase the number of primary autogenous fistulae, Silva and colleagues[27] in 1997 described the routine use of duplex scanning for preoperative access planning of superficial venous transposition of forearm veins for autogenous hemodialysis access. They reported a series of 89 patients in whom arteries and veins were identified with duplex scanning as suitable for primary arteriovenous fistulae. After the superficial venous transposition procedure, 91% of the fistulae matured to be used for hemodialysis access.[27] The primary patency rate was 84% at 1 year and 69% at 2 years.[27] The beneficial impact of a preoperative duplex ultrasound assessments was reported in 1998.[8] Silva and associates[8] demonstrated a dramatic improvement in their autogenous fistula rate with the institution of the protocol of routine use of duplex scanning for preoperative access planning. The group's autogenous fistula rate was 14% before the institution of the protocol and 63% after the protocol was established.[8] Table 118-2 demonstrates the three general areas where the superficial veins are found and the rates at which they were used in this study.[27] Note that the minority (15%) of the transpositions were accomplished through a single incision with the artery and vein in close proximity. Approximately half of transposed veins arose from the volar surface of the forearm, and a third were harvested from the dorsal aspect of the forearm.[27]

Lower Extremity Venous Transpositions

The upper extremity is the preferred site for hemodialysis access, with the lower extremity generally being reserved for use once upper extremity options have been exhausted. If the extremity is not suitable for fistula creation, a prosthetic graft can be placed. However, there is a concern about increased thrombosis and been infection rates in thigh hemodialysis grafts, which have reported as high as 55% and 35%, respectively.[28] Tashjian and coworkers,[29] reviewing their experience with 73 femoral artery–based hemodialysis grafts, found a primary patency rate of 71% and secondary patency rate of 83% at 1 year.[29] The infection rate in this series was 22%.

Venous transpositions in the lower extremity using both the greater saphenous vein (GSV) and the superficial femoral vein (SFV) have been described.[30,31] The use of translocated greater saphenous and superficial femoral veins in the leg have theoretical benefits similar to those of venous translocations in the upper extremity. The venous conduits are long and generally of good caliber and are less prone to infection than prosthetic grafts. Importantly, only one anastomosis is required, as the more central venous segment maintains its native connection with the common femoral vein.

The superficial femoral vein, part of the deep venous system, has a diameter in the range of 6 to 10 mm, has relatively thick walls, and has been used for a wide variety of vascular reconstructions.[32] Gradman and colleagues[31] reported a retrospective analysis of 25 patients who underwent arteriovenous construction using superficial femoral veins. Eighteen of the patients underwent SFV transposition, and 7 were given a composite loop fistula of SFV and PTFE. The cumulative primary fistula patency rate was 78% at 6 months and 73% at 1 year. The cumulative secondary patency rate was 91% at 5 months and 86% at 1 year. There were no fistula infections, but the rate of major wound complications was 28%. Eight patients required secondary procedures for symptomatic steal syndrome, and one patient ultimately needed an above-knee amputation after development of ipsilateral compartment syndrome.[31]

The saphenous vein has been utilized for arterial reconstructions in virtually all vascular beds and in the construction of arteriovenous access in both the upper and lower extremities. The greater saphenous vein has been used to create an autogenous fistula in the upper thigh in a looped configuration and an arterial anastomosis with the common femoral or superficial femoral artery.[30,33-35] Although described more than 30 years ago, this configuration is seldom used.[35] Illig and colleagues,[30] noting that the incidence of infection can be as high as 40% in traditional saphenous vein harvest, have utilized an endoscopic vein harvest technique in combination with creation of a transposed saphenous vein arteriovenous fistula.

Table 118-2	Superficial Venous Transpositions of the Forearm

TRANSPOSITION PERFORMED	% OF TOTAL

Type A
  Artery and vein in immediate proximity
  Single incision
  Superficial subcutaneous transposition only
	15

Type B
  Dorsally located vein transposed to volar surface artery
  Separate incisions
  Superficial subcutaneous transposition
	33

Type C
  Volar vein transposed to mid forearm volar surface
  Separate incisions
  Superficial subcutaneous transposition
	52

From Silva MB Jr, Hobson RW II, Pappas PJ, et al: Vein transposition in the forearm for autogenous hemodialysis access. J Vasc Surg 26:981-988, 1997.

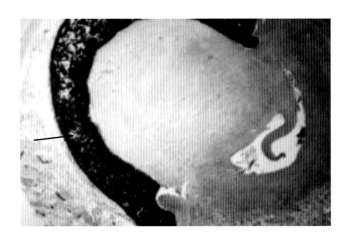

FIGURE 119-1 Transverse section through the venous anastomosis of an expanded polytetrafluoroethylene graft (*arrow*). The lumen is almost completely filled with neointimal hyperplasia. This lesion is the most common cause of graft failure and is difficult to dilate with an angioplasty balloon.

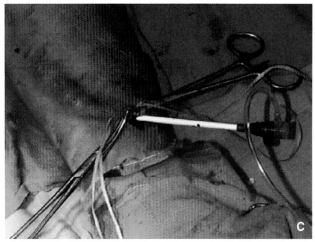

FIGURE 119-3C. The traditional open approach is to pass a Fogarty catheter proximally and distally through a graftotomy. Many surgeons simply open the graft through the venous anastomosis to facilitate subsequent patching. We favor making a graftotomy remote from the venous anastomosis, to permit ease of imaging the entire graft. Surgical cutdown over the apex of a forearm loop polytetrafluoroethylene graft has been performed. The graft has been encircled with a Romel for control. A No. 4 Fogarty embolectomy catheter is used to thrombectomize the venous anastomosis first and then the arterial anastomosis with the arterial plug. Shown in this illustration, when the thrombectomy has been completed, a hemostatic sheath is inserted into both ends of the graft, and angiography is performed.

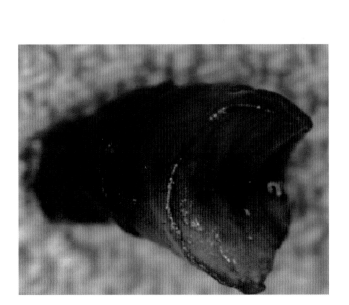

FIGURE 119-4 The arterial plug is thrombolysis resistant and consists of compact layers of fibrin and red blood cells.

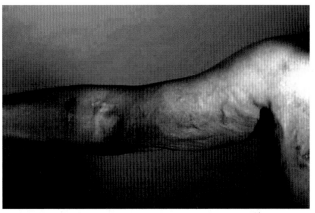

FIGURE 120-4 Development of marked upper arm and chest venous collaterals shortly after creation of an arteriovenous access.

■ TECHNIQUES OF VENOUS TRANSPOSITIONS

Patient Assessment and Selection of Optimal Site

The patient evaluation and preoperative assessment are the most important steps in the establishment of durable hemodialysis access. First, the best available site, based on optimal arterial inflow and venous outflow, is selected. We prefer an autogenous fistula over a prosthetic graft, the forearm over the upper arm, and the nondominant arm over the dominant arm. Visual inspection and physical examination of the upper extremities are performed but may be inadequate to assess certain aspects, especially vein size and quality as well as adequacy of central venous outflow. Therefore, duplex scanning is used to screen all patients. Table 118-3 summarizes the noninvasive criteria used to identify suitable arteries and veins for venous transposition procedures. A vein diameter of 2.5 mm is acceptable for superficial venous transposition of the forearm. The translocated brachial-basilic fistula may not be ideally suited for patients with obese arms or veins with a diameter less than 4 mm.

A tourniquet is placed on the mid-forearm. The examination begins at the wrist, and after dilatation with gentle tapping and stroking, the veins are insonated with a 5- or 7-MHz scanning ultrasound probe. The veins are evaluated for diameter, compressibility, and continuity with the upper arm veins. Patency of the deep system and continuity with patent axillary and subclavian veins are verified. The largest-diameter superficial vein of good quality is mapped with skin markings. Next, the arterial anatomy of the upper extremity is evaluated with duplex scanning, and the diameter of the target artery is measured. Bilateral arm pressures are recorded, and the palmar arch is assessed for patency. The target artery diameter should be greater than 2 mm and the artery should have no obliterating calcification.

Brachial-Basilic Transposition

The brachial-basilic transposition is usually performed with either local anesthesia using 1% lidocaine and intravenous sedation or regional anesthesia using an interscalene nerve block. The entire arm and ipsilateral axilla and shoulder are sterilely prepared. The basilic vein is first identified anterior to the medial epicondyle of the humerus, and through a longitudinal incision along the medial aspect of the upper arm to the axilla, the basilic vein is exposed. The median cutaneous nerve is close to the basilic vein and should be preserved. Venous branches are ligated and divided as the basilic vein is mobilized to its junction with the brachial vein. The brachial artery can be exposed through the same incision or through a separate incision. Vessel loops are loosely encircled around the brachial artery proximally and distally.

Next, the basilic vein is divided near the antecubital fossa and then flushed and distended with heparinized saline. A sterile marking pen is used to mark the vein along its entire length to help avoid twisting during passage through the subcutaneous tunnel created anteriorly between the axilla and antecubital fossa. Approximately 3000 units of intravenous heparin is administered, and then proximal and distal control of the brachial artery is obtained with the vessel loops. An end-to-side anastomosis with the brachial artery is then constructed with 6-0 polypropylene suture. After completion of the anastomosis, the fistula is inspected for a thrill. If a thrill is not present, a technical or structural problem is suspected that will require correction. The subcutaneous tissues and skin are closed with absorbable suture.

Superficial Venous Transposition of the Forearm

The superficial venous transposition of the forearm is performed in the operating suite, and the usual anesthetic of choice is local 1% lidocaine infusion supplemented with intravenous sedation. Lidocaine with epinephrine is avoided because of its vasoconstrictive properties. The entire arm is sterilely prepared, and the procedure is performed by the surgeon and the assistant in the seated position. The use of surgical magnifying lenses with 2.5× magnification is routine.

Once the skin and subcutaneous tissue overlying the vein have been properly anesthetized, a longitudinal incision is made directly over the vein, beginning at the distal extent of the previously mapped and marked vein. The incision proceeds toward the antecubital fossa for a distance of at least 15 cm (Fig. 118-2). A 3-0 silk suture ligature is used to ligate the portion of vein remaining in its distal bed, and the

Table 118-3	Noninvasive Criteria for Selection of Arteries and Veins for Dialysis Access Procedures
Venous examination	Venous luminal diameter > 2.5 mm
	Absence of segmental stenosis
	Continuity with the deep system in the upper arm
	Absence of ipsilateral central venous stenosis or occlusion
Arterial examination	Arterial lumen diameter > 2.0 mm
	Absence of obliterative calcification
	Absence of blood pressure differential > 20 mm Hg
	Patent palmar arch

Adapted from Silva MB Jr, Hobson RW II, Pappas PJ, et al: A strategy for increasing of autogenous hemodialysis access procedures: Impact of preoperative noninvasive evaluation. J Vasc Surg 27:302-308, 1998.

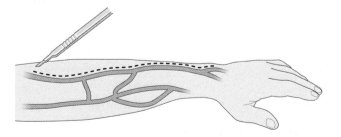

FIGURE 118-2 Incision along length of vein marked by duplex ultrasonography. (From Silva MB, Hobson RW, Pappas PJ, et al: Vein transposition in the forearm for autogenous hemodialysis access. J Vasc Surg 26:982, 1997.)

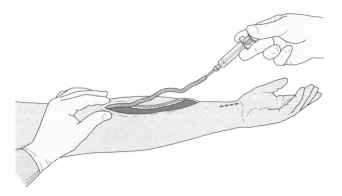

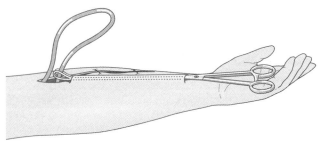

FIGURE 118-4 Construction of subcutaneous tunnel. (From Silva MB, Hobson RW, Pappas PJ, et al: Vein transposition in the forearm for autogenous hemodialysis access. J Vasc Surg 26:983, 1997.)

FIGURE 118-3 Complete dissection of the vein and dilatation with heparinized saline. A separate radial artery incision is marked. (From Silva MB, Hobson RW, Pappas PJ, et al: Vein transposition in the forearm for autogenous hemodialysis access. J Vasc Surg 26:982, 1997.)

vein is transected at the wrist. The vein is dissected free from its surrounding tissue so that it may be completely transposed to a superficial tunnel in the midportion of the volar aspect of the forearm. Most venous branches along the length of the vein are ligated and divided; however, those that will not interfere with transposition are left intact in order to maximize outflow. Heparinized saline is flushed through the open end of the vein with digital compression for occlusion of outflow at the antecubital fossa (Fig. 118-3). This step results in substantial dilatation of the freed segment of vein. The vein is wrapped in a heparin-saline–soaked sponge, and attention is then turned to the arterial dissection.

The segment of artery that has been preoperatively identified as suitable for inflow is then exposed. Usually, the radial artery is identified between the brachial radialis and flexor carpi radialis tendons. The superficial branch of the radial nerve is located lateral to the radial artery, and this nerve is separated from the radial artery by the brachial radialis muscle. The nerve is sensory at this level, and care must be taken not to injure it. Concomitant veins run parallel to the artery on either side. These should be carefully dissected free from the artery, facilitating identification of the numerous small arterial branches. Although there are no arterial branches typically on the anterior aspect of the artery, several paired arterial branches usually leave the radial artery on each side, and they must be addressed. We ligate these in continuity, with the ligature placed approximately 2 mm away from the radial artery to avoid impingement once dilatation has occurred. Vessel loops are placed proximally and distally along the artery for vascular control.

A tunneling instrument is passed through the subcutaneous tissues to develop a superficial tunnel (Fig. 118-4). The vein is marked along its length with a sterile marking pen to facilitate passage through the tunnel without twisting or kinking. Once the vein has been passed through the subcutaneous tunnel (Fig. 118-5) and hemostasis has been ensured, the patient is typically given 3000 units of intravenous heparin, and a 1- to 2-mm arteriotomy is made with a No. 11 blade scalpel on the volar surface of the artery. The arteriotomy is extended to approximately 15 to 20 mm with fine Potts scissors. With an 18-gauge angiocatheter, the artery is locally heparinized by injection of heparinized saline distally and then proximally while the vessel loops are simultaneously opened.

An end-to-side anastomosis is performed with either 7-0 polypropylene with a double-armed CV1 needles. Alternatively, Gore-Tex polytetrafluoroethylene suture (W. L. Gore & Associates, Flagstaff, Ariz) CV6 on TT-9 needles can be used. Before completion of the anastomosis, vascular dilators are used to size both the vein and the radial artery. This step has the benefit of allowing enlargement of blood vessels in in spasm from vessel loops and manipulation. Self-retaining retractors are not used, because the portion of the retractor above the skin level is cumbersome and the greater distance above the anastomosis line makes suturing more difficult.

After the anastomosis is constructed, it is essential that a thrill be felt within the vein. Absence of a thrill indicates a probable technical or anatomic defect and requires further investigation with exploration of the anastomosis. Wounds are closed with a running subcuticular absorbable stitch (Fig. 118-6). Care is taken to maintain strict atraumatic technique during handling of the skin edges to limit wound complications. Adhesive strips or tape applied directly to the skin are not used.

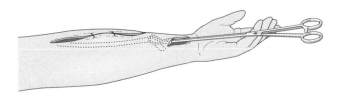

FIGURE 118-5 Vein transposed through mid-forearm volar subcutaneous tissues. (From Silva MB, Hobson RW, Pappas PJ, et al: Vein transposition in the forearm for autogenous hemodialysis access. J Vasc Surg 26:983, 1997.)

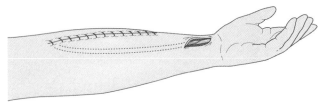

FIGURE 118-6 Completed fistula. The mid-forearm volar location facilitates cannulation and comfortable arm positioning during dialysis. (From Silva MB, Hobson RW, Pappas PJ, et al: Vein transposition in the forearm for autogenous hemodialysis access. J Vasc Surg 26:984, 1997.)

Follow-up

Adequate arterialization of the vein usually occurs within 8 to 12 weeks. Hand exercises are advocated to encourage fistula maturation. Before the initial use of the access by our dialysis access personnel, the patient is re-evaluated in the noninvasive laboratory, and the sites most suitable for needle insertion are marked on the skin to facilitate initial needle cannulation.

■ SECONDARY INTERVENTIONS IN AUTOGENOUS FISTULAE

Few published series have focused on re-intervention of failing or nonmaturing autogenous arteriovenous fistulae, and most of those that are reported are focused on the traditional radial-cephalic arteriovenous fistula. Recognizing this fact, Hingorani and colleagues[36] reviewed their experience with salvage procedures in the management of nonfunctioning or nonmaturing arteriovenous fistulae in a series of patients that included fistulae based in the upper arm. The distribution of fistulae that required salvage procedures were 37% radial-cephalic, 47% brachial-cephalic, and 16% brachial-basilic. Seventy-five procedures, both open and endovascular, were performed in 46 patients (49 fistulae). Seventeen patients underwent 26 balloon angioplasties, and 20 patients had vein patch angioplasty. The group performed 12 fistula revisions to a more proximal level and four vein interposition grafts. Although the total number of subsequent procedures required for percutaneously treated fistulae was higher than that for open repair, there was no statistical difference between primary patency rates. The group concluded that salvage procedures may allow maturation and extend the lifespan of arteriovenous fistulae for hemodialysis.

The beneficial effect of secondary interventions on the maturation and maintenance of autogenous arteriovenous fistulae has been demonstrated by Berman and Gentile.[37] They placed 170 autogenous fistulae in 163 patients—115 brachial-cephalic, 47 radial-cephalic, and 8 brachial-basilic. Secondary procedures for failure to mature were required in 9 patients and for failure of previously functioning fistulae in 6 patients. A functional access was achieved in 90% of patients, and these researchers demonstrated a 10% improvement in accomplishing or maintaining functional autogenous access through secondary procedures.[37]

In a series of arm cephalic and basilic vein arteriovenous fistulae that encompassed 109 brachial-cephalic and 63 brachial-basilic arteriovenous fistulae, Ascher and colleagues[25] reported thrombosis in 12% and 6%, respectively (no statistical difference). No thrombosed fistula in either group was treated with thrombolysis or thrombectomy. Within the brachial-cephalic group, 15 secondary interventions were performed: six balloon angioplasties, five patch angioplasties, two superficial elevation procedures, and one extension to the jugular vein for subclavian vein thrombosis. There were seven secondary interventions in the brachial-basilic group: five balloon angioplasties and two patch angioplasties.[25]

In the series of 89 patients with superficial venous transposition of forearm veins after duplex mapping for establishment of hemodialysis access, Silva and associates[27]

reported a total of 18 failed fistulae.[27] With surgical revision, 4 were successfully salvaged, and 6 were converted to ipsilateral prosthetic grafts (three forearm, three upper arm). Additionally, access was established on the other arm in five patients (three autogenous fistulae, two prosthetic grafts).[27]

■ CONCLUSION

The goals of DOQI and a shift toward all-autogenous hemodialysis access cannot be met with traditional arteriovenous access. Venous transpositions give dialysis patients more autogenous options. Institutional strategies of preoperative noninvasive vascular assessments and utilization of venous transposition procedures can be effective in increasing autogenous access in the dialysis population.

■ REFERENCES

1. NKF-DOQI clinical practice guidelines for vascular access. National Kidney Foundation–Dialysis Outcomes Quality Initiative. Am J Kidney Dis 30:S150-S191, 1997.
2. III. NKF-K/DOQI Clinical Practice Guidelines for Vascular Access: Update 2000. Am J Kidney Dis 37:S137-S181, 2001.
3. Lok CE, Oliver MJ: Overcoming barriers to arteriovenous fistula creation and use. Semin Dial 16:189-196, 2003.
4. Huber TS, Ozaki CK, Flynn TC, et al: Prospective validation of an algorithm to maximize native arteriovenous fistulae for chronic hemodialysis access. J Vasc Surg 36:452-459, 2002.
5. Hakaim AG, Nalbandian M, Scott T: Superior maturation and patency of primary brachiocephalic and transposed basilic vein arteriovenous fistulae in patients with diabetes. J Vasc Surg 27:154-157, 1998.
6. Mendes RR, Farber MA, Marston WA, et al: Prediction of wrist arteriovenous fistula maturation with preoperative vein mapping with ultrasonography. J Vasc Surg 36:460-463, 2002.
7. Palder SB, Kirkman RL, Whittemore AD, et al: Vascular access for hemodialysis: Patency rates and results of revision. Ann Surg 202:235-239, 1985.
8. Silva MB Jr, Hobson RW, Pappas PJ, Jamil Z, et al: A strategy for increasing use of autogenous hemodialysis access procedures: Impact of preoperative noninvasive evaluation. J Vasc Surg 27:302-307, 1998.
9. Kherlakian GM, Roedersheimer LR, Arbaugh JJ, et al: Comparison of autogenous fistula versus expanded polytetrafluoroethylene graft fistula for angioaccess in hemodialysis. Am J Surg 152:238-243, 1986.
10. Kinnaert P, Vereerstraeten P, Toussaint C, van Geertruyden J: Nine years' experience with internal arteriovenous fistulas for haemodialysis: A study of some factors influencing the results. Br J Surg 64:242-246, 1977.
11. Limet RR, Lejeune GN: Evaluation of 110 subcutaneous arteriovenous fistulae in 100 chronically hemodialysed patients. J Cardiovasc Surg (Torino) 15:573-576, 1974.
12. Rohr MS, Browder W, Frentz GD, McDonald JC: Arteriovenous fistulas for long-term dialysis: Factors that influence fistula survival. Arch Surg 113:153-155, 1978.
13. Ascher E, Gade P, Hingorani A, et al: Changes in the practice of angioaccess surgery: Impact of dialysis outcome and quality initiative recommendations. J Vasc Surg 31:84-92, 2000.
14. Miller A, Holzenbein TJ, Gottlieb MN, et al: Strategies to increase the use of autogenous arteriovenous fistula in end-stage renal disease. Ann Vasc Surg 11:397-405, 1997.
15. Sidawy AN, Gray R, Besarab A, et al: Recommended standards for reports dealing with arteriovenous hemodialysis accesses. J Vasc Surg 35:603-610, 2002.
16. LoGerfo FW, Menzoian JO, Kumaki DJ, Idelson BA: Transposed basilic vein-brachial arteriovenous fistula: A reliable secondary-access procedure. Arch Surg 113:1008-1010, 1978.

17. Dagher F, Gelber R, Ramos E, Sadler J: The use of basilic vein and brachial artery as an A-V fistula for long term hemodialysis. J Surg Res 20:373-376, 1976.

18. Dagher FJ, Gelber R, Reed W: Basilic vein to brachial artery, arteriovenous fistula for long-term hemodialysis: A five year follow-up. Proc Clin Dial Transplant Forum 10:126-129, 1980.

19. Dagher FJ: The upper arm AV hemoaccess: Long term follow-up. J Cardiovasc Surg (Torino) 27:447-449, 1986.

20. Coburn MC, Carney WI Jr: Comparison of basilic vein and polytetra-fluoroethylene for brachial arteriovenous fistula. J Vasc Surg 20:896-902, 1994.

21. Murphy GJ, White SA, Knight AJ, et al: Long-term results of arterio-venous fistulas using transposed autologous basilic vein. Br J Surg 87:819-823, 2000.

22. Taghizadeh A, Dasgupta P, Khan MS, et al: Long-term outcomes of brachiobasilic transposition fistula for haemodialysis. Eur J Vasc Endovasc Surg 26:670-672, 2003.

23. Matsuura JH, Rosenthal D, Clark M, et al: Transposed basilic vein versus polytetrafluorethylene for brachial-axillary arteriovenous fistulas. Am J Surg 176:219-221, 1998.

24. Gormus N, Ozergin U, Durgut K, et al: Comparison of autologous basilic vein transpositions between forearm and upper arm regions. Ann Vasc Surg 17:522-525, 2003.

25. Ascher E, Hingoran A, Gunduz Y, et al: The value and limitations of the arm cephalic and basilic vein for arteriovenous access. Ann Vasc Surg 15:89-97, 2001.

26. Brescia MJ, Cimino JE, Appel K, Hurwich BJ: Chronic hemodialysis using venipuncture and a surgically created arteriovenous fistula. N Engl J Med 275:1089-1092, 1966.

27. Silva MB Jr, Hobson RW, Pappas PJ, et al: Vein transposition in the forearm for autogenous hemodialysis access. J Vasc Surg 26:981-986, 1997.

28. Bhandari S, Wilkinson A, Sellars L: Saphenous vein forearm grafts and gortex thigh grafts as alternative forms of vascular access. Clin Nephrol 44:325-328, 1995.

29. Tashjian DB, Lipkowitz GS, Madden RL, et al: Safety and efficacy of femoral-based hemodialysis access grafts. J Vasc Surg 35:691-693, 2002.

30. Illig KA, Orloff M, Lyden SP, Green RM: Transposed saphenous vein arteriovenous fistula revisited: New technology for an old idea. Cardiovasc Surg 10:212-215, 2002.

31. Gradman WS, Cohen W, Haji-Aghaii M: Arteriovenous fistula construction in the thigh with transposed superficial femoral vein: Our initial experience. J Vasc Surg 33:968-975, 2001.

32. Huber TS, Ozaki CK, Flynn TC, et al: Use of superficial femoral vein for hemodialysis arteriovenous access. J Vasc Surg 31:1038-1041, 2000.

33. Gorski TF, Nguyen HQ, Gorski YC, et al: Lower-extremity saphenous vein transposition arteriovenous fistula: An alternative for hemodialysis access in AIDS patients. Am Surg 64:338-340, 1998.

34. Kinnaert P, Vereerstraeten P, Toussaint C, van Geertruyden J: Saphenous vein loop fistula in the thigh for maintenance hemodialysis. World J Surg 3:95-98, 132-133, 1979.

35. May J, Tiller D, Johnson J, Stewart J, Sheil AG: Saphenous-vein arteriovenous fistula in regular dialysis treatment. N Engl J Med 280:770, 1969.

36. Hingorani A, Ascher E, Kallakuri S, et al: Impact of reintervention for failing upper-extremity arteriovenous autogenous access for hemo-dialysis. J Vasc Surg 34:1004-1009, 2001.

37. Berman SS, Gentile AT: Impact of secondary procedures in autogenous arteriovenous fistula maturation and maintenance. J Vasc Surg 34:866-871, 2001.

Chapter

Management of Thrombosed Dialysis Access

119

ALAN B. LUMSDEN, FACS
RUTH L. BUSH, MD
PETER H. LIN, MD
ERIC K. PEDEN, MD

In the United States, long-term hemodialysis for end-stage renal failure affects at least 250,000 patients. Patients with renal failure today are older and have a high incidence of diabetes mellitus as a causative factor in renal disease. Because kidney allografts are a limited and rare commodity, the percentage of patients with chronic renal failure on hemodialysis is greater than 35%. Of all dialysis patient admissions, 20% are related to access site problems, and the most common complication leading to failure of a vascular access site is thrombosis. Ballard and colleagues[1] found that 18% of the total surgical caseload was related to the treatment of dialysis access complications in a 4-year single-institution review of angioaccess procedures. A large portion of the cost of treatment of dialysis patients relates to provid-

ing, preserving, and maintaining arteriovenous (AV) access for hemodialysis.

Prosthetic AV access thrombosis is a frequent complication that occurs at a rate of 0.5 to 0.8 episodes per year. AV access thrombosis alone accounts for a major source of hospital admissions, increasing hospital costs, patient morbidity, and physician frustration. Thrombosed grafts often require rescue procedures to extend the life of the graft and make the most use of the limited available access sites. Salvage procedures of thrombosed prosthetic dialysis shunts may be performed with conventional surgical or endovascular techniques or a combination of both techniques. Many techniques for declotting have been used, including open surgical thrombectomy, percutaneous pharmacologic or mechanical thrombectomy, and pharmacomechanical techniques. Despite the various treatment options, no individual declotting modality has proved superior. Long-term patencies after a single revascularization procedure are meager (median <90 days).

The reason for prosthetic AV access thrombosis is multifactorial and includes the formation of intimal hyperplasia, adequacy of the patient's arteries and veins, prosthetic material choice, actual access site and graft anatomic configuration, intrinsic coagulation state, systemic blood pressure, and cardiac output. Prosthetic AV access using either polytetrafluoroethylene (PTFE) or the more recently introduced polyurethane graft has lower patency rates compared with autogenous AV access. The secondary patency rates tend to be slightly higher, however, as a result of multiple revisions in attempts to maximize the longevity of each individual access. Data from the U.S. Renal Data System Dialysis Morbidity and Mortality Study Wave 2, which contained a random sample of dialysis patients initiating dialysis in 1996 and early 1997, included evaluations of failures and revisions among 2247 newly placed hemodialysis accesses.[2] In a cohort of 1574 prosthetic AV accesses, there was a 41% greater risk of failure than with autogenous AV access and a 91% higher chance of needing a revision. PTFE grafts had a 2-year primary patency rate of 24.6% (versus 39.8% for autogenous AV access; $P < .001$) with equivalent secondary patency rates (64.3% versus 59.5%; $P = .24$).

■ CLINICAL EVALUATION OF THE THROMBOSED ACCESS

A great deal of information can be gained from taking a detailed access history and careful clinical examination of the patient:

1. How many accesses have been placed previously, how long did they last, and how often were they revised? This is particularly important for the affected limb.

2. Have there been catheters placed? Did they work well, were they difficult to place, and has there been any arm swelling? Again, the emphasis is on the affected side. These questions may glean useful information on the status of the central veins.

3. Extremity examination should focus on the type of access previously placed, how it was revised (e.g., extension from a forearm access may consume upper arm vein), and whether there is any evidence of infection in existing grafts and the height in the axilla of previous venous anastomoses (very high anastomoses are revised more easily using a catheter-based approach than an open surgical approach). Type and geometry of the graft dictate where the graft should be accessed for thrombus removal.

4. A history of hypercoagulable states, lupus, or sickle cell tends to decrease graft patency.

Venous Anastomotic Lesion

The principal cause of access graft failure is development of a stenosis at the venous anastomosis. This venous anastomotic lesion is actively proliferative and contains a large amount of smooth muscle cells and ground substance (Fig. 119-1). It can be extraordinarily difficult to dilate and tends to recoil after balloon angioplasty. High-pressure balloons are designed specifically to dilate this lesion because of this well-recognized difficulty. Despite using high pressures (20 to 30 atm), it may prove impossible to resolve the "waist" that is usually regarded as the determination of a successful outcome (Fig. 119-2).

It is clear that all venous anastomotic lesions are not equal, varying from short segment focal lesions to extensive stenoses with near-total obliteration of the outflow venous

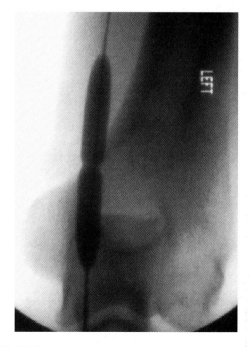

FIGURE 119-2 Despite the use of high-pressure angioplasty balloons (20 atm), it can be difficult to dilate the stenosis. Persistent "waisting" of the balloon is observed in this study.

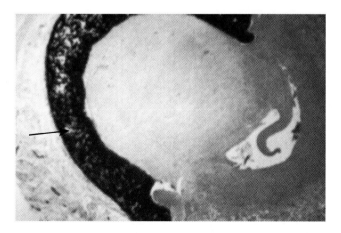

FIGURE 119-1 Transverse section through the venous anastomosis of an expanded polytetrafluoroethylene graft (*arrow*). The lumen is almost completely filled with neointimal hyperplasia. This lesion is the most common cause of graft failure and is difficult to dilate with an angioplasty balloon. (See color figure in this section.)

segment over considerable lengths. The lesions can be classified based on the number of stenoses and anatomic location, severity, and length of stenosis or occlusion. Subclavian and brachiocephalic lesions are more likely to be immediate technical failures compared with axillary or more proximal lesions. The duration of efficacy also is less for long venous lesions and subclavian lesions than for other venous stenoses. In 27% of lesions, high-pressure balloons are required to dilate the stenosis. Even with high-pressure balloons, lesions resistant to dilatation are encountered, and pressures greater than 10 atm are required in 20% of cases.

The mechanism of action of percutaneous transluminal angioplasty in hemodialysis-associated stenoses has been examined using intravascular ultrasound. Vessel dissection occurred in 16% cases, stretching occurred in 50%, but significant elastic recoil occurred in 50%. This is different from the mechanism of action in arterial stenoses, where dissection of the plaque may be the primary mode of therapeutic efficacy.

To prolong graft life and decrease the frequency of interventions, graft surveillance within dialysis units is recommended. Measurements of venous resistance, defined by various clinical and hemodialysis recirculation parameters, can lead to recognition of an outflow problem before thrombosis occurs. If followed by a subsequent venogram and percutaneous dilatation of identified stenoses, correction is easier and more expedient for the patient and surgeon. Stenoses are identified as the inciting lesion in more than 90% of cases at the time of percutaneous thrombectomy or thrombolysis with the culprit lesion being at or near the venous anastomosis.[3,4] In a retrospective study of a single dialysis unit graft surveillance policy, patients in whom early intervention was undertaken had a better graft survival (15.8 months versus 6.3 months, $P < .01$) than patients who were treated after prosthetic AV access thrombosis had occurred.[5] In a study by Lumsden and associates,[6] all patients in a single dialysis unit with prosthetic AV access using PTFE bridge grafts were subject to a surveillance duplex ultrasound, and patients found to have a perigraft (in the graft or the adjacent artery and vein) stenosis of greater than 50% underwent angiography.[6] Interventions were performed on a randomized basis for stenosis greater than 50%. There were no significant differences in 6-month or 12-month patency rates. Cost estimates of duplex ultrasound and interventions along with equivalent patency rates led these authors to conclude that a policy of prosthetic AV access surveillance and prophylaxis is expensive and does not lead to improved patency.

The high costs of hospitalization and treatment of thrombosed AV access require effective, yet less invasive outpatient procedures. Recent years have seen a sudden increase in the development of percutaneous mechanical devices that function via mechanical dissolution, fragmentation, or aspiration of clot. Postprocedural dialysis can be performed immediately, reducing the number of central venous catheters necessary with their inherent difficulties. The clinical success rates of mechanical thrombectomies are usually between 71% and 100%. The incidence of serious complications of percutaneous treatment is low. This chapter reviews several of these modern techniques, including the role of the thrombosed dialysis graft as an endovascular model for vascular surgeons seeking new percutaneous skills.[7]

■ THROMBOSED GRAFT: THREE MANAGEMENT PRINCIPLES

The three management principles for the thrombosed graft are as follows:

1. Complete thrombus removal
2. Total graft imaging
3. Identification and correction of all significant stenoses

Regardless of the approach selected, all three principles must be applied to result in optimal graft revision. Compromise, particularly in imaging and lesion identification, is partly responsible for the dismal patency data often reported.

■ SURGICAL THROMBECTOMY

Open surgical thrombectomy alone typically is not adequate for successful treatment of thrombosed prosthetic AV access, unless there has been a clear-cut inciting event, such as external compression or hypotension. Development of a stenosis at the venous end is usually the provocative lesion resulting in thrombosis, and local revision of the graft-to-vein anastomosis needs to be done to prolong graft survival. Thrombectomies are performed in the sterile environment in an operating room generally under local anesthesia with systemic heparin given (3000 to 4000 U) or injection of heparinized solution in the venous inflow and outflow and in the body of the access after thrombectomy is completed. There are two approaches to performing open thrombectomy. One is to perform thrombectomy rapidly via a short incision, make a transverse graftotomy, remove the thrombus, and identify the lesion (Figs. 119-3 and 119-4). The transverse graftotomy can be made in any readily accessible portion of the graft. Alternatively, many surgeons anticipate that in most cases the offending lesion is at the venous anastomosis and expose the anastomosis, opening it longitudinally with the anticipation that a patch will be necessary (Fig. 119-5). Thrombectomy is typically done with a No. 4 Fogarty embolectomy catheter (see Fig. 119-3); first, the venous end is declotted, then the arterial plug is removed (see Fig. 119-4). The plug is inspected carefully to ensure the meniscus that represents where the clot abuts against arterial flow has been included. After complete clot removal, a patch angioplasty with either PTFE or Dacron is performed (see Fig. 119-5), or an interposition bypass graft is placed. A patch angioplasty may be partially sewn in place without performing the arterial thrombectomy. This maneuver is reserved until just before placement of the final sutures in the patch. In doing this, bleeding is controlled, the graft should not rethrombose during sewing of the patch, and dissection is minimized.

Surgical revision has been compared with transluminal angioplasty coupled with thrombectomy.[8] In a retrospective review, 24 patients undergoing 28 angioplasty procedures were compared with 24 patients undergoing 33 surgical graft revisions. There were no significant differences found in success rates, primary patency rates, or secondary patency rates. The angioplasty patients experienced shorter hospital stays and less anesthetic requirements, however. Another study by Bitar and colleagues[9] also showed equivocal results in comparison of the two treatment modalities with similar

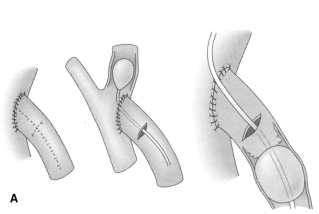

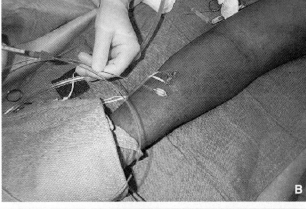

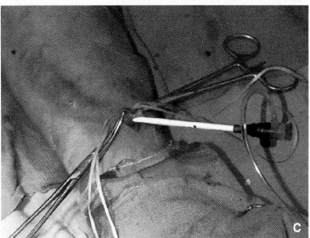

FIGURE 119-3 A, The traditional open approach is to pass a Fogarty catheter proximally and distally through a graftotomy. Many surgeons simply open the graft through the venous anastomosis to facilitate subsequent patching. **B,** We favor making a graftotomy remote from the venous anastomosis, to permit ease of imaging the entire graft. Surgical cutdown over the apex of a forearm loop polytetrafluoroethylene graft has been performed. The graft has been encircled with a Romel for control. A No. 4 Fogarty embolectomy catheter is used to thrombectomize the venous anastomosis first and then the arterial anastomosis with the arterial plug. **C,** When the thrombectomy has been completed, a hemostatic sheath is inserted into both ends of the graft, and angiography is performed. (See color figure in this section.)

FIGURE 119-4 The arterial plug is thrombolysis resistant and consists of compact layers of fibrin and red blood cells. (See color figure in this section.)

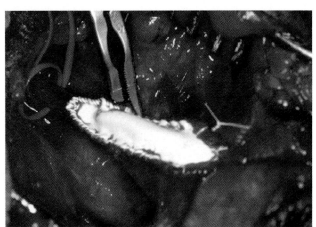

FIGURE 119-5 A longitudinal incision is made onto the graft and extended down onto the venous outflow tract. A prosthetic patch is used to create a patch angioplasty onto the venous anastomotic stenosis.

patency rates and complications. From these two reviews, balloon angioplasty can be recommended only as an alternative to surgical revision in the salvage of prosthetic AV access grafts.

■ ENDOVASCULAR MANAGEMENT

Percutaneous techniques have become commonplace in the management of thrombosed grafts. The caveat exists that these endovascular maneuvers be applied only in grafts that have formerly functioned. Early graft failure is generally attributed to technical failure or inadequate inflow and outflow vessels for support, unless prolonged hypotension or graft compression can be identified as having occurred. Otherwise, these cases normally require surgical revision. Patients in whom there is a need for urgent dialysis (fluid overload or electrolyte abnormality) or an existing contraindication to iodinated contrast material or thrombolysis should have a temporary double-lumen catheter inserted for immediate treatment.

■ THROMBOLYSIS

In 1985, Zeit and Cope[10] first described the use of thrombolytic agents in thrombosed prosthetic AV access. Twenty-six patients were treated 33 times with a streptokinase dilution introduced into the graft via multiple needle puncture sites. A functioning access was obtained in 73%, although surgical correction of a stenosis or pseudo-aneurysm was necessary in 30%. Subsequently, pulse-spray thrombolysis was introduced in 1989 with urokinase (Abbott Laboratories, Abbott Park, Ill).[11]

In a study that included 29 thrombosed dialysis AV grafts, infusion catheters were inserted using the crossing catheters technique, one directed toward the arterial anastomosis and the other directed toward the venous anastomosis, which ensured that the entire graft was treated.[11] A starting bolus of 250,000 U of urokinase was used, mixed with heparin; additional dosing was performed on an as-needed basis for residual clot. This technique of pharmacomechanical thrombolysis would reveal venous stenoses that were then dilated and the arterial plug was macerated with a balloon catheter. In these patients, a 100%

technical success rate was achieved. Flow was restored in 19 minutes, and time for total lysis was 49 minutes. Roberts and coworkers[12] performed a larger review of the pulse-spray technique in 1993. They reviewed 209 thrombosed grafts treated with crossing catheters and found 99% to be patent and functioning at the conclusion of the procedure. The average procedural duration was 40 minutes. This treatment option was believed to be safe, expeditious, and effective. The "crossed catheter" technique has since been the "gold standard" for thrombolysis of thrombosed PTFE grafts (Fig. 119-6), until the advent and widespread use of mechanical thrombectomy devices in more recent years.

The "lyse-and-wait" technique was later popularized by Cynamon and associates[13] in 1997 (Figs. 119-7 and 119-8). With this modification of pharmacomechanical thrombolysis, the graft was instilled with lytic agent, initially 250,000 U, and the patient waited in the interventional preoperative area. The angiography suite was available for use while the time-consuming portion of the case was being performed (i.e., the actual time for lysis). The original description involved using sheaths that could tolerate high flow rates (>500 mL/min) so that the patient could undergo immediate hemodialysis without waiting for puncture site homeostasis. Overall, with the "lyse-and-wait" technique, operator, room, and fluoroscopy times all are greatly reduced. This type of declotting has been studied with urokinase and, after this lytic agent was removed from the market, tissue plasminogen activator.[13-16]

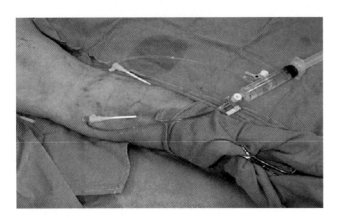

FIGURE 119-6 Arterial and venous sheaths are inserted into a forearm loop graft.

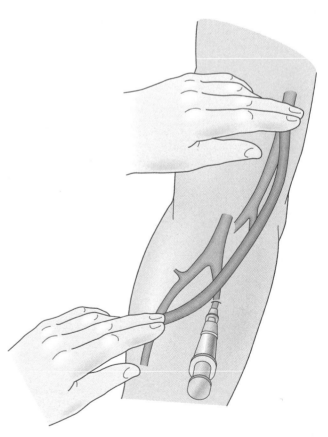

FIGURE 119-7 Lyse and wait technique. The surgeon slowly injects 250,000 IU of urokinase or 2 mg of tissue plasminogen activator mixed with 5000 U of heparin in 5 mL of normal saline.

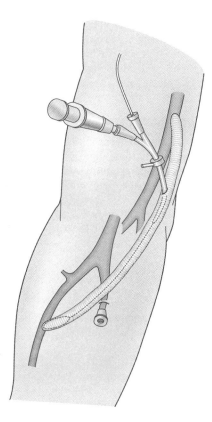

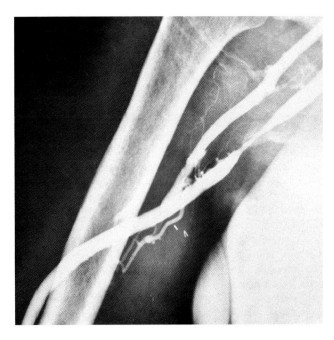

FIGURE 119-9   Angiogram shows a typical venous anastomotic stenosis.

FIGURE 119-8   When the patient enters the interventional suite, the graft is accessed using the crossed catheter technique with a 5F sheath close to the venous anastomosis and directed toward the artery. A Fogarty catheter is used to displace the plug from the arterial anastomosis, which is allowed to pass into the central veins. A second sheath is inserted into the graft close to the arterial end and directed toward the venous anastomosis. The entire graft, arterial anastomosis, and venous outflow can be studied rapidly via the dual sheaths. Through this, angioplasty of a venous anastomotic stenosis or central venous stenosis can be performed.

To perform this technique, a heparin and lytic agent mixture is prepared and instilled into the graft via an 18-gauge needle with an assistant compressing the arterial and the venous outflow. In a review of 21 graft declottings in 17 patients, Vogel and colleagues[14] performed their initial angiographic graft evaluation at an average of 86 minutes after the administration of 6667 U of urokinase. The graft angiogram, via the indwelling needle, was performed only when an interventional suite became available between other cases. Technical and clinical success, as defined by the ability to undergo hemodialysis, was achieved in 95% of cases. This group showed that very-low-dose thrombolytic therapy was effective in graft thrombectomy, resulting in a decrease in cost and hemorrhagic complications.

■ PERCUTANEOUS MECHANICAL THROMBECTOMY

Multiple different percutaneous mechanical thrombectomy (PMT) devices now exist that have been tested and approved by the Food and Drug Administration for use in hemodialysis grafts. Their use is only beginning to be widespread by treating physicians, however. PMT devices allow for

expeditious clot removal with a decrease in the frequency, dose, and duration of lytic usage. By decreasing overall procedural time and eliminating a surgical incision, it is argued that patients often can go straight from the interventional suite to the dialysis unit. This also can be accomplished by surgical thrombectomy and outflow patch or jump graft. These patients also can be dialyzed immediately after surgery.

Essential to all interventional procedures performed on acutely thrombosed hemodialysis grafts are the quality and patency of the native venous system, including the central veins. A venogram must be performed first to document patency of the runoff veins or collateral channels before thrombectomy is begun. Two vascular sheaths may be inserted into the prosthetic AV access—one toward the arterial inflow and the other toward the venous outflow (see Fig. 119-6). The diagnostic venogram usually reveals a focal high-grade venous stenosis as the inciting lesion leading to prosthetic AV access thrombosis (Fig. 119-9). We prefer to treat any venous anastomotic lesions before declotting; when the graft thrombus and arterial plug are removed, adequate outflow exists, avoiding rethrombosis.

A complete discussion of all the currently available PMT devices is beyond the scope of this chapter. A few representative methods are presented with individual data. Additionally, the devices are approved for use in prosthetic AV access, but not autogenous AV access. One of the current Food and Drug Administration–approved devices is the AngioJet rheolytic catheter (Possis Medical, Inc, Minneapolis, Minn). This mechanical thrombectomy system fits through a 6F sheath and over a 0.035-inch guide wire. The theoretical principle of this device is based on the Venturi effect. Rapidly flowing saline jets (8000 psi) are directed backward from the tip of the device, rather than outward to the vessel wall, to reduce intimal injury. The thrombus is drawn into the vacuum created by these rapidly flowing jets and then out the catheter to a collection bag. In a prospective, randomized trial comparing surgical thrombectomy with AngioJet thrombectomy in thrombosed hemodialysis grafts, 153 patients were studied with follow-up of 6 months.[17] There was no difference between the groups in their ability to undergo hemodialysis treatment, and there was no difference in the primary patency rates. The surgical group did have more major complications, however, primarily wound related.

An Arrow-Trerotola device (Arrow International, Reading, Pa) is basically an over-the-wire rotating fragmentation basket that macerates clot, which is then removed via an aspiration port. The remaining arterial plug is removed at the conclusion of graft declotting with a standard Fogarty embolectomy catheter. Rocek and colleagues[18] evaluated this type of "mechanical thrombolysis" in a preliminary report of seven patients. The procedures took an average of 126 minutes, there were no major complications, and the primary patency at 6 months was 60%. The authors concluded that this technique was rapid and effective; however, they tested it in autogenous native fistula, which most likely accounts for the above-average primary patency rate. Lazzaro and colleagues[19] studied a much larger group (50 patients) prospectively 3 months after using the Arrow-Trerotola catheter solely (they also removed the arterial plug with this device) in thrombosed grafts. These authors used historical controls for comparison in which the Fogarty catheter portion of the procedure was performed. They showed no differences in either technical success or 3-month patency rates, showing that the additional catheter maneuver was not necessary for sufficient functioning of this device.

Conversely, Sofocleous and associates[20] evaluated the Amplatz thrombectomy device and compared it with pulse-spray thrombolysis. The Amplatz percutaneous rotational device homogenizes and debulks thrombus using a high-speed impeller, which creates a vortex action (Microvena Corp., White Bear Lake, Minn). In 126 episodes of graft occlusion in 79 patients, the patients were divided almost equally between the two treatment modalities. Although the technical success rates were similar, the Amplatz device was associated with a significantly higher local complication rate. This fact along with the technical difficulties the authors cited in using the 8F device led to conclusions limiting its use.

The most recent entrant into the percutaneous clot management arena is the Trellis catheter. This device is unique in that it combines a mechanical clot disruption system with the ability to infuse lytic agents that can be isolated within the graft by occlusion balloons. This device has significant potential appeal, but further experience and data are needed before any recommendations can be made.

Overall, despite the PMT device chosen, there are some general principles for the interventionist treating patients with thrombosed prosthetic AV access. The age of the thrombus is of particular importance because acute, fresh (<3 days old) thrombus is removed much more successfully than chronic, organized, fibrosed clot. Adjunctive thrombolytic agent may facilitate removal, however. There are no data to support the addition of thrombolytics to PMT; nonetheless, intuitively this combined approach makes

sense. Also, as the device is extended past the graft into the native vessels, damaging wall contact may occur. The PMTs that use a saline jet spray may incite less endothelial damage. The advantages of these devices over local thrombolysis are a more rapid establishment of a patent lumen, only a single catheterization session, fewer laboratory tests for monitoring the fibrinolytic effect, and decreased chance of remote bleeding. Advantages over traditional balloon thrombectomy include the use of fluoroscopic guidance and the ability to perform immediate arteriography; over-the-wire passage of the device, which should minimize the incidence of arterial perforation and pseudoaneurysm formation; and probably lesser endothelial damage. Additionally, immediate percutaneous correction of the underlying lesion that caused the thrombosis is possible (Fig. 119-10).

■ COMBINED OPEN THROMBECTOMY AND BALLOON ANGIOPLASTY

A more recent alternate approach combines open and catheter-based techniques (see Fig. 119-3). The principles of this approach include the following:

1. Balloon catheter thrombectomy through a small transverse graft incision remote from the arterial and the venous anastomosis
2. Angiographic imaging of the entire graft, including arterial anastomosis and the entire venous outflow tract, via hemostatic sheaths inserted through the graftotomy
3. Balloon angioplasty of graft and anastomotic or venous outflow tract stenoses

■ ENDOVASCULAR STENTING

Percutaneous stenting attempts to preserve hemodialysis grafts. No clear advantage over angioplasty alone has been seen, however, following stent placement after percutaneous graft recanalization.[21-26] Quinn and associates[22] placed 25 self-expanding stents in 19 patients with a technical success rate of 90%. Primary patency rate at 2 years was 25% with a secondary patency of 34%. This compares poorly with the 2-year reported primary and secondary patency rates of prosthetic AV grafts at 50% and 78%.[27] Vorwerk and colleagues[24] showed grafts with stents placed to have a 76% 3-month patency, decreasing to 31% at 1 year. With repeat interventions, the patency rates improved to 86% at 1 year. Overall, stenoses in vascular grafts tend to recur and be in variable locations, contributing to the difficulty in maintaining a functioning graft. Patients with long segment venous outflow stenosis or occlusion have a significantly worse patency rate than patients with only a focal venous anastomotic stenosis.[28]

■ CONCLUSION

Salvage of a thrombosed prosthetic AV access may be accomplished with either surgical or endovascular techniques or a combination of the two. Long-term function of

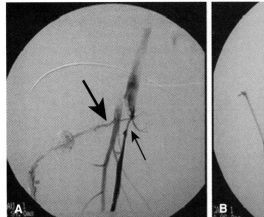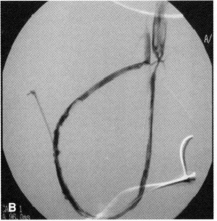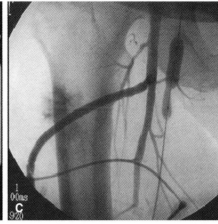

FIGURE 119-10 Thrombosed femoral loop polytetrafluoroethylene graft. **A,** The larger arrow is pointing toward the arterial end, and the smaller arrow is pointing toward a high-grade venous anastomotic stenosis seen on initial diagnostic angiogram. **B,** Femoral graft after initial run with the AngioJet percutaneous thrombectomy device. Notice two sheaths in either side of the graft for declotting the arterial and venous ends. **C,** Angioplasty of the venous outflow stenosis; a tight waist is seen during insufflation of the balloon.

the thrombosed graft is currently difficult to obtain with any treatment modality.[28] It is crucial that open thrombectomy and percutaneous thrombectomy be carefully evaluated by imaging the entire graft, arterial anastomosis, and venous outflow all the way to the right atrium. Endovascular techniques for dealing with the venous anastomosis will continue to evolve. Prosthetic AV access with PTFE grafts represents an ideal, safe endovascular training ground for surgeons wishing to incorporate catheter-based skills into their patient management armamentarium.

■ REFERENCES

1. Ballard JL, Bunt TJ, Malone JM: Major complications of angioaccess surgery. Am J Surg 164:229-232, 1992.
2. Gibson KD, Gillen DL, Caps MT, et al: Vascular access survival and incidence of revisions: A comparison of prosthetic grafts, simple autogenous fistulas, and venous transposition fistulas from the United States Renal Data System Dialysis Morbidity and Mortality Study. J Vasc Surg 34:694-700, 2001.
3. Beathard GA: Mechanical versus pharmacomechanical thrombolysis for the treatment of thrombosed dialysis access grafts. Kidney Int 45:1401-1406, 1994.
4. Turmel-Rodrigues L, Pengloan J, Baudin S, et al: Treatment of stenosis and thrombosis in haemodialysis fistulas and grafts by interventional radiology. Nephrol Dial Transplant 15:2029-2036, 2000.
5. Roberts AB, Kahn MB, Bradford S, et al: Graft surveillance and angioplasty prolongs dialysis graft patency. J Am Coll Surg 183:486-492, 1996.
6. Lumsden AB, MacDonald MJ, Kikeri D, et al: Cost efficacy of duplex surveillance and prophylactic angioplasty of arteriovenous ePTFE grafts. Ann Vasc Surg 12:138-142, 1998.
7. Lumsden AB, Hughes JD, MacDonald MJ, Ofenloch JC: The thrombosed arteriovenous graft: An endovascular model for vascular surgeons. Cardiovasc Surg 5:401-407, 1997.
8. Schwartz CI, McBrayer CV, Sloan JH, et al: Thrombosed dialysis grafts: Comparison of treatment with transluminal angioplasty and surgical revision. Radiology 194:337-341, 1995.
9. Bitar G, Yang S, Badosa F: Balloon versus patch angioplasty as an adjuvant treatment to surgical thrombectomy of hemodialysis grafts. Am J Surg 174:140-142, 1997.
10. Zeit RM, Cope C: Failed hemodialysis shunts: One year of experience with aggressive treatment. Radiology 154:353-356, 1985.
11. Bookstein JJ, Fellmeth B, Roberts A, et al: Pulsed-spray pharmaco-mechanical thrombolysis: Preliminary clinical results. AJR Am J Roentgenol 152:1097-1100, 1989.
12. Roberts AC, Valji K, Bookstein JJ, Hye RJ: Pulse-spray pharmaco-mechanical thrombolysis for treatment of thrombosed dialysis access grafts. Am J Surg 166:221-226, 1993.
13. Cynamon J, Lakritz PS, Wahl SI, et al: Hemodialysis graft declotting: Description of the "lyse and wait" technique. J Vasc Interv Radiol 8:825-829, 1997.
14. Vogel PM, Bansal V, Marshall MW: Thrombosed hemodialysis grafts: Lyse and wait with tissue plasminogen activator or urokinase compared to mechanical thrombolysis with the Arrow-Trerotola Percutaneous Thrombolytic Device. J Vasc Interv Radiol 12:1157-1165, 2001.
15. Duszak R Jr, Sacks D: Pitfalls that may contribute to "lyse and wait" declotting failures [letter; author reply]. J Vasc Interv Radiol 9:660, 661, 1998.
16. Duszak R Jr, Sacks D: Dialysis graft declotting with very low dose urokinase: Is it feasible to use "lyse and wait"? J Vasc Interv Radiol 10:123-128, 1999.
17. Vesely TM, Williams D, Weiss M, et al: Comparison of the angiojet rheolytic catheter to surgical thrombectomy for the treatment of thrombosed hemodialysis grafts. Peripheral AngioJet Clinical Trial. J Vasc Interv Radiol 10:1195-1205, 1999.
18. Rocek M, Peregrin JH, Lasovickova J, et al: Mechanical thrombolysis of thrombosed hemodialysis native fistulas with use of the Arrow-Trerotola percutaneous thrombolytic device: Our preliminary experience. J Vasc Interv Radiol 11:1153-1158, 2000.
19. Lazzaro CR, Trerotola SO, Shah H, et al: Modified use of the Arrow-Trerotola percutaneous thrombolytic device for the treatment of thrombosed hemodialysis access grafts. J Vasc Interv Radiol 10:1025-1031, 1999.
20. Sofocleous CT, Cooper SG, Schur I, et al: Retrospective comparison of the Amplatz thrombectomy device with modified pulse-spray pharmacomechanical thrombolysis in the treatment of thrombosed hemodialysis access grafts. Radiology 213:561-567, 1999.
21. Patel RI, Peck SH, Cooper SG, et al: Patency of Wallstents placed across the venous anastomosis of hemodialysis grafts after percutaneous recanalization. Radiology 209:365-370, 1998.
22. Quinn SF, Schuman ES, Hall L, et al: Venous stenoses in patients who undergo hemodialysis: Treatment with self-expandable endovascular stents. Radiology 183:499-504, 1992.

23. Zaleski GX, Funaki B, Rosenblum J, et al: Metallic stents deployed in synthetic arteriovenous hemodialysis grafts. AJR Am J Roentgenol 176:1515-1519, 2001.

24. Vorwerk D, Guenther RW, Schurmann K: Stent placement on fresh venous thrombosis. Cardiovasc Interv Radiol 20:359-363, 1997.

25. Hoffer EK, Sultan S, Herskowitz MM, et al: Prospective randomized trial of a metallic intravascular stent in hemodialysis graft maintenance. J Vasc Interv Radiol 8:965-973, 1997.

26. Gray RJ, Horton KM, Dolmatch BL, et al: Use of Wallstents for hemodialysis access-related venous stenoses and occlusions untreatable with balloon angioplasty. Radiology 195:479-484, 1995.

27. Munda R, First MR, Alexander JW, et al: Polytetrafluoroethylene graft survival in hemodialysis. JAMA 249:219-222, 1983.

28. Marston WA, Criado E, Jaques PF, et al: Prospective randomized comparison of surgical versus endovascular management of thrombosed dialysis access grafts. J Vasc Surg 26:373-381, 1997.

Chapter

Nonthrombotic Complications of Arteriovenous Access for Hemodialysis

120

ERIC D. ADAMS, MD
ANTON N. SIDAWY, MD, MPH

■ BACKGROUND

End-stage renal disease (ESRD) is an increasingly common diagnosis in the United States. The American Kidney Foundation now lists it as the ninth leading cause of death. Although hemodialysis had its start in the 1960s by the introduction of the technique at the University of Washington, the numbers treated were relatively small. Prior to 1973 the total number of patients on hemodialysis was 13,000. That same year saw the passage of the End-Stage Renal Disease Program of Medicare, which provided financial support to renal failure patients. By 1980 there were more than 50,000 patients on dialysis, and by 1986 the number was 87,000.[1] Data from the 1999 U.S. Renal Data System (USRDS) showed 194,000 patients receiving renal dialysis.[2] This trend is likely to continue as the population gets older and the incidence of diabetes mellitus in the overall population increases. The overall incidence is 180 per million and continues to rise at a rate of 7.8% per year.[3] The incidence for those older than 75 years of age rose even faster at 9.5% between 1996 and 2000.[4] Most patients with ESRD are treated with hemodialysis rather than peritoneal dialysis or renal transplant. Hemodialysis patients outnumber those on peritoneal dialysis or renal transplant patients by almost 2:1.[4] The year 2000 saw more than 83,000 new patients beginning hemodialysis.

Costs for renal dialysis continue to rise accordingly. Costs for treatment of ESRD patients was estimated at $8.6 billion in 1991, or an annual cost of $47,000 per patient.[5] Not reflected in this number are additional expenses for outpatient drugs and supplies, cost of disability, and Social Security payments.[6] USRDS data from 2000 reveal a cost of more than $11 billion per year. Medicare parts A and B

payments per patient per month in 1999 ranged from $4,931 ($59,173 per annum) for patients younger than 44 years of age without diabetes up to $6,233 ($74,796 per annum) for a patient older than 75 years of age with diabetes.[4] It is believed that one third of the cost of maintenance hemodialysis is related to establishing and preserving vascular access.[5] Vascular access dysfunction was the leading indication for hospitalization in the population of patients undergoing dialysis in 1993.[7]

The Dialysis Outcome Quality Initiative (DOQI) guidelines published by the National Kidney Foundation provide recommendations for optimal clinical practices aimed at improving dialysis outcome and patient survival. In an effort to standardize both the nomenclature used to describe autogenous and nonautogenous arteriovenous (AV) accesses as well as their complications, the Committee on Reporting Standards for Arteriovenous Access of the Society for Vascular Surgery (SVS) and the American Association for Vascular Surgery (AAVS) published their report.[3] The nomenclature used by the Reporting Standards document is used throughout this chapter to describe access for hemodialysis. The discussion of complications from the creation and use of hemodialysis access is related to the DOQI guidelines. The Reporting Standards document recognizes eight categories of complications from the creation or use of hemodialysis access. These include thrombosis (discussed in Chapter 119), bleeding, infection, pseudoaneurysm, noninfectious fluid collections, steal syndrome, venous hypertension, and neuropathy. The physician charged with establishing hemodialysis access or with management of patients on maintenance hemodialysis should be knowledgeable about all of these potential complications.

■ BLEEDING

Bleeding difficulties can plague the surgeon during the creation of a new AV access or during the revision of an older one. Prolonged bleeding from needle puncture sites is another source of problems in the hemodialysis patient. The Reporting Standards document grades the severity of bleeding from grades 0 to 3, as follows:

Grade 0: No bleeding
Grade 1: Resolves without treatment
Grade 2: Medical therapy needed to correct coagulation abnormality
Grade 3: Intervention needed

Factors Contributing to a Bleeding Diathesis

Morgagni in 1764 was the first to recognize the association between kidney dysfunction and a bleeding tendency.[8,9] Riesman made the observation again in 1907 with his description of a bleeding tendency seen in the course of Bright's disease.[10] Patients on hemodialysis have the additional risk factor for bleeding of periodic heparin administration. Subdural hematoma, hemopericardium, gastrointestinal bleeding, bleeding into the anterior chamber of the eye, parathyroids, retroperitoneum, and mediastinum all have been described in patients on chronic hemodialysis.[10] There is no close relationship between the degree of azotemia and bleeding complications, but as a general rule, the risk of bleeding increases markedly when the blood urea nitrogen concentrations exceed 100 mg/dL. Certain medications are known to worsen bleeding tendencies in patients with ESRD as well. Beta-lactam antibiotics (i.e., penicillins and cephalosporins) have a half-life that is prolonged in renal failure and at high levels have been shown to cause platelet dysfunction. At extremely high serum levels, penicillins alter antithrombin III activity, causing heparin-like abnormalities.[11] Low-molecular-weight heparins are mainly eliminated by the kidneys, and their use in hemodialysis patients can be difficult to adjust correctly.[12] Skin puncture bleeding time is a reliable predictor of clinical bleeding in the setting of uremia.[13,14]

The defect in hemostasis seen in the setting of uremia is multifactorial. Although some of the defect arises from chronic anemia, other factors also play an important role. At normal hematocrit levels, red blood cells occupy the center of the blood stream, with platelets and plasma more concentrated at the periphery and able to react readily with the endothelium. In anemia the rheology of the blood changes and the blood acts like more of a classic Newtonian fluid with platelets and red blood cells evenly mixed.[13,15,16] Most research has pointed to platelet dysfunction as the most prominent defect in uremia.[8,9,17,18] Platelets of patients with uremia exhibit a decrease in glycoprotein (GP) Ib,[19] the receptor for von Willebrand factor (vWF). Furthermore, GPIIb-IIIa function of platelets is impaired, most likely the result of a conformational change and fibrinogen-ligand binding defect of GPIIb-IIIa.[18] Excessive nitric oxide (NO) production by uremic vessels, perhaps secondary to uncleared guanidinosuccinic acid, has been implicated as the previously mysterious factor inducing the changes in platelet function.[9] The final defect seen in uremic patients is the increased endothelial production of prostaglandin I_2, a vasodilator with antiplatelet effects.[10,15]

Treatment of Bleeding Diathesis

Treatment of bleeding in the hemodialysis patient can be addressed by several means. Adequate dialysis itself can improve platelet function. Maintenance of an adequate hematocrit by use of erythropoietin gives both a margin of safety should there be any bleeding as well as favorably affects the rheology of the blood-facilitating platelet function. Recombinant human erythropoietin (rHuEPO) also induces an increase in GPIIb-IIIa expression.[18]

Intraoperative or postoperative bleeding can be dealt with by the administration of 0.3 to 0.4 µg/kg of 1-deamino-8-D-arginine vasopressin (DDAVP). The DDAVP should be diluted in saline and administered as a short (30-minute) infusion.[10] DDAVP releases factor VIII:vWF from storage sites into the plasma and increases the proportion circulating as large multimers.[20] The effect of DDAVP should be apparent in 30 minutes and lasts up to 8 hours. Tachyphylaxis to DDAVP typically develops after the second dose once stores of VIII:vWF are exhausted.[21] Some evidence exists that DDAVP may act through transiently decreasing protein C activity as well.[8]

Cryoprecipitate, 10 units, can also be administered intraoperatively or postoperatively to control the coagulopathy acutely. It contains large amounts of VIII:vWF multimers and fibrinogen. The effect lasts approximately 24 hours.[20] Persistent oozing during surgery or after dialysis may be secondary to continued heparinization. Protamine can be administered up to 0.01 mg of protamine per unit of heparin to reverse the anticoagulant effect of heparin. Use of activated factor VII has been used with success if all the earlier discussed measures fail to arrest the bleeding but carries with it the risk of systemic thrombosis.[12]

The use of transdermal estradiol is safe and effective in providing longer term procoagulant effects.[22] Oral conjugated estrogens can also be used with the same effect at the dose of 2.5 to 25 mg or 0.6 mg/kg intravenously.[15] It is thought that the effect may occur by antagonizing the synthesis of NO.[23] The effect of estrogens can be seen within 6 hours[24] but does not manifest fully for 5 to 7 days. The effect can last for 14 days.[15]

Bleeding in the hemodialysis patient can be difficult to manage once it starts. Strategies advocated to avoid bleeding include stopping aspirin or nonsteroidal anti-inflammatory drugs for 1 week prior to surgery. Optimally, the surgery should be performed 24 hours after dialysis to allow for recovery of platelet function. Patients facing major surgery should be placed on transdermal estrogen (100 µg/24 hours) for 2 weeks prior to the procedure. Intravenous estrogen can be used if a more urgent operation is required.[16] Hemodialysis patients are also often malnourished to some degree,[21] and supplemental vitamin K can be administered as needed. Use of rHuEPO should be universal.

Bleeding in the postoperative period in most cases should be addressed by returning the patient to the operating room and exploring the operative site for evidence of surgical bleeding. Pharmacologic adjuncts as described earlier, particularly the use of protamine sulfate to reverse the effects of heparin, should be considered if the initial procedure involved heparinization. DDAVP to improve platelet function should also be used liberally but not as a substitute for surgical exploration. Bleeding from access puncture sites can be problematic as well. Prolonged bleeding, or bleeding that occurs after discharge from the dialysis center, can be significant enough to prompt patients to seek attention in the emergency department. Rarely does bleeding from this cause require operative intervention, however. Bleeding should be controlled by direct pressure over the point of blood loss. The pressure applied should be enough to stop the bleeding without obstructing blood flow through the access itself. Generally direct pressure applied in this manner controls the bleeding within 30 minutes or less. If the patient has just finished a dialysis session, protamine sulfate may be useful to counter any remaining heparin effects. DDAVP can also be helpful. If bleeding after dialysis is a consistent problem, consideration should be given to a venous outflow obstruction and an investigation with either a duplex ultrasound or venogram undertaken.

■ INFECTION

Infection is common in prosthetic hemodialysis accesses but is also seen in autogenous accesses.[4] Infection is the second leading cause for access loss and can cause significant morbidity or even mortality. Infectious complications of all types are the second leading cause of death in dialysis patients, accounting for 15% to 36%.[6,25-27] Impaired humoral and cellular immunity, nutritional deficiencies, and type of vascular access are thought to be among the major determinants.[28] Because autogenous AV accesses, once functioning, have a better patency than prosthetic accesses and are less prone to infection, the DOQI guidelines recommended increasing the relative proportion (percentage) of hemodialysis patients with autogenous accesses. The Reporting Standards document recommends reporting infections as early (<30 days) versus late (>30 days), culture positive or negative, and identifying the site of the infection (para-anastomotic/mid-AV access/outflow veins). The timing of the infection as well as its location and type of access (autogenous vs. prosthetic) determines how the infection is addressed. The severity of infection recognizes how significant an access infection can be and is graded as follows:

Grade 0: None
Grade 1: Resolved with antibiotic treatment
Grade 2: Loss of AV access because of ligation, removal of bypass
Grade 3: Loss of limb

The bacteriology of hemodialysis-related infections shows a predominance of gram-positive organisms, with *Staphylococcus aureus* being the most common isolate. Gram-negative organisms account for roughly another 25%, and a smaller percentage are polymicrobial.[29,30] Two reports exist of infection with *Clostridium perfringems*.[31,32] The implications of infection with *S. aureus* can be profound. One study of staphylococcal infections in this setting showed that complications occurred in 44%, and 14% of those patients died. Infective endocarditis, osteomyelitis, and septic arthritis were the most common complications. Because of the risks associated with access infections, antibiotics that cover both gram-positive and gram-negative organisms should be initiated as soon as the suspicion of access-related infection is entertained. Most commonly,

vancomycin and gentamicin are chosen because of their broad spectrum and ease of dosing. Accordingly, hemodialysis patients have been recognized for the development of vancomycin resistance.[33] Also several authors have pointed out slower in-vitro killing rates for these antibiotics when compared with beta-lactam antibiotics.[34] In centers where the prevalence of methicillin-resistant *S. aureus* is low, nafcillin, oxacillin, or cefazolin should be used in place of vancomycin.[35,36]

The National Kidney Foundation's DOQI Guideline 30 recommends less than 10% use of catheters for chronic hemodialysis. At the time of the initial publication only small studies were available to support that recommendation.[27] Initial reports showed low rates of bacteremia with tunneled catheters, but the duration of use was short.[37] Since then several large studies[38,39] have shown the dramatically increased infection rate of catheter-based access. Stevenson and associates[27] looked at their experience from 111,383 dialysis sessions over a 2-year period and found 471 (0.4%) access infections. Tunneled catheters accounted for 270 (57%) of them and 73% of the blood stream infections. Only 2% of the patients in their series were dialyzed using nontunneled catheters, but these still accounted for 10% of the total infection rate. Analysis of their data revealed that the relative risk of infection strikingly correlated with the access type used. Nontunneled catheters had the highest risk with relative risk versus autogenous AV access of 32.6. Tunneled catheters were next with a relative risk of 13.6. Prosthetic AV access showed a relative risk of 2.2.[27] Other studies corroborate these findings. The Centers for Disease Control and Prevention performed surveillance of 800 dialysis patients and found that independent risk factors for vascular site infection included the use of catheter for access, specific dialysis center, and albumin level of less than 3.5.[40] A study of 988 hemodialysis patients in France[38] also identified catheter versus autogenous AV access as an independent risk factor. A study of *S. aureus* infections in hemodialysis patients that showed 67% of all the access-related infections occurred in patients with a catheter access.[41] As would be predicted, the incidence of infection for nontunneled catheters rises with duration of use. For internal jugular lines, Oliver and colleagues[42] showed a risk of 10% after 4 weeks. Others have shown similar results,[43,44] with one report demonstrating a higher than 50% catheter-related bacteremia rate by the second month.[45]

Management of catheter infection can be complicated by the frequent lack of other access sites. Patients dialyzed with catheters are often doing so for lack of other access options. This has led to attempts at catheter salvage. In general exit-site infections (defined as crusting, induration, or tenderness adjacent to catheter exit site) can be managed conservatively with careful cleaning and topical antibiotics.[35,46] Tunnel infections (tenderness, erythema, or induration > 2 cm from the catheter exit site with or without concomitant blood stream infection) are best treated with catheter removal and 3 or more weeks of parenteral antibiotics.[47,48] The acute onset of fever, chills, or hyperglycemia in a patient with a hemodialysis catheter and no localizing signs is generally considered to be a catheter-related infection until proven otherwise. In an older or immunocompromised patient, the signs may be less obvious and include only hypothermia, lethargy, hypoglycemia, and confusion. In some cases metastatic infections may be the first presenting sign.[46] Blood cultures should be obtained both through the catheter and from peripheral blood. These paired quantitative cultures can be helpful in determining if the catheter is the source of bacteremia. Catheters yielding a 5- to 10-fold higher colony count than cultures from the peripheral blood are predictive of catheter infection.[49]

In cases of complicated catheter infection such as tunnel infection or metastatic infections such as bacterial endocarditis, septic arthritis or osteomyelitis, the catheter must be removed immediately and long-term antibiotics begun. In uncomplicated cases salvage has been attempted. Marr and coworkers looked at 41 patients who developed 62 episodes of catheter-related infections as defined by the presence of bacteremia.[29] In 38 instances salvage was attempted. Ultimately, only 12 catheters (31%) were salvaged, but they found no increase in metastatic infectious complications in those patients in whom salvage was attempted. No attempt at catheter exchange over a guide wire was attempted in that series. Other authors have pointed out that the presence of biofilms on the catheter surface may play a role in the failure to cure catheter infections.[44] Robinson and associates reported on catheter exchange in a cohort of 23 patients and obtained an 80% salvage rate.[50] Beathard[48] used guide wire exchange with new tunnel creation if needed and had success in more than 75%. In all cases parenteral antibiotics were administered for at least 3 weeks.

DOQI Guideline 29 suggests increasing to 50% the percentage of patients dialyzing with autogenous AV accesses. This is based both on the better long-term patency and the diminished infection risk. The average life span of a prosthetic AV access is only 2 years, and 20% of them are lost due to infection.[6] A prospective study conducted in the 1980s of 18 Canadian dialysis centers showed the probability of an access infection in 12 months was 4.5% of autogenous AV access versus 19.7% for prosthetic AV access.[51] Jaar and colleagues conducted a longitudinal cohort study using USRDS data looking at 4005 hemodialysis patients. They found a relative risk for infection of 1.35 for prosthetic access versus autogenous.[28] For polytetrafluoroethylene (PTFE) grafts, S. aureus bacteremia recurred more often than with autogenous access (44% vs. 7.1%).[41]

Infections involving an autogenous AV access can present as either diffuse cellulitis or focal abscess. Most episodes respond to a 2- to 4-week course of antibiotics alone. Those associated with an abscess require drainage of the abscess itself and prolonged antibiotics. Those involving the endovasculature of the autogenous access itself also require a prolonged course (4 to 6 weeks) of parenteral antibiotics.[52] Recurrent infections may require ligation of the access. The bacteriology of autogenous access infection does not seem to differ from other graft infections and can be treated with similar antimicrobial agents. The likelihood of metastatic infection seems to be related more to the causative organism than to the type of access.

Treatment of prosthetic AV access infections may involve complex, difficult clinical decisions. If only local signs of infection are seen without a skin opening or sinus and no bacteremia is demonstrated, a trial of parenteral antibiotics is reasonable, especially if this coincides with placement of the access or after manipulation such as a surgical revision. Antibiotics should be continued for at least 2 weeks.[52]

Failure to improve requires excision of at least all unincorporated graft. Infections involving the anastomosis require excision of the graft, even when the graft appears to be incorporated, because of the risk of anastomotic disruption.[53] Palder and colleagues in 1985 showed that in more than half of the cases of prosthetic access infection, only a discrete portion of the graft was involved.[54] Infections can present as a focal area of erythema or sinus. In these cases an attempt can be made to resect only that portion of the graft that is involved. Schwab and coworkers presented the largest series to date with 17 cases managed with segmental resection in 12 patients.[55] In each case the infection involved only one section of the graft and not the anastomosis. They describe excluding the area of infection with a transparent occlusive dressing and exploring the graft through clean incisions proximal and distal to the infected segment. If the graft was incorporated and free of infection, a new PTFE graft was anastomosed to the cut ends of the graft and tunneled through noninfected tissue planes and the incisions closed primarily. The infected portion of the graft was then removed through the sinus tract and the skin left open. With this technique, 94% of the infections were eradicated, though in several instances the patients developed subsequent infections in other portions of the same graft. Raju reported a 90% salvage rate in his smaller series using the same technique.[56]

Infections that appear to be focal in nature and occur 30 or more days beyond surgical placement can be treated as described earlier. However, any infection that takes place within the first 30 days after graft implantation and that involves the graft should be treated by complete excision of the graft and placement of a new access elsewhere.[52,55]

Unresolved is the issue of what to do with the abandoned prosthetic AV graft in the face of persistent bacteremia. Removal of a thrombosed, noninfected prosthetic AV access has not been thought to be necessary,[57] since removal of an incorporated graft can be difficult and somewhat bloody. A study looking at hemodialysis patients with abandoned prosthetic AV grafts in place found a surprisingly high percentage of those access sites to be infected.[57] The authors concluded that in the face of a fever of unknown origin in patients with a clotted prosthetic access, an indium scan should be obtained. If positive, the clotted access should be removed.

■ PSEUDOANEURYSM

Pseudoaneurysms are associated with an increased risk of graft thrombosis, pain, cosmetic problems, infection, bleeding, and difficulty accessing the graft.[58] The presence of a pseudoaneurysm does not imply the presence of infection. The thrice-weekly trauma to vessels or prosthetic graft leads eventually to the overlying skin becoming scarred and ischemic. Pseudoaneurysm formation in PTFE AV grafts is relatively uncommon but well documented, occurring in 2% to 10% of grafts.[59] Tissue ingrowth into the graft is thought to limit pseudoaneurysm development. Poorly incorporated grafts or those that are subjected to lacerations from large needle puncture may develop perigraft hematoma or pseudoaneurysm.[59] Autogenous fistula may also form pseudoaneurysms but at a lower rate than PTFE grafts.[60]

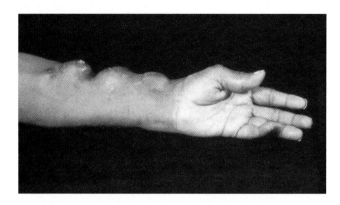

FIGURE 120-1 Multiple asymptomatic pseudoaneurysms resulting several years after creation of an autogenous wrist (Brescia-Cimino) arteriovenous fistula.

The presence or the size of a pseudoaneurysm alone is not necessarily a reason for intervention. Treatment is typically reserved for enlarging pseudoaneurysms or changes in the overlying skin that might predispose these patients to aneurysm rupture.[59] At other times, the size becomes problematic for the dialysis technician to obtain cannulation (Fig. 120-1).

Traditionally, management involves either resection of the pseudoaneurysm with placement of an interposition graft or a bypass around the lesion. While the new segment is allowed to incorporate, dialysis can be continued using the nonreplaced, already incorporated segment of the access. However, sometimes multiple pseudoaneurysms are found along the length of the access. In that situation it is rather difficult to perform segmental replacement of the affected area; rather, the whole length of the access needs to be replaced or bypassed. Usually, both arterial and venous ends of the aneurysmal graft can be preserved and the new graft segment is anastomosed in an end-to-end fashion to the remaining ends. While the new graft segment is allowed to incorporate, the patient needs to be dialyzed by a tunneled or nontunneled catheter. To avoid placement of temporary catheters, the length of the access can be replaced in two settings, replacing first the segment with the larger or more ominous pseudoaneurysm. While the first replaced segment is allowed to incorporate, dialysis is performed through the nonreplaced segment and then dialysis is performed through the new incorporated segment while the second segment is replaced. Obviously, this requires two surgical procedures. The risk of performing two surgical procedures with multiple anastomoses should be discussed and compared with the risk of replacing the whole graft and using a catheter for continued dialysis.

Several series[58,61] have been reported repairing pseudoaneurysms by using covered stents. Results have been variable. The largest series reported to date involved 10 patients treated endovascularly using a Wallgraft stent. One patient had thrombosis of the graft on postoperative day 1, one thrombosed at 3 weeks, and one did so at 3 months. The authors noted that most patients continued to have a palpable pulse through the aneurysm for a few days after placement, which then stopped. Ultrasound at 6-month follow-up showed no flow outside of the graft in 7 patients.[59] Larger series with longer follow-up periods are required to see if the less-invasive endovascular techniques can be used as a reliable alternative to open surgical repair.

■ SEROMA

A perigraft seroma, sometimes referred to as a "weeping graft," is a relatively rare complication of synthetic vascular prosthesis. The Reporting Standards of the SVS/AAVS[3] grade the severity of these complications from grade 0 to 3, as follows:

Grade 0: No collection
Grade 1: Observed, resolves
Grade 2: Involves aspiration or surgical drainage
Grade 3: Results in loss of the graft

Noninfectious fluid collections surrounding hemodialysis accesses can represent hematoma, perigraft seroma, or lymphocele. Small hematomas and lymphoceles can be expected to resolve over time with simple observation; however, treatment of a perigraft seroma usually requires operative intervention, and even then treatment is sometimes unsuccessful.

Perigraft seromas have been reported with both Dacron and PTFE grafts most commonly when placed in subcutaneous locations. Schanzer in his overview of complications notes that in prosthetic AV accesses, the seroma always occurs in proximity to the arterial anastomosis.[62,63] The active transudation of serum-like fluid can be observed when the graft is exposed at that point. By definition the fluid is persistent, sterile, and confined within a nonsecretory fibrous pseudomembrane surrounding the graft.[64] The exact incidence of this complication is not known, but reports for prosthetic grafts placed at all locations range from 8 cases seen of 1674 PTFE grafts (0.48%)[65] to as high as 5 of 118 extra-anatomic bypasses (4.2%).[66] Perigraft seromas generally appear within the first month after placement of the prosthetic AV access, though they can occur as late as several years afterward. They generally are painless but tend to enlarge over time, leading to difficulty with needle placement or, occasionally, stretching and thinning of the overlying skin with local pressure symptoms.[65] The mass itself is filled with serous or gelatinous material.

Several theories exist as to the etiology of perigraft seroma formation. Szilagyi attributed the process to transudation of serum through excessively porous grafts perhaps due to a focal defect at the time of manufacture.[67] Blumenburg and associates[64] as well as Bolton and Cannon[62] postulated that "wetting" of the graft by inadvertent soaking of the graft in tissue fluid or blood might cause seepage. Also organic solvents such as alcohol and povidone-iodine can cause increased porosity and permeability to serum. Others have postulated an immunologic or allergic reaction to the graft.[66] Ahn and coworkers demonstrated that serum samples from patients with a perigraft seroma inhibited fibroblast growth, whereas sera from normal controls and those with incorporated grafts did not.[68] With serial testing, Ahn's group found that serum from a patient with a perigraft seroma initially inhibited fibroblast growth but no longer did so once the graft was removed. In another patient in whom the graft was not removed and the seroma eventually resolved, the serum also changed from inhibitory to normal when the seroma resolved.[66] Sladen and associates described successfully treating two cases of perigraft seroma with plasmapheresis.[69]

A variety of treatments for this problem have been described. Anecdotal reports exist for success placing microfibrillar collagen (Avitene) around the graft after repeated attempts at aspiration had failed.[66,70,71] Borrero and Doscher[65] reported on eight cases of perigraft seroma surrounding PTFE grafts. Patients were treated with surgical extirpation of the entire seroma, including the portion attached to the graft. They reported success in six of the eight cases leaving the original graft in place. Blumenberg and colleagues, who surveyed the North American Chapter of the Society for Cardiovascular Surgery and reported on 279 cases from the 320 surgeons who responded, collected the largest series. Modalities of treatment included serial aspiration, observation, incision and drainage, cyst removal, and graft replacement. Graft replacement yielded the highest cure rate at 92%. Observation alone had essentially the same success rate as aspiration (68% vs. 69%). Aspiration, however, led to infection or graft thrombosis in 8%. Cyst removal as advocated by Borrero and Doscher[65] had a 72% success, but infection or thrombosis occurred in 12%. Incision and drainage had only a 53% success rate, with persistence of the seroma in 40% and infection or thrombosis in 7%.[64] Based largely on the results of this study, the authors recommend segmental resection of the involved segment in patients with an enlarging or symptomatic perigraft seroma. An interposition graft of conduit made from a different composition, ideally through a new tunnel, should be used to restore continuity.[63,68,72-74] Aspiration should be reserved for cases in which there is diagnostic doubt.[72]

■ STEAL

The first description of ischemic vascular steal after an AV access was in 1969 by Storey and associates, who described it following a Bescia-Cimino hemodialysis access.[75] Vascular steal after AV access creation is remarkably common if one uses the definition of reversal of flow in the inflow artery distal to the anastomosis. Kwun and colleagues demonstrated reversal of flow in 73% of autogenous AV access and in 91% of prosthetic access.[76] Duncan and coworkers, in a study of Brescia-Cimino fistulae, showed evidence of reduced blood pressure in the fingers in 80%.[77] Despite the frequency of demonstrable alterations in flow, a symptomatic steal syndrome is much less common. Although some coolness in the hand and mild tingling in the fingers are reported in about 10% of new accesses, most have symptoms that resolve spontaneously after a period of several weeks. The incidence of clinically significant steal has been reported to be as low as 1% for autogenous AV accesses placed distally in the forearm to as much as 9% for prosthetic grafts.[63,78] The Reporting Standards document[3] suggests grading steal from 0 to 3 and in general terms defines those patients in whom intervention is needed as follows:

Grade 0: No steal
Grade 1: Mild (cool extremity with few symptoms but demonstrable by flow augmentation with access occlusion)—no treatment needed
Grade 2: Moderate (intermittent ischemia only during dialysis/claudication)—intervention sometimes needed
Grade 3: Severe (ischemic pain at rest / tissue loss)—intervention mandatory

Deciding which patients need intervention for steal syndrome requires clinical judgment. As Berman and associates pointed out, symptomatic ischemic steal syndrome related to a functioning dialysis AV graft or fistula poses two challenges to access surgeons: (1) preservation of uninterrupted vascular access and (2) resolution of the distal ischemia.[79] Many patients experience transient mild symptoms such as coolness of the hand as well as numbness and paresthesia of one or more fingers. Pain and stiffness of the fingers can also occur.[78,80] These symptoms can be present during dialysis or worsen with dialysis. These symptoms can be watched with the expectation that most will resolve within a few weeks or not progress. If it is decided to observe the patient because the symptoms are deemed mild, one should insist the patient return for follow-up on a regular and frequent basis because worsening of the symptoms can happen quickly and the patient may be left with permanent injury such as muscle atrophy. As implied earlier, some patients have more severe symptoms, either immediately after access creation or developing over time. Most reports show that between half and two thirds of the patients who develop steal do so within the first 30 days.[79,81] Rest pain or motor impairment immediately after surgery requires immediate reoperation.[82-85] Symptoms such as progressive numbness or pain, pallor of the hand, diminished sensation, ischemic ulcers, progressive dry gangrene, and atrophy of the hand muscle all demand intervention.[78] Strictly neurologic changes in the hand or forearm must be differentiated from entrapment neuropathies such as carpal tunnel syndrome, diabetic or uremic neuropathy, and ischemic monomelic neuropathy (IMN). Bone pain from hyperparathyroidism can mimic neuropathic symptoms as well.[86] Physical examination findings such as a warm hand and presence of a palpable radial pulse distal to the inflow anastomosis suggest a diagnosis other than steal. Electrodiagnostic and nerve conduction studies (NCSs) can assist in making a more precise diagnosis.[78,82-84,87-89]

A variety of diagnostic studies have been used to confirm the diagnosis of ischemic steal in hemodialysis patients. Absence of a palpable pulse distal to the arterial anastomosis in the absence of clinical symptoms is not an indication for intervention. One study found absent radial pulse in one third of 180 accesses of whom only 7 developed clinical steal.[85] Berman and associates[79] studied digital photoplethysmography (PPG) in 12 patients. In 10 of the 12 the PPG showed flat digital waveforms in the affected extremity with return of pulsatile waveforms with access compression. The two patients who did not demonstrate flattening of the signals at rest had symptoms during dialysis. When PPG was tested during dialysis for both of those patients, the waveforms were flattened.[79] Others have reported similar findings with both PPG and pneumatic plethysmography.[90,91] Katz and Kohl reported on six patients with steal, all of whom were interrogated with duplex ultrasound prior to surgery. All six patients had obvious clinical symptoms of hand ischemia and all showed diminished Doppler waveforms in the radial and ulnar arteries that augmented with manual compression of the access.[92] Digital pulse oximetry can also be used to aid in the confirmation of steal. Halevy and colleagues[102] reported on five patients with AV access and symptoms of steal but normal physical examination. Pulse oximetry measured oxygen saturations were low in all but rose to 90% saturation with compression of the access.

Lazarides and coworkers studied the arterial pressure distal to an access and found that low pressure alone is not an indication for correction of steal. They used a systolic pressure index (SPI) comparing the postoperative forearm systolic pressure divided by the contralateral forearm pressure. In a prospective trial they found that 14% of their patients had both mild or moderate symptoms and a critical ischemia level (SPI < 0.4). Half of these patients improved symptomatically over time, as did their SPI.[85] They recommended following serial SPI for those with an index less than 0.5 and doing serial NCSs. They concluded that doing serial NCSs might detect patients likely to develop IMN.

No preoperative test has been shown to reliably predict who will develop steal, though there are several anatomic and patient factors that make the entity more likely.[93-95] Factors that place the patient at risk for development of symptomatic steal include age older than 60 years, multiple operations on the same limb, diabetes, use of a prosthetic graft, and the use of the brachial artery versus a more distal artery as the donor vessel.[91,96,97] Berman and associates showed that only 3 (0.3%) of 884 patients who had otherwise normal preoperative arterial examinations could have potentially been identified as being at risk for ischemia by segmental or digital pressure evaluation before surgery. They concluded that this low yield does not justify routine testing beyond physical examination prior to access placement.[79]

Recommended preoperative evaluation includes a thorough physical examination. This should include obtaining pressures in both arms to rule out inflow stenosis. A pressure difference of more than 20 mm Hg is considered significant.[79] Prior to construction of an access at the wrist, an Allen test should be uniformly performed to confirm the presence of adequate collateral circulation through the palmar arch. The test is performed by elevating the arm with the fist clenched and compressing both the radial and ulnar arteries. Pressure over one is then released and the hand is observed for the flush of reperfusion. The test is repeated, next time releasing the other artery. Results can be difficult to interpret in those with significant anemia or very dark skin pigmentation. Significantly calcified vessels as are often seen in diabetics can also make compression of the arteries difficult. A variation on the study is to perform the evaluation with a hand-held Doppler. A triphasic flow augmenting with collateral compression is a normal study and no further evaluation is necessary.[80] The pathogenesis of symptomatic steal has been well described by Miles.[96] She pointed out that the low-pressure run-off afforded by the access causes

reversal of the flow from digital and palmar arch arteries through the portion of the artery distal to the arterial anastomosis. In patients with preexisting athero-occlusive narrowing of the palmar arch vessels and digital arteries, even mild degrees of flow reversal may cause symptomatic steal. In the radial location, end artery-to-end vein configuration eliminates the retrograde flow, but flow rates with this configuration are usually lower than with end vein-to-side artery or side to side.[98] In the brachial location, end-arterial fistulae are not possible since the distal brachial artery and its branches provide conduits for distal flow.[96]

Treatment options for vascular steal after access placement include ligation of the access, various maneuvers to limit the flow through the graft, and *d*istal *r*evascularization and *i*nterval *l*igation—the DRIL procedure.

Ligation of the access is the surest method of eliminating the steal phenomenon but obviously requires the creation of a new access in a different site. Several methods have been described to salvage the access by limiting the flow through it. Each of them is designed to effectively increase the resistance through the fistula to thereby favor antegrade arterial flow distal to the arterial anastomosis. One group suggested lengthening the access with an interposition graft to increase the overall resistance.[99] Although intuitively sound, the length required to increase the resistance is difficult to calibrate and may differ at different flow rates. Rivers and colleagues reported good results in five patients in whom steal was treated by suture plication of a proximal portion of the access and monitoring pulse volume recordings during surgery.[91] Other authors have suggested an effectively similar technique of placing a band around the access and tightening it until the desired result is achieved.[90] The banding procedure involves narrowing the lumen of the conduit over 1 cm or more rather than simple suture stenosis (Fig. 120-2). Several authors point out that a short stenosis produces little decrease in flow until critical stenosis is reached, at which point resistance increases exponentially and the turbulence generated likely promotes a greater

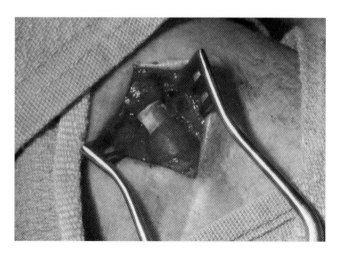

FIGURE 120-2 Banding of arteriovenous fistula for steal. Bands of 1 cm or more in width create less turbulence. Intraoperative assessment with digital plethysmography or color duplex can be used to assess adequate flow limitation.

tendency to thrombose. Making the band wider is thought to allow more accurate adjustments in flow with possibly less turbulent flow.

Procedures designed to narrow the access have been described using a variety of intraoperative assessment tools including digital plethysmography,[90,100] angiodynography,[101] pulse oximetry,[102] and color duplex.[102] However, despite careful intraoperative assessment, long-term results of banding have been disappointing. Odland and coworkers reported on a series of patients banded using photoplethysmography and used target endpoints of digital artery pressures of 50 mm Hg or a digital/brachial index of 0.6. They reported patency rates of 62% at 6 months and 38% at 12 months.[100] DeCaprio and associates reported on 11 patients treated with banding. In all but one of these patients, the access occluded within 6 months (9% patency).[103] Wilcox and colleagues described the hemodynamics of vascular steal and gave some insight as to why techniques used to increase resistance are likely to lead to thrombosis. They point out that in large accesses, defined as having a diameter greater than 75% of that of the donor artery, the blood flow tends to be independent of access resistance and diameter. Flow is determined primarily by the relative resistances of the peripheral vascular bed, the donor artery, and collateral circulation. Limitation of flow by increasing resistance, then, must narrow the conduit sufficiently to convert a large, flow-independent access to a small, flow-dependent access, the natural history of which is to thrombose.[97]

The technique of DRIL as originally described by Schanzer and colleagues[81,104] has come to be called the conservative approach to the problem of steal.[95] The technique involves creation of a bypass graft originating from the native artery proximal to the inflow anastomosis and ending in an outflow artery distal to the inflow anastomosis. A ligature is then placed on the artery distal to the inflow anastomosis but proximal to the distal anastomosis of the bypass graft (Fig. 120-3). The bypass effectively reduces resistance in the peripheral circulation as well as the total system by acting as a low-resistance collateral in parallel. By reducing the ratios of resistance between the systemic circulation and the access, the brachial access fraction is decreased and peripheral perfusion is augmented. Failure to ligate the native artery distal to the inflow anastomosis of the access could allow augmentation of retrograde flow.[97]

A preoperative arteriogram should always be obtained prior to embarking on a DRIL operation. The arteriogram can demonstrate which outflow vessel looks to be the dominant one supplying the forearm and hand as well as demonstrating a possible inflow stenosis that might need to be addressed. Certain technical factors need to be observed for success. An area of reduced pressure exists in the artery just proximal to the fistula. This has been called a *pressure sink*.[97] It exists because the large capacitance of the venous outflow causes the pressure to fall off rapidly with the pressure on the venous side of the access approximating central venous pressure within 1 cm of the anastomosis. Locating the origin of the bypass graft 3 to 5 cm above the inflow anastomosis of the access is sufficient to avoid this pressure sink and avoids the need to approach the artery through a reoperative field.[79,81,97] Although using autogenous vein material is preferred, the procedure has been done

successfully with both autogenous vein and prosthetic.[79,81] The distal anastomosis should be constructed to the dominant distal outflow vessel.

Reported long-term results have been excellent for the DRIL procedure. Schanzer and associates reported on 14 patients, all of whom had an access originating from the brachial artery; 13 of those patients had complete recovery of function, including healing of gangrenous lesions.[81] The 1-year patency of the access was 81.7%, and all the bypass grafts remained open. Berman and colleagues reported on 21 patients with limb salvage and graft patency of 100% and 94% by life-table analysis.[79] Knox and coworkers published the largest series to date with 55 patients. In that series 90% had substantial or complete resolution of ischemic hand symptoms and 15 of 20 with digital ischemia healed completely. Access patency rate was 83% at 1 year and 80% of the bypass grafts were open at 4 years.[105] It would appear from these studies that the DRIL procedure has a good success rate for symptomatic relief and good durability in this difficult patient population.

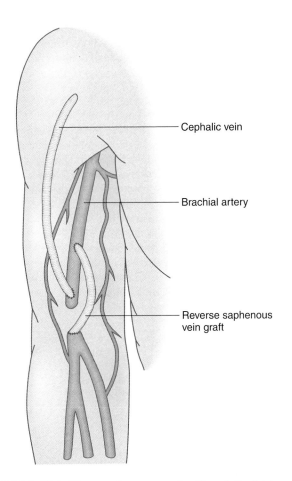

FIGURE 120-3 Diagram of upper arm brachiocephalic fistula and brachial artery bypass with interval brachial artery ligation. In this case, the brachial artery was divided below the origin of the fistula and distal anastomosis of the vein bypass graft was performed end-to-end to the distal brachial artery. (From Knox R, Berman S, Hughes J, et al: Distal revascularization-interval ligation: A durable and effective treatment for ischemic steal syndrome after hemodialysis access. J Vasc Surg 36:250-256, 2002.)

■ VENOUS HYPERTENSION

Venous hypertension manifested by minimal arm swelling is quite common in hemodialysis patients with upper extremity access. The manifestations can be more severe, with a few cases even developing venous ulceration leading to digit or even hand loss. The latter is rare, with one report citing only 1 instance of 800 accesses and another citing only 4 of 516.[106,107] Symptoms of venous hypertension can be seen in patients with incompetent venous valves and in patients with a venous outflow obstruction. The Reporting Standards document recommends grading the severity from Grade 0 to 3, as follows:

Grade 0: None
Grade 1: Mild (minimal symptoms, discoloration, minimal extremity swelling)—no treatment needed
Grade 2: Moderate (intermittent discomfort, severe swelling) —intervention usually needed
Grade 3: Severe (persistent discomfort with hyperpigmentation, persistent swelling, severe or massive, venous ulceration)—intervention mandatory

In the first group the symptoms are related to reflux through incompetent venous valves. Venous hypertension of the hand following a side-to-side Brescia-Cimino fistula was first described in 1975.[107] The findings include those found in classic venous stasis disease of the lower extremity— swelling, induration, hyperpigmentation, and even ulceration.[106,108,109] Findings are usually more prominent on the thumb and index finger.[108] Severe symptoms are seen almost exclusively in patients who have undergone side-to-side AV anastomoses. The findings usually develop slowly over 1 to 2 years after creation of the access and follow a slowly progressive course. Venous hypertension leads to increased transcapillary pressures driving fluid into the interstitium. If significant enough, this edema can interfere with finger function and limit joint mobility. The overall tissue edema has been implicated in the increased incidence of carpal tunnel syndrome seen in hemodialysis patients.[80]

Treatment must include limitation of retrograde flow through the incompetent veins. Initially sacrifice of the access was advocated[107,110,111] but in most cases ligation of the tributary veins to the access will resolve the symptoms. In a side-to-side wrist fistula, simple ligation of the vein on the hand side of the access converts the fistula from a side-to-side fistula to a side artery-to-end vein and resolve the problem.

More problematic can be the second group of patients in whom venous hypertension develops when an AV access is established ipsilateral to a proximal venous outflow obstruction. It is estimated that up to 40% of patients who undergo a subclavian or brachiocephalic vein catheterization will develop a venous stenosis.[112] Most of these patients remain asymptomatic[113,114] but if an AV access is placed on the same side, the dramatically increased flow can result in venous hypertension manifested by almost immediate arm swelling, pain, or access failure. The arm swelling can lead to cyanosis and even ulcerations in extreme cases.[115] Distended collateral vessels may be visible on the shoulder and chest (Figs. 120-4 and 120-5). In some cases, collateral flow may be sufficient for the patient to remain asymptomatic, but this is unpredictable. To avoid this complication, Rutherford[80] and others have recommended duplex scanning of all patients who have had a proximal vein cannulation—particularly a subclavian line. Some lesions may be inadequately visualized with this technique secondary to poor ultrasound windows. In these cases a venogram obtained by direct puncture of the access should be obtained with attention directed to the venous anastomosis and the central venous circulation. If central venous occlusion is confirmed, placement of AV access in the ipsilateral limb should be avoided.

Some edema of the limb is expected after construction of either an autogenous or prosthetic access. Generally, the

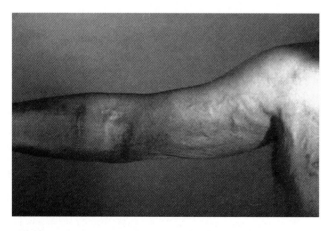

FIGURE 120-4 Development of marked upper arm and chest venous collaterals shortly after creation of an arteriovenous access. (See color figure in this section.)

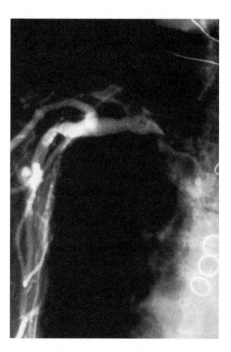

FIGURE 120-5 Venogram from the same patient as in Figure 120-4 revealing subclavian vein stenosis. Patients who have had prior subclavian catheters should have an evaluation of their proximal venous anatomy prior to creation of an ipsilateral access.

edema subsides to a large extent within several weeks. The magnitude of initial postoperative swelling varies depending on the configuration of the access placed with more proximal accesses producing more marked swelling. Of those patients with persistent edema, approximately 25% have a significant central venous lesion.[116]

To address outflow obstruction leading to venous hypertension after an access has been created, the DOQI guidelines[35] suggest only two solutions—sacrifice of the access or the use of angioplasty or stenting for central lesions. We believe this is an incomplete description of the reasonable choices available. The use of endovascular treatments for central lesion offers the potential to address a difficult anatomic problem with little morbidity and often in an outpatient scenario. Unfortunately the procedure cannot be performed in all patients and the results may not be long lasting. A series looking at patients treated with only angioplasty revealed primary symptomatic relief of only 36% at 1 year, but this number increased to 86% with repeated treatments.[117] Another series employed stents in these central lesions and reported a 68% primary patency rate and a 93% secondary patency.[118] A more recent study looking at long-term results of stent placement[119] also pointed out the relatively low primary patency rate and that 62% required some reintervention within the first 12 months. They concluded that stents provided a temporary benefit, but patients with a reasonable life expectancy should be considered for alternative therapy.

A variety of surgical techniques have been described to alleviate the symptoms from central venous obstruction. The first venous reconstruction described for central venous obstruction came in 1976 by Doty and Baker, who described a reconstruction of the inferior vena cava using a spiraled saphenous vein graft.[120] Others have described using a prosthetic graft from subclavian vein to the right atrium. One report even cited the use of the femoral vein as an outflow vessel.[121] Fortunately most patients can be managed by procedures that do not require entering the thoracic cavity or lengthy extra-anatomic bypasses. For lesions of the subclavian medial to the internal jugular vein an autologous internal jugular to internal jugular vein crossover technique has been described.[122] For the more common stenosis seen lateral to the internal jugular, an ipsilateral internal jugular turn-down technique can be used[123] or we find a technically easier procedure that preserves the internal jugular to be a subclavian-to-ipsilateral internal jugular bypass using 6-mm PTFE. The latter can be done under local anesthesia and, with a functioning AV access, has had very satisfactory long-term patency (Fig. 120-6).[124]

■ NEUROPATHY

Neuropathy is a common finding among hemodialysis patients. Causes can be systemic such as uremia or diabetes as well as mechanical such as entrapment of compartment syndromes. The Reporting Standards document[3] sets out four gradations of severity to describe neuropathy related to hemodialysis access as follows:

Grade 0: No symptoms
Grade 1: Mild, intermittent sensory changes (pain/paresthesia/ numbness with sensory deficit)

Grade 2: Moderate, persistent sensory changes
Grade 3: Severe, sensory changes and progressive loss of motor function (movement/strength/muscle wasting)

The major causes of neuropathy in the hemodialysis patient include uremic neuropathy, diabetic neuropathy, mononeuropathies from anatomic compression such as occurs in carpal tunnel syndrome, and the uncommon but important IMN that can occur acutely after access creation. Hand pain and numbness are not uncommon with long-standing dialysis fistulae or shunts.[80]

The most common neuropathy seen in patients new to dialysis is uremic polyneuropathy. It is seen in 50% to 70% of patients on long-term hemodialysis.[82,125] Although the pathogenesis is unclear, the most consistent finding is axonal degeneration with secondary segmental demyelination. These changes are most severe distally.[82,126-129] Men are affected more often than women. The most common manifestation is burning dysesthesias of the feet, although distal aberrant sensations of swelling and burning in the fingers are also described. Dysesthesias may be accompanied by slowly progressive weakness and atrophy.[82] Physical examination findings include impaired vibratory sensation in the lower extremities and loss of deep tendon reflexes in the Achilles tendon. Advanced cases show loss of distal touch and position senses. Several studies have demonstrated that initiation of dialysis tends to improve but not necessarily eliminate the symptoms over time. The nerve conduction velocities tend to stabilize but not improve.[82,88,130,131] Worsening of symptoms over time is an indication of inadequate dialysis. Interestingly, a well-functioning transplant graft completely reverses all the changes in 6 to 12 months, and the symptoms begin to improve within a few days.[132-134] For the surgeon tasked with creation of a new access for hemodialysis, the importance of this entity lies in differentiating it from other causes of neuropathy and documenting its presence or absence preoperatively.

Carpal tunnel syndrome occurs with greater frequency in dialysis patients than the general population. Warren and

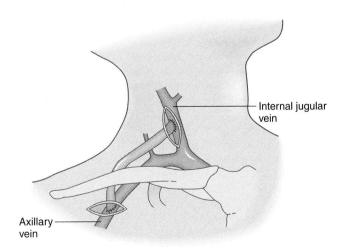

FIGURE 120-6 Subclavian to ipsilateral internal jugular bypass using 6-mm polytetrafluoroethylene to bypass subclavian stenosis. This procedure can be done under local anesthesia with good long-term patency.

Otieno are credited with documenting the first case of carpal tunnel syndrome in a hemodialysis patient in 1975.[135] Since then numerous series have been published showing an increased incidence in this population with reports ranging from 0.6% to 30%.[136-138] Symptoms are the same as for those not on dialysis. Patients complain of tingling dysesthesias in the median nerve distribution, particularly bothersome at night. Hemodialysis patients, however, often complain of worse symptoms during their dialysis sessions.[82] This is thought to be due to a combination of relative ischemia and compression from venous hypertension and edema.[139] Recent attention has been focused on levels of serum β_2-microglobulin as the cause of the increased incidence of carpal tunnel in this population. β_2-Microglobulin is not cleared by even long-term hemodialysis. It is deposited as amyloid in periarticular tissues leading to arthropathy as well as carpal tunnel syndrome.[136,139-141] However, in one study that looked at nerve conduction velocities in 46 hemodialysis patients and studied both the arm used for hemodialysis access and the contralateral arm, more median nerve dysfunction was seen on the contralateral side. Of the eight patients with the disorder, only one had it on the side of the access.[139] This and other studies lend support to the idea that the carpal tunnel and other entrapment neuropathies seen in hemodialysis patients have more to do with systemic influences than local ones such as edema.

Surgeons and other physicians caring for the hemodialysis patient need to be alert for the early symptoms of carpal tunnel syndrome because several studies demonstrate improved functional recovery if the nerve is decompressed early.[142,143] Once motor or sensory deficits develop, symptoms respond poorly if at all.[139] The likelihood of developing carpal tunnel syndrome is thought to increase with increasing time on dialysis. Although Bicknell and group[139] found it in 8% after only 3 years, most other series have shown very few cases until 3 or more years on dialysis. The overall trend is for increasing numbers seen with increasing length of time on dialysis. Halter and associates[144] found an incidence of 50% after 5 years on dialysis, and Bicknell and group[139] found a 46% incidence at 5 or more years. Other compressive mononeuropathies such as cubital and Guyon's tunnel syndromes have also been described in the hemodialysis population.[136,145,146]

IMN is a distinctive syndrome of nerve injury resulting from acute vascular compromise in an extremity.[147] Although rare, surgeons need to be aware of it because failure to recognize the syndrome in a timely fashion leads to irreversible, often profound, neurologic deficits in median, radial, and ulnar nerves of the affected extremity. Although a few reports exist in the literature of this entity occurring in the lower extremities,[83,148,149] most have been described in patients with diabetes mellitus who have undergone creation of an autogenous or prosthetic dialysis access arising from the brachial artery.[147] Bolton and coworkers[150] first described the entity in 1979 and a more detailed description came in 1983. Wilbourn and associates coined the term *IMN*. The entity is seen almost exclusively in older diabetic patients with preexisting peripheral neuropathy and most have a history of peripheral vascular disease. The condition is not seen in accesses originating distal to the brachial artery.[78,96,147]

The clinical presentation of IMN is that of acute pain, weakness, or paralysis of the muscles of the hand and forearm, often with prominent sensory loss and dysesthesiae. Symptoms begin within hours of creation of an access in the brachiocephalic or antecubital region.[78,82,89,96,147,151] IMN can be distinguished from a more classic vascular steal syndrome by absence of other signs of vascular insufficiency. The hand is warm, and there are no signs of muscle infarction such as pain with passive stretch of the muscles or pain with palpation over the muscles of the forearm themselves. Distal pulses are usually preserved. Creatine phosphokinase values remain normal and the digital pressure index is higher than 0.3.[84] Although the symptoms of IMN are present almost immediately, diagnosis is often delayed. Symptoms are attributed to patient positioning, surgical trauma, or anesthetic complications.[84] Symptoms of acute limb pain, distal weakness, and sensory loss in the immediate postoperative period should prompt an immediate evaluation of the arm to rule out hematoma or direct nerve damage. If these are absent, then the diagnosis of IMN needs to be considered and addressed.

The pathogenesis of IMN is likely related to preexisting marginal distal tissue perfusion in some diabetics. The additional flow requirements imposed by a proximal shunt cannot be compensated, leading to ischemia of the nerves. The ischemia is transient or insufficient to cause muscle or skin necrosis but results in severe ischemic nerve injury. There is general agreement that the ischemic threshold of peripheral nerves is lower than that of muscle.[83] Dyck and colleagues in 1972 studied the morphology of fiber degeneration related to occluded vessels and found the antecubital area to be a "watershed" area for the vasae nervorum of the three upper limb nerves.[152] Hye and Wolf pointed out that recent studies have implicated nerve ischemia as a cause of diabetic polyneuropathy. It is likely that preexisting ischemia and damage to the neural tissue are responsible for a lowered threshold for ischemic injury.[84]

Electrophysiologic studies of these patients support the hypothesis of IMN being a steal syndrome involving only the nerves. NCSs done acutely (as soon as 1 hour afterward) can show a motor conduction block and conduction slowing.[147] These acute changes are not due to demyelination but rather are thought to be due to retraction of myelin from the node of Ranvier, a reversible process if the ischemia is reversed early.[147] Late changes on NCSs and electromyography seen in IMN are suggestive of axon-loss lesions of motor and sensory nerves. The findings are similar to a dying-back axonal degenerating polyneuropathy, but it involves only one limb. Wilbourn and coworkers[83] found the motor and sensory responses to be low or unobtainable on NCSs and that the sensory amplitudes are usually more severely affected. Evidence of denervation is more severe distally with a proximal gradient.[84]

Because IMN represents a form of steal, treatment of the syndrome must include either ligation of the access or correction of the steal physiology. Even with early access closure, paralysis and pain may be permanent or only partially reversible.[84,89,96,153] Wytrzes and associates[89] described two patients who underwent a banding procedure several weeks after initial access placement, both of whom showed some improvement in function over time as well as a third patient who had ligation of the access. Hye and

Wolf[84] described two patients who had ligation of their shunts at 2 and 7 days after surgery. In all cases there remained considerable motor dysfunction. Ideally IMN is best treated by avoidance of the procedures likely to lead to the syndrome, such as placing the inflow of the access as distal as possible in the extremity and avoiding the brachial artery for inflow. This condition was not observed in accesses placed distal to this artery. If distal access cannot be achieved, careful clinical observation is mandatory should a brachial artery-based access be required, especially in a diabetic patient.

■ CONCLUSION

ESRD is an increasingly common diagnosis in the United States, and most of these patients are treated with hemodialysis. The most common problem confronting the vascular surgeon and interventionalist is thrombosis of AV access. In addition to thrombosis, physicians caring for hemodialysis patients must have a working knowledge of the other complications these patients can face. Infection of access sites can lead to loss of access, sepsis, and even death. Unrecognized steal can lead to unremitting pain, progressive neurologic dysfunction in the affected extremity, and even limb loss. Neuropathies are relatively common, and careful documentation of their presence preoperatively can prevent diagnostic confusion. Following the DOQI guidelines will help reduce some of the morbidity for hemodialysis patients.

■ REFERENCES

1. Cloonan CC, Gatrell CB, Cushner HM: Emergencies in continuous dialysis patients: Diagnosis and management. Am J Emerg Med 8:134-148, 1990.
2. NIH, US Renal Data System: USRDS 1999 Annual Data Report. Bethesda, MD, National Institutes of Health, National Institute of Diabetes and Digestive and Kidney Diseases, 1999.
3. Sidawy AN, Gray R, Besarab A, et al: Recommended standards for reports dealing with arteriovenous hemodialysis accesses. J Vasc Surg 35:603-610, 2002.
4. NIH, US Renal Data System: USRDS 2002 Annual Data Report. Bethesda, MD, National Institutes of Health, National Institute of Diabetes and Digestive and Kidney Diseases, 2002.
5. McCann RL: Axillary grafts for difficult hemodialysis access. J Vasc Surg 24:457-462, 1996.
6. Morbidity and Mortality of Dialysis. NIH Consensus Statement. Washington, DC, National Institutes of Health, 1993, pp 1-33.
7. Feldman, H.I., Held PJ, Hutchinson JT, et al: Hemodialysis vascular access morbidity in the United States. Kidney Int 43:1091-1096, 1993.
8. Akpolat T, Ozdemir O, Arik N, et al: Effect of desmopressin (DDAVP) on protein C and protein C inhibitors in uremia. Nephron 64:232-234, 1993.
9. Noris M, Remuzzi G: Uremic bleeding: Closing the circle after 30 years of controversies? Blood 94:2569-2574, 1999.
10. Andrassy K, Ritz E: Uremia as a cause of bleeding. Am J Nephrol 5:313-319, 1985.
11. Andrassy K, Weischedel E, Ritz E, et al: Bleeding in uremic patients after carfenicillin. Thromb Haemost 36:115-126, 1976.
12. Ng HJ, Koh LP, Lee LH: Successful control of post-surgical bleeding by recombinant factor VIIa in a renal failure patient given low molecular weight heparin and aspirin. Ann Hematol 82:257-258, 2003.
13. Livio M, Gotti E, Marchesi D, et al: Uremic bleeding: role of anaemia and beneficial effect of red cell transfusions. Lancet 2:1013, 1982.
14. Steiner RW, Coggins C, Carvalho ACA: Bleeding time in uremia: A useful test to assess clinical bleeding. Am J Hematol 7:107, 1979.
15. Janssen MJFM, van der Meulen J: The bleeding risk in chronic haemodialysis: Preventive strategies in high-risk patients. Neth J Med 48:198-207, 1996.
16. Sloand JA: Long-term therapy for uremic bleeding. Int J Artif Organs 19:439-440, 1996.
17. Salvati F, Liani M, Golato M: Long-term therapy for uremic bleeding: Effects of conjugate estrogens on the expression of platelet surface receptors for von Willebrand factor and fibrinogen (GPIb and GPIIb/IIIa glycoproteins). Int J Artif Organs 20:184-185, 1997.
18. Gawaz MP, Dobos G, Spath M, et al: Impaired function of platelet membrane glycoprotein IIb-IIIa in end-stage renal disease. J Am Soc Nephrol 5:36-46, 1994.
19. Sloand EM, Sloand JA, Prodouz K, et al: Reduction of platelet glycoprotein Ib in uremia. Br J Haematol 77:375-381, 1991.
20. Wolfson AB, Singer I: Hemodialysis-related emergencies: II. J Emerg Med 6:61-70, 1987.
21. Dember LM: Critical care issues in the patient with chronic renal failure. Crit Care Clin 18:421-440, 2002.
22. Sloand JA, Schiff MJ: Beneficial effect of low-dose transdermal estrogen on bleeding time and clinical bleeding in uremia. Am J Kidney Dis 26:22-26, 1995.
23. Zoja C, Noris M, Coma D, et al: L-Arginine, the precursor of nitric oxide, abolishes the effect of estrogens on bleeding time in experimental uremia. Lab Invest 65:479-483, 1991.
24. Livio M, Mannucci PM, Vigano G, et al: Conjugated estrogens for the management of bleeding associated with renal failure. N Engl J Med 315:731-735, 1986.
25. Butterly DW, Schwab SJ: Dialysis access infections. Curr Opin Nephrol Hypertens 9:631-635, 2000.
26. Mailloux LU, Bellucci AG, Wilkes BM, et al: Mortality in dialysis patients: Analysis of the causes of death. Am J Kidney Dis 18:326-335, 1991.
27. Stevenson KB, Hannah EL, Lowder CA, et al: Epidemiology of hemodialysis vascular access infections from longitudinal infection surveillance data: Predicting the impact of NKF-DOQI Clinical Practice Guidelines for Vascular Access. Am J Kidney Dis 39:549-555, 2002.
28. Jaar BG, Hermann JA, Furth SL, et al: Septicemia in diabetic hemodialysis patients: Comparison on incidence, risk factors, and mortality with non-diabetic hemodialysis patients. Am J Kidney Dis 35:282-292, 2000.
29. Marr KA, Sexton DJ, Conlon PJ, et al: Catheter-related bacteremia and outcome of attempted catheter salvage in patients undergoing hemodialysis. Ann Intern Med 127:275-280, 1997.
30. Saad TF: Bacteremia associated with tunneled, cuff hemodialysis catheters. Am J Kidney Dis 34:1114-1124, 1999.
31. Claeys LGY, Matamoros R: Anaerobic cellulitis as the result of *Clostridium perfringens*: A rare cause of vascular access graft infection. J Vasc Surg 35:1287-1288, 2002.
32. Oliveras A, Orfila A, Inigo V: *Clostridium perfringens*: An unusual pathogen infecting arteriovenous shunts for dialysis. Nephron 80:479, 1998.
33. Update: *Staphylococcus aureus* with reduced susceptibility to vancomycin—United States. MMWR Morb Mortal Wkly Rep 46:813-815, 1997.
34. Kong L: Recurrent *S. aureus* bacteremia: Pulse field gel electrophoresis findings in 28 consecutive patients. Toronto, Canada, International Conference on Antimicrobial Agents and Chemotherapy, 1997.
35. Gray RJ, Sands JJ (eds): Dialysis Access. Philadelphia, Lippincott Williams & Wilkins, 2002.
36. Fogel MA, Nussbaum PB, Feintzeig ID, et al: Cefazolin in chronic hemodialysis patients: A safe and effective alternative to vancomyin. Am J Kidney Dis 32:401-409, 1998.

37. Schwab SJ, Buller GL, McCann RL, et al: Prospective evaluation of a Dacron cuffed hemodialysis catheter for prolonged use. Am J Kidney Dis 11:166-169, 1988.

38. Hoen B, Paul-Dauphin A, Hestin D, et al: EPIBACDIAL: A multicenter prospective study of risk factors for bacteremia in chronic hemodialysis patients. J Am Soc Nephrol 9:869-876, 1998.

39. Hoen B, Kessler M, Hestin D, et al: Risk factors for bacterial infections in chronic hemodialysis adult patients: A multicentre prospective survey. Nephrol Dial Transplant 10:377-381, 1995.

40. Tokars JI, Light P, Anderson J, et al: A prospective study of vascular access infections at seven outpatient hemodialysis centers. Am J Kidney Dis 37:1232-1240, 2001.

41. Marr KA, Kong L, Fowler VG, et al: Incidence and outcome of *Staphylococcus aureus* bacteremia in hemodialysis patients. Kidney Int 54:1684-1689, 1998.

42. Oliver MJ, Callery SM, Thorpe KE, et al: Risk of bacteremia from temporary hemodialysis catheters by site of insertion and duration of use. Kidney Int 58:2543-2545, 2000.

43. Kairaitis LK, Gottlieb T: Outcome and complications of temporary hemodialysis catheters by site of insertion and duration of use. Nephrol Dial Transplant 14:1710-1714, 1999.

44. Schwab SJ, Beathard G: The hemodialysis catheter conundrum: Hate living with them, but can't live without them. Kidney Int 56:1-17, 1999.

45. Hung KY, et al: Infection associated with double-lumen catheterization for temporary haemodialysis: Experience with 168 cases. Nephrol Dial Transplant 10:247-251, 1995.

46. Nassar GM, Ayus JC: Infectious complications of the hemodialysis access. Kidney Int 60:1-13, 2001.

47. Favero MS, Alter MJ, Tokars JI, et al: Dialysis-associated infections and their control. In Bennett JV, Brachman PS (eds): Hospital Infections. Philadelphia, Lippincott-Raven, 1998, pp 357-380.

48. Beathard GA: Management of bacteremia associated with tunneled-cuffed hemodialysis catheters. J Am Soc Nephrol 10:1045-1049, 1999.

49. Fan ST, Teoh-Chan CH, Lau KF: Evaluation of central venous catheter sepsis by differential quantitative blood culture. Eur J Clin Microbiol Infect Dis 8:142-144, 1989.

50. Robinson D, Suhocki P, Schwab SJ: Treatment of infected tunneled venous access hemodialysis catheters with guidewire exchange. Kidney Int 53:1792-1794, 1998.

51. Churchill D, Taylor DW, Cook RJ, et al: Canadian Hemodialysis Morbidity Study. Am J Kidney Dis 19:214-234, 1992.

52. Stevenson KB: Management of hemodialysis vascular access infections. In Gray RJ (ed): Dialysis Access. Philadelphia, Lippincott Williams & Wilkins, 2002, pp 98-106.

53. Bennion RS, Wilson SE, Williams RA: Vascular prosthetic infection. Infect Surg 1:45-55, 1982.

54. Palder SB, Kirkman RL, Whittemore AD, et al: Vascular access for hemodialysis. Ann Surg 202:235-239, 1985.

55. Schwab DP, Taylor SM, Cull DL, et al: Isolated arteriovenous dialysis access graft segment infection: The results of segmental bypass and partial graft excision. Ann Vasc Surg 14:63-66, 2000.

56. Raju S: PTFE grafts for hemodialysis access: Techniques for insertion and management of complications. Ann Surg 206:666-673, 1987.

57. Ayus JC, Sheikh-Hamad D: Silent infection in clotted hemodialysis access grafts. J Am Soc Nephrol 9:1314-1317, 1998.

58. Ryan JM: Using a covered stent (Wallgraft) to treat pseudoaneurysms of dialysis grafts and fistulas. AJR Am J Radiol 180:1067-1071, 2002.

59. Najibi S, Bush RL, Terremani TT, et al: Covered stent exclusion of dialysis access pseudoaneurysms. J Surg Res 106:15-19, 2002.

60. Zibari GB, Rohr MS, Landreneau MD, et al: Complications from permanent hemodialysis vascular access. Surgery 104:681-686, 1988.

61. Hausegger KA, Tiessenhausen K, Klimpfinger M, et al: Aneurysms of hemodialysis access grafts: Treatment with covered stents—a report of three cases. Cardiovasc Intervent Radiol 21:334, 1998.

62. Bolton W, Cannon JA: Seroma formation associated with PTFE vascular grafts used as arteriovenous fistulae. Dial Transplant 10:60-68, 1981.

63. Schanzer H: Overview of complications and management after vascular access creation. In Gray RJ (ed): Dialysis Access. Philadelphia, Lippincott Williams & Wilkins, 2002, pp 93-97.

64. Blumenberg RM, Galfand ML, Dale WA: Perigraft seromas complicating arterial grafts. Surgery 97:194-203, 1985.

65. Borrero E, Doscher W: Chronic perigraft seromas in PTFE grafts. J Cardiovasc Surg 29:46-49, 1988.

66. Ahn SS, Machleder HI, Gupta R, et al: Perigraft seroma: Clinical, histologic, and serologic correlates. Am J Surg 154:173-178, 1987.

67. Szilagyi DE: In discussion of Kaupp et al: Graft infection or graft rejection? Arch Surg 114:1422, 1979.

68. Ahn SS, Williams DE, Thye DA, et al: The isolation of a fibroblast growth inhibitor associated with perigraft seroma. J Vasc Surg 20:202-208, 1994.

69. Sladen JG, Mandl MA, Grossman L, et al: Fibroblast inhibition: A new and treatable cause of graft failure. Am J Surg 149:587-590, 1985.

70. Rhodes VJ: Perigraft seroma: Simple solution to a difficult problem. J Vasc Surg 3:939, 1986.

71. Blumenberg RM: Invited commentary in lymph fistulas and seromas. In Dale WA (ed): Management of Vascular Surgical Problems. New York, McGraw-Hill, 1985, pp 293-298.

72. Lewis P, Wolfe JHN: Lymphatic fistula and perigraft seroma. Br J Surg 80:410-411, 1993.

73. Eid A, Lyass S: Acute perigraft seroma simulating anastomotic bleeding of a PTFE graft applied as an arteriovenous shunt for hemodialysis. Ann Vasc Surg 10:290-291, 1996.

74. Claessens F, Van den Brande P: Treatment of two cases of perigraft seroma with fistulization to the skin. Acta Chir Belg 94:116-119, 1994.

75. Storey BG, George CR, Stewart JH, et al: Embolic and ischemic complications after anastomosis of radial artery to cephalic vein. Surgery 66:325-327, 1969.

76. Kwun KB: Hemodynamic evaluation of angioaccess procedures for hemodialysis. Vasc Surg 13:170-177, 1979.

77. Duncan H, Ferguson L, Faris I: Incidence of the radial steal syndrome in maladies with Brescia fistula hemodialysis: Its clinical significance. J Vasc Surg 4:144-147, 1986.

78. Miles AM: Upper limb ischemia after vascular access surgery: Differential diagnosis and management. Semin Dial 13:312-315, 2000.

79. Berman SS, Gentile AT, Glickman MH, et al: Distal revascularization-interval ligation for limb salvage and maintenance of dialysis access in ischemic steal syndrome. J Vasc Surg 26:393-404, 1997.

80. Rutherford RB: The value of noninvasive testing before and after hemodialysis access in the prevention and management of complications. Semin Vasc Surg 10:157-161, 1997.

81. Schanzer H, Skadany M, Haimov M: Treatment of angioaccess-induced ischemia by revascularization. J Vasc Surg 16:861-866, 1992.

82. Pirzada NA, Morgenlander JC: Peripheral neuropathy in patients with chronic renal failure: A treatable source of discomfort and disability. Postgrad Med 102:249-261, 1997.

83. Wilbourn AJ, Furlan AJ, Hulley W, et al: Ischemic monomelic neuropathy. Neurology 33:447-451, 1983.

84. Hye RJ, Wolf YG: Ischemic monomelic neuropathy: An under-recognized complication of hemodialysis access. Ann Vasc Surg 8:578-582, 1994.

85. Lazarides MK, Staramos DN, Panagopoulos GN, et al: Indications for the surgical treatment of angioaccess-induced arterial "steal." J Am Coll Surg 187:422-426, 1998.

86. Pelle MT, Miller F III: Dermatologic manifestations and management of vascular steal syndrome in hemodialysis patients with arteriovenous fistulas. Arch Dermatol 138:1296-1298, 2002.

87. Laaksonen S, Netsarinne K, Voipio-Pulkki LM, et al: Neurophysiologic parameters and symptoms in chronic renal failure. Muscle Nerve 25:884-890, 2002.

88. Ogura T, Makinodan A, Kubo T, et al: Electrophysiological course of uraemic neuropathy in hemodialysis patients. Postgrad Med J 77:451-454, 2001.

89. Wytrzes L, Markley HG, Fisher M, et al: Brachial neuropathy after brachial artery-antecubital vein shunts for chronic hemodialysis. Neurology 37:1398-1400, 1987.

90. Mattson WJ: Recognition and treatment of vascular steal secondary to hemodialysis prostheses. Am J Surg 154:198-201, 1987.

91. Rivers SP, Scher LA, Veith FJ: Correction of steal syndrome secondary to hemodialysis access fistulas: A simplified quantitative technique. Surgery 112:593-597, 1992.

92. Katz S, Kohl RD: The treatment of hand ischemia by arterial ligation and upper extremity bypass after angioaccess surgery. J Am Coll Surg 183:239-242, 1996.

93. Knox RC, Berman SS, Hughes JD, et al: Distal revascularization-interval ligation: A durable and effective treatment for ischemic steal syndrome after hemodialysis. J Vasc Surg 36:250-256, 2002.

94. Goff CD, Sato DH, Bloch PH, et al: Steal syndrome complicating hemodialysis access procedures: Can it be predicted? Ann Vasc Surg 14:138-144, 2000.

95. Sessa C, Pecher M, Maurizi-Balsan J, et al: Critical hand ischemia after angioaccess surgery: Diagnosis and treatment. Ann Vasc Surg 14:583-593, 2000.

96. Miles AM: Vascular steal syndrome and ischemic monomelic neuropathy: Two variants of upper limb ischemia after hemodialysis vascular access surgery. Nephrol Dial Transplant 14:297-300, 1999.

97. Wixon CL, Hughes JD, Mills JL: Understanding strategies for the treatment of ischemic steal syndrome after hemodialysis access. J Am Coll Surg 191:301-310, 2000.

98. Johnson G Jr, Dart CH Jr, Peters RM, et al: The importance of venous circulation in arteriovenous fistula. Surg Gynecol Obstet 123:995-1000, 1966.

99. West JC, Evans RD, Kelley SE, et al: Arterial insufficiency in hemodialysis access procedures: Reconstruction by an interposition PTFE conduit. Am J Surg 153:300-301, 1987.

100. Odland MD, Kelly PH, Ney AL, et al: Management of dialysis-associated steal syndrome complicating upper extremity arteriovenous fistulas: Use of intraoperative digital photoplethysmography. Surgery 110:664-669, 1991.

101. Jain KM, Simoni EJ, Munn JS: A new technique to correct vascular steal secondary to hemodialysis grafts. Surg Gynecol Obstet 175:183-184, 1992.

102. Halevy A, Halpern Z, Negri M, et al: Pulse oximetry in the evaluation of the painful hand after arteriovenous fistula creation. Vasc Surg 14:537-539, 1991.

103. DeCaprio JD, Valentine RJ, Kakish HB, et al: Steal syndrome complicating hemodialysis access. Cardiovasc Surg 5:648-653, 1997.

104. Schanzer H, Schwartz M, Harrington E, et al: Treatment of ischemia due to "steal" by arteriovenous fistula with distal artery ligation and revascularization. J Vasc Surg 7:770-773, 1988.

105. Knox RC, Berman SS, Hughes JD, et al: Distal revascularization-interval ligation: A durable and effective treatment for ischemic steal syndrome after hemodialysis. J Vasc Surg 36:250-256, 2002.

106. Irvine C, Holt P: Hand venous hypertension complicating arteriovenous fistula construction for haemodialysis. Clin Exp Dermatol 14:289-290, 1989.

107. Haimov M, Baez A, Noff M, et al: Complications of arteriovenous fistulae for hemodialysis. Arch Surg 110:708-712, 1975.

108. Brakman M, Faber WR, Zeegelaar JE, et al: Venous hypertension of the hand caused by hemodialysis shunt: Immunofluorescence studies of pericapillary cuffs. J Am Acad Dermatol 31:23-26, 1994.

109. Deshmukh N: Venous ulceration of the hand secondary to a Cimino fistula. Mil Med 158:752-753, 1993.

110. Bogaert AM, Vanholder R, De Roose J: Pseudo-Kaposi's sarcoma as a complication of Cimino-Brescia arteriovenous fistulas in hemodialysis patients. Nephron 46:170-173, 1987.

111. Wood ML, Reilly GD, Smith GT: Ulceration of the hand secondary to a radial arteriovenous fistula: A model for varicose ulceration. BMJ 287:1167-1168, 1983.

112. Lumsden AB, MacDonald MJ, Isiklar H, et al: Central venous stenosis in the hemodialysis patient: Incidence and efficacy of endovascular treatment. Cardiovasc Surg 5:504-509, 1997.

113. Vanherweghem JL, Yassine T, Goldman M, et al: Subclavian vein thrombosis: A frequent complication of subclavian vein cannulation for hemodialysis. Clin Nephrol 26:235-238, 1986.

114. Abruahma AF, Sadler DL, Robinson PA: Axillary subclavian vein thrombosis: Changing patterns of etiology, diagnostic, and therapeutic modalities. Am Surg 57:101-107, 1991.

115. Davis RP, Lipsig LJ, Connolly MM, et al: Varicose ulcer of the upper extremity. Surgery 98:616-618, 1985.

116. Schwab SJ, Quarles LD, Middleton JP, et al: Hemodialysis-associated subclavian vein stenosis. Kidney Int 33:1156-1159, 1988.

117. Wisselink W, Money SR, Becker MO, et al: Comparison of operative reconstruction and percutaneous balloon dilation for central venous obstruction. Am J Surg 166:200-205, 1993.

118. Shoenfeld R, Hermans H, Novick A, et al: Stenting of proximal venous obstructions to maintain hemodialysis access. J Vasc Surg 19:532-539, 1994.

119. Oderich GSC, Treiman GS, Schneider P, et al: Stent placement for treatment of central and peripheral venous obstruction: A long-term multi-institutional experience. J Vasc Surg 32:760-769, 2000.

120. Doty DB, Baker WH: Bypass of superior vena cava with spiral vein graft. Ann Thorac Surg 22:490-493, 1976.

121. Ayarragaray JEF: Surgical treatment of hemodialysis-related central venous stenosis or occlusion: Another option to maintain vascular access. J Vasc Surg 37:1043-1046, 2003.

122. Hoballah JJ, Eid GM, Nazzal MM, et al: Contralateral internal jugular vein interposition for salvage of a functioning arteriovenous fistula. Ann Vasc Surg 14:679-682, 2000.

123. Puskas JD, Gertler JP: Internal jugular to axillary vein bypass for subclavian vein thrombosis in the setting of brachial arteriovenous fistula. J Vasc Surg 19:939-942, 1994.

124. Currier CB Jr, Widder S, Ali A, et al: Surgical management of subclavian and axillary vein thrombosis in patients with a functioning arteriovenous fistula. Surgery 100:25-28, 1985.

125. Burn DJ, Bates D: Neurology and the kidney. J Neurol Neurosurg Psychiatry 65:810-821, 1998.

126. Ahonen RE: Peripheral neuropathy in uremic patients and in renal transplant recipients. Acta Neuropathol 54:43-53, 1981.

127. Bolton CF, McKeown MJ, Chen R, et al: Sub-acute uremic and diabetic polyneuropathy. Muscle Nerve 20:59-64, 1997.

128. Rosales RL, Navarro J, Izumo S, et al: Sural nerve morphology in asymptomatic uremia. Eur Neurol 28:156-160, 1988.

129. Said G, Boudier L, Selva J, et al: Different patterns of uremic polyneuropathy: Clinicopathologic studies. Neurology 33:567-574, 1983.

130. Nielson VK: The peripheral nerve function in chronic renal failure: VIII. Longitudinal course during terminal renal failure and regular hemodialysis. Acta Med Scand 195:155-162, 1974.

131. Bolton CF, Lindsay RM, Linton AL: The course of uremic neuropathy during chronic hemodialysis. Can J Neurol Sci 2:332-333, 1975.

132. Bolton CF, Baltzan MA, Baltzan BR: Effects of renal transplantation on uremic neuropathy: A clinical and electrophysiologic study. N Engl J Med 284:1170-1175, 1971.

133. Nielsen VK: The peripheral nerve function in chronic renal failure: VIII. Recovery after renal transplantation—clinical aspects. Acta Med Scand 195:163-170, 1974.

134. Aminoff MJ (ed): Neurological Aspects of Renal Failure. New York, Churchill Livingstone, 1989.

135. Warren DJ, Otieno LS: Carpal tunnel syndrome in patients on intermittent haemodialysis. Postgrad Med J 51:450, 1975.

136. Borman H, Akinbingol G, Maral T, et al: Entrapment neuropathy of the upper extremity in hemodialysis patients. Plast Reconstr Surg 109:2598-2599, 2002.

137. Hussein MM, Mooij JM, Roujouleh H, et al: Observations in a Saudi Arabian dialysis population over a 13-year period. Nephrol Dial Transplant 9:1072, 1994.

138. Jadoul M, Garbar C, Noel H, et al: Histological prevalence of beta-2 microglobulin amyloidosis in hemodialyis: A prospective post-mortem study. Kidney Int 51:1928, 1997.

139. Bicknell JM, Lim AC, Raroque HG Jr, et al: Carpal tunnel syndrome, subclinical median mononeuropathy, and peripheral polyneuropathy: Common early complications of chronic peritoneal dialysis and hemodialysis. Arch Phys Med Rehabil 72:378-381, 1991.

140. Gejyo F, Odani S, Yamada T, et al: Beta-2 microglobulin: A new form of amyloid protein associated with chronic hemodialysis. Kidney Int 30:385-390, 1986.

141. Tzamaloukas A: Carpal tunnel syndrome in patients on chronic hemodialysis. Dial Transplant 17:525-526, 1988.

142. Semple JC, Cargill AO: Carpal tunnel syndrome: Results of surgical decompression. Lancet 1:918-919, 1969.

143. Naito M, Ogata K, Goya T: Carpal tunnel syndrome in chronic renal dialysis patients: Clinical evaluation of 62 hands and results of operative treatment. J Hand Surg 12:366-374, 1987.

144. Halter SK, DeLisa JA, Stolov WC, et al: Carpal tunnel syndrome in chronic renal dialysis patients. Arch Phys Med Rehabil 62:197-201, 1981.

145. Borgatti PP, Lusenti T, Franco V, et al: Guyon's syndrome in a long-term hemodialysis patient. Nephrol Dial Transplant 6:734, 1991.

146. Konishiike T, Hashizuma H, Nishida K, et al: Cubital tunnel syndrome in a patient on long-term dialysis. J Hand Surg 19:636, 1994.

147. Kaku DA, Malamut RI, Frey DJ, et al: Conduction block as an early sign of reversible injury in ischemic monomelic neuropathy. Neurology 43:1126-1130, 1993.

148. Honet JC, Wajszczuk WJ, Rubenfire M, et al: Neurological abnormalities in the legs after use of intra-aortic balloon pump: Report of six cases. Arch Phys Med Rehabil 56:346-352, 1975.

149. Levin KH: AAEM case no. 19: Ischemic monomelic neuropathy. Muscle Nerve 12:791-795, 1989.

150. Bolton CF, Driedger AA, Lindsay RM: Ischaemic neuropathy in uraemic patients caused by bovine arteriovenous shunt. J Neurol Neurosurg Psychiatry 42:810-814, 1979.

151. Adams JP: Arteriovenous shunts and nerve damage. Lancet 1:211, 1981.

152. Dyck PJ, Conn DL, Okazaki H: Necrotizing angiopathic neuropathy: Three-dimensional morphology of fiber degeneration related to the sites of occluded vessels. Mayo Clin Proc 47:461-475, 1972.

153. Redfern AB, Zimmerman NB: Neurologic and ischemic complications of upper extremity vascular access for dialysis. J Hand Surg 20A:199-204, 1995.

THE MANAGEMENT OF SPLANCHNIC VASCULAR LESIONS AND DISORDERS

JAMES M. SEEGER, MD

Chapter

Physiology and Diagnosis of Splanchnic Arterial Occlusion

121

MARK C. WYERS, MD
ROBERT M. ZWOLAK, MD, PhD

The primary goal of initial attempts at surgical treatment for mesenteric ischemia was removal of infarcted bowel before the patient was moribund. In 1951 Klass,[1] the first surgeon to focus on the restoration of arterial blood supply in an attempt to salvage the bowel, performed the first reported superior mesenteric artery (SMA) embolectomy for acute mesenteric ischemia (AMI). The next 2 decades produced more such reports and increasing success with SMA thromboembolectomy. In 1958, Shaw and Maynard[2] published the first report of a successful thromboendarterectomy for the treatment of acute SMA thrombosis. Successful outcome after treatment of acute thrombotic SMA occlusion remained elusive, with mortality rates of 70% to 90%.

Aakhus[3] was an early proponent of angiography as a means to establish the diagnosis of mesenteric occlusive disease to help prevent bowel infarction. Early and liberal use of angiography was embraced more widely in the early 1970s, as championed by Boley and colleagues[4] and Clark and Gallant.[5] With this aggressive approach, these authors showed a reduction in the mortality rate to approximately 50%. Other major advancements during the second half of the 20th century included an increased knowledge of pathophysiology and clinical presentation of splanchnic arterial occlusive disease and refinement of open surgical revascularization techniques for the management of splanchnic arterial occlusion. Delay in diagnosis remains the greatest obstacle to reduction of morbidity and mortality surrounding this disease. This chapter focuses on normal and variant splanchnic anatomy, physiology, pathophysiology, and diagnosis of surgically important forms of

mesenteric arterial occlusion. Nonocclusive and venous causes of mesenteric ischemia are considered separately in other chapters of this section.

■ ANATOMY

The abdominal aorta has its embryologic origin in the primitive dorsal aorta. The primitive ventral aorta regresses, as do most of the ventral segmental arteries, during the fourth week of gestation. The 10th, 13th, and 21st primitive ventral segmental arteries persist, however, and give rise to the celiac artery, SMA, and inferior mesenteric artery (IMA), which supply arterial blood to the primitive foregut (celiac artery), midgut (SMA), and hindgut (IMA).[6] Anatomic variations in the visceral anatomy result from aberrances in the regression of the primitive ventral aorta and ventral segmental arteries (Fig. 121-1). The relative frequency of these variations is based on autopsy studies and is summarized in Table 121-1.

The celiac artery in most cases arises in a horizontal or slightly caudad fashion from the ventral aorta at the level of 12th thoracic or 1st lumbar vertebra. The classic pattern of this artery involves three branching arteries—left gastric, splenic, and common hepatic—configured as a true trifurcation (25%) or, more commonly, with the left gastric branching first (65% to 75%). The next most common variation is the additional presence of a fourth branch, either a dorsal pancreatic or the middle colic artery (5% to 10%). The remaining variations, including a single celiacomesenteric trunk, are much less common, each accounting for less than 1% of cases. Hepatic artery anatomy is highly variable

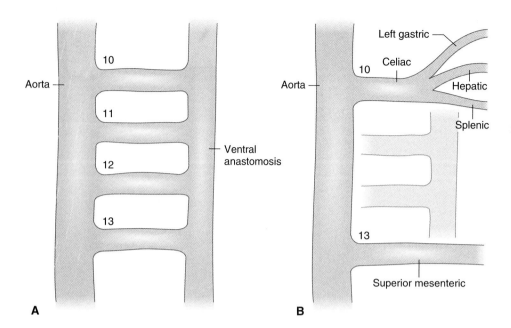

FIGURE 121-1 Embryology of the celiac artery and superior mesenteric artery (SMA). The 11th and 12th ventral anastomoses (**A**) regress, leaving the 10th ventral anastomosis to form the celiac and the 13th ventral anastomosis to form the SMA (**B**). (From Kadir S: Atlas of Normal and Variant Angiographic Anatomy. Philadelphia, WB Saunders, 1991.)

beyond its origin with 18% to 20% of hepatic branches originating from the SMA rather than the celiac artery. The common hepatic artery does this with the lowest frequency (2.5%), whereas a replaced or accessory right or left hepatic artery originating from the SMA is relatively common (14% to 18%) and may be clinically significant when considering revascularization strategies.

The SMA origin is located approximately at the level of the first lumbar vertebra at a distance of 0.2 to 2 cm inferior to the celiac artery. Typically the first branch is the inferior pancreaticoduodenal artery, which completes an important collateral pathway with the celiac artery via the superior pancreaticoduodenal and gastroduodenal arteries. The middle colic artery is usually the second SMA branch. It divides subsequently into right and left branches. The former connects with the ascending branch of the right colic artery, which arises from a more distal point on the SMA. The latter connects with the ascending branch of the left colic, running immediately adjacent to the splenic flexure to form an important SMA-IMA collateral named the *marginal artery of Drummond*. This artery should be distinguished from the meandering mesenteric artery (arc of Riolan), which courses radially through the mid-portion of the mesenteric arcade, near the inferior mesenteric vein. A variable number[10-15] of jejunal and ileal branches originates from the left side of the SMA as it courses toward the right lower quadrant. This arrangement is clinically significant because the typical SMA embolus lodges just beyond the first few jejunal branches as the SMA tapers, sparing the proximal jejunum from ischemia. This pattern contrasts with an acute thrombotic occlusion, which commonly blocks the SMA at its origin and causes widespread ischemia, including most of the small bowel and right colon.

The IMA typically arises from the left anterolateral aspect of the aorta at the level of the third lumbar vertebra and divides into the left colic and two or three sigmoidal branches. The ascending left colic branch forms the lower portion of the marginal artery of Drummond. The terminal branches of the sigmoidal arteries form the left and right superior rectal arteries, which complete collateral pathways to the internal iliac arteries via the middle rectal and internal pudendal arteries.

The splanchnic circulation is characterized by a wide network of collateral blood pathways that impart redundancy and resultant protection from ischemia or infarction in settings of segmental arterial occlusion. The primary

Table 121-1	Normal and Variant Vascular Anatomy
VESSEL	**INCIDENCE (%)**
Celiac Axis	
Classic, three vessel	65-75
Classic plus dorsal pancreatic artery	5-10
Common celiacomesenteric trunk	<1
Hepatic Artery	
Common hepatic from celiac artery	75
Common hepatic from SMA	2.5
Replaced right hepatic artery	17-18
Replaced left hepatic artery	15-18
Accessory right hepatic artery	7-8
Accessory left hepatic artery	2.5
Left Gastric Artery	
From celiac artery	90
From aorta	3
Right Gastric Artery	
From proper hepatic artery	40
From left or middle hepatic artery	40
From right hepatic artery	10
From gastroduodenal artery	8

SMA, superior mesenteric artery.

Adapted from Rosenblum JD, Boyle CM, Schwartz LB: The mesenteric circulation: Anatomy and physiology. Surg Clin North Am 77:293, 1997.

collaterals between the main mesenteric arteries are fairly constant. The celiac artery and SMA are connected by the superior and inferior pancreaticoduodenal arteries; the SMA and IMA, by the marginal artery of Drummond; and the IMA and hypogastric arteries, by the superior and middle rectal arteries. Other less constant collateral pathways, including the arch of Bühler (celiac-SMA), the arch of Barkow (celiac-SMA), and the arch of Riolan (SMA-IMA), also may be present.

■ PHYSIOLOGY

Changes in the resistance of mesenteric arterioles account for wide fluctuations in splanchnic blood flow, which can range from 10% to 35% of cardiac output (300 to 1200 mL/min.)[7,8] Most of this variability of mesenteric blood flow is accounted for by changes in flow to the small intestine. Duplex studies of SMA flow have shown an increase in SMA vessel diameter that peaks 45 minutes after a 1000-calorie meal. Correspondingly the SMA flow velocity increases significantly from a mean velocity of 22.2 cm/sec to a mean of 57 cm/sec,[9] and the Doppler waveform changes from a high-resistance triphasic morphology in the fasting state to a low-resistance pattern with high end-diastolic flow after a meal. In contrast, flow to the liver in the fed state increases primarily as a function of portal venous flow rather than any increase in flow through the fairly constant, low-resistance hepatic artery. A mixed caloric meal produces a greater increase in SMA flow than equal caloric loads of fat, glucose, or protein alone.[10] Actual intestinal absorption of nutrients also is required to initiate the vasomotor response that leads to this intestinal hyperemia,[11] whereas nonabsorbed substances or water have little effect on mesenteric blood flow.

Splanchnic Blood Flow Control

Numerous intrinsic and neurohormonal control mechanisms contribute to the regulation of mesenteric vascular tone.[11] Intrinsic autoregulation of blood flow by the splanchnic vessels is thought to occur in response to acute reductions in perfusion pressure (myogenic). Proposed mechanisms that result in the preservation of splanchnic tissue perfusion include direct arteriolar smooth muscle relaxation and a metabolic response to adenosine and other metabolites of mucosal ischemia.[12] In addition, intestinal mucosa extracts increasing amounts of oxygen during hypoperfusion[13] to preserve mucosal integrity during periods of metabolic insult. In in vitro human intestinal preparations, oxygen consumption remains fairly constant until flow decreases to a critical level of about 30 mL/min/100 grams (Fig. 121-2).[13]

Extrinsic neural and hormonal mechanisms also contribute to the control of intestinal blood flow. These mechanisms include the sympathetic nervous system, the renin-angiotensin axis, and vasopressin. Sympathetic tone is provided largely by the preganglionic cholinergic fibers of the greater splanchnic nerves, which synapse in the paired celiac ganglia adjacent to the celiac axis. Stimulation of the postganglionic adrenergic fibers of the celiac ganglia results in mesenteric artery and arteriolar vasoconstriction. Parasympathetic fibers of the vagi also innervate the intestine, but probably exert little effect on the mesenteric

vasculature.[14] Decreases in extracellular volume stimulate the renin-angiotensin axis, causing mesenteric vasoconstriction through the direct action of angiotensin II and indirectly via adrenergic potentiation. The putative importance of the renin-angiotensin axis in mediating selective mesenteric vasoconstriction has been re-emphasized more recently[15] and is likely responsible for the increased mesenteric resistance that accompanies nonpulsative cardiopulmonary bypass. Finally, loss of blood volume and hyperosmolarity result in stimulation of the neurohypophysis and release of vasopressin (antidiuretic hormone) from the pituitary gland, causing mesenteric vasoconstriction and venorelaxation. An understanding of these mechanisms has led to the therapeutic use of vasopressin in patients with bleeding from portal hypertension, which, by causing mesenteric vasoconstriction and venorelaxation, is effective in reducing portal venous pressures and bleeding.

■ PATHOPHYSIOLOGY

It is a common belief that two of the three mesenteric arteries must be involved with significant occlusive disease to cause symptoms of chronic mesenteric ischemia (CMI), and that the SMA must be one of the two. The slow progression of atherosclerotic occlusions is such that collateral pathways usually have time to develop so that single-vessel mesenteric vascular disease rarely results in symptoms. Isolated celiac artery or IMA narrowing or occlusion is almost always well tolerated. In contrast, single-vessel disease is more likely to cause ischemia if it represents a complete, sudden SMA occlusion, or if there is an SMA stenosis combined with previously interrupted collateral pathways. For this reason, a history of previous abdominal surgery, especially with regard to previous bowel resection, is important in the workup of CMI. In this situation, collateral flow from the celiac artery and IMA may not be adequate to prevent significant gut ischemia, and the patient with a solitary SMA occlusion and clear-cut symptoms of CMI should be considered for single-vessel SMA revascularization.

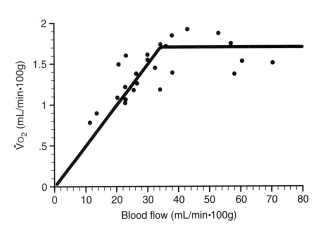

FIGURE 121-2 Relation between intestinal blood flow and oxygen consumption. (From Desai TR, Sisley AC, Brown S, Gewertz BL: Defining the critical limit of oxygen extraction in the human small intestine. J Vasc Surg 23:832, 1996.)

Similarly, isolated celiac artery stenosis is found in patients with the median arcuate ligament syndrome.[16] If all other causes of abdominal pain have been exhausted, patients with this rare entity may be treated successfully with an operation to release the celiac artery compression caused by the median arcuate ligament and the diaphragmatic crura. In straightforward cases, this may be accomplished laparoscopically, but in an equal number of patients celiac endarterectomy or patch angioplasty is necessary to achieve improved blood flow. The cohort of patients with median arcuate ligament syndrome is generally young, and complete resolution of debilitating symptoms may be achieved with adequate treatment.

Except for the aforementioned two unusual patient groups, development of CMI symptoms is almost always due to progression of disease in at least two of the three visceral arteries to severe stenosis or occlusion, such that collateral circulation is no longer sufficient to maintain adequate gut perfusion. Autopsy studies have shown that the incidence of 50% or greater stenosis in at least one mesenteric artery occurs in 6% to 10% of the population.[17] The incidence of 50% or greater asymptomatic celiac artery or SMA stenosis in patients undergoing arteriography for other peripheral vascular disease may be 27%.[18] The incidence of symptomatic CMI is much less than that, however, and these reports underscore the ability of mesenteric collaterals to maintain splanchnic perfusion until multiple severe stenoses or occlusions are present. Although the true natural history of such incidental, asymptomatic mesenteric arterial lesions is unknown, in one report 86% of patients with more advanced three-vessel mesenteric atherosclerosis experienced vague abdominal discomfort symptoms, experienced frank mesenteric ischemia, or died during a 2.6-year mean follow-up.[19] Although these authors suggested that prophylactic treatment of asymptomatic patients with advanced mesenteric atherosclerosis should be considered, particularly at the time of aortoiliac reconstruction for occlusive or aneurysmal disease, no consensus has been reached.

■ DIAGNOSIS

The clinical presentation of the patient suspected of having AMI or CMI guides the choice of specific diagnostic modality. The clinical presentation and diagnosis of patients with AMI, CMI, mesenteric venous occlusion, and non-occlusive mesenteric ischemia are discussed in detail in the other chapters in this section. This discussion focuses primarily on newer diagnostic tests and specific imaging modalities used to evaluate the splanchnic arterial circulation in a patient suspected of having mesenteric ischemia. Regardless, diagnostic or confirmatory imaging should not delay timely surgical exploration in patients with acute presentations or when peritonitis is suspected.

Laboratory Evaluation

Blood tests are helpful in the management of patients with mesenteric ischemia. These serum markers are completely insensitive and nonspecific, however, for the diagnosis of mesenteric ischemia.[20,21] One blood test that may offer some promise as a diagnostic tool for AMI is an enzyme immunoassay for elevated levels of intestinal fatty acid binding protein. First discovered in rodents,[22] the human homologue also was found to be elevated in cases of documented bowel infarction.[23] Clinical experience with this test is limited, and it needs to be evaluated further.

Abdominal Plain Radiographs

Abdominal plain radiographs are normal in 25% of patients with AMI.[24] Ileus may be an early finding consistent with mesenteric ischemia, however, and advanced cases of intestinal ischemia may show evidence of bowel wall edema ("thumbprinting") or pneumatosis.

Computed Tomography

Several authors have described the use of ultrafast multidetector row computed tomography arteriography (MDCTA) for the evaluation of AMI and CMI.[25-29] The widespread availability of these newest generation computed tomography (CT) scanners represents a potential change in the diagnostic algorithm for the workup of AMI and offers the advantage of speed compared with angiography. A significant amount of information can be obtained about the central arterial and venous circulation with MDCTA. Accurate timing of contrast injection and fine slices through the upper abdomen usually provide excellent visualization of the celiac artery and SMA. CT also offers the ability to exclude other causes of abdominal pain and some ability to assess bowel perfusion. The exact timing of intravenous contrast administration is tailored to the specific clinical question. The use of traditional oral "positive" contrast agents detracts from image quality, and most visceral computed tomography angiography (CTA) protocols recommend the use of a "negative" oral contrast agent, such as water (500 to 750 mL), given immediately before the scan. Administration of a negative contrast agent prevents image artifact from pooled areas of high opacification within the intestinal tract and enhances the ability to see bowel wall enhancement (or lack thereof) in the late arterial phase of the contrast bolus.[30] Main branches of the celiac artery and SMA are seen remarkably well using MDCTA because of thinner collimation (0.5 to 1.5 mm) and overlapping data acquisition. MDCTA reduces the amount of volume averaging and creates higher quality three-dimensional volume sets for reformatting and interpretation (Figs. 121-3 and 121-4).

Initial interest in so-called biphasic CT was generated in the evaluation of pancreatic and hepatic lesions and included an arterial phase and a delayed phase that is timed based on visualization of the portal venous system. Biphasic CT has been applied more recently to detect the early findings seen in AMI. The same scan is used to detect arterial narrowings or occlusions and to assess associated changes in bowel wall thickness, pneumatosis, mucosal enhancement pattern, or bowel wall enhancement pattern that support the diagnosis of AMI. Kirkpatrick and associates[31] sought to improve on a previous retrospective report that used single-detector helical CT.[32] These investigators evaluated prospectively 62 patients suspected to have AMI who underwent biphasic MDCTA. Similar to the previous study, no single CT finding was sensitive and specific (Table 121-2). Twenty-six

Table 121-2   Analysis of Computed Tomography Findings

CT FINDING	PATIENTS WITH AMI (n = 26)	CONTROL GROUP (n = 36)	SENSITIVITY (%)	SPECIFICITY (%)
Pneumatosis intestinalis	11	0	42	100
SMA or combined celiac and IMA occlusion*	5	0	19	100
Arterial embolism	3	0	12	100
SMA or portal venous gas	3	0	12	100
Focal lack of bowel wall enhancement	11	1	42	97
Free intraperitoneal air	5	2	19	94
Superior mesenteric or portal venous thrombosis	4	2	15	94
Solid-organ infarction	4	2	15	94
Bowel obstruction	3	2	12	94
Bowel dilatation	17	6	65	83
Mucosal enhancement	12	7	46	81
Bowel wall thickening	22	10	85	72
Mesenteric stranding	23	14	88	61
Ascites	19	24	73	33

*Patients with celiac and IMA occlusion also had evidence of distal disease in the SMA distribution.
AMI, acute mesenteric ischemia; CT, computed tomography; IMA, inferior mesenteric artery; SMA, superior mesenteric artery.

From Kirkpatrick ID, Kroeker MA, Greenberg HM: Biphasic CT with mesenteric CT angiography in the evaluation of acute mesenteric ischemia: initial experience. Radiology 229:91, 2003.

patients had AMI confirmed at surgical exploration or based on pathologic examination, however, and the interpreting radiologist identified correctly all of these patients as having AMI. An additional four CT scans interpreted as showing AMI turned out to be false-positive studies, with ultimate diagnosis of Crohn's disease (n = 2), neutropenic enterocolitis (n = 1), and infectious enterocolitis (n = 1). The initial interpretation had a sensitivity of 100% and specificity of 89% for the diagnosis of AMI. In the same study, CTA visualization was judged to be satisfactory in all cases up to second-order branches of the celiac artery and the SMA. Angiography was available in only three patients, but correlated well with the CTA findings (see Fig. 121-4).

Arteriography

Traditional multiplanar aortography is the definitive diagnostic study for AMI and offers several treatment options depending on the specific pathology, including injection of intra-arterial vasodilators,[33] thrombolysis,[34] and angioplasty with or without stenting.[35] As vascular surgeons become accomplished interventionalists, and as intraoperative fluoroscopy improves, confirmatory diagnostic arteriography can be accomplished in the operating room followed by immediate surgical exploration. This unified approach can limit delay in surgical exploration and revascularization. With respect to evaluation for CMI, angiography remains the "gold standard" for diagnostic imaging and preoperative planning based on superior image resolution, ability to visualize collateral flow direction, and identification of disease in the distal portions of the splanchnic arterial bed.

Duplex Ultrasonography

Duplex ultrasonography accurately identifies high-grade stenoses of the celiac artery and SMA. It is the noninvasive diagnostic study of choice in patients with symptoms suggesting CMI. Similar to most specialized duplex applications, however, a significant amount of expertise is required of the vascular technologist. Careful attention to proper angle correction is crucial to avoid falsely elevated velocities.[36] In addition, to minimize interference from overlying bowel gas, the study is best performed after an overnight fast. Pre–ultrasound scan dosing of simethicone also may improve visualization. In nonselected patient groups, adequate visualization may be 60%,[37] but in more selected studies of patients thought to have CMI, the reported technical adequacy approaches 100%.[38,39] The ability of duplex ultrasonography to identify anatomic anomalies has not been tested extensively, but in the Dartmouth validation study, duplex prospectively identified most anomalies that ultimately were confirmed by arteriography. This identification requires a thorough understanding of the more common anatomic variants by the vascular technologist along with careful attention to the subtleties of B-mode images, colorflow, and Doppler waveform characteristics.

Authors from the Oregon Health Sciences University and from Dartmouth were the first to propose duplex criteria for the diagnosis of splanchnic artery stenosis or occlusion in 1991.[10,40] Both groups have since published validation studies for their criteria, and the diagnostic thresholds have been published for peak systolic velocity (PSV) and end-diastolic velocity (EDV). For the SMA, a PSV greater than 275 cm/sec had a sensitivity of 92% and a specificity of 96% for a greater than 70% angiographic stenosis.[41] An EDV of greater than 45 cm/sec had a sensitivity of 90% and a specificity of 91% for a stenosis greater than 50%.[39] For the celiac artery, a PSV greater than 200 cm/sec had a sensitivity of 90% and specificity of 91% for a stenosis of greater than 70%.[41] Retrograde hepatic artery flow is 100% predictive of a severe celiac artery stenosis or occlusion.[39,42] Celiac EDV greater than 55 cm/sec had a 93% sensitivity and 100% specificity for a greater than 50% stenosis. A third group[38] published a similar confirmatory study, which confirmed the previously published systolic and diastolic criteria for 50% or greater stenoses, focusing more heavily on several diastolic thresholds, including early diastolic velocity, peak diastolic velocity, and EDV.[38] The duplex parameters tested

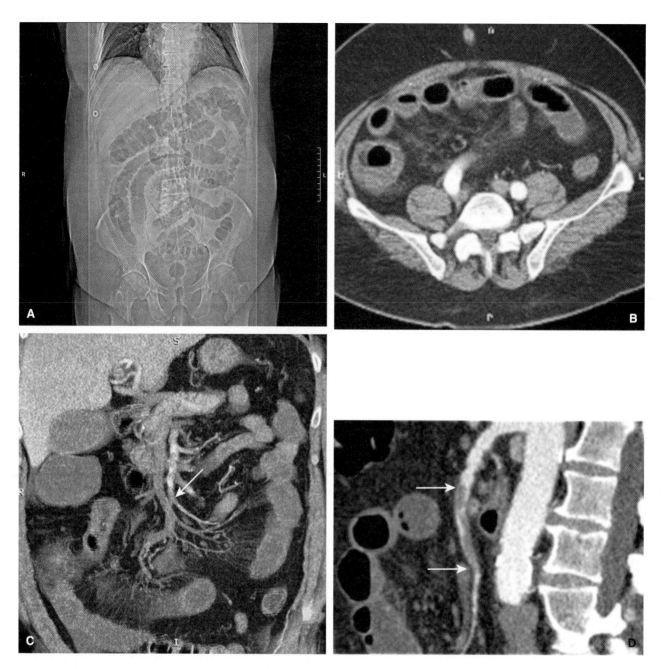

FIGURE 121-3 Biphasic multidetector CTA of acute superior mesenteric artery (SMA) embolus. **A,** Scout projection shows ileus pattern. **B,** Associated bowel wall thickening in region of cecum and distal small intestine; **C** and **D,** Filling defect beyond the SMA origin is shown with relative sparing of the first several jejunal branches. (From Fleischmann D: Multiple detector-row CT angiography of the renal and mesenteric vessels. Eur J Radiol 45[Suppl 1]: S79, 2003.)

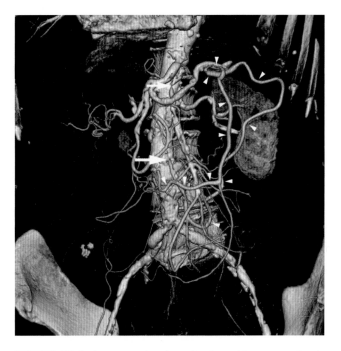

FIGURE 122-2 Anteroposterior view of patient with acute on chronic intestinal ischemia due to superior mesenteric artery occlusion (*small arrow*). In this case, the inferior mesenteric artery (*large arrow*) fills the superior mesenteric artery distribution in a retrograde fashion via a large meandering artery (*arrowheads*).

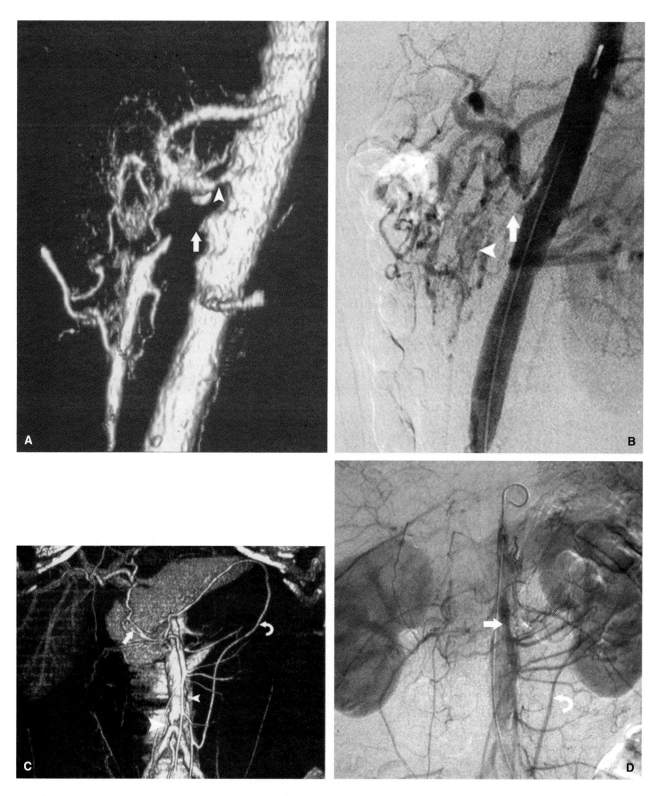

FIGURE 121-4 Volume-rendered multidetector CT arteriography images (**A** and **B**) and conventional digital subtraction angiography (**C** and **D**) of chronic mesenteric ischemia. In the upper images (lateral view), the celiac artery is stenotic, and the proximal superior mesenteric artery is occluded with reconstitution distally. In the lower images (anteroposterior), excellent detail allows visualization of the pancreaticoduodenal collaterals *(straight arrow)* and arch of Riolan *(curved arrow)*. (From Kirkpatrick ID, Kroeker MA, Greenberg HM: Biphasic CT with mesenteric CT angiography in the evaluation of acute mesenteric ischemia: Initial experience. Radiology 229:91, 2003.)

Table 121-3 Prospective Validation Studies of Mesenteric Diagnostic Criteria

AUTHOR (YEAR)	STENOSIS THRESHOLD (%)	SMA	SENSITIVITY (%)	SPECIFICITY (%)	CELIAC	SENSITIVITY (%)	SPECIFICITY (%)
Moneta (1993)[41]	≥70	PSV ≥275	92	96	PSV ≥200	90	91
	≥70	EDV ≥55	88	94	EDV ≥55	58	77
Zwolak (1998)[39]	≥50	PSV ≥300	60	100	PSV ≥200	93	94
	≥50	EDV ≥45	90	91	EDV ≥55	93	100
Perko (1997)[38]	≥50	PSV ≥275	93	80	PSV ≥200	94	94
	≥50	EDV ≥50	100	100	EDV ≥100	100	100

EDV, end-diastolic velocity; PSV, peak systolic velocity; SMA, superior mesenteric artery.

in these three studies are the most frequently employed clinically and are summarized in Table 121-3. The difference in stenosis thresholds selected by these groups is not likely as significant as it would seem at face value. This apparent discrepancy is reconciled by the fact that both validation studies[39,41] included relatively few patients who had angiographic stenoses in the 50% to 70% range. More patients with this degree of moderate stenosis would have been needed to distinguish patients within this group more effectively.

Postprandial duplex scanning in symptomatic patients adds little to the overall accuracy of fasting examinations. Although there is clear evidence that splanchnic arterial flow in normal patients is measurably increased after a meal, this effect is less pronounced in patients with known 70% or greater SMA stenosis. In a study by Gentile and associates,[43] the overall accuracy of the postprandial examination was reduced at 91% compared with 96% accuracy attained by the fasting examination. These investigators concluded that the postprandial examination may be applicable only in selected patients to help confirm negative studies. In clinical practice, however, it is difficult to justify a duplicate postprandial examination when the initial fasting examination has an overall accuracy of 96% and a negative predictive value of 99%.

Magnetic Resonance Imaging

Magnetic resonance imaging (MRI) of the splanchnic vessels is an evolving technology. MRI is theoretically appealing because it is noninvasive, avoids the risk of allergic reaction and nephrotoxicity associated with iodinated contrast agents, and may not be as operator dependent as duplex ultrasound. MRI of the mesenteric vasculature can incorporate functional and anatomic evaluations of CMI. Functional assessment has been investigated by several groups using noncontrast, cine cardiac gated phase contrast magnetic resonance angiography (MRA) to correlate superior mesenteric vein (SMV) and SMA flow rates.[44-47] Burkart and coworkers[47] showed that patients with CMI ($n = 10$) had a reduced rate of postprandial flow augmentation ($64\% \pm 28\%$; $P = .02$) compared with healthy controls ($n = 10$). In a similar study, Li and colleagues[44,48] showed that the combination of paired flow measurements taken 30 minutes after a meal in the SMA and the SMV provided

more information about collateral flow and that the ratio of SMV and SMA flow decreases with increasing disease severity. In a canine model of AMI and porcine model of CMI, Li and colleagues[49] and Chan and associates[50] used phase contract MRA to show that there is decreased postprandial blood oxygenation in the SMV, and that this is a sensitive indicator of ischemia. These types of analyses may provide physiologic information to confirm the diagnosis of CMI suspected clinically. Preprandial and postprandial comparisons in human subjects may provide the ability to distinguish the overall adequacy of arterial blood flow. Li and colleagues[17] were successful at distinguishing patients with CMI from patients without CMI using only SMV blood T2 measurements. In healthy patients, the postprandial SMV T2 measurements increased compared with fasting, whereas the same measurement decreased in symptomatic CMI patients ($P < .0001$).

Anatomic imaging of the visceral vessels relies on contrast-enhanced MRI techniques; noncontrast three-dimensional phase-contrast MRA identifies only 66% of angiographic stenoses and creates some false-positive results.[51] Rapid bolus intravenous administration of a T1-shortening agent (e.g., gadolinium diethylenetriaminepenta-acetic acid) paired with a rapid, three-dimensional gradient recalled echo sequence allows consistent imaging of the splanchnic circulation with minimal flow artifact. Commercially available data acquisition protocols are available, and the three-dimensional dataset can be postprocessed with techniques such as maximal intensity projection, curved planar reformation, and volume rendering, which distill the data into more readily comprehensible images (Fig. 121-5). Two studies addressed the accuracy of three-dimensional contrast-enhanced MRA in evaluating percent stenosis in the celiac artery, SMA, and IMA. The most common error was overestimation of the stenosis (Fig. 121-6). The weakness of MRA is its relatively poor spatial resolution that, even on the best systems, is limited to 1 mm³. Gadolinium-enhanced MRA currently does not provide sufficient resolution to show distal emboli; nonocclusive, low-flow states; small vessel occlusion; or vasculitis.[52] Meaney and associates[53] evaluated 14 patients with CMI; three-dimensional contrast-enhanced MRA had a sensitivity of 100% and a specificity of 87% in the overall detection of 50% or greater visceral artery stenosis. The lack of specificity was due to the false-positive diagnosis of IMA

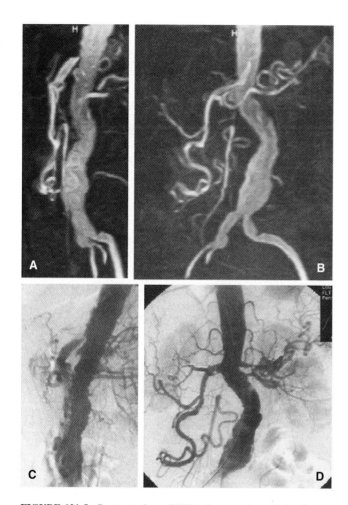

FIGURE 121-5 Contrast-enhanced MRA of mesenteric occlusive disease. **A** and **B,** Lateral and anteroposterior maximum intensity projection (MIP) images show focal celiac artery stenosis and superior mesenteric artery occlusion with reconstitution via pancreaticoduodenal collaterals. **C** and **D,** Lateral and anteroposterior arteriograms of the same patient confirm the MRA findings. (From Laissy JP, Trillaud H, Douek P: MR angiography: Non-invasive vascular imaging of the abdomen. Abdom Imaging 27:488, 2002.)

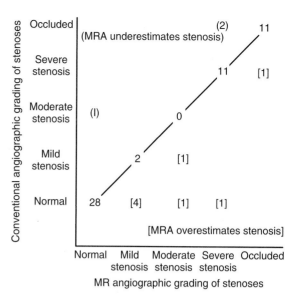

FIGURE 121-6 The MRA grading accuracy for celiac artery (CA), superior mesenteric artery (SMA), and inferior mesenteric artery (IMA) (n = 63) in 26 patients with prospective conventional angiographic correlation. Numbers on solid line represent the number of arteries in which results of MRA and conventional angiography agreed. Numbers in parentheses represent the number of arteries in which MRA resulted in underestimation of the degree of stenosis. Numbers in brackets represent the number of arteries in which MRA resulted in overestimation of the degree of stenosis. (From Carlos RC, Stanley JC, Stafford-Johnson D, Prince MR: Interobserver variability in the evaluation of chronic mesenteric ischemia with gadolinium-enhanced MR angiography. Acad Radiol 8:879, 2001.)

stenoses. Looking only at the subset of celiac artery and SMA data, the sensitivity and specificity were 100% for the detection of 50% or greater stenosis. In a similar, more recent study by Carlos and colleagues,[52] two blinded observers reviewed gadolinium-enhanced MRA studies and compared them with conventional arteriography in 26 patients suspected to have CMI. The overall accuracies for the detection of 50% or greater stenosis or occlusion in the celiac artery, SMA, or IMA were 95% and 97%. Kappa statistic was generated and used to evaluate interobserver agreement and was excellent for the celiac artery (kappa = .90) and the SMA (kappa = .92), but was only moderate for the IMA (kappa = .48).

Secondary signs of mesenteric ischemia, such as indurated fat or bowel wall thickening, which are routinely delineated by CT, are more difficult to assess with MRI. In general, the anatomic evaluation of the mesenteric arteries is limited to the proximal celiac artery and SMA only, and the evaluation of SMA branches or IMA is limited by the spatial resolution of MRI techniques. Overall, MRA is not practical in the setting of AMI because of time delay, and its utility in CMI depends on the quality of the instrumentation, the sophistication of the software, and the skill of the interpreting radiologist.

■ SUMMARY

The diagnosis of occlusive mesenteric ischemia requires a thorough understanding of the anatomy, physiology, and pathophysiology of the mesenteric circulation. Early diagnosis is crucial to minimize the associated high mortality rates. We recommend two diagnostic algorithms (Figs. 121-7 and 121-8) that advocate the liberal use of angiography. Duplex ultrasound is an especially important tool in evaluation of CMI, and biphasic MDCTA has an evolving role in the emergent evaluation of AMI.

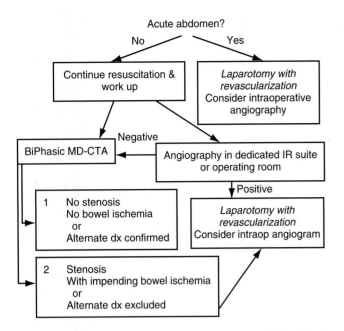

FIGURE 121-7 Acute occlusive mesenteric ischemia—initial clinical evaluation/resuscitation. IR, interventional radiology; MDCTA, multidetector CT arteriography.

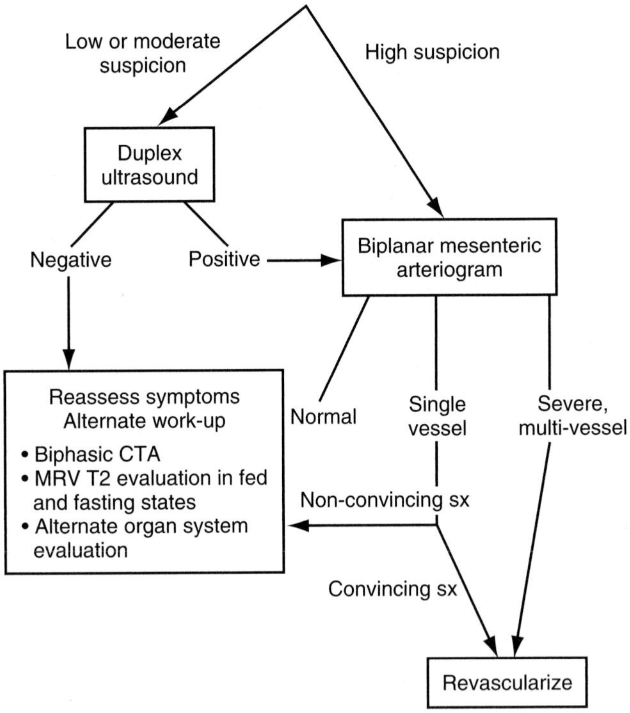

FIGURE 121-8 Chronic mesenteric ischemia—patient with chronic mesenteric ischemia symptoms. MRV, magnetic resonance venography.

■ REFERENCES

1. Klass AA: Embolectomy in acute mesenteric occlusion. Ann Surg 134:913, 1951.
2. Shaw RS, Maynard EP 3rd: Acute and chronic thrombosis of the mesenteric arteries associated with malabsorption: A report of two cases successfully treated by thromboendarterectomy. N Engl J Med 258:874, 1958.
3. Aakhus T: The value of angiography in superior mesenteric artery embolism. Br J Radiol 39:928, 1966.
4. Boley SJ, Sprayregen S, Veith FJ, Siegelman SS: An aggressive roentgenologic and surgical approach to acute mesenteric ischemia. Surg Ann 5:355, 1973.
5. Clark RA, Gallant TE: Acute mesenteric ischemia: Angiographic spectrum. AJR Am J Roentgenol 142:555, 1984.
6. Kadir S: Atlas of Normal and Variant Angiographic Anatomy. Philadelphia, WB Saunders, 1991.
7. Rapp JH, Reilly LM, Qvarfordt PG, et al: Durability of endarterectomy and antegrade grafts in the treatment of chronic visceral ischemia. J Vasc Surg 3:799, 1986.
8. Schwartz LB, Purut CM, O'Donohoe MK, et al: Quantitation of vascular outflow by measurement of impedance. J Vasc Surg 14:353, 1991.
9. Jager K, Bollinger A, Valli C, Ammann R: Measurement of mesenteric blood flow by duplex scanning. J Vasc Surg 3:462, 1986.
10. Moneta GL, Yeager RA, Dalman R, et al: Duplex ultrasound criteria for diagnosis of splanchnic artery stenosis or occlusion. J Vasc Surg 14:511, 1991.
11. Qamar MI, Read AE, Skidmore R, et al: Transcutaneous Doppler ultrasound measurement of coeliac axis blood flow in man. Br J Surg 72:391, 1985.
12. Rosenblum JD, Boyle CM, Schwartz LB: The mesenteric circulation: Anatomy and physiology. Surg Clin North Am 77:289, 1997.
13. Desai TR, Sisley AC, Brown S, Gewertz BL: Defining the critical limit of oxygen extraction in the human small intestine. J Vasc Surg 23:832, 1996.
14. Granger DN, Richardson PD, Kvietys PR, Mortillaro NA: Intestinal blood flow. Gastroenterology 78:837, 1980.
15. Reilly PM, Bulkley GB: Vasoactive mediators and splanchnic perfusion. Crit Care Med 21(2 Suppl):S55, 1993.
16. Carey JP, Stemmer EA, Connolly JE: Median arcuate ligament syndrome: Experimental and clinical observations. Arch Surg 99:441, 1969.
17. Li KC, Dalman RL, Wright GA: In vivo flow-independent T2 measurements of superior mesenteric vein blood in diagnosis of chronic mesenteric ischemia: A preliminary evaluation. Acad Radiol 6:530, 1999.
18. Valentine RJ, Martin JD, Myers SI, et al: Asymptomatic celiac and superior mesenteric artery stenoses are more prevalent among patients with unsuspected renal artery stenoses. J Vasc Surg 14:195, 1991.
19. Thomas JH, Blake K, Pierce GE, et al: The clinical course of asymptomatic mesenteric arterial stenosis. J Vasc Surg 27:840, 1998.
20. Kolkman JJ, Groeneveld AB: Occlusive and non-occlusive gastrointestinal ischaemia: A clinical review with special emphasis on the diagnostic value of tonometry. Scand J Gastroenterol 225(Suppl):3, 1998.
21. Kurland B, Brandt LJ, Delany HM: Diagnostic tests for intestinal ischemia. Surg Clin North Am 72:85, 1992.
22. Gollin G, Marks C, Marks WH: Intestinal fatty acid binding protein in serum and urine reflects early ischemic injury to the small bowel. Surgery 113:545, 1993.
23. Kanda T, Fujii H, Tani T, et al: Intestinal fatty acid-binding protein is a useful diagnostic marker for mesenteric infarction in humans. Gastroenterology 110:339, 1996.
24. Smerud MJ, Johnson CD, Stephens DH: Diagnosis of bowel infarction: A comparison of plain films and CT scans in 23 cases. AJR Am J Roentgenol 154:99, 1990.
25. Horton KM, Fishman EK: 3D CT angiography of the celiac and superior mesenteric arteries with multidetector CT data sets: Preliminary observations. Abdom Imaging 25:523, 2000.
26. Laghi A, Iannaccone R, Catalano C, Passariello R: Multislice spiral computed tomography angiography of mesenteric arteries. Lancet 358:638, 2001.

27. Lee R, Tung HK, Tung PH, et al: CT in acute mesenteric ischaemia. Clin Radiol 58:279, 2003.
28. Zandrino F, Curone P, Benzi L, Musante F: Value of an early arteriographic acquisition for evaluating the splanchnic vessels as an adjunct to biphasic CT using a multislice scanner. Eur Radiol 13:1072, 2003.
29. Fleischmann D: Multiple detector-row CT angiography of the renal and mesenteric vessels. Eur J Radiol 45(suppl 1):S79, 2003.
30. Horton KM, Fishman EK: Multi-detector row CT of mesenteric ischemia: Can it be done? Radiographics 21:1463, 2001.
31. Kirkpatrick ID, Kroeker MA, Greenberg HM: Biphasic CT with mesenteric CT angiography in the evaluation of acute mesenteric ischemia: Initial experience. Radiology 229:91, 2003.
32. Taourel PG, Deneuville M, Pradel JA, et al: Acute mesenteric ischemia: Diagnosis with contrast-enhanced CT. Radiology 199:632, 1996.
33. Meilahn JE, Morris JB, Ceppa EP, Bulkley GB: Effect of prolonged selective intramesenteric arterial vasodilator therapy on intestinal viability after acute segmental mesenteric vascular occlusion. Ann Surg 234:107, 2001.
34. Savassi-Rocha PR, Veloso LF: Treatment of superior mesenteric artery embolism with a fibrinolytic agent: Case report and literature review. Hepatogastroenterology 49:1307, 2002.
35. Kasirajan K, O'Hara PJ, Gray BH, et al: Chronic mesenteric ischemia: Open surgery versus percutaneous angioplasty and stenting. J Vasc Surg 33:63, 2001.
36. Rizzo RJ, Sandager G, Astleford P, et al: Mesenteric flow velocity variations as a function of angle of insonation. J Vasc Surg 11:688, 1990.
37. Sabba C, Ferraioli G, Sarin SK, et al: Feasibility spectrum for Doppler flowmetry of splanchnic vessels: In normal and cirrhotic populations. J Ultrasound Med 9:705, 1990.
38. Perko MJ, Just S, Schroeder TV: Importance of diastolic velocities in the detection of celiac and mesenteric artery disease by duplex ultrasound. J Vasc Surg 26:288, 1997.
39. Zwolak RM, Fillinger MF, Walsh DB, et al: Mesenteric and celiac duplex scanning: A validation study. J Vasc Surg 27:1078, 1998.
40. Bowersox JC, Zwolak RM, Walsh DB, et al: Duplex ultrasonography in the diagnosis of celiac and mesenteric artery occlusive disease. J Vasc Surg 14:780, 1991.
41. Moneta GL, Lee RW, Yeager RA, et al: Mesenteric duplex scanning: A blinded prospective study. J Vasc Surg 17:79, 1993.
42. Labombard FE, Musson A, Bowersox JC, et al: Hepatic artery duplex as an adjunct in the evaluation of chronic mesenteric ischemia. J Vasc Tech 16:7, 1992.
43. Gentile AT, Moneta GL, Lee RW, et al: Usefulness of fasting and postprandial duplex ultrasound examinations for predicting high-grade superior mesenteric artery stenosis. Am J Surg 169:476, 1995.
44. Li KC, Hopkins KL, Dalman RL, Song CK: Simultaneous measurement of flow in the superior mesenteric vein and artery with cine phase-contrast MR imaging: Value in diagnosis of chronic mesenteric ischemia: Work in progress. Radiology 194:327, 1995.
45. Burkart DJ, Johnson CD, Ehman RL: Correlation of arterial and venous blood flow in the mesenteric system based on MR findings. 1993 ARRS Executive Council Award. AJR Am J Roentgenol 161:1279, 1993.
46. Burkart DJ, Johnson CD, Morton MJ, et al: Volumetric flow rates in the portal venous system: Measurement with cine phase-contrast MR imaging. AJR Am J Roentgenol 160:1113, 1993.
47. Burkart DJ, Johnson CD, Reading CC, Ehman RL: MR measurements of mesenteric venous flow: prospective evaluation in healthy volunteers and patients with suspected chronic mesenteric ischemia. Radiology 194:801, 1995.
48. Li KC, Wright GA, Pelc LR, et al: Oxygen saturation of blood in the superior mesenteric vein: In vivo verification of MR imaging measurements in a canine model: Work in progress. Radiology 194:321, 1995.
49. Li KC, Pelc LR, Dalman RL, et al: In vivo magnetic resonance evaluation of blood oxygen saturation in the superior mesenteric vein as a measure of the degree of acute flow reduction in the superior mesenteric artery: Findings in a canine model. Acad Radiol 4:21, 1997.
50. Chan FP, Li KC, Heiss SG, Razavi MK: A comprehensive approach using MR imaging to diagnose acute segmental mesenteric ischemia in a porcine model. AJR Am J Roentgenol 173:523, 1999.
51. Wasser MN, Geelkerken RH, Kouwenhoven M, et al: Systolically gated 3D phase contrast MRA of mesenteric arteries in suspected mesenteric ischemia. J Comput Assist Tomogr 20:262, 1996.
52. Carlos RC, Stanley JC, Stafford-Johnson D, Prince MR: Interobserver variability in the evaluation of chronic mesenteric ischemia with gadolinium-enhanced MR angiography. Acad Radiol 8:879, 2001.
53. Meaney JF, Prince MR, Nostrant TT, Stanley JC: Gadolinium-enhanced MR angiography of visceral arteries in patients with suspected chronic mesenteric ischemia. J Magn Reson Imaging 7:171, 1997.

Treatment of Acute Intestinal Ischemia Caused by Arterial Occlusions

122

ERIN M. MOORE, MD
ERIC D. ENDEAN, MD

In 1933, Hibbard and Swenson[1] reported a 70% mortality for acute intestinal infarction. Advances in surgical and critical care have improved the outcomes in many areas of medicine, but unfortunately, the same cannot be said for acute mesenteric ischemia; patients with this disorder continue to have high mortality. A number of factors have prevented improvements in outcomes for patients with acute intestinal ischemia, including an increasingly aged population, more severe illness among patients coming to treatment, and the lack of younger patients with rheumatic heart disease as the cause of mesenteric arterial embolization.[2] Additionally, ischemic times as short as 3 hours can produce significant damage to the bowel mucosa, initiating a cascade of events such as reperfusion injury via oxygen-derived free radicals, acute inflammatory response, hypovolemia, and multisystem organ dysfunction.

Typically, though not exclusively, acute mesenteric ischemia affects the elderly, who often have other co-morbid conditions and little physiologic reserve. Too often an elderly patient is admitted for vague abdominal pain. As evaluation for the etiology of this pain proceeds, a surgeon is finally called because growing leukocytosis, acidosis, hypotension, or bloody diarrhea and the development of sepsis mandates surgical exploration. Upon exploratory laparotomy, the disastrous finding of extensive bowel infarction is encountered.[3,4] At that point, often little can be done for the patient, and even patients who survive extensive bowel resection are left with debilitating short-gut symptoms and a lifetime of special dietary requirements.

Early diagnosis appears to be the key factor that will ultimately improve outcomes. However, patients with intestinal ischemia often present with signs and symptoms that may not lead the practitioner to immediately suspect mesenteric ischemia. As a result, patients may undergo an evaluation that may be thorough but that is not performed with the urgency demanded by the underlying pathology. A delay in definitive diagnosis as a systematic evaluation proceeds then leads to a critical delay in treatment. By the time the patient has obvious signs and symptoms of ischemic bowel, such as acidosis, hypotension, and peritoneal signs, damage to the bowel is often far advanced. The solution to an earlier diagnosis ultimately requires a high index of suspicion on the part of the physician evaluating a patient with the potential for acute mesenteric ischemia.

When considering the diagnosis of acute mesenteric ischemia, it is also important to specify the cause of the ischemia. Nonocclusive mesenteric ischemia and venous thrombosis (detailed in Chapters 123 and 125) carry specific requirements for evaluation and intervention, and venous occlusive disease has a somewhat more optimistic prognosis. The situation is different for intestinal ischemia due to acute arterial obstruction. A review of the last 10 years' literature reveals a mortality in excess of 80% to 95% in some studies,[5,6] although later reviews show some evidence of progress, with mortality rates between 30% and 60% (Table 122-1).[7,8] However, the collated mortality figures since the experience reported by Ottinger and Austen[9] in 1967 generally paint a persistently grim picture for patients who are diagnosed and treated late in the course of disease. The better outcomes reported in later studies imply hope for the patient whose physician maintains vigilance and rapidly evaluates, resuscitates, and intervenes to ensure a favorable recovery. This chapter focuses on the evaluation and management of such patients. It is important to note that the extreme nature of this disease state implies that most of the steps presented are performed simultaneously, with aggressive resuscitation in anticipation of immediate surgical therapy.

■ ETIOLOGY OF ACUTE MESENTERIC ISCHEMIA

The two common etiologies of acute intestinal ischemia as caused by arterial occlusion are embolization to and thrombosis of the superior mesenteric artery. Each of these conditions is discussed in detail, as the treatment of patients with these two different problems may differ significantly.

Mesenteric Arterial Embolism

An embolus to the superior mesenteric artery is the cause of acute occlusive mesenteric ischemia in approximately half of all cases. Most emboli arise from a cardiac source. In these instances, a previous history of cardiac disease (congestive heart failure or recent myocardial infarction), atrial arrhythmia, or valvular disease can be elicited via the patient history. Patients with a cardiac source of emboli may

Table 122-1	Collated Mortality Associated with Treatment of Acute Intestinal Ischemia due to Acute Arterial Occlusion by Embolus or Thrombosis		
STUDY*	**PUBLICATION YEAR**	**NO. OF PATIENTS**	**MORTALITY**
Park et al[8]	2002	53	17/53 (32)
Endean et al[15]	2001	43	26/43 (60)
Foley et al[7]	2000	21	5/21 (24)
Mamode et al[6]	1999	57	46/57 (81)
Newman et al[38]	1998	24	18/24 (75)
Urayama et al[39]	1998	25	10/25 (40)
Klempnauer et al[40]	1997	48	38/48 (79)
Voltolini et al[41]	1996	47	34/47 (72)
Konturek et al[5]	1996	28	27/28 (96)
Deehan et al[42]	1995	43	30/43 (70)
Levy et al[43]	1990	45	20/45 (44)
Batellier et al[12]	1990	82	35/82 (43)
Bapat et al[44]	1990	24	7/24 (29)
Finucane et al[45]	1989	32	22/32 (69)
Sitges-Serra et al[46]	1988	25	14/25 (56)
Wilson et al[11]	1987	61	57/61 (93)
Bergan et al[47]	1987	14	11/14 (79)
Lazaro et al[48]	1986	23	6/23 (27)
Andersson et al[49]	1984	53	45/53 (85)
Sachs et al[10]	1982	30	23/30 (77)
Hertzer et al[50]	1978	9	6/9 (67)
Krausz & Manny[51]	1978	40	31/40 (78)
Kairaluoma et al[52]	1977	32	29/32 (91)
Boley et al[53]	1977	19	10/19 (53)
Smith & Patterson[54]	1976	17	15/17 (88)
Singh et al[55]	1975	26	21/26 (81)
Slater & Elliott[56]	1972	4	4/4 (100)
Ottinger et al[9]	1967	51	43/51 (84)
Collated experience		976	650/976 (67)

*Superscript numbers indicate chapter references.

also have a history of embolization to other locations either prior to or simultaneous with the mesenteric embolus. Increased use of anticoagulant medications is slowly reducing the number of cases in which a cardiac source is to blame and, as previously noted, rheumatic valvular disease as a source of cardiac emboli is also less commonly seen in modern practice.

Other sources of emboli have also been seen, including arterio-arterial emboli from such conditions as aneurysms and proximal atherosclerotic aortic disease and iatrogenic emboli created during intra-arterial manipulation of catheters and wires such as occurs during cardiac and peripheral angiography procedures.[10-12] The arterio-arterial emboli tend to be smaller and therefore lodge in the more distal mesenteric circulation. As a result, these emboli are likely to affect bowel in more localized areas, in contrast to the diffuse bowel ischemia that develops when the proximal mesenteric vessel is occluded, as is most common in patients with mesenteric emboli from a cardiac source. Nonetheless, like Klass, who first described the triad of abdominal pain, gut emptying, and a cardiac source for embolization,[13] the practicing surgeon must consider the diagnosis of mesenteric embolus in any patient with preexisting cardiac disease or recent arterial catheterization who presents with sudden onset of severe abdominal pain.

Mesenteric Arterial Thrombosis

Thrombosis of a visceral artery accounts for approximately 25% of all causes of acute mesenteric ischemia. Autopsy studies demonstrate a 6% to 10% incidence of mesenteric artery atherosclerosis in the general population,[14] yet the number of mesenteric revascularization procedures performed does not approach this level. It also remains unclear which patients with significant mesenteric artery stenosis are at risk for the development of acute mesenteric ischemia. The immediate cause of the visceral artery thrombosis may be a low-flow state that leads to thrombosis or sudden expansion of plaque (e.g., intraplaque hemorrhage) that results in abrupt narrowing of the artery. In the latter case, the underlying mesenteric atherosclerotic plaque may not have been hemodynamically significant enough to stimulate the development of collateral pathways, and with sudden occlusion of the visceral vessel, profound intestinal ischemia results. Typically, most individuals with preocclusive mesenteric atherosclerotic disease are women about 70 years old who often have vascular disease in other locations and commonly have a history of prior vascular intervention. Some have a history of postprandial abdominal pain and antecedent weight loss related to food avoidance suggestive of intestinal angina. However, in a 2001 series, only 20% of patients with mesenteric thrombosis had prior symptoms that were suggestive of chronic intestinal ischemia.[15]

■ DIAGNOSIS OF ACUTE MESENTERIC ISCHEMIA

In general, simple laboratory and radiographic imaging studies cannot confirm or exclude the diagnosis of acute mesenteric ischemia. The clinician therefore must learn the typical patterns of presentation for patients who are subsequently found to have this problem. As previously noted, most patients are elderly, and a consistent finding is the abrupt onset of severe, continuous abdominal pain that is not well localized. The onset of pain may or may not be accompanied by gut emptying, such as vomiting, a bowel movement, or diarrhea. Early in the course, the abdominal findings are normal, leading to the hallmark of acute mesenteric ischemia—pain out of proportion to the physical examination. With time, however, as bowel ischemia progresses to bowel infarction and perforation, peritoneal findings are compatible with an acute abdomen.

Acute bowel ischemia causes a number of laboratory abnormalities, but laboratory findings are nonspecific. The serum amylase concentration may be elevated because of increased peritoneal absorption as amylase leaks from ischemic bowel. A serum lactate elevation may be found, but its presence often implies that severe ischemia or bowel infarction has occurred. Acute mesenteric ischemia also results in dysfunction of the bowel cell membrane enzymes and allows sodium, followed by water, to enter the cells. Clinically this is seen as fluid sequestration in the bowel wall and manifests as hemoconcentration and signs of hypovolemia. Perhaps the most common laboratory abnormality encountered is a persistent and often profound leukocytosis, many times in excess of 15,000 cells per mm[3].

In up to 10% of patients with acute mesenteric ischemia, however, the white blood cell count is within the normal range, and some patients even have neutropenia.

Plain radiographs may be helpful in identifying other serious intra-abdominal disease, such as small bowel obstruction or free air due to a perforated viscus, but typically, plain abdominal series demonstrate no abnormalities until late in the clinical course in patients with acute mesenteric ischemia. Late findings such as distended bowel loops with air-fluid levels and thickening of the bowel wall are sometimes present; even later, gas within the mesenteric venous circulation is a finding that portends a very grave prognosis. Duplex ultrasonographic evaluation of the mesenteric vessels has also been suggested as a noninvasive technique to evaluate the mesenteric vessels in patients with possible acute mesenteric arterial occlusion. However, best results are obtained when the patient has fasted before the duplex examination and has received simethicone to decrease bowel gas, and such patient preparation is obviously impossible in the emergency setting. Additionally, duplex scanning is very operator dependent, and many facilities do not have vascular technologists readily available at all hours to perform such evaluations.

In contrast, computed tomography (CT) using an intravenous contrast agent is now generally available at all hours and can demonstrate failure of the proximal mesenteric vessel to opacify, bowel wall edema, and stranding in the mesentery—all clues that lead to the correct diagnosis. As the technology for multidetector CT has evolved, numerous researchers have proposed its use as a fast, effective, and noninvasive way to determine the status of the mesenteric circulation.[16-18] Diseases such as superior mesenteric artery occlusion and pneumatosis within the bowel wall can be quickly discerned on axial CT scanning (Fig. 122-1), whereas three-dimensional CT reconstructions enable evaluation of even more complex vascular anatomy (Fig. 122-2). It remains to be seen whether the widespread use of CT scanning will lead to earlier diagnosis and treatment for patients with acute mesenteric ischemia, and additional studies will be required to establish a reproducible protocol for its use. Regardless, as previously mentioned, a high index of suspicion in a patient with suggestive historical and clinical findings remains key to the diagnosis of acute mesenteric ischemia, and to date, angiography remains the "gold standard" for the imaging of mesenteric occlusion.

Angiography in Patients with Acute Mesenteric Ischemia

Preoperative angiography is definitive in confirming or excluding the diagnosis of mesenteric occlusive disease, and angiographic findings can demonstrate the cause of the mesenteric arterial occlusion. In the case of mesenteric thrombosis, the thrombus generally occurs at or near the origin of the superior mesenteric artery, and complete absence of opacification of the superior mesenteric artery circulation is therefore the usual angiographic finding (Fig. 122-3). This finding corresponds to the typical findings at operation, in which ischemia is found to involve the bowel from the ligament of Treitz to the mid-transverse colon (Fig. 122-4A). In contrast, an embolus usually lodges at an arterial branch point, as a result sparing the proximal branches of the superior mesenteric artery, and a meniscus may also be noted at the point where the embolus has lodged (Fig. 122-5). Findings at laparotomy are consistent with the sparing of the proximal branches, and typically, the proximal jejunum and possibly the ascending colon remain viable, while the middle and distal jejunum and ileum are ischemic

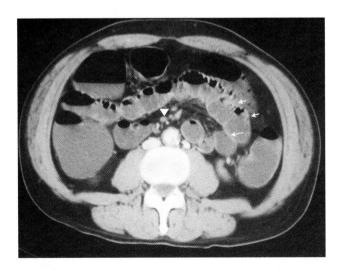

FIGURE 122-1 Contrast-enhanced computed tomography scan of the abdomen demonstrating nonenhancement of the superior mesenteric artery (SMA) due to occlusion (*arrowhead*), and the subtle findings of pneumatosis within the bowel wall (*arrows*). This patient required urgent exploration, bowel resection, and SMA bypass.

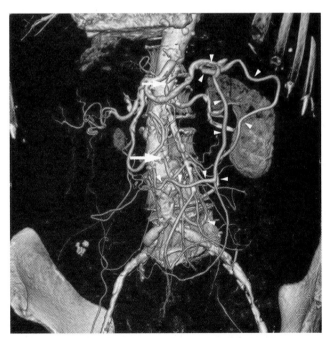

FIGURE 122-2 Anteroposterior view of patient with acute on chronic intestinal ischemia due to superior mesenteric artery occlusion (*small arrow*). In this case, the inferior mesenteric artery (*large arrow*) fills the superior mesenteric artery distribution in a retrograde fashion via a large meandering artery (*arrowheads*).

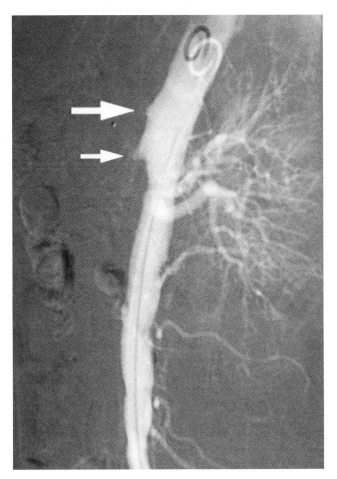

FIGURE 122-3 Lateral aortogram of a patient with acute intestinal ischemia due to superior mesenteric artery thrombosis. There is abrupt occlusion just distal to the origin of the vessel (*small arrow*). Note also the proximal occlusion of the celiac origin (*large arrow*).

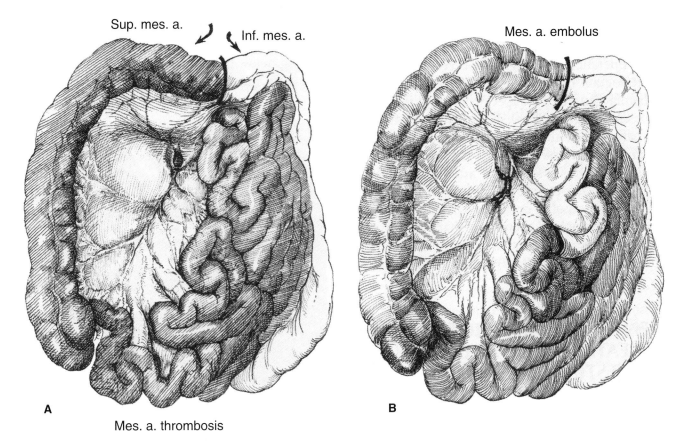

Sup. mes. a.   Inf. mes. a.

Mes. a. embolus

A

Mes. a. thrombosis

B

FIGURE 122-4 A, Ischemic bowel seen with superior mesenteric artery (Sup. mes. a.) thrombosis. Note that the ischemia begins at or slightly above the ligament of Treitz. **B,** Typical distribution of ischemia with superior mesenteric artery embolism. There is sparing of the proximal jejunum due to more distal occlusion. Inf., inferior. (From Bergan JJ: Recognition and treatment of intestinal ischemia. Surg Clin North Am 47:109, 1967).

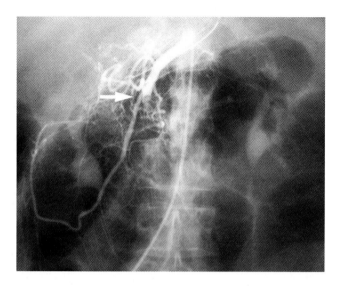

FIGURE 122-5 Selective arteriogram in a patient with acute intestinal ischemia due to superior mesenteric artery embolus. Note that flow is spared in the proximal jejunal branches and that there is visible thrombus at the site of occlusion (*arrow*).

(Fig. 122-4B). Preoperative angiography is also useful for the planning of surgical treatment, especially in identifying appropriate sites for the proximal anastomosis if a bypass is required, and endovascular treatment options such as thrombolysis and angioplasty may also be considered at the time of angiography in appropriate patients. In addition, some researchers have suggested that the mesenteric vasoconstriction that persists after revascularization should be treated with postoperative selective infusion of a vasodilator such as papaverine or tolazoline.[19,20]

The primary disadvantage to the use of preoperative angiography in patients in whom acute mesenteric ischemia is suspected is delay of definitive treatment. Because an angiogram is an invasive procedure, clinicians often spend time deliberating its need; also, the study is often needed after normal working hours, so delays are incurred in the wait for on-call personnel to arrive. It also takes time to complete the angiogram itself, varying with the expertise of the radiographer.

In light of these considerations, which patients presumed to have acute mesenteric ischemia should undergo mesenteric angiography? The first factor to consider is the general condition of the patient. Most patients who have infarcted bowel due to mesenteric embolus or thrombosis also have tachycardia, hypotension, and peritoneal signs. In such patients, it is most prudent to proceed directly to the operating room after expeditious resuscitation. If it becomes important to obtain angiographic information during the laparotomy, on-table angiography can be done. On the other hand, mesenteric angiography should probably be performed in patients who present with abdominal pain in the absence of other clinical findings that would imply intestinal infarction. Ultimately, the decision to obtain an angiogram is based on a number of interrelated factors: the availability of the study, the clinical circumstances, the stability of the patient, the certainty of the diagnosis, and the availability of an operating room.

■ TREATMENT

Initial Management

Patients who present with acute mesenteric ischemia often have volume depletion due to sequestration of fluid within the ischemic bowel wall. Some fluid is also lost if patients have experienced vomiting or diarrhea. Aggressive correction of fluid and electrolyte balance is thus required before treatment. Because these patients often have co-morbid medical conditions such as cardiac dysfunction, renal failure, and pulmonary insufficiency, invasive monitoring should be considered. A baseline electrocardiogram should also be obtained, because a finding of atrial fibrillation would support an embolus as the cause of the ischemia. Systemic anticoagulation with heparin should be started to prevent distal propagation of thrombus, and parenteral broad-spectrum antibiotics given because the mucosal barrier to the gut flora is broken down with mesenteric ischemia. The decision is then made whether to obtain a mesenteric arteriogram or to proceed directly to surgery without any further diagnostic studies (as described previously).

Endovascular Therapy

As previously discussed, mesenteric arterial thrombosis is usually due to atherosclerotic mesenteric arterial stenosis and that mesenteric arterial thrombosis and embolization potentially could be treated with thrombolysis and systemic anticoagulation. It may therefore seem reasonable to consider treating patients with acute mesenteric ischemia due to such lesions with thrombolysis, angioplasty, and stenting, particularly considering the high mortality associated with surgical treatment of this problem. Furthermore, since VanDeinse and colleagues[21] first reported their experience with percutaneous transluminal angioplasty in the treatment of mesenteric ischemia, some investigators have promoted endovascular treatment as a first-line therapy for mesenteric occlusive disease.[22] Simonetti and associates have reported on seven patients who presented with acute occlusive mesenteric ischemia.[23] However, only five cases were amenable to angioplasty, fibrinolysis, or both. Of those five patients, four showed clinical improvement without need for operation. Other groups have reported even more limited success in the endovascular management of patients with acute mesenteric ischemia.[24,25]

Endovascular treatment of patients with acute mesenteric ischemia also may expose the patient to the risk of ongoing ischemic damage during the wait for the thrombolytic therapy to have an effect. Furthermore, acute bowel ischemia may result in mucosal slough, leaving a large raw surface area, so that infusion of thrombolytic agents directly into the superior mesenteric artery vessel could result in significant gastrointestinal hemorrhage. Finally, the status of the bowel integrity cannot be addressed through angiographic techniques, and early recognition and resection of ischemic bowel that may progress to perforation are essential to avoid potentially disastrous clinical deterioration. Percutaneous intervention followed by laparoscopic evaluation of bowel integrity as a minimally invasive approach to mesenteric ischemia has been reported,[26] but such evaluation requires advanced laparoscopic skill for careful manipulation of the entire bowel to ensure that all areas of intestine are viable and to avoid further injury to marginally perfused segments. Currently, the best candidates for endovascular treatment of acute mesenteric ischemia may be patients with angiographic findings of good collateral circulation, minimizing the chance of bowel infarction during attempted thrombolysis. As discussed previously, however, there are no reliable studies to either exclude or confirm the presence of ongoing bowel ischemia, and either laparoscopic evaluation or open laparotomy would seem necessary in virtually all cases to confirm that the bowel is viable. Thus, at present, despite the appeal of treating these very ill patients in a "less invasive" manner, support for the safety and efficacy of such an approach is lacking.

Surgical Therapy

The abdomen is explored through a generous midline incision, typically extending from xiphoid to pubic symphysis, although a bilateral subcostal incision with a midline extension to the xiphoid could be considered if a bypass from the supraceliac aorta to the superior mesenteric artery is thought to be necessary. The initial steps in the laparotomy are to determine or confirm the cause and extent of the mesenteric occlusive disease, particularly in patients who have not undergone preoperative mesenteric arteriography, and to assess the viability of the bowel. As previously noted, the extent and pattern of bowel ischemia can offer valuable clues concerning the cause of bowel ischemia, thereby aiding in planning for revascularization.

The initial assessment of bowel viability is made by visual inspection, with an attempt to differentiate between ischemic but potentially viable bowel and infarcted bowel. Bowel necrosis is characterized by bowel wall that is an ashen, dull gray color, lacking the normal glistening sheen. Peristalsis also does not occur in infarcted segments of intestine, but its presence does not exclude significant ischemia. Unfortunately, some patients have such obvious, extensive bowel infarction that after resection they would be left with insufficient bowel to sustain life. In such cases, it is appropriate to close without attempting to restore blood flow or resect the infarcted bowel.

The appearance of the bowel can be deceiving, however; bowel that is nearing irreversible necrosis can be deceptively normal in appearance, and bowel that appears severely ischemic may be viable after revascularization. Thus, in all but the case of obvious catastrophic bowel necrosis, the surgeon should proceed with revascularization before resecting any intestine unless faced with an area of frank necrosis or perforation and peritoneal soilage. In the latter case, resection of the affected bowel and containment of the spillage should be achieved rapidly before revascularization. Mesenteric embolectomy and superior mesenteric artery bypass are the alternatives for mesenteric revascularization in patients with acute mesenteric ischemia, and the specific technique performed is determined by the disease encountered. Regardless, preparation and draping of all patients undergoing laparotomy for presumed acute mesenteric ischemia should include both lower extremities at least to the knee to allow for possible saphenous or superficial femoral vein harvest for bypass.

Superior Mesenteric Artery Embolectomy

Exposure of the superior mesenteric artery for embolectomy is achieved by retraction of the omentum and transverse colon cephalad and the small bowel and its mesentery inferiorly (Fig. 122-6). An incision is made in the small bowel mesentery near the root of the mesentery, directly over the area where the superior mesenteric vessels lie. Careful dissection in the mesentery initially reveals the superior mesenteric vein, or its tributaries that in turn lead to the main venous trunk. The superior mesenteric artery lies to the left of and inferior to the vein.

A segment of the proximal superior mesenteric artery and its branches (jejunal branches and the middle colic artery) are controlled. The artery is opened transversely if direct repair after embolectomy is planned, or longitudinally if bypass grafting is potentially required, as the graft can be readily anastomosed at this site (Fig. 122-7A). Some surgeons prefer longitudinal arteriotomy in all cases of acute ischemia, though closure of the vessel in the absence of bypass may require vein patch angioplasty. Proximal embolectomy is performed with a 3 or 4 French (F) balloon catheter. With extraction of the embolus, pulsatile inflow should be expected.

Distal embolectomy is performed with a smaller catheter, typically 2 or 3 F (see Fig. 122-7B). Great care must be taken to avoid damage or rupture of the fragile mesenteric arteries and subsequent hemorrhage into the bowel mesentery. Difficulty in passing a catheter down multiple branches of

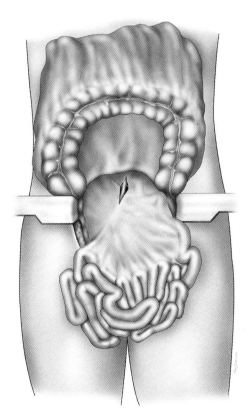

FIGURE 122-6 Superior mesenteric artery embolectomy. After retraction of the transverse colon cephalad and the small bowel caudad, the artery is exposed via a longitudinal incision at the root of the mesentery.

small size adds to the complexity of performing the distal embolectomy. An alternative or adjunct to balloon embolectomy of the distal mesenteric vessels is for the surgeon to place a hand on either side of the mesentery and "milk" thrombotic material out of the vessels. When all thrombus is removed, the arteriotomy is closed primarily or with vein patch, and flow is reestablished (see Fig. 122-7C and D).

Superior Mesenteric Artery Bypass

Thrombectomy alone does not reestablish adequate perfusion of the ischemic bowel in patients with thrombosis of the proximal superior mesenteric artery due to atherosclerotic occlusive disease, so a bypass is required. Considerations to be made concerning such bypasses are the type of conduit to be used and the origin of the graft. In a patient with chronic mesenteric ischemia, often the best procedure is a prosthetic bypass graft, with construction of the proximal anastomosis to the supraceliac aorta. However, if ischemic bowel of questionable viability, obviously infarcted bowel requiring resection, or perforated bowel is present in a patient with acute mesenteric ischemia, the use of prosthetic graft material risks later graft infection and is generally contraindicated. In such cases, autogenous vein (greater saphenous, superficial femoral, or arm vein) is preferred as the conduit.

The infrarenal aorta is often used as the site for the proximal anastomosis for such bypasses by many surgeons, because exposure of the supraceliac aorta is unfamiliar and time consuming. Use of the infrarenal site poses two potential problems. First, patients who have mesenteric ischemia due to thrombosis of the superior mesenteric artery often also have extensive atherosclerosis that involves the infrarenal aorta, the presence of which would preclude clamping and use of this site for the proximal anastomosis for a mesenteric bypass. An additional inflow site for a retrograde mesenteric bypass graft is an iliac vessel; alternatively, an endarterectomy of the infrarenal aorta or of the superior mesenteric artery origin can be considered.[27] However, endarterectomy of the infrarenal aortic or superior mesenteric artery may be technically more challenging than an antegrade bypass from the supraceliac aorta. A second problem with a bypass that originates from the infrarenal aorta is that although the aorta and the superior mesenteric artery are in close proximity anatomically, their exposure requires that they be distracted from each other, and this requirement creates a problem in determining the correct graft length to prevent graft kinking.

Creation of an antegrade aortomesenteric bypass may be preferable when the preceding situations arise. The gastrohepatic ligament is divided to gain access to the aorta as it passes through the diaphragmatic hiatus. The graft is anastomosed to the aorta in an end-to-side fashion and is then tunneled behind the pancreas. The distal anastomosis is created in an end-to-side fashion to the superior mesenteric artery in an area that is free of disease. Potential pitfalls may be encountered with this technique. First, the acuity of the operative situation and the presence of nonviable bowel typically obligate the use of autogenous conduit rather than prosthetic material. The area through which the vein is tunneled can be snug, increasing the risk of compression of a thin-walled vein graft. Second, unlike the exposure of the infrarenal aorta, exposure of the supraceliac aorta and the retropancreatic tunnel is less often performed, resulting in less familiarity with the anatomy. This problem leads to longer operative time, which is not well tolerated by the patient. Finally, supraceliac cross-clamping may cause further hypoperfusion to bowel and kidneys, causing additional ischemic injury. Nonetheless, when the patient has a heavily diseased infrarenal aortoiliac anatomy, antegrade bypass may be the preferred option.

The exposure of the superior mesenteric artery for a retrograde mesenteric arterial bypass from the infrarenal aorta is similar to that previously described for performing a superior mesenteric artery embolectomy. The infrarenal aorta is exposed in the standard fashion by retraction of the omentum and transverse colon cephalad and the small bowel caudad and to the patient's right. The ligament of Treitz is divided, and the retroperitoneum is opened between the duodenum and the inferior mesenteric vein. If the aorta is soft enough, a side-biting clamp can be used to partially occlude the aorta; however, proximal and distal occluding clamps are often required. The proximal anastomosis is created so that the graft is directed cephalad and the duodenum is allowed to fall back to its normal position with the graft looped over the duodenum. This technique attempts to create a graft that is longer than needed and to position the graft so that it follows the course of a lazy C to prevent the graft from kinking (Fig. 122-8A). As the small bowel is retracted caudally, the graft is positioned over the exposed superior mesenteric artery. The distal anastomosis is then created in an end-to-side fashion, and flow is reestablished to the intestine. An alternative graft configuration involves the use of a short conduit that courses from the lateral infrarenal aorta directly to the superior mesenteric artery (see Fig. 122-8B). The aorta is controlled with a side-biting clamp or with proximal and distal aortic clamps, and a diagonal incision is made in the left anterolateral aorta as the site of the proximal anastomosis. The graft is then directed across the anterior surface of the aorta to the proximal superior mesenteric artery. Care must be taken to avoid any redundancy within the graft that would predispose it to kinking and occlusion (see Fig. 122-8B).

Determination of Intestinal Viability

After revascularization has been accomplished, the viability of the bowel must be reassessed. The bowel should be covered with laparotomy pads moistened in warm saline and should be left covered for 15 to 20 minutes prior to this final assessment of viability. Initial clinical evaluation of the bowel then consists of assessment for visible and palpable pulsations in the mesenteric arcade, normal color and appearance of the bowel wall, peristalsis, and bleeding from cut surfaces. Each of these is subjective in nature and prone to inaccuracy; with the use of clinical criteria alone, bowel viability has been reported to be successfully determined with a sensitivity of only 82% and a specificity of 91%.[28] More objective and potentially more accurate methods for determination of intestinal viability include detection of Doppler signals on the antimesenteric border of the bowel wall, inspection of the bowel under a Wood's lamp after injection of fluorescein, infrared photoplethysmography, surface oximetry, and laser tissue flowmetry.

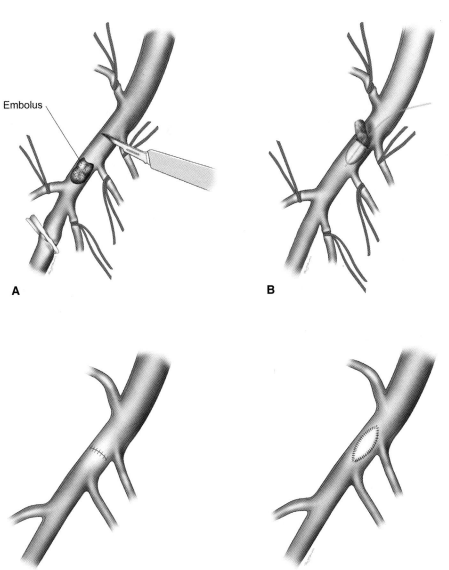

Embolus

A

B

C

D

FIGURE 122-7 A, Transverse arteriotomy is performed here proximal to the suspected embolus. **B,** Balloon extraction of the embolic material is then performed. **C,** Transverse arteriotomy is closed primarily. **D,** Alternative longitudinal incision may require vein patch angioplasty.

Wright and Hobson[29] reported that absence of pulsatile signals on the antimesenteric border of the intestine with a continuous-wave 9 to 10 MHz Doppler ultrasound probe implies a nonviable segment, and the clinical usefulness of this technique in determining bowel viability has been demonstrated in multiple studies.[28,30,31] However, discrimination between viable and nonviable bowel with this means is not always precise, because pulsatile Doppler signals may be present in perfused but nonviable bowel and mesenteric vasoconstriction after reperfusion may limit the detection of Doppler signals in ischemic but viable bowel.

Bowel that is perfused fluoresces when exposed to a Wood's lamp after intravenous fluorescein injection, and complete lack of fluorescence is diagnostic of nonviable bowel. The variation between these extremes, however, is broad and imperfect, and once the fluorescein has been administered, a second administration to reassess bowel perfusion is not possible. Quantification of the level of fluorescence with a high degree of accuracy with the use of a perfusion fluorometer has been demonstrated,[32] but special equipment requirements and technical considerations have made this less attractive for clinical use.

Surface oximetry has been evaluated in a canine model to predict anastomotic healing in segments of intestine with varying degrees of ischemia.[33] Pulse oximetry has similarly been tested in canine models and found to be equivalent to surface oximetry in assessing the degree of bowel ischemia.[34] Limited clinical experience with use of pulse oximetry using a special probe adapted to the bowel to assess intraoperative bowel viability has also been reported from eastern Europe.[35] Finally, infrared photoplethysmography, which detects changes in tissue blood volume by measurement of the scatter of light from erythrocyte-containing tissues, has been suggested by some to be on a parity with Doppler and fluorescein methods for determination of bowel viability.[36]

Only one study, performed more than 20 years ago, has compared the use of clinical judgment, fluorescein injection, and Doppler signals to determine intestinal viability in a prospective, controlled fashion. Bulkley and coworkers,[28] in

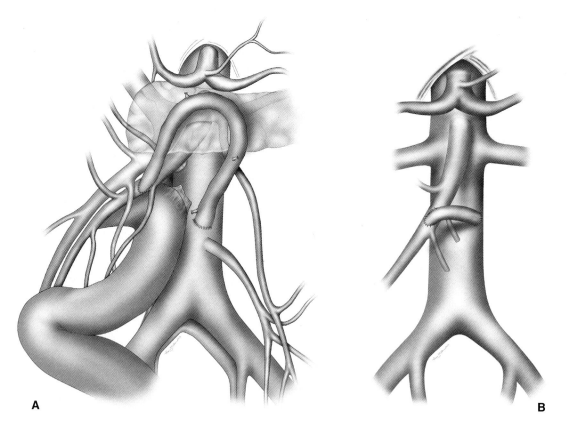

A

B

FIGURE 122-8 A, Superior mesenteric artery bypass is performed via a lazy C-loop graft over the course of the duodenum to avoid kinking. **B,** Short-segment bypass from the left anterolateral aorta to the superior mesenteric artery in an end-to-side manner. The graft is short and without redundancy. It should be noted that supraceliac aortomesenteric bypass can also be performed in cases of difficult infrarenal aortic disease.

a study of 78 intestinal segments in 28 consecutive patients, demonstrated clinical judgment to be as reliable as the other methods examined. Furthermore, Whitehill and associates[37] found that Doppler ultrasound evaluation, photoplethys-mography, and fluorescein injection may be too sensitive in some cases for accurate determination of bowel viability, yielding false-positive results by detecting levels of flow below what was needed to sustain tissue viability. Thus, ultimately, accurate determination of intestinal viability remains a product of clinical judgment aided by a com-bination of objective tests. Decision-making about which bowel to resect is also affected by the length of the segment involved as well as the need to preserve as much bowel length as possible. If the remaining segment would be short (i.e., less than 150 cm) or ischemic areas span multiple close intervals, creating the possible need for multiple areas of resection and significant intestinal loss, resection should be preferentially deferred to a second-look procedure.

Second-Look Surgery

There often are areas in which intestinal viability is questionable even after reperfusion and careful assessment of bowel viability. For preservation of as much bowel as possible, any areas of bowel that are clearly not infarcted are left and are reexamined during a second-look laparotomy. The decision for this second laparotomy is made at the time of initial operation, and this plan is essentially inviolate

regardless of the clinical status of the patient. The ends of the bowel where resection has taken place are stapled closed and dropped into the abdomen without performance of an anastomosis. The abdomen is closed, and the patient is taken to the intensive care unit, where fluid resuscitation and correction of acidosis and coagulopathy are continued.

The patient is returned to the operating room 12 to 36 hours later, and the abdomen is reexplored. By this time, the viability of the bowel will have declared itself, and additional bowel that is not viable is resected. Mesenteric blood flow is reassessed, and the bowel anastomoses are performed. Further return trips to the operating room for reevaluation may be needed, depending on the surgeon's confidence in viability of the bowel. Alternatively, if a patient has been doing well but demonstrates unexplained complications such as acidosis, hemodynamic instability, and abdominal pain, a second-look laparotomy should be seriously considered. This is often a difficult decision but may be lifesaving, allowing the surgeon to address an intra-abdominal catastrophe before irreversible physiologic changes develop.

Management of Extensive Bowel Infarction

Even with attempts to conserve as much bowel as possible, some patients have short-bowel syndrome. Typically, short-bowel syndrome develops when the patient retains less than 150 to 200 cm of small bowel. The presence or absence of functional colon and a competent ileocecal valve also are determinants of the severity of symptoms. Rapid transit time through the intestinal tract leads to dehydration, electrolyte disorders, malabsorption, and inadequate nutritional uptake. Over time, the small bowel, especially the ileum, adapts by developing taller villi and increasing in diameter to provide for a larger absorptive area. Many patients need parenteral nutrition for some time as the bowel adapts. Specific vitamin, mineral, and nutrient requirements are encountered, depending on the segments of bowel that have been resected. Other physiologic consequences, such as increased oxalate absorption leading to nephrolithiasis, must be accounted for in dietary management. Coherent postoperative management frequently must be performed in concert with a gastroenterologist who is well versed in the long-term treatment of such patients.

■ SUMMARY

Acute mesenteric ischemia remains a disease associated with a high mortality. Early diagnosis followed by prompt definitive treatment is needed if there is to be any chance for patient survival. Unfortunately, no noninvasive diagnostic tests or studies reliably confirm or exclude the diagnosis of acute mesenteric ischemia. Rather, the clinician must have a high index of suspicion when faced with a patient who has acute onset of abdominal pain and the pain is out of proportion to the physical findings on abdominal examination. Preoperative angiography, although not always necessary, is helpful to making a definitive diagnosis and planning the operation. Ischemia caused by embolus is treated with embolectomy, and that caused by thrombosis most often requires bypass but can also be treated with endarterectomy. Bowel viability is assessed after restoration of blood flow. Obviously infarcted bowel is resected, and bowel segments that are of uncertain viability are left in the abdomen and subsequently assessed at a second-look laparotomy in an attempt to limit the amount of bowel resection required. Patients with this disorder are critically ill, and careful attention to all facets of their care, including diagnosis, operative care and postoperative critical care, is required for best outcomes.

■ REFERENCES

1. Hibbard JS, Swenson PC, Levin AG: Roentgenology of experimental mesenteric vascular occlusion. Arch Surg 26:20, 1933.
2. Bergan J, Flinn WR, McCarthy WJ III, et al: Acute mesenteric ischemia. In Bergan JJ, Yao JST (eds): Vascular Surgical Emergencies. Philadelphia, Grune & Stratton, 1987.
3. Parks DA, Jacobson ED: Physiology of the splanchnic circulation. Arch Intern Med 145:1278-1281, 1985.
4. Schoenberg MH, Younes M, Haglund U, et al: Participation of oxygen radicals in pathogenesis of postischemic tissue damage. Langenbecks Arch 93(Suppl):59-62, 1985.
5. Konturek A, Cichon S, Gucwa J, et al: Acute intestinal ischemia. In material of the III Clinic of General Surgery, Collegium Medicum at the Jagellonian University [Polish]. Przegl Lek 53:719-721, 1996.
6. Mamode N, Pickford I, Leiberman P: Failure to improve outcome in acute mesenteric ischaemia: Seven year review. Eur J Surg 64:611-616, 1998.
7. Foley MI, Moneta GL, Abou-Zamzam AM, et al: Revascularization of the superior mesenteric artery alone for treatment of intestinal ischemia. J Vasc Surg 32:37-47, 2000.
8. Park WM, Gloviczki P, Cherry KJ, et al: Contemporary management of acute mesenteric ischemia: Factors associated with survival. J Vasc Surg 35:445-452, 2002.
9. Ottinger L, Austen WB: A study of 136 patients with mesenteric infarction. Surg Gynecol Obstet 124:251-261, 1967.
10. Sachs SM, Morton JH, Schwartz SI: Acute mesenteric ischemia. Surgery 92:646-653, 1982.
11. Wilson C, Gupta R, Gilmour DG, et al: Acute superior mesenteric ischaemia. Br J Surg 74:279-281, 1987.
12. Batellier J, Kieny R: Superior mesenteric artery embolism: Eighty-two cases. Ann Vasc Surg 4:112-116, 1990.
13. Bergan JJ: Diagnosis of acute intestinal ischemia. Semin Vasc Surg 3:143-148, 1990.
14. Croft RJ, Menon GP, Marston A: Does intestinal angina exist? A critical study of obstructed visceral arteries. Br J Surg 68:316-318, 1981.
15. Endean ED, Barnes S, Kwolek CJ, et al: Surgical management of thrombotic acute intestinal ischemia. Ann Surg 6:801-808, 2001.
16. Fleischmann D: Multiple detector-row CT angiography of the renal and mesenteric vessels. Eur J Radiol 45(Suppl):79-87, 2003.
17. Horton KM, Fishman EK: Multi-detector row CT of mesenteric ischemia: Can it be done? Radiographics 21:1463-1473, 2001.
18. Laghi A, Iannaccone R, Catalano C, et al: Multislice spiral computed tomography angiography of mesenteric arteries. Lancet 358:638-639, 2001.
19. Siegelman SS, Sprayregan S, Boley SJ: Angiographic diagnosis of mesenteric arterial vasoconstriction. Radiology 112:533-542, 1974.
20. Gray BH, Sullivan TM: Mesenteric vascular disease. Curr Treat Options Cardiovasc Med 3:195-206, 2001.
21. VanDeinse WH, Zawacki JK, Phillips D: Treatment of acute mesenteric ischemia by percutaneous transluminal angioplasty. Gastroenterology 91:475-478, 1986.
22. Steinmetz E, Tatou E, Favier-Biavoux C, et al: Endovascular treatment as first choice in chronic intestinal ischemia. Ann Vasc Surg 16:693-699, 2002.
23. Simonetti G, Lupattelli L, Urigo F, et al: Interventional radiology in the treatment of acute and chronic mesenteric ischemia. Radiol Med (Torino) 84:98-105, 1992.
24. Calin GA, Calin S, Ionescu R, et al: Successful local fibrinolytic treatment and balloon angioplasty in superior mesenteric arterial embolism: A case report and literature review. Hepatogastroenterology 50:732-734, 2003.
25. Yamaguchi T, Saeki M, Iwasaki Y, et al: Local thrombolytics therapy for superior mesenteric artery embolism: Complications and long-term clinical follow-up. Radiat Med 17:27-33, 1999.
26. Leduc FJ, Pestieau SR, Detry O, et al: Acute mesenteric ischaemia: Minimal invasive management by combined laparoscopy and percutaneous transluminal angioplasty. Eur J Surg 166:345-347, 2000.
27. Rapp JH, Reilly LM, Qvarfordt PG, et al: Durability of endarterectomy and antegrade grafts in the treatment of chronic visceral ischemia. J Vasc Surg 3:799-806, 1986.
28. Bulkley GB, Zuidema GD, Hamilton SR, et al: Intraoperative determination of small intestinal viability following ischemic injury. Ann Surg 193:628-637, 1981.
29. Wright CB, Hobson RW: Prediction of intestinal viability using Doppler ultrasound technique. Am J Surg 129:642-645, 1975.
30. O'Donnell JA, Hobson RW: Operative confirmation of Doppler ultrasound evaluation of intestinal ischemia. Surgery 87:109-112, 1980.
31. Cooperman M, Pace WG, Martin EW, et al: Determination of viability of ischemic intestine by Doppler ultrasound. Surgery 83:705-710, 1978.
32. Carter MS, Fantini GA, Sammartano RJ, et al: Qualitative and quantitative fluorescein fluorescence in determining intestinal viability. Am J Surg 147:117-121, 1984.
33. Locke R, Hauser CJ, Shoemaker WC: The use of surface oximetry to assess bowel viability. Arch Surg 119:1252-1256, 1984.
34. MacDonald PH, Dinda PK, Beck IT, et al: The use of oximetry in determining intestinal blood flow. Surg Gynecol Obstet 176:451-458, 1993.

35. Szilagyi S: Pulse oximetry in the study of the viability of the intestines and the microcirculation in intestinal anastomosis (preliminary report) [Hungarian]. Orv Hetil 135:1531-1534, 1994.

36. Pearce WH, Jones DN, Warren GH, et al: The use of infrared photoplethysmography in identifying early intestinal ischemia. Arch Surg 122:308-310, 1987.

37. Whitehill TA, Pearce WH, Rosales C, et al: Detection thresholds of nonocclusive intestinal hypoperfusion by Doppler ultrasound, photoplethysmography, and fluorescein. J Vasc Surg 8:28-32, 1988.

38. Newman TS, Maguson TH, Ahrendt SA, et al: The changing face of mesenteric infarction. Am Surg 64:611-616, 1998.

39. Urayama H, Ojtake H, Kawakama T, et al: Acute mesenteric vascular occlusion: Analysis of 39 patients. Eur J Surg 164:195-200, 1998.

40. Klempnauer J, Grotheus F, Bektas H, et al: Long-term results after surgery for acute mesenteric ischemia. Surgery 121:239-243, 1997.

41. Voltolini F, Pricolo R, Naldini G, et al: Acute mesenteric ischemia: Analysis of 47 cases. Minerva Chir 51:285-292, 1996.

42. Deehan DJ, Heys SD, Brittenden J, et al: Mesenteric ischaemia: Prognostic factors and influence of delay upon outcome. J R Coll Surg Edinb 40:112-115, 1995.

43. Levy PJ, Krausz MM, Manny J: Acute mesenteric ischemia: Improved results—a retrospective analysis of ninety-two patients. Surgery 107:372-380, 1990.

44. Bapat RD, Aiyer PM, Relekar RG, et al: Ischemic bowel disease. Indian J Gastroenterol 9:19-22, 1990.

45. Finucane PM, Arunachalam T, O'Dowd J, et al: Acute mesenteric infarction in elderly patients. J Am Geriatr Soc 37:355-358, 1989.

46. Sitges-Serra A, Mas X, Roqueta F, et al: Mesenteric infarction: An analysis of 83 patients with prognostic studies in 44 cases undergoing massive small-bowel resection. Br J Surg 75:544-548, 1988.

47. Bergan JJ, McCarthy WJ, Flinn WR, et al: Nontraumatic mesenteric vascular emergencies. J Vasc Surg 5:903-909, 1987.

48. Lazaro T, Sierra L, Gesto R, et al: Embolization of the mesenteric arteries: Surgical treatment in twenty-three consecutive cases. Ann Vasc Surg 4:112-116, 1990.

49. Andersson R, Parsson H, Isaksson B, et al: Acute intestinal ischemia: A 14 year retrospective investigation. Acta Chir Scand 150:217-221, 1984.

50. Hertzer NR, Beven EG, Humphries AW: Acute intestinal ischemia. Am Surg 44:744-749, 1978.

51. Krausz MM, Manny J: Acute superior mesenteric arterial occlusion: A plea for early diagnosis. Surgery 82:856-866, 1977.

52. Kairaluoma MI, Karkola P, Heikkinen D, et al: Mesenteric infarction. Am J Surg 133:188-193, 1977.

53. Boley SJ, Sprayregan S, Siegelman SS, et al: Initial results from an aggressive roentgenological and surgical approach to acute mesenteric ischemia. Surgery 82:848-855, 1977.

54. Smith S, Patterson LT: Acute mesenteric infarction. Am J Surg 42:562-567, 1976.

55. Singh RP, Shah RC, Lee ST: Acute mesenteric vascular occlusion: A review of thirty-two patients. Surgery 78:613-617, 1975.

56. Slater H, Elliott PW: Primary mesenteric infarction. Am J Surg 123:309-311, 1972.

Chapter

Diagnosis and Treatment of Nonocclusive Mesenteric Ischemia

123

TINA R. DESAI, MD

HISHAM S. BASSIOUNY, MD

Acute mesenteric ischemia may result from arterial embolization, arterial or venous thrombosis, or nonocclusive mesenteric ischemia (NOMI). Nonocclusive mesenteric ischemia, caused by primary splanchnic vasoconstriction, accounts for 20% to 30% of cases of acute mesenteric ischemia and is associated with mortality rates of up to 70% of cases.[1-3] NOMI is associated with cardiopulmonary bypass, shock states, and the use of vasoactive medications (digoxin, α-adrenergic agents, vasopressin). Poor prognosis from NOMI is related to a number of factors, including delay in diagnosis, significant associated co-morbidities, and an incomplete understanding of the pathophysiology of this process. The recent improvement in survival may be attributed to advances in critical care and a higher index of suspicion for NOMI. Early arteriographic diagnosis and subsequent therapy offer the best chance for better outcomes and survival.

■ PATHOPHYSIOLOGY

NOMI was initially described as a postmortem observation of small intestinal gangrene in patients who had shown no evidence of arterial or venous occlusive disease.[4,5] Early reports by Cohen,[6] Wilson and Qualheim,[7] and Ende[8] as well as subsequent characterization by Boley and colleagues[9,10] described this diagnosis in patients with severe cardiac failure. These observations formed the basis for the hypothesis that cardiac failure, peripheral hypoxemia, paradoxical splanchnic vasospasm, and reperfusion injury may all contribute to the development of NOMI.

Mesenteric vasospasm, usually in the distribution of the superior mesenteric artery (SMA), is a sine qua non of NOMI. Perhaps resulting from excessive sympathetic activity during cardiogenic shock or hypovolemia, the vasospasm represents a homeostatic mechanism that attempts to maintain cardiac and cerebral perfusion at the expense of visceral and peripheral organs. Vasopressin and angiotensin are the likely neurohormonal mediators of this process.[11,12]

The intestinal circulation possesses extensive protective mechanisms to preserve oxygen delivery to tissues. Over a wide range of blood pressure, intestinal blood flow can be maintained as a result of an autoregulatory response mediated by local and systemic factors leading to arteriolar smooth muscle relaxation and vasodilatation.[13] Even after this pressure-flow autoregulatory limit has been reached, further maximization of oxygen extraction can preserve oxygen consumption until a critical pressure of 40 mm Hg is reached.[14] Below this critical pressure, oxygen consumption declines and ischemia ensues. Pathologic findings characteristic of intestinal ischemia begin at the mucosal villus tip and progress over hours to affect the remainder of the mucosa, submucosa, and muscularis.

Once mesenteric vasospasm is initiated, it may persist even after correction of the initiating event. Although intestinal autoregulation may initially offset reductions in blood flow, the autoregulatory capacity is exceeded after several hours.[15] The exact mechanism of persistence of vasospasm is unknown, but it plays an important role in the development and maintenance of occlusive and nonocclusive mesenteric ischemia as well as reperfusion phenomena complicating mesenteric revascularization.[16]

The use of digitalis has historically been associated with the development of NOMI. In early reports, digitalis use was noted in a majority of patients with this diagnosis. Experimental models have demonstrated that digoxin preparations alter mesenteric vasoreactivity by stimulating arterial and venous smooth muscle cell contraction in vitro and in vivo[17] and may enhance mesenteric arteriolar vasoconstriction in the setting of acute venous hypertension.[18] In the current era, use of vasoactive medications such as epinephrine, norepinephrine, and vasopressin have also been associated with the development of NOMI.[11,12,19]

Studies of reperfusion injury after mesenteric ischemia may further delineate mechanisms relevant to NOMI. As a consequence of restoration of oxygenated blood flow to hypoxic tissues, release of reactive oxygen species can result in significant cellular membrane injury, increased capillary permeability, and connective tissue degradation. Subsequent failure of intestinal autoregulation and paradoxic vasoconstriction may ensue, resulting in tissue injury. The degree of ischemia-reperfusion injury appears to be related to the frequency as well as duration of ischemic episodes. Clark and Gewertz demonstrated that two 15-minute periods of low flow followed by reperfusion resulted in more severe histologic injury than a single 30-minute period of ischemia. NOMI results in an analogous scenario, whereby hypoperfusion may be partial and occasionally repetitive. Episodic reperfusion is thought to prime the ischemic tissue with leukocytes that are attracted to and produce reactive oxygen species.[20] This concept is further supported by studies demonstrating attenuation of ischemia-reperfusion injury by reperfusion with leukopenic blood or blockade of endothelial cell surface receptors for leukocyte adherence.[21,22] Reports of NOMI after elective mesenteric revascularization have associated this syndrome with reperfusion phenomena, further supporting reperfusion injury in the pathogenesis of NOMI.[16]

CLINICAL PRESENTATION

It is estimated that acute mesenteric ischemia is responsible for 1:1000 of all hospital admissions, with NOMI constituting 20% of these cases. The incidence of NOMI may be declining with improvements in the care of critically ill patients and the widespread use of systemic vasodilators in cardiac intensive care. Agents such as calcium channel blockers and nitroglycerin compounds may serve to improve cardiac hemodynamics and help prevent mesenteric vasospasm. The clinical diagnosis of NOMI requires a high index of suspicion in elderly patients with any of the following risk factors: acute myocardial infarction with shock; congestive heart failure; arrhythmia; hypovolemia related to burns, sepsis, trauma, pancreatitis, or hemorrhage; and the administration of a splanchnic vasoconstrictor such as α-adrenergic agents, vasopressin, or digitalis. Later studies have indicated that NOMI also occurs at a higher rate in patients undergoing hemodialysis and may be associated with hypoperfusion occurring during dialysis.[23] Early diagnosis of NOMI and treatment prior to the development of intestinal infarction are the most important variables determining survival.

Abdominal pain out of proportion to physical findings is characteristic of acute mesenteric ischemia, but this symptom may be absent in 20% to 25% of cases of NOMI.[24] When present, the pain is usually severe but may be variable in intensity, character, and location. In the absence of pain, symptoms of unexplained abdominal distention and gastrointestinal bleeding may be the earliest indicators of ischemia. Fever, diarrhea, nausea and vomiting, and diminished bowel sounds are other common but nonspecific manifestations. Diffuse or localized abdominal tenderness, rebound, and rigidity are ominous signs heralding transmural infarction and peritonitis. Occasional patients may present with shock or sepsis of unknown etiology.

DIAGNOSIS

A high index of suspicion in patients with appropriate risk factors and early angiography are crucial to the diagnosis and early treatment of NOMI. Hematologic and serologic abnormalities are frequently detected during the course of acute mesenteric insufficiency but are nonspecific. Leukocytosis ($\geq 15,000$ cells/mm^3) with a left shift and hemoconcentration due to extracellular fluid loss into the intestine and peritoneal cavity are common. Elevated amylase concentrations in the serum or peritoneal fluid, metabolic acidosis, and hyperphosphatemia may also be seen.[25] Late elevations of serum glutamic-oxaloacetic transaminase, lactate dehydrogenase, and creatine phosphokinase often indicate intestinal infarction.

Plain abdominal radiography is useful in excluding other causes of abdominal pain, such as a perforated viscus and bowel obstruction. Normal abdominal radiographic findings in a patient with pain out of proportion to physical findings are suggestive of early ischemia and should prompt consideration of diagnostic arteriography. Findings of ileus, bowel wall edema ("thumbprinting," a gasless abdomen), and intramural or portal air appear late in the course of NOMI and suggest intestinal infarction. Positive abdominal radiographic findings are noted in only 20% to 60% of cases.[26]

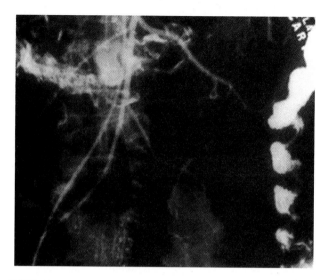

FIGURE 123-1 Angiographic appearance of mesenteric vasospasm in nonocclusive mesenteric ischemia. Note the pruning of distal branches of the superior mesenteric artery.

Similarly, computed tomography (CT) may also be utilized expediently to rule out other abnormalities in the setting of nonspecific abdominal pain or distention. CT findings in the setting of nonocclusive mesenteric ischemia are, again, nonspecific, until late manifestation of intestinal infarction. The CT scan may also be useful in delineating the origin of the mesenteric arteries to detect occlusive disease and in diagnosing mesenteric venous or portal venous thrombi. Duplex ultrasonography is of minimal use in the setting of acute mesenteric ischemia, because the examination is commonly difficult secondary to the presence of abdominal pain and significant bowel gas. If technically feasible, this study may provide information regarding the patency of the proximal SMA, but visualization of primary or secondary branches of the SMA is difficult, if not impossible.

Definitive diagnosis of NOMI requires expedient arteriography of the aorta and mesenteric vessels, including anteroposterior, lateral, and delayed venous phase views with selective celiac artery and SMA injections. This study can rule out other causes of mesenteric ischemia and establish the definitive diagnosis of NOMI. If time allows, arteriography should be considered even when a decision has been made to proceed with exploratory laparotomy in order to determine a cause for the acute mesenteric ischemia and to formulate an optimal operative strategy. Oral and rectal contrast studies should be avoided in the patient in whom NOMI is suspected because they interfere with arteriography. Siegelman and colleagues[2] have described the following four reliable arteriographic criteria for the diagnosis of mesenteric vasospasm: (1) narrowing of the origins of multiple branches of the SMA, (2) "string-of-sausages" sign: alternating dilation and narrowing of the intestinal branches (Fig. 123-1), (3) spasm of the mesenteric arcades, and (4) impaired filling of the intramural branches.

Exploratory laparoscopy may be useful in a minority of patients who present for abdominal exploration. Laparoscopic evaluation may be helpful in excluding other causes of peritonitis,[27] but the role of this procedure in the diagnosis of NOMI is limited to examination of the serosal surface of the intestine and is, thus, useful only in advanced cases in which transmural infarction has occurred.

■ MANAGEMENT

Successful treatment of NOMI depends on early diagnosis, established by liberal use of mesenteric arteriography in patients with appropriate risk factors, before the onset of mesenteric infarction. Expedient management of precipitating factors such as cardiac events and shock states is essential, as is rapid hemodynamic stabilization before diagnostic evaluation and definitive therapy. Systemic vasoconstrictors such as α-adrenergic agents and vasopressin should be avoided and are preferably replaced by vasodilators that diminish cardiac preload and afterload.

Pharmacologic management is central to treatment of NOMI and is achieved by selective intra-arterial infusion of papaverine into the SMA. Boley and colleagues[28,29] have described an effective treatment algorithm that starts with intra-arterial papaverine initiated at a dose of 30 to 60 mg/hr. Subsequent management depends on the patient's clinical response. If abdominal pain resolves, arteriography is repeated after 30 minutes to document resolution of vasospasm. Papaverine infusion is continued for 24 hours, as is close monitoring of the patient. Because papaverine is metabolized primarily in the liver, hypotension is uncommon, but careful monitoring of the blood pressure, heart rate, and rhythm is appropriate. If a sudden decrease in blood pressure is noted, papaverine infusion should be substituted with saline, and a plain abdominal radiograph obtained to confirm position of the catheter. Finally, heparin sodium is chemically incompatible with papaverine and should not be infused simultaneously through the same catheter. In the case of resolved abdominal symptoms, second arteriography is advisable prior to the cessation of papaverine unless the risk of contrast nephropathy precludes it (Fig. 123-2).

If peritoneal signs develop or abdominal pain fails to resolve despite papaverine infusion, emergent celiotomy is indicated. Additional signs of increasing leukocytosis, metabolic acidosis, gastrointestinal bleeding, or free intraperitoneal or intramural air also support urgent celiotomy. The goals of the operation are assessment of bowel viability, resection of obviously infarcted intestine, and determination of the need for a second-look procedure after 24 hours. Assessment of bowel viability may be made on the basis of gross appearance (dull gray or black), intraoperative Doppler evaluation, or fluorescein injection and inspection with a Wood lamp[30] (as described in detail in Chapter 122). The finding of bowel of questionable viability mandates a second-look laparotomy in 24 to 48 hours, irrespective of clinical improvement in the immediate postoperative period. Intestinal continuity is restored after bowel resection if the margins are viable; otherwise, exteriorization is advised.

Intraoperative hypothermia should be avoided to help alleviate vasospasm. This can be accomplished by peritoneal lavage with warm saline and maintenance of the ambient operating room temperature at or above 75° F. Papaverine infusion is continued both during and after surgery until either bowel viability is confirmed during the second-look procedure or second angiography demonstrates relief of vasospasm. Careful attention to fluid management in the

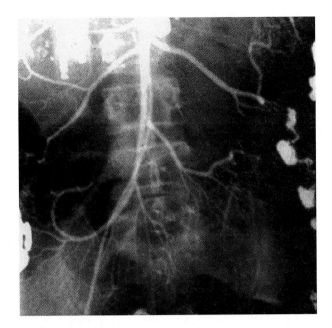

FIGURE 123-2 Selective arteriography of the superior mesenteric artery after 24 hours of treatment with intra-arterial papaverine demonstrates resolution of vasospasm.

perioperative period is essential. Systemic anticoagulation is unnecessary in patients with NOMI unless there is associated angiographic evidence of thromboembolism. Broad-spectrum antibiotics should be administered to minimize septic complications related to bacterial translocation and peritonitis.

■ SUMMARY

NOMI is an infrequently diagnosed condition that may develop in association with systemic low-flow states and vasoconstrictive pharmacologic intervention. If left untreated, prolonged mesenteric arterial hypoperfusion and ischemia may ultimately lead to intestinal infarction and patient demise. A high index of suspicion, early arteriographic diagnosis, correction of underlying hypovolemia, improving cardiac output, and selective mesenteric intra-arterial vasodilator therapy are often successful in reversing the underlying splanchnic vasoconstriction. Continued advances in the management of critically ill patients will likely decrease the prevalence of NOMI and its morbid consequences.

■ REFERENCES

1. Berger RW, Bulkley GB, Hamilton SR: Intestinal gangrene associated with heart disease. Surg Gynecol Obstet 113:522-529, 1961.
2. Siegelman SS, Sprayregen S, Boley SJ: Angiographic diagnosis of mesenteric arterial vasoconstriction. Radiology 112:533-542, 1974.
3. Wilson GSM, Block J: Mesenteric vascular occlusion. Arch Surg 73:330-345, 1956.
4. Case records of the Massachusetts General Hospital: Case 35082. N Engl J Med 240:308-310, 1949.
5. Haglund U, Lundgren O: Non-occlusive acute intestinal vascular failure. Br J Surg 66:155-158, 1979.
6. Cohen EB: Infarction of the stomach. Am J Med 11:645, 1951.
7. Wilson R, Qualheim RE: A form of acute hemorrhagic enterocolitis afflicting chronically ill individuals: A description of twenty cases. Gastroenterology 27:431-444, 1954.
8. Ende N: Infarction of the bowel in cardiac failure. N Engl J Med 258:879-881, 1958.
9. Boley SJ, Feinstein FR, Sammartano R, et al: New concepts in the management of emboli of the superior mesenteric artery. Surg Gynecol Obstet 153:561-569, 1981.
10. Boley SJ, Brandt LJ, Veith FJ: Ischemic disorders of the intestines. Curr Probl Surg 15:1-85, 1978.
11. Bailey RW, Bulkley GB, Hamilton SR, et al: Protection of the small intestine from nonocclusive mesenteric ischemic injury due to cardiogenic shock. Am J Surg 153:108-116, 1987.
12. McNeill JR, Stark RD, Greenway CV: Intestinal vasoconstriction after hemorrhage: Roles of vasopressin and angiotensin. Am J Physiol 219:1342-1347, 1970.
13. Mesh CL, Gewertz BL: The effect of hemodilution on blood flow regulation in normal and postischemic intestine. J Surg Res 48:183-189, 1990.
14. Desai TR, Sisley AC, Brown S, Gewertz BL: Defining the critical limit of oxygen extraction in the human small intestine. J Vasc Surg 23:832-838, 1996.
15. Boley SJ, Regan JA, Tunick, PA: Persistent vasoconstriction: A major factor in nonocclusive mesenteric ischemia. Current Topics in Surgical Research 3:425-430, 1971.
16. Gewertz BL, Zarins CK: Postoperative vasospasm after antegrade mesenteric revascularization: A report of three cases. J Vasc Surg 14:382-385, 1991.
17. Mikkelsen E, Andersson KE, Pedersen OL: Effects of digoxin on isolated human peripheral arteries and veins. Acta Pharmacol Toxicol (Copenh) 45:249-456, 1979.
18. Kim EH, Gewertz BL: Chronic digitalis administration alters mesenteric vascular reactivity. J Vasc Surg 5:382-389, 1987.
19. Studer W, Wu X, Siegemund M, Seeberger M: Resuscitation from cardiac arrest with adrenaline/epinephrine or vasopressin: Effects on intestinal mucosal tonometer pCO(2) during the postresuscitation period in rats. Resuscitation 53:201-207, 2002.
20. Harlan JM, Killen PD, Senecal FM, et al: The role of neutrophil membrane glycoprotein GP-150 in neutrophil adherence to endothelium in vitro. Blood 66:167-178, 1985.
21. Luscinskas FW, Brock AF, Arnaout MA, Gimbrone MA Jr: Endothelial-leukocyte adhesion molecule-1-dependent and leukocyte (CD11/CD18)-dependent mechanisms contribute to polymorpho-nuclear leukocyte adhesion to cytokine-activated human vascular endothelium. J Immunol 142:2257-2263, 1989.
22. Mileski WJ, Winn RK, Harlan JM, Rice CL: Transient inhibition of neutrophil adherence with the anti-CD18 monoclonal antibody 60.3 does not increase mortality rates in abdominal sepsis. Surgery 109:497-501, 1991.
23. John AS, Tuerff SD, Kerstein MD: Nonocclusive mesenteric infarction in hemodialysis patients. J Am Coll Surg 190:84-88, 2000.
24. Howard TJ, Plaskon LA, Wiebke EA, et al: Nonocclusive mesenteric ischemia remains a diagnostic dilemma. Am J Surg 171:405-408, 1996.
25. Jamieson WG, Lozon A, Durand D, Wall W: Changes in serum phosphate levels associated with intestinal infarction and necrosis. Surg Gynecol Obstet 140:19-21, 1975.
26. Tomchik FS, Wittenberg J, Ottinger LW: The roentgenographic spectrum of bowel infarction. Radiology 96:249-260, 1970.
27. Serreyn RF, Schoofs PR, Baetens PR, Vandekerckhove D: Laparoscopic diagnosis of mesenteric venous thrombosis. Endoscopy 18:249-250, 1986.
28. Boley SJ, Sprayregan S, Siegelman SS, Veith FJ: Initial results from an aggressive roentgenological and surgical approach to acute mesenteric ischemia. Surgery 82:848-855, 1977.
29. Boley SJ, Sprayregen SS, Veith FJ: An aggressive roentgenologic and surgical approach to acute mesenteric ischemia. In Nyhus LM (ed): Surgery Annual. New York, Appleton-Century-Crofts, 1973.
30. Gorey TF: Tests for intestinal viability. In Marston A (ed): Vascular Diseases of the Intestinal Tract. Baltimore, Williams & Wilkins, 1986.

Chronic Mesenteric Ischemia

124

THOMAS S. HUBER, MD, PhD

W. ANTHONY LEE, MD

JAMES M. SEEGER, MD

Chronic mesenteric ischemia (CMI) is a life-threatening problem that can result in death from inanition or bowel infarction. The incidence of CMI is quite low, and, accordingly, experiences of individual surgeons and institutions are usually limited. It has been estimated that only about 340 open revascularizations for CMI are performed annually in nonfederal hospitals throughout the United States.[1] Johnston and colleagues[2] reported that mesenteric bypasses accounted for less than 0.5% of all peripheral vascular procedures performed in their academic medical center. The optimal treatment remains poorly defined, and many of the issues regarding the means of revascularization (open versus endovascular), the type of open procedure (endarterectomy versus antegrade bypass versus retrograde bypass), the number of vessels to be revascularized (one versus two versus three), and the optimal bypass conduit (prosthetic versus saphenous vein versus superficial femoral vein) that were debated during the 1980s and 1990s remain unanswered. Despite these limitations, it is incumbent on vascular surgeons to expedite the diagnosis and treatment of patients with CMI because of the severity of the underlying problem and the frequent diagnostic delays before referral.

■ PATHOPHYSIOLOGY AND ETIOLOGY

The underlying pathophysiology of CMI is the failure to achieve postprandial hyperemic intestinal blood flow. In normal individuals, intestinal blood flow increases after eating, with the maximal increase occurring at 30 to 90 minutes.[3,4] This hyperemic response lasts 4 to 6 hours and varies with the size and composition of the meal.[4,5] Most of the hyperemic blood flow goes to the small bowel and pancreas with little increase detected in the stomach and colon.[6] There is a corresponding marked postprandial increase in the end-diastolic flow velocities of the superior mesenteric artery (SMA) by duplex ultrasound, whereas there is little change in the end-diastolic velocities of the celiac axis, presumably because of the relative low resistance in the splenic and hepatic circulation at baseline. In the presence of hemodynamically significant arterial stenoses, the postprandial hyperemic response is attenuated. This attenuated response results in a relative imbalance between the tissue supply and demand for oxygen and other metabolites, leading to the onset of postprandial pain or "mesenteric angina." The postprandial hyperemic flow changes return to normal after mesenteric revascularization.[7]

There is an extensive collateral network between the three visceral vessels and the internal iliac arteries (Fig. 124-1). The celiac axis and SMA collateralize through the superior (celiac axis) and inferior (SMA) pancreatico-duodenal arteries with the direction of flow contingent on the location of the significant stenosis. The SMA and inferior mesenteric artery (IMA) collateralize through the meandering artery and the marginal artery of Drummond. The meandering artery is the most significant collateral vessel and connects the ascending branch of the left colic with the middle branch of the middle colic. It lies at the base of the mesentery and is at risk of being ligated along with the inferior mesenteric vein during exposure of the infrarenal aorta. The IMA communicates with the internal iliac artery via the hemorrhoidal branches and may represent a more important collateral than originally appreciated.[2] This collateral pathway may be disrupted during sigmoid colectomy or infrarenal aortic aneurysm repair.

The presence of significant arterial occlusive disease in two of the three visceral vessels usually is required before patients become symptomatic given the extensive collateral network. It has been contended that this is an absolute requirement,[8] and this myth has been propagated throughout many surgical textbooks. It is possible, however, to have symptomatic mesenteric arterial occlusive disease in the presence of isolated celiac axis or SMA disease if the collateral pathways are insufficient.[9] This situation is usually due to the presence of hemodynamically significant disease in the SMA as might be predicted from the postprandial hyperemic response. Greater than 90% of patients undergoing open surgical revascularization for mesenteric ischemia in several large clinical series had significant stenosis or occlusions of the SMA, and greater than 80% had significant disease in the celiac axis and the SMA.[10]

Atherosclerosis is the leading cause of the visceral artery occlusive disease that leads to CMI. A variety of other causes, including fibromuscular disease, aortic dissections, neurofibromatosis, rheumatoid arthritis, Takayasu's arteritis, radiation injury, Buerger's disease, systemic lupus, and drugs (e.g., cocaine, ergots), have been incriminated and merit investigation in the appropriate clinical setting, although they are significantly less common. Patients with visceral artery occlusive disease often have concomitant renal artery occlusive disease or a pattern consistent with "central aortic" disease. Visceral artery occlusive disease is relatively common, however, in contradistinction to mesenteric ischemia. Wilson and associates[11] reported from

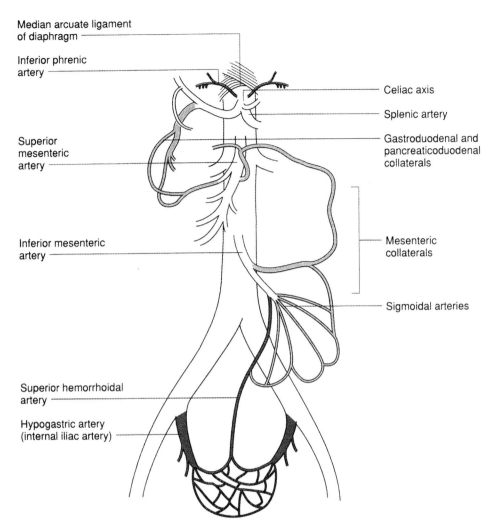

Median arcuate ligament
of diaphragm

Inferior phrenic
artery

Superior
mesenteric
artery

Inferior mesenteric
artery

Superior hemorrhoidal
artery

Hypogastric artery
(internal iliac artery)

Celiac axis

Splenic artery

Gastroduodenal and
pancreaticoduodenal
collaterals

Mesenteric
collaterals

Sigmoidal arteries

FIGURE 124-1 A diagram of the collateral pathways for the mesenteric vessels. The celiac axis and superior mesenteric arteries communicate through the superior and inferior pancreaticoduodenal arteries. The superior and inferior mesenteric arteries communicate through the meandering artery and the marginal artery of Drummond, with the meandering artery serving as the dominant collateral. The inferior mesenteric artery communicates with the internal iliac artery through the hemorrhoidal vessels. (From Zelenock GB: Visceral occlusive disease. In Greenfield LJ [ed]: Surgery: Scientific Principles and Practice. Philadelphia, Lippincott Williams & Wilkins, 2001, p 1691.)

a population study using duplex ultrasound that 17.5% of individuals older than 65 years of age had a critical stenosis of at least one of the visceral vessels (celiac, 15%; celiac/SMA, 1.3%; SMA, 0.9%). Additionally, unselected autopsy studies have reported that the incidence of a 50% or greater stenosis in one of the three visceral vessels is 6% to 10%,[12] whereas 27% of the patients undergoing arteriography before peripheral arterial reconstruction have a greater than 50% stenosis of the SMA or celiac axis.[13]

The natural history of CMI is presumably death from inanition or bowel infarction. This natural history has not been well characterized because patients usually undergo revascularization after diagnosis, and there is no untreated or "control" group. The natural history of asymptomatic, mesenteric artery occlusive disease is even less well characterized. Thomas and coworkers[14] attempted to define the natural history of asymptomatic stenoses among 980 patients undergoing mesenteric arteriography during a 7-year period. They reported that 4 of 15 patients with significant (≥50%) stenoses of all three visceral arteries developed mesenteric ischemia during a mean follow-up of 2.6 years. Notably, mesenteric ischemia did not occur in any of the patients with involvement of fewer than three vessels. They concluded

that prophylactic revascularization should be considered in this high-risk group with triple-vessel disease, and that it should be routine before aortic reconstruction. Additional justification for prophylactic revascularization in patients with mesenteric arterial occlusive disease is provided by the observation that 15% to 50% of patients with acute mesenteric ischemia (AMI) secondary to thrombosis of existing occlusive disease do not have any antecedent warning signs.[15,16] Infarction of the bowel after aortic surgery in patients with preexisting mesenteric arterial occlusive disease also has been reported[17] and used to justify staged or simultaneous repair and revascularization.

■ PRESENTATION AND DIAGNOSIS

Patients referred for evaluation of CMI are fairly characteristic, and the diagnosis usually is suggested by the initial visual inspection. The typical patient is a cachectic, middle-aged woman with a strong smoking history who presents with abdominal pain and weight loss. CMI is one of the few cardiovascular disorders more common in women. A study from the Nationwide Inpatient Sample examining outcome after revascularization for CMI reported that the mean patient age was 66 ± 11 years (SD), and that 76% were women—both within the range of the multiple institutional series.

Abdominal pain is usually the symptom that precipitates presentation to either a primary care physician or a gastroenterologist. There are no specific characteristics of the pain associated with CMI, however. The pain usually involves the mid-epigastric region with occasional radiations through to the back and often is described as either dull or colicky. The quality of the pain is distinctly different from that associated with peritonitis, which suggests bowel perforation. The onset of the pain usually occurs 15 to 30 minutes after eating and lasts 1 to 3 hours. This presentation is consistent with the underlying pathophysiology and the abnormal postprandial hyperemic blood flow response. The etiology of the pain itself is unclear and has been attributed to arterial "steal" from the gastric circulation and various ischemic mediators.[18] The pain may progress along the spectrum from intermittent pain associated with certain types and quantities of food to consistent, unremitting pain that likely forebodes bowel infarction. Pain may be absent at the time of presentation because patients develop adaptive strategies to relieve or reduce it.

The net effect of the abdominal pain is that patients avoid certain food types or eating altogether and ultimately lose weight. This specific behavioral response has been termed "food fear." The weight loss is due to inadequate nutritional intake rather than an absorption problem as might be hypothesized.[19] The mean weight loss in many large clinical series ranges from 20 to 30 lb.[2,20,21] Many affected individuals are thin at the time of onset of symptoms and cachectic at the time of diagnosis and treatment. There is no consistent bowel pattern associated with CMI. Some patients develop constipation as a result of food avoidance, whereas others develop intermittent diarrhea. AMI is a profound cathartic.

Physical examination is not enlightening for making the diagnosis of CMI except for the generalized appearance in the characteristic patient. Patients often have evidence of systemic vascular disease and abdominal bruits, although both are fairly nonspecific. The apparent absence of systemic vascular disease on physical examination does not preclude the diagnosis of CMI. The patient's vascular disease may be isolated to the central aortic region.

A patient with CMI usually undergoes an extensive medical workup before the ultimate, correct diagnosis is made. This extensive diagnostic workup usually includes an esophagogastroduodenoscopy, a colonoscopy, an ultrasound, and a computed tomography (CT) scan; frequently, patients also undergo cholecystectomy. This diagnostic evaluation usually exceeds a calendar year from the onset of symptoms to the correct diagnosis[22-25] and a mean of 2.8 diagnostic tests.[24] The diagnostic evaluation is confounded by the fact that CMI may lead to gastroparesis, gastric ulceration, gastroduodenitis, and gallbladder dysmotility. Commonly the patient's abdominal pain, weight loss, and generalized "failure to thrive" are attributed to any one of these pathologic processes during the course of the diagnostic evaluation. Gastric ulceration and gastroduodenitis, to a lesser extent, are so common that they are almost pathognomonic for CMI.[2,20,26] They are likely sequelae of gastric ischemia because they occur in areas of reduced

perfusion,[27,28] are refractory to medical management, and resolve after revascularization.

The diagnosis of CMI requires the proper clinical scenario, a confirmatory imaging study, and the exclusion of other potential causes of abdominal pain. Most patients referred for evaluation of CMI usually already have undergone an extensive, prolonged workup as outlined earlier, and the diagnosis is obvious if not already confirmed. The differential diagnosis of abdominal pain is extensive, however, and CMI is fairly low on this list. Foremost on the list of differential diagnoses of abdominal pain and weight loss should be an intra-abdominal malignancy until proved otherwise. Patients should likely undergo an esophagogastroduodenoscopy, colonoscopy, abdominal ultrasound, and abdominal CT scan early in their workup to exclude the more common potential causes of their complaints.

Mesenteric duplex ultrasound is an excellent screening tool for occlusive disease in the celiac axis and SMA with sensitivities and specificities relative to contrast arteriography of 80% or greater.[29] The IMA is difficult to visualize and not routinely included as part of the examination. Mesenteric duplex is technically challenging, operator dependent, and not universally available. The examination is complicated by the deep location of the vessels, respiratory variation, the strict need for a Doppler angle of 60%, and the presence of intra-abdominal gas. Moneta and colleagues[29] reported that a peak systolic flow velocity of greater than 275 cm/sec and greater than 200 cm/sec in the SMA and celiac axis correspond to greater than 70% stenoses. Similarly, Zwolak and colleagues[30] reported that end-diastolic velocities of greater than 45 cm/sec in the SMA and greater than 55 cm/sec in the celiac axis correspond to greater than 50% stenoses. It is incumbent on each institution, however, to develop and validate its own criteria for significant stenoses. Several groups have attempted to develop a duplex-based "stress test" for mesenteric artery occlusive disease by imaging the vessels after a mixed composition meal, although its clinical utility is unclear.[31,32] Mesenteric duplex examination has proved to be an excellent postoperative technique to image the mesenteric bypass grafts.[33]

Standard contrast arteriography is the definitive imaging test for mesenteric artery occlusive disease (Fig. 124-2). It serves to confirm the mesenteric duplex findings and plan the operative procedure and affords an opportunity for intervention. The mesenteric arterial occlusive disease from atherosclerosis is essentially "aortic spillover." Consequently the celiac axis and SMA lesions are usually orificial and the more distal extent of the vessels spared or uninvolved. This usually holds true in the presence of a complete orificial occlusion even when the distal vessels are not seen with contrast arteriography. Involvement of the distal vasculature suggests a nonatherosclerotic process, such as cocaine or ergot ingestion. The presence of well-developed collateral channels between the visceral vessels supports the diagnosis of mesenteric ischemia and attests to the hemodynamic significance of the ostial lesions. It is relatively common to see concomitant renal artery occlusive disease, and these findings support the concept of a "central aortic" atherosclerotic process. It is imperative that a lateral arteriogram be obtained at the time of the diagnostic study, and this

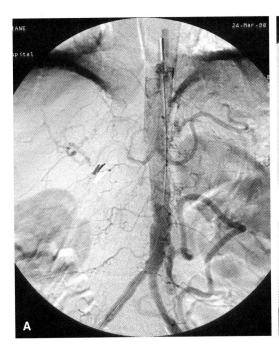
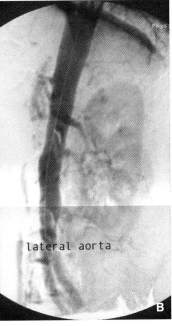

FIGURE 124-2 **A,** Anteroposterior contrast arteriogram of the aorta, visceral vessels, and proximal common iliac arteries. The branches of the celiac axis are visualized, although neither the superior mesenteric artery nor the inferior mesenteric artery is seen. Similarly, neither renal artery is seen, although there are bilateral nephrograms. Note the large meandering artery. **B,** Corresponding lateral arteriogram. There is a high-grade proximal celiac artery stenosis. The origin of the superior mesenteric artery is occluded, but it appears to reconstitute distally. Both renal arteries are patent.

requirement should be communicated to the physician performing the arteriogram if he or she is not the treating physician. Small visceral artery aneurysms are seen occasionally on arteriogram in the collateral branches, specifically the pancreaticoduodenal artery. These are presumably flow-related aneurysms similar to aneurysms seen in the splenic artery in patients with portal hypertension.[34] It is usually not necessary to catheterize the visceral vessels selectively given the orificial distribution of the occlusive disease. Rarely, mesenteric angioplasty or stenting or both may serve as a diagnostic study for patients with mesenteric arterial occlusive disease and atypical symptoms.

The role of magnetic resonance arteriography [7,35] and CT arteriography in the diagnosis of mesenteric arterial occlusive disease is undefined. Both imaging modalities offer great promise and the potential to replace standard contrast arteriography. It has been our anecdotal impression, however, that many of the claims espoused by the proponents of these modalities have not been realized for either the mesenteric circulation or the other vascular beds. Both modalities likely require an institutional champion committed to providing the best quality images. Magnetic resonance arteriography has been used as an adjunct to mesenteric duplex in our own practice. We have felt compelled to obtain standard contrast arteriograms, however, when the clinical history is suspicious and the magnetic resonance arteriogram is normal or equivocal.

■ INDICATIONS AND TREATMENT STRATEGIES

All patients with CMI should undergo revascularization. The goals of treatment are to reduce pain, prevent bowel infarction, and allow patients to regain weight and restore

nutritional reserves. Despite the theoretical appeal, there is likely no role for long-term parenteral alimentation and noninterventional therapies even in patients who are relatively high risk because of other comorbidities. The postprandial pain can be relieved by not eating, and total parenteral nutrition (TPN) may allow patients to regain weight and restore nutritional status. The potential for bowel infarction is not alleviated, however, and lifetime dependence on TPN is not practical in terms of convenience, expense, and the risk of catheter-related complications. Rheudasil and associates[36] reported that a significant percentage of the patients in their series who were hospitalized with CMI on TPN and awaiting bypass developed AMI.

The optimal means of revascularization for patients with CMI has been actively debated for the past few decades, and this debate has become more intense with the emergence of the endovascular approach. The pivotal questions are the type of revascularization (endovascular versus open) and the type and configuration of open revascularization. There is no consensus regarding these issues, and resolution does not seem imminent given the relative infrequency of the problem and the limited surgeon and institutional experience. There are no randomized, controlled trials comparing the various treatment strategies. Most of the relevant reports are retrospective studies of patients undergoing revascularization for AMI and CMI using a variety of techniques, bypass configurations, and conduits. Long-term patency of the reconstructions has not been documented objectively in most reports. Relief of symptoms is one of the treatment goals. It is impossible to compare the various reconstructions without objective data because symptom-free survival is not the same as graft patency. McMillan and associates[37] reported that the sensitivity for symptomatic follow-up as a surrogate for graft patency was only 33%.

The indication for revascularization in asymptomatic patients with known mesenteric arterial occlusive disease is unresolved as noted earlier. Thomas and colleagues[14] have reported that patients with involvement of all three visceral vessels represent a group at high risk for bowel infarction, and anecdotal reports have documented poor outcomes in patients with untreated visceral artery occlusive disease after aortic reconstructions.[17] Revascularization should be considered in these settings, although the justification in the literature is weak, and any prophylactic intervention has to be balanced against the treatment-associated mortality and morbidity rates, which are significant. Patients with untreated visceral artery occlusive disease should be followed closely and counseled regarding the symptoms that merit presentation. All episodes of significant abdominal pain require investigation and should be associated with a low threshold for intervention.

Endovascular treatment has a tremendous amount of appeal for patients with CMI because it is less invasive and has the potential to reduce morbidity, mortality, length of hospital stay, and cost. The long-term outcome after endovascular treatment is unclear, however, and is a major concern given the patient's life expectancy and the potential catastrophic complications associated with vessel thrombosis. The visceral atherosclerotic lesions are likely "aortic spillover" that may not be amenable to angioplasty, although this concept of aortic spillover has been challenged by several more recent reports.[21,38] Similar renal artery orificial lesions have been treated effectively with the addition of an endoluminal stent. In contrast to the renal arteries, the stenotic or occlusive lesions in the SMA may extend several centimeters beyond the orifice and may be less ideal candidates for endovascular therapy. The meta-analysis by Kasirajan and coworkers[39] of the endovascular treatment of visceral occlusive disease suggested that open, surgical revascularization was superior.

The ongoing issues with regards to open revascularization for patients with CMI include the type of revascularization, the number of vessels to be revascularized, and the optimal conduit. The techniques of reimplantation, endarterectomy, and bypass all have been employed successfully, and each possesses theoretical advantages. Mesenteric bypass either antegrade from the supraceliac aorta or retrograde from the infrarenal aorta and common iliac artery has emerged as the most common treatment, with the current debate being the specific configuration. The theoretical advantages of the antegrade bypass include the fact that supraceliac aorta is frequently uninvolved with atherosclerosis and that the limbs of the graft follow a direct path and maintain prograde flow. The theoretical advantages of the retrograde bypass include the fact that infrarenal aorta and common iliac artery are easier and faster to expose and generally more familiar to most vascular surgeons. There is less hemodynamic instability and potential for distal embolization with the infrarenal aortic/iliac clamp application. It is usually possible to occlude the supraceliac aorta partially, while performing the proximal anastomosis of the antegrade bypass. One major disadvantage of the retrograde bypass is the obligatory course of the graft and its potential to kink, which is even more problematic for vein conduits. The graft must transition from the aorta, which sits posterior in the abdomen, to the SMA, which sits more anterior and includes a near 180-degree turn.

Inherent to the debate about the type of bypass procedure to be performed is the number of vessels to be revascularized. Multivessel revascularization offers the theoretical advantage that if one bypass fails, the patient does not develop recurrent symptoms or acute intestinal ischemia. Hollier and colleagues[23] reported in 1981 that the recurrence rate after mesenteric revascularization was inversely related to the number of vessels revascularized, and that it exceeded 50% if only a single vessel was repaired. Proponents of the retrograde bypass to the SMA alone emphasize that the procedure revascularizes the primary vessel of concern, that multivessel reconstructions add to the complexity of the procedure, and, most importantly, that the more recent series have not shown a significant clinical advantage for multivessel bypass. Park and associates[40] reported a follow-up study from the same institution as the original report from Hollier and colleagues,[23] which stated they have "maintained a degree of faithfulness" to the multivessel revascularization concept, although they no longer believe that reconstructing the IMA is essential.

Prosthetic and autogenous conduits have been used with the various mesenteric bypass procedures, although reports comparing the long-term patency rates for the two different conduits have been inconclusive.[24,37,41,42] Kihara and associates[41] reported that the patency rates for vein grafts were significantly lower than the rates for prosthetic grafts by univariate analysis, but multivariate analysis showed that patient gender (patency—female greater than male) rather than conduit was responsible for the observed difference. Saphenous vein conduits may be at risk for developing stenoses given the relative high flow rate through the visceral vessels. Modrall and colleagues[42] reported that the symptomatic recurrence rate after mesenteric bypass was lower in patients who underwent reconstruction using superficial femoral vein compared with saphenous vein. The superficial femoral vein may represent an ideal conduit for mesenteric bypass when a prosthetic conduit is contraindicated given its mean diameter of 7 mm[43] and relatively thick wall. Harvesting the superficial femoral vein adds a significant amount of time and complexity to the procedure, however.

Reported perioperative and long-term outcomes after open and endovascular revascularization for patients with CMI are shown in Tables 124-1 and 124-2. Although some of the reports include patients with CMI and AMI and a variety of different procedures, several conclusions can be reached. The technical and immediate clinical success rates for endovascular treatment of visceral artery occlusive lesions are quite good and range from 81% to 100% and 77% to 100%. The SMA alone, the celiac artery alone, or the two in combination were treated throughout the various reports, and technical success was usually defined as less than 30% residual stenosis. The technical success rate for open repair is irrelevant given the nature of the procedure, but is essentially 100%. The corresponding immediate clinical success rate for open revascularization was inconsistently reported, but likewise essentially 100%. The mortality and complication rates seemed to be lower for the endovascular treatment. The ranges for the mortality and complication rates (open revascularization, mortality 0 to 11%, complications 12% to 66%; endovascular revascularization, mortality 0 to 11%, complications 0 to 40%) were

Table 124-1 Perioperative and Long-Term Outcome After Open Surgical Revascularization for Chronic Mesenteric Ischemia

AUTHOR	YEAR	N	INDICATION (% CMI)	OPERATION	TECHNICAL SUCCESS	MORTALITY (%)	COMPLICATION (%)	IMMEDIATE CLINICAL SUCCESS (%)	LONG-TERM CLINICAL SUCCESS— OBJECTIVE* (%)	PATENCY— OBJECTIVE* (%)	5-YEAR SURVIVAL— OBJECTIVE* (%)
Johnston et al[2]	1995	21	100	AB—5, RB—16	NA	0	19	NA	NA	NA	79
McMillan et al[37]	1995	25	64	AB—10, RB—15	NA	Overall—12, CMI—6, AMI—22	Overall—30, CMI—12, AMI—57	NA	NA	5 yr primary—89	75
Moawad et al[59]	1997	24	100	AB—17, RB—7	NA	4	NA	NA	NA	5 yr primary—78	71
Mateo et al[24]	1999	85	100	RB—34, AB—24, EA—19, Other—2	NA	8	33	100	5 yr—87	NA	64
Kihara et al[41]	1999	42	100	AB—35, RB—1, EA—4, other—2	NA	10	30	NA	3 yr—86	3 yr primary—65, 3 yr secondary—67	70
Foley et al[10]	2000	49	52	RB—43, AB—6	NA	Overall—12, CMI—3, AMI—24	NA	100	NA	5 yr assisted primary—79	61
Jimenez et al[20]	2002	47	100	AB—47	NA	11	66	100	NA	5 yr primary—69, 5 yr assisted primary—96, 5 yr secondary—100	74
Park et al[40]	2002	98	100	AB—77, RB—14, EA—1, other—2	NA	5	NA	98	5 yr—92	NA	62
Cho et al[60]	2002	48	52	AB/RB—30, EA—18	NA	Overall—29, CMI—4, AMI—57	Overall—60	NA	5 yr—79	5 yr primary—57	54

*Objective—life-table or Kaplan-Meier.
AB, antegrade bypass; AMI, acute mesenteric ischemia; CMI, chronic mesenteric ischemia; EA, endarterectomy; NA, not available; RB, retrograde bypass.

Table 124-2   Perioperative and Long-Term Outcome After Endovascular Revascularization for Chronic Mesenteric Ischemia

AUTHOR	YEAR	N	INDICATION (% CMI)	OPERATION	TECHNICAL SUCCESS (%)	MORTALITY (%)	COMPLICATION (%)	IMMEDIATE CLINICAL SUCCESS (%)	LONG-TERM CLINICAL SUCCESS—OBJECTIVE* (%)	PATENCY—OBJECTIVE* (%)	5-YEAR SURVIVAL—OBJECTIVE* (%)
Hallisey et al[61]	1995	16	88	PTA—15, PTA/stent—1	88	Overall—6, CMI—0	Overall—6	Overall—88, CMI—93	NA	NA	NA
Allen et al[62]	1996	19	100	PTA—19	95	5	5	79	NA	NA	NA
Maspes et al[63]	1998	23	100	PTA—23	90	0	9	77	NA	NA	NA
Nyman et al[64]	1998	5	80	PTA—2, PTA/stent—3	100	0	40	100	NA	NA	NA
Sheeran et al[65]	1999	12	100	PTA/stent—12	92	8	0	92	18 mo primary—74, 18 mo assisted primary—83	NA	NA
Kasirajan et al[39]	2001	28	100	PTA—5, PTA/stent—23	100	11	18	NA	3 yr—66	NA	60
Steinmetz et al[38]	2002	19	100	PTA—12, PTA/stent—7	100	0	16	94	NA	NA	NA
Cognet et al[66]	2002	16	100	PTA—11, PTA/stent—5	100	0	12	100	NA	NA	NA
Pietura et al[67]	2002	6	100	PTA—5, PTA/stent—1	100	0	NA	100	NA	NA	NA
Matsumoto et al[21]	2002	33	100	PTA—21, PTA/stent—12	81	0	16	88	NA	NA	NA
Sharafuddin et al[68]	2003	25	84	PTA/stent—25	96	4	12	88	4 yr primary—72, 4 yr assisted primary—92	30 mo primary—65, 30 mo assisted primary—82	NA

*Objective—life-table or Kaplan-Meier.
CMI, chronic mesenteric ischemia; NA, not available; PTA, percutaneous transluminal angioplasty.

similar, although the adverse outcomes in the endovascular reports seemed to cluster at the lower end of the range, and the magnitude of the complications themselves were less. The mortality and complication rates reported from the institutional series for open revascularization were comparable to the 15% mortality and 45% complication rates reported across the United States by Derrow and colleagues[1] from a 20% U.S. sample. Mateo and associates[24] reported that the complication rates, including mortality, were significantly increased by simultaneous aortic repair, complete revascularization, and the presence of preoperative renal insufficiency. The long-term clinical success (5 years, range 79% to 92%), graft patency (5 years, primary patency, range 57% to 89%), and patient survival (5 years, range 54% to 79%) after open revascularization as objectively documented with either the life-table or the Kaplan-Meier method all are quite good. The same outcome measures are poorly documented after endovascular treatment. The limited available objective data suggest, however, that these long-term measures are comparable. Among the reports objectively documenting the outcome after retrograde/ antegrade bypasses and prosthetic/vein bypasses, no differences in patency were found (i.e., patency of antegrade bypass comparable to retrograde bypass). Many other relevant outcome measures, such as cost, hospital and intensive care unit length of stay, and return to normal weight, were not consistently reported in the multiple series. Foley and associates[10] and Jimenez and coworkers[20] reported mean lengths of stay of 19 days and 32 days after open revascularization for mesenteric ischemia. Kasirajan and colleagues[39] reported a median length of stay of 5 and 13 days after endovascular and open revascularization, although this difference was not significant. Matsumoto and coworkers[21] reported that most patients were discharged to home within 72 hours after endovascular revascularization and that they did not require treatment in the intensive care unit. Jimenez and coworkers[20] reported the patients' mean weight was 103% of their ideal body weight at 6 months postoperatively compared with the preoperative value of 87%.

■ OPERATIVE TECHNIQUE AND PERIOPERATIVE MANAGEMENT

Open Revascularization

Preoperative Evaluation

The preoperative evaluation for patients undergoing open revascularization for CMI is similar to that for other major vascular surgical procedures. All active medical conditions should be optimized, although extensive medical workups are likely unnecessary given the relative sense of urgency and life-threatening nature of CMI. Patients with visceral artery occlusive disease likely also have systemic vascular disease, particularly coronary artery disease as shown by the landmark study by Hertzer and coworkers.[44] Extensive cardiac workups are likely unnecessary and should be dictated by the patient's underlying symptoms, with cardiac catheterization reserved for patients with either unstable angina or a change in their anginal pattern. The specific

cardiac workup likely should be dictated by institutional preference or the algorithm for noncardiac surgery published by the American Heart Association.[45] Operative planning is facilitated by a conventional contrast arteriogram of the aorta and visceral vessels, although this is usually the definitive diagnostic study that precipitates the revascularization. Some type of imaging study of the supraceliac aorta should be obtained if antegrade bypass is planned to ensure that it is a suitable inflow site. Our current preference is a standard contrast CT scan. Ankle-brachial indices and vein surveys of the saphenous and superficial femoral veins are routinely obtained to quantify the level of lower extremity arterial occlusive disease and to identify all available autogenous conduits in the event that a prosthetic conduit is contraindicated. The management of oral feedings in the preoperative period is dictated by the severity and extent of the patient's abdominal pain. Patients with minimal postprandial pain are allowed to continue to eat, although they are counseled to avoid large meals or types of food that exacerbate their symptoms. On the other end of the spectrum, patients with continuous abdominal pain are made nothing per mouth (NPO) with the exception of medications. Patients hospitalized during the preoperative period are started on TPN. The operative intervention is not delayed in an attempt to replete the nutritional stores, given the ongoing risk of developing AMI and the anecdotal impression that patients with CMI do not metabolize the parenteral nutrition adequately. No bowel preparation is used in the immediate preoperative period because of the theoretical concerns of precipitating AMI.

Antegrade Aortoceliac/superior Mesenteric Artery Bypass

The antegrade aortoceliac/superior mesenteric artery bypass (Fig. 124-3) can be performed using either a midline or bilateral subcostal incision with the choice contingent on surgeon preference. The midline incision is slightly easier and faster to close, and the structures that need to be exposed during the procedure are all in the midline. A bilateral subcostal incision with a midline extension to the xiphoid provides the optimal exposure to the upper abdomen, however. It is particularly helpful in large men because of the posterior location and the corresponding depth of the supraceliac aorta. The abdomen should be explored per routine to rule out any other intra-abdominal pathology and to assess the status of the bowel. We do not persist too long with this maneuver or take down extensive adhesions if the bowel is viable, unless there is some uncertainty about the diagnosis.

The supraceliac aorta is exposed by taking down the left triangular ligament of the liver and reflecting the left lateral segment to the patient's right. The retraction of the left lateral segment and the exposure itself is facilitated using a self-retaining retractor, such as a Bookwalter, and placing the patient in a reverse Trendelenburg position. The gastrohepatic ligament is incised, although care should be used during this maneuver because a replaced left hepatic artery from the left gastric artery is seen approximately 25% of the time and courses through the ligament.[46] The esophagus and stomach are retracted to the patient's left. Care should be used throughout the procedure to avoid

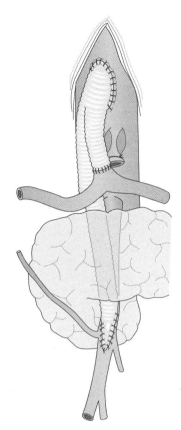

FIGURE 124-3 An antegrade aortoceliac/superior mesenteric artery bypass is shown. The proximal anastomosis is performed to the supraceliac aorta, and the limbs of the graft are oriented on top of each other. The celiac anastomosis is performed in an end-to-end fashion, whereas the superior mesenteric anastomosis is performed end-to-side. The body of the graft should be left as short as possible because the distance from the aorta to the celiac anastomosis is so short. The inferior limb to the superior mesenteric artery is tunneled deep to the pancreas.

injuring the esophagus, although it usually can be identified easily by the presence of a nasogastric tube or transesophageal echocardiography probe. The posterior peritoneum can be incised and the aorta exposed directly. This exposure can be facilitated by incising the median arcuate ligament and the crus of the diaphragm. Occasionally the pleura of the lung is entered while incising the crus. This is usually obvious and of little consequence, although a chest radiograph should be obtained in the immediate postoperative period to confirm that the lungs are fully expanded. A sufficient length of supraceliac aorta should be dissected free to facilitate clamp application. It is not necessary to dissect the aorta circumferentially throughout the length, where it is anticipated that the clamp will be applied. It can be helpful, however, to place an umbilical tape around the aorta to facilitate the initial clamp application and to serve as a handle should difficulties arise.

The celiac axis can be exposed by dissecting caudad along the anterior surface of the aorta. This exposure requires incising the remaining fibers of the diaphragm and the dense, fibrous neural tissue known as the celiac ganglion that surrounds the proximal celiac axis. It is our preferred technique to dissect the origin of the celiac axis and its proximal branches circumferentially to facilitate performing

the anastomosis in an end-to-end fashion. Alternatively the common hepatic, proper hepatic, and gastroduodenal arteries can be dissected circumferentially, and the distal anastomosis can be performed in an end-to-side configuration, although the orientation of the limb and the anastomosis are more challenging.

A suitable segment of the SMA for the distal anastomosis can be exposed using a variety of techniques. In our preferred approach, the artery is dissected free immediately caudad to the inferior border of the pancreas. This dissection can be facilitated by entering the lesser sac by incising the gastrocolic ligament or by retracting the lesser curve of the stomach inferiorly and going through the gastrohepatic ligament. The SMA sits relatively deep within the retroperitoneal tissue in patients with a moderate amount of retroperitoneal fat and should not be mistaken for a dilated collateral. Locating the artery is facilitated by identifying the adjacent superior mesenteric vein, which courses on its right lateral side. Approximately 2 to 3 cm of the artery should be dissected to facilitate the anastomosis, but caution should be used during this step because the multiple branches of the artery are friable and easily injured. The SMA also may be approached elevating the transverse colon and incising the root of its mesentery. The artery lies adjacent to the superior mesenteric vein within the mesenteric fat and can be identified by tracing the middle colic artery retrograde. The SMA can be approached laterally by completely mobilizing the fourth portion of the duodenum after incising the ligament of Treitz and the other peritoneal attachments. After exposure of the SMA, a retropancreatic tunnel is created to facilitate passage of the bypass limb. It is usually possible to create this tunnel using gentle, bimanual finger dissection between the exposed supraceliac aorta and the SMA. This should be done with caution because the tunnel courses adjacent to the portal vein and beneath the splenic vein. A straight aortic clamp can be passed through the tunnel and left in place to facilitate later passage of the limb.

The proximal anastomosis to the supraceliac aorta usually can be performed by only partially occluding the vessel using numerous side-biting clamps. In our own practice, we use a Lambert-Kaye clamp that has been modified with a clamp-locking device that secures the tips. When it is not possible to use a partially occluding clamp because of calcification or atherosclerotic involvement of the aorta or both, two straight aortic clamps are usually sufficient. Before clamp application, the patients are given systemic heparinization (100 U/kg), started on renal protective doses of dopamine (3 to 5 μg/kg/min), and given 25 g of mannitol as an antioxidant and to induce diuresis. Our conduit of choice is a bifurcated Dacron graft with a body diameter of 12 mm and limb diameters of 7 mm (12 × 7). Grafts in this size are not universally available, however, and can be substituted with ones measuring 12 × 6 or 14 × 7. Polytetrafluoroethylene and autogenous conduits are likely suitable substitutes because the optimal conduit has not been defined. An arteriotomy is made along the longitudinal axis of the aorta, and the graft is spatulated in such a fashion that the limbs of the graft are oriented on top of each other (in contrast to the case of an aortobifemoral graft, in which the limbs are oriented side by side). The body of the graft should be as short as possible with the heel of the anastomosis essentially being the start of the inferior limb. This is necessary because the distance between the aortic anastomosis and the celiac anastomosis is short. Occasionally a limited endarterectomy of the aorta is necessary, although caution should be exercised to avoid creating an aorta that is so thin that it will not hold sutures. The proximal anastomosis can be challenging in large patients, in whom the aorta is deep relative to the abdominal wall. These difficulties can be partially reduced by placing retracting stay sutures in the lateral aspects of the aortotomy (3 and 9 positions of the clock) and by placing the sutures using a single bite technique.

The anastomoses to the celiac axis and the SMA are performed using fairly standard techniques. The cephalad limb of the graft is used for the celiac anastomosis, whereas the caudad limb is tunneled deep to the pancreas with the assistance of the previously placed aortic clamp. The celiac anastomosis usually is performed in an end-to-end fashion after suture ligating the stump at its origin, whereas the anastomosis to the SMA usually is configured in an end-to-side fashion. In our own practice, we have used only continuous-wave Doppler to interrogate the completed bypasses and have justified our approach by the excellent long-term outcomes.[20] Oderich and coworkers[47] have advocated intraoperative duplex ultrasound after visceral revascularization and reported that persistent ultrasound abnormalities are associated with risk of early graft failure, reintervention, and death. The retroperitoneal tissue over the SMA anastomosis is closed, although we have not routinely attempted to cover the proximal anastomosis. We do not routinely revascularize the IMA.

Retrograde Aortosuperior Mesenteric Artery Bypass

Many of the principles outlined for the antegrade bypass are relevant to the retrograde approach (Fig. 124-4). Several technical points merit further comment. The proximal anastomosis can be positioned on the proximal right common iliac artery, the infrarenal aorta, or the proximal left common iliac artery with the order of preference in descending order as listed. The ultimate choice is contingent on the anatomic lie of the graft and the degree of atherosclerosis and arterial occlusive disease in the vessels. The inflow vessels are exposed by incising the overlying retroperitoneal tissue in the standard fashion for an infrarenal abdominal aortic aneurysm repair, and the anastomosis is frequently hooded down the right common iliac artery with the heel of the graft placed on the distal aorta immediately before its bifurcation. Foley and associates[10] described cutting off one limb of a bifurcated graft and using the body to construct a generous hood for the proximal anastomosis. The proximal anastomosis usually is performed first, but some authors have proposed the opposite order to simplify tunneling the graft.[48] The SMA is exposed by reflecting the fourth portion of the duodenum after incising the ligament of Treitz and the other peritoneal attachments as outlined earlier. The distal anastomosis can be performed in either an end-to-end or end-to-side fashion, but the anatomic course of the graft is often more favorable if performed in an end-to-end fashion. Either a 6-mm or 7-mm diameter Dacron graft is a suitable conduit, although a comparable sized,

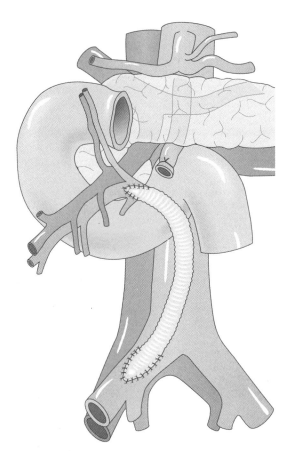

FIGURE 124-4 A retrograde aorta/superior mesenteric artery bypass is shown. The proximal anastomosis is performed in an end-to-side fashion to the proximal right common iliac artery. The distal anastomosis is performed in an end-to-end fashion to the superior mesenteric artery after mobilization of the ligament of Treitz and the other duodenal peritoneal attachments. The bypass graft takes a gentle curve or C loop as it transitions posterior to anterior and caudad to cephalad.

externally supported polytetrafluoroethylene graft is likely a reasonable alternative and holds some theoretical appeal because of its ability to avoid kinking. The graft should be tunneled in such a fashion that it forms a gentle curve or C loop between the two anastomoses as it traverses caudad to cephalad and posterior to anterior. The loop should be configured such that the SMA anastomosis can be constructed in an antegrade fashion. It is imperative that the graft does not kink and that the anastomoses are tension-free. The retroperitoneal tissue over the aorta, the ligament of Treitz, and the peritoneum over the SMA all are reapproximated to exclude the graft from contact with the intestine after interrogating the graft with the continuous-wave Doppler. Some authors have suggested further that the omentum be mobilized and used to protect the graft.[49]

Postoperative Care

The immediate postoperative care for patients undergoing revascularization for CMI frequently is complicated by the development of multiple organ dysfunction and is distinctly different from that associated with most other abdominal vascular procedures, such as aortic reconstruction for aorto-iliac occlusive disease. This propensity to develop multiple organ dysfunction likely accounts for the prolonged intensive care unit and total hospital length of stays and is one of the leading causes of death in the postoperative period.[50] The responsible mechanism is likely the visceral ischemia and reperfusion phenomenon inherent to the revascularization. This process has been reported to induce a complex response involving several interrelated inflammatory mediators that have the potential to cause local and distant organ injury.[48] In a detailed study, Harward and colleagues[50] characterized the individual organ system dysfunction after revascularization for AMI and CMI. They reported that the serum hepatic transaminases increased 90-fold to 100-fold immediately postoperatively and did not normalize for 7 to 10 days, that the platelet counts decreased to less than 40,000 U within 12 to 24 hours and remained abnormal for the first 3 to 6 days, and that the prothrombin and partial thromboplastin times increased and stayed elevated also for 3 to 6 days. Perhaps most notably, these investigators reported that most patients developed a significant pulmonary injury characterized by an elevated mean shunt fraction and a radiographic picture of acute respiratory distress syndrome that manifested 1 to 3 days postoperatively and persisted for 5 to 8 days. A report from Jimenez and colleagues[20] documented a 64% incidence of multiple organ dysfunction and a 53% incidence of prolonged mechanical ventilation after antegrade revascularization for CMI, which further supported the findings by Harward and colleagues.

The optimal early patient management strategy after mesenteric revascularization is to support the individual organ systems until the dysfunction resolves. Not all patients develop organ dysfunction, but the incidence is high and unpredictable. The optimal ventilator management is unresolved. We usually have extubated patients in the early postoperative period when they satisfy the weaning criteria and have been reluctant to maintain them on mechanical ventilation in anticipation that they may develop lung injury. Frequently these patients need to be reintubated and started back on mechanical ventilation, however. Thrombocytopenia and coagulopathy usually are managed expectantly with platelet or plasma transfusions reserved for severely depressed platelet counts or any clinical evidence of bleeding. The report by Harward and colleagues suggested that the inherent coagulopathy after mesenteric revascularization was not responsive to vitamin K. Patients should be maintained on TPN throughout the postoperative period until bowel function returns. TPN is particularly important given the fact that most patients are severely malnourished. Patients may have a prolonged ileus after revascularization and require TPN for some time. The bypass should be interrogated before discharge to confirm the technical adequacy of the reconstruction. A variety of imaging studies, including mesenteric duplex, contrast arteriography, magnetic resonance arteriography, and CT angiography, are suitable. We prefer mesenteric duplex, although examination in the early postoperative period frequently is compromised by the persistent ileus and the presence of bowel gas. Patients with significant acute changes in their clinical status also should undergo visceral imaging to confirm that their bypass is patent. It can be difficult to differentiate multiple organ dysfunction that is a

sequela of the ischemia and reperfusion injury from AMI secondary to graft thrombosis. Serum lactate levels may be helpful in this setting.

All patients who undergo revascularization for CMI require long-term follow-up. The long-term survival, relief from symptoms, and objectively documented graft patency rates all are quite good. Patients are seen frequently in the early postoperative period until all their active issues resolve, then at 6-month intervals thereafter with mesenteric duplex imaging to confirm graft patency and to identify any graft or anastomotic related problems. Objective assessment of graft patency is crucial and significantly better than the return of symptoms that has been used as a surrogate marker.[37] All abnormalities on duplex imaging merit further investigation with additional imaging or intervention or both. Diarrhea is a common complaint after revascularization and can persist for several months. It is more common in patients with preoperative diarrhea and can be so severe that it necessitates TPN. Jimenez and colleagues[20] reported that 33% of the patients in their series experienced significant postoperative diarrhea, and that it persisted more than 6 months in 24%. Kihara and associates[41] reported that patients had almost 2 stools/day (1.9 ± 0.4) after revascularization for CMI. The etiology of the diarrhea is unclear but may be related to intestinal atrophy, bacterial overgrowth, or disruption of the mesenteric neuroplexus.

Endovascular Revascularization

Preoperative Evaluation

The preoperative evaluation before endovascular treatment of mesenteric occlusive lesions in patients with CMI is essentially the same as that for open revascularization. Patients should be prepared to undergo emergent, open revascularization if a complication should arise, although this is unusual, and patients who are not amenable to endovascular revascularization usually can be scheduled for elective or semielective open repair. Patients with a contrast allergy should be treated with an appropriate steroid preparation. Patients with an elevated serum creatinine level who are considered candidates for standard contrast administration (serum creatinine 1.5 to 2 mg/dL) should receive gentle hydration and N-acetyl cysteine, although their benefits are unsubstantiated.

Diagnostic and Interventional Technique

Percutaneous access can be obtained through either the femoral or the brachial arteries (Fig. 124-5). The primary consideration for the particular approach should be the a priori likelihood of a therapeutic intervention except for patients with known anatomic limitations, such as iliofemoral or subclavian artery occlusive disease. The femoral approach is more familiar to most surgeons, it is associated with a lower incidence of vascular injury, and it is closer to the target artery, allowing the use of proportionately shorter guide wires and catheters. It should be used only when the possibility of a therapeutic intervention is remote, however, because of the orientation of the

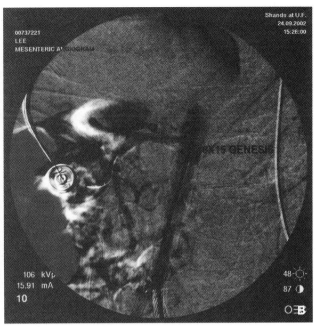

FIGURE 124-5   A, Lateral arteriogram of the celiac axis and superior mesenteric artery. Note the occluded celiac axis and severe proximal stenosis in the superior mesenteric artery. **B,** Completion study after angioplasty and stenting of the superior mesenteric artery stenosis. A balloon-expandable stent (Genesis) 6 mm in diameter and 15 mm in length was used.

mesenteric vessels. The angle between the mesenteric vessels and the aorta is fairly acute and directed caudally. The vector forces of a catheter directed from the femoral artery are opposite to the angle of the mesenteric vessels, and its pushability is compromised. These mechanical factors may be attenuated by the use of appropriate guiding catheters and stiffer wires. It may be difficult, if not impossible, however, to cross a tight stenosis through this approach, and guide wire access may be permanently lost during a crucial step of the procedure. The brachial approach overcomes these limitations and is the obvious choice in patients with severe aortoiliac occlusive disease. The change in catheter mechanics from the cephalad approach is sufficient to overcome the increased physical distance and need for longer devices and allows greater pushability for target vessel engagement. Additional disadvantages of the brachial approach (other than those cited as advantages of the femoral approach) include the limited maximal sheath size possible without use of a surgical cutdown (7F for men and 6F for women), the risk of embolic stroke, and difficulty gaining access to the descending thoracic aorta in patients with a tortuous arch. Although aortic access may be obtained easily from either brachial artery, the left brachial approach is preferred because of the risk of carotid embolization with prolonged catheterization across the innominate artery.

The visceral arteriogram is initiated by accessing the left brachial artery near the medial head of the humerus using a micropuncture technique (21-gauge needle, 0.018-inch wire) and a short 5F introducer sheath. A combination of a floppy-tipped guide wire (e.g., Bentson) and a pigtail angiographic catheter is used to direct the catheter into the

descending thoracic aorta, because an undirected guide wire would pass into the ascending arch in most cases from this approach. All catheters and guide wires should have a working length of at least 80 cm and up to 240 cm. The initial diagnostic arteriogram is obtained by positioning a pigtail catheter at the level of the 12th thoracic (T12) vertebral body. A flush aortogram is performed in anteroposterior and lateral projections using 20 mL of contrast agent at an injection rate of 15 mL/sec. Because most lesions in the SMA and celiac axis are orificial and located in the proximal 2 cm, selective catheterization usually is not necessary, unless a distal lesion is suspected or the extent of the lesion cannot be determined. In the presence of severe lesions or frank occlusions, the acquisition interval should be prolonged to allow for late filling via known collateral pathways. Provided that either the SMA or the celiac axis is patent, further visualization of the stenotic or occluded vessel, including the distal extent of the lesion, can be obtained by selectively cannulating the patent vessel (contrast volume of 10 to 15 mL at a rate of 7 mL/sec) because of the extensive collateral network between the two vessels. When the SMA and the celiac axis are severely stenotic or occluded, their distal extent can be visualized further by selectively cannulating the IMA. The median arcuate ligament may extrinsically compress the proximal celiac axis. This extrinsic compression can be differentiated from an intrinsic lesion by obtaining provocative inspiratory and expiratory phase images. A greater than 50% diameter reduction of the SMA usually is considered clinically significant regardless of whether or not the celiac axis is involved. In contrast, the diagnosis of mesenteric ischemia should be questioned in the presence of an isolated celiac axis stenosis.

Symptomatic stenoses of the visceral vessels can be treated at the time of the diagnostic arteriogram. Similar to renal artery lesions, the orificial stenoses in the mesenteric vessels are refractory to angioplasty alone, and primary stenting is recommended. Balloon angioplasty with selective stenting is reserved for mid-segment lesions. Balloon-expandable stents are preferred over self-expanding ones because of their superior radial force and controlled deployment. Although stent foreshortening historically has been described as a characteristic of self-expanding stents, balloon-expandable stents also can foreshorten 5% to 15% depending on the cell design, and this must be taken into account in the selection of stent length and positioning during deployment.

After a decision to proceed with intervention is made, a 90-cm straight 6F guiding sheath is advanced to the orifice of the SMA. This requires passing a stiffer guide wire (e.g., Rosen, Boston Scientific Corp., Natick, Mass) into the abdominal aorta and removing the pigtail catheter and the short 5F sheath. The SMA is always treated before the celiac axis even in the presence of significant disease in both vessels. A single intravenous bolus of heparin (5000 U) is administered, and no attempt is made to monitor the activated clotting time or to make weight-based dose adjustments. A combination of a 100-cm 5F angled catheter (e.g., multipurpose angiographic) and an angled hydrophilic guide wire (e.g., Glidewire, (Boston Scientific Corp., Natick, Mass) is used to cross the stenosis. This catheter is exchanged for a 4F hydrophilic catheter (e.g., Glidecatheter, (Boston Scientific Corp., Natick, Mass) that is advanced through the lesion over the guide wire.

The hydrophilic guide wire is removed, and a selective arteriogram is performed using only manual injection to rule out a tandem lesion and, more importantly, to confirm that the catheter is intravascular and that the vessel has not been injured by the guide wire/catheter manipulations. Intra-arterial nitroglycerin (200 to 400 µg) or papaverine (10 to 15 mg) may be administered to relieve any vasospasm and dilate the distal bed, although it is not usually necessary. A pressure gradient between the artery and the aorta can be measured by simultaneously transducing the coaxial 4F catheter and the 6F guiding sheath if the hemodynamic significance of the lesion is questionable. A mean gradient greater than 5 mm Hg or a peak systolic gradient greater than 10 mm Hg is considered significant. A guide wire is re-introduced through the catheter after the selective arteriogram or pressure measurements, and its tip is advanced as far distal as possible. It is imperative that the position of the guide wire tip be monitored closely throughout the procedure because it may inadvertently perforate or dissect the target vessel. This is particularly problematic during celiac axis interventions because the guide wire is positioned in either the hepatic or the splenic artery in the anteroposterior projection, whereas the actual intervention is performed in the lateral projection. A control arteriogram is obtained through the guiding sheath to localize the lesion. It is crucial to optimize the projection angle (lateral versus anterior oblique) to locate properly the true orifice relative to the aorta. Although a dilator with the guiding sheath may be used to "dotter" the stenosis, predilatation with a 5 mm × 20 mm angioplasty balloon is easier and potentially less traumatic. The target artery diameter may be estimated

using electronic calipers, but a 6- to 7-mm diameter stent (including 10% oversizing) is sufficient for most patients. A segment of the target vessel beyond any post-stenotic dilatation should be used as the reference. The guiding sheath is advanced gently over the balloon beyond the stenosis. A 15-mm or 20-mm long balloon-expandable stent of appropriate diameter is delivered to the site of the predilated lesion, and the sheath is retracted just proximal to the balloon. A repeat control arteriogram is obtained, and the stent is deployed with its proximal extent protruding roughly 2 mm into the aortic lumen to ensure complete coverage of the entire proximal extent of the "aortic" lesion. Adjunctive techniques, including proximal molding or funneling of the stent with larger balloons, have been described, but are rarely necessary.

It is important that the depth of conscious sedation be modulated so that the patient is sufficiently awake to detect any significant pain during the procedure. Although mild discomfort in the mid-epigastrium and back is typical, significant pain is an important indicator of overdilatation and may serve as a precursor to artery rupture. The balloon should be deflated if patients experience significant pain. After stent deployment, the balloon is carefully removed while guide wire access is maintained. A selective arteriogram is performed through the guiding sheath to confirm adequate stent placement and expansion. If the stent appears undersized or incompletely expanded, and the patient was comfortable during the initial deployment, postdilatation with a larger balloon (usually 0.5 or 1 mm larger) and a follow-up arteriogram are performed. Technical endpoints of success include less than 10% residual stenosis and brisk flow of contrast material distally without dissection or extravasation.

Recanalization of occluded mesenteric vessels is similar to that for other arterial beds and may be attempted if the total length of the occlusion is less than 2 cm and an orificial "stump" is present. Although the occlusions are almost always orificial, it is important to determine that the distal artery is patent and to establish the extent of the occlusion using the techniques outlined earlier, because the extent of the occlusion has an impact on the probability of a successful recanalization. A stump is beneficial because the orifice of the vessels may be hard to localize in the presence of a flush occlusion. It is difficult to engage a supporting catheter to facilitate guide wire entry in the presence of a flush occlusion. Provided that the occlusion is amenable to recanalization, a hydrophilic guide wire with a medium-stiff shaft (e.g., Roadrunner, (Cook Ine., Bloomington, Ind) combined with an angled selective or guiding catheter, is used to probe the occluded orifice gently. After guide wire access is obtained, it is crucial to pass a catheter (e.g., 4F Glidecatheter) across the occlusion and into the patent distal segment to confirm that the guide wire passed into the lumen of the vessel. The remaining portions of the procedure were outlined earlier, although predilatation with primary stenting is recommended.

Postoperative Care

The postoperative care after mesenteric angioplasty and stenting is comparable to that after renal and aortoiliac artery endovascular procedures. Early in our endovascular experience, a patient developed multiple organ dysfunction typically associated with open revascularization. Multiple organ dysfunction has been uncommon more recently and should raise the concern that the endovascular procedure was unsuccessful. Patients are admitted to the hospital for overnight observation and started on clopidogrel for 30 days (75 mg/day) with the first dose given in the recovery room (150 mg). They are allowed to resume a regular diet within 4 to 6 hours. Most patients notice a marked improvement of postprandial symptoms shortly after the procedure. A fasting mesenteric duplex ultrasound is obtained on the morning after the procedure to serve as a baseline. Elevated velocities are noted occasionally in the duplex scan despite a technically satisfactory arteriographic result and complete resolution of the preoperative symptoms. The explanation for these abnormal duplex findings is unclear, although we have elected to follow the patient's clinical course in this setting and repeat only the arteriogram or intervention (or both) if there is a significant change. Magnetic resonance arteriography is not helpful in this setting because of the signal dropout from the metallic stent. A repeat duplex examination is performed at 1 month, and aspirin (325 mg/day) is substituted for the clopidogrel at that time. The subsequent follow-up with serial duplex is comparable to that outlined for open revascularization.

■ ADDITIONAL CONSIDERATIONS

Aortic Reconstruction and Mesenteric Revascularization

Patients with visceral artery occlusive disease who require aortic reconstruction represent a relatively high-risk population in terms of their potential for adverse postoperative outcome, and consideration should be given to revascularization before aortic reconstruction even in asymptomatic patients. Simultaneous open aortic reconstruction and mesenteric revascularization likely should be avoided unless absolutely necessary. Mateo and associates[24] reported that the complication rate, including mortality, after mesenteric bypass was increased when aortic reconstructions were performed simultaneously, whereas McAfee and colleagues[51] reported that most deaths in their series occurred after combined procedures. An alternative approach includes staged procedures with either endovascular or open mesenteric revascularization performed as the initial step. Endovascular revascularization may be ideal in this setting because of its purported lower complication rates. In the few instances when simultaneous open revascularization and aortic reconstruction are necessary, the procedure likely should be performed using the retrograde technique owing to its comparative simplicity and minimal additional dissection. Foley and associates[10] reported that retrograde mesenteric bypass and aortic reconstruction was not associated with an increased mortality rate.

Median Arcuate Ligament Syndrome

The median arcuate ligament of the diaphragm compresses the origin of the celiac axis in a significant proportion of individuals, and this compression is augmented by full expiration.[52,53] The contribution of this celiac axis compression to the development of mesenteric ischemia or chronic abdominal pain is uncertain, however, and likely minimal. There is little theoretical justification to believe that this compression could lead to ischemic symptoms given the rich collateral network between the celiac axis and the SMA and the fact that the SMA is usually the most significant visceral vessel in terms of gut perfusion. The diagnosis of symptomatic celiac axis compression resulting from the median arcuate ligament is a diagnosis of exclusion. Reilly and coworkers[54] identified several criteria that may predict relief after surgical therapy for the median arcuate ligament syndrome including female gender, postprandial pain, weight loss greater than 20 lb, absence of psychiatric or drug abuse history, and arteriographic findings of celiac axis compression with post-stenotic dilatation or collateral flow or both. Effective treatment requires decompression of the median arcuate ligament and visceral artery bypass. Endovascular treatment alone is ineffective and likely contraindicated because of the refractory, extrinsic compression of the celiac origin by the ligament.

Remedial Procedures After Open Surgical Mesenteric Revascularization

Remedial, open surgical revascularization for recurrent symptoms of CMI is occasionally necessary, although quite rare, given the excellent graft patency rates. The surgical options include the antegrade and the retrograde bypasses with the choice contingent on the distribution of the occlusive disease and the original procedure. A failed retrograde bypass from the infrarenal aorta to the SMA usually can be remediated with the traditional antegrade bypass from the supraceliac aorta to the celiac axis and the SMA. This bypass usually requires siting the SMA anastomosis distal to the original one and obviates the concern about the course of the retrograde graft that may have contributed to the initial failure. A failed antegrade bypass usually can be redone or converted to a retrograde bypass. The latter option is much simpler, but the overriding principle in this setting should be to optimize the potential long-term success and graft patency, rather than minimize the operative procedure. It is unusual for both limbs of an antegrade bypass to fail. This scenario suggests a problem at the proximal aortic anastomosis. In the more common scenario, single limb failure is usually due to either a stenosis at the distal anastomosis from intimal hyperplasia or a technical problem from tunneling or kinking of the graft. The anastomotic problem can be corrected by graft thrombectomy and revision of the anastomosis with a vein patch or a new interposition graft. Problems related to tunneling the graft usually require excising the redundant segment or replacing the limb or both. "Redo" mesenteric bypass and particularly a redo antegrade bypass may be technically challenging because of the earlier dissection and the development of adhesions. In addition to siting the visceral artery anastomosis further distal, the procedure can be simplified by using the original cuff of the main body to avoid placing additional sutures in the supraceliac aorta.

In the unusual scenario that the traditional antegrade and retrograde bypasses are not feasible, a variety of potential bypass configurations or alternative repair techniques are possible. The descending thoracic aorta can serve as an alternative inflow source, whereas alternative distal targets include the hepatic artery, the splenic artery, the distal SMA, and the named branches of the SMA. Stenoses of the SMA and the celiac axis occasionally can be repaired using patch angioplasty alone, or the vessels may be directly reimplanted onto the aorta depending on the location of the lesion. Schneider and colleagues[55] reported a small series of isolated IMA revascularizations for CMI. They stated that the revascularization was sufficient to relieve the symptoms and prevent bowel infarction, although it required a well-developed collateral pathway.

The role of endovascular treatment for failing or failed mesenteric bypass grafts remains to be determined, although a few, more recent studies have shown that the techniques are feasible.[56,57] The treatment of restenosis after previous endovascular or open surgical revascularization is essentially the same as described for a de novo stenosis. Lesions that have undergone previous angioplasty alone should be routinely stented. Previously stented lesions and restenosis involving surgical grafts may be treated with balloon angioplasty with stenting or re-stenting reserved for recoil or other balloon failures. Endovascular treatment of a stenosis at the suture line of a prosthetic graft theoretically could disrupt the suture line and result in a pseudoaneurysm. The use of special "cutting" balloons (atherotomes) to predilate intimal hyperplastic stenoses and initiate a cleavage plane before conventional balloon angioplasty holds some promise and may improve early technical success and longer term patency.

Nonatherosclerotic Causes of Chronic Mesenteric Ischemia

The nonatherosclerotic causes of CMI are rarely encountered, and the clinical experience is limited. Fibromuscular dysplasia may involve the visceral vessels. Symptomatic stenoses have been reported to be amenable to balloon angioplasty and associated with a reasonable outcome.[58] Involvement of the visceral vessels from any of the multiple inflammatory arteritides may lead to CMI. The effective treatment in this setting is contingent on controlling or arresting the underlying inflammatory process and requires a multidisciplinary approach including a rheumatologist. Revascularization should be delayed until the underlying disease process is arrested or at least controlled. The stenotic lesions may be more distal on the arterial tree than the more common ostial atherosclerotic lesions. Open surgical revascularization may require dissecting the SMA distal in the small bowel mesentery well beyond the takeoff of the middle colic vessel. The distal anastomosis at this level can be facilitated by patching the artery with saphenous vein, then implanting the prosthetic graft on the generous vein patch. Every attempt to preserve the small, friable branches of the SMA should be made.

■ REFERENCES

1. Derrow AE, Seeger JM, Dame DA, et al: The outcome in the United States after thoracoabdominal aortic aneurysm repair, renal artery bypass, and mesenteric revascularization. J Vasc Surg 34:54, 2001.
2. Johnston KW, Lindsay TF, Walker PM, Kalman PG: Mesenteric arterial bypass grafts: Early and late results and suggested surgical approach for chronic and acute mesenteric ischemia. Surgery 118:1, 1995.
3. Fara JW: Postprandial mesenteric hyperemia. In Shepard AP, Granger DN (eds): Physiology of the Intestinal Circulation. New York, Raven Press, 1984, p 99.
4. Moneta GL, Taylor DC, Helton WS, et al: Duplex ultrasound measurement of postprandial intestinal blood flow: Effect of meal composition. Gastroenterology 95:1294, 1988.
5. Siregar H, Chou CC: Relative contribution of fat, protein, carbohydrate, and ethanol to intestinal hyperemia. Am J Physiol 242:G27, 1982.
6. Bond JH, Prentiss RA, Levitt MD: The effects of feeding on blood flow to the stomach, small bowel, and colon of the conscious dog. J Lab Clin Med 93:594, 1979.
7. Li KC, Whitney WS, McDonnell CH, et al: Chronic mesenteric ischemia: Evaluation with phase-contrast cine MR imaging. Radiology 190:175, 1994.
8. Mikkelsen WP: Intestinal angina: Its surgical significance. Am J Surg 94:262, 1957.
9. Taylor LM, Moneta GL, Porter JM: Treatment of chronic visceral ischemia. In Rutherford RB (ed): Vascular Surgery, 5th ed. Philadelphia, WB Saunders, 2000, p 1532.
10. Foley MI, Moneta GL, Abou-Zamzam AM Jr, et al: Revascularization of the superior mesenteric artery alone for treatment of intestinal ischemia. J Vasc Surg 32:37, 2000.
11. Wilson DB, Hansen KJ, Pearce JD, et al: Prevalence of mesenteric artery disease in the elderly. J Vasc Surg 40:45, 2004.
12. Croft RJ, Menon GP, Marston A: Does 'intestinal angina' exist? A critical study of obstructed visceral arteries. Br J Surg 68:316, 1981.
13. Valentine RJ, Martin JD, Myers SI, et al: Asymptomatic celiac and superior mesenteric artery stenoses are more prevalent among patients with unsuspected renal artery stenoses. J Vasc Surg 14:195, 1991.
14. Thomas JH, Blake K, Pierce GE, et al: The clinical course of asymptomatic mesenteric arterial stenosis. J Vasc Surg 27:840, 1998.
15. Levy PJ, Krausz MM, Manny J: Acute mesenteric ischemia: Improved results—a retrospective analysis of ninety-two patients. Surgery 107:372, 1990.
16. Stoney RJ, Cunningham CG: Acute mesenteric ischemia. Surgery 114:489, 1993.
17. Connolly JE, Stemmer EA: Intestinal gangrene as the result of mesenteric arterial steal. Am J Surg 126:197, 1973.
18. Poole JW, Sammartano RJ, Boley SJ: Hemodynamic basis of the pain of chronic mesenteric ischemia. Am J Surg 153:171, 1987.
19. Marston A, Clarke JM, Garcia GJ, Miller AL: Intestinal function and intestinal blood supply: A 20 year surgical study. Gut 26:656, 1985.
20. Jimenez JG, Huber TS, Ozaki CK, et al: Durability of antegrade synthetic aortomesenteric bypass for chronic mesenteric ischemia. J Vasc Surg 35:1078, 2002.
21. Matsumoto AH, Angle JF, Spinosa DJ, et al: Percutaneous transluminal angioplasty and stenting in the treatment of chronic mesenteric ischemia: Results and longterm followup. J Am Coll Surg 194:S22, 2002.
22. Calderon M, Reul GJ, Gregoric ID, et al: Long-term results of the surgical management of symptomatic chronic intestinal ischemia. J Cardiovasc Surg (Torino) 33:723, 1992.
23. Hollier LH, Bernatz PE, Pairolero PC, et al: Surgical management of chronic intestinal ischemia: A reappraisal. Surgery 90:940, 1981.
24. Mateo RB, O'Hara PJ, Hertzer NR, et al: Elective surgical treatment of symptomatic chronic mesenteric occlusive disease: Early results and late outcomes. J Vasc Surg 29:821, 1999.
25. Rapp JH, Reilly LM, Qvarfordt PG, et al: Durability of endarterectomy and antegrade grafts in the treatment of chronic visceral ischemia. J Vasc Surg 3:799, 1986.
26. Van Damme H, Jacquet N, Belaiche J, et al: Chronic ischaemic gastritis: An unusual form of splanchnic vascular insufficiency. J Cardiovasc Surg (Torino) 33:451, 1992.
27. Sales J, Norton L, Nolan P, et al: Gastric mucosal ischemia in experimental stress ulcer. J Surg Res 18:65, 1975.

28. Shirazi S, Mueller TM, Hardy BM: Canine gastric acid secretion and blood flow measurement in hemorrhagic shock. Gastroenterology 73:75, 1977.

29. Moneta GL, Lee RW, Yeager RA, et al: Mesenteric duplex scanning: A blinded prospective study. J Vasc Surg 17:79, 1993.

30. Zwolak RM, Fillinger MF, Walsh DB, et al: Mesenteric and celiac duplex scanning: A validation study. J Vasc Surg 27:1078, 1998.

31. Boley SJ, Brandt LJ, Veith FJ, et al: A new provocative test for chronic mesenteric ischemia. Am J Gastroenterol 86:888, 1991.

32. Gentile AT, Moneta GL, Lee RW, et al: Usefulness of fasting and postprandial duplex ultrasound examinations for predicting high-grade superior mesenteric artery stenosis. Am J Surg 169:476, 1995.

33. Flinn WR, Rizzo RJ, Park JS, Sandager GP: Duplex scanning for assessment of mesenteric ischemia. Surg Clin North Am 70:99, 1990.

34. Lee PC, Rhee RY, Gordon RY, et al: Management of splenic artery aneurysms: The significance of portal and essential hypertension. J Am Coll Surg 189:483, 1999.

35. Burkart DJ, Johnson CD, Reading CC, Ehman RL: MR measurements of mesenteric venous flow: Prospective evaluation in healthy volunteers and patients with suspected chronic mesenteric ischemia. Radiology 194:801, 1995.

36. Rheudasil JM, Stewart MT, Schellack JV, et al: Surgical treatment of chronic mesenteric arterial insufficiency. J Vasc Surg 8:495, 1988.

37. McMillan WD, McCarthy WJ, Bresticker MR, et al: Mesenteric artery bypass: Objective patency determination. J Vasc Surg 21:729, 1995.

38. Steinmetz E, Tatou E, Favier-Blavoux C, et al: Endovascular treatment as first choice in chronic intestinal ischemia. Ann Vasc Surg 16:693, 2002.

39. Kasirajan K, O'Hara PJ, Gray BH, et al: Chronic mesenteric ischemia: Open surgery versus percutaneous angioplasty and stenting. J Vasc Surg 33:63, 2001.

40. Park WM, Cherry KJ Jr, Chua HK, et al: Current results of open revascularization for chronic mesenteric ischemia: A standard for comparison. J Vasc Surg 35:853, 2002.

41. Kihara TK, Blebea J, Anderson KM, et al: Risk factors and outcomes following revascularization for chronic mesenteric ischemia. Ann Vasc Surg 13:37, 1999.

42. Modrall JG, Sadjadi J, Joiner DR, et al: Comparison of superficial femoral vein and saphenous vein as conduits for mesenteric arterial bypass. J Vasc Surg 37:362, 2003.

43. Hertzberg BS, Kliewer MA, DeLong DM, et al: Sonographic assessment of lower limb vein diameters: Implications for the diagnosis and characterization of deep venous thrombosis. AJR Am J Roentgenol 168:1253, 1997.

44. Hertzer NR, Beven EG, Young JR, et al: Coronary artery disease in peripheral vascular patients: A classification of 1000 coronary angiograms and results of surgical management. Ann Surg 199:223, 1984.

45. Eagle KA, Berger PB, Calkins H, et al: ACC/AHA guideline update for perioperative cardiovascular evaluation for noncardiac surgery—executive summary: A report of the American College of Cardiology/American Heart Association Task Force on Practice Guidelines (Committee to Update the 1996 Guidelines on Perioperative Cardiovascular Evaluation for Noncardiac Surgery). Circulation 105:1257, 2002.

46. Cho KJ, Varma MK: Arteriographic evaluation of splanchnic artery occlusive disease. In Ernst CB, Stanley JC (eds): Current Therapy in Vascular Surgery. St. Louis, Mosby, 2001, p 661.

47. Oderich GS, Panneton JM, Macedo TA, et al: Intraoperative duplex ultrasound of visceral revascularizations: Optimizing technical success and outcome. J Vasc Surg 38:684, 2003.

48. Kagan SA, Myers SI: Acute embolic and thrombotic mesenteric ischemia. In Ernst CB, Stanley JC (eds): Current Therapy in Vascular Surgery. St. Louis, Mosby, 2001, p 675.

49. Kazmers A: Operative management of acute mesenteric ischemia: Part 1. Ann Vasc Surg 12:187, 1998.

50. Harward TR, Brooks DL, Flynn TC, Seeger JM: Multiple organ dysfunction after mesenteric artery revascularization. J Vasc Surg 18:459, 1993.

51. McAfee MK, Cherry KJ Jr, Naessens JM, et al: Influence of complete revascularization on chronic mesenteric ischemia. Am J Surg 164:220, 1992.

52. Lindner HH, Kemprud E: A clinicoanatomical study of the arcuate ligament of the diaphragm. Arch Surg 103:600, 1971.

53. Taylor DC, Moneta GL, Cramer MM: Extrinsic compression of the celiac artery by the median arcuate ligament of the diaphragm: diagnosis by duplex ultrasound. J Vasc Tech 11:236, 1987.

54. Reilly LM, Ammar AD, Stoney RJ, Ehrenfeld WK: Late results following operative repair for celiac artery compression syndrome. J Vasc Surg 2:79, 1985.

55. Schneider DB, Nelken NA, Messina LM, Ehrenfeld WK: Isolated inferior mesenteric artery revascularization for chronic visceral ischemia. J Vasc Surg 30:51, 1999.

56. Howd A, Loose H, Chamberlain J: Transluminal angioplasty in the treatment of mesenteric vein graft stenosis. Cardiovasc Interv Radiol 10:43, 1987.

57. Levy PJ, Haskell L, Gordon RL: Percutaneous transluminal angioplasty of splanchnic arteries: An alternative method to elective revascularisation in chronic visceral ischaemia. Eur J Radiol 7:239, 1987.

58. Golden DA, Ring EJ, McLean GK, Freiman DB: Percutaneous transluminal angioplasty in the treatment of abdominal angina. AJR Am J Roentgenol 139:247, 1982.

59. Moawad J, McKinsey JF, Wyble CW, et al: Current results of surgical therapy for chronic mesenteric ischemia. Arch Surg 132:613, 1997.

60. Cho JS, Carr JA, Jacobsen G, et al: Long-term outcome after mesenteric artery reconstruction: A 37-year experience. J Vasc Surg 35:453, 2002.

61. Hallisey MJ, Deschaine J, Illescas FF, et al: Angioplasty for the treatment of visceral ischemia. J Vasc Interv Radiol 6:785, 1995.

62. Allen RC, Martin GH, Rees CR, et al: Mesenteric angioplasty in the treatment of chronic intestinal ischemia. J Vasc Surg 24:415, 1996.

63. Maspes F, Mazzetti DP, Gandini R, et al: Percutaneous transluminal angioplasty in the treatment of chronic mesenteric ischemia: Results and 3 years of follow-up in 23 patients. Abdom Imaging 23:358, 1998.

64. Nyman U, Ivancev K, Lindh M, Uher P: Endovascular treatment of chronic mesenteric ischemia: Report of five cases. Cardiovasc Interv Radiol 21:305, 1998.

65. Sheeran SR, Murphy TP, Khwaja A, et al: Stent placement for treatment of mesenteric artery stenoses or occlusions. J Vasc Interv Radiol 10:861, 1999.

66. Cognet F, Ben Salem D, Dranssart M, et al: Chronic mesenteric ischemia: Imaging and percutaneous treatment. Radiographics 22:863, 2002.

67. Pietura R, Szymanska A, El Furah M, et al: Chronic mesenteric ischemia: Diagnosis and treatment with balloon angioplasty and stenting. Med Sci Monit 8:R8, 2002.

68. Sharafuddin MJ, Olson CH, Sun S, et al: Endovascular treatment of celiac and mesenteric arteries stenoses: Applications and results. J Vasc Surg 38:692, 2003.

Intestinal Ischemia Caused by Venous Thrombosis

125

MARK D. MORASCH, MD

Splanchnic vein occlusion, commonly known as *mesenteric venous thrombosis* (MVT), is a rare disorder with a broad range of clinical presentations. Although relatively infrequent and often benign, MVT is an important cause of acute mesenteric ischemia that in rare cases can be lethal. This form of acute intestinal ischemia was first reported by Elliot in 1895[1] and was described in detail as distinct from mesenteric arterial occlusion by Warren and Eberhard in 1935.[2] Early authors reported significant mortality rates associated with the disease. Today, because of its often insidious presentation and because of the potential for delayed diagnosis, MVT remains a formidable disease entity with significant morbid implications. Prompt recognition is important because early and aggressive treatment may limit progression of the thrombotic process.

MVT, which usually involves the superior mesenteric and splenic veins and less commonly the inferior mesenteric and portal veins, is largely considered to be the least common cause of acute mesenteric ischemia. MVT is responsible for less than 10% of clinically significant cases of mesenteric ischemia and is found in fewer than 1 in 1000 laparotomies.[3,4] Rius and colleagues[5] reported that 0.38% of laparotomies for acute abdomen revealed mesenteric infarction, and only 17% of those were the result of splanchnic venous occlusion.[5] In another study by Ottinger and Austen,[6] MVT was found in less than 1% of patients with mesenteric ischemia. In autopsy studies, MVT has been found in 0.2% to 2% of the population.[2,6] Because MVT may not be suspected and not be diagnosed in many patients, its true incidence is unknown, but the incidence

of symptomatic MVT over a more contemporary 20-year period was reported to be 2 in 100,000 admissions in one report.[7] MVT can occur at any age and in either sex, but it seems to be more common in the 50s and 60s, and there seems to be a slight male preponderance.[8,9]

Earlier reports suggested that the mortality rate for MVT could be 50%. These figures likely were biased by the fact that most cases were detected at the time of laparotomy or autopsy, and because modern diagnostic modalities were still undeveloped. More contemporary reports have found MVT much less likely to be fatal than other forms of mesenteric ischemia (Table 125-1).[2,4,10-12] In addition, the widespread use of computed tomography (CT) has led to more frequent diagnosis of benign, subclinical acute, subacute, and chronic forms of MVT.[11]

The clinical presentation of patients with acute or subacute MVT depends on the extent and location of the splanchnic thrombus. Diagnosis should be suspected when acute abdominal symptoms develop in patients with prior thrombotic episodes or a documented coagulopathy. Patients may be mildly symptomatic, sometimes even asymptomatic, or they may present with signs and symptoms consistent with an acute, catastrophic surgical illness. Commonly, patients with MVT present with anorexia and some abdominal pain; this can be sudden in onset, but frequently begins insidiously and worsens progressively. The pain is commonly nonspecific and generalized; point tenderness or rebound would be ominous signs and should be expected only in patients who have developed transmural bowel ischemia. Abdominal distention is often present, but

Table 125-1 Literature Review of Acute Mesenteric Venous Thrombosis: Management and Mortality

AUTHOR (YEAR)	NO. PATIENTS	BOWEL RESECTION	NONOPERATIVE	ANTICOAGULATION	30-DAY MORTALITY
Sack (1982)[37]	9	9	0	6	2 (22%)
Wilson (1987)[10]	16	10	3	6	8 (50%)
Montany (1988)[12]	6	5	1	6	3 (50%)
Clavien (1988)[38]	12	12	0	12	5 (42%)
Kaleya (1989)[7]	22	22	0	22	7 (32%)
Harward (1989)[39]	16	5	11	7	3 (19%)
Levy (1990)[40]	21	19	2	17	8 (38%)
Grieshop (1991)[41]	15	5	10	9	2 (13%)
Rhee (1994)[4]	53	30	19	33	14 (27%)
Morasch (2001)[11]	23	8	14	19	7 (30%)

tympany on examination may be disproportionately lacking secondary to mesenteric and bowel wall edema and to sequestrated intraluminal and intraperitoneal fluid.

More than half of patients with clinically significant MVT report abdominal pain and distention that has been present for 1 week to 1 month, and another quarter report abdominal pain that has lasted for much longer. Mathews and White[13] found that 50% of patients had pain 5 to 30 days before seeking medical attention; 27% reported abdominal pain for more than 1 month. Some patients have reported a symptom complex consistent with MVT that has lasted for much longer periods, even years, before having the correct diagnosis made.[11]

Diarrhea is present in one third or more of patients with MVT. Occult gastrointestinal bleeding is noted in more than half of patients diagnosed with MVT, whereas gross gastrointestinal bleeding is rare and is usually a sign of an advanced process involving transmural bowel infarction or a chronic form of the disease that has led to a variceal hemorrhage.[14]

In our series, 16% of our patients developed peritonitis from intestinal necrosis, but only two patients died from massive bowel infarction.[15] Declining mortality rates may be the result of earlier diagnosis and more aggressive treatment; it is also possible, however, that we now more readily diagnose a more benign form of the disease because of widespread use of CT. Improved image resolution of high-speed CT scanners and magnetic resonance imaging likely has added to the sensitivity for diagnosing MVT. An apparent increase in the incidence of MVT along with declining mortality may be due to improved diagnostic capabilities rather than an actual increase in disease frequency. Patients with the chronic form of the disease do not have the sequelae of ischemic bowel; rather, they most often present with late complications of the portal or splenic vein thrombosis, which can include variceal bleeding.[14]

Traditionally an objective diagnosis of MVT has been difficult to establish. Although routine blood work often shows some irregularities, and x-rays are abnormal in three quarters of patients, laboratory tests or plain abdominal films do not provide a diagnosis of intestinal ischemia caused by splanchnic venous occlusion. A mild leukocytosis with a left shift and a slightly elevated lactate dehydrogenase level are the only laboratory abnormalities consistently present. Laboratory values suggesting hemoconcentration and dehydration are expected, but these are nonspecific findings in patients who present with MVT. Other laboratory values, such as serum electrolytes and amylase, often are unremarkable. Plain films of the abdomen usually show a nondescript ileus-type pattern with dilated, fluid-filled bowel loops. *Thumbprinting,* or gas in the portal system, is suggestive of severe or advanced disease.

The diagnosis of MVT usually requires a high clinical index of suspicion followed by some form of noninvasive abdominal imaging. MVT should be considered in patients presenting with vague abdominal pain, especially patients with known hypercoagulable disorders, history of deep venous thrombosis, or prior splenectomy. These patients should undergo fine-columnation, contrast-enhanced CT with close attention to the mesenteric venous phase, magnetic resonance venography, or a vascular ultrasound.

CT established a diagnosis in more than 90% of the patients in our series who underwent the test. Contrast-enhanced abdominal CT is known to detect ovarian venous thrombosis, portal venous thrombosis, and MVT accurately. Acute thrombus in the superior mesenteric vein is evident on CT as a central lucency devoid of contrast and surrounded by a well-defined, enhancing, inflamed, and thickened vein wall (Fig. 125-1). Other CT findings include superior mesenteric vein dilatation, persistent enhancement of thickened bowel wall, and a well-developed collateral venous circulation with cavernous transformation in the splanchnic veins in more chronic cases. When the triad of thrombus within the superior mesenteric vein, thickened small bowel wall, and free fluid in the peritoneal cavity is identified on CT, at least one author has suggested that bowel infarction is likely and that laparotomy is indicated.[3] Portal gas or pneumatosis intestinalis strongly suggests the presence of transmural bowel infarction. Because of the accuracy and simplicity of CT, we no longer recommend venous phase angiography as a primary diagnostic modality.[14]

Similar to contrast-enhanced CT, contrast-enhanced magnetic resonance imaging with magnetic resonance venography is sensitive and specific for the detection of MVT. The magnetic resonance techniques are simple and consist of steady-state, balanced gradient echo pulse sequences in axial and coronal planes. These sequences are followed by pregadolinium and postgadolinium, contrast-enhanced, fat-suppressed, gradient echo imaging in the same axial and coronal planes. Although the information can be obtained by postcontrast three-dimensional magnetic resonance angiography techniques, simple breath-held two-dimensional acquisitions are sufficient and less challenging to perform. Because a dynamic magnetic resonance angiography sequence is not crucial, breath-held two-dimensional imaging can be performed 3 and 10 minutes after infusion when the contrast material is homogeneously concentrated in the blood pool. Venous occlusion appears as a typical flow void on reconstructed magnetic resonance

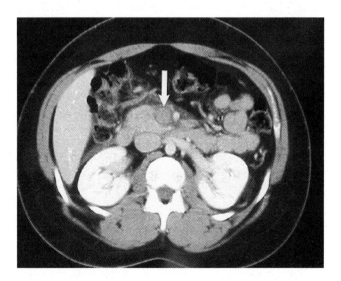

FIGURE 125-1 CT scan shows typical mesenteric venous thrombosis *(arrow).*

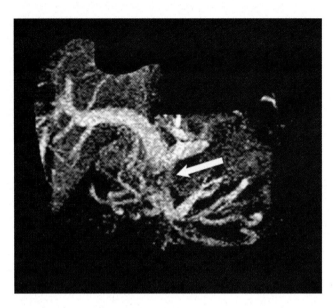

FIGURE 125-2 Magnetic resonance venography shows occlusion (*arrow*).

Table 125-2	Conditions Associated with Mesenteric Venous Thrombosis

Direct injury
   Abdominal trauma (blunt and penetrating)
   Postsurgical (particularly postsplenectomy)
   Intra-abdominal inflammatory states (pancreatitis, inflammatory bowel)
   Peritonitis and abdominal abscess

Local venous congestion or stasis
   Portal hypertension/cirrhosis of the liver
   Congestive heart failure
   Hypersplenism

Hypercoagulable states
   Protein C and protein S deficiency
   Antithrombin III deficiency
   Activated protein C resistance (factor V Leiden gene mutation)
   Presence of the 20210 A allele of the prothrombin gene
   Methylenetetrahydrofolate reductase mutations
   Neoplasms (particularly pancreatic and colonic)
   Oral contraceptive use
   Polycythemia vera
   Heparin-induced thrombocytopenia
   Lupus anticoagulant/antiphospholipid syndrome

venograms (Fig. 125-2), whereas the thickened vein wall and a thrombus-filled lumen enhance differentially on transaxial and coronal slice imaging. Prominent bowel wall and perimesenteric enhancement are nonspecific findings that also can be seen with MVT. Different T2-weighted sequences also can show edema and ascites when present.

Duplex ultrasound often can detect intravenous echogenic thrombus, enlargement of the splanchnic veins, abnormal or absent flow within the splanchnic vein lumen, and lack of compressibility or respiratory variation in the thrombosed vein wall. The portal vein is usually less than 13 mm in diameter in normal adults, whereas it distends greater than 15 mm when acutely thrombosed.[3] High-definition ultrasound can show the thickening of the inflamed mesenteric vein wall. Abdominal duplex can be limited, however, if the bowel is distended with gas. Also, the results of ultrasound are known to vary because this test notoriously depends on the skills of the technician.

A variety of acquired and inherited hypercoagulable states are known to be associated with MVT (Table 125-2).[8,15-18] The most commonly associated induced hypercoagulable states include prior abdominal surgery; history of endoscopic sclerotherapy; neoplastic diseases (particularly pancreatic and colon cancers) and associated chemotherapeutic agents; and acquired thrombophilic blood disorders, such as antiphospholipid syndrome, hyperhomocysteinemia, and heparin-induced thrombocytopenia. Postsplenectomy thrombocytosis (early and late) and polycythemia vera also have been associated with MVT. Additionally, the use of oral contraceptive agents is thought to be responsible for approximately 5% of MVT cases (9% to 18% of cases in women).[9,19]

Deficiencies of the vitamin K–dependent coagulation inhibitors—proteins S and C (which account for about 5% of all venous thromboses)—and antithrombin III deficiency (which accounts for another 2% of all venous thrombotic events) are genetic risk factors that commonly have been identified in patients diagnosed with MVT.[20-25] Other genetic variances that have been reported to be associated with MVT include activated protein C resistance with factor V Leiden gene mutation, methylenetetrahydrofolate reductase mutations, and presence of the 20210 A allele of the prothrombin gene.[21,26,27]

A past medical history of thromboses or a family history of pathologic thrombophilia in combination with abdominal complaints should increase the index of suspicion for MVT. A hypercoagulable state is far more likely to be found in patients diagnosed with MVT than in patients found to have lower extremity deep venous thrombosis. In an update of our 2001 review, 37 of 41 patients (90%) had an identifiable hypercoagulable state, and 54% of the patients in this series had some form of acquired or heritable hematologic thrombophilic disorder associated with hypercoagulability. Some authors have chosen to classify MVT into primary and secondary forms, with the latter reserved for patients with a clearly defined underlying cause. We have elected to do away with this classification scheme because we believe that a careful search would define an underlying etiology in virtually every case.

Although the natural history of MVT is unknown and often relates directly to the extent of the thrombosis and to the underlying etiology, it does not seem to have the same ominous prognosis that has been associated with arterial occlusion. Nonetheless, if left undiagnosed and untreated, there is a distinct mortality associated with MVT. In complicated cases, at surgery or autopsy, the affected segments of bowel appear markedly edematous and darkly reddened. The mesentery is thick and rubbery, and the thrombotic process appears segmental. Foregut and colonic involvement are rare because of the many venous collaterals that drain the esophagus, stomach, and large bowel.[28] Sequestered volumes of third-space fluid are usually much more extensive than with mesenteric arterial occlusive diseases. This often massive sequestration of third-space fluid accounts for the significant volume requirements noted in

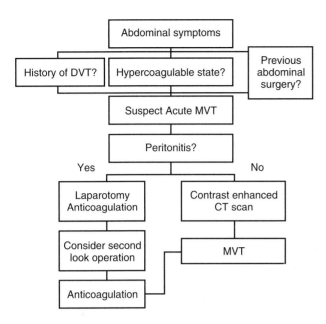

FIGURE 125-3 Management of acute mesenteric ischemia. DVT, deep venous thrombosis; MVT, mesenteric venous thrombosis.

patients who present with extensive MVT. Because of this potential for massive sequestration of third-space fluid, we have found invasive monitoring with a pulmonary artery catheter to be useful in complicated cases.

In our review, treatment ranged from close patient observation and bowel rest with or without anticoagulation to extensive bowel resection with venous thrombectomy. At present, we agree with most authors, who recommend conservative management for most MVT patients.[29-32] Conservative management includes bowel rest and aggressive anticoagulation with heparin and warfarin (Coumadin) (Fig. 125-3). Early anticoagulation with heparin followed by warfarin, usually for life, is recommended to limit thrombosis and reduce the likelihood of recurrent symptoms. Patients found to have asymptomatic or chronic MVT serendipitously on imaging performed for other indications should be evaluated for hypercoagulable disorders and should be considered for lifelong anticoagulation therapy. Full thrombophilia screening should be performed in all patients diagnosed with MVT, and the thrombophilic disorder should be treated properly with anticoagulation when indicated; most of these patients should have a good long-term prognosis.

Our published review also included four patients who underwent attempted treatment with thrombolytic agents and two patients who had attempted surgical or interventional venous thrombectomy. Thrombolysis has been attempted with systemic intravenous or intramesenteric arterial administration of thrombolytic agents and with directed infusions into the mesenteric veins via a transhepatic route.[33-36] None of the four patients who were treated with thrombolysis at our institution (two treated with intra-arterial urokinase infused via the superior mesenteric artery, one treated with transhepatic administration of tissue plasminogen activator, and one who underwent transhepatic mechanical thrombectomy with intramesenteric venous

urokinase infusion) developed significant radiographic evidence of decreased clot burden or were thought to have had hastened clinical improvement. Thrombolytic therapy carries risk for hemorrhage and has been reported elsewhere to have a low rate of radiographic or clinical success unless initiated soon after the thrombotic process begins.[15] Venous thrombectomy and intra-arterial or transhepatic thrombolysis should be reserved for only the most dire circumstances and only when the perceived short-term and long-term benefits outweigh the potential immediate risks involved because most patients improve with observation and anticoagulation alone.

The recognition and management of MVT remains a clinical challenge. MVT is a rare disease entity, and the patient presentation can be vague and varied. Prompt diagnosis may limit the severity of MVT, and treatment is almost always supportive and includes prompt patient anticoagulation. Finally, a specific hypercoagulable disorder must be sought and aggressively treated when it has been identified.

■ REFERENCES

1. Elliott JW: The operative relief of gangrene of intestine due to occlusion of the mesenteric vessels. Ann Surg 21:9-23, 1895.
2. Warren S, Eberhard TP: Mesenteric venous thrombosis. Surg Gynecol Obstet 61:102-121, 1935.
3. Kazmers A: Intestinal ischemia caused by venous thrombosis. In Rutherford RB (ed): Vascular Surgery, 5th ed. Philadelphia, WB Saunders, 2000, pp 1524-1531.
4. Rhee RY, Gloviczki P, Mendonca CT, et al: Mesenteric venous thrombosis: Still a lethal disease in the 1990s. J Vasc Surg 20:688-697, 1994.
5. Rius X, Escalante JF, Llaurado MJ, et al: Mesenteric infarction. World J Surg 3:489-493, 1979.
6. Ottinger LW, Austen WG: A study of 136 patients with mesenteric infarction. Surg Gynecol Obstet 124:251-261, 1967.
7. Kaleya RN, Boley SJ: Mesenteric venous thrombosis. In Najarian JS, Delaney JP (eds): Progress in Gastrointestinal Surgery. Chicago, Year Book Medical Publishers, 1989, pp 417-425.
8. Hassan HA, Raufman J-P: Mesenteric venous thrombosis. South Med J 92:558-562, 1999.
9. Kumar S, Sarr MG, Kamath PS: Mesenteric venous thrombosis. N Engl J Med 345:1683-1688, 2001.
10. Wilson C, Walker ID, Davidson JF, Imrie CW: Mesenteric venous thrombosis and antithrombin III deficiency. J Clin Pathol 40:906-908, 1987.
11. Morasch MD, Ebaugh JL, Chiou AC, et al: Mesenteric venous thrombosis: A changing clinical entity. J Vasc Surg 34:680-684, 2001.
12. Montany PF, Finley RK: Mesenteric venous thrombosis. Am Surg 54:161-166, 1988.
13. Mathews JE, White RR: Primary mesenteric venous occlusive disease. Am J Surg 122:579-583, 1971.
14. Condat B, Pessione F, Denninger MH, et al: Recent portal or mesenteric venous thrombosis: Increased recognition and frequent recanalization on anticoagulant therapy. Hepatology 32:466-470, 2000.
15. Morasch MD: Mesenteric venous thrombosis: Current concepts in diagnosis and treatment. In Pearce WH, Matsumura JS, Yao JST (eds): Trends in Vascular Surgery. Chicago, Precept Press, 2002, pp 473-478.
16. Gordon MB, Beckman JA: Successful anticoagulation with hirudin in a patient with mesenteric venous thrombosis and multiple coagulation abnormalities. Vasc Med 5:159-162, 2000.
17. Feenstra J, Vermeer RJ, Stricker BH: Mesenteric venous thrombosis attributed to docetaxel. Am J Clin Oncol 23:353-354, 2000.
18. Marie I, Levesque H, Lecam-Duchez V, et al: Mesenteric venous thrombosis revealing both factor II G20212A mutation and hyperhomocysteinemia related to pernicious anemia. Gastroenterology 118:237-238, 2000.

19. Hassan HA: Oral contraceptive-induced mesenteric venous thrombosis with resultant intestinal ischemia. J Clin Gastroenterol 29:90-95, 1999.

20. Wakefield TW: Coagulation and disorders of hemostasis. In Sidawy AN, Sumpio BE, DePalma RG (eds): The Basic Science of Vascular Disease. New York, Futura, 1997, pp 477-501.

21. Mitani M, Kuwabara Y, Kawamura H, et al: Mesenteric venous thrombosis associated with protein C deficiency. J Gastroenterol 34:387-389, 1999.

22. Amitrano L, Brancaccio V, Guardascione MA, et al: High prevalence of thrombophilic genotypes in patients with acute mesenteric vein thrombosis. Am J Gastroenterol 96:146-149, 2001.

23. Kato M, Iida S, Sato M, et al: Superior mesenteric venous thrombosis associated with a familial missense mutation (Pro626Leu) in the SHBG-like domain of the protein S molecule. Int J Hematol 75:100-103, 2002.

24. Matsushita I, Hanai H, Sato Y, et al: Protein-losing enteropathy caused by mesenteric venous thrombosis with protein C deficiency. J Clin Gastroenterol 30:94-97, 2000.

25. Lau LL, McMurray AH: Mesenteric venous thrombosis in protein S deficiency: Case report and literature review. Ulster Med J 68:33-35, 1999.

26. Bergenfeldt M, Svensson PJ, Borgstrom A: Mesenteric vein thrombosis due to factor V Leiden gene mutation. Br J Surg 86:1059-1062, 1999.

27. Zuazu-Jausoro I, Sanchez I, Fernandez MC, et al: Portal mesenteric venous thrombosis in a patient heterozygous for the 20210 A allele of the prothrombin gene. Haematologica 83:1129-1130, 1998.

28. Bramwit DN, Hummel WC: The superior venous and inferior mesenteric veins as collateral channels in inferior vena cava obstruction. Radiology 92:90-91, 1968.

29. Brunaud L, Antunes L, Collinet-Adler S, et al: Acute mesenteric venous thrombosis: Case for nonoperative management. J Vasc Surg 34:673-679, 2001.

30. Choudhary AM, Grayer D, Nelson A, Roberts I: Mesenteric venous thrombosis: A diagnosis not to be missed! J Clin Gastroenterol 31:179-182, 2000.

31. Chong AK, So JB, Ti TK: Use of laparoscopy in the management of mesenteric venous thrombosis. Surg Endosc 15:1042, 2001.

32. McGurgan P, Holohan M, McKenna P, Gorey TF: Idiopathic mesenteric thrombosis following caesarean section. Ir J Med Sci 169:149, 2000.

33. Sehgal M, Haskal ZJ: Use of transjugular intrahepatic portosystemic shunts during lytic therapy of extensive portal splenic and mesenteric venous thrombosis: Long-term follow-up. J Vasc Interv Radiol 11:61-65, 2000.

34. Rundback JH: Mesenteric venous thrombosis: Successful treatment by intraarterial lytic therapy. J Vasc Interv Radiol 10:98-99, 1999.

35. Ludwig DJ, Hauptmann E, Rosoff L Jr, Neuzil D: Mesenteric and portal vein thrombosis in a young patient with protein S deficiency treated with urokinase via the superior mesenteric artery. J Vasc Surg 30:551-554, 1999.

36. Tateishi A, Mitsui H, Oki T, et al: Extensive mesenteric vein and portal vein thrombosis successfully treated by thrombolysis and anticoagulation. J Gastroenterol Hepatol 16:1429-1433, 2001.

37. Sack J, Aldrete JS: Primary mesenteric venous thrombosis. Surg Gynecol Obstet 154:205-208, 1982.

38. Clavien PA, Harder F: Mesenteric venous thrombis. Helv Chir Acta 55:29-34, 1988.

39. Harward TRS, Green D, Bergan JJ, et al: Mesenteric venous thrombosis. J Vasc Surg 9:328-333, 1989.

40. Levy PJ, Krausz MM, Manny J: The role of second-look procedure in improving survival time for patients with mesenteric venous thrombosis. Surg Gynecol Obstet 170:287-291, 1990.

41. Grieshop RJ, Dalsing MC, Ckirit DF, et al: Acute mesenteric venous thrombosis: Revisited in a time of diagnostic clarity. Am J Surg 57:573-578, 1991.

Chapter

126

Portal Hypertension:
Surgical Management of Its Complications

KAJ JOHANSEN, MD, PhD

■ BACKGROUND

Portal hypertension, usually arising either from hepatic cirrhosis or (uncommonly) a structural abnormality of the portomesenteric or hepatic venous circulation, remains a significant medical and public health problem. Cirrhosis of the liver and its complications ranks 12th among all causes of mortality in North America[1]: bleeding resulting from esophagogastric varices is the leading cause of death worldwide from gastrointestinal (GI) hemorrhage. In the developing world such bleeding, usually arising as a consequence of schistosomal or viral infection of the liver, is a leading cause of nontraumatic mortality and morbidity among adults.

Development of the surgical portosystemic shunt (PSS) in the 1940s and 1950s was a major component in the evolution of vascular surgery. Remarkably, however, contemporary technologic developments in clinical pharmacology, interventional radiology, and endoscopy have profoundly altered—and diminished—the surgeon's role in the management of hepatic cirrhosis and portal hypertension. Operative management is much less commonplace in the care of variceal bleeders—to the extent that American Board of Surgery examiners are now discouraged from asking candidates questions about surgical therapy for portal hypertension. The fourth edition of this text (1994) extensively discussed portal hypertension in five chapters covering 34 pages. For this sixth edition, the author recommended, and the editorial board agreed on, a single chapter of 10 pages.

However, as for all varieties of GI hemorrhage, surgeons must continue to be available when bleeding is torrential and uncontrollable or when the lack of available gastroenterologic or interventional radiologic expertise requires emergency surgical intervention. Further, as discussed subsequently, it may well be that the therapeutic pendulum has swung too far away from surgical involvement for certain of these patients. This chapter, therefore, represents a contemporary view of the diagnosis and management of portal hypertension and its complications, emphasizing those areas in which surgical involvement remains important and potentially crucial.

■ PATHOPHYSIOLOGY

Total hepatic blood flow approximates 2000 mL/min, 80% of which passes into and through the liver via the porto-mesenteric circulation and 20% via the hepatic artery and its branches. Normal portal venous pressure is 5 mm Hg.

When an obstruction to portomesenteric venous blood flow occurs—such as a portal vein thrombosis (PVT), intra-hepatic compression or occlusion of venous radicles (such as occurs in Laënnec's cirrhosis) or in a posthepatic scenario (e.g., Budd-Chiari syndrome)—portal venous pressure rises sharply. (An uncommon cause of a rise in portal hyper-tension may result from an increase in total hepatic *inflow*, such as might occur with a hepatoportal or splenic arterio-venous fistula.) The development of portal hypertension is defined by an increase in the wedged hepatic vein pressure to greater than 12 mm Hg. This is an important threshold number, for it is widely agreed that variceal hemorrhage is unlikely at a portal pressure gradient of below 12 mm Hg.[2]

It has traditionally been thought that the basis for the development of portal hypertension, and the specific level to which portal pressure rises, is determined primarily by mechanical obstruction of the hepatic sinusoid by the scarring/reparative process inherent in hepatic cirrhosis. Such a view is not difficult to comprehend given the some-time profound fibrosis seen on histologic examination of cirrhotic liver. Indeed, investigation of various antifibrotic agents (e.g., penicillamine) has been a conceptually attrac-tive investigative effort in the context of a potential pharma-cologic treatment for cirrhosis.[3]

However, recent investigation has suggested a more dynamic basis for portal hypertension than a simple mechanical/obstructive explanation. Most relevant here appear to be alterations in the nitric oxide (NO)/nitric oxide synthase (NOS) pathway.[4] Current evidence suggests that the degree of portal hypertension in cirrhosis is based on an excess of NOS activity in the splanchnic venous circulation (leading to vasodilation and increased portomesenteric blood flow) but paradoxically an intrahepatic diminution of NO, resulting in vasoconstriction and increased portal pressure.[4,5] An overflow of NO shunted into the systemic circulation is thought to result in the hyperdynamic circu-latory state seen in advanced cirrhosis. The marked interest in NO donors or inhibitors elsewhere in the body, such as in the pulmonary circulation,[6] may result in the elucidation of agents that can lower portal hypertension by their direct impact either on the splanchnic venous circulation or on intrahepatic portal venous capacitance.

Other physiologic pathways thought to have the potential for fruitful exploration regarding underlying physiology of portal hypertension in cirrhosis include: hyperactivity of the sympathetic nervous system,[7] abnormalities of prosta-

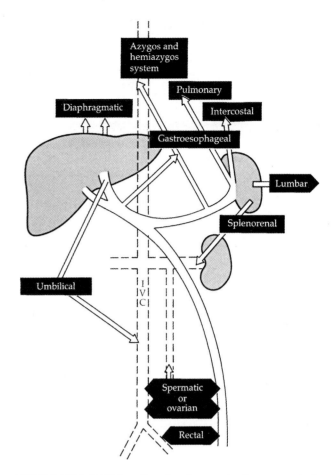

FIGURE 126-1 Multiple collateral pathways arise in response to the development of portal hypertension. Most important clinically, from the perspective of variceal hemorrhage, are pathways from the portal vein to the azygos or hemiazygos system via the gastroesophageal variceal plexus and those communicating with hemorrhoidal tributaries of the hypogastric venous circuit. IVC, inferior vena cava. (From Sherlock S: The portal venous system and portal hypertension. In Diseases of the Liver and Biliary System, 8th ed. Oxford, Blackwell, 1989, p 166.)

glandin production and metabolism,[8] and vasodilation due to certain neuropeptides.[9]

As for all other venous beds in the body, the development of portal venous hypertension results in development of a multipotential collateral bed (Fig. 126-1). Although many of the collaterals that develop as a response to the hyperten-sive portal system are clinically silent (e.g., those in the abdominal wall or in the retroperitoneum), a number of col-lateral pathways, either natural or iatrogenic, may be of clinical significance.

Most important, of course, are venous collaterals that develop between the portal and splenic veins in the abdomen and the azygos/hemiazygos circulation in the thorax, especially the mediastinum. When fully developed these collaterals, which course in the submucosa of the duode-num and stomach en route to the lower and middle aspects of the esophagus, become clinically relevant as gastric and esophageal varices. Because the splanchnic venous system, including its tributaries and its branches, is devoid of valves, the same high pressure is distributed throughout the system—meaning that a portal vein pressure of 40 to

50 mm Hg resulting from severe hepatic cirrhosis can be measured in the varices protruding out into the lumen of the lower esophagus or the fundus of the stomach.

Although the precise mechanism by which varices actually bleed remains obscure, a combination of a thin-walled vein under extremely high venous pressures, combined with the not-uncommon coagulation and platelet defects found in cirrhotics, can obviously result in substantial and even torrential bleeding once the mucosa overlying varix wall is breached.

Other clinically important collateral pathways decompressing the hypertensive portomesenteric circulation include communications to the middle and inferior hemorrhoidal veins (resulting in rectal varices) and collateralization between the reopened umbilical vein and branches of the internal mammary and inferior epigastric veins (presenting as prominent abdominal wall varicosities known as a *caput medusae*). Important iatrogenic sites of such portomesenteric venous collateralization occur at any point where the gut becomes adherent to the parietal peritoneum or where stomata (e.g., colostomies, ileostomies) are attached to the abdominal wall. (A unifying anatomic principle for the development of such varices is their location at the interface between the splanchnic and systemic venous circulations.)

■ CLINICAL PRESENTATIONS

Most patients presenting with bleeding complications of portal hypertension experience painless hematemesis. It is not uncommon for such patients to manifest their underlying advanced end-stage liver disease (ESLD) with signs such as jaundice, ascites, portomesenteric encephalopathy (PSE), or, alternatively, manifestations of the underlying condition that led to their problem (e.g., signs of acute alcoholism, delirium tremens). A much smaller percentage of individuals present with hematochezia or melena. Because of the frequently markedly elevated venous pressure within esophagogastric varices, and these patients' concurrent platelet and coagulation defects, bleeding may be brisk and even exsanguinating. Patients not uncommonly present in shock from variceal hemorrhage, and the mortality rate from a first variceal hemorrhage still exceeds 30%.[10]

A second determinant of choice of management and resultant and clinical outcome is the cirrhotic patient's physiologic state, encoded in scoring systems for hepatocellular function and overall clinical status. Child class (Table 126-1) and Pugh scores (Table 126-2) continue to be

accepted as having substantial predictive accuracy regarding clinical outcome following various interventions to treat complications of cirrhosis and portal hypertension.

■ PORTAL HYPERTENSIVE BLEEDING: ACUTE CARE

Because the acute mortality rate, and the long-term morbidity, associated with bleeding from portal hypertension is extraordinarily high, it is likely that patients with variceal hemorrhage should be resuscitated, stabilized, and then transferred to a regional center for specialized care. However, this assertion is unproven.

Because, as noted, the mortality risk associated with an initial variceal hemorrhage approaches one in three, an aggressive approach to such patients is obligatory. In fact, simultaneous resuscitation, diagnosis, and (if possible) bleeding control are the hallmark of optimal therapy in this setting. Installation of large-bore intravenous lines, admission to an intensive care unit, serial monitoring of hematocrit, and administration of appropriate volumes of crystalloid, blood and fresh frozen plasma should go hand in hand with the obtaining of blood tests relevant to liver disease (and other disorders); virtually simultaneously emergency upper endoscopy (esophagogastroduodenoscopy [EGD]) should take place as soon as possible.

EGD is crucial in patients whose GI hemorrhage potentially arises from portal hypertension for both diagnostic and therapeutic reasons. First, up to a third of patients with portal hypertension and GI bleeding do so from a nonportal hypertensive source, such as peptic ulcer disease, gastritis, or Mallory-Weiss tear.[11] Directing therapeutic modalities toward portal hypertension when in fact the patient needs treatment for a bleeding duodenal ulcer obviously is fruitless.

Second, in that group of individuals whose GI tract bleeding is indeed due to portal hypertension, EGD provides an accurate description of the specific identity, anatomic locale, and extent of the bleeding site.

Third, presuming suitable targets, expertise, and equipment, EGD offers an unparalleled opportunity to halt variceal hemorrhage at the bedside. This may be carried out by the performance of endoscopic variceal sclerotherapy (EVS), endoscopic variceal ligation (EVL) with rubber bands, or on occasion a combination of these two therapies. Both EVS and EVL can be highly effective; a randomized,

Table 126-1 Child Classification

FACTORS	CATEGORY		
	A	B	C
Bilirubin (mg/dL)	<2.0	2.0-3.0	>3.0
Albumin (mg/dL)	>3.5	3.0-3.5	<3.0
Ascites	None	Reversible	Refractory
Encephalopathy	None	Minimal	Spontaneous
Nutrition (muscle mass)	Normal	Fair	Poor

Table 126-2 Pugh Score*

FACTORS	POINTS FOR INCREASING ABNORMALITY		
	1	2	3
Encephalopathy (grade)	Normal (0)	1 or 2	3 or 4
Albumin (mg/dL)	>3.5	2.8-3.5	<2.8
Bilirubin (mg/dL)	1.0-2.0	2.0-3.0	>3.0
Ascites	Absent	Slight	Significant
Prothrombin time (seconds prolonged)	1.4	4-6	>6

*Grade A = 5 or 6 points; grade B = 7-9 points; grade C = 10-15 points.

controlled trial has suggested that band ligation is more effective and has fewer complications than does injection sclerotherapy.[12] Emergency endoscopic therapy is associated in more than 90% of cases with cessation of variceal hemorrhage. Control of a specific bleeding varix by injection or rubber band ligation is commonly the basis for cessation of bleeding; concurrent administration of vasoconstrictor medications, clotting factors, and/or platelets surely helps. The not-infrequent concurrence of hypovolemia and shock likely contributes to bleeding cessation as well.

An important adjunctive treatment, universally used and likely of substantial relevance although not confirmed statistically, is the utilization of various pharmacologic vasoconstrictors or venodilators that reduce portal tributary blood flow and, therefore, portal pressure. In longest use has been intravenous vasopressin (standard dosage, 0.4 µ/min) now commonly used in conjunction with intravenous nitroglycerin (standard dosage, 10 to 20 µg/min) administered to diminish the coronary arterial vasoconstrictive effects of vasopressin.

More often administered in contemporary practice is octreotide, a synthetic somatostatin analogue (standard dosage, 25 to 50 µg intravenous bolus followed by 25 to 50 µg/hr). Both vasopressin (or vasopressin/nitroglycerin) and octreotide have been demonstrated to reduce the portal pressure gradient and to be associated with a significant reduction in blood loss and early variceal rebleeding.[13,14] Octreotide is the drug of choice for initial control of variceal bleeding in most centers in North America. Neither pharmacologic approach, however, has been independently associated with prolongation of survival in patients in whom it has been administered. Another somatostatin analogue, terlipressin, used widely in Europe but not approved by the U.S. Food and Drug Administration, has been associated with a statistically significant prolongation of survival—presumably from its effect on diminishing the magnitude of the initial variceal hemorrhage and the likelihood of early recurrence of hemorrhage.[13,14]

In approximately 5% of patients with variceal hemorrhage, bleeding is torrential enough that it cannot be controlled by endoscopic means, even in the presence of pharmacologic vasoconstrictor/venodilating agents. In such circumstances the use of an esophagogastric balloon tamponade device (Sengstaken-Blakemore) may be life saving.[15] Once inserted, these devices can be used to control esophagogastric variceal hemorrhage for up to 48 hours, after which tamponade must be released at least temporarily to avoid esophageal or gastric fundal mucosal necrosis: Great care must be maintained to ensure that the deflated gastric balloon of the device is indeed in the stomach before inflating it, since esophageal perforation is commonplace (and generally lethal) if the device is inflated in the lower esophagus. Since the most common complications associated with esophagogastric balloon tamponade relate to pulmonary aspiration, endotracheal intubation and mechanical ventilation are an obligatory part of management of patients in whom esophagogastric balloon tamponade is being used.

Emergency operative therapy—either portacaval shunt or esophagogastric devascularization—has generally been considered to be imprudent as an initial intervention because of excessive early postoperative mortality rates. In a center where patients with variceal hemorrhage can be quickly conducted to the operating room without time being wasted on extensive diagnostic or therapeutic maneuvers, mortality associated with emergency portacaval shunt may be expected to reach the remarkably low levels reported by Orloff and Bell.[16]

■ DEFINITIVE CARE

As noted, the combination of successful endoscopic therapy, administration of pharmacologic agents designed to lower portal pressure, and restitution of volume and blood-clotting factors generally results in cessation of hemorrhage and stabilization of the variceal bleeder. Although clinicians' tendency too frequently is simply resuscitate the patient, perhaps initiate an alcohol rehabilitation program, and discharge the patient, such instincts should be vigorously resisted. Failing definitive therapy, more than 70% of those whose variceal bleeding is initially controlled will rebleed, each episode being associated with a greater than 50% likelihood of mortality. Thus, exploiting the index hospitalization to initiate one or another form of semipermanent protection against variceal rebleeding is crucial.

Of the various forms of therapy designed to provide definitive control of bleeding, particular advantages or disadvantages may be present with each of the following options: long-term pharmacologic administration of beta-blocking agents, chronic endoscopic variceal therapy, transjugular intrahepatic portosystemic shunt (TIPS), surgical shunts, and orthotopic liver transplantation (OLT). To a great extent the choice for one form or another of such definitive therapy depends on available expertise and, even more important, on the patient's general overall and specific hepatocellular functional status. The following sections summarize the decision-making processes regarding each of these potential therapeutic approaches.

Chronic Beta Blockade

The administration of a nonselective beta blocker can significantly reduce the portal pressure gradient, and the chronic administration of such agents has become a mainstay both of primary presentation of bleeding in cirrhotics with varices, as well as the secondary prophylaxis of patients who have bled from esophagogastric varices.[2,17] Randomized, controlled trials of beta-blocking agents suggest a statistically significant reduction in the incidence of recurrent variceal hemorrhage.[17,18] However, such patients so treated still have a greater than 50% likelihood of a recurrent variceal hemorrhage, making beta blockade alone an inadequate preventive measure against variceal bleeding.

Up to 30% of cirrhotic patients are intolerant of the side effects of beta blockade—especially in view of the significant hepatopulmonary syndrome that can occur with far-advanced cirrhosis.[19] Additionally, the fact that beta blockade, which reduces basal heart rate and significantly inhibits the ability to generate a reflex tachycardia in response to the hypovolemia that might result with variceal rehemorrhage, is also a significant concern to be maintained about the chronic use of beta blockade in cirrhotics with esophagogastric varices. Isosorbide mononitrate alone[20] or in concert with beta blockade[21] can mitigate some concerns about the use of beta-blocking agents used alone in the primary and secondary prevention of variceal hemorrhage.

Chronic Endoscopic Therapy

An important and widely used adjunct for secondary prophylaxis of variceal hemorrhage is chronic variceal therapy—either by injection or by rubber band ligation. This approach, carried out on a serial basis until complete eradication of varices is demonstrated, is highly effective and has been associated with a significant reduction in mortality from variceal hemorrhage. The approach works most effectively with esophageal varices; it is less demonstrably useful in patients with gastric varices and is not useful at all for portal hypertensive gastropathy.

A cumulative risk of complications present with chronic endoscopic therapy, including esophageal stricture, esophageal mucosal ulceration, gastroesophageal reflux disease, and esophageal perforation with mediastinitis. Chronic variceal therapy has been associated with portal and splenic vein thrombosis; conceptually, obliteration of gastroesophageal variceal pathways might be expected to raise portal pressure and the risk of bleeding, such as from gastric varices, but this is not a proven concern. Chronic recurrent endoscopic therapy is best carried out in compliant patients who live near the medical center; those who are noncompliant or cannot be because they live in rural regions distant from the medical center have an excessive risk of variceal hemorrhage[22] and should be treated by other means (see later).

Transjugular Portosystemic Shunt

One of the fruits of the endovascular revolution of the past 20 years has been the development of a minimally invasive interventional radiologic means of constructing a transhepatic portosystemic shunt. The technique was developed experimentally by Rosch and associates[23] in the 1960s and initially carried out in humans by Colapinto and colleagues[24] in 1983: by 1995 the technology and the therapeutic approach had matured enough that several large series had been presented.[25-27] TIPS is performed in the interventional radiology suite commonly (although not exclusively) with the patient under general anesthesia. "Road-mapping" imaging techniques and ultrasonographic guidance are used to assist the operator's angiographic needle in crossing liver parenchyma between the hepatic vein (usually the right one) and the right branch of the portal vein. Once access has been gained to the portal vein, the parenchymal tract between the hepatic vein and the portal vein is dilated and then stented. Adjunctive coil embolization of the left gastric vein and other potential variceal sources can be carried out simultaneously.

TIPS technology and capabilities have matured to the extent that the technical success rate of the procedure exceeds 95%, and early technical morbidity and mortality is uncommon. Because portomesenteric circulation is immediately decompressed, variceal hemorrhage halts immediately and TIPS may not infrequently be life saving because of this. TIPS has also been found useful in the management of medically intractable ascites, hepatic hydrothorax, and the hepatorenal syndrome.[28-30] TIPS has had a particularly beneficial effect in ESLD patients who commence variceal bleeding while awaiting liver transplantation.[31] Such patients were previously destined to a high likelihood of immediate mortality or at best of having their bleeding halted by an emergency surgical shunt (even if successful at halting hemorrhage, a procedure of major magnitude that may irretrievably complicate consideration of a future OLT).

The important morbidity (and mortality) associated with TIPS relates paradoxically to the fact that (1) it works too well and (2) its beneficial effects are short lived.

PSSs have long been recognized to be associated with accelerated liver failure—especially manifested by the acute neuropsychiatric deterioration termed *PSE*. Recent animal and human investigation has clearly documented that this phenomenon occurs as a consequence of the severity of hepatocellular dysfunction *and* the degree of portosystemic shunting. Unfortunately, the incidence of new PSE in patients successfully treated with TIPS approximates 25%,[32] likely in part because TIPS has commonly been used in patients with far-advanced hepatocellular dysfunction, and because the portal decompression associated with TIPS (usually via a 10-mm stent) is near total. If liver transplantation is not carried out with alacrity in such patients, their PSE may prove intractable and they will either die as a consequence or the TIPS channel will need to be blocked by coil embolization.[33]

The second major complication that significantly reduces TIPS' clinical utility is its lack of durable patency. Although the basis for the technique's rapid failure rate is likely multifactorial, its predictably rapid stenosis/occlusion rate has been reproduced in all large series so far, with the likelihood of variceal rebleeding or TIPS occlusion/stenosis exceeding 50% within 1 year after insertion.[34] It is clear that close angiographic or (perhaps) duplex sonographic surveillance can alert the clinician to an impeding TIPS failure, thereby permitting a repeat intervention before complete occlusion and/or repeat variceal hemorrhage—but this requires a resource-intensive approach in a patient population that is notoriously noncompliant and undependable.

Newer technologies for keeping TIPS channels more durably patent are under investigation. A PTFE-graft covered stent has appeared to have reasonably favorable results in early investigations.[35]

Surgical Shunts

Surgical portal decompression procedures ("shunts") were developed in the 1940s and were one of the first clinical manifestations of the burgeoning specialty of vascular surgery (Fig. 126-2). Surgical shunts are extraordinarily effective: 90% to 95% of shunted patients are permanently protected from recurrent variceal hemorrhage. Only belatedly, in randomized, control trials carried out in the 1960s and 1970s.[36-39] did it become clear that standard total shunts (i.e., those that completely decompress the portal, system) fail to improve overall survival, notwithstanding their success at permanently halting variceal bleeding. Improvement in mortality from variceal hemorrhage in such patients is almost exactly balanced by a sharp increase in death from accelerated liver failure. Worse, a marked increase in

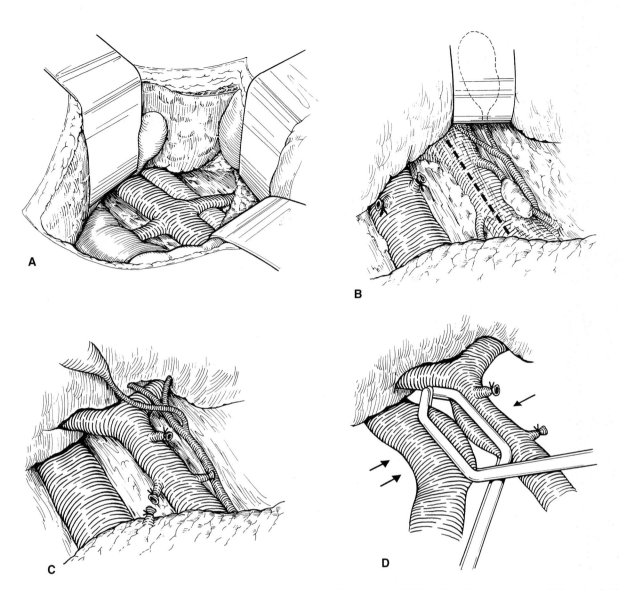

FIGURE 126-2 Portacaval shunt. **A,** An extensive Kocher maneuver is performed to expose the infrahepatic inferior vena cava caudally to a point just below the renal veins. **B,** Exposing the portal vein is best approached by incising the peritoneum over the lateral hepatoduodenal ligament *(hatched line)*; alternatively, careful dissection of a prominent, anteriorly placed lymph node may expose the portal vein. **C,** Mobilization of the portal vein by careful ligature and division of one or more medially directed coronary veins (two are depicted here) and a constant, large posterolateral portal vein tributary from the head of the pancreas. **D,** Properly mobilized inferior vena cava and portal vein can be readily approximated for side-to-side anastomosis using apposing Satinsky clamps. (**A-D,** From Johansen K, Helton WS: The relief of portal hypertension. In Yao JST, Jamieson CW [eds]: Rob and Smith's Operative Surgery, 5th ed. London, Chapman & Hall, 1994.)

Continued

incapacitating PSE makes a return to functional status for survivors of operative portacaval shunts problematic in many cases.

Is there a way that the traditional total shunt can be modified so that this procedure's permanent protection against variceal bleeding can be maintained yet the risk of acceleration of liver failure and PSE can be mitigated? Various attempts at refining the standard total shunt demonstrated some promise. Warren and others developed the distal splenorenal shunt (DSRS) (Fig. 126-3) as a means by which the morbidity of the standard shunt could be avoided.[40,41] Although the selectivity (maintenance of antegrade portal vein flow) in most DSRS patients is not maintained,[42] long-term follow-up demonstrates significant protection against variceal rebleeding and a reduced risk of PSE in many patients so treated.

More recently Collins and coworkers[43] and Johansen[44] have developed the concept of *partial* portal decompression—construction of a shunt that decompresses the hypertensive portal system, but only to a portacaval pressure gradient that is physiologic yet still less than the threshold level of 12 mm Hg below which variceal bleeding does not occur. Follow-up studies demonstrate that this approach does indeed protect against variceal rebleeding yet with a markedly reduced likelihood of liver failure and PSE.[43-45]

Many good-risk cirrhotic patients with complications of

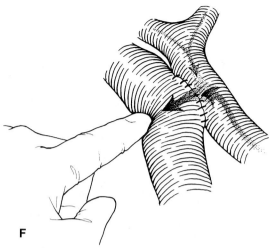

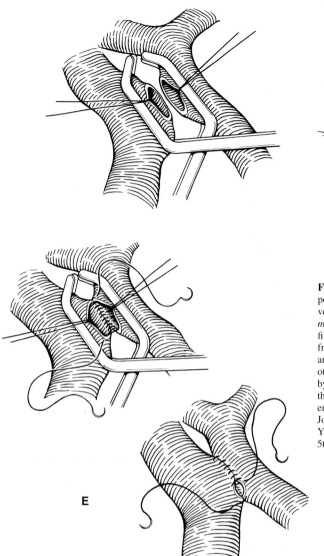

F

E

FIGURE 126-2, cont'd   Portacaval shunt. **E,** Completing the portacaval anastomosis: *Top,* A parallel cavotomy and portal venotomy are carried out, and stay sutures are placed as shown; *middle,* after starting the anastomotic suture (a 4-0 or 5-0 mono-filament stitch) at the top, the posterior walls are anastomosed from within using the first "arm" of the stitch; and *bottom,* the anterior closure is accomplished from the outside using the other arm of the stitch. **F,** Patency of the shunt can be assessed by palpation of the inferior vena cava wall opposite the shunt; a thrill is frequently noted. Pressures should be measured to ensure that portal decompression is adequate. (**E** and **F,** From Johansen K, Helton WS: The relief of portal hypertension. In Yao JST, Jamieson CW [eds]: Rob and Smith's Operative Surgery, 5th ed. London, Chapman & Hall, 1994.)

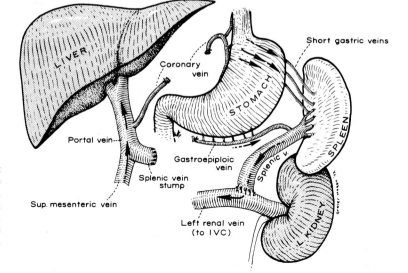

FIGURE 126-3   Conceptually, the distal splenorenal shunt of Warren and colleagues[40,41] combines decompression of the esophagogastric variceal complex via the short gastric veins, the spleen, and the splenic vein into the left renal vein with maintenance of a high-pressure portomesenteric circulation. This latter state results from closure of the central end of the splenic vein as well as meticulous ligation of all potential right-to-left coronary and gastroepiploic venous collaterals. IVC, inferior vena cava.

portal hypertension are referred for TIPS. Because Child classes A and B patients survive for prolonged periods (especially if they stop drinking), TIPS is demonstrably a poor management option. Helton and associates demonstrated in a case-control study comparing Child A and B patients that those undergoing TIPS had a vastly greater likelihood of rebleeding, recurrent hospitalization, and repeat intervention than those undergoing surgical shunt.[46] Zacks and colleagues' decision analysis suggested hugely excessive costs—more than $150,000 per life-year saved—if TIPS is used for portal decompression in good-risk cirrhotics.[47]

Liver Transplantation

Replacement with a new liver is curative for portal hypertension and its complications. However, the well-publicized and steadily worsening shortage of donor livers make this optimal therapy mostly irrelevant for the vast majority of patients with the bleeding (or other) complications of cirrhosis and portal hypertension. Most patients with alcohol-induced ESLD are not candidates for OLT, primarily because they are either still drinking (most liver transplantation services require at least 6 months of proven alcohol abstinence before transplantation will be considered) or because such patients have far-advanced organ dysfunction elsewhere—cardiomyopathy, pancreatitis, central nervous system deterioration, and so forth. For those cirrhotic patients who are able to undergo OLT, graft and patient survival rates are approximately 80% at 2 years and do not differ from those values in patients undergoing transplantation for reasons other than those associated with portal hypertension.

In patients who are actual or potential candidates for OLT, treatment with TIPS is much to be preferred over chronic endoscopic therapy or, especially, surgical PSS. The latter approach, although it no longer absolutely interdicts OLT and no longer has a significant negative effect on posttransplant mortality,[48] nevertheless significantly increases the complexity of the subsequent transplant operation.[49] This is most true of prior shunt procedures carried out in the hilum of the cirrhotic liver, although complications such as PVT may follow on DSRS or other peripheral shunts and thereby also complicate a later attempt at liver transplantation.

■ UNCOMMON TYPES OF PORTAL HYPERTENSION

One circumstance in which surgical involvement and expertise continues to be obligatory is in the setting of partial or complete thrombosis of the extrahepatic splanchnic or hepatic venous system. This occurs occasionally in the neonatal setting (usually due to septic pylephlebitis that results in thrombosis of the portal vein) but most commonly in contemporary clinical practice among subjects with various hypercoagulable (prothrombotic) states.[50] PVT per se does not warrant prophylactic intervention against future complications of portal hypertension: Natural history studies show that the course of such patients is set primarily by that of their underlying hematologic disorder, and less than 5% suffer lethal portal hypertensive bleeding.[51] If such bleeding

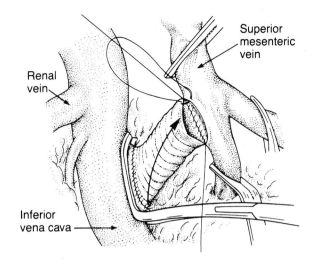

FIGURE 126-4 Mesocaval shunt. Anastomosis of a graft to the infrarenal inferior vena cava has been accomplished, and the anastomosis to the posterolateral superior mesenteric vein has been partially completed. Giving the prosthetic graft approximately a 30% clockwise twist (*solid arrow over graft*) accommodates the different vectors of the superior mesenteric vein and the inferior vena cava and eliminates any risk of kinking of the graft.

does occur and cannot be controlled by the usual "medical" means, mesocaval shunting—best with autogenous vein[52] or externally supported PTFE grafts (Fig. 126-4)[53] is the optimal approach. The pathologic clotting tendency that led to the problem in the first place makes the risk of shunt thrombosis high: chronic anticoagulation may be required.

Particularly vexing to manage are patients with portal hypertensive bleeding in the presence of diffuse splanchnic venous thrombosis. With the portal, splenic, and superior mesenteric veins occluded, no TIPS or surgical shunt is possible. Medical management, such as endoscopic therapy, is often stymied because of variceal bleeding in remote sites, such as the duodenum, proximal jejunum, and colon. Proper management of such patients includes operative approaches to diminish total splanchnic blood flow (e.g., splenectomy) and to halt variceal bleeding where it occurs (e.g., transgastric esophageal staple transection, radical proximal gastric devascularization). Sugiura and Futagawa advanced the concept of a two-stage operative approach including esophageal devascularization via a left thoracotomy followed several weeks later by laparotomy, splenectomy, and proximal gastric devascularization.[54] Orloff and associates[55] has championed radical esophagogastrectomy as an effective palliative procedure in this setting, whereas Orozco,[56] Caps,[57] and their coworkers have promoted a single-stage left-upper quadrant devascularization approach.

Diffuse thrombosis of the hepatic veins can result in abdominal pain, ascites formation, and, over time, hepatic necrosis—the Budd-Chiari syndrome. Many such patients have an underlying hypercoagulable state. If detected early, catheter-directed thrombolysis and hepatic vein angioplasty can reverse the process.[58] In established Budd-Chiari syndrome the proper management depends on the degree of hepatocellular deterioration as manifest by liver function studies and biopsy. A useful algorithm, as advanced by

Bismuth and Sherlock[59] and Langer and colleagues,[60] is to carry out large-bore side-to-side portacaval shunt when liver biopsy abnormalities are relatively minor. However, when far-advanced hepatic centrilobular necrosis is present on liver biopsy, liver transplantation may be the best alternative.

■ REFERENCES

1. Anonymous: National Center for Health Statistics. US Department of Health and Human Services, 2003.
2. Bosch J, Garcia-Pagan JC: Prevention of variceal rebleeding. Lancet 361:452-954, 2003.
3. Bavdekar AR, Bhave SA, Pradhan AM, et al: Long-term survival in Indican childhood cirrhosis treated with D-penicillamine. Arch Dis Child 74:32-35, 1996.
4. Vallance P, Moncada S: Hyperdynamic circulation in cirrhosis: A role for nitric oxide. Lancet 337:776-778, 1991.
5. Sogni P, Moreau R, Gadano A, Lebrec D: The role of nitric oxide in the hyperdynamic circulatory syndrome associated with portal hypertension. J Hepatol 23:218-224, 1995.
6. Moncada S, Palmer R, Higgs E: Nitric oxide: Physiology, pathophysiology, and pharmacology. Pharmacol Rev 43:109-142, 1991.
7. Gaudin C, Braillon A, Poo JL, et al: Plasma catecholamines in patients with presinusoidal portal hypertension: Comparison with cirrhotic patients and non portal hypertensive subjects. Hepatology 13:913-916, 1991.
8. Oberti F, Sogni P, Cailmail S, et al: Role of prostacyclin in hemodynamic alterations in conscious rats with extrahepatic or intrahepatic portal hypertension. Hepatology 18:621-627, 1993.
9. Lebrec D, Bataille C, Bercoff E, Valla D: Hemodynamic changes in patients with portal vein obstruction. Hepatology 3:550-553, 1982.
10. Graham D, Smith JL: The course of patients after variceal hemorrhage. Gastroenterology 80:800-809, 1981.
11. Jensen DM, Kovacs TOG, Jutabha R, et al: Prospective study of the causes and outcomes of severe UGI hemorrhage in cirrhotics [Abstract]. Gastrointest Endosc 49:AB167, 1999.
12. Laine L, Cook D: Endoscopic ligation compared with sclerotherapy for treatment of esophageal variceal bleeding: A meta-analysis. Ann Intern Med 123:280-287, 1995.
13. Bosch J: Medical treatment of portal hypertension. Digestion 59:547-555, 1998.
14. Chan LY, Sung JJY: The role of pharmaco-therapy for acute variceal hemorrhage in the era of endoscopic hemostasis. Aliment Pharmacol Ther 11:45-50, 1997.
15. Avgerinos A, Armonis A: Balloon tamponade technique and efficacy in variceal haemorrhage. Scand J Gastroenterol 207(Suppl):11-16, 1994.
16. Orloff MJ, Bell RH Jr: Long-term survival after emergency portacaval shunting for bleeding varices in patients with alcoholic cirrhosis. Am J Surg 151:176-182, 1986.
17. D'Amico G, Pagliaro L, Bosch J: The treatment of portal hypertension: A meta-analytic review. Hepatology 22:332-354, 1995.
18. D'Amico G, Pagliaro L, Bosch J: Pharmacological treatment of portal hypertension: An evidence-based approach. Semin Liver Dis 19:475-505, 1999.
19. Yao EH, Kong MC, Hsue GL, et al: Pulmonary function changes in cirrhosis of the liver. Am J Gastroenterol 82:352, 1987.
20. Garcia-Pagan JC, Villanueva C, Vila MC, et al: Isosorbide mononitrate in the prevention of first variceal bleed in patients who cannot receive beta-blockers. Gastroenterology 121:908-914, 2001.
21. Gournay J, Masliah C, Martin T, et al: Isosorbide mononitrate and propranolol compared with propranolol alone for the prevention of variceal rebleeding. Hepatology 31:1239-1245, 2000.
22. Rikkers LF, Jin G, Burnett DA, et al: Shunt surgery versus endoscopic sclerotherapy for variceal hemorrhage: Late results of a randomized trial. Am J Surg 165:27, 1993.
23. Rosch J, Hanafee WN, Snow H: Transjugular portal venography and radiologic portacaval shunt: An experimental study. Radiology 92:1112-1115, 1969.
24. Colapinto RF, Stronell RD, Gildiner M, et al: Formation of intrahepatic portosystemic shunts using a balloon dilatation catheter: Preliminary clinical experience. AJR Am J Roentgenol 140:709, 1983.
25. Richter GM, Noeldge G, Palmaz JC, et al: Transjugular intrahepatic portacaval stent shunt: Preliminary clinical results. Radiology 174:1027, 1990.
26. Zemel G, Katzen BT, Becker GJ, et al: Percutaneous transjugular portosystemic shunt. JAMA 266:390, 1991.
27. LaBerge JM, Somberg KA, Lake JR, et al: Two-year outcome following transjugular intrahepatic portosystemic shunt for variceal bleeding: Results in 90 patients. Gastroenterology 108:1143-1151, 1995.
28. Ochs A, Rossle M, Haag K, et al: The transjugular intrahepatic portosystemic stent-shunt for refractory ascites. N Engl J Med 332:1192-1197, 1995.
29. Gordon FD, Anastopoulos HT, Crenshaw W, et al: The successful treatment of symptomatic refractory hepatic hydrothorax with transjugular intrahepatic portosystemic shunt. Hepatology 25:1366-1369, 1997.
30. Guevara M, Gines P, Bandi JC, et al: Transjugular intrahepatic portosystemic shunt in the hepatorenal syndrome: Effects on renal function and vasoactive systems. Hepatology 28:416-422, 1998.
31. Ring EJ, Lake JR, Roberts JP, et al: Using percutaneous intrahepatic portosystemic shunts to control variceal bleeding prior to liver transplantation. Ann Intern Med 116:304, 1992.
32. Somberg KA, Riegler JL, Doherty M, et al: Hepatic encephalopathy following transjugular intrahepatic portosystemic shunts (TIPS): Incidence and risk factors. Hepatology 16:122A, 1992.
33. Kerlan RK Jr, LaBerge JM, Baker EL, et al: Successful reversal of hepatic encephalopathy with intentional occlusion of transjugular intrahepatic portosystemic shunts. J Vasc Intervent Radiol 6:917, 1995.
34. Sanyal AJ, Freedman AM, Luketic VA, et al: The natural history of portal hypertension after transjugular intrahepatic portosystemic shunts. Gastroenterology 112:1040, 1997.
35. Saxon RR, Timmermans HA, Uchida BT, et al: Stent-grafts for revision of TIPS stenoses and occlusions: A clinical pilot study. J Vasc Intervent Radiol 8:539-544, 1997.
36. Jackson FC, Perrin EB, Felix WR, et al: A clinical investigation of the portacaval shunt: V. Survival analysis of the therapeutic operation. Ann Surg 174:672-701, 1971.
37. Resnick RH, Iber FL, Ishihara AM, et al: A controlled study of the portacaval shunt. Gastroenterology 67:843, 1974.
38. Rueff B, Degos F, Degos JD, et al: A controlled study of therapeutic portacaval shunt in alcoholic cirrhosis. Lancet 1:655, 1976.
39. Reynolds TB, Donovan AJ, Mikkelson WP, et al: Results of a 12-year randomized trial of portacaval shunt in patients with alcoholic liver disease and bleeding varices. Gastroenterology 89:1005, 1981.
40. Warren WD: Control of variceal bleeding: Reassessment of rationale. Am J Surg 145:8, 1983.
41. Warren WD, Millikan WJ, Henderson JM, et al: Splenopancreatic disconnection: Improved selectivity of distal splenorenal shunt. Ann Surg 204:346, 1986.
42. Belghiti J, Grenier P, Nouel O, et al: Long-term loss of Warren's shunt selectivity: Angiographic demonstration. Arch Surg 116:1121, 1981.
43. Collins JC, Ong MJ, Rypins EB, Sarfeh IJ: Partial portacaval shunt for variceal hemorrhage: Longitudinal analysis of effectiveness. Arch Surg 133:590-592, 1998.
44. Johansen KH: Prospective comparison of partial versus total portal decompression for bleeding esophageal varices. Surg Gynecol Obstet 175:528, 1992.
45. Zervos EE, Goode SE, Rosmurgy AS: Immediate and long-term portal hemodynamic consequences of small-diameter H-graft portacaval shunt. J Surg Res 74:71-75, 1998.
46. Helton WS, Maves R, Wicks K, Johansen K: Transjugular intrahepatic portosystemic shunt versus surgical shunt in good-risk cirrhotic patients. Arch Surg 136:17-20, 2001.

47. Zacks SL, Sandler RS, Biddle AK, et al: Decision analysis of transjugular intrahepatic portasystemic shunt versus distal splenorenal shunt for portal hypertension. Hepatology 29:1399-1405, 1999.

48. Abou Jaoude MM, Almavi WY: Liver transplantation in patients with previous portasystemic shunt. Transplant Proc 33:2723-2725, 2001.

49. Mazzaferro V, Todo S, Tzakis AG, et al: Liver transplantation in patients with previous portosystemic shunt. Am J Surg 160:111, 1990.

50. Schafer AL: The hypercoagulable state. Ann Intern Med 102:814, 1985.

51. Janssen HCA, Wijnhoud A, Haagsma EB, et al: Extrahepatic portal vein thrombosis: Aetiology and determinants of survival. Gut 49:720-724, 2001.

52. Stipa S, Ziparo V, Anza M, et al: A randomized controlled trial of mesentericocaval shunt with autologous jugular vein. Surg Gynecol Obstet 153:353, 1981.

53. Paquet KJ, Mercado MA, Gad HA: Surgical procedures for bleeding esophagogastric varices when sclerotherapy fails: A prospective study. Am J Surg 160:43-47, 1990.

54. Sugiura M, Futagawa S: Results of 636 esophageal transections with paraesophagogastric devascularization in the treatment of esophageal varices. J Vasc Surg 1:254-260, 1984.

55. Orloff MJ, Orloff MS, Daily PO, Girard B: Long-term results of radical esophagogastrectomy for bleeding varices due to unshuntable extrahepatic portal hypertension. Am J Surg 167:96-103, 1984.

56. Orozco H, Takahashi T, Mercado MA, et al: The Sugiura procedure for patients with hemorrhagic portal hypertension secondary to extrahepatic portal vein thrombosis. Surg Gynecol Obstet 173:45-48, 1991.

57. Caps MT, Helton WS, Johansen K: Left-upper-quadrant devascularization for "unshuntable" portal hypertension. Arch Surg 131:834-839, 1996.

58. Peltzer MY, Ring EJ, LaBerge JM, et al: Treatment of Budd-Chiari by a transjugular intrahepatic portosystemic shunt. J Vasc Intervent Radiol 4:263, 1993.

59. Bismuth H, Sherlock DJ: Portosystemic shunting versus liver transplantation for the Budd-Chiari syndrome. Ann Surg 214:581, 1991.

60. Hemming AW, Langer B, Greig P, et al: Treatment of Budd-Chiari syndrome with portosystemic shunt or liver transplantation. Am J Surg 171:176, 1996.

THE MANAGEMENT OF RENOVASCULAR DISORDERS

KIMBERLEY J. HANSEN, MD

Renovascular Disease:
An Overview

127

KIMBERLEY J. HANSEN, MD

■ HISTORICAL BACKGROUND

Renovascular Hypertension

Goldblatt[1] defined a causal relationship between renovascular disease and hypertension through his innovative work published in 1934; however, Bright,[2] of Guy's Hospital, London, first called attention to a potential association between hypertension and renal disease 100 years earlier. Bright[2] observed that patients with "dropsy" and albuminuria during life had shrunken kidneys and an enlarged heart (cardiac hypertrophy) at autopsy. He suggested that the altered quality of the blood so affected the small circulation as to render greater action necessary to force the blood through the terminal divisions of the vascular system.

Although Bright failed to recognize the relationship between increased blood pressure and cardiac hypertrophy, his observations stimulated many theories. Among these theories was Traube's[3] speculation that the elevated blood pressure led to increased myocardial work and subsequent hypertrophy. Stimulated by Bright's observations and subsequent hypotheses, several investigators described experimental models intended to recreate the clinical lesions observed in the kidney and heart. In 1879, Growitz and Israel[4] produced acute occlusion of one renal artery and performed contralateral nephrectomy to decrease functioning renal mass. Although these investigators created what they thought was cardiac hypertrophy in some animals, elevated blood pressures occurred in none.

Lewinski[5] might have predated Goldblatt's observations had his experiments included blood pressure measurements. In 1880, he reported that 6 of 25 dogs developed cardiac hypertrophy after partial constriction of the renal arteries. In 1905, Katzenstein[6] created hypertension in dogs by producing partial occlusion of the renal arteries, although complete occlusion after torsion of the renal pedicle did not produce elevated blood pressures. Katzenstein[6] showed that the elevated pressures returned to normal when constricting rubber bands were removed. He concluded mistakenly, however, that the blood pressure changes were not related to a chemically mediated mechanism. In 1898, Tigerstedt and Bergman[7] published the landmark description of a renal pressor substance in rabbits, a crude extract they termed *renin*. Although their work was confirmed in 1911 by Senator,[8] these and other investigators did not consider renin central to the pathogenesis of hypertension.

In 1934, Goldblatt[1] showed that constriction of the renal artery produced atrophy of the kidney and hypertension in the dog. As a clinical pathologist, Goldblatt noticed that extensive vascular disease was often present at autopsy in patients with hypertension and was frequently severe in the renal arteries: "Contrary, therefore, to what I had been taught, I began to suspect that the vascular disease comes first and, when it involves the kidneys, the resultant impairment of the renal circulation probably, in some way, causes elevation of the blood pressure."[1] Goldblatt's elegant experiments introduced a new era by showing that renal artery stenosis could produce a form of hypertension corrected by nephrectomy.

In 1938, Leadbetter and Burkland[9] described the first successful treatment of this correctable form of hypertension. These authors cured a 5-year-old child with severe hypertension by removing an ischemic ectopic kidney. The photomicrographs published from that renal artery specimen were the first documentation of a renovascular origin of hypertension. In subsequent years, numerous patients were treated by nephrectomy based on the findings of hypertension and a small kidney on intravenous pyelogram. In 1956, Smith[10] reviewed 575 such cases and found that only 26% of patients were cured of hypertension by nephrectomy.

Table 127-1   Results of Univariate Analysis for Renovascular Disease and Associated Factors

VARIABLE*	PARTICIPANTS WITH RVD (n = 57)	PARTICIPANTS WITHOUT RVD (n = 777)	ODDS RATIO	95% CONFIDENCE INTERVAL	P VALUE
Age†	78.7 ± 5.7	77.1 ± 4.9	1.35	1.05, 1.73	.018
Gender (male)			1.70	0.99, 2.92	.053
Female (%)	29 (51)	281 (36)	—	—	—
Male (%)	28 (49)	496 (64)	—	—	—
Race			0.97	0.51, 1.85	.933
African-American (%)	13 (23)	181 (23)	—	—	—
White and other (%)	44 (77)	596 (77)	—	—	—
Systolic blood pressure‡	142 ± 20	134 ± 21	1.42	1.10, 1.82	.007
Diastolic blood pressure‡	73 ± 11	72 ± 10	1.11	0.85, 1.45	.444
Clinical hypertension (%)	30 (53)	306 (39)	1.71	0.99, 2.93	.052
Diabetes	10 (18)	161 (21)	0.81	0.40, 1.65	.567
Smoking	28 (49)	355 (46)	1.13	0.66, 1.94	.647
Hypercholesterolemia (%)	8 (14)	152 (18)	0.67	0.31, 1.45	.313
Elevated LDL-C (%)	11 (20)	125 (17)	1.23	0.62, 2.45	.551
Decreased HDL-C (%)	16 (29)	119 (16)	2.17	1.18, 4.00	.013
Obesity	21 (37)	224 (29)	1.44	0.82, 2.52	.202

*Age at time of renal duplex sonography.
†Odds ratio per 5-year increase.
‡Odds ratio per standard deviation increase.
HDL-C, high-density lipoprotein cholesterol; LDL-C, low-density lipoprotein cholesterol; RVD, renovascular disease.

From: Hansen KJ, Edwards MS, Craven TE, et al: Prevalence of renovascular disease in the elderly: A population based study. J Vasc Surg 36:443, 2002.

This finding led him to suggest that nephrectomy should be limited to strictly urologic indications.

In 1954, Freeman[11] performed an aortic and bilateral renal artery thromboendarterectomy in a hypertensive patient, which resulted in resolution of the hypertension. This first cure of hypertension by renal revascularization combined with widespread use of aortography was followed with enthusiastic reports describing blood pressure benefit after renal revascularization.[12-15] Nevertheless, by 1960, it became apparent that renal revascularization in hypertensive patients with renal artery stenosis was associated with beneficial blood pressure response in fewer than half of individuals. These clinical results fostered general pessimism regarding the value of operative renal artery reconstruction for the treatment of hypertension.

Contemporary operative management of renovascular hypertension began with the introduction of tests of functional significance. Split renal function studies by Howard and Connor,[16] Stamey and associates,[17] Page and Helmes,[18] and others[19-21] identified the role of the renin-angiotensin system in blood pressure control, describing the pathophysiology of renovascular hypertension. After accurate assays for plasma renin activity became available, physicians could predict accurately which renal artery lesion was producing renovascular hypertension.

Renovascular Renal Insufficiency

Until the current era, the pathophysiology and management of renovascular disease focused solely on hypertension; contemporary reports have emphasized the relationship between renovascular disease and renal insufficiency.[22-30] The term *ischemic nephropathy* has been adopted to recognize this relationship. By definition, ischemic nephropathy describes the presence of severe occlusive disease of the extraparenchymal renal artery in combination with

excretory renal insufficiency. In 1962, Morris and associates[31] reported on eight azotemic patients with global renal ischemia who had improved blood pressure and renal function after renal revascularization. Dean, Libertino, and Novick and their groups[23-26] found a similar beneficial function response when bilateral renal lesions were corrected in azotemic patients. These early reports and the reports that followed suggested that ischemic nephropathy could mediate renal insufficiency that was rapidly progressive, contributing to end-stage renal disease. The diagnosis and management of renovascular disease contributing to renal insufficiency are discussed in detail in Chapter 130.

■ PREVALENCE

The actual contribution of renovascular disease to hypertension or renal insufficiency was uncertain because the prevalence of renovascular disease was unknown. Past prevalence estimates of renovascular disease were extrapolated from case series autopsy examinations or angiography obtained to evaluate diseases of the aorta or peripheral circulation.[31-38] More recently, the population-based prevalence of renovascular disease has been estimated in participants of the National Heart, Lung and Blood Institute–sponsored Cardiovascular Health Study. This is a longitudinal, prospective, population-based study of coronary heart disease and stroke in elderly men and women. This population-based study showed that hemodynamically significant renovascular disease was present in 6.8% of this elderly, free-living cohort.[39] Multivariate analysis showed increasing participant age (P = .028; odds ratio 1.44; 95% confidence interval 1.03, 1.73) and increasing systolic blood pressure at baseline (P = .007; odds ratio 1.44; 95% confidence interval 1.10, 1.87) were significantly and independently associated with the presence of renovascular disease (Table 127-1). Renal insufficiency

Table 127-2 Prevalence of Renovascular Hypertension in 74 Hypertensive Children

	0-5 YEARS	6-10 YEARS	11-15 YEARS	16-20 YEARS
Total no. children	9	9	29	27
Essential	2	5	24	21
Correctable	7 (78%)	4 (44%)	5 (17%)	6 (22%)

From Lawson JD, Boerth RF, Foster JH, Dean RH: Diagnosis and management of renovascular hypertension in children. Arch Surg 112:1307, 1977.

Table 127-3 Renal Duplex Sonography in 629 Adults with New Hypertension

	RVD PRESENT (%)	RVD ABSENT (%)	TOTAL
All Patients	154 (24)	475 (76)	629 (100)
>60 yr and DBP ≥110 mm Hg	98 (52)	91 (48)	189 (30)
DBP ≥110 mm Hg and SCr ≥2 mg/dL	53 (71)	22 (29)	75 (12)

DBP, diastolic blood pressure; RVD, renovascular disease; SCr, serum creatinine.

was associated with renovascular disease, but only when renal artery disease coexisted with significant hypertension. Contrary to prior assumptions, renovascular disease showed no significant relationships with gender or ethnicity.[39]

Considering the general population, the prevalence of renovascular disease in the 90 million persons with hypertension in the United States is probably low. Renovascular disease is thought to account for 3% to 5% of hypertension among all persons with increased blood pressure. Renovascular hypertension is associated with severe increases in blood pressure, however. Consequently, its presence in the numerous people with mild hypertension is probably negligible. In contrast, renovascular disease is frequently the cause in people with severe systemic hypertension (diastolic blood pressure >105 mm Hg).

Severe hypertension, particularly at the extremes of age, has the highest probability of being renovascular hypertension. A review of 74 consecutive children evaluated for hypertension over a 5-year period showed that 78% of the children younger than 5 years old had a correctable renin-mediated cause (Table 127-2).[40] After children, the next group that is most likely to have renovascular hypertension is the elderly. In the 1996 academic year, our center screened 629 hypertensive adults for renovascular disease (Table 127-3). Overall, 25% of subjects screened showed significant renal artery disease; however, 52% of subjects older than 60 with diastolic pressure greater than 110 mm Hg had significant renal artery stenosis or occlusion. When serum creatinine was elevated in conjunction with these age and blood pressure findings, 71% of subjects showed hemodynamically significant renovascular disease. In half of this latter subgroup, renovascular disease was present in both kidneys.

Among hypertensive patients with excretory renal insufficiency, the prevalence of renovascular disease (i.e., ischemic nephropathy) also varies. In a series of randomly selected patients 45 to 75 years old with serum creatinine greater than 2.0 mg/dL evaluated at our center, 14% showed unsuspected renovascular disease.[41] In a prospective study of 90 consecutive patients older than 50 with new-onset end-stage renal disease who presented for long-term renal replacement therapy, 22% had renal artery stenosis or occlusion (Table 127-4).[42] In contrast to the population-based study of prevalent disease, dialysis-dependent ischemic nephropathy showed significant ethnic differences. Overall, 40% of white patients in the atherosclerotic age range with end-stage renal failure had unsuspected

renovascular disease. Twenty percent had global renal ischemia consistent with potentially reversible dialysis-dependent renal failure (see Table 127-4).[42]

These data suggest that people with hypertension or renal insufficiency do not show equal risk for the presence of renovascular disease, renovascular hypertension, or ischemic nephropathy. Rather, the probability of finding clinically significant renal artery disease correlates with age, severity of hypertension, and presence and severity of renal insufficiency. Consequently the search for renovascular disease should be directed toward the children or adults in the atherosclerotic age range who have severe hypertension, especially when severe hypertension is combined with excretory renal insufficiency. *Severity of hypertension* refers to the level of blood pressure *without medication* and does not relate to the difficulty of medical control.

Past attempts to discriminate between essential and renovascular hypertension have focused on the value of demographic factors and physical findings to guide further diagnostic study. The Cooperative Study of Renovascular Hypertension is the best study to date that compared the

Table 127-4 Prevalence of Dialysis-Dependent Ischemic Nephropathy Among 45 Patients with New End-Stage Renal Disease

	RENOVASCULAR DISEASE PRESENT	RENOVASCULAR DISEASE ABSENT
No. patients (%)	10 (22%)	35 (78%)
Whites only	10 (40%)	15 (60%)
Type RVD		
Bilateral	5	
Unilateral	5	
Occlusion	4	
Mean age (yr)*	69.4 ± 2.5	64.1 ± 1.5
Gender		
Male	5	15
Female	5	20
Ethnicity†		
African-American	0	20
White	10	15

*P = .07.
†P = .002.
RVD, renovascular disease.

Modified from Appel RG, Bleyer AJ, Reavis S, Hansen KJ: Renovascular disease in older patients beginning renal replacement therapy. Kidney Int 48:171, 1995.

clinical characteristics of essential and renovascular hypertension.[43] In that study, the prevalence of certain clinical characteristics in 339 patients with essential hypertension was compared with their prevalence in 175 patients with renovascular hypertension secondary to atherosclerotic lesions (91 patients) or fibromuscular dysplasia (84 patients). The significant differences identified in the Cooperative Study of Renovascular Hypertension are summarized in Table 127-5.[43] Several characteristics show statistically significant differences between the two varieties of hypertension, but *none* has sufficient negative predictive value to exclude individuals from further investigation for renovascular disease. The finding of an epigastric bruit in a young woman with severe hypertension strongly suggests a renovascular cause for the elevated blood pressure; however, the absence of these clinical features does not rule out renovascular disease. Consequently, clinical criteria should *not* be used to eliminate patients from further diagnostic study.

The decision for diagnostic evaluation should be based on the severity of the hypertension. Mild hypertension has a minimal chance of being renovascular in origin, whereas the more severe the hypertension, the greater the probability that it is from a correctable renovascular cause. With this in mind, our center evaluates all persons with severe hypertension for renovascular disease, especially individuals at the extremes of age and especially when hypertension is associated with excretory renal insufficiency.

■ PATHOPHYSIOLOGY

The renin-angiotensin system is one of the mechanisms by which mammals regulate homeostasis. The active hormone products of the system act to regulate body fluid volumes, electrolyte composition, and tissue perfusion pressure. Physiologically the renal renin-angiotensin system may function as a short-term regulator of arterial pressure

Table 127-5 Clinical Characteristics in Essential Hypertension and Renovascular Hypertension

| | ESSENTIAL HYPERTENSION (339 Cases) | | RENOVASCULAR HYPERTENSION | | | |
| | | | Atherosclerotic (91 Cases) | | Fibromuscular (84 Cases) | |
	%	Years	%	Years	%	Years
History						
Average age		41		48		35
<20 yr	2		1		14	
Average duration		3.1		1.9		2
<1 yr	10		23		19	
>10 yr	23		12		10	
Average age at onset		35		46		33*
>50 yr	7		39		3*	
<20 yr	12		2		16*	
Sex (female)	40		34		81	
Race (black)	29		7		10	
Acceleration of hypertension	13		23		14	
Family History						
Hypertension	67		68*		41	
Stroke	37		44*		22	
Neither of foregoing	19		30*		46	
Symptoms						
Nocturia	38		55		35	
Weakness, fatigue	32		49		42*	
Angina						
Headache						
All of foregoing	0		14		10	
Previous vascular occlusive disease	10		20		6	
Physical Evaluation						
Body habitus						
Obese	38		17		11	
Thin	6		13*		30	
Fundi (grades 3 and 4)	12		26		10*	
Bruit						
Abdomen	6		38		55	
Flank	1		8		20	
Abdomen or flank	7		41		57	

*Differences are statistically different at the 5% level except where so designated.

From Simon N, Franklin SS, Bleifer KH, Maxwell MH: Clinical characteristics of renovascular hypertension. JAMA 220:1209, 1972.

and body fluid volumes. Renin-angiotensin system genes have been identified in virtually all the cardiovascular and reproductive systems of mammals.[44] This tissue renin-angiotensin system may be involved primarily in the regulation of cell functions related to growth and cell-to-cell communication. The circulating renin-angiotensin system is an example of endocrine regulation, whereas the tissue renin-angiotensin system may reflect paracrine and autocrine hormones.[45] Although there is no consensus as to the relative importance of the endocrine and paracrine functions of the circulating and tissue renin-angiotensin systems, emerging data favor an important participation of tissue-derived angiotensin peptides in cardiac and vascular pathology.[45,46]

Renovascular hypertension is an entity in which the blood pressure elevation is caused by hypoperfusion of the kidney with concomitant decreases in renal blood flow. Stenosis of the renal artery may affect a single kidney, but bilateral stenosis may be found also, particularly in subjects with atherosclerotic renal artery disease (see Chapter 130). The presence of a contralateral intact kidney has a significant effect on the mechanisms accounting for the evolution of renovascular hypertension and ischemic nephropathy. In general, the mechanisms contributing to the initial rise in arterial pressure may be considered as volume and vasoconstrictor systems. The initial stimulus of renal hypoperfusion causes an activation of the renin-angiotensin system that translates to the release of renin with an attendant increase in the circulating levels of angiotensin II (Ang II). Volume expansion due to Ang II–mediated sodium retention is incompletely counteracted by a natriuretic response from the opposite intact kidney, which responds to the increase in blood pressure with a pressure natriuresis.[47,48] This anatomy is considered the primary example of vasoconstriction hypertension because the contralateral kidney can negate partially the contribution from volume expansion. The absence of the intact kidney or bilateral renal artery stenosis eliminates, however, the compensatory pressure-induced natriuresis. In this condition, severe hypertension results from the combined effects of volume expansion and peripheral vasoconstriction.

The progression of hypertension over time reflects an adjustment of homeostatic mechanisms to the elevation of arterial pressure. The activation of neurogenic mechanisms by Ang II increases cardiac output, but this effect is progressively replaced by a sustained increase in peripheral vascular resistance.[49] The cardiovascular system responds to the sustained increase in arterial pressure by adaptive structural changes of the heart and peripheral blood vessels. The restructuring of the cardiovascular system in terms of left ventricular hypertrophy and vascular hypertrophy may become the predominant mechanism by which hypertension is sustained.[50] These structural changes are mediated by the multiple actions of Ang II and the activation of other vasopressor systems.

It would be simplistic to think that the above-enumerated factors provide a complete description of the mechanisms activated by the onset of renal hypoperfusion. In the clinical context, the pathophysiology of renal hypertension may be characterized by a sustained elevation in peripheral vascular resistance that is mediated by activation of the renin-angiotensin and the sympathetic nervous systems and their concomitant contribution to vascular endothelial dysfunction. Although the contribution of increased secretion of renin and Ang II production is a sustaining stimulus for the hemodynamic and hormonal response, the actions of Ang II on the vascular endothelium may be of greatest importance in sustained blood pressure elevation. The renin-angiotensin and sympathetic nervous system seem to act in concert to regulate the integrated hormonal response that operates to regulate sodium and potassium balance and arterial pressure.

It is well accepted that renovascular hypertension is caused by an increased activity of the renin-angiotensin system produced initially by hypersecretion of renin from juxtaglomerular apparatus of the ischemic kidney. As hypertension evolves into a chronic stage, however, vascular hypertrophy may become an essential mechanism for the maintenance of elevated blood pressure and peripheral vascular resistance. The effect of hypertension on precapillary resistant vessels triggers a myogenic response that is evidenced by the combination of hypertrophy and hyperplasia of the vascular smooth muscle.[50,51] This response augments vascular reactivity to pressor agents. There also is evidence that renin may be trapped in structural elements of the vascular wall.[52] Local production of Ang II of tissue renin-angiotensin systems may contribute to the remodeling of resistance vessels.[42] Angiotensin-converting enzyme exists in the plasma membrane of vascular endothelial and smooth muscle cells. The necessary components for the production of Ang II may be found in vascular and cardiac tissue. In the chronic phases of the hypertension process, hypersecretion of renin from the ischemic kidney may be of lesser importance than increased production of vascular Ang II as the mechanism that sustains the elevation in arterial pressure.

The pathophysiology of renovascular renal insufficiency (i.e., ischemic nephropathy) is incompletely understood.[53] The earliest clinical reports[44] suggested a "glomerular filtration failure" based on hypoperfusion of the kidney, but the molecular basis for ischemic nephropathy is poorly characterized. Similar to renovascular hypertension, the renin-angiotensin system likely contributes to ischemic nephropathy through its paracrine effects—intrarenal angiotensin peptides increase efferent arteriolar tone.[54] In the presence of a pressure-reducing renal artery lesion, this paracrine effect increases glomerular capillary pressure to support glomerular filtration. In contrast to these positive effects, angiotensin peptides also have been shown to promote tubulointerstitial injury in the presence of a renal artery lesion.[55] This observation is supported by induction of transforming growth factor-β and interstitial platelet-derived growth factor-β, which are associated with increased extracellular matrix and interstitial fibrosis.[56-59] The disruption of tubular cytoskeleton and the loss of tubular membrane polarity also have been suggested. Besides these potentially reversible contributors to excretory renal insufficiency, an atherosclerotic renovascular lesion can serve as a source for atheroemboli.[60] The inability to distinguish potentially reversible ischemic nephropathy from irreversible renal parenchymal disease has enormous clinical importance. Recovery of renal function after renovascular intervention has proved to be the strongest predictor of dialysis-free survival.[29,30]

■ EVALUATION AND DIAGNOSIS

The general evaluation of all hypertensive subjects should include a careful medical history, physical examination, serum electrolytes (including creatinine), and electrocardiogram. The electrocardiogram reveals the extent of secondary myocardial hypertrophy and associated heart disease. Serum electrolytes and serial serum potassium determinations can effectively exclude patients with primary aldosteronism if potassium levels are greater than 3.0 mEq/dL. Finally, estimation of renal function is mandatory for all patients. Primary renal parenchymal disease may mediate renal dysfunction and hypertension. Conversely, hypertension from any cause may produce intrarenal arteriolar nephrosclerosis and mediate decreased excretory renal function.

A noninvasive screening test that accurately identifies renal artery disease in all individuals does not exist yet (see Chapter 128).[61] Isotope renography is proposed as a valuable screening test; however, the methods employed and the criteria for interpretation are continuously modified with the hope of improving the sensitivity and specificity.[62] Current isotope renography uses a variety of radiopharmaceuticals before and after exercise or angiotensin-converting enzyme inhibition (i.e., captopril). As described in Chapter 128, only captopril renography has gained widespread use and acceptance as a useful screening tool for renovascular disease.

Currently available screening tests can be broadly characterized as *functional* (relying on some feature of the renin-angiotensin axis) or *anatomic* (providing a renal artery image or associated hemodynamic data). With the exception of captopril renography, studies that rely on the renin-angiotensin axis have been associated with an unacceptable rate of false-negative results. Consequently, our center emphasizes direct screening methods.[63]

Of the direct screening methods in current use described in Chapter 128, our center has chosen renal duplex sonography as the preliminary study of choice for renovascular hypertension and ischemic nephropathy. Through continued improvements in software and probe design, renal duplex has proved an accurate method to identify hemodynamically significant renal artery occlusive disease. It is ideally suited to the evaluation of anatomic renovascular disease in the contemporary patient population.[64] When duplex is used as a screening study, preparation is minimal (an overnight fast), and there is no need to alter antihypertensive medications. The examination poses no risk to residual excretory renal function, and overall accuracy is not affected adversely by concomitant aortoiliac disease. These considerations are important because more than 80% of contemporary patients have at least mild renal insufficiency combined with aortoiliac atherosclerosis.

During the past 14 years, our center has performed more than 15,000 renal duplex studies to screen for renovascular disease among hypertensive subjects ranging in age from 2 to 91. Overall, technically "satisfactory" studies (defined as complete main renal artery Doppler interrogation from aortic origin to renal hilum) were obtained in 92% of patients and 96% of kidneys examined.[64] Although these rates of success are not influenced by patient age, extent of disease, or presence of renal insufficiency, these results require examination by a skilled sonographer.

The utility of renal duplex sonography is shown by the results from our first prospective validity analysis in 74 consecutive patients who had 77 conventional cut-film angiograms of 148 kidneys.[64] Renal duplex correctly identified the presence of hemodynamically significant renal artery stenosis or occlusion in 41 of 44 patients with angiographically proven lesions and produced no false-positive findings. Among 122 kidneys with single renal arteries, renal duplex sonography provided 95% sensitivity, 98% specificity, 98% positive predictive value, 94% negative predictive value, and overall accuracy of 96%. These results were adversely affected in the 14 patients who had 20 kidneys with multiple renal arteries (Table 127-6).[64] Diastolic features of the renal artery spectral analysis correlated significantly and inversely with estimated glomerular filtration ($r = .30773$; $P = .009$); however, parameters from the Doppler spectral analysis did not correlate with hypertension or renal function response in patients submitted to renovascular repair. The study provides accurate anatomic information, but Doppler parameters should not be used as the sole measure to predict response after renal artery intervention.

Judging from this experience, renal duplex sonography seems to be a valuable study for lesions of the main renal artery when the screened population shows 20% to 40% prevalence of renovascular disease. A negative duplex examination effectively excludes ischemic nephropathy because the primary consideration is global renal ischemia secondary to main renal artery disease. When renal duplex is used to screen for renovascular hypertension, however, multiple or polar renal arteries and their associated disease

Table 127-6	Renal Duplex Sonography: Comparative Analysis Parameter Estimates and 95% Confidence Intervals		
GROUP	**N**	**MEASURE**	**ESTIMATE**	**95% CI**
All kidneys	142 (kidneys)	Sensitivity	0.88	0.84, 0.92
		Specificity	0.99	0.97, 1.00
		PPV	0.98	0.96, 0.99
		NPV	0.92	0.89, 0.95
		Accuracy	0.91	0.87, 0.95
Kidneys with single renal artery	122 (kidneys) 148 (kidneys)	Sensitivity	0.93	0.90, 0.96
		Specificity	0.98	0.96, 1.00
		PPV	0.98	0.96, 1.00
		NPV	0.94	0.91, 0.97
		Accuracy	0.91	0.87, 0.95
Kidneys with multiple renal arteries	21 (arteries)	Sensitivity	0.67	0.53, 0.81
		Specificity	1.00*	—
		PPV	1.00*	—
		NPV	0.79	0.68, 0.90
		Accuracy	0.86	0.76, 0.96
All patients	74 (subjects)	Sensitivity	0.93	0.87, 0.99
		Specificity	1.00*	—
		PPV	1.00*	—
		NPV	0.91	0.84, 0.98
		Accuracy	0.96	0.91, 1.00

*Estimated standard error is 0; confidence level is inestimable.
CI, confidence interval; NPV, negative predictive value; PPV, positive predictive value.

From Hansen KJ, Tribble RW, Reavis SW, et al: Renal duplex sonography: Evaluation of clinical utility. J Vasc Surg 12:227, 1990.

are potential limitations. Despite enhanced recognition of multiple arteries provided by Doppler color-flow ultrasonography, only 40% of these accessory renal vessels are identified. Overall, 17% of patients treated for renovascular hypertension by our center have polar renal artery disease, and in 11% of patients, polar disease constitutes the sole source of renovascular hypertension; this is important, particularly when children and young adults are considered. For these individuals, we proceed with angiography when hypertension is severe or poorly controlled, despite a negative duplex result.

The use of angiography as a screening study for renovascular hypertension is controversial. These issues are discussed completely in Chapters 128 and 131. We perform angiography as a screening study when renal duplex is technically incomplete or branch/polar renal artery disease is suspected in an individual with severe hypertension. It is widely recognized that angiography can aggravate renal failure in patients with severe renal insufficiency, especially when secondary to diabetic nephropathy (see Chapter 58). Nevertheless, this risk would seem justified in patients who have severe or accelerated hypertension and in patients with positive renal duplex sonography results. In these circumstances, the benefit derived from the identification and correction of a functionally significant renovascular lesion exceeds the risk of angiography.

When a unilateral renal artery lesion is confirmed by angiography, its functional significance should be defined. Renal vein renin assays and split renal function studies have proved valuable in assessing the functional significance of renovascular disease (see Chapter 128). Neither renal vein renin assays nor split renal function studies have great value, however, when severe bilateral disease or disease to a solitary kidney is present. In these latter circumstances, the decision for intervention is based on the severity of the renal artery lesions, the severity of hypertension, and the degree of associated renal insufficiency. Finally, urologic split renal function studies are no longer performed (the reader is referred to earlier texts describing their use).[65] At present, renal vein renin assays are used most commonly to establish the presumptive diagnosis of renovascular hypertension. Proper patient preparation and performance of renal vein renin assays are crucial to obtaining valid results.

■ MANAGEMENT OPTIONS

The question of what constitutes optimal management of renovascular disease contributing to hypertension or renal insufficiency is unanswerable. There are no prospective, randomized trials that compare available treatment options. In the absence of level I data, advocates of medical management, percutaneous transluminal renal angioplasty (PTRA), or operative intervention cite selective clinical data to support their particular views.

Most physicians evaluate patients for renovascular hypertension only when medications are not tolerated or hypertension remains severe and poorly controlled. The study by Hunt and Strong[66] is the most informative one available to assess the comparative value of medical therapy and operation. In this nonrandomized study, the results of operative treatment in 100 patients were compared with the

results of drug therapy in 114 similar patients. After 7 to 14 years of follow-up, 84% of the operated group was alive compared with 66% in the drug therapy group. Of the 84 patients alive in the operated group, 93% were cured or significantly improved compared with only 21% of patients alive in the drug therapy group. Compared with surgical management, death during follow-up was twice as common in the medically treated group, resulting in differences that were statistically significant in patients with either atherosclerosis or fibromuscular dysplasia of the renal artery.

Additional prospective data regarding medical therapy for renovascular hypertension suggest that decrease in kidney size and renal function may occur despite satisfactory blood pressure control. Dean and colleagues[67] reported the results of serial renal function studies performed on 41 patients with renovascular hypertension (i.e., hypertension and positive functional studies) secondary to atherosclerotic renal artery disease who were randomly selected for nonoperative management (Table 127-7). In 19 patients, serum creatinine levels increased 25% to 120%. The glomerular filtration rates decreased 25% to 50% in 12 patients, and 14 patients (37%) lost more than 10% of renal length. In 4 patients (12%), a significant stenosis progressed to total occlusion. Overall, 17 patients (41%) had deterioration of renal function or loss of renal size that led to operation, and one patient required removal of a previously reconstructible kidney. Of the 17 patients in whom renal function deteriorated, 15 had acceptable control of blood pressure during the period of nonoperative observation. This experience suggested that progressive decline of renal function in medically treated patients with atherosclerotic renovascular disease and renovascular hypertension occurs despite medical blood pressure control.

The detrimental changes that may occur during medical therapy alone are often cited as supporting evidence for intervention for all renovascular lesions. However, the only prospective angiographic data were obtained from patients with *proven* renovascular hypertension (i.e., significant renal artery lesions, severe hypertension as positive physiologic studies). Accordingly, these data should not be applied to an asymptomatic patient (see Chapter 130). Our indications for interventional management include all patients with severe, difficult-to-control hypertension.[39,68] This includes patients with complicating factors, such as branch lesions and extrarenal atherosclerotic disease, including patients with

Table 127-7	Changes in Excretory Renal Function During Medical Management of Renovascular Hypertension in 41 Patients

CHANGE	NO. AFFECTED (%)
Decreased by 25-49%	11 (37)
Decreased ≥50%	1 (3)
No change ± 24%	14 (47)
Improved ≥25%	4 (13)
Total	*30 (100)*

From Dean RH, Kieffer RW, Smith BM, et al: Renovascular hypertension: Anatomic and renal function changes during drug therapy. Arch Surg 116:1408, 1981.

associated cardiovascular disease that would be improved by blood pressure reduction. Young patients whose hypertension is moderate, who have no associated end-organ disease, and who have an easily correctable atherosclerotic or dysplastic main renal artery lesion also are candidates for operative intervention. The chance for cure of moderate hypertension is quite good in such patients, and it remains to be proved that medical blood pressure control is equivalent to the cure of hypertension. Finally, no evidence exists that age, type of renovascular lesion (whether atherosclerotic or dysplastic), duration of hypertension, or presence of bilateral lesions accurately estimates operative risk or the likelihood of successful surgical management. Consequently the presence or absence of these factors should not be used as determinants of intervention.

Chapter 131 provides a comprehensive review of endovascular treatment for renovascular disease. In my view, experience with the liberal use of percutaneous balloon angioplasty has helped to clarify its role as a useful therapeutic option in the treatment of renovascular hypertension; however, accumulated data argue for its selective application. In this regard, percutaneous transluminal angioplasty of nonorificial atherosclerotic lesions and medial fibroplasia of the main renal artery seems to yield results comparable to the results of operative repair. In contrast, suboptimal lesions for PTRA include congenital lesions, fibrodysplastic lesions involving renal artery branches, and ostial atherosclerotic lesions. Treatment of these lesions with PTRA is associated with inferior results and increased risk of complications.

Endoluminal stenting of the renal artery as an adjunct to PTRA was first introduced in the United States in 1988 as part of a multicenter trial.[69] During this same period, the Palmaz and Wallstents were being used in Europe. Currently, no stent has Food and Drug Administration approval for renal use in the United States. The most common indications for their use seem to be (1) elastic recoil of the vessel immediately after angioplasty, (2) renal artery dissection after angioplasty, and (3) restenosis after angioplasty. With 263 patients entered, results from the multicenter trial showed cure or improvement of hypertension in 61% of patients at 1 year. At follow-up of less than 1 year, angiographic restenosis occurred in 32.7% of patients. Recognizing the poor immediate success of PTRA alone for ostial atherosclerosis, primary placement of endoluminal stents has been advised for these lesions.[70]

Table 127-8 summarizes single-center reports with renal function and angiographic follow-up after treatment of ostial atherosclerosis by PTRA combined with endoluminal stents.[70-84] These studies differ in regard to criteria for ostial lesions, evaluation of the clinical response to intervention, and parameters for significant restenosis. Despite these differences, these cumulative results provide the best available estimates of early hypertension response, change in renal function, and primary patency. From these data, immediate technical success was observed in 99% of patients, and beneficial blood pressure response (cured and improved) was observed in 63%. Only 15% of patients with renal insufficiency showed improved excretory renal function, however, whereas 16% of patients were worsened after intervention. During angiographic follow-up ranging from 5.8 to 16.4 months, restenosis was observed in 21% of patients. Based on available data, PTRA with endoluminal stenting of ostial atherosclerosis seems to yield blood pressure, renal function, and anatomic results that are inferior to contemporary surgical results.[68,76,77] No studies to date have examined long-term renal function results or dialysis-free survival after either primary or secondary PTRA with or without stents. For these reasons, I believe that open operative repair is the initial treatment of choice for good-risk patients with ostial renal artery atherosclerosis when hypertension combined with renal insufficiency is present.

Table 127-8   Results After Primary Renal Artery Stent Placement for Ostial Atherosclerotic Renal Artery Stenosis

FIRST AUTHOR (YEAR)	PATIENTS WITH OSTIAL LESIONS (n)	PATIENTS WITH RENAL DYSFUNCTION (n)	RENAL FUNCTION RESPONSE (%)			HYPERTENSION RESPONSE (%)			RESTENOSIS (%)
			Improved	Unchanged	Worsened	Cured	Improved	Failed	
Rees (1991)[70]	28	14	36	35	29	11	54	36	39
Hennequin (1994)[71]	7	2	0	50	50	0	100	0	43
Raynaud (1994)[72]	4	3	0	33	67	0	50	50	33
MacLeod (1995)[73]	22	13	15	85		0	31	69	20
van de Ven (1995)[74]	24	NR	33	58	8	0	73	27	13
Blum (1997)[75]	68	20	0	100	0	16	62	22	17
Rundback (1998)[76]	32	32	16	53	31	NR	NR	NR	26
Fiala (1998)[77]	21	9	0	100	0	53		47	65
Tuttle (1998)[78]	129	74	16	75	9	2	46	52	14
Gross (1998)[79]	30	12	55	27	18	0	69	31	12
Rodriguez-Lopez (1999)[80]	82	NR	No change in mean SCr			13	55	32	26
van de Ven (1999)[81]	40	29	17	55	28	15	43	42	14
Baumgartner (2000)[82]	21	NR	33	42	25	43		57	20
Giroux (2000)[83]	34	23	70		30	53		47	NR
Lederman (2001)[84]	286	106	8	78	14	70		30	21
Totals	*828*	*337*	*15*	*69*	*16*	*5*	*58*	*37*	*21*

NR, not reported; SCr, serum creatinine.

REFERENCES

1. Goldblatt H: Studies on experimental hypertension. J Exp Med 59:346, 1934.
2. Bright R: Cases and observations illustrative of renal disease accompanied with the secretion of albuminous urine. Guy Hosp Rep 1:388, 1936.
3. Traube L: Über den zusammenhang von herz und nieren krankheiten. In Hirschwald A (ed): Gesammelte Beiträge zur Pathologie und Physiologie, vol 2. Berlin, 1871, p 290.
4. Growitz P, Israel O: Experimentelle Untersuchung über den Zusammenhand zwischen Nierenerkrangung und Herzhypertrophie. Arch Pathol Anat 77:315, 1879.
5. Lewinski L: Ueber den Zusammenhang zwischen Nierenschrumpfung und Herzhypertrophie. Z Klin Med 1:561, 1880.
6. Katzenstein M: Experimenteller Beitrag zur Erkenntnis der bei Nephritis auftretenden Hypertrophie des linken Herzens. Virchows Arch 182:327, 1905.
7. Tigerstedt R, Bergman PG: Niere und Kreislauf. Skand Arch Physiol 8:223, 1898.
8. Senator H: Ueber die Beziehungen des Nierenkreislaufs zum arteriellen Blutdruck und über die Ursachen der Herzhypertrophie bei Nierenkrankheiten. Z Klin Med 72:189, 1911.
9. Leadbetter WFG, Burkland CE: Hypertension in unilateral renal disease. J Urol 39:611, 1938.
10. Smith HW: Unilateral nephrectomy in hypertensive disease. J Urol 76:685, 1956.
11. Freeman N: Thromboendarterectomy for hypertension due to renal artery occlusion. JAMA 157:1077, 1954.
12. DeCamp PT, Birchall R: Recognition and treatment of renal arterial stenosis associated with hypertension. Surgery 43:134, 1958.
13. Morris GC Jr, Cooley DA, Crawford ES, et al: Renal revascularization for hypertension: Clinical and physiological studies in 32 cases. Surgery 48:95, 1960.
14. Abelson DS, Haimovici H, Hurwitt ES, Seidenberg B: Splenorenal arterial anastomoses. Circulation 14:532, 1956.
15. Luke JC, Levitan BA: Revascularization of the kidney in hypertension due to renal artery stenosis. AMA Arch Surg 79:269, 1959.
16. Howard JE, Connor TB: Use of differential renal function studies in the diagnosis of renovascular hypertension. Am J Surg 107:58, 1964.
17. Stamey TA, Nudelman IJ, Good PH, et al: Functional characteristics of renovascular hypertension. Medicine (Baltimore) 40:347, 1961.
18. Page IH, Helmes OM: A crystalline pressor substance (angiotensin) resulting from the reaction between renin and renin activator. J Exp Med 71:29, 1940.
19. Bruan-Memendez E, Fasciolo JC, Lelois LF, et al: La substancia hypertensora de la sangre del rinon, isquemiado. Rev Soc Argent Biol 15:420, 1939.
20. Lentz KE, Skeggs LT Jr, Woods KR, et al: The amino acid composition of hypertensin II and its biochemical relationship to hypertensin I. J Exp Med 104:183, 1956.
21. Tobian L: Relationship of juxtaglomerular apparatus to renin and angiotensin. Circulation 25:189, 1962.
22. Bengtsson U, Bergentz SE, Norback B: Surgical treatment of renal artery stenosis with impending uremia. Clin Nephrol 2:222, 1974.
23. Dean RH, Englund R, Dupont WD, et al: Retrieval of renal function by revascularization: Study of preoperative outcome predictors. Ann Surg 202:367, 1985.
24. Dean RH, Lawson JD, Hollifield JW, et al: Revascularization of the poorly functioning kidney. Surgery 85:44, 1979.
25. Libertino JA, Zinman L: Revascularization of the poorly functioning and nonfunctioning kidney. In Novick AC, Stratton RA (eds): Vascular Problems in Urologic Surgery. Philadelphia, WB Saunders, 1982, p 173.
26. Novick AC, Pohl MA, Schreiber M, et al: Revascularization for preservation of renal function in patients with atherosclerotic renovascular disease. J Urol 129:907, 1983.
27. Scoble JE, Maher ER, Hamilton G, et al: Atherosclerotic renovascular disease causing renal impairment—a case for treatment. Clin Nephrol 31:119, 1989.
28. Zinman L, Libertino JA: Revascularization of the chronic totally occluded renal artery with restoration of renal function. J Urol 118:517, 1977.
29. Hansen KJ, Cherr GS, Craven TE, et al: Management of ischemic nephropathy: Dialysis-free survival after surgical repair. J Vasc Surg 32:472, 2000.
30. Cherr GS, Hansen KJ, Craven TE, et al: Surgical management of atherosclerotic renovascular disease. J Vasc Surg 35:236, 2002.
31. Morris GC Jr, Debakey ME, Cooley DA: Surgical treatment of renal failure of renovascular origin. JAMA 182:609, 1962.
32. Schwartz CJ, White TA: Stenosis of the renal artery: An unselected necropsy study. BMJ 5422:1415, 1964.
33. Holley KE, Hunt JC, Brown AL Jr, et al: Renal artery stenosis: A clinical-pathologic study in normotensive and hypertensive patients. Am J Med 37:14, 1964.
34. Choudhri AH, Cleland JG, Rowlands PC, et al: Unsuspected renal artery stenosis in peripheral vascular disease. BMJ 301:1197, 1990.
35. Wilms G, Marchal G, Peene P, Baert AL: The angiographic incidence of renal artery stenosis in the arteriosclerotic population. Eur J Radiol 10:195, 1990.
36. Wachtell K, Ibsen H, Olsen MH, et al: Prevalence of renal artery stenosis in patients with peripheral vascular disease and hypertension. J Hum Hypertens 10:83, 1996.
37. Metcalfe W, Reid AW, Geddes CC: Prevalence of angiographic atherosclerotic renal artery disease and its relationship to the anatomical extent of peripheral vascular atherosclerosis. Nephrol Dial Transplant 14:105, 1999.
38. Valentine RJ, Clagett GP, Miller GL, et al: The coronary risk of unsuspected renal artery stenosis. J Vasc Surg 18:433, 1993.
39. Hansen KJ, Edwards MS, Craven TE, et al: Prevalence of renovascular disease in the elderly: A population-based study. J Vasc Surg 36:443, 2002.
40. Lawson JD, Boerth R, Foster JH, Dean RH: Diagnosis and management of renovascular hypertension in children. Arch Surg 112:1307, 1977.
41. O'Neil EA, Hansen KJ, Canzanello VJ, et al: Prevalence of ischemic nephropathy in patients with renal insufficiency. Am Surg 58:485, 1992.
42. Appel RG, Bleyer AJ, Reavis S, Hansen KJ: Renovascular disease in older patients beginning renal replacement therapy. Kidney Int 48:171, 1995.
43. Simon N, Franklin SS, Bleifer KH, Maxwell MH: Clinical characteristics of renovascular hypertension. JAMA 220:1209, 1972.
44. Dzau VJ, Re R: Tissue angiotensin system in cardiovascular medicine: A paradigm shift? Circulation 89:493, 1994.
45. Ferrario CM, Moriguchi A, Brosnihan KB: Angiotensin mechanisms in hypertension. In Ganten D, DeJong W (eds): Handbook of Hypertension. Amsterdam, Elsevier, 1998, p 441.
46. Dzau VJ: Local expression and pathophysiological role of renin-angiotensin in the blood vessels and heart. Basic Res Cardiol 88 (Suppl 1):1, 1993.
47. Cowley AW Jr, Roman RJ: The pressure-diuresis-natriuresis mechanism in normal and hypertensive states. In Zanchetti A, Tarazi RC (eds): Handbook of Hypertension, vol 8. London, Elsevier Science Publishers, 1986, p 295.
48. Guyton AC, Coleman TG, Bower JD, Granger HJ: Circulatory control in hypertension. Circ Res 27(Suppl 2):135, 1970.
49. Ferrario CM: Contribution of cardiac output and peripheral resistance to experimental renal hypertension. Am J Physiol 226:711, 1974.
50. Pipinos II, Nypaver TJ, Moshin SK, et al: Response to angiotensin inhibition in rats with sustained renovascular hypertension correlates with response to removing renal artery stenosis. J Vasc Surg 28:167, 1998.
51. Folkow B: Physiological aspects of primary hypertension. Physiol Rev 62:347, 1982.

52. Swales JD, Abramovici A, Beck F, et al: Arterial wall renin. J Hypertens 1(Suppl):17, 1983.

53. Textor SC, Tarazi RC, Novick AC, et al: Regulation of renal hemodynamics and glomerular filtration in patients with renovascular hypertension during converting enzyme inhibition with captopril. Am J Med 76:29, 1984.

54. Hricik DE, Browning PJ, Kopelman R, et al: Captopril-induced functional renal insufficiency in patients with bilateral renal-artery stenoses or renal-artery stenosis in a solitary kidney. N Engl J Med 308:373, 1983.

55. Kobayashi S, Ishida A, Moriya H, et al: Angiotensin II receptor blockade limits kidney injury in two-kidney, one-clip Goldblatt hypertensive rats with special reference to phenotypic changes. J Lab Clin Med 133:134, 1999.

56. Kim S, Ohta K, Hamaguchi A, et al: Contribution of renal angiotensin II type I receptor to gene expressions in hypertension-induced renal injury. Kidney Int 46:1346, 1994.

57. Johnson RJ, Alpers CE, Yoshimura A, et al: Renal injury from angiotensin II-mediated hypertension. Hypertension 19:464, 1992.

58. Eddy AA: Molecular insights into renal interstitial fibrosis. J Am Soc Nephrol 7:2495, 1996.

59. Maschio G, Alberti D, Janin G, et al: Effect of the angiotensin-converting-enzyme inhibitor benazepril on the progression of chronic renal insufficiency. The Angiotensin-Converting-Enzyme Inhibition in Progressive Renal Insufficiency Study Group. N Engl J Med 334:939, 1996.

60. Scoble JE: Atherosclerotic nephropathy. Kidney Int 71(Suppl):S106, 1999.

61. Svetkey LP, Himmelstein SI, Dunnick NR, et al: Prospective analysis of strategies for diagnosing renovascular hypertension. Hypertension 14:247, 1989.

62. Nally JV Jr, Chen C, Fine E, et al: Diagnostic criteria of renovascular hypertension with captopril renography: A consensus statement. Am J Hypertens 4:749S, 1991.

63. Dean RH, Benjamin ME, Hansen KJ: Surgical management of renovascular hypertension. Curr Probl Surg 34:209, 1997.

64. Hansen KJ, Tribble RW, Reavis SW, et al: Renal duplex sonography: Evaluation of clinical utility. J Vasc Surg 12:227, 1990.

65. Dean RH, Rhamy RK: Split renal function studies in renovascular hypertension. In Stanley JC, Ernst CB, Fry WJ (eds): Renovascular Hypertension. Philadelphia, WB Saunders, 1984, p 135.

66. Hunt JC, Strong CG: Renovascular hypertension: Mechanisms, natural history and treatment. Am J Cardiol 32:562, 1973.

67. Dean RH, Kieffer RW, Smith BM, et al: Renovascular hypertension: Anatomic and renal function changes during drug therapy. Arch Surg 116:1408, 1981.

68. Hansen KJ, Starr SM, Sands RE, et al: Contemporary surgical management of renovascular disease. J Vasc Surg 16:319, 1992.

69. Rees CR: Renovascular interventions. 21st Annual Meeting Society of Cardiovascular and Interventional Radiology, Seattle, WA, March, 1996, p 311.

70. Rees CR, Palmaz JC, Becker GJ, et al: Palmaz stent in atherosclerotic stenoses involving the ostia of the renal arteries: Preliminary report of a multicenter study. Radiology 181:507, 1991.

71. Hennequin LM, Joffre FG, Rousseau HP, et al: Renal artery stent placement: Long-term results with the Wallstent endoprosthesis. Radiology 191:713, 1994.

72. Raynaud AC, Beyssen BM, Turmel-Rodrigues LE, et al: Renal artery stent placement: Immediate and midterm technical and clinical results. J Vasc Interv Radiol 5:849, 1994.

73. MacLeod M, Taylor AD, Baxter G, et al: Renal artery stenosis managed by Palmaz stent insertion: Technical and clinical outcome. J Hypertens 13:1791, 1995.

74. van de Ven PJ, Beutler JJ, Kaatee R, et al: Transluminal vascular stent for ostial atherosclerotic renal artery stenosis. Lancet 346:672, 1995.

75. Blum U, Krumme B, Flugel P, et al: Treatment of ostial renal-artery stenoses with vascular endoprostheses after unsuccessful balloon angioplasty. N Engl J Med 336:459, 1997.

76. Rundback JH, Gray RJ, Rozenblit G, et al: Renal artery stent placement for the management of ischemic nephropathy. J Vasc Interv Radiol 9:413, 1998.

77. Fiala LA, Jackson MR, Gillespie DL, et al: Primary stenting of atherosclerotic renal artery ostial stenosis. Ann Vasc Surg 12:128, 1998.

78. Tuttle KR, Chouinard RF, Webber JT, et al: Treatment of atherosclerotic ostial renal artery stenosis with the intravascular stent. Am J Kidney Dis 32:611, 1998.

79. Gross CM, Kramer J, Waigand J, et al: Ostial renal artery stent placement for atherosclerotic renal artery stenosis in patients with coronary artery disease. Cathet Cardiovasc Diagn 45:1, 1998.

80. Rodriguez-Lopez JA, Werner A, Ray LI, et al: Renal artery stenosis treated with stent deployment: Indications, technique, and outcome for 108 patients. J Vasc Surg 29:617, 1999.

81. van de Ven PJ, Kaatee R, Beutler JJ, et al: Arterial stenting and balloon angioplasty in ostial atherosclerotic renovascular disease: A randomised trial. Lancet 353:282, 1999.

82. Baumgartner I, von Aesch K, Do DD, et al: Stent placement in ostial and nonostial atherosclerotic renal arterial stenoses: A prospective follow-up study. Radiology 216:498, 2000.

83. Giroux MF, Soulez G, Therasse E, et al: Percutaneous revascularization of the renal arteries: Predictors of outcome. J Vasc Interv Radiol 11:713, 2000.

84. Lederman RJ, Mendelsohn FO, Santos R, et al: Primary renal artery stenting: Characteristics and outcomes after 363 procedures. Am Heart J 142:314, 2001.

Renal Artery Imaging and Physiologic Testing

128

JOSHUA W. BERNHEIM, MD

K. CRAIG KENT, MD

■ OVERVIEW

Renal artery stenosis (RAS) is the most common cause of secondary hypertension; its prevalence in patients with hypertension is estimated to range from 1% to 5%.[1-5] In patients with associated atherosclerosis in other vascular beds, the prevalence may be significantly higher.[6] Harding and associates[7] studied the renal arteries in 1235 patients at the time of coronary angiography and found a 30% incidence of renal artery disease. In most cases, atherosclerosis or fibromuscular dysplasia is the cause. There has been increased focus on the diagnosis and treatment of renovascular disease because this form of hypertension is potentially curable. Control of hypertension has been associated with a reduction in patient morbidity and mortality.

Owing to the advent of multiple new antihypertensive agents and the aging of the population, patients with atherosclerotic renal artery stenosis (RAS) are presenting later in the course of their disease and with more advanced renal dysfunction. This trend has increased the association of ischemic nephropathy and RAS. It is estimated from angiographic studies that ischemic nephropathy may be a contributing factor in 43% of patients referred for dialysis or renal transplantation.[8-13]

It has become crucial to identify accurate methods for diagnosing RAS. Although contrast angiography remains the "gold standard," because of its invasiveness and attendant risks, it is not an appropriate screening test for all patients thought to have renovascular hypertension or ischemic nephropathy. Consequently, many noninvasive modalities have been developed that can be used to evaluate this disease process. The noninvasive tests can be divided into tests that rely on an evaluation of the *physiologic* sequelae of renovascular disease (e.g., captopril test, captopril scintigraphy, renal vein renins) and tests that directly *image* the renal artery (duplex ultrasonography, magnetic resonance angiography [MRA], and sequential helical computed tomography [spiral CT]). This chapter reviews and discusses the current knowledge of available renal artery imaging modalities and physiologic testing.

■ ARTERIOGRAPHY

Despite technologic advances in noninvasive methods for evaluating the renal arteries, definitive diagnosis of renal artery pathology continues to depend on visualization of renal artery anatomy with angiographic techniques. After a diagnosis of renal vascular disease is established, decisions regarding surgical or endovascular treatments are based in part on the arteriographic appearance of the lesion. An understanding of angiographic techniques for evaluation of the renal arteries is crucial.

Technique

Arteriography can be performed with film-screen or digital subtraction techniques. In film-screen arteriography, multiple sequential x-ray images are recorded on 14 × 14 inch film during the intra-arterial injection of contrast material. The images are reviewed after the film is developed. This approach is rarely used now. With digital subtraction angiography (DSA), multiple sequential fluoroscopic images acquired by an image intensifier are electronically converted to digital form and stored. An image obtained before contrast injection, the *mask,* is electronically subtracted from images containing contrast material. Only the contrast material is visualized. The images are displayed immediately on a 1024 × 1024 matrix screen for review. The DSA images can be modified via the computer and stored on computer disk or printed.

DSA is sensitive to motion artifact because it involves the subtraction of one image from another. Any movement between images degrades image quality. Patient cooperation is necessary, and carefully titrated conscious sedation is often helpful. For patients with large amounts of bowel gas, the intravenous administration of glucagon (0.5 to 1 mg) before image acquisition also improves evaluation of the abdominal aorta and its branches by decreasing peristalsis. Small amounts of movement usually can be compensated for by manually shifting the subtracted mask image relative to the contrast-enhanced images.

Evaluation of the renal arteries usually begins with an aortic injection of contrast material. A 5F multiple side-hole catheter is placed into the aorta through a femoral or brachial artery approach[14] using a modified Seldinger technique.[15] Contrast material is injected with an automatic power injector while sequential images are recorded. The rate and volume of contrast injection and the rate of image acquisition are determined and specific for each patient. In general, a contrast injection of 10 to 20 mL/sec for 2 seconds is usually adequate. Images usually are acquired at a rate of three per second for 3 to 5 seconds, followed by a rate of one to two images per second for the next 5 seconds. These images allow assessment of the arterial, the nephrographic, and occasionally the venous phases of flow.

For optimal visualization of the renal arteries, attention to several technical details is required. Multiple catheters have been designed to optimize opacification of the renal arteries during an injection into the aorta.[16,17] The catheter should be positioned with the side holes at the level of the renal arteries, usually between the first and second lumbar vertebrae. Ideally the catheter should be positioned low enough to avoid filling of the superior mesenteric artery and its branches, which may overlap and obscure the renal arteries. The number of renal arteries is highly variable; multiple arteries supplying a single kidney are seen in 20% to 30% of patients.[18-20] The right renal artery usually arises cephalad to the left. The right renal artery usually arises from the anterolateral surface of the aorta, whereas the left arises from the posterolateral surface.[18,21,22] When imaged from an anteroposterior projection, the proximal renal arteries can be obscured by overlap with the contrast-filled aorta.

Because of variability in the number and origins of the renal arteries, many studies have attempted to establish the optimal rotational projection for acquiring images.[23-27] Most often, images are acquired in anteroposterior and shallow left anterior oblique projections. Verschuyl and coworkers[23] performed a detailed analysis of the angles at which the renal arteries originate from the aorta using axial images from CT scans. They found that a 15- to 20-degree left anterior oblique projection most frequently showed the origins of the renal arteries without overlap of the contrast-filled aorta. The next most useful projections were anteroposterior, followed by a 40-degree left anterior oblique view.[24] A projection error of 10 degrees was sufficient to obscure a significant length of the renal artery. As noninvasive imaging modalities have gained popularity to screen for disease of the renal arteries, cross-sectional imaging is increasingly available before arteriography. Careful evaluation of noninvasive images often allows a prediction of the precise projection that would best depict the renal arteries. This approach can save unnecessary injections of contrast material in patients who are already at high risk for contrast nephropathy.

Aortography with optimized technique usually provides adequate evaluation of the main renal arteries and the segmental and subsegmental branches.[28-31] In some cases, selective catheterization of the renal arteries[32] allows better visualization of the orifice and distal branches without overlap from the aorta or other vessels. Catheterization of the renal artery usually is performed with a preshaped Cobra, Omni Selective, or Simmons (all three manufactured by Angio Dynamics, Queensbury, NY) type of catheter, with hand injection of contrast material or power injection of 3 to 6 mL of contrast material per second for 1 to 2 seconds. Selective renal arteriography limits the total volume of contrast material used for imaging in renal vessels in multiple obliquities. Selective arteriography also provides the opportunity to evaluate the hemodynamic effects of a stenosis. This evaluation can be accomplished with direct pressure measurements proximal and distal to the lesion.[33,34] The ability to measure pressures across a RAS is valuable and is not available with noninvasive imaging modalities.

Numerous new technologies currently are being investigated and warrant mention. Traditional image acquisition involves a phosphorus-based image intensifier, which detects x-ray beams and creates an analog image, which is converted into digital information for display and manipulation. Newer systems use a solid-state system that detects x-rays and creates a digital image directly; this allows higher resolution with lower radiation dosages and simplified and more accurate postacquisition image processing. Three-dimensional DSA is another revolutionary technique in which the tube makes a single rotation around the area of interest before contrast administration, resulting in the acquisition of a mask. A second revolution is performed that coincides with an injection of intra-arterial contrast material. The mask is subtracted from the contrast image, and three-dimensional reconstructions are created. This technique combines the three-dimensional capabilities of MRA and CT angiography with the higher resolution of DSA. A turn of the tube can take 4 seconds, and two revolutions are required to obtain an image, so motion artifact is a potential problem. In addition, the arteries to be imaged need to be opacified for an entire 4-second revolution, necessitating injection of larger volumes of contrast material. The benefit of these new technologies is expected to become more evident as they are introduced into clinical practice over the next few years.

Complications of Arteriography

The risks of aortography and selective renal arteriography can be substantial and may include complications related to the arterial puncture (e.g., hematoma, pseudoaneurysm), contrast-induced nephropathy, and cholesterol embolization. These risks are more prevalent when arteriography is performed in patients with advanced atherosclerosis, severe hypertension, or renal insufficiency,[35] all frequent comorbidities with RAS. The prevalence of these complications in this specific patient group is not well understood because large published studies of conventional angiography generally include "uncomplicated patients" who have only renovascular hypertension and normal renal function. The complications of angiography are often insidious and difficult to assess accurately, especially retrospectively. Among 2374 patients who underwent contrast angiography as part of the Cooperative Study of Renovascular Hypertension,[36] a fatality rate of 0.11%, a nonfatal major complication rate of 1.2%, and a minor complication rate of 2.7% were observed. The authors of this study relied on self-reporting by radiologists at many different centers. The subjects were principally patients who had normal renal function.

Contrast nephropathy is discussed in detail in Chapter 58. The incidence of contrast-induced nephropathy varies significantly and has been reported to range from 0 to 7%, with the largest studies reporting an average incidence of 3%.[37] Risk factors for the development of acute contrast-induced nephrotoxicity include dehydration,[38] renal insufficiency,[39-43] and diabetes mellitus.[41,43,44] In some studies, the combination of diabetes and renal insufficiency has been shown to increase the risk to 20% to 50% depending on the degree of preexisting renal dysfunction.[45] Diabetic patients with renal insufficiency are at highest risk. In patients who do not have risk factors, acute contrast-induced nephrotoxicity is usually transient.[41,42,46-49]

Atheroembolism is an increasingly recognized complication of renal arteriography. It tends to be underdiagnosed because it is an insidious disorder that is difficult to identify with certainty without performing a biopsy.[50] Only the most fulminant cases are recognized clinically. Although clinical studies generally have reported a low incidence (1.4% in one large series[51]), autopsy studies found evidence of atheroemboli in 25% to 30% of patients who died within 6 months after cardiac catheterization or aortography.[52] Patients with widespread atherosclerotic disease and preexisting renal insufficiency—precisely the population at risk for ischemic nephropathy—are the patients who are most susceptible to atheroembolism.

Although conventional angiography can detect the anatomic presence of a renal artery lesion, it does not provide data on the physiologic or hemodynamic significance. Also, because conventional angiography provides only a two-dimensional image and does not allow imaging of the renal artery in multiple planes, it can be difficult to determine the precise degree of stenosis. Even when multiple views are obtained, it can be difficult to identify accurately the origin of a tortuous renal artery that arises from a severely diseased aorta. Despite these limitations, if the index of suspicion for RAS is high and the patient has reasonably acceptable renal function, it may be appropriate in certain circumstances to proceed directly to conventional angiography without performing a noninvasive study.

Contrast Material

Intravascular administration of contrast material has been established as a risk factor for the development of renal insufficiency.[53,54] Factors that appear to increase the risk of renal dysfunction include use of high volumes of contrast material[55-59] and use of high-osmolar contrast.[60] Iodixanol, an isosmolar contrast agent available since the late 1990s, may provide reduced risk.[61] There also may be an advantage to non-ionic contrast material. In a prospective, randomized, double-blinded, multicenter trial involving 1196 patients undergoing cardiac angiography, Rudnick and colleagues[39] found that the use of a non-ionic contrast agent did not influence the incidence of renal failure in the study population as a whole. In patients with the highest risk (i.e., patients with renal insufficiency with or without diabetes), the use of non-ionic contrast was beneficial. Patients with renal insufficiency receiving diatrizoate (ionic) were 3.3 times more likely to develop acute nephrotoxicity compared with patients receiving iohexol (non-ionic).

Several measures to prevent acute contrast-induced nephrotoxicity have been evaluated, including pretreatment with mannitol, diuretics, calcium channel blockers, theophylline, or dopamine (see Chapter 58). No significant benefit of any of these agents over simple infusion of saline has been shown yet.[62] Two agents that have received a great deal of attention are N-acetyl cysteine and fenoldopam. In a landmark study in 2000, Tepel and coworkers[63] evaluated N-acetyl cysteine in a randomized, prospective, placebo-controlled study comprising 83 patients with chronic renal insufficiency. Two percent of patients in the treatment arm developed a significant increase in serum creatinine versus 21% of the control patients. Several subsequent studies have validated the efficacy of N-acetyl cysteine.[64-67] The mechanism of N-acetyl cysteine's protective effect is poorly understood but may be related to increased nitric oxide production and decreased oxidative stress.[68] Although conflicting studies in the literature show no benefit,[69-72] the benign nature and low cost of this agent have led to its widespread and liberal application.

Despite the failure of dopamine infusion to prevent contrast-induced nephropathy,[73,74] Bakris and colleagues[75] showed in a dog model that fenoldopam mesylate, a selective dopamine-1 receptor antagonist, prevented the decrease in glomerular filtration rate (GFR) and renal blood flow associated with intravenous contrast injection. In 2001, Hunter and coworkers[76] reported a series of 29 patients with diabetes and renal insufficiency who received fenoldopam before angiography. Only one patient experienced an increase in creatinine. Tumlin and colleagues,[77] in a randomized trial, showed a significant benefit to fenoldopam infusion. Other studies, including a randomized, controlled trial involving 315 patients with baseline renal insufficiency (CONTRAST investigators),[78] have failed to show benefit, however. Because use of fenoldopam is more involved and costlier than N-acetyl cysteine, it has not gained popularity. Larger randomized, multicenter trials are needed to confirm its benefit.

For patients at significant risk for contrast-induced nephrotoxicity or who have an allergy to iodinated contrast material, exposure can be drastically limited or entirely avoided if carbon dioxide (CO_2) is used as the contrast agent. Intravascular CO_2 was first used for the diagnosis of pericardial effusions in the 1950s.[79] Extensive animal testing established its intravascular use to be safe, even with the administration of massive volumes.[80,81] CO_2 passes rapidly through the capillary bed and is absorbed or routed through the venous system back to the heart and eliminated through the lungs.[82] Repeated, large-volume CO_2 injections made at frequent intervals can produce a "vapor lock," which rarely can cause transient ischemia. In addition, injection of CO_2 into the intracranial circulation has never been proved safe in humans, and its use in animals has resulted in unexplained complications.[83] It also is crucial to prevent room air from entering the injection system to avoid an air embolus. Several technical factors become important when using CO_2. Ideally a dedicated CO_2 injector should be used, but some authors have been successful in creating "homemade" systems, using great care to avoid contamination with air and overinjection.[84] Ample time between injections should be allowed for clearance of the bolus—usually 2 to 3 minutes to prevent vapor lock. Volumes of 25 to 80 mL over 1 second are usually adequate to image the abdominal aorta. An attempt should be made to keep total volumes less than 400 mL. Elevation of the kidney of interest facilitates filling of the vessel owing to the buoyancy of the gas. Movement of bowel gas, a bigger problem than with standard angiography, can be minimized by the administration of an antiperistaltic agent.

It is widely believed that gas entry into the mesenteric circulation causes the abdominal bloating, pressure, and cramps that patients sometimes experience during injections. End-hole catheters may produce a smoother bolus than flush catheters when using CO_2 because they do not break up the "bubble." Stacking of consecutive images is often helpful because of the rapid transit of the gaseous contrast in the arterial system. CO_2 results in images with lower resolution than with contrast angiography; however, with experience CO_2 can be used effectively for renal artery imaging.[85-93] If necessary, supplemental views with a limited volume of low-osmolar iodinated contrast material can be acquired after the optimal projection has been determined with CO_2.[85,88,94,95] In this manner, optimal high-quality images of the renal arteries can be obtained with 2 to 10 mL of contrast material. Angiograms of diagnostic quality are obtained in 79% to 95% of patients, with sensitivity and specificity of 83% and 99%.[96,97]

Another potential alternate contrast material is gadopentetate dimeglumine (gadolinium), which is the contrast agent routinely used during magnetic resonance imaging (MRI). Gadopentetate dimeglumine does not pose a risk of nephrotoxicity,[98-100] but it costs approximately four times more than low-osmolar iodinated contrast material. Adverse reactions have been reported and include nausea, headache, and dizziness in 3% of patients and signs of asymptomatic hemolysis in 1% to 3%.[101,102] These side effects are minor, however, and often self-limited. Also, hypocalcemia has been observed in patients who have received large quantities of gadolinium. It is recommended that doses not exceed 0.25 mmol/kg because larger doses have not been proved safe.[103-105] Ailawadi and colleagues[101] reported adequate visualization in 38 renal arteries that were evaluated only with gadolinium. There were no adverse effects on renal function in any of the patients studied. The major obstacles to the widespread adoption of gadolinium-based agents in renal artery imaging are lower contrast resolution and the high cost of these agents. In high-risk patients, gadolinium remains an effective alternative to iodinated contrast material.

■ NONINVASIVE RENAL ARTERY IMAGING

An ideal noninvasive imaging study would serve as an accurate screening tool for RAS and a means for delineating renal anatomy before arterial reconstruction. Other attributes of the ideal imaging technique are minimal expense, excellent accuracy, good reproducibility, and low complication rate. In recent years, numerous, less invasive renal artery imaging strategies have been evaluated. Each has its advantages and disadvantages, but overall these studies are safer than conventional angiography. As opposed to the traditional screening tests that rely on physiologic criteria (i.e., captopril test, radionuclide renography, renal vein renins), noninvasive imaging studies require no preprocedural adjustments in a patient's medication or diet. Also, their accuracy is not diminished by renal insufficiency. Noninvasive imaging techniques also can supply detailed anatomic information that potentially might obviate the need for preoperative angiography.

In all investigations of noninvasive imaging modalities to date, contrast angiography has been used as the standard of comparison. Because of the previously mentioned limitations of conventional angiography, there is no true standard. Clinicians who have worked extensively with noninvasive imaging modalities realize that, under some circumstances (particularly because of the three-dimensional capabilities of many of these techniques), these studies may be more revealing and accurate than contrast angiography. The ultimate test of any imaging technique designed to screen for RAS is its capability of identifying which patients would respond clinically to renal artery revascularization.

It is difficult to obtain consensus on the diagnostic accuracy and utility of the various noninvasive methods of renal artery imaging. For each modality, investigators have employed a variety of approaches and techniques. Compounding this problem is the fact that the parameters of reporting often vary from one institution to another. In many studies, the threshold for determining significant RAS is 50%. Most clinicians reserve intervention for renal artery lesions that are greater than 70%, however. Finally, patients entered into these studies are almost exclusively patients who have been referred for angiography. This "selected" population tends to have a high prevalence of renal artery disease. It is difficult to extrapolate from the results of these studies to a patient cohort that is being screened, because disease is much less prevalent in the latter group.

Duplex Ultrasonography

Duplex ultrasonography is the imaging modality that has been most intensively investigated. Duplex ultrasonography combines direct visualization of the renal artery via B-mode imaging with Doppler measurement of the velocity of blood flow. This combination affords anatomic evaluation and hemodynamic assessment of the renal vessels.[106] Duplex ultrasonography also allows simultaneous measurement of kidney size. Resistive indices of the segmental arteries can be measured by duplex scanning; these values also may be useful in predicting response to renal revascularization.

Technical Considerations

Because of the depth of the renal arteries and their location in the retroperitoneum, it is difficult with B-mode imaging to assess directly the luminal anatomy along the entire length of the renal artery and its branches. Instead, ultrasound is used to locate the main renal artery. After the renal artery is identified, Doppler measurements can be sampled sequentially at regular intervals along its length and in the kidney itself. These measurements are processed into spectral velocity waveforms using fast Fourier transform analysis (Fig. 128-1). A significant stenosis is indicated by an increase in velocity, which reflects acceleration of the blood as it crosses the area of narrowing. Alternatively, with indirect techniques, a proximal stenosis can be inferred from an abnormal Doppler waveform in the more distal segmental arteries of the kidney.

The main renal artery should be examined with the patient fasting to avoid interference from overlying bowel gas. A low-frequency transducer (range 2 to 3.5 Hz) should be used, and Doppler-shifted signals should be obtained at less than a 60-degree angle to the artery. It is essential to survey the entire renal artery, including the proximal, middle, and distal portions. If the artery is not examined carefully throughout its length, significant stenoses, especially stenoses that are the consequence of fibromuscular

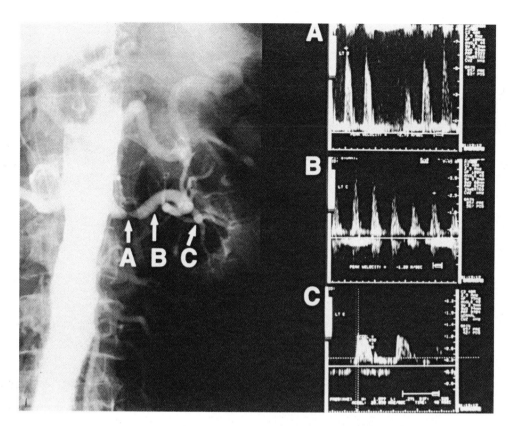

FIGURE 128-1 Duplex ultrasound spectral analysis and corresponding angiogram for a patient with unilateral renal artery stenosis. *Arrows A, B,* and *C* indicate the approximate sites along the renal artery where the Doppler measurements were obtained.

disease (which can be focal or distal or both), may be missed. The examination can be performed without discontinuing antihypertensive medications and is appropriate even for patients who have advanced renal insufficiency.

Numerous parameters have been reported for the identification of a hemodynamically significant main RAS.[107-111] The most widely accepted criteria are (1) a ratio of the peak systolic velocity in the renal artery to the peak systolic velocity in the adjacent aorta greater than 3.5:1 and (2) a peak systolic velocity in the renal artery greater than 180 to 200 cm/sec in association with post-stenotic turbulence. In numerous studies, these criteria have correlated with an "angiographic stenosis" of greater than 60%. An end-diastolic velocity (EDV) 150 cm/sec or greater may signify an 80% or greater angiographic stenosis.[112] The absence of a flow signal in the renal artery signifies an occlusion.

Direct interrogation of the renal arteries is a labor-intensive and time-consuming undertaking that requires a dedicated and experienced technologist and a cooperative patient. In centers where this test has been developed and studied extensively, excellent results have been obtained. In one of the earliest large studies, Hansen and coworkers[113] evaluated 74 consecutive patients with duplex ultrasonography and conventional angiography. Duplex ultrasonography predicted the presence of a main RAS greater than 60% with a sensitivity of 93% and specificity of 98% when only kidneys with single renal arteries were evaluated. When patients with multiple renal arteries also were considered, the sensitivity decreased to 88%, although the specificity remained high (99%). Other centers also have reported sensitivities that range from 84% to 98% and specificities of 90% to 98% for the detection of angiographically significant

main RAS.[114-119] The exact site of the renal artery lesion can be accurately ascertained in 80% to 95% of patients.[153]

Other investigators have been unable to duplicate these excellent results. Sensitivities of 0 and rates of inadequate examinations of 40% have been reported.[120-123] There are many limitations to duplex ultrasonography that may account for these variations in accuracy. Frequently encountered technical difficulties include inability to identify the main renal artery because of overlying fat or bowel gas, difficulty interrogating the entire length of the renal artery, and inability to obtain an optimal angle of insonation. Traditional duplex ultrasonography techniques do not allow accurate identification of accessory renal arteries,[120,124] which may be present in 30% of kidneys.[125] This information may be clinically important because stenosis of an accessory renal artery is frequently the cause of reversible renovascular hypertension.

Numerous attempts have been made to overcome these limitations. The most studied of these is the method of indirect Doppler evaluation of the distal renal arterial tree. Through a flank approach, segmental waveforms are obtained at the hilum and the upper, middle, and lower poles of the kidney. The presence of a more proximal high-grade renal artery lesion is inferred when a *tardus* or *parvus* waveform is observed in the distal vessels (Fig. 128-2). The hemodynamic significance of these lesions is determined by evaluating the acceleration time (normal value <0.07 second), acceleration index (normal value >3 m/sec^2), and waveform pattern recognition. Many published series have shown this technique to have excellent accuracy in predicting angiographically significant RAS.[126-130] Radermacher and associates[126] used this tech-

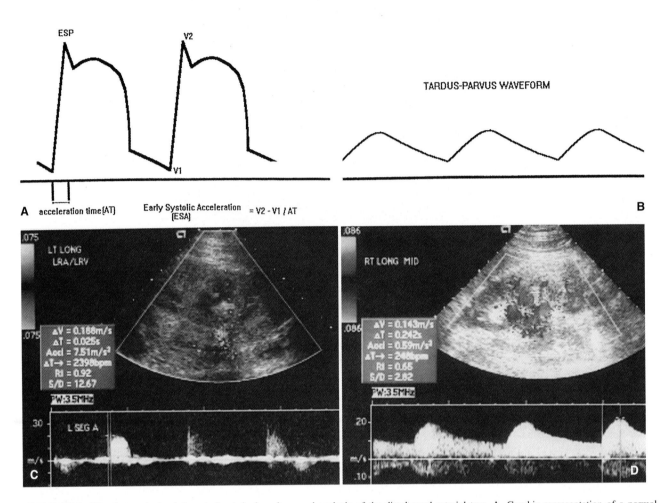

FIGURE 128-2 Waveforms obtained from indirect duplex ultrasound analysis of the distal renal arterial tree. **A,** Graphic representation of a normal waveform. **B,** Graphic representation of an abnormal waveform that would indicate the presence of significant renal artery stenosis. **C,** Waveform represents a normal study; the acceleration time (AT) was calculated to be 0.025 sec (normal <0.07 sec), and the acceleration index (AI) was 7.51 m/sec^2 (normal >3 m/sec^2). **D,** Waveform represents a highly abnormal study suggestive of renal artery stenosis with an AT of 0.242 sec and AI of 2.46 m/sec^2.

nique as an adjunct when direct evaluation of the renal artery failed or was difficult. With this approach, these investigators eliminated technical failures with a resultant decrease in the time required to perform the test. In other studies using indirect Doppler techniques, a measurement called the *resistive index* (RI) has been used as a criterion for RAS (normal RI <0.70). This value, which estimates the state of renal arterial resistance, is defined as follows:

$$RI = \frac{\text{Peak systolic shift} - \text{minimum diastolic shift}}{\text{Peak systolic shift}}$$

This measurement has decreased specificity because it also can be elevated in the presence of medical renal disease, decreased cardiac output, or perinephric or subcapsular fluid collections. Others have used the RI not as a tool to determine the presence of RAS, but as a predictor of response to renal revascularization. The higher the RI, the more likely the kidney is affected by severe underlying nephrosclerosis or glomerulosclerosis. It is hypothesized that these kidneys are unlikely to benefit from revascularization. Radermacher and associates[131] reported on 131 patients who underwent successful renal revascularization. Patients who had a RI greater than 0.8 were highly unlikely to benefit from surgery or angioplasty. Such patients experienced less improvement in blood pressure and more frequent deterioration of renal function. In contrast, most patients with lower RIs benefited, with 94% experiencing a decline in blood pressure and only 3% progressing to dialysis.[131]

Indirect techniques have many potential advantages over direct interrogation of the renal artery. Segmental waveform analysis is much less time-consuming, and the results may be less dependent on operator experience than the results derived from direct renal artery interrogation. Because the examination is performed from a lateral approach, adequate data can be obtained even in obese patients and patients who have excessive bowel gas. Accessory renal artery disease can be identified by a damped waveform isolated to a kidney pole.[132]

Disadvantages of the indirect technique include the inability to distinguish a severe stenosis from an obstruction and the lack of information regarding the exact location of a stenotic lesion. The systolic features of renal artery spectral analysis are affected by increased renovascular resistance (see Fig. 128-1). Increased resistance may change distal renal artery acceleration time or acceleration index in 40% of hemodynamically significant stenoses associated with renal insufficiency.[107,113] In preliminary studies, several investigators have shown that the sensitivity of this technique can be enhanced by using an ultrasound contrast agent or by administration of captopril before the study.[133-135] Many centers, including our own, have begun to perform direct examination of the renal arteries and indirect segmental waveform analysis routinely.

Emerging Strategies

Other strategies have been employed to improve the accuracy of main renal artery interrogation. In a few preliminary studies, intravenous contrast agents significantly enhanced the diagnostic accuracy of duplex ultrasonography. These agents may decrease examination time and increase accuracy by allowing (1) easier identification of the main renal artery and (2) detection of a larger percentage of accessory renal arteries. Claudon and associates[136] reported that intravenous administration of SH U 508A (Levovist) before duplex examination increased the number of technically successful studies from 64% to 84%. Contrast administration also seemed to increase accuracy, with 70% of enhanced scans correlating with angiography versus only 52% of nonenhanced studies. Although the overall accuracy of duplex ultrasonography in this trial was less than what has been reported in other single-institution studies, these results may be representative of what can be achieved at centers without special expertise in renal duplex ultrasonography. At least in this setting, contrast agents seem to improve accuracy. Although ultrasound contrast agents may prove to be adjuncts in the evaluation of RAS by duplex ultrasonography, larger, more thorough studies must be conducted to determine their definitive role.

Other Clinical Applications

In addition to being a screening tool, duplex ultrasonography has proved useful for numerous other clinical applications. Because it is noninvasive and can assess kidney size and the degree of stenosis, duplex ultrasonography has become the procedure of choice for following patients with documented renal artery disease who are being treated medically.[137,138] Duplex ultrasonography also can be used to monitor long-term patency after surgical reconstruction of the renal arteries. Studies have confirmed that a normal postoperative duplex scan is highly predictive of a patent bypass graft.[139,140] Because of their size and position adjacent to the abdominal aorta, aortorenal grafts are often easier to assess than native renal arteries. Hepatorenal, splenorenal, and iliorenal bypasses are more difficult to study, but a skilled technician often can successfully scan even these.

Duplex ultrasonography also has been used intraoperatively to detect and allow correction of technical problems that occasionally complicate renal artery bypass or endarterectomy.[125,141] The superficial location of the transplanted kidney also makes this study well suited for investigating suspected transplant RAS.[142-144] Finally, duplex ultrasonography has been used to evaluate the results and long-term patency after percutaneous renal angioplasty or stenting or both.[145,146]

One drawback of duplex ultrasonography is that it does not provide the necessary anatomic information that would allow surgical intervention without first obtaining a contrast angiogram. Duplex ultrasonography is accurate in detecting celiac artery stenoses,[147] however, and this information may be useful in patients with severely diseased aortas when hepatorenal or splenorenal bypass is being considered.

Renal artery duplex ultrasonography is an excellent screening test for hemodynamically significant RAS in centers where the appropriate technical expertise is available. Of the various alternatives for noninvasive imaging, duplex ultrasonography is the least expensive. Adding indirect techniques and using contrast agents may increase its accuracy and reproducibility further, which would make it a more widely acceptable study for RAS screening. In addition, measurement of the RI has shown promise in predicting which patients will respond to revascularization.

Magnetic Resonance Angiography

MRA also has been extensively evaluated as a method for noninvasively evaluating RAS. MRA can show vascular anatomy and generate an image that is similar in appearance to that obtained by conventional angiography (Fig. 128-3). In contrast to conventional angiography, however, MRA does not require arterial puncture or nephrotoxic agents. In contrast to the traditional physiologic studies for RAS, there is no need to discontinue antihypertensive medications, which interfere with the renin-angiotensin system, and the accuracy of MRA does not diminish because of renal dysfunction. The similarity of the images generated by MRA and by conventional angiography increases the comfort level of clinicians. There are significant differences in these images, however, and the interpretation of renal MRA requires specific expertise and experience.

The physics of MRA is complex, and a complete description of this technique is beyond the scope of this chapter. The clinician should have a basic understanding of the fundamental principles that underlie MRA, however, to recognize its advantages and limitations. Numerous different MRA techniques can be used to image the renal arteries.[148,149] In early studies, two imaging techniques were employed: *time of flight* (TOF) and *phase contrast* (PC). With both, protons in tissue and blood are charged when the body is exposed to a magnetic field. The protons emit a signal that is registered as a visual image. TOF imaging relies on flow-related enhancement to image the renal arteries. With multiple magnetic pulses delivered at short intervals, stationary protons are "saturated" so that they no longer yield signal, whereas moving protons yield maximal

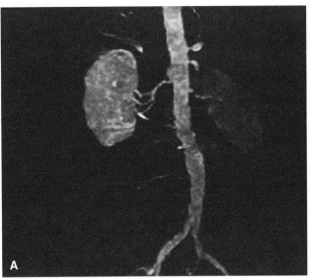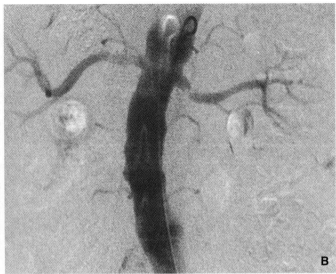

FIGURE 128-3   A, Three-dimensional gadolinium-enhanced magnetic resonance angiogram shows severe left renal artery stenosis. **B,** The corresponding conventional contrast angiogram from the same patient.

signal. PC imaging relies on the differences in phase shift between moving and stationary protons.

More recently, a third approach called *three-dimensional gadolinium-enhanced MRA* has become the standard of care in renal artery MRI. With this technique, many of the shortcomings of TOF and PC MRA have been overcome, including (1) saturation effects that can make vessels with relatively slow flow appear stenotic; (2) turbulence-induced signal loss, which results in overestimation of stenoses; and (3) long imaging times. Rather than image individual protons in flowing blood, this method allows direct visualization of the contrast agent filling the lumen similar to conventional angiography. When this technique was initially developed, long acquisition times (approximately 2 to 3 minutes) were necessary; however, distal and accessory arteries could not be assessed accurately owing to respiration artifact. More recently, rapid bolus injections used with suspended respiration have produced slightly poorer resolution, but less pronounced respiratory artifact.

Data from MRA are compiled initially as multiple, thin, contiguous cross-sectional slices. The slices are converted into a three-dimensional data set, which can be used to create projections in any orientation that look like conventional angiograms. The most commonly used reconstruction technique is called a *maximal intensity projection* (MIP).[150] In contrast to conventional angiography, MRA allows data to be projected in multiple planes (axial, coronal, sagittal, oblique). This flexibility is particularly useful for investigating the renal ostium and tortuous renal arteries. To assess the degree of stenosis accurately, it is necessary to examine the nonreformatted axial images because the reformatting process, although it produces visually satisfying images, often can lead to overestimation or underestimation of the degree of stenosis.

In addition to defining the anatomy, attention has focused on the use of MRA to evaluate several physiologic parameters. PC flow measurements, assessment of

gadolinium clearance, and detection of turbulent flow resulting in signal loss in nonenhanced studies all may be used to detect the physiologic sequelae of RAS.[151-155] The clinical applicability of these techniques awaits further investigation.

Clinical Experience

Using a breath-holding, three-dimensional gadolinium-enhanced method, DeCobelli and coworkers[156] achieved 100% sensitivity and 97% specificity for RAS greater than 50%. Using these same techniques, they correctly identified significantly more accessory renal arteries than could be found using a PC technique. Many other investigators also have reported excellent results with three-dimensional gadolinium-enhanced MRA.[157-162] Hany and coworkers[163] reported the largest series to date, which included a comparison of 103 patients who underwent gadolinium-enhanced MRA and contrast angiography. Using this technique, these investigators reported a sensitivity and specificity of 93% and 90%. Using a combination of anatomic images from gadolinium-enhanced MRA and physiologic data from cine PC MRI, Schoenberg and colleagues[164] also showed excellent correlation between MRI and digital angiography in the evaluation of RAS.

Because of the high degree of accuracy associated with MRA and its ability to image arterial anatomy, in certain cases surgeons may proceed directly to operation for RAS without preoperative conventional contrast angiography.[165] This advantage has become less relevant as angioplasty and endoluminal stents have become widely applied to RAS. MRA remains an important screening test for renal artery disease, however. MRA also has been evaluated for detection of RAS in transplants, although not as thoroughly as has duplex ultrasonography. Although the accuracy has been satisfactory when MRA is used for this purpose, false-positive findings occur frequently.[166-168] Another potential

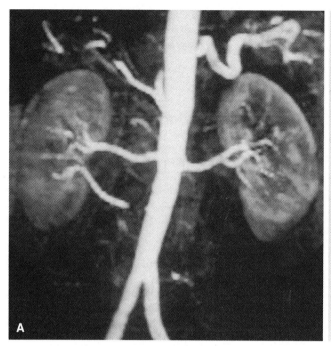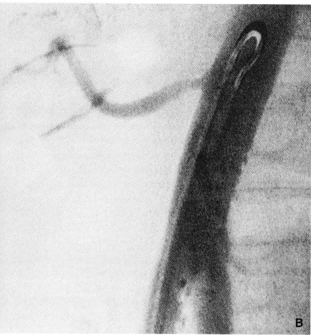

FIGURE 128-4 A, Three-dimensional gadolinium-enhanced magnetic resonance angiogram shows severe ostial accessory renal artery stenosis. **B,** The conventional contrast angiogram of the same accessory renal artery reveals only a mild lesion. Pull-back pressures revealed no gradient across the ostium of this renal artery.

advantage of MRA is its ability to obtain functional and anatomic data.[169] Several investigators have been able to estimate split renal function accurately with clearance of gadolinium contrast agents using a method similar to conventional radionuclide renography.[170-172] Others have used gated MRI techniques to assess accurately renal blood flow in patients with renal artery disease.[173,174] It is also possible to obtain the rates of tissue diffusion and perfusion; both of these measurements may help to delineate the physiologic significance of RAS.[175]

Although the popularity of MRA for noninvasive imaging is increasing, it has many limitations. False-positive scans are common (Fig. 128-4). MRA has a general tendency to overestimate the degree of stenosis. Although images may appear strikingly detailed, they do not strictly correlate with luminal anatomy. Breath-holding, three-dimensional gadolinium-enhanced MRA is now the MRA technique most often used for imaging the renal vasculature. Although it seems to afford superior resolution of accessory and branch renal arteries, few patients with fibromuscular or other distal renal artery lesions have been studied. MRA is not the screening test of choice for patients who may harbor such lesions. Three-dimensional gadolinium-enhanced MRA also requires patients to hold their breath for a short time, which may be difficult for patients with significant cardiac or pulmonary disease. Some patients are unable to tolerate the study because of claustrophobia. MRA also is contraindicated in patients with pacemakers, cerebral aneurysm clips, or intraocular metal devices. Neighboring surgical clip artifact can produce signal voids and false-positive studies. Finally, although it is not always evident when reviewing published reports, considerable expertise is required to obtain high-quality images and proper interpretation.

The most striking aspect of MRA, as used to detect proximal renovascular disease, is its extremely low false-negative rate. In most series, *sensitivity* is almost 100%, which makes it an excellent screening tool for suspected ischemic nephropathy secondary to atherosclerotic disease of the main renal artery. Because of this high negative predictive value, a clinician can be confident that with a normal MRA study, functionally significant renal artery disease is exceedingly unlikely. Because of its current tendency to overestimate the degree of stenosis, MRA is less accurate than conventional contrast angiography in defining high-grade RAS; however, MRA technology is continually evolving, and the images are expected to continue to improve.

Helical (Spiral) Computed Tomography

Helical CT has emerged as a promising technique for identifying RAS. Spiral CT employs a rotating gantry, which allows numerous images to be acquired over a relatively brief time. For arterial imaging, intravenous iodinated contrast material is injected through a peripheral vein. After an appropriate delay to allow passage of the contrast agent into the renal arterial circulation, a series of thin cuts are obtained throughout the aorta at the level of the renal arteries. Rapid acquisition of data afforded by spiral CT allows multiple images to be made precisely at the moment when the contrast medium passes through the renal vessels.

Many technical variables must be optimized if the renal arteries are to be imaged adequately by spiral CT.[176] Several of these parameters (collimation, table speed, pitch) determine the interval at which cuts are acquired. These variables are adjusted so that sections are taken at 2- to 3-mm intervals,[177] which afford a resolution of approximately 0.5 mm (whereas that for MRA is 1 to 1.5 mm). It is also necessary to adjust the rate of injection and the interval between peripheral injection and renal artery imaging. Optimizing both of these timing variables allows maximal enhancement of the renal arteries by contrast medium. If the contrast bolus arrives in the renal arteries too early, the volume of contrast is inadequate for complete visualization of the renal vessels. If the bolus arrives after imaging has begun, contrast returning from the renal vein might obscure the renal artery. The importance of precise timing has led many investigators to administer a test bolus using 15 to 20 mL of contrast material. Interval imaging over 30 seconds allows the physician to estimate when contrast enhancement of the renal vessels is maximal. Breath holding longer than 20 seconds is required during image acquisition. It is essential that patients remain immobile for these studies because motion artifact reduces the quality of the images. The entire study takes only 20 to 30 minutes.

After the raw images are acquired, postprocessing is the next step. Initially the data are interpolated into axial sections, then reconstructed images are rendered. This time-consuming process takes 30 to 90 minutes for an experienced radiologist or technician. Although many reconstructive techniques exist, the techniques currently available on most commercial CT systems are MIP and surface-shaded display (SSD). Images provided by these two techniques differ, as does the information they relay.[178] MIP is a method wherein the raw data are reconstructed using the maximum-intensity signal along each ray through the data set (Fig. 128-5A and B). MIP enhances visual distinction between the blood vessel and background tissue. The images are two-dimensional, however, and depth relationships are not apparent, and overlapping vessels are not clearly delineated. Displaying multiple MIP images minimizes this problem. SSD has the advantage of three-dimensional representation of anatomic relationship (Fig. 128-5C). Depending on the chosen threshold, however, SSD can exaggerate stenoses, and surrounding structures can produce artifacts that obscure arterial anatomy. Generally, MIP is the more accurate of the two techniques, although SSD is the more visually "pleasing." When one is determining renal artery anatomy and degree of stenosis, images from all available modalities should be reviewed. In addition to the MIP and SSD reconstructions, much information can be obtained by examining the original axial data or by using multiplanar reformats. Such a complete analysis allows repeated confirmation of the degree of stenosis, which improves diagnostic accuracy.

Regardless of which technique is used, the major hindrance of helical CT is arterial calcification. In MIP-formatted images, calcium obscures the vessel lumen. Atherosclerotic disease can be inferred by the presence of calcium, but the degree of stenosis cannot be gauged accurately. In SSD-formatted images, it is impossible to differentiate calcium from contrast medium. Calcified atheromas blend with intraluminal contrast and create the image of a widely patent vessel. Numerous calcium suppression techniques have been studied, but they have marginal utility.

Although helical CT has been less widely studied than MRA or duplex ultrasonography, numerous centers with experience in helical CT have produced favorable results.[179-183] Wittenberg and coworkers[184] prospectively compared helical CT and conventional angiography in 82 consecutive patients suspected to have renal artery disease. Helical CT detected stenoses greater than 50% with sensitivity of 96% and specificity of 99%. Five adrenal masses were incidentally detected. In 50 patients with suspected renovascular disease, Deregi and coworkers[185] found helical CT to have sensitivity of 100% and specificity of 98% for main renal artery lesions more extensive than 50%. The two false-positive results in this study were related to difficulty imaging the right main renal artery adjacent to the vena cava. When accessory renal arteries were included in this evaluation, the sensitivity decreased to 88%. Kim and associates[186] studied 50 patients with CT angiography, and conventional CT. These authors reported a 90% sensitivity and a 97% specificity for CT angiography in the detection of RAS greater than 50%.

In addition to its great accuracy, other advantages of helical CT include the ability to determine renal size, cortical thickness, and, potentially, kidney perfusion.[187] It also affords simultaneous evaluation for aortic aneurysms and adrenal gland anatomy in patients suspected to have secondary hypertension.[188-190] In contrast to MRA, helical CT can be used to assess the patency of renal arteries that have been treated with endoluminal stents.

The principal drawback of spiral CT for imaging renal arteries is the necessity for iodinated contrast medium. For most studies, 120 to 150 mL of contrast agent is required. This is a quantity significantly greater than that required for digital subtraction angiography (15 to 20 mL if selective renal images need not be obtained). For this reason, helical CT may not be appropriate for the increasing number of patients with renal insufficiency who undergo screening for renal artery disease.

Similar to duplex ultrasonography and MRA, helical CT does not produce satisfactory images of accessory renal arteries.[177] Although these arteries often can be identified, the extent to which they are diseased is difficult to assess owing to poor resolution. Because branch renal arteries tend to lie in a single plane, they too are often inadequately imaged by helical CT. Even with these limitations, CT may be more accurate than MRA for detecting lesions related to fibromuscular disease. Other drawbacks of spiral CT include long postprocessing times, inability to image patients who weigh more than 125 kg, and a general tendency to produce false-positive results. False-positive images can result from incomplete opacification of the renal arteries secondary to poor timing of a contrast bolus, overlying calcification, or artifact from adjacent tissue. Despite these limitations, for patients with relatively normal renal function and in centers with appropriate experience and expertise, spiral CT offers an accurate, less invasive assessment of renal artery anatomy.

■ FUNCTIONAL STUDIES

In 1934, Goldblatt and associates[191] made the seminal discovery that constriction of the renal artery in a dog caused an elevation in blood pressure proportional to the degree of

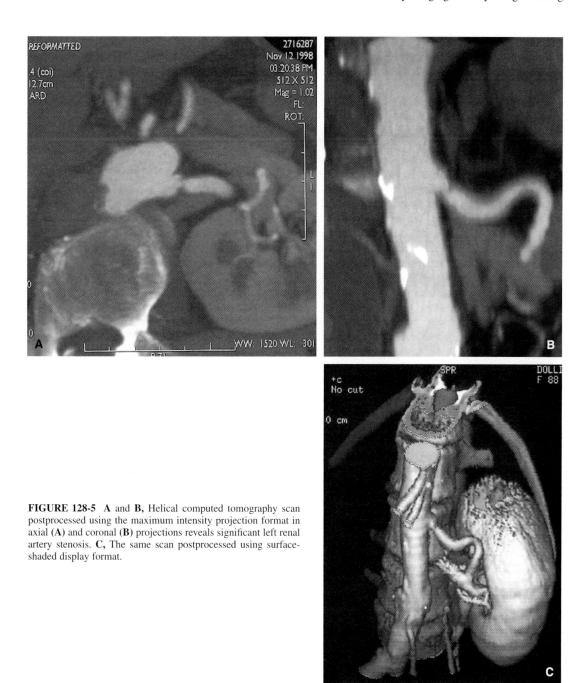

FIGURE 128-5 A and **B,** Helical computed tomography scan postprocessed using the maximum intensity projection format in axial (**A**) and coronal (**B**) projections reveals significant left renal artery stenosis. **C,** The same scan postprocessed using surface-shaded display format.

constriction. Subsequent models were devised that clarified further the pathophysiology of different patterns of renal artery obstruction. Stenosis of a single renal artery and consequent renal hypoperfusion leads to the release of renin and an increase in the level of angiotensin. Angiotensin produces direct vasoconstriction and sodium and fluid retention. Patients with a normal functioning contralateral kidney are able to correct for this volume expansion partially with a compensatory natriuresis.

A variety of noninvasive physiologic tests have been developed and evaluated. An accurate noninvasive physiologic test could serve as a screening test for RAS. A physiologic test could prove functional significance in patients who are found to have anatomic evidence of RAS and improve the success of revascularization. Despite the plethora of physiologic studies that have been evaluated and used clinically, the perfect test remains elusive. Studies that are currently available are evaluated here.

Renal Vein Renins

Intravenous pyelography and plasma vein renin levels are mentioned only for their historical significance. Neither intravenous pyelography nor plasma vein renin level is currently used, and neither was found to predict patients with RAS. Renal vein renins are still used as a method for detecting RAS in some centers. Catheterization of the renal veins is an involved and invasive procedure, which is not appropriate for screening. Renal vein renins have been proposed as a method for determining which patients with RAS would respond favorably to revascularization. Patients with renin-induced renovascular hypertension have high renin levels in the venous drainage of the affected kidney and suppressed renin levels in the contralateral renal vein. Many investigators have found a correlation between renal vein renins and a favorable response to surgery. The usefulness of this test is limited, however, because absence of a significant difference in renal vein renins does not always correlate with lack of benefit of revascularization. Of patients with a negative test, 57% still have improvement after renal reconstruction.[192-194] As might be anticipated, patients with bilateral RAS often fail to lateralize. Selective sampling often misses accessory renal artery stenoses that produce renin hypersecretion in only a segment of the affected kidney, especially if there is separate venous drainage for that segment. This test is still used occasionally with the caveat that a positive study is meaningful, whereas a negative study should be placed in the context of the patient's overall clinical presentation.

Radionuclide Renography

A variety of radioisotopes can be used to determine renal blood flow and GFR. In addition, images obtained can be used to estimate kidney size. Interest in using nuclear scintigraphy to diagnose RAS was renewed with the addition of angiotensin-converting enzyme (ACE) inhibitors to the regimen. Protocols for the test vary among institutions. Typically, after similar preparation to that used for non–ACE-enhanced scans, 25 to 50 mg of captopril is given after a baseline scan, and repeat images are obtained 60 minutes later. In a kidney affected with RAS, the angiotensin II–induced vasoconstriction of the efferent arteriole is acutely reduced, decreasing the GFR in that kidney selectively; this is shown by a decrease in the relative GFR in the affected kidney compared with a baseline scan. The normal kidney responds with an increase in perfusion. Criteria that suggest RAS are delayed time to maximal uptake (>11 minutes) in the affected kidney, significant asymmetry in uptake between kidneys, cortical retention of radionuclide with captopril, and marked reduction of GFR after captopril.[195]

Initial reports of this technique were quite promising. Setaro and coauthors,[196] in a study of 90 patients, showed a sensitivity of 91% and a specificity of 94% in the detection of RAS greater than 50%. Several other investigators have reported similar results.[197,198] Although a significant improvement over scintigraphy alone, captopril scanning is less reliable in patients with significant parenchymal disease or bilateral stenoses. In a large European trial, the positive predictive value of this test decreased from 88% to 57% in patients with plasma creatinine greater than 1.5 mg/dL.[199] Currently, ACE inhibitor renography continues to play a role in screening of patients with suspected renovascular hypertension. A normal captopril renogram makes the diagnosis of unilateral RAS highly unlikely.[200] A positive finding suggests a high likelihood of renovascular hypertension in subjects with preserved renal function. ACE

inhibitor renography cannot rule out RAS, however, in an azotemia patient or in patients with bilateral disease. Both subgroups are among the most important patients who require treatment.

■ SUGGESTED PARADIGM FOR DIAGNOSIS OF SUSPECTED RENAL ARTERY DISEASE

Renal artery disease is a complex disorder that can have many causes and different clinical presentations. A rigid diagnostic approach to suspected RAS is neither possible nor advisable. Instead, it is more prudent to adopt a flexible strategy that is based on each patient's clinical presentation and on "local expertise" with the various diagnostic modalities. General recommendations for the diagnostic approach to patients thought to have RAS follow.

When there is strong clinical suspicion of renovascular hypertension, and fibromuscular disease is the presumed cause, it may be appropriate to proceed directly to contrast angiography because of the relatively high incidence of distal and accessory renal artery lesions. No noninvasive imaging study currently available provides the necessary precision in detecting these lesions.

A traditional functional or physiologic diagnostic test can be used to verify the diagnosis and predict response to revascularization in patients who have normal renal function, who have suspected unilateral stenoses, and who can tolerate temporary withdrawal of certain antihypertensive medications. The number of patients thought to have RAS who have impaired renal function or who cannot discontinue hypertensive medications is increasing. These patients are not optimal candidates for physiologic testing, and noninvasive renal artery imaging is advisable for them. Which noninvasive modality should be used is largely a matter of local expertise. If there is a vascular laboratory with a dedicated technician who has documented proficiency with renal artery duplex ultrasonography, this would be the diagnostic modality of choice. Alternatively, if there is a radiologist with experience in three-dimensional gadolinium-enhanced MRA, MRA may be more appropriate. Experience with spiral CT is less extensive than with the other two modalities, but further development of this technique is expected to make it a viable approach in selected patients with normal renal function. Although technologic advances will continue to improve the accuracy of noninvasive imaging for suspected RAS, sound clinical judgment is still paramount to the diagnosis and evaluation of this complicated disorder.

■ REFERENCES

1. Pickering TG: Diagnosis and evaluation of renovascular hypertension: Indications for therapy. Circulation 83(Suppl I):I-147-I-154, 1991.
2. Mann SJ, Pickering TG: Detection of renovascular hypertension: State of the art 1992. Ann Intern Med 117:845-853, 1992.
3. Lewin A, Blaufox MD, Castle H, et al: Apparent prevalence of curable hypertension in the hypertension detection and follow-up program. Arch Intern Med 145:451-455, 1985.
4. Berglund G, Andersson O, Wilhelmsen L: Prevalence of primary and secondary hypertension in a random population sample. BMJ 2:554-556, 1976.

5. Bech K, Hilden T: The frequency of secondary hypertension. Acta Med Scand 195:65-79, 1975.

6. Olin JW, Melia M, Young JR, et al: Prevalence of atherosclerotic renal artery stenosis in patients with atherosclerosis elsewhere. Am J Med 88(1N):46N-51N, 1990.

7. Harding MB, Smith LR, Himmelstein SI, et al: Renal artery stenosis: Prevalence and associated risk factors in patients undergoing routine cardiac catheterization. J Am Soc Nephrol 2:1608-1616, 1992.

8. Greco BA, Breyer JA: Atherosclerotic ischemic renal disease. Am J Kidney Dis 29:167-187, 1997.

9. Scoble JE, Maher ER, Hamilton G: Atherosclerotic renovascular disease causing renal impairment—a case for treatment. Clin Nephrol 31:119-120, 1989.

10. Kahn IH, Catto GRD, Edward N: Influence of coexisting disease on survival in renal-replacement therapy. Lancet 341:415-418, 1993.

11. Mailloux LU, Napolitano B, Bellucci AG: Renal vascular disease causing end-stage renal disease, incidence, clinical correlates, and outcomes: A 20-year clinical experience. Am J Kidney Dis 24:622-629, 1994.

12. Appel RG, Bleyer AJ, Reavis S, et al: Renovascular disease in older patients beginning renal replacement therapy. Kidney Int 48:171-176, 1995.

13. Simon P, Benarbia S, Charasse C, et al: Ischemic renal diseases have become the most frequent causes of end stage renal disease in the elderly. Arch Mal Coeur Vaiss 91:1065-1068, 1998.

14. Hawkins IF Jr: "Mini-catheter" technique for femoral run-off and abdominal arteriography. Am J Roentgenol Radium Ther Nucl Med 116:199-203, 1972.

15. Seldinger SI: Catheter replacement of the needle in percutaneous arteriography. Acta Radiol 39:368-376, 1953.

16. Ovitt TW, Amplatz K: Semiselective renal angiography. AJR Am J Roentgenol 119:767-769, 1973.

17. Yedlicka JW Jr, Carlson JE, Hedlund LF, et al: Nonselective and semiselective catheters for renal artery evaluation: Experimental study. J Vasc Interv Radiol 2:273-276, 1991.

18. Bauer FW, Robbins SL: A postmortem study comparing renal angiograms and renal artery casts in 58 patients. Arch Pathol 83:307-314, 1967.

19. Boijsen E: Angiographic studies of the anatomy of single and multiple renal arteries. Acta Radiol 183(Suppl):23-129, 1959.

20. Pick JW, Anson BJ: The renal vascular pedicle: An anatomical study of 430 body halves. J Urol 44:411-434, 1940.

21. Keen EN: Origin of renal arteries from the aorta. Acta Anat (Basel) 110:285-286, 1981.

22. Odman P, Ranninger K: The location of the renal arteries: An angiographic and postmortem study. Am J Roentgenol Radium Ther Nucl Med 104:283-286, 1968.

23. Verschuyl EJ, Kaatee R, Beek FJ, et al: Renal artery origins: Best angiographic projection angles. Radiology 205:115-120, 1997.

24. Verschuyl EJ, Kaatee R, Beek FJ, et al: Renal artery origins: Location and distribution in the transverse plane at CT. Radiology 203:71-75, 1997.

25. Gerlock AJ Jr, Goncharenko V, Sloan OM: Right posterior oblique: The projection of choice in aortography of hypertensive patients. Radiology 127:45-48, 1978.

26. Harrington DP, Levin DC, Garnic JD, et al: Compound angulation for the angiographic evaluation of renal artery stenosis. Radiology 146:829-831, 1983.

27. Garcier JM, De Fraissinette B, Filaire M, et al: Origin and initial course of the renal arteries: A radiological study. Surg Radiol Anat 23:51-55, 2001.

28. Kaufman SL, Chang R, Kadir S, et al: Intraarterial digital subtraction angiography in diagnostic arteriography. Radiology 151:323-327, 1984.

29. Working Group on Renovascular Hypertension: Detection, evaluation, and treatment of renovascular hypertension: Final report. Arch Intern Med 147:820-829, 1987.

30. Caridi JG, Devane AM, Hawkins IF Jr, Newman R: Examination of renal donors as outpatients using intraarterial digital subtraction

angiography and a pigtail catheter. AJR Am J Roentgenol 169:537-539, 1997.

31. Sherwood T, Ruutu M, Chisholm GD: Renal angiography problems in live kidney donors. Br J Radiol 51:99-105, 1978.

32. Meaney TF, Dustan HP: Selective renal arteriography in the diagnosis of renal hypertension. Circulation 28:1035-1041, 1963.

33. Nahman NS Jr, Maniam P, Hernandez RA Jr, et al: Renal artery pressure gradients in patients with angiographic evidence of atherosclerotic renal artery stenosis. Am J Kidney Dis 24:695-699, 1994.

34. Carter SA, Ritchie GW: Measurement of renal artery pressures by catheterization in patients with and without renal artery stenosis. Circulation 33:443-449, 1966.

35. Wilcox CS: Ischemic nephropathy: Noninvasive testing. Semin Nephrol 16:43-52, 1996.

36. Reiss MD, Bookstein JJ, Bleifer KH: Radiologic aspects of renovascular hypertension: Part 4. Arteriographic complications. JAMA 221:374-378, 1972.

37. Rudnick MR, Berns JS, Cohen RM, Goldfarb S: Nephrotoxic risks of renal angiography: Contrast media-associated nephrotoxicity and atheroembolism—a critical review. Am J Kidney Dis 24:713-727, 1994.

38. Eisenberg RL, Bank WO, Hedgock MW: Renal failure after major angiography can be avoided with hydration. AJR Am J Roentgenol 136:859-861, 1981.

39. Rudnick MR, Goldfarb S, Wesler L, et al: Nephrotoxicity of ionic and nonionic contrast media in 1196 patients: A randomized trial. The Iohexol Cooperative Study. Kidney Int 47:254-261, 1995.

40. D'Elia JA, Gleason RE, Alday M, et al: Nephrotoxicity from angiographic contrast material: A prospective study. Am J Med 72:719-725, 1982.

41. Lautin EM, Freeman NJ, Schoenfeld AH, et al: Radiocontrast-associated renal dysfunction: Incidence and risk factors. AJR Am J Roentgenol 157:49-58, 1991.

42. Moore RD, Steinberg EP, Powe NR, et al: Nephrotoxicity of high-osmolality versus low-osmolality contrast media: Randomized clinical trial. Radiology 182:649-655, 1992.

43. Berns AS: Nephrotoxicity of contrast media. Kidney Int 36:730-740, 1989.

44. Barrett BJ, Parfrey PS, Vavasour HM, et al: Contrast nephropathy in patients with impaired renal function: High versus low osmolar media. Kidney Int 41:1274-1279, 1992.

45. Huber W, Schipek C, Ilgmann K, et al: Effectiveness of theophylline prophylaxis of renal impairment after coronary angiography in patients with chronic renal insufficiency. Am J Cardiol 91:1157-1162, 2003.

46. Schwab SJ, Hlatky MA, Pieper KS, et al: Contrast nephrotoxicity: A randomized controlled trial of a nonionic and an ionic radiographic contrast agent. N Engl J Med 320:149-153, 1989.

47. Harris KG, Smith TP, Cragg AH, Lemke JH: Nephrotoxicity from contrast material in renal insufficiency: Ionic versus nonionic agents. Radiology 179:849-852, 1991.

48. Parfrey PS, Griffiths SM, Barrett BJ, et al: Contrast material-induced renal failure in patients with diabetes mellitus, renal insufficiency, or both: A prospective controlled study. N Engl J Med 320:143-149, 1989.

49. Taliercio CP, Vlietstra RE, Ilstrup DM, et al: A randomized comparison of the nephrotoxicity of iopamidol and diatrizoate in high risk patients undergoing cardiac angioplasty. J Am Coll Cardiol 17:384-390, 1991.

50. Thadhani RI, Carnargo CA, Xavier FJ, et al: Atheroembolic renal failure after invasive procedures: Natural history based on 52 histologically proven cases. Medicine 74:350-358, 1995.

51. Fukumoto Y, Tsutsui H, Tsuchihashi M, et al; Cholesterol Embolism Study (CHEST) Investigators: The incidence and risk factors of cholesterol embolization syndrome, a complication of cardiac catheterization: A prospective study. J Am Coll Cardiol 42:211-216, 2003.

52. Ramirez G, O'Neill WM, Lambert R, Bloomer HA: Cholesterol embolization: A complication of angiography. Arch Intern Med 138:1430-1432, 1978.

53. Hou SH, Bushinsky DA, Wish JB, et al: Hospital-acquired renal insufficiency: A prospective study. Am J Med 74:243-248, 1983.

54. Shusterman N, Strom BL, Murray TG, et al: Risk factors and outcome of hospital-acquired acute renal failure: Clinical epidemiologic study. Am J Med 83:65-71, 1987.

55. Taliercio CP, Vlietstra RE, Fisher LD, Burnett JC: Risks for renal dysfunction with cardiac angiography. Ann Intern Med 104:501-504, 1986.

56. Manske CL, Sprafka JM, Strony JT, Want Y: Contrast nephropathy in azotemic diabetic patients undergoing coronary angiography. Am J Med 89:615-620, 1990.

57. Cigarroa RG, Lange RA, Williams RH, Hillis LD: Dosing of contrast material to prevent contrast nephropathy in patients with renal disease. Am J Med 86(6 Pt 1):649-652, 1989.

58. Gomes AS, Baker JD, Martin-Paredero V, et al: Acute renal dysfunction after major arteriography. AJR Am J Roentgenol 145:1249-1253, 1985.

59. Martin-Paredero V, Dixon SM, Baker JD, et al: Risk of renal failure after major angiography. Arch Surg 118:1417-1420, 1983.

60. Barrett BJ, Carlisle EJ: Meta-analysis of the relative nephrotoxicity of high- and low-osmolality iodinated contrast media. Radiology 188:171-178, 1993.

61. Jakobsen JA: Renal effects of iodixanol in healthy volunteers and patients with severe renal failure. Acta Radiol 36(Suppl 399):191-195, 1995.

62. Rudnick MR, Berns JS, Cohen RM, Goldfarb S: Nephrotoxic risks of renal angiography: Contrast media-associated nephrotoxicity and atheroembolism—a critical review. Am J Kidney Dis 24:713-727, 1994.

63. Tepel M, van der Giet M, Schwarzfeld C, et al: Prevention of radiographic-contrast-agent-induced reductions in renal function by acetylcysteine. N Engl J Med 343:180-184, 2000.

64. Kay J, Chow WH, Chan TM, et al: Acetylcysteine for prevention of acute deterioration of renal function following elective coronary angiography and intervention: A randomized controlled trial. JAMA 289:553-558, 2003.

65. Diaz-Sandoval LJ, Kosowsky BD, Losordo DW: Acetylcysteine to prevent angiography-related renal tissue injury (the APART trial). Am J Cardiol 89:356-358, 2002.

66. Shyu KG, Cheng JJ, Kuan P: Acetylcysteine protects against acute renal damage in patients with abnormal renal function undergoing a coronary procedure. J Am Coll Cardiol 40:1383-1388, 2002.

67. MacNeill BD, Harding SA, Bazari H, et al: Prophylaxis of contrast-induced nephropathy in patients undergoing coronary angiography. Catheter Cardiovasc Interv 60:458-461, 2003.

68. Efrati S, Dishy V, Averbukh M, et al: The effect of N-acetylcysteine on renal function, nitric oxide, and oxidative stress after angiography. Kidney Int 64:2182-2187, 2003.

69. Durham JD, Caputo C, Dokko J, et al: A randomized controlled trial of N-acetylcysteine to prevent contrast nephropathy in cardiac angiography. Kidney Int 62:2202-2207, 2002.

70. Briguori C, Manganelli F, Scarpato P, et al: Acetylcysteine and contrast agent-associated nephrotoxicity. J Am Coll Cardiol 40:298-303, 2002.

71. Boccalandro F, Amhad M, Smalling RW, Sdringola S: Oral acetylcysteine does not protect renal function from moderate to high doses of intravenous radiographic contrast. Catheter Cardiovasc Interv 58:336-341, 2003.

72. Allaqaband S, Tumuluri R, Malik AM, et al: Prospective randomized study of N-acetylcysteine, fenoldopam, and saline for prevention of radiocontrast-induced nephropathy. Catheter Cardiovasc Interv 57:279-283, 2002.

73. Stevens MA, McCullough PA, Tobin KJ, et al: A prospective randomized trial of prevention measures in patients at high risk for contrast nephropathy: Results of the PRINCE study. J Am Coll Cardiol 33:403-411, 1999.

74. Wiesberg LS, Kurnik PB, Kurnik BRC: Risk of radiocontrast nephropathy in patients with and without diabetes mellitus. Kidney Int 45:259-265, 1994.

75. Bakris GL, Lass NA, Glock D: Renal hemodynamics in radiocontrast medium-induced renal dysfunction: A role for dopamine-1 receptors. Kidney Int 56:206-210, 1999.

76. Hunter DW, Chamsuddin A, Bjarnason H, Kowalik K: Preventing contrast-induced nephropathy with fenoldopam. Tech Vasc Interv Radiol 4:53-56, 2001.

77. Tumlin JA, Wang A, Murray PT, Mathur VS: Fenoldopam mesylate blocks reductions in renal plasma flow after radiocontrast dye infusion: A pilot trial in the prevention of contrast nephropathy. Am Heart J 143:894-903, 2002.

78. Stone GW, McCullough PA, Tumlin JA, et al: Fenoldopam mesylate for the prevention of contrast-induced nephropathy: A randomized controlled trial. JAMA 290: 2284-2291, 2003.

79. Paul RE, Durant TM, Oppenheimer MJ, Stauffer HM: Intravenous carbon dioxide for intracardiac gas contrast in the roentgen diagnosis of pericardial effusion and thickening. AJR Am J Roentgenol 78:223-224, 1957.

80. Oppenheimer MJ, Durant DM, Stauffer H, et al: Cardiovascular-respiratory effects and associated changes in blood chemistry. Am J Physiol 186:325-334, 1956.

81. Moore RM, Braselton CW: Injections of air and carbon dioxide into a pulmonary vein. Ann Surg 112:212-218, 1940.

82. Hawkins IF Jr, Wilcox CS, Kerns SR, Sabatelli FW: CO2 digital angiography: A safer contrast agent for renal vascular imaging? Am J Kidney Dis 24:685-694, 1994.

83. Coffey R, Quisling RG, Mickle JP, et al: The cerebrovascular effects of intra-arterial CO2 in quantities required for diagnostic imaging. Radiology 151:405-410, 1984.

84. Hawkins IF, Caridi JG, Kerns SR: Plastic bag delivery system for hand injection of carbon dioxide. AJR Am J Roentgenol 165:1-3, 1995.

85. Seeger JM, Self S, Harward TR, et al: Carbon dioxide gas as an arterial contrast agent. Ann Surg 217:688-698, 1993.

86. Harward TR, Smith S, Hawkins IF, Seeger JM: Follow-up evaluation after renal artery bypass surgery with use of carbon dioxide arteriography and color-flow duplex scanning. J Vasc Surg 18:23-30, 1993.

87. Schreier DZ, Weaver FA, Frankhouse J, et al: A prospective study of carbon dioxide-digital subtraction vs standard contrast arteriography in the evaluation of the renal arteries. Arch Surg 131:503-508, 1996.

88. Kerns SR, Hawkins IF Jr: Carbon dioxide digital subtraction angiography: Expanding applications and technical evolution. AJR Am J Roentgenol 164:735-741, 1995.

89. Weaver FA, Pentecost MJ, Yellin AE, et al: Clinical applications of carbon dioxide/digital subtraction arteriography. J Vasc Surg 13:266-273, 1991.

90. Hawkins IF, Caridi JG: Carbon dioxide (CO2) digital subtraction angiography: 26-year experience at the University of Florida. Eur Radiol 8:391-402, 1998.

91. Miller FJ, Mineau DE, Koehler PR, et al: Clinical intra-arterial digital subtraction imaging: Use of small volumes of iodinated contrast material or carbon dioxide. Radiology 148:273-278, 1983.

92. Kriss VM, Cottrill CM, Gurley JC: Carbon dioxide (CO2) angiography in children. Pediatr Radiol 27:807-810, 1997.

93. Hawkins IF: Carbon dioxide digital subtraction arteriography. AJR Am J Roentgenol 139:19-24, 1982.

94. Spinosa DJ, Matsumoto AH, Angle JF, et al: Safety of CO(2)- and gadodiamide-enhanced angiography for the evaluation and percutaneous treatment of renal artery stenosis in patients with chronic renal insufficiency. AJR Am J Roentgenol 176:1305-1311, 2001.

95. Dowling K, Kan H, Siskin G, et al: Safety of limited supplemental iodinated contrast administration in azotemic patients undergoing CO2 angiography. J Endovasc Ther 10:312-316, 2003.

96. Beese RC, Bees NR, Belli AM: Renal angiography using carbon dioxide. Br J Radiol 73:3-6, 2000.

97. Harward TR, Smith S, Hawkins IF, Seeger JM: Follow-up evaluation after renal artery bypass surgery with use of carbon dioxide arteriography and color-flow duplex scanning. J Vasc Surg 18:23-30, 1993.

98. Prince MR, Arnoldus C, Frisoli JK: Nephrotoxicity of high-dose gadolinium compared with iodinated contrast. J Magn Reson Imaging 6:162-166, 1996.

99. Niendorf HP, Haustein J, Cornelius I, et al: Safety of gadolinium-DTPA: Extended clinical experience. Magn Reson Med 22:222-232, 1991.

100. Haustein J, Niendorf HP, Krestin G, et al: Renal tolerance of gadolinium-DTPA/dimeglumine in patients with chronic renal failure. Invest Radiol 27:153-156, 1992.

101. Ailawadi G, Stanley JC, Williams DM, et al: Gadolinium as a nonnephrotoxic contrast agent for catheter-based arteriographic evaluation of renal arteries in patients with azotemia. J Vasc Surg 37:346-352, 2003.

102. Neindorf HP, Seifert W: Serum iron and serum bilirubin after administration of gad-DTPA dimeglumine: A pharmacologic study in healthy volunteers. Invest Radiol 23:S275-S280, 1988.

103. Prince MR, Arnoldus C, Frisoli JK: Nephrotoxicity of high dose gadolinium compared with iodinated contrast material. J Magn Reson Imaging 6:162-166, 1996.

104. Arsenault TM, King BF, Marsh JW Jr, et al: Systemic gadolinium toxicity in patients with renal insufficiency and renal failure: Retrospective analysis of initial experience. Mayo Clin Proc 71:1150-1154, 1996.

105. Haustein J, Niendorf HP, Krestin G, et al: Renal tolerance of gadolinium-DTPA/dimeglumine in patients with chronic renal failure. Invest Radiol 27:153-156, 1992.

106. Burns PN: The physical principles of Doppler and spectral analysis. J Clin Ultrasound 15:567-590, 1987.

107. Olin JW: Role of duplex ultrasonography in screening for significant renal artery disease. Urol Clin North Am 21:215-226, 1994.

108. Schwerk WB, Restrepo IK, Stellwaag M, et al: Renal artery stenosis: Grading with image-directed Doppler US evaluation of renal resistive index. Radiology 190:785-790, 1994.

109. Postma CT, van Aalen J, De Boo T, et al: Doppler ultrasound scanning in the detection of renal artery stenosis in hypertensive patients. Br J Radiol 65:857-860, 1992.

110. Bardilli M, Jensen G, Volkmann R, Aurell M: Non-invasive ultrasound assessment of renal artery stenosis by means of the Gosling pulsatility index. J Hypertens 10:985-999, 1992.

111. Kohler TR, Zierler RE, Martin RL, et al: Noninvasive diagnosis of renal artery stenosis by ultrasonic duplex scanning. J Vasc Surg 4:450-456, 1988.

112. Olin JW: Atherosclerotic renal artery disease. Cardiol Clin 20:547-562, 2002.

113. Hansen KJ, Tribble RW, Reavis SW, et al: Renal duplex sonography: Evaluation of clinical utility. J Vasc Surg 12:227-236, 1990.

114. Olin JW, Piedmonte MA, Young JR, et al: The utility of duplex ultrasound scanning of the renal arteries for diagnosing significant renal artery stenosis. Ann Intern Med 122:833-838, 1995.

115. Taylor DC, Kettler MD, Moneta G, et al: Duplex ultrasound scanning in the diagnosis of renal artery stenosis: A prospective evaluation. J Vasc Surg 7:363-369, 1988.

116. Hoffmann U, Edwards JM, Carter S, et al: Role of duplex scanning for the detection of atherosclerotic renal artery disease. Kidney Int 39:1232-1239, 1991.

117. Simoni C, Balestra G, Bandini A, Rusticali F: [Doppler ultrasound in the diagnosis of renal artery stenosis in hypertensive patients: A prospective study]. G Ital Cardiol 21:249-255, 1991.

118. Handa N, Fukunaga R, Etani H, et al: Efficacy of echo-Doppler examination for the evaluation of renovascular disease. Ultrasound Med Biol 14:1-5, 1988.

119. Nchimi A: Duplex ultrasound as first-line screening test for patients suspected of renal artery stenosis: Prospective evaluation in high-risk group. Eur Radiol 13:1413-1419, 2003.

120. Desberg AL, Paushter DM, Lammert GK, et al: Renal artery stenosis: Evaluation with color Doppler flow imaging. Radiology 177:749-753, 1990.

121. Lewis BD, James EM: Current applications of duplex and color Doppler ultrasound imaging: Abdomen. Mayo Clin Proc 643:1158-1169, 1984.

122. Robertson R, Murphy A, Dubbins PA: Renal artery stenosis: The use of duplex ultrasound as a screening technique. Br J Radiol 61:196-201, 1988.

123. Mollo M, Pelet V, Mouawad J, et al: Evaluation of colour duplex ultrasound scanning in diagnosis of renal artery stenosis, compared to angiography: A prospective study on 53 patients. Eur J Vasc Endovasc Surg 14:305-309, 1997.

124. Berland LL, Koslin DB, Routh WD, Keller FS: Renal artery stenosis: prospective evaluation of diagnosis with color duplex US compared with angiography. Radiology 174:421-423, 1990.

125. Cochran ST, Krasny RM, Danovitch GM, et al: Helical CT angiography for examination of living renal donors. AJR Am J Roentgenol 168:1569-1573, 1997.

126. Radermacher J, Chavan A, Schaffer J, et al: Detection of significant renal artery stenosis with color Doppler sonography: Combining extrarenal and intrarenal approaches to minimize technical failure. Clin Nephrol 53:333-343, 2000.

127. Platt JF: Doppler ultrasound of the kidney. Semin Ultrasound CT MRI 18:22-32, 1997.

128. Stavros AT, Parker SH, Yakes WF, et al: Segmental stenosis of the renal artery: Pattern recognition of tardus and parvus abnormalities with duplex sonography. Genitourin Radiol 184:487-492, 1992.

129. Nazzal MMS, Hoballah JJ, Miller EV, et al: Renal hilar Doppler analysis is of value in the management of patients with renovascular disease. Am J Surg 174:164-168, 1997.

130. Halpern EJ, Needleman L, Nack TL, East SA: Renal artery stenosis: Should we study the main renal artery or segmental vessels? Radiology 195:799-804, 1995.

131. Radermacher J, Chavan A, Bleck J, et al: Use of Doppler ultra-sonography to predict the outcome of therapy for renal-artery stenosis. N Engl J Med 344:410-417, 2001.

132. Hall NJ, Thorpe RJ, MacKechnie SG: Stenosis of the accessory renal artery: Doppler ultrasound findings. Australas Radiol 39:73-77, 1995.

133. Oliva VL, Soulez G, Lesage D, et al: Detection of renal artery stenosis with Doppler sonography after administration of captopril: Value of early systolic rise. AJR Am J Roentgenol 171:169-175, 1998.

134. Rene PC, Oliva VL, Bui BT, et al: Renal artery stenosis: Evaluation of captopril. Radiology 196:675-679, 1995.

135. Missouris CG, Allen CM, Balen FG, et al: Noninvasive screening for renal artery stenosis with ultrasound contrast enhancement. J Hypertens 14:519-524, 1996.

136. Claudon M, Plouin PF, Baxter GM, et al: Renal arteries in patients at risk of renal arterial stenosis: Multicenter evaluation of the echo-enhancer SH U 508A at color and spectral Doppler US. Levovist Renal Artery Stenosis Study Group. Radiology 21:739-746, 2000.

137. Strandness DE: Natural history of renal artery stenosis. Am J Kidney Dis 24:630-635, 1994.

138. Guzman RP, Zierler RE, Isaacson JA, et al: Renal atrophy and arterial stenosis. Hypertension 23:346-350, 1994.

139. Taylor DC, Moneta GL, Strandness DE: Follow-up of renal artery stenosis by duplex ultrasound. J Vasc Surg 9:410-415, 1989.

140. Eidt JF, Fry RE, Clagett GP, et al: Postoperative follow-up of renal artery reconstruction with duplex ultrasound. J Vasc Surg 8:667-673, 1988.

141. Lantz EJ, Charboneau JW, Hallett JW, et al: Intraoperative color-Doppler sonography during renal artery revascularization. AJR Am J Roentgenol 162:847-852, 1994.

142. Duda SH, Erley CM, Wakat JP, et al: Posttransplant renal artery stenosis—outpatient intra-arterial DSA versus color aided duplex Doppler sonography. Eur J Radiol 16:95-101, 1993.

143. Sagalowsky A, McQuitty DM: The assessment and management of renal vascular hypertension after kidney transplantation. Semin Urol 12:221-223, 1994.

144. Snider JF, Hunter DW, Moradian GP, et al: Transplant renal artery stenosis: Evaluation with duplex sonography. Radiology 172:1027-1030, 1989.

145. Blum U, Drumme B, Flugel P, et al: Treatment of ostial renal artery stenosis with vascular endoprostheses after unsuccessful balloon angioplasty. N Engl J Med 336:459-465, 1997.

146. Guzman RP, Zierler RE, Isaacson JA, et al: Renal atrophy and arterial stenosis: A prospective study with duplex ultrasound. Hypertension 23:346-350, 1994.

147. Harward TRS, Smith S, Seeger JM: Detection of celiac axis and superior mesenteric artery occlusive disease with use of abdominal duplex scanning. J Vasc Surg 17:738-745, 1993.

148. Gedroyc WM: Magnetic resonance angiography of renal arteries. Urol Clin North Am 21:201-214, 1994.

149. Grist TM: Magnetic resonance angiography of renal artery stenosis. Am J Kidney Dis 24:700-712, 1994.

150. Borrello JA: Renal MR angiography. Genitourin Imaging 5:83-93, 1997.

151. Müller MF, Prasad PV, Bimmler D, et al: Functional imaging of the kidney by means of the apparent diffusion coefficient. Radiology 193:711-715, 1994.

152. Roberts DA, Detre JA, Bolinger L, et al: Renal perfusion in humans: MR imaging with spin tagging of arterial water. Radiology 196:281-286, 1995.

153. Prasad PV, Kim D, Kaiser AM, et al: Noninvasive comprehensive characterization of renal artery stenosis by combination of STAR angiography and EPISTAR perfusion imaging. Magn Reson Med 38:776-787, 1997.

154. Niendorf ER, Grist TM, Lee FT, et al: Rapid in vivo measurement of single-kidney extraction fraction and glomerular filtration rate with MR imaging. Radiology 206:791-798, 1998.

155. Schoenberg SO, Knopp MV, Bock M, et al: Renal artery stenosis: Grading of hemodynamic changes with MR CINE phase-contrast flow measurements. Radiology 203:45-53, 1997.

156. DeCobelli F, Vanzuli A, Sironi S, et al: Renal artery stenosis: Evaluation with breath-hold, three-dimensional, dynamic, gadolinium-enhanced versus three-dimensional, phase-contrast MR angiography. Radiology 205:689-695, 1997.

157. Leung DA, Nany TF, Debatin JF: Three-dimensional contrast enhanced magnetic resonance angiography of the abdominal arterial system. Cardiovasc Intervent Radiol 21:1-10, 1998.

158. Prince MR, Narasimhan DL, Stanley JC, et al: Breath-hold gadolinium-enhanced MR angiography of the abdominal aorta and its branches. Radiology 197:785-792, 1995.

159. Steffens JC, Link J, Crassner J, et al: Contrast enhanced centered breath-hold MR angiography of the renal arteries and the abdominal aorta. J Magn Reson Imaging 7:617-622, 1997.

160. Hany TF, Debatin JF, Leung DA, Pfammatter T: Evaluation of the aortoiliac and renal arteries: Comparison of breath-hold contrast-enhanced three-dimensional MR angiography with conventional catheter angiography. Radiology 204:357-362, 1997.

161. Rieumont MJ, Kaufman JA, Geller SC, et al: Evaluation of renal artery stenosis with dynamic gadolinium enhanced MR angiography. AJR Am J Roentgenol 169:39-44, 1997.

162. Holland GA, Dougherty L, Carpenter JP, et al: Breath-hold ultrafast three-dimensional gadolinium-enhanced MR angiography of the aorta and the renal and other visceral abdominal arteries. AJR Am J Roentgenol 166:971-981, 1996.

163. Hany TF, Leung DA, Pfammatter T, Debatin JF: Contrast-enhanced magnetic resonance angiography of the renal arteries. Invest Radiol 33:653-665, 1998.

164. Schoenberg SO, Knopp MV, Londy F, et al: Morphologic and functional magnetic resonance imaging of renal artery stenosis: A multireader tricenter study. J Am Soc Nephrol 13:158-169, 2002.

165. Prince MR: A gadolinium enhanced MR aortography. Radiology 191:155-164, 1994.

166. Gedroyc WM, Negus R, Al-Kutoubi A, et al: Magnetic resonance angiography of renal transplants. Lancet 339:789-791, 1992.

167. Johnson DB, Lerner CA, Prince MR, et al: Gadolinium-enhanced magnetic resonance angiography of renal transplants. Magn Reson Imaging 15:13-20, 1997.

168. Loubeyre P, Cahen R, Grozel F, et al: Transplant renal artery stenosis: Evaluation of diagnosis with magnetic resonance angiography compared with color duplex sonography and arteriography. Transplantation 62:446-450, 1996.

169. Bennett HF, Li D: MR imaging of renal function. Magn Reson Imaging Clin N Am 5:107-126, 1997.

170. Taylor J, Summers PE, Keevil SF, et al: Magnetic resonance renography: Optimization of pulse sequence parameters and Gd-DPTA dose, comparison with radionuclide renography. Magn Reson Imaging 15:637-649, 1997.

171. Grenier N, Trillaud H, Combe C, et al: Diagnosis of renovascular hypertension: Feasibility of captopril-sensitized dynamic MR imaging and comparison with captopril scintigraphy. AJR Am J Roentgenol 16:835-843, 1996.

172. Ros PR, Gauger J, Stoupis C, et al: Diagnosis of renal artery stenosis: Feasibility of combining MR angiography, MR renography, and gadopentetate based measurements of glomerular filtration rate. AJR Am J Roentgenol 165:1447-1451, 1995.

173. Cortsen M, Peterson LJ, Stahlberg F, et al: MR velocity mapping measurement of renal artery blood flow in patients with impaired kidney function. Acta Radiol 37:79-84, 1996.

174. Lundin B, Cooper TG, Meyer RA, Potchen J: Measurement of total and unilateral renal blood flow by oblique angle velocity encoded 2D-cine magnetic resonance angiography. Magn Reson Imaging 11:51-59, 1993.

175. Powers TA, Lorenz CH, Holburn GE, Price RK: Renal artery stenosis: In vivo perfusion MR imaging. Radiology 178:543-548, 1991.

176. Rubin GD: Spiral (helical) CT of the renal vasculature. Semin Ultrasound CT MR 17:374-397, 1996.

177. Brink JA, Lim JT, Wang G, et al: Technical optimization of spiral CT for depiction of renal artery stenosis: In vitro analysis. Radiology 194:157-163, 1995.

178. Rubin GD, Dake MD, Napel S, et al: Spiral CT of renal artery stenosis: Comparison of three-dimensional rendering techniques. Radiology 190:181-189, 1994.

179. Rubin GD, Dake MD, Napel SA, et al: Three-dimensional spiral CT angiography of the abdomen: Initial clinical experience. Radiology 186:147-152, 1993.

180. Galanski M, Prokop M, Schaefer C, et al: Renal artery stenosis: Spiral CT angiography. Radiology 189:185-192, 1993.

181. Kaatee R, Beek FJ, de Lange EE, et al: Renal artery stenosis: Detection and quantification with spiral CT angiography versus optimized digital subtraction angiography. Radiology 205:121-127, 1997.

182. Farres MT, Lammer J, Schima W, et al: Spiral computed tomographic angiography of the renal arteries: A prospective comparison with intravenous and intra-arterial digital subtraction angiography. Cardiovasc Intervent Radiol 19:101-106, 1996.

183. Cikrit DF, Harris JV, Hemmer DG, et al: Comparison of spiral CT scan and arteriography for evaluation of renal and visceral arteries. Ann Vasc Surg 10:109-116, 1996.

184. Wittenberg G, Kenn W, Tschammler A, et al: Spiral CT angiography of renal arteries: Comparison with angiography. Eur Radiol 9:546-551,1999.

185. Deregi JP, Elkohen M, Deklunder G, et al: Helical CT angiography compared with arteriography in the detection of renal artery stenosis. AJR Am J Roentgenol 167:495-501, 1996.

186. Kim TS, Chung JW, Park JH, et al: Renal artery evaluation: Comparison of spiral CT angiography to intra-arterial DSA. J Vasc Interv Radiol 9:553-559, 1998.

187. Lerman LO, Taler SJ, Textor SC, et al: Computed tomography derived intrarenal blood flow in renovascular and essential hypertension. Kidney Int 49:846-854, 1996.

188. Gomes MN, Davros WJ, Zeman RK: Preoperative assessment of abdominal aortic aneurysm: The value of helical and three-dimensional computed tomography. J Vasc Surg 20:367-375, 1994.

189. Todd GJ, Nowygrod R, Benvenisty A, et al: The accuracy of CT scanning in the diagnosis of abdominal and thoracoabdominal aortic aneurysms. J Vasc Surg 13:302-310, 1991.

190. Elkohen M, Deregi JP, Deklunder G, et al: A prospective study of helical computed tomography angiography versus angiography for the detection of renal artery stenosis in hypertensive patients. J Hypertens 14:525-528, 1996.
191. Goldblatt H, et al: Studies on experimental hypertension: I. The production of elevation of the systolic blood pressure by means of renal ischemia. J Exp Med 59:347, 1934.
192. Marks LS, Maxwell MH: Renal vein renin: Value and limitations in the prediction of operative results. Urol Clin North Am 2:311-325, 1975.
193. Smith MC, Dunn MJ: Renovascular and renal parenchymal hypertension. In Brenner BM, Rector FC Jr (eds): The Kidney, 3rd ed. Philadelphia, WB Saunders, 1986, p 1221.
194. Pickering TG, Sos TA, Vaughan ED Jr, Laragh JH: Differing patterns of renal vein renin secretion in patients with renovascular hypertension, and their role in predicting the response to angioplasty. Nephron 44(Suppl 1): 8-11, 1986.
195. Nally JV, Chen C, Fine E, et al: Diagnostic criteria of renovascular hypertension with captopril renography—a consensus statement. Am J Hypertens 4:749S-752S, 1991.
196. Setaro JF, Saddler MC, Chen CC, et al: Simplified captopril renography in diagnosis and treatment of renal artery stenosis. Hypertension 18:289-298, 1991.
197. Dondi M: Captopril renal scintigraphy with 99mTc mercaptor acetyltriglycine (99mTc-MAG3) for detecting renal artery stenosis. Am J Hypertens 4:737S-740S, 1991.
198. Marks SJ, Pickering TG, Sos TA, et al: Captopril renography in the diagnosis of renal artery stenosis: Accuracy and limitations. Am J Med 90:30-39, 1991.
199. Nally JV: Provocative captopril testing in the diagnosis of renovascular hypertension [abstract]. Urol Clin North Am 21:227-234, 1994.
200. Woolfson RG, Neild GH: Renal nuclear medicine: Can it survive the millennium? Nephrol Dial Transplant 13:12-14, 1998.

Chapter

Renal Artery Fibrodysplasia and Renovascular Hypertension

129

DARREN B. SCHNEIDER, MD
JAMES C. STANLEY, MD
LOUIS M. MESSINA, MD

Arterial *fibrodysplasia* encompasses a heterogeneous group of arterial dysplastic lesions of unknown etiology that affect segments of small and medium-sized muscular arteries.[73,88] Fibrodysplastic lesions have been described in virtually every artery. The dysplastic process usually results in a stenosis but may cause aneurysm formation. The most commonly affected vessel is the renal artery, first reported by McCormick and colleagues,[59] who used the term *fibromuscular dysplasia* in 1958 to describe renal artery stenoses in three patients with hypertension. The renal artery stenosis affecting the first patient cured of renovascular hypertension, reported by Leadbetter and Burkland[51] in 1938, was, in retrospect, fibromuscular dysplasia.

Occlusive renal artery lesions are the most common cause of surgically correctable hypertension. Although the precise incidence of renovascular hypertension has not been defined, its clinical importance has been clearly established. Fibrodysplastic renal artery stenoses, which affect up to 0.5% of the general population, are second only to atherosclerotic stenoses as the most frequent cause of renovascular hypertension. This overview of renal artery fibrodysplasia describes its pathology and clinical manifestations as well as the indications for therapeutic intervention, drug therapy, and percutaneous transluminal angioplasty and the role of surgical therapy for lesions causing renovascular hypertension.

■ PATHOLOGY

Arterial dysplasia is categorized according to the principal layer of arterial wall involvement, and these groupings correlate with angiographic findings[31] and progression of renovascular disease. The four most commonly encountered dysplastic lesions of the renal arteries are (1) *intimal fibroplasia*, (2) *medial hyperplasia*, (3) *medial fibroplasia*, and (4) *perimedial dysplasia*.[37,85] The first two represent distinctly different pathologic processes, whereas the latter two may be a continuum of the same disease. *Developmental stenoses* represent a fifth distinct and unusual form of renal artery dysplasia.[87]

Intimal Fibroplasia

Intimal fibroplasia accounts for 5% of all fibrodysplastic renal artery lesions. It affects children and young adults of both sexes equally. Intimal fibroplasia occurs morphologically as long, irregular tubular stenoses of the main renal artery in younger patients and as smooth focal stenoses in older patients.[86] Progression of intimal fibroplasia in most patients occurs more slowly than that of medial fibroplasia.

Medial Hyperplasia

Medial hyperplasia is found in fewer than 1% of fibrodysplastic renal artery lesions. Angiographically similar to intimal hyperplasia, it is seen most often in women aged 30 to 50 years. Medial hyperplasia usually occurs as an isolated lesion in the midportion of the main renal artery. One study utilized the presence or absence of smooth muscle hyperplasia to classify fibrodysplastic lesions.[2] The presence of smooth muscle hyperplasia is associated with a shorter duration of hypertension, fewer aneurysms, and less extension of disease into branch vessels as well as a better response to surgical intervention. These features suggest that hyperplastic lesions may be precursors of advanced and more widespread fibrodysplastic lesions instead of representing a distinct pathologic process.

Medial Fibroplasia

Medial fibroplasia constitutes approximately 85% of all dysplastic renal artery lesions and manifests most commonly in white women in the third or fourth decade of life. It occurs most frequently in the renal arteries. Medial fibroplasia is bilateral in 55% of patients; when it is unilateral, it affects the right side in 80% of cases.[86] Lesions usually affect the distal main renal artery, with extension into branch vessels in approximately 25% of cases.

The angiographic appearance of medial fibroplasia is the classic "string of beads." Aneurysms larger than the adjacent artery wall, alternating with luminal weblike projections, are responsible for this presentation. A pathologic study of isolated renal artery aneurysms demonstrated that most have evidence of fibrodysplastic disease, usually unaccompanied by a clinical presentation of renovascular hypertension.[38] Progression of medial fibroplasia appears to be less common than that of perimedial dysplasia.[31]

Perimedial Dysplasia

Perimedial dysplasia, characterized by accumulation of elastic tissue at the media-adventitia junction, is seen in 10% of arterial dysplastic lesions. This lesion is seen in younger women whose angiograms reveal either focal stenoses or multiple stenoses of the main renal artery, without the intervening aneurysmal dilatations seen typically in medial fibroplasia. Perimedial dysplasia is usually associated with marked stenoses severe enough to cause renovascular hypertension.[31]

■ ETIOLOGY

Although the origin of arterial fibrodysplasia remains unclear, three factors appear to play important etiologic roles: (1) hormonal influences, (2) arterial wall ischemia, and (3) mechanical stresses.[86] The higher incidence of arterial dysplasia in women during their reproductive years contrasts with the protective effects of estrogen in human atherosclerosis. Similarly, the antiproliferative effect of estrogen on vascular smooth muscle at both the cellular[43] and arterial levels[104] is contrary to the predilection for arterial dysplasia in women. Oral contraceptives and pregnancies are not significant risk factors for arterial fibrodysplasia,[86] although multiparity has been associated with other degenerative vascular lesions, such as splenic artery aneurysms.

Vessel wall ischemia may contribute to the development of arterial dysplasia.[73] Vasa vasorum of muscular arteries originate from branch points of the parent arteries and supply oxygen and nutrients to the arterial wall. The most commonly affected vessels—the renal, internal carotid, and external iliac arteries—all have long segments that are free of branches and thus have few vasa vasorum. Arterial dysplasia may develop as a result of ischemia of the artery wall secondary to injury to the sparse vasa vasorum of these vessels. Animal studies demonstrate that occlusion of the vasa vasorum induces formation of dysplastic lesions.[77] The media-adventitia junction, where nutrient flow from vasa vasorum is most critical, is also the site of lesions of perimedial dysplasia and peripheral medial fibroplasia.

The unique stresses to which certain long muscular arteries (e.g., internal carotid artery, renal arteries) are subject suggests that mechanical forces may also play a role in development of arterial dysplasia. Repeated stretching of vessels may trigger a fibroproliferative response. This hypothesis is supported by the finding of predominantly right-sided lesions in unilateral fibromuscular disease. The right renal artery is longer than the left and may be subject to greater axial stretch, particularly because the right kidney is known to be subjected to ptosis more than the left, and ptosis in general is more common in women than men.

■ CLINICAL MANIFESTATIONS AND INDICATION FOR TREATMENT

The prevalence of renovascular hypertension in the population with elevated blood pressure is low ($\approx$2% to 5%). Hypertension caused by arterial fibrodysplasia is even less common.[52] The first decision in a reasonable management algorithm depends on the ability to recognize clinical clues of renovascular hypertension secondary to fibrodysplasia (Fig. 129-1).[24] Hypertension in pediatric patients that is unaccompanied by obvious renal disease and the sudden onset of diastolic hypertension greater than 115 mm Hg in women younger than 45 years are two dominant clinical features of renovascular hypertension. Elevated blood pressure in this group of patients tends to be refractory to simple medical management. Furthermore, if the disease affects either arteries to both kidneys or one artery to a solitary kidney, impaired renal function may result from the use of angiotensin-converting enzyme (ACE) inhibitors. Renovascular hypertension secondary to arterial fibrodysplasia is rare in African Americans.[46]

Other clinical findings may be more common in patients with renovascular hypertension than in those with essential hypertension; unfortunately, such findings are not pathognomonic of this disease.[75] For instance, younger children and infants with renovascular hypertension frequently exhibit failure to thrive, whereas hyperkinesis,

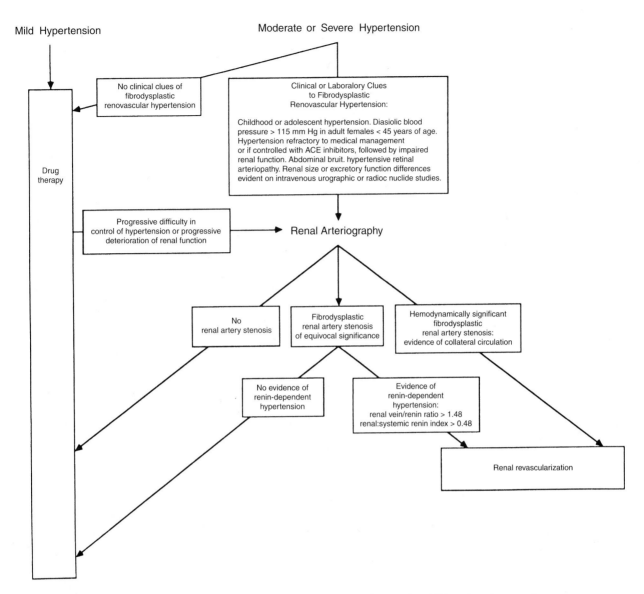

FIGURE 129-1 Management algorithm for fibrodysplastic renovascular hypertension. ACE, angiotensin-converting enzyme.

seizure disorders, cephalalgia, and easy fatigability often affect older children and adolescents.[106] Adults with renovascular hypertension secondary to fibrodysplasia often present with lethargy. Abdominal bruit and hypertensive retinal arteriolar changes may be common findings for patients with renal artery fibrodysplasia, but they are not specific enough to distinguish these patients from those with essential hypertension.

Certain characteristics of children with renal fibrodysplasia are noteworthy. In an earlier report reflecting the experience at the University of Michigan, renal arterial fibrodysplasia causing renovascular hypertension in children showed atypical medial-perimedial dysplasia, often with secondary intimal fibroplasia, in 88% of the renal artery stenoses encountered.[90] The classic string-of-beads appearance of medial fibrodysplasia that occurs in adults was not observed in any child in that series. In a later series, 33 boys and 24 girls whose mean age was 9.5 and 12 years, respectively, presented with an average duration

of hypertension of 14.2 months. The mean preoperative blood pressures were 181 mm Hg systolic/117 mm Hg diastolic without medication and 158/104 mm Hg with drug therapy.[94]

In contrast, the adults treated for renal artery fibrodysplasia at the same institution were 133 women and 11 men, with mean ages of 39.1 and 30.5 years, respectively.[90] The average duration of hypertension in this adult group was 42.5 months. Blood pressures without therapy averaged 206/122 mm Hg, which fell to an average of 184/111 mm Hg with drug treatment. Later reports of adult patients undergoing treatment for renal fibrodysplasia show a distinct change in the presentation and outcome.[3,68] Adult patients are now significantly older, experience a longer duration of hypertension, more frequently demonstrate extrarenal atherosclerosis, and have fibrodysplasia of renal artery branch vessels. These changes in the presentation of the patient population have greatly influenced treatment patterns and outcome.

■ INDICATIONS FOR TREATMENT OF RENAL FIBRODYSPLASIA

Indications for treatment of renal fibrodysplasia depend largely on age at presentation. Because the incidence of essential hypertension is negligible in infants and children, most instances of hypertension in this patient population represent a renovascular etiology.[92,94] The presence of modest or severe blood pressure elevations in a pediatric patient is sufficient justification to undertake detailed diagnostic studies in search of a correctable cause of hypertension. One exception is the occasional child who has evidence of significant underlying renal parenchymal disease. In pediatric patients, catheter angiography is the most important diagnostic study when renovascular hypertension is suspected.

Specific indications for intervention in adults are as follows:

- Presence of moderate to severe hypertension
- A hemodynamically significant renal artery stenosis
- Evidence of the functional importance of the stenosis

The dramatic improvement in drug therapy for hypertension over the last two decades has raised the threshold for intervention for renovascular hypertension, most likely accounting for the observed increase in average age at presentation and duration of hypertension in these patients. However, this improvement often makes determination of the functional significance of renal fibrodysplasia more challenging, because these older patients have a higher frequency of essential hypertension.[3] Nonetheless, clinical clues are the most cost-effective way of identifying patients for screening for renovascular hypertension (see Fig. 129-1). The most commonly employed screening studies are renal duplex ultrasonography, magnetic resonance angiography (MRA), and radionuclide scans. Once a patient has been identified on the basis of clinical clues or the use of screening studies, catheter angiography is the most useful test for assessing the hemodynamic and functional significance of renal artery dysplastic occlusive disease.[82-84]

A number of angiographic features can be used to determine the hemodynamic significance of dysplastic renal artery stenosis. Demonstration of collateral vessels as a manifestation of a significant stenosis has been important in this regard.[26] Collateral vessels circumventing a renal artery stenosis usually develop when the pressure gradient across the stenosis approaches 10 mm Hg. This same gradient is generally accepted as being associated with an increased release of renin from the juxtaglomerular apparatus of the kidney. In this way, the demonstration via pharmaco-angiographic techniques using epinephrine and acetylcholine that the nonparenchymal renal artery branches are functioning as collateral vessels has been helpful in establishing the significance of many equivocal renal artery stenoses.[10]

Renin assays have also been important in determining functional significance of equivocal renal artery stenoses (see Fig. 129-1). Renin assays are most useful for patients who have medically controlled hypertension and in older patients with arterial fibrodysplasia and diffuse extrarenal atherosclerosis.[3] For young patients with poorly controlled hypertension or threatened ischemic nephropathy, such as those with arterial fibrodysplasia affecting a solitary kidney or those with severe bilateral stenoses, the diagnosis may also be made via renin profiling with the *renal systemic renin index* (RSRI).

The *renal vein renin ratio* (RVRR), which compares renin activity in the venous effluent from the ischemic and contralateral kidneys, has not been a highly predictive test, largely because of the frequent occurrence of bilateral disease, in which case the RVRR may revert toward 1.0.[26,53] Although the RVRR is considered abnormal when it exceeds 1.48, lower ratios occur in approximately 15% to 20% of patients whose hypertension is eventually found to have a renovascular cause.[53,82,86]

An alternative calculation of each kidney's renin secretory activity can be expressed as the RSRI.[52,86] One can calculate this index by subtracting the systemic renin activity from renal vein renin activity and dividing the remainder by the systemic renin activity:

$$\frac{\text{renal vein renin} - \text{systemic renin}}{\text{systemic renin}}$$

Renin hypersecretion is defined as an RSRI above 0.48. *Suppression of renin secretion* by a kidney is defined as an RSRI below 0.24, usually approaching 0.0. This method of evaluating each kidney's renin secretory activity indexed to the systemic renin concentration provides a more accurate identification of patients likely to be improved or cured after operation.[82,83] Absolute and relative renin activities do not appear to vary among children and adults with renal arterial fibrodysplasia.[82,98] ACE inhibitors have been used to enhance the sensitivity of these calculations in documenting the existence of renovascular hypertension.[64,102]

Drug Therapy

Improved antihypertensive drug therapy has had an important effect on the management of hypertension for patients with renovascular hypertension secondary to renal artery fibrodysplasia.[105,108] Current principles underlying drug therapy for renovascular hypertension are based on the now well-known pathophysiology of hypertension secondary to a functionally significant renal artery stenosis. Renin-angiotensin–mediated vasoconstriction is the primary mechanism of hypertension in patients with unilateral renal artery stenosis and a normal contralateral kidney. Under these circumstances, the sodium retention and hypervolemia that results from the direct effect of angiotensin II, as well as angiotensin II–induced aldosterone secretion, is compensated by a natriuresis of the normal contralateral kidney. In the setting of bilateral renal artery stenoses, and thus an impaired capacity for natriuresis, renin-angiotensin-aldosterone–mediated sodium retention and hypervolemia are the dominant pathophysiologic mechanisms of hypertension. Similarly, sodium retention and hypervolemia constitute an important mechanism of hypertension in the presence of a unilateral stenosis and either contralateral parenchymal disease or renal absence due to agenesis or previous nephrectomy.

Hypertension in most patients with renal artery fibrodysplasia can be controlled with the appropriate pharmacologic intervention. The following issues may influence the long-term therapeutic effectiveness of drug therapy for hypertension:

- Drug side effects.
- Patient compliance.
- Whether blood pressure control is achieved at the expense of diminished renal function, occurring as a direct effect of the drug or as unrecognized insidious progression of renal artery occlusive disease.

In this last regard, ischemic nephropathy was not observed in earlier studies of young patients with renal artery fibrodysplasia. However, ischemic nephropathy has been reported in some studies of both surgical and angioplasty outcomes.[3,71]

In patients with documented renovascular hypertension, a beta-blocking agent is often the first drug given. Inhibition of renin secretion by beta-blocking agents is the principal means of blood pressure reduction in these patients.[12] In instances of refractory hypertension, often as the result of bilateral renal artery stenoses, the addition of a diuretic agent may be used to compensate for the hypervolemic state that exists in these patients. A thiazide is usually used in this circumstance. In the subgroup of patients with impaired renal function, a loop diuretic such as furosemide may be needed to achieve an effective diuresis. ACE inhibitors and angiotensin II antagonists have become highly effective agents in the management of hypertension in general and renovascular hypertension in particular.[1,14,29,39] These agents may be supplemented by both beta-blockers and diuretics in instances of refractory hypertension. Calcium-channel blockers have been used to supplement ACE inhibitors in the management of renovascular hypertension. Finally, in most cases of severe hypertension, clonidine or vasodilators such as hydralazine are utilized.

It is recognized that when ACE inhibitors are used to treat renovascular hypertension, renal function may become impaired.[16] Impairment occurs most often in patients with bilateral renal artery stenosis as well as in patients with a stenosis affecting a solitary kidney.[40] In these circumstances, a severe reduction in the glomerular filtration rate occurs, because the primary effect of the ACE inhibitors in the kidney is to mediate efferent arteriolar vasodilatation, thereby reducing the effective driving pressure across the glomerulus.

Percutaneous Transluminal Renal Angioplasty

Although the first successful percutaneous transluminal angioplasty (PTA), reported in 1978 by Gruntzig and colleagues,[35] involved the dilatation of an atherosclerotic renal artery stenosis, this technique was soon recognized to be effective in the treatment of fibrodysplastic lesions.[4,33,34,57,72,74,101] For a variety of reasons, percutaneous transluminal renal angioplasty (PTRA) has become the dominant mode of treatment of renal arterial dysplasia at most institutions.

PTRA is performed after aortography and selective renal arteriographic studies have defined the severity and extent of renal artery stenosis. Femoral or brachial approaches may be used for PTRA. The renal artery itself is usually entered by means of a selective catheter over a hydrophilic guidewire. The guidewire is exchanged for a Rosen wire, which is positioned within a renal artery branch. A guiding catheter or sheath is generally used to facilitate balloon introduction and for the injection of contrast agent during PTRA. PTRA is performed with a standard angioplasty balloon with a diameter equal to the nondiseased renal artery. Completion angiography is then undertaken through the guiding catheter or sheath. Angioplasty is deemed technically successful when preexisting pressure gradients across the stenosis are abolished and anatomic documentation of an adequate dilatation is apparent.[76,101]

Intravenous heparin is typically administered before PTRA to prevent renal artery thrombosis. Instillation of nitroglycerin directly into the renal artery is also useful to prevent vasospasm. Low-profile (0.018-in. or smaller) and rapid-exchange systems may facilitate percutaneous treatment of difficult renal artery lesions. The role of distal protection devices to prevent embolism during PTRA remains unclear. The majority of fibrodysplastic lesions may be treated with PTRA alone, and stent placement is reserved for rescue in failed PTRA or renal artery dissection.

The mechanism by which balloon angioplasty increases the diameter of fibrodysplastic arteries is similar to that used during dilatation of atherosclerotic arteries. As the balloon is inflated, the artery wall is stretched, separating the intima from underlying structures, splitting the media, and stretching the adventitia beyond its elastic recoil. The dilated artery gradually undergoes a fibroproliferative reparative process, and a neointima is formed.

Approximately 85% of adult patients with renal artery fibrodysplasia and renovascular hypertension benefit from PTRA (Table 129-1); however, the effectiveness and complication rates for this procedure vary widely. This variation may in part reflect differences in patient age and the type of renal artery fibrodysplasia that is being treated. For instance, PTRA is less effective in patients with intimal fibroplasia or perimedial dysplasia and for developmental lesions. The best results with transluminal renal angioplasty are obtained in adult patients who have unilateral medial fibroplasia.

The results of transluminal renal angioplasty for renal artery fibrodysplasia in pediatric patients are less salutary.[20,93] Most studies show that attempts to dilate proximal ostial lesions, especially those associated with neurofibromatosis or aortic anomalies, are likely to be unsuccessful.[49,61,62] In one series involving children, 60% of unsuccessful angioplasties resulted in nephrectomy.[106] However, later reports show a higher rate of short-term and long-term success.[13]

An overall complication rate after renal angioplasty, as reflected in review of 624 procedures, averaged 11%, ranging from 2.5% to 38.5%.[56,79] In contrast to atherosclerosis, mortality after PTRA of renal arterial dysplasia is extremely rare.[9] However, certain complications are more common, in particular arterial dissection and perforation.

Table 129-1   Results of Percutaneous Transluminal Angioplasty for Renovascular Hypertension due to Fibrodysplasia in Adults

STUDY (YEAR)*	NO. PATIENTS	POSTANGIOPLASTY STATUS (%)†			LENGTH OF FOLLOW-UP (mo)
		Cure	Improvement	Failure	
Martin et al (1985)[58]	26	58	35	8	60
Luscher et al (1986)[54]	28	50	39	11	15
Hagg et al (1987)[36]	18	33	22	44	36
Rodriguez-Perez et al (1994)[71]	27	43	48	10	60
Cluzel et al (1994)[17]	20	68	16	15	19
Bonelli et al (1995)[9]	105	22	41	37	43
Davidson et al (1996)[18]	23	52	22	26	6
Birrer et al (2002)[8]	27	—	74‡	26	12

*Superscript numbers indicate chapter references.
†Criteria for blood pressure response are defined in cited publications. Data are expressed to nearest 1%.
‡Cured or improved.

Transluminal renal angioplasty is contraindicated in patients who have renal artery stenosis associated with macro-aneurysms, extensive branch vessel disease, or complex dissections. In these latter circumstances, the frequency of angioplasty-related complications is high. Trends in outcome after PTRA parallel those after surgical management.[3,9] Failures correlate with longer duration of hypertension and older age of patients at the time of presentation for treatment.

Surgical Therapy

Operative Technique

Adequate exposure is critical to the performance of successful arterial reconstructive surgery for renal artery fibrodysplasia. Either a supraumbilical transverse or midline incision can be used. The transverse incision extends from opposite the midclavicular line to the midaxillary line on the side of renal artery reconstruction. An advantage of a transverse abdominal incision is that the handling of instruments is perpendicular to the longitudinal access of the body.

Midline incisions extend from the xiphoid process to the pubic symphysis. After the peritoneal cavity has been entered and its contents explored, the intestines are displaced to the other side of the abdomen. In children and infants, proper exposure is more easily obtained if the intestines are eviscerated.

During *right-sided* reconstructions, the surgeon exposes the renal artery and vein as well as the inferior vena cava and aorta by incising the lateral attachments of the colon from the hepatic flexure to the cecum and by reflecting the right colon, duodenum, and pancreas medially in an extended Kocher-like maneuver. This measure provides excellent exposure of the midabdominal aorta, vena cava, and distal renal artery and vein (Fig. 129-2). Dissection of the renal artery should begin in its midportion just lateral to the vena cava, usually requiring superior retraction of the renal vein. The vein should be dissected carefully from surrounding tissues, and small venous branches, such as those to the adrenal gland, should be ligated and transected. If the more distal renal artery is dissected first, troublesome injury to small arterial and venous branches is more likely to occur. When one is treating developmental right-sided ostial lesions, the vena cava may be retracted laterally, and the proximal renal artery exposed near its origin. Ligation and division of adjacent lumbar veins facilitates mobilization of the vena cava and exposure of the proximal right renal artery.

For *left-sided* reconstructions, the surgeon exposes the renal vessels using a retroperitoneal dissection similar to that performed on the right with reflection of the viscera, including the left colon, medially. Such a retroperitoneal approach offers better visualization of the middle and distal renal vessels than an anterior exposure through the mesocolon at the root of the mesentery. Exposure of the left renal artery usually requires mobilization of the renal vein with ligation and transection of the gonadal branch inferiorly and adrenal venous branches superiorly.

The infrarenal aorta is dissected circumferentially for approximately 5 cm, just below the origin of the renal arteries. A large-diameter aorta can be occluded partially,

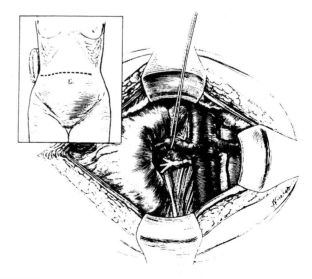

FIGURE 129-2 Operative approach through a transverse supraumbilical abdominal incision, with an extraperitoneal dissection and reflection of the colon and foregut structures providing exposure of the renal and great vessels.

although in most instances total aortic occlusion is required. Systemic anticoagulation is accomplished by intravenous (IV) administration of heparin, 100 to 150 units/kg, prior to clamping of the aorta. A linear aortotomy is created, with a length approximately two to three times the graft diameter. Whenever possible, the saphenous vein is harvested so that a branch is included at its caudal end. This branch is incised so that its orifice is connected to the lumen of the main trunk. A generous anastomotic circumference is created by this branch patch maneuver, which allows for a more perpendicular origin of the vein graft from the aorta (Fig. 129-3). To perform the vein graft–aorta anastomosis, the surgeon uses a 4-0 or 5-0 polypropylene suture. In certain patients, other sites of origin for renal grafts are preferable, with hepatic, splenic, and common iliac arteries being the nonaortic vessels from which grafts most often originate.[15]

The graft is then positioned for the renal anastomosis. The most direct route for *right-sided* aortorenal grafts is in a retrocaval position originating from a lateral aortotomy. However, some grafts may be less likely to kink when taken from an anterolateral aortotomy and carried in front of the inferior vena cava and then posterior to the renal vessels. The choice of antecaval or retrocaval graft positioning must be individualized. Grafts to the *left kidney* are usually positioned beneath the left renal vein. The aortic clamp should be left in place during completion of the renal anastomosis. To remove it and to place an occluding device on a vein graft itself might injure the conduit.

Next, the renal anastomosis is performed. The proximal renal artery is clamped, transected, and ligated. Before antegrade renal artery blood flow is interrupted, a sustained diuresis should be established, usually by IV administration of 12.5 g of mannitol. Preformed collateral vessels in these patients usually provide adequate blood flow to maintain kidney viability during renal artery occlusion. Microvascular clamps, developing tensions ranging from 30 to 70 gm, are favored over conventional vascular clamps or elastic slings for occlusion of distal renal vessels. The microvascular clamps have less potential to cause vessel injury and, because of their very small size, do not obscure the operative field.

For a graft–renal artery anastomosis, an end-to-end anastomosis is preferred to an end-to-side one. It is facilitated by spatulation of the graft posteriorly and the renal artery anteriorly (see Fig. 129-3). This allows visualization of the artery's interior, such that inclusion of intima with each stitch is easily accomplished. In adults, the surgeon completes the anastomosis using a continuous suture of 6-0 polypropylene. In pediatric patients, three or four sutures are interrupted to provide for anastomotic growth. If the vessels are less than 2 mm in diameter, the anastomosis is best completed with individual interrupted sutures around the entire circumference. Spatulated anastomoses are ovoid and, with healing, are less likely to develop strictures (Fig. 129-4).

After the aortic and renal anastomoses are completed, the vascular clamps are removed, antegrade renal blood flow is re-established, and the heparin effect is reversed with slow IV administration of 1.2 mg of protamine sulfate for each 100 units of heparin given previously. Assessment of the reconstruction is undertaken with duplex scanning

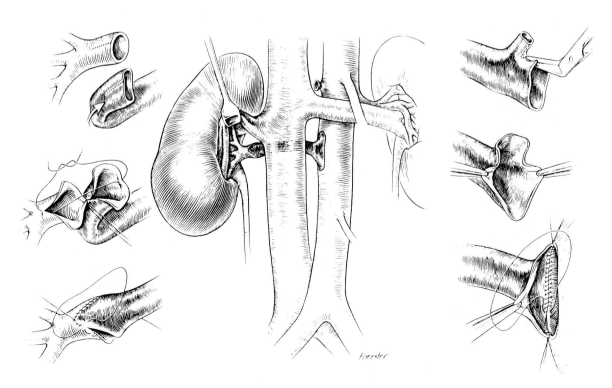

Foerster

FIGURE 129-3 Technique of end-to-end graft–renal artery anastomosis after spatulation of the artery anteriorly and the graft posteriorly, and end-to-side graft-aorta anastomosis after creation of a common orifice between a branch and the central lumen of the saphenous vein.

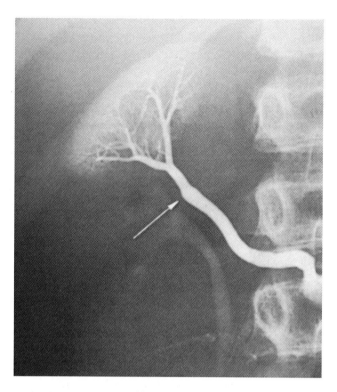

FIGURE 129-4 Autogenous saphenous vein aortorenal bypass to a segmental artery. Note the ovoid appearance of the renal anastomosis (*arrow*). (From Fry WJ, Ernst CB, Stanley JC, Brink BE: Renovascular hypertension in the pediatric patient. Arch Surg 107:692, 1973. Copyright 1973, American Medical Association.)

or through evaluation of flow with a directional Doppler device. Although intraoperative arteriography is seldom necessary, postoperative arteriography should be performed in all patients before discharge to establish the adequacy of the reconstructive procedure and to provide a baseline for continued graft follow-up.

In the treatment of fibrodysplastic renovascular disease, autologous vein grafts are usually preferred for reconstructions in adults,[82] and autologous hypogastric artery grafts are favored for bypass procedures in children (Fig. 129-5).[66,78,95] The hypogastric artery may also be used in adult reconstructions.[45,48] Vein grafts are procured carefully, handled gently, and irrigated cautiously with heparinized blood prior to implantation. Procurement of the hypogastric artery for use as an interposition graft proceeds in a similar manner, with the surgeon taking care not to cause excessive vessel wall trauma. Synthetic grafts of fabricated polyester (Dacron) or expanded polytetrafluoroethylene (ePTFE) may also be used for main renal artery reconstructive procedures,[35,38] but these conduits are less compliant and are technically more difficult to use when revascularizations involve small dysplastic segmental vessels.

Arterial dilatation, alone or in conjunction with a bypass procedure, is sometimes used for treatment of intraparenchymal intimal and medial fibrodysplastic stenoses. After the renal artery is exposed in a manner similar to that noted previously, the patient receives systemic anticoagulation therapy, and rigid cylindrical-tipped dilators are advanced through a transverse arteriotomy in the main renal artery. Dilators are thoroughly

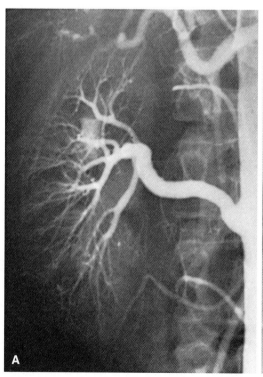
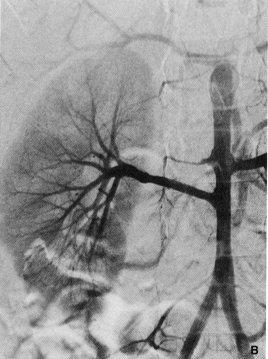

FIGURE 129-5 A, Autogenous saphenous vein aortorenal graft. **B,** Autogenous iliac artery aortorenal graft. (**A** from Stanley JC, Graham LM: Renovascular hypertension. In Miller DC, Roon AJ [eds]: Diagnosis and Management of Peripheral Vascular Disease. Menlo Park, CA, Addison-Wesley, 1981, p 321; **B** from Stanley JC, Zelenock GB, Messina LM, et al: Pediatric renovascular hypotension: A thirty-year experience of operative treatment. J Vasc Surg 21:212, 1995.)

lubricated with heparinized blood or a silicone solution to lessen intimal drag. The stenotic area is progressively dilated in increments of 0.5 mm by careful passage of increasingly larger dilators. Dilators 1.0 mm larger than the diameter of the normal proximal artery should not be used because they may disrupt the vessel wall. The role of operative dilatation of fibrodysplastic renal artery stenoses using standard axial balloon catheters remains uncertain.

An increasing proportion of patients undergoing surgical management of renal artery fibrodysplasia are found to have complex renal artery branch vessel disease.[3,65] The method of repair depends on whether the disease extends beyond the primary renal artery bifurcation. In situ repair can be accomplished for virtually all lesions that do not extend beyond the primary bifurcation into second- or third-order branches. Ex vivo repair is often used for more extensive patterns of complex disease.[2,5,97,103]

For the more proximal segmental disease pattern, three alternative methods of repair can be applied. The first calls for separate implantations of the renal arteries into a single conduit. This is usually accomplished with a proximal end-to-side anastomosis and a distal end-to-end anastomosis to an autograft. If a nonreversed branching segment of saphenous vein in which the valves have been cut or a hypogastric artery with its branches is used as the bypass conduit, separate graft–renal artery anastomoses may be undertaken in an end-to-end manner.

In the second method, an in situ anastomosis of the involved renal arteries is performed in a side-to-side manner so as to form a common orifice. The autograft is then anastomosed to the single channel created by this arterial union (Fig. 129-6).

The third method involves implantation of an affected artery, beyond its diseased segment, into an adjacent normal artery in an end-to-side manner. Such an anastomosis usually involves second-order branches of the renal artery (Fig. 129-7), but implantation may be undertaken into the main renal artery if the anastomosis can be fashioned without tension.

Ex vivo repairs require mobilization of the entire kidney, including the accompanying vasculature and ureter to the pelvis.[5,6] The renal artery and vein are controlled with vascular clamps and transected, allowing the kidney to be placed on the abdominal wall. A tourniquet around the intact ureter prevents collateral blood flow to the kidney. Lactated Ringer's solution at 4° C is used to flush the kidney until the venous effluent has cleared. The kidney is connected to the perfusion manifold of the dissecting platform, which has been placed on the lower abdominal wall (Fig. 129-8).[65] Hypothermic perfusion is begun, with monitoring by a perfusionist, and the kidney surface is cooled to 8° to 12° C.

Meticulous dissection of the renal artery is undertaken to the distal level of visible and palpable disease. After the renal artery branches are mobilized, an iliac artery arterial autograft is excised and flushed with lactated Ringer's solution. Sequential branch anastomoses are performed end-to-end with fine interrupted sutures (Fig. 129-9).[65] For vessels smaller than 2 mm in diameter, anastomoses are performed over a metal dilator to prevent an anastomotic narrowing. After the perfusion cannulas are disconnected, the reconstructed kidney is repositioned in the retroperi-

toneum. The proximal aortic anastomosis is performed in an end-to-side manner, and the renal vein is reanastomosed to the transected proximal renal vein on the left or to a new site on the lateral vena cava on the right. The venous clamps, followed by the arterial clamps, are removed, and the ureteral tourniquet is released, after which the kidney can be reperfused.

Current indications for in situ versus ex vivo repair have become better defined. In general, in situ repair is appropriate when a patient has two kidneys requiring primary operation limited to the first renal bifurcation. Ex vivo repair with hypothermic perfusion has the advantage of uncompromised exposure beyond the limits of complex branch disease and should be applied in the following situations:

- Reoperation for failed prior renal arterial repairs
- Multiple branch artery lesions in a solitary kidney
- Extension of branch vessel disease into the renal hilus
- Certain branch artery stenoses in children
- Traumatic injuries involving the renal hilus
- Stenoses involving multiple renal arteries

In these circumstances, the inserted branched arterial autograft allows the restoration of nearly normal renal artery anatomy. A durable repair, essential for the younger patients affected by this pattern of disease who anticipate a normal lifespan after renal revascularization, is achieved.

Alternative means of revascularization may be appropriate in select circumstances. In the case of left-sided lesions in adults, an in situ splenorenal bypass offers an alternative to aortorenal bypass.[47,63] However, before undertaking the latter, one must document that the proximal celiac artery is not involved with an occlusive lesion that might perpetuate the hypertensive state following such a bypass. Splenorenal bypasses for treatment of pediatric renovascular stenoses should be avoided. Results from this approach in these younger patients have been very poor.[67] This low success rate may reflect the small splenic artery caliber in children but is more likely due to proximal celiac artery stenoses.[87]

Treatment of pediatric orificial renal artery stenoses deserve comment, in that aortic reimplantation of the vessel beyond its disease has become favored over bypass procedures.[19,92,94] The vessel is transected beyond the stenotic segment and spatulated anteriorly and posteriorly so as to provide a generous patch for implantation (Fig. 129-10). For arteries 2 to 3 mm in diameter, the anastomosis should be performed with multiple interrupted sutures. The kidney may be mobilized medially during these reconstructions to reduce any potential tension on the reimplanted renal artery.

Operative treatment of fibrodysplastic renovascular hypertension associated with aortic hypoplasia or coarctation is often complex (Fig. 129-11). Thoracoabdominal bypasses and local aortoplasties are the most common aortic operations, with concomitant renal artery construction performed in a standard manner.[32,36] The reported operative mortality rate for these extensive operations approaches 8%, but nearly 90% of the survivors benefit from such interventions.[32,60]

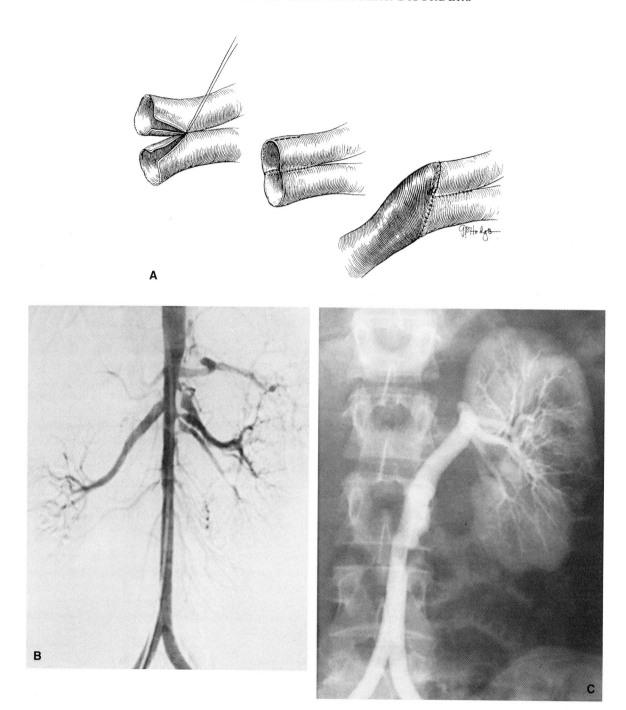

FIGURE 129-6 A, Revascularization of multiple renal arteries with side-to-side anastomoses of affected vessels followed by the anastomosis of a vein graft to their common orifice. **B** and **C,** Preoperative and postoperative arteriograms of this type of repair, with three vessels joined together before being anastomosed to a vein graft. (**A** from Ernst BC, Fry WJ, Stanley JC: Surgical treatment of renovascular hypertension: Revascularization with autogenous vein. In Stanley JC, Ernst CB, Fry WJ [eds]: Renovascular Hypertension. Philadelphia, WB Saunders, 1984, p 284; **B** and **C** from Stanley JC, Fry WJ: Pediatric renal artery occlusive disease and renovascular hypertension: Etiology, diagnosis and operative treatment. Arch Surg 116:669, 1981. Copyright 1981, American Medical Association.)

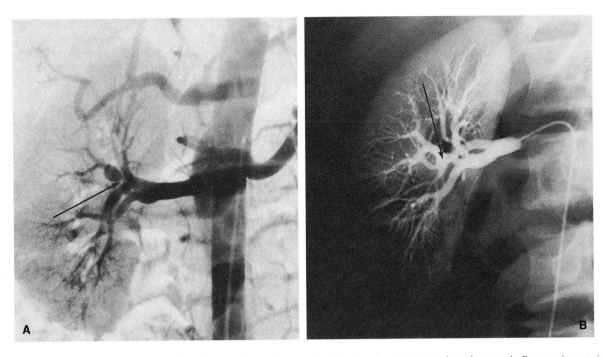

FIGURE 129-7 Reimplantation of segmental renal artery, beyond its stenosis, into the adjacent segmental renal artery. **A,** Preoperative arteriogram documenting stenosis and post-stenotic dilatation (*arrow*). **B,** Postoperative arteriogram demonstrates widely patent anastomosis (*arrow*). (**A** and **B** from Stanley JC, Zelenock GB, Messina LM, et al: Pediatric renovascular hypertension: A thirty-year experience of operative treatment. J Vasc Surg 21:212, 1995.)

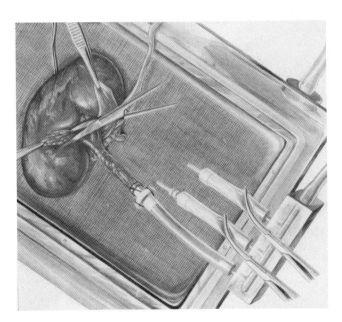

FIGURE 129-8 Illustration of dissection of renal hilus ex vivo. Kidney is perfused through one cannula on the perfusion manifold of the dissection platform. (From Murray SP, Kent CK, Salvatierra O, et al: Complex branch renovascular disease: Management options and late results. J Vasc Surg 20:338, 1984.)

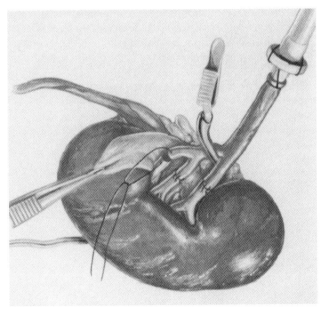

FIGURE 129-9 Ex vivo multibranched arterial autograft repair. Two of three branch anastomoses are completed, and the lowest one is being sutured. (From Murray SP, Kent CK, Salvatierra O, et al: Complex branch renovascular disease: Management options and late results. J Vasc Surg 20:338, 1984.)

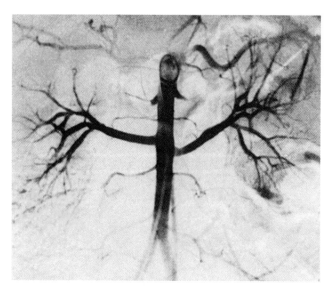

FIGURE 129-10 Reimplantation of main renal arteries beyond orificial stenosis into the aorta. (From Stanley JC, Zelenock GB, Messina LM, et al: Pediatric renovascular hypertension: A thirty-year experience of operative treatment. J Vasc Surg 21:212, 1995.)

Complications

The critical consequences of graft stenosis or occlusion, including loss of the kidney, attest to the importance of a properly planned and executed initial renal reconstructive procedure.[27,32] Reoperations for complications of renal artery reconstructive surgery undertaken for renal artery fibrodysplasia in children and adults entail secondary nephrectomy rates up to 60% and 39%, respectively.[91]

The incidence of early postoperative aortorenal vein graft thrombosis is 2% to 7%.[3] Early postoperative thrombosis after arterial autografts appears to be less frequent.[55,65,96] Postoperative graft thrombosis occurs more commonly in small-diameter arteries and branch vessel reconstructions. Many experienced surgeons emphasize the importance of intraoperative duplex ultrasound assessment to determine the technical adequacy of the renal revascularization and early correction of significant defects at the time of primary procedure.[3]

Arteriography is essential to assess the status of small branch vessel reconstructions and equivocal reconstructions. When clinical circumstances suggest early postoperative graft occlusion, such as episodic hypertension, arteriography is the diagnostic study of choice. Radionuclide studies are of limited use in detecting postoperative graft occlusions, in that many kidneys have extensive preexisting collateral circulation that provides for relatively normal renal function and perfusion patterns despite acutely occluded grafts.

Late anastomotic stenoses have become less common with improved vascular surgical techniques. In particular, the creation of generous ovoid graft–renal artery anastomoses has reduced the frequency of this complication. Nevertheless, late graft stenoses may be a consequence of intimal hyperplasia, clamp injury, and overzealous advancement of large dilators through stenoses or "sounding of segmental vessels." Overall, late vein graft stenoses can be encountered in up to 8% of aortorenal vein grafts.[22,25] Late stenoses of aortorenal arterial autografts are rare.[44,65,96]

Late vein graft dilatation, documented in 20% to 44% of aortorenal saphenous vein grafts, usually appears as a nonprogressive, uniform increase in vein graft diameter.[23,80] Marked aneurysmal changes affect approximately 2% of aortorenal grafts in adults[80] and 20% of vein grafts placed in

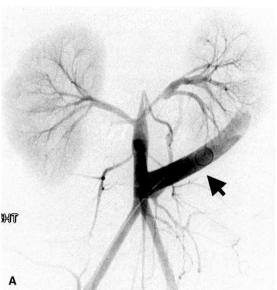
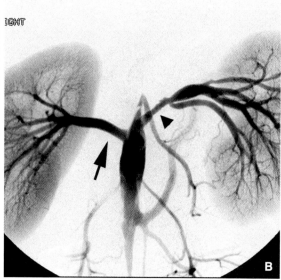

FIGURE 129-11 Complex renal reconstructive procedure for middle aortic syndrome (**A**) by prosthetic thoracoabdominal bypass (*arrow*) and (**B**) reimplantation of right renal artery (*arrow*) and hypogastric artery bypass to the left renal artery.

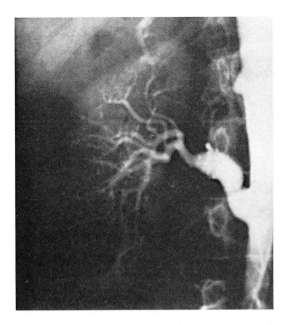

FIGURE 129-12 Aneurysmal dilatation of an autogenous saphenous vein aortorenal graft. This complication is most likely to affect pediatric patients. (From Stanley JC, Ernst CB, Fry WJ: Fate of 100 aortorenal vein grafts: Characteristics of late graft expansion, aneurysmal dilatation, and stenosis. Surgery 74:931, 1973.)

pediatric patients[84] (Fig. 129-12). Other investigators have reported a lower incidence of this complication.[23] The predisposition for dilatation of vein grafts in children may reflect anatomic variations in the number and distribution of the vasa vasorum in their veins. The veins in children may be particularly susceptible to ischemic injury during transplantation. Expansion and aneurysmal dilatation have also occurred with renovascular reconstructions using autogenous arterial grafts, but the frequency of this complication is much lower than that in veins.[23,96] Luminal thrombus formation and distal embolization of microthrombi can occur in aneurysmal veins and are the reason some surgeons advocate replacement or plication of dilated vein grafts.[89]

Outcome of Surgical Therapy

Beneficial outcomes after operative intervention for renovascular hypertension are directly proportional to the accurate identification of appropriate surgical candidates and performance of an appropriate reconstructive procedure. The Cooperative Study of Renovascular Hypertension was undertaken nearly three decades ago in an attempt to define the optimal diagnostic and therapeutic management of renal artery occlusive disease. The less than optimal results from the Cooperative Study probably reflect errors in patient selection and early technical failures.[28,30] The overall results from 577 surgical procedures undertaken in 520 patients with all forms of renovascular hypertension were 51%, cure; 15%, improvement; and 34%, failure. As surgical techniques and new methods in patient selection evolved, overall results improved.[81] Patients with renal artery fibrodysplasia were more likely to show favorable response to operative intervention than those with atherosclerotic disease.

The results of surgical treatment of renal artery fibrodysplasia document excellent outcomes for control of arterial hypertension. During the 1980s and 1990s, between 90% and 95% of properly selected patients either were cured of or gained more control over their renovascular hypertension (Tables 129-2 and 129-3). These results relate to the evolution of better reconstructive techniques, as evidenced by the reduction of primary nephrectomy rates.[16,83] In addition, operative mortality rates approached 0 in most series of surgical treatment of renal arterial fibrodysplasia. Thus, the mortality rate of 3.4%, as noted for the surgical treatment of renal artery fibrodysplasia in the Cooperative Study, would be unacceptable in contemporary practice.

Finally, although renal failure secondary to renal artery fibrodysplasia is much less common than that seen secondary to atherosclerotic disease, long-term follow-up shows excellent preservation of renal function.[3,21,107]

A distinct change in the clinical profile, clinical evaluation, and operative management of patients with renal artery fibrodysplasia has been documented in many

		POSTOPERATIVE STATUS (%)†			
STUDY (YEAR)*	**NO. PATIENTS**	**Cure**	**Improvement**	**Failure**	**OPERATIVE MORTALITY RATE (%)**
Buda et al (1976)[11]	42	76	14	10	NA
Bergentz et al (1979)[7]	40	66	24	10	0
Lawrie et al (1980)[49]	113	43	24	33	0‡
Jakubowski et al (1981)[42]	75	63	24	13	0
Stanley and Fry (1981)[84]	114	55	39	6	0
Stoney et al (1981)[96]	77	66	32	1	0
Novick et al (1987)[68]	104	63	30	7	0
vanBockel (1987)[103]	53	53	34	11	1.9
Anderson et al (1995)[3]	40	33	57	10	0
Reiher et al (2000)[70]	101	36	31	33	2

Table 129-2 Results of Surgical Therapy for Renovascular Hypertension due to Fibrodysplasia in Adults

*Superscript numbers indicate chapter references.
†Criteria for blood pressure response are defined in cited publications.
‡No deaths in 100 isolated renal reconstructions; data on 13 patients with associated arteriosclerosis unavailable.
NA, not available.

Table 129-3 Results of Surgical Treatment of Renovascular Hypertension due to Fibrodysplasia in Children

STUDY (YEAR)*	NO. PATIENTS	NO. ARTERIAL RECONSTRUCTIONS	NO. NEPHRECTOMIES	NO. SECONDARY PROCEDURES	POSTOPERATIVE STATUS (%)†			OPERATIVE MORTALITY RATE (%)
					Cure	Improvement	Failure	
Stoney et al (1975)[95]	14	10	4	2	86	7	0	7
Lawson et al (1977)[50]‡	21	15	8	4	68	24	8	0
Novick et al (1978)[67]	27	22	11	5	59	18.5	18.5	4
Kaufman (1979)[44]	26	19		7	84.5	7.5	4	4
Stanley et al (1995)[94]§	57	50	7	14	79	19	2.0	0

*Superscript numbers indicate chapter references.
†Criteria for blood pressure response are defined in cited publications. Data are expressed to nearest 0.5%.
‡Results include data from 4 patients with parenchymal disease treated by nephrectomy. A more recent but less detailed review includes 28 patients with cure, improvement, and failure rates of 72%, 21%, and 7%, respectively.[11]
§Results include data from 6 patients treated at University of Texas Southwestern Medical Center at Dallas.

centers.[3,65,68] Patients presenting for treatment are significantly older, have had a longer duration of hypertension, and have a higher prevalence of extrarenal atherosclerosis. Most significantly, a higher frequency of branch vessel involvement requiring complex repairs is found consistently. At the University of California, San Francisco, patients presenting with a complex branch vessel pattern secondary to arterial fibrodysplasia had solitary kidneys in 18% of cases; 9% needed concomitant aortic replacement, and 10% represented failure of previous operations. Thus, although the overall beneficial response rate remains similar to that in earlier reports, the cure rate is generally lower, reflecting the changes in the overall clinical profile of the patients.

Outcome after management of complex branch renal artery disease deserves special comment. A report from the University of California, San Francisco, describing outcome in 68 consecutive patients with complex branch vessel disease was notable for a renal salvage rate of 98.8%.[99,100] No operative deaths occurred. Renal function and control of blood pressure were assessed at a mean follow-up of 7.5 years. Of the 68 patients, 46% underwent follow-up angiography at a mean of 52 months after operation. No evidence of late graft failure was documented. Hypertension was cured or improved in 51 of the 53 patients (96%) with a proven patent reconstruction. Renal function was improved in 4 patients with ex vivo repairs, unchanged in 59 patients, and worse in only 3 patients, all of whom had undergone in situ repair.

■ REFERENCES

1. Aldigier J, Plouin PF, Guyene TT, et al: Comparison of the hormonal and renal effects of captopril in severe essential and renovascular hypertension. Am J Cardiol 49:1447, 1982.
2. Alimi Y, Mercier C, Pellissier JF, et al: Fibromuscular disease of the renal artery: A new histopathologic classification. Ann Vasc Surg 6:220, 1992.
3. Anderson CA, Hansen KJ, Benjamin ME, et al: Renal artery fibromuscular dysplasia: Results of current surgical therapy. J Vasc Surg 22:207, 1995.
4. Baumgartner I, Triller J, Mahler F: Patency of percutaneous transluminal renal angioplasty: A prospective sonographic study. Kidney Int 51:798, 1997.
5. Belzer FO, Raczkowski A: Ex vivo renal artery reconstruction with autotransplantation. Surgery 92:642, 1982.
6. Benjamin SP, Dustan HP, Gifford RW Jr, et al: Stenosing renal artery disease in children: Clinicopathologic correlation in 20 surgically treated cases. Cleve Clin Q 43;197, 1976.
7. Bergentz SE, Ericsson BF, Husberg B: Technique and complications in the surgical treatment of renovascular hypertension. Acta Chir Scand 145:143, 1979.
8. Birrer M, Do DD, Mahler F, et al: Treatment of renal artery fibromuscular dysplasia with balloon angioplasty: A prospective follow-up study. Eur J Vasc Endovasc Surg 23:146, 2002.
9. Bonelli FS, McKusick MA, Textor SC, et al: Renal artery angioplasty: Technical results and clinical outcome in 320 patients. Mayo Clin Proc 70:1041, 1995.
10. Bookstein JJ, Walter JF, Stanley JC, et al: Pharmacoangiographic manipulation of renal collateral blood flow. Circulation 54:328, 1976.
11. Buda JA, Baer L, Parra-Carrillo J, et al: Predictability of surgical response in renovascular hypertension. Arch Surg 111:1243, 1976.
12. Buhler FR, Laragh JH, Baer L, et al: Propranolol inhibition of renin secretion. N Engl J Med 287:1209, 1972.
13. Casalini E, Sfondrini M, Fossali E: Two-year clinical follow-up of children and adolescents after percutaneous transluminal angioplasty for renovascular hypertension. Invest Radiol 30:1, 1995.
14. Case DB, Atlas SA, Marion RM, et al: Long-term efficacy of captopril in renovascular and essential hypertension. Am J Cardiol 49:1440, 1982.
15. Chibaro EA, Libertino JA, Novick AC: Use of the hepatic circulation for renal revascularization. Ann Surg 199;406, 1984.
16. Chrysant SG, Dunn M, Marples M, et al: Severe reversible azotemia from captopril therapy: Report of three cases and review of the literature. Arch Intern Med 143:347,1983.
17. Cluzel P, Raynaud A, Beyssen B, et al: Stenoses of renal branch arteries in fibromuscular dysplasia: Results of percutaneous transluminal angioplasty. Radiology 193:227, 1994.
18. Davidson R, Barri Y, Wilcox CS: Predictors of cure of hypertension in fibromuscular renovascular disease. Am J Kidney Dis 28:334, 1996.
19. Dean RH: Renovascular hypertension during childhood. In Dean RH, O'Neil JA Jr (eds): Vascular Disorders of Childhood. Philadelphia, Lea & Febiger, 1983, p 77.
20. Dean RH, Benjamin ME, Hansen KJ: Surgical management of renovascular hypertension. In Wells SA Jr (ed): Current Problems in Surgery. St. Louis, Mosby-Year Book, Inc, 1997, pp 209-316.

21. Dean RH, Englund R, Dupont WD, et al: Retrieval of renal function by revascularization: Study of preoperative outcome predictors. Ann Surg 202:367, 1985.

22. Dean RH, Krueger TC, Whiteneck JM, et al: Operative management of renovascular hypertension: Results after a follow-up of fifteen to twenty-three years. J Vasc Surg 1:234, 1984.

23. Dean RH, Wilson JP, Burko H, et al: Saphenous vein aortorenal bypass grafts: Serial arteriographic study. Ann Surg 130:469, 1974.

24. Detection, evaluation and treatment of renovascular hypertension: Final report. Working Group on Renovascular Hypertension. Arch Intern Med 147:820, 1987.

25. Ekelund J, Gerlock J Jr, Goncharenko V, et al: Angiographic findings following surgical treatment for renovascular hypertension. Radiology 126:345, 1978.

26. Ernst CB, Bookstein JJ, Montie J, et al: Renal vein renin ratios and collateral vessels in renovascular hypertension. Arch Surg 104:496, 1972.

27. Foster JH, Dean RH, Pinkerton JA, et al: Ten years' experience with surgical management of renovascular hypertension. Ann Surg 177:755, 1973.

28. Foster JH, Maxwell SS, Bleifer KH, et al: Renovascular occlusive disease: Results of operative treatment. JAMA 231:1043, 1975.

29. Franklin SS, Smith RD: A comparison of enalapril plus hydrochlorothiazide with standard triple therapy in renovascular hypertension. Nephron 44(Suppl 1):73, 1986.

30. Franklin SS, Young JD Jr, Maxwell MH, et al: Operative morbidity and mortality in renovascular disease. JAMA 231:1148, 1975.

31. Goncharenko V, Gerlock AJ, Shaff MI, et al: Progression of renal artery fibromuscular dysplasia in 42 patients as seen on angiography. Radiology 139:45, 1981.

32. Graham LM, Zelenock GB, Erlandson EE, et al: Abdominal aortic coarctation and segmental hypoplasia. Surgery 86:519, 1979.

33. Grim CE, Luft FC, Yune HY, et al: Percutaneous transluminal dilatation in the treatment of renal vascular hypertension. Ann Intern Med 95:439, 1981.

34. Grim CE, Yune HY, Donahue JP, et al: Unilateral renal vascular hypertension: Surgery vs. dilation. Vasa 11:367, 1982.

35. Gruntzig A, Vetter W, Meier B, et al: Treatment of renovascular hypertension with percutaneous transluminal dilatation of a renal artery stenosis. Lancet 1(8068):801, 1978.

36. Hagg A, Aberg H, Eriksson I, et al: Fibromuscular dysplasia of the renal artery: Management and outcome. Acta Chir Scand 153:15, 1987.

37. Harrison EG, McCormack LJ: Pathologic classification of renal artery disease in renovascular hypertension. Mayo Clin Proc 46:161, 1971.

38. Henriksson C, Bjorkerud S, Nilson AE, Pettersson S: Natural history of renal artery aneurysm elucidated by repeated angiography and pathoanatomical studies. Eur Urol 11:244, 1985.

39. Hodsman GP, Brown JJ, Cummings AMM, et al: Enalapril in treatment of hypertension with renal artery stenosis: Changes in blood pressure, renin, angiotensin I and II, renal function, and body composition. Am J Med 77:52, 1984.

40. Hricik DE, Browning PK, Kopelman R, et al: Captopril-induced renal insufficiency in patients with bilateral renal-artery stenosis or renal-artery stenosis in a solitary kidney. N Engl J Med 308:373, 1983.

41. Hunt JC, Strong CG: Renovascular hypertension: Mechanisms, natural history and treatment. Am J Cardiol 32:562, 1973.

42. Jakubowski HD, Eigler FW, Montag H: Results of surgery in fibrodysplastic renal artery stenosis. World J Surg 5:859, 1981.

43. Karas RH, Caur W, Tassi L, Mendelsohn ME: Inhibition of vascular smooth muscle cell growth by estrogen. Circulation 88:I-325, 1993.

44. Kaufman JJ: Renovascular hypertension: The UCLA experience. J Urol 112:139, 1979.

45. Kaufmann JJ: Long-term results of aortorenal Dacron grafts in the treatment of renal artery stenosis. J Urol 111:298, 1974.

46. Keith TA III: Renovascular hypertension in black patients. Hypertension 4:438, 1982.

47. Khauli RB, Novick AC, Ziegelbaum M: Splenorenal bypass in the treatment of renal artery stenosis: Experience with sixty-nine cases. J Vasc Surg 2:547, 1985.

48. Lagneau P, Michel JB, Charrat JM: Use of polytetrafluoroethylene grafts for renal bypass. J Vasc Surg 5:738, 1987.

49. Lawrie GM, Morris GC Jr, Soussou ID, et al: Late results of reconstructive surgery for renovascular disease. Ann Surg 191:528, 1980.

50. Lawson JD, Boerth R, Foster JH, et al: Diagnosis and management of renovascular hypertension in children. Arch Surg 122:1307, 1977.

51. Leadbetter WFG, Burkland CE: Hypertension in unilateral renal disease. J Urol 39:611, 1938.

52. Lewin A, Blaufox MD, Castle H, et al: Apparent prevalence of curable hypertension in the Hypertension Detection and Follow-up Program. Arch Intern Med 145:424, 1985.

53. Luscher TF, Greminger P, Kuhlmann TJ, et al: Renal venous renin determinations in renovascular hypertension: Diagnostic and prognostic value in unilateral renal artery stenosis treated by surgery or percutaneous transluminal angioplasty. Nephron 44(Suppl 1):17, 1986.

54. Luscher TF, Keller HM, Imhof HG, et al: Fibromuscular hyperplasia: Extension of the disease and therapeutic outcome: Results of the University Hospital Zurich Cooperative Study on Fibromuscular Hyperplasia. Nephron 44(Suppl 1):109, 1986.

55. Lye CR, String ST, Wylie EJ, et al: Aortorenal arterial auto-grafts: Late observations. Arch Surg 110:1321, 1975.

56. Mahler F, Triller J, Weidmarim P, et al: Complications in percutaneous transluminal dilation of renal arteries. Nephron 44(Suppl 1): 60, 1986.

57. Martin EC, Diamond NG, Casarella WJ: Percutaneous transluminal angioplasty in non-atherosclerotic disease. Radiology 135:27, 1980.

58. Martin LG, Price RB, Casarella WJ, et al: Percutaneous angioplasty in clinical management of renovascular hypertension: Initial and long-term results. Radiology 155:629, 1985.

59. McCormick LJ, Hazard JB, Poutasse EF: Obstructive lesions of the renal artery associated with remediable hypertension. Am J Pathol 34:582,1958.

60. Messina LM, Reilly LM, Goldstone J, et al: Middle aortic syndrome: Effectiveness and durability of complex revascularization techniques. Ann Surg 204:331, 1986.

61. Millan VG, McCauley J, Kopelman RI, et al: Percutaneous transluminal renal angioplasty in nonatherosclerotic renovascular hypertension: Long-term results. Hypertension 7:668, 1985.

62. Miller GA, Ford KK, Braum SD, et al: Percutaneous transluminal angioplasty vs. surgery for renovascular hypertension. Am J Roentgenol 144:447, 1985.

63. Moncure AC, Brewster DC, Darling RC, et al: Use of the splenic and hepatic arteries for renal revascularization. J Vasc Surg 3:196, 1986.

64. Muller FB, Sealey JF, Case DB, et al: The captopril test for identifying disease in hypertensive patients. Am J Med 80:633, 1986.

65. Murray SP, Kent CK, Salvatierra O, et al: Complex branch renovascular disease: Management options and late results. J Vasc Surg 20:338, 1994.

66. Novick AC, Steward BH, Straffon RA, et al: Autogenous arterial grafts in the treatment of renal artery stenosis. J Urol 118:919, 1977.

67. Novick AC, Straffon RA, Steward BH, et al: Surgical treatment of renovascular hypertension in the pediatric patient. J Urol 119:794, 1978.

68. Novick AC, Ziegelbaum M, Vidt DG, et al: Trends in surgical revascularization for renal artery disease: Ten years' experience. JAMA 257:498, 1987.

69. Palubinskis AJ, Ripley HR: Fibromuscular hyperplasia in extra renal arteries. Radiology 82:451, 1964.

70. Reiher L, Pfeiffer T, Sandmann W: Long-term results after surgical reconstruction for renal artery fibromuscular dysplasia. Eur J Vasc Endovasc Surg 20:556, 2000.

71. Rodriguez-Perez JC, Plaza C, Reyes R, et al: Treatment of renovascular hypertension with percutaneous transluminal angioplasty: Experience in Spain. J Vasc Interv Radiol 5:101, 1994.

72. Saffitz JE, Totty WG, McClennan BL, et al: Percutaneous transluminal angioplasty: Radiological-pathological correlation. Radiology 141:651, 1981.

73. Sarkar R, Messina LM: Renovascular disease: Pathology of renal artery occlusive disease. In Ernst CB, Stanley JC (eds): Current Therapy of Vascular Surgery, 3rd ed. St. Louis, CV Mosby, 1985, p 764.

74. Schwarten DE, Yune HY, Klatte EC, et al: Clinical experience with percutaneous transluminal angioplasty (PTA) of stenotic renal arteries. Radiology 135:601, 1980.

75. Simon N, Franklin SS, Bleifer KH, et al: Clinical characteristics of renovascular hypertension. JAMA 220:1209, 1972.

76. Sos TA, Saddekini S, Pickering TG, et al: Technical aspects of percutaneous transluminal angioplasty in renovascular disease. Nephron 44(Suppl 1):45, 1986.

77. Sottiurai V, Fry WJ, Stanley JC: Ultrastructural characteristics of experimental arterial medial fibroplasia induced by vasa vasorum occlusion. J Surg Res 24:169, 1978.

78. Stanley JC: Renal vascular disease and renovascular hypertension in children. Urol Clin 11:451, 1984.

79. Stanley JC: Surgery of failed percutaneous transluminal renal artery angioplasty. In Bergan JJ, Yao JST (eds): Reoperative Arterial Surgery. Orlando, FL, Grune & Stratton, 1986, p 441.

80. Stanley JC, Ernst CB, Fry WJ: Fate of 100 aortorenal vein grafts: Characteristics of late graft expansion, aneurysmal dilation, and stenosis. Surgery 74:931, 1973.

81. Stanley JC, Ernst CB, Fry WJ: Surgical treatment of renovascular hypertension: Results in specific patient subgroups. In Stanley JC, Ernst CB, Fry WJ (eds): Renovascular Hypertension. Philadelphia, WB Saunders, 1984, p 363.

82. Stanley JC, Fry WJ: Renovascular hypertension secondary to arterial fibrodysplasia in adults: Criteria for operation and results of surgical therapy. Arch Surg 110:922, 1975.

83. Stanley JC, Fry WJ: Surgical treatment of renovascular hypertension. Arch Surg 112:1291, 1977.

84. Stanley JC, Fry WJ: Pediatric renal artery occlusive disease and renovascular hypertension: Etiology, diagnosis and operative treatment. Arch Surg 116:669, 1981.

85. Stanley JC, Gewertz BL, Bove EL, et al: Arterial fibrodysplasia: Histopathologic character and current etiologic concepts. Arch Surg 110:561, 1975.

86. Stanley JC, Gewertz BL, Fry WJ: Renal systemic renin indices and renal vein renin ratios as prognostic indicators in remedial renovascular hypertension. J Surg Res 20:149, 1976.

87. Stanley JC, Graham LM, Whitehouse WM Jr, et al: Developmental occlusive disease of the abdominal aorta, splanchnic and renal arteries. Am J Surg 142:190, 1981.

88. Stanley JC, Wakefield TW: Arterial fibrodysplasia. In Rutherford RJ, (ed): Vascular Surgery, 5th ed, vol 1. Philadelphia, WB Saunders, 2000, p 387.

89. Stanley JC, Whitehouse WM Jr, Graham LM: Complications of renal revascularization. In Bernhard VM, Towne JB (eds): Complications in Vascular Surgery. New York, Grune & Stratton, 1980, p 189.

90. Stanley JC, Whitehouse WM Jr, Graham LM, et al: Operative therapy of renovascular hypertension. Br J Surg 69(Suppl):S63, 1982.

91. Stanley JC, Whitehouse WM Jr, Zelenock GB, et al: Re-operation for complications of renal artery reconstructive surgery undertaken for treatment of renovascular hypertension. J Vasc Surg 2:133, 1985.

92. Stanley P, Gyepes MT, Olson DL, et al: Renovascular hypertension in children and adolescents. Radiology 129:123, 1978.

93. Stanley P, Hieshima G, Mehringer M: Percutaneous transluminal angioplasty for pediatric renovascular hypertension. Radiology 153:101, 1984.

94. Stanley JC, Zelenock GB, Messina LM, et al: Pediatric renovascular hypertension: A thirty-year experience of operative treatment. J Vasc Surg 21:212, 1995.

95. Stoney RJ, Cooke PA, String ST: Surgical treatment of renovascular hypertension in children. J Pediatr Surg 10:631, 1975.

96. Stoney RJ, DeLuccia N, Ehrenfeld WK, et al: Aortorenal arterial autografts: Long-term assessment. Arch Surg 116:1416, 1981.

97. Stoney RJ, Silane M, Salvatierra O: Ex vivo renal artery reconstruction. Arch Surg 113:1272, 1978.

98. Stringer DA, deBruyn R, Dillion MJ, et al: Comparison of aortography, renal vein renin sampling, radionuclide scans, ultrasound and the IVU in the investigation of childhood renovascular hypertension. Br J Radiol 57:111, 1984.

99. Surur MF, Sos TA, Saddekini S, et al: Intimal fibromuscular dysplasia and Takayasu arteritis: Delayed response to percutaneous transluminal angioplasty. Radiology 157:657, 1985.

100. Tegtmeyer CJ, Elson J, Glass TA, et al: Percutaneous transluminal angioplasty: The treatment of choice for renovascular hypertension due to fibromuscular dysplasia. Radiology 143:631, 1982.

101. Tegtmeyer CJ, Sos TA: Techniques of renal angioplasty. Radiology 161:577, 1986.

102. Thibonnier M, Joseph A, Sassano P, et al: Improved diagnosis of unilateral renal artery lesions after captopril administration. JAMA 251:56, 1984.

103. vanBockel JH, van Schilfgaarde R, Felthuis W, et al: Long-term results of in situ and extracorporeal surgery for renovascular hypertension caused by fibrodysplasia. J Vasc Surg 6:355, 1987.

104. Vargas R, Wroblewska B, Rego A, et al: Oestradiol inhibits smooth muscle cell proliferation of pig coronary artery. Br J Pharmacol 09:612, 1993.

105. Vidt DG: Advances in the medical management of renovascular hypertension. Urol Clin 11:417, 1984.

106. Watson AR, Balfe JW, Hardy BE: Renovascular hypertension in childhood: A changing perspective in management. J Pediatr 106:366, 1985.

107. Whitehouse WM Jr, Kazmers A, Zelenock GB, et al: Chronic total renal artery occlusion: Effects of treatment on secondary hypertension and renal function. Surgery 89:753, 1981.

108. Zweifler AJ, Julius S: Medical treatment of renovascular hypertension. In Stanley JC, Ernst CB, Fry WJ (eds): Renovascular Hypertension. Philadelphia, WB Saunders, 1980, p 231.

Atherosclerotic Renovascular Disease and Ischemic Nephropathy

130

KIMBERLEY J. HANSEN, MD
DAVID B. WILSON, MD
RICHARD H. DEAN, MD

The introduction of new antihypertensive agents and percutaneous transluminal angioplasty (PTA) with endoluminal stenting has changed many attitudes regarding the role of surgical intervention for atherosclerotic renovascular disease.[1-5] These treatment alternatives, combined with the increasingly older patient population evaluated for renovascular disease, have led many physicians to limit surgical intervention to patients with severe hypertension despite maximal medical therapy, to patients demonstrating anatomic failures or disease patterns not amenable to balloon angioplasty and stenting, or to patients with renovascular disease complicated by renal excretory insufficiency.[6] As a consequence of these changing attitudes and treatment strategies, the demography of the contemporary patient population has also changed.[1,2,7,8] Current patient groups are characterized by diffuse extrarenal atherosclerosis complicated by end-organ damage and renal insufficiency.[1,2] Consequently, the current strategy, indications, and contemporary results of surgical management differ significantly from those in earlier reported series.[1-3,9-11] In addition to the traditional concerns regarding renovascular hypertension, these observations also emphasize the relationship between renovascular occlusive disease and excretory renal dysfunction. This relationship, described by the term *ischemic nephropathy*, defines the presence of anatomically severe occlusive disease of the extraparenchymal renal artery in a patient with excretory renal insufficiency.[1]

Three patient groups can be considered for reconstruction of atherosclerotic renovascular disease to improve renal function. The first group is represented by the patient with normal global renal function who is found to have a nonfunctioning kidney during evaluation for renovascular hypertension. Renal artery occlusion frequently characterizes this group. In this instance, overall renal function is maintained by the contralateral normal kidney, and the clinical question is whether to perform a nephrectomy or renal artery repair. The second group is characterized by the patient with azotemic ischemic nephropathy. In this patient, renal artery intervention must address the possibility of retrieving significant excretory function compared with the risk of worsening residual function as well as the associated higher risk in operative morbidity and mortality. The third group is characterized by the patient with dialysis-dependent ischemic nephropathy representing end-stage, end-organ dysfunction. Despite general pessimism regard-

ing recovery of renal function in this setting, the group reaching dialysis dependence demonstrates the greatest potential improvement in quality and quantity of life from successful renal artery intervention.[12]

■ RENAL ARTERY OCCLUSION WITHOUT AZOTEMIA

The Patient with Hypertension

Hypertension in the patient with renal artery occlusion can be treated equally well by revascularization and nephrectomy. However, the most desirable management would result in both blood pressure and renal function benefits. When the potential for improved renal function exists, the price of nephrectomy with the loss of functioning renal mass may be greater than the benefit derived from a favorable blood pressure response.[2] The practical value of this premise is demonstrated by progression of mild contralateral renal artery lesions to hemodynamically severe lesions in 35% to 40% of patients within 5 years of unilateral operative repair.[13,14] When such patients are treated by nephrectomy for renal artery occlusion and their contralateral renal disease progresses, global renal function is threatened. Intervention must then be performed in azotemic patients who are at risk for dialysis-dependent renal failure. Moreover, the atherosclerotic renal artery disease in the remaining kidney may not develop in a manner that is clinically recognized or may develop at a site that is not amenable to correction. Conversely, an overly aggressive approach to repair of renal artery occlusion sometimes leads to revascularization of a kidney in which no beneficial function or blood pressure response can be achieved. In this instance, primary nephrectomy would be simpler and safer than revascularization with control of hypertension.

Given these considerations, we have limited nephrectomy to cases of renal artery occlusion in which a kidney contributing to severe hypertension has an unreconstructible renal artery and demonstrates negligible renal function on isotopic renography. The value of this management philosophy is demonstrated by the results obtained in 95 consecutive patients (52 women and 43 men with a mean age of 63 years) treated for 100 consecutive atherosclerotic renal artery occlusions.[15] Cut-film angiography demonstrated

Table 130-1	Comparison of Operative Results for Patient Groups Treated for Renal Artery Occlusion (RA-OCC) and Renal Artery Stenosis (RAS)		
	RA-OCC (n = 95)	RAS (n = 302)	*P* VALUE
Perioperative mortality (%)	5.3	4.0	.59
Hypertension response (%)			.52
Cured	11	13	
Improved	80	74	
No change	9	13	
Renal function response (%)*			.20
Improved	49	41	
No change/ worsened	51	59	

*Preoperative serum creatinine value ≥ 1.3 mg/dL.

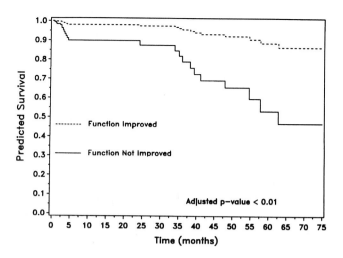

FIGURE 130-1 Predicted survival among patients with renal artery occlusion with improved or unimproved renal function after operative renal artery repair. (From Oskin TC, Hansen KJ, Deitch JS, et al: Chronic renal artery occlusion: Nephrectomy versus revascularization. J Vasc Surg 29:140-149, 1999. Used by permission.)

distal renal artery reconstitution in 69% and a nephrogram in 62% of cases. Neither distal renal artery reconstitution nor nephrogram was demonstrated in 25% of kidneys. Overall, 75 renal artery occlusions were treated with direct aortorenal reconstruction, and 25 nephrectomies were performed. After surgical renal artery repair, mortality rates were similar for renal artery revascularization and nephrectomy (2.8% and 12%, respectively; P = .11) and did not differ from those for 302 patients treated during the same period for atherosclerotic renal artery stenosis (5.3% and 4.0%, respectively; P = .59; Table 130-1).[15] Blood pressure response among the 90 operative survivors was considered cured in 11%, and improved in 80%; failure to improve blood pressure occurred in 9% of patients. Importantly, the rates of beneficial blood pressure response were equivalent after revascularization and nephrectomy (92% and 87%, respectively). However, significant improvement in estimated glomerular filtration rate (EGFR) was observed only after revascularization (P < .01) and after nephrectomy if contralateral revascularization was included (P = .02). A significant increase in EGFR was not observed when nephrectomy alone was performed. Most importantly, improved excretory renal function demonstrated a significant and independent association with better postoperative survival after operation (Fig. 130-1).

Absence of preoperative nephrogram or distal renal artery reconstitution did not preclude revascularization in half the kidneys with occluded renal arteries. In fact, 8 of 21 patients (38%) with neither preoperative nephrogram nor distal renal artery reconstitution underwent operative reconstruction, resulting in beneficial blood pressure response and improved renal function in 75%. Preoperative kidney length was less in the patients undergoing nephrectomy (7.3 ± 1.4 cm) than in those undergoing revascularization (8.2 ± 1.5 cm), but length alone did not preclude revascularization. Nine of 16 kidneys shorter than 7 cm were revascularized, with beneficial blood pressure response in all and improved renal function in 44%.

Because the lower limits of renal function retrieval are not well defined for atherosclerotic renovascular disease but progression of contralateral renal artery disease is common, these data argue that nephrectomy should be limited and should be applied selectively. Patients with severe hypertension in whom the kidney responsible for hypertension

has an unreconstructible vessel and negligible excretory renal function should be considered for nephrectomy. This conservative approach is supported by the equivalent blood pressure response and improved renal function response observed after renal artery revascularization. Moreover, improved renal function after operation confers a significant and independent survival advantage. Conversely, when significant renal function exists in the occluded kidney, the price of nephrectomy with loss of functioning renal mass may be greater than the benefit from improved blood pressure control.[2] Exception to this premise occurs only when hypertension is uncontrolled with maximal drug therapy, resulting in overt end-organ damage, and nephrectomy leads to blood pressure cure.[1] In children, limited use of nephrectomy is of even greater importance because 50% of such patients demonstrate significant contralateral renal artery disease over time.[16]

In summary, renal artery revascularization in the patient with renal artery occlusion and renovascular hypertension without azotemia should be considered whenever the distal vessel is identified and appears normal on angiography. If the vessel is not visualized on angiography, the distal vessel is explored prior to nephrectomy. When a normal distal vessel is demonstrated, renal revascularization is performed. With this approach, repair rather than nephrectomy is performed in 50% of such cases. Conversely, if the distal renal artery and segmental branches demonstrate atherosclerosis during exploration, these findings correlate with intrarenal nephrosclerosis and poor blood pressure and renal function response. In such cases, a primary nephrectomy is performed if renal function has proved negligible (<10%) on preoperative isotope renography.

The Patient Without Hypertension

This aggressive approach to renal revascularization does not extend to prophylactic repair of renal artery stenosis or occlusion in normotensive patients. In such patients, the

Table 130-2   Angiographic Progression of Renal Artery Atherosclerosis

| MEAN FOLLOW-UP (mo) | NO. | IPSILATERAL LESIONS | | PERCENTAGE OF CONTRALATERAL LESIONS EXHIBITING PROGRESSION |
		Percentage Exhibiting Progression	Percentage Progressing to Occlusion	
29-35*	85	44	16	—
28†	35	—	12	17

*Data from Wollenweber J, Sheps SG, Davis GD: Clinical course of atherosclerotic renovascular disease. Am J Cardiol 21:60-71, 1968; and Schreiber MJ, Pohl MA, Novick AC: The natural history of atherosclerotic and fibrous renal artery disease. Urol Clin North Am 11:383-392, 1984.

†Data from Dean, RH, Kieffer RW, Smith BM, et al: Renovascular hypertension: Anatomic and renal function changes during drug therapy. Arch Surg 166:1408-1415, 1981.

term *prophylactic repair* indicates that renal revascularization is performed before the occurrence of any clinical sequelae related to the lesion. By definition, therefore, patients considered for prophylactic renal artery repair have neither hypertension nor reduced excretory renal function. Correction of an atherosclerotic renal artery lesion assumes that (1) a significant percentage of such asymptomatic patients will survive to the point that the renal lesion would cause hypertension or renal dysfunction and (2) preemptive correction is necessary to prevent an untreatable adverse event. On the basis of available data, we do not perform prophylactic renal artery intervention either as an isolated catheter-based or open procedure or a procedure combined with planned aortic repair.

This management philosophy is based on angiographic data from three studies regarding the anatomic progression of atherosclerotic renovascular disease causing hypertension, which are summarized in Table 130-2.[17-19] Of patients with renovascular hypertension, ipsilateral progression of renovascular atherosclerosis occurred in 44%, and 12% progressed to have total occlusion during medical management. However, only 1 (3%) of these patients had untreatable loss of a previously reconstructible renal artery.[19] In the absence of hypertension, one must assume that the renal artery lesion first progresses anatomically to become functionally significant (i.e., to produce hypertension). On the basis of the preceding data, progression of a silent renal artery lesion to produce renovascular hypertension could be expected in approximately 44% of normotensive patients.

If one assumes that the incident of renovascular hypertension is managed medically, the next consideration is the frequency of decline in renal function. Among 30 patients with renovascular hypertension in one study who were randomly assigned to medical management, significant loss of renal function—reflected by at least 25% decrease in glomerular filtration rate (GFR)—occurred in 40% of patients during 15 to 24 months of follow-up.[19] Medical management was considered to have failed in these patients, who underwent operative renal artery repair. However, 13% of the patients continued to exhibit progressive deterioration in renal function after operation. Therefore, in 36% of the patients with renovascular hypertension who were randomly assigned to medical management, loss of renal function could have been prevented by an earlier operation. Moreover, one must consider how many of these patients who demonstrate a decline in kidney function during medical management experience restoration of function after surgery. In this regard, reports suggest that renal function is

restored by renovascular repair in 58% to 67% of properly selected patients.[2,20]

The importance of these issues considered in context of prophylactic renal revascularization can be demonstrated by considering 100 hypothetical patients without hypertension in whom an unsuspected renal artery lesion is demonstrated before open aortic repair (Table 130-3). If the renal artery lesion is not repaired prophylactically, in approximately 44 patients the lesion will progress anatomically and renovascular hypertension will subsequently develop. Sixteen (36%) of these 44 patients may experience a preventable reduction in renal function during follow-up. However, delayed operation will restore function in 11 (67%) of these 16 patients. In theory, therefore, only 5 of the hypothetical 100 patients receive unique benefit from prophylactic intervention. This unique benefit should be considered in terms of the associated morbidity and mortality of renal artery repair. In our center, the operative mortality associated with the surgical treatment of isolated renal artery disease alone is approximately 1%, but combined aortorenal reconstruction is associated with a 5% to 6% perioperative mortality.[3-8,10,11,13,15-22] If direct aortorenal methods of reconstruction are employed in conjunction with intraoperative completion duplex ultrasonography, the early technical failure rate is less than 1%, and late failures of reconstruction can be expected in 3%

Table 130-3   Comparison of Risk to Estimated Benefit for Prophylactic Renal Revascularization in 100 Hypothetically Normotensive Patients

BENEFIT OR RISK	NO. PATIENTS
Benefit	
Progression to RVH (44/100 or 44%)	44
Patients with RVH who lose renal function (16/44 or 36%)	16
Renal function restored by later operation (11/16 or 67%)	11
Renal function not restored by later operation (5/16 or 33%)	5
Unique benefit	*5 patients*
Risk (combined aortorenal reconstruction):	
Operative mortality (5.5%)	5
Early technical failure (0.5%)	1
Late failure of revascularization (4.0%)	4
Adverse outcome	*10 patients*

RVH, renovascular hypertension.

to 4% of renal artery repairs.[3] Therefore, adverse results could be expected in 10 of these 100 patients after combined aortorenal repair. Theoretically, then, prophylactic renal artery repair could provide unique benefit in only 5 patients but could potentially produce an adverse outcome in up to 10 patients. On the basis of available data, we find no justification for prophylactic renal artery surgery either as an independent procedure or as a procedure performed in combination with aortic repair. This same management strategy is applied to catheter-based renal artery intervention.

■ AZOTEMIC ISCHEMIC NEPHROPATHY

The azotemic patient with atherosclerotic renovascular disease more clearly resembles the patient with end-organ damage than does the patient with normal renal function. Retrieval of function has immediate practical significance in the azotemic patient; however, the hazard of accelerating renal failure to dialysis dependence by ineffective intervention has limited widespread enthusiasm for surgical treatment of these patients.

In 1962, Morris and associates[23] reported on eight azotemic patients with global renal ischemia who experienced improved blood pressure and renal function after renal revascularization. Novick and colleagues[20] found a similar beneficial function response when bilateral renal lesions were corrected in azotemic patients. Nevertheless, data regarding the prevalence, clinical presentation, or natural history of azotemic ischemic nephropathy are lacking or incomplete. Circumstantial evidence, however, suggests that it may be a more common cause of renal insufficiency in the atherosclerotic age group than was previously recognized. In a 1992 study of randomly selected azotemic patients with serum creatinine ≥ 2 mg/dL, 14% had unsuspected renovascular disease.[24] Compared with patients without renal artery disease, patients with ischemic nephropathy were older and had a higher prevalence of extrarenal atherosclerosis. Each of these clinical characteristics is compatible with the demographic features of patients with proven ischemic nephropathy after surgical treatment.[2,12,25-27] Collectively, these data argue that renovascular disease may be either the primary cause or an important secondary accelerant of renal insufficiency in more patients than is commonly recognized.[12]

The changes in renal function associated with azotemic ischemic nephropathy are demonstrated by a retrospective review of data collected from 58 consecutive patients with ischemic nephropathy who underwent operative renal artery repair.[25] The rate of decline in renal function during the period before and after intervention and the immediate effect of surgery on excretory function were examined. Patients with preoperative serum creatinine ≥ 1.8 mg/dL and at least three sequential measurements for calculations of EGFR changes during the 6 months before operation (n = 32) were included. These data were used to describe the preoperative rate of decline in EGFR and postoperative rate of decline among surgical survivors as a function of response to operation.

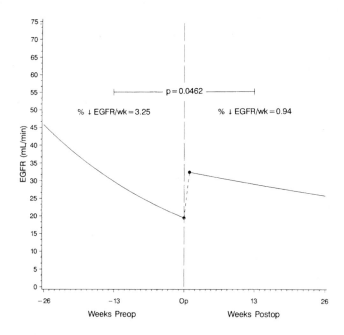

FIGURE 130-2 Percentage decrease in estimated glomerular filtration rate (EGFR) per week for the entire group during the 6 months before (preop; n = 50) and after (postop; n = 32) operation. The immediate effect of operation on EGFR is also depicted. The *P* values for differences are determined with use of the t-test for unpaired data. Note the improvement in the slope of decline in EGFR after operation. (From Dean RH, Tribble RW, Hansen KJ, et al: Evolution of renal insufficiency in ischemic nephropathy. Ann Surg 213:446, 1991. Used by permission.)

Patient ages ranged from 52 to 79 years (mean, 69 years). On the basis of serum creatinine values, preoperative EGFR averaged 23.9 mL/min/m². Comparison of the immediate preoperative EGFR with the immediate postoperative EGFR for the entire group demonstrated significant increase in response to operation (23.9 vs. 32.7 mL/min/m²; *P* = .001). Figure 130-2 demonstrates the preoperative and postoperative rates of change and immediate improvement in EGFR for the entire group. For all patients, a 3.25% per week decrease in EGFR was observed before operation, which differed significantly from the 0.94% per week decline after operation. However, this decrease in the rate of decline following surgical repair was observed *only* in patients who had immediate improvement in excretory renal function after operation (Figs. 130-2 and 130-3). Furthermore, immediate improvement was observed only in patients who had shown rapid decline in EGFR in the 6 months preceding surgery (see Fig. 130-3). In patients with slow preoperative decline in EGFR, there was no immediate improvement in function and no change in the rate of decline in EGFR after intervention (Fig. 130-4). Unfortunately, the variance in individual slopes of change in EGFR prevented the determination of a critical rate of decline that would predict retrieval of renal function by operation. Nevertheless, rapidly deteriorating renal function in a hypertensive patient should alert the physician to the possibility of ischemic nephropathy and supports the likelihood of function benefit after operative repair of atherosclerotic renovascular disease.

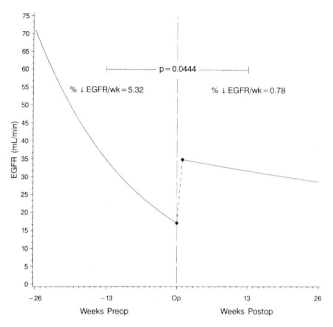

FIGURE 130-3   Percentage decline in estimated glomerular filtration rate (EGFR) per week during the 6 months before (preop; n = 23) and after (postop; n = 25) operation in the group of patients with proven ischemic nephropathy. Each patient had at least a 20% improvement in EGFR after operation. The immediate effect of operation on EGFR in this group is also depicted. The P values for differences are determined with use of the t-test for unpaired data. Note the improvement in the slope of decline in EGFR after operation in this group. This improvement confirmed a causal relationship between the atherosclerotic renovascular disease and renal insufficiency. (From Dean RH, Tribble RW, Hansen KJ, et al: Evolution of renal insufficiency in ischemic nephropathy. Ann Surg 213:446, 1991. Used by permission.)

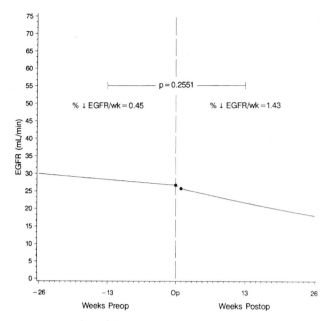

FIGURE 130-4   Percent decline in estimated glomerular filtration rate (EGFR) per week during the 6 months before (preop; n = 18) and after (postop; n = 8) operation in the group of patients who had no immediate benefit in EGFR after operation. The P values for differences are determined with use of the t-test for unpaired data. Note the absence of improvement in the rate of deterioration of EGFR after operation in this group. (From Dean RH, Tribble RW, Hansen KJ, et al: Evolution of renal insufficiency in ischemic nephropathy. Ann Surg 213:446, 1991. Used by permission.)

When data were analyzed collectively, renal artery repair was shown to have a beneficial effect on both immediate EGFR and the rate of decline in EGFR. However, when data were analyzed with respect to response after operation, beneficial effect of operation on the rate of deterioration of EGFR was seen only in patients who experienced an immediate improvement in EGFR after operation. This observation may have important clinical significance, because the detrimental effect of atherosclerotic renovascular disease may arise from one of two causes. First, the lesion may limit glomerular perfusion to a degree that it contributes to "glomerular filtration failure" and decreased excretory function.[23] Second, it may be the source of atheroembolism that destroys functioning renal parenchyma. These data suggest that correction of renal artery atherosclerosis causing reversible ischemia will both provide an immediate improvement in EGFR and slow the postoperative rate of decline. Conversely, when the lesion is not producing reversible ischemia, as evidenced by the absence of improvement in EGFR immediately after operation, no decrease in the rate of decline in EGFR will be realized after operation. This experience emphasizes the rapid decline in renal function among patients with proven ischemic nephropathy and demonstrates the immediate benefit of operation on EGFR and its subsequent rate of deterioration in azotemic patients. Although the biases inherent to this

retrospective analysis limit the power of these observations, the rate of deterioration in EGFR was rapid and entirely consistent with early entry into end-stage renal disease (ESRD) and dialysis dependence.

■ DIALYSIS-DEPENDENT ISCHEMIC NEPHROPATHY

End-stage renal disease requiring long-term renal replacement therapy is the final clinical expression of ischemic nephropathy. In this instance, identification of dialysis-dependent ischemic nephropathy is a clinical imperative, because both quality and quantity of life are adversely affected. Nevertheless, dialysis-dependent ischemic nephropathy is uncommonly sought, and the associated renovascular disease less commonly corrected.[12,26,28,29] In part, this situation reflects general pessimism about retrieval of excretory renal function and the risk inherent to operative intervention in patients who are dependent on dialysis.

Despite this general pessimism, circumstantial evidence suggests that ischemic nephropathy is a more common cause of end-stage renal failure than previously recognized. In a 1986 survey, 73% of patients with ESRD were in the atherosclerotic age group.[30] In a report by Mailloux and coworkers,[31] ischemic nephropathy causing dialysis dependence increased from 6.7% for the period between 1978 and 1981 to 16.5% for the period between 1982 and 1985. The median age of onset of ESRD for this group was the highest among all groups.

These data are supported by a prospective study from our center. During a 7-month period, all patients 50 years and older presenting for chronic renal replacement therapy were screened for atherosclerotic renovascular disease by renal duplex sonography. Of 90 consecutive patients, 53 agreed to undergo the study and among these patients, 45 studies were technically adequate to delineate the presence or absence of renovascular disease.[32] Nonparticipants were significantly older than participants (70.3 ± 1.7 vs. 65.0 ± 1.1 years; P = .007), but otherwise, the two groups demonstrated no significant differences in race, gender, or clinical diagnosis. Overall, significant renovascular disease was noted in 15 of 92 kidneys (16%), including four renal artery occlusions. Ten of 45 participants (22%) demonstrated renal artery stenosis or occlusion, including bilateral disease in 5 patients. When demographic characteristics of participants with and without renal artery disease were compared, age and race differed significantly. Older white patients presenting for chronic renal replacement therapy were significantly more likely to have renovascular disease. Among white participants, 40% demonstrated hemodynamically significant renal artery stenosis or occlusion. In 20% of white participants, both kidneys were involved. Moreover, participants with renovascular disease had higher rates of tobacco abuse (P = .04) and extrarenal atherosclerosis (P = .005) than those without renovascular disease. The results from this prospective study indicate that renovascular disease may exist in a significant minority of older patients beginning long-term renal replacement therapy. Advanced age, white race, tobacco abuse, and extrarenal atherosclerosis characterized individuals with dialysis-dependent ischemic nephropathy requiring chronic renal replacement therapy.[32]

The significance of these findings is demonstrated by both recovery of renal function and improvement in patient survival after operative renal artery repair in dialysis-dependent patients. From January 1987 through December 1999, 40 of 500 patients treated at our centers for atherosclerotic renovascular disease were considered permanently dialysis-dependent.[1] Analysis of the rate of change in EGFR before and after operation and the impact of function retrieval are available for the first 20 consecutive patients.[26] This group of 20 patients (6 women, 14 men; mean age 66 years) had been dialysis-dependent from 1 to 9 weeks (mean, 3.4 weeks) prior to operation. Each patient had severe hypertension and evidence of diffuse extrarenal atherosclerosis. Direct aortorenal reconstruction was performed in each patient without perioperative or in-hospital deaths. Sixteen of 20 patients (80%) were initially removed from hemodialysis. For these 16 patients, postoperative EGFR ranged from 9.0 to 56.1 mL/m² (mean, 32.4 mL/min/m²). Two of 16 patients with a modest increase in EGFR resumed hemodialysis 4 and 6 months after surgery. Outcome was determined by the site of renovascular disease and the extent of repair. Removal from dialysis was more likely after bilateral or complete renal artery repair (15 of 16 patients) than after unilateral repair (1 of 4 patients; P = .01). The estimated rate of decline before and after

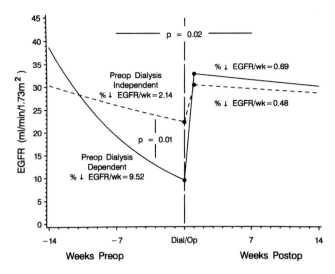

FIGURE 130-5   Percent decline in estimated glomerular filtration rate (EGFR) per week before and after operation for azotemic (*broken line*) and dialysis-dependent (*solid line*) patients. Although the rate of decline in EGFR was significantly greater for dialysis-dependent patients, the return of renal function was very similar. Note the decrease in the rate of decline of EGFR for both azotemic and dialysis-dependent groups after operation. (From Hansen KJ, Thommason RB, Craven TE, et al. Surgical management of dialysis-dependent ischemic nephropathy. J Vasc Surg 21:197-211, 1995. Used by permission.)

operation in dialysis-dependent patients compared with patients with azotemic ischemic nephropathy is depicted in Figure 130-5. Permanent removal from dialysis was associated with a rapid preoperative rate of decline in EGFR (mean slope $\log^e$ EGFR: −0.1393 ± 0.0340 off dialysis; −0.0188 ± 0.0464 on dialysis; P = .04). Immediate increase in EGFR after operation was inversely correlated with the severity of intrarenal atherosclerosis (rank correlation: −0.57; 95% confidence interval [CI], −0.83-0.10). Although the rate of decline in preoperative EGFR was significantly greater than that observed for azotemic patients, the return in renal function and decrease in the postoperative decline in EGFR were very similar for the two groups. Death during follow-up was associated with dialysis dependence; two deaths occurred among 14 patients off dialysis, whereas 5 of 6 dialysis-dependent patients died (P < .01). The product-limit estimates for follow-up survival as a function of dialysis status are illustrated in Figure 130-6. For those patients remaining on dialysis after operation, median survival was only 7 months.

Applying the premise that significant renal artery disease is prevalent in the atherosclerotic population and may cause excretory renal insufficiency that can progress to ESRD and dialysis dependence, we currently screen for ischemic nephropathy in all hypertensive patients older than 50 years who present with newly recognized renal insufficiency.[3,27-29] As described in Chapter 127, our preferred screening method is renal duplex sonography.[27,33] Renal duplex sonography has demonstrated an overall accuracy of 96% for establishing the presence or absence of main renal artery stenosis or occlusion.[33] In the search for a renovascular cause of renal insufficiency, normal results of renal duplex scanning performed by an experienced sonographer exclude ischemic

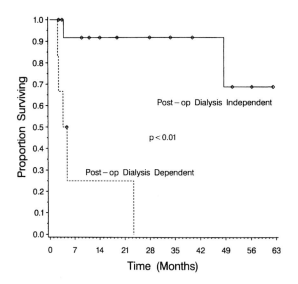

FIGURE 130-6 Product-limit estimate of patient survival according to dialysis status after operation (n = 20). (From Hansen KJ, Thomason RB, Craven TE, et al: Surgical management of dialysis-dependent ischemic nephropathy. J Vasc Surg 21:197-211, 1995. Used by permission.)

nephropathy. If the study is obtained to evaluate for a renovascular cause for hypertension, however, normal findings do not exclude branch or polar renal artery disease. Consequently, we limit the use of conventional angiography in patients with renal insufficiency to those with either positive renal duplex scanning findings or severe, poorly controlled hypertension.

Unfortunately, once ischemic nephropathy is identified, most issues regarding anticipated function retrieval in a particular patient remain poorly defined.[3,25,34,35] We observed that the site of disease and operation and the rate of decline in preoperative EGFR differed between patients with and without improved renal function after operation. Although angiographic findings consistent with intrarenal atherosclerosis were inversely correlated with change in EGFR, this feature did not differ significantly in patients on and off dialysis after operation. Zinman and Libertino[36] have found preoperative renal biopsy a useful predictor of functional retrieval in their series of patients, but we have not found the procedure worthwhile. Having identified hyalinized glomeruli in open biopsy specimens from kidneys with adequate renal function and from kidneys with marked improvement in excretory function after operation, we abandoned the technique as misleading and potentially hazardous.[2,28]

The role of repair of unilateral renal artery stenosis in patients with renal insufficiency of any degree is uncertain. Even greater uncertainty surrounds the role of renal artery repair in the normotensive patient with renal insufficiency. In this case, the issue is whether renovascular disease sufficient to cause renal failure can exist without activating the renin-angiotensin system and raising blood pressure. This clinical scenario has the greatest practical importance for the patient who is normotensive as a consequence of antihypertensive agents. In the setting of renal artery disease, the contribution of potent diuretics, angiotensin-converting enzyme (ACE) inhibitors, and angiotensin

receptor blockers to renal dysfunction is widely recognized. Otherwise, in the complete absence of hypertension, the physiologic importance of renal artery disease as a cause of renal insufficiency must remain suspect.[29]

CONTEMPORARY RESULTS OF OPERATIVE INTERVENTION

To examine the changes that have occurred in both the patient population presenting for operative management and the results of operation over the past three decades, we have reviewed our recent operative experience. During the last 15-year period, over 800 patients have had operative renal artery repair. The first 500 consecutive patients treated for atherosclerotic renovascular disease have already been described.[1,2] This group included 246 men and 254 women, with ages ranging from 34 to 88 years (mean age, 65 ± 9 years). Severe or uncontrolled hypertension was present in all of these patients (mean, 200 ± 35 mm Hg systolic/104 ± 21 mm Hg diastolic; mean number of medications required, 2.6 ± 1.1). Hypertension had been recognized for 1 to 57 years (mean duration, 10.0 ± 9.1 years). Evidence of at least one manifestation of extrarenal atherosclerotic damage was present in 451 patients (90%) with atherosclerotic renovascular disease: cardiac disease (70%), cerebrovascular disease (32%), or aortoiliac disease (64%).

Ischemic nephropathy, defined as a serum creatinine level of 1.8 mg/dL or greater after the removal of high-dose diuretics, ACE inhibitors, and receptor blockers, was present in 244 patients (49%) with atherosclerotic renovascular disease, including 40 patients dependent on dialysis.[1,2]

Two hundred three patients (41%) had clinically significant unilateral renal artery disease and 297 (59%) had global renal artery disease (276 patients with bilateral disease; 21 patients with disease of a solitary kidney). Methods of operative repair are described in Table 130-4. Renal revascularization combined with aortic or mesenteric reconstruction was performed in 196 patients (39%); 76 patients underwent combined repair of clinically significant aortic occlusive disease; and 57 patients had repair

Table 130-4	Summary of Operative Management of Atherosclerotic Renovascular Disease in 500 Patients	
PROCEDURE	**NO. KIDNEYS**	
Aortorenal bypass		*384*
Vein	204	
PTFE	159	
Polyester (Dacron)	21	
Splanchnorenal bypass		*13*
Reimplantation		*56*
Endarterectomy		*267*
Nephrectomy		*56*
Primary	13	
Contralateral	43	
Total no. kidneys operated		*776*

PTFE, polytetrafluoroethylene.

Adapted from Cherr GS, Hansen KJ, Craven TE, et al: Surgical management of atherosclerotic renovascular disease. J Vasc Surg 35:236-245, 2002.

of an abdominal aortic aneurysm. Sixty-three patients had combined repair of both aortic occlusive and aneurysmal disease.

Perioperative morbidity (excluding perioperative deaths) occurred in 81 patients (16%)—myocardial infarction in 15 patients, stroke in 5, significant arrhythmia in 22, and pneumonia in 36. Five patients had worsening renal function after operation that resulted in permanent dialysis dependence within 1 month of surgery. The mean preoperative serum creatinine level and EGFR for these 5 patients were 3.4 mg/dL and 20.2 mL/min/m², respectively. Nine patients who were dialysis dependent before renal revascularization continued to require renal replacement therapy after operation.

Follow-up data were available for 99% of survivors of surgery. During follow-up (mean, 56 months; range, 1-159 months), there were 171 deaths, giving estimated 5- and 10-year survival rates of 69.0% and 33.6%, respectively, for all patients. Product limits of time to death or dialysis are depicted in Figure 130-7. Cardiovascular events accounted for the majority (74%) of late deaths, including coronary artery disease (41%) and stroke (9%). Twenty-four percent of late deaths occurred from treatment of or complications from aneurysmal disease or noncoronary atherosclerosis. Cancer accounted for 12% of deaths, lung disease for 6%, and other causes for 8%. Thirty-eight percent of patients who died during follow-up required renal replacement therapy prior to death.

Table 130-5 summarizes the proportional hazard regression analysis for time to death from all causes. Factors significantly and independently associated with increased risk of death from all causes included poor preoperative renal function, diabetes mellitus, history of myocardial infarction or stroke, severe aortic occlusive disease, greater age, and renal function worsened after operation. Prior myocardial revascularization, blood pressure cured, and increased systolic blood pressure favored survival; these associations were significant and independent of other parameters.

On follow-up, 218 nonfatal cardiovascular events occurred in 139 patients (28%). They included angina (49 patients), myocardial infarction (29 patients), percutaneous transluminal coronary angioplasty (19 patients), and coronary artery bypass graft (22 patients). Cerebrovascular events

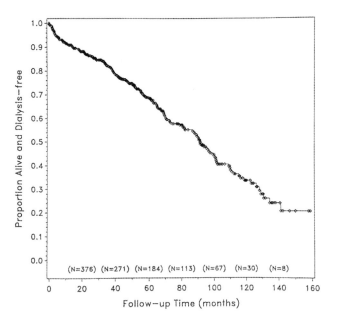

FIGURE 130-7   Product-limit estimates of time to death or dialysis for all patients with atherosclerotic renovascular disease. (From Cherr GS, Hansen KJ, Craven TE, et al: Surgical management of atherosclerotic renovascular disease. J Vasc Surg 35:236-245, 2002. Used by permission.)

were transient ischemic attacks (18 patients), stroke (22 patients), and carotid endarterectomy (27 patients). Lower extremity revascularization was required in 11 patients. Other vascular reconstructions performed were aortomesenteric reconstruction (5 patients), thoracoabdominal aortic aneurysm repair (7 patients), and renal revascularization for progression of contralateral atherosclerotic-renovascular disease (12 patients). Multivariate analysis showed that only preoperative angina ($P = .001$; odds ratio [OR], 2.18; 95% CI, 1.25-3.84) had a significant and independent association with late cardiovascular morbidity. Neither blood pressure nor renal function response demonstrated an association with follow-up cardiovascular morbidity. However, vascular reconstruction during follow-up was predicted by male gender ($P = .009$; OR, 2.10; 95% CI, 1.21-3.67) and combined aortorenal repair ($P = .008$; OR, 2.36; 95% CI, 1.26-4.46).

Table 130-5	Proportional Hazards Regression Model for All Causes of Death Among 455 Atherosclerotic Patients				
VARIABLE*	**BETA**	**STANDARD ERROR**	**HAZARD RATIO**	**95% CONFIDENCE INTERVAL**	***P* VALUE**
Preoperative EGFR	−0.5121	0.1066	0.60	0.49-0.74	.001
Age	0.1988	0.0906	1.22	1.02-1.46	.028
Diabetes mellitus	0.5618	0.2017	1.75	1.18-2.60	.005
Prior myocardial infarction	0.3913	0.1712	1.48	1.06-2.07	.022
Prior PTCA/CABG	−0.5082	0.2392	0.60	0.38-0.96	.034
Prior stroke	0.4159	0.2112	1.52	1.00-2.29	.049
Severe aortic occlusive disease	0.4008	0.1731	1.49	1.06-2.10	.021
Blood pressure cured	−0.6328	0.2844	0.53	0.30-0.93	.026
Postoperative systolic blood pressure	−0.1994	0.0928	0.82	0.68-0.98	.032
Postoperative EGFR worse	0.5121	0.2321	1.67	1.06-2.63	.027

*All variables significant at $P < .10$ included.
CABG, coronary artery bypass graft; EGFR, estimated glomerular filtration rate (mL/min·m²); PTCA, percutaneous transluminal coronary angioplasty.

From Cherr GS, Hansen KJ, Craven TE, et al: Surgical management of atherosclerotic renovascular disease. J Vasc Surg 35:236-245, 2002.

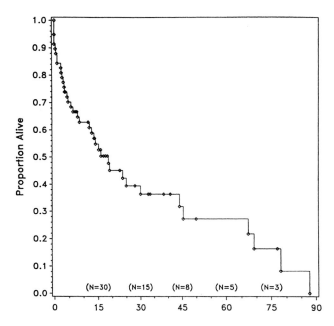

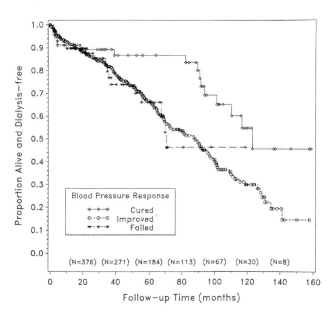

FIGURE 130-8 Graphic depiction of the product-limit estimates of time to death after onset of dialysis dependence. (From Cherr GS, Hansen KJ, Craven TE, et al: Surgical management of atherosclerotic renovascular disease. J Vasc Surg 35:236-245, 2002. Used by permission.)

FIGURE 130-9 Product-limit estimates of time to death or dialysis according to blood pressure response to operation. (From Cherr GS, Hansen KJ, Craven TE, et al: Surgical management of atherosclerotic renovascular disease. J Vasc Surg 35:236-245, 2002. Used by permission.)

Eighty-four patients progressed to eventual dialysis dependence during follow-up. Of these, 65 patients (77%) died. Cause of death in patients requiring renal replacement therapy were coronary artery disease (39%), noncoronary atherosclerosis (37%), stroke (9%), cancer (7%), lung disease (4%), and other (4%). Figure 130-8 depicts the estimated survival for patients after initiation of renal replacement therapy. The median survival after dialysis dependence was 18.6 months, and 27% of patients were alive at 5 years. In 10 patients progressing to dialysis dependence, renal duplex scanning identified anatomic failure of 13 renal artery repairs.

Overall, 389 patients underwent 1295 intraoperative and postoperative renal duplex sonography evaluations of 622 renal artery repairs. Intraoperative revision of major B-scan defects was required in 7.1% of repairs. Restenosis or thrombosis of 24 renal artery repairs (3.9%) occurred in 20 patients (5.0%) evaluated with postoperative duplex scanning.

Among the 477 patients surviving surgical repair, blood pressure response was considered cured in 12%, improved in 73%, and failed in 15%. The preoperative and post operative blood pressure values and medication requirements for each group are listed in Table 130-6. Compared with the results of blood pressure improved and failed, blood pressure cured was significantly and independently associated with better dialysis-free survival ($P = .011$; OR, 0.52; 95% CI, 0.30-0.88). Although improved blood pressure was associated with significant postoperative decreases in blood pressure and medication requirements (blood pressure, 205/107 vs. 147/81; $P < .0001$; medications, 2.8 vs. 1.7, $P < .0001$), these differences were *not* associated with better dialysis-free survival. The product-limit estimates of dialysis-free survival according to postoperative blood pressure response are depicted in Figure 130-9.

In all the patients who survived surgery, there was a significant increase in postoperative EGFR compared with

Table 130-6	Blood Pressure Response to Operation for Atherosclerotic Renovascular Disease in 472 Patients*				
	NO. PATIENTS	**BLOOD PRESSURE (SYSTOLIC/DIASTOLIC, mm Hg)**		**NO. MEDICATIONS**	
RESPONSE	**(%)**	**Preoperative**	**Postoperative†**	**Preoperative**	**Postoperative†**
Cured	57 (12)	195 ± 35/103 ± 22	137 ± 16/78 ± 9	2.0 ± 1.1	0 ± 0†
Improved	345 (73)	205 ± 35/107 ± 21	147 ± 21/81 ± 11	2.8 ± 1.1	1.7 ± 0.8†
Failed	70 (15)	182 ± 30/87 ± 13	158 ± 28/82 ± 12	2.0 ± 0.9	2.0 ± 0.9
All	472 (100)	201 ± 35/104 ± 22	148 ± 22/81 ± 11	2.6 ± 1.1	1.6 ± 0.9†

*Blood pressure and medications are mean ± standard deviation.
†$P < .0001$ as compared with preoperative value, except diastolic blood pressure value in failed group, for which $P = .001$.

Adapted from Cherr GS, Hansen KJ, Craven TE, et al: Surgical management of atherosclerotic renovascular disease. J Vasc Surg 35:236-245, 2002.

Table 130-7	Renal Function Response Versus Preoperative Serum Creatinine Level for Atherosclerotic Renovascular Disease in 469 Patients				
RENAL FUNCTION RESPONSE	**PREOPERATIVE SERUM CREATININE VALUE (mg/dL)***				
	<1.8	**1.8-2.9**	**≥3.0**	**DIALYSIS-DEPENDENT**	**TOTAL**
Improved	71 (29%)	75 (54%)	29 (58%)	28 (76%)	203 (43%)
No Change	142 (58%)	52 (38%)	17 (34%)	9 (24%)	220 (47%)
Worse	31 (13%)	11 (8%)	4 (8%)	0 (0%)	46 (10%)

*$P < .0001$ for rate of improved response compared with preoperative serum creatinine value.

Adapted from Cherr GS, Hansen KJ, Craven TE, et al: Surgical management of atherosclerotic renovascular disease. J Vasc Surg 35:236-245, 2002.

preoperative EGFR (preoperative, 41.1 ± 23.9 mL/min/m²; postoperative, 48.2 ± 25.5 mL/min/m²; $P < .0001$). Among individual patients, 43% had improved renal function, 47% had unchanged function, and 10% had worsened function after surgical repair. Twenty-eight patients (70%) requiring renal replacement therapy before operation were permanently removed from dialysis after surgery. A greater proportion of patients with higher preoperative serum creatinine level or worse renal function progressing to dialysis dependence before surgery had improved postoperative renal function (Table 130-7). This association between increased preoperative serum creatinine level and improved postoperative renal function was significant ($P < .0001$).

Progression to death or dialysis demonstrated significant associations with both preoperative parameters and postoperative blood pressure and renal function response. Table 130-8 summarizes the proportional hazard regression analysis for time to death or dialysis during follow-up.

Preoperative factors significantly and independently associated with death or dialysis included diabetes mellitus, severe aortic occlusive disease, and poor renal function. Significant and independent associations were noted for blood pressure cured and survival compared with blood pressure improved or worsened. Moreover, improved postoperative renal function demonstrated significant and independent associations with better dialysis-free survival compared with renal function unchanged. The relationship between each category of renal function response and dialysis-free survival demonstrated significant interactions with preoperative renal function. In patients with renal function unchanged by operation, those with poor preoperative renal function had a higher risk of death or dialysis after surgery. In patients whose renal function worsened after operation, higher risk of death or dialysis was significant for those with preoperative renal function at median values of EGFR or greater. These significant and independent interactions are

Table 130-8	Proportional Hazards Regression Model of Time to Death or Dialysis for 460 Atherosclerotic Patients				
VARIABLE*	**BETA**	**STANDARD ERROR**	**HAZARD RATIO**	**95% CONFIDENCE INTERVAL**	**P VALUE**
Preoperative EGFR	0.8555	0.1198	0.43	0.34-0.54	0.001
Diabetes mellitus	0.5313	0.1959	2.14	1.15-3.97	0.007
Prior myocardial infarction	0.3095	0.1646	1.36	0.99-1.88	0.060
Prior PTCA/CABG	0.3733	0.2190	0.69	0.45-1.06	0.088
Prior stroke	0.4068	0.2001	1.50	1.02-2.22	0.042
Severe aortic occlusive disease	0.5078	0.1689	1.66	1.19-2.31	0.003
Preoperative systolic blood pressure	0.2329	0.0848	0.79	0.67-0.94	0.006
Blood pressure cured	0.6637	0.2711	0.52	0.30-0.88	0.014
Postoperative EGFR—no change:	0.9259	0.3659	—	—	—
Preoperative EGFR = 25 (25th percentile)			1.49	1.04-2.13	0.028
Preoperative EGFR = 38 (median)			1.12	0.79-1.61	0.524
Preoperative EGFR = 53 (75th percentile)			0.83	0.48-1.42	0.495
IA preoperative EGFR × postoperative EGFR: not changed	0.5047	0.2461	—	—	0.032
Postoperative EGFR—worsened:	0.1070	0.5324	—	—	—
Preoperative EGFR = 25 (25th percentile)			1.45	0.81-2.60	0.211
Preoperative EGFR = 38 (median)			1.68	1.02-2.74	0.040
Preoperative EGFR = 53 (75th percentile)			1.95	1.06-3.61	0.032
IA preoperative EGFR × postoperative EGFR: worsened	0.2549	0.2969	—	—	0.032

*All variables significant at $P < .10$ included.

CABG, coronary artery bypass graft; EGFR, estimated glomerular filtration rate (mL/min/m²); IA, interaction term; PTCA, percutaneous transluminal coronary angioplasty.

Adapted from Cherr GS, Hansen KJ, Craven TE, et al: Surgical management of atherosclerotic renovascular disease. J Vasc Surg 35:236-245, 2002.

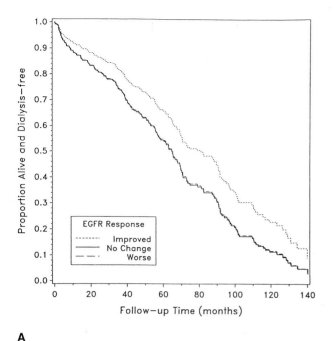

A

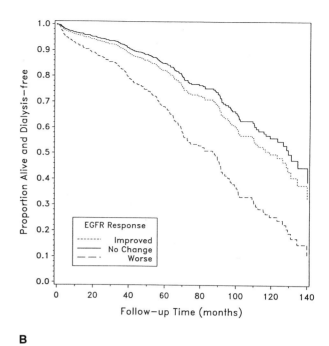

B

FIGURE 130-10 Predicted dialysis-free survival according to postoperative renal function response for patients with preoperative EGFRs of 25 mL/min/m^2 (25th percentile, **A**) or 39 mL/min/m^2 (median value, **B**). The interaction between preoperative EGFR and renal function response for dialysis-free survival was significant and independent. (From Cherr GS, Hansen KJ, Craven TE, et al: Surgical management of atherosclerotic renovascular disease. J Vasc Surg 35:236-245, 2002. Used by permission.)

shown for predicted dialysis-free survival according to postoperative renal function in Figure 130-10.

Contemporary patient demographics, surgical management, and response to operation for the first 157 patients with atherosclerotic renovascular disease are contrasted with a previously reported experience in Table 130-9.[1,3,21] Clearly, the current atherosclerotic patient population includes individuals who presented for treatment with more advanced disease. Specifically, patients in the current group presented with hypertension of longer duration. Likewise, the current group presented at an older age for treatment than the patients in the previous report. The much higher incidence of ischemic nephropathy (49% vs. 8%) and the lower cure rates after operative correction of renovascular disease may be influenced by this longer duration of drug therapy before intervention.

■ EFFECT OF BLOOD PRESSURE AND RENAL FUNCTION RESPONSE ON EVENT-FREE SURVIVAL

The rationale for treatment of atherosclerotic renovascular disease is to improve event-free survival. Hypertension response has been the primary outcome measure for the vast majority of intervention studies for atherosclerotic renovascular disease. Because the relationship between adverse cardiovascular events and blood pressure has long been considered quantitative, the lack of association between improved blood pressure response and cardiovascular morbidity or mortality rate in atherosclerotic

patients was an unexpected finding. In the absence of validating studies, this observation may reflect limitations in the grading system for blood pressure response. Blood pressure response was categorized to account for both magnitude change in diastolic pressure and change in the number of antihypertensive medications, but neither change

Table 130-9	Comparison of Earlier Surgical Experience with Contemporary Experience	
	1961-1972*	**1987-1999†**
No. patients	122	
Mean age (years)	50	65
Duration of hypertension (years)	5.1	10.0
Renal artery repair (%):		
Unilateral	80	59
Bilateral	20	41
Combined‡	13	39
Ischemic nephropathy (%):		
Not dependent on dialysis	8	49
Dependent on dialysis	0	8
Graft failure (%)	16	3
Hypertension response (%):		
Cured	53§	12
Improved	36§	73
No change		

*Data adapted from Foster JH, Dean RH, Pinkerton JA, Rhamy RK: Ten years experience with the surgical management of renovascular hypertension. Ann Surg 177:755-766, 1973.
†Data from Cherr GS, Hansen KJ, Craven TE, et al: Surgical management of atherosclerotic renovascular disease. J Vasc Surg 35:236-245, 2002.
‡Combined aortic repair for occlusive or aneurysmal disease.
§Hypertension response, excluding technical failures.

in systolic pressure nor change in class or dose of anti-hypertensive medication was considered. However, when the changes in systolic, diastolic, and pulse pressures were considered as continuous variables, no significant associations between improved blood pressure response and morbidity or mortality were noted. For patients considered improved, the observed decrease in mean systolic and diastolic blood pressure of 58 and 26 mm Hg, respectively, demonstrated no apparent association with cardiovascular morbidity, death from all causes, or cardiovascular death. These results suggest that the quantitative association between blood pressure and survival observed in population-based studies may not apply to the current patient group characterized by atherosclerotic renovascular disease. In this latter regard, the presence of atherosclerotic renovascular disease in combination with diffuse atherosclerosis and renal insufficiency may limit the survival benefit conferred by improved blood pressure control in all but those patients cured of hypertension.

Similar observations have been made between clinical response and outcome after treatment for atherosclerotic renovascular disease contributing to ischemic nephropathy.[2] Among patients in whom ischemic nephropathy was defined as a preoperative serum creatinine of ≥1.8 mg/dL, preoperative EGFR and renal function response to operation were the strongest predictors of dialysis-free survival. Compared with patients whose renal function was unchanged or worsened, only patients with improved renal function after operation demonstrated increased survival free of dialysis dependence. These same relationships exist for the entire patient group with atherosclerotic renovascular disease; however, they are strongest for patients with poor pre-operative excretory renal function. Moreover, when all patients with atherosclerotic renovascular disease were considered, increased severity of preoperative hypertension was associated with improved dialysis-free survival. This observation suggests a possible change in the pathologic sequelae of importance in atherosclerotic renovascular disease. In this shifted paradigm, severe hypertension could be viewed as the key preoperative characteristic favoring clinical benefit, whereas renal function after operation could be considered the key response—the primary determinant of dialysis-free survival. Viewed in this way, future trials that examine the best method of management of atherosclerotic renovascular disease should consider early renal function response as a primary parameter and surrogate for survival free of dialysis.

Once atherosclerotic renovascular disease is identified in combination with severe hypertension and excretory renal insufficiency, discriminating predictors of cured blood pressure or improved renal function are lacking. Results from renal vein systemic renin index have been proposed to predict hypertension cure.[11] Although we advocate the use of renal vein renin assays to guide management in selected cases of unilateral renal artery disease, whether considered as index or ratio values, lateralizing renin assays have predicted blood pressure benefit but not cure.[3] Similarly, renal function response in patients with atherosclerotic renovascular disease is uncertain after renal artery intervention.[2] Later studies have described significant correlation between parameters derived from renal parenchymal Doppler spectral analysis and response to intervention.[37,38] Despite extensive experience with these techniques, we have not been able to reproduce these results at our center. In our clinical experience, factors favoring recovery of renal function after operation have included severe preoperative hypertension, bilateral or global atherosclerotic renovascular disease due to high-grade (>95%) stenosis or renal artery occlusion, and rapidly deteriorating renal function.[2,3,15,26,39] When these features were expressed in their final form as dialysis-dependent ischemic nephropathy, 70% of patients who underwent surgery were removed from dialysis dependence. Given the effect of renal function on both quality and quantity of life, the definition of predictors of function response after intervention for atherosclerotic renovascular disease should be a primary focus of future investigation.

For the contemporary group of 500 patients reviewed here, beneficial hypertension response did not convey improvement in estimated survival.[1,2] This finding contrasted sharply with the outcome of 71 patients who underwent operative management of renovascular hypertension 15 to 23 years previously.[40] Complete follow-up was available in 66 of the 68 patients who survived operation. Comparison of the initial blood pressure response to operation (1 to 6 months postoperatively) with the blood pressure status at the time of death or current date (up to 23 years later) showed that the effect of operative treatment was maintained over long-term follow-up (Fig. 130-11). In those patients who required second renovascular operations for recurrent hypertension during follow-up, the majority of the operations were performed for the management of contralateral renal artery lesions that had progressed to functional significance. For this group of patients, beneficial blood pressure response was associated with better estimated survival than failed response. Although the subgroup of "nonresponders" was small, they experienced a more rapid death rate during follow-up (Fig. 130-12). This fact suggested that when long-term follow-up was considered, inadequate management of renovascular hypertension may leave the patient at higher risk of cardiovascular death.

There are several potential explanations why our contemporary patient group has not demonstrated a similar improvement in estimated survival after improved blood pressure response. First, the average follow-up for the contemporary group of 500 patients is much shorter (mean, 17 vs. 3 years). Second, the contemporary group was significantly older at the time of initial intervention (mean age, 50 vs. 69 years), with significantly more extrarenal atherosclerotic disease (40% vs. 95%). Finally, and perhaps most importantly, 49% of current patients demonstrated ischemic nephropathy.

In contrast to blood pressure response, renal function response among contemporary patients showed a significant and independent association with follow-up survival.[14] Global renal disease submitted to complete renal artery repair after rapid decline in excretory renal function is associated with the best opportunity for recovery of renal function.[1-3,25,26,39] In addition, patients with improved renal function have demonstrated a significant decrease in the rate of decline in EGFR after renal artery repair.[25,26] In the

FIGURE 130-11 Bar graphs comparing initial benefit with late blood pressure response in the respective types of lesions. Numbers of patients in each outcome group are written inside the bars. AS, atherosclerosis; C, cured; F, failed; FMD, fibromuscular dysplasia; I, improved. (From Dean RH, Krueger TC, Whiteneck JM, et al: Operative management of renovascular hypertension: Results after a follow-up of fifteen to twenty-three years. J Vasc Surg 1:234-242, 1984. Used by permission.)

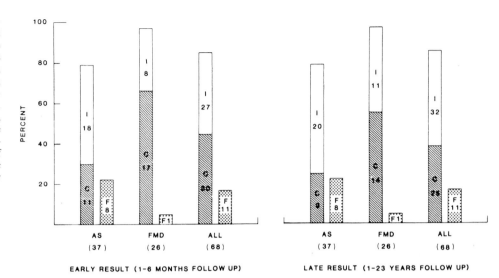

EARLY RESULT (1-6 MONTHS FOLLOW UP)   LATE RESULT (1-23 YEARS FOLLOW UP)

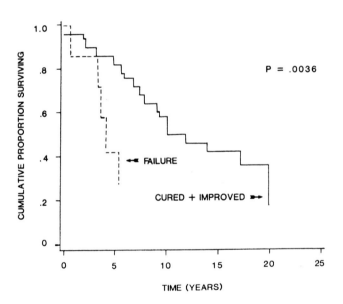

FIGURE 130-12 Kaplan-Meier life-table analysis: Estimated survival by blood pressure response to operation in 37 arteriosclerotic patients. Deaths are from cardiovascular causes. (From Dean RH, Krueger TC, Whiteneck JM, et al: Operative management of renovascular hypertension. J Vasc Surg 1:234, 1984. Used by permission.)

case of primary renal artery repair, patients with ischemic nephropathy whose renal function is unchanged or worsened after repair remain at risk for dialysis dependence during follow-up.[3,14] The clinical significance of these observations is expressed in both the quality and quantity of patient survival after intervention. Initiation of postoperative dialysis dependence both profoundly decreases a patient's vigor and independence and contributes significantly to an increased risk for death during follow-up.[3,26,31] In the contemporary patient population, the single strongest risk factor for death during follow-up has been progression to dialysis-dependent renal failure.

■ OPERATIVE STRATEGY

As discussed earlier, we do not recommend prophylactic renal revascularization; however, empiric renal artery repair is appropriate in selected circumstances. The term *empiric repair* implies that hypertension, renal dysfunction, or both are present, although a causal relationship between the renal artery lesion and these clinical sequelae has not been established. Repair of unilateral renal artery disease may be appropriate as an independent or combined procedure in the presence of negative functional studies when (1) hypertension remains severe and uncontrollable with maximal drug therapy, (2) the patient is relatively young and without significant risk factors for operation, and (3) the probability of long-term patency is greater than 95%. In these circumstances, correction of a renal artery lesion may be justified in order to eliminate all possible causes of hypertension before assigning a patient a higher risk of adverse cardiovascular events. However, because the probability of blood pressure benefit is lower in such a patient, morbidity from the procedure must also be predictably low. Although we have undertaken unilateral renal artery repair in patients with renal insufficiency without positive functional test results, such procedures have been performed as a part of a clinical research study on ischemic nephropathy. Unilateral repair for ischemic nephropathy cannot be recommended as a clinically proven therapeutic intervention. We frequently correct bilateral renovascular disease without prior functional assessment in patients with severe hypertension, renal insufficiency, or both. However, we do not proceed with empiric renal artery repair as an independent procedure if the hypertension is mild and if renal insufficiency is not present.

The incidental finding of renal artery disease during angiographic evaluation of either occlusive or aneurysmal aortic disease commonly produces a therapeutic dilemma. Although concern about leaving uncorrected anatomic disease in juxtaposition to an aortic reconstruction has led to a liberal approach to simultaneous renal reconstruction or catheter-based intervention in many centers, the application of a selective approach to such combined procedures is more appropriate. As discussed earlier, we consider hypertension a prerequisite for renal artery repair. If the patient is normotensive, intervention should be limited to the aortic procedure. If unilateral renal artery stenosis is found in a hypertensive patient, simultaneous renal revascularization should be performed when functional significance is demonstrated by positive renal vein renin assays. When hypertension is severe or poorly controlled, renal intervention may be undertaken empirically without functional study even though the blood pressure benefit is less predictable.

When a patient has bilateral renal artery stenoses and hypertension, the decision to combine renal artery repair with correction of the aortic disease is based on the severity of both the hypertension and the renovascular lesions. When the two renal artery lesions consist of severe disease on one side and only mild or moderate disease on the other, the patient is treated as if only a unilateral lesion exists. If both lesions are only moderately severe (stenosis reducing diameter by 60% to 80%), renal revascularization is undertaken only if the hypertension is severe. In contrast, if both renal artery lesions are severe (> 80% stenosis) and the patient has drug-dependent hypertension, bilateral simultaneous renal revascularization is performed. In this instance, renovascular hypertension secondary to severe bilateral renal artery stenoses is particularly severe and difficult to control. Furthermore, at least mild renal insufficiency is often present. Because azotemia usually parallels the severity of hypertension, a patient who presents with severe azotemia but only mild hypertension usually has renal parenchymal disease. Characteristically, renovascular hypertension associated with severe azotemia or dialysis dependence is associated with total renal artery occlusions or with very severe bilateral stenoses. When considering combined repair of incidentally identified bilateral renal artery disease with open correction of aortic disease, one should evaluate these clinical parameters with respect to this characteristic presentation. In such situations, combined renal artery repair at the time of open aortic surgery is indicated to improve excretory renal function. A beneficial blood pressure response is a secondary goal. Such indications appear justified in light of the observed increase in estimated survival associated with improved renal function despite the greater morbidity and mortality of a combined aortorenal procedure.

Applying this premise, the operative mortality rate in our center for "combined aortorenal procedures" parallels that of other contemporary experiences (Table 130-10).[22,41-53] Review of our operative mortality rates and clinical characteristics in this current experience with "combined procedure," "renal procedure alone," and "aortic procedure alone" groups suggests that operative risk is affected by the stage of a patient's atherosclerosis and the complexity of the procedure. The prevalence of end-organ damage, such as azotemia and heart disease, and the frequency of extrarenal atherosclerosis were greater in the "combined" and "renal alone" groups than in the "aortic alone" group.[22] Although the operative mortality rate of the "combined" group was higher (5.3%) than that of the "renal alone" group (1.7%), the difference is not statistically significant. In contrast, the "combined" operative death rate was statistically higher

than the "aortic alone" rate (0.7%). These two observations suggest that stage of disease and magnitude of operation both may affect operative risk, providing further support for empiric, but not prophylactic, renovascular repair.

Otherwise, operative strategy for atherosclerotic renovascular disease involves correction of all significant renal artery lesions at a single operation. This approach recognizes that the magnitude of renal function benefit varies directly with the site and extent of disease. Staged repairs are undertaken only when bilateral branch reconstruction is required. Direct aortorenal reconstruction (i.e., bypass, endarterectomy, or reimplantation) is preferred over indirect or splanchnorenal repair. In part, this preference reflects the demography of the atherosclerotic patient population—40% have concomitant stenosis of the celiac axis, 59% require bilateral renovascular reconstruction, and 39% undergo combined aortic repair.[1] For reasons discussed previously, nephrectomy is reserved for unreconstructible renovascular disease in a nonfunctioning kidney contributing to severe hypertension.[15] Recognizing the strong, independent relationship of renal function with dialysis-free survival, we do not remove kidneys that are providing less than 20% overall excretory function as shown by isotope renography. As discussed in detail in Chapter 132, regardless of the method of renal artery reconstruction, each repair is evaluated with intraoperative duplex sonography at completion.

■ CONSEQUENCE OF FAILED RENAL ARTERY REPAIR

Advocates of medical management, PTA, and stenting or surgical reconstruction for atherosclerotic renovascular disease typically cite selected clinical results to support their respective views. Reports that examine failure of interventional management by either PTA and stenting or operative repair emphasize the techniques required to re-establish renal artery patency and the immediate blood pressure response to secondary treatment.[54-57] For both PTA and operative repair, data regarding renal function response and event-free survival after remedial management of failed renal artery intervention remain incomplete. Analysis of the consequences of failed renal artery repair in consecutive patients treated at our center from January 1987 to July 1997 provides additional information in this regard. Among these primary procedures, 80 were performed for congenital lesions or fibromuscular dysplasia (FMD), fibromuscular dysplasia and 454 were performed for atherosclerotic renovascular disease. Unilateral procedures were performed in 269 patients and bilateral procedures in 265, yielding a total of 720 renal artery reconstructions during this period.[14] On mean follow-up of 27 months, a failed renal artery repair was identified in 20 patients with recurrent hypertension (12 patients) or recurrent hypertension with worsening excretory renal function (8 patients).[14]

This subgroup included 9 women and 11 men, ranging in age from 12 to 77 years (mean, 54 years) treated for either FMD (6 patients), atherosclerosis (13 patients), or coarctation of the abdominal aorta.[14] Prior to primary renovascular reconstruction, each patient had hypertension (mean blood pressure, 198/111 mm Hg; mean number of

Table 130-10   Comparison of Major Series of Combined Aortorenal Reconstruction

STUDY (YEAR)*	CITY	MEAN PATIENT AGE (yr)	NO. PATIENTS	RENAL REPAIR (%)		HTN RESPONSE (%)†	PERIOPERATIVE MORTALITY (%)
				Unilateral	Bilateral		
Allen et al (1993)[41]	St. Louis	66.3	102	83	17	86	5
McNeil et al (1994)[42]	Mobile, AL	64	101	64	36	74	1
Huber et al (1995)[43]	Gainesville, FL	—	56	—	—	—	8.9
Brothers et al (1995)[44]	Charleston, SC	63	70	59	41	—	16
Cambria et al (1995)[45]	Boston	67.5	100	81.5	18.5	68	6.5
Darling et al (1995)[46]	Albany	69.3	73	—	—	27	2.7
Benjamin et al (1996)[22]	Winston-Salem, NC	62.5	133	47	53	63	5.3
Kulbaski et al (1998)[47]	Atlanta	63	43	56	44	50	4.7
Jean-Claude et al (1999)[48]	San Francisco	67.5	77	48	52	—	5.8
Hassen-Khodja et al (2000)[49]	Nice, France	66.7	39	69	31	44	2.6
Taylor et al (2000)[50]	Greenville	64	31	39	61	100	6
Tsoukas et al (2001)[51]	Cleveland	69	73	79	21	63	8.2
Ballard (2001)[52]	Loma Linda, CA	70	16	0	100	67	0
Checinski et al (2002)[53]	Poznan, Poland	59	53	—	—	87	9.4

*Superscript numbers indicate chapter references.
†Represents the total patients with hypertension (HTN) cured or improved.

medications, 3). Preoperative serum creatinine values ranged from 0.7 to 3.3 mg/dL (mean, 1.6 mg/dL). Seven patients were considered to have ischemic nephropathy, including 1 patient dependent on dialysis. Failed percutaneous balloon angioplasty preceded primary operative intervention in 4 patients (1 for fibromuscular dysplasia, 3 for atherosclerosis). Twenty-two of 24 failed primary reconstructions were treated with secondary operative intervention. Four patients had bilateral procedures (including repair to a solitary kidney), 15 patients had unilateral procedures, and 1 patient declined reoperation. Secondary operative intervention included 5 renal artery bypasses, 5 patch angioplasties, 2 hepatorenal bypasses, and 10 nephrectomies for unreconstructible disease.

Secondary management was influenced by the type of primary repair, the presence of postoperative stenosis or thrombosis, and whether clinical failure occurred early or late after primary operation.[14] All three early failures required nephrectomy. Of the remaining 21 repairs that failed between 2 and 36 months, 9 were associated with thrombosis and 12 were secondary to stenosis. Thrombosis was significantly more common than recurrent stenosis in the first postoperative year (89% vs. 33%; $P = .050$). Two early thromboses (2 and 4 months after surgery) were ex vivo reconstructions. Each failure led to renal infarction and recurrent hypertension requiring nephrectomy. Two ex vivo reconstructions failed after recurrent branch stenosis or degenerative change in a patch angioplasty. Each was

treated with "redo" ex vivo repair and patch angioplasty. The remaining 7 primary repairs (6 renal artery bypasses, 1 thromboendarterectomy) became thrombosed 4 to 30 months after repair (mean, 9.8 months). For these seven failures, five nephrectomies were performed to control hypertension. In each case, the kidney provided less than 5% renal function as shown by isotope renography. Two thrombosed repairs in a single patient were revised with thrombectomy and patch angioplasty; this patient had been removed from dialysis by the primary operation and was returned to dialysis after bilateral failure.

Blood pressure responses after primary and secondary operative interventions were equivalent. In contrast to blood pressure, renal function responses after primary and secondary repair differed significantly (Table 130-11). Renal function after primary repair was improved in 10 (59%) patients, including 1 patient removed from dialysis dependence, unchanged in 5 (29%) patients, and worsened in 2 (12%) patients. Eventual renal function response in all 20 patients after secondary operative intervention was classified as improved in 2 (10%) patients, unchanged in 10 (50%) patients, and worse in 8 (40%) patients, including 7 dialysis-dependent patients ($P = .015$). Of the subgroup of patients with atherosclerotic renovascular disease, renal function was improved in 1 patient and unchanged in 5; 7 patients were eventually dialysis dependent. Eventual renal function response was not associated with the extent of primary renal artery disease or repair, thrombosis or

Table 130-11 Comparison of Eventual Results of Reoperation (n = 20) with Results from Primary Intervention Only (n = 514)

	PRIMARY INTERVENTION ONLY	SECONDARY INTERVENTION		*P* VALUE
		Initial	**Eventual**	
Perioperative mortality (%)	3.6	0	0	.999
Hypertension response (%):				
Cured	19	24	15	.808
Improved	71	70	80	
No change	10	6	5	
Renal function response (%):				
Improved	34	59	10	.003
No change	53	29	50	
Worsened	13	12	40	
Eventual dialysis dependence (%)	4	0	35	< .001

From Hansen KJ, Deitch JA, Oskin TC: Renal artery repair: Consequence of operative failures. Ann Surg 227:678-689, 1998.

stenosis, or secondary renal artery repair or nephrectomy. However, eventual renal function response demonstrated a significant association with the presence of preoperative ischemic nephropathy ($P = .039$) and bilateral failure of primary repair ($P = .007$).

The product-limit estimates for dialysis-free survival for patients requiring secondary intervention and patients having only primary renovascular repair are shown in Figure 130-13. Patients requiring secondary intervention demonstrated a significant and independent higher risk of eventual dialysis dependence (relative risk [RR], 12.6; 95% CI, 4.5-34.9; $P \le .001$) and decreased dialysis-free survival (RR, 2.4; 95% CI, 1.1-5.4; $P = .035$). Whether failed balloon angioplasty with stenting demonstrates similar associations with eventual dialysis dependence is not known.

Our methods for evaluation and treatment of renovascular disease were described earlier. However, this experience with failed renal artery repairs reinforces two important issues. First, the irretrievable loss of excretory renal function observed after failed renal artery repair supports the view that renal revascularization should be performed for clear clinical indications but not as a "prophylactic" procedure in the absence of either hypertension or renal insufficiency.[1,3,22] Second, the direct aortorenal reconstructions utilized in these patients are durable. The short length and high blood flow characterizing aortorenal repair favor prolonged patency. Consequently, most failures of repair reflect errors in surgical technique or judgment.

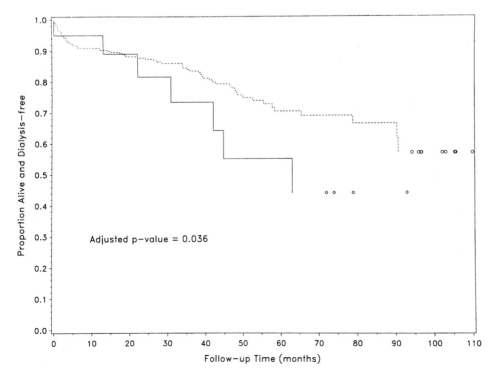

FIGURE 130-13 Product-limit estimates of dialysis-free survival for 20 patients requiring secondary renal artery operation (*solid line*) and 514 patients having primary renal artery repair only (*broken line*) with adjusted *P* value. Operative failure was associated with a significant and independent decrease in dialysis-free survival. (From Hansen KJ, Deitch JS, Oskin TC, et al: Renal artery repair: Consequences of operative failures. Ann Surg 227:678-689, 1998. Used by permission.)

Both the consequence of failed PTRA and its role after failed operative repair are uncertain. In this series of failed operative repairs, balloon angioplasty was utilized in 7 of 20 patients before either primary (4 patients, 6 arteries) or secondary (3 patients, 5 arteries) operative intervention. As a primary procedure for atherosclerotic lesions, balloon angioplasty is frequently associated with focal plaque dissection and disruption of the intima and media. As a consequence of the resulting periarterial fibrosis, subsequent operative procedures often resemble secondary procedures after failed operative repair.[58] In patients with failed operative repair, the technical challenges posed by secondary operative intervention may make percutaneous treatment particularly appealing.[56,59,60] In this group, balloon dilatation was applied to five renal arteries after failed primary operative repair. In each case, percutaneous angioplasty was considered a technical success but failed 1 to 8 months later. Given the paucity of data regarding balloon angioplasty after failed operative repair, secondary operative intervention should be considered the preferred, albeit challenging, method of remedial management.

■ SPECIAL ISSUES

Renovascular Disease in the Elderly

Adults in the fifth decade of life with severe hypertension of recent onset are frequently considered representative of the population with renovascular hypertension. In contrast, many reported experiences have confirmed that hypertension of renal origin is most commonly caused by renovascular occlusive disease at the extremes of age.[9,61,62] However, the value of diagnostic evaluation and intervention for atherosclerotic renovascular disease in the elderly beyond the seventh decade of life is debated. Some surgeons argue that renal artery disease in the elderly represents only one component of a widespread atherosclerotic process associated with advanced and irreversible renal and nonrenal atherosclerotic damage, which decreases the opportunity for improvement in blood pressure while raising the risk of surgical intervention.[62]

This pessimistic argument is amplified when one considers that contemporary patients in the seventh and eighth decades of life are characterized by hypertension of long duration, overt extrarenal atherosclerosis, and renal insufficiency.[63,64] Consequently, elderly patients with hypertension are often systematically excluded from diagnostic evaluation and surgical management of significant renovascular disease.[62] When one considers that the population with atherosclerosis evaluated for renal artery disease is an increasingly older group, the question of renal artery intervention in elderly patients has importance.[10] In this regard, 230 patients, 60 years of age and older, underwent operative renal artery repair at our center from January 1987 through June 1995.[39] There were 117 men and 113 women in their seventh (153 patients), eighth (70 patients), or ninth (7 patients) decades of life (range, 60-86 years; mean, 68 years). Significant hypertension was present in all patients, ranging from 280/190 mm Hg to 178/90 mm Hg (mean, 202/102 mm Hg). Fifty patients had a normal serum creatinine value (<1.2 mg/dL), 76 patients had mild renal insufficiency (1.3 to 1.9 mg/dL), and 104

patients had severe insufficiency (>2.0 mg/dL), including 23 patients who had been dialysis dependent for 10 to 31 days prior to operation.

All patients underwent direct aortorenal reconstruction.[39] Simultaneous aortic reconstruction was required in 95 patients. All hemodynamically significant disease was corrected surgically. Among 366 kidneys operated, only six nephrectomies were performed. Thirteen patients died in the hospital or within 30 days of surgery, yielding a perioperative mortality of 6%. Of these, 10 patients died after complex renovascular procedures combined with aortic reconstruction. Significant perioperative (30-day) morbidity that extended hospitalization occurred in 61 patients (27%). Overall, beneficial blood pressure response was observed in 86%, and renal function improved in 43%, including 18 of 23 patients removed from dialysis. During a mean follow-up of 29 months, there were 28 deaths. Twenty-five deaths during follow-up occurred from a presumed cardiovascular cause. Multivariate analysis demonstrated that preoperative renal insufficiency and a preoperative history of congestive heart failure were significant and independent predictors of death during follow-up among these elderly patients. Moreover, survival rate was significantly higher for patients whose renal function improved after operation than for those whose renal function did not improve ($P = .001$).

Many of the controversies surrounding decisions for evaluation and surgical management of atherosclerotic renovascular disease causing hypertension and renal insufficiency are illustrated by this group of elderly patients and the results of our management. As shown by this experience, elderly patients often have hypertension of long duration and extensive extrarenal atherosclerosis. These features have been reported by others to diminish beneficial blood pressure response to renal revascularization.[62,63] Similarly, nonrenal organ-specific damage as a result of diffuse atherosclerosis has been recognized to significantly raise the risk of cardiovascular morbidity and mortality associated with surgery. In addition, renovascular hypertension associated with diffuse vascular disease, as seen in these elderly patients, has been associated with decreased long-term survival in both patients who have had surgery and those who have not.[40,65,66] As a result of these reports indicating a reduced chance for cure of hypertension, a raised risk for operative morbidity and mortality, and a diminished long-term survival regardless of surgical intervention, many investigators have advised a conservative diagnostic and nonsurgical approach in patients with hypertension beyond the fifth or sixth decade of life.[10,62,63] Conversely, the investigators evaluate all patients with severe hypertension, regardless of chronologic age or associated atherosclerosis, if the patients would be otherwise considered candidates for correction of renal artery disease or a significant renal artery lesion is defined. Preoperative evaluation is designed to identify those parameters that contribute independently to increased postoperative mortality.

Renovascular Disease in the Diabetic Patient

The value of surgical correction of atherosclerotic renovascular disease in the diabetic patient is uncertain. On the basis of a decreased rate of beneficial blood pressure response, early reports cited diabetes mellitus as a relative contraindication to operative renal artery repair.[62,67] Moreover, the results of surgical intervention to retrieve excretory renal function in the diabetic patient with renal insufficiency are more unpredictable, because the relative contributions to renal insufficiency of ischemic nephropathy and renal parenchymal disease (e.g., diabetic nephropathy) are poorly defined.[29,68] The uncertainties regarding surgical intervention in this setting led us to review our experience with surgical management of atherosclerotic renal artery disease in 54 consecutive diabetic adults.[69] This patient group consisted of 37 women and 17 men ranging in age from 52 to 78 years (mean, 64 ± 6.0 years). Each patient was hypertensive (mean blood pressure, $213 \pm 29/103 \pm 21$ mm Hg; mean number of medications, 3), and each was diabetic. Sixteen patients had required insulin, and 38 patients had required oral agents, for control of hyperglycemia for 3 to 24 years (mean duration: 12.6), and 11 patients had been diabetic for more than 10 years. No patient had been diagnosed with diabetes mellitus prior to the fourth decade of life. Ischemic nephropathy was present in 45 patients (82%; mean serum creatinine, 2.4 mg/dL; 3 patients dialysis-dependent). On the basis of preoperative urinalysis from morning specimens, proteinuria was present in 36 patients (67%). Thirteen patients had trace to 30 mg/dL urinary protein, whereas 23 patients had >100 mg/dL. Seven patients had persistent proteinuria exceeding 300 mg/dL and in each case demonstrated nephrotic range proteinuria from a 24-hour urine collection.

Among the 50 patients surviving operation, 72% of patients had a beneficial blood pressure response.[69] Blood pressure response demonstrated no significant association with patient age, duration of hypertension or diabetes, or requirement for insulin. Renal function response was improved in 17 of the 42 (40%) patients with ischemic nephropathy who survived the operation, including 3 removed from dialysis. Blood pressure response showed no change in 18 (43%) patients and was worsened in 7 patients (17%). Unlike in patients without diabetes, change in EGFR demonstrated no significant relationship to the site of disease or extent of operation in these diabetic patients. Similarly, neither the presence nor severity of preoperative proteinuria nor the angiographic grade of nephrosclerosis was significantly associated with change in EGFR after operation.

The product-limit estimates demonstrated that preoperative EGFR was significantly and inversely associated with time to dialysis or death on follow-up ($P = .03$).[69] Although blood pressure response did not demonstrate a significant association with dialysis dependence or death during follow-up, renal function response to operation was important. Diabetic patients who demonstrated improved renal function after operation had a significantly lower risk of death or dialysis than patients whose renal function was unchanged or worsened ($P = .01$). When considered in context of all 500 atherosclerotic patients managed at our center, the diabetic patients have demonstrated a significant and independent increased risk of eventual dialysis dependence and death from all causes compared with nondiabetic patients (see Tables 130-5 and 130-8). At this time, the presence of diabetes mellitus must be considered an important confounding factor in the management of atherosclerotic renovascular disease.

Renovascular Disease in African-Americans

Hypertension in African-American patients differs in a quantitative sense from that observed in white patients. Hypertension in black persons occurs with greater frequency, with greater severity, and at a younger age than in white persons.[70] In addition, elevated blood pressure at any level is associated with greater cardiovascular morbidity and renal disease in black patients.[71] Many putative mechanisms have been suggested to account for this aggressive form of hypertension, which imply that hypertension in African-Americans is intrinsically different from that in white persons.[72] Although these mechanisms remain speculative, it has generally been accepted that correctable renovascular disease and renovascular hypertension occur infrequently in African-Americans.[73-75] Moreover, the greater end-organ damage at any level of hypertension along with the perceived low prevalence of renovascular hypertension has limited enthusiasm for the investigation and treatment of renovascular disease in African-Americans.

Comparison of 28 African-Americans with 370 white patients undergoing surgery for atherosclerotic renovascular disease at our center revealed no significant differences in severity or duration of hypertension between the two groups.[76] Overall, black patients had a greater prevalence of clinically detectable cardiovascular disease and demonstrated a significantly higher prevalence of left ventricular hypertrophy than white patients ($P = .02$). More extensive renovascular disease was noted among African-Americans; bilateral disease was present in 68% of black patients and 54% of white patients ($P = .16$). Moreover, African-Americans demonstrated higher serum creatinine levels (mean, 2.5 vs. 2.1 mg/dL, respectively; $P = .25$). Ischemic nephropathy was present in 57% of black patients and in 40% of white patients.

Despite the tendency to greater prevalence of cardiovascular disease, more extensive renal disease, and more severe renal dysfunction in black patients, the beneficial blood pressure response was similar for black and white patients (70% vs. 89% benefited).[76] Although the proportion of patients with improved renal function after surgery did not differ significantly (59% vs. 42% improved), African-Americans demonstrated a significantly greater decline in serum creatinine values (0.74-mg/dL vs. 0.14-mg/dL decrease; $P < .05$). Unlike in the white cohort, equivalent and significant improvement was observed in African-Americans regardless of the site of disease or extent of operation.

Data derived from 7200 African-American adults referred to a tertiary hypertension clinic demonstrated that renovascular hypertension was present in only 0.2%.[74] A low prevalence for renovascular hypertension among hypertensive black persons was also suggested by the Cooperative Study of Renovascular Hypertension.[74,77] Although African-Americans constituted 30% of the study sample, only 8% of the patients with renal artery stenosis were black. Foster and associates[73] described a lower prevalence of renal artery stenosis in black women than in white women. Moreover, no case of advanced renovascular disease was found in black men, compared with a 30% prevalence in white men.[73,74] Given the apparent rarity of renovascular disease and renovascular hypertension in

African-Americans, these researchers suggested that hypertensive African-Americans should not be subjected to extensive investigation for renal artery disease.

By contrast, a population-based study of the prevalence has demonstrated no association with ethnicity.[74,78] Although renal artery disease may occur with equal frequency in black and white persons, this is not to say that renovascular hypertension contributes equally to hypertension in the two groups. We reviewed the results from renal duplex scanning studies obtained to screen for renovascular disease among 629 consecutive subjects, 127 black (20%) and 502 white (80%). Twelve percent of black and 28% of white subjects had renovascular disease according to duplex scanning criteria ($P < .001$).[33,74] This highly significant difference between black and white people should be considered in context of the selection criteria for study. The primary clinical criteria prompting renal duplex scanning examination for the entire group was severe or poorly controlled hypertension. Because severe essential hypertension occurs more commonly in African-Americans, proportionately fewer black patients would be expected to demonstrate renovascular disease when screened according to these selection criteria.

On the basis of our findings, we believe that clinicians should search for a renovascular cause of severe hypertension without regard to race. Although proportionately fewer black patients demonstrate renovascular hypertension, the beneficial effects of operative renovascular repair are demonstrated by our surgical experience. Especially gratifying was the observed improvement in excretory renal function in the black cohort. Both unilateral and bilateral renal reconstructions were associated with significantly improved renal function, which in turn was significantly greater than the improvement observed among white patients.

■ REFERENCES

1. Cherr GS, Hansen KJ, Craven TE, et al: Surgical management of atherosclerotic renovascular disease. J Vasc Surg 35:236-245, 2002.
2. Hansen KJ, Cherr GS, Craven TE, et al: Management of ischemic nephropathy: Dialysis-free survival after surgical repair. J Vasc Surg 32:472-481, 2000.
3. Hansen KJ, Starr SM, Sands RE, et al: Contemporary surgical management of renovascular disease. J Vasc Surg 16:319-330, 1992.
4. Maxwell MH, Waks AU: Evaluation of patients with renovascular hypertension. Hypertension 6:589-592, 1984.
5. Cumberland DC: Percutaneous transluminal angioplasty: A review. Clin Radiol 34:25-38, 1983.
6. Vaughan ED, Case DB, Pickering TG, et al: Indication for intervention in patients with renovascular hypertension. Am J Kidney Dis 5:A136, 1985.
7. Libertino JA, Flam TA, Zinman LN, et al: Changing concepts in surgical management of renovascular hypertension. Arch Intern Med 148:357-359, 1988.
8. Novick AC, Ziegelbaum M, Vidt DG, et al: Trends in surgical revascularization for renal artery disease: Ten years' experience. JAMA 257:498-501, 1987.
9. Foster JH, Maxwell MH, Franklin SS, et al: Renovascular occlusive disease: Results of operative treatment. JAMA 231:1043-1048, 1975.
10. Hansen KJ, Ditesheim JA, Metropol SH, et al: Management of renovascular hypertension in the elderly population. J Vasc Surg 10:266-273, 1989.
11. Stanley JC, Fry WJ: Surgical treatment of renovascular hypertension. Arch Surg 112:1291-1297, 1977.
12. Ferrario CM (ed): Ischemic Nephropathy: Clinical Curiosity or Neglected Imperative? Council for High Blood Pressure Newsletter. American Heart Association, 1993.
13. Dean RH, Wilson JP, Burko H, Foster JH: Saphenous vein aortorenal bypass grafts: Serial arteriographic study. Ann Surg 180:469-478, 1974.
14. Hansen KJ, Deitch JS, Oskin TC, et al: Renal artery repair: Consequence of operative failures. Ann Surg 227:678-689, 1998.
15. Oskin TC, Hansen KJ, Deitch JS, et al: Chronic renal artery occlusion: Nephrectomy versus revascularization. J Vasc Surg 29:140-149, 1999.
16. Lawson JD, Boerth R, Foster JH, Dean RH: Diagnosis and management of renovascular hypertension in children. Arch Surg 112:1307-1316, 1977.
17. Wollenweber J, Sheps SG, Davis GD: Clinical course of atherosclerotic renovascular disease. Am J Cardiol 21:60-71, 1968.
18. Schreiber MJ, Pohl MA, Novick AC: The natural history of atherosclerotic and fibrous renal artery disease. Urol Clin North Am 11:383-392, 1984.
19. Dean RH, Kieffer RW, Smith BM, et al: Renovascular hypertension: Anatomic and renal function changes during drug therapy. Arch Surg 116:1408-1415, 1981.
20. Novick AC, Pohl MA, Schreiber M, et al: Revascularization for preservation of renal function in patients with atherosclerotic renovascular disease. J Urol 129:907-912, 1983.
21. Foster JH, Dean RH, Pinkerton JA, Rhamy RK: Ten years experience with the surgical management of renovascular hypertension. Ann Surg 177:755-766, 1973.
22. Benjamin ME, Hansen KJ, Craven TE, et al: Combined aortic and renal artery surgery: A contemporary experience. Ann Surg 223:555-565, 1996.
23. Morris GC, Debakey ME, Cooley DA: Surgical treatment of renal failure of renovascular origin. JAMA 182:609, 1962.
24. O'Neil EA, Hansen KJ, Canzanello VJ, et al: Prevalence of ischemic nephropathy in patients with renal insufficiency. Am Surg 58:485-490, 1992.
25. Dean RH, Tribble RW, Hansen KJ, et al: Evolution of renal insufficiency in ischemic nephropathy. Ann Surg 213:446-455, 1991.
26. Hansen KJ, Thomason RB, Craven TE, et al: Surgical management of dialysis-dependent ischemic nephropathy. J Vasc Surg 21:197-211, 1995.
27. Hansen KJ, Reavis SW, Dean RH: Duplex scanning in renovascular disease. Geriatr Nephrol Urol 6:89, 1996.
28. Jacobson HR: Ischemic renal disease: An overlooked clinical entity? Kidney Int 34:729-743, 1988.
29. Rimmer JM, Gennari FJ: Atherosclerotic renovascular disease and progressive renal failure. Ann Intern Med 118:712-719, 1993.
30. NC Kidney Council: Annual Report. Raleigh, NC, the Council, 1986.
31. Mailloux LU, Bellucci AG, Mossey RT, et al: Predictors of survival in patients undergoing dialysis. Am J Med 84:855-862, 1988.
32. Appel RG, Bleyer AJ, Reavis S, Hansen KJ: Renovascular disease in older patients beginning renal replacement therapy. Kidney Int 48:171-176, 1995.
33. Hansen KJ, Tribble RW, Reavis SW, et al: Renal duplex sonography: Evaluation of clinical utility. J Vasc Surg 12:227-236, 1990.
34. Towne JB, Bernhard VM: Revascularization of the ischemic kidney. Arch Surg 113:216-218, 1978.
35. Dean RH, Lawson JD, Hollifield JW, et al: Revascularization of the poorly functioning kidney. Surgery 85:44-52, 1979.
36. Zinman L, Libertino JA: Revascularization of the chronic totally occluded renal artery with restoration of renal function. J Urol 118:517-521, 1977.
37. Cohn EJ Jr, Benjamin ME, Sandager GP, et al: Can intrarenal duplex waveform analysis predict successful renal artery revascularization? J Vasc Surg 28:471-480, 1998.
38. Radermacher J, Chavan A, Bleck J, et al: Use of Doppler ultrasonography to predict the outcome of therapy for renal-artery stenosis. N Engl J Med 344:410-417, 2001.
39. Hansen KJ, Benjamin ME, Appel RG, et al: Renovascular hypertension in the elderly: Results of surgical management. Geriatr Nephrol Urol 6:3-11, 1996.

40. Dean RH, Krueger TC, Whiteneck JM, et al: Operative management of renovascular hypertension: Results after a follow-up of fifteen to twenty-three years. J Vasc Surg 1:234-242, 1984.

41. Allen BT, Rubin BG, Anderson CB, et al: Simultaneous surgical management of aortic and renovascular disease. Am J Surg 166:726-732, 1993.

42. McNeil JW, String ST, Pfeiffer RB Jr: Concomitant renal endarterectomy and aortic reconstruction. J Vasc Surg 20:331-336, 1994.

43. Huber TS, Harward TR, Flynn TC, et al: Operative mortality rates after elective infrarenal aortic reconstructions. J Vasc Surg 22:287-293, 1995.

44. Brothers TE, Elliott BM, Robison JG, Rajagopalan PR: Stratification of mortality risk for renal artery surgery. Am Surg 61:45-51, 1995.

45. Cambria RP, Brewster DC, L'Italien G, et al: Simultaneous aortic and renal artery reconstruction: Evolution of an eighteen-year experience. J Vasc Surg 21(6):916-924, 1995.

46. Darling RC III, Shah DM, Chang BB, Leather RP: Does concomitant aortic bypass and renal artery revascularization using the retroperitoneal approach increase perioperative risk? Cardiovasc Surg 3:421-423, 1995.

47. Kulbaski MJ, Kosinski AS, Smith RB III, et al: Concomitant aortic and renal artery reconstruction in patients on an intensive antihypertensive medical regimen: Long-term outcome. Ann Vasc Surg 12:270-277, 1998.

48. Jean-Claude JM, Reilly LM, Stoney RJ, Messina LM: Pararenal aortic aneurysms: The future of open aortic aneurysm repair. J Vasc Surg 29:902-912, 1999.

49. Hassen-Khodja R, Sala F, Declemy S, et al: Renal artery revascularization in combination with infrarenal aortic reconstruction. Ann Vasc Surg 14:577-582, 2000.

50. Taylor SM, Langan EM III, Snyder BA, et al: Concomitant renal revascularization with aortic surgery: Are the risks of combined procedures justified? Am Surg 66:768-772, 2000.

51. Tsoukas AI, Hertzer NR, Mascha EJ, et al: Simultaneous aortic replacement and renal artery revascularization: The influence of preoperative renal function on early risk and late outcome. J Vasc Surg 34:1041-1049, 2001.

52. Ballard JL: Renal artery endarterectomy for treatment of renovascular hypertension combined with infrarenal aortic reconstruction: Analysis of surgical results. Ann Vasc Surg 15:260-266, 2001.

53. Checinski P, Gabriel M, Dzieciuchowicz L, et al: Renovascular hypertension—simultaneous aortic and renal artery reconstruction. Langenbecks Arch Surg 387:161-165, 2002.

54. Erturk E, Novick AC, Vidt DG, Cunningham R: Secondary renal revascularization for recurrent renal artery stenosis. Cleve Clin J Med 56:427-431, 1989.

55. Fowl RJ, Hollier LH, Bernatz PE, et al: Repeat revascularization versus nephrectomy in the treatment of recurrent renovascular hypertension. Surg Gynecol Obstet 162:37-42, 1986.

56. Novick AC: Percutaneous transluminal angioplasty and surgery of the renal artery. Eur J Vasc Surg 8:1-9, 1994.

57. Stanley JC, Whitehouse WM Jr, Zelenock GB, et al: Reoperation for complications of renal artery reconstructive surgery undertaken for treatment of renovascular hypertension. J Vasc Surg 2:133-144, 1985.

58. Dean RH, Callis JT, Smith BM, Meacham PW: Failed percutaneous transluminal renal angioplasty: Experience with lesions requiring operative intervention. J Vasc Surg 6:301-307, 1987.

59. Erdoes LS, Berman SS, Hunter GC, Mills JL: Comparative analysis of percutaneous transluminal angioplasty and operation for renal revascularization. Am J Kidney Dis 27:496-503, 1996.

60. Libertino JA, Beckmann CF: Surgery and percutaneous angioplasty in the management of renovascular hypertension. Urol Clin North Am 21:235-243, 1994.

61. Hunt JC, Strong CG: Renovascular hypertension: Mechanisms, natural history and treatment. Am J Cardiol 32:562-574, 1973.

62. Shapiro AP, Perez-Stable E, Scheib ET, et al: Renal artery stenosis and hypertension: Observations on current status of therapy from a study of 115 patients. Am J Med 47:175-193, 1969.

63. Ernst CB, Stanley JC, Marshall FF, Fry WJ: Renal revascularization for arteriosclerotic renovascular hypertension: Prognostic implications of focal renal arterial vs. overt generalized arteriosclerosis. Surgery 73:859-867, 1973.

64. Lawrie GM, Morris GC Jr, Soussou ID, et al: Late results of reconstructive surgery for renovascular disease. Ann Surg 191:528-533, 1980.

65. van Bockel JH, van Schilfgaarde R, Felthuis W, et al: Surgical treatment of renovascular hypertension caused by arteriosclerosis. II: Influence of preoperative risk factors and postoperative blood pressure response on late patient survival. Surgery 101:468-477, 1987.

66. Delin K, Aurell M, Granerus G, et al: Surgical treatment of renovascular hypertension in the elderly patient. Acta Med Scand 211:169-174, 1982.

67. Shapiro AP, Perez-Stable E, Moutsos SE: Coexistence of renal arterial hypertension and diabetes mellitus. JAMA 192:813-816, 1965.

68. Connolly JO, Higgins RM, Walters HL, et al: Presentation, clinical features and outcome in different patterns of atherosclerotic renovascular disease. QJM 87:413-421, 1994.

69. Hansen KJ, Lundberg AH, Benjamin ME, et al: Is renal revascularization in diabetic patients worthwhile? J Vasc Surg 24:383-392, 1996.

70. Calhoun DA, Oparil S: Racial differences in the pathogenesis of hypertension. Am J Med Sci 310(Suppl 1):S86-S90, 1995.

71. Flack JM, Neaton JD, Daniels B, Esunge P: Ethnicity and renal disease: Lessons from the Multiple Risk Factor Intervention Trial and the Treatment of Mild Hypertension Study. Am J Kidney Dis 21(Suppl 1):31-40, 1993.

72. Jamerson KA: Prevalence of complications and response to different treatments of hypertension in African Americans and white Americans in the U.S. Clin Exp Hypertens 15:979-995, 1993.

73. Foster JH, Oates JA, Rhamy RK, et al: Detection and treatment of patients with renovascular hypertension. Surgery 60:240, 1966.

74. Detection, evaluation, and treatment of renovascular hypertension: Final report. Working Group on Renovascular Hypertension. Arch Intern Med 147:820-829, 1987.

75. Albers FJ: Clinical characteristics of atherosclerotic renovascular disease. Am J Kidney Dis 24:636-641, 1994.

76. Deitch JS, Hansen KJ, Craven TE, et al: Renal artery repair in African-Americans. J Vasc Surg 26:465-472, 1997.

77. Simon N, Franklin SS, Bleifer KH, Maxwell MH: Clinical characteristics of renovascular hypertension. JAMA 220:1209-1218, 1972.

78. Hansen KJ, Edwards MS, Craven TE, et al: Prevalence of renovascular disease in the elderly: A population-based study. J Vasc Surg 36:443-451, 2002.

Endovascular Treatment of Renovascular Disease

MICHAEL J. COSTANZA, MD
RICHARD J. STRILKA, MD, PhD
MATTHEW S. EDWARDS, MD
MARSHALL E. BENJAMIN, MD

The treatment of renovascular disease is currently in a state of evolution. Surgical revascularization through the use of bypass or endarterectomy represents the "gold standard" and has demonstrated excellent long-term durability and clinical results in terms of hypertension management and improvement of renal function.[1-3] However, the morbidity and mortality associated with surgical revascularization are significant, even when the operations are performed in centers with extensive experience.[1-4] Not surprisingly, endovascular techniques for renal revascularization, including percutaneous transluminal angioplasty with or without endoluminal stenting (PTAS), have emerged as another option for the treatment of occlusive renovascular disease.[5-10] These techniques provide the potential benefits of decreased morbidity, mortality, recovery times, and hospital resource utilization with the major potential drawback of decreased durability.[11-38] Controversy persists, however, regarding the appropriate application of surgical and endovascular therapy in the treatment of renovascular disease, with proponents of each modality citing selected literature to support their position. This chapter provides an overview of the technical aspects of the performance of endovascular renal revascularization as well as current data concerning the technical results, clinical outcomes, and associated complications.

■ CONTRAST ANGIOGRAPHY OF THE RENAL ARTERIES

Despite advances in diagnostic imaging and functional testing that allow for the noninvasive identification of patients with renovascular disease (Fig. 131-1),[39-46] the formulation of a surgical or endovascular therapeutic plan continues to depend on visualization of the renal artery anatomy with angiographic techniques. Therefore, contrast arteriography of the renal arteries should be considered an integral component of the therapeutic armamentarium for clinically significant renal artery lesions. Contrast arteriography of the renal arteries is discussed in detail in Chapter 128. However, certain points bear repeating here as they have particular application in the performance of endovascular revascularization of the renal arteries.

■ CONSIDERATIONS FOR USE OF CONTRAST AGENTS

Patients with known renovascular disease typically have a high prevalence of associated medical co-morbidities, including diabetes mellitus, congestive heart failure, chronic renal insufficiency, and diuretic-induced intravascular volume depletion. These conditions may require alterations in the usual routines for patient preparation and use of iodinated contrast agents. It has been clearly demonstrated that use of iodinated contrast agents can lead to impairment of excretory renal function.[47] The resulting impairment may be permanent, and the risk of this complication is highest in individuals with preexisting dehydration,[48] renal

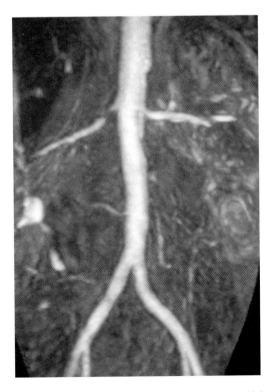

FIGURE 131-1 Magnetic resonance image demonstrating high-grade bilateral renal artery stenosis, worse on the right than the left.

Table 131-1	Treatment Protocol for Patients with Renal Dysfunction

Preprocedure hydration
N-Acetylcysteine, 600 mg PO bid, given either the day before or the day of the procedure
Use of minimal amount of contrast agent
Use of diluted contrast agent
Combining contrast study with gadopentetate dimeglumine or CO_2
Postprocedure hydration
Evaluation of renal function after procedure

insufficiency,[49-54] and diabetes mellitus.[55-57] Previous investigations have demonstrated that higher volumes of iodinated contrast agent[58-60] and higher contrast agent osmolarity[49,61] may also raise the risk of postprocedure impairment of renal function. Reports have also shown a lower risk of renal functional impairment after angiography with the periprocedural use of acetylcysteine.[62-64]

It is our policy to prepare all patients for aortorenal arteriography with saline hydration (limited in patients with significant heart failure) and periprocedural administration of acetylcysteine (Table 131-1). Furthermore, the use of low-osmolarity iodinated contrast agents should be considered routine in such patients, and special attention should be paid to limiting the volumes infused. In patients with moderate to severe preexisting renal insufficiency, carbon dioxide[65-69] and gadopentetate dimeglumine[70-74] can also be used as intra-arterial contrast agents to limit or completely eliminate the use of iodinated contrast agents (Fig. 131-2). It is our practice to use carbon dioxide or gadopentetate dimeglumine to initially localize and selectively cannulate the renal artery in patients with moderate to severe renal insufficiency, and then to use iodinated contrast agents in small volumes to definitively plan and perform the required intervention.

■ ANGIOGRAPHIC TECHNICAL CONSIDERATIONS

Femoral arterial access, when possible, is the most versatile and lowest-risk option. Either femoral artery provides adequate access for nonselective renal arteriography. Selective renal cannulation however, may be facilitated by accessing the femoral artery contralateral to the renal artery to be addressed. This technique takes advantage of the fact that the catheter will preferentially track to the contralateral aortic wall, facilitating catheter tip cannulation of the renal ostia (Fig. 131-3). Brachial artery access is a useful alternative in patients with downsloping renal

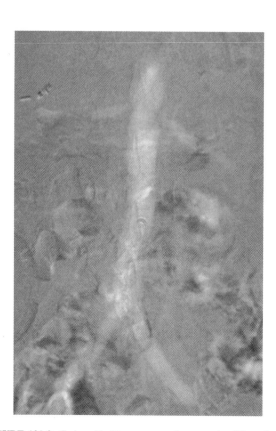

FIGURE 131-2 Carbon dioxide aortogram demonstrating bilateral renal artery stenosis in a patient with severe renal dysfunction.

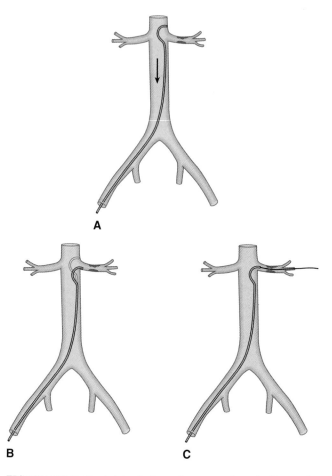

FIGURE 131-3 Contralateral femoral access often facilitates the selective renal cannulation as illustrated. (From Schneider PA: More about how to get where you are going: Selective catheterization. In Campbell B [ed]: Endovascular Skills: Guidewires, Catheters, Arteriography, Balloon Angioplasty, Stents. St. Louis, Quality Medical Publishing, 1998, p 71.)

arteries or in whom femoral access is not advisable. The left brachial artery is preferred, to avoid crossing the origin of the right common carotid artery. Access may be established with percutaneous or open techniques. Percutaneous brachial access is associated with a higher risk of complications[75] and smaller permissible sheath and catheter sizes. We perform an open exposure of the brachial artery for such access, carrying out puncture, cannulation, and closure under direct vision.

Aortography and selective renal arteriography, using multiple projections, are necessary to fully examine the renal arteries and juxtarenal aorta. In addition, the interlobar and intralobar arteries within the renal parenchyma, as well as the nephrogram and overall size of the kidney, should be closely examined. Initial anteroposterior (AP) images of the visceral aorta are obtained with power contrast injections through a multiple–side-hole flush catheter (Fig. 131-4) positioned just beneath the diaphragm at the level of the first lumbar vertebra. These initial AP views provide an overview of the renal artery and perivisceral aortic anatomy. All further nonselective images of the renal arteries should be obtained by repositioning of the catheter to a location below the origin of the superior mesenteric artery to prevent contrast agent opacification of the visceral vessels, which might obscure anatomic details of the renal arteries (Fig. 131-5). The ostia of the renal arteries are usually on the posterolateral aspect of the aorta. Therefore, lesions within the renal ostia frequently are not seen or appear insignificant in an AP aortogram, due to overlap of the contrast-filled aorta. Oblique aortography, or oblique selective renal arteriography, projects these portions of the vessel in profile and often better identifies any lesions (Fig. 131-6). The most useful projections to visualize the renal ostia are usually moderate ipsilateral anterior oblique views (10 to 20 degrees).[76-78] Steeper oblique views may be necessary in certain patients. Previously obtained axial images of the renal origins (i.e., computed tomography [CT] images) may allow for better estimation of the necessary obliquity and thus may allow use of smaller amounts of iodinated contrast agent and ionizing radiation.

Lesions within the body of the renal artery may require selective arteriographic views for full delineation. Selective cannulation is usually performed with an angled catheter such as a Cobra, SOS, or renal double-curve catheter, in combination with a steerable guidewire. There are several catheters of varying configurations offering advantages to particular anatomic situations (Fig. 131-7). The Bernstein and JB1 catheters, for example, may be useful in selecting renal arteries that are angled cephalad as they leave the aorta. The more typical downsloping arteries may be better accessed with the Sos or Simmons catheter. Prior to selective renal artery cannulation, it is our practice to administer intravenous heparin.

Once the guidewire and catheter are gently advanced into the renal artery ostia, a hand injection of contrast agent should be performed to ensure an intraluminal position. Selective images (Fig. 131-8) can then be obtained using low-volume power or hand-injected images (we favor the latter). The proximal third of the left renal artery usually courses anteriorly, the middle third transversely, and the distal third posteriorly, whereas the right renal artery pursues a more consistent posterior course. Oblique and cranial-caudad rotated images may be necessary to fully delineate lesions in the various segments. For example, the delicate septal lesions of fibromuscular dysplasia (FMD) may be unrecognizable or may appear insignificant in the AP projection, whereas an oblique projection demonstrates their true severity (Fig. 131-9).

■ ADJUNCTIVE MEASURES

The performance of arteriographic imaging of the renal arteries also provides the opportunity to employ other measures to assess the hemodynamics and anatomy of

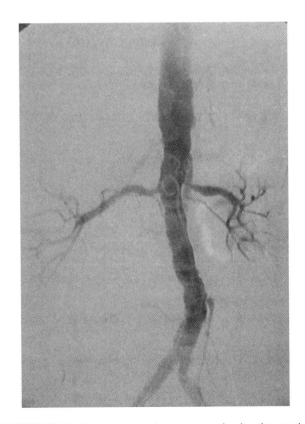

FIGURE 131-5 Flush anteroposterior aortogram showing the superior mesenteric artery overshadowing an ostial left renal artery stenosis.

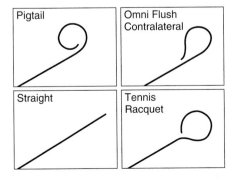

FIGURE 131-4 Drawing of four commonly used diagnostic flush catheters.

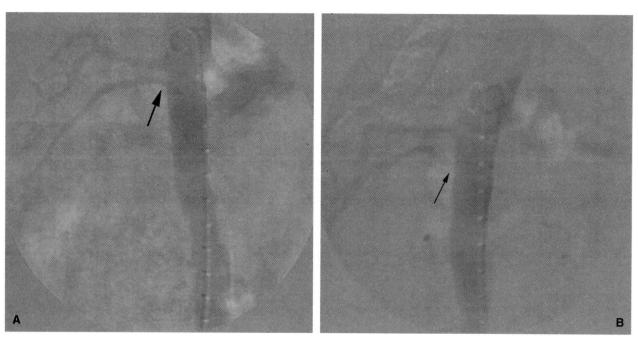

FIGURE 131-6   A, Normal-appearing renal arteries in the anteroposterior (AP) view. **B,** In the oblique projection, a significant stenosis is now evident in the right (inferior) accessory renal artery.

a renal artery lesion. The hemodynamic effects of an angiographically detected stenosis or treatment can be assessed by means of direct pressure measurements proximal and distal to the lesion.[79] Additional anatomic information can be obtained through the use of intravascular ultrasonography. The use and performance of intravascular ultrasonography is discussed in detail in Chapter 128. Intravascular ultrasonography of the renal artery can provide detailed information regarding plaque morphology, vessel size, and potential dissection flaps to complement data gained through arteriography.[80-82]

■ ARTERIOGRAPHIC FINDINGS

As mentioned earlier, the current role for contrast arteriography in the treatment of renovascular disease lies mainly within the realm of therapy rather than diagnosis. Angiography is most commonly performed to assess a renal artery lesion previously defined by renal duplex ultrasonography, CT angiography (CTA), or magnetic resonance angiography (MRA) prior to, or as part of, a therapeutic intervention. Most clinically significant renal artery lesions are caused by atherosclerotic disease or FMD, with a small minority being secondary to other forms of renal artery pathology. Each pathologic entity has specific imaging characteristics and treatment considerations.

FIGURE 131-7 Various selective catheters commonly used to cannulate a renal artery.

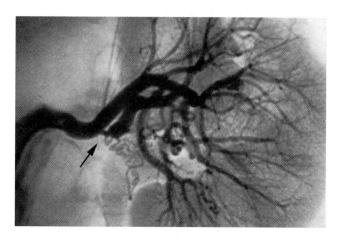

FIGURE 131-8 Selective renal arteriogram showing branch stenosis and nearby collateral vessel formation.

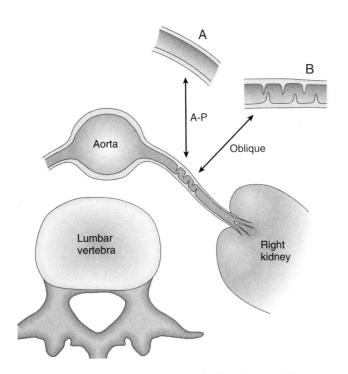

FIGURE 131-9 Schematic diagrams showing how the septa of fibromuscular dysplasia may be (**A**) missed in the anteroposterior (A-P) projection, but (**B**) apparent in an oblique plane. (From Dean RH, Benjamin ME, Hansen KJ: Surgical management of renovascular hypertension. Curr Probl Surg 34:209-308, 1997.)

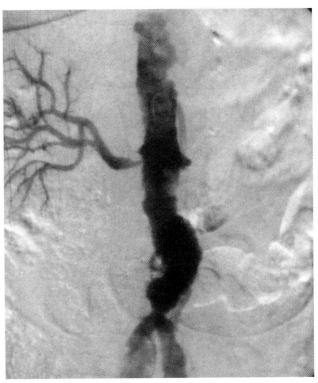

FIGURE 131-10 This anteroposterior flush aortogram demonstrates severe combined renal and aortic occlusive disease. One can appreciate the "spillover" of aortic plaque into the renal origins. Note that the left renal artery is occluded.

■ ATHEROSCLEROTIC RENOVASCULAR DISEASE

Among all renovascular lesions, atherosclerosis of the renal artery is the most common etiology, being the causative lesion in roughly two thirds of cases.[83] Affected patients are most frequently elderly with additional medical co-morbidities and other manifestations of atherosclerosis.[84-87] Atherosclerotic renal lesions generally represent a continuation of a process that begins in the aorta, and "spills over" into the origin of the renal vessels (Fig. 131-10). These lesions are characterized by an eccentric, irregular narrowing of the ostium and proximal portion of the renal artery. Lesions are limited to the ostia and proximal renal artery in more than 80% of cases, and the two sides are affected equally.[88,89] The aortic lesion origin has important implications for the treatment of atherosclerotic renovascular disease. Placement of an endovascular stent into the proximal renal artery, without the aortic origin of the plaque taken into consideration, may result in residual or recurrent disease. Occlusions of the renal artery are also common in patients with clinically significant lesions and frequently occur in the setting of contralateral renal artery stenosis.[90,91]

■ FIBROMUSCULAR DYSPLASIA

Fibromuscular dysplasia is discussed in detail in Chapter 129. The term is used to describe a group of histologically distinct forms of renal artery wall disease most commonly affecting the main renal artery and its branches. FMD of the renal artery, with resultant renal artery stenosis, is the culprit lesion in approximately 25% to 30% of treated cases of renovascular hypertension.[92] The lesions are usually described according to the layer of the artery wall most predominantly involved. Described categories are medial fibroplasia, perimedial dysplasia, and intimal fibroplasia. Medial fibroplasia is the most common variant, representing 85% of recognized cases. Medial fibroplasia is encountered almost exclusively in women, most commonly in the third or fourth decade of life. The arteriographic pattern associated with medial fibroplasia most frequently appears as a "string of beads" (Fig. 131-11) due to weblike stenotic areas with intervening areas of post-stenotic dilatation or microaneurysms. These lesions are frequently unilateral and they can also produce aneurysms or dissections of the renal arteries.[93-95] Stenotic medial fibroplastic lesions of the main renal artery are among the most favorable for treatment by endovascular means. In our view, however, the presence of branch vessel disease or aneurysms precludes endovascular treatment.

Perimedial dysplasia accounts for approximately 15% of cases of FMD, with the most common appearance being one of multiple irregular stenoses without microaneurysms.[96] Intimal fibroplasia is the least common entity, representing less than 5% of recognized cases of FMD. The lesions of intimal fibroplasia are typically smooth concentric stenoses.[96]

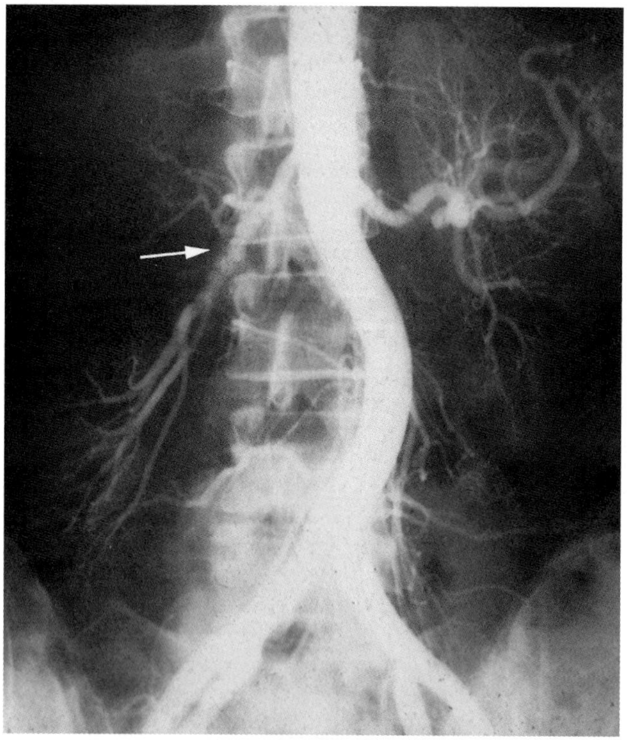

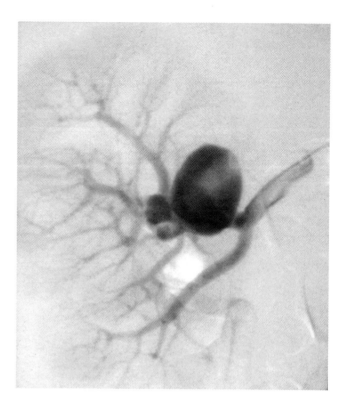

FIGURE 131-11 The typical angiographic "string-of-beads" appearance of fibromuscular dysplasia of the renal artery.

FIGURE 131-12 Selective renal arteriogram demonstrating a large renal artery aneurysm.

These latter two categories of FMD tend to have less favorable responses to endovascular treatment.

■ OTHER PATHOLOGIC LESIONS OF THE RENAL ARTERY

Other causes of renovascular hypertension and ischemic nephropathy exist, but they are rare. They include renal artery aneurysms, traumatic lesions, dissections, arteriovenous malformations, and congenital lesions.

Renal artery aneurysms are discussed in detail in Chapter 133. They can occur in patients of all ages and may contribute to renovascular hypertension.[97,98] As an aneurysm enlarges, it may impede flow in adjacent normal renal branches and thus may activate the renin-angiotensin system, or the aneurysm may be associated with the presence of an occult renal artery stenosis. Aneurysms may involve the main renal artery but are more commonly located at the branch points of the renal vessels (Fig. 131-12). Selective arteriographic views, often with multiple oblique and cranial-caudal projections, are required to fully characterize these lesions. Although case reports of endovascular treatment of renal artery aneurysms using covered stents or coil embolization have been reported,[99,100] the preferred method of repair for these lesions remains surgical.

Renal artery trauma is discussed in detail in Chapter 134. Renovascular injuries may be secondary to penetrating or blunt trauma, blunt injuries being more common. The patient may present with hematuria or complaints of abdominal or back pain secondary to renal infarct. Most commonly, the diagnosis is made when a CT scan performed with

intravascular contrast agent reveals "nonenhancement" of the involved kidney (Fig. 131-13A) Pathologically, the renal artery injury typically represents a dissection or myointimal flap that may narrow the renal vessel or cause acute occlusion (Fig. 131-13B). In general, the role of arteriography in the evaluation of renal trauma is diagnostic. However, in selected cases, endovascular stenting may be employed to stabilize a traumatic dissection or flap in an unstable patient. Renal artery trauma may also lead to acute or delayed presentation of arteriovenous fistulae secondary to injuries to both the renal artery and vein. These lesions can occur as a result of blunt, penetrating, or iatrogenic renal artery injuries. Renal arteriovenous fistulae may result in hematuria, high-output cardiac failure, or renovascular hypertension.[101] Endovascular treatment of these lesions is described in Chapter 133.[102]

Spontaneous dissections of the renal artery may also occur, and they are discussed in detail in Chapter 134. They may be limited to the renal artery or they may be an extension of an aortic dissection. Isolated renal artery dissections are rare but are most commonly associated with FMD, blunt trauma, or iatrogenic catheter injuries.[103] Angiographically, dissection usually appears as a myointimal flap with a narrow true lumen and a dilated irregular false lumen.[104,105] Endovascular treatment of spontaneous renal artery dissections has also been described.

Lesions of the renal artery may also be congenital. Childhood renal artery lesions are frequently classified as FMD. In reality, though, the majority of these lesions are congenital or developmental in origin, representing a developmental failure of all layers of the arterial wall

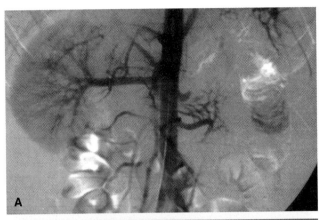

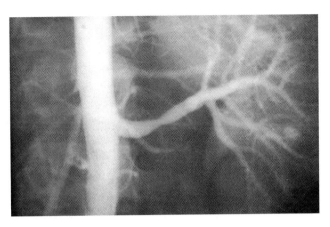

FIGURE 131-14 Flush aortogram demonstrating a congenital left renal artery stenosis; the patient's right kidney had been surgically removed during childhood.

FIGURE 131-13 A, Flush aortogram showing an acute occlusion of the left renal artery secondary to blunt trauma. B, Intraoperative photograph in the same patient showing the intimal disruption that was causing the acute occlusion.

(Fig. 131-14).[106] These hypoplastic lesions respond poorly to endovascular techniques and should be managed with open surgical repair when treatment is indicated.

Clinically significant renovascular disease may also be associated with other rare conditions, including Takayasu's disease,[107] arteriovenous malformations,[108,109] irradiation,[110] polyarteritis nodosa,[111] and congenital fibrous bands.[112]

■ ENDOVASCULAR TREATMENT OF RENOVASCULAR DISEASE

Patient Management and Preparation

Patient preparation is similar to that routinely practiced for diagnostic arteriography. Patients are instructed to take no solid food by mouth after midnight the evening before endovascular therapy is planned. If patients are taking

warfarin, they are told not to take it for at least 4 days prior to the procedure. Aspirin or clopidogrel (plavix) is continued. Intravenous fluids and acetylcysteine are administered the evening before the procedure, with care taken to avoid fluid overload in patients with impaired cardiac function (see Table 131-1). Patients take their routine medications, with the exception of angiotensin-converting enzyme inhibitors and angiotensin receptor antagonists, on the morning of the procedure with a sip of water. In patients in whom stent placement is considered a possibility, first-generation cephalosporin antibiotics are administered intravenously 30 minutes prior to the procedure. After the intervention, patients are observed in the hospital overnight for access site problems and severe alterations in blood pressure. Acetylcysteine is continued throughout the hospital stay, and oral administration of clopidogrel is instituted the evening after the procedure. Patients continue to take clopidogrel for at least 30 days and aspirin indefinitely.

Therapeutic Intervention

Once the diagnostic portion of the procedure is completed, the images obtained are closely examined and correlated with the patient's clinical presentation. Intra-arterial pressure measurements can occasionally be misleading in the renal location. Because most renal arteries are approximately 5 to 6 mm in diameter, a lesion that causes a stenosis that reduces the vessel diameter by more than 60% leaves only 2.0 to 2.5 mm of residual lumen. A 4F or 5F diagnostic catheter may completely occlude the residual lumen, thus resulting in a pressure measurement distal to the stenosis that is falsely low in this "end artery." This problem may be alleviated with the use of newly developed pressure wires, but their expense may prohibit their routine use. It is our practice to combine the anatomic arteriographic information with the functional significance of the lesion as determined by either renal vein renin assays or duplex scanning.

Table 131-2 summarizes some of the materials commonly used for endovascular renal artery angioplasty and stenting. Once the decision for endovascular intervention is made, the patient is systemically heparinized and the 5F diagnostic catheter and introducer sheath are exchanged over a

Table 131-2   Typical Supplies for Renal Artery Intervention

Guidewires	Starting guidewire	Bentson	145-cm length; 0.35-in. diameter
	Selective guidewire	Magic Torque	180-cm length; 0.35-in. (marker tip)
		Thruway	190-cm length; 0.18-in. diameter (radiopaque shapeable tip)
		Glidewire	180-cm length; 0.35-in. diameter (angled tip)
	Exchange guidewire	Rosen	180-cm length; 0.35-in. diameter (J tip)
Catheter	Flush catheter	Omni-flush	65-cm length; 5 Fr
	Selective catheter	Cobra C1, C2	65-, 80-cm length; 5 Fr
		Contra 2	65-cm length; 5 Fr
		SOS Omni 2	80-cm length; 5 Fr
Sheath	Selective guide	Pinnacle-Destination	45-cm length; 6 Fr
		Flexor check-flow ANL2 introducer	45-cm length; 6 Fr
Balloon	Balloon angioplasty	Balloon	Balloon: 1.5-, 2-cm length; 4-, 5-, 6-, 7-mm diameter; 4, 5 Fr Catheter shaft: 75-cm length
Stent*	Balloon- expandable stent (premounted)	Genesis	Stent: 5-, 6-, 7-mm diameter; 12- to 29-mm length Shaft: 80-cm length
		NiRRoyal	Stent: 4-, 5-, 6-, 7-mm diameter; 14-,19-mm length Shaft: 90-cm length
		Express-Biliary LD	Stent: 5-, 6-, 7-, 8-mm diameter; 17-mm length Shaft: 75-, 135-cm length

*No stents listed have been approved by the U.S. Food and Drug Administration for routine use in renal arteries.

0.035-inch guidewire, for an access platform that that will provide secure renal artery access for the therapeutic intervention. Direct pressure is used for hemostasis and wire control during this sheath exchange. Most contemporary angioplasty and stenting devices pass through a 6F lumen. Access options include the use of guide sheaths and guide catheters.

Common to both of these options is the provision of a long segment of mechanical support for guidewire placement and maintenance within the renal artery for easy, maneuverable, low-friction passage of therapeutic devices within the protective sheath to the renal artery. These systems vary in shape and diameter with multiple configurations to facilitate renal artery access (Fig. 131-15). We prefer the Pinnacle Destination Renal Guiding Sheath (Terumo Medical Corp, Elkton, MD/Boston Scientific, Natick, MA). This 6F sheath is extremely soft, kink resistant, and flexible, and it comes in straight and "hockey-stick" configurations.

Through this sheath, a curved "selective" catheter designed to facilitate renal artery access is passed. This is usually a Simmons or Sos catheter. Sometimes a Contra 2 flush catheter, which we commonly use in the performance of the diagnostic portion of the procedure, can be used to select the renal artery, eliminating a catheter exchange (Fig. 131-16). After the tip of the guiding catheter is positioned at or within the ostium of the renal artery, guidewire access to the lesion is obtained, frequently employing the "road-mapping" features of contemporary digital imaging software packages (Fig. 131-17).

It is important during all subsequent manipulations to refrain from advancing the sheath beyond the orifice of the renal artery as its nontapered tip may injure the renal artery. Depending upon the lesion type, severity, and location, a 0.35-, 0.18-, or 0.14-inch guidewire with a floppy, radiopaque tip is chosen. There are intuitive advantages to the use of the smaller guidewire systems, in terms of crossing tighter stenoses, limiting renal artery

trauma, and liberation of emboli, but these remain to be proved. We prefer to use a 0.18-inch system when therapeutic intervention is necessary. Our preferred guidewire is the Thruway guidewire (Boston Scientific, Natick, MA). This 0.18-inch guidewire has a short taper and a very floppy, radiopaque, 5-cm-long tip. The guidewire also has a silicon coating to ease catheter exchanges. Generally, a guidewire approximately 180 cm in length is adequate for renal interventions. The working shaft of the guidewire is usually stiff enough to allow for the selective catheter to be removed and the introducer sheath to be advanced to the renal artery orifice without loss of guidewire access. The guidewire is gently advanced across the lesion into the distal renal artery. Once it is in place, the guidewire and access platform are secured and remain there until the intervention and any post-intervention imaging are complete.

With the guidewire secured distal to the lesion, therapeutic intervention may proceed. A large array of options currently exists in terms of available angioplasty and stenting products. Coaxial systems (entire catheter over the wire, requiring an assistant to control the wire during intervention, or catheter exchange) and monorail or rapid-exchange (only distal portion of catheter over the wire, allowing for single-operator control of the wire during intervention and catheter exchange) are available for renal artery intervention. Regardless of the system chosen, the principles of intervention remain the same.

Transluminal angioplasty of the renal artery may be the sole therapy for a renal artery lesion or as a means to predilate a lesion to allow for the passage of an endoluminal stent. Angioplasty may also be employed for the treatment of recurrent renal stenoses after surgical or endovascular therapy. Angioplasty is effective stand-alone therapy in most cases of main renal artery disease (FMD and nonostial atherosclerosis) but is frequently ineffective for atherosclerotic ostial and proximal renal artery disease. Angioplasty balloon size is chosen according to quantitative angiographic

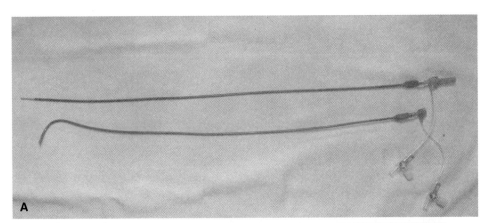

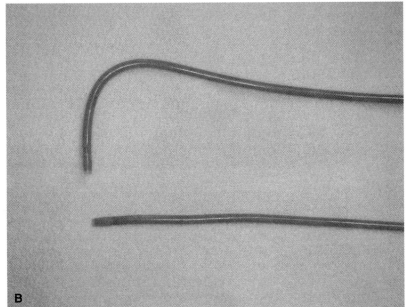

FIGURE 131-15 A and B, Straight and angled 6F introducer sheaths.

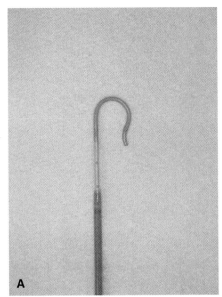

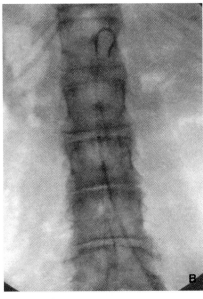

FIGURE 131-16 A, Contra 2 flush catheter within a 6F introducer sheath, on back table for illustration. B, Contra 2 flush catheter within introducer sheath now placed within the aorta from a left femoral approach.

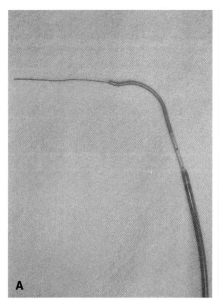

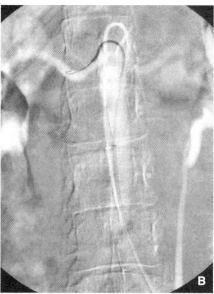

FIGURE 131-17 A, Contra 2 flush catheter over an 0.18-inch guidewire placed through the introducer sheath, on back table for illustration. **B,** With use of road-mapping techniques, the Contra 2 catheter is used to select the right renal artery, and the 0.18-inch guidewire is advanced into the right renal artery.

images. Direct cut-film images with ball-bearing or marker catheter references can be used as well as quantitative software packages that are available on most contemporary digital angiographic systems. In general, the angioplasty balloon should be slightly larger than the adjacent normal artery for primary treatment and somewhat smaller for use in lesion predilatation. For predilating lesions prior to endoluminal stent placement, it is our general practice to employ a 4 × 20–mm low-profile angioplasty balloon to facilitate stent passage (Fig. 131-18). This generally allows for a less traumatic passage of the stent and also helps to estimate the stent diameter and length.

During inflation of the angioplasty balloon, the aortic origin of most ostial plaques can be localized from a "waist," and the image can be centered over a bony landmark to facilitate subsequent stent placement. It is not unusual for the patient to experience some discomfort during balloon inflation. However, this should quickly resolve when the balloon is deflated. Should it persist, renal artery trauma (either dissection or rupture) should be suspected. It is our practice to slowly inflate the balloon to its fully inflated profile at the rated nominal pressure and hold the inflation for 30 to 45 seconds prior to deflation. After complete deflation of the balloon, confirmed by intermittent fluoroscopic imaging, the balloon is removed, and selective angiography is repeated to assess lesion response and survey for complications. It is imperative that guidewire access be maintained until the end of the procedure to allow for the treatment of any suboptimal results, such as dissection or residual stenoses.

Endovascular stent placement may be performed either as a primary procedure or as a secondary procedure in

FIGURE 131-18 A, An angioplasty balloon, placed over an 0.18-inch wire, both within the introducer sheath, on back table for illustration. **B,** Introducer sheath is positioned at the renal ostium, and predilatation of a renal lesion is performed with 4 × 20–mm angioplasty balloon over the 0.18-inch wire. A small "waist" is seen in the area of the stenosis.

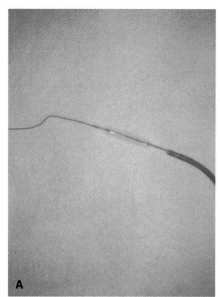

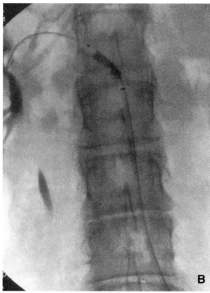

FIGURE 131-19 The NiRRoyal balloon-expandable stent.

response to suboptimal results of angioplasty. Most FMD lesions and nonostial atherosclerotic lesions respond well to angioplasty alone. However, secondary stent placement should be considered for nonostial lesions that do not respond appropriately to angioplasty. Secondary stent placement is typically performed to address elastic recoil, residual stenosis (≥30%), pressure gradients (≥10 mm Hg), and myointimal flaps or dissections. Balloon-expandable stents (Express Biliary LD, Genesis, and NiRRoyal) (Fig. 131-19) and, less commonly, self-expanding stents (Wallstent, Precise, and Aurora) can be employed in the renal artery. In general, balloon-expandable stents demonstrate greater radial strength whereas self-expanding stents demonstrate greater flexibility and conform to the shape of the renal artery. We use balloon-expandable stents primarily in the treatment of ostial atherosclerotic lesions to take advantage of their greater radial strength and precise placement.

In general, the technical aspects of stent placement parallel the performance of transluminal angioplasty.

Frequent small hand injections of contrast agent through the guiding sheath are employed to direct the stent into position across the lesion before deployment of the stent (Fig. 131-20). After the stent has been deployed, one can abut and support the stent with the introducer sheath as the angioplasty balloon is withdrawn. A completion angiogram is performed while wire access to the renal artery is maintained. This is accomplished by passing a second wire and flush catheter through the introducer (Fig. 131-21). Stent placement with 1 to 2 mm extending into the aorta is preferred for the treatment of ostial or proximal renal artery lesions (Fig. 131-22).[8,113-115] Frequent hand injection of contrast agent through the guiding sheath allows for precise placement of the stent and helps avoid malpositioning. A stent placed too far into the artery does not support the true renal orifice and is prone to residual or recurrent disease.[8,113-115] Because disease can recur and may not respond to further endovascular attempts, one should use the shortest possible stent needed to support the lesion. In addition, a stent that extends well out into the distal renal artery (Fig. 131-23) can make later surgical options more difficult and carries a higher failure rate. Conversely, a stent placed too far into the aorta may expose the patient to the risk of future distal embolic events (Fig. 131-24).

A balloon-expandable stent is deployed by inflation of the angioplasty balloon on which it is mounted. In the past, such a stent had to be crimped and hand mounted on the angioplasty balloon, making its delivery somewhat insecure. With these early stents, total sheath coverage of the stent during placement was typically required. Fortunately, currently available stent systems come securely premounted with low-profile delivery systems capable of passage through most lesions without difficulty or with minimal predilatation. We deploy these stents with 1- to 2-mm extension into the aorta, guided by anatomic information provided by previous positioning over bony landmarks.

Although not commonly employed, self-expanding stents can also be used in the treatment of renovascular disease. The deployment of a self-expanding stent is accomplished by the retraction of an outer membrane of the delivery

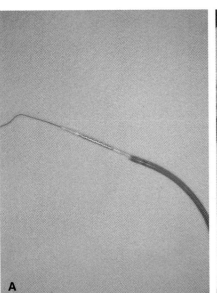

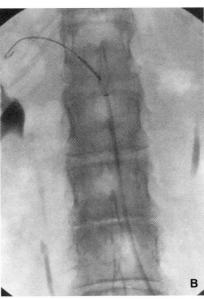

FIGURE 131-20 A, A typical premounted stent over an 0.18-inch wire within a 6F introducer sheath, on back table for illustration. **B,** The premounted stent (over an 0.18-inch wire) has been placed across a lesion in the right renal artery. Precise stent position is verified by "puffing" contrast agent through the sheath.

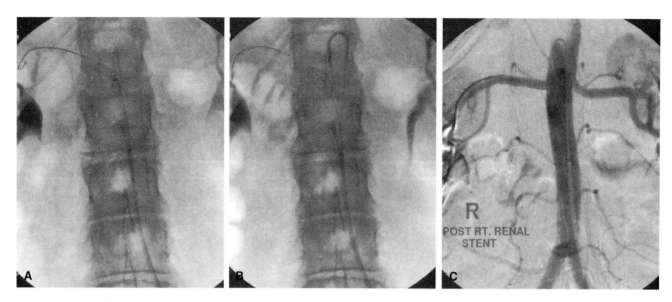

FIGURE 131-21 A, After stent deployment, the guiding introducer sheath has been positioned to abut and support the renal stent as the balloon (which was used to expand the stent) is withdrawn. **B,** While the 0.18-inch wire access is maintained within the right renal artery, a second "buddy" wire and flush catheter are placed within the introducer sheath. **C,** The flush aortogram verifies correct placement of the right renal artery stent before the 0.18-inch wire is withdrawn.

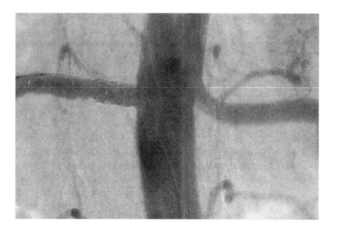

FIGURE 131-22 Final magnified view showing the proper positioning of the stent with 1- to 2-mm extension into the aorta.

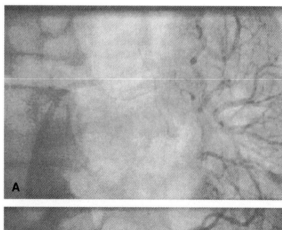

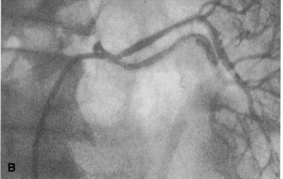

FIGURE 131-23 A, Anteroposterior view of a self-expanding right renal stent extending well out into the distal aspect of the inferior branch of the renal artery. **B,** One can also see that the stent was placed across the origin of the superior branch of the artery.

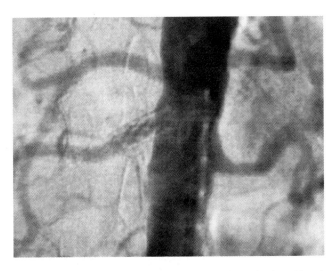

FIGURE 131-24 Example of a malpositioned renal stent that is positioned too far within the aorta.

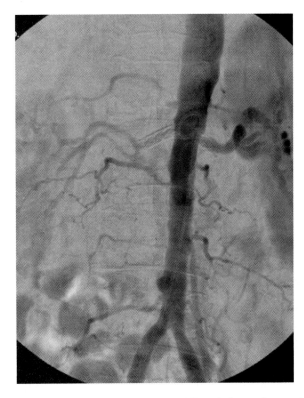

FIGURE 131-25 Example of recurrent bilateral "in-stent" stenosis, worse on the right than on the left, 4 years after stent placement.

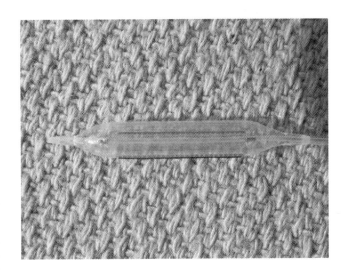

FIGURE 131-26 The cutting balloon.

device to expose the stent. Care must be taken during the deployment to ensure that foreshortening of the stent does not compromise coverage of the lesion. After a stent is deployed, there may be residual narrow areas within it that require balloon dilatation. These areas may be visible upon non-contrast fluoroscopic evaluation of the stent or detected during postdeployment selective renal angiography.

After all therapeutic measures are complete, pressure gradients may be remeasured or intravascular ultrasonography may be performed to assess the technical result and survey for undetected defects. When a satisfactory result has been obtained, guidewire and sheath access may be removed, and hemostasis secured. Although bilateral renal interventions (i.e., angioplasty or stent placement) can be performed at a single setting, we prefer to perform these interventions in stages, when possible, to avoid administration of large volumes of contrast agent.

Postoperative Care and Follow-Up

After renal artery stenting, most patients are treated with 30 days of clopidogrel (Plavix), aspirin, or both. Aspirin therapy is then continued indefinitely in the absence of contraindications to its use. Renal artery duplex ultrasonography is performed at the time of the first office visit, in 2 weeks.[116,117] Renal artery duplex scanning is performed every 4 months for 2 years and then yearly thereafter to check for recurrent disease.

Recurrent Disease and In-Stent Restenosis

Disease can recur after renal stenting, and the incidence of this problem is discussed extensively later in this chapter. Disease that recurs within the stent can be a particularly challenging problem (Fig. 131-25). Although it has been suggested that the recurrent lesion "can always be ballooned," our experience with this approach has been less than optimal. The etiology of this lesion is most often intimal hyperplasia, so repeat balloon angioplasty generally does little to improve the lesion.

For recurrent lesions, initial dilatation with a "cutting" balloon is extremely useful to release fibrous scar tissue of the restenosis lesion and allow for subsequent larger-diameter dilatation with a conventional angioplasty balloon. The cutting balloon (Boston Scientific, Natick, MA) consists of a noncompliant balloon with three or four atherotomes (microsurgical blades) mounted longitudinally on its outer surface (Fig. 131-26). When the cutting balloon is inflated, the atherotomes score the intimal hyperplasia within the stent. The balloon is then rotated and re-inflated to score the lesion in multiple planes. This technology has been used in coronary arteries for several years, but its use has also been studied with renal artery in-stent restenosis.[118] A larger balloon may then be used to enlarge the stent and is the usual mode of therapy. Repeat stent placement may then be performed, if necessary.

■ RESULTS OF ENDOVASCULAR TREATMENT OF RENOVASCULAR DISEASE

Interpreting the reported results for renal artery angioplasty and stenting is challenging. Even after hundreds of reports on the subject, it is not entirely clear how angioplasty and stenting compare with surgical or medical management. The absence of universal reporting standards further complicates matters by making it difficult to compare the results of different studies. Nevertheless, a review of the available prospective studies, as well as a number of large clinical series, offers the best method for describing the contemporary results of renal artery angioplasty and stenting.

■ TREATMENT OF ATHEROSCLEROTIC RENOVASCULAR DISEASE

Technical Success

Because atherosclerotic renal artery ostial stenosis is continuous with the atherosclerotic disease within the aorta, the treatment of these lesions with balloon angioplasty alone has been associated with low technical success rates because of the resistance of the aortic plaque and elastic recoil.[119-122] Endoluminal stents can overcome the resistance of the aortic plaque and the tendency for elastic recoil characteristic of these ostial lesions. As a result, the use of stents has improved the technical success rates of endovascular therapy for atherosclerotic renovascular disease. Tuttle and colleagues[29] reported a 98% technical success rate for angioplasty and stent placement in 148 atherosclerotic renal artery ostial lesions. They found that only 11% of ostial lesions showed a satisfactory response (defined as less than 30% residual stenosis) after balloon angioplasty alone. In a later randomized prospective study of atherosclerotic ostial renal artery stenosis, van de Ven and associates[33] found that primary stenting resulted in a significantly higher rate of technical success and a lower incidence of restenosis than balloon angioplasty alone. The use of primary or selective stent placement in the treatment of atherosclerotic renal artery stenosis has resulted in technical success rates of 88% to 100% in several observational series. Gill and Fowler[123] defined technical success as <10% residual stenosis and reported a 95% technical success rate in 126 atherosclerotic renal lesions treated with endovascular angioplasty and stenting. The only technical failures in their series reflected difficulties with guidewire access or stent misplacement.

Clinical Success

To be considered successful, a renal artery intervention should improve a patient's quality of life, decrease the chances of adverse cardiovascular or renal events, and increase survival. Patients with renovascular hypertension have higher mortality rates as a result of cardiovascular events than age-matched patients with essential hypertension.[124,125] Therefore, the success of an intervention to treat renal artery stenosis should be judged, in part, on its ability to reduce the rate of adverse cardiovascular events. Guidelines for the reporting of renal artery revascularization suggest that clinical events, including overall mortality, cardiovascular mortality, and nonfatal cardiovascular events, should be the gold standard for examining the effects of renal artery interventions.[126] Unfortunately, few studies using these clinical outcome markers have been performed. Consequently, the hypertension and renal function benefit reported by most published series must be considered, rather than the incidence of adverse cardiovascular events or the estimated survival.

Endovascular Therapy and Blood Pressure Response

Three randomized controlled studies have been completed that compared endovascular therapy with medical treatment for renovascular hypertension. These offer the best available data concerning the efficacy of endovascular therapy for hypertension management. In 1998, the Essai Multicentrique Medicaments vs Angioplastie (EMMA) Study Group was the first to publish in this regard. These investigators reported on 23 patients randomly assigned to undergo angioplasty and 26 patients randomly assigned to medical hypertension treatment.[127] Their study, limited to patients with unilateral renal artery stenosis, was unable to demonstrate a statistically significant lowering of the blood pressure. The angioplasty group, however, did show improvement in hypertension control, as evidenced by a reduction in the amount of antihypertensive medications required. It is interesting to note that 7 patients in the medically treated group underwent angioplasty because of uncontrollable hypertension.

The second prospective, randomized study comparing endovascular and medical treatments was reported by the Scottish and Newcastle Renal Artery Stenosis Collaborative Group in 1998.[128] In this report, 55 patients were randomly assigned to either angioplasty or antihypertensive therapy. Patients with both unilateral and bilateral renal artery stenosis were included. The Group concluded that there was a modest improvement in blood pressure control, but that this benefit was confined to patients with bilateral disease. No patient, however, was cured of hypertension.

The largest prospective, randomized study reported to date was performed by the Dutch Renal Artery Stenosis Intervention Cooperative Study Group.[129] A total of 106 patients were randomly assigned to either drug therapy or angioplasty for the treatment of renovascular hypertension. At 12 months after treatment, there was no significant difference in either systolic or diastolic blood pressure between the two treatment groups. The Study Group concluded that angioplasty has little advantage over antihypertensive therapy.

Nordmann and coworkers[130] have subsequently performed a meta-analysis of these randomized controlled studies. They reviewed data from 210 patients. Renal artery angioplasty was associated with a lower blood pressure and lower antihypertensive medication requirements as well as a higher renal artery patency rate at 12 months of follow-up. Angioplasty was not associated with a beneficial renal functional response, although these studies were not specifically designed to address this issue. From this meta-analysis, the investigators concluded that balloon angioplasty has a modest but significant effect on blood pressure control.

Another meta-analysis, this time of the retrospective literature, was performed by Leertouwer and associates[11] and reported in 2000. In this meta-analysis, data from 14 articles* involving 678 patients treated with renal artery stenting were combined with data from 10 articles[6,117,127,128,133-138] involving 644 patients treated with angioplasty alone. Renal artery stenting had a high (98%) technical success rate. The overall hypertension cure rate was 20%, and 49% of the patients had improved blood pressure control. The restenosis rate was 17% at 6 to 29 months. However, when percutaneous transluminal renal angioplasty (PTRA) with stenting was compared with angioplasty alone, the restenosis rate was significantly lower for stenting (17% vs. 26%; $P < .001$). These results are consistent with those reported by van de Ven and associates.[33]

Table 131-3 summarizes 27 contemporary case series reporting results of blood pressure response after primary stent placement for treatment of atherosclerotic renal artery stenosis.[12-38] Published between 1991 and 2001, these series collectively describe the treatment of 1808 patients. The indication for endovascular intervention was hypertension, renal insufficiency, or a combination of the two. Each study demonstrated a decline in the mean systolic and diastolic blood pressures after treatment. The percentage of patients cured ranged from 0 to 30% (average, 10%), and the percentage of patients experiencing improved blood pressure control ranged from 5% to 93% (average, 51%). Each series demonstrated a high technical success rate, ranging from 88% to 100%. These results are consistent with those in the meta-analysis by Leertouwer and associates.[11]

There has only been one prospective, randomized controlled study comparing endovascular treatment with open surgery repair for the treatment of renovascular hypertension. In 1993, Weibull and colleagues[141] reported on 58 patients with renovascular hypertension randomly assigned to undergo either surgery or angioplasty. An angiogram was performed in each patient at 10 days, 1 year, and 2 years after treatment. At 24 months, the primary patency rate was 75% in the PTRA group, versus 96% in the surgery group. Secondary patency rates were 90% in the PTRA group and 97% in the surgery group. Hypertension was cured or improved in approximately 90% of the patients

in both groups, and the treatment response rates in the two cohorts were not statistically different. It must be noted, however, that more than half of the patients failed angioplasty and were reassigned to the surgical group for revascularization. On the basis of these results, the investigators recommended angioplasty as the treatment of choice for selected renovascular lesions contributing to renovascular hypertension with aggressive follow-up and repeat intervention (endovascular and surgical) as needed. Interestingly, however, Wong and coworkers[142] have found that a beneficial blood pressure response after open surgical repair for failed angioplasty may be less than in those who undergo primary surgical repair without prior PTRA. Moreover, surgery may be made technically more demanding after an endovascular procedure, especially after the placement of an endoluminal stent.[142]

Endovascular Therapy and Renal Function Response

Several factors hinder an accurate assessment of the effect of renal artery angioplasty and stenting on renal function. No prospective studies have been performed to compare renal function after medical, surgical, and endovascular treatments of renal artery stenosis. Most observational series report results from a diverse group of patients whose renal function response varies widely. Interpreting the existing renal function response data is further complicated by the fact that the serum creatinine value, the most commonly employed measure of renal function in these studies, is an insensitive method of detecting changes in renal function, especially in patients with values less than 1.2 mg/dL.

Nevertheless, treatment benefit with respect to renal function has been reported in several retrospective studies as a decrease or stabilization of serum creatinine value during clinical follow-up. Bush and coworkers[38] reported that serum creatinine value had decreased by more than 20% or was unchanged (within 20% of baseline) in 51 of 69 (70%) patients treated with renal artery stenting after an average of 20 months of follow-up. The overall mean postoperative creatinine value did not change in a subset of 50 patients with preprocedure renal insufficiency, and all patients with extreme preprocedure renal dysfunction (defined as serum creatinine >4.0 mg/dL) required dialysis during the follow-up period. Similar results were reported by three other groups.[37,143,144] In these retrospective series, renal function was reported as improved in 13% to 31% of patients, stabilized in 42% to 60% of patients, and deteriorated in 24% to 31% of patients. Ramos and associates[145] reported a significant increase in the overall mean glomerular filtration rate (GFR) in a subgroup of 50 patients with renal impairment (defined as GFR < 50 mL/min) treated with renal artery angioplasty and stent placement. However, the severity of the renal impairment is difficult to discern from their report, because they did not include the exact numbers of patients with improved, unchanged, and worsened renal function after stent placement.

Watson and colleagues[146] attempted to isolate the direct effects of renal artery stenting on renal function by studying patients with global renal ischemia, defined as severe stenosis of all renal arteries. The researchers sought to improve upon

Table 131-3   Results After Primary Renal Artery Stent Placement for Atherosclerotic Renal Artery Stenosis

STUDY (YEAR)*	NO. PATIENTS	TECHNICAL SUCCESS (%)	NO. PATIENTS WITH RENAL DYSFUNCTION	RENAL FUNCTION RESPONSE (%)			HYPERTENSION RESPONSE (%)			RESTENOSIS (%)	MAJOR COMPLICATIONS (%)
				Improved	Unchanged	Worsened	Cured	Improved	Failed		
Rees et al (1991)[12]	28	96	14	36	36	29	11	5	36	39	18
Wilms et al (1991)[13]	10	80	1	0	100	0%	30	40	30	22	18
Kuhn et al (1991)[14]	8	92	n/r	n/r	n/r	n/r	22	34	44	17	13
Joffre et al (1992)[15]	11	91	4	50	50	0	27	64	9	18	13
Hennequin et al (1994)[16]	15	100	6	20	40	40	7	93	0	27	19
Raynaud et al (1994)[17]	15	100	7	0	43	57	7	43	50	13	13
MacLeod et al (1995)[18]	28	100	16	25	75		0	40	60	17	19
van de Ven et al (1995)[19]	24	100	n/r	33	58	8	0	73	27	13	13
Dorros et al (1995)[20]	76	100	29	28	28	45	6	46	48	25	11
Henry et al (1996)[21]	55	100	10	20	80		18	57	24	9	3
Iannone et al (1996)[22]	63	99	29	36	46	18	4	35	61	14	32
Harden et al (1997)[23]	32	100	32	35	35	29	n/r	n/r	n/r	13	19
Blum et al (1997)[24]	68	100	20	0	100	0	16	62	22	17	0
Boisclair et al (1997)[25]	33	100	17	41	35	24	6	61	33	0	21
Rundback et al (1998)[26]	45	94	45	18	53	30	n/r	n/r	n/r	26	9
Fiala et al (1998)[27]	21	95	9	0	100	0		53	47	65	19
Dorros et al (1998)[28]	163	99	63	No change in mean SCr			1	42	57	n/r	14
Tuttle et al (1998)[29]	120	98	74	16	75	9	2	46	52	14	4
Gross et al (1998)[30]	30	100	12	55	27	18	0	69	31	13	n/r
Henry et al (1999)[31]	200	99	48	29	67	2	19	61	20	11	2
Rodriguez-Lopez et al (1999)[32]	108	98	32	No change in mean SCr			13	55	32	26	12
van de Ven et al (1999)[33]	40	88	29	17	55	28	15	43	42	14	30
Baumgartner et al (2000)[34]	64	95	n/r	33	42	25		43	57	28	9
Giroux et al (2000)[35]	30	95	21		76	24		53	47	n/r	n/r
Perkovic et al (2001)[36]	148	97	99	8	56	36	n/r	n/r	n/r	29	7
Lederman et al (2001)[37]	300	100	111	8	78	14		70	30	21	2
Bush et al (2001)[38]	73	89	50	23	51	26	n/r	n/r	n/r	n/r	9
Totals	*1808*	*98*	*778*	*20*	*59*	*21*	*10*	*51*	*39*	*19*	*9*

*Superscript numbers indicate chapter references.
n/r, not reported; SCr, serum creatinine.

serum creatinine value as an endogenous analyte of overall renal function to evaluate endovascular treatment effects in patients with unilateral disease. They assessed renal function by comparing the slopes of regression lines derived from the reciprocal of serum creatinine value versus time, plotted before and after stent deployment. At a mean follow-up of 20 months, the regression slope became positive (suggesting improved renal function) in 18 patients (72%) and became less negative (suggesting stabilization) in 7 patients (28%).

Several issues regarding the effects of renal stenting on renal function remain unresolved. A review of the endovascular series cited in Table 131-3 shows that the majority of patients had no change in serum creatinine value after renal artery stenting.[12-38] Whether or not an unchanged serum creatinine value should be considered beneficial remains unclear. Yutan and colleagues[147] reported that 88% of their patients treated for renal dysfunction showed improvement or stabilization of serum creatinine value after angioplasty, stenting, or both. However, this clinical benefit was sustained in only 25% of the patients over a 5-year follow-up period. The other 75% of patients in that series continued to have renal function deterioration, defined as dialysis dependence, death due to renal-related causes, or a rise in serum creatinine values to more than 20% higher than postprocedure concentrations. These results contrast sharply with reports of surgical treatment for renal dysfunction, which demonstrate 5-year dialysis-free survival rates of 55%.[2] Furthermore, in this surgical series, patients experiencing no change in renal function after revascularization experienced rates of death and dialysis dependence during follow-up that were similar to those of patients with worsened renal function after revascularization.[2] These findings raise serious questions about the concept of "stabilized" renal function.

The effect of endovascular treatment with renal stenting on patient survival also remains unclear. Dorros and colleagues[28] reported decreased or stabilized serum creatinine values in 60% to 71% of patients followed for 4 years after renal artery stenting. Survival was associated with baseline creatinine values, in that 3-year survival was 92% in patients with baseline serum creatinine values ≤ 1.4 mg/dL, 74% in those with baseline values ranging from 1.5 to 1.9 mg/dL, and 51% in those with baseline values ≥ 2.0 mg/dL. In this series, improvement or stabilization of renal function after endovascular treatment resulted in greater survival for patients with renal dysfunction. Unfortunately, though, these results appear inferior to survival rates reported after surgical revascularization for ischemic nephropathy.[2]

Consistent in all studies of renal function after stenting is the finding that renal function worsens after intervention in a significant percentage of the patients treated. Ideally, renal artery intervention by either endovascular or operative treatment would be applied to patients with the highest likelihood of clinical benefit. Several retrospective series have examined potential predictors of renal functional response after endovascular treatment of renovascular disease. Burket and colleagues[148] examined several clinical and radiographic variables, but did not find any significant predictors of clinical response to renal angioplasty and stenting. In a small study, Gill-Leertouwer and associates[149] demonstrated that preoperative scintigraphy with lateraliza-tion to the affected kidney was predictive of renal benefit 1 year after stenting. Radermacher and coworkers[150] and Mukherjee and colleagues[151] showed that a low resistive index (< 80 and < 75, respectively) correlated with clinical benefit in the treatment of renal artery stenosis. Cohn and associates[152] examined the relationship between clinical success after renal revascularization and the parenchymal diastolic/systolic ratio measured on duplex scanning. Their findings suggested that a low diastolic/systolic ratio correlated with clinical failure after intervention for renal artery stenosis.

In summary, the effect of endovascular treatment on renal function is uncertain. Although the serum creatinine value is an imperfect measure of renal function, most studies demonstrate short- and intermediate-term improvement or stabilization in serum creatinine values after endovascular treatment of renovascular disease. This clinical response appears to be most consistent in patients with mild or moderate renal insufficiency and is less likely in patients with severe preprocedure renal dysfunction. It is still unclear whether endovascular treatment associated with immediate benefit results in improved survival or decreased adverse cardiovascular events for these patients. Future studies that incorporate direct measures of renal function, long-term follow-up, and outcome predictors are essential to resolve these issues.

Restenosis

Restenosis continues to be a weakness of renal artery angioplasty and stenting. Despite initial technical success rates that exceeded 95%, four reports have documented high rates of restenosis that ranged from 14% to 37%.[37,123,145,147] In most cases, restenosis results from neointimal fibrous hyperplasia that is amenable to further endovascular treatment. Bax and colleagues[153] successfully treated 20 in-stent renal artery stenoses with repeat angioplasty procedures in 18 cases and a second stent in 2 cases. The 6- and 12-month patency rates after this intervention were 93% and 76%, respectively. The technical limits of repeat angioplasty and the risk of additional neointimal fibrosis with a second stent has prompted the search for alternative endovascular techniques for treating restenosis. Atherectomy[154] and cutting balloon angioplasty[155] have been described in case reports. Endovascular brachytherapy may offer another treatment approach for restenosis. Stoeteknuel-Friedi and associates,[156] who treated restenosis in 11 patients with repeat angioplasty and endovascular brachytherapy, reported an 80% stenosis-free patency rate at 1 year.

Treatment of Fibromuscular Dysplasia

Balloon angioplasty appears to be an acceptable treatment for patients with FMD of the medial fibroplasia type involving the main renal artery. In this group of patients, evidence supports balloon angioplasty as a treatment associated with clinical benefit and low morbidity. Tegtmeyer and colleagues[157] successfully treated 85 renal artery stenoses in 66 patients with FMD. Hypertension was cured or improved in all but 1 patient (98%), and the 14 patients with elevated creatinine values had improvement or stabilization of renal function after renal angioplasty. De Fraissinette and associates[158] reported somewhat different blood pressure response results in a series of older patients with FMD (mean age, 59 years) who had long-standing hypertension (average duration, 13 years). After an average follow-up of 39 months, hypertension was cured in 14% and improved in 74%. Results of these series support the general consensus that primary angioplasty without mandatory stent placement can be used to treat medial fibroplasia of the main renal artery with initial technical success rates of 94% to 100%. Furthermore, a beneficial clinical response was seen in these patients after endovascular intervention, and this response was greater in those who were younger with a shorter duration of hypertension.

The durability of balloon angioplasty for the treatment of renal FMD has not been well defined. Few studies have included surveillance imaging studies of the treated renal artery, relying instead on follow-up clinical assessment. The usefulness of clinical follow-up has been questioned by studies that have shown a discrepancy between clinical and anatomic results.[159] To examine the issue of restenosis after balloon angioplasty for FMD, Birrer and colleagues[139] used serial duplex sonography evaluations to prospectively monitor 31 renal artery lesions treated with endovascular treatment for 1 year. They reported a cumulative 23% restenosis rate at 12 months. These results suggest that although angioplasty has a high rate of initial technical and clinical success in the treatment of FMD, the rate of restenosis may approach that observed in the treatment of atherosclerotic renovascular disease.

Complications of Endovascular Therapy

General complications of endovascular arterial intervention are discussed in detail in Chapters 54 and 58. In a meta-analysis performed by Leertouwer and colleagues,[11] the reported range of complication rates after endovascular renal intervention was 0 to 40%, with a calculated mean rate of 11%. The most frequently reported complications involved arterial access sites with hematoma formation or puncture site trauma. Severe complications, which occurred in 9% of the compiled cases, included renal failure, segmental renal infarction, perinephric hematoma, and renal artery thrombosis or occlusion. The mean mortality rate—death within the first month after angioplasty and stenting—was 1%. Fortunately, occlusion of a main renal artery was uncommon. Ivanovic and coworkers[140] reported similar results in a single-center retrospective review of complications after endovascular treatment with renal artery stenting. Major complications occurred after 15 of 179 procedures (8.4%) and included renal infarction, permanently increased serum creatinine value, dialysis dependence, need for blood transfusion or surgical intervention, and deep venous thrombosis. These investigators were not able to demonstrate any association between pretreatment characteristics and subsequent major complications. They did observe, however, that patients with renal site or renal function complications tended to be older and to have higher serum creatinine values. Two patients (1.1%) in their series died within 30 days of endovascular treatment, although neither death was considered secondary to the intervention.

■ SUMMARY

The optimal treatment for patients with renal artery disease remains controversial. Advocates of medical, endovascular, or surgical treatment each support their opinions with selected clinical data. Like other types of minimally invasive therapy, endovascular treatment of renal artery disease is associated with less morbidity and allows for an earlier return to normal activity. However, the benefits of a less invasive approach must be carefully weighed against the limitations of the technique, and the results compared objectively with the results and outcomes associated with open surgical therapy. The available data suggest that for the treatment of renovascular hypertension, endovascular therapy may have a beneficial effect on blood pressure, similar to that of surgical revascularization. However, for the treatment of worsening renal failure or ischemic nephropathy, the functional response obtained from endovascular treatment does not appear to be equivalent to that reported from surgical series. In addition, survival of patients undergoing endovascular treatment appears to be inferior to that of patients treated surgically. The reasons for these disparate results are unclear. Recurrent stenosis also remains a problem. Available data suggest that restenosis occurs in approximately 15% to 20% of patients at 1 year and that its treatment may lead to functional responses that are inferior to the results of treatment for primary disease.

In summary, when faced with a patient with symptomatic renovascular disease, the vascular surgeon must carefully consider the patient's co-morbid risks for the planned intervention, the likelihood of a beneficial response, and the durability of the technique before recommending either endovascular or surgical therapy. Despite the large volume of literature on the subject, it appears that a large multicenter, prospective, randomized trial comparing medical treatment, endovascular angioplasty and stenting, and surgical revascularization is required to finally define the appropriate applications for each modality.

■ REFERENCES

1. Cambria RP, Brewster DC, L'Italien GJ, et al: The durability of different reconstructive techniques for atherosclerotic renal disease. J Vasc Surg 20:76-85, 1994.
2. Cherr GS, Hansen KJ, Craven TE, et al: Surgical management of atherosclerotic renovascular disease. J Vasc Surg. 35:236-245, 2002.
3. Novick AC: Long-term results of surgical revascularization for renal artery disease. Urol Clin North Am 28:827-831, 2001.
4. Derrow AE, Seeger JM, Dame DA, et al: The outcome in the United States after thoracoabdominal aortic aneurysm repair, renal artery bypass, and mesenteric revascularization. J Vasc Surg. 34:54-61, 2001.
5. Tegtmeyer CJ, Kellman CD, Ayers C: Percutaneous transluminal angioplasty of the renal artery. Results and long-term follow-up. Radiology 153:77-84, 1984.
6. Bonelli FS, McKusick MA, Textor SC, et al: Renal artery angioplasty: Technical results and clinical outcome in 320 patients. Mayo Clin Proc 70:1041-1052, 1995.
7. Dorros G, Jaff M, Mathiak L, He T; Multicenter Registry Participants: Multicenter Registry Palmaz stent renal artery stenosis revascularization registry report: Four-year follow-up of 1,058 successful patients. Catheter Cardiovasc Interv 55:182-188, 2002.

8. Blum U, Krumme B, Flugel P, et al: Treatment of ostial renal-artery stenosis with vascular endoprostheses after unsuccessful balloon angioplasty. N Engl J Med 336:459-465, 1997.

9. Rundback JH, Manoni T, Rozenblit GN, et al: Balloon angioplasty or stent placement in patients with azotemic renovascular disease: A retrospective comparison of clinical outcomes. Heart Dis 1:121-125, 1999.

10. Sacks D, Rundback JH, Martin LG: Renal angioplasty/stent placement and hypertension in the year 2000. J Vasc Interv Radiol 11:949-953, 2000.

11. Leertouwer TC, Gussenhoven EJ, Bosch JL, et al: Stent placement for renal arterial stenosis: Where do we stand? A meta-analysis. Radiology 216:78-85, 2000.

12. Rees CR, Palmaz JC, Becker GJ, et al: Palmaz stent in atherosclerotic stenoses involving the ostia of the renal arteries: Preliminary report of a multicenter study. Radiology 181:507-514, 1991.

13. Wilms GE, Peene PT, Baert AL, et al: Renal artery stent placement with use of the Wallstent endoprosthesis. Radiology 179:457-462, 1991.

14. Kuhn FP, Kutkuhn B, Torsello G, Modder U: Renal artery stenosis: Preliminary results of treatment with the Strecker stent. Radiology 180:367-372, 1991.

15. Joffre F, Rousseau H, Bernadet P, et al: Midterm results of renal artery stenting. Cardiovasc Intervent Radiol 15:313-318, 1992.

16. Hennequin LM, Joffre FG, Rousseau HP, et al: Renal artery stent placement: Long-term results with the Wallstent endoprosthesis. Radiology 191:619-621, 1994.

17. Raynaud AC, Beyssen BM, Turmel-Rodrigues LE, et al: Renal artery stent placement: Immediate and midterm technical and clinical results. J Vasc Interv Radiol Nov- 5:849-858, 1994.

18. MacLeod M, Taylor AD, Baxter G, et al: Renal artery stenosis managed by Palmaz stent insertion: Technical and clinical outcome. J Hypertens 13:1791-1795, 1995.

19. van de Ven PJ, Beutler JJ, Kaatee R, et al: Transluminal vascular stent for ostial atherosclerotic renal artery stenosis. Lancet 346:672-674, 1995.

20. Dorros G, Jaff M, Jain A, et al: Follow-up of primary Palmaz-Schatz stent placement for atherosclerotic renal artery stenosis. Am J Cardiol 75:1051-1055, 1995.

21. Henry M, Amor M, Henry I, et al: Stent placement in the renal artery: Three-year experience with the Palmaz stent. J Vasc Interv Radiol 7:343-350, 1996.

22. Iannone LA, Underwood PL, Nath A, et al: Effect of primary balloon expandable renal artery stents on long-term patency, renal function, and blood pressure in hypertensive and renal insufficient patients with renal artery stenosis. Cathet Cardiovasc Diagn 37:243-250, 1996.

23. Harden PN, MacLeod MJ, Rodger RS, et al: Effect of renal-artery stenting on progression of renovascular renal failure. Lancet 349:1133-1136, 1997.

24. Blum U, Krumme B, Flugel P, et al: Treatment of ostial renal-artery stenoses with vascular endoprostheses after unsuccessful balloon angioplasty. N Engl J Med 336:459-465, 1997.

25. Boisclair C, Therasse E, Oliva VL, et al: Treatment of renal angioplasty failure by percutaneous renal artery stenting with Palmaz stents: Midterm technical and clinical results. AJR Am J Roentgenol 168:245-251, 1997.

26. Rundback JH, Gray RJ, Rozenblit G, et al: Renal artery stent placement for the management of ischemic nephropathy. J Vasc Interv Radiol 9:413-420, 1998.

27. Fiala LA, Jackson MR, Gillespie DL, et al: Primary stenting of atherosclerotic renal artery ostial stenosis. Ann Vasc Surg 12:128-133, 1998.

28. Dorros G, Jaff M, Mathiak L, et al: Four-year follow-up of Palmaz-Schatz stent revascularization as treatment for atherosclerotic renal artery stenosis. Circulation 98:642-647, 1998.

29. Tuttle KR, Chouinard RF, Webber JT, et al: Treatment of atherosclerotic ostial renal artery stenosis with the intravascular stent. Am J Kidney Dis 32:611-622, 1998.

30. Gross CM, Kramer J, Waigand J, et al: Ostial renal artery stent placement for atherosclerotic renal artery stenosis in patients with coronary artery disease. Cathet Cardiovasc Diagn 45:1-8, 1998.

31. Henry M, Amor M, Henry I, et al: Stents in the treatment of renal artery stenosis: Long-term follow-up. J Endovasc Surg 6:42-51, 1999.

32. Rodriguez-Lopez JA, Werner A, Ray LI, et al: Renal artery stenosis treated with stent deployment: Indications, technique, and outcome for 108 patients. J Vasc Surg 29:617-624, 1999.

33. van de Ven PJ, Kaatee R, Beutler JJ, et al: Arterial stenting and balloon angioplasty in ostial atherosclerotic renovascular disease: A randomised trial. Lancet 353:282-286, 1999.

34. Baumgartner I, von Aesch K, Do DD, et al: Stent placement in ostial and nonostial atherosclerotic renal arterial stenoses: A prospective follow-up study. Radiology 216:498-505, 2000.

35. Giroux MF, Soulez G, Therasse E, et al: Percutaneous revascularization of the renal arteries: Predictors of outcome. J Vasc Interv Radiol 11:713-720, 2000.

36. Perkovic V, Thomson KR, Mitchell PJ, et al: Treatment of renovascular disease with percutaneous stent insertion: Long-term outcomes. Australas Radiol 45:438-443, 2001.

37. Lederman RJ, Mendelsohn FO, Santos R, et al: Primary renal artery stenting: Characteristics and outcomes after 363 procedures. Am Heart J 142:314-323, 2001.

38. Bush RL, Najibi S, MacDonald MJ, et al: Endovascular revascularization of renal artery stenosis: Technical and clinical results. J Vasc Surg 33:1041-1049, 2001.

39. Tan KT, van Beek EJ, Brown PW, et al: Magnetic resonance angiography for the diagnosis of renal artery stenosis: A meta-analysis. Clin Radiol 57:617-624, 2002.

40. Qanadli SD, Soulez G, Therasse E, et al: Detection of renal artery stenosis: Prospective comparison of captopril-enhanced Doppler sonography, captopril-enhanced scintigraphy, and MR angiography. AJR Am J Roentgenol 177:1123-1129, 2001.

41. Lin CC, Shiau YC, Li TC, et al: Usefulness of captopril renography to predict the benefits of renal artery revascularization or captopril treatment in hypertensive patients with diabetic nephropathy. J Diabetes Complications 16:344-346, 2002.

42. Karanikas G, Becherer A, Wiesner K, et al: ACE inhibition is superior to angiotensin receptor blockade for renography in renal artery stenosis. Eur J Nucl Med Mol Imaging 29:312-318, 2002.

43. Johansson M, Jensen G, Aurell M, et al: Evaluation of duplex ultrasound and captopril renography for detection of renovascular hypertension. Kidney Int 58:774-782, 2000.

44. Ugar O, Serdengecti M, Karacalioglu O, et al: Comparison of Tc-99m EC and Tc-99m DTPA captopril scintigraphy to diagnose renal artery stenosis. Clin Nucl Med 24:553-560, 1999.

45. Motew SJ, Cherr GS, Craven TE, et al: Renal duplex sonography: Main renal artery versus hilar analysis. J Vasc Surg 32:462-471, 2000.

46. Hansen KJ, Tribble RW, Reavis SW, et al: Renal duplex sonography: Evaluation of clinical utility. J Vasc Surg 12:227-236, 1990.

47. Shusterman N, Strom BL, Murray TG, et al: Risk factors and outcome of hospital-acquired acute renal failure: Clinical epidemiologic study. Am J Med 83:65-71, 1987.

48. Eisenberg RL, Bank WO, Hedgock MW: Renal failure after major angiography can be avoided with hydration. AJR Am J Roentgenol 136:859-861, 1981.

49. Rudnick MR, Goldfarb S, Wexler L, et al: Nephrotoxicity of ionic and nonionic contrast media in 1196 patients: A randomized trial. Iohexol Cooperative Study. Kidney Int 47:254-261, 1995.

50. D'Elia JA, Gleason RF, Alday M, et al: Nephrotoxicity from angiographic contrast material: A prospective study. Am J Med 72:719-725, 1982.

51. Lautin EM, Freeman NJ, Schoenfeld AH, et al: Radiocontrast-associated renal dysfunction: Incidence and risk factors. AJR Am J Roentgenol 157:49-58, 1991.

52. Lautin EM, Freeman NJ, Schoenfeld AH, et al: Radiocontrast-associated renal dysfunction: A comparison of lower-osmolality and conventional high-osmolality contrast media. AJR Am J Roentgenol 157:59-65, 1991.

53. Moore RD, Steinberg EP, Powe NR, et al: Nephrotoxicity of high-osmolality versus low-osmolality contrast media: Randomized clinical trial. Radiology 182:649-655, 1992.

54. Steinberg EP, Moore RD, Powe NR, et al: Safety and cost effectiveness of high-osmolality as compared with low-osmolality contrast material in patients undergoing cardiac angiography. N Engl J Med 326:425-430, 1992.

55. Barret BJ, Parfrey PS, Vavasour HM, et al: A comparison of nonionic, low-osmolality radiocontrast agents with ionic, high-osmolality agents during cardiac catheterization. N Engl J Med 326:431-436, 1992.

56. Barrett BJ, Parfrey PS, McDonald JR, et al: Nonionic low-osmolality versus ionic high-osmolality contrast material for intravenous use in patients perceived to be at high risk: Randomized trial. Radiology 183:105-110, 1992.

57. Taliercio CP, Vlietstra RE, Fisher LD, Burnett JC: Risks for renal dysfunction with cardiac angiography. Ann Intern Med 104:501-504, 1986.

58. Cigarroa RG, Lange RA, Williams RH, Hillis LD: Dosing of contrast material to prevent contrast nephropathy in patients with renal disease. Am J Med 86:649-652, 1989.

59. Gomes AS, Baker JD, Martin-Paredero V, et al: Acute renal dysfunction after major arteriography. AJR Am J Roentgenol 145:1249-1253, 1985.

60. Martin-Paredero V, Dixon SM, Baker JD, et al: Risk of renal failure after major angiography. Arch Surg 118:1417-1420, 1983.

61. Barrett BJ, Carisie EJ: Metaanalysis of the relative nephrotoxicity of high- and low-osmolality iodinated contrast media. Radiology 188:171-178, 1993.

62. Tepel M, van der Giet M, Schwarzfeld C, et al: Prevention of radiographic-contrast-agent-induced reductions in renal function by acetylcysteine. N Engl J Med 343:180-184, 2000.

63. Baker CS, Wragg A, Kumar S, et al: A rapid protocol for the prevention of contrast-induced renal dysfunction: The RAPPID study. J Am Coll Cardiol 41:211-218, 2003.

64. Kay J, Chow WH, Chan TM, et al: Acetylcysteine for the prevention of acute deterioration of renal function following elective coronary angiography and intervention: A randomized controlled trail. JAMA 289:553-558, 2003.

65. Hawkins IF Jr, Wilcox CS, Kerns SR, Sabatelli FW: CO2 digital angiography: A safer contrast agent for renal vascular imaging? Am J kidney Dis 24:685-694, 1994.

66. Seeger JM, Self S, Harward TR, et al: Carbon dioxide gas as an arterial contrast agent. Ann Surg 217:697-698, 1993.

67. Schreier DZ, Weaver FA, Frankhouse J, et al: A prospective study of carbon dioxide-digital subtraction vs standard contrast arteriography in the evaluation of the renal arteries. Arch Surg 131:503-508, 1996.

68. Weaver FA, Penecost MJ, Yellin AE, et al: Clinical applications of carbon dioxide/digital subtraction arteriography. J Vasc Surg 13:266-273, 1991.

69. Frankhouse JH, Ryan MG, Papanicolaou G, et al: Carbon dioxide/digital subtraction arteriography-assisted transluminal angioplasty Ann Vasc Surg 9:448-452, 1995.

70. Bloem JL, Wondergem J: Gd-DTPA as a contrast agent in CT. Radiology 171:578-579, 1989.

71. Kinno Y, Odagiri K, Andoh K, et al: Gadopentetate dimeglumine as an alternative contrast material for use in angiography. AJR Am J Roentgenol 160:1293-1294, 1993.

72. Matchett WJ, Mcfarland DR, Russell DK, et al: Azotemia: Gadopentetate dimeglumine as contrast agent at digital subtraction angiography. Radiology 201:569-571, 1996.

73. Kaufman JA, Geller SC, Waltman AC: Renal insufficiency: Gadopentetate dimeglumine as a radiographic contrast agent during peripheral vascular interventional procedures. Radiology 198:579-581, 1996.

74. Ailawadi G, Stanley JC, Williams DM, et al: Gadolinium as a nonnephrotic contrast agent for catheter-based arteriographic evaluation of renal arteries in patients with azotemia. J Vasc Surg 37:346-352, 2003.

75. Grollman JH Jr, Marcus R: Transbrachial arteriography: Techniques and complications. Cardiovasc Intervent Radiol 11:32-35, 1988.

76. Verschuyl EJ, Kaatee R, Beek FJ, et al: Renal artery origins: Best angiographic projection angles. Radiology 205:115-120, 1997.

77. Verschuyl EJ, Kaatee R, Beek FJ, et al: Renal artery origins: Location and distribution in the transverse plane at CT. Radiology 203:71-75, 1997.

78. Gerlock AJ Jr, Goncharenko V, Sloan OM: Right posterior oblique of choice in aortography of hypertensive patients. Radiology 127:45-48, 1978.

79. Nahman NS Jr, Maniam P, Hernandez RA Jr, et al: Renal artery pressure gradients in patients with angiographic evidence of atherosclerotic renal artery stenosis. Am J Kidney Dis 24:695-699, 1994.

80. Sheikh KH, Davidson CJ, Newman GE, et al: Intravascular ultrasound assessment of the renal artery. Ann Intern Med 115:22-25, 1991.

81. Sheikh KH, Kisslo K, Davidson CJ: Interventional applications of intravascular ultrasound imaging: Initial experience and future perspectives. Echocardiography 7:433-441, 1990.

82. Leertouwer TC, Gussenhoven EJ, van Jaarsveld BC, et al: In-vitro validation, with histology, of intravascular ultrasound in renal arteries. J Hypertens 17:271-277, 1999.

83. 1995 update of the working group reports on chronic renal failure and renovascular hypertension. National High Blood Pressure Education Program Working Group. Arch Intern Med 156:1938-1947, 1996.

84. Hansen KJ, Edwards MS, Craven TE, et al: Prevalence of renovascular disease in the elderly: A population-based study. J Vasc Surg 36:443-451, 2002.

85. Olin JW, Melia M, Young JR, et al: Prevalence of atherosclerotic renal artery stenosis in patients with atherosclerosis elsewhere. Am J Med 88(1N):46N-51N, 1990.

86. Choudhri AH, Cleland JG, Rowlands PC, et al: Unsuspected renal artery stenosis in peripheral vascular disease. BMJ 301:1197-1198, 1990.

87. Valentine RJ, Clagett GP, Miller GL, et al: The coronary risk of unsuspected renal artery stenosis. J Vasc Surg 18:433-440, 1993.

88. Bookstein JJ, Abrams HL, Buenger RE, et al: Radiographic aspects of renovascular hypertension. 3: Appraisal of arteriography. JAMA 221:368-374, 1972.

89. McCormack LJ, Poutasse EF, Meaney TF, et al: A pathologic-arteriographic correlation of renal arterial disease. Am Heart J 72:188-198, 1966.

90. Cherr GS, Hansen KJ, Craven TE, et al: Surgical management of atherosclerotic renovascular disease. J Vasc Surg 35:236-245, 2002.

91. Hansen KJ, Cherr GS, Craven TE, et al: Management of ischemic nephropathy: Dialysis-free survival after surgical repair. J Vasc Surg 32:472-482, 2000.

92. Dean RH, Benjamin ME, Hansen KJ: Surgical management of renovascular hypertension. Curr Probl Surg 34:209-308, 1997.

93. Kincaid OW, Davis GD, Hallerman FJ, Hunt JC: Fibromuscular dysplasia of the renal arteries: Arteriographic features, classification, and observation on natural history of the disease. Am J Roentgenol Radium Ther Nucl Med 104:271-282, 1968.

94. Wylie EJ, Perloff D, Wellington JS: Fibromuscular hyperplasia of the renal arteries. Ann Surg 156:592-609, 1962.

95. Alimi Y, Mercier C, Pellissier JF, et al: Fibromuscular disease of the renal artery: A new histopathologic classification. Ann Vasc Surg 6:220-224, 1992.

96. McCormack LJ, Noto TJ Jr, Meaney TF, et al: Subadventitial fibroplasia of the renal artery, a disease of young women. Am Heart J 73:602-614, 1967.

97. Henke PK, Cardneau JD, Welling TH 3rd, et al: Renal artery aneurysms: A 35-year clinical experience with 252 aneurysms in 168 patients. Ann Surg 223:454-463, 2001.

98. Pfeiffer T, Reiher L, Grabitz K, et al: Reconstruction for renal artery aneurysm: Operative techniques and long term results. J Vasc Surg 37:293-300, 2003.

99. Tan WA, Chough S, Saito J, et al: Covered stent for renal artery aneurysm. Cathet Cardiovasc Interv 52:106-109, 2001.

100. Halloul Z, Buerger T, Grote R, Meyer F: Selective embolization of a renal artery aneurysm. Vasa 29:285-287, 2000.

101. Morin RP, Dunn EJ, Wright CB: Renal arteriovenous fistulas: A review of etiology, diagnosis, and management. Surgery 99:114-118, 1986.

102. Sprouse LR 2nd, Hamilton IN Jr: The endovascular treatment of a renal arteriovenous fistula: Placement of a covered stent. J Vasc Surg 36:1066-1068, 2002.

103. Gewertz BL, Stanley JC, Fry WJ: Renal artery dissections. Arch Surg 112:409-414, 1977.

104. Lee JT, White RA: Endovascular management of blunt traumatic renal artery dissection. J Endovasc Ther 9:354-358, 2002.

105. Starnes BW, O'Donnell SD, Gillespie DL, et al: Endovascular management of renal ischemia in a patient with acute aortic dissection and renovascular hypertension. Ann Vasc Surg 16:368-374, 2002.

106. Stanley JC: Renal vascular disease and renovascular hypertension in children. Urol Clin North Am 11:451-463, 1984.

107. Kerr GS, Hallahan CW, Giordano J, et al: Takayasu arteritis. Ann Intern Med 120:919-929, 1994.

108. Lupattelli T, Garaci FG, Manenti G, et al: Giant high-flow renal arteriovenous fistula treated by percutaneous embolization. Urology 61:837, 2003.

109. Rimon U, Garniek A, Golan G, et al: Endovascular closure of a large renal arteriovenous fistula. Cathet Cardiovasc Interv 59:66-70, 2003.

110. Staab GE, Tegtmeyer CJ, Constable WC: Radiation-induced renovascular hypertension. Am J Roentgenol 126:634-637, 1976.

111. Fleming RJ, Stern LZ: Multiple intraparenchymal renal artery aneurysms in polyarteritis nodosa. Radiology 84:100-103, 1965.

112. Silver D, Clements JB: Renovascular hypertension from renal artery compression by congenital bands. Ann Surg 183:161-166, 1976.

113. Henry M, Amor M, Henry I, et al: Stent placement in the renal artery: Three-year experience with Palmaz stent. J Vasc Interv Radiol 7:343-350, 1996.

114. Rundback JH, Jacobs JM: Percutaneous renal artery stent placement for hypertension and azotemia: Pilot study. Am J Kidney Dis 28:214-219, 1996.

115. Boisclair C, Therasse E, Oliva VL, et al: Treatment of renal angioplasty failure by percutaneous renal artery stenting with Palmaz stents: Midterm technical and clinical results. AJR Am J Roentgenol 168:24-51, 1997.

116. Hudspeth DA, Hansen KJ, Reavis SW, et al: Renal duplex sonography after treatment of renovascular disease. J Vasc Surg 18:381-388, 1993.

117. Tullis MJ, Zierler RE, Glickerman DJ, et al: Results of percutaneous transluminal angioplasty for atherosclerotic renal artery stenosis: A follow up study with duplex ultrasonography. J Vasc Surg 25:46-54, 1997.

118. Munneke GJ, Engelke C, Morgan RA, Belli AM: Cutting balloon angioplasty for resistant renal artery in-stent restenosis. J Vasc Interv Radiol 13:327-331, 2002.

119. Sos TA, Pickering TG, Sniderman K, et al: Percutaneous transluminal renal angioplasty in renovascular hypertension due to atheroma or fibromuscular dysplasia. N Engl J Med 309:274-279, 1983.

120. Canzanello VJ, Milan VG, Spiegel JE, et al: Percutaneous transluminal renal angioplasty in management of atherosclerotic renovascular hypertension: Results in 100 patients. Hypertension 13:163-172, 1989.

121. Martin LG, Cork RD, Kaufman SL: Long-term results of angioplasty in 110 patients with renal artery stenosis. J Vasc Interv Radiol 3:619-626, 1992.

122. Eldrup-Jorgensen J, Harvey HR, Sampson LN, et al: Should percutaneous transluminal renal angioplasty be applied to ostial renal artery atherosclerosis? J Vasc Surg 21:909-915, 1995.

123. Gill KS, Fowler RC: Atherosclerotic renal arterial stenosis: Clinical outcomes of stent placement for hypertension and renal failure. Radiology 226:821-826, 2003.

124. Simon N, Franklin SS, Bleifer KH, Maxwell MH: Clinical characteristics of renovascular hypertension. JAMA 220:1209-1218, 1972.

125. Maxwell MH, Bleifer KH, Franklin SS, Varady PD: Cooperative study of renovascular hypertension: Demographic analysis of the study. JAMA 220:1195-1204, 1972.

126. Rundback JH, Sacks D, Kent KC, et al: Guidelines for the reporting of renal artery revascularization in clinical trials. Circulation 106:1572-1585, 2002.

127. Plouin PF, Chatellier G, Darne B, Raynaud A: Blood pressure outcome of angioplasty in atherosclerotic renal artery stenosis: A randomized trial. Essai Multicentrique Medicaments vs Angioplastie (EMMA) Study Group. Hypertension 31:823-829, 1998.

128. Webster J, Marshall F, Abdalla M, et al: Randomized comparison of percutaneous angioplasty vs continued medical therapy for hypertension patients with atheromatous renal artery stenosis. Scottish and Newcastle Renal Artery Stenosis Collaborative Group. J Hum Hypertens 12:329-335, 1998.

129. Van Jaarsveld BC, Krijnen P, Pieterman H, et al: The effect of balloon angioplasty on hypertension in atherosclerotic renal-artery stenosis. Dutch Renal Artery Stenosis Intervention Cooperative Study Group. N Engl J Med 342:1007-1014, 2000.

130. Nordmann AJ, Woo K, Parkes R, Logan AG: Balloon angioplasty or medical therapy for hypertensive patients with atherosclerotic renal artery stenosis? A meta-analysis of randomized controlled trials. Am J Med 114:44-50, 2003.

131. White CJ, Ramee SR, Collins TJ, et al: Renal artery stent placement: Utility in lesions difficult to treat with balloon angioplasty. J Am Coll Cardiol 30:1445-1450, 1997.

132. Shannon HM, Gillespie IN, Moss JG: Salvage of the solitary kidney by insertion of a renal artery stent. AJR Am J Roentgenol 171:217-222, 1998.

133. Hoffman O, Carreres T, Sapoval MR, et al: Ostial renal artery stenosis angioplasty: Immediate and mid-term angiographic and clinical results. J Vasc Interv Radiol. 9:65-73, 1998.

134. Karagiannis A, Douma S, Voyiatzis K, et al: Percutaneous transluminal renal angioplasty in patients with renovascular hypertension: Long-term results. Hypertens Res 18:27-31, 1995.

135. Jensen G, Zachrisson BF, Delin K, et al: Treatment of renovascular hypertension: One year results of renal angioplasty. Kidney Int 48:1936-1945, 1995.

136. Eldrup-Jorgensen J, Harvey HR, Sampson LN, et al: Should percutaneous transluminal renal artery angioplasty be applied to ostial renal artery atherosclerosis? J Vasc Surg 21:909-914, 1995.

137. von Knorring J, Edgren J, Lepantalo M: Long-term results of percutaneous transluminal angioplasty in renovascular hypertension. Acta Radiol 37:36-40, 1996.

138. Baumgartner I, Triller J, Mahler F: Patency of percutaneous transluminal renal angioplasty: A prospective sonographic study. Kidney Int 51:798-803, 1997.

139. Birrer M, Do DD, Mahler F, et al: Treatment of renal artery fibromuscular dysplasia with balloon angioplasty: A prospective follow-up study. Eur J Vasc Endovasc Surg 23:146-152, 2002.

140. Ivanovic V, McKusick MA, Johnson CM, et al: Renal artery stent placement: Complications at a single tertiary care center. J Vasc Interv Radiol 14:217-225, 2003.

141. Weibull H, Bergqvist D, Bergentz S, et al: Percutaneous transluminal renal angioplasty versus surgical reconstruction of atherosclerotic renal artery stenosis: A prospective randomized study. J Vasc Surg 18:841-852, 1993.

142. Wong JM, Hansen KJ, Oskin TC, et al: Surgery after failed percutaneous renal artery angioplasty. J Vasc Surg 30:468-483, 1999.

143. Gill KS, Fowler RC: Atherosclerotic renal arterial stenosis: Clinical outcomes of stent placement for hypertension and renal failure. Radiology 226:821-826, 2003.

144. Beutler JJ, Van Ampting JM, Van de Ven PJ, et al: Long-term effects of arterial stenting on kidney function for patients with ostial atherosclerotic renal artery stenosis and renal insufficiency. J Am Soc Nephrol 12:1475-1481, 2001.

145. Ramos F, Kotilar C, Alvarez D, et al: Renal function and outcome of PTRA and stenting for atherosclerotic renal artery stenosis. Kidney Int 63:276-282, 2003.

146. Watson PS, Hadjipetrou P, Cox SV, et al: Effect of renal artery stenting on renal function and size in patients with atherosclerotic renovascular disease. Circulation 102:1671-1677, 2000.

147. Yutan E, Glickerman DJ, Caps MT, et al: Percutaneous transluminal revascularization for renal artery stenosis: Veterans Affairs Puget Sound Health Care System experience. J Vasc Surg 34:685-693, 2001.

148. Burket MW, Cooper CJ, Kennedy DJ, et al: Renal artery angioplasty and stent placement: Predictors of a favorable outcome. Am Heart J 139:64-71, 2000.

149. Gill-Leertouwer TC, Gussenhoven EJ, Bosch JL, et al: Predictors of clinical success at one year following renal artery stent placement. J Endovasc Ther 9:495-502, 2002.

150. Radermacher J, Chavan A, Bleck J, et al: Use of Doppler ultrasonography to predict the outcome of therapy for renal artery stenosis. N Engl J Med 344:410-417, 2001.

151. Mukherjee D, Bhatt DL, Robbins M, et al: Renal artery end-diastolic velocity and renal artery resistance index as predictors of outcome after renal stenting. Am J Cardiol 88:1064-1066, 2001.

152. Cohn EJ Jr, Benjamin ME, Sandager GP, et al: Can intrarenal duplex waveform analysis predict successful renal artery revascularization? J Vasc Surg 28:471-480, 1998.

153. Bax L, Mali WPTM, Van de Ven PJG, et al: Repeated intervention for in-stent restenosis of the renal arteries. J Vasc Interv Radiol 13:1219-1224, 2002.

154. Rao BH, Chandra KS: Renal artery in-stent restenosis: Treatment with high speed rotational atherectomy. Indian Heart J 52:205-206, 2000.

155. Munneke GJ, Engelke C, Morgan RA, Belli AM: Cutting balloon angioplasty for resistant renal artery in-stent restenosis. J Vasc Interv Radiol 13:327-331, 2002.

156. Stoeteknuel-Friedi S, Do DD, Von Briel C, et al: Endovascular brachytherapy for prevention of recurrent renal in-stent restenosis. J Endovasc Ther 9:350-353, 2002.

157. Tegtmeyer CJ, Selby JB, Hartwell GD, et al: Results and complications of angioplasty in fibromuscular disease. Circulation 83:I155-I161, 1991.

158. De Fraissinette B, Garcier JM, Dieu V, et al: Percutaneous transluminal angioplasty of dysplastic stenoses of the renal artery: Results on 70 adults. Cardiovasc Intervent Radiol 26:46-51, 2003.

159. Oertle M, Do DD, Baumgartner I, et al: Discrepancy of clinical and angiographic results in the follow-up of percutaneous transluminal renal angioplasty. Vasa 27:154-157, 1998.

Chapter

Open Surgical Repair of Renovascular Disease

132

KIMBERLEY J. HANSEN, MD

JUAN AYERDI, MD

MATTHEW S. EDWARDS, MD

A variety of open operative techniques have been used to correct renal artery disease. From a practical standpoint, three basic operations have been most commonly utilized: aortorenal bypass, renal artery thromboendarterectomy, and renal artery reimplantation. Although each method may have its proponents, no single approach provides optimal repair for all types of renovascular disease. Aortorenal bypass using saphenous vein is probably the most versatile technique; however, thromboendarterectomy is especially useful for orificial atherosclerosis involving multiple renal arteries. Occasionally, the renal artery is sufficiently redundant to allow reimplantation—probably the simplest technique and one particularly appropriate to renal artery disease in children.

■ PREOPERATIVE PREPARATION

Antihypertensive medications are reduced during the preoperative period to the minimum necessary for blood pressure control. Frequently, patients who have required large doses of multiple medications for hypertension management need much less such management while hospitalized at bed rest. If continued therapy is required, vasodilators (e.g., amlodipine) and selective β-adrenergic blocking agents (i.e., atenolol or metoprolol) are useful. Combination of these agents with general anesthesia has few adverse effects on hemodynamics. If an adult's diastolic blood pressure exceeds 120 mm Hg, it is essential that the operative treatment be postponed until the blood pressure is brought under control. In this instance, the combination of intravenous sodium nitroprusside and esmolol is administered in an intensive care setting with continuous intra-arterial blood pressure monitoring. Similarly, in the patient with significant heart disease, pulmonary artery wedge pressure, cardiac index, and oxygen delivery are monitored to maintain optimal cardiac performance before and after operation.

Certain measures are used in almost all renal artery operations. Mannitol is administered intravenously in 12.5-g doses early in the operation. Repeated doses are administered before and after periods of renal ischemia, up to a total dose of 1 gm per kilogram patient body weight. Just prior to renal artery cross-clamping, 100 units of heparin per kilogram body weight is given intravenously and systemic anticoagulation is verified with measurement of activated clotting time. Unless required for hemostasis, protamine is not routinely administered for reversal of heparin at the completion of the operation.

■ MOBILIZATION AND DISSECTION

A xiphoid-to-pubis midline abdominal incision is made for operative repair of atherosclerotic renal artery disease. The last 1 or 2 cm of the proximal incision is made so as to course to one side of the xiphoid to obtain full exposure of the upper abdominal aorta and renal branches. Some type of fixed mechanical retraction is also advantageous, particularly when combined aortorenal procedures are required. Otherwise, extended flank and subcostal incisions are reserved for unilateral fibrodysplastic lesions or splanchnorenal bypass.

When the supraceliac aorta is utilized as an inflow source for unilateral aortorenal bypass, an extended flank incision is useful. With the ipsilateral flank elevated, the incision extends from the opposite semilunar line into the flank bisecting the abdominal wall between the costal margin and iliac crest. A left or right visceral mobilization allows access to the renal vasculature and the aortic crus. The crus can be divided, and an extrapleural dissection of the descending thoracic aorta can provide access to the T9-T10 thoracic aorta for proximal control and anastomosis.[1,2]

When the midline xiphoid-to-pubis incision is used, the posterior peritoneum overlying the aorta is incised longitudinally and the duodenum is mobilized at the ligament of Treitz (Fig. 132-1). During this maneuver, it is important to identify visceral collaterals that course at this level. Finally, the duodenum is reflected to the patient's right to expose the left renal vein. Extending the posterior peritoneal incision to the left along the inferior border of the pancreas allows entry of an avascular plane posterior to the pancreas (see Fig. 132-1) to expose the entire left renal hilum. This exposure is of special importance when there are distal renal artery lesions to be managed (Fig. 132-2A). The left renal artery lies posterior to the left renal vein. In some cases, the vein can be retracted cephalad to expose the artery; in other cases, caudal retraction of the vein provides better access. Usually, the gonadal and adrenal veins, which enter the left renal vein, must be ligated and divided to facilitate exposure

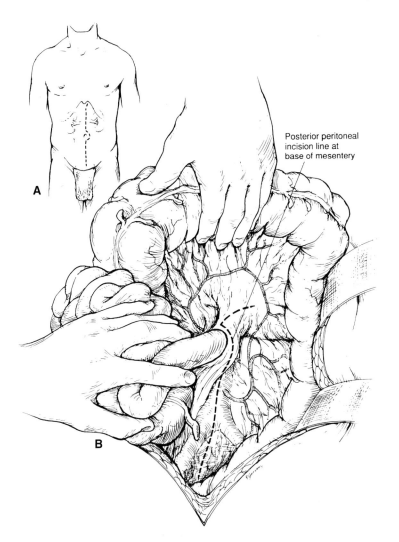

Posterior peritoneal
incision line at
base of mesentery

A

B

FIGURE 132-1 Exposure of the aorta and left renal hilum through the base of the mesentery. Extension of the posterior peritoneal incision to the left, along the inferior border of the pancreas, provides entry to an avascular plane behind the pancreas. This allows excellent exposure of the entire left renal hilum as well as the proximal right renal artery. (From Benjamin ME, Dean RH: Techniques in renal artery reconstruction: Part I. Ann Vasc Surg 10:306-314, 1996.)

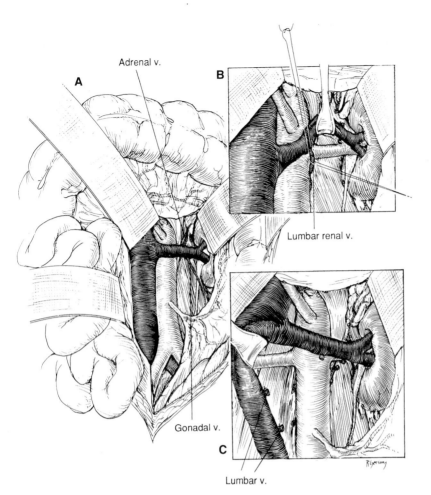

Adrenal v.

Lumbar renal v.

Gonadal v.

Lumbar v.

FIGURE 132-2 A, Exposure of the proximal right renal artery through the base of the mesentery. **B,** Mobilization of the left renal vein by ligation and division of the adrenal, gonadal, and lumbar renal veins allows exposure of the entire left renal artery to the hilum. **C,** Two pairs of lumbar vessels have been ligated and divided to allow retraction of the vena cava to the right, revealing adequate exposure of the proximal renal artery disease. (From Benjamin ME, Dean RH: Techniques in renal artery reconstruction: Part I. Ann Vasc Surg 10:306-314, 1996.)

of the distal artery. Frequently, a lumbar vein enters the posterior wall of the left renal vein, and it can be injured easily unless special care is taken (Fig. 132-2B). The proximal portion of the right renal artery can be exposed through the base of the mesentery by retraction of the left renal vein cephalad and the vena cava to the patient's right (Fig. 132-2C). However, the distal portion of the right renal artery is best exposed by mobilization of the duodenum and right colon medially; the right renal vein is mobilized and usually retracted cephalad in order to expose the artery.

Branch renal arteries on the right are exposed with colonic and duodenal mobilization. First, the hepatic flexure is mobilized at the peritoneal reflection (Fig. 132-3). With the right colon retracted medially and inferiorly, a Kocher maneuver mobilizes the duodenum and pancreatic head to expose the inferior vena cava and right renal vein (Fig. 132-4). Typically, the right renal artery is located just inferior to the accompanying vein, which can be retracted superiorly to provide best exposure. Though accessory vessels may arise from the aorta or iliac vessels at any level, all arterial branches coursing anterior to the vena cava should be considered accessory right renal branches and carefully preserved (Fig. 132-5).

When bilateral renal artery lesions are to be corrected and when correction of a right renal artery lesion or bilateral lesions is combined with aortic reconstruction, these exposure techniques can be modified. Aortic exposure may

be extended through mobilization of the base of the small bowel mesentery exposure to allow complete evisceration of the entire small bowel, right colon, and transverse colon. For this extended exposure, the posterior peritoneal incision begins with division of the ligament of Treitz and proceeds along the base of the mesentery to the cecum and then along the lateral gutter to the foramen of Winslow (Fig. 132-6A). The inferior border of the pancreas is fully mobilized to allow entry of a retropancreatic plane, thereby exposing the aorta to a point above the superior mesenteric artery. Through this modified exposure, simultaneous bilateral renal endarterectomies, aortorenal grafting, or renal artery attachment to the aortic graft can be performed with complete visualization of the entire aorta and its branches. Another useful technique for suprarenal aortic exposure is partial division of both diaphragmatic crura as they pass behind the renal arteries to their paravertebral attachment. This partial division of the crura allows the aorta above the superior mesenteric artery to be easily visualized and mobilized for suprarenal cross-clamping (Fig. 132-6B).

■ AORTORENAL BYPASS

Three types of materials are available for aortorenal bypass: autologous saphenous vein, autologous hypogastric artery, and synthetic prosthetic. The decision as to which graft is used depends on a number of factors. In most instances, we

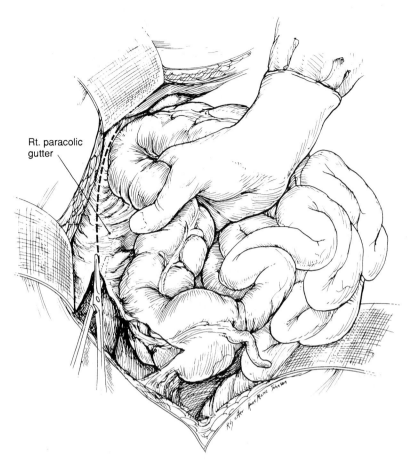

Rt. paracolic
gutter

FIGURE 132-3 Exposure of the distal right renal artery begins with mobilization of the ascending colon. (From Benjamin ME, Dean RH: Techniques in renal artery reconstruction: Part I. Ann Vasc Surg 10:306-314, 1996.)

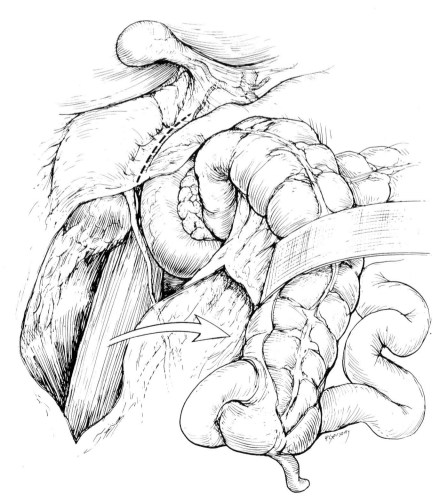

FIGURE 132-4 With the right colon mobilized medially, a Kocher maneuver exposes the right renal hilum. (From Benjamin ME, Dean RH: Techniques in renal artery reconstruction: Part I. Ann Vasc Surg 10:306-314, 1996.)

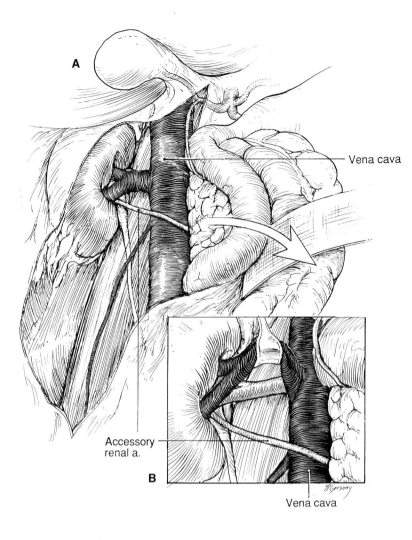

FIGURE 132-5 **A,** Not uncommonly, an accessory right renal artery arises from the anterior aorta and crosses anterior to the vena cava. **B,** The right renal vein is typically mobilized superiorly for exposure of the distal right renal artery. (From Benjamin ME, Dean RH: Techniques in renal artery reconstruction: Part I. Ann Vasc Surg 10:306-314, 1996.)

Vena cava

Accessory renal a.

B

Vena cava

use the saphenous vein preferentially. However, if the vein is small (less than 4 mm in diameter) or sclerotic, the hypogastric artery or a synthetic graft may be preferable. A 6-mm, thin-walled polytetrafluoroethylene graft is quite satisfactory when the distal renal artery is of sufficient caliber ($\geq$4 mm). Hypogastric artery autograft is preferred for aortorenal bypass in children when reimplantation is not possible.[3,4]

When an end-to-side renal artery bypass is performed, the anastomosis between the renal artery and the graft is performed first (Fig. 132-7A). Polymeric silicone (Silastic) vessel loops can be used to occlude the renal artery distally. This method of vessel occlusion has special application to renal reconstruction. In contrast to vascular clamps, these slings are essentially atraumatic to the delicate renal artery and avoid the presence of clamps in the operative field. Furthermore, when tension is applied to the slings, they lift the vessel out of the retroperitoneal soft tissue for better visualization. During creation of the anastomosis, the length of the arteriotomy should be at least three times the diameter of the smaller conduit to guard against late suture-line stenosis (Fig. 132-7B). A 6-0 or 7-0 monofilament polypropylene continuous suture is employed under loupe magnification.

After the renal artery anastomosis is completed, the occluding clamps and slings are removed from the artery,

and a small bulldog clamp is placed across the vein graft adjacent to the anastomosis. The aortic anastomosis is then performed (Fig. 132-7C), with removal of an ellipse of the anterolateral aortic wall. In most instances, an end-to-end anastomosis between the graft and distal renal artery provides a better reconstruction (Fig. 132-7D). In this regard, we routinely employ end-to-end renal artery anastomosis for the majority of renal revascularizations. In combined reconstructions, the proximal anastomosis is performed first and the distal renal anastomosis second to limit renal ischemia. Regardless of the type of distal anastomosis, the proximal aortorenal anastomosis is best performed after excision of an ellipse of aortic wall. This is especially important when the aorta is relatively inflexible owing to atherosclerotic involvement. A 5.2-mm aortic punch applied two to three times creates a very satisfactory ellipse in most instances.

■ THROMBOENDARTERECTOMY

In cases of ostial atherosclerosis of both renal artery origins, simultaneous bilateral endarterectomies may be the most suitable procedure. Endarterectomy may be either transaortic or transrenal. In the latter instance, the aortotomy is made transversely and is carried across the aorta and into the renal artery to a point beyond the visible atheromatous

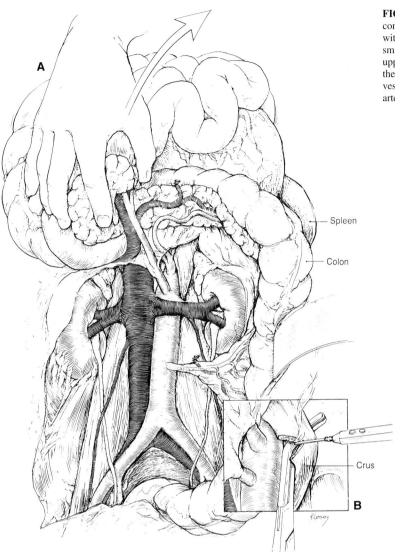

A

Spleen

Colon

Crus

B

FIGURE 132-6 A, For bilateral renal artery reconstruction, combined with aortic repair, extended exposure can be obtained with mobilization of the cecum and ascending colon. The entire small bowel and right colon are then mobilized to the right upper quadrant and placed on to the chest wall. B, Division of the diaphragmatic crus exposes the origin of the mesenteric vessels. (From Benjamin ME, Dean RH: Techniques in renal artery reconstruction: Part I. Ann Vasc Surg 10:306-314, 1996.)

disease (Fig. 132-8). With this method, the distal endarterectomy can be assessed and tacked down with mattress sutures under direct vision if necessary. After completion of the endarterectomy, the arteriotomy is closed. In most patients, this closure is performed with a synthetic patch to ensure that the proximal renal artery is widely patent.

For the majority of renal endarterectomies, the transaortic technique is used. The transaortic method is particularly applicable in patients with multiple renal arteries that demonstrate ostial disease. In this instance, all visible and palpable renal artery atheromas should end within one centimeter of their aortic origin. Transaortic endarterectomy is performed through a longitudinal aortotomy with sleeve endarterectomy of the aorta and eversion endarterectomy of the renal arteries (Fig. 132-9). When combined aortic replacement is planned, the transaortic endarterectomy is performed through the transected aorta. When using the transaortic technique, the surgeon must mobilize the renal arteries extensively to allow eversion of the vessel into the aorta. This allows the distal endpoint to be completed under direct vision. When the aortic atheroma is divided flush with the adventitia, tacking sutures are not required.

Like thromboendarterectomy at all sites, the procedure is contraindicated by the presence of either preaneurysmal degeneration of the aorta or transmural calcification. The latter condition is subtle and can be missed unless careful attention is given to gentle palpation of the aorta. Aortic atheroma complicated by transmural calcification feels like fine-grade sandpaper on palpation. Endarterectomy in this setting is characterized by numerous sites of punctate bleeding after blood flow is restored.

■ RENAL ARTERY REIMPLANTATION

After the renal artery has been dissected from the surrounding retroperitoneal tissue, the vessel may be somewhat redundant. When the renal artery stenosis is orificial and there is sufficient vessel length, the renal artery can be transected and reimplanted into the aorta at a slightly lower level. The renal artery must be spatulated and a portion of the aortic wall removed, as in renal artery bypass (Fig. 132-10). This technique has particular application in children with orificial lesions in whom the need for graft material can be avoided; however, it is suitable for selected

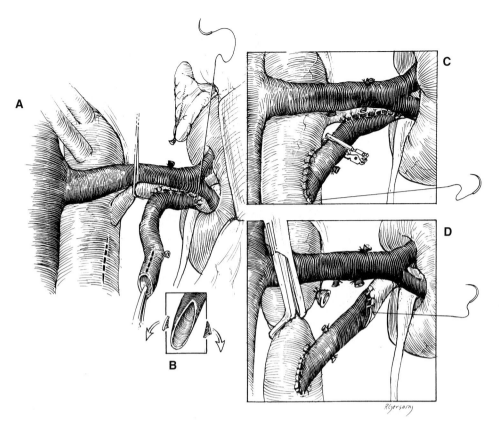

FIGURE 132-7 Technique for end-to-side (**A** to **C**) and end-to-end (**D**) aortorenal bypass grafting. The length of arteriotomy is at least three times the diameter of the artery to prevent recurrent anastomotic stenosis. For the anastomosis, 6-0 or 7-0 monofilament polypropylene sutures are made in continuous fashion under loupe magnification. If the apex sutures are placed too deeply or with excess advancement, stenosis can be created, posing a risk of late graft thrombosis. (From Benjamin ME, Dean RH: Techniques in renal artery reconstruction: Part I. Ann Vasc Surg 10:306-314, 1996.)

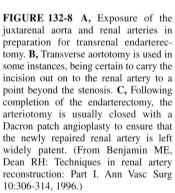

FIGURE 132-8 A, Exposure of the juxtarenal aorta and renal arteries in preparation for transrenal endarterectomy. **B,** Transverse aortotomy is used in some instances, being certain to carry the incision out on to the renal artery to a point beyond the stenosis. **C,** Following completion of the endarterectomy, the arteriotomy is usually closed with a Dacron patch angioplasty to ensure that the newly repaired renal artery is left widely patent. (From Benjamin ME, Dean RH: Techniques in renal artery reconstruction: Part I. Ann Vasc Surg 10:306-314, 1996.)

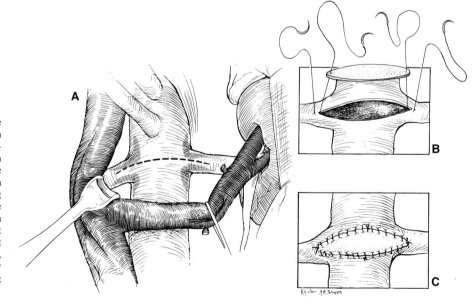

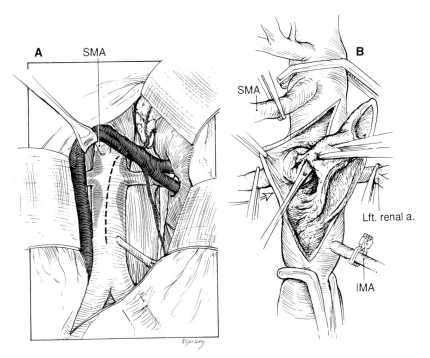

FIGURE 132-9 Exposure for a longitudinal transaortic endarterectomy is through the standard transperitoneal approach. The duodenum is mobilized from the aorta laterally in standard fashion or, for more complete exposure, the ascending colon and small bowel are mobilized. SMA, superior mesenteric artery. **A,** *Dotted line* shows the location of the aortotomy. **B,** The plaque is transected proximally and distally, and with eversion of the renal arteries, the atherosclerotic plaque is removed from each renal ostium. The aortotomy is typically closed with a running 4-0 or 5-0 polypropylene suture. IMA, inferior mesenteric artery. (From Benjamin ME, Dean RH: Techniques in renal artery reconstruction: Part I. Ann Vasc Surg 10:306-314, 1996.)

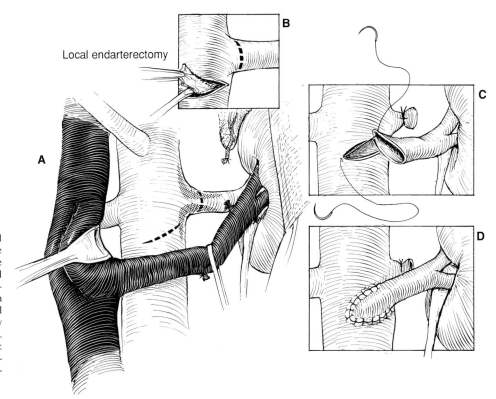

FIGURE 132-10 A, When the renal artery is redundant and the disease orificial, the vessel usually can be reimplanted at a lower level. Local endarterectomy (**B**) allows for placement of the monofilament suture in the aortic wall (**C**). The native renal artery is then ligated, proximally spatulated, and reimplanted (**D**). (From Benjamin ME, Dean RH: Techniques in renal artery reconstruction: Part II. Ann Vasc Surg 10:409-414, 1996.)

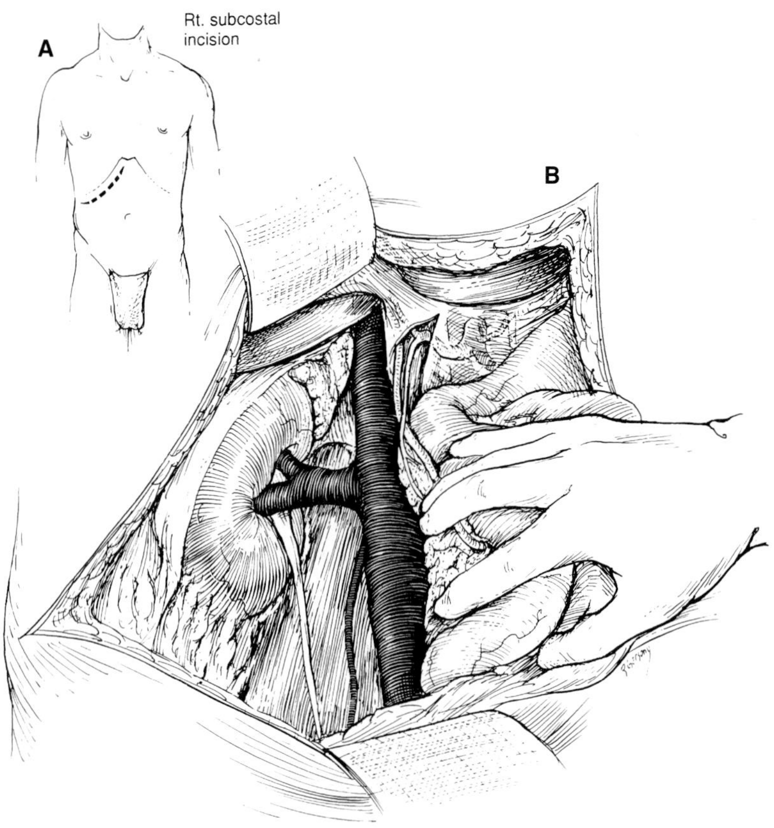

Rt. subcostal
incision

A

B

FIGURE 132-11 **A**, and **B**, In preparation for extra-anatomic reconstruction of the right renal artery, the common hepatic artery and proximal gastroduodenal artery are exposed in the hepatoduodenal ligament. Exposure would typically be through a right subcostal skin incision. (From Benjamin ME, Dean RH: Techniques in renal artery reconstruction: Part II. Ann Vasc Surg 10:409-414, 1996.)

atherosclerotic lesions as well.[5] When performed during combined aortic replacement in adults, the renal artery–graft anastomosis is usually performed first, after the proximal aortic anastomosis, and is followed by distal aortic reconstruction.

■   SPLANCHNORENAL BYPASS

Splanchnorenal bypass and other indirect revascularization procedures have received greater attention as an alternative method for renal revascularization.[6] We do not believe that these procedures demonstrate durability equivalent to that of direct aortorenal reconstructions, but they are useful in a carefully selected subgroup of patients at high risk for direct repair.[7]

Hepatorenal Bypass

A right subcostal incision is used to perform hepatorenal bypass.[6] The lesser omentum is incised to expose the hepatic artery both proximal and distal to the gastroduodenal artery (Fig. 132-11). Next, the descending duodenum is mobilized with a Kocher maneuver, the inferior vena cava is identified, the right renal vein is identified, and the right renal artery is encircled either cephalad or caudad to the renal vein.

A greater saphenous vein graft is usually used to construct the bypass. The hepatic artery anastomosis of the vein graft can be placed at the site of the amputated stump of the gastroduodenal artery; however, this vessel may serve as an important collateral vessel for intestinal perfusion. Therefore, the proximal anastomosis is usually made to the common hepatic artery. After completion of this anastomosis, the renal artery is transected and brought anterior to the vena cava for end-to-end anastomosis to the graft (Fig. 132-12).

Splenorenal Bypass

Splenorenal bypass can be performed through a midline or a left subcostal incision.[6,7] The posterior pancreas is mobilized by reflection of the inferior border cephalad. A retropancreatic plane is developed, and the splenic artery is mobilized from the left gastroepiploic artery to the level of its branches. The left renal artery is exposed cephalad to the left renal vein after division of the adrenal vein. After the splenic artery has been mobilized, it is divided distally, spatulated, and anastomosed end-to-end to the transected renal artery (Fig. 132-13).

■   EX VIVO RECONSTRUCTION

In part, operative strategy for renal artery repair is determined by the exposure required and the anticipated period of renal ischemia. When reconstruction can be accomplished with less than 40 minutes of ischemia, an in-situ repair is undertaken without special measures for renal preservation. When longer periods of ischemia are anticipated, one of two techniques for hypothermic preservation of the kidney are

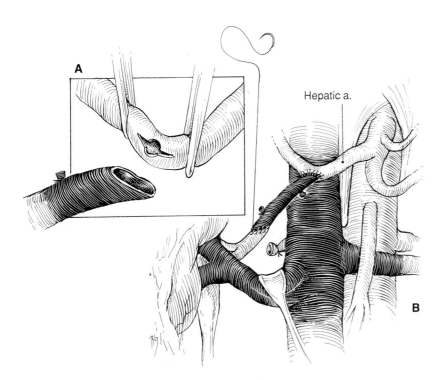

FIGURE 132-12 The reconstruction is completed using a saphenous vein interposition graft between the side of the hepatic artery (**A**) and the distal end of the transected right renal artery (**B**). (From Benjamin ME, Dean RH: Techniques in renal artery reconstruction: Part II. Ann Vasc Surg 10:409-414, 1996.)

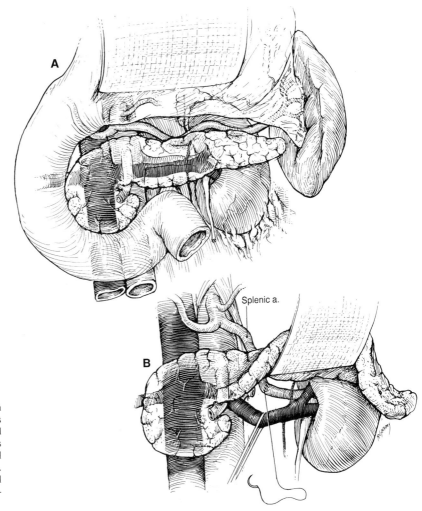

FIGURE 132-13 A, Exposure of the left renal hilum in preparation for splenorenal bypass. **B,** The pancreas has been mobilized along its inferior margin and retracted superiorly. The transected splenic artery is anastomosed end-to-end to the transected left renal artery. A splenectomy is not routinely performed. (From Benjamin ME, Dean RH: Techniques in renal artery reconstruction: Part II. Ann Vasc Surg 10:409-414, 1996.)

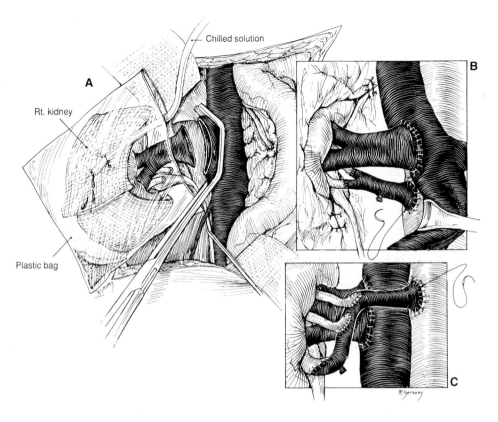

FIGURE 132-14 A, An ellipse of the vena cava containing the renal vein origin is excised by placement of a large partially occluding clamp. After ex vivo branch repair, the renal vein can then be reattached without risk of anastomotic stricture. **B,** The kidney is repositioned in its native bed after ex vivo repair. Gerota's fascia is reattached to provide stability to the replaced kidney. Arterial reconstruction can be accomplished via end-to-end anastomoses (as in **B**) or occasionally with a combination of end-to-end and end-to-side anastomoses (**C**). (From Benjamin ME, Dean RH: Techniques in renal artery reconstruction: Part II. Ann Vasc Surg 10:409-414, 1996.)

considered—renal mobilization without renal vein transection and ex vivo repair with orthotopic replacement in the renal fossa.[8]

Ex vivo management is necessary when extensive exposure is required for prolonged periods. Patients in whom extensive and prolonged exposure is needed are those with fibromuscular dysplasia and aneurysms or stenoses involving renal artery branches; with renal artery dissection and branch occlusion; with congenital arteriovenous fistulae of renal artery branches requiring partial resection; and with failure of a prior reconstruction to the distal renal artery. Several methods of ex vivo hypothermic perfusion and reconstruction are available. A midline xiphoid-to-pubic incision is used for most renovascular procedures and is preferred when autotransplantation of the reconstructed kidney or combined aortic reconstructions are to be performed. When isolated branch renal repair is planned with orthotopic replacement, an extended flank incision is made parallel to the lower rib margin and carried to the posterior axillary line, as described earlier. This latter method is our preferred approach for ex vivo reconstructions. The ureter is always mobilized to the pelvic brim. An elastic sling is placed around the ureter to prevent perfusion from ureteric collaterals and subsequent renal rewarming.

Gerota's fascia is opened with a cruciate incision, and the kidney is completely mobilized and the renal vessels divided (Fig. 132-14). The kidney is placed in a plastic sling and perfused with a chilled renal preservation solution. Continuous perfusion during the period of total renal ischemia is possible with perfusion pump systems and may be superior for prolonged renal preservation.[9] However,

simple intermittent flushing with a chilled preservation solution provides equal protection during the shorter periods (2 to 3 hours) required for ex vivo dissection and branch renal artery reconstructions. For this technique, we refrigerate the preservative overnight, add other components (Table 132-1) immediately before use to make up a liter of solution, and hang the chilled (5° to 10° C) solution at a height of at least 2 m. Immediately after the kidney is removed from the renal fossa, 300 to 500 mL of solution is flushed through the kidney until the venous effluent is

Table 132-1	Solution for Cold Perfusion Preservation of the Kidney*
Composition (gm/L):	
K_2HPO_4	7.4
KH_2PO_4	2.04
KCl	1.12
$NaHCO_3$	0.84
Ionic concentration (mEq/L):	
Potassium	115
Sodium	10
Phosphate (HPO_4^-)	85
Phosphate ($H_2PO_4^-$)	15
Chlorideate	15
Bicarbonate	10
Additives at time of use to 930 mL of solution:	
50% dextrose	70 mL
Sodium heparin	2000 units

*Electrolyte solution for kidney preservation supplied by Travenol Labs, Inc., Deerfield, IL.

clear. As each anastomosis is completed, the kidney is perfused with 150 to 200 mL more solution. In addition to maintaining satisfactory hypothermia, periodic perfusion demonstrates suture line leaks that are repaired prior to reimplantation.

As a supplement to perfusion, surface hypothermia is used during ex vivo renal artery reconstruction. The kidney is placed in ice slush, and liter bottles of chilled normal saline solution are used to create a constant drip of chilled saline. With this technique, renal core temperatures are maintained at 10° C or below throughout the period of reconstruction. Even though it is an accepted method after ex vivo reconstruction, autotransplantation to the iliac fossa is unnecessary for most ex vivo reconstructions. This technique was adopted from renal transplant surgery. Reduction in the magnitude of the operative exposure, manual palpation of the transplanted kidney, and ease of removal when treatment of rejection has failed are all practical reasons for placing the transplanted kidney into the recipient's iliac fossa. However, none of these advantages applies in the patient requiring autogenous ex vivo reconstruction. In this latter patient group, the factors most important relate to those improving the long-term patency after renal artery repair.

Because many ex vivo procedures are performed in relatively young patients, the durability of the operation must be measured in terms of decades. For this reason, attachment of the kidney to the iliac arterial system within or below sites that are susceptible to subsequent atherosclerosis subjects the repaired vessels to disease that may threaten their long-term patency. Moreover, subsequent management of peripheral vascular disease may be complicated by the presence of the autotransplanted kidney. Finally, if the kidney is replaced in the renal fossa and the renal artery graft is properly attached to the aorta at a proximal infrarenal site, the result should mimic that of the standard aortorenal bypass and, thus, should carry a high probability of technical success and long-term durability.

■ INTRAOPERATIVE ASSESSMENT

Provided that the best method of reconstruction is chosen for renal artery repair, the short course and high blood flow rates characteristic of renal reconstruction favor patency. Consequently, flawless technical repair plays a dominant role in determining postoperative success.[10-12] The negative impact of technical errors unrecognized at operation is implied by the fact that we have observed no late thromboses of renovascular reconstructions in arteries that were free of disease after 1 year.[13]

Intraoperative assessment of most arterial reconstructions has been made with intraoperative angiography.[14,15] This method has serious limitations, however, when applied to upper aortic and branch aortic reconstruction. Angiography provides static images and provides evaluation of anatomy in only one projection.[16,17] In addition, arteriolar vasospasm in response to injection of contrast agent may falsely suggest distal vascular occlusion. Finally, coexisting renal insufficiency is present in 75% of patients with atherosclerotic renovascular disease encountered in contemporary practice, increasing the risk of postoperative contrast nephropathy.

Intraoperative Duplex Ultrasonography

These risks and the inherent limitations of completion angiography are not demonstrated by intraoperative duplex ultrasonography.[18] Because the ultrasound probe can be placed immediately adjacent to the vascular repair, high carrying frequencies may be used to provide excellent B-scan detail sensitive to 1.0-mm anatomic defects. Once imaged, the defects can be viewed in a multitude of projections during conditions of uninterrupted, pulsatile blood flow. In addition to excellent anatomic detail, important hemodynamic information is obtained from the spectral analysis of the Doppler-shifted signal proximal and distal to the imaged defect.[18] Freedom from static projections, the absence of potentially nephrotoxic contrast material, and the hemodynamic data provided by Doppler spectral analysis make duplex scanning a very useful intraoperative method to assess both renovascular and mesenteric repairs.

In order to realize these advantages of intraoperative duplex scanning, close cooperation between the vascular surgeon and the vascular technologist is required for accurate intraoperative assessment. Although the surgeon is responsible for manipulating the probe head to acquire optimal B-scan images of the vascular repair at likely sites of technical error, proper power and time gain adjustments are best made by an experienced technologist. Close cooperation is likewise required to obtain complete pulse-Doppler sampling associated with abnormalities on B-scan. While the surgeon images areas of interest at an optimal insonating angle, the technologist sets the Doppler sample's depth and volume and estimates blood flow velocities from the Doppler spectrum analyzer. Finally, the participation of the vascular technologist during intraoperative assessment enhances his or her ability to perform satisfactory surveillance duplex scanning during follow-up. Intraoperative duplex scanning assessment and the routine participation of a vascular technologist have yielded a scan time of 5 to 10 minutes and a 98% study completion rate.[18,19]

Currently, we use a 10/5.0 MHz compact linear array probe with Doppler color flow designed specifically for intraoperative assessment. The probe is placed within a sterile sheath with a latex tip containing sterile gel. After the operative field is flooded with warm saline, B-scan images are first obtained in longitudinal projection. Care is taken to image the entire upper abdominal aorta and renal artery origins along the entire length of the repair. All defects seen in longitudinal projection are imaged in transverse projection to confirm their anatomic presence and to estimate associated luminal narrowing. Doppler samples are then obtained just proximal and distal to imaged lesions in longitudinal projection, so as to determine their potential contribution to flow disturbance. Our criteria for major B-scan defects associated with greater than 60% diameter-reducing stenosis or occlusion have been validated in a canine model of graded renal artery stenosis (Table 132-2).[18] They have also proved valid in a retrospective study when preoperative radiographic studies were compared with intraoperative duplex scans obtained prior to surgical repair.[19]

In the first validity analysis of intraoperative duplex scanning, we used the modality to assess 57 renovascular reconstructions in 35 patients who underwent unilateral (13 patients) or bilateral (22 patients) repair.[18] Direct aortorenal methods of reconstruction included renal artery bypass

Table 132-2	Intraoperative Doppler Velocity Criteria for Renal Artery Repair	
B-SCAN DEFECT	**DOPPLER CRITERIA**
Minor: stenosis reduces diameter by <60%	PSV from entire artery <1.8 m/sec
Major: stenosis reduces diameter by ≥60%	Focal PSV ≥1.8 m/sec and distal turbulent waveform
Occlusion	No Doppler-shifted signal from renal artery B-scan image
Inadequate study	Failure to obtain Doppler samples from entire arterial repair

PSV, peak systolic velocity.

Modified from Hansen KJ, O'Neill EA, Reavis SW, et al: Intraoperative duplex sonography during renal artery reconstruction. J Vasc Surg 14:364-374, 1991.

(RAB) in 29 patients (20 saphenous vein, 5 polytetrafluoroethylene [PTFE], 4 polyethylene [Dacron]), reimplantation in 7 repairs, transrenal thromboendarterectomy (TEA) with PTFE patch angioplasty in 13 repairs, and transaortic TEA in 8 repairs. Branch renal artery repair was performed in 6 cases (5 in vivo, 1 ex vivo), and combined aortic replacement in 14.

Average time for intraoperative duplex scanning was 4.5 minutes, and studies provided complete B-scan and Doppler information in 56 of 57 repairs (98%).[18] Duplex ultrasonography findings were considered normal in 44 repairs (77%), but B-scan defects were present in 13 (23%). Six of these B-scan defects (11%) had Doppler spectra with focal increases in peak systolic velocity (PSV) of 1.8 m/sec or more with post-stenotic turbulence. These defects were defined as major, and each underwent immediate operative revision (Fig. 132-15); in each case, a significant defect was discovered during revision and corrected. Seven B-scan defects without Doppler spectral abnormality were defined as minor and were not repaired.

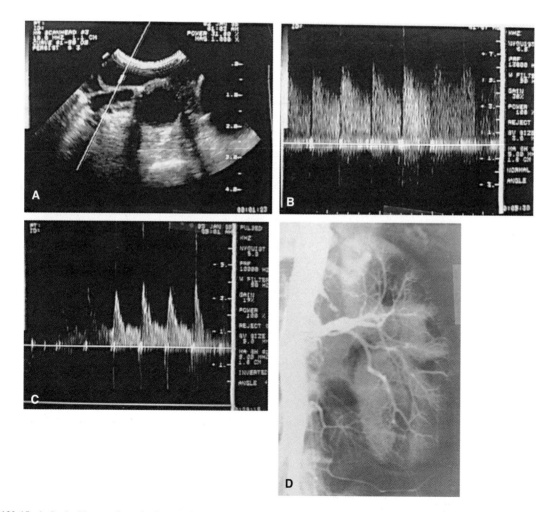

FIGURE 132-15 A, Sagittal image of a major B-scan defect. **B,** This intimal flap at the proximal anastomosis demonstrated a focal increase in renal artery peak systolic velocity (RA-PSV), which was 3.1 m/sec. **C,** After revision, RA-PSV was decreased to 1.1 m/sec. **D,** Follow-up angiogram demonstrated a widely patent anastomosis. This patient was cured of hypertension. (From Hansen KJ, O'Neil EA, Reavis SW, et al: Intraoperative duplex sonography during renal artery reconstruction. J Vasc Surg 14:364-374, 1991.)

At a mean follow-up of 12.4 months, the status of 55 renal artery reconstructions in 34 patients was determined by either surface renal duplex scanning or renal angiography. Forty-two of 43 renal artery repairs with normal intraoperative duplex scanning findings and 6 of 6 repairs with minor B-scan defects were patent and free of critical stenosis. Of the 6 revisions prompted by abnormal B-scan and Doppler criteria for a major defect, 4 were patent without stenosis, 1 showed restenosis, and 1 was occluded. In the cases of restenosis and occlusion, duplex scanning was not repeated after revision. With application of these criteria, intraoperative duplex scanning was 86% sensitive and 100% specific for technical defects associated with postoperative stenosis and occlusion of direct aortorenal repairs. These anatomic results were supported by the clinical response to operation. Eighty-six percent of hypertensive patients demonstrated a favorable blood pressure response, whereas 63% of patients with renal insufficiency demonstrated improved renal function after surgery.

Since this initial evaluation, we have examined the results of intraoperative duplex scanning in 249 renal artery repairs with anatomic follow-up evaluation.[19] Complete B-scan and Doppler information was obtained in 241 of 249 renal artery repairs. Intraoperative assessment was normal in 157, but 84 (35%) repairs demonstrated one or more B-scan defects. Twenty-five of the defects (10%) had focal increases in PSV higher than 1.8 m/sec with turbulent distal waveform and were therefore defined as major. Each major B-scan defect prompted immediate operative revision, and in each case, a significant defect was discovered. B-scan defects defined as minor were not repaired. At 12-month follow-up, renal artery patency free of critical stenosis was demonstrated in 97% of patients with normal duplex scanning studies, 100% of those with minor B-scan defects, and 88% of those with revised major B-scan defects, providing an overall patency rate of 97%. Of the 5 repair failures with normal intraoperative B-scan findings, 3 had occurred after ex vivo branch renal artery repair.

Designation of B-scan defects according to Doppler velocity criteria provides accurate information to guide decisions regarding intraoperative revision. However, special circumstances deserve comment. Unlike surface duplex scanning, in which the Doppler sample volume is large relative to the renal artery diameter, a small Doppler sample volume can be accurately positioned within mid-center stream flow. Despite a small, centered Doppler sample, renal artery repairs demonstrate at least moderate spectral broadening. Transaortic endarterectomy gives the audible Doppler signal an oscillating characteristic, which is normal and is not associated with anatomic defects. In addition, an occasional intraoperative study demonstrates PSVs that exceed criteria for critical stenosis even though there is no anatomic defect. In these cases, the PSVs are elevated uniformly throughout the repair and there is no focal velocity change and no distal turbulent waveform. This scenario is most commonly encountered immediately after renal artery reconstruction for nonatherosclerotic renovascular disease. Moreover, renovascular repair to a solitary kidney frequently demonstrates increased velocities throughout. Finally, an increase in PSV is observed in

transition from the main renal artery to the segmental renal vessels after branch renal artery repair, but no distal turbulent waveform is observed.

In addition to these systolic spectral abnormalities, changes may be observed in the diastolic features of the Doppler spectra in the absence of technical error. Abnormal diastolic spectra may be observed after revascularization of chronic renal ischemia. Reflecting increased vascular resistance in response to reperfusion, these spectra demonstrate abbreviated systolic flow, short systolic acceleration times, and decreased diastolic flow. This picture can mimic distal embolic catastrophe, but it is distinguished from embolization by spectral changes observed after intraarterial administration of a vasodilator. Given intra-arterially at the site of repair, 60 mg of papaverine relieves this reactive vasospasm. In this instance, the Doppler spectral signature characteristic for the renal artery usually appears within 5 minutes.

Finally, some B-scan abnormalities observed in conjunction with renal endarterectomy deserve comment. Infrequently, an irregular B-scan abnormality evolves during performance of a completion scan. This B-scan finding may be associated with either increased or decreased (blunted) PSVs but reflects formation of intra-arterial thrombus. Unlike acute venous thrombus, which is usually echolucent, acute arterial thrombus is characterized by irregular echogenic material. Regardless of the associated PSV estimates, the endarterectomy site is reopened and revised immediately. Lastly, a B-scan defect otherwise minor according to PSV criteria may be revised because of its location and appearance. A mobile flap greater than 2 mm in length at the distal endpoint of an endarterectomy site is usually revised on the basis of its mere presence and the potential for dissection or thrombosis.

■ ANATOMIC RESULTS OF OPERATIVE MANAGEMENT

The cumulative operative experience from January 1987 through June 1997 at our center is summarized in Table 132-3.[20] Over this 10.5-year period, 720 renovascular reconstructions and 57 primary nephrectomies were performed in 534 patients, with application of the management

Table 132-3	Summary of Operative Management (n = 534 patients)		
Total renal reconstructions:			720
Aortorenal bypass:		445	
Vein		288	
Polytetrafluoroethylene		127	
Polyester (Dacron)		19	
Hypogastric artery:		11	
Ex vivo	33		
Reimplantation		52	
Thromboendarterectomy		223	
Total nephrectomies		57	
Total kidneys operated			777

From Hansen KJ, Deitch JA, Oskin TC: Renal artery repair: Consequence of operative failures. Ann Surg 227:678-690, 1998.

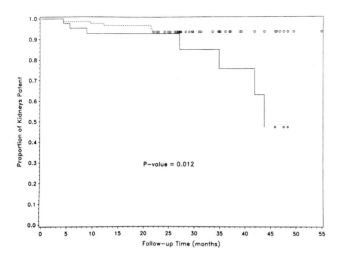

FIGURE 132-16 Comparison of estimated patency of direct aortorenal repair (*solid line*) with development of significant disease in unrepaired native renal arteries (*broken line*). (From Hansen KJ, Deitch JS, Oskin TC, et al: Renal artery repair: Consequence of operative failures. Ann Surg 227:678-690, 1998.)

philosophy and operative techniques described. Postoperative stenosis or thrombosis occurred in 3.3% of renal artery repairs, resulting in recurrent hypertension and declining renal function in 3.7% of patients at mean follow-up of 36 months. However, because complete anatomic failure of repair (i.e., thrombosis) may result in blood pressure benefit equivalent to nephrectomy, anatomic failure is potentially more common than the rate of recurrent hypertension or reoperation.[18] To examine our rate of anatomic failure, we reviewed the results of 227 postoperative duplex studies in 128 consecutive patients.[20] Over a mean follow-up of 22 months, 6 of 177 operative renal artery repairs (3.4%) underwent stenosis, whereas hemodynamically significant disease developed in 7 of 59 contralateral, unoperated arteries (11.9%). Overall, the incidence of follow-up stenosis was significantly greater for unoperated renal arteries than for surgical repairs (Fig. 132-16; *P* = .020). Compared with other reports describing failure of renovascular repair,[11,21,22] these results support the techniques of operative management described.

■ REFERENCES

1. Fry RE, Fry WJ: Suprailiac aortorenal bypass with saphenous vein for renovascular hypertrophy. Surg Gynecol Obstet 168:181-182, 1989.
2. Novick AL: Use of the thoracic aorta for renal arterial reconstruction. J Vasc Surg 19:605-609, 1994.
3. Dean RH, Benjamin ME, Hansen KJ: Surgical management of renovascular hypertension. Curr Probl Surg 34:209-308, 1997.
4. Stoney RJ, Olofsson PA: Aortorenal arterial autografts: The last two decades. Ann Vasc Surg 2:169-173, 1988.
5. Fry WJ, Ernst CB, Stanley JC, et al: Renovascular hypertension in the pediatric patient. Arch Surg 107:692-698, 1973.
6. Moncure AC, Brewster DC, Darling RC, et al: Use of the splenic and hepatic arteries for renal revascularization. J Vasc Surg 3:196-203, 1986.
7. Fergany A, Kolettis P, Novick AL: The contemporary role of extra-anatomic surgical renal revascularization in patients with atherosclerotic renal artery disease. J Urol 153:1798-1802, 1995.
8. Dean RH, Meacham PW, Weaver FA: Ex vivo renal artery reconstructions: Indications and techniques. J Vasc Surg 49:546-552, 1986.
9. Salvatierra O Jr, Olcott C IV, Stoney RJ: Ex vivo renal artery reconstruction using perfusion preservation. J Urol 119:16-19, 1978.
10. Dean RH, Wilson JP, Burko H, et al: Saphenous vein aortorenal bypass grafts: Serial angiographic study. Ann Surg 180:469-478, 1974.
11. Stanley JC, Ernest CB, Fry WJ: Fate of 100 aortorenal vein grafts: Characteristics of late graft expansion, aneurysmal dilatation, and stenosis. Surgery 74:931-944, 1973.
12. Dean RH: Complications of renal revascularization. In Bernhard VM, Towne JB (eds): Complications in Vascular Surgery, 2nd ed. Orlando, FL, Grune & Stratton, 1985, p 229-246.
13. Dean RH, Krueger TC, Whiteneck JM, et al: Operative management of renovascular hypertension. J Vasc Surg 1:234-242, 1984.
14. Plecha FR, Pories WJ: Intraoperative angiography in the immediate assessment of arterial reconstruction. Arch Surg 105:902-907, 1972.
15. Courbier R, Jausseran JM, Reggi M: Detection complications of direct arterial surgery. Arch Surg 112:1115-1118, 1977.
16. Okuhn SP, Reilly LM, Bennett JR, et al: Intraoperative assessment of renal and visceral artery reconstruction: The role of duplex scanning and spectral analysis. J Vasc Surg 5:137-147, 1987.
17. Goldstone J: Intraoperative assessment of renal and visceral arterial reconstruction using Doppler and duplex imaging. In Ernst CB, Stanley JC (eds): Current Therapy in Vascular Surgery, 2nd ed. Philadelphia, BC Decker, 1991, p 872.
18. Hansen KJ, O'Neil EA, Reavis SW, et al: Intraoperative duplex sonography during renal artery reconstruction. J Vasc Surg 14:364-374, 1991.
19. Hansen KJ, Reavis SW, Dean RH: Duplex scanning in renovascular disease. Geriatr Nephrol Urol 6:89, 1996.
20. Hansen KJ, Deitch JA, Oskin TC: Renal artery repair: Consequence of operative failures. Ann Surg 227:678-690, 1998.
21. Stanley JC, Whitehouse WM, Zelenock GB, et al: Reoperation for complications of renal artery reconstructive surgery undertaken for treatment of renovascular hypertension. J Vasc Surg 2:133-144, 1985.
22. Svetkey LP, Kadir S, Dunnick NR, et al: Similar prevalence of renovascular hypertension in selected blacks and whites. Hypertension 17:678-683, 1991.

Renal Artery Aneurysms and Arteriovenous Fistulae

133

KEITH D. CALLIGARO, MD
MATTHEW J. DOUGHERTY, MD

Renal artery aneurysms and renal arteriovenous fistulae (AVFs) are rare entities, but they are encountered frequently enough that vascular surgeons need to be well acquainted with the natural history, diagnosis, and management of these lesions. Endovascular interventions represent the newest advances for treatment of some of these lesions. Aneurysms and AVFs are discussed separately because they rarely occur concomitantly and their clinical course and treatment differ.

■ RENAL ARTERY ANEURYSMS

Even in referral centers, few vascular surgeons have extensive experience with the clinical management of renal artery aneurysms.[57,87] Autopsy studies have revealed an incidence of renal artery aneurysms of 0.01% to 0.09%, which is probably an underestimation because these lesions may be small, intrarenal, or not specifically sought.[11,57] In two studies, renal artery aneurysms were documented in 0.73% (7/965) to 0.97% (83/8525) of arteriograms.[23,95] Conversely, these two reports may overestimate the prevalence of these lesions. If renal artery aneurysms were present in almost 1% of patients undergoing abdominal aortography, vascular surgeons would be expected to have a far greater experience diagnosing and treating these lesions than has been reported to date. At Pennsylvania Hospital in Philadelphia, we have documented renal artery aneurysms in only 0.12% (1/845) of consecutive abdominal aortograms performed at our hospital. Renal artery aneurysms are bilateral in about 10% of cases.[57,95] If fibrodysplastic cases are omitted, there is an equal incidence in males and females.[14,57,87]

Because of the lack of controlled data, controversy persists regarding the indications for repair of asymptomatic renal artery aneurysms. The optimal method of repair is also controversial. Types of renal artery aneurysms, their clinical manifestations, indications for repair, and techniques of both traditional surgical and newer endovascular interventions are reviewed.

Types of Renal Artery Aneurysms

Types of renal artery aneurysms include (1) true (saccular and fusiform); (2) false; (3) dissecting; and (4) intrarenal.

True Aneurysms

More than 90% of true renal artery aneurysms are extraparenchymal.[25,53,87,88] Peak incidence occurs in patients between the ages of 40 and 60 years. Stanley and colleagues have suggested that true aneurysms are probably due to either atherosclerosis or a congenital defect.[87,88] Although arteriosclerotic changes have been identified in most aneurysms in patients with multiple lesions, this is not a uniform finding, suggesting that arteriosclerosis may not be the most important factor in the genesis of renal artery aneurysms. These aneurysms are more likely due to a congenital medial degenerative process with weakness of the elastic lamina.[14,88] Lesions typically occur at the primary or secondary renal artery bifurcations and are rarely confined only to the main trunk of the renal artery. As discussed later, this finding makes surgical repair challenging.

Approximately 75% of true renal artery aneurysms are saccular. This type of renal artery aneurysm is usually less than 5 cm in diameter,[72] although some have been reported as large as 9 cm.[7,22,53] Saccular aneurysms occur almost invariably at the main renal artery bifurcation.[14] Fusiform aneurysms are usually associated with atherosclerosis or are a result of a post-stenotic dilation distal to a hemodynamically significant renal artery stenosis, the latter occurring due to atherosclerosis or fibromuscular disease.[14,25,73,74] Fusiform aneurysms are generally less than 2 cm in diameter and usually affect the main renal artery trunk.[25]

Arterial fibrodysplasia is often a direct contributor to the development of aneurysm.[87,88] Medial fibroplasia is typically associated with multiple stenoses and post-stenotic dilation of the distal two thirds of the renal artery. Renal artery aneurysms in association with fibromuscular dysplasia are generally only a few millimeters in diameter. The typical angiographic appearance of a renal artery involved with medial fibroplasia is a "string of beads." Larger aneurysms can also occur, however, and in one study renal artery macroaneurysms were found in 9.2% of adults with fibromuscular dysplasia.[88]

A rare cause of renal artery aneurysms is Ehlers-Danlos syndrome. This disorder is associated with extreme arterial fragility and spontaneous rupture.[58]

False Aneurysms

False aneurysms of the renal artery arise from blunt or penetrating trauma and occasionally from iatrogenic causes such as renal artery catheterization. They represent contained ruptures of the renal artery, with only inflammatory and fibrous tissue encasing the leak.

Dissections

Spontaneous dissections confined to the renal artery that do not arise from the adjacent aorta are rare; however, primary dissections causing pseudoaneurysms affect the renal arteries more than any other peripheral artery.[27,31,42,56,73,87] Poutasse[73] and Stanley and coworkers[88] reported that 14 of 57 cases of renal artery aneurysms were due to spontaneous dissections. An intimal defect of the renal artery due to atherosclerosis is probably the underlying cause of spontaneous renal artery dissections causing aneurysms, along with dysplastic renovascular disease and trauma.[25] The incidence of dissection in patients with fibrodysplastic renal arteries ranges from 0.5% to 9.0%.[27,87] Dissection often extends into the branches of the renal artery and may pose particularly challenging reconstruction problems.

Traumatic renal artery dissections can occur secondary to blunt abdominal trauma or catheter-induced injury. Blunt trauma accounts for the higher prevalence of dissection in men and is more likely to result in right-sided injuries, possibly because of ptosis-related physical stresses affecting the renal pedicle.[87] Blunt trauma can cause renal artery dissections by either severe stretching of the artery with fracture of the intima or compression of the artery against the vertebra. Renal artery dissection caused by guide wires or catheters can occur but is rare, being observed in only 4 of 2200 selective renal artery arteriograms.[27]

Intrarenal Aneurysms

Fewer than 10% of renal artery aneurysms are intraparenchymal.[53,88] Intrarenal aneurysms are usually multiple and may be congenital, associated with collagen vascular disease, or post-traumatic. They may be associated with AVFs, possibly as a result of spontaneous closure of a fistula. Intrarenal aneurysms can occur with polyarteritis nodosa and are usually in the renal cortex.[34,85]

Clinical Manifestations

Most renal artery aneurysms are asymptomatic and found on imaging studies such as arteriography, ultrasonography, and computed tomography (CT) performed to investigate other intra-abdominal pathology.[22,35,87] Magnetic resonance (MR) angiography can also delineate renal artery aneurysms.[92] Clinical manifestations of renal artery aneurysms include rupture, hypertension, pain, and hematuria. In one series, only 11 (34%) of 32 patients who underwent surgery for renal artery aneurysms presented with symptoms.[22]

Rupture

The most dreaded complication of renal artery aneurysm is rupture. Patients with this complication present with manifestations similar to other intra-abdominal arterial ruptures, including syncope, abdominal or flank pain, abdominal distention, and possibly a pulsatile mass. Occasionally, an intact renal artery aneurysm presents with abdominal or flank pain, discomfort, or fullness, symptoms that are presumed to reflect acute aneurysmal expansion.

Hypertension

Renal artery aneurysms may be associated with severe hypertension. Macroaneurysms were found in 2.5% of arteriograms performed for evaluation of hypertension.[88]

Renal artery aneurysms may cause renovascular hypertension by distal embolization with segmental hypoperfusion and renin-mediated vasoconstriction and fluid retention. Compression of an adjacent renal artery branch or luminal stenosis due to extensive thrombus may also lead to renin-mediated hypertension. Frequently there is a significant renal artery stenosis causing a post-stenotic fusiform aneurysm, and the renal artery stenosis is responsible for the hypertension. Saccular and intrarenal aneurysms are much less likely to be associated with hypertension.

Dissection

Patients with renal artery aneurysms caused by dissection may present with severe flank pain, hematuria, or acute hypertension, although most dissections are asymptomatic. An intravenous pyelogram may reveal nonfunction or diminished function of the involved kidney but is rarely the first test ordered unless urolithiasis is considered likely to be causing the symptoms. Contrast or MR angiography is essential to detect dissection.

Hematuria

Intrarenal aneurysms may rupture into calices.[11] In addition to pain, microscopic or gross hematuria may occur.

Collecting System Obstruction

Renal artery aneurysms rarely cause obstruction of the collecting system. Although main renal artery aneurysms may be large, they are usually not near enough to the caliceal system to cause obstruction. Intrarenal aneurysms tend to be too small to cause significant collecting duct obstruction. However, a 9-cm renal artery aneurysm has been documented to cause hydronephrosis.[7]

Indications for Intervention

Indications to repair a renal artery aneurysm are related to (1) the risk of rupture, (2) hypertension, (3) acute dissection, and (4) other clinical symptoms.

Rupture

Rupture of a renal artery aneurysm is an indication for emergency intervention, as with virtually any arterial aneurysm. Probably fewer than 3% of renal artery aneurysms rupture.[87,88] This complication is associated with a mortality rate of approximately 10% in males and nonpregnant females.[30,37,87,88] In a hemodynamically stable patient, an emergent CT scan may reveal the pathology and allow the surgeon to further plan the operative repair. However, if a hypotensive elderly patient presents to the emergency department with abdominal pain and a tender, distended abdomen and does not respond to fluid resuscitation, emergency exploration for a presumptive diagnosis of a ruptured abdominal aneurysm may be indicated.

Prevention of rupture is the most common indication for intervention of an asymptomatic renal artery aneurysm. Traditionally, repair of renal artery aneurysms has been recommended for aneurysms greater than 2.0 cm in diameter.[25,74] Likelihood of rupture of a renal artery aneurysm is controversial because the natural history has not been delineated. Most reports are retrospective reviews of incidentally discovered intact renal artery aneurysms in autopsy series or collections of ruptured aneurysms without full details concerning their size and presence or absence of calcification. Harrow and Sloane reported one of the highest rates of rupture of renal artery aneurysms, noting 14 ruptures in 100 cases.[33] In another series of 126 renal artery aneurysms, 6 ruptured.[55] Many authorities believe that there are no good data to support the belief that the larger the renal artery aneurysm, the more likely it is to rupture.[25,57,69,87,88]

Most other series of asymptomatic renal artery aneurysms in men and nonpregnant women report a much lower incidence of rupture. Only 1 of 62 patients with aneurysms 4.0 cm or smaller in diameter ruptured after follow-up from 1 to 17 years.[37] None of 19 small aneurysms in another series ruptured.[30] A group of 21 patients were observed for an average of about 3 years without rupture.[35] In another series of 18 patients with renal artery aneurysms less than 2.6 cm who were followed up for 1 to 16 years, none ruptured.[57] There were no ruptures in a series of 32 patients (who eventually underwent surgery) of renal artery aneurysms, which ranged from 0.7 to 9.0 cm.[22] Of 83 renal artery aneurysms found on arteriography from a series in Sweden, 69 were followed up without surgery, and none ruptured or became symptomatic after a mean of 4.3 years of follow-up.[95] In a pooled analysis, there were no ruptures in more than 200 renal artery aneurysms observed for up to 17 years.[14] One must keep in mind that there was obvious selection bias in following up many of these aneurysms (i.e., small size) and that many of the larger aneurysms were repaired.

Besides aneurysm size, other factors may play a role in the consideration of elective surgery for asymptomatic renal artery aneurysms. Calcification of the aneurysm has been thought to protect from rupture. Poutasse suggested that a heavily calcified renal artery aneurysm may be less likely to rupture than a noncalcified or minimally calcified one.[74] In a review of cases through 1959, 14 of 100 noncalcified aneurysms ruptured.[33] In a more recent series, 15 of 18 ruptured renal artery aneurysms were noncalcified.[36] In a series of 62 solitary aneurysms less than 4.0 cm in diameter, however, one third were not calcified, and only one aneurysm in the entire series ruptured between 1 and 17 years of follow-up.[37] Because of these conflicting data, some authorities believe that presence or absence of calcification is not relevant to predict risk of rupture.[87]

Most authorities agree, however, that pregnancy is associated with a significant increased risk of rupture of a renal artery aneurysm.[15,22,87,88] Pregnancy may increase the risk of rupture because of the hyperdynamic state with increased blood volume and cardiac output, hormonal influences on the aneurysm, and increased intra-abdominal pressure due to the gravid uterus.[57,88] Cohen and Shamash reported 18 cases of rupture during pregnancy.[15] In another series of 18 patients having surgery for renal artery aneurysms,[57] the only two ruptures were in females at childbirth; both of these aneurysms measured only 1.0 cm in diameter.[57] In a review of 43 ruptured renal artery aneurysms,[36] 35 (81%) occurred in women; 21 of the 35 women in this series were younger than 40 years of age, and

18 were pregnant. Of the 18 aneurysms of known size, 3 ruptured when they were smaller than 2.0 cm.[36]

Of note, rupture of renal artery aneurysms in pregnancy has been associated with a maternal mortality rate of 55% and a fetal death rate of 85%.[15,86] Risk of renal artery rupture is small, however, even in pregnant women. In a series of 19,600 autopsies of pregnant women, no ruptured renal artery aneurysms were found.[55] This report did not indicate the number of unruptured renal artery aneurysms in this population, however, so the risk of rupture remains uncertain. We agree with others that there are enough data to support an aggressive surgical approach for pregnant women with renal artery aneurysms of any size.

Essentially all false renal artery aneurysms of recent onset should be repaired because of the high likelihood of rupture.[25] In the rare instance when a chronic contained rupture of a small false aneurysm is found months or years later, however, and the pseudoaneurysm has thrombosed, careful follow-up is probably all that is warranted.

Renal artery aneurysms associated with fibrodysplastic disease may be associated with a higher risk of rupture because of the thin-walled nature of these aneurysms, although firm data supporting this concern are lacking.[25] Certainly, renal artery aneurysms in men or women beyond childbearing age that are less than 2.0 in diameter due to fibrodysplastic disease should be studied closely.[25]

In summary, our recommendation concerning elective repair of asymptomatic renal artery aneurysms in men and women beyond childbearing age is based on the data just presented and on the well-documented history of other abdominal arterial aneurysms. General guidelines for repair of asymptomatic abdominal aneurysms include (1) infrarenal aortic aneurysms greater than 5.0 to 5.5 cm in diameter; (2) common iliac aneurysms greater than 3.0 cm; and (3) splenic artery aneurysms greater than 3.0 cm.[89] On the other hand, surgery is recommended for visceral artery aneurysms of any size.[89] Although various hemodynamic factors may play a role in other intra-abdominal aneurysms, and despite the relative paucity of data suggesting a high risk of rupture for renal artery aneurysms, it seems prudent to recommend repair of renal artery aneurysms greater than 3.0 cm in diameter in good-risk patients when there is reasonable certainty that nephrectomy will not be required.[33,69] This suggested guideline remains controversial since others have taken a more conservative approach, reserving repair for aneurysms larger than 4.0 cm.[102] As previously mentioned, any renal artery aneurysm in women of childbearing age should be repaired.

Hypertension

Although the prevalence of hypertension in patients with renal artery aneurysms is approximately 80% in several series, there is no conclusive evidence that the aneurysms themselves are the direct cause of hypertension unless there is an associated stenosis or compression of an adjacent artery.[22,57,88] In a series of 39 patients with renal artery aneurysms, 33 had diastolic hypertension, but in only 9 (23%) did the hypertension prove to be of renovascular origin.[57] In a more recent series of 16 patients with extraparenchymal renal artery aneurysms, 12 (75%) had renovascular hypertension.[3] The indication for surgical intervention for renovascular hypertension due to renal artery stenosis secondary to atherosclerosis should continue to be failure of medical management, namely diastolic blood pressure greater than 90 to 100 mm Hg despite three antihypertensive medications. The same criteria for surgical intervention for renovascular hypertension secondary to atherosclerosis as described in Chapter 130 should probably be applied when renal artery aneurysm is present. The stenotic artery along with the aneurysm must be repaired. Our current evaluation of these patients primarily relies on the clinical scenario, exclusion of other causes of secondary hypertension, documentation of significant renal artery stenoses, and occasional use of captopril renal scans.[100]

Dissection

Emergent intervention is required for dissections that cause renal artery aneurysms and threaten the viability of the kidney. Nephrectomies are frequently required in these cases, however, because of the extensive damage to the renal branch vessels and the limited time available to salvage a previously healthy kidney that will not tolerate prolonged periods of ischemia. If hypertension is the only manifestation of a chronic dissection, and the hypertension is well controlled by blood pressure medications, or if the patient is asymptomatic and a renal artery dissection is found incidentally (without an associated aneurysm), surgery is probably not justified.[88]

Other Clinical Manifestations

If a patient with an intact renal artery aneurysm, as documented by CT or MR imaging, is symptomatic as manifested by abdominal or flank pain or fullness, then repair is indicated regardless of the previously mentioned criteria. Symptoms may be a harbinger of impending rupture, but even if not, medical treatment will not relieve these symptoms. Embolization to the renal parenchyma may also account for these symptoms.[53]

Treatment

Ruptured Renal Artery Aneurysm

If emergent surgery is required for a ruptured renal artery aneurysm, a midline approach and supraceliac aortic control are generally required. A sizable juxtarenal hematoma does not allow safe aortic exposure and clamping immediately above the renal arteries. If proximal control of the renal artery itself can be obtained, the supraceliac clamp can then be removed. If the bleeding is quickly controlled and the patient is clearly hemodynamically stable, and if the proximal and distal renal arteries lend themselves to a relatively quick and straightforward bypass, consideration can be given to reconstruction.

In most cases, however, nephrectomy is required because of the instability of the patient, the prolonged ischemia of the kidney, and the technical and time-consuming nature of surgical repair with a bypass.[73,87,88,104] If the aneurysm extends into the renal parenchyma or if a "bench" repair of the kidney is required, the patient is generally best treated by nephrectomy as long as the contralateral kidney is known to be intact with normal function. Of note, a stable patient with a ruptured true or false renal artery aneurysm may potentially be treated with newer endovascular techniques. Routh and associates reported thrombosis of a leaking saccular aneurysm using Gianturco coils, thrombin, and bucrylate.[79]

Elective Repair of Renal Artery Aneurysm

Even in the elective situation, repair of a renal artery aneurysm is usually more challenging than revascularization for a renal artery stenosis. Most renal artery aneurysms extend past the bifurcation of the main renal arteries and frequently extend into the renal parenchyma. An associated renal artery stenosis must be repaired in conjunction with the aneurysm. For in-situ repairs of a renal artery aneurysm, exposure of the left kidney can be obtained through a retroperitoneal approach with a transverse left supraumbilical incision. The right kidney can be exposed through a transperitoneal approach with a Kocher maneuver to reflect the right colon and duodenum medially or occasionally with a subcostal incision.

Several methods have been used to repair renal artery aneurysms. The most straightforward technique for saccular aneurysms involves aneurysmorrhaphy with primary repair or patching. In three combined series of patients undergoing surgical repair for renal artery aneurysms, about one third (6/18, 3/10, 6/23) of renal artery aneurysms were able to be repaired in this manner.[22,53,57] If this technique is not possible, we and others prefer autologous tissue bypasses such as saphenous vein if the graft can be anastomosed to the distal part of the main trunk of the renal artery or to the most proximal branches.[22,25]

Another method of in-situ repair includes use of bifurcated internal iliac artery autograft.[64] The proximal anastomosis of the graft is usually the infrarenal aorta. Useful alternatives include a splenorenal bypass for a left-sided renal artery aneurysm and hepatorenal bypass for a right-sided aneurysm.

If multiple-branch vessels are involved, and especially if the cause of the renal artery aneurysm is dissection resulting in a friable vessel, extracorporeal or bench surgery may be required.[8,21] Ex-vivo surgery requires nephrectomy, followed by hypothermic perfusion of the kidney with a heparinized renal preservation solution. The kidney can then be autotransplanted to its original bed, as Dean and associates prefer,[19] or the iliac fossa. Perfusion is carried out through the main renal artery to preserve the kidney while selected branches are individually repaired and other branches perfused. This technique is recommended when renal ischemia is projected to exceed 45 minutes or when exposure of small renal branches is required.

For renal autotransplantation into the iliac fossa, a flank incision with a retroperitoneal approach is used for exposure of the kidney, ureter, and iliac artery. Gonadal and adrenal veins are divided to obtain an adequate length of renal vein. If the reconstruction can be safely performed by placing the kidney on the anterior abdominal wall, the ureter does not need to be divided. The procedure is occasionally best performed at a separate table, however, after dividing the ureter and removing the kidney from the operative field. Ex-vivo repair is also discussed in Chapter 132.

The kidney may be perfused with a heparinized crystalloid solution, such as Collins solution or lactated Ringer's solution with 1000 units of heparin/L with 12.5 g of mannitol, while the kidney is wrapped with gauze and placed in a chilled solution at 4° C.[8,25,48] The use of continuous pulsatile perfusion is controversial.[8]

The most common arterial reconstruction is an end-to-side anastomosis of a small renal artery branch to the main renal artery or a side-to-side anastomosis of two small renal arteries to create a common inflow channel with a single lumen of larger diameter, which can then be anastomosed to the renal artery or vein. Because the small branches of the main renal artery are often involved with the aneurysm, an autologous graft is preferred to reconstruct these lesions. The internal iliac artery is an excellent choice in these reconstructions because of its multiple small side branches.[64,69] The saphenous vein, however, also functions well. The renal artery and vein are then anastomosed end-to-side to the external iliac vessels or to the renal vein and aorta in the kidney's original bed.[8,25] The clamps are removed from the venous anastomosis first. A ureteroneocystostomy is constructed if the ureter was divided after the vessels were anastomosed.

When performed for proper indications by well-trained surgeons, repair of renal artery aneurysms should be associated with low morbidity and mortality.[48,53,84,87] In a series of 12 patients operated on for renal artery aneurysms, there was no mortality and only 1 patient required reoperation for a ureteral stenosis.[84] Ex-vivo repairs have also been shown to be safe and effective by Dean[19] and others.[8] Murray and coworkers reported a series of 11 patients with renal artery aneurysms successfully treated using ex-vivo repair.[64] Another series of 8 aneurysms were all successfully repaired with the ex-vivo technique without deaths or complications.[98] In a review of ex-vivo repairs, postoperative mortality rates ranged from 0 to 9.6%.[86] Bifurcated internal iliac artery autograft was highly successful in a series of 11 patients, most with fibrodysplastic aneurysms, treated by in-situ or bench repair.[64] In a series of 35 repairs of renal artery aneurysms treated by in-situ repair, ex-vivo repair, or nephrectomy, there was no mortality and only 1 postoperative graft occlusion.[22]

An exciting new approach to treat renal artery aneurysms includes use of endovascular techniques.[10,44,69,94] Renal artery aneurysms have been treated with transcatheter embolization with detachable platinum coils, which occluded the aneurysms but maintained renal flow.[94,99] Another patient in whom a renal artery aneurysm occurred after percutaneous renal biopsy was successfully treated by embolization.[68] In one of the largest series of endovascular repairs that has been reported, Klein and coworkers treated 12 renal artery aneurysms using endovascular selective embolization with nondetachable microcoils or Guglielmo's detachable coils.[44] Eight aneurysms were located in the bifurcation of the main renal artery, 2 were in the main renal artery, and 2 were intrarenal. All 12 aneurysms were successfully occluded with only two minor complications. The authors concluded that endovascular treatment of renal artery aneurysms with microcoils is as safe as but less invasive than surgical treatment.[44]

Placement of endovascular grafts across a renal artery aneurysm is also possible. A patient with fibrodysplastic disease and a 1.5-cm saccular aneurysm was treated by percutaneous placement of a polytetrafluoroethylene (PTFE) stent-graft that remained patent at 1-year follow-up with normalization of blood pressure.[10] Another patient with a 2.5-cm saccular left renal artery aneurysm was successfully treated by endoluminal grafting with a coronary stent-graft that remained patent after 12 months' follow-up.[9] An 86-year-old woman presented with a ruptured aneurysm involving the distal right main renal artery and was successfully treated with a coronary stent-graft.[83] It remains to be seen whether partial occlusion of renal artery aneurysms will prevent enlargement and later rupture, although early data are encouraging.

Fibromuscular Dysplasia

Post-stenotic dilations resulting from fibromuscular disease can be treated by balloon angioplasty of the stenotic lesions, although in these cases the primary indication for treatment is the stenotic lesions. When the lesions extend into the branches of the main renal artery, surgery can yield excellent results. Dean and coworkers reported 24 patients with fibromuscular disease, many of whom had branch aneurysms; all but 1 did well.[19]

Intrarenal Aneurysms

Intrarenal aneurysms represent particularly challenging lesions. Frequently a partial nephrectomy is required.[47] Intrarenal aneurysms in association with polyarteritis nodosa have also been successfully treated with renal artery embolization with preservation of the kidney.[80]

■ RENAL ARTERIOVENOUS MALFORMATIONS AND FISTULAE

Arteriovenous malformations (AVMs) and AVFs are uncommon lesions that can be associated with hematuria, hypertension and renal dysfunction, high-output congestive heart failure, and even rupture. More than 200 cases have been reported since the first description in 1928.[63] Fistulae may be congenital or acquired. Multiple diagnostic modalities are now available, although conventional selective arteriography remains the standard. Many asymptomatic lesions do not require treatment. Symptomatic lesions have previously been treated surgically, but endovascular treatment has now supplanted surgery in most cases.

Etiology

Congenital Arteriovenous Malformations

True congenital AVMs of the kidney are quite rare, with an incidence of only 0.04%.[13] In a large series, only 1 congenital AVM was noted in 30,000 autopsies.[17] These lesions represent approximately one fourth of all renal AVFs.[43,54] The right kidney is more frequently involved than the left, and although multiple lesions may occur, a single focus is more common.[19] The angiographic appearance of lesions is similar to AVMs elsewhere, with large coils of dilated vessels. Though Piquet and colleagues describe a single artery feeding all but advanced cases,[71] others describe multiple connections of arterial branches and venous tributaries.[63]

An early "blush" is noted and correlates with the degree of arteriovenous shunting, which is variable. These lesions have been described as "cirsoid," or varix-like, and are generally focal and located in the renal medulla. AVMs are not neoplastic, but enlargement presumably can occur based on vessel dilation and hypertrophy associated with high-flow volume from arteriovenous shunting. Symptomatic AVMs have been reported in pregnancy,[28,63] and it is thought that the hyperdynamic state of the gravida leads to increased AVM flow and symptoms.

Histologically, involved vessels have irregular fibrosis or intimal hyperplasia as well as medial hypertrophy. Focal intraparenchymal hemorrhage may be noted in the lamina propria beneath the transitional epithelium of the collecting system.[24]

Acquired Arteriovenous Fistulae

Spontaneous Acquired AVFs may occur spontaneously. Spontaneous AVFs have been documented in association with fibromuscular dysplasia[62] and are thought to develop when a dysplastic or aneurysmal renal artery erodes into a neighboring vein.[39] This may also occur with renal malignancy, and indeed significant arteriovenous shunting is a hallmark of renal cell carcinoma.[103] With arteriography, it can be difficult to differentiate a renal malignancy from a congenital or acquired AVF, although CT and MR imaging generally reveal a mass distinct from renal parenchyma in malignancy. As with AVMs, symptoms depend on the degree of shunting.

Traumatic Traumatic AVFs are the most common lesions, accounting for more than 70% of all renal AVFs.[63] These lesions may occur after nephrectomy related to erosion of the arterial stump into the vein with mass ligature,[17,77,90] after renal artery angioplasty,[63] after blunt[101] or penetrating[77] trauma, nephrostomy,[38] and, most commonly, after percutaneous renal biopsy. With routine use of needle biopsy for the diagnosis of rejection in renal allografts, the incidence of acquired AVF has grown. Although only 1% to 2% of patients who undergo needle biopsy develop a symptomatic AVF,[49,96] the true incidence of AVF is 15% to 18% when arteriography is routinely used.[59,75]

Ozbek and colleagues[67] found AVFs in 8 (12.5%) of 64 patients monitored by color-duplex ultrasonography, whereas only 5.0% developed AVFs in the study of Rollino and associates.[78] In the prospective study of Merkus and colleagues, who used routine color-duplex surveillance, 10% of patients undergoing biopsy developed AVFs.[59] In their series, the development of AVFs correlated with bleeding dysfunction (elevated bleeding time or diminished platelet count), supporting the idea that inadequate intraparenchymal hemostasis leads to the development of a channel between artery and vein that subsequently enlarges. Others have reported fewer fistulae and bleeding complications with automated small-gauge needles rather than the standard 14-gauge core biopsy technique.[45,76]

Clinical Presentation

The majority of both congenital and acquired AVFs do not produce clinical symptoms, and increasingly lesions are noted incidentally in studies done for other reasons. The most common symptom of congenital AVM is hematuria, occurring in 72% of cases.[17] Hematuria occurs when subepithelial varices erode transitional epithelium into the collecting system. Dramatic presentation with massive hematuria can occur,[12,28,61] although minor or microscopic hematuria is more common.

Hypertension occurs in congenital AVM and is the primary abnormality in most acquired AVFs described as symptomatic. The hypertension is renin mediated, based on diminished glomerular filtration pressure distal to the fistula because of arterial "steal."[38,54,82] Renal dysfunction is not usually noted except in transplant patients, where diminished parenchymal flow in the solitary kidney is not masked by a functional contralateral kidney.[32]

Some patients have been discovered to have AVF when undergoing radiographic evaluation for vague abdominal or flank symptoms. Although AVFs are generally painless, intermittent perilumbar discomfort has been reported in some patients.[90,103] This discomfort has generally been associated with hematuria and may represent renal colic.

Dyspnea and other symptoms of congestive heart failure may be the primary complaint of some patients, more commonly with acquired lesions, and only those lesions with a large communication between artery and vein. This "high-output" type of heart failure is manifest by tachycardia, left ventricular hypertrophy and cardiomegaly, and a palpable thrill in the flank. A continuous abdominal bruit is a hallmark of acquired AVF and is frequently noted with congenital AVM as well.

Retroperitoneal or intra-abdominal hemorrhage occurs rarely with AVM and AVF.[6,12] Patients present with severe abdominal and flank pain and shock, a clinical picture indistinguishable from ruptured abdominal aortic aneurysm.

Diagnosis

Excretory urography has been performed in many patients presenting with hematuria or flank pain. A filling defect may be noted in the kidney, and dilated vessels can compress the collecting system, although these findings are not specific. Although helpful to exclude more common causes of hematuria such as nephrolithiasis, intravenous pyelography is of limited use in the diagnosis of AVF.

CT can usually define AVFs and AVMs within the kidney, but it is not always possible to differentiate these lesions from other hypervascular abnormalities such as renal cell carcinoma. Similarly, radionuclide imaging can demonstrate early augmented perfusion, but differentiation from malignancy is not possible.[106] Ultrafast CT with angiographic reconstruction has significantly improved noninvasive imaging of AVF and AVM.[70] Likewise, contrast-enhanced MR angiography allows for three-dimensional reconstruction that can provide visualization not possible with conventional angiography.[4]

Color-duplex imaging is of growing importance in the diagnosis of AVM and AVF. Because it is inexpensive and noninvasive, it is the ideal study for screening purposes.

Color-duplex imaging has been used liberally to assess for AVF after percutaneous renal biopsy.[26,59,67] Marked turbulence is noted on color examination, and Doppler spectral analysis reveals elevation of peak systolic flow velocity (PSV) and a larger increase in end-diastolic flow velocity (EDV) compared with the normal renal artery, with a resultant low "resistive index"[26,67]:

$$(PSV - EDV) \div PSV$$

Arteriography has been and remains the definitive diagnostic modality for renal AVMs and AVFs. Rapid opacification of the inferior vena cava is noted. Depending on the size of the fistula, the nephrogram may be diminished distal to the AVF. With congenital AVM, multiple segmental and interlobar arteries communicate with varix-like veins, whereas a single arterial communication is generally present with acquired AVF.[17] Although a relatively expensive and invasive diagnostic study, unlike other modalities, arteriography alone offers the opportunity for definitive therapy.

Treatment: Medical, Surgical, and Endovascular

The majority of both congenital and acquired AVFs do not cause symptoms and do not require treatment. Patients may become symptomatic even many years after the occurrence or diagnosis of AVF and should be closely observed for the development of hypertension, hematuria, or high-output cardiac failure.

Most AVFs occurring after percutaneous renal biopsy close spontaneously.[5,38,59,60,67] This is particularly true of AVFs discovered early after biopsy by color-duplex ultrasonography. Periodic duplex surveillance, along with clinical follow-up for the development of hypertension or renal insufficiency, is indicated. If a postbiopsy AVF persists at 1 year, it is not likely to close spontaneously,[49] although intervention should still be reserved for the development of symptoms.[32,59]

Although hypertension related to AVF may be readily controlled with angiotensin-converting enzyme inhibitors,[62] as with renal artery stenosis, the long-term effect on renal function is not known. In most published reports, patients with hypertension have undergone surgical or endovascular therapy; thus, the natural history of medically treated patients with hypertension secondary to AVF remains undefined.

For patients with symptomatic AVF, surgery had been the standard treatment for many years and may still be the best option in certain circumstances.[46,91] Except for very peripheral lesions, a transperitoneal approach is preferred to establish proximal arterial and venous control at the renal pedicle. Owing to the frequent presence of thin-walled, dilated veins and channels, surgery can be challenging. Ex-vivo repair for a large, complex renal artery aneurysm causing an AVF in a patient with fibromuscular dysplasia has been reported.[97] With surgery, ligation of the feeding vessel or vessels alone is often not possible, and frequently partial or total nephrectomy is required. The resultant loss of functional renal mass, as well as the morbidity of the operation itself, makes endovascular treatment a more attractive approach.

There are now more than 2 decades of experience with percutaneous arterial embolization therapy for congenital and acquired AVFs.[93] Because renal arteries are "end arteries," they are especially amenable to therapeutic occlusion. In earlier reports, autologous clot was used as the embolic material, but recanalization and recurrence of AVF are possible, and thrombus has been supplanted by other materials, including gelatins, glues, alcohols, silicon, steel and platinum coils, and detachable balloons.[5,6,18,37,43,105] The development of coaxial catheter systems has allowed for highly selective embolization, which can preserve renal function. Loss of functional renal parenchyma has been reported to be between 0% and 30% with modern techniques.

In general, smaller AVFs are treated with glues or macroparticles, whereas coils and balloons have been used for larger vessel fistulae (Fig. 133-1).[81] Because Gelfoam and autologous clot resorb, recanalization with recurrence of symptoms can occur in up to 50% of cases.[20,65] For this reason and a perception that microcoils are associated with less indiscriminate embolization than glues and alcohols, recent trends favor the use of microcoils even for smaller AVF and AVM.[5,6,37]

Very large AVFs may present a technical challenge for treatment due to the risk of central embolization, and some authors recommend surgery in this setting.[46,52,91,107] Others have reported success in this setting using the Amplatz "spider" device to provide a scaffolding that can then engage other embolic materials.[43,77] Staging the procedure, first with large coils followed weeks later by smaller coils and other materials to close off persistent flow channels, may also be an effective strategy.[29] As very large arteriovenous communications tend to be at the renal pedicle rather than intraparenchymal, surgical treatment is feasible and probably preferable for good-risk patients.

Complications of embolization are unusual but not insignificant. In addition to arterial access site morbidity and contrast toxicity, pulmonary or peripheral arterial embolization can occur. This is usually related to improper selection and delivery of embolic materials. Large AVFs require large agents such as coils or detachable balloons, but even these can embolize centrally. Gelfoam, alcohol, and various glues may be more appropriate for very small communications, but delivery is less precise and more renal parenchymal infarction seems to occur with these materials.[38] It is common for patients to have fever, leukocytosis, and even hypertension after embolization, which is transient and presumed to be secondary to renal infarction.[75] Embolization itself was reported to cause massive collecting system hemorrhage in one case, but this was successfully managed with further embolization.[41] With modern techniques, success is achieved with endovascular treatment in more than 80% of patients[32] and clearly is the treatment of choice for symptomatic congenital or acquired AVF.

■ SUMMARY

Congenital renal AVMs and acquired AVFs are uncommon and often asymptomatic. When symptoms of hematuria, hypertension, renal dysfunction, high-output congestive heart failure, or rupture occur, treatment is mandated.

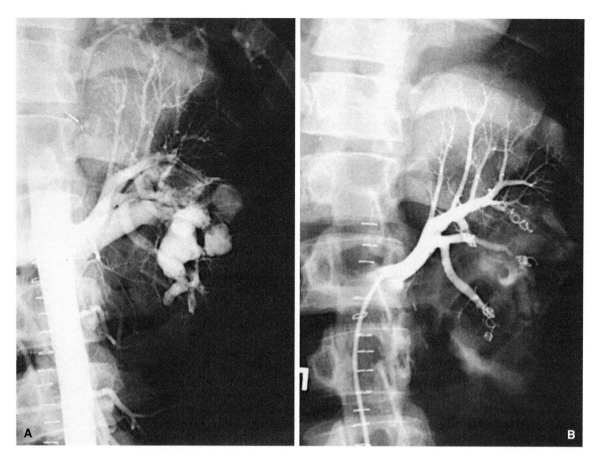

FIGURE 133-1 A, Arteriogram showing a post-traumatic arteriovenous fistula. This patient suffered a stab wound to the flank and presented with hematuria. **B,** After Gianturco coil embolization of multiple arterial branches, venous communication is no longer present. Hematuria resolved, and the patient recovered uneventfully.

Endovascular embolization is the treatment of choice, with surgical ligation or nephrectomy indicated only when embolization is unsafe or unsuccessful.

■   REFERENCES

1. Alcazar R, de la Torre M, Peces R: Symptomatic intrarenal arteriovenous fistula detected 25 years after percutaneous renal biopsy: Case report. Nephrol Dial Transplant 11:1346-1348, 1996.
2. Armstrong A, Birch B, Jenkins J: Renal arteriovenous fistula following blunt trauma: Case report. Br J Urol 73:321-322, 1994.
3. Arroyo Bielsa A, Porto Rodriguez J, Gesto Castromil R: Extraparenchymal renal artery aneurysms: Is hypertension an indication for revascularization surgery? Ann Vasc Surg 16:339, 2002.
4. Bagga H, Bis KG: Contrast-enhanced MR angiography in the assessment of arteriovenous fistula after renal transplant biopsy. AJR Am J Roentgenol 172:1509-1511, 1999.
5. Beaujeux R, Boudjema K, Ellero B, et al: Endovascular treatment of renal allograft postbiopsy arteriovenous fistula with platinum microcoils. Transplantation 57:311-314, 1994.
6. Beaujeux R, Saussine C, Al-Fakir A, et al: Superselective endovascular treatment of renal vascular lesions. J Urol 153:14-17, 1995.
7. Bernhardt J, Zwicker C, Hering M, et al: A major renal artery aneurysm as the cause of a hydronephrosis with renovascular hypertension. Urol Int 57:237, 1996.
8. Brayman KL, Gincherman Y, Levy MM, et al: Ex vivo reconstruction of the renal artery for aneurysm and other abnormalities of renal vascular anatomy. In Calligaro KD, Dougherty MJ, Dean RH (eds): Modern Management of Renovascular Hypertension and Renal Salvage. Baltimore, Williams & Wilkins, 1996, p 269.
9. Bruce M, Kuan YM: Endoluminal stent-graft repair of a renal artery aneurysm. J Endovasc Ther 9:359, 2002.
10. Bui BT, Oliva VL, Leclerc G, et al: Renal artery aneurysm: Treatment with percutaneous placement of a stent-graft. Radiology 195:181, 1995.
11. Charron J, Belanger R, Vauclair R, et al: Renal artery aneurysm: Polyaneurysmal lesion of kidney. Urology 5:1, 1975.
12. Chivate J, Blewitt R: Congenital renal arteriovenous fistula: Case report. Br J Urol 71:358-359, 1993.
13. Cho KJ, Stanley JC: Non-neoplastic congenital and acquired renal arteriovenous malformations and fistulas. Radiology 129:333-343, 1978.
14. Cinat M, Yoon P, Wilson SE: Management of renal artery aneurysms. Semin Vasc Surg 9:236, 1996.
15. Cohen JR, Shamash FS: Ruptured renal artery aneurysms during pregnancy. J Vasc Surg 6:51, 1987.
16. Coppes M, Anderson R, Mueller D, et al: Arteriovenous fistula: A complication following renal biopsy of suspected bilateral Wilms' tumor. Med Pediatr Oncol 28:455-461, 1997.
17. Crotty K, Orihuela E, Warren M: Recent advances in the diagnosis and treatment of renal arteriovenous malformations and fistulas. J Urol 150:1355-1359, 1993.
18. Cursio R, Choquenet C, Brunner P: Successful transarterial embolization of idiopathic renal arteriovenous fistula. Minerva Chir 56:321-323, 2001.

19. Dean RH, Meachum PW, Weaver FA: Ex vivo renal artery reconstructions: Indications and techniques. J Vasc Surg 4:546, 1986.
20. Defrayne L, Govaere F, Vanlangenhove P, et al: Cirsoid renal arteriovenous malformation treated by endovascular embolization with N-butyl 2-cyanoacrylate. Eur Radiol 10:772-775, 2000.
21. Dubernard JM, Martin X, Gelet A, et al: Aneurysms of the renal artery: Surgical management with special reference to extracorporeal surgery and autotransplantation. Eur Urol 11:26, 1985.
22. Dzsinich C, Gloviczki P, McKusick MA, et al: Fibromuscular dysplasia and surgical management of renal artery aneurysm. Cardiovasc Surg 1:243, 1993.
23. Erdsman G: Angionephrography and suprarenal angiography. Acta Radiol 155(Suppl):104, 1957.
24. Fogazzi G, Moriggi M, Fontanella U: Spontaneous renal arteriovenous fistula as a cause of haematuria. Nephrol Dial Transplant 12:350-356, 1997.
25. Fry WF: Renal artery aneurysm. In Ernst CB, Stanley JC (eds): Current Therapy in Vascular Surgery. Philadelphia, BC Decker, 1987, p 363.
26. Gainza F, Minguela I, Lopez-Vidaur I, et al: Evaluation of complications due to percutaneous renal biopsy in allografts and native kidneys with color-coded Doppler sonography. Clin Nephrol 43:303-308, 1995.
27. Gewertz BL, Stanley JC, Fry WJ: Renal artery dissections. Arch Surg 112:409, 1977.
28. Gopalakrishnan G, Al-Awadi K, Bhatia V, Mahmoud A: Renal arteriovenous malformation presenting as haematuria in pregnancy: Case report. Br J Urol 75:110-111, 1995.
29. Gralino BJ, Bricker DL: Staged endovascular occlusion of giant idiopathic renal arteriovenous fistula with platinum microcoils and silk suture threads. J Vasc Interv Radiol 13:747-752, 2002.
30. Hageman JH, Smith RF, Szilagyi DD, et al: Aneurysms of the renal artery: Problems of prognosis and surgical management. Surgery 84:563, 1978.
31. Hare WSC, Kincaid-Smith P: Dissecting aneurysms of the renal artery. Radiology 97:255, 1970.
32. Harrison K, Nghiem H, Coldwell D, Davis C: Renal dysfunction due to an arteriovenous fistula in a transplant recipient. J Am Soc Nephrol 5:1300-1306, 1994.
33. Harrow BR, Sloane JA: Aneurysm of renal artery: Report of five cases. J Urol 81:35, 1959.
34. Hekali P, Kivisaara L, Standerskjold-Nordenstam CG, et al: Renal complications of polyarteritis nodosa: CT findings. J Comput Assist Tomogr 9:333, 1985.
35. Henriksson C, Bjorkerud S, Nilson AE, et al: Natural history of renal artery aneurysm elucidated by repeated angiography and pathoanatomic studies. Eur Urol 11:244, 1985.
36. Hidai H, Kinoshita Y, Murayama T, et al: Rupture of renal artery aneurysm. Eur Urol 11:249, 1985.
37. Hubert JP Jr, Pairolero PC, Kazmier FJ: Solitary renal artery aneurysms. Surgery 88:557, 1980.
38. Huppert P, Duda S, Erley C, et al: Embolization of renal vascular lesions: Clinical experience with microcoils and tracker catheters. Cardiovasc Intervent Radiol 16:361-367, 1993.
39. Imray TJ, Cohen AJ, Hahn L: Renal arteriovenous fistula associated with fibromuscular dysplasia. Urology 23:378-381, 1989.
40. Kajbafzadeh A, Broumand B: Arteriovenous fistula following nephrectomy: Case report. Eur Urol 31:112-114, 1997.
41. Kamai T, Saito K, Hirokawa M, et al: A case of gross hematuria arising during embolization for renal arteriovenous malformation. Urol Int 58:55-57, 1997.
42. Kaufman JJ, Coulson WF, Lecky JW, et al: Primary dissecting aneurysms of renal artery: Report of a case causing reversible renal hypertension. Ann Surg 177:259, 1973.
43. Kearse W Jr, Joseph A, Sabanegh E Jr: Transcatheter embolization of large idiopathic renal arteriovenous fistula: Case report. J Urol 151:967-969, 1994.
44. Klein GE, Szolar DH, Breinl E, et al: Endovascular treatment of renal artery aneurysm with conventional non-detachable microcoils and Guglielmi detachable coils. Br J Urol 79:852, 1997.
45. Kolb L, Velosa J, Bergstralh E, Offord K: Percutaneous renal allograft biopsy: A comparison of two needle types and analysis of risk factors. Transplantation 57:1742-1746, 1994.
46. Kumar U, German K, Blackford H, Dux A: Perioperative use of a balloon-occluding arterial catheter in renal arteriovenous malformation. Br J Urol 77:312-313, 1996.
47. Kyle VN: Renal artery aneurysms. Can Med Assoc J 98:815, 1968.
48. Lacombe M: Ex situ repair of complex renal artery lesions. Cardiovasc Surg 2:767, 1994.
49. Lawen JD, van Buren CT, Lewis RM, Kahan BD: Arteriovenous fistulas after renal allograft biopsy: A serious complication in patients beyond one year. Clin Transplant 4:357-369, 1990.
50. Lee W, Lee E: Arteriovenous fistula and renal artery stenosis in a transplant kidney [Letter to the Editor]. Nephron 69:190-192, 1995.
51. Leong K, Boey M, Feng P: Renal arteriovenous fistula following kidney biopsy in systemic lupus erythematosus. Singapore Med J 34:327-328, 1993.
52. Lord RSA, Cherian SM, Ozmen J: Massive renal arteriovenous fistula presenting as a pulsatile abdominal mass. Cardiovasc Surg 8:164-166, 2000.
53. Lumsden AB, Salam TA, Walton KG: Renal artery aneurysm: A report of 28 cases. Cardiovasc Surg 4:185, 1996.
54. McAlhany JC Jr, Black HC Jr, Hanback LD Jr, Yarbrough DR III: Renal arteriovenous fistula as a cause of hypertension. Am J Surg 122:117-120, 1971.
55. McCarron JP Jr, Marshall VF, Whitsell JC II: Indications for surgery on renal artery aneurysms. J Urol 114:177, 1975.
56. McCormack LJ, Poutasse EF, Meaney TF, et al: A pathologic arteriographic correlation of renal arterial disease. Am Heart J 72:188, 1966.
57. Martin RS III, Meacham PW, Ditesheim JA, et al: Renal artery aneurysm: Selective treatment for hypertension and prevention of rupture. J Vasc Surg 9:26, 1989.
58. Mattar SG, Kumar AG, Lumsden AB: Vascular complications in Ehlers-Danlos syndrome. Am Surg 60:827, 1994.
59. Merkus J, Zeebregts C, Hoitsma A, et al: High incidence of arteriovenous fistula after biopsy of kidney allografts. Br J Surg 80:310-312, 1993.
60. Messing E, Kessler R, Kavaney PB: Renal arteriovenous fistulas. Urology 8:101-103, 1976.
61. Mori K, Koga S, Nishikido M, et al: Spontaneous rupture of an aneurysmal intrarenal arteriovenous fistula. Urol Int 70:83-84, 2003.
62. Morimoto A, Nakatani A, Matsui K, et al: A unique case of renovascular hypertension caused by combined renal artery disease: Case report. Hypertens Res 18:255-257, 1995.
63. Motta J, Breslin D, Vogel F, et al: Congenital renal arteriovenous malformation in pregnancy presenting with hypertension: Case report. Urology 44:911-914, 1994.
64. Murray SP, Kent C, Salvatierra O, et al: Complex branch renovascular disease: Management options and late results. J Vasc Surg 20:338, 1994.
65. Nakamura H, Uchida H, Kuroda C, et al: Renal aorto-venous malformations: Transcatheter embolization and follow-up. AJR Am J Roentgenol 137:113-116, 1981.
66. Oleaga JA, Grossman RA, McLean GK, et al: Arteriovenous fistula of a segmental renal artery branch as a complication of percutaneous angioplasty. AJR Am J Roentgenol 136:988-989, 1981.
67. Ozbek S, Memis A, Killi R, et al: Image-directed and color Doppler ultrasonography in the diagnosis of postbiopsy arteriovenous fistulas of native kidneys. J Clin Ultrasound 23:239-242, 1995.
68. Pall AA, Reid AW, Allsion MEM: Renal artery aneurysm six years after percutaneous renal biopsy: Successful treatment by embolization. Nephrol Dial Transplant 7:883, 1992.
69. Panayiotopoulos YP, Assadourian R, Taylor PR: Aneurysms of the visceral and renal arteries. Ann R Coll Surg Engl 78:412, 1996.

70. Peces R, Gorostidi M, Garcia-Gala J, et al: Giant saccular aneurysm of the renal artery presenting as malignant hypertension. J Hum Hypertens 5:465-466, 1991.

71. Piquet P, Trainier P, Garibotti F, et al: Aneurysmes des arteres renales et fistules arterioveineuses renales. In Kieffer E (ed): Chirurgie des Arteres Renales. Paris, AERCV, 1993, pp 237-250.

72. Pliskin MJ, Dresner ML, Hassell LH, et al: A giant renal artery aneurysm diagnosed postpartum. J Urol 144:1459, 1990.

73. Poutasse EF: Renal artery aneurysms: Their natural history and surgery. J Urol 95:297, 1966.

74. Poutasse EF: Renal artery aneurysms. J Urol 43:113, 1975.

75. Reilly K, Shapiro M, Haskal Z: Angiographic embolization of a penetrating traumatic renal arteriovenous fistula. J Trauma 41:763-765, 1996.

76. Riehl J, Maigatter S, Kierdorf H, et al: Percutaneous renal biopsy: Comparison of manual and automated puncture techniques with native and transplant kidneys. Nephrol Dial Transplant 9:1568-1574, 1994.

77. Robinson D, Teitelbaum G, Pentecost M, et al: Transcatheter embolization of an aortocaval fistula caused by residual renal artery stump from previous nephrectomy: A case report. J Vasc Surg 17:794-797, 1993.

78. Rollino C, Garofalo G, Roccatello D, et al: Colour-coded Doppler sonography in monitoring native kidney biopsies. Nephrol Dial Transplant 9:1260-1263, 1994.

79. Routh WD, Keller FS, Gross GM: Transcatheter thrombosis of a leaking saccular aneurysm of the main renal artery with preservation of renal blood flow. AJR Am J Roentgenol 154:1097, 1990.

80. Sachs D, Langevitz P, Moraq B, et al: Polyarteritis nodosa and familial Mediterranean fever. Br J Rheumatol 26:139, 1987.

81. Saliou C, Raynaud A, Blanc F, et al: Idiopathic renal arteriovenous fistula: Treatment with embolization. Ann Vasc Surg 12:75-77, 1998.

82. Schmid T, Sandbichler P, Ausserwinkler M, et al: Vascular lesions after percutaneous biopsies of renal allografts. Transplant Int 2:56-58, 1989.

83. Schneidereit NP, Lee S, Morris DC, Chen JC: Endovascular repair of a ruptured renal artery aneurysm. J Endovasc Ther 10:71, 2003.

84. Seki, T Koyanagi T, Togashi M, et al: Experience with revascularizing renal artery aneurysms: Is it feasible, safe, and worth attempting? J Urol 158:357, 1997.

85. Sellar RJ, Mackay IG, Buist TA: The incidence of microaneurysms in polyarteritis nodosa. Cardiovasc Intervent Radiol 9:123, 1986.

86. Sicard GA, Reilly JM, Picus DD, et al: Alternatives in renal revascularization. Curr Probl Surg 32:569, 1995.

87. Stanley JC: Natural history of renal artery stenosis and aneurysms. In Calligaro KD, Dougherty MJ, Dean RH (eds): Modern Management of Renovascular Hypertension and Renal Salvage. Baltimore, Williams & Wilkins, 1996, p 15.

88. Stanley JC, Rhodes EL, Gewertz BL, et al: Renal artery aneurysms: Significance of macroaneurysms exclusive of dissections and fibrodysplastic mural dilations. Arch Surg 110:1327, 1975.

89. Stanley JC, Zelenock GB: Splanchnic artery aneurysms. In Rutherford RB (ed): Vascular Surgery, 4th ed. Philadelphia, WB Saunders, 1995, p 1124.

90. Steffens J, Defreyne L, Kramann B, et al: Selective transcatheter embolization of a pediatric postnephrectomy arteriovenous fistula: Case report. Urol Int 53:99-101, 1994.

91. Takatera H, Nakamura M, Nakano E, et al: Renal arteriovenous fistula associated with a huge renal vein dilatation. J Urol 137:722, 1987.

92. Takebayashi S, Ohno T, Tanaka K, et al: MR angiography of renal vascular malformations. J Comput Assist Tomogr 18:596, 1994.

93. Takebayashi S, Hosaka M, Masahiko K, et al: Transarterial embolization and ablation of renal arteriovenous malformations: Efficacy and damages in 30 patients with long-term followup. J Urol 159:696-701, 1998.

94. Tateno T, Kubota Y, Sasagawa I, et al: Successful embolization of a renal artery aneurysm with preservation of renal blood flow. Int Urol Nephrol 28:283, 1996.

95. Tham G, Ekelund L, Herrlin K, et al: Renal artery aneurysms: Natural history and prognosis. Ann Surg 197:348, 1983.

96. Thistlethwaite JR Jr, Woodle ES, Mayes JT, et al: Aggressive needle biopsy protocol prevents loss of renal allografts to undetected rejection during early post-transplant dysfunction. Transplant Proc 21:1890-1892, 1989.

97. Torres G, Terramani T, Weaver F: Ex vivo repair of a large renal artery aneurysm and associated arteriovenous fistula. Ann Vasc Surg 16:141-144, 2002.

98. Toshino A, Oka A, Kitajima K, et al: Ex vivo surgery for renal artery aneurysms. Int J Urol 3:421, 1996.

99. Tshomba Y, Deleo G, Ferrari S, et al: Renal artery aneurysm: Improved renal function after coil embolization. J Endovasc Ther 9:54, 2002.

100. Turpin S, Lambert R, Querin S, et al: Radionuclide captopril renography in postpartum renal artery aneurysms. J Nucl Med 37:1368, 1996.

101. van der Zee J, van den Hoek J, Weerts J: Traumatic renal arteriovenous fistula in a 3-year-old girl, successfully treated by percutaneous transluminal embolization. J Pediatr Surg 30:1513-1514, 1995.

102. Van Way CW III: Renal artery aneurysms and arteriovenous fistulae. In Rutherford RB (ed): Vascular Surgery, 4th ed. Philadelphia, WB Saunders, 1995, p 1438.

103. Vasavada S, Manion S, Flanigan RC, et al: Renal arteriovenous malformations masquerading as renal cell carcinoma. Urology 46:716-721, 1995.

104. Vaughan TJ, Barry WF, Jeffords DL, et al: Renal artery aneurysms and hypertension. Radiology 99:287, 1971.

105. Wikholm G, Svendsen P, Herlitz H, et al: Superselective transarterial embolization of renal arteriovenous malformations of cryptogenic origin. Scand J Urol Nephrol 28:29-33, 1994.

106. Yeo E, Low J: Intrarenal arteriovenous fistula simulating a hypervascular renal tumor on radionuclide renal imaging. Clin Nucl Med 20:549-564, 1995.

107. Ziani M, Valignat C, Lopez J, et al: Renal arteriovenous malformation requiring surgery in Rendu-Osler-Weber disease (hereditary hemorrhagic telangiectasia). J Urol 164:1292-1293, 2000.

Acute Renovascular Occlusive Events

134

TINA R. DESAI, MD

NAVYASH GUPTA, MD

BRUCE L. GEWERTZ, MD

Acute events involving the renal vessels include acute renal artery occlusion secondary to embolism, thrombosis or renal artery dissection, renal artery trauma, and renal vein thrombosis. The clinical management of these diverse entities is discussed less frequently than that of chronic renovascular disease and renovascular hypertension, yet proper decision making can make a substantial difference in outcomes.

The diverse mechanisms responsible for each presentation further complicate the clinical situation. For example, penetrating trauma to the renal vessels usually requires emergent operative repair to prevent life-threatening hemorrhage, whereas blunt injury to the renal artery from impact or acceleration/deceleration phenomenon requires a more precise diagnostic approach directed to salvage renal function. The increased use of angioplasty and stenting in the treatment of chronic occlusive renovascular disease is associated with a low rate of acute occlusion, but these patients represent a unique subgroup of patients who are difficult to treat.

■ ACUTE RENAL ARTERY EMBOLISM

Embolic occlusion of the renal artery is a relatively rare occurrence. Traube described a case of embolic renal artery occlusion in 1856,[1] but this entity gained notice in the modern era only in 1940 when Hoxie and Coggin reported 205 cases of renal infarction found at autopsy.[2] This study involved a total of 14,411 autopsies, yielding an incidence of 1.5% of renal infarction from either embolic or thrombotic events.

Most renal artery emboli originate from the left side of the heart in association with atrial fibrillation, mitral valvular disease, and acute myocardial infarction. Suprarenal aneurysms and ulcerative atherosclerotic plaques ("shaggy aorta") can also embolize to the renal arteries. Although embolization of aneurysmal contents can occur spontaneously, atheroemboli more frequently result from manipulation of angiographic catheters within the aorta. In these circumstances, the ischemic insult is exacerbated by the distal impact of microscopic debris and the adverse effect of nephrotoxic contrast. As many as 30% of renal artery emboli of cardiac origin are bilateral. Simultaneous emboli to other visceral, extremity, and brachiocephalic vessels are also common. In instances of atheroembolism, bilateral embolization is even more common (>75%).

The classic clinical presentation of renal artery embolism may not be manifest until renal ischemia progresses to infarction.[3] Common presenting symptoms include flank pain, back or abdominal pain, hypertension, hematuria, and nausea and vomiting. In cases of acute occlusion of both renal arteries or renal artery occlusion in a solitary kidney, anuria and acute renal failure may develop. A low-grade fever may also be present. Leukocytosis and elevated lactate dehydrogenase levels are often evident on laboratory evaluation. Urinalysis frequently reveals erythrocytes, leukocytes, and proteinuria. These nonspecific findings are rarely ascribed to renal pathology, and frequent delays in diagnosis result in an overall low rate of renal salvage.

Additional diagnostic studies are frequently obtained because the diagnosis of acute renal artery occlusion is rarely clear based on clinical signs alone. Intravenous pyelography may reveal absent or poor function depending on the degree of renal artery obstruction. Renal nuclear medicine studies also may demonstrate impaired renal perfusion. Unfortunately, both of these studies are not definitive and provide no anatomic information. Since any delay in diagnosis adversely affects renal salvage, renal arteriography should be undertaken as the initial diagnostic study whenever acute renal artery occlusion is considered. This study frequently demonstrates an abrupt occlusion of the renal artery or multiple emboli within branches with limited collateralization. Frequently, bilateral emboli or additional emboli to visceral vessels may be evident.

Arteriography not only demonstrates the diagnosis of renal artery occlusion, but the degree of atherosclerotic disease and the pattern of collateral blood flow to the distal renal artery can help differentiate between renal artery embolus and thrombosis. In centers where access to duplex ultrasonography is readily available, this study may be useful as a screening study.[4]

Appropriate selection of patients for intervention is dependent on the duration and severity of renal ischemia, the site of the embolus, the status of the contralateral kidney, and underlying cardiopulmonary risk factors. In the past, renal salvage was thought unlikely in patients presenting with symptoms of prolonged duration (>12 hours) with no evidence of ipsilateral renal perfusion. In particular, patients with distal branch emboli or severe cardiopulmonary risk factors were rarely considered operative candidates; anticoagulation alone was recommended. In the current era, the evolution of thrombolytic therapy and improvements in operative and perioperative management have allowed a more aggressive approach to these patients.[5] Successful renal artery reconstructions have been reported well after 12 hours of incomplete ischemia.[6]

It is now well accepted that most patients with early presentations of embolic occlusion should be considered for revascularization by operative embolectomy or catheter-directed thrombolytic therapy. Surgical intervention is preferable in good-risk patients with partial renal artery occlusion, bilateral renal artery emboli, or an embolus to a solitary kidney. Operative mortality is significantly reduced by preoperative correction of metabolic derangements and fluid resuscitation.

Exposure of the left kidney can be gained via a retroperitoneal approach through a transverse left supraumbilical incision. With some effort even the right renal artery can be exposed through this route, although most surgeons prefer a midline transperitoneal approach with an extended Kocher maneuver for right renal exposure.[7] The renal vein is gently retracted, and the renal artery is dissected free. If the renal artery is free of significant atherosclerotic disease and of sufficient size (>4 mm), a transverse arteriotomy can be made allowing proximal and distal passage of embolectomy catheters. The arteriotomy can be closed primarily with interrupted 6-0 sutures or with a vein patch. If the renal artery is unsuitable for arteriotomy, a transverse aortotomy can be performed at the level of the renal artery and an embolectomy catheter passed distally and thromboembolic debris cleared. The aortotomy can usually be closed primarily. If atherosclerotic disease of the renal artery is encountered, the aortotomy can be extended across the renal ostium, endarterectomy performed, and the arteriotomy closed with a patch.

Complete extraction of embolic material can be difficult to assess in the operating room. Although intraoperative arteriography remains an option, the nephrotoxicity of contrast material and other technical difficulties in adequately visualizing the in-situ kidney make this approach less attractive. Intraoperative duplex ultrasonography avoids these potential complications and has been used with some success (see Chapter 132). Diuretics, mannitol, and renal dose dopamine or fenoldopam are advisable following revascularization.[8] Finally, because the renal parenchyma can swell considerably after revascularization, partial renal decapsulation may be considered in extreme cases.[9] The true benefits of this adjunctive procedure are not known.

Catheter-directed thrombolytic therapy has been employed with increasing frequency in the management of patients with renal artery embolism. This technique offers the theoretical advantage of avoiding operative stress in an acutely ill patient and certainly avoids trauma to the renal artery. It may offer particular advantage in patients with distal branch emboli. Although hemorrhagic complications have been reported with the use of streptokinase, urokinase, and tissue plasminogen activator, no major bleeding complications were encountered in one reported series of 10 patients with acute renal artery occlusion.[10] Of the two patients in this series with renal artery embolism, perfusion was restored in both, but renal function was preserved only in one. These results are comparable to Ouriel and colleagues' series[10a] of 13 patients with renal artery embolism treated with open operation.

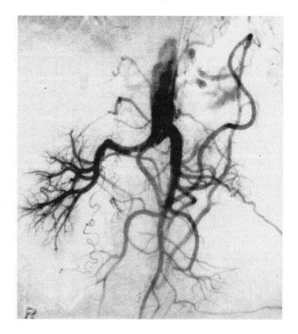

FIGURE 134-1 Patient with thrombotic occlusion of severely diseased aorta with proximal propagation of clot to left renal artery. Severe hypertension was more prominent presenting symptom than lower limb ischemia which was mitigated by collaterals to common femoral arteries.

■ RENAL ARTERY THROMBOSIS

Acute thrombosis of the renal artery occurs most commonly in patients with advanced atherosclerotic disease of the aorta and its branches. This event may be clinically silent if adequate collateral circulation to the distal renal artery from ureteral, lumbar, adrenal, or capsular vessels already exists.[11] However, in patients with only one functional kidney or poor renal reserve, renal artery thrombosis may present with both severe hypertension and the acute onset of oliguric renal failure.[12] Renal artery thrombosis may also complicate percutaneous transluminal renal angioplasty, which is being used more commonly to treat atherosclerotic renal artery stenosis.[13,14] Patients at highest risk for periprocedural thrombosis are those with significant abdominal aortic atherosclerosis and associated ostial renal artery stenosis (Fig. 134-1).[15] The increased use of stenting in cases of suboptimal angioplasty has decreased the overall incidence of acute thrombosis. In a recent report by Morris and coworkers,[6] 6 of 212 patients suffered acute occlusion after renal artery angioplasty and stenting, presumably from intimal injury or dissection. All of these were successfully treated nonoperatively with either thrombolysis or additional stenting.

Both renal ultrasonography and angiography can aid in establishing the diagnosis. If adequate collateral arterial supply is present, arteriography may reveal retrograde filling of the distal renal arterial tree. This finding, in combination with documentation of renal perfusion by isotope renography, are excellent prognostic signs even if excretory function is markedly reduced.[15] Most importantly, unlike the treatment of renal artery embolism, correction of renal artery thrombosis superimposed on a preexistent severe occlusive lesion rarely mandates an urgent operative

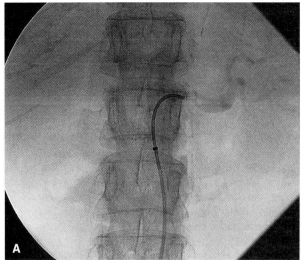
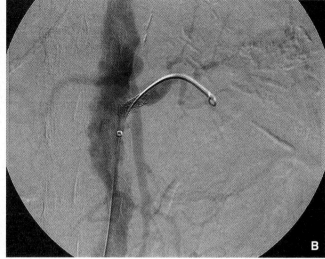

FIGURE 134-2 **A,** Occluded left renal artery in a patient presenting with acute renal failure requiring hemodialysis (the right kidney was atrophic with a chronically occluded right renal artery). **B,** The occlusion was traversed with a wire, allowing angioplasty and stenting of the left renal artery. The patient required no further dialysis after the procedure.

approach. Any metabolic derangements should be corrected and the appropriate evaluation of cardiac and other risk factors should be carried out. Although patients may require dialysis during this period, it has been the experience of many centers that this does not preclude considerable recovery of renal function following revascularization, even if the procedure is delayed by weeks.[16,17]

Surgical revascularization options include aortorenal bypass with saphenous vein or synthetic grafts.[18-20] In patients with severe atherosclerosis of the abdominal aorta, extra-anatomic bypasses including hepatorenal bypass, splenorenal bypass or iliorenal bypass may be preferable. Revascularization can yield dramatic results with almost immediate recovery of renal function in a majority of appropriately selected patients.[16]

Thrombolysis with angioplasty and stent placement may also have a role in these patients.[21] Intervention can be executed at the time of arteriogram and thrombolysis may reveal an underlying stenosis that can then be angioplastied and stented (Fig. 134-2). Primary stenting should be undertaken in these vessels with a previous complete occlusion. In small published series, initial success rates approaching 60% are reported, although long-term patency and durability of renal function recovery are yet unknown with these new techniques.[22-24] In some patients, primary angioplasty and stenting without thrombolysis may be undertaken if wire traversal of the acute occlusion is possible and a patent distal artery exists.

■ RENAL ARTERY DISSECTION

Renal artery dissections can be categorized into primary and secondary lesions. Primary lesions are associated with underlying renal artery disease, such as fibromuscular dysplasia (FMD) or atherosclerosis, and occur spontaneously. Secondary dissections result from either blunt trauma or interventional procedures involving selective renal artery catheterization. Aortic dissection can also present with acute renal ischemia if the intimal flap obstructs the renal artery, the dissection extends into the renal artery, or if an artery originates from a false lumen that becomes thrombosed.

Renal artery dissections are often clinically silent yet they can result in a broad spectrum of consequences including renal infarction and the acute onset of severe hypertension. The clinical course is largely dictated by the degree of renal artery obstruction and the presence or absence of preformed arterial collateral vessels. Treatment is appropriately individualized depending on the severity of symptoms and the anatomic nature of the lesion.

It is thought that renal arteries are the most common site of primary dissection involving peripheral vessels.[25] Nonetheless, spontaneous dissection of the renal artery is relatively rare and usually occurs in the setting of FMD, advanced atherosclerosis, or other arteritides (Fig. 134-3).[26] The clinical characteristics of patients suffering from dissections represent the underlying diseases: young women are most commonly affected in the case of dysplastic lesions and older individuals are affected with generalized atherosclerosis. Most spontaneous dissections are clinically silent so the precise incidence of complications related to these lesions is difficult to assess. Symptomatic dissections typically present with upper abdominal or flank pain (92%), hematuria (33%), and onset of severe hypertension (100%).[27] The hypertension produced by spontaneous dissection of the renal artery is often severe and difficult to control and usually requires multidrug therapy. Although there are isolated reports of spontaneous recovery with normalization of blood pressure, this phenomenon is far less common in localized dissection than in instances of aortic dissection extending into or excluding the renal arteries.[28] Histopathologic examination suggests, in fact, that unlike typical aortic dissections, spontaneous renal artery dissection channels often do not communicate with the vessel

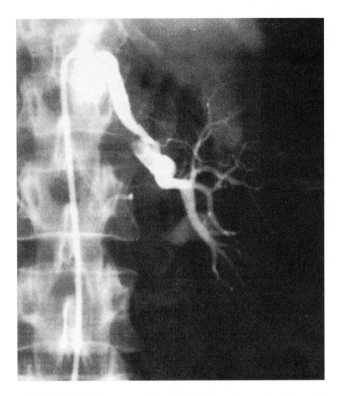

FIGURE 134-3 Spontaneous dissection in left renal artery in patient with acute onset of severe hypertension. Such highly stenotic dissections require operative treatment (From Gewertz BL, Stanley JC, Fry WJ: Renal artery dissections. Arch Surg 112:409-414, 1977.)

lumen but rather represent intramural hematoma formation along a deeper medial plane.[29] Hence, true "re-entry" is less likely. Post-traumatic dissections in previously normal vessels also present with obstruction unassociated with re-entry. Their etiology is different from spontaneous dissections because they usually begin with an intimal tear and extend along subintimal or superficial medial planes.

Although isotope renography may be helpful in determining the presence of renal ischemia, this information does not aid in planning operative repair and is not helpful in identifying which patients are most amenable to treatment (i.e., those with patent but stenosed renal arteries with adequate antegrade renal perfusion to maintain patent distal vasculature). Duplex ultrasonography may be helpful in the identification of abnormalities of the renal arteries, but this technique is ill suited to reliably distinguish between intrinsic atherosclerotic or fibromuscular disease and dissection. Selective arteriography remains the diagnostic test of choice and should be used in every case to define the nature and extent of the lesion and suitability for repair.

Limited dissection without significant main renal artery stenosis or hypertension is best treated expectantly. In symptomatic patients with severe hypertension, most experienced surgeons advocate renal artery revascularization unless irreversible renal ischemia has occurred or the dissection extends into renal artery parenchymal branches. Although partial or total nephrectomy usually results in resolution of hypertension, the high incidence of bilaterality

in renal artery dissection (>20%) and in the related FMD (>50%) argues strongly for maximal renal salvage attempts.

Operative repair of renal artery dissection is challenging and invariably requires control of at least the primary branches of the renal artery regardless of the apparent limits of the dissection. When the dissection does not extend past the first branch point, in-situ repair is almost always feasible. In contrast, repair of dissection extending into the secondary branches is best performed with ex-vivo techniques (Fig. 134-4). In a series of patients with extensive dissections reported by Reilly and associates, temporary preservation with reimplantation was used successfully in six of seven reconstructions.[30] Intraoperative duplex ultrasonography is most useful in assessing the technical success of the repair in the small hilar branches.

Prior to the widespread application of percutaneous interventional procedures, the incidence of secondary (iatrogenic) dissections was very low. In 1976, Gewertz and associates documented only four instances of renal artery dissection among a total of 11,000 abdominal arteriograms, including more than 2000 selective renal catheterizations.[29] With increased application of renal artery angioplasty, the frequency of secondary dissection has predictably increased, although its precise incidence is not known.[31] Virtually all balloon dilations create a dissection when the plaque or dysplastic lesion is fractured; hence, the practical definition of a postangiographic dissection must include a limitation of blood flow from occlusion or stenosis. Using these criteria, collected series of angioplasties estimate an incidence of approximately 4% of main and branch renal artery dissections with less than half of these requiring surgery.[32-35] Many limited dissections are managed at the time of angioplasty and stenting, and in the absence of sequelae, may not even be recorded as a complication. Provided wire control is maintained across the lesion, stenting can effectively tack down the dissection, preventing further propagation. Loss of wire control across the lesion and area of dissection may require urgent operation to revascularize the kidney.

In instances of extensive dissection with main renal artery or major branch occlusion, urgent operation is appropriate. Results are far less favorable than those of elective renal artery revascularization but are probably comparable to outcomes after operative treatment of spontaneous dissections. Highly experienced renovascular surgeons have noted the unique challenges of operating on dissected renal arteries, including the dense periarterial inflammatory response that greatly complicates distal repairs even with the ex-vivo technique.[13]

Aortic dissection associated with renal ischemia represents a particularly difficult problem. Ischemic complications of aortic dissection are associated with a high mortality, particularly when they involve the mesenteric or renal arteries,[36-39] and operations to repair visceral aortic dissection in the acute setting have significant morbidity. Endovascular treatment of these lesions may provide a less invasive technique that can restore renal artery blood flow. Balloon fenestration of an aortic flap to restore blood flow into the lumen supplying the affected renal artery with or without additional stenting of the aorta or renal artery to maintain perfusion has been described with acceptable initial results.[40,41]

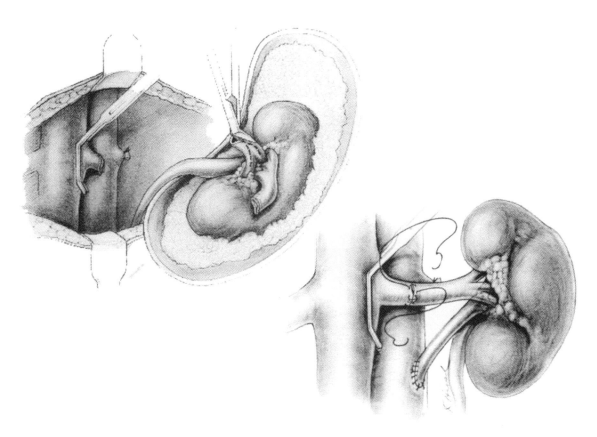

FIGURE 134-4 Technique for ex-vivo repair of distal left renal artery dissection. The kidney is flushed with renal preservation solution and placed on ice during repair to minimize ischemic injury. Bypass with autologous vein or artery is completed (*lower right*) and vein is reanastomosed.

■ ACUTE RENAL VEIN THROMBOSIS

Renal vein thrombosis is an unusual clinical entity that rarely requires operative intervention. Renal vein thrombosis is seen in two discrete patient populations: adults with nephrotic syndrome and neonates with severe dehydration.[42,43] The morbidity associated with renal vein thrombosis is primarily related to the underlying condition producing the coagulopathic state.

The nephrotic syndrome results in loss of low-molecular-weight proteins in the urine, decreased antithrombin III levels, and thrombocytosis, all of which contribute to a hypercoagulable state.[44] A contracted intravascular volume and hemoconcentration also lead to renal vein stasis. Other conditions occasionally associated with renal vein thrombosis in adults include pregnancy, use of oral contraceptives, neoplasms (especially renal cell carcinoma), sickle cell anemia, and trauma.

Adults with acute renal vein thrombosis present with acute-onset flank pain, hematuria, proteinuria, and impairment of renal function. Rarely, venous congestion of the kidney can cause hemorrhagic infarction and rupture. In these unusual cases, severe retroperitoneal hemorrhage may require urgent nephrectomy.

Neonatal renal vein thrombosis occurs in infants who are severely dehydrated secondary to diarrhea or vomiting or in septic states.[45] Infants of diabetic mothers may be predisposed to this disorder due to hyperglycemia and solute diuresis.[46] Children present with sudden onset of abdominal distention, flank mass, hematuria, and proteinuria. In advanced cases of bilateral renal vein thrombosis, infants can suffer progressive renal insufficiency.

Diagnosis can be established by duplex ultrasonography, which demonstrates renal enlargement with distortion of the parenchymal pattern, renal vein dilation, and thrombus within the renal vein. Computed tomography (CT) may also be helpful in establishing the diagnosis, although it requires the administration of potentially nephrotoxic contrast agents. Magnetic resonance imaging avoids contrast administration and may prove to be the test of choice in the future especially in adults.[47]

Management in both the adult and pediatric populations is primarily supportive and directed toward treatment of underlying metabolic abnormalities and correction of any potentially reversible hypercoagulable state. Hydration and immediate heparin anticoagulation followed by warfarin anticoagulation for 6 months are standard. A longer period of anticoagulation is indicated in patients with nephrotic syndrome. More recently, thrombolytic therapy has been used, via either renal venous or arterial infusion. This approach is most attractive in patients with bilateral renal vein thrombosis or venous thrombosis of a solitary kidney. Operative thrombectomy of renal vein thrombosis is limited to those few patients with rapidly declining renal function in whom thrombolytic therapy is contraindicated or unsuccessful.

Both the underlying hypercoagulable state and the presence of thrombus along the vena cava substantially increase the likelihood of pulmonary embolus in these patients. If pulmonary emboli are documented, strong consideration should be given to placement of a suprarenal filter in addition to anticoagulation. Although filter placement has the theoretical disadvantage of predisposing to vena caval thrombosis, the incidence of this complication appears to be quite low.

■ RENAL ARTERY TRAUMA

Renal artery trauma is unusual. Penetrating abdominal or lower thoracic injuries result in renal pedicle laceration in less than 7% of cases while it is estimated that blunt abdominal trauma leads to disruption, dissection, or occlusion of the renal artery in less than 4% of seriously injured patients.[48] Although management strategies for these two types of injuries are somewhat different, results from all treatments are not particularly good.

The mechanisms of renal artery injury with penetrating trauma are unambiguous. Nonetheless, in such gunshot and stab wounds, management is still complicated by the likelihood that the renal parenchyma and other vital structures are injured simultaneously. In contrast, diagnosis and management of blunt trauma reflect the two distinct patterns of injury.[49] In *direct injuries* from contact sports or motor vehicle accidents, anterior blows to the mid-abdomen compress the right renal artery as it crosses the vertebral column (Fig. 134-5). In *indirect injuries*, acceleration/deceleration forces accompanying high-speed collisions stretch both renal pedicles and can disrupt the vessels or rupture the intima, the least elastic portion of vessel. Intimal

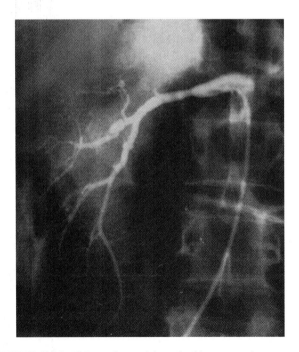

FIGURE 134-5 Right renal artery injury after blunt trauma demonstrates dissection of the main renal artery both primary branches (From Gewertz BL, Stanley JC, Fry WJ: Renal artery dissections. Arch Surg 112:409-414, 1977.)

tears can lead to acute renal artery thrombosis or a more stable yet obstructive dissection.[29]

Owing to these divergent mechanisms of injury, the diagnosis and treatment of penetrating and blunt trauma differ substantially. Patients with hypotension and/or exsanguinating hemorrhage from penetrating truncal injury require immediate operative exploration. In such situations, control of associated hepatic, splenic, and major vascular injury is mandatory. Surgical decision making relative to the kidneys is enhanced if the patient is stable enough to undergo a "single-shot" intravenous pyelogram in the operating room prior to opening any hematoma in the retroperitoneum. Although such studies may not necessarily differentiate a renal parenchymal laceration from a pedicle injury, the presence of a functional contralateral kidney can be confirmed.

If nonrenal injuries are controlled and the patient's condition is stable, vascular repair of an injured renal pedicle can be considered. Most commonly, this requires an aortorenal bypass to the débrided distal renal artery. Unfortunately, circumstances usually do not allow for such repairs; renal artery lacerations or transections are rarely the only serious injury, and most patients' overall conditions mandate the most rapid resolution for the problem, which is nephrectomy.

The diagnosis of renal artery injury following blunt trauma is based on the routine inclusion of thoracic and abdominal vascular imaging in the initial assessment of any patient suffering a high-speed accident. A history of such an injury is a more compelling indication for such an evaluation than any specific sign or symptom. In fact, up to 25% of patients with renal pedicle injuries have no urinary findings, supporting the observation that the presence of hematuria or flank pain reflects associated renal contusions, not the status of the renal vessels.[50] In the past, aggressive utilization of arteriography was the only reliable method of screening for such injuries.[51,52] More recently, CT with helical scanning techniques has supplanted arteriography in many large centers.[53,54]

Successful emergency reconstruction of renal artery injuries in the setting of blunt trauma is rare. Stables and associates reported that only 2 of 26 renal artery injuries could be successfully reconstructed.[55] Clark and colleagues reported only a 17% restoration of function in 12 kidneys revascularized after injury.[49] In truth, this dismal outlook more likely reflects the common association of other life-threatening injuries, especially of the aortic isthmus, spleen, and liver, which detract from the attention given renal artery injuries.

■ REFERENCES

1. Traube L: Uber den Zusammenhang von Herz und Nieren Krakheiten. In Hirschwald A (ed): Gesammelte Beitrage zur Pathologie und Physiologie. Berlin, 1856, 77.
2. Hoxie HJ, Coggin CB: Renal infarction: Statistical study of two hundred five cases and detailed report of an unusual case. Arch Intern Med 65:587, 1940.
3. Nicholas GG, DeMuth WE Jr: Treatment of renal artery embolism. Arch Surg 119:278-281, 1984.
4. Platt JF: Duplex Doppler evaluation of acute renal obstruction. Semin Ultrasound CT MR 18:147-153, 1997.

5. Fischer CP, Konnak JW, Cho KJ, et al: Renal artery embolism: Therapy with intra-arterial streptokinase infusion. J Urol 125: 402-404, 1981.

6. Morris CS, Bonnevie GJ, Najarian KE: Nonsurgical treatment of acute iatrogenic renal artery injuries occurring after renal artery angioplasty and stenting. AJR Am J Roentgenol 177:1353-1357, 2001.

7. Shah DM, Darling RC III, Chang BB, et al: Access to the right renal artery from the left retroperitoneal approach. Cardiovasc Surg 4:763-765, 1996.

8. Schwartz LB, Gewertz BL: The renal response to low-dose dopamine. J Surg Res 45:574-588, 1988.

9. Stone HH, Fulenwider JT: Renal decapsulation in the prevention of post-ischemic oliguria. Ann Surg 186:343-355, 1977.

10. Salam TA, Lumsden AB, Martin LG: Local infusion of fibrinolytic agents for acute renal artery thromboembolism: Report of ten cases. Ann Vasc Surg 7:21-26, 1993.

10a. Ouriel K, Andrus CH, Ricotta JJ, et al: Acute renal artery occlusion: When is revascularization justified? J Vasc Surg 5:348-355, 1987.

11. Abrams HL, Cornell SH: Patterns of collateral flow in renal ischemia. Radiology 84:1001-1012, 1965.

12. Hall SK: Acute renal vascular occlusion: An uncommon mimic. J Emerg Med 11:691-700, 1993.

13. Dean RH, Callis JT, Smith BM, Meacham PW: Failed percutaneous transluminal renal angioplasty: Experience with lesions requiring operative intervention. J Vasc Surg 6:301-307, 1987.

14. Komeyama T: Successful fibrinolytic therapy using tissue plasminogen activator in acute renal failure due to thrombosis of bilateral renal arteries. Urol Int 51:177-180, 1993.

15. Gilbert LA, Katz N, Mandal AK, et al: Acute proximal occlusion of a nonaneurysmal abdominal aorta and renal arteries detected by renal imaging. Clin Nucl Med 22:231-234, 1997.

16. Dean RH, Tribble RW, Hansen KJ, et al: Evolution of renal insufficiency in ischemic nephropathy. Ann Surg 213:446-455, 1991.

17. Higgins RM, Goldsmith DJ, Charlesworth D, et al: Elective rather than emergency intervention for acute renal artery occlusion with anuria. Nephron 68:265-267, 1994.

18. Dean RH: Surgery for renovascular hypertension. In Bergen JJ, Yao JST (eds): Operative Techniques in Vascular Surgery. New York, Grune & Stratton, 1980, pp 81-87.

19. Chaikof EL: Revascularization of the occluded renal artery. Semin Vasc Surg 9:218-220, 1996.

20. Fujitani RM, Murray SP: Surgical methods for renal revascularization. Semin Vasc Surg 9:198-217, 1996.

21. Ellis D, Kaye RD, Bontempo FA: Aortic and renal artery thrombosis in a neonate: Recovery with thrombolytic therapy. Pediatr Nephrol 11:641-644, 1997.

22. Dwyer KM, Vrazas JL, Lodge RS, et al: Treatment of acute renal failure caused by renal artery occlusion with renal artery angioplasty. Am J Kidney Dis 40:189-194, 2002.

23. Kadir S, Watson A, Burrow C: Percutaneous transcatheter recanalization in the management of acute renal failure due to sudden occlusion of the renal artery to a solitary kidney. Am J Nephrol 7:445-449, 1987.

24. Louden JD, Leen GL, Cove-Smith R: Systemic thrombolysis for bilateral atherosclerotic renal artery occlusion resulting in prolonged recovery of renal function. Nephrol Dial Transplant 13:2924-2926, 1998.

25. Foord AG, Lewis RD: Primary dissecting aneurysms of the peripheral and pulmonary arteries: Dissecting hemorrhage of the media. Arch Pathol 68:553-577, 1956.

26. Englund GW: Primary dissecting aneurysm of the renal artery: Report of a case and review of the literature. Am J Clin Pathol 45:472-479, 1966.

27. Smith BM, Holcomb GW III, Richie RE, Dean RH: Renal artery dissection. Ann Surg 200:134-146, 1984.

28. Park JH, Chung JW, Cho YK, et al: Percutaneous fenestration of aortic dissection: Salvage of an ischemic solitary left kidney. Cardiovasc Intervent Radiol 20:146-148, 1997.

29. Gewertz BL, Stanley JC, Fry WJ: Renal artery dissections. Arch Surg 112:409-414, 1977.

30. Reilly LM, Cunningham CG, Maggisano R, et al: The role of arterial reconstruction in spontaneous renal artery dissection. J Vasc Surg 14:468-479, 1991.

31. Anwar YA, Sullivan ED, Chen HH, White WB: Abrupt, severe hypertension associated with dissection of a renal artery during selective catheterization. J Hum Hypertens 11:533-536, 1997.

32. Martinez AG, Novick AC, Hayes JM: Surgical treatment of renal artery stenosis after failed percutaneous transluminal angioplasty. J Urol 144:1094-1096, 1990.

33. Tegtmeyer CJ, Selby JB, Hartwell GD, et al: Results and complications of angioplasty in fibromuscular disease. Circulation 83:I155-I161, 1991.

34. Rees CR, Palmaz JC, Becker GJ, et al: Palmaz stent in atherosclerotic stenoses involving the ostia of the renal arteries: Preliminary report of a multicenter study. Radiology 181:507-514, 1991.

35. Martin LG, Casarella WJ, Alspaugh JP, Chuang VP: Renal artery angioplasty: Increased technical success and decreased complications in the second 100 patients. Radiology 159:631-634, 1986.

36. Miller DC, Mitchell RS, Oyer PE, et al: Independent determinants of operative mortality for patients with aortic dissections. Circulation 70:I153-I164, 1984.

37. Cambria RP, Brewster DC, Gertler J, et al: Vascular complications associated with spontaneous aortic dissection. J Vasc Surg 7:199-209, 1988.

38. Fann JI, Sarris GE, Mitchell RS, et al: Treatment of patients with aortic dissection presenting with peripheral vascular complications. Ann Surg 212:705-713, 1990.

39. Doroghazi RM, Slater EE, De Santis RW, et al: Long-term survival of patients with treated aortic dissection. J Am Coll Cardiol 3:1026-1034, 1984.

40. Slonim SM, Nyman U, Semba CP, et al: Aortic dissection: Percutaneous management of ischemic complications with endovascular stents and balloon fenestration. J Vasc Surg 23:241-253, 1996.

41. Vedantham S, Picus D, Sanchez LA, et al: Percutaneous management of ischemic complications in patients with type-B aortic dissection. J Vasc Interv Radiol 14:181-194, 2003.

42. Baum NH, Moriel E, Carlton CE Jr: Renal vein thrombosis. J Urol 119:443-448, 1978.

43. Arneil GC, MacDonald AM, Sweet EM: Renal venous thrombosis. Clin Nephrol 1:119-131, 1973.

44. Brumfitt W, O'Brien W: Renal vein thrombosis with nephrotic syndrome and renal failure. BMJ 12:751-752, 1956.

45. Jones JE, Reed JF Jr: Renal vein thrombosis and thrombocytopenia in a newborn infant. J Pediatr 67:681-682, 1965.

46. Avery ME, Oppenheimer EH, Gordon HH: Renal-vein thrombosis in newborn infants of diabetic mothers: Report of two cases. N Engl J Med 256:1134-1138, 1957.

47. Dietrich RB, Kangarloo H: Kidneys in infants and children: Evaluation with MR. Radiology 159:215-221, 1986.

48. Brown MF, Graham JM, Mattox KL, et al: Renovascular trauma. Am J Surg 140:802-805, 1980.

49. Clark DE, Georgitis JW, Ray FS: Renal arterial injuries caused by blunt trauma. Surgery 90:87-96, 1981.

50. Grablowsky OM, Goff JB, Schlegel JU, Weichert RF III: Renal artery thrombosis following blunt trauma: Report of four cases. Surgery 67:895-900, 1970.

51. Itzchak Y, Adar R, Mozes M, Deutsch V: Occlusion of renal and visceral arteries following blunt abdominal trauma: Angiographic observations. J Cardiovasc Surg (Torino) 15:383-388, 1974.

52. Marks LS, Brosman SA, Lindstrom RR, Fay R: Arteriography in penetrating renal trauma. Urology 3:18-22, 1974.

53. Nunez D Jr, Becerra JL, Fuentes D, Pagson S: Traumatic occlusion of the renal artery: Helical CT diagnosis. AJR Am J Roentgenol 167:777-780, 1996.

54. Fang YC, Tiu CM, Chou YH, Chang T: A case of acute renal artery thrombosis caused by blunt trauma: Computed tomographic and Doppler ultrasonic findings. J Formos Med Assoc 92:356-358, 1993.

55. Stables DP, Rouche RF, de Villiers van Niekerk JP, et al: Traumatic renal artery occlusion: Twenty-one cases. J Urol 115:229-233, 1976.

MANAGEMENT OF EXTRACRANIAL CEREBROVASCULAR DISEASE

WILLIAM C. KRUPSKI, MD

Chapter

Fundamental Considerations in Cerebrovascular Disease

135

WESLEY S. MOORE, MD

Stroke is the third leading cause of death in the United States each year. It is the second leading cause of cardiovascular death and the most common cause of death as a result of neurologic disorders. The incidence of new stroke is approximately 160 per 100,000 population per year.[59,63] In addition to death, the disability following cerebral infarction must be considered from the standpoint of the crippling effect on the patient as well as the socioeconomic burden on the patient, his or her family, and society. Reviews of the financial impact of stroke for calendar year 1999 were estimated to be $45.3 billion of direct and indirect cost.[2,94]

The earliest report linking stroke with extracranial vascular disease is credited to Gowers, who in 1875 described a patient with right hemiplegia and blindness in the left eye.[37] He attributed this syndrome to an occlusion of the left carotid artery in the neck. Several similar reports soon followed.[9,12,41] In 1914, Hunt emphasized that extracranial carotid artery occlusive disease was a possible cause of stroke.[54] He noted that the cervical portions of the carotid arteries were not examined routinely postmortem and urged that thorough examination of this portion of the circulatory system be carried out during autopsy. Furthermore, he believed that transient cerebral ischemia was tantamount to intermittent claudication of the brain and represented a prodrome to a major stroke.

In spite of these early reports, work in this field remained relatively dormant until Moniz and coworkers reported in 1937 that arteriography could be used to diagnose carotid artery occlusion.[76] Johnson and Walker reviewed 101 cases of carotid occlusion diagnosed by arteriography and advocated either carotid arterectomy or cervical ganglionectomy

to relieve cerebral vasospasm, which they believed to be a major cause of subsequent disability following the initial stroke.[56] Strully and associates are credited with the first attempt at endarterectomy of a totally occluded carotid artery; however, this was unsuccessful.[93]

The first report of a successful surgical procedure on the extracranial carotid artery appeared in 1954: Eastcott and colleagues described their experience with a patient who had episodes of transient hemispheric cerebral ischemic attacks.[22] She was found to have an atherosclerotic lesion at the carotid bifurcation that was treated with a resection and primary anastomosis. A later publication by DeBakey[16] and one of Carrea and coworkers[10] cite operative procedures reportedly performed at earlier dates, but the report of Eastcott and colleagues must be credited as the most influential in bringing the possibility of carotid artery repair to medical attention. Vascular surgery had progressed to a point at which surgical repair of this lesion was rapidly accepted, and subsequently carotid endarterectomy has become one of the most common and successful operations performed on the vascular system.

The surgical approach to cerebrovascular disease is predicated on the relief of symptoms of cerebral dysfunction and the prevention of cerebral infarction or stroke by excision of a critical lesion in the extracranial carotid artery. There was a major international debate concerning the efficacy of carotid endarterectomy in stroke prevention when one considers the combination of perioperative risk and late results. It has been shown that an aggressive surgical approach to cerebrovascular disease can be justified only when the operation can be performed with sufficiently low rates of morbidity and mortality for the longevity and quality of survival of patients with cerebrovascular atherosclerosis to be materially altered, when compared with the results of medical management alone.[26,48,80,81,95]

■ EPIDEMIOLOGY AND NATURAL HISTORY OF CEREBROVASCULAR DISEASE

Knowledge of the incidence and natural history of hemispheric transient ischemic attacks (TIAs) and strokes in a given population is of paramount importance not only in understanding the magnitude of the problem but also in designing a program of diagnosis, treatment, and prevention. The magnitude of the problem dictates its investigative priority, and knowledge of the natural history is fundamental in evaluating and comparing the impact of various therapeutic interventions.

The objective of all therapeutic intervention is to prevent cerebral infarction. Episodes of transient cerebral ischemia usually are considered benign events, but they are harbingers of subsequent stroke, neurologic disability, or death.

Cerebral Infarction

There is considerable variability concerning the incidence of stroke, depending on the year of reporting, geographic location, and racial and gender mix of patients. For example, there has been a steady decline in mortality from cerebrovascular disease in the United States dating back to 1915.[105] This decline in mortality may or may not translate into a true decline in stroke incidence. The reason for the decline in stroke mortality is difficult to ascertain. It may be something as simple as a more accurate diagnosis of stroke on a death certificate, or it may represent a true change in the incidence of the disease. Finally, various interventions, ranging from control of hypertension to the use of aspirin and other antiplatelet drugs to carotid endarterectomy, must be interpreted accordingly.

There have been several population studies designed to look at stroke incidence. The Rochester, Minnesota, population study (from 1955 to 1969) emphasized the influence of advancing age on the progressive incidence of cerebral infarction.[68] The age group of 55 to 64 years had a cerebral infarction rate of 276.8 per 100,000 population per year; the age group of 65 to 74 years had an incidence of 632 per 100,000 population per year; and the older than-75-year age group had a stroke rate of 1786.4 per 100,000 population per year. Analysis of the cerebral infarction rate divided by sex distribution indicated that in men the rate was approximately 1.5 times as great as that in women of the same age. Six months following survival from cerebral infarction, only 29% of the patients in the Rochester study had normal cerebral function; 71% continued to have manifestations of neurologic dysfunction. In the latter group, 4% required total nursing care, 18% were disabled but capable of contributing to self-care, and 10% were aphasic. Of those patients who suffered a fatal stroke, 38% died of the initial stroke, 10% died of a subsequent stroke, and 18% died from complications of coronary artery disease. The chance of a recurrent stroke within 1 year of the initial stroke was 10%, and

the chance of a recurrent stroke within 5 years of the initial attack was 20%.

Wolfe and colleagues, in 1989, reported data from the Framingham study.[106] They reviewed the experience from three successive decades beginning in 1953. They noted a decline of *stroke fatality* in both men and women. However, the 10-year prevalence rate of stroke actually rose, and the *incidence* of stroke rose in men from 5.7% to 7.6% to 7.9% without any apparent change in women. The investigators suggested that the case fatality rates may result from changes in diagnostic criteria, a lessening in stroke severity, or improved care of stroke patients. Nonetheless, they clearly show that there was not a declining incidence.[106]

Wallace's studied the natural history of stroke in 188 patients in the city of Goulburn, Australia.[101] The overall incidence of stroke for all ages was 330 per 100,000 population per year. During a 24-month interval, he accumulated 158 cases of stroke, of which 101 were presumed to be due to cerebral infarction. The mortality rate of the first attack was 37%, and the recurrence rate among survivors was 35%. The mortality rate with the first recurrence was 35%, but the mortality rate for subsequent recurrences in survivors of a first recurrence was 65%.

Baker and colleagues reported a series of 430 hospitalized patients who survived their initial cerebral infarction.[4] The mortality rate from the initial stroke was not described. However, the overall mortality rate for the 430 survivors during the interval of study was 40%. On a life table, the mortality rate was 10% per year of patients at risk. The cumulative 5-year mortality rate was 50%. Twenty-three percent of subsequent deaths were due to recurrent cerebral infarction. Of the 430 survivors of the initial stroke, 26% developed a subsequent recurrent cerebral infarction, and 20% experienced new TIAs. Because some patients have both TIA and stroke, a combined 38% were reported to develop a new neurologic event: stroke, transient cerebral ischemia, or both. Of the 113 patients who developed a new cerebral infarction, 62% died.

Sacco and coworkers, reviewing the stroke data from the Framingham, Massachusetts, population, noted an alarmingly high incidence of recurrent cerebral infarction in the same anatomic region.[89] Among 394 patients surviving an initial stroke, 84 second and 27 third strokes were reported. The cumulative 5-year recurrent stroke rate in the male population was 42%. Thus, the recurrent stroke rate, following an initial stroke, is approximately 9% per year.

These data indicate that cerebral infarction produces significant morbidity and mortality in the United States. Of particular interest is the remarkably high rate of recurrence of cerebral infarction in patients following their first stroke, if no intervention has taken place. Most of the recurrences appear to occur within the first year of the initial event. Not only is the rate of recurrence with progressive neurologic deterioration high but also the death rate with subsequent infarction is considerable.

Transient Ischemic Attacks

To discuss the incidence and significance of TIAs, one must define the type and anatomic distribution of the event. Those reports that combine focal neurologic events with those of global symptoms such as dizziness and vertigo cloud the

Table 135-1	Average Annual Incidence* of New Transient Ischemic Attacks in a Previously Asymptomatic Population					
	ROCHESTER STUDY		FRAMINGHAM STUDY		LEHIGH VALLEY STUDY	
AGE, yr	Male	Female	Male	Female	Male	Female
45-54	21	12	56	15	85	48
55-64	96	50	114	49	—	—
65-74	263	192	184	142	244	151

*Expressed in number per 100,000 population.

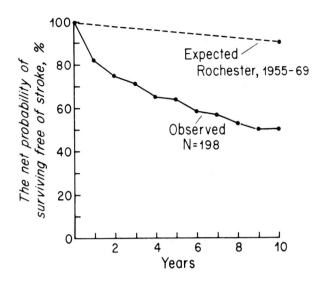

FIGURE 135-1 Conditional probability of surviving free of stroke after first transient ischemic attack (TIA), if the patients survive. Expected survivorship is for a population of the given age and sex and is based on the stroke incidence rates of the Rochester, Minnesota, study for 1955 through 1969. (From Whisnant JP, Matsumoto N, Elveback LR: Transient cerebral ischemic attacks in a community: Rochester, Minnesota, 1955 through 1969. Mayo Clin Proc 48:194, 1973.)

issue and lead to erroneous conclusions because the natural history and prognosis of the two types of attacks are quite different. Most investigators agree that TIAs producing focal neurologic deficits have a greater risk for subsequent cerebral infarction.[34] For purposes of this discussion, therefore, TIAs are considered those that produce transient focal neurologic deficit, in either the anterior or the posterior circulation.

Because many patients with TIAs never reach a hospital, studies of hospital populations are not an accurate reflection of the disease. Studies that review the overall incidence in *specific communities* give a far better view of the incidence and natural history of the event. There have been several such population studies, and these are cited in the text and among the references.[67] One of the most important studies has been carried out using Rochester, Minnesota, as a population base and reported by members of the staff of the Mayo Clinic. Their reports evaluated two time intervals: 1945 to 1954 and 1955 to 1969.[68,103] In the Rochester, Minnesota, population, the incidence of TIAs amounted to 31 patients per 100,000 population per year for all ages, with a rapidly rising incidence associated with advancing age. The incidence of new attacks in the 65- to 74-year-old age group was 200 patients per 100,000 population per year. As in the instance of cerebral infarction, there was also a higher incidence of TIAs in men than in women of the same age group at a ratio of 1.3:1. Table 135-1 compares the average annual incidence of first TIA per 100,000 population in three population studies: Rochester, Minnesota; Framingham, Massachusetts; and Lehigh Valley, Pennsylvania.

Reviewing the natural history of patients with TIA reveals somewhat conflicting data. This is due, primarily, to the lack of definition of the underlying lesion present in the patient population manifesting transient cerebral ischemia. For example, if one population has a large preponderance of patients with high-grade stenoses, composed of soft plaque with ulceration, there is likely to be a much higher subsequent stroke rate than there would be if the population consisted of a large number of patients with low-grade to medium stenoses. Nonetheless, considerable information is to be gained by looking at some of the general population studies with regard to TIA outcome. In the Rochester, Minnesota, study, the probability of surviving free of stroke 5 years after the onset of TIA was only 64%. Conversely, the incidence of stroke was 36% during follow-up. Fifty-one percent of the strokes occurred within the first year after the

onset of TIAs (Fig. 135-1). In the stroke population, the authors noted that, in addition to advancing age, the three major predisposing factors for cerebral infarction were transient ischemia, hypertension, and cardiac disease.

In an excellent review of the available literature, Wiebers and Whisnant[104] noted that of the available studies, the reported annual stroke incidence in patients with TIA ranged from 5.3% to 8.6% per year for the first 5 years. They concluded that the average annual stroke rate among TIA patients was 7% per year for the first 5 years or that approximately one third of patients with TIA will suffer a stroke within 5 years of onset.[104]

The definition of TIA as opposed to stroke is quite arbitrary. If the neurologic deficit lasts less than 24 hours, it is defined as a TIA. If it lasts more than 24 hours it is presumably a stroke. New data suggest that a large proportion of TIAs are actually small strokes. Toole, in his Willis lecture, reminded us that TIA patients suffer a large number of cerebral infarctions that go unrecognized from a clinical perspective. These lesions can now be identified by better brain imaging techniques.[98] Further evidence suggesting that a TIA is actually a small stroke is provided by the observations of Grigg and colleagues, who correlated cerebral infarction and atrophy as a function of TIAs and percent stenosis.[38] In patients who presented with transient episodes of monocular blindness, the incidence of cerebral infarction, as documented by computed tomographic (CT) scanning, rose from 2% in patients with mild stenoses to 58% in patients with high-grade, so-called asymptomatic stenoses. In addition, the incidence of cerebral atrophy showed a parallel increase.[38] With these observations, the benignity of transient cerebral ischemia is called into question. Thus, the need to identify so-called asymptomatic lesions and treat them before TIAs (probably small strokes) occur becomes more important.

Asymptomatic Lesions of the Carotid Artery

Asymptomatic, potentially critical lesions of the carotid bifurcation can be divided into two categories: preocclusive stenoses resulting in hemodynamic compromise; and large, grossly irregular or ulcerative lesions, independent of hemodynamic compromise but with the potential of releasing emboli into the cerebral circulation. In the past few years, the natural history of these lesions has been better defined as a result of several retrospective studies as well as new prospective studies.

The asymptomatic carotid stenosis was the original asymptomatic lesion to be identified as a potential cause of stroke. Stenotic lesions now can be readily identified in screening programs that use noninvasive testing. The natural history of these lesions, however, remains variable and controversial. Three prospective, randomized trials were initiated to determine the efficacy (or lack thereof) of carotid endarterectomy in patients with asymptomatic, hemodynamically significant carotid stenosis.

The European study (Casanova) reported no benefit of carotid endarterectomy when compared with medical management alone.[108] Unfortunately, the study was hampered by serious methodologic flaws in that a large number of patients in the control group were removed and operated on but were counted as medically managed in an intent-to-treat design. Furthermore, the reasons that the patients were removed from the control group, including TIAs, were not considered treatment failures.[108]

The Veterans Affairs Department reported that the combined incidence of ipsilateral neurologic events (TIA plus stroke) was 8% in the surgery group in contrast with 20.6% in the medical group ($P < .001$). Unfortunately, the study was not designed to look for differences in stroke alone.[48]

The Asymptomatic Carotid Atherosclerosis Study (ACAS) is the largest of the trials on asymptomatic carotid stenosis. The trial is now complete and has provided definitive evidence to support the benefit of carotid endarterectomy versus medical management alone in patients with carotid stenosis that equals or exceeds 60% diameter reduction by angiography. In 1994, the Data Safety and Monitoring Committee called a halt to the study far earlier than anticipated and informed the investigators and the public that an endpoint had been reached in favor of carotid endarterectomy. With a mean follow-up of 2.7 years (4657 patient-years of observation), the 5-year risk for ipsilateral stroke, any perioperative stroke, and death was 5.1% for the surgical patients and 11% for patients treated medically alone. This represents an absolute risk reduction of 5.9% and a relative risk reduction of 53% in favor of carotid endarterectomy.[95] The benefit of carotid endarterectomy compared with medical management alone was made possible by low operative morbidity and mortality rates. Of patients actually undergoing carotid endarterectomy, the combined neurologic morbidity and mortality was 1.52%. Thus, careful selection of surgeons and institutions that participated in the study and that could perform this operation safely contributed in large part to the outcome favoring operation.[80]

Perhaps one of the most important arguments in favor of prophylactic repair of asymptomatic lesions is based on a review of various populations of stroke patients. Careful histories from patients who have suffered a stroke reveal that only 30% to 50% of patients had antecedent TIAs. That means that up to one half of patients who developed stroke proceeded from an asymptomatic lesion one day to a stroke the next.

The early leaders in the aggressive surgical approach to the asymptomatic stenoses are Thompson and colleagues, who in 1978 described their experience with 138 patients who presented with asymptomatic bruits and who were followed without operation.[96-98] They noted that 37 of these patients developed TIAs and required endarterectomy. Another 24 patients (17%) presented with stroke without antecedent TIA. From these data, the investigators argue that the imminence of stroke is significant in the asymptomatic patient, and they recommended prophylactic operation when an appropriate lesion is identified.[96-98] The weakness of this argument lies in the fact that the data do not have angiographic substantiation of the nature of the lesion that was present in the patients that were being followed, nor were noninvasive observations made to determine whether a hemodynamically significant stenosis was present. Perhaps a more impressive series was reported by Kartchner and McRae in 1977, in which they followed 147 patients who had oculoplethysmographic and phonoangiographic evidence of carotid stenosis.[60] Without carotid operation, 17 of these 147 patients, or approximately 12%, suffered an acute stroke.

Two fairly new prospective studies have been reported. Roederer and colleagues studied 167 asymptomatic patients with cervical bruit using duplex scanning.[85] They noted that progression of a lesion to compromise the lumen by 80% or more carried a 35% risk of stroke, TIA, or occlusion within 6 months and a 46% event rate at 12 months. Further, they noted that 89% of all events were preceded by a disease progression to greater than 80% stenosis. This probably represents an underestimate of risk in view of the fact that 96 of the 167 patients underwent carotid endarterectomy during the study interval.

The second important natural history study was carried out by Chambers and Norris.[11] These investigators have followed the natural history of 500 patients with asymptomatic carotid bruits in whom the carotid arteries were characterized by Doppler scanning. The patients were restudied every 6 months. In patients identified as having carotid stenoses in excess of 75%, the neurologic event rate was 18% per year and the completed stroke rate was 5% per year. The completed stroke rate without antecedent TIA was 3% per year.

The arguments against an aggressive approach to asymptomatic carotid stenosis are best exemplified in a report by Humphries and colleagues from the Cleveland Clinic.[53] They followed 168 patients with 182 carotid stenoses for an average of 32 months and noted that 26 patients developed TIAs and underwent surgical correction, whereas only 4 patients developed a stroke before operative intervention could be considered. This report suggested that asymptomatic stenosis is a relatively benign lesion and that an imminent stroke will usually be heralded by an antecedent TIA. It is of interest that Humphries' colleagues at the Cleveland Clinic, in spite of this report, continue to advocate prophylactic operation on the asymptomatic stenosis.

In addition to the asymptomatic stenosis, the asymptomatic ulceration in the absence of major concomitant stenosis has been identified as a lesion of potential stroke risk. Our group has carried out a retrospective review of nonstenotic ulcerative lesions that were identified at the time of angiography as being performed for contralateral symptomatic lesions.[77] Because it had been our group's practice not to operate on the asymptomatic ulcer, we had the opportunity to examine the natural history of 67 patients with ulcerative lesions in 72 carotid arteries. The ulcer size was semiquantitatively described as small (group A), medium (group B), or large (group C). In the initial series, 40 lesions were classified as group A and 32 lesions were combined group B and group C. The follow-up of these patients was expressed in the life-table format in which the event of stroke was looked at as a function of duration of follow-up. Our follow-up extended for approximately 7 years. In this group, only one patient in the small ulcer series (group A) went on to have a stroke. There were, however, 10 strokes in the group with larger ulceration, and this produced a stroke rate that averaged 12.5% per year of follow-up.

The report was challenged by a retrospective review carried out by Kroener and colleagues, who confirmed the benign prognosis of small ulcers in group A but could not find a significant stroke risk in group B ulcers.[62] It is of interest that their series excluded patients with the large ulcers, group C, since it had been their practice to operate routinely on those with a very large carotid ulceration. More recently, our group reviewed yet another series and included data from their original report. This yielded 153 asymptomatic, nonstenotic ulcerative lesions of the carotid bifurcation in 141 patients. During the course of the study, with follow-up extending up to 10 years, 3% of patients in group A, 21% of patients in group B, and 19% of patients in group C had hemispheric strokes without antecedent transient ischemia on the side appropriate to the lesion. The interval stroke rates were 4.5% per year for group B and 7.5% per year for group C.[20] Because the interval stroke rate among patients with asymptomatic ulcers was comparable with the stroke rate among patients with TIA, my associates and I have made the recommendation that prophylactic operation be carried out in patients who are good surgical candidates when they have an identifiable group B or C ulceration.

With the publication of the results of the ACAS study, the controversy concerning management of patients with asymptomatic high-grade carotid stenoses has been resolved. Provided that a surgeon can offer a patient a carotid endarterectomy with a stroke morbidity and mortality of less than 1.5%, those patients will clearly fare better than if they were treated with medical management alone. However, not every critic of asymptomatic carotid stenosis intervention has been satisfied. Currently, there is yet another prospective, randomized trial in progress in Europe. This will be a large multicenter trial. The design of this trial has been published, but results are not yet available.[43]

■ PATHOLOGY

The primary pathologic entity responsible for disease in the extracranial cerebrovascular system is *atherosclerosis*, which accounts for approximately 90% of lesions in

the extracranial system seen in the Western world. The remaining 10% include such entities as fibromuscular dysplasia, arterial kinking as a result of elongation, extrinsic compression, traumatic occlusion, intimal dissection, the inflammatory angiopathies, and migraine. Radiation-induced arteriosclerotic change of the extracranial carotid artery has become a recognized entity. Other rare entities, usually involving intracranial vessels, include fibrinoid necrosis, amyloidosis, polyarteritis, allergic angiitis, Wegener's granulomatosis, granulomatous angiitis, giant cell arteritis, amphetamine-associated arteritis, infectious arteritis, and moyamoya disease.[28] Embolization of cardiac origin is a major entity, but for purposes of this presentation it is not considered a primary manifestation of arterial disease of the extracranial system.

Atherosclerosis

The atherosclerotic plaque consists of nodular deposition of fat, primarily cholesterol, in the arterial intima. An associated inflammatory response results in fibroblastic proliferation (Fig. 135-2). In addition, calcium salts may be precipitated in the primary fatty plaque, producing various degrees of calcification of the lesion. The lesion may enlarge as a result of progression of the atheromatous process, or it may be altered by a sudden intraplaque hemorrhage causing precipitous enlargement and possibly occlusion. With either slow or rapid enlargement, there may be a rupture of the intimal lining, with discharge of degenerative atheromatous debris into the lumen of the vessel. Following such an atheromatous discharge, an open cavity remains within the central portion of the lesion. This cavity, or so-called ulcer, can be the nidus for platelet aggregation or thrombus formation or the outlet for further degenerative plaque egress (Fig. 135-3). If the aggregates within the ulcer are only loosely attached, they can be swept into the arterial blood stream as secondary arterial emboli.

Atheromatous lesions characteristically occur at branches or arterial bifurcations. The common sites include (1) the points of takeoff for the branches of the aortic arch; (2) the origins of the vertebral artery from the subclavian artery; (3) the bifurcation of the common carotid artery and, particularly, the carotid bulb; (4) the carotid siphon; and (5) the origins of the anterior and middle cerebral arteries. The course of the basilar artery may also be studded with atheromatous beads, often corresponding to the origins of major branches, including the posterior cerebral arteries. All these locations are of clinical importance, but the relative frequency of involvement of each potential site influences the frequency of occurrence of various clinical manifestations. The predilection of the carotid bifurcation for atheromatous plaquing has been extensively studied and appears to be related to arterial geometry, velocity profile, and wall shear stress.[107] The relative distribution has been studied both by angiography and at the time of autopsy (Figs. 135-4 to 135-6).

Without question, the most common location of significant lesions is the carotid bifurcation. The ratio of extracranial to intracranial lesions is in excess of 2:1. Blaisdell and associates, in a review of aortocranial angiograms of 300 patients, noted that 33% of lesions seen on angiography were distributed intracranially or in

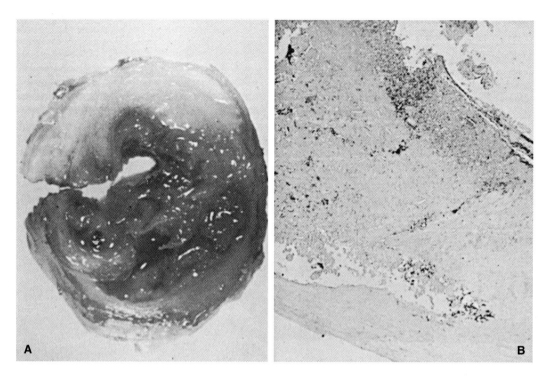

FIGURE 135-2   A, Cross section through a proliferative arteriosclerotic plaque taken at the bifurcation of the common carotid artery. Note the tiny lumen that remains. The material is glistening and consists primarily of cholesterol and necrotic atheromatous debris. **B,** Microscopic section at ×10 magnification. The atheromatous portion of the diseased intima is at the upper part of the photograph. The small spaces or clefts distributed throughout the intimal lesion represent cholesterol crystals.

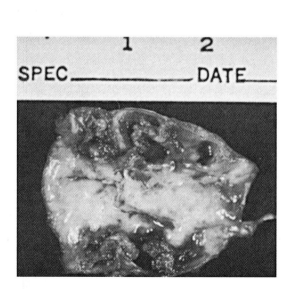

FIGURE 135-3   Atherosclerotic plaque removed from a carotid bifurcation and opened longitudinally to demonstrate the cavities, or ulcers, produced by evacuation of atheromatous debris. These ulcers continue to harbor degenerative atheromatous debris, platelet aggregate material, and thrombus.

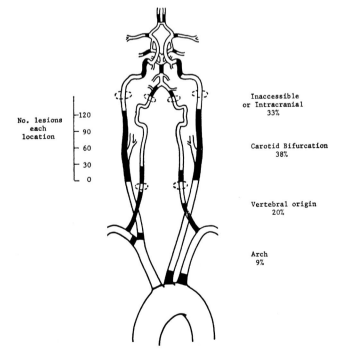

FIGURE 135-4   Location and incidence of significant atherosclerotic lesions. The length of the dark area at each location (measured against the scale at left) corresponds to the number of lesions detected by arteriography in this series. (From Blaisdell FW, Hall AD, Thomas AN, Ross SJ: Cerebrovascular occlusive disease: Experience with panarteriography in 300 consecutive cases. Calif Med 103:321, 1965.)

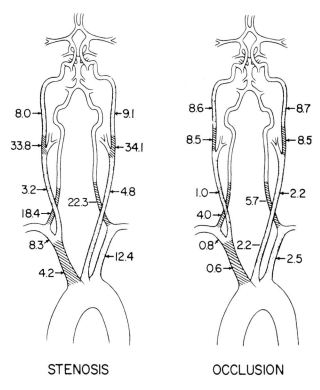

STENOSIS   OCCLUSION

FIGURE 135-5 Frequency distribution of arterial lesions at surgically accessible sites (4748 patients). (From Hass WK, Fields WS, North RR, et al: Joint study of extracranial arterial occlusion: II. Arteriography, techniques, sites, and complications. JAMA 203:961-968, 1968.)

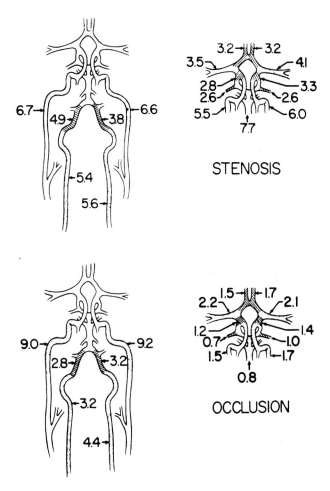

STENOSIS

OCCLUSION

FIGURE 135-6 Frequency distribution of surgically inaccessible lesions. (From Hass WK, Fields WS, North RR, et al: Joint study of extracranial arterial occlusion: II. Arteriography, techniques, sites, and complications. JAMA 203:961-968, 1968.)

locations that were inaccessible to direct surgical repair.[7] The remaining 67% were extracranial, with 38% of all lesions located at the carotid bifurcation, 20% at vertebral origins, and 9% at the origin of the branches of the aortic arch. Hass and coworkers, reviewing the arteriograms of 4748 patients followed in the joint study of extracranial arterial occlusive disease, reported a similar distribution.[46]

Arterial Elongation, Tortuosity, and Kinking

Sixteen percent to 21% of the carotid arteriograms of adults demonstrate some degree of elongation of the internal carotid artery in its cervical portion. The extent can vary from a mild tortuosity to as much as a 360-degree coil (Fig. 135-7). On occasion, excessive redundancy of the vessel produces kinking with apparent compromise of blood flow (Fig. 135-8).[84] These changes are attributed to either congenital or acquired factors. The carotid artery is formed from the third aortic arch and the dorsal aorta. During embryonic development, the carotid normally is redundant or kinked. As the heart descends into the thorax, the carotid artery is stretched and the redundancy is eliminated. Some redundancy may remain until further growth takes place, as evidenced by a redundancy rate as high as 43% seen in arteriograms of infants.[90,102] The acquired form of carotid redundancy is attributed to a manifestation of atherosclerosis that produces lengthening of the affected vessels leading to redundancy and, ultimately, to anatomic kinking. Carotid tortuosity and kinkings are discussed in detail in Chapter 144.

Fibromuscular Dysplasia

The pathology of this entity is discussed in detail in Chapter 142.

Extrinsic Compression

Extrinsic compression of the cervical arteries carrying blood to the brain is seen most often in the vertebral arteries as they course through the bony vertebral canal. Hyperostoses, or bone spurs, related to the cervical transverse processes can impinge on the vertebral artery and result in compression.[3,5,45,92]

Another source of external compression can be caused by neoplasms within the neck. Tumors can surround the carotid artery and invade its wall.

Radiation-Induced Carotid Stenosis

It has been long recognized experimentally that external radiation can produce an arterial injury.[66] With the increasing use of cervical radiation to treat neoplasia, we are now beginning to see patients with radiation-induced atherosclerotic change producing symptomatic carotid artery disease.[25,70]

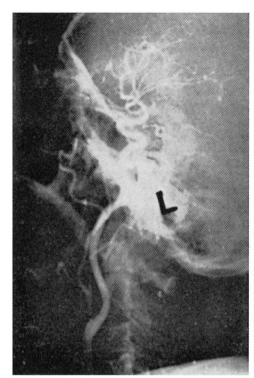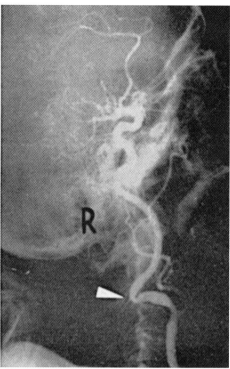

FIGURE 135-7 Carotid arteriograms showing bilateral coiling of circular configuration at level of base of skull (*arrow* shows 360-degree coil). No aneurysmal dilation is present in the proximal segment of arteries. (From Weibel J, Fields WS: Tortuosity, coiling, and kinking of the internal carotid artery: I. Etiology and radiographic anatomy. Neurology 15:7, 1965.)

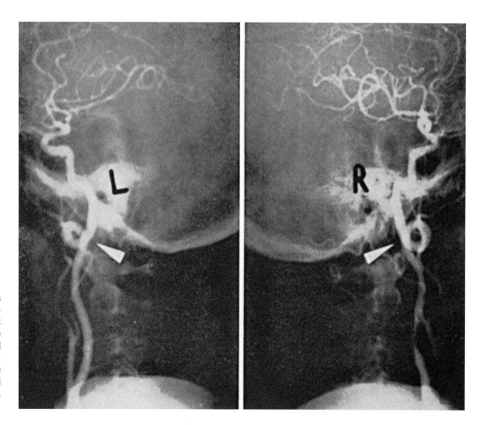

FIGURE 135-8 Carotid arteriograms demonstrating mild post-stenotic aneurysmal dilation and kinking of the right internal carotid artery *(arrowheads)*. The left internal carotid artery has S-shaped tortuosity. (From Weibel J, Fields WS: Tortuosity, coiling, and kinking of the internal carotid artery: I. Etiology and radiographic anatomy. Neurology 15:7, 1965.)

Postoperative Restenosis of the Carotid Artery

The pathology of this lesion is discussed in detail in Chapter 145.

Traumatic Occlusion and Spontaneous Intimal Dissection

Blunt craniocervical trauma, as a result of either a direct blow or the indirect effect of sudden head and neck extension, has been reported to produce occlusion of the internal carotid artery.[32,33,52,91] Angiographic and autopsy studies suggest that the most likely mechanism for this phenomenon is a tear of the intima followed by an acute intimal dissection, resulting in an occlusion of the lumen with secondary thrombosis. Spontaneous intimal dissection in the absence of trauma can also occur (Fig. 135-9).

Inflammatory Arteriopathies

Inflammatory conditions are rare, but they should be kept in mind during the evaluation of patients with cerebrovascular symptoms. Takayasu's disease is an inflammatory arteriopathy that involves the major trunks of the aortic arch. This is most frequently seen in women and occurs with greatest frequency in Asia and the Middle East; it has also been reported with some frequency in Latin America, but it is less common in North America and Europe. The lesion produces occlusion of major branches of the aortic arch with

the concomitant physical findings and varying symptomatic manifestations.[57] One dramatic finding on examination is often the total absence of extremity pulses; hence, the common synonym for this condition is *pulseless disease*. The central nervous system may also be involved in the systemic collagen vascular diseases, which include periarteritis nodosa, lupus erythematosus, and temporal arteritis (see also Chapter 28). Chapter 144 further discusses carotid arteriopathies.

Migraine

The vasospasm associated with migraine prodrome can cause transient neurologic dysfunction. The visual symptoms associated with the prodrome, the so-called scintillating scotoma, on occasion can be mistaken or misinterpreted as amaurosis fugax. There are also documented cases of permanent neurologic damage resulting from the prolonged phase of cerebral vasospastic prodrome.

■ PATHOGENETIC MECHANISMS OF CEREBRAL DYSFUNCTION

In addition to a knowledge of the various pathologic lesions that can affect the extracranial system, an understanding of the mechanism by which a lesion produces symptoms, either transient or permanent, is of particular importance when planning a diagnostic evaluation and selecting appropriate therapy.

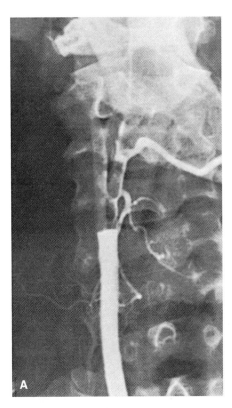
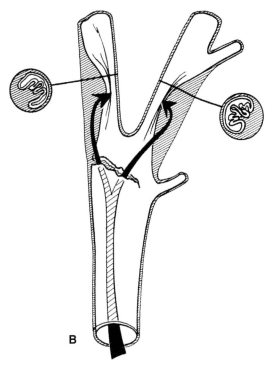

FIGURE 135-9 A, Right carotid arteriogram of a 32-year-old man who experienced a sudden episode of left hemiparesis. Carotid arteriography demonstrates a sharp cutoff contrast at the carotid bifurcation with faint visualization of the internal and external carotid arteries beyond. Subsequent exploration of this region revealed a spontaneous transverse intimal tear with subintimal dissection of blood and distal occlusion. **B,** Artist's concept of an intimal tear with subintimal dissection of blood and occlusion of the lumen. The *insets* of the internal and external carotid arteries in cross section graphically demonstrate luminal compromise by subintimal dissection.

Lateralizing Transient Ischemic Attacks

Several theories have been proposed to explain ischemic events that are transient in nature. These have included cerebral angiospasm, mechanical reduction of cerebral blood flow secondary to a critical arterial lesion, cerebral emboli originating from arteriosclerotic plaques, cervical arterial kinking or compression, polycythemia, anemia, and the transient shunting of blood away from the brain such as is seen in the subclavian steal syndrome.[19,72,74] The theory of cerebral vasospasm was held to be an important mechanism in the not-too-distant past. Therapy that was advocated to treat symptoms that were due to cerebral vasospasm included carotid arterectomy or cervical sympathetic ganglionectomy.[56]

Eastcott and colleagues spoke out against the vasospastic theory, stating that it would be difficult to conceive of spasm involving just those few vessels that were required to produce repetitive ischemic attacks, while the remaining cerebral vessels were left unaffected.[22] Rothenberg and Corday[86] produced experimental evidence against the angiospasm theory, and Millikan[74] pointed out that potent vasodilators such as 5% carbon dioxide mixed with 95% oxygen and cervical sympathectomy were not effective in preventing or treating attacks of transient cerebral ischemia. Two theories emerged as the primary explanation for transient ischemic events: (1) the arterial stenotic theory (mechanical flow reduction) and (2) the cerebral embolic theory.

During the early experience with carotid artery disease, most surgeons accepted the concept that arterial stenosis, producing reduced cerebral blood flow, represented the mechanism for transient cerebral ischemia.[64] For example, Crawford and coworkers stated that the criterion for carotid endarterectomy should be the presence of a pressure gradient across a stenosis involving the internal carotid artery.[15] These workers measured the carotid artery pressure during operation; if a gradient was present across a stenotic lesion, an endarterectomy was performed. If no gradient could be documented, the artery was not opened, since it was assumed that the patient's symptoms might be due to something other than a lesion in the carotid artery. On the basis of this experience, the investigators stated that at least a 50% stenosis, as measured in one projection of an arteriogram, was necessary to justify operation on the carotid artery. In their opinion, a gradient indicated not only decreased flow in that artery but also a decrease in total cerebral blood flow.

This concept was affirmed by other investigators.[17,18,49] Haller and Turrell stated that cerebral ischemia as a result of carotid artery disease was purely the result of mechanical flow obstruction and that surgical treatment should be directed at relief of this obstruction.[42] They concluded that lesions that failed to produce a pressure gradient did not constitute a significant threat to the patient. The mechanical concept of transient cerebral ischemia is appealing, particularly when surgeons are used to treating stenotic or obstructive arteries in other locations. The concept of transient ischemia has been likened to intermittent claudication of the brain. However, with the advent of techniques for the measurement of cerebral blood flow, it has been determined that the cerebral perfusion rate is relatively constant due to autoregulation. For this reason, it is difficult to understand how a constant stenosis could produce intermittent reduction in blood flow. In an attempt to explain this inconsistency, several investigators suggested that TIAs may result from intermittent episodes of systemic hypotension or decreased cardiac output in patients with stenosed or occluded cerebral arteries.[14,19,55]

In spite of the wide acceptance of the hemodynamic theory, there appeared increasing evidence to dispute it. In 1963, Adams and associates studied cerebral blood flow in patients with carotid and vertebral artery stenoses.[1] They found that cerebral blood flow, prior to carotid artery surgery, was normal and that endarterectomy did not produce any change or increase in hemispheric cerebral blood flow. Brice and colleagues measured carotid artery blood flow at the time of ligation for intracranial aneurysm and found that blood flow was not reduced until a stenosis of 84% to 93% was produced.[8] In view of these observations, those who advocate operating on an artery that is only 50% stenotic would have to offer some justification other than the improvement of blood flow. Furthermore, the intermittent nature of ischemic attacks is difficult to reconcile with the presence of a constant stenosis, since there is no significant variation in the demand for cerebral blood flow.

Some workers stated that transient reduction in blood pressure or cardiac output associated with a stenosis might cause neurologic symptoms. Kendall and Marshall studied 37 patients who had frequent TIAs.[61] They were unable to reproduce these symptoms with deliberately induced systemic hypotension. Similar experience was reported by others.[22,27] Russell and Cranstone noted that ophthalmic pressures did not diminish in patients with associated ischemic attacks and carotid artery stenosis.[87] When total occlusion of the internal carotid artery occurred, the ophthalmic artery pressure fell transiently but then rapidly returned to normal levels as collateral circulation became effective. Several workers have noted that TIAs disappear at the time of carotid occlusion.[21,88] It is unlikely that transient cerebral ischemia results from mechanical reduction of blood flow through a stenosed artery when the symptoms can be relieved by total occlusion of the same vessel. A similar phenomenon has been observed by surgeons who noted that occlusion of the common carotid artery under local anesthesia at the time of carotid endarterectomy is usually well tolerated.

Several investigators have stated that hemispheric TIAs can best be explained as a manifestation of cerebral embolization.[40,41,51,74] Atheromatous plaques in the extracranial arteries can be a source of either atheromatous or platelet emboli. The fact that atheromatous plaques can be a source of emboli was first reported by Panum in 1862.[82] Flory reported a series of autopsies in which emboli from atheroma were detected in kidneys, spleen, and thyroid.[31] The presence of emboli, confirmed microscopically, produced areas of infarction in the affected organs. Although Chiari, in 1905,[12] suggested that carotid artery lesions could produce cerebral emboli, this was not documented conclusively until 1947.[73] Handler, studying embolization of atheromatous material in a series of autopsy cases, noted that there was a frequent occurrence of encephalomalacia in patients who demonstrated atheroma embolism to other parts of the body.[44] Prior support for the embolic cause of transient cerebral ischemia came from the reports of Millikan and associates in 1955[75] and Fisher in 1958,[29] who noted that TIAs could be virtually eliminated if the patients were placed on anticoagulant therapy. In examining the ocular fundus of patients with carotid artery stenosis, Fisher described a "boxcar" effect in the retinal arteries.[30] He did not arrive at a definite explanation for this phenomenon but suggested that it might represent embolic material in the retinal arteries and that transient cerebral ischemia might be due to the same type of embolism. Hollenhorst described a series of patients with "bright plaques" in the retinal vessels and suggested that these were cholesterol crystals from eroded atheromatous plaques.[50] Russell observed two patients presenting with transient monocular blindness and concluded that this phenomenon was due to retinal emboli composed of friable thrombus.[88] He stated that if this observation were correct, thrombotic microemboli carried to the brain might be responsible for the TIAs often associated with carotid artery disease.

McBrien and coworkers performed a histologic examination of retinal vessels of a patient who had been having transient monocular blindness.[69] These workers noted that the material within the vessels was indeed microembolic and consisted of platelets, a few leukocytes, and a small quantity of lipid material. Julian and associates reported a series of patients in whom ulceration was seen in carotid plaques at the time of operation.[58] They postulated that thrombotic material within the ulcer might embolize and cause episodes of transient cerebral ischemia. Ehrenfeld and colleagues reported a series of patients with carotid stenosis and intermittent monocular blindness.[23] They found that the ocular phenomenon as well as the cerebral ischemic attacks stopped following carotid endarterectomy.

Additional evidence for the embolic theory of transient cerebral ischemia comes from the fact that ischemic attacks stop abruptly when carotid stenosis progresses to occlusion, provided the patient does not go on to have a major stroke. The cessation of TIAs presumably occurs because the route

for embolic material to the brain has been obstructed, not because of the establishment of collateral circulation.[21,87] The relationship between transient cerebral ischemia and emboli has been difficult to prove on the basis of operative results, because the criterion for operation dictates that a hemodynamically significant carotid stenosis be present before an operation is performed.

After reviewing the overwhelming evidence in favor of the embolic theory, our group realized that the presence of a hemodynamically significant stenosis is probably not necessary for the release of embolic material. Rather, the nature of the plaque itself would be the important factor. Atherosclerotic plaques whose consistency leads to degeneration with atheromatous fragmentation or whose surface characteristics are irregular or ulcerated, thus forming a suitable nidus for platelet aggregation, are the necessary requirements for emboli. Our group began to operate on patients with so-called nonstenotic ulcerative lesions who were experiencing hemispheric TIAs. In two subsequent publications, we described prompt relief without recurrence of transient ischemic phenomena following removal of the low-profile or nonstenotic ulcerative lesion.[78,79] These reports represented the first surgical series in which the lesions removed did not have associated stenosis or compromise in blood flow and in which, therefore, the relief of symptoms could be construed to be due not to the augmentation of blood flow but rather to the removal of the ulcerated plaque as a source of cerebral emboli.

From this discussion, it seems evident that the primary mechanism responsible for episodes of transient monocular or hemispheric symptoms associated with atherosclerotic lesions is cerebral emboli originating from the plaque surface. These emboli may consist of atheromatous debris, platelet aggregates, or thrombus. Embolization may occur either at the time an atheromatous plaque ruptures into the luminal surface and dislodges atheromatous contents into the blood stream, or from secondary platelet or thrombus aggregation within the irregularity or ulceration on the surface of the plaque (Figs. 135-10 to 135-16).

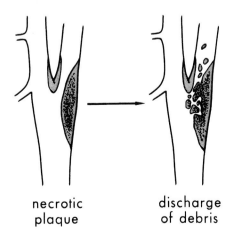

necrotic
plaque

discharge
of debris

FIGURE 135-10 Graphic representation of the process by which a bulky atheromatous lesion undergoes central degeneration with subsequent discharge of atheromatous debris into the arterial lumen and embolization to the brain.

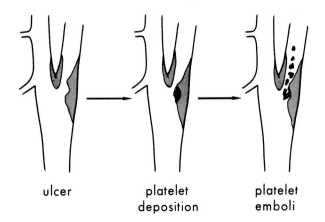

ulcer

platelet
deposition

platelet
emboli

FIGURE 135-11 An irregular or ulcerated surface on an arterial sclerotic plaque can provide a nidus for deposition of platelet aggregate material. These platelet aggregates can be dislodged into the arterial lumen and can embolize to the intracranial circulation.

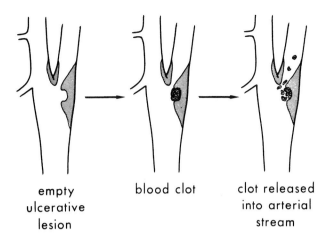

empty
ulcerative
lesion

blood clot

clot released
into arterial
stream

FIGURE 135-12 An empty ulcerative lesion can also be filled with mature thrombus material. The thrombus can be dislodged by the arterial stream or by manipulation, thus releasing clot into the arterial lumen with subsequent cerebral embolization.

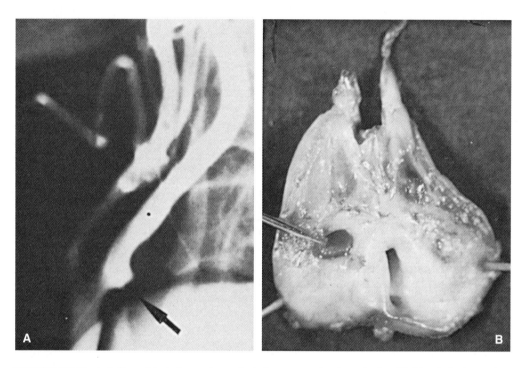

FIGURE 135-13 A, Left carotid arteriogram in a patient who was experiencing episodes of left hemispheric transient cerebral ischemia. The *arrow* points to a posterior outpouching of the internal carotid artery just beyond the bifurcation. This finding was interpreted as being an ulcerative atherosclerotic lesion. **B,** Atherosclerotic plaque that corresponds to the angiographically demonstrated lesion. It was removed from the carotid bifurcation, and the pointer indicates the ulcerative lesion containing remnants of mature thrombus.

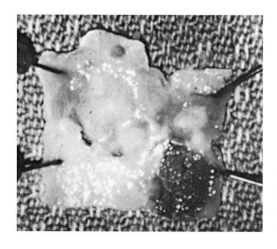

FIGURE 135-14 Example of an atherosclerotic plaque removed from the carotid bifurcation and opened out for visualization of the luminal surface. In the lower right-hand corner, a mature thrombus is loosely adherent to a very superficial ulceration.

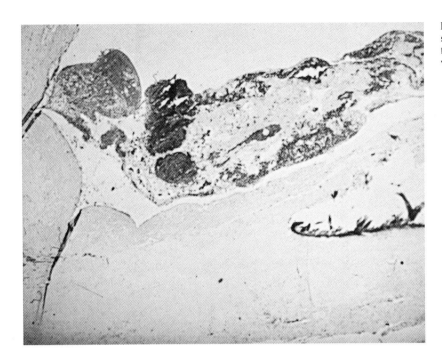

FIGURE 135-15 Microscopic section through a superficial ulcerating atheromatous plaque. Loose fibrin platelet thrombus material is demonstrated within the ulcer crater.

One question often posed by those who doubt the embolic theory is "if these episodes are embolic, why is the same pattern of neurologic dysfunction frequently reproduced in a carbon-copy fashion? Shouldn't the recipient site be random if the cause is really embolization?" The answer to this question is related to the fluid mechanics associated with laminar blood flow. If the source of emboli from an ulcerated atheromatous plaque is located at one point on the arterial wall circumference, embolic discharge into the blood stream will inevitably be carried to the same terminal branch because of the characteristics of laminar blood flow. This phenomenon was nicely demonstrated by Millikan.[74] During experiments on cerebral embolization, he introduced tiny metal beads through a needle placed in the internal carotid artery in monkeys. This method of introduction is analogous to a point source of atheromatous embolization. Autopsy studies of these experimental animals demonstrated that the metallic embolic beads would inevitably stack up, one behind the other, in the same cortical branch (Fig. 135-17).

Lateralizing Ischemic Attacks with Concomitant Internal Carotid Occlusion

Although most territorial TIAs are probably caused by emboli of arterial origin that pass through a patent internal carotid artery, we do see patients who experience these symptoms in the presence of a known and totally occluded internal carotid artery. Two possible explanations for these phenomena exist: (1) emboli may come from collateral sources or (2) marginally perfused brain tissue, distal to the internal carotid artery occlusion, may temporarily fall below

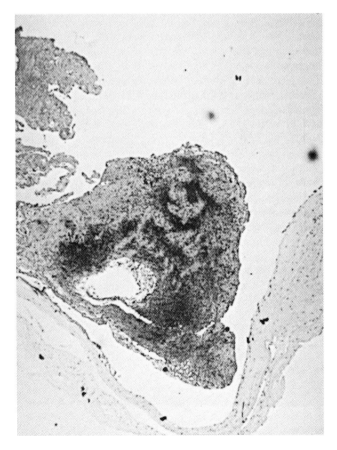

FIGURE 135-16 Microscopic section taken through a deeper ulcerating lesion of an atheromatous plaque removed from the carotid bifurcation. An organizing thrombus, only loosely attached, is seen partially filling the ulcer crater.

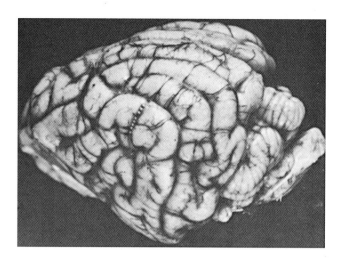

FIGURE 135-17 Brain of monkey removed following experimental embolization with ball bearings. The ball bearings were introduced from a point source in the carotid artery. Note that all the ball bearings lodged in a single cortical branch. (Courtesy of Clark Millikan, MD, Department of Neurology, Mayo Clinic, Rochester, Minn.)

the minimal threshold of perfusion to maintain function. The external carotid artery is a well-recognized source of collateral blood flow and a recently recognized source of emboli. Ulcerated plaques at the carotid bifurcation can release emboli into the external carotid artery, where they pass retrograde via collateral communications to the ophthalmic artery and subsequently to the carotid siphon and into branches of the middle cerebral artery.[13,47] Barnett and colleagues have identified the "stump" of the occluded internal carotid artery as a source of emboli to the external carotid artery.[6] This stump serves as a functional ulcer feeding emboli to a major collateral branch.

Emboli can also reach the hemisphere ipsilateral to an internal carotid artery occlusion from the opposite carotid artery or from the vertebral-basilar system.

Finally, marginally perfused brain, distal to an internal carotid artery occlusion, is more susceptible to temporary alterations in systemic blood pressure. In this instance, the cerebral vasculature is maximally vasodilated and therefore does not have the capacity to autoregulate in response to a drop in blood pressure. There is a direct and linear relationship between blood pressure and perfusion.

Nonlateralizing Transient Ischemic Attacks

Nonlateralizing ischemic attacks, such as dizziness, vertigo, ataxia, or syncope, may represent symptoms that are associated with brain stem or posterior circulation dysfunction. Because these attacks are often precipitated by postural changes, the mechanism is presumed to be flow related rather than a consequence of emboli. To make this connection between symptoms and lesions, it is necessary to have either occlusive lesions of several extracranial vessels involving both anterior and posterior circulation or a critical lesion in the vertebral-basilar distribution, with an effective anatomic disconnection between anterior and posterior blood flow.

One variant of posterior circulation ischemia occurs with subclavian steal syndrome. The anatomic lesion and the collateral circulatory response to arm ischemia have been described previously. It is easy to associate brain stem ischemic symptoms that occur with arm exercise in the presence of an ipsilateral subclavian artery occlusion: Blood is diverted away from the vertebral-basilar system as a result of retrograde flow down the ipsilateral vertebral artery. This diversion occurs because the vertebral artery now functions as a collateral channel for the exercising upper extremity. For this to occur, however, the principal or dominant vertebral artery must be on the side of the subclavian stenosis or occlusion. If the dominant vertebral artery is on the opposite side and a smaller vertebral artery is on the side of subclavian occlusion, it is not physiologically possible for a small artery to steal a sufficient quantity of blood from the posterior circulation because the opposite or dominant vertebral artery can more than make up the difference. Similarly, if the dominant vertebral artery is on the side of a total subclavian artery occlusion and the opposite vertebral artery is either small or absent, it is possible to have these symptoms in the absence of arm exercise because, in this instance, the subclavian artery stenosis or occlusion becomes a de-facto vertebral artery stenosis or occlusion and compromises blood flow through this dominant vessel to the brain stem.[24,71]

It is probable that emboli may occur in association with atherosclerotic plaques in the vertebral-basilar system, but the exact nature of the clinical consequences of such an event is not clear at present.

Completed Stroke

The completed stroke represents an area of brain infarction. Cerebral infarction can result from embolic occlusion of a critical vessel, thrombosis of an end vessel, or an acute deprivation of blood flow as a result of proximal arterial occlusion with inadequate collateral contribution through the circle of Willis.[83]

The mechanism of embolic occlusion of a distal cerebral vessel is essentially the same as that of a hemispheric TIA. Why one embolic event results in transient symptoms on one occasion and produces an area of cerebral infarction at a later time is the subject of considerable speculation. Presumably, the variables that operate during any one embolic event must include the size of the embolus, the nature of the embolic material, and the final location of the embolic fragment. A large embolus clearly presents a major threat of infarction, since the likelihood of subsequent fragmentation or rapid clot lysis is reduced. Similarly, if the embolic material is composed of platelet aggregates or thrombus, the chances of fragmentation or lysis with prompt restoration of blood flow are good, whereas if the embolus is composed of an atheromatous fragment, the chances of permanent end-vessel occlusion and subsequent infarction are increased significantly. Finally, if the embolus lodges in a critical location such as the internal capsule, the time during which the ischemic changes are reversible is likely to be shorter and the neurologic dysfunction that occurs with such a critical embolization is likely to be more prominent.

Evidence using CT scanning and magnetic resonance imaging also indicates that what is clinically a transient ischemic event is actually cerebral infarction in a small focal zone that is compensated for function by adjacent tissue.

It is likely that intracerebral thrombosis is caused by one of two mechanisms. The first is related to intracranial atheromatosis, with branch vessel occlusion occurring in association with a critical stenotic lesion. The second mechanism results from propagation of thrombus from the internal carotid artery distal to the proximal atheromatous stenosis.

The top of the column of thrombus in the internal carotid artery can literally spill into the middle cerebral artery and cause occlusion and cerebral infarction. This mechanism has not been recognized uniformly, but it can be deduced from the sequence of events that takes place with carotid thrombosis.

An atheromatous lesion located at the origin of the internal carotid artery slowly and progressively causes a reduction of blood flow as the lesion produces a further compromise of cross-sectional luminal area. Ultimately, the lesion approaches a critical compromise, following which the flow is so reduced that thrombosis occurs. When this happens, there may be no sequelae, or the patient may suffer a cerebral infarction with major neurologic deficit.

Because flow is reduced just prior to occlusion, it is unreasonable to assume that the tiny flow through the vessel before occlusion is really that important and that the absence of this tiny flow will make the difference between live functioning brain and cerebral infarction. In some patients, when thrombosis occurs, the column of clot probably progresses up to the first major branch, such as the ophthalmic artery, and stops. In this instance, the clinical consequence of stroke is unlikely, and this sequence represents the events that occur in patients who later are found to have an asymptomatic carotid occlusion. In other patients, the clot may not stop at the siphon branches but may progress through the siphon to the takeoff of the middle cerebral artery. If some of this clot "spills over" or is carried by collateral blood flow, thrombotic occlusion of a major intracranial artery will occur and cerebral infarction will be the consequence, resulting in a major stroke (Fig. 135-18). This phenomenon has been demonstrated at autopsy in patients who died shortly after a critical event. If the patient lives for a considerable time after the initial stroke, the propagated thrombus will usually undergo lysis back to the branches of the siphon and no clue will remain at subsequent autopsy to demonstrate the actual events that occurred.

On occasion, a modest atheromatous lesion of the internal carotid artery may undergo sudden intraplaque hemorrhage. This produces an acute occlusion (Fig. 135-19). This precipitate event causes an acute change in circulatory dynamics. Occlusion of this type produces acute ischemia, and probably infarction, in the distribution of that artery. Likewise, thrombosis and propagation, as described earlier, may also take place with the same consequences.

Stroke-in-Evolution

The stroke-in-evolution, in contrast to a simple acute stroke, is one in which the resultant neurologic deficit progressively worsens by a series of discrete exacerbations occurring over

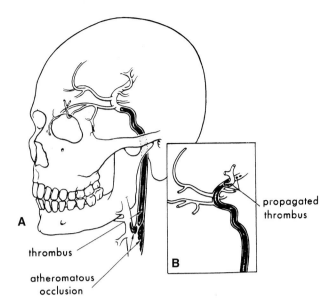

FIGURE 135-18 **A,** Artist's concept of the events following carotid occlusion. The thrombus within the internal carotid artery ascends to the first branch of that artery, the ophthalmic artery. At this point, the thrombus stops and the remaining portion of the intracranial circulation is not compromised. **B,** An alternative sequence of events in which the thrombus does not stop at the ophthalmic artery but progresses up to the terminal branches of the internal carotid artery, so that thrombus material spills over and propagates into the middle cerebral artery, producing cerebral infarction.[35,36]

a period of hours or days. The exact mechanism for this type of progression is unknown. Several hypotheses can be speculated on to explain this pattern. One might be a series of infarct-producing emboli from a bulky, friable, carotid bifurcation lesion. These emboli, occurring serially, would result in a series of events that produce a progressively worsening neurologic deficit.[35,36] Another explanation might be a series of thromboemboli coming off the top of a thrombotic column in an occluded internal carotid artery. A third possibility might involve the dynamics of the infarct zone, such as secondary thrombosis or occlusion of a neighboring vessel in the brain substance as the result of edema, or expansion of the original infarct zone as a consequence of central hemorrhage, although this last mechanism is probably unlikely.

Deterioration of Intellectual Function

The relationship between intellectual dysfunction with cerebrovascular disease is a hotly debated issue among neurologists. Many believe that dementia is not a manifestation of vascular disease, but others do not share this concept. The subjective responses of patients following carotid thromboendarterectomy are interesting. Patients often report an improvement in intellectual function following successful operation, which may be manifested as improved ability to carry out mathematical operations, improved reading comprehension, better conversational ability, and so forth. The patients' observations usually are shared by their friends or relatives.[100]

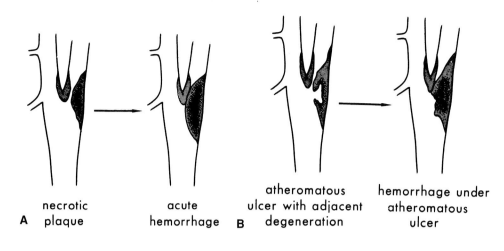

FIGURE 135-19 A, Artist's concept of spontaneous hemorrhage within an atherosclerotic plaque resulting in sudden acute occlusion of the internal carotid artery. **B,** A similar phenomenon can occur within the depths of an atheromatous ulcer, producing acute cessation of blood flow.

necrotic
A plaque

acute
hemorrhage **B**

atheromatous
ulcer with adjacent
degeneration

hemorrhage under
atheromatous
ulcer

If we accept the notion that intellectual abilities are a function of cerebral performance, and that reduced blood flow, either from proximal arterial occlusive disease or from distal embolization, can impair cerebral function, it is reasonable to assume that multiple thromboembolic events in the areas of the brain, silent with regard to motor and sensory functions but important to intellectual function, may be affected adversely by decreased arterial perfusion. Areas that may be so affected include the frontal lobes. If the embolic or ischemic events persist, intellectual deterioration may result in time. Our group has followed several such patients who, when arteriograms were finally performed, demonstrated loss of multiple branches in the distribution of the anterior cerebral artery. Our group has also had experience with patients who were somnolent when first examined, being aroused with great difficulty, and in whom there were multiple extracranial stenoses or occlusions. Repair or bypass of these lesions resulted in a prompt return to a normal level of consciousness and a resumption of previous intellectual function.

In evaluating the status of patients after cerebrovascular operations, the surgeon must be careful to avoid taking credit for seeming intellectual improvement as a result of the effect of operation. The patient who is told that a major occlusive lesion was removed from a critical artery going to his or her brain may, following operation, exhibit a brightness and jubilation because he or she believes that the brain is now going to work better. Improved intracranial function may be a sham effect of operation, but correction of multiple cerebral occlusive lesions with intellectual improvement is an undeniable observation.

■ REFERENCES

1. Adams JE, Smith MC, Wylie EJ: Cerebral blood flow and hemodynamics in extracranial vascular disease: Effect of endarterectomy. Surgery 53:449, 1963.
2. American Heart Association: 1999 Economic Cost of Cardiovascular Diseases. Dallas, American Heart Association, 1999.
3. Bakay L, Leslie EV: Surgical treatment of vertebral artery insufficiency caused by cervical spondylosis. J Neurosurg 23:596, 1965.
4. Baker RN, Schwartz WS, Ramseyer JC: Prognosis among survivors of ischemic stroke. Neurology (Minneap) 18:933, 1968.
5. Balla JI, Langford KH: Vertebral artery compression in cervical spondylosis. Med J Aust 1:284, 1967.
6. Barnett HJM, Peerless SJ, Kaufmann JCE: "Stump" on internal carotid artery—a source for further cerebral embolic ischemia. Stroke 9:448, 1978.
7. Blaisdell FW, Hall AD, Thomas AN, et al: Cerebrovascular occlusive disease: Experience with panarteriography in 300 consecutive cases. Calif Med 103:321, 1965.
8. Brice JG, Dowsett DJ, Lowe RD: Hemodynamic effects of carotid artery stenosis. BMJ 3:1363, 1964.
9. Cadwalader WB: Unilateral optic atrophy and contralateral hemiplegia consequent on occlusion of the cerebral vessels. JAMA 59:2248, 1912.
10. Carrea R, Molins M, Murphy G: Surgical treatment of spontaneous thrombosis of the internal carotid artery in the neck: Carotid-carotid anastomosis—report of a case. Acta Neurol Lat Am 1:71, 1955.
11. Chambers BR, Norris JW: Outcome in patients with asymptomatic neck bruits. N Engl J Med 315:860, 1986.
12. Chiari H: Ueber das Verhalten des Teilungswinkels der Carotid communis bei der Endarteriitis chronica deformans. Verh Dtsch Ges Pathol 9:326, 1905.
13. Connolly JE, Stemmer EA: Endarterectomy of the external carotid artery. Arch Surg 106:799, 1973.
14. Corday E, Rothenberg S, Weiner SM: Cerebral vascular insufficiency: An explanation of the transient stroke. Arch Intern Med 98:683, 1956.
15. Crawford ES, DeBakey ME, Blaisdell FW, et al: Hemodynamic alterations in patients with cerebral arterial insufficiency before and after operation. Surgery 48:76, 1960.
16. DeBakey ME: Successful carotid endarterectomy for cerebrovascular insufficiency: Nineteen-year follow-up. JAMA 233:1083, 1975.
17. DeBakey ME, Crawford ES, Fields WS: Surgical treatment of patients with cerebral arterial insufficiency associated with extracranial arterial occlusive lesions. Neurology (Minneap) 11:145, 1961.
18. DeBakey ME, Crawford ES, Cooley DA, et al: Cerebral arterial insufficiency: One- to 11-year results following arterial reconstructive operation. Ann Surg 161:921, 1965.
19. Denny-Brown D: Recurrent cerebrovascular episodes. Arch Neurol 2:194, 1960.
20. Dixon S, Pais SO, Raviola C, et al: Natural history of nonstenotic asymptomatic ulcerative lesions of the carotid artery: A further analysis. Arch Surg 117:1493, 1982.
21. Drake WE Jr, Drake MAL: Clinical and angiographic correlates of cerebrovascular insufficiency. Am J Med 45:253, 1968.
22. Eastcott HHG, Pickering GW, Robb CG: Reconstruction of internal carotid artery in a patient with intermittent attacks of hemiplegia. Lancet 2:994, 1954.

23. Ehrenfeld WK, Hoyt WF, Wylie EJ: Embolization and transient blindness from carotid atheroma. Surgical considerations. Arch Surg 93:787, 1966.

24. Eklof B, Schwartz SI: Effects of subclavian steal and compromised cephalic blood flow on cerebral circulation. Surgery 68:431, 1969.

25. Elerding SC, Fernandez RN, Grotta JC, et al: Carotid artery disease following external cervical irradiation. Ann Surg 194:609, 1981.

26. European Carotid Surgery Trialists' Collaborative Group: MRC European Carotid Surgery Trial: Interim results for symptomatic patients with severe (70-99%) or with mild (0-29%) carotid stenosis. Lancet 337:1235, 1991.

27. Fazekas JF, Alman RW: The role of hypotension in transitory focal cerebral ischemia. Am J Med Sci 248:567, 1964.

28. Feigin I, Budzilovich GN: The general pathology of cerebrovascular disease. In Vinken PJ, Bruyn GW (eds): Handbook of Clinical Neurology, Part I. Amsterdam, North-Holland, 1972.

29. Fisher CM: The use of anticoagulants in cerebral thrombosis. Neurology 8:311, 1958.

30. Fisher CM: Observations of the fundus oculi in transient monocular blindness. Neurology (Minneap) 9:333, 1959.

31. Flory CM: Arterial occlusions produced by emboli from eroded aortic atheromatous plaques. Am J Pathol 21:549, 1945.

32. Garg AG, Gordon DS, Taylor AR, et al: Internal carotid artery thrombosis secondary to closed craniocervical trauma. Br J Surg 55:4, 1968.

33. Gee W, Kaupp HA, McDonald KM, et al: Spontaneous dissection of internal carotid arteries. Arch Surg 115:944, 1980.

34. Goldner JC, Whisnant JP, Taylor WF: Long-term prognosis of transient cerebral ischemic attacks. Stroke 2:160, 1971.

35. Goldstone J, Moore WS: Emergency carotid artery surgery in neurologically unstable patients. Arch Surg 111:1284, 1976.

36. Goldstone J, Moore WS: A new look at emergency carotid artery operations for the treatment of cerebrovascular insufficiency. Stroke 9:599, 1978.

37. Gowers WR: On a case of simultaneous embolism of central retinal and middle cerebral arteries. Lancet 2:794, 1875.

38. Grigg MJ, Papadakas K, Nicolaides AM, et al: The significance of cerebral infarction and atrophy in patients with amaurosis fugax and transient ischemic attacks in relation to internal carotid artery stenosis: A preliminary report. J Vasc Surg 7:215, 1988.

39. Grunnet ML: Cerebrovascular disease: Diabetes and cerebral atherosclerosis. Neurology (Minneap) 13:486, 1963.

40. Gunning AJ, Pickering GW, Robb-Smith AHT, et al: Mural thrombosis of the internal carotid artery and subsequent embolism. Q J Med 33:155, 1964.

41. Guthrie LG, Mayou S: Right hemiplegia and atrophy of left optic nerve. Proc R Soc Med 1:180, 1908.

42. Haller JA Jr, Turrell R: Studies on effectiveness of endarterectomy in treatment of carotid insufficiency. Arch Surg 85:637, 1962.

43. Halliday AM, Thomas D, Mansfield A: The Asymptomatic Carotid Surgery Trial (ACST): Rationale and design. Eur J Vasc Surg 8:703, 1994.

44. Handler FP: Clinical and pathological significance of atheromatous embolization, with emphasis on an etiology of renal hypertension. Am J Med 20:366, 1956.

45. Hardin CA, Williamson WP, Steegmann AT: Vertebral artery insufficiency produced by cervical osteoarthritic spurs. Neurology (Minneap) 10:855, 1960.

46. Hass WK, Fields WS, North RR, et al: Joint study of extracranial arterial occlusion: II. Arteriography, techniques, sites, and complications. JAMA 203:961, 1968.

47. Hertzer NR: External carotid endarterectomy. Surg Gynecol Obstet 153:186, 1981.

48. Hobson RW II, Weiss DG, Fields WS, et al: Efficacy of carotid endarterectomy for asymptomatic carotid stenosis, for The Veterans Affairs Asymptomatic Cooperative Study Group. N Engl J Med 328:221, 1993.

49. Hohf RP: The clinical evaluation and surgery of internal carotid insufficiency. Surg Clin North Am 47:1:71, 1967.

50. Hollenhorst RW: Significance of bright plaques in the retinal arteries. JAMA 178:23, 1961.

51. Hollenhorst RW: Vascular status of patients who have cholesterol emboli in the retina. Am J Ophthalmol 61:1159, 1966.

52. Houck WS, Jackson JR, Odom DL, et al: Occlusion of the internal carotid artery in the neck secondary to closed trauma to the head and neck: A report of two cases. Ann Surg 159:219, 1964.

53. Humphries AW, Young JR, Santilli PM, et al: Unoperated, asymptomatic significant internal carotid artery stenosis. Surgery 80:695, 1976.

54. Hunt JR: The role of the carotid arteries in the causation of vascular lesions of the brain, with remarks on certain special features of the symptomatology. Am J Med Sci 147:704, 1914.

55. Hutchinson EC, Yates PO: Caroticovertebral stenosis. Lancet 1:2, 1957.

56. Johnson HC, Walker AE: The angiographic diagnosis of spontaneous thrombosis of internal and common carotid arteries. J Neurosurg 8:631, 1951.

57. Judge RD, Currier RD, Gracie WA, et al: Takayasu's arteritis and the aortic arch syndrome. Am J Med 32:379, 1962.

58. Julian OC, Dye WS, Javid H, et al: Ulcerative lesions of the carotid artery bifurcation. Arch Surg 86:803, 1963.

59. Kannel WB: Epidemiology of cerebrovascular disease: An epidemiologic study of cerebrovascular disease. In American Neurological Association and American Heart Association: Cerebral Vascular Diseases. New York, Grune & Stratton, 1966, pp 53-66.

60. Kartchner MM, McRae LP: Noninvasive evaluation and management of the "asymptomatic" carotid bruit. Surgery 82:840, 1977.

61. Kendall RE, Marshall J: Role of hypertension in the genesis of transient focal cerebral ischemic attacks. BMJ 2:344, 1963.

62. Kroener JM, Dorn PL, Shoor PM, et al: Prognosis of asymptomatic ulcerating carotid lesions. Arch Surg 115:1387, 1980.

63. Kuller LH, Cook LP, Friedman GD: Survey of stroke epidemiology studies. Stroke 3:579, 1972.

64. Landolt AM, Millikan CH: Pathogenesis of cerebral infarction secondary to mechanical carotid artery occlusion. Stroke 1:52, 1970.

65. LeNet M: Le cout des malaides cardio-vasculaires. Coeur et Santé 33(Suppl), Edition Medicale (Commission Paritaire No. 55920). Paris, 1982.

66. Lindsay S, Entenman C, Ellis EE, Geraci CL: Aortic arteriosclerosis in the dog after localized aortic irradiation with electrons. J Circ Res 10:61, 1962.

67. Marshall J: The natural history of transient cerebrovascular ischemic attacks. Q J Med 131:309, 1964.

68. Matsumoto N, Whisnant JP, Kurland LT, et al: Natural history of stroke in Rochester, Minnesota, 1955 through 1969: An extension of a previous study, 1945 through 1954. Stroke 4:20, 1973.

69. McBrien DJ, Bradley RD, Ashton N: The nature of retinal emboli in stenosis of the internal carotid artery. Lancet 1:697, 1963.

70. McCready RA, Hyde GL, Bivins BA, et al: Radiation-induced arterial injuries. Surgery 93:306, 1983.

71. McLaughlin JS, Linberg E, Attar A, et al: Cerebral vascular insufficiency: Syndromes of reversed blood flow in vessels supplying the brain. Am Surg 33:317, 1967.

72. Meyer JS: Occlusive cerebrovascular disease: Pathogenesis and treatment. Am J Med 30:577, 1961.

73. Meyer WW: Cholesterinkrystallembolie kleiner Organarterien und ihre Folgen. Virchows Arch Pathol Anat 314:616, 1947.

74. Millikan CH: The pathogenesis of transient focal cerebral ischemia. Circulation 32:438, 1965.

75. Millikan CH, Siekert RG, Shick RM: Studies in cerebrovascular disease: V. The use of anticoagulant drugs in the treatment of intermittent insufficiency of the internal carotid arterial system. Proc Staff Meet Mayo Clin 30:578, 1955.

76. Moniz E, Lima A, deLacerda R: Hemiplegies par thrombose de la carotide interne. Presse Med 45:977, 1937.

77. Moore WS, Boren C, Malone JM, et al: Natural history of nonstenotic asymptomatic ulcerative lesions of the carotid artery. Arch Surg 113:1352, 1978.

78. Moore WS, Hall AD: Ulcerated atheroma of the carotid artery: A cause of transient cerebral ischemia. Am J Surg 116:237, 1968.

79. Moore WS, Hall AD: Importance of emboli from carotid bifurcation in pathogenesis of cerebral ischemic attacks. Arch Surg 101:708, 1970.

80. Moore WS, Young B, Baker WH, et al: Surgical results: A justification of the surgeon selection process from the ACAS trial. J Vasc Surg 23:323, 1996.

81. North American Symptomatic Carotid Endarterectomy Trial Collaborators: Beneficial effect of carotid endarterectomy in symptomatic patients with high-grade carotid stenosis. N Engl J Med 325:445, 1991.

82. Panum PL: Experimentelle Beitrage zur Lehre von der Embolie. Virchows Arch (Pathol Anat) 25:308, 1862.

83. Paulson OB: Cerebral apoplexy (stroke) pathogenesis, pathophysiology, and therapy as illustrated by regional blood flow measurements in the brain. Stroke 2:327, 1971.

84. Quattlebaum JK Jr, Wade JS, Whiddon CM: Stroke associated with elongation and kinking of the carotid artery: Long-term follow-up. Ann Surg 177:572, 1973.

85. Roederer GO, Langlois YE, Jager KA, et al: The natural history of carotid arterial disease in asymptomatic patients with cervical bruits. Stroke 15:605, 1984.

86. Rothenberg SF, Corday E: Etiology of the transient cerebral stroke. JAMA 164:2005, 1957.

87. Russell RW, Cranstone WI: Ophthalmodynamometry in carotid artery disease. J Neurol Neurosurg Psychiatry 24:281, 1961.

88. Russell RWR: Observations on the retinal blood-vessels in monocular blindness. Lancet 2:1422, 1961.

89. Sacco RL, Wolf PA, Kannel WB, et al: Survival and recurrence following stroke in the Framingham study. Stroke 13:290, 1982.

90. Sarkari NBS, Holmes JM, Bickerstaff ER: Neurological manifestations associated with internal carotid loops and kinks in children. J Neurol Neurosurg Psychiatry 33:194, 1970.

91. Schneider RC, Lemmen LJ: Traumatic internal carotid artery thrombosis secondary to nonpenetrating injuries to the neck: A problem in the differential diagnosis of craniocerebral trauma. J Neurosurg 9:495, 1952.

92. Sheehan S, Bauer RB, Meyer JS: Vertebral artery compression in cervical spondylosis: Arteriographic demonstration during life of vertebral artery insufficiency due to rotation and extension of the neck. Neurology (Minneap) 10:968, 1960.

93. Strully KJ, Hurwitt ES, Blankenberg HW: Thromboendarterectomy for thrombosis of the carotid artery in the neck. J Neurosurg 10:474, 1953.

94. Taylor TN, Davis PH, Torner JC, et al: Lifetime cost of stroke in the United States. Stroke 27:1459, 1996.

95. The Executive Committee for the Asymptomatic Carotid Atherosclerosis (ACAS) Study: Endarterectomy for asymptomatic carotid artery stenosis. JAMA 273:1421, 1995.

96. Thompson JE, Austin DJ, Patman RD: Carotid endarterectomy for cerebrovascular insufficiency: Long-term results in 592 patients followed up to thirteen years. Ann Surg 172:663, 1970.

97. Thompson JE, Patman RD: Endarterectomy for asymptomatic carotid bruits. Surg Digest 7:9, 1972.

98. Thompson JE, Patman RD, Talkington CM: Asymptomatic carotid bruit. Ann Surg 188:308, 1978.

99. Toole JF: The Willis Lecture: Transient ischemic attacks, scientific method, and new realities. Stroke 22:99-104, 1991.

100. Vitale JH, Pulos SM, Okada A, et al: Relationships of psychological dimensions to impairment in a population with cerebrovascular insufficiency. J Nerv Ment Dis 158:456, 1974.

101. Wallace DC: A study of the natural history of cerebral vascular disease. Med J Aust 1:90, 1967.

102. Weibel J, Fields WS: Tortuosity, coiling, and kinking of the internal carotid artery: I. Etiology and radiographic anatomy. Neurology (Minneap) 15:7, 1965.

103. Whisnant JP, Fitzgibbons JP, Kurland LT, et al: Natural history of stroke in Rochester, Minnesota, 1945 through 1954. Stroke 2:11, 1971.

104. Wiebers DO, Whisnant JP: In Warlow C, Morris PJ (eds): Transient Ischemic Attacks. New York, Marcel Dekker, 1982, p 8.

105. Wolfe PA, Kannel WB, McGee DL: Epidemiology of strokes in North America. Stroke 1:19, 1986.

106. Wolfe PA, O'Neal A, D'Agostino RV, et al: Declining mortality, not declining incidence of stroke: The Framingham Study. Stroke 20:29, 1989.

107. Zarins CK, Giddens DP, Bharadvaj BK, et al: Carotid bifurcation atherosclerosis: Quantitative correlation of plaque localization with flow velocity profiles and wall shear stress. J Circ Res 53:502, 1983.

108. The Casanova Study Group: Carotid surgery versus medical therapy in asymptomatic carotid stenosis. Stroke 22:1229, 1991.

Diagnostic Evaluation and Medical Management of Patients with Ischemic Cerebrovascular Disease

136

KERSTIN BETTERMANN, MD, PhD
JAMES F. TOOLE, MD

■ ISCHEMIC STROKE

Cerebrovascular disease is the leading cause of disability in adults and the third leading cause of death in the United States. Worldwide it is the second leading cause of death.[1] Yearly more than 750,000 patients in the United States and more than 15 million patients globally are diagnosed with new or recurrent stroke.[2] Because age is one of the major risk factors and the population segment of persons aged 65 years or older is rapidly growing, the stroke rate will dramatically increase.[3] The number of stroke patients, however, is probably even significantly higher, because many patients with transient ischemic attack (TIA) or stroke do not seek medical attention.[4]

Approximately 20% to 30% of all ischemic infarcts are due to atherosclerotic changes of the major extracranial and intracranial cerebral blood vessels. Atherothrombotic plaque within these arteries can cause progressive stenosis resulting in turbulence, diminished flow and pressure, or distal embolism, any of which can result in infarction. For example, if perfusion pressure falls below the threshold of collateral vasculature and compensation of central autoregulation, a narrowed internal carotid artery (ICA) can become symptomatic.

Major risk factors for atherosclerosis include hypertension, diabetes mellitus, hyperlipidemia, obesity, and elevated homocysteine levels. Furthermore, coronary artery and peripheral vascular disease are markers of generalized atherosclerosis, as are sedentary life style, inflammatory mediators, fibrinogen, genetic predisposition, and other, yet to be identified risk factors.

About 30% of all infarcts have a cardioembolic origin, estimated to reach close to 50% in patients younger than 40 years of age, of which congenital anomalies and atrial fibrillation are the most common. About 40% of acute strokes have no known cause.[5] Etiologies for stroke are listed for overview in Table 136-1.

Occurrence of Ischemic Events

Awareness of TIA as a medical emergency in the general population is poor.[6-8] Even in hospitalized patients, stroke and TIA are frequently missed or treatment is delayed due to seemingly benign phenomena, such as pure sensory symptoms, dizziness, and unsteadiness or vague visual complaints. Patients with TIAs are frequently discharged from the emergency department without further diagnostic workup, other than a normal head computed tomographic (CT) scan, which places such persons at increased risk to develop recurrent TIAs or infarction. Recurrence rate of infarction is estimated to be 4% to 8% within the first month, 12% to 13% at 1 year, and 24% to 29% after 5 years. The long-term risk following a TIA is 3% to 10% in 1 month, 10% to 14% after 1 year, and 25% to 40% after 5 years.[9-12]

Extracranial Atherosclerosis and Ischemic Stroke

The risk for patients with TIA due to extracranial occlusive disease is even greater,[13,14] especially in symptomatic carotid artery stenosis.[15] Therefore, appropriate candidates for endarterectomy need to be identified early to prevent recurrence of ischemic events.

In 1996 more than 130,000 carotid endarterectomies (CEAs) were performed in the United States.[16] Almost all patients are asymptomatic when operated on; however, most have had a TIA in the past that brought them to medical attention. The proportion of patients operated who have never had symptoms with stenosis increased from 16% in 1990-1994 to 45% during 1995-2000.[17] Yet, major controversy continues regarding the decision whether a person who has never had symptoms should undergo CEA for stroke prevention.[18]

Patients with extracranial atherosclerotic disease come to medical attention because they have been found to have a carotid murmur that sometimes can be correlated to significant carotid stenosis by ultrasound, or because they were symptomatic from a stroke or TIA. During an acute ischemic event it is important to clarify, if possible, whether the neurologic symptoms represent evolving infarct or TIA. It is crucial to localize symptoms and findings on neurologic examination to a specific vascular territory to determine whether an ICA stenosis is the cause.

Table 136-1   Etiology of Ischemic Stroke

Atherosclerosis
    Vascular thrombus in extracranial vessels (CCA, ICA,
      vertebral arteries)
    Intracranial atherosclerotic disease affecting large cerebral arteries
    Intracranial microangiopathy (ischemic small-vessel disease)
Embolic stroke
    Cardioembolic stroke
      Arrhythmias, especially atrial fibrillation
      Cardiac disease with low cardiac output and cardiac thrombus
      Endocarditis
      Patent foramen ovale ± aneurysm and paradoxical embolus
      Atrial myxoma
      Valvular disease
    Arterioarterial emboli from vascular thrombus or aneurysm
Hemodynamic compromise with decrease in systemic blood pressure
  and cerebral perfusion
Hematologic diseases
    Sickle cell anemia
    Coagulopathy
      Factor Leyden V deficiency and clotting disorders
      Protein C and S deficiency
      Lupus anticoagulant
      Antiphospholipid syndrome
      Paraneoplastic
      Pregnancy
    Polycythemia
    Thrombocytosis
Vascular disease
    Vasculitis
      Connective tissue disease
        Sjögren's disease
        Systemic lupus erythematosus
        Wegener's granulomatosis
        Sneddon's syndrome
        Panarteritis nodosa

        Churg-Strauss syndrome
        Neuro-Behçet's disease
        Isolated CNS vasculitis
        Takayashu's disease
        Moyamoya disease
    Infections
      Herpes simplex encephalitis
      Neurosyphilis
      HIV
      Chagas' disease
    Neoplasms
      Lymphoproliferative disease
      Angioendotheliosis
    Radiation induced
    Toxin and drug induced
      Cocaine
      Amphetamines
Trauma
Dissection
Venous disease
Migraine and vasospasm
Metabolic disease
    Mitochondrial disease
      MELAS
      MERF
    Homocysteinemia
    Others
Hereditary/degenerative diseases
    Marfan syndrome
    Fibromuscular vascular disease
    Rendu-Weber-Osler syndrome
    CADASIL and other inherited microangiopathies
    Amyloid angiopathy
    Dolichoectasia

CCA, common carotid artery; ICA, internal carotid artery; HIV, human immunodeficiency virus; MELAS, mitochondrial myopathy, encephalopathy, lactic acidosis and stroke-like episodes; MERF, familial mitochondrial encephalomyopathy; CADASIL, cerebral autosomal dominant arteriopathy with subcortical infarcts and leukoencephalopathy.

Classification of Cerebral Ischemic Events

Ischemic cerebrovascular events are defined as TIA, cerebral infarction with transient signs, or infarction with varying degrees of disability. These definitions rest purely on clinical assessment and the time course. Based on definitions formulated in the 1950s, any sudden focal neurologic event lasting less than 24 hours is termed *TIA* and has often been considered a relatively benign, nonfatal secondary clinical endpoint. Naturally the differential diagnosis of these transient ischemic events is quite broad.[19]

Neuroimaging modalities, especially brain magnetic resonance (MR) imaging with diffusion-weighted (DW) and perfusion-weighted (PW) imaging can identify subtle brain injury shortly after onset of ischemia.[20,21] Ischemic brain injury on DW-MR imaging done within 72 hours of the clinical event correlates well with event duration. DW-MR imaging demonstrates that brain injury is present in about 50% of patients with clinical symptoms lasting longer than 1 hour and in 70% of patients with events lasting 12 to 24 hours.[22] Therefore it is misleading to assume that TIAs are benign. Proposals for a newer definition of stroke versus TIA include findings on MR imaging,[23,24] in addition to the traditional symptom-oriented ones. TIA is then defined as a sudden focal neurologic event lasting at least 10 minutes,

but less than 24 hours, without evidence of acute ischemic brain injury on DW-MR imaging consisting of acute onset of motor signs or sensory symptoms, language disturbance, blindness, diplopia, ataxia, dysarthria, vertigo, confusion, or memory loss.[25,26] As a general rule, patients presenting with signs and symptoms lasting longer than 1 hour very likely have nonreversible brain injury.

■ CLINICAL PRESENTATIONS

Based on history, neurologic examination, and neuroimaging studies, usually a cranial CT, the topography of stroke, classic stroke syndromes, and possible stroke etiologies can be identified. This is important in choosing effective preventive therapies and in treating underlying medical problems. The following is an abbreviated approach to typical clinical presentations caused by infarcts in the distribution of major cerebral arteries or observed in typical stroke constellations. First and foremost, patients who present with TIA should be hospitalized to undergo further diagnostic workup and appropriate therapy.

Internal Carotid Artery

Most ischemic strokes caused by extracranial vascular disease are due to atherosclerosis. Atherosclerotic vascular changes

Table 136-2 Signs and Symptoms of ICA-Related Ischemic Events

VASCULAR TERRITORY	SYMPTOMS	SIGNS
ICA	Transient monocular visual changes lasting about 3-5 minutes and presenting as Blindness Blurry or foggy vision Blind spots, colors, shapes Tunnel vision In only 10-15%, curtain-like blindness ascending or descending throughout visual field Rarely headaches	Amaurosis fugax Rarely Horner's syndrome
MCA	Difficulties in comprehension or language production, difficulties performing motor tasks or calculations, incoordination, numbness/tingling on one side of body, weakness in arm and leg	Aphasia, head and eye deviation toward lesion, apraxia, neglect, anosognosia, contralateral sensory deficit, contralateral paresis, confusional states
ACA	Numbness/tingling on one side of body, weakness of leg more than arm, difficulties walking	Contralateral sensory deficit, contralateral paresis, apathy, mutism, reduced spontaneity, gait apraxia, urinary incontinence

ICA, internal carotid artery; MCA, middle cerebral artery; ACA, anterior carotid artery.

are mainly observed at the carotid bifurcation, the siphon, at both locations (tandem lesion), or at the origin of the ophthalmic artery. Atherothrombotic plaque can induce brain infarcts by stenosis or occlusion resulting from perfusion failure, or it can cause thromboembolic events. In younger patients infarcts are often caused by dissection of the ICA. In ICA dissections the vessel lumen usually remains patent although stenosed. Over time the clot may resorb, the false passage close, and normal flow be re-established. Patients with acute dissections are placed on anticoagulation for 3 months to prevent emboli. However, the process of dissection may continue. Angioplasty with stent placement may be used to close the false vessel lumen. If the artery becomes occluded, bypass surgery may become necessary.

If collateral blood flow, mainly via the external carotid artery, is inadequate, occlusion of the ICA can produce extensive infarction involving the territories of the anterior and medial cerebral artery, which represents about two thirds of one entire brain hemisphere. This results in contralateral hemiparesis and hemisensory disturbance; bilateral visual hemifield loss (homonymous hemianopsia); and cortical findings, such as inability to talk (aphasia). Rapidly progressive ICA occlusion often presents with headaches, Horner's syndrome, and fluctuating neurologic symptoms of contralateral sensory dysfunction or paresis. These are often associated with arterial dissection. To avoid devastating infarction, preliminary warning signs (Table 136-2) must be recognized and patients be managed appropriately.

Middle Cerebral Artery

Infarction in the middle cerebral artery (MCA) territory is commonly caused by emboli that originate from the ipsilateral carotid artery, the aortic arch, or the heart. Large infarcts involving the entire MCA territory result in right or left hemispheric symptoms and present with contralateral hemiparesis, hemianesthesia, as well as head and eye deviation toward the infarcted side. In most right-handed

persons the left is the language dominant hemisphere. Strokes in the left MCA distribution therefore result in aphasias and in a variety of neuropsychological symptoms depending on their topography, such as inability to execute complex motor tasks without the presence of weakness, incoordination, or sensory deficit (apraxia). Right hemispheric strokes are characterized by neglect of stimuli presented to the left side, confusional states, or anosognosia (patient's inability to perceive own bodily dysfunction).

Anterior Cerebral Artery

Infarcts in the distribution of the anterior cerebral artery (ACA) are unusual and can be due to vasospasm following subarachnoid hemorrhage, arteriosclerosis, or emboli originating from the ICA or the heart.[27] The typical clinical presentation is characterized by paresis and sensory disturbance of the contralateral lower extremity, urinary incontinence, apathy, mutism, reduced spontaneity, and inability to walk (gait apraxia).

Posterior Cerebral Artery

Atherosclerosis of the posterior cerebral artery (PCA) is less common. Most infarcts in this territory are caused by emboli originating in the basilar and the vertebral arteries. About 10% to 15% of patients have a complete territory infarct, but most are restricted to its branches. The complete territory infarct involves mesencephalon, thalamus, occipital, and temporal lobes. The main clinical presentation is a homonymous visual field cut. Some patients are conscious of the visual field cut, others describe blind spots or blurred vision, and some patients are unaware of their visual impairment. Cortical blindness results from bilateral occipital infarcts. Some of these patients deny their blindness (Anton's syndrome). Other PCA territory defects result in loss of reading (alexia), recognizing faces (prosopagnosia), changes in color perception, confusional states, amnesia, and/or visual hallucinations.

Vertebrobasilar Arteries

Most ischemic infarcts within the distribution of the posterior circulation are due to atherosclerotic disease. Other less common etiologies include aneurysms, causing emboli or local compression of cranial nerves or the brain stem, or dissections mainly affecting the extracranial portion of the vertebral artery. Despite its connection with the anterior circulation via the circle of Willis, collateral blood supply is generally poor. Therefore acute occlusions of the vertebral or basilar arteries frequently result in complete ischemic infarcts of the brain stem or cerebellum. Because of the brain stem anatomy, placing crucial structures tightly together, even small infarcts can result in dramatic and often life-threatening neurologic dysfunction.

Typical clinical presentations, indicating posterior brain stem ischemia, include "crossed findings" on neurologic examination, that is, ipsilateral cranial nerve palsy causing facial numbness and weakness on the side of the infarct and sensory symptoms and weakness in extremities contralateral to the infarct due to long tract infarction. For example, the relatively common lateral medullary syndrome that is caused by an acute occlusion of the posterior inferior cerebellar artery, a branch of the vertebral artery, is characterized by decreased or absent sensation for temperature and pain in the face ipsilateral, and on the half of the body contralateral, to the infarct. Vertigo, nausea, vomiting, imbalance, especially when presenting with double vision (diplopia), perioral numbness, and hiccups are typical clinical findings in patients with acute posterior circulation ischemia and require emergent diagnostic workup and management.

Watershed Infarcts

Usually cerebral vessels compensate for systemic hypotension via autoregulation, resulting in maintenance of adequate cerebral perfusion pressure. If autoregulation fails, watershed infarcts can result. These occur typically in areas of critical cerebral perfusion at the border of vascular territories localized between the ACA and MCA, and the MCA and PCA territories (Fig. 136-1).

In watershed infarcts the lumen of the artery immediately supplying the territory is normal, but a greater than 80% proximal stenosis, usually of the ICA or very proximal intracranial arteries, causes a cerebral perfusion pressure deficit if systemic blood pressure decreases too much. Extremely low blood pressures, or hypotension in concert

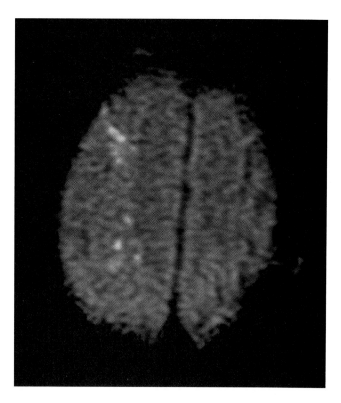

FIGURE 136-1 Diffusion-weighted brain MR imaging demonstrating acute right hemispheric watershed infarctions.

with critical proximal stenosis, can cause acute cerebral hypoperfusion. Proximal high-grade stenosis of greater than 80% can induce failure of distal autoregulation due to loss of the central vasomotor reserve. It is therefore essential to evaluate patients for orthostatic hypotension measuring blood pressure in the supine, sitting, and standing positions. Typical clinical presentations of watershed infarcts are presented in Table 136-3.

Lacunar Infarcts

Lacunar infarcts, measuring less than 1.5 cm in diameter, are caused by angiopathy of small penetrating arteries found in the brain stem, the basal ganglia, and the deep white matter of the brain and are quite common.[28] Causes are hypertension, diabetes mellitus, and elevated homocysteine levels.[29] About 20 lacunar syndromes have been described.[30]

Table 136-3 Clinical Presentations of Watershed Infarcts	
ACA/MCA WATERSHED INFARCT	**MCA/PCA WATERSHED INFARCT**
Contralateral sensory disturbance and hemiparesis of face and arm more than leg	Decreased sensation contralateral side of body
Hemiparesis	Sensory disturbance and hemiparesis contralaterally
Paresis of arm only	Aphasia (Wernicke type)
Aphasia (transcortical motor aphasia)	Hemineglect
Decreased level of consciousness	Homonymous quadrantanopsia
Seizures	Seizures

ACA, anterior carotid artery; MCA, middle cerebral artery; PCA, posterior carotid artery.

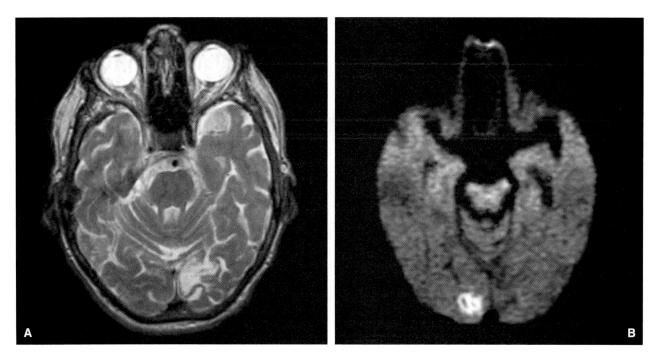

FIGURE 136-2 Assessment of stroke acuity based on MR imaging. **A,** Patient with chronic infarctions showing as hyperintense signals on this T2-weighted MR imaging. Acute infarctions are not yet visible on this imaging sequence. **B,** Diffusion-weighted brain MR imaging of the same patient. An acute infarction can be seen in the right occipital lobe. Old infarcts are no longer detectable.

The four most important include pure motor stroke (isolated weakness on one side of body), pure sensory stroke (isolated sensory disturbance of one side of body), ataxic hemiparesis (weakness of the leg more than arm with ipsilateral ataxia), and dysarthria clumsy hand syndrome (dysarthric speech, arm and facial weakness). Microangiopathy of the white matter can induce multiple small infarcts that are usually clinically silent and have diffuse borders. These small lesions can merge to larger areas and are termed *leukoencephalopathy* or *leukoariosis*, easily visible on MR imaging. If leukoariosis is extensive, it can produce cognitive impairment, gait disturbances, and parkinson-like features. These patients should undergo screening for stroke risk factors.

■ DIAGNOSTIC STUDIES IN ISCHEMIC STROKE

Past medical, family, and social history all give indications to the possible underlying causes of a stroke. Patients are screened for typical risk factors of atherosclerosis. The neurologic examination focuses on consciousness, orientation, speech, presence of neglect, evaluation of cranial nerves, strength, sensory loss, reflexes, coordination, and ability to walk. Further diagnostic workup depends on history, presence of risk factors, and age.

Auscultation of the carotid arteries for bruits is important because the presence of bruits warrants further diagnostic workup. Overall the degree of stenosis does not correlate well with the loudness of the murmur. The most ominous murmur is soft, high pitched, and present throughout the entire cardiac cycle. Murmurs originating from the internal versus the external carotid artery are characterized by their presence in both systole and diastole and their increase in intensity or duration with compression of the superficial temporal, facial or occipital arteries, during which blood is diverted from the external to the ICA.

Neuroimaging

After a comprehensive history and a general and neurologic examination, a cranial CT or MR imaging should be ordered to differentiate between hemorrhage and infarct. After 24 hours most ischemic events can be visualized on CT; however, even in the presence of an extensive ischemic stroke, CT might be completely normal. Other caveats are that other intracranial pathologic processes such as malignancies may be missed and that it is difficult to determine the age of infarcts precisely.

MR scan using DW and PW imaging, together with standard T1- and T2-weighted sequences, is a better tool to determine the temporal course of ischemia (Fig. 136-2). In the acute stroke phase MR imaging can differentiate between the ischemic core, visible within minutes on DW-MR imaging, which, if left untreated, will typically enlarge over time progressing to infarction and a larger area of hemodynamic compromise visible on PW-MR imaging. This is known as *perfusion/diffusion mismatch*, and the region of mismatch has been considered to be a marker of the ischemic penumbra.[31]

Based on these MR imaging techniques as well as single-photon emission CT, positron emission tomography, CT angiography, and CT perfusion, neuroimaging studies may help in the future to identify those candidates for thrombolytic therapy who will benefit most from acute therapeutic interventions[32] and those who might benefit from receiving thrombolytic therapy beyond the therapeutic 3-hour time window for tissue plasminogen activator (t-PA).[33] MR and CT angiography and CT perfusion studies are excellent methods for noninvasive evaluation of the intracranial and extracranial vessels. Advancement in MR angiography flow quantification will soon provide additional hemodynamic information, as well as visualization of vascular anatomy, which is standard now.[34,35]

Laboratory Studies

Further workup depends on history and age of the patient. In most patients older than 60 years of age, basic laboratory studies are indicated and include a complete blood count with differential, prothrombin time, fibrinogen, basic metabolic panel, fasting lipid profile, sedimentation rate, hemoglobin A1c, and homocysteine level. Stroke in the young or unusual presentations should trigger more extensive workup since a magnitude of potential etiologies can be responsible for ischemic stroke in this population (see Table 136-1). Laboratory studies should be extended to include a urinary drug screen; a rheumatologic panel; evaluation for thrombophilia and coagulopathy with thrombophilia screen; and evaluation for lupus anticoagulant, anticardiolipin antibodies, and antiphospholipid antibodies.

Ultrasound

Further diagnostic studies depend on the results of these screening tests. Especially older patients with cardiac disorders should be placed on telemetry for evaluation of atrial fibrillation. The incidence and prevalence of atrial fibrillation increase progressively with age, and a high proportion of ischemic strokes in the elderly is due to atrial fibrillation.[36,37] Additional workup should include transthoracic echocardiography to evaluate for cardiac disease and cardiac thrombus and to calculate the ejection fraction. The echocardiogram should include an agitated saline bubble study to detect possible cardiac shunt as source of paradoxical emboli. If the image quality of the transthoracic echocardiogram allows only limited view, or if it is essential to gain a better view of the left atrium, a transesophageal echocardiogram should be performed.

Evaluation of the major extracranial and intracranial vessels is done by transcranial Doppler (TCD) studies and carotid duplex with B-mode imaging, which has the ability to detect and characterize atherothrombotic plaque, measure intima media thickness, and determine the degree of vascular stenosis.[38] In combination with TCD it provides additional information on flow dynamics, presence or absence of collateral circulation, and central vascular reserve. TCD studies can be used to detect emboli in the MCA, originating from the heart, the aorta, or the carotid system (Fig. 136-3).

Carotid and TCD studies are supplementary to MR or CT angiographies. Additionally TCD and carotid duplex are

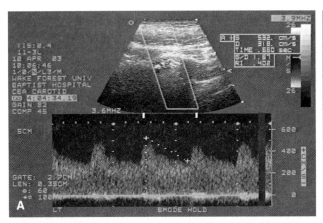
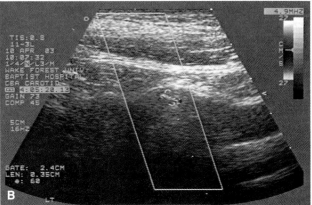
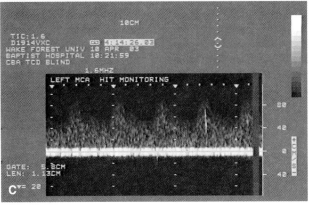

FIGURE 136-3 Neuroultrasound in carotid artery disease. **A** and **B,** Color duplex of high-grade internal carotid artery stenosis demonstrating high-flow velocities and a significantly decreased residual vessel lumen within the area of stenosis. **C,** Transcranial Doppler study (TCD) for microemboli detection. The TCD of the middle cerebral artery (MCA) shows a typical high-intensity transient signal within the otherwise normal spectral display of flow within the MCA indicating the presence of emboli. (See color figure in this section.)

used to evaluate the efficacy of acute thrombolytic therapy,[39] and future developments may result in ultrasound-based fragmentation and lysis of clot.[40]

If carotid artery stenosis is found during carotid ultrasound studies, it is important to determine whether the patient is a candidate for CEA. Carotid duplex studies are an excellent tool with which to detect plaques and stenosis, when used under the strict guidelines provided by credentialing bodies and technical quality control. However, ultrasound may overestimate the degree of stenosis if contralateral occlusion of the ICA is present because of compensatory increased flow velocity.[41]

Cerebral angiography is seldom, if ever, performed in three projections for accurate delineation of the true lumen, which could be achieved by adding oblique to the standard anteroposterior and lateral projections. MR imaging and ultrasound are more accurate techniques for this purpose because they allow three-dimensional imaging. Furthermore they are superior techniques for the assessment of plaque size and morphology.[42,43] Angiography has a combined mortality and morbidity of 0.5% to 4% in patients with atherosclerosis,[44,45] so that many medical centers today perform CEAs based on MR angiography and carotid duplex studies. Whether MR angiography alone or in combination with carotid artery duplex can completely replace cerebral angiography before performing endarterectomy is still being ascertained.[46-48] More recent reviews suggest that with advancement of ultrasound and MR angiography scanners and newer technology, noninvasive tests also yield very high sensitivity and specificity.[49] MR angiography still has limitations due to overestimation of the degree of stenosis and production of flow artifacts, which results in misclassification of patients.[50,51] The accuracy of carotid duplex ultrasound is highly operator dependent and cannot reliably differentiate between 99% stenosis and occlusion, which is crucial for surgical decision making. The combination of both imaging modalities can provide accurate diagnosis of carotid artery stenosis noninvasively. However, noninvasive imaging must be properly validated against cerebral angiography within individual centers.[52] If noninvasive imaging is used, patients undergoing CEA should also undergo additional evaluation of the intracranial circulation by MR angiography and TCD because otherwise tandem lesions and other significant intracranial disease might be missed.

Measurement Methods for Internal Carotid Artery Stenosis

Cerebral angiography remains the referential standard for determination of the carotid artery stenosis degree. The two major studies on CEA in symptomatic patients[35,36] unfortunately used different methods to measure the degree of stenosis (Fig. 136-4): The European Carotid Surgery Trial (ECST) measured the degree of stenosis locally at the level of the smallest lumen,[53] and the North American Symptomatic Carotid Endarterectomy Trial (NASCET)[54] measured the smallest lumen at the level of the stenosis and compared it with the lumen of the carotid artery distally to the carotid bulb as devised by Blaisdell and associates.[55,56]

A severe stenosis is defined as a 70% to 99% distal degree of stenosis in NASCET and an 85% to 99% local stenosis in ECST. A moderate stenosis corresponds to a 50% to 69% stenosis in NASCET and a 75% to 84% stenosis in ECST. Given that the benefit of surgery increases with the degree of stenosis, it is important to measure the stenosis as exactly as possible and to know the point of reference for measurement.

■ MANAGEMENT OF CAROTID ARTERY STENOSIS

Symptomatic Stenosis

Generally carotid artery stenosis is classified into asymptomatic or symptomatic disease, although this differentiation seems arbitrary because transient neurologic symptoms of ICA stenosis are often vague and subjective, can occur during sleep, or might not even be recognized by the patient or caregivers. From this standpoint a theoretical argument could be made that all patients with high-grade carotid stenosis should be treated comparably.[57] However, current clinical management differs for patients with symptomatic versus asymptomatic carotid stenosis.

Typically neurologic symptoms caused by ICA disease consist of monocular vision changes, contralateral hemiparesis, or hemisensory deficits (which might be restricted to the face and upper extremity) and cortical dysfunction,

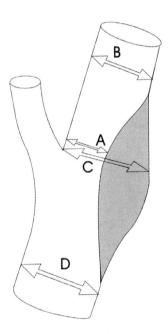

FIGURE 136-4 Degree of carotid artery stenosis as measured in the North American Symptomatic Carotid Endarterectomy Trial (NASCET) and the European Carotid Surgery Trial (ECST). NASCET used the distal reference point, measuring the residual lumen (A) in comparison to the normal distal internal carotid artery (ICA) lumen (B). ECST measured the residual ICA lumen (A) compared with the local estimated diameter of the carotid bulb (C). Local degree of stenosis = C − A/C. Distal degree of stenosis = B − A/B. Degree of common carotid artery stenosis = D − A/D.

such as aphasia, inability to write (agraphia) and calculate (acalculia) and perform motor tasks (apraxia), or hemineglect. Visual symptoms, as well as the presence of cortical findings, help distinguish these events from symptoms due to lacunar infarcts, which are caused by microangiopathy and managed medically. To determine if even a high-grade carotid artery stenosis is symptomatic, thorough history and neurologic evaluation are crucial. Due to its brief duration and subjective symptoms, it can be impossible to determine with certainty that the patient had a TIA. It is at times also difficult to differentiate between TIA, complicated migraine, and simple partial seizures. A spreading of symptoms in a distal to proximal fashion in one extremity might suggest a migraine equivalent in the absence of headache, or a jacksonian type of seizure expression. Involuntary movements of an extremity may be due to epilepsy, but limb shaking due to decreased cerebral perfusion has also been observed during TIAs.[58,59]

Based on the major clinical trials of endarterectomy versus medical management for symptomatic carotid stenosis and their subsequent meta-analyses,[60-65] patients with symptomatic stenosis ≥ 70% (measurement method used in ECST) or ≥ 85% (measurement method used in NASCET), absence of significant comorbidities, high risk for stroke, and access to an experienced team with low surgical complication rate should undergo CEA. High-risk patients include those with cardiac disease, high-grade stenosis, irregular plaque with ulceration and hemorrhage, cerebral versus ocular ischemic event, and an ischemic event within the last 2 months. The efficacy of CEA depends on the degree of stenosis and perioperative complication rate. ECST and NASCET data indicate higher perioperative complication rates for patients with cerebral ischemic versus retinal events, for patients with crescendo TIA or stroke-in-evolution, for early intervention within the first week following a stroke, for patients with active coronary artery disease, and for women. Perioperatively, the risk of stroke or death is higher in the surgical group than in the medically managed group, but both studies demonstrate significant risk reduction in rate of stroke and death after 2 years following CEA for high-grade stenosis. NASCET showed an absolute risk reduction of 12.5% for 70% to 99% stenosis and a 5% risk reduction for 50% to 69% stenosis. ECST demonstrates an absolute risk reduction of 12.9% for 70% to 99% stenosis and only moderate benefit for patients with 50% to 69% stenosis. CEA in patients with high-grade carotid stenosis near occlusion has probably no benefit.[61] Newer studies challenge the results of NASCET regarding the benefits of CEA in women, suggesting comparable outcomes and benefits for women as previously observed in men.[64]

Asymptomatic Stenosis

In about 75% of all cases, carotid artery stenosis is asymptomatic. For both asymptomatic and symptomatic stenoses, the risk of stroke increases, depending on the degree of stenosis. The incidence of stroke is about 1% to 2% annually in patients with a 50% to 75% asymptomatic stenosis, 6% per year with a 75% to 90% stenosis, and more than 8% in patients with ≥ 90% stenosis.[65] Controversy

exists regarding surgical management of patients with ≥ 60% stenosis who are otherwise not at increased risk for stroke.[66-68] So far five prospective studies that examined the efficacy of CEA in asymptomatic carotid stenosis have been published.[66,69-73] The Carotid Artery Stenosis with Asymptomatic Narrowing Operation Versus Aspirin (CASANOVA) trial showed no benefit of CEA and had a high 6.9% perioperative risk for stroke or death.[70,71] The Veterans Affair study showed no significant difference in outcome (stroke or death) between the surgical and the aspirin-treated group. The prospective, randomized study of Clagett and colleagues[69] did not include enough study subjects, and the study design does not fulfill current standards of clinical trials. The Mayo Asymptomatic Carotid Endarterectomy (MACE) study was terminated early secondary to the unacceptable high rate of myocardial infarction in the surgical treatment arm, in which patients did not receive aspirin.

There is probably a consensus that patients with asymptomatic stenosis but rapid progression of atherosclerotic carotid disease, stenosis greater than 90%, and impending carotid occlusion with poor collateral flow are at high risk for stroke and should undergo urgent surgery.

Based on the results from the Asymptomatic Carotid Atherosclerosis Study (ACAS),[66,67] which represents the largest and most influential study to date, most healthy male patients with asymptomatic carotid artery stenosis ≥ 60% and no coronary artery disease should undergo CEA. The relative risk reduction of stroke in surgically treated men over 5 years compared to the study arm treated with aspirin is 66%. CEA in women is less clear, because their perioperative complication rate in ACAS was higher (3.6%) compared to men (1.7%). However, those differences have been recently questioned.[64] The ACAS enrolled 1662 patients with asymptomatic carotid artery stenosis of 60% to 99%; 825 patients were randomized into the surgical group undergoing CEA and additionally received 325 mg of aspirin daily. Both treatment arms received 325 mg of aspirin per day. The relative risk reduction following surgery compared to medical treatment was 53%. The absolute risk reduction for ipsilateral stroke and perioperative death and stroke in all patients undergoing surgery was 5.1%. The difference between the surgical and the nonsurgical treatment arm was significant for all ipsilateral TIAs and stroke but nonsignificant for prevention of major stroke or death. Most significant benefits from CEA compared to medical treatment with aspirin were observed for reduction of ipsilateral TIA or perioperative TIA or stroke or death. Reduction of TIAs has important consequences because ischemic events frequently precede complete infarct. Multiple TIAs originating from one arterial source necessitate urgent CEA, which has a higher risk for poor outcome than does elective endarterectomy. Elective CEA can thus prevent these ischemic events with lower perioperative risk.

Based on the current data, not all patients with asymptomatic carotid artery stenosis ≥ 60% should undergo surgery. The perioperative risk must be minimal to achieve an optimal risk-benefit ratio.[74] In the ACAS the operative mortality (0.14%) and the risk of stroke and death (1.5%) were very low compared to the numbers observed in routine

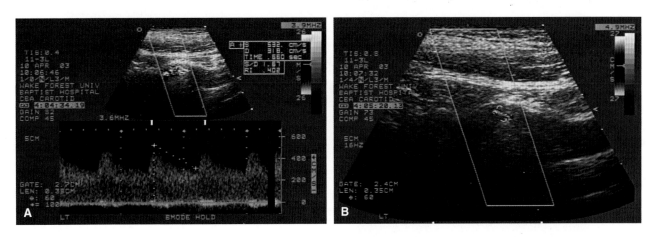

FIGURE 136-3 Neuroultrasound in carotid artery disease. **A** and **B,** Color duplex of high-grade internal carotid artery stenosis demonstrating high-flow velocities and a significantly decreased residual vessel lumen within the area of stenosis.

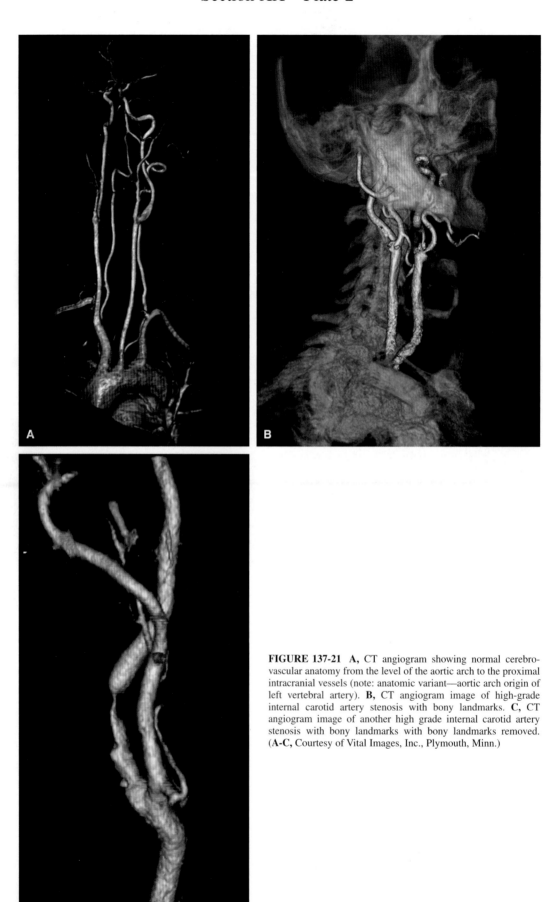

FIGURE 137-21 A, CT angiogram showing normal cerebro-vascular anatomy from the level of the aortic arch to the proximal intracranial vessels (note: anatomic variant—aortic arch origin of left vertebral artery). **B,** CT angiogram image of high-grade internal carotid artery stenosis with bony landmarks. **C,** CT angiogram image of another high grade internal carotid artery stenosis with bony landmarks with bony landmarks removed. (**A-C,** Courtesy of Vital Images, Inc., Plymouth, Minn.)

practice where the risk of stroke and death is up to three times higher than in ACAS and the operative mortality is up to eight times higher than in ACAS.[15] Some authors[75] suggest therefore to postpone CEA until the stenosis progresses to ≥ 80%. Asymptomatic patients with moderate stenosis who are otherwise not at high risk should be monitored for plaque progression with regular carotid duplex studies every 6 to 12 months while on preventive antiplatelet therapy. If atherosclerosis progresses despite best medical therapy, these patients should undergo endarterectomy.

To choose patients for endarterectomy based only on clinical classification into symptomatic versus asymptomatic patients with carotid artery stenosis would be an oversimplification. Even in clinically asymptomatic patients with high-grade stenosis, cranial CT shows that 15% of these patients have ischemic strokes.[76] In the ACAS, 21 patients in the surgical arm and 24 patients in the medical treatment arm died from myocardial infarct and 8 patients in both groups died from stroke. The evidence of asymptomatic coronary artery disease in this population is very high. About 20% to 40% of patients with TIA or cerebral infarct have abnormal provocative tests for silent cardiac ischemia. In patients with asymptomatic and symptomatic carotid artery stenosis, abnormal provocative tests for myocardial ischemia were found in 25% to 60%,[77] demonstrating that this population is at highest risk for cardiovascular death. The short-term risk for myocardial infarct or cardiovascular death within 3 months of admission for TIA or infarct is 2% to 5%, and the intermediate risk between 1 month to 2 years is estimated to be 1.5% to 5%.[77] The long-term risk for myocardial infarct in this population, however, is about 30%.[77]

The question remains, what keeps an atheromatous plaque asymptomatic and which plaque features or additional tests would predefine appropriate surgical candidates, even if they are clinically asymptomatic. In both symptomatic and asymptomatic carotid stenosis, microemboli to the brain can be detected on TCD studies of the MCA, although more frequently in symptomatic patients.[78,79] Both groups show expression of vascular adhesion molecules involved in the destabilization of atherosclerotic plaque, but possibly different patterns in activations of these factors can be observed in high- compared to low-risk patients.[80,81]

In summary, patients in good health with hemodynamic significant stenosis who are otherwise at high risk for stroke should undergo CEA, in our opinion, if the surgical and perioperative risks of mortality and morbidity can be kept low.

Timing of Surgery from a Neurologic Standpoint

The question of when to perform surgery following a stroke remains controversial. Likewise, timing of surgery in patients with progressive stroke (stroke-in-evolution) or frequently recurring ischemic events (crescendo TIA) remains unanswered. Because early studies on CEAs showed an increased risk of intracerebral hemorrhage and mortality due to surgery within the first few weeks following an ischemic infarct, it was recommended to delay surgery by

4 to 6 weeks.[82,83] However, postponing surgery may place patients at risk for recurrence of cerebrovascular events.[84-86] Both the ECST and NASCET confirmed the extensive literature that the risk is highest within the first weeks following an ischemic event, with a 30-day stroke risk of 4.9% for patients with severe stenosis who were in the medical treatment arm. Therefore, delay of surgery in neurologically stable patients is not advised. A subset of patients might actually benefit from acute surgery,[87,88] and neuroimaging studies such as MR imaging or Doppler studies assessing cerebrovascular reactivity could be helpful to identify appropriate candidates for acute surgery in the future.[89,90] On the other hand a recent meta-analysis of CEA studies published between 1980 and 2000[91] demonstrated that the mortality and risk for stroke is about 20% when patients with stroke-in-evolution or crescendo TIA undergo endarterectomy in the acute phase. In summary, based on current scant data, no recommendation regarding surgery in the acute phase can be made. Further prospective studies are necessary to provide safe-practice guidelines for different subgroups of stroke patients to determine preoperatively who is at high risk for poor outcome and who will have significant benefit from surgery.

Perioperative Medical Management

Currently anticoagulation with intravenous heparin in acute stroke and high-grade carotid artery stenosis is recommended before and after CEA and stenting to prevent reischemia or complete arterial occlusion within the first 2 weeks.[92,93] Intraoperatively or postoperatively, most neurologic complications in CEA are due to thromboembolism. Therefore we suggested to continue intravenous heparin and aspirin throughout the early postoperative phase.[93] If risk factors for atherosclerosis, such as hypertension, elevated homocysteine levels, or hyperlipidemia are present, they are medically treated as indicated. Patients also should be treated with antiplatelet agents as discussed in a later section for long-term stroke prevention.

Whether anticoagulation can prevent arterial occlusion preoperatively in high-grade carotid artery stenosis is unclear, and acute stroke patients on systemic anticoagulation may be at increased risk for secondary hemorrhagic transformation. In the NASCET and ECST, patients were not anticoagulated but were treated with aspirin. Data from the NASCET revealed increased risk of stroke with increase degree of stenosis, but then again decrease in risk approaching subtotal stenosis.[94] Current guidelines for preoperative management recommend the use of antiplatelet therapy before CEA or angioplasty with stenting.[95-97]

Anesthesia

At our institution endarterectomies are routinely performed under local cervical block anesthesia. In comparison to general anesthesia the perioperative risk for stroke is significantly lower in patients undergoing CEA with cervical block[98] and the frequency of arrhythmias and acute myocardial infarction is reduced.[99] Local anesthesia allows intraoperative monitoring of the neurologic status reducing strokes induced by clamping ischemia. It facilitates surgical techniques and intraoperative management to be modified according to the neurologic status and significantly reduces the need for carotid artery shunting.[98] Patients have a lower perioperative complication rate and can be discharged sooner from the hospital.

After endarterectomy patients are evaluated neurologically. Patients without complications of surgery are able to ambulate and are being discharged after 48 hours following CEA under local anesthesia. They are placed on antiplatelet therapy for long-term stroke prevention.

Postoperative Ultrasound Monitoring

There are no clear guidelines on when to perform follow-up ultrasound studies after endarterectomy. Some suggest to screen patients for presence and magnitude of embolic events using TCD within the first 24 hours because perioperative stroke occurs frequently during the early postoperative phase.[100] Clinically silent microemboli detected by TCD correlate with recent symptomatic cerebral ischemia, plaque instability, and thrombus formation.[101,102] Early postsurgical TCD monitoring can help detect patients at high risk for stroke after endarterectomy and allows rapid intervention such as taking the patient back for surgery or starting anticoagulation.

Postsurgical carotid duplex should be performed 2 to 6 weeks after the endarterectomy to evaluate the CEA site and to differentiate between recurrent and residual stenosis. If the CEA site is unremarkable, follow-up duplex should then be performed in 6 months to 1 year and then annually. If there is moderate contralateral disease or evidence for recurrent stenosis, scanning may be performed at 6- to 12-month intervals depending on the severity and progression of atherosclerosis.[103] Patients also should have long-term neurologic follow-up annually or more frequently if there is evidence for rapid disease progression.

Neurologic Complications of Carotid Endarterectomy and Restenosis

In the acute perioperative time period risks due to surgery by far outweigh the benefits, which are measurable only several years following the procedure. Most preoperative complications occur in the immediate postsurgical phase. The most important causes include dislodgement of carotid artery embolism with subsequent TIA/stroke, ischemia induced by clamping of the artery during the procedure, development of postoperative thrombus, and reperfusion syndrome in the presence of disturbed cerebrovascular autoregulation. Reperfusion injury results in cerebral edema secondary to disruption of the blood-brain barrier or in intracranial hemorrhage. Close monitoring and treatment of blood pressure are therefore essential. Clinically reperfusion injury manifests itself by headaches, seizures, altered mental status, and focal neurologic symptoms.

Perioperative morbidity due to surgery and use of anesthesia varies widely between medical centers from as low as less than 1% to up to 10% and mortality varies between 0.1% to 1%. Taking into account the additional morbidity rate of about 1% and mortality rate of about 0.3%

due to cerebral angiography, many physicians remain hesitant to perform surgery. Poor outcome might be caused by poor patient selection, anesthesia, inadequate surgical technique, or irreducible risk inherent to surgery. In about 1% of cases, reperfusion injury with rapid reinstitution of normal blood pressure and volume flow through a presurgical tightly stenosed artery can result in potentially devastating intracranial hemorrhage.

Cranial nerve palsies secondary to the procedures are observed in up to 5% of patients and involve the hypoglossal, recurrent laryngeal, or the facial nerve. Usually these cranial nerve lesions have a high rate of spontaneous recovery over several months.[104]

Despite successful surgery and complete plaque removal, asymptomatic restenosis at the procedure site can be observed in up to 8% of patients. About 3% of patients become symptomatic from the restenosed carotid artery. Biopsy studies of recurrent arterial lesions demonstrated intimal smooth muscle cell proliferation, not recurrence of atherothrombotic plaque as the underlying cause.

Multiple Vascular Lesions

Patients with general atherosclerosis frequently present with multiple vascular lesions requiring intervention. In these situations surgical decision making is more complicated and in general the most threatening vascular lesion regarding mortality and morbidity should primarily be addressed by surgery.

Bilateral Carotid Artery Stenosis

Each procedure carries its own risk for mortality and morbidity, and the cumulative risk increases with the number of surgeries. If patients have bilateral carotid artery stenosis, it is generally recommended to perform CEA only on the symptomatic side and closely monitor the patient for disease progression on the other side with serial carotid duplex studies in long-term follow-up. Some suggest to repair both sides, irrespective if the stenosis is symptomatic, if the narrowing is critical. Under these circumstances initially the side with the higher degree of stenosis is reconstructed, followed by the other side in at least 6 weeks later.

Simultaneous surgery of both arteries should be avoided due to the increased risk of mortality and morbidity and higher complication rate secondary to tissue swelling, airway obstruction, and the possibility of bilateral palsies of the recurrent laryngeal nerve.

Occlusion of One Carotid Artery and Significant Stenosis of the Other Artery

The prognosis for an asymptomatic carotid artery occlusion is generally poor.[105] In unilateral occlusions occurring within 1 week, flow can be re-established in less than 20% of patients. Risk of recanalization procedures is especially high in patients with large cerebral infarcts with a mortality rate up to 50%.[106] In patients with asymptomatic carotid stenosis and contralateral occlusion, CEA does not result in long-term benefit but may be potentially harmful.[107]

Tandem Lesions

Lesions at the carotid artery bifurcation are oftentimes associated with significant ipsilateral intracranial artery stenosis at the siphon. Frequently the intracranial lesion is inaccessible. It is important to assess the hemodynamic changes due to the tandem lesion and the stenosis degree of both lesions. If the intracranial stenosis exceeds the extracranial one, CEA should be avoided, because it does not improve flow through the distal segment. Given the results of the Warfarin-Aspirin Symptomatic Intracranial Disease (WASID) study,[108] patients with symptomatic intracranial stenosis in this situation might benefit most from anticoagulation with warfarin.

Coronary Endarterectomy and Coronary Artery Bypass Graft

Because the population of the elderly presenting with atherosclerosis is rapidly increasing and atherosclerosis affects multiple vessels, management of patients with combined coronary and carotid artery disease is a growing concern for cardiac and vascular surgeons.

Neurologically asymptomatic patients who are selected for elective CEA should have a thorough preoperative cardiac evaluation. If significant coronary artery stenosis is found and if feasible, percutaneous angioplasty should be performed before the CEA. In patients requiring coronary artery bypass graft (CABG), some favor to approach cardiac and carotid vascular lesions during one session,[109] whereas others opt to postpone the CEA several weeks following the CABG.[110] In patients with coronary artery occlusive disease presenting with symptomatic carotid artery stenosis, the decision making is more complex. The perioperative risk for adverse outcome is highest in patients undergoing simultaneous coronary and carotid artery surgery for symptomatic carotid stenosis and should therefore best be avoided whenever clinically possible.[111,112] From results of current clinical trials it remains unclear, if the increased postoperative stroke rate and mortality in combined surgery are due to the additional CEA, or whether concurrent CEA actually reduces the overall long-term risk for stroke. In general CABG in patients with symptomatic carotid artery stenosis should be delayed for at least 2 to 3 weeks.[113] However, controversy over these question continues, and we refer to the existing extensive literature.

■ MEDICAL TREATMENT OF ISCHEMIC STROKE

Acute Stroke Therapies

Thrombolytic treatment modalities for acute ischemic stroke encompass the use of intravenous t-PA and intra-arterial lysis. Both are limited by a relatively short window of opportunity for therapeutic intervention and multiple contraindications. Currently only about 1% to 3% of all acute stroke patients receive t-PA,[114] and despite its extended time window of 6 hours, the use of intra-arterial thrombolysis requires nonreadily available expertise, generally limited to tertiary medical centers, and is mainly investigational at this time.[115]

Further developments in acute stroke research will involve the experimental use of neuroprotective agents, hypothermia, and hyperbaric oxygenation as emerging alternative or adjunct acute treatment modalities.

Acute Intra-arterial Thrombolytic Therapy

Neuroradiologic developments of new catheterization equipment, high-resolution imaging, and improved contrast agents allow feasible and safe access to extracranial blood vessels and major vessels of the circle of Willis for angioplasty and stenting as well as application of intra-arterial thrombolytics, such as t-PA or prourokinase. Randomized trials comparing the thrombolytic agent prourokinase given intra-arterially plus intravenous heparin with intra-arterial placebo plus intravenous heparin[116] demonstrated a higher partial or complete recanalization rate of the occluded MCA than that observed with t-PA (58% and 66% in treatment groups vs. 14% in placebo groups), but the Prolyse in Acute Cerebral Thromboembolism (PROACT) I study did not show significant improvement in neurologic outcome. In the PROACT II study the effect on neurologic outcome was moderate, with 40% of prourokinase-treated versus 25% of placebo group patients having mild or no disability. Asymptomatic intracranial hemorrhage occurred in 27% of patients on high-dose heparin (100 U/kg bolus followed by 1000 U of heparin per hour) plus prourokinase (6 mg) and in 7% of patients on lower dose heparin (2000 U bolus followed by 500 U/h) plus prourokinase (PROACT I) and in 10.9% of patients on higher dose prourokinase (9 mg) plus low-dose heparin.[117] Limitations in intra-arterial thrombolysis at this time are due to a 6-hour therapeutic time window from symptom onset to treatment, contraindications comparable to intravenous t-PA use, and the rate of intracranial hemorrhage.[118,119]

Acute Intravenous Thrombolytic Therapy

For patients presenting acutely within 3 hours after stroke onset and who have no contraindications, the application of intravenous t-PA is now approved by the U.S. Food and Drug Administration and represents the standard of acute medical care. In 1995 the National Institute of Neurological Disorders and Stroke (NINDS) study demonstrated that t-PA, given to ischemic stroke patients within 3 hours, resulted in an 11% to 13% absolute improvement of neurological outcome (i.e., minimal or no disability at 3 months).[114] Although there is ongoing controversy on effectiveness and timing of t-PA treatment,[120-122] several recent studies confirmed a significant benefit for neurologic outcome.[123-125] In selected patients the 3-hour time window may be extended to 6 hours in the future.[126]

For acute ischemic stroke patients who are potential candidates for t-PA treatment, rapid diagnostic workup is essential. A rather complex medical system has to be in place and function flawlessly, from emergency medical system activation to emergent CT, to evaluation by emergency department personnel, to activation of an acute stroke

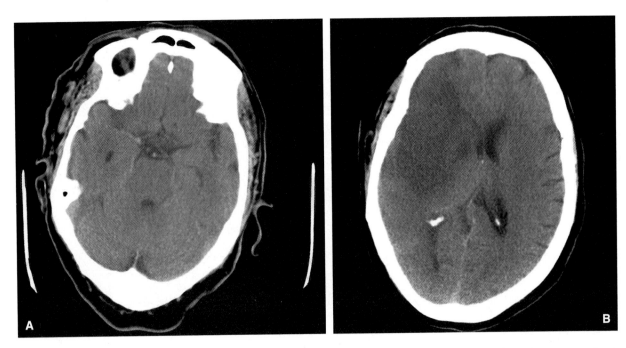

FIGURE 136-5 Evolution of acute brain infarct. The patient had sudden onset of left hemiplegia 2 hours prior to presentation to the emergency department. **A,** The initial head CT showed a dense right middle cerebral artery (MCA) but was otherwise unremarkable. **B,** Head CT of same patient taken 12 hours after initial scan, showing large right MCA territory infarct.

team. Goal is keep the "door to needle time" as brief as possible, and ideally management of stroke patients takes place in the intensive care of a specialized stroke unit because long-term prognosis for improved neurologic outcome is better at specialized stroke centers.[127]

On arrival in the emergency department, patients undergo head CT imaging to evaluate for ischemic versus hemorrhagic infarct and for early signs of ischemia-related changes on CT scan (Fig. 136-5).

The determination of exact onset time of stroke symptoms, preferably verified by a third-party history, is necessary. Patients are placed on a cardiac monitor with continuous noninvasive monitoring of blood pressure. Basic laboratory studies, especially complete blood count, coagulation studies, glucose, and pregnancy test in women of childbearing age are performed. A complete history with emphasis on screening for potential contraindications is obtained, and the patient undergoes a complete general physical and neurologic examination. The neurologic status is evaluated using the National Institutes of Health Stroke Scale (NIHSS). The neurologic examination focuses on level of alertness and orientation and screening for aphasia analyzing spontaneous speech, comprehension, naming, and repetition, horizontal eye movements, pupillary reaction, facial droop and its severity, presence of weakness and decreased sensation in limbs, reflex side-to-side differences, Babinski responses, and ataxia.

There are several contraindications obtained from the medical history or the examination or due to abnormalities on laboratory studies for t-PA treatment (Table 136-4). Increased risk for intracranial hemorrhage exists for very large strokes, found clinically in patients with an NIHSS score greater than 22 or if the initial head CT shows major

early signs of infarct, such as effacement of white/gray matter differentiation or an early hypodense area. On the other hand, patients with big strokes potentially have the most benefit from successful early t-PA treatment.[128-130]

Management of Hypertension

Management of hypertension in the acute phase is essential, because the systemic pressures should not exceed systolic values of 185 mm Hg and diastolic values of 110 mm Hg. Often patients present with severely elevated blood pressure in the initial phase of stroke. Acutely, we prefer the use of antihypertensives such as labetalol or nitroprusside (Table 136-5).

However, if the blood pressure remains difficult to control despite intense antihypertensive treatment, t-PA should not be given. In the acute phase of an ischemic infarct, too aggressive treatment of hypertension must be avoided because the potentially viable brain tissue or penumbra around the infarct core has partly or completely lost vascular autoregulation and requires elevated cerebral perfusion pressure to maintain its viability. With too aggressive blood pressure therapy during the acute stroke phase, the area of infarcted brain tissue can further extend. Acutely, systemic blood pressure should be adjusted to ranges of 150 to 170 mm Hg systolic and 90 to 100 mm Hg diastolic.

Except in emergency situations, central or arterial lines, nasogastric tube insertion and urinary catheterization should be avoided until 30 minutes after t-PA infusion. Noncompressible venous, arterial, or muscular puncture sites, from which bleeding can occur, are contraindications for thrombolytic therapy.

Table 136-4	Checklist for Administration of t-PA for Thrombolysis in Acute Ischemic Stroke*		
CONTRAINDICATIONS		**NO**	**YES†**
History			
1. Only minor or rapidly improving neurologic symptoms		_____	_____
2. Clinical presentation worrisome for SAH		_____	_____
3. Pure sensory symptoms, pure ataxia or a motor score of 1 in NIHSS		_____	_____
4. Rapid improvement in neurologic status before initiation of t-PA		_____	_____
5. Concurrent serious medical illness		_____	_____
6. Seizure in the setting of symptom onset		_____	_____
7. Active systemic bleeding		_____	_____
8. Major surgery or trauma in last 14 days		_____	_____
9. Head trauma, intracranial surgery, or prior stroke in last 3 months		_____	_____
10. GI or urinary tract hemorrhage in last 21 days		_____	_____
11. Recent arterial puncture at noncompressible site		_____	_____
12. Recent lumbar puncture		_____	_____
13. History of cerebral vascular malformation		_____	_____
14. Any history of intracranial hemorrhage		_____	_____
15. Pericarditis after myocardial infarct		_____	_____
16. Pregnancy		_____	_____
Laboratory			
1. Intracranial hemorrhage or SAH on brain scan			
2. Sustained BP > 185/110 mm Hg or aggressive treatment to maintain BP within acceptable range		_____	_____
3. Abnormal serum glucose (<50 or >400 mg/dL)		_____	_____
4. Platelet count <100,000		_____	_____
5. Elevated aPTT		_____	_____
6. INR >1.5		_____	_____
7. ECG changes consistent with acute myocardial infarct		_____	_____
8. Positive drug screen		_____	_____

*Eligibility criteria: (1) clinical diagnosis of acute ischemic stroke and onset time of symptoms within 3 hours of t-PA administration; (2) age 18 years or older.
†Any check in the "yes" column makes patient not eligible for t-PA.
t-PA, tissue plasminogen activator; SAH, subarachnoid hemorrhage; NIHSS, National Institutes of Health Stroke Scale; GI, gastrointestinal; BP, blood pressure; aPTT, activated partial thromboplastin time; INR, International Normalized Ratio; ECG, electrocardiogram.

Following the application of t-PA, patients need to stay in an intensive care unit for at least 24 hours for observation of respiration, coagulation, cardiovascular, and neurologic status. Patients should receive no food or fluids by mouth because many stroke patients have dysphagia and are at increased risk for aspiration, aspiration pneumonia, and acute respiratory distress syndrome following a stroke.[131] After 24 hours a repeat head CT is performed to evaluate for development of intracranial hemorrhage or cerebral edema,

potentially requiring acute neurosurgical intervention. If the CT scan does not show hemorrhage, severe cerebral edema, or hydrocephalus, especially in large ischemic infarcts, the patient can be triaged to an acute care stroke unit or to a regular stroke ward. If indicated, systemic anticoagulation with intravenous heparin or antiplatelet therapy can be initiated at this point.

Management of Patients Presenting Beyond the t-PA Window

Most stroke patients present beyond the time frame for acute thrombolytic therapy, sometimes after weeks, following an acute ischemic event. Initially patients undergo head CT to screen for ischemic versus hemorrhagic infarct and to differentiate from other sources causing sudden onset of neurologic symptoms, such as acute hemorrhage into undiagnosed central nervous system neoplasm. Basic laboratory studies, chest radiograph, and 12-lead electrocardiogram are done. A complete medical and neurologic history and examination are performed, and patients receive the diagnostic workup described earlier.

Table 136-5	Management of Hypertension in Acute Stroke

1. Nitroprusside drip (0.5 mg/kg/min) for diastolic blood pressure >150 mm Hg

2. For systolic blood pressure >230 mm Hg or diastolic values 121-140 mm Hg, labetalol 20 mg intravenously over 1-2 minutes, which can be repeated every 10 minutes, up to a maximum of 150 mg

3. For systolic blood pressures between 180-230 mm Hg or diastolic blood pressures of 105-120 mm Hg on two readings 5-10 minutes apart, labetalol 10 mg intravenously over 1-2 minutes, which can be repeated every 10-20 minutes, up to maximum dose of 150 mg.

Clinical assessment is important to judge the severity of a stroke and the required level of medical care. Patients can be divided into those with mild, moderate and severe ischemic stroke. Patients with mild stroke can be admitted to a regular stroke unit bed, with frequent neurologic checks every 4 hours within the first 24 hours, then every 8 hours, bedside swallowing evaluation by speech pathology or trained nursing staff, and initiation of bladder and bowel protocols. Moderate stroke patients need to be admitted to a regular room or acute care of a stroke unit, depending on cardiovascular-respiratory status and level of consciousness. Patients should undergo vital sign and neurologic checks every 4 hours, screening for dysphagia, respiratory care, and deep venous thrombosis prophylaxis and prophylaxis for gastrointestinal bleeding. Patients with severe stroke are admitted to the acute care stroke unit or to intensive care because they can have rapid mental status changes and develop cerebral edema, arrhythmia, or other medical complications.

NEUROLOGIC COMPLICATIONS FOLLOWING ISCHEMIC STROKE

Cerebral edema can develop rapidly following large infarcts, especially within the first 24 to 48 hours, and can result in brain herniation. Early intervention is necessary and should be started when the patient is obtunded but can still be aroused. Patients are treated with osmotherapy and hyperventilation on mechanical ventilators. The goal of hyperventilation is to maintain the PCO_2 at 35 to 40 mm Hg. Hyperventilation induces alkalosis, resulting in vasoconstriction and decrease in cerebral perfusion. But several hours after hyperventilation, metabolic compensation for respiratory alkalosis takes place, and continuation of hyperventilation in this situation might even increase intracranial pressure and decrease blood supply to the brain. Mannitol (20% solution) is given intravenously with a bolus of 1 g/kg body weight with the goal to keep serum osmolality greater than 280 mOsm/L and often is kept in the 295- to 305-mOsm/L range. Mannitol acts as an osmotic diuretic, reducing brain volume by drawing free water out of the tissue and into the circulation, where it is renally excreted. Repeat dosing can be given at 0.25 to 0.5 g/kg as needed, generally every 6 to 8 hours. If mannitol is initiated, blood pressure, serum sodium, serum osmolality, and renal function need to be closely monitored. All of these therapeutic measures, however, have only temporary effect,[132-135] and controversy exists regarding the benefit of osmotherapy and hyperventilation.[136-138] The use of other osmotic agents, steroids, barbiturates, or hypothermia is also controversial.[139]

Another risk of large ischemic infarcts is hemorrhagic transformation. Hemorrhages can consist of isolated petechial bleeds without relevance or can consist of confluent petechial hemorrhages involving more than one third of the infarcted brain tissue. These hemorrhages can produce mass effect. There is evidence that hemorrhagic transformation is seen more frequently after cardioembolic stroke.[140] If major intracranial hemorrhages develop, early intubation and possible ventriculostomy are necessary. Specific inhibition of t-PA is usually not indicated, due to the short half-life of thrombolytics. Warfarin can be antagonized emergently with fresh frozen plasma or within 6 to 12 hours with vitamin K. The use of protamine sulfate for reversal of systemic anticoagulation with heparin is potentially complicated by bradycardia, hypotension, dyspnea, and anaphylactic reactions.

All stroke patients who are dysarthric or aphasic or have at least a moderate stroke should undergo a formal swallowing evaluation at the bedside and possible pharyngeal function study, if indicated. Patients who fail the swallowing evaluation require feeding per nasogastric tube initially to avoid aspiration. If they fail a repeat study after several days, placement of a percutaneous endoscopic gastrostomy tube is usually indicated. Depending on their neurologic deficits, most patients need to be assessed early by physical and occupational therapists and should be evaluated for possible extended rehabilitation following the acute hospital stay. Early rehabilitation following stroke is essential for optimal neurologic recovery.[141]

PHARMACOLOGIC TREATMENT OF STROKE

Despite the high incidence, morbidity, and mortality rates of ischemic stroke, the overall available data on pharmacologic management, relying on clinical evidence derived from statistically powerful, prospective, randomized, multicenter trials, are scant.[142,143] Although general guidelines are available, specific indications for pharmacologic agents exist for only relatively few circumscribed clinical scenarios.

Systemic Anticoagulation with Intravenous Heparin

Currently, few indications for systemic anticoagulation in acute ischemic stroke remain (Table 136-6). Even for part of these indications controversy continues because only limited study data exist. Guidelines for anticoagulation in acute stroke and for cardiac arrhythmia are published by several organizations.[144-146]

Table 136-6	Current Indications for Intravenous Heparin in Acute Ischemic Stroke

Cardioembolic stroke with high recurrence risk
    Artificial heart valve
    Atrial fibrillation
    Cardiac disease with mural or left atrial thrombus
Vascular dissection
Coagulopathy
    Protein C deficiency
    Protein S deficiency
    Activated protein C resistance
    Factor Leyden V deficiency
Symptomatic high-grade extracranial and intracranial stenosis
Stroke-in-evolution, crescendo TIA
Sinus-venous thrombosis
Preoperative symptomatic internal carotid artery stenosis

TIA, transient ischemic attack.

Anticoagulation with Subcutaneous Heparin

Low-molecular-weight heparin in stroke patients prevents deep venous thrombosis and pulmonary edema. Several trials studied the effect of low-molecular-weight heparin given subcutaneously for prevention of recurrent ischemic stroke.[145-148] In summary the current data show no benefit of low-molecular-weight heparin or heparinoids for stroke prevention in acute ischemic infarcts. There are no data available regarding possible preventive effects of low-molecular-weight fractionated or unfractionated heparin or heparinoids in patients with cardioembolic stroke or evolving stroke. The risk of systemic or cerebral hemorrhage was increased in patients receiving low-molecular-weight heparin.

Warfarin

Patients with cardioembolic stroke or TIA due to atrial fibrillation, mural or left atrial thrombus, artificial heart valve, patent foramen ovale with aneurysm, and coagulopathy need life-long anticoagulation. Patients with symptomatic extracranial dissection or sinus-venous thrombosis require temporary systemic anticoagulation. Data of the WASID study[149] demonstrated a significant reduction in stroke risk for patients with 50% to 99% intracranial stenosis on warfarin compared to aspirin. Although used in clinical practice for patients with severe extracranial disease who cannot undergo CEA, there are no data from randomized control trials to comment on the appropriateness of using warfarin in this clinical situation.

Antiplatelet Therapy

Treatment options with antiplatelet therapies include aspirin, dipyridamole, clopidogrel, and ticlopidine. Antiplatelet agents for stroke prevention are usually initiated after TIA or ischemic stroke, after CEA, or in patients with intracranial or extracranial atherosclerosis.

Aspirin

Aspirin is the least expensive antiplatelet medication for stroke prevention and continues to be the first-choice antiplatelet agent of physicians for stroke prevention. Its mechanisms of action is irreversible inhibition of the platelet cyclooxygenase that lasts about 7 to 10 days and has a rapid onset of action—within 15 to 30 minutes.[150] Aspirin decreases platelet aggregation but does not inhibit the proliferative response leading to atherosclerosis.

The CAST study[151] showed a relative risk reduction of 12% for stroke and death within 4 weeks following acute stroke in patients receiving 160 mg of aspirin a day, compared to placebo. The placebo-controlled International Stroke Trial (IST)[146] demonstrated a small but significant reduction of early reinfarct rate within 2 weeks of ischemic stroke in the aspirin-treated group. The meta-analysis of both studies[152] showed a relatively small absolute risk reduction rate for reinfarct and death in the acute phase with doses of 160 to 300 mg of aspirin.

A meta-analysis of 10 studies examining the efficacy of aspirin for secondary stroke prevention[153] demonstrated that aspirin can significantly reduce the risk of stroke, myocardial infarction, and vascular death. The relative risk reduction was 13% for vascular events, when comparing aspirin to placebo. The Aspirin and Carotid Endarterectomy (ACE) trial[154] showed that relatively low doses of aspirin at 81 and 325 mg daily had lower risk of vascular events than high doses of aspirin (650 and 1300 mg/day). Major limitations of aspirin are due to gastrointestinal side effects that are less pronounced with smaller doses of aspirin. Overall aspirin is a relatively weak protective agent, and aspirin monotherapy might soon be replaced by combination therapy of dipyridamole and aspirin or other agents.

Clopidogrel

Clopidogrel is relatively expensive antiplatelet agent. It irreversibly inhibits platelet aggregation. The main study examining its efficacy for stroke prevention was the Clopidogrel Versus Aspirin in Patients at Risk of Ischemic Events (CAPRIE) trial.[155] Results of the CAPRIE study showed that clopidogrel was slightly more effective than aspirin in preventing ischemic stroke in patients with generalized atherosclerosis. Compared to aspirin, clopidogrel resulted only in an absolute stroke risk reduction of 0.5% in all study patients on clopidogrel. No significant preventive effect on ischemic infarct, myocardial infarct, or vascular death was observed in the study subpopulation of stroke patients. At this time clopidogrel monotherapy should be used for stroke prevention in patients who cannot tolerate aspirin. The effect of the combination therapy of clopidogrel and aspirin versus aspirin monotherapy is currently investigated. Clopidogrel is an excellent add-on agent to aspirin for patients with coronary artery or peripheral vascular disease.[156] Generally, in patients with generalized atherosclerosis, aspirin and clopidogrel combination therapy is therefore indicated.

Although there are not enough study data available to comment on this use, some authorities advocate a loading dose of 300 mg of clopidogrel in patients with crescendo TIA or stroke-in-evolution because an 80% platelet inhibition can already be observed after only 5 hours following its application.[157]

Dipyridamole

Dipyridamole reversibly inhibits platelet adhesion, and in combination with aspirin there is a synergistic antiplatelet effect by concomitant inhibition of platelet adhesion and aggregation.

The European Stroke Prevention Study (ESPS) 2 analyzed the effect of dipyridamole, aspirin, and combination therapy of both medications compared with placebo.[158] Dipyridamole monotherapy lowered the risk of stroke by 16%, and the combination therapy of aspirin and dipyridamole reduced the stroke event rate by 37% over 2 years. Combination therapy with aspirin and dipyridamole therefore seems to be superior to aspirin monotherapy. Head-to-head comparison for secondary stroke prevention comparing combination therapy of low-dose aspirin and dipyridamole with aspirin and clopidogrel are currently under way.

Ticlopidine

Ticlopidine is an irreversible inhibitor of platelet aggregation. It is highly effective in preventing ischemic infarcts in patients with previous TIA or stroke with a relative risk reduction of 23% for stroke, myocardial infarct, and vascular death in the "intention to treat" analysis of the Canadian-American Ticlopidine Study (CATS).[159] The Ticlopidine Aspirin Stroke Study (TASS)[160] demonstrated a 21% relative risk reduction for stroke and a 21% relative risk reduction for the combined endpoints of stroke and death. A meta-analysis of this trial[161] showed that ticlopidine is significantly more effective in stroke prevention in patients without severe carotid artery stenosis than aspirin. However, it has the potential to induce neutropenia. Recently ticlopidine has become a drug of second choice for stroke prevention due to its risk of agranulocytosis and the need for monitoring the neutrophil count.

Combination Therapy and Aspirin Failure

In patients with recurrent cerebral ischemic events that occurred while they were on aspirin or another antiplatelet agent, a different medication regimen is indicated. Therapeutic alternatives include changing to another antiplatelet agent or using combination therapy of antiplatelet agents, such as aspirin and clopidogrel or aspirin and dipyridamole. In patients on aspirin, an increase of the dose might be beneficial because there is a genetically determined dose-dependent responsiveness to the drug. The responsiveness to aspirin is also influenced by concurrent medical disease, individual metabolism, and drug interactions with other medications.

■   RISK FACTOR MODIFICATION

As holds true for secondary stroke prevention overall, it is essential to modify risk factors for atherosclerosis in patients with carotid artery stenosis. Thromboembolic disease of the carotid artery is frequently a marker for systemic atherosclerosis. Therefore, the general principles for risk factor modification such as tobacco cessation or adequate treatment of hypertension, hyperlipidemia, diabetes mellitus, and high homocysteine levels should be followed in ischemic stroke patients. Many patients should probably be evaluated by a multidisciplinary team because they have significant morbidity and mortality from cardiac and peripheral vascular disease as well. In the ACAS,[66] 24 of 825 patients in the surgical arm of the study died from myocardial infarction, and 8 of 825 patients from stroke.

The severity of carotid artery stenosis is a predictor of cerebral and cardiac ischemic events and the presence of peripheral vascular disease. Because atherosclerosis is a generalized disease, intervention directed toward a carotid plaque or carotid artery stenosis is a supplement to general medical management and modifications of underlying risk factors. Screening of patients for atherosclerosis could include measurement of the ankle-brachial index, intima media thickness, and plaque on ultrasound B-mode imaging, measurement of arterial distensibility, emboli detection on TCD, and angiographic or transesophageal echocardiography-based evaluation of the aortic arch. In the near future advances in molecular genetics may help identify genes that can induce susceptibility for atherosclerotic disease and ischemic stroke.[162,163]

Acknowledgments   We wish to express our special thanks to Dr. Ralph Hicks for his meticulous bibliographic work and his ideas and outstanding ongoing support during the preparation of this chapter.

■   REFERENCES

1. World Health Organization (WHO): Surveillance in brief: Update of noncommunicable diseases and mental health surveillance activities. Issue No. 5, Geneva, WHO, 5:1-5, 2003. Available at *www.who.int/entity/ncd_surveillance/media.org.*
2. American Heart Association: Heart and Stroke Facts Statistics—1999: Statistical Supplement. Dallas, American Heart Association.
3. Howard G, Howard VJ: Stroke incidence, mortality, and prevalence. In Gorelick PB, Alter M (eds): The Prevention of Stroke. New York, Panthenon, 2002, pp 1-11.
4. Reeves MJ, Hogan JG, Rafferty AP: Knowledge of stroke risk factors and warning signs among Michigan adults. Neurology 59:1547-1552, 2002.
5. Sacco RL, Ellenberg JH, Mohr JP, et al: Infarcts of undetermined cause: The NINCDS Stroke Data Bank. Ann Neurol 25:382-390, 1989.
6. Johnson SC, Fayad PB, Gorelick PB, et al: Prevalence and knowledge of transient ischemic attacks among U.S. adults. Neurology 60:1429-1434, 2003.
7. Shelton JE, Gaines KJ: Patients' attitudes towards TIA. Va Med Q 122:24-28, 1995.
8. Toole JF: Transient ischemic attack: Awareness and prevalence in the community. Health Rep 6:121-125, 1994.
9. Feinberg WM, Albers GM, Barner HJM, et al: Predictors of mortality and recurrence after hospitalized cerebral infarction in an urban community. The Northern Manhattan Stroke Study. Stroke 25:1320-1335, 1994.
10. Sacco RL: Risk factors, outcomes, and stroke subtypes for ischemic stroke. Neurology 49(Suppl 4):S39-S44, 1997.
11. Sacco RL, Shi T, Zamanillo MC, Kargman DE: Predictors of mortality and recurrence after hospitalized cerebral infarction in an urban community. The Northern Manhattan Stroke Study. Neurology 44:626-634, 1994.
12. Broderick J, Brott T, Kotharl R, et al: The Greater Cincinnati/Northern Kentucky Stroke Study: Preliminary first-ever and total incidence rates of stroke among blacks. Stroke 29:415-421, 1998.
13. Mohr JP, Caplan LR, Melski JW, et al: The Harvard Cooperative Stroke Registry: A prospective registry. Neurology 28:754-762, 1978.
14. Russo LS: Carotid system transient ischemic attacks: Clinical, racial, and angiographic correlations. Stroke 12:470, 1981.
15. NASCET Collaborators: Beneficial effect of carotid endarterectomy in symptomatic patients with high-grade carotid stenosis. N Engl J Med 325:445, 1991.
16. Tu JV, Hannan EL, Anderson GM, et al: The fall and rise of carotid endarterectomy in the United States and Canada. N Engl J Med 339:1441-1447, 1998.
17. Bond R: High morbidity and mortality due to endarterectomy. Cerebrovasc Dis 16(Suppl 4):1-125, 2003.
18. Halm EA, Chassin MR, Tuhrim S, et al. Revisiting the appropriateness on carotid endarterectomy. Stroke 34:1464-1471, 2003.
19. Waxman SG, Toole JF: Temporal profile resembling TIA in the setting of cerebral infarction. Stroke 14:433-437, 1983.
20. Rovira A, Rovira-Gols A, Pedraza S, et al: Diffusion-weighted MR imaging in the acute phase of transient ischemic attacks.. AJNR Am J Neuroradiol 23:77-83, 2002.
21. Kamal AK, Segal AZ, Ulu AM: Quantitative diffusion-weighted MR imaging in transient ischemic attacks. AJNR Am J Neuroradiol 23:1533-1538, 2002.

22. Kidwell CS, Alger JR, Di Salle F, et al: Diffusion MRI in patients with transient ischemic attacks. Stroke 3012:1174-1180, 1999.

23. Toole JF: The Willis Lecture: Transient, ischemic attacks, scientific method, and new realities. Stroke 22:99-104, 1991.

24. Albers GW, Caplan LR, Easton JD, et al, for the TIW Working Group: Transient ischemic attack: Proposal for a new definition. N Engl J Med 347:1713-1716, 2002.

25. Guidelines for the management of transient ischemic attacks. From the Ad Hoc Committee on Guidelines for the Management of Transient Ischemic Attacks of the Stroke Council of the American Heart Association. Stroke 25:1320-1335, 1994.

26. Albers GW, Hart RG, Lutsep HL, et al: AHA Scientific Statement. Supplement to the guidelines for the management of transient ischemic attacks: A statement from the Ad Hoc Committee on Guidelines for the Management of Transient Ischemic Attacks of the Stroke Council of the American Heart Association. Stroke 30:2502-2511, 1999.

27. Rodda RA: The arterial patterns associated with internal carotid disease and cerebral infarcts. Stroke 17:69-75, 1986.

28. Foulkes MA, Wolf PA, Price TR, et al: The Stroke Data Bank: Design, methods, and baseline characteristics. Stroke 19:547-554, 1988.

29. Evers S, Koch HG, Grotemeyer KH, et al: Features, symptoms, and neurophysical findings in stroke associated with hyperhomocysteinemia. Arch Neurol 54:1276-1282, 1997.

30. Fisher CM: Lacunar strokes and infarcts: A review. Neurology 32:871-876, 1982.

31. Warach S: Measurement of the ischemic penumbra with MRI: It's about time. Stroke 34:2533-2534, 2003.

32. Heiss WD, Thiel A, Winhuisen L, et al: Functional imaging in the assessment of capability for recovery after stroke. J Rehabil Med 41(Suppl):27-33, 2003.

33. Albers G: Expanding the window for thrombolytic therapy in acute stroke: The potential role of acute MRI for patient selection. Stroke 30:2230-2237, 1999.

34. Rutgers DR, Blankensteijn JD, van der Grond J: Preoperative MRA flow quantification in CEA patients: Flow differences between patients who develop cerebral ischemia and patients who do not develop cerebral ischemia during cross-clamping of the carotid artery. Stroke 31:3021-3028, 2000.

35. Long Q, Xu XY, Collins MW, et al: The combination of magnetic resonance angiography. Crit Rev Biomed Eng 26:227-274, 1998.

36. Chen J, Rich MW: Atrial fibrillation in the elderly. Curr Treat Options Cardiovasc Med 5:355-367, 2003.

37. Wang TJ, Massaro JM, Levy D, et al: A risk score for predicting stroke or death in individuals with new-onset atrial fibrillation in the community: The Framingham Heart Study. JAMA 290:1049-1056, 2003.

38. Weinberger J, Tegeler CH, McKinney WM, et al: Ultrasonography for diagnosis and management of carotid artery atherosclerosis. J Neuroimaging 5:237-243, 1995.

39. Christou I, Felberg RA, Demchuk AM, et al: Intravenous tissue plasminogen activator and flow improvement in acute ischemic stroke patients with internal carotid artery occlusion. J Neuroimaging 12:119-123, 2002.

40. Daffertshofer M, Hennerici M: Ultrasound in the treatment of ischemic stroke. Lancet Neurol 2:283-290, 2003.

41. Busttsil SJ, Franklin DP, Youkey JR, Elmore JR: Carotid duplex overestimation of stenosis due to severe contralateral disease. Am J Surg 172:147-148, 1996.

42. Pan XM, Saloner D, Reilly LM, et al: Assessment of carotid artery stenosis by ultrasonography, conventional angiography, and magnetic resonance angiography: Correlation with in vivo measurement of plaque stenosis. J Vasc Surg 21:82-89, 1995.

43. Elgersma OEH, Wüst AFJ, Buijs PC, et al: Multidirectional depiction of internal carotid arterial stenosis: Three-dimensional time-of-flight MR angiography versus rotational and conventional digital subtraction angiography. Radiology 216:511-516, 2000.

44. Executive Committee for the Asymptomatic Carotid Atherosclerosis study: Endarterectomy for asymptomatic carotid artery stenosis. JAMA 273:1421-1428, 1995.

45. Hankey GJ, Warlow CP, Molyneux AJ: Complications of cerebral angiography for patients with mild carotid territory ischemia being considered for carotid endarterectomy. J Neurol Neurosurg Psychiatry 53:542-548, 1990.

46. Blakeley DD, Oddone EZ, Hasselblad V: Noninvasive carotid artery testing: A meta-analytic review. Ann Intern Med 122:360-367, 1995.

47. Kallmes DF, Omary RA, Dix JE, et al: Specificity of MR angiography as a confirmatory test of carotid artery stenosis. AJNR Am J Neuroradiol 17:1501-1506, 1996.

48. Westwood ME, Kelly S, Berry E, et al: Use of magnetic resonance angiography to select candidates with recently symptomatic carotid stenosis for surgery: Systematic review. BMJ 324:198-202, 2002.

49. Nederkoorn PJ, vab der Graaf Y, Hunink MGM: Duplex ultrasound and magnetic resonance angiography compared with digital subtraction angiography in carotid artery stenosis: A systemic review. Stroke 34:1324-1332, 2003.

50. Johnston DCC, Goldstein LB: Clinical carotid endarterectomy decision making: Noninvasive vascular imaging versus angiography. Neurology 56:1009-1015, 2001.

51. Wardlow JM, Lewis SC, Humphrey P, et al: How does the degree of stenosis affect the accuracy and interobserver variability of magnetic resonance angiography? J Neurol Neurosurg Psychiatry 71:155-160, 2001.

52. Rothewell PM: Analysis of agreement between measurements of continuous variables: General principles and lessons from studies of imaging of carotid stenosis. J Neurol 451:825-834, 2000.

53. European Carotid Surgery Trialist's Collaborative Group: Randomized trial of endarterectomy for recently symptomatic carotid stenosis: Final results of the MRC European Carotid Surgery Trial (ECST). Lancet 351:1379-1387, 1998.

54. Barnett HJM, Taylor DW, Elizsziw M, et al, for the North American Symptomatic Carotid Endarterectomy Trial Collaborators: Benefit of carotid endarterectomy in patients with symptomatic moderate or severe stenosis. N Engl J Med 339:1415-1425, 1998.

55. Blaisdell, WF, Claus RH, Galbraith JG, et al: Joint study of extracranial arterial occlusion. JAMA 209:1889-1895, 1969.

56. Toole JF, Castaldo JE: Accurate measurement of carotid stenosis: Chaos in methodology. J Neuroimaging 4:222-230, 1994.

57. Toole JF: Medical and surgical management of carotid stenosis. In Toole JF (ed): Cerebrovascular Disease, 5th ed. Philadelphia, Lippincott Williams & Wilkins, 1999, pp 40-59.

58. Leira AD, Ajax T, Adams HP Jr: Limb-shaking carotid transient ischemic attacks successfully treated with modification of the antihypertensive regimen. Arch Neurol 54:904-905, 1997.

59. Firlik AD, Firlik KS, Yonas H: Physiological diagnosis and surgical treatment of recurrent limb shaking: Case report. Neurosurgery 39:607-611, 1996.

60. North American Symptomatic Carotid Endarterectomy Trial (NASCET): Methods, patient characteristics, and progress. Stroke 22:711-720, 1991.

61. European Carotid Surgery Trialist's Collaborative Group (ECST): MRC European Carotid Surgery Trial. Interim results for symptomatic patients with severe (70-99%) or with mild (0-29%) carotid stenosis. Lancet 337:1235-1243, 1991.

62. European Carotid Surgery Trialist's Collaborative Group: Endarterectomy for moderate symptomatic carotid stenosis: Interim results from the MRC European Carotid Surgery Trial. Lancet 347:1591-1593, 1996.

63. Rothwell PM, Gutnikov SA, Warlow CP, et al: Reanalysis of the final results of the European Carotid Surgery Trial. Stroke 34:514-523, 2003.

64. Mattos MA Summer DS, Bohannon WT, et al: Carotid endarterectomy in women: Challenging the results from ACAS and NASET. Ann Surg 234:438-446, 2001.

65. Toole JF, Chambless LE, Heiss G, et al: Prevalence of stroke and transient ischemic attacks in the Atherosclerosis Risk in Communities (ARIC) study. Ann Epidemiol 3:500-503, 1993.

66. Asymptomatic Carotid Atherosclerosis Study Group (ACAS): Study design for randomized prospective trial of carotid endarterectomy for asymptomatic atherosclerosis. Stroke 20:844-849, 1989.

67. Mayberg MR, Winn HR: Endarterectomy for asymptomatic carotid artery stenosis. JAMA 273:1285-1291, 1995.

68. Warlow C: Endarterectomy for asymptomatic carotid stenosis? Lancet 345:1254-1255, 1995.

69. Clagett GP, Youkey JR, Brigham RA, et al: Asymptomatic cervical bruit and abnormal ocular pneumoplethysmography: A prospective study comparing two approaches to management. Surgery 96:823-830, 1984.

70. CASANOVA Study Group: Carotid surgery versus medical therapy in asymptomatic carotid stenosis. J Neurol 237:129-161, 1990.

71. CASANOVA Study Group: Carotid surgery versus medical therapy in asymptomatic carotid stenosis. Stroke 22:1229-1235, 1991.

72. Mayo Asymptomatic Carotid Endarterectomy Study Group (MACE): Results of a randomized controlled trial of carotid endarterectomy for asymptomatic carotid stenosis. Mayo Clin Proc 67:513-518, 1992.

73. Hobson RW II, Weiss DG, Fields WS, et al: Efficacy of carotid endarterectomy for asymptomatic carotid stenosis. The Veterans Affairs Cooperative Study Group. N Engl J Med 328:221-227, 1993.

74. Cusi C, Candelise L: Is carotid endarterectomy effective and safe in asymptomatic patients with carotid stenosis? Neuroepidemiology 22:153-154, 2003.

75. Fleck JD, Biller J: Carotid endarterectomy for symptomatic and asymptomatic carotid stenosis. In Gorelick PB, Alter M (eds): The Prevention of Stroke. New York, Parthenon, 2002, pp 223-232.

76. Brott T, Tomsick T, Feinberg W, et al: Baseline silent cerebral infarction in the Asymptomatic Carotid Atherosclerosis Study. Stroke 25:1122-1129, 1994.

77. Adams RJ, Chimowitz MI, Alpert JS, et al: Stroke Council and the Council on Clinical Cardiology of the American Heart Association, American Stroke Association: Coronary risk evaluation in patients with transient ischemic attack and ischemic stroke: A scientific statement for healthcare professionals from the Stroke Council and the Council on Clinical Cardiology of the American Heart Association/American Stroke Association. Circulation 108:1278-1290, 2003.

78. Marcus HS, Thomson ND, Brown MM: Asymptomatic cerebral embolic signals in symptomatic and asymptomatic carotid artery disease. Brain 118:1005-1011, 1995.

79. Sieble M, Kleinschmidt A, Sitzer M, et al: Cerebral microembolism in symptomatic and asymptomatic high-grade internal carotid artery stenosis. Neurology 44:615-618, 1994.

80. Tan KT, Blann AD: To stroke or not to stroke: Is ICASM-1 or CRP the answer? [Editorial] Neurology 60:1884-1885, 2003.

81. Nuotio K, Lindsberg PJ, Carpén O: Adhesion molecule expression in symptomatic and asymptomatic carotid stenosis. Neurology 60:1890-1899, 2003.

82. Caplan LR, Skillman J, Ojemann R, Fields WS: Intracerebral hemorrhage following carotid endarterectomy: A hypertensive complication? Stroke 9:457-460, 1978.

83. Giordano JM, Trout HH III, Kozloff L, DePalma RG: Timing of carotid artery endarterectomy after stroke. J Vasc Surg 2:250-254, 1985.

84. Dosick SM, Whalen RC, Gale SS, Brown OW: Carotid endarterectomy in the stroke patient: Computerized axial tomography to determine timing. J Vasc Surg 2:214-219, 1985.

85. Khanna HL, Garg AG: Seven hundred seventy-four carotid endarterectomies for strokes and transient ischaemic attacks: Comparison of results of early vs. late surgery. Acta Neurochir Suppl (Wien) 42:103-106, 1988.

86. Gassecki AP, Ferguson GG, Eliasziw M, et al: Early endarterectomy for severe carotid artery stenosis after a nondisabling stroke: Results from the North American Symptomatic Carotid Endarterectomy Trial. J Vasc Surg 20:288-295, 1994.

87. McPherson CM, Woo D, Cohen PL, et al. Early carotid endarterectomy for critical carotid artery stenosis after thrombolysis therapy in acute ischemic stroke in the middle cerebral artery. Stroke 32:2075-2080, 2001.

88. Blaser T, Hofmann K, Buerger T, et al: Risk of stroke, transient ischemic attack, and vessel occlusion before endarterectomy in patients with symptomatic severe carotid stenosis. Stroke 33:1057-1062, 2002.

89. Krishnamurthy S, Tong D, McNamara KP, et al: Early carotid endarterectomy after ischemic stroke improves diffusion/perfusion mismatch on magnetic resonance imaging: Report of two cases. Neurosurgery 52:238-242, 2003.

90. Bond R, Rerkasem K, Rothwell PM: Systematic review of the risks of carotid endarterectomy in relation to the clinical indication for and timing of surgery. Stroke 34:2290-2303, 2003.

91. Nehler MR, Moneta GL, McConnell DB, et al: Anticoagulation followed by elective carotid surgery in patients with repetitive transient ischemic attacks and high-grade stenosis. Arch Surg 128:1117-1123, 1993.

92. Eckstein HH, Schmacher H, Dorler A, et al: Carotid endarterectomy and intracranial thrombolysis: Simultaneous and staged procedures in ischemic stroke. J Vasc Surg 29:459-471, 1999.

93. Inzitari D, Eliasziw M, Gates P, et al: The causes and risk of stroke in patients with asymptomatic internal-carotid artery stenosis. N Engl J Med 342:1693-1700, 2000.

94. Finlay JM, Tucker WS, Ferguson GG, et al: Guidelines for the use of carotid endarterectomy: Current recommendations from the Canadian Neurosurgical Society. Can Med Assoc J 157:653-659, 1997.

95. Moore WS, Mohr JP, Najafi H, et al: Carotid endarterectomy: Practice guidelines. Reports of the Ad Hoc Committee to the Joint Council of the Society for Vascular Surgery and the North American Chapter of the International Society for Cardiovascular Surgery. J Vasc Surg 15:469-479, 1992.

96. Vitek JJ, Roubin GS, Al-Mubarek N, et al: Carotid artery stenting: Technical considerations. AJNR Am J Neuroradiol 21:1736-1743, 2000.

97. Yadav JS: Management practices in carotid artery stenting. Cerebrovasc Dis 11(Suppl 2):18-22, 2001.

98. Fiorani P, Sbarigia E, Speziale F, et al: General anesthesia versus cervical block and perioperative complications in carotid artery surgery. Eur J Vasc Endovasc Surg 13:37-42, 1997.

99. Allen BT, Anderson CB, Rubin BG, et al: The influence of anesthetic technique on perioperative complications after carotid endarterectomy. J Vasc Surg 19:834-843, 1994.

100. Levi CR, O'Malley HM, Fell G, et al: Transcranial Doppler-detected cerebral microembolism following carotid endarterectomy: High microembolic signal loads predict postoperative cerebral ischaemia. Brain 120:621-629, 1997.

101. Harrison MJ, Pugsley W, Newman S, et al: Detection of middle cerebral emboli during coronary artery bypass surgery using transcranial Doppler sonography. Stroke 21:1512, 1990.

102. vanZuilen E, Moll FL, Vermeulen FEE, et al: Detection of cerebral microemboli by means of transcranial Doppler monitoring before and after carotid endarterectomy. Stroke 27:210-213, 1995.

103. Ricotta JJ, DeWeese JA: Is routine carotid ultrasound surveillance after carotid endarterectomy worthwhile? Am J Surg 172:140-143, 1996.

104. Maroulis J, Karkanevatos A, Papakostas K, et al: Cranial nerve dysfunction following carotid endarterectomy. Int Angiol 19:237-241, 2000.

105. Rautenbertg W, Mess W, Hennerici M: Prognosis of asymptomatic carotid occlusion. J Neurol Sci 98:213-220, 1990.

106. Friedman SG, Riles TS, Lamparello PJ, et al: Surgical therapy for the patient with internal carotid artery occlusion and contralateral stenosis. J Vasc Surg 6:856-861, 1987.

107. Baker WH, Howard VJ, Howard G, et al: Effect of contralateral occlusion on long-term efficacy of endarterectomy in the Asymptomatic Carotid Atherosclerosis Study (ACAS). Stroke 31:2330-2334, 2000.

108. Benesch CG, Chimowitz MI, for the WASID Investigators: Best treatment for intracranial arterial stenosis? 50 years of uncertainty. Neurology 55:465-466, 2000.

109. Ricotta JJ, Char DJ, Cuadra SA, et al: Modeling stroke risk after coronary artery bypass and combined coronary artery bypass and carotid endarterectomy. Stroke 34:1212-1217, 2003.

110. Chimowitz MI, Kokkinos J, Strong J, et al: The Warfarin-Aspirin Symptomatic Intracranial Disease Study. Neurology 45:1488-1493, 1995.

111. Brenner BJ, Brief DK, Alpert J, et al: The risk of stroke in patients with asymptomatic carotid stenosis undergoing cardiac surgery: A follow-up study. J Vasc Surg 5:269-279, 1987.

112. Gasparis AP, Ricotta L, Cuadra SA, et al: High-risk carotid endarterectomy: Fact or fiction. J Vasc Surg 37:40-46, 2003.

113. Ricotta JJ, Wall LP: Treatment of patients with combined coronary and carotid atherosclerosis. J Cardiovasc Surg 44:363-369, 2003.

114. Tissue plasminogen activator for acute ischemic stroke. The National Institute of Neurological Disorders and Stroke rt-PA Stroke Study Group. N Engl J Med 333:1581-1587, 1995.

115. Randall RT, Furlan AJ, Roberts H, et al: Trial design and reporting standards for intra-arterial cerebral thrombolysis for acute ischemic stroke. Stroke 34:e109-e137, 2003.

116. del Zoppo G, Higashida R, Furlan A, et al: PROACT: A phase II randomized trial of recombinant pro-urokinase by direct arterial delivery in acute middle cerebral artery stroke. Stroke 29:4-11, 1998.

117. Furlan A, Higashida R, Wechsler L, et al: Intra-arterial prourokinase for acute ischemic stroke: The PROACT II study: A randomized controlled trial. PROlyse in Acute Cerebral Thromboembolism. JAMA 282:2003-2011, 1999.

118. Kase CS, Furlan AJ, Wechsler LR, et al: Cerebral hemorrhage after intra-arterial thrombolysis for ischemic stroke: The PROACT II trial. Neurology 57:1603-1610, 2001.

119. Bendszus M, Urbach H, Ries F, Solymosi L: Outcome after local intra-arterial fibrinolysis compared with the natural course of patients with a dense middle cerebral artery on early CT. Neuroradiology 40:54-58, 1998.

120. Suarez JI, Sunshine JL, Tarr R, et al: Predictors of clinical improvement, angiographic recanalization, and intracranial hemorrhage after intra-arterial thrombolysis for acute ischemic stroke. Stroke 30:2094-2100, 1999.

121. Hacke W, Kaste M, Fieschi C, et al: Randomised double-blind placebo-controlled trial of thrombolytic therapy with intravenous alteplase in acute ischemic stroke (ECASS II). Second European-Australasian Acute Stroke Study Investigators. Lancet 352:1245-1251, 1998.

122. Clark WM, Wissman S, Albers GW, et al: Recombinant tissue-type plasminogen activator (Alteplase) for ischemic stroke 3 to 5 hours after symptom onset. The Atlantis study: A randomized controlled trial. Alteplase Thrombolysis for Acute Noninterventional Therapy in Ischemic Stroke. JAMA 282:2019-2026, 1999.

123. Tanne D, Bates VE, Verro P, et al: Initial clinical experience with IV tissue plasminogen activator for acute ischemic stroke: A multicenter survey: The t-PA Stroke Survey Group. Neurology 53:424-427, 1999.

124. Buchan AM, Barber PA, Newcommon N, et al: Effectiveness of t-PA in acute ischemic stroke: Outcome relates to the appropriateness. Neurology 54:679-684, 2000.

125. Kent D, Bluhmki E, Selker H: Beyond the three-hour time window: Multivariable patient selection for thrombolytic therapy in acute ischemic stroke. 2003 12th European Stroke Conference. Cerebrovasc Dis 16(Suppl 4):274, 2003.

126. Ringelstein EB, Busse O. Grond M: Akutversorgung von Patienten mit zerebralen Insulten. D Aerztbl 35:875-877, 1999.

127. Jorgenson HS, Nakayama H, Raaschou HO, et al: The effect of a stroke unit: Reductions in mortality, discharge rate to nursing home, length of hospital stay, and cost: A community-based study. Stroke 26:1178-1182, 1995.

128. Manelfe C, Larrue V, von Kummer R, et al: Association of hyperdense middle cerebral artery sign with clinical outcome in patients treated with tissue plasminogen activator. Stroke 30:769-772, 1999.

129. Fiorelli M, von Kummer R: Early ischemic changes on computed tomography in patients with acute stroke. JAMA 287:2361-2362, 2002.

130. Silver FL, Norris JW, Lewis AJ, Hachinski VC: Early mortality following stroke: A prospective review. Stroke 15:492-496, 1984.

131. Laffey JG, Kavanagh BP: Hypocapnia. N Engl J Med 343:53, 2002.

132. Muizelaar JP, Marmarou A, Ward JD, et al: Adverse effects of prolonged hyperventilation in patients with severe head injury: A randomized clinical trial. J Neurosurg 75:731-739, 1991.

133. Dennis LJ, Mayer SA: Diagnosis and management of increased intracranial pressure. Neurol India 49(Suppl 1):S37-S50, 2001.

134. Jafar JJ, Johns LM, Mullan SF: The effect of mannitol on cerebral blood flow. J Neurosurg 64:754-759, 1986.

135. Kaufmann AM, Cardoso ER: Aggravation of vasogenic cerebral edema by multiple-dose mannitol. J Neurosurg 77:584-589, 1992.

136. Polderman KH, van de Kraats G, Dixon JM, et al: Increases in spinal fluid osmolarity induced by mannitol. Crit Care Med 31:584-590, 2003.

137. Yundt KD, Diringer MN: The use of hyperventilation and its impact on cerebral ischemia in the treatment of traumatic brain injury. Crit Care Clin 13:163-184, 1997.

138. Garcia-Sola R, Pulido P, Capilla P: The immediate and long-term effects of mannitol and glycerol: A comparative experimental study. Acta Neurochir (Wien) 109:114-121, 1991.

139. Node Y, Nakazawa S: Clinical study of mannitol and glycerol on raised intracranial pressure and on their rebound phenomenon. Adv Neurol 52:359-363, 1990.

140. Alexandrov AV, Black SE, Ehrlich LE, et al: Predictors of hemorrhagic transformation occurring spontaneously and on anticoagulants in patients with acute ischemic stroke. Stroke 28:1198-1202, 1997.

141. Musicco M, Emberti L, Nappi G, Caltagirone C; for the Italian Multicenter Study on Outcomes of Rehabilitation of Neurological Patients: Early and long-term outcome of rehabilitation in stroke patients: The role of patient characteristics, time of initiation, and duration of interventions. Arch Phys Med Rehabil 84:551-558, 2003.

142. Coull BM, Williams LS, Goldstein LB, et al: Anticoagulants and antiplatelet agents in acute ischemic stroke: REPORT of the Joint Stroke Guideline Development Committee of the American Academy of Neurology and the American Stroke Association (a division of the American Heart Association). Neurology 59:13-22, 2002.

143. European Stroke Initiative recommendations for stroke management. European Stroke Council, European Neurological Society and European Federation of Neurological Societies. Cerebrovasc Dis 10:335-351, 2000.

144. Eagle KA, Berger PB, Calkins H, et al: ACC/AHA guideline update for perioperative cardiovascular evaluation for noncardiac surgery-executive summary: A report of the American College of Cardiology/American Heart Association Task Force on Practice Guidelines (Committee to Update the 1996 Guidelines on Perioperative Cardiovascular Evaluation for Noncardiac Surgery). J Am Coll Cardiol 39:542-553, 2002.

145. Kay R, Wong KS, Yu YL, et al: Low-molecular-weight heparin for the treatment of acute ischemic stroke. N Engl J Med 333:1588-1593, 1995.

146. The International Stroke Trial (IST): A randomized trial of aspirin, subcutaneous heparin, both, or neither among 19,435 patients with acute ischemic stroke. International Stroke Trial Collaborative Group. Lancet 349:1569-1581, 1997.

147. Hommel M, for the FISS Investigators Group. Fraxiparine in ischemic stroke study (FISS-BIS). Cerebrovasc Dis 8:63, 1998.

148. Low-molecular-weight heparinoid, ORG 10172 (danaproid), and outcome after acute ischemic stroke: A randomized controlled trial. The Publications Committee for the Trial of ORG 10172 in Acute Stroke Treatment (TOAST) Investigators. JAMA 279:1265-1272, 1998.

149. Benesch CG,. Chimowitz MI: Best treatment for intracranial arterial stenosis? 50 years of uncertainty. The WASID Investigators. Neurology 554:465-466, 2000.

150. Schafer AI: Antiplatelet therapy. Am J Med 101:199-209, 1996.

151. CAST: Randomised placebo-controlled trial of early aspirin use in 20,000 patients with acute ischaemic stroke. CAST (Chinese Acute Stroke Trial) Collaborative Group. Lancet 349:1641-1649, 1997.

152. Chen ZM, Sandercock P, Pan HC, et al: Indications for early aspirin use in acute ischemic stroke: A combined analysis of 40 000 randomized

patients from the Chinese acute stroke trial and the international stroke trial. On behalf of the CAST and IST collaborative groups. Stroke 6:1240-1249, 2000.

153. Albers GW, Tijssen JG: Antiplatelet therapy: New foundations for optimal treatment decisions. Neurology 53(Suppl 4):S25-S31, 1999.

154. Taylor DW, Barnett HJ, Haynes RB, et al: Low-dose and high-dose acetylsalicylic acid for patients undergoing carotid endarterectomy: A randomised controlled trial. ASA and Carotid Endarterectomy (ACE) Trial Collaborators. Lancet 353:2179-2184, 1999.

155. A randomized, blinded trial of clopidogrel versus aspirin in patients at risk of ischemic events (CAPRIE). CAPRIE Steering Committee. Lancet 348:1329-1339, 1996.

156. Yusuf S, Zhao F, Mehta SR, et al: Clopidogrel in Unstable Angina to Prevent Recurrent Events Trial Investigators. Effects of clopidogrel in addition to aspirin in patients with acute coronary syndromes without ST-segment elevation. N Engl J Med 345:494-502, 2001.

157. Mills DC, Puri R, Hu CJ, et al: Clopidogrel inhibits the binding of ADP analogues to the receptor mediating inhibition of platelet adenylate cyclase. Arterioscler Thromb 12:430-436, 1992.

158. Diener HC, Cunha L, Forbes C, et al: European Stroke Prevention Study: II. Dipyridamole and acetylsalicylic acid in the secondary prevention of stroke. J Neurol Sci 143:1-13, 1996.

159. Gent M, Blakely JA, Easton JD, et al: The Canadian American Ticlopidine Study (CATS) in thromboembolic stroke. Lancet 1:1215-1220, 1989.

160. Hass WK, Easton JD, Adams HP Jr, et al: A randomized trial comparing ticlopidine hydrochloride with aspirin for the prevention of stroke in high-risk patients. Ticlopidine Aspirin Stroke Study Group. N Engl J Med 321:501-507, 1989.

161. Grotta JC, Norris JW, Kamm B: Prevention of stroke with ticlopidine: Who benefits most? TASS Baseline and Angiographic Data Subgroup. Neurology 42:111-115, 1992.

162. Skvortsova VI, Limboorskaia SA, Slominskii PA, et al: [Association between Bam HI RFLP p53 gene polymorphism and brain infarction volume in patients with atherothrombotic ischemic stroke] Cerebrovasc Dis 16(Suppl 8):24-29, 2003.

163. Gretarsdottir S, Thorleifsson G, Reynisdottir ST, et al: The gene encoding phosphodiesterase 4D confers risk of ischemic stroke. Nat Genet 35:131-138, 2003.

Chapter

Anatomy and Angiographic Diagnosis of Extracranial and Intracranial Vascular Disease

137

LARRY-STUART DEUTSCH, MD, CM, FRCPC, FACR

■ ARTERIAL ANATOMY: EXTRACRANIAL AND INTRACRANIAL VASCULAR SYSTEM

Aortic Arch and Its Branches

The surgical approach to the diagnosis and treatment of cerebrovascular disease requires an understanding of the vascular anatomy that begins with the aortic arch and ends with the principal intracranial arteries. The normal aortic arch curves smoothly upward into the superior mediastinum, running from right to left and anterior to posterior, with its apex at approximately the mid-manubrium. It passes to the left of the trachea, arching over the pulmonary artery bifurcation and the left main stem bronchus, descending to the left of the esophagus. The ligamentum arteriosum, the fibrous remnant of the fetal ductus arteriosus, tethers the concave undersurface of the aortic arch to the proximal left main pulmonary artery, attaching at a point usually just distal to the left subclavian artery.

In approximately 95% of all individuals, the aortic arch gives rise to three major branches: the right brachiocephalic trunk (formerly designated the *innominate artery*), the left common carotid artery, and the left subclavian artery (Fig. 137-1). One of the most common variants is a common ostial origin of the brachiocephalic and left common carotid arteries, which occurs in approximately 10% of individuals and has been termed a *bovine trunk* because of its occurrence in that animal. However, a true trunk of more than a few millimeters in length that then divides into the right brachiocephalic and left common carotid arteries is relatively rare. Origination of the left vertebral artery directly from the aorta proximal to the left subclavian artery is another common anatomic variant, occurring in approximately 5% of individuals (Fig. 137-2).

True anomalies of the aortic arch are actually rare, present in less than 2% of adults. Anomalies, such as double aortic arch; interrupted arch; right-sided arch, especially the mirror image branching form; and cervical arch, are often associated with complex congenital heart disease. Symptoms caused by pressure on the trachea or esophagus often require surgical correction in neonates or children. Because routine surgical correction of such anomalies is relatively recent, few of these patients have reached an age when they would be subject to the most common cerebrovascular disease, atherosclerosis. Indeed, even when

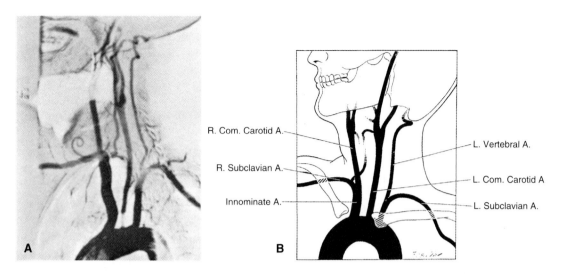

R. Com. Carotid A.

R. Subclavian A.

Innominate A.

L. Vertebral A.

L. Com. Carotid A

L. Subclavian A.

FIGURE 137-1 **A,** An arch aortogram demonstrating the three primary branches of the aortic arch: the innominate artery, the left common (Com) carotid artery, and the left subclavian artery. **B,** Artist's concept of an arch aortogram illustrating the three primary branches of the aortic arch and their pertinent anatomic relationships.

these patients eventually do develop clinically significant occlusive cerebrovascular disease, it is most likely to be simple atherosclerotic carotid bifurcation disease amenable to conventional surgical thromboendarterectomy. However, as endovascular therapies, especial carotid angioplasty, stenting and the use of distal embolic protection devices gain acceptance, catheterization and device deployment may be challenging.

The most common aortic arch anomaly compatible with long-term survival is the aberrant right subclavian artery that originates from the proximal descending thoracic aorta and passes posterior to the esophagus (Fig. 137-3). Unless this anomaly causes dysphagia in the neonatal period, it may escape detection until the patient is examined angiographically later in life. A diverticulum often accompanies the origin of an aberrant right subclavian artery, called *Kommerelli's diverticulum*; it can become aneurysmal, with rupture or compressive symptoms. Simple right aortic arches with normal branching, uncomplicated right arches with mirror image branching, and mirror image arches associated with thoracic situs inversus are sufficiently uncommon that many surgeons and angiographers will never actually encounter a case even in a busy clinical practice.

Right Brachiocephalic Trunk

The right brachiocephalic trunk (innominate artery) is the first major branch of the thoracic aorta and the largest of its branches. It originates in the superior mediastinum posterior to the mid-point of the sternal manubrium and passes superiorly and posteriorly for a distance of 4 to 6 cm, then bifurcates into the right common carotid and right subclavian arteries in the root of the neck posterior to the right sternoclavicular joint. Whereas the proximal segments of the other major branches of the aortic arch are usually relatively straight, the right brachiocephalic trunk and the proximal segments of the right common carotid and subclavian arteries are often rather tortuous, particularly in

elderly patients. Such tortuosity, especially when it involves the right subclavian artery at the base of the neck, often can mimic aneurysmal dilation on physical examination as well as angiography and ultrasound. Fortunately, both computed tomography (CT) and magnetic resonance (MR) angiography with their ability to display multiple views of the same image are quite useful in differentiating tortuosity from true aneurysmal dilation of the subclavian aneurysm.

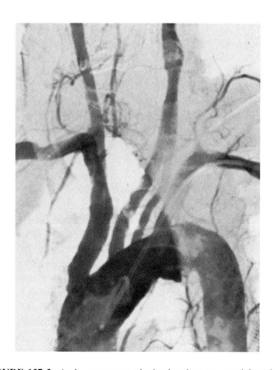

FIGURE 137-2 Arch aortogram obtained using an arterial catheter inserted via the left subclavian artery. Visualization of the primary branches of the aortic arch demonstrates that the left vertebral artery originates from the arch between the left common carotid and the left subclavian arteries.

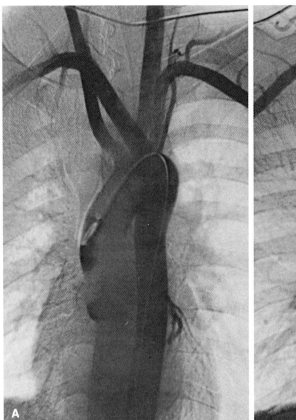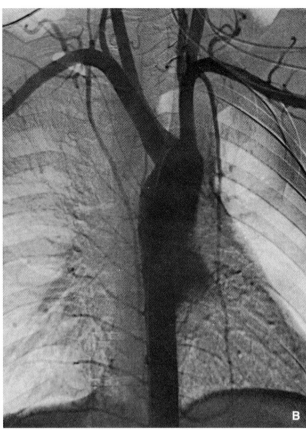

FIGURE 137-3 A and **B,** An arch aortogram demonstrating the first branch of the aortic arch to be an isolated right common carotid artery. An aberrant right subclavian artery originates just distal to the left subclavian artery and courses posterior to all of the other major branches of the aortic arch.

Subclavian Arteries

The right subclavian artery originates from the right brachiocephalic trunk and arches laterally and posteriorly, passing behind the anterior scalene muscle. The left subclavian artery originates directly from the aorta and is usually its third branch. It ascends vertically within the mediastinum, then arches laterally in the root of the neck, also to pass behind the anterior scalene muscle. Both subclavian arteries pass immediately above the dome of the pleura. The principal branches of the subclavian arteries arise from the segment proximal to the medial border of the anterior scalene muscle and consist of the vertebral, internal mammary, thyrocervical, and costocervical arteries (Fig. 137-4). The vertebral and internal mammary arteries have a highly constant relationship, originating directly opposite each other, with the vertebral artery arising from the cephalad aspect and the internal mammary artery arising from the anteroinferior aspect. The subclavian arteries then exit from the neck by passing over the superior surface of the first rib posterior to the clavicle, in close relationship to the lower portion of the brachial plexus. After they pass the lateral aspect of the first rib, these vessels are designated the *axillary arteries*. Although the vertebral artery is the primary subclavian branch that contributes to the cerebral circulation, the other branches may become important sources of collateral supply in the setting of vertebral artery stenoses.

Common Carotid Arteries

The right common carotid artery originates from the right brachiocephalic trunk in the base of the neck, whereas the left common carotid artery originates directly from the aortic arch in the mediastinum. However, the anatomy of the cervical segments is virtually identical on both sides (Fig. 137-5). The common carotid arteries ascend in the neck, running anterior to the transverse processes of the cervical vertebrae and separated from them by the anterior scalene, longus coli, and capitis muscles and by the sympathetic trunks. The common carotid artery usually bifurcates into the external and the internal carotid arteries near the superior horn of the thyroid cartilage (at approximately vertebrae C2-C3), although there is considerable variation in the level of this bifurcation. The carotid arteries bifurcate at the same level in only 28% of cases; in 50%, the left bifurcation is higher than the right one, whereas the reverse is present in the remaining 22%. Throughout their cervical course, the common and internal carotid arteries are enclosed in a fibrous sheath (deemed the *carotid sheath*), which also encompasses the internal jugular vein and the vagus nerve.

External Carotid Arteries

The external carotid artery is usually smaller than the internal carotid artery and originates anterior and medial to

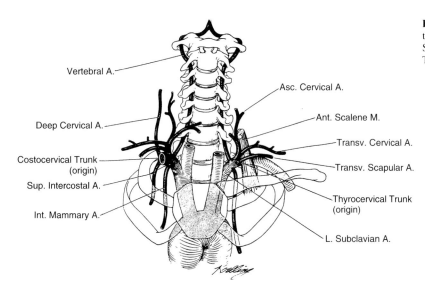

FIGURE 137-4 Artist's concept of the relationships of the subclavian arteries and their primary branches. Sup, Superior; Int, Internal; Asc, Ascending; Ant, Anterior; Transv, Transverse; L, Left.

it, passing laterally to ascend just posterior to the ramus and neck of the mandible and superficial to the styloid process. It supplies the face, scalp, oronasopharynx, skull, and meninges through four major branch vessel groups: (1) anterior branches (superior thyroid, lingual, facial, transverse facial); (2) posterior branches (occipital and auricular); (3) ascending branches (ascending pharyngeal); and (4) terminal branches (superficial temporal, internal maxillary) (Fig. 137-6). These vessels are of significance to the cerebral circulation in the setting of carotid or vertebral artery occlusive disease, where they can become important sources of collateral blood supply.

One of the most common collateral routes involves distal anastomoses between the pterygopalatine branches of the internal maxillary artery and the ethmoidal branches of the ophthalmic artery system (Fig. 137-7). Other important collateral pathways include anastomoses between orbitonasal branches of the facial artery and orbital branches of the ophthalmic artery, anastomoses between anterior branches of the superficial temporal artery and ethmoidal branches of the ophthalmic artery, and anastomoses between ascending pharyngeal branches of the external carotid artery and muscular branches of the vertebral artery.

Internal Carotid Arteries

The internal carotid artery is divided into five major segments: carotid bulb, cervical, petrous, cavernous, and cerebral (Fig. 137-8). The *carotid bulb*, literally a focal bulbous dilation, is located at the origin of the internal carotid artery.

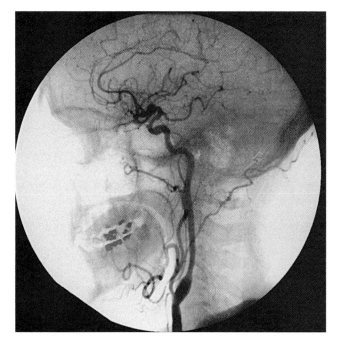

FIGURE 137-5 A selective injection of the left common carotid artery outlines the common carotid artery as it bifurcates into the internal and external carotid arteries within the mid-cervical region.

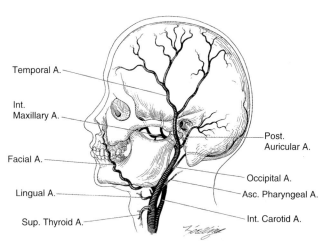

FIGURE 137-6 Artist's concept of the distribution of the external carotid artery with its major branches visualized. Int, Internal; Sup, Superior; Post, Posterior; Asc, Ascending.

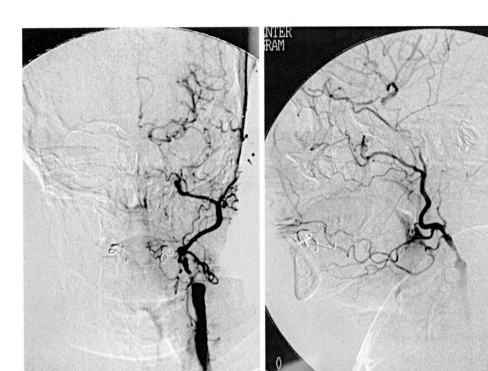

FIGURE 137-7 Anteroposterior (**A**) and lateral (**B**) views of an angiogram showing occlusion of the left internal carotid artery at its origin, with filling of the intracranial carotid system via collateral vessels providing retrograde flow in the ophthalmic artery.

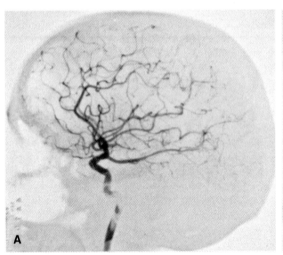

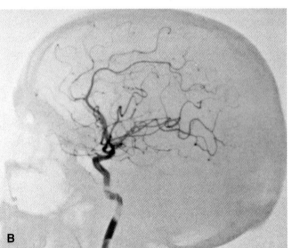

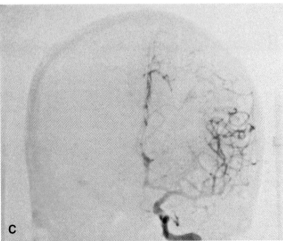

FIGURE 137-8 A, Left carotid arteriogram, shown in a lateral projection, demonstrating a common anatomic variant, posterior cerebral artery originating directly from the internal carotid artery, also known as a fetal origin. **B,** Right carotid arteriogram presented in a lateral projection and showing the terminal distribution into the anterior and middle cerebral branches. **C,** Anteroposterior projection of a left carotid arteriogram demonstrating filling of the anterior cerebral artery (ACA) in the midline and the branches of the middle cerebral artery (MCA) in the lateral or parietal region.

It is a relatively constant feature, although its shape and size vary considerably among individuals. The *cervical* segment has no significant branches and ascends in the neck immediately anterior to the transverse processes of the cervical vertebrae and their associated muscles. The internal carotid artery then enters the skull via the carotid canal, traversing the *petrous* portion of the temporal bone in a slightly medial direction and separated from the middle ear structures by only a thin layer of bone. The petrous segment also has no major branches, although there are minor branches that anastomose with small pterygopalatine branches of the internal maxillary artery that can become sources of collateral supply in the setting of occlusive disease.

The *cavernous* segment of the internal carotid artery is called the *carotid siphon* because of its gentle, S-shaped configuration as it passes through the cavernous sinus along the sella turcica toward the anterior clinoid process. Along its course through the cavernous sinus it often indents the wall of the sphenoid sinus, sometimes separated from the sinus cavity by only dura and sinus mucosa. Although this segment has several minor branches, the ophthalmic artery is the cavernous segment branch of primary clinical significance since it can become an important collateral route to the intracranial circulation in the setting of extracranial occlusive disease of the internal carotid artery, and because hemodynamic or embolic phenomena can produce amaurosis fugax. Thus, the ophthalmic artery is the first branch of the internal carotid artery of major clinical importance.

The *cerebral* segment of the internal carotid artery is relatively short. After traversing the dura mater medial to the anterior clinoid process, it passes superolaterally to divide into the anterior and middle cerebral arteries (MCAs).

Vertebral Arteries

The vertebral artery is the first branch of the subclavian artery. It takes a relatively straight course, entering the transverse foramen of C6 and passing cranially through the transverse foramina of C6-C1. Because the transverse foramen of the atlas is lateral to that of the axis, it passes laterally between the axis and the atlas. It then runs posteromedially along the arch of the atlas lateral to the atlanto-occipital joint. After passing the atlas, it turns sharply cephalad to enter the cranium via the foramen magnum. Within the skull, the paired vertebral arteries pass medially along the inferior surface of the brain stem to unite into a single midline vessel, the basilar artery (Fig. 137-9).

Although the carotid arteries are of similar size bilaterally, considerable asymmetry is frequent in the vertebral system, even including absence of one of the vertebral arteries. The left vertebral artery is dominant in approximately 50% of individuals, whereas the right one is dominant in 25%, and they are of roughly equal caliber in the remaining 25%. These variations are of little or no clinical significance except in cases of subclavian artery disease proximal to the vertebral origin. A moderate degree of tortuosity and smooth variation in caliber of the intracranial vertebral arteries is common even in young individuals and is also of no clinical significance.

The cervical portion of the vertebral arteries supplies multiple small segmental branches to the spinal cord,

cervical vertebrae, and adjacent muscles. The anastomotic connections between these small vertebral artery branches and the occipital and ascending pharyngeal branches of the external carotid artery system form potential collateral routes in the event of development of vertebral or carotid occlusive disease (Figs. 137-10 and 137-11).

The intracranial portion of the vertebral artery gives rise to the anterior and posterior spinal arteries, the penetrating medullary arteries, and the complex posterior inferior cerebellar artery, which supplies the inferior surface of the cerebellum.

Basilar Artery

The basilar artery is a relatively short mid-line vessel formed by the union of the vertebral arteries along the inferior surface of the pons. It runs along the pons, dividing into the left and right posterior cerebral arteries (PCAs). In its short course, it gives rise to several important paired sets of arteries, including the anterior inferior cerebellar arteries, the internal auditory arteries, multiple small pontine arteries, and the superior cerebellar arteries (Fig. 137-12). These branch vessels are important sources of blood supply to the brain and play important roles in the plethora of symptoms associated with vertebrobasilar insufficiency.

Middle Cerebral Artery

The MCA (Fig. 137-13) is generally larger in caliber than the anterior cerebral artery (ACA), and its initial segment forms a relatively straighter pathway from the internal carotid artery than the corresponding segment of the ACA.

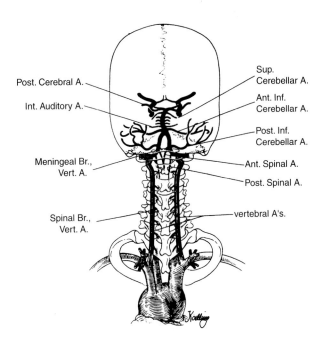

Post. Cerebral A.

Int. Auditory A.

Meningeal Br., Vert. A.

Spinal Br., Vert. A.

Sup. Cerebellar A.

Ant. Inf. Cerebellar A.

Post. Inf. Cerebellar A.

Ant. Spinal A.

Post. Spinal A.

vertebral A's.

FIGURE 137-9 Artist's concept of the relationship of the vertebral arteries as they enter the root of the neck and ascend within the vertebral canal en route to joining at the brain stem to form the basilar artery. The significant cervical and cranial branches are labeled. Post, Posterior; Int, Internal; Vert, Vertical; Sup, Superior; Ant inf, Anterior inferior.

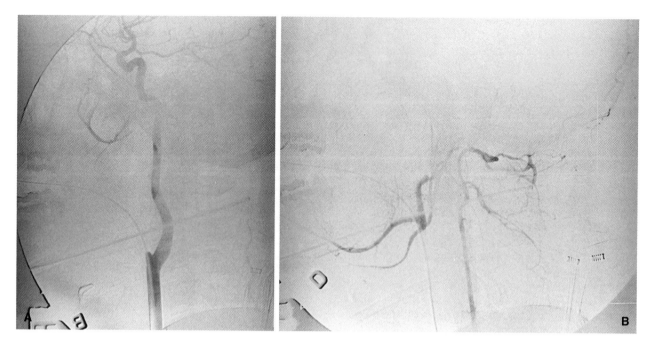

FIGURE 137-10 A, Carotid angiogram showing occlusion of the external carotid artery at its origin, with collateral flow to the internal maxillary artery system via orbital collaterals (not shown). **B,** Vertebral angiogram showing collateral flow to the external carotid artery system via anastomoses between deep muscular branches of the vertebral artery and the ascending pharyngeal artery and similar branches communicating with the occipital artery.

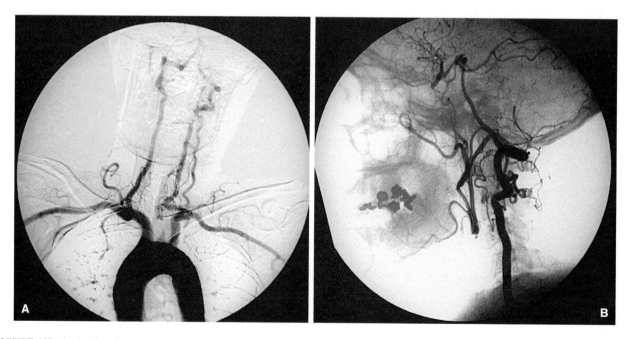

FIGURE 137-11 A, Thoracic aortogram showing total occlusion of both the right and left common carotid arteries. **B,** Selective injection of the right vertebral artery shows extensive collateral supply to the right external carotid artery via cervical branches of the vertebral artery. These vessels are normally so small that they are not routinely visualized on angiography. The large size of the vessels indicates that the occlusion is chronic, as it takes weeks to months for such small vessels to dilate to their present size. The intracranial portions of the right internal carotid artery fill via the posterior communicating artery, a key part of the circle of Willis. Although not documented by selective angiography, the collateral supply pattern is similar on the patient's left side.

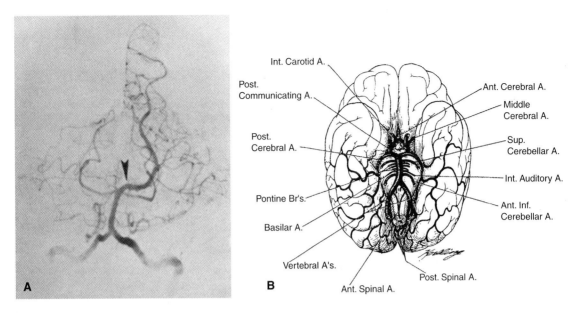

FIGURE 137-12 A, Vertebral-basilar arteriogram demonstrating the confluence of both vertebral arteries as they form the basilar artery running along the brain stem. Note that on the left side the basilar artery terminates in the posterior cerebral artery, but on the right side the terminal branch is the right superior cerebellar artery. This occurred because the right posterior cerebral artery originated from the carotid artery in this patient. **B,** Artist's concept of the relationship of the vertebral-basilar system to the brain stem. All the major branches of the terminal vertebral arteries and the extent of the basilar arteries are named. Int, Internal; Post, Posterior; Ant, Anterior; Sup, Superior; Inf, Inferior.

For this reason, most of the emboli originating in, or traversing, the carotid system lodge in branches of this vessel. The initial (M1) segment of the MCA is straight and runs laterally along the inferior surface of the anterior perforated substance of the brain toward the sylvian fissure, which separates the temporal lobe from the frontoparietal lobes. Numerous short, straight, vertical lenticulostriate arteries arise from this segment to supply the basal ganglia and adjacent structures. The MCA branches in the sylvian fissure; its branches bend upward to run over the surface of the insula, then turn inferiorly again to emerge onto the cortical surfaces of the temporal and frontoparietal lobes. This pathway forms a characteristic, upwardly convex "genu," or kneelike, curvature.

There is considerable variation in the course of the MCA branches as they emerge from the sylvian fissure; however, they form three general groups: (1) the anterior temporal artery; (2) the anterior group, including the orbitofrontal and operculofrontal arteries; and (3) the posterior group, including the posteroparietal, angular, and posterior temporal arteries. Although extracranial-intracranial (EC-IC) bypass procedures have fallen out of favor because of the unfavorable report of the EC/IC Bypass Study in 1985, these MCA branches do provide a fortuitously convenient bypass pathway because of their accessibility on the surface of the brain and the close proximity of the overlying superficial temporal artery branches of the external carotid system.

Anterior Cerebral Artery

The ACA begins at the bifurcation of the internal carotid artery (Fig. 137-14). Its initial segment is the short, straight (A1) segment that runs anteromedially just above the optic chiasm. Several medial lenticulostriate arteries originate from this segment. The A1 segment communicates with its opposite counterpart across the interhemispheric fissure via the short but important anterior communicating artery, the anterior component of the circle of Willis. A reciprocal size relationship between the A1 segment and the anterior

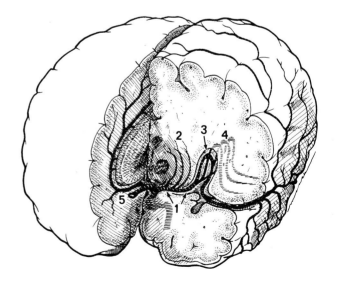

FIGURE 137-13 Artist's concept showing the relationship of the middle cerebral artery (MCA) to adjacent structures (the sylvian fissure has been exaggerated to emphasize that the MCA loops over the insula). 1, M1 (horizontal) segment. The "genu" is the upward curve of the MCA branches into the sylvian fissure. 2, Lateral lenticulostriate arteries. 3, Sylvian fissure. 4, MCA branches within the depths of the sylvian fissure. 5, ACA. (From Osborn AG: Introduction to Cerebral Angiography. Hagerstown, Md, Harper & Row, 1980.)

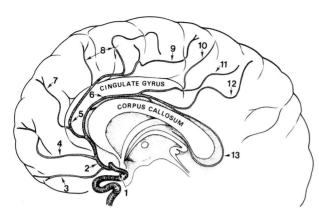

FIGURE 137-14 Artist's concept showing the relationship of the anterior cerebral artery (ACA) to adjacent structures. 1, A1 (horizontal) segment. 2, ACA in front of lamina terminalis. 3, Orbitofrontal artery. 4, Frontopolar artery. 5, Callosomarginal artery. 6, Pericallosal artery. (From Osborn AG: Introduction to Cerebral Angiography. Hagerstown, Md, Harper & Row, 1980.)

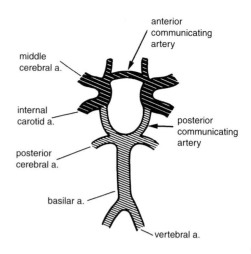

FIGURE 137-15 The classic intact circle of Willis forms a distribution manifold balancing the anterior (*dark shading*) inflow with the posterior (*light shading*) inflow; however, many variations occur, and the circle is often incomplete.

communicating artery is common; a relatively hypoplastic A1 segment is usually accompanied by a large-caliber anterior communicating artery. In such cases, both ACAs are preferentially dependent on a single internal carotid system and thus are especially sensitive to flow disturbances and other abnormalities in the corresponding carotid artery.

Beyond the origin of the anterior communicating artery, the ACA turns abruptly upward to pass around the genu of the corpus callosum. As it passes the genu, it gives rise to the pericallosal artery, which runs posteriorly along the superior surface of the corpus callosum, and the callosomarginal artery, which runs along the cingulate sulcus roughly parallel to the pericallosal artery. The branches of these vessels supply the inner aspects of the frontal and parietal cortex in the interhemispheric fissure and end by passing over the superior margins of the interhemispheric fissure to supply a small band of cortical tissue along the anterior two thirds of the frontal and parietal lobes. Although the ACA and its branches are of considerable functional significance, they are largely inaccessible to the vascular surgeon because of their location deep within the interhemispheric fissure.

Circle of Willis

The circle of Willis is a unique vascular ring that encircles the diencephalon, including the sella turcica and pituitary. The A1 segments of the ACAs and the anterior communicating artery form the anterior portion of the ring and connect the internal carotid systems with each other. The short posterior communicating arteries originate from the internal carotid arteries at or near the bifurcation into ACA and MCAs. The posterior communicating arteries run posteriorly to connect with the corresponding proximal segments of the PCAs, thus connecting the internal carotid system, which is the anterior circulation, with the vertebral-basilar system, which is the posterior circulation (Fig. 137-15).

The circle of Willis, as described, effectively forms an arterial manifold that balances the inflow coming from the internal carotid and vertebral arteries with the outflow to the ACA, MCA, and PCAs (see Fig. 137-11). However, only 20% of individuals actually have the "textbook" symmetrical circle of Willis; hypoplasia of one or more components occurs in most individuals. Hypoplasia, or absence of one or both posterior communicating arteries, occurs in approximately 25% to 30% of cases, thus effectively isolating the anterior and posterior circulations. Anomalies of the anterior communicating artery, including hypoplasia, absence, or duplication, occur in approximately 10% of individuals. Hypoplasia of the A1 segments occurs in approximately 25% of cases, making both ACA systems preferentially dependent on a single internal carotid artery. Hypoplasia of the initial (P1) segment of the PCA, with primary or sole flow to the PCA via an enlarged posterior communicating artery from the internal carotid artery, occurs in approximately 15% to 20% of cases and is termed a *fetal origin*. Persistence of additional fetal communications between the carotid and the vertebral-basilar systems, including the trigeminal, otic, hypoglossal, and proatlantal intersegmental arteries, also occurs but is relatively rare.

The frequency of variations in the textbook arrangement of the circle of Willis often explains seemingly paradoxical ischemic or embolic neurovascular abnormalities. Such variations are also of considerable practical clinical significance because they imply that existence of the textbook collateral routes cannot be simply assumed before surgical or endovascular interventions such as carotid endarterectomy or stenting are undertaken. Unless routine shunting is employed during surgery, adequate collateral supply must therefore be proved by preoperative angiography or intraoperative hemodynamic or electroencephalographic monitoring or both. Even in the case of endovascular therapy, such as carotid artery angioplasty and stenting, with its very short inflation times and correspondingly short ischemic periods, knowledge of the collateral supply is essential for assessing procedural risk.

■ ANGIOGRAPHIC DIAGNOSIS AND ENDOVASCULAR TREATMENT

Noninvasive Alternatives to Cerebral Angiography

The surgical aphorism, "There is no such thing as a *little* operation," applies equally well to angiography and, indeed, to all invasive medical procedures. Although remarkably free of serious complications, angiography is not a simple laboratory test nor is it an inexpensive screening examination. Although certainly uncommon, complications, when they do occur, can be permanent and devastating. Accordingly, the angiographer should function as a consultant specialist able to evaluate the indications and contraindications of the proposed procedure with regard to the patient's overall medical history and physical status, as well as the specific details of the present illness and the proposed treatment. Furthermore, as a consultant specialist, the angiographer should also provide guidance in the selection of appropriate noninvasive imaging prior to, or instead of, angiography.

The approach to investigation and management of intracranial vascular lesions has changed significantly over the past decade, largely as a result of dramatic advances in imaging technology. High-resolution CT and MR imaging have virtually replaced angiography as primary diagnostic modalities. Nuclear medicine brain scanning for the investigation of intracranial mass lesions, once a core technology, is such a nonspecific low-resolution technique that it is now of historic interest only, and radioisotope cerebral perfusion studies, which are still the routine method for determination of brain death, may also be replaced by MR perfusion imaging (Figs. 137-16 and 137-17). Positron emission tomography (PET) scanning, with its ability to image and quantify regional metabolic function and thus provide information about the functional significance of certain lesions, is also a rapidly emerging imaging technology likely to become another mainstream modality, although there are still significant cost and availability issues that limit the potential usefulness of PET scanning as a clinical tool.

Similarly, the approach to the investigation and management of extracranial cerebrovascular disease has also changed considerably. Noninvasive duplex Doppler screening evaluations of the cervical carotid circulation can now be performed effectively and inexpensively using a combination of high-resolution gray scale ultrasound imaging, to delineate anatomic detail, and color-coded pulsed Doppler ultrasound scanning, to estimate the hemodynamic significance of lesions identified by anatomic imaging (Fig. 137-18). Power Doppler imaging, a relative newcomer to the noninvasive imaging arsenal, creates a two-dimensional color-coded flow map by using the integrated power of the Doppler spectrum, rather than mean Doppler frequency, and is thus inherently more sensitive to low-flow states. This

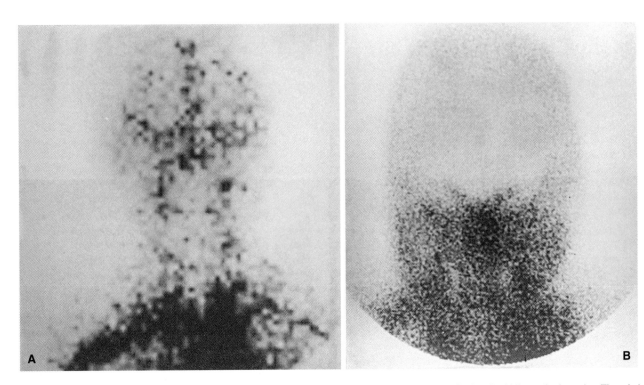

FIGURE 137-16 A, Normal isotope brain flow study showing filling of the internal carotid, anterior cerebral, and middle cerebral arteries. The relative paucity of flow to the facial regions is simply a reflection of preferential flow to the intracranial circulation. **B,** Abnormal isotope brain flow study with no detectable flow in the area of the anterior or middle cerebral arteries, indicating ischemic brain death, associated with severe cerebral edema. Increased isotope activity in the facial regions represents increased flow in the external carotid artery branches, which fill preferentially because there is no longer any significant flow to the intracranial vessels. (**A** and **B,** Courtesy of Felix Wang, MD, Nuclear Medicine Section, University of California, Irvine Medical Center, Orange, Calif.)

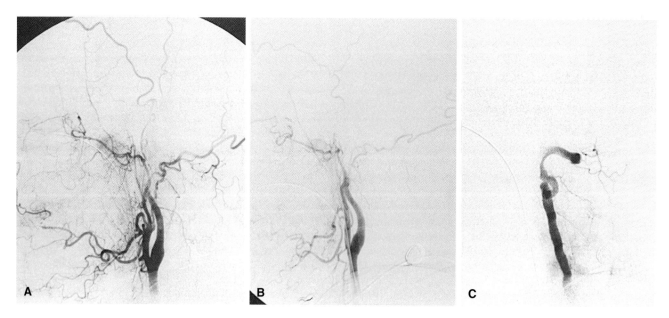

FIGURE 137-17 Angiograms of a 30-year-old female patient with intracranial hemorrhage that was thought to be due to a ruptured aneurysm or arteriovenous malformation. The patient was on a respirator and being maintained in barbiturate coma to minimize brain injury, which masked the occurrence of brain death. The angiogram shows no intracranial blood flow via right internal carotid artery (**A**), left internal carotid artery (**B**), or left vertebral artery (**C**). (**A-C,** Courtesy of David D. Kidney, MD, Vascular and Interventional Radiology Section, University of California, Irvine Medical Center, Orange, Calif.)

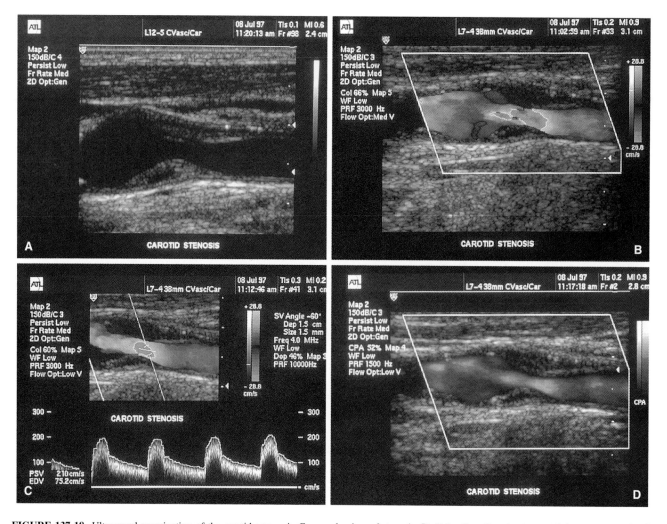

FIGURE 137-18 Ultrasound examination of the carotid artery. **A,** Gray scale view of stenosis. **B,** Color-flow Doppler image of the same stenosis. **C,** Doppler flow velocity measurements used to grade the approximate severity of the stenosis. **D,** Power Doppler image of the same stenosis. (**A-D,** Courtesy of Philips Medical Systems, Bothell, Wash.)

makes it a useful adjunct to the conventional duplex Doppler examination in differentiating near-occlusive stenoses from total occlusions, one of the more challenging and clinically significant tasks in noninvasive carotid imaging. (See Chapter 138 for more details on the use of ultrasound techniques in the evaluation of cerebrovascular disease.)

Although supraorbital and transcranial Doppler ultrasound examinations provide information about the state of the intracranial portions of the carotid circulation, the circle of Willis, and some of the common collateral circulation pathways not evaluated by duplex Doppler scanning, these examinations have a far steeper learning curve than does duplex Doppler ultrasound and they are far more operator dependent. Accordingly, although they have been used to advantage in some noninvasive vascular laboratories and in monitoring downstream embolization during carotid surgery or endovascular intervention, they are not routinely available in most centers. Similarly, oculoplethysmography, a technique that measured pulsatility in the eye in an effort to assess patency of the internal carotid supply to the ophthalmic artery, once a common examination, is a technique now solely of historical interest.

MR imaging, described in the previous edition of this text simply as a "noninvasive imaging technique that shows promise for use in evaluating the cerebrovascular circulation," is rapidly becoming one of the basic primary tools for evaluation of extracranial cerebrovascular disease in many institutions. Initially, MR imaging techniques were used to obtain vascular images by simply varying pulse sequences and signal sampling methods so as to exploit various aspects of the differences between the physical properties of blood, especially flowing blood, and adjacent tissues. However, the addition of intravenously injected magnetic contrast agents permits images to be made with shorter acquisition times and better signal-to-noise ratio, making the use of contrast enhancement a commonly used technique in cerebrovascular MR imaging. Mathematically "stacking" multiple closely spaced cross-sectional "slice" images of the area of interest enables creation of two- and three-dimensional images of vessels that can then be displayed in many different formats as MR "angiograms," some of which closely resemble conventional contrast angiograms (Figs. 137-19 and 137-20).

Although MR angiography images look similar to conventional radiographic contrast angiograms, it is important to remember that the physical basis of MR angiography is quite different from that of conventional contrast angiography. Factors affecting MR angiography image quality include flow direction, velocity, vessel size, turbulence (chaotic flow), vortices (localized areas of direction reversal), boundary layer flow separation, pulsatility, elasticity, capacitance, and peripheral impedance. Vessel tortuosity, as well as the intravascular disturbances of flow encountered in the region of a lesion such as a carotid bifurcation stenosis, include complex and unpredictable combinations of most of these flow phenomena, leading to imaging artifacts that can be difficult to evaluate, and may lead to overestimation of the severity of some stenotic lesions. Thus, although MR angiography is a highly sophisticated technique capable of impressive image quality, and use of MR angiography in the evaluation of extracranial

cerebrovascular disease should now be considered a first-line technique employed prior to or in place of conventional radiographic angiography, an understanding of the physical basis of this imaging technique is essential to its use, and these images should not be viewed as being identical to conventional angiograms or simply as a replacement for conventional angiograms. Instead, MR angiography should be thought of as a first-line noninvasive examination that may eliminate the need for a conventional angiogram in a particular patient if it provides images of sufficient diagnostic quality to adequately delineate the relevant anatomy and determine the presence or absence of significant pathology. Even in situations where an MR angiography study fails to provide a complete diagnostic examination sufficient for clinical decision making, it is nevertheless useful as a guide to planning subsequent angiography. MR angiography is also a very expensive, technology-intensive imaging technique, and image quality is highly dependent on factors such as field strength,

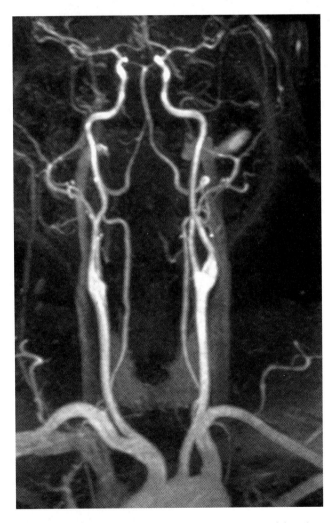

FIGURE 137-19 MR angiogram demonstrating the extracranial cerebrovascular systems from the level of the aortic arch to the proximal intracranial vessels. (Courtesy of Rosalind Dietrich, MD, Department of Radiology, University of California, San Diego, San Diego, Calif.)

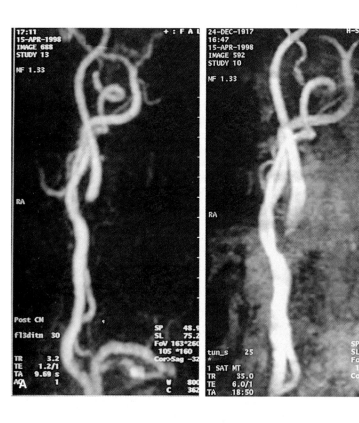

FIGURE 137-20 MR angiography images of a near-occlusive internal carotid artery stenosis. **A** employed conventional time-of-flight technique (three-dimensional [3D]-TOF) and required several minutes of data acquisition. **B** was acquired in less than 10 seconds using first-pass gadolinium intravenous contrast-enhanced technique. Although newer noncontrast pulse sequences and data processing methods enable faster imaging, contrast enhanced methods generally provide higher quality images and substantially faster imaging than unenhanced methods. Surgery was performed without further diagnostic imaging. (**A** and **B,** Courtesy of William G. Bradley, Jr., MD, PhD, FACR, Professor and Chair, Department of Radiology, University of California, San Diego, San Diego, Calif.)

imaging coil design, and computational power. Thus, the quality and the utility of MR angiography depend to a considerable degree on the specifics of the equipment actually in use at a particular site as well as the expertise of the people using it. In addition, unlike contrast angiography, which employs relatively stable technologies, the pace of MR development is still rapid and the cost of acquiring new equipment or upgrades at that pace is prohibitive for many institutions, making the relative value of MR angiography with regard to alternative imaging modalities a local decision.

CT in the form of CT angiography can also be applied to the task of noninvasive extracranial cerebrovascular examination (Fig. 137-21). Like MR angiography, it also employs the mathematical manipulation of multiple, closely spaced, cross-sectional "slice" images to reconstruct two-dimensional and three-dimensional depictions of vessels. Unlike MR angiography techniques, which generally employ contrast agents of very low nephrotoxicity that are virtually free of hypersensitivity reactions, CT angiography techniques do require the use of iodinated contrast agents of the same sort as those used for conventional angiography. Although modern low-osmolarity radiographic contrast agents and the use of adjunctive renal protection agents such as fenoldopam have made the use of radiographic contrast far less worrisome than in the past, the use of contrast agents in CT angiography still involves consideration of the same issues as in the case of conventional contrast angiography.

Like MR angiography, CT angiography has also improved dramatically since the last edition of this text. The advent of spiral scanning, which involves continuous motion of the

x-ray tube and detector system around the patient while at the same time moving the patient through the scanning gantry, greatly reduced scanning times, which enables faster imaging and higher resolution with a corresponding decrease in motion artifact. Multislice scanning that couples spiral scanning with the use of multiple x-ray detector rows has yet again increased resolution and scanning speed, so much so that the quality of CT angiography is now quite similar to that of conventional angiography. Four-slice scanners were introduced only a few years ago but shortly thereafter were replaced by 8-slice scanners and are now being replaced by 16-slice scanners, with higher density scanners being actively developed by most manufacturers. The pace of development in CT scanner technology, especially in the area of multislice scanning and computational power, has created an issue similar to that encountered in evaluating the utility of MR angiography in that it is also difficult for an institution to keep pace with the cycle of new product and upgrade developments. Thus, determining the relative value of CT angiography with regard to alternative imaging modalities is also a local decision.

As the physics of CT imaging is essentially the same as that employed in conventional angiography (i.e., transmission x-ray absorption), the interpretation of CT angiography images and the understanding of artifacts is generally more straightforward than the interpretation of MR angiography images. However, although the artifacts due to the physics of CT angiography imaging are less troublesome than those of MR angiography, understanding the nature of potential artifacts is as essential to the use of CT angiography as it is to MR angiography. Specifically, the

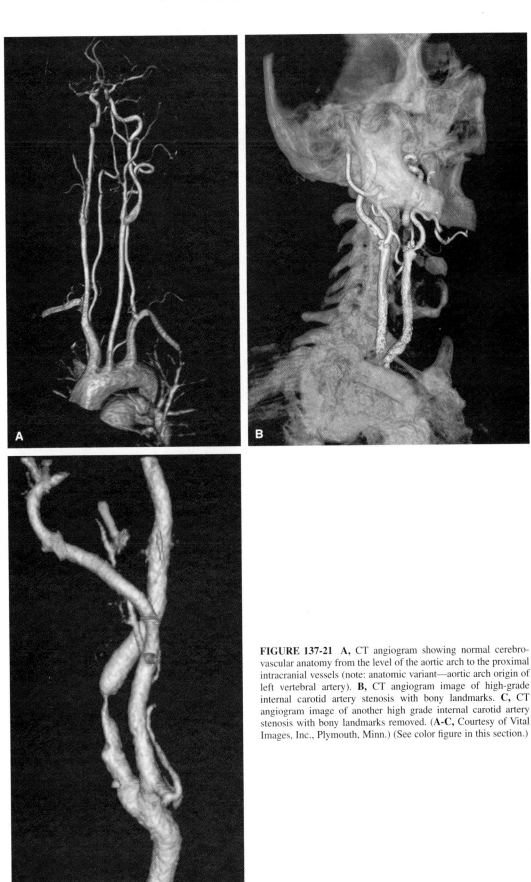

FIGURE 137-21 A, CT angiogram showing normal cerebrovascular anatomy from the level of the aortic arch to the proximal intracranial vessels (note: anatomic variant—aortic arch origin of left vertebral artery). **B,** CT angiogram image of high-grade internal carotid artery stenosis with bony landmarks. **C,** CT angiogram image of another high grade internal carotid artery stenosis with bony landmarks removed. (**A-C,** Courtesy of Vital Images, Inc., Plymouth, Minn.) (See color figure in this section.)

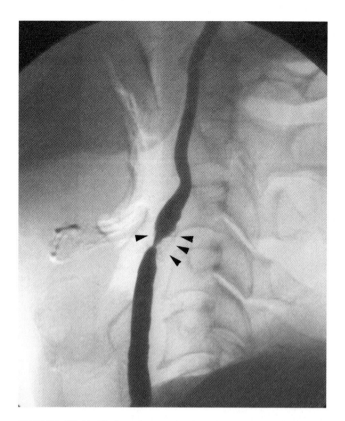

FIGURE 137-22 High-grade stenosis of the internal carotid artery and occlusion of the external carotid artery associated with a densely calcified plaque (*arrowheads* pointing left). The severity of the stenosis is indicated by a well-demarcated high-velocity jet (*arrowhead* pointing right) created as the contrast flows through this tight narrowing. This jet is the visual analog of the high-velocity flow distal to a hemodynamically significant stenosis often encountered on ultrasound imaging. Angiography would have been unnecessary in this setting had the referring surgeons been willing to operate on the basis of ultrasound findings.

presence of calcification, a common accompaniment to atheromatous disease, though a conceptually simple artifact, can be troublesome, so much so that considerable research and development effort is being spent on the design of computational and imaging technologies aimed at dealing with the presence of calcification. Indeed, the difficulty of dealing with calcification has often been touted as one of the principal advantages of MR angiography over CT angiography.

Although there are definite differences in the applicability, sensitivity, specificity, spatial resolution, and ability to provide physiologic information, the ultimate choice of which noninvasive modality (ultrasound, MR angiography, or CT angiography) to employ is determined by technical factors, economics, and availability. Ultrasound currently still has a commanding lead as a first-line noninvasive screening and evaluation modality, simply because of its relatively low cost and widespread availability, especially in the screening of asymptomatic individuals (Fig. 137-22). However, in many institutions, MR angiography or CT angiography, depending on local factors, has become the first-line technique when dealing with symptomatic individuals.

Indications and Contraindications for Cerebral Angiography

The choice of whether to rely on noninvasive testing or angiography in the investigation and management of patients with cerebrovascular lesions depends largely on the question of lesion type, location, and symptoms, together with local resources and expertise.

The incidence of asymptomatic nonvascular lesions of the intracranial central nervous system (e.g., tumors) is sufficiently low that routine noninvasive screening is rarely warranted. However, with the exception of systemic conditions known to be associated with intracranial vascular lesions such as Osler-Weber-Rendu syndrome and carotid artery fibromuscular dysplasia, the true incidence of asymptomatic intracranial vascular lesions (e.g., arteriovenous malformations [AVMs] and aneurysms) is not well known. Generally, however, such patients do not come to medical attention until they have become symptomatic, often in a catastrophic manner associated with intracranial hemorrhage. In such patients, CT or MR scanning is often useful as a guide to planning angiographic investigation, but prompt angiography is the definitive procedure for establishing the diagnosis and planning therapy, especially because many benign intracranial vascular lesions (e.g., vascular malformations and aneurysms) are amenable to endovascular therapy.

In any event, noninvasive (CT and MR imaging) delineation and characterization of symptomatic intracranial mass lesions is generally so reliable that angiography is used primarily as a tool in planning or administering therapy rather than as a purely diagnostic tool. Indeed, over the past decade, advances in microcatheter technologies and both liquid as well as solid embolic agents and devices have made the endovascular approach to the treatment of AVMs and aneurysms the method of choice in most situations rather than surgical clipping or resection. In the case of lesions not amenable to definitive endovascular treatment, mapping of the associated vascular supply and drainage can be vital to a successful surgical outcome, and transcatheter embolization of feeding vessels, though it may not always constitute definitive therapy, can be a useful adjunct to surgery.

The ideal strategy to use in determining the relative roles of noninvasive testing and angiography when dealing with extracranial cerebrovascular disease is still controversial, although much of the intellectual dust has begun to settle. Angiographic *screening* of asymptomatic individuals even in specific high-risk groups is now unjustifiable, because the low cost, accuracy, and widespread availability of ultrasound examination make this noninvasive modality the logical choice for the initial imaging evaluation of asymptomatic patients. Unlike intracranial vascular lesions, asymptomatic extracranial lesions, specifically hemodynamically significant carotid stenoses, occur with sufficient frequency that selective noninvasive screening is reasonable in specific at-risk patient populations. Ultrasound techniques permit relatively inexpensive screening of asymptomatic patients in groups identified to be at risk for developing cerebrovascular symptoms by several prospective, randomized studies.

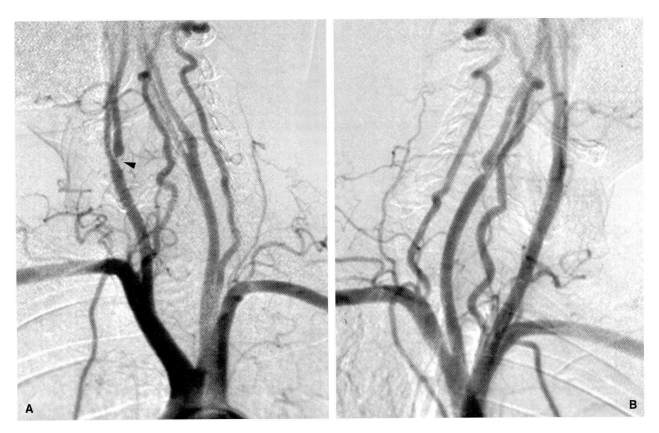

FIGURE 137-23 Left anterior oblique (LAO) view (**A**) of high-grade ostial right internal carotid artery stenosis (*arrowhead*) that is not well visualized in the right anterior oblique (RAO) view (**B**) and could thus be easily underestimated on that view illustrating the importance of multiple-view angiography.

The appropriate imaging evaluation for symptomatic patients, however, remains controversial. Many surgeons still lack confidence in the reliability of noninvasive testing, insisting on the "gold standard" of angiography before subjecting the patient to the risks of operative intervention. In contrast, many angiographers and surgeons think that the risks of angiography, though admittedly low, do not justify adding the risks of preoperative angiography to those of the operative intervention if noninvasive imaging is able to provide an unequivocal diagnosis. On the other hand, when the noninvasive examination is either negative or equivocal in the face of appropriate symptoms and a high clinical index of suspicion, proceeding to contrast angiography is, at least for the present, the standard of care. This is especially true in situations where nonocclusive mural disease such as ulceration responsible for an embolic episode is suspected but sufficiently subtle that it cannot be reliably detected on ultrasound, MR angiography, or CT angiography.

The choice of a specific noninvasive modality (i.e., ultrasound, MR angiography or CT angiography) is a more complex issue and is still for practical purposes largely a compromise among efficacy, cost, availability, and local expertise.

The development and now widespread dissemination of reliable, broadly applicable noninvasive imaging techniques, a basically positive development, like many other recent developments in modern medical care, may also create some new problems. As the need for conventional catheter angiography declines, so too will the opportunity for house staff training in this area, eventually leading to a situation where cerebral angiography, even simple carotid angiography, may not be routinely available in many practice settings.

The Basic Examination Plan

Once a decision has been made that noninvasive imaging is insufficient to form the basis for definitive therapy, consideration needs to be focused on determining the optimal plan for angiographic investigation. From the standpoint of the vascular surgeon, most angiography of the cerebrovascular system is performed for the evaluation of atheromatous (atherosclerotic) occlusive disease of the carotid system in the region of the carotid bifurcation because this is the most common location of this common disease. Nevertheless, a complete examination must allow for the possibility that the disease process may not be confined to that region and that it may not even be atherosclerotic in nature.

Multiview imaging and examination of the inflow and outflow are the basic principles in the angiographic evaluation of any vascular system (Fig. 137-23). Therefore, a complete examination of the cerebrovascular system ideally should include delineation of the aortic arch origins

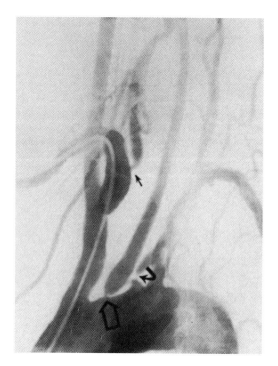

FIGURE 137-24 Arch aortogram (subtraction film). The right vertebral artery (*straight arrow*) and left common carotid artery (*open arrow*) are both stenotic. The left vertebral artery (*curved arrow*) arises from the aorta and is also stenotic. A decreased pulse in the left carotid artery was not recognized prior to this examination.

of the great vessels and their major branches, the cervical and intracranial segments of the carotid and vertebral arteries, and the major intracranial branches of these vessels. This can be accomplished by first obtaining a nonselective arch aortogram to demonstrate the aortic arch origins of the great vessels and their major branches.

Omission of the preliminary nonselective aortic arch angiogram is unwise when investigating patients for occlusive vascular disease, even when selective angiography of the carotid arteries is planned. Ostial disease of the principal aortic arch branch vessels is sufficiently common that failure to detect such lesions prior to selective catheterization needlessly exposes patients to the risks of embolization associated with markedly irregular atheromatous plaques or cerebral ischemia associated with traversing high-grade stenoses (Fig. 137-24).

Failure to detect significant atherosclerotic lesions at the aortic origin of the great vessels, whether they be hemodynamically significant stenoses or sources of emboli, also exposes patients to the risk of undergoing operative procedures that may not fully address the cause of their problems. In addition, the aortogram serves as a road map for use in selective catheterization of the right and left common carotid arteries, which should then be examined at least to the level of the intracranial carotid bifurcation. Whether selective vertebral artery angiography or more detailed views of the intracranial circulation are also obtained depends on the specifics of the clinical situation.

Several variations of the basic examination have gained wide acceptance. High-quality, nonselective, biplanar oblique arch aortograms showing the cerebrovascular system from the level of the aortic arch to the level of the proximal major intracranial branches are often sufficient to evaluate the extracranial occlusive disease of the cerebrovascular system. Such examinations are usually adequate for the evaluation of atherosclerotic occlusive disease, because significant atherosclerotic disease distal to the carotid siphon is relatively uncommon, although disease at that level is not uncommon. Furthermore, avoidance of selective catheterization does materially decrease the incidence of procedure-related neurologic complications. Obviously, both carotid bifurcations must be well demonstrated; otherwise, the examination should be supplemented by selective angiography of one or both carotid arteries. Similarly, failure to find an occlusive lesion that explains the patient's symptoms indicates the need for selective catheterization and a more detailed search aimed at finding nonocclusive ulcerative disease that could account for the symptomatology. Disease of the vertebral-basilar system may also require supplemental selective angiography with views designed to show the vertebral-basilar junction. Because the basilar artery is formed by the union of the right and left vertebral arteries, it is rarely necessary to perform selective angiography of both vertebral arteries.

Reporting Conventions

The criteria for reporting percentage stenosis is simple throughout the cerebrovascular system (i.e., comparison of residual lumen diameter with adjacent normal-vessel diameter), except in the internal carotid artery where the variable configuration of the carotid bulb has been approached in a number of ways, not all of which make hemodynamic sense. The North American Symptomatic Carotid Endarterectomy Trial (NASCET) and the Asymptomatic Carotid Artery Study (ACAS) both confirmed the effectiveness of carotid endarterectomy for preventing stroke in patients who have significant carotid stenosis. These studies addressed both the clinical approach to treating occlusive carotid disease and the methods of measuring stenoses. Specifically, both studies adopted the convention of reporting percentage stenoses by dividing the minimal diameter of the stenoses by the diameter of the normal carotid segment distal to the stenosis.

Before that strict definition was adopted, most radiologists reported percentage stenosis by comparing the stenosis to the *expected* maximal diameter of the carotid bulb—obviously an imagined estimate (truly a "guesstimate"). The NASCET/ACAS convention was rapidly and uniformly adopted in North America and has now become a virtual worldwide standard. The method makes physiologic sense, and it is based on precise measurements, not estimates. Although the NASCET criteria introduced a measure of precision, the fact that angiography is still basically a two-dimensional projection image introduces one important variable: specifically, the fact that lesions are rarely symmetrical and thus appear to be of varying severity depending on the angle from which they are viewed. The generally accepted convention in this regard is to report the most severe degree of narrowing seen in the various imaging views obtained during the examination. Although many angiography laboratories employ systems capable of three-dimensional (3D) imaging, this is a technique that is far from universally available. Thus, although 3D images with their ability to determine the true degree of narrowing are certainly appealing from a theoretical point of view, there is no established frame of reference for evaluating their clinical significance, because the body of experience on which most clinical decisions are made is still based on conventional two-dimensional methods.

■ RADIOGRAPHIC EQUIPMENT AND IMAGING TECHNIQUES

Specific Considerations for Cerebrovascular Angiography

High-resolution image-intensified video fluoroscopic units equipped with high-output x-ray generators and rapid-sequence imaging capabilities are now standard equipment, enabling angiographers to routinely visualize and manipulate small-caliber catheters with ease. However, simultaneous biplane angiographic imaging capability, though often considered desirable because of the reduction in contrast dosage and procedure time achieved by simultaneous multiview imaging, is relatively uncommon even in larger institutions simply because of its expense and complexity. In fact, the decline in diagnostic neuroangiographic procedures, occasioned by the advent of high-resolution CT and MR imaging techniques, often results in replacement of older biplane units by newer single-plane units because of significant cost differences and the lack of importance of simultaneous biplane angiography in other areas of the body. Thus, biplane units are now found mostly in institutions where there is a sufficient volume of endovascular neuroradiologic interventions to justify their high cost.

One of the most significant technical advances in cerebrovascular angiography has been widespread deployment of modern digital imaging equipment since the early 1990s, including both digital angiography (DA) and digital subtraction angiography (DSA) capabilities. High-resolution digitized images are obtained directly from the fluoroscopic image intensifier; these images can then be manipulated by computer to enhance image contrast or subtract background detail from contrast-filled vessels. Both DA and DSA images are composed of a fixed number of pixels (picture elements), creating an important tradeoff between field of view and resolution. Because resolution is at least partially dependent on the pixel density per unit area, it can be improved by using the magnification modes of the image intensifier at the expense of reducing the field of view to a specific region of interest. In that manner, a given number of image pixels span a smaller anatomic region, thus showing the region in greater detail. It is, of course, important to differentiate true physical magnification obtained in this manner, which yields a real improvement in resolution at the expense of field of view, from simple digital enlargement of the display screen image, which magnifies the picture and may make some things easier to see but does not actually alter resolution.

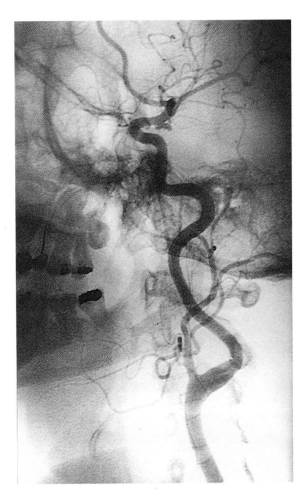

FIGURE 137-25 Digital angiography (DA) of the carotid artery. Because this is a nonsubtracted image, it is relatively immune to the sort of motion artifacts that can severely degrade a digital subtraction angiography (DSA) image. However, because it is also a digital image, the DA image can be manipulated to enhance various details using the viewing station computer system, just like a DSA image. (Courtesy of Julius Grollman, MD, Little Company of Mary Hospital, Torrance, Calif.)

DA images, unlike those of DSA, are basically conventional fluoroscopic images recorded digitally for storage and enhancement (Fig. 137-25). DSA, in contrast, is an image subtraction process conceptually similar to conventional film subtraction, which makes the appearance of an image dependent on the accuracy of the subtraction process, as well as the lack of motion between the initial noncontrast "mask" image and subsequent images. These are assumed to be identical except for the presence of intravascular contrast media. In the ideal situation, all structures not containing contrast agents are eliminated from the image after film or DSA subtraction processing, leaving an image composed solely of contrast-filled vessels.

In the case of film subtraction, the mask is actually a photographic reversal of an angiographic film taken prior to the injection of contrast media, made by copying that film onto a special film that accurately renders the various shades of an image in the mathematically opposite shades of the gray scale. When the mask film is superimposed on a film containing contrast medium, the images cancel except for the contrast-filled vessels. In the case of DSA, the mask is simply a precontrast digital image, and subtraction is just a point-by-point mathematical process. Of course, as conventional x-ray filming devices used for angiography become less common, the concept of film subtraction will become yet another of those once common techniques now of largely historic interest only.

Image subtraction techniques, whether digital or film based, almost always introduce slight differences between the precontrast mask and the contrast-filled images, caused primarily by motion, make the subtraction less than perfect, leaving faint residual images of bone and soft tissue. Although the presence of these faint images associated with imperfections in the subtraction process might at first seem undesirable, the residual background images are actually quite useful in providing a visual frame of reference for what would otherwise be a difficult-to-evaluate "disembodied" image of a vessel—allowing, for example, estimation of the location of the carotid bifurcation with respect to the cervical vertebrae or angle of the mandible. For that reason, modern DSA systems include some capability to subtract a variable percentage of the original image pixel values, thus leaving residual landmark images of whatever intensity the examiner desires (Fig. 137-26).

Because the basic assumption inherent in both DSA and film image subtraction is the absence of any change in the image other than the appearance of radiographic contrast material within the vascular system, these techniques require a considerable degree of patient cooperation. Motion such as simple head and neck movement, swallowing, or breathing creates artifacts in the subtraction process. Simple translational movement artifacts can be eliminated by shifting the precontrast and postcontrast injection images relative to each other to compensate for such movements. Artifacts that are due to complex motion, such as swallowing or breathing, are nonuniform across the image field of view and cannot be totally eliminated by simple image shifting. When such artifacts overlie an area of interest, they can cause significant diagnostic uncertainty. Although satisfactory results often can be obtained even in the presence of motion artifacts by simple correlation of the information obtained from different images in a sequence, as well as images obtained in different views, this is not always possible, especially in patients unable to cooperate.

DSA provides far better contrast resolution than either DA or standard photographic x-ray film technique. Visualization of vessels is possible with much less contrast material (or much more dilute material) than that required by film technique, which was the basis for early efforts at intravenous DSA. Injection of contrast material through a small right atrial catheter, introduced via a percutaneous antecubital venipuncture, held out the promise of rapid, low-cost, low-risk outpatient angiographic carotid artery screening. However, problems with motion artifacts are much more frequent with venous injection than with arterial injection, because there is a much longer period between the onset of the subjective sensations resulting from the

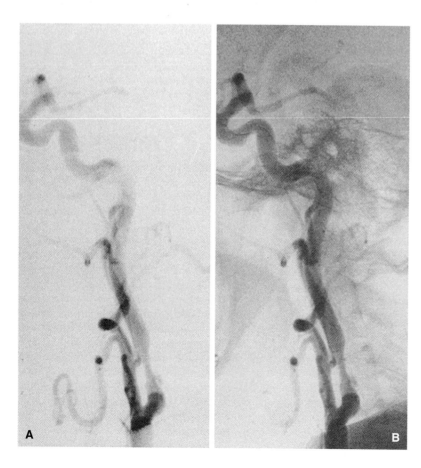

FIGURE 137-26 A and **B,** Digital subtraction angiography (DSA) showing an ulcerated plaque that narrows the proximal internal carotid artery. Owing to the lack of motion artifact, background subtraction is virtually complete. Although this shows the lesion to advantage, it also makes orientation difficult. Reducing the degree of background subtraction in the same DSA image produces an image that contains useful background landmarks.

injection and filling of the vessels of interest than there is with arterial injection. Dispersal and dilution of the contrast bolus in patients with low cardiac output also tended to degrade image quality. For these reasons, the percentage of diagnostic quality studies proved to be disappointing, and the technique has been virtually abandoned. In addition, the advent of small-caliber (4 and 5 French), high-flow arterial catheters and the judicious use of vessel closure devices has substantially reduced arterial puncture site complications and postprocedure recovery times, making outpatient arterial angiography convenient for both patients and providers.

Although intravenous DSA imaging of the cerebrovascular system has justifiably fallen out of favor in most applications, it does have utility in those rare circumstances that involve combined upper and lower extremity peripheral vascular disease of such severity that direct arterial access is impractical. Intravenous DSA studies may well be prudent in this very small cohort of patients; however, direct translumbar aortic puncture with the patient in the prone position, a technique once popular for lower extremity angiography and now largely of historical interest, can still be used to gain direct arterial access for both selective and nonselective angiography of the head and neck vessels.

Consideration of the relative merits of conventional photographic x-ray film and DSA or DA techniques is interesting in that it involves important theoretical considerations. DSA provides contrast resolution far superior to that of standard photographic x-ray film, whereas film is capable of considerably better spatial resolution than either DA or DSA. In contrast, DA and DSA are far more efficient and convenient than film. In the early days of digital angiographic imaging, this was an important tradeoff. When very fine detail and the detection of nonocclusive disease, such as ulceration or fibromuscular dysplasia, was the principal concern, angiographers often opted for conventional film techniques in preference to digital imaging. However, the advent of high-resolution digital imaging systems and the use of supplemental high-magnification views when appropriate have made it practical to achieve spatial resolution with digital techniques that provide diagnostic accuracy equivalent to conventional film techniques.

Although a comparison of these techniques based solely on the physics of imaging still shows that film provides better spatial resolution, the nature of the images is such that the ability to detect disease is not significantly different when using either of these techniques. Now that the practical clinical equivalence has been established with regard to spatial resolution, the differences in contrast resolution, speed, and convenience weigh even more in favor of digital imaging techniques. Perhaps the best example of this advantage is the classic problem of differentiating a total occlusion from a near-total occlusion, in which distal flow cannot be shown with certainty on a conventional film angiogram but can be detected on a DSA study, owing to the superior contrast resolution of the DSA technique.

Although still not generally available, most of the recent product offerings for digital angiography include an option for creating three-dimensional views similar in appearance to those produced by CT angiography and MR angiography techniques. Three-dimensional DSA images are constructed from a data set gathered by moving the imaging system (e.g., an angiographic C-arm with its x-ray tube and image intensifier) through an arc around the patient while injecting contrast in the vessel of concern and using mathematical image reconstruction methods similar to those used in CT angiography and MR angiography. Although still not available in most institutions, three-dimensional rotational angiography has generated considerable interest because it enables depiction of asymmetrical lesions from multiple angles with a single contrast injection, minimizing the chance of missing a significant focal ulceration or a severe but asymmetrical stenosis due to the necessity of doing only a limited injection with conventional single-view angiographic imaging technique.

Solid-state flat panel x-ray detectors, though only recently introduced to the marketplace, are another recent technical development likely to have considerable impact on the quality of DSA and DA images. Despite the "high-tech" nature of current digital x-ray imaging, these techniques still rely on an image produced using conventional video-coupled image intensifier tubes. These massive vacuum tube structures employ phosphor screens that convert x-ray energy impinging on their large field input screens to light, then to electrons, and focus the electrons onto a much smaller output phosphor that in turn again produces light, which is in turn converted to a video signal by a camera focused on the output screen. The process of focusing the large-input image onto a smaller output screen is the process actually responsible for amplifying the light level, hence the term *intensifier*. Although the development of the video-coupled image intensifier tube was the development that made digital video imaging technology possible, the system suffers from many problems including geometric distortion and a limited dynamic range, that is, the maximum range of x-ray intensities that they can accurately detect. Solid-state detector systems, on the other hand, are flat panel detector systems that generate the image directly on the surface that receives the x-ray beam eliminating geometric distortion. Furthermore, they have a dynamic range that is far greater than conventional systems, which eliminates many of the imaging artifacts that angiographers have dealt with for years by introducing various types of filters into the x-ray beam to "even out" the image and thereby reduce the range of x-ray intensities to ensure that the resulting image falls within the dynamic range of the image intensifier system. In addition, by virtue of being much smaller than the conventional image intensifier systems, they allow significant reductions in equipment size, although real reductions in equipment size must still await the development of some device that could also replace the large and rather heavy x-ray tubes required to produce these radiographic images.

No matter what type of system is used to produce the images, both DA and DSA images are available on the computer console immediately after contrast injection, unlike conventional photographic x-ray films, which require chemical processing; thus, DA and DSA techniques are much more convenient to use than conventional film technique and allow an examination to progress considerably faster. Thus, although an understanding of film techniques and resolution issues is of importance in understanding how all of these images are made and used, the practical choices have already been made by market forces. Film-based angiography, for many sound reasons, is a dying technique. Indeed, most manufacturers no longer offer conventional photographic x-ray filming devices, and most of the current angiographic units still equipped with conventional filming devices are rapidly nearing the end of their useful life cycle.

Technical Aspects of Cerebrovascular Angiography

Prior to the advent of selective catheterization via peripheral vascular access routes, direct-puncture carotid angiography was routinely employed. The technique is simple, quick, and relatively safe, although, by definition, it limits the scope of examination, making assessment of the proximal vessel segment virtually impossible. Direct cannulation is accomplished by puncturing the common carotid artery low in the neck, using a thin-walled cannula equipped with a hollow stylet. Single-wall or double-wall (puncture and pull-back) techniques are acceptable. Once the vessel has been successfully punctured, as shown by brisk blood flow through the cannula, the cannula is advanced a short distance into the vessel over a soft-tipped guide wire. Between injections, the cannula is plugged with a blunt-tipped obturator to prevent thrombus formation in the cannula; frequent flushing and meticulous injection techniques are also essential. Numerous needle, cannula, and sheath combinations have been designed for this purpose, and most work well. However, like the motion picture *The Exorcist*, which included a very graphic scene involving a direct-puncture carotid angiogram, the technique is now largely of historical interest only.

The development of small-caliber, high-torque catheters that can be introduced via remote access sites (e.g., femoral, axillary, or brachial arteries) and easily manipulated into the cerebral vessels has completely eliminated the use of direct-puncture carotid angiography, because it allows the entire cerebrovascular system to be studied with a single puncture. In addition to the obvious technical advantages of this method, it also involves far less patient anxiety than does the direct-puncture technique. A detailed discussion of the techniques and materials used for cerebrovascular angiography is beyond the scope of this text; however, just as there are strong personal preferences regarding surgical

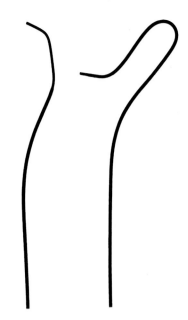

FIGURE 137-27 *Left,* Headhunter catheter—an advancement catheter. *Right,* Simmons' sidewinder catheter—a withdrawal catheter.

instruments among surgeons, catheter choice is often a matter of both technical and personal preference among radiologists. The development of small-caliber (4 and 5 French), high-flow, high-torque preshaped catheters available in a wide range of curve shapes and sizes has virtually eliminated the use of "homemade" heat-shaped polyethylene catheters once popular among neuroradiologists.

Although the variety of catheter shapes is too numerous to discuss in detail, there are two basic classes of catheter shape: advancement and withdrawal (Fig. 137-27). Advancement catheters are designed to be advanced into the vessel of choice by a combination of torque and guide wire manipulations. Withdrawal catheters, typified by the shepherd's crook-shaped Simmons' sidewinder catheter, are used by advancing beyond the vessel ostium and withdrawing to engage the tip in the vessel ostium (Fig. 137-28). Thus, withdrawal catheters are advanced out of a

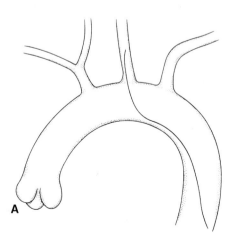
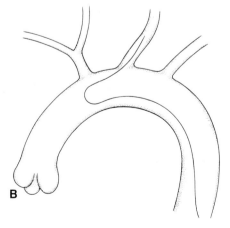

FIGURE 137-28 A, Headhunter catheter advanced into the left common carotid artery. **B,** Simmons' sidewinder catheter withdrawn into the left common carotid artery. Note that the angulation of this vessel would have made advancement catheterization with the headhunter catheter difficult.

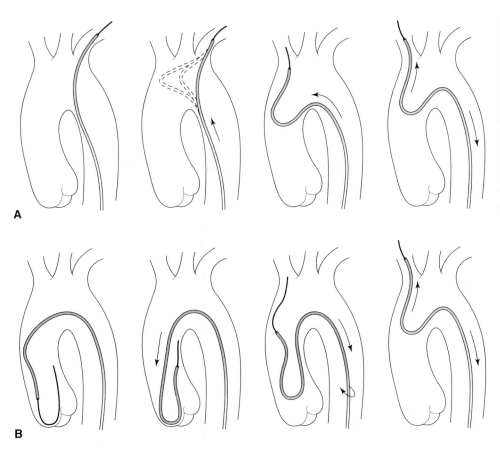

A

B

FIGURE 137-29 A, Simmons' side-winder catheter re-formed, with the left subclavian artery used as a pivot point. **B,** Catheter re-formed using a guide wire looped on the aortic valve to redirect the catheter tip. This maneuver should be done rapidly to avoid prolapsing across the valve into the left ventricle. If prolapse occurs, the catheter is simply withdrawn and the maneuver repeated. Re-forming the catheter can also be done using the contralateral common iliac artery, the renal artery, or the superior mesenteric artery, although such maneuvers are somewhat more difficult than those shown.

vessel and withdrawn into it. The withdrawal catheters are particularly useful when the angulation of the proximal segment of the branch vessel makes direct advancement difficult. Although they are easy to use, withdrawal catheters have the disadvantage of requiring a re-forming maneuver to regain their special shape after being introduced into the vessel over a guide wire in a relatively straight configuration (Fig. 137-29). The choice of catheter shape depends largely on the anatomy and tortuosity of the vessels to be traversed (Fig. 137-30).

For reasons of convenience and safety, most angiographers prefer the percutaneous femoral artery approach popularized by Dr. Sven Seldinger. However, when that approach proves to be impractical because of severe ileofemoral vascular disease, cerebral angiography can be carried out successfully via percutaneous axillary (Fig. 137-31), brachial, or even translumbar catheterization. Withdrawal catheters are generally used as part of the transaxillary approach, and the right axillary artery is generally chosen because it greatly simplifies selective catheterization of the right common carotid artery.

Numerous acceptable radiographic contrast agents are available for use in cerebrovascular angiography. These agents fall into the following three broad categories:

- Ionic
- Low osmolarity (low dissociation)
- Non-ionic

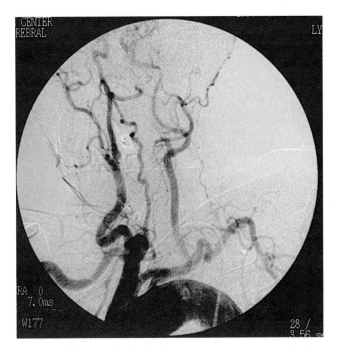

FIGURE 137-30 Marked tortuosity in this elderly patient makes selective catheterization of the internal carotid and vertebral arteries extremely difficult, requiring the use of a Simmons' sidewinder III catheter to negotiate the reverse curves encountered en route to the vessels. (Simmons' catheters are designated as I to III depending on the length of the reverse direction segment, with III being the longest.)

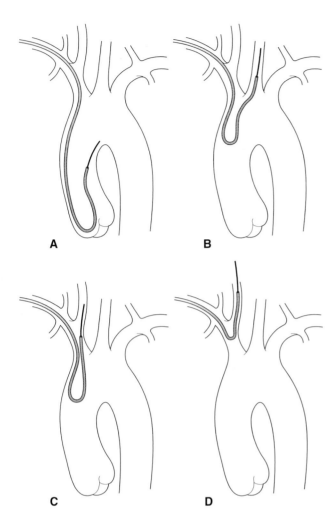

FIGURE 137-31 Selective catheterization of the cerebral vessels can be accomplished from the right brachial approach using a withdrawal type of catheter (Simmons' sidewinder II or III). **A,** The catheter is re-formed as usual, via the aortic valve (see also Fig. 137-29). **B-D,** The catheter can then be directed toward any of the cerebral vessels by a combination of catheter and guide wire manipulations. Selective catheterization of the vertebral arteries is more difficult than catheterization of the carotids, especially on the left side. When selective catheterization of a vertebral artery cannot be accomplished, injection of radiographic contrast material in the adjacent subclavian artery using an occlusive pressure cuff on the ipsilateral arm will usually yield a diagnostic quality angiogram.

In general, the negative chronotropic and inotropic cardiac effects, as well as the neurotoxicity, nephrotoxicity, allergic potential, and subjective discomfort associated with ionic agents, are greater than those associated with the low-osmolarity and non-ionic agents. Many angiographers continued to use ionic agents until recently, except in patients considered to be at increased risk for adverse events due to advanced age or a prior history of allergic reaction to contrast material or significant cardiac or renal disease, due simply to significant cost differences in these agents. However, over the past few years market forces and reimbursement policies determined by various government and private payers have begun to drive down the effective cost of the non-ionic and low-osmolarity agents, resulting in a general shift toward use of these agents. However,

although these newer agents are safer than conventional ionic agents, they are not completely free of risk for the same types of adverse events. Contrast-induced nephropathy, hypersensitivity reactions, and thrombus formation when blood is allowed to mix with contrast in the injection system are still matters of concern.[3a] Minimizing the total contrast dose to the extent that the clinical imaging problem will permit, and employing renal protection measures including preprocedure hydration and other strategies including bicarbonate infusion, in patients with preexisting renal dysfunction (generally defined for practical purposes as a creatinine > 1.5 mg/dL), are simple but highly effective measures. Steroid and antihistamine premedication of patients with significant atopic histories or a history of a prior contrast reaction is still important despite the much lower incidence of such reactions with these contrast agents. Similarly, careful attention to the handling of injection and flush syringes in an effort to avoid allowing blood and contrast to mix is also important. Although this can certainly be done with conventional open-bowl technique, use of a closed-system manifold equipped with a valve system that allows flush solutions, waste collection, and contrast to be isolated from each other makes this a much easier task. Although use of a closed manifold system may also be useful in angiography elsewhere in the body, it is far more important in cerebral angiography due to the consequences of even a small embolus in this territory; after all, as the old saying goes, *kidneys may be important, but they don't think.*

■ COMPLICATIONS OF CEREBROVASCULAR ANGIOGRAPHY

Most complications of cerebrovascular angiography are associated with the puncture site or the administration of radiographic contrast material and have already been discussed elsewhere in this text. Furthermore, most of the access site complications (e.g., hematoma as a result of ineffective postwithdrawal hemostasis or delayed puncture site bleeding and occlusion as a result of excessive postwithdrawal pressure on the vessel) can be avoided by careful technique and a refusal to delegate this important phase of the procedure to an assistant or a mechanical compression device. Although simple manual compression applied correctly is remarkably effective in achieving hemostasis, consideration should also be given to the use of one of the many different vessel closure devices in patients who are at higher risk than normal for puncture site bleeding owing to local atheromatous disease, hypertension, or the inability to cooperate.

Fortunately, neurologic complications are relatively uncommon during cerebral angiography, although they are certainly not rare. Transient neurologic deficits (transient ischemic attacks [TIAs]) have been reported to occur with a frequency of approximately 1.0%, whereas permanent neurologic sequelae average closer to 0.5%. However, the angiography-related stroke rate in the multicenter, prospective and randomized ACAS study was 1.2% despite the fact that the study centers were all carefully selected institutions with a history of low complication and high technical success rates. Furthermore, although many investigators have made a distinction between these two types of events for purposes of reporting complication rates, transient neurologic events and permanent strokes are essentially variations of the same phenomenon, making it best to simply regard the aggregate as the appropriate measure of safety to employ when assessing risk and establishing quality of care threshold values. Although these may seem to be low complication rates when compared with other invasive procedures, neurologic complications can be devastating, making even these relatively low complication rates a significant reason to favor the use of noninvasive imaging alternatives whenever practical.

Although some angiographers employ routine anticoagulation during cerebral angiography, no studies have shown a definite beneficial effect in reducing neurologic complications. Unlike the case in coronary angiography, anticoagulation is not routinely employed during diagnostic cerebral angiography. However, as is often the case for surgical procedures, there is a direct correlation between the duration of the procedure and the incidence of complications. This fact is of special relevance to academic institutions in which the educational requirements of the house staff and the safety of the patient must be carefully balanced. Although the importance of the clinical information might dictate continuation of the study in some situations, the occurrence of a neurologic complication, even if relatively transient, should generally halt the angiographic study, at least until a complete neurologic assessment is performed and consultation with the referring physician is obtained to determine whether the clinical situation justifies the risk of continuing the procedure.

Although there are no studies actually documenting the relative risks of using an automated injector, as opposed to hand injection of contrast during selective cerebral angiography, there is certainly a significant body of opinion that hand injection is safer because it allows operators to immediately cease injecting if they perceive any change in resistance. On the other hand, there is an equally significant body of opinion that the use of automated injectors is as safe as hand injection and permits much better imaging due to more uniform injection bolusing. Whether hand injection actually prevents complications such as injection-induced dissections or indeed any other procedural complication has never been determined, and selection of one or the other technique seems to be primarily a matter of prior training and "*gut feeling.*" However, the trend toward use of smaller 4-French catheters instead of 5-French catheters may not be an optimal choice in cerebral angiography as opposed to other areas of the body. In the case of hand injection, the increased resistance to flow associated with the physics of the smaller catheter lumen makes it correspondingly more difficult to achieve an injection flow rate adequate to provide optimal vessel opacification, thus compromising diagnostic quality. In the case of the automated injector, the increased resistance can easily be overcome, but it comes at the expense of a higher velocity jet of contrast exiting the catheter to achieve the same flow rate as achieved with the larger 5-French catheters.

Fortunately, the incidence of vessel dissections related to selective cerebral angiography is very low ($\approx 0.4\%$), and although significant adverse effects can occur, the outcome is generally benign. Nevertheless, simple measures aimed at reducing the risk of vessel dissection should be almost instinctive for experienced operators. When preparing to inject contrast, a small amount of blood should be aspirated into the syringe in the case of hand injection, or into the injector connection tube in the case of an automated injector, both to make sure that air emboli are not present and to make sure that the catheter is free within the vessel lumen, not abutting the vessel wall where the force of the injection could create a subintimal channel. Catheters should also be positioned within vessels so as to avoid directing the stream toward the wall rather than toward the downstream lumen, a consideration of importance when catheterizing tortuous vessels. Likewise, guide wire manipulations should be done with care and should generally involve the use of soft, floppy-tipped guide wires in vascular territories where the consequences of vessel injury are significant, such as the cerebral circulation.

Although there are varying opinions regarding the level of sedation desirable in noncerebral angiography, there is a general consensus that sedation is generally undesirable for most cerebrovascular angiographic procedures and should be avoided so as not to mask neurologic complications. Obviously this is a clinical decision; some patients are so anxious that light sedation is essential to achieve appropriate cooperation, and some patients are so neurologically impaired that general anesthesia and muscle paralysis are essential to achieve a study of diagnostic quality.

■ GOAL-DIRECTED ANGIOGRAPHIC PROCEDURES

The precise design of an angiographic study must balance the information needs of the referring physician with the risks and benefits to the patient. Thus, the following discussion is divided into five major subgroups of patients:

- Asymptomatic
- Symptomatic
- Injured
- Stroke-in-evolution
- Postoperative

The Asymptomatic Patient

Asymptomatic patients are considered for cerebrovascular evaluation only because they are at high risk for neurologic events due some preexisting condition known to be associated with significant cerebrovascular disease. As previously discussed, angiography is rarely indicated as a first-line investigation in asymptomatic individuals because noninvasive imaging is generally sufficient to detect the presence of a significant lesion in such patients. Indeed, a normal noninvasive imaging study is usually adequate to redirect the clinical investigation without resorting to invasive angiography. However, conventional angiography may be appropriate if the pretest probability of a significant lesion is high due to other factors and noninvasive imaging proves inadequate for technical reasons. Of course, performing angiography presupposes that the patient is a

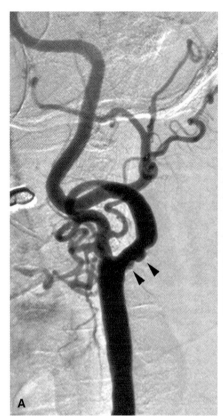

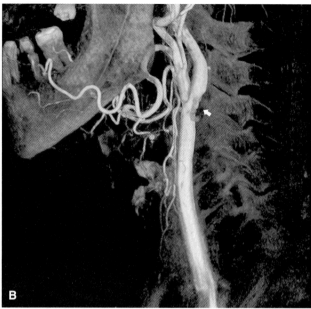

FIGURE 137-32 A, Selective angiogram showing irregular shallow ulceration of the proximal internal carotid artery. **B,** CT angiogram showing similar irregular shallow ulcerations. (**A** and **B,** Courtesy of Philips Medical Systems, Bothell, Wash.)

good candidate for surgical or endovascular intervention. In the unusual situation where conventional catheter-based angiography is indeed appropriate for an asymptomatic patient, comprehensive angiography is essential because there is no clinical information that would otherwise focus attention on a specific vessel. The angiogram should include at least two views of the aortic arch and cervical great vessels to the level of the proximal intracranial vessels, supplemented by selective catheterization and angiography of any vessels not adequately visualized on the nonselective aortogram.

The Symptomatic Patient

As indicated previously, many surgeons think that angiography is unnecessary in symptomatic patients with unequivocal findings of occlusive or ulcerative atheromatous disease on duplex Doppler ultrasound, MR angiography, or CT angiography, whereas others are equally convinced that the accuracy of the noninvasive techniques is not sufficient to determine the need for surgery. In any event, once it has been determined that angiography is indicated, comprehensive angiography is generally desirable in most situations because angiography limited solely to the suspect vessel is likely to be inadequate owing to the propensity for vascular occlusive disease of various etiologies (atherosclerosis, fibromuscular dysplasia, and arteritis) to occur at multiple sites. The general plan of examination is similar to that used in the asymptomatic patient; however, additional views of

clinically suspect areas may be required to complete the examination, especially in the detection of nonocclusive ulcerative disease that might serve as a site of thrombus/embolus formation (Fig. 137-32) or nonatheromatous occlusive disease (e.g., arteritis), in which the specific location of occlusive lesions and the patterns of collateral flow may be important in determining therapy. In symptomatic patients, absence of atheromatous occlusive or ulcerative disease at the carotid bifurcation also necessitates a detailed examination of the aortic arch vessels and the intracranial vessels, particularly the region of the carotid siphon.

Comprehensive angiography including the aortic arch as well as both the extracranial and intracranial circulation is especially important when dealing with nonatheromatous occlusive disease. Although the various types of occlusive arteritis are uncommon and patients with these ailments may never be encountered even in a busy vascular surgery practice, it is important to recognize these entities because they often require a coordinated approach that may include both surgical revascularization as well as medical management.

Fibromuscular dysplasia is the most common of the nonatheromatous occlusive diseases affecting the cerebral circulation, specifically the extracranial carotid arteries. It occurs in approximately 1% of the population and is seen in approximately 0.6% of carotid angiograms. It has a 3:1 male-to-female predominance and occurs in patients in their mid-20s to mid-50s. Although there are histologically distinct intimal, medial, and subadventitial forms, the symptoms and angiographic appearance are similar. Patients with carotid fibromuscular dysplasia present with ischemic/embolic symptoms similar to those seen in patients with ordinary atheromatous occlusive disease (e.g., TIAs and stroke), although there is a 30% incidence of accompanying intracranial aneurysms and a 10% to 20% incidence of spontaneous carotid artery dissection as well, making it essential to study both the extracranial and intracranial circulation in the patients (see Chapter 142 for further detail). Angiographically, the characteristic appearance, seen in the medial variety of the lesion, is the so-called string of beads, consisting of a closely spaced sequence of focal moderate- to high-grade narrowings. The etiology of fibromuscular dysplasia is unknown, and there is no specific medical therapy; thus, the mainstay of treatment is either endovascular or surgical dilation.

Although fibromuscular dysplasia involves the carotid arteries in approximately 60% of patients with the disease, it is often first recognized due to symptoms associated with ischemia in other vascular territories, principally the renal arteries and, to a lesser extent, the celiac, mesenteric, and lumbar arteries. Thus, when fibromuscular dysplasia is found in other vascular territories, the carotid arteries should also be evaluated by angiography. High-resolution CT angiography or MR angiography, and occasionally ultrasound, may well depict the lesions of fibromuscular dysplasia without the need for conventional angiography; however, very high-resolution imaging may be needed to definitively rule out the presence of fibromuscular dysplasia. Thus, the absence of such findings on noninvasive imaging cannot be considered conclusive with the current state of these technologies.

Giant cell, or "temporal," arteritis, often thought to be the vascular manifestation of the complex systemic autoimmune disease polymyalgia rheumatica, occurs in approximately 1:3000 individuals older than 50 years of age. Pathologically, this is a disease of the elastic media associated with macrophage and giant cell infiltration and the release of factors that stimulate occlusive intimal hyperplasia. Tenderness and pain in the facial temporal region are frequent complaints. Other symptoms depend on the severity of the occlusive lesions and their specific location and include headache, jaw, or tongue pain, especially with eating and speaking, and visual disturbances. Although surgical revascularization is occasionally necessary, this is usually a self-limiting disease that responds well to steroid therapy and generally lasts 1 to 2 years (see also Chapter 28 for further detail). Angiography is largely a procedure of eliminating other types of occlusive disease in this entity, because findings range from apparently normal vessels to subtle smoothly tapering narrowings or occlusions. Ultrasound often shows a characteristic perivascular "halo," but biopsy is the definitive diagnostic technique.

Takayasu's arteritis, also called *pulseless disease* because of its propensity to affect the larger brachiocephalic vessels (Fig. 137-33), including the subclavian arteries as well as the aorta and pulmonary arteries, occurs in 2 to 3 people per million per year and has a 9:1 female-to-male predominance usually affecting Asian women in their 20s and 30s, but it can also be seen in non-Asians as well.

This condition is discussed in Chapter 26. Like giant cell arteritis, this is also a disease of large vessels with elastic media rather than intracranial vessels. Symptoms vary widely from one patient to another and range from headaches to TIAs and stroke or upper extremity "claudication," depending simply on the distribution of affected vessels and the functional territory rendered ischemic by the offending lesions. Treatment includes surgical revascularization as well as steroids and antineoplastic antimetabolite agents (e.g., methotrexate, azathioprine, and even cyclophosphamide); however, even with treatment the disease tends to be progressive and fatal within a few years, although long-term survival has been reported. Angiographically, the lesions of Takayasu's arteritis tend to have smoothly tapering surfaces, unlike the irregular lesions usually seen with atheromatous disease, but they can also present with a corkscrew pattern reminiscent of fibromuscular dysplasia.

Moyamoya disease, literally a translation of the Japanese term for "puff of smoke," is a rare disease seen more often in children than adults. The disease is characterized by focal occlusive lesions of the distal internal carotid arteries and adjacent segments of the circle of Willis as well as the

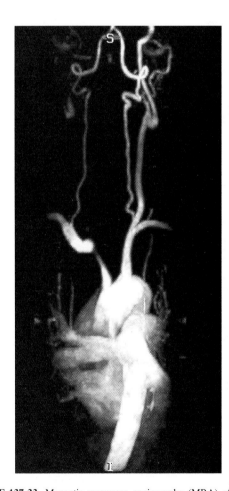

FIGURE 137-33 Magnetic resonance angiography (MRA) of a patient with Takayasu's arteritis showing a severe focal stenosis of the right brachiocephalic artery associated with occlusion of the adjacent right common carotid artery. (Courtesy of William G. Bradley, Jr., MD, PhD, Department of Radiology, University of California, San Diego, San Diego, Calif.)

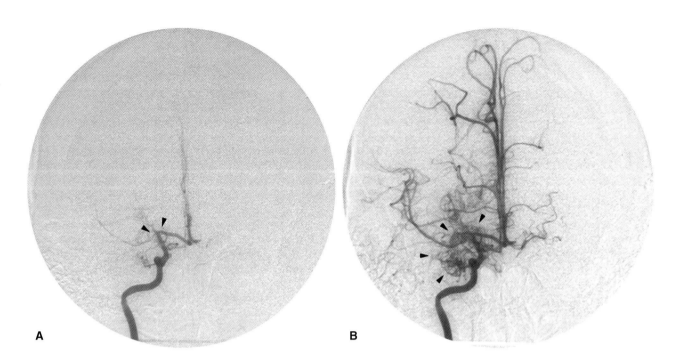

FIGURE 137-34   A, Occluded right middle cerebral artery visualized on early angiographic images in a young female patient with moyamoya disease. **B,** Classic "cloud of smoke" small-caliber collateral vessels reconstituting flow to the middle cerebral artery. (**A** and **B,** Courtesy of Irwin Walot, MD, Los Angeles County Harbor-UCLA Medical Center Department of Radiology, University of California, Torrance, Calif.)

proximal portions of the adjacent MCA, ACA, and PCA branches (Fig. 137-34). The abundance of collaterals of extremely small caliber is responsible for the characteristically indistinct puff-of-smoke appearance on angiography. Symptoms include ischemic strokes, TIAs often associated with exercise and hyperventilation, as well as progressive intellectual impairment in children and hemorrhagic stroke in adults. Although EC-IC bypass surgery yields disappointing results in the treatment of atheromatous carotid disease, it is the procedure of choice in moyamoya disease and often yields excellent long-term results. The etiology of moyamoya disease is still uncertain, and there is no specific medical treatment; in fact, this disease may actually be a result of early trauma rather than a true inflammatory disease.

When dealing with ordinary atheromatous occlusive disease in a symptomatic patient, the finding of a seemingly occluded carotid or vertebral artery, especially on nonselective arch angiography (Fig. 137-35), is a special case. Because there is a major difference in the approach to a total occlusion and to a near-total occlusion, definitive resolution of the issue is essential. In such cases, selective injection of the vessel in question should be performed with imaging that provides both early and late views of the area, to differentiate total occlusion from near-total occlusion with very slow faint antegrade filling of the distal vessel segment (Fig. 137-36) or retrograde collateral filling (Fig. 137-37).

Although image subtraction techniques applied to nonselective arch aortograms may be useful in the evaluation of collateral filling patterns and the detection of low-volume filling distal to a near-total obstruction, they can also introduce motion artifacts that are difficult to evaluate.

Selective injection presents a maximal opacification dose of undiluted contrast material to the suspect area, whereas nonselective arch angiography, of necessity, involves significant dilution of the contrast bolus. Once a near-total occlusion has been confirmed, prompt anticoagulation generally should be instituted because there is a definite, although poorly quantified, risk of occlusion of such lesions after angiography.

Patients who have recently had a completed stroke thought to be a consequence of atherosclerotic carotid disease constitute a special case of the symptomatic patient. Determining whether angiography is appropriate and when it should be performed depends on the determination of whether surgery or endovascular intervention would be of benefit in prevention of additional neurologic events in that vascular territory. Basically, the decision involves assessment of the extent of the infarct in relation to the residual at-risk vascular territory. In the presence of a significant residual at-risk vascular territory, noninvasive assessment is the first logical step, with angiography reserved for situations in which the noninvasive testing fails to yield an unequivocal result.

The presence of a recent cerebral infarct implies a defect in the blood-brain barrier; thus, on principle, direct injection of a neurotoxic agent such as radiographic contrast material probably should be avoided unless benefit significantly outweighs the risk (although the actual magnitude of the risk in such circumstances has never been well established). Indeed, there are few definitive data as to when angiography can be safely performed in the poststroke patient. The persistence of parenchymal CT contrast enhancement, which implies a defect in the blood-brain barrier, can last for

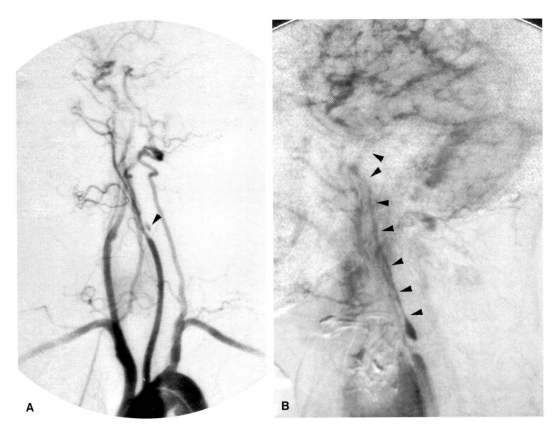

FIGURE 137-35 A, Early film from nonselective aortic arch angiogram showing a near-occlusive stenosis of the proximal left internal carotid artery with such slow flow that only a small segment of the vessel can be visualized (*arrowhead*). **B,** Late film from the same angiogram showing slow flow and poor filling of the internal carotid artery segment (*arrowheads*) distal to the stenosis, the classic "string sign" indicative of an almost completely occlusive lesion. The apparent small size of the vessel is an artifact of low-perfusion pressure; the actual size of the vessel cannot be accurately determined from the angiogram in the presence of this near-occlusive lesion.

as long as 6 weeks. Therefore, although the decision is based on anecdotal experience and extrapolation of the significance of the CT enhancement data, a delay of about 6 weeks probably constitutes an appropriate waiting period, particularly in patients with substantial neurologic deficits.

Finally, the human body is not simply a collection of isolated systems—failure to detect demonstrable anatomic disease in the presence of symptoms suggesting ischemic or embolic cerebrovascular pathology mandates a search for other sources of emboli or hemodynamic insufficiency, with particular attention to structural heart disease (e.g., valve disease, infarcted areas with mural thrombus) and arrhythmias.

The Injured Patient

Angiographic examination of the injured patient involving trauma to the extracranial or intracranial cerebral circulation, or both, constitutes an important exception to the rule of completeness because there is usually a premium on expeditious diagnosis and treatment. Even the so-called stable patient rapidly can become unstable. Because single-system injury is uncommon, the angiographer must participate in the radiologic and nonradiologic evaluation of the patient as a member of a team able to coordinate and

prioritize various investigations and treatments. The need for angiographic evaluation depends on patient condition and the location and type of injury as well as the management approach of the trauma surgeons caring for the patient (Fig. 137-38) and the potential for endovascular treatment such as embolization to occlude a bleeding branch vessel or implantation of a endograft to treat disruption at a surgically inaccessible site (Figs. 137-39 and 137-40). Angiography of superficial facial injuries is not usually required, since physical examination is generally quite accurate and surgical exploration is straightforward. Deep, penetrating facial injuries, in contrast, may well require angiography for both diagnosis and treatment involving transcatheter embolization because such injuries can involve relatively inaccessible structures.

Most surgeons agree as to the need for angiographic evaluation of neck injuries to zone I (angle of jaw–base of skull) and zone III (cricoid-clavicle) since these areas present significant problems in surgical exposure. The need for angiographic evaluation of injuries to zone II (cricoid-angle of jaw) is far more controversial, since this is an area relatively amenable to prompt surgical exploration. Despite the controversy, some of which is economic and logistic in nature, angiography of zone II injuries still seems like a worthwhile step in the stable patient because it can

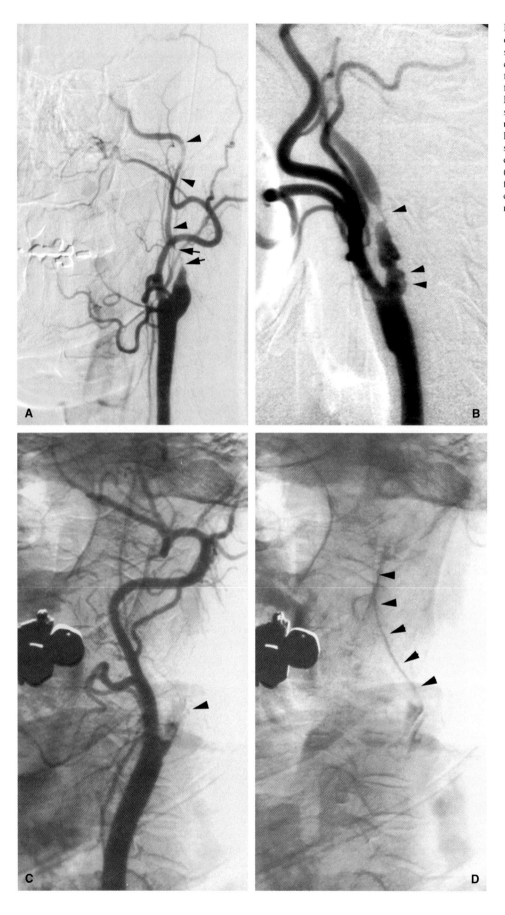

FIGURE 137-36 A, Selective angiogram showing a very high-grade stenosis of the proximal internal carotid artery (*arrowheads*) with slow flow distal to the lesion, the mild form of an occlusive "string sign." **B,** Similar mild form of the string sign accompanied by significant ulceration proximal to the stenotic lesion (*arrowheads*). **C,** Another selective angiogram showing a near-occlusive stenosis on early images (*arrowhead*), and **D** shows delayed flow in the vessel distal to the lesion on a later image (*arrowheads*), a more severe form of the string sign.

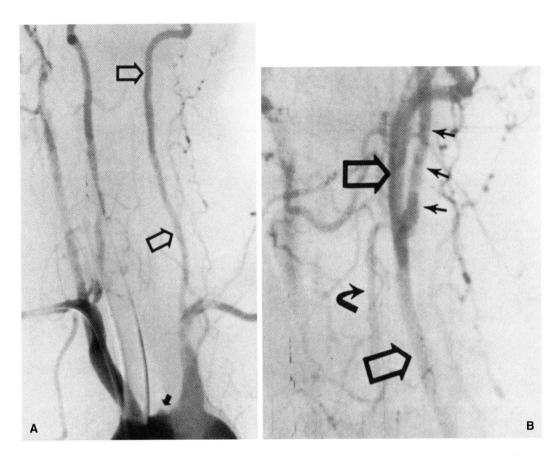

FIGURE 137-37 Occluded left common carotid artery with patent internal and external carotid branches. **A,** Arch aortogram, early film. The left common carotid is occluded (*solid arrow*). The left vertebral artery is outlined by *open arrows*. **B,** Arch aortogram, delayed film (close-up view). The vertebral artery is again outlined by *open arrows*. The internal carotid (*straight arrows*) is filled via the external carotid. The chief collateral pathway is the superior thyroid artery (*curved arrow*).

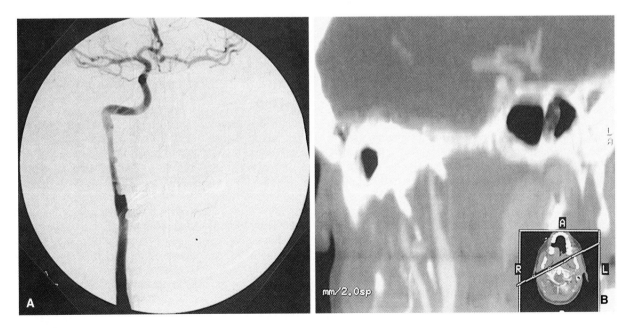

FIGURE 137-38 **A,** Angiogram of the right internal carotid artery, showing a dissection resulting from motor vehicle trauma. In view of the fact that the contralateral internal carotid artery sustained a total occlusion during the accident as well as the relatively inaccessible location of the lesion, which extended to the skull base behind the mandible, both operative and endovascular interventions were considered high-risk options. **B,** For that reason, the patient was anticoagulated and followed with serial CT angiography examinations.

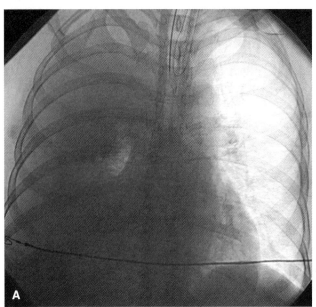

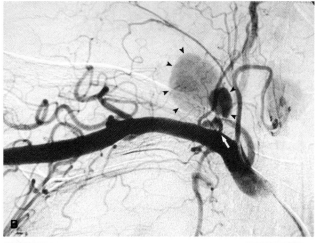

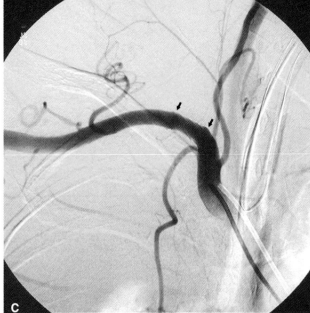

FIGURE 137-39 A, Massive hemothorax in a young male gunshot victim. **B,** Multilobulated pseudoaneurysm (*black arrowheads*) originating from traumatic disruption of the cephalad margin of the right subclavian artery (*white arrow*). **C,** Subclavian artery effectively sealed by implantation of a covered stent endoprosthesis (Wallgraft) at a site where surgical access would have been difficult. (**A-C,** Courtesy of Sue Hanks, MD, Los Angeles County—USC Medical Center, Los Angeles, Calif.)

easily diagnose unsuspected vascular injuries or eliminate unnecessary explorations. Once the role of angiography in the overall management of the patient has been determined, a study plan for the areas subjected to trauma should be formulated on the basis of the anatomy and mode of injury.

The most common cerebrovascular injuries of interest to the vascular surgeon that require emergency angiographic evaluation are the penetrating injuries of the neck. Although stab wounds may at first seem relatively limited in scope, a small entry wound can easily hide more extensive underlying trauma. For that reason, angiographic evaluation of a stab wound should involve at least selective angiography of the cervical segments of the ipsilateral carotid or vertebral arteries, or both. If an injury is detected, views of the intracranial circulation, including the contralateral supply, generally should be obtained to evaluate collateral flow pathways. Knowledge of the collateral flow becomes especially important when the injury occurs in a region

where surgical access is difficult, such as the zone III area just below the base of the skull, in which case ligation of an injured vessel may be preferable to repair if the collateral flow patterns permit sacrificing the vessel in question (Fig. 137-41).

The trajectory of a bullet within tissue, especially in a complex area such as the neck, is virtually impossible to reconstruct. Furthermore, the extent of both direct and shock wave injury is also difficult to determine simply by physical examination. If the path of injury is clearly confined to one side, ipsilateral selective angiography of the cervical segments of the carotid or vertebral arteries is usually sufficient; however, if there is any doubt as to whether the bullet crossed the mid-line, bilateral angiography should be performed. As in the case of stab wound injuries, the detection of a cervical segment injury strongly suggests the need for delineation of the intracranial circulation and potential collateral pathways.

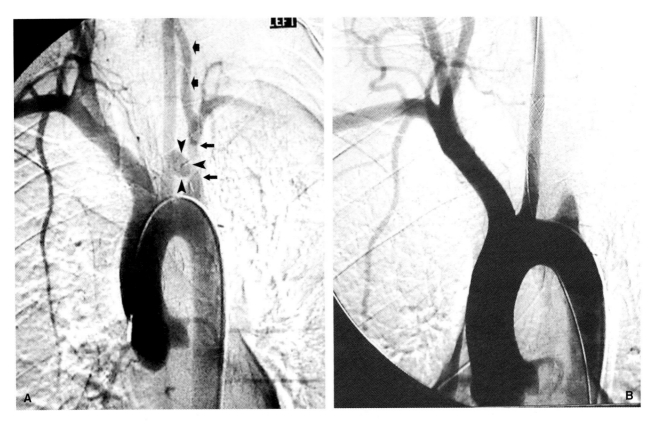

FIGURE 137-40 A, Young male gunshot victim treated by left subclavian artery ligation (*small arrows*) and carotid-to-subclavian bypass (*broad arrows*) at another hospital who subsequently developed a left carotid artery pseudoaneurysm (*arrowheads*). **B,** Pseudoaneurysm of the left carotid was treated by implantation of a covered stent endoprosthesis (Wallgraft), as his medical condition had deteriorated to a point where conventional surgical repair presented an unacceptable level of risk. (Note that the left subclavian artery is not visualized on current image filled via carotid-to-subclavian graft on later images of this angiogram). (**A** and **B,** Courtesy of Sue Hanks, MD, Los Angeles County—USC Medical Center, Los Angeles, Calif.)

The absence of an angiographically detectable abnormality or the presence of a minor irregularity such as localized bulging or indistinctness, which might be overlooked on routine diagnostic angiography, should be considered highly suspect in the traumatized patient, especially for high-velocity wounds, and the suspect area should be carefully evaluated with additional views as needed. This is especially true if there are clinical, physical, or radiographic findings suggesting significant trauma, such as hypotension or a soft tissue swelling indicating the presence of a hematoma (Fig. 137-42). Such findings should raise the examiner's index of suspicion because they may be the only evidence of a major vascular injury temporarily hidden by the tamponade of a precarious clot. However, additional views and selective catheterization obviously should be undertaken with considerable care, because these maneuvers may well pinpoint the injury, revealing its true significance by initiating bleeding at the injury site and suddenly destabilizing the situation (Fig. 137-43). Urgent surgical intervention is required in such situations; however, simple local compression may be sufficient to stop bleeding long enough to transport the patient to the operating room. Temporary hemostasis can often be obtained quickly by catheterizing the injured vessel with either an angioplasty or soft occlusion balloon placed across the injury site and inflated to a low pressure sufficient to provide both proximal and distal vascular control. If ligation rather than primary repair is contemplated, the same outcome can also be achieved safely and effectively in the angiography suite by placing embolic coil occlusive devices proximal and distal to the injury site.

Zone I injuries add a special consideration to planning the angiographic evaluation, since these injuries may actually involve intrathoracic structures such as the arch origins of the great vessels. Thus, a thoracic aortogram prior to selective catheterization should be obtained in low zone I injuries. Likewise, a thoracic aortogram prior to selective angiography is advisable in the elderly patient, in whom unsuspected atherosclerotic occlusive disease may make selective catheterization a greater risk or compromise the efficacy of the intended surgical repair.

Direct blunt trauma to the neck and acceleration-deceleration injuries such as those sustained in motor vehicle or pedestrian-vehicle accidents present a difficult clinical problem. If there are obvious physical signs of significant injury or neurologic signs that cannot be explained on the basis of head injury, angiography is usually indicated in the acute setting. Similarly, should the patient experience a delayed neurologic event that might be referable to traumatic vascular injury, prompt angiographic evaluation is also indicated. Although ultrasound, MR angiography, or CT angiography may be useful in detection

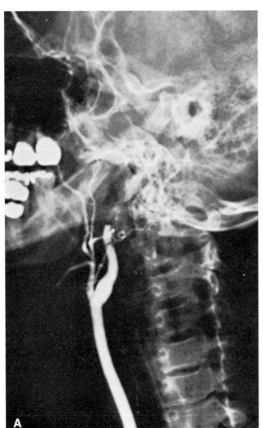
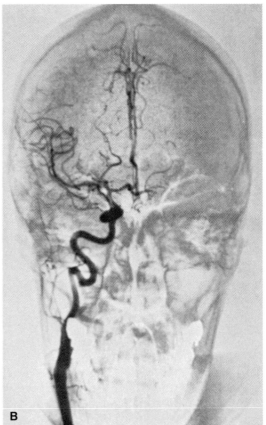
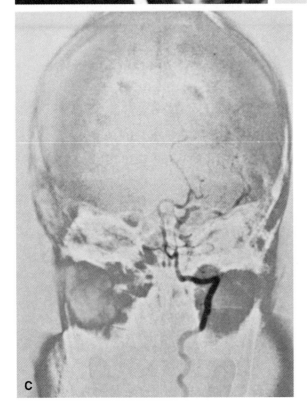

FIGURE 137-41 A, Selective left common carotid angiogram of a young woman stabbed in the neck just below the base of the skull during a violent rape assault. The left common carotid artery is totally occluded, but there is no evidence of extravasation. **B,** Selective right common carotid angiogram showing flow to right middle cerebral artery (MCA) as well as both right and left anterior carotid arteries. The flow "pseudo-occlusion" of the left MCA is caused by inflow of unopacified blood to the left MCA arising from the posterior circulation. **C,** Selective left vertebral injection showing normal posterior circulation as well as supply to the left MCA. Demonstration of adequate flow from the contralateral and posterior circulations allowed safe ligation of the left internal carotid artery just below the base of the skull rather than a difficult reconstruction. (Examination of the vessel at surgery showed it to be occluded by thrombus, presumably as the result of an intimal disruption associated with violent neck motion and trauma to the vessel at the atlanto-occipital joint; no penetrating injury was found.)

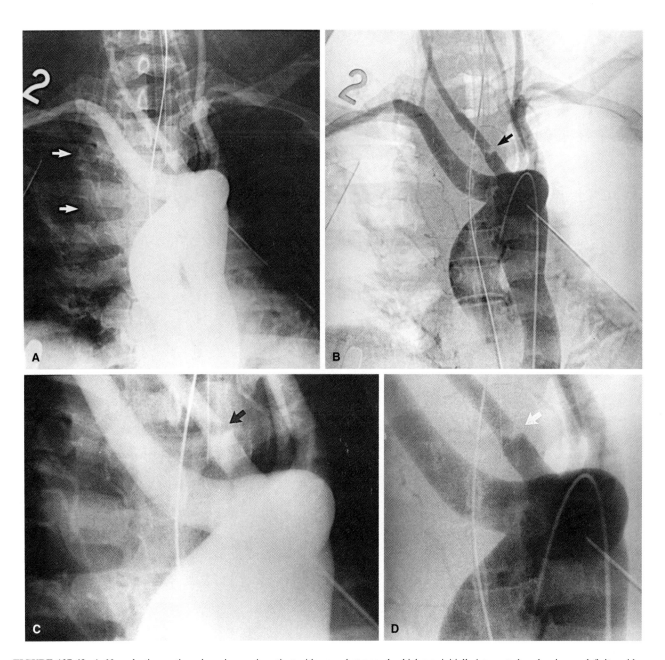

FIGURE 137-42 A, Nonselective aortic arch angiogram in patient with a gunshot wound, which was initially interpreted as showing no definite evidence of a major vascular injury despite the presence of a large right superior mediastinal soft tissue density indicating the presence of a large hematoma (*arrows*). (Note that the aberrant right subclavian artery is a normal anatomic variant.) **B,** Film subtraction of the same angiogram revealing partial transection of the right common carotid artery (*arrow*). Although, in retrospect, this lesion may indeed have been seen on the unsubtracted angiogram, the allowance made for radiographic shadows of underlying bony structures effectively desensitized the examiner, precluding detection of this highly significant injury. **C,** Unsubtracted magnification view of the same area makes the injury (*arrow*) far more obvious, as does magnification film subtraction (**D**). (**A-D,** Courtesy of Irwin Walot, MD, Department of Radiology, Los Angeles County Harbor-UCLA Medical Center, University of California, Torrance, Calif.)

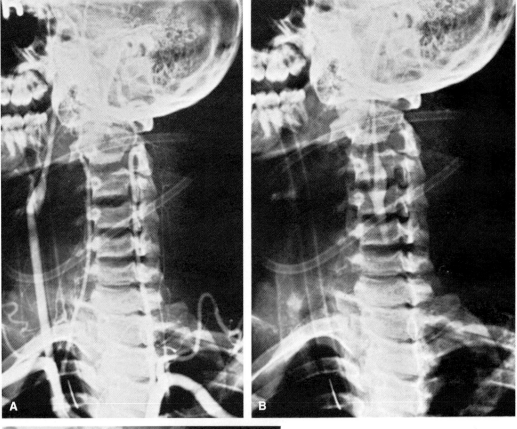

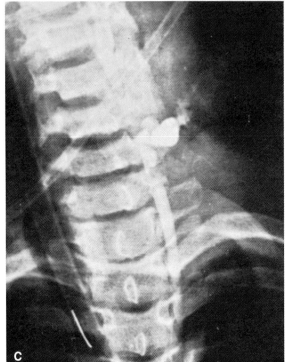

FIGURE 137-43 A, Arch aortogram showing apparent absence of the left common carotid artery. **B,** Late film from arch aortogram showing retrograde collateral filling of the left common carotid artery. **C,** Selective left common carotid angiogram demonstrating precise location of injury (stab wound) and unequivocal extravasation.

of occult dissections or occlusions in such patients, small but nevertheless clinically significant injuries may be difficult to detect without the use of conventional angiography

In the case of intracranial vascular trauma, CT scanning is usually the primary evaluation modality, followed by angiography if the CT scan suggests that a salvageable situation still exists. Diagnosis and treatment of such injuries are usually the province of the neurosurgeon rather than the vascular surgeon and, as such, are beyond the scope of this discussion.

The Patient with Stroke-in-Evolution

The crescendo TIA syndrome, in which ischemic neurologic events occur with ominously increasing frequency although they completely resolve in the intervals between TIAs, should be considered an urgent presentation of the symptomatic patient. Stroke-in-evolution is another dangerous entity, consisting of an event with ongoing neurologic symptoms that do not completely resolve but may wax and wane. Whereas many investigators have attempted to place arbitrary time limits on the definition of stroke-in-evolution, the distinction between it and crescendo TIAs is far from clear. Attempting to make that distinction may even be counterproductive because waiting to determine whether the event will resolve also may forfeit the opportunity to provide timely therapy.

Treatment, and hence the angiographic approach to the stroke-in-evolution, is changing. Over the past several years, a new concept of the pathophysiology of ischemic stroke has gained acceptance, in which irreversible neurologic damage does not occur as an all-or-none phenomenon. In some instances, prompt restoration of flow can restore brain viability and neurologic function. Whether this represents the presence of an ischemic penumbra surrounding a smaller but irrevocably infarcted core of tissue, as opposed to a potentially viable but "stunned" volume of neurons, is unclear, but it may be that both of these mechanisms occur. In fact, while still unproved, it seems likely that progression from a stunned but completely viable state to the infarcted core with viable penumbra is the basic mode of evolution for all strokes. Indeed, an understanding of the factors affecting the time course would help explain the variation in the clinical course of individual patients. In any event, stroke-in-evolution seems to be analogous to a myocardial infarction, in which a period of ischemic viability exists between the inciting event and irreversible infarction, during which restoration of flow will restore function and either prevent or minimize the extent of myocardial, or in this case, neurologic damage.

The emergency treatment of stroke-in-evolution is a logical outgrowth of advances in the treatment of acute myocardial infarction and peripheral vascular disease. Progress in the understanding of the pathophysiology of myocardial infarction since 1980 has led to the establishment of regionalized acute care cardiac centers organized around the concept of providing rapid and effective treatment. Current practice in acute cardiac care, based on the concept of salvageable myocardium, represents a dramatic shift from the passive rest, recovery, and rehabili-tation approach to myocardial infarction of the 1970s that was predicated on the paradigm of irreversible damage. This strategy is now being applied to patients with acute strokes. We know that "time is myocardium"; we need to recognize that "time is brain" and educate our colleagues in other specialties to this critically important concept. The concept of a "brain attack" should engender a similar response to a "heart attack." Prompt restoration of cerebral perfusion is critical to outcome; thus, every aspect of the treatment plan must be directed toward preserving neurons and restoring blood flow as rapidly as possible.

The one practical difference that exists between myocardial infarction and cerebral infarction is the occurrence of both hemorrhagic and ischemic infarcts in the brain. Obviously, thrombolytic therapy must be avoided in the setting of hemorrhage, but this diagnosis can be made easily using CT scanning, because hemorrhage, unlike bland cerebral infarction, is detectable as soon as it occurs. Since ischemic infarction accounts for approximately 75% of all strokes, reperfusion induced by thrombolysis is widely applicable. Although diffusion-weighted MR scanning is far more sensitive than CT at detecting the early signs of infarction, this is of little significance in developing a brain attack treatment protocol because there is sufficient evidence to indicate that thrombolysis is effective if instituted early in the absence of intracranial hemorrhage, and CT scanning does an excellent job of detecting intra-cranial hemorrhage.

Although there are few data defining the so-called window of opportunity (i.e., the interval between onset of symptoms and irreversible damage), most authorities think that perfusion must be restored within 4 to 6 hours to provide maximal benefit. Indeed, although the interval of irreversible cerebral ischemia is still undetermined, there is evidence from both animal and human experiments that delayed thrombolysis is ineffective and also extends infarction due to hemorrhage.

Can intravenous thrombolysis produce results comparable to catheter-directed intra-arterial thrombolytic techniques? (a question similar to the controversy encountered in the cardiac care arena). Logistics and economics dictate that emergency treatment of stroke by simple intravenous infusion is less expensive and more widely available even in major metropolitan areas than are the specialized personnel and equipment needed to provide subselective cerebral angiography and catheter-directed thrombolysis. Although data comparing the efficacy of acute stroke interventions suggest that catheter-directed therapy is probably more effective than intravenous therapy, there are numerous reports as to the efficacy of intravenous thrombolysis and it is largely a matter of resource availability when choosing which approach to use. In most settings a brain attack treatment program simply has to rely on intravenous treatment for practical reasons.

Strategy for Thrombolytic Therapy

From a purely technical standpoint, subselective catheter-directed thrombolysis does appear to be more effective than intravenous thrombolysis. Fortunately, unlike endovascular occlusion of intracranial AVMs and aneurysms for which considerable experience and a knowledge of functional neuroanatomy (including the innumerable potential routes of collateral circulation) is required, restoring cerebral perfusion is far easier.

Preservation of normal neurons is another area of active research. Because it is not yet possible to differentiate ischemic from hemorrhagic infarcts before hospitalization, prehospital administration of intravenous thrombolytic agents is unsafe. In addition, experiments in cardiac reperfusion models have shown that simply reperfusing myocardium with blood can produce cell damage that limits therapeutic benefit in proportion to the duration of the ischemia. Whether a "neuroplegia" agent conceptually similar to cardioplegia is possible is another topic of active research.

Although catheter-directed thrombolysis may never be the mainstay of emergency stroke treatment due to logistic and economic factors, the work done in catheter-directed thrombolysis explains why emergency carotid endarterectomy surgery has had such disappointing results in the care of patients with stroke-in-evolution syndrome. Until the advent of catheter-directed thrombolytic treatment for stroke-in-evolution, there had actually been little reason to perform cerebral angiography in the setting of acute ischemic stroke. (Obviously, if one is dealing with stroke due to subarachnoid or certain specific types of intracerebral hemorrhage, there is a premium on obtaining prompt angiographic diagnosis to detect intracranial aneurysms or AVMs amenable to endovascular or surgical therapy.) As angiographic experience has grown in this area, it is clear that most ischemic infarcts are due to thrombi or emboli lodged in branches of the MCA or, less commonly, the ACA, not thrombotic occlusion at the site of atheromatous carotid disease.

The Postoperative Patient

Routine intraoperative "completion angiography" following carotid endarterectomy has become common, although there is still some controversy as to its indication. Irregularities of the endarterectomy margins and intimal fractures ("clamp defects") are common and are of little clinical significance. Furthermore, such irregularities are likely to disappear when the vessel heals. However, the presence of an unsuspected and potentially occlusive intimal flap or an endarterectomy that fails to traverse the area of stenosis fully is of considerable significance and therefore best detected when correction involves simply reopening an already exposed vessel and repairing the defect. Although completion angiography has become commonplace, some surgeons have chosen to employ routine angioscopic evaluation or intraoperative duplex ultrasonography, since these techniques may be even more sensitive than conventional angiography in the detection of correctable technical problems.

The occurrence of an acute neurologic event in the immediate postoperative period is best treated by prompt re-exploration when it occurs in the same vascular territory, rather than accepting the delays inherent in obtaining angiography even in the most efficient centers. If re-exploration fails to reveal a correctable surgical problem, however, intraoperative angiography is essential. Once the immediate postoperative period has passed, the occurrence or recurrence of symptoms in a patient who has recently undergone carotid endarterectomy mandates angiographic evaluation of both the operative site and the downstream vascular territory subject to embolization from that area. If the surgery is not recent (>6 months previously), evaluation should be as thorough as in the case of a patient who has not yet had surgery, because of the possible development of new lesions or the exacerbation of previously mild lesions.

■ ENDOVASCULAR PROCEDURES

Over the past decade, angiography, once primarily a diagnostic modality in the management of intracranial cerebrovascular disease, has become an essential therapeutic modality. Indeed, endovascular treatments for intracranial aneurysms and AVMs have gained general acceptance owing to their high degree of success, as well as to the corresponding limitations of conventional surgical therapy in such cases. Indeed, endovascular treatment is now widely accepted as the preferred first-line management for intracranial aneurysms and AVMs. Similarly, catheter-directed thrombolysis, despite limitations with regard to availability, has also become important in the management of acute stroke.

In contrast to the situation encountered in treating intracranial vascular lesions, the excellent results and low morbidity of extracranial cerebrovascular surgery, specifically carotid endarterectomy, at first would seem to make endovascular therapies nothing more than valuable adjunctive techniques with specific but limited application. However, it is now apparent that carotid angioplasty and stenting are techniques with the *potential* to fundamentally alter basic treatment paradigms, and that there are many technical and market forces as well as patient preference considerations that make this an attractive technique *if* it indeed proves to have efficacy and safety outcomes similar to those achieved for carotid endarterectomy. The potential for rapid growth and use of what many still perceive as an unverified technique and the financial ramifications of that trend have engendered so much concern that the U.S. Medicare Administration, at the time of this writing, limits payment to procedures performed as part of formal clinical trials involving appropriate Institutional Review Board oversight and the issuance of a U.S. Food and Drug Administration investigational device exemption. Approval in patients at high risk for carotid endarterectomy is expected.

Unfortunately, much of the initial debate followed specialty "turf" lines. Vascular surgeons, who generally stand ready to be convinced by real evidence, remained skeptical in view of what they saw as already well-documented favorable outcomes for conventional carotid endarterectomy. Interventional radiologists, usually strong proponents of endovascular alternatives to conventional open surgery, also tended to remain skeptical, seeing carotid angioplasty as a technique with benefits in limited applications, such as recurrent stenosis following carotid endarterectomy, stenosis due to radiation-induced fibrosis, fibromuscular dysplasia (Fig. 137-44), carotid disease in the setting of a hostile surgical field associated with major prior

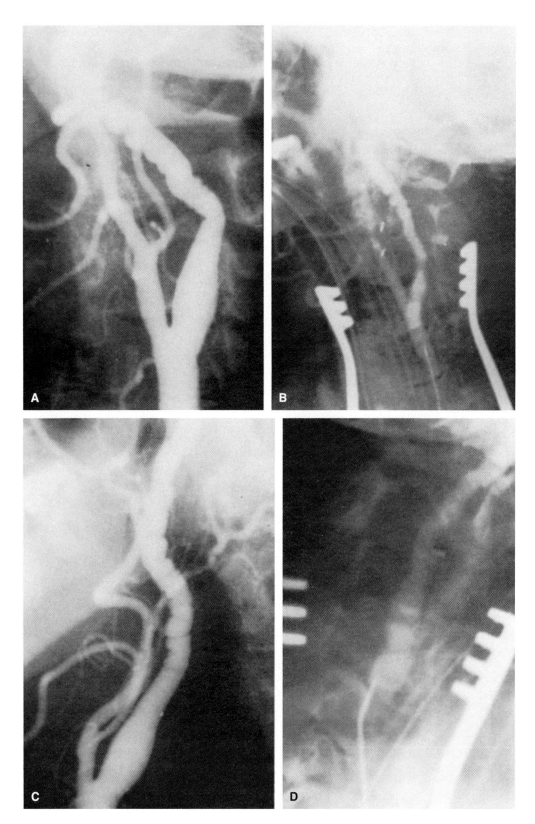

FIGURE 137-44 A, Preoperative left common carotid angiogram showing multiple diaphragm-like stenoses of fibromuscular dysplasia. **B,** Intraoperative completion angiogram following two attempts at dilation using rigid dilators, documenting the presence of residual stenoses and irregularities. **C,** Preoperative right common carotid angiogram documenting similar lesions. **D,** Intraoperative completion angiogram following dilation using transluminal balloon angioplasty catheter, showing no significant residual stenoses.

head and neck surgery, and unusually high carotid bifurcations. Because carotid endarterectomy can be accomplished with either general anesthesia or local anesthesia and mild conscious sedation also means that almost no patients are too ill to undergo this procedure. This fact reinforces the attitude of both the surgeons and the radiologists.

Interventional cardiologists, in contrast, have been the major proponents in this area, often to the dismay of their surgical and radiologic colleagues. Of particular concern to their colleagues was the fact that many patients were initially routed toward angioplasty and stenting simply as a result of referral patterns that did not include either surgeons or radiologists in the evaluation or management decisions. The early and dramatic surge in enthusiasm for this procedure among interventional cardiologists was viewed as a matter of some concern by their colleagues in other specialties as well as third-party payers. Indeed, the once numerous 1- and 2-day courses given as "how-to" sessions, with many of the proponents presenting their material in a "don't try this at home" manner that actually encouraged exactly that sort of approach, did nothing to alleviate this concern. Fortunately, reason and genuine scientific investigation have largely replaced the initial "anything goes" enthusiasm and the techniques are now the subjects of collaborative well-designed, mutispecialty clinical investigations that fortunately transcend the old turf lines.

Leaving the thorny, albeit significant, turf issues aside, carotid angioplasty is certainly a technique that now deserves substantive critical evaluation (Fig. 137-45). Prior to the advent of distal protection devices, it seemed unlikely to be a technique that could compete solely on its technical merits. Early reports from capable individuals indicated complication rates (significant neurologic deficits and death) ranging from 5% to 7%, in contrast to surgical carotid endarterectomy in which stroke complication rates of 1% to 2% are the norm. However, critical comparisons using a combined adverse event measure (death, stroke, and myocardial infarction) show that the overall complication rates for carotid angioplasty/stenting with distal protection actually tend to be significantly lower for angioplasty/stenting than endarterectomy, owing in part to the higher incidence of cardiovascular morbidity in the surgery cohort. Long-term follow-up data are still largely unavailable, making durability of an initially favorable result an important unknown.

With the universal switch to low-profile catheter and guide wire systems that occurred a few years ago and the development of a number of different investigational distal protection devices designed to eliminate the almost inevitable, although not always clinically apparent, downstream embolization that occurs with endovascular carotid interventions, carotid angioplasty/stenting has gained a new maturity as a clinical technique. Now that the technology has matured, a number of prospective, randomized trials have been undertaken in an effort to put the technique on a solid intellectual footing so that the real merits vis-à-vis conventional surgery can be determined scientifically. The Stenting and Angioplasty with Protection

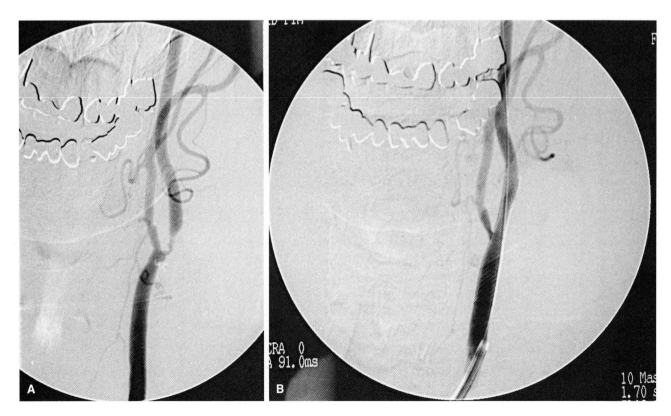

FIGURE 137-45 **A,** Left carotid angiogram showing high-grade stenosis in the proximal internal carotid artery, which recurred after two prior carotid endarterectomies. **B,** Angiogram following balloon catheter angioplasty and deployment of a self-expanding stent (Wallstent).

in Patients at High Risk for Endarterectomy (SAPPHIRE) trial, which compared the short-term results of carotid angioplasty/stenting with distal protection to endarterectomy in high-risk patients, showed a clear and significant advantage to the endovascular approach. Similarly, preliminary results of the Carotid Revascularization Endarterectomy Versus Stent Trial (CREST) and Acculink for Revascularization of Carotids in High-Risk Patients Registry (ARCHeR) have also tended to support the efficacy and safety of the technique, at least in the short term, especially in high-risk patients.

In the previous edition of this text the statement was made that "one can only speculate as to how this issue will be resolved and whether carotid angioplasty and stenting will merit a brief historical footnote or its own chapter in the next edition of this textbook." It is now clear that this is an important and promising area of clinical investigation with a high likelihood of permanently altering the approach to treatment of occlusive carotid artery disease. (See Chapter 140 for a more thorough discussion of this significant and rapidly evolving technique.)

■ A SIGNIFICANT PARADIGM SHIFT

Since the last edition of this text, there has been a significant shift in the role of angiography as it applies to the investigation and treatment of cerebrovascular disease, especially the occlusive carotid artery type. Angiography is no longer a routine first-line technique; noninvasive imaging employing varying choices of ultrasound, MR angiography, and CT angiography, depending on local resources, is now the standard of care in many situations. Angiography is already, or will surely soon become, a second-line investigation aimed primarily toward dealing with complex diagnostic problems not adequately handled by the noninvasive imaging modalities. In addition, routine use of endovascular interventions in the treatment of intracranial AVMs and aneurysms as well as the advent of second-generation approaches to carotid artery angioplasty/stenting, especially low-profile systems and distal protection devices, have also shifted the focus in angiography from diagnosis to treatment.

■ REFERENCES

1. Ahuja A, Blatt GL, Guterman LR, Hopkins LN: Angioplasty for symptomatic radiation-induced extracranial carotid artery stenosis: Case report. Neurosurgery 36:399-403, 1995.
2. Appleyard RF, Cohn LH: Myocardial stunning and reperfusion injury in cardiac surgery. J Card Surg 8(2 Suppl):316-324, 1993.
3a. Asif A, Preston RA, Roth D: Radiocontrast-induced nephropathy. Am J Ther 10:137-147, 2003.
3. Arlart I, Bongartz GM: Magnetic Resonance Angiography. Darmstadt, Springer-Verlag, 1996.
4. Babatasi G, Massetti M, Theron J, Khayat A: Asymptomatic carotid stenosis in patients undergoing major cardiac surgery: Can percutaneous carotid angioplasty be an alternative? Eur J Cardiothorac Surg 11:547-553, 1997.
5. Baker CS, Wragg A, Kumar S, et al: A rapid protocol for the prevention of contrast-induced renal dysfunction: The RAPPID study. J Am Coll Cardiol 41:2114-2118, 2003.
6. Balousek PA, Knowles HJ, Higashida RT, del Zoppo GJ: New interventions in cerebrovascular disease: The role of thrombolytic therapy and balloon angioplasty. Opin Cardiol 11:550-557, 1996.
7. Baum S, Abrams HL (eds): Abrams Angiography: Vascular and Interventional Radiology. Philadelphia, Lippincott-Raven, 1996.
8. Ben-Menachem Y: Angiography in Trauma: A Work Atlas. Philadelphia, WB Saunders, 1981.
9. Bergeon P, Rudondy P, Benichou H, et al: Transluminal angioplasty for recurrent stenosis after carotid endarterectomy: Prognostic factors and indications. Int Angiol 12:256-259, 1993.
10. Berry E, Kelly S, Westwood ME, et al: The cost-effectiveness of magnetic resonance angiography for carotid artery stenosis and peripheral vascular disease: A systematic review. Health Technol Assess 6:1-155, 2002.
11. Bettmann MA, Katzen BT, Whisnant J, et al: Carotid stenting and angioplasty: A statement for healthcare professionals from the Councils on Cardiovascular Radiology, Stroke, Cardio-Thoracic and Vascular Surgery, Epidemiology, and Prevention, and Clinical Cardiology, American Heart Association. Stroke 29:336-338, 1998.
12. Buckberg GD: Update on current techniques of myocardial protection. Ann Thorac Surg 60:805-814, 1995.
13. Busch E, Kruger K, Allegrini PR, et al: Reperfusion after thrombolytic therapy of embolic stroke in the rat: Magnetic resonance and biochemical imaging. J Cereb Blood Flow Metab 18:407-418, 1998.
14. Cebul RD, Snow RJ, Pine R, et al: Indications, outcomes, and provider volumes for carotid endarterectomy. JAMA 279:1282-1287, 1998.
15. Chaturvedi S, Policherla PN, Femino L: Cerebral angiography practices at U.S. teaching hospitals: Implications for carotid endarterectomy. Stroke 28:1895-1897, 1997.
16. Chuang YM, Chao AC, Teng MM, et al: Use of CT angiography in patient selection for thrombolytic therapy. Am J Emerg Med 21:167-172, 2003.
17. Cloft HJ, Jensen ME, Kallmes DF, Dion JE: Arterial dissections complicating cerebral angiography and cerebrovascular interventions. AJNR Am J Neuroradiol 21:541-545, 2000.
18. Comerota AJ, Eze AR: Intraoperative high-dose regional urokinase infusion for cerebrovascular occlusion after carotid endarterectomy. J Vasc Surg 24:1008-1016, 1996.
19. del Zoppo GJ, Higashida RT, Furlan AJ, et al: PROACT: A phase II randomized trial of recombinant pro-urokinase by direct arterial delivery in acute middle cerebral artery stroke. PROACT Investigators. Prolyse in Acute Cerebral Thromboembolism. Stroke 29:4-11, 1998.
20. del Zoppo GJ: Thrombolysis in acute stroke. Neurologia 10(Suppl 2):37-47, 1995.
21. Derdeyn CP, Powers WJ, Moran CJ, et al: Role of Doppler ultrasound in screening for carotid atherosclerotic disease. Radiology 197:635-643, 1995.
22. Dorros G: Carotid stenting: A gordian knot to be unraveled. J Invasive Cardiol 15:139-144, 2003.
23. Elgersma OE, Buijs PC, Wust AF, et al: Maximum internal carotid arterial stenosis: Assessment with rotational angiography versus conventional intraarterial digital subtraction angiography. Radiology 213:777-783, 1999.
24. Executive Committee for the Asymptomatic Carotid Atherosclerosis Study: Endarterectomy for asymptomatic carotid artery stenosis. JAMA 273:1421-1428, 1995.
25. Ferguson RD, Ferguson JG: Carotid angioplasty: In search of a worthy alternative to endarterectomy. Arch Neurol 53:696-698, 1996.
26. Fujitani RM, Kafie F: Screening and preoperative imaging of candidates for carotid endarterectomy. Semin Vasc Surg 12:261-274, 1999.
27. Gagne PJ, Matchett J, MacFarland D, et al: Can the NASCET technique for measuring carotid stenosis be reliably applied outside the trial? J Vasc Surg 24:449-455, 1996.
28. Gasecki AP, Ferguson GG, Eliasziw M, et al: Early endarterectomy for severe carotid artery stenosis after a nondisabling stroke: Results from the North American Symptomatic Carotid Endarterectomy Trial. J Vasc Surg 20:288-295, 1994.
29. Golledge J, Wright R, Pugh N, Lane IF: Colour-coded duplex assessment alone before carotid endarterectomy. Br J Surg 83:1234-1237, 1996.

30. Hacke W, Kaste M, Fieschi C, et al: Intravenous thrombolysis with recombinant tissue plasminogen activator for acute hemispheric stroke: The European Cooperative Acute Stroke Study. JAMA 274:1017-1025, 1995.

31. Handa J, Handa H: Progressive cerebral arterial occlusive disease: Analysis of 27 cases. Neuroradiology 3:119, 1974.

32. Higashida RT, Tsai FY, Halbach VV, et al: Interventional neurovascular techniques in the treatment of stroke: State-of-the-art therapy. Intern Med 237:105-115, 1995.

33. Ishikawa K: Natural history and classification of occlusive thromboarthropathy (Takayasu's disease). Circulation 57:27, 1978.

34. Jayakrishnan VK, White PM, Aitken D, et al: Subtraction helical CT angiography of intracranial and extracranial vessels: Technical considerations and preliminary experience. AJNR Am J Neuroradiol 24:451-455, 2003.

35. Johnston DC, Goldstein LB: Clinical carotid endarterectomy decision making: Noninvasive vascular imaging versus angiography. Neurology 56:1009-1015, 2001.

36. Jordan WD Jr, Roye GD, Fisher WS III, et al: A cost comparison of balloon angioplasty and stenting versus endarterectomy for the treatment of carotid artery stenosis. J Vasc Surg 27:16-22, 1998.

37. Jordan WD Jr, Schroeder PT, Fisher WS, McDowell HA: A comparison of angioplasty with stenting versus endarterectomy for the treatment of carotid artery stenosis. Ann Vasc Surg 11:2-8, 1997.

38. Kachel R: Results of balloon angioplasty in the carotid arteries. J Endovasc Surg 3:22-30, 1996.

39. Kadir S: Diagnostic Angiography. Philadelphia, WB Saunders, 1986.

40. Kadir S: Atlas of Normal and Variant Angiographic Anatomy. Philadelphia, WB Saunders, 1991.

41. Kent KC, Kuntz KM, Patel MR, et al: Perioperative imaging strategies for carotid endarterectomy: An analysis of morbidity and cost-effectiveness in symptomatic patients. JAMA 274:888-893, 1995.

42. Kini AS, Mitre CA, Kim M, et al: A protocol for prevention of radiographic contrast nephropathy during percutaneous coronary intervention: Effect of selective dopamine receptor agonist fenoldopam. Cathet Cardiovasc Interv 55:169-173, 2002.

43. Kwiatkowski TG, Libman RB, Frankel M, et al: Effects of tissue plasminogen activator for acute ischemic stroke at one year. National Institute of Neurological Disorders and Stroke rt-PA Stroke Study Group. N Engl J Med 340:1781, 1999.

44. Landis DM, Tarr RW, Selman WR: Thrombolysis for acute ischemic stroke. Neurosurg Clin North Am 8:219-226, 1997.

45. Lanzer P, Rösch J: Vascular Diagnostics. Darmstadt, Springer-Verlag, 1994.

46. Lautin EM, Freeman NJ, Schoenfeld AH, et al: Radiocontrast-associated renal dysfunction: A comparison of lower-osmolality and conventional high-osmolality contrast media. AJR Am J Roentgenol 157:59-65, 1991. [erratum in: AJR Am J Roentgenol 157:895, 1991].

47. Lee TT, Solomon NA, Heidenreich PA, et al: Cost-effectiveness of screening for carotid stenosis in asymptomatic persons. Ann Intern Med 126:337-346, 1997.

48. Link J, Brossmann J, Grabener M, et al: Spiral CT angiography and selective digital subtraction angiography of internal carotid artery stenosis. AJNR Am J Neuroradiol 17:89-94, 1996.

49. Link J, Brossmann J, Penselin V, et al: Common carotid artery bifurcation: Preliminary results of CT angiography and color-coded duplex sonography compared with digital subtraction angiography. AJR Am J Roentgenol 168:361-365, 1997.

50. Magarelli N, Scarabino T, Simeone AL, et al: Carotid stenosis: A comparison between MR and spiral CT angiography. Neuroradiology 40:367-373, 1998.

51. Mani RL, Eisenberg RL, McDonald EJ, et al: Complications of catheter cerebral angiography: Analysis of 5000 procedures: I. Criteria and incidence. AJR Am J Roentgenol 131:861, 1978.

52. Marek J, Mills JL, Harvich J, et al: Utility of routine carotid duplex screening in patients who have claudication. Vasc Surg 24:572-577, 1996.

53. Mathur A, Dorros G, Iyer SS, et al: Palmaz stent compression in patients following carotid artery stenting. Cathet Cardiovasc Diagn 41:137-140, 1997.

54. Mathur VS, Swan SK, Lambrecht LJ, et al: The effects of fenoldopam, a selective dopamine receptor agonist, on systemic and renal hemodynamics in normotensive subjects. Crit Care Med 27:1832-1837, 1999.

55. Matillon Y (ed): MR-angiography, CT-angiography, and Doppler ultrasonography in preoperative investigation of proximal stenosis of the cervical internal carotid artery. National Agency for Accreditation and Evaluation in Health, Government of France, June 2001.

56. McMinn RMH, Hutchings RT, Logan BM: Color Atlas of Head and Neck Anatomy. St. Louis, Mosby-Year Book, 1994.

57. Mintz EP, Gruberg L: Radiocontrast-induced nephropathy and percutaneous coronary intervention: A review of preventive measures. Expert Opin Pharmacother 4:639-652, 2003.

58. Moll R, Dinkel HP: Value of the CT angiography in the diagnosis of common carotid artery bifurcation disease: CT angiography versus digital subtraction angiography and color-flow Doppler. Eur J Radiol 39:155-162, 2001.

59. Mori E, Tabuchi M, Yoshida T, Yamadori A: Intracarotid urokinase with thromboembolic occlusion of the middle cerebral artery. Stroke 19:802-812, 1988.

60. Muller M, Bartylla K, Rolshausen A, et al: Influence of the angiographic internal carotid artery stenosis assessment method on indicating carotid surgery. Vasa 27:24-28, 1998.

61. Murphy KJ, Rubin JM: Power Doppler: It's a good thing. Semin Ultrasound CT MR 18:13-21, 1997.

62. Nederkoorn PJ, Elgersma OE, Mali WP, et al: Overestimation of carotid artery stenosis with magnetic resonance angiography compared with digital subtraction angiography. J Vasc Surg 36:806-813, 2002.

63. Nederkoorn PJ, Mali WP, Eikelboom BC, et al: Preoperative diagnosis of carotid artery stenosis: Accuracy of noninvasive testing. Stroke 33:2003-2008, 2002.

64. Nederkoorn PJ, van der Graaf Y, Eikelboom BC, et al: Time-of-flight MR angiography of carotid artery stenosis: Does a flow void represent severe stenosis? AJNR Am J Neuroradiol 23:1779-1784, 2002.

65. Nederkoorn PJ, van der Graaf Y, Hunink MG: Duplex ultrasound and magnetic resonance angiography compared with digital subtraction angiography in carotid artery stenosis: A systematic review. Stroke 34:1324-1332, 2003.

66. Osborn AG: Diagnostic Neuroradiology. St. Louis, Mosby-Year Book, 1999.

67. Padayachee TS, Cox TC, Modaresi KB, et al: The measurement of internal carotid artery stenosis: Comparison of duplex with digital subtraction angiography. Eur J Vasc Endovasc Surg 13:180-185, 1997.

68. Paddock-Eliasziw LM, Eliasziw M, Barr HW, Barnett HJ: Long-term prognosis and the effect of carotid endarterectomy in patients with recurrent ipsilateral ischemic events. North American Symptomatic Carotid Endarterectomy Trial Group. Neurology 47:1158-1162, 1996.

69. Patel SG, Collie DA, Wardlaw JM, et al: Outcome, observer reliability, and patient preferences if CTA, MRA, or Doppler ultrasound were used, individually or together, instead of digital subtraction angiography before carotid endarterectomy. J Neurol Neurosurg Psychiatry 73:21-28, 2002.

70. Phillips CD, Bubash LA: CT angiography and MR angiography in the evaluation of extracranial carotid vascular disease. Radiol Clin North Am 40:783-798, 2002.

71. Romanes GJ (ed): Cunningham's Manual of Practical Anatomy: Head, Neck, and Brain. London, Oxford University Press, 1986.

72. Roubin GS, Yadav S, Iyer SS, Vitek J: Carotid stent-supported angioplasty: A neurovascular intervention to prevent stroke. Am J Cardiol 78:8-12, 1996.

73. Schmidt WA, Kraft HE, Vorpahl K, et al: Color-duplex ultrasonography in the diagnosis of temporal arteritis. N Engl J Med 337:1336-1342, 1997.

74. Sivaguru A, Venables GS, Beard JD, Gaines PA: European Carotid Angioplasty Trial. J Endovasc Surg 3:16-20, 1996.

75. Skolnick AA: Rapid clot-dissolving drugs promising for stroke. JAMA 269:195-198, 1993.
76. Smith DC, Smith LL, Hasso AN: Fibromuscular dysplasia of the internal carotid artery treated by operative transluminal balloon angioplasty. Radiology 155:645, 1985.
77. Stark DD, Bradley WG (eds): Magnetic Resonance Imaging, 3rd ed. St. Louis, Mosby-Year Book, 1999.
78. Steinke W, Ries S, Artemis N, et al: Power Doppler imaging of carotid artery stenosis: Comparison with color-Doppler flow imaging and angiography. Stroke 28:1981-1987, 1997.
79. Streifler JY, Eliasziw M, Fox AJ, et al: Angiographic detection of carotid plaque ulceration: Comparison with surgical observations in a multicenter study. North American Symptomatic Carotid Endarterectomy Trial. Stroke 25:1130-1132, 1994.
80. The EC/IC Bypass Study Group: Failure of extracranial-intracranial arterial bypass to reduce the risk of ischemic stroke. N Engl J Med 313:1191, 1985.
81. Theron JG, Payelle GG, Coskun O, et al: Carotid artery stenosis: Treatment with protected balloon angioplasty and stent placement. Radiology 201:627-636, 1996.
82. Townsend TC, Saloner D, Pan XM, Rapp JH: Contrast material-enhanced MRA overestimates severity of carotid stenosis, compared with 3D time-of-flight MRA. J Vasc Surg 8:36-44, 2003.
83. Vale FL, Fisher WS III, Jordan WD Jr, et al: Carotid endarterectomy performed after progressive carotid stenosis following angioplasty and stent placement: Case report. J Neurosurg 87:940-943, 1997.
84. Vanninen RL, Manninen HI, Partanen PK, et al: How should we estimate carotid stenosis using magnetic resonance angiography? Neuroradiology 38:299-305, 1996.
85. Westwood ME, Kelly S, Berry E, et al: Use of magnetic resonance angiography to select candidates with recently symptomatic carotid stenosis for surgery: Systematic review. BMJ 324:198, 2002.
86. Westwood ME, Kelly S, Berry E, et al: Use of magnetic resonance angiography to select candidates with recently symptomatic carotid stenosis for surgery: Systematic review. BMJ 324:198, 2002.
87. Wikstrom J, Johansson LO, Rossitti S, et al: High-resolution carotid artery MRA: Comparison with fast dynamic acquisition and duplex ultrasound scanning. Acta Radiol 43:256-261, 2002.
88. Wildermuth S, Knauth M, Brandt T, et al: Role of CT angiography in patient selection for thrombolytic therapy in acute hemispheric stroke. Stroke 29:935-938, 1998.
89. Willinsky RA, Taylor SM, TerBrugge K, et al: Neurologic complications of cerebral angiography: Prospective analysis of 2,899 procedures and review of the literature. Radiology 227:522-528, 2003.
90. Yadav JS, Roubin GS, Iyer S, et al: Elective stenting of extracranial carotid arteries. Circulation 95:376-338, 1997.
91. Yin D, Carpenter JP: Cost-effectiveness of screening for asymptomatic carotid stenosis. J Vasc Surg 27:245-255, 1998.
92. Yuh EL, Jeffrey RB Jr, Birdwell RL, et al: Virtual endoscopy using perspective volume-rendered three-dimensional sonographic data: Technique and clinical applications. AJR Am J Roentgenol 172:1193-1197, 1999.

Chapter

The Role of Noninvasive Studies in the Diagnosis and Management of Cerebrovascular Disease

138

MICHAEL A. RICCI, MD
MARYANNE WATERS, RN, RVT
DEBORAH PEATE, RVT

Carotid endarterectomy (CEA) has been proven efficacious for both symptomatic and asymptomatic internal carotid artery (ICA) stenosis,[1-4] and carotid stents[5] are also showing some promise. The need for accurate, safe screening and diagnosis of carotid bifurcation disease has become even more important. Concepts once thought to be unassailable, such as pre-endarterectomy contrast angiography, are now being challenged.[6] Yet, a multitude of diagnostic tests, combinations of tests, diagnostic algorithms, and opinions may leave the student of vascular diseases bewildered and frustrated.

■ HISTORY OF NONINVASIVE TESTING

A complete history of the development of ultrasound technologies for cerebrovascular diagnosis was documented by Strandness in 1993.[7] The clinical use of ultrasound for vascular diagnosis began in the mid-1960s when a continuous-wave Doppler device was developed at the University of Washington and subsequently marketed as the *Dopotone*.[7] The device had a single transducer connected to a speaker to produce an audible output of the detected frequency shift, representing the presence or absence of blood flow. With some experience, the user could subjectively estimate the quality of the received signal as normal or abnormal. However, listeners could not be sure of the vessel they were interrogating since any vessel within the path of the ultrasound signal could be heard. An objective analog display was lacking and the direction of flow was unable to be determined. These obstacles were overcome by workers at the University of Washington[7] when changes in the direction of flow were recognized as positive and negative Doppler frequency shifts, which could be separated electronically. Twenty-five years later, the inability to detect flow direction seems inconceivable, but

Section

XX

the use of this *pulsed Doppler* technique allowed the study of complex flow patterns, such as the pattern seen at the carotid bulb, which ultimately had clinical diagnostic implications.

Early clinical use of the *Doppler flowmeter* was suggested by Brockenbrough.[8] Through a sequence of maneuvers, the periorbital Doppler examination evaluated the direction of flow in branches of the ophthalmic artery (OA) and collateral vessels to predict ICA stenosis. Unfortunately, this simple, inexpensive test did not prove reliable enough for all users. The fundamental principle was sound, however, and forms the basis of today's transcranial Doppler (TCD) examinations.

To gain widespread acceptance, two additional innovations were needed for the advancement of ultrasound for clinical use. The first was a successful means to convert Doppler frequency shifts to an analog form, fast Fourier transform spectral analysis; and the second was successful imaging of the vascular system with B-mode or gray-scale ultrasound, which forms the basis of the modern *duplex scanner*. Many technical electronic modifications followed that improved the image, Doppler ultrasound quality, and reproducibility of testing, while clinicians defined diagnostic criteria and expanded indications for its use.

The next significant advance came in the late 1970s with the development of color-flow imaging. Though the addition of color by itself does not add to the accuracy of diagnostic criteria, it does function as an aid in defining complex flow patterns. Tortuous vessels, flow disturbances, and even routine examinations are facilitated today by real-time color-flow patterns within the vessel under investigation. The present-day duplex scanner is built on 40 years of technical innovations and clinical experience that followed each innovation.

Ocular pneumoplethysmography (OPG) is another non-invasive test developed in the 1970s to indirectly diagnose carotid artery stenosis. Two different OPG methods have been used.[9,10] Kartchner and associates[9] developed a method, later known as *OPG-Kartchner*, to detect the arrival of the pulse wave in the eye. A stenosis on one side would introduce a delay in the arrival of the pulse wave. Using fluid-filled eye cups held in place with 40 to 50 mm Hg of suction and photodetectors on each earlobe, a delay in the arrival of one pulse wave compared to the contralateral eye would indicate a unilateral stenosis of 70% or more. A delay in both eyes compared to the earlobes would indicate a bilateral stenosis. Though initial studies were promising,[9] this method fell out of use, suffering from the inaccuracies inherent in any indirect test.

The second method, *OPG-Gee*, was also developed around the same time but used an entirely different methodology.[10] This method measured the OA pressure by applying sustained pressure to fluid-filled eyecups. The OPG-Gee test was abnormal if a difference in OA pressure of 5 mm Hg or more between the eyes was observed, if the pressure difference was between 1 and 4 mm Hg and the ratio of the OA pressure to the brachial pressure was less than 0.66, or if the pressures in each eye were equal and the ratio was less than 0.6. This indirect test also showed excellent results[11] and was used commonly for screening and as a monitor during carotid surgery. However, OPG-Gee also suffered from the inadequacies of indirect testing and was replaced by duplex scanning in routine clinical practice.

Other minimally invasive techniques also have been used that improved the diagnosis of extracranial carotid disease, such as intravenous digital subtraction angiography (IVDSA). Because IVDSA avoided an arterial puncture and outpatient examinations (at a time when intra-arterial angiography still necessitated a hospital admission), there were lower costs and no risk of arterial complications. Initial interest waned, however, because of large contrast loads and unsatisfactory images in a substantial number of patients.[12] More recent techniques of IVDSA have superior images; however, the reliability and low cost of duplex scanning have supplanted the need for IVDSA.

Other minimally invasive techniques using spiral or helical computed tomographic angiography (CTA)[13] or magnetic resonance angiography (MRA)[14] have been examined as additional methods to evaluate the carotid system. CTA requires contrast injection, whereas MRA may be performed with or without non-ionic contrast agents, as discussed later in this chapter.

■ DUPLEX SCANNING

Equipment

A pivotal improvement to cerebrovascular diagnosis is the modern duplex scanner, which produces gray-scale images, velocity spectral analysis, and color-flow images. A bare minimum modern ultrasound system consists of a color monitor, a computer processor to manage the huge volume of data and calculations generated by scanning, and ultrasound transducers of different frequencies. Although most ultrasound systems automatically preset the system settings to optimize performance based on the selected transducer and test to be performed, adjustments may be made to the pulse repetition frequency, gain, and power depending on circumstances. The transducer's transmitting frequency may vary from 2.5 to 12.0 MHz, with the lower frequencies allowing greater tissue penetration. For cerebrovascular examinations, usually a 5.0- or 7.5-MHz frequency is selected.

Strandness[15] listed the essential system elements for cerebrovascular duplex as (1) high-resolution images; (2) a small Doppler sample volume, about 3 mm³ at an operating range of 25 mm, to permit sampling in four sites across the vessel; (3) real-time spectral analysis that permits a display from −3 kHz to +7 kHz; (4) hard copy output for image and spectral analysis; (5) automatic display of the angle of incidence of the Doppler ultrasound beam; and (6) conversion of frequency to angle-adjusted velocity.

Technique

A thorough understanding of the anatomy of the carotid artery system (see Chapter 137) as well as Doppler physics (see Chapter 16), hemodynamics, and physiology and physiology (see Chapter 9) is necessary before beginning a duplex scan. With the examiner at the head, patients should be positioned supine with their head turned away from the side being examined. The examination should include both longitudinal and transverse views throughout. Scanning with the 5.0- or 7.5-MHz transducer should begin low in the neck with the common carotid artery (CCA) and proceed distally to the carotid bulb, external carotid artery (ECA), and ICA. Each step in the examination sequence should be carried out in the same fashion each time to be sure no step is left out. At each level, the spectral velocity analysis, color-flow pattern, and gray-scale image are analyzed. After completion of the carotid system examination, the transducer is rocked posteriorly to look for the vertebral artery (VA). Direction of flow and velocity in this vessel should be recorded. The examination is then repeated on the opposite side.

The color-flow pattern simplifies the examination and may help identify suspicious areas. The presence of a *jet*, a focal color change indicating very high velocities, can identify an area of stenosis to be interrogated with Doppler spectral analysis. A color change indicating reversed flow at the end of systole is normal in the CCA, ECA, and ICA bulb, but more pronounced color changes or a "mosaic" of colors may indicate turbulence in the region of a stenosis. In the vertebral system, reversal of flow may indicate a pathologic obstruction of the subclavian artery. Sometimes turbulence created by a stenosis may produce a *color bruit* as tissue adjacent to the artery reverberates and creates pixels of color (indicating movement) outside the vessel.

The location of plaque should be noted, but estimates of the degree of stenosis based on the gray-scale image should be avoided. Advances in technology may eventually improve our ability to estimate stenosis from images alone. Beebe and coauthors,[16] in a prospective comparison of ultrasound images to angiography, showed a positive predictive value (PPV) of 94% with stenoses of 70% to 99%. In the CCA, significant plaque may occasionally be identified, but agreement regarding diagnostic criteria in the vessel is lacking. At the opposite end of the vessel, it is also important to identify the distal end of the plaque in the ICA to be sure that the lesion is completely surgically accessible, particularly if CEA is to be performed without angiography.

A search for ulcerations should be performed. Sometimes these are more easily seen with gray-scale imaging (without color). The ability to see ulcerations, however, is variable, and many authors have pointed out that duplex scanning is not a reliable method. Overall detection rates range in the 50th to 60th percentile compared to surgical specimens,[17,18] and color-flow imaging has not improved on this.[18] However, Comerota and colleagues[17] suggested that ulcerations may be more reliably detected when the degree of stenosis is less than 50%. In their experience, ulcers that were missed by both duplex scanning as well as angiography were more likely to be accompanying significant stenoses and have little impact on clinical decision making. The absence of ulceration on duplex scans[17,18] or arteriography[19] does not mean that an ulcer does not exist.

Additionally, during duplex scanning, the plaque characteristics (hard, calcific plaque, soft, hemorrhagic plaque, or heterogeneous plaque [which has elements of both]) should also be noted. Calcific plaque may prevent the transmission of ultrasound, creating shadowing artifacts. Some surgeons

think that plaque hemorrhage (producing soft plaque) places the patient at risk for stroke and that this finding should be considered when selecting patients for CEA.[20-22] Considerable variability may exist between examiners describing plaque morphology[23]; however, these findings should be interpreted with caution and validated within individual laboratories.

Although each of these aspects is important during the cerebrovascular duplex examination, the most important aspect of diagnosis is the spectral analysis. The B-mode or color image serves to direct the placement of the Doppler for sampling. Multiple samples from the midstream of the vessel being interrogated should routinely be obtained. The angle of incidence of the ultrasound beam should be kept at 60 degrees or less. Any subsequent scans should be performed at the same angle. Spectral analysis should first be obtained low in the CCA and in its mid and distal portions, in the ECA, through the carotid bulb, and throughout the ICA. Specific parameters to be recorded include peak systolic velocity (PSV), end diastolic velocity (EDV), the ratio of the PSV in the ICA and CCA (PSV ICA/CCA), and the ratio of the EDV in the ICA and CCA (EDV ICA/CCA). Obviously, any areas suspicious for stenosis on the basis of the color pattern should be thoroughly investigated. The spectral profile in the CCA typically demonstrates a mix of the low-resistance pattern seen in the ICA (flow through diastole) and the high-resistance pattern (no flow during diastole) of the ECA (Fig. 138-1). A high-resistance profile in the CCA may be the first clue to an ICA occlusion. As noted earlier, a brief flow reversal in the carotid bulb is a normal finding. In addition, there is a narrow spectrum of velocities in undiseased vessels known as a *spectral window* (see Fig. 138-1). Stenosis within the bulb and ICA produces turbulence that diminishes or obliterates the window with *spectral broadening*, one of the earlier signs of stenosis. Spectral broadening can also be artificially generated if the sample volume is too large or the sample is too close to the vessel wall (as opposed to midstream sample) or in tortuous vessels. In addition, if the gain is too high, the spectral window will be obliterated with artificially elevated velocities. The gain should be set to a minimal but discernable amount of background noise.

Diagnostic Criteria

Various criteria have been developed for the duplex diagnosis of carotid artery disease, but the two most commonly used are those from Strandness[15] or Zwiebel (Table 138-1).[24,25] Zwiebel indicated that more precise categorization of the degree of stenosis by duplex ultrasound was possible with the use of systolic and diastolic velocities as well as velocity ratios.[24] Strandness[15] reported a sensitivity of 99% and a specificity of 84%; Bandyk and coworkers[26] reported 96% accuracy using these criteria to detect stenosis greater than 50%, with 97% accuracy in the detection of occlusion. However, it is important that these criteria are validated in the individual vascular laboratory.[27-32] Whether the same ultrasound system is used in different laboratories[28,30] or if the same personnel use different systems,[27] it is clear that variations can be seen,

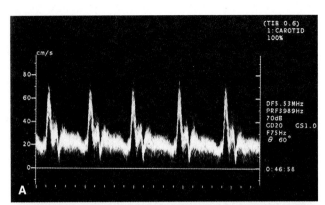

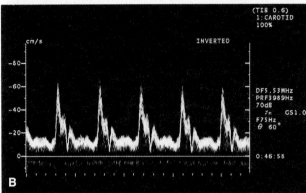

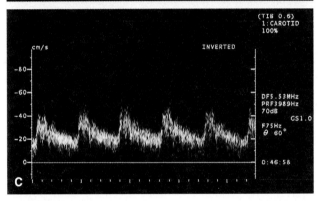

Table 138-1   Criteria for Duplex Diagnosis of ICA Stenosis

STRANDNESS CRITERIA[15]		ZWIEBEL CRITERIA[25]	
Stenosis, %	Characteristics	Stenosis, %	Characteristics
Normal	PSV < 125 cm/sec No SB Flow reversal in bulb	0	PSV < 110 cm/sec EDV < 40 cm/sec PSV ICA/CCA < 1.8 EDV ICA/CCA < 2.4 SB < 30 cm/sec
1-15	PSV < 125 cm/sec No or minimal SB Flow reversal in bulb absent	1-39	PSV < 110 cm/sec EDV < 40 cm/sec PSV ICA/CCA < 1.8 EDV ICA/CCA < 2.4 SB < 40 cm/sec
16-49	PSV > 125 cm/sec Marked SB	40-59	PSV < 130 cm/sec EDV < 40 cm/sec PSV ICA/CCA < 1.8 EDV ICA/CCA < 2.4 SB < 40 cm/sec

50-79	PSV > 125 cm/sec
	EDV < 140 cm/sec
		60-79	PSV > 130 cm/sec
			EDV > 40 cm/sec
			PSV ICA/CCA
			  > 1.8
			EDV ICA/CCA
			  > 2.4
			SB > 40 cm/sec

80-99	PSV > 125 cm/sec
	EDV > 140 cm/sec
		80-99	PSV > 250 cm/sec
			EDV > 100 cm/sec
			PSV ICA/CCA
			  > 3.7
			EDV ICA/CCA
			  > 5.5
			SB > 80 cm/sec

Occlusion	No flow	Occlusion	No flow

SB, spectral broadening; PSV, peak systolic velocity; EDV, end-diastolic velocity; ICA, internal carotid artery; CCA, common carotid artery.

FIGURE 138-1 Normal fast Fourier transform FFT spectral analysis patterns seen in the common (CCA) (**A**), external (ECA) (**B**), and internal (ICA) carotid arteries (**C**). The ECA demonstrates minimal flow during diastole, indicating a high-resistance peripheral vascular bed, and a prominent dicrotic notch. The ICA supplies the low-resistance bed in the brain and demonstrates flow throughout diastole. The CCA demonstrates a mix of the patterns from the ICA and ECA. Note the absence of signals below the peak velocities recorded in the ICA, an area known as the *spectral window.*

even when the same patients are scanned.[27] Efforts to improve upon existing diagnostic accuracy are continuously ongoing.[33-35] An abnormal carotid duplex is shown in Figure 138-2.

Criteria for identifying normal and abnormal VAs have also been determined and are listed in Table 138-2.[36] Others also have studied the VAs with duplex and found duplex scanning to be accurate and reproducible.[37-39] de Bray and coauthors[37] suggested that duplex scanning was a reasonable first step to evaluate patients who suffered vertebrobasilar strokes, reporting accuracy of 71% and a

specificity of 99% (for stenosis > 70%). These authors used ultrasound-derived diameter reduction or a segmental velocity increase of more than 20% rather than the criteria listed in Table 138-2.[37] Additional evaluation of vertebral lesions, particularly when planning surgery, requires conventional angiography.[40]

Special modification of the standard criteria is necessary in the presence of a contralateral severe stenosis (>70%) or complete occlusion. In this situation, flow through the ipsilateral carotid system is increased to compensate for the contralateral flow obstruction. van Everdingen and coworkers[41] measured volume flow in the ICA of symptomatic patients with MRA flow quantification. Those with high flow (2 SD greater than the mean of controls, equivalent to > 274 mL/min) had an increase in the PSV (statistically significant correlation coefficient of 0.75), compared with volume flow in the control group where flow was significantly increased in vessels with up to 69% stenosis when the contralateral ICA had a greater than

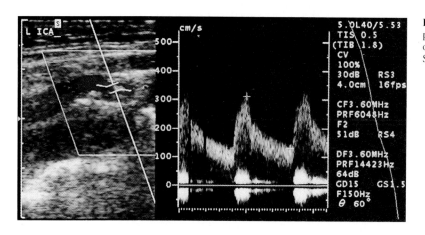

FIGURE 138-2 Abnormal carotid duplex with elevated peak systolic velocity of 309 cm/sec and diastolic velocity of 128 cm/sec consistent with 50% to 79% stenosis by Strandness criteria.

70% stenosis or occlusion. This led to an overestimation of the ipsilateral stenosis if standard velocity criteria are used.[41] Not surprisingly, flow may be increased in the ipsilateral or contralateral VA as well.[42] It is important that this phenomenon is recognized and accommodated, particularly when severe bilateral disease is present, since downgrading of a stenosis may follow CEA.[43]

Spadone and associates[44] first pointed out that the PSV and EDV was increased in the ICA contralateral to severe stenosis or occlusion. The effect was most prominent in the (ipsilateral) 50% to 79% category, but the correlations between velocity and stenosis were widely scattered. Subsequently, Fujitani and coworkers[45] modified the standard Strandness criteria (Table 138-3) after reviewing the duplex scans of 154 patients who had angiographic evidence of unilateral ICA occlusion. The modified criteria were 97.5% accurate in detecting 80% to 99% stenosis and 96.9% accurate in detecting 50% to 79% stenosis contra-lateral to ICA occlusion (Tables 138-3 and 138-4).

Slightly different criteria were developed by AbuRahma and coworkers,[46] who evaluated the Strandness criteria,[15] the criteria developed by Fujitani and coworkers,[45] and two additional modifications based on velocity or ICA/CCA ratios. AbuRahma and coworkers identified 356 arteries with more than 50% stenosis by duplex scanning. Angiography revealed stenosis ≥ 50% in 247 arteries: 97 had 80% to 99% stenosis and 39 had complete occlusion. They found that the Strandness criteria[15] were less reliable under these

conditions (see Table 138-4). Their results with the criteria of Fujitani and coworkers[45] were acceptable, but new PSV ICA/CCA ratios were unreliable (see Table 138-4). For 50% to 79% stenosis, the criteria of Fujitani and coworkers[45] and the authors' new criteria[46] were comparable with 97% accuracy with high sensitivity, specificity, and predictive values (see Table 138-4). For 80% to 99% stenosis, both criteria were good, with a slight edge in accuracy to the criteria of AbuRahma: 96% vs. 94%.[46] AbuRahma and coworkers[46] included both hemodynamically significant stenosis and occlusion in contrast to Fujitani and colleagues,[45] who only included occlusions. The former approach may actually have greater clinical applicability. Adoption of the criteria of AbuRahma[46] or Fujitani[45] is recommended, but individual laboratories should correlate their results, as emphasized earlier.

Another application that has prompted modifications to the standard diagnostic criteria is the desire to correlate duplex scanning with major clinical trials.[47] Since large-scale clinical trials of CEA have shown the benefit of the procedure in both symptomatic patients[1,2] with greater than 70% ICA stenosis and asymptomatic patients[3] with greater than 60% stenosis, several authors have tried to correlate duplex with these results.[29,48-54] The European Carotid Surgery Trialist (ECST)[1] and North American Symptomatic Carotid Endarterectomy Trial (NASCET)[2] studies, which concluded that CEA was effective for symptomatic patients with ICA stenosis ≥ 70%, used different measurements of angiographic stenosis. The NASCET measured the residual lumen at the point of maximal stenosis within the ICA with reference to the normal distal ICA beyond the bulb. The ECST study measured the same residual lumen of the ICA compared to the estimated diameter of the carotid bulb. The same stenosis measured by the NASCET method would produce a more severe stenosis than the ECST method. The Asymptomatic Carotid Atherosclerosis Study (ACAS)[3] of CEA in asymptomatic patients used the same measurement technique as NASCET. Thus, these randomized trials used cutoff values that were different than the widely used duplex diagnostic criteria (see Table 138-1).

To reconcile these differences, Moneta and coworkers[51] reviewed 184 patent ICAs that were scanned within 1 week of angiography, with the degree of stenosis measured by the NASCET method. Though they measured several criteria,

Table 138-2	Criteria for Duplex Diagnosis of Vertebral Artery Stenosis[36]	
HEMODYNAMIC ASSESSMENT	**DOPPLER SIGNAL QUALITY**	**SYSTOLIC VELOCITY**
Strong	Good	>40 cm/sec
Normal	Good	20-40 cm/sec
Moderately damped	Fair, systolic damping	12-20 cm/sec
Severely damped	Poor, nearly absent	<12 cm/sec
Occlusion	Absent	0
Subclavian steal	Fair to good, blood pressure cuff on ipsilateral arm reverses flow	Reversed

Table 138-3   Criteria for Diagnosis of ICA Stenosis with Contralateral Severe Stenosis or Occlusion

	CRITERIA			
STENOSIS, %	Strandness[15]	Fujitani et al[45]	AbuRahma et al[46]	Carotid Ratios[46]
Normal	PSV < 125 cm/sec No SB Flow reversal in bulb	PSV < 125 cm/sec No SB	PSV < 125 cm/sec No SB	PSV < 125 cm/sec No SB
1-15	PSV < 125 cm/sec No or minimal SB Flow reversal in bulb absent	PSV < 125 cm/sec Minimal SB	PSV < 125 cm/sec Minimal SB	ICA/CCA PSV < 1.5
16-49	PSV > 125 cm/sec Marked SB	PSV > 125 cm/sec EDV < 155 cm/sec Minimal SB	PSV < 140 cm/sec EDV < 140 cm/sec	ICA/CCA PSV < 1.5
50-79	PSV > 125 cm/sec EDV < 140 cm/sec	PSV > 140 cm/sec EDV < 155 cm/sec Marked SB	PSV ≥ 140 cm/sec EDV < 140 cm/sec	ICA/CCA PSV ≥ 1.5 EDV < 100 cm/sec
80-99	PSV > 125 cm/sec EDV > 140 cm/sec	PSV > 140 cm/sec EDV > 155 cm/sec Marked SB	PSV > 140 cm/sec EDV > 140 cm/sec	ICA/CCA PSV ≥ 1.8 EDV > 100 cm/sec
Occlusion	No flow	No flow	No flow	No flow

SB, spectral broadening; PSV, peak systolic velocity; EDV, end-diastolic velocity; CCA, common carotid artery; ICA, internal carotid artery.

Modified from Ricci MA: The changing role of duplex scan in the management of carotid bifurcation disease and endarterectomy. Semin Vasc Surg 11:3-11, 1998.

Table 138-4   Accuracy of Modified Duplex Diagnostic Criteria with Contralateral Severe Stenosis or Occlusion

AUTHOR	CRITERIA	ACCURACY, %	SENSITIVITY, %	SPECIFICITY, %	PPV, %	NPV, %
50-79% Stenosis						
Fujitani[45]	Fujitani: PSV > 140 cm/sec, EDV < 155 cm/sec	71	84	70	28	97
AbuRahma[46]	Fujitani: PSV > 140 cm/sec, EDV < 155 cm/sec	97	99	98	98	95
	Strandness: PSV > 125 cm/sec, EDV < 140 cm/sec	83	100	56	78	100
	AbuRahma: PSV ≥ 140 cm/sec, EDV < 100 cm/sec	97	97	98	99	95
	Ratios: ICA/CCA ≥ 1.5, EDV < 100 cm/sec	76	96	44	73	86
80-99% Stenosis						
Fujitani[45]	Fujitani: PSV > 140 cm/sec, EDV > 155 cm/sec	96	91	97	89	98
AbuRahma[46]	Fujitani: PSV > 140 cm/sec, EDV > 155 cm/sec	94	96	92	92	96
	Strandness: PSV > 125 cm/sec, EDV > 140 cm/sec	76	100	53	68	100
	AbuRahma: PSV > 140 cm/sec, EDV > 140 cm/sec	96	100	92	92	100
	Ratios: ICA/CCA ≥ 1.8, EDV > 100 cm/sec	71	96	47	64	92
All >50% Stenosis						
Fujitani[45]	Fujitani	74	97	57	62	96
	Fujitani	92	88	100	100	83
	Strandness	74	100	33	71	100
	AbuRahma	97	96	100	100	94
	Ratios	77	100	40	73	100

PSV, peak systolic velocity; PPV, positive predictive value; NPV, negative predictive value; EDV, end-diastolic velocity; ICA, internal carotid artery; CCA, common carotid artery.

Modified from Ricci MA: The changing role of duplex scan in the management of carotid bifurcation disease and endarterectomy. Semin Vasc Surg 11:3-11, 1998.

the maximum accuracy to determine 70% to 99% ICA stenosis was 88% accurate with PSV $\geq$ 325 cm/sec or ICA/CCA $\geq$ 4.0. Of these, they recommended the use of the ICA/CCA $\geq$ 4.0 as the best predictor of 70% to 99% angiographic stenosis because of the greater sensitivity (91% vs. 83%). Faught and coworkers[50] used a PSV $\geq$ 130 cm/sec and EDV $\geq$ 100 cm/sec and found 95% accuracy in detecting 70% to 99% ICA stenosis with those criteria in a retrospective review of 770 carotid bifurcations. They validated these criteria in a prospective study as well.[48] Neale and coworkers[29] used another set of criteria (PSV $\geq$ 270 cm/sec and EDV $\geq$ 110 cm/sec) and found an accuracy of 93% and sensitivity of 96%. AbuRahma and coinvestigators[52] detected 70% to 99% stenosis by using a PSV $\geq$ 150 cm/sec and an EDV of $\geq$ 90 cm/sec. They had an accuracy of 92%, a PPV of 91%, and a negative predictive value of 92%. Since each of these investigations reported excellent results, the decision is left to individual vascular laboratories to select and, as noted earlier, internally validate criteria. However, these criteria are not a replacement for standard diagnostic criteria but are merely a supplement to aid clinical decision making. Care must be exercised to not "mix and match" criteria but to use a standardized approach validated in individual laboratories.

To determine criteria that might best predict greater than 60% ICA stenosis, Moneta and coworkers[49] evaluated 352 carotid bifurcations and found that a PSV $\geq$ 260 cm/sec and an EDV $\geq$ 70 cm/sec together were the best predictors because of the highest overall accuracy (90%), sensitivity (84%), and specificity (94%). However, if they turned the question around and first asked which criteria would produce a PPV of 95%, a different result was found. In that case, a PSV $\geq$ 290 cm/sec and an EDV $\geq$ 80 cm/sec produced a PPV of 95%, but with lower sensitivity (78%). AbuRahma and coworkers[52] used a PSV greater than 150 cm/sec and an EDV of greater than 65 cm/sec to detect greater than 60% ICA stenosis with 90% accuracy (PPV of 96%). Remember, however, that internal validation is most important.

Indications for Cerebrovascular Duplex

The following generally accepted indications for cerebrovascular duplex examinations have been established:

1. Cervical bruit in asymptomatic patient[55]
2. Amaurosis fugax[55]
3. Focal transient ischemic attacks[55]
4. Cerebrovascular accident in a potential candidate for CEA[55]
5. Follow-up of known stenoses (>20%) in asymptomatic patient[15,55-57]
6. Follow-up after CEA[15,55,57-61]
7. Intraoperative assessment of CEA[62,63]
8. CEA without arteriography[15,64,65]
9. Drop attacks (rare indications)[55]

Several of these indications merit further discussion. Strandness[15] has made recommendations for follow-up of known stenoses that are asymptomatic (or lesions contralateral to an operated side). For patients who have less

than 50% stenosis, a follow-up duplex scan at yearly intervals is adequate. For those with moderate stenosis of 50% to 79%, a surveillance scan every 6 months is appropriate, though progression to more than 80% stenosis may prompt consideration for CEA.[15,57]

Historically, vascular surgeons have followed up CEA results with regular duplex scans. However, extended follow-up examinations may not be necessary or cost-effective. Restenosis after CEA is uncommon, occurring in 10% or less of all cases.[58-60] Coe and associates[58] found that only 15% of 88 CEAs had restenosis of more than 50%, with symptoms in two patients. Only 7.9% of 449 patients developed severe restenosis in the study by Ricotta and colleagues,[60] and 1.1% developed symptoms. Mackey and associates[59] reviewed 1053 postoperative duplex scans on 348 carotid arteries in 258 patients with an average follow-up of 52.6 $\pm$ 2.3 months. Only 56 arteries (16.1%) developed a restenosis greater than 50%. Of these, 46.4% occurred within 3 years of surgery, with 41% developing more than 5 years postoperatively. Thus, many authors recommended a single postoperative study, at 6 to 12 months after surgery,[57,59,61] whereas Ricotta and associates[60] suggested a single study 1 to 2 months postoperatively. Strandness also recommended a single postoperative study at 3 months.[15] Thus, routine postoperative surveillance at 3- to 6-month intervals no longer seems warranted in the absence of a specific indication, such as contralateral stenosis.

Investigators have suggested that intraoperative assessment of CEA may reduce the likelihood of restenosis.[61-63,66] Surgeons performing such examinations should have the requisite ultrasound skills to perform and interpret the intraoperative examination.[67] Baker and coworkers[62] found that 17% of patients who had abnormal completion duplex scans had no corrective action taken and developed restenoses (>75%) compared to 4.3% of patients who had normal post-CEA duplex scans ($P < 0.001$).

The importance of intraoperative completion duplex scanning was demonstrated by the clinical outcomes seen by Kinney and associates.[66] These authors prospectively studied 461 CEAs and correlated the results of intraoperative assessment by ultrasound, arteriography, and/or clinical inspection with stroke as the endpoint. The CEA site was assessed by duplex scan alone in 142 cases, by duplex scan and arteriography in 268 cases, or by clinical inspection alone in 51 cases. Based on these intraoperative assessments, 5.6% of CEAs were revised. Perioperative morbidity was similar in cases with normal, mildly abnormal, or no duplex: 6 strokes (1.3%), 12 transient neurologic deficits (2.6%), and 6 deaths (1.3 %). However, the postoperative development of greater than 50% ICA stenosis or occlusion was increased ($P < .007$) in patients with residual duplex abnormalities or when no duplex was performed. In those patients with late restenosis or occlusion, the risk of stroke was increased (3/35) compared with patients without restenosis (3/426; $P = .00016$). Additionally, when a normal intraoperative duplex examination was obtained, patients had a significantly lower rate of *late* ipsilateral stroke compared with the other patients ($P = .04$). Other authors found that intraoperative correction of abnormal duplex results prevented late stenosis.[61,63] These studies indicate that intraoperative duplex scanning is an effective means to detect abnormalities and prevent late restenosis as well as stroke in the long-term after CEA.

The performance of CEA without angiography has also enhanced the importance of duplex scanning. As the reliability and reproducibility of duplex scanning increased, it became apparent that the duplex scan could provide all the information the surgeon needed to plan the operation, without the risks of arteriography, particularly stroke.[64,68] Ricotta and associates[68] found that arteriography in patients with hemispheric symptoms did not add to the management of two thirds of their patients. In a retrospective review of 83 patients, Dawson and coworkers[69] found that clinical presentation and duplex findings were adequate for management in 87%. In the remaining 13%, arteriography was needed for those that had technically inadequate duplex scans, an atypical disease pattern, or an ICA stenosis less than 50%. A subsequent prospective study by this group revealed that arteriography affected clinical management in only 1 (1%) of 94 cases.[70]

Moore and coworkers[64] also prospectively evaluated 85 patients with duplex scans and arteriograms. Duplex correctly characterized 159 (93.5%) of 170 carotid arteries; hemodynamically significant stenosis was determined correctly by duplex scans in 100%. These authors then performed 32 CEAs in 29 patients without angiography, confirming the duplex-predicted lesion in every case. No perioperative strokes occurred. Kuntz and coworkers[65] actually demonstrated a lower 5-year risk of stroke with duplex scanning as the sole preoperative test compared to angiography (6.35% vs. 7.12%).

The two major questions that must be addressed when performing CEA without preoperative arteriography are (1) whether the accuracy of carotid duplex is comparable to arteriography and (2) whether arteriography, with its risks, and costs, can be safely eliminated? Surgeons planning CEA without arteriography should be well versed in the interpretation and pitfalls of carotid duplex scanning.[6,15,67,71] Our policy at the University of Vermont is that the surgeon must be present during the scan (even if it needs to be repeated) or must review videotapes personally. Only vascular laboratories that have adequate, regular quality assurance programs and proven track records should attempt to use duplex as the sole preoperative test before CEA.

Eliminating arteriography, which carries a risk of stroke between 1% and 6%, reduces the overall risk of treatment for carotid stenosis. However, the possibility of a proximal source for emboli should be remembered, since the aortic arch or CCA in the chest is a blind spot for duplex scanning. In addition, duplex scans cannot detect carotid siphon stenosis, intracranial aneurysms, or a brain tumor, which could be a source of hemispheric symptoms. Fortunately, carotid siphon disease is unlikely the source of symptoms, and a stenosis there does not impact significantly on the clinical decision to perform CEA.[15,72] Likewise, intracranial aneurysms can be seen in 1% to 2% of patients undergoing arteriography, but most are small and are unlikely to be affected by CEA.[73] Finally, advanced cerebral imaging techniques make concern about occult brain tumors less relevant.[64]

CEA without arteriography can be safely performed if the following criteria are met[6,70,71]:

1. The vascular laboratory duplex accuracy is known (ongoing quality assurance).
2. The duplex scan is technically adequate.
3. Vascular anomalies, kinks, or loops are not present.
4. The CCA is free of significant disease.
5. The distal ICA is free of significant disease (i.e., localized to the carotid bifurcation).

Potential pitfalls include patients with recurrent stenosis, nonhemispheric symptoms, or ICA stenosis of less than 50%.[69,70] In addition, when bilateral disease is present following CEA of the symptomatic or more severe side, repeat duplex is essential because of the possibility of changes in classification, as discussed earlier.[43,74] These postoperative changes may also be more pronounced in the presence of a stenotic VA.[75]

One final area that should be addressed for carotid duplex scanning is diagnosis and screening for blunt and penetrating wounds to the carotid artery.[76,77] Carotid duplex following trauma is a difficult examination in the face of edema, hematoma, uncooperative patients, and the bustling activity around a multitrauma patient. Only experienced examiners and interpreters should attempt this. Davis and coworkers[77] suggested that duplex scanning should be the primary screening modality for suspected carotid injury and dissection. In a prospective evaluation, Fry and colleagues[76] studied carotid duplex scanning after blunt and penetrating cervical trauma. Fifteen patients had a duplex scan followed by arteriography. Of these, 11 patients had a region of interest in zone II and four in zone III. Duplex scan correctly identified the single injury demonstrated by arteriography and correctly identified the remaining 14 normal studies. These investigators then performed duplex scans for the next 85 patients, but arteriography was performed only when the duplex scan was abnormal. In this group, 62 patients had potential injuries in zone II and the remainder in zone III. Seven arterial injuries identified by duplex scan were confirmed by arteriography. The remaining 76 patients with normal duplex scans had no sequelae for up to 3 weeks postdischarge. Savings of $1252 per case accrued when carotid duplex was used instead of arteriography. The potential benefits of duplex scanning in this difficult situation are comparable to the benefits seen when duplex scanning is used in the management of atherosclerotic carotid artery disease.

■ TRANSCRANIAL DOPPLER EXAMINATION

Since the early 1980s, TCD has been used as an inexpensive, noninvasive diagnostic tool to evaluate the hemodynamics of the intracranial arteries. Originally, studies were performed using a low-frequency 2-MHz-range gated pulsed nonimaging Doppler probe coupled with an analog output to display positive and/or negative frequency shifts and audio generator.[78] Later, the addition of high-resolution imaging, particularly color flow-imaging, spectral analysis, and

Table 138-5 Normal Velocity, Depth, and Direction of TCD Measured Blood Flow[80]

WINDOW	ARTERY	MEAN VELOCITY, cm/sec	DEPTH, mm	FLOW DIRECTION
Transtemporal	MCA	62 ± 12	40-50	Toward
	ACA	50 ± 12	65-75	Away
	PCA	42 ± 10	60-70	P1 toward, P2 away
Transorbital	Terminal ICA	39 ± 9	55-65	Toward
	ICA siphon	42 ± 11	60-80	Bidirectional
	Ophthalmic	21 ± 5	46-55	Toward
Transforaminal	Vertebral	36 ± 10	60-70	Away
	Basilar	39 ± 10	80-100	Away
Submandibular	Extracranial ICA	Variable	50	Away

TCD, transcranial Doppler; MCA, middle cerebral artery; ACA, anterior cerebral artery; PCA, posterior cerebral artery; ICA, internal carotid artery.

power Doppler, added greatly to the performance and accuracy of TCD.

TCD studies are performed to detect intracranial stenotic lesions, occlusions, assessment of vasospasm, and the associated complex flow patterns in the presence of collateralization. The quality of TCD examinations is based, in large part, on the sonographer's level of experience and confidence performing the examination. The significant attenuation of the ultrasound beam as it travels through the temporal bone is a technical factor that can affect the quality of TCD studies. Despite the relative thinness of the temporal bone, approximately 10% of all patients scanned may have inaccessible vessels because of increased bone density and inner table thickness.[79]

Intracranial vessels are accessed via four standard windows of the skull: transtemporal, transorbital, suboccipital, and submandibular. Anatomic landmarks assist in identifying vessels, whereas color-flow duplex aids in accurate sampling of the vessels. Accurate identification is dependent on several factors: the window used, the vessel/sample volume depth, the direction of flow related to the probe, and the relative flow velocities (Table 138-5).[80] In a normal patient, the direction of flow in any given vessel remains a constant; however, when scanning via the transtemporal window the display of the complete circle of Willis and contralateral flow may also be seen. This may be confusing because contralateral flows are color coded and spectrally displayed opposite to the conventional pattern. Traditionally antegrade flow is displayed above the baseline, represents flow toward the probe, and is conventionally coded red, whereas retrograde flow is displayed below the baseline, represents flow away from the probe, and is coded blue. In general, cerebral flows decrease from anterior to posterior:

Middle cerebral artery (MCA) > anterior cerebral artery (ACA) > posterior cerebral artery (PCA) = basilar artery (BA) = VA

Unlike extracranial carotid studies, vessel walls are not adequately seen during TCD examinations; thus, mean velocities (MVs) obtained assume 0-degree Doppler angle. Fortunately, most intracranial vessels lie in an axial plane relative to the ultrasound beam. The MV or time-averaged velocity is automatically calculated via spectral analysis and refers to all velocity values over one cardiac cycle. Mean flows are useful because they have less individual variability as compared to peak systolic or end-diastolic values.[81]

Technique

TCD examinations begin with the patient placed in a supine position. A 2- to 3-MHz phased-array pulsed Doppler transducer is placed over the temporal bone above the zygomatic arch with the orientation mark of the probe directed to the face. Proper orientation of the image places the ipsilateral hemisphere at the top of the screen and the contralateral hemisphere at the bottom, with anterior circulation displayed on the left and posterior circulation on the right. It is important to begin by positively identifying the midline by locating one of several landmarks: the contralateral bony wall, the falx, a thin linear and highly reflective interface, or the mesencephalon or peduncles (a heart-shaped hypoechoic structure). Midline identification is crucial because relative vessel depths change as a result of midline shifts.

Using a transtemporal window and gray-scale imaging, the bright bony landmarks of the lesser wing of the sphenoid and petrous ridge are used as a guide to locate the MCA. This location is also used frequently as a reference for finding the ACA, terminal ICA, and PCA. Color flow is then used to define the vessel, and Doppler information is gathered by "walking" through the vessel, a methodical and thorough sampling at incremental depths. A small sample volume of 3.5 mm is used and, depending on the vessel length, at least one sample is taken at a specific depth. The highest MV is recorded. Evaluation of the "prebranching" or M1 segment of the MCA begins in the proximal portion, just beyond the terminal ICA, with additional sampling in the mid and distal vessel. Flow is normally directed toward the transducer. One additional sample is taken in the "postbranching" or M2 segment where the smaller vessels are seen coursing away from the transducer.

The terminal ICA is identified by angling the transducer inferiorly from the proximal M1 segment. The foramen lacerum is used as a bony landmark, and bright reflections are seen completely surrounding the vessel. With slight rotation of the probe, color flow defines a cane-shaped vessel that has essentially an antegrade flow but may display ambiguous color due to tortuosity.

Identification of the ACA is made by slightly angling the transducer in an anterior and superior direction from the MCA. This locates the bifurcation of the MCA/ACA with characteristic bidirectional flow pattern and aids in identifying the ACA, which courses toward the midline and away from the transducer. This vessel has a precommunicating or A1 horizontal segment and a postcommunicating or A2 segment, with the A1 segments of each hemisphere connected via the anterior communicating artery (ACoA).

From the MCA reference, angling the transducer posteriorly and inferiorly allows an evaluation of the PCA. The PCA is divided into two segments and is named relative to the junction with the posterior communication artery (PCoA). Because the PCA wraps around the mesencephalic brain stem or cerebral peduncles, the precommunicating or P1 segment is directed toward the transducer, with the postcommunicating or P2 segment directed away from the transducer.

The transorbital window allows the ultrasound beam to pass through the globe of the eye, optic canal, and the superior orbital fissure for evaluation of the OA, and the carotid siphon, the cavernous portion of the intracranial ICA. The probe orientation marker is placed facing the midline, and gel is placed over the closed eyelid. Patients are asked to look inferiorly and toward their nose because this helps to identify the optic canal and nerve. Angling the transducer medially, the OA is visualized as it courses in a medial-to-lateral direction, and a sample is taken to a depth of 4 to 5 cm, where no other intracranial vessels lie. Flow is normally directed toward the transducer; however, in the presence of ipsilateral ICA occlusion, direction of flow may be reversed. When evaluating the OA, lower acoustic power output is used. Unlike the 100% acoustic output required to penetrate the bony vault, low attenuation of the beam through the orbit and thin orbital plate allows minimizing the output to approximately 10%, limiting ultrasound exposure to the eye.

Maintaining the same probe position, the sample volume depth is increased to evaluate the carotid siphon. Evaluation of the carotid siphon reveals flow both toward and away from the transducer. Because of the tortuosity of the siphon, flow in the parasellar segment is toward the transducer, bidirectional in the "genu segment" and directed away from the transducer in the supraclinoid segment.

VA and BAs are evaluated via the suboccipital window. With the patient's head slightly flexed, the transducer is placed at the base of the occipital bone with the ultrasound beam directed toward the bridge of the nose. The ultrasound beam passes through the foramen magnum, and both VAs will be seen coursing over the transverse processes of the atlas and atlanto-occipital joint. These vessels converge to form the BA, which may be tortuous and is often deviated toward the dominant side, with flows directed away from the probe.

The submandibular window allows for evaluation of the distal extracranial ICA. The ICA and ECA are seen as an inverted-V configuration, with Doppler flows away from the probe. The value obtained in this segment of the ICA is compared with the MCA velocity to obtain the hemispheric index (HI), a velocity ratio used in the assessment of vasospasm.[82]

Diagnostic Criteria

Interpretation of TCD findings is based on direction of flow, MVs, spectral information, waveform configuration, and pulsatility index (PI) (see Table 138-5).[80] Identification of a hemodynamically significant stenosis is based on the fundamentals of Doppler arterial assessment, including a focally elevated (mean) velocity with comparison of the pre-stenotic segment, post-stenotic turbulence, and a distally dampened waveform. Specific to TCD studies, a hemodynamically significant stenosis is identified based on an MV elevation of more than 80 cm/sec in adjacent vessel segments, a greater than 30 cm/sec differential compared to the contralateral side, and a drop in PI.[83] Asymmetry of hemispheric flow patterns and musical murmurs or vibrations may also be present.

Positive identification of an intracranial occlusion is a more difficult task. Absent Doppler and color-flow data from specific depths within the vessel is highly suspicious. In the presence of a technically adequate study (meaning all other ipsilateral vessels were adequately seen and interrogated), this would be consistent with an occlusion. Verification should be done via the same window on the contralateral side, and in the presence of an occlusion, compensatory flow increases and/or reversals may be present provided the anterior and posterior communicating arteries are patent.

Pulsatility is used to describe the configuration of a waveform using degree of variability in the velocities during a cardiac cycle. Differences between the peak systolic and end-diastolic values are used, and the closer the two values are, the lower the pulsatility, and conversely the greater the difference, the higher the pulsatility. The Gosling PI is used to quantify the waveform by calculating the difference between the maximum and minimum velocities divided by the mean flow velocity over one cardiac cycle. Normal PI values are from 0.5 to 1.1 due to the low resistance of the brain with constant forward flow during diastole.[84,85]

Vasospasm is a condition that may be detected by TCD, such as when it accompanies subarachnoid hemorrhage following intracerebral aneurysm rupture.[82,84] TCD evaluation is based primarily on MVs and the HI, the MCA/ICA velocity ratio (Table 138-6).[82,85] Vasospasm can occur in other cerebral arteries and can be complicated by coexisting

Table 138-6	TCD Velocities Within MCA Representing Vasospasm[82,85]	
MEAN MCA VELOCITY, cm/sec	**MCA/ICA VELOCITY RATIO**	**INTERPRETATION**
<120	<3	No evidence of vasospasm
>120	3-4	Mild vasospasm
120-200	4-6	Moderate vasospasm
>200	>6	Severe vasospasm

MCA, middle cerebral artery; TCD, transcranial Doppler; ICA, internal carotid artery.

proximal disease, increased ICP, and mass effect.[86-88] Vasospasm most often occurs between 2 and 17 days, with maximum severity between 7 to 12 days.[89] Patients are generally followed every other day with TCD examinations starting with the first postevent or postoperative day. If evidence of vasospasm is detected or if there is a clinical change in the patient's condition, TCD exams will be performed every day.[84]

Indications

A TCD examination is a valuable tool in assessing the presence of stenosis in the intracranial vessels, which is the cause of about 10% of ischemic strokes in the United States.[2] The most common sites of stenosis occurring in the intracranial arteries are the carotid siphon, terminal ICA bifurcation, which is the origin of the MCA and ACA, M1 segment of the MCA, proximal VAs, distal BAs and the origin of the PCA. It has also been suggested that TCD should be used to follow symptomatic MCA stenoses, of which 32% may progress.[90,91]

TCD examinations have been used to monitor microembolic events during surgical procedures[92,93] or to assess collateral flow during CEA.[94] These microemboli may result in cognitive impairment or silent strokes.[95] However, although monitoring with TCD is informative, the application of this technology does not yet have a demonstrated role in preventing microemboli or changing the clinical outcome.

Patients afflicted with sickle cell anemia possess a significant threat for stroke by 20 years of age. The source for most of these events is the large vessels of the circle of Willis, specifically the terminal ICA, MCA, and ACA. Children normally exhibit higher MVs in the MCA (130 to 170 cm/sec). Those who exhibited MVs greater than 200 cm/sec revealed a significantly increased risk for stroke of 40% within the next 3 years. Thus, TCD may be an important means to monitor these patients, focusing on velocity trends in their anterior intracranial vessels.[96]

The American Academy of Neurology has reported the established value of TCD for the following clinical situations[97]:

1. Detecting severe stenosis (>65%) in the major basal intracranial arteries
2. Assessing patterns and extent of collateral circulation in patients with known regions of severe stenosis or occlusion
3. Evaluation and follow-up of patients with cerebral vasoconstriction of any cause, especially after subarachnoid hemorrhage
4. Detecting arteriovenous malformations and studying their supply arteries and flow patterns
5. Assessing patients with suspected brain death[98]

In addition, the American Academy of Neurology notes that several areas are under investigation but not yet established[97]:

1. Assessing patients with migraine
2. Monitoring during surgical procedures
3. Evaluating patients with dilated vasculopathies such as fusiform aneurysms

4. Assessing pharmacologic responses of cerebral arteries
5. Evaluating children with vasculopathies, such as sickle cell anemia, moyamoya disease, and neurofibromatosis

Pitfalls and Limitations

TCD requires an experienced examiner, perhaps even more than other noninvasive Doppler examinations. Thorough understanding of anatomy, principles of imaging, and optimization of the ultrasound system all factor into the quality of the examination.

Anatomical variants may occur that may mislead the examiner. Only 18% to 54% of people have a normal circle of Willis.[99,100] The most common variation is a hypoplastic or tortuous ACA, which occurs in approximately 25% of the population.[100] The PCA is usually the terminal branch of the BA, but 15% to 40% of the population have an origin from the terminal ICA or MCA, deriving flow entirely from that vessel.[99] Other common variants include an absent anterior communicating artery, early branching of the MCA, and a hypoplastic VA associated with a tortuous BA.[99-101] As noted earlier, particularly in light of anatomic variants, occlusion of intracranial vessels can be difficult to diagnose.

As noted previously for extracranial carotid duplex examinations, there is some need to validate results in individual laboratories. The normal TCD velocities are, in fact, a *range* of velocities and are subject to variability in equipment but also in individual patients due to age, hypertension, and several other factors.[86,102,103] Owing to the combination of all of these factors, TCD studies may present challenges to even the most experienced sonographer.

■ COMPUTED TOMOGRAPHIC ANGIOGRAPHY

Spiral or helical CTA allows the acquisition of images from a large volume of tissue in a short time as the system continuously moves the patient while rotating the x-ray tube within the gantry. This technique may allow better vascular images to be generated than conventional CT because the speed of data acquisition allows scanning to be completed with higher levels of circulating contrast material. Postprocessing of images with volume-rendering methods (maximal intensity projection [MIP]) and three-dimensional (3D) reconstructions allows image generation not seen with conventional techniques.[13,104,105] CTA has the advantage of minimal patient discomfort, low radiation doses, a brief examination time with low operator dependence, good delineation of calcified plaques, and lower cost than angiography.[105] CTA has been applied as a minimally invasive method of diagnosis for cerebrovascular disease.

Technique and Results

Multiple variations of the technique, timing of image acquisition, contrast volume, and other factors have been published.[104,106-111] In brief, the patient is supine while 2- to 3-mm sections are performed from C2 to C6 with continuous data acquisition. Patients are asked to breathe quietly and avoid swallowing. Often a set of images without contrast is obtained first. A volume of contrast material (75 to 120 mL) is injected into an arm vein with a 20- to 25-second scan delay (or a delay determined by computer-assisted techniques) after the start of contrast administration. Axial images and/or 3D reconstructions are produced on the CT workstation when the examination is complete. Reconstructions are typically done using MIP after deleting bony structures.

Although the fast-scanning technique minimizes motion artifacts, calcifications produce imaging artifacts, particularly when MIP reconstruction is attempted. These artifacts may be incorrectly diagnosed as stenoses.[105] In addition, interpretation may be complicated by the numerous vascular structures in this region. Other factors that may produce suboptimal images are poor timing or inadequate volume of contrast material.[105,106]

CTA has been favorably compared to contrast arteriography. Dillon and associates[107] characterized the degree of stenosis as mild, moderate, severe, or occluded and found that there was agreement in 41 (82%) of 50 carotid arteries. Leclerc and coworkers,[108] using six categories (normal, <30%, 30% to 70%, >70%, near occlusion, and occlusion) found agreement with contrast arteriography in 95%. These authors also thought that MIP reconstructions, when technically possible, offered a more reliable estimate of stenosis. Unfortunately, 10 of 40 arteries they evaluated were unable to be reconstructed because of calcifications. Simeone and coworkers[109] compared 80 arteries imaged with CTA to intra-arterial digital subtraction angiography (DSA). When classified as normal, 1% to 29%, 30% to 69%, 70% to 99%, or occlusion, accuracy was 96% with 88% sensitivity and 100% specificity. Cinat and colleagues, using greater than 60% ICA stenosis as a cutoff, found CTA compared to angiography had an accuracy of 89%, a negative predictive value of 88%, and a PPV 89%.[104,111] In contrast to others,[106] they found that CTA identified plaque characteristics such as ulcerations, occlusion, fatty plaques, calcifications, and fibrosis. In that study, CTA underestimated two short-segment stenoses. CTA has also been suggested as a reliable means to detect carotid occlusions[112] or evaluate the VAs[113] and aortic arch,[114] although less data are available supporting these applications. CTA does have the concern of contrast-induced renal dysfunction that, although it cannot be ignored, seems relatively rare.[111]

■ MAGNETIC RESONANCE ANGIOGRAPHY

MRA has been developed as another noninvasive (or minimally invasive) method to evaluate the carotid system. This technique does not require the use of contrast, a major advantage over CTA or conventional angiography. MRA uses pulses of radiofrequency energy to excite protons of primarily hydrogen (water molecules) within a magnetic field. The characteristic spin produces a radiofrequency echo of the original signal. Tissue produces a signal, whereas air and bone do not. There are multitudes of protocols that can generate images of blood flow or flow velocity. The protocols in common clinical usage use MIP technology to reconstruct images of vessels and, frequently,

are combined with imaging studies of the brain. Though there are few contraindications to MRA, patients with implanted metallic or electronic devices, such as pacemakers, cannot undergo MRI or MRA.

Technique and Results

The usual clinical MRA method is the time-of-flight (TOF) technique that relies on flow-related enhancement.[14,115] Stationary tissue becomes saturated with the radiofrequency pulses, whereas blood moving through the field of interest provides unsaturated echoes that produce a strong signal from the vessel. Through different methods, the signal in the vessel can be maximized. Both 2D and 3D techniques are used to acquire data. The 2D technique acquires data with sequential thin transverse slices, whereas the 3D TOF technique acquires data in any plane. The 2D method allows blood to flow quickly through the scanning slice and not become saturated with radiofrequency signals compared to a 3D method obtaining images in a sagittal plane. The 2D TOF method produces better visualization of slowly moving blood, which may be useful when attempting to distinguish between a tight stenosis and occlusion. On the other hand, the 3D method can image vessels in any direction, is less susceptible to turbulence-generated artifacts, can image plaque, and has better image resolution,[14,116,117] as demonstrated in Figure 138-3. The 3D TOF method may also allow the injection of gadolinium that may enhance areas of slow flow. Sophisticated enhancements and refinements will doubtless continue to improve MRA-generated images.[118]

During the first pass of a gadolinium contrast agent injection, rapid acquisition of data with 3D TOF techniques gives greater spatial resolution and reduces artifacts from low flow, radiofrequency saturation, and areas of turbulence.[117,119-121] The contrast agent is primarily an extracellular component but not strictly intravascular, so that the timing of the initial bolus is critical to avoid more widespread distribution and venous overlay that can obscure the diagnosis. This contrast-enhanced technique has gained almost universal acceptance, though a recent report suggests accuracy is higher *without* the use of contrast.[122]

The more recent studies of MRA demonstrate good results when this technique is used for the carotid artery.[14,116,117,123,124] MRA has the advantage of demonstrating the intracerebral vessels, if the clinician believes that this is an important piece of information prior to CEA. Remonda and coworkers found that contrast-enhanced MRA was in agreement with conventional angiography in 93% of cases with 70% to 99% ICA stenosis. All internal carotid occlusions (n = 28) and seven of nine pseudo-occlusions were accurately detected with MRA.[117] The tendency for MRA to overestimate the degree of stenosis is a generally recognized pitfall in interpretation and a precise estimate of stenosis is difficult to obtain with MRA.[124-126] Routine MRA does not reveal ulcerations with a high degree of accuracy and, overall, as a single diagnostic test, it has not been considered a sensitive technique to determine the need for surgery. Others have suggested that MRA may be used to evaluate the aortic arch[127] or postendarterectomy carotid arteries.[128] It is imperative that individual institutions

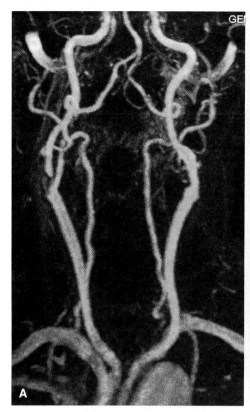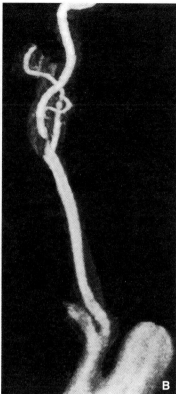

FIGURE 138-3 Three-dimensional MRA images showing arch view with both carotid and vertebral systems (**A**) and isolated right carotid system showing significant internal carotid artery stenosis (**B**).

correlate their results with MRA compared to conventional angiography, particularly since there are such variations in MRA technique.

■ COMPARISONS BETWEEN IMAGING MODALITIES

The imaging modalities discussed earlier are noninvasive tests that will not replace conventional contrast or digital subtraction arteriography entirely, but there are several approaches that have been recommended to severely limit its use and avoid the attendant expense and risk.[40,65,123,129-134] First, although contrast and DSA are considered the gold standard for the diagnosis of cerebrovascular disease, this modality may underestimate the degree of stenosis[135] and does not accurately detect ulceration.[136] In addition, there is both interobserver and intraobserver variability in determining the degree of stenosis.[137] This 5% to 15% difference can affect comparisons between different test methods. For instance, an arteriogram reported as 78% stenosis could be read by a different radiologist as a 71% to 85% stenosis, based on the 9% interobservation noted by Young and colleagues.[137] A duplex scan interpreted as 80% to 99% stenosis might be considered correct if one radiologist reads the arteriogram and incorrect if read by another. Even if one considers the 78% stenosis as an "absolute," is that really clinically significant from an 80% to 99% stenosis by duplex scan? Moderate stenoses, which may be a pitfall of duplex scanning and CTA, may be even more problematic.[105] One should always be cognizant, however,

that arteriogram interpretations with exact stenosis determinations may imply a somewhat artificial degree of precision.

No clinical studies have yet compared arteriography with all three noninvasive modalities (duplex scanning, CTA, and MRA). A unique attempt to compare arteriography, duplex scanning, and MRA with surgical specimens was carried out by Pan and coworkers,[135] who studied 31 CEA specimens that were removed en bloc at the time of surgery with contrast DSA, 3D MRA, and color-flow duplex imaging. They used the ECST method[1] to estimate stenosis since the distal ICA diameter could not be determined in the specimens. The gold standard for comparison was the surgical specimen, with the diameters determined by high-resolution MRI. Data were then analyzed by placing in-vivo measurements from each modality and the specimen measurement in the following categories: 1% to 39%, 40% to 59%, 60% to 79%, 80% to 99%, and occluded.

The 31 measurements from the ex-vivo specimens were found to be 40% to 59% in 2 specimens, 60% to 79% in 6, and 80% to 99% in the remaining 23. A diagnostic match was found in 76% of MRAs, 75% of duplex scans, and only 57% of arteriograms. MRA was more likely to overestimate stenosis (17%) than duplex (14%) or arteriography (6%). On the other hand, arteriography was most likely to *underestimate* the degree of stenosis (37% vs. 11% for duplex and 7% for MRA). Of the 23 specimens with 80% to 99% stenosis, MRA was accurate in 95%, duplex in 90%, and arteriography in 52%. Overall, the correlation of the ex-vivo measurement with the in-vivo modalities was better for duplex ultrasound ($r = 0.80$) and MRA ($r = 0.76$) than arteriography ($r = 0.56$). This study confirms the reliability of duplex scanning and MRA to determine critical stenosis and points out the pitfalls of relying on arteriography as an absolute gold standard.

■ CLINICAL RECOMMENDATIONS

Based on the NASCET[2] experience with duplex ultrasound, it has been suggested that contrast arteriography must be performed prior to CEA. In addition to the significant methodologic problems with the use of duplex ultrasound in that trial, the earlier discussion points out many of the problems and pitfalls with arteriography. Presently, no test can give an absolute value for the degree of stenosis in every carotid artery. The mere fact that large, randomized clinical trials measuring the degree of stenosis in different ways, all found a clinical benefit to CEA indicates that there is a range of stenoses where the benefit from CEA can be recognized.[1-4] The surgeon's clinical judgment and familiarity with the accuracy and pitfalls of each diagnostic modality are the most important factors in determining the appropriateness of CEA. Although arteriography will continue to play a vital role in cerebrovascular diagnosis, an appropriate role at the present time should be when noninvasive tests do not give a clear diagnosis or when diagnoses other than carotid occlusive disease are suspected.

Several authors have suggested that duplex scanning may be used as the single preoperative diagnostic test prior to CEA in symptomatic or asymptomatic patients.[6,40,55,64,70,71] The accuracy of the laboratory must be known, the individual scan should be technically adequate, the CCA should be free of disease, and the ICA should be free of significant anomalies and disease-free distally. If those conditions are met, CEA can be carried out without the risk of arteriography or the expense of other invasive or noninvasive tests. Inadequate imaging should prompt additional confirmatory noninvasive testing (MRA or CTA) or arteriography.[138] Since one of the pitfalls of duplex imaging is distinguishing the nearly occluded carotid from one that is completely occluded, in patients with symptoms in the hemisphere ipsilateral to a duplex-detected occlusion, confirmation of the occlusion with MRA, CTA, or arteriography is recommended, since in this instance the consequences of error are potentially devastating.

An alternative approach that has been suggested is the combination of duplex scanning and MRA.[129,130,134,139,140] In that case, the tendency of MRA to overestimate the degree of stenosis should be balanced by the duplex examination. Overall, this combination of tests has been reported to be accurate in selecting patients for surgery. Although this approach is more expensive than duplex alone, the combination remains less expensive than arteriography.

■ REFERENCES

1. MRC European Carotid Surgery Trial: Interim results for symptomatic patients with severe (70-99%) or with mild (0-29%) carotid stenosis. European Carotid Surgery Trialists' Collaborative Group. Lancet 337:1235-1243, 1991.

2. Beneficial effect of carotid endarterectomy in symptomatic patients with high-grade carotid stenosis. North American Symptomatic Carotid Endarterectomy Trial Collaborators. N Engl J Med 325:445-453, 1991.

3. Endarterectomy for asymptomatic carotid artery stenosis. Executive Committee for the Asymptomatic Carotid Atherosclerosis Study. JAMA 273:1421-1428, 1995.

4. Randomised trial of endarterectomy for recently symptomatic carotid stenosis: Final results of the MRC European Carotid Surgery Trial (ECST). Lancet 351:1379-1387, 1998.

5. Qureshi AI, Knape C, Maroney J, et al: Multicenter clinical trial of the NexStent coiled sheet stent in the treatment of extracranial carotid artery stenosis: Immediate results and late clinical outcomes. J Neurosurg 99:264-270, 2003.

6. Strandness DE Jr: Angiography before carotid endarterectomy—no. Arch Neurol 52:832-833, 1995.

7. Strandness DE Jr: Historical aspects. In Strandness DE Jr (ed): Duplex Scanning in Vascular Disorders, 2nd ed. New York, Raven, 1993, pp 1-26.

8. Brockenbrough EC: Screening for the prevention of stroke: Use of a Doppler flowmeter. Brochure by Alaska/Washington Regional Medical Program, 1969.

9. Kartchner MM, McRae LP, Morrison FD: Noninvasive detection and evaluation of carotid occlusive disease. Arch Surg 106:528-535, 1973.

10. Gee W, Oller DW, Amundsen DG, Goodreau JJ: Ocular plethysmography in carotid artery disease. Med Instrum 8:244-248, 1974.

11. Gee W, Oller DW, Amundsen DG, Goodreau JJ: The asymptomatic carotid bruit and the ocular pneumoplethysmography. Arch Surg 112:1381-1388, 1977.

12. Crocker EF Jr, Tutton RH, Bowen JC: The role of intravenous digital subtraction angiography in the evaluation of extracranial carotid artery disease: Can the decision for carotid artery surgery be made solely on the basis of its findings? J Vasc Surg 4:157-163, 1986.

13. Napel S, Marks MP, Rubin GD, et al: CT angiography with spiral CT and maximum image projection. Radiology 185:607-610, 1992.

14. Anderson CM, Haacke EM: Approaches to diagnostic magnetic resonance carotid angiography. Semin Ultrasound CT MR 13:246-255, 1992.

15. Strandness DE Jr: Extracranial arterial disease. In Strandness DE Jr (ed): Duplex Scanning in Vascular Disorders, 2nd ed. New York, Raven, 1993, pp 113-158.

16. Beebe HG, Salles-Cunha SX, Scissons RP, et al: Carotid arterial ultrasound scan imaging: A direct approach to stenosis measurement. J Vasc Surg 29:838-844, 1999.

17. Comerota AJ, Katz ML, White JV, Grosh JD: The preoperative diagnosis of the ulcerated carotid atheroma. J Vasc Surg 11:505-510, 1990.

18. Sitzer M, Muller W, Rademacher J, et al: Color-flow Doppler-assisted duplex imaging fails to detect ulceration in high-grade internal carotid artery stenosis. J Vasc Surg 23:461-465, 1996.

19. Eikelboom BC, Riles TR, Mintzer R, et al:. Inaccuracy of angiography in the diagnosis of carotid ulceration. Stroke 14:882-885, 1983.

20. Imparato AM, Riles TS, Mintzer R, Baumann FG: The importance of hemorrhage in the relationship between gross morphologic characteristics and cerebral symptoms in 376 carotid artery plaques. Ann Surg 197:195-203, 1983.

21. Sabetai MM, Tegos TJ, Nicolaides AN, et al: Hemispheric symptoms and carotid plaque echomorphology. J Vasc Surg 31:39-49, 2000.

22. AbuRahma AF, Wulu JT Jr, Crotty B: Carotid plaque ultrasonic heterogeneity and severity of stenosis. Stroke 33:1772-1775, 2002.

23. Arnold JA, Modaresi KB, Thomas N, et al: Carotid plaque characterization by duplex scanning: Observer error may undermine current clinical trials. Stroke 30:61-65, 1999.

24. Zwiebel WJ: Spectrum analysis in carotid sonography. Ultrasound Med Biol 13:625-636, 1987.

25. Zwiebel WJ: Doppler evaluation of carotid stenosis. In Zwiebel WJ (ed): Introduction to Vascular Ultrasonography. Philadelphia, WB Saunders, 1992, pp 123-132.

26. Bandyk DF, Levine AW, Pohl L, Towne JB: Classification of carotid bifurcation disease using quantitative Doppler spectrum analysis. Arch Surg 120:306-314, 1985.

27. Fillinger MF, Baker RJ Jr, Zwolak RM, et al: Carotid duplex criteria for a 60% or greater angiographic stenosis: Variation according to equipment. J Vasc Surg 24:856-864, 1996.

28. Alexandrov AV, Vital D, Brodie DS, et al: Grading carotid stenosis with ultrasound: An interlaboratory comparison. Stroke 28:1208-1210, 1997.

29. Neale ML, Chambers JL, Kelly AT, et al: Reappraisal of duplex criteria to assess significant carotid stenosis with special reference to reports from the North American Symptomatic Carotid Endarterectomy Trial and the European Carotid Surgery Trial. J Vasc Surg 20:642-649, 1994.

30. Criswell BK, Langsfeld M, Tullis MJ, Marek J: Evaluating institutional variability of duplex scanning in the detection of carotid artery stenosis. Am J Surg 176:591-597, 1998.

31. Curley PJ, Norrie L, Nicholson A, et al: Accuracy of carotid duplex is laboratory specific and must be determined by internal audit. Eur J Vasc Endovasc Surg 15:511-514, 1998.

32. Hwang CS, Shau WY, Tegeler CH: Doppler velocity criteria based on receiver operating characteristic analysis for the detection of threshold carotid stenoses. J Neuroimaging 12:124-130, 2002.

33. Leonardo G, Crescenzi B, Cotrufo R, et al: Improvement in accuracy of diagnosis of carotid artery stenosis with duplex ultrasound scanning with combined use of linear array 7.5 MHz and convex array 3.5 MHz probes: Validation versus 489 arteriographic procedures. J Vasc Surg 37:1240-1247, 2003.

34. Rasmussen TE, Panneton JM, Kalra M, et al: Intraoperative use of a new angle-independent Doppler system to measure arterial velocities after carotid endarterectomy. J Vasc Surg 37:374-380, 2003.

35. Bluth EI, Sunshine JH, Lyons JB, et al: Power Doppler imaging: Initial evaluation as a screening examination for carotid artery stenosis. Radiology 215:791-800, 2000.

36. Bendick PJ, Jackson VP: Evaluation of vertebral arteries with duplex ultrasonography. J Vasc Surg 3:523-530, 1986.

37. de Bray JM, Pasco A, Tranquart F, et al: Accuracy of color-Doppler in the quantification of proximal vertebral artery stenoses. Cerebrovasc Dis 11:335-340, 2001.

38. Bluth EI, Merritt CR, Sullivan MA, et al: Usefulness of duplex ultrasound in evaluating vertebral arteries. J Ultrasound Med 8:229-235, 1989.

39. Bartels E, Flugel KA: Advantages of color Doppler imaging for the evaluation of vertebral arteries. J Neuroimaging 3:229-233, 1993.

40. Ricci MA: Evaluating cerebrovascular symptoms. In Rutherford JC (ed): Decision Making in Vascular Surgery. Philadelphia, WB Saunders, 2001, pp 22-26.

41. van Everdingen KJ, van der Grond J, Kappelle LJ: Overestimation of a stenosis in the internal carotid artery by duplex sonography caused by an increase in volume flow. J Vasc Surg 27:479-485, 1998.

42. Nicolau C, Gilabert R, Garcia A, et al: Effect of internal carotid artery occlusion on vertebral artery blood flow: A duplex ultrasonographic evaluation. J Ultrasound Med 20:105-111, 2001.

43. Ray SA, Lockhart SJ, Dourado R, et al: Effect of contralateral disease on duplex measurements of internal carotid artery stenosis. Br J Surg 87:1057-1062, 2000.

44. Spadone DP, Barkmeier LD, Hodgson KJ, et al: Contralateral internal carotid artery stenosis or occlusion: Pitfall of correct ipsilateral classification—a study performed with color-flow imaging. J Vasc Surg 11:642-649, 1990.

45. Fujitani RM, Mills JL, Wang LM, Taylor SM: The effect of unilateral internal carotid arterial occlusion upon contralateral duplex study: criteria for accurate interpretation. J Vasc Surg 16:459-468, 1992.

46. AbuRahma AF, Richmond BK, Robinson PA, et al: Effect of contralateral severe stenosis or carotid occlusion on duplex criteria of ipsilateral stenoses: comparative study of various duplex parameters. J Vasc Surg 22:751-762, 1995.

47. Ricci MA: The changing role of duplex scan in the management of carotid bifurcation disease and endarterectomy. Semin Vasc Surg 11:3-11, 1998.

48. Hood DB, Mattos MA, Mansour A, et al: Prospective evaluation of new duplex criteria to identify 70% internal carotid artery stenosis. J Vasc Surg 23:254-262, 1996.

49. Moneta GL, Edwards JM, Papanicolaou G, et al: Screening for asymptomatic internal carotid artery stenosis: Duplex criteria for discriminating 60% to 99% stenosis. J Vasc Surg 21:989-994, 1995.

50. Faught WE, Mattos MA, van Bemmelen PS, et al: Color-flow duplex scanning of carotid arteries: New velocity criteria based on receiver operator characteristic analysis for threshold stenoses used in the symptomatic and asymptomatic carotid trials. J Vasc Surg 19:818-828, 1994.

51. Moneta GL, Edwards JM, Chitwood RW, et al: Correlation of North American Symptomatic Carotid Endarterectomy Trial (NASCET) angiographic definition of 70% to 99% internal carotid artery stenosis with duplex scanning. J Vasc Surg 17:152-159, 1993.

52. AbuRahma AF, Robinson PA, Strickler DL, et al: Proposed new duplex classification for threshold stenoses used in various symptomatic and asymptomatic carotid endarterectomy trials. Ann Vasc Surg 12:349-358, 1998.

53. Bonig L, Weder B, Schott D, et al: Prediction of angiographic carotid artery stenosis indexes by colour Doppler-assisted duplex imaging: A critical appraisal of the parameters used. Eur J Neurol 7:183-190, 2000.

54. Koga M, Kimura K, Minematsu K, Yamaguchi T: Diagnosis of internal carotid artery stenosis greater than 70% with power Doppler duplex sonography. AJNR Am J Neuroradiol 22:413-417, 2001.

55. Strandness DE Jr: Indications for and frequency of noninvasive testing. Semin Vasc Surg 7:245-250, 1994.

56. AbuRahma AF, Thiele SP, Wulu JT Jr: Prospective controlled study of the natural history of asymptomatic 60% to 69% carotid stenosis according to ultrasonic plaque morphology. J Vasc Surg 36:437-442, 2002.

57. Strandness DE Jr: Screening for carotid disease and surveillance for carotid restenosis. Semin Vasc Surg 14:200-205, 2001.

58. Coe DA, Towne JB, Seabrook GR, et al: Duplex morphologic features of the reconstructed carotid artery: Changes occurring more than five years after endarterectomy. J Vasc Surg 25:850-857, 1997.

59. Mackey WC, Belkin M, Sindhi R, et al: Routine postendarterectomy duplex surveillance: Does it prevent late stroke? J Vasc Surg 16:934-940, 1992.

60. Ricotta JJ, O'Brien MS, DeWeese JA: Natural history of recurrent and residual stenosis after carotid endarterectomy: Implications for postoperative surveillance and surgical management. Surgery 112:656-663, 1992.

61. Roth SM, Back MR, Bandyk DF, et al: A rational algorithm for duplex scan surveillance after carotid endarterectomy. J Vasc Surg 30:453-460, 1999.

62. Baker WH, Koustas G, Burke K, et al: Intraoperative duplex scanning and late carotid artery stenosis. J Vasc Surg 19:829-833, 1994.

63. Mansour MA, Webb KM, Kang SS, et al: Timing and frequency of perioperative carotid color-flow duplex scanning: A preliminary report. J Vasc Surg 29:833-837, 1999.

64. Moore WS, Ziomek S, Quinones-Baldrich WJ, et al: Can clinical evaluation and noninvasive testing substitute for arteriography in the evaluation of carotid artery disease? Ann Surg 208:91-94, 1988.

65. Kuntz KM, Skillman JJ, Whittemore AD, Kent KC: Carotid endarterectomy in asymptomatic patients—is contrast angiography necessary? A morbidity analysis. J Vasc Surg 22:706-716, 1995.

66. Kinney EV, Seabrook GR, Kinney LY, et al: The importance of intraoperative detection of residual flow abnormalities after carotid artery endarterectomy. J Vasc Surg 17:912-923, 1993.

67. Ricci MA, Rutherford RB: Qualifications of the physician in the vascular diagnostic laboratory. In AbuRhama JB (ed): Noninvasive Vascular Diagnosis. London, Springer-Verlag, 2000, pp 19-22.

68. Ricotta JJ, Holen J, Schenk E, et al: Is routine angiography necessary prior to carotid endarterectomy? J Vasc Surg 1:96-102, 1984.

69. Dawson DL, Zierler RE, Kohler TR: Role of arteriography in the preoperative evaluation of carotid artery disease. Am J Surg 161:619-624, 1991.

70. Dawson DL, Zierler RE, Strandness DE Jr, et al: The role of duplex scanning and arteriography before carotid endarterectomy: A prospective study. J Vasc Surg 18:673-683, 1993.

71. Moore WS: For severe carotid stenosis found on ultrasound, further arterial evaluation is unnecessary. Stroke 34:1816-1817, 2003.

72. Roederer GO, Langlois YE, Chan AR, et al: Is siphon disease important in predicting outcome of carotid endarterectomy? Arch Surg 118:1177-1181, 1983.

73. Orecchia PM, Clagett GP, Youkey JR, et al: Management of patients with symptomatic extracranial carotid artery disease and incidental intracranial berry aneurysm. J Vasc Surg 2:158-164, 1985.

74. Abou-Zamzam AM Jr, Moneta GL, Edwards JM, et al: Is a single preoperative duplex scan sufficient for planning bilateral carotid endarterectomy? J Vasc Surg 31:282-288, 2000.

75. Welch HJ, Murphy MC, Raftery KB, Jewell ER: Carotid duplex with contralateral disease: The influence of vertebral artery blood flow. Ann Vasc Surg 14:82-88, 2000.

76. Fry WR, Dort JA, Smith RS, et al: Duplex scanning replaces arteriography and operative exploration in the diagnosis of potential cervical vascular injury. Am J Surg 168:693-696, 1994.

77. Davis JW, Holbrook TL, Hoyt DB, et al: Blunt carotid artery dissection: Incidence, associated injuries, screening, and treatment. J Trauma 30:1514-1517, 1990.

78. Aaslid R, Markwalder TM, Nornes H: Noninvasive transcranial Doppler ultrasound recording of flow velocity in basal cerebral arteries. J Neurosurg 57:769-774, 1982.

79. Grolimund P: Transmission of ultrasound through the temporal bone. In Aaslid R (ed): Transcranial Doppler Sonography. New York, Springer-Verlag, 1986, pp 10-21.

80. Ringelstein E: A practical guide to transcranial Doppler sonography. In Weinberger J (ed): Noninvasive Imaging of Cerebrovascular Disease. New York, Alan R. Liss, 1989, pp 75-121.

81. Hennerici M, Rautenberg W, Sitzer G, Schwartz A: Transcranial Doppler ultrasound for the assessment of intracranial arterial flow velocity: I. Examination technique and normal values. Surg Neurol 27:439-448, 1987.

82. Lindegaard KF, Nornes H, Bakke SJ, et al: Cerebral vasospasm diagnosis by means of angiography and blood velocity measurements. Acta Neurochir (Wien) 100:12-24, 1989.

83. Ley-Pozo J, Ringelstein EB: Noninvasive detection of occlusive disease of the carotid siphon and middle cerebral artery. Ann Neurol 28:640-647, 1990.

84. Newell D, Douville C: Cerebral vasospasm. J Vasc Tech 24:53-57, 2000.

85. Lindegaard KF, Bakke SJ, Grolimund P, et al: Assessment of intracranial hemodynamics in carotid artery disease by transcranial Doppler ultrasound. J Neurosurg 63:890-898, 1985.

86. Giller CA, Lam M, Roseland A: Periodic variations in transcranial Doppler mean velocities. J Neuroimaging 3:160-162, 1993.

87. Sloan M: Transcranial Doppler monitoring of a vasospasm after subarachnoid hemorrhage. In Tegeler C, Babakian VL, Gomez CR (eds): Neurosonology. St. Louis, Mosby, 1996, pp 156-171.

88. Klingelhofer J, Dander D, Holzgraefe M, et al: Cerebral vasospasm evaluated by transcranial Doppler ultrasonography at different intracranial pressures. J Neurosurg 75:752-758, 1991.

89. Weir B, Grace M, Hansen J, Rothberg C: Time course of vasospasm in man. J Neurosurg 48:173-178, 1978.

90. Arenillas JF, Molina CA, Montaner J, et al: Progression and clinical recurrence of symptomatic middle cerebral artery stenosis: A long-term follow-up transcranial Doppler ultrasound study. Stroke 32:2898-2904, 2001.

91. Schwarze JJ, Babikian V, DeWitt LD, et al: Longitudinal monitoring of intracranial arterial stenoses with transcranial Doppler ultrasonography. J Neuroimaging 4:182-187, 1994.

92. Rudolph JL, Pochay V, Treanor P, et al: Brain distribution of microemboli during coronary artery bypass graft surgery. Heart Surg Forum 6:206, 2003.

93. Babikian VL, Cantelmo NL: Cerebrovascular monitoring during carotid endarterectomy. Stroke 31:1799-1801, 2000.

94. Babikian VL, Schwarze JJ, Cantelmo NL, et al: Collateral flow changes through the anterior communicating artery during carotid endarterectomy. J Neurol Sci 138:53-59, 1996.

95. Babikian VL, Wijman CA: Brain embolism monitoring with transcranial Doppler ultrasound. Curr Treat Options Cardiovasc Med 5:221-232, 2003.

96. Jones AM, Seibert JJ, Nichols FT, et al: Comparison of transcranial color Doppler imaging (TCDI) and transcranial Doppler (TCD) in children with sickle-cell anemia. Pediatr Radiol 31:461-469, 2001.

97. Assessment: Transcranial Doppler. Report of the American Academy of Neurology, Therapeutics and Technology Assessment Subcommittee. Neurology 40:680-681, 1990.

98. Kirkham FJ, Levin SD, Padayachee TS, et al: Transcranial pulsed Doppler ultrasound findings in brain stem death. J Neurol Neurosurg Psychiatry 50:1504-1513, 1987.

99. Hodes PJ, Campoy F, Riggs HE, Bly P: Cerebral angiography: Fundamentals in anatomy and physiology. AJR Am J Roentgenol 70:61-82, 1953.

100. Riggs HE, Rupp C: Variation in form of circle of Willis: The relation of the variations to collateral circulation—anatomic analysis. Arch Neurol 8:8-14, 1963.

101. Nonoshita-Karr L, Fujioka K: Transcranial Doppler sonography freehand examination techniques. J Vasc Tech 24:9-16, 2000.

102. Kirkham FJ, Padayachee TS, Parsons S, et al: Transcranial measurement of blood velocities in the basal cerebral arteries using pulsed Doppler ultrasound: Velocity as an index of flow. Ultrasound Med Biol 12:15-21, 1986.

103. Arnolds BJ, von Reutern GM: Transcranial Doppler sonography: Examination technique and normal reference values. Ultrasound Med Biol 12:115-123, 1986.

104. Cinat ME, Pham H, Vo D, et al: Improved imaging of carotid artery bifurcation using helical computed tomographic angiography. Ann Vasc Surg 13:178-183, 1999.

105. Scaroni R, Cardaioli G, Pelliccioli GP, Gallai V: Spiral computed tomography angiography (SCTA) and color-coded duplex ultrasound (CCDUS): Two complementary diagnostic techniques for assessment of extracranial cerebral artery stenosis. Clin Exp Hypertens 24:659-668, 2002.

106. Castillo M, Wilson JD: CT angiography of the common carotid artery bifurcation: Comparison between two techniques and conventional angiography. Neuroradiology 36:602-604, 1994.

107. Dillon EH, van Leeuwen MS, Fernandez MA, et al: CT angiography: Application to the evaluation of carotid artery stenosis. Radiology 189:211-219, 1993.

108. Leclerc X, Godefroy O, Pruvo JP, Leys D: Computed tomographic angiography for the evaluation of carotid artery stenosis. Stroke 26:1577-1581, 1995.

109. Simeone A, Carriero A, Armillotta M, et al: Spiral CT angiography in the study of the carotid stenoses. J Neuroradiol 24:18-22, 1997.

110. Corti R, Ferrari C, Roberti M, et al: Spiral computed tomography: A novel diagnostic approach for investigation of the extracranial cerebral arteries and its complementary role in duplex ultrasonography. Circulation 98:984-989, 1998.

111. Cinat M, Lane CT, Pham H, et al: Helical CT angiography in the preoperative evaluation of carotid artery stenosis. J Vasc Surg 28:290-300, 1998.

112. Verro P, Tanenbaum LN, Borden NM, et al: CT angiography in acute ischemic stroke: Preliminary results. Stroke 33:276-278, 2002.

113. Farres MT, Grabenwoger F, Magometschnig H, et al: Spiral CT angiography: Study of stenoses and calcification at the origin of the vertebral artery. Neuroradiology 38:738-743, 1996.

114. Park JH, Chung JW, Lee KW, et al: CT angiography of Takayasu arteritis: Comparison with conventional angiography. J Vasc Interv Radiol 8:393-400, 1997.

115. Szabo K, Gass A, Hennerici MG: Diffusion and perfusion MRI for the assessment of carotid atherosclerosis. Neuroimaging Clin North Am 12:381-390, 2002.

116. Morasch MD, Gurjala AN, Washington E, et al: Cross-sectional magnetic resonance angiography is accurate in predicting degree of carotid stenosis. Ann Vasc Surg 16:266-272, 2002.

117. Remonda L, Senn P, Barth A, et al: Contrast-enhanced 3D MR angiography of the carotid artery: Comparison with conventional digital subtraction angiography. AJNR Am J Neuroradiol 23:213-219, 2002.

118. Hassouna MS, Faraf AA, Hushek S, Moriarty T: Statistical-based approach for extracting 3D blood vessels from TOF-MyRA data. In Randy E, Ellis TMP (eds): Medical Image Computing and Computer-Assisted Intervention, November 15-18, 2003, Montreal, Springer-Verlag, 2003, pp 681-687.

119. Bongartz GM, Boos M, Winter K, et al: Clinical utility of contrast-enhanced MR angiography. Eur Radiol 7(Suppl 5):178-186, 1997.

120. Sundgren PC, Sunden P, Lindgren A, et al: Carotid artery stenosis: Contrast-enhanced MR angiography with two different scan times compared with digital subtraction angiography. Neuroradiology 44:592-599, 2002.

121. Wikstrom J, Johansson LO, Rossitti S, et al: High-resolution carotid artery MRA: Comparison with fast dynamic acquisition and duplex ultrasound scanning. Acta Radiol 43:256-261, 2002.

122. Townsend TC, Saloner D, Pan XM, Rapp JH: Contrast material-enhanced MRA overestimates severity of carotid stenosis, compared with 3D time-of-flight MRA. J Vasc Surg 38:36-40, 2003.

123. Back MR, Wilson JS, Rushing G, et al: Magnetic resonance angiography is an accurate imaging adjunct to duplex ultrasound scan in patient selection for carotid endarterectomy. J Vasc Surg 32:429-440, 2000.

124. Nederkoorn PJ, Elgersma OE, Mali WP, et al: Overestimation of carotid artery stenosis with magnetic resonance angiography compared with digital subtraction angiography. J Vasc Surg 36:806-813, 2002.

125. Nederkoorn PJ, van der Graaf Y, Eikelboom BC, et al: Time-of-flight MR angiography of carotid artery stenosis: Does a flow void represent severe stenosis? AJNR Am J Neuroradiol 23:1779-1784, 2002.

126. Cosottini M, Pingitore A, Puglioli M, et al: Contrast-enhanced three-dimensional magnetic resonance angiography of atherosclerotic internal carotid stenosis as the noninvasive imaging modality in revascularization decision making. Stroke 34:660-664, 2003.

127. Carpenter JP, Holland GA, Golden MA, et al: Magnetic resonance angiography of the aortic arch. J Vasc Surg 25:145-151, 1997.

128. Stuckey SL, Gilford EJ, Smith PJ, Kean M: Magnetic resonance angiography findings in the early post-carotid endarterectomy period. Australas Radiol 39:350-355, 1995.

129. Back MR, Rogers GA, Wilson JS, et al: Magnetic resonance angiography minimizes need for arteriography after inadequate carotid duplex ultrasound scanning. J Vasc Surg 38:422-431, 2003.

130. Borisch I, Horn M, Butz B, et al: Preoperative evaluation of carotid artery stenosis: Comparison of contrast-enhanced MR angiography and duplex sonography with digital subtraction angiography. AJNR Am J Neuroradiol 24:1117-1122, 2003.

131. Friese S, Krapf H, Fetter M, et al: Ultrasonography and contrast-enhanced MRA in ICA-stenosis: Is conventional angiography obsolete? J Neurol 248:506-513, 2001.

132. Johnston DC, Goldstein LB: Clinical carotid endarterectomy decision making: Noninvasive vascular imaging versus angiography. Neurology 56:1009-1015, 2001.

133. Johnston DC, Eastwood JD, Nguyen T, Goldstein LB: Contrast-enhanced magnetic resonance angiography of carotid arteries: Utility in routine clinical practice. Stroke 33:2834-2838, 2002.

134. Nederkoorn PJ, Mali WP, Eikelboom BC, et al: Preoperative diagnosis of carotid artery stenosis: Accuracy of noninvasive testing. Stroke 33:2003-2008, 2002.

135. Pan XM, Saloner D, Reilly LM, et al: Assessment of carotid artery stenosis by ultrasonography, conventional angiography, and magnetic resonance angiography: Correlation with ex vivo measurement of plaque stenosis. J Vasc Surg 21:82-89, 1995.

136. Estol C, Claasen D, Hirsch W, et al: Correlative angiographic and pathologic findings in the diagnosis of ulcerated plaques in the carotid artery. Arch Neurol 48:692-694, 1991.

137. Young GR, Humphrey PR, Shaw MD, et al: Comparison of magnetic resonance angiography, duplex ultrasound, and digital subtraction angiography in assessment of extracranial internal carotid artery stenosis. J Neurol Neurosurg Psychiatry 57:1466-1478, 1994.

138. Erdoes LS, Marek JM, Mills JL, et al: The relative contributions of carotid duplex scanning, magnetic resonance angiography, and cerebral arteriography to clinical decision making: A prospective study in patients with carotid occlusive disease. J Vasc Surg 23:950-956, 1996.

139. Lee KS: What workup should we require for a patient who has had one TIA and demonstrates 80% carotid stenosis? J Neurosurg Anesthesiol 8:305-307, 1996.

140. Turnipseed WD, Kennell TW, Turski PA, et al: Combined use of duplex imaging and magnetic resonance angiography for evaluation of patients with symptomatic ipsilateral high-grade carotid stenosis. J Vasc Surg 17:832-840, 1993.

Indications, Surgical Technique, and Results for Repair of Extracranial Occlusive Lesions

139

WILLIAM C. KRUPSKI, MD
WESLEY S. MOORE, MD

The primary objective of surgery for extracranial disorders is prevention of stroke. Carotid artery operations are warranted when surgery improves the natural history of the disease and provides a safe and more effective alternative to medical management. Selecting patients for operation requires the identification of specific patient subsets at high risk for stroke.

Although the symptomatic manifestations of cerebrovascular lesions can be frightening, annoying, and occasionally disabling, opinions differ as to whether transient ischemic attacks (TIAs) produce irreversible brain injury. Thus, prevention or relief of TIAs is viewed as an important secondary objective.

■ INDICATIONS FOR OPERATIVE REPAIR

Indications for operation can be derived from three sources: (1) retrospective reviews; (2) prospective, randomized trials; and (3) position/consensus statements.

Indications Based on Retrospective Reviews

Reports that document the natural history of disease, usually subdivided by symptomatic status, are compared with reports concerning immediate and long-term results of operation. If operative results, including 30-day morbidity/mortality and long-term reduction of amaurosis fugax, TIAs, and strokes, are less with operation than with medical treatment, then operation can be justified. The following is an analysis of operative indications by symptomatic status.

Transient Ischemic Attacks

When associated with an appropriate lesion, hemispheric or monocular TIAs have been the most readily accepted indications for carotid endarterectomy.

Most of the early natural history studies were performed without characterization of the underlying arterial lesion. Nevertheless, it is safe to say that the stroke risk in the untreated patient with TIAs is at least 10% within the first year of symptom onset and continues at the rate of about 6% per year, declining after 3 years.[67,158] In contrast, the stroke risk in the hemisphere ipsilateral to carotid endarterec-

tomy in the same patient group falls to less than 1% per year.[13,34,48,74,85,90,142,153] Provided that carotid endarterectomy by an individual surgeon can be performed with a low stroke morbidity and mortality, TIAs are a compelling indication for operation.

Stroke with Recovery

Because many patients who suffer strokes are only mildly disabled and may enjoy complete or nearly complete recovery, such patients require careful evaluation to discover a lesion that places them at risk for recurrent stroke. The natural history of this group of patients with respect to the annual recurrent stroke rate is approximately 9% per year.[5,47,127,132] The risk for recurrent stroke does not decrease after 3 years as occurs in patients with a TIA. Antiplatelet drugs are relatively ineffective in reducing this recurrence rate.[76] In contrast, carotid endarterectomy has successfully lowered the recurrent stroke rate to less than 2% per year.[93,98,145]

Patients who recover after completed strokes require careful assessment to determine the presence of a continuing, unstable causative lesion. For example, a patient who has recovered from a left hemisphere stroke and is found to have a significant stenosis of the left internal carotid artery is at high risk for subsequent left hemispheric stroke. In contrast, if the same patient has total occlusion of that artery, carotid endarterectomy is no longer feasible.

Review of operative outcomes in patients operated on after strokes reveals that the operative morbidity and mortality rates will be higher in this group of patients; therefore, they require special management (see Operative Technique).

Whether a patient who has made an *incomplete* recovery from a prior stroke is a candidate for carotid endarterectomy requires considerable experience and prudent judgment. In general, the patient who has been devastated by a stroke is not a candidate for carotid endarterectomy. Conversely, the patient who has had a mild stroke with complete or nearly complete recovery is an excellent candidate. The decision for operation for the in-between categories depends on a variety of factors, including how much neurologic function the patient has left to lose, his or her general functional status, the presence of medical comorbidities, and the patient's life expectancy.

Stroke-in-Evolution

The patient with stroke-in-evolution represents the highest risk for either medical or surgical management. Appropriately timed and appropriately performed carotid endarterectomy in such patients who are carefully selected dramatically improves the natural history of this disorder. In contrast, the risk of mortality and the risk of major stroke are predictably high. Operation on these patients should be performed only by those teams that have had considerable experience in managing this category of patient and can accept the added risk to achieve an important benefit.[61,101]

Global Ischemia

Patients who present with symptoms of global cerebral ischemia most often have these symptoms on the basis of decreased cardiac output secondary to arrhythmia or myocardial ischemia. Often the surgical dictum, "The dizzy surgeon operates on the dizzy patient for carotid disease," applies. However, a few patients who have *multiple* lesions involving the extracranial arteries manifest global ischemia and do benefit from correction of one or more of these lesions.[81]

Subclavian Steal Syndrome

Although many patients demonstrate an anatomic subclavian steal syndrome by angiography (i.e., reversed flow through the ipsilateral vertebral artery), only a few have symptoms produced by extremity exercise on the side of the subclavian artery stenosis or occlusion. Those patients who fall into the latter category or those who have a dominant vertebral artery on the side of the proximal subclavian lesion may be candidates for subclavian artery revascularization.[8]

Progressive Intellectual Dysfunction

Progressive intellectual dysfunction represents an extremely controversial indication for carotid endarterectomy. Nonetheless, many anecdotal reports document improved intellectual function after carotid endarterectomy. Decreased intellectual function can occur because of flow or as a summating effect of multiple emboli to centers of the brain responsible for cognitive abilities, independent of motor or sensory findings. In properly selected patients, intervention by carotid endarterectomy *may* improve intellectual function or prevent its further deterioration.

Asymptomatic Carotid Stenosis

Asymptomatic carotid stenosis is one of the most common indications for carotid endarterectomy. It is also the most controversial. Recently, several publications have provided surgeons with considerable natural history data that were previously unavailable. It is now safe to state that the risk of stroke in patients with a carotid artery stenosis in excess of 75% is about 3% to 5% per year of follow-up. Most of these strokes occur without warning symptoms.[25,100] Many authorities have recommended that patients with carotid stenoses in excess of 75% who are otherwise in satisfactory medical condition and have a reasonable life expectancy

undergo prophylactic carotid endarterectomy if the operation can be performed safely in the hands of the individual surgeon.[73,104] Operative morbidity and mortality rate for this indication should be less than 3%.

The average late stroke rate in the distribution of the operated artery is 0.3% per year.[146] In a 10-year experience at the University of California at Los Angeles (UCLA), there were no late strokes in the distribution of the operated artery, with a mean follow-up of 54 months.[55]

Asymptomatic Ulceration

Patients who are discovered by angiography to have ulcerative lesions of the carotid artery have an increased risk of subsequent stroke when treated expectantly.[108] This risk rises progressively as the size and complexity of the ulceration increase.

Retrospective natural history studies have divided ulcers into three categories: A, B, and C.[108] Quantitation of A, B, and C ulcers is performed by examining an unmagnified lateral projection of a carotid arteriogram.[37] If the product of the length and depth of the ulcer is obtained, an A ulcer is one that is 10 mm² or less; a B ulcer varies from 10 to 40 mm²; and a C ulcer exceeds 40 mm² or is cavernous or compound.

Retrospective natural history studies suggest that the stroke rate in patients with asymptomatic A ulcers is insignificant. Of note, the stroke rate in patients with asymptomatic C ulcers exceeds 7.5% per year.[37] According to these retrospective data, patients with a C ulcer on arteriogram who are acceptable surgical risks warrant consideration for prophylactic carotid endarterectomy. The decision whether to operate on the patient with a B ulcer depends on the experience of the operating team and the individual conviction of the importance of this lesion. There is no place for surgery for patients with the asymptomatic A ulcer. These recommendations are somewhat controversial because the key studies, which originated from UCLA, have not been corroborated by other centers.

Prospective, Randomized Trials

Symptomatic Patients

Three prospective, randomized trials have provided definitive data concerning indications for carotid endarterectomy in symptomatic patients.[49,95,116] Patients with *hemispheric* or *monocular* TIAs or prior mild stroke with a 70% or greater stenosis have clear indications for carotid endarterectomy. Patients with *crescendo* TIAs in the presence of a 50% or greater stenosis benefit from operation. Symptomatic patients with stenoses of less than 30% showed no benefit from operation in one study.[49] Symptomatic patients with stenoses ranging from 30% to 69% are still being evaluated in two randomized trials.[49,116] Preliminary results from the North American Symptomatic Carotid Endarterectomy Trial (NASCET) for symptomatic patients with 50% to 69% carotid stenoses were reported at the 1998 meeting of the American Heart Association (see Results).

Three prospective, randomized trials in asymptomatic patients with carotid stenoses have been completed. The

CASANOVA Study Group concluded that no benefit was to be derived from carotid endarterectomy in the asymptomatic patient.[24] High-risk patients were excluded, and 118 (57%) of 206 patients randomized to medical treatment were systematically withdrawn as they became "high risk" and were treated surgically. In an intent-to-treat analysis, however, they were counted as if they were treated medically. Therefore, no conclusions can be drawn from this study.

The Veterans Affairs Cooperative Study has reported definitive results.[78] Carotid endarterectomy plus aspirin was more effective than aspirin alone in reducing the combined incidence of TIAs and stroke in patients with asymptomatic stenosis of 50% or more, which was the study's hypothesis. The number of patients randomized ($n = 444$) was insufficient to make a definitive statement about stroke prevention alone, although the trend was clearly in favor of operation.

Results of the Asymptomatic Carotid Atherosclerosis Study (ACAS) were published in 1995.[3] Acquisition of patients began in November 1987 and ended in December 1992, with randomization of 1622 men and women with asymptomatic carotid stenoses of between 60% and 99%. According to Kaplan-Meier projections at 5 years, the risk of ipsilateral stroke for the medical group was 11% and 5.1% for the surgical group. This represents a relative risk reduction of 53% and an absolute risk reduction of about 1% per year.

Consensus Statements Affecting Indications

Several organizations have published position papers or consensus statements based on the collective opinion of recognized experts. These include an ad hoc committee report from the Joint Council of the two national vascular societies[111] and the Rand Corporation.[94] Most recently, the American Heart Association convened a consensus conference, and its report has been published.[106] Table 139-1 summarizes the current indications for carotid endarterectomy and compares the recommendations from retrospective reviews, the Rand panel, the Joint Council position statement, and the prospective, randomized trials.[105]

■ CONTRAINDICATIONS TO OPERATIVE REPAIR

An aggressive surgical approach is contraindicated if the general condition of the patient includes a serious illness that will materially shorten the normal life expectancy. In addition to this general reservation, some patients have specific neurologic complications that prohibit operation or make its postponement advisable. These include the patient who presents acutely with a major stroke and has not yet begun to recover. Another is one who has had a major stroke in the past and is so devastated by neurologic dysfunction or altered level of consciousness that operation is inadvisable.

Table 139-1   Current Indications for Carotid Endarterectomy

	SOURCE OF RECOMMENDATION			
PATIENTS	Retrospective Data Analysis	Rand Panel	Joint Council*	Randomized Trials
Symptomatic				
Single focal TIA (>70% stenosis)	Yes	Yes	Yes	Yes
Multiple focal TIAs with				
>70% stenosis	Yes	Yes	Yes	Yes
>50% stenosis with ulceration	Yes	Yes	Yes	NA
50-69% stenosis†	Yes	Yes	Yes	NA
30-49% stenosis†	Yes	Yes	Yes	NA
<30% stenosis with or without ulcer†	Yes	Yes	Yes	No
Previous stroke (mild), ipsilateral				
>70% stenosis	Yes	Yes	Yes	Yes
>50% with large ulcer	Yes	Yes	Yes	NA
30-69% with and without ulcer	Yes	Yes	Yes	NA
Evolving stroke				
>70% stenosis	Yes	Yes	Yes	NA
Global symptoms				
>70% carotid stenosis with uncorrectable vertebrobasilar disease	Yes	Yes	Yes	NA
Asymptomatic				
>70% stenosis with contralateral occlusion or high-grade stenosis	Yes	Yes	Yes	NA
>70% unilateral stenosis	Yes	No	Yes	NA
Large ulcer with >50% stenosis	Yes	No	NA	NA

*Joint Council of the Society for Vascular Surgery and the International Society for Cardiovascular Surgery (North American Chapter).
†Patients receiving aspirin therapy.
NA, not available; TIA, transient ischemic attack.

From Moore WS: Carotid endarterectomy for prevention of stroke. West J Med 159:37-43, 1993.

During early experience with carotid surgery, emergency operation for acute stroke was relatively common.[126] However, emergency thromboendarterectomy of an acutely occluded carotid artery frequently resulted in conversion of an ischemic cerebral infarction to a hemorrhagic cerebral infarction, resulting in death.[139] These findings were particularly dramatized in the first randomized cooperative study involving operation for carotid artery disease.[17] In addition, endarterectomy after acute stroke in a diseased but open internal carotid artery, prior to neurologic recovery, often resulted in an exacerbation of the neurologic deficit, presumably because of an increase in localized cerebral edema and its attendant adverse consequences. After recent major neurologic injury, it is better to wait for the patient to reach a plateau of recovery before proceeding with elective carotid endarterectomy.[120]

■ OPERATIVE TECHNIQUE

Surgery of the Carotid Bifurcation

Anesthesia and Positioning of the Patient

Operations on the carotid bifurcation were originally, and often still are, performed using local or cervical block anesthesia. Local anesthesia has the advantage of allowing the surgeon to evaluate the patient's cerebral tolerance to trial carotid clamping. When the carotid clamp is temporarily applied, the patient is asked to speak and move the extremities of the appropriate side as evidence of adequate collateral cerebral circulation to support brain function during the time required to remove the lesion. For this reason, a number of surgeons continue to advocate local anesthesia as the anesthetic technique of choice.

The disadvantages of local anesthesia primarily relate to patient anxiety. If the patient becomes restless or agitated, this will also disturb the surgical team. Finally, when a difficult lesion is encountered, extended operating time may exceed the forbearance of the average patient under local anesthesia.

General anesthesia has the following three major advantages:

1. The anesthesiologist has better control of the patient's airway and ventilatory mechanics.
2. Halogenated anesthetic agents can increase cerebral blood flow and, at the same time, decrease cerebral metabolic demand.[27] This combined effect may increase tolerance to temporary carotid artery clamping.
3. The sleeping, anesthetized patient can undergo comfortably whichever exacting procedure is required without disturbing the operating field and the surgical team.

Positioning the patient is an important aspect of preparing for a carotid endarterectomy. The patient is placed supine on the operating table with the neck slightly hyperextended. This may be accomplished by placing a folded sheet under the shoulders. Excessive hypertension actually makes exposure more difficult by tightening the sternocleidomastoid muscle and by restricting the mobility of the common carotid artery and carotid bifurcation. Once

the head is extended, it is then gently turned to the side opposite that of operation.

Many patients in the age group appropriate for carotid artery disease may have a significant degree of cervical arthritis. Care must be taken to avoid neck injury with rotation. If the patient's blood pressure is stable, flexing the operating table and introducing a 10- to 20-degree reverse Trendelenburg inclination brings the patient's neck into best perspective, reducing venous pressure and minimizing incisional bleeding (Fig. 139-1).

Two incisions have been employed for exposure of the carotid bifurcation. The first is a vertical incision parallel to the anterior border of the sternocleidomastoid muscle, along a line connecting the sternoclavicular junction with the mastoid process. The surgeon decides its exact length and placement along this imaginary line by noting the position of the carotid bifurcation and the extent of the lesion on the lateral projection of the carotid arteriogram (Fig. 139-2). This determination is also made solely by the use of carotid duplex ultrasound scans. The incision is deepened through the platysmal layer to gain access to the investing fascia in the interval between the sternocleidomastoid muscle and

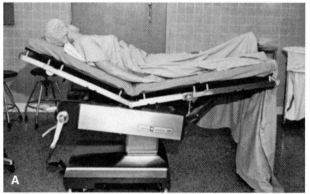
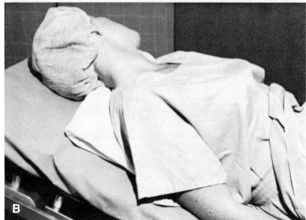

FIGURE 139-1 **A,** The optimal operating table adjustment for carotid bifurcation endarterectomy. The table is flexed 10- to 20-degrees in the reverse Trendelenburg position to bring the patient into a semirecumbent position. **B,** The neck is mildly hyperextended by introducing a folded sheet under the patient's shoulders. Finally, the patient's head is turned to the side opposite the operation. The neck on the side of operation is now exposed to best surgical advantage.

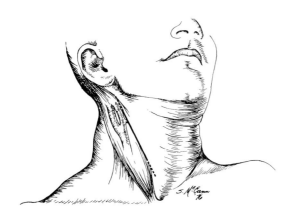

FIGURE 139-2 Placement of a vertical incision along the anterior border of the sternocleidomastoid muscle in relationship to the underlying carotid artery bifurcation.

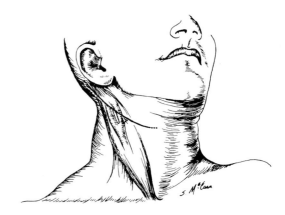

FIGURE 139-3 The alternative incision placed obliquely in a skin crease over the carotid bifurcation. The dissection is carried down through the platysma, and subplatysmal flaps are developed in the superior and inferior aspects of the incision to convert the exposure of the carotid bifurcation to a vertical approach.

the trachea. We prefer this incision because it parallels the carotid artery. If the surgeon needs to gain additional exposure of the proximal or distal part of the vessel, extension of the incision is simple and easy.

The second incision employed for exposure of the carotid bifurcation is oblique and is placed in one of the skin creases over the side of the neck (Fig. 139-3). It is deepened through the platysma, and the subplatysmal space between the sternocleidomastoid muscle and the trachea is mobilized. The advantage of this incision is that it may produce a more cosmetically acceptable scar than that resulting from the vertical incision. The disadvantages are that (1) it is necessary to raise skin flaps and (2) it is more difficult to gain additional proximal or distal arterial exposure because the direction of the incision is oblique to the direction of the artery.

After exposure, the investing fascia is incised along the anterior border of the sternocleidomastoid muscle, and the muscle is then mobilized to expose the underlying carotid sheath (Fig. 139-4). The carotid sheath is incised low on the neck, and the dissection is directed along the medial aspect of the internal jugular vein. The vein is retracted laterally to expose the common carotid artery (Fig. 139-5). The vagus nerve is usually the most posterior occupant of the carotid sheath, but occasionally it may spiral to take an anterior position at the point where the sheath is opened. This anomaly should be anticipated, and the surgeon should take care to avoid injuring the nerve when the sheath is initially incised.

The medial aspect of the jugular vein is exposed until the common facial vein is seen coursing obliquely across the common carotid artery and draining into the jugular vein.

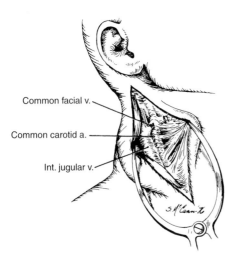

FIGURE 139-4 The relationship of the internal jugular vein and common carotid artery within the carotid sheath. The major tributary to the internal jugular vein at this level is the common facial vein. Division of the common facial vein consistently gives access to the carotid bifurcation.

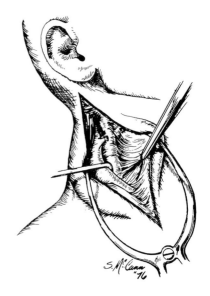

FIGURE 139-5 Following mobilization of its anteromedial aspect, the internal jugular vein is retracted laterally, giving clear exposure to the underlying common carotid artery.

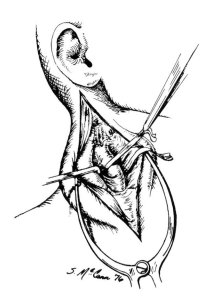

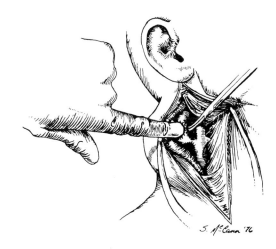

FIGURE 139-7 The internal carotid artery is mobilized well above the diseased intima. This fact is confirmed by careful palpation of the relatively normal internal carotid artery against the surface of the right-angle clamp.

FIGURE 139-6 The mobilized common carotid artery with the surrounding umbilical tape. The dissection toward the internal and external carotid arteries has begun.

The common facial vein is a constant landmark for the carotid bifurcation and represents the venous analogue of the external carotid artery. The vein is mobilized, suture ligated, and divided (Fig. 139-6). When the vein is divided, the carotid artery can be appropriately visualized. The common carotid artery is mobilized circumferentially and encircled with polymeric silicone (Silastic) tape. The periarterial dissection continues superiorly to expose the carotid bifurcation. As soon as the bifurcation is identified, if a sinus bradycardia occurs, 1 to 2 mL of 1% lidocaine may be injected into the tissues between the external and the internal carotid arteries to block the nerves to the carotid sinus. Some surgeons routinely anesthetize the carotid sinus to prevent this phenomenon.

Particular care must be taken during this part of the dissection to avoid undue manipulation or palpation of the carotid bifurcation and bulb of the internal carotid artery. Because this is the location of the atheromatous lesion and because the lesion may be quite friable or contain thrombotic or atheromatous debris, manipulation may cause dislodgment with subsequent cerebral embolization and stroke. Some surgeons have described this requirement for gentleness as "dissecting the patient away from the carotid, not vice versa."

The internal carotid artery is mobilized to a point well above the palpable atheromatous lesion, where it is unquestionably soft and not diseased (Fig. 139-7). The same is done for the external carotid artery, with care taken not to injure the superior thyroid branch. In patients with a high carotid bifurcation or a lesion that goes relatively far up the internal carotid artery, the surgeon obtains additional exposure by carefully dividing the tissues in the crotch formed by the internal and the external carotid arteries. This maneuver should be performed between clamps because, on occasion, the ascending pharyngeal artery can be located in this position. The tissues in this crotch often act as a suspensory ligament of the carotid bifurcation and, once

divided, allow the bifurcation to drop down, making further mobilization of the internal carotid artery possible.

The 12th cranial nerve should always be identified when the internal carotid artery is mobilized. It passes obliquely through the upper portion of the field, just superior to the bulb of the carotid artery, on its way to innervate the tongue (Fig. 139-8). Injury to this nerve causes a lateral deviation of the tongue toward the side of operation when the patient attempts to extrude the tongue. This also produces difficulty with initiation of swallowing. Should additional exposure of the internal carotid artery be necessary, mobilization and division of the posterior belly of the digastric muscle may be required (Fig. 139-9).

Determination of Cerebral Tolerance to Carotid Cross-Clamping

Once the carotid bifurcation is exposed but before endarterectomy can be started, a decision must be made regarding the method of maintaining cerebral flow during carotid occlusion. The time-honored technique for

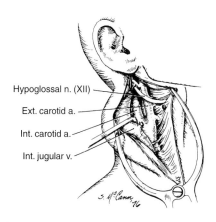

Hypoglossal n. (XII)

Ext. carotid a.

Int. carotid a.

Int. jugular v.

FIGURE 139-8 The relationship of the 12th cranial nerve to the upper extent of the dissection of the carotid bifurcation.

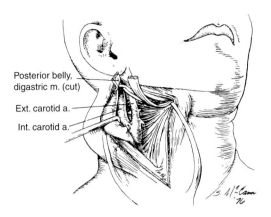

FIGURE 139-9 When the carotid bifurcation is high or when the lesion extends for an unusual distance up the internal carotid artery, additional distal exposure of the internal carotid artery can be obtained by division of the posterior belly of the digastric muscle.

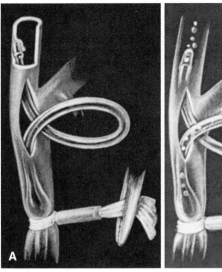
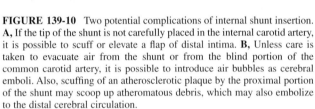

FIGURE 139-10 Two potential complications of internal shunt insertion. **A,** If the tip of the shunt is not carefully placed in the internal carotid artery, it is possible to scuff or elevate a flap of distal intima. **B,** Unless care is taken to evacuate air from the shunt or from the blind portion of the common carotid artery, it is possible to introduce air bubbles as cerebral emboli. Also, scuffing of an atherosclerotic plaque by the proximal portion of the shunt may scoop up atheromatous debris, which may also embolize to the distal cerebral circulation.

determining the safety of temporary carotid clamping is trial occlusion with local anesthesia. The common, external, and internal carotid arteries are occluded for 3 minutes. During this time, the patient is asked to talk and move the arm and leg on the side affected by the carotid lesion. If there is no evidence of weakness or disturbance of consciousness, the intracranial circulation is judged to be adequate and operation can proceed without additional circulatory support. Adequate cerebral collateral circulation is found in approximately 85% to 90% of patients tested. In the 10% to 15% in whom circulation is inadequate, an internal shunt must be employed.

Local anesthesia and trial occlusion constitute a very satisfactory technique. If the surgeon prefers general anesthesia, an alternative method for determining the safety of temporary carotid occlusion must be employed. Many surgeons who use general anesthesia prefer to insert an internal shunt routinely. This does not identify selectively the individual patient who requires such circulatory support, but it has the advantage of "playing it safe" by providing additional flow to all patients.[147] The disadvantage is that the presence of an internal shunt makes the performance of endarterectomy somewhat more cumbersome. It also compromises precise visualization of the distal endpoint and introduces the potential complications inherent in the use of the shunt.

These complications include scuffing or disruption of the distal intima during shunt insertion and the possible introduction of air or thrombotic emboli through the shunt when flow is reconstituted (Fig. 139-10). In a personal series (W.S.M), surgical patients without a shunt had a postoperative neurologic complication rate of 1.5%, whereas those with a shunt had a neurologic complication rate of 5%. Because of such experiences, we prefer to reserve the use of an internal shunt for those selected few patients with inadequate collateral circulation when it is clearly indicated and justified. We prefer not to expose the remaining majority of patients to the small but finite increased risk of shunt use when there is no need to provide the additional cerebral blood flow.

The next question is how to identify inadequate collateral blood flow in patients undergoing general anesthesia. Several methods have been attempted, such as the measurement of ipsilateral jugular venous oxygen tension.[91] The hypothesis on which this test is based states that patients with adequate collateral blood flow would have a higher oxygen tension in the venous blood draining from that segment than those patients with inadequate blood flow. This test proved to be inexact because, owing to the anatomy of the venous-sinus system, the venous drainage from the brain is a mixture of blood from both hemispheres.[85]

Another suggested method is electroencephalographic monitoring during operation. Initial experience with this technique was disappointing, owing to the effect of general anesthesia on electroencephalographic tracing.[64] More recently, however, the technique was reintroduced and has now become a standard method by which adequacy of cerebral blood flow is monitored.[4,153] This test is somewhat cumbersome because of the instrumentation involved and the expertise needed to interpret the electroencephalographic tracing. Nonetheless, several centers use it with enthusiasm and with excellent results.

Many surgeons have noted that patients who tolerate carotid cross-clamping also have excellent back-bleeding from the internal carotid artery through the arteriotomy when the clamps are released. Some investigators have used this observation to determine the adequacy of collateral blood flow and shunt requirement. This method can work in the hands of the experienced surgeon who has developed the ability to judge back-flow; however, it is a qualitative rather than a quantitative observation, and as such cannot be taught.

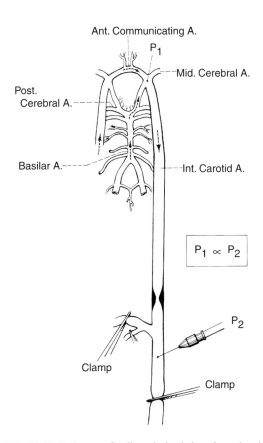

Ant. Communicating A.

P_1

Mid. Cerebral A.

Post. Cerebral A.

Basilar A.

Int. Carotid A.

$$P_1 \propto P_2$$

P_2

Clamp

Clamp

FIGURE 139-11 Pathways of collateral circulation about the circle of Willis. Perfusion pressure at the middle cerebral artery (P_1). Internal carotid back pressure as measured at the bifurcation (P_2). Being a closed, unbranched fluid system, P_2 is proportional to P_1. Ant, Anterior; Mid, Middle; Int, Internal. (From Moore WS, Hall AD: Carotid artery back pressure. Arch Surg 99:702, 1969.)

Recognizing the validity of the observation of back-flow, in 1966 the author (W.S.M.) and his colleagues set about to develop a method of quantitation. The results of this clinical research have led to the introduction of the *internal carotid artery back-pressure determination* as a means of estimating collateral cerebral blood flow. These investigators reasoned that a relationship existed between the intracranial collateral blood flow and perfusion pressure. Measurement of the back-pressure down the proximally clamped internal carotid artery is an indirect measurement of the perfusion pressure that is present on the ipsilateral side of the circle of Willis (Fig. 139-11). Our group initially validated the technique by measuring back-pressure in a series of 36 patients undergoing 48 carotid thromboendarterectomies under local anesthesia. The patients' conscious response to trial occlusion was correlated with the measured value of internal carotid artery back-pressure. Of the 48 carotid arteries tested, 43 had back-pressures that ranged from 25 to 88 mm Hg. In each instance, the patient maintained full motor and intellectual function. Three patients were intolerant of trial occlusion, and their internal carotid artery back-pressure ranged from 12 to 24 mm Hg. These observations led the investigators to conclude that 25 mm Hg under ambient conditions of Pco_2 and the patient's normal blood pressure was the minimal safe level. All patients with

back-pressures below 25 mm Hg required an internal shunt, and the carotid arteries of those with pressures above 25 mm Hg could be occluded temporarily without additional cerebral circulatory support.[109]

Other investigators reported similar results using carotid artery back-pressure of 40 mm Hg.[44,69] The validity of carotid back-pressure measurements to determine the need for temporary shunt placement in patients under general anesthesia has been confirmed, but one group of patients constitute an exception to the back-pressure criteria—those who have had a previous cerebral infarction. Patients who have suffered a previous stroke often experience a temporary exacerbation of neurologic deficit when a shunt is not used, because patients with a previous cerebral infarction have a surrounding zone of relative ischemia that is being perfused through collateral channels, the *ischemic penumbra*. These collateral channels have a variably higher resistance to flow; therefore, this group of patients has a greater perfusion pressure requirement to maintain flow to the ischemic penumbra than those with normal circulatory patterns.[112]

In patients with a previous cerebral infarction, in our opinion, shunts should be used routinely regardless of the measured back-pressure. The temporary shunt is indicated for all patients with a prior history of cerebral infarction as well as for those with a back-pressure of less than 25 mm Hg. Patients undergoing operations for TIAs or asymptomatic carotid stenosis in whom the back-pressure is greater than 25 to 40 mm Hg do not require a shunt. Using these criteria, the author's group (W.S.M.) then carried out a series of 172 carotid endarterectomies in 153 patients with a 0.6% overall neurologic morbidity rate that included postoperative TIAs as well as infarction. In 74% of cases, the operation was performed without an internal shunt, whereas 26% required internal shunt support.[82]

The technique for measuring internal carotid back-pressure is quite simple and has been validated by others.[69,80] After the carotid bifurcation is mobilized, 5000 to 10,000 units of heparin is administered intravenously. A 22-gauge needle is bent at a 45-degree angle and is connected via rigid pressure tubing to a pressure transducer. The bent portion of the needle is then inserted into the common carotid artery so that it rests in a position that is axial to the artery and does not impinge on the posterior wall. Systemic arterial pressure is measured in this manner, before clamping and compared with radial artery pressure being monitored via a catheter placed earlier. The common carotid artery, proximal to the needle, is then clamped.

A second clamp is placed on the external carotid artery. This leaves the needle in continuity with a static column of blood that is open to the internal carotid artery. Even though the needle is placed proximal to the carotid stenosis, pressure equalizes on both sides of the carotid stenosis because there is no blood flow. The residual pressure or internal carotid artery back-pressure is then recorded (Fig. 139-12).

In an effort to reduce further the need for internal shunt, investigation was conducted into possible methods of increasing cerebral blood flow during carotid surgery. The methods attempted include inducing arterial hypertension and manipulating arterial Pco_2.[45,84,157] Increasing arterial blood pressure by use of vasopressor drugs increases

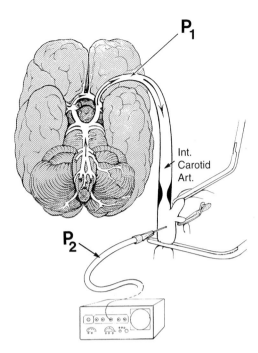

FIGURE 139-12 Relationship of middle cerebral to internal carotid perfusion pressure is represented. With common and external carotid arteries clamped, back-pressure distal to the internal carotid artery is in direct continuity with the middle cerebral artery. Therefore, P_2 is essentially equal to P_1. Int, Internal. (From Moore WS, Yee JM, Hall AD: Collateral cerebral blood pressure: An index of tolerance to temporary carotid occlusion. Arch Surg 106:520, 1973.)

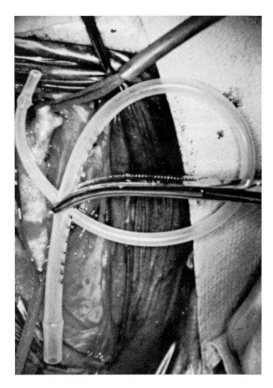

FIGURE 139-13 A Javid shunt prior to placement. We prefer this type of inlying shunt because its size is appropriate to provide maximal flow, and the proximal and distal diameter expansions reduce the possibility of inadvertent displacement while the shunt is functioning.

perfusion pressure in collateral channels and, presumably, increases collateral blood flow. There is, however, a price to be paid for this benefit in the form of increasing afterload on the myocardium. Because most of these patients have associated coronary artery disease, the net result may be an increased risk of myocardial damage. It is preferable to use an internal shunt in a few more patients rather than risk increasing the incidence of myocardial infarction.

Increasing P_{CO_2} (hypercapnia) effectively induces cerebral vasodilation.[79,121] For this reason, many surgeons employ hypercapnia to increase cerebral blood flow during carotid occlusion. However, there is evidence to suggest that the cerebral vasculature in areas of decreased cerebral perfusion is already maximally dilated. Hypercapnia not only fails to increase cerebral blood flow where it is needed but also, by producing cerebral vasodilation in the opposite hemisphere, causes a redistribution of blood flow with a reduced collateral contribution from the normally perfused hemisphere. Therefore, some investigators have suggested that the reverse approach be employed (i.e., a reduction of P_{CO_2}, or hypocapnia), to cause cerebral vasoconstriction on the normally perfused side so that collateral redistribution will be from the normal to the ischemic side. The experimental data in the literature are contradictory, and the information is inadequate on which to base a conclusion about the relative merits of hypocapnia versus hypercapnia. Because the back-pressure data originally were obtained using normocapnia, we prefer to continue using normocapnia to avoid confusing the interpretation of back-pressure values.

Internal Shunt Placement

A shunt is a valuable surgical adjunct that, properly used, can reduce the incidence of neurologic complications in those patients who depend on continued flow through the carotid artery that is undergoing repair. An improperly placed shunt, however, can be the source of several complications that may lead to permanent neurologic damage. Once it has been decided to use an internal shunt, the operating surgeon should take a few minutes to describe the technique to the team and make certain that the proper shunt and appropriate instruments are immediately available to minimize ischemia time between carotid clamping and shunt placement.

The *Javid shunt* is still popular because of the appropriate diameter, length, and smooth finish of the ends to be inserted into the artery (Fig. 139-13). A modified Rumel tourniquet may be used to anchor the shunt, by drawing an umbilical tape encircling the common and internal carotid arteries through a short segment of rubber tubing, and "snugging down" on the rubber tube clamp to draw the umbilical sling firmly around the internal shunt within the artery (Fig. 139-14). Alternatively, specially fashioned Javid shunt clamps are available.

A longitudinal arteriotomy is begun on the posterior lateral part of the common carotid artery, well proximal to the lesion. The arteriotomy is extended through the lesion, into the carotid bulb, and beyond into the internal carotid artery as far as necessary to clear the obvious diseased intima. The distal end of the shunt is placed in the internal

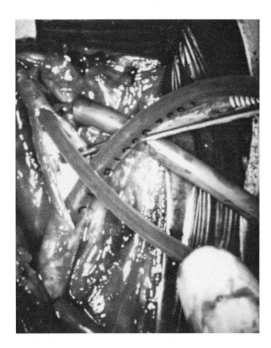

FIGURE 139-14 A functioning shunt in place. The shunt is held in position by a proximal and distal sling tourniquet.

carotid artery, which is then allowed to back-bleed and fill the shunt with blood. The proximal part of the shunt is passed into the common carotid artery. This passage is made with the shunt actively back-bleeding to dissipate any air from the common carotid segment. Several insertions and withdrawals of the shunt may be required to flush all the air out of the blind segment.

The shunt is then clamped, the tourniquet about the shunt within the common carotid artery is tightened, and the clamp on the common carotid artery is released. At this point, the clamp on the shunt tubing is slowly opened and the translucent tubing is carefully observed for air bubbles

and atheromatous debris. If no bubbles or debris is seen, the shunt is fully opened and the operation can proceed. The complications of an internal shunt include scuffing of the distal arterial intima, embolization of atheromatous debris or air, and poor distal endpoint management (Fig. 139-15).

Scuffing of the intima can be minimized by using the polyethylene shunt tubing with a smooth, rounded tip specifically manufactured for this purpose. Atheroma embolization can be avoided by making an arteriotomy large enough to prevent scooping up of atheromatous debris at the time the proximal portion of the shunt is inserted into the common carotid artery. Air emboli can be prevented by careful evacuation of the air at the time of shunt insertion. Problems with distal endpoint management can be reduced by opening the internal carotid artery as far as necessary to ensure direct visualization of a smooth endpoint (Fig. 139-16).

In another technique of shunting, the distal end of the shunt is placed in the external rather than the internal carotid artery.[92] This method augments, to a variable degree, cerebral collateral blood flow through the external carotid artery-ophthalmic artery-internal carotid artery route, which has the advantage of keeping the shunt out of the internal carotid artery and reducing the problems with distal endpoint management (Fig. 139-17). This alternative technique is less well established.

Bifurcation Endarterectomy

One of the most critical details of endarterectomy is the selection of an appropriate endarterectomy plane. The optimal plane of dissection lies between the diseased intima and the circular fibers of the arterial media (Fig. 139-18). A carotid endarterectomy performed in this plane allows for a smooth, distal tapering of endpoint. It is easy to get into the plane between the arterial media and the adventitia. Although this is an easily dissectible plane, obtaining a smooth, tapering endpoint is more difficult because of the increased thickness of the relatively normal intima and media at the termination point of dissection in the internal

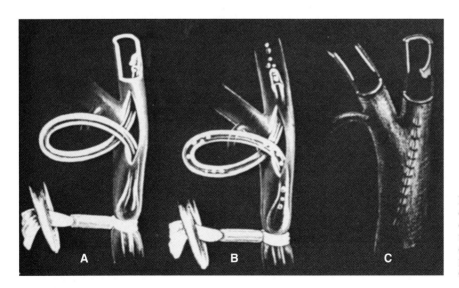

FIGURE 139-15 The three potential complications of an internal shunt. **A,** Scuffing of the distal intima. **B,** Embolization of air or atherothrombotic debris. **C,** Poor visualization of the distal endpoint so that an intimal flap is left, producing the risk of subsequent thromboembolic complications.

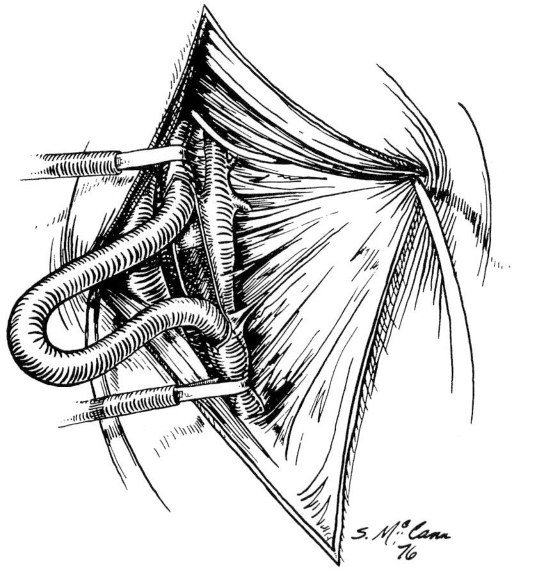

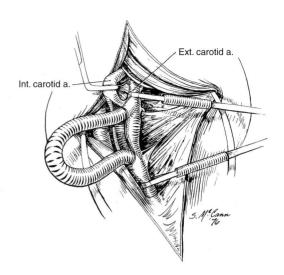

FIGURE 139-17 Technique of placing the distal end of the shunt in the external carotid artery to provide free access to the internal carotid artery. This is an alternative way to minimize problems with endpoint management.

FIGURE 139-16 Appearance of the carotid bifurcation with the shunt in place following bifurcation endarterectomy. The distal portion of the arteriotomy extends far enough up the internal carotid artery to permit direct visualization of the distal endpoint.

carotid artery. Because of this thickness, there is often a shelf or a step-up in the internal carotid artery, which may require the use of sutures to tack down the endpoint. We believe that it is disadvantageous to use tacking sutures and prefer to achieve a smooth, tapered endpoint that occurs naturally within a proper dissection plane.

Once the proper plane is established in the common carotid artery, dissection is continued with a dissector circumferentially about the artery. The circumferential

dissection is completed with a right-angle clamp, making it possible to identify the same dissection plane on the opposite side of the artery (Fig. 139-19). The atheromatous lesion is then sharply divided at its most proximal limit in the common carotid artery. The circumferential dissection is then carried to the external carotid artery, where a core of diseased intima is carefully developed by eversion of the artery and then gently removed.

The final and most important part of the dissection can now proceed up the internal carotid artery. Care is taken to advance equal distances circumferentially up the internal carotid artery. The specimen suddenly becomes free at a point where the intima becomes relatively normal, leaving a

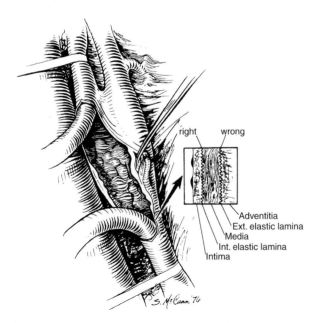

FIGURE 139-18 The proper endarterectomy dissection plane. The optimal plane lies between the diseased intima and the media at the level of the internal elastic lamina.

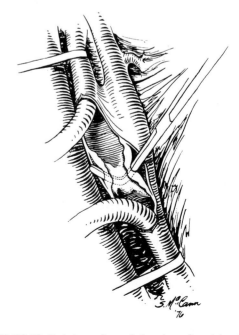

FIGURE 139-19 Technique of completing circumferential mobilization of the atheromatous lesion by using the closed jaws of a right-angle clamp.

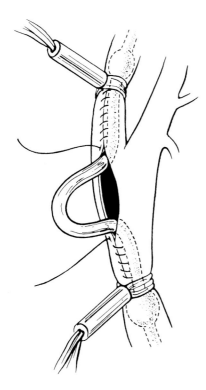

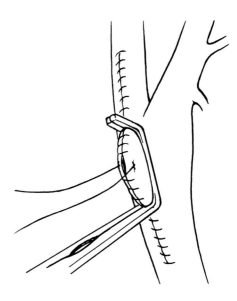

FIGURE 139-21 Application of a partially occluding pediatric vascular clamp permits restoration of blood flow to the internal and external carotid arteries while the final portion of the arteriotomy closure is completed after removal of the internal shunt.

FIGURE 139-20 Partial closure of the arteriotomy with a suture beginning at each end. The arteriotomy is closed as far as the emergence of the internal shunt will permit.

smooth, tapering endpoint. The intimectomized surface of the carotid bifurcation is then generously irrigated with heparinized saline solution, and any loose bits of debris or tiny strips of media are carefully removed. The proximal and distal endpoints in the internal and external carotid arteries are irrigated under direct vision to make certain that there are no floating intimal flaps. A free edge of intima that floats is gently picked at with the tip of a fine clamp.

This part of the operation must not be hurried. If the patient has adequate collateral circulation, increased clamp time is not a problem. If collateral circulation is inadequate, a shunt should have been employed so that the operation can be done in a careful, unhurried fashion.

Once the endarterectomy is complete, the next step is closure. If a shunt has not been employed, a careful primary closure can be performed with 6-0 polypropylene suture. Tiny, closely placed, continuous stitches restore the normal contour of the artery without narrowing. If the arteriotomy was carried high up on a small or attenuated internal carotid artery, closure with a patch of vein or prosthetic material is desirable. Reports concerning recurrent carotid stenosis suggest that the use of a patch in patients with small arteries, particularly women, can minimize both early and late recurrence of stenosis.[72]

If an internal shunt has been employed, the closure is somewhat encumbered and the technique must be modified. A suture line is begun at the distal portion of the arteriotomy on the internal carotid artery and carried down to the common carotid artery. A second suture is then started proximally and is continued as far as the emergence of the plastic shunt will permit. The loop of the internal shunt then

emerges between the two sutures (Fig. 139-20). The shunt is then removed, each vessel is carefully flushed, and a partially occluding pediatric vascular clamp is applied to approximate the remaining open portion of the arteriotomy. Flow is restored initially to the external carotid artery to flush any possible residual air or debris into that vessel. Flow is then restored to the internal carotid artery, and the surgeon makes a final closure of the arteriotomy by approximating the tissue held in place with the pediatric vascular clamp (Fig. 139-21).

Endarterectomy of an external carotid artery stenosis, in the presence of a totally occluded internal carotid artery, can be performed in the same manner as a carotid bifurcation endarterectomy.[32] In this instance, the arteriotomy extends from the common carotid artery onto the external carotid artery (Fig. 139-22). It may be more convenient to detach the occluded internal carotid artery, in which case the arteriotomy passes through the opening left by this detachment. This has the advantage of eliminating the stump of the internal carotid artery at the time of arteriotomy closure.

Several techniques are available for the correction of coiling, kinking, or tortuosity of the internal carotid artery (see Chapter 144).[115] These include (1) resection of a segment of the internal carotid artery, (2) reimplantation of the internal carotid artery in a more proximal location, and (3) resection of a segment of the common carotid artery (Fig. 139-23). If an arteriosclerotic lesion is present in the carotid bifurcation, a thromboendarterectomy must be performed in combination with one of the shortening procedures.

Verification of the Technical Result

The surgeon who performs carotid endarterectomy has one chance to get it right. Thus, it is helpful to have some objective means of verifying the technical result. The most

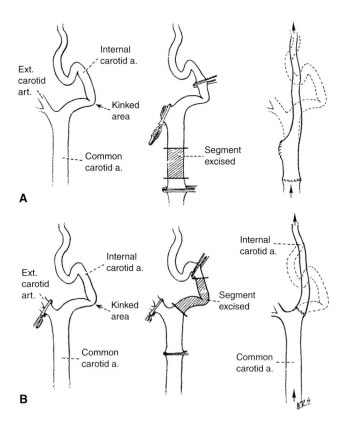

FIGURE 139-22 An endarterectomy of the external carotid artery can be carried out through an arteriotomy. It begins on the common carotid artery and extends through the stenotic lesion in the external carotid artery. Because the internal carotid artery is totally occluded, the lesion in this vessel can be ignored.

direct method is a *completion angiogram*. Other techniques include visualization with intraoperative *B-mode ultrasonography* and *waveform analysis* with continuous Doppler ultrasound.

The technique of operative completion angiography is both simple and effective. A 20-gauge needle is bent at a 45-degree angle so as to allow the needle to be placed into the artery and for it to lie axial to the direction of the artery and minimize the risk of a subintimal injection. A 10-mL syringe is filled with angiographic contrast material and is connected to the needle with flexible tubing. A film is placed beneath the patient's head and neck, either in a sterile cassette holder or slid into the film slot of the operating table. A portable x-ray machine can be used, and the 10 mL of full-strength contrast material is rapidly injected at the time the film is exposed. This yields an excellent quality of image of the carotid bifurcation and the cervical carotid artery. The anatomic result of operation can thus be verified.

Any defect or intimal flap in the internal carotid artery can be corrected before a thromboembolic complication occurs. If an unsatisfactory endpoint of the external carotid artery appears, it should be corrected as well. If the angiographic appearance is satisfactory, the heparin can be reversed with protamine prior to closure, although some surgeons do not reverse heparin with protamine because of potential adverse reactions to this drug.

Surgery of the Vertebral Artery

The clinical manifestations, indications, technique, and results of surgical repair of the vertebral artery are detailed

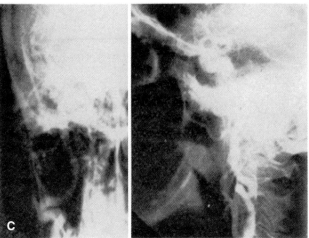

FIGURE 139-23 A, Indirect relief of a kinked internal carotid artery by resection of a portion of the common carotid artery. **B,** Direct relief of a kinked internal carotid artery by resection and end-to-end anastomosis. **C,** Markedly redundant and kinked left internal carotid artery in a 55-year-old man with intermittent attacks of right hemiparesis. Ext, External. (**A-C,** From Najafi H, Javid H, Dye WS, et al: Kinked internal carotid artery: Clinical evaluation and surgical correction. Arch Surg 89:134, 1964.)

in Chapter 141. For the sake of continuity, a brief discourse concerning the reconstruction of orificial lesions of the vertebral artery is presented here.

Most lesions involving the vertebral artery are atheromatous plaques of the subclavian artery that encroach on the lumen of the vertebral artery origin. This area is best exposed through a supraclavicular incision centered over the clavicular head of the sternocleidomastoid muscle. The

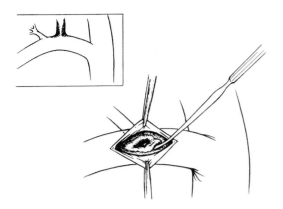

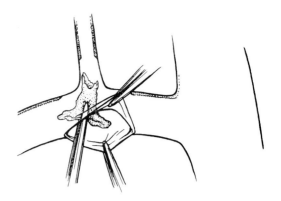

FIGURE 139-24 The trans-subclavian approach to vertebral artery endarterectomy. The *inset* demonstrates the vertebral artery stenosis in profile, emphasizing that the origin of the lesion is within the subclavian artery. A longitudinal arteriotomy is made on the posteroinferior aspect of the subclavian artery opposite the vertebral artery orifice. An endarterectomy is started at the base of the vertebral artery plaque within the subclavian artery.

FIGURE 139-25 Separation of the atheromatous core from the distal intima within the vertebral artery and its dislocation into the subclavian artery as it is removed.

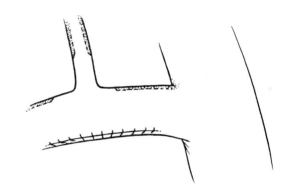

FIGURE 139-26 The final appearance following trans-subclavian endarterectomy, leaving a widely patent vertebral artery and showing the closure of the subclavian arteriotomy.

incision is deepened through the platysmal layer, and the clavicular head of the sternocleidomastoid muscle is divided. The scalene fat pad is dissected along its inferior margin and retracted superiorly, together with the omohyoid muscle. The anterior scalene muscle is identified, and the phrenic nerve lies obliquely along this muscle. The phrenic nerve is mobilized, and the anterior scalene muscle is divided.

The subclavian artery is now identified. The vessel is mobilized circumferentially, and an umbilical sling is applied. Mobilization of the subclavian artery continues proximally. At a point where the subclavian artery arches toward the mediastinum, the vertebral artery can be identified on the superior portion of the subclavian artery and the internal mammary artery identified on the inferior margin, opposite the takeoff of the vertebral artery. The vertebral artery branch can be mobilized carefully, and the proximal subclavian artery is dissected as far proximal as possible.

The atherosclerotic plaque, encroaching on the vertebral artery orifice, can be handled in one of two ways. If the plaque primarily involves the orifice and does not extend into the artery itself, a most satisfactory technique is a trans-subclavian artery endarterectomy. The subclavian artery is clamped proximally and distally, and a longitudinal incision is made along its anteroinferior aspect approximately 3 mm from the vertebral artery. A thromboendarterectomy plane is established in the subclavian artery, and a circular intimal button is developed around the vertebral artery orifice (Fig. 139-24). The atheromatous lesion is then carefully cored out to achieve a clean distal endpoint (Fig. 139-25). The area is flushed with saline solution, the artery is back-bled, and closure of the subclavian arterotomy is accomplished with a simple running suture of 6-0 polypropylene (Fig. 139-26). After a completion angiogram, the wound is closed in layers.

If the lesion extends up the vertebral artery for a short distance or if it was not possible to achieve a clean endpoint

with trans-subclavian endarterectomy, a direct vertebral thromboendarterectomy can be accomplished through a vertical arteriotomy extending from the subclavian artery through the vertebral artery orifice and up to a point distal to the atheromatous lesion. After the endarterectomy, the arteriotomy should be closed with vein patch angioplasty (Fig. 139-27).

Surgery of Occlusive Lesions of the Aortic Arch

Occlusive lesions at the level of the aortic arch account for fewer than 10% of operations on the extracranial vascular tree. Early in the experience with cerebrovascular surgery, these lesions were repaired by a transthoracic or trans-mediastinal approach.[29,32,44] These approaches used either endarterectomy of the affected vessel or bypass graft. These operations were occasionally associated with significant morbidity and mortality rates. Less direct techniques have been described that enabled the surgeon to revascularize a branch of the aortic arch without entering either the thorax or the mediastinum to expose its proximal extent.[110]

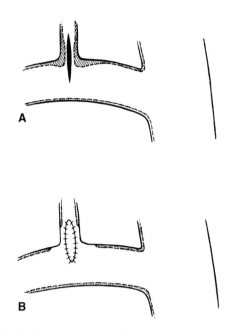

FIGURE 139-27 A, Technique of direct vertebral artery thromboendarterectomy through a vertical arteriotomy incision. **B,** Following endarterectomy, the arteriotomy in the vertebral artery is closed with a vein patch.

Stenoses or Occlusion of the Subclavian Artery

Lesions of the subclavian artery can be repaired in one of the following four ways:

1. Bypass graft from the ipsilateral common carotid artery to the subclavian artery distal to the site of an occlusive lesion
2. Transposition of the subclavian artery to the side of the common carotid artery (the most preferable method)
3. Subcutaneous bypass graft extending from the opposite, unaffected axillary artery to the axillary artery distal to the subclavian lesion[14,30,126]
4. Mediastinal approach to the subclavian artery, with repair by either thromboendarterectomy or bypass graft from the ascending aorta to a point distal to the obstructing lesion

Carotid-Subclavian Bypass

The carotid-subclavian bypass is best performed through a supraclavicular approach to the subclavian artery.[36] Once the subclavian artery is mobilized, the common carotid artery is easily exposed through the same incision. The sternocleidomastoid muscle is mobilized along its posterior extent to visualize the carotid sheath, which is opened, and the common carotid artery is mobilized for a short distance. An 8-mm polyester (Dacron) graft or a 6-mm polytetrafluoroethylene graft can be used for bypass. The patient receives systemic anticoagulation with 5000 units of heparin. The back-pressure from the proximally clamped common carotid artery is measured. If the collateral back-pressure or residual pressure is greater than 25 mm Hg, a second distal clamp is applied to the common carotid artery. A longitudinal incision is made, and an anastomosis is constructed between the end of the graft and the side of the common carotid artery.

After appropriate flushing of the graft, a clamp is placed on the proximal portion of the graft and carotid artery blood flow is restored. The distal graft is then brought to the side of the subclavian artery at a convenient location, and an end-to-side anastomosis is constructed in a similar manner (Fig. 139-28). The wound is closed in layers, and the operation is complete. If carotid back-pressure is less than 25 mm Hg, a carotid shunt can be used and subsequently withdrawn through the graft on completion of the anastomosis.

Subclavian Artery Transposition

Subclavian artery transposition has three advantages. It is an autogenous reconstruction, has only one anastomosis, and carries the best long-term patency. The common carotid and subclavian arteries are exposed and mobilized as described previously. The subclavian artery must be mobilized well proximal to the vertebral and internal mammary arteries, which are both carefully preserved. The subclavian artery is then divided proximally, and the proximal stump is oversewn. The distal end, proximal to the vertebral artery, is then sutured end-to-side to the common carotid artery.

Axillary-Axillary Bypass

The axillary-axillary bypass is an alternative procedure to the carotid-subclavian bypass. Both axillary arteries are exposed through infraclavicular incisions. The wound is deepened through the fascia. The sternal and clavicular portions of the pectoralis major muscle are split to expose the insertion of the pectoralis minor muscle. This muscle may be divided to provide additional access to the axillary artery (Fig. 139-29).

Thromboendarterectomy or Bypass Graft

A bypass graft is sutured end-to-side to the donor axillary artery, brought subcutaneously across the sternum, and anastomosed end-to-side to the recipient axillary artery (Fig. 139-30). The advantage of this technique over subclavian-carotid bypass is that temporary interruption of common carotid artery blood flow is avoided; however, two incisions are needed, it uses a longer graft, and it is somewhat less cosmetically acceptable because the graft passes subcutaneously over the sternum.

Common Carotid Artery Occlusive Lesions

The primary cause of an occlusion of the common carotid artery is an atheromatous plaque involving its bifurcation with retrograde thrombosis. The thrombus extends down to the innominate artery bifurcation on the right side or to the level of the aortic arch on the left side. Some common carotid artery occlusions are due to lesions that begin at the level of the aortic arch and produce an antegrade thrombosis. Finally, a few occlusions of the common carotid

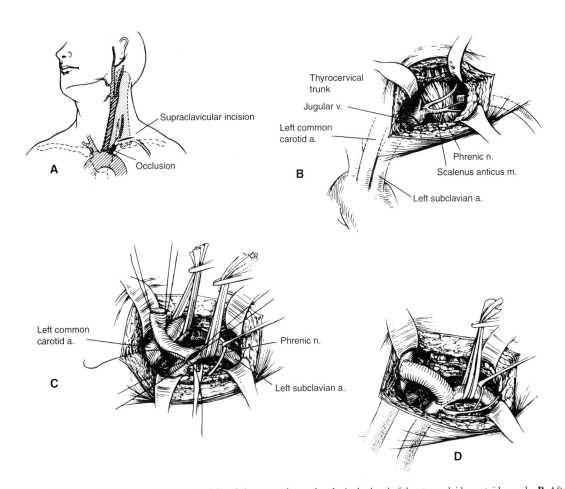

FIGURE 139-28 A, Placement of the supraclavicular incision. It is centered over the clavicular head of the sternocleidomastoid muscle. **B,** After division of the clavicular head of the sternocleidomastoid muscle, the relationships of the phrenic nerve, scalenus anticus, and subclavian artery are demonstrated. **C,** After mobilization of the carotid and subclavian arteries, preparation is made for a graft connection. **D,** Completion of the subclavian-carotid artery bypass is demonstrated and points out the close proximity of the two arteries and the short length of graft that is required. (**A-D,** From Moore WS, Malone JM, Goldstone J: Extrathoracic repair of branch occlusions of the aortic arch. Am J Surg 132:249, 1976.)

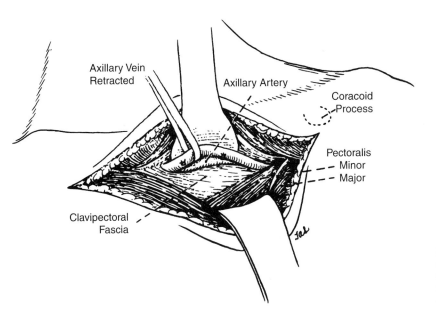

FIGURE 139-29 Surgical exposure of the axillary artery. (From Mozersky DJ, Sumner DS, Barnes RW, Strandness DE: Subclavian revascularization by means of a subcutaneous axillary-axillary graft. Arch Surg 106:20, 1973.)

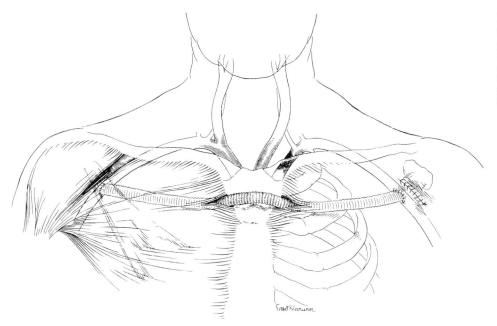

FIGURE 139-30 Diagrammatic representation of placement of the axillary-axillary graft. (From Snider RL, Porter JM, Eidemiller LR: Axillary-axillary artery bypass for the correction of subclavian artery occlusive disease. Ann Surg 180: 888, 1974.)

artery are due to lesions in its mid-portion, with both antegrade and retrograde propagation (Fig. 139-31).

Occlusions produced by retrograde thrombosis can be treated by late retrograde thrombectomy in combination with bifurcation endarterectomy.[107] Occlusions produced by more proximal lesions can be bypassed with a subclavian-to-carotid bypass or a carotid-to-carotid bypass. The authors approach these lesions by initially exposing the carotid bifurcation in the usual manner. A bulky atheromatous plaque at the carotid bifurcation confirms the mechanism of carotid artery occlusion to be retrograde clot propagation. The internal carotid artery may be kept open by flow between the internal and the external carotid arteries.

If the internal carotid artery is occluded, one can depend on the external carotid artery to be patent beyond the superior thyroid branch. An arteriotomy should be made on the common carotid artery, proximal to the atheromatous lesion. By carefully opening the vessel, one can identify a plane that exists between the organized thrombus and the intact intima of the common carotid artery. The organized thrombotic cord can be mobilized circumferentially and then divided at a convenient portion within the arteriotomy. A smooth loop endarterectomy stripper can be used to develop the plane between thrombus and intima in a retrograde fashion. Usually, several gentle passes free the thrombus down to the level of the aortic arch or innominate bifurcation and allow the thrombotic cord to be pushed out of the arteriotomy by pulsatile blood flow. A clamp is then applied to the common carotid artery, once inflow is established. A standard bifurcation endarterectomy is then performed.

If the internal carotid artery is occluded, it should be removed to avoid a blind stump that may serve as a source of further emboli. The arteriotomy is closed, and flow is restored to the external carotid artery (Fig. 139-32).

If the lesion that produced common carotid artery occlusion is located at a more proximal location or if the thrombotic cord cannot be removed by retrograde thrombectomy, a subclavian-carotid bypass can be performed in a manner identical to that described for a carotid-subclavian bypass. If a lesion is also present in the ipsilateral subclavian artery, a bypass graft in the opposite common carotid artery can be used for inflow.

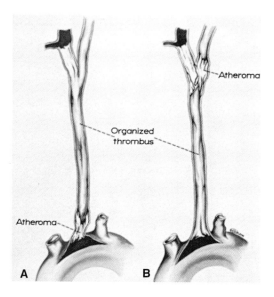

FIGURE 139-31 Occlusion of the common carotid artery can be produced by an atheromatous lesion at the origin of the common carotid artery (**A**), with antegrade thrombosis to involve the carotid bifurcation, or, more commonly, by an atheromatous lesion at the common carotid bifurcation (**B**) with retrograde thrombosis down to the level of the aortic arch.

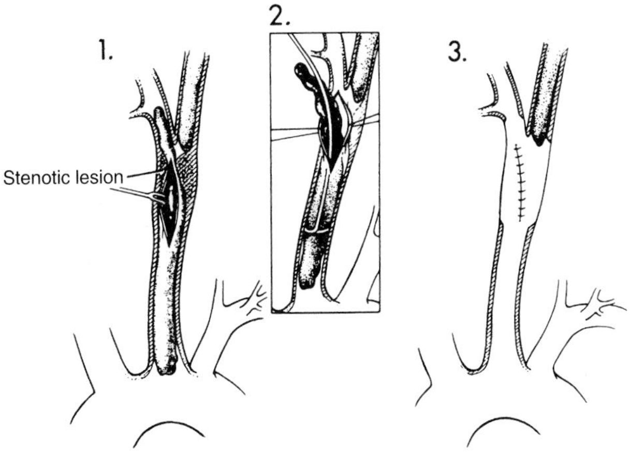

FIGURE 139-32 *Step 1,* An arteriotomy is made in the common carotid artery to begin separating the organized thrombus from the arterial wall. *Step 2,* A flexible wire-loop stripper is passed over the organized thrombus to free its entire length. *Step 3,* After removal of the occlusive arteriosclerotic plaque at the carotid bifurcation, the outflow of the external carotid artery is restored and the arteriotomy is closed. (From Moore WS, Malone JM, Goldstone MD: Extrathoracic repair of branch occlusions of the aortic arch. Am J Surg 132:249, 1976.)

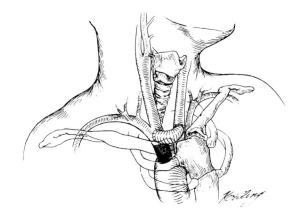

FIGURE 139-33 Bypass graft from the left carotid to the right carotid artery as a means of bypassing an innominate artery occlusion. (From Moore WS, Malone JM, Goldstone J: Extrathoracic repair of branch occlusions of the aortic arch. Am J Surg 132:249, 1976.)

Occlusive Lesions of the Innominate Artery

Lesions of the innominate artery are best treated directly through a median sternotomy. This can be achieved with either an open endarterectomy or a bypass graft from the ascending aorta to the innominate artery bifurcation.[31]

If the patient's general condition is so poor as to prohibit a median sternotomy, occlusive lesions of the innominate artery can be treated by a carotid-carotid bypass (Fig. 139-33). Alternative methods include left subclavian-to-right carotid bypass, subclavian-subclavian bypass, or axillary-axillary arterial bypass.

Occlusive Lesions of All Three Arch Vessels

It is rare for a patient to present with occlusive lesions involving all three major arch trunks. When this occurs, the patient is at high risk for major complications associated either with the natural history of the disease or with revascularization. The temptation to carry out a total revascularization at one operative procedure should be avoided. In these patients, autoregulatory control of the cerebral circulation has been lost. A total revascularization places the patient at high risk for intracerebral hemorrhage as a result of hyperperfusion syndrome.

In general, it is much better to stage the reconstruction of patients with this complex series of lesions, using either a direct or an extrathoracic approach. A direct approach would consist of an aortic-innominate bypass or innominate endarterectomy. This then establishes reperfusion of the right carotid and right subclavian systems. Subsequent revascularization, if required, can be achieved by various combinations of extrathoracic repair, such as carotid-carotid bypass or by axillary-axillary bypass in combination with subclavian-carotid bypass.[114]

If the patient is not a suitable candidate for a mediastinal approach, revascularization can be carried out by means of

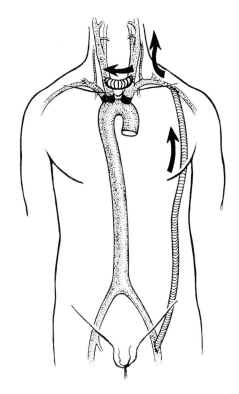

FIGURE 139-34 Artist's concept of subcutaneous bypass grafts from the right femoral to the right axillary arteries in combination with a graft from the right carotid to left carotid arteries. (From Moore WS, Malone JM, Goldstone J: Extrathoracic repair of branch occlusions of the aortic arch. Am J Surg 132:249, 1976.)

a femoral-axillary bypass if there is an intact aortofemoral system.[107,141] A subcutaneous bypass from the femoral artery to the right axillary artery establishes blood flow to the right vertebral and right carotid arteries through retrograde perfusion. If necessary, a subsequent right carotid-to-left carotid artery bypass can be added to complete the extrathoracic revascularization of the arch vessels (Fig. 139-34).

■ RESULTS

Medical Management

The principles of medical management of cerebrovascular disease are discussed in Chapter 136. Several important points, however, are emphasized here.

Anticoagulation

In patients with atrial fibrillation, anticoagulation has been of benefit in preventing strokes and other thromboembolic events. Five randomized clinical trials have been published documenting this effect.[65] Patients with atrial fibrillation randomized to placebo had an average ischemic stroke rate of 5% per year. In contrast, warfarin anticoagulation reduced the risk of thromboembolism substantially. Such results have revived interest in anticoagulation for the prevention of stroke in patients with extracranial cerebrovascular disease.

Initial clinical studies of oral anticoagulation for prevention of anterior circulation strokes carried out in the 1970s showed little benefit. Whisnant and colleagues from the Mayo Clinic performed a retrospective study in 1973 that showed a reduction in strokes in patients treated with oral anticoagulation.[158] The risk of stroke within 5 years in control patients was approximately 40% and was reduced to 20% after anticoagulation. However, the stroke rate in treated patients is still higher than rates reported from both retrospective and prospective series of surgically treated patients.

Conflicting reports have come from Sweden regarding the efficacy of anticoagulation in cerebrovascular disease. Link and associates reported an increased incidence of stroke when anticoagulation therapy was discontinued in patients who presented with carotid territory TIAs; these results prompted a recommendation for long-term treatment with warfarin.[87] In contrast, Torrent and Anderson found more deaths in stroke patients treated with anticoagulants because of serious bleeding complications related to length of treatment, hypertension, and inadequate patient compliance.[152]

Five small prospective, randomized trials compared anticoagulation (approximate International Normalized Ratio, 1.7 to 4.0) to antiplatelet agents in patients with TIAs and minor strokes.[6,21,56,119,123] However, these trials were small, with poorly defined entry and outcome criteria and short follow-up. In part because of the low occurrence rate of strokes, none of these studies showed a clear reduction in the incidence of strokes by anticoagulation, and aggregate results remain inconclusive. Moreover, in two of these studies,[6,123] mortality was higher in the anticoagulated group of patients owing to bleeding complications. At present, chronic oral anticoagulation agents should not be the initial treatment for patients with carotid territory cerebrovascular disease.

Antiplatelet Treatment

At least 10 randomized trials have compared aspirin with placebo for prevention of stroke in patients with TIAs and minor and major strokes (Table 139-2).[1,18,22,53,54,131,140,143,155] The first of these studies was published in 1977 by Fields and colleagues.[53] This American trial randomized patients with cerebrovascular symptoms to 650 mg of aspirin twice daily versus placebo. Half the patients had operable carotid artery stenoses. After 6 months of follow-up, there was a statistically significant benefit for aspirin treatment when the endpoints of death, cerebral or retinal infarction, and TIAs were combined. There was no significant difference in any single endpoint, however. A second part of this trial involved aspirin treatment versus placebo in patients who eventually underwent endarterectomy.[54] With these same endpoints, there was no significant benefit of aspirin treatment at 24-month follow-up. When non-stroke-related deaths were eliminated, aspirin was beneficial.

The Canadian Cooperative Study of aspirin versus placebo for patients with symptomatic extracranial cerebrovascular disease is perhaps the most widely quoted of the antiplatelet trials in which 585 patients were randomized.[22] About 65%

Table 139-2 Randomized, Prospective Trials of Antiplatelet Agents in Treatment of Cerebrovascular Disease

TRIAL	YEAR	ENTRY CRITERIA	ENDPOINT (24 MONTHS)	GROUPS	NO. OF PATIENTS	OUTCOME Percentage	OUTCOME Significance
Canadian Study[22]	1978	TIA	Stroke or death	Sulfinpyrazone 200 mg qid	115	23	P = placebo
				ASA 325 mg qid	98	15	P = .005
				Both	102	8	P = ASA alone
				Placebo	91	19	—
Fields et al[53]	1976	TIA	Stroke or death	ASA 650 mg bid	88	19	—
				Placebo	90	27	P = .18
AICLA (French)[18,*20]	1983	TIA, stroke	Stroke	ASA 330 mg tid	198	7	P = .05
				ASA (330 mg) + DP (75 mg) tid	202	8	P = ASA alone
				Placebo	204	13	—
American-Canadian Study[1]	1985	TIA	Stroke or death	ASA 325 mg qid	442	8.2	—
				ASA (325 mg) + DP (75 mg) qid	448	8.6	P = NS

*Men only.

TIA, transient ischemic attack; DP, dipyridamole; ASA, aspirin; AICLA, Accidents, Ischemiques, Cerebraux Lies a l'Atherosclerose; NS, not significant.

had ischemic events in carotid artery territories, 25% had vertebral-basilar insufficiency, and 10% had both. After 12 to 57 months of follow-up, aspirin reduced the risk of continuing TIAs, stroke, or death by 19%, whereas sulfinpyrazone had no significant benefit. When male patients were analyzed separately, the risk reduction was even higher. In women, there was no significant reduction in stroke or death rates in any of the four treatment regimens.

In 1983, the French AICLA trial was published.[18] Six hundred four patients were randomized to aspirin (990 mg/day), placebo, or aspirin (990 mg/day) plus dipyridamole (225 mg/day). Most of these patients had completed minor strokes, and patients with severe carotid stenoses and women younger than 50 years of age were excluded from the study. Endpoints were fatal and nonfatal strokes. Both aspirin and aspirin-dipyridamole produced reduction in endpoints compared with placebo by about 60% at 3-year follow-up (10.5% vs. 18%). Although this trial shows a general benefit of antiplatelet treatment for cerebrovascular disease, its exclusion criteria call into question its applicability to patients with significant carotid stenoses.

Also in 1983, the Danish Cooperative Study of aspirin in the prevention of stroke in patients with TIAs appeared.[140] Two hundred three patients with TIAs were treated with aspirin ($n = 101$) or placebo ($n = 102$). After an average follow-up of 25 months, there was no statistically significant difference between groups with respect to the primary endpoints of stroke or death (aspirin, 20.8%; placebo, 16.7%). There was a trend toward fewer myocardial infarctions in the aspirin group, but statistical significance was not achieved because of the relatively small sample size.[41]

The American-Canadian Cooperative Study is one of the largest to examine aspirin treatment of symptomatic cerebrovascular disease.[1] Eight hundred ninety patients were randomized to aspirin (1300 mg/day) alone or aspirin (1300 mg/day) plus dipyridamole (300 mg/day). After 1 to 5 years of follow-up, endpoints (stroke, retinal infarction, or death) were nearly identical in the two groups, leading investigators to conclude that the addition of dipyridamole to aspirin was of no supplemental benefit. The cumulative risk of stroke in both groups was about 20% at 4 years, averaging 5% per year.

In 1987, the Swedish Cooperative Study of high-dose aspirin after minor stroke was published.[143] Five hundred five patients were randomized to aspirin (1500 mg/day) or placebo within 3 weeks of stroke. After an average follow-up of 2 years, there was no difference in stroke recurrence rate or death between groups. Moreover, the risk of TIA or myocardial infarction was not reduced in the aspirin group.

Sze and colleagues reported a meta-analysis of these trials shortly after they had all appeared. These investigators concluded that aspirin produced a nonsignificant reduction in stroke rate of 15% compared with placebo.[144] When aspirin was combined with sulfinpyrazone or dipyridamole, a 39% reduction of stroke was observed, but there was a 350% increase in peptic ulcer or gastrointestinal hemorrhage. Men enjoyed a "trend" in stroke reduction with aspirin treatment, regardless of regimen, but a measurable decrease in the incidence of stroke by aspirin treatment alone or in combination could not be established.

Another meta-analysis examined additional studies of aspirin for treatment of patients with peripheral vascular disease, some of which used stroke as an endpoint; this report was not limited to review of cerebrovascular trials. This publication reported an overall reduction in nonfatal strokes of 22% and a 25% reduction in the combined endpoints of nonfatal stroke, myocardial infarctions, or vascular death.[2] Examination of individual series, however, shows several inconsistencies, which may in part be explained by methodologic differences and insufficient sample sizes producing type II statistical errors. There appears to be a sex difference in responsiveness to aspirin, with men experiencing more therapeutic benefit than women.[22,53,54] This difference may also be artifactual due to the small number of women entered into the trials and their inherent lower event rates. More recent studies have shown equal therapeutic benefits in men and women.[136]

There is ongoing controversy regarding the optimal dose of aspirin for treatment of cerebrovascular disease. As indicated earlier, the large clinical trials all used relatively high doses of aspirin. However, we have shown that high doses of aspirin produce high complication rates (chiefly gastrointestinal bleeding and other gastrotoxicity), and patients assigned to high doses of aspirin have low compliance.[95] Aspirin also probably increases the risk of intracerebral hemorrhage.[97] Variability in the pharmacologic response to aspirin contributes to the debate regarding appropriate dosage. For example, as little as 20 mg of aspirin in some individuals completely acetylates platelet cyclooxygenase and ablates platelet aggregation,[156] whereas even 1300 mg in other individuals may not achieve this effect.[70] The factors inciting platelet aggregation may determine the efficacy of low-dose aspirin.[151] Moreover, in-vitro measurement of platelet aggregation in patients taking aspirin may not correlate with prevention of in-vivo cerebrovascular events.[70]

Several trials have examined lower doses of aspirin in patients with peripheral vascular and cerebrovascular disease. The *Dutch TIA trial* randomized 3135 patients with TIA or minor stroke to 283 mg or 30 mg of aspirin daily.[40] Using endpoints of vascular death, stroke, or myocardial infarction, there was no difference between the two groups (15.2% in the 283-mg group vs. 14.7% in the 30-mg group). Predictably, the incidence of major bleeding complications was low in both groups (3.2% and 2.6%, respectively).

The *Swedish Aspirin Low-Dose Trial* (SALT) showed a significant beneficial effect of a daily aspirin dose of 75 mg/day compared with placebo.[133] This dose of aspirin reduced the risk of vascular death, stroke, or myocardial infarction by 17% versus placebo. The incidence of significant hemorrhagic complications was low in the aspirin group (3%) but significantly higher than the placebo group (1.3%). Although low-dose aspirin is much safer than high-dose aspirin, bleeding complications are not eliminated.

The *United Kingdom-Transient Ischemic Attack (UK-TIA)* study compared medium-dose aspirin (300 mg/day) to high-dose aspirin (1200 mg/day).[155] The two doses were equally effective for prevention of strokes. High-dose aspirin was associated with a 5% risk of major bleeding complications, compared with 3% for the low-dose aspirin. Most U.S. physicians seem to favor medium-dose aspirin (325 mg/day) for secondary stroke prevention, whereas Canadians endorse high-dose (>1000 mg/day) and Europeans advocate low-dose aspirin (30 to 75 mg/day).

Table 139-3   Randomized, Prospective Trials of Thienopyridine Derivatives in the Treatment of Cerebrovascular Ischemic Events

TRIAL	YEAR	ENTRY CRITERIA	ENDPOINT (24 MONTHS)	GROUPS	NO. OF PATIENTS	OUTCOME	
						Percentage	Significance
Canadian-American Ticlopidine Study (CATS)[58]	1978	Stroke	Stroke, MI, death	ASA (325 mg) + DP (75 mg) qid	448	8.6	P = NS
				Ticlopidine 250 mg bid	525	18	—
				Placebo	528	25	—
TASS[67]	1989	TIA, stroke	Stroke or death	Ticlopidine 250 mg bid	1515	10	—
				ASA 650 mg bid	1519	12	P = .048
Clopidogrel Versus Aspirin for the Prevention of Ischemic Events (CAPRIE)[23]	1996	Stroke, MI, PVD	Stroke, MI, amputation, death	Clopidogrel 75 mg qd	17,636	10.6	—
				ASA 325 mg qd	17,519	11.2	P = .043

DP, dipyridamole; ASA, aspirin; TIA, transient ischemic attack; MI, myocardial infarction; PVD, peripheral vascular disease; NS, not significant.

Ticlopidine hydrochloride is a potent antiplatelet agent that does not inhibit the thromboxane A_2 pathway for platelet aggregation like aspirin does, nor does it affect prostacyclin production by vascular endothelium. Instead, it inhibits the adenosine diphosphate (ADP) pathway in platelet aggregation and adhesion.[99] It has no analgesic characteristics.[138] Maximal antiplatelet effect occurs after 5 days of treatment, and normal platelet activity returns 4 to 8 days after discontinuation.[88] Serious side effects are associated with administration of ticlopidine, including a 2.4% incidence of neutropenia, 20% incidence of diarrhea, and 10% incidence of rash.[58,68]

Most cases of ticlopidine-induced neutropenia occur during the first 3 months of therapy; after the first 3 months of treatment, the incidences of mild and moderate neutropenia are no different for ticlopidine, aspirin, and placebo. It is impossible to predict which patients will develop neutropenia, so white blood cell differential counts must be performed every 2 weeks beginning from the second week to the end of the third month of therapy.[138] In contrast to ticlopidine, clopidogrel, which has an identical mechanism of action, does not produce neutropenia.[23]

Three large clinical trials have evaluated ticlopidine and clopidogrel for secondary prevention of stroke and vascular events (Table 139-3).[23,58,67] In the *Ticlopidine Aspirin Stroke Study* (TASS), 3069 patients with TIAs or minor strokes were randomized to ticlopidine or aspirin.[67] After an average follow-up of 3 years, 13% of patients taking aspirin (1300 mg/day) had strokes versus 10% of patients taking ticlopidine (500 mg/day). This results in a relative risk reduction of 21%, but the absolute reduction in risk of stroke is only 1% per year with ticlopidine therapy compared with aspirin therapy.[129] These data are confounded by including "aspirin failures" (i.e, patients whose initial qualifying event occurred while they were taking aspirin) in the ticlopidine group, thus potentially biasing the study against aspirin. In addition, a significantly elevated level of cholesterol was noted in patients taking ticlopidine.

In the *Canadian-American Ticlopidine Study* (CATS), patients with minor thromboembolic strokes were randomized to 250 mg of ticlopidine twice a day (n = 525) or

placebo (n = 528) and followed for an average of 2 years.[58] Ticlopidine produced a relative risk of reduction for recurrent stroke of 30%; strokes occurred at a rate of 15.3% per year in the placebo group versus 10.8% per year in the ticlopidine group. The drug was equally effective in men and women. Severe neutropenia occurred in four patients taking ticlopidine (0.8%) and one patient taking placebo (0.2%).

Results of a randomized, blinded trial of *Clopidogrel* (75 mg once daily) *versus Aspirin* (325 mg once daily) in *Patients at Risk for Ischemic Events* (CAPRIE) were published in 1996.[23] This extremely large multicenter trial enrolled 19,185 patients, with more than 6300 in clinical subgroups of those with atherosclerotic vascular disease manifested as either recent ischemic stroke, recent myocardial infarction, or symptomatic peripheral arterial disease. Patients were studied 1 to 3 years, with a mean follow-up of 1.9 years. In the entire group, ischemic stroke, myocardial infarction, or vascular death occurred in 939 patients taking clopidogrel (17,636 patient-years) and in 1021 patients taking aspirin (17,519 patient-years), for a relative risk reduction of 8.7% (P = .04).

In the subgroup of patients who were enrolled because they had suffered strokes, 6054 were assigned to aspirin treatment and 5979 were assigned to clopidogrel. There were 315 versus 338 fatal and nonfatal recurrent strokes in the clopidogrel (n = 6054) versus aspirin (n = 5979) groups, respectively, for a relative risk reduction of 7.3% (P = .26). Although the adverse side effects or rash or diarrhea were slightly more common in the clopidogrel group, gastrointestinal symptoms and bleeding and abnormal liver function studies occurred more commonly in patients taking aspirin. Moreover, there was no difference in major bleeding, intracranial hemorrhage, or neutropenia between the treatment groups. Thus, it appears that clopidogrel is at least as safe as medium-dose aspirin and is safer than ticlopidine, but the indications for preferential use of clopidogrel instead of aspirin are unclear at present, at least for patients with symptomatic cerebrovascular disease.

A combination of low-dose aspirin and ticlopidine has been reported in a small study.[154] Patients with symptomatic cerebrovascular disease were randomized to combination therapy (aspirin 81 mg/day plus ticlopidine 100 mg/day, medium-dose aspirin 300 mg/day), or placebo. Platelet aggregation by ADP, arachidonate, and platelet-activating factor was markedly inhibited by combination therapy, and in-vivo platelet activation was decreased, as evidenced by lowered plasma concentrations of beta thromboglobulin and platelet factor IV (released by aggregating platelets). Bleeding time was significantly increased by combination therapy compared with the other groups. However, such profound platelet inhibition potentially could result in an increase in the risk of hemorrhagic complications.[33] The author (W.C.K.) has had anecdotal experience operating on patients who were taking both aspirin and ticlopidine preoperatively, and operative blood loss seemed substantially greater than in patients taking only aspirin or ticlopidine alone.

Surgical Management

Nonrandomized Studies of Carotid Endarterectomy

Symptomatic and Asymptomatic Carotid Artery Stenosis
It is readily apparent from examining individual, institutional, and cooperation studies of carotid endarterectory for various indications reported in the literature that results vary, but such nonrandomized studies provided important data to develop the hypothesis that underlies the prospective, randomized trials of carotid endarterectomy for both symptomatic and asymptomatic carotid artery stenosis—namely, that this procedure is a safe and effective treatment for these disorders.

Analysis of the outcomes of carotid endarterectomy, as performed in nonrandomized studies, is crucial for the determination of the appropriateness of operation in any given institution or by any given surgeon. The importance of low perioperative morbidity and mortality for carotid endarterectomy cannot be overemphasized. For example, using retrospective chart reviews, Easton and Sherman reported surgical morbidity and mortality of 21% in community hospitals in Springfield, Illinois.[42] This unacceptably high rate is often quoted by opponents of surgical intervention. Indeed, when 1 of every 5 patients undergoing carotid endarterectomy has an adverse outcome, the operation cannot be recommended. In contrast, operative morbidity and mortality rates as low as 0.1% have been reported. Such differences in adverse outcomes underscore the importance of internal review to establish local morbidity and mortality rates. An updated review of the Springfield experience with carotid endarterectomy in 1983 revealed a reduction in stroke and death rate to 5%.[103]

Late follow-up provided by nonrandomized reports has confirmed that carotid endarterectomy is a durable procedure. One of the leaders in cerebrovascular surgery, Dr. J. E. Thompson, and colleagues reviewed their own results of carotid endarterectomies in 592 patients followed for up to 13 years.[148] Operative mortality for the last 476 consecutive operations was 1.47%, and stroke rate was 2.7%. Overall, late mortality was 30%; half of deaths were due to cardiac disease, and only 3.9% occurred from stroke. Of those patients who had a preoperative stroke as an indication for carotid endarterectomy, 88.9% were normal or improved at follow-up. Of those patients who had TIAs

preoperatively, 81% had no further attacks and only 7 patients (3.3%) eventually experienced permanent deficits. Two of these 7 patients suffered strokes on the side contralateral to the carotid endarterectomy.

In a later report, Thompson and colleagues described long-term results in 132 patients undergoing 167 carotid endarterectomies for asymptomatic carotid stenoses.[150] There were no perioperative deaths, and permanent neurologic deficits occurred in only 2 patients (1.2%). At a mean follow-up of 55 months, 90.9% of the patients remained asymptomatic. Six patients (4.5%) had TIAs, five from the unoperated side. Strokes occurred in 4.6%. Although not truly a "control" group (because many patients were denied surgery because of prohibitive operative risk and other factors), 1328 contemporaneous patients had asymptomatic stenoses and did not undergo carotid endarterectomy. Only 55.8% remained asymptomatic; 26.8% had TIAs; and 17.4% suffered strokes.

A Belgian series from 1980 reported late outcomes in 141 patients followed for up to 16 years after carotid endarterectomy.[135] Forty-three patients operated on for asymptomatic carotid stenoses were followed for an average of 5.4 years; there were no deaths and 1 stroke referable to the contralateral carotid artery. Twenty-five patients presented with symptomatic stenoses and contralateral carotid occlusions; in mean follow-up of 7.3 years, only two patients had strokes (8%). Of 70 symptomatic patients without contralateral occlusions, only 6 had strokes, for an overall rate of 8.6%. A similar stroke rate of less than 2% per year was reported by Field in a series of 400 endarterectomies.[51]

Riles and associates compared 146 patients who underwent unilateral carotid endarterectomy (with nonstenotic contralateral carotid arteries) with 86 patients who underwent bilateral carotid endarterectomy.[125] Both groups were followed for a mean of 4.3 years. No significant differences existed between groups with respect to age, gender, neurologic status, or associated illnesses, and all patients were treated with aspirin postoperatively. Seventeen new strokes occurred in the first group, of which only six involved the hemisphere ipsilateral to the carotid endarterectomy. In the second group, there were four new strokes. The cumulative stroke rates at 5 years by life-table analysis were 17.6% and 5.6%, respectively ($P < .05$).

Hertzer and Arison reported the Cleveland Clinic experience with 329 patients followed a minimum of 10 years after carotid endarterectomy.[71] In 126 patients who underwent carotid endarterectomy for asymptomatic stenoses, the incidence of stroke in the ipsilateral cerebral hemisphere was 9%, less than 1% per year. Two hundred three patients operated on for symptomatic carotid artery stenoses had a late ipsilateral stroke incidence of 6%. The overall ipsilateral stroke risk was 10% at 10 years. Late strokes were most common among hypertensive patients (31%), patients whose indication for carotid endarterectomy was stroke (31%), and patients with uncorrected contralateral stenosis (42%). Patients with uncorrected contralateral stenosis had a contralateral late stroke incidence of 36%, compared with 8% in patients who underwent elective staged bilateral carotid endarterectomies.

The Cleveland Clinic group also provided useful retrospective data regarding the late risk of stroke with respect to degree of stenosis.[73,74] Two hundred eleven patients presented with symptomatic carotid artery stenosis; 126 were treated nonoperatively, and 85 underwent carotid endarterectomy. In patients with greater than 70% carotid artery stenosis treated medically, the stroke rate was 31% at 5 years compared with 7% in similar patients treated surgically.[74] Surgically treated patients with 50% stenosis also enjoyed improved outcomes compared with medically treated patients (5-year stroke rate of 3% vs. 28%, respectively). Of 290 asymptomatic patients, 195 were treated expectantly and 95 underwent carotid endarterectomy.[73] Five-year stroke incidence was 15% in the expectant group and 14% in the surgical group. However, patients with greater than 70% stenosis had a 24% to 33% 5-year stroke risk with nonoperative treatment versus 7% to 12% for those having prophylactic endarterectomies. Although neither of these studies was prospective or randomized, the results are consistent with findings from cooperative trials inspired by such descriptive data.

Completed Strokes The natural history of patients with completed stroke and good neurologic recovery justifies therapeutic carotid endarterectomy, with most reports citing an annual risk of recurrent stroke between 6% and 12%. Carotid endarterectomy is beneficial in these patients. Rubin and colleagues reported no ipsilateral strokes in 95 patients studied from 6 to 72 months after surgery for completed strokes.[130] Operative morbidity and mortality was 2.7%; annual cumulative stroke risk was thus 0.64%. Not all reports have corroborated such favorable results, however. For example, Bardin and coworkers reported a cumulative stroke rate of 20% at 5 years in 127 patients who underwent carotid endarterectomy for minor strokes.[7] Perioperative morbidity and mortality was 7%. Almost one third of patients died or suffered a stroke as a result of or in spite of carotid endarterectomy.

The indication and timing of carotid endarterectomy for acute stroke remain controversial. Bruetman and colleagues[20] first described disastrous results after carotid endarterectomy for acute stroke, describing autopsy findings of intracerebral hemorrhage with blood in the subarachnoid space and ventricles. Wylie and coworkers corroborated these adverse outcomes in an independent study 1 year later.[163] They reported nine patients operated on for acute stroke; catastrophic hemorrhages occurred in five of these patients (56%), three of whom had attempted revascularization after complete carotid artery occlusions.

In 1969, Rob described a 29% perioperative mortality rate following revascularization after carotid occlusions; only 21% of operated patients were benefited by surgery.[126] The mortality rate of operation during the acute phase of cerebral infarction was 42% in the Joint Study for Extracranial Arterial Disease, the first prospective, multicenter study of carotid endarterectomy.[12,16] Other investigators have noted similar findings.[60,149] Of note, many of the reported unfavorable results occurred in patients who presented with profound neurologic deficits and diminished consciousness, and many operations of acutely occluded arteries were performed in patients with neurologic deficits who had diminished consciousness. In addition, many operations for acutely occluded arteries were performed after a prolonged interval. Nevertheless, dismal consequences after carotid endarterectomy for acute strokes led

most authorities to recommend delaying operative intervention for at least 30 days or more.[52,60,118,128]

The reasons for "conversion of a white to red infarction" (i.e., hemorrhage occurring in a bland thrombotic cerebral infarction) are multifactorial. Probably the most important principle is restoration of normotensive blood flow to vessels that have lost the ability to autoregulate.[140] This vasomotor paralysis with maximal vasodilation regardless of perfusion pressures extends to vessels supplying peri-infarct tissue in the ischemic penumbra.[62,86] When the ability for blood vessels to autoregulate is lost, blood flow becomes passively dependent on blood pressure.[126] The combination of hypertension, which often accompanies acute stroke, and loss of autoregulation produces elevated perfusion pressures that are capable of precipitating small vessel disruption and hemorrhage both within and adjacent to the area of infarction. Several experimental animal studies support this hypothesis.[66,102]

Currently, neither computed tomography (CT) nor magnetic resonance imaging (MRI) reliably distinguishes areas of reversible ischemia (penumbra) and irreversible brain cell death (infarction). Wing and associates reported that CT brain scan indicates loss of integrity of the blood-brain barrier, suggesting that the reperfusion produced by carotid endarterectomy may be associated with increased risk of hemorrhage transformation.[161] When the CT brain scans in patients did not show enhancement after strokes, Ricotta and colleagues found that only 1 (6%) of 17 patients deteriorated neurologically after carotid endarterectomy, whereas 15 (88%) of 17 improved.[124] In contrast, when the CT scan remained enhancing, only 5 patients (50%) improved, whereas 4 (40%) deteriorated. Similar findings were reported by the Cleveland Clinic group.[89]

Postponing operation until CT scans "normalize" has disadvantages, however. Dosick and colleagues found that waiting 4 to 6 weeks for observation after acute stroke resulted in a 21% incidence of recurrent stroke.[39] Based on these findings, these investigators proceeded directly to surgery (within 2 weeks of onset) in patients with acute strokes who had no bleeding, as shown on CT scans. This strategy resulted in no perioperative morbidity and mortality in 110 patients. Whitney and associates reported similar results in 28 patients who presented with small, fixed neurologic deficits undergoing endarterectomy an average of 11 days from onset of symptoms.[160] Only one postoperative death and no new neurologic deficits occurred in this small group of patients. Other studies have confirmed the relative safety of early endarterectomy after small, fixed deficits, but the ideal algorithm remains unsettled because reported series are small and nonrandomized.[111,159]

Stroke-in-Evolution Stroke-in-evolution is a variety of acute stroke in which the initial deficit is followed by varying degrees of resolution and deterioration. An Ad Hoc Committee to the Joint Council of the North American chapter of the International Society for Cardiovascular Surgery defined this entity as a variation of acute stroke in which neurologic changes begin with "one level of deficit and in a progressive or stuttering fashion the deficit worsens."[111] After excluding intracranial hemorrhage by CT scans, heparin anticoagulation should be initiated, but despite medical management, the prognosis is poor.

Improved results have been reported in patients presenting with stroke-in-evolution treated surgically.[61,101] Mentzer and associates reported 17 patients with stroke-in-evolution who underwent emergency carotid endarterectomy.[101] Seventy percent had complete recovery, 24% remained unchanged, and none were worse after carotid endarterectomy.[101] One patient died, for an overall mortality rate of 6%. This compared favorably with a parallel group of 20 patients with stroke-in-evolution treated medically. Mortality in the medical group was 15%, with 55% of the remaining patients having permanent moderate to severe neurologic deficits. In a review of the literature, 55% of patients having emergency carotid endarterectomy for stroke-in-evolution showed improvement, 25% showed no change, and 10% were worse after surgery.[111] Average mortality was about 10%.

Patients presenting with stroke-in-evolution should undergo emergency CT scans to exclude intracranial bleeding. After a high-risk carotid lesion has been identified in a patient with stroke-in-evolution or crescendo TIAs, well-performed carotid endarterectomy carries the best prognosis for neurologic recovery. However, the patient and the family must understand that the procedure has the highest mortality and morbidity for all carotid endarterectomy indications, and some patients' neurologic conditions will worsen in the perioperative period.

External Carotid Artery Revascularization   Surgical revascularization of the external carotid artery is indicated in rare patients. The importance of the external carotid artery as a major collateral pathway to the cerebral circulation has been well demonstrated, particularly in the presence of an ipsilateral internal carotid artery occlusion.[134,164] Neurologic symptoms may arise owing to a stenosis at the origin of the external carotid artery either from emboli or hemodynamic compromise. Emboli may also originate from the cul-de-sac created by an occluded internal stump.

The Cleveland Clinic group reported 42 external carotid artery endarterectomies in 37 patients.[117] Temporary shunting and patch angioplasty were used in two thirds of the cases. Thirty procedures were primary external carotid artery reconstructions (limited operations) and 12 were reoperations or were combined with subclavian or intracranial bypass (extended operations). There were significant differences in outcomes between these two groups. Four patients (33%) in the extended operations group suffered perioperative ipsilateral hemispheric strokes versus none in the limited operations group. Three late strokes, one ipsilateral and two contralateral at 1, 16, and 33 months, respectively, occurred after external carotid artery reconstruction. Five additional patients required further therapy (anticoagulation, reoperation, or bypass) for recurrent symptoms. Appropriately, the authors urged caution and careful patient selection for external carotid artery revascularization.

Halstuk and colleagues analyzed the outcomes of 36 patients undergoing external carotid artery revascularization, noting a 13.8% stroke rate and a 2.7% mortality rate.[63] In addition, 14.2% of patients suffered a late stroke on follow-up. The combination of bilateral carotid occlusion and preoperative fixed neurologic deficit was found to predict the highest perioperative morbidity (37%). In a literature review in this paper, the authors described perioperative neurologic morbidity of 14.3% in 126 reported patients.

In another literature review, Gertler and Cambria found 23 series reporting cases in which external carotid artery reconstruction was undertaken.[59] Two hundred eighteen external carotid artery revascularizations were performed in the 23 series. Of the patients, 83% enjoyed resolution of symptoms, with another 7% showing improvement. Perioperative mortality was 3%, with a 5% perioperative neurologic morbidity. Increased perioperative adverse outcomes were associated with a severely diseased contralateral carotid artery and in symptomatic patients with internal carotid artery occlusion. The best results were obtained when surgery was performed to relieve specific hemispheric or retinal symptoms, as opposed to nonspecific neurologic complaints or previous stroke. Vertebral artery occlusive disease did not affect outcome.

External carotid artery reconstruction should be reserved for symptomatic patients with significant orificial external carotid artery stenoses whose intracerebral circulation can be demonstrated by ipsilateral injection of contrast on arteriogram, thus providing a potential conduit for emboli or suitable anatomy for cerebral hemodynamic compromise. The presence of a fixed neurologic deficit, bilateral internal carotid artery occlusion, or severe intracranial arterial disease increases the morbidity of external carotid artery revascularization, and medical therapy may be warranted in these cases.

■ RANDOMIZED STUDIES OF CAROTID ENDARTERECTOMY

Symptomatic Carotid Artery Stenosis

The first prospective, randomized multicenter study of surgical versus medical treatment for extracranial carotid occlusive disease began in 1959.[12] The Joint Study of Extracranial Arterial Occlusion randomized 1225 patients, with 621 having carotid endarterectomy and 604 treated with "best medical therapy" (not necessarily including antiplatelet agents). In many but not all instances, best medical therapy included anticoagulation. The groups were well matched with respect to symptoms, demographics, associated diseases, and angiographic patterns of disease, but mortality rates, according to the patient's clinical presentation and the angiographic pattern of disease, revealed significant differences.

At 43 months of follow-up, the survival rate was higher than 80% in the surgical group but only 50% in the medical group for patients who had unilateral carotid artery stenosis and no other surgically accessible lesion. In 316 patients who had hemispheric TIAs without residual deficit as an indication for entrance into the study (including patients with unilateral stenosis, bilateral stenosis, and unilateral stenosis with contralateral occlusion), the incidence of subsequent TIAs or strokes was lower in the surgical group. Moreover, most adverse neurologic events occurred in the ipsilateral hemisphere in medical patients and the contralateral hemisphere in surgical patients. These differences were all statistically significant. By today's standards, the perioperative neurologic morbidity and mortality rates were strikingly high at 8%. Nevertheless, this randomized study confirmed the beneficial effects of carotid endarterectomy described in nonrandomized series. The popularity of carotid endarterectomy rose so much that the number of these procedures performed in non-Veterans Affairs hospitals increased from 15,000 in 1971 to 107,000 in 1985.[122]

Despite the overwhelming preponderance of evidence, mostly from nonrandomized studies as described earlier, that carotid endarterectomy is safe and effective therapy for symptomatic carotid artery stenosis, reports such as the one by Easton and Sherman[42] from Springfield, Illinois, and the failure of extracranial to intracranial bypasses to improve outcomes in symptomatic patients with complete carotid occlusions[43] led to an abundance of negative publicity concerning carotid endarterectomy in the late 1980s. In addition to alarm over high complication rates in community hospitals and suspected lack of efficacy, there was concern over indications for surgery and marked regional variations in the number of carotid endarterectomies performed.[19] Numerous editorials appeared appealing for more restrained treatment of carotid artery stenosis and for development of randomized clinical trials to resolve the question.[11,26]

Three clinical trials of carotid endarterectomy in symptomatic patients have now been partially or fully completed; results were published in 1991.[55,95,116] These investigations are (1) the NASCET, (2) the European Carotid Surgery Trial (ECST), and (3) the Department of Veterans Affairs Symptomatic Trial (VAST). The trial design and methods differed among studies. One of the shortcomings of all three trials is that they used nonstandardized ultrasound examinations and relied primarily on arteriographic findings to determine patient eligibility and degree of stenosis. In addition, the two largest studies used different methods of determining eligibility and measuring degree of carotid stenosis by arteriogram (see Chapter 136; Fig. 136-4). The formula for calculating percent stenosis is

$$(1 - S/D) \times 100$$

where S is the diameter of the stenosis at the narrowest part of the artery and D is the diameter of the "normal artery."

In NASCET and VAST, the distal internal carotid artery just beyond the stenosis was used as the "denominator (D)" (i.e., the normal-sized artery) for determination of percent stenosis; in ECST, determination of percent stenosis was based on estimation of the diameter of the normal carotid bulb as the denominator (D). Thus, a lesion that NASCET measured as 70% was about 85% in ECST. A 50% stenosis in NASCET was 70% to 75% in ECST.

North American Symptomatic Carotid Endarterectomy Trial

NASCET was conducted at 50 clinical centers throughout the United States and Canada, stratifying patients into 30% to 69% carotid stenosis and 70% to 99% stenosis.[116] The surgical results of the vascular surgeons or neurosurgeons in NASCET were reviewed by the surgical committee before each center was certified as acceptable, and morbidity and mortality rates had to be 5% or less. Patients were eligible for randomization who had TIAs or minor strokes within 3

Table 139-4	Baseline Characteristics of the NASCET Study	
	MEDICAL (*n* = 331)	**SURGICAL** (*n* = 328)
Median age (yr)	66	65
Sex		
Male	69%	68%
Female	31%	32%
Race		
White	89%	93%
Black	4%	2%
Other	7%	5%
Antithrombotic medications	85%	85%
TIA at entry	69%	67%
Stroke at entry	31%	33%
Ipsilateral stenosis		
70-79%	43%	40%
80-89%	33%	38%
90-99%	24%	22%
Contralateral 70-99% stenosis	9%	8%

NASCET, North American Symptomatic Carotid Endarterectomy Trial; TIA, transient ischemic attack.

months of entry into the study. Aspirin (1300 mg/day or less if poorly tolerated) was the primary medical therapy, along with control of hypertension, hyperlipidemia, and diabetes. Aspirin was also given to surgical patients; the details of operative intervention were not standardized.

Follow-up protocol was rigorous. In addition to determinations by surgeons in the immediate postoperative period and at 30 days, an independent neurologic evaluation was performed by participating neurologists at 30 days, every 3 months for the first year, and every 4 months in ensuing years. Duplex ultrasonography was performed 1 month postoperatively and after neurologic symptoms. Repeat arteriograms were obtained if clinically indicated.

In the 70% to 99% carotid stenosis subset, between January 1988 and February 1991, 659 patients were randomized: 328 in the surgical group and 331 in the medical group. Table 139-4 describes the baseline characteristics of the two groups. In February 1991, after only 18 months of mean follow-up, the Data and Safety Monitoring Board prematurely stopped the enrollment of patients with 70% to 99% stenoses by invoking the predetermined stopping rule, and the National Institutes of Health issued a "clinical alert" informing physicians of the results. Patients in the medical arm of this subset of the study were advised to undergo carotid endarterectomy. Altogether, these were highly unusual measures that emphasized the importance of findings.

Table 139-5 summarizes the results for patients in both NASCET groups.[116] The total adverse event rate for surgical patients was 5.8% during the first 30 days compared with 3.3% in medically treated patients. The 30-day major stroke and death event rates were 2.1% and 0.9% in the surgical and medical groups, respectively. The cumulative risk of an ipsilateral stroke was 9% for surgically treated patients and 26% in those randomized to medical therapy, which represented an absolute risk reduction of 17% and a relative risk reduction of 65% (P < .001). The number of patients needed to treat to prevent stroke in 2 years is 6. The risk of

| **Table 139-5** | First Adverse Events for the Patients in the Two Arms of the NASCET Study at Two Years of Follow-Up |

| | EVENTS (EVENT RATE, %)* | | | |
EVENT	Medical Patients (n = 331)	Surgical Patients (n = 328)	ABSOLUTE DIFFERENCE (% ± SE)	RELATIVE RISK REDUCTION, %
Any ipsilateral stroke	61 (26)	26 (9)	17 ± 3.5†	65
Any stroke	64 (27.6)	34 (12.6)	15 ± 3.8†	54
Any stroke or death	73 (32.3)	41 (15.8)	16.5 ± 4.2†	51
Major or fatal ipsilateral stroke	29 (13.1)	8 (2.5)	10.6 ± 2.6†	81
Any major or fatal stroke	29 (13.1)	10 (3.7)	9.4 ± 2.7†	72
Any major stroke or death	38 (18.1)	19 (8.0)	10.1 ± 3.5‡	56

*Event rates were determined by Kaplan-Meier estimates for survival. "Death" refers to mortality from all causes. All events from the time of randomization to the first 30 days in the surgical group and 32 days in the medical group are included, along with subsequent events defining treatment failure.
†$P < .001$ for the comparison of the treatment groups.
‡$P < .01$ for the comparison of the treatment groups.
NASCET, North American Symptomatic Carotid Endarterectomy Trial.

a major or fatal ipsilateral stroke in the surgical group was 2.5% versus 13.1% in the medical group, representing a relative risk reduction of 81% ($P < .001$). For patients who did not die or have a major stroke within 30 days of randomization, the 2-year stroke risk was 1.6% versus 12.2% in surgically versus medically treated patients, respectively.

The degree of stenosis correlated profoundly with the risk of stroke in NASCET. In a subset analysis, Morgenstern and colleagues showed progressively increasing surgical benefit in the 8th, 9th, and 10th deciles.[113] The results of this analysis are portrayed in Figure 139-35. Symptomatic patients with 90% to 94% stenoses have the greatest medical risk and the most surgical benefit. Less difference between medical and surgical treatment (only 4.4% at 1 year in those with a "string sign") is seen in patients with near occlusion, presumably because excellent collateral development was relatively protective, and the conduit for large emboli is

substantially narrowed (Fig. 139-36).

NASCET continued to randomize symptomatic patients with less than 70% carotid stenosis until December 1996. All patients were then followed for 1 additional year. The results of this phase of the trial have been presented at the annual meeting of the American Heart Association, and subsequently published.[9a] In brief, there was definite but moderate benefit for carotid endarterectomy in symptomatic patients in this subset.[9] Although carotid endarterectomy was not associated with a reduction in major or fatal stroke, there was a statistically significant 39% relative risk reduction for any stroke in surgically treated patients with 50% to 69% carotid stenoses. The number needed to treat to prevent 1 stroke in 5 years was 15 patients. There appeared to be no significant benefit of carotid endarterectomy in those with less than 50% stenoses. With respect to long-term survival, there was no significant benefit in (1) women or (2) those who presented with retinal symptoms compared with

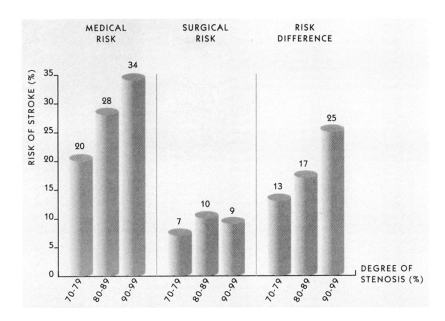

FIGURE 139-35 Estimates of risk of stroke at 2 years by degree of stenosis by deciles, as determined by Kaplan-Meier statistics from the North American Symptomatic Carotid Endarterectomy Trial (NASCET). The risk of stroke is similar for all deciles of stenosis in surgically treated patients; in contrast, the risk of stroke increases with deciles in medically treated patients. (From Barnett HJM, Meldrum HE, Elaiasziw M: Lessons from the symptomatic trials for the management of asymptomatic disease. In Caplan LR, Shifrin EG, Nicolaides AN, Moore WAS [eds]: Cerebrovascular Ischaemia Investigation and Management. London, Med-Orion, 1996, p 385.)

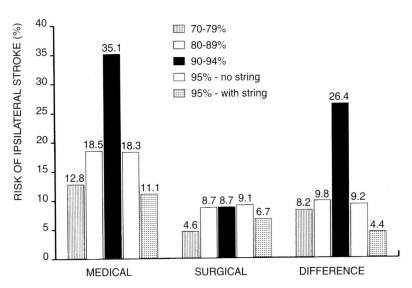

FIGURE 139-36 Estimates of ipsilateral stroke at 1 year by degree of stenosis according to Kaplan-Meier statistical analysis of North American Symptomatic Carotid Endarterectomy Trial (NASCET) data. 95% = near occlusion. (From Morgenstern LB, Fox AJ, Sharpe BL, et al: The risks and benefits of carotid endarterectomy in patients with near-occlusion of the carotid artery. Neurology 48:911, 1997.)

those with hemispheric events. There was little benefit in patients who were enrolled for hemispheric TIAs versus those with completed minor strokes.

Once again, it is important to emphasize that the NASCET results were not based on duplex ultrasound findings. NASCET's ultrasound/arteriography findings were subject to an error of approximately 15%.[46] In contrast to the Asymptomatic Carotid Atherosclerosis Study (ACAS, see later), the arteriographic complications in NASCET were low, occurring in only 0.6% of 2885 conventional cerebral angiograms.

European Carotid Surgery Trial

Over a 10-year period, a total of 2518 patients with carotid territory nonincapacitating strokes, TIAs, or retinal infarctions were randomized to either medical or surgical treatment with an average follow-up of nearly 3 years. The study was conducted in 80 medical centers in 14 countries. In contrast with NASCET, medical treatment was not specified but rather left to the discretion of the treating physician. In addition, in NASCET the qualifying event had to occur within 120 days of randomization, in comparison with a 6-month interval in ECST. Another major difference between ECST and NASCET is that ECST allowed participating centers to enter only the patients for whose treatment they had uncertainty, thus calling into question the true "randomized" status of ECST. A ratio of 1:2 of patients randomized into the medical-to-surgical arms also emphasizes the problematic design of ECST.

Finally, the arteriographic measurement differences between ECST and NASCET have been discussed. This difference "diluted" the ECST results so that about 350 patients who would be classified as having less than 70% stenosis by NASCET criteria were included in the "severe" ECST group.

Seven hundred seventy-eight patients with 70% to 99% carotid stenosis were randomized to carotid endarterectomy versus medical treatment in ECST.[49] There was a disappointing 30-day perioperative morbidity and mortality rate for surgical intervention of 7.5%, but despite this high rate of adverse outcomes, the results favored carotid endarterectomy for the severe stenosis subgroup. After 3 years of follow-up, the risk of an ipsilateral stroke was an additional 2.8% in the carotid endarterectomy group versus 16.8% in the medical group, for a sixfold risk reduction (P < .0001). The risk of death, ipsilateral stroke, or any other stroke was 12.3% in surgical patients compared with 21.9% of patients in the medical group (P < .01) at 3 years. Among those with severe stenosis, only 3.7% of surgical patients had disabling strokes, compared with an incidence of 8.4% in the medical arm. A total 3-year risk of any disabling or fatal stroke was 6% versus 11% in the surgical and medical groups, respectively.

Patients in the mild carotid stenosis category (0% to 29%) had a very small 3-year risk of ipsilateral stroke, so that the surgical risks were not outweighed by its benefits.[49] Thus, randomization in this group was stopped in 1991. More than 2000 patients with 30% to 69% carotid stenosis were enrolled in ECST. In a preliminary report of the results in this group, there was no significant benefit from endarterectomy, according to the measurement method used in this trial.[50] The perioperative complication rate was 7.6%. Again, it must be emphasized that a substantial number of patients in this subgroup would have had less than 50% stenoses by NASCET criteria.

Veterans Affairs Symptomatic Trial

The Department of Veterans Affairs randomized multicenter trial of carotid endarterectomy for patients with symptomatic carotid stenosis was terminated in 1991 after publication of the other trials described earlier.[95] Only 189 patients were randomized in 16 university-affiliated Veterans Affairs Medical Centers. In contrast to the other trial, TIAs were included as endpoints in this trial. After a mean follow-up of 11.9 months, the risk of a neurologic event for patients in the surgical group was 7.7% compared with 19.4% in the medical group (P = .011).

Thus, all three randomized trials of symptomatic patients with high-grade stenoses showed significant benefit for carotid endarterectomy compared with nonsurgical treatment.

Asymptomatic Carotid Artery Stenosis

Through population-based studies, it has been well established that an asymptomatic carotid bruit is associated with a low risk of stroke.[75,162] Norris and colleagues[115a] reported bruits in stenoses of only 20%; when the degree of stenosis was less than 50%, the annual percentage rate of stroke was only 1.3%. In contrast, when carotid stenosis was greater than 75%, the annual stroke rate was 3.3%; moreover, the combined TIA, stroke, cardiac, and vascular death event rate was 25.3% in this group. Based on such findings, investigators focused on functional stenosis, using noninvasive screening tests such as ocular pneumoplethysmography and duplex scanning.[15,57]

Despite excellent results from nonrandomized series of carotid endarterectomy in asymptomatic patients, as discussed previously, even greater disagreement existed regarding carotid endarterectomy for asymptomatic stenoses than for symptomatic disease. This controversy gave rise to four randomized clinical trials, discussed next, on the efficacy of carotid endarterectomy in patients with asymptomatic carotid stenosis.[24,50,78,96]

Carotid Surgery Versus Medical Therapy in the Asymptomatic Carotid Stenosis Trial

The first published results of a randomized, controlled trial of carotid endarterectomy for asymptomatic carotid stenosis are those of the Carotid Surgery Versus Medical Therapy in Asymptomatic Carotid Stenosis (CASANOVA) Study Group.[24] This multicenter trial compared surgical and medical treatment in 410 patients with asymptomatic carotid stenosis ranging from 50% to 90%. Arteriography was performed in all patients. Two hundred six patients underwent carotid endarterectomy and received aspirin postoperatively; 204 patients received aspirin therapy alone. All patients also received 75 mg of dipyridamole three times daily. Patients in the medical group who had bilateral carotid stenoses of 90% or more were immediately referred for carotid endarterectomy, thus negating the influence of surgical management in patients most likely to experience neurologic events. In addition, carotid endarterectomy was performed in the medical group when the stenosis progressed to 90%, if bilateral internal carotid artery stenosis greater than 50% developed, or if the patient had TIAs in the brain supplied by the randomized internal carotid artery.

Minimum follow-up was 3 years. A total of 334 carotid endarterectomies were performed, including 118 in the medically treated patients who were analyzed by "intent to treat" in the medical group. Twenty percent of patients randomized to the medical group underwent carotid endarterectomy immediately (30 patients as part of the protocol for bilateral lesions and 10 in violation of the protocol). An additional 20% of patients in the medical group underwent endarterectomy performed by protocol in follow-up. The authors concluded that there was no benefit of the procedure in patients with asymptomatic stenoses, but the many methodologic errors in this study invalidate the findings—as admitted by the authors in their response[35] to a critical editorial.[137] In the final analysis, the best thing about the CASANOVA study is its catchy title.

Mayo Clinic Asymptomatic Carotid Endarterectomy Trial

In 1992, results of an attempted randomized trial of carotid endarterectomy for asymptomatic carotid stenoses at the Mayo Clinic were published.[96] Only 71 patients were randomized to carotid endarterectomy versus medical treatment during a 30-month period. Too few neurologic events occurred in this small group of patients to permit analysis of efficacy of these treatments. In addition, the trial was terminated because significantly more adverse cardiac events occurred in the surgical group. These cardiac events may have been related to absence of aspirin therapy in the patients undergoing carotid endarterectomy.

The Veterans Affairs Asymptomatic Trial

In 1986, the Department of Veterans Affairs launched the Cooperative Study on Asymptomatic Carotid Stenosis (Clinical Studies Program No. 167) to determine the role of carotid endarterectomy in the treatment of asymptomatic carotid stenosis.[78] The trial was conducted in 11 university-affiliated Veterans Affairs Medical Centers. Endpoints were TIAs, transient monocular blindness, and stroke. A total of 444 men (mean age, 64.5 years) with asymptomatic internal carotid stenoses of 50% or more (lumen diameter reduction on arteriogram as calculated by NASCET criteria) were randomized to optimal medical care, including aspirin plus carotid endarterectomy ($n = 211$, surgical group) or optimal medical care alone ($n = 233$, medical group). All patients initially received aspirin at a dose of 1300 mg/day, but this dose was lowered for many patients who were intolerant of aspirin.[77,83] Patients were followed by a neurologist and a vascular surgeon for a mean follow-up of 47.9 months.

The 30-day operative mortality for the surgical group was 1.9% (4 of 211 patients). Three deaths occurred from myocardial infarction, and one resulted from myocardial infarction followed by stroke. The incidence of nonfatal perioperative stroke was 2.4% (5 of 211 patients). Three nonfatal strokes occurred after arteriography (3 of 714, 0.4%). When all complications of arteriography were assigned to the surgical group, the permanent stroke and death rate within 30 days of randomization was 4.7% for patients randomized to carotid endarterectomy. In comparison, in the medical group, 1 patient committed suicide (0.4%) and 2 patients had neurologic events (one stroke, one TIA; 0.9%).

The combined incidence of ipsilateral neurologic events was 8% in the surgical group and 20.6% in the medical group ($P < .001$, Fig. 139-37). The incidence of ipsilateral stroke alone was 4.7% in the surgical group and 9.4% in the medical group ($P = .056$). Although this 2:1 "trend" in stroke reduction by carotid endarterectomy in asymptomatic patients is interesting, the results of the study were unconvincing to many clinicians.[10] Nevertheless, the Veterans Affairs trial was the first to demonstrate a reduction in neurologic events in patients undergoing prophylactic carotid endarterectomy for significant asymptomatic carotid artery stenosis.

Asymptomatic Carotid Atherosclerosis Study

The ACAS is the largest published randomized trial of carotid endarterectomy versus medical treatment for

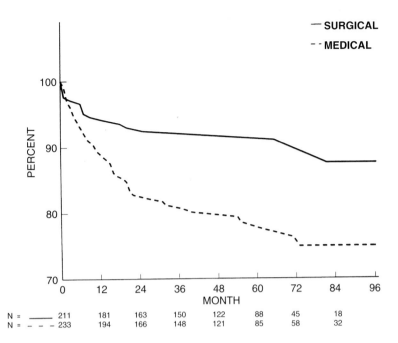

— SURGICAL

- - MEDICAL

N = ——— 211   181   163   150   122   88   45   18
N = – – – 233   194   166   148   121   85   58   32

FIGURE 139-37 Event-free rates for ipsilateral stroke and transient ischemic attach (TIA) or amaurosis fugax in the Veterans Affairs Cooperative Study (Clinical Studies Program No. 167) by Kaplan-Meier analysis. The numbers of patients (N) remaining event-free and in the study at the beginning of each 12-month period are provided beneath the graph. Treatment group comparisons by the log-rank test showed significant differences in favor of the surgical group ($P < .001$). (From Hobson RW, Weiss DG, Fields WAS, et al: Efficacy of carotid endarterectomy for asymptomatic carotid stenosis. N Engl J Med 3288:221, 1993.)

asymptomatic carotid stenosis.[50] This National Institutes of Health-sponsored study is similar in design to the Veterans Affairs cooperative study. Arteriography was not absolutely mandated in ACAS if the participating institutions' noninvasive determination of degree of carotid stenosis had been validated. A 60% luminal reduction was considered significant in ACAS. The advantages of ACAS are inclusion of both men and women and enrollment of a large sample. Acquisition of patients began in November 1987 and was completed in December 1992. A total of 1662 men and women were randomized, nearly four times the sample size of the Veterans Affairs study. In the middle of the study, the ACAS trialists changed their statistical analysis to observe stroke alone rather than the combined endpoints of stroke plus TIAs.

In 1964, the results of ACAS were reported. The 30-day perioperative stroke and mortality rate was 2.3%. Of note, the risk of stroke from arteriography alone was a surprisingly high 1.2%. When data were extrapolated to 5 years using Kaplan-Meier projections, the primary outcome of ipsilateral stroke was 5.1% for the surgical group and 11% for the medical group, representing a relative risk reduction of 53% ($P = .006$). The absolute risk reduction was only about 1% per year; this was a much less dramatic reduction than that demonstrated in the symptomatic trials.

■ SUMMARY

Based on published data, carotid endarterectomy remains the treatment of choice for carotid artery stenosis in appropriate patients with atherosclerotic lesions. The low morbidity and mortality rates described in both nonrandomized and randomized series for both symptomatic and asymptomatic patients must be equaled in studies of percutaneous transluminal angiography, and this is certainly not the case at this time.[38] Data on percutaneous transluminal angioplasty and stenting are presented in Chapter 140.

A number of industry-supported trials have been reported, but prospective, randomized trials will be needed to settle the growing debate over carotid endarterectomy versus carotid stenting.

■ REFERENCES

1. American-Canadian Cooperative Study Group: Persantine aspirin trial in cerebral ischemia: II. Endpoint results. Stroke 16:406, 1985.
2. Antiplatelet Trialists' Collaboration: Secondary prevention of vascular disease by prolonged antiplatelet treatment. BMJ 296:320, 1988.
3. Asymptomatic Carotid Artery Stenosis Group: Study design for randomized prospective trial of carotid endarterectomy for asymptomatic atherosclerosis. Stroke 20:844, 1989.
4. Baker JD, Gluecklich B, Watson CW, et al: An evaluation of electroencephalographic monitoring for carotid study. Surgery 78:787, 1975.
5. Baker RN, Schwart WS, Ramseyer JC: Prognosis among survivors of ischemic stroke. Neurology 18:933, 1968.
6. Baker RN, Schwartz WS, Rose AS: Transient ischemic strokes: A report of a study of anticoagulant therapy. Neurology 16:841, 1964.
7. Bardin JA, Bernstein EF, Humber BB, et al: Is carotid endarterectomy beneficial in the prevention of recurrent stroke? Arch Surg 117:1401, 1982.
8. Barner HB, Rittenhouse EA, Willman VL: Carotid-subclavian bypass for "subclavian steal syndrome." J Thorac Cardiovasc Surg 55:773, 1968.
9. Barnett HJM: An update on NASCET and ECST. In Branchereau A, Jacobs M (eds): New Trends and Developments in Carotid Artery Disease. Armonk, NY, Futura, 1998, p 107.
9a. Barnettt HJM, Taylor DW, Eliasziw M, et al: North American Symptomatic Carotid Endarterectomy Trial Collaborators: Benefit of carotid endarterectomy in patients with symptomatic moderate or severe stenosis. N Engl J Med 339:1415-1425, 1998.
10. Barnett HJM, Haines SJ: Carotid endarterectomy for asymptomatic carotid stenosis. N Engl J Med 328:276, 1993.
11. Barnett HJM, Plum F, Walton JN: Carotid endarterectomy: An expression of concern. Stroke 15:941, 1984.

12. Bauer RG, Meyer JS, Fields WAS, et al: Joint study of extracranial arterial occlusion: III. Progress report of controlled study of long-term survival in patients with and without operation. JAMA 208:509, 1969.

13. Bernstein EF, Humber PB, Collins GM, et al: Life expectancy and late stroke following carotid endarterectomy. Ann Surg 198:80, 1983.

14. Bergan JJ, Dean RH, Yao JS: Use of the axillary artery in complex cerebral revascularization. Surgery 77:338, 1975.

15. Blackshear WM Jr, Phillips DJ, Thiele BL, et al: Detection of carotid occlusive disease by ultrasonic imaging and pulsed Doppler spectral analysis. Surgery 86:698, 1979.

16. Blaisdell FW, Clauss RH, Galbraith JG, et al: Joint study of extracranial artery occlusion: IV. A review of surgical considerations. JAMA 209:1889, 1969.

17. Blaisdell FW, Lim RJ Jr, Hall AD: Technical result of carotid endarterectomy: Arteriographic assessment. Am J Surg 114:239, 1967.

18. Bousser MG, Eschwege E, Haguenau M, et al: "AICLA" controlled trial of aspirin and dipyridamole in the secondary prevention of atherosclerothrombotic cerebral ischemia. Stroke 14:5, 1983.

19. Brooke R, Park E, Chassin M, et al: Carotid endarterectomy for elderly patients: Predicting complications. Ann Intern Med 113:747, 1990.

20. Bruetman ME, Fields WS, Crawford ES, et al: Cerebral hemorrhage in carotid artery surgery. Arch Neurol 9:458, 1963.

21. Buren A, Ygge J: Treatment program and comparison between anticoagulants and platelet aggregation inhibitors after transient ischemic attack. Stroke 12:578, 1981.

22. Canadian Cooperative Study Group: A randomized trial of aspirin and sulfinpyrazone in threatened stroke. N Engl J Med 299:53, 1978.

23. CAPRIE Steering Committee: A randomized, blinded trial of clopidogrel versus aspirin in patients at risk of ischaemic events (CAPRIE). Lancet 348:1329, 1996.

24. The CASANOVA Study Group: Carotid surgery versus medical therapy for asymptomatic carotid stenosis. Stroke 22:1229, 1991.

25. Chambers BR, Norris JW: Outcome in patients with asymptomatic neck bruits. N Engl J Med 315:860, 1986.

26. Chambers BR, Norris JW: The case against surgery for asymptomatic carotid stenosis. Stroke 15:964, 1984.

27. Christensen MS, Hoedi-Rasmussen K, Lassen NA: Cerebral vasodilatation by halothane anesthesia in man and its potentiation by hypotension and hypercapnia. Br J Anaesth 39:927, 1967.

28. Connolly JE, Stemmer EA: Endarterectomy of the external carotid artery: Its importance in the surgical management of extracranial cerebrovascular occlusive disease. Surgery 106:799, 1973.

29. Crawford ES, DeBakey ME, Morris GC Jr, et al: Surgical treatment of occlusion of the innominate, common carotid, and subclavian arteries: A 10-year experience. Surgery 65:17, 1969.

30. Dardik H, Dardik I: Axillo-axillary bypass with cephalic vein for correction of subclavian steal syndrome. Surgery 76:143, 1974.

31. Davis JB, Grove WJ, Julian OC: Thrombotic occlusion of the branches of the aortic arch—Martorell's syndrome: Report of a case treated surgically. Ann Surg 144:124, 1956.

32. DeBakey ME, Crawford ES, Cooley DA, et al: Surgical considerations of occlusive disease of the innominate, carotid, subclavian, and vertebral arteries. Ann Surg 149:690, 1959.

33. DeCaterina R, Sicari R, Bernini W, et al: Benefit/risk profile of combined antiplatelet therapy with ticlopidine and aspirin. Thromb Haemost 65:504, 1991.

34. DeWeese JA, Rob CG, Satran R, et al: Results of carotid endarterectomy for transient ischemic attacks five years later. Ann Surg 178:258, 1973.

35. Diener HC: Response to Letter to the Editor. Stroke 23:918, 1992.

36. Diethrich EB, Garrett HE, Ameriso J, et al: Occlusive disease of the common carotid and subclavian arteries treated by carotid-subclavian bypass: Analysis of 125 cases. Am J Surg 113:800, 1967.

37. Dixon S, Pais SO, Raviola C, et al: Natural history of nonstenotic asymptomatic ulcerative lesions of the carotid artery. Arch Surg 117:1493, 1982.

38. Dorros G: Carotid arterial obliterative disease: Should endovascular revascularization (stent-supported angioplasty) today supplant carotid endarterectomy? J Intervent Cardiol 9:257, 1996.

39. Dosick SM, Whalen RC, Gale SS, Brown OW: Carotid endarterectomy in the stroke patient: Computerized axial tomography to determine timing. J Vasc Surg 2:214, 1985.

40. The Dutch TIA Study Group: A comparison of two doses of aspirin (30 mg vs 283 mg a day) in patients after a transient ischemic attack or minor ischemic stroke. N Engl J Med 325:1261, 1991.

41. Dyken ML: Transient ischemic attacks and aspirin, stroke, and death: Negative studies and type II error [Editorial]. Stroke 14:2, 1983.

42. Easton JD, Sherman DG: Stroke and mortality rate in carotid endarterectomy—228 consecutive operations. Stroke 8:565, 1977.

43. EC/IC Bypass Study Group: Failure of extracranial-intracranial arterial bypass to reduce the risk of ischemic stroke: Results of an international randomized trial. N Engl J Med 313:1191, 1985.

44. Ehrenfeld WK, Chapman ED, Wylie EJ: Management of occlusive lesions of the branches of the aortic arch. Am J Surg 118:236, 1969.

45. Ehrenfeld WK, Hamilton FN, Larson CP Jr, et al: Effect of CO_2 and systemic hypertension on downstream cerebral arterial pressure during carotid endarterectomy. Surgery 67:87, 1970.

46. Eliasziw M, Rankin RN, Fox AJ, et al: Accuracy and prognostic consequences of ultrasonography in identifying severe carotid artery stenosis. Stroke 26:1745, 1995.

47. Enger E, Boyesen S: Long-term anticoagulant therapy in patients with cerebral infarction: A controlled clinical study. Acta Med Scand 178(Suppl 438):1, 1965.

48. Eriksson SE, Link H, Alm A, et al: Results from eighty-eight consecutive prophylactic carotid endarterectomies in cerebral infarction and transitory ischemic attacks. Acta Neurol Scand 63:209, 1981.

49. European Carotid Surgery Trialists' Collaborative Group: Medical Research Council European Carotid Surgery Trial: Interim results for symptomatic patients with severe (70-99%) or with mild (0-29%) carotid stenosis. Lancet 337:1235, 1991.

50. The Executive Committee for the Asymptomatic Carotid Atherosclerosis Study: Endarterectomy for asymptomatic carotid artery stenosis. JAMA 273:1421, 1995.

51. Field PL: Effective stroke prevention with carotid endarterectomy: A series of 400 cases with two-year follow-up. International Vascular Symposium Program and Abstracts. New York, Macmillan, 1981, p 528.

52. Fields WAS: Selection of stroke patients for arterial reconstructive surgery. Am J Surg 125:527, 1973.

53. Fields WAS, Lemak N, Frankowski RF, Hardy RJ: Controlled trial of aspirin in cerebral ischemia. Stroke 8:301, 1977.

54. Fields WAS, Lemak N, Frankowski RF, Hardy RJ: Controlled trial of aspirin in cerebral ischemia: II. Surgical results. Stroke 9:309, 1978.

55. Freischlag JA, Hanna D, Moore WS: Improved prognosis for asymptomatic carotid stenosis with prophylactic carotid endarterectomy. Stroke 23:479, 1992.

56. Garde A, Samuelsson K, Fahlgran H, et al: Treatment after transient ischemic attacks: A comparison between anticoagulant drug and inhibition of platelet aggregation. Stroke 14:677, 1983.

57. Gee W, Mehigan JT, Wylie EJ: Measurement of collateral cerebral hemispheric blood pressure by ocular pneumoplethysmography. Am J Surg 130:121, 1975.

58. Gent M, Blakeley JA, Easton JC, and CATS Group: The Canadian-American Ticlopidine Study (CATS) in thromboembolic stroke. Lancet 1:1215, 1989.

59. Gertler JP, Cambria RP: The role of external carotid endarterectomy in the treatment of ipsilateral internal carotid occlusion: Collective review. J Vasc Surg 6:158, 1987.

60. Giordano JM, Trout HM III, Kozloff L, DePalma RG: Timing of carotid endarterectomy after stroke. J Vasc Surg 2:350, 1985.

61. Goldstone J, Moore WS: Emergency carotid artery surgery in neurologically unstable patients. Arch Surg 111:1284, 1976.

62. Hachinski V, Norris JW: The reversibility of cerebral ischemia. In Hachinski V, Norris JW: The Acute Stroke. Philadelphia, FA Davis, 1985, p 41.

63. Halstuk KS, Baker WH, Littooy FN: External carotid endarterectomy. J Vasc Surg 1:398, 1984.

64. Harris EJ, Brown WH, Pavy RN, et al: Continuous electroencephalographic monitoring during carotid artery endarterectomy. Surgery 62:441, 1967.

65. Hart RG: Cardiogenic embolism to the brain. Lancet 339:589, 1992.

66. Harvey J, Rasmussen T: Occlusion of the middle cerebral artery. Arch Neurol Psychiatry 66:20, 1951.

67. Hass WK, Easton JD, Adams HP Jr, et al: Ticlopidine Aspirin Stroke Study Group: A randomized trial comparing ticlopidine hydrochloride with aspirin for the prevention of stroke in high-risk patients. N Engl J Med 321:501, 1989.

68. Hass WK, Jonas S: Caution: Falling rock zone: An analysis of the medical and surgical management of threatened stroke. Proc Inst Med Chicago 33:80, 1980.

69. Hays RJ, Levinson SA, Wylie EJ: Intraoperative measurement of carotid back pressure as a guide to operative management for carotid endarterectomy. Surgery 72:953, 1972.

70. Helgason CM, Tortorice KL, Winkler SR, et al: Aspirin response and failure in cerebral infarction. Stroke 24:345, 1993.

71. Hertzer NR, Arison R: Cumulative stroke and survival ten years after carotid endarterectomy. J Vasc Surg 2:661, 1985.

72. Hertzer NR, Beven EG, O'Hara PJ, et al: A prospective study of vein patch angioplasty during carotid endarterectomy. Ann Surg 206:628, 1987.

73. Hertzer NR, Flanagan RA Jr, O'Hara PJ, et al: Surgical versus nonoperative treatment of asymptomatic carotid stenosis. Ann Surg 204:163, 1986.

74. Hertzer NR, Flanagan RA Jr, O'Hara PJ, et al: Surgical versus nonoperative treatment of symptomatic carotid stenosis. Ann Surg 204:154, 1986.

75. Heyman W, Wilkinson WE, Heyden S, et al: Risk of stroke in asymptomatic persons with cervical arterial bruits: A population study in Evans County, Georgia. N Engl J Med 302:838, 1980.

76. High-dose acetylsalicylic acid after cerebral infarction: A Swedish Cooperative Study. Stroke 18:325, 1987.

77. Hobson RW, Krupski WC, Weiss DG, et al: Influence of aspirin in the management of asymptomatic carotid artery stenosis. J Vasc Surg 17:257, 1993.

78. Hobson RW II, Weiss DG, Fields WS, et al: Efficacy of carotid endarterectomy for asymptomatic carotid stenosis. N Engl J Med 328:221, 1993.

79. Homi J, Humphries AW, Young JR, et al: Hypercarbic anesthesia in cerebrovascular surgery. Surgery 59:57, 1966.

80. Hughes RK, Bustos M, Byrne JP Jr: Internal carotid artery pressures: A guide for use of shunt during carotid repair. Arch Surg 109:494, 1974.

81. Humphries AW, Young JR, Beven EG, et al: Relief of vertebrobasilar symptoms by carotid endarterectomy. Surgery 57:48, 1965.

82. Hunter GC, Sieffert G, Malone JM, et al: The accuracy of carotid back pressure as an index for shunt requirement: A reappraisal. Stroke 13:319, 1982.

83. Krupski WC, Weiss DG, Rapp JH, et al: Adverse effects of aspirin in the treatment of asymptomatic carotid artery stenosis. J Vasc Surg 16:588, 1992.

84. Larson CP: Anesthesia and control of the cerebral circulation. In Wylie EJ, Ehrenfeld WK (eds): Extracranial Occlusive Cerebrovascular Disease. Philadelphia, WB Saunders, 1970.

85. Larson CP, Ehrenfeld WK, Wade JG, et al: Jugular venous oxygen saturation as an index of adequacy of cerebral oxygenation. Surgery 62:31, 1967.

86. Lassen WA: The luxury-perfusion syndrome and its possible relation to acute metabolic acidosis localized within the brain. Lancet 2:1113, 1996.

87. Link H, Lebram G, Johannson I, Radberg C: Prognosis in patients with infarction and TIA in carotid territory during and after anticoagulant therapy. Stroke 10:529, 1979.

88. Lips JPM, Sixma JJ, Schiphorst ME: The effect of ticlopidine administration to humans on binding of adenosine diphosphate to blood platelets. Thromb Res 17:19, 1980.

89. Little JR, Moufarrij NA, Furlan AJ: Early carotid endarterectomy after cerebral infarction. Neurosurgery 24:334, 1989.

90. Lord RSA: Later survival after carotid endarterectomy for transient ischemic attacks. J Vasc Surg 1:512, 1984.

91. Lyons C, Clark LC Jr, McDowell H, et al: Cerebral venous oxygen content during carotid thrombointimectomy. Ann Surg 106:561, 1964.

92. Machleder HI, Barker WF: External carotid artery shunting during carotid endarterectomy. Arch Surg 108:785, 1974.

93. Makhoul RG, Moore WS, Colburn MD, et al: Benefit of carotid endarterectomy following prior stroke. J Vasc Surg 18:666, 1993.

94. Matchar DB, Goldstein LB, McCory DC, et al: Carotid Endarterectomy: A Literature Review and Ratings of Appropriateness and Necessity. Santa Monica, Calif, Rand Corporation, 1992.

95. Mayberg MR, Wilson SE, Yatsu F, et al, for the Veterans Affairs Cooperative Studies Program 309 Trialist Group: Carotid endarterectomy and prevention of cerebral ischemia in symptomatic carotid stenosis. JAMA 266:3289, 1991.

96. The Mayo Asymptomatic Carotid Endarterectomy Study Group: Results of a randomized controlled trial of carotid endarterectomy for asymptomatic carotid stenosis. Mayo Clin Proc 67:513, 1992.

97. Mayo NE, Levy R, Goldberg MS: Aspirin and hemorrhagic stroke. Stroke 212:1213, 1991.

98. McCullough JL, Mentzer RM, Harman PK, et al: Carotid endarterectomy after a completed stroke: Reduction in long neurologic deterioration. J Vasc Surg 2:7, 1985.

99. McTavish D, Faulds D, Goa K: Ticlopidine A: An updated review of its pharmacology and therapeutic use in platelet-dependent disorders. Drugs 40:238, 1990.

100. Meissner I, Wiebers DO, Whisnant JP, et al: The natural history of asymptomatic carotid artery occlusive lesions. JAMA 258:2704, 1987.

101. Mentzer RN, Finkelmeir BA, Crosby LK, Wellons MA Jr: Emergency carotid endarterectomy for fluctuating neurologic deficits. Surgery 89:60, 1981.

102. Meyer JS: Importance of ischemic damage to small vessels in experimental cerebral infarcts. J Neuropathol Exp Neurol 17:571, 1958.

103. Modi JR, Finch WT, Sumner DS: Update of carotid endarterectomy in two community hospitals: Springfield revisited. Stroke 14:128, 1983.

104. Moneta GL, Taylor DC, Nicholls SC, et al: Operative versus nonoperative management of asymptomatic high-grade internal carotid artery stenosis: Improved results with endarterectomy. Stroke 18:1005, 1987.

105. Moore WS: Carotid endarterectomy for prevention of stroke. West J Med 159:37, 1993.

106. Moore WS, Barnett MJ, Beebe HE, et al: Guidelines for carotid endarterectomy: A multidisciplinary consensus statement from the Ad Hoc Committee, American Heart Association. Stroke 26:188, 1995.

107. Moore WS, Blaisdell FW, Hall AD: Retrograde thrombectomy for chronic occlusion of the common carotid artery. Arch Surg 95:664, 1967.

108. Moore WS, Boren C, Malone JM, et al: Natural history of nonstenotic asymptomatic ulcerative lesions of the carotid artery. Arch Surg 113:1352, 1978.

109. Moore WS, Hall AD: Carotid artery back pressure. Arch Surg 99:702, 1969.

110. Moore WS, Malone JM, Goldstone J: Extrathoracic repair of branch occlusions of the aortic arch. Am J Surg 132:249, 1976.

111. Moore WS, Mohr JP, Najafi H, et al: Carotid endarterectomy: Practice guidelines. J Vasc Surg 15:469, 1992.

112. Moore WS, Yee JM, Hall AD: Collateral cerebral blood pressure: An index of tolerance to temporary carotid occlusion. Arch Surg 106:520, 1973.

113. Morgenstern LB, Fox LJ, Sharpe BL, et al: The risks and benefits of carotid endarterectomy in patients with near occlusion of the carotid artery. Neurology 48:911, 1997.

114. Mozersky DJ, Barnes RW, Sumner DS, et al: The hemodynamics of the axillary-axillary bypass. Surg Gynecol Obstet 135:925, 1972.

115. Najafi H, Javid H, Dye WS, et al: Kinked internal carotid artery: Clinical evaluation and surgical correction. Arch Surg 89:134, 1964.

115a. Norris JW: Head and neck bruits in stroke prevention. In Norris JW, Machinski VC (eds): Prevention of Stroke. New York, Springer-Verlag, 1991, p 103.

116. North American Symptomatic Carotid Endarterectomy Trial Collaborators: Beneficial effect of carotid endarterectomy in symptomatic patients with high-grade carotid stenosis. N Engl J Med 325:445, 1991.

117. O'Hara PJ, Hertzer NR, Beven EG: External carotid revascularization: Review of a 10-year experience. J Vasc Surg 2:709, 1985.

118. Ojemman RG, Crowell RM, Robertson GH, Fisher CM: Surgical treatment of extracranial carotid disease. Clin Neurosurg 22:214, 1975.

119. Olsson JE, Brechter C, Backolund H, et al: Anticoagulant vs. antiplatelet therapy as prophylactic against cerebral infarction in transient ischemic attacks. Stroke 11:4, 1980.

120. Piotowski JJ, Bernhard VM, Rubin JR, et al: Timing of carotid endarterectomy after acute stroke. J Vasc Surg 11:45, 1990.

121. Pistolese GR, Citone G, Faraglia V: Effects of hypercapnia on cerebral blood flow during the clamping of the carotid arteries in surgical management of cerebrovascular insufficiency. Neurology (Minneap) 21:95, 1971.

122. Pokras JR, Dyken ML: Dramatic changes in the performance of endarterectomy for diseases of the extracranial arteries of the head. Stroke 10:1289, 1988.

123. Report of the Veterans Administration Cooperative Study of Arteriosclerosis: An evaluation of anticoagulant therapy in the treatment of cerebrovascular disease. Neurology 11:132, 1961.

124. Ricotta JJ, Ouriel K, Green RM, DeWeese JA: Use of computerized cerebral tomography in the selection of patients for elective and urgent carotid endarterectomy. Ann Surg 202:783, 1985.

125. Riles TS, Imparato AM, Mintaer R, Baumann FS: Comparison of results of bilateral and unilateral carotid endarterectomy five years after surgery. Surgery 91:258, 1982.

126. Rob CG: Operation for acute completed stroke due to thrombosis of the internal carotid artery. Surgery 65:862, 1969.

127. Robinson RW, Demirel M, LeBeau RJ: Natural history of cerebral thrombosis: Nine- to nineteen-year follow-up. J Chronic Dis 21:221, 1968.

128. Rosenthal D, Borrero E, Clark MD, et al: Carotid endarterectomy after reversible ischemic neurologic deficit or stroke: Is it of value? J Vasc Surg 8:527, 1988.

129. Rothrock JF, Hart RG: Ticlopidine use and threatened stroke: A clinical perspective. West J Med 160:43, 1994.

130. Rubin JR, Goldstone J, McIntyre KE, et al: The value of carotid endarterectomy in reducing the morbidity and mortality of recurrent stroke. J Vasc Surg 4:443, 1986.

131. Ruether R, Dorndorf W: Aspirin in patients with cerebral ischemia and normal angiograms or nonsurgical lesions: The results of a double-blind trial. In Breddin K, Dorndorf W, Lowe D, et al (eds): Acetylsalicylic Acid in Cerebral Ischemia and Coronary Heart Disease. Stuttgart, Schattauer, 1978, pp 97.

132. Sacco RL, Wolf PA, Kannel WB, et al: Survival and recurrence following stroke: The Framingham Study. Stroke 13:290, 1982.

133. The SALT Collaborative: Swedish aspirin low-dose trial (SALT) of 75 mg aspirin as secondary prophylaxis after cerebrovascular ischemic events. Lancet 338:1345, 1991.

134. Schuler JJ, Flanigan B, DeBord JR, et al: The treatment of cerebral ischemia by external carotid artery revascularization. Arch Surg 118:567, 1983.

135. Sergeant PT, Derom F, Berzsenyi G, et al: Carotid endarterectomy for cerebrovascular insufficiency: Long-term follow-up of 141 patients followed up to 16 years. Acta Chir Belg 79:309, 1980.

136. Silvenius J, Laakso M, Pentilla IM, et al: The European Stroke Prevention Study: Results according to sex. Neurology 41:1189, 1991.

137. Solis MM, Ranval TJ, Barone GW, et al: The CASANOVA Study: Immediate surgery versus delayed surgery for moderate carotid stenosis [Letter]? Stroke 23:917, 1992.

138. Solomon DH, Hart RG: Antithrombotic therapies to prevent stroke. In Zierler RE (ed): Surgical Management of Cerebrovascular Disease. New York, McGraw-Hill, 1995, p 237.

139. Solomon RA, Loftus CM, Quest DO, Correll JW: Incidence and etiology of intracerebral hemorrhage following carotid endarterectomy. J Vasc Surg 64:29, 1986.

140. Sorenson PA, Pedersen H, Marquardsen J, et al: Acetylsalicylic acid in the prevention of stroke in patients with reversible cerebral ischemia attacks: A Danish cooperative study. Stroke 14:15, 1983.

141. Sproul G: Femoral-axillary bypass for cerebrovascular insufficiency. Arch Surg 103:746, 1971.

142. Stewart G, Ross-Russell RW, Browse NL: The long-term results of carotid endarterectomy for transient ischemic attacks. J Vasc Surg 4:600, 1986.

143. Swedish Cooperative Study: High-dose acetylsalicylic acid after cerebral infarction. Stroke 18:325, 1987.

144. Sze PC, Reitman D, Pincus MM, et al: Antiplatelet agents in the secondary prevention of stroke: Meta-analysis of the randomized control trials. Stroke 19:436, 1988.

145. Takolander RJ, Bergentz SE, Ericsson BF: Carotid artery surgery in patients with minor stroke. Br J Surg 70:13, 1982.

146. Thompson JE: Carotid endarterectomy for asymptomatic carotid stenosis: An update. J Vasc Surg 13:669, 1991.

147. Thompson JE: Cerebral protection during carotid endarterectomy. JAMA 202:1046, 1967.

148. Thompson JE, Austen DJ, Patman RD: Carotid endarterectomy for cerebrovascular insufficiency: Long-term results in 592 patients followed up to 13 years. Ann Surg 172:663, 1970.

149. Thompson JE, Austen DJ, Patman RD: Endarterectomy of the totally occluded carotid artery for stroke. Arch Surg 95:791, 1967.

150. Thompson JE, Patman RD, Talkington CM: Asymptomatic carotid bruit: Long-term outcome of patients having endarterectomy compared with unoperated controls. Ann Surg 188:308, 1978.

151. Tohgi H, Konno S, Tamura K, et al: Effects of low-to-high doses of aspirin on platelet aggregatability and metabolites of thromboxane A_2 and prostacyclin. Stroke 23:1400, 1992.

152. Torrent A, Anderson B: The outcome of patients with transient ischemic attacks and stroke treated with anticoagulation. Acta Med Scand 208:359, 1980.

153. Trojaborg W, Boysen G: Relation between EEG, regional cerebral blood flow, and internal carotid artery pressure during carotid endarterectomy. Electroencephalogr Clin Neurophysiol 34:61, 1973.

154. Uchiyama S, Sone R, Nagayama T, et al: Combination therapy with low-dose aspirin and ticlopidine in cerebral ischemia. Stroke 20:1643, 1989.

155. UK-TIA Study Group: United Kingdom transient ischaemic attack (UK-TIA) aspirin trial: Final results. J Neurol Neurosurg Psychiatry 54:1044, 1991.

156. Van Gijn J: Aspirin: Dose and indications in modern stroke. Neurol Clin 10:193, 1992.

158. Waltz AG: Effect of blood pressure on blood flow in ischemic and in nonischemic cerebral cortex. Neurology (Minneap) 18:613, 1968.

158. Whisnant JP, Matsumoto M, Elveback LR: The effect of anticoagulant therapy on the prognosis of patients with transient cerebral ischemic attacks in a community—Rochester, Minnesota, 1965-1969. Mayo Clin Proc 48:844, 1973.

159. Whitemore AD, Ruby ST, Couch MP, Mannick JA: Early carotid endarterectomy in patients with small, fixed neurologic deficits. J Vasc Surg 1:795, 1984.

160. Whitney DG, Kahn EM, Estes JW, Jones CE: Carotid artery surgery without a temporary indwelling shunt: 1917 consecutive procedures. Arch Surg 115:1393, 1980.

161. Wing SD, Norman D, Pollock JA, Newton TH: Contrast enhancement of cerebral infarcts in computed tomography. Radiology 121:89, 1979.

162. Wolf PA, Kannel WB, Sorlie P, McNamara P: Asymptomatic carotid bruit and the risk of stroke. JAMA 245:1442, 1981.

163. Wylie EJ, Hein MF, Adams JE: Intracranial hemorrhage following surgical revascularization for treatment of acute stroke. J Neurosurg 21:212, 1964.

164. Zarins CK, DelBaccaro EJ, Johns L, et al: Increased cerebral blood flow after external carotid artery revascularization. Surgery 89:730, 1981.

Chapter

Carotid Angioplasty and Stenting

140

TIMOTHY M. SULLIVAN, MD, FACS

HARRY CLOFT, MD, PhD

Cerebrovascular accident is the third leading cause of death in the United States, surpassed only by heart disease and malignancy.[1] Stroke accounts for 10% to 12% of all deaths in industrialized countries. Almost one in four men and one in five women aged 45 years can expect to have a stroke if they live to 85 years of age. In a population of 1 million, 1600 people will have a stroke each year. Only 55% of these survive 6 months, and a third of the survivors have significant problems caring for themselves. As our population ages, the total number of people afflicted with stroke will continue to rise unless historic stroke rates decline in the future.[2]

The etiology of stroke is multifactorial. Ischemic stroke accounts for about 80% of all first-ever strokes, whereas intracerebral hemorrhage and subarachnoid hemorrhage are responsible for 10% and 5%, respectively. Of those strokes that are ischemic in nature, most are linked to complications of atheromatous plaques. The most frequent site of such an atheroma is the carotid bifurcation. Although the prevention of stroke in the general population has largely focused on the control of hypertension, a substantial number of strokes are preventable by the identification and treatment of carotid disease, especially as the population ages.

Surgical endarterectomy of high-grade carotid lesions, both symptomatic and asymptomatic, has been identified as the treatment of choice for stroke prophylaxis in most patients when compared to "best medical therapy" (risk factor reduction and antiplatelet agents), as proven by the North American Symptomatic Carotid Endarterectomy Trial (NASCET) and the Asymptomatic Carotid Atherosclerosis Study (ACAS).[3,4] More careful inspection of their respective results suggest that the risk of disabling stroke or death was 1.9% in NASCET, with a 3.9% risk of minor stroke. In ACAS, the risk of major stroke or death was 0.6% when one excludes the 1.2% risk of stroke caused by diagnostic arteriography. Subsequently, carotid endarterectomy (CEA)

has been performed in increasing numbers of patients and now represents the most frequent surgical procedure performed by vascular surgeons. Despite the proven efficacy of CEA in the prevention of ischemic stroke, great interest has been generated in carotid angioplasty and stenting (CAS) as an alternative to surgical therapy. This chapter examines the indications, techniques, and results of this novel therapy.

■ CAROTID ENDARTERECTOMY

The era of CEA was ushered in by the report of Eastcott and associates in 1954. They treated a 66-year-old woman who had 33 episodes of transient cerebral ischemia; following the operation, her symptoms resolved.[5] Despite publication of satisfactory surgical results, the efficacy of CEA came into question during the 1970s and 1980s. Among Medicare beneficiaries, the frequency of CEA declined from 1985 (61,273 per annum) to 1989 (46,571).[6] It was not until the 1990s that randomized trials of best medical therapy versus CEA were undertaken. Following publication of the NASCET and ACAS results, the volume of CEA in the United States rose dramatically; again, among Medicare recipients, the incidence rose to 108,275 in 1996 following release of data from these trials. The *Dartmouth Atlas of Vascular Health Care* reported that the number of CEAs performed between 1995 and 1997 nearly doubled, from 62,000 to 114,000 annually.[7]

With the advent of CAS, CEA has again come under attack, despite its proven efficacy and durability in stroke prevention in patients with high-grade stenosis of the internal carotid artery (ICA).[8] Proponents of CAS have suggested that the results of NASCET and ACAS are not achievable in general practice outside selected centers of excellence. The question is a reasonable one; if the combined stroke and death rate of CEA in asymptomatic patients were more than 3%, there would be little benefit of operation in the asymptomatic population.[9] Both ACAS and NASCET included good-risk patients on the basis of reasonable life expectancy (so as to be available for follow-up) and exclusion of other potential causes of stroke (such as atrial fibrillation). Exclusion criteria included previous carotid surgery, prior myocardial infarction (MI), congestive heart failure, renal failure, unstable angina, and those requiring combined CEA and coronary bypass procedures. Tables 140-1 and 140-2 list inclusion and exclusion criteria for several important CEA and CAS trials. A review of 25 studies reporting 30-day stroke and death rates by Rothwell and associates[10] found a mortality rate of 1.3% in asymptomatic patients and 1.8% in symptomatic patients. The combined stroke and death rates were 3% in asymptomatic patients and 5.2% in those presenting with symptomatic carotid stenosis.

A number of studies have focused on NASCET and ACAS eligibility as they relate to the results of CEA in the general population. Lepore and colleagues[11] from the Ochsner Clinic reviewed 366 CEAs performed at their institution over a 2-year period. Surprisingly, 46% were found to be "high risk" based on NASCET and ACAS ineligibility. Their cohort included 60% who presented with asymptomatic carotid stenosis; the remaining 40% had focal ipsilateral symptoms at presentation. The overall stroke and death rate (combined stroke + mortality [CSM]) was 2.5%; trial-eligible good-risk patients had a CSM of 1.5%, and the remainder (trial ineligible) had a CSM of 3.6%. Although there was a trend toward higher neurologic morbidity in trial-ineligible patients, this difference did not reach statistical significance ($P = 0.17$). These authors concluded that ineligibility for NASCET or ACAS should not be employed as a *de facto* indication for CAS. Illig and co-workers[12] examined the results of CEA at the University of Rochester in 857 patients. Stroke or death at 30 days occurred in 2.1%. Rates were similar in patients excluded from (2.7%) or included in (1.6%) NASCET and ACAS and in patients eligible (3.1%) or ineligible (2.1%) for ACCULINK for Revascularization of Carotids in High-Risk Patients (ARCHeR), a CAS registry. These rates did not differ according to whether exclusion or inclusion was based on anatomic risk, medical risk, or protocol exclusion; however, there was a trend toward worse outcome in the high medical risk subgroup. Stroke and death rates were similar according to age, gender, repeat procedure, or the presence of contralateral occlusion.

Mozes and associates[13] examined the results of 776 consecutive CEAs from the Division of Vascular Surgery at the Mayo Clinic in Rochester, Minnesota. Patients were categorized as high risk based on the inclusion and exclusion criteria for the Stenting and Angioplasty with Protection in Patients at High Risk for Endarterectomy (SAPPHIRE) trial of CAS with cerebral embolic protection. Of 776 CEAs, 323 (42%) were considered high risk based on the criteria listed in Table 140-3. Clinical presentation was similar in the high- and low-risk groups (Table 140-4). The overall postoperative stroke rate was 1.4% (symptomatic, 2.9%; asymptomatic, 0.9%). When comparing high- and low-risk CEAs, there was no statistical difference in stroke rate. Factors associated with significantly increased stroke risk were cervical radiation therapy,

class III/IV angina, symptomatic presentation, and age ≤ 60 years. Overall mortality was 0.3% (symptomatic, 0.5%; asymptomatic, 0.2%), not significantly different between the high- (0.6%) and low-risk groups (0.0%). Non-Q MI was more frequent in the high-risk group (3.1% vs. 0.9%; $P < 0.05$). Of note, the *only* MIs that occurred in the entire series were nontransmural (non-Q). A composite cluster of adverse clinical events (death, stroke, and MI) was more frequent in the symptomatic high-risk group (9.3% vs. 1.6%; $P < 0.005$) but not in the asymptomatic cohort. There was a trend for more major cranial nerve injuries in patients with local risk factors, such as high carotid bifurcation, reoperation, and cervical radiation therapy (4.6% vs. 1.7%; $P < 0.13$). In 121 patients, excluded on the base of synchronous or immediate subsequent operations (who would have also been excluded from SAPPHIRE), the overall stroke (1.65%; $P = 0.69$), death (1.65%; $P = 0.09$), and MI (0.83%; $P = 0.71$) rates were not significantly different from the study population. The authors concluded that SAPPHIRE-eligible high-risk patients could undergo CEA with stroke and death rates well within accepted standards and that patients with local risk factors were at higher risk for cranial nerve injuries, not necessarily stroke. These data bring into question the application of CAS as an alternative to CEA, even in high-risk patients.

Although the previously cited studies do not support the premise that operative risk is higher in patients excluded from NASCET and ACAS or in trials of CAS in high-risk patients, there may in fact be categories of patients in whom CEA may not be optimal therapy. Hertzer and colleagues[14] described the Cleveland Clinic experience for 2228 consecutive CEA procedures in 2046 patients from 1989 to 1995. The stroke and mortality rates for CEA as an isolated procedure were exemplary at 1.8% and 0.5%, respectively, for a combined rate of 2.3%. In addition, no statistical difference was found in stroke and mortality rates for asymptomatic patients, those presenting with hemispheric transient ischemic attack (TIA), or those operated for stroke with minimal residua. Those patients having combined CEA and coronary artery bypass graft (CABG) had higher rates of perioperative stroke (4.3%) and death (5.3%) than those patients having isolated CEA. Carotid reoperations were also associated with higher stroke (4.6%) and death (2.0%) rates. These data again lend credence to the idea that CEA can be performed safely in large groups of unselected patients but may give some insight into categories of patients who are at increased risk for operative intervention.

A follow-up study from the Cleveland Clinic by Ouriel and coworkers, including Hertzer,[15] attempted to identify a subgroup of patients who, on retrospective analysis, were at increased risk for CEA and therefore might be better served by CAS. Three thousand sixty-one CEAs were examined from a prospective database over a 10-year period. A high-risk cohort was identified, based on the presence of severe coronary artery disease (requiring angioplasty or bypass surgery within the 6 months prior to CEA), history of congestive heart failure, severe chronic obstructive pulmonary disease, or renal insufficiency (serum creatinine > 3.0 mg/dL) (Figs. 140-1 and 140-2). The rate of the composite endpoint of stroke/death/ MI was 3.8% for the entire group (stroke 2.1%, MI 1.2%, and death 1.1%). This composite endpoint occurred in 7.4% of those considered

Table 140-1   Definition of High-Risk Carotid Endarterectomy (CEA): Major Exclusion Criteria of NASCET/ACAS and Major Inclusion Criteria for Population-Based Studies on High-Risk CEA and for the SAPPHIRE Study

	EXCLUSION CRITERIA		INCLUSION CRITERIA			
	NASCET	**ACAS**	**Ouriel et al (2001)**	**Jordan et al (2002)**	**Gasparis et al (2003)**	**SAPPHIRE**
Age (yr)	>79	>79	—	—	≥80	>80
History	Contralateral CEA <4 mo Major surgical procedure <1 mo Stroke-in-evolution	Major surgical procedure <1 mo Stroke-in-evolution	—	Major vascular procedure <1 mo	—	—
Comorbidities Cardiac	Unstable angina Atrial fibrillation Valvular heart disease Symptomatic CHF MI <6 mo	Unstable angina Atrial fibrillation Valvular heart disease Symptomatic CHF	PTCA/CABG <6 mo History of CHF	Coronary procedure <1 mo CABG <6 wk Angina, NYHA class III/IV EF <30% MI <4 wk	NYHA functional class III/IV Canadian CVA heart failure functional class III/IV CABG <6 mo	Open heart surgery <6 wk MI <4 wk Angina CCS class III/IV CHF class III/IV EF <30% Abnormal cardiac stress test
Pulmonary	Lung failure	Lung failure with impact on 5-yr survival	Severe COPD	FEV$_1$ <1 L Home oxygen	Steroid dependency Oxygen dependency	Chronic oxygen therapy Resting Po$_2$ ≤60 mm Hg Baseline hematocrit ≥50% FEV$_1$ or DLco ≤50% predicted
Renal	Kidney failure	Cr >3 mg/dL	Cr >3 mg/dL	—	Cr ≥3 mg/dL	—
Other	Uncontrolled HTN Uncontrolled DM Liver failure Cancer, <50% 5-yr survival	>180 systolic, 115 diastolic BP (mm Hg) Fasting glucose >400 mg/dL Liver failure Cancer, <50% 5-yr survival Active ulcer disease Warfarin	—	—	—	—
Anatomic criteria	Previous ipsilateral CEA Tandem lesion > target stenosis	Previous ipsilateral CEA Tandem lesion > target stenosis Cervical radiation treatment	—	Previous ipsilateral CEA Cervical radiation treatment Contralateral carotid occlusion High cervical lesion Lesion below the clavicle	Previous ipsilateral CEA Cervical radiation treatment Contralateral carotid occlusion Cervical radiation treatment High cervical lesion	Previous ipsilateral CEA Severe tandem lesion Cervical radiation treatment Contralateral carotid occlusion High cervical lesion (at least C2) Lesion below the clavicle Contralateral laryngeal palsy

CHF, chronic heart failure; MI, myocardial infarction; HTN, hypertension; DM, diabetes mellitus; Cr, creatinine; BP, blood pressure; PTCA, percutaneous transluminal coronary angioplasty; CABG, coronary artery bypass graft; COPD, chronic obstructive pulmonary disease; NYHA, New York Heart Association; Canadian CVA, Canadian Cardiovascular Association; CCS, Canadian Cardiovascular Society; EF, ejection fraction; Po$_2$, partial oxygen pressure; FEV$_1$, forced expiratory volume in 1 second; DLco, diffusing capacity of the lung for carbon monoxide; C2, second cervical vertebra.

Table 140-2	Exclusion Criteria of the SAPPHIRE Trial

Acute stroke (≤48 hr)

Staged elective procedure (within 30 days following the CEA)
    Elective percutaneous intervention
    Contralateral CEA
    Other elective operation

Synchronous operation
    CCA angioplasty/stenting or bypass
    Cardiac operation
    Noncardiac operation

Intracranial pathology
    Intracranial mass
    Aneurysm >9 mm
    Arteriovenous malformation
    Ventriculoperitoneal shunt

CEA, carotid endarterectomy; CCA, common carotid artery.

Table 140-3	Number and Frequency of High-Risk Criteria in All Carotid Endarterectomies*

HIGH-RISK CRITERIA	NUMBER (PERCENTAGE)
Positive cardiac stress test	109 (14)
Age >80 yr	85 (11)
Contralateral carotid occlusion	66 (9)
Pulmonary dysfunction	56 (7)
High carotid bifurcation	36 (5)
Carotid reoperation	27 (3)
Left ventricular EF < 30%	11 (1.4)
NYHA class III/IV CHF	11 (1.4)
NYHA class III/IV angina	8 (1)
Cervical radiation therapy	6 (<1)
Recent (<6 wk) cardiac operation	4 (<1)
Contralateral laryngeal nerve palsy	2 (<1)
Recent (< 4 wk) MI	1 (<1)

*n = 776; 84 operations were associated with more than one high-risk criterion.
EF, ejection fraction; CHF, chronic heart failure; NYHA, New York Heart Association; MI, myocardial infarction.

Table 140-4	Demographics and Frequency of Clinical Variables in Patients with High- and Low-Risk Carotid Endarterectomy		
	HIGH-RISK	LOW-RISK	P
Number	323	453	—
Presentation	—	—	—
Asymptomatic	73%	73%	NS
TIA/amaurosis fugax	23%	22%	NS
Stroke	4%	5%	NS
Demographics			
Mean age	73 yr	70 yr	<0.0001
Male gender	67%	60%	<0.05
CV risk factors			
Smoking	71%	71%	NS
Arterial hypertension	88%	83%	NS
Dyslipidemia	76%	81%	NS
Diabetes mellitus	24%	24%	NS
Chronic CAD	55%	44%	0.01
Diagnostic studies			
Cardiac stress test	67%	47%	0.0001
Duplex US	97%	99%	NS
MRA	25%	22%	NS
Angiography	16%	11%	0.05
Operative technique			
Shunt	22%	13%	0.001
Patch	87%	89%	NS
Eversion CEA	2%	3%	NS

CEA, carotid endarterectomy; TIA, transient ischemic attack; CV, cardiovascular; CAD, coronary artery disease; US, ultrasonography; MRA, magnetic resonance angiography; NS, not significant.

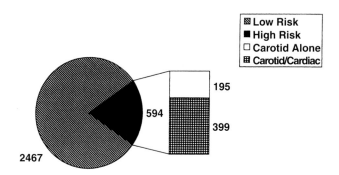

FIGURE 140-1 Proportion of patients by risk category. (From Ouriel K, Hertzer NR, Beven EG, et al: Preprocedural risk stratification: Identifying an appropriate population for carotid stenting. J Vasc Surg 33:728-732, 2001.)

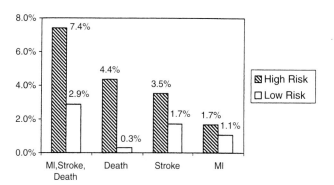

FIGURE 140-2 Rate of perioperative events in low- and high-risk subgroups. MI, myocardial infarction. (From Ouriel K, Hertzer NR, Beven EG, et al: Preprocedural risk stratification: Identifying an appropriate population for carotid stenting. J Vasc Surg 33:728-732, 2001.)

high risk (n = 594, 19.4%), significantly higher than in those in the low-risk (n = 2467, 80.6%) category (2.9%; P = 0.008). Patients in the high-risk group were further subdivided into those who had CEA alone and those in whom CEA was combined with CABG. Not surprisingly, the incidence of the composite endpoint was greater in those having combined CEA/CABG than those having CEA as an isolated procedure. In those having CEA alone, the risk of death was significantly greater in the high-risk group (P < 0.001). Importantly, however, although the risk of the combined endpoint stroke/death/MI was greater in the high-risk group, this difference did not reach statistical significance (P = 0.078) In addition, the rates of the individual endpoints of MI and stroke did not differ statistically between the high- and low-risk groups. These data from the Cleveland Clinic vascular surgery registry seem to support the notion that patients enrolled in the multicenter trials of CEA (NASCET and ACAS) were likely similar to the low-risk group, whereas those in the high-risk group may not in fact have had such stellar outcomes if included in multicenter trials. Other authors have called into question the idea of "high-risk" CEA; conflicting data exist as to factors such as high lesions, reoperations, cervical radiation, and contralateral carotid occlusion.[16-22] Subsequent trials have therefore focused on medically compromised, high-risk patients as those who may benefit from an alternative procedure such as CAS.

■ CAROTID ANGIOPLASTY AND STENTING

History of CAS

ICA stenosis has been demonstrated to be safely and efficaciously treated with CEA in NASCET and ACAS, as described earlier. The use of angioplasty and stenting techniques in the coronary and peripheral circulation stimulated an interest in the application of this technology to the carotid circulation, especially in those patients who are poor surgical candidates.

Andreas Gruntzig pioneered the technique of balloon angioplasty in the coronary circulation in 1977.[23] By 1980, reports of balloon angioplasty in the carotid arteries were published.[24,25] The first stents were implanted for ischemic heart disease in 1986,[26] and by the 1990s several investigators had reported the application of stents to the carotid circulation. Since these early reports, CAS has advanced to the level of investigation by clinical trials.

Indications

The following basic indications for CAS do not differ from those of standard surgical carotid endartectomy:

1. Asymptomatic lesions that fall within the 80% to 99% range on duplex ultrasound, which correlates with an angiographic stenosis of at least 60%—Most clinical trials of CAS in asymptomatic patients require an *angiographic* stenosis of at least 80% for study inclusion.
2. Symptomatic patients (hemispheric TIA, amaurosis fugax, or stroke with minimal residua) with at least a 70% angiographic stenosis—Patients with symptomatic, ulcerated stenoses greater than 50% may benefit from endarterectomy; this has not yet been extrapolated to carotid intervention.

A list of the possible indications for CAS in high-risk patients and relative contraindications to the procedure are listed in Tables 140-5 and 140-6.

Results of CAS

Short-Term Results

The short-term results of CAS are largely dependent on the presence or absence of cerebral embolization. With the relatively recent addition of cerebral protection to the procedure, associated stroke risk seems to have decreased. Admittedly, however, improvements in devices and technology have created a "moving target," making evaluation of results difficult at best. Nevertheless, a reasonable summary of the procedure, as it exists today, can be created from the available literature.

A list of studies, encompassing 40 case series and more than 17,000 procedures, is shown in Table 140-7.[27-66]

Table 140-5	Indications for Carotid Angioplasty/Stenting in High-Risk Patients

Severe cardiac disease
    Requiring coronary PTA or CABG
    History of congestive heart failure
Severe chronic obstructive pulmonary disease
    Requiring home oxygen
    FEV_1 <20% predicted
Severe chronic renal insufficiency
    Serum creatinine >3.0 mg/dL
    Currently on dialysis
Prior carotid endarterectomy (restenosis)
    Contralateral vocal cord paralysis
Surgically inaccessible lesions
    At or above C2
    Inferior to the clavicle
Radiation-induced carotid stenosis
Prior ipsilateral radical neck dissection

PTA, percutaneous transluminal angioplasty; CABG, coronary artery bypass graft; FEV_1, forced expiratory volume in 1 second.

Table 140-6	Limitations of and Contraindications to Carotid Angioplasty/Stenting

Inability to obtain femoral artery access
Unfavorable aortic arch anatomy
Severe tortuosity of the common or internal carotid arteries
Severely calcified/undilatable stenoses
Lesions containing fresh thrombus
Extensive stenoses (longer than 2 cm)
Critical (>99%) stenoses
Lesions adjacent to carotid artery aneurysms
Contrast-related issues
    Chronic renal insufficiency
    Previous life-threatening contrast reaction
Preload dependent states—severe aortic valvular stenosis

One of the first peer-reviewed manuscripts reporting on the results of a large cohort of patients was in 1997 by Yadav and associates[28] from the University of Alabama at Birmingham (UAB). A total of 107 patients (126 arteries) were treated; 59% were symptomatic, and many were referred from local vascular surgeons. All patients were treated with balloon-expandable stents without cerebral protection. Amazingly, there were only two major strokes, 7 minor strokes, and one death at 30 days, for a CSM of 7.9%. Of note, 77% of their patients would not have been eligible for NASCET or ACAS (inferring that these patients were unfit for standard CEA); Jordan and colleagues,[67] reporting from the same institution, found that 72% of 120 CEA procedures performed during a similar period would also have been excluded from these two pivotal trials.

Expanding on the Birmingham experience, Roubin and coworkers[38] subsequently reported on patients treated at

UAB and at Lenox Hill Hospital in New York. Six hundred four arteries were treated in 528 consecutive patients over a 5-year period, including patients treated with both balloon-expandable and self-expanding stents, with and without cerebral protection devices. The overall 30-day CSM was 8.1% (for 528 patients) and included a 5.5% rate of minor stroke, 1.6% major stroke rate, and 1% rate of non-neurologic death. When divided into yearly intervals, the risk of stroke and death reached a maximum of 12.5% in the period ending September 1997 and fell to a minimum of 3.2% the following year. This rather dramatic change in results likely represents improvements in technology (protection devices, stents, guide wires) as well as an improved ability of the investigators to select appropriate patients for intervention.

The Carotid and Vertebral Artery Transluminal Angioplasty Study (CAVATAS),[35] published in June 2001,

Table 140-7 Current Results of Carotid Angioplasty/Stenting				
AUTHOR, YEAR	**NO. OF ARTERIES**	**PERCENTAGE SYMPTOMATIC**	**CEREBRAL PROTECTION**	**STROKE + DEATH, %**
Diethrich 1996	117	28	No	7.3
Yadav 1997	126	59	No	7.9
Henry 1998	174	35	Mixed	2.9
Teitelbaum 1998	25	68	No	27.3
Bergeron 1999	99	44	No	2
Shawl 2000	192	61	No	2.9
Malek 2000	28	100	No	3.6
Roubin 2001	604	52	Mixed	7.4
Ahmadi 2001	298	38	Mixed	3.0
CAVATAS 2001	251	96	No	10
Brooks 2001	53	100	No	0
d'Audiffret 2001	68	30	Mixed	5.8
Chakhtoura 2001	50	39	No	2.2
Leger 2001	8	38	No	0
Dietz 2001	43	100	Yes	5
Baudier 2001	50	98	Mixed	6
Reimers 2001	88	36	Yes	2.3
Pappada 2001	27	93	Mixed	3.7
Paniagua 2001	69	16	No	5.6
Criado 2002	135	40	Mixed	2
Guimaraens 2002	194	92	Yes	2.6
Al-Mubarak 2002	164	48	Yes	2
Bonaldi 2002	71	100	Mixed	5.6
Kao 2002	118	75	No	4.2
Whitlow 2002	75	56	Yes	0
Qureshi 2002	73	37	Mixed	4.1
Macdonald 2002	50	84	Yes	6
Stankovic 2002	102	37	Mixed	0
Kastrup 2003	100	63	Mixed	5
Cremonisi 2003	442	57	Yes	1.1
Terada 2003	87	80	Yes	2.3
Bowser 2003	52	60	No	5.7
Wholey 2003	12,392	53	Mixed	4.75
Becquemin 2003	114	33	Mixed	7.0
Dabrowski 2003	73	Not stated	Mixed	5.5
Cernetti 2003	104	26	Yes	4
Bush 2003	51	29	No	2
Gable 2003	31	69	No	3
Lal 2003	122	45	Mixed	3.3
SAPPHIRE 30-DAY	565	30	Yes	6.2%
TOTAL	**17,485**			**4.7**

reported the results of a randomized trial of surgery versus angioplasty (with and without stenting) for the treatment of patients with symptomatic carotid and vertebral artery stenosis: 251 patients were randomized to the endovascular arm and 253 into the surgical arm. Although the two procedures were essentially equivalent in their abilities to prevent (or cause, as it turned out) stroke, both treatments did so at an unacceptably high level; the combined endpoint of death or any stroke was achieved in 10% of patients in both groups. In addition, 20% of patients treated with angioplasty or stenting had severe restenosis or occlusion at 1 year. The authors conclude that endovascular techniques are better than surgery because they avoid a neck incision and the risk of general anesthesia. Had the results from the surgical cohort approached those of the NASCET, however, it is likely that the trial would have been suspended in favor of surgery. This trial has several other flaws that make it essentially irrelevant in current clinical practice. It was selective and nonconsecutive, only 26% of the patients in the endovascular group had stents placed (most had angioplasty alone), and no cerebral protection devices were used. As such, the conclusions reached are probably not applicable to current, state-of-the-art carotid angioplasty practice.

A report from Criado and associates[46] describes their experience with CAS in a vascular surgery practice. During a 40-month period from 1997 to 2001, 135 procedures were performed, largely (60%) in asymptomatic patients. The rate of complications was quite acceptable at 2%, and only one patient had a significant restenosis at 16 months' mean follow-up. Perhaps more important, these 132 patients represented 41% of those being treated for carotid disease in their vascular/endovascular practice. Although this seems extraordinarily high, it may simply be a bellwether of things to come in the practice of vascular surgery and underscores the importance of multispecialty involvement in this new technology.

Results from the SAPPHIRE trial of CAS in high-risk patients were published in October 2004. This trial, which included a group randomized to CAS ($n = 167$) or CEA ($n = 167$), is the only industry-sponsored U.S. Food and Drug Administration (FDA)-approved trial to date that did in fact randomize patients. A separate registry was compiled of patients thought to be too high risk for surgery and underwent CAS ($n = 406$) or who were not suitable candidates for CAS and underwent CEA ($n = 7$). The study sought to evaluate the combined endpoint of major adverse events including stroke, death, and MI. Inclusion and exclusion criteria for the study are listed in Tables 140-1 and 140-2. Patients were independently evaluated by a certified neurologist before and after the procedure. This trial was designed to test the hypothesis that CAS *was not inferior* to CEA. Most of the randomized patients were asymptomatic; of the group randomized to CAS, 29.9% were symptomatic, and in the group randomized to CEA, 27.7% were symptomatic. At 30 days, the risk of stroke (CAS, 3.1%, CEA, 3.3%; $P > 0.99$) in the two groups was almost identical. One patient in the CAS group (0.6%) and three patients in the CEA group (2.0%) died within 30 days; this difference did not reach statistical significance ($P = 0.36$). When periprocedural MI was examined, more patients in the

CEA group suffered this complication (6.6%) than in the CAS group (4.4%), a difference that did reach significance ($P < 0.05$). Of note, most of the MIs were non-Q, identified on routine postprocedure laboratory studies, including 3 of 3 in the CAS group and 8 of 10 in the CEA cohort. The combined endpoint death/stroke/MI did not reach statistical significance (CAS, 4.4%; CEA, 9.9%; $P = 0.08$). At 1 year, those endpoints that reached statistical significance included major ipsilateral stroke (CAS, 0%; CEA, 3.5%; $P = 0.02$) and MI (CAS, 2.5%; CEA, 8.1%; $P = 0.03$). In addition, the combined endpoint at 1 year favored the CAS group (12.0% vs. 20.1% $P = 0.05$). The reported results in the stent registry group included 20 strokes (4.9%), 9 deaths (2.2%), and 7 periprocedural MIs (1.7%) at 30 days. These results will likely be used to support FDA approval of the stent and filter protection device used in this important study.[66] The ARCHeR trial[69] represents another industry-sponsored study of a stent and protection device; it differs from SAPPHIRE in that it is a registry of high-risk patients rather than a randomized trial. Preliminary results have been released. The incidence of the composite endpoint (stroke/death/MI) was 7.7%, which included a 5.3% stroke risk; the risk of stroke or death was 6.6% at 30 days. Patients having CAS for restenosis following CEA had an extremely low risk of stroke (0.7%); those patients with end-stage renal disease had an extraordinarily high risk (28%).

Proximal common carotid artery (CCA) lesions are relatively uncommon when compared with bifurcation lesions but may be well treated with angioplasty and stenting. In the author's (T.M.S.) experience, most are treated via CCA cutdown, retrograde angioplasty, and placement of a balloon-expandable stent. Of 14 consecutive procedures performed at the Cleveland Clinic,[68] one was converted to carotid-subclavian transposition following iatrogenic dissection and two other procedures resulted in stroke secondary to ICA thrombosis. In both cases, which were performed in conjunction with re-do bifurcation endarterectomies, the CCA was patent at the time of surgical re-exploration and ICA thrombectomy. Although the carotid stent procedure was not likely implicated, caution is urged when performing these combined procedures.

Stent Implantation, Restenosis, and Duplex Follow-Up

Stent implantation within the ICA may be associated with angiographic and morphologic changes in the ICA. Berkefeld and associates[70] retrospectively evaluated deviations in stented ICAs. They defined maximum extension of ICA tortuosity from the axis of the CCA as *ICA offset*. A straight course of the ICA was associated with low offset values, whereas a tortuous ICA was associated with high offset angles. Stents, by their relatively stiff nature, tended to straighten the angle between the CCA and the ICA; in five cases of self-expanding Wallstent placement, the tortuous segments of the ICA were simply "transferred" to a segment above the stent. This was associated with kinking of the ICA at the end of the stent and often caused constant or increased offset despite the presence of a stent. The ideal stent has enough stiffness and radial force to adequately maintain lumen diameter following angioplasty while not inducing

ICA kinking by transferring tortuosity to a more distal part of the artery. Morphologic changes also occur in the external carotid artery (ECA) following CAS. During angioplasty, plaque in the proximal ICA and distal CCA is often displaced toward the origin of the ECA, causing iatrogenic stenosis. In addition, most stents are placed from the ICA into the CCA, covering the origin of the ECA. In a study of 112 consecutive patients having CAS with Wallstents, Willfort-Ehringer and colleagues[71] found a 17.5% incidence of ECA stenosis immediately following CAS, increasing to 38% at 2 years. Five ECA occlusions (4.7%) were registered at 2 years. Although not clinically significant in this series, the ECA may be an important collateral to the intracranial circulation, especially with ipsilateral ICA restenosis or occlusion.

Many of the initial reports with CAS were described using balloon-expandable stainless-steel stents. At the time, they were the only devices available for peripheral or carotid intervention. Subsequently, Wallstents were used because of their ease of deliverability and self-expanding nature. Although the initial experience using this relatively crude technology was promising, reports began to surface suggesting that balloon-expandable stents were subject to deformation.[28,72-74] Yadav, in his original report of CAS in 107 patients,[28] discovered two patients having restenosis secondary to deformation of balloon-expandable stents. Wholey and coworkers[75] compared balloon-mounted and self-expanding stents in more than 500 patients. Forty-eight percent of 520 stents were bare metal balloon-expandable stents; the remainder were self-expanding. The rates of stroke and death at 30 days and 3 years were almost identical for the two stent types. Vessel patency at 3 years was slightly greater in the balloon-expandable stent group (96.3% vs. 92.0%; $P = .042$). The authors concluded that both stent types were satisfactory but, because of vulnerability to compression, balloon-expandable stents were not favored.

Initial experimental studies with intravascular stents in dog coronary arteries[76] showed that the stent, which is inherently thrombogenic, is initially covered by a thin layer of thrombus. This layer is replaced over time with a proliferation of cellular neointima that reached its maximum thickness at 8 weeks. At 1 week postimplantation, the stents were covered by an immature endothelial layer. The neointimal layer eventually became more sclerotic and less cellular. Healing of carotid stents has been examined by duplex ultrasound. Three phases of stent incorporation have been identified: (1) an early "unstable" period immediately after stent implantation with an echolucent layer of thrombus; (2) a phase characterized by ingrowth of neointima (1 to 12 months); and finally (3) a stable phase after 2 years.[77] Restenosis following stent implantation is typically secondary to intimal hyperplasia and is likely related to the degree of arterial injury.[78] Control of the second phase of stent healing may be important in preventing clinically significant restenosis.

Restenosis has proven to be a substantial clinical problem following endovascular therapy in a number of vascular beds, including the coronary and renal arteries. Prior to the routine use of stents in conjunction with angioplasty (percutaneous transluminal angioplasty [PTA]), Crawley

and associates[79] followed 12 patients with symptomatic carotid stenosis treated with PTA alone. The immediate angioplasty result decreased the mean percent stenosis from 82% to 51%. Six of the 12 showed further improvement in lumen diameter greater than 14% at 1 year, from a mean stenosis immediately post-PTA of 47% to 28% at follow-up angiography. Obviously, there is substantial arterial remodeling that occurs following carotid PTA. Schillinger and colleagues,[80] in a prospective study of 108 patients having CAS (with stenting), found restenosis of more than 50% in six patients (14%). Elevated levels of C-reactive protein (CRP) at 48 hours' postintervention, indicative of a systemic inflammatory response, correlate strongly with restenosis at 6 months ($P = 0.01$). Both residual stenosis of 10% to 30% and restenosis following prior stent implantation were independent predictors of restenosis in this study. Khan and coworkers[81] identified, in a series of 222 patients having successful carotid artery stenting, a number of factors that were predictive of restenosis. By univariate analysis, female gender and age older than 75 years were statistically predictive of restenosis; by multivariate analysis, older age, female gender, implantation of multiple stents, and postprocedural percent stenosis were associated with an increased risk of restenosis. Christiaans and associates[82] also identified loss of proximal stent apposition as a risk factor for restenosis. In addition, in their series, most restenoses were found on routine follow-up and were asymptomatic, a finding confirmed by Lal and colleagues.[83] These studies suggest that a number of patient-related and procedure-related factors are associated with restenosis following CAS. Table 140-8 includes those studies* in which restenosis rates were defined following CAS. Although the reported incidence of restenosis is quite variable, ranging from 1.8% to 75%, most studies report restenosis rates between 5% and 10% at 12 to 24 months.

Owing to the nature of CAS—the plaque is not removed but is simply displaced—the duplex criteria used to follow patients post-CEA may not apply. Robbin and associates,[84] reporting on patients treated at the UAB by Yadav and colleagues, prospectively studied 170 stented carotid arteries. Prospective duplex criteria for stenosis included peak systolic velocity greater than 125 cm/sec, ICA/CCA ratio greater than 3, and intrastent doubling of velocity. Although few stents showed significant restenosis, duplex was able to accurately identify restenosis and correlated with angiographic findings at 1 year.

In a study that included blinded comparison of carotid angiograms at completion of CAS and 24-hour duplex ultrasound studies in 114 patients, Ringer and colleagues[85] found little correlation between the two modalities. Using two standard criteria for high-grade stenosis (A, peak in-stent velocity > 125 cm/sec; B, ICA/CCA > 3) and two customized criteria (C, peak in-stent velocity > 170 cm/sec; D, ICA/CCA > 2), they found 61 patients who met at least one of these criteria for high-grade stenosis immediately following CAS. None of these 61 had more than 50%

*References 27-32, 34, 35, 37-41, 43-47, 50, 51, 55-60, 64, 65, 71, 75, 82, and 88-91.

Table 140-8	Incidence of Restenosis Following Carotid Angioplasty/Stenting		
AUTHOR, YEAR	**NO. OF ARTERIES**	**FOLLOW-UP**	**RESTENOSIS/ OCCLUSION, %**
Diethrich 1996	110	8 mo	3.4
Yadav 1997	81	6 mo	4.9
Teitelbaum 1998	26	6 mo	14.3
Henry 1998	174	13 mo	2.3
Bergeron 1999	99	13 mo	3
Malek 2000	28	14 mo	25
Cremonesi 2000	119	6-36 mo	5.0
CAVATAS 2001	251	12 mo	14
Roubin 2001	520	36 mo	3.1
Ahmadi 2001	320	12 mo	8
D'Audiffret 2001	83	16 mo	7.2
Chakhtoura 2001	50	18 mo	8
Leger 2001	8	20 mo	75
Paniagua 2001	62	17 mo	5.7
Dietz 2001	43	20 mo	2.3
Baudier 2001	54	34 mo	28
Pappada 2001	27	6-37 mo	3.7
Criado 2002	135	16 mo	3
Guimarens 2002	194	12 mo	4.1
Kao 2002	129	16 mo	3.1
Bonaldi 2002	71	1 yr	8
Willfort 2002	279	1 yr	3
Stankovic 2002	100	1 yr	3.4
Shawl 2002	343	26 mo	2.7
Gable 2003	31	28 mo	6
Cernetti 2003	104	24 mo	1.8
Dabrowski 2003	80	12 mo	7.5
Becquemin 2003	114	15 mo	7.5
Wholey 2003	12,392	36 mo	1.7
Khan 2003	179	12 mo	6.7
Christiaans 2003	217	48 mo	21
Wholey 2003	520	36 mo	8
DeBorst 2003	217	8 mo	1.8
Lal 2003	122	60 mo	6.4
Bush 2003	51	12 mo	2
Bowser 2003	52	34 mo	16

residual stenosis by angiography at the completion of their procedure. Most strikingly, in those patients found to have recurrent stenosis in follow-up, in-stent peak systolic velocities and ICA/CCA had increased by more than 80% when compared to their immediate postprocedure study. These authors conclude that strict velocity criteria for restenosis is less reliable than changes in velocity over time. Clearly, based on these data, a baseline duplex following CAS, which can be correlated with the completion angiogram and followed over time, is imperative. This policy will lead to fewer false-positive duplex studies.

Lal and coworkers,[86] from Hobson's group in New Jersey, found that among several duplex criteria, post-CAS peak systolic velocity correlated best with angiography in 90 stented arteries. A mean residual angiographic stenosis of 4.2% ± 9.7% correlated with an ICA peak systolic velocity of 123 ± 30 cm/sec. They concluded that a peak systolic velocity 150 cm/sec or lower correlates with a "normal" lumen (0 to 19% stenosis) following CAS. Contrast-enhanced color-coded duplex ultrasound using an ultrasound contrast

agent, administered intravenously, that produces air-filled microbubbles may be a promising technique on the horizon for imaging post-CAS arteries, producing images comparable to contrast angiography.[87]

From the data presented, several recommendations regarding follow-up in patients having CAS can be made, including the following:

1. Duplex ultrasound follow-up of stented carotid arteries is an important tool to identify patients with restenosis. Early restenosis is typically secondary to myointimal hyperplasia.
2. Because follow-up duplex ultrasound studies may be difficult to interpret based on traditional velocity criteria, a baseline study is imperative; this must be correlated with the degree of residual stenosis at the completion of the CAS procedure. Subsequent studies are performed at 3, 6, and 12 months, and at 6- to 12-month intervals thereafter.

Current evidence suggests that a peak systolic velocity of 150 cm/sec or lower in the ICA correlates with a normal vessel (0 to 19% stenosis). Elevation of the peak systolic velocity and the ICA/CCA (>80% increase) may be an even more important criterion in determining significant restenosis following CAS. Identification of high-grade restenosis typically warrants further evaluation with contrast angiography. Most patients having recurrent stenosis complicating CAS can be safely treated with repeat angioplasty (Fig. 140-3).[37,40,128]

Technical Aspects of CAS

Anatomy

The anatomy of the cerebral circulation, from the aortic arch to the capillary level, is important to the planning of CAS. Several anatomic considerations are particularly germane to the procedure. The configuration of the aortic arch is perhaps the first anatomic challenge to consider. With advancing age, the apex of the arch tends to become displaced further distally. This change in arch configuration tends to make selective catheterization of the brachiocephalic vessels more challenging and influences the choice of catheter to be used (Fig. 140-4A). The operator should become familiar with a variety of selective catheters; we tend to prefer the Simmons II catheter because it provides for "deep" cannulation of the CCA, facilitating ultimate passage of a guide wire for delivery of a sheath. As the level of the origin of the object vessel increases in distance from the dome of the arch, the degree of difficulty in obtaining guide wire and sheath access increases. Examples of arches of varying complexity are shown in Figure 140-4B. Cannulation of a left CCA arising from a common brachiocephalic trunk (bovine arch) may be particularly difficult to access and should be identified on preprocedural contrast- or magnetic resonance (MR) angiography. Especially when starting to perform these interventions, a complete study, including the aortic arch and origins of the brachiocephalic trunks, is essential.

The presence of any tandem lesions along the course of the cerebral circulation is likewise important in treatment

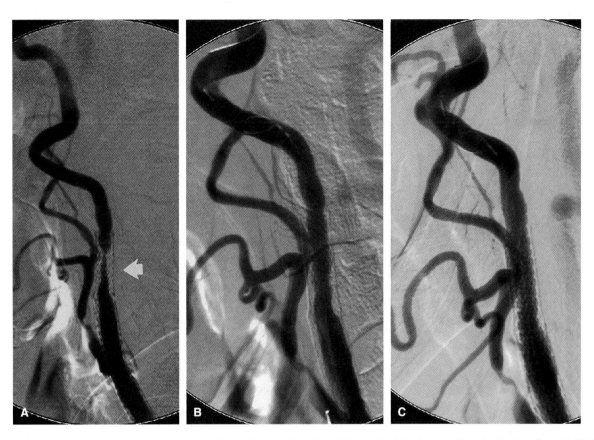

FIGURE 140-3 A, High-grade restenosis of the internal carotid artery (*arrowhead*) 11 months following carotid angioplasty/stenting with Wallstent. **B,** Following angioplasty alone. **C,** Following placement of nitinol stent. Note filter protection device in distal internal carotid.

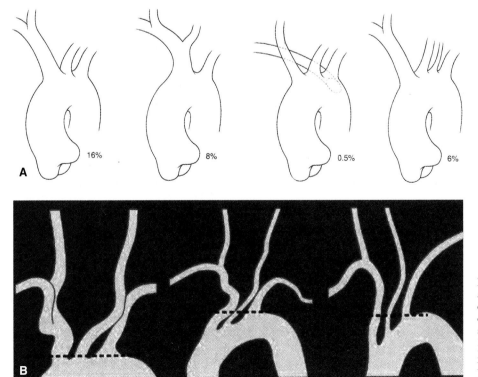

FIGURE 140-4 A, Normal variations of aortic arch configuration. **B,** Increasingly complex aortic arches, making common carotid artery cannulation and sheath passage more difficult. (**A,** From Berguer R, Kieffer E: Surgery of the Arteries to the Head. New York, Springer-Verlag, 1992; **B,** From Criado F: Mastering carotid intervention. Endovasc Today 2:65, 2003.)

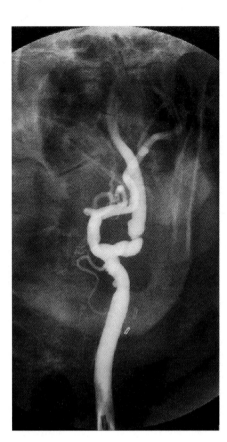

FIGURE 140-5 High-grade internal carotid artery stenosis. Tortuosity of the distal common and proximal internal carotid arteries precluded safe coronary angioplasty/stenting.

planning. Proximal CCA lesions may require intervention prior to ICA revascularization to provide safe access to the ICA. Tortuosity of the ICA is also relevant; although most ICAs are relatively straight, extreme tortuosity may preclude safe passage of a guide wire or protection device and may exclude patients from safe intervention (Fig. 140-5). The anatomy and configuration of the ECA are typically not an important consideration in carotid intervention, even when this vessel is iatrogenically stenosed or covered with a bare stent.

Finally, collateral circulation (or lack thereof) through the circle of Willis is an important consideration that may profoundly influence procedural strategy. The status of the contralateral ICA, the vertebrobasilar system, and the intracranial collaterals may affect the type of embolic protection to be used. Anatomic variations in the circle of Willis are the rule rather than the exception. A "complete" circle is present in less than half of all cases. Common variations include a hypoplastic (10%) or absent A1 segment, and plexiform (10% to 33%) or duplicated (18%) anterior communicating artery. Anomalies of the posterior portion of the circle of Willis occur in half of all cases, including a hypoplastic (33%) or absent posterior communicating artery.[92] Careful attention should be paid, on pre-procedure angiography or intracranial MR angiography, to the anterior and posterior communicating arteries (Fig. 140-6). Patients with limited collateral circulation may

develop reversible neurologic symptoms with inflation of a protection balloon or during angioplasty of the target lesion. They may also be at higher risk for permanent neurologic deficits because their limited collateral blood supply will be less likely to compensate for any iatrogenic arterial occlusions complicating the procedure.

General Considerations

There is currently a paucity of well-controlled data regarding the safety and efficacy of CAS; as such, our practice has been limited to treating those patients deemed high risk for CEA, accounting for 10% to 20% of all patients having intervention (surgical or endovascular) for carotid disease at the Mayo Clinic at Rochester. Symptomatic patients with greater than 50% angiographic stenosis and asymptomatic patients with greater than 80% angiographic stenosis are considered for intervention, either surgical or percutaneous. Table 140-5 suggests what are reasonable criteria for patients at increased risk for CEA and may serve as a general guide for those embarking on a program of carotid stenting. Relative contraindications to CAS are also included in Table 140-6. In our opinion, these procedures should be performed by physicians with a thorough knowledge of the pathophysiology and natural history of carotid disease and by those with current expertise in peripheral, cardiac, or neurointerventional procedures. For those unable to participate in FDA-approved trials, the procedure should be performed as part of a local Institutional Review Board (IRB)-approved protocol with dispassionate oversight, independent preprocedure and postprocedure neurologic examination, and prospective case review. In addition, development of a carotid stenting program may help facilitate cooperation among those specialties with a desire to participate in this high-profile arena. A team of experienced personnel should be assembled (including one or two physicians and a technician) to ensure patient safety, maximize exposure within a small cadre of operators, and avoid duplication of effort. All patients considered for carotid stent-supported angioplasty (CSSA) should have informed consent and counseling regarding the risks/benefits vis-à-vis CEA and best medical therapy and a clear understanding as to the investigational nature of the procedure. In addition, they must agree to regular and careful follow-up examinations.

Preprocedure Preparation

For those with limited experience in carotid intervention, a diagnostic arch, carotid, and cerebral angiogram (done well in advance of the proposed intervention) is suggested; a high-quality MR angiography that includes the aortic arch may substitute. This allows for careful, unhurried evaluation of the aortic arch and brachiocephalic origins, which is imperative in determining the ease or difficulty of sheath/guide access to the CCAs, which is an absolute key to procedural success. If the brachiocephalic trunk (innominate) or left CCAs originate in a location more than two "CCA diameters" (≈2 cm) below the dome of the aortic arch, one should anticipate some difficulty with access. In addition, measurements of lesion length, maximum percent stenosis, and CCA and ICA diameter can be determined by

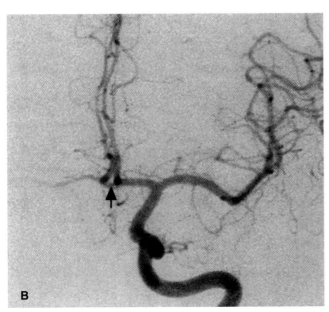

FIGURE 140-6 A, The circle of Willis. A1, horizontal portion, anterior cerebral artery; ACoA, anterior communicating artery; A2, vertical anterior cerebral artery segment; ICA, internal carotid artery; MCA, middle carotid artery; SCA, superior cerebellar artery; OA, ophthalmic artery; ON, ophthalmic nerve; PCoA, posterior communicating artery; P1, posterior cerebral artery; P2, ambient posterior cerebral artery segment; BA, basilar artery; CN, cranial nerve. **B,** Anterior communicating artery (*arrow*) **C,** Posterior communicating artery (*small arrows*), and posterior cerebral artery (*large arrow*) identified from contrast injection in the ICA. (**A-C,** From Osborn A: Diagnostic Cerebral Angiography, 2nd ed. Philadelphia, Lippincott Williams & Wilkins, 1999.)

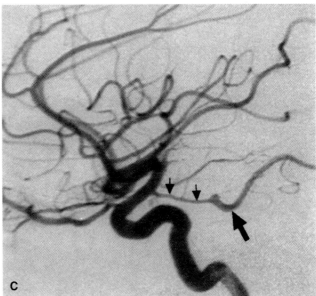

placing a radiopaque marker of known diameter in the field of view. Ball-bearings of progressively increasing diameter (2 through 7 mm) are ideal. These measurements allow for preprocedure selection of balloons and stents and facilitate a smoother, more efficient procedure, which ultimately accomplishes the main goal: patient safety and exemplary results.

All patients should have a careful history and physical examination, paying close attention to comorbid medical conditions and femoral pulses (which impact access). A complete neurologic examination should be performed by a certified neurologist. In addition to the preprocedure arteriogram/MR angiograph, a duplex ultrasound should be performed in an accredited vascular laboratory, ideally by the same laboratory that will be performing the follow-up examinations. We prefer to treat patients with aspirin 325 mg daily for at least 1 week prior to their procedure, in addition to clopidogrel (Plavix) 75 mg daily for at least 3 days prior. All patients receive antibiotics (typically 1 g of cefazolin IV) immediately prior to their procedure.

Procedural Details

Regardless of the exact physical location of the procedure, access to high-quality imaging equipment is mandatory; portable C-arms are less adequate for this purpose. Our procedures are performed in the neuroradiology suite, which has the advantage of biplane imaging. This arrangement avoids duplication of effort and equipment, and the room is staffed by knowledgeable personnel and by a certified registered nurse anesthetist (CRNA), who monitors the patient with electrocardiogram, blood pressure, and pulse oximetry continuously. Patients are placed in a supine position; both groins are prepared routinely. The head is placed in a cradle and gently secured to decrease patient motion during critical portions of the procedure. The procedure is performed with the patient awake, although minimal sedation is acceptable in particularly anxious subjects.

Our technique for CAS has evolved with time. The procedure, in its current iteration, is performed in the following steps, with few exceptions. Although one must, of course, be able to make adjustments to unanticipated situations, we encourage the operators to standardize the procedure as much as possible.

1. Retrograde femoral access with a 5-French sheath
2. Full heparin anticoagulation (typically 100 mg/kg body mass) after arterial access is gained and prior to manipulation of catheters in the aortic arch and brachiocephalic vessels
3. Following selective catheterization of the ipsilateral mid-distal CCA (typically with a Simmons II catheter), a selective arteriogram of the carotid bifurcation is performed, paying careful attention to choose a view that provides minimal overlap of the ICA and ECAs and provides maximum visualization of the target lesion. A complete cerebral arteriogram, if not performed previously, is performed as a baseline and to identify intracranial pathology such as aneurysms and arteriovenous communications.
4. We have used two techniques for advancing a sheath into the CCA: (a) The preferred technique is to place an exchange-length guide wire into the terminal branches of the ECA; our personal favorite is a stiff, angled glide wire (realizing that sheath exchange over this wire, given its lubricious nature, can be tricky). The diagnostic catheter and 5-French sheath are removed (while maintaining constant visualization of the guide wire in the ECA during this process), and a long (70 to 90 cm, depending on patient body habitus) 6-French sheath is advanced, with its dilator, into the CCA. If larger (>8 mm diameter) stents are to be used, a 7-French sheath may be required to allow for contrast injection around the stent delivery system. Care must be taken to identify the tip of the dilator, which is not radiopaque, because it may extend a significant distance from the end of the sheath, depending on the brand of sheath used. Obviously, inadvertently advancing the dilator into the carotid bulb may have disastrous consequences. In patients with short CCAs or low bifurcations, the sheath can be advanced over the dilator once the sheath edge (radiopaque marker) is past the origin of the CCA. (b) Alternatively, the long sheath can be advanced into the transverse arch over a guide wire. The dilator is removed, and an appropriate selective diagnostic catheter is advanced into the CCA. This catheter must be substantially longer than the sheath, typically 100 cm or longer. A stiff guide wire is then advanced into the ECA. Using the wire *and* catheter for support (by pinning both at the groin), the sheath (without dilator) is advanced into the CCA. This technique may be advantageous in "hostile" arches, in that the catheter and wire provide more support than a wire alone but risks "snowplowing" the edge of the sheath at the junction of the aortic arch and the innominate or left CCA (without the protection of the sheath dilator), causing dissection or distal embolization. One should not underestimate the importance of gaining and maintaining sheath access to the distal CCA: once the 0.035-inch guide wire is removed (and ultimately exchanged for a 0.014-inch wire), support for angioplasty and stent placement is provided solely by the sheath. If the sheath backs up into the aortic arch during the interventional procedure, it is virtually impossible to advance it into the CCA over a 0.014-inch guide wire or protection device. Patient selection and recognition of which arches to avoid are paramount to success. In particularly difficult arches, deep inspiration or expiration may facilitate sheath advancement by subtly changing the configuration of the brachiocephalic origins once guide wire access has been obtained. Alternatively, in patients in whom a sheath *cannot* be advanced into the CCA, a preshaped guiding sheath or catheter can be seated in the proximal CCA; although potentially facilitating an otherwise impossible intervention, guiding catheters provide a less stable position and should be used only if no other reasonable alternative exists.
5. For patients with an occluded ECA, sheath access to the CCA may be difficult. We have used two techniques to overcome this challenge: (a) a stiff 0.035-inch wire with a preshaped "J" can be placed into the distal CCA, taking care to avoid the bulb and bifurcation. The J-configuration prevents guide wire traversal of the lesion. A stiff wire with a shapeable tip can be used to the same end. (b) Alternatively, a wire with variable diameter (0.018-inch tip, enlarging to 0.035-inch more proximally) can to used to cross the ICA lesion, giving additional guide wire support to facilitate sheath advancement. Although a reasonable option, this technique ultimately necessitates crossing the target lesion twice.
6. Once the sheath is in place, the guide wire and dilator are removed. We prefer to attach the sheath sidearm to a slow, continuous infusion of heparin-saline solution to avoid stagnation of blood in the sheath. A selective angiogram of the carotid bifurcation is then performed through the sheath, again demonstrating the area of maximal stenosis, the extent of the lesion, and normal ICA and CCA above and below the lesion. Roadmapping, if available, is helpful in crossing the lesion with an embolic protection device or guide wire. Most procedures are now performed with the aid of an embolic protection device.
7. It is wise to have determined an activated clotting time (ACT) prior to crossing the lesion and performing CAS.

For patients in whom balloon occlusion of the ICA is being used for embolic protection, an ACT maintained at > 300 seconds is desired. If a filter-type device or standard guide wire is employed, an ACT > 250 seconds is likely sufficient. The interventional team should discuss, in detail, the steps that will subsequently be performed, so that all members are "on the same page." Balloons should be flushed and prepared (with special care to remove all air from the system in the unlikely event of balloon rupture), the stent opened and on the table, and the crossing guide wire/embolic protection device prepped. For de-novo lesions, we typically administer atropine (0.5 to 1 mg intravenously) as prophylaxis against bradycardia during balloon inflation in the carotid bulb; for restenoses following CEA, this may not be necessary. The monitoring nurse/CRNA should be alerted that balloon inflation may cause significant hemodynamic instability (bradycardia, hypotension).

8. The guide wire/embolic protection device (0.014-inch) is advanced across the lesion, with the aid of roadmapping. Care should be taken when inserting the device through the sheath valve because the tip can be damaged at this juncture. If a protection device is used, it should be deployed into the distal extracranial ICA, just prior to the horizontal petrous segment. For balloon occlusion devices, *absence* of flow in the ICA must be demonstrated; for filter devices, apposition of the device to the ICA must be documented, along with flow in the ICA through the device (and should be documented after each step during the intervention, to detect a filter occluded with debris) (Figs. 140-7 and 140-8).

9. The lesion is predilated with a 5.0-mm angioplasty balloon, typically with a monorail or "rapid-exchange" platform. The balloon can be advanced into the distal CCA prior to crossing the lesion with the guide wire/protection device to save time. Typically, relatively low inflation pressures (4 to 6 mm Hg) are required to achieve balloon profile. After the predilation balloon is removed, another bifurcation angiogram is performed through the sheath (unless distal balloon occlusion is used, in which case the ICA will not be visualized; in these circumstances, the distal stent must be placed based on predetermined bony landmarks and the location of the CCA bifurcation).

10. The stent is then deployed after confirmation of accurate position. Our current preference is to use nitinol stents, most commonly extending an 8-10 mm (diameter) × 30 mm (length) stent from the ICA into the CCA, covering the ECA origin. Nitinol stents may have a tendency to "jump" distally when deployed rapidly (despite manufacturers' claims to the contrary), which may cause one to miss the target lesion. As such, we typically expose/deploy two or three stent rings and wait for 5 to 7 seconds, allowing the distal stent to become fully expanded, well opposed and attached to the ICA above the lesion. Subsequently, the remainder of the stent can be deployed more rapidly with little worry that it will migrate. The diameter of the stent must be sized to the largest portion of the vessel, typically the distal CCA (and not the ICA); it is important to avoid unopposed stent in the CCA, which may

become a nidus for thrombus formation. Unconstrained stent diameter should be at least 10% (≈1 to 2 mm) larger than the maximum CCA diameter. On occasion, the lesion is limited to the ICA well above the carotid bifurcation, allowing for a shorter stent isolated to the ICA.

11. If necessary, the lesion is postdilated with a 5-mm balloon; larger balloons are rarely necessary. Our tendency has been to predilate with a larger balloon (5-mm diameter), avoiding postdilation if possible. A residual stenosis of 10% or so is completely acceptable; the goal is protection from embolic stroke, not necessarily a perfect angiographic result.

12. A completion angiogram of the carotid bulb/bifurcation and distal extracranial ICA is performed *prior to* removing the guide wire/device wire to ensure that a dissection or occlusion has not occurred. Severe vasospasm can sometimes be encountered (and can mimic dissection). Watchful waiting and, on occasion, administration of vasodilators through the sheath (nitroglycerin in 100-µg aliquots) usually resolve this problem. On occasion, the wire must be removed before spasm will resolve completely, but this should be undertaken only after dissection is excluded. After the wire is removed, a completion angiogram of the carotid and intracranial circulation is performed in two views.

13. We typically do not reverse the heparin anticoagulation; we obtain access-site hemostasis with a percutaneous closure device.

Following the procedure, patients are monitored in the recovery area for approximately 30 minutes and then transferred to a monitored floor. Admission to an intensive care unit is typically not necessary. Patients are allowed to ambulate in 2 to 3 hours if a closure device is used and allowed to resume a regular diet. An occasional patient suffers prolonged hypotension from carotid sinus stimulation; this can be managed with judicious fluid administration, pharmacologic treatment of bradycardia, and occasionally intravenous pressors such as dopamine. A rare patient experiences prolonged hypotension that must be treated with oral agents; phenylephrine and midodrine are both acceptable for this purpose.

A duplex ultrasound is obtained prior to hospital discharge as a baseline study. Subsequent ultrasound examinations are performed at 6 weeks, 6 months, 1 year, and yearly thereafter. Neurologic evaluation is performed at approximately 24 hours postprocedure, and then following the schedule of duplex studies. Patients are treated with aspirin for life and clopidogrel for 4 to 6 weeks.

Regardless of the exact technique used for CSSA, like surgical CEA, proper patient selection, procedural standardization, and meticulous attention to detail are mandatory for success.

Cerebral Protection during CAS

Stroke remains the most devastating complication of procedures, both surgical and interventional, directed at the extracranial carotid artery. Although a number of etiologies for stroke have been described, most are due to cerebral embolization of atheromatous debris or thrombus. Riles and

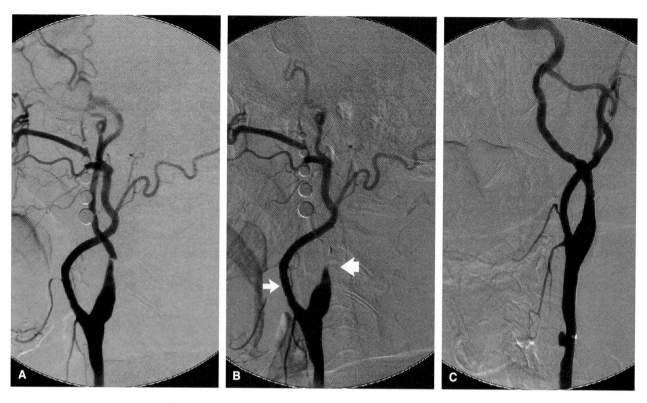

FIGURE 140-7 A, High-grade symptomatic recurrent stenosis, left internal carotid artery (ICA). **B,** Occlusion of the ICA (*large arrow*) with PercuSurge device. Flow remains through the external carotid artery. Note ball bearings to assist in device sizing (*small arrow*). **C,** Completion angiogram following nitinol stent placement and aspiration of static column of blood in ICA.

associates[93] examined the results of 3062 CEAs performed over a 26-year period from 1965 to 1991 at New York University Medical Center. Sixty-six procedures (2.2%) were associated with stroke. They identified 20 different mechanisms for stroke, including ischemia during carotid artery clamping ($n = 10$), thrombosis and embolism ($n = 25$), and intracranial hemorrhage ($n = 12$). During the study period, although the overall risk of stroke decreased from 2.7% (1965-1979) to 1.5% (1986-1991), postoperative thrombosis and embolism remained the most common cause. These thromboembolic strokes were thought to be largely preventable with meticulous technique and minimal manipulation of the target lesion. Although CEA can be performed without mobilization and dissection of the carotid bulb, the same cannot be said for CAS, where the lesion must be crossed with a guide wire, balloon, and stent for treatment to occur. Hence the development of devices to prevent atheromatous embolization during critical portions of the procedure. Most would predict that unprotected angioplasty and stenting of high-grade, ulcerated carotid lesions would produce stroke rates of at least 25%. Nevertheless, even with relatively crude equipment and a lack of cerebral protection, early series of CAS produced stroke rates far below this level. Jordan and colleagues[94] evaluated patients having CEA and CAS (prior to the availability of cerebral embolic protection) with transcranial Doppler (TCD). During CEA procedures ($n = 76$), there was a mean of 8.8 emboli per stenosis (range 0 to 102), whereas in the CAS group ($n = 40$), there were, on average, 74 emboli per stenosis ($P = 0.0001$). The mean number of emboli in patients having neurologic events was 85.1; in those without events, the average number of emboli detected by TCD was 59.0 (Fig. 140-9).

Even when cerebral emboli do not produce major stroke, they may in fact cause substantial cognitive impairment. Gaunt and coworkers,[95] in a prospective study of 100 patients monitored with TCD during CEA, found that microemboli were detected during 92% of procedures. Although most emboli were characteristic of air (and not associated with adverse clinical events), more than 10 particulate emboli correlated with significant deterioration in postoperative cognitive function. Fearn and associates[96] studied 70 patients undergoing cardiac surgery with cardiopulmonary bypass, measuring cognitive function at 1 week, 2 months, and 6 months after surgery. Elderly patients having urologic surgery served as controls. More than 200 emboli were detected by TCD in 40 patients, principally during aortic clamping and release, when bypass was initiated, and during defibrillation. Emboli were associated with memory loss ($P < .02$). In addition, cognitive function deteriorated more in the test patients than the urologic controls but recovered by 2 months. Rapp and colleagues,[97] in a rat model, studied the effect of atheroemboli of varying sizes on neuronal cell death. Those animals having been subjected to particles less than 200 μm had no evidence of brain injury at 1 and 3 days, whereas those exposed to particles measuring between 200 and 500 μm showed a scattered pattern of neuronal cell death at necropsy. At 7

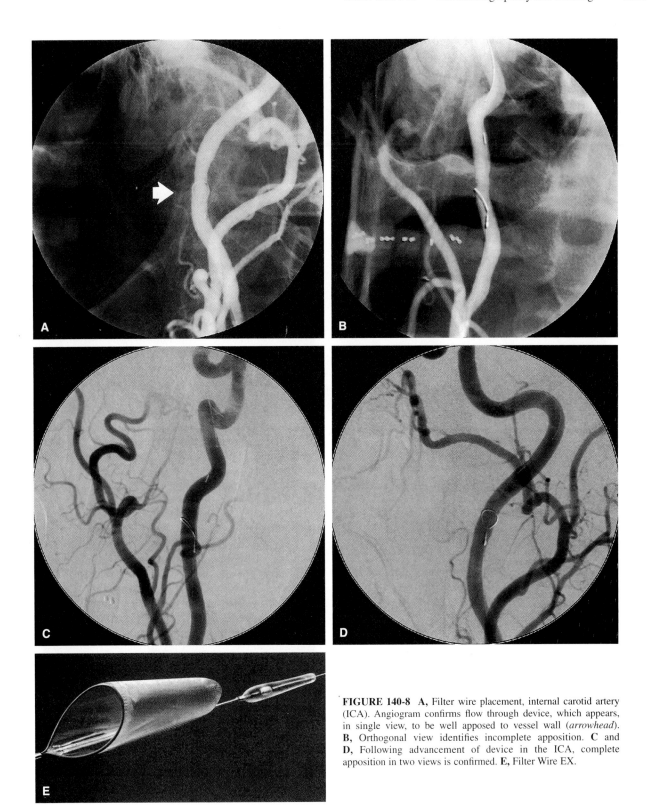

FIGURE 140-8 A, Filter wire placement, internal carotid artery (ICA). Angiogram confirms flow through device, which appears, in single view, to be well apposed to vessel wall (*arrowhead*). **B,** Orthogonal view identifies incomplete apposition. **C** and **D,** Following advancement of device in the ICA, complete apposition in two views is confirmed. **E,** Filter Wire EX.

days postembolization, however, both groups showed evidence of cell death. These findings suggest that although the brain may have a substantial tolerance for small emboli in the acute setting, even particles smaller than 200 μm have deleterious effects at later time points. If extrapolated to humans, the implications for embolic protection during

CAS seem obvious. To this end, Jaeger and coworkers[98] evaluated 67 patients undergoing CAS with diffusion-weighted magnetic resonance (MR) imaging before and after their procedure. Although the neurologic status of only one patient deteriorated following the procedure, MR imaging showed new ipsilateral ischemic lesions in 20,

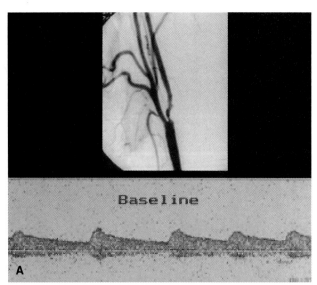

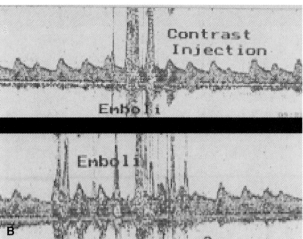

FIGURE 140-9 **A,** Baseline carotid arteriogram and transcranial Doppler (TCD) in symptomatic patient with cervical radiation and previous radical neck dissection, treated prior to advent of cerebral protection. **B,** TCD identifies high-intensity transient signals through middle cerebral artery with contrast injection and balloon dilatation.

representing 29% of the study population; new *contralateral* lesions occurred in 9%. These data suggest that microembolization is frequent following unprotected CAS and that the incidence of clinically silent cerebral ischemia is substantial.

A number of investigators have studied the embolic potential of carotid plaques in ex-vivo models. Ohki and associates,[99] in a model of CAS using human atherosclerotic plaque in a flow chamber, found that substantial numbers of particles were released from these lesions during angioplasty; most were captured by an experimental filter device. Of note, the filter device itself produced very few particles, due to its low crossing profile. Bicknell and colleagues[100] studied the embolic potential of human carotid plaques during experimental angioplasty. An average of 133 emboli per angioplasty were measured; lesion severity correlated with increased maximum size of embolic particles ($P = .012$). Patients having been placed on statin

therapy more than 4 weeks preoperatively had significantly fewer emboli of smaller size ($P = .022$). In the clinical arena, Tubler and colleagues,[101] using a distal balloon-occlusion system during CAS, found that the median number of particles, their maximum diameter, and their maximum area were significantly higher in patients who had periprocedural neurologic complications. Three phases of the procedure are associated with an increased risk of embolization: predilation, stent deployment, and postdilation.[102]

Devices for Cerebral Embolic Protection

The use of embolic protection in large numbers of patients has been described in the coronary vascular bed, where interventional procedures on diseased aorto-coronary saphenous vein grafts are associated with a 20% risk of periprocedural complications, largely related to distal embolization of atheromatous debris. The Saphenous Vein Graft Angioplasty Free of Emboli Randomized (SAFER) trial[103] reported on the first multicenter, randomized study evaluating the use of distal embolic protection during saphenous vein graft interventions. Eight hundred one patients were randomized to angioplasty and stenting with or without distal balloon protection. The composite primary endpoint (death, MI, emergency coronary bypass, target lesion revascularization) was observed in 16.5% of the control patients compared to 9.6% of test subjects ($P = .004$), largely driven by decreases in MI and decrease in distal embolization. These dramatic results suggest that lesions of high embolic potential (e.g., carotid bifurcation) may benefit from some type of embolic protection. Coggia and associates,[104] in an ex-vivo model of angioplasty, confirmed the findings of other investigators that emboli occur at several stages of carotid intervention and stressed that techniques of cerebral protection should be effective from the earliest parts of the procedure.

Three types of embolic protection are currently available for use in the carotid artery, either as part of FDA-approved clinical trials, or "off-label" use of devices approved for noncarotid use. These include distal balloon occlusion, distal filter protection, and reversal of ICA flow. Theron and colleagues[105] were the first to report on the use of an angioplasty technique involving temporary occlusion of the internal carotid artery during manipulation of ulcerated plaques. They subsequently reported on a triple-coaxial catheter system allowing angioplasty with cerebral protection in 13 patients.[106] Cholesterol crystals, ranging in size from 600 to 1200 μm, were aspirated at the time of intervention. The PercuSurge Guardwire, which is approved for aortocoronary saphenous vein graft intervention, has been used in the Medtronic AVE Self-Expanding Carotid Stent System with Distal Protection in the Treatment of Carotid Stenosis (MAVERIC) trial of carotid intervention, and has been used extensively during off-label carotid intervention outside of FDA-approved clinical trials. Advantages of this device include its low profile and ease of crossing the target lesion, its procedural simplicity, and its ability to aspirate large particulate debris following intervention. Disadvantages include potential incomplete occlusion of the internal carotid artery in patients with particularly large arteries (the device can be inflated from 3- to 6-mm diameter) and inability to aspirate exceptionally large particles into the suction catheter following intervention.[101] In addition, as flow is diverted into the ECA, emboli may travel by this route and into the ipsilateral middle cerebral artery via periorbital and ophthalmic artery collaterals.[107] Finally, a small percentage of patients with an incomplete circle of Willis and an "isolated" cerebral hemisphere may be intolerant of even temporary internal carotid occlusion. Whitlow and coworkers[108] evaluated the PercuSurge device in 75 CAS procedures. Four patients (5%) developed transient neurologic symptoms during balloon occlusion that resolved with deflation and restoration of internal carotid flow. Embolic material was aspirated from the internal carotid in all patients; no patients suffered major or minor stroke at 30 days.

A great deal of interest in filter protection devices has been generated in an attempt to trap large particulate debris while maintaining flow in the ICA; this not only provides continued cerebral perfusion during intervention but also allows angiography of the target vessel during various phases of the procedure. The pore size of all currently available filters is greater than 100 μm; as such they allow passage of smaller particles that may not cause clinically significant neurologic events, but which may cause silent neuronal injury. These filters may also be difficult to pass across particularly severe stenoses due to their larger profile when compared to balloon occlusion devices. Filters that are not completely apposed to the vessel wall may allow emboli to pass around the device and into the distal cerebral circulation. Reimers and associates[42] reported on CAS in 86 lesions using three different filter devices. In three cases, the filter could not be advanced across the lesion. More than half of the successfully deployed filters contained macroscopic embolic material, and only one patient (1.2%) suffered a neurologic complication (minor stroke).

Ohki and colleagues[109] reported on the use of a device that induces reversal of flow in the ICA by occluding the common and ECAs via balloon occlusion of the ECA and creation of a temporary arteriovenous shunt between the ICA and the femoral vein. This device, although potentially more cumbersome than other protection devices, may in fact produce "complete" protection by preventing *any* emboli from traveling to the intracranial circulation (Fig. 140-10).

New and coworkers[110] reported their experience with 1202 CAS procedures from 1994 to 2002. During the study period, 33% of patients had a cerebral protection device used during their procedures. The overall stroke rate was 4.4%; the risk of stroke reached its maximum during the period from September 1996 to September 1997 (9.1%) and reached its nadir during the final year of the study (0.6%). The authors conclude that improvements in technique, equipment, and pharmacotherapy and the use of neuroprotection have contributed significantly to improvements in results. In a series by Parodi and associates,[111] 46 patients were treated with CAS; in 25, cerebral protection was used.

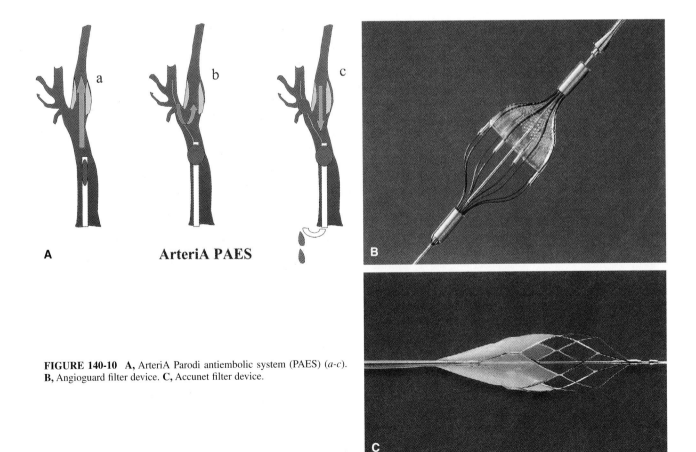

FIGURE 140-10 A, ArteriA Parodi antiembolic system (PAES) (*a-c*). **B,** Angioguard filter device. **C,** Accunet filter device.

Two neurologic events (9.5%) occurred in the unprotected cohort. There were no events in the protected group. Although the small numbers of patients prevented meaningful statistical analysis, they concluded that cerebral protection is technically feasible and effective in preventing neurologic complications during CAS. A review of the worldwide CAS experience (see Table 140-7) shows that the overall risk of stroke, in more than 17,000 procedures, is 4.7%. When one examines these results more closely, the risk of stroke for those series reporting procedures performed without cerebral protection (1270 procedures, stroke risk 5.3%) were not statistically different than those using cerebral protection in all cases (1812 procedures, stroke risk 3.4%) or those using occasional protection (14,403 procedures, stroke risk 4.8%). Protection devices are not without potential problems and complications, including abrupt vessel closure secondary to iatrogenic dissection, inability to retrieve the device, transient loss of consciousness, and tremors and fasciculations secondary to device-induced cerebral ischemia.[112] Nevertheless, it seems reasonable, based on the available evidence, to consider embolic cerebral protection devices in most cases of CAS.

Pharmacologic Adjuncts for the Prevention of Intraprocedural Stroke

The pharmacologic prevention of thromboembolic events during CAS is modeled after the literature regarding prevention of these events during percutaneous coronary interventions. Intravenous heparin should be administered to maintain an ACT of at least 250 to 300 seconds. Antiplatelet therapy consists of aspirin and clopidogrel orally prior to the procedure and for 1 month following.[113-117] Antiplatelet therapy with glycoprotein IIB-IIIA antagonists has been shown to reduce thromboembolic complications during percutaneous coronary procedures.[118] Although there has been some interest in applying these agents to patients undergoing CAS,[119,120] early data suggest that they offer no significant benefit[121] and may increase the risk of intracerebral hemorrhage.[122]

Complications Following CAS

Embolic stroke is the most common serious complication reported for CAS; its incidence may be affected by the use of cerebral protection devices. Advanced age and the presence of long or multiple lesions have been implicated as independent predictors of stroke.[123] As with most procedures, there is a significant learning curve that must be overcome.[34] Other complications have also been cited, including prolonged bradycardia and hypotension,[124] deformation of balloon-expandable stents,[28,72-74] stent thrombosis,[125] and Horner's syndrome.[126] Cerebral hyperperfusion with associated seizures and intracranial hemorrhage have also been reported.[127]

Acute Stroke Intervention Following CAS

Despite the use of cerebral protection devices, acute stroke is the most common complication described following CAS. Ischemic stroke complicating CAS is generally due to thromboembolism. The embolus may be composed of atheroma, chronic thrombus that was adherent to the atherosclerotic plaque, acute thrombus that formed during the intervention, or a combination of all three. The composition of this material has implications for the treatment of acute stroke. Although thrombus may be amenable to lysis, treatment of an atheromatous embolus with thrombolytic agents is typically not efficacious and exposes the patient to the risk of hemorrhage. Unfortunately, it is generally not possible to know the composition of such emboli at the time that a therapeutic decision must be made. The available literature regarding interventional treatment of acute ischemic stroke provides us with only a limited amount of information to guide the treatment of patients having this complication following CAS.

The only acute intervention approved by the FDA for acute ischemic stroke is the intravenous infusion of recombinant tissue plasminogen activator (rt-PA).[129] Patients who are undergoing CAS are not good candidates for intravenous rt-PA infusion for several reasons. First, they are generally anticoagulated with heparin, which is a relative contraindication for the use of rt-PA. Second, they have generally been treated with antiplatelet agents (aspirin and clopidogrel) that may further increase their risk of intracranial hemorrhage. Finally, the embolus, by its potentially multifactorial nature, may not be amenable to venous infusion of this agent.

Since intravenous lytic therapy is generally contraindicated in patients with acute stroke complicating CAS, consideration is often given to intra-arterial thrombolysis. Because no drugs or devices are approved by the FDA for intra-arterial treatment, such therapy is not standard. Intra-arterial therapy has historically been most commonly usd to treat patients who have an occlusion of a major anterior circulation artery (ICA or middle cerebral artery) or the basilar artery. The amount of time a patient can tolerate an arterial occlusion without permanent neurologic deficit depends on the presence of residual circulation to the affected area. Variability in degree of occlusion and collateral circulation probably accounts for much of the variability in outcome in patients treated with lytic techniques. As more time passes following the onset of symptoms, the chance of neurologic improvement decreases and the chance of hemorrhagic complications increases. Intra-arterial therapy for anterior circulation ischemia should begin within 6 hours of symptom onset. The use of intra-arterial stroke interventions necessitates the patient being at an experienced stroke center with immediate access to cerebral angiography and neurointervention (Fig. 140-11).

Several agents have been used for the intra-arterial treatment of acute ischemic stroke. Urokinase[130-132] was the most commonly used drug for this purpose until its removal from the market in 1999. It has recently been reintroduced and might once again become available for the acute treatment of ischemic stroke. The use of urokinase is supported by a small number of case series.

Trials have been performed to evaluate the efficacy of the urokinase precursor prourokinase. Prolyse in Acute Cerebral Thromboembolism (PROACT) I[133] was a phase II prospective, randomized, placebo-controlled study to evaluate the intra-arterial administration of recombinant

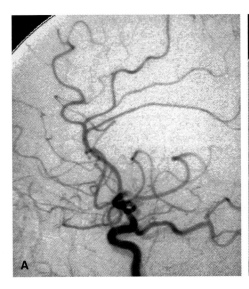
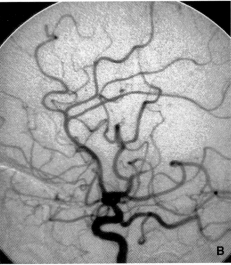

FIGURE 140-11 A, Iatrogenic embolus to a large middle cerebral artery branch as a complication of carotid angioplasty/stenting. **B,** Successful intra-arterial thrombolysis using recombinant tissue plasminogen activator.

prourokinase as a treatment for acute ischemic stroke due to middle cerebral artery occlusion. Recanalization was significantly associated with prourokinase treatment ($P = 0.085$). Intracerebral hemorrhage occurred in 15% of the patients treated with prourokinase and in 7% of control patients (not statistically significant). High-dose adjuvant heparin therapy was associated with a high risk of intracerebral hemorrhage compared to low-dose heparin therapy. PROACT II[134] was a phase III, randomized, placebo-controlled trial to evaluate the efficacy of intra-arterial prourokinase in patients with stroke less than 6 hours' duration secondary to occlusion of the middle cerebral artery. Low-dose heparin was used during the intervention. There was a significant improvement in outcome associated with prourokinase treatment, with 40% of the 121 patients treated with prourokinase and 25% of the 59 control patients having modified Rankin Score = 0 to 2 at 90 days ($P = 0.043$). Recanalization of the middle cerebral artery occurred in 66% of patients treated with prourokinase and in 18% of patients in the control group ($P < 0.001$). Intracranial hemorrhage with neurological deterioration within 24 hours of treatment occurred in 10% of patients treated with prourokinase and in 2% of the control patients. There was no difference in overall mortality between patients treated with urokinase and placebo. Prourokinase is not currently available for clinical use because it was not approved by the FDA.

Because urokinase and prourokinase have been unavailable, and because rt-PA is widely available, most centers in the United States have been using this agent for intra-arterial stroke therapy. The intra-arterial use of rt-PA is largely based on its availability and its acceptance as an intravenous agent for acute ischemic stroke. It is unclear if the PROACT II results can be extrapolated to intra-arterial therapy. The Emergency Management of Stroke (EMS) bridging trial was a phase I trial designed to evaluate the feasibility of combined intravenous and local intra-arterial rt-PA.[135] Angiographic recanalization rates 2 hours after the start of intra-arterial infusion suggest that combined intravenous and intra-arterial infusions may be more effective than intra-arterial therapy alone. The efficacy of such regimens remains to be proven.

Patients who develop thromboemboli during endovascular procedures (excluding cases of CAS) are an interesting subset of patients, because we can be quite certain that the thrombus is acute in nature. In a series of 9 patients having intraprocedural thromboemboli, intra-arterial lysis with rt-PA resulted in successful recanalization in only 4 (44%).[136] This study suggests that perhaps fibrinolytic drugs such as rt-PA are not the optimal approach for platelet-rich, acute intra-arterial thromboemboli. Early experience in similar cases with intravenous abciximab,[137,138] a potent antiplatelet agent, suggests that the recanalization rate is higher with this agent than with rt-PA.

To date, we know of only one report directed specifically at the treatment of acute embolic stroke complicating CAS. Wholey and coworkers[139] reported a series of five patients suffering acute ischemic strokes complicating CAS who were treated with intra-arterial thrombolytic therapy. Angiographic improvement was noted in four, but only two improved clinically.

Because intra-arterial administration of thrombolytic drugs is not always successful in recanalizing an artery, attempts are being made to remove emboli by mechanical means. Angioplasty of clot with balloons[140,141] and retrieval of emboli with snares[142,143] have been successful in recanalizing arteries in small case series. Devices specifically designed to remove thromboemboli from the cerebral circulation are currently being developed, and one such device has already been approved for use in Europe. Mechanical removal of emboli will likely be the only means to restore flow when an embolus is composed of atheroma or chronic thrombus.

■ FUTURE DIRECTIONS

Based on the preliminary results of clinical trials of CAS in high-risk patients, it appears that the results of this procedure may in fact be equivalent to CEA in this subgroup. The addition of cerebral protection, along with improvements in stents and better patient selection will likely add to its safety. The next logical question to be asked is "Can good-risk patients be safely treated with CAS?" The Carotid Revascularization Endarterectomy versus Stent Trial (CREST)[144] will attempt to provide a definitive answer. This important study contrasts the relative efficacy of CEA and CAS in preventing primary outcomes of stroke, MI, or death at 30 days, and ipsilateral stroke at 4 years' follow-up. The primary criteria for eligibility are carotid stenosis of at least 50% and hemispheric TIA or non-disabling stroke. It is anticipated that 2500 patients will be randomized. Secondary outcomes include (1) establishing the differential efficacy in men and women, (2) contrasting morbidity and mortality rates, (3) identifying restenosis rates, (4) establishing health-related quality of life and cost-effectiveness, and (5) identifying subgroups of patients at differential risk for CEA or CAS. Enrollment is currently underway; CAS procedures will be performed with cerebral protection and self-expanding stents. The outcome is not anticipated for a number of years, but randomization is the only way to definitively answer the question at hand.

Next, what about asymptomatic patients? The Society for Vascular Surgery and the Stroke Council of the American Heart Association (AHA) have published practice guidelines for CEA that outline "acceptable" rates of stroke and death (CSM) following CEA.[145] For patients presenting with TIAs or prior stroke, 5% is the upper limit of acceptability; for asymptomatic patients, the bar is raised to 3% CSM. Examining the results of SAPPHIRE more closely, where the risk of stroke or death in symptomatic randomized patients was 2.1 %, the results are favorable. For asymptomatic randomized patients (which represented nearly two thirds of the cohort randomized to CAS), whereas many nonrandomized case series meet the standard set by the AHA, SAPPHIRE does not, with a CSM of 5.8%.[66] Perhaps, then, asymptomatic high-risk patients should be treated medically unless the operator can show results that meet or exceed AHA guidelines.

Regardless of the outcome of CREST, CAS has gained in popularity since its inception. A partial list of ongoing or recently completed industry-sponsored clinical trials of CAS are presented in Table 140-9. Further study regarding cost of devices, relative cost as compared to CEA, reimbursement (which currently does not exist from most payors outside of FDA-approved trials), and long-term

Table 140-9 Carotid Artery Stenting Update

STUDY	SPONSOR	SAMPLE SIZE, *n*	STUDY DESIGN	RESULTS	STATUS
ARCHeR	Guidant	437	High-risk registry	30-day results; stent patients: MACE = 7.8%; Acculink success rate = 97.8%	FDA approval
ARCHeR RX	Guidant	145	High-risk registry	NA	Enrollment completed
BEACH	Boston Scientific	480 (400 evaluable)	High-risk registry	NA	Enrollment completed
CABERNET	EndoTex	380	High-risk registry	NA	Enrolling
CREATE	ev3	400	High-risk registry	NA	Information not provided
CREST	NIH and Guidant	2500	Randomized multicenter trial for symptomatic, CEA-eligible patients	NA	Enrolling
MAVErIC Int'l	Medtronic	51	Outside U.S. high-risk registry	30-day results: MACE = 5.9%	CE Mark approved
MAVErIC II	Medtronic	99 (Phase I) 399 (Phase II)	U.S. IDE high-risk registry	30-day phase I results: MACE = 4%	Enrollment completed; currently in 1-yr follow-up
PASCAL	Medtronic	115	Symptomatic and asymptomatic patients	30-day results: MACE = 8%	Enrollment completed; currently in 1-yr follow-up
SAPPHIRE	Cordis	724*	Randomized (CEA and CAS) multicenter trial of high-risk patients; evaluated by multi-disciplinary team	30-day results: (1) stent patients, MACE = 5.8%; (2) surgical patients, MACE = 12.6%, *P* = .04; AngioGuard XP success rate = 98.6%	Trial completed. Results published (see reference 66)
SECuRITY	Abbott Vascular Devices	320	High-risk registry	NA	Enrollment complete

*Randomized *n* = 310; Stent Registry (Surgical Refusal) = 407; Surgical Registry (Stent Refusal) = 7.
MACE, major adverse cardiac event; NA, not applicable. See text for other terms.

outcomes will be necessary to determine its ultimate usefulness in the treatment of patients with carotid disease. Patient preference will also play a significant role, especially as CAS receives increasing attention in the lay press.[146] In addition, training and credentialing are important issues that must be dealt with on both the national and local levels, especially for physicians and specialties that have not traditionally been involved in the practice of cervicocerebral angiography and carotid intervention.

CAS is an evolving technique that shows significant promise in the treatment of patients with carotid occlusive disease. CEA remains, however, the treatment of choice for most patients with bifurcation disease, both symptomatic and asymptomatic. Certain high-risk subsets, especially those with cardiopulmonary disease and those with surgically unfavorable lesions, may benefit from endovascular therapy at the present time.

Although tremendous enthusiasm has been generated for CAS, especially by nonsurgeons, it remains an investigational procedure and has yet to be proven equivalent or superior to CEA for most patients. As noted in the AHA Science Advisory[147] in 1998, we must remember the first tenet of medicine: *primum non nocere*—first, do no harm. Only through carefully designed clinical trials with dispassionate oversight can we determine the role of CAS in the treatment of patients with carotid disease.

■ REFERENCES

1. U.S. Bureau of the Census: Statistical Abstract of the United States: 1992, 112th ed. Washington, DC, U.S. Printing Office, 1993.
2. Bonita R: Epidemiology of stroke. Lancet 339:342-344, 1992.
3. North American Symptomatic Carotid Endarterectomy Trial Collaborators: Beneficial effect of carotid endarterectomy in symptomatic patients with high-grade carotid stenosis. N Engl J Med 325:445-453, 1991.
4. Executive Committee for the Asymptomatic Carotid Atherosclerosis Study: Endarterectomy for asymptomatic carotid artery stenosis. JAMA 273:1421-1428, 1995.
5. Eastcott HHG, Pickering GW, Robb CG: Reconstruction of the internal carotid artery in a patient with intermittent attacks of hemiplegia. Lancet 2:994-996, 1954.
6. Hsia DC, Krushat WM, Moscoe LM: Epidemiology of carotid endarterectomies among Medicare beneficiaries. J Vasc Surg 16:201-208, 1992.
7. Huber TS, Seeger JM: Dartmouth Atlas of Vascular Health Care review: Impact of hospital volume, surgeon volume, and training on outcome. Vasc Surg 34:751-756, 2001.
8. Menzoian JO: Presidential address: Carotid endarterectomy, under attack again! J Vasc Surg 37:1137-1141, 2003.
9. Chaturvedi S, Aggarwal R, Murugappan A: Results of carotid endarterectomy with prospective neurologist follow-up. Neurology 55:769-772, 2000.
10. Rothwell PM, Slattery J, Warlow CP: A systematic comparison of the risks of stroke and death due to carotid endarterectomy for symptomatic and asymptomatic stenosis. Stroke 27:266-269, 1996.
11. Lepore MR, Sternbergh C, Salartash K, et al: Influence of NASCET/ACAS trial eligibility on outcome after carotid endarterectomy. J Vasc Surg 34:581-586, 2001.
12. Illig KA, Zhang R, Tanski W, et al: Is the rationale for carotid angioplasty and stenting in patients excluded from NASCET/ACAS or eligible for ARCHeR justified? J Vasc Surg 37:575-581, 2003.
13. Mozes G, Sullivan T, Torres-Russotto D, et al: Carotid endarterectomy in SAPPHIRE-eligible high-risk patients: Implications for selecting patients for carotid angioplasty and stenting. J Vasc Surg 39:958-965, 2004.
14. Hertzer NR, O'Hara PJ, Mascha EJ, et al: Early outcome assessment for 2228 consecutive carotid endarterectomy procedures: The Cleveland Clinic experience from 1989 to 1995. J Vasc Surg 26:1-10, 1997.
15. Ouriel K, Hertzer NR, Beven EG, et al: Preprocedural risk stratification: Identifying an appropriate population for carotid stenting. J Vasc Surg 33:728-732, 2001.
16. Rockman CB, Riles TS, Landis R, et al: Redo carotid surgery: An analysis of materials and configurations used in carotid reoperations and their influence on perioperative stroke and subsequent recurrent stenosis. J Vasc Surg 29:72-80, 1999.
17. Kashyap VS, Moore WS, Quinones-Baldrich WJ: Carotid artery repair for radiation-associated atherosclerosis is a safe and durable procedure. J Vasc Surg 29:90-96, 1999.
18. Sundt TM Jr, Houser OW, Sharbrough FW, Messick JM Jr: Carotid endarterectomy: Results, complications, and monitoring techniques. Adv Neurol 16:97-119, 1977.
19. Rothwell PM, Slattery J, Warlow CP: Clinical and angiographic predictors of stroke and death from carotid endarterectomy: Systematic review. BMJ 315:1571-1577, 1997.
20. Gasparis AP, Ricotta L, Cuadra SA, et al: High-risk carotid endarterectomy: Fact or fiction? J Vasc Surg 37:40-46, 2003.
21. Jordan WD, Alcocer F, Wirthlin DJ, et al: High-risk carotid endarterectomy: Challenges for carotid stent protocols. J Vasc Surg 35:16-22, 2002.
22. Reed AB, Gaccione P, Belkin M, et al: Preoperative risk factors for carotid endarterectomy: Defining the patient at high risk. J Vasc Surg 37:1191-1199, 2003.
23. Gruntzig A: Transluminal dilatation of coronary artery stenosis. Lancet 1:263, 1978.
24. Kerber CW, Cromwell LD, Loehden OL: Catheter dilatation of proximal carotid stenosis during distal bifurcation endarterectomy. AJNR Am J Neuroradiol 1:348-349, 1980.
25. Mullan S, Duda EE, Patronas NJ: Some examples of balloon technology in neurosurgery. J Neurosurg 52:321-329, 1980.
26. Goy JJ, Eeckhout E: Intracoronary stenting. Lancet 351:1943-1949, 1998.
27. Diethrich EB, Ndiaye M, Reid DB: Stenting in the carotid artery: Initial experience in 110 patients. J Endovasc Surg 3:42-62, 1996.
28. Yadav JS, Roubin GS, Iyer S, et al: Elective stenting of the extracranial carotid arteries. Circulation 95:376-381, 1997.
29. Henry M, Amor M, Masson I, et al: Angioplasty and stenting of the extracranial carotid arteries. J Endovasc Surg 5:293-304, 1998.
30. Teitelbaum GP, Lefkowitz MA, Giannotta SL: Carotid angioplasty and stenting in high-risk patients. Surg Neurol 50:300-312, 1998.
31. Malek AM, Higashida RT, Phatouros CC, et al: Stent angioplasty for cervical carotid artery stenosis in high-risk symptomatic NASCET-ineligible patients. Stroke 31:3029-3033, 2001.
32. Bergeron P, Becquemin JP, Jausseran JM, et al: Percutaneous stenting of the internal carotid artery: The European CAST I study. Carotid Artery Stent Trial. J Endovasc Surg 6:155-159, 1999.
33. Shawl F, Kadro W, Domanski MJ, et al: Safety and efficacy of elective artery stenting in high-risk patients. J Am Coll Cardiol 35:1721-1728, 2000.
34. Ahmadi R, Willfort A, Lang W, et al: Carotid artery stenting: effect of learning curve and intermediate term morphological outcome. J Endovasc Ther 8:539-546, 2001.
35. Endovascular versus surgical treatment in patients with carotid stenosis in the Carotid and Vertebral Artery Transluminal Angioplasty Study (CAVATAS): A randomised trial. Lancet 357:1729-1737, 2001.
36. Brooks WH, McClure RR, Jones MR: Carotid angioplasty and stenting versus carotid endarterectomy: Randomized trial in a community hospital. J Am Coll Cardiol 38:1589-1595, 2001.
37. d'Audiffret A, Desgranges P, Kobeiter H, Becquemin JP: Technical aspects and current results of carotid stenting. J Vasc Surg 33:1001-1007, 2001.

38. Roubin GS, New G, Iyer SS, et al: Immediate and late clinical outcomes of carotid artery stenting in patients with symptomatic and asymptomatic carotid artery stenosis: A 5-year prospective analysis. Circulation 103:532-537, 2001.

39. Chakhtoura EY, Hobson RW II, Goldstein J, et al: In-stent restenosis after carotid angioplasty-stenting: Incidence and management. J Vasc Surg 33:220-226, 2001.

40. Leger AR, Neale M, Harris JP: Poor durability of carotid angioplasty and stenting for treatment of recurrent artery stenosis after carotid endarterectomy: An institutional experience. J Vasc Surg 33:1008-1014, 2001.

41. Paniagua D, Howell M, Strickman N, et al: Outcomes following extracranial carotid artery stenting in high-risk patients. J Invas Cardiol 13:375-381, 2001.

42. Reimers B, Corvaja N, Moshiri S, et al: Cerebral protection with filter devices during carotid artery stenting. Circulation 104:12-15, 2001.

43. Dietz A, Berkefeld J, Theron JG, et al: Endovascular treatment of symptomatic carotid stenosis using stent placement: Long-term follow-up of patients with a balanced surgical risk/benefit ratio. Stroke 32:1855-1859, 2001.

44. Baudier JF, Licht PB, Roder O, Andersen PE: Endovascular treatment of severe symptomatic stenosis of the internal carotid artery: Early and late outcome. Eur J Vasc Endovasc Surg 22:205-210, 2001.

45. Pappada G, Marina R, Fiori L, et al: Stenting of atherosclerotic stenoses of the extracranial carotid artery. Acta Neurochir (Wien) 143:1005-1011, 2001.

46. Criado FJ, Lingelbach JM, Ledesma DF, Lucas PR: Carotid artery stenting in a vascular surgery practice. J Vasc Surg 35:430-434, 2002.

47. Guimaraens L, Sola MT, Matali A, et al: Carotid angioplasty with cerebral protection and stenting: Report of 164 patients (194 carotid percutaneous transluminal angioplasties). Cerebrovasc Dis 13:114-119, 2002.

48. Al-Mubarak N, Colombo A, Gaines PA, et al: Multicenter evaluation of carotid artery stenting with a filter protection system. J Am Coll Cardiol 39:841-846, 2002.

49. Bonaldi G: Angioplasty and stenting of the cervical carotid bifurcation: Results of a 4-year series. Neuroradiology 44:164-174, 2002.

50. Stankovic G, Liistro F, Moshiri S, et al: Carotid artery stenting in the first 100 consecutive patients: Results and follow-up. Heart 88:381-386, 2002.

51. Kao HL, Lin LY, Lu CJ, et al: Long-term results of elective stenting for severe carotid artery stenosis in Taiwan. Cardiology 97:89-93, 2002.

52. Whitlow PL, Lylyk P, Londero H, et al: Carotid artery stenting protected with an emboli containment system. Stroke 33:1308-1314, 2002.

53. Qureshi AI, Suri MF, New G, et al: Multicenter study of the feasibility and safety of using the Memotherm carotid arterial stent for extracranial carotid artery stenosis. J Neurosurg 96:830-836, 2002.

54. Macdonald S, Venables GS, Cleveland TJ, Gaines PA: Protected carotid stenting: Safety and efficacy of the MedNova NeuroShield filter. J Vasc Surg 35:966-972, 2002.

55. Gable DR, Bergamini T, Garrett WV, et al: Intermediate follow-up of carotid artery stent placement. Am J Surg 185:183-187, 2003.

56. Wholey MH, Al-Mubarek N, Wholey MH: Updated review of the global carotid artery stent registry. Catheter Cardiovasc Interv 60:259-266, 2003.

57. Lal BK, Hobson RW II, Goldstein J, et al: In-stent recurrent stenosis after carotid artery stenting: Life-table analysis and clinical relevance. J Vasc Surg 38:1162-1169, 2003.

58. Cernetti C, Reimers B, Picciolo A, et al: Carotid artery stenting with cerebral protection in 100 consecutive patients: Immediate and two-year follow-up results. Ital Heart J 4:695-700, 2003.

59. Becquemin JP, Ben El Kadi H, Desgranges P, Kobeiter H: Carotid stenting versus carotid surgery: A prospective cohort study. J Endovasc Ther 10:687-694, 2003.

60. Dabrowski M, Bielecki D, Golebiewski P, Kwiecinski H: Percutaneous internal carotid artery angioplasty with stenting: Early and long-term results. Kardiol Pol 58:469-480, 2003.

61. Kastrup A, Skalej M, Krapf H, et al: Early outcome of carotid angioplasty and stenting versus carotid endarterectomy in a single academic center. Cerebrovasc Dis 15:84-89, 2003.

62. Cremonesi A, Manetti R, Setacci F, et al: Protected carotid stenting: Clinical advantages and complications of embolic protection devices in 442 consecutive patients. Stroke 34:1936-1933, 2003.

63. Terada T, Tsuura M, Matsumoto H, et al: Results of endovascular treatment of internal carotid artery stenoses with a newly developed balloon protection catheter. Neurosurgery 53:617-623, 2003.

64. Bowser AN, Bandyk DF, Evans A: Outcome of carotid stent-assisted angioplasty versus open surgical repair of recurrent carotid stenosis. J Vasc Surg 38:432-438, 2003.

65. Bush RL, Lin PH, Bianco CC, et al: Carotid artery stenting in a community setting: Experience outside of a clinical trial. Ann Vasc Surg 17:629-634, 2003.

66. Yadav J, Wholey M, Kuntz R, et al; for the SAPPHIRE Investigators: Protected carotid-artery stenting versus endarterectomy in high-risk patients. N Engl J Med 351:1493-1501, 2004.

67. Jordan WD, Schroeder BS, Fisher WK, McDowell HA: A comparison of angioplasty with stenting with endarterectomy for the treatment of carotid artery stenosis. Ann Vasc Surg 11:2-8, 1997.

68. Sullivan TM, Gray BH, Bacharach JM, et al: Angioplasty and primary stenting of the subclavian, innominate, and common carotid arteries in 83 patients. J Vasc Surg 28:1059-1065, 1998.

69. Wholey M, for the ARCHeR Investigators: Data presented at the American College of Cardiology, 2003.

70. Berkefeld J, Martin JB, Théron JG, et al: Stent impact on the geometry of the carotid bifurcation and the course of the internal carotid artery. Neuroradiology 44:67-76, 2002.

71. Willfort-Ehringer A, Ahmadi R, Gruber D, et al: Effect of carotid artery stenting on the external carotid artery. J Vasc Surg 38:1039-1044, 2003.

72. Roubin GS, Yadav S, Iyer SS, Vitek J: Carotid stent-supported angioplasty: A neurovascular intervention to prevent stroke. Am J Cardiol 78:8-12, 1996.

73. Rosenfield J, Schainfeld R, Pieczak A, et al: Restenosis of endovascular stents from stent compression. J Am Coll Cardiol 29:328-338, 1997.

74. Johnson SP, Fujitani RM, Lyendecker JR, Joseph FB: Stent deformation and intimal hyperplasia complicating treatment of a post-carotid endarterectomy intimal flap with a Palmaz stent. J Vasc Surg 25:764-768, 1997.

75. Wholey MH, Wholey MH, Tan WA, et al: A comparison of balloon-mounted and self-expanding stents in the carotid arteries: Immediate and long-term results of more than 500 patients. J Endovasc Ther 10:171-181, 2003.

76. Schatz RA, Palmaz JC, Tio FO, et al: Balloon-expandable intracoronary stents in the adult dog. Circulation 76:450-457, 1987.

77. Willfort-Ehringer A, Ahmadi R, Gschwandtner ME, et al: Healing of carotid stents: A prospective duplex ultrasound study. J Endovasc Surg 10:636-642, 2003.

78. Sullivan TM, Ainsworth SD, Langan, EM, et al: Effect of endovascular stent strut geometry on vascular injury, myointimal hyperplasia, and restenosis. J Vasc Surg 36:142-149, 2002.

79. Crawley F, Clifton A, Markus H, Brown MM: Delayed improvement in carotid artery diameter after carotid angioplasty. Stroke 28:574-579, 1997.

80. Schillinger M, Exner M, Mlekusch W, et al: Acute-phase response after stent implantation in the carotid artery: Association with 6-month in-stent restenosis. Radiology 227:516-521, 2003.

81. Khan MA, Liu MW, Chio FL, et al: Predictors of restenosis after successful carotid artery stenting. Am J Cardiol 92:895-897, 2003.

82. Christiaans MH, Ernst JMPG, Suttorp MJ, et al: Restenosis after carotid angioplasty and stenting: A follow-up study with duplex ultrasonography. Eur J Vasc Endovasc Surg 26:141-144, 2003.

83. Lal BK, Hobson RW, Goldstein J, et al: In-stent recurrent stenosis after carotid artery stenting: Life table analysis and clinical relevance. J Vasc Surg 38:1162-1169, 2003.

84. Robbin ML, Lockhart ME, Weber TM, et al: Carotid artery stents: Early and intermediate follow-up with Doppler US. Radiology 205:749-756, 1997.

85. Ringer AJ, German JW, Guterman LR, Hopkins LN: Follow-up of stented carotid arteries by Doppler ultrasound. Neurosurgery 51:639-643, 2002.

86. Lal BK, Hobson RW, Goldstein J, Chakhtura E: Carotid artery stenting: Is there a need to revise ultrasound velocity criteria? J Vasc Surg 39:58-66, 2004.

87. Yoshida K, Nozaki K. Kikuta K, et al: Contrast-enhanced carotid color-coded duplex sonography for carotid stenting follow-up assessment. AJNR Am J Neuroradiol 24:992-995, 2003.

88. Cremonesi A, Castriota F, Manetti R, et al: Endovascular treatment of carotid atherosclerotic disease: Early and late outcome in a non-selected population. Ital Heart J 1:801-809, 2000.

89. Shawl FA: Carotid artery stenting: Acute and long-term results. Curr Opin Cardiol 17:671-676, 2002.

90. Khan MA, Liu MW, Chio FL, et al: Predictors of restenosis after successful carotid artery stenting. Am J Cardiol 92:895-897, 2003.

91. de Borst GJ, Ackerstaff GA, Mauser HW, Moll FL: Operative management of carotid artery in-stent restenosis: First experiences and duplex follow-up. Eur J Vasc Endovasc Surg 26:137-140, 2003.

92. Osborn A: Diagnostic Cerebral Angiography, 2nd ed. Philadelphia, Lippincott Williams & Wilkins, 1999, p 111.

93. Riles TS, Imparato AM, Jacobowitz GR, et al: The cause of perioperative stroke after carotid endarterectomy. J Vasc Surg 19:206-214, 1994.

94. Jordan WD, Voellinger DC, Doblar DD, et al: Microemboli detected by transcranial Doppler monitoring in patients during carotid angioplasty versus carotid endarterectomy. Cardiovasc Surg 7:33-38, 1999.

95. Gaunt ME, Martin PJ, Smith JL, et al: Clinical relevance of intraoperative embolization detected by transcranial Doppler ultrasonography during carotid endarterectomy: A prospective study of 100 patients. Br J Surg 81:1435-1439, 1994.

96. Fearn SJ, Pole R, Wesnes K, et al: Cardiopulmonary support and physiology. J Thorac Cardiovasc Surg 121:1150-1160, 2001.

97. Rapp JH, Pan XM, Sharp FR, et al: Atheroemboli to the brain: Size threshold for causing acute neuronal cell death. J Vasc Surg 32:68-76, 2000.

98. Jaeger HJ, Mathias DK, Hauth E, et al: Cerebral ischemia detected with diffusion-weighted MR imaging after stent implantation in the carotid artery. AJNR Am J Neuroradiol 23:200-207, 2002.

99. Ohki T, Marin ML, Lyon RT, et al: Ex vivo human carotid artery bifurcation stenting: Correlation of lesion characteristics with embolic potential. J Vasc Surg 27:463-471, 1998.

100. Bickness CD, Cowling MG, Clark MW, et al: Carotid angioplasty in a pulsatile flow model: Factors affecting embolic potential. Eur J Vasc Endovasc Surg 26:22-31, 2003.

101. Tübler T, Schlüter M, Dirsch O, et al: Balloon-protected carotid artery stenting: Relationship of periprocedural neurological complications with the size of particulate debris. Circulation 104:2791-2796, 2001.

102. Al-Mubarak N, Roubin GS, Vitek JJ, et al: Effect of the distal-balloon protection system on macroembolization during carotid stenting. Circulation 104:1999-2002, 2001.

103. Baim DS, Wahr D, George B, et al: Randomized trial of a distal embolic protection device during percutaneous intervention of saphenous vein aorto-coronary bypass grafts. Circulation 105:1285-1290, 2002.

104. Coggia M, Goëau-Brissonière, Duval J-L, et al: Embolic risk of the different stages of carotid bifurcation balloon angioplasty: An experimental study. J Vasc Surg 31:550-557, 2000.

105. Theron J, Raymond J, Casasco A, Courtheoux P: Percutaneous angioplasty of atherosclerotic and postsurgical stenosis of carotid arteries. AJNR Am J Neuroradiol 8:495-500, 1987.

106. Theron J, Courtheoux P, Alachkar, et al: New triple-coaxial catheter system for carotid angioplasty with cerebral protection. AJNR Am J Neuroradiol 11:869-874, 1990.

107. Al-Mubarak N, Vitek JJ, Iyer S, et al: Embolization via collateral circulation during carotid stenting with the distal balloon protection system. J Endovasc Ther 8:354-357, 2001.

108. Whitlow PL, Lylyk P, Londero H, et al: Carotid artery stenting protected with an emboli containment system. Stroke 22:1308-1314, 2002.

109. Ohki T, Parodi J, Veith FJ, et al: Efficacy of a proximal occlusion catheter with reversal of flow in the prevention of embolic events during carotid artery stenting: An experimental analysis. J Vasc Surg 33:504-509, 2001.

110. New G, Roubin GS, Iyer SS, Dangas G, et al: Outcomes from carotid artery stenting in over 1,000 cases from a single group of operators. J Am Coll Cardiol 41(Suppl A):868, 2003.

111. Parodi JC, LaMura R, Ferriera LM, et al: Initial evaluation of carotid angioplasty and stenting with three different cerebral protection devices. J Vasc Surg 32:1127-1136, 2000.

112. Cremonesi A, Manetti R, Setacci F, et al: Protected carotid stenting: Clinical advantages and complications of embolic protection devices in 442 consecutive patients. Stroke 34:1936-1943, 2003.

113. Ragosta M, Karve M, Brezynski D, et al: Effectiveness of heparin in preventing thrombin generation and thrombin activity in patients undergoing coronary intervention. Am Heart J 137:250-257, 1999.

114. Deleted in revision.

115. Mehta SR, Yusuf S, Peters RJ, et al: Effects of pretreatment with clopidogrel and aspirin followed by long-term therapy in patients undergoing percutaneous coronary intervention: The PCI-CURE study. Lancet 358:527-533, 2001.

116. Steinhubl SR, Berger PB, Mann JT III, et al: Early and sustained dual oral antiplatelet therapy following percutaneous coronary intervention: A randomized controlled trial. JAMA 288:2411-2420, 2002.

117. Bhatt DL, Kapadia SR, Bajzer CT, et al: Dual antiplatelet therapy with clopidogrel and aspirin after carotid artery stenting. J Invas Cardiol 13:767-771, 2001.

118. Moliterno DJ, Chan AW: Glycoprotein IIb/IIIa inhibition in early intent-to-stent treatment of acute coronary syndromes: EPISTENT, ADMIRAL, CADILLAC, and TARGET. J Am Coll Cardiol 41(4 Suppl S):49S-54S, 2003.

119. Schneiderman J, Morag B, Gerniak A, et al: Abciximab in carotid stenting for postsurgical carotid restenosis: Intermediate results. J Endovasc Ther 7:263-272, 2000.

120. Kapadia SR, Bajzer CT, Ziada KM, et al: Initial experience of platelet glycoprotein IIb/IIIa inhibition with abciximab during carotid stenting: A safe and effective adjunctive therapy. Stroke 32:2328-2332, 2001.

121. Hofmann R, Kerschner K, Steinwender C, et al: Abciximab bolus injection does not reduce cerebral ischemic Complications of elective carotid artery stenting: a randomized study. Stroke 33:725-727, 2002.

122. Qureshi AI, Suri MF, Ali Z, et al: Carotid angioplasty and stent placement: A prospective analysis of perioperative complications and impact of intravenously administered abciximab. Neurosurgery 50:466-475, 2002.

123. Mathur A, Roubin GS, Iyer SS, et al: Predictors of stroke complicating carotid artery stenting. Circulation 97:1239-1245, 1998.

124. Leisch F, Kerschner K, Hofmann R, et al: Carotid sinus reactions during carotid artery stenting: Predictors, incidence, and influence on clinical outcome. Cathet Cardiovasc Interv 58:516-523, 2003.

125. Bush RL, Bhama JK, Lin PH, Lumsden AB: Transient ischemic attack due to early carotid stent thrombosis: Successful rescue with rheolytic thrombectomy and systemic abciximab. J Endovasc Ther 10:870-874, 2003.

126. Ringer AJ, Fessler RD, Quereshi AI, et al: Horner's syndrome after carotid artery stenting: Case report. Surg Neurol 54:439-443, 2000.

127. McCabe DJ, Brown MM, Clifton A: Fatal cerebral reperfusion hemorrhage after carotid stenting. Stroke 30:2483-2486, 1999.

128. Chakhotura EY, Hobson RW, Goldstein J, et al: In-stent restenosis after carotid angioplasty: Incidence and management. J Vasc Surg 33:220-226, 2001.

129. Generalized efficacy of t-PA for acute stroke. Subgroup analysis of the NINDS t-PA Stroke Trial. Stroke 28:2119-2125, 1997.

130. Wijdicks EF, Nichols DA, Thielen KR, et al: Intra-arterial thrombolysis in acute basilar artery thromboembolism: The initial Mayo Clinic experience. Mayo Clin Proc 72:1005-1013, 1997.

131. Jungreis CA, Wechsler LR, Horton JA: Intracranial thrombolysis via a catheter embedded in the clot. Stroke 20:1578-1580, 1989.

132. Barr JD, Mathis JM, Wildenhain SL, et al: Acute stroke intervention with intra-arterial urokinase infusion. J Vasc Interv Radiol 5:705-713, 1994.

133. del Zoppo GJ, Higashida RT, Furlan AJ, et al: PROACT: A phase II randomized trial of recombinant pro-urokinase by direct arterial delivery in acute middle cerebral artery stroke. PROACT Investigators. Prolyse in Acute Cerebral Thromboembolism [see comments]. Stroke 29:4-11, 1998.

134. Furlan A, Higashida R, Wechsler L, et al: Intra-arterial prourokinase for acute ischemic stroke. The PROACT II study: a randomized controlled trial. Prolyse in Acute Cerebral Thromboembolism. JAMA 282:2003-2011, 1999.

135. Lewandowski CA, Frankel M, Tomsick TA, et al: Combined intravenous and intra-arterial r-TPA versus intra-arterial therapy of acute ischemic stroke: Emergency Management of Stroke (EMS) Bridging Trial. Stroke 30:2598-2605, 1999.

136. Hahnel S, Schellinger PD, Gutschalk A, et al: Local intra-arterial fibrinolysis of thromboemboli occurring during neuroendovascular procedures with recombinant tissue plasminogen activator. Stroke 34:1723-1728, 2003.

137. Cloft HJ, Samuels OB, Tong FC, Dion JE: Use of abciximab for mediation of thromboembolic complications of endovascular therapy. AJNR Am J Neuroradiol 22:1764-1767, 2001.

138. Workman MJ, Cloft HJ, Tong FC, et al: Thrombus formation at the neck of cerebral aneurysms during treatment with Guglielmi detachable coils. AJNR Am J Neuroradiol 23:1568-1576, 2002.

139. Wholey MH, Tan WA, Toursarkissian B, et al: Management of neurological complications of carotid artery stenting. J Endovasc Ther 8:341-353, 2001.

140. Nakano S, Iseda T, Yoneyama T, et al: Direct percutaneous transluminal angioplasty for acute middle cerebral artery trunk occlusion: An alternative option to intra-arterial thrombolysis. Stroke 33:2872-2876, 2002.

141. Ueda T, Sakaki S, Nochide I, et al: Angioplasty after intra-arterial thrombolysis for acute occlusion of intracranial arteries. Stroke 29:2568-2574, 1998.

142. Kerber CW, Barr JD, Berger RM, Chopko BW: Snare retrieval of intracranial thrombus in patients with acute stroke. J Vasc Interv Radiol 13:1269-1274, 2002.

143. Wikholm G: Transarterial embolectomy in acute stroke. AJNR Am J Neuroradiol 24:892-894, 2003.

144. Hobson RW: CREST: Background, design, and current status. J Vasc Surg 13:139-143, 2000.

145. Moore W, Mohr JP, Najafi H, et al: Carotid endarterectomy: Practice guidelines. Report of the Ad Hoc Committee to the Joint Council of the Society for Vascular Surgery and the North American Chapter of the International Society for Cardiovascular Surgery. J Vasc Surg 15:469-479, 1992.

146. Sternberg S: Stents in Neck Can Prevent Stroke. USA Today, November 20, 2002.

147. Bettman MA, Katzen BT, Whisnant J, et al: AHA Science Advisory. Carotid stenting and angioplasty. Circulation 97:121-123, 1998.

Chapter

141

Vertebrobasilar Ischemia:
Indications, Techniques, and Results of Surgical Repair

MARK D. MORASCH, MD
RAMON BERGUER, MD, PhD

■ INDICATIONS

Direct surgery on the vertebral artery (VA) to correct stenosis or occlusion may be indicated for two types of patients: (1) those with vertebrobasilar ischemia (VBI), to increase blood flow to the basilar territory or to prevent further embolization and (2) those with extensive, severe, and symptomatic extracranial disease, to increase total brain blood flow.

Two mechanisms are recognized in the causation of VBI: microembolization and low flow. VBI may be due to *microembolization* from the heart or, more frequently, from the arteries leading to the basilar artery (innominate, proximal subclavian, and vertebral arteries). These patients may present with transient ischemic attacks (TIAs) or strokes in the territory supplied by the basilar artery. The importance of the *embolic* mechanism as a cause of vertebrobasilar symptoms has been emphasized in clinical and anatomopathologic studies.[1,2] This information, derived from autopsy studies and magnetic resonance (MR) imaging, identifies small infarcts in the brain stem and cerebellum (previously not visualized by computed tomography [CT] scanning) and their source in selective arteriograms showing the offending lesions in the subclavian or vertebral arteries. Patients with embolic VBI develop multiple infarcts in the brain stem, cerebellum, and, occasionally, posterior cerebral artery territory and have a high incidence of stroke. Microembolization is the cause of VBI in approximately 30% of patients.[1]

The *low-flow* mechanism of VBI is better recognized and more frequent than the embolic one. Patients with low-flow VBI present with TIA in the territory of the basilar artery because they lack appropriate inflow from the VA and have inadequate compensation from the carotid territory. Low-flow VBI, manifested as TIA, is usually caused by stenosis or occlusion of the VA. Although most of these lesions are atherosclerotic plaques, the VA may also be compressed extrinsically by osteophytes adjacent to the VA canal.

For patients with low-flow VBI, it is essential to rule out systemic causes of VBI before advising arteriography. In the later years of life, VA stenosis is not an uncommon arteriographic finding, and dizziness is a common complaint. However, the presence of both in a patient cannot be assumed to be a cause-effect relationship. Common systemic causes of low-flow VBI are orthostatic hypotension, poorly regulated antihypertensive therapy, arrhythmias, heart failure, malfunction of pacemakers, and anemia.

The evaluation of patients with VBI should include a number of specific steps. The precise circumstances associated with development of symptoms should be ascertained. Symptoms often appear on standing in older individuals with poor sympathetic control of their venous tone, which causes excessive pooling of blood in the veins of the leg. This is particularly common in patients with diabetes who have diminished sympathetic venoconstrictor reflexes. We use an arbitrary 20-mm Hg systolic pressure drop on rapid standing as the criterion for a diagnosis of orthostatic hypotension causing low-flow in the vertebrobasilar system. In these cases the pressure drop triggers the symptoms of VBI.

Patients may relate their symptoms to turning or extending their heads. These dynamic symptoms usually appear when turning the head to one side. Frequently, the mechanism here is extrinsic compression of the VA, usually the dominant or the only one, by arthritic bone spurs.[3] To differentiate this mechanism from dizziness or vertigo secondary to labyrinthine disorders that appear with head or body rotation, the patient should attempt to reproduce the symptoms by turning the head *slowly* and then repeating the maneuver, but this time *briskly*, as when shaking the head from side to side. In labyrinthine disease, the sudden inertial changes caused by the latter maneuver result in immediate symptoms and nystagmus. Conversely, in extrinsic VA compression, a short delay occurs before the patient fears for his or her balance.

Demonstration of extrinsic dynamic compression of the VA, usually by osteophytes, requires an arteriogram. This is performed either with the patient sitting up, by means of bilateral brachial injections, or with the patient supine in Trendelenburg's position with the head resting against a block if the femoral route is used. In these positions, intended to exert axial compression of the cervical vertebrae, the angiographer should obtain the specific rotation or extension of the head that provokes the symptoms. When the patient is rendered symptomatic, the arteriographic injection will demonstrate the extrinsic compression that developed with the head rotation or extension. The reason to position the patient either sitting up or in 25 degrees of Trendelenburg is to mimic the effects of the weight of the head on the spine. With the patient standing, the weight of the head acting on the cervical spine changes its curvature and decreases the distance between C1 and C7. This longitudinal compression of the spine often enhances the extrinsic compression effects caused by osteophytic spurs.[4]

In the work-up of patients with VBI an MR scan is preferable to a CT scan of the brain to rule out a brain tumor and to assess the integrity of the brain. Brain stem infarctions are often missed by CT scan because they tend to be small and the resolution of the CT scan in the brain stem is poor. In patients who are candidates for VA reconstruction, MR brain scans are performed preoperatively to ascertain whether infarctions have taken place in the vertebrobasilar territory.

Excessive use of antihypertensive medications can also cause low-flow VBI by decreasing the perfusion pressure and inducing severe orthostatic hypotension. An ambulatory 24-hour electrocardiogram (Holter monitor) is obtained in all patients evaluated for low-flow VBI. Sometimes patients with VBI secondary to arrhythmias acknowledge the association of palpitations with the appearance of VBI symptoms, the latter being secondary to decreased cardiac output resulting from the arrhythmia.

Physical examination can alert the physician to the possibility of a subclavian steal in patients with brachial pressure differences greater than 25 mm Hg or with diminished or absent pulses in one arm. The diagnosis of reversal of VA flow can be made accurately by noninvasive indirect methods[5] and demonstrated directly by duplex imaging of the reversal of flow in the VA.

Any systemic mechanism that decreases the mean pressure of the basilar artery may be responsible for the syndrome of low-flow VBI. Affected individuals may or may not have concomitant VA stenosis or occlusion. In some patients, the cause of the drop in mean arterial pressure can be corrected by readjustment in their antihypertensive medication, by administration of antiarrhythmic drugs, or by insertion of a cardiac pacemaker. In patients with orthostatic hypotension, the problem may not respond to medical treatment and only the reconstruction of a diseased or occluded VA will render the patient asymptomatic in the face of persistent oscillations of blood pressure secondary to poor sympathetic venous tone. Rheologic factors, such as increased viscosity (polycythemia) and decreased oxygen-carrying capacity (anemia), may exacerbate or cause VBI in patients with severe VA occlusive disease.

The second major indication for VA reconstruction pertains to patients who have extensive extracranial disease with one or both internal carotid arteries occluded and who have global manifestations of cerebrovascular ischemia. In these patients the carotid arteries may be occluded or involved with severe siphon stenosis, making a direct revascularization via the internal carotid arteries impossible or inadvisable, and reconstruction of the VA may offer the best option for re-establishment of adequate cerebral blood flow. In patients with global ischemia, the VAs are important pathways for cerebral revascularization when they are critically stenosed or occluded. In the latter case, they can often be revascularized at skull base with a distal reconstruction. In this latter group, demonstration of normal-sized posterior communicating arteries increases the likelihood of successfully correcting global ischemic symptoms.

In VA reconstructions done for hemodynamic symptoms, the minimal anatomic requirement to justify a VA reconstruction is stenosis greater than 60% diameter in both VAs if both are patent and complete, or the same degree of stenosis in the dominant VA if the opposite VA is

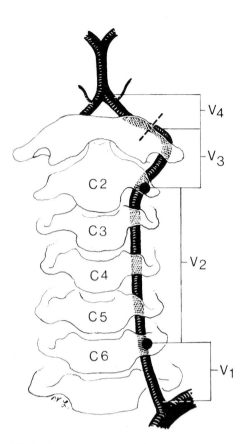

FIGURE 141-1 The four segments of the vertebral (V) artery. (From Berguer R: Surgical management of the vertebral artery. In Moore WS [ed]: Surgery for Cerebrovascular Disease. New York, Churchill Livingstone, 1986.)

hypoplastic (ending in a posteroinferior cerebellar artery) or occluded. In addition, a normal VA is sufficient to perfuse adequately the basilar artery, regardless of a stenosis in the contralateral VA. In patients with VBI secondary to microembolism and appropriate lesions in a vertebral (or subclavian) artery, the potential source of the embolus

needs to be eliminated regardless of the status of the contralateral VA.

In our series of VA reconstructions, 96% of patients presented with neurologic symptoms (TIA or stroke) and 4% were asymptomatic. The neurologic symptoms were referable to the hemispheres in 4% and to the vertebrobasilar system in 60% and were considered global in 30%.

■ ARTERIOGRAPHIC EVALUATION

The arteriographic investigation of VA pathology necessitates systematic positions and projections to evaluate the vertebrobasilar system from its origin to the top of the basilar artery. The VA is described in four segments, each with specific radiologic and pathologic features (Fig. 141-1).

Arteriographic evaluation begins with an arch view, which determines the presence or absence of VA on each side. It shows whether one VA is dominant (generally the left) and whether any of the VA has an abnormal origin. The most common anomalous origin is the left VA, originating from the arch (6%). A much rarer variant is the right VA arising from the innominate or right common carotid artery (Fig. 141-2), which occurs in patients with a retroesophageal right subclavian artery. Arch views must be obtained in at least two projections: right and left posterior obliques. Usually these two views display well the *first segment* (V1) of the VA, from its origin to the transverse process of C6. Occasionally additional oblique views may be required (see later).

The most common atherosclerotic lesion of the VA is stenosis of its origin. This lesion may be missed in standard arch views because of superimposition of the subclavian artery over the first segment of the VA. Additional oblique projections may be needed to "throw off" the subclavian artery to obtain a clear view of the origin of the VA (Fig. 141-3). The presence of a post-stenotic dilation in the first centimeter of the VA suggests that there may be a significant stenosis at its origin hidden by an overlying subclavian artery. Redundancy and kinks are common, but only very

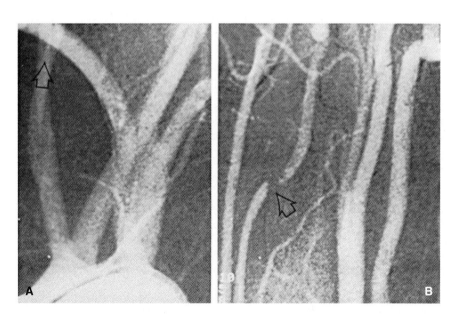

FIGURE 141-2 Arch injection in a 33-year-old woman with vertebrobasilar ischemia. **A,** The right vertebral artery (VA) and the right external carotid artery arise from a long common right carotid trunk *(arrow)*. The right internal carotid artery is congenitally absent. The right subclavian arises as the last branch of the aorta. **B,** The right VA, which has an anomalous origin, enters the spine at a high level (C4) and is severely compressed *(arrow)* at this level on head rotation.

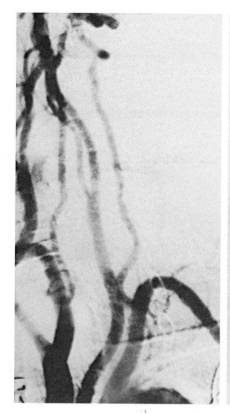
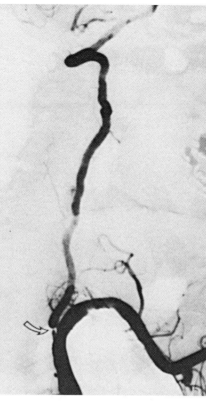

FIGURE 141-3 A severe stenosis *(arrow)* of a dominant left vertebral artery seen only after additional oblique rotation of the patient *(right)*. (From Berguer R: Role of vertebral artery surgery after carotid endarterectomy. In Bergan JJ, Yao JST [eds]: Reoperative Arterial Surgery. Orlando, Grune & Stratton, 1986, pp 555-564.)

severe kinks associated with post-stenotic dilations can be related to low-flow symptoms.

Visualization of the *second segment* (V2) of the VA, from C6 to the top of the transverse process of C2, is accomplished in the oblique arch views in conjunction with selective subclavian injections. The point of entry of the artery in the spine is determined, and an abnormally low entry at the level of C7 instead of C6 should be noted. This finding is associated with a short V1 segment of the VA, which suggests inadequate length will be available if one is considering its eventual transposition to the common carotid artery. The level of entry into the spine is best determined in unsubtracted views. Extrinsic compression by musculotendinous structures is common in VA with an abnormally high level of entry into the spine, usually C4 or C5 (see Fig. 141-2). This is due to the sharp angulation resulting from the abnormal level of entry.

The most common pathology of the V2 segment is extrinsic compression of the VA by osteophytes.[3] In patients with dynamic symptoms prompted by neck rotation, the V2 segment must be evaluated with arteriograms taken with the neck in right and left rotation with the weight of the head—or an equivalent force—acting on the cervical spine (see later). The VA may be normal in one projection and occluded by extrinsic compression in the other (Fig. 141-4). The agent of compression may be bone (an osteophyte) or tendon (longus colli). The V2 and V3 segments are frequent sites for traumatic or spontaneous arteriovenous fistulae because the fixation of the adventitia of the VA to the periosteum of the foramina makes the former vulnerable to luxation/subluxation of the vertebrae or to fractures of their lateral mass. The close proximity of the artery to its surrounding venous plexus results in an arteriovenous fistula whenever the artery and the vain are damaged in continuity. The VA may tear completely or incompletely (dissection) as a consequence of stretch injury after brisk rotation or hyperextension of the neck.

The *third segment* of the VA (V3) extends from the top of the transverse process of C2 to the atlanto-occipital membrane. After crossing this membrane, the artery enters the foramen magnum at the base of the skull and becomes intradural. The first two cervical vertebrae are the most mobile of the spine. About 50% of the neck rotation occurs between C1 and C2. The VA is redundant at this level to allow for the arc of displacement of the transverse process of the atlas (≈80 degrees) to which the VA is attached. The most common problems at this level are arterial dissection, arteriovenous fistulae, and arteriovenous aneurysms. Dissection may be associated with fibromuscular dysplasia or occur in a normal artery after seemingly trivial trauma (Fig. 141-5). Dissection of a VA may result in stenosis, thrombosis, distal embolization, and pseudoaneurysmal dilation. Arteriovenous fistula results from rupture of the wall of the VA into its surrounding venous plexus. In long-standing fistulae the pulsatile mass formed by the fistula and its dilated venous channels is called an *arteriovenous aneurysm.*

The VA may be compressed in the *pars atlantica* of the third segment between the occipital ridge and the arch of the atlas. In these patients the symptoms of low-flow VBI are usually precipitated by head extension or rotation.

An anatomic finding crucial for surgical strategy is that when the VA is occluded proximally it usually reconstitutes at the V3 segment via collateral blood vessels linking

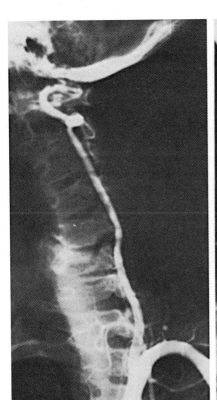
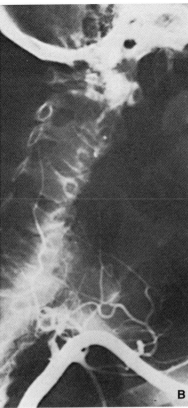

FIGURE 141-4 A patient with a single vertebral artery showing minimal extrinsic compression (**A**) when the neck is rotated to the right and occlusion (**B**) when the neck is rotated to the left. (**A** and **B**, From Berguer R: Surgical management of the vertebral artery. In Moore WS [ed]: Surgery for Cerebrovascular Disease. New York, Churchill Livingstone, 1986.)

the occipital artery with the VA at this level (Fig. 141-6). Because of this collateral network, the distal (V3 + V4) vertebral and basilar arteries usually remain patent despite a proximal VA occlusion.

The *fourth segment* (V4) is infrequently affected by atherosclerosis. Finally, the basilar artery (Fig. 141-7) should be clearly seen in a lateral projection. Subtracted views are needed to eliminate the temporal bone density in the lateral projection. In the Towne anteroposterior view, routinely used in neuroradiology, the basilar artery is foreshortened and therefore the resolution is poor. Advanced atherosclerotic disease of the basilar artery contraindicates reconstruction of VA lesions.

■ SURGICAL TECHNIQUES

With rare exceptions, most reconstructions of the VA are performed to relieve either an orificial stenosis (V1 segment) or stenosis, dissection, or occlusion of its intraspinal component (V2 and V3 segments).[6]

Although in the 1970s Berguer and colleagues advocated the correction of proximal VA disease by subclavian-vertebral bypass,[7,8] they currently seldom use this technique, reserving it for uncommon anatomic circumstances such as (1) contralateral carotid occlusion that increases the risk of clamping the only carotid supply during VA-carotid transposition and (2) a short V1 segment with the VA entering the foramen transversarium of C7. This anatomic variant

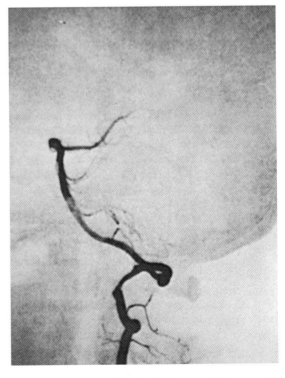

FIGURE 141-5 Intramural dissection of the vertebral artery at the V3 segment in a 40-year-old woman with Klippel-Feil syndrome and subluxation of the atlantoaxial joint.

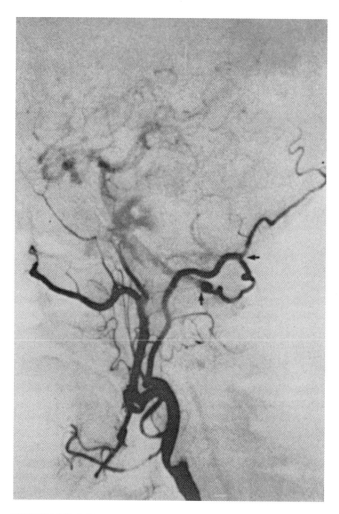

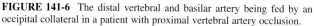

FIGURE 141-6 The distal vertebral and basilar artery being fed by an occipital collateral in a patient with proximal vertebral artery occlusion.

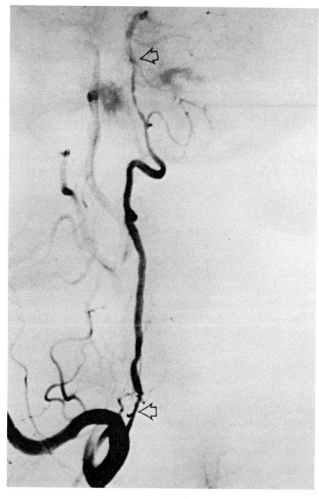

FIGURE 141-7 Arteriogram showing atheromatous disease of the V1 and V4 segments *(arrowheads)* of the vertebral artery and of the basilar artery.

provides inadequate length to transpose the VA to the common carotid artery. For disease involving the origin of the VA, we routinely perform a transposition of this vessel into the common carotid artery, which is a simpler and more elegant solution than a subclavian-VA bypass. The common carotid artery is more accessible than the subclavian artery, and this procedure needs only one anastomosis and no vein graft.

For disease involving any level at or above the transverse process of C6, we routinely carry the reconstruction to the C2-C1 level (V3 segment). This reconstruction is usually a common carotid to distal VA bypass,[9-12] although other techniques (see later) may be required in specific circumstances. Bypasses above the level of C1 (suboccipital) are technically demanding and have been required in only 4% of cases of distal VA reconstruction. There is no reason to approach the VA for reconstruction in its V2 portion (C6-C2), where the exposure is poorer than that obtained in the V3 segment. In addition, reconstruction of the VA at the level of C2-C1 bypasses most potential areas of extrinsic compression by osteophytes.

Transposition of the Vertebral Artery into the Common Carotid Artery

If the VA operation is performed as an isolated procedure, the incision is supraclavicular approaching the VA between the heads of the sternocleidomastoid muscle (Fig. 141-8). The omohyoid muscle is divided. The jugular vein and vagus nerve are retracted laterally, and the carotid sheath is entered. The carotid artery should be exposed proximally as far as possible; this is facilitated if the surgeon temporarily stands at the head of the patient and looks down into the mediastinum.

After the carotid artery is mobilized, the sympathetic chain is identified running behind and parallel to it. On the left side, the thoracic duct is divided between ligatures, avoiding transfixion sutures that will result in lymph leaks. The proximal end of the thoracic duct is doubly ligated. Accessory lymph ducts—often seen on the right side—are identified, ligated, and divided. The entire dissection is confined medial to the prescalene fat pad that covers the scalenus anticus muscle and phrenic nerve. These latter

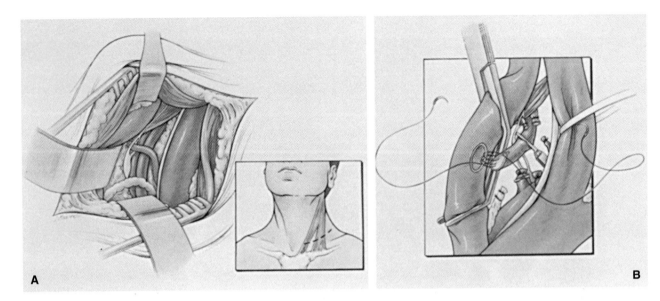

FIGURE 141-8   A, Access to the proximal vertebral artery (VA) between the sternocleidomastoid muscle bellies. **B,** Transposition of the proximal VA to the posterior wall of the common carotid artery. (**A** and **B,** From Berguer R, Kieffer E: Surgery of the Arteries to the Head. New York, Springer-Verlag, 1992.)

structures are left unexposed lateral to the field. The inferior thyroid artery runs transversely across the field, and it is ligated and divided.

The vertebral vein is next identified emerging from the angle formed by the longus colli and scalenus anticus and overlying the VA and, at the bottom of the field, the subclavian artery. Unlike its sister artery, the vertebral vein has branches. It is ligated in continuity and divided. Below the vertebral vein lies the VA. It is important to identify and avoid injury to the adjacent sympathetic chain. The VA is dissected superiorly to the tendon of the longus colli and interiorly to its origin in the subclavian artery. The VA is freed from the sympathetic trunk resting on its anterior surface without damaging the trunk or the ganglionic rami. To preserve the sympathetic trunks and the stellate or intermediate ganglia resting on the artery, usually requires freeing the VA from these structures and, after dividing its origin, the latter is transposed anterior to the sympathetics.

Once the artery is fully exposed, an appropriate site for reimplantation in the common carotid artery is selected. The patient is given systemic heparin. The distal portion of the V1 segment of the VA is clamped below the edge of the longus colli with a microclip placed vertically to indicate the orientation of the artery and to avoid axial twisting during its transposition. The proximal VA is closed with a transfixion of 5-0 polypropylene immediately above the stenosis at its origin. The artery is divided at this level, and its proximal stump is further secured with a hemoclip. The artery is then brought to the common carotid artery and its free end is spatulated for anastomosis.

The carotid artery is then cross-clamped. An elliptical defect of approximately 5 × 7 mm is created in the posterolateral wall of the common carotid artery with an aortic punch. The anastomosis is performed in open fashion with continuous 6-0 or 7-0 polypropylene suture, avoiding any tension on the VA, which tears easily. Before completion of the anastomosis, the suture slack is

tightened appropriately with a nerve hook, standard flushing maneuvers are performed, and the suture is tied, re-establishing flow.

When a simultaneous carotid endarterectomy is planned (Fig. 141-9), the VA is approached through the standard carotid incision extended inferiorly to the head of the clavicle. With this approach, the sternocleidomastoid muscle is lateral and the field is a bit narrower than when the VA is approached between the heads of the sternocleidomastoid. The remaining steps of the operation are as described previously.

Distal Vertebral Artery Reconstruction

Reconstruction of the distal VA is generally done at the C1-C2 level. Rarely the reconstruction is done at the C1-C0 level using a posterior approach. Although various techniques can be applied to revascularize the VA in its V3 segment (between the transverse processes of C1 and C2), the approach to the VA at this level is the same for all procedures.[11-13]

The incision is anterior to the sternocleidomastoid muscle, the same as in a carotid operation, and is carried superiorly to immediately below the earlobe (Fig. 141-10). The dissection proceeds between the jugular vein and the anterior edge of the sternocleidomastoid, exposing the spinal accessory nerve. The nerve is followed distally as it joins the jugular vein and crosses in front of the transverse process of C1, which can be easily felt by the operator's finger. This necessitates freeing and retracting the digastric muscle upward or dividing it.

The next step involves the identification of the levator scapula muscle by removal of the fibrofatty tissue overlying it. With the anterior edge of the levator scapula identified, the surgeon searches for the anterior ramus of C2. With the ramus as a guide, a right-angle clamp is slid over the ramus, elevating the levator scapula, which is transected (Fig. 141-11).

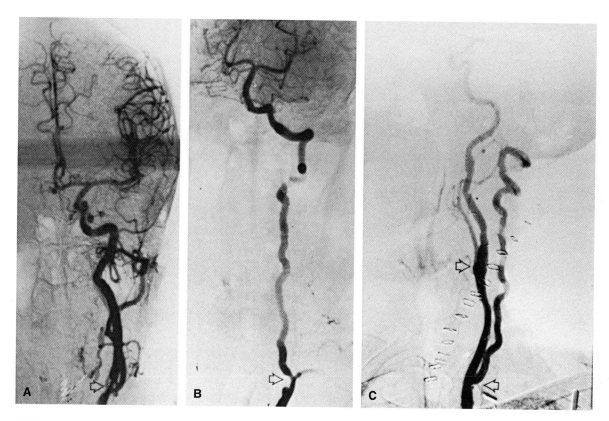

FIGURE 141-9 **A** and **B,** Arteriogram in a patient with left hemispheric transient symptoms showing carotid and vertebral (dominant) arterial stenoses *(arrowheads).* **C,** Arteriogram obtained 2 days after left carotid endarterectomy and transposition of the left vertebral artery into the left common carotid artery *(arrowheads).*

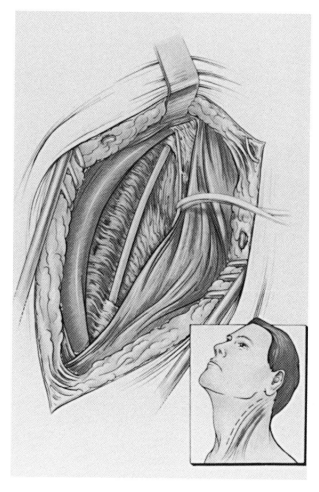

FIGURE 141-10 Retrojugular approach and isolation of the spinal accessory nerve. (From Berguer R, Kieffer E: Surgery of the Arteries to the Head. New York, Springer-Verlag, 1992.)

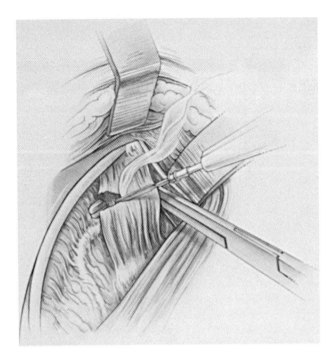

FIGURE 141-11 Dividing the levator scapula over the C2 ramus. The vagus, internal jugular vein, and internal carotid artery are anterior to the muscle. (From Berguer R, Kieffer E: Surgery of the Arteries to the Head. New York, Springer-Verlag, 1992.)

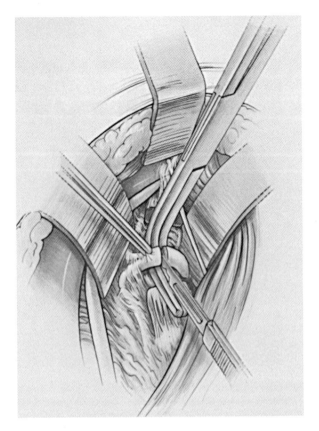

FIGURE 141-12 Dividing the anterior ramus of C2 to expose the underlying vertebral artery running perpendicular to the former. (From Berguer R, Kieffer E: Surgery of the Arteries to the Head. New York, Springer-Verlag, 1992.)

The proximal stump of the levator is excised up to its insertion on the C1 transverse process. The C2 ramus divides into three branches after crossing the VA. The artery runs below, in contact with the nerve and perpendicular to it. The surgeon cuts the ramus (Fig. 141-12) before its branching; underneath it, the VA can be identified.

The dissection of the artery at this level is best accomplished with loupe magnification, advisable for all VA reconstructions. The artery is freed from the surrounding veins with extreme care because hemorrhage is difficult to control at this level. Before encircling the artery with fine silicone (Silastic) vessel loops, one must ensure that a collateral from the occipital collateral artery does not enter the posterior aspect of the VA at the location at which the surgeon is dissecting. Tearing this important collateral vessel (Fig. 141-13) complicates the preparation of the distal VA unnecessarily. Once the VA is encircled, the distal common carotid artery is dissected and prepared to receive a saphenous vein graft. There is no need to dissect the carotid bifurcation. The location selected for the proximal anastomosis of the saphenous vein graft on the common carotid artery should not be too close to the bifurcation because cross-clamping at this level may fracture underlying atheroma.

A saphenous vein graft of appropriate length is obtained and prepared. A valveless segment facilitates back-bleeding of the VA after completion of the distal anastomosis. The patient is given intravenous heparin. The VA is elevated by gently pulling the loop and is occluded with a small J-clamp that isolates this segment for an end-to-side anastomosis. The VA is opened longitudinally with a coronary knife for a length adequate to accommodate the spatulated end of the

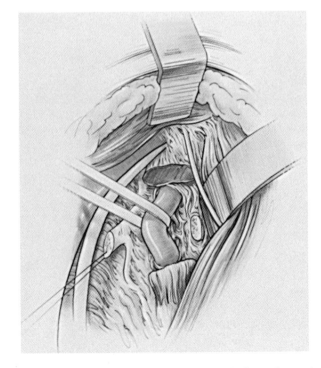

FIGURE 141-13 After the vertebral venous plexus is dissected away, the vertebral artery is slung with a polymeric silicone (Silastic) loop for clamping and anastomosis. (From Berguer R, Kieffer E: Surgery of the Arteries to the Head. New York, Springer-Verlag, 1992.)

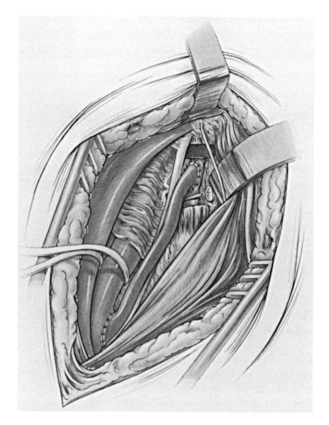

FIGURE 141-14 A completed common carotid artery to distal vertebral artery bypass using saphenous vein. (From Berguer R, Kieffer E: Surgery of the Arteries to the Head. New York, Springer-Verlag, 1992.)

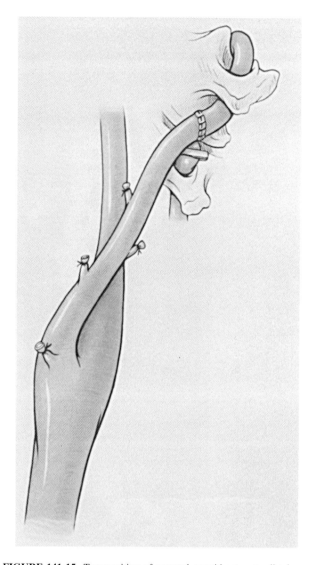

FIGURE 141-15 Transposition of external carotid artery to distal vertebral artery. (From Berguer R, Kieffer E: Surgery of the Arteries to the Head. New York, Springer-Verlag, 1992.)

vein graft. The end-to-side anastomosis is done with continuous 7-0 polypropylene and fine needles. The distal anastomosis is assessed for back-flow, and, if satisfactory, a Heifitz clip is placed in the vein graft proximal to the anastomosis, resuming flow through the VA.

The proximal end of the graft is passed beneath the jugular vein and in proximity to the side of the common carotid artery. The common carotid artery is then cross-clamped, an elliptical arteriotomy is made in its posterior wall with an aortic punch, and the proximal vein graft is anastomosed end-to-side to the common carotid artery with continuous 6-0 polypropylene (Fig. 141-14). Before the anastomosis is completed, standard flushing maneuvers are performed, the suture is tied, and flow is re-established. Next, the VA is occluded with a clip immediately below the anastomosis so as to avoid competitive flow or the potential for recurrent emboli.

Variations on Technique

The distal VA may also be revascularized via the external carotid artery (ECA) either directly by means of a transposition of the ECA to the distal VA or by anastomosis of the proximal end of a graft to the ECA. The transposition of the ECA to the distal VA (Figs. 141-15 and 141-16) requires a carotid bifurcation free of disease and a long ECA trunk. ECAs that divide early often are too small to match the caliber of the VA. If the trunk of the ECA is of adequate size

and length to reach the VA, the ECA is skeletonized by dividing all its branches. The ECA is then rotated over the internal carotid artery and beneath the jugular vein to construct an end-to-side anastomosis to the distal VA at the C1-C2 level. After completion of this anastomosis, the VA is permanently occluded with a clip immediately below the anastomosis.

A patient may have a segment of saphenous vein that is of appropriate diameter but of insufficient length to bridge the distance between the common carotid artery and the distal VA. In this case, the proximal ECA can be used as the inflow source for the vein graft. This technique is particularly useful when the contralateral internal carotid artery is occluded and one wishes to avoid clamping the common carotid supplying the only patent internal carotid artery. If a vein bypass graft is used between the ECA and the distal VA, it should be placed with the proper amount of tension and assessed with the neck rotated back to the neutral position to avoid kinking.

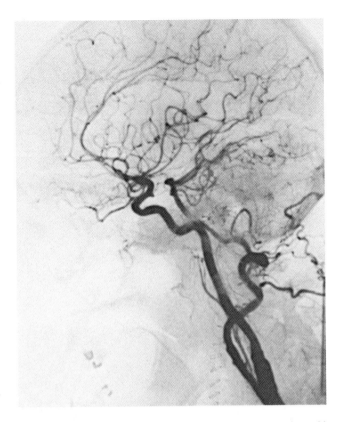

FIGURE 141-16 Arteriogram of a transposition of the external carotid artery to the distal vertebral artery. This patient had a previous internal carotid endarterectomy. (From Berguer R, Kieffer E: Surgery of the Arteries to the Head. New York, Springer-Verlag, 1992.)

In patients younger than 35 years of age without atherosclerosis, the cause of VA occlusion is usually trauma (subluxation, injury), fibromuscular dysplasia, or deliberate ligation (during a Blalock-Taussig procedure) (Fig. 141-17). These patients usually have patent internal carotid arteries, and collaterals to the distal VA develop via an enlarged ECA branch (occipital). These collaterals may nevertheless be too small to provide adequate flow into the basilar system. Under these circumstances, if the occipital artery is sufficiently enlarged, it can be directly anastomosed to the distal VA (Fig. 141-18). This strategy should also be considered in patients who do not have a satisfactory saphenous vein. If the patient is at risk for atherosclerosis, however, one should ensure that the origin of the ECA is not stenotic.

Another method of revascularization of the distal VA is the transposition of this vessel into the distal cervical internal carotid artery below the transverse process of C1 (Fig. 141-19). This technique is particularly applicable for patients with inadequate saphenous veins or in whom the ECA cannot be used because of unsuitable anatomy or disease of the carotid bifurcation. This is a straightforward end-to-side anastomosis between the distal VA and the distal cervical internal carotid artery. This procedure, however, is contraindicated in patients with contralateral internal carotid artery occlusion in whom the risk of cerebral ischemia during the anastomosis would be prohibitive.

A small group of patients have disease up to the level of C1 and require revascularization in the last segment of extracranial VA.[14] To accomplish this, the VA must be

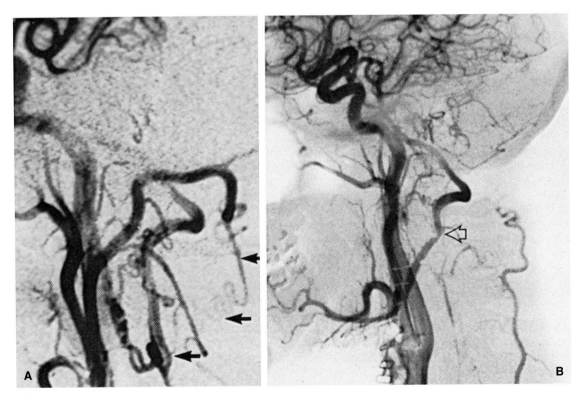

FIGURE 141-17 A, Occlusion of the proximal vertebral artery (bilaterally) (*arrows*) in a young patient with congenital heart disease who underwent bilateral Blalock-Taussig procedures with ligation of both proximal VAs. **B,** Postoperative arteriogram showing an occipital-to-distal vertebral artery anastomosis (*arrowhead*).

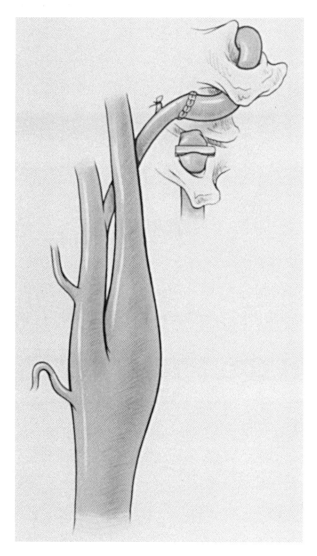

FIGURE 141-18 Transposition of the occipital artery to the distal vertebral artery. (From Berguer R, Kieffer E: Surgery of the Arteries to the Head. New York, Springer-Verlag, 1992.)

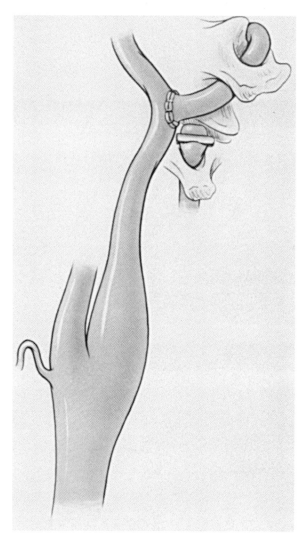

FIGURE 141-19 Transposition of the distal vertebral artery to the cervical internal carotid artery. (From Berguer R, Kieffer E: Surgery of the Arteries to the Head. New York, Springer-Verlag, 1992.)

exposed in its pars atlantica, where the artery runs parallel to the lamina of the atlas before entering the foramen magnum.

The approach to the suboccipital segment of the distal VA is posterior. The patient lies prone in the "park-bench" position. The incision is racket-shaped with a horizontal segment below the occipital bone from the midline laterally to the level of the sternocleidomastoid. There the incision becomes oblique and follows the posterior belly of the sternocleidomastoid muscle. The superficial nucchal muscle layer (splenius capitis and semispinalis) is transected (Fig. 141-20). The accessory spinal nerve is isolated laterally below the sternocleidomastoid muscle. The transverse process of C1 is located by palpation. The short posterior muscles between the atlas and occipital bone (obliquus capitis and rectus capitis posterior major) are divided (Fig. 141-21). The artery can now be seen enveloped by a dense venous plexus (Fig. 141-22) from which it is extricated by bipolar coagulation and microligature of these

veins. The artery can be exposed from its emergence at the top of C1 to the dura mater (Fig. 141-23). Through the same posterior approach, the internal carotid artery can be isolated posterior and medial to the sternocleidomastoid after mobilization and retraction of the hypoglossal and vagus nerves that, at this level, cover its posterior wall. The distal anastomosis of the vein graft to the VA is performed first. The vein is allowed to distend over the lamina of the atlas and into its site of anastomosis at the posterior wall of the internal carotid artery (Figs. 141-24 and 141-25).

■ RESULTS

The author's group's experience with reconstruction of the VA comprises 421 reconstructions, of which 280 were proximal and 141 were distal operations. Fifty VA reconstructions were performed in combination with a carotid operation.

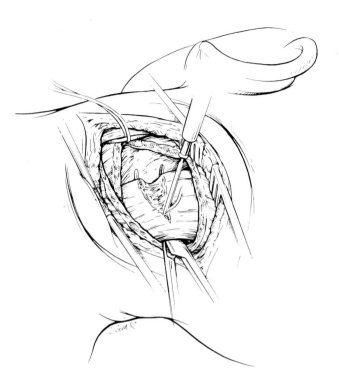

FIGURE 141-20 Posterior approach to the suboccipital segment of the distal vertebral artery: division of the splenius capitis and semispinalis.

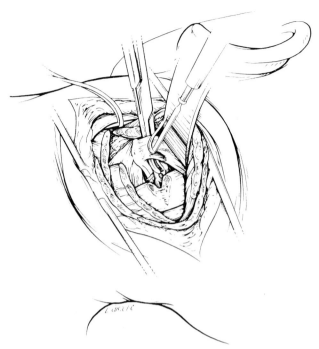

FIGURE 141-21 Posterior approach to the suboccipital vertebral artery: division of the obliquus and rectus capitis.

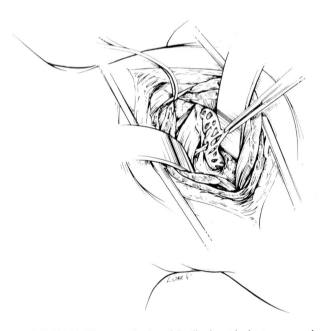

FIGURE 141-22 The pars atlantica of the distal vertebral artery exposed and surrounded by a dense venous plexus.

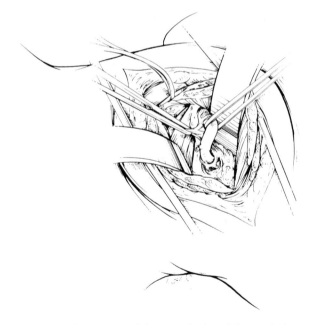

FIGURE 141-23 Exposure of the pars atlantica of the vertebral artery from its exit from the transverse foramen of C1 to its entrance in the dura mater.

Proximal Vertebral Artery Reconstruction

Among patients undergoing proximal operations, there were no deaths or stroke in those who had only a vertebral reconstruction. When the proximal VA reconstruction was combined with a carotid operation, the observed stroke and death rates increased to 5.7%.

There were four instances of immediate postoperative thrombosis (1.4%). Three of the four patients had vein grafts interposed between the VA and the common carotid due to a short V1 segment. The grafts kinked and thrombosed. With better attention to avoidance of injury to the sympathetic chain, the incidence of mostly temporary Horner's syndrome has decreased to 8.4% in the last 118 patients.

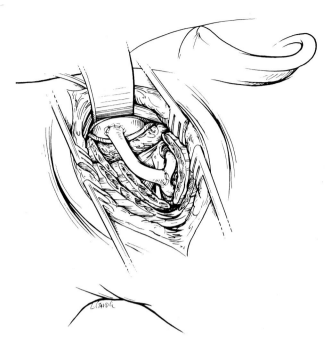

FIGURE 141-24 A distal cervical internal carotid to suboccipital vertebral bypass.

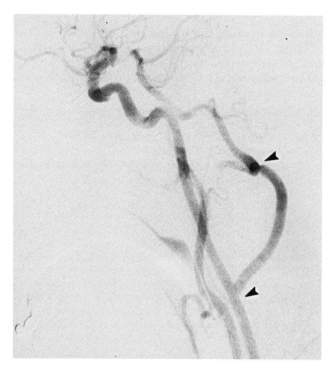

FIGURE 141-25 Bypass from mid-cervical internal carotid artery to suboccipital vertebral artery (*arrowheads*).

Lymphocele was also a common complication early in our experience. By avoiding transfixion sutures and securely ligating the thoracic duct and any accessory ducts, this complication practically has been eliminated. There was one postoperative hemorrhage necessitating reoperation in a patient in whom the origin of the VA was occluded with a hemoclip that became dislodged. A 5-0 transfixion ligature has been used routinely since then.

The cumulative patency rate of proximal VA reconstruction at 10 years is 92%.

Distal Vertebral Artery Reconstruction

Operations on the distal VA carry higher stroke and death rates than operations on the proximal VA (Table 141-1). Among 141 distal operations, there were seven strokes, five of which resulted in deaths: Three patients had brain stem strokes and deaths related to the procedure. Two died of a large hemispheric infarction.

Routine intraoperative postreconstruction arteriography was not used for the first part of our series. In the first 53 distal reconstructions done before January 1991, there were three stroke/deaths (4.5%) and an 11% rate of immediate postoperative thrombosis. After the introduction of routine intraoperative arteriography in 1991, we have performed an additional 88 distal vertebral reconstructions and, in this group, there was only one stroke/death (1.1%) and a 1.1% rate of immediate postoperative thrombosis. Although the improved results partly reflect a learning curve, they are primarily the consequence of correction of technical flaws that are identified by arteriography during the operation.

The cumulative patency rate for distal vertebral reconstruction at 5 years is 80%. Similar to patients undergoing standard carotid endarterectomies, 70% of the patients undergoing distal VA reconstruction are dead at 5-year follow-up, mostly from cardiac disease. Freedom from stroke among survivors at 5 years is 97%. In this group, symptoms were cured in 71% of patients and improved in 16% of patients.

It is appropriate to consider our experience in two periods. Before 1991, our problems were related to a learning curve for new procedures and unfamiliar territory. Our indications also changed during this time. In 1991, we started using routine intraoperative arteriography and we had the continuous availability of a dedicated vascular anesthesia team and of MR technology. Our protocols and indications have not changed since then. Table 141-1 shows the difference in the rates of strokes and deaths for this period. The data since January 1991 reflect the management, risk, and outcomes of VA reconstruction today.

Table 141-1	Rates of Stroke and Death for All Vertebral Artery Reconstructions Before and Since January 1991			
	BEFORE 1/91 (N = 215)		**SINCE 1/91 (N = 206)**	
	No.	Percentage	No.	Percentage
Stroke	9	4.1	3	1.4
Death	7	3.2	1	0.4
Death/stroke	11	5.1	3	1.4

■ SUMMARY

VA reconstruction can be accomplished with minimal morbidity in its proximal segment and with a combined stroke/death rate of less than 1.1% in its distal segment. This intervention achieves excellent protection from stroke in the posterior brain.

■ REFERENCES

1. Caplan LR, Tettenborn B: Embolism in the posterior circulation. In Berguer R, Caplan LR (eds): Vertebrobasilar Arterial Disease. St. Louis, Quality Medical, 1992, pp 52-65.
2. Pessin MS: Posterior cerebral artery disease and occipital ischemia. In Berguer R, Caplan LR (eds): Vertebrobasilar Arterial Disease. St. Louis, Quality Medical, 1992, pp 66-75.
3. Bauer RB: Mechanical compression of the vertebral arteries. In Berguer R, Bauer RB (eds): Vertebrobasilar Arterial Occlusive Disease: Medical and Surgical Management. New York, Raven, 1984, pp 45-71.
4. Ruotolo C, Hazan H, Rancurel G, Kieffer E: Dynamic arteriography. In Berguer R, Caplan LR (eds): Vertebrobasilar Arterial Disease. St. Louis, Quality Medical, 1992, pp 116-123.
5. Berguer R, Higgins RF, Nelson R: Noninvasive diagnosis of reversal of vertebral artery flow. N Engl J Med 302:1349, 1980.
6. Berguer R, Kieffer E: Surgery of the Arteries to the Head. New York, Springer-Verlag, 1992.
7. Berguer R, Andaya LV, Bauer RB: Vertebral artery bypass. Arch Surg 111:976, 1976.
8. Berguer R, Bauer RB: Vertebral artery reconstruction: A successful technique in selected patients. Ann Surg 193:441, 1981.
9. Edwards WH, Mulherin JL Jr: The surgical approach to significant stenosis of vertebral and subclavian arteries. Surgery 87:20, 1980.
10. Malone JM, Moore WS, Hamilton R, et al: Combined carotid-vertebral vascular disease. Arch Surg 115:783, 1980.
11. Roon AJ, Ehrenfeld WK, Cooke PB, et al: Vertebral artery reconstruction. Am J Surg 138:29, 1979.
12. Berguer R: Distal vertebral artery bypass: Technique, the occipital connection and potential uses. J Vasc Surg 2:621, 1985.
13. Kieffer E, Rancurel G, Richart T: Reconstruction of the distal cervical vertebral artery. In Berguer R, Bauer RB (eds): Vertebrobasilar Arterial Occlusive Disease: Medical and Surgical Management. New York, Raven, 1984, pp 265-289.
14. Berguer R: Revascularization of the vertebral arteries. In Nyhus L, Baker RJ, Fischer JE (eds): Mastery of Surgery. Boston, Little, Brown, 1997, p 1937.
15. Berguer R, Morasch M, Kline RA: A review of 100 consecutive reconstructions of the distal vertebral artery for embolic and hemodynamic disease. J Vasc Surg 27:852-859, 1998.

Chapter

Endovascular and Surgical Management of Extracranial Carotid Fibromuscular Arterial Dysplasia

142

PETER A. SCHNEIDER, MD

Fibromuscular dysplasia (FMD) is a nonatheromatous degenerative process of unknown etiology that involves long, unbranched segments of medium-sized arteries, such as the renal artery, the internal carotid artery, the external iliac artery, and the splenic and hepatic arteries (in order of frequency).[1-3] Although this disease has been described in Chapter 27, certain aspects pertinent to its involvement of the extracranial cerebral arteries are summarized here.

FMD is found in 0.25% to 0.68% of consecutive cerebral arteriograms.[4,5] In one series of 2000 carotid operations, it was the identified pathology in 3.4% of cases.[6] In another sizeable series of carotid operations, rigid dilation for FMD was performed in less than 1%.[7] Among the four distinct types of FMD, the internal carotid artery is most often affected by medial fibroplasia, which results in an arteriographic appearance resembling a "string of beads"

(Fig. 142-1) and constitutes 80% to 95% of the lesions.[4,6,8,9] In one large series,[4] medial fibroplasia was seen in 89%, with a fusiform narrowing in 7% and an eccentric septum-like lesion in 4%. The arterial segments involved tend to be more distal than that with arteriosclerosis, in the mid and distal segments of the extracranial internal carotid artery. The artery is often elongated, tortuous, and occasionally kinked. Carotid FMD is bilateral in 39% to 86% of reported cases.[1,4,10,11] Women predominate in most series and constitute 60% to 90% of patients.[1,6,10-15]

■ CLINICAL PRESENTATION

Extracranial cerebral artery FMD may present as either an incidental finding without symptoms or as the cause of neurologic events. Symptomatic presentations in large,

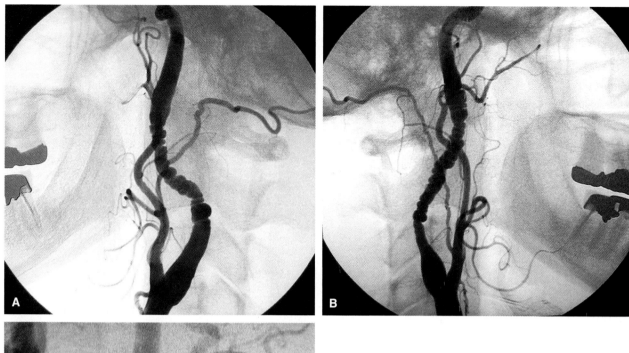

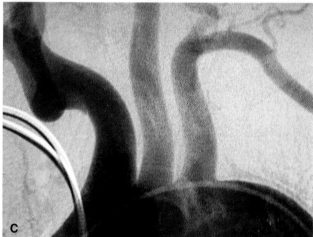

FIGURE 142-1 **A** and **B,** Carotid arteriogram demonstrating the classic appearance of fibromuscular dysplasia in the usual location opposite the C1-C3 vertebral bodies and intervening disks. Note the low bifurcation and long internal carotid artery. The lesions are present bilaterally in this 43-year-old woman. **C,** The aortic arch shows no evidence of disease, and the arch branches originate near the top of the arch.

contemporary series of treated patients demonstrate the capacity of FMD to cause transient ischemic attack (TIA), stroke, and disability (Table 142-1). Stroke was the initial finding in 12% to 27% of patients, hemispheric TIA occurred in 31% to 42%, and amaurosis fugax was present in 22% to 28%.[6,15,16] Other series were similar with respect to presenting symptoms.[12,17,18]

■ NATURAL HISTORY

Many series have documented the potential for carotid FMD to present with symptoms, but the natural history of asymptomatic lesions is not clear. In one series of 79 patients, most of whom were found to have carotid FMD incidentally on cerebral angiogram (0.6% of the total), only three patients (4%) subsequently suffered a cerebral

Table 142-1	Presenting Symptoms in Patients with Extracranial Fibromuscular Arterial Dysplasia		
	SCHNEIDER et al* (*n* = 115)	**CHICHE et al†** (*n* = 70)	**MOREAU et al‡** (*n* = 58)
Hemispheric TIA (%)	42	36	31
Hemispheric stroke (%)	23	27	12
Amaurosis fugax (%)	22	NA	28
Vertebrobasilar TIA or stroke (%)	NA	45	22

*Data from Schneider PA, Cunningham CG, Ehrenfeld WK, et al: Fibromuscular dysplasia of the carotid artery. In Veith FJ, Hobson RW, Williams RA, Wilson SE (eds): Vascular Surgery: Principles and Practice. New York, McGraw-Hill, 1994, pp 711-717.
† Chiche L, Bahnini A, Koskas F, et al: Occlusive fibromuscular disease of the arteries supplying the brain: Results of surgical treatment. Ann Vasc Surg 11:496-504, 1997.
‡Data from Moreau P, Albat B, Thevenet A: Fibromuscular dysplasia of the internal carotid artery: Long-term results. J Cardiovasc Surg 34:465-472, 1993.
TIA, transient ischemic attack; NA, not available.

ischemic event during an average follow-up of 5 years.[13] When small groups of asymptomatic patients were studied prospectively, fewer than 10% of patients went on to experience new neurologic symptoms.[2,10,13] Nevertheless, two series have shown that about a third of these lesions demonstrate significant angiographic progression with time.[2,12] None of these studies has followed a significant number of *high-grade* asymptomatic stenoses, in which the risk of stroke would be expected to be higher.

Most reported cases of symptomatic carotid FMD have been treated with dilation of the corresponding artery. There is no study in which a large number of patients with carotid FMD who presented with focal cerebral ischemic events were observed expectantly. In one series, 13 patients who presented with either TIA (10 patients) or stroke (3 patients) did not undergo surgical correction of carotid FMD but instead were observed. Only one patient remained symptomatic.[19] Some have suggested that symptomatic lesions should not be considered for operation until their natural history is better understood.[19,20] However, this advice is not useful, since there is no way to define the natural history of these rare lesions. At present, we are left with a rare cause of focal cerebral ischemic events caused by extracranial carotid stenosis, which can be repaired with a fairly simple open operation or a percutaneous balloon dilation.

■ ASSOCIATED LESIONS

Concurrently presenting lesions that frequently complicate the management of carotid FMD include (1) atherosclerotic occlusive disease at the carotid bifurcation, (2) extracranial carotid artery aneurysms, (3) carotid artery dissection, (4) vertebral artery FMD, (5) intracranial aneurysms and occlusive disease, and (6) renal artery FMD.

Atherosclerotic Occlusive Disease

Ipsilateral atheromatous carotid bifurcation disease is present in as many as 20% of individuals.[6,21] Although it may not always be possible to attribute symptoms to one lesion or the other, when atherosclerotic and fibromuscular dysplastic lesions present together in the same symptomatic artery, they are usually treated simultaneously. In a series of 72 operations for extracranial FMD, carotid endarterectomy was performed as part of a combined procedure in 14 patients (19%).[6]

Extracranial Carotid Artery Aneurysms

Extracranial carotid artery aneurysms are uncommon, and those associated with FMD are rare. Among 130 extracranial carotid aneurysms in one literature review, 2.3% were associated with FMD.[22] In a single institution series of 15 carotid aneurysms, one third were thought to be caused by FMD, and most were successfully managed with resection and replacement grafting.[23]

Carotid Artery Dissection

FMD may play a role in the development of spontaneous dissection of the carotid artery. This often catastrophic event is responsible for 4% of strokes and is associated with fibrodysplasia in approximately 15% of cases.[24-26] In a series of 50 patients undergoing surgery for carotid dissection, 12% had FMD as the etiology and were treated with either graduated rigid dilation or vein graft replacement.[27] FMD is often suggested among the potential etiologic mechanisms of spontaneous carotid dissection.[8,28-30] However, reports of spontaneous dissection occurring subsequent to the identification of asymptomatic carotid FMD are not available. The structural abnormality of the arterial wall in FMD and its association with spontaneous dissection suggest that dilation of the artery may pose an increased risk of perioperative dissection. Nevertheless, dissection is an unusual complication of dilation.[1,6,15,31]

Vertebral Artery Disease

Vertebral artery FMD is identified in 7% to 38% of those with carotid lesions and occasionally presents as an isolated finding.[6,12,15] Vertebral artery disease is usually located at the level of the C2 vertebral body and does not extend intracranially.[9] FMD has been associated with vertebral artery dissection following neck or spine manipulation.[32] Fortunately, it is rarely responsible for symptoms and does not usually complicate the management of the internal carotid lesion. One series reported 32 patients with vertebrobasilar TIA and stroke due to vertebral artery FMD.[15] Among 12 vertebral artery reconstructions performed, half were for isolated vertebral FMD and half were performed at the time of rigid dilation of a carotid lesion. The most frequently employed operative approach was a vein bypass to the distal vertebral artery.

Intracranial Aneurysms and Occlusive Disease

Intracranial aneurysms, another expression of the dysplastic process, are found in at least 10% and as many as 51% of patients with internal carotid FMD (≈20% on average).[10,12] Not only do these pose an independent threat of rupture and subarachnoid hemorrhage but their natural history has the potential to be worsened by relieving a proximal stenosis. In one series, intracranial aneurysms and extracranial FMD each caused half the symptoms, and in another, half the strokes were due to aneurysm rupture.[10,19] In most studies, however, intracranial aneurysms produced one quarter to one third of the rate of neurologic symptoms caused by the cervical carotid lesion.[2]

Intracranial aneurysms should be treated on their own individual merits (e.g., size, presenting symptoms, coexistence of hypertension), just as the cervical fibrodysplastic lesions should, with primary attention directed toward the most threatening lesion. The presence of a small, asymptomatic intracranial aneurysm should not dissuade the vascular surgeon from repairing a threatening cervical lesion.

The supraclinoid vasculature may also be affected by occlusive disease that suggests FMD as the etiology. This occurs rarely, primarily in young and middle aged women without other apparent etiologic factors. There may be associated evidence of FMD of the cervical internal carotid artery.[33]

Renal Artery Disease

Renal artery FMD coexists in 8% to 40% of patients with carotid FMD.[2,6,16] It is an additional threat in patients with intracranial aneurysms since it often presents with severe hypertension. Because renal artery FMD generally responds well to percutaneous balloon angioplasty, the possibility of coexistent renal artery involvement should be considered prior to the treatment of carotid stenosis (see Chapter 129).

■ DIAGNOSTIC EVALUATION

Most asymptomatic patients with a carotid bruit and those with hemispheric or nonfocal neurologic symptoms undergo carotid duplex scanning. Duplex may reveal velocity elevation resulting from FMD, but the lesion may be missed because it is located more distally than the usual atherosclerotic plaque.[9,34] Catheter-based contrast arteriography is the best way to evaluate FMD of the extracranial cerebral arteries. No other method provides the anatomic detail provided by arteriography. Many cases of carotid FMD are discovered during arteriography.[9,35] When carotid FMD is identified, intracranial vascular anatomy should be evaluated to check for the presence of intracranial aneurysms as well as contralateral carotid stenosis and vertebral artery disease. Magnetic resonance (MR) angiography has not been particularly useful in the diagnostic evaluation of FMD, but it may be beneficial for follow-up of known FMD.[35] Patients with symptomatic carotid FMD should undergo computed tomography or MR imaging of the brain.

■ TREATMENT

Because of the lack of sophisticated data on carotid FMD, the following challenges frequently arise in its management and must be considered during the treatment planning stage.

1. One of the key driving factors in the treatment of carotid bifurcation atherosclerosis, the degree of stenosis, is not possible to determine with any reliability in carotid FMD. This makes the severity of the disease in a given patient extremely difficult to assess. This factor also compromises the follow-up of asymptomatic patients.
2. It is not always possible to determine which of two concurrently presenting lesions is causing cerebral symptoms, as is the case when carotid FMD presents with coexistent, significant bifurcation atherosclerosis. These lesions are usually treated simultaneously.
3. When symptomatic carotid FMD is treated, it can be a challenge to decide how to manage a contralateral severe but asymptomatic lesion. Although asymptomatic lesions seem to have a generally benign course, this may not be the case in a patient who suffered a stroke on the contralateral side due to the same pathology.
4. Carotid FMD patients often present with nonfocal symptoms, some of which may be due to global ischemia. The indications for intervention in this situation are ambiguous.
5. The presence of an intracranial aneurysm may alter the treatment sequence or the surgical approach.
6. The presence of hypertension from renal artery FMD may complicate any procedure performed for carotid FMD.

7. Percutaneous transluminal angioplasty (PTA) has been successful for the treatment of renal artery FMD, and carotid angioplasty and stenting has a growing role in the management of carotid disease; however, the results and durability of balloon angioplasty and stent placement for carotid FMD are not known. Some patients may be better served with a percutaneous approach, but it is not yet possible to use data to guide patient selection for these different treatments.

Indications for Intervention

On the basis of the relative safety and effectiveness of surgical intervention (see later), operative management is appropriate for lesions causing focal ischemic events (hemispheric or ocular) or episodes of cerebral hypoperfusion. The lesion that presents with a focal cerebral ischemic event has declared itself and remains a significant threat. Hypoperfusion is rare but can occur in the setting of critical bilateral carotid FMD or even unilateral disease when there is a significant defect in the circle of Willis. High-surgical-risk, symptomatic patients should be considered for percutaneous balloon angioplasty, especially if cerebral protection devices are available. It is not clear whether carotid balloon angioplasty should be accompanied by stent placement in FMD. Stent placement is usually not required following PTA in renal artery FMD because results are excellent without stents and the patients are usually otherwise young and healthy with good life expectancy. However, stents are routinely placed when carotid bifurcation stenosis is treated percutaneously and there is some likelihood that stent placement after PTA helps to stabilize flaps and disrupted dysplastic tissue. There is little experience with PTA for FMD. Since there is a low prevalence of these cases, some time will be required to determine the role of PTA.

Arterial Repair: Rationale and Results

Methods of mechanical intervention advocated for the treatment of carotid FMD include the following:

- Open, graduated, rigid dilation
- Open transluminal balloon dilation with outflow control
- PTA (with or without stent placement, with or without cerebral protection devices)

The usual fibrodysplastic lesion encountered in the internal carotid artery responds to mechanical dilation. Over the past several decades, this has been performed with relative success and safety by means of rigid dilators of progressively enlarging sizes passed antegrade into the internal carotid artery with outflow control.[1,6,14-18] This approach permits gentle disruption of the obstructive webs while allowing associated debris to be flushed out of the artery.

The results of three large, contemporary series of surgically managed patients are presented in Tables 142-2 and 142-3. These reports consist primarily of patients undergoing rigid carotid dilation but also include some instances of carotid replacement and vertebral revascularization.[6,15,16] The risk of perioperative stroke for surgical treatment in these series ranged from 1.4% to 2.6%. TIA

Table 142-2 Results of Surgical Treatment of Extracranial Fibromuscular Arterial Dysplasia

	SCHNEIDER et al* (*n* = 115)	CHICHE et al† (*n* = 70)	MOREAU et al‡ (*n* = 58)
Operations	168	78	72
Operative stroke (%)	1.7	2.6	1.4
Operative TIA (%)	6.0	7.7	1.4
Operative death (%)	0	1.3	0

*Data from Schneider PA, Cunningham CG, Ehrenfeld WK, et al: Fibromuscular dysplasia of the carotid artery. In Veith FJ, Hobson RW, Williams RA, Wilson SE (eds): Vascular Surgery: Principles and Practice. New York, McGraw-Hill, 1994, pp 711-717.
† Chiche L, Bahnini A, Koskas F, et al: Occlusive fibromuscular disease of the arteries supplying the brain: Results of surgical treatment. Ann Vasc Surg 11:496-504, 1997.
‡Data from Moreau P, Albat B, Thevenet A: Fibromuscular dysplasia of the internal carotid artery: Long-term results. J Cardiovasc Surg 34:465-472, 1993.
TIA, transient ischemic attack; NA, not available.

Table 142-3 Late Follow-Up after Surgical Treatment of Extracranial Fibromuscular Arterial Dysplasia

	SCHNEIDER et al* (*n* = 115)	CHICHE et al† (*n* = 70)	MOREAU et al‡ (*n* = 58)
Follow-up (mean yr)	1-17	7 (1-15)	13 (6-22)
Recurrent stenosis (%)	2.3	0	0
Late occlusion (%)	0.6	0	2.8
Late stroke (%)	1.2	2.9	3.8
Death (other causes) (%)	NA	8.6	13.2

*Data from Schneider PA, Cunningham CG, Ehrenfeld WK, et al: Fibromuscular dysplasia of the carotid artery. In Veith FJ, Hobson RW, Williams RA, Wilson SE (eds): Vascular Surgery: Principles and Practice. New York, McGraw-Hill, 1994, pp 711-717.
† Chiche L, Bahnini A, Koskas F, et al: Occlusive fibromuscular disease of the arteries supplying the brain: Results of surgical treatment. Ann Vasc Surg 11:496-504, 1997.
‡Data from Moreau P, Albat B, Thevenet A: Fibromuscular dysplasia of the internal carotid artery: Long-term results. J Cardiovasc Surg 34:465-472, 1993.
NA, not available.

occurred in 1.4% to 7.7%, and perforation occurred twice in 318 operations (0.6%).[6,16] Cranial nerve injuries, most of which were transient, resulted from extensive distal operative exposure of the internal carotid artery and were reported to occur in 5.1% to 16.7% of cases.[6,15]

Excellent long-term follow-up data are available (see Table 142-3). Late stroke developed in 1.2% to 3.8% of patients, and nearly all late deaths (up to 22 years) were due to non-neurologic causes. In one series,[15] 94% of patients underwent duplex scanning (mean follow-up, 7 years). The actuarial rates of primary patency, survival, and stroke-free survival were 94%, 96%, and 94%, respectively, at 5 years and 94%, 82%, and 88%, respectively, at 10 years. When follow-up angiography is obtained, it usually demonstrates a normal-sized lumen (Fig. 142-2).

When the length of the diseased internal carotid artery extends too distally to be dissected out and ensure adequate control of manual dilation, some authors have advised balloon angioplasty combined with open, outflow control.[36-39] The benefit of this approach is the opportunity for a controlled dilation while maintaining the ability to back-bleed the artery and avoid embolization of debris from the dilated lesion. Among a small number of patients from different reports, it appears that early results with this approach may be comparable to those of rigid dilation.

PTA may be a reasonable approach for carotid FMD.[40,41] The rationale for this approach is based on the success of PTA in the treatment of renal artery FMD and the dramatic improvement in the technology that supports balloon angioplasty and stenting of carotid bifurcation

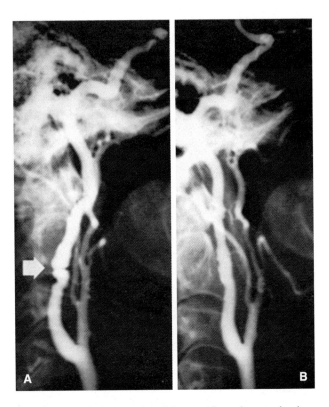

FIGURE 142-2 A, Preoperative right carotid arteriogram showing a localized zone of fibromuscular dysplasia characterized by an intraluminal diaphragm *(arrow).* **B,** Postoperative right carotid arteriogram following graduated intraluminal dilation. The carotid lumen is now widely patent.

atherosclerosis. Balloon angioplasty has fewer complications than open surgery of the renal artery and provides reasonable long-term results. The development of distal cerebral protection devices has made the percutaneous approach to carotid FMD conceptually much more appealing. However, it is not clear whether this approach can be readily applied to carotid FMD. The emboli produced by PTA may consist of disrupted tissue and be quite large. Balloon angioplasty may cause dissection. Carotid stent placement may be challenging since many of these patients have redundancy, kinks, and coils of the cervical internal carotid artery. There is only limited experience with stent placement near the base of the skull. In addition, no one knows the implications of stent placement in patients with life expectancy of many decades, as is the case with many FMD patients. In contrast, surgical dilation of the carotid lesion is a simple, safe operation in a generally younger population with fewer comorbid conditions. The open operation for carotid FMD appears to be safer than carotid endarterectomy.

Unfortunately, it is not possible at present to develop a balanced approach since few data are available regarding perioperative complications or longer-term success. Since 1981, a few dozen patients have been reported in the literature as having undergone balloon angioplasty for carotid FMD, usually as part of larger series of angioplasty patients.[31,41-44] In one case report,[31] postangioplasty carotid dissection resulted in a stroke; in other reports, however, no specific mention was made of periprocedural complications. No follow-up is available beyond the perioperative period.

■ SURGICAL TECHNIQUE

Exposure is similar to that for carotid endarterectomy except that *higher* internal carotid artery exposure is usually required to ensure that safe dilation is carried out under direct vision. The posterior belly of the digastric muscle may be divided, but subluxation of the mandible is rarely required. If the distal internal carotid artery is not accessible, balloon angioplasty should be considered. The normal arterial segment above the highest point of involvement is apparent by direct inspection, and the internal carotid artery is encircled at this point.

The surgeon should take care not to manipulate the intervening segment of the internal carotid artery as it is gently exposed throughout its length. Stump pressures or electroencephalographic monitoring is *not* ordinarily needed for this brief procedure but may be indicated if a more extensive procedure is planned (e.g., bifurcation endarterectomy, correction of redundancy, or interposition grafting). Except in such unusual circumstances, a shunt is unnecessary.

Heparin is administered (75 to 100 U/kg) prior to interrupting flow. A single 500-mL unit of dextran 40, at 25 mL/hr, beginning at the time of operation and continued during the immediate postoperative period, may help prevent early deposition of thrombotic material on the inner surfaces of the arteriotomy and the fractured septa. The common carotid artery is cross-clamped. Traction on a Silastic "sling" placed around the internal carotid artery just above the bifurcation is performed to straighten the artery. A short arteriotomy is made in the internal carotid artery at the base of the bulb. Graduated metal dilators are then gently passed up the straightened internal carotid artery, beginning with a 1.5-mm-diameter probe and progressing up to a 3.5-mm-, or, occasionally, a 4.0-mm-diameter probe (Fig. 142-3). There is usually a series of "giving" sensations felt as each septal stenosis is gently fractured for the first time, but this is not felt thereafter.

The procedure is terminated after the segment has been gently stretched to full diameter throughout its course. This can usually be observed under direct vision. It is important not to exceed this gentle stretching and, therefore, not to proceed beyond a 4-mm diameter. Back-bleeding following passage of the dilators should be thorough because large debris are sometimes retrieved. The short arteriotomy is rapidly closed with a simple running suture of 6-0 polypropylene. Careful interrogation of the entire segment with a Doppler probe or duplex scanner after restoration of flow ensures patency without turbulence or residual defect.

Poor candidates for this operation include patients with lesions that are too distal to be exposed and patients who have contraindications to open surgery. In these cases, the options are open exposure for PTA with outflow control or, more likely, transfemoral PTA with a cerebral protection device with stent placement for dissection.

When there is significant associated bifurcation atherosclerosis, a concomitant endarterectomy or carotid bifurcation stent may be performed. If an open approach is planned, the initial arteriotomy is *longitudinal*. If severe elongation and kinking are present, such that the kinking cannot be ruled out as a cause of hypoperfusion episodes (particularly position-related syncope), an oblique arteriotomy, initially placed anteriorly at the base of the carotid bulb at the bifurcation, can be extended circumferentially after the dilation procedure; it is then carried longitudinally down the common carotid artery, allowing the internal carotid to be translocated downward until it is straightened and anastomosed at this lower position. Another option is to resect or imbricate a segment of artery to remove the redundancy.

■ ENDOVASCULAR TECHNIQUE

The diagnostic evaluation for carotid FMD is likely to include an arch aortogram and carotid and cerebral arteriogram. This is a valuable tool in planning carotid PTA. Most of the carotid FMD patients are young, and they are much more likely than other vascular patients to have an arch favorable for percutaneous carotid artery access. The carotid arteries frequently arise from the superior aspect of the arch (see Fig. 142-1). The carotid artery sheath may be placed in the distal common carotid artery since the bifurcation is usually not diseased. Use of a cerebral protection device is highly desirable. If a distal occlusion balloon or filter is used, placement is likely to be in the petrous carotid or above, so that it is distal to the disease. This segment of the internal carotid artery is more prone to spasm and dissection than is the extracranial segment so caution should be exercised. FMD generally covers a longer distance of the internal carotid artery than does carotid atherosclerosis and therefore may require a longer balloon (4 cm) or multiple inflations of a shorter (2 cm) balloon. The

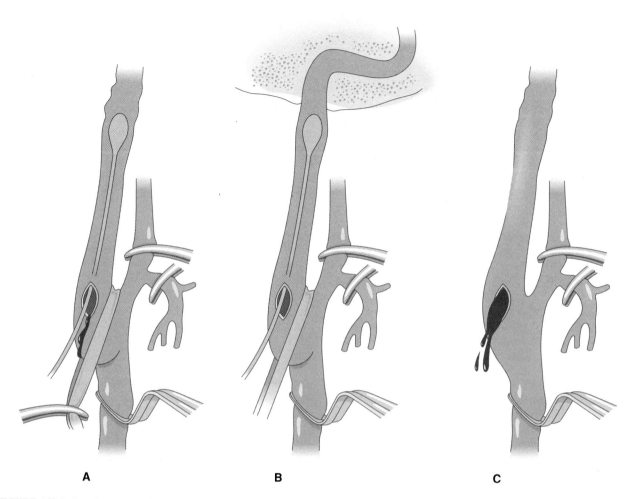

A   **B**   **C**

FIGURE 142-3 Drawing representing the main features of the operative technique. **A,** Straightening of the carotid artery with downward traction on a Silastic sling. **B,** Gentle, graduated dilation of the internal carotid artery from 2 to 4 mm. Passage of the dilator to the bony canal at the base of the skull is shown. **C,** Back-bleeding of the artery to remove dislodged debris. (**A-C,** From Wylie EJ, Stoney RJ, Ehrenfeld WK, Effeney DJ: Nonatherosclerotic diseases of the extracranial carotid arteries. In Manual of Vascular Surgery. New York, Springer-Verlag, 1986, pp 184-185.)

balloon should be undersized slightly to the intended diameter of the artery to help avoid dissection or rupture. Fortunately, most extracranial carotid FMD is medial fibroplasia, which is amenable to dilation and less likely to include aneurysmal dilation. For FMD lesions that contain aneurysmal segments, PTA is probably not advisable. Given a track record of success with PTA of FMD lesions in other locations, primary stent placement is probably not warranted. However, if dissection, residual stenosis, or flaps are present on completion arteriography, stents should be considered. Smaller stents are used than what is usually the case with bifurcation disease, since self-expanding stents are sized for the distal internal carotid artery (5 or 6 mm) rather than the common carotid artery (8 or 10 mm). Kinks, coils, and redundancy are common in FMD. These configurations present unique situations for stenting. Stent placement in a kink should be performed cautiously since the extra curvature is usually transferred to another segment of the artery and may exacerbate a kink in that area. Stent placement in a coil should be avoided altogether.

■ SUMMARY

More than half the patients present with cerebral ischemic events. Fewer than half of these patients will have suffered infarcts, and only half of the latter will be left with significant neurologic deficits (i.e., ~10% of the total). The natural history of incidentally identified lesions is more benign, with one third showing angiographic progression but less than one tenth ultimately producing cerebral ischemic symptoms.

Surgical dilation of carotid FMD is safe and effective, and any surgeon who obtains excellent results with carotid endarterectomy can expect reasonable results with this procedure. It is appropriate to operate on lesions producing focal hemispheric or ocular ischemic events or on critical stenoses that cause hypoperfusion symptoms. An aggressive posture with asymptomatic lesions, however, can be justified only for unusually threatening combinations of lesions (e.g., operating on one of two severe bilateral stenoses). Associated intracranial aneurysms should be managed according to their own merits and should not be allowed to compromise valid indications for operation on the cervical lesion. Balloon angioplasty carries a small but definite risk of thromboembolic events, and there are insufficient data to clarify the indications for its use. The recent development of cerebral protection devices and stents is likely to make PTA an excellent treatment option for many patients.

It is possible to develop a logical, selective management approach based on much that is known and to apply it to individual patients based on their clinical findings, operative risk, and longevity outlook.

■ REFERENCES

1. Effeney DJ: Surgery for fibromuscular dysplasia of the carotid artery: Indications, technique, and results. In Moore WS (ed): Surgery for Cerebrovascular Disease. New York, Churchill Livingstone, 1987, pp 525-533.
2. Stanley JC, Wakefield TW: Arterial fibrodysplasia. In Rutherford RB (ed): Vascular Surgery, 3rd ed. Philadelphia, WB Saunders, 1990, pp 245-265.
3. Begelman SM, Olin JW: Nonatherosclerotic arterial disease of the extracranial cerebrovasculature. Semin Vasc Surg 13:153-164, 2000.
4. Osborn AG, Anderson RE: Angiographic spectrum of cervical and intracranial fibromuscular dysplasia. Stroke 8:617, 1977.
5. Houser OW, Baker HL: Fibrovascular dysplasia and other uncommon diseases of the cervical carotid artery: Angiographic aspects. AJR Am J Roentgenol 104:201, 1968.
6. Moreau P, Albat B, Thevenet A: Fibromuscular dysplasia of the internal carotid artery: Long-term results. J Cardiovasc Surg 34:465-472, 1993.
7. Taylor SM, Langan EM, Snyder BA, et al: Nonendarterectomy procedures of the carotid artery: A five-year review. Am Surg 65:323-327, 1999.
8. Fisicaro M, Tonizzo M, Mucelli RP, et al: Fibromuscular dysplasia: A case report of multivessel vascular involvement. Int Angiol 13:347-350, 1994.
9. Furie DM, Tien RD: Fibromuscular dysplasia of arteries of the head and neck: Imaging findings. AJR Am J Roentgenol 162:1205-1209, 1994.
10. Mettinger KL, Ericson K: Fibromuscular dysplasia and the brain: I. Observations on angiographic, clinical, and genetic characteristics. Stroke 13:46, 1982.
11. Schievink WI, Bjornsson J: Fibromuscular dysplasia of the internal carotid artery: A clinicopathological study. Clin Neuropathol 15:2-6, 1996.
12. So EL, Toole JF, Dalal P, et al: Cephalic fibromuscular dysplasia in 32 patients: Clinical findings and radiologic features. Arch Neurol 38:619, 1981.
13. Corrin LS, Sandok BA, Houser OW: Cerebral ischemic events in patients with carotid artery fibromuscular dysplasia. Arch Neurol 38:616, 1981.
14. Morris GC Jr, Lechter A, DeBakey ME: Surgical treatment of fibromuscular disease of the carotid arteries. Arch Surg 96:636, 1968.
15. Chiche L, Bahnini A, Koskas F, et al: Occlusive fibromuscular disease of the arteries supplying the brain: Results of surgical treatment. Ann Vasc Surg 11:496-504, 1997.
16. Schneider PA, Cunningham CG, Ehrenfeld WK, et al: Fibromuscular dysplasia of the carotid artery. In Veith FJ, Hobson RW, Williams RA, Wilson SE (eds): Vascular Surgery: Principles and Practice. New York, McGraw-Hill, 1994, pp 711-717.
17. Starr DS, Lawrie GM, Morris GC: Fibromuscular disease of carotid arteries: Long-term results of graduated internal dilatation. Stroke 12:196, 1981.
18. Collins GJ, Rich NM, Clagett GP, et al: Fibromuscular dysplasia of the internal carotid arteries: Clinical experience and follow-up. Ann Surg 194:89, 1981.
19. Stewart MT, Moritz MW, Smith RB, et al: The natural history of carotid fibromuscular dysplasia. J Vasc Surg 3:305, 1986.
20. Patman RD, Thompson JE, Talkington CM, et al: Natural history of fibromuscular dysplasia of the carotid artery. Stroke 2:135, 1980.
21. Effeney DJ, Ehrenfeld WK: Extracranial fibromuscular disease. In Rutherford RB (ed): Vascular Surgery, 3rd ed. Philadelphia, WB Saunders, 1990, pp 1412-1417.
22. Miyauchi M, Shionoya S: Aneurysm of the extracranial internal carotid artery caused by fibromuscular dysplasia. Eur J Vasc Surg 5:587-591, 1991.
23. Coffin O, Maiza D, Galateau-Salle F, et al: Results of surgical management of internal carotid artery aneurysm by the cervical approach. Ann Vasc Surg 11:482-490, 1997.
24. Rhee RY, Gloviczki P, Cherry KJ, et al: Two unusual variants of internal carotid artery aneurysms due to fibromuscular dysplasia. Ann Vasc Surg 10:481-485,1996.
25. Hart RG, Easton JD: Dissections of cervical and cerebral arteries. Neurol Clin 1:155, 1983.
26. Luscher TF, Lie JT, Stanson AW, et al: Arterial fibromuscular dysplasia. Mayo Clin Proc 62:931-952, 1987.
27. Muller BT, Luther B, Hort W, et al: Surgical treatment of 50 carotid dissections: Indications and results. J Vasc Surg 31:980-988, 2000.
28. DeOcampo J, Brillman J, Levy DI: Stenting: A new approach to carotid dissection. J Neuroimag 7:187-190, 1997.
29. Manninen HU, Koivisto T, Saari T, et al: Dissecting aneurysms of all four cervicocranial arteries in fibromuscular dysplasia: Treatment with self-expanding endovascular stents, coil embolization, and surgical ligation. AJNR Am J Neuroradiol 18:1216-1220, 1997.
30. Klufas RA, Hsu L, Barnes PD, et al: Dissection of the carotid and vertebral arteries: Imaging with MR angiography. AJR Am J Roentgenol 164:673-677, 1995.
31. Jooma R, Bradshaw JR, Griffith HB: Intimal dissection following percutaneous transluminal carotid angioplasty for fibromuscular hyperplasia. Neuroradiology 27:181-182, 1985.
32. Haldeman S, Kohlbeck FJ, McGregor M: Risk factors and precipitating neck movements causing vertbrobasilar artery dissection after trauma and spinal manipulation. Spine 15:785-794, 1999.
33. Cloft HJ, Kallmes DF, Snider R, et al: Idiopathic supraclinoid and internal carotid bifurcation steno-occlusive disease in young American adults. Neuroradiology 41:772-776, 1999.
34. Arning C: Nonatherosclerotic disease of the cervical arteries: Role of ultrasonography for diagnosis. Vasa 30:160-167, 2001.
35. Russo CP, Smoker WRK: Nonatheromatous carotid artery disease. Neuroimaging Clin North Am 6:811-830, 1996.
36. Smith LL, Smith DC, Killeen JD, et al: Operative balloon angioplasty in the treatment of internal carotid artery fibromuscular dysplasia. J Vasc Surg 6:482-487, 1987.
37. de Smul G, Bostoen H: Operative balloon dilatation of fibromuscular dysplasia of the internal carotid artery: Two case reports. Acta Chir Belg 95:139-143, 1995.
38. Ballard JL, Guinn JE, Killeen D, et al: Open operative balloon angioplasty of the internal carotid artery: A technique in evolution. Ann Vasc Surg 9:390-393, 1995.
39. Lord RSA, Graham AR, Benn IV: Radiologic control of operative carotid dilation: Aneurysm formation following balloon dilation. Cardiovasc Surg 27:158-161, 1986.
40. Brown MM: Balloon angioplasty for cerebrovascular disease. Neurol Res 14:159-163, 1992.
41. Motarjeme A: Percutaneous transluminal angioplasty of the supra-aortic vessels. J Endovasc Surg 3:171-181, 1996.
42. Hasso AN, Bird CR, Zinke DE, et al: Fibromuscular dysplasia of the internal carotid artery: Percutaneous transluminal angioplasty. AJNR Am J Neuroradiol 2:175-180, 1981.
43. Tsai FY, Matovich V, Hiesheima G, et al: Percutaneous transluminal angioplasty of the carotid artery. AJNR Am J Neuroradiol 7:349-358, 1986.
44. Theron JG, Payelle GG, Coskun O, et al: Carotid artery stenosis: Treatment with protected balloon angioplasty and stent placement. Radiology 201:627-636, 1996.

Aneurysms of the Extracranial Carotid Artery

JERRY GOLDSTONE, MD

Occlusive and ulcerated atherosclerotic lesions of the cervical carotid arteries are extremely common. Aneurysms of these vessels are rare, particularly in comparison with the frequency of aneurysms involving the *intracranial* carotid arteries and their branches and the frequency of aneurysms that occur throughout the rest of the arterial system. From 1927 to 1947, only five carotid aneurysms were encountered at the Hospital of the University of Pennsylvania, and Reid noted only 12 cases in a 30-year survey at the Johns Hopkins Hospital through 1922.[34,57] McCollum and associates at Baylor University reported 37 aneurysms treated over a 21-year period during which approximately 8500 operations for arterial aneurysms of all types were performed in the same institution.[42] These lesions are also rare when compared with the number of operations performed for carotid occlusive disease. Only six extracranial carotid aneurysms were repaired by Painter and associates at the Cleveland Clinic over a 7-year interval during which more than 1500 patients were treated for carotid occlusive disease.[52] More recently published data by El-Sabrout and Cooley from the Texas Heart Institute included 67 extracranial carotid aneurysms between 1960 and 1995, during which 7394 peripheral aneurysms were repaired and 4491 carotid operations were performed.[18] This 1.34% relative incidence of extracranial carotid aneurysms is nearly identical to the 1.25% reported by Rosset and associates from Marseilles, France, in the same year.[61]

Overall, about 2600 aneurysms of all types of the extracranial carotid arteries have been reported. Because of the rarity of these aneurysms, it is impossible to define their true incidence or to determine whether their frequency is increasing; however, with the widespread use of angiography, duplex ultrasound, and other imaging modalities, they clearly are being recognized more often than before. This is borne out by two reports from the Mayo Clinic. The first included six carotid aneurysms identified between 1936 and 1963,[56] and the second included 25 aneurysms treated from 1950 to 1990.[7] The rarity of these lesions also makes it difficult to be certain about their relative etiologies, natural history, and treatment outcomes, but the cumulative experience indicates that all of these are changing. Nevertheless, in spite of their rarity, extracranial carotid aneurysms should be considered in the differential diagnosis of a mass in the neck or posterior pharynx.

■ LOCATION

The common carotid artery, particularly at its bifurcation, is the most frequently reported site of true aneurysm formation

in the extracranial carotid system; the internal carotid artery is the next most common; and the external carotid is the least common (Figs. 143-1 to 143-9).[1,20,50,61,63] However, location varies with etiology, and the relative proportion of the various causes of these aneurysms is changing. For example, atherosclerotic aneurysms usually occur at or near the carotid bifurcation, whereas those caused by blunt trauma usually involve the high cervical portion of the internal carotid artery. In the Texas Heart Institute series, 17 (74%) of 23 of the atherosclerotic aneurysms occurred in the common carotid artery and/or its bifurcation.[18] Pseudoaneurysms that develop after previous carotid procedures are obviously located at the site of the procedure, namely the bifurcation.

■ ETIOLOGY

There are many causes of extracranial carotid aneurysms, and the relative frequency of each has changed over the years. Syphilis, tuberculosis, and other local infections were the most common causes 50 years ago, but they are rare today because of the widespread availability of antibiotics. Instead, dissection, atherosclerosis, trauma, and previous carotid surgery are the cause of most extracranial carotid aneurysms in current practice.

Atherosclerosis

Atherosclerosis is now the most frequently reported pathologic process associated with extracranial carotid artery aneurysms, occurring in up to 70% of the aneurysms in some published series, but averaging around 40%.[13,17,19,46,52,76,80] These are *true aneurysms*. The histologic features are typically atherosclerotic (often termed *degenerative*), with disruption of the internal elastic lamina and thinning of the media. Grossly, these aneurysms tend to be fusiform rather than saccular and are most commonly located at the bifurcation of the common carotid artery or the proximal internal carotid artery, where occlusive atherosclerotic plaques are quite common. Atherosclerotic aneurysms that do not involve the carotid bifurcation are frequently *saccular*. Most affected patients have severe arterial hypertension. Most bilateral, nontraumatic, extracranial carotid aneurysms are this type.[3]

Arterial Dysplasia

Arterial dysplasia, usually the fibromuscular variant, was the most frequent cause in three contemporary series of

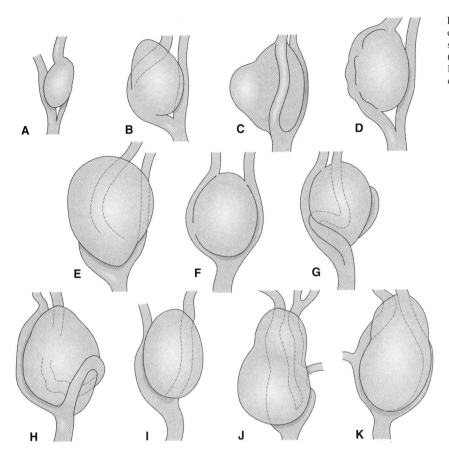

FIGURE 143-1 Artist's depiction of aneurysms of the extracranial internal carotid artery (**A-K**), showing variations in size and configuration. (From Alexander E Jr, Wigser SM, Davis CH: Bilateral extracranial aneurysms of the internal carotid artery. J Neurosurg 25:437, 1966.)

extracranial carotid aneurysms.[33,58] It accounted for 12 (50%) of 24 in that of Faggioli and colleagues,[20] 13 (52%) of 25 in that of Rosset and coworkers,[61] and 9 (60%) of 15 in that of Coffin and associates. However, postoperative aneurysms were not included in either of the last two of these reports. These dysplastic aneurysms may be caused by, or be the cause of, dissections of the internal carotid artery.

Trauma

Another major and increasingly frequent cause of carotid aneurysms is trauma,[15,35,65] both penetrating and blunt. The resulting transmural carotid disruption leads to the formation of these *false aneurysms* (pseudoaneurysms).

Penetrating Trauma

Penetrating wounds involving the carotid arteries can lead to two important vascular sequelae: (1) arteriovenous fistula (aneurysm) and (2) false aneurysm. Arteriovenous fistula was more common than false aneurysm in reports from World War II, although earlier reports indicated a higher incidence of false aneurysm, probably because the causative injuries were produced by low-velocity, low-energy-releasing missiles or by penetrating hand-driven weapons.[20,77] The decreased number of such cases reported since the mid-1930s may be due to the high initial mortality rate

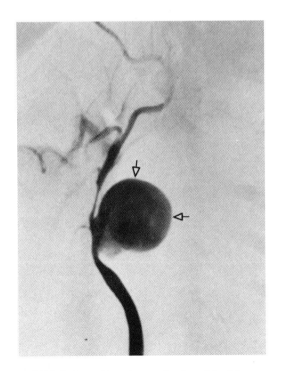

FIGURE 143-2 Left carotid arteriogram showing a 3.5 × 4.0 cm aneurysm arising from the left carotid artery adjacent to the common carotid bifurcation (*arrows*). The left internal carotid is occluded. (From Margolis MT, Stein RL, Newton TH: Extracranial aneurysms of the internal carotid artery. Neuroradiology 4:78, 1972.)

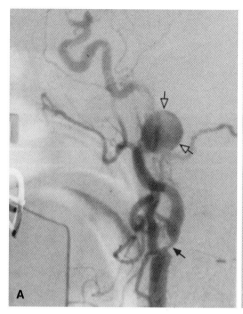
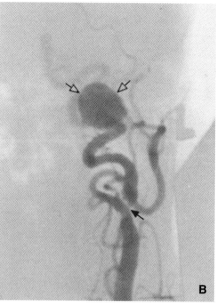

FIGURE 143-3 Left common carotid arteriogram showing a 1.8 × 2.0 cm aneurysm of the left internal carotid artery (*open arrows*) extending up to the base of the skull, associated with stenosis of the origin of the internal artery (*closed arrows*). **A,** Lateral projection. **B,** Anteroposterior projection. (**A** and **B,** From Margolis MT, Stein RL, Newton TH: Extracranial aneurysms of the internal carotid artery. Neuroradiology 4:78, 1972.)

associated with neck wounds produced by modern high-velocity weapons when they involve the region of the internal carotid artery. Such injuries to an area so closely related anatomically to the base of the skull are often lethal. In the Vietnam conflict, nearly all the patients who survived to be treated for carotid injuries were wounded by relatively low-velocity fragments from land mines, rockets, mortars, or grenades.

Direct carotid puncture for arteriography also can result in the formation of a false carotid aneurysm, but this technique is now rarely used for cerebral angiography. However, accidental puncture of the common carotid artery is a well-described complication of percutaneous cannulation of the internal jugular vein, and subsequent pseudo-

aneurysms are all too familiar to most vascular surgeons.

Nonpenetrating Trauma

Blunt or nonpenetrating trauma, although more often the cause of thrombosis of the injured vessel, can be associated with the development of false aneurysms. Blunt trauma of the carotid artery produces a spectrum of injury, including spasm, intimal and medial tears, and partial or complete severance of the vessel.[75] Disruption of the continuity of the arterial wall is required to produce any false aneurysm, and carotid false aneurysms are formed by the same sequence of events. This results in formation of a periarterial hematoma that is contained and confined by fascial planes. The center

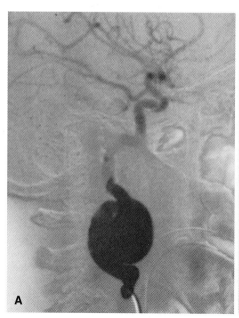
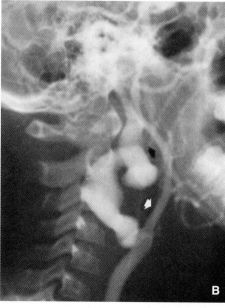

FIGURE 143-4 Right internal carotid arteriogram demonstrating fusiform aneurysm and looping of the proximal right internal carotid artery. (From Margolis MT, Stein RL, Newton TH: Extracranial aneurysms of the internal carotid artery. Neuroradiology 4:78, 1972.)

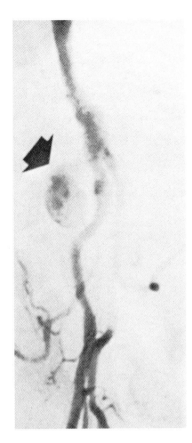

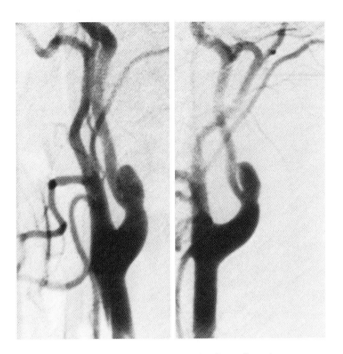

FIGURE 143-5 Left carotid arteriogram showing a false aneurysm adjacent to a carotid endarterectomy site *(arrowhead)*. (From Ehrenfeld WK, Hays RJ: False aneurysm after carotid endarterectomy. Arch Surg 104:288, 1972.)

FIGURE 143-6 Left carotid arteriogram showing a dissecting aneurysm of the proximal internal carotid artery caused by arteriographic catheter injury.

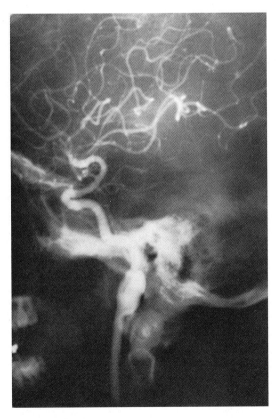

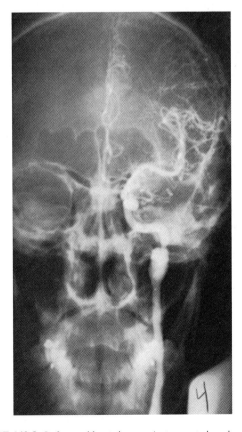

FIGURE 143-7 Left carotid arteriogram (lateral view) showing a traumatic internal carotid pseudoaneurysm involving a typical location in the distal internal carotid artery.

FIGURE 143-8 Left carotid arteriogram (anteroposterior view) of the same patient as in Figure 143-7.

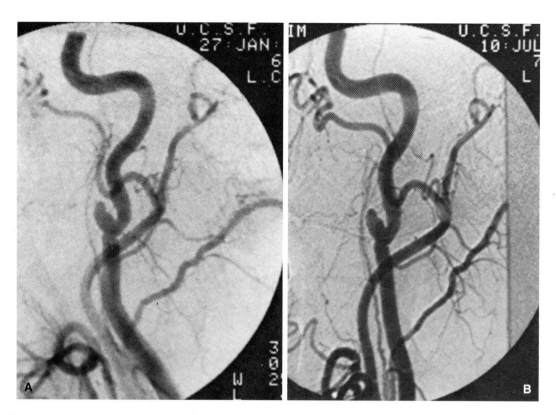

FIGURE 143-9 **A,** Left carotid arteriogram showing a traumatic pseudoaneurysm of the distal internal carotid artery. **B,** Left carotid arteriogram of the same patient, 6 months later, showing no change in the size of the aneurysm.

of the hematoma becomes a cavity composed of blood and laminated thrombus communicating with the arterial lumen. The fibrotic reaction that is initiated in the surrounding tissues assists in containing the aneurysm.

Hyperextension and rotation of the neck can cause stretching and compression of the distal extracranial internal carotid artery on the transverse process of the second and third cervical vertebrae, producing disruption of the wall and subsequent aneurysm formation or intimal fracture and dissection or thrombosis.[59,75] Similarly, the extreme displacement of the tissues of the neck that can occur during motor vehicle accidents and other trauma may stretch or disrupt the artery at its points of fixation to bone at the base of the skull.

The styloid process has been implicated in the pathophysiology of these blunt carotid injuries because it rotates with the skull on the dens, whereas the artery moves with the cervical spine.[68,78] In addition, when mandibular fracture is associated with blunt cervical trauma, bone fragments may penetrate the arterial wall, with subsequent development of one or more false aneurysms. Most of these blunt injuries are located high in the neck near the base of the skull, making them difficult to approach surgically, in contrast with carotid aneurysms that are due to penetrating trauma, which most often involve the common carotid artery.

Dissection

Dissection of the extracranial internal carotid artery can

occur after penetrating or blunt injury to the neck, inadvertent intraoperative trauma, percutaneous or catheter angiography, and chiropractic manipulation or spontaneously without obvious cause (see Chapter 144).[5,17,22,23,27,43,45,51,78] Nearly 20% of patients with dissecting aneurysms of the carotid artery have fibromuscular dysplasia of the involved or contralateral carotid vessel, and in nearly 10% they are bilateral. Many of the trauma-related dissections are associated with motor vehicle accidents, and it is believed that a significant proportion are not detected during the initial evaluation of the trauma patient.

Typical angiographic findings of dissection include a tapered narrowing in the mid or distal cervical internal carotid artery ("string sign") as well as a localized saccular aneurysm or cylindrical dilation in the dissected segment. Very focal lesions and total occlusions can also occur. The vertebral artery can also be affected by dissection. These dissecting aneurysms develop as a result of a break in the intima followed by hemorrhage into the media, which enlarges the vessel wall and reduces the caliber of the true lumen. If the hemorrhage dissects into the plane between the media and the adventitia, an aneurysm forms. About 30% of carotid dissections are associated with aneurysm formation. These lesions are often associated with hemicrania and Horner's syndrome in addition to transient or fixed neurologic deficits.

Surgery

False aneurysms can also occur after carotid bifurcation

endarterectomy for cerebrovascular insufficiency.[13,28,48,56] Nineteen (51%) of 37 cases in the series by McCollum and associates[42] and 38 (57%) in that of El-Sabrout and Cooley[18] fall into this category. *Staphylococcus aureus* has been the most commonly cultured causative organism. About 50% of the reported cases have occurred after endarterectomy in which a synthetic patch was used. Most often, these pseudoaneurysms have been attributed to the presence of infection or suture failure. However, pseudoaneurysms can also occur when a vein patch is used and after endarterectomy with primary closure. Although the incidence of false aneurysm is low, significant morbidity is associated with these pseudoaneurysms. Surgical trauma to the carotid artery during tonsillectomy or drainage of a peritonsillar abscess can also lead to pseudoaneurysm formation. Other even rarer causes of carotid pseudoaneurysm formation are connective tissue diseases such as vasculo-Behçet's disease.

Infection

Prior to the development of antibiotics, most extracranial carotid aneurysms were caused by infection resulting from either syphilis or contiguous pharyngeal or cervical infection.[34,66,77] In fact, in their 1949 review, Kirby and associates stated that "at least 90% of all aneurysms of the common carotid artery are due to syphilis."[34] The near disappearance of syphilitic arteritis accounts for the rarity of syphilitic aneurysms today, but infectious or mycotic aneurysms caused by other organisms still occur.[2,37,49] Additional etiologic processes include intravenous drug use, penetrating trauma, dental extraction, and catheter-based angiographic procedures.

In the 19th century, during streptococcal epidemics children were frequently seen with profuse oropharyngeal bleeding from infective aneurysms of the internal carotid artery. Cervical carotid aneurysms may protrude through the relatively thin pharyngeal constrictor muscles into the posterolateral pharyngeal wall, where they can rupture or where the true nature of these mycotic aneurysms may not be recognized until an unsuspecting physician drains a "peritonsillar abscess," only to be met with a gush of blood. Horner's syndrome and generalized sepsis can also occur. *S. aureus* has been the most frequent organism responsible for mycotic carotid aneurysms in recent years, but *Escherichia coli*, *Klebsiella*, *Corynebacterium* species, *Proteus mirabilis*, and *Yersinia enterocolitica* have also been reported. *Salmonella* species, which are a frequent pathogen in other arterial mycotic aneurysms, are less common in this location.[12,21,25,31,60]

The presence of a pulsatile neck mass associated with fever and pain should strongly suggest the diagnosis of a mycotic carotid artery aneurysm. Sources of infection include septicemia with involvement of the vasa vasorum, septic emboli within the lumen, and direct extension of infection from contiguous sites. This is obviously not a common problem today, although heroin addicts are especially susceptible to these nonsyphilitic, infectious aneurysms.[37,42,57]

Miscellaneous Causes

Other well-documented but even less common causes of carotid aneurysm include cystic medial necrosis, Marfan syndrome, Takayasu's arteritis, and idiopathic medial arteriopathy.[6,36,44,60,70,71,73,75] Several carotid aneurysms have been thought to be congenital because of their occurrence early in life, bilaterality, saccular shape, the presence of a defect in the media of the vessel similar to the "berry" type of intracranial aneurysm, and the absence of pathologic or clinical features characteristic of other entities.[26,47] Thus, carotid aneurysm should also be in the differential diagnosis of a painless neck mass in a young adult.[39]

■ NATURAL HISTORY

The natural history of extracranial carotid aneurysms is uncertain because these lesions are rare and because no single institution has had a large clinical experience with them. There are only seven single-institution reports that have 25 or more cases. These include series of 25,[7] 25,[61] 28,[55] 37,[42] 38,[47] 41,[67] and 67[18] cases, the largest being from the Texas Heart Institute. Thus, only estimates of natural history can be made, based on multiple case reports, small series, and collected reviews. Unfortunately, most of these include aneurysms of all types, and results have not always been correlated with specific causes; as a result, information regarding specific etiologic mechanisms is even more fragmentary. Furthermore, because these reports describe only aneurysms requiring medical attention, it is impossible to determine the number that were never detected. Although routine autopsy studies suggest the incidence is low, the available information suggests that the natural history of these lesions is generally unfavorable.

Winslow's 1926 report revealed a 71% mortality rate from rupture, thrombosis, or embolism in 35 untreated patients, compared with a 30% mortality rate in those patients who underwent proximal carotid ligation, the only surgical treatment available at that time.[77] More contemporary reviews have substantiated this poor prognosis of untreated patients and have emphasized the high incidence of neurologic symptoms.[32,60,65] For example, Zwolak and coworkers reported a stroke rate of 50% for atherosclerotic aneurysms followed up without surgery.[80] Aneurysm rupture is rare.

An especially high incidence of complications and death with mycotic and postsurgical pseudoaneurysms is documented in several reviews and case reports.[21,25,31,39,60] Conversely, some small, high cervical traumatic aneurysms remain stable or even become smaller when observed for long periods (see Fig. 143-9). Therapy must therefore be individualized, with the major objective being prevention of severe neurologic complications in atherosclerotic aneurysms and hemorrhage and thrombosis from mycotic aneurysms.[50]

■ CLINICAL FEATURES

Pulsatile Mass

The symptoms of extracranial carotid aneurysms vary according to their location, size, and etiology. Small internal carotid aneurysms may be asymptomatic, but most cervical carotid aneurysms (30%) are identified by the finding of a pulsating mass in the neck just below the angle of the mandible. Systolic bruits are present in many of these patients, especially the elderly, but there is often no evidence of other atherosclerotic lesions. These aneurysms may be painful, tender, or asymptomatic. They are occasionally recognized as a pulsating tumor of the tonsillar fossa or pharynx, with little or no manifestation of their presence externally in the neck.

The classic paper by Shipley's group[66] emphasized that aneurysms of the internal carotid present inwardly into the throat, whereas those of the common carotid present outwardly in the neck. The absence of cervical swelling in the former is attributed to the dense, deep cervical fascia and muscles attached to the styloid process anteriorly and the cervical vertebrae posteriorly that crowd the gradually dilating aneurysm inward toward the tonsillar fossa, where the thin superior pharyngeal constrictor muscle and mucous membrane offer only minimal resistance to inward protrusion. The level at which the common carotid bifurcates also influences the point of appearance, for with a low bifurcation even an internal carotid aneurysm is likely to be visible and palpable externally in the neck.

Because aneurysms that arise at or proximal to the carotid bifurcation are readily palpable, they usually pose no diagnostic difficulty; however, those arising from the internal carotid near the base of the skull can and do cause diagnostic problems. A chronic unilateral swelling of the posterior pharynx should raise the level of suspicion, especially when other physical signs are lacking, bizarre, or atypical. Otolaryngologists often are the first to see these lesions. A high index of suspicion usually leads to computed tomography (CT), magnetic resonance (MR) imaging, or angiography, which are nearly always diagnostic when an aneurysm is present.

Symptoms

Most patients with extracranial carotid aneurysms are symptomatic, with the larger lesions tending to produce the most severe symptoms, but even small carotid aneurysms can be symptomatic.

Pain

Overall, pain probably is the most common local symptom.[32] It was prominent in 40% of patients in a reported series from the Mayo Clinic.[7] Some patients have aching in the neck, retro-orbital pressure, or throbbing headaches. Glossopharyngeal compression can account for auricular pain, and radiation into the occipital area also occurs. Dissection can cause acute, severe cervical, retro-orbital, or hemicranial pain.[65]

Dysphagia

The mass of an aneurysm can cause compression of adjacent structures. Dysphagia secondary to the bulk of the lesion or to compression of the nerve supply to the pharynx is a frequent symptom.

Cranial Nerve Compression

Aneurysms arising near the carotid canal may compress other nerves and produce severe recurrent facial pain, fifth and sixth cranial nerve palsies, deafness, and occa-

sionally Horner's syndrome. Vagal compression may cause hoarseness.[41] Oculosympathetic paresis and intermittent facial pain (Raeder's paratrigeminal syndrome) in some cases have been caused by a carotid aneurysm at the base of the skull.[35]

Central Nervous System Dysfunction

Most reports indicate that central neurologic deficits are the most common symptoms produced by carotid aneurysms.[59] This reflects the high percentage of atherosclerotic aneurysms in many series.[7,14,54,55] These lesions tend to produce either transient ischemic attacks or strokes occurring in more than 40% of patients. Transient neurologic deficits occur about twice as often as completed strokes.[46,76,80] Most neurologic events are due to embolization of thrombotic material emanating from the aneurysmal wall, but some are caused by diminished flow when a large aneurysm compresses the internal carotid artery when the head is turned to certain positions. Occasionally, concomitant carotid bifurcation occlusive disease accounts for focal neurologic events. Dizziness, tinnitus, and other nonlocalizing symptoms have also been reported.

Hemorrhage

Hemorrhage is now a rare manifestation of carotid aneurysm. In earlier reports, many of these aneurysms were first noticed because of hemorrhage from the pharynx, ear, or nose. Bleeding of this type is usually from an internal carotid artery aneurysm or from infected false aneurysms after carotid endarterectomy. If rupture occurs into the oropharynx, the bleeding can be massive and can lead to suffocation and death. Most fatalities have usually been preceded by repeated episodes of hemorrhage that were improperly recognized or treated. Mycotic aneurysms are especially susceptible to rupture and bleeding.[50]

■ DIFFERENTIAL DIAGNOSIS

The most frequently encountered lesion that must be distinguished from an extracranial carotid aneurysm is a kinked or coiled carotid artery (see Chapter 144).[34,53] This usually involves the common carotid artery, producing a pulsatile mass at the base of the neck, typically on the right side, in obese, hypertensive, older women. This lesion has been referred to by Bergan and Hoehn as *evanescent cervical pseudoaneurysm*.[4] It is much more common than bona fide aneurysms in this location, from which it can be readily distinguished by the characteristic location and by the nature of the pulsation, which is parallel to the long axis of the vessel, in contrast to the pulsation of an aneurysm, which typically is expansile at right angles to the axis of the parent vessel. Soft tissue radiographs of the neck may reveal linear calcification in an atherosclerotic aneurysm but usually not in a tortuous artery. Duplex ultrasonography readily defines the lesion.

Redundant length also causes sigmoid curves, loops, and coils of the internal carotid artery higher in the neck. These usually are discovered by angiography because their high cervical location renders them nonpalpable.

A prominent carotid bifurcation in a patient with a thin

Extracranial Carotid Aneurysms

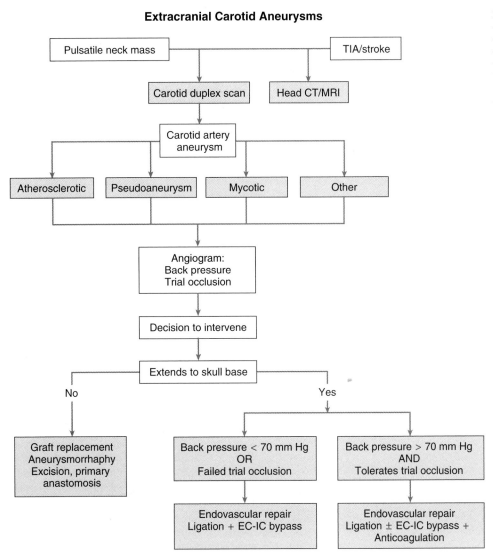

FIGURE 143-10 Algorithm for the diagnosis and management of extracranial carotid aneurysms. MI, myocardial infarction; EC-IC, external carotid-to-internal carotid. (Modified from Rothstein J, Goldstone J: Carotid artery aneurysm. In Cronenwett JL, Rutherford RB [eds]: Decision Making in Vascular Surgery. Philadelphia, WB Saunders, 2001, p 54.)

neck can also be mistaken for a carotid aneurysm, as can carotid body tumors, enlarged lymph nodes, branchial cleft cysts, and cystic hygromas. Careful physical examination should identify these entities correctly, but more objective modalities are useful in confirming the diagnosis.

Ultrasonography (B mode with or without Doppler spectral analysis) should establish the correct diagnosis of those aneurysms low enough in the neck to be evaluated with this technique (Fig. 143-10). However, aneurysms in the distal part of the extracranial internal carotid artery are usually not seen with routine duplex scanning protocols. Other methods are needed, specifically CT and MR scanning, that document the size and nature these aneurysms.[16] The CT anatomy of the neck, nasopharynx, and parapharyngeal spaces is well known, and carotid aneurysms deforming these areas should be clearly differentiated from other mass lesions, particularly if bolus contrast injection and dynamic scanning are employed. MR imaging is equally effective and may be the method of choice when dissection is the suspected cause, owing to the method's unique ability to identify old blood in the dissection plane. Recently, ultra-fast (spiral) CT scans have

also been shown to be highly accurate for diagnosis of dissection.

Even if the diagnosis of extracranial carotid aneurysm is made by one of the imaging techniques described, angiography is necessary to obtain the detailed vascular anatomy necessary for the planning of surgical treatment; angiography should also be performed in virtually all patients in whom an aneurysm is suspected and cannot be excluded by other diagnostic methods.[46] It is best accomplished by the transfemoral selective technique that provide high-quality, detailed views of both carotid and vertebral arteries as well as the intracranial vessels. As they do with aneurysms in other locations, conventional angiograms (including digital subtraction) may underestimate the size of carotid aneurysms as a result of the presence of mural thrombus. Angiography serves not only to define the extent of the aneurysm and its relationship to bony structures, especially the base of the skull, but also to provide anatomic information that will allow establishment of a probable etiology for the aneurysm. In addition, angiography allows measurement of carotid artery back ("stump")-pressure and a period of temporary carotid occlusion. This is done using an end-hole, balloon occlusion catheter in patients who are awake, anticoagulated, and at their baseline blood pressure. The trial typically lasts 30 minutes during which the back-pressure is measured electronically while the patient is monitored for development of any neurologic deficits. Finally, angiography is an essential prerequisite for attempts at endovascular repair of any carotid aneurysm but is usually performed during the same angiographic session.

MR angiography can also provide definitive diagnostic information and has the obvious advantage of being noninvasive and thus free from stroke risk. Excellent multiplanar images of the extracranial as well as the intracranial vasculature can be obtained (see Chapter 22). Early experience with spiral CT with three-dimensional image reconstruction (CT angiography) has been favorable for other types of carotid lesions and may prove useful for aneurysms as well (see Chapters 21).

■ TREATMENT

The treatment of extracranial carotid aneurysms has evolved with the specialty of vascular surgery. The choice of treatment depends on the size, location, and etiologic mechanism of the lesion in question and also on the overall condition of the patient. Treatment must, therefore, be individualized. As noted previously, some small, traumatic, distal internal carotid aneurysms may remain stable or even shrink when observed for a long period, but most require treatment to relieve local symptoms and to prevent new or recurrent neurologic events and the rare case of rupture.[9]

For most patients, the primary objective of treatment is the prevention of permanent neurologic deficits that arise from atheroembolism or thromboembolism. This can best be accomplished by resection of the aneurysm and restoration of arterial continuity. Unfortunately, these goals are not always possible.

Ligation

In 1552, Ambroise Paré published the first account of operative ligation of the common carotid artery to control massive hemorrhage from a laceration of the artery. His patient had aphasia and a contralateral monoplegia. In 1805, Astley Cooper performed the first common carotid ligation for an aneurysm of the artery. Hemiplegia developed on the eighth postoperative day, and the patient died 13 days later. Cooper later accomplished the first successful treatment of a cervical carotid aneurysm by proximal ligation, and this, coupled occasionally with distal ligation and extirpation, remained the procedure of choice until Matas developed the technique of endoaneurysmorrhaphy.

In 1926, Winslow was able to report that the death rate from cervical carotid aneurysms had decreased from 71% with conservative therapy to 30% following ligation, and in 1951 ligation was still recommended as the treatment of choice despite the unpredictability of the outcome.[77] Modifications such as the use of partially constricting bands rather than complete occlusion were used by some surgeons to lessen the danger of cerebral ischemia. Kirby and coworkers pointed out the dangers of such procedures and

made an unsuccessful attempt to resect a syphilitic carotid aneurysm in 1949.[34]

The subsequent development of reconstructive vascular techniques has eliminated ligation as a procedure of choice. Ligation now should be limited to aneurysms of the internal carotid artery that extend distally to the base of the skull so that distal control of the vessel cannot be obtained, making resection with arterial reconstruction impossible. Even then, however, successful reconstructions can often be accomplished using special maneuvers to increase exposure, such as drilling away portions of the petrous and mastoid bones.[61] Ligation of the vessel may be necessary in emergency situations when rupture has occurred, especially if infection is the cause.

Ligation results in thrombosis from the level of the interruption up to the origin of the first major intracranial collateral artery, usually the ophthalmic artery, thereby obliterating the aneurysm. When this method is used, however, neurologic deficits occur in 30% to 60% of the patients, and half of such patients die.[8,34] This may be the result of acute cerebrovascular insufficiency due to inadequate collateral circulation or, more commonly, distal clot propagation and embolization. Gradual carotid occlusion with devices such as the Selverstone clamp has not eliminated this problem.

In an effort to avoid this complication, numerous techniques have been developed for preoperative determination of the adequacy of cerebral collateral circulation. The carotid compression tests (e.g., Matas' test) all have proved unreliable, as has the observation of intracerebral cross-filling seen on angiography or by transcranial Doppler examination. Intraoperative measurement of the back-pressure in the temporarily occluded internal carotid artery has been shown by several authors to be an excellent predictor of tolerance of temporary carotid occlusion in patients with occlusive disease, and it can be applied similarly to patients with aneurysms. The oculopneumoplethysmograph (OPG-Gee), when used with carotid compression, is also able to determine the internal carotid back-pressure and can provide this information preoperatively.[24] However, these instruments are no longer available in most medical centers. Alternatively, carotid artery back-pressure, as discussed earlier, can be measured at the time of angiography by means of a catheter with an inflatable balloon proximal to a measuring port. Both methods correlate closely with carotid back-pressure measured intraoperatively. A carotid back-pressure in excess of 60 to 70 mm Hg suggests the presence of sufficient collateral cerebral perfusion to enable a patient to withstand carotid ligation without development of an ischemic neurologic deficit.

Careful analysis of the results of carotid ligation reveals a substantial number of patients who experience hemiplegia hours to days after the procedure. Because this sequela most probably represents propagation of clot, from the top of the thrombus column in the internal carotid artery, into the distal branches of the internal carotid artery rather than acute cerebrovascular insufficiency, heparin anticoagulation should be maintained for 7 to 10 days when carotid ligation is performed. When carotid ligation is required but collateral cerebral perfusion is inadequate, an extracranial-to-intracranial arterial bypass procedure should be considered. The superficial temporal-middle cerebral bypass was the most commonly performed procedure of this type, but concerns about the volume of flow through the superficial temporal artery have led to the use of saphenous vein grafts as the preferred method of minimizing the risk of irreversible cerebral ischemia.

Wrapping

External wrapping of the aneurysm, suggested by Thompson and Austin more than 40 years ago, has been used as an alternative to ligation when resection was not feasible.[72] These authors used fascia lata, but prosthetic materials seem equally well suited. Wrapping may control the expansion of the aneurysm and may limit the risk of rupture, but it is not reliable for reducing the more significant risks of embolism or thrombosis. This method is not appropriate except in the most unusual circumstances. Of note, it was also usually unsuccessful for treatment of abdominal aortic aneurysms.

Endoaneurysmorrhaphy

Originally described by Matas, endoaneurysmorrhaphy has largely been replaced by more modern reconstructive vascular techniques, but it still is useful for some fusiform aneurysms that are unresectable because they extend to the base of the skull. This technique can be performed over an internal shunt wedged into the carotid foramen to control back-bleeding. Some saccular aneurysms may also be treatable by localized arterial repair, and several mycotic aneurysms have been treated by a modification of this technique employing débridement of the arterial wall and autogenous patch angioplasty.[25,31,60]

Resection

Resection of the aneurysm with restoration of flow is the preferred method of treatment.[10,11,47,61,65,79] It is indicated for accessible lesions of the common carotid and proximal third of the internal carotid artery. More distal lesions usually present difficulties in gaining distal control, and other methods often must be employed.[61,67] A small saccular aneurysm with a narrow neck can be managed by aneurysmectomy and primary closure or patch angioplasty. Fusiform lesions and saccular lesions with large necks are not as suitable for this type of local repair. They should be resected, and arterial continuity should be re-established.

The first report of resection of a carotid aneurysm with primary anastomosis was that of Shea and associates in 1955, although the first successful procedure of this type was performed by Dimtza in 1952.[58] Beall and associates performed the first prosthetic graft replacement for this lesion in 1959. In subsequent years, there have been numerous reports of successful carotid aneurysm resection with re-establishment of arterial continuity, and this should be the objective of all such procedures. Redundancy of the carotid vessels allows resection and primary anastomosis to be performed in more than 50% of cases, especially when the aneurysm is small.

Anastomosis of the proximal external carotid artery to the more distal internal carotid artery has been successfully used to bridge an internal carotid defect resulting from aneurysm excision. A spatulated anastomosis using interrupted suture technique diminishes the likelihood of anastomotic narrowing. When inadequate length of vessels precludes primary anastomosis, interposition grafts must be used. Prosthetic and autogenous (artery or vein) grafts have been used with equally good results, although an autogenous conduit is preferable whenever infection is a possibility.

Large aneurysms and aneurysms involving the most distal internal carotid artery are especially challenging technically. Exposure of the upper end of the internal carotid may be enhanced by several maneuvers, including the following:

1. Division of the sternocleidomastoid muscle from its mastoid attachment and elevation or resection of the parotid gland
2. Division of the digastric muscle
3. Removal of the styloid process and its attached muscles
4. Use of intraluminal balloons (usually as an intraluminal shunt)—to control distal internal carotid back-bleeding
5. Subluxation of the mandible by any of several techniques—can increase the width of exposure of the distal field at the base of the skull by approximately 1 cm.[10,11,14,55,65] Nearly equal advantage can be gained by using a nasotracheal rather than an endotracheal tube for administration of general anesthesia.
6. Drilling and removing portions of the inferior surface of the petrous portion of the temporal bone—this usually requires an interdisciplinary team that includes nonvascular surgeons with experience in skull base surgery.[56]

Complete excision of large lesions risks injury to cranial nerves, including the facial, vagus, spinal accessory, hypoglossal, and glossopharyngeal nerves. Profound disturbances in swallowing can occur as a result of injury to pharyngeal muscular branches arising from the vagus, superior laryngeal, and glossopharyngeal nerves. Although these are usually temporary deficits, they can be severely disturbing to affected patients and the cause of considerable postoperative morbidity. To minimize these problems, the surgeon must use extreme care when dissecting these structures, and a bipolar cautery should be employed for hemostasis. The surgeon should also pay attention to gentle handling of the aneurysm itself to prevent dislodgement and downstream embolization of a mural thrombus.

Methods of cerebral protection during the period of carotid occlusion required for repair of carotid aneurysms are the same as those used during bifurcation endarterectomy for occlusive disease. Some surgeons employ electroencephalographic monitoring or cerebral blood flow measurements.[46,65,69] Others selectively use an internal shunt based on back-pressure criteria. Routine shunting is advocated by many surgeons because of the longer time required for this type of carotid reconstruction compared with that required for endarterectomy. The shunt may also be helpful by serving as a stent during construction of the anastomoses. Hypothermia, induced hypertension, and hypercapnia or hypocapnia are unnecessary and confusing adjuncts.

With modern vascular surgical techniques, correction of most extracranial carotid aneurysms should be possible with a high rate of success and an acceptable rate of neurologic complications. Results vary widely depending on the type, size, and location of the aneurysm. In general, surgical therapy is associated with a mortality rate of about 2%, although mortality rates as high as 40% have been reported for carotid ligation for infected postendarterectomy false aneurysms. The central neurologic morbidity rate ranges from 6% to 20%; it is highest in atherosclerotic cases, and this rate is obviously higher than that associated with the treatment of occlusive carotid bifurcation atherosclerosis. Cranial nerve dysfunction occurs in about 20% of patients. Fortunately, most of these defects are transient.

More specific outcome data are available from current reports. Among the 67 cases reported by El-Sabrout and Cooley, there were 4 deaths (6%), 5 strokes (7.5%), and a combined mortality and stroke rate of 10.4%.[18] Cranial nerve deficits occurred in 4 patients (6%). Rosset and associates' smaller series of 25 patients had no deaths, 1 stroke (4%), and 1 permanent cranial nerve palsy, although 11 patients (44%) had temporary nerve deficits, some of which persisted for as long as 7 months.[61] It is important to realize that most of these problems were in patients whose lesions were near or at the skull base and also that none had postoperative false aneurysms. This differs from El-Sabrout and Cooley's series in which only 5 aneurysms involved the distal portion of the carotid artery and the majority (56.7%) were pseudoaneurysms resulting from previous carotid bifurcation operations. El-Sabrout and Cooley's article also included a review of the data from the 13 largest single-center series reported from 1950 to 1995. There were 392 total cases. Those treated nonoperatively had a combined stroke and/or death rate of 21%. Treatment with carotid ligation was associated with an 11% stroke/death rate, whereas those treated with surgical reconstruction had a combined major stroke and death rate of only 9%. These data indicate that the surgical treatment of extracranial carotid aneurysms, although technically challenging, can be carried out with acceptably low morbidity and mortality. However, the results are not nearly as good as those for carotid bifurcation occlusive disease.

Endovascular Therapy

The recent development of endovascular techniques and technologies has permitted successful treatment, with maintenance of patency, of even the most challenging distal as well as more proximal carotid aneurysms. Higashida and colleagues have definitively treated several high-cervical true and false aneurysms with intravascular detachable silicone balloons and platinum coils inserted via a transfemoral route.[29,30] This has resulted in obliteration of the aneurysm and preservation of cervical carotid patency and flow. In several other patients with acute pseudo-aneurysms that were due to trauma or tumor erosion, these investigators obliterated the aneurysm by trapping it between two balloons: one was placed in the cavernous carotid artery below the ophthalmic artery but beyond the inferolateral and meningohypophyseal trunk, and a second

one was placed just proximal to the aneurysm. As with surgical ligation, test occlusion to document tolerance to permanent carotid occlusion is obviously mandatory prior to this method of treatment. Stents have also been successfully employed for the treatment of carotid dissections. Most patients should receive antiplatelet and or antithrombotic therapy for 6 weeks following endovascular repair to facilitate re-endothelialization of the treated surface.

Although neurologic complications have followed this form of therapy, the long-term results have been encouraging. This procedure should be considered in the treatment of carefully selected patients with difficult and dangerous aneurysms, especially those at the skull base. Despite the advances in skull base surgery, the associated morbidity may be substantial with some of the special techniques required to gain adequate exposure at that location. Endovascular treatment avoids such problems by reaching the lesion entirely through an intraluminal route.[27,39] For either true or false aneurysms, covered stents can be used to reinforce the vessel wall, thereby reducing the risk of rupture. By excluding the mural thrombus, they also reduce the risk of downstream embolization. Bare stents can be placed across the neck of a saccular aneurysm to promote aneurysm thrombosis while maintaining vessel patency. If thrombosis does not occur, thrombogenic coils can be placed into the aneurysm through the interstices of the stent. As experience grows and endoluminal devices and techniques improve, it is likely that endoluminal therapy will become the treatment of choice for most extracranial carotid aneurysms that extend more than a short distance beyond the carotid bifurcation. However, in spite of the seeming popularity of this form of treatment, long-term follow-up data, in terms of stent migration, stenosis, thrombosis and neurologic events, are not available.

■ REFERENCES

1. Agrifoglio M, Rona P, Spirito R, et al: External carotid artery aneurysms. J Cardiovasc Surg 30:942, 1989.
2. Angle N, Dorafshar AH, Ahn SS: Mycotic aneurysm of the internal carotid artery: A case report. Vasc Endovascular Surg 37:213, 2003.
3. Bemelman M, Donker DN, Ackerstaff RG, Moll FL: Bilateral extracranial aneurysm of the internal carotid artery: A case report. Vasc Surg 35:225, 2001.
4. Bergan JJ, Hoehn JG: Evanescent cervical pseudoaneurysms. Ann Surg 162:213, 1965.
5. Biller J, Hingtgen WL, Adams HP Jr, et al: Cervicocephalic arterial dissections: A ten-year experience. Arch Neurol 43:1234, 1986.
6. Bour P, Taghavi I, Bracard S, et al: Aneurysms of the extracranial internal carotid artery due to fibromuscular dysplasia: Results of surgical management. Ann Vasc Surg 6:205, 1992.
7. Bower TC, Pairolero PC, Hallett JW Jr, et al: Brachiocephalic aneurysm: The case for early recognition and repair. Ann Vasc Surg 5:125, 1991.
8. Brackett CE Jr: The complications of carotid artery ligation in the neck. J Neurosurg 10:91, 1953.
9. Busuttil RW, Davidson RK, Foley KT, et al: Selective management of extracranial carotid artery aneurysms. Am J Surg 140:85, 1980.
10. Carrel T, Bauer E, von Segesser L, et al: Surgical management of extracranial carotid artery aneurysms: Analysis of six cases. Cerebrovasc Dis 1:49, 1991.
11. Coffin O, Maiza D, Galateau-Salle F, et al: Results of surgical

management of internal carotid artery aneurysms by the cervical approach. Ann Vasc Surg 11:482, 1997.

12. Dawson KJ, Stansby G, Novell JR, Hamilton G: Mycotic aneurysm of the cervical carotid artery due to *Salmonella enteritidis.* Eur J Vasc Surg 6:327, 1992.

13. Dehn TCB, Taylor GW: Extracranial carotid artery aneurysms. Ann R Coll Surg Engl 66:247, 1984.

14. de Jong KP, Zondervan PE, van Urk H: Extracranial carotid artery aneurysms. Eur J Vasc Surg 3:557, 1989.

15. Deysine M, Adiga R, Wilder JR: Traumatic false aneurysm of the cervical internal carotid artery. Surgery 66:1004, 1969.

16. Duvall ER, Gupta KL, Vitek JJ, et al: CT demonstration of extracranial carotid artery aneurysms. J Comput Assist Tomogr 10:404, 1986.

17. Ehrenfeld WK, Wylie EJ: Spontaneous dissection of the internal carotid artery. Arch Surg 111:1294, 1976.

18. El-Sabrout R, Cooley DA: Extracranial carotid artery aneurysms: Texas Heart Institute experience. J Vasc Surg 31:823, 2000.

19. Ekestrom S, Bergdahl L, Huttunen H: Extracranial carotid and vertebral artery aneurysms. Scand J Thorac Cardiovasc Surg 17:135, 1983.

20. Faggioli GL, Freyrie A, Stella A, et al: Extracranial internal carotid artery aneurysms: Results of a surgical series with long-term follow-up. J Vasc Surg 23:587, 1996.

21. Ferguson LJ, Fell G, Buxton B, Royle JP: Mycotic cervical carotid aneurysm. Br J Surg 71:245, 1984.

22. Fisher CM, Ojemann RG, Roberson GH: Spontaneous dissection of cervicocerebral arteries. J Can Sci Neurol 5:9, 1978.

23. Friedman WA, Day AK, Guisling RG, et al: Cervical carotid dissecting aneurysms. Neurosurgery 7:207, 1980.

24. Gee W, Mehigan JT, Wylie EJ: Measurement of collateral cerebral hemispheric blood pressure by ocular pneumoplethysmography. Am J Surg 130:121, 1975.

25. Grossi RJ, Onofrey D, Tvetenstrand C, Blumenthal J: Mycotic carotid aneurysm. J Vasc Surg 6:81, 1987.

26. Hammon JW Jr, Silver D, Young WF Jr: Congenital aneurysm of the extracranial carotid arteries. Ann Surg 176:777, 1972.

27. Hacein-Bey L, Connolly ES Jr, Duong H: Treatment of inoperable carotid aneurysms with endovascular occlusion after extracranial-intracranial bypass surgery. Neurosurgery 41:1225, 1997.

28. Hejhal L, Hejhal J, Firt P, et al: Aneurysms following endarterectomy associated with patch graft angioplasty. J Cardiovasc Surg 15:620, 1974.

29. Higashida RT, Hieshima GB, Halbach VV, et al: Cervical carotid artery aneurysms and pseudoaneurysms. Acta Radiol 369:591, 1986.

30. Higashida RT, Hieshima GB, Halbach VV, et al: Intravascular detachable balloon embolization of intracranial aneurysms. Acta Radiol 369:594, 1986.

31. Jebara VA, Acar C, Dervanian P, et al: Mycotic aneurysms of the carotid arteries: Case report and review of the literature. J Vasc Surg 14:215, 1991.

32. Kaupp HA, Haid SP, Gurayj MN, et al: Aneurysms of the extracranial carotid artery. Surgery 72:946, 1972.

33. Kawada T, Oki A, Iyano K, et al: Surgical treatment of atherosclerotic and dysplastic aneurysms of the extracranial internal carotid artery. Ann Thorac Cardiovasc Surg 8:183, 2002.

34. Kirby CK, Johnson J, Donald JG: Aneurysm of the common carotid artery. Ann Surg 130:913, 1949.

35. Klein GE, Szolar DH, Raith J: Posttraumatic extracranial aneurysm of the internal carotid artery: Combined endovascular treatment with coils and stents. AJNR Am J Neuroradiol 18:1261, 1997.

36. Latter DA, Ricci MA, Forbes RDC, Graham AM: Internal carotid artery aneurysm and fan's syndrome. Can J Surg 32:463, 1989.

37. Ledgerwood AM, Luca CE: Mycotic aneurysm of the carotid artery. Arch Surg 109:496, 1974.

38. Lim YM, Lee SA, Kim DK, Kim GE: Aneurysm of the extracranial internal carotid artery presenting as the syndrome of glossopharyngeal pain and syncope. J Neurol Neurosurg Psychiatry 73:87, 2002.

39. Lueg EA, Awerbuck D, Forte V: Ligation of the common carotid artery for the management of a mycotic pseudoaneurysm of an extracranial

40. Margolis MT, Stein RL, Newton TH: Extracranial aneurysms of the internal carotid artery. Neuroradiology 4:78, 1972.

41. Mathews J, Yeong CC, Reddy KT, Kent SE: Bilateral aneurysms of the extracranial internal carotid artery presenting as vocal fold palsy. J Laryngol Otol 115:663, 2001.

42. McCollum CH, Wheeler WG, Noon GP, et al: Aneurysms of the extracranial carotid artery: Twenty-one years' experience. Am J Surg 137:196, 1979.

43. McNeill DH Jr, Driesbach J, Marsden RJ: Spontaneous dissection of the internal carotid artery: Its conservative management with heparin sodium. Arch Neurol 37:54, 1980.

44. Miyauchi M, Shionoya S: Aneurysm of the extracranial internal carotid artery caused by fibromuscular dysplasia. Eur J Vasc Surg 5:587, 1991.

45. Mokri B, Sundt TM Jr, Houser OW: Spontaneous internal carotid dissection, hemicrania, and Horner's syndrome. Arch Neurol 36:677, 1979.

46. Mokri B, Piepgras DG, Sundt TM, et al: Extracranial internal carotid artery aneurysms. Mayo Clin Proc 57:310, 1982.

47. Moreau P, Albat B, Thevent, A: Surgical treatment of extracranial internal carotid aneurysm. Ann Vasc Surg 8:409, 1994.

48. Motte S, Wautrecht JC, Bellens B, et al: Infected false aneurysm following carotid endarterectomy with vein patch angioplasty. J Cardiovasc Surg 28:734, 1987.

49. Nader R, Mohr G, Sheiner NM, et al: Mycotic aneurysm of the carotid bifurcation in the neck: Case report and review of the literature. Neurosurgery 48:1152, 2001.

50. Nicholson ML, Horrocks M: Leaking carotid artery aneurysm. Eur J Vasc Surg 2:197, 1988.

51. O'Connell BK, Towfighi J, Brennan RW, et al: Dissecting aneurysms of head and neck. Neurology 35:993, 1985.

52. Painter TA, Hertzer NR, Beven EG, et al: Extracranial carotid aneurysms: Report of six cases and review of the literature. J Vasc Surg 2:312, 1985.

53. Perdue GD, Barreca JP, Smith RB III, et al: The significance of elongation and angulation of the carotid artery: A negative view. Surgery 77:45, 1975.

54. Petrovic P, Avramov S, Pfau J, et al: Surgical management of extracranial carotid artery aneurysms. Ann Vasc Surg 5:506, 1991.

55. Pratschke E, Schafer K, Reimer J, et al: Extracranial aneurysms of the carotid artery. Thorac Cardiovasc Surg 28:354, 1980.

56. Raptis S, Baker SR: Infected false aneurysms of the carotid arteries after carotid endarterectomy. Eur J Vasc Endovasc Surg 11:148, 1996.

57. Reid MR: Aneurysms in the Johns Hopkins Hospital. Arch Surg 12:1, 1926.

58. Rhee RY, Gloviczki P, Cherry KJ Jr, Eswards WD: Two unusual variants of internal carotid aneurysms due to fibromuscular dysplasia. Ann Vasc Surg 10:481, 1996.

59. Rhodes EL, Stanley JC, Hoffman GL, et al: Aneurysms of extracranial carotid arteries. Arch Surg 111:339, 1976.

60. Rice HE, Arabi S, Kremer R, Needle D, Johansen K: Ruptured *Salmonella* mycotic aneurysm of the extracranial carotid artery. Ann Vasc Surg 11:416, 1997.

61. Rosset E, Albertini JN, Magnan PE, et al: Surgical treatment of extracranial internal carotid artery aneurysms. J Vasc Surg 31:713, 2000.

62. Rothstein JH, Goldstone J: Carotid artery aneurysm. In Cronenwett JL, Rutherford RB (eds): Decision Making in Vascular Surgery. Philadelphia, WB Saunders, 2001, p 54.

63. Schechter DC: Cervical carotid aneurysms: I. N Y State J Med 79:892, 1979.

64. Schechter DC: Cervical carotid aneurysms: II. N Y State J Med 79:1042, 1979.

65. Schiervink W, Piepgras D, McCaffrey TV, Mokri B: Surgical treatment of extracranial internal carotid artery dissecting aneurysms. Neurosurgery 35:809, 1994.

66. Shipley AM, Winslow N, Walker WW: Aneurysm in the cervical portion of the internal carotid artery: An analytical study of the cases

recorded in the literature between August 1, 1925, and July 31, 1936: Report of two new cases. Ann Surg 105:673, 1937.

67. Skau T, Hillman J, Harder H, Magnuson B: Surgical treatment of distal extracranial internal carotid artery aneurysms involving the base of the skull: A multidisciplinary approach. Eur J Vasc Endovasc Surg 20:308, 2000.

68. Stonebridge PA, Clason AE, Jenkins AM: Traumatic aneurysm of the extracranial internal carotid artery due to hyperextension of the neck. Eur J Vasc Surg 4:423, 1990.

69. Sundt TM Jr, Pearson BW, Piepgras DG, et al: Surgical management of aneurysms of the distal extracranial internal carotid artery. J Neurosurg 64:169, 1986.

70. Sztajzel R, Hefft S, Girardet C: Marfan's syndrome and multiple extracranial aneurysms. Cerebrovasc Dis 11:346, 2001.

71. Tabata M, Kitagawa T, Saito T, et al: Extracranial carotid aneurysm in Takayasu's arteritis. J Vasc Surg 34:739, 2001.

72. Thompson JE, Austin DJ: Surgical management of cervical carotid aneurysms. Arch Surg 74:80, 1957.

73. Un-Sup K, Friedman EW, Werther LJ, et al: Carotid artery aneurysm associated with nonbacterial suppurative arteritis. Arch Surg 106:865, 1973.

74. van Sambeek MR, Segren CM, van Dijk LC, et al: Endovascular repair of an extracranial internal carotid artery aneurysm complicated by heparin-induced thrombocytopenia and thrombosis. J Endovasc Ther 7:353, 2000.

75. Welling RE, Kakkasseril JS, Peschiera J: Pseudoaneurysm of the cervical internal carotid artery secondary to blunt trauma. J Trauma 25:1108, 1985.

76. Welling RE, Taha A, Goel T, et al: Extracranial carotid artery aneurysms. Surgery 93:319, 1983.

77. Winslow N: Extracranial aneurysm of the internal carotid artery. Arch Surg 13:689, 1926.

78. Zelenock GB, Kazmers A, Whitehouse WM, et al: Extracranial internal carotid artery dissections. Arch Surg 117:425, 1982.

79. Zhang Q, Duan ZQ, Xin SJ, et al: Management of extracranial carotid artery aneurysms: Seventeen years' experience. Eur J Vasc Endovasc Surg 18:162, 1999.

80. Zwolak RM, Whitehouse WM, Knake JE, et al: Atherosclerotic extracranial carotid artery aneurysms. J Vasc Surg 1:415, 1984.

Chapter

Uncommon Disorders Affecting the Carotid Arteries

144

WILLIAM C. KRUPSKI, MD

Never bet against atherosclerosis.

Edwin J. (Jack) Wylie

Although atherosclerotic occlusive disease is the most common disorder of the extracranial cerebrovasculature, there are many other processes with which the surgeon dealing with the cerebrovascular disorders must be familiar. Because these conditions are rare, large studies are unavailable, and their management must be based on the experience of several select authorities and anecdotal reports. Several relatively uncommon disorders, including carotid aneurysms, extracranial fibromuscular disease, and vertebrobasilar insufficiency, have been discussed in the three previous chapters. This chapter addresses the clinical presentation and management of carotid artery coils and kinks, carotid body tumors, carotid sinus syndrome (CSS), carotid artery dissection, radiation-induced carotid arteritis and stenosis, adjacent malignancy and infection, vasculitis (including Takayasu's arteritis and temporal arteritis), moyamoya disease, and extracranial-intracranial (EC-IC) bypass.

■ CAROTID ARTERY KINKS AND COILS

Anatomists first described elongated and distorted carotid arteries in autopsy specimens in the mid-1700s.[201] In 1898, Kelly reported finding large, pulsating vessels in the pharynx in the proximity of tortuous internal carotid arteries (ICAs).[110] In the early 1900s, there were numerous reports describing fatal hemorrhage after injury to tortuous carotid arteries during tonsillectomy or adenoidectomy.[39,59,102,213] Riser and colleagues in France first described cerebrovascular symptoms related to redundant kinked carotid arteries in 1951.[191] These investigators described a patient with an elongated carotid artery that was straightened by affixing the artery to the sheath of the sternocleidomastoid muscle. Subsequently, the patient remained asymptomatic.

In 1956, Hsu and Kistin reported the first direct surgical repair of a kinked carotid artery.[97] In 1959, Quattlebaum and associates described three patients who presented with hemiplegia and kinked carotid arteries.[184] The patients were treated by resection and reanastomosis of the common carotid artery, with relief of symptoms.

Alleviation of cerebrovascular symptoms by surgical repair of tortuous kinked and coiled carotid arteries is a controversial topic. Numerous angiographic and autopsy studies have shown that carotid redundancy is not uncommon and that most individuals with this anatomic variant remain asymptomatic.[92] Although most carotid kinks and coils are incidental findings with no clinical significance, there does appear to be a subset of patients whose anatomy produces cerebrovascular symptoms as a direct consequence of carotid angulation.

Pathophysiology

Kinks and coils of the ICA may be developmental or acquired. In both types, the carotid artery is excessively long in fixed space, resulting in redundancy and tortuosity of the vessel. The redundancy may occur in coronal, transverse, or sagittal planes. Usually the ICA is affected, but occasionally kinks and coils are seen in the common carotid artery as well. The ICA usually assumes an S shape, but single and even double complete loops have been described. When the elongation becomes acutely angulated, a carotid kink may be present; kinks are often associated with atherosclerotic plaque or arterial stenoses (Fig. 144-1).

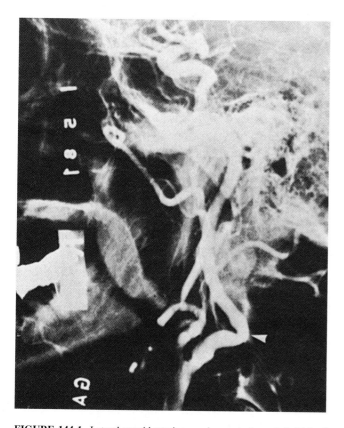

FIGURE 144-1 Lateral carotid arteriogram demonstrating a tight kink of the internal carotid artery *(arrowhead)*. The external carotid artery is also elongated and tortuous.

The congenital coils seen in children may result from faulty descent of the heart and great vessels within the mediastinum during embryologic development. The carotid artery is formed by the third aortic arch and the dorsal aorta. During embryologic development, there is a prominent bend at the junction of these vessels. The carotid artery is quite tortuous. As the heart descends into the thorax, these vessels straighten, but kinking can occur if the straightening process is incomplete. Alternatively, tortuosity may result from excessive lengthening of the carotid as the cervical skeletal elongates. Normally, one process keeps pace with the other, establishing the correct length of the carotid artery. A greater frequency of bilateral carotid coiling in children (~50%) than in adults supports this hypothesis.

Carotid coils in adults occur more frequently in elderly people in whom atherosclerosis is also frequently present. Coiling may be acquired from excessive elongation of the artery with age, and the elongated artery may have thinning of the media and fragmentation of elastic lamina. Often, one carotid artery is more prominently coiled than the other; this disorder is bilateral in only 25% of adults. A kink in the carotid artery may be a consequence of degeneration of the arterial wall, loss of elasticity, or hypertension-induced elongation due to increased intraluminal pressure. Support for this hypothesis is provided by the occurrence of kinks in older individuals who frequently have hypertension as well as atherosclerotic disease. In most instances, atherosclerotic plaques are present proximal to ICA kinks. These plaques can fix the vessel and promote tortuosity. Alternatively, fascial bands can tether the artery. These bands, which represent remnants of the embryonic aortic arch, cross the ICA at or above the bifurcation and become fibrotic with increasing age. As the involved carotid arteries elongate with age, they become fixed between two points by the arch and these external bands. Thus, a kink usually is located in the ICA 2 to 3 cm beyond the bifurcation.

Carotid kinks occur four times more commonly in women than in men.[234] This increased predominance in women may explain the greater frequency with which older hypertensive women, in contrast to men, are thought to have carotid aneurysms when they actually have tortuous carotid or subclavian vessels. Bergan and Hoen have described this physical finding as the "evanescent cervical pseudoaneurysm."[15]

Incidence

The true incidence of kinks and coils of the carotid artery is unknown since most patients with this anatomy remain asymptomatic. In a review of anatomic studies in patients who died of other causes, Cairney described a 30% prevalence.[26] Most recent reports are based on arteriographic studies in elderly individuals with cerebrovascular symptoms. One of the largest angiographic series was reported by Weibel and Fields from the Methodist Hospital in Houston, Texas.[241] In 2453 carotid angiograms performed in 1438 patients, tortuosity of the carotid artery was observed in 489 (35%), coiling in 88 (6%), and kinking in 65 (5%). Among 76 patients with coiled carotid arteries, 40 (53%) had bilateral involvement, and 15 (28%) of 53 patients with kinked carotid arteries had bilateral involvement.

In another large review, Metz and coworkers analyzed 1000 consecutive carotid arteriograms.[152] These investigators defined a kink as angulation between two vessel segments of 90 degrees or less, or formation of a complete loop. Kinked carotid arteries were found in patients of every decade examined (1st through 8th), but most cases occurred between ages 41 and 70 years. In all, 161 patients (16%) had some degree of kinking. Sixty patients (6%) had severe kinking (angle < 30 degrees); of these, 14 (23%) had cerebrovascular symptoms (stroke, $n = 8$; single transient ischemic attack [TIA], $n = 2$; recurrent TIA, $n = 4$).

Acquired kinking may occur after carotid endarterectomies. In a series of 308 patients who had undergone carotid artery operations, Najafi and associates reported a 5% incidence of carotid artery kinking.[168] Vannix and associates reported 15 cases of postendarterectomy kinking in 312 carotid reconstructions, resulting in an incidence of 4.8%.[234] Busuttil and colleagues described kinks in 10 (1.4%) of 670 carotid operations during a 13-year period.[23]

Clinical Presentation

In children, carotid coils have rarely been associated with neurologic symptoms; however, in adults, kinks are much more commonly responsible for neurologic manifestations in patients with elongated carotid arteries.[199] Because cerebrovascular flow is not compromised by carotid loops or coils, these findings are often of no clinical significance in adults. However, kinks in the carotid artery are more likely to produce luminal narrowing and flow abnormalities. In addition to hemodynamic abnormalities, carotid artery kinking may produce turbulent blood flow and subsequently lead to intimal ulceration and embolization. Symptoms, therefore, are usually similar to those caused by atherosclerotic disease of the carotid bifurcation, and patients may present with strokes, hemispheric TIAs, or amaurosis fugax. Kinks in the vertebral artery may produce vertebrobasilar insufficiency, with symptoms of ataxia, diplopia, bilateral paresthesias, vertigo, dysarthria, or drop attacks.

A peculiar feature of symptoms caused by carotid artery kinks is an association with head turning. Quattlebaum and associates have described the occurrence of symptoms as patients turn their heads sideways.[185] Ipsilateral rotation produces greatest flow reduction, but even contralateral rotation and neck flexion/extension may exaggerate the kink and reduce blood flow.[220] In some patients, head rotation produces total occlusion of an otherwise patent, but redundant, carotid artery. Thus, when focal neurologic deficits can be reproduced by head motion, the clinician should suspect a carotid or vertebral artery kink.

Diagnosis

Carotid kinks and coils cannot be reliably diagnosed by physical examination, although occasionally a prominent pulsation suggestive of a carotid aneurysm may be palpated in the neck. The mass is due to the tissue volume occupied by the carotid kink or coil; it is accentuated by head rotation if the kink involves the ICA. Occasionally, the kink can be palpated intraorally in a tonsillar fossa.[201] In the presence of a carotid kink a bruit may be present or may develop when the patient's head is turned to the side.

Historically, noninvasive studies, including oculoplethysmography, technetium-pertechnetate brain scans, and electroencephalography, were used to identify patients who might have carotid kinks that are hemodynamically significant.[91,92,131,199,220,229] Although positional testing using these tests might be helpful in identifying hemodynamically significant kinking, the incidence of false-positive studies has not been established; therefore, all positive tests must be corroborated by angiography. Thus, definitive diagnosis of carotid kinks and coils requires four-vessel cerebral arteriography. Multiple views are necessary, with patients in neutral, flexion, extension, and rotation positions. It is most important that the arteriogram be performed with the head in a position thought to produce neurologic symptoms.

Treatment

Because the natural history of carotid kinks and coils is uncertain and because of the relatively small number of patients identified with symptomatic disease, observation is recommended in asymptomatic patients. When symptoms are corroborated by arteriographic findings in symptomatic patients, hemodynamic alterations may be implicated, and surgical correction is indicated.[45,180]

Simple surgical tethering of the elongated redundant and tortuous kinked or coiled carotid artery (arteriopexy) is inadequate treatment because it does not correct the redundancy. Several surgical options have been recommended for the correction of the ICA kink: (1) a long-patch angioplasty; (2) ICA resection and reanastomosis; (3) ICA resection and saphenous vein interposition; (4) ICA reimplantation into the side of the common carotid artery; and (5) resection and reanastomosis of a portion of the common carotid.[37,67,214,220,234] Although some have recommended ligation and division of the external carotid artery when performing common carotid resection, Poindexter and colleagues have advocated preservation of this potential collateral vessel (Fig. 144-2).[180]

A more anatomic procedure than common carotid resection involves resection of the kinked portion of the ICA and reanastomosis with or without patch angioplasty. The disadvantage of this technique is performing the procedure (resection) on the smaller ICA, a difficulty that is occasionally posed when the kink is close to the base of the skull (Fig. 144-3). Alternatively, the ICA may be detached from its bifurcation and reanastomosed more proximally to the common carotid artery (Fig. 144-4). During the operation, regardless of the technique chosen, the patient's head should be turned to be sure that the rearranged anatomy will not produce a new kink.

Although there are no large individual series, the collective results of operations for carotid kinks in patients with symptomatic disease have been good. Approximately 80% of patients have been rendered asymptomatic, with an approximate 5% perioperative stroke and mortality rate.[91,185,220,234] Patients operated on for lateralizing symptoms have better outcomes than patients operated on for global ischemic symptoms.

■ CAROTID BODY TUMORS

In 1743, Von Haller first described the carotid body.[238] Reigner first attempted resection of a carotid body tumor in

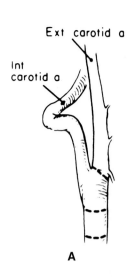

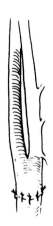

FIGURE 144-2 A, Resection of the common carotid artery with external (Ext) carotid artery ligation and division to remove a kink from the internal (Int) carotid artery. **B,** If the external carotid artery is also redundant, as shown in Figure 144-1, it may not require ligation as part of this maneuver.

1880, but the patient did not survive.[188] Maydl was the first to resect a carotid body tumor in 1886, but the patient became aphasic and hemiplegic.[146] In 1903, Scudder performed the first successful removal of a carotid body tumor in the United States, with preservation of the carotid artery and avoidance of significant nerve injury.[206] As of this writing, more than 900 cases have been reported in the literature.* The controversy regarding the biologic behavior and surgical management of carotid body tumors is reflected in the voluminous literature on the subject.

Physiology

The carotid body is a chemoreceptor located in the bifurcation of the common carotid artery, in the adventitia of its posterior medial surface. It is attached by a thin strand of adventitia known as *Meyer's ligament*, which also carries its

*See References 16, 42, 44, 62, 69, 98, 123, 149, 150, 189, 196, and 244.

blood supply that arises from the external carotid artery in most cases. The carotid body is derived from both mesodermal elements of the third branchial arch and neural elements originating from the neural crest ectoderm.[183] These neural crest cells further differentiate into forerunners of paraganglionic cells. Because cells in the neural crest migrate in close association with autonomic ganglion cells, neoplasms have been called *paragangliomas*. Mulligan introduced the term *chemodectoma* from the Greek words *chemia* (infusion), *dechesthai* (to receive), and *oma* (tumor).[166] The terms *paraganglioma* and *chemodectoma* are often used interchangeably.

Histologically, cervical chemodectomas resemble the normal architecture of the carotid body. The tumors are highly vascular, and between the many capillaries are clusters of cells called *Zellballen* (cell balls) (Fig. 144-5). One of the cell types represented is a "sustentacular," or supporting, cell. The other is the epithelioid, or chief, cell, which has finely granular eosinophilic cytoplasm. Cytochemical techniques have demonstrated epinephrine, norepinephrine, and serotonin in these cells.[79] Although there are reports of

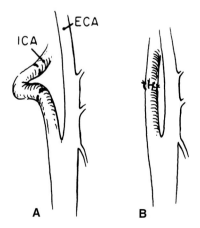

FIGURE 144-3 A, Segmental resection of a length of the internal carotid artery (ICA). **B,** Reanastomosis of the ICA using meticulous interrupted suture technique. ECA, external carotid artery.

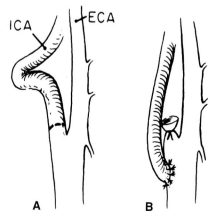

FIGURE 144-4 A, Transection of the kinked internal carotid artery (ICA) at its origin with the external carotid artery (ECA). **B,** Reimplantation onto the more proximal common carotid artery.

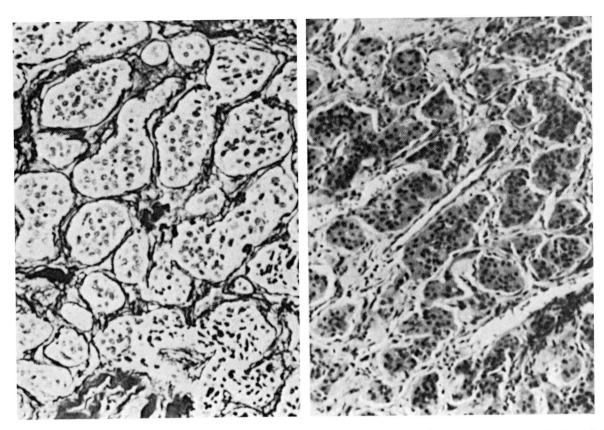

FIGURE 144-5 Cross-sectional photomicrographs of a carotid body tumor. **Left,** Reticulin stain accentuates the characteristic Zellballen (cell nests). Clusters of darkly stained red blood cells mark numerous small blood vessels. **Right,** On hematoxylin-eosin staining, the cell nests are shown to be separated by fibrous septa containing numerous small vascular spaces. The tumor cells have moderately abundant, finely granular eosinophilic cytoplasm, indistinct cell borders, and round-to-oval nuclei. (×125.) (From Krupski WC, Effeney DJ, Ehrenfeld WK, Stoney RJ: Cervical chemodectoma: Technical considerations and management options. Am J Surg 144:218, 1982.)

functioning tumors producing hypertension in the carotid and jugular bodies,[64,133] this is extremely unusual. In contradistinction, retroperitoneal chemodectomas often secrete catecholamines, and more than 60% of patients with such tumors present with a *pressor amine syndrome*.[27] In the absence of hypertension, screening studies for catecholamine metabolites in patients with cervical chemodectoma are unwarranted.

Paragangliomas are classified as *chromaffin* and *nonchromaffin*. Chromaffin-positive cells possess the ability to produce catecholamines. Initially, carotid body tumors were thought to be nonchromaffin paragangliomas, but recent studies have demonstrated some chromaffin-positive secretory granules, suggesting that the carotid body is capable of secreting catecholamines.[183] However, at most, 5% of carotid body tumors are endocrinologically active.[41,73,130]

It has been suggested that carotid body tumors may be a part of the neurocristopathies that occur in various combinations, such as *multiple endocrine neoplasia* (MEN) types 1 and 2. Secondary tumors are common in patients with carotid body tumors, including pheochromocytomas. MEN 1 and 2 involve tissues that are also derived from the neural crest, such as the medulla of the thyroid.[19] The carotid body has extremely high blood flow and oxygen consumption, averaging approximately 0.2 L/g/min, which is more than is required by the brain, thyroid, and heart.[153]

The carotid body is responsive primarily to hypoxia and, to a lesser degree, to hypercapnia and acidosis. Stimulation of the carotid body produces an increase in respiratory rate, tidal volume, heart rate, and blood pressure together with vasoconstriction, and production of circulating catecholamines.[62] Of note, the incidence in carotid body tumors is increased in individuals living at high altitudes and in patients subjected to chronic hypoxia.[34,197] The afferent input to the carotid body is via the glossopharyngeal nerve to the reticular formation of the medulla.[30]

Pathology

The normal carotid body measures approximately 5 × 3 × 2 mm, similar to the size of a grain of wheat.[28,153] Its only known pathology is neoplasia. Carotid body tumors are the most common of the nonchromaffin paragangliomas. Paragangliomas may be located at the base of the skull, in the nasopharynx, and throughout the body cavities. They are known as *glomus jugulare, glomus intravagale, glomus aorticum, glomus ciliare,* and *Zuckerkandl bodies.* They also are found in various locations in the retroperitoneum (Fig. 144-6). Synonyms for carotid body tumor include chemodectoma, endothelioma, glomus caroticum, perithelioma, chromaffinoma, and nonchromaffin paraganglioma. *Carotid body tumor* is the preferred term in current usage, however.

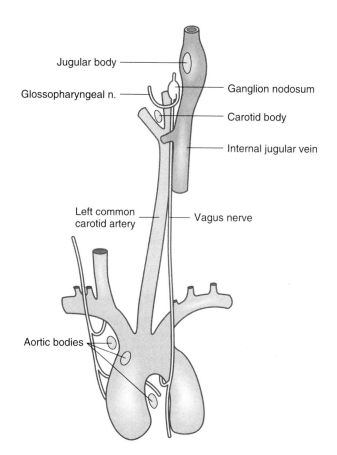

FIGURE 144-6 Anatomic location of chemoreceptive tissues. (From Krupski WC, Effeney DJ, Ehrenfeld WK, Stoney RJ: Cervical chemodectoma: Technical considerations and management options. Am J Surg 144:217, 1982.)

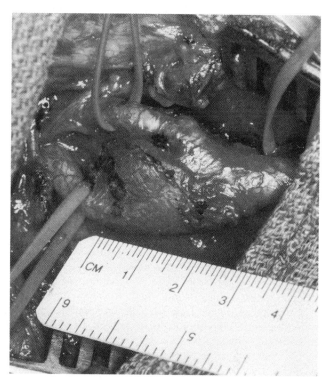

FIGURE 144-7 Operative photograph taken during resection of a small carotid body tumor. Vessel loops encircle the common *(right)*, external *(left upper)*, and internal *(left lower)* carotid arteries.

Macroscopically, carotid body tumors are well circumscribed, rubbery, and reddish brown. Their microscopic appearance has been described earlier. Despite the well-circumscribed nature of carotid body tumors, there is no true capsule.[105,183] As the tumor grows, the carotid bifurcation is progressively distorted, and the internal and external carotid arteries are "splayed" (Fig. 144-7).

The renowned Mayo Clinic surgeon Shamblin and his colleagues[207] described the following anatomic groups of carotid body tumors:

- *Group I* consists of relatively small tumors, which are minimally attached to the carotid vessels; surgical excision is not difficult.
- *Group II* tumors are larger, with moderate attachments. These tumors can be resected, but many patients require a temporary intraluminal carotid shunt.
- *Group III* tumors are very large neoplasms that encase the carotid arteries and often require arterial resection and grafting.

Biologic Behavior

Carotid body tumors may be sporadic or familial. In the more common *sporadic* form, there is a 5% incidence of bilateral carotid body tumors.[105,150,207] In the *familial* form of carotid body tumors, transmission is by an autosomal dominant pattern.[82] In the familial form, there is a 32% incidence of bilateral tumors.[82,86] Screening of family members is strongly recommended in these cases, because the ease of resection is related to size of the tumor.

The malignant potential of carotid body tumors is controversial. The reported rates of malignancy range from 2% to 50% in the medical literature.[31,69,130,186,207,218] Malignant potential cannot be predicted by nuclear pleomorphism or mitotic activity. Dissemination can become apparent many years after the initial diagnosis.[79,207,218] Because the malignant potential of carotid body tumors cannot be predicted by histologic markers, this determination can be made only by the presence of lymph nodes or distant metastases. Metastatic spread generally occurs in regional lymph nodes. Metastases have also been described to the kidney, thyroid, pancreas, cerebellum, lungs, bone, brachial plexus, abdomen, and breast.[56,186,193,244] Metastases should not be confused with multicentricity of paragangliomas at other sites in the body.[47] Most authorities estimate that the metastatic rate of carotid body tumors is approximately 5%.[98,130,193,207]

Most carotid body tumors grow slowly and exhibit benign characteristics. Many patients may survive for long periods without surgical treatment, but these tumors can cause significant disability and death, even without malignancy. Death due to asphyxia and intracranial extension of carotid body tumors has been described.[44,142,163] Martin and colleagues noted a death rate of about 8% in untreated patients.[142] Some authors have reported palliation using radiation therapy alone, but most agree that this is not acceptable primary treatment.[130,142,149,207] Complications from radiation therapy include osteonecrosis of the mandible, carotid radiation arteritis, and laryngeal injury. Even after prolonged disease-free intervals, local recurrence following surgical resection has also been described.[142,218] Predictors of future biologic behavior are the severity of symptoms and the size of the carotid body tumors at the time of diagnosis.[123]

Incidence

Because of the rarity of carotid body tumors, their incidence is difficult to determine. Hallett and associates reported one of the largest experiences in 1988, in which 153 cervical paragangliomas were treated over a 50-year period (from 1935 to 1985) at the Mayo Clinic.[86] This experience far surpassed the experience at most busy centers but accounted for only at most three or four patients with this disorder per year. There are conflicting reports with respect to gender prevalence; some citations show a male predominance, whereas others note a 3:1 female predominance.[86] In familial carotid body tumors, there appears to be an equal distribution between men and women, thus supporting an autosomal mode of genetic transmission. Although cases have been reported in patients ranging in age from the 2nd to the 8th decade, most tumors become apparent in the 5th decade of life.

Clinical Presentation

Most commonly, patients present with a painless swelling in the neck, located at the angle of the mandible. The mass has often been present for several years, and some male patients may first become aware of it because their shirt collars become tight. Other nonspecific symptoms may include neck or ear pain, local tenderness, hoarseness, dysphasia, or tinnitus. Typically, many years may elapse between initial recognition of the mass and surgical treatment.[123,207] Although cranial nerve dysfunction in unoperated carotid body tumors is unusual, symptoms from vagal, hypoglossal, and cervical sympathetic nerve impingement have been described.[42,178] Patients rarely have lateralizing central neurologic symptoms or signs, although they may describe dizziness.[16] Because approximately 5% of tumors may have neurosecretory activity, some patients describe symptoms of dizziness, flushing, palpitations, tachycardia, arrhythmias, headache, diaphoresis, and photophobia. Neuroendocrine activity obviously has anesthetic implications.[250]

The most notable finding on physical examination is a neck mass located below the angle of the mandible, which is laterally mobile but vertically fixed because of its attachment to the carotid bifurcation. The mass is often pulsatile due to its close relationship to the carotid artery. A bruit may be audible due to impingement of the artery, but this is a nonspecific finding because atherosclerosis is frequently present in this location as well. Rarely, patients demonstrate neurologic abnormalities caused by vagal or hypoglossal nerve involvement; even more unusual is the patient who presents with Horner's syndrome. The mass is usually nontender, rubbery, firm, and noncompressible. Because of the 5% incidence of bilaterality even in nonfamilial tumors, the opposite side of the neck should be

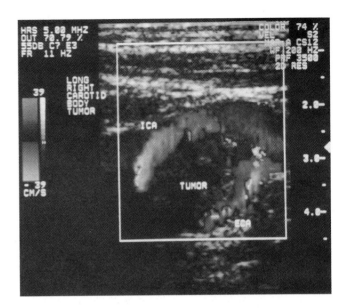

FIGURE 144-8 Characteristic duplex color-flow image of a carotid body tumor. The internal (ICA) and external carotid artery (ECA) branches are splayed by the tumor mass. The tumor may exhibit a very active mixed-signal pattern representing the extensive vascularity of the tumor.

carefully palpated as well; this is especially important when familial tumors are suspected.[86]

Diagnosis

Although history and physical findings are helpful, the diagnosis of carotid body tumor is included in the differential diagnosis of numerous other causes of neck masses, including lymphomas, metastatic tumors, carotid artery aneurysms, thyroid lesions, submandibular salivary gland tumors, and branchial cleft cysts. The vascularity of carotid body tumors is important in several ways. First, percutaneous needle aspiration or incisional biopsy is strongly contraindicated, because these procedures may result in massive hemorrhage, pseudoaneurysm formation, and carotid thrombosis.[178,218] Second, duplex scanning with color-flow imaging usually documents the highly vascularized mass in the area of the carotid bifurcation.[80,221,249] Characteristically, tumors separate the internal and external carotid arteries, widening the bifurcation (Fig. 144-8). The vascularity of carotid body tumors is readily shown by color-flow imaging, which differentiates them from the relatively nonvascular masses listed earlier. In addition, duplex scanning can provide information on the tumor dimensions and demonstrate any coexistent carotid occlusive disease. Third, the concept of preoperative embolization of these tumors is based on the blood loss that may be associated with tumor resection.

The carotid body normally obtains its blood supply from the external carotid artery, but as the tumor grows, contributions from the ICA, vertebral artery, and thyrocervical trunk can develop.[31,251] Because patients may demonstrate such unusual blood supply, thereby complicating exposure and hemostasis, angiography remains the gold standard for the diagnosis and management of carotid body tumors.

Bilateral angiography is important for the evaluation of concurrent atherosclerosis, collateral flow, and identification of multicentric disease.

Both computed tomography (CT) scans and magnetic resonance (MR) scans have been useful in evaluating cervical masses. Although differentiation between aneurysm and neoplasm may be difficult, dynamic or rapid-sequencing CT improves this differentiation.[210] MR imaging may be superior to CT scanning for demonstrating the relationship of the carotid body tumors to adjacent structures.[177,237] MR imaging can readily differentiate carotid body tumors from other soft tissue lesions at the base of the skull because of the highly vascular nature of these lesions. Both CT and MR scans can demonstrate the size and extent of the tumor and help plan proper surgical exposure.

Treatment

Because of the 5% or greater incidence of metastases and the unrelenting growth of unresected tumors (which tends to encase the adjacent neurovascular structures, making delayed surgery more hazardous), the mainstay of treatment for carotid body tumors is complete surgical excision. Early removal of small, asymptomatic tumors decreases the incidence of cranial nerve and carotid artery injuries. Unfortunately, most carotid body tumors, when discovered, are in Shamblin's group II and III at the time of clinical presentation.[123] As indicated previously, radiation therapy for carotid body tumors has been largely unsatisfactory, except for local control of residual or recurrent disease.[204,233] Radiation therapy prior to surgery makes operative treatment more difficult. Chemotherapy has no role.

The role of preoperative embolization of highly vascular carotid body tumors is controversial. Preoperative embolization has been reported by some to decrease vascularity and improve the safety of surgical excision, with lower operative blood loss and decreased technical difficulties.[127,192,215] However, percutaneous embolization may produce thrombosis of the ICA or cerebral embolization.[179]

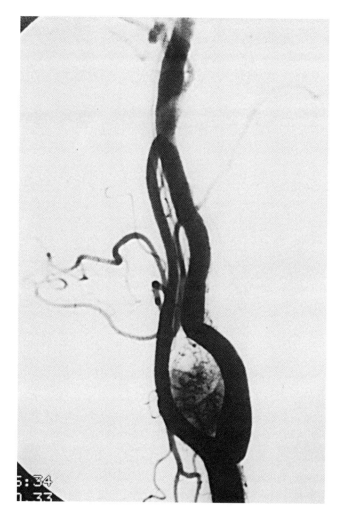

FIGURE 144-9 Selective carotid arteriogram demonstrating the classic characteristics of a carotid body tumor. The bifurcation is widened by the tumor; note the contrast density of the "tumor blush" that portrays the highly vascular nature of these tumors.

Surgical Technique

As discussed earlier, arteriography is essential for diagnosis and to provide information about carotid artery anatomy and the vascular supply of the carotid body tumor (Fig. 144-9). Cranial nerve function should be evaluated carefully prior to operation. Despite increased improvements in technique, the incidence of postoperative nerve damage has not been substantially reduced. Catecholamine screening should be reserved for those few individuals who present with a history suggesting endocrine activity and for those with bilateral tumors, which are thought to be more likely to produce neurosecretory activity.

The anatomic and technical details of operations for carotid body tumors are similar to those for carotid endarterectomy. Because blood loss can be substantial, an autotransfusion device should be available, reducing the requirements for bank blood. Extremely large tumors extending toward the base of the skull may require subluxation of the temporomandibular joint to facilitate distal carotid artery exposure. A suitable saphenous vein should be available, since complicated arterial reconstruction is required in up to 25% of cases. Carotid shunts also should be available if clamping of the ICA is necessary because of low carotid back-pressure, intraoperative electroencephalographic changes, or other indications of inadequate cerebral perfusion. Avoidance of cranial nerve injury may be achieved by meticulous dissection around the tumor and by the use of bipolar electrocautery to minimize conductive heat injury to adjacent nerves.

General endotracheal anesthesia is preferable. Nasotracheal intubation may be required if temporomandibular subluxation is anticipated. Patient positioning is identical to that for carotid endarterectomy. A longitudinal incision along the anterior border of the sternocleidomastoid muscle curving behind the ear usually gives adequate exposure. However, large tumors are more easily excised with a modified-T neck incision (Fig. 144-10). An alternative incision in front of the ear, with parotid gland mobilization and facial nerve preservation, can facilitate distal ICA exposure. The first tenet of vascular surgery, which is to obtain distal and proximal arterial control, should be

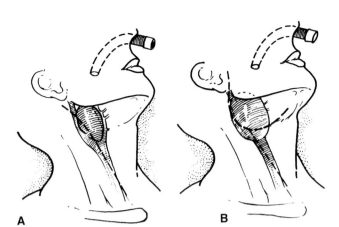

FIGURE 144-10 Operative incisions appropriate for carotid body tumor resection. The nasotracheal tube allows for greater distraction of the mandible, if required. **A,** Incision for small tumor (Shamblin I). **B,** Incision for medium and large tumors (Shamblin II and Shamblin III). (**A** and **B,** From Hallett JW: Carotid body tumor resection. In Bergan JJ, Yao JST [eds]: Techniques in Arterial Surgery. Philadelphia, WB Saunders, 1990, p 214.)

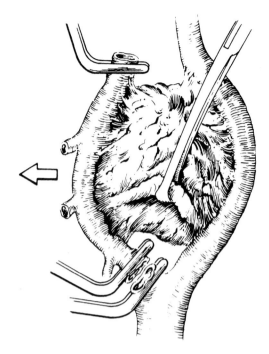

FIGURE 144-11 Ligation and division of the external carotid artery facilitates control of the carotid body tumor blood supply and aids in mobilizing large tumors. The vessel is removed with the tumor. (From Krupski WC, Effeney DJ, Ehrenfeld WK, Stoney RJ: Cervical chemodectoma: Technical considerations and management options. Am J Surg 144:219, 1982.)

followed. However, control of the external carotid artery may be especially difficult because it gives rise to the blood supply of the tumor.

Occasionally, with very large tumors, the distal ICA cannot be exposed and arterial reconstruction is impossible. In this case, sacrifice of the ICA may be required. However, ligation of the internal common carotid artery results in a stroke incidence ranging from 23% to 50% and a mortality rate of 14% to 64%.[143,164] When carotid ligation is anticipated preoperatively, temporary occlusion of the carotid artery in the awake patient during preoperative arteriography helps predict the outcome of ligation. Alternatively, oculopneumoplethysmography may be useful in evaluating the cerebral collateral circulation and the patient's ability to tolerate carotid artery occlusion.[70]

After proximal and distal arterial control has been obtained, the tumor should be mobilized circumferentially to assess the extent of disease. The hypoglossal and vagus nerves must be identified and protected during this dissection. Resection should not be carried out within the media of the vessels. This can lead to a weakened wall, predisposing the patient to intraoperative hemorrhage or postoperative carotid blowout. Instead, the plane of dissection should be periadventitial, in a so-called white line described by Gordon-Taylor.[75] Unfortunately, this white line is often difficult to find, particularly because carotid body tumors do not have a true capsule and do not shave off the arterial wall easily.

The tumor should be removed beginning at the inferior extent and continuing cephalad. Two particular areas of difficulty are the carotid bifurcation and the posterior surface, which often encompasses the superior laryngeal nerve. Tumors may extend quite high. The posterior belly of the digastric muscle should then be divided, preferably at its insertion into the mastoid groove. The digastric muscle should also be divided to improve exposure and resection of the stylomandibular ligament when access to the most distal ICA is required.

If the proper plane between the tumor and the carotid artery cannot be developed because of transmural tumor invasion of the arterial wall, carotid resection may be required. When this is necessary, a segment of greater saphenous vein harvested from the thigh can be used as an interposition graft. In some cases, earlier ligation and division of the external carotid artery may reduce blood flow and facilitate further resection of the tumor (Fig. 144-11).[123] The clamped external carotid artery can then be used as a "handle" to assist in mobilization of the shrunken tumor. Reconstruction of the external carotid artery following tumor removal is not necessary, and the external carotid stump may be oversewn.

The liberal use of arteriography and modern surgical techniques have reduced the risk of postoperative stroke in carotid body tumor resection from approximately 30% to less than 5%. However, the incidence of cranial nerve injury remains strikingly high, ranging from 20% to 40%.[86,123,178] Because of the high incidence of cranial nerve injury, some have questioned the appropriateness of surgical treatment, because many of these tumors may be small and slow growing. However, because the morbidity of surgical removal is lowest when the tumors are small, generally they should be removed soon after diagnosis to minimize the risk of postoperative nerve dysfunction (Fig. 144-12).

Most patients do well after curative resection of malignant carotid body tumors. Survival of patients after tumor resection is equivalent to that of sex- and age-matched controls. Metastatic disease develops in fewer than 2% of patients undergoing resection, and only 6% of patients

FIGURE 144-12 Postoperative photograph taken after resection of the carotid body tumor shown in Figure 144-7. The adventitia of the carotid arteries is intact; the external carotid artery is preserved.

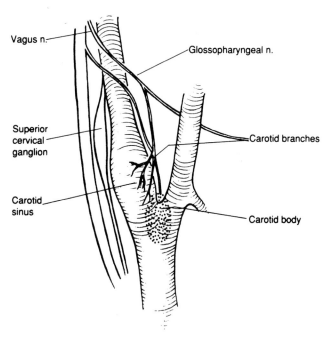

FIGURE 144-13 Diagram of the carotid sinus and the carotid body. The nerve of Hering is shown as it courses to the glossopharyngeal nerve. (From Hollinshead WH: Anatomy for surgeons. In The Head and Neck, Vol 1. New York, Hoeber & Harper, 1958.)

experience recurrence after complete resection.[164] Periodic clinical observation is indicated in patients with carotid body tumors to detect multicentric or recurrent disease. Those with interposition grafts should undergo duplex scanning periodically to identify graft stenoses. Finally, examination of the patient's first-degree relatives is advisable in cases of suspected familial carotid body tumors.

■ CAROTID SINUS SYNDROME

The carotid sinus is located at the distal end of the common carotid artery as it branches into the internal and external carotid arteries. It is a localized area of dilation where the tunica media is thinner and the adventitia is thicker than elsewhere in the arterial wall. The *carotid sinus* must be differentiated from the *carotid bulb*. The carotid bulb is a fusiform enlargement of the first portion of the ICA, immediately adjacent to the bifurcation of the common carotid artery (Fig. 144-13). The carotid sinus is a collection of sensory nerve endings, with an unusual amount of elastic tissue where smooth muscle cells are scarce. The carotid sinus is baroreceptor tissue; when stimulated by increased intraluminal pressure, it produces reflex bradycardia and decreased blood pressure. The nerve of Hering arises from the glossopharyngeal nerve and has been designated the *carotid sinus nerve*. It supplies the carotid sinus and the carotid body, and it synapses with the cardioinhibitory and vasomotor centers in the medulla through efferent fibers that are carried in the vagus nerve. (Some anatomists have

labeled this the *nerve of de Castro.*) The nerve of Hering may descend either on the surface of the ICA or between the internal and external carotid artery branches.

CSS consists of syncope caused by carotid sinus hypersensitivity. Patients experience the sudden onset of bradycardia and hypotension. Although the syndrome has been attributed to a hypersensitive carotid sinus, the true pathophysiology is unknown. CSS occurs in elderly patients, most commonly men; it is associated with atherosclerosis, diabetes, hypertension, and coronary artery disease.[202,243] The existence of this syndrome has been questioned, because denervation of one or both carotid sinuses does not produce prolonged and permanently increased blood pressure in patients who have undergone carotid endarterectomy. Thus, CSS must be differentiated from far more common causes of syncope in the elderly—arrhythmias, vertebrobasilar insufficiency, hypoglycemia, orthostatic hypotension, vasovagal attacks, aortic stenosis, and, probably most commonly, overmedication with antihypertensives. It has been estimated that fewer than 1% of elderly patients with syncope have CSS.[108]

A unique finding in patients with CSS is that direct carotid sinus massage or pressure at the carotid artery reproduces symptoms that may be related to both *heart rate-independent* factors and *heart rate-dependent* factors.[78] It is interesting that right-sided hypersensitivity is more frequent than left-sided hypersensitivity. One third of patients describe a prodrome before syncope, and one third have retrograde amnesia. In approximately half of patients, syncope may be precipitated by head movement.[113] Many patients are taking antihypertensive agents and other medications that block compensatory heart rate. If possible,

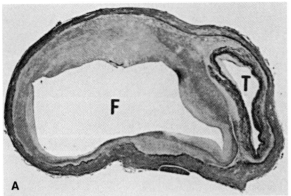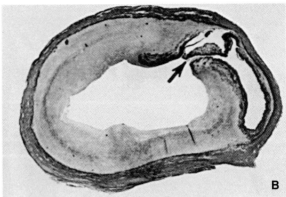

FIGURE 144-14 A, Cross section through an aneurysmal segment of a dissected extracranial internal carotid artery. Note the true lumen (T) with its surrounding intact internal elastic lamina. The false lumen (F) is formed within the media. The external elastic lamina and adventitia surround both lumina. Numerous blood vessel elements are present in the outer vessel wall. **B,** An adjacent cross section reveals the actual intimal tear *(arrow)* and an entry/reentry point of communication between the true and false lumina. (**A** and **B,** From Mokri M: Dissections of cervical and cephalic arteries. In Meyer FB [ed]: Sundt's Occlusive Cerebrovascular Disease. Philadelphia, WB Saunders, 1994, p 46.)

discontinuation of these medications is efficacious. Carotid body denervation has been suggested in the past for patients with CSS.[3,35] Currently, carotid body denervation is not recommended because patients have better results when cardiac pacemakers are implanted.[21]

Of historical interest is a report by Nakayama that bilateral carotid body excision controlled carbon dioxide retention in patients with asthma.[169] Nakayama reported success in 65% of a staggering 3914 patients who underwent the procedure. Because chemoreceptive tissue exists throughout the body, however, partial excision would be expected to be of little benefit. Follow-up studies demonstrated deleterious effects of this procedure; it has subsequently been abandoned.[248]

■ CAROTID ARTERY DISSECTION

Arterial dissection consists of intimal disruption, with extravasation of blood into layers of the arterial wall producing luminal stenosis, occlusion, or aneurysm formation (Fig. 144-14).[155] Carotid artery dissections are of two types: (1) "spontaneous" dissection, which occurs presumably without cause, and (2) "all others," which include dissections for which a precipitating cause can be identified. However, distinction between these types is imprecise. Unquestionably, dissection of the cervical segment of the carotid artery may occur as a result of penetrating or blunt trauma. In fact, the first case of extracranial dissection of the ICA was described (more than a century ago) in a patient who sustained a blunt, nonpenetrating trauma.[235] Seventy years elapsed before the next case was reported.[27] Subsequently, many cases of both traumatic and spontaneous dissection of the carotid artery have been reported.*

In addition to blunt trauma associated with automobile accidents, other mechanisms have produced ICA dissections, including fist fights, boxing, falls, direct neck trauma, accidental hanging, diagnostic carotid compression, and chiropractic manipulative therapy.[157] Hyperextension and rotation of the neck may produce intimal tears by stretching the ICA against the transverse processes of the second and third cervical vertebrae (Fig. 144-15).[253]

Spontaneous carotid dissections were first described by Jentzer in 1954.[106] Five years later, Anderson and Schechter described a second case of spontaneous carotid dissection.[5] Since that time, almost 300 cases have been reported, but the true incidence is difficult to determine because the diagnosis is easily missed in patients who have minimal or no symptoms.[77] In an early series of carotid dissections reported by Ehrenfeld and Wylie, the term *spontaneous dissection* was popularized because a history of recent past cervical trauma or unusual head position or movement preceding the onset of symptoms was not described for any of their group of 19 patients.[52] Despite that publication, controversy continues as to whether or not carotid dissection truly occurs in a spontaneous fashion. In some cases, the role of trivial trauma cannot be entirely excluded. For example, carotid dissection has been described after "bottoms-up" drinking; whiplash injuries; head turning while leading a parade; diving into water; childbirth; paroxysms of coughing, retching, or vomiting; and "head banging" during punk rock dancing.[60,89,103,230,242]

The misleading term *dissecting aneurysm* has often been applied to any arterial dissection with or without aneurysmal dilation. In fact, aneurysmal dilation in initial stages rarely is present. As the intramural hematoma dissects the vessel wall and expands toward the adventitia, aneurysmal dilation can occur as a late complication.

Pathology

As the hematoma dissects into the vessel wall, it creates a false lumen within the media. Dissections may be in close proximity to the arterial lumen *(subintimal dissections)* or

*See References 4, 12, 52, 60, 68, 76, 89, 94, 106, 137, 154, 156, 158, 175, 222, 230, 242, 253, and 254.

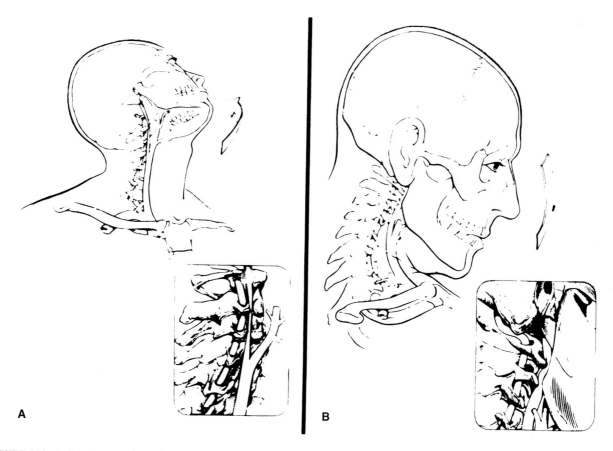

FIGURE 144-15 A, Hyperextension and rotation of the head subject the opposite carotid artery to stretching and compression injury (1) by the lateral mass of the first cervical vertebra (C1) or the transverse processes of C2 and C3 (**B**); (2) by direct compression between the angle of the mandible and the transverse processes of C2 and C3 through extreme flexion of the head on the neck; or (3) by fracture or posterior dislocation of the mandible. (**A** and **B,** From Mokri M: Dissections of cervical and cephalic arteries. In Meyer FB [ed]: Sundt's Occlusive Cerebrovascular Disease. Philadelphia, WB Saunders, 1994, p 59.)

to the adventitia *(subadventitial dissections).* Occasionally, rupture occurs back into the arterial lumen, creating a "double-lumen" or a "reentry" phenomenon. The false lumen may compress and narrow the true lumen or may expand toward the adventitia, causing aneurysmal dilation.[137]

In general, the pathogenesis of spontaneous dissection of the ICA artery is unclear in most patients. Atherosclerotic changes in the vessels of patients suffering this disorder are unusual. However, carotid artery dissections have been noted and are associated with Marfan syndrome and fibromuscular dysplasia (FMD) of the ICA.[4,10,156,190,252] The usual location of the intimal tear, the starting point of the dissection, is within 2 to 4 cm of the bifurcation. Thus, it arises in the carotid bulb. In general, the dissection stops at the entrance of the carotid into the carotid canal, but exceptions do exist. Dissections into the cavernous and petrous portions of the ICA have been described.

In spontaneous dissection, histologic abnormalities of the artery are difficult to detect unless arterial resection is required because of extensive arterial pathology, such as in FMD or Marfan syndrome. As is usually encountered in dissections, direct communication between the hematoma and arterial lumen cannot be demonstrated. Subtle luminal irregularities remote from the site of dissection have

been noted.[94] The significance of these irregularities is unclear, and they may represent an early form of FMD. This was substantiated when Wirth and coworkers described such irregularities, which ultimately proved to be a type of FMD.[247]

Epidemiology

The true incidence of carotid dissection is unknown. ICA dissection occurs in all age groups, but it is more common in young adults. The mean patient age ranges from 41 to 51 years but tends to be lower in those sustaining known traumatic dissections.[18,89] Hypertension is present in about 40% of patients, in contrast to the lower incidence (14% to 20%) found in the general population in age- and sex-matched controls.

Dissections are often multiple and involve both cervical and visceral arteries in some patients.[154] There is an increased incidence of intracranial aneurysms in patients with carotid artery dissections.[203] In addition, familial intracranial aneurysm and carotid artery dissections have been reported, suggesting the occurrence of a primary arteriopathy in some of these patients.[158] Preference for one gender or side has not been clearly demonstrated.[7,151]

Clinical Presentation

Carotid artery dissections often produce multiple symptoms. This multiplicity of symptoms makes the diagnosis difficult, and the disorder can easily be missed in trauma patients who present with an altered level of consciousness. The principal manifestation in patients with spontaneous carotid dissection is pain, which usually occurs as unilateral headache, particularly in the anterior aspect of the head or in the orbital and periorbital regions. Headaches may also be diffuse or bilateral; they are usually described as steady and nonthrobbing, with fluctuations in intensity. Neck pain occurs much less frequently than does headache. When it does occur, it is often associated with headache and is usually unilateral in the anterolateral aspect of the neck. Patients rarely report scalp tenderness ipsilateral to the headache.

There is discrepancy in the literature with respect to the frequency of central neurologic symptoms associated with carotid dissection. TIAs, stroke, or both have been reported in one third to three fourths of patients with this disorder.[18,68,89,157] The most common combination of symptoms associated with spontaneous carotid dissection is unilateral headache followed by delayed cerebral ischemic symptoms.[162] Mechanisms for hemispheric neurologic deficits include emboli due to platelet aggregates and thrombus formation at sites of intimal damage. Flow reduction from luminal stenosis has also been postulated as a potential mechanism for neurologic symptoms. Subarachnoid hemorrhage can also occur in patients who suffer intracranial carotid artery dissection.[63]

The third most common clinical presentation in patients with spontaneous carotid dissection is *oculosympathetic paresis*, which may occur minutes to days after the onset of headaches. The oculosympathetic paresis of dissection of the ICA consists of incomplete Horner's syndrome, so that facial sweating is unaffected. The cause of this presentation is presumed to be involvement of the sympathetic fibers that accompany the ICA, with sparing of the external carotid plexus that produces facial sweating.

Palsies of other lower cranial nerves have also been described, with dysgeusia (involvement of the chorda tympani branch of cranial nerve VII), slurred speech (involvement of cranial nerve XII), and dysphagia (involvement of cranial nerves IX and X).[129,154] The precise mechanism of lower cranial nerve palsies is unknown. Proposed mechanisms include direct compression of the lower cranial nerves below the jugular foramen by the dissected artery. Alternatively, an anomalous artery that originates from the petrous or extrapetrous ICA in the neck may be compromised, thus affecting the vascular supply to the nearby cranial nerves. A third proposed mechanism is compromise of an anomalous ascending pharyngeal artery, which arises from the cervical ICA that supplies the lower cranial nerves. Cranial nerve XII is most commonly involved.[159]

Headache, focal cerebral ischemic symptoms, oculosympathetic paresis, and peripheral nerve symptoms may occur in various combinations in patients with dissections of the ICA. Two more distinct syndromes are (1) unilateral headache associated with ipsilateral oculosympathetic paresis, and (2) unilateral headache accompanying delayed focal cerebral ischemic events. Involvement of lower cranial nerves is much less common.

Diagnosis

As with atherosclerotic carotid artery stenosis, evaluation of carotid dissections should begin with a carotid duplex scan. Although ICA dissections usually occur distal to the carotid bifurcation at about the C2 vertebral level (beyond the range of carotid ultrasonography), the Doppler signal of the proximal ICA or of the common carotid artery is usually abnormal and suggestive of distal stenosis or occlusion.[12,254] Because the patients are usually young, they do not often have significant coexistent atherosclerosis. Occasionally, the image demonstrates the intimal flap.

Recently, MR imaging has played an increasing role in the diagnosis of ICA and vertebral artery dissections. Diagnosis of arterial dissection is made when both the arterial lumen and the intramural hematoma are shown. The lumen appears as a dark, circular area resulting from flow void, which is usually smaller than the normal ICA caliber. The intramural hematoma appears hyperintense and bright in both T1- and T2-weighted images, surrounding the area of flow void as a bright crescent.[195,205] Advances in MR angiography also have added to the diagnostic capabilities of MR imaging. MR imaging, in combination with MR angiography, eventually may be the modality of choice for most cases of carotid and vertebral artery dissections.

Despite advances in these newer modalities, angiography remains the gold standard for the diagnosis of carotid artery dissection. Arteriography demonstrates the origin of the dissection, the extent of dissection, the presence of distal embolization, and collateral blood flow. The arteriographic appearances of carotid dissections vary, depending on severity and extent. Typical features include luminal stenosis, decreased flow in the ICA and middle cerebral artery, tapered occlusion, distal branch occlusions, abrupt reconstitution of the lumen, intimal flaps, and aneurysm of the extracranial arterial segment.

Luminal stenosis is the most common angiographic finding. It usually is elongated, tapered, and irregular and extends to the base of the skull and the carotid canal. The length of dissection is usually 2 to 4 cm, localized to the level of the first and second cervical vertebral bodies.[162] Reconstitution of the lumen is also fairly common. This usually occurs at the entrance of the ICA into the carotid canal (Fig. 144-16). The elongated, tapered narrowing has been described as a "string sign" by Ojemann and colleagues.[175]

Aneurysms occur in about one third of ICAs involved by dissection. They are usually located in the upper cervical and subcranial regions (Fig. 144-17).[161] Emboli occluding distal cervical branches occur in about 10% of patients; in about 25% of cases, dissections of the ICAs are bilateral.

Natural History

Most patients who present with carotid dissection do well. Seventy-eight percent to 92% of patients recover when they either had mild symptoms or were asymptomatic.[89,151,157]

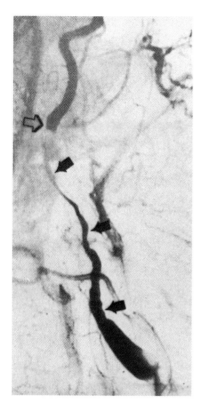

FIGURE 144-16 Dissection of the cervical segment of the internal carotid artery. Note the elongated, narrowed, and tapered luminal stenosis *(solid arrows)*, a finding frequently seen in association with extracranial dissections. Another common feature of this entity, fairly abrupt reconstitution of the carotid lumen at the base of the skull *(open arrow)*, is also shown. (From Mokri M: Dissections of cervical and cephalic arteries. In Meyer FB [ed]: Sundt's Occlusive Cerebrovascular Disease. Philadelphia, WB Saunders, 1994, p 51.)

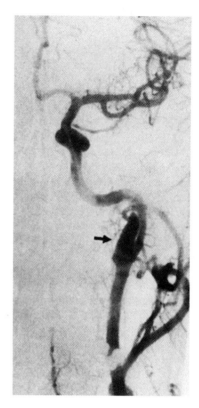

FIGURE 144-17 Finger-like aneurysm formation along a point of dissection of the cervical segment of the internal carotid artery *(arrow)* lying parallel to the course of the vessel. (From Mokri M: Dissections of cervical and cephalic arteries. In Meyer FB [ed]: Sundt's Occlusive Cerebrovascular Disease. Philadelphia, WB Saunders, 1994, p 51.)

Those who present with fixed neurologic deficits do less well, with a 40% rate of return of good function.[18] Traumatic dissections are more likely to result in fixed neurologic deficits than are spontaneous dissections.

In contrast to neurologic signs, oculosympathetic paresis resolves less frequently. It persists in two thirds of patients as a result of permanent damage to the sympathetic fibers in the ICA plexus. Clinical Horner's syndrome, however, is usually quite mild and does not create significant functional or esthetic problems. Headaches resolve in 95% of patients, three fourths of whom recover within 3 months. Residual dissection with aneurysm formation may produce persistent headache. Angiographically, stenoses of the ICA either completely resolve or significantly improve in approximately 85% of patients; complete resolution occurs in more than half of patients, and significant improvement occurs in 30%.[94,160] Although recanalization of a completely occluded vessel can occur, this is uncommon. Aneurysms resolve or diminish in size in two thirds of involved vessels, and these aneurysms rarely rupture. Recurrence of dissection in the same vessel is extremely rare.

In summary, spontaneous dissection of the ICA is associated with a relatively good prognosis. Complete or excellent clinical recovery occurs in 85% of patients, and stenotic lesions improve or completely resolve in 85% of vessels. Most aneurysms resulting from dissection resolve angiographically or diminish in size.

Treatment

Because carotid dissection is uncommon and there are no controlled studies regarding treatment, the proper therapy for extracranial dissection of the ICA has not been firmly established. Although Ehrenfeld and Wylie originally recommended operative treatment, they also recognized the unfavorable outcomes associated with surgical intervention in many cases.[52] In many instances, surgical revascularization was limited by technical difficulties involved in obtaining distal control. This discouraging early surgical experience, in conjunction with the remarkably favorable results of nonoperative therapy, has led most authorities to recommend anticoagulation as standard management. Surgical intervention is performed only when medical therapy fails and when the lesion is surgically accessible.[18] Surgical intervention may include thrombectomy, progressive intraluminal dilation, endarterectomy, intimectomy, or graft interposition.

Carotid ligation has also been suggested for patients with recurrent embolization, with or without concomitant EC-IC bypass, depending on carotid back-pressure and collateral circulatory status. Carotid stump pressure at or above 70 mm Hg is thought to be satisfactory to permit safe carotid ligation.[52] Most authorities recommend anticoagulation with heparin and then warfarin (Coumadin) for a period of 3 to 4 months, followed by antiplatelet treatment for a similar period.[89,162]

Treatment of patients with traumatic carotid dissections is even less unequivocally established. Presentation and angiographic findings are similar to those of patients with spontaneous dissections of the ICA, with the exception that fixed neurologic deficits are more common. This is thought to be due to an increased incidence of distal embolization. If there is apparent potential for thromboembolism in patients with traumatic ICA dissections, anticoagulation should be strongly considered. However, this may not be advisable because of hemorrhagic risk owing to concomitant traumatic injuries.

Most patients who survive the initial episode do well. Traumatic dissections result in aneurysms or chronic luminal irregularities more frequently than do spontaneous dissections.[154] Compared with the spontaneous group, fewer patients with traumatic dissections are asymptomatic at follow-up. Although both traumatic and spontaneous dissections of the carotid arteries have a good prognosis, the outcome is less favorable in the traumatic group. Nevertheless, initial anticoagulation therapy followed by repeat angiography within a few months appears to be the most reasonable strategy for these patients.

■ VASCULITIS

Cerebral vasculitis—or arteritis—is really a spectrum of disorders including lymphoid granuloma, collagen diseases, giant cell arteritis (temporal arteritis), Takayasu's disease, and Behçet's disease.[55,95,226,239] The focus here is cerebral vasculitis. A number of these disorders are more broadly described in Chapters 26 to 28. Arteritis is an inflammatory process resulting in necrosis of the structural elements of the vessel wall. Obliteration of the lumen produces ischemia of dependent tissues as the terminal event. The course of vasculitis is usually quite variable, with unusual and varied clinical presentations. Vasculitis may affect blood vessels of any type, location, or size. The nomenclature and classification of vasculitis in the literature are quite confusing. Moreover, there is no definitive laboratory test or pathognomonic or clinical sign for most of these syndromes. The diagnosis depends on a combination of clinical, radiologic, laboratory, and histologic information.

Cerebrovascular arteritis is generally classified as *primary* or *secondary*. Primary vasculitis manifests only as vascular disease; secondary vasculitis complicates an underlying systemic primary illness.[118] Theories abound regarding the etiology of arteritis. Most authorities implicate humoral and cellular autoimmune mechanisms.[200] Circulating antibody complexes invade arterial walls, with triggering of the complement cascade. Polymorphonuclear leukocytes become activated and infiltrate the vessel wall, engulfing the immune complexes and producing damaging enzymes. Several primary types of vasculitis are characterized by granulomas; this finding weakens the immune complex model but does not exclude it, and it increases the likelihood of a cellular-mediated or combined mechanism.

Cerebral vasculitis can portray almost all central nervous signs and symptoms; the clinical presentation depends on whether the arteritis is primary or secondary. Women patients outnumber men by 2:1, and half of the patients are younger than 50 years of age. Focal neurologic deficits, including TIAs and strokes, often result from focal cerebral vasculitis. Cranial nerve palsies, especially when multiple, simulate vertebrobasilar insufficiency, producing diplopia, visual changes, dysphagia, tinnitus, vertigo, syncope, and headache. Diagnosis is further confused by the frequent angiographic appearance of luminal "beading" suggestive of FMD or arterial dissections.[128] Because angiography has a resolution of only 100 to 200 μm, vasculitis cannot reliably be excluded on the basis of a negative arteriogram.[111]

Treatment of arteritis usually requires steroids and anti-inflammatory drugs. However, because vasculitis is uncommon, the nomenclature is unstandardized, the diagnosis is empirical, and no control series exists regarding optimal treatment.

Giant Cell Arteritis

Giant cell arteritis is a generalized vasculitis that usually affects medium and large arteries in elderly patients, more commonly in women than men. Because granulomas typify the histology of this disorder, it has also been known as *granulomatous arteritis*. In addition, because it has been described in patients with rheumatoid arthritis, it has been called *polymyalgia rheumatica*. Classically, giant cell arteritis presents as temporal arteritis with headache, scalp tenderness, jaw claudication, and visual disturbances. Polymyalgia rheumatica, a systemic variety of giant cell arteritis, has been identified with increasing frequency due to a higher incidence of suspicion.

The lesions of giant cell arteritis occur in medium- to large-caliber arteries throughout the body. Most often, the aortic arch and the extracranial carotid arteries are involved. The inflammatory process consists of invasion of lymphocytes and plasma cells, with edema and fragmentation of the internal elastic lamina and deposition of multinucleated foreign body giant cells appearing late in the course of the disease. Gradually, the media is entirely replaced by connective tissue. The most prominent findings of giant cell arteritis are disruptions of the elastic lamina and media, with foreign body reaction leading to granulomatous degeneration. Lesions are typically short and segmental, with normal artery between lesions. Biopsy confirms the diagnosis but is not always accurate because of inadequate sample size.[13]

Giant cell arteritis, temporal arteritis, and Takayasu's arteritis all are characterized by necrotizing changes within the vessel wall, with giant cell granuloma formation. In addition, mild fever, malaise, weight loss, and an elevated erythrocyte sedimentation rate (ESR) accompany these disorders. Approximately 25% to 50% of patients have fever and weight loss.[28] The demography of these disorders is quite different, however. *Temporal arteritis* affects the elderly and responds promptly to early treatment. *Takayasu's arteritis* occurs in young individuals (mostly women) but has a much poorer prognosis. Giant cell or granulomatous arteritis is confined primarily to the central nervous system. It occurs in all ages in both sexes, and the prognosis is poor. Temporal arteritis is usually classified as a form of giant cell arteritis, illustrating the confusing nomenclature.

Giant cell arteritis appears almost exclusively in Caucasians.[14] Nordborg and Bengtsson reported the average incidence in Sweden of giant cell arteritis to be 6.7 per 100,000 inhabitants.[172] In individuals 50 years of age or older, the yearly incidence rose to 18.3 per 100,000 inhabitants, with 25 cases per 100,000 inhabitants in women and 9.4 per 100,000 in men.

Similar statistics were reported by investigators at the Mayo Clinic. In Olmstead County, Minnesota, giant cell arteritis occurred in 17 per 100,000 individuals older than 50 years of age.[139] Women were three times more likely to have giant cell arteritis than men. In both the Swedish and American studies, the incidence of giant cell arteritis in women appears to be increasing, whereas in men the rate is stable or decreasing.

Clinical Presentation

Typically, giant cell arteritis (which most commonly presents as temporal arteritis) produces a flulike syndrome, with low-grade fever, lassitude, and headache. After the initial event, patients often complain of jaw claudication, diffuse joint aches, and tender temporal arteries. In 20% to 60% of patients, amaurosis fugax, scintillating scotomata, diplopia, or permanent visual loss occurs in the second or third month. Laboratory findings are nonspecific. They may include an elevated ESR, mild thrombocytosis, leukocytosis, normocytic anemia, and elevations of prothrombin time, alkaline phosphatase, and transaminases. Patients with active disease may occasionally have a normal ESR. ESR elevation may be unmasked once anti-inflammatory drugs are discontinued.[107]

Temporal arteritis usually involves the branches of the external carotid artery, including the facial, occipital, internal maxillary, and especially the superficial temporal arteries. In addition, the posterior ciliary and ophthalmic arteries are frequently affected. Arteritis in the superficial temporal artery is probably responsible for the typical headache and ocular symptoms. Headache is a characteristic feature of those patients with temporal arteritis with external carotid artery involvement.

In the polymyalgia rheumatic variety, pain occurs in the muscles of the shoulder girdle in about 60% of patients.[28] When the superficial temporal artery or other external carotid branches are involved, the vessel is usually extremely tender to palpation, with spontaneous pain made worse by palpation. The vessel is often cordlike and difficult to compress, with reduced or absent pulsations. Often the overlying skin is swollen, erythematous, and warm. Pain may not be limited to the temporal area but may be facial, occipital, or diffuse. Duplex ultrasonography may be useful to localize a portion of the superficial temporal artery for biopsy, which is the preferred method for diagnosis. Characteristically, the involved segment has abnormal flow velocities.

Mumenthaler reported a 62% incidence of sudden and complete visual loss.[167] The mechanism of blindness involves loss of blood supply to the optic nerve because of occlusion of branches of the ophthalmic artery, usually the posterior ciliary arteries. It is not uncommon for the clinical course to progress to blindness in less than 24 hours, and recovery of vision almost never occurs even after institution of steroids and anti-inflammatory agents.[76] Persistent blindness is likely due to the inability to stop progressive thrombosis of the involved artery. On funduscopic examination, the retina appears pale, with decreased flow in the retinal vessels, diminished vessel size, and papilledema.

The temporal artery biopsy should include a 4- to 7-cm-long specimen, particularly when the artery is grossly normal because of intermittent distribution of lesions. Some authorities have recommended contralateral biopsy when the first biopsy is negative and the clinical suspicion is high.[57,85] Hall and Hunder reported a 14% incidence of positive contralateral biopsies.[85] In contrast, Klein and colleagues reported a series of 60 patients who underwent bilateral biopsies with only three cases of unilateral involvement.[120]

As indicated previously, angiography may miss lesions. When present, characteristic findings include tapered narrowings with post-stenotic dilation, vessel occlusion, and collateral vessel formation. Despite localization to the head, many arteries throughout the body are often involved. The aorta is involved in one half of affected patients, and the carotid and vertebral arteries also show typical changes.[246] The coronary and visceral arteries are affected less commonly. Thoracic aortic dissection and aneurysm formation have also been reported.[107,219]

Treatment

Because of the potential for rapid onset of permanent visual loss, temporal arteritis is considered to be a medical emergency. Steroids should be started immediately, followed by temporal artery biopsy. Positive biopsy results are not changed by 2 to 3 days of steroid treatment.[53,57,107] However, Allison and Gallagher reported that the positive biopsy rate fell from 60% to less than 10% after 1 week of steroid therapy.[2]

Arterial reconstruction is rarely necessary for patients with giant cell arteritis. Surgical indications may include aneurysm formation, aortic valvular incompetence, aortic dissection, or persistent ischemia after adequate medical therapy. Elective procedures ideally should be delayed until the disease becomes quiescent, because graft occlusion is common when operation is performed during the active phase of arteritis.[107]

The prognosis for patients with giant cell arteritis is good when they are treated expeditiously. The disease is generally self-limited and does not adversely influence life expectancy. Andersson and associates reported a survival rate similar to that of the general population in a series of 90 patients with giant cell arteritis followed for 9 to 16 years.[6]

Takayasu's Arteritis

A case of Takayasu's arteritis may have first been recognized as early as 1761, when Margagni described the autopsy findings in a 40-year-old woman with absent radial pulses, a thickened proximal aorta, lower thoracic aortic stenoses, cardiac hypertrophy, and pulmonary edema.[46] In

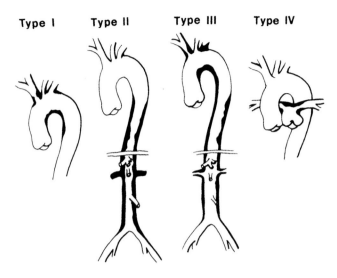

FIGURE 144-18 Classification system used to categorize the four types of arterial involvement in Takayasu's arteritis as determined by arteriography. (From Cottrell ED, Smith LL: Management of uncommon lesions affecting the extracranial vessels.)

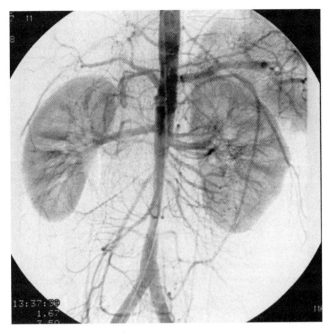

FIGURE 144-19 Abdominal aortogram demonstrating pathologic aortic anatomy as seen in a patient with type III Takayasu's arteritis. Note the narrowed infrarenal aortic segment and the prominent meandering mesenteric artery (superior mesenteric artery to inferior mesenteric artery collateral). The patient had diminished femoral artery pulses and depressed bilateral lower extremity segmental limb pressures.

1908, Takayasu, a Japanese ophthalmologist, described a young Japanese woman who presented with progressive visual loss, vertigo, syncope, conjunctival injection, retinal arteriovenous anastomoses, and alopecia.[226] A colleague of Takayasu, Onishi, noted that the retinal changes were associated with absent pulses in the upper extremities, and Takayasu's disease became known as *pulseless disease*.[117] A descriptive term is *obliterative brachiocephalic arteritis*, because involvement of the aortic arch and vessels is a prominent feature.

Although it was initially thought that there was a predilection for this condition in Asians, it is now clear that Takayasu's arteritis occurs in all races and age groups, but it is more common in women in the 2nd and 3rd decades of life.[72] It may occur as late as the 4th decade, however. In a 13-year population study at the Mayo Clinic of individuals of Olmstead County, Minnesota, three cases of Takayasu's disease were noted, for an incidence of 2.6 per million per year.[83]

Takayasu's arteritis involves the aortic arch and great vessels. Cerebral ischemia has been considered to be the most life-threatening complication of this disorder,[101] but reports from countries other than Japan have stressed a relatively greater involvement of other, more distal aortic segments, as well as the pulmonary and coronary arteries (see also Chapter 26). Accordingly, Lupi-Herrera,[138] Ueno,[232] and their colleagues have described four distinct classifications of Takayasu's disease (Fig. 144-18).

- *Type I* is Takayasu's original description involving the aortic arch and great vessels; roughly 20% to 40% of patients have this distribution of disease, which results in signs and symptoms of cerebrovascular insufficiency, including visual abnormalities.
- Another 20% to 40% of patients with Takayasu's disease have a middle aortic syndrome *(type II)* in which the distal thoracic and visceral abdominal aorta is affected;

these patients present with mesenteric ischemia and symptoms of postprandial pain, fear of food, weight loss, and renal artery stenosis or occlusion with hypertension (Fig. 144-19).
- Most patients, 50% to 65%, have *type III*, which involves both the aortic arch and the abdominal aorta. These patients may present with both cerebrovascular and lower extremity symptoms as well as hypertension.
- Only 10% of patients have *type IV* Takayasu's disease in which the pulmonary arteries are involved.

Pathophysiology

Patients with Takayasu's arteritis typically present with three distinct clinical phases. The *first phase* is characterized by prodromal symptoms that are primarily constitutional: malaise, anorexia, fatigue, weight loss, anemia, myalgias, fevers, and night sweats. Because of these vague symptoms, it was long thought that a causal relationship existed between Takayasu's arteritis and tuberculosis and other indolent chronic infections. This was particularly true in Third World countries, such as China, where large numbers of patients with this disorder were referred from rural areas with lower living standards and where infections were especially common.

The *second phase* revolves around inflammation of blood vessels, in which discomfort in the region of the involved arteries is described by patients. In the *third*, or "burned out," *phase*, patients present with symptoms of ischemia caused by arterial stenosis, embolization, or occlusion and, less commonly, aneurysm formation.

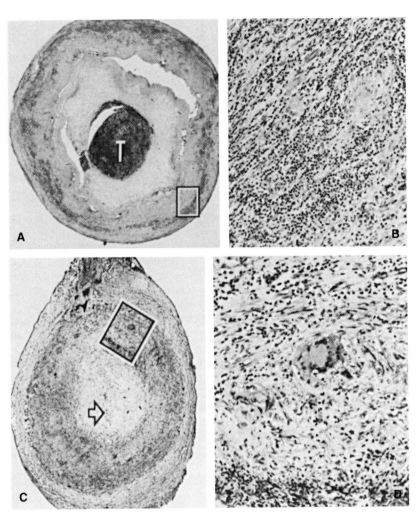

FIGURE 144-20 Photomicrographs of Takayasu's arteritis of the carotid artery (**A** and **B**) and temporal arteritis (**C** and **D**). (**A**, ×16; **B**, ×160; **C**, ×40; **D**, ×160.) Both are granulomatous giant cell arteritides, as shown in **B** (boxed area of **A**) and in **D** (boxed area of **C**) at higher magnifications. Thrombosis (T) and occlusive proliferation *(arrow)* are common complications (hematoxylin-eosin). (**A-D**, From Lie JT: Pathology of occlusive disease of the extracranial arteries. In Meyer FB [ed]: Sundt's Occlusive Cerebrovascular Disease. Philadelphia, WB Saunders, 1994, p 39.)

Pathologic changes of Takayasu's arteritis include inflammation of all three layers of the arterial wall (intima, media, and adventitia) (Fig. 144-20). In the inflammatory stage of the disease, macrophages and giant cells are abundant, and acute lesions show edema of the wall and lymphocytic infiltration. The elastic lamina becomes fragmented. However, despite the large number of giant cells, caseation and cavitation are absent. Patchy involvement of the vessel, with frequent "skip" areas, is characteristic, and diseased segments show varying amounts of intimal thickening and narrowing. In the latter stages of disease, fibrous scarring of the media and adventitia occurs along the length of the vessel in conjunction with degeneration of the media and deposition of ground substance in the intima.[46,194,236] Eventually, thrombosis occurs, occasionally followed by recanalization. Deterioration of the arterial wall with aneurysm formation also may develop.

Clinical Presentation

As would be expected from the distribution of lesions and phases of the clinical course, the clinical presentation of patients with Takayasu's disease can vary. Signs and symptoms of ischemia may occur early in the course or may not appear until many years after onset of systemic inflam-matory symptoms. The patient's symptoms are completely dependent on location of the lesions in Takayasu's arteritis. Aortic involvement may result in renovascular hypertension, mesenteric ischemia, and lower extremity insufficiency. Aortic arch and brachiocephalic involvement produces TIAs, visual impairment, stroke, and effort fatigue of the upper extremities. In the Mayo Clinic series of 32 patients with Takayasu's disease, 14 (45%) presented with symptoms of upper extremity vascular insufficiency, and 30 (94%) had multiple bruits.[83] Visual symptoms, including amaurosis fugax, diplopia, and blurred vision, have been described in about one third of patients.[84] In patients with pulmonary involvement, pulmonary hypertension, dyspnea on exertion, and pleuritic chest pain may develop. Ascending aortic involvement may also produce aortic valvular insufficiency owing to aneurysm formation.

The diagnosis of Takayasu's disease relies on a careful clinical evaluation and a high index of suspicion. The ESR is usually elevated in the inflammatory phase of the disease, but it may be normal in the burned-out phase or when patients are treated with anti-inflammatory agents and steroids. Angiography is essential to document the extent of the disease and to confirm the diagnosis. Typically, angiograms show stenosis or occlusion of the proximal extracranial cerebral arteries in the vicinity of the aorta

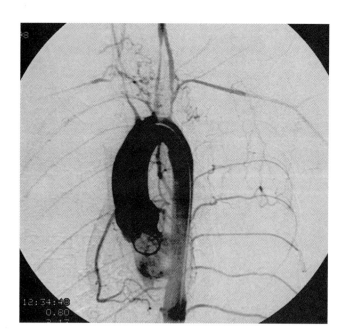

FIGURE 144-21 Arch aortogram from a young woman with Takayasu's arteritis. This demonstrates a critical uniform narrowing of the innominate artery, leading to a complete occlusion at its bifurcation. There is a tight stenosis of the left common carotid artery at its mid-portion; the left subclavian orifice is nearly occluded.

(Fig. 144-21). In a series of 244 angiograms reviewed by Liu, 85% of lesions were purely stenotic, 2% were aneurysmal, and the rest were a combination of both.[134]

Serial angiography may be necessary to determine the progress and extent of disease. Ultrasonography may also be used in the detection and follow-up of carotid lesions in patients with Takayasu's arteritis.[20,22,140] The so-called macaroni sign is characteristic of Takayasu's disease. This is described as diffuse, circumferential vessel thickening in the common carotid artery, which decreases as the disease becomes quiescent.[140]

Ishikawa has reviewed the clinical course of 96 Japanese patients with Takayasu's arteritis.[99] Diagnostic criteria included one *obligatory* criterion (age of 40 years or younger at diagnosis or at onset of characteristic signs and symptoms of 1 month's duration); two *major* criteria (left and right subclavian artery lesions); and nine *minor* criteria (elevated ESR, common carotid tenderness, hypertension, aortic regurgitation, and lesions of the pulmonary artery, left mid-common carotid artery, distal brachiocephalic trunk, descending thoracic aorta, and abdominal aorta). In 60 of 64 patients with active disease, these criteria were fulfilled. In 21 of the 32 patients with inactive disease they were not, producing an overall sensitivity of 84%. In addition to the obligatory criteria, the presence of two major criteria, or one major plus two or more minor criteria, or four or more minor criteria suggested the high possibility of Takayasu's disease.

Natural History

The course of Takayasu's arteritis is unpredictable. In his reviews of this disorder, Ishikawa noted that prognosis of Takayasu's arteritis was dependent on the presence of

complications and the severity of disease.[99,100] Patients with hypertension, retinopathy, aortic valvular insufficiency, and aneurysm formation, in conjunction with a progressive clinical course, had a 6-year survival rate of only 55%. Conversely, patients without these complications and with stable disease had a 6-year survival rate of 98%. In the Mayo Clinic study, Hall and colleagues reported a 5-year survival rate of 94%.[83] Death was most commonly due to congestive heart failure, stroke, myocardial infarction, or renal failure.

Treatment

Takayasu's arteritis is probably best managed by intensive treatment with steroids and anti-inflammatory agents, which should be given at a high initial dosage and, then, depending on response, gradually tapered to a maintenance dose. Most patients can discontinue steroid therapy eventually, but others may require maintenance steroids for 5 years or more. In patients without any response to clinical steroids after 3 months, cyclophosphamide therapy should be added.[209]

Long-term anticoagulation therapy has also been recommended, but the results are inconclusive and for the most part disappointing. In the Mayo Clinic series, 29 patients with active Takayasu's disease were treated with oral prednisone.[83] Substantial reduction in systemic inflammatory symptoms occurred in all patients within days to weeks. Eight of 16 patients with absent pulses had return of pulses, and 13 patients were able to discontinue steroids after duration of therapy of only 22 months. Not all studies have reported such dramatic improvement and regression of the lesion, as shown by angiography, by treatment with corticosteroids.[209,212,240]

Up to one third of patients with chronic advanced Takayasu's arteritis require surgery for palliation or prevention of ischemic complications. However, the role of surgical intervention is controversial, and multiple questions exist regarding timing, efficacy, and durability. Whenever possible, operative intervention should be delayed until the active phase of the disease has passed.[72,83] Ideally, patients should not be taking corticosteroids or cyclophosphamide, but often discontinuation of these agents is impossible.

Transmural disease involves all layers of the vessel wall. Endarterectomy or patch angioplasty is not recommended. Instead, interposition grafting should be performed when necessary. Suture lines should not be placed in diseased segments to avoid false aneurysms and stenoses.[115,181]

Giordano and coworkers reported excellent results in selected patients.[72] In 21 vascular surgery operations performed on 10 patients with Takayasu's arteritis, there were no deaths. Seven of these procedures were for cerebral revascularization; during an average follow-up of 5 years, no strokes occurred.

Multiple operations are often required in these patients.[209] All patients require close postoperative surveillance because of the frequent development of anastomotic stenoses, which can occur as early as 1 or 2 years after the initial operation.

Radiation-Induced Carotid Arteritis and Stenosis

In 1899, Gassman reported vascular endothelial edema and perforation with subsequent luminal narrowing after radiation therapy.[66] Cade described rupture of irradiated arteries in 1940.[25] Radiation-induced atherosclerosis in large blood vessels was reported by Thomas and Forbus in 1959.[228] In the mid-1970s, numerous reports associated cerebral ischemic cerebrovascular disease and cervical irradiation.[40,132,211] These reports highlighted the general absence of significant atherosclerotic risk factors in patients who developed carotid atherosclerosis after cervical irradiation. In addition, patients tended to be younger and had an unusual distribution of occlusive disease in that arterial lesions were limited to the field of radiation.

When irradiated, small vessels develop plaque-like thickening of the intima owing to the collection of fluid, with foam cells and hyaline material between the endothelium and the internal elastic membrane.[208] These plaques narrow the lumen and decrease perfusion to local tissue. Fonkalsrud and colleagues have divided changes that occur in irradiated arteries into *acute* and *chronic* phases, based on experiments in dogs.[61] After a 10-day total dose of 4000 cGy of radiation, endothelial injury was demonstrated within 48 hours. Changes included nuclear disruption, deposition of fibrin, and cell sloughing. The media was minimally affected, and the adventitia showed only mild fibrosis and hemorrhage. After 2 to 3 weeks, endothelium regenerated, whereas the media and adventitia demonstrated marked necrosis and hemorrhage. After 4 months, the endothelial surface became thickened and irregular, the media and adventitia continued to fibrose, and the regeneration of endothelium in conjunction with the fibrosis of the media-adventitia narrowed the lumen.

These pathologic changes predisposed vessels to thrombosis and lipid accumulation. This intimal cell injury model was similar to other studies involving direct endothelial injury to produce experimental atherosclerosis. A high-cholesterol diet administered after radiation therapy accelerates atheromatous changes in animal models.[74,147] Later, pathologic changes to the media and adventitia are responsible for the total vessel involvement, which may be secondary to injury to the vasa vasorum. The common carotid artery has a predilection for radiation-induced changes, particularly in patients with hypercholesteremia.[135] Irradiation-induced occlusive vascular disease takes three patterns.[24] The first pattern consists of intimal damage producing mural thrombosis occurring within the first 5 years after irradiation. The second pattern occurs at about 10 years and consists of fibrotic occlusion. Twenty years after irradiation, periarterial fibrosis and accelerated atherosclerosis occur.

Although clinically and angiographically these lesions are indistinguishable from those of atherosclerosis, there are certain characteristic features of radiation-induced disease. Often, the narrowing is diffuse rather than focal, as is seen in standard atherosclerosis.[144] Symptoms often develop at an earlier age in patients with radiation-induced disease than with non-radiation-induced atherosclerosis, and patients are less likely to have associated coronary or other vascular disease, since irradiation injuries are localized to the irradiated areas.[17,24,54,135]

Despite all this extensive investigation, it is still unclear whether radiation induces atherosclerosis or accelerates its formation in susceptible individuals. All studies using duplex scans of carotid arteries in patients who have received cervical radiation have shown significant progression of disease compared with controls.[58,165] One MR imaging study has corroborated these findings.[36]

Clinical Presentation

McCready and associates described 20 patients with radiation-induced arterial injuries.[147] Two patterns of the disease were described: (1) luminal occlusion and (2) arterial disruption. Atypical stenoses or occlusions occurred in 6 patients from 7 to 24 years after radiation. Three of these patients presented with symptoms of cerebrovascular disease after neck irradiation, and 3 patients had iliofemoral disease with severe lower extremity ischemia after pelvic radiation. Carotid disruptions occurred in 7 patients. All had undergone resection of the primary tumor and radical neck dissection 3 to 8 weeks following 5000 to 6500 cGy of cervical radiation. Infection was present in the vicinity of the carotid arteries in all patients, manifested by disrupted skin flaps or oral cutaneous fistulae. Arterial rupture occurred from 14 days to 16 weeks after the initial operation. A similar experience was reported by Marcial-Rojas and Castro, who described 6 patients with carotid artery rupture following treatment for head and neck carcinomas.[141] Necrosis of skin flaps in association with salivary fistulae preceded arterial ruptures.

Treatment

Several questions must be answered before surgical intervention for radiation-induced carotid artery occlusive disease is undertaken.

1. What is the estimated life expectancy with respect to the underlying malignancy?
2. Will an incision through irradiated skin heal primarily without added risk of infection?
3. To what extent are the carotid artery and neighboring nerves entrapped in postirradiation scar tissue?
4. Has the artery adjacent to the irradiated tumor been affected by radiation arteritis or accelerated atherosclerosis?[29]

If the probability of death from the malignancy outweighs the risk of a vascular event, surgical revascularization should be reconsidered. Because irradiated skin heals poorly, use of myocutaneous flaps for coverage is often warranted. Radiation may produce progressive small vessel and connective tissue changes in the epidermis that result in atrophy. The epidermis loses hair follicles, sebaceous glands, and sweat glands, and normal tissues are gradually replaced with dense fibrous tissue. Radiation dermatitis and hyperkeratosis may occur. The net result is thin, poorly nourished skin that heals unpredictably.

The transmural radiation damage to vessels obliterates the normal cleavage plane in the vessel wall, rendering endarterectomy difficult.[17,135] Thus, most authorities recommend bypass grafting of diseased segments. Reversed saphenous vein interposition grafts may be used, although extra-anatomic grafts or bypass grafts originating from the ascending aorta are required to avoid diseased segments. Autogenous tissue is preferable to prosthetic graft to avoid infection, but kinking of vein grafts in the neck may be a problem. After vascular repair, it is mandatory to have good tissue coverage, which may require rotational or advancement myocutaneous flaps.

In patients who present very late after irradiation, accelerated atherosclerosis may produce symptoms. These patients generally can undergo routine endarterectomy, but the surgeon must proceed with care through irradiated tissues.

Atkinson and coworkers concluded that carotid endarterectomy after cervical irradiation was technically more demanding, but feasible, and produced good long-term results.[8] They reported nine carotid endarterectomies, with an average follow-up of 49 months. One patient who underwent primary closure of the arteriotomy experienced TIAs postoperatively; two patients suffered transient cranial nerve palsies. The authors stated that the arterial dissection was more difficult because of periarterial fibrosis and that the endarterectomy was complicated by strong adherence of the plaque to the vessel wall. They also noted that after removal of the lesion, the arterial wall was attenuated more than usual, and segmental resection and reconstruction were required.[9] It is advisable to close the arteriotomy using a patch to help prevent future stenoses of the irradiated vessel.[96]

Predictably, patients who sustained carotid artery rupture after irradiation have a poor prognosis. In series reported by McCready and colleagues, ligation of the vessel resulted in stroke or death in five of nine patients.[148] Two of nine patients in the McCready study and two of six patients who suffered carotid rupture reported by Marcial-Rojas and Castro[141] presented with a sentinel bleed followed by exsanguinating hemorrhage. When a sentinel bleeding episode occurs, the authors recommend prompt surgical exploration and carotid ligation if no neurologic deficits are produced by carotid cross-clamping. Otherwise, EC-IC bypass with autogenous graft is recommended, with the subclavian artery used as the inflow source.

■ ADJACENT MALIGNANCY AND INFECTION

Patients with malignant tumors of the head and neck may present with primary or metastatic involvement of structures adjacent to the carotid artery. Fortunately, actual invasion of the carotid artery occurs in only 5% of these patients.[112] Because it provides only a two-dimensional view of the arterial lumen, arteriography cannot determine whether or not a malignancy has invaded the carotid artery. When the contrast column is narrowed, external compression, rather than invasion, may be present, whereas normal appearance can mislead the surgeon to think that there is no vessel wall involvement. When invasion is suspected, however, particularly with large, symptomatic tumors, angiography provides important anatomic information regarding coexistent carotid artery disease, collateral blood flow, and relevant anatomy. In addition, a stump pressure can be measured by inserting a balloon catheter in the proximal ICA.[176] CT scans show the proximity of lesions to the carotid artery but cannot identify invasion. MR imaging is promising and may best visualize tissue planes and give anatomic data in multiple projections.

Conley first reported resection of the carotid artery involved with tumor.[38] In 1981, Olcott and colleagues described six patients who presented with tumor invasion of the carotid artery.[176] The authors excised the carotid artery with the tumor and used saphenous vein interposition grafts for reconstructions. There were no operative deaths and no neurologic deficits in the immediate postoperative period, although hemiparesis developed in one patient on the 4th postoperative day and eventually cleared. Subsequent arteriography showed a patent graft with no obvious source of embolus in this patient.

In 1988, Biller and associates reported 26 patients who underwent carotid resection and graft replacement for recurrent cancer of the head and neck.[17] Seven percent of patients who received grafts suffered postoperative neurologic events; the postoperative mortality rate was 15%. The authors stated that as of 1986, only 60 cases of carotid artery resection and graft placement had been reported in the English literature.

In 1989, McCready and associates reported 16 patients with advanced cervical carcinomas, 3 of whom were treated with simple ligation of the carotid; each suffered postoperative TIAs that resolved.[148] Thirteen patients were treated with resection of the involved carotid and saphenous vein interposition grafting. There were two postoperative strokes and one postoperative death in the series. Preoperative cerebral angiography and a Javid shunt were used in all patients to determine collateral flow, and all arteries were closed with myocutaneous flaps using the greater pectoral muscle.[148]

Often carotid involvement can be assessed only at the time of operation. Occasionally, even when a carotid artery is not actually invaded, the dissection of tumor strips the vessel and weakens it beyond repair. In these cases as well as in those of carotid invasion, a saphenous vein interposition graft is advisable. Occasionally, reconstruction is impossible, and ligation is necessary. Measurement of the carotid back-pressure at operation can assist in determining tolerance of carotid interruption. Ehrenfeld and associates have shown that a back-pressure of 50 mm Hg indicates acceptable collateral flow, but 70 mm Hg is safer.[51] Patients with carotid back-pressure of less than this have significant neurologic morbidity. Many of the patients who sustain strokes after carotid ligation experience delayed neurologic symptoms.[51,164] These delayed strokes are probably thromboembolic due to propagation of thrombus into the middle cerebral artery. Thus, when possible, after ligation of the ICA, the patient should receive anticoagulation therapy for at least 7 to 10 days. In contrast to the low stroke rate for atherosclerotic disease, after arterial reconstruction these patients have stroke rates ranging from 7% to 20%.[8,38,136,176]

Infection of the carotid artery following head and neck surgery or after endarterectomy is a rare but potentially life-threatening problem. Hematogenous dissemination can also be a source for carotid artery infection.[116] Forty patients with carotid artery rupture sustained permanent neurologic damage, and 30% died despite rapid and prompt treatment.[187] Carotid artery blowouts (ruptures) occur in 3% of patients after operation for head and neck cancer.[114] Wound infection, salivary leaks, skin flap necrosis, and radiation are contributing factors to this postoperative problem. Of note, a sentinel bleed is often present prior to massive exsanguination.

Patients who present with carotid artery infection require rapid surgical intervention. Wound and blood cultures with directed antibiotic selection are advisable, but definitive operative intervention should not be postponed pending these results. If time permits, angiography is useful to identify relevant anatomy and document collateral circulation. Likewise, carotid back-pressure can be measured in preparation for possible carotid ligation. Reconstruction should employ autogenous tissue, thus avoiding proximity of interposition grafts within the area of infection. Wide débridement of infected tissue and flap coverage are also important.

■ MOYAMOYA DISEASE

Moyamoya disease is a rare cerebrovascular disorder in which there is progressive stenosis in the arteries of the circle of Willis. Initially, the disease involves the intracranial vessels of both cerebral hemispheres and then may progress to involve one or both of the middle cerebral and posterior cerebral arteries. As the disease progresses, an abnormal capillary network develops at the base of the brain. These vascular changes may result in ischemic strokes in children and cerebral hemorrhages in adults.

Moyamoya disease was first described by Takeuchi and Shimizu in 1957 as "bilateral hypogenesis of the ICAs."[227] In 1968, Kudo introduced this disorder in the English literature as "spontaneous occlusion of the circle of Willis, a disease apparently confined to the Japanese."[124] In that same year, Nishimoto and Takeuchi described 96 cases that occurred in Japanese individuals.[171] Suzuki and Takaku first coined the term *moyamoya disease* in 1969, employing the Japanese word *moyamoya* to describe the typical "puff of smoke" appearance of the abnormal capillary network at the base of the skull.[225]

The cause is unknown. There is no evidence that the disorder is inflammatory or autoimmune, but an episode of infection (often upper respiratory) is frequently antecedent. The disease does not affect large vessels and has no relationship to extracranial cervical arteries. The disease slowly and progressively occludes the major trunks of the intracerebral arteries, beginning at the carotid artery in the cavernous sinus. The formation of abnormally small moyamoya vessels distal to the carotid narrowings is now considered to be a secondary process that attempts to develop collateral circulation.[124,231] At autopsy, characteristic findings include intimal thickening and medial thinning of affected intracranial arteries without inflammatory infiltrates.[87] There have been reports of familial cases and a higher incidence in individuals with Down syndrome.[65,119]

Because moyamoya disease does not affect large vessels and is unrelated to the extracranial cervical arteries, it is not amenable to treatment by the vascular surgeon. It is of interest, nevertheless, because it is occasionally visualized on angiograms brought to the attention of the vascular surgeon because it produces symptoms similar to those of extracranial carotid disease and because of its unusual name.

Clinical Presentation

Moyamoya disease has a biphasic distribution of age of onset, affecting individuals in the 1st and 4th decades of life. In 1979, according to national statistics in Japan, 518 cases were registered; the overall female-to-male ratio was about 1:5.[170] The clinical presentations between juvenile and adult types are distinctly different. In the juvenile type, children usually present with ischemic events, such as repetitive TIAs or a completed stroke.

Typically, cerebral ischemia is induced by crying, coughing, or straining. Seizures are also common, occurring in about 14% of affected individuals. In adults with moyamoya disease, hemorrhage from the fragile abnormal vessels is the most prominent clinical feature. In 70% to 80% of patients, bleeding occurs in the ventricles, thalamus, and basal ganglia. Hemorrhage may be either subarachnoid or intracerebral.

Adults have a slightly worse prognosis than children do. Nishimoto reported 39 deaths (7.5%) in the 518 patients previously cited.[170] Adults had a mortality rate of 10% and children had a mortality rate of 4.3%. Intracranial bleeding was the cause of death in 56% of children and 63% of adults. Few have examined the natural history of patients who present with TIAs because most of these patients go on to treatment. In 1985, Kurokaw and colleagues observed 47 patients who presented with TIAs; in most, TIAs disappeared, but one half to two thirds of the patients showed deterioration in cognitive function over 5 to 10 years.[125] There is also an increased incidence of intracranial aneurysms in patients with moyamoya disease. The aneurysms are characteristically in the posterior circulation.[126]

Diagnosis

Imaging

CT and MR scans may reveal multiple dilated abnormal vessels in the basal ganglia or thalamus, occlusion or narrowing of the major arteries of the circle of Willis, ischemic infarction (predominantly in the watershed of the brain parenchyma), or intracerebral hemorrhages.[32] Cerebral blood flow studies have also been described for diagnosis of this disorder. Ogawa and colleagues reported that the distribution of cerebral blood flow was greater to the occipital regions, whereas normally blood flow is predominantly to the frontal lobes.[173] In addition, the response to hypotension/hypocapnia, which requires vasodilation, is severely impaired in contrast to a relatively preserved response to hypertension and hypercapnia.[174]

Stages

Arteriography is the standard for diagnosis of moyamoya disease (Fig. 144-22). Suzuki and Takaku have described the following six distinct stages[225]:

- In *stage I*, stenosis of the carotid artery is present at its suprasellar portion, usually occurring bilaterally.
- In *stage II*, the carotid artery is narrow, and moyamoya vessels begin to develop at the base of the brain.

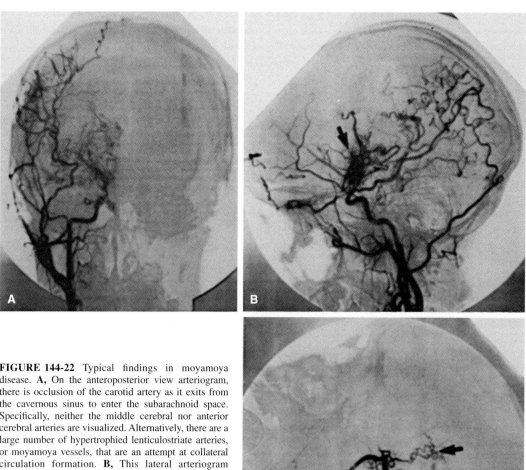

FIGURE 144-22 Typical findings in moyamoya disease. **A,** On the anteroposterior view arteriogram, there is occlusion of the carotid artery as it exits from the cavernous sinus to enter the subarachnoid space. Specifically, neither the middle cerebral nor anterior cerebral arteries are visualized. Alternatively, there are a large number of hypertrophied lenticulostriate arteries, or moyamoya vessels, that are an attempt at collateral circulation formation. **B,** This lateral arteriogram demonstrates only filling of the posterior cerebral arterial complex. The middle cerebral and anterior cerebral arteries are not visualized. Alternatively, there is the "puff-of-smoke" appearance of the large number of moyamoya vessels *(arrow).* **C,** The vertebral injection demonstrates some attempt at collateral blood flow to the anterior circulation *(arrow).* (**A-C,** From Ueki K, Meyer FB: Moyamoya disease. In Meyer FB [ed]: Sundt's Occlusive Cerebrovascular Disease. Philadelphia, WB Saunders, 1994, p 467.)

- In *stage III*, these abnormal moyamoya vessels become more prominent as major arteries in the anterior circulation become severely stenotic or occluded; at this stage, the diagnosis is usually confirmed.
- In *stage IV*, the moyamoya vessels extend to all components of the circle of Willis, including the posterior cerebral arteries.
- In *stage V*, the moyamoya vessels begin to diminish.
- By *stage VI*, they disappear completely. In stage VI, the cerebral hemisphere receives blood through abnormal EC-IC anastomoses.

These changes are almost always bilateral, and if angiographic abnormalities are unilateral, the case is considered questionable.

This puff-of-smoke angiographic pattern is mimicked in other conditions, including generalized atherosclerosis, radiation arteritis, trauma, sickle cell anemia, and even tuberculous meningitis.[88] In 1975, Debrun and coworkers described moyamoya disease as the end stage of a number of conditions that may result in this nonspecific angiographic pattern rather than representing a discrete clinical entity.[43]

Treatment

In 1983, Suzuki and Kodoma proposed perivascular sympathectomy and superior cervical ganglionectomy to produce both intracranial and extracranial vasodilation for treatment of moyamoya disease.[224] Currently, most surgeons use some sort of intracranial procedure to treat this rare disease. The most popular is *superficial temporal artery-to-middle cerebral artery* (STA-MCA) anastomosis, which was proposed by Krayenbuhl for treatment of moyamoya disease in 1975.[122] Additional procedures include *encephalomyo-synangiosis* and *encephaloduroarteriosynangiosis*.

Encephalomyosynangiosis, proposed by Matsushima and coworkers in 1981, consists of suturing a patent superficial temporal artery along the longitudinal dural defect to approximate the artery to the brain surface.[145] Encephalomyosynangiosis, used by Karasawa and associates in 1977, consists of suturing the temporalis muscle to surgical dural defects, approximating the muscles to the surface of the brain.[109] Most of the procedures are indirect anastomotic operations, the goal of which is developing neovascularization from the extracranial arterial and soft tissue systems to the ischemic brain. Reportedly, the operations are easier and safer to perform than STA-MCA bypass, especially in small children.

In general, results of operation in children are better than in adults because the primary purpose of these revascularization techniques is to prevent brain ischemia. When applied to the adult or hemorrhagic type of moyamoya disease, they are less likely to reduce the risk of bleeding despite the expectation of retarding development of abnormal moyamoya vessels.

■ EXTRACRANIAL-INTRACRANIAL BYPASS

Because the international multicenter, randomized study of EC-IC bypass failed to show improved outcome in the surgical group, this operation has largely fallen into disfavor.[50]

Microvascular anastomosis was first successfully performed in experimental models in the 1960s.[48,104] The first EC-IC bypass was by Donaghy and Yasargil in 1967 when they performed an STA-MCA anastomosis.[48] In 1978, Samson and Boone introduced use of the occipital or middle meningeal artery when the superficial temporal artery is inadequate.[198] In 1987, Hopkins and colleagues developed bypass procedures for posterior circulation revascularization.[93] Spetzler and associates first used a saphenous vein graft from the external carotid artery, subclavian artery, or proximal superficial temporal artery to provide a high-flow conduit.[217]

EC-IC bypass was originally designed to treat patients with ICA occlusion or intracranial occlusive lesions, such as siphon stenosis or middle cerebral artery occlusion. These lesions are not amenable to standard extracranial carotid procedures.[223] Several nonrandomized studies suggested long-term resolution of ischemic symptoms after EC-IC bypass.[33,90]

The EC-IC Bypass Study

Despite the apparent success of numerous uncontrolled and nonrandomized studies supporting the use of EC-IC bypass for cerebrovascular disease, the definitive study awaited funding by the National Institutes of Health, the results of which were initiated in 1977 and published in 1985.[50] This international, multicenter, randomized, prospective study included patients who had one or more TIAs or minor completed strokes in the carotid distribution within 3 months of entering the study.

One of the following ipsilateral lesions was present: (1) occlusion of the ICA; (2) stenosis of the ICA at or above the C2 vertebral body; or (3) stenosis or occlusion of the middle cerebral artery. All patients received 325 mg of aspirin four times per day and were randomized to best medical care (aspirin plus risk factor control) or to the same regimen with the addition of EC-IC bypass. Mean follow-up was 55.8 months, and endpoints included fatal or nonfatal stroke. Secondary analysis involved ipsilateral stroke, death from any cause, and functional status. A total of 1377 patients were randomized: 714 to best medical care and 663 to surgery.

Postoperative mortality was only 0.6%, and major stroke morbidity was 2.5%. The angiographically confirmed bypass patency rate was 96%. In the 5-year follow-up, perioperative nonfatal and fatal strokes occurred slightly more frequently and earlier in patients who had surgery compared with the best medical care group. Subset analysis did not identify a specific group that was preferentially benefited by EC-IC bypass, including those with bilateral carotid occlusion and middle cerebral artery occlusion. In fact, the group of patients with severe middle cerebral artery stenosis had a significantly worse outcome when treated operatively than those treated medically, suggesting that the bypass actually caused the strokes by precipitating proximal middle cerebral artery occlusion.

Unfortunately, the EC-IC bypass study was riddled with methodologic flaws.[11,216] Two features of the study conspired to weaken its validity. First, there was a strikingly low stroke rate of the medically treated patients, suggesting that patients with a lower stroke risk were selected for randomization and inclusion. Second, and perhaps more important, a substantial number of patients had EC-IC bypasses at the participating medical centers without being offered randomization. Thus, it would appear that only relatively stable, low-risk patients were entered into the trial, whereas patients who were at most risk for stroke were excluded from nonoperative management, presumably because surgeons felt that they were at "excessive risk." Although these criticisms have been addressed by participants of the EC-IC bypass study, the conclusions of the study will forever be questioned by some. Nevertheless, after this international trial was published, there was a marked reduction in the number of EC-IC bypasses performed. For example, in one center in which 70 such cases were performed annually, only four have been performed annually in recent years.[217]

It is noteworthy that several important clinical categories of cerebrovascular disease were not included in the EC-IC bypass cohort. These included patients with ischemic ocular syndromes, moyamoya disease, vertebrobasilar insufficiency, and chronic low-perfusion syndromes.[109,216] In addition, some authorities consider patients as candidates for this operation (1) who have persistent or progressive cerebrovascular symptoms despite maximal medical therapy and who have demonstrated cerebral hemodynamic insufficiency, and also (2) those with therapeutic carotid occlusion who failed temporary balloon test occlusion. Findings of those patients with "hemodynamic insufficiency" may be accomplished using a number of special studies, including xenon CT, transcranial Doppler, single-photon emission tomography, and positron emission tomography.[49,71,81,182,245] Use of various vasodilator stimulants (CO_2, acetazolamide) has also been suggested to select patients for this procedure.[49,121,245] The technique of EC-IC bypass is beyond the scope of this chapter. Interested readers are referred to numerous treatises on this topic.

■ REFERENCES

1. Albert G, cited by Staats EF, Brown RL, Smith RR: Carotid body tumors: Benign and malignant. Laryngoscope 76:907, 1966.

2. Allison MC, Gallagher PJ: Temporal artery biopsy and corticosteroid treatment. Ann Rheum Dis 43:416, 1984.

3. Almquist A, Gornick C, Benson DW Jr, et al: Carotid sinus hypersensitivity: Evaluation of the vasodepressor component. Circulation 71:927, 1985.

4. Anderson CA, Collins JG Jr, Rich HM, et al: Spontaneous dissection of the internal carotid artery associated with fibromuscular dysplasia. Am Surg 46:263, 1980.

5. Anderson RM, Schecter MM: A case of spontaneous dissecting aneurysm of the internal carotid artery. J Neurol Neurosurg Psychiaty 22:195, 1959.

6. Andersson R, Malmvall E, Bengtsson BA: Long-term survival in giant cell arteritis, including temporal arteritis and polymyalgia rheumatica: A follow-up study of 90 patients treated with corticosteroids. Acta Med Scand 220:361, 1986.

7. Anson J, Crowell RM: Cervicocranial arterial dissection. Neurosurgery 29:89, 1991.

8. Atkinson DP, Jacobs LA, Weaver AW: Elective carotid resection for squamous cell carcinomas of the head and neck. Am J Surg 148:483, 1984.

9. Atkinson JL, Sundt TM Jr, Dale AJ, et al: Radiation-associated atheromatous disease of the cervical carotid artery: Report of 7 cases and review of the literature. Neurosurgery 24:171, 1989.

10. Austin MG, Schaefer RF: Marfan's syndrome with unusual blood vessel manifestations: Primary media necrosis dissection of right innominate, right carotid, and left carotid arteries. Arch Pathol 64:205, 1957.

11. Awad IA, Spetzler RF: Extracranial-intracranial arterial bypass surgery: A critical analysis in light of the International Cooperative Study. Neurosurgery 19:655, 1986.

12. Bashour TT, Crew JP, Dean M, et al: Ultrasonic imaging of common carotid artery dissection. J Clin Ultrasound 13:210, 1985.

13. Bengtsson BA: Incidence of giant cell arteritis. Acta Med Scand 658 (Suppl):15, 1987.

14. Bengtsson BA, Andersson R: Giant cell and Takayasu's arteritis. Curr Opin Rheumatol 3:15, 1991.

15. Bergan JJ, Hoen JG: Evanescent cervical pseudoaneurysm. Ann Surg 162:213, 1965.

16. Bergdahl L: Carotid body tumours. Scand J Thorac Cardiovasc Surg 12:275, 1978.

17. Biller HF, Urken M, Klawson W, et al: Carotid artery resection and bypass for neck carcinoma. Laryngoscope 98:181, 1988.

18. Bogousslavsky J, Despland PA, Regli F: Spontaneous carotid dissection with acute stroke. Arch Neurol 44:137, 1987.

19. Bolande RP: The neurocristopathies: A unifying concept of disease arising in the neural crest development. Hum Pathol 5:409, 1976.

20. Bond JR, Charboneau JW, Stanson AW: Takayasu's arteritis: Carotid duplex and sonographic appearance, including color Doppler imaging. J Ultrasound Med 9:625, 1990.

21. Brignole M, Menozzi C, Lolli G, et al: Long-term outcome of paced and non-paced patients with severe carotid sinus syndrome. Am J Cardiol 69:1039, 1992.

22. Buckley A, Southwood T, Culham G, et al: The role of ultrasound in the evaluation of Takayasu's arteritis. J Rheumatol 18:1073, 1991.

23. Busuttil RW, Memsic L, Thomas DS: Coiling and kinking of the carotid artery. In Rutherford RB (ed): Vascular Surgery, 4th ed. Philadelphia, WB Saunders, 1995, p 1588.

24. Butler MS, Lane RHS, Webster JHH: Irradiation injury to large arteries. Br J Surg 67:341, 1980.

25. Cade S: Malignant Disease and Its Treatment by Radium. Baltimore, Williams & Wilkins, 1940, p 161.

26. Cairney J: Tortuosity of the cervical segment of the internal carotid artery. J Anat 59:87, 1924.

27. Cairns H: Vascular aspects of head injuries. Lisboa Med 19:375, 1942.

28. Callow AD (ed): Surgery of the Carotid and Vertebral Arteries. Baltimore, Williams & Wilkins, 1996, p 152.

29. Callow AD (ed): Surgery of the Carotid and Vertebral Arteries. Baltimore, Williams & Wilkins, 1996, p 136.

30. Carpenter MB: Human Neuroanatomy, 7th ed. Baltimore, Williams & Wilkins, 1976, p 345.

31. Chambers RG, Mahoney WD: Carotid body tumors. Am J Surg 116:554, 1968.

32. Chang KH, Yi JG, Han MH, et al: MR imaging finding of moyamoya disease. J Korean Med Sci 5:85, 1990.

33. Chater N, Popp J: Microsurgical vascular bypass for occlusive cerebrovascular disease: Review of 100 cases. Surg Neurol 6:114, 1976.

34. Chedid A, Jao W: Hereditary tumors of the carotid bodies and chronic obstructive pulmonary disease. Cancer 33:1635, 1974.

35. Cheng LH, Norris CW: Surgical management of the carotid sinus syndrome. Arch Otolaryngol 97:395, 1973.

36. Chung TS, Yousem DM, Lexa FJ, Markiewicz DA: MRI of carotid angiopathy after therapeutic radiation. J Comput Assist Tomogr 18:533, 1994.

37. Collins PS, Orecchia P, Gomez E: A technique for correction of carotid kinks and coils following endarterectomy. Ann Vasc Surg 5:116, 1991.

38. Conley JJ: Free autogenous vein graft to the internal and common carotid arteries in the treatment of tumors of the neck. Ann Surg 137:205, 1953.

39. Connolly JH: Large pulsating vessels in the right portion of the posterior pharyngeal wall partially concealed behind the right tonsil in a boy aged five. Proc R Soc Med (Laryngol Sect) 7:25, 1913.

40. Conomy JP, Kellermeyer RW: Delayed cerebrovascular consequences of therapeutic radiation: A clinicopathologic study of a stroke associated with radiation-related carotid arteriopathy. Cancer 36:1702, 1975.

41. Crowell WT, Grizzle WE, Siegel AL: Functional carotid paragangliomas: Biomedical, ultrastructural, and histochemical correlation with clinical symptoms. Arch Pathol Lab Med 106:599, 1982.

42. Davidge-Pitts KJ, Pantanowitz D: Carotid body tumors. Surg Annu 16:203, 1984.

43. Debrun CT, Sauvegrain J, Goutieres F: Moyamoya, a nonspecific radiologic syndrome. Neuroradiology 8:241, 1975.

44. Dent TL, Thompson NW, Fry J: Carotid body tumors. Surgery 80:365, 1976.

45. Desai B, Toole JF: Kinks, coils, and carotids: A review. Stroke 6:649, 1975.

46. Di Giacomo V: A case of Takayasu's disease occurred over 200 years ago. Angiology 35:750, 1984.

47. Dockerty MB, Love JG, Patton MM: Non-chromaffin paraganglioma of the middle ear: Report of a case in which the clinical aspects were those of a brain tumor. Proc Staff Meet Mayo Clin 26:25, 1961.

48. Donaghy RMP, Yasargil MG: Microvascular Surgery. St. Louis, CV Mosby, 1967.

49. Durham SR, Smith HA, Rutigliano MJ, Yonas H: Assessment of cerebral vasoreactivity and stroke risk using Xe CT acetazolamide challenge. Stroke 22:138, 1991.

50. The EC-IC Bypass Study Group: Failure of extracranial-intracranial arterial bypass to reduce the risk of ischemia stroke: Results of an international randomized trial. N Engl J Med 313:1191, 1985.

51. Ehrenfeld WR, Stoney RJ, Wylie EJ: Relation of carotid stump pressure to safety of carotid arterial ligation. Surgery 93:299, 1983.

52. Ehrenfeld WR, Wylie EJ: Spontaneous dissection of the internal carotid artery. Arch Surg 111:1294, 1976.

53. Ehsan M, Lange RK, Waxman J: Overdiagnosis of temporal arteritis. South Med J 74:1198, 1981.
54. Elerding SC, Fernandez RN, Gotta JC, et al: Carotid artery disease following cervical irradiation. Ann Surg 194:609, 1981.
55. Faer MJ, Mead JH, Lynch RD: Cerebral granulomatous angiitis. Case report and literature review. AJR Am J Roentgenol 129:463, 1977.
56. Fanning JP, Woods FM, Christian HJ: Metastatic carotid body tumor: Report of a case with review of the literature. JAMA 185:49, 1963.
57. Fauchald P, Rygvold O, Oystese B: Temporal arteritis and polymyalgia rheumatica: Clinical and biopsy findings. Ann Intern Med 77:845, 1972.
58. Feehs RS, McGuirt WF, Bond MG, et al: Irradiation; A significant risk factor for carotid atherosclerosis. Arch Otolaryngol Head Neck Surg 117:1135, 1991.
59. Fisher AGT: Sigmoid tortuosity of the internal carotid artery and its relation to tonsil and pharynx. Lancet 2:128, 1915.
60. Fisher CM, Ojemann RG, Roberson GH: Spontaneous dissection of cervicocerebral arteries. Can J Neurol Sci 5:9, 1978.
61. Fonkalsrud EW, Sanchez M, Zerubavel R, et al: Serial changes in arterial structure following radiation therapy. Surg Gynecol Obstet 145:389, 1977.
62. Frey CF, Karoll RP: Management of chemodectomas. Am J Surg 111:536, 1966.
63. Friedman AH, Drake CG: Subarachnoid hemorrhage from intracranial dissecting aneurysm. J Neurosurg 60:325, 1984.
64. Fries JC, Chamberlin JA: Extra-adrenal pheochromocytoma: Literature review and report of a cervical pheochromocytoma. Surgery 63:268, 1968.
65. Fukushima Y, Kondo Y, Kuroki Y, et al: Are Down syndrome patients predisposed to moyamoya disease? Eur J Pediatr 144:516, 1986.
66. Gassman A: Zur Histologie der Röntgenulcera. Fortschr Geb Roentgenstr 2:199, 1899.
67. Gates JD, Murphy MP, Lipson WE: Autogenous patching of a kinked internal carotid artery. Surgery 123:483, 1998.
68. Gauthier G, Rohr J, Wildi E, Megret M: Spontaneous dissecting aneurysm of the internal carotid artery: General review of 205 published cases with ten personal cases. Schweiz Arch Neurol Psychiatr 136:53, 1985.
69. Gaylis H, Mieny CJ: The incidence of malignancy in carotid body tumours. Br J Surg 64:885, 1977.
70. Gee W, Mehigan JT, Wylie EJ: Measurement of collateral cerebral hemispheric blood pressure by ocular pneumoplethysmography. Am J Surg 130:121, 1975.
71. Gibbs JM, Leeders KL, Wiser RJS, Jones T: Evaluation of cerebral perfusion in patients with carotid artery occlusion. Lancet 2:310, 1984.
72. Giordano JM, Leavitt RY, Hoffman G, Fauci AS: Experience with surgical treatment of Takayasu's disease. Surgery 109:252, 1991.
73. Glenner GG, Crout JR, Roberts WC: A functional carotid body-like tumor secreting levarterenol. Arch Pathol 73:66, 1962.
74. Gold H: Production of atherosclerosis in the rat: Effect of x-ray and a high-fat diet. Arch Pathol 71:268, 1961.
75. Gordon-Taylor G: On carotid body tumours. Br J Surg 28:163, 1940.
76. Graham E, Holland A, Avery A, Russell RWR: Prognosis in giant cell arteritis. BMJ 282:269, 1981.
77. Graham JM, Miller T, Stinnett DM: Spontaneous dissection of the common carotid artery: Case report and review of the literature. J Vasc Surg 7:811, 1988.
78. Griebenow R, Kramer L, Steffen HM, et al: Quantification of the heart rate-dependent vasopressor component in carotid sinus syndrome. Klin Wochenschr 67:1132, 1989.
79. Grimley PM, Glenner GG: Histology and ultra-structure of carotid body paragangliomas: Comparison with a normal gland. Cancer 20:473, 1967.
80. Gritzmann N, Herold C, Haller J, et al: Duplex sonography for tumors of the carotid body. Cardiovasc Intervent Radiol 10:280, 1987.
81. Grubb RL Jr, Ratcheson RA, Raichle MD, et al: Regional cerebral blood flow and oxygen utilization in superficial temporal middle cerebral artery anastomosis patients. J Neurosurg 50:733, 1979.
82. Grufferman S, Gillman AB, Pasternak LR, et al: Familial carotid body tumors: Case report and epidemiologic review. Cancer 46:2116, 1980.
83. Hall S, Barr W, Lie JT, et al: Takayasu's arteritis: A study of 32 North American patients. Medicine 64:89, 1985.
84. Hall S, Buchbinder R: Takayasu's arteritis. Rheum Dis Clin North Am 16:411, 1990.
85. Hall S, Hunder GG: Is temporal artery biopsy prudent? Mayo Clin Proc 59:793, 1984.
86. Hallett JW Jr, Nora JD, Hollier LH, et al: Trends in neurovascular complications of surgical management for carotid body and cervical paragangliomas: A 50-year experience with 153 tumors. J Vasc Surg 7:284, 1988.
87. Hanakita J, Kondo A, Ishikawa J, et al: An autopsy case of "moyamoya" disease. No Shinkei Geka 10:531, 1982.
88. Hardy RC, Williams RG: Moyamoya disease and cerebral hemorrhage. Surg Neurol 21:507, 1984.
89. Hart RG, Easton JD: Dissections of the cervical and cerebral arteries. Neurol Clin 1:155, 1983.
90. Heilbrun MP, Reichman OH, Anderson RE, Roberts DW: Regional cerebral blood flow studies following middle cerebral artery anastomosis. J Neurosurg 43:706, 1975.
91. Henly WW, Cooley DA, Gordon WB, et al: Tortuosity of the internal carotid artery: Report of seven cases treated surgically. Postgrad Med 31:133, 1962.
92. Herrschaft P, Duus P, Glenn F, et al: Preoperative and postoperative cerebral flow in patients with carotid artery stenoses. In Lanfitt TW, McHenry LCM Jr, Reivich M (eds): Cerebral Circulation and Metabolism. New York, Springer-Verlag, 1975, p 276.
93. Hopkins L, Martin N, Hadley M, et al: Vertebrobasilar insufficiency: II. Microsurgical treatment of intracranial vertebrobasilar disease. J Neurosurg 66:662, 1987.
94. Houser OW, Mokri B, Sundt TM Jr, et al: Spontaneous cervical cephalic arterial dissection and its residuum: Angiographic spectrum. AJNR Am J Neuroradiol 5:27, 1984.
95. Hunder GG: Giant cell (temporal) arteritis. Rheum Dis Clin North Am 16:399, 1990.
96. Hurley JJ, Nordestgaard AG, Woods JJ: Carotid endarterectomy with vein patch angioplasty for radiation-induced symptomatic atherosclerosis. J Vasc Surg 14:419, 1991.
97. Hsu I, Kistin AD: Buckling of the great vessels. Arch Intern Med 98:712, 1956.
98. Irons GB, Weiland LH, Brown WL: Paragangliomas of the neck: Clinical and pathological analysis of 116 cases. Surg Clin North Am 57:575, 1977.
99. Ishikawa K: Diagnostic approach and proposed criteria for the clinical diagnosis of Takayasu's arteriopathy. J Am Coll Cardiol 12:964, 1986.
100. Ishikawa K: Natural history and classification of occlusive thromboaortopathy (Takayasu's disease). Circulation 57:27, 1978.
101. Ishikawa K: Survival and morbidity after diagnosis of occlusive thromboarthropathy (Takayasu's disease). Am J Cardiol 47:1026, 1981.
102. Jackson JL: Tortuosity of the internal carotid artery in its relation to tonsillectomy. Can Med Assoc J 29:475, 1933.
103. Jackson MA, Hughes RC, Ward SP, McInnes EG: "Headbanging" and carotid dissection. BMJ 287:1262, 1983.
104. Jacobson JH II, Suarez E: Microsurgery in anastomosis of small vessels. Surg Forum 11:243, 1960.
105. Javid H, Chawla SK, Dye WS, et al: Carotid body tumors: Resection or reflection. Arch Surg 111:344, 1976.
106. Jentzer A: Dissecting aneurysm of the left internal carotid artery. Angiology 5:232, 1954.
107. Joyce JW: Giant cell arteritis. In Ernst CB, Stanley JC (eds): Current Therapy in Vascular Surgery, 2nd ed. Philadelphia, BC Decker, 1991, p 173.
108. Kapoor WN, Karpf M, Wieand S: A prospective evaluation and follow-up of patients with syncope. N Engl J Med 309:197, 1983.

109. Karasawa J, Kikuchi H, Furuse S, et al: A surgical treatment of "moyamoya" disease, "encephalo-myo synangiosis." Neurol Med Chir 17:29, 1977.

110. Kelly AB: Large pulsating vessels in the pharynx. Glasgow Med J 49:28, 1898.

111. Kendall B: Vasculitis in the central nervous system: Contribution of angiography. Eur Neurol 23:472, 1984.

112. Kennedy JT, Krause CJ, Loevy S: The importance of tumor attachment to the carotid artery. Arch Otolaryngol 103:70, 1977.

113. Kenny RA, Traynor G: Carotid sinus syndrome: Clinical characteristic in elderly patients. Age Ageing 20:449, 1991.

114. Ketcham AS, Hoyle RC: Spontaneous carotid artery hemorrhage after head and neck surgery. Am J Surg 110:649, 1965.

115. Kieffer E, Bahnini A: Aortic lesions in Takayasu's disease. In Bergan JJ, Yao JST (eds): Aortic Surgery. Philadelphia, WB Saunders, 1989, p 111.

116. Killeen JD, Smith LL: Management of contiguous malignancy, radiation damage, and infection involving the carotid artery. Semin Vasc Surg 4:123, 1991.

117. Kimoto S: The history and present status of aortic surgery in Japan, particularly for aortitis syndrome. J Cardiovasc Surg 20:107, 1979.

118. Kissel JT: Neurologic manifestations of vasculitis. Neurol Clin 7:655, 1989.

119. Kitahara T, Ariga N, Yamaura A, et al: Familial occurrence of moyamoya disease: Report of three Japanese families. J Neurol Neurosurg Psychiatry 42:208, 1979.

120. Klein RG, Campbell RJ, Hunder GG, Carney JA: Skip lesions in temporal arteritis. Mayo Clin Proc 51:504, 1976.

121. Kleiser B, Widder B: Course of carotid occlusions with impaired cerebrovascular reactivity. Stroke 23:171, 1992.

122. Krayenbuhl HA: The moyamoya syndrome and the neurosurgeon. Surg Neurol 4:353, 1975.

123. Krupski WC, Effeney DJ, Ehrenfeld WK, Stoney RJ: Cervical chemodectoma: Technical considerations and management options. Am J Surg 144:215, 1982.

124. Kudo T: Spontaneous occlusion of the circle of Willis: A disease apparently confined to Japanese. Neurology 18:485, 1968.

125. Kurokawa T, Tomita S, Ueda K, et al: Prognosis of occlusive disease of the circle of Willis (moyamoya disease) in children. Pediatr Neurol 1:274, 1985.

126. Kwak R, Ito S, Yamamoto N, et al: Significance of intracranial aneurysms associated with moyamoya disease: I. Neurol Med Chir (Tokyo) 24:97, 1984.

127. Lamuraglia GM, Fabian RL, Brewster DC, et al: The current surgical management of carotid body paragangliomas. J Vasc Surg 15:1038, 1992.

128. Launes J, Ivanainen M, Erkininjuntti T, et al: Isolated angiitis of the central nervous system. Acta Neurol Scand 74:108, 1986.

129. Lee NS, Jones HR Jr: Extracranial cerebrovascular disease. Cardiol Clin 9:523, 1991.

130. Lees CD, Levine HL, Beven EG, Tucker HM: Tumors of the carotid body: Experience with 41 operative cases. Am J Surg 142:362, 1981.

131. Leipzig TJ, Dohrmann GJ: The tortuous or kinked carotid artery: Pathogenesis and clinical considerations. Surg Neurol 25:478, 1986.

132. Levinson SA, Close MB, Ehrenfeld WK, Stoney RJ: Carotid artery occlusive disease following external cervical irradiation. Arch Surg 107:395, 1973.

133. Levit SA, Sheps SG, Espinosa RE, et al: Catecholamine-secreting paraganglioma of glomus-jugular region resembling pheochromocytoma. N Engl J Med 281:805, 1969.

134. Liu YQ: Radiology of aortoarteritis. Radiol Clin North Am 23:671, 1985.

135. Lofftus CM, Biller J, Hart MN, et al: Management of radiation-induced accelerated carotid atherosclerosis. Arch Neurol 44:711, 1987.

136. Lore JM, Boulos EJ: Resection and reconstruction of the carotid artery in metastatic squamous cell carcinoma. Am J Surg 142:437, 1981.

137. Luken MG III, Ascherl GF Jr, Correll JW, et al: Spontaneous dissecting aneurysms of the extracranial internal carotid artery. Clin Neurosurg 26:353, 1979.

138. Lupi-Herrera E, Sanchez GT, Horwitz S, et al: Pulmonary artery involvement in Takayasu's arteritis. Chest 63:69, 1975.

139. Machado EB, Michet CJ, Ballard DJ, et al: Trends and incidents and clinical presentation of temporal arteritis in Olmstead County, Minnesota, 1950-1985. Arthritis Rheum 31:745, 1988.

140. Maed H, Handa N, Matsumoto M, et al: Carotid lesions detected by B-mode ultrasonography in Takayasu's arteritis: "Macaroni sign" as an indicator of the disease. Ultrasound Med Biol 17:695, 1991.

141. Marcial-Rojas RA, Castro JR: Irradiation injury to elastic arteries in the course of treatment for neoplastic disease. Ann Otol 71:945, 1962.

142. Martin CE, Rosenfeld L, McSwain B: Carotid body tumors: A 16-year follow-up of seven malignant cases. South Med J 66:1236, 1973.

143. Martinez SA, Oller DW, Gee W, et al: Elective carotid artery resection. Arch Otolaryngol 101:744, 1975.

144. Mathes SJ, Alexander J: Radiation injury. Surg Oncol Clin North Am 5:809, 1996.

145. Matsushima Y, Fukai N, Tanaka K, et al: A new surgical treatment of moyamoya disease in children: A preliminary report. Surg Neurol 15:313, 1981.

146. Maydl: Cited by Byrne JJ: Carotid body and allied tumors. Am J Surg 95:371, 1958.

147. McCready RA, Hyde GL, Bivens BA, et al: Radiation-induced arterial injuries. Surgery 93:306, 1982.

148. McCready RA, Miller KS, Hamaker RC, et al: What is the role of carotid arterial resection in the management of advanced cervical cancer? J Vasc Surg 10:274, 1989.

149. McGuirt WF, Harker LA: Carotid body tumors. Arch Otolaryngol 101:58, 1975.

150. McIlrath DC, Remine WH: Carotid body tumors. Surg Clin North Am 43:1135, 1963.

151. Meissner I, Mokri B: Vascular diseases of the cervical carotid artery. Cardiovasc Clin 22:161, 1992.

152. Metz H, Murray-Leslie RM, Bannister RG, et al: Kinking of the internal carotid artery in relation to cerebrovascular disease. Lancet 1:424, 1961.

153. Meyer FB, Sundt TM Jr, Pearson BW: Carotid body tumors: A subject review and suggested surgical approach. J Neurosurg 64:377, 1986.

154. Mokri B: Traumatic and spontaneous extracranial internal carotid artery dissections. J Neurol 237:356, 1990.

155. Mokri B: Dissection of cervical and cephalic arteries. In Meyer FB (ed): Sundt's Occlusive Cerebrovascular Disease. Philadelphia, WB Saunders, 1994, p 46.

156. Mokri B, Okazaki H: Cystic medial necrosis and internal carotid artery dissection in a Marfan sibling: Partial expression of Marfan syndrome. J Stroke Cerebrovasc Dis 2:100, 1992.

157. Mokri B, Piepgras DG, Houser OW: Traumatic dissections of the extracranial internal carotid artery. J Neurosurg 68:189, 1988.

158. Mokri B, Piepgras DG, Wiebers DO: Familial occurrence of spontaneous dissection of the internal carotid artery. Stroke 18:246, 1987.

159. Mokri B, Schievink WI, Olsen KD, Piepgras DG: Spontaneous dissection of the cervical internal carotid artery: Presentation with lower cranial nerve palsies. Arch Otolaryngol Head Neck Surg 118:431, 1992.

160. Mokri B, Houser OW, Sundt TM Jr, et al: Spontaneous dissection of the internal carotid arteries: Clinical presentation and angiographic features [Abstract]. Ann Neurol 12:84, 1982.

161. Mokri B, Sundt TM Jr, Houser OW, et al: Spontaneous internal carotid dissection, hemicrania, and Horner's syndrome. Arch Neurol 36:677, 1979.

162. Mokri B, Sundt TM, Houser OW, et al: Spontaneous dissection of the cervical internal carotid artery. Ann Neurol 19:126, 1986.

163. Monro RS: Natural history of carotid body tumors and their diagnosis and treatment. Br J Surg 37:445, 1950.

164. Moore OS, Karlan M, Sigler L: Factors influencing the safety of carotid ligation. Am J Surg 118:666, 1969.
165. Moritz MW, Higgins RF, Jacobs JR: Duplex imaging and incidence of carotid radiation injury after high-dose radiotherapy for tumors of the head and neck. Arch Surg 125:1181, 1990.
166. Mulligan RM: Syllabus of Human Neoplasms. Philadelphia, Lea & Febiger 1950, p 98.
167. Mumenthaler M: Cranial arteritis. In Vinken PJ, Bruyn GD, Klawans HL, Toole JF (eds): Handbook of Clinical Neurology. Vol 5. Vascular Diseases, Part III. New York, Elsevier Science, 1986, p 341.
168. Najafi H, Javid H, Dye WS: Kinked internal carotid artery. Arch Surg 89:135, 1964.
169. Nakayama K: Surgical removal of the carotid body for bronchial asthma. Dis Chest 40:595, 1961.
170. Nishimoto A: Moyamoya disease. Neurol Med Chir (Tokyo) 19:221, 1979.
171. Nishimoto A, Takeuchi S: Abnormal cerebrovascular network related to the internal carotid arteries. J Neurosurg 29:255, 1968.
172. Nordborg E, Bengtsson BA: Epidemiology of biopsy-proven giant cell arteritis (GCA). J Intern Med 227:233, 1990.
173. Ogawa A, Nakamura N, Yoshimoto T, et al: Cerebral blood flow in moyamoya disease: I. Correlation with age and regional distribution. Acta Neurochir (Wien) 105:30, 1990.
174. Ogawa A, Nakamura N, Yoshimoto T, et al: Cerebral blood flow in moyamoya disease: II. Autoregulation and CO_2 response. Acta Neurochir (Wien) 105:107, 1990.
175. Ojemann RG, Fisher CM, Rich JC: Spontaneous dissecting aneurysm of the internal carotid artery. Stroke 3:434, 1972.
176. Olcott CN, Fee WE, Enzmann DR, et al: Planned approach to management of malignant invasion of the carotid artery. Am J Surg 142:123, 1981.
177. Olsen WL, Dillon WP, Kelly WM, et al: MR imaging of paragangliomas. AJR Am J Roentgenol 148:201, 1987.
178. Padberg FT Jr, Cady B, Persson AV: Carotid body tumor: The Lahey Clinic experience. Am J Surg 145:526, 1983.
179. Pandya SK, Nagpal RD, Desai AP, Purohit AT: Death following external carotid arterial embolization for a functioning glomus jugular chemodectoma. J Neurosurg 48:1030, 1978.
180. Poindexter JM Jr, Patel KR, Clauss RH: Management of kinked extracranial cerebral arteries. J Vasc Surg 6:127, 1987.
181. Pokrovsky AV, Sultanaliev TA, Spiridonov AA: Surgical treatment of vasorenal hypertension in non-specific aorto-arteritis (Takayasu's disease). J Cardiovasc Surg 24:111, 1983.
182. Powers WJ, Tempel L, Grubb RL Jr: Influence of cerebral hemodynamics on stroke risk: One-year follow-up of 30 medically treated patients. Ann Neurol 25:325, 1989.
183. Pryse-Davies J, Dawson IMP, Westbury G: Some morphological histochemical and chemical observations on chemodectomas and the normal carotid body, including a study of the chromaffin reaction and possible ganglion cell elements. Cancer 17:185, 1964.
184. Quattlebaum JK Jr, Upson ET, Neville RL: Stroke associated with elongation and kinking of the internal carotid artery. Ann Surg 150:824, 1959.
185. Quattlebaum JK Jr, Wade JS, Whiddon CM: Stroke associated with elongation and kinking of the carotid artery: Long-term follow-up. Ann Surg 177:572, 1973.
186. Rangwala F, Sylvia LC, Becker SM: Soft tissue metastases of a chemodectoma: A case report and review of the literature. Cancer 42:2865, 1978.
187. Razack MS, Sako K: Carotid artery hemorrhage of ligation in head and neck cancer. J Surg Oncol 19:189, 1982.
188. Reigner: Cited by Lahey FH, Warren KW: A long-term appraisal of carotid tumors with remarks on their removal. Surg Gynecol Obstet 92:481, 1951.
189. Ridge BA, Brewster DC, Darling RC, et al: Familial carotid body tumors: Incidence and implications. Ann Vasc Surg 7:190, 1993.
190. Ringel SP, Harrison SH, Norenberg MD, et al: Fibromuscular dysplasia: Multiple "spontaneous" dissecting aneurysms of the major cervical arteries. Ann Neurol 1:301, 1977.
191. Riser MM, Gelraud J, Ducoudray J, et al: Dolicho-carotide interne avec syndrome vertigineux. Rev Neurol (Paris) 85:145, 1951.
192. Robison JG, Shagets FW, Beckett WC Jr, et al: A multidisciplinary approach to reducing morbidity and operative blood loss during resection of carotid body tumor. Surg Gynecol Obstet 168:166, 1989.
193. Romanski R: Chemodectoma (non-chromaffinic paraganglioma) of the carotid body with distant metastases with illustrative case. Am Pathol 30:1, 1954.
194. Rose G, Sinclair-Smith CC: Takayasu's arteritis: A study of 16 autopsy cases. Arch Pathol Lab Med 104:231, 1980.
195. Rothrock JF, Lim V, Press G, et al: Serial magnetic resonance and carotid duplex examinations in the management of carotid dissection. Neurology 39:686, 1989.
196. Rush BF: Familial bilateral carotid body tumors. Ann Surg 147:633, 1963.
197. Saldana MJ, Salem LE, Travezan R: High altitude hypoxia and chemodectomas. Hum Pathol 4:251, 1973.
198. Samson DS, Boone S: Extracranial-intracranial (EC/IC) arterial bypass: Past performance and current concepts. Neurosurgery 3:79, 1978.
199. Sarkari NBS, Holmes JM, Bickerstaff ER: Neurological manifestation associated with internal carotid loops and kinks in children. J Neurol Neurosurg Psychiaty 33:194, 1970.
200. Savage CO, Ng YC: The etiology and pathogenesis of major systemic vasculitides. Postgrad Med J 62:627, 1986.
201. Schechter DC: Dolichocarotid syndrome: Cerebral ischemia related to cervical carotid artery redundancy with kinking: I, II. Stat Med 79:1391, 1979.
202. Schellack J, Fulenwider JT, Olson RA, et al: The carotid sinus syndrome: A frequently overlooked cause of syncope in the elderly. J Vasc Surg 4:376, 1986.
203. Schevink WI, Mokri B, Piepgras DG: Angiographic frequency of saccular intracranial aneurysms in patients with spontaneous cervical artery dissection. J Neurosurg 76:62, 1992.
204. Schild SE, Foote RL, Buskirk S, et al: Results of radiotherapy for chemodectomas. Mayo Clin Proc 67:537, 1992.
205. Schwaighofer BW, Kline MV, Lynden PD, et al: MR imaging of vertebrobasilar vascular disease. J Comput Assist Tomogr 14:895, 1990.
206. Scudder CL: Tumor of the intercarotid body: A report of one case, together with all cases in literature. Am J Med Sci 126:1384, 1903.
207. Shamblin WR, ReMine WH, Sheps SG, et al: Carotid body tumor (chemodectoma): Clinicopathologic analysis of ninety cases. Am J Surg 122:732, 1971.
208. Shehan JF: Foam cell plaques in the interna elastica of irradiated small arteries. Arch Pathol 37:297, 1944.
209. Shelhamer JH, Volkman DJ, Parrillo JE, et al: Takayasu's arteritis and its therapy. Ann Intern Med 103:121, 1985.
210. Shugar MA, Mafee MF: Diagnosis of carotid body tumors by dynamic computerized tomography. Head Neck Surg 4:518, 1982.
211. Silverberg JD, Brit RH, Goffinet DR: Radiation-induced carotid artery disease. Cancer 41:130, 1978.
212. Sise MJ, Connihan CM, Shackford SR: The clinical spectrum of Takayasu's arteritis. Surgery 104:905, 1988.
213. Skillern PG: Anomalous internal carotid artery and its clinical significance in operations of the tonsils. JAMA 60:172, 1913.
214. Smith BM, Starnes VA, Maggart MA: Operative management of the kinked carotid artery. Surg Gynecol Obstet 162:70, 1986.
215. Smith RF, Shetty PC, Reddy DJ: Surgical treatment of carotid paragangliomas presenting unusual technical difficulties: The value of preoperative embolization. J Vasc Surg 7:631, 1988.
216. Spetzler R, Hadley M: Extracranial-intracranial bypass grafting: An update. In Wilkins R, Rengachary S (eds): Neurosurgery, Update II: Vascular, Spinal, Pediatric, and Functional Neurosurgery. New York, McGraw-Hill, 1991, p 197.
217. Spetzler RF, Selman WR, Roski RA, et al: Cerebral revascularization during barbiturate coma in primates and humans. Surg Neurol 17:111, 1982.

218. Staats EF, Brown RL, Smith RR: Carotid body tumors, benign and malignant. Laryngoscope 76:907, 1966.

219. Stanson AW, Klein RG, Hunder GG: Extracranial angiographic findings in giant cell (temporal) arteritis. AJR Am J Roentgenol 127:957, 1976.

220. Stanton PE Jr, McClusky DA Jr, Lamis PA: Hemodynamic assessment and surgical correction of kinking of the internal carotid artery. Surgery 84:793, 1978.

221. Steinke W, Hennerici M, Aulich A: Doppler color-flow imaging of carotid body tumors. Stroke 20:1574, 1989.

222. Stringer WL, Kelly DL Jr: Traumatic dissection of extracranial internal carotid artery. Neurosurgery 6:123, 1980.

223. Sundt TM, Whistman JP, Piepgras DG, et al: Techniques, results, complications, and follow-up in superficial temporal artery to middle cerebral artery bypass pedicles. In Meyer FB (ed): Sundt's Occlusive Cerebrovascular Disease, 2nd ed. Philadelphia, WB Saunders, 1994, p 436.

224. Suzuki J, Kodoma H: Moyamoya disease: A review. Stroke 14:104, 1983.

225. Suzuki J, Takaku A: Cerebrovascular "moyamoya" disease: Disease showing abnormal netlike vessels in the base of brain. Arch Neurol 20:288, 1969.

226. Takayasu M: A case with peculiar changes of the central retinal vessels. Acta Soc Ophthalmol Jpn 12:554, 1908.

227. Takeuchi K, Shimizu K: Hypoplasia of the bilateral internal carotid arteries. Brain Nerve (Tokyo) 9:37, 1957.

228. Thomas E, Forbus WB: Irradiation injury to the aorta and the lung. Arch Pathol 67:256, 1959.

229. Trackler RT, Mikulicich AG: Diminished cerebral perfusion resulting from kinking of the internal carotid artery. J Nucl Med 15:634, 1974.

230. Trosch RM, Hasbani M, Brass LM: "Bottoms-up" dissection [Letter]. N Engl J Med 320:1564, 1989.

231. Ueki K, Meyer FB: Moyamoya disease. In Meyer FB (ed): Sundt's Occlusive Cerebrovascular Disease, 2nd ed. Philadelphia, WB Saunders, 1994, p 466.

232. Ueno A, Awane Y, Wakabayashi A, et al: Successfully operated obliterative brachiocephalic arteritis (Takayasu's) associated with elongated coarctation. Jpn Heart J 93:94, 1977.

233. Valdagni R, Amichetti M: Radiation therapy of carotid body tumors. Am J Clin Oncol 13:45, 1990.

234. Vannix RS, Joergenson FJ, Carter R: Kinking of the internal carotid artery: Clinical significance and surgical management. Am J Surg 134:82, 1977.

235. Verneuil M: Contusions multiples délire violate, hémiplégia à droite, signes de compression cérébrale. Bull Acad Natl Med (Paris) 1:46, 1872.

236. Vinijchaikul K: Primary arteritis of the aorta and its main branches (Takayasu's arteriopathy): A clinicopathologic autopsy study of 8 cases. Am J Med 43:15, 1967.

237. Vogl T, Brunning R, Schedel H, et al: Paragangliomas of the jugular bulb and carotid body: MR imaging with short sequences and Gd-DTPA enhancement. AJR Am J Roentgenol 153:583, 1989.

238. Von Haller: Cited by Gratiot JH: Carotid tumors: A collective review. Abstr Surg 7:117, 1943.

239. Waddington MM, Ring BA: Syndromes of occlusions of middle cerebral artery branches: Angiographic and clinical correlation. Brain 91:685, 1968.

240. Weaver FA, Yellin AE, Campen DH: Surgical procedures in the management of Takayasu's arteritis. J Vasc Surg 12:429, 1990.

241. Weibel J, Fields WS: Tortuosity, coiling, and kinking of the internal carotid artery: Relationship of morphological variation to cerebrovascular insufficiency. Neurology 15:462, 1965.

242. Weibers DO, Mokri B: Internal carotid artery dissection after childbirth. Stroke 16: 956, 1988.

243. Weidemann G, Grotz J, Bewermeyer H, et al: High resolution real-time ultrasound of the carotid bifurcation in patients with hyperactive carotid sinus syndrome. J Neurol 232:318, 1985.

244. Westbrook KC, Guillamondequi OM, Medellin H, et al: Chemodectomas of the neck: Selective management. Am J Surg 124:760, 1972.

245. Widder B: The Doppler CO_2 test to exclude patients not in need of extracranial-intracranial bypass surgery. J Neurol Neurosurg Psychiatry 28:449, 1965.

246. Wilkinson IMS, Russell RWR: Arteries of the head and neck in giant cell arteritis: A pathological study to show the pattern of arterial involvement. Arch Neurol 27:378, 1972.

247. Wirth FP, Miller WA, Russell AP: Atypical fibromuscular hyperplasia: Report of two cases. J Neurosurg 54:685, 1981.

248. Wood JB, Frankland AW, Eastcott HHG: Bilateral removal of carotid bodies for asthma. Thorax 20:570, 1965.

249. Worsey MJ, Laborde AL, Bower T, et al: A evaluation of color duplex scanning in the primary diagnosis and management of carotid body tumors. Ann Vasc Surg 6:90, 1992.

250. Wright DJ, Pandya A, Noel F: Anesthesia for carotid body tumour resection. Anaesthesia 34:806, 1979.

251. Yaghami I, Shariat S, Shamloo M: Carotid body tumors. Radiology 97:559, 1970.

252. Youl BD, Coutlellier A, Dubois B, et al: Three cases of spontaneous extracranial vertebral artery dissection. Stroke 21:618, 1990.

253. Zelenock GB, Kazmers A, Whitehouse WM Jr, et al: Extracranial internal carotid artery dissections: Noniatrogenic traumatic lesions. Arch Surg 117:425, 1982.

254. Zirkel PK, Wheeler JR, Gregory RT, et al: Carotid involvement in aortic dissection diagnosed by duplex scanning. J Vasc Surg 1:700, 1984.

Complications Following Carotid Endarterectomy and Perioperative Management

145

TIMOTHY F. KRESOWIK, MD

Carotid endarterectomy (CEA) has been one of the most scrutinized peripheral vascular procedures. There have been a number of well-designed, randomized, prospective clinical trials that have documented the efficacy of CEA compared to medical therapy for patients with moderate to severe carotid stenosis both with and without symptoms.[1-7] These prospective trials have also provided the best documentation of perioperative complication rates. The efficacy of the procedure in specific populations is dependent on achieving perioperative complication rates that are comparable to or superior to the complication rates observed in the trials. The complication rates in the trials can be looked on as "achievable benchmarks" since they were a compilation of the results across a large number of surgeons and institutions. It is incumbent on every physician discussing CEA with a patient to be familiar with the risks and benefits of the procedure. The randomized trials have provided a valid prediction of the natural history of the disease with medical therapy alone. The risks of the procedure presented to the patient should be those that are achieved in the setting the patient would have the procedure, that is, specific to the institution and/or surgeon. The availability of this information is obviously dependent on a system to document complication rates in every institution where the procedure is performed.

In addition to being aware of the institution or surgeon specific complication rates, a clinician involved in the care of patients with carotid occlusive disease should be involved in continuous quality improvement. Every institution and surgeon should be striving for benchmark performance. Obviously, an important component of achieving optimal results for CEA is technical perfection in the operating room. Perioperative care processes are also an important contributor to CEA quality improvement. Physicians caring for patients undergoing CEA should be familiar with the evidence base for or against specific care processes employed during the perioperative period. Optimal results are achieved only when a system is in place to ensure that every patient undergoing CEA receives all the therapeutic interventions that have an evidence linkage to better outcomes.

■ COMPLICATIONS

The risk of CEA can be stratified in multiple ways. There are perioperative or immediate complications and late (after 30-day) complications. Immediate complications can be characterized as central neurologic, local (neck), and systemic. CEA is a prophylactic operation with essentially one purpose: the prevention of stroke (alleviation of disabling symptoms being a rare additional indication). Postoperative stroke is thus the most important complication. Obviously, death is an equally serious adverse event. Strokes or deaths following CEA are usually expressed together as a combined event rate. Important local complications are cranial nerve injury and hemorrhage. The most frequent systemic aberration associated with CEA is temporary alteration in blood pressure control with both hypotension and hypertension occurring. Since coronary artery disease is common in patients with carotid stenosis, perioperative myocardial infarction (MI) is always a concern. The most common late complication is recurrent carotid stenosis. Suture line or patch disruption associated with infection is a rare but serious late complication.

Central Neurologic Complications or Death

Perioperative Stroke or Death

Perioperative stroke is usually combined with mortality and expressed as the combined event rate. The combined event rate implies that an individual patient would count only as one adverse event in calculating the rate even if he or she suffered a stroke that was fatal. In other words the combined event rate is the mortality rate plus the nonfatal stroke rate. A stroke is usually defined as a new or worsened central neurologic deficit that lasts longer than 24 hours. This would also include ischemic events in the distribution of the ophthalmic artery (retinal stroke). Transient neurologic deficits (<24 hours) may also occur but are not usually considered major complications. This is particularly true in the patient with a prior stroke, as the effect of anesthesia may temporarily make a preexisting neurologic deficit appear worse. Perioperative stroke should be distinguished from ipsilateral cranial nerve deficits (see later) that may be mistaken for a stroke by the novice observer.

It would seem useful to describe the severity of strokes when reporting this complication because the severity obviously has tremendous implications for the patient. In some of the prospective trials, major or disabling stroke has been distinguished from minor stroke. Part of the problem in using this distinction in other settings is standardization of the definition of major versus minor stroke. In studies with prospective data collection, a standardized stroke severity

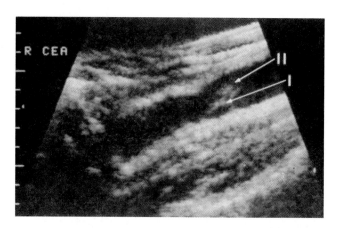

FIGURE 145-1 Intraoperative ultrasound following carotid endarterectomy (CEA) demonstrating an intimal flap (I) with a platelet thrombus (II) at the internal carotid endpoint. This type of defect could result in a thromboembolic postoperative stroke if uncorrected. (From Kresowik TF, Hoballah JJ, Sharp WJ, et al: Intraoperative B-mode ultrasonography is a useful adjunct to peripheral arterial reconstruction. Ann Vasc Surg 7:35, 1993.)

scale can be used, but these scales are often not applicable to retrospective data collection because of missing data elements.

The convention in reporting postoperative complication rates is to include all events that occur within 30 days of the operative event. Since CEA is usually associated with a very brief hospitalization, calculation of a true 30-day complication rate requires follow-up data beyond the hospital stay. When comparing reported results it is important to determine whether the reported complication rate includes events that occur within 30 days but beyond the initial hospital stay.

To prevent and appropriately manage postoperative stroke, it is useful to understand the timing and pathophysiology of these events. In most large series describing the etiology of perioperative stroke, the majority (60% to 80%) of strokes are delayed; that is, the patient is confirmed to be neurologically intact at the completion of the procedure.[8-13] Most of these postoperative events occur in the first 24 hours following the operation and are attributed to endarterectomy site thrombosis and/or embolism from the endarterectomy site (Fig. 145-1). These observations suggest that technical defects are the most common cause of perioperative stroke. A combination of technical perfection and appropriate perioperative antithrombotic therapy would appear to be important in achieving the best outcomes for CEA. Other less common causes of stroke from CEA include ischemia at the time of carotid clamping and embolism during dissection or embolism from remote sites.

The high frequency of endarterectomy site technical defects and thromboembolism as a cause of early postoperative stroke dictates an aggressive approach toward evaluation and management of patients who develop a new neurologic deficit following CEA. The traditional approach to this scenario has been emergent reoperation and exploration of the endarterectomy site.[14,15] Thrombectomy for acute thrombosis of the endarterectomy site with restoration of flow is associated with a high percentage of reversal of

the neurologic deficit. With ready availability of good-quality color-duplex technology it is possible to rapidly rule out internal carotid thrombosis or major technical defects without reoperation. In the absence of thrombosis or endarterectomy site technical defects, emergent angiography to evaluate the intracranial circulation should be considered. Although systemic thrombolytic therapy should generally be avoided, intra-arterial thrombolytic therapy may be a reasonable option for documented intracerebral embolism in this setting.[16,17]

Hyperperfusion/Cerebral Hemorrhage

One of the most frustrating complications of CEA is what has been referred to as *hyperperfusion syndrome*.[18-35] The classic full-blown hyperperfusion syndrome consists of unilateral headache, seizure activity, and cerebral hemorrhage. Hyperperfusion syndrome commonly peaks at 2 to 7 days following operation and thus often after the patient has been discharged from the hospital. Cerebral hemorrhage occurred in 0.2% to 0.8% of cases in several well-documented large series of CEA.[11,20,22-24] Most cerebral hemorrhage in these series was attributed to hyperperfusion syndrome. A documented clinically apparent hyperperfusion syndrome with and without hemorrhage occurs in 2% to 3% of patients.[30-32] Imaging and cerebral flow studies have demonstrated edema, microhemorrhage, and supranormal cerebral blood flow in patients with the clinical presentation of hyperperfusion (Figs. 145-2 and 145-3). Epileptiform activity ipsilateral to the CEA or frank seizures are associated with the syndrome.[19,21,25,35] Hyperperfusion is thought to be a consequence of disturbed cerebral autoregulation that develops in the territory of a carotid stenosis. Most reports of hyperperfusion syndrome have associated the syndrome with correction of very high-grade carotid stenoses, especially in the presence of contralateral occlusion or high-grade stenosis, although the syndrome has been described in the absence of these risk factors.[30] Uncontrolled hypertension is an additional risk factor. Hyperperfusion syndrome is extremely frustrating for the surgeon since it does not appear related to the technical performance of the procedure. With prevention of clamp-associated hypoperfusion through selective or routine shunting and avoidance of technical defects, cerebral hyperperfusion becomes an increasingly important cause of postoperative strokes.

Although the rarity of severe hyperperfusion syndrome in most surgical practices limits the available evidence for prevention or treatment recommendations, extra attention to blood pressure control would certainly be appropriate in patients at risk (very high-grade stenosis or severe bilateral disease). In patients who develop ipsilateral headache following CEA, a cerebral imaging study should be obtained. A magnetic resonance (MR) imaging scan with T2 weighting and cerebrospinal fluid signal suppression (fluid attenuation inversion recovery) in addition to gadolinium-enhanced imaging and MR angiography is likely the most sensitive study for the typical changes associated with hyperperfusion (see Fig. 145-2). A noncontrast computed tomographic (CT) scan (see Fig. 145-3) documents hemorrhage if it is present and may indicate edema, although it is less sensitive than MR imaging.

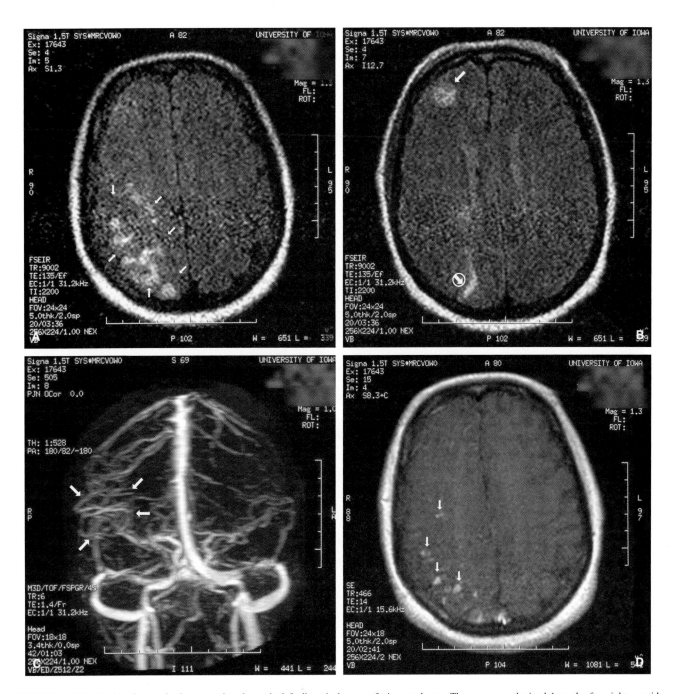

FIGURE 145-2 MR imaging study demonstrating the typical findings in hyperperfusion syndrome. The scan was obtained 1 week after right carotid revascularization. The patient presented with severe right-sided headache for several days followed by a seizure. **A,** T2-weighted study with cerebrospinal fluid signal suppression (fluid attenuation inversion recovery [FLAIR]). The *arrows* indicate the easily visualized areas of cerebral edema. **B,** Another cut using the same technique demonstrating an area of hemorrhage in the frontal lobe (*arrow*) and edema posteriorly (*circled arrow*). **C,** Gadolinium-enhanced MR angiogram demonstrating right-sided vasodilation (*arrows*). **D,** T1-weighted post-gadolinium image demonstrating the dilated vessels (*arrows*).

Patients with cerebral edema or microhemorrhage might be admitted to the hospital for seizure precautions and aggressive blood pressure management. An electroencephalogram may identify patients with subclinical seizure activity for whom seizure medication prophylaxis may be appropriate. Although antiplatelet therapy is highly desired following CEA, temporarily discontinuing antithrombotic therapy may be prudent in patients with confirmed hyperperfusion syndrome.

Reported Results of Carotid Endarterectomy

When comparing the reported results of CEA, there are a number of dataset characteristics that should be examined. Complication data collected prospectively tend to be more reliable than data collected retrospectively. Complication rates based on administrative (claims) data can be highly misleading. Recording of complications other than mortality in these administrative sets is often incomplete.

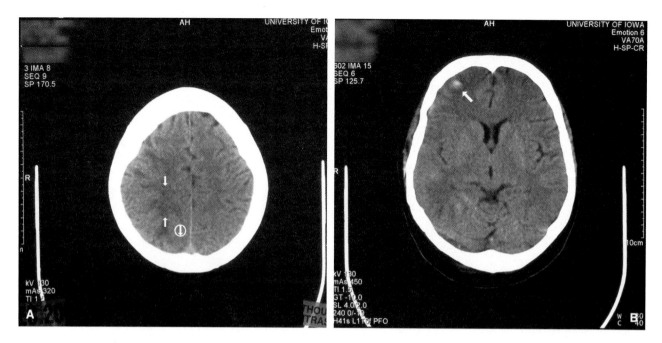

FIGURE 145-3 Noncontrast CT scan from the same patient depicted in Figure 145-2. **A,** The right-sided white matter (*arrows*) is less dense (darker) than the left side, suggesting edema. There is a gray matter area of hypodensity (*circled arrow*), also suggesting edema. **B,** Another cut from the same study showing the frontal lobe hemorrhage (*arrow*).

Since the major purpose of administrative data is the determination of payment, the incentive to record a complication is influenced by whether or not it would alter the payment amount. Datasets based on voluntary reporting (registries) may have the advantage of prospective collection but are limited by under-reporting or lack of participation by providers with suboptimal outcomes. Administrative datasets and registries often address only the initial hospitalization and thus do not necessarily reflect 30-day outcomes.

The randomized, prospective trials likely provide the best documentation of multi-institution CEA results (Table 145-1). In these trials specific outcome endpoints were defined and preoperative and postoperative neurologic examinations were performed. Accurate 30-day outcomes

were prospectively collected and reported. The randomized clinical trials do not necessarily reflect the community-wide results of CEA. Surgeons who participated in the trials had to meet entry criteria, as did the patients. Patients older than 79 years of age were excluded from the Asymptomatic Carotid Atherosclerosis Study (ACAS) and from the initial phase (before 1991) of the North American Symptomatic Carotid Endarterectomy Study (NASCET). Patients with significant medical comorbidities, remote ipsilateral symptoms or stroke, and vertebrobasilar symptoms were excluded from the symptomatic and asymptomatic trials.

Community-wide reports of CEA results reflecting procedures performed since 1990 are displayed in Table 145-2.[36-42] All the reports included in Table 145-2 used medical record review to determine outcomes and reported

Table 145-1	Reported 30-Day Outcomes for CEA from Randomized Clinical Trials				
STUDY, PUBLICATION DATE	**POPULATION**	**STUDY PERIOD**	**NO. OF PROCEDURES***	**MORTALITY, %**	**COMBINED EVENT RATE,† %**
Symptomatic					
ECST, 1998[5]	Symptomatic, 0-99% stenosis	1981-1994	1745	1.0	7.0
NASCET, 1999[11]	Symptomatic, 30-99% stenosis	1987-1996	1415	1.1	6.5
VA Symptomatic, 1991[3]	Symptomatic, 50-99% stenosis	1988-1991	90	3.3	5.5
Asymptomatic					
ACAS, 1995[12]	Asymptomatic, 60-99% stenosis	1987-1993	721	0.1	1.5
VA Asymptomatic, 1990[13]	Asymptomatic, 50-99% stenosis	1983-1987	203	2.0	4.5

*The number of procedures used to determine the event rate was the actual number of procedures performed. Patients who were randomized to the surgical group but did not undergo the procedure (included in the intention-to-treat analysis) were excluded.
†ECST defined stroke as new deficits lasting > 7 days; the other studies defined stroke as new deficits lasting > 24 hours.
CEA, carotid endarterectomy.

Table 145-2	Reported 30-Day Outcomes for CEA from Community Surveys Based on Retrospective Medical Record Reviews				
STUDY AUTHORS, DATE	POPULATION	STUDY PERIOD	NO. OF PROCEDURES	MORTALITY, %	COMBINED EVENT RATE,* %
Bratzler et al, 1996[36]	Eight community hospitals	1993-1994	774	1.6	4.9
Karp et al,1998[37]	Georgia Medicare patients	1993	1945	1.9	4.7
Cebul et al, 1998[38]	Ohio Medicare patients	1993-1994	678	1.8	4.7*
Kucey et al, 1998[39]	Eight Toronto hospitals	1994-1996	1280	1.8	6.3
Kresowik et al, 2000[40]	Iowa Medicare patients	1994	2063	2.2	6.6
Kresowik et al, 2001[41]	10 state Medicare patients	1995-1996	10561	1.5	5.2
Kresowik et al, 2004[42]	10 state Medicare patients	1998-1999	10379	1.3	5.0

*In the Ohio Medicare study, stroke was defined as a new deficit still present at hospital discharge. All the other reports depicted in this table used a >24-hour definition of stroke.
CEA, carotid endarterectomy.

30-day outcomes. Reported results from administrative databases and registries were not included because of the previously mentioned limitations. The results displayed in Table 145-2 do exclude patients undergoing combined CEA and coronary artery bypass grafting (CABG). All of the series in Table 145-2, with the exception of one,[39] are from the U.S. Medicare population. This means that nondisabled patients younger than 65 years of age would not be included.

Even in the randomized trials, there were some differences in the endpoint definitions. The European Carotid Surgery Trial (ECST) defined a postoperative stroke as a new deficit lasting more than 1 week. The other trials used a "greater than 24-hour duration" definition for distinguishing postoperative stroke from transient ischemic attacks (TIAs). Definitions of major or disabling stroke versus minor or nondisabling stroke are even more variable. In a large Medicare-population retrospective medical record review of CEA complications, we used a definition of major stroke based on a disability in walking, talking, or eating.[41] Patients who suffered a new postoperative neurologic deficit that resulted in the need for assistance with walking or eating or had aphasia were considered to have a major stroke. Table 145-3 displays the breakdown of stroke severity in the NASCET, ECST, ACAS, and the 10-state Medicare review. The timing of disability determination (NASCET and ACAS 30 days, ECST 6 months, 10-state Medicare 5 days) likely accounts for some of the variation in the ratio of disabling to nondisabling strokes in these studies. In NASCET and ACAS only one third of the strokes were found to be disabling.

Table 145-3 also provides the rates of stroke-related versus non-stroke-related death in the same reports. There is more consistency in the ratio between stroke-related and non-stroke-related death in these reports than in stroke classification. It is apparent that approximately half of the deaths associated with CEA appear to be related to stroke. Most non-stroke-related death is cardiac in origin. These facts illustrate the importance of patient selection and cardiac management in optimizing the outcomes of CEA. Comparison of the ACAS and VA asymptomatic trials (see Table 145-1) also demonstrates the impact of cardiac disease on overall outcomes. The threefold higher combined event rate seen in the VA asymptomatic trial versus ACAS is largely due to the 2.0% versus 0.1% mortality rate observed in these two trials. All the perioperative deaths in the VA asymptomatic trial were cardiac related.

Although many factors may impact the risk of CEA, by far the most important is the indication or symptom status of the patient.[43] The NASCET and ACAS surgical results indicate that the risk of stroke or death from CEA is four times greater in symptomatic (6.5%) that asymptomatic patients (1.5%). It is important to understand that the definition used for symptomatic in the NASCET trial included only patients who had experienced a relatively *recent* (within 120-day) hemispheric TIA, stroke, or ipsilateral transient monocular blindness (amaurosis fugax). In many of the reports that address symptom status, patients are stratified only into symptomatic and asymptomatic subgroups. There are a significant number of patients undergoing CEA whose symptomatic status does not fall into

Table 145-3	Perioperative Stroke Severity and Cause of Death Following CEA			
STUDY*	DISABLING STROKE (NONFATAL), %	NONDISABLING STROKE (NONFATAL), %	STROKE DEATH, %	NONSTROKE DEATH, %
NASCET[11]	1.8	3.7	0.6	0.5
ECST[5]	2.6	3.5	0.6	0.4
ACAS[12]	0.5	1.0	0.0	0.1
10-state Medicare[41]	2.5	1.2	0.6	0.9

*NASCET and ACAS defined a stroke as any new deficit lasting > 24 hours; disability was determined at 30 days. ECST defined a stroke as any new deficit lasting > 7 days: disability was determined at 6 months. The 10-state Medicare study defined a stroke as any new deficit lasting > 24 hours; disability was determined at 5 days.
CEA, carotid endarterectomy.

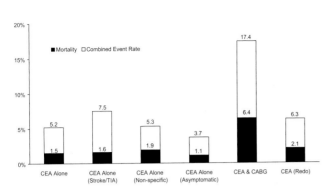

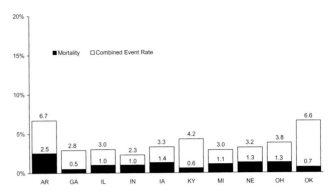

FIGURE 145-4 Combined event rate (30-day) following carotid endarterectomy (CEA) by indication and type of procedure. The event rates are based on complete retrospective medical record (hospital chart) review, review of medical records from readmissions within 30 days, and query of the Social Security database to determine any out-of-hospital deaths within 30 days. Two clinicians independently validated all adverse outcomes. The results are from review of 10,561 CEA procedures performed in 10 states on Medicare patients between June 1, 1995, and May 30, 1996. CEA alone represents first-time procedures performed not in conjunction with coronary artery bypass grafting (CABG); CEA and CABG are combined procedures in the same operative setting, and CEA (redo) are repeat operations for recurrent stenosis. Indications in the CEA alone subset are stratified by transient ischemic attack (TIA)/stroke (ipsilateral hemispheric TIA or stroke within 90 days prior to the procedure), nonspecific (global ischemia, contralateral hemispheric events, vertebrobasilar events or remote ipsilateral events), and asymptomatic (no prior history of TIA or stroke in any distribution). (From Kresowik TF, Bratzler D, Karp HR, et al: Multistate utilization, processes, and outcomes of carotid endarterectomy. J Vasc Surg 33:227-234, 2001.)

FIGURE 145-5 Combined event rate (30-day) in asymptomatic carotid endarterectomy alone in Medicare patients in 10 states by state. The outcomes were determined by complete medical record review of 3891 total CEA procedures (smallest individual state sample was 289) performed between June 1, 1995, and May 30, 1996, on asymptomatic patients. (From Kresowik TF, Bratzler D, Karp HR, et al: Multistate utilization, processes, and outcomes of carotid endarterectomy. J Vasc Surg 33:227-234; 2001.)

either the NASCET or ACAS definitions. In our review of the Medicare CEA results in 10 states we combined the patients not meeting NASCET/ACAS definitions (e.g., those with global, vertebrobasilar, contralateral, or remote ipsilateral hemispheric symptoms) into a nonspecific subgroup.[41] This subgroup made up almost 40% of the procedures in our study. The nonspecific subgroup had a 30% lower combined event rate than the patients with recent hemispheric symptoms and a 30% higher combined event rate than asymptomatic patients (Fig. 145-4). It would seem that reported results for CEA should be stratified in at least three categories—asymptomatic, recent ipsilateral hemispheric symptoms (NASCET), and a nonspecific group—to provide valid comparisons between reports.

There is significant variability in the outcomes of CEA even when risk adjustment and common definitions of endpoints are used. Figure 145-5 depicts the statewide combined event rate in asymptomatic patients for the 10 different states in our initial Medicare CEA review. It can be seen that there was as much as a threefold variation in outcomes between states. A follow-up review in the same states 3 years later did demonstrate improvement in outcomes.[42] In at least one state (Georgia) in the follow-up time period, the statewide combined event rate for asymptomatic patients was 1.5%.[42] This event rate is identical to the combined event rate observed in the ACAS trial and demonstrates that this level of surgical proficiency can be achieved across an entire state. Unfortunately, variation in outcomes between states persisted, and most statewide results did not reach the ACAS benchmark outcomes.

Another important variable in predicting the risk of CEA is whether it is performed as a solitary procedure or combined with coronary artery bypass grafting (CEA/CABG). The risk of stroke or death following the combined procedure may be as much as three times higher than CEA performed as a solitary procedure (see Fig. 145-4).[41] Most strokes that occur following the combined procedure are not in the distribution of the operated carotid.[44] Most of the increased risk associated with the combined procedure is likely due to the addition of the risk of stroke or death from the CABG. Patients who undergo the combined procedure usually have extensive disease and thus are at higher risk for stroke or death than typical patients undergoing either CEA or CABG alone. This is the likely explanation for the fact that the adverse event rate for combined CEA/CABG exceeds the sum of the adverse event rates observed in typical series of CEA or CABG alone procedures. The optimal management of patients with combined coronary and carotid disease remains controversial. It should be clear that outcomes from reports that include a significant percentage of the combined procedure should not be compared to reports where the combined procedure was excluded. Procedures done for recurrent stenosis should probably also be analyzed separately, although it is not evident that the risk of stroke or death is higher in these procedures than primary CEA.[41,45-47] The risk of local complications appears to be higher for redo procedures.[48]

In summary, several variables should be considered in evaluating or reporting results of CEA. Prospective data collection with clear indication and adverse outcome definitions as well as outcome reporting for the first 30 days following the procedure should be considered the gold standard. Lacking prospective data collection, complete medical record review with standardized definitions of adverse outcomes is necessary for valid assessment of outcomes other than mortality. The symptomatic status of the patients should be stratified into at least three levels: recent TIA/stroke, nonspecific, and asymptomatic. Primary CEA alone procedures should be considered separately from

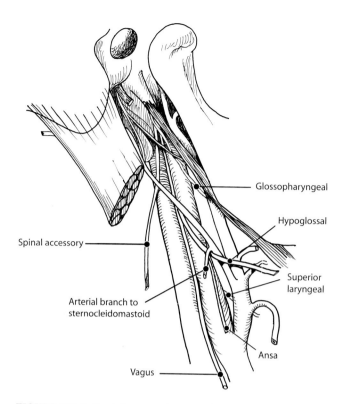

FIGURE 145-6 Cranial nerves that may be injured during carotid endarterectomy. The line drawing depicts the typical relationship of cranial nerves to the carotid bifurcation. (Modified from Kresowik TF: Carotid endarterectomy. In Scott-Conner CEH, Dawson DL [eds]: Operative Anatomy. Philadelphia, Lippincott, Williams & Wilkins, 2003, p 64.)

combined CEA/CABG and redo procedures. These same standards of reporting should be equally applicable to endovascular (angioplasty/stent) cerebrovascular procedures.

Local Complications

Although the major focus on risks of CEA is usually on stroke or mortality, local complications can cause significant morbidity or even mortality. Cranial nerve injury should be considered a mostly preventable complication. Many cranial nerve injuries go undetected, but some may cause vocal or swallowing dysfunction. Wound hematomas can be a serious complication through compromise of the airway. Infection is a rare complication of a CEA wound but can be devastating if a suture line or patch closure is involved.

Cranial Nerve Injury

The typical location and course of the cranial nerves encountered during CEA are seen in Figures 145-6 and 145-7. The reported incidences of cranial nerve injuries associated with CEA series have been generally in the 2% to 15% range, but some have reported even higher incidences (in the 25% to 30% range) when routine pharyngeal function studies and laryngoscopy are performed.[49-63] Some of the nerve dysfunction uncovered in prospective studies was associated with no or minimal symptoms and thus would have been missed if only symptomatic patients were

tabulated. In the NASCET trial the incidence of cranial nerve injury was 8.6% (hypoglossal 3.7%, vagus 2.5%, marginal mandibular 2.2%), with 92% of the deficits classified as mild.[11] The cranial nerve injury rate in ACAS was 4.9%.[12] Almost all cranial nerve injuries associated with CEA are transient, with complete recovery in 90% to 99% of patients. This suggests that the nerve dysfunction is related to blunt injury rather than to inadvertent division of the nerves. Prevention of nerve injury requires knowledge of the cranial nerve anatomy as well as care with use of forceps, clamps, and retractors. Bipolar cautery may be preferred to unipolar cautery to reduce the likelihood of nerve injury from cauterization. The most common cranial nerve injuries during CEA appear to be the vagus, hypoglossal, and marginal mandibular branch of the facial nerve. This is not surprising since these are the nerves that are usually encountered in the typical CEA dissection field. Some series report the vagus as the most common injury and others the hypoglossal.[49-63] Because of the difficulty associated with operating in a previously dissected field, it is not surprising that operations for recurrent carotid stenosis are associated with a higher incidence of cranial nerve injury.[48]

Vagus Nerve   The vagus nerve passes into the neck through the jugular foramen along with the glossopharyngeal and spinal accessory nerves. The usual course of the vagus is within the carotid sheath, lateral and posterior to the internal and common carotid arteries. The nerve may course more anteriorly, especially proximally along the common carotid artery, so care should be taken when first opening the carotid sheath. To avoid a clamp injury to the vagus, the nerve usually has to be mobilized off the posterolateral aspect of the common and internal carotid arteries. It is important to avoid inadvertent forceps injury to the vagus during dissection of the carotid vessels. Although the vagus contains somatic and visceral afferent and efferent fibers, the most important deficit associated with vagus injury at the level of a CEA dissection is recurrent laryngeal nerve dysfunction. The recurrent laryngeal nerve supplies motor function of the vocal cord and thus ipsilateral vocal cord paralysis occurs after a complete vagal injury. Vocal cord paralysis usually results in hoarseness, impaired phonation, and an ineffective cough. Even a transient vagal injury may be especially important in the circumstance of bilateral CEA. Bilateral recurrent laryngeal nerve palsy may result in airway obstruction or inability to protect the airway depending on the position of the paralyzed cords. Simultaneous bilateral CEA is avoided because of this potential, and many would recommend laryngoscopy to document vocal cord function between staged bilateral CEA procedures.

Hypoglossal Nerve   The hypoglossal nerve descends anteriorly and medially to the internal carotid, usually looping anteriorly over the external carotid to supply the tongue musculature. The descending branch of the ansa cervicalis (providing motor function to the strap muscles) travels with the proximal hypoglossal and usually exits from the hypoglossal as it crosses the carotid vessels to descend anterior and parallel to the common carotid. Mobilization of the hypoglossal may require division of either the

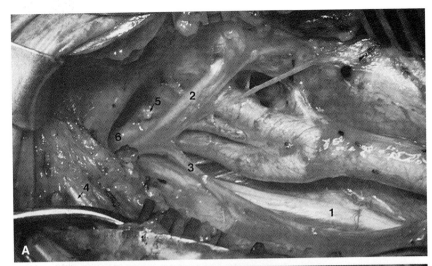

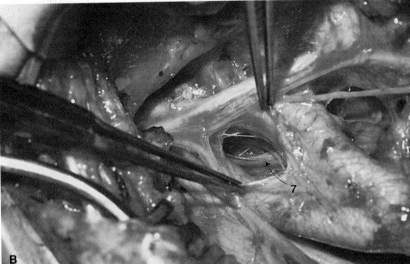

FIGURE 145-7 Operative photograph depicting nerves in the vicinity of the carotid bifurcation. **A,** Vagus (1), hypoglossal (2), ansa hypoglossi (3), greater auricular (4), divided vascular bundle to sternocleidomastoid muscle (5), and occipital branch of external carotid artery (6). **B,** Superior laryngeal nerve (7).

descending branch or transverse branches of the ansa cervicalis arising from the cervical plexus. Division of the ansa is not associated with a noticeable neurologic deficit. Typically there is a vascular pedicle containing an arterial branch from the external carotid artery looping over the hypoglossal nerve to supply the sternocleidomastoid muscle. Division of this vascular pedicle during the dissection usually allows the hypoglossal nerve to ascend superiorly and medially, providing adequate access to the internal carotid and carotid bifurcation for a CEA. Hypoglossal nerve injury results in ipsilateral tongue palsy with impaired annunciation and deglutition.

Facial Nerve   The marginal mandibular nerve is the most inferior coursing branch of the facial nerve. This branch typically travels along the inferior ramus of the mandible but may drop lower in the neck. Injury to the marginal mandibular may occur in the case of a very low course of the nerve or more commonly from retractor compression against the mandible. The marginal mandibular supplies motor fibers to the facial muscles at the corner of the mouth. Marginal mandibular palsy may lead to both a cosmetic (drooping at corner of the mouth) and functional (drooling) deficit.

Other Nerves   Other nerve injuries less commonly associated with CEA include the superior laryngeal nerve, greater auricular nerve, spinal accessory nerve, glossopharyngeal nerve, and sympathetic chain. The superior laryngeal nerve arises from the vagus above the level of the typical CEA dissection. The nerve runs posterior to the internal and external carotid and then pierces the cricothyroid membrane to provide sensory function to the larynx and motor function to the tensors of the vocal cord. Superior laryngeal nerve dysfunction may be asymptomatic, but voice fatigue or alteration in sound quality may be noted, especially in patients who have occupations or hobbies requiring public speaking or singing.[49-51] The superior laryngeal nerve may be encountered during a dissection in the vicinity of the carotid bifurcation or of the proximal branches of the external carotid (e.g., superior thyroid). The sympathetic chain is also deep to the carotid vessels.

Horner's syndrome from injury to the inferior sympathetic ganglion is rare unless a high dissection is required. The glossopharyngeal nerve is rarely encountered during a CEA because it is adjacent to the internal carotid only very high in the neck. If unusually distal dissection of the internal carotid is required, the glossopharyngeal nerve may be injured.[64] The glossopharyngeal nerve lies posterior to the styloid process and the muscles arising from it. The nerve supplies sensation to the pharynx, and the muscles innervated by the glossopharyngeal elevate the larynx and pharynx during swallowing. Glossopharyngeal nerve injury can be a devastating functional injury because of marked impairment of swallowing and recurrent aspiration. Spinal accessory nerve injury is rare following CEA.[65] The spinal accessory nerve runs lateral to the carotid sheath but may be encountered if the dissection wanders lateral to the internal jugular vein or injury could occur from a retractor. Spinal accessory nerve dysfunction is associated with denervation of the trapezius and serratus anterior muscles leading to shoulder pain, shoulder drop, difficulty in elevating the arm past horizontal, and winging of the scapula. The greater auricular nerve provides sensory function to the external ear and may be encountered at the superior end of the skin incision, especially if carried lateral to the medial border of the sternocleidomastoid muscle. Paresthesia and hypesthesia of the ear can result from injury to the greater auricular.[52] Transverse sensory nerve fibers have to be divided during the typical CEA skin incision, and at least transient hypesthesia of the skin medial to the incision is common. This is most commonly noticed by men because of shaving.

Hemorrhage

The use of perioperative antiplatelet therapy and intra-operative heparinization are both associated with better overall outcomes (reduction of stroke and mortality rate) for CEA. It seems obvious that the use of antithrombotic therapy may increase the risk of perioperative wound hemorrhage. Some degree of neck wound hematoma is not uncommon following CEA, but serious bleeding requiring a return to the operating room is unusual, occurring in 1% to 3% of cases.[11,41,66,67] Perioperative hypertension is a risk factor for hematoma formation, and control of blood pressure may be the most important modifiable risk factor. The impact of reversal of heparin on the incidence of wound hematoma is unclear, and heparin reversal has the potential for increasing thromboembolic complications.[66,68-71] The most serious sequelae associated with wound hemorrhage is airway compromise.[72] This can occur as a result of a hematoma deviating and compressing the larynx and/or diffuse hemorrhage into the laryngeal soft tissue (Fig. 145-8). This complication accounted for two of the seven non-stroke-related deaths in the NASCET trial.[11] A heightened awareness of this possibility, close observation of a patient with any degree of wound hematoma, and a relatively low threshold for hematoma drainage are certainly warranted. Any patient with a neck hematoma causing tracheal deviation and/or respiratory difficulty should have the hematoma evacuated. Emergent opening of the wound at the bedside may rarely be necessary to establish an airway and can be life saving. Some surgeons routinely employ temporary suction drainage in an attempt to reduce the incidence of neck hematomas, although there is not a high level of evidence supporting this practice.[73]

It is extremely rare to have a suture line disruption lead to massive hemorrhage following CEA. However, a still uncommon but well-described hemorrhagic complication associated with CEA is disruption of a vein patch. Most large series where routine patching with vein is employed have reported this complication, with an incidence of 0.1% to 0.7%.[74-77] The complication appears to be associated with the use of poorer quality or at least a more thin-walled vein, for example, ankle as opposed to thigh saphenous vein. The authors of these reports have almost universally described central necrosis of the vein patch with massive hemorrhage. Since the complication often occurs after discharge from the hospital, there has been a high case-fatality rate. It would seem prudent to choose a good-quality vein for patching if an autogenous patch is to be used. Most surgeons have abandoned the use of ankle-level saphenous vein as a CEA patch and use thigh saphenous if vein patching is performed.

Infection

Infection is an uncommon complication of CEA. The vascularity of the neck as well as the relatively thin subcutaneous layer likely is responsible for the low incidence of wound infection. The incidence of wound infection following CEA is difficult to determine from the

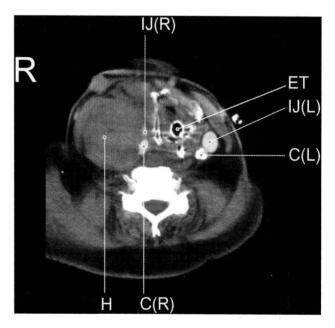

FIGURE 145-8 CT image of the lower neck in a patient with a large hematoma following a right carotid endarterectomy (CEA). The marked shift and compression of the airway are well visualized. The IJ(R) is compressed by the hematoma. This patient had a cardiac event following CEA and was already intubated when he experienced marked hypertension during resuscitation and subsequent hematoma development. Imaging studies are not necessary to make the clinical diagnosis of potential airway compromise from a post-CEA hematoma and should not delay hematoma evacuation. H, hematoma; C(R), right carotid; C(L), left carotid; IJ(R), right internal jugular; IJ(L), left internal jugular; ET, endotracheal tube.

literature. Since subcutaneous hemorrhage can cause incisional erythema mimicking cellulitis, the diagnosis may be overestimated if only clinical signs are used to characterize infection. In the NASCET trial wound infection was reported in 2.0%, with two thirds of cases classified as mild (no delay in discharge or return to the operating room).[11] It is unlikely that these "mild" wound infections were associated with purulence and thus the incidence was likely overestimated. Many large series do not even mention wound infection as an observed complication.

Systemic Complications

Systemic complications are more common than local complications following CEA. The most common systemic complication is hemodynamic instability. Either hypertension or hypotension can occur. Because of the high incidence of coronary artery disease in the population of patients with carotid occlusive disease, cardiac complications are always a concern.

Hemodynamic Instability

The hemodynamic instability associated with CEA is likely related to the carotid baroreceptor, although cerebral ischemia/reperfusion may play a role.[78-82] Dissection of the carotid bifurcation may lead to either transient or permanent dysfunction of the carotid sinus nerve. Absent or decreased carotid baroreceptor activity is thought to be a contributor to the hypertension seen following CEA. Conversely, the hypotension associated with CEA is thought to be related to hyperactivity of the carotid baroreceptor. The assumed mechanism is an increased sensitivity of the baroreceptor associated with chronic stenosis related to the build-up of carotid plaque leading to decreased compliance of the wall of the carotid bulb.[83] Theoretically the setpoint of the baroreceptor adjusts to the chronic decreased compliance. Immediately following CEA, there is a sudden restoration of compliance of the vessel wall leading to hyperactivity of the carotid baroreceptor. The hyperactive baroreceptor leads to bradycardia and hypotension. In almost all cases the hemodynamic instability is transient and rarely persists beyond 24 hours.

The use of local or regional rather than general anesthesia appears to be associated with a lower incidence of hemodynamic instability following CEA.[84-86] Some surgeons, irrespective of the method of anesthesia, routinely inject the vicinity of the carotid bifurcation with local anesthetic in an attempt to block the carotid sinus nerve. There is no good evidence to support this practice.[87-89] There does appear to be an increased incidence of hemodynamic instability in patients who have poorly controlled hypertension prior to the procedure. It seems prudent to delay an elective CEA in any patient with poorly controlled hypertension until medical management results in better control.

Myocardial Infarction

The reported incidence of MI accompanying CEA is dependent on the method of perioperative surveillance for myocardial ischemia and the definition of MI. If only symptomatic MI is included, the incidence is much lower than if silent infarction is documented with routine electrocardiogram (ECG) or enzyme surveillance. The incidence also depends on the patient population and the aggressiveness of preoperative screening and treatment of coronary artery disease. These variables make it difficult to compare reports in the literature unless prospective data collection with standardized screening protocols and similar patient populations is involved. The severity of the MI also has tremendous implications for the patient. The impact of a large transmural MI resulting in impaired ventricular function is obviously quite different from an event characterized by minimal troponin elevation with no symptoms. Irrespective of these differences in documentation, myocardial ischemic events are the most frequent non-neurologic complication associated with CEA.

In the NASCET trial there were 5 (0.4%) perioperative cardiac deaths.[90] There were 11 (0.8%) nonfatal MIs; in addition, a 1.6% arrhythmia, 1.0% congestive heart failure, and a 1.3% angina rate were observed. In the ACAS trial there was one (0.1%) cardiac death and three (0.4%) perioperative MIs reported.[12] Routine cardiac enzyme screening was not part of either trial, so it is likely that the reported incidence of MI would have been higher if all patients had perioperative cardiac enzyme screening. The NASCET and ACAS trials excluded patients with recent cardiac events or unstable cardiac disease. The higher rates of cardiac events in the NASCET trial compared to ACAS demonstrates that symptomatic patients are not only at higher risk for perioperative neurologic events than asymptomatic patients but also have a higher cardiac event rate.

Late Complications

Almost all of the procedural related morbidity from CEA occurs in the early postoperative period. CEA is a highly durable procedure with excellent long-term protection against ipsilateral stroke. Complications requiring intervention at the operative site are unusual. The most common late complication is recurrent stenosis. Although some degree of intimal thickening and possibly luminal narrowing occurs not infrequently, high-grade recurrent stenosis or symptomatic recurrence is rare. Aneurysmal dilation of the endarterectomized carotid is extremely rare, although vein patch dilation has been described. False aneurysms are also rare and usually associated with infection of a prosthetic patch.

Recurrent Stenosis

Recurrent stenosis following CEA is usually categorized into early and late recurrence. The typical angiographic appearance of a recurrent stenosis from intimal hyperplasia is seen in Figure 145-9. Early recurrence should be distinguished from residual stenosis, but this requires routine intraoperative completion imaging or at least an imaging study within the first postoperative month.[91,92] Residual stenosis may account for as much as one third of "recurrent" disease.[93,94] Technical defects observed at the time of the original procedure are associated with a higher incidence of recurrent stenosis even when the defects would not be characterized as a residual stenosis.[95,96] Intimal

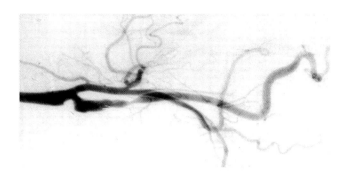

FIGURE 145-9 Intra-arterial digital subtraction arteriogram demonstrating the typical appearance of early recurrent stenosis from intimal hyperplasia following carotid endarterectomy. This patient had a recurrent stenosis at the distal endpoint despite patch angioplasty. (Courtesy of B. A. Ballinger, M.D.)

hyperplasia leading to some degree of recurrent stenosis can occur within 3 months and is usually apparent by 6 months, although it may continue to progress.[97] Early recurrence histologically is due to smooth muscle and fibroblast proliferation with deposition of a collagen-rich extracellular matrix.[98] Early recurrent stenosis due to intimal hyperplasia may regress and rarely progresses to occlusion in the first 2 years.[99-101] The smooth, firm surface is readily distinguishable from typical carotid atherosclerosis, and the less frequent association with symptoms is likely due to the lower embolic potential.[102] Recurrence that first becomes apparent after 2 years is considered late recurrence. Late recurrence is usually more consistent with typical atherosclerosis and appears to have a higher stroke risk than early recurrence.[103,104] The distinction between early and late recurrence is somewhat artificial in that intimal hyperplasia can be a precursor to the more typical complex atherosclerotic plaque.

The reported incidence of recurrent stenosis is dependent on the definition of recurrence. Some degree of thickening of the endarterectomized wall occurs in almost all cases and must be considered part of the normal vascular wall response. Meta-analysis of reports on recurrent stenosis suggests that the cumulative incidence of residual/recurrent stenosis is 10% at 2 years and 17% at 10 years.[103] The rate of development of recurrent stenosis is highest in the first year after surgery and then decreases dramatically.[103] In the ACAS trial, the residual/recurrent stenosis rate ($\geq$60%) was observed in 12% of patients at 5 years of follow-up using duplex criteria with a positive predictive value of 0.95.[94]

Numerous reports have suggested that recurrent stenosis is more common in women.[93,100,104-106] This has been attributed to many factors including gender differences in the hormonal environment but may be explained by the fact that women have generally smaller vessels than men. Patching has been shown to decrease the likelihood of a significant recurrence.[94,103] In the ACAS report, patching was associated with a decrease in recurrent stenosis incidence by 70% to 80%.[94] Even those who do not recommend universal patching suggest that all women should have patch angioplasty as an endarterectomy closure because of the increased likelihood of recurrence in women. Other factors that have been associated with an increased

risk of recurrent disease include smoking, hyperlipidemia, and hypertension.[95,107,108] There is no clear evidence that the use of antiplatelet therapy reduces the likelihood of recurrent stenosis following CEA.[108,109]

Significant early recurrent stenosis following CEA may occur in up to 10% of patients by 2 years, but elimination of residual stenoses and routine patching would appear to decrease this expected incidence to less than 2%. Atherosclerotic risk factor management may reduce the likelihood of recurrent disease. Early recurrent stenosis can likely be observed initially because of the possibility of regression and the low stroke risk. Recurrent lesions that progress to high-grade stenoses should be treated as one would treat similar primary lesions, that is, intervention for symptomatic patients and good-risk asymptomatic patients. Endovascular stenting may be a reasonable or even preferred option in the treatment of recurrent lesions because of the increased risk of cranial nerve injury with redo procedures and the apparently lower embolic risk of intimal hyperplastic lesions.[110] Open surgical repair of a recurrent carotid stenosis should at a minimum include patch angioplasty. Interposition grafting should be considered in secondary recurrent procedures or for extensive first-time recurrences.

False Aneurysms

The common practice of using monofilament suture for arteriotomy closure reduces the likelihood of a suture line infection as a complication of wound infection and the incidence of false aneurysm formation. The late occurrence of a true or false aneurysm of an endarterectomy site in the absence of infection or use of silk sutures is extremely rare.[111,112] Because of the previously mentioned potential complication of vein patch disruption and the lack of evidence suggesting that vein is superior to prosthetic patch closure, prosthetic patches are being increasingly used during CEA. The use of prosthetic material obviously increases the risk of a serious complication if infection does occur. Infection involving the prosthetic material can lead to a false aneurysm or frank disruption.[113-116] Infection can also cause false aneurysm formation in association with a vein patch.[111] Fortunately, the risk of patch infection remains very low and the benefits of patching outweigh the risk. The use of a prosthetic patch during CEA certainly means that systemic antibiotic prophylaxis is appropriate because of the serious nature of an infectious complication. If an infected false aneurysm is encountered following CEA, the optimal management is removal of any prosthetic material, débridement of infected tissue, and autologous reconstruction.[113-115,117] Ligation of the carotid should be avoided if at all possible because of the high likelihood of neurologic morbidity.

■ PERIOPERATIVE MANAGEMENT

Surgical technique is extremely important in minimizing complications associated with CEA. However, the value of adjunctive medical therapy in achieving benchmark outcomes should not be minimized. Technical perfection does not ensure a complication-free outcome. Antithrombotic therapy, optimal medical management of coronary artery disease, and appropriate perioperative hemodynamic monitoring and management all are essential processes to consider in CEA performance improvement.

Antithrombotic Therapy

The cornerstone of antithrombotic therapy for CEA is antiplatelet therapy. Perioperative and long-term postoperative antiplatelet therapy are both important. Anticoagulation (e.g., heparin) during the procedure is useful in preventing intraoperative thromboembolic complications.

Antiplatelet Therapy

There is an extensive evidence base supporting the role of antiplatelet therapy in preventing thromboembolic events in cerebrovascular disease.[118,119] It is important to recognize that antiplatelet therapy should be used perioperatively, that is, adequate antiplatelet activity should be ensured during the procedure. Preoperative antiplatelet agent use (within 1 day prior to operation) was associated with a 27% risk reduction for perioperative stroke or death in the multistate CEA experience.[41] Preoperative and postoperative administration of aspirin was part of the protocol for the surgical arm in the major randomized trials.[1-7] The benefit from antiplatelet therapy in terms of reducing the risk of perioperative thromboembolic events outweighs any increased risk of bleeding complications. Surgeons should specifically address the issue of preoperative aspirin use for CEA with patients, primary care physicians, nursing professionals, and anesthesiologists. It is not uncommon for patients to be instructed to hold all antiplatelet therapy prior to non-vascular procedures. This recommendation may inadvertently be extended to CEA by other health care professionals involved in preparing a patient for the procedure, unless it is specifically addressed preferably as part of a written protocol.

Aspirin therapy has been the most widely studied agent. Other agents such as ticlopidine and clopidogrel have not been specifically evaluated for risk/benefit in the CEA setting. It is certainly the impression of most surgeons that clopidogrel use perioperatively carries a higher bleeding risk than aspirin. Given the extensive experience with aspirin and the lack of compelling evidence to suggest superiority of the other agents in the perioperative setting, it may be appropriate to switch patients taking other agents to aspirin therapy alone preoperatively. However, an urgent CEA in a symptomatic patient should probably not be delayed solely because of recent use of alternative antiplatelet agents. Some surgeons have used intravenous low-molecular-weight dextrose (dextran) in the perioperative period as antithrombotic therapy.[120] There is no clear evidence to support or refute this practice, but its use should probably be an addition to aspirin therapy rather than a substitute for it.

The optimum dosage of aspirin in the perioperative period has been a subject of debate. There is a theoretical basis that lower dose aspirin may inhibit thromboxane production but not prostacyclin production. On the other hand, a retrospective analysis of the NASCET trial data for the surgical group suggested that the patients on 650 mg/day or more had fewer combined events than those on 325 mg

or less.[4] A prospective, randomized trial of various perioperative aspirin dosage regimens for CEA contradicted the retrospective observation and found that combined events were lower in patients receiving 81 to 325 mg of aspirin daily than those receiving 650 to 1300 mg.[121] Based on the available evidence, an aspirin dose in the 80- to 325-mg/day range seems to be appropriate for CEA patients. Antiplatelet therapy should be continued following the operation. In addition to the possible benefit in preventing further neurologic events, the close association of carotid occlusive disease and coronary artery disease certainly would justify the use of lifetime antiplatelet use in the CEA patient population.

Anticoagulation

The use of intraoperative heparin anticoagulation is almost universal, although there is no randomized, prospective trial comparing CEA with and without the use of systemic heparin. In our multistate CEA analysis, systemic heparin was used in more than 98% of cases.[41] There was evidence of a benefit of the use of heparin with a 50% risk reduction in stroke or mortality compared to the no-heparin group. Although the use of heparin should be considered standard therapy, there is no consensus on the dosage regimen or the practice of protamine reversal.[122-126] Regimens vary from fixed doses (e.g., 3000 to 5000 units) to dosage based on body weight (e.g., 100 to 150 units/kg). Surgeons employing the lower fixed doses of heparin are more likely to avoid heparin reversal. Some retrospective studies have suggested that heparin reversal increased the likelihood of thromboembolic events, but this has not been unequivocally confirmed in prospective trials, although the small size of the trials does not preclude a type II statistical error.[125-127] On the other hand, there is no clear evidence that avoiding heparin reversal leads to an increase in major bleeding complications.[125,126] Given the current evidence, it is hard to make a firm recommendation about a specific anticoagulation dose/reversal regimen.

It is my practice to use a fixed dose of heparin (5000 units). Adequate anticoagulation is confirmed with an intraoperative activated clotting time (ACT) because of the possible variable response to heparin. Supplemental heparin is given to ensure an ACT of greater than 200 seconds or twice control. Since protamine reversal has the potential for increased thromboembolic risk and other adverse consequences including allergy and hypotension, reversal of heparin is not employed.

There is no evidence supporting the use of heparin beyond the operative period or of long-term anticoagulation with warfarin. The increased bleeding risks associated with postoperative anticoagulation and the lack of proven benefit suggest that it should be avoided unless other indications for anticoagulation (hypercoaguable state, mechanical heart valve, chronic atrial fibrillation) are present.

Cardiac Assessment and Therapy

Coronary artery disease is common in patients with carotid occlusive disease. The extent of preoperative cardiac evaluation should depend on the indication for the CEA and the patient's cardiac symptom status. There is no evidence that a program of *routine* coronary artery imaging or stress testing accompanied by coronary artery intervention prior to CEA is justified.[128] Patients who present with TIA or stroke and high-grade carotid stenosis should not have CEA delayed solely for purposes of a cardiac evaluation in the absence of concomitant cardiac symptoms. Defining the role of stress testing in a patient with asymptomatic carotid occlusive disease is more difficult. The therapeutic benefit of CEA in the asymptomatic patient is dependent not only on the procedure being performed at a low level of patient risk but also on a reasonable life expectancy for the patient. Identification of physiologically significant coronary artery disease, even in the absence of symptoms, could alter the decision to recommend CEA or endovascular carotid treatment. Decision making has to be individualized, including any decision to proceed with coronary angiography and/or intervention if significant coronary artery disease is suggested on a stress evaluation. Endovascular or surgical intervention for coronary artery disease would be inappropriate solely (i.e., in the absence of other indications) to "allow" a patient to have an intervention for an asymptomatic carotid stenosis.

A preoperative resting ECG should certainly be considered the minimum cardiac work-up prior to CEA. The preoperative ECG provides a baseline for intraoperative and perioperative monitoring. Although, as discussed earlier, routine stress evaluation prior to CEA is hard to justify, routine perioperative assessment for coronary ischemic events may be appropriate. The CEA itself serves as a cardiac "stress" evaluation. Monitoring with ECG and/or myocardial enzyme testing may identify asymptomatic cardiac events. In the current environment of early discharge, the occurrence of a cardiac event may identify the patient in need of further monitoring. The occurrence of a cardiac event may also have implications for the future treatment of the patient. Those patients who experience perioperative cardiac events may benefit from a more extensive cardiac evaluation, medical therapy, or, in some cases, endovascular/surgical intervention for their coronary artery disease to extend life expectancy and thus the benefit of their carotid procedure.

Even in the absence of documented coronary artery disease preoperatively, routine perioperative beta-blocker therapy may be appropriate in all CEA patients. Beta blockade perioperatively has been shown to reduce the incidence of coronary artery events following both cardiac and noncardiac surgical procedures in patients with established coronary artery disease.[129] Since the incidence of coronary artery disease in patients with carotid occlusive disease is high, it may be appropriate to routinely use perioperative beta blockade in all CEA patients. The low risk and cost of perioperative beta blockade would not justify the use of cardiac stress testing or imaging solely to identify patients for whom beta blockade is indicated. A typical perioperative beta-blocker regimen (e.g., metoprolol 50 mg twice daily) is generally started preoperatively and continued for 30 days postoperatively

Hemodynamic Monitoring and Management

Given the hemodynamic instability associated with CEA, direct, continuous arterial pressure monitoring is usually employed during the procedure. Continuous monitoring of the arterial pressure allows for rapid response to any aberrations. Patients may develop focal cerebral ischemia associated with carotid clamping that may be reversed by an intervention to raise blood pressure and improve collateral flow. Systemic blood pressure elevation is the normal physiologic response to cerebral ischemia associated with carotid clamping. For this reason, hypertension during the period of carotid clamping is not treated unless it reaches dangerous levels or is associated with myocardial stress. After restoration of flow, intervention for continued hypertension is indicated. Hypertension during the immediate post-CEA period may increase the risk of local bleeding complications. In addition, as discussed previously, the disturbed cerebral autoregulation that may be associated with carotid stenosis may increase the risk of cerebral edema or hemorrhage from hypertension. Hypertensive therapy should generally employ rapid-acting, short half-life intravenous agents to allow optimum titration to normal blood pressure levels and avoid wide swings in blood pressure.

Hypotension following CEA is attributed to overactivity of the carotid baroreceptor and is usually accompanied by bradycardia. Since large blood loss is unusual during CEA, repeated fluid bolus administration, in the absence of documented volume depletion, is usually not the ideal response to perioperative hypotension. Excess fluid administration could potentially lead to later problems with fluid overload. Since the hypotension is likely due to an autonomic nervous system response, drug therapy is appropriate. Atropine is certainly a reasonable response to hypotension accompanied by marked bradycardia. An intravenous agent with alpha-adrenergic activity (e.g., phenylephrine) used as a continuous infusion to treat hypotension is a good choice so that the agent can be titrated to the patient's changing requirements. It is unclear that mild to moderate hypotension in an alert, neurologically intact patient, without evidence of cardiac ischemia, needs to be treated.

Hospital Resource Management

At one time, it was routine for patients to be admitted to the intensive care following CEA because of the possibility of hemodynamic instability and increased risk of cardiac complications. In more recent times, hospital resource pressures caused many to challenge this practice. It has been demonstrated by many groups over the last 20 years that most CEA patients can be managed without admission to the intensive care unit.[130-133] It is unusual for a patient who was initially stable to develop delayed hemodynamic instability following CEA. This allows patients to be triaged in the postanesthesia care unit based on their initial postoperative course. Those patients with hemodynamic changes requiring intervention may need care in a unit that has the capability of continuous blood pressure monitoring and use of vasoactive infusions.

Hospital stays of 3 to 7 days for "monitoring" following CEA was also not an uncommon practice 20 years ago. The need for hospitalization periods of this length has also been challenged. Although delayed complications (myocardial ischemia, stroke) can occur, there is no evidence that prolonged hospitalization of all patients will prevent these late complications. It has been clearly demonstrated that most patients can be discharged on the day following operation.[134-136] Some have even advocated same-day surgery for selected patients.[137] However, it would seem that a period of observation of 12 to 24 hours following CEA is appropriate to allow rapid intervention for progressive wound hematoma or endarterectomy site thrombosis. The possibility of hyperperfusion syndrome does suggest caution in discharging patients who have poorly controlled hypertension or who develop unilateral headache following the procedure. Any program of early discharge following CEA should obviously include comprehensive patient education regarding potentially worrisome symptoms that would warrant immediate medical attention.

Risk Factor Modification

Although it is not always considered to be in the purview of the surgeon, the opportunity to influence the patient's risk profile for progressive atherosclerosis and recurrent disease should not be overlooked.[138] Standard atherosclerotic risk factors (smoking, hypertension, and hyperlipidemia) should at a minimum be discussed with the patient. Patients should be educated about the association of carotid occlusive disease with coronary disease and the common risk factors for future cardiac events. The need for an operative intervention may be the event that finally gets the patient to stop smoking. Understanding the importance of control of hypertension and hyperlipidemia in preventing recurrent or new atherosclerotic disease may encourage a patient to be more compliant with therapy. Carotid occlusive disease may be the initial presenting sign of atherosclerosis, and it should not be assumed that the patient has had appropriate lipid testing and treatment. Patients and their primary care physician should be encouraged to identify and treat hyperlipidemia consistent with the goals for secondary prevention, that is, target low-density lipoprotein cholesterol levels of less than 100 mg/dL.

■ REFERENCES

1. Beneficial effect of carotid endarterectomy in symptomatic patients with high-grade carotid stenosis. North American Symptomatic Carotid Endarterectomy Trial Collaborators. N Engl J Med 325:445-453, 1991.
2. MRC European Carotid Surgery Trial: Interim results for symptomatic patients with severe (70-99%) or with mild (0-29%) carotid stenosis. European Carotid Surgery Trialists' Collaborative Group. Lancet 337:1235-1243, 1991.
3. Mayberg MR, Wilson SE, Yatsu F, et al: Carotid endarterectomy and prevention of cerebral ischemia in symptomatic carotid stenosis. Veterans Affairs Cooperative Studies Program 309 Trialist Group. JAMA 266:3289-3294, 1991.
4. Barnett HJ, Taylor DW, Eliasziw M, et al: Benefit of carotid endarterectomy in patients with symptomatic moderate or severe stenosis. North American Symptomatic Carotid Endarterectomy Trial Collaborators. N Engl J Med 339:1415-1425, 1998.
5. Randomised trial of endarterectomy for recently symptomatic carotid stenosis: Final results of the MRC European Carotid Surgery Trial (ECST). Lancet 351:1379-1387, 1998.
6. Endarterectomy for asymptomatic carotid artery stenosis. Executive Committee for the Asymptomatic Carotid Atherosclerosis Study. JAMA 273:1421-1428, 1995.
7. Hobson RW II, Weiss DG, Fields WS, et al: Efficacy of carotid endarterectomy for asymptomatic carotid stenosis. The Veterans Affairs Cooperative Study Group. N Engl J Med 328:221-227, 1993.
8. Riles TS, Imparato AM, Jacobowitz GR, et al: The cause of perioperative stroke after carotid endarterectomy. J Vasc Surg 19:206-216, 1994.
9. Hamdan AD, Pomposelli FB Jr, Gibbons GW, et al: Perioperative strokes after 1001 consecutive carotid endarterectomy procedures without an electroencephalogram: Incidence, mechanism, and recovery. Arch Surg 134:412-415, 1999.
10. De Borst GJ, Moll FL, Van de Pavoordt HD, et al: Stroke from carotid endarterectomy: When and how to reduce perioperative stroke rate? Eur J Vasc Endovasc Surg 21:484-489, 2001.
11. Ferguson GG, Eliasziw M, Barr HW, et al: The North American Symptomatic Carotid Endarterectomy Trial: Surgical results in 1415 patients. Stroke 30:1751-1758, 1999.
12. Young B, Moore WS, Robertson JT, et al: An analysis of perioperative surgical mortality and morbidity in the asymptomatic carotid atherosclerosis study. ACAS Investigators. Asymptomatic Carotid Artheriosclerosis Study. Stroke 27:2216-2224, 1996.
13. Towne JB, Weiss DG, Hobson RW II: First-phase report of cooperative Veterans Administration asymptomatic carotid stenosis study: Operative morbidity and mortality. J Vasc Surg 11:252-259, 1990.
14. Novick WM, Millili JJ, Nemir P Jr: Management of acute postoperative thrombosis following carotid endarterectomy. Arch Surg 120:922-925, 1985.
15. Painter TA, Hertzer NR, O'Hara PJ, et al: Symptomatic internal carotid thrombosis after carotid endarterectomy. J Vasc Surg 5:445-451, 1987.
16. Chalela JA, Katzan I, Liebeskind DS, et al: Safety of intra-arterial thrombolysis in the postoperative period. Stroke 32:1365-1369, 2001.
17. Barr JD, Horowitz MB, Mathis JM, et al: Intraoperative urokinase infusion for embolic stroke during carotid endarterectomy. Neurosurgery 36:606-611, 1995.
18. Bernstein M, Fleming JF, Deck JH: Cerebral hyperperfusion after carotid endarterectomy: A cause of cerebral hemorrhage. Neurosurgery 15:50-56, 1984.
19. Youkey JR, Clagett GP, Jaffin JH, et al: Focal motor seizures complicating carotid endarterectomy. Arch Surg 119:1080-1084, 1984.
20. Solomon RA, Loftus CM, Quest DO, Correll JW: Incidence and etiology of intracerebral hemorrhage following carotid endarterectomy. J Neurosurg 64:29-34, 1986.
21. Reigel MM, Hollier LH, Sundt TM Jr, et al: Cerebral hyperperfusion syndrome: A cause of neurologic dysfunction after carotid endarterectomy. J Vasc Surg 5:628-634, 1987.
22. Schroeder T, Sillesen H, Boesen J, et al: Intracerebral haemorrhage after carotid endarterectomy. Eur J Vasc Surg 1:51-60, 1987.
23. Piepgras DG, Morgan MK, Sundt TM Jr, et al: Intracerebral hemorrhage after carotid endarterectomy. J Neurosurg 68:532-536, 1988.
24. Pomposelli FB, Lamparello PJ, Riles TS, et al: Intracranial hemorrhage after carotid endarterectomy. J Vasc Surg 7:248-255, 1988.
25. Kieburtz K, Ricotta JJ, Moxley RT III: Seizures following carotid endarterectomy. Arch Neurol 47:568-570, 1990.
26. Ouriel K, Shortell CK, Illig KA, et al: Intracerebral hemorrhage after carotid endarterectomy: Incidence, contribution to neurologic morbidity, and predictive factors. J Vasc Surg 29:82-89, 1999.
27. Henderson RD, Phan TG, Piepgras DG, Wijdicks EF: Mechanisms of intracerebral hemorrhage after carotid endarterectomy. J Neurosurg 95:964-969, 2001.
28. Hosoda K, Kawaguchi T, Shibata Y, et al: Cerebral vasoreactivity and internal carotid artery flow help to identify patients at risk for hyperperfusion after carotid endarterectomy. Stroke 32:1567-1573, 2001.
29. Schaafsma A, Veen L, Vos JP: Three cases of hyperperfusion syndrome identified by daily transcranial Doppler investigation after carotid surgery. Eur J Vasc Endovasc Surg 23:17-22, 2002.

30. Ascher E, Markevich N, Schutzer RW, et al: Cerebral hyperperfusion syndrome after carotid endarterectomy: Predictive factors and hemodynamic changes. J Vasc Surg 37:769-777, 2003.

31. Coutts SB, Hill MD, Hu WY: Hyperperfusion syndrome: Toward a stricter definition. Neurosurgery 53:1053-1060, 2003.

32. Ogasawara K, Yukawa H, Kobayashi M, et al: Prediction and monitoring of cerebral hyperperfusion after carotid endarterectomy by using single-photon emission computerized tomography scanning. J Neurosurg 99:504-510, 2003.

33. Breen JC, Caplan LR, DeWitt LD, et al: Brain edema after carotid surgery. Neurology 46:175-181, 1996.

34. Hosoda K, Kawaguchi T, Ishii K, et al: Prediction of hyperperfusion after carotid endarterectomy by brain SPECT analysis with semiquantitative statistical mapping method. Stroke 34:1187-1193, 2003.

35. Naylor AR, Evans J, Thompson MM, et al: Seizures after carotid endarterectomy: Hyperperfusion, dysautoregulation or hypertensive encephalopathy? Eur J Vasc Endovasc Surg 26:39-44, 2003.

36. Bratzler DW, Oehlert WH, Murray CK, et al: Carotid endarterectomy in Oklahoma Medicare beneficiaries: Patient characteristics and outcomes. Journal—Oklahoma State Medical Association. 89:423-429, 1996.

37. Karp HR, Flanders WD, Shipp CC, et al: Carotid endarterectomy among Medicare beneficiaries: A statewide evaluation of appropriateness and outcome. Stroke 29:46-52, 1998.

38. Cebul RD, Snow RJ, Pine R, et al: Indications, outcomes, and provider volumes for carotid endarterectomy. JAMA 279:1282-1287, 1998.

39. Kucey DS, Bowyer B, Iron K, et al: Determinants of outcome after carotid endarterectomy. J Vasc Surg 28:1051-1058, 1998.

40. Kresowik TF, Hemann RA, Grund SL, et al: Improving the outcomes of carotid endarterectomy: Results of a statewide quality improvement project. J Vasc Surg 31:918-926, 2000.

41. Kresowik TF, Bratzler D, Karp HR, et al: Multistate utilization, processes, and outcomes of carotid endarterectomy. J Vasc Surg 33:227-235, 2001.

42. Kresowik TF, Bratzler DW, Kresowik RA, et al: Multistate improvement in process and outcomes of carotid endarterectomy. J Vasc Surg 39:372-380, 2004.

43. Bond R, Rerkasem K, Rothwell PM: Systematic review of the risks of carotid endarterectomy in relation to the clinical indication for and timing of surgery. Stroke 34:2290-2301, 2003.

44. Brown KR, Kresowik TF, Chin MH, et al: Multistate population-based outcomes of combined carotid endarterectomy and coronary artery bypass. J Vasc Surg 37:32-39, 2003.

45. Coyle KA, Smith RB III, Gray BC, et al: Treatment of recurrent cerebrovascular disease: Review of a 10-year experience. Ann Surg 221:517-524, 1995.

46. Mansour MA, Kang SS, Baker WH, et al: Carotid endarterectomy for recurrent stenosis. J Vasc Surg 25:877-883, 1997.

47. Hill BB, Olcott CT, Dalman RL, et al: Reoperation for carotid stenosis is as safe as primary carotid endarterectomy. J Vasc Surg 30:26-35, 1999.

48. AbuRahma AF, Jennings TG, Wulu JT, et al: Redo carotid endarterectomy versus primary carotid endarterectomy. Stroke 32:2787-2792, 2001.

49. Hertzer NR, Feldman BJ, Beven EG, Tucker HM: A prospective study of the incidence of injury to the cranial nerves during carotid endarterectomy. Surg Gynecol Obstet 151:781-784, 1980.

50. Liapis CD, Satiani B, Florance CL, Evans WE: Motor speech malfunction following carotid endarterectomy. Surgery 89:56-59, 1981.

51. Evans WE, Mendelowitz DS, Liapis C, et al: Motor speech deficit following carotid endarterectomy. Ann Surg 196:461-464, 1982.

52. Dehn TC, Taylor GW: Cranial and cervical nerve damage associated with carotid endarterectomy. Br J Surg 70:365-368, 1983.

53. Massey EW, Heyman A, Utley C, et al: Cranial nerve paralysis following carotid endarterectomy. Stroke 15:157-159, 1984.

54. Forssell C, Takolander R, Bergqvist D, et al: Cranial nerve injuries associated with carotid endarterectomy: A prospective study. Acta Chir Scand 151:595-598, 1985.

55. Krupski WC, Effeney DJ, Goldstone J, et al: Carotid endarterectomy in a metropolitan community: Comparison of results from three institutions. Surgery 98:492-499, 1985.

56. Downs AR, Jessen M, Lye CR: Peripheral nerve injuries during carotid endarterectomy. Can J Surg 30:22-24, 1987.

57. Knight FW, Yeager RM, Morris DM: Cranial nerve injuries during carotid endarterectomy. Am J Surg 154:529-532, 1987.

58. Aldoori MI, Baird RN: Local neurological complication during carotid endarterectomy. J Cardiovasc Surg (Torino) 29:432-436, 1988.

59. Maniglia AJ, Han DP: Cranial nerve injuries following carotid endarterectomy: An analysis of 336 procedures. Head Neck 13:121-124, 1991.

60. Schauber MD, Fontenelle LJ, Solomon JW, Hanson TL: Cranial/cervical nerve dysfunction after carotid endarterectomy. J Vasc Surg 25:481-487, 1997.

61. Zannetti S, Parente B, De Rango P, et al: Role of surgical techniques and operative findings in cranial and cervical nerve injuries during carotid endarterectomy. Eur J Vasc Endovasc Surg 15:528-531, 1998.

62. Ballotta E, Da Giau G, Renon L, et al: Cranial and cervical nerve injuries after carotid endarterectomy: A prospective study. Surgery 125:85-91, 1999.

63. Maroulis J, Karkanevatos A, Papakostas K, et al: Cranial nerve dysfunction following carotid endarterectomy. Int Angiol 19:237-241, 2000.

64. Rosenbloom M, Friedman SG, Lamparello PJ, et al: Glossopharyngeal nerve injury complicating carotid endarterectomy. J Vasc Surg 5:469-471, 1987.

65. Tucker JA, Gee W, Nicholas GG, et al: Accessory nerve injury during carotid endarterectomy. J Vasc Surg 5:440-444, 1987.

66. Kunkel JM, Gomez ER, Spebar MJ, et al: Wound hematomas after carotid endarterectomy. Am J Surg 148:844-847, 1984.

67. Welling RE, Ramadas HS, Gansmuller KJ: Cervical wound hematoma after carotid endarterectomy. Ann Vasc Surg 3:229-231, 1989.

68. Treiman RL, Cossman DV, Foran RF, et al: The influence of neutralizing heparin after carotid endarterectomy on postoperative stroke and wound hematoma. J Vasc Surg 12:440-446, 1990.

69. Dorman BH, Elliott BM, Spinale FG, et al: Protamine use during peripheral vascular surgery: A prospective randomized trial. J Vasc Surg 22:248-256, 1995.

70. Fearn SJ, Parry AD, Picton AJ, et al: Should heparin be reversed after carotid endarterectomy? A randomised prospective trial. Eur J Vasc Endovasc Surg 13:394-397, 1997.

71. Mauney MC, Buchanan SA, Lawrence WA, et al: Stroke rate is markedly reduced after carotid endarterectomy by avoidance of protamine. J Vasc Surg 22:264-270, 1995.

72. Munro FJ, Makin AP, Reid J: Airway problems after carotid endarterectomy. Br J Anaesth 76:156-159, 1996.

73. Beard JD, Mountney J, Wilkinson JM, et al: Prevention of postoperative wound haematomas and hyperperfusion following carotid endarterectomy. Eur J Vasc Endovasc Surg 21:490-493, 2001.

74. Riles TS, Lamparello PJ, Giangola G, Imparato AM: Rupture of the vein patch: A rare complication of carotid endarterectomy. Surgery 107:10-12, 1990.

75. Tawes RL Jr, Treiman RL: Vein patch rupture after carotid endarterectomy: A survey of the Western Vascular Society members. Ann Vasc Surg 5:71-73, 1991.

76. O'Hara PJ, Hertzer NR, Krajewski LP, Beven EG: Saphenous vein patch rupture after carotid endarterectomy. J Vasc Surg 15:504-509, 1992.

77. Yamamoto Y, Piepgras DG, Marsh WR, Meyer FB: Complications resulting from saphenous vein patch graft after carotid endarterectomy. Neurosurgery 39:670-676, 1996.

78. Bove EL, Fry WJ, Gross WS, Stanley JC: Hypotension and hypertension as consequences of baroreceptor dysfunction following carotid endarterectomy. Surgery 85:633-637, 1979.

79. Ahn SS, Marcus DR, Moore WS: Post-carotid endarterectomy hypertension: Association with elevated cranial norepinephrine. J Vasc Surg 9:351-360, 1989.

80. Cafferata HT, Merchant RF Jr, DePalma RG: Avoidance of post-carotid endarterectomy hypertension. Ann Surg 196:465-472, 1982.

81. Englund R, Dean RH: Blood pressure aberrations associated with carotid endarterectomy. Ann Vasc Surg 1:304-309, 1986.

82. Skydell JL, Machleder HI, Baker JD, et al: Incidence and mechanism of post-carotid endarterectomy hypertension. Arch Surg 122:1153-1155, 1987.

83. Akinola A, Mathias CJ, Mansfield A, et al: Cardiovascular, autonomic, and plasma catecholamine responses in unilateral and bilateral carotid artery stenosis. J Neurol Neurosurg Psychiatry 67:428-432, 1999.

84. Corson JD, Chang BB, Leopold PW, et al: Perioperative hypertension in patients undergoing carotid endarterectomy: Shorter duration under regional block anesthesia. Circulation 74:I1-I4, 1986.

85. Hartsell PA, Calligaro KD, Syrek JR, et al: Postoperative blood pressure changes associated with cervical block versus general anesthesia following carotid endarterectomy. Ann Vasc Surg 13:104-108, 1999.

86. Sternbach Y, Illig KA, Zhang R, et al: Hemodynamic benefits of regional anesthesia for carotid endarterectomy. J Vasc Surg 35:333-339, 2002.

87. Maher CO, Wetjen NM, Friedman JA, Meyer FB: Intraoperative lidocaine injection into the carotid sinus during endarterectomy. J Neurosurg 97:80-83, 2002.

88. Elliott BM, Collins GJ Jr, Youkey JR, et al: Intraoperative local anesthetic injection of the carotid sinus nerve: A prospective, randomized study. Am J Surg 152:695-699, 1986.

89. Fearn SJ, Mortimer AJ, Faragher EB, McCollum CN: Carotid sinus nerve blockade during carotid surgery: A randomised controlled trial. Eur J Vasc Endovasc Surg 24:480-484, 2002.

90. Paciaroni M, Eliasziw M, Kappelle LJ, et al: Medical complications associated with carotid endarterectomy. North American Symptomatic Carotid Endarterectomy Trial (NASCET). Stroke 30:1759-1763, 1999.

91. Kinney EV, Seabrook GR, Kinney LY, et al: The importance of intraoperative detection of residual flow abnormalities after carotid artery endarterectomy. J Vasc Surg 17:912-923, 1993.

92. Lipski DA, Bergamini TM, Garrison RN, Fulton RL: Intraoperative duplex scanning reduces the incidence of residual stenosis after carotid endarterectomy. J Surg Res 60:317-320, 1996.

93. Ricotta JJ, O'Brien-Irr MS: Conservative management of residual and recurrent lesions after carotid endarterectomy: Long-term results. J Vasc Surg 26:963-972, 1997.

94. Moore WS, Kempczinski RF, Nelson JJ, Toole JF: Recurrent carotid stenosis: Results of the asymptomatic carotid atherosclerosis study. Stroke 29:2018-2025, 1998.

95. Reilly LM, Okuhn SP, Rapp JH, et al: Recurrent carotid stenosis: A consequence of local or systemic factors? The influence of unrepaired technical defects. J Vasc Surg 11:448-460, 1990.

96. Bandyk DF, Kaebnick HW, Adams MB, Towne JB: Turbulence occurring after carotid bifurcation endarterectomy: A harbinger of residual and recurrent carotid stenosis. J Vasc Surg 7:261-274, 1988.

97. Thomas M, Otis SM, Rush M, et al: Recurrent carotid artery stenosis following endarterectomy. Ann Surg 200:74-79, 1984.

98. Clagett GP, Robinowitz M, Youkey JR, et al: Morphogenesis and clinicopathologic characteristics of recurrent carotid disease. J Vasc Surg 3:10-23, 1986.

99. Carballo RE, Towne JB, Seabrook GR, et al: An outcome analysis of carotid endarterectomy: The incidence and natural history of recurrent stenosis. J Vasc Surg 23:749-754, 1996.

100. Healy DA, Zierler RE, Nicholls SC, et al: Long-term follow-up and clinical outcome of carotid restenosis. J Vasc Surg 10:662-669, 1989.

101. Samson RH, Showalter DP, Yunis JP, et al: Hemodynamically significant early recurrent carotid stenosis: An often self-limiting and self-reversing condition. J Vasc Surg 30:446-452, 1999.

102. O'Donnell TF Jr, Callow AD, Scott G, et al: Ultrasound characteristics of recurrent carotid disease: Hypothesis explaining the low incidence of symptomatic recurrence. J Vasc Surg 2:26-41, 1985.

103. Frericks H, Kievit J, van Baalen JM, van Bockel JH: Carotid recurrent stenosis and risk of ipsilateral stroke: A systematic review of the literature. Stroke 29:244-250, 1998.

104. Das MB, Hertzer NR, Ratliff NB, et al: Recurrent carotid stenosis: A five-year series of 65 reoperations. Ann Surg 202:28-35, 1985.

105. Ouriel K, Green RM: Clinical and technical factors influencing recurrent carotid stenosis and occlusion after endarterectomy. J Vasc Surg 5:702-706, 1987.

106. Bernstein EF, Torem S, Dilley RB: Does carotid restenosis predict an increased risk of late symptoms, stroke, or death? Ann Surg 212:629-636, 1990.

107. Hertzer NR, Martinez BD, Benjamin SP, Beven EG: Recurrent stenosis after carotid endarterectomy. Surg Gynecol Obstet 149:360-364, 1979.

108. Clagett GP, Rich NM, McDonald PT, et al: Etiologic factors for recurrent carotid artery stenosis. Surgery 93:313-318, 1983.

109. Lindblad B, Persson NH, Takolander R, Bergqvist D: Does low-dose acetylsalicylic acid prevent stroke after carotid surgery? A double-blind, placebo-controlled randomized trial. Stroke 24:1125-1128, 1993.

110. Hobson RW II, Goldstein JE, Jamil Z, et al: Carotid restenosis: Operative and endovascular management. J Vasc Surg 29:228-238, 1999.

111. Bergamini TM, Seabrook GR, Bandyk DF, Towne JB: Symptomatic recurrent carotid stenosis and aneurysmal degeneration after endarterectomy. Surgery 113:580-586, 1993.

112. Branch CL Jr, Davis CH Jr: False aneurysm complicating carotid endarterectomy. Neurosurgery 19:421-425, 1986.

113. Raptis S, Baker SR: Infected false aneurysms of the carotid arteries after carotid endarterectomy. Eur J Vasc Endovasc Surg 11:148-152, 1996.

114. Naylor AR, Payne D, London NJ, et al: Prosthetic patch infection after carotid endarterectomy. Eur J Vasc Endovasc Surg 23:11-16, 2002.

115. Rockman CB, Su WT, Domenig C, et al: Postoperative infection associated with polyester patch angioplasty after carotid endarterectomy. J Vasc Surg 38:251-256, 2003.

116. Borazjani BH, Wilson SE, Fujitani RM, et al: Postoperative complications of carotid patching: Pseudoaneurysm and infection. Ann Vasc Surg 17:156-161, 2003.

117. El-Sabrout R, Reul G, Cooley DA: Infected postcarotid endarterectomy pseudoaneurysms: Retrospective review of a series. Ann Vasc Surg 14:239-247, 2000.

118. Collaborative overview of randomised trials of antiplatelet therapy: I. Prevention of death, myocardial infarction, and stroke by prolonged antiplatelet therapy in various categories of patients. Antiplatelet Trialists' Collaboration. BMJ 308:81-106, 1994.

119. Lindblad B, Persson NH, Takolander R, Bergqvist D: Does low-dose acetylsalicylic acid prevent stroke after carotid surgery? A double-blind, placebo-controlled randomized trial. Stroke 24:1125-1128, 1993.

120. Naylor AR, Hayes PD, Allroggen H, et al: Reducing the risk of carotid surgery: A 7-year audit of the role of monitoring and quality control assessment. J Vasc Surg 32:750-759, 2000.

121. Taylor DW, Barnett HJ, Haynes RB, et al: Low-dose and high-dose acetylsalicylic acid for patients undergoing carotid endarterectomy: A randomised controlled trial. ASA and Carotid Endarterectomy (ACE) Trial Collaborators. Lancet 353:2179-2184, 1999.

122. Wakefield TW, Lindblad B, Stanley TJ, et al: Heparin and protamine use in peripheral vascular surgery: A comparison between surgeons of the Society for Vascular Surgery and the European Society for Vascular Surgery. Eur J Vasc Surg 8:193-198, 1994.

123. Poisik A, Heyer EJ, Solomon RA, et al: Safety and efficacy of fixed-dose heparin in carotid endarterectomy. Neurosurgery 45:434-442, 1999.

124. Treiman RL, Cossman DV, Foran RF, et al: The influence of neutralizing heparin after carotid endarterectomy on postoperative stroke and wound hematoma. J Vasc Surg 12:440-446, 1990.
125. Dorman BH, Elliott BM, Spinale FG, et al: Protamine use during peripheral vascular surgery: A prospective randomized trial. J Vasc Surg 22:248-256, 1995.
126. Fearn SJ, Parry AD, Picton AJ, et al: Should heparin be reversed after carotid endarterectomy? A randomised prospective trial. Eur J Vasc Endovasc Surg 13:394-397, 1997.
127. Mauney MC, Buchanan SA, Lawrence WA, et al: Stroke rate is markedly reduced after carotid endarterectomy by avoidance of protamine. J Vasc Surg 22:264-270, 1995.
128. Kresowik TF, Hoballah JJ, Sharp WJ, Corson JD: Cardiac screening tests prior to lower extremity revascularization: Routine versus selective application. Semin Vasc Surg 10:55-60, 1997.
129. Auerbach AD, Goldman L: Beta-blockers and reduction of cardiac events in noncardiac surgery: Scientific review. JAMA 287:1435-1444, 2002.
130. O'Brien MS, Ricotta JJ: Conserving resources after carotid endarterectomy: Selective use of the intensive care unit. J Vasc Surg 14:796-802, 1991.
131. Morasch MD, Hodgett D, Burke K, Baker WH: Selective use of the intensive care unit following carotid endarterectomy. Ann Vasc Surg 9:229-234, 1995.
132. Back MR, Harward TR, Huber TS, et al: Improving the cost-effectiveness of carotid endarterectomy. J Vasc Surg 26:456-464, 1997.
133. Rigdon EE, Monajjem N, Rhodes RS: Criteria for selective utilization of the intensive care unit following carotid endarterectomy. Ann Vasc Surg 11:20-27, 1997.
134. Kaufman JL, Frank D, Rhee SW, et al: Feasibility and safety of 1-day postoperative hospitalization for carotid endarterectomy. Arch Surg 131:751-755, 1996.
135. Angevine PD, Choudhri TF, Huang J, et al: Significant reductions in length of stay after carotid endarterectomy can be safely accomplished without modifying either anesthetic technique or postoperative ICU monitoring. Stroke 30:2341-2346, 1999.
136. Syrek JR, Calligaro KD, Dougherty MJ, et al: Five-step protocol for carotid endarterectomy in the managed health care era. Surgery 125:96-101, 1999.
137. Sheehan MK, Baker WH, Littooy FN, e al: Timing of postcarotid complications: A guide to safe discharge planning. J Vasc Surg 34:13-16, 2001.
138. Biller J, Feinberg WM, Castaldo JE, et al: Guidelines for carotid endarterectomy: A statement for healthcare professionals from a Special Writing Group of the Stroke Council, American Heart Association. Circulation 97:501-509, 1998.

THE MANAGEMENT OF VENOUS DISORDERS

PETER GLOVICZKI, MD

Introduction and General Considerations

PETER GLOVICZKI, MD

> *Chronic ulceration of the lower extremity following deep venous thrombosis is a condition that undoubtedly has plagued the human race since man assumed the erect position.*

Robert R. Linton (1953)

Acute and chronic venous diseases are among the most prevalent medical conditions worldwide. Acute venous thromboembolism is a serious and frequently lethal disease, whereas chronic venous insufficiency can be the source of considerable discomfort, disability, and loss of working days. Venous diseases of the lower limbs, as noted by Linton[1] in 1953, are greatly influenced by the erect position of the human race, and impairment of return of venous blood to the heart against gravity contributes to the development of both acute venous thrombosis and chronic venous insufficiency. Manifestations of chronic venous disease, including varicosity, pain, swelling, skin changes, and leg ulcers, have long been known to humankind, and attempts to treat them date back thousands of years.

■ HISTORICAL BACKGROUND

1550 BC to 200 AD: Venous Discoveries

The fascinating history of venous surgery has been the subject of many reviews and monographs.[2-9] The first written record of varicose veins and suggestions on treatment were found in the Ebers papyrus around 1550 BC.[4] The first illustration of a varicose vein, discovered in Athens at the foot of the Acropolis, dates back to the 4th century BC. It is a commonly reproduced votive tablet that shows a large leg with a serpentine varicose vein on its medial aspect (Fig. 146-1). Extensive description of venous ulceration was found in the work of Hippocrates, entitled *De ulceribus*, in which he stated that "in the case of an ulcer, it is not expedient to stand, more especially if the ulcer is situated in the leg."[10] Hippocrates recognized that incisions around large ulcers do not heal well, and he suggested puncturing the ulcer to stimulate healing. According to Browse and colleagues,[6] Hippocrates made the first reference to compressive dressing when he instructed, "if necessary, cut out the ulcer and then compress it to squeeze out the blood and humours."

The first ligation of blood vessels was described by members of the Alexandrian School of Medicine in Egypt around 270 BC.[3] Celsus,[11] a Roman physician in the 1st century AD, treated varicose veins by excision and cauterization and described ligation of bleeding veins and division of veins between ligatures. Galen, in the 2nd century, used silk ligature to tie off blood vessels and suggested that varicose veins should be treated by incision and avulsion with the use of hooks.[12] It was not until several centuries after Galen that major new discoveries in medicine were documented.

FIGURE 146-1 Votive tablet found at the base of the Acropolis in Athens, Greece, dating back to the 4th century BC. It was dedicated to Dr. Amynos by his patient, Lysimachidis of Acharnes. This is the earliest known illustration of a varicose vein.

14th to 20th Century: Progress in Anatomy and Physiology

In the 14th century, Maitre Henri de Mondeville[13] followed the advice of Hippocrates and successfully used bandages on limbs with ulcerations to "drive back the evil humours." The 15th century brought new interest in venous anatomy, as illustrated in Leonardo da Vinci's drawings of the human body (Fig. 146-2), and in the 16th century, the anatomy of the venous system was presented in great details in the works of Andreas Vesalius (Fig. 146-3). The presence of venous valves was probably first mentioned by J. B. Canano, who described the valvular fold in the azygos vein in 1547.[14] Browse and colleagues[6] give credit to Saloman Alberti in 1585 for the first drawing of a valve in a vein (Fig. 146-4), but the first full description of the valves was given by Hieronymus Fabricius de Aquapendente,[15] professor of anatomy of the renowned medical school of Padua, in 1603 (Fig. 146-5). Browse and colleagues[6] suggest, however, that Fabricius, a teacher of William Harvey, demonstrated the valves in public dissections as early as 1579. Fabricius also wrote on the surgical treatment of varicose veins in his book *Opera chirurgica*, published in 1593.

Stimulated by the work of Fabricius and by his own observations on the venous circulation of the arm (Fig. 146-6), William Harvey[16] published his monumental discovery of the circulation in 1628. He wrote that his demonstration "clearly established that the blood moves in the veins from parts below to those above and to the heart, and not in the opposite way."

Accurate reports on acute venous thrombosis were published much later than descriptions of varicosities. It was

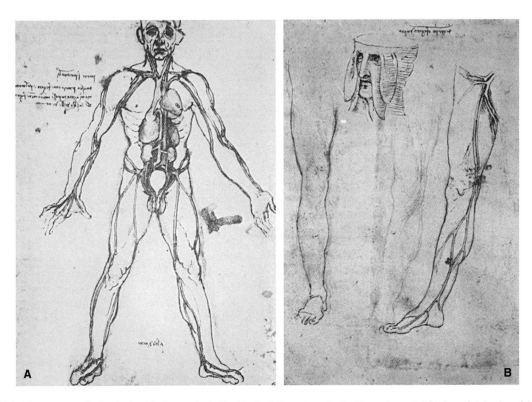

FIGURE 146-2 The anatomy of veins depicted by Leonardo da Vinci in the 15th century. **A,** The "tree of vessels." **B,** Superficial veins of the lower limb.

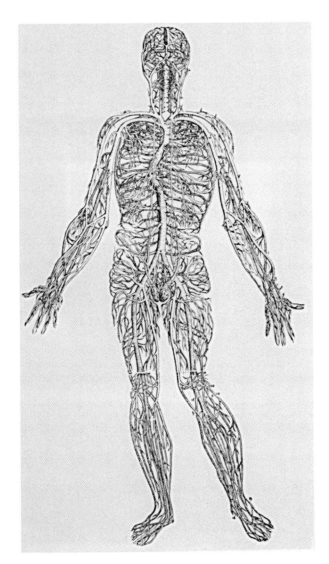

FIGURE 146-3   The venous system, as depicted by Andreas Vesalius in 1543. (From Works of Andreas Vesalius of Brussels, World Publishing Co, Cleveland and New York, 1950.)

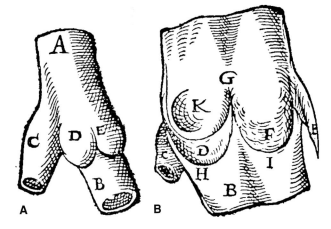

FIGURE 146-4   The first known depiction of venous valves. **A,** Outside depiction of a valve stationed just distal to the origin of a venous tributary. **B,** Inside drawing of a pair of valve leaflets. (From Alberti S: De valvulis membraneis quorundam vasorum: Tres orations. Norimb, 1585. Reprinted in Browse NL, Burnand KG, Thomas ML: Diseases of the Veins: Pathology, Diagnosis, and Treatment. London, Edward Arnold, 1988, p 6.)

not until 1810 that Ferriar[17] described a patient with phlegmasia alba dolens, but he still presumed that the condition was caused by lymphatic obstruction. The relationship between phlegmasia alba dolens and acute *deep venous thrombosis* (DVT) was established by Davis[18] in 1822; he also recognized the relationship between venous thrombosis and childbirth. Anatomic studies on the venous system in the 1800s were definitive in most aspects (Figs. 146-7 through 146-9), and information on management of venous disease also rapidly accumulated. Brodie,[19] in 1846, described his test of venous valvular incompetence and used compression bandages to treat venous ulcers. Unna's[20] description of an elastic plaster dressing with a glycerine-gelatin mixture, known as the Unna boot, in 1854 gave further impetus to nonoperative management.

Virchow[21] described his revolutionary discovery of the three main causes of DVT—changes in the venous wall, stasis of venous blood, and changes in the blood coagulation—in his book *Die Cellular Pathologie.* His depiction of propa-

gation of thrombus in the deep veins and pulmonary emboli changed our understanding of DVT (Fig. 146-10). In 1864, the French physician Pravaz initiated sclerotherapy and injected perchloride of iron to sclerose varicose veins using hypodermic needles, as described previously by Francis Rynd.[6] John Gay's[22] *Lettsomian Lectures,* published in 1866, are most important because they contain accurate descriptions of perforating veins in patients with varicosity and ulcerations and emphasize that treatment of varicose veins results in healing of ulcers (Fig. 146-11). Gay clearly understood that permanent changes occur in the deep veins as a result of venous thrombosis.

20th Century Landmarks

Surgical treatment of DVT at the end of the 19th century consisted of proximal ligation of the greater saphenous vein, as described by Trendelenburg[23] in 1891. In the early 20th century, stripping of the saphenous veins was added to proximal ligation. Keller[24] described an internal stripper in 1905, and Charles H. Mayo[25] used an external ringed vein stripper in 1906. Babcock's[26] contribution was the development of a flexible internal saphenous stripper soon thereafter. Reconstructive venous surgery dates back to 1877, when Eck first performed anastomoses between the portal vein and the inferior vena cava; in 1906, Carrel and Guthrie[27] described their first attempts at venous anastomoses. John Homans,[28] in 1917, introduced the terms *venous stasis* and *post-thrombotic syndrome* and classified varicose veins as primary and post-thrombotic.[28,29]

The first attempts at phlebography by injection of strontium bromide were made by Berberich and Hirsch[30] in 1923, although it was not until 1938 that Dos Santos[31] in Lisbon described a usable technique of contrast phlebography in humans. Bauer[32-34] performed phlebographies regularly in patients to study DVT. The fibrinolytic effect of *Streptococcus* was first described in 1933 by Tillett and Garner,[35] and heparin was first used successfully in humans

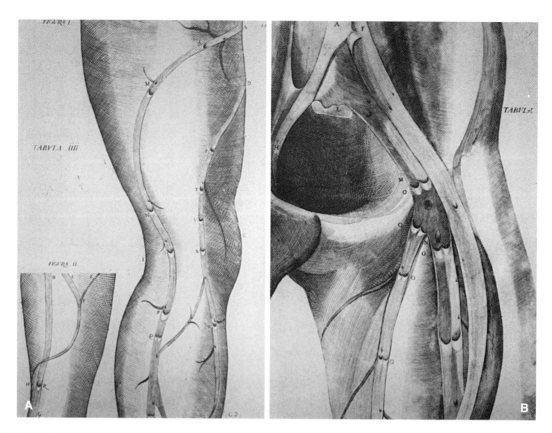

FIGURE 146-5 The first full description of venous valves by Hieronymus Fabricius de Aquapendente. **A,** Venous valves in the superficial veins of the lower limb. **B,** Venous valves in the superficial and deep veins of the lower limbs and pelvis. (From Fabricius Hieronymus de Aquapendente: Anatomici Patavini de Venarum Ostiolis [Valves of veins]. In Laufman H [ed]: The Veins. Austin, Tex, Silvergirl, Inc, 1986, p 14.)

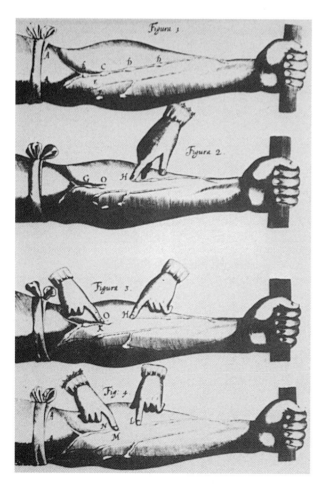

FIGURE 146-6 Illustrations from "De Motu Cordis" of William Harvey, published in 1628. The observations depicted in the drawings persuaded Harvey of unidirectional blood flow in the veins toward the heart. They are also the first known illustrations of the strip test to confirm valvular competence.

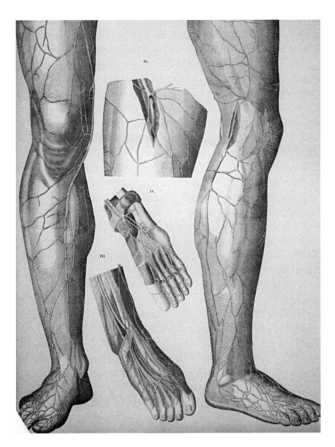

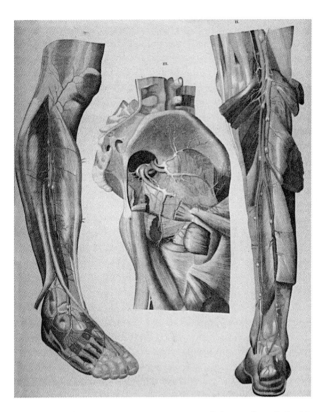

FIGURE 146-7 Illustrations of superficial veins of the legs from the 19th century. (From Oesterreicher JH: Atlas of Human Anatomy. Cincinnati, A. E. Wilde and Co, 1879.)

FIGURE 146-8 Illustration of the anatomy of deep veins of the hip, thigh, and leg. (From Oesterreicher JH: Atlas of Human Anatomy. Cincinnati, A. E. Wilde and Co, 1879.)

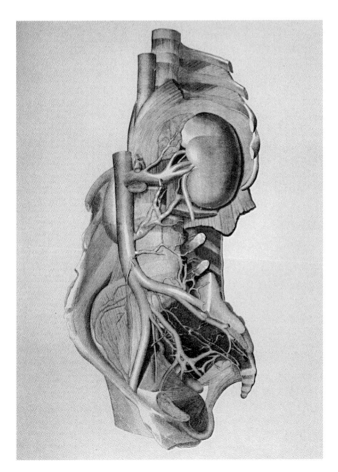

FIGURE 146-9 Anatomy of the common iliac vein and the vena cava. Note the "nutcracker" position of the left renal vein between the superior mesenteric artery and the aorta. (From Oesterreicher JH: Atlas of Human Anatomy. Cincinnati, A. E. Wilde and Co, 1879.)

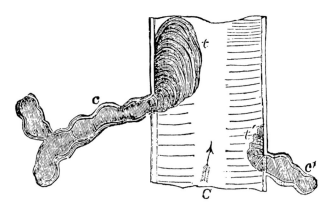

FIGURE 146-10 Venous thrombi protruding into a deep vein from side branches. (From Virchow's Die Cellular Pathologie, 1860.)

by Craafoord[36,37] in 1937. Bauer[33] also showed the beneficial effect of heparin on DVT in 1941. Details of a coagulation cascade were first reported by MacFarlane and Biggs[38] in 1946, and the Hungarian-born Geza De Takats,[39] practicing in Chicago, was the first to use low-dose heparin for the prevention of DVT. Research by Tillett and associates[40] on the beneficial effect of streptokinase in venous thrombosis, published in 1955, started the era of thrombolysis in the management of acute venous thromboembolism.

The first attempts at venous thrombectomy date back to 1926, when Basy[41] performed thrombectomy in a patient with axillary vein thrombosis. The technique of surgical thrombectomy was described by Leriche and Geisendorf[42] in 1939; in the same year, Oschner and DeBakey[43] suggested the terms *phlebothrombosis* and *thrombophlebitis* in a major review of the topic.

Prominent figures in perforating vein surgery included Robert R. Linton,[44] who described subfascial ligation of incompetent communicating veins in 1938 (Fig. 146-12), and Frank Cockett, who suggested the term "ankle blow-out syndrome" for varicose ulcers and described, with Jones,[45] his technique of extrafascial ligation of incompetent perforators. Cockett's book, cowritten with Dodd, was the first standard textbook of the treatment of venous disease.[46] The work of the Austrian Robert May and colleagues[47] on perforating veins, along with May and Thurner's description of the *iliac vein compression syndrome*, also must be mentioned here.

Venous reconstructive surgery developed as a result of extensive experimental work in the middle of the 20th century. To improve patency of grafts placed in the venous system, Jean Kunlin and associates, in France, suggested the use of a distal arteriovenous fistula (Fig. 146-13A) and ring suspension of venous anastomoses (Fig. 146-13B).[48,49] Deep venous reconstruction was first performed successfully in a patient with superficial femoral vein occlusion in 1954 by Warren and Thayer.[50] In 1958, Palma and coworkers[51]

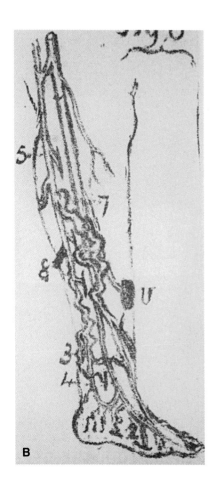

ON

VARICOSE DISEASE

OF THE

LOWER EXTREMITIES

AND ITS ALLIED DISORDERS :

SKIN DISCOLORATION,

INDURATION, AND ULCER:

BEING THE

LETTSOMIAN LECTURES...

DELIVERED BEFORE THE

MEDICAL SOCIETY OF LONDON

IN 1867, BY

JOHN GAY, F.R.C.S.,

SURGEON TO THE GREAT NORTHERN HOSPITAL, CONSULTING SURGEON TO THE
KARLSWOOD IDIOT ASYLUM, ETC., ETC.

" Disséquer en anatomie, faire des expériences en physiologie, suivre les maladies, et ouvrir les cadavres en médecine, c'est là une triple voie hors laquelle il ne peut y avoir d'anatomiste, de physiologiste, ni de médecin."

BRIQUET.

LONDON:
JOHN CHURCHILL AND SONS,
NEW BURLINGTON STREET.
1868.

A

B

FIGURE 146-11 A, Front page of the Lettsomian Lectures of John Gay. **B,** Illustrations of the medial leg veins by John Gay. Note the posterior arch vein and three perforating veins (5, 8, and 4), which are clearly depicted. (From Gay J: On Varicose Disease of the Lower Extremities: Lettsomian Lecture. London, Churchill, 1868.)

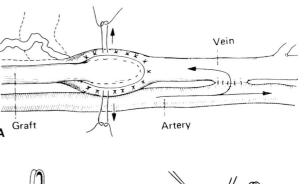

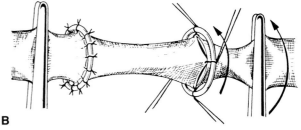

FIGURE 146-13 **A,** Kunlin's drawing on a distal arteriovenous fistula to improve blood flow in a graft placed in the venous system. (From Kunlin J: Les greffes veineuses. Lisbon, Congres Soc Internat de Chirurgie, September 1953.) **B,** External support of venous interposition graft by suspension of the anastomoses on rings, as suggested by Kunlin. (From Kunlin J, Kunlin A, Richard S, Tregouet T: Le remplacement et l'anastomose latero-laterale des veines par greffon avec sutures suspendue par des anneaux: Etude experimentale. J Chir (Paris) 85:305, 1953.)

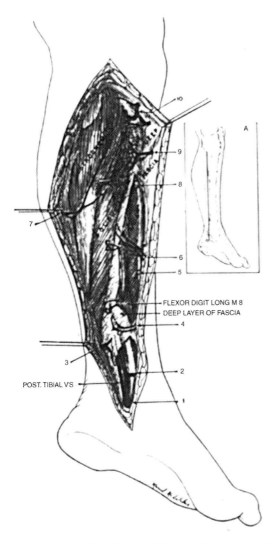

FLEXOR DIGIT LONG M 8
DEEP LAYER OF FASCIA

POST. TIBIAL V'S

FIGURE 146-12 Linton's technique of ligation of the communicating veins. (From Linton RR: The communicating veins of the lower leg and the operative technic for their ligation. Ann Surg 107:582, 1938.)

described an operation of a femorofemoral bypass using the greater saphenous vein to relieve an iliac vein obstruction. The pioneer work by Dale and coworkers[52] accelerated prosthetic replacement of large veins.

Kistner's[53] important contribution in 1968 began the era of venous valve reconstructions to treat deep venous incompetence (Fig. 146-14).[53] In the past three decades, the introduction of endovascular interventions and the use of thrombolysis, venous angioplasty, and stents have rapidly improved our ability to reconstruct the deep venous system.[54] Minimally invasive endoscopic surgical procedures (Fig. 146-15) have also been introduced and added to our armamentarium to treat patients with venous disease.[55]

■ STATE OF THE ART IN THE 21ST CENTURY

In the United States each year, more than 250,000 people experience acute DVT and at least 50,000 suffer from pulmonary embolism.[56] High-probability lung scans

document pulmonary emboli in 25% to 51% of the patients with DVT, even in the absence of respiratory symptoms.[57,58]

Although new information on the pathophysiology of acute DVT has emerged, including venous thrombogenesis and the early course of the disease, the basic mechanism of thrombosis, as described by Virchow[21] more than a century ago, has remained valid. In Chapter 147 of this book, Meissner from the University of Washington, Seattle, and Eugene Strandness, Jr, summarize our current understanding of the pathophysiology of DVT, giving an update on coagulation and fibrinolysis and relaying new data regarding the role of the venous endothelium. Our understanding of primary hypercoagulable states has advanced considerably with discovery of natural anticoagulants, including antithrombin III, protein C, protein S, and the tissue factor pathway inhibitors. Resistance to activated protein C has received increased attention. It is now recognized that factor V Leiden mutation is present in 94% of individuals with activated protein C resistance and that this mutation has an autosomal dominant mode of inheritance.[59] This is an important discovery, because approximately 25% of people with Leiden V mutation have venous thrombosis by age 50 years. In addition, the prevalence of activated protein C resistance in patients with DVT has varied from 10% to 65%.[59,60]

Duplex ultrasonography scanning has extended our knowledge in many areas of venous disease, including the natural history of acute DVT. Multiple studies have confirmed that recanalization is early, with the greatest reduction in thrombus load occurring within 3 months and complete resolution in more than half of patients by 9 months. Recanalization of thrombus, however, can continue for months to years after the acute event.

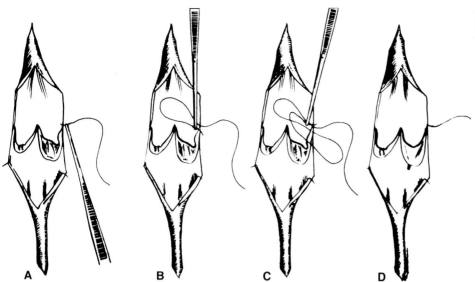

FIGURE 146-14 A through **D,** Illustrations of repair of incompetent femoral vein valves by Kistner.

Readers will benefit greatly from the expert overview in Chapter 148 by Cook and Meissner, who describe the clinical presentation and risk factors of DVT and provide sound and practical guidelines for efficient and cost-effective diagnostic evaluation. These writers emphasize that clinical assessment in patients with suspected DVT is notoriously inaccurate. To establish the diagnosis, duplex ultrasonography has replaced venography as the primary imaging modality for DVT evaluation.[61,62] Magnetic resonance venography is used with growing frequency to evaluate central and pelvic vein thrombosis.[63] D-dimer assays are sensitive for DVT and provide the best information in patients for whom the disease has a low probability.[64,65] The most promising clinical strategy for improving diagnostic accuracy incorporates clinical criteria, D-dimer assays, and ultrasound examination. Ultrasonography is used most effectively as the primary diagnostic modality in patients with high probability for DVT, and as confirmatory testing in patients with low or intermediate probability for DVD but positive D-dimer assay results.

In the past two decades, evidence-based medicine has transformed clinical research, and retrospective clinical reviews and nonrandomized trials have been replaced by large multicenter randomized studies to provide level I evidence of treatment efficacy. Such clinical trials are discussed by Pineo and Hull in Chapter 149, on the prevention and medical management of acute DVT. Credible evidence now supports the effectiveness of low-molecular-weight heparins in both the prevention and the treatment of DVT. Low-molecular-weight heparin given subcutaneously once or twice daily is as effective as or more effective than unfractionated heparin in preventing thrombosis,[66-72] and superior in decreasing bleeding.[66,67] The greater efficacy of outpatient treatment of acute DVT with low-molecular-weight heparin in comparison with conventional intravenous unfractionated heparin given in hospital also has been documented in several clinical studies.[73-75] Low-molecular-weight heparins replaced unfractionated heparin for both the prevention and outpatient treatment of acute DVT.

Progress in invasive management of acute DVT has also been considerable. Additional evidence for both early and late efficacy of surgical thrombectomy has been collected, and in the last decade, the popularity of minimally invasive endovascular techniques has rapidly transformed management algorithms of acute venous disease. Experts present the rationales for both surgical thrombectomy (Chapter 151)

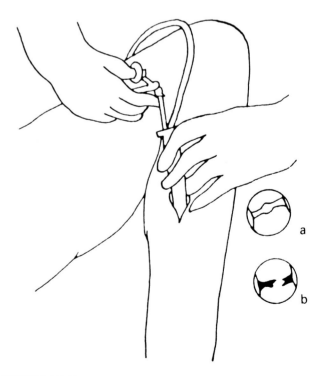

FIGURE 146-15 The first illustration of endoscopic subfascial perforator vein surgery by Hauer in 1985. (From Hauer G: The endoscopic subfascial division of the perforating veins—preliminary report [German]. Vasa 14:59, 1985.)

and catheter-directed thrombolysis (Chapter 150), used with or without additional endovascular techniques, such as mechanical thrombectomy, angioplasty, and stents. Open surgical thrombectomy is rarely performed, although in the experience by Plate and colleagues with more than 200 operations, mortality was 1% and no fatal pulmonary embolism occurred; the long-term benefit of surgical treatment is also supported by a prospective, randomized study from Sweden.[76,77]

A multicenter venous registry for catheter-directed thrombolysis collected data on almost 500 patients.[78] Significant lysis with catheter-directed thrombolysis (>50%) was achieved in 80% of patients, and complete lysis in one third. Preliminary data indicate better results for (1) iliofemoral than for femoropopliteal thrombosis, (2) patients with acute (<10 days) presentation, and (3) patients with the first episode of DVT. Mortality (0.4%) and pulmonary embolism (1.2%) were rare. These data support the use of catheter-directed thrombolysis in carefully selected patients with iliofemoral DVT. In phlegmasia cerulea dolens, surgery is preferred, whereas in phlegmasia alba dolens, catheter-directed thrombolysis is attempted first, unless there are contraindications to fibrinolysis. To restore patency of the thrombosed veins more rapidly, percutaneous mechanical thrombectomy devices have been used alone or combined with thrombolysis, with increasing frequency. If these techniques can achieve similar immediate results without raising the risk of rethrombosis and pulmonary embolism, the duration of treatment and in-hospital care and the overall cost will be reduced.

Prevention of pulmonary embolism by placement of inferior vena caval filters, discussed in Chapter 152, remains an effective method in patients with DVT who cannot undergo anticoagulation or who had documented pulmonary embolism in spite of adequate anticoagulation. Indications for filter placement in trauma patients still are not fully defined, and level I evidence on routine filter placement is not available. The standard for comparison of all the devices remains the stainless steel Greenfield filter, which, in a study observing nearly 500 patients over 12 years, had a 4% rate of recurrent embolism and a long-term filter patency rate of 98%.[79] Rectenwald, Proctor, and Wakefield discuss in detail the different types of removable IVC filters, the technique of placement, and their extended indications.[80]

The management of superficial thrombophlebitis continues to be controversial, and most surgeons remain cautious, advocating high ligation in patients with proximal great saphenous vein thrombophlebitis to prevent pulmonary embolism. Others, however, have collected valuable data to support full anticoagulation for prevention of thrombus extension or development of new thrombi in the deep veins and avoidance of pulmonary embolism. As emphasized by Ralph DePalma in Chapter 153, recurrent thrombophlebitis requires thorough investigation for an underlying thrombotic disorder, malignancy, and, in young smokers, Buerger's disease.

Post-thrombotic syndrome develops in 29% to 79% of patients after an acute episode of DVT.[81] Primary valvular incompetence and, less frequently, congenital venous anomalies are additional causes of chronic venous insufficiency. Recent epidemiologic studies are not available; in the United States, however, it is estimated that at least 25 million people have varicosities, 2 to 6 million have more advanced forms of chronic venous insufficiency (swelling, skin changes), and about 500,000 have venous ulcers.[82]

Current theories of the pathophysiology of chronic venous insufficiency are presented by Peter Pappas in Chapter 154. Macrocirculatory and microcirculatory changes are described for the two main forms of chronic venous insufficiency—primary valvular incompetence and post-thrombotic syndrome. It is clear now that varicose vein formation has a genetic component that is linked to environmental stimuli. Susceptible patients experience vein wall fibrosis and loss of valvular competence that lead to venous hypertension. It has also become evident that a large percentage of patients with deep venous insufficiency do not have a known history of DVT. Arguments for and against the different theories, such as fibrin cuff, tissue hypoxia, local neural control, and white blood cell trapping, are presented.[83-86] The transmission of high venous pressures to the microcirculation causes extravasation of macromolecules and red blood cells, which serves as the underlying stimulus for inflammatory injury.[87,88] Activation of the microcirculation results in cytokine and growth factor release, leading to leukocyte migration into the interstitium. Fibroblast proliferation diminishes with disease progression, ultimately leading to senescence and poor ulcer healing.

In Chapter 155, Frank Padberg presents a practical approach to definitive diagnosis of chronic venous disease using the updated CEAP (clinical, etiologic, anatomic, pathophysiologic) classification that has been accepted worldwide.[89,90] He describes clinical presentations in each class and suggests different levels of diagnostic evaluation. As in the diagnosis of acute venous disease, duplex scanning has become important in diagnosis of chronic venous obstruction and in confirming the presence of superficial and deep venous valvular incompetence. The modality has also been used to localize perforating veins and confirm their incompetence. Ascending and descending venography is reserved now in chronic venous disease for patients who are candidates for endovascular or surgical intervention.[91]

Nonoperative management in patients who are compliant with therapy remains highly effective in controlling symptoms and promoting healing of venous ulcers.[92-94] Leg elevation, elastic and nonelastic bandages and stockings, paste gauze boots, and intermittent compression pumps are elements of compression therapy. Drug treatment in the United States awaits clinical trials; in Europe, the most commonly used drugs are fibrinolytic agents, flavonoids, pentoxifylline, and prostaglandin E_1. For topical ulcer treatment, a bioengineered product made from human foreskin has been reported to show effectiveness in inducing ulcer healing.[95] The author of Chapter 156, Gregory Moneta from Oregon Health Sciences University, offers a critical analysis on nonoperative management, but admits that ulcer healing can be prolonged and in some cases painful and that recurrence of venous ulceration remains a significant problem.[96] Still, compression therapy continues to be the standard against which all other therapies for venous ulcer and chronic venous insufficiency should be compared.

Chapter 157, on the management of varicose veins, reflects the lifelong experience devoted to this subject by chapter author John Bergan, a noble scholar of venous surgery. Bergan guides us masterfully to finding the appropriate balance among surgery, new endovenous interventions, and sclerotherapy, a technique that in the past decade has received growing and well-deserved recognition. Until recently, great saphenous vein reflux has been best treated by high ligation and stripping of the segment that demonstrates reflux, usually from the groin to the knee.[97,98] Radiofrequency ablation of the saphenous vein[99,100] and endovenous laser therapy,[101] however, are important new techniques that have already replaced stripping in many centers. Large varicose clusters are best treated by removal or foam sclerotherapy.[102] Other vessels, especially those with telangiectasia, may be subjected to conventional sclerotherapy.

Chapter 158 discusses progress in perforating vein surgery with emphasis on a minimally invasive new technique, subfascial endoscopic perforator surgery (SEPS).[103-105] The contributing role of perforating veins in the pathophysiology of venous ulcers remains a topic of debate.[106] Available studies have documented that roughly two thirds of patients with chronic venous insufficiency have incompetent perforating veins and that about 70% of cases are of moderate to major hemodynamic significance.[107] Interruption of incompetent perforating veins in this group of patients contributes to improvement in ambulatory venous hypertension and calf muscle pump function. Two publications for the North American Registry confirmed the safety of SEPS, but mid-term results also reflected higher rates of ulcer recurrence in patients with post-thrombotic syndrome.[108,109] Level I evidence is still required not only to confirm the effectiveness of surgical treatment over medical management but also to ascertain the contributory role of perforators to the development of venous ulcers. The European randomized trial failed to confirm the greater effectiveness of SEPS compared with superficial vein surgery alone. Duplex scanning–guided sclerotherapy of perforating veins is promising and deserves further evaluation.

Current techniques and results of reconstruction of deep vein valves are presented by Michael Dalsing in Chapter 159. Patients with either post-thrombotic syndrome or primary valvular incompetence in whom venous ulcerations recurred in spite of nonoperative management or correction of superficial vein reflux are candidates for valve reconstruction. Currently used techniques include internal valvuloplasty, external and transcommissural valvuloplasty with or without angioscopic control, prosthetic sleeve in situ placed around the dilated valve station, and axillary vein transfer. The last is still the mainstay in patients with destroyed valves. The best results have been reported with internal valvuloplasty, which appeared to be durable with few recurrences 3 or 4 years after surgery.[110-113] Hemodynamic improvement using ambulatory venous pressure measurements and air plethysmography has also been documented after valve reconstructions. Percutaneous valve substitutes are on the horizon, and if they are successful, we may experience a true revolution in deep venous reconstructions.

Venous grafting for iliocaval occlusion has been performed with increasing frequency with the use of polytetrafluoroethylene grafts, frequently with an arteriovenous fistula (see Chapter 160).[114-116] Still, the most popular venous reconstructive operation remains the Palma procedure.[117]

The suprapubic saphenous femorofemoral bypass can be performed in patients with unilateral iliac vein occlusion. Clinical improvement after the Palma-Dale procedure has been observed in 75% to 86% of patients.[115-120] In one report on 50 consecutive cases, the cumulative 5-year patency rate was 75%.[119]

Neglén and Raju have developed a school of venous surgery in Jackson, Mississippi. In Chapter 161, they share with us a unique experience with iliac vein stenting for both nonthrombotic and post-thrombotic disease.[121,122]

More on advances made in the fields of thrombolysis, percutaneous transluminal angioplasty (PTA), and endoluminal stenting to recanalize chronic large vein occlusions is presented by the experienced Stanford group in Chapter 162. Dake discusses advances in radiologic imaging and catheter-based interventional procedures that now offer safe, less invasive, and effective treatment alternatives for patients with iliocaval or superior vena caval occlusion.[54] Advantages and disadvantages of the different stents used in large veins, such as the Gianturco Z-stents, the Palmaz stent, and the Wallstent, are discussed, and indications for each are suggested. The role of transluminal angioplasty has changed; it is used now most commonly for predilatation before stenting.

With improvement of imaging techniques and the ability to detect abdominal, retroperitoneal, and pelvic tumors at an earlier stage,[123] vascular surgeons are faced more and more commonly with problems of primary and secondary tumors invading the inferior vena cava.[124-128] In Chapter 163, Bower from the Mayo Clinic provides guidelines for diagnosis and management of primary venous leiomyosarcomas, renal cancers, and metastatic liver and adrenal tumors that invade the vena cava. Tumor resection can be combined with caval reconstruction, using polytetrafluoroethylene grafts with external ring support, yielding excellent rates of early graft patency. Postoperative quality of life, even if survival in many patients is limited, can be improved by caval reconstruction.

The last chapter in this section discusses evaluation and surgical management of superior vena cava syndrome. It is appropriate to conclude with the treatment of this venous disease, because few areas of reconstructive venous surgery provide more satisfying experience than reconstruction of the superior vena cava or innominate veins, with the use of either autologous or prosthetic grafts. Relief from severe, frequently incapacitating symptoms of superior vena caval obstruction after surgery is instantaneous; the benefit, because of high flow and favorable conditions, is generally long-lasting.[129,130] Patients with nonmalignant disease have excellent long-term outcome; survival and graft patency in patients with malignant disease are determined by the nature of the underlying tumor.[131] Progress in venous stenting has reduced the number of surgical candidates for superior vena caval bypass, and the operation is reserved for patients in whom stenting fails or who are not candidates for endovascular treatment.

This entirely revised, new venous section of the 6th edition of *Vascular Surgery* brings the readers the very best currently offered on management of acute and chronic venous diseases. Open venous surgery still has its well-deserved place in the treatment of venous disease, but minimally invasive endovenous technology is growing by leaps and bounds. A noble goal of the authors of this section has also been to inspire investigators of the 21st century to intensify basic and clinical research in the evaluation and treatment of venous disease. Future editions of this volume will testify whether this mission has been accomplished.

■ REFERENCES

1. Linton RR: The post-thrombotic ulceration of the lower extremity: Its etiology and surgical treatment. Am J Surg 107:415, 1953.

2. Major RH: A History of Medicine, vol 1. Oxford, Blackwell Scientific, 1954.

3. Anning ST: Historical aspects. In Dodd H, Cockett FB (eds): The Pathophysiology and Surgery of Veins of the Lower Limb. Edinburgh, Livingstone, 1956.

4. Majno G: The Healing Hand. Cambridge, MA, Harvard University Press, 1975.

5. Laufman H: The Veins. Austin, Silvergirl, 1986.

6. Browse NL, Burnand KG, Lea TM: Diseases of the Veins. London, EH Arnold, 1988, p 1.

7. Bergan JJ, Ballard JL: Historical perspectives. In Gloviczki P, Bergan JJ (eds): Atlas of Endoscopic Perforator Vein Surgery. London, Springer-Verlag, 1998, p 5.

8. Bergan JJ, Cho JS, Weber J, Gloviczki P: Profiles. In Gloviczki P, Bergan JJ (eds): Atlas of Endoscopic Perforator Vein Surgery. London, Springer-Verlag, 1998.

9. Negus D: Leg Ulcers: A Practical Approach to Management. London, Butterworth-Heinemann, 1995, p 3.

10. Hippocrates: The Genuine Works of Hippocrates, vol 2. Adams EF, trans. New York, Wm Wood & Co, 1886, p 305.

11. Celsus AC: Of Medicine (in Eight Books). Grieve J, trans. London, Wilson & Durham, 1756.

12. Walsh J: Galen's writings and influences inspiring them. Ann Med Hist Part I:14, 1934.

13. Mondeville H: de Chirurgie de Maitre Henri de Mondeville, Composé de 1306 à 1320. Nicalse A, trans. Paris, Alcan, 1893.

14. Friedenwald H: Amatus lusitanus. Bull Inst Hist Med 5:644, 1937.

15. Fabricius de Aquapendente, H: Anatomici Patavini de Venarum Ostiolis [Valves of veins]. In Laufman H (ed): The Veins. Austin, Silvergirl, 1986, p 14.

16. Harvey W: Exercitatio Anatomica de Motu Cordis et Sanguini in Animalibus. Frankfurt, W Fitzer, 1628.

17. Ferriar J: An affectation of the lymphatic vessels hitherto misunderstood. Medical Histories and Reflections 3:129, 1810.

18. Davis DD: The proximate cause of phlegmasia dolens. Med Chir Trans 12:419, 1822.

19. Brodie BC: Lectures Illustrative of Various Subjects in Pathology and Surgery. London, Longman, Brown, Green & Longman, 1846.

20. Unna PG: Ueber Paraplaste eine neue Form Medikamentoser Pflaster. Wien Med Wochenschr 46:1854, 1896.

21. Virchow R: Die Cellular Pathologie. Berlin, Verlag von August Hirschwald, 1859.

22. Gay J: On Varicose Disease of the Lower Extremities: Lettsomian Lecture. London, Churchill, 1866.

23. Trendelenburg F: Uber die Unterbindung der Vena Saphena magna bie Unterschenkel Varicen. Beitr Z Clin Chir 7:195, 1891.

24. Keller WL: A new method of extirpating the internal saphenous and similar veins in varicose conditions. N Y Med J 82:385, 1905.

25. Mayo CH: Treatment of varicose veins. Surg Gynecol Obstet 2:385, 1906.

26. Babcock WW: A new operation for extirpation of varicose veins of the leg. N Y Med J 86:153, 1907.

27. Carrel A, Guthrie CC: Uniterminal and biterminal venous transplantation. Surg Gynecol Obstet 2:266, 1906.

28. Homans J: The operative treatment of varicose veins and ulcers, based upon a classification of these lesions. Surg Gynecol Obstet 22:143, 1916.

29. Homans J: The aetiology and treatment of varicose ulcers of the leg. Surg Gynecol Obstet 24:300, 1917.

30. Berberich J, Hirsch S: Die roentgenographische Darstellung der Arterien und Venen am lebenden Menschen. Klin Wochenschr 2:2226, 1923.

31. Dos Santos JC: La phlébographie directe: Conception, technique, premier résultats. J Int Chir 3:625, 1938.

32. Bauer G: A venographic study of thromboembolic patients. Acta Chir Scand 84, Suppl 61, 1940.

33. Bauer G: Venous thrombosis: Early diagnosis with aid of phlebography and abortive treatment with heparin. Arch Surg 43:463, 1941.

34. Bauer G: A roentgenological and clinical study of the sequels of thrombosis. Acta Chir Scand 86:Suppl 74, 1942.

35. Tillett WS, Garner RL: The fibrinolytic activity of haemolytic streptococci. J Exp Med 58:485, 1933.

36. Crafoord C: Heparin and post-operative thrombosis. Acta Chir Scand 82:319, 1939.

37. Crafoord C, Jorpes E: Heparin as a prophylactic against thrombosis. JAMA 116:2831, 1941.

38. MacFarlane RG, Biggs R: Observations on fibrinolysis, spontaneous activity associated with surgical operations and trauma. Lancet 2:862, 1946.

39. De Takats G: Anticoagulant therapy in surgery. JAMA 142:527, 1950.

40. Tillett WS, Johnson AJ, McCarty WR: The intravenous infusion of the streptococcal fibrinolytic principle (streptokinase) into patients. J Clin Invest 34:169, 1955.

41. Basy L: Thrombose de la veine axillaire droite (thrombo-phlébite par effort): Phlébotomie, ablation de caillots, suture de la veine. Mem Acad Chir 52:529, 1926.

42. Leriche R, Geisendorf W: Résultats d'une thrombectomie précoce avec résection veineuse dans une phlébite grave des deux membres inférieurs. Presse Med 47:1239, 1939.

43. Oschner A, DeBakey M: Therapy of phlebothrombosis and thrombophlebitis. South Surg 8:269, 1939.

44. Linton RR: The communicating veins of the lower leg and the operative technique for their ligation. Ann Surg 107:582, 1938.

45. Cockett FB, Jones DE: The ankle blow-out syndrome: A new approach of the varicose ulcer problem. Lancet 1:17, 1953.

46. Dodd H, Cockett FB (eds): The Pathophysiology and Surgery of Veins of the Lower Limb. Edinburgh, Livingstone, 1956.

47. May R, Partsch H, Staubesand J (eds): Perforating Veins. Munchen, Urban & Schwarzenberg, 1979.

48. Kunlin J: Les greffes veineuses. Lisbon, Congres Soc Internat de Chirurgie, September 1953.

49. Kunlin J, Kunlin A, Richard S, Tregouet T: Le remplacement et l'anastomose latéro-latérale des veines par greffon avec sutures suspendue par des anneaux: Etude expérimentale. J Chir (Paris) 85:305, 1953.

50. Warren R, Thayer T: Transplantation of the saphenous vein for postphlebitic stasis. Surgery 35:867, 1954.

51. Palma EC, Risi F, De Campo F: Tratamiento de los trastornos postflebiticos mediante anastomosis venosa safeno-femoral contro-lateral. Bull Soc Surg Uruguay 29:135, 1958.

52. Dale WA, Harris J, Terry RB: Polytetrafluoroethylene reconstruction of the inferior vena cava. Surgery 95:625, 1984.

53. Kistner RL: Surgical repair of a venous valve. Straub Clin Proc 34:41, 1968.

54. Rosch J, Petersen BD, Lakin PC: Venous stents: Indications, techniques, results. In Perler BA, Becker GJ (eds): Vascular Intervention: A Clinical Approach. New York, Thieme, 1998, p 706.

55. Hauer G: The endoscopic subfascial division of the perforating veins—preliminary report [German]. Vasa 14:59, 1985.

56. Anderson FA Jr, Wheeler HB, Goldberg R, et al: A population-based perspective of the hospital incidence and case-fatality rates of deep vein thrombosis and pulmonary embolism: The Worcester Deep Venous Thrombosis Study. Arch Intern Med 151:933, 1991.

57. Jick H, Derby LE, Myers MW, et al: Risk of hospital admission for idiopathic venous thromboembolism among users of postmenopausal oestrogens. Lancet 348:981, 1996.

58. Nicolaides AN, Irving D: Clinical factors and the risk of deep venous thrombosis. In Nicolaides AN (ed): Thromboembolism: Aetiology, Advances in Prevention and Management. Lancaster, UK, MTP Press, 1975.

59. Simioni P, Prandoni P, Lensing AW, et al: The risk of recurrent venous thromboembolism in patients with an Arg506→Gln mutation in the gene for factor V (factor V Leiden). N Engl J Med 336:399, 1997.

60. Ridker PM, Glynn RJ, Miletich JP, et al: Age-specific incidence rates of venous thromboembolism among heterozygous carriers of factor V Leiden mutation. Ann Intern Med 126:528, 1997.

61. Meissner MH, Manzo RA, Bergelin RO, et al: Deep venous insufficiency: The relationship between lysis and subsequent reflux. J Vasc Surg 18:596, 1993.

62. Comerota AJ, Katz ML, Greenwald LI, et al: Venous duplex imaging: Should it replace hemodynamic tests for deep venous thrombosis? J Vasc Surg 11:53, 1990.

63. Carpenter JP, Holland GA, Baum RA, Owen RS: Magnetic resonance venography for detection of deep venous thrombosis: Comparison with contrast venography and duplex Doppler ultrasonography. J Vasc Surg 18:734, 1993.

64. Rowbotham BJ, Carrol P, Whitaker AN, et al: Measurement of crosslinked fibrin derivatives: Use in the diagnosis of venous thrombosis. Thromb Haemost 57:59-61, 1987.

65. Ginsberg JS, Kearon C, Douketis J, et al: The use of D-dimer testing and impedance plethysmographic examination in patients with clinical indications of deep vein thrombosis. Arch Intern Med 157:1077, 1997.

66. Kakkar VV, Cohen AT, Edmonson RA, et al: Low molecular weight versus standard heparin for prevention of venous thromboembolism after major abdominal surgery. Lancet 341:259, 1993.

67. Kakkar VV, Boeckl O, Boneau B, et al: Efficacy and safety of a low molecular weight heparin and standard unfractionated heparin for prophylaxis of postoperative venous thromboembolism: European Multicenter Trial. World J Surg 21:2, 1997.

68. Bergqvist D, Matzsch T, Brumark U, et al: Low molecular weight heparin given the evening before surgery compared with conventional low dose heparin in prevention of thrombosis. Br J Surg 75:888, 1988.

69. Caen JP: A randomized double-blinded study between a low molecular weight heparin, Kabi 2154 and standard heparin, in the prevention of deep vein thrombosis in general surgery: A French Multicentre Trial. Thromb Haemost 59:216, 1988.

70. Bergqvist D, Burmark US, Flordal PA, et al: Low molecular weight heparin started before surgery as prophylaxis against deep vein thrombosis: 2500 versus 5000 XaI units in 2070 patients. Br J Surg 82:496, 1995.

71. Nurmohamed MT, Verhaeghe R, Haas S, et al: A comparative trial of a low molecular weight heparin (Enoxaparin) versus standard heparin for the prophylaxis of postoperative deep vein thrombosis in general surgery. Am J Surg 169:567-571, 1995.

72. Efficacy and safety of enoxaparin versus unfractionated heparin for prevention of deep vein thrombosis in elective cancer surgery: A double-blind randomized multicentre trial with venographic assessment. ENOXACAN Study Group. Br J Surg 84:1099, 1997.

73. Levine M, Gent M, Hirsh J, et al: A comparison of low molecular weight heparin administered primarily at home with unfractionated heparin administered in the hospital for proximal deep vein thrombosis. N Engl J Med 334:677, 1996.

74. Koopman MMW, Prandoni P, Piovella F, et al: Treatment of venous thrombosis with intravenous unfractionated heparin administered in the hospital as compared with subcutaneous low molecular weight heparin administered at home. N Engl J Med 334:682, 1996.

75. Low molecular weight heparin in the treatment of patients with venous thromboembolism. The Columbus Investigators. N Engl J Med 337:657, 1997.

76. Plate G, Einarsson E, Ohlin P, et al: Thrombectomy with temporary arteriovenous fistula: The treatment of choice in acute iliofemoral venous thrombosis. J Vasc Surg 1:867, 1984.

77. Plate G, Akesson H, Einarsson E, et al: Long-term results of venous thrombectomy combined with a temporary arteriovenous fistula. Eur J Vasc Surg 4:483, 1990.

78. Mewissen MW: Data presented at the Venous Registry Investigators Meeting, San Diego, September 1997.

79. Greenfield LJ, Michna BA: Twelve-year clinical experience with the Greenfield vena cava filter. Surgery 104:706, 1988.

80. Wicky S, Doenz F, Meuwly JY, et al: Clinical experience with retrievable Günther tulip vena cava filters. J Endovasc Ther 10:994, 2003.

81. Salzman EW, Hirsh J: The epidemiology, pathogenesis, and natural history of venous thrombosis. In Colman RW, Hirsh J, Mardr VJ, Salzman EW (eds): Hemostasis and Thrombosis: Basic Principles and Clinical Practice, 3rd ed. Philadelphia, JB Lippincott, 1994.

82. Coon WW, Willis PW, Keller JB: Venous thromboembolism and other venous disease in the Tecumseh Community Health Study. Circulation 48:839, 1973.

83. Burnand KG, Whimster I, Naidoo A, Browse NL: Pericapillary fibrin in the ulcer-bearing skin of the leg: The cause of lipodermatosclerosis and venous ulceration. Br Med J 285:1071, 1982.

84. Thomas PR, Nash GB, Dormandy JA: Increased white cell trapping in the dependent legs of patients with chronic venous insufficiency. J Mal Vasc 15:35, 1990.

85. Saharay M, Shields DA, Porter JB, et al: Leukocyte activity in the microcirculation of the leg in patients with chronic venous disease. J Vasc Surg 25:265, 1997.

86. Scott HJ, Coleridge Smith PD, Scurr JH: Histologic study of white blood cells and their association with lipodermatosclerosis and venous ulceration. Br J Surg 78:210, 1991.

87. Pappas PJ, DeFouw DO, Venezio LM, et al: Morphometric assessment of the dermal microcirculation in patients with chronic venous insufficiency. J Vasc Surg 26:784, 1997.

88. Pappas PJ, Fallek SR, Garcia A, et al: Role of leukocyte activation in patients with venous stasis ulcers. J Surg Res 59:553, 1995.

89. Porter JM, Moneta GL: Reporting standards in venous disease: An update. International Consensus Committee on Chronic Venous Disease. J Vasc Surg 21:635, 1995.

90. The Consensus Group: Classification and grading of chronic venous disease in the lower limb: A consensus statement. Vasc Surg 30:5, 1996.

91. Kistner RL: Definitive diagnosis and definitive treatment in chronic venous disease: A concept whose time has come. J Vasc Surg 24:703, 1996.

92. Mayberry JC, Moneta GL, DeFrang RD, Porter JM: The influence of elastic compression stockings on deep venous hemodynamics. J Vasc Surg 13:91, 1991.

93. Mayberry JC, Moneta GL, Taylor LM, Porter JM: Fifteen-year results of ambulatory compression therapy for chronic venous ulcers. Surgery 109:575, 1991.

94. O'Donnell TF, Rosenthal DA, Callow AD, Ledig BL: The effect of elastic compression on venous hemodynamics in postphlebitic limbs. JAMA 242:2766, 1979.

95. Falanga V, Margolis D, Alvarez O, et al: Rapid healing of venous ulcers and lack of clinical rejection with an allogenic cultured human skin equivalent. Human Skin Equivalent Investigations Group. Arch Dermatol 134:293, 1998.

96. Erickson CA, Lanza DJ, Karp DL, et al: Healing of venous ulcers in an ambulatory care program: The roles of chronic venous insufficiency and patient compliance. J Vasc Surg 22:629, 1995.

97. Dwerryhouse S, Davies B, Harradine K, Earnshaw JJ: Stripping the long saphenous vein reduces the rate of reoperation for recurrent varicose veins: Five-year results of a randomized trial. J Vasc Surg 29:589, 1999.

98. Rutgers PH, Kitslaar PJ: Randomized trial of stripping versus high ligation combined with sclerotherapy in the treatment of the incompetent greater saphenous vein. Am J Surg 168:311, 1994.

99. Merchant RF, DePalma RG, Kabnick LS: Endovascular obliteration of saphenous reflux: A multicenter study [see comments]. J Vasc Surg 35:1190, 2002.

100. Lurie F, Creton D, Ekloff B, et al: Prospective randomized study of endovenous radiofrequency obliteration (closure procedure) versus ligation and stripping in a selected patient population (EVOLVeS Study). J Vasc Surg 38:207, 2003.

101. Min RJ, Khilnani N, Zimmet SE, Steven E: Endovenous laser treatment of saphenous vein reflux: Long-term results. J Vasc Interv Radiol 14:991, 2003.

102. Hamel-Desnos C, Desnos P, Wollmann J, et al: Evaluation of the efficacy of polidocanol in the form of foam compared with liquid foam in sclerotherapy of the greater saphenous vein: Initial results. Dermatol Surg 29:1170, 2003.

103. Pierik EGJM, Wittens CHA, van Urk H: Subfascial endoscopic ligation in the treatment of incompetent perforating veins. Eur J Vasc Endovasc Surg 9:38, 1995.

104. Gloviczki P, Bergan JJ: Atlas of Endoscopic Perforator Vein Surgery. London, Springer-Verlag, 1998.

105. Kalra M, Gloviczki P, Noel AA, et al: Subfascial endoscopic perforator vein surgery in patients with post-thrombotic venous insufficiency—Is it justified? Vasc Endovasc Surg 36:41, 2002.

106. Burnand K, O'Donnell T, Lea MT, Browse NL: Relationship between post-phlebitic changes in deep veins and results of surgical treatment of venous ulcers. Lancet 1(7966):936, 1976.

107. Zukovsky AJ, Nicolaides AN, Szendro G, et al: Haemodynamic significance of incompetent calf perforating vein. Br J Surg 78:625, 1991.

108. Gloviczki P, Bergan JJ, Menawat SS, et al: Safety, feasibility, and early efficacy of subfascial endoscopic perforator surgery (SEPS): A preliminary report from the North American Registry. J Vasc Surg 25:94, 1997.

109. Gloviczki P, Bergan JJ, Rhodes JM, et al: Mid-term results of endoscopic perforator vein interruption for chronic venous insufficiency: Lessons learned from the North American Subfascial Endoscopic Perforator Surgery (NASEPS) Registry. J Vasc Surg 29:489, 1999.

110. Masuda E, Kistner RL: Long-term results of venous valve reconstruction: A 14- to 21-year follow-up. J Vasc Surg 19:391, 1994.

111. Raju S: New approaches to the diagnosis and treatment of venous obstruction. J Vasc Surg 4:42, 1986.

112. Raju S, Fredericks RK, Neglen PN, Bass JD: Durability of venous valve reconstruction techniques for "primary" and postthrombotic reflux. J Vasc Surg 23:357, 1996.

113. Sottiurai VS: Results of deep-vein reconstruction. Vasc Surg 31:276, 1997.

114. Gloviczki P, Pairolero PC, Toomey BJ, et al: Reconstruction of large veins for nonmalignant venous occlusive disease. J Vasc Surg 16:750, 1992.

115. Gruss JD: Venous bypass for chronic venous insufficiency. In Bergan JJ, Yao JST (eds): Venous Disorders. Philadelphia, WB Saunders, 1991, p 316.

116. Jost CJ, Gloviczki P, Cherry KJ, et al: Surgical reconstructions of iliofemoral veins and the inferior vena cava for nonmalignant occlusive disease. J Vasc Surg 33:320, 2001.

117. Palma EC, Esperon R: Vein transplants and grafts in the surgical treatment of the postphlebitic syndrome. J Cardiovasc Surg 1:94, 1960.

118. Dale WA, Harris J: Cross-over vein grafts for iliac and femoral venous occlusion. J Cardiovasc Surg 10:458, 1969.

119. Halliday P, Harris J, May J: Femoro-femoral crossover grafts (Palma operation): A long-term follow-up study. In Bergan JJ, Yao JST (eds): Surgery of the Veins. Orlando, FL, Grune & Stratton, 1985, p 241.

120. AbuRahma AF, Robinson PA, Boland JP: Clinical hemodynamic and anatomic predictors of long-term outcome of lower extremity venovenous bypasses. J Vasc Surg 14:635, 1991.

121. Raju S, Owen S Jr, Neglén P: The clinical impact of iliac venous stents in the management of chronic venous insufficiency. J Vasc Surg 35:8, 2002.

122. Neglén P, Raju S: Proximal lower extremity chronic venous outflow obstruction: Recognition and treatment. Semin Vasc Surg 15:57, 2002.

123. Stanson AW, Breen JF: Computed tomography and magnetic resonance imaging. In Gloviczki P, Yao JST (eds): Handbook of Venous Disorders: Guidelines of the American Venous Forum. London, Chapman & Hall, 1996, p 190.

124. Dzsinich C, Gloviczki P, van Heerden JA, et al: Primary venous leiomyosarcoma: A rare but lethal disease. J Vasc Surg 15:595, 1992.

125. Bower TC: Primary and secondary tumors of the inferior vena cava. In Gloviczki P, Yao JST (eds): Handbook of Venous Disorders: Guidelines of the American Venous Forum, 1996, pp 529-550.

126. Bower TC, Nagorney DM, Toomey BJ, et al: Vena cava replacement for malignant disease: Is there a role? Ann Surg 7:51, 1993.

127. Bower TC, Nagorney DM, Cherry KJ Jr, et al: Replacement of the inferior vena cava for malignancy: An update. J Vasc Surg 31:270, 2000.

128. Neves RJ, Zincke H: Surgical treatment of renal cancer with vena cava extension. Br J Urol 59:390, 1987.

129. Alimi YS, Gloviczki P, Vrtiska TJ, et al: Reconstruction of the superior vena cava: Benefits of postoperative surveillance and secondary endovascular interventions. J Vasc Surg 27:287, 1998.

130. Kalra M, Gloviczki P, Andrews JC, et al: Open surgical and endovascular treatment of superior vena cava syndrome caused by non-malignant disease. J Vasc Surg 38:215, 2003.

131. Dartevelle PG, Chapelier AR, Pastorino U, et al: Long-term follow-up after prosthetic replacement of the superior vena cava combined with resection of mediastinal-pulmonary malignant tumors. J Thorac Cardiovasc Surg 102:259, 1991.

Pathophysiology and Natural History of Acute Deep Venous Thrombosis

147

MARK H. MEISSNER, MD
EUGENE STRANDNESS, JR, MD

The complications of acute deep venous thrombosis (DVT), pulmonary embolism (PE), and the post-thrombotic syndrome are important not only as the most common preventable cause of hospital death[89] but also as a source of substantial long-term morbidity.[11,28,197] An understanding of the underlying epidemiology, pathophysiology, and natural history of DVT is essential in guiding appropriate prophylaxis, diagnosis, and treatment. Recognition of the underlying risk factors and an appreciation of the multifactorial nature of DVT may facilitate the identification of situations likely to provoke thrombosis in high-risk individuals as well as the further evaluation of those with unexplained thromboembolism. An understanding of the natural history of DVT is similarly important in defining the relative risk and benefits of anticoagulation as well as the duration of treatment in individual patients.

Components of the pathophysiologic triad initially described by Rudolf Virchow remain applicable today. However, an improved understanding of the coagulation and fibrinolytic systems as well as the role of the vascular endothelium in thrombosis and hemostasis has led to the identification of new prethrombotic conditions and also a more thorough appreciation of previously recognized risk factors. Furthermore, accurate and repeatable noninvasive diagnostic methods, such as duplex ultrasonography, have allowed the pathophysiology to be related to the natural history of DVT. It now appears that many venous thrombi arise from the convergence of several risk factors against a background of imbalanced coagulation and fibrinolysis. Similar factors defining the balance between recanalization of the venous lumen and recurrent thrombotic events also may be important determinants of long-term outcome after an episode of acute DVT.

■ EPIDEMIOLOGY

Precise definition of the incidence of acute DVT is complicated by the clinically silent nature of most thromboses in hospitalized patients as well as by the nonspecific signs and symptoms.[6,31,69,94] The incidence depends on the population studied, the intensity of screening, and the accuracy of the diagnostic tests employed. Autopsy studies, which are biased by inclusion of the very sick and old, have reported the prevalence of DVT to be 35% to 52%.[61,118] Most clinical trials and studies on the incidence of acute DVT have focused on specific inpatient groups, such as postoperative patients. Although useful in defining risk factors for acute DVT, such studies provide few data regarding the overall prevalence of acute DVT. Community-based studies may provide a better estimate of overall prevalence but frequently suffer from a lack of objective documentation of DVT. Extrapolating data from a longitudinal community-based study, Coon and associates[28] calculated an incidence of 250,000 cases of acute DVT per year in the United States. These results, however, were based largely on questionnaires and clinical findings suggestive of previous DVT. Community-based studies of venographically documented symptomatic DVT have reported a yearly incidence of 1.6 per 1000 residents.[153] Among men, the cumulative probability of suffering a thromboembolic event is estimated to be 10.7% by the age of 80 years.[72]

Later epidemiologic data from the Olmsted County project in Minnesota found that the overall average age- and sex-adjusted annual incidence of venous thromboembolism (VTE) was 117 per 100,000 (DVT, 48 per 100,000; PE, 69 per 100,000), with higher age-adjusted rates among men than women (130 vs. 110 per 100,000, respectively).[248] The incidence of PE decreased in the past decades, but the incidence of DVT remained constant for males across all age strata, decreased for females younger than 55 years, and increased for women older than 60 years.

VTE is a major national health problem, especially among the elderly, with an overall age- and sex-adjusted incidence of more than 1 per 1000 each year. Silverstein and colleagues[248] estimated that at least 201,000 new cases of VTE occur in this country annually, of which 107,000 are DVT alone and 94,000 are PE (with or without DVT). Of the total (201,000), 30% of the affected patients die within 30 days, and one fifth suffer sudden death due to PE.

■ PATHOPHYSIOLOGY

Venous Thrombogenesis

As initially postulated by Virchow, three factors are of primary importance in the development of venous thrombosis: (1) abnormalities of blood flow, (2) abnormalities of blood, and (3) vascular injury. These tenets have subsequently been refined, and it currently appears that flow abnormalities determine the localization of venous thrombi, that abnormalities of blood may include aberrations of both the coagulation and fibrinolytic systems, and that biologic injury to the venous endothelium is potentially more important than gross trauma. It also clear, however, that the origin of DVT is frequently multifactorial, with components of Virchow's triad assuming variable importance in individual patients.

Mechanical venous injury clearly plays a role in thrombosis associated with direct venous trauma,[39,207] hip arthroplasty,[193,202] and central venous catheters.[235] Central venous cannulation is largely responsible for the increasing incidence of upper extremity thrombosis, whereas similar venous injury is presumably responsible for the observation that 57% of thrombi occurring after hip arthroplasty arise from the femoral vein rather than the usual site in the calf.[202] However, the importance of mechanical venous injury in other situations is questionable. Focal venous injury cannot account for the observations that thromboses in trauma patients are more commonly bilateral (77%) than unilateral (23%) and may be as common in an injured limb as in an uninjured limb.[192] Neither do mechanical crush injuries in animal models usually cause thrombosis, even when followed by stasis.[5,212] Overt endothelial injury likely is neither necessary nor sufficient to cause thrombosis in the absence of other stimuli.[212,231]

The potential role of biochemical injury to the venous endothelium has only lately become apparent.[125] The normal venous endothelium is antithrombotic, producing prostaglandin I_2 (PGI_2, prostacyclin), glycosaminoglycan cofactors of antithrombin, thrombomodulin, and tissue-type plasminogen activator (t-PA).[22] However, the endothelium may become prothrombotic under some conditions, producing tissue factor, von Willebrand factor, and fibronectin. It is conceivable that some thrombotic risk factors act through production of a procoagulant endothelium. Microscopic changes in the endothelial surface associated with greater endothelial permeability and leukocyte adhesion have been demonstrated in response to distant surgical injury.[204] Induction of procoagulant activity, suppression of anticoagulant mechanisms, and exposure of neutrophil receptor ligands may accompany such endothelial perturbation.[147,203]

Associated inflammatory cells may be capable of both initiating and amplifying thrombosis.[228] The importance of cytokine-mediated expression of tissue factor procoagulant activity under clinical conditions is unknown, but both interleukin-1 (IL-1) and tumor necrosis factor (TNF) may induce fibrin deposition through a combination of endothelial procoagulant expression and fibrinolytic depression.[138,147,210] TNF also may downregulate endothelial thrombomodulin expression, further converting the endothelium from an antithrombotic to a procoagulant state.[228] In such situations, Virchow's concept of venous injury may be more important at the molecular than the macroscopic level.

Regardless of etiology, most venous thrombi originate in areas of low blood flow, either in the soleal veins of the calf[61,95,150] or behind valve pockets.[191] Furthermore, many risk factors for acute DVT are associated with immobilization and slow venous flow, and several mechanisms have

been advanced to explain the role of stasis in thrombogenesis. In comparison with pulsatile flow, static streamline flow is associated with profound hypoxia at the depths of the venous valve cusps and may induce endothelial injury.[70] The effects of hypoxia in cultured endothelial cells have been noted to include stimulation of cytokine production and leukocyte adhesion molecule expression,[194] perhaps accounting for the adhesion and migration of leukocytes observed in association with stasis.[211] Furthermore, stasis also allows the accumulation of activated coagulation factors and the consumption of inhibitors at sites prone to thrombosis. Stasis in the large veins may be particularly important, because the low surface-to-volume ratio may prevent interaction with endothelial inhibitory pathways, particularly the endothelium-bound thrombomodulin–protein C system.[210]

Despite these observations, there is little evidence that stasis can activate coagulation, and in isolation, stasis appears to be an inadequate stimulus for thrombosis.[14,211] Experimental ligation of the rabbit jugular vein for intervals of 10 to 60 minutes has consistently failed to cause thrombosis.[5,211,232] From a clinical perspective, activation of coagulation during hip arthroplasty is associated with manipulation of the femoral component rather than simply occlusion of the femoral vein.[193] Stasis should thus perhaps be viewed as a permissive factor in venous thrombosis, localizing activated coagulation to thrombosis-prone sites.

Activation of coagulation appears to be critical in the pathogenesis of DVT. The coagulation cascade functions through serial activation of zymogens in the intrinsic and tissue factor pathways, with the ultimate generation of thrombin by the prothrombinase complex. Antithrombin and the thrombomodulin–protein C systems are the primary inhibitors of coagulation, whereas the fibrinolytic system serves to further limit fibrin deposition. Although the hemostatic system is continuously active, thrombus formation is ordinarily confined to sites of local injury by a precise balance between activators and inhibitors of coagulation and fibrinolysis. A prethrombotic state may result either from imbalances in the regulatory and inhibitory systems or from activation exceeding antithrombotic capacity.[3]

Although measurement of zymogen levels and in vitro clotting assays has not proved fruitful in defining prethrombotic states, identification of activated coagulation has been facilitated by the development of sensitive assays for stable byproducts of thrombin activation.[7] The most useful of these byproducts are:

- Prothrombin fragment F_{1+2}, generated by factor Xa in the cleavage of prothrombin to thrombin
- Fibrinopeptide A, formed in the thrombin-mediated conversion of fibrinogen to fibrin
- Thrombin-antithrombin complex, formed by the combination of thrombin with its primary inhibitor

Increased levels of these markers have been described in association with risk factors such as surgery,[96,103] oral contraceptives,[171,226] and malignancy.[50]

Just as the combination of stasis and injury may be ineffective in causing thrombosis without low levels of activated coagulation factors,[5] activated coagulation alone may be insufficient to provoke thrombosis. Ordinarily, activated coagulation factors are rapidly cleared from the circulation. When localized in regions of stasis, however, the coagulation cascade allows activated factors to rapidly amplify the thrombotic stimulus, leading to platelet aggregation and fibrin formation.[5,210] DVT thus appears to be a multifactorial phenomenon, with convergence of several pathologic factors often required to produce a thrombotic event.[179]

Although infusion of activated coagulation factors alone may not cause thrombosis, infusion of TNF and antibody to protein C, combined with low flow and subtle catheter injury, consistently produces proximal venous thrombosis in a baboon model.[228] In a similar fashion, the thrombogenic potential of hip arthroplasty derives from the combination of injury to the femoral vein, venous occlusion, and measurable activation of coagulation during placement of the femoral component.[193] The existence of a prethrombotic state prior to the precipitation of overt thrombosis is also well recognized.[7,159] Increased thrombin activity may precede the development of a positive duplex leg scan result in surgical patients by several days,[159] whereas thrombosis in patients with congenital thrombophilias is often precipitated by events such as injury, surgery, and pregnancy.[177]

Early Course

Against this pathophysiologic background, the factors contributing to clinically important thrombosis have been most thoroughly evaluated in the valve pockets of the lower extremity veins. In flow models, primary and secondary vortices are produced beyond the valve cusps, which tend to trap red cells in a low shear field near the apex of the cusp.[98] The early nidus for thrombus formation likely consists of red blood cell aggregates forming within these eddies; however, these aggregates are probably transient until stabilized by fibrin in the setting of locally activated coagulation. The further events in the evolution of these thrombi have been described by Sevitt[190,191] in a series of detailed histologic studies.

Once formed in the valve pocket, early thrombi may become adherent to the endothelium near the apex of the valve cusp. These valve pocket thrombi appear to form on structurally normal endothelium and largely to spare the valve cusp. Laminated appositional growth may then occur outward from the apex of the cusp, with propagation beyond the valve pocket probably depending on the relative balance between activated coagulation and thrombolysis. Once luminal flow is disturbed, prograde and retrograde propagation may occur.

Clinical symptoms, present in a minority of hospitalized patients, develop only when a sufficient fraction of the venous outflow is occluded. If present, such symptoms appear 24 to 36 hours after the first appearance of thrombus detectable by radioactive iodine (^{125}I)–fibrinogen scanning.[95] Conversely, early thrombi may fail to propagate, with evidence of aborted thrombi appearing as endothelialized fibrin fragments within the valve pockets.[190,191] A significant number of these early thrombi spontaneously resolve after serial ^{125}I-fibrinogen scanning.[42,94]

Table 147-1	Risk Factors for Acute Deep Venous Thrombosis (DVT) and Pulmonary Embolism (PE)	
RISK FACTOR FOR DVT OR PE	**ODDS RATIO**	**95% CONFIDENCE INTERVAL**
Hospitalization:		
With recent surgery	21.72	9.44-49.93
Without recent surgery	7.98	4.49-14.18
Trauma	12.69	4.06-39.66
Malignant neoplasm:		
With chemotherapy	6.53	2.11-20.23
Without chemotherapy	4.05	1.93-8.52
Prior central venous catheter or pacemaker	5.55	1.57-19.58
Prior superficial vein thrombosis	4.32	1.76-10.61
Neurologic disease with extremity paresis	3.04	1.25-7.38
Varicose veins:		
Age 45 yr	4.19	1.56-11.30
Age 60 yr	1.93	1.03-3.61
Age 75 yr	0.88	0.55-1.43
Congestive heart failure:		
Thromboembolism not categorized as a cause of death at postmortem	9.64	2.44-38.10
Thromboembolism categorized as a cause of death at postmortem	1.36	0.69-2.68

Adapted from Heit JA, Silverstein MD, Mohr DN, et al: Risk factors for deep vein thrombosis and pulmonary embolism: A population-based case-control study. Arch Intern Med. 160:809, 2000.

■ RISK FACTORS

DVT occurring in the setting of a recognized risk factor is often defined as *secondary*, whereas that occurring in the absence of risk factors is termed *primary* or *idiopathic*.[26] Recognized risk factors for DVT are listed in Table 147-1.

The high incidence of acute DVT in hospitalized patients, the availability of objective diagnostic tests, and the existence of clinical trials evaluating prophylactic measures have allowed identification of high-risk groups in this population. In contrast, the risk factors for acute DVT have been less well defined in population-based studies. Substantial differences, however, have been noted in the distribution of risk factors between inpatients and outpatients.[164] Malignancy, surgery, and trauma within the previous 3 months remain significant risk factors for outpatient thrombosis, whereas the frequency of surgery and malignancy is higher among inpatients with DVT.[26,157] Approximately 47% of outpatients with a documented DVT have one or more recognized risk factors[26]; the incidence of VTE increases along with the number of risk factors.[4] Although some investigators have found the risk of acute DVT to be significantly higher only for those with three or more risk factors,[157] others have reported the relative risk to increase progressively from 2.4 in those with one risk factor to more than 20 among subjects with three or more risk factors.[179] Heit and colleagues[239,240] identified the following independent risk factors for VTE: increasing age, male gender, surgery, trauma, hospital or nursing home confinement, malignancy, neurologic disease with extremity paresis, central venous catheter or transvenous pacemaker, prior superficial vein thrombosis, and varicose veins. Among women, risk factors include pregnancy, oral contraceptives, and hormone replacement therapy. Independent predictors for recurrent DVT, which occurs within 10 years in as many as 30% of cases, include increasing age, obesity, malignant neoplasm, and extremity paresis.

Age

VTE occurs in both the young and the elderly, although a higher incidence has consistently been associated with advanced age. Some investigators have identified precise cutoff points at which the risk of DVT is raised, whereas others have reported a progressive increase with advancing age. In a community-based study of phlebographically documented DVT, the yearly incidence of DVT was noted to increase progressively from almost 0 in childhood to 7.65 cases per 1000 in men and 8.22 cases per 1000 in women older than 80 years.[153] The incidence of DVT increased 30-fold from age 30 years to 80 or more years. Rosendaal[179] similarly noted an incidence of 0.006 per 1000 children younger than 14 years, which rose to 0.7 per 1000 among adults 40 to 54 years old, and Hansson and colleagues[72] found the prevalence of objectively documented thromboembolic events among men to increase from 0.5% at age 50 years to 3.8% at age 80 years.

The influence of age on the incidence of VTE is likely multifactorial. The number of thrombotic risk factors increases with age, three or more risk factors being present in only 3% of hospitalized patients younger than 40 years but in 30% of those 40 years and older.[4] Furthermore, it appears that the number of risk factors required to precipitate thrombosis decreases with age.[179] This possibility may be related to an acquired prethrombotic state associated with aging, because higher levels of thrombin activation markers are found among older people.[209] Advanced age also has been associated with anatomic changes in the soleal veins and with more pronounced stasis in the venous valve pockets.[61,129]

Venous diseases, including VTE, are usually regarded as rare in children younger than 10 years.[28] Population-based studies have suggested an incidence of 0.006 per 1000 children younger than 14 years,[179] whereas the incidence in hospitalized children younger than 18 years has been estimated to be 0.05%.[178] Early mobilization and discharge may partially explain the lower incidence in children.[178] The diagnosis, however, is often not considered in pediatric patients, and few studies have systematically evaluated children for DVT.

VTE in children is almost always associated with recognized thrombotic risk factors,[17,27,179,234] and multiple risk factors are often required to precipitate thrombosis.[179] Venous thrombosis is more common in some pediatric populations, such as children hospitalized in the intensive care unit, those with spinal cord injuries, and those undergoing prolonged orthopedic immobilization, although the incidence is substantially lower than in corresponding adult populations. DVT may occur in as many as 3.7% of pediatric patients immobilized in halo-femoral traction for preoperative treatment of scoliosis,[116] 4% of children

hospitalized in the intensive care unit,[37] and 10% of children with spinal cord injuries.[128,172] Symptomatic postoperative DVT is regarded as unusual in children, although there are few data from studies employing routine surveillance,[148] and autopsy-identified PE is approximately four times more frequent in pediatric patients who have undergone surgery than in the general pediatric medical population.[17] Other thrombotic risk factors noted in hospitalized children are local infection and trauma, immobilization,[234] inherited hypercoagulable states,[179] oral contraceptive use,[9] lower limb paresis,[116] and the use of femoral venous catheters.[37]

Immobilization

Many of the clinical circumstances in which thromboembolism occurs support the role of immobilization as a risk factor. Stasis in the soleal veins and behind the valve cusps is exacerbated by advancing age and inactivity of the calf muscle pump,[129] both of which are associated with an increased risk of DVT. The prevalence of lower extremity DVT in autopsy studies also parallels the duration of bed rest, with an increase during the first 3 days of confinement and a rapid rise to very high levels after 2 weeks. DVT was found in 15% of patients dying after 0 to 7 days of bed rest, in comparison with 79% to 94% of those dying after 2 to 12 weeks.[61] Preoperative immobilization is similarly associated with a twofold higher risk of postoperative DVT,[195] and DVT among stroke patients is significantly more common in paralyzed or paretic extremities (53% of limbs) than in nonparalyzed limbs (7%).[229] Patients with neurologic disease and extremity paresis or plegia have a threefold higher risk for DVT and PE that is independent of hospital confinement.[239]

Travel

Immobilization as a thrombotic risk factor has been extended now to include prolonged travel, particularly the "economy class syndrome," which occurs in people who have sat in a cramped position during extended aircraft flights.[32] Several case series have reported the occurrence of PE in relation to extended travel,[32,82,115,156,182,208] although none has rigorously examined the prevalence relative to the occurrence in the general population, and few have thoroughly reported the presence of coexisting risk factors. A high prevalence of preexisting venous disease and other thrombotic risk factors in this group of patients has sometimes been noted.[208,209] The questionable importance of prolonged travel is supported by observations that extreme degrees of venous stasis alone may fail to produce thrombosis[231] and that no consistent rheologic or prothrombotic changes have been demonstrated during prolonged travel.[113,209] However, the observation that PE is the second leading cause of travel-related death, accounting for 18% of 61 deaths, suggests that such a relationship cannot be excluded.[182] After a consensus meeting in 2001, the World Health Organization published the following conclusions[236]:

- An association probably exists between air travel and venous thrombosis.

- Such an association is likely to be small and mainly affects passengers with additional risk factors for VTE.
- Similar links may exist for other forms of travel.
- The available evidence does not permit an estimation of actual risk.

More evidence that establishes a connection between travel and DVT and PE has accumulated. In a case-control study, Ferrari and associates[237] found that long distance travel increased the risk of DVT with an odds ratio (OR) of 4.0, and Samama[246] made similar observations (OR 2.3). Scurr and colleagues[247] found a 10% risk of calf DVT in patients who traveled without compression stockings. Lapostolle and coworkers[243] observed that over an 86-month period, 56 of 135.3 million airline passengers had severe PE. The frequency among those who traveled more than 5000 km was 150 times as high as the frequency among those who traveled less than 5000 km. In another case-control study, Paganin and associates[245] observed a high incidence of VTE in patients with risk factors for DVT who traveled long distances. In particular, history of previous VTE (OR 63.3), recent trauma (OR 13.6), presence of varicose veins (OR 10), obesity (OR 9.6), immobility during flight (OR, 9.3), and cardiac disease (OR 8.9) increased the risk of DVT. These investigators concluded that low mobility during flight was a striking modifiable risk factor for development of PE and that travelers with risk factors should increase their mobility.

Hughes and colleagues[241] provided evidence that the frequency of VTE is increased even in travelers otherwise at low to moderate risk. In a prospective study that involved 878 long distance air travelers, the frequency of VTE was 1.0% (9/878; 95% confidence interval [CI], 0.5-1.9), which included four cases of PE and five of DVT. Two of the patients traveled in business class, five used aspirin, and four wore compression stockings. We agree with these researchers that traditional risk factors and prophylactic measures in air travel–related VTE need further investigation.

History of Venous Thromboembolism

Approximately 23% to 26% of patients presenting with acute DVT have a previous history of thrombosis,[153,164] and histologic studies confirm that acute thrombi are often associated with fibrous remnants of previous thrombi in the same or nearby veins.[189] Depending on sex and age, population-based studies have demonstrated that recurrent thromboembolism occurs in 1 of every 11 to 50 persons with a previous episode of thromboembolism.[28] The risk of recurrent thromboembolism is higher among patients with idiopathic DVT.[198] The relative importance of disordered venous hemodynamics, residual damage to the venous wall, and underlying abnormalities of the coagulation and fibrinolytic systems in recurrent thrombosis is unknown. However, primary hypercoagulability appears to have a significant role in many recurrences. Simioni and associates[198] reported the cumulative incidence of recurrent thrombosis among patients who are heterozygous for the factor V Leiden mutation to be 40% at 8 years of follow-up, 2.4-fold higher than in patients without the mutation.

Den Heijer and colleagues[38] estimated that 17% of recurrent thromboembolic events may be due to hyperhomocyst(e)inemia. A similar relationship between impaired fibrinolysis and recurrent DVT has been suggested by several investigators, although the methodologic validity of these findings has been questioned.[169]

Malignancy

A recognized malignancy is present in 19% to 30% of patients with DVT.[140,153,164] Approximately 15% of malignancies are complicated by VTE, with a substantially higher prevalence in autopsy studies.[50] An association between mucin-secreting gastrointestinal tumors and thrombosis has long been recognized. However, carcinoma of the lung is more prevalent and is now the most common tumor associated with VTE, accounting for one quarter of cases.[175] Although more than half the tumors underlying episodes of VTE are located in the genitourinary and gastrointestinal systems,[153] thrombosis has been reported to accompany a wide variety of malignancies. The frequency of any individual malignancy probably depends on referral patterns, treatment, and intensity of screening.

DVT may also herald a previously undetected malignancy in 3% to 23% of patients with idiopathic thrombosis.[29,140,167] In another 5% to 11% of patients, malignancy appears within 1 to 2 years of presentation for DVT.[152,153,167] Although small studies have reported no difference between patients in whom diagnostic studies confirm or exclude thromboembolism,[29,67] several other series have documented a significantly higher risk of malignancy in patients with idiopathic DVT. Among such patients, 7.6% have been noted to have a malignancy during follow-up, with an odds ratio of 2.3 in comparison with those with secondary thrombosis.[167] The incidence of occult malignancy diagnosed within 6 to 12 months of an idiopathic DVT is 2.2 to 5.3 times higher than that expected from general population estimates.[152,201] Recurrent idiopathic DVT is associated with a 9.8-fold higher risk than that for secondary thrombosis, a subsequent malignancy being identified in 17.1% of patients with the vascular disorder.[167]

The thrombogenic mechanisms associated with cancer may be heterogeneous, but likely they involve release of substances that directly or indirectly activate coagulation. Tissue factor and cancer procoagulant, a cysteine protease activator of factor X, are the primary tumor cell procoagulants; associated macrophages may also produce procoagulants as well as inflammatory cytokines.[49,176] As many as 90% of patients with cancer have abnormal coagulation parameters, including increased levels of coagulation factors, elevated fibrinogen or fibrin degradation products, and thrombocytosis.[48,50,176] Elevated fibrinogen values and thrombocytosis are the most common abnormalities, perhaps reflecting an overcompensated form of intravascular coagulation.[45,175] Levels of the coagulation inhibitors antithrombin, protein C, and protein S also may be reduced in malignancy.[176]

The clinical significance of these abnormalities is suggested by observations that markers of activated coagulation are elevated in the majority of patients with solid tumors and leukemia.[45,50,51,176] Fibrinopeptide A levels

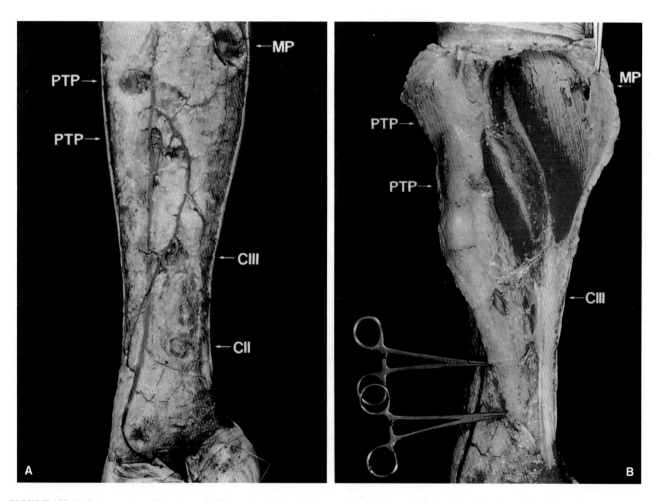

FIGURE 158-4 Corrosion cast of leg veins. **A,** Skin and a portion of subcutaneous fat were removed. **B,** Fascia has been incised and rolled anteriorly to expose the superficial posterior compartment. Note that only the lower paratibial perforator and Cockett III perforators are now accessible in the superficial posterior compartment. MP, muscle perforator; PTP, paratibial perforator; CII, Cockett II; CIII, Cockett III. (From Mozes G, Gloviczki P, Menawat SS, et al: Surgical anatomy for endoscopic subfascial division of perforating veins. J Vasc Surg 24:800-808, 1996.)

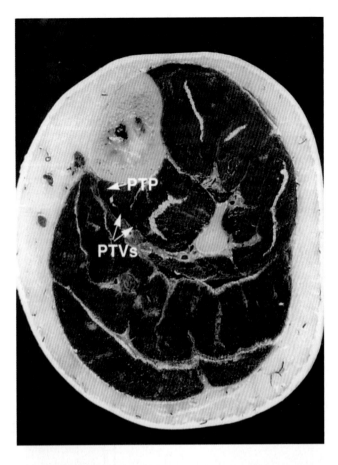

FIGURE 158-5 Cross section of the upper third of the leg. Note a paratibial perforating vein (PTP) passing between the periosteum of the tibia and the fascia of the superficial posterior compartment. Veins were filled with blue Latex. PTVs, posterior tibial veins. (From Mozes G, Gloviczki P, Menawat SS, et al: A surgical anatomy for endoscopic subfascial division of perforating veins. J Vasc Surg 24:800-808, 1996.)

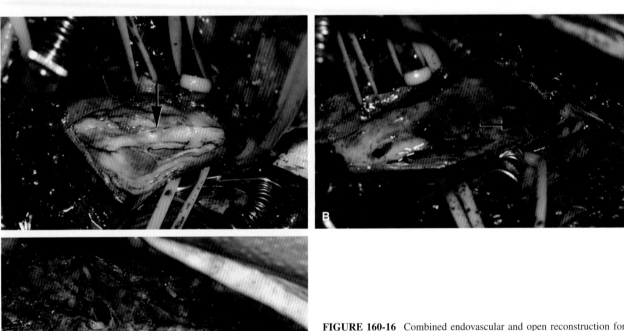

FIGURE 160-16 Combined endovascular and open reconstruction for chronic iliofemoral venous occlusion. **A,** Note old recanalized thrombus *(arrow)* in the common femoral vein. **B,** The old thrombus was excised and the iliofemoral vein was stented with Wallstents. **C,** The femoral vein was closed with bovine pericardial patch.

reflect tumor activity, decreasing or increasing in response to treatment or progression of disease, suggesting that tumor growth and thrombin generation are intimately related.[45,176] Furthermore, these levels may fail to normalize after administration of heparin to patients with cancer and DVT, perhaps explaining why their DVT may be refractory to anticoagulants.[175]

VTE is also associated with the treatment of some cancers. DVT complicates 29% of general surgical procedures for malignancy.[24] Preoperative activation of the coagulation system, as reflected by elevated thrombin-antithrombin complex values, is associated with a 7.5-fold greater risk of postoperative DVT.[48,51] Some chemotherapeutic regimens also predispose to DVT, and thrombotic complications may be as common as the more widely recognized infectious complications.[117] VTE has been reported in up to 6% of patients undergoing treatment for non-Hodgkin's lymphoma, in 17.5% of those receiving therapy for breast cancer, and in patients being treated for germ cell tumors.[40] Among patients with stage II breast cancer, thrombosis was significantly more common in those randomly assigned to 36 weeks of chemotherapy (8.8%) than in those receiving only 12 weeks of treatment (4.9%).[117] Potential thrombogenic mechanisms associated with chemotherapy include direct endothelial toxicity, induction of a hypercoagulable state, reduced fibrinolytic activity, tumor cell lysis, and use of central venous catheters.[25,40] Some intravenous chemotherapeutic agents are associated with activation of coagulation and increased markers of thrombin generation, a response that is blocked by pretreatment with heparin.[44]

Surgery

The high incidence of postoperative DVT, as well as the availability of easily repeatable, noninvasive diagnostic tests such as ^{125}I-labeled fibrinogen scanning, has allowed a greater understanding of the risk factors associated with surgery than in most other conditions. Surgery constitutes a spectrum of risk that is influenced by patient age, coexistent thrombotic risk factors, type of procedure, extent of surgical trauma, length of procedure, and duration of postoperative immobilization.[23,125] The type of surgical procedure is particularly important.[195] The overall incidence of DVT is approximately 19% in patients undergoing general surgical operations, 24% in those having elective neurosurgical procedures; and 48%, 51%, and 61% among those undergoing surgery for hip fracture, hip arthroplasty, and knee arthroplasty, respectively.[23] On the basis of these data, patients can be classified as being at low, moderate, or high risk for thromboembolic complications, as shown in Table 147-2.

Approximately half of postoperative lower extremity thrombi detected by ^{125}I-labeled fibrinogen scanning develop in the operating room, with the remainder occurring over the next 3 to 5 days.[95] However, the risk for development of DVT does not end uniformly at hospital discharge. In one study, 51% of the thromboembolic events occurring in patients undergoing gynecologic surgical procedures occurred after initial discharge.[122] Similarly, up to 25% of patients undergoing abdominal surgery have been noted to have DVT within 6 weeks of discharge.[187]

Heit and associates[238] found a nearly 22-fold higher risk of DVT and PE among patients who were hospitalized following previous surgery.

All components of Virchow's triad may be present in the surgical patient—perioperative immobilization, transient changes in coagulation and fibrinolysis, and the potential for gross venous injury, as exemplified by hip arthroplasty. Immobilization is associated with a reduction in venous outflow and capacitance during the early postoperative period.[218] Surgery is also accompanied by a transient, low-level hypercoagulable state, presumably mediated by the release of tissue factor, which is marked by a rise in thrombin activation markers shortly after the procedure begins.[96] The thrombogenic potential of surgical procedures appears to differ, with greater rises in thrombin activation markers during hip arthroplasty than after laparotomy.[193] Increased levels of plasminogen activator inhibitor-1 (PAI-1) are also associated with a decrease in fibrinolytic activity on the first postoperative day, the "postoperative fibrinolytic shutdown."[47,103] The relationship between impaired fibrinolysis and postoperative DVT may be particularly important,[169] with preoperative and early postoperative elevations in PAI-1 correlating with the development of thrombosis in orthopedic patients.[47]

Trauma

Despite improvements in trauma care and thromboembolism prophylaxis, DVT remains a significant source of morbidity and mortality in the injured patient. The prevalence of DVT among autopsied trauma casualties has been reported to be 62% to 65%,[71,192] comparable to the 58% incidence among injured patients in modern venographic series.[58] Substantially lower DVT rates, ranging from 4% to 20%,[19,105,106,146,183,219] have been noted in series employing duplex ultrasonography, although many patients were receiving prophylaxis and the limitations of ultrasound in screening asymptomatic patients are well recognized. Recent trauma was the second most common risk factor for thromboembolism in the Olmsted County study by Heit and associates,[238] being associated with nearly a 13-fold increase in risk.

Although the risk of DVT may be less than 20% in as few as 8% of injured patients,[58] certain subgroups are at particularly high risk. Age (OR 1.05 for each 1-year

CATEGORY	CHARACTERISTICS
Low	Age < 40 yr, no other risk factors, uncomplicated abdominal/thoracic surgery
	Age > 40 yr, no other risk factors, minor elective abdominal/thoracic surgery < 30 min
Moderate	Age > 40 yr, abdominal/thoracic surgery > 30 min
High	History of recent thromboembolism
	Abdominal or pelvic procedure for malignancy
	Major lower extremity orthopedic procedure

Table 147-2 Risk of Postoperative Deep Venous Thrombosis

From Hull RD, Raskob GE, Hirsh J: Prophylaxis of venous thromboembolism. Chest 89(Suppl):374S, 1986.

increment), blood transfusion (OR 1.74), surgery (OR 2.30), fracture of the femur or tibia (OR 4.82), and spinal cord injury (OR 8.59) have been significantly associated with the development of DVT in this population.[58] Other reported risk factors are a hospital stay longer than 7 days,[146] increased Injury Severity Score (ISS),[76,146] Trauma Injury Severity Score (TRISS) of 85 or less,[146] pelvic fractures,[106] major venous injury,[39,207] presence of femoral venous lines,[107] the duration of immobilization,[105,106,146] and prolongation of the partial thromboplastin time.[105]

As with postoperative DVT, several pathophysiologic elements may be responsible for the high incidence of DVT in trauma patients. Immobilization by skeletal fixation, paralysis, and critical illness are obviously associated with venous stasis, whereas mechanical injury is important after direct trauma and central venous cannulation. Less well appreciated is the hypercoagulable state after depletion of coagulation inhibitors and components of the fibrinolytic system. Fibrinopeptide A levels rise after injury,[56] consistent with activation of coagulation, whereas fibrinolytic activity has been found to increase initially and then decrease.[57,97]

Primary Hypercoagulable States

Primary hypercoagulable states represent discrete genetic mutation. They include inherited deficiencies of the naturally occurring anticoagulants antithrombin (antithrombin III), protein C, and protein S; resistance to activated protein C (APC); hyperhomocyst(e)inemia; and several potential defects in fibrinolysis. Overall, 42% to 46% of patients with a lower extremity DVT can be characterized as thrombophilic on this basis, and a positive family history is associated with a relative risk of 2.9 for VTE.[13,77] Most of the thrombotic events occurring in association with these disorders are venous in origin.[185] Although occasionally associated with thrombosis in unusual sites, hypercoagulable states appear to be less important as a risk factor for upper extremity thrombosis, with a prevalence (15%) similar to that in control populations.[78] Heterozygous protein C and protein S deficiencies have also been associated with warfarin (Coumadin)–induced skin necrosis.[145]

The natural anticoagulation systems, including antithrombin, the protein C system, and tissue factor pathway inhibitor, are the primary inhibitors of thrombin generation and activity.[145] Antithrombin inhibits thrombin as well as factors Xa, IXa, XIa, and XIIa, actions that are accelerated by heparin and heparin-like glycosaminoglycans on the endothelial surface. The protein C–protein S–thrombomodulin system is a negative feedback system initiated by the binding of thrombin to thrombomodulin at the endothelial surface, with subsequent activation of protein C and degradation of activated factors V and VIII. Factors Va and VIIIa function as critical cofactors for factors Xa and IXa, respectively, increasing their activity more than 1000-fold.[33] Protein S, approximately 60% of which is bound to C4b-binding protein, in its free form functions as a nonenzymatic cofactor of activated protein C. In addition to congenital deficiencies, acquired deficiencies of antithrombin, protein C, and protein S may accompany liver disease, the nephrotic syndrome, disseminated intravascular coagu-

lation (DIC), and chemotherapy with L-asparaginase.[145] Thrombotic tendencies caused by abnormalities of tissue factor pathway inhibitor have not yet been described.[185]

Primary deficiencies of the coagulation inhibitors antithrombin, protein C, and protein S are present in approximately 0.5% of healthy subjects.[233] Although these deficiencies are generally regarded as autosomal dominant traits, the observation that some heterozygotes are minimally affected but homozygotes have severe thrombotic manifestations suggests a recessive component in some types of protein C deficiency.[33] In aggregate, these three deficiencies may be associated with 5% to 10% of thrombotic events.[33] Patients with heterozygous deficiency states often present with a first thrombotic event before age 40 years, approximately 50% of such events being related to predisposing situations such as surgery or trauma.[63] Associated thrombotic episodes are often recurrent and may occur at unusual sites, such as in the mesenteric and cerebral veins.[123]

However, the phenotypic expression of these deficiencies may vary both within and between families. A multitude of mutations in the genes coding for these proteins may lead to either quantitative (type I) or qualitative (type II) deficiencies.[1] A type III protein S deficiency is further characterized by low levels of free protein S with normal total antigen levels.[33] Although approximately 50% of individuals with these deficiencies may have a history of venous thrombosis,[63,123] the frequency of thrombotic manifestations within different kindreds may range from 15% to 100% for antithrombin deficiency[185] and is less than 50% in some protein C–deficient families.[1,185] It has been hypothesized that multigene interactions may be partially responsible for such phenotypic variability.[185] The factor V Leiden mutation may be particularly important in this regard, with a higher frequency of thrombotic manifestations among the 9.5% to 19% of protein C heterozygotes who also carry this mutation.[1,123]

Resistance to activated protein C, characterized by the failure of exogenous activated protein C to prolong the activated partial thromboplastin time, was initially described in 1993. It is now recognized that a single-point mutation in the factor V gene, resulting in replacement of arginine 506 with glutamine (factor V Leiden; FV:R506Q), is present in 94% of individuals with activated protein C resistance.[10,33,123] Factor Va is inactivated by protein C–mediated cleavage at the Arg 306 and Arg 506 sites; this mutation thus renders factor Va less sensitive to degradation by activated protein C. The factor V Leiden mutation has an autosomal dominant mode of inheritance and is at least ten times more common than other inheritable defects.[33,109] The frequency of the mutation shows significant geographic variability, with 8.8% of Europeans being carriers.[174] Heterozygotes for the factor V Leiden mutation carry a fivefold to tenfold higher risk of thrombosis, which is an additional ten times higher in homozygotes.[33,123] Approximately 25% of individuals with the factor V Leiden mutation sustain a thrombosis by age 50 years, and the prevalence of activated protein C resistance among patients with DVT has varied from 10% to 65%.[185]

Several other primary coagulation disorders may also be associated with heritable thrombophilia. A recently identified point mutation at position 20210 in the prothrombin gene (G to A) has been associated with increased prothrombin levels and a thrombotic tendency. This mutation, present in 7.1% of patients with confirmed DVT and 1.8% of controls, carries a fourfold higher risk of DVT.[77] Although less clearly established than for arterial disease, hyperhomocyst(e)inemia may be related to VTE.[38,52]

Finally, several disorders of plasmin generation, including dysplasminogenemia, hypoplasminogenemia, decreased synthesis or release of t-PA, and increased PAI-1, have been associated with recurrent familial thromboembolism.[145,185] However, critical review of the literature has suggested that methodologic problems make this relationship inconclusive at present.[169]

Pregnancy

The frequency of VTE in young women has been noted to be higher than that in men, with half of first episodes in women younger than 40 years being associated with pregnancy.[28] Although the absolute numbers may be small, thromboembolism during pregnancy and the puerperium is associated with higher rates of preterm delivery and perinatal mortality,[217] whereas PE is second only to abortion as a cause of maternal mortality.[99] Population-based studies, often relying on clinical diagnosis, have suggested that VTE complicates 0.1% to 0.7% of pregnancies.[28,122,217] However, this incidence has been disputed, with studies that employ objective documentation of clinically suspected thromboembolism suggesting a lower incidence of 0.013% to 0.029%.[15,99] Recurrent thromboembolism may complicate 4% to 15% of subsequent pregnancies.[216]

Although the third trimester has often been associated with the greatest thrombotic risk,[216] some studies suggest that objectively documented thromboses are distributed among all three trimesters.[62] The risk of thrombosis appears to be two to three times greater during the puerperium, with a rate of 2.3 to 6.1 per 1000 deliveries.[179,217]

The inherited thrombophilias constitute an additional risk for pregnancy-associated thromboembolism,[160,179,216,222] complicating 4% of pregnancies in women with congenital anticoagulant deficiencies.[55] Anticoagulant factor deficiencies, lupus anticoagulant, or fibrinolytic deficiencies have been reported in 20% of patients with pregnancy-related thrombosis.[36] The factor V Leiden mutation may be particularly important in this regard, because resistance to activated protein C has been identified in up to 59% of patients with pregnancy-related thromboembolism.[74,81] The risk of puerperal DVT also increases with maternal age, suppression of lactation, hypertension, and assisted delivery but not with the number of pregnancies.[122,215,217]

DVT in pregnancy has been attributed to an acquired prethrombotic state in combination with impaired venous outflow due to uterine compression; 81% to 97% of documented thromboses have been isolated to the left leg.[36,62,216] A variety of coagulation factors, including fibrinogen and factors II, VII, VIII, and X, are increased during pregnancy.[8] Perhaps more important, protein S levels are decreased by 50% to 60% early during pregnancy, with free protein S levels comparable to those in hereditary heterozygous protein S deficiency.[2,124] Fibrinolytic activity has also been reported to diminish during pregnancy.[8]

Oral Contraceptives and Hormonal Therapy

As suggested by case reports in the early 1960s, case-control and population-based studies have now established the use of oral contraceptives as an independent risk factor for the development of DVT. Most studies have reported odds ratios of 3.8 to 11.0 for idiopathic thrombosis,[170,180,181,206] an unweighted summary relative risk among 18 controlled studies being 2.9.[110] Approximately one quarter of idiopathic thromboembolic events among women of childbearing age have been attributed to oral contraceptives.[181] The risk of hospital admission for a thromboembolic event, including cerebral thrombosis, has been estimated to be 0.4 to 0.6 per 1000 for oral contraceptive users, compared with 0.05 to 0.06 for non-users.[53,170,225] Early studies also suggested that thromboembolism is responsible for approximately 2% of deaths in young women, with contraceptive-associated mortality rates of 1.3 and 3.4 per 100,000 among women aged 20 to 34 and 35 to 44 years, respectively.[90] The increased risk of thromboembolism appears to diminish soon after oral contraceptives are discontinued and is independent of the duration of use.[66,68,158,170,181]

Risk is correspondingly higher when oral contraceptive use is combined with other factors, such as surgery[66] and inherited inhibitor deficiencies.[160] The factor V Leiden mutation may be particularly important in this regard; resistance to activated protein C has been reported in up to 30% of patients with contraceptive-associated thromboembolism.[74] The use of third-generation oral contraceptives may act synergistically with the factor V Leiden mutation, raising thromboembolic risk 30- to 50-fold.[13,75,221]

Thromboembolic risk may be related both to the dose of estrogen and the type of progestin in contraceptive preparations. Preparations containing less than 30 to 50 µg of estrogen are associated with less thrombotic risk; the relative risks of intermediate-dose (50 µg of estrogen) and high-dose (>50 µg of estrogen) contraceptives is 1.5 and 1.7 times, respectively, that of low-dose preparations (<50 µg of estrogen).[59,60] Although no clear dose-response relationship has been demonstrated for progestin potency and DVT, third-generation contraceptives containing the progestin desogestrel, norgestimate, or gestodene have been associated with a twofold higher risk of VTE than second-generation drugs.[75,221] The risk of VTE among users of third-generation oral contraceptives may be up to eight times that of young women who do not use oral contraceptives. However, the higher risk associated with third-generation progestins has been questioned based on the possible confounding effects of age and other prescribing biases.[53]

Estrogenic compounds also increase the risk of VTE when used for lactation suppression,[215] in treatment of carcinoma of the prostate, and as postmenopausal replacement therapy.[68] Although estrogen doses used for postmenopausal replacement therapy are approximately one sixth those in oral contraceptives, some data support an increased thromboembolic risk at these doses as well. Several studies have now reported a twofold to fourfold higher risk among women taking hormone replacement therapy.[35,68,92,162,223] This increased risk is greatest during the first year of treatment.[92,162,223] However, given the relative infrequency of thromboembolism, this risk represents only 1 or 2 additional cases of thromboembolism per year in every 10,000 women in this age group.

Estrogen in pharmacologic doses is associated with alterations in the coagulation system that may contribute to this thrombotic tendency. Such alterations include decreases in PAI-1[184] and increases in blood viscosity, fibrinogen, plasma levels of factors VII and X, and platelet adhesion and aggregation.[170,171,226] An associated prethrombotic state is implied by rises in markers of activated coagulation occurring in conjunction with elevations of circulating factor VIIa[171] and decreases in antithrombin and protein S inhibitor activity.[124,171,226,233] The extent to which antithrombin and protein S are depressed is significantly less with lower-estrogen preparations.[233]

Blood Group

There also appears to be a consistent relationship between thromboembolic risk and the ABO blood groups, with a higher prevalence of blood type A and correspondingly lower prevalence of blood type O among patients with thromboembolism. In comparison with the types in blood donors, deficits of type O have been noted in both Belgian and Swedish patients with DVT.[153,230] In reviewing the literature, Mourant and colleagues[144] similarly found the relative incidence of type A to be 1.41 times higher among patients with thromboembolism than among controls. The effect of blood type was greater in young women who were taking oral contraceptives or were pregnant; the relative incidence of type A among patients with thromboembolism was 3.12 in those taking oral contraceptives and 1.85 in those who were pregnant. Jick and colleagues[93] estimated the relative risk of thromboembolism among patients with type A blood in comparison with patients with type O to vary from 1.9 in medical patients to 3.2 in young women taking oral contraceptives. A relationship between soluble endothelial cell markers and ABO blood group is known to exist, with significantly lower levels of von Willebrand factor among those with type O blood.[12]

Geography and Ethnicity

There are also geographic differences in the frequency of VTE. The incidence of postoperative DVT in Europe has been noted to be approximately twice that in North America.[23,24] Higher rates of thromboembolism have also been noted in the interior United States than on either coast.[104] Autopsy series suggest that although the prevalence of thromboembolism is identical among American black and white patients, it is significantly higher than in a matched Ugandan black population.[213] A similar autopsy series noted the prevalence of thromboembolism to be 40.6% in Boston and 13.9% in Kyushu, Japan.[65]

Unfortunately, regional variations in underlying medical and surgical conditions as well as in prophylactic measures and diagnostic methods may confound any apparent differences in the incidence of thromboembolism among different ethnic groups. Nevertheless, it is certainly conceivable that true differences among ethnic groups might also arise from either genetic or environmental factors. Such differences seem likely on the basis of recognized geographic differences in the spectrum of mutations leading to congenital anticoagulant deficiencies.[1] Such theoretical concerns are also supported by geographic variability in the incidence of the factor V Leiden mutation. The factor V Leiden allele has a prevalence of 4.4% in Europeans, corresponding to a carrier rate of 8.8%, but the allele has not been identified in Southeast Asian or African populations.[174]

Central Venous Catheters

The use of central venous cannulation for hemodynamic monitoring, infusion catheters, and pacemakers has been associated with a rising frequency of DVT. This is particularly true for upper extremity thrombi, as many as 65% of which are related to central venous cannulation.[79] Although the incidence of symptomatic thrombosis may be low, studies employing objective surveillance have reported thrombosis to occur with a mean incidence of 28% after subclavian cannulation.[83] This risk also extends to femoral venous catheters; ipsilateral thrombosis develops in 12% of patients undergoing placement of large-bore catheters for trauma resuscitation.[137]

Experimental studies in rats suggest that the catheter itself, associated vascular injury, and stasis contribute to the development of early perigraft thrombus in virtually all cases.[235] Catheter material appears to be an important determinant of thromboembolism[131,142]; polytetrafluoroethylene (Teflon) and heparin-bonded catheters are associated with thrombosis in fewer than 10% of cases.[46] Other determinants of thrombosis are catheter diameter, number of venipuncture attempts, duration of catheter placement, and composition of the infusate.[83]

Heit and colleagues[238] found that current or recent placement of a central venous catheter and previous placement of a transvenous pacemaker were strongly associated with upper extremity DVT, with more than a 5-fold higher risk. Although the risk associated with central venous catheterization may reflect risk from co-morbid conditions, the investigators controlled the study for most conditions in which such catheters would probably be used.[238]

Inflammatory Bowel Disease

Clinical series have reported VTE to complicate inflammatory bowel disease (IBD) in 1.2% to 7.1% of cases.[91,108] Such thromboses frequently occur among young patients, are more common with active disease, and may affect unusual sites, such as the cerebral veins.[91,108] Although there are anecdotal reports of VTE in patients with IBD and primary hypercoagulable states, most cases are not associated with inherited inhibitor deficiencies, antiphospholipid antibodies, or the factor V Leiden mutation. The significance of thrombocytosis and elevations of factor V, VIII, and fibrinogen during active episodes of IBD is unclear, because all are acute-phase reactants.[108]

Other coagulation abnormalities, including depressed antithrombin values, elevated PAI-1 values, and presence of anticardiolipin antibodies, have been inconsistently reported.[224] However, fibrinopeptide A elevations in IBD suggest that active inflammation is associated with activation of coagulation, possibly mediated by endotoxin-induced monocyte activation.[108,224]

Systemic Lupus Erythematosus

The syndrome of arterial and venous thrombosis, recurrent abortion, thrombocytopenia, and neurologic disease may complicate systemic lupus erythematosus (SLE) when accompanied by the presence of antiphospholipid antibodies.[84] Lupus anticoagulant and anticardiolipin antibodies may be seen in association with SLE; with other autoimmune disorders; with non-autoimmune disorders, such as syphilis and acute infection, with drugs, including chlorpromazine, procainamide, and hydralazine; and with great age.[121]

Lupus anticoagulant is present in 34% of patients with SLE, and anticardiolipin antibodies in 44%, in comparison with 2% and 0% to 7.5%, respectively, of the general population.[121] Among patients with SLE, those with lupus anticoagulant are at a sixfold higher risk for VTE, whereas those with anticardiolipin antibodies are at a twofold greater risk.[227] The incidence of arterial or venous thrombosis is 25% in patients with lupus anticoagulant and 28% in patients with anticardiolipin antibodies.[121] The relationship between antiphospholipid antibodies and thrombosis is much less clear in non-SLE disorders.

Varicose Veins and Superficial Thrombophlebitis

Varicose veins have also been included as a risk factor for acute DVT, frequently only as a marker of either previous DVT or venous stasis.[149] Most studies evaluating thrombotic risk have been performed in inpatients with other major risk factors for DVT. Such studies have inconsistently supported varicose veins as a risk factor in postoperative DVT and after stroke or myocardial infarction.[127,149,180,229] The importance of varicose veins in otherwise healthy outpatients has been questioned by some researchers.[20] Varicose veins were not identified as independent risk factor for DVT in a study of young women.[225] The few studies evaluating outpatients have suggested that varicose veins are either not a risk factor for DVT[26] or are an independent risk factor only among women and patients older than 65 years.[157] Consistent with this observation, some studies of postmenopausal women have reported varicose veins or superficial thrombophlebitis to be associated with odds ratios of 3.6 to 6.9 for the development of thromboembolism.[162,223]

Heit and associates[238] found, however, that varicose veins were independent predictors of DVT. These investigators also confirmed that age is an important factor in these patients, reporting a higher correlation between DVT and varicosity in young patients. For example, 45-year-old patients with varicose veins had a fourfold higher risk of VTE, 60-year-old patients had a twofold greater risk, and 75-year-old patients had no increase in risk. This group also found that patients with previous superficial vein thrombosis were more than four times more likely to have DVT or PE.[238]

Other Risk Factors

Traditional risk factors for VTE have included obesity and cardiac disease; however, the evidence supporting these risk factors remains equivocal at present. Among postmenopausal women, a body mass index of greater than 25 to 30 kg/m^2 has been associated with a significantly increased risk,[92,162] although obesity has not proved uniformly to be an independent risk factor in high-risk situations. Some investigators have reported obesity to be associated with a twofold greater risk for postoperative DVT,[95] although multifactorial analysis by others has not shown obesity to constitute an independent risk.[149] Obesity (and past tobacco smoking) was not an independent risk factor of DVT in the Olmsted County study[238] and has not been proved to be a risk factor for the development of DVT after stroke.[229] Obesity has been a risk factor, however, for recurrent DVT.[239,240]

Systemic hypercoagulability, congestive heart failure, and enforced bed rest theoretically may predispose patients who are hospitalized with acute myocardial infarction to DVT. The incidence of DVT in this population has been reported to be 20% to 40%, with an overall average of 24%.[23,111,127] Some investigators have noted the incidence of DVT to be higher among patients in whom myocardial infarction was confirmed (34%) than in those in whom the diagnosis was excluded (7%). However, other researchers[151] have found a high incidence of ^{125}I-fibrinogen scanning–detected thrombosis both among patients with myocardial infarction (38%) and among those with other severe illnesses but without confirmed infarction (62%). The prevalence of PE among autopsied patients has also not differed substantially from that in other patients dying while hospitalized.[65,213]

Although Kotilainen and colleagues[111] found the incidence of DVT to be similar in patients in whom myocardial infarction was confirmed (21%) and excluded (25%), a substantially higher incidence was noted among those older than 60 years with congestive heart failure (54%), a finding that has been confirmed by others.[199] However, the evidence supporting congestive heart failure as an independent risk factor for DVT is also conflicting. A variety of thromboembolic complications account for nearly half the deaths among patients who did not undergo anticoagulation after hospitalization for congestive heart failure, but congestive heart failure has not been identified as an independent risk factor for postoperative DVT.[195] The balance of evidence suggests that severely ill medical patients are at significant risk for VTE,[80] although it is difficult to define precisely the additional risk associated with cardiac disease in these patients.

■ NATURAL HISTORY

Histologic Evolution

Although venous thrombi were once regarded as relatively static structures that changed little over time, it is now clear that they undergo a dynamic evolution beginning soon after their formation. The venous lumen is most often re-established after a thrombotic event, although the factors responsible for this re-establishment and the nomenclature to be employed remain the subject of debate. Often referred to interchangeably as *recanalization* or *spontaneous lysis*, this is a complex series of both cellular and humoral processes. Animal models afford an opportunity for serial evaluation of the histologic evolution of a thrombus, although artifacts introduced by a variety of injuries or generation in a static column of blood may limit correlation with the event as observed in humans.

Disappearance and early regeneration of the underlying endothelium has been reported for some experimental models,[154,200] whereas other workers have reported the endothelium to remain intact.[186] In either case, this endothelium or neoendothelium appears to be fibrinolytically active, with clearing of the thrombus–vein wall interface within 4 days.[154] At this time, small, endothelium-lined clefts become visible between the thrombus and vein wall.[54,186] As in the initial stages of thrombosis, white blood cells appear to be intimately involved in the process of recanalization.

An early neutrophil infiltrate is largely replaced by monocytes within 6 days of thrombosis.[43] This progressive monocyte infiltration is accompanied by early signs of organization at the vein wall interface as well as an increase in tissue-type plasminogen activator (t-PA) and urokinase-type plasminogen activator (u-PA) activity within the thrombus.[155] Although t-PA activity within distal vein walls also rises soon after thrombosis, the greatest t-PA activity is associated with the infiltrating monocytes rather than with the luminal endothelium.[155,200] Thrombolysis is marked by a progressive thinning and loss of fibrin strands, with disappearance of red blood cells.[196] Complete resolution of experimental thrombi in the rat, leaving only an endothelialized subintimal streak, is observed within 21 days.[155] Rapid recanalization of experimental thrombi has been also observed in other animal models.[54,186]

Although precise aging and serial histologic evaluation of human thrombi are difficult, the lesions appear to follow a similar course. Thrombus organization begins in the attachment zone, with the infiltration of fibroblasts, monocytes, and capillary sprouts and the migration of surfacing cells over the thrombus.[30,189,190] These migrating endothelial cells have previously been regarded as important in recanalization, with endothelium-derived t-PA causing the activation of thrombus-bound plasminogen and contributing to peripheral fragmentation of the thrombus.[188] However, the animal models described earlier raise questions about the relative importance of monocytes and the endothelium as sources of plasminogen activator. Furthermore, the degree to which recanalization depends on cell-mediated local thrombolysis, versus systemic thrombolysis, has not been completely defined. Although changes in systemic t-PA levels have been observed to parallel the resolution of thrombus, rising 1 to 2 weeks after presentation and

returning to baseline within 24 to 36 weeks, these levels are not clearly related to the extent of thrombus resolution.[101]

Regardless of the mechanism, progressively enlarging pockets are formed between the thrombus and vein wall through a combination of fibrinolysis, thrombus retraction, and peripheral fragmentation.[189] These pockets are lined by flat cells, presumably derived from the endothelium, which invade the thrombus and may initiate organization and fragmentation in unattached zones.[188,190] The primary factor limiting the extent of recanalization may be the extent of fibrous anchoring to the vein wall.[188] Although the most common outcome is a restored venous lumen with fibroelastic intimal thickening at the site of initial thrombus attachment, residual fibrous synechiae are present in 3% to 11% of specimens.[188]

Thrombus Evolution as Determined by Noninvasive Studies

Unlike in animal models employing a transient stimulus to thrombosis, the relative balance between organization, thrombolysis, propagation, and rethrombosis determines outcome after human thrombosis. From a clinical perspective, the most important events after thrombosis are recanalization and recurrent thrombosis. However, the relative importance, frequency, and rate of these processes were not possible to define until the development of noninvasive technology that permitted serial examinations of patients.

Impedance plethysmography was the first widely available noninvasive test permitting serial evaluations of venous outflow obstruction due to an acute DVT. Although this test could not distinguish between recanalization and the development of collateral venous outflow, results of such studies were found to normalize in 67% of patients by 3 months and in 92% of patients by 9 months.[85] Venous duplex ultrasonography, which permits individual venous segments to be observed over time, has further documented that recanalization does occur in most patients after an episode of acute DVT. In 21 patients monitored prospectively with duplex scanning, recanalization was evident in 44% of patients at 7 days and in 100% of patients by 90 days after the acute event.[100] The percentage of initially involved segments that remained occluded decreased to a mean of 44% by 30 days and 14% by 90 days (Fig. 147-1).

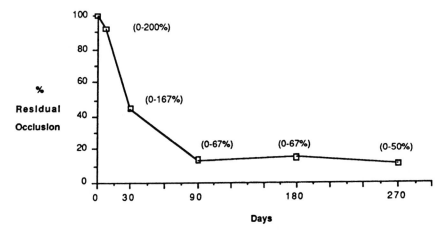

FIGURE 147-1 Mean percentage of initially occluded segments remaining occluded at follow-up among 21 patients with acute deep venous thrombosis (percentage residual occlusion = number of segments occluded at follow-up ÷ number of segments occluded at presentation). Numbers in parentheses are the ranges for individual cases, with numbers greater than 100% indicating extension of the initial thrombus. (From Killewich LA, Bedford GR, Beach KW, et al: Spontaneous lysis of deep venous thrombi: Rate and outcome. J Vasc Surg 9:89, 1989.)

Van Ramshorst and associates[220] similarly noted an exponential decrease in thrombus load over the first 6 months after femoropopliteal thrombosis. Most recanalization occurred within the first 6 weeks, with flow re-established in 87% of 23 completely occluded segments during this interval. Killewich and colleagues[101] reported a linear decrease in thrombus load by which at 24 to 36 weeks, only 26% of the original thrombus remained. Using a somewhat different approach, measuring thrombus thickness when maximally compressed, Prandoni and coworkers[165] noted the most significant reduction in thrombus mass over the first 3 months after thrombosis—62% in the common femoral vein and 50% in the popliteal vein. In aggregate, these studies confirm the histologic findings that recanalization begins early after an episode of acute DVT, with the greatest reduction in thrombus load occurring within 3 months of the event. Complete thrombus resolution has been reported in 56% of patients monitored for 9 months.[101] However, recanalization may continue, albeit at a slower rate, for months to years after the acute event.[126,165]

Recurrent thrombotic events appear to compete with recanalization early after an acute DVT. The importance of such events is well recognized clinically, although their frequency in patients studied prospectively has only recently been described. Most clinical studies have included both recurrent DVT and PE, with rates depending on treatment, location of thrombus, and duration of follow-up. Among patients with proximal DVT, recurrent thromboembolic events have been reported in 5.2% of patients who were treated with standard anticoagulation measures for 3 months,[88] compared with 47% of patients who were inadequately treated with a 3-month course of low-dose subcutaneous heparin.[87] Proximal propagation may also complicate isolated calf vein thrombosis in up to 23% of untreated patients.[163]

Despite the significance of these observations, studies employing serial noninvasive follow-up examinations suggest that these studies may underestimate the incidence of new thrombotic events. In the acute setting, Krupski and colleagues[112] found ultrasonographic evidence of proximal propagation in 38% of 24 patients being treated with intravenous heparin. In a larger series of 177 patients, most of whom were treated with standard anticoagulation measures, recurrent thrombotic events were observed in 52% of patients.[133] New thrombi were observed in 6% of uninvolved contralateral extremities, whereas propagation of thrombi to new segments occurred in 30% of involved limbs and rethrombosis of a partially occluded or recanalized segment in 31% of extremities. Propagation to new segments in the ipsilateral limb tended to occur as an early event at a median of less than 40 days after presentation, whereas rethrombosis and extension to the contralateral limb tended to occur sporadically as later events.

■ COMPLICATIONS

Pulmonary Embolism

Pulmonary embolism, with its attendant mortality, is the most devastating complication of acute DVT. Inadequate treatment of proximal lower extremity venous thrombosis is associated with a 20% to 50% risk of clinically significant

recurrent thromboembolism,[173] with approximately 90% of thromboemboli arising from the lower extremity veins.[63,89] Symptomatic PE may also complicate 7% to 17% of proximal upper extremity thrombi.[21,41,78,79,83] As for acute DVT, the majority of pulmonary emboli may be clinically silent. High-probability lung scan results may be obtained in 25% to 51% of patients with documented DVT in the absence of pulmonary symptoms,[86,139] and some autopsy series have reported the combination of PE and DVT to be 1.8 times more common than proximal DVT alone.[118] The presence of symptomatic PE may depend not only on the amount of the pulmonary circulation occluded but also on the patients' underlying cardiopulmonary reserve.

Unfortunately, estimates of the prevalence of symptomatic PE are less reliable, because the diagnosis is difficult to establish ante mortem.[180] Rates reported from studies of autopsied and hospitalized patients are probably overestimates and are significantly influenced by the detail of dissection, whereas community-based studies that exclude chronically and seriously ill individuals may yield underestimates. Extrapolation from autopsy studies—PE causes or contributes to approximately 15% of hospital deaths—suggests that 150,000 to 200,000 deaths per year occur from PE in the United States.[27,34] In contrast, community-based studies have suggested a lower prevalence, 64,000 cases per year in the United States.[28] Combining autopsy data and a number of observations concerning the natural history of PE, Dalen and Alpert[34] calculated an incidence of 630,000 episodes of symptomatic PE per year.

Death occurs within 1 hour of presentation in 11% of patients with symptomatic PE, and in 30% of those surviving 1 hour but in whom the diagnosis of PE is not made.[34] The 1-week survival rate after a PE is only 71%, and almost 25% of all cases of PE essentially manifest as sudden death.[238] Mortality among patients with an appropriate diagnosis and treatment has been reported to be only 8% to 9%. Among the survivors, early resolution of abnormal lung scans has been documented in several series employing routine follow-up studies.[86] Chronic cor pulmonale is rare after PE, generally occurring after repeated, often silent, emboli.[34]

The Post-thrombotic Syndrome

Although less dramatic than PE, development of the post-thrombotic syndrome is responsible for a greater degree of chronic socioeconomic morbidity. Data regarding the prevalence of the post-thrombotic syndrome may be more accurate than those for PE, which are largely derived from hospitalized patients.[27] As many as 29% to 79% of patients may have long-term manifestations, such as pain, edema, hyperpigmentation, or ulceration, after an episode of acute DVT.[119,168,205] Coon and associates[28] have estimated that severe post-thrombotic changes are present in 5% of the U.S. population, corresponding to a prevalence of between 6 and 7 million individuals with stasis changes and 400,000 to 500,000 with leg ulcers.

Severe manifestations of the post-thrombotic syndrome are a consequence of ambulatory venous hypertension, which is determined by a number of factors, including valvular reflux, persistent venous obstruction, and the anatomic distribution of these abnormalities. The pathophysiology and natural history of chronic venous insufficiency are reviewed

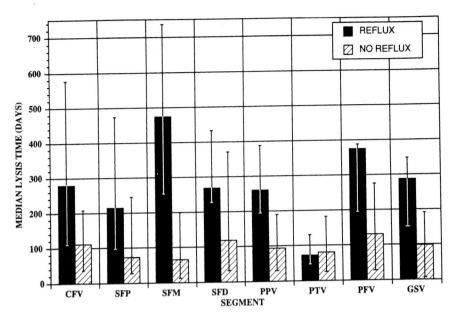

FIGURE 147-2 Median time (± interquartile range) from thrombosis to complete recanalization, stratified according to ultimate reflux status. Median times are 2.3 to 7.3 times longer among segments in which reflux developed, in all but the posterior tibial veins. CFV, common femoral vein; GSV, greater saphenous vein; PFV, profunda femoris vein; PPV, popliteal vein; PTV, posterior tibial vein; SFD, superficial femoral vein; SFM, midsuperficial femoral vein; SFP, proximal superficial femoral vein. (From Meissner MH, Manzo RA, Bergelin RO, et al: Deep venous insufficiency: The relationship between lysis and subsequent reflux. J Vasc Surg 18:596, 1993.)

in Chapter 144. However, despite the importance of valvular reflux in post-thrombotic sequelae, valvular destruction does not appear to be universally associated with recanalization, and as many as one third of patients may remain free of chronic symptoms after an episode of acute DVT. Only 69% of involved extremities and 33% to 59% of initially thrombosed segments show evidence of reflux on duplex ultrasonography 1 year after the event.[126]

Such clinical observations are supported by histologic evidence that thrombus organization rarely involves the valve cusps. In most cases, the thrombus is separated from the valve cusp by a clear zone postulated to arise from the local fibrinolytic activity of the valvular endothelium.[64,188,190] This protective mechanism appears to fail in approximately 10% of cases in which thrombus adherence to the valve cusp is noted.[188,190] Initial thrombus adherence presumably accounts for the histologic findings in established post-

thrombotic syndrome; approximately 50% of popliteal valves in such extremities demonstrate thrombus formation on the valve leaflets, usually on the surface facing the valve sinus, with associated loss of the endothelium and basement membrane.[18]

Most investigators have not found a clear relationship between the extent of thrombus on initial presentation and ultimate clinical outcome.[16,73,134,141,166] However, several factors in the early natural history of a thrombotic event do appear to influence the ultimate development of valvular incompetence and eventual post-thrombotic manifestations. The rate of recanalization and recurrent thrombotic events appear to be important determinants of valvular competence. Depending on the segment involved, venous segments developing reflux have been noted to require 2.3 to 7.3 times longer for complete recanalization than segments in which valve function is preserved (Fig. 147-2).[135]

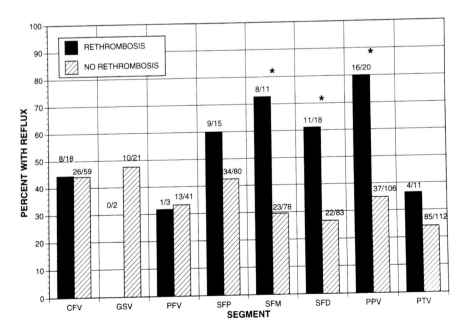

FIGURE 147-3 Reflux incidence in initially involved venous segments with and without subsequent rethrombosis. Numbers above *bars* indicate the number of segments in which reflux was observed divided by the number of segments in which reflux could be definitively assessed. Differences between segments with and without rethrombosis are statistically significant (*P < .005) for the midsuperficial femoral vein (SFM), distal superficial femoral vein (SFD), and popliteal vein (PPV) segments. CFV, common femoral vein; GSV, greater saphenous vein; PFV, profunda femoris vein; PTV, posterior tibial vein; SFP, proximal superficial femoral vein. (From Meissner MH, Caps MT, Bergelin RO, et al: Propagation, rethrombosis and new thrombus formation after acute deep venous thrombosis. J Vasc Surg 22:558, 1995.)

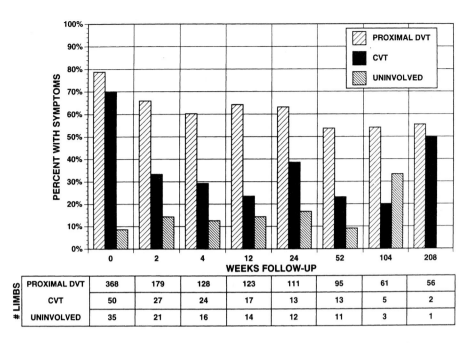

FIGURE 147-4 Prevalence of symptoms (edema, pain, hyperpigmentation, or ulceration) during follow-up among extremities with proximal deep venous thrombosis, extremities with isolated calf vein thrombosis (CVT), and uninvolved limbs contralateral to a calf vein thrombosis. The prevalence of symptoms in the three groups is significantly different at 12 months ($P = .004$). The table shows the total number of extremities within each group evaluated at each follow-up interval. (From Meissner MH, Caps MT, Bergelin RO, et al: Early outcome after isolated calf vein thrombosis. J Vasc Surg 26:749, 1997.)

Recurrent thrombotic events are also detrimental to valve competence. Reflux may develop in 36% to 73% of segments with rethrombosis, a rate considerably higher than that in segments without rethrombosis (Fig. 147-3).[133] Consistent with these observations, Prandoni and associates[166] have noted a sixfold higher risk of post-thrombotic syndrome among patients with recurrent thrombosis.

In a 25-year population-based retrospective cohort study, Mohr and coworkers[244] found chronic venous insufficiency developed in 245 of 1527 patients with DVT or PE; 1-year, 5-year, 10-year, and 20-year cumulative incidence rates were 7.3%, 14.3%, 19.7%, and 26.8%, respectively.[244] By 20 years, the cumulative incidence of venous ulcers was 3.7%. In patients 40 years or younger, venous stasis syndrome was 3.0-fold more likely in those with proximal DVT than in those with distal-only DVT (95% confidence interval, 1.6-fold to 4.7-fold). This study was important to confirm that the cumulative incidence of venous stasis syndrome continues to rise for 20 years after VTE.

Mortality After Acute Deep Venous Thrombosis

DVT is associated with a high frequency of co-morbid medical conditions, and the rate of early death after a lower extremity thrombosis is substantial. Piccioli and coworkers[164] noted a 3-month mortality rate of 19%, with no deaths due to PE. Kniffen and colleagues[104] reported a similar mortality (21%) during the first year after an acute DVT but noted that the survival curve after 1 year parallels that of an age-, sex-, and race-matched population. Higher short-term mortality rates have been seen in patients with upper extremity DVT, who tend to be more ill, with an increased prevalence of metastatic malignancy.[78,214] Six-month mortality may be as high as 48% among patients with upper extremity DVT, compared with 13% in those with a lower extremity thrombosis.[78]

■ CALF VEIN THROMBOSIS

Thrombosis isolated to the deep veins of the calf is often differentiated from that involving the proximal veins because of perceived differences in the associated rates of PE and post-thrombotic complications. Noninvasive studies do suggest that such isolated thrombi recanalize more rapidly than proximal thrombi,[135] with a mean 50% reduction in thrombus load by 1 month and complete recanalization within 1 year.[132] The frequency of reflux in involved calf vein segments is also lower than in proximal venous segments.[135] However, propagation to more proximal segments also occurs in 15% to 23% of limbs with thrombosis confined to the calf veins.[94,114,120,132] In a review of the subject, Kearon[242] found that in the absence of treatment, about one fourth to one third of symptomatic, isolated calf vein thrombosis extend to involve the proximal veins.

Clinical data suggest that although the incidence of acute and long-term complications may be less than after proximal venous thrombosis, isolated calf vein thrombi are not entirely benign. Although prior embolization of more proximal thrombus cannot be excluded, concurrent PE has been noted in approximately 10% of patients with calf vein thrombosis when clinical suspicion is supplemented by objective tests,[132,136,161] and in up to 33% of patients in series employing routine ventilation-perfusion lung scans.[102,143] Even if clinically significant emboli are presumed to arise only from proximal thrombus extension, a 20% rate of proximal propagation in untreated calf vein thrombosis theoretically would be associated with a 2% risk of fatal PE and a 5% to 10% risk of symptomatic recurrent thromboembolism.[173]

Although perhaps less common than after proximal thrombosis, post-thrombotic symptoms may also complicate isolated calf vein thrombosis. Persistent symptoms of pain and swelling at 1 year have been noted in 23% of extremities with calf vein thrombosis, compared with 54% of those with proximal thrombosis and 9% of uninvolved limbs

(Fig. 147-4).[132] In contrast, Prandoni and colleagues[168] found the rates of mild (21%) and severe (5%) post-thrombotic sequelae 45 months after the acute event to be similar among patients with isolated calf and proximal venous thromboses. Other researchers have reported post-thrombotic symptoms in 38% of patients after a mean follow-up of 3.4 years[130] and 47% after 5 to 10 years.[119]

■ REFERENCES

1. Aiach M, Gandrille S, Emmerich J: A review of mutations causing deficiencies of antithrombin, protein C, and protein S. Thromb Haemost 74:81, 1995.

2. Alving BM, Comp PC: Recent advances in understanding clotting and evaluating patients with recurrent thrombosis. Am J Obstet Gynecol 167:1184, 1992.

3. Amiral J, Fareed J: Thromboembolic diseases: Biochemical mechanisms and new possibilities of biological diagnosis. Semin Thromb Hemost 22(Suppl 1):41, 1996.

4. Anderson FA, Wheeler HB, Goldberg RJ, et al: The prevalence of risk factors for venous thromboembolism among hospital patients. Arch Intern Med 152:1660, 1992.

5. Aronson DL, Thomas DP: Experimental studies on venous thrombosis: Effect of coagulants, procoagulants and vessel contusion. Thromb Haemost 54:866, 1985.

6. Barnes RW, Wu KK, Hoak JC: Fallibility of the clinical diagnosis of venous thrombosis. JAMA 234:605, 1975.

7. Bauer KA, Rosenberg RD: The pathophysiology of the prethrombotic state in humans: Insights gained from studies using markers of hemostatic system activation. Blood 70:343, 1987.

8. Beller FK, Ebert C: The coagulation and fibrinolytic enzyme system in pregnancy and the puerperium. Eur J Obstet Gynecol Reprod Biol 13:177, 1982.

9. Bernstein D, Coupey S, Schonberg SK: Pulmonary embolism in adolescents. Am J Dis Child 140:667, 1986.

10. Bertina RM, Koeleman BPC, Koster T, et al: Mutation in blood coagulation factor V associated with resistance to activated protein C. Nature 369:64, 1994.

11. Biland L, Widmer LK: Varicose veins (VV) and chronic venous insufficiency (CVI): Medical and socioeconomic aspects: Basle study. Acta Chir Scand (Suppl) 544:9, 1988.

12. Blann AD, Daly RJ, Amiral J: The influence of age, gender, and ABO blood group on soluble endothelial cell markers and adhesion markers. Br J Haematol 92:498, 1996.

13. Bloemenkamp KWM, Rosendaal FR, Helmerhorst FM, et al: Enhancement by factor V Leiden mutation of risk of deep-vein thrombosis associated with oral contraceptives containing a third generation progestagen. Lancet 346:1593, 1995.

14. Breddin HK: Thrombosis and Virchow's triad: What is established? Semin Thromb Hemost 15:237, 1989.

15. Brickner LA, Scannell KA, Ackerson L: Pregnancy-related thromboembolism [letter]. Ann Intern Med 127:164, 1997.

16. Browse NL, Clemenson G, Thomas ML: Is the postphlebitic leg always postphlebitic? Relation between phlebographic appearances of deep-vein thrombosis and late sequelae. Br Med J 281(6249):1167, 1980.

17. Buck JR, Connors RH, Coon WW, et al: Pulmonary embolism in children. J Pediatr Surg 16:385, 1981.

18. Budd TW, Meenaghan MA, Wirth J, et al: Histopathology of veins and venous valves of patients with venous insufficiency syndrome: Ultrastructure. J Med 21:181, 1990.

19. Burns GA, Cohn SM, Frumento RJ, et al: Prospective ultrasound evaluation of venous thrombosis in high-risk trauma patients. J Trauma 35:405, 1993.

20. Campbell B: Thrombosis, phlebitis, and varicose veins. Br Med J 312:198, 1996.

21. Campbell CB, Chandler JG, Tegtmeyer CJ, et al: Axillary, subclavian, and brachiocephalic obstruction. Surgery 82:816, 1977.

22. Carter CJ, Anderson FA, Wheeler HB: Epidemiology and pathophysiology of venous thromboembolism. In Hull RD, Raskob GE, Pineo GF (eds): Venous Thromboembolism: An Evidence-based Atlas. Armonk, NY, Futura, 1996, p 3.

23. Clagett GP, Anderson FA, Heit J, et al: Prevention of venous thromboembolism. Chest 108(Suppl):312S, 1995.

24. Clagett GP, Reisch JS: Prevention of venous thromboembolism in general surgical patients: Results of meta-analysis. Ann Surg 208:277, 1988.

25. Clarke CS, Otridge BW, Carney DN: Thromboembolism: A complication of weekly chemotherapy in the treatment of non-Hodgkin's lymphoma. Cancer 66:2027, 1990.

26. Cogo A, Bernardi E, Prandoni P, et al: Acquired risk factors for deep-vein thrombosis in symptomatic outpatients. Arch Intern Med 154:164, 1994.

27. Coon WW: Epidemiology of venous thromboembolism. Ann Surg 186:149, 1977.

28. Coon WW, Willis PW, Keller JB: Venous thromboembolism and other venous disease in the Tecumseh Community Health Study. Circulation 48:839, 1973.

29. Cornuz J, Pearson SD, Creager MA, et al: Importance of findings on the initial evaluation for cancer in patients with symptomatic idiopathic DVT. Ann Intern Med 125:785, 1996.

30. Cox JST: The maturation and canalization of thrombi. Surg Gynecol Obstet 116:593, 1963.

31. Cranley JJ, Canos AJ, Sull WJ: The diagnosis of deep venous thrombosis: Fallibility of clinical symptoms and signs. Arch Surg 111:34, 1976.

32. Cruickshank JM, Gorlin R, Jennett B: Air travel and thrombotic episodes: The economy class syndrome. Lancet 2(8609):497, 1988.

33. Dahlback B: Inherited thrombophilia: Resistance to activated protein C as a pathogenic factor of venous thromboembolism. Blood 85:607, 1995.

34. Dalen JE, Alpert JS: Natural history of pulmonary embolism. Prog Cardiovasc Dis 17:259, 1975.

35. Daly E, Vessey MP, Hawkins MM, et al: Risk of venous thromboembolism in users of hormone replacement therapy. Lancet 348:977, 1996.

36. de Boer K, Buller HR, ten Cate JW, et al: Deep vein thrombosis in obstetric patients: Diagnosis and risk factors. Thromb Haemost 67:4, 1992.

37. DeAngelis GA, McIlhenny J, Willson DF, et al: Prevalence of deep venous thrombosis in the lower extremities of children in the intensive care unit. Pediatr Radiol 26:821, 1996.

38. den Heijer M, Blom HJ, Gerrits WB, et al: Is hyperhomocysteinaemia a risk factor for recurrent venous thrombosis? Lancet 345:882, 1995.

39. Dennis JW, Menawat S, Von Thron J, et al: Efficacy of deep venous thrombosis prophylaxis in trauma patients and identification of high-risk groups. J Trauma 35:132, 1993.

40. Doll DC, Ringenberg QS, Yarbro JW: Vascular toxicity associated with antineoplastic agents. J Clin Oncol 4:1405, 1986.

41. Donayre CE, White GH, Mehringer SM, et al: Pathogenesis determines late morbidity of axillosubclavian vein thrombosis. Am J Surg 152:179, 1986.

42. Doouss TW: The clinical significance of venous thrombosis of the calf. Br J Surg 63:377, 1976.

43. Downing LJ, Streiter RM, Kadell AM, et al: Neutrophils are the initial cell type identified in deep venous thrombosis-induced vein wall inflammation. ASAIO J 42:M677, 1996.

44. Edwards RL, Klaus M, Matthews E, et al: Heparin abolishes the chemotherapy-induced increase in plasma fibrinopeptide A levels. Am J Med 89:25, 1990.

45. Edwards RL, Rickles FR, Moritz TE, et al: Abnormalities of blood coagulation tests in patients with cancer. Am J Clin Pathol 88:596, 1987.

46. Efsing HO, Lindblad B, Mark J, et al: Thromboembolic complications from central venous catheters: A comparison of three catheter materials. World J Surg 7:419, 1983.

47. Eriksson BI, Eriksson E, Risberg B: Impaired fibrinolysis and post-operative thromboembolism in orthopedic patients. Thromb Res 62:55, 1991.

48. Falanga A, Barbui T, Rickles FR, et al: Guidelines for clotting studies in cancer patients. For the Scientific and Standardization Committee of the Subcommittee on Haemostasis and Malignancy, International Society of Thrombosis and Haemostasis. Thromb Haemost 70:540, 1993.

49. Falanga A, Gordon SG: Isolation and characterization of cancer procoagulant: A cysteine proteinase from malignant tissue. Biochemistry 24:5558, 1985.

50. Falanga A, Ofosu FA, Oldani E, et al: The hypercoagulable state in cancer patients: Evidence for impaired thrombin inhibitions. Blood Coagul Fibrinolysis 5(Suppl 1):S19, 1994.

51. Falanga A, Ofosu FA, Cortelazzo S, et al: Preliminary study to identify cancer patients at high risk of venous thrombosis following major surgery. Br J Haematol 85:745, 1993.

52. Falcon CR, Cattaneo M, Panzeri D, et al: High prevalence of hyperhomocyst(e)inemia in patients with juvenile venous thrombosis. Arterioscler Thromb 14:1080, 1994.

53. Farmer RD, Lawrenson RA, Thompson CR, et al: Population-based study of risk of venous thromboembolism associated with various oral contraceptives. Lancet 349:83, 1997.

54. Flanc C: An experimental study of the recanalization of arterial and venous thrombi. Br J Surg 55:519, 1968.

55. Friederich PW, Sanson B-J, Simioni P, et al: Frequency of pregnancy-related venous thromboembolism in anticoagulant factor-deficient women: Implications for prophylaxis. Ann Intern Med 125:955, 1996.

56. Gando S, Tedo I, Kubota M: Posttrauma coagulation and fibrinolysis. Crit Care Med 20:594, 1992.

57. Garcia Frade LJ, Landin L, Avello AG, et al: Changes in fibrinolysis in the intensive care patient. Thromb Res 47:593, 1987.

58. Geerts WH, Code KI, Jay RM, et al: A prospective study of venous thromboembolism after major trauma. N Engl J Med 331:1601, 1994.

59. Gerstman BB, Piper JM, Freiman JP, et al: Oral contraceptive oestrogen and progestin potencies and the incidence of deep venous thromboembolism. Int J Epidemiol 19:931, 1990.

60. Gerstman BB, Piper JM, Tomita DK, et al: Oral contraceptive estrogen dose and the risk of deep venous thromboembolic disease. Am J Epidemiol 133:32, 1991.

61. Gibbs NM: Venous thrombosis of the lower limbs with particular reference to bed rest. Br J Surg 45:209, 1957.

62. Ginsberg JS, Brill-Edwards PB, Burrows RF, et al: Venous thrombosis during pregnancy: Leg and trimester of presentation. Thromb Haemost 67:519, 1992.

63. Girolami A, Prandoni P, Simioni P, et al: The pathogenesis of venous thromboembolism. Haematologica 80(Suppl):25, 1995.

64. Glas-Greenwalt P, Dalton BC, Astrup T: Localization of tissue plasminogen activator in relation to morphological changes in human saphenous veins used as coronary artery bypass autografts. Ann Surg 181:431, 1975.

65. Gore I, Hirst AE: Myocardial infarction and thromboembolism. Arch Intern Med 113:323, 1964.

66. Greene GR, Sartwell PE: Oral contraceptive use in patients with thromboembolism following surgery, trauma, or infection. Am J Public Health 62:680, 1972.

67. Griffin MR, Stanson AW, Brown ML, et al: Deep venous thrombosis and pulmonary embolism: Risk of subsequent malignant neoplasms. Arch Intern Med 147:1907, 1987.

68. Grodstein F, Stampfer MJ, Manson JE, et al: Prospective study of exogenous hormones and risk of pulmonary embolism in women. Lancet 348:983, 1996.

69. Haeger K: Problems of acute deep venous thrombosis. Angiology 20:219, 1969.

70. Hamer JD, Malone PC, Silver IA: The PO$_2$ in venous valve pockets: Its possible bearing on thrombogenesis. Br J Surg 68:166, 1981.

71. Hamilton T, Angevine D: Fatal pulmonary embolism in 100 battle casualties. Mil Surg 99:450, 1946.

72. Hansson PO, Welin L, Tibblin G, et al: Deep vein thrombosis and pulmonary embolism in the general population:'The Study of Men Born in 1913.' Arch Intern Med 157:1665, 1997.

73. Heldal M, Seem E, Sandset PM, et al: Deep vein thrombosis: A 7-year follow-up study. J Intern Med 234:71, 1993.

74. Hellgren M, Svensson PJ, Dahlback B: Resistance to activated protein C as a basis for venous thromboembolism associated with pregnancy and oral contraceptives. Am J Obstet Gynecol 173:210, 1995.

75. Helmerhorst FM, Bloemkamp KWM, Rosendaal FR, et al: Oral contraceptives and thrombotic disease: Risk of venous thromboembolism. Thromb Haemost 78:327, 1997.

76. Hill SL, Berry RE, Ruiz AJ: Deep venous thrombosis in the trauma patient. Am Surg 60:405, 1994.

77. Hillarp A, Zoller B, Svensson PJ, et al: The 20210 A allele of the prothrombin gene is a common risk factor among Swedish outpatients with verified deep venous thrombosis. Thromb Haemost 78:990, 1997.

78. Hingorani A, Ascher E, Hanson J, et al: Upper extremity versus lower extremity deep venous thrombosis. Am J Surg 174:214, 1997.

79. Hingorani A, Ascher E, Lorenson E, et al: Upper extremity deep venous thrombosis and its impact on morbidity and mortality rates in a hospital-based population. J Vasc Surg 26:853, 1997.

80. Hirsch D, Ingenito E, Goldhaber S: Prevalence of deep venous thrombosis among patients in medical intensive care. JAMA 274:335, 1995.

81. Hirsch DR, Mikkola KM, Marks PW, et al: Pulmonary embolism and deep venous thrombosis during pregnancy or oral contraceptive use: Prevalence of factor V Leiden. Am Heart J 131:1145, 1996.

82. Homans J: Thrombosis of the deep leg veins due to prolonged sitting. N Engl J Med 250:148, 1954.

83. Horattas MC, Wright DJ, Fenton AH, et al: Changing concepts of deep venous thrombosis of the upper extremity: Report of a series and review of the literature. Surgery 104:561, 1988.

84. Hughes GR, Harris NN, Gharavi AE: The anticardiolipin syndrome. J Rheumatol 13:486, 1986.

85. Huisman MV, Buller HR, ten Cate JW: Utility of impedance plethysmography in the diagnosis of recurrent deep-vein thrombosis. Arch Intern Med 148:681, 1988.

86. Huisman MV, Buller HR, ten Cate JW, et al: Unexpected high prevalence of silent pulmonary embolism in patients with deep venous thrombosis. Chest 95:498, 1989.

87. Hull R, Delmore T, Genton E, et al: Warfarin sodium versus low-dose heparin in the treatment of venous thrombosis. N Engl J Med 301:855, 1979.

88. Hull RD, Raskob GE, Hirsch J, et al: Continuous intravenous heparin compared with intermittent subcutaneous heparin in the initial treatment of proximal-vein thrombosis. N Engl J Med 315:1109, 1986.

89. Hull RD, Raskob GE, Hirsh J: Prophylaxis of venous thromboembolism: An overview. Chest 89(Suppl):374S, 1986.

90. Inman WHW, Vessey MP: Investigation of deaths from pulmonary, coronary, and cerebral thrombosis and embolism in women of child-bearing age. Br Med J 2(599):193, 1968.

91. Jackson LM, O'Gorman PJ, O'Connell J, et al: Thrombosis in inflammatory bowel disease: Clinical setting, procoagulant profile and factor V Leiden. Q J Med 90:183, 1997.

92. Jick H, Derby LE, Myers MW, et al: Risk of hospital admission for idiopathic venous thromboembolism among users of postmenopausal oestrogens. Lancet 348:981, 1996.

93. Jick H, Westerholm B, Vessey MP, et al: Venous thromboembolic disease and ABO blood type. Lancet 1(7594):539, 1969.

94. Kakkar VV, Flanc C, Howe CT, et al: Natural history of post-operative deep-vein thrombosis. Lancet 2(7614):230, 1969.

95. Kakkar VV, Howe CT, Nicolaides AN, et al: Deep vein thrombosis of the leg: Is there a "high risk" group? Am J Surg 120:527, 1970.

96. Kambayashi J, Sakon M, Yokota M, et al: Activation of coagulation and fibrinolysis during surgery, analyzed by molecular markers. Thromb Res 60:157, 1990.

97. Kapsch DN, Metzler M, Harrington M, et al: Fibrinolytic response to trauma. Surgery 95:473, 1984.

98. Karino T, Motomiya M: Flow through a venous valve and its implications for thrombus formation. Thromb Res 36:245, 1984.

99. Kierkegaard A: Incidence and diagnosis of deep vein thrombosis associated with pregnancy. Acta Obstet Gynecol Scand 62:239, 1983.

100. Killewich LA, Bedford GR, Beach KW, et al: Spontaneous lysis of deep venous thrombi: Rate and outcome. J Vasc Surg 9:89, 1989.

101. Killewich LA, Macko RF, Cox K, et al: Regression of proximal deep venous thrombosis is associated with fibrinolytic enhancement. J Vasc Surg 26:861, 1997.

102. Kistner R, Ball J, Nordyke R, et al: Incidence of pulmonary embolism in the course of thrombophlebitis of the lower extremities. Am J Surg 124:169, 1972.

103. Kluft C, Verheijen JH, Jie AFH, et al: The post-operative fibrinolytic shutdown: A rapidly reverting acute phase pattern for the fast-acting inhibitor of tissue-type plasminogen activator after trauma. Scand J Clin Lab Invest 45:605, 1985.

104. Kniffen WD, Baron JA, Barrett J, et al: The epidemiology of diagnosed pulmonary embolism and deep venous thrombosis in the elderly. Arch Intern Med 154:861, 1994.

105. Knudson MM, Collins JA, Goodman SB, et al: Thromboembolism following multiple trauma. J Trauma 32:2, 1992.

106. Knudson MM, Lewis FR, Clinton A, et al: Prevention of venous thromboembolism in trauma patients. J Trauma 37:480, 1994.

107. Knudson MM, Morabito D, Paiement GD, et al: Use of low molecular weight heparin in preventing thromboembolism in trauma patients. J Trauma 41:446, 1996.

108. Koenigs KP, McPhedran P, Spiro HM: Thrombosis in inflammatory bowel disease. J Clin Gastroenterol 9:627, 1987.

109. Koster T, Rosendaal FR, Briet E, et al: Venous thrombosis due to poor anticoagulant response to activated protein C: Leiden thrombophilia study. Lancet 342:1503, 1993.

110. Koster T, Small R-A, Rosendaal FR, et al: Oral contraceptives and venous thromboembolism: A quantitative discussion of the uncertainties. J Intern Med 238:31, 1995.

111. Kotilainen M, Ristola P, Ikkala E, et al: Leg vein thrombosis diagnosed by ^{125}I-fibrinogen test after acute myocardial infarction. Ann Clin Res 5:365, 1973.

112. Krupski WC, Bass A, Dilley RB, et al: Propagation of deep venous thrombosis by duplex ultrasonography. J Vasc Surg 12:467, 1990.

113. Landgraf H, Vanselow B, Schulte-Huermann D, et al: Economy class syndrome: Rheology, fluid balance, and lower leg edema during a simulated 12-hour long distance flight. Aviat Space Environ Med 65:930, 1994.

114. Lagerstedt CI, Olsson C, Fagher BO, et al: Need for long-term anticoagulant treatment in symptomatic calf vein thrombosis. Lancet 2(8454):515, 1985.

115. Lederman JA, Keshavarzian A: Acute pulmonary embolism following air travel. Postgrad Med J 59:104, 1983.

116. Leslie IJ, Dorgan JC, Bentley G, et al: A prospective study of deep vein thrombosis of the leg in children on halo-femoral traction. J Bone Joint Surg [Br] 63:168, 1981.

117. Levine MN, Gent M, Hirsh J, et al: The thrombogenic effect of anticancer drug therapy in women with stage II breast cancer. N Engl J Med 318:404, 1988.

118. Lindblad B, Sternby NH, Bergqvist D: Incidence of venous thromboembolism verified by necropsy over 30 years. Br Med J 302:709, 1991.

119. Lindner D, Edwards J, Phinney E, et al: Long-term hemodynamic and clinical sequelae of lower extremity deep vein thrombosis. J Vasc Surg 4:436, 1986.

120. Lohr J, Kerr T, Lutter K, et al: Lower extremity calf thrombosis: To treat or not to treat? J Vasc Surg 14:618, 1991.

121. Love PE, Santoro SA: Antiphospholipid antibodies: Anticardiolipin and the lupus anticoagulant in systemic lupus erythematosus (SLE) and in non-SLE disorders. Ann Intern Med 112:682, 1990.

122. Macklon NS, Greer IA: Venous thromboembolic disease in obstetrics and gynaecology: The Scottish experience. Scot Med J 41:83, 1996.

123. Makris M, Rosendaal FR, Preston FE: Familial thrombophilia: Genetic risk factors and management. J Intern Med 242(Suppl 740):9, 1997.

124. Malm J, Laurell M, Dahlback B: Changes in plasma levels of vitamin K-dependent proteins C and S and of C4b-binding protein during pregnancy and oral contraception. Br J Haematol 68:437, 1988.

125. Mammen EF: Pathogenesis of venous thrombosis. Chest 102(Suppl): 640S, 1992.

126. Markel A, Manzo RA, Bergelin RO, et al: Valvular reflux after deep vein thrombosis: Incidence and time of occurrence. J Vasc Surg 15:377, 1992.

127. Maurer BJ, Wray R, Shillingford JP: Frequency of venous thrombosis after myocardial infarction. Lancet 2(7739):1385, 1971.

128. McBride WJ, Gadowski GR, Keller MS, et al: Pulmonary embolism in pediatric trauma patients. J Trauma 37:913, 1994.

129. McLachlin AD, McLachlin JA, Jory TA, et al: Venous stasis in the lower extremities. Ann Surg 152:678, 1960.

130. McLafferty R, Moneta G, Passman M, et al: Late clinical and hemodynamic sequelae of isolated calf vein thrombosis. J Vasc Surg 27:50, 1998.

131. McLean Ross AH, Griffith CDM, Anderson JR, et al: Thromboembolic complications with silicone elastomer subclavian catheters. J Parenter Enteral Nutr 6:61, 1982.

132. Meissner MH, Caps MT, Bergelin RO, et al: Early outcome after isolated calf vein thrombosis. J Vasc Surg 26:749, 1997.

133. Meissner MH, Caps MT, Bergelin RO, et al: Propagation, rethrombosis, and new thrombus formation after acute deep venous thrombosis. J Vasc Surg 22:558, 1995.

134. Meissner MH, Caps MT, Zierler BK, et al: Determinants of chronic venous disease after acute deep venous thrombosis. J Vasc Surg 28:826, 1998.

135. Meissner MH, Manzo RA, Bergelin RO, et al: Deep venous insufficiency: The relationship between lysis and subsequent reflux. J Vasc Surg 18:596, 1993.

136. Menzoin J, Sequeira J, Doyle J, et al: Therapeutic and clinical course of deep venous thrombosis. Am J Surg 146:581, 1983.

137. Meredith JW, Young JS, O'Neil EA, et al: Femoral catheters and deep venous thrombosis: A prospective evaluation with venous duplex sonography. J Trauma 35:187, 1993.

138. Merton RE, Hockley D, Gray EP, et al: The effect of interleukin 1 on venous endothelium—an ultrastructural study. Thromb Haemost 66:725, 1991.

139. Monreal M, Barroso R-J, Ruiz Manzano J, et al: Asymptomatic pulmonary embolism in patients with deep vein thrombosis: Is it useful to take a lung scan to rule out this condition? J Cardiovasc Surg 30:104, 1989.

140. Monreal M, Lafoz E, Casals A, et al: Occult cancer in patients with deep venous thrombosis: A systematic approach. Cancer 67:541, 1991.

141. Monreal M, Martorell A, Callejas J, et al: Venographic assessment of deep vein thrombosis and risk of developing post-thrombotic syndrome: A prospective trial. J Intern Med 233:233, 1993.

142. Monreal M, Raventos A, Lerma R, et al: Pulmonary embolism in patients with upper extremity DVT associated to venous central lines—a prospective study. Thromb Haemost 72:548, 1994.

143. Moreno-Cabral R, Kistner R, Nordyke R: Importance of calf vein thrombophlebitis. Surgery 80:735, 1976.

144. Mourant AE, Kopec AC, Domaniewska-Sobczak K: Blood groups and blood clotting. Lancet 1(7692):223, 1971.

145. Nachman RL, Silverstein R: Hypercoagulable states. Ann Intern Med 119:819, 1993.

146. Napolitano LM, Garlapati VS, Heard SO, et al: Asymptomatic deep venous thrombosis in the trauma patient: Is an aggressive screening protocol justified? J Trauma 39:651, 1995.

147. Nawroth PP, Handley DA, Esmon CT, et al: Interleukin 1 induces endothelial cell procoagulant while suppressing cell-surface anticoagulant activity. Proc Natl Acad Sci U S A 83:3460, 1986.

148. Nguyen LT, Laberge JM, Guttman FMA: Spontaneous deep vein thrombosis in childhood and adolescence. J Pediatr Surg 21:640, 1986.

149. Nicolaides AN, Irving D: Clinical factors and the risk of deep venous thrombosis. In Nicolaides AN (ed): Thromboembolism: Aetiology, Advances in Prevention and Management. Lancaster, UK, MTP Press, 1975.

150. Nicolaides AN, Kakkar VV, Field ES, et al: The origin of deep vein thrombosis: A venographic study. Br J Radiol 44:653, 1971.

151. Nicolaides AN, Kakkar VV, Renney JTG, et al: Myocardial infarction and deep venous thrombosis. Br Med J 1(746):432, 1971.

152. Nordstrom M, Lindblad B, Anderson H, et al: Deep venous thrombosis and occult malignancy: An epidemiological study. Br Med J 308(6933):891, 1994.

153. Nordstrom M, Lindblad B, Bergqvist D, et al: A prospective study of the incidence of deep-vein thrombosis within a defined urban population. J Intern Med 232:155, 1992.

154. Northeast AD, Burnand KG: The response of the vessel wall to thrombosis: The in vivo study of venous thrombolysis. Ann N Y Acad Sci 667:127, 1992.

155. Northeast AD, Soo KS, Bobrow LG, et al: The tissue plasminogen activator and urokinase response in vivo during natural resolution of venous thrombus. J Vasc Surg 22:573, 1995.

156. Anonymous: Thromboembolism and air travel [letter]. Lancet 2(8614): 797, 1988.

157. Oger E, Leroyer C, Le Moigne E, et al: The value of risk factor analysis in clinically suspected deep venous thrombosis. Respiration 64:326, 1997.

158. Olivieri O, Friso S, Manzato F, et al: Resistance to activated protein C, associated with oral contraceptive use: Effect of formulations, duration of assumption, and doses of oestro-progestins. Contraception 54:149, 1996.

159. Owen J, Kvam D, Nossel HL, et al: Thrombin and plasmin activity and platelet activation in the development of venous thrombosis. Blood 61:476, 1983.

160. Pabinger I, Schneider B, Inhibitors GS, Go N: Thrombotic risk of women with hereditary antithrombin III-, protein C-, and protein S-deficiency taking oral contraceptive medication. Thromb Haemost 71:548, 1994.

161. Passman M, Moneta G, Taylor L, et al: Pulmonary embolism is associated with the combination of isolated calf vein thrombosis and respiratory symptoms. J Vasc Surg 25:39, 1997.

162. Perez Gutthann S, Garcia Rodriguez LA, Castellsague J, et al: Hormone replacement therapy and risk of venous thromboembolism: Population based case-control study. Br Med J 314:796, 1997.

163. Philbrick JT, Becker DM: Calf deep venous thrombosis: A wolf in sheep's clothing? Arch Intern Med 148:2131, 1988.

164. Piccioli A, Prandoni P, Goldhaber SZ: Epidemiologic characteristics, management, and outcome of deep venous thrombosis in a tertiary-care hospital: The Brigham and Women's Hospital DVT Registry. Am Heart J 132:1010, 1996.

165. Prandoni P, Cogo A, Bernardi E, et al: A simple ultrasound approach for detection of recurrent proximal vein thrombosis. Circulation 88:1730, 1993.

166. Prandoni P, Lensing A, Cogo A, et al: The long-term clinical course of acute deep venous thrombosis. Ann Intern Med 125:1, 1996.

167. Prandoni P, Lensing AW, Buller HR, et al: Deep-vein thrombosis and the incidence of subsequent symptomatic cancer. N Engl J Med 327:1128, 1992.

168. Prandoni P, Villalta S, Polistena P, et al: Symptomatic deep-vein thrombosis and the post-thrombotic syndrome. Haematologica 80(Suppl):42, 1995.

169. Prins MH, Hirsch J: A critical review of the evidence supporting a relationship between impaired fibrinolytic activity and venous thromboembolism. Arch Intern Med 15:1721, 1991.

170. Oral contraceptive use and venous thromboembolic disease, surgically confirmed gall-bladder disease, and breast tumors. Boston Collaborative Drug Surveillance Program. Lancet 1(7817):1399, 1973.

171. Quehenberger P, Loner U, Kapiotis S, et al: Increased levels of activated factor VII and decreased plasma protein S activity and circu-lating thrombomodulin during use of oral contraceptives. Thromb Haemost 76:729, 1996.

172. Radecki RT, Gaebler-Spira D: Deep vein thrombosis in the disabled pediatric population. Arch Phys Med Rehabil 75:248, 1994.

173. Raskob G: Calf-vein thrombosis. In Hull RD, Raskob GE, Pineo GF (eds): Venous Thromboembolism: An Evidence-based Atlas. Armonk, NY, Futura, 1996, p 307.

174. Rees DC, Cox M, Clegg JB: World distribution of factor V Leiden. Lancet 346:1133, 1995.

175. Rickles FR, Edwards RL: Activation of blood coagulation in cancer: Trousseau's syndrome revisited. Blood 62:14, 1983.

176. Rickles FR, Levine M, Edwards RL: Hemostatic alterations in cancer patients. Cancer Metast Rev 11:237, 1992.

177. Ridker PM, Glynn RJ, Miletich JP, et al: Age-specific incidence rates of venous thromboembolism among heterozygous carriers of factor V Leiden mutation. Ann Intern Med 126:528, 1997.

178. Rohrer MJ, Cutler BS, MacDougall E, et al: A prospective study of the incidence of deep venous thrombosis in hospitalized children. J Vasc Surg 24:46, 1996.

179. Rosendaal FR: Thrombosis in the young: Epidemiology and risk factors: A focus on venous thrombosis. Thromb Haemost 78:1, 1997.

180. Salzman EW, Hirsh J: The epidemiology, pathogenesis, and natural history of venous thrombosis. In Colman RW, Hirsh J, Marder VJ, Salzman EW (eds): Hemostasis and Thrombosis: Basic Principles and Clinical Practice, 3rd ed. Philadelphia, JB Lippincott, 1994, p 1275.

181. Sartwell PE, Masi AT, Arthes FG, et al: Thromboembolism and oral contraceptives: An epidemiologic case-control study. Am J Epidemiol 90:365, 1969.

182. Sarvesvaran R: Sudden natural deaths associated with commercial air travel. Med Sci Law 26:35, 1986.

183. Satiani B, Falcone R, Shook L, et al: Screening for major deep vein thrombosis in seriously injured patients: A prospective study. Ann Vasc Surg 11:626, 1997.

184. Scarabin P-Y, Plu-Bureau G, Zitoun D, et al: Changes in haemostatic variables induced by oral contraceptives containing 50 µg or 30 µg oestrogen: Absence of dose-dependent effect of PAI-1 activity. Thromb Haemost 74:928, 1995.

185. Schafer AI: Hypercoagulable states: Molecular genetics to clinical practice. Lancet 344:1739, 1994.

186. Scott GBD: A quantitative study of the fate of occlusive red venous thrombi. Br J Exp Pathol 49:544, 1968.

187. Scurr JH: How long after surgery does the risk of thromboembolism persist? Acta Chir Scand Suppl 556:22, 1990.

188. Sevitt S: The mechanisms of canalisation in deep vein thrombosis. J Pathol 110:153, 1973.

189. Sevitt S: The vascularisation of deep-vein thrombi and their fibrous residue: A post-mortem angiographic study. J Pathol 111:1, 1973.

190. Sevitt S: Organization of valve pocket thrombi and the anomalies of double thrombi and valve cusp involvement. Br J Surg 61:641, 1974.

191. Sevitt S: The structure and growth of valve-pocket thrombi in femoral veins. J Clin Pathol 27:517, 1974.

192. Sevitt S, Gallagher N: Venous thrombosis and pulmonary embolism: A clinico-pathological study in injured and burned victims. Br J Surg 48:475, 1961.

193. Sharrock NE, Go G, Harpel PC, et al: The John Charnley Award: Thrombogenesis during total hip arthroplasty. Clin Orthop 319:16, 1995.

194. Shreeniwas R, Koga S, Karakurum M, et al: Hypoxia-mediated induction of endothelial cell interleukin-1α: An autocrine mechanism promoting expression of leukocyte adhesion molecules on the vessel surface. J Clin Invest 90:2333, 1992.

195. Sigel B, Ipsen J, Felix WR: The epidemiology of lower extremity deep venous thrombosis in surgical patients. Ann Surg 179:278, 1974.

196. Sigel B, Swami V, Can A, et al: Intimal hyperplasia producing thrombus organization in an experimental venous thrombosis model. J Vasc Surg 19:350, 1994.

197. Silva MDC: Chronic venous insufficiency of the lower limbs and its socio-economic significance. Int Angiol 10:152, 1991.

198. Simioni P, Prandoni P, Lensing AW, et al: The risk of recurrent venous thromboembolism in patients with an Arg506→Gln mutation in the gene for factor V (factor V Leiden). N Engl J Med 336:399, 1997.

199. Simmons AV, Sheppard MA, Cox AF: Deep venous thrombosis after myocardial infarction: Predisposing factors. Br Heart J 35:623, 1973.

200. Soo KS, Northeast AD, Happerfield LC, et al: Tissue plasminogen activator production by monocytes in venous thrombolysis. J Pathol 178:190, 1996.

201. Sorensen HT, Mellemkjaer L, Steffensen FH, et al: The risk of a diagnosis of cancer after primary deep venous thrombosis or pulmonary embolism. N Engl J Med 338:1169, 1998.

202. Stamatakis JD, Kakkar VV, Sagar S, et al: Femoral vein thrombosis and total hip replacement. Br J Med 2(6081):223, 1977.

203. Stewart GJ: Neutrophils and deep venous thrombosis. Haemostasis 23(Suppl 1):127, 1993.

204. Stewart GJ, Stern HS, Lynch PR, et al: Responses of canine jugular veins and carotid arteries to hysterectomy: Increased permeability and leukocyte adhesions and invasion. Thromb Res 20:473, 1980.

205. Strandness DE, Langlois Y, Cramer M, et al: Long-term sequelae of acute venous thrombosis. JAMA 250:1289, 1983.

206. Strolley PD, Tonascia JA, Tockman MS, et al: Thrombosis with low-estrogen oral contraceptives. Am J Epidemiol 102:197, 1975.

207. Sue LP, Davis JW, Parks SN: Iliofemoral venous injuries: An indication for prophylactic caval filter placement. J Trauma 39:693, 1995.

208. Symington IS, Stack BHR: Pulmonary thromboembolism after travel. Br J Dis Chest 71:147, 1977.

209. Tardy B, Tardy-Poncet B, Bara L, et al: Effects of long travels in sitting position in elderly volunteers on biologic markers of coagulation activity and fibrinolysis. Thromb Res 83:153, 1996.

210. Thomas D: Venous thrombogenesis. Br Med Bull 50:803, 1994.

211. Thomas DP, Merton RE, Hockley DJ: The effect of stasis on the venous endothelium: An ultrastructural study. Br J Haematol 55:113, 1983.

212. Thomas DP, Merton RE, Wood RD, et al: The relationship between vessel wall injury and venous thrombosis: An experimental study. Br J Haematol 59:449, 1985.

213. Thomas WA, Davies JNP, O'Neal RM, et al: Incidence of myocardial infarction correlated with venous and pulmonary thrombosis and embolism. Am J Cardiol 5:41, 1960.

214. Tilney NL, Griffiths HJG, Edwards EA: Natural history of major venous thrombosis of the upper extremity. Arch Surg 101:792, 1970.

215. Tindall VR: Factors influencing puerperal thromboembolism. J Obstet Gynaecol Br Commonw 75:1324, 1968.

216. Toglia MR, Weg JG: Venous thromboembolism during pregnancy. N Engl J Med 335:108, 1996.

217. Treffers PE, Huidekoper BL, Weenink GH, et al: Epidemiological observations of thromboembolic disease during pregnancy and in the puerperium, in 56,022 women. Int J Gynaecol Obstet 21:327, 1983.

218. Tripolitis AJ, Bodily KC, Blackshear WM, et al: Venous capacitance and outflow in the post-operative patient. Ann Surg 190:634, 1979.

219. Upchurch GR Jr, Demling RH, Davies J, et al: Efficacy of subcutaneous heparin in prevention of venous thromboembolic events in trauma patients. Am Surg 61:749, 1995.

220. van Ramshorst B, van Bemmelen PS, Honeveld H, et al: Thrombus regression in deep venous thrombosis: Quantification of spontaneous thrombolysis with duplex scanning. Circulation 86:414, 1992.

221. Vandenbroucke JP, Helmerhorst FM, Bloemenkamp KW, et al: Third-generation oral contraceptive and deep venous thrombosis: From epidemiologic controversy to new insight in coagulation. Am J Obstet Gynecol 177:887, 1997.

222. Vandenbrouke JP, van der Meer FJM, Helmerhorst FM, et al: Factor V Leiden: Should we screen oral contraceptive users and pregnant women? BMJ 313:1127, 1996.

223. Varas-Lorenzo C, Garcia-Rodriguez LA, Cattaruzzi C, et al: Hormone replacement therapy and the risk of hospitalization for venous thromboembolism: A population-based study in southern Europe. Am J Epidemiol 147:387, 1998.

224. Vecchi M, Cattaneo M, de Franchis R, et al: Risk of thromboembolic complications in patients with inflammatory bowel disease: Study of hemostasis measurements. Int J Clin Lab Res 21:165, 1991.

225. Vessey MP, Doll R: Investigation of relation between use of oral contraceptives and thromboembolic disease. Br Med J 2(599):199, 1968.

226. von Kaulla E, Droegemueller W, Aoki N, et al: Antithrombin III depression and thrombin generation acceleration in women taking oral contraceptives. Am J Obstet Gynecol 109:868, 1971.

227. Wahl DG, Guillemin F, de Maistre E, et al: Risk for venous thrombosis related to antiphospholipid antibodies in systemic lupus erythematosus—a meta-analysis. Lupus 6:467, 1997.

228. Wakefield TW, Greenfield LJ, Rolfe MW, et al: Inflammatory and procoagulant mediator interactions in an experimental baboon model of venous thrombosis. Thromb Haemost 69:164, 1993.

229. Warlow C, Ogston D, Douglas AS: Deep venous thrombosis of the legs after strokes: Part I-Incidence and predisposing factors. Br Med J 1(6019):1178, 1976.

230. Wautrecht JC, Galle C, Motte S, et al: The role of ABO blood groups in the incidence of deep vein thrombosis [letter]. Thromb Haemost 79:688, 1998.

231. Wessler S: Thrombosis in the presence of vascular stasis. Am J Med 33:648, 1962.

232. Wessler S, Reimer SM, Sheps MC: Biologic assay of a thrombosis-inducing activity in human serum. J Appl Physiol 14:943, 1959.

233. Winkler UH, Holscher T, Schulte H, et al: Ethinylestradiol 20 versus 30 μg combined with 150 μg desogestrel: A large comparative study of the effects of two low-dose oral contraceptives on the hemostatic system. Gynecol Endocrinol 10:265, 1996.

234. Wise RC: Spontaneous lower extremity venous thrombosis in children. Am J Dis Child 126:766, 1973.

235. Xiang DZ, Verbeken EK, Van Lommel ATL, et al: Composition and formation of the sleeve enveloping a central venous catheter. J Vasc Surg 28:260, 1998.

236. Eklof B: Air travel related venous thromboembolism—an existing problem that can be prevented? Cardiovasc Surg 10:95, 2002.

237. Ferrari E, Chevalier T, Chapelier A, Baudouy M: Travel as risk factor for thromboembolic disease: A case control study. Chest 115:440, 1999.

238. Heit JA, Silverstein MD, Mohr DN, et al: Predictors of survival after deep vein thrombosis and pulmonary embolism: A population-based cohort study. Arch Intern Med 159:445, 1999.

239. Heit JA, Silverstein MD, Mohr DN, et al: Risk factors for deep vein thrombosis and pulmonary embolism: A population-based case-control study. Arch Intern Med 160:809, 2000.

240. Heit JA, Silverstein MD, Mohr DN, et al: The epidemiology of venous thromboembolism in the community. Thromb Haemost 86:452, 2001.

241. Hughes RJ, Hopkins RJ, Hill S, et al: Frequency of venous thromboembolism in low to moderate risk long distance air travellers: The New Zealand Air Traveller's Thrombosis (NZATT) study. Lancet 362:2039, 2003.

242. Kearon C: Natural history of venous thromboembolism. Circulation 107(Suppl):22, 2003.

243. Lapostolle F, Surget V, Borron SW: Severe pulmonary embolism associated with air travel. N Engl J Med 345:779, 2001.

244. Mohr DN, Silverstein MD, Heit JA, et al: The venous stasis syndrome after deep venous thromboembolism or pulmonary embolism: A population-based study. Mayo Clin Proc 75:1249, 2000.

245. Paganin F, Bourde A, Yvin JL, et al: Venous thromboembolism in passengers following a 12-h flight: A case-control study. Aviat Space Environ Med 74(12):1277-1280, 2003.

246. Samama MM: An epidemiological study of risk factors for deep vein thrombosis in medical outpatients. Arch Intern Med 160:3415, 2000.

247. Scurr JH, Machin SJ, Balley-King S, et al: Frequency and prevention of symptomless deep-vein thrombosis in long-haul flights: A randomized trial. Lancet 357:1485, 2001.

248. Silverstein MD, Heit JA, Mohr DN, et al: Trends in the incidence of deep vein thrombosis and pulmonary embolism: A 25-year population-based study. Arch Intern Med 158:585, 1998.

Clinical and Diagnostic Evaluation of the Patient with Deep Venous Thrombosis

148

JUDITH COOK, MD

MARK H. MEISSNER, MD

Approximately 1 million patients annually undergo investigation for suspected acute deep venous thrombosis (DVT) in North America.[1,2] The consequences of acute DVT and its treatment make the accurate and timely diagnosis of DVT particularly important. An untreated proximal DVT is associated with a 30% to 50% risk of pulmonary embolism (PE),[3] with a concomitant 12% mortality rate,[3] whereas unnecessary treatment of DVT incurs the risk, inconvenience, and expense of anticoagulation. Unfortunately, the diagnosis of DVT based on clinical signs and symptoms alone is inaccurate; in up to half of patients with the classic findings of pain, swelling, and tenderness, a DVT is not confirmed by diagnostic testing.[4-7] The use of confirmatory testing in the diagnosis and treatment of DVT is therefore of paramount importance.

Several strategies for the diagnosis of acute DVT have accordingly been developed, many of which are primarily of historical interest. Contrast venography has historically been the "gold standard" for the diagnosis of acute DVT. However, venography is inconvenient and expensive, and it may cause significant discomfort.[8,9] Although still of value as a confirmatory test in situations of diagnostic uncertainty, and in the setting of clinical trials requiring the detection of asymptomatic DVT, contrast venography has largely been replaced by less invasive tests.

Impedance plethysmography (IPG) was the first widely available noninvasive test for DVT and correlates a reduction in venous outflow with the presence of proximal DVT.[10] Although the sensitivity and specificity of IPG exceed 90% for occlusive proximal DVT, it is less sensitive for calf DVT and nonocclusive thrombus, cannot provide specific anatomic information, and has a 5% false-positive rate.[11-14] Radiolabeled fibrinogen was formerly used to detect DVT by external scintillation counting of circulating ^{125}I-fibrinogen that had been incorporated into thrombi.[15] This method was reported to have 100% sensitivity and 94% specificity for calf thrombi. Unfortunately, its sensitivity above midthigh is only 60% owing to background radiation from the trunk.[16] Furthermore, the 24-hour delay and the risk of blood-borne disease from fibrinogen donors have made this test obsolete.[17]

Thermography is similarly only of historical importance. DVT typically raises the surface skin temperature 1° C, a difference that can be detected with the use of sensitive instruments incorporating infrared or liquid crystal technology.[18] However, increased skin temperature is very nonspecific, and although thermography has a sensitivity of 83% to 87%, its specificity is only 39% to 55%.[19]

Duplex ultrasonography is currently the most widely used noninvasive tool for the diagnosis of DVT.[20] Although duplex scanning is accurate for the diagnosis of acute DVT, a thorough understanding of its limitations is required (see Chapter 17). Other approaches, notably the determination of pretest probability and measurement of plasma D-dimer levels, have been more recently incorporated into diagnostic strategies for acute DVT. Like duplex ultrasonography, however, these strategies have limitations that must be clearly understood. Ultimately, the strengths of the available modalities are complementary, and they can be combined into effective and efficient algorithms for DVT diagnosis.

■ DIAGNOSTIC MODALITIES

Clinical Evaluation

Signs and symptoms of acute DVT most often prompt referral for diagnostic testing. However, the clinical presentation of an acute DVT may vary from the absence of symptoms to massive swelling and cyanosis with impending venous gangrene (phlegmasia cerulea dolens). Signs and symptoms commonly attributed to acute DVT include pain, edema, erythema, tenderness, fever, prominent superficial veins, pain with passive dorsiflexion of the foot (Homans' sign), and peripheral cyanosis. The most common presenting symptoms have a wide range of reported sensitivities and specificities; calf pain has a sensitivity of 75% to 91% and a specificity of 3% to 87%, and calf swelling, a sensitivity of 35% to 97% and a specificity of 8% to 88%.[5,6,21-24]

Unfortunately, the diagnosis of DVT based on clinical signs and symptoms alone is notoriously inaccurate. Of patients referred to the vascular laboratory for exclusion of DVT, results of ultrasonography are positive in only 12% to 31%.[25-27] Others have found as many as 46% of patients with classic signs or symptoms of DVT to have negative venography findings.[6] Furthermore, up to 50% of patients with acute DVT may lack any specific sign or symptom.[28,29]

The presence of underlying risk factors also influences the likelihood of acute DVT. Bed rest due to illness or recent surgery is a well-recognized risk factor for DVT.[28] Although recent operation is associated with the development of DVT in almost 40% of patients, a similar history can be elicited in up to 35% of patients with negative ultrasonography results.[27] Malignancy carries a threefold higher risk for the development of DVT,[27] perhaps owing to the production of procoagulant proteins by certain tumors.[30] A prior history of DVT or PE also increases the risk of subsequent DVT formation.[31,32] Although some studies have suggested that gender may be a risk factor for DVT,[27] others have not demonstrated such a difference but have shown a higher number of female referrals for DVT testing.[25,33] The importance of specific thrombotic risk factors is reviewed in Chapter 147.

Markel and associates[27] evaluated the predictive values of patient risk factors and clinical signs and symptoms. When they considered bed rest, surgery, malignancy, and a history of DVT or PE, approximately 80% of patients with a DVT were found to have at least one risk factor, 40% had two, and almost 10% had three.[27] A history of swelling or edema was the most common clinical sign, present in 83% of patients with a DVT, compared with 63% of those without. Limb pain was less common, present in 51% and 41% of patients with and without DVT, respectively. The combination of a prior history of DVT, malignancy, and bed rest had a positive predictive value of 67%. If edema was also present, the predictive value rose to 75%. Cyanosis was present in only 6% and 2% of patients with and without DVT, respectively. Nonetheless, when cyanosis was combined with the previously identified clinical characteristics, the probability of DVT increased to 94%. However, the specificity of these observations is limited and would be associated with a prohibitive false-positive rate in all but the most narrowly defined of clinical settings.

The accuracy of the clinical signs and symptoms of DVT also differs between inpatients and outpatients. Inpatients more often have just undergone surgery or are critically ill, whereas outpatients are less likely to have had recent surgery, trauma, or a prior DVT.[25] Additionally, the incidence of DVT is lower among outpatients but specific leg symptoms are more common in this group.[25] Given the lower incidence of disease in outpatients, it is perhaps not surprising that the absence of certain risk factors, signs, and symptoms has been shown to have a high negative predictive value in this group.[26] The triad consisting of duration of symptoms greater than 7 days, no history of cancer, and a differential thigh circumference less 3 cm in outpatients had a negative predictive value of 95% (sensitivity 86%, specificity 52.4%); unfortunately, the positive predictive value was only 28.6%. When applied prospectively to an outpatient cohort over 5 months, this model yielded a 96.7% negative predictive value.[26] The same model, however, had only a 75% negative predictive value when applied in the inpatient setting.

Criado and Burnham[25] similarly evaluated clinical presentation.[25] A difference in calf circumference of less than 2 cm demonstrated a negative predictive value of 85% among outpatients, and of 93% in inpatients. When combined with the absence of risk factors including surgery, trauma, malignancy, history of DVT, or hypercoagulable state, the negative predictive values of the absence of swelling were 97% in outpatients and 92% in inpatients. Applying this approach retrospectively, Criado and Burnham[25] found that the diagnosis of DVT would have been missed in 3 of 610 outpatients and 15 of 916 inpatients. Other investigators have shown that isolated joint pain and cellulitis are almost never associated with a DVT.[34]

Despite these observations, the diagnosis of DVT based only on signs or symptoms and patient risk factors remains inaccurate. At best, the utility of certain clinical characteristics can be defined by the negative predictive value of their absence, and this fact is as much related to the infrequency of disease in some patient populations, particularly outpatients, as it is to the accuracy of any particular feature. Nonetheless, withholding treatment on the basis of clinical observations only poses a significant risk of thromboembolism, in that 2% to 4% of outpatients and up to 8% of inpatients would have untreated DVT.[25,26]

Venography

Historically, ascending venography has been the "gold standard" confirmatory test for acute DVT. Accordingly, it is the test to which all other diagnostic modalities should be compared. Rabinov and Paulin[8] published the seminal article on the technique of ascending venography in 1972. The technique requires bilateral pedal vein cannulation and sequential limb imaging with oblique and lateral projections after intravenous administration of a contrast agent. Serial tourniquet placement or Valsalva's maneuver may be required to facilitate adequate venous opacification. Definitive filling defects present in well-opacified veins constitute a positive result. Inadequate opacification of the superficial or deep venous systems constitutes a nondiagnostic study.[8]

More than 50% of patients with clinical manifestations compatible with DVT have negative venography results,[9,35] and the clinical validity of withholding anticoagulation after such a result has been confirmed in appropriate management trials. In a study by Hull and colleagues,[35] 160 patients with negative venography results were monitored for 3 months.[35] Fewer than 2% developed clinical manifestations of recurrent thromboembolism, and there was no associated mortality. Two patients (1.3%) experienced new symptoms with a confirmed DVT within 8 days.

Despite its accuracy, venography has several limitations. In a series of more than 300 venograms, venipuncture was unsuccessful in 2.3% of studies, and venous opacification was inadequate in another 2.3%.[36] In 10% to 30% of studies, all venous segments are not visualized, and certain segments, such as the profunda femoral and iliac veins, were infrequently seen.[37] In the upper extremity, venography does not demonstrate the internal jugular vein and often fails to identify venous segments beyond an obstruction.[38,39] Furthermore, when venography is performed without fluoroscopy, the rate of interobserver variability approaches 10%.[40]

In addition to these technical considerations, venography also consumes considerable time and resources. The procedure requires the presence of both a technologist and radiologist and cannot always be performed urgently.

Furthermore, the patient must be sufficiently stable for transportation to the radiology suite. Injection of the contrast agent can be painful, although the pain can be decreased with the use of non-ionic media.[9,41] Systemic contrast agent reactions may occur in 1% to 3% of patients,[42] and extravasation into the tissues can result in mild to severe skin necrosis.[43] Contrast agents are irritating to the venous endothelium, although less so when non-ionic, and may cause thrombosis in 1.3% to 9% of patients.[9,35,44] Despite its diagnostic reliability, the limitations and potential complications of venography have spurred interest in noninvasive imaging modalities for acute DVT.

Duplex Ultrasonography

Venous duplex ultrasonography has now replaced venography as the most widely used diagnostic test for acute DVT. Duplex scanning is noninvasive, widely available, and portable with minimal potential for complications (see Chapter 17). Evaluation of the lower extremities includes an assessment of venous compressibility, intraluminal echoes, venous flow characteristics, and luminal color filling. Among these, venous incompressibility is the most widely used and objective criterion for the diagnosis of DVT.[45] Incompressibility has excellent sensitivity and specificity for the detection of proximal DVT. Reviewing 18 studies using a variety of ultrasound techniques, Kearon[1] reported a weighted mean sensitivity and specificity of 97% and 94%, respectively, with mean positive and negative predictive values of 97% and 98%, respectively, for proximal DVT. Cogo and associates[46] prospectively compared compression and Doppler ultrasonography techniques for detection of proximal DVT, with confirmatory venography in all patients.[46] In comparison to Doppler ultrasonography, compression ultrasonography had better sensitivity for both proximal DVT (100% vs. 89%) and all DVT (95% vs. 76%). The specificity values for the two techniques were high, 100% for compression and 98% for Doppler. Although compression ultrasonography appears superior to standardized Doppler ultrasonography, incompressibility used in combination with the absence of phasic flow and visible thrombus can achieve a sensitivity of 95% and specificity of 83%.[47] Furthermore, despite the accuracy of compression alone in the diagnosis of proximal DVT, the technique has substantial limitations in the evaluation of the calf veins. However, the use of color flow imaging significantly improves the accuracy of detecting isolated calf vein thrombosis.

Despite its utility, duplex ultrasonography does have some well-recognized limitations. Among studies limited to the proximal veins, the results are indeterminate or nondiagnostic in 1% to 6% of patients.[48,49] Adequate evaluation of the tibial and peroneal veins may be impeded by large calf size, edema, or operator experience but is aided by the use of color-flow Doppler ultrasonography.[50,51] Difficult compressibility and musculoskeletal structures may similarly limit evaluation of the iliac, superficial femoral, and upper extremity veins. Messina and colleagues[51] reported adequate visualization of both the common and external iliac veins in 47% of patients and of the external iliac alone in 79% with color-flow duplex scanning.

In the design of strategies for the diagnosis of acute DVT with duplex ultrasonography, the extent of examination is among the most controversial areas and has significant implications with respect to diagnostic accuracy, patient convenience, and utilization of vascular laboratory resources. Various protocols incorporating the use of limited or more thorough assessments of the lower extremity veins and single versus serial examinations have been proposed for the diagnostic evaluation of DVT. The validity of these various protocols in many ways depends on the importance attached to the detection of isolated calf vein thrombosis. Compression ultrasonography techniques applied only to the common femoral vein and popliteal fossa may leave isolated calf vein thrombi undetected in up to 29% of cases.[52,53] However, DVT usually starts in the calf,[53,54] and isolated calf thrombi have a 20% to 28% rate of progression to the proximal venous segments.[54-56] Such progression usually occurs within 1 week.[12,57] Without treatment, PE may develop in 8% to 34% of patients with isolated calf vein thrombosis,[58] with an associated mortality of up to 15%.[29] Unfortunately, the sensitivity and specificity of ultrasonography for detecting calf vein thrombosis are variable, ranging from 11% to 100% and 90% to 100%, respectively.[59] Thus, diagnostic protocols employing compression ultrasonography limited to the proximal venous segments are based on two assumptions: (1) isolated calf vein thrombosis that does not extend is of little clinical importance and (2) proximal extension of calf vein thrombosis more than a week after presentation is unusual.

Early algorithms using compression ultrasonography limited to the proximal veins required two additional studies, at day 2 and day 7 or 8, after negative results of an initial examination.[60,61] Thromboembolic events within 3 months of serially negative results ranged from 1.3% to 1.5%, and an average of 1.3 to 1.6 additional hospital visits were required per patient.[60,61] Birdwell and associates[62] evaluated a protocol requiring only one additional test between days 5 and 7. Ten percent of all abnormal results were obtained on the second study. There were no thromboembolic events during the wait for a follow-up study. Only 2 of 335 patients (0.6%) had an adverse event, one a new DVT and the other a nonfatal PE. The negative predictive value of negative results for two consecutive ultrasonography examinations was 99.4%. In a study of 1703 patients, Cogo and associates[63] evaluated a similar protocol using one additional test at day 7. Their protocol included examination of the distal popliteal veins but not the calf veins. The cumulative thromboembolic rate at 6 months was 0.7%, including two PEs, one of which occurred during the week prior to the second ultrasound examination.[63] The second examination diagnosed an additional 3% of patients, compared with 7% for the more limited technique.[60,61,63] Extension of the examination to include the distal popliteal vein resulted in a diagnosis of 6.3% of patients on the initial examination, and the average patient needed only 0.8 extra tests. There was, however, an increased risk of false-positive results, with a positive predictive value of 98% in the common femoral vein but only 79% in the distal popliteal vein.

The premise that isolated, nonextending calf vein thrombosis is inconsequential is still controversial. Although the embolic potential of thrombosis that remains confined to the calf may be lower than for proximal DVT, concurrent PE has been demonstrated in 11% to 33% of patients with isolated calf vein thrombus.[58,64] Also, the risk of the post-thrombotic syndrome after isolated calf vein thrombus is not insignificant. The prevalence of valvular incompetence and venous reflux at 1 year is 24%.[64] Furthermore, risk and inconvenience are associated with protocols requiring follow-up evaluations to assess for proximal thrombus extension. Thus, a complete ultrasonography protocol including evaluation of the calf veins has been advocated by some investigators. Although the sensitivity of compression ultrasonography for calf vein thrombosis is variable, it has been reported as high as 91% compared with venography.[65] Protocols including complete evaluation of the calf veins have been compared with limited compression ultra-sonography examination of the proximal veins. In one study, 27% of all abnormal results were from calf vein thrombosis.[66] Limited examination failed to detect 7.3% of proximal thromboses as well as the 27% of patients with isolated calf vein thrombosis.[66] The complete examination technique added an average of 4 to 5 minutes per extremity.[66]

The clinical validity of withholding anticoagulation on the basis of a single, technically adequate ultrasonography examination including the calf veins has been confirmed. Such protocols require serial examinations only in patients with equivocal examination results. A retrospective study of 128 patients found only a single DVT and no PE in the 3 months after negative results of a complete ultrasonography examination.[67] Schellong and coworkers[68] reported a 0.3% thromboembolism rate 3 months after negative results of a complete compression ultrasonography study.[68] Other investigators found a similarly low 0.5% incidence of thromboembolic events 3 months after negative compression study results.[69] Further-more, the complete compression ultrasonography examination identified a causative diagnosis in 42% of patients in whom no DVT was found.[69]

In more than 400 patients evaluated with a complete ultrasound protocol, Wolf and colleagues[52] reported four adverse events (1.1%) during a 3-month follow-up period: one PE, 1 patient with early recurrent symptoms (within 1 week) and a documented DVT, and 2 patients with late recurrent or progressive symptoms (4 to 6 weeks) and documented DVT. Other studies using the complete ultrasonography protocol have found the rate of PE to be 0, and the rate of DVT to be 0 to 0.3% 3 months after a negative study result.[70,71] Although indeterminate test results have been reported in as few as 2% of patients,[68,69] other researchers have reported 18% to 22% of examination results to be equivocal in the calf veins.[52,70] However, regardless of the rate of indeterminate studies, a single, technically adequate study including the calf veins does appear to reliably and safely exclude a diagnosis of DVT.

Unfortunately, the majority of patients referred for exclusion of DVT have negative study results. In patients referred for extremity symptoms, ultrasonography demonstrates DVT in the symptomatic leg in only 20% to 32%[45,53] and DVT isolated to the asymptomatic leg in less than 2%.[72,73] Single institutions have reported the annual costs of negative venous ultrasonography results to exceed

$600,000.[25] Although protocols employing serial examinations limited to the proximal veins are safe, their cost-effectiveness remains dubious.[74] The cost per life saved of a single follow-up study is $390,000, and that of a second follow-up study is $3.5 million.[75] Complete ultrasonography protocols may reduce the need for serial ultrasonography testing, but the longer time needed for this technique consumes vascular laboratory resources, and a substantial subset of patients with equivocal results may still need serial studies. The use of adjunctive measures, such as clinical risk stratification and D-dimer measurements, have now been extensively evaluated as tools to decrease the burden of negative ultrasound study results.

Other Imaging Modalities

Although duplex scanning is both noninvasive and inexpensive, its does have limitations, including a limited ability to assess the iliac and central venous circulation.[48,49] The rapid development of many other imaging modalities may have applications to the venous system that overcome at least some of these limitations. Computed tomography (CT) pulmonary angiography is becoming widely utilized for the diagnosis of PE, and with the introduction of computed tomography venography (CTV), a single CT scan may become a practical test for DVT and PE. CTV performed at the time of CT pulmonary angiography adds only 3 to 5 minutes to the study.[76] In comparison with venous ultra-sonography, CTV has been reported to have sensitivities of 98% to 100%, specificities of 94% to 100%, and positive and negative predictive values of 92% and 100% for pelvic and thigh thrombosis.[77-80]

Peterson and colleagues,[81] however, found that CTV is specific but not sensitive for DVT, with a sensitivity of 71% and a specificity of 93%. The corresponding positive and negative predictive values were 53% and 97%, respectively. Stover and associates[82] reported a 50% false-positive rate for CTV detection of pelvic DVT compared with contrast venography. Also, CTV has not been investigated for the detection of isolated calf vein thrombosis. Although the modality may have clinical utility in patients with PE, and thus a higher pretest probability for DVT, its precise role has yet to be defined. Additionally, the cost to the patient may be as much as six times higher than that of duplex scanning.[81]

Magnetic resonance imaging (MRI) has also been used for imaging the venous system. Conventional MRI, using spin-echo imaging, can detect central venous thrombi[83,84] and, through its ability to identify acute perivascular edema, can provide information about the age of a thrombus.[85] A prospective comparison of MRI with standard venography for proximal DVT demonstrated a sensitivity of 90%, a specificity of 100%, and a κ level of agreement of 0.752.[85] Unfortunately, although conventional MRI has reasonably high sensitivity and specificity values for detecting central and iliac vein thrombus, it is time-intensive, requiring up to 45 minutes for scanning, and is thus subject to motion artifact.[85]

Flow-sensitive MRI techniques, or magnetic resonance venography (MRV), have been developed specifically for imaging the venous circulation. MRV takes advantage of the ability of magnetic resonance to distinguish stationary from moving signals. Various protocols have been employed, including noncontrast MRV techniques such as time-of-flight (TOF) and phase-contrast techniques as well as contrast-enhanced MRV (CE MRV). TOF and phase contrast MRV rely on flow-related enhancement and velocity shifts to provide signals from flowing blood.[86] Postprocessing techniques allow creation of three-dimensional images analogous to those provided by conventional venography.[86] As for MR arteriography, CE MRV uses rapid three-dimensional sequences after a timed injection of a contrast agent and postprocessing algorithms to remove the arterial signal.[86]

TOF has been used as the primary noncontrast MRV modality for DVT. Carpenter and associates[87] compared TOF MRV with duplex ultrasonography and contrast venography of the inferior vena cava and proximal lower extremity veins. The sensitivity and specificity values for MRV and duplex scanning were identical, 100% and 96%, respectively. Positive predictive values for MRV and duplex scanning were 90% and 94%, respectively, and both had 100% negative predictive value.[87] Another study comparing TOF MRV and duplex scanning with contrast venography for DVT in the vena cava and iliac and femoropopliteal veins demonstrated superior sensitivity and specificity for MRV (100% and 100%, respectively) compared with color Doppler ultrasonography (87% and 83%, respectively).[88] Furthermore, MRV was 95% sensitive and 99% specific in detecting the proximal extent of DVT, compared with 46% sensitivity and 100% specificity, respectively, for color Doppler ultrasonography.[88]

Disadvantages of TOF techniques include slow acquisition times and susceptibility to flow artifacts in parallel vessels (i.e., the common iliac veins).[89] Furthermore, in order to reduce imaging times, acquisition frequently requires imaging gaps of up to 1 cm.[89] CE MRV overcomes these disadvantages through the use of three-dimensional acquisition. Additionally, the inflammatory changes associated with acute DVT cause gadolinium to accumulate in the vein wall and perivenous tissue. This characteristic enhancement pattern fades with thrombus organization,[90] allowing differentiation of acute from chronic DVT. In comparison with venography, CE MRV has been shown to have a sensitivity of 100% for iliac and femoral vein DVT, with corresponding specificities of 100% and 97%.[89] Furthermore, CE MRV has been shown to more reliably depict the proximal extent of DVT than venography.[89]

MRV technology has distinct disadvantages that limit its utility as either a screening or routine diagnostic test for DVT. The cost of MRV is 1.4 times that of contrast venography and 2.5 times that of duplex scanning.[87] MRV also has limitations in imaging of the calf veins. The paired nature of the tibial veins and their proximity to arteries creates significant artifacts during postprocessing.[86,91] Although flow augmentation (compression and decompression techniques) has been combined with ultrafast imaging to achieve a sensitivity of 87% and a specificity of 97% for infrapopliteal venous thrombi,[92] MRV for lower leg DVT is not widely available. Nonetheless, MRV may be complementary to duplex in some clinical circumstances. The increased ability of MRV to detect the proximal extent

of venous thrombus may affect clinical decision-making.[88,89] The accuracy of MRV in the imaging of the iliac and central venous circulation makes it useful for evaluation of pelvic or central venous thrombosis.[93] In up to 27% of patients with PE and a negative ultrasonography result, MRV demonstrates pelvic or inferior vena cava thrombosis.[94] Compared with venography without selective catheterization, MRV has also been shown to be superior in detecting hypogastric vein thrombosis.[87] In the future, the ability to combine pulmonary MRA and MRV of the lower extremities may provide a valuable diagnostic tool for venous thromboembolic disease.

Newer radiopharmaceuticals have also been approved for the imaging of DVT. ^{99m}Tc-apcitide is a complex of the radionuclide technetium Tc 99m and apcitide, a small synthetic peptide that binds the glycoprotein IIb/IIIa receptor on activated platelets and is specific for acute thrombus.[95,96] Imaging with ^{99m}Tc-apcitide has the advantage of being functional rather than relying on anatomic structural changes in the vein. Hence, it may avoid some of the pitfalls associated with venography and ultrasonography. Imaging is typically performed 10 to 60 minutes after peripheral venous administration of the radionuclide, and venous segments both above and below the knee may be targeted.[97]

^{99m}Tc-apcitide scintigraphy has been compared with standard venography in phase 3 clinical trials. Sensitivity, specificity, and agreement for ^{99m}Tc-apcitide scanning compared with contrast venography ranged from 59% to 81%, 65% to 77%, and 66% to 74%, respectively.[98] Because venography results may be positive in chronic as well as acute DVT, ^{99m}Tc-apcitide scanning was investigated in a subset of patients with acute symptoms (less than 3 days) and no prior history of DVT or PE. In this setting, sensitivity, specificity, and agreement ranged from 83% to 100%, 69% to 83%, and 76% to 87%, respectively.[98] Furthermore, over a disease prevalence range of 20% to 50%, ^{99m}Tc-apcitide scanning had a negative predictive value of 90% to 97%.[98] Another study found excellent accuracy for ^{99m}Tc-apcitide scintigraphy compared with ultrasonography, with a sensitivity of 92% and a specificity of 82% to 90%.[99] Although this modality shows promise for diagnostic evaluation of DVT, management studies with follow-up after a negative ^{99m}Tc-apcitide scanning result have not been performed. Anticoagulation therapy should not be withheld on the basis of a negative ^{99m}Tc-apcitide scintigraphy result alone. The utility of this study may also be limited by the availability and cost of scintigraphy in a particular hospital setting. However, ^{99m}Tc-apcitide scanning may be useful in patients with indeterminate ultrasonography results and contraindications to contrast venography.

D-Dimer Assays

D-dimers are products of the degradation of cross-linked fibrin by plasmin (Fig. 148-1). Diagnostic assays for D-dimer have been based on the development of monoclonal antibodies capable of differentiating degradation products of fibrin and fibrinogen. D-dimer blood levels reflect the presence of intravascular fibrin and are

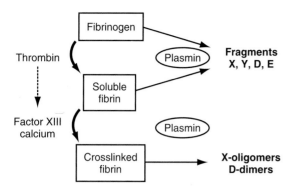

FIGURE 148-1 D-dimer is a specific plasmin-mediated breakdown product of cross-linked fibrin. Thrombin converts fibrinogen into soluble fibrin. Activated factor XIII (by thrombin) in the presence of calcium then cross-links the fibrin polymer. Plasmin cleavage of fibrinogen or soluble fibrin produces degradation products—fragments X, Y, D and E. Plasmin cleavage of cross-linked fibrin produces different degradation products: X-oligomers and D-dimers. Thus, while fibrinogen degradation products may be elevated when no thrombus is present (i.e., from plasmin acting on fibrinogen or soluble fibrin), D-dimer is specific for fibrinolysis.

sensitive for the diagnosis of venous thromboembolism. When measured by enzyme-linked immunosorbent assay (ELISA), the reference standard, sensitivity for the diagnosis of DVT is as high as 96.8%.[100] Unfortunately, these measurements are also quite nonspecific, with specificities as low as 35.2%.[100,101] Elevated D-dimer values are also associated with disseminated intravascular coagulation, malignancy, postoperative states, preeclampsia, infection, and recent trauma.[102] The specificity of D-dimer measurements also diminishes with patient age.[103,104] The high sensitivity of D-dimer measurements makes it theoretically possible to exclude a diagnosis of DVT on the basis of a negative result. However, owing to the low specificity and positive predictive value, a positive D-dimer assay result requires confirmatory testing.

Several assays, with notable differences in sensitivity and efficiency, have been developed for the measurement of D-dimer levels. The sensitivity of different assays varies between 60% and 96%.[104,105] There are currently four methods of measuring D-dimer levels in blood: conventional membrane ELISA, microplate ELISA, latex agglutination, and whole blood agglutination assays. The ELISA assays have higher sensitivities, whereas the agglutination assays have higher specificity. Conventional ELISA assays (e.g., Asserachrom, Enzygnost, and Fibrinostika) are the most sensitive but are time consuming and suitable only for batch analysis.[101,104] Although simpler to perform, traditional qualitative latex agglutination assays (e.g., Minutex), with sensitivities less than 80%, are too insensitive for clinical use.[106-108] Although whole blood or red cell agglutination assays (e.g., SimpliRED) may be more specific than the latex agglutination assays, with specificities exceeding 90% in some studies, they likewise have sensitivities near 80%.[108,109] Several rapid semiquantitative assays can yield results within 1 hour, with sensitivities equivalent to those of ELISA.[108,110] The rapid quantitative assays (e.g., VIDAS, Tinaquant, and Liatest) appear to have the best combination of convenience, sensitivity, and specificity.[108]

The performance of all available assays is limited by the extent of thrombosis,[111] duration of symptoms,[108] and the prior use of anticoagulants.[103] Their sensitivity for isolated calf vein thrombosis is 1.6% to 7.8% lower than that for proximal venous thrombosis.[108,111,112] The assay result may also be negative when the interval between thrombosis and presentation exceeds 2 to 3 weeks. Decreased specificity owing to co-morbid diseases and reduced sensitivity due to the use of anticoagulant prophylaxis combine to limit the accuracy of D-dimer measurements in hospitalized patients.[101] For example, D-dimer value has been reported to have specificity values of 0 in patients with malignancy and only 18% in patients who have recently had surgery.[113] D-dimer measurement therefore has little diagnostic utility in unselected inpatients, particularly those who are older than 60 years or have been hospitalized for more than 3 days.[104] Depending on the assay used, D-dimer results are falsely negative in 15% to 29% of inpatients.[105]

Given its limitations, D-dimer measurement is most valuable as an adjunct to other diagnostic modalities, such as duplex ultrasonography and determination of pretest probability. D-dimer assays have been incorporated into two general diagnostic strategies. The first strategy uses D-dimer measurements to confirm initial negative results of noninvasive tests to reduce the need for serial diagnostic studies.[114] Withholding anticoagulation has been shown to be safe in patients with a single negative proximal venous ultrasonography result in combination with a negative D-dimer assay result. The second strategy utilizes D-dimer measurement as an initial test to triage patients for further diagnostic testing. Because patients with normal results might require no further testing, this strategy is potentially useful in reducing utilization of the vascular laboratory. Although sensitivity is of great importance in such diagnostic algorithms, specificity is also important as a determinant of exclusion efficiency.[107] Assays with a very low specificity require additional diagnostic testing in most patients. Exclusion tests are most beneficial when specificity is high and disease prevalence is low.[108]

■ DIAGNOSTIC TESTING AND PRETEST PROBABILITY

The clinical utility of many diagnostic tests is described in terms of their sensitivity and specificity, which are defined in terms of true and false positive and negative results (Table 148-1). This information is important in validating and establishing the accuracy of any diagnostic test. However, sensitivity and specificity are independent of disease prevalence; from a clinical perspective, the positive and negative predictive values of a test are more important. The positive predictive value is the percentage of patients with positive results who truly have the disease, and the negative predictive value is the percentage of patients with negative results who do not (see Table 148-1).

Unfortunately, it is not widely appreciated that, according to Bayes' theorem, the accuracy of any diagnostic test is related to the pretest probability of disease. In contrast to the traditional concepts of sensitivity and specificity, Bayesian analysis formally incorporates preexisting external information into the interpretation of data.[115] Bayes' theorem

AU: Figure 2 was actually a table so was reassigned as Table 1 in the chapter.

Table 148-1	Defining Sensitivity, Specificity, and Predictive Values of a Test*			
TEST	**DISEASE PRESENT**	**DISEASE ABSENT**		
Positive result	True-positive (TP)	False-positive (FP)	Positive predictive value	$= \dfrac{TP}{(TP + FP)}$
Negative result	False-negative (FN)	True-negative (TN)	Negative predictive value	$= \dfrac{TN}{(FN + TN)}$
Sensitivity	$\dfrac{TP}{(TP + FN)}$			
Specificity		$\dfrac{TN}{(FP + TN)}$		

*Sensitivity and specificity are defined in terms of true and false positive and negative results. *Sensitivity* thus reflects the accuracy of a test in positively identifying a disease among patients who actually have the disease, and *specificity* reflects the ability to accurately exclude a disease in patients who do not have the disease. The *positive predictive value* is the percentage of the patients with positive test results who truly have the disease; and the *negative predictive value* is the percentage of the patients with negative test results who truly do not have the disease.

provides a method of inverting conditional probability statements—that is, if the probability (P) of x given y [P(x|y)] is known, what is the probability of y given x [P(y|x)]? For any diagnostic test for DVT, this method allows determination of the probability that a patient with a positive study result has a DVT [post-test probability of disease = P(DVT|Positive Test)] if the probability that a patient with a DVT will have a positive study is known [P(Positive Test|DVT)]. The probability that a patient with a positive or negative study actually does or does not have a DVT is given by the expressions:

$$P(DV \mid \text{Positive Test}) =$$
$$P(\text{Positive Test} \mid DVT) \times \frac{P(DVT)}{P(\text{Positive Test})}$$

$$P(\text{No DVT} \mid \text{Negative Test}) =$$
$$P(\text{Negative Test} \mid \text{No DVT}) \times \frac{P(\text{No DVT})}{P(\text{Negative Test})}$$

The probability of DVT given a positive study [P(DVT|Positive Test] and that of no DVT given a negative study [P(No DVT|Negative Test)] correspond to the positive and negative predictive values, respectively. It is clear that both of these values depend on how likely the diagnosis of DVT [P(DVT)] is in a given patient.

The importance of disease prevalence and pretest probability of disease is exemplified by duplex ultrasonography. Using a weighted mean sensitivity and specificity of 97% and 94%,[1] we can derive the positive and negative predictive values of duplex ultrasonography in groups with a variable pretest probability of disease (Table 148-2). Although the negative predictive value of venous duplex scanning is very good in populations with a disease prevalence of 10% or less, the predictive value of a positive result is poor. These theoretical considerations have been confirmed in clinical trials. The positive predictive value of an abnormal venous ultrasonography result is 100% in patients with a high pretest probability of disease, compared with only 63% to 82% for those with a low pretest probability.[116,117] Similarly, the negative predictive value of a normal proximal venous ultrasonography result is only 77.8% to 82% in patients with a high pretest probability of disease, compared with 97.8% to 99.7% in patients with a

low pretest probability.[117,118] Thus, although a normal scan result in a patient with a low pretest probability essentially excludes a diagnosis of DVT, a positive result must be viewed with suspicion, and many investigators have recommended confirmatory venography in this setting.[117]

The sensitivity of duplex ultrasonography also appears to be related to the pretest probability of disease. These differences in the accuracy of ultrasonography are probably related to the frequency of small, nonocclusive proximal thrombi and isolated calf vein thrombi in groups with different pretest probabilities of disease. For ultrasonography examinations restricted to the proximal veins, the sensitivity is greater than 90% in patients with a high pretest probability of disease but only 67% in those with a low pretest probability.[116] This situation is exemplified by differences in accuracy reported for asymptomatic and symptomatic patients. Among asymptomatic orthopedic patients, the sensitivity and specificity of ultrasonography for proximal DVT have been reported to be 62% and 97%, respectively.[119] The positive and negative predictive values of duplex scanning at various sensitivities in groups with different pretest probabilities of disease are illustrated in Figure 148-2. Although the positive predictive values in symptomatic and asymptomatic patients are similar, the lower sensitivity in asymptomatic patients significantly reduces the negative predictive value.

Similar considerations apply to the utility of D-dimer measurements. D-dimer testing is most appropriate in outpatients with a low pretest probability of disease, in whom the negative predictive value is 99% to 100%, and withholding anticoagulation therapy in this population carries a less than 1% risk of thromboembolism at 3 months.[101] Unfortunately, the diagnostic performance of D-dimer measurement is poor in those with a higher probability of disease. Although the negative predictive value of D-dimer testing (96.2%) is equivalent to that of compression ultrasonography (97.8%) in inpatients with low pretest probability of DVT, it is only 89% and 33%, respectively, in patients with moderate and high pretest probabilities.[118] Others have reported that up to 20% of patients with a high pretest probability of DVT have an objectively confirmed DVT despite a negative D-dimer result.[101] The high number of false-positive results precludes effective use of D-dimer measurement in patients with high pretest probability of DVT.[120]

Table 148-2 | Predictive Value of Venous Ultrasonography Based on Pretest Probability*

PRETEST PROBABILITY [P(DVT)]	POSITIVE PREDICTIVE VALUE [P(DVT | POSITIVE US)]	NEGATIVE PREDICTIVE VALUE [P(NO DVT | NEGATIVE US)]
0.02	0.25	1.00
0.05	0.46	1.00
0.1	0.64	1.00
0.15	0.74	0.99
0.2	0.80	0.99
0.25	0.84	0.99
0.3	0.87	0.99
0.35	0.90	0.98
0.4	0.92	0.98
0.45	0.93	0.97
0.5	0.94	0.97
0.55	0.95	0.96
0.6	0.96	0.95
0.65	0.97	0.94
0.7	0.97	0.93
0.75	0.98	0.91
0.8	0.98	0.89
0.85	0.99	0.85
0.9	0.99	0.78
0.95	1.00	0.62
1	1.00	0.00

DVT, deep venous thrombosis; P, probability; US, ultrasonography (result).
*Assumes 97% sensitivity, 94% specificity.

From Meissner MH: Off hours vascular laboratory utilization. In Pearce WH, Matsumura JS, Yao JST (eds): Trends in Vascular Surgery. Chicago, Precept Press, 2003, pp 47-60. Reproduced with permission.

These theoretical considerations have several implications with respect to the diagnostic utility of tests for acute DVT. First, the incidence of DVT in many ultrasonography validation studies was as high as 25%, but in many laboratories, the incidence has declined to less than 10%.[121] At the University of Washington, the frequency of positive ultrasonography results has declined from 25% in 1986 through 1990 to 11% in 1995.[122] According to Bayes' theorem, this change theoretically reduces the overall positive predictive value from 84% to less than 65% (see Table 148-2). Furthermore, this decreased yield has most likely resulted from greater referral of patients with low pretest probability of DVT, in whom the sensitivity, and thus the negative predictive value, is also reduced. The wide variability in the positive and negative predictive values of duplex ultrasonography and D-dimer measurements based on pretest probability has profound implications for clinical outcomes. Current clinical strategies attempt to incorporate clinical risk assessment and an assessment of pretest probability with these modalities.

■ **CLINICAL ASSESSMENT, PRETEST PROBABILITY, AND COMBINED DIAGNOSTIC STRATEGIES**

Despite the nonspecific nature of the signs and symptoms of acute DVT, objective clinical models have been developed that allow stratification of patients on the basis of the pretest probability of disease. Empiric risk stratification is a subjective approach that relies on clinician judgment to assess an individual patient's risk of DVT. Conversely, explicit criteria stipulate a predefined number of elements with a fixed value, with risk stratification based on a cumulative score. Despite observations that empiric risk stratification may be as accurate as explicit criteria,[23,124] empiric models are difficult to institutionalize and have problems with reproducibility. Agreement between empiric assessment and use of an explicit risk model is poor to fair

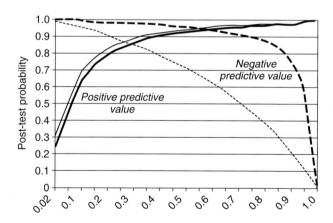

FIGURE 148-2 Positive and negative predictive value of venous ultrasonography in populations with a variable pretest probability of disease at different diagnostic accuracies. The solid lines show the positive predictive value and the dashed lines the negative predictive values. The heavy lines correspond to the sensitivity and specificity of ultrasound reported in symptomatic patients (97% sensitivity, 94% specificity) while the thin lines represent those reported in asymptomatic orthopedic patients (62% sensitivity, 97% specificity). (From Meissner MH: Off hours vascular laboratory utilization. In Pearce WH, Matsumura JS, Yao JST [eds]: Trends in Vascular Surgery. Chicago, Precept Press, 2003, pp 47-60. Reproduced with permission.)

Table 148-3 Stratification of Pretest Probability

CLINICAL FEATURE	SCORE
Active cancer (treatment ongoing or within previous 6 months or palliative)	1
Paralysis, paresis, or recent plaster immobilization of the lower extremities	1
Recently bedridden > 3 days or major surgery within 4 weeks	1
Localized tenderness along the distribution of the deep venous system	1
Entire leg swollen	1
Calf swelling by more than 3 cm compared with the asymptomatic leg (measured 10 cm below tibial tuberosity)	1
Pitting edema (greater in the symptomatic leg)	1
Collateral superficial veins (nonvaricose)	1
Alternative diagnosis as likely as or more likely than that of deep vein thrombosis	−2

Low probability ≤ 0 points; Moderate probability 1-2 points; High probability ≥ 3 points.

Modified from Wells PS, Anderson DR, Bormanis J, et al: Value of assessment of pretest probability of deep-vein thrombosis in clinical management. Lancet 350:1795-1798, 1997. Reprinted with permission.

(κ = 0.32 to 0.56).[123,125] Moreover, explicit models based on objective criteria appear to classify a greater number of patients into low and high pretest probability categories. This is important because it best identifies those patients least likely and most likely to have DVT.[123]

Successful models for determination of pretest probability have included the presence of recognized thrombotic risk factors and the probability of alternative diagnoses as well as objective clinical signs. Using an early clinical model for symptomatic outpatients, Wells and associates[116] were able to define groups with low, moderate, and high pretest probability of disease having DVT prevalences of 5%, 33%, and 85%, respectively. This probability model has subsequently been refined and simplified to incorporate eight clinical features or risk factors, each given a score of 1 if present, and the likelihood of an alternative diagnosis, for which 2 points are subtracted from the total score (Table 148-3).[125] Patients with ≤ 0 points are classified as having a low pretest probability, those with 1 or 2 points moderate probability, and those with ≥ 3 points high probability. A

valid alternative diagnosis, which is the most subjective of the nine components of the model, is present in 56% of those without DVT, compared with only 17% of those with a confirmed DVT.[120] Cellulitis and musculoskeletal disorders account for half to three quarters of these diagnoses.[114,120] When present, an alternative diagnosis lowers the clinical probability level in 85% of patients.

The Wells clinical probability model has been validated in several prospective trials and has excellent reproducibility (κ = 0.75),[120] even in comparing providers with different backgrounds.[117] It is critical to note, however, that most trials have included only outpatients without a previous history of venous thromboembolism. The incidence of DVT among outpatients with different pretest probabilities is shown in Table 148-4. In the specific setting of the emergency department, the incidence of DVT in patients with low pretest probability is only 2% to 3%.[120] This model has also been validated in hospitalized patients,[118] although the frequency of patients with low pretest probability is lower among inpatients and the incidence of DVT in these patients is higher (Table 148-5). Unfortunately, although clinical probability strategies may be useful in limiting the need for serial ultrasonography examinations in the event of a negative initial result, the 5% prevalence of DVT likely precludes completely eliminating ultrasonography even in patients with low pretest probability.

A combined strategy using an assessment of clinical probability, D-dimer measurement, and venous ultrasonography holds the greatest promise of safely limiting the number of negative ultrasound results. Algorithms can be designed in which at least some patients can be initially managed on the basis of D-dimer results (Fig. 148-3). This clinical strategy is based on the observation that the negative predictive value of D-dimer assays approaches 100% in outpatients with a low pretest clinical probability.[120,128] Because 23% to 50% of outpatients can be stratified into the low pretest probability group,[116,121,127] this approach can significantly reduce resource utilization. It is important to note that such strategies require a D-dimer assay with a sensitivity approaching 100%, have been evaluated only in outpatients, and have generally excluded patients with a previous history of DVT, clinical suspicion of PE, and preceding use of anticoagulants, or a combination of these features.

Table 148-4 Outpatient Incidence of Deep Venous Thrombosis (DVT)

STUDY*	TOTAL NO. PATIENTS	LOW PROBABILITY No. Patients	% with DVT	MODERATE PROBABILITY No. Patients	% with DVT	HIGH PROBABILITY No. Patients	% with DVT
Wells et al[117]	593	329 (55.0%)	3	193 (32.5%)	17	71 (12%)	75
Schutgens et al[126]	812	201 (24.8%)	12.9	332 (40.9%)	37.7	279 (34.3%)	59.5
Anderson et al[109]	214	118 (55.4%)	3.4	66 (30.5%)	13.6	30 (14.0%)	50
Dryjski et al[121]	66	7 (10%)	0	23 (35%)	0	36 (55%)	16.7
Bucek et al[127]	176	99 (56%)	2	—	—	—	—
Total	1861	754 (40.1%)	5.7	614 (36.4%)	26.7%	416 (24.7%)	57.7

*Superscript numbers indicate chapter references.

Modified from Meissner MH: Off hours vascular laboratory utilization. In Pearce WH, Matsumura JS, Yao JST (eds): Trends in Vascular Surgery. Chicago, Precept Press, 2003, pp 47-60. Reproduced with permission.

Table 148-5 Pretest Probability of Deep Venous Thrombosis in Outpatients and Hospitalized Patients (Inpatients)*

PROBABILITY	POINTS	OUTPATIENTS[117]		INPATIENTS[118]	
		No. of Patients (%)	DVT Incidence (%)	No. of Patients (%)	DVT Incidence (%)
Low	≤0	55.5%	3	33%	10
Moderate	1-2	32.5%	17	47.3%	19.7
High	≥3	12%	75	19%	76

*Superscript numbers indicate chapter references.

From Meissner MH: Off hours vascular laboratory utilization. In Pearce WH, Matsumura JS, Yao JST (eds): Trends in Vascular Surgery. Chicago, Precept Press, 2003, pp 47-60. Reproduced with permission.

In the emergency department setting, Anderson and colleagues[109] showed that, when used in combination with pretest probability, the negative predictive value of D-dimer measurements was 100%, 94.1%, and 86.7% in patients with low, moderate, and high pretest probabilities, respectively. The data further suggested that urgent diagnostic imaging could be safely deferred for at least 24 hours without anticoagulation in patients with low and moderate probabilities and with empiric therapy consisting of subcutaneous or intravenous unfractionated heparin in patients with high probability. These investigators concluded that diagnostic imaging might not be necessary in the patient with low clinical probability of DVT and a negative D-dimer result, although further testing was prudent in the patient with moderate or high probability. Others have similarly found the combination of a low clinical probability and negative D-dimer result to have a negative predictive value of 100% and to require no further diagnostic testing.[101,127]

Dryjski and coworkers[121] evaluated 66 patients with D-dimer assays and pretest probability assessment. No thrombi were identified in patients with low or moderate pretest probability, and the researchers concluded that further diagnostic testing was unnecessary in patients with low to moderate probability and negative D-dimer results.

Although the number of high-probability patients was higher than in many other series, confining venous ultrasonography to patients with a positive D-dimer result or high pretest probability reduced the number of referrals by 23%. In the largest management trial to date, Schutgens and associates[126] evaluated such a combined diagnostic approach in 812 patients, reserving the use of ultrasonography for patients with a high pretest probability score or an abnormal D-dimer result. The incidence of venous thromboembolism during 3 months of follow-up was only 0.6% among the 176 patients (22%) with a low or moderate pretest probability and normal D-dimer result (negative predictive value 99.4%). This study suggests that it may be safe to withhold anticoagulation in both low- and moderate-probability patients with negative D-dimer assay results. The total number of ultrasonography examinations required for outpatients referred with a suspicion of DVT was reduced by 29%.

These data suggest that outpatients without a previous history of DVT who have no symptoms of PE and are not taking anticoagulants can be safely managed with a combination of pretest probability assessment, D-dimer assay, and selective venous ultrasonography. Among patients managed according to such algorithms, the incidence of thromboembolism during 3 months of follow-up is

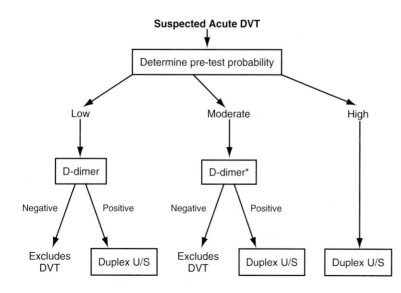

FIGURE 148-3 Diagnostic algorithm incorporating combined clinical probability / D-dimer determination and venous duplex ultrasonography. Patients with high pretest probability are triaged directly to ultrasound. If a sensitive D-dimer assay is used,* patients with non-high (low and moderate) pretest probability and a negative D-dimer can be managed without further diagnostic testing. If a less sensitive D-dimer assay is used, moderate pretest probability patients should be triaged to duplex. (From Meissner MH: Off hours vascular laboratory utilization. In Pearce WH, Matsumura JS, Yao JST [eds]: Trends in Vascular Surgery. Chicago, Precept Press, 2003, pp 47-60. Reproduced with permission.)

less than the 1.3% incidence after negative venography[35] and equivalent to the 0.6% to 0.7% rate after serially negative ultrasonography examinations.[62,63] Patients with low pretest probability and a negative D-dimer result likely require no further diagnostic testing. Duplex scanning is required in patients with high pretest probability regardless of D-dimer results.

Unfortunately, the evaluation of patients with moderate pretest probability remains somewhat unclear, and they have variously been managed according to the algorithms for low-probability[121,126] or high-probability[109,112] patients. Appropriate management of these patients likely depends on the sensitivity of the D-dimer assay. If an assay with limited sensitivity, such as the whole blood agglutination assay, is used, up to 6% of patients with moderate pretest probability may have DVT despite a negative D-dimer result.[109] However, if a more sensitive assay is used, negative predictive values may approach 99.6% in this group.[126] Moderate-probability patients can probably be managed as low-probability patients, that is, without further diagnostic testing, if a sensitive D-dimer assay result is within the normal range. However, they should be managed as high-probability patients if only a relatively insensitive assay is available. Given the variability in disease prevalence and available D-dimer assays, local validation of these algorithms at the time they are instituted is appropriate.

Diagnostic strategies for inpatients are less well developed. The negative predictive value of D-dimer measurement combined with pretest probability has been noted to be as high as 97.2%,[112] but this strategy has not been validated in prospective management trials. Although pretest risk stratification is possible, the incidence of DVT in low-probability inpatients may be as high as 10%.[118] Furthermore, as discussed previously, the utility of inpatient D-dimer testing is substantially less because both sensitivity and specificity are decreased. Most hospitalized patients with a clinical suspicion of DVT therefore need confirmatory diagnostic testing.

■ SUMMARY

Although DVT is a common disease with potentially life-threatening consequences, its signs and symptoms are nonspecific. Clinical assessment in patients with suspected DVT is notoriously inaccurate. The diagnosis therefore requires confirmatory testing that is often resource intensive. Historically, venography has been the gold standard for such testing. Although accurate, it has many limitations and has potential for complications. Venography is currently reserved for clinical situations involving indeterminate ultrasonography findings in most institutions. Duplex ultrasonography has replaced venography as the primary imaging modality for DVT evaluation. Unfortunately, ultrasonography has become overutilized in many institutions, straining scarce resources and compromising diagnostic accuracy. MRV has utility for evaluating central and pelvic vein thrombosis, but other imaging modalities, including CT and nuclear medicine, are not widely used in current clinical paradigms. D-dimer assays, a relatively new diagnostic modality, can be sensitive for DVT, but sensitivity and specificity also depend highly on patient

population. The best clinical utility for D-dimer assays is in patients with low probability of DVT.

The most promising clinical strategy for improving diagnostic accuracy incorporates clinical criteria, D-dimer assays, and ultrasonography examination. In such an algorithm, clinical characteristics are used to stratify patients into groups with low, moderate, and high probability of disease, and D-dimer screening is used in the low-probability and possibly the moderate-probability patients. Ultrasonography is used as a primary diagnostic modality in patients with high probability of DVT and as confirmatory testing in other patients with positive D-dimer assay results.

■ REFERENCES

1. Kearon C, Julian JA, Math M, et al: Noninvasive diagnosis of deep venous thrombosis: McMaster Diagnostic Imaging Practice Guidelines Initiative. Ann Intern Med 128:663-677, 1998.
2. Strothman G, Blebea J, Fowl RJ: Contralateral duplex scanning for deep venous thrombosis is unnecessary in patients with symptoms. J Vasc Surg 22:543-547, 1995.
3. Anderson FA, Wheeler HB, Goldberg RJ, et al: A population-based perspective of the hospital incidence and case-fatality rates of deep vein thrombosis and pulmonary embolism. Arch Intern Med 151:933-938, 1991.
4. Barnes RW, Wu KK, Hoak JC: Fallibility of the clinical diagnosis of venous thrombosis. JAMA 234:605-607, 1975.
5. Cranley JJ, Canos AJ, Sull WJ: The diagnosis of deep venous thrombosis: Fallibility of clinical symptoms and signs. Arch Surg 111:34-36, 1976.
6. Haeger K: Problems of acute deep venous thrombosis. I: The interpretation of signs and symptoms. Angiology 20:219-223, 1969.
7. Kakkar VV, Flanc C, Howe CT, et al: Natural history of post-operative deep-vein thrombosis. Lancet 2(7614):230-233, 1969.
8. Rabinov K, Paulin S: Roentgen diagnosis of venous thrombosis in the leg. Arch Surg 104:134-144, 1972.
9. Bettman MA, Robbins A, Braun SD, et al: Contrast venography of the leg: Diagnostic efficacy, tolerance, and complication rates with ionic and nonionic contrast media. Radiology 165:113-116, 1987.
10. Wheeler HB, O'Donnel JA, Anderson FA, Benedict K: Occlusive impedance phlebography: A diagnostic procedure for venous thrombosis and pulmonary embolism. Prog Cardiovasc Dis 17:199-205, 1974.
11. Hull RD, Taylor DW, Hush J, et al: Impedance plethysmography: The relationship between venous filling and sensitivity and specificity for proximal vein thrombosis. Circulation 58:898-902, 1978.
12. Hull RD, Hirsch J, Carter CF, et al: Diagnostic efficacy of impedance plethysmography for clinically suspected deep-vein thrombosis. Ann Intern Med 102:21-28, 1985.
13. Wheeler HB, Anderson FA, Cardullo PA, et al: Suspected deep vein thrombosis: Management by impedance plethysmography. Arch Surg 177:1206-1209, 1982.
14. Patterson RB, Fowl RJ, Keller KD, et al: The limitations of impedance plethysmography in the diagnosis of deep vein thrombosis. J Vasc Surg 9:725-730, 1989.
15. Flanc C, Kakkar VV, Clarke MB: The detection of venous thrombosis of the legs using ^{125}I-labelled fibrinogen. Br J Surg 55:742-747, 1968.
16. Negus D, Pinto DJ, Le Quense LP, et al: ^{125}I-labelled fibrinogen in the diagnosis of deep-vein thrombosis and its correlation with phlebography. Br J Surg 55:835-839, 1968.
17. Lemoine JR, Moser KM: Radiolabelled fibrinogen and impedance plethysmography in the diagnosis of deep vein thrombosis. Vasc Surg 11:216-218, 1977.
18. Wheeler HB, Anderson FA: Diagnostic methods for deep vein thrombosis. Haemostasis 25:6-26, 1995.

19. Holmgren K, Jacobsson H, Johnsson H, Lofsjogard-Nilsson E: Thermography and plethysmography, a non-invasive alternative to venography in the diagnosis of deep vein thrombosis. J Intern Med 228:29-33, 1990.

20. Sumner DS, Mattos MA: Diagnosis of Deep Vein Thrombosis with Real Time Color and Duplex Scanning. St. Louis, Mosby, 1993.

21. Hull R, Hirsch J, Sackett DL, Stoddard G: Cost effectiveness of clinical diagnosis, venography, and noninvasive testing in patients with symptomatic deep vein thrombosis. N Engl J Med 304:1561-1567, 1981.

22. Cooperman M, Martin EW, Satiani B, et al: Detection of deep venous thrombosis by impedance plethysmography. Am J Surg 137:242-254, 1979.

23. Peters SH, Jonker JJ, deBoer AC, Ottolander GJ: Home diagnosis of deep vein thrombosis with impedance plethysmography. Thromb Haemost 48:297-300, 1982.

24. Johnson WC: Evaluation of newer techniques for the diagnosis of venous thrombosis. J Surg Res 16:473-481, 1974.

25. Criado E, Burnham CB: Predictive value of clinical criteria for the diagnosis of deep vein thrombosis. Surgery 122:578-583, 1997.

26. Nypaver TJ, Shepard AD, Kiell CS, et al: Outpatient duplex scanning for deep vein thrombosis: Parameters predictive of a negative study result. J Vasc Surg 18:821-826, 1993.

27. Markel A, Manzo RA, Bergelin R, Strandness DE: Acute deep vein thrombosis: Diagnosis, localization, and risk factors. J Vasc Med Biol 3:432-439, 1991.

28. McLachlin JA, Richards T, Paterson JC: An evaluation of clinical signs in the diagnosis of deep venous thrombosis. Arch Surg 85:738-744, 1962.

29. Sevitt S, Gallagher N: Venous thrombosis and pulmonary embolism: A clinico-pathological study in injured and burned victims. Br J Surg 48:475-489, 1961.

30. Goldhaber SZ, Buring JE, Hennekens CH: Cancer and venous thromboembolism. Arch Intern Med 147:216, 1987.

31. Barker NW, Nygaard KK, Walters W, Priestley JT: A statistical study of post-operative venous thrombosis and pulmonary embolism: Predisposing factors. Proc Mayo Clin 16:17-21, 1941.

32. Kakkar VV, Howe CT, Nicolaides AN, Clarke MB: Deep vein thrombosis of the leg: Is there a "high risk" group? Am J Surg 120:527-530, 1970.

33. Beebe HG, Scissons RP, Salles-Cunha SX, et al: Gender bias in use of venous ultrasonography for diagnosis of deep vein thrombosis. J Vasc Surg 22:538-542, 1995.

34. Glover JL, Bendick PJ: Appropriate indications for venous duplex ultrasonic examinations. Surgery 120:725-731, 1996.

35. Hull R, Hirsh J, Sackett DL, et al: Clinical validity of a negative venogram in patients with clinically suspected venous thrombosis. Circulation 64:622-625, 1981.

36. Nadich J, Feinberg A, Karp-Harman H, et al: Contrast venography: Reassessment of its role. Radiology 168:97-100, 1988.

37. Browse NL, Thomas ML: Source of non-lethal pulmonary emboli. Lancet 1(7851):258-259, 1974.

38. Baxter GM, Kincaid W, Jeffrey RF, et al: Comparison of colour Doppler ultrasound with venography in the diagnosis of axillary and subclavian vein thrombosis. Br J Radiol 64:777-781, 1991.

39. Falk RL, Smith DF: Thrombosis of upper extremity thoracic inlet veins: Diagnosis with duplex Doppler sonography. Am J Roentenol 149:677-682, 1987.

40. Sauerbrei E, Thomson JG, McLachlan MS, et al: Observer variation in lower limb venography. J Can Assoc Radiol 32:28-29, 1981.

41. Lea Thomas M, Walters HL, Briggs GM: A double-blind comparative study of the tolerance of sodium and meglumine ioxaglate (Hexabrix) with meglumine iothalamate (Conray) in ascending phlebography of the leg. Australas Radiol 26:288-290, 1982.

42. Crummy AB, Stieghortst MF, Turski PA, et al: Digital subtraction angiography: Current status and use of intra-arterial injection. Radiology 145:303-307, 1986.

43. Redman HC: Deep venous thrombosis: Is contrast venography still the "gold standard"? Radiology 168:277-278, 1988.

44. Lea Thomas M, Keeling FP, Piaggio RB, Treweeke PS: Contrast agent induced thrombophlebitis: Iopamidol versus meglumine iothalamate. Br J Radiol 57:205-207, 1984.

45. Lensing AW, Prandoni P, Brandjes D, et al: Detection of deep-vein thrombosis by real-time B-mode ultrasonography. N Engl J Med 320:342-345, 1989.

46. Cogo A, Lensing AWA, Prandoni P, et al: Comparison of real-time B-mode ultrasonography and Doppler ultrasound with contrast venography in the diagnosis of venous thrombosis in symptomatic outpatients. Thromb Haemost 70:404-407, 1993.

47. Killewich LA, Bedford GR, Beach KW, Strandness DE: Diagnosis of deep venous thrombosis: A prospective study comparing duplex scanning to contrast venography. Circulation 79:810-814, 1989.

48. Lewis BD, James EM, Welch TJ, et al: Diagnosis of acute deep venous thrombosis of the lower extremities: Prospective evaluation of color Doppler flow imaging versus venography. Radiology 192:651-655, 1994.

49. Vaccaro JP, Cronan JJ, Dorfman GS: Outcome analysis of patients with normal compression US exams. Radiology 175:645-649, 1990.

50. Mattos MA, Melendres G, Sumner DS, et al: Prevalence and distribution of calf vein thrombosis in patients with symptomatic deep venous thrombosis: A color-flow duplex study. J Vasc Surg 24:738-744, 1996.

51. Messina LM, Sarpa MS, Smith MA, et al: Clinical significance of routine imaging of iliac and calf veins by color flow duplex scanning in patients suspected of having acute lower extremity deep venous thrombosis. Surgery 114:921-927, 1993.

52. Wolf B, Nichols DM, Duncan JL: Safety of a single duplex scan to exclude deep venous thrombosis. Br J Surg 87:1525-1528, 2000.

53. Cogo A, Lensing AW, Prandoni P, Hirsch J: Distribution of thrombosis in patients with symptomatic deep vein thrombosis: Implications for simplifying the diagnostic process with compression ultrasound. Arch Intern Med 153: 2777-2780, 1993.

54. Philbrick JT, Becker DM: Calf deep venous thrombosis: A wolf in sheep's clothing? Arch Intern Med 148:2131-2138, 1988.

55. Lohr JM, James KV, Deshmukh RM, et al: Calf vein thrombi are not a benign finding. Am J Surg 170:86-90, 1995.

56. Lagerstedt CI, Olsson C, Fagher BO, et al: Need for long-term anticoagulant treatment in symptomatic calf vein thrombosis. Lancet 2(8454):515-518, 1985.

57. Huisman MV, Buller HR, ten Cate JW, Vreeken J: Serial impedance plethysmography for suspected deep venous thrombosis in outpatients: The Amsterdam General Practitioner Study. N Engl J Med 314:832-828, 1986.

58. Moreno-Cabral R, Kistner RL, Nordyke RA: Importance of calf vein thrombophlebitis. Surgery 80:735-742, 1976.

59. Fraser JD, Anderson DR: Deep venous thrombosis: Recent advances and optimal investigation with US. Radiology 211:9-24, 1999.

60. Sluzewski M, Koopman MMW, Schuur KH, et al: Influence of negative ultrasound findings on the management of in- and outpatients with suspected deep-vein thrombosis. Eur J Radiol 13:174-177, 1991.

61. Heijboer H, Buller HR, Lensing AWA, et al: A comparison of real-time compression ultrasonography with impedance plethysmography for the diagnosis of deep-vein thrombosis in symptomatic outpatients. N Engl J Med 329:1365-1369, 1993.

62. Birdwell B, Raskob G, Whitsett T, et al: The clinical validity of normal compression ultrasonography in outpatients suspected of having deep venous thrombosis. Ann Intern Med 128:1-7, 1998.

63. Cogo A, Lensing AWA, Koopman MMW, et al: Compression ultrasonography for diagnostic management of patients with clinically suspected deep vein thrombosis: Prospective cohort study. BMJ 316:617-620, 1998.

64. Meissner M, Caps M, Bergelin R, et al: Early outcome after isolated calf vein thrombosis. J Vasc Surg 26:749-756, 1997.

65. Elias A, Le Corff G, Bouvier J, et al: Value of real time B mode ultrasound imaging in the diagnosis of deep vein thrombosis of the lower limbs. Int Angiol 6:175-182, 1987.

66. Badgett DK, Comerota MC, Khan MN, et al: Duplex venous imaging: Role for a comprehensive lower extremity examination. Ann Vasc Surg 14:73-76, 2000.

67. Noren A, Lindmarker P, Rosfors S: A retrospective follow-up study of patients with suspected deep vein thrombosis and negative results of colour duplex ultrasound. Phlebography 12:56-59, 1997.

68. Schellong SM, Schwarz T, Halbritter K, et al: Complete compression ultrasonography of the leg veins as a single test for the diagnosis of deep vein thrombosis. Thromb Haemost 89:228-234, 2003.

69. Elias A, Mallard L, Elias M, et al: A single complete ultrasound investigation of the venous network for the diagnostic management of patients with a clinically suspected first episode of deep venous thrombosis of the lower limbs. Thromb Haemost 89:221-227, 2003.

70. Noren A, Ottosson E, Rosfors S: Is it safe to withhold anticoagulation based on a single negative color duplex examination in patients with suspected deep venous thrombosis? A prospective 3-month follow-up study. Angiology 53:521-527, 2002.

71. Cornuz J, Pearson SD, Polak JF: Deep venous thrombosis: Complete lower extremity venous US evaluation in patients with known risk factors—outcome study. Radiology 211:637-641, 1999.

72. Sheiman RG, McArdle CR: Bilateral lower extremity US in the patients with unilateral leg symptoms of deep venous thrombosis: Assessment of need. Radiology 194:171-173, 1995.

73. Naidich JB, Torre JR, Pellorito JS, et al: Suspected deep venous thrombosis: Is US of both legs necessary? Radiology 200:429-431, 1996.

74. Kim HM, Kuntz KM, Cronan JJ: Optimal management strategy for use of compression US for deep venous thrombosis in symptomatic patients: A cost-effective analysis. Acad Radiol 7:67-76, 2000.

75. Hillner BE, Philbrick JT, Becker DM: Optimal management of suspected lower-extremity deep vein thrombosis. Arch Intern Med 152:165-175, 1992.

76. Loud PA, Grossman ZD, Klippenstein DL, et al: Combined CT venography and pulmonary angiography: A new diagnostic technique for suspected thromboembolic disease. AJR Am J Roentgenol 170:951-954, 1998.

77. Walsh G, Redmond S: Does addition of CT pelvic venography to CT pulmonary angiography protocols contribute to the diagnosis of pulmonary thromboembolic disease? Clin Radiol 57:462-465, 2002.

78. Coche EE, Hamoir XL, Hammer FD, et al: Using dual-detector helical CT angiography to detect deep venous thrombosis in patients with suspicion of pulmonary embolism. AJR Am J Roentgenol 176:1035-1039, 2001.

79. Loud PA, Katz DS, Bruce DA, e al: Deep venous thrombosis with suspected pulmonary embolism: Detection with combined CT venography and pulmonary angiography. Radiology 219:498-502, 2001.

80. Begemann PGC, Bonacker M, Kemper J, et al: Evaluation of the deep venous system in patients with suspected pulmonary embolism with multi-detector CT: A prospective study in comparison to Doppler sonography. J Comput Assist Tomogr 27:399-409, 2003.

81. Peterson DA, Kaverooni EA, Wakefield TW, et al: Computed tomographic venography is specific but not sensitive for diagnosis of acute lower extremity deep venous thrombosis in patients with suspected pulmonary embolus. J Vasc Surg 34:798-804, 2001.

82. Stover MD, Morgan SJ, Bosse MJ, et al: Prospective comparison of contrast-enhanced computed tomography versus magnetic resonance venography in the detection of occult deep pelvic vein thrombosis in patients with pelvic and acetabular fractures. J Orthop Trauma 16:613-621, 2002.

83. Erdman WA, Weinreb JC, Cohen JM, et al: Venous thrombosis: Clinical and experimental MR imaging. Radiology 161:233-238, 1986.

84. Hricak H, Amparo EG, Fisher MR, et al: Abdominal venous system: Assessment using MR. Radiology 156:415-422, 1985.

85. Erdman WA, Jayson HT, Redman HC, et al: Deep venous thrombosis of extremities: Role of MR imaging in the diagnosis. Radiology 174:425-431, 1990.

86. Butty S, Hagspiel KD, Leung DA, et al: Body MR venography. Radiol Clin North Am 40:899-919, 2002.

87. Carpenter JP, Holland JA, Baum RA, et al: Magnetic resonance venography for the detection of deep venous thrombosis: Comparison with contrast venography and duplex Doppler ultrasonography. J Vasc Surg 18:734-741, 1993.

88. Laissy JP, Cinqualbre A, Loshkajian A, et al: Assessment of deep venous thrombosis in the lower limbs and pelvis: MR venography versus duplex Doppler sonography. AJR Am J Roentgenol 167:971-975, 1996.

89. Fraser DGW, Moody AR, Davidson IR, et al: Deep venous thrombosis: Diagnosis by using venous enhanced subtracted peak arterial MR venography versus conventional venography. Radiology 226:812-820, 2003.

90. Froelich JB, Prince MR, Greenfield LJ, et al: "Bull's-eye" sign on gadolinium-enhanced magnetic resonance venography determines thrombus presence and age: A preliminary study. J Vasc Surg 26:809-816, 1997.

91. Larsson EM, Sunden P, Olsson CG, et al: MR venography using an intravascular contrast agent: Results from a multicenter phase 2 study of dosage. AJR Am J Roentgenol 180:227-232, 2003.

92. Evans AJ, Sostman HD, Knelson MH, et al: 1992 ARRS Executive Council Award: Detection of deep venous thrombosis: Prospective comparison of MR imaging with contrast venography. AJR Am J Roentgenol 161:131-139, 1993.

93. Spritzer CE, Arata MA, Freed KS: Isolated deep venous thrombosis: Relative frequency as detected with MR imaging. Radiology 219:521-525, 2000.

94. Stern JP, Abehsera M, Grenet D, et al: Detection of pelvic vein thrombosis by magnetic resonance angiography in patients with acute pulmonary embolism and normal lower limb compression ultra-sonography. Chest 122:112-121, 2002.

95. Muto P, Lastoria S, Varella P, et al: Detecting deep venous thrombosis with technetium-99m-labeled synthetic peptide P280. J Nucl Med 36:1384-1391, 1995.

96. Pearson DA, Lister-James J, McBride WJ, et al: Thrombus imaging using technetium-99m-labeled high potency GPIIb/IIIa receptor agonists: Chemistry and initial biological studies. J Med Chem 39:1372-1382, 1996.

97. Carretta RF: Scintigraphic imaging of lower-extremity acute venous thrombosis. Adv Ther 15:315-322, 1998.

98. Taillefer R, Edell S, Innes G, Lister-James J: Acute thrombo-scintigraphy with 99Tc-apcitide: Results of the phase 3 multicenter trial comparing 99Tc-apcitide scintigraphy with contrast venography for imaging acute DVT. J Nucl Med 41:1214-1223, 2000.

99. Bates SH, Lister-James J, Julian JM, et al: Imaging characteristics of a novel technetium Tc 99m-labeled platelet glycoprotein IIb/IIIa receptor antagonist in patients with acute deep vein thrombosis or a history of deep vein thrombosis. Arch Intern Med 163:452-456, 2003.

100. Horellou M-H, Conard J, Samama MM: Venous Thromboembolism: An Evidence-Based Atlas. Armonk, NY, Futura, 1996.

101. Kelly J, Hunt BJ: Role of D-dimers in diagnosis of venous thrombo-embolism. Lancet 359:456-458, 2002.

102. Gaffney PJ, Creighton LJ, Callus MJ, Thorpe R: Monoclonal antibodies to crosslinked fibrin degradation products (XL-FDP). II: Evolution in a variety of clinical conditions. Br J Haematol 68:91-96, 1988.

103. Schutgens REG, Esseboom EU, Haas FJLM, et al: Usefulness of a semiquantitative D-dimer test for the exclusion of deep venous thrombosis in outpatients. Am J Med 112:617-621, 2002.

104. Brotman DJ, Segal JB, Jani JT, et al: Limitations of D-dimer testing in unselected inpatients with suspected venous thromboembolism. Am J Med 114:276-282, 2003.

105. Larsen TB, Stoffersen E, Christensen CS, Laursen B: Validity of D-dimer tests in the diagnosis of deep vein thrombosis: A prospective comparative study of three quantitative assays. J Intern Med 252:36-40, 2002.

106. Carter CJ, Doyle DL, Dawson N, et al: Investigations into the clinical utility of latex D-dimer in the diagnosis of deep venous thrombosis. Thromb Haemost 69:8-11, 1993.

107. de Moerloose P: D-dimer assays for the exclusion of venous thromboembolism: Which test for which diagnostic strategy? Thromb Haemost 83:180-181, 2000.

108. van der Graaf F, van den Borne H, van der Kolk M, et al: Exclusion of deep venous thrombosis with D-dimer testing: Comparison of 13 D-dimer methods in 99 outpatients suspected of deep venous thrombosis using venography as reference standard. Thromb Haemost 85:191-198, 2000.

109. Anderson DR, Wells PS, Stiell I, et al: Management of patients with suspected deep vein thrombosis in the emergency department: Combining use of a clinical diagnosis model with D-dimer testing. J Emerg Med 19:225-230, 2000.

110. Wahlander K, Tengborn L, Hellstrom M, et al: Comparison of various D-dimer tests for the diagnosis of deep venous thrombosis. Blood Coag Fibrinol 10:121-126, 1999.

111. Philbrick JT, Heim S: The D-dimer test for deep venous thrombosis: Gold standards and bias in negative predictive values. Clin Chem 49:570-574, 2003.

112. Aschwanden M, Labs KH, Jeanneret C, et al: The value of rapid D-dimer testing combined with structured clinical evaluation for the diagnosis of deep vein thrombosis. J Vasc Surg 30:929-935, 1999.

113. Shitrit D, Levi H, Huerta M, et al: Appropriate indications for venous duplex scanning based on D-dimer assay. Ann Vasc Surg 16:304-308, 2002.

114. Tick LW, Ton E, van Voorthuizen T, et al: Practical diagnostic management of patients with clinically suspected deep vein thrombosis by clinical probability test, compression ultrasonography, and D-dimer test. Am J Med 113:630-635, 2002.

115. Grunkemeir GL, Payne N: Bayesian analysis: A new statistical paradigm for new technology. Ann Thorac Surg 74:1901-1908, 2002.

116. Wells PS, Hirsh J, Anderson DR, et al: Accuracy of clinical assessment of deep-vein thrombosis. Lancet 345:1326-1330, 1995.

117. Wells PS, Anderson DR, Bormanis J, et al: Value of assessment of pretest probability of deep-vein thrombosis in clinical management. Lancet 350:1795-1798, 1997.

118. Wells PS, Anderson DR, Bormanis J, et al: Application of a diagnostic clinical model for the management of hospitalized patients with suspected deep-vein thrombosis. Thromb Haemost 81:493-497, 1999.

119. Wells P, Lensing A, Davidson B, et al: Accuracy of ultrasound for the diagnosis of deep venous thrombosis in asymptomatic patients after orthopedic surgery. Ann Intern Med 122:47-53, 1995.

120. Shields GP, Turnipseed S, Panacek EA, et al: Validation of the Canadian clinical probability model for acute venous thrombosis. Acad Emerg Med 9:561-566, 2002.

121. Dryjski M, O'Brien-Irr MS, Harris LM, et al: Evaluation of a screening protocol to exclude the diagnosis of deep venous thrombosis among emergency department patients. J Vasc Surg 34:1010-1015, 2001.

122. Zierler BK: Screening for acute DVT: Optimal utilization of the vascular diagnostic laboratory. Semin Vasc Surg 14:206-214, 2001.

123. Miron MJ, Perrier A, Bounameaux H: Clinical assessment of suspected deep vein thrombosis: Comparison between a score and empirical assessment. J Intern Med 247:249-254, 2000.

124. Perrier A, Desmarais S, Miron MJ, et al: Non-invasive diagnosis of venous thromboembolism in outpatients. Lancet 353:190-195, 1999.

125. Wells PS, Hirsh J, Anderson DR, et al: A simple clinical model for the diagnosis of deep-vein thrombosis combined with impedance plethysmography: Potential for an improvement in the diagnostic process. J Intern Med 243:15-23, 1998.

126. Schutgens RE, Ackermark P, Haas FJ, et al: Combination of a normal D-dimer concentration and a non-high pretest clinical probability score is a safe strategy to exclude deep venous thrombosis. Circulation 107:593-597, 2003.

127. Bucek RA, Koca N, Reiter M, et al: Algorithms for the diagnosis of deep-vein thrombosis in patients with low clinical pretest probability. Thromb Res 105:43-47, 2002.

128. Cornuz J, Ghali WA, Hayoz D, et al: Clinical prediction of deep venous thrombosis using two risk assessment methods in combination with rapid quantitative D-dimer testing. Am J Med 112:198-203, 2002.

Prevention and Medical Treatment of Acute Deep Venous Thrombosis

149

GRAHAM F. PINEO, MD
RUSSELL D. HULL, MBBS, MSc

Deep venous thrombosis (DVT) most commonly arises in the deep veins of the calf muscles or, less commonly, in the proximal deep veins of the leg. DVT confined to the calf veins is associated with a low risk of clinically important pulmonary embolism.[1-3] However, without treatment, approximately 20% of calf vein thrombi extend into the proximal venous system, where they may pose a serious and potentially life-threatening disorder.[3-5] Untreated proximal venous thrombosis is associated with a 10% risk of fatal pulmonary embolism and at least a 50% risk of pulmonary embolism or recurrent venous thrombosis.[1-3] Furthermore, the post-thrombotic syndrome is associated with extensive proximal venous thrombosis and carries its own long-term morbidity.

It is now well established that clinically important pulmonary emboli arise from thrombi in the proximal deep veins of the legs.[3,6-9] Other, less common sources of pulmonary embolism are the deep pelvic veins, the renal veins, the inferior vena cava, the right heart, and, occasionally, the axillary veins. The clinical significance of pulmonary embolism depends on the size of the embolus and the cardiorespiratory reserve of the patient.

■ PREVENTION OF VENOUS THROMBOEMBOLISM

There are two approaches to the prevention of fatal pulmonary embolism, primary and secondary. Primary prophylaxis is carried out with the use of either drugs or physical methods that are effective for preventing DVT. Secondary prevention involves the early detection and treatment of subclinical venous thrombosis through screening of postoperative patients with objective tests that are sensitive for venous thrombosis. Primary prophylaxis is preferred in most clinical circumstances. Furthermore, prevention of DVT and pulmonary embolism is more cost-effective than treatment of the complications when they occur.[10-14] Secondary prevention through case-finding studies should never replace primary prophylaxis. It should be reserved for patients in whom primary prophylaxis is either contraindicated or ineffective.

The prevention of thrombosis can be directed toward the three components of Virchow's triad—blood flow, factors within the blood itself, and the vascular endothelium. Some methods act on all three, resulting in a reduction of venous stasis, prevention of the hypercoagulable state induced by tissue trauma and other factors, and protection of the endothelium. Whichever method is used, prophylaxis should be initiated before induction of anesthesia if possible, as it has been demonstrated that the thrombotic process commences intraoperatively[15] and may persist for days or weeks after surgery.

For patients undergoing general surgical procedures, the pattern of practice based on numerous clinical trials has been to start prophylaxis 2 hours preoperatively with either unfractionated heparin or low-molecular-weight heparin (LMWH). This approach has been shown to be both effective and safe and, indeed, has resulted in a significant decrease in the incidence of fatal pulmonary embolism in surgical patients.[15-20] For patients undergoing high-risk orthopedic surgical procedures, such as total hip or total knee replacement and surgery for hip fracture because of concern about excess bleeding, commencement of prophylaxis has been delayed. Thus, in Europe, prophylaxis is started 10 to 12 hours preoperatively, whereas in North America, prophylaxis is usually started 12 to 24 hours postoperatively. This difference in patterns of practice may account for the difference in the rates of postoperative venous thrombosis and bleeding in Europe and North America.

There is now good evidence that the timing of the initial administration of a prophylactic agent has a significant effect on the incidence of postoperative venous thrombosis.[21-23] In one study, starting an LMWH (dalteparin) at half the daily dose within 2 hours of hip replacement surgery, followed by a further half dose 6 to 8 hours later, and then using the usual daily dose once a day was associated with a significantly lower incidence of venous thrombosis than that for placebo or warfarin.[22] The incidence of venographically proven DVT was 14.6% with LMWH, compared with 25.8% for warfarin started the evening before surgery ($P = .006$). The incidence of proximal venous thrombosis was similar in the two LMWH groups. Although there was no difference in the incidence of major bleeding, patients given preoperative LMWH had more bleeding complications involving the operative site, and a higher percentage required postoperative transfusions. No difference in the incidence of major bleeding was reported by the principal investigators; however, assessment of major bleeding from time 0 to day 8 by the central adjudication committee identified a higher incidence of major bleeding in the patients in whom LMWH was started preoperatively compared with either the postoperative LMWH group or the warfarin group.

Hull and colleagues[23] systematically reviewed the results of two studies comparing the early initiation of LMWH with warfarin and those of two previous studies comparing warfarin prophylaxis with LMWH started 12 hours preoperatively or 12 to 24 hours postoperatively. These investigators showed that the incidence of postoperative venous thrombosis was significantly lower in the two clinical trials starting prophylaxis in close proximity to surgery than in the studies in which LMWH was started either 12 hours preoperatively or 12 to 24 hours postoperatively (Figs. 149-1 through 149-3).[23] There was no increase in the incidence of major bleeding. Starting LMWH (enoxaparin) no more than 8 hours postoperatively also led to a significantly lower incidence of venous thrombosis in patients undergoing total knee replacement than starting warfarin on the night of surgery, although there was a higher incidence of total bleeding rates with LMWH.[24]

The regimen of LMWH started 4 to 6 hours after surgery at half the usual high-risk dose and then continuing with the usual high-risk dose the following day was included in the most recent American College of Chest Physicians (ACCP) recommendations for patients undergoing elective hip replacement.[20] As discussed later, there has been concern about the associated use of neuraxial anesthesia and LMWH prophylaxis because of a cluster of occurrences of spinal hematoma.[25] This intriguing difference between the incidences of bleeding complications in Europe and the United States may arise from local practice patterns with a predominant tendency toward once-daily LMWH prophylaxis in Europe and twice-daily prophylaxis using a higher total daily dose in the United States. Because half the usual high-risk dose of the LMWH is administered in the close postoperative proximity regimen and the average time of initiation after spinal anesthesia was 9 hours, the close postoperative proximity regimen may be a safe approach in conjunction with spinal anesthesia.

Without prophylaxis, the frequency of fatal pulmonary embolism ranges from 0.1% to 0.8% in patients undergoing elective general surgery,[26-28] from 2% to 3% in patients undergoing elective hip replacement,[29] and from 4% to 7% in patients undergoing surgery for a fractured hip.[30] The need for prophylaxis after elective hip replacement has been questioned because of the low incidence of fatal pulmonary embolism (PE) in patients participating in clinical trials.[31] However, review of data from the National Confidential Enquiry into Peri-Operative Deaths (NCEPOD) indicates that PE continues to be the most common cause of death after total hip replacement surgery; PE was confirmed at autopsy in 35% of patients who died.[32] Factors raising the risk of postoperative venous thrombosis include advanced age, malignancy, previous venous thromboembolism, obesity, heart failure, and paralysis.

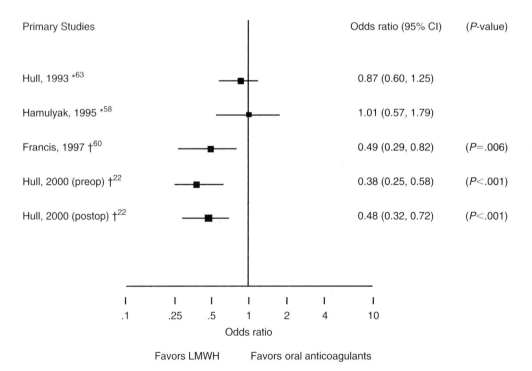

FIGURE 149-1 Primary study odds ratios for all deep venous thrombosis. Odds ratios are indicated by *boxes. Horizontal lines* represent 95% confidence intervals. Odds ratios less than 1.0 favor low-molecular-weight heparin(s) (LMWH); odds ratios greater than 1.0 favor oral anticoagulants. *Study using remote timing prophylaxis. †Study using close proximity timing prophylaxis. (Adapted from Hull RD, Pineo GF, Stein PD, et al: Timing of initial administration of low-molecular-weight heparin prophylaxis against deep vein thrombosis in patients following elective hip arthroplasty. Arch Intern Med 160:1952-1960, 2001.)

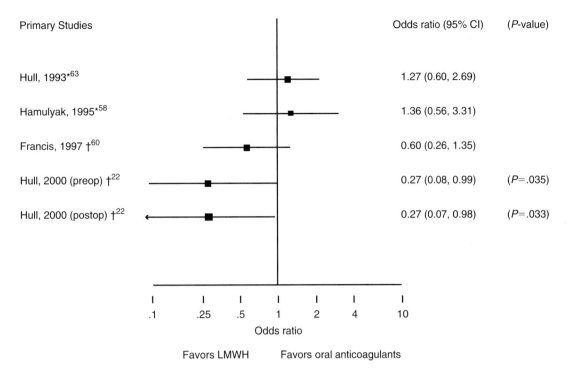

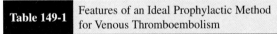

FIGURE 149-2   Primary study odds ratios for proximal deep venous thrombosis. Odds ratios are indicated by *boxes. Horizontal lines* represent 95% confidence intervals. Odds ratios less than 1.0 favor low-molecular-weight heparin(s) (LMWH); odds ratios greater than 1.0 favor oral anticoagulants. *Study using remote timing prophylaxis. †Study using close proximity timing prophylaxis. (Adapted from Hull RD, Pineo GF, Stein PD, et al: Timing of initial administration of low-molecular-weight heparin prophylaxis against deep vein thrombosis in patients following elective hip arthroplasty. Arch Intern Med 160:1952-1960, 2001.)

The ideal prophylactic agent is described in Table 149-1. Prophylactic measures most commonly used are low-dose or adjusted-dose unfractionated heparin, LMWH, oral anticoagulant (International Normalized Ratio [INR] 2.0 to 3.0), and intermittent pneumatic compression. The pentasaccharide fondaparinux (Arixtra) has now been approved for use in the United States for patients undergoing surgery for total hip or total knee replacement or for hip fracture.

There has also been concern about the use of regional anesthesia, in the form of intraspinal or epidural anesthesia or analgesia, and prophylactic anticoagulants. Spinal hematomas have been reported with the use of intravenous or subcutaneous heparin and warfarin treatment, but most of these complications occurred in patients with complex clinical problems.[33] With the advent of LMWH and the greater use of regional anesthesia, concern was raised about the potential risk of neuraxial damage due to bleeding when the two regimens are used together. Surveys among anesthetists in Europe suggested that the likelihood of spinal hematoma in this setting is remote.[34,35] However, experience in the United States with the use of neuraxial anesthesia and analgesia and the postoperative administration of LMWH has resulted in a number of case reports of spinal hematoma, many of which caused permanent neurologic damage.[25] Many of these occurred with continued epidural analgesia, many of the procedures were traumatic, and several patients had been taking nonsteroidal anti-inflammatory drugs. Other risk factors appear to be age more than 75 years and female gender. At this stage, the U.S. Food and Drug

Table 149-1	Features of an Ideal Prophylactic Method for Venous Thromboembolism

Effective compared with placebo or active approaches
Safe
Good compliance with patient, nurses, and physicians
Ease of administration
No need for laboratory monitoring
Cost-effective

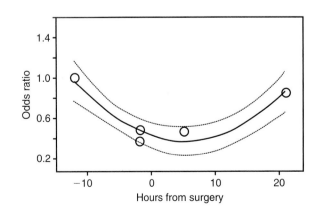

FIGURE 149-3   Quadratic fit for study odds ratio for deep venous thrombosis versus the number of hours from surgery for the first dose of low-molecular-weight heparin. The upper and lower *dashed lines* indicate the 95% confidence intervals for the true odds ratio. (Adapted from Hull RD, Pineo GF, Stein PD, et al: Timing of initial administration of low-molecular-weight heparin prophylaxis against deep vein thrombosis in patients following elective hip arthroplasty. Arch Intern Med 160:1952-1960, 2001.)

Administration (FDA) has recommended caution when neuraxial anesthesia is used in the presence of LMWH prophylaxis. The American Association of Regional Anesthesia Consensus Conference has reviewed these issues, and new guidelines have been published.[36]

Extended Out-of-Hospital Prophylaxis

It is widely recognized that the risk of development of DVT increases after total hip arthroplasty.[37] The need for in-hospital prophylaxis has been firmly established. The Sixth ACCP Consensus Conference on Antithrombotic Therapy recommends anticoagulant prophylaxis for at least 7 to 10 days after elective total hip replacement surgery.[20] Although thromboprophylaxis is routinely administered to patients undergoing total hip replacement, it is commonly stopped at the time of hospital discharge. In an epidemiologic study by White and colleagues, however, a large linked hospital discharge database revealed that the mean lengths of hospital stay after primary and revision total hip arthroplasty were 6.9 and 8.0 days, respectively. The period of risk for the development of venous thromboembolism was shown to extend well beyond this initial hospital stay. In this study of hip arthroplasty patients, White and colleagues[38] report that 76% of thromboembolic cases were diagnosed after hospital discharge. The median time for diagnosing these thrombo-

embolic events was 17 days after hip arthroplasty. The median time for diagnosing venous thromboembolism after total knee arthroplasty was 7 days, suggesting that extended prophylaxis may not be required in patients undergoing this procedure.

For major orthopedic surgery, current recommendations from the Sixth ACCP Consensus Conference on Antithrombotic Therapy are that the use of extended out-of-hospital prophylaxis in patients undergoing total hip arthroplasty with LMWH may reduce the incidence of clinically important venous thromboembolism and that this approach be used, at least for high-risk patients.[20] Because of uncertainty regarding cost-effectiveness, this is currently a grade 2A recommendation.[20]

There have been six randomized clinical trials comparing extended LMWH prophylaxis with placebo in patients undergoing total hip replacement who have received either LMWH (enoxaparin or dalteparin) or warfarin for in-hospital prophylaxis.[39-43] All of these trials indicated that DVT rates were lower with extended prophylaxis. A systematic review of all six clinical trials demonstrated not only a significantly lower rate in both total and proximal DVT, as shown by bilateral venography, but also a significantly lower rate of symptomatic venous thromboembolism during the treatment period.[44] There was no major bleeding in the out-of-hospital phase of any of these trials, indicating that the risk-to-benefit ratio strongly favored extended prophylaxis (Figs, 149-4 through 149-6).

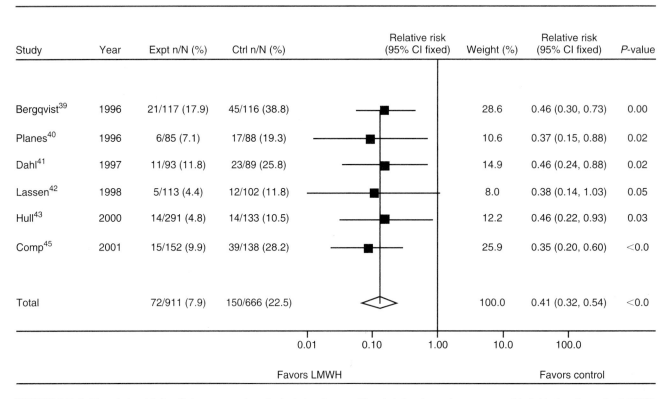

Study	Year	Expt n/N (%)	Ctrl n/N (%)	Relative risk (95% CI fixed)	Weight (%)	Relative risk (95% CI fixed)	*P*-value
Bergqvist[39]	1996	21/117 (17.9)	45/116 (38.8)		28.6	0.46 (0.30, 0.73)	0.00
Planes[40]	1996	6/85 (7.1)	17/88 (19.3)		10.6	0.37 (0.15, 0.88)	0.02
Dahl[41]	1997	11/93 (11.8)	23/89 (25.8)		14.9	0.46 (0.24, 0.88)	0.02
Lassen[42]	1998	5/113 (4.4)	12/102 (11.8)		8.0	0.38 (0.14, 1.03)	0.05
Hull[43]	2000	14/291 (4.8)	14/133 (10.5)		12.2	0.46 (0.22, 0.93)	0.03
Comp[45]	2001	15/152 (9.9)	39/138 (28.2)		25.9	0.35 (0.20, 0.60)	<0.0
Total		72/911 (7.9)	150/666 (22.5)		100.0	0.41 (0.32, 0.54)	<0.0

0.01   0.10   1.00   10.0   100.0

Favors LMWH   Favors control

FIGURE 149-4 The relative risk for all deep venous thrombosis during the out-of-hospital time interval; summary and individual study results. LMWH, low-molecular-weight heparin(s). (Adapted from Hull RD, Pineo GF, Francis C, et al; North American Fragmin Trial Investigators: Low-molecular-weight heparin prophylaxis using dalteparin extended out-of-hospital vs in-hospital warfarin/out-of-hospital placebo in hip arthroplasty patients: A double-blind, randomized comparison. Arch Intern Med 160:2208-2215, 2000, with permission.)

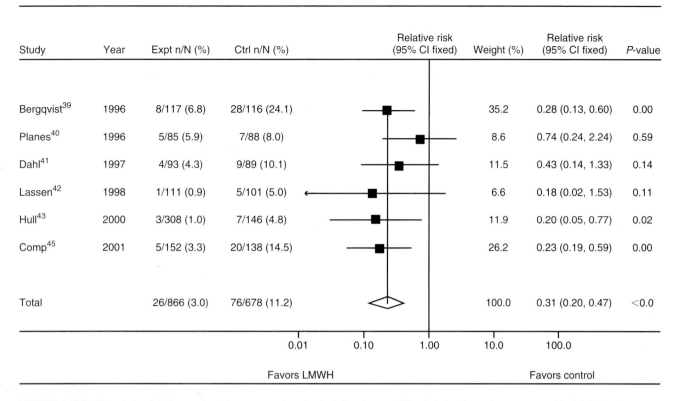

FIGURE 149-5 The relative risk for proximal deep venous thrombosis during the out-of-hospital time interval; summary and individual study results. LMWH, low-molecular-weight heparin(s). (Adapted from Hull RD, Pineo GF, Francis C, et al: Low-molecular-weight heparin prophylaxis using dalteparin extended out-of-hospital vs in-hospital warfarin/out-of-hospital placebo in hip arthroplasty patients: A double-blind, randomized comparison. North American Fragmin Trial Investigators. Arch Intern Med 160:2208-2215, 2000, with permission.)

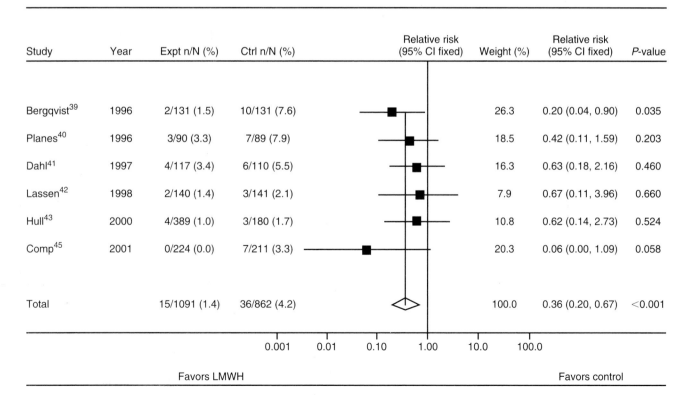

FIGURE 149-6 The relative risk for symptomatic venous thromboembolism during the out-of-hospital time interval; summary and individual study results. LMWH, low-molecular-weight heparin(s). (Adapted from Hull RD, Pineo GF, Francis C, et al: Low-molecular-weight heparin prophylaxis using dalteparin extended out-of-hospital vs in-hospital warfarin/out-of-hospital placebo in hip arthroplasty patients: A double-blind, randomized comparison. North American Fragmin Trial Investigators. Arch Intern Med 160:2208-2215, 2000, with permission.)

The NNT (number needed to be treated) provides a useful public health overview.[43] One study comparing out-of-hospital LMWH prophylaxis with out-of-hospital placebo in patients having elective hip arthroplasty in the United States and Canada found that only 24 to 28 patients required out-of-hospital LMWH prophylaxis to prevent one new episode of out-of-hospital proximal venous thrombosis.[43]

From a population perspective, extended prophylaxis prevents 41 cases of proximal DVT for every 1000 patients having elective hip surgery. Even if the death rate is as low as 8% in these 41 cases, extended prophylaxis will allow the saving of about 3.5 lives per 1000 patients undergoing elective hip surgery by preventing fatal PE. Although a 0.35% mortality rate is low, it would be recognized that these deaths are preventable; for every 500,000 patients undergoing elective hip surgery in North America, extended prophylaxis would save 1750 lives. Even a death rate as low as 0.1% still reflects 500 lives saved.[43]

On the basis of the findings of these studies, extended prophylaxis with LMWH is effective and safe in the prevention of DVT after total hip arthroplasty. The use of LMWH prophylaxis is associated with substantive risk reductions. Thus, the recommended 7- to 10-day prophylaxis regimen after total hip arthroplasty is suboptimal.

The optimal duration of extended prophylaxis remains uncertain. The intervals of extended out-of-hospital prophylaxis that were evaluated in the randomized clinical trials using venographic endpoints ranged from 19 to 28 days.[39-45] This interval is in harmony with the finding that patients with venographically confirmed symptomatic DVT after hip surgery in whom prophylaxis was stopped at hospital discharge were re-admitted, on average, 17 days after surgery.[38] Thus, in all patients undergoing elective hip surgery, 19 to 28 days would seem a reasonable duration for extended LMWH prophylaxis. Two economic analyses have indicated that out-of-hospital antithrombotic prophylaxis with LMWH after total hip replacement is cost effective.[46]

Samama and coworkers[47] compared extended prophylaxis with acenocoumarol and LMWH for 30 days after total hip replacement.[47] DVT rates were similar but there was significantly more bleeding with acenocoumarol. Extended prophylaxis to day 28 in patients undergoing total knee replacement did not yield significantly lower rates of venous thrombosis than 7 to 10 days of prophylaxis with LMWH.

In patients undergoing cancer surgery, extended prophylaxis to 25 to 31 days with LMWH was superior to prophylaxis for 6 to 10 days.[48] Extended prophylaxis is currently being studied in patients undergoing surgery for hip fracture and in high-risk medical patients. The advent of effective oral agents will simplify the approach to extended prophylaxis, but concerns about cost will remain a problem.

Specific Prophylactic Measures

Patterns of clinical practice in the prevention of venous thromboembolism and the appropriate use of anticoagulants for the treatment of thrombotic disease have been influenced very strongly by recent consensus conferences.[20,49] Recommendations from the Sixth ACCP Consensus Conference on Antithrombotic Therapy and the International Consensus Statement on the Prevention of Venous Thromboembolism have been published. Guyatt and colleagues[50] applied rules of evidence for assessing the literature to all recommendations regarding prevention and treatment of venous thrombosis, thereby indicating which recommendations were based on rigorous randomized trials, which were based on extrapolation of evidence from related clinical disorders, and which were based only on nonrandomized clinical trials or case series.[50]

Low-Molecular-Weight Heparin

A number of LMWHs have been evaluated by randomized clinical trials in moderate-risk general surgical patients, including many who underwent cancer surgery.[18,19,51-54] In randomized clinical trials comparing LMWHs with low-dose unfractionated heparin, the LMWHs given once or twice daily have been shown to be as effective or more effective in preventing thrombosis.[18,19,21,52-54] In most of the trials, similarly low frequencies of bleeding for LMWH and low-dose unfractionated heparin were documented, although the incidence of bleeding was significantly lower in the LMWH group, as evidenced by a reduction in the incidence of wound hematoma, severe bleeding, and the number of patients requiring re-operation for bleeding.[18,19]

A number of randomized controlled trials have been performed to compare LMWH with either unfractionated heparin or warfarin for the prevention of venous thrombosis after total hip replacement. Results of the latest trials using bilateral venography are shown in Table 149-2.[22,55-63] The drugs under investigation and their dosage schedules vary from one clinical trial to another, making comparisons among trials difficult. Furthermore, it has been shown that even within the same clinical trial, there can be considerable intercenter variability.[63] Major bleeding rates and definitions of major bleeding vary among trials as well.

Although the number of patients undergoing total knee replacement now equals the number undergoing total hip replacements, there have been fewer trials for prophylaxis after knee replacement. Results of clinical trials comparing LMWH with warfarin are shown in Table 149-3.[24,58,63-66] Although the rates of DVT with LMWH are significantly lower than those with warfarin, the rates continue to be high.

Multiple meta-analyses have shown that LMWH and unfractionated heparin are equally effective in preventing venous thrombosis in general surgery,[67-70] but LMWH is more effective in orthopedic surgery. Bleeding rates were higher with unfractionated heparin in patients undergoing general surgery.

Two decision analyses compared the cost-effectiveness of enoxaparin and warfarin in patients undergoing hip replacement.[71,72] Although enoxaparin was more expensive than low-dose warfarin, the former's cost-effectiveness compared favorably with that of other medical interventions. An economic evaluation of LMWH versus warfarin prophylaxis after total hip or knee replacement identified that LMWH was cost effective.[73]

Studies have also shown that LMWH is superior to low-dose unfractionated heparin in patients suffering multiple trauma[74] and is equally effective in medical patients.[75,76]

Table 149-2 Recent Randomized Trials of Low-Molecular-Weight Heparin vs. Heparin or Warfarin Prophylaxis for Deep Venous Thrombosis (DVT) after Hip Replacement Surgery: Total Rates of DVT and Major Bleeding

STUDY*	TREATMENT	NO. PATIENTS	TOTAL RATE OF DVT (%)	TOTAL RATE OF MAJOR BLEEDING (%)
Levine et al[62]	Enoxaparin	258	19.4	3.3
	Unfractionated heparin	263	23.3	5.7
Leyvraz et al[55]	Nadroparin	198	12.6	0.5
	Unfractionated heparin	199	16.0	1.5
Eriksson et al[56]	Dalteparin	67	30.2	1.4†
	Unfractionated heparin	68	42.4	7.4
Planes et al[57]	Enoxaparin	120	12.5	1.6
	Heparin	108	25.0	0
Colwell et al[61]	Enoxaparin	136	21.0	4.0
	Enoxaparin	136	6.0	1.0
	Heparin	142	1.5	6.0
Hull et al[63]	Tinzaparin	332	21.0	2.8
	Warfarin	340	23.0	1.5
Hamulyak et al[58]	Nadroparin	195	13.8	1.5‡
	Warfarin	196	13.8	2.3
Francis et al[60]	Dalteparin	192	15.0	2.0
	Warfarin	190	26.0	1.0
Hull et al[22]	Dalteparin	496	10.7	2.8
	Dalteparin	487	13.1	1.8
	Warfarin	489	24.0	2.0

*Superscript numbers indicate chapter references.
†Serious bleeding.
‡Clinically important plus minor bleeding for combined hip and knee replacement patients.

Table 149-3 Randomized Controlled Trials of Low-Molecular-Weight Heparin Prophylaxis vs. Warfarin for Deep Venous Thrombosis (DVT) after Total Knee Replacement: Total Rates of DVT and Major Bleeding

STUDY*	TREATMENT	NO. PATIENTS	TOTAL RATE OF DVT (%)	TOTAL RATE OF MAJOR BLEEDING (%)
Hull et al[63]	Tinzaparin	317	45.0	0.9
	Warfarin	324	54.0	2.0
Leclerc et al[65]	Enoxaparin	206	37.0	2.1
	Warfarin	211	52.0	1.8
Heit et al[66]	Ardeparin	232	27.0†	7.9‡
	Warfarin	222	38.0	4.4
Hamulyak et al[58]	Nadroparin	65	24.6	1.5§
	Warfarin	61	37.7	2.3
Fitzgerald et al[24]	Enoxaparin	173	38.0	5.2
	Warfarin	176	59.0	2.3

*Superscript numbers indicate chapter references.
†Venogram on operated leg only
‡Overt bleeding—total
§Clinically important and minor bleeding for combined hip and knee replacement patients.

Low-Dose Unfractionated Heparin

The effectiveness of low-dose unfractionated heparin for preventing DVT after general surgery has been established by multiple randomized clinical trials.[17-19] Low-dose subcutaneous heparin is usually given in a dose of 5000 units 2 hours preoperatively and then every 8 or 12 hours postoperatively. Most of the patients in these trials underwent abdominothoracic surgery, particularly for gastrointestinal disease, but patients having gynecologic and urologic surgery as well as mastectomies and vascular procedures were also included. Pooled data from meta-analyses confirm that low-dose heparin significantly reduces the incidence of all DVT, proximal DVT, and all pulmonary emboli, including fatal pulmonary emboli.[17,67-70] An international multicenter trial also established the effectiveness of low-dose heparin for preventing fatal PE, a clinically and significantly striking reduction from 0.7% to 0.1% ($P < .005$).[16]

The incidence of major bleeding complications is not raised by low-dose heparin, but there is an increase in minor wound hematomas. The platelet count should be monitored regularly in all patients taking low-dose heparin to detect the rare but significant development of heparin-induced thrombocytopenia.

Intermittent Leg Compression

The use of intermittent pneumatic leg compression prevents venous thrombosis by enhancing blood flow in the deep veins of the legs, thereby avoiding venous stasis. It also raises blood fibrinolytic activity, which may contribute to its antithrombotic properties. Intermittent pneumatic leg compression is effective for preventing venous thrombosis after cardiac surgery[77] and in patients undergoing neurosurgery.[78-80] In patients undergoing hip surgery, intermittent pneumatic compression of the calf is effective for preventing calf vein thrombosis, but it is less effective against proximal vein thrombosis than warfarin sodium.[81,82] Intermittent pneumatic compression of the calf was found to decrease the rate of venous thrombosis after knee replacement.[83,84]

Intermittent pneumatic compression is virtually free of clinically important side effects and offers a valuable alternative in patients who have a high risk of bleeding. It may produce discomfort in the occasional patient and should not be used in patients with overt leg ischemia due to peripheral vascular disease. A variety of well-accepted, comfortable, and effective intermittent pneumatic devices are currently available that may be applied preoperatively, at the time of operation, or in the early postoperative period. These devices should be used until the patient is fully ambulatory, with only temporary removal for nursing care or physiotherapy.

With a shortened hospital stay, use of intermittent pneumatic compression becomes of limited value. A greater problem, however, is one of compliance with the therapy.[85,86] In addition to poor compliance, a study documented the fact that key outcome-related parameters such as the rate of pressure rise and the maximum pressure applied to various parts of the leg were less than anticipated most of the time in patients undergoing intermittent pneumatic compression after elective hip surgery.[86] Disappointingly, an intensive nursing training program did not improve these outcomes.

Graduated-Compression Stockings

Graduated-compression stockings offer a simple, safe, and moderately effective form of thromboprophylaxis. It is by no means clear how graduated-compression stockings achieve a thromboprophylactic effect. It has been shown that they increase the velocity of venous blood flow, so their use is recommended in patients at low risk for thromboembolism and as an adjunct in those with medium or high risk.[87-89] The only major contraindication is peripheral vascular disease. The majority of studies in patients undergoing general abdominal and gynecologic procedures have shown a reduction in the incidence of DVT with graduated-compression stockings. A comprehensive meta-analysis concluded that, in studies using objective methods, there was a highly significant risk reduction—

68%—in patients at moderate risk of postoperative thromboembolism in whom the stockings were used.[89] However, there is no conclusive evidence that graduated-compression stockings are effective in reducing the incidence of fatal and nonfatal PEs. It is not known whether wearing graduated-compression stockings after hospital discharge is efficacious. Graduated-compression stockings may be useful in preventing the postphlebitic syndrome after an episode of proximal DVT[90] and in reducing the likelihood of thrombosis during prolonged airline travel.[91]

Oral Anticoagulants

For prophylaxis, oral anticoagulants (coumarin derivatives) can be commenced preoperatively, at the time of surgery, or in the early postoperative period.[92] Oral anticoagulant therapy commenced at the time of surgery or in the early postoperative period may not prevent small venous thrombi from forming during or soon after surgery, because the antithrombotic effect is not achieved until the third or fourth postoperative day. However, oral anticoagulants are effective in inhibiting the extension of these thrombi, thereby preventing clinically important venous thromboembolism.

A number of studies have compared the postoperative use of warfarin after total hip or total knee replacement surgery with that of LMWH[22,24,58,60,61,63] and intermittent pneumatic compression,[82,93] showing little or no difference in the incidence of postoperative venous thrombosis or bleeding. Later studies using earlier intervention with LMWH, however, have demonstrated superior efficacy over the use of warfarin, closely controlled using a warfarin nomogram.[22] Another clinical trial using clinical endpoints for venous thromboembolism demonstrated superior efficacy of LMWH although the majority of patients taking warfarin had an INR less than 2.[61]

Turpie and colleagues[104] reported that results of a regimen in which warfarin was initiated 7 to 10 days preoperatively to prolong prothrombin time (PT) 1.5 to 3.0 seconds, and then less intense warfarin therapy was started the night of surgery, were similar to those of a regimen in which warfarin was started the night before surgery.[104]

In patients with hip fractures, warfarin was more effective than either aspirin or placebo.[94] Compared with placebo, very low doses of oral anticoagulants (warfarin 1mg per day) decreased the postoperative thrombosis rate in patients undergoing gynecologic surgery or major general surgery.[95] Very low-dose warfarin, however, did not provide protection against DVT after hip or knee replacement.[96]

Other Agents

Although meta-analyses indicate that aspirin decreases the frequency of venous thrombosis following general or orthopedic surgery, this reduction is significantly less than that obtained with other agents.[97] Interest in the use of aspirin in patients with hip fracture was fueled by the awareness that this agent significantly reduces the incidence of stroke and myocardial infarction in this patient population. The Pulmonary Embolism Prevention (PEP) trial compared aspirin and placebo in a large number of patients undergoing surgery for hip fracture.[98] Although there was extensive contamination of results because of other prophylactic measures, the PEP trial showed a significant decrease in fatal PE with the use of aspirin, whereas the rates of fatal and nonfatal cardiovascular events and all-cause mortality were no different. Wound-related and gastrointestinal bleeding and the need for blood transfusions were all significantly more frequent in the aspirin-treated patients. Aspirin cannot be recommended for the prevention of venous thrombosis in high-risk patients.[20] Also, although intravenous dextran has been shown to be effective in the prevention of venous thrombosis following major orthopedic surgery, it is cumbersome, expensive, and associated with significant side effects. It has, therefore, been replaced by other agents.

New Antithrombotic Agents

For many years, unfractionated heparin and warfarin were the only agents available for the prevention and treatment of thrombotic disorders. Then the LMWHs found their place in the physicians' armamentarium. A plethora of new specific antithrombotic agents have now been described, and a number have been used in phase 2 and phase 3 clinical trials. The most advanced of these agents are inhibitors of factor X, factor II (thrombin), or the factor VIIa–tissue factor complex. Heparin and LMWH can be made available for absorption by the oral route, and a large phase 3 study has been completed comparing the efficacy and safety of oral heparin and LMWH in patients undergoing total hip replacement. Only the pentasaccharide fondaparinux (Arixtra) has been approved for clinical use by the FDA. These agents and a number of other innovative antithrombotic agents are under extensive study for the prevention and treatment of both venous and arterial thrombotic disorders, and more information about them will become available soon.

Fondaparinux is a highly selective factor X inhibitor with a high affinity for antithrombin. When fondaparinux binds to antithrombin, it induces a conformational change that markedly increases the rate of factor Xa inhibition. When antithrombin then binds to activated factor X, the fondaparinux is released and thus continues the process. Inhibition of Xa leads to less generation of thrombin, but unlike other antithrombotic agents, fondaparinux does not inhibit other coagulation proteins or affect platelet function or aggregation. Fondaparinux has a long half-life (17 hours), permitting once-daily dosing. This agent has the further advantage of being a wholly synthetic molecule, so it is not dependent on animal sources as the heparins are, and it does not produce heparin-associated antibodies. Of some concern is the fact that the antithrombotic activity of fondaparinux cannot be blocked by any of the known agents, and the FDA has mandated that caution be used in elderly patients, who may have decreased renal function, because of a concern about possible drug accumulation. It has been suggested that differences in efficacy and safety between Arixtra and the comparator may have been influenced by factors such as the timing of the first dose of the drug after surgery.[99]

In a dose-finding study, fondaparinux was shown to have a highly reproducible and linear dose-dependent inhibition of thrombosis as well as to be associated with a dose-dependent increase in major bleeding episodes.[100] Fondaparinux has been compared with the LMWH enoxaparin in more than 7000 patients undergoing orthopedic proce-

dures in four phase 3 clinical trials.[100-104] The fondaparinux protocol was the same in all four studies (i.e., 2.5 mg SC started 6 hours after the operation, with the second injection 12 hours or longer after the first). Enoxaparin regimens were different. A 40-mg dose was started an average of 18 hours postoperatively in patients with hip fracture; a 30-mg twice-daily dose was started an average of 21 hours postoperatively in patients undergoing knee replacement; a 40-mg dose was started 12 hours preoperatively in the European hip replacement study; and a 30-mg twice-daily dose was started a mean of 13 hours postoperatively in the North American hip replacement study. In the hip fracture study, there was a significant decrease in both total and proximal DVT rates with fondaparinux with no difference in the major bleeding rates, although minor bleeding was increased with fondaparinux.[101] In the knee replacement study, there was a significant decrease in the total DVT rates with fondaparinux, although proximal DVT rates were similar; however, there was a significant increase in the rate of major bleeding, as indicated by the bleeding index, in the fondaparinux group. In the European total hip replacement study, there were significant decreases in both total and proximal DVT rates in the fondaparinux group, whereas in the North American study, there was a significant difference in rates of venographically proven distal DVT but not in rates of proximal DVT. In both studies, the bleeding index was similar in the two groups. When all studies were pooled, there was a significant decrease in both total and proximal DVT rates with fondaparinux but no difference in the incidence of symptomatic events.[105] The incidence of major bleeding was increased in the fondaparinux group.[105]

The specific direct thrombin inhibitors melagatran (subcutaneous form) and ximelagatran (oral form) have undergone extensive study. In the first study, subcutaneous melagatran in three doses was given twice daily for 2 days beginning immediately before surgery, the second dose being on the evening of surgery; on day 3, oral ximelagatran in three different doses was started and was continued in a twice-daily fashion for 6 to 9 days.[106] The control agent was dalteparin, 5000 units, started the evening before surgery and continued daily. Bilateral venography showed there was no difference in total or proximal DVT rates among the various groups. In the second study (METHRO II), a combination of subcutaneous melagatran, started immediately before surgery and continued twice daily for 2 to 3 days in four dose levels, was followed by ximelagatran in four different doses given orally twice daily and compared with dalteparin, 5000 units, started the evening before surgery.[107] A highly significant dose-dependent decrease in DVT rates was seen for both the patients undergoing total hip replacement and those having total knee replacement. Also, a dose-dependent decrease in rates of proximal DVT and PE was found in the total population. Total bleeding rates were not significantly different in the treatment groups.

In a phase 3 study in patients undergoing total hip replacement surgery, ximelagatran 24 mg twice daily was compared with enoxaparin 30 mg twice daily, both initiated the morning after surgery.[108] Enoxaparin-treated patients had significantly fewer events of venous thromboembolism (venographic and symptomatic venous thromboembolism) compared with the ximelagatran-treated patients. Bleeding rates were low and comparable between the groups. A study comparing ximelagatran 24 mg twice daily with warfarin in patients undergoing total knee replacement surgery has recently been reported.[109]

When unfractionated heparin or LMWH is given orally, there is little evidence of absorption, in that there is little if any change in the levels of various coagulation factors, including factor Xa levels. However, if a carrier agent such as sodium *N*-[8-(2-hydroxy-benzoyl) amino] caprylate (SNAC) is combined with unfractionated heparin, absorption is significantly greater than that of unfractionated heparin without the carrier.[109,110] In a phase 2 study, SNAC heparin was shown to have a significant antithrombotic effect compared with subcutaneous LMWH.[111] A large international clinical trial has been carried out comparing a regimen comprising two doses of SNAC heparin started 6 hours postoperatively and given three times daily by mouth with enoxaparin, 30 mg twice daily, started 12 to 24 hours postoperatively. The results of this clinical trial will become available soon. The technology is also available for delivering LMWH by the oral route in either the liquid or the dry form. Therefore, in spite of the development of a host of new oral antithrombotic agents, there may well be a role for oral heparin and oral LMWH in both prevention and treatment of thrombotic disorders, particularly in the out-of-hospital setting following discharge.

Specific Recommendations for Prophylaxis

The recommended primary prophylactic approach depends on the patient's risk category and in surgical patients, the type of surgery. In assessing the literature relating to the prevention of venous thromboembolism, we have used the grades of evidence as defined by Guyatt and colleagues.[50] They can be summarized as follows:

- *Level I*: Randomized trials with low levels of false-positive (a) and false-negative (b) errors
- *Level II*: Randomized trials with high levels of false-positive (a) and false-negative (b) errors
- *Level III*: Nonrandomized concurrent cohort studies
- *Level IV*: Nonrandomized historical cohort studies
- *Level V*: Case series

Unless indicated, all recommendations in the following section are based on level I evidence.[20,49]

High Risk-Patients

Elective Hip Replacement   Several approaches to prophylaxis are effective in patients undergoing elective hip replacement. Subcutaneous LMWH given once or twice daily is effective and safe.[20,49] Several such agents are approved for use in Europe and North America. At present in North America, these agents are approved for postoperative use only. Prophylaxis with oral anticoagulant dosages adjusted to maintain an INR of 2.0 to 3.0 is effective and is associated with a low risk of bleeding. Other effective approaches are adjusted-dose subcutaneous unfractionated heparin and intermittent pneumatic compression.[20,49] However, rates of proximal venous thrombosis are higher for intermittent pneumatic compression than for high-risk doses of pharmacologic prophylaxis.

Elective Knee Replacement   The current prophylaxis of choice for elective knee replacement is LMWH given once or twice daily starting after operation.[20,49] Oral anticoagulants are less effective than LMWH, and intermittent pneumatic compression was shown in earlier studies to be an effective and useful alternative.

Hip Fractures   Two approaches to prophylaxis in hip fracture are available, oral anticoagulation (INR = 2.0 to 3.0) or fixed-dose subcutaneous LMWH started preoperatively.[20,50] The combined use of intermittent pneumatic compression with LMWH or warfarin may provide additional benefit in certain patients (not level I evidence).

Multiple Trauma   Multiple trauma represents a high risk for thrombosis. LMWH is the prophylaxis of choice.[20,54] Intermittent pneumatic compression has been recommended, when feasible, because it has no risk for bleeding.[20] Other alternatives are low-dose unfractionated heparin or warfarin, based on extrapolation from other high-risk situations, such as hip fracture and hip replacement surgery. Insertion of an inferior vena cava filter has been recommended for very high-risk situations in which anticoagulants may be contraindicated, but this recommendation is based on level V data.

Acute Spinal Cord Injury Associated with Paralysis   LMWH is the most effective prophylaxis.[20,49] Adjusted-dose heparin has also been shown to be effective. Low-dose heparin and intermittent pneumatic compression are less effective. Combining intermittent pneumatic compression with LMWH or adjusted-dose heparin may provide additional benefit, but this is not supported by data.

Moderate-Risk Patients

Neurosurgery   Patients undergoing neurosurgery should receive intermittent pneumatic compression. This approach may be used in conjunction with graduated-compression stockings. Low-dose heparin is an acceptable alternative.[20,49]

General Abdominal, Thoracic, or Gynecologic Surgery   In moderate-risk patients undergoing general abdominal, thoracic, or gynecologic surgery, the use of subcutaneous low-dose unfractionated heparin (5000 units every 8 or 12 hours) or subcutaneous LMWH is recommended.[20,49] Subcutaneous LMWH is as effective as subcutaneous heparin for prophylaxis and has the advantage of a once-daily injection. An alternative recommendation is the use of intermittent pneumatic compression until the patient is ambulatory. This method is indicated in patients at high risk for bleeding. Pharmacologic methods may be combined with graduated-compression stockings in selected patients.

Low-Risk Patients

Apart from early ambulation, specific prophylaxis is usually not recommended for low-risk patients, except in certain circumstances.[20,49] It is the clinical custom in some countries to use graduated-compression stockings, but this use is not based on evidence from clinical trials.

Medical Patients

Medical patients should be classified as having low, moderate, or high risk for venous thromboembolism according to the underlying medical condition and other co-morbid factors, such as immobility, previous DVT, and cancer. Low-risk patients should be considered for graduated-compression stockings. For patients with myocardial infarction who have no other significant risk factors, anticoagulation with heparin or warfarin is recommended.[20,49] In the presence of congestive heart failure, pulmonary infection or pneumonia, either low-dose heparin or LMWH is recommended.[20,49,112] For patients with ischemic stroke and lower limb paralysis, low-dose heparin or LMWH is recommended.[20,50] Intermittent pneumatic compression may be used for high-risk patients who are at high risk of bleeding, although this is not based on clinical trial data.

In a multicenter study in acutely ill medical patients (including those with congestive heart failure, acute respiratory failure, and medical conditions associated with at least one additional risk factor for venous thromboembolism), LMWH (enoxaparin) 40 mg daily was shown to significantly decrease the incidence of venographically demonstrated DVT compared with enoxaparin 20 mg and placebo.[113] Prophylaxis was continued for 6 to 14 days. The observed benefit with the 40-mg dose was maintained at 3 months. There was no difference in death rates or in the incidence of major bleeding.

A clinical trial is under way in high-risk medical patients to determine whether extended prophylaxis with enoxaparin out to day 38 is superior to initial prophylaxis for 9 to 14 days with an ultrasonographic endpoint. Similarly, another study has been completed but not yet reported that compared LMWH (dalteparin) for 14 days with a placebo in high-risk medical patients also with an ultrasonographic endpoint.[114] At this time, there have been no studies that are adequately powered to show a difference in efficacy between unfractionated heparin and LMWH in high-risk medical patients.

■ ANTICOAGULANT THERAPY FOR VENOUS THROMBOEMBOLISM

Anticoagulant drugs (heparin, LMWH, and warfarin) are the mainstay in the management of venous thromboembolism. The anti-Xa inhibitor fondaparinux (Arixtra) and the antithrombin agent ximelagatran (Exanta), which could be on the market, may modify the current approach to treatment of VTE.

Objectives of treatment in patients with VTE are:

- To prevent death from PE
- To prevent recurrent VTE
- To prevent the post-thrombotic syndrome

The use of graduated-compression stockings has been shown to significantly reduce the incidence of post-thrombotic syndrome.[90] Furthermore, the incidence of post-thrombotic syndrome has been diminishing, suggesting that the more efficient treatment of VTE and the prevention of recurrent DVT are having a positive effect on this complication.

Heparin Therapy

The anticoagulant activity of unfractionated heparin depends on a unique pentasaccharide which binds to antithrombin III (ATIII) and potentiates the inhibition of thrombin and activated factor X (Xa) by ATIII.[115-117] About one third of all heparin molecules contain the unique pentasaccharide sequence, regardless of whether they are low- or high-molecular-weight fractions.[115-117] It is the pentasaccharide sequence that confers the molecular high affinity for ATIII.[115-117] In addition, heparin catalyzes the inactivation of thrombin by another plasma co-factor, cofactor II, which acts independently of ATIII.[117]

Heparin has a number of other effects. They include the release of tissue factor pathway inhibitor, binding to numerous plasma and platelet proteins, endothelial cells, and leukocytes, suppression of platelet function, and an increase in vascular permeability.[115] The anticoagulant response to a standard dose of heparin varies widely among patients. This variation makes it necessary to monitor the anticoagulant response to heparin, by either the activated partial thromboplastin time (aPTT) or heparin blood levels and to titrate the dose in the individual patient.[117]

The accepted anticoagulant therapy for VTE is a combination of continuous intravenous heparin and oral warfarin. The duration of initial intravenous heparin therapy has been reduced to 5 days, thus shortening the hospital stay and leading to significant cost savings.[118,119] The simultaneous use of initial heparin and warfarin has become clinical practice for all patients with venous thromboembolism who are medically stable. Exceptions are patients who require immediate medical or surgical intervention, such as in thrombolysis or insertion of a vena cava filter, and patients at very high risk of bleeding. Heparin is continued until the INR has been within the therapeutic range (2.0 to 3.0) for 2 consecutive days.[120]

Experimental studies and clinical trials have established that the efficacy of heparin therapy depends on achievement of a critical therapeutic level of heparin within the first 24 hours of treatment.[121-123] Data from three consecutive double-blinded clinical trials indicate that failure to achieve the therapeutic aPTT threshold by 24 hours was associated with a 23.3% rate of subsequent recurrent venous thromboembolism, compared with a rate of 4% to 6% for patients in whom a therapeutic aPTT was achieved at 24 hours.[122,123] The recurrences occurred throughout the 3-month follow-up period and could not be attributed to inadequate oral anticoagulant therapy.[122] The critical therapeutic level of heparin, as measured by the aPTT, is 1.5 times the mean of the control value or the upper limit of the normal aPTT range.[121-123] This level corresponds to a heparin blood value of 0.2 to 0.4 U/mL on the protamine sulfate titration assay and to a value of 0.35 to 0.70 on the anti–factor Xa assay.

However, there is wide variability in the aPTT and in heparin blood levels measured with different reagents and even with different batches of the same reagent.[117,124] It is therefore vital for each laboratory to establish the minimal therapeutic level of heparin, as measured by the aPTT, that will provide a heparin blood level of at least 0.35 U/mL on the anti-factor Xa assay for each batch of thromboplastin reagent being used, particularly for reagents provided by

Table 149-4 Heparin Protocol

1. Administer initial intravenous heparin bolus: 5000 U.

2. Administer continuous intravenous heparin infusion: commence at 42 mL/hr of 20,000 U (1680 U/hr) in 500 mL of two-thirds dextrose and one-third saline (a 24-hour heparin dose of 40,320 U), except in the following patients, in whom heparin infusion is commenced at a rate of 31 mL/hr (1240 U/hr, a 24-hour dose of 29,760 U):
   - Patients who have undergone surgery within the previous 2 weeks.
   - Patients with a previous history of peptic ulcer disease or gastrointestinal or genitourinary bleeding.
   - Patients with recent stroke (i.e., thrombotic stroke within 2 weeks previously).
   - Patients with a platelet count $< 150 \times 10^9$/L.
   - Patients with miscellaneous reasons for a high risk of bleeding (e.g., hepatic failure, renal failure, or vitamin K deficiency)

3. Adjust heparin dose according to activated partial thromboplastin time (aPTT). The aPTT is measured in all patients as follows:
   a. 4-6 hours after commencement of heparin; the heparin dose is then adjusted.
   b. 4-6 hours after the first dosage adjustment.
   c. Then, as indicated by the nomogram for the first 24 hours of therapy.
   d. Thereafter, once daily, unless the aPTT value is subtherapeutic,* in which case the aPTT test is repeated 4-6 hours after the heparin dose is increased.

*Subtherapeutic = aPTT < 1.5 times the mean normal control value for the thromboplastin reagent being used.

different manufacturers.[117]

Although there is a strong correlation between subtherapeutic aPTT values and recurrent thromboembolism, the relationship between supratherapeutic aPTT values and bleeding (aPTT ratio 2.5 or more) is less definite.[122] Indeed, bleeding during heparin therapy is more closely related to underlying clinical risk factors than to elevation of the aPTT above the therapeutic range.[122] Studies now confirm that body weight and age greater than 65 years are independent risk factors for bleeding in patients receiving heparin.

Numerous audits of heparin therapy indicate that administration of intravenous heparin is fraught with difficulty and that the clinical practice of using an ad hoc approach to heparin dose titration frequently results in inadequate therapy. The use of a prescriptive approach or protocol for administering intravenous heparin therapy has been evaluated in two prospective studies in patients with venous thromboembolism.[121,123,124]

In one clinical trial for the treatment of DVT, patients were given either intravenous heparin alone followed by warfarin or intravenous heparin simultaneously with warfarin.[119] The heparin nomogram is summarized in Tables 149-4 and 149-5. Only 1% of patients in the heparin group and 2% in the heparin and warfarin group were undertreated for more than 24 hours. Recurrent venous thrombo-

embolism (objectively documented) occurred infrequently in both groups (7%), at rates similar to those previously reported. These findings demonstrated that inadequate therapy was avoided in most patients and that the heparin protocol resulted in effective delivery of heparin therapy in both groups.

In another clinical trial, a weight-based heparin dosage nomogram was compared with a standard care nomogram (Table 149-6).[123] Patients on the weight-adjusted heparin nomogram received a starting dose of 80 IU/kg as a bolus and 18 IU/kg/hr as an infusion. The heparin dose was adjusted to maintain an aPTT of 1.5 to 2.3 times control. In the weight-adjusted group, 89% of patients achieved the therapeutic range within 24 hours, compared with 75% in the standard care group. The risk of recurrent VTE was higher in the standard care group, supporting the previous observation that subtherapeutic heparin dosages during the initial 24 hours are associated with a higher incidence of recurrences. This study included patients with unstable angina and arterial thromboembolism in addition to VTE, suggesting that the principles applied to a heparin nomogram for the treatment of venous thromboembolism may be generalizable to other clinical conditions. Continued use of the weight-based nomogram has been similarly effective.

Table 149-5 Intravenous Heparin Dose Titration Nomogram According to Activated Partial Thromboplastin Time (aPTT)

aPTT (sec)	RATE CHANGE (mL/hr)	DOSE CHANGE (IU/24hr)*	ADDITIONAL ACTION
≤45	+6	+5760	Repeat aPTT† in 4-6 hr
46-54	+3	+2880	Repeat aPTT in 4-6 hr
55-85	0	0	None‡
86-110	−3	−2880	Stop heparin sodium treatment for 1hr; repeat aPTT 4-6 hr after restarting heparin treatment
>110	−6	−5760	Stop heparin treatment for 1 hr; repeat aPTT 4-6 hr after restarting heparin treatment

*Heparin sodium concentration 20,000 IU in 500 mL = 40 IU/mL.
†With the use of Actin-FS thromboplastin reagent (Dade, Mississauga, Ontario, Canada).
‡During the first 24 hours, repeat aPTT in 4-6 hours. Thereafter, the aPTT is determined once daily, unless the value is subtherapeutic.

Adapted from Hull RD, Raskob GE, Rosenbloom D, et al: Optimal therapeutic level of heparin therapy in patients with venous thrombosis. Arch Intern Med 152:1589, 1992, with permission.

Table 149-6	Weight-Based Nomogram for Initial Intravenous Heparin Therapy*	
	DOSE (IU/kg)	
Initial	80 bolus, then 18/hr	
aPTT (sec):		
<35 (<1.2×)	80 bolus, then 4/hr	
35-45 (1.2-1.5×)	40 bolus, then 2/hr	
46-70 (1.5-2.3×)	No change	
71-90 (2.3-3.0×)	Decrease infusion rate by 2/hr	
>90 (>3.0×)	Hold infusion 1hr, then decrease infusion rate by 3/hr	

*Figures in parentheses show comparison with control.
aPTT, activated partial thromboplastin time.

Adapted from Raschke RA, Reilly BM, Guidry JR, et al: The weight based heparin dosing nomogram compared with a 'standard care' nomogram. Ann Intern Med 119:874-881, 1993, with permission.

Complications of Heparin Therapy   The main adverse effects of heparin therapy are bleeding, thrombocytopenia, and osteoporosis. Patients at particular risk are those who have experienced recent surgery or trauma and those with other clinical factors predisposing to bleeding with heparin therapy, such as peptic ulcer, occult malignancy, liver disease, hemostatic defects, weight, age more than 65 years, and female gender.[117]

The management of bleeding in patients on heparin therapy depends on the location and severity of bleeding, the risk of recurrent VTE, and the aPTT. Heparin should be discontinued temporarily or permanently. Patients with recent VTE may be candidates for insertion of an inferior vena cava filter. If urgent reversal of heparin effect is required, protamine sulfate can be administered.[117]

Heparin-induced thrombocytopenia is a well-recognized complication of heparin therapy,[125-128] usually occurring within 5 to 10 days after heparin treatment has started. Approximately 1% to 2% of patients receiving unfractionated heparin experience a drop in platelet count to less than the normal range or a 50% fall in the platelet count within the normal range. In the majority of cases, this mild to moderate thrombocytopenia appears to be a direct effect of heparin on platelets and is of no consequence. However, approximately 0.1% to 0.2% of patients receiving heparin demonstrate an immune thrombocytopenia mediated by immunoglobulin G antibody directed against a complex of platelet factor 4 and heparin.[126]

The development of thrombocytopenia may be accompanied by arterial thrombosis or DVT, which may lead to serious consequences, such as death and limb amputation.[128] The diagnosis of heparin-induced thrombocytopenia, with or without thrombosis, must be made on clinical grounds, because the assays with the highest sensitivity and specificity are not readily available and have a slow turnaround time for results.

When the diagnosis of heparin-induced thrombocytopenia is made, heparin in all forms must be stopped immediately.[125-128] In patients who need ongoing anticoagulation, several alternatives exist. The agents most extensively used include the heparinoid danaparoid,[127] hirudin,[128] and the specific antithrombin argatroban.[128]

Danaparoid is available for limited use on compassionate grounds, and hirudin and argatroban have now been approved for use in the United States and Canada. Warfarin may be used but should not be started until one of the previous agents has been used for 3 or 4 days to suppress thrombin generation. Insertion of an inferior vena cava filter is seldom indicated.

Osteoporosis has been reported in patients receiving unfractionated heparin in dosages of 20,000 U/day (or more) for more than 6 months.[117] Demineralization can progress to the fracture of vertebral bodies or long bones, and the defect may not be entirely reversible.[117]

Low-Molecular-Weight Heparin

Heparin currently in clinical use is polydispersed unmodified heparin, with a mean molecular weight ranging from 10 to 16 kD. Low-molecular-weight derivatives of commercial heparin, with a mean molecular weight of 4 to 5 kD, have now been prepared.[129,130]

The commercially available LMWHs are made by different processes (such as nitrous acid, alkaline, or enzymatic depolymerization) and differ chemically and pharmacokinetically.[129,130] The clinical significance of these differences, however, is unclear, and there have been very few studies comparing LMWHs with respect to clinical outcomes.[130] The doses of the various LMWHs have been established empirically and are not necessarily interchangeable. Therefore, at this time, the effectiveness and safety of each of the LMWHs must be tested separately.[130]

The LMWHs differ from unfractionated heparin in numerous ways. Of particular importance are greater bioavailability (>90% after subcutaneous injection), prolonged half-life, and predictable clearance, all of which enable once- or twice-daily injection, and a predictable antithrombotic response based on body weight, permitting treatment without laboratory monitoring.[117,129,130] Other possible advantages are the ability of LMWHs to inactivate platelet-bound factor Xa, their resistance to inhibition by platelet factor IV, and their decreased effect on platelet function and vascular permeability (possibly accounting for less hemorrhagic effects at comparable antithrombotic doses).

It was hoped that the LMWHs would have fewer serious complications, such as bleeding, heparin-induced thrombocytopenia, and osteoporosis than unfractionated heparin.[129-131] Evidence is accumulating that these complications are indeed less serious and less frequent with the use of LMWH. LMWH has been approved for the prevention and treatment of venous thromboembolism in pregnancy. These drugs do not cross the placenta, and small case series suggest that they may be both effective and safe. The LMWHs all cross-react with unfractionated heparin and therefore cannot be used as alternative therapy in patients who demonstrate heparin-induced thrombocytopenia. The heparinoid danaparoid, which possesses a 10% to 20% cross-reactivity with heparin, can be safely used in patients who show no cross-reactivity.

Several different LMWHs are available for the prevention and treatment of VTE in various countries. Four LMWHs are approved for clinical use in Canada, and three LMWHs have been approved for use in the United States.

Table 149-7	Predominantly Outpatient Treatment of Proximal Deep Venous Thrombosis (DVT) with Low-Molecular-Weight Heparin vs. Inpatient Treatment with Intravenous Heparin		
STUDY*	**TREATMENT**	**RECURRENT DVT**	**MAJOR BLEEDING**
Koopman et al[139]	Nadroparin	14/202 (6.9%)	1/202 (0.5%)
	Heparin	17/198 (8.6%)	4/198 (2.0%)
Levine et al[140]	Enoxaparin	13/247 (5.3%)	5/247 (2.0%)
	Heparin	17/253 (6.7%)	3/253 (1.2%)
Columbus Study[141]	Reviparin	27/510 (5.3%)	16/510 (3.1%)
	Heparin	24/511 (4.9%)	12/511 (2.3%)

*Superscript numbers indicate chapter references.

In a number of early clinical trials (some of which were dose-finding), LMWH given by subcutaneous or intravenous injection was compared with continuous intravenous unfractionated heparin with repeat venography at day 7-10 being the primary endpoint.[117] These studies demonstrated that LMWH was at least as effective as unfractionated heparin in preventing extension or increasing resolution of thrombi on repeat venography.

Subcutaneous unmonitored LMWH has been compared with continuous intravenous heparin in a number of clinical trials for the treatment of proximal DVT using long-term follow-up as an outcome measure.[132-137,139-142] These studies have shown that LMWH is at least as effective and safe as unfractionated heparin in the treatment of proximal DVT. Pooling of the most methodologically sound studies indicates a significant advantage for LMWH in the reduction of major bleeding and mortality.[136] More recent studies have indicated that LMWH used predominantly out-of-hospital was as effective and safe as intravenous unfractionated heparin given in-hospital (Table 149-7).[139-141] Two clinical trials showed that LMWH was as effective as intravenous heparin in the treatment of patients presenting with PE.[138,143] Economic analysis of treatment with LMWH versus intravenous heparin demonstrated that LMWH was cost-effective for treatment in-hospital as well as out-of-hospital.[143] As these agents become more widely available for treatment, they have replaced intravenous unfractionated heparin in the initial management of patients with VTE.

Long-term LMWH has been compared with warfarin therapy in patients presenting with proximal DVT.[144-146] Although these studies differ in design and doses of LMWH, they do indicate that LMWH is a useful alternative to warfarin therapy, particularly in patients who have recurrence of VTE while on therapeutic doses of warfarin (e.g., in the cancer population).

Coumarin Therapy

Pharmacokinetics and Pharmacodynamics of Warfarin

There are two distinct chemical groups of oral anticoagulants, the 4-hydroxy coumarin derivatives (e.g., warfarin sodium) and the indane-1,3-dione derivatives (e.g., phenindione).[147] The coumarin derivatives are the oral anticoagulants of choice because they are associated with fewer nonhemorrhagic side effects than the indanedione derivatives. In North America, the most commonly used agent is coumarin (Coumadin), but various generic forms of warfarin sodium have also been introduced.

Warfarin, a racemic mixture of stereoisomers (R and S forms), is highly water soluble and is highly bioavailable.[148] Peak absorption occurs around 90 minutes, and the half-life is between 36 and 42 hours. Warfarin is highly protein bound (primarily to albumin), and only the non–protein-bound material is biologically active. Any drug or chemical that is also bound to albumin may displace warfarin from its protein binding sites and thereby increase the biologically active material.[148] Warfarin is metabolized in the liver by the p450 (CYP2C9) system of enzymes. Interference with the CYP2C9 enzymes by various drugs or a mutation in the gene coding for one of the common CYP2C9 enzymes can markedly interfere with the metabolism of warfarin.[149]

The anticoagulant effect of warfarin is mediated by the inhibition of the vitamin K–dependent gamma-carboxylation of coagulation factors II, VII, IX, and X.[146-148] This results in the synthesis of immunologically detectable but biologically inactive forms of these coagulation proteins. Warfarin also inhibits the vitamin K–dependent gamma-carboxylation of proteins C and S[148,149] as well as of protein Z.[150] Protein C circulates as a proenzyme that is activated on endothelial cells by the thrombin-thrombomodulin complex to form activated protein C.[151] Activated protein C in the presence of protein S inhibits activated factor VIII and activated factor V activity.[152] Therefore, vitamin K antagonists such as warfarin create a biochemical paradox by producing an anticoagulant effect owing to the inhibition of procoagulants (factors II, VII, IX, and X) and a potentially thrombogenic effect by impairing the synthesis of naturally occurring inhibitors of coagulation (proteins C and S).[152] Heparin or LMWH and warfarin treatment should overlap by 4 to 5 days when warfarin treatment is initiated in patients with thrombotic disease. The role of protein Z in the coagulation process is less definite.

The anticoagulant effect of warfarin is delayed until the normal clotting factors are cleared from the circulation, and the peak effect does not occur until 36 to 72 hours after its administration.[152] During the first few days of warfarin therapy, the prothrombin time (PT) reflects mainly the depression of factor VII, which has a half-life of 5 to 7 hours. Equilibrium levels of factors II, IX, and X are not reached until about 1 week after the initiation of therapy. The use of small initial daily doses (e.g., 5 mg) is the preferred approach to initiation of warfarin treatment.[153] The dose-response relationship to warfarin therapy varies widely among individuals, and therefore the dose must be carefully monitored to prevent overdosing or underdosing.

A number of factors influence the anticoagulant response of warfarin in individual patients; they include inaccuracies in laboratory testing and noncompliance of patients, but more importantly reflect the influence of dietary changes or the influence of drugs that interfere with the metabolism of warfarin. The availability of vitamin K can be influenced by dramatic changes in dietary intake or by drugs such as antibiotics, which interfere with the synthesis of vitamin K in the gastrointestinal tract.[154] A wide variety of drugs may interact with warfarin. However, a critical appraisal of the literature reporting such interactions indicates that the evidence substantiating many of the claims is limited.[155] Aspirin is particularly problematic because it (1) interferes with platelet function, (2) displaces warfarin from its protein binding, thus augmenting its biologic activities, and (3) as with the nonsteroidal anti-inflammatory drugs (NSAIDs), may cause gastric erosions, thus creating a site for bleeding. Nonetheless, in certain patients, the use of aspirin and warfarin is indicated to improve efficacy even though bleeding may be somewhat increased. It is important that patients be warned against taking any new drugs without the knowledge of their attending physician, and it is prudent to monitor the INR more frequently when any drug (including natural compounds) is added to or withdrawn from the regimen of a patient being treated with an oral anticoagulant.

Laboratory Monitoring and Therapeutic Range

The laboratory test most commonly used to measure the effects of warfarin is the one-stage PT measurement. The PT is sensitive to reduced activity of factors II, VII, and X but is insensitive to reduced activity of factor IX. Confusion about the appropriate therapeutic range has occurred because the different tissue thromboplastins used for measuring the PT vary considerably in sensitivity to the vitamin K–dependent clotting factors and in response to warfarin.[156,157]

In order to promote standardization of the PT for monitoring oral anticoagulant therapy, the World Health Organization (WHO) developed an international reference thromboplastin from human brain tissue and recommended that the PT ratio be expressed as the International Normalized Ratio, or INR. The INR is the PT ratio obtained by testing a given sample using the WHO reference thromboplastin. For practical clinical purposes, the INR for a given plasma sample is equivalent to the PT ratio obtained using a standardized human brain thromboplastin known as the Manchester Comparative Reagent, which has been widely used in the United Kingdom. Thromboplastins with a high sensitivity are in current use. In fact, many centers have been using the recombinant tissue factor, which has an International Sensitivity Index value 0.9 to 1.0, giving an INR equivalent to the prothrombin time ratio.

Warfarin is administered in an initial dose of 5 mg per day for the first 2 days, and the daily dose is then adjusted according to the INR. Heparin or LMWH therapy is discontinued on the fifth day after initiation of warfarin therapy, provided that the INR is prolonged into the recommended therapeutic range (INR 2.0 to 3.0) for at least 2 consecutive days.[120] Frequent INR determinations are required initially to establish therapeutic anticoagulation.

Once the anticoagulant effect and patient's warfarin dose requirements are stable, the INR should be monitored every 1 to 3 weeks throughout the course of warfarin therapy. However, if there are factors that may produce an unpredictable response to warfarin (e.g., concomitant

drug therapy), the INR should be monitored more frequently to minimize the risk of complications due to poor anticoagulant control.[147,153]

Adverse Effects of Oral Anticoagulants

Bleeding

The major side effect of oral anticoagulant therapy is bleeding.[158] A number of risk factors have been identified that predispose to bleeding with oral anticoagulant therapy.[158-160] The most important factor influencing bleeding risk is the intensity of the INR.[158-161] Other factors are a history of bleeding, previous history of stroke or myocardial infarction, hypertension, renal failure, diabetes, and a decreased hematocrit.[160] Efforts have been made to quantify the bleeding risk according to these underlying clinical factors.[159] Fihn and coworkers[159] reported that introduction of a multicomponent intervention combining patient education and alternative approaches to the maintenance of the INR resulted in a lower frequency of major bleeding in the patients in the intervention group. Furthermore, INR values in patients in the intervention group were within the therapeutic range significantly more often than values of patients in the standard care group.

In a retrospective cohort study of patients with an INR greater than 6.0, it was shown that a prolonged delay in the return of the INR to therapeutic range was seen in patients whose INR exceeded 4.0 after two doses of warfarin were withheld, patients with an extreme elevation of the INR, and older patients, particularly those with decompensated congestive heart failure and active cancer.[159] Numerous randomized clinical trials have demonstrated that the rate of clinically important bleeding is lower when the targeted INR is 2.0 to 3.0 and that bleeding increases exponentially when the INR rises above 4.5 or 5.0.[157,161,162] There is a strong negative relationship between the percentage of time that patients have INR values within the targeted range and the rates of both bleeding and recurrent thrombosis.

Oral anticoagulant therapy in elderly patients presents further problems.[163,164] Many of these patients require long-term anticoagulants because of their underlying clinical conditions, which increase with age, but they are also more likely to have underlying causes for bleeding, including the development of cancer, intestinal polyps, renal failure, and stroke, and they are more prone to falling. The daily requirements for warfarin to maintain the therapeutic INR also decreases with age, presumably owing to decreased clearance of the drug.[165] Therefore, before initiation of oral anticoagulant treatment in elderly patients, the risk-to-benefit ratio of treatment must be considered. If such a patient is started on oral anticoagulant therapy, careful attention to the INR is required.

Patients with cancer are more likely to bleed with oral anticoagulant treatment.[163] Compared with patients receiving oral anticoagulants who do not have cancer, patients with cancer have a higher incidence of both major and minor bleeding, and cessation of anticoagulant therapy is more frequently due to bleeding. In one study, patients with cancer had a higher thrombotic complication rate and a higher bleeding rate regardless of the INR, whereas bleeding in patients without cancer was seen only when the INR was greater than 4.5. Safer and more effective anticoagulant therapy is required for the treatment of VTE in patients with cancer.[166]

Management of Over-Anticoagulation

The approach to the patient with an elevated INR depends on the extent of elevation of the INR and the clinical circumstances.[153] Options available to the physician include temporary discontinuation of warfarin treatment, administration of vitamin K, and administration of blood products, such as fresh-frozen plasma and prothrombin concentrate, to replace the vitamin K–dependent clotting factors. If the rise in INR is mild and the patient is not bleeding, no specific treatment is necessary other than reduction in the warfarin dose. The INR can be expected to decrease during the next 24 hours with this approach.

With more marked increase of the INR in patients who are not bleeding, treatment with small doses of vitamin K_1 (e.g., 1 mg), given either orally or by subcutaneous injection, could be considered.[153,167,168] With very marked increase in the INR, particularly in a patient who is either actively bleeding or at risk for bleeding, the coagulation defect should be corrected. Vitamin K can be given intravenously, subcutaneously, or orally.[167] When possible, the oral route is preferred. If ongoing anticoagulation with warfarin is planned, then repeated small doses of vitamin K should be given, so that there is no problem with warfarin resistance.[166,167]

Reported side effects of vitamin K include flushing, dizziness, tachycardia, hypotension, dyspnea, and sweating.[147] Intravenous administration of vitamin K_1 should be performed with caution to avoid inducing an anaphylactoid reaction. The risk of anaphylactoid reaction can be reduced by slow administration of vitamin K_1. In most patients, intravenous administration of vitamin K_1 has a demonstrable effect on the INR within 6 to 8 hours and corrects the elevated INR within 12 to 24 hours. Because the half-life of vitamin K_1 is less than that of warfarin sodium, a second course of vitamin K_1 may be necessary. If bleeding is very severe and life-threatening, vitamin K therapy can be supplemented with concentrates of factors II, VII, IX, and X.

When bleeding occurs in a patient receiving oral anticoagulants, it is important to consider the site of bleeding. Bleeding from the upper gastrointestinal tract is commonly seen in such patients, and the concomitant use of other medications is often a factor. Once the bleeding is controlled, the necessary investigations must be carried out to identify bleeding lesions in the gastrointestinal or genitourinary tract, which are often unsuspected.[169] Johnsen and colleagues[170] have reviewed the various protocols for the perioperative management of patients receiving oral anticoagulants.

Long-Term Treatment of Venous Thromboembolism

Patients with established DVT or PE require long-term anticoagulant therapy to prevent recurrent disease.[120,171] Warfarin therapy is highly effective and is preferred in most patients. Adjusted-dose subcutaneous heparin or LMWH is the treatment of choice when long-term oral anticoagulants are contraindicated, such as in pregnancy, and for the long-term treatment of patients in whom oral anticoagulant therapy proves to be very difficult to control.[171] In patients with proximal DVT, long-term therapy with warfarin reduces the frequency of objectively documented recurrent VTE from 47% to 2%. The use of a less intense warfarin regimen (INR 2.0 to 3.0) markedly lowers the risk of bleeding, from 20% to 4%, without loss of effectiveness in comparison with more intense warfarin regimens.[157] With the improved safety of oral anticoagulant therapy using a less intense warfarin regimen, interest in evaluating the long-term treatment of thrombotic disorders has been renewed.

Optimal Duration of Oral Anticoagulants After a First Episode of Venous Thromboembolism

It has been recommended that all patients with a first episode of VTE receive warfarin therapy for at least 3 to 6 months. Attempts to decrease the treatment to 4 weeks or 6 weeks resulted in higher rates of recurrent VTE in comparison with either 12 or 24 weeks of treatment (11% to 18% recurrent VTE in the following 1 to 2 years).[172-174] Most of the recurrent thromboembolic events occurred in the 6 to 8 weeks immediately after anticoagulant treatment was stopped, and the incidence was higher in patients with continuing risk factors, such as cancer and immobilization.[175] Treatment with oral anticoagulants for 6 months reduced the incidence of recurrent thromboembolic events, but there was a cumulative incidence of recurrent events at 2 years (11%) and an ongoing risk of recurrent VTE of approximately 5% to 6% per year.[174]

In patients with a first episode of idiopathic VTE treated with intravenous heparin followed by warfarin for three months, continuation of warfarin for 24 months led to a significant lower incidence of recurrent DVT compared with placebo.[175] In a further trial comparing 3 months and 12 months of oral anticoagulant therapy after the occurrence of a first episode of idiopathic proximal DVT, patients who were treated for only 3 months had a higher incidence of recurrence of VTE during the subsequent 12 months than patients who continued to receive anticoagulants for 12 months.[176] However, the cumulative hazard of recurrent VTE at 36 months was the same in the two groups. The incidence of recurrence after discontinuation of treatment was 5.1% per patient-year in patients in whom oral anticoagulant therapy was discontinued after 3 months and 5.0% per patient-year in patients who received 12 months of oral anticoagulant therapy. The VTE recurred in the initially unaffected leg more than half the time, suggesting that the recurrences were related to a hypercoagulable state and that the duration of anticoagulant therapy did not influence the ultimate recurrence rate.[176]

Venous thromboembolism should be considered a chronic disease with a continued risk of VTE often associated with minor provocation.[177] The continued risk of recurrent thromboembolism even with 12 months of treatment after a first episode of DVT has encouraged the development of clinical trials evaluating the effectiveness of long-term anticoagulant treatment (beyond 6 months). In one trial, patients with documented proximal DVT with or without the diagnosis of thrombophilia who had received adequate anticoagulation were randomly assigned to receive either coumarin with a targeted INR of 1.5 to 2 or an identical placebo. This study showed that the lower-intensity warfarin regimen significantly decreased the incidence of recurrent VTE on follow-up with no added risk for major bleeding.[178] In another study, however, two regimens of warfarin therapy, one with a targeted INR of 1.5 to 2 and the other with a targeted INR of 2 to 3, were compared in similar patient populations. Results indicated that the usual INR of 2 to 3 resulted in a significantly lower incidence of recurrent VTE with no added risk for bleeding.[179] Therefore, at this time, there is no justification for the use of the less intense warfarin regimen.

Optimal Duration of Oral Anticoagulant Treatment in Patients with Recurrent Venous Thromboembolism

In a multicenter clinical trial, Schulman and associates[181] randomly assigned patients with a first recurrent episode of VTE to receive either 6 months of oral anticoagulants or continuation of such therapy indefinitely, with a targeted INR of 2.0 to 2.85. The analysis was reported at 4 years. VTE recurred in 20.7% of patients receiving anticoagulants for 6 months but in only 2.6% of patients undergoing indefinite treatment ($P < .001$). However, the rates of major bleeding were 2.7% for 6 months of therapy and 8.6% for indefinite therapy. In the indefinite therapy group, two of the major hemorrhages were fatal, whereas there were no fatal hemorrhages in the 6-month therapy group. Extending the duration of oral anticoagulants for approximately 4 years significant decreased the incidence of recurrent VTE, but with a higher incidence of major bleeding. Without a mortality difference, the risk of hemorrhage versus the benefit of decreased recurrent thromboembolism with the use of extended warfarin treatment remains uncertain and requires further clinical trials.

The Sixth ACCP Consensus Conference on Antithrombotic Therapy yielded the following recommendations.[120] Oral anticoagulant therapy should be continued for at least 3 months to prolong the prothrombin time to a targeted INR of 2.5 (range, 2.0 to 3.0). Patients with reversible or time-limited risk factors can be treated for 3 to 6 months. Patients with a first episode of idiopathic VTE should be treated for at least 6 months. It should be noted that these recommendations antedated the results of the study by Agnelli and colleagues.[177] Patients with recurrent VTE or a continuing risk factor, such as cancer, antithrombin deficiency, or the antiphospholipid syndrome, should be treated indefinitely. Patients with activated protein C resistance (factor V Leiden mutation) should probably receive indefinite treatment if they have recurrent disease, are homozygous for the gene, or have multiple thrombophilic conditions. Accumulated evidence indicates that symptomatic isolated calf vein thrombosis should be treated with anticoagulants for at least 3 months.[120]

■ THROMBOLYTIC THERAPY FOR VENOUS THROMBOEMBOLISM

Several studies have demonstrated that the mortality from PE can be decreased by heparin. Treatment with intravenous heparin and oral anticoagulants reduces the mortality rate to less than 5%, which may be further lowered with the use of LMWH. In the Prospective Investigation of Pulmonary Embolism Diagnosis (PIOPED), only 10 of 399 (2.5%) patients who had angiographically confirmed PE died.[182] However, patients who present with acute massive PE and hypotension have a mortality rate of approximately 20%. For such patients, the appropriate use of thrombolytic agents has a role.

Several trials have compared thrombolytic drugs with heparin.[182-187] Outcome measures for accelerated thrombolysis included quantitative measures on second pulmonary angiograms, quantitative scores on second pulmonary perfusion scans, and measures of pulmonary vascular resistance. Although all studies demonstrated superiority of thrombolysis (and in particular with tissue-type plasminogen activator [t-PA]) in radiographic and hemodynamic abnormalities within the first 24 hours, this advantage was short lived.[183]

Two systematic reviews have compared thrombolytic therapy with heparin treatments.[186,187] In one study, the composite endpoint of death and recurrent PE was lower with the use of thrombolytic agents, but the risk of major bleeding was higher.[186] Both of these studies indicated that until the proper randomized clinical trials have been carried out, thrombolytic therapy should be used only in patients with massive PE complicated by shock.[186-188]

Two thrombolytic agents have been approved by the FDA for the treatment of acute PE. The dosage schedules are as follows:

■ Streptokinase, 250,000 units over 30 min, followed by 100,000 units h^{-1} for 24 hr
■ Recombinant tissue plasminogen activator (rt-PA), 100 mg administered over 2 hr.

Anticoagulation with heparin or LMWH is usually commenced when the aPTT is less than two times the control.

■ INFERIOR VENA CAVAL INTERRUPTION

Early approaches to inferior vena caval interruption included ligation or plication using external clips. Both procedures were accompanied by an operative mortality rate of 12% to 14%, a recurrent pulmonary emboli rate of 4% to 6%, and an occlusion rate of 67% to 69%. These complications gave rise to the development of catheter-inserted intraluminal filters. An ideal filter is one that is easily and safely placed percutaneously, is biocompatible and mechanically stable, is able to trap emboli without causing occlusion of the vena cava, does not require anticoagulation, and is not ferromagnetic (i.e., does not cause artifacts on magnetic resonance imaging). Although there is as yet no ideal filter, several types are available; they are discussed in detail in Chapter 152. They include the Greenfield stainless-steel filter, the titanium Greenfield filter, the bird's nest filter, the Vena Tech filter, and the Simon-Nitinol filter. In experienced hands, these devices can be quickly and safely inserted under fluoroscopic control. One filter (the Antheor TU 50-125 Medi-Tech, Boston Scientific Corp.) can be inserted temporarily in conjunction with thrombolytic therapy and then removed. The follow-up data available to date show that the Greenfield filter has had the best performance record, so any future comparative studies should use this filter as the standard.[189]

The main indications for vena caval filters are contra-indications to anticoagulants, recurrent PE despite adequate anticoagulation, and for prophylactic placement in high-risk patients. In the last category are patients with cor pulmonale or a previous history of PE who have been put in high-risk situations, such as acetabular fracture, and patients who have cancer. A more controversial indication for the prophylactic insertion of a filter is emergency surgery occurring within the first 4 weeks of the start of anticoagulant therapy after thrombolytic therapy.

In the past, the detection of a free-floating thrombus by ultrasonography examination has been regarded as an indication for either thrombectomy or insertion of an inferior vena cava filter.[190] An important study compared the clinical outcomes of patients who did and did not have a free-floating thrombus in a proximal leg vein.[191] There was no difference in the incidence of PE or death between the two groups. The researchers concluded that the routine insertion of inferior vena cava filters in patients with free-floating thrombi cannot be supported. This statement is in keeping with an earlier observation that free-floating thrombi become attached to the vein wall rather than embolizing. In a further study, patients with proximal DVT were randomly assigned to receive either an inferior vena cava filter or anticoagulant treatment alone.[192] All patients were treated with heparin followed by oral anticoagulant therapy for 3 months. At 10 days, there was a significant difference in incidence of PE, but no difference in mortality. Extended follow-up at 1 to 2 years showed a (nonsignificant) increase in the incidence of PE in the control group, but a higher incidence of recurrent DVT in the vena cava filter group and no difference in mortality.[193]

■ CONCLUSION

Over the past 20 years, a large number of trials have studied the diagnosis, prevention, and treatment of VTE. Clinical practice has dramatically changed in response. A number of studies are currently under way to explore new approaches to diagnosis and treatment; they include the use of pretest clinical probabilities and the D-dimer assay, the role of spiral computed tomography, and determination of the optimal management using LMWH and newer anticoagulants such as pentasaccharide and specific antithrombin agents. Longer duration of anticoagulant therapy with LMWH or warfarin is aimed at decreasing the rate of recurrent DVT and PE and decreasing the incidence of the post-thrombotic syndrome. The role of thrombolytic therapy in patients with submassive or massive PE remains controversial, and further randomized clinical trials are needed.

■ REFERENCES

1. Hull RD, Hirsh J, Carter CJ, et al: Diagnostic efficacy of impedance plethysmography for clinically suspected deep vein thrombosis: A randomized trial. Ann Intern Med 102:21-28, 1985.
2. Huisman MV, Buller HR, ten Cate JW, Vreeken J: Serial impedance plethysmography for suspected deep venous thrombosis in outpatients. The Amsterdam General Practitioner Study. N Engl J Med 314:823-828, 1986.
3. Kakkar VV, Howe CT, Flanc C, Clarke MB: Natural history of postoperative deep vein thrombosis. Lancet 2(7614):230-233, 1969.
4. Lagerstedt CI, Olsson CG, Fagher BO, et al: Need for long term anticoagulant treatment in symptomatic calf vein thrombosis. Lancet 2(8454):515-518, 1985.
5. Lohr JM, James KV, Deshmukh RM, Hasselfeld KA: Calf vein thrombi are not a benign finding. Am J Surg 170:86-90, 1995.
6. Moser KM, Le Moine JR: Is embolic risk conditioned by location of deep venous thrombosis? Ann Intern Med 94:439-444, 1981.
7. Sevitt S, Gallagher N: Venous thrombosis and pulmonary embolism: A clinico-pathological study in injured and burned patients. Br J Surg 48:475-489, 1961.
8. Mavor GE, Galloway JMD: The iliofemoral venous segment as a source of pulmonary emboli. Lancet 1:871-874, 1967.
9. Hull RD, Hirsh J, Carter CJ, et al: Diagnostic value of ventilation-perfusion lung scanning in patients with suspected pulmonary embolism. Chest. 88:819-828, 1985.
10. Salzman EW, Davies GC: Prophylaxis of venous thromboembolism: Analysis of cost-effectiveness. Ann Surg 191:207-218, 1980.
11. Hull R, Hirsh J, Sackett DL, Stoddart GL: Cost-effectiveness of primary and secondary prevention of fatal pulmonary embolism in high risk surgical patients. CMAJ 127:990-995, 1982.
12. Oster G, Tuden RL, Colditz GA: A cost-effectiveness analysis of prophylaxis against deep vein thrombosis in major orthopedic surgery. JAMA 257:203-208, 1987.
13. Bergqvist D, Jonsson B: Cost-effectiveness of prolonged out-of-hospital prophylaxis with low-molecular-weight heparin following total hip replacement. Haemostasis 30(Suppl 2):130-135, 2000.
14. Hauch O, Khattar SC, Jorensen LN: Cost-benefit analysis of prophylaxis against deep vein thrombosis in major orthopaedic surgery. Semin Thromb Hemost 17(Suppl 3):280-283, 1991.
15. Sharnoff JG, Deblassio G: Prevention of fatal postoperative thromboembolism by heparin prophylaxis. Lancet 2(7681):1006-1007, 1970.
16. Prevention of fatal postoperative pulmonary embolism by low doses of heparin. An international multicentre trial. Lancet 2(7924):45-51, 1975.
17. Collins R, Scrimgeour A, Yusef S, Peto R: Reduction in fatal pulmonary embolism and venous thrombosis by perioperative administration of subcutaneous heparin. N Engl J Med 318:1162-1173, 1988.
18. Kakkar VV, Cohen AT, Edmonson RA, et al: Low molecular weight versus standard heparin for prevention of venous thromboembolism after major abdominal surgery. Lancet 341:259-265, 1993.
19. Kakkar VV, Boeckl O, Boneau B, et al: Efficacy and safety of a low molecular weight heparin and standard unfractionated heparin for prophylaxis of postoperative venous thromboembolism: European multicenter trial. World J Surg 21:2-9, 1997.
20. Geerts WH, Heit JA, Clagett GP, et al: Prevention of venous thromboembolism. Chest 199:132S-175S, 2001.
21. Bergqvist D, Burmark US, Flordal PA, et al: Low molecular weight heparin started before surgery as prophylaxis against deep vein thrombosis: 2500 versus 5000 XaI units in 2070 patients. Br J Surg 82:496-501, 1995.
22. Hull RD, Pineo GF, Francis C, et al: Low-molecular-weight heparin prophylaxis using dalteparin in close proximity to surgery vs. warfarin in hip arthroplasty patients. Arch Intern Med 160:2199-2207, 2000.
23. Hull RD, Pineo GF, Stein PD, et al: Timing of initial administration of low-molecular-weight heparin prophylaxis against deep vein

thrombosis in patients following elective hip arthroplasty. Arch Intern Med 160:1952-1960, 2001.

24. Fitzgerald RH Jr, Spiro TE, Trowbridge AA, et al; Enoxaparin Clinical Trial Group: Prevention of venous thromboembolic disease following primary total knee arthroplasty: A randomized, multicenter, open-label, parallel-group comparison of enoxaparin and warfarin. J Bone Joint Surg Am 83:900-906, 2001.

25. Horlocker TT, Heit JA: Low molecular weight heparin: Biochemistry, pharmacology, perioperative prophylaxis regimens, and guidelines for regional anesthetic management. Anesth Analg 85:874-885, 1997.

26. Kakkar VV, Adams PC: Preventive and therapeutic approach to thromboembolic disease and pulmonary embolism: Can death from pulmonary embolism be prevented ? J Am Coll Cardiol 8(Suppl B): 146B-158B, 1986.

27. Skinner DB, Salzman EW: Anticoagulant prophylaxis in surgical patients. Surg Gynecol Obstet 125:741-746, 1967.

28. Shephard RM Jr, White HA, Shirkey AL: Anticoagulant prophylaxis of thromboembolism in post-surgical patients. Am J Surg 112:698-702, 1966.

29. Coventry MB, Nolan DR, Beckenbaugh RD: "Delayed" prophylactic anticoagulation: A study of results and complications in 2,012 total hip arthroplasties. J Bone Joint Surg Am 55:1487-1492, 1973.

30. Eskeland G, Solheim K, Skjorten F: Anticoagulant prophylaxis, thromboembolism and mortality in elderly patients with hip fracture: A controlled clinical trial. Acta Chir Scand 131:16-29, 1966.

31. Murray DW, Britton AR, Bulstrode CJK: Thromboprophylaxis and death after total hip replacement. J Bone Joint Surg Br 78: 863-870, 1996.

32. Campling EA, Devlin HB, Hoile RW, Lunn JN: The report of the National Confidential Enquiry into Perioperative Deaths (NCEPOD). London, HM30, 1991/92.

33. Vandermeulen EP, Van Aken H, Vermylen J: Anticoagulants and spinal-epidural anesthesia. Anesth Analg 79:1165-2277, 1994.

34. Bergqvist D, Matzsch T, Jendteg S, et al: The cost-effectiveness of prevention of post-operative thromboembolism. Acta Chir Scand Suppl 556:36-41, 1990.

35. Dahlgren N, Tornebrandt K: Neurological complications after anaesthesia: A follow-up of 18,000 spinal and epidural anaesthetics performed over three years. Acta Anaesthesiol Scand 39:872-880, 1995.

36. Horlocker TT, Weder DJ, Benzon H, et al: Regional anesthesia in the anticoagulated patient: Defining the risks (the second ASRA Consensus Conference on Neuraxial Anesthesia and Anticoagulation). Reg Anesth Pain Med 28:163-166, 2003.

37. Dahl OE, Aspelin T, Arnesen H, et al: Increased activation of coagulation and formation of late deep venous thrombosis following discontinuation of thromboprophylaxis after hip replacement surgery. Thromb Res 80:299-306, 1995.

38. White RH, Romano PS, Zhou H, et al: Incidence and time course of thromboembolic outcomes following total hip or knee arthroplasty. Arch Intern Med 158:1525-1531, 1998.

39. Bergqvist D, Benoni G, Bjorgell O, et al: Low molecular weight heparin (enoxaparin) as prophylaxis against venous thromboembolism after total hip replacement. N Engl J Med 335:696-700, 1996.

40. Planes A, Vochelle N, Darmon JY, et al: Risk of deep-venous thrombosis after hospital discharge in patients having undergone total hip replacement: Double-blind randomized comparison of enoxaparin versus placebo. Lancet 348:224-228, 1996.

41. Dahl OE, Andreassen G, Aspelin T, et al: Prolonged thrombo-prophylaxis following hip replacement surgery—results of a double-blind, prospective, randomized, placebo-controlled study with dalteparin (Fragmin). Thromb Haemost 77:26-31, 1997.

42. Lassen MR, Borris LC, Anderson BS, et al: Efficacy and safety of prolonged thromboprophylaxis with a low-molecular-weight heparin (dalteparin) after total hip arthroplasty: The Danish Prolonged Prophylaxis (DaPP) study. Thromb Res 89:281-287, 1998.

43. Hull RD, Pineo GF, Francis C, et al: Low-molecular-weight heparin prophylaxis using dalteparin extended out-of-hospital vs in-hospital warfarin/out-of-hospital placebo in hip arthroplasty patients: A double-blind, randomized comparison. North American Fragmin Trial Investigators. Arch Intern Med 160:2208-2215, 2000.

44. Hull RD, Pineo GF, Stein PD, et al: Extended out-of-hospital low-molecular-weight heparin prophylaxis against deep venous thrombosis in patients after elective hip arthroplasty: A systematic review. Ann Intern Med 135:858-869, 2001.

45. Comp PC, Spiro TE, Friedman RJ, et al: Prolonged enoxaparin therapy to prevent venous thromboembolism after primary hip or knee replacement. J Bone Joint Surg Am 83:336-345, 2001.

46. Sarasin FP, Bounameaux H: Out of hospital antithrombotic prophylaxis after total hip replacement: Low-molecular-weight heparin, warfarin, aspirin or nothing? A cost-effectiveness analysis. Thromb Haemost 87:586-592, 2002.

47. Samama CM, Vray M, Barré J, et al: Extended venous thromboembolism prophylaxis after total hip replacement: A comparison of low-molecular-weight heparin with oral anticoagulant. Arch Intern Med 162:2191-2196, 2002.

48. Bergqvist D, Agnelli G, Cohen AT, et al: Duration of prophylaxis against venous thromboembolism with enoxaparin after surgery for cancer. N Engl J Med 346:975-980, 2002.

49. Nicolaides AN, Breddin HK, Fareed J, et al: Prevention of venous thromboembolism: International Consensus Statement. Guidelines compiled in accordance with the scientific evidence. Int Angiol 20:1-37, 2001.

50. Guyatt G, Schünemann H, Cook D, et al: Grades of recommendation for antithrombotic agents. Chest 119(Suppl):3S-7S, 2001.

51. Bergqvist D, Matzsch T, Burmark U, et al: Low molecular weight heparin given the evening before surgery compared with conventional low dose heparin in prevention of thrombosis. Br J Surg 75:888-891, 1988.

52. Caen JP: A randomized double-blind study between a low molecular weight heparin Kabi 2154 and standard heparin in the prevention of deep vein thrombosis in general surgery: A French multicentre trial. Thromb Haemost 59:216-220, 1988.

53. Nurmohamed MT, Verhaeghe R, Haas S, et al: A comparative trial of a low molecular weight heparin (enoxaparin) versus standard heparin for the prophylaxis of postoperative deep vein thrombosis in general surgery. Am J Surg 169:567-571, 1995.

54. Efficacy and safety of enoxaparin versus unfractionated heparin for prevention of deep vein thrombosis in elective cancer surgery: A double-blind randomized multicentre trial with venographic assessment. ENOXACAN Study Group. Br J Surg 84:1099-1103, 1997.

55. Leyvraz PF, Bachmann F, Hoek J, et al: Prevention of deep vein thrombosis after hip replacement: Randomised comparison between unfractionated heparin and low molecular weight heparin. BMJ 303:543-548, 1991.

56. Eriksson BL, Kälebo P, Anthymyr BA, et al: Prevention of deep vein thrombosis and pulmonary embolism after total hip replacement. J Bone Joint Surg Am 73:484-493, 1991.

57. Planes A, Vochelle N, Fagola M, et al: Prevention of deep vein thrombosis after total hip replacement: The effect of low molecular weight heparin with spinal and general anaesthesia. J Bone Joint Surg Br 73:418-422, 1991.

58. Hamulyak K, Lensing AW, van der Meer J, et al: Subcutaneous low-molecular-weight heparin or oral anticoagulants for the prevention of deep-vein thrombosis in elective hip and knee replacement? Thromb Haemost 74:1428-1431, 1995.

59. Torholm C, Broeng L, Jorgensen PS, et al: Thromboprophylaxis by low-molecular-weight heparin in elective hip surgery: A placebo controlled study. J Bone Joint Surg Br 73:434-438, 1991.

60. Francis CW, Pellegrini VD Jr, Totterman S, et al: Prevention of deep vein thrombosis after total hip arthroplasty: Comparison of warfarin and dalteparin. J Bone Joint Surg Am 79:1365-1372, 1997.

61. Colwell CW Jr, Collis DK, Paulson R, et al: Comparison of enoxaparin and warfarin for the prevention of venous thromboembolic disease after total hip arthroplasty. J Bone Joint Surg Am 81:932-940, 1999.

62. Levine MN, Hirsh J, Gent M, et al: Prevention of deep vein thrombosis after elective hip surgery: A randomized trial comparing low molecular weight heparin with standard unfractionated heparin. Ann Intern Med 114:545-551, 1991.

63. Hull RD, Raskob GE, Pineo GF, et al: A comparison of subcutaneous low molecular weight heparin with warfarin sodium for prophylaxis against deep vein thrombosis after hip or knee implantation. N Engl J Med 329:1370-1376, 1993.

64. Leclerc JR, Geerts WH, Desjardins L, et al: Prevention of deep vein thrombosis after major knee surgery: A randomised, double-blind trial comparing a low molecular weight heparin fragment (enoxaparin) to placebo. Thromb Haemost 67:417-423, 1992.

65. Leclerc JR, Geerts WH, Desjardins L, et al: Prevention of venous thromboembolism after knee arthroplasty: A randomized, double-blind trial comparing enoxaparin with warfarin. Ann Intern Med 124:619-626, 1996.

66. Heit JA, Berkowitz SD, Bona R, et al: Efficacy and safety of low molecular weight heparin (ardeparin sodium) compared to warfarin for the prevention of venous thromboembolism after total knee replacement surgery: A double blind, dose ranging study. Thromb Haemost 77:32-38, 1997.

67. Leizorovicz A, Haugh MC, Chapuis FR, et al: Low molecular weight heparin in prevention of perioperative thrombosis. BMJ 305:913-920, 1992.

68. Nurmohamed MT, Rosendaal FR, Buller HR, et al: Low-molecular-weight heparin versus standard heparin in general and orthopaedic surgery: A meta-analysis. Lancet 340:152-156, 1992.

69. Koch A, Bouges S, Ziegler S, et al: Low molecular weight heparin and unfractionated heparin in thrombosis prophylaxis after major surgical intervention: Update of previous meta-analyses. Br J Surg 84:750-759, 1997.

70. Palmer AJ, Koppenhagen K, Kirchhof B, et al: Efficacy and safety of low molecular weight heparin, unfractionated heparin and warfarin for thrombo-embolism prophylaxis in orthopaedic surgery: A meta-analysis of randomised clinical trials. Haemostasis 27:75-84, 1997.

71. O'Brien BJ, Anderson DR, Goeree R: Cost-effectiveness of enoxaparin versus warfarin prophylaxis against deep vein thrombosis after total hip replacement. Can Med Assoc J 150:1083-1089, 1994.

72. Menzin J, Colditz GA, Regan MM, et al: Cost-effectiveness of enoxaparin vs. low dose warfarin in the prevention of deep vein thrombosis after total hip replacement surgery. Arch Intern Med 155:757-764, 1995.

73. Hull RD, Raskob GE, Pineo GF, et al: Subcutaneous low-molecular-weight heparin vs warfarin for prophylaxis of deep vein thrombosis after hip or knee implantation: An economic perspective. Arch Intern Med 157:298-303, 1997.

74. Geerts WH, Jay RM, Code KI, et al: A comparison of low dose heparin with low molecular weight heparin as prophylaxis against venous thromboembolism after major trauma. N Engl J Med 335:701-707, 1996.

75. Harenberg J, Roebruck P, Heene DL: Subcutaneous low molecular weight heparin versus standard heparin and the prevention of thromboembolism in medical inpatients. The Heparin Study in Internal Medicine Group. Haemostasis 26:127-139, 1996.

76. Bergmann JF, Neuhart E: A multicenter randomized double-blind study of enoxaparin compared with unfractionated heparin in the prevention of venous thromboembolic disease in elderly inpatients bedridden for an acute medical illness. Thromb Haemost 7:529-534, 1996.

77. Ramos R, Salem BI, De Pawlikowski MP, et al: The efficacy of pneumatic compression stockings in the prevention of pulmonary embolism after cardiac surgery. Chest 109:82-85, 1996.

78. Turpie AG, Gallus A, Beattie WS, Hirsh J: Prevention of venous thrombosis in patients with intracranial disease by intermittent pneumatic compression of the calf. Neurology 27:435-438, 1977.

79. Turpie AGG, Delmore T, Hirsh J, et al: Prevention of venous thrombosis by intermittent sequential calf compression in patients with intracranial disease. Thromb Res 16:611-616, 1979.

80. Skillman JJ, Collins RE, Coe NP, et al: Prevention of deep vein thrombosis in neurosurgical patients: A controlled, randomized trial of external pneumatic compression boots. Surgery 83:354-358, 1978.

81. Hull RD, Raskob GE, Gent M, et al: Effectiveness of intermittent pneumatic leg compression for preventing deep vein thrombosis after total hip replacement. JAMA 263:2313-2317, 1990.

82. Francis CW, Pellegrini VD Jr, Marder VJ, et al: Comparison of warfarin and external pneumatic compression in prevention of venous thrombosis after total hip replacement. JAMA 267:2911-2915, 1992.

83. Hull RD, Delmore TJ, Hirsh J, et al: Effectiveness of intermittent pulsatile elastic stockings for the prevention of calf and thigh vein thrombosis in patients undergoing elective knee surgery. Thromb Res 16:37-45, 1979.

84. McKenna R, Galante J, Bachmann F, et al: Prevention of venous thromboembolism after total knee replacement by high-dose aspirin or intermittent calf and thigh compression. BMJ 280:514-517, 1980.

85. Comerota AJ, Katz ML, White JV: Why does prophylaxis with external pneumatic compression for deep vein thrombosis fail? Am J Surg 164:265-268, 1992.

86. Haddad FS, Kerry RM, McEwan JA, et al: Unanticipated variations between expected and delivered pneumatic compression therapy after elective hip surgery: A possible source of variation in reported patient outcomes. J Arthroplasty 16:37-46, 2001.

87. Meyerowitz BR, Nelson R: Measurement of the velocity of blood in lower limb veins with and without compression surgery. Surgery 56:481-486, 1964.

88. Sigel B, Edelstein AL, Felix WR: Compression of the deep vein system of the lower leg during inactive recumbency. Arch Surg 106:38-43, 1973.

89. Wells PS, Lensing AWA, Hirsh J: Graduated compression stockings in the prevention of postoperative venous thromboembolism: A meta-analysis. Arch Intern Med 154:67-72, 1994.

90. Brandjes DPM, Buller HR, Heijboer H, et al: Randomised trial of effect of compression stockings in patients with symptomatic proximal vein thrombosis. Lancet 349:759-762, 1997.

91. Scurr JH, Machin SJ, Bailey-King S, et al: Frequency and prevention of symptomless deep-vein thrombosis in long-haul flights: A randomised trial. Lancet 357:1485-1489, 2001.

92. Francis CW, Pellegrini VD Jr, Leibert KM, et al: Comparison of two warfarin regimens in the prevention of venous thrombosis following total knee replacement. Thromb Haemost 75:706-711, 1996.

93. Paiement GD, Wessinger SJ, Waltman WC, Harris WH: Low dose warfarin versus external pneumatic compression for prophylaxis against venous thromboembolism following total hip replacement. J Arthroplasty 2:23-26, 1987.

94. Powers PJ, Gent M, Jay RM, et al: A randomized trial of less intense postoperative warfarin or aspirin therapy in the prevention of venous thromboembolism after surgery for fractured hip. Arch Intern Med 149:771-774, 1989.

95. Poller L, McKernan A, Thomson JM, et al: Fixed minidose warfarin: A new approach to prophylaxis against venous thrombosis after major surgery. BMJ 295:1309-1312, 1987.

96. Dale C, Gallus A, Wycherley A, et al: Prevention of venous thrombosis with minidose warfarin after joint replacement. BMJ 303:224, 1991.

97. Collaborative overview of randomized trials of antiplatelet therapy. III: Reduction in venous thrombosis and pulmonary embolism by antiplatelet prophylaxis among surgical and medical patients. Antiplatelet Trialists' Collaboration. BMJ 308:235-246, 1994.

98. Prevention of pulmonary embolism and deep vein thrombosis with low dose aspirin: Pulmonary Embolism Prevention (PEP) Trial. Lancet 355:1295-1302, 2000.

99. Hull RD, Pineo GF: A synthetic pentasaccharide for the prevention of deep-vein thrombosis. N Engl J Med 345:291, 2001.

100. Turpie AGG, Gallus AS, Hoek JA; Pentasaccharide Investigators: A synthetic pentasaccharide for the prevention of deep-vein thrombosis after total hip replacement. N Engl J Med 344:619-625, 2001.

101. Eriksson BI, Bauer KA, Lassen MR, et al: Fondaparinux compared with enoxaparin for the prevention of venous thromboembolism after hip-fracture surgery. N Engl J Med 345:1298-1304, 2001.

102. Bauer KA, Eriksson BI, Lassen MR, et al: Fondaparinux compared with enoxaparin for the prevention of venous thromboembolism after elective knee surgery. N Engl J Med 345:1305-1310, 2001.

103. Lassen MR, Bauer KA, Eriksson BI, et al; European Pentasaccharide Hip Elective Surgery Study (EPHESUS) Steering Committee: Postoperative fondaparinux versus preoperative enoxaparin for prevention of venous thromboembolism in elective-hip-replacement surgery: A randomised double-blind comparison. Lancet 359:1715-1720, 2002.

104. Turpie AGG, Bauer KA, Eriksson BI, Lassen MR; PENTATHLON 2000 Study Steering Committee: Postoperative fondaparinux versus post-operative enoxaparin for prevention of venous thromboembolism after elective-hip-replacement surgery: A randomized double-blind trial. Lancet 359:1721-1726, 2002.

105. Bounameaux H, Perneger T: Fondaparinux: A new synthetic pentasaccharide for thrombosis prevention. Lancet 359:1710-1711, 2002.

106. Eriksson BI, Lindbratt S, Kalebo P, et al: METHRO II: Dose-response study of the novel oral, direct thrombin inhibitor, H 376/95 and its subcutaneous formulation melagatran, compared with dalteparin as thromboembolic prophylaxis after total hip or total knee replacement. Haemostasis 30(Suppl 1):20, 2000.

107. Eriksson BI, Arfwidsson A-C, Frison L, Eriksson UG, et al: A dose-ranging study of the oral direct thrombin inhibitor, ximelagatran, and its subcutaneous form, melagatran, compared with dalteparin in the prophylaxis of thromboembolism after hip or knee replacement: METHRO I. Thromb Haemost 87:231-237, 2002.

108. Colwell CW Jr, Berkowitz SD, Davidson BL, et al: Comparison of ximelagatran, an oral direct thrombin inhibitor, with enoxaparin for the prevention venous thromboembolism following total hip replacement: A randomized double-blind study. J Thromb Haemost 1:2119-2130, 2003.

109. Francis CW, Davidson BI, Berkowitz SD, et al: Ximelagatran versus warfarin for the prevention of venous thromboembolism after total knee arthroplasty. Ann Intern Med 137:648-655, 2002.

110. Baughman RA, Kapoor SC, Agarwal RK, et al: Oral delivery of anticoagulant doses of heparin: A randomized, double-blind, controlled study in humans. Circulation 98:1610-1615, 1998.

111. Berkowitz SD, Kosutic G, Marder VJ, et al: Oral heparin administration with a novel drug delivery agent (SNAC) in healthy volunteers and patients undergoing elective total hip arthroplasty. J Thromb Haemost 1:1914-1919, 2003.

112. Mismetti P, Laporte-Simitsidis S, Tardy B, et al: Prevention of venous thromboembolism in internal medicine with unfractionated or low-molecular-weight heparins: A meta-analysis of randomised clinical trials. Thromb Haemost 83:14-19, 2000.

113. Samama MM, Cohen AT, Darmon JY, et al: A comparison of enoxaparin with placebo for the prevention of venous thromboembolism in acutely ill medical patients. Prophylaxis in Medical Patients with Enoxaparin Study Group. N Engl J Med 341:793-800, 1999.

114. Leizorovicz A, Cohen AT, Turpie AGG, et al: A randomized placebo controlled trial of dalteparin for the prevention of venous thromboembolism in 3706 acutely ill medical patients: The PREVENT medical thromboprophylaxis study. J Thromb Haemost 1:abstract OC396, 2003.

115. Lane DA: Heparin binding and neutralizing protein. In Lane DA, Lindahl U (eds): Heparin: Chemical and Biological Properties, Clinical Applications. Boca Raton, FL, CRC Press, 1989, pp 363-391.

116. Rosenberg RD, Lam L: Correlation between structure and function of heparin. Proc Natl Acad Sci 76:1218-1222, 1979.

117. Hirsh J, Warkentin TE, Shaugnessy SG, et al: Heparin and low-molecular-weight heparin: Mechanisms of action, pharmacokinetics, dosing considerations, monitoring, efficacy and safety. Chest 119(Suppl):64S-94S, 2001.

118. Gallus A, Jackaman J, Tillett J, et al: Safety and efficacy of warfarin started early after submassive venous thrombosis or pulmonary embolism. Lancet 2(8519):1293-1296, 1986.

119. Hull RD, Raskob GE, Rosenbloom D, et al: Heparin for 5 days as compared with 10 days in the initial treatment of proximal venous thrombosis. N Engl J Med 322:1260-1264, 1990.

120. Hyers T, Agnelli G, Hull R, et al: Antithrombotic therapy for venous thromboembolic disease. Chest 119(Suppl):176S-193S, 2001.

121. Hull RD, Raskob GE, Rosenbloom D, et al: Optimal therapeutic level of heparin therapy in patients with venous thrombosis. Arch Intern Med 152:1589-1595, 1992.

122. Hull RD, Raskob GE, Brant RF, et al: The importance of initial heparin treatment on long-term clinical outcomes of antithrombotic therapy. Arch Intern Med 157:2317-2321, 1997.

123. Raschke RA, Reilly BM, Guidry JR, et al: The weight based heparin dosing nomogram compared with a 'standard care' nomogram. Ann Intern Med 119:874-881, 1993.

124. Raschke R, Hirsh J, Guidry JR: Suboptimal monitoring and dosing of unfractionated heparin in comparative studies with low-molecular-weight heparin. Ann Intern Med 138:720-723, 2003.

125. Kelton JG: Heparin-induced thrombocytopenia. Haemostasis 16:173-186, 1986.

126. Greinacher A, Eichler P, Lubenow N, et al: Heparin-induced thrombo-cytopenia with thromboembolic complications: Meta-analysis of two prospective trials to assess the value of parenteral treatment with lepirudin and its therapeutic aPTT range. Blood 96: 846, 2000.

127. Warkentin TE, Chong BH, Greinacher A: Heparin-induced thrombo-cytopenia: Towards consensus. Thromb Haemost 79:1-7, 1998.

128. Warkentin TE: Heparin-induced thrombocytopenia: Pathogenesis and management. Br J Haematol 121:535-565, 2003.

129. Barrowcliffe TW, Curtis AD, Johnson EA, et al: An international standard for low molecular weight heparin. Thromb Haemost 60:1-7, 1988.

130. Weitz JI: Low molecular weight heparins. N Engl J Med 337:688-698, 1997.

131. Shaughnessy SG, Young E, Deschamps P, Hirsh J: The effects of low molecular weight and standard heparin on calcium loss from fetal rat calvaria. Blood 86:1368-1373, 1995.

132. Hull RD, Raskob GE, Pineo GF, et al: Subcutaneous low molecular weight heparin compared with continuous intravenous heparin in the treatment of proximal vein thrombosis. N Engl J Med 326:975-988, 1992.

133. Prandoni P, Lensing AW, Buller HR, et al: Comparison of subcutaneous low molecular weight heparin with intravenous standard heparin in proximal deep vein thrombosis. Lancet 339:441-445, 1992.

134. Lopaciuk S, Meissner AJ, Filipecki S, et al: Subcutaneous low molecular weight heparin versus subcutaneous unfractionated heparin in the treatment of deep vein thrombosis: A Polish multicentre trial. Thromb Haemost 68:14-18, 1992.

135. Simonneau G, Charbonnier B, Decousus H, et al: Subcutaneous low molecular weight heparin compared with continuous intravenous unfractionated heparin in the treatment of proximal deep vein thrombosis. Arch Intern Med 153:1541-1546, 1993.

136. Gould MK, Dembitzer AD, Doyle RL, et al: Low-molecular-weight heparins compared with unfractionated heparin for treatment of acute deep venous thrombosis: A meta-analysis of randomized, controlled trials. Ann Intern Med 130:800-809, 1999.

137. Van den Belt AG, Prins MH, Lensing AW, et al: Fixed dose subcutaneous low-molecular-weight heparin for venous thromboembolism. Cochrane Database Syst Rev CD001100, 2000.

138. Simonneau G, Sors H, Charbonnier B, et al: A comparison of low molecular weight heparin with unfractionated heparin for acute pulmonary embolism. N Engl J Med 337:663-669, 1997.

139. Koopman MMW, Prandoni P, Piovella F, et al: Treatment of venous thrombosis with intravenous unfractionated heparin administered in the hospital as compared with subcutaneous low molecular weight heparin administered at home. N Engl J Med 334:682-687, 1996.

140. Levine M, Gent M, Hirsh J, et al: A comparison of low molecular weight heparin administered primarily at home with unfractionated heparin administered in the hospital for proximal deep vein thrombosis. N Engl J Med 334:677-681, 1996.

141. Low-molecular-weight heparin in the treatment of patients with venous thromboembolism. The Columbus Investigators. N Engl J Med 337:657-662, 1997.

142. Hull RD, Raskob GE, Brant RF, et al: Low-molecular-weight heparin versus heparin in the treatment of patients with pulmonary embolism. American-Canadian Thrombosis Study Group. Arch Intern Med 160:229-236, 2000.

143. Hull RD, Raskob GE, Rosenbloom D, et al: Treatment of proximal vein thrombosis with subcutaneous low molecular weight heparin vs. intravenous heparin: An economic perspective. Arch Intern Med 157:289-294, 1997.

144. van der Heijden JF, Hutten BA, Buller HR, et al: Vitamin K antagonists or low-molecular-weight heparin for the long term treatment of symptomatic venous thromboembolism. Cochrane Database Sys Rev CD002001, 2000.

145. Kakkar VV, Gebska M, Kadziola Z, et al: Low-molecular-weight heparin in the acute and long-term treatment of deep vein thrombosis. Thromb Haemost 89:674-680, 2003.

146. Breddin HK, Hach-Wunderle V, Nakov R, et al: Effects of a low-molecular-weight heparin on thrombus regression and recurrent thromboembolism in patients with deep-vein thrombosis. N Engl J Med 344:626, 2001.

147. Hirsh J, Dalen JE, Anderson D, et al: Oral anticoagulants: Mechanism of action, clinical effectiveness, and optimal therapeutic range. Chest 119(Suppl):8S-21S, 2001.

148. Vermeer C: Gamma-carboxylglutamate-containing proteins and the vitamin K-dependent carboxylase. Biochem J 266:625-636, 1990.

149. Loebstein R, Yonath H, Peleg D, et al: Interindividual variability in sensitivity to warfarin: Nature or nurture? Clin Pharmacol Ther 27:159-164, 2000.

150. Broze GJ: Protein Z-dependent regulation of coagulation. Thromb Haemost 86:8-13, 2001.

151. Clouse LH, Comp PC: The regulation of haemostasis: The protein C system. N Engl J Med 314:1298-1304, 1986.

152. Fiore LD, Scola MA, Cantillon CE, et al: Anaphylactoid reactions to vitamin K. J Thromb Thrombol 11:175-183, 2001.

153. O'Reilly RA, Aggeler PM: Studies on coumarin anticoagulant drugs: Initiation of warfarin therapy without a loading dose. Circulation 38:169-177, 1968.

154. Ansell J, Hirsh J, Dalen J, et al: Managing oral anticoagulant therapy. Chest 119:22S-38S, 2001.

155. Lipsky JJ: Antibiotic-associated hypoprothrombinaemia. J Antimicrob Chemother 21:281-300, 1998.

156. Wells PS, Holbrook AM, Crowther R, Hirsh J: Warfarin and its drug/food interactions: A critical appraisal of the literature. Ann Intern Med 121:676-683, 1994.

157. Poller L, Taberner DA: Dosage and control of oral anticoagulants: An international survey. Br J Haematol 51:479-485, 1982.

158. Hull R, Hirsh J, Jay R, et al: Different intensities of oral anticoagulant therapy in the treatment of proximal vein thrombosis. N Engl J Med 307:1676-1681, 1982.

159. Fihn SD, Mcdonnell M, Martin D, et al: Risk factors for complications of chronic anticoagulation: A multicenter study. Ann Intern Med 118:511-519, 1993.

160. Beyth RJ, Quinn L, Landefeld CS: A multicomponent intervention to prevent major bleeding complications in older patients receiving warfarin. Ann Intern Med 133:687-695, 2000.

161. Hylek EM, Regan S, Go AS: Clinical predictors of prolonged delay in return of the International Normalized Ratio to within the therapeutic range after excessive anticoagulation with warfarin. Ann Intern Med 135:393-400, 2001.

162. Cannegieter SC, Rosendaal FR, Wintzen AR, et al: The optimal intensity of oral anticoagulant therapy in patients with mechanical heart valve prostheses: The Leiden artificial valve and anti-coagulation study. N Engl J Med 333:11-17, 1995.

163. Hylek EM, Skates SJ, Sheehan MA, et al: An analysis of the lowest effective intensity of prophylactic anticoagulation for patients with nonrheumatic atrial fibrillation. N Engl J Med 335:540-589, 1995.

164. Henderson MC, White RHL: Anticoagulation in the elderly. Curr Opin Pulm Med 7:365-370, 2001.

165. Palareti G, Hirsh J, Legnani C, et al: Oral anticoagulation treatment in the elderly. Arch Intern Med 160:470-478, 2000.

166. Gage BF, Fihn SD, White RH: Management and dosing of warfarin therapy. Am J Med 109:481-488, 2000.

167. Palareti G, Legnani C, Lee A, et al: A comparison of the safety and efficacy of oral anticoagulation for the treatment of venous thromboembolic disease in patients with or without malignancy. Thromb Haemost 84:805-810, 2000.

168. Crowther MA, Julian J, McCarty D, et al: Treatment of warfarin-associated coagulopathy with oral vitamin K: A randomized controlled trial. Lancet 356:1551-1553, 2000.

169. Bussey HI: Managing excessive warfarin anticoagulation. Ann Intern Med 135:460-462, 2001.

170. Johnsen SP, Sorensen HT, Mellemkjoer L, et al: Hospitalisation for upper gastrointestinal bleeding associated with use of oral anticoagulants. Thromb Haemost 86:563-568, 2001.

171. Dunn AS, Turpie AGG: Perioperative management of patients receiving oral anticoagulants. Arch Intern Med 163:901-908, 2003.

172. Hull RD, Delmore TJ, Genton E, et al: Warfarin sodium versus low-dose heparin in the long-term treatment of venous thrombosis. N Engl J Med 301:855-858, 1979.

173. Optimum duration of anticoagulation for deep vein thrombosis and pulmonary embolism. Research Committee of the British Thoracic Society. Lancet 340:873-876, 1992.

174. Levine MN, Hirsh J, Gent M, et al: Optimal duration of oral anticoagulation therapy: A randomized trial comparing four weeks with three months of warfarin in patients with proximal deep vein thrombosis. Thromb Haemost 74:606-611, 1995.

175. Schulman S, Rhedin AS, Lindmarker P, et al: A comparison of six weeks with six months of oral anticoagulation therapy after a first episode of venous thromboembolism. N Engl J Med 332:1661-1665, 1995.

176. Kearon C, Gent M, Hirsh J, et al: Extended anticoagulation prevented recurrence after a first episode of idiopathic venous thromboembolism. N Engl J Med 340:901-907, 1999.

177. Agnelli G, Prandoni P, Santamaria MG, et al: Three months versus one year of oral anticoagulants therapy for idiopathic deep venous thrombosis. N Engl J Med 345:165-169, 2001.

178. Schafer A: Venous thrombosis is a chronic disease. N Engl J Med 340:955-956, 1999.

179. Ridker PM, Goldhaber SZ, Danielson E, et al: Long-term, low-intensity warfarin therapy for the prevention of recurrent venous thromboembolism. N Engl J Med 348:1425-1434, 2003.

180. Kearon C, Ginsberg JS, Kovacs MJ, et al: Comparison of low-intensity warfarin therapy with conventional-intensity warfarin therapy for long-term prevention of recurrent venous thromboembolism. N Engl J Med 349:631-639, 2003.

181. Schulman S, Granqvist S, Holmstrom M, et al: The duration of oral anticoagulant therapy after a second episode of venous thromboembolism. N Engl J Med 336:393-398, 1997.

182. Value of the ventilation/perfusion scan in acute pulmonary embolism: Results of the Prospective Investigation Of Pulmonary Embolism Diagnosis (PIOPED). The PIOPED Investigators. JAMA 263:2753-2759, 1990.

183. Arcasoy SM, Kreit JW: Thrombolytic therapy of pulmonary embolism. Chest 155:1695-1707, 1999.

184. Goldhaber SZ, Haire WD, Feldstein ML, et al: Alteplase versus heparin in acute pulmonary embolism: Randomized trial assessing right ventricular function and pulmonary perfusion. Lancet 341:507-511, 1993.

185. Konstantinides S, Geibel A, Heusel G, et al: Heparin plus alteplase compared with heparin alone in patients with submassive pulmonary embolism. N Engl J Med 347:1143-1150, 2002.

186. Hamel E, Pacouret G, Vincentelli D, et al: Thrombolysis or heparin therapy in massive pulmonary embolism with right ventricular dilation. Chest 120:120-125, 2001.

187. Agnelli G, Becattini C, Kirschstein T: Thrombolysis or heparin in the treatment of pulmonary embolism. Arch Intern Med 162:2537-2541, 2002.

188. Thabut G, Thabut D, Myers RP, et al: Thrombolytic therapy of pulmonary embolism: A meta-analysis. J Am Coll Cardiol 40:1660-1667, 2002.

189. Dalen JE: The uncertain role of thrombolytic therapy in the treatment of pulmonary embolism. Arch Intern Med 162:2521-2523, 2002.

190. Greenfield LJ: Evolution of venous interruption for pulmonary thromboembolism. Arch Surg 127:622-626, 1992.

191. Baldridge ED, Martin MA, Welling RE: Clinical significance of free floating venous thrombi. J Vasc Surg 11:62-67, 1990.

192. Pacouret G, Alison D, Pottier JM, et al: Free floating thrombus and embolic risk in patients with angiographically confirmed proximal deep venous thrombosis. Arch Intern Med 157:305-308, 1997.

193. Decousus H, Leizorovicz A, Parent F, et al: A clinical trial of vena caval filters in the prevention of pulmonary embolism in patients with proximal deep vein thrombosis. N Engl J Med 338:409-415, 1998.

Chapter

Catheter-Based Interventions for Acute Deep Venous Thrombosis

150

ANTHONY J. COMEROTA, MD, FACS

ZAKARIA I. ASSI, MD

■ BACKGROUND

Acute deep venous thrombosis (DVT) represents a disease spectrum ranging from asymptomatic calf vein thrombosis to the painful, blue, swollen limb of phlegmasia cerulea dolens resulting from extensive multisegment DVT.[1] Although patient presentation and extent of venous thrombosis vary considerably, treatment is usually uniform for all severities of disease, with anticoagulation being the mainstay.[2]

Advances in anticoagulation have included low-molecular-weight heparins,[3] observations that longer duration (indefinite) oral anticoagulation for patients with idiopathic venous thromboembolism is beneficial,[4,5] and the development of pentasaccharides[6] and oral thrombin inhibitors.[7] Investigation of oral thrombin inhibitors for the treatment of DVT continues, but they have not yet been approved for this indication.

Physicians have traditionally divided acute DVT into calf vein thrombosis (infrapopliteal) and proximal DVT (popliteal vein and above). In patients with isolated calf DVT, anticoagulation for 6 to 12 weeks is recommended.[2] If anticoagulation cannot be given, serial venous duplex ultrasonography examinations of the lower extremity should be performed during the ensuing 2 weeks to monitor whether proximal extension of the clot occurs. This recommendation is based on the results of a randomized trial demonstrating a 29% incidence of recurrent venous

thromboembolic complications in patients with isolated calf DVT who were not treated and no venous thromboembolic complications in patients who received anticoagulation for 3 months.[8]

In all patients with proximal DVT, anticoagulation is recommended.[2] Numerous randomized trials have shown that low-molecular-weight heparin is at least as effective as if not superior to unfractionated heparin.[3] When this agent is given subcutaneously on a weight-adjusted basis, blood test monitoring is not necessary. Patients can be treated as outpatients, thereby remaining ambulatory and facing a lower risk of heparin-induced thrombocytopenia. The important issue of proper duration of oral anticoagulation is being clarified. Data have emerged from randomized trials that demonstrate superiority of indefinite oral anticoagulation after a first-time idiopathic venous thromboembolic event.[4,5]

Unfortunately, most physicians treat all cases of proximal DVT the same. Often, there is no differentiation of patients with iliofemoral DVT from those with infrainguinal DVT, and little or no attention is given to treatment options that reduce or eliminate thrombus burden. This approach results in needlessly high post-thrombotic morbidity in patients with iliofemoral DVT. A number of investigators have documented the virulence of the post-thrombotic sequelae in this relevant subset of patients.[9-11] Akesson and colleagues[9] have shown that 95% of patients with iliofemoral DVT treated with anticoagulation alone have ambulatory venous hypertension at 5 years, and 90% suffer symptoms of chronic venous insufficiency. During this relatively short follow-up, 15% of the patients in their study already had venous ulceration, and another 15% had the debilitating symptom of venous claudication.

■ POST-THROMBOTIC CHRONIC VENOUS INSUFFICIENCY

The underlying pathophysiology of the post-thrombotic syndrome is ambulatory venous hypertension.[12] During exercise (walking), the venous pressure in the lower extremity should drop to less than 50% of the standing venous pressure. In patients with the post-thrombotic syndrome, the ambulatory pressure drops very little, and in those with persistent proximal venous occlusion, the ambulatory pressures may rise above the standing pressure, leading to symptoms of venous claudication. The pathologic components of ambulatory venous hypertension are venous obstruction and venous valve incompetence. Shull and associates[13] and Johnson and coworkers[14] have confirmed that after acute DVT, patients with combined obstruction and valvular incompetence suffer the most severe post-thrombotic morbidity.

Technology has advanced to the level at which assessment of venous valvular function is accurate. The timing of valve closure can be measured to small fractions of a second. However, relative venous obstruction is not reliably quantified with standard technology. The use of intravascular ultrasonography appears to be helpful in evaluating the anatomy of proximal venous obstructive lesions.[15] Physiologic testing has not kept pace with similar advances in other areas of the vascular tree. Paradoxically, vascular laboratories have traditionally tested the hemodynamics of venous obstruction with patients in the resting supine position and their legs elevated. This is the standard position to measure maximal venous outflow. However, the pathophysiology of chronic venous disease is defined in the upright, exercising patient. Phlebograms of post-thrombotic recanalized veins frequently document "patency," and noninvasive studies may show normal maximal venous outflow values, giving the mistaken impression that venous obstruction contributes little to post-thrombotic morbidity.

This problem is clearly illustrated by the patient represented in Figure 150-1, who had a post-thrombotic venous ulcer and underwent a classic Linton procedure. Noninvasive testing showed the patient to have valvular incompetence but a normal 3-second maximal venous outflow. An ascending phlebogram was officially interpreted as *"the classic tree barking appearance of chronic venous disease. However, there is no evidence of venous obstruction."* The day after the noninvasive evaluation and ascending phlebogram, the patient underwent surgery. As part of the procedure, the femoral vein was ligated just below its junction with the profunda femoris vein. A cross-section of the divided femoral vein is shown in Figure 150-1, along with the corresponding level of the ascending phlebogram. The vein demonstrates multiple recanalization channels of the previously thrombosed vein. Although patency was

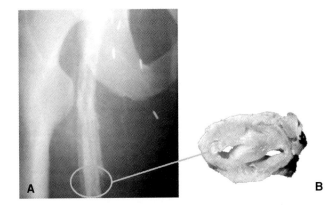

FIGURE 150-1 The ascending phlebogram of a patient with the post-thrombotic syndrome 10 years after acute iliac and femoral deep venous thrombosis shows the classic "tree barking" appearance of chronic venous disease with recanalization of the previously thrombosed vein. The formal radiographic report indicated "no obstruction" of the deep venous system. An impedance plethysmography performed the morning of the phlebography demonstrated a normal 3-second maximal venous outflow. The cross-section of the femoral vein at the point of ligation and division during a classic Linton procedure shows multiple recanalization channels and significant luminal obstruction. Although substantially contributing to ambulatory venous hypertension in the exercising patient; this marked extent of obstruction was not detected by reduced venous outflow with the leg in a resting and elevated position.

restored, there is clear evidence of considerable luminal obstruction. The phlebogram substantially underestimates the degree of venous obstruction. This example illustrates the underappreciation of the contribution of chronic venous obstruction to the pathophysiology of post-thrombotic venous insufficiency. Although the medical profession has developed techniques to measure relative degrees of arterial obstruction with great precision, the same has not yet occurred on the venous side of the circulation.

■ CONCEPT OF THROMBUS REMOVAL

Growing evidence supports the concept that early thrombus resolution after acute DVT is associated with improved outcome. This evidence includes experimental data, findings of natural history studies of acute DVT treated with anticoagulation, venous thrombectomy data, and observations regarding catheter-directed thrombolysis.

Cho and colleagues[15] and Rhodes and associates[16] have used a canine experimental model of acute DVT to compare the results of urokinase infusion, placebo, and mechanical thrombectomy. They demonstrated that thrombolysis with urokinase preserves valve function and endothelium-dependent relaxation both immediately and at 4 weeks. There was less residual thrombus in veins treated with urokinase, thereby maintaining the veins' structural and functional integrity.

A number of excellent observations have been published by the investigators at the University of Washington regarding the natural history of acute DVT treated with anticoagulation.[17-20] They observed that persistent obstruction of proximal veins was associated with distal valve incompetence. The combination of venous obstruction and valve incompetence was associated with the most severe post-thrombotic morbidity. Spontaneous clot lysis restores venous patency. An important observation was that early lysis preserved valve function in the previously thrombosed vein. Interestingly, these investigators defined "early lysis" as lysis occurring up to 90 days from diagnosis.

Early trials of systemic thrombolytic therapy for proximal DVT demonstrated that only 45% of patients had substantial or complete lysis. Those whose clot was successfully lysed had a significant reduction in post-thrombotic morbidity and preservation of venous valve function.[21] Goldhaber and coworkers,[22] who reviewed the results from eight trials of systemic streptokinase treatment for acute DVT, found that moderate or significant thrombolysis was achieved 2.9 times more often among patients treated with thrombolytic therapy than among patients treated with heparin; however, there was a 3.8-fold risk of major bleeding in those receiving thrombolytic therapy.

The Scandinavian investigators randomly assigned patients with iliofemoral DVT to undergo either venous thrombectomy plus femoral arteriovenous fistula and anticoagulation or anticoagulation alone. Follow-up reports at 6 months,[23] 5 years,[24] and 10 years[25] demonstrated clear benefit in patients who underwent venous thrombectomy. Early thrombus removal resulted in better patency of the iliofemoral venous system, lower venous pressures, less edema, and fewer post-thrombotic symptoms.

The aggregate of the above observations support the concept that thrombus removal in patients with acute iliofemoral DVT results in significantly less post-thrombotic morbidity. Despite the favorable results of contemporary venous thrombectomy, few vascular surgeons in the United States are willing to perform the operation, and most physicians are unwilling to accept the higher risk of bleeding complications with lytic therapy. Therefore, thrombolysis for acute DVT is infrequently recommended.

■ CATHETER-DIRECTED (INTRATHROMBUS) THROMBOLYSIS

Catheter-based techniques that deliver the plasminogen activator into the thrombus can accelerate thrombolysis, increasing the likelihood of a successful outcome while decreasing bleeding complications. The basic mechanism of thrombolysis is activation of fibrin-bound plasminogen.[26] When circulating GLU-plasminogen binds to fibrin, it is modified to LYS-plasminogen, which has greater affinity for plasminogen activators. When delivered into the thrombus, plasminogen activators efficiently activate LYS-plasminogen. Intrathrombus delivery protects plasminogen activators from neutralization by circulating plasminogen activator inhibitors and protects plasmin from neutralization by circulating α_2-antiplasmins.

A number of reports have emerged supporting favorable outcomes for catheter-directed thrombolysis. Three of the larger reports demonstrate an 80% to 85% success rate (Table 150-1).[27-29] Initial success rates might have been higher if treatment had been restricted to patients with acute iliofemoral DVT. However, treatment of patients with more distal and chronic venous thrombosis led to a higher failure rate and a lower overall success rate, which are reflected in the data. In these three studies, 422 patients were treated with remarkably consistent rates of success and complications. Catheter-directed urokinase was used in each of these studies. Underlying iliac vein stenoses were treated with balloon angioplasty, stenting, or both to achieve unobstructed drainage into the vena cava and reduce the risk of recurrent thrombosis (Fig. 150-2).

Major bleeding occurred in 5% to 10% of cases, with the majority being puncture site bleeding. Fortunately, intracranial bleeding was rare, occurring in only three patients in the National Venous Registry and resulting in the death of one.[28] Pulmonary embolism occurred in 1% of the patients in the series reported by Bjarnason and associates[27] and in the National Venous Registry,[28] and fatal

Table 150-1	Results of Catheter-Directed Thrombolysis with Urokinase in Three Contemporary Series: Efficacy and Complications*		
	BJARNASON et al[27] (n = 77)	MEWISSEN, et al[28] (n = 287)	COMEROTA et al[29] (n = 58)
Efficacy:			
Initial success (%):	79	83	84
Iliac	63	64	78
Femoral	40	47	—
Primary patency rate at 1 yr (%):			
Iliac	63	64	78
Femoral	40	47	—
Iliac stent: patency rate at 1yr (%):			
With stent	54	74	89
Without stent	75	53	71
Complication rate (%):			
Major bleed	5	11	9
Intracranial bleed	0	< 1	0
Pulmonary embolism	1	1	0
Fatal pulmonary embolism	0	0.2	0
Death secondary to lysis	0	0.4	0

*Superscript numbers indicate chapter references.

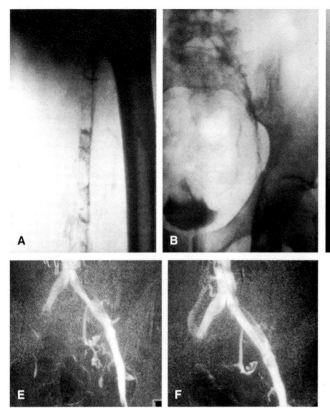

FIGURE 150-2 A, Initial phlebogram of patient with extensive iliofemoral deep vein thrombosis presenting with a swollen, painful left leg. **B,** Intrathrombus catheter positioned via ultrasonography-guided popliteal vein access. Urokinase was infused at 160,000 IU/hr diluted in 80 mL of saline (2,000 IU/mL). **C,** The patient had a good clinical and phlebographic result after catheter-directed urokinase infusion. **D,** After 36 hours, the thrombus was resolved, uncovering a stenosis of the left common iliac vein. **E** and **F,** After balloon angioplasty and stenting with a 14-mm Wallstent, the patient has unobstructed venous drainage into the vena cava. She remained asymptomatic and had normal valve function 1 year after treatment.

pulmonary embolism occurred in only 1 patient out of the 422. Therefore, death as a result of catheter-directed thrombolysis was rare.

Until 1999, the majority of the experience with catheter-directed thrombolysis for acute DVT was with urokinase. In 1999, urokinase was removed from the market owing to concerns about the source of neonatal kidneys as well as whether the manufacturing procedures adequately protected against transmission of viral disease. Subsequently, clinicians have used catheter-directed alteplase[30-32] and reteplase[33] with similarly good results.

Verhaeghe and coworkers[30] treated 24 patients with acute iliofemoral DVT with intrathrombus alteplase at a dose of 3 mg/hr. The mean treatment dose was 86 mg (range 45 to 174 mg). The volume of infusate per hour in which the alteplase was delivered was not reported. The investigators recorded a 75% success rate. The most common complication was puncture site bleeding requiring blood transfusion in 25%. Shortell and associates[31] treated 31 patients with either urokinase (n = 23) or recombinant tissue-type plasminogen activator (rt-PA) (n = 8). Success rates were equivalent (77% for rt-PA and 81% for urokinase), with shorter time to lysis in the rt-PA–treated patients. Bleeding rates were equivalent in the two groups, and no pulmonary emboli were observed.

Chang and colleagues[32] reported an intriguing use of rt-PA in 10 patients (12 legs) with acute DVT. rt-PA was administered by intrathrombus bolus, pulse-spray infusion using no more than 50 mg per treatment. This was repeated for up to four daily sessions. Results in this preliminary report were excellent; 11 patients (90% of legs) had significant or complete lysis, and the remaining patient had 50% to 75% lysis. Although the average total dose of rt-PA was 106 mg, bleeding complications were minor, and no patient had a decrease in hematocrit value greater than 2%. This technique is deserving of further study to evaluate whether other investigators can obtain similarly good results.

Castaneda and associates[33] evaluated the efficacy and safety of reteplase in 13 patients with iliofemoral DVT and 2 patients with femoral-popliteal DVT. Intrathrombus reteplase was infused at a dose of 1 mg/hr in the first 5 patients and 0.5 mg/hr subsequently. A subtherapeutic heparin dose, at 300 to 500 U/hr, was also infused. The total dose of reteplase ranged from 2.5 U to 42 U with the median dose of 16.5 U. All patients had successful lysis. The median infusion time was 29 hours. No major bleeding complications were observed, and no patient required blood transfusion.

It is revealing to take a closer look at the efficacy results reported in the National Venous Registry,[28] because they represent a cross-sectional experience from centers in the United States. Of the 287 patients treated in the 63 academic and community centers, 66% had acute DVT, 16% had chronic DVT, and 19% had an acute episode superimposed on a chronic condition. Seventy-one percent of the patients presented with iliofemoral DVT, and 25% with femoral-popliteal DVT. Catheter-directed thrombolysis with intrathrombus infusion of urokinase was the preferred approach. Phlebographic evaluation showed that 31% of patients had complete lytic success and 52% had 50% to 99% lytic success; in 17% of patients, less than 50% of the thrombus was dissolved. Interestingly, in the subgroup of patients with acute, first-time iliofemoral DVT, 65% of the patients enjoyed complete clot lysis.

Overall, thrombosis-free survival was observed in 65% of patients at 6 months and in 60% at 12 months. There was a significant correlation ($P < .001$) of thrombosis-free survival with the results of initial therapy. Seventy-eight percent of the patients with complete clot resolution had patent veins at 1 year compared with 37% of those in whom less than 50% of the clot was dissolved. Interestingly, in the subgroup of patients with acute, first-time iliofemoral DVT who had successful thrombolysis, 96% of the veins remained patent at 1 year. In addition to sustained patency, early success directly correlated with valve function at 6 months. Sixty-two percent of patients with less than 50% thrombolysis had venous valvular incompetence, whereas 72% of patients who had complete lysis had normal valve function ($P < .02$).

These objectively documented treatment outcomes provided an opportunity to evaluate whether catheter-directed thrombolysis improved the quality-of-life over the long term compared with anticoagulation alone. After constructing and validating a quality-of-life questionnaire,[34] Comerota and colleagues[35] compared results in 68 patients treated with catheter-directed urokinase for iliofemoral DVT and 30 patients treated with anticoagulation alone because of physician preference. All patients were candidates for thrombolytic therapy. Patients were queried at 16 and 22 months after treatment. Those treated with catheter-directed urokinase enjoyed a significantly better quality of life than those treated with anticoagulation alone. Not surprisingly, the quality-of-life results were directly related to the initial success of thrombolysis. Patients who had a successful lytic outcome ($\geq 50\%$ lysis) reported a significantly better Health Utilities Index, better physical functioning, less stigma of chronic venous disease, less health distress, and fewer overall post-thrombotic symptoms (Table 150-2). Patients in whom catheter-directed thrombolysis failed and patients treated with anticoagulation alone had similar outcomes. These data offer a compelling argument for a prospective randomized trial of catheter-directed thrombolysis compared with anticoagulation alone in patients with acute iliofemoral DVT.

Indeed, a prospective randomized trial comparing catheter-directed intrathrombus urokinase and anticoagulation versus anticoagulation alone was initiated. The TOLEDO trial (Thrombolysis Of Lower Extremity Deep vein thrombosis Or anticoagulation) was approved by the FDA. The hypotheses of the study are as follows:

1. Catheter-directed intrathrombus infusion of urokinase plus anticoagulation will be associated with significantly better early clot lysis than anticoagulation alone.
2. Early clot lysis will be associated with a significantly improved quality of life at 1 year.

This phase 4, multicenter, open-label trial was planned to randomly assign 150 patients in a 2:1 ratio, with 2 patients receiving catheter-directed intrathrombus urokinase for every 1 receiving standard anticoagulation. Primary endpoints were patency of the iliofemoral venous system at 5 days and quality of life at 1 year. Multiple secondary endpoints were to be recorded, among them patency of the iliofemoral venous segment at 30 days, venous valve function at 6 months and 1 year, quality of life at 3 months and 24 months, and venous disease severity score at 12 months. Safety parameters including bleeding complications, pulmonary embolism, and death were monitored.

We believed that the results of this trial would support the strategy of catheter-directed thrombolysis for acute iliofemoral DVT in patients who have no contraindication to thrombolytic therapy. If a contraindication to lytic therapy exists, a contemporary venous thrombectomy followed by long-term anticoagulation should be considered (Fig. 150-3). Ambulatory patients who suffer iliofemoral DVT and whose thrombus is removed, thereby allowing unobstructed venous drainage from the leg into the vena cava, have a significantly better outcome than patients treated with anticoagulation alone. Unfortunately, the manufacture of urokinase has been terminated, thereby placing the TOLEDO trial on hold, pending the design and funding of a trial using an alternative plasminogen activator.

■ TECHNIQUE OF CATHETER-DIRECTED THROMBOLYSIS

The technique of catheter-directed thrombolysis for iliofemoral DVT has evolved during the past several years.

Table 150-2	Quality-of-Life Outcome at 16 Months After Treatment of Iliofemoral Deep Venous Thrombosis: Successful Lysis vs. Anticoagulation		
	SUCCESSFUL LYSIS (n = 43)	**ANTICOAGULATION (n = 30)**	**P VALUE**
Health Utilities Index	0.83	0.74	.032
Role functioning physical	75.68	58.59	.013
Treatment satisfaction	86.59	81.72	.490
Stigma	85.98	71.32	.033
Health distress	82.48	64.11	.007
Overall symptoms	78.55	55.56	<.001

From Comerota AJ, Thromb RC, Mathias S, et al: Catheter-directed thrombolysis for iliofemoral deep venous thrombosis improves health-related quality of life. J Vasc Surg 32:130-137, 2000.

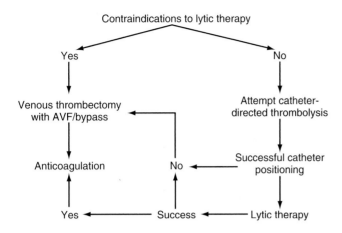

FIGURE 150-3   Algorithm for the contemporary treatment of iliofemoral deep venous thrombosis.

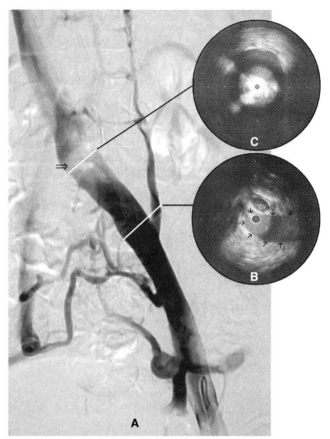

FIGURE 150-4   The potential value of intravascular ultrasonography is illustrated in this patient whose phlebogram (**A**) shows obstruction (compression) of the left common iliac vein by the right common iliac artery (*open arrow*). **B,** Intravascular ultrasonogram proximal to the area of compression shows the vein lumen (v) and collateral vein (cv). At the point of maximal compression (**C**) the vein lumen is obliterated.

The preferred approach is through an ultrasonography-guided popliteal vein puncture with antegrade passage of a long infusion catheter. The physician can incorporate adjunctive mechanical thrombectomy techniques through this approach if desired.

If the popliteal vein is thrombosed, an additional catheter is placed through an ultrasonography-guided posterior tibial vein puncture. This technique maximizes the chance of restoring patency to the popliteal vein. Long-segment infusion catheters can be used such that 40 to 80 cm of thrombus can be continuously treated during the infusion.

During the past several years, a conceptual evolution has occurred in catheter-directed thrombolysis. Infusion volumes of the lytic infusate have increased. It is our preference to increase the volume of lytic infusion to 80 to 100 mL per hour. The larger volume is intended to saturate the thrombus, exposing more fibrin-bound plasminogen to the plasminogen activator. Because activation of fibrin-bound plasminogen is not dose dependent, the trend has been to reduce the dose of plasminogen activator while increasing the volume of infusate. Phlebograms obtained at 12-hour intervals are used to monitor the success of lysis. Vena caval filters are not routinely used but are recommended for the patient with free-floating thrombus in the vena cava. A retrievable filter can be used in the patient in whom temporary protection is recommended.

After successful thrombolysis, the venous system is evaluated for areas of stenosis. The stenosis is commonly observed in the left common iliac vein, where it is compressed by the right common iliac artery. The addition of intravascular ultrasonography has improved the evaluation of iliac vein compression and the precision of stent deployment for correction of these lesions (Fig. 150-4).[36] Residual areas of stenosis must be corrected; otherwise the patient faces a high risk of recurrent thrombosis. Balloon angioplasty and stenting improve venous return and reduce the risk of rethrombosis. Single stents in the common iliac vein have been associated with excellent patency. It is our recommendation that these stents be almost as large as the normally anticipated diameter of the common iliac vein.

PERCUTANEOUS MECHANICAL THROMBECTOMY

Although thrombolysis and venous thrombectomy have demonstrated better outcomes than standard anticoagulation, each has potential complications and cannot be applied to all patients. The concept of using a percutaneous mechanical thrombectomy device to remove venous clot is appealing. The clot burden in patients with iliofemoral DVT is usually significant. A percutaneous mechanical thrombectomy device might significantly shorten the duration of lytic therapy by reducing the clot burden, or ideally, remove all thrombus and fully restore patency. This should reduce the risks of major bleeding complications, shorten hospital stay, and reduce or eliminate the need to monitor patients in an intensive care unit.

The three main disadvantages of percutaneous mechanical thrombectomy are (1) the risk of damaging venous endothelium and vein valves, (2) fragmentation of thrombus with pulmonary embolism, and (3) increased procedure time (compared with catheter-directed thrombolysis).

Although a number of percutaneous thrombectomy devices have been approved for the management of a clotted hemodialysis access, none has been approved for acute DVT. Several devices have been used "off-label" for this

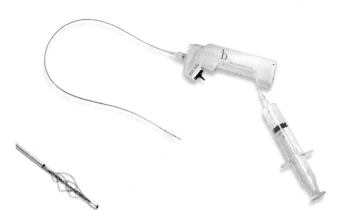

FIGURE 150-5 The Fino catheter (Bacchus Vascular, Santa Clara, CA).

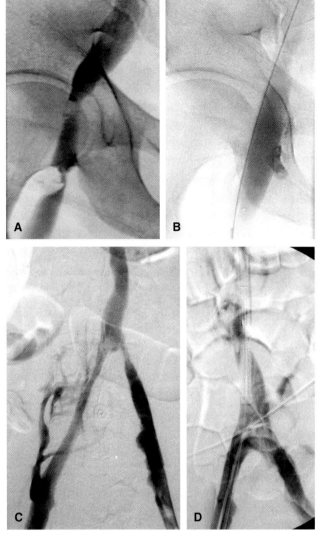

FIGURE 150-6 **A,** Phlebogram of femoral vein following catheter-directed infusion of recombinant tissue-type plasminogen activator (rt-PA) (110 mg) and rheolytic thrombectomy with the AngioJet catheter. A chronic thrombus remains attached to the femoral vein wall, causing stenosis. **B,** Phlebogram after thrombectomy with the Fino catheter. **C,** Iliocavogram of the same patient showing chronic thrombus at the level of the caval bifurcation and proximal left common iliac vein after catheter-directed use of rt-PA (110 mg) and rheolytic thrombectomy. **D,** Phlebogram of the vena caval bifurcation after extraction of the chronic thrombus with the Fino catheter.

indication, either alone or combined with plasminogen activators, and new devices are being designed specifically for percutaneous venous thrombectomy. Included in this review are only those devices with potential application for venous thrombectomy.

The Solera catheter (Bacchus Vascular, Santa Clara, CA) is a new 7F over-the-wire device that uses a 10-mm fixed outer basket containing an inner rotating spiral wire. The wire cleaves the thrombus trapped within the basket and delivers it proximally, where a manually activated suction removes the clot. This device is approved for synthetic hemodialysis grafts but has been used in patients with acute venous thrombosis.

A similar device from the same manufacturer (the Fino catheter; see Fig. 150-5) is currently under trial in patients with acute DVT. Preliminary results in 29 patients with iliofemoral DVT have demonstrated a 65% efficacy. The Fino catheter is believed to be less traumatic to the endothelium and the venous valves because of its protective basket. It retrieves fragmented thrombus through a central channel, which aspirates fragments as well as transporting them via an Archimedes' screw technology. Although the experience with this catheter is limited, it has demonstrated ability to remove acute thrombus as well as subacute and chronic thrombus remaining after an extended period of catheter-directed thrombolysis and failed rheolytic thrombectomy (Fig. 150-5). The application of this device in patients with acute DVT will be delayed, as clinical trials have been postponed.

A third device, the Trellis catheter (Bacchus Vascular, Santa Clara, CA), is a hybrid that isolates the thrombosed vein segment between two occluding balloons. A lytic agent is infused into the thrombus between the occluding balloons. The intervening catheter shaft assumes a sine-wave configuration and spins at 15,000 rpm. After 10 to 15 minutes, the liquefied thrombus and remaining fragments are aspirated. Subsequent venous segments are treated if necessary. The advantage of such a device is its ability to incorporate mechanical and pharmacologic therapies, even in patients with a contraindication to thrombolytic therapy, because the infusate is aspirated. An additional advantage is the potential for reduced risk of pulmonary embolism.

The Helix Clot Buster (Microvena, White Bear Lake, MN), which was formally known as the Amplatz Thrombec-

tomy Device, is a rotational recirculation device designed to fragment thrombus and pulverize the resulting particles through the action of a hydrodynamic vortex at the catheter tip. This vortex pulls thrombus into the tip, where it is macerated. The impeller rotates up to 150,000 rpm, thereby generating a strong recirculation vortex. This device uses negative aspirating pressure around the catheter tip and high-pressure jets along the shaft. It has been approved by the U.S. Food and Drug Administration (FDA) for use in clotted hemodialysis grafts. Several investigators have reported using the Helix Clot Buster to successfully treat patients with iliocaval thrombosis, but there have also been reports of transient oxygen desaturation and pulmonary embolism.[37,38]

The AngioJet Rheolytic Thrombectomy System (Posis Medical, Minneapolis, MN) is a hydraulic recirculation device generating high-pressure jets that are responsible for the hydrodynamic vortex created to macerate or liquefy thrombus, allowing its aspiration (Fig. 150-6). The catheter has a large lumen for evacuation of debris and for passage of a guidewire. A second, smaller lumen is through a stainless steel tube that projects beyond the tip of the catheter in the shape of a transverse loop for delivery of a pulsatile perfusion solution from a drive pump. This generally produces a fluid stream of 8000 to 10,000 psi. The space between the distal loop and the end-hole of the aspiration lumen is an area of low pressure created by the Venturi effect of the high-velocity jets. This hydrodynamic recirculation at the catheter tip entrains adjacent thrombus, macerating and liquefying it and thereby allowing its evacuation from the vessel through the catheter's effluent lumen.

The Oasis Thrombectomy System (Boston Scientific, Quincy, MA) and the Hydrolyser Percutaneous Thrombectomy Catheter (Cordis, Miami, FL) are devices similar in design to the AngioJet with modest modifications.

Although a large experience has not been reported with any specific device, the AngioJet appears to be the most commonly used percutaneous mechanical thrombectomy device for acute DVT. Kasirajan and associates[39] treated 14 patients with acute iliofemoral DVT using the AngioJet catheter. In 14% of the patients, more than 90% thrombus was removed with percutaneous mechanical thrombectomy alone; in 43% of patients, 50% to 90% thrombus extraction was achieved; and in the remaining 43%, more than 50% of thrombus remained. Nine patients with less than 90% thrombus removal underwent catheter-directed thrombolysis after percutaneous mechanical thrombectomy; in 7 of these 9 patients, thrombolysis achieved significant improvement, in that more than 90% of the thrombus was removed at completion of therapy. The thrombolytic agents used were urokinase, rt-PA (alteplase), and reteplase (Retavase). Average lysis time was 20 hours, and no significant bleeding complications were observed.

Hemolysis occurs with the high-pressure hydraulic recirculation devices, resulting in discoloration of the patients' urine due to renal excretion of the hemoglobin pigment. Generally, this excretion is of little clinical consequence unless the patient has underlying renal insufficiency, in which case there may be an added nephrotoxic effect. Generally, a limit on the volume of infusate is recommended by the manufacturer, approximately 600 mL.

A potentially serious complication associated with mechanical or pharmacomechanical thrombectomy (thrombolysis) is pulmonary embolism. Kinney and associates[40] performed a prospective evaluation of pulse-spray pharmacomechanical thrombolysis of clotted hemodialysis grafts. They evaluated the incidence of pulmonary embolism in patients treated with urokinase pulse spray versus heparinized saline. Because hemodialysis grafts are in direct communication with the venous circulation and they are somewhat smaller than proximal veins with acute DVT, the observations made in this study can be expected to be magnified when similar treatment is applied to patients with acute DVT. New pulmonary embolism (documented by ventilation-perfusion lung scans) occurred in 18% of patients treated with a urokinase pulse-spray solution and in 64% of patients treated with a heparinized saline pulse-spray solution ($P = .04$). Although all cases of pulmonary embolism were asymptomatic, quantitative global pulmonary perfusion analyses showed that treatment with urokinase improved flow to the pulmonary segments, whereas treatment with the saline solution reduced perfusion.

Greenberg and colleagues[41] developed a vascular thrombosis model to compare mechanical, pharmacomechanical, and pharmacologic thrombolysis procedures. Their findings are consistent with anecdotal clinical observations as well as those reported by Kinney and associates[40] in their randomized study. Greenberg and colleagues[41] demonstrated that pulse-spray mechanical thrombectomy was associated with the largest number and greatest size of distal emboli. Using urokinase in the solution diminished the number and size of distal emboli and increased the speed of reperfusion. Catheter-directed lysis alone was associated with the slowest reperfusion but the fewest distal emboli.

Vendantham and coworkers[42] reported their experience with lower extremity venous thrombolysis and adjunctive mechanical thrombectomy. They used a variety of devices coupled with catheter-directed urokinase, rt-PA, and reteplase. They reported an overall procedural success of 82%, with 14% of the patients experiencing a major bleeding complication. Mechanical thrombectomy alone was associated with minimal thrombus removal when it was used initially, whereas it was associated with substantial thrombus removal when used after catheter-directed thrombolysis ($P = .006$). These investigators documented significant shortening of lytic infusions when combined pharmacomechanical thrombolysis was used.

■ SUMMARY

The overwhelming body of evidence indicates that patients with extensive, acute DVT do better with thrombus removal compared with anticoagulation alone. Effective anticoagulation is necessary to avoid recurrent venous thrombosis. Level I evidence from a randomized clinical trial should establish the proper role of catheter-directed thrombolysis in the management of patients with extensive DVT.

If percutaneous mechanical techniques can achieve similar immediate results without increasing the risk of rethrombosis or pulmonary embolism, the duration of treatment and in-hospital care as well as the overall cost will be reduced.

A natural question that follows is whether patients with infrainguinal venous thrombosis should be offered catheter-directed thrombolysis or percutaneous mechanical thrombectomy in addition to anticoagulation. Because the clot is limited to the infrainguinal venous segments in the majority of patients with proximal DVT, this is an area appropriate for prospective investigation.

■ REFERENCES

1. Comerota AJ: Venous thromboembolism. In Rutherford RB (ed): Vascular Surgery, 4th ed. Philadelphia, WB Saunders, 1995, pp 1785 1814.

2. Hyers TM, Agnelli G, Hull RD, et al: Antithrombotic therapy for venous thromboembolic disease. Sixth ACCP Consensus Conference on Antithrombotic Therapy. Chest 119(Suppl):176S-193S, 2001.

3. Lensing AWA, Prins MH, Davidson BL, et al: Treatment of deep venous thrombosis with low molecular weight heparins: A meta-analysis. Arch Intern Med 155:601-607, 1995.

4. Ridker PM, Goldhaber SZ, Danielson E, et al: Long-term, low-intensity warfarin therapy for the prevention of recurrent venous thromboembolism. N Engl J Med 348:1425-1434, 2003.

5. Kearon C, Ginsberg JS, Kovacs MJ, et al: Comparison of low-intensity warfarin therapy with conventional-intensity warfarin therapy for long-term prevention of recurrent venous thromboembolism. N Engl J Med 349:631-639, 2003.

6. Turpie AG, Bauer KA, Eriksson BI, Lassen MR: Fondaparinux vs enoxaparin for the prevention of venous thromboembolism in major orthopedic surgery: A meta-analysis of 4 randomized double-blind studies. Arch Intern Med 162:1833-1840, 2002.

7. Heit JA, Colwell CWJ, Francis CW, et al: Comparison of the oral direct thrombin inhibitor with enoxaparin as prophylaxis against venous thromboembolism after total knee replacement: A phase 2 dose-finding study. Arch Intern Med 161:2215-2222, 2001.

8. Lagerstedt CI, Olsson CG, Fagher BO, et al: Need for long term anticoagulant treatment in symptomatic calf-vein thrombosis. Lancet 2:515-518, 1985.

9. Akesson H, Brudin L, Dahlstron JA, et al: Venous function assessed during a 5-year period after acute ilio-femoral venous thrombosis treated with anticoagulation. Eur J Vasc Surg 4:43-48, 1990.

10. O'Donnell TF, Browse NL, Burnand KG, et al: The socioeconomic effects of an iliofemoral venous thrombosis. J Surg Res 22:483-488, 1977.

11. Hill SL, Martin D, Evans P: Massive vein thrombosis of the extremities. Am J Surg 158:131-135, 1989.

12. Nicolaides AN, Schull K, Fernandes E, et al: Ambulatory venous pressures: New information. In Nicolaides AN, Yao JST (eds): Investigation of Vascular Disorders. New York, Churchill Livingstone, 1981, pp 488-494.

13. Shull KC, Nicolaides AN, Fernandes E, et al: Significance of popliteal reflux in relation to ambulatory venous pressure and ulceration. Arch Surg 114:1304-1306, 1979.

14. Johnson BF, Manzo RA, Bergelin RO, et al: Relationship between changes in the deep venous system and the development of the postthrombotic syndrome after an acute episode of lower limb deep vein thrombosis: A one-to-six year follow-up. J Vasc Surg 21:307-313, 1995.

15. Cho JS, Martelli E, Mozes G, et al: Acute effects of thrombolysis and thrombectomy on valvular competence, thrombogenicity, morphology and function of canine veins. J Vasc Surg 28:787-799, 1998.

16. Rhodes JM, Cho JS, Gloviczki P, et al: Thrombolysis for experimental deep venous thrombosis maintains valvular competence and vasoreactivity. J Vasc Surg 31:1193-1205, 2000.

17. Killewich LA, Bedford GE, Beach KW, et al: Spontaneous lysis of deep venous thrombi: Rate and outcome. J Vasc Surg 9:89-97, 1989.

18. Markel A, Manzo R, Bergelin R, et al: Valvular reflux after deep vein thrombosis: Incidence and time of occurrence. J Vasc Surg 15:377-384, 1992.

19. Meissner MH, Manzo RA, Bergelin RO, et al: Deep venous insufficiency: The relationship between lysis and subsequent reflux. J Vasc Surg 18:596-605, 1993.

20. Caps MT, Manzo RA, Bergelin RO, et al: Venous valvular reflux in veins not involved at the time of acute deep vein thrombosis. J Vasc Surg 22:524-531, 1995.

21. Comerota AJ, Aldridge SA: Thrombolytic therapy for acute deep vein thrombosis. Semin Vasc Surg 5:76-84, 1992.

22. Goldhaber SZ, Buring JE, Lipnick RJ, et al: Pooled analysis of randomized trials of streptokinase and heparin in phlebographically documented acute DVT. Am J Med 76:393-397, 1984.

23. Plate G, Einarsson E, Ohlin P, et al: Thrombectomy with temporary arteriovenous fistula: The treatment of choice in acute iliofemoral venous thrombosis. J Vasc Surg 1:867-876, 1984.

24. Plate G, Akesson H, Einarsson E, et al: Long-term results of venous thrombectomy combined with a temporary arterio-venous fistula. Eur J Vasc Surg 4:483-489, 1990.

25. Plate G, Eklof B, Norgren L, et al: Venous thrombectomy for iliofemoral vein thrombosis: 10-year results of a prospective randomized study. Eur J Vasc Endovasc Surg 14:367-374, 1997.

26. Alkjaersig N, Fletcher AP, Sherry S: The mechanism of clot dissolution by plasmin. J Clin Invest 38:1086, 1959.

27. Bjarnason H, Kruse JR, Asinger DA, et al: Iliofemoral deep venous thrombosis: Safety and efficacy outcome during 5 years of catheter-directed thrombolytic therapy. J Vasc Interv Radiol 8:405-418, 1997.

28. Mewissen MW, Seabrook GR, Meissner MH, et al: Catheter-directed thrombolysis for lower extremity deep venous thrombosis: Report of a national multicenter registry. Radiology 211:39-49, 1999.

29. Comerota AJ, Kagan SA: Catheter-directed thrombolysis for the treatment of acute iliofemoral deep venous thrombosis. Phlebology 15:149-155, 2001.

30. Verhaeghe R, Stockx L, Lacroix H, et al: Catheter-directed lysis of iliofemoral vein thrombosis. Eur Radiol 7:996-1001, 1977.

31. Shortell CK, Queiroz R, Johansson M, et al: Safety and efficacy of limited-dose tissue plasminogen activator in acute vascular occlusion. J Vasc Surg 34:854-859, 2001.

32. Chang R, Cannon RO, Chen CC, et al: Daily catheter-directed single dosing of t-PA in treatment of acute deep venous thrombosis of the lower extremity. J Vasc Interv Radiol 12:247-252, 2001.

33. Castaneda F, Li R, Young K, et al: Catheter-directed thrombolysis in deep venous thrombosis with use of Reteplase: Immediate results and complications from a pilot study. J Vasc Interv Radiol 13:577-580, 2002.

34. Mathias SD, Prebil LA, Patterman CG, et al: A health related quality-of-life measure in patients with deep vein thrombosis: A validation study. Drug Info J 33:1173-1187, 1999.

35. Comerota AJ, Thromb RC, Mathias S, et al: Catheter-directed thrombolysis for iliofemoral deep venous thrombosis improves health-related quality of life. J Vasc Surg 32:130-137, 2000.

36. Forauer AR, Gemmete GG, Dasika NL, et al: Intravascular ultrasound in the diagnosis and treatment of iliac vein compression (May-Thurner) syndrome. J Vasc Interv Radiol 13:523-527, 2002.

37. Delomez M, Bereji J, Willoteau S, et al: Mechanical thrombectomy in patients with deep venous thrombosis. Cardiovasc Interv Radiol 24:42-48, 2001.

38. Ulfacker R: Mechanical thrombectomy in acute and subacute thrombosis with the use of Amplatz device: Arterial and venous applications. J Vasc Interv Radiol 8:923-932, 1997.

39. Kasirajan K, Gray B, Ouriel K: Percutaneous AngioJet thrombectomy in the management of extensive deep venous thrombosis. J Vasc Interv Radiol 12:179-185, 2001.

40. Kinney TB, Valji K, Rose SC, et al: Pulmonary embolism from pulse-spray pharmacomechanical thrombolysis of clotted hemodialysis grafts: Urokinase versus heparinized saline. J Vasc Interv Radiol 11:1143-1152, 2000.

41. Greenberg RK, Ouriel K, Srivastava S, et al: Mechanical versus chemical thrombolysis: An in vitro differentiation of thrombolytic mechanisms. J Vasc Interv Radiol 11:199-205, 2000.

42. Vendantham S, Vesely TM, Parti N, et al: Lower extremity venous thrombolysis with adjunctive mechanical thrombectomy. J Vasc Interv Radiol 13:1001-1008, 2002.

Surgical Thrombectomy for Acute Deep Venous Thrombosis

151

BO EKLOF, MD, PhD

ROBERT B. RUTHERFORD, MD, FACS, FRCS (GLASG)

The options for early removal of an acute thrombus in the iliofemoral veins are as follows:

- Catheter-directed thrombolysis (CDT)
- A combination of percutaneous mechanical "thrombectomy" (PMT), using one of a number of mechanical devices, with or without thrombolysis (PMT ± CDT)
- Open surgical thrombectomy

Chapter 150 addresses the first two options. In this chapter, the technique and results of thrombectomy are presented. We propose that if catheter-based interventions fail or are contraindicated, surgical thrombectomy is a valid alternative, primarily in patients with acute iliofemoral vein thrombosis (IFVT).

■ RATIONALE FOR EARLY THROMBUS REMOVAL

When deep venous thrombosis (DVT) occurs, the goals of therapy are (1) to prevent the extension or recurrence of DVT, (2) to prevent pulmonary embolism (PE), and (3) to minimize the early and late sequelae of DVT. Antithrombotic therapy can accomplish the first two goals (see Chapter 149), but it contributes little or nothing to the third. In patients with massive iliofemoral DVT, progressive swelling of the leg can lead to a condition known as phlegmasia cerulea dolens (literally, painful blue swelling) and to increased compartment pressure, which can progress to venous gangrene and, occasionally, to limb loss. Later, the development of severe post-thrombotic syndrome (PTS) can result from persistent obstruction of the venous outflow, loss of valvular competence, or both, and pulmonary embolism can lead to chronic pulmonary hypertension.

Most clinicians seem to focus on the initial results of the treatment, that is, preventing PE, the propagation of the thrombus, or DVT recurrence. Randomized clinical trials published in the literature brought evidence that antithrombotic therapy, particularly low-molecular-weight heparin (LMWH), can achieve these goals. This issue is amply reviewed in Chapter 149, and it is not our intention to refute it. However, there is a lack of appreciation that the endpoint in these randomized clinical trials has not been prevention of post-thrombotic sequelae. Furthermore, there is apparently also a lack of appreciation of how different the natural history of IFVT is from that of more distal DVT as well as a lack of understanding of the different pathophysiologic changes that occur with time after DVT, and of their relative contribution to the pathogenesis and severity of the PTS. These aspects are reviewed in detail in this chapter, to provide a selective basis for the decision to opt for early thrombus removal.

Pathophysiologic Changes Associated with Deep Venous Thrombosis

For details on the pathophysiology and natural history of acute DVT, the readers are referred to Chapter 147. For the reader to understand the rationale for early thrombectomy, however, we must review some of the changes associated with DVT. On the basis of the presence or absence of residual venous disease after DVT, patients can be assigned into four groups: those with normal veins and complete recovery (neither residual obstruction nor valvular incompetence), those with residual obstruction, those with valvular incompetence, and those with both outflow obstruction and valvular incompetence. Noninvasive testing has shown that less than 20% of those with documented DVT recover completely and have neither significant obstruction nor reflux.[1] In a 5-year follow-up of 20 patients treated with anticoagulation alone in a Swedish prospective, randomized study of patients with acute IFVT, there was residual iliac vein obstruction in 70% of patients, and valvular incompetence and muscle pump dysfunction developed in *all* patients, creating severe venous hypertension and PTS.[2] However, the overall outcome of DVT, in terms of disturbed venous physiology, depends to a great extent on the location of the thrombosed segments and the extent of involvement—that is, of single or multiple segments.

The location relates to the likelihood of recanalization of the thrombosed segment, which decreases as one moves proximally in the lower extremity. Venographic studies, which were commonly performed only in the 1950s and 1960s, showed that close to 95% of popliteal or tibial thromboses completely recanalize[3] and that at least 50% of femoral venous thromboses recanalize.[4] In contrast, the minority of iliofemoral thromboses (less than 20%) completely recanalize and result in a normal, unobstructed lumen.[5] However, although only 20% of the iliac vein segments involved in IFVT completely recanalize, another

60% *partly* recanalize or at least develop adequate collateral vessels so that they do not test positive for obstruction on noninvasive study. Thus, in reality, only about 20% have occlusion significant enough to produce symptoms detectable on noninvasive physiologic testing, if time (3-6 months) is allowed for complete resolution. Nevertheless, a significant degree of obstruction persists for these 3 to 6 months in the *majority* of patients with iliofemoral venous thrombosis.

What is not well appreciated is that proximal obstruction, even if it is ultimately relieved by partial recanalization or collateral development, can lead to progressive breakdown of distal valves, resulting in reflux. This issue is important, because if the distal venous valves (and particularly those in the popliteal vein) remain competent, the post-thrombotic sequelae are relatively modest and controllable by conservative measures.[6] The severity of post-thrombotic sequelae correlates with the level of ambulatory venous pressure (AVP), as shown by Nicolaides and associates.[7] It is impressive how steadily the frequency of ulceration climbs with rising levels of AVP. This observation suggests that anything that significantly lowers AVP will reduce the severity of the post-thrombotic sequelae, and vice versa. Nicolaides and Sumner[8] have also shown that the highest levels of AVP are found in patients with *both* obstruction and reflux. These two observations underscore a major point to be made in regard to the disturbed pathophysiology associated with iliofemoral venous thrombosis and the pathogenesis of post-thrombotic sequelae. Obstruction alone rarely causes venous claudication, usually resulting in increased swelling with activity. Valvular incompetence alone causes most of the "stasis sequelae" (pigmentation, lipodermatosclerosis and ulceration), but these too can be managed, in the compliant patient, with elastic stockings and elevation. However, patients with both obstruction and valvular incompetence have severe post-thrombotic sequelae, so severe that conservative management is difficult even in compliant patients.

The importance of the proximal obstruction for the development of distal valvular incompetence has been carefully studied by Strandness and his group (Chapter 147). In a series of articles, they have shown the following:

- From 20% to 50% of initially uninvolved distal veins became incompetent by 2 years
- The combination of reflux and obstruction, as opposed to either alone, correlated with the severity of symptoms, which were present in 55% of symptomatic patients
- 25% of all venous segments developed reflux in time; 32% of these segments were documented to not have been previously involved with thrombosis
- In a study of the posterior tibial veins located below a popliteal segment involved with thrombosis, 55% of the distal veins became incompetent if the segment remained obstructed, compared with 7.5% of those below a popliteal vein that recanalized

These changes in the distal veins occur early enough that they cannot be blamed on proximal valvular reflux, although it also comes into play with time. Thus, it would appear that the early relief of obstructing thrombus by thrombolysis or thrombectomy should prevent more extensive post-thrombotic sequelae if only by protecting the distal veins

against progressive valvular incompetence. This point has not been well recognized, not only in terms of basic pathogenesis but also in judging the results of thrombolysis and thrombectomy; critics of these procedures have largely ignored the restoration of proximal patency while focusing on the presence or absence of valve reflux.

New data published on the inflammatory response to DVT underscore the importance of early thrombus removal. Downing and colleagues[9] in Ann Arbor have shown that the leukocyte adhesion molecule P-selectin activates the leukocytes emigrating into the venous wall, creating an inflammation that destroys the venous wall and the valves. See-Tho and Harris[10] from Stanford showed, in another experimental model, that if the thrombus is removed early, the inflammatory changes are reversible.

Finally, although modern venous reconstructive valvuloplasty can achieve good long-term results in *primary* venous disease with severe reflux, the results of vein segment transfer and autologous vein transplantation in *secondary* (i.e., post-thrombotic) venous disease are much less promising.[11] Therefore, there are less suitable late interventions for the venous derangements typically seen in patients with severe PTS. The common mistake is for clinicians to treat all patients with DVT with anticoagulation alone, and belatedly refer those who complain of severe pain and swelling during follow-up for consideration of thrombolysis or thrombectomy—too late for them to achieve the goals of such procedures. *The conclusions from this and all the other studies cited here are clear: Early removal of the thrombus conveys significant benefits, and the earlier the removal, the better the outcome.*

■ DIAGNOSIS

Whether DVT is suspected on the basis of pain, discoloration, or swelling of one leg or during the search for a source for PE, the diagnosis can be confirmed by duplex scanning using color-flow imaging (fully discussed in Chapter 148). Clinical signs are more likely to be present in proximal DVT—in other words, IFVT—but there may be no apparent swelling in patients confined to bed rest, and the first signs may be those of PE (pleuritic chest pain, shortness of breath, hemoptysis; see also Chapter 152). Duplex scanning should evaluate not only the femoral and popliteal veins but the iliac and calf veins as well; otherwise, 30% of DVTs will be missed. Venography is mainly used now when catheter-directed interventions or surgical thrombectomy is indicated, to guide and monitor the procedure. Standard ascending venography using foot vein injection may miss isolated iliac vein thrombosis unless an adequate load of contrast agent is infused (see Chapter 19). In cases of IFVT with extension into the iliac vein without visualization of the upper end of the thrombus, a femoral venogram from the contralateral side is performed to visualize the inferior vena cava and determine the upper extent of thrombus extension.

■ TREATMENT

The treatment of patients with DVT until recently consisted of in-hospital bed rest with leg elevation and anticoagulation using intravenous unfractionated heparin for at least 5 days, accompanied by oral warfarin, which was started simultaneously and continued for at least 3 months. This therapy has shifted now from the use of unfractionated heparin to injections of LMWH without monitoring; instead, a weight-determined dosage is administered mostly on an outpatient basis. The U.S. Food and Drug Administration (FDA) approved this treatment for DVT in 1999. The rationale and effectiveness of this new approach are well discussed in Chapter 149. One potentially serious consequence of this trend is that the evidence of its cost-effectiveness may lull clinicians into the convenient practice of treating all patients with DVT in this manner, so that the outpatient treatment of DVT may circumvent the opportunity to apply thrombus-removing interventions to appropriately selected patients who have IFVT.

■ INDICATIONS FOR INTERVENTION

Early thrombus removal has clear benefit in two categories of patients with IFVT falling at the two ends of the clinical spectrum—active healthy patients with good longevity, to prevent or mitigate potentially severe late post-thrombotic sequelae, and patients with massive swelling and phlegmasia cerulea dolens, to mitigate early morbidity and prevent progression to venous gangrene. Older patients with significant intercurrent disease and serious co-morbidities, who are unlikely to be active and live a long life, and patients with distal (popliteal or calf vein) thrombosis should be treated with anticoagulant therapy. Late post-thrombotic sequelae are not likely to be an issue with them. Even these patients, however, if faced with the threat of venous gangrene, may merit an attempt at prompt thrombus removal.

In terms of the choice of the method of thrombus removal, catheter-directed techniques are appropriate for achieving the first goal, by removing obstructing thrombus and thereby preserving valve function, although the latter result has been presumed rather than proved. These techniques and their results are fully discussed in Chapter 150. In the patients identified as having indications for intervention, however, if catheter access cannot be achieved, thrombus removal or dissolution is unsuccessful or does not progress satisfactorily, or concomitant anticoagulation is contraindicated (e.g., IFVT in young peripartum women, and certain postoperative or trauma patients), surgical thrombectomy is an appropriate choice (Fig. 151-1).

■ SURGICAL THROMBECTOMY

Historical Background

The history of venous thrombectomy in the United States is quite interesting and reveals misconceptions that underscore its current infrequent use. John Homans,[12] an advocate for division of the femoral vein to prevent PE, first suggested thrombectomy in a paper entitled "Exploration and Division of the Femoral and Iliac Veins in the Treatment of Thrombophlebitis of the Leg," which he presented at the New England Surgical Society in 1940. Homans discussed indications for thrombectomy with or without ligation of the femoral vein, the technique, the complications, and the importance to prevent reflux.

However, the modern era of thrombectomy in the United States started in 1954, with Howard Mahorner's[13] paper, "New Management for Thrombosis of Deep Veins of Extremities," in which he advocated thrombectomy followed by restoration of vein lumen and regional heparinization. He presented 6 patients of whom 5 had an excellent result, with rapid disappearance of leg swelling, very little late morbidity, and minimal leg edema. There was no PE prior or subsequent to surgery. He claimed that this

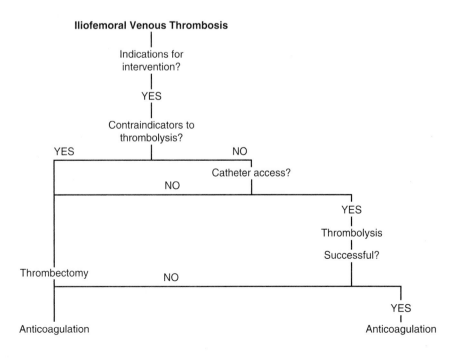

FIGURE 151-1 An algorithm summarizing the application of either thrombectomy or catheter-directed thrombolysis to selected patients with iliofemoral venous thrombosis, as discussed in the text.

method restored vein function with preservation of the vein lumen and vein valves. In a follow-up paper in 1957, Mahorner and colleagues[14] reported on 16 patients in whom thrombectomy was performed in 14 legs and 2 arms; excellent results were achieved in 12 patients, good results in 2, and poor results in 2. The enthusiasm for thrombectomy created by Mahorner's reports received strong support from Haller and Abrams[15] in 1963. They described 45 patients with IFVT who underwent thrombectomy. Of 34 patients with a short history (<10 days) of IFVT, excellent bidirectional flow was established in 31 (91%). At follow-up after an average of 18 months, 26 of these 31 patients (84%) had normal legs; ascending venography was performed in 13 patients, 11 of whom were shown to have normal patency of the deep venous system (85%).

Enthusiasm quickly subsided, however, after Lansing and Davis[16] presented their 5-year follow-up of Haller and Abrams' patients in 1968. Only 17 of the 34 patients (50%) in the Haller and Abrams series who had had a short history of IFVT were interviewed, but 16 of them were found to have swelling of the leg requiring stockings, and 1 patient had an ulcer. Ascending venography in the supine position was performed in 15 patients, showing patent veins but "the involved area of the deep venous system was found to be incompetent in all cases and there were no functioning valves."[16]

Unfortunately, the flaws in the Lansing and Davis study were not recognized. The first is they studied only half of the original cohort, likely those who returned with symptoms. Second, the incompetence of the valves in the femoral and popliteal veins cannot reliably be assessed by an ascending venographic study in the supine position. Third, the outstanding late patency of the thrombectomized veins was

completely ignored. In a 1970 paper, "Iliofemoral Venous Thrombosis: Reappraisal of Thrombectomy," Edwards and colleagues[17] argued with Lansing and Davis's results, concluding that "venous thrombectomy offers an effective and safe method of restoring flow in the deep venous system; when the thrombus is less than 10 days in duration and is of the iliofemoral segment, thrombectomy is recommended; venograms at operation to determine the patency of the deep venous system will aid in complete removal of the thrombus and give a basis for later comparison and evaluation of long-term patency." In the discussion of this report, Lansing repeated his findings from the 5-year follow-up, still questioning the value of thrombectomy, but Haller, who was never consulted about the follow-up study, stated that during a recent visit to Louisville, Kentucky (where the operations were performed), he had studied 17 patients in whom total removal of the thrombus had been possible, and none had significant residual edema. Despite this rebuttal, the impact of the Lansing study, combined with that of a subsequent one-page report by Karp and Wylie[18] of 10 patients, in whom 8 had reocclusion of the femoral vein before discharge (even though all had phlegmasia cerulea dolens and extensive thrombosis) was profound: Only a few series on thrombectomy were subsequently published from the United States, in spite of the fact that they all showed very good clinical results in more than 75% of patients. There seems, however, to be renewed interest in thrombectomy in the United States, as judged from the current American textbooks in vascular surgery. This revival is based mainly on positive reports from Europe and Japan. The results of reported U.S. experiences with thrombectomy are summarized in Tables 151-1 and 151-2.[19-32]

Table 151-1   Iliofemoral Venous Thrombectomy in the United States Before Lansing and Davis (1968)

STUDY (YEAR)*	NO. PATIENTS	PERIOPERATIVE MORTALITY No. (%)	NO. FATAL PULMONARY EMBOLISMS	POSTOPERATIVE VENOGRAPHY (%)	CLINICAL SUCCESS (%)
Mahorner et al[14] (1957)	14	1 (7)	0	39	85
DeWeese et al[19] (1960)	11	3 (27)	1	—	75
Haller and Abrams[15] (1963)	34[†]	3 (9)	0	58	84
	11[‡]	3 (27)	2	50	13
DeWeese[20] (1964)	29	4 (14)	1	64	80
Bradham and Buxton[21] (1964)	16	3 (19)	1	62	100
Kaiser et al[22] (1965)	48	9 (19)	0	—	82
Hafner et al[23] (1965)	49[§]	1 (2)	1	—	86
Smith[24] (1965)	18	1 (6)	1	24	82
Fogarty et al[25] (1966)	31	0 (0)	0	55	89
Karp and Wylie[18] (1966)	10	— —	—	80	—
Britt[26] (1966)	16	0 (0)	0	—	42
Wilson and Britt[27] (1967)	36	1 (3)	1	31	39
Total	*323*	*29 (9)*	*8*	*—*	*71*

*Superscript numbers indicate chapter references.
[†]Symptoms for less than 10 days.
[‡]Symptons 14-21 days.
[§]With venous interruption in 41 cases.

From Eklof B, Kistner RL: Is there a role for thrombectomy in iliofemoral venous thrombosis? Semin Vasc Surg 9:34-45, 1996.

Table 151-2 Iliofemoral Venous Thrombectomy in the United States After Lansing and Davis (1968)

STUDY (YEAR)*	NO. PATIENTS	PERIOPERATIVE MORTALITY No. (%)	NO. FATAL PULMONARY EMBOLISMS	POSTOPERATIVE VENOGRAPHY (%)	CLINICAL SUCCESS (%)
Harris and Brown[28] (1968)	17	0 (0)	0	100	88
Mahorner[29] (1969)	93	6 (6)	1	+	83
Barner et al[30] (1969)	70	12 (17)	1	29	76
Edwards et al[17] (1970)	58	1 (2)	0	+	80
Stephens[31] (1976)	16	0 (0)	0	—	75
Kistner and Sparkuhl[32] (1979)	77	0 (0)	0	74	86

*Superscript numbers indicate chapter references.

From Eklof B, Kistner RL: Is there a role for thrombectomy in iliofemoral venous thrombosis? Semin Vasc Surg 9:34-45, 1996.

Surgical Technique

The first thrombectomy for IFVT was performed by Läwen of Germany in 1937.[33] Surgery today is performed under general anesthesia, with positive end-expiratory pressure at 10 cm H$_2$O added during manipulation of the thrombus to prevent PE. The skin of the involved leg, contralateral groin, and abdomen is prepared for surgery. A longitudinal incision is made in the groin to expose the great saphenous vein (GSV), which is followed to its confluence with the common femoral vein (CFV), which in turn is dissected up to the inguinal ligament. The superficial femoral artery is dissected 3 to 4 cm below the femoral bifurcation for construction of an arteriovenous fistula (AVF).

In *primary* IFVT, in which the thrombus originates in the iliac vein and subsequently progresses distally, a longitudinal venotomy is made in the CFV, and a venous Fogarty thrombectomy catheter is passed upward through the thrombus into the inferior vena cava (IVC). The balloon is inflated and withdrawn, these maneuvers being repeated until no more thrombotic material can be extracted. With the balloon left inflated in the common iliac vein, a suction catheter is introduced to the level of the internal iliac vein to evacuate thrombi from this vein. Backflow is not a reliable sign of thrombus clearance, because a proximal valve in the external iliac vein may be present in 25% of cases, preventing retrograde flow in a cleared vein. On the other hand, backflow from the internal iliac vein and its tributaries can be excellent despite a remaining occlusion of the common iliac vein. Therefore, an intraoperative completion venogram is mandatory. An alternative is the use of an angioscope, which enables removal of residual thrombus material under direct vision. In cases of early IFVT, the distal thrombus is usually readily extruded through the venotomy by means of manual massage of the leg distally, starting at the foot. The Fogarty *venous* catheter, with soft flexible tip, can sometimes be advanced in retrograde fashion without significant trauma. The aim is to remove all fresh thrombi from the leg. The venotomy is closed with continuous suture, and an AVF is created with the saphenous vein, which is anastomosed end-to-side to the superficial femoral artery (Fig. 151-2). An intraoperative venogram is performed through a catheter inserted in a branch of the AVF. After a satisfactory completion venogram, the wound

is closed in layers without drainage. Intraoperative blood salvage with rapid retransfusion has been very helpful to decrease blood loss during the operation.

In IFVT *secondary* to ascending thrombosis from the calf, the thrombus in the femoral vein may be old and adherent to the venous wall. The chance of preserving valve function has been already lost, and the opportunity to restore patency significantly diminished. A femoral segment without functioning valves leads in time to distal valve dysfunction, much as does failure to achieve proximal patency. However, a patent iliac venous outflow plus a competent profunda collateral system usually achieves normal venous function. Therefore, if iliac patency is established but the thrombus in the femoral vein is too old to remove, it is preferable to ligate the femoral vein. If normal flow cannot be re-established in the femoral vein, we recommend extending the incision distally and exploring the orifices of the deep femoral branches. These are isolated, and venous flow is restored with a small Fogarty catheter. The femoral vein is then ligated distal to the profunda branches. In a 13-year follow-up after femoral vein ligation in this setting, Masuda and colleagues[34] found excellent clinical and physiologic results without PTS. Finally, if the completion venogram shows evidence of iliac vein compression, which can occur in about 50% of cases of left-sided IFVT, we recommend intraoperative iliac angioplasty and stenting.

If phlegmasia cerulea dolens is the indication for intervention, because of the threat of impending venous gangrene, we start the operation with fasciotomy of the calf compartments in order to release the pressure and improve the circulation immediately.

If there is extension of the thrombus into the IVC, the vena cava is approached transperitoneally through a subcostal incision. The IVC is exposed by medial deflection of the ascending colon and duodenum. Depending on the venographic findings relative to the top of the thrombus, the IVC is controlled, usually just below the renal veins. The IVC is opened, and the thrombus is removed by massage, especially of the iliac venous system. Then, if the femoral segment is involved, the operation is continued in the groin as previously described. When laparotomy is contraindicated in patients in poor condition, a vena cava filter of the

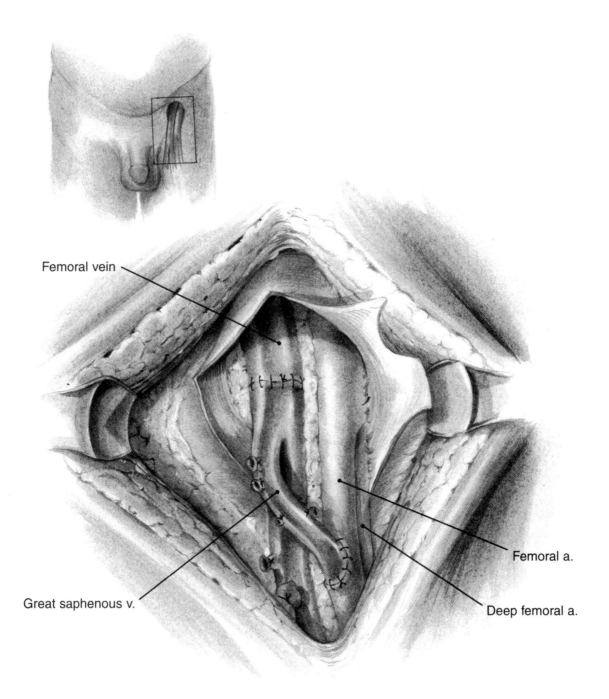

FIGURE 151-2 After complete thrombectomy, an arteriovenous fistula is constructed using the proximal 10 cm of the great saphenous vein, which is divided and anastomosed end-to-side to the superficial femoral artery. (From Eklof B: Arteriovenous fistulas as an adjunct to venous surgery. Semin Vasc Surg 13:20, 2000.)

Greenfield type can be introduced before the thrombectomy to protect against fatal PE. We have no experience using retrievable vena cava filters.

Heparin therapy is continued at least 5 days postoperatively. Warfarin therapy is started the first postoperative day and continued routinely for 6 months. The patient is ambulated the day after the operation while wearing a compression stocking and is usually discharged after a week, to return after 6 weeks for closure of the fistula.

The objectives of a temporary AVF are to increase blood flow in the thrombectomized iliac segment to prevent immediate rethrombosis, to allow time for healing of the endothelium, and to promote development of collateral vessels in case of incomplete clearance or immediate rethrombosis of the iliac segment. Usually, the AVF is performed between the saphenous vein and the superficial femoral artery. More distally placed AVFs do not function, in our experience.

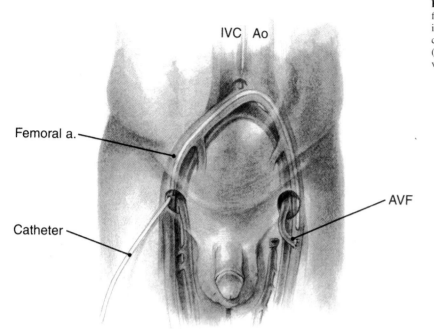

FIGURE 151-3 Before closure of the arteriovenous fistula at 6 weeks, an arteriovenogram is performed, in which the femoral artery on the contralateral side is catheterized to the level of the arteriovenous fistula. (From Eklof B: Arteriovenous fistulas as an adjunct to venous surgery. Semin Vasc Surg 13:20, 2000.)

A new percutaneous technique for fistula closure was developed by Endrys and colleagues[35] in Kuwait. A catheter is inserted through a puncture of the femoral artery on the other, surgically untouched side and is positioned at the fistula level (Fig. 151-3). Prior to release of a coil, an arteriovenogram can be performed to evaluate the patency of the iliac vein and vena cava, which is of prognostic value (Figs. 151-4 and 151-5). More than 10% of patients have been shown to have remaining significant stenosis of the iliac vein despite initially successful surgery. A percutaneous, transvenous angioplasty and stenting can be performed under the protection of the AVF, which is closed 4 weeks later.

Results and Complications of Surgical Management

Mortality

One of the reasons that induced surgeons to abandon thrombectomy in the 1960s, when its ability to achieve patency and preserve valve function was challenged by the two papers as already described,[16,18] was the high mortality associated with early thrombectomy. Surgery still bears a risk, but with today's great improvements in anesthesia, perioperative monitoring, and intensive care, results are significantly better. In the first author's (BE) series of more than 200 patients, only 2 died. One patient succumbed in an acute respiratory failure due to chronic pulmonary fibrosis; autopsy did not show any fresh PE. The other patient had an IVC extension of the thrombus and preoperatively undetected cirrhosis of the liver; the patient died of multiorgan failure on the 32nd postoperative day, after intra-abdominal hemorrhage and shock due to over-anticoagulation.

Pulmonary Embolism

Earlier reports of high mortality due to fatal PE have not been borne out in our experience. In the first author's experience (BE), there have been no cases of fatal PE in the perioperative period. To avoid this problem, a preoperative venogram to exclude IVC extension of thrombus is

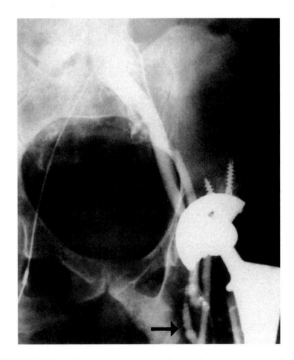

FIGURE 151-4 An arteriovenogram shows the arteriovenous fistula (*arrow*) with normal morphology of the iliac vein and distal inferior vena cava. (From Eklof B: Arteriovenous fistulas as an adjunct to venous surgery. Semin Vasc Surg 13:20, 2000.)

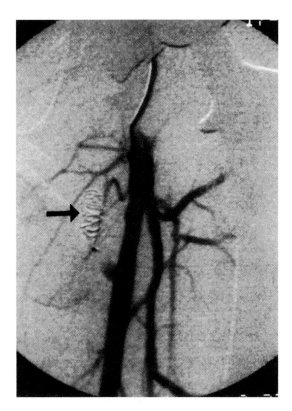

FIGURE 151-5 If the proximal venous system is patent without signs of stenosis or occlusion, the arteriovenous fistula is occluded using coils (*arrow*), with a second arteriogram to confirm closure. (From Eklof B: Arteriovenous fistulas as an adjunct to venous surgery. Semin Vasc Surg 13:20, 2000.)

Table 151-3	Thrombectomy with Temporary Arteriovenous Fistula: Early Iliac Vein Patency	
STUDY (YEAR)*	**NO. PATIENTS**	**PATENT ILIAC VEIN (%)**
Delin et al[39] (1982)	13	85
Plate et al[38] (1984)	31	87
Piquet et al[40] (1985)	92	80
Einarsson et al[41] (1986)	51	88
Juhan et al[42] (1987)	42	93
Vollmar and Hutschenreiter[43] (1989)	93	82
Kniemeyer et al[44] (1990)	185	96
Neglén et al[45] (1991)	48	89
Total	*555*	*88*

*Superscript numbers indicate chapter references.

From Eklof B, Kistner RL: Is there a role for thrombectomy in iliofemoral venous thrombosis? Semin Vasc Surg 9:34-45, 1996.

essential; such an extension can be fractured and dislodged during manipulation with the Fogarty catheter. Eklof and his group (from the Swedish series) do not use a separate balloon catheter to occlude the IVC but routinely ask the anesthetist to apply positive end-expiratory pressure (PEEP) during the operative manipulation of the thrombosed iliac vein. In a prospective randomized study from Sweden, perfusion scan results were positive on admission in 45% of all patients, with additional defects seen after 1 week in 11% and after 4 weeks in 12% of the conservatively treated group, and in 20% after 1 week and none after 4 weeks of the patients treated with thrombectomy and AVF.[36] Mavor and Galloway[37] demonstrated that incomplete clearance of the thrombus in the iliac vein *raised* the incidence of rethrombosis and PE. In the Swedish series, no additional perfusion defects developed beyond the first week after thrombectomy with AVF. Because the AVF effectively prevented rethrombosis, the fistula can be assumed to have contributed to the low incidence of postoperative PE.

Early Morbidity After Thrombectomy

The rate of early rethrombosis of the iliac vein varies. In a retrospective study from Hawaii, the rate was 34% in primary, descending IFVT (8 of 24) and 18% in secondary, ascending IFVT (6 of 33) without use of temporary AVF.[32] In a prospective randomized study from Sweden in which AVF was used, 13% of patients had early rethrombosis of

the iliac vein.[38] This low rate of early rethrombosis for thrombectomy with use of a temporary AVF is corroborated by a series of 555 patients showing 12% rethrombosis (Table 151-3).[39-45] Important aspects of the protocol to avoid this complication are as follows:

- Rarely operating in patients whose symptoms of iliac obstruction began more than 7 days previously
- Use of a Fogarty catheter to clear the external and common iliac vein with special attention to the internal iliac vein
- Direct caval approach when the IVC is involved
- Intraoperative venography or venoscopy to demonstrate clearance of the iliac vein
- Liberal indications for and early performance of decompressive leg fasciotomy in patients with phlegmasia cerulea dolens
- Use of a temporary AVF
- Early ambulation with the patient wearing compression stockings
- Carefully monitored postoperative administration of anticoagulants

Postoperative bleeding with hematoma formation in the groin was not uncommon in the Swedish series (Eklof and his group), despite drainage of the wound, because full anticoagulation with heparin was continued for 5 days after operation. To avoid compression of the vein with risk of thrombosis and infection, the hematomas should be evacuated.

Early rethrombosis was previously common, but with the use of the temporary AVF, the rate is now 12%. If there is an immediate reocclusion of the iliac vein, a re-exploration with a second thrombectomy is performed. In selected cases in which iliac outflow patency cannot be restored, angioplasty and stenting or a femorofemoral crossover bypass graft is considered to prevent retrograde formation of thrombus and subsequent valve incompetence.

Venous gangrene is very rare and, in most cases, due to underlying malignancy. With liberal indications for fasciotomy in phlegmasia cerulea dolens, it can be prevented.

Table 151-4	Thrombectomy with Temporary Arteriovenous Fistula: Clinical Results		
STUDY (YEAR)*	NO. PATIENTS	FOLLOW-UP (mo)	CLINICAL SUCCESS (%)
Poilleux et al[46] (1975)	27	—	78
Plate et al[38] (1984)	31	6	42
Piquet et al[40] (1985)	82	51	51
Einarsson et al[41] (1986)	55	10	75
Juhan et al[42] (1987)	36	12-48	93
Gänger et al[47] (1989)	17	91	88
Winter et al[48] (1989)	100	12	64
Kniemeyer et al[44] (1990)	147	43	51
Plate et al[49] (1990)	19	60	37
Rasmussen et al[50] (1990)	25	20	68
Loeprecht et al[51] (1991)	112	36	59
Neglén et al[45] (1991)	37	24	83
Törngren et al[52] (1991)	63	66	43
Juhan et al[53] (1997)[†]	44	60	82
Juhan et al[53] (1997)[†]	16	120	81

*Superscript numbers indicate chapter references.
[†]Data updated by author.

From Eklof B, Kistner RL: Is there a role for thrombectomy in iliofemoral venous thrombosis? Semin Vasc Surg 9:34-45, 1996.

Table 151-5	Thrombectomy with Temporary Arteriovenous Fistula: "Long-Term" Iliac Vein Patency		
STUDY (YEAR)*	NO. PATIENTS	FOLLOW-UP (mo)	PATENT ILIAC VEIN (%)
Plate et al[38] (1984)	31	6	76
Piquet et al[40] (1985)	57	39	80
Einarsson et al[41] (1986)	58	10	61
Vollmar[54] (1986)	93	53	82
Juhan et al[42] (1987)	36	12-48	93
Törngren et al[55] (1988)	54	19	54
Plate et al[49] (1990)	19	60	77
Rasmussen et al[50] (1990)	24	20	75
Neglén et al[45] (1991)	34	24	88
Juhan et al[53] (1997)[†]	44	60	84
Juhan et al[53] (1997)[†]	16	120	80

*Superscript numbers indicate chapter references.
[†]Data updated by author.

From Eklof B, Kistner RL: Is there a role for thrombectomy in iliofemoral venous thrombosis? Semin Vasc Surg 9:34-45, 1996.

Groin infection was common until they (Eklof's group) improved preoperative hygiene and added prophylactic antibiotics. Lymphorrhea is still seen but it usually stops after 2 to 3 weeks. In two elderly patients in the Swedish series, previously known to have compromised cardiac function, the AVF caused high-output cardiac failure, which responded immediately to closure of the fistula. There has been some concern that the AVF might increase venous pressure and produce limb swelling. We found no increase in iliac vein pressure without residual outflow obstruction. This finding stresses the importance of ensuring unobstructed proximal venous outflow.

"Late" Results

There are few studies on "long-term" results after thrombectomy with AVF. There are eight studies of clinical results in 521 patients with more than 2 years of follow-up in which "clinical success" is claimed in 62% of cases (Table 151-4).[46,53] Five studies of iliac vein patency in 247 patients with more than 2 years of follow-up show an 82% patency rate (range, 77% to 88%; Table 151-5).[54,55] Five studies of femoropopliteal valvular competence in 259 patients with more than 2 years of follow-up report a 60% competency rate (range 36% to 84%; Table 151-6).[56]

In a prospective, randomized study from Sweden comparing thrombectomy plus AVF with conservative treatment using anticoagulation alone, a highly significant difference in the number of asymptomatic patients after 6 months was found, with 42% in the surgical group versus 7% in the conservatively treated group.[39,49,57] At 5 years, 37% of the operated patients were asymptomatic, compared with 18% of the conservatively treated group. At 10 years,

54% of patients in the surgical group were basically asymptomatic (CEAP classifications 0 to 2) compared with 23% in the conservative treatment group; however, the difference was not statistically significant with so few patients with this late follow-up. Rate of iliac vein patency at 6 months was 76% in the surgical group compared with 35% in the conservative treatment group, as demonstrated on venography. This significant difference was upheld after 5 and 10 years, with 77% and 77% patency in the surgical group, respectively, compared with 30% and 47% in the conservative group, respectively. The rate of femoropopliteal valvular competence at 6 months was 52% in the surgical group compared with 26% in the conservatively treated group, as monitored by descending venography with

Table 151-6	Thrombectomy with Temporary Arteriovenous Fistula: "Long-Term" Competence of the Femoropopliteal Vein		
STUDY (YEAR)*	NO. PATIENTS	FOLLOW-UP (mo)	COMPETENCE (%)
Plate et al[38] (1984)	31	6	52
Einarsson et al[41] (1986)	53	10	42
Gänger et al[47] (1989)	17	91	82
Kniemeyer et al[44] (1990)	147	43	44
Plate et al[49] (1990)	14	60	36
Neglén et al[45] (1991)	37	24	56
Kniemeyer et al[56] (1992)	37	55	84
Juhan et al[53] (1997)[†]	44	60	84
Juhan et al[53] (1997)[†]	16	120	56

*Superscript numbers indicate chapter references.
[†]Data updated by author.

From Eklof B, Kistner RL: Is there a role for thrombectomy in iliofemoral venous thrombosis? Semin Vasc Surg 9:34-45, 1996.

Valsalva maneuver; a statistically significant difference. After 5 years, the patients who underwent thrombectomy had significantly lower AVPs, improved venous emptying (as shown on plethysmography), and a better calf pump function with less reflux, as measured by foot volumetry. Combining the results of all functional tests shows that 36% of the surgical patients had normal venous function, compared with 11% of the conservatively treated group. These differences were not statistically significant owing to loss of patients to follow-up. At 10 years, duplex scanning found popliteal reflux in 32% in the surgical group compared with 67% in the conservative treatment group. Six patients who had a successful thrombectomy 10 years before, without obstruction of the iliac vein (May-Thurner) at the time of surgery, were all asymptomatic with patent iliac veins, and 50% had competent popliteal veins.

■ SUMMARY

Prompt early removal of the thrombus is indicated to avoid the late PTS in active patients with acute IFVT. The first line of treatment is CDT, or PMT plus CDT, with or without adjunct procedures such as angioplasty and stenting. When there are contraindications to or failure to achieve catheter access or adequate lysis with these techniques, thrombectomy with a temporary AVF is an appropriate alternative in patients qualifying for intervention in the first place—that is, active, healthy patients with reasonable longevity and short duration of IFVT. These interventions are not justified in chronically ill, bedridden, high-risk, or aged patients or in those with serious intercurrent disease or limited life expectancy, except when performed for limb salvage in patients with phlegmasia cerulea dolens in whom elevation and anticoagulation do not prevent the development of an acute compartment syndrome and progression to venous gangrene.

■ REFERENCES

1. Lindner DJ, Edwards JM, Phinney ES, et al: Long-term hemodynamic and clinical sequelae of lower extremity deep vein thrombosis. J Vasc Surg 4:436, 1986.
2. Åkesson H, Brundin L, Dahlström JA, et al: Venous function assessed during a 5 year period after acute iliofemoral venous thrombosis treated with anticoagulation. Eur J Vasc Surg 4:43, 1990.
3. Arenander E: Varicosity and ulceration of the lower limb: A clinical follow-up study of 247 patients examined phlebographically. Acta Chir Scand 12:135, 1957.
4. Thomas ML, McAllister V: The radiological progression of deep venous thrombosis. Radiology 99:37, 1971.
5. Mavor GE, Galloway JMD: Iliofemoral venous thrombosis: Pathological considerations and surgical management. Br J Surg 56:45, 1969.
6. Schull KC, Nicolaides AN, Fernandes é Fernandes J, et al: Significance of popliteal reflux in relation to ambulatory venous pressure. Arch Surg 114:1304, 1979.
7. Nicolaides AN, Hussein MK, Szendro G, et al: The relation of venous ulceration with ambulatory venous pressure measurements. J Vasc Surg 17:414, 1993.
8. Nicolaides AN, Sumner DS (eds): Investigation of Patients with Deep Vein Thrombosis and Chronic Venous Insufficiency. Los Angeles, Med-Orion Publishing, 1991.
9. Downing LJ, Wakefield TW, Strieter RM, et al: Anti-P-selectin antibody decreases inflammation and thrombus formation in venous thrombosis. J Vasc Surg 25:816, 1997.
10. See-Tho K, Harris EJ Jr: Thrombosis with outflow obstruction delays thrombolysis and results in chronic wall thickening of rat veins. J Vasc Surg 28:115, 1998.
11. Kistner RL: Valve repair and segment transposition in primary valvular insufficiency. In Bergan JJ, Yao JST (eds): Venous Disorders. Philadelphia, WB Saunders, 1991, p 261.
12. Homans J: Exploration and division of the femoral and iliac veins in the treatment of thrombophlebitits of the leg. JAMA 224:179, 1941.
13. Mahorner H: New management for thrombosis of deep veins of extremities. Am Surg 20:487, 1954.
14. Mahorner H, Castleberry JW, Coleman WO: Attempts to restore function in major veins which are the site of massive thrombosis. Ann Surg 146:510, 1957.
15. Haller JAJ, Abrams BL: Use of thrombectomy in the treatment of acute iliofemoral venous thrombosis in forty-five patients. Ann Surg 158:561, 1963.
16. Lansing AM, Davis WM: Five-year follow-up study of iliofemoral venous thrombectomy. Ann Surg 168:620, 1968.
17. Edwards WH, Sawyers JL, Foster JH: Iliofemoral venous thrombosis: Reappraisal of thrombectomy. Ann Surg 171:961, 1970.
18. Karp RB, Wylie EJ: Recurrent thrombosis after iliofemoral venous thrombectomy. Surg Forum 17:147, 1966.
19. DeWeese JA, Jones TI, Lyon J, Dale WA: Evaluation of thrombectomy in the management of iliofemoral venous thrombosis. Surgery 47:140, 1960.
20. DeWeese JA: Thrombectomy for acute iliofemoral venous thrombosis. J Cardiovasc Surg 5:703, 1964.
21. Bradham RR, Buxton JT: Thrombectomy for acute iliofemoral venous thrombosis. Surg Gynecol Obstet 119:1271, 1964.
22. Kaiser GC, Murray RC, Willman VL, et al: Iliofemoral thrombectomy for venous occlusion. Arch Surg 90:574, 1965.
23. Hafner CD, Cranley JJ, Krause RJ, et al: Venous thrombectomy: Current status. Ann Surg 161:411, 1965.
24. Smith GW: Therapy of iliofemoral venous thrombosis. Surg Gynecol Obstet 121:1298, 1965.
25. Fogarty TJ, Dennis D, Krippaehne WW: Surgical management of iliofemoral venous thrombosis. Am J Surg 112:211, 1966.
26. Britt LG: Iliofemoral veno-occlusive disease: Results with thrombectomy in 16 cases. Am Surg 32:103, 1966.
27. Wilson H, Britt LG: Surgical treatment of iliofemoral thrombosis. Ann Surg 165:855, 1967.
28. Harris EJ, Brown WH: Patency of the thrombectomy for iliofemoral thrombosis. Ann Surg 167:91, 1968.
29. Mahorner H: Results of surgical operations for venous thrombosis. Surg Gynecol Obstet 129:66, 1969.
30. Barner HB, Willman VL, Kaiser GC, et al: Thrombectomy for iliofemoral venous thrombosis. JAMA 28:2442, 1969.
31. Stephens GGL: Current opinion on iliofemoral venous thrombectomy. Am Surg 42:108, 1976.
32. Kistner RL, Sparkuhl MD: Surgery in acute and chronic venous disease. Surgery 85:31, 1979.
33. Läwen A: Uber Thrombectomie bei Venenthrombose und Arteriespasmus. Zentralbl Chir 64:961, 1937.
34. Masuda EM, Kistner RL, Ferris EB: Long-term effects of superficial femoral vein ligation: Thirteen-year follow-up. J Vasc Surg 16:741, 1992.
35. Endrys J, Eklof B, Neglén P, et al: Percutaneous balloon occlusion of surgical arteriovenous fistulae following venous thrombectomy. Cardiovasc Intervent Radiol 12:226, 1989.
36. Plate G, Ohlin P, Eklof B: Pulmonary embolism in acute iliofemoral venous thrombosis. Br J Surg 72 912, 1985.
37. Mavor GE, Galloway JMD: The iliofemoral venous segment as a source of pulmonary emboli. Lancet 1(7495):871, 1967.
38. Plate G, Einarsson E, Ohlin P, et al: Thrombectomy with temporary arteriovenous fistula: The treatment of choice in acute iliofemoral venous thrombosis. J Vasc Surg 1:867, 1984.
39. Delin A, Swedenborg J, Hellgren M, et al: Thrombectomy and arteriovenous fistula for iliofemoral venous thrombosis in fertile women. Surg Gynecol Obstet 154:69, 1982.

40. Piquet P, Tournigand P, Josso B, et al: Traitement chirurgical des thromboses ilio-caves: Exigences et resultats. In Kieffer E (ed): Chirurgie de la Veine Cave Inferieure et de ses Branches. Paris, Expansion Scientifique Francaise, 1985, p 210.

41. Einarsson E, Albrechtsson U, Eklof B: Thrombectomy and temporary AV-fistula in iliofemoral vein thrombosis: Technical considerations and early results. Int Angiol 5:65, 1986.

42. Juhan C, Cornillon B, Tobiana F, et al: Patency after iliofemoral and iliocaval venous thrombectomy. Ann Vasc Surg 1:529, 1987.

43. Vollmar J, Hutschenreiter S: Surgical treatment of acute thromboembolic disease: The role of vascular endoscopy. In Veith FJ (ed): Current Critical Problems in Vascular Surgery. St. Louis, Quality Medical Publishing, 1989, p 154.

44. Kniemeyer HW, Merckle R, Stuhmeier K, et al: Chirurgische Therapie der akuten und embolisierenden tiefen Beinvenenthrombose—Indikation, technisches Prinzip, Ergebnisse. Klin Wochenschr 68:1208, 1990.

45. Neglén P, Al-Hassan HK, Endrys J, et al: Iliofemoral venous thrombectomy followed by percutaneous closure of the temporary arteriovenous fistula. Surgery 110:493, 1991.

46. Poilleux J, Chermet J, Bigot JM, et al: Les thromboses veineuses iliofemorales recentes. Ann Chir 29:713, 1975.

47. Gänger KH, Nachbur BH, Ris HB, et al: Surgical thrombectomy versus conservative treatment for deep venous thrombosis: Functional comparison of long-term results. Eur J Vasc Surg 3:529, 1989.

48. Winter C, Weber H, Loeprecht H: Surgical treatment of iliofemoral vein thrombosis. Technical aspects: Possible secondary interventions. Int Angiol 8:188, 1989.

49. Plate G, Åkesson H, Einarsson E, et al: Long-term results of venous thrombectomy combined with a temporary arterio-venous fistula. Eur J Vasc Surg 4:483, 1990.

50. Rasmussen A, Mogensen K, Nissen FH, et al: Acute iliofemoral venous thrombosis: Twenty-six cases treated with thrombectomy, temporary arteriovenous fistula and anti-coagulants. Ugeskr Laeger 152:2928, 1990.

51. Loeprecht H, Weber H, Krawielitzky B: Indikationen zur Gefässchirurgischen Behandlung der Iliofemoralvenenthrombose. In Maurer PC, Doorler J, von Sommoggy S (eds): Gefässchirurgie in Fortschritt: Neuenentwicklungen, Kontroversen, Grenzen, Perspektiven. Stuttgart, Georg Thieme Verlag, 1991, p 180.

52. Törngren S, Bremme K, Hjertberg R, et al: Late results of thrombectomy for iliofemoral venous thrombosis. Phlebology 6:249, 1991.

53. Juhan CM, Alimi YS, Barthelemy TJ, et al: Late results of iliofemoral venous thrombectomy. J Vasc Surg 25:417, 1997.

54. Vollmar JF: Advances in reconstructive venous surgery. Int Angiol 5:117, 1986.

55. Törngren S, Swedenborg J: Thrombectomy and temporary arteriovenous fistula for ilio-femoral venous thrombosis. Int Angiol 7:14, 1988.

56. Kniemeyer HW, Sandmann W, Schwindt C, et al: Thrombectomy with AV-fistula: The better alternative to prevent recurrent pulmonary embolism. Presented at the 4th Annual Meeting of the American Venous Forum, Coronado, CA, February 26-28, 1992.

57. Plate G, Eklof B, Norgren L, et al: Venous thrombectomy for iliofemoral vein thrombosis: 10-year results of a prospective randomized study. Eur J Endovasc Surg 14:367, 1997.

Chapter

Vena Caval Interruption Procedures

152

JOHN E. RECTENWALD, MD

LAZAR J. GREENFIELD, MD

PETER K. HENKE, MD

MARY C. PROCTOR, MS

THOMAS W. WAKEFIELD, MD

■ HISTORICAL PERSPECTIVE

John Hunter performed the first femoral vein ligation for thrombophlebitis in 1784. However, not until 1893 did Bottini report successful ligation of the inferior vena cava (IVC) to prevent pulmonary embolism (PE). In the United States, venous ligation was also the earliest surgical technique used. Bilateral common femoral vein ligation was undertaken first as suggested by Homans, but an unacceptable incidence of recurrent PE and lower extremity venous stasis sequelae led to abandonment of the procedure. Ligation of the infrarenal inferior vena cava provided theoretical control of the final common path to the pulmonary circulation for most emboli and was commonly performed until the late 1960s. However, high postoperative mortality, recurrent PE, and adverse lower extremity sequelae were unacceptable outcomes.

Nasbeth and Moran[1] and Amador and coworkers[2] reported mortality rates after IVC ligation of 19% and 39%, respectively; rates were highest in patients with underlying cardiac disease (41% and 19%, respectively). Among patients who had normal cardiac function and who were classified as good preoperative risks, an operative mortality rate of 4% was still observed; cited causes included recurrent PE arising at the site of caval ligation and phlegmasia cerulea dolens. In follow-up studies, Ferris and colleagues[3] found recurrent PE in 3 of 20 patients within 2 months of vena caval ligation. Although thrombus can form above the ligation, large ovarian and ascending lumbar venous collateral vessels were the probable conduits for

Table 152-1	Indications for Insertion of a Vena Caval Filter
Absolute indications	Deep venous thrombosis or documented thromboembolism in a patient who has a contraindication to anticoagulation Recurrent thromboembolism despite adequate anticoagulation Complications of anticoagulation that have forced therapy to be discontinued Immediately after pulmonary embolectomy Failure of another form of caval interruption, demonstrated by recurrent thromboembolism
Relative indications	A large free-floating iliofemoral thrombus demonstrated on venography in a high-risk patient A propagating iliofemoral thrombus despite adequate anticoagulation Septic pulmonary embolism Chronic pulmonary embolism in a patient with pulmonary hypertension and cor pulmonale A patient who has occlusion of more than 50% of the pulmonary vascular bed and would not tolerate any additional thrombus Severe ataxia and risk of falling

emboli from lower extremity sources, because acute thrombi were present below the ligation site in 40% to 50% of cases. Lower extremity sequelae in the series reported by Nasbeth and Moran[1] included leg edema (40%), development of new varicose veins (20%), stasis pigmentation (18%), leg discomfort (14%), disabling venous claudication (14%), and ulceration (6%).

Later data have also suggested an underappreciation of cardiac output limitation after vena caval ligation in patients without preexisting heart disease. Miller and Staats,[4] in an exercise and gas exchange study of such patients, found significant impairment of cardiac output secondary to inadequate venous return.

Against this background, the first techniques to provide filtration of emboli without vena caval occlusion evolved. For more than a decade, vena caval suture, staple plication, and externally applied clip devices were used to provide a limited orifice flow through the IVC.[5-7] These techniques added the morbidity of general anesthesia and laparotomy. Although IVC clips are still being applied at the time of surgery in some instances, there is considerably less morbidity if an intracaval filter is placed preoperatively. Despite promising early patency data, high rates of caval occlusion with external devices were noted after a relatively short follow-up.[8-10]

The development of transvenous approaches with the use of local anesthesia was the next logical step. The earliest transvenous approaches demonstrated the ease of access to the vena cava with local anesthesia and fluoroscopy. Although various devices were developed, the Mobin-Uddin umbrella became the most popular because it could be readily positioned below the renal veins. However, its use was found to cause a high rate of subsequent vena caval thrombosis and was associated with additional complications of proximal thrombus formation and occasional migration into the pulmonary artery.[11] It was withdrawn from the market, and a new generation of devices was developed to facilitate placement, achieve reliable capture of thromboemboli, and maintain long-term caval patency.

■ INDICATIONS FOR VENA CAVAL FILTER PLACEMENT

Currently accepted indications for insertion of an inferior vena caval filter are (1) documented deep venous thrombosis (DVT) or PE in a patient with a recognized contraindication to anticoagulation, (2) recurrent PE and DVT despite adequate anticoagulation, (3) bleeding complications requiring

that anticoagulation therapy for DVT or PE be discontinued, (4) for prevention of further PE after pulmonary embolectomy, and (5) failure of another form of caval interruption as demonstrated by recurrent thromboembolism (Table 152-1).

Case-selective or relative indications include the presence of iliofemoral thrombosis with a 5-cm or longer free-floating tail. Although this indication has been questioned by a prospective trial,[12] thrombus with a 5-cm free-floating tail may still be prudently treated with a vena caval filter. Other such indications are septic PE, chronic PE in a patient with cor pulmonale, a high-risk patient (e.g., one who has significant cardiopulmonary disease, occlusion of more than 50% of the pulmonary bed, or both) who would not tolerate any recurrent thromboembolism, and severe ataxia, putting a patient at risk for falls while undergoing anticoagulation therapy.

Because long-term favorable experience with the Greenfield vena caval filter has accumulated, there have been suggestions to liberalize the indications for filter insertion. Two new uses for vena caval filters have been suggested. As a method of PE prophylaxis, they have been placed in patients who have sustained massive trauma and remain at high risk for thromboembolism but do not actually have the disease.[13-15] Some physicians, such as Cohen and colleagues,[16] Lossef and Barth,[17] and Rosen and colleagues,[18] advocate the use of filters in patients with malignancy who are at risk for PE or who have thromboembolism. Each of these indications remains unproven in randomized studies, but its efficacy is suggested in smaller series.

Recommendations have included the routine use of the filter for DVT instead of anticoagulation in high-risk general surgical patients, in older patients, and in pregnant women with DVT or PE.[16,19] Additional studies are required to determine whether the risk of anticoagulation outweighs the risk of filter placement alone in these patient groups and, in particular, with long-term follow-up. At present, most authorities recommend the use of appropriate anticoagulation to control the underlying thrombotic disorder in patients who are eligible for anticoagulant therapy.

■ STAINLESS STEEL GREENFIELD FILTER

The current benchmark for performance of transvenous vena caval filters is the stainless steel Greenfield filter, for which 20 years of long-term follow-up is available.[20] The Greenfield filter was developed to maintain caval patency

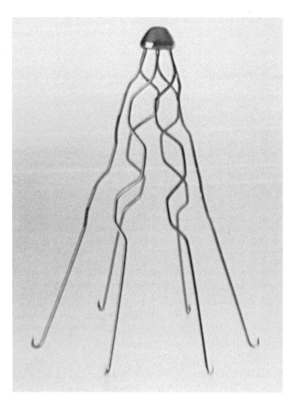

FIGURE 152-1 Original stainless steel Greenfield filter introduced in 1972 for mechanical protection against pulmonary thromboembolism.

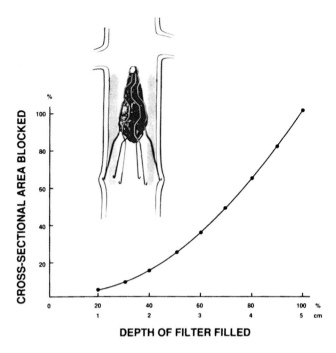

FIGURE 152-2 Relationship between the volume of thrombus trapped within the filter and the percentage of cross-section occluded.

after trapping emboli and to preserve prograde caval flow, avoiding stasis and facilitating lysis of the trapped emboli (Fig. 152-1). The cone-shaped filter is 4.6 cm long from apex to base. The base is formed by the filter's six legs, which provide for caval fixation by means of small, recurved hooks at their distal ends. The spacing between the legs is 2 mm at the apex of the cone and a maximum of 5 to 6 mm at the base when the device is expanded, depending on IVC size. The spacing between limbs is such that the filter effectively traps most emboli 3 mm or more in diameter.[21]

The conical geometry allows progressive central filling while maintaining circumferential blood flow, thus avoiding progressive venous thrombosis, caval obstruction, and venous hypertension. When thrombus fills the filter to 70% of its depth, only 49% of the cross-sectional area is blocked. Experience has shown that no distal venous pressure increase occurs until 80% of the filter is filled with clot, at which point more than 64% of the cross-sectional area is blocked (Fig. 152-2). These design features result in superior patency rates and a minimal incidence of stasis sequelae. In addition, an unexpected result of flow preservation is the evidence of progressive lysis of the trapped thrombus over time.

The stainless steel Greenfield filter demonstrates a 4% rate of recurrent embolism over a 12-year period of observation in 469 patients, and a long-term filter patency rate of 98%.[22] Similar results have been obtained in other follow-up series, with long-term patency rates in excess of 95%.[11,23] The 20-year experience demonstrated the same low rate of recurrent PE and high rate of caval patency as

seen in the earlier reports,[24] reinforcing the durability of findings for this device. This high level of patency has allowed placement of the Greenfield filter above the level of the renal veins when needed because of thrombus at that level or in pregnant women to avoid contact between the gravid uterus and the filter. The results for suprarenal filter placement are quite comparable, with a 100% long-term patency rate in the 22 patients studied in the series of 69 filters placed at this level since 1976.[25]

The patency rate of the Greenfield filter does not depend on prolonged anticoagulation, and the termination of anticoagulant therapy is dictated by the patient's underlying thrombotic disorder. The associated complications include misplacement due to premature discharge or inaccurate fluoroscopic control of the carrier, rare limb penetration of the cava, and filter limb fracture. Although it is possible to retrieve a misplaced device, misplacements into the renal, hepatic, or iliac veins have not caused functional problems. The only functional consequence of venous misplacement may be inadequate prophylaxis against PE.

Because of its reliable preservation of caval patency, the filter has adapted well to a variety of unusual clinical problems, such as the rare need for placement in the superior vena cava (SVC). The filter has also been a useful adjunct in the successful management of septic thrombophlebitis. This is possible because preserved prograde venous flow through the filter permits in-vivo sterilization of any infected thrombus within it via parenteral antibiotic treatment.[26]

Technical Considerations for Filter Insertion

The procedure is usually performed under fluoroscopy, which can be achieved either in the operating room with a C-arm fluoroscope, or in the radiology suite or endovascular operating room, where better imaging can be obtained. A preoperative selective venacavogram should be obtained and should be available for review at the time of filter insertion.[27]

In some cases, it may be desirable to place the filter with the use of intravascular ultrasound (IVUS) in order to image the vena cava, determine its true diameter, and locate the renal and other tributary veins. IVUS as a sole imaging modality for vena cava filter placement has been evaluated and, although promising, requires precise technique.[28] Proposed IVUS-guided filter placement was inaccurate by more than 3 cm in 3 of the 34 patients studied, owing to movement of surgical drapes and error in assembly of the filter device. Nonetheless, the advantages of the use of IVUS for filter placement are attractive. IVUS avoids transfer of sick patients in intensive care to the operating room or fluoroscopy suite and the use of nephrotoxic contrast agent, and potentially reduces overall cost of the procedure. A transfemoral route for IVUS to guide filter placement may be preferred over the transjugular route to achieve more accurate placement.[29] Examples of patient situations that might make this useful are severely unstable patients who cannot be moved from the intensive care unit, pregnant patients who are at risk from irradiation, and patients with a contraindication to contrast medium.

The use of external duplex ultrasonography to guide placement of vena cava filters has also been investigated. Advantages of using external ultrasound rather than venacavography to guide filter placement are similar to those for IVUS. After a report of an initial safety and feasibility study,[30] Connors and colleagues[31] evaluated the use of duplex scanning to guide placement of vena cava filters in 325 patients. Duplex scanning was used in placing IVC filters in 203 patients; in 41 patients, placement was not possible because of unsuitable anatomy or IVC thrombosis, or because the IVC was poorly visualized on ultrasonography. Technical complications occurred in 12 patients (4%)—filter misplacement in 6 patients (2%), access site thrombosis in 1 patient (<1%), filter migration in 1 patient (<1%), and IVC occlusion in 3 patients (1%). Pulmonary emboli occurred after filter placement in 1 patient with a misplaced filter. There were no deaths or septic complications, and the average hospital charges related to duplex scanning were $2388 less than those for fluoroscopic placement.[31]

The Greenfield filters are designed for either surgical or percutaneous placement. Prior to being discontinued, the 24F design was placed at a similar overall expense and complication rate.[32] Regardless of the method of delivery, it is important to ensure the security of the device before delivery. This is achieved by the over-the-wire technique with the 24F design, and the protective sheath used with titanium. The newest percutaneous filter also uses a sheath and an over-the-wire system to prevent misplacement. In the majority of cases, the ideal level for placement is L2 or L3; however, placement in the suprarenal IVC or SVC may be indicated in some situations.

The radiographic diameter of the vena cava should be measured, with correction for magnification, which can be as much as 25% to 30%. Very large venae cavae (> 30 mm in diameter) may be found in patients with right-sided heart failure. In these patients, it is safer to introduce separate filters into each iliac vein. Fortunately, the vena cava is narrower in the anteroposterior diameter than it is in the transverse diameter, providing an additional measure of security for fixation.

Thrombus within the vena cava should not be allowed to contact the filter, because such contact would lead to propagation of thrombus through the filter and above the level of mechanical protection. If thrombus does extend to the level of the renal veins or if the distal IVC is thrombosed, the filter should be placed at the level of T12, above the renal veins. After removal of the carrier system and the guidewire, a follow-up abdominal radiograph is obtained to confirm the position of the filter. Often, a discrepancy is noted between the fluoroscopic impression of the level of the filter and the filter level indicated by the abdominal radiograph; this difference is due to slight parallax of the fluoroscopic image.

■ PERCUTANEOUS FILTER DEVICES

Percutaneous insertion of devices designed to provide effective filtration of thromboemboli in the vena cava offers a number of potential advantages for the patient, including reductions in discomfort, insertion time, and procedural cost because of the use of the radiology suite rather than the operating room.[6] A newer technique is use of single-wall needles to limit the risk of puncturing the femoral artery during the attempt to enter the vein. Ultrasonography guidance has also been used when the internal jugular vein has been the selected site for placement. Enlarging the skin incision permits expansion of the tract by either a balloon or dilators to allow the insertion of a larger sheath.

Percutaneously inserted caval devices are customarily placed through the right femoral vein, but they may also be inserted through the neck by way of the jugular vein. The latter route is less desirable because of the risk of air embolism. Although the left femoral approach is more challenging because of more difficult anatomy, it has also been used as an access site. With introduction of the flexible delivery system for the percutaneous stainless steel filter, the left femoral vein has been used with greater ease and success.

Initial efforts at percutaneous introduction of the standard 24F carrier system of the stainless steel Greenfield filter required a very large sheath (28F) and prolonged compression of the insertion site; it resulted in a 30% to 40% incidence of insertion site venous thrombosis.[33] This complication led to the enthusiastic proliferation of many innovative devices that could be inserted percutaneously using smaller-diameter delivery systems (Fig. 152-3) in an effort to retain the advantage of percutaneous insertion while minimizing the incidence of insertion site venous thrombosis. Despite the insertion of large numbers of these alternative filter devices (Fig. 152-4), it has been difficult to obtain accurate follow-up information to compare their effectiveness (Table 152-2).

Percutaneous Filter Insertion Technique

With local anesthesia, a 4-mm stab incision is made over the right femoral vein, which is entered with a thin-walled needle that allows passage of a 0.035-inch guidewire

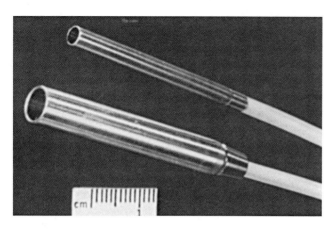

FIGURE 152-3 Comparison of the carriers used for the available models of the Greenfield filter: the 12 French (F) carrier for the modified-hook titanium Greenfield filter (*top*) and the 24F carrier for the stainless steel Greenfield filter (*bottom*).

(Fig. 152-5). The guidewire is passed into the upper reaches of the IVC, after which the dilator-sheath system is introduced and passed into the IVC (Fig. 152-6). The dilator is withdrawn, and the preloaded carrier is passed under fluoroscopic control through the sheath to the desired level of filter placement (Fig. 152-7). If resistance is encountered at the level of the common iliac vein as it angles out of the pelvis, the sheath and carrier should be advanced together, which will usually facilitate passage.

Once the carrier has been seen to exit from the sheath, the base of the sheath is secured to the carrier and the filter tip is positioned at the desired level of introduction (Fig. 152-8). As a unit, the carrier catheter and sheath are retracted to release the filter. The carrier and sheath are then withdrawn, and gentle pressure is applied to the insertion site. An additional advantage to the use of the sheath-carrier is that premature discharge of the filter would be into the sheath rather than into the patient. The filter is preloaded into the carrier system, obviating concern about crossed limbs.

Many percutaneously placed IVC filters are currently in use, but few with long-term performance data. Most studies of these filters are small, and many are retrospective. Percutaneously placed IVC filters in current use are reviewed in the following sections and in Table 152-2.

Bird's Nest Filter

In 1984, Roehm and coworkers[34] reported the use of a percutaneously placed intracaval bird's nest filter that consisted of four stainless steel wires preshaped into a crisscrossing array of nonmatching bends. Placement of such a complex array was intended to provide multiple barriers to thromboemboli. Each of these wires is 25 cm long, is 0.18 mm in diameter, and ends in a strut that is connected to a fixation hook. One strut is Z-shaped, so that a pusher wire can be attached.

As initially described, the device was preloaded into an 8F (polytetrafluoroethylene) catheter. Problems with

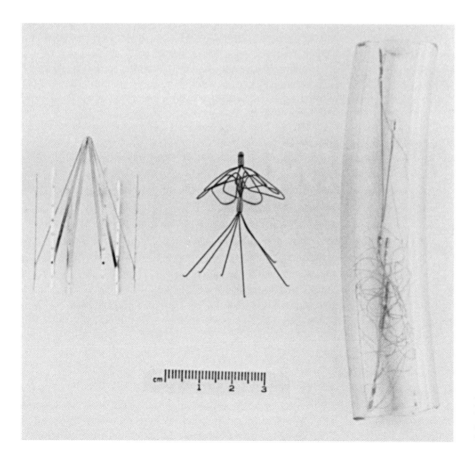

FIGURE 152-4 Commercially available vena caval filter devices: The Vena Tech filter (*left*), the Simon nitinol filter (*center*), and the bird's nest filter (*right*).

Table 152-2   Comparison of Inferior Vena Caval Filters*

PARAMETER	GREENFIELD STAINLESS STEEL[22]	GREENFIELD TITANIUM[61]	VENA TECH[50]	BIRD'S NEST[35]	SIMON NITINOL[45]	GÜNTHER TULIP[73]	TRAPEASE[67]	RECOVERY NITINOL[78]
Type and year of evaluation	Registry (1988)	Clinical trial (1991)	Clinical trial (1990)	Clinical trial (1988)	Clinical trial (1990)	Registry (2001)	Clinical trial (2003)	Clinical trial (2002)
Duration	12 years	30 days	1 year	6 months	6 months	5-420 days	0-24 months	5-134 days
Number of patients	469	186 (154 at follow-up)	97 (77 at follow-up)	568 (440 at 6 months)	224 (102 at follow-up)	90 (39 patients with filter not removed, 25 with follow-up)	189 (152 at 24 months)	32
Rate of recurrent pulmonary embolism (%)	4	3	2	2.7 (33-67 in subset with objective follow-up)	4 based on those with follow-up	None	None suspected	None
Caval patency rate (%)	98	100	92	97	81	99	98.50	100
Filter patency rate (%)	98	Not reported	63 without thrombus	81	Not reported	95.00	98.50	100
Rate of deep venous thrombosis at insertion site (%)	41 (percutaneous)	8.70	23	Few reported clinically	11	None	None	None
Migration rate (%)	35; >3 mm	11; > 9 mm	14; >10 mm	9 with original model	1.2 in those with follow-up	None	None	3 (one filter); >20 mm
Penetration rate (%)	Not reported	1	Not reported	None reported	0.6 in those with follow-up	None reported	0.50	None
Misplacement rate (%)	4	0.50	Not reported	Not reported	Not reported	2.20	Not reported	6.2 (filter tilt >15 degrees)
Rate of incomplete opening (%)	Not seen	2	6	Not reported	Not reported	Not reported	Not reported	3 (unable to advance filter through sheath in one case)
Means of follow-up	Physical exam, IVC scan, x-ray study, noninvasive vascular exam	Physical exam, x-ray study, CT, noninvasive vascular exam	Objective data vary by site (cavogram, CT, duplex scanning, x-ray study)	Phone interview; objective data are random and available for only 40 of 440	Clinical, x-ray, laboratory test	Clinical, duplex scanning, and CT in indicated patients	Clinical, duplex scanning, and CT in indicated patients	Clinical, duplex scanning, and CT in indicated patients
Retrieval rate	Not applicable.	Not applicable	Not applicable	Not applicable	Not applicable	98 by 10 days	Not applicable, only case reports	100 up to 134 days

*Superscript numbers indicate chapter references.
CT, computed tomography; IVC, inferior vena cava; mm, millimeter.

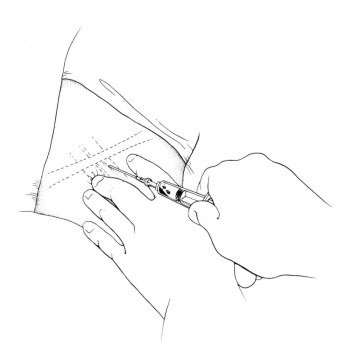

FIGURE 152-5 Percutaneous needle insertion into the common femoral vein is shown medial to the femoral artery, which is palpated with the middle finger. (From Greenfield LJ: Percutaneous placement of the Greenfield filter. In Vanoer Salm TJ, Cutler BS, Wheeler HB [eds]: Atlas of Bedside Procedures, 2nd ed. Boston, Little, Brown, 1988, pp 107-110.)

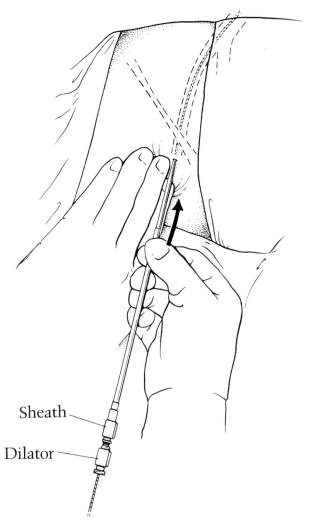

Sheath

Dilator

FIGURE 152-6 The dilator with attached sheath is passed under fluoroscopic guidance over the guidewire to the desired level of discharge of the filter. The dilator and guidewire are withdrawn, leaving the sheath in place. The sheath should then be flushed with heparinized saline. Digital control of the sheath orifice is necessary to minimize blood loss. (From Greenfield LJ: Percutaneous placement of the Greenfield filter. In Vanoer Salm TJ, Cutler BS, Wheeler HB [eds]: Atlas of Bedside Procedures, 2nd ed. Boston, Little, Brown, 1988, pp 107-110.)

proximal migration of this model led to redesign of the struts in 1986, with a stiffer, 0.46-mm wire used in an attempt to improve fixation. This modification required a concomitant increase in diameter of the catheter system to 12F. During placement of this modified device, the pusher is used to set the first group of hooks into the caval wall; the wires are then extruded with the goal of closely packing the formed loops into a 7-cm–long segment of IVC (see Fig. 152-4). Finally, the second group of hooks is pushed into the caval wall. The pusher is then disengaged by being unscrewed from the filter, and the catheter is withdrawn.

Purported but unproven advantages of this device are:

- The ability to trap smaller emboli by virtue of the tighter meshing of wires
- Avoidance of the need for intraluminal centering with this configuration
- The ability to accommodate to venae cavae as large in diameter as 40 mm
- The possibility that wires may be able to occlude nearby collateral vessels
- The lack of radially oriented struts, which limits the tendency toward caval wall penetration

A series of 481 patients in whom the bird's nest filter was placed was reported on in 1988.[35] Only 37 patients with the filter in place 6 months or longer had been studied by venacavography or ultrasonography, so long-term data are limited. Of these patients, 7 (19%) had an occluded vena cava. Three patients underwent pulmonary angiography for suspicion of recurrent embolism, which was confirmed in one case (3%). As indicated previously, the original model showed a troublesome tendency to migrate proximally despite what appeared to be adequate placement. This problem was encountered in 5 patients and resulted in the death of 1; 10 days after placement in this patient, the filter was discovered to be embedded within a massive pulmonary embolus. In a later series of 32 patients in whom the modified strut version was used, three instances of proximal migration were encountered.[36] Two of these occurred within 24 hours of placement and could be corrected by angiographic manipulation. The third instance was not detected until 6 months after insertion, at which point the filter could not be repositioned from the right side of the heart, where it had become embedded.

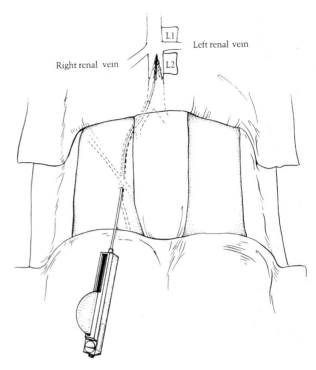

FIGURE 152-8 The carrier tip should be positioned under fluoroscopic guidance at the level of L2-L3. The operator releases the locking mechanism on the control handle by moving the control tab to the left with the thumb. The control tab is then pulled backward to uncover the filter, which is discharged within the vena cava. Once the filter has been discharged, no attempt should be made to alter its position. (From Greenfield LJ: Percutaneous placement of the Greenfield filter. In Vanoer Salm TJ, Cutler BS, Wheeler HB [eds]: Atlas of Bedside Procedures, 2nd ed. Boston, Little, Brown, 1988, pp 107-110.)

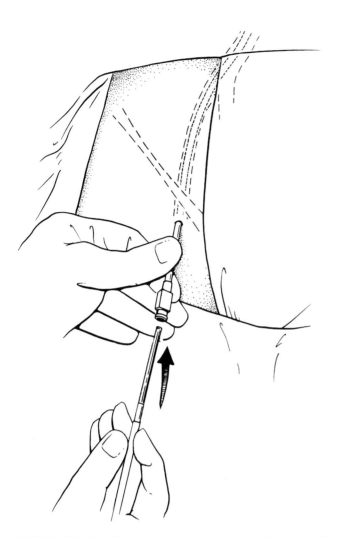

FIGURE 152-7 The filter carrier is introduced into the sheath, and if difficulty is encountered in exiting from the pelvis, both carrier and sheath should be advanced together. The carrier should be advanced through the sheath until the sheath hub contacts the control handle, to prevent release of the filter into the sheath. (From Greenfield LJ: Percutaneous placement of the Greenfield filter. In Vanoer Salm TJ, Cutler BS, Wheeler HB [eds]: Atlas of Bedside Procedures, 2nd ed. Boston, Little, Brown, 1988, pp 107-110.)

Longer-term clinical follow-up of the bird's nest filter in a relatively small group of patients has been reported by Nicholson and colleagues.[37] Seventy-eight consecutive patients with bird's nest filters placed between 1989 and 1994 were recalled for assessment and imaging studies. Imaging consisted of abdominal radiography, color duplex ultrasound evaluation and computed tomography (CT) of the abdomen in the 52 patients that were still alive at the time of the study. According to this study, recurrent pulmonary embolism occurred in 1.3% of patients, and IVC occlusion in 4.7%. Although no filter migration was noted, wire prolapse was visualized in 70% by abdominal plain film. CT showed asymptomatic penetration of the vena caval wall in 85.3% of the patients studied.

Until recently, aortic penetration from the bird's nest filters was not recorded in the literature. However, this event appears to be a potential complication with the bird's nest

filter as it is with filters of other designs.[38] In this particular case, aortic penetration of a bird's nest filter resulted in a clinically significant aortic pseudoaneurysm from penetration of one of the filter struts, which required repair.

The rate of IVC occlusion associated with the bird's nest device appears to be similar to that for other vena cava filters, although estimates range from 0 to 19%.[35,39-41] A retrospective study of 140 patients with bird's nest filters has been reported in the literature. Ninety-three patients were contacted, 7 of whom (7%) were found to have caval thrombosis, 5 with duplex scanning, 2 on the basis of clinical symptoms despite anticoagulation.[42] Although this study may underestimate the rate of IVC thrombosis, the results are comparable to but slighter higher than the rate associated with Greenfield filters.

Simon Nitinol Filter

Nitinol is a nickel-titanium alloy that can be drawn into a straight wire. Although pliable when cooled, it is rapidly transformed into a previously imprinted rigid shape on warming to body temperature. Although a filter composed of this alloy was initially described in 1977, the preliminary results of a multicenter clinical trial were not available until 1989.[43]

The filter design makes use of a 28-mm dome of eight overlapping loops, below which six diverging legs form a cone (see Fig. 152-4). Each leg has end-hooks designed to engage the caval wall. Insertion of this filter requires that iced normal saline be continuously infused through a 9F delivery system to keep the filter cooled. During placement, the cooled filter wire is rapidly advanced by the feeder pump and discharged from the storage catheter. Purportedly, the filter then instantly reshapes itself into its predetermined configuration and locks into place.

The small delivery system has made the Simon nitinol vena cava filter an attractive device for percutaneous placement. In addition, its compact design allows it to be used in patients in whom the distance between the iliac bifurcation and the renal veins is relatively short. However, this same feature may account for the higher than average vena cava occlusion rate associated with the filter.[44]

Of the 103 placements recorded in the initial multicenter trial, detailed information is available on only 44.[43] During a limited follow-up period, 2 patients sustained recurrent PE (5%). In 1 patient, thrombus propagating above the filter was seen on venacavography. There were seven cases of confirmed vena caval occlusion, and in two cases, occlusion was suspected on the basis of clinical findings, yielding an overall caval occlusion rate of 18%. Five patients (11%) had stasis sequelae. Insertion site thrombosis was seen in 5 of 18 patients (28%) studied with ultrasonography. Proximal migration of the filter was noted in 1 patient.

A subsequent report on the use of this device in 224 patients indicated that of the 102 individuals followed up and the 65 in whom 6-month follow-up evaluations had been completed, 4 patients had experienced recurrent embolism (4%) and 1 had died (1%). In addition, there were 20 documented caval occlusions (20%).[45] A smaller series of 20 patients had follow-up information in 16 patients for an average of 14 months. Caval penetration was seen in 5 patients (31%), caval thrombosis was seen in 4 patients (25%), filter migration into the pulmonary artery was found in 1 patient, and filter leg fracture was noted in 2 patients.[4]

In a 1998 series on the long-term performance of the Simon nitinol filter, Poletti and colleagues[46] reported 114 consecutive patients in two institutions with an average follow-up of 27 months (range, 3-63 months) after placement. These investigators prospectively evaluated 38 patients with previously placed nitinol filters by means of abdominal radiography, duplex scanning, and abdominal CT. The remaining patients were retrospectively evaluated from follow-up clinical data. Five patients (4.4%) suffered recurrent PE. DVT was documented in 5.3%, with thrombosis at the access site noted in 3.5%. Filter migration was not found in any of the patients, but the IVC thrombosis rate was 3.5%. The nitinol filter was found to have penetrated the vena cava in 95% of patients and to be in contact with adjacent organs in 76%; however, all of these findings were asymptomatic. Sixty-three percent of filters were eccentrically positioned within the vena cava, and 16% were found to have partial filter disruption that did not appear to affect filter function.[46]

In 2001, Wolfe and associates[47] documented a slightly higher recurrent PE rate, 7.7%, and evidence of vena cava penetration in all 117 patients they studied, although as in the Poletti study, there were no sequelae. Filter strut fracture was noted in 2.9% of patients, and 19% had eccentrically oriented filters. There was no case of IVC thrombosis in this study.[47]

Vena Tech Filters

The Vena Tech filter, introduced in 1986, is a stamped, cone-shaped filter made of Phynox, a material with properties similar to the alloy Elgiloy, which is used in temporary cardiac pacing wires. The filter cone consists of six angled radial prongs, each of which is connected to a hooked stabilizing strut; this array is designed to center and immobilize the device within the vena cava (see Fig. 152-4). It is generally inserted via a right internal jugular approach by means of a 12F catheter system that is positioned over a guidewire, although alternative approaches, such as through the inferior epigastric vein, have been described.[48] After the filter is pushed through the entire length of the insertion catheter, it is released by quick withdrawal of the catheter.

Placement of the Vena Tech filter was described in the "oversized IVC," but the filter was placed in a position below the renal veins, where the vena cava measured less than 28 mm in diameter.[49] This study was conducted in only four patients and without any complications, migration, or occlusion, suggesting that bi–iliac vein filter could be avoided with use of this technique.

The initial reported experience with the Vena Tech filter was from France, where the design was introduced as the LGM filter.[50] In a series of 100 patients, the indication for filter placement was thromboembolism in 77%, prophylaxis in iliocaval thrombosis in 13%, and contraindication to anticoagulation in 9%. As a result, most patients continued anticoagulation therapy after filter placement. In 100 attempted percutaneous insertions via the jugular route, 98 filters were discharged and 82 were positioned correctly. Eight filters had a 15-degree or greater tilt, 5 did not open completely, and 3 other filters had both conditions, resulting in a 16% incidence of malposition. The investigators commented that many of these instances of malpositioning occurred early in their experience and might have been operator dependent. Recurrent PE was seen in 2 patients (2%), both of whom had incompletely opened filters. One-year follow-up demonstrated seven caval occlusions (8%). Twenty-nine per cent of patients had lower extremity edema despite the use of support stockings. Migration of the device both proximally to the renal veins (4%) and distally to the iliac veins (9%) was observed.

Another small series reported a 2.5% incidence of recurrent embolism and an occlusion rate of 8%.[51] There was a 13% rate of either tilting or incomplete opening, and a similar rate of distal migration. A later experience with this filter showed an occlusion rate of 22%.[52] Breakage of stabilizer struts has also been reported in individual cases.[53] Long-term studies of this device by Crochet and associates[54] have demonstrated that there has been a 37% incidence of filter occlusion with this device over time, and laboratory studies in sheep demonstrated a strong association between duration of placement and increased amounts of hyperplastic tissue, which could be seen as early as 8 weeks after placement.

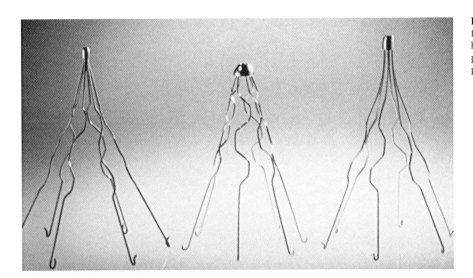

FIGURE 152-12 The three marketed Greenfield filters have similar conical shapes, which have demonstrated long-term protection from pulmonary embolism while maintaining caval patency in more than 95% of cases.

In 2001, a small French multicenter prospective trial was conducted to evaluate the nitinol TrapEase IVC filter.[66] A total of 65 patients who had DVT with recurrent PE, free-floating thrombus, or both with a contraindication to anticoagulation (37 patients), or with complications in achieving adequate anticoagulation (28 patients) were enrolled in 12 centers throughout Europe and Canada. The patients were evaluated at 10 days, and 1, 3, and 6 months with clinical examination, abdominal radiography, duplex scanning, and abdominal CT. The investigators noted a 95.4% technical success rate in filter placement and a clinical success rate of 100% at 6 months (no symptomatic PE). They noted no filter migration, filter fracture, vessel wall penetration, or insertion site thrombosis during this short time. Two patients had early (within 30 days) IVC thrombosis; one case was symptomatic (1.5%) and was treated with thrombolysis, and the other was asymptomatic. The full 6-month follow-up was completed in only 42 of the 65 patients owing to 23 deaths unrelated to the filter.

A second study of the filter, although retrospective, is interesting. Schutzer and coworkers[67] retrospectively reviewed 189 consecutively infrarenal TrapEase filter placements at a single institution over 22 months. The filter was successfully deployed in all cases. Although follow-up evaluations were performed only when clinically indicated, the study appears to confirm the symptomatic vena cava thrombosis rate of 1.5% (3 patients).[67] The investigators also noted a single retroperitoneal hemorrhage potentially caused by filter placement. This is also the first study to report a symptomatic PE after TrapEase filter placement.

Although neither of the preceding studies documented filter migration, there has been one case report in the literature of intracardiac migration of the TrapEase filter, suggesting that it can occur.[68] In addition, the symptomatic IVC thrombosis rate documented in the two previous studies is well within acceptable limits, but later reports to the FDA of IVC thrombosis associated with the TrapEase filter[69] are very concerning. Whether this finding represents effective filtering of multiple small thrombi or a large PE resulting in filter occlusion and IVC thrombosis, or is a potential adverse

consequence of the filter's design is currently unknown. IVC occlusion rates may also be influenced by the methodology of studies—whether all patients are screened for IVC thrombosis or only those patients with apparent venous insufficiency. In any case, more follow-up data are needed to fully evaluate the risks associated with the TrapEase filter.

Günther Tulip Filter

The Günther Tulip filter was approved for use in the United States in 2001, although it has been used in Europe since 1992. It is used primarily as an IVC filter although it has been placed in the SVC.[70] The filter is composed of Elgiloy and employs a conical design with an apical hook for manipulation or removal. The filter is made of 0.4-mm–diameter wires with four elongated wire loops that

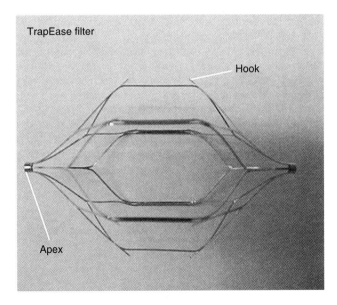

FIGURE 152-13 The TrapEase vena cava filter.

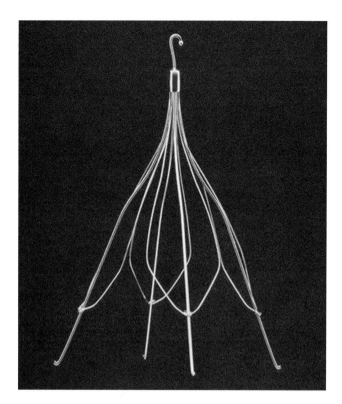

FIGURE 152-14   The Günther Tulip vena cava filter.

extend three quarters of the way from the apex to the hooked ends of the four main cross-struts. The filter is fixed to the vena cava by means of 1-mm hooks at the inferior ends of the four main cross-struts (Fig. 152-14).[56] The filter may be placed either through a preloaded 80-cm femoral 8.5F sheath or through a manually loaded 45-cm jugular sheath. In the United States, the filter is approved by the FDA only as a permanent device, but it is currently being used as a retrievable filter in Europe and Canada.

The initial results with the Günther Tulip filter in early studies were somewhat mixed,[71,72] and there is surprisingly little data on the long-term performance of the filter in the literature, because most studies focused on short-term performance and filter retrieval. When a permanent filter is required, the Günther Tulip filter is frequently removed and replaced with a different type of permanent filter.[73]

One study that evaluated the long-term performance of the Günther Tulip filter had a mean follow-up of 136 days (range, 3 days to 3 years), with follow-up longer than 180 days in only 30 patients.[74] This study used an older stainless steel version of the filter and reports the results of filter placement in 83 patients. There is complete follow-up on 75 of the patients; two filters were removed without complication within 11 days, and 6 patients were lost to follow-up. The investigators noted recurrent PE in 3 patients (4%, one fatal), filter tilting in 3 patients (4%, 1 to 90 degrees causing asymptomatic vena cava penetration), overall silent penetration in 2 patients (2.7%), complete caval obstruction in 5 patients (6.7%), and partial caval obstruction in 3 patients (4%). They found no insertion site thrombosis, and migration of the filter occurred in only 3 patients (4%).

A second, smaller study with a total enrollment of 15 patients, which was designed to evaluate filter retrieval, included a subgroup of 5 patients in whom the Günther Tulip filter was left in place owing to a continued contraindication to anticoagulation and filter retrieval. Of these 5 patients with mean follow-up of 39 days (10 to 94 days), 1 patient had an IVC thrombosis to the level of the filter. The remaining patients had no thrombosis, recurrent PE, or filter migration.[75]

Millward and colleagues[73] expanded upon their earlier smaller study, reporting results of the placement of Günther Tulip filters from eight hospitals and in 90 patients. The indications for vena cava filter placement were for PE or DVT with a contraindication for anticoagulation in 83 patients, prophylaxis for proximal free-floating thrombus in 1 patient, and prophylaxis with no DVT or PE in 6 patients (major trauma in 4, major preoperative risk in 2). Filter retrieval was attempted in 52 patients with 53 filters and was successful with 52 filters. The duration of filter implantation was 2 to 25 days, with a mean implantation time of 9 days. The 51 patients were monitored for a mean of 103 days after filter retrieval. Four patients (8%) required re-insertion of a permanent filter from 17 to 167 days after filter removal, because of either bleeding from anticoagulation or requirement for further surgery. Of the patients in whom the filters were successfully retrieved, 1 patient had recurrent DVT at 230 days after filter retrieval. In the 39 patients in whom the filter was not retrieved (with a mean follow-up of 85 days), two filter occlusions (5%) were noted. No other complications of filter placement were described.

The latest study reviewed 75 Günther Tulip filter placements. The rate of technically successful insertion was 97.3%. Of the initial 71 patients, 18 died from unrelated causes, and 6 were too ill to undergo retrieval of the filter. Of the 49 patients in whom filter retrieval was planned, retrieval was successful in only 35 (81%), because of large trapped thrombi in the other 14 patients. The mean implantation time for retrieved filters was 8.2 days (range, 1 to 13 days). Delivery tilt was observed in 16% of retrieved filters. Filter tilt and migration were noted in 22% of non-retrieved filters with a mean follow-up time of 30 months. The investigators noted no other complications associated with the Günther Tulip filter.[76]

Recovery Nitinol Filter

The Recovery nitinol filter is the latest device design tested in humans. The filter is constructed of 12 0.13-mm nitinol wires that extend from a nitinol sleeve. These 12 wires are divided into six separate arms and six legs with fixation hooks that create a two-tiered conical device whose arms and legs extend from the apex of the device (Fig. 152-15). The filter's arms extend to 30.5 mm resting diameter, and the legs to a resting diameter of 32 mm. The filter is 40 mm in length. It is inserted through a 6F femoral sheath and can be retrieved through a 10F jugular sheath. The retrieval implement is a specially designed conical device (15 mm when open) with nine metal claws covered by a polyurethane cover.[77] The filter is intended for use in venae cavae 28 mm in diameter or smaller.

Given the recent development of the Recovery nitinol filter, there is only one report in the literature of the device

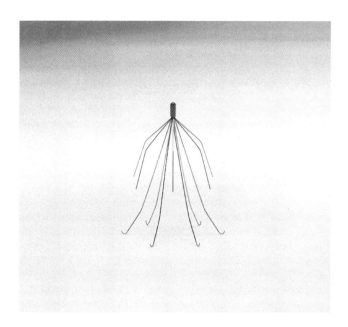

FIGURE 152-15 The Recovery nitinol filter. (Reprinted with permission from Asch MR: Initial experience in humans with a new retrievable inferior vena cava filter. Radiology 225:835-844, 2002.)

placed in 32 patients.[78] The indications for filter placement were typical. The filter was placed successfully in all 32 patients and retrieved in all patients in whom removal was attempted (n = 24). The mean implantation time was rather long, at 53 days (range, 5 to 134 days). There were no recurrent PEs in any of the patients enrolled in the study, with evidence of captured thrombus in seven filters, and there was no evidence of insertion-site thrombosis. One filter migrated 4 cm cephalad due to a large captured thromboembolus. Obviously, the combination of the filter's migration on capturing a large thrombus and the ease with which the filter may be retrieved after long periods of implantation in the IVC raise concerns about the device's ability to adequately adhere to the vena cava wall. Further investigation of this potentially promising device is needed.

Temporary and Retrievable Filters

Interest in a vena cava filter that could be removed in whole or part has been expressed by some orthopedic and trauma surgeons and is the subject of intense investigation today. The rationale is simple. In many cases, there is a very limited period of risk, and surgeons do not want to leave a permanent device in a young person with years of life expectancy.

The drive for a retrievable filter was greatly accelerated by a study describing the only randomized prospective clinical trial to evaluate the overall efficacy of vena cava filters (the PREPIC trial).[79] In this study, 400 patients with DVT were randomly assigned to placement of one of four types of vena cava filters (Vena Tech-LGM, titanium Greenfield, Cardial, or bird's nest) or no filter. All patients received either low-molecular-weight or unfractionated heparin. Patients were monitored for up to 2 years with ventilation-perfusion scans initially and clinical assessments

throughout the follow-up period. In essence, this study showed that at day 12 of the study, there was a significantly lower rate of PE in patients with vena cava filters (1.1% vs. 4.8%), but that at 2 years, there was no difference between the groups. Additionally, patients in the vena cava filter group experienced a higher rate of recurrent DVT (20.8% vs. 11.6%), possibly related to the presence of the filter itself.

Although this study makes no effort to compare the different filters employed, its findings do suggest that the benefit of vena cava filters may apply early in the presence of DVT and that filters may promote recurrent DVT at later times. Both of these points support the concept of retrievable filters.

Follow-up data for the patients enrolled in the PREPIC trial at 5 years[80] and 8 years[81] are interesting. The initial beneficial effect of vena cava filters endured but still did not affect overall mortality rates of the groups, which remained similar at about 50%. Recurrent DVT, which occurred at a higher rate in the filter group at 2 years, was found in 53 patients (34.7%) assigned to the filter group and 39 patients (27.3%) in the group without filters at 5 years ($P = .06$). At 8 years, the recurrent DVT rate in the filter group remained unchanged at 53 patients (37.1%) but increased to 40 patients (27.3%) in the no-filter group ($P = .08$). These unpublished 5- and 8-year data suggest that there is no significant difference in the rate of DVT in the group with filters in the long-term, in contrast to findings of the initial study.[79]

Proponents of retrievable filters also argue that many patients (such as trauma victims and orthopedic patients) require protection from a PE for only a short time. Permanent presence of a filter would put an otherwise healthy patient, remote from the trauma or orthopedic surgery, at risk for the complications associated with long-term filter placement, such as filter migration, fracture, vena cava penetration, and IVC occlusion, a risk that may rise over time.

By definition, temporary filters are filters that remain connected extracorporeally by means of a catheter or sheath and may be considered useful if thromboembolectomy is being performed or for very transient contraindications for anticoagulation. Temporary filters have been in use in Europe but have not been approved in the United States. The results of one large multicenter registry investigating several temporary vena cava filters were not encouraging.[82] Of the 188 patients undergoing temporary filter placement, 4 died of pulmonary embolism during filter protection, and filter thrombosis occurred in 16%. As would be expected of a device anchored extracorporeally, filter dislocation was also a problem. Although not seen in this study, the risk of infection also limits use of temporary filter devices. Despite these results, there are numerous case reports of the use of temporary vena cava filters in pregnancy,[83] trauma,[84] and in the SVC.[85]

Current trends in North America suggest that there will be a very limited role for temporary filters in the daily routine of most surgeons and interventionists. Emphasis has instead been placed on new filter designs that are categorized as retrievable. Retrievable filters are placed much like permanent filters but are designed to be removed through a separate percutaneous procedure at a later time.

Several permanent filters currently are available that have been modified with apical hooks for retrieval and potential use as retrievable filters. These filters, as a whole, can be left in place as permanent filter devices but retain the option of retrieval via a right internal jugular approach.

Timing of retrievable filter removal has been somewhat problematic, with conflicting animal and human data. Most manufacturers of retrievable filters currently recommend removal no later than 10 days after placement, and most early studies with these filters adhere to this recommendation. The 10-day time limit for removal appears to be based on data from animal studies that evaluated the extent to which the filter incorporated itself into the vena cava. In the case of the Günther Tulip filter, studies in dogs and pigs reveal significant difficulty in retrieving the filter after 3 weeks because of incorporation of the filter into the vena caval wall.[86,87] In humans, however, there are reports of removal of the Günther Tulip filter as late as 67 days after placement.[88] Other investigators have chosen to reposition the filter several times within the 10-day period in order to extend the time the Günther Tulip can be safely left in place.[88] Unfortunately, repositioning a filter many times for this reason increases the cost and potentially exposes the patient to greater complications. Devices such as the Recovery nitinol filter may be advantageous in this concern. Clearly, the field of retrievable filters is evolving, and further study on how long a retrievable filter can be left in place and then safely removed with minimal risk to the patient is needed.

Retrievable vena caval filters have been successfully utilized in treatment and prophylaxis of PE in young trauma patients who cannot undergo anticoagulation.[89] Placement of retrievable filters in this group of patients (young age, temporary immobilization, presence of fractures or splenic and hepatic injuries, expectant surgical management) makes sense and avoids the potential pitfalls of permanent vena cava filter placement, such as vena cava occlusion, recurrent DVT, and filter migration.

■ VENA CAVAL INTERRUPTION IN TRAUMA PATIENTS

Trauma patients identified as being at high risk for DVT and subsequent PE (>21 to 54 times the risk in the general trauma population) are candidates for prophylactic IVC filter placement. This is a relative indication for filter placement. Those at highest risk include patients with (1) severe head injury and coma, (2) spinal cord injuries with neurologic deficit, and (3) pelvic and long bone fractures.[15] Therapeutically, and more recently prophylactically, placed IVC filters have been increasingly used in this group of patients over the last decade, with good results and minimal complications.

Wojcik and associates[90] reported a series of 105 blunt trauma victims who were treated with permanent IVC filters for treatment of DVT and prophylaxis, with a mean follow-up of 29 months.[90] In this series, there were no PEs in the patients in whom filters were placed, and no patients experienced any clinically identifiable complications related to insertion of the vena caval filters. In follow-up, the researchers noted minimal migration of only one filter and one vena cava occlusion (0.95%). However, 11 patients

(10.4%) experienced symptoms of leg swelling after hospital discharge, and 28 of the 64 patients with prophylactically placed vena caval filters had a DVT after filter placement.

Other studies report similar results with early prophylactic placement of vena cava filters in trauma victims. In one study of Greenfield filters placed within 48 hours, PE-related mortality decreased from 17% to 2.5%, and in only 2 of 40 patients did significant venous stasis of the lower extremities develop.[14] One significant criticism of this study is the rather high baseline PE rate in trauma patients (17%). A follow-up to this study, by the same investigators, demonstrated similar results, with no documented PEs. Thirteen patients in the historically matched control group (13 out of 216; 6%), however, had PEs, 9 of which were fatal. The differences in the rate of PE and PE-related death between the treatment and control groups were highly statistically significant.[13] Unfortunately, prophylactic placement of IVC filters did not influence the overall mortality rate, which was similar in the treatment and control groups.

These and other data appear to support prophylactic placement of vena cava filters in trauma patients at high risk for DVT and PE. These patients are generally young with a defined period during which they are at risk for PE. It is intuitive that the use of a retrievable filter in this select group might be beneficial, thereby treating the potential PE and decreasing or eliminating the risks of long-term filter placement. This intuitive judgment, however, must be borne out by further studies.

■ VENA CAVAL INTERRUPTION IN MALIGNANT DISEASE

Since Trousseau[91] first described an association between PE and cancer in 1865, studies have confirmed that patients with malignant disease are at increased risk of PE. The reported incidence of PE in the literature is somewhere between 7% and 50% in patients with malignancy.[92] In fact, two studies have estimated the risks of PE to be approximately 3.6-fold higher in patients with cancer than in patients without malignancy.[93,94] Unfortunately, these same patients at increased risk for DVT and PE also appear to be at higher risk of bleeding while undergoing anticoagulation therapy.[93,95,96]

Debate in the literature on the role of vena caval filters in patients with malignant disease began in the 1990s[17,18] and continues today. Although the filters are commonly used in cancer patients with contraindications to anticoagulation or with recurrent PE, attempts to address the question have not led to a definitive answer.

A retrospective study reported in 2002 questioned the clinical benefit of vena caval filter placement in patients with malignant disease. Jarrett and colleagues[97] reported the outcomes in 116 patients over an 8-year period (1993-2000) who underwent Greenfield filter placement. These patients had a wide array of primary tumors (25 gastrointestinal, 24 lung, 14 breast, 14 gynecologic, 12 prostate, 8 hematologic, 4 genitourinary, and 15 other tumors), and indications for filter placement were standard. Procedural complications were negligible. Two patients had clinically apparent recurrent PEs, and an additional two patients had progressive

DVT after vena caval filter placement. Life-table analysis of the patients in this study revealed survival rates of 68.8% at 30 days, 49.4% at 3 months, and 26.8% at 1 year. Of the 91 patients with stage IV disease, 42 had died at 6 weeks, and only 13 were alive at 1 year. The investigators suggest that vena caval filter placement may not clinically benefit the patient with cancer and may not be a cost-effective measure, given the overall survival rates.

A second retrospective study was conducted in an attempt to determine whether patients with cancer benefit from placement of vena cava filters.[92] Ninety-nine patients were enrolled in this study. Lin and coworkers[92] noted that in 55% of patients, PE was the presenting symptom of newly metastatic disease, and that in 12% of patients, the diagnosis of PE predated the diagnosis of malignancy. Acute PE was present in 52% of patients at cancer diagnosis, and 34% of the patients' PEs were associated with new metastases. The researchers identified several risk factors for the 40% rate of recurrent PE in these patients: the presence of new metastasis (odds ratio [OR], 3.3), history of PE (OR, 10.6), and multiple neutropenic episodes ($P = .04$). Mean survival in this study was 30 months; survival was significantly worse in patients who had PE at cancer diagnosis and were unable to tolerate anticoagulant therapy in conjunction with vena caval filter placement. This study suggests there may be a benefit to the placement of vena caval filters in the subgroup of patients who have newly diagnosed metastatic disease or a history of PE, or who experience multiple episodes of neutropenia, assuming that their quality of life and life expectancy are reasonable.

In order to answer the question of the cost-effectiveness of vena caval filter placement in patients with cancer, Marcy and colleagues[98] retrospectively reviewed data on a total of 30 patients treated from 1994 to 2000 at one hospital. Six of the 30 patients expired before discharge, and 2 died from renal vein thrombosis after suprarenal IVC filter placement. Nevertheless, 76% of patients were alive at 1 month, 56% at 3 months, and 40% at 6 months, with an improved quality of survival in at least 53% of the patients. The investigators argue that the low complication rate and low cost relative to the mean cost of hospitalization for PE (2%) favor IVC filter placement if it is medically indicated.

Clearly, the issues of placing prophylactic vena cava filters in patients with malignancy are complex. It appears that there may be a subgroup of patients who will benefit from placement of filters early in the course of their disease. Patients with cancer who have the standard indications for filter placement should not be denied the procedure on a fiscal basis.

■ VENA CAVAL INTERRUPTION IN SEPSIS

Septic patients are at risk for DVT and subsequent thromboembolism, but the FDA guidelines for intravascular filters state that "filters should not be implanted in patients with risk of septic embolism."[99] In the case of a septic patient with a contraindication to anticoagulation, the physician must choose between placing a vena cava filter in contravention to FDA guidelines and leaving the patient at serious and increased risk of PE. This dictum has now been challenged.

A review of a large registry of 2600 patients in whom Greenfield filters had been placed over a 15-year period suggests that filter placement may be a safe method of PE prophylaxis in septic patients.[100] Identifying 175 patients with the diagnosis of sepsis at the time of vena cava filter placement, the investigators reviewed survival rates, adverse events, and recurrent sepsis or clinical sequelae of filter placement. They noted an initial 33% mortality rate in the study group; however, the mortality leveled out over time, suggesting that the cause of death is related not to filter placement but rather to the process of sepsis itself. No filters were removed from any patient, and the recurrent PE rate was 1.7%. Interestingly, the patients who underwent anticoagulation in addition to vena cava filter placement faired significantly better than those that did not.

There are several reasons that sepsis may not negatively influence outcomes in septic patients in whom filters are placed. The filters employed in this study are made of titanium and stainless steel, both inert materials, and in early animal studies, septic thrombus captured in these filters has been shown to be sterilized with administration of appropriate antibiotics.[101,102] In these studies, either embolized septic thrombi or thrombi infected after capture by the filter were sterilized by administration of appropriate intravenous antibiotics.

Thus, it appears that vena cava filter placement in septic patients receiving appropriate antibiotics, especially patients with contraindications to anticoagulation, may be of benefit, given the hypercoagulable state associated with the disease process.

■ SUMMARY

There is considerable ingenuity in the numerous devices now available for clinical use as vena caval filters. The primary objective—to provide a safe and effective device for temporary or permanent implantation—should lead to continued evolution of materials and design. The standard for comparison, however, should remain the stainless steel Greenfield filter, for which long-term follow-up data are available beginning with its introduction in 1972. It seems clear that advances in retrievable filters will affect the current practice patterns of the surgeon and the interventionist, but the long-term safety and efficacy of the conical design of the Greenfield filter suggest that a new design may not be needed. The benefits of retrievable filters are largely theoretical at this point and need to be proved by well-designed studies.

In the overall management of the patient with thrombotic disease, it is imperative to understand that any filtration device plays only a limited role, to provide protection against PE. The physician who treats the patient must assume the responsibility for the ongoing management and long-term follow-up of the underlying thrombotic disorder.

■ REFERENCES

1. Nasbeth D, Moran J: Reassessment of the role of inferior vena cava ligation in thromboembolism. N Engl J Med 273:1250-1253, 1965.
2. Amador E, Ting K, Crane C: Ligation of inferior vena cava for thromboembolism. JAMA 206:441-443, 1968.

3. Ferris EJ, Vittimberga J, Byrne JJ, et al: The inferior vena cava ligation and plication: A study of collateral routes. Radiology 89:1-10, 1967.

4. Miller TD, Staats BA: Impaired exercise tolerance after inferior vena caval interruption. Chest 93:776-780, 1988.

5. Adams JT, De Weese JA: Partial interruption of the inferior vena cava with a new plastic clip. Surg Gynecol Obstet 123:1087-1088, 1966.

6. Hye RJ, Mitchell AT, Dory CE, et al: Analysis of the transition to percutaneous placement of Greenfield filters. Arch Surg 125:1550-1553, 1990.

7. Spencer F: Plication of the vena cava for pulmonary embolism. Surgery 62:388-392, 1967.

8. Askew AR, Gardner AM: Long-term follow-up of partial caval occlusion by clip. Am J Surg 140:441-443, 1980.

9. Couch NP, Baldwin SS, Crane C: Mortality and morbidity rates after inferior vena caval clipping. Surgery 77:106-112, 1975.

10. DeMeester TR, Rutherford R, Blazek J: Plication of the inferior vena cava for thromboembolism. Surgery 62:56-65, 1967.

11. Cimochowski GE, Evans RH, Zarins CK, et al: Greenfield filter versus Mobin-Uddin umbrella: The continuing quest for the ideal method of vena caval interruption. J Thorac Cardiovasc Surg 79:358-365, 1980.

12. Pacouret G, Alison D, Pottier JM, et al: Free-floating thrombus and embolic risk in patients with angiographically confirmed proximal deep venous thrombosis: A prospective study. Arch Intern Med 157:305-308, 1997.

13. Khansarinia S, Dennis JW, Veldenz HC, et al: Prophylactic Greenfield filter placement in selected high-risk trauma patients. J Vasc Surg 22:231-235, 1995.

14. Rodriguez JL, Lopez JM, Proctor MC, et al: Early placement of prophylactic vena caval filters in injured patients at high risk for pulmonary embolism. J Trauma 40:797-802, 1996.

15. Rogers FB, Shackford SR, Wilson J, et al: Prophylactic vena cava filter insertion in severely injured trauma patients: Indications and preliminary results. J Trauma 35:637-641, 1993.

16. Cohen JR, Tenenbaum N, Citron M: Greenfield filter as primary therapy for deep venous thrombosis and/or pulmonary embolism in patients with cancer. Surgery 109:12-15, 1991.

17. Lossef SV, Barth KH: Outcome of patients with advanced neoplastic disease receiving vena caval filters. J Vasc Interv Radiol 6:273-277, 1995.

18. Rosen MP, Porter DH, Kim D: Reassessment of vena caval filter use in patients with cancer. J Vasc Interv Radiol 5:501-506, 1994.

19. Fink JA, Jones BT: The Greenfield filter as the primary means of therapy in venous thromboembolic disease. Surg Gynecol Obstet 172:253-256, 1991.

20. Greenfield LJ, McCurdy JR, Brown PP, Elkins RC: A new intracaval filter permitting continued flow and resolution of emboli. Surgery 73:599-606, 1973.

21. Verstraete M: Thrombolytic treatment. BMJ 311:582-583, 1995.

22. Greenfield LJ, Michna BA: Twelve-year clinical experience with the Greenfield vena caval filter. Surgery 104:706-712, 1988.

23. Gomez GA, Cutler BS, Wheeler HB: Transvenous interruption of the inferior vena cava. Surgery 93:612-619, 1983.

24. Greenfield LJ, Proctor MC: Twenty-year clinical experience with the Greenfield filter. Cardiovasc Surg 3:199-205, 1995.

25. Greenfield LJ, Cho KJ, Proctor MC, et al: Late results of suprarenal Greenfield vena cava filter placement. Arch Surg 127:969-973, 1992.

26. Peyton JW, Hylemon MB, Greenfield LJ, et al: Comparison of Greenfield filter and vena caval ligation for experimental septic thromboembolism. Surgery 93:533-537, 1983.

27. Danetz JS, McLafferty RB, Ayerdi J, et al: Selective venography versus nonselective venography before vena cava filter placement: Evidence for more, not less. J Vasc Surg 38:928-934, 2003.

28. Gamblin TC, Ashley DW, Burch S, Solis M: A prospective evaluation of a bedside technique for placement of inferior vena cava filters:

Accuracy and limitations of intravascular ultrasound. Am Surg 69:382-386, 2003.

29. Matsuura JH, White RA, Kopchok G, et al: Vena caval filter placement by intravascular ultrasound. Cardiovasc Surg 9:571-574, 2001.

30. Neuzil DF, Garrard CL, Berkman RA, et al: Duplex-directed vena caval filter placement: Report of initial experience. Surgery 123:470-474, 1998.

31. Connors MS III, Becker S, Guzman RJ, et al: Duplex scan-directed placement of inferior vena cava filters: A five-year institutional experience. J Vasc Surg 35:286-291, 2002.

32. Bhatia RS, Collingwood P, Bartlett P: Radiologic versus surgical placement of vena cava filters: A comparative study of cost, time and complications. Can Assoc Radiol J 49:79-83, 1998.

33. Kantor A, Glanz S, Gordon DH, Sclafani SJ: Percutaneous insertion of the Kimray-Greenfield filter: Incidence of femoral vein thrombosis. AJR Am J Roentgenol 149:1065-1066, 1987.

34. Roehm JO Jr, Gianturco C, Barth MH, Wright KC: Percutaneous transcatheter filter for the inferior vena cava: A new device for treatment of patients with pulmonary embolism. Radiology 150:255-257, 1984.

35. Roehm JO Jr, Johnsrude IS, Barth MH, Gianturco C: The bird's nest inferior vena cava filter: Progress report. Radiology 168:745-749, 1988.

36. McCowan T, Ferris EJ, Keifsteck J: Retrieval of dislodged bird's nest inferior vena cava filter: Progress report. J Interv Radiol 3:179, 1988.

37. Nicholson AA, Ettles DF, Paddon AJ, Dyet JF: Long-term follow-up of the bird's nest IVC filter. Clin Radiol 54:759-764, 1999.

38. Campbell JJ, Calcagno D: Aortic pseudoaneurysm from aortic penetration with a bird's nest vena cava filter. J Vasc Surg 38:596-599, 2003.

39. Mohan CR, Hoballah JJ, Sharp WJ, et al: Comparative efficacy and complications of vena caval filters. J Vasc Surg 21:235-245, 1995.

40. Becker DM, Philbrick JT, Selby JB: Inferior vena cava filters: Indications, safety, effectiveness. Arch Intern Med 152:1985-1994, 1992.

41. Lord RS, Benn I: Early and late results after bird's nest filter placement in the inferior vena cava: Clinical and duplex ultrasound follow up. Aust N Z J Surg 64:106-114, 1994.

42. Thomas JH, Cornell KM, Siegel EL, et al: Vena caval occlusion after bird's nest filter placement. Am J Surg 176:598-600, 1998.

43. Simon M, Athanasoulis CA, Kim D, et al: Simon nitinol inferior vena cava filter: Initial clinical experience. Work in progress. Radiology 172:99-103, 1989.

44. Leask RL, Johnston KW, Ojha M: In vitro hemodynamic evaluation of a Simon nitinol vena cava filter: Possible explanation of IVC occlusion. J Vasc Interv Radiol 12:613-618, 2001.

45. Dorfman GS: Percutaneous inferior vena caval filters. Radiology 174:987-992, 1990.

46. Poletti PA, Becker CD, Prina L, et al: Long-term results of the Simon nitinol inferior vena cava filter. Eur Radiol 8:289-294, 1998.

47. Wolfe F, Thurnher S, Lammer J: [Simon nitinol vena cava filters: Effectiveness and complications]. Rofo Fortschr Geb Rontgenstr Neuen Bildgeb Verfahr 173:924-930, 2001.

48. Danikas D, Theodorou SJ, Ginalis EM, et al: Vena cava filter placement using a cutdown of the superficial epigastric vein. Vasc Endovascular Surg 36:381-384, 2002.

49. Millward SF, Aquino J Jr, Peterson RA: Oversized inferior vena cava: Use of a single Vena Tech–LGM filter. Can Assoc Radiol J 47:272-274, 1996.

50. Ricco JB, Crochet D, Sebilotte P, et al: Percutaneous transvenous caval interruption with the "LGM" filter: Early results of a multicenter trial. Ann Vasc Surg 2:242-247, 1988.

51. Maquin P, Fajadet E, Carver D: LGM and Gunther: Two complementary vena cava filters. Radiology 173:476, 1988.

52. Millward SF, Marsh JI, Peterson RA, et al: LGM (Vena Tech) vena cava filter: Clinical experience in 64 patients. J Vasc Interv Radiol 2:429-433, 1991.

53. Awh MH, Taylor FC, Lu CT: Spontaneous fracture of a Vena-Tech inferior vena caval filter. AJR Am J Roentgenol 157:177-178, 1991.

54. Crochet DP, Stora O, Ferry D, et al: Vena Tech-LGM filter: Long-term results of a prospective study. Radiology 188:857-860, 1993.

55. Crochet DP, Brunel P, Trogrlic S, et al: Long-term follow-up of Vena Tech-LGM filter: Predictors and frequency of caval occlusion. J Vasc Interv Radiol 10:137-142, 1999.

56. Kinney TB: Update on inferior vena cava filters. J Vasc Interv Radiol 14:425-440, 2003.

57. Greenfield LJ, Savin MA: Comparison of titanium and stainless steel, Greenfield vena caval filters. Surgery 106:820-828, 1989.

58. Greenfield LJ, Cho KJ, Pais SO, Van Aman M: Preliminary clinical experience with the titanium Greenfield vena caval filter. Arch Surg 124:657-659, 1989.

59. Greenfield LJ, Cho KJ, Tauscher JR: Evolution of hook design for fixation of the titanium Greenfield filter. J Vasc Surg 12:345-353, 1990.

60. Sherman PM, Soares GM, Dick EJ, et al: In vivo evaluation of the effects of gravitational force (+Gz) on over-the-wire stainless steel Greenfield inferior vena cava filter in swine. Cardiovasc Intervent Radiol 26:386-394, 2003.

61. Greenfield LJ, Cho KJ, Proctor M, et al: Results of a multicenter study of the modified hook-titanium Greenfield filter. J Vasc Surg 14:253-257, 1991.

62. Greenfield LJ, Proctor MC, Cho KJ, et al: Extended evaluation of the titanium Greenfield vena caval filter. J Vasc Surg 20:458-464, 1994.

63. Cho KJ, Greenfield LJ, Proctor MC, et al: Evaluation of a new percutaneous stainless steel Greenfield filter. J Vasc Interv Radiol 8:181-187, 1997.

64. Nutting C, Coldwell D: Use of a TrapEase device as a temporary caval filter. J Vasc Interv Radiol 12:991-993, 2001.

65. Davison BD, Grassi CJ: TrapEase inferior vena cava filter placed via the basilic arm vein: A new antecubital access. J Vasc Interv Radiol 13:107-109, 2002.

66. Rousseau H, Perreault P, Otal P, et al: The 6-F nitinol TrapEase inferior vena cava filter: Results of a prospective multicenter trial. J Vasc Interv Radiol 12:299-304, 2001.

67. Schutzer R, Ascher E, Hingorani A, et al: Preliminary results of the new 6F TrapEase inferior vena cava filter. Ann Vasc Surg 17:103-106, 2003.

68. Porcellini M, Stassano P, Musumeci A, Bracale G: Intracardiac migration of nitinol TrapEase vena cava filter and paradoxical embolism. Eur J Cardiothorac Surg 22:460-461, 2002.

69. U.S. Food and Drug Administration, Center for Devices and Radiological Health: MAUDE database. Online at: www.accessdata.fda.gov/scripts/cdrh/cfdocs/cfMAUDE/search.cfm.

70. Nadkarni S, Macdonald S, Cleveland TJ, Gaines PA: Placement of a retrievable Gunther Tulip filter in the superior vena cava for upper extremity deep venous thrombosis. Cardiovasc Intervent Radiol 25:524-526, 2002.

71. Grabenwoger F, Dock W, Metz V, et al: [Percutaneous transluminal implantation of the Gunther cava filter: Experience based on 22 patients]. Rofo Fortschr Geb Rontgenstr Neuen Bildgeb Verfahr 155:405-408, 1991.

72. Schweizer J, Altmann E, Schmidt PK, et al: [Experiences with the Gunther filter]. Z Gesamte Inn Med 46:483-485, 1991.

73. Millward SF, Oliva VL, Bell SD, et al: Gunther Tulip retrievable vena cava filter: Results from the Registry of the Canadian Interventional Radiology Association. J Vasc Interv Radiol 12:1053-1058, 2001.

74. Neuerburg JM, Gunther RW, Vorwerk D, et al: Results of a multicenter study of the retrievable Tulip Vena Cava Filter: Early clinical experience. Cardiovasc Intervent Radiol 20:10-16, 1997.

75. Millward SF, Bhargava A, Aquino J Jr, et al: Gunther Tulip filter: Preliminary clinical experience with retrieval. J Vasc Interv Radiol 11:75-82, 2000.

76. Wicky S, Doenz F, Meuwly JY, et al: Clinical experience with retrievable Günther tulip vena cava filters. J Endovasc Ther 10:994-1000, 2003.

77. Brountzos EN, Kaufman JA, Venbrux AC, et al: A new optional vena cava filter: Retrieval at 12 weeks in an animal model. J Vasc Interv Radiol 14:763-772, 2003.

78. Asch MR: Initial experience in humans with a new retrievable inferior vena cava filter. Radiology 225:835-844, 2002.

79. Decousus H, Leizorovicz A, Parent F, et al: A clinical trial of vena caval filters in the prevention of pulmonary embolism in patients with proximal deep-vein thrombosis: Prevention du Risque d'Embolie Pulmonaire par Interruption Cave Study Group. N Engl J Med 338:409-415, 1998.

80. Laporte S, Decousus H: A randomized clinical trial of vena cava filters in the prevention of pulmonary embolism in patients with proximal deep-vein thrombosis: Preliminary results of a long-term follow-up. J. Thromb Haemost Suppl 1, 2001. Abstract OC 961.

81. Decousus H: Eight-year follow-up of a randomized trial investigating vena cava filters in the prevention of PE in patients presenting a proximal DVT: The PREPIC trial. J Thromb Haemost 1 (Suppl 1), 2003. Abstract OC440.

82. Lorch H, Welger D, Wagner V, et al: Current practice of temporary vena cava filter insertion: A multicenter registry. J Vasc Interv Radiol 11:83-88, 2000.

83. Nakajima O, Arishiro K, Kani K, et al: Massive deep vein thrombosis after cesarean section treated with a temporary inferior vena cava filter: A case report. J Cardiol 36:337-342, 2000.

84. Backus CL, Heniford BT, Sing RF: Temporary vena cava filter placement for pulmonary embolism. J Am Osteopath Assoc 102:555-556, 2002.

85. Watanabe S, Shimokawa S, Shibuya H, et al: Superior vena caval placement of a temporary filter: A case report. Vasc Surg 35:59-62, 2001.

86. Neuerburg JM, Handt S, Beckert K, et al: Percutaneous retrieval of the Tulip vena cava filter: Feasibility, short- and long-term changes in an experimental study in dogs. Cardiovasc Intervent Radiol 24:418-423, 2001.

87. de Gregorio MA, Gimeno MJ, Tobio R, et al: Animal experience in the Gunther Tulip retrievable inferior vena cava filter. Cardiovasc Intervent Radiol 24:413-417, 2001.

88. Millward S: Re: Temporary IVC filtration before patent foramen ovale closure in a patient with paradoxic embolism. J Vasc Interv Radiol 14:937, 2003.

89. Offner PJ, Hawkes A, Madayag R, et al: The role of temporary inferior vena cava filters in critically ill surgical patients. Arch Surg 138:591-594, 2003.

90. Wojcik R, Cipolle MD, Fearen I, et al: Long-term follow-up of trauma patients with a vena caval filter. J Trauma 49:839-843, 2000.

91. Trousseau A: Phlegmasia alba dolens. Clin Med Hotel Dieu de Paris 94, 1865.

92. Lin J, Proctor MC, Varma M, et al: Factors associated with recurrent venous thromboembolism in patients with malignant disease. J Vasc Surg 37:976-983, 2003.

93. Gitter MJ, Jaeger TM, Petterson TM, et al: Bleeding and thromboembolism during anticoagulant therapy: A population-based study in Rochester, Minnesota. Mayo Clin Proc 70:725-733, 1995.

94. Prandoni P, Lensing AW, Piccioli A, et al: Recurrent venous thromboembolism and bleeding complications during anticoagulant treatment in patients with cancer and venous thrombosis. Blood 100:3484-3488, 2002.

95. Krauth D, Holden A, Knapic N, et al: Safety and efficacy of long-term oral anticoagulation in cancer patients. Cancer 59:983-985, 1987.

96. Ihnat DM, Mills JL, Hughes JD, et al: Treatment of patients with venous thromboembolism and malignant disease: Should vena cava filter placement be routine? J Vasc Surg 28:800-807, 1998.

97. Jarrett BP, Dougherty MJ, Calligaro KD: Inferior vena cava filters in malignant disease. J Vasc Surg 36:704-707, 2002.

98. Marcy PY, Magne N, Gallard JC, et al: Cost-benefit assessment of inferior vena cava filter placement in advanced cancer patients. Support Care Cancer 10:76-80, 2002.

99. U.S. Food and Drug Administration, Center for Devices and Radiological Help: Guidance for Cardiovascular Intravascular Filter 510(K) Submissions. Online at: www.fda.gov/cdrh/ode/24.html/

100. Greenfield LJ, Proctor MC: Vena caval filter use in patients with sepsis: Results in 175 patients. Arch Surg 138:1245-1248, 2003.

101. Scott JH, Anderson CL, Shankar PS: Septicemia from infected caval "umbrella." JAMA 243:1133-1134, 1980.

102. Peyton JW, Hylemon MB, Greenfield LJ, et al: Comparison of Greenfield filter and vena caval ligation for experimental septic thromboembolism. Surgery 93:533-537, 1983.

Chapter

Superficial Thrombophlebitis:
Diagnosis and Management

153

RALPH G. DE PALMA, MD

The seriousness of thrombosis involving the superficial venous system had long been underestimated. Although superficial venous thrombophlebitis (SVT) causes significant discomfort, it had been considered a benign and self-limiting condition; in many instances, this is so. However, SVT can progress to involve the deep venous system in some patients and can also cause pulmonary embolism (PE). The incidence of progression to these complications, according to a 2001 literature review,[1] ranges from 0.75% to 40% for association with or progression to deep venous thrombosis (DVT). For PE, estimates ranged from 0 to 17% depending on the studies quoted. The availability of more sophisticated and sensitive screening methods, such as duplex scanning and lung scanning, yields higher figures in the later studies. The recognition of etiology and predisposing risk factors in particular cohorts has also contributed to such estimates. The estimate from a report published in 1996, that superficial thrombophlebitis can progress to DVT in as many as 11% of cases, was likely reasonable.[2]

SVT can be caused by trauma such as catheter insertion, direct intimal injury, infection, and, more commonly, stasis within saphenous varices. It can also be promoted by abnormalities in blood coagulation or thrombophilias. SVT, particularly in what appears to be a normal venous system, may signal the presence of abnormalities in levels of antithrombin III and protein C or S.[3] An important relationship between oral contraceptives[4,5] and pregnancy[6] and SVT occurs in women of childbearing age, particularly those with abnormal activated protein C. An equally relevant association with certain malignancies has also long been noted. Specific procoagulant factors have been identified in acute lymphocytic leukemia[7] and cholangiocarcinoma.[8] In considering factors leading to SVT, the clinician must remember that all the components constituting *Virchow's triad*—namely, intimal injury, stasis, and changes in blood coagulation—exist. The challenge for the clinician is to discern the possible contribution of each factor and to treat, when possible, the underlying etiology of SVT in individual cases. This chapter provides guidance to accomplish these goals.

■ ETIOLOGY AND CLINICAL PRESENTATIONS

Traumatic Thrombophlebitis

SVT can develop after direct injury, usually of an extremity. A tender cord along the course of a vein, juxtaposing the area of trauma, usually signals its presence. Ecchymosis is often present, indicating extravasation of blood associated with the injury. Thrombophlebitis at the site of an intravenous infusion is the result of irritating drugs, hypertonic solutions, and, less commonly, intimal injury caused by the catheter, particularly when the access device remains in place in a peripheral vein for an extended period. This presentation of SVT is seen in hospitalized patients or in ambulatory individuals who are using drugs or undergoing drug therapy. Redness, pain, and tenderness usually signal its development while the infusion is in progress. The thrombotic vein segment remains as a cord or lump for days or weeks after cessation of intravenous therapy.

Thrombophlebitis in Varicose Veins

Superficial thrombophlebitis frequently occurs in varicose veins: this may be a common antecedent to progression to DVT. The process extends the length of the saphenous vein or, more frequently, remains segmentally confined.

Sometimes SVT involves cluster varicosities well away from the main saphenous trunk. Although thrombosis may occur after local trauma, the process more often appears in varicosities without antecedent cause, likely as a result of stasis. Thrombophlebitis manifests as a tender, hard nodule surrounded by a zone of erythema in a previously noted varicose vein. Rarely, bleeding occurs if an inflammatory reaction extends through the vein wall and skin at the ankle. Localized thrombosis and woody induration, sometimes with thrombosed superficial veins, surround venous stasis ulcers, owing to round cell inflammation and cytokine elaboration.

Thrombophlebitis and Infection

DeTakats[9] in 1932 speculated that dormant infection in varicose veins was a factor in the development of thrombophlebitis, which might be exacerbated after operations, injection treatments, trauma, or exposure to radiation therapy. Altemeier and colleagues[10] suggested that the presence of L-forms and other atypical bacterial forms in the blood play an etiologic role in thrombophlebitis and recommended administration of tetracycline. This drug might act to decrease the inflammatory response rather than acting as an antibiotic. Septic phlebitis caused by intravenous cannulation is a special case clearly related to an infectious process. It is a serious, potentially lethal complication.

Aerobic and anaerobic as well as mixed infections have been seen in SVT.[11] Aerobic organisms include *Staphylococcus aureus*, *Pseudomonas*, and *Klebsiella*; anaerobic bacteria include *Peptostreptococcus*, *Propionibacterium*, *Bacteroides fragilis*, *Prevotella*, *Fusobacterium*, and, more recently, fungi such as *Fusarium proliferatum*.[12] With SVT in children and neonates as well as in elderly people, septicemia might manifest in one third of patients. Most patients exhibit localizing signs, but a search with a high index of suspicion should be made of intravenous sites in older people and infants with unexplained fevers. Treatment involves discontinuation of cannulation, prompt excision of suppurating veins, and administration of appropriate systemic antibiotics.[13]

Migratory Thrombophlebitis

Migratory thrombophlebitis was first described by Jadioux in 1845 as an entity characterized by repeated thrombosis of superficial veins at varying sites, commonly involving the lower extremity.[14] The association with carcinoma was first reported by Trousseau in 1856. Sproul[15] emphasized that migratory thrombophlebitis was particularly prevalent with carcinoma of the tail of the pancreas. Migratory phlebitis occurs in vasculitides, such as polyarteritis nodosa (periarteritis nodosa) and Buerger's disease. Buerger[16] initially noted phlebitis in 8 of his 19 patients, and SVT has been reported in 43% of 255 patients monitored for extended periods.[17] Upper extremity involvement occurs in Buerger's disease. Inflammatory lesions mimicking migratory phlebitis include erythema nodosum, erythema induratum, and Behçet's disease.[18,19]

Mondor's Disease: Thrombophlebitis of Superficial Veins of the Breast

Superficial thrombophlebitis involving the veins at the anterolateral aspect of the upper portion of the breast or in the region extending from the lower portion of the breast across the submammary fold toward the costal margin and the epigastrium is known as Mondor's disease. Characteristically, a tender, cordlike structure can be demonstrated by tensing the skin, as with elevation of the arm. As in other cases of thrombophlebitis, a search for malignancy may be indicated. Mondor's disease occurs after breast surgery, with use of oral contraceptives, with hereditary protein C deficiency, and in the presence of anticardiolipin antibodies.[20]

Unusual Forms

Thrombophlebitis of the dorsal penile vein, a rare condition, is also called penile Mondor's disease. Main etiologic factors are prolonged excessive sexual intercourse, hernia operations, and, as with other forms of superficial thrombophlebitis, involvement of the deep veins.[21] Duplex scanning is also needed in this condition to rule out concomitant DVT,[22] as should be done in any case of SVT. Therapy consists of nonsteroidal anti-inflammatory drugs (NSAIDs) as well as dorsal penile vein resection for cases not responding to medical therapy.

Another unusual form of superficial thrombophlebitis has been described in the palmar digital veins in five women, with vein involvement over the proximal interphalangeal joints.[23] In all women, no history of trauma was elicited, and no underlying cause was noted. Four of the five were treated with excision, and histopathologic examination confirmed the diagnosis.

■ DIAGNOSIS

The initial diagnosis of SVT is usually made from physical examination. The patient complains of a painful, cordlike structure along the course of the affected vein. Perivenous inflammation frequently gives rise to redness and induration of variable degrees along the course of the vein. Duplex scanning of lower extremity involvement should be used to determine the extent of the thrombus in the superficial vein as well as to provide critical information about extension into the deep venous system (Fig. 153-1).

Lutter and associates[24] reported that 12% of 186 patients with superficial thrombophlebitis of the great saphenous vein above the knee had simultaneous extension of thrombophlebitis into the deep venous system. Bounameaux and Reber-Wassem[25] described association of SVT with deep venous thrombosis, with reported frequencies of 12% to 44%. In their database, 31 cases of SVT, or 5.6%, with a confidence interval of 3.8% to 7.9%, were associated with DVT. During a 3-month follow-up, thromboembolic events were detected in 1.7%. In Sullivan and colleagues'[1] review of six series of above-knee SVT, involving a total of 246 patients who were treated medically or surgically, extension

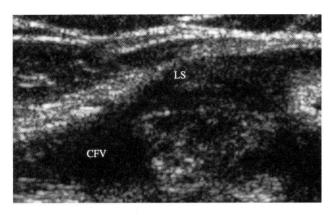

FIGURE 153-1 Duplex ultrasonography scan of saphenous vein thrombophlebitis extending into the deep venous system at the saphenofemoral junction. Patient is a 65-year-old man with carcinoma of the prostate; first presentation was dyspnea due to pulmonary embolism.

into the deep venous system subsequently occurred in 3.4% of patients surgically treated and in 2.2% of those treated medically, as documented by duplex scanning surveillance. The wide range of rates of DVT associated with SVT on initial presentation (0.75% to 40%) probably reflects a heterogeneous population, as does the association of venous thromboembolism with pulmonary embolism, at rates of 0 to 14%. The prevalence of thrombophilias associated with SVT has been estimated to be 35%,[26] along with a tight association of SVT with varicose veins (50% to 93%).[27,28] Andreozzi and Verlato[29] reported that in 21 patients studied prospectively with lung scanning, high probability of PE was present in 7 of their 21 patients, although only 1 had clinical symptoms. The risk of PE did not appear equal in patients with and without thrombus approaching the saphenofemoral junction, suggesting that clot can readily enter into the deep system through major channels such as the Hunterian or Boyd perforators.

It appears difficult to provide relevant expected incidences of DVT or PE from current data; an estimate might be somewhere in the low double digits for progression to DVT, and possibly the same for undetected PE. The salient point is that almost all patients should undergo duplex scanning immediately upon presentation as well as serial examinations at intervals after initiation or discontinuation of interventions. Phlebography is not needed to confirm the diagnosis; in fact, this procedure might make the process worse. Duplex scanning is highly specific and sensitive for guiding operative interventions.[30] Phlebography might be considered to examine iliocaval involvement if the clinical picture suggests such involvement, but either computed tomography of the iliocaval veins or magnetic resonance imaging can also be used.

■ TREATMENT

The treatment of SVT depends on its etiology and extent as well as the severity of symptoms. As mentioned, duplex scanning gives an accurate appraisal of the extent and distribution of superficial and possible deep venous

involvement. For the superficial, highly localized, mildly tender area of thrombophlebitis involving a varicose vein cluster, well away from the main saphenous trunk, treatment with aspirin and the use of elastic support usually suffice. Patients are encouraged to continue their usual daily activities.[31] With localized varicosities or when symptoms persist, phlebotomy with clot removal or excision of the involved segment can speed recovery.

More extensive involvement, as indicated by severe pain, redness, and diffuse brawny induration, has been treated traditionally with bed rest, elevation of the extremity, and application of massive warm, wet compresses. The last measure seems to be more effective with the use of a large, bulky dressing, consisting of a blanket and plastic sheeting, followed by an aquathermal pad. Initial brief immobilization may be as beneficial as the moist heat in some cases. Appropriate elastic support is indicated when the patient becomes ambulatory. Antibiotics are indicated when an ulcer or lymphangitis accompanies or appears to complicate SVT.

Although past wisdom suggested saphenectomy or saphenofemoral junction ligation, particularly when the great saphenous vein involvement extended high into the thigh, a 1995 report described nonoperative treatment of 20 patients with saphenofemoral junctional thrombophlebitis.[27] Significantly, 40% of the patients already had concurrent deep venous involvement, indicating the need for full heparin anticoagulation in a hospital setting followed by warfarin therapy for 6 months. In a later report,[32] superficial saphenous thrombophlebitis extended into the common femoral vein in 8.6% of patients; among these, 10% of patients had pulmonary emboli.[32] The investigators in this study recommended standard anticoagulation for SVT.

Andreozzi and Verlato[29] are performing a prospective study based on the association of SVT with or progression of SVT to DVT in an estimated 17% to 40% of patients. The availability of low-molecular-weight heparin will make a difference in the long-term approach to SVT, but the duration and intensity of treatment have yet to be determined.[33,34] In the few studies reviewed, 6 to 12 days has been suggested. One might note here that if surgery is planned, preoperative unfractionated heparin would be desired as its effects can be measured and controlled intraoperatively as needed. Several centers have recommended surgical management, some in combination with the use of anticoagulants.[35-38] Sullivan and colleagues'[1] meta-analysis of one prospective randomized level 1 study[39] and four level 5 studies concluded that no definite conclusions can be drawn for selection of either treatment. They recommended further study.

When serial duplex scans reveal ascending superficial thrombophlebitis, I have selectively followed a surgical approach to the saphenofemoral junction in suitable candidates or immediately post partum, with good outcomes. One can meticulously expose the saphenofemoral junction, perform flush ligation, and occasionally remove encroaching thrombus from the deep venous system. It is crucial not to provoke embolization by obtaining early and atraumatic control of the saphenofemoral junction. External or internal stripping of the involved long saphenous segment may be used to complete the procedure and speed recovery. In other instances (in elderly or immobilized patients), standard anticoagulation is a safe alternative. At this time, it is not possible to provide a formulaic approach to selection of anticoagulation or surgery in individual cases. As in any operative intervention, the clinician must use an individual approach and clinical intelligence for case selection. After a week, duplex scanning should be done to assess results and also to ensure that no DVT has occurred. At this time, neither intelligent case selection for operative intervention nor anticoagulation can be criticized.

As emphasized previously, suppurative thrombophlebitis due to a catheter or cannula insertion demands immediate aggressive surgical treatment. Such treatment consists of excision of the involved vein, leaving the wound open, and administration of appropriate systemic antibiotic therapy.

■ PROGNOSIS AND LONG-TERM MANAGEMENT

The prognosis of patients with superficial thrombophlebitis depends on its etiology, extent of involvement, and whether or not there is concomitant extension into the deep venous system. Deep extension is not ubiquitous but occurs in certain cases with varying frequencies. As repeatedly emphasized, SVT requires initial duplex scanning and then serial duplex examinations for surveillance. When SVT persists or recurs, the search for coagulation abnormalities, including measurements of protein C, protein S, and antithrombin III and detection of activated protein C resistance, is indicated. Such screening, although costly, is important in young women in whom superficial thrombophlebitis occurs while they are using oral contraceptives. A final caution exists in vascular laboratory reporting of "superficial" femoral vein thrombophlebitis,[40] which, in actuality, is a misnomer for deep venous involvement. Although such confusion is unlikely among surgeons, the primary care community might be misled and doubly deceived into believing that the prognosis for a patient with such a report is relatively less serious. Consistent use of the new venous terminology (using the term *femoral vein* instead of "superficial femoral vein") will ensure proper management of patients with deep venous thrombosis.

■ REFERENCES

1. Sullivan V, Denk PM, Sonnad SS, et al: Ligation versus anticoagulation: Treatment of above-knee superficial thrombophlebitis not involving the deep venous system. J Am Coll Surg 193:556, 2001.
2. Chengelis D, Berdick PJ, Glover JL, et al: Progression of superficial venous thrombosis to deep vein thrombosis. J Vasc Surg 24:745, 1996.
3. Pabinger I, Schneider B: Thrombotic risk in hereditary antithrombin III, protein C, and protein S deficiency. Arterioscler Thromb Vasc Biol 16:742, 1996.
4. Girolami A, Simioni P, Girolami B, et al: Homozygous patients with APC resistance may remain paucisymptomatic or asymptomatic during oral contraception. Blood Coagul Fibrinolysis 7:590, 1996.
5. Samama MM, Simon D, Horellou MH, et al: Diagnosis and clinical characteristics of inherited activated protein C resistance. Haemostasis 26(Suppl 4):325, 1996.
6. Cook G, Walker ID, McCall F, et al: Familial thrombophilia and activated protein C resistance: Thrombotic risk in pregnancy. Br J Haematol 87:873, 1994.
7. Bilgrami S, Greenberg BR, Weinstein RE, et al: Recurrent venous thrombosis as the presenting manifestation of acute lymphocytic leukemia. Med J Pediatr Oncol 24:40, 1995.
8. Martins EP, Flemming RA, Garrido MC, et al: Thrombophlebitis, dysplasia, and cholangiocarcinoma in primary sclerosing cholangitis. Gastroenterology 107:537, 1994.
9. DeTakats G: "Resting infection" in varicose veins: Its diagnosis and treatment. Am J Med Sci 184:57, 1932.
10. Altemeier WA, Hill EO, Fullen WD: Acute recurrent thromboembolic disease: A new concept of etiology. Ann Surg 170:547, 1969.
11. Brook I, Frazier EH: Aerobic and anaerobic microbiology of superficial suppurative thrombophlebitis. Arch Surg 131:95, 1996.
12. Murray CK, Beckius ML, McAllister K: *Fusarium proliferatum* superficial suppurative thrombophlebitis. Mil Med 168:426, 2003.
13. Kahn EA, Correa AS, Baker CJ: Suppurative thrombophlebitis in children: A ten-year experience. Pediatr Infect Dis J 16:63, 1997.
14. Glasser ST: Principles of Peripheral Vascular Surgery. Philadelphia, FA Davis, 1959.
15. Sproul EE: Carcinoma and venous thrombosis: Frequency of association of carcinoma in body or tail of pancreas with multiple venous thrombosis. Am J Cancer 34:566, 1938.
16. Buerger L: The veins in thromboangiitis obliterans: With particular reference to arteriovenous anastomosis as a cure for the condition. JAMA 52:1319, 1909.
17. Shionoya S: Buerger's Disease: Pathology, Diagnosis and Treatment. Nagoya, Japan, University of Nagoya Press, 1990.
18. Sagdic R, Ozer ZG, Saba D, et al: Venous lesions in Behçet's disease. Eur J Vasc Endovasc Surg 11:537, 1996.
19. Cho KH, Kim YG, Yang SG, et al: Inflammatory nodules of the lower legs: A clinical and histological analysis of 234 cases. J Dermatol 24:522, 1997.
20. Wester JP, Kuenen BC, Menwissen OJ: Mondor's disease as the first thrombotic event in hereditary protein C deficiency and anticardiolipin antibodies. Neth J Med 50:85, 1997.
21. Sasso F, Gulino G, Bsar M, et al: Penile Mondor's disease, an underestimated pathology. Br J Urol 77:729, 1996.
22. Shapiro RJ: Superficial dorsal penile vein thrombosis (penile Mondor's phlebitis): Ultrasound diagnosis. J Clin Ultrasound 24:272, 1996.
23. Lanzetta M, Morrison WA: Spontaneous thrombosis of palmar digital veins. J Hand Surg 21:410, 1996.
24. Lutter KS, Kerr TM, Roedersheimer LR, et al: Superficial thrombophlebitis diagnosed by duplex scanning. Surgery 110:42, 1991.
25. Bounameaux H, Reber-Wassem MA: Superficial deep vein thrombosis: A controversial association. Arch Intern Med 157:1822, 1997.
26. Hansen JN, Ascer E, DePippo, P et al: Saphenous vein thrombophlebitis: A deceptively benign disease. J Vasc Surg 27:677, 1998.
27. Ascer E, Lorenson E, Pollina RM, et al: Preliminary results of a nonoperative approach to saphenofemoral junctional thrombophlebitis. J Vasc Surg 22:616, 1995.
28. Jorgensen JO, Hanel KC, Morgan AM, et al: The incidence of deep venous thrombosis in patients with superficial thrombophlebitis of the lower limbs. J Vasc Surg 18:70, 1993.
29. Andreozzi GM, Verlato F: Superficial thrombophlebitis. Minerva Cardioangiol 48:9, 2000.
30. Lohr JM, McDevitt DT, Lutter KS, et al: Operative management of greater saphenous thrombophlebitis involving the saphenofemoral junction. Am J Surg 164:269, 1992.
31. Cranley JJ: Thrombophlebitis in obstetrics and gynecology. In Rakel RE (ed): Conn's Current Therapy. Philadelphia, WB Saunders, 1984.
32. Blumenberg RM, Barton E, Gelfand ML, et al: Occult deep venous thrombosis complicating superficial thrombophlebitis. J Vasc Surg 27:338, 1998.
33. Partsch H: Diagnosis and therapy of thrombophlebitis with special consideration of low molecular weight heparin. Hamostaseologie 22:154, 2002.
34. Kalodiki E, Nicolaides AN: Superficial thrombophlebitis and low-molecular weight heparin. Angiology 53:659, 2002.

35. Murgia AP, Cisno C, Pansini GC, et al: Surgical management of ascending saphenous thrombophlebitis. Int Angiol 18:343, 1999.

36. Beatty J, Fitzridge R, Benveniste G, Greenstein D: Acute superficial thrombophlebitis: Does emergency surgery have a role? Int Angiol 21:93, 2002.

37. Denzel C, Lang W: Diagnosis and therapy of progressive thrombophlebitis of epifascial leg veins. Zentralbl Chir 126:374, 2001.

38. Rohrbach N, Mouton WG, Naef M, et al: Morbidity in superficial thrombophlebitis and its potential surgical prevention. Swiss Surg 9:15, 3003.

39. Belcaro G, Nicolaides AN, Errichie BM, et al: Superficial thrombophlebitis of the legs: A randomized, controlled, follow-up study. Angiology 50:523, 1999.

40. Bundens WP, Bergan JJ, Halasz NA, et al: The superficial femoral vein: A potentially lethal misnomer. JAMA 274:1296, 1995.

Chapter

The Pathophysiology of Chronic Venous Insufficiency

154

PETER J. PAPPAS, MD

BRAJESH K. LAL, MD

JOAQUIM J. CERVEIRA, MD

WALTER N. DURAN, PhD

Ten percent to 35% of adults in the United States have some form of chronic venous disorder, ranging from spider veins and simple varicosities, to the most advanced form of chronic venous insufficiency (CVI), venous ulcers, which affect 4% of people older than 65 years.[1,2] Because of the high prevalence of the disease, the population-based costs to the U.S. government for CVI treatment and venous ulcer care has been estimated to exceed $1 billion a year. In addition, 4.6 million work-days per year are lost to chronic venous disease.[3,4] The recurrent nature of the disease, the high cost to the health care system, and the ineffectiveness of current treatment modalities underscore the need for CVI-related research. The past decade has further defined the role of leukocyte-mediated injury and elucidated the role of inflammatory cytokines in lower extremity dermal disease. In addition, several laboratories have performed investigations of pathologic alterations in cellular function and the molecular regulation of these processes observed in patients with CVI. In this chapter, we discuss the pathophysiology of varicose veins and advanced CVI leading to venous ulcerations. We also describe in detail the alterations in the microcirculation that lead to venous ulcers and the molecular regulation of inflammatory damage to the lower extremity dermis caused by persistent ambulatory venous hypertension.

■ THE VENOUS MACROCIRCULATION

Unlike arteries, veins are thin-walled, low-pressure conduits whose function is to return blood from the periphery to the heart. Muscular contractions in the upper and lower extremities propel blood forward, and a series of intra-

luminal valves prevent retrograde flow or reflux. Venous reflux is observed when valvular destruction or dysfunction occurs. Valvular reflux causes a rise in ambulatory venous pressure and a cascade of pathologic events that manifest clinically as varicose veins, lower extremity edema, pain, itching, skin discoloration, and, in the severest form, venous ulceration. These clinical signs and symptoms collectively refer to chronic venous disorders; manifestations specific to abnormal venous function are known as *chronic venous insufficiency* (CVI).[5] Classification of chronic venous disorders according to the signs and severity of the disease is discussed in detail in Chapter 155.

Primary valvular incompetence can involve all veins participating in the *macrocirculation*: the superficial, the deep, and the perforating venous systems, alone or in combination. In patients with post-thrombotic syndrome, destruction of the valves results in secondary valvular incompetence. Chronic obstruction of deep veins due to previous deep venous thrombosis (DVT) is another important cause of persistent ambulatory venous hypertension. The role of the perforating veins is still a subject of much debate; it is discussed in detail in Chapter 158, where the distribution of venous reflux in advanced CVI is also presented.

■ VARICOSE VEINS

Etiology

Age, gender, pregnancy, weight, height, race, diet, bowel habits, occupation, posture, previous DVT, and genetics have all been proposed as predisposing factors for varicose vein formation.[6] Except for previous DVT and genetics, there is poor evidence for a causative relationship between these predisposing factors and the formation of varicose veins.

The Role of Genetics

There are few reported epidemiologic investigations that suggest a relationship between varicose vein formation and a genetic predisposition.[7,8] It was previously thought that axial destruction of venous valves led to transmission of ambulatory venous hypertension, causing reflux and varix formation.[6] However, Labropoulos and associates[9] reported that the most common location for initial varicose vein formation was in the below-knee great saphenous vein (GSV) and its tributaries, followed by the above-knee GSV, and the saphenofemoral junction. Their study clearly indicates that vein wall degeneration with subsequent varix formation can occur in any segment of the superficial and deep systems at any time and suggests a genetic component to the disease.

In 1969, Gunderson and Hauge[7] reported on the epidemiology of varicose veins observed in the vein clinic in Malmo, Sweden, over 2 months. Of 250 patients, 154 women and 24 men provided complete survey information about their parents and siblings. Although biased by the predominance of women and a dependence on survey data, this report suggested that patients with varicose veins had a higher likelihood of varicosities if their fathers had varicose veins. Furthermore, risk of varicose vein development increases if both parents had varicosities. Cornu-Thenard and associates[8] prospectively examined 67 patients and their parents. Patients' non-affected spouses and parents were used as controls, for a total of 402 subjects.[8] These investigators reported that the risk of development of varicose veins was 90% if both parents were affected, 25% for males and 62% for females if one parent was affected, and 20% if neither parent was affected. These data suggest an autosomal dominant with variable penetrance mode of genetic transmission. The lower incidence in males with an affected parent and the spontaneous development in patients without affected parents suggest that males are more resistant to varix formation and that other multifactorial causes in patients with predispositions to the disease must exist. To further elucidate the genetic component of the disease, molecular analyses with gene chip technologies is required. The chromosome responsible for the disease and its protein byproducts are currently unknown.

The Role of Deep Venous Thrombosis

An injury to the venous endothelium or local procoagulant environmental factors lead to thrombus formation in the venous system. It is currently well accepted that a venous thrombus initiates a cascade of inflammatory events that contribute to or cause vein wall fibrosis.[10] Thrombus formation at venous confluences and valve pockets leads to activation of neutrophils and platelets. Activation of these cells results in formation of inflammatory cytokines, procoagulants, and chemokines, causing thrombin activation and further clot formation. Production of inflammatory mediators creates a cytokine-chemokine gradient, prompting leukocyte invasion of the vein wall at the thrombus wall interface and from the surrounding adventitia. Upregulation of adhesion molecules perpetuates this process, eventually leading to vein wall fibrosis, valvular destruction, and alteration of vein wall architecture.[10,11] Although the mechanisms associated with vein wall damage secondary to venous thrombosis are beginning to be unraveled, the majority of varicose veins occur in patients with no prior history of DVT. The etiology of primary varicose veins continues to be a mystery.

Vein Wall Anatomy and Histopathology

Whatever the initiating event, several unique anatomic and biochemical abnormalities have been observed in patients with varicose veins. The walls of both normal and varicose GSVs are characterized by three distinct muscle layers. The media contains an inner longitudinal and an outer circular layer, but the adventitia contains a loosely organized outer longitudinal layer.[12-14] In normal GSVs, these muscle layers are composed of smooth muscle cells (SMCs), which appear spindle-shaped (contractile phenotype) when examined with electron microscopy (Fig. 154-1).[15] These cells lie in close proximity to one another, are in parallel arrays, and are surrounded by bundles of regularly arranged collagen fibers.

In varicose veins, the orderly appearance of the muscle layers of the media is replaced by an intense and disorganized deposition of collagen.[15-17] Collagen deposits separate the normally closely opposed SMCs and are particularly striking in the media. SMCs appear elliptical rather than spindle-shaped and demonstrate numerous collagen-containing vacuoles, imparting a secretory phenotype (Fig. 154-2).[15] What causes SMCs to dedifferentiate from a contractile to a secretory phenotype is currently unknown. Ascher and coworkers[18,19] theorized that SMC dedifferentiation may be related to dysregulation of apoptosis. These investigators reported a decrease in the pro-apoptotic mediators bax and PARP (poly ADP-ribose polymerase) in the adventitia of varicose veins compared

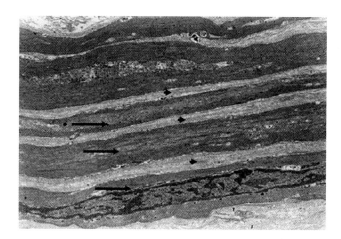

FIGURE 154-1 Electron micrograph of normal great saphenous vein (×11,830). Note organized structure of alternating smooth muscle cells (*long arrows*) with spindle-shaped contractile phenotype, interspersed with longitudinally arranged collagen bundles (*short arrows*).

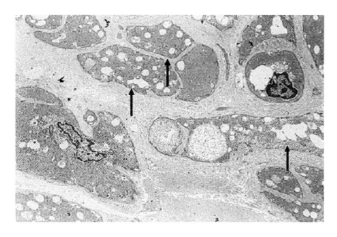

FIGURE 154-2   Electron micrograph of varicosed great saphenous vein (×4240). Smooth muscle cells exhibit prominent vacuoles (*arrows*) and an elliptical appearance consistent with a secretory phenotype. Smooth muscle cells are separated by diffusely deposited collagen bundles, which impart a disorganized architectural appearance to the vein wall.

with normal veins. Although no difference in these mediators was observed in the media or intima of varicose veins, a decrease in SMC turnover was postulated as a possible cause of the increase in secretory phenotype. Increased phosphorylation of the retinoblastoma protein, an intracellular regulator of cellular proliferation and differentiation, has been observed in varicose veins and may similarly contribute to this process.[13]

Vein wall remodeling has been consistently observed in histologic varicose vein specimens.[12,14-17,20] Gandhi and associates[20] quantitatively demonstrated higher collagen content and lower elastin content in varicose compared with normal GSVs. The net increase in the collagen-elastin ratio suggested an imbalance in connective tissue matrix regulation. As a result, several investigators have observed alterations in matrix metalloproteinase (MMP) and fibrinolytic activity in varicose veins. Tissue inhibitor of matrix metalloproteinases-1 (TIMP-1) and MMP-1 protein levels are higher at the saphenofemoral junction than in normal controls, whereas MMP-2 levels are lower.[21,22] No overall differences in MMP-9 protein or activity levels have been identified. However, the number of cells expressing MMP-9 as shown by immunohistochemistry has been reported to be elevated in varicose veins compared with normal veins.[22,23] There are conflicting reports about the role of plasmin activators and their inhibitors. Shireman and colleagues[24] reported that urokinase plasminogen activator (u-PA) levels are three to five times higher than normal in the media of vein specimens cultured in an organ bath system. They noted no differences in tissue-type plasminogen activator (t-PA) or plasmin activator inhibitor-1 (PAI-1) levels. However, other investigations using enzyme zymography have demonstrated a decrease in u-PA and t-PA activity in varicose veins.[22,25] These data suggest that the plasminogen activators may play a role in MMP activation, leading to vein wall fibrosis and varix formation; however, further research into the mechanisms regulating vein wall fibrosis is clearly needed.

Abnormal Vein Wall Function in Varicose Veins

What effect vein wall fibrosis has on venous function needs further elucidation. The contractile responses of varicose and normal GSV rings to noradrenaline, potassium chloride, endothelin, calcium ionophore A23187, angiotensin II, and nitric oxide have been evaluated by several researchers.[26,27] These studies have demonstrated decreased contractility of varicose veins when stimulated by noradrenaline, endothelin, and potassium chloride. Similarly, endothelium-dependent and endothelium-independent relaxations after administration of A23187 and nitric oxide administration, respectively, are diminished in varicose compared with normal GSVs. The mechanisms responsible for decreased varicose vein contractility appear to be receptor mediated.[27,28] Utilizing sarafotoxin 6c (selective pharmacologic inhibitor of endothelin B) and competitive inhibition receptor assays with ^{131}I-labeled endothelin-1, Barber and associates[28] have observed fewer endothelin B receptors in varicose veins than in normal GSVs.

Feedback inhibition of receptor production secondary to increased endothelin-1 is postulated to mediate the lower receptor content in varicose vein walls. Other possible mechanisms for decreased contractility appear related to levels of cyclic AMP (cAMP) and the ratio of prostacyclin to thromboxane A_2.[29] Cyclic AMP levels are higher in varicose vein specimens than in normal GSVs. In addition, the ratio of prostacyclin to thromboxane A_2 is higher in varicose veins, although no differences in absolute protein levels were observed between normal veins and varicosities. Whether venodilatation of varicosities is caused by diminished endothelin receptor levels and responsiveness to cAMP or a secondary effect of varix formation is not known. It is clear, however, that with the development of vein wall fibrosis, varicose veins demonstrate diminished contractile properties, probably exacerbating the development of ambulatory venous hypertension.

■ HISTORICAL THEORIES OF CHRONIC VENOUS INSUFFICIENCY

In the 20th century, numerous theories were postulated regarding the etiology and pathophysiology of CVI and the cause of venous ulceration. The venous stasis, arteriovenous fistula, and diffusion block theories have been disproved over time and are discussed here for historical interest only. The etiology of dermal skin disease is primarily a chronic inflammatory process, and the events regulating these events are discussed later.

Venous Stasis Theory

In 1917, John Homans[30] published a manuscript titled "The etiology and treatment of varicose ulcer of the leg." This work was a clinical treatise on the diagnosis and management of patients with CVI. Homans coined the term *post-phlebitic syndrome* and speculated on the cause of venous ulceration. He stated, "Overstretching of the vein walls and destruction of the valves upon which the mechanism principally depends bring about a degree of surface stasis which obviously interferes with the nutrition of the skin and subcutaneous tissues.... It is to be expected, therefore, that skin which is bathed under pressure in stagnant venous blood will readily form permanent, open sores or ulcers."[30] This statement resulted in a generation of investigators trying to seek a causal relationship among hypoxia, stagnant blood flow, and the development of CVI.

The first investigator to address the question of hypoxia and CVI scientifically was Alfred Blalock.[31] He obtained venous samples from the femoral, greater saphenous, and varicose veins in 10 patients with CVI isolated to one limb and compared the oxygen content in those veins to that in samples taken from corresponding veins in the other limb. Seven of the patients had active ulcers at the time. All samples were collected in the recumbent and standing positions. He reported that in patients with unilateral CVI, the oxygen content was higher in the femoral vein of the affected limb. He speculated that this observation might be reflective of greater venous flow rather than stagnation.

Arteriovenous Fistula Theory

The concept of increased venous flow in the dermal venous plexus was expanded upon by Pratt,[32] who reported that increased venous flow in patients with CVI could be clinically observed. He attributed the development of venous ulceration to the presence of arteriovenous connections and coined the term *arterial varices*. He reported that in a series of 272 patients with varicose veins who underwent vein ligation, 24% had arteriovenous connections. Fifty percent of the recurrences in 61 patients occurred in those in whom arteriovenous communications had been identified clinically from the presence of arterial pulsations in venous conduits. Pratt[32] hypothesized that increased venous flow shunted nutrient- and oxygen-rich blood away from the dermal plexus, leading to areas of ischemia and hypoxia and resulting in venous ulceration. Pratt's clinical observations, however, have never been confirmed with objective scientific evidence. Experiments with radioactively labeled microspheres have never demonstrated shunting and have therefore cast serious doubts on the validity of this theory.

Diffusion Block Theory

Hypoxia and alterations in nutrient blood flow were again proposed as the underlying etiology of CVI in 1982 by Burnand and colleagues.[33] These investigators performed a study in which skin biopsies were obtained from 109 limbs of patients with CVI and 30 limbs from patients without CVI. Foot vein pressures were measured in the patients with CVI at rest and after 5, 10, 15, and 20 heel raises. Vein pressure measurements were then correlated with the number of capillaries observed on histologic section. Burnand and colleagues[33] reported that venous hypertension was associated with higher numbers of capillaries in the dermis of patients with CVI.

Whether the histologic sections represented true increases in capillary quantity or an elongation and dis-

tension of existing capillaries was not answered by that study. However, in a canine hind limb model, the same investigators were able to induce enlargement in the number of capillaries with experimentally induced hypertension.[34] This important investigation was one of the first studies to demonstrate a direct effect of venous hypertension on the venous microcirculation. In a later study, Browse and Burnand[35] noted that the enlarged capillaries observed on histologic examination exhibited pericapillary fibrin deposition and coined the term *fibrin cuff*. They speculated that venous hypertension led to widening of endothelial gap junctions, with subsequent extravasation of fibrinogen leading to the development of fibrin cuffs. They also theorized that the cuffs acted as a barrier to oxygen diffusion and nutrient blood flow, resulting in epidermal cell death. Although pericapillary cuffs do exist, it has never been demonstrated that they act as a barrier to nutrient flow or oxygen diffusion.

Leukocyte Activation

Dissatisfaction with the fibrin cuff theory and subsequent observations of lower numbers of circulating leukocytes in blood samples obtained from GSVs in patients with CVI led Coleridge Smith and colleagues[36] to propose the leukocyte trapping theory. According to the theory, circulating neutrophils are trapped in the venous microcirculation secondary to venous hypertension. The subsequent sluggish capillary blood flow leads to hypoxia and neutrophil activation. Neutrophil activation results in degranulation of toxic metabolites with subsequent endothelial cell damage. The ensuing heterogeneous capillary perfusion causes alterations in skin blood flow and eventual skin damage. The problem with the leukocyte trapping theory is that neutrophils have never been directly observed to obstruct capillary flow, therefore casting doubt on its validity. However, there is significant evidence that leukocyte activation plays a major role in the pathophysiology of CVI.

Role of Leukocyte Activation and Function

In 1988, Thomas and associates[37] reported that 24% fewer white cells left the venous circulation after a period of recumbency and that packed red blood cell volume was higher in patients with CVI compared with normal patients. They also noted that the relative number of white cells was significantly lower than in control patients and those with primary varicose veins (28% vs. 5%; $P < .01$). These researchers concluded that the decrease in white cell number was due to leukocyte trapping in the venous microcirculation secondary to venous hypertension. They further speculated that trapped leukocytes may become activated, resulting in release of toxic metabolites that damage the microcirculation and overlying skin. These important observations were the first to implicate abnormal leukocyte activity in the pathophysiology of CVI.

The importance of leukocytes in the development of dermal skin alterations was emphasized by Scott and coworkers.[38] These investigators obtained punch biopsy specimens from patients with primary varicose veins, with lipodermatosclerosis, and with lipodermatosclerosis and healed ulcers and reported the median number of white blood cells per high-power field (40× magnification) in each group. No patients with active ulcers were included in the study, and no attempt was made to identify the type of leukocytes. The investigators reported that in patients with primary varicose veins, lipodermatosclerosis, and healed ulceration, there was a median of 6, 45, and 217 white blood cells per mm^3, respectively. This study demonstrated a correlation between clinical severity of disease and the number of leukocytes in the dermis of patients with CVI.

The types of leukocytes involved in the skin changes seen in dermal venous stasis are controversial. T lymphocytes, macrophages, and mast cells have been observed on immunohistochemical and electron-microscopic examinations.[39,40] The variation in types of leukocytes observed may reflect the types of patients investigated. Wilkinson and colleagues[39] performed biopsies in patients with erythematous and eczematous skin changes, whereas Pappas and associates[40] evaluated predominantly older patients with dermal fibrosis. In patients with eczematous skin changes, there may be an autoimmune component to the CVI, whereas patients with dermal fibrosis may experience pathologic alterations consistent with chronic inflammation and altered tissue remodeling.

■ THE VENOUS MICROCIRCULATION

Endothelial Cell Characteristics

Numerous investigations have attempted to evaluate the microcirculation of patients with CVI.[40,41-44] The majority of the studies were qualitative descriptions of vascular abnormalities, which lacked uniformity of biopsy sites and patient stratification. Prior to 1997, it was widely accepted that endothelial cells from the dermal microcirculation appeared abnormal, contained Weibel-Palade bodies, were edematous, and demonstrated widened interendothelial gap junctions.[43] On the basis of these descriptive observations, it was assumed that the dermal microcirculation of patients with CVI has functional derangements related to permeability and ulcer formation. These earlier observations have been refuted by Pappas and associates,[40] who performed a quantitative morphometric analysis of the dermal microcirculation in patients with CVI. This investigation indicated that interendothelial gap junctions in patients with CVI were very tight, suggesting that edema formation was secondary to other mechanisms. These investigators speculated that tissue edema may be secondary to increased transendothelial vesicle transport, formation of transendothelial channels, and alterations in the glycocalyx lining the junctional cleft; they based their speculation on the appearance of capillary endothelial cells and the number of vacuoles observed with electron microscopy.[40] Furthermore, endothelial cells appeared metabolically active, consistent with endothelial cell activation and perivascular cuff formation.

Types and Distribution of Leukocytes

In the study just described, Pappas and associates[40] reported that the most striking differences in cell type and distribution were mast cells and macrophages (Fig. 154-3). In both

gaiter and thigh biopsy specimens, mast cell numbers were two to four times greater around arterioles and postcapillary venules in patients with CEAP class 4 and class 5 disease than in control subjects ($P < .05$). Similarly, macrophages demonstrated increased numbers around arterioles and postcapillary venules (PCVs) in patients with class 5 and class 6 disease, respectively ($P < .05$). Surprisingly, lymphocytes, plasma cells, and neutrophils were not present in the immediate perivascular space. Fibroblasts were the most common cells observed in both gaiter and thigh biopsy specimens.

It was speculated that mast cells and macrophages may function to regulate tissue remodeling that results in dermal fibrosis.[40] The mast cell enzyme chymase is a potent activator of matrix metalloproteinases 1 and 3 (collagenase and stromelysin).[45-47] In an in-vitro model using the human mast cell line HMC-1, these cells were reported to spontaneously adhere to fibronectin, laminin, and collagen types I and III, all of which are components of the perivascular cuff (see later).[47] Chymase also causes release of latent transforming growth factor-β_1 (TGF-β_1) secreted by activated endothelial cells, fibroblasts, and platelets from extracellular matrices.[48] Release and activation of TGF-β_1 initiates a cascade of events in which macrophages and fibroblasts are recruited to wound healing sites and are stimulated to produce fibroblast mitogens and connective tissue proteins, respectively.[49] Mast cell degranulation leading to TGF-β_1 activation and macrophage recruitment

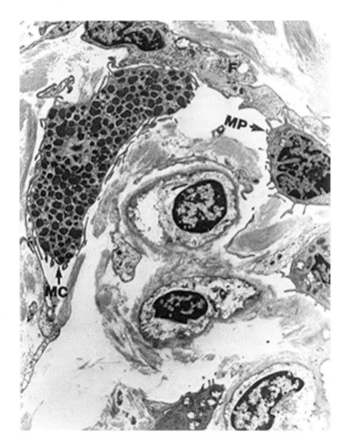

FIGURE 154-3 Electron micrograph (×4300) of mast cells (MC), macrophages (MP), and fibroblast (F) surrounding a central capillary from dermal biopsy of a patient with CEAP class 4 chronic venous insufficiency.

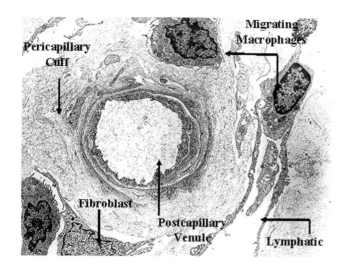

FIGURE 154-4 Electron micrograph (×4300) of a well-developed perivascular cuff in close proximity to a fibroblast in a patient with CEAP class 6 chronic venous insufficiency. *Long arrow* points to macrophages that appear to be entering a lymphatic lumen.

may explain why reduced mast cell and higher macrophage numbers were observed in patients with class 6 disease. Macrophage migration, as evidenced by the frequent appearance of cytoplasmic tails in perivascular macrophages, further substantiates the concept of inflammatory cytokine recruitment (Fig. 154-4).

Alterations in Extracellular Matrix

Once leukocytes have migrated to the extracellular space they localize around capillaries and postcapillary venules. The perivascular space is surrounded by extracellular matrix (ECM) proteins and forms a perivascular "cuff." Adjacent to these perivascular cuffs and throughout the dermal interstitium is an intense and disorganized collagen deposition.[33,40] Perivascular cuffs and the accompanying collagen deposition are the sine qua non of the dermal microcirculation in patients with CVI (see Fig. 154-4). The perivascular cuff was originally thought to be the result of fibrinogen extravasation and erroneously referred to as a "fibrin cuff."[5] It is now known that the cuff is a ring of ECM proteins consisting of collagen types I and III, fibronectin, vitronectin, laminin, tenascin, and fibrin.[50]

The role of the cuff and its cell of origin are not completely understood. The investigation by Pappas and associates[40] suggested that the endothelial cells of the dermal microcirculation are responsible for cuff formation, The cuff was once thought to be a barrier to oxygen and nutrient diffusion; however, evidence now suggests that cuff formation is an attempt to maintain vascular architecture in response to increased mechanical load.[51] Although perivascular cuffs may function to preserve microcirculatory architecture, several pathologic processes may be related to cuff formation. Immunohistochemical analyses have demonstrated transforming TGF-β_1 and α_2-macroglobulin in the interstices of perivascular cuffs.[52] It has been suggested that these "trapped" molecules are abnormally distributed in the dermis, leading to altered tissue remodel-

ing and fibrosis. Cuffs may also serve as a lattice for capillary angiogenesis, explaining the capillary tortuosity and increased capillary density observed in the dermis of patients with CVI.

Pathophysiology of Stasis Dermatitis and Dermal Fibrosis

The mechanisms modulating leukocyte activation, fibroblast function, and dermal extracellular matrix alterations were the focus of investigation in the 1990s. CVI is a disease of chronic inflammation due to a persistent and sustained injury secondary to venous hypertension. It is hypothesized that the primary injury is extravasation of macromolecules (i.e., fibrinogen and α_2-macroglobulin) and red blood cells (RBCs) into the dermal interstitium.[33,34,42,43,52] RBC degradation products and interstitial proteins are potent chemoattractants and presumably represent the initial underlying chronic inflammatory signal responsible for leukocyte recruitment. It has been assumed that these cytochemical events are responsible for the increased expression of intercellular adhesion molecule-1 (ICAM-1) on endothelial cells of microcirculatory exchange vessels observed in CVI dermal biopsy specimens.[39,53] ICAM-1 is the activation-dependent adhesion molecule utilized by macrophages, lymphocytes, and mast cells for diapedesis. As stated previously, all of these cells have been observed with immunohistochemistry and electron microscopy in the interstitium of dermal biopsy specimens.[39,40]

Cytokine Regulation and Tissue Fibrosis

Several investigators have attempted to identify cytokines and growth factors involved in the pathophysiology of CVI. As stated previously, CVI is a chronic inflammatory disease characterized by leukocyte recruitment, tissue remodeling, and dermal fibrosis. These physiologic processes are prototypical of disease states regulated by TGF-β_1. TGF-β_1 is present in pathologic quantities in the dermis of patients with CVI and increases with disease severity.[54] TGF-β_1 is secreted by interstitial leukocytes and bound to dermal fibroblasts and extracellular matrix proteins (Figs. 154-3, 154-5, and 154-6). Whether or not perivascular cuffs bind TGF-β_1 is controversial.[54] Higley and colleagues[52] reported a positive TGF-β_1 staining response in perivascular cuffs and an absence of TGF-β_1 in the provisional matrix of the venous ulcer compared with healing donor skin graft sites. They concluded that TGF-β_1 was abnormally "trapped" in the perivascular cuff and therefore unavailable for normal granulation tissue development. No TGF-β_1 binding to perivascular cuffs was observed by Pappas and associates.[54] Differences between the two studies may relate to biopsy site selection. Higley and colleagues[52] sampled the edges and bases of chronic, nonhealing venous ulcers, whereas Pappas and associates[54] took samples 5 to 10 cm away from active ulcers. Therefore, findings of the former study reflect the biology of chronic wound healing, and those of the latter study suggest active tissue remodeling in response to a chronic injury stimulus.

The distribution and location of several other growth factors in the skin of patients with CVI have also been investigated. Peschen and coworkers[55] reported on the role

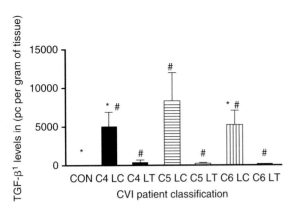

FIGURE 154-5 Bar graph demonstrating differences in active transforming growth factor-β1 protein concentration between and within chronic venous insufficiency (CVI) groups in comparison with control subjects. *, Control vs. CEAP Class 4 and Class 6 ($P \le .05$); #, Lower calf vs. lower thigh biopsies within each class ($P \le .02$). Con, control; C4, C5, C6, CEAP Class 4, Class 5, and Class 6.

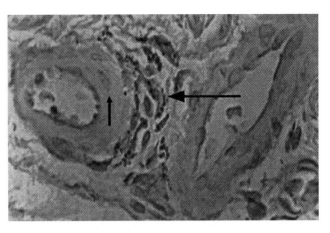

FIGURE 154-6 Immunohistochemistry (×575) of dermal skin biopsy demonstrating transforming growth factor-β1–positive granules (*long arrow*) in leukocytes surrounding a perivascular cuff and leukocytes migrating through a perivascular cuff (*short arrow*).

of platelet-derived growth factor receptors α and β (PDGFR-α and PDGFR-β) and vascular endothelial growth factor (VEGF).[55] Skin biopsy specimens from 30 patients were separated into five groups according to disorder—reticular veins, venous eczema, skin pigmentation, lipodermatosclerosis, and active leg ulcers—with a total of 6 patients in each group. Specimens were studied with immunohistochemistry, and the extent of immunoreactivity was assessed with a scoring system by two blinded reviewers. The investigators reported that expressions of PDGFR-α, PDGFR-β, and VEGF were markedly higher in the stroma of the patients with CVI with eczema and active ulcers than in that of patients with reticular veins and pigmentation changes only. To a lesser extent, patients with lipodermatosclerosis demonstrated immunoreactivity to PDGFR-α, PDGFR-β, and VEGF as well. Expressions of PDGFR-α and PDGFR-β were considerably elevated in the capillaries, surrounding fibroblasts, and inflammatory cells of patients with venous eczema. In addition, immunoreactivity was higher in dermal fibroblasts, smooth muscle cells, and vascular cells of patients with lipodermatosclerosis than in patients with reticular veins only. The greatest expressions of PDGFR-α and PDGFR-β were observed in mesenchymal cells and vascular endothelial cells of patients with active venous ulcers. VEGF immunoreactivity correlated with disease severity. VEGF-positive capillary endothelial cells and pericapillary cells were higher in patients with venous eczema, lipodermatosclerosis, and active venous ulceration, respectively.

In a subsequent investigation, these researchers reported that with progression of CVI dermal disease, the endothelial cell expression of ICAM-1 and vascular adhesion molecule-1 (VCAM-1) and their corresponding leukocyte ligands, leukocyte function–associated antigen-1 (LFA-1) and very late activation antigen-4 (VLA-4) increased.[53] On the basis of these observations, Peschen and coworkers[53] speculated that leukocyte recruitment, capillary proliferation, and interstitial edema in patients with CVI may be regulated through PDGF and VEGF through upregulation of adhesion

molecules, leading to leukocyte recruitment, diapedesis, and release of chemical mediators.

In summary, the preceding investigations indicate that progression of CVI dermal disease is mediated by a cascade of inflammatory events. Venous hypertension causes extravasation of macromolecules, such as fibrinogen and red blood cells, that act as potent inflammatory mediators. These mediators cause an upregulation of adhesion molecules and the expression of growth factors like PDGF and VEGF, which result in leukocyte recruitment. Monocytes and mast cells travel to the site of injury, activating or releasing TGF-β1 and probably other undiscovered chemicals as well. What effect growth factor binding has on fibroblast and endothelial cell function was the focus of numerous investigations in the 1990s.

Dermal Fibroblast Function

Several studies have reported aberrant phenotypic behavior of fibroblasts isolated from edges of venous ulcer compared with fibroblasts obtained from ipsilateral thigh biopsy specimens of normal skin in the same patients. Hasan and colleagues[56] compared the ability of venous ulcer fibroblasts to produce αI procollagen mRNA and collagen after stimulation with TGF-β1.[56] These investigators were not able to demonstrate differences in αI procollagen mRNA levels after stimulation with TGF-β1 between the venous ulcer fibroblasts and the normal fibroblasts (control). However, collagen production was increased by 60% in a dose-dependent manner in controls, whereas venous ulcer fibroblasts were unresponsive. This unresponsiveness was associated with a fourfold decrease in TGF-β1 type II receptors. In a follow-up report, Kim and associates[57] indicated that the decrease in TGF-β1 type II receptors was associated with a decrease in phosphorylation of the TGF-β1 receptor substrates SMAD 2 and 3 as well as p42/44 mitogen–activated protein kinases. A similar investigation reported a decrease in collagen production by venous ulcer fibroblasts and similar amounts of fibronectin production compared with normal controls.[58]

Stanley and colleagues[59] further delineated fibroblast responsiveness to growth factors. These investigators characterized the proliferative responses of venous ulcer fibroblasts when stimulated with basic fibroblastic growth factor (bFGF), epidermal growth factor (EGF), and interleukin-1β (IL-1β). In their first study, they reported that venous ulcer fibroblast growth rates were markedly suppressed when stimulated with bFGF, EGF, and IL-1β. In a follow-up investigation, the investigators noted that the previously observed growth inhibition could be reversed with bFGF.[60] Lal and associates[61] reported that the proliferative responses of CVI fibroblasts to TGF-β₁ correlated with disease severity. Fibroblasts from patients with CEAP class 2 or 3 disease retain their agonist-induced proliferative capacity. Class 4 and class 5 fibroblasts demonstrated diminished agonist-induced proliferation, whereas class 6 (venous ulcer) fibroblasts did not proliferate after TGF-β₁ stimulation, confirming the observations made by previous investigators. Phenotypically, venous ulcer fibroblasts appeared large and polygonal and exhibited varied nuclear morphologic features, whereas normal fibroblasts appeared compact and tapered with well-defined nuclear morphologic features. Venous ulcer fibroblasts appeared morphologically similar to fibroblasts undergoing cellular senescence. Therefore, the blunted growth response of CVI venous ulcer fibroblasts appears related to development of cellular senescence.[59,62]

Other characteristics of senescent cells are an overexpression of matrix proteins such as fibronectin (cFN) and enhanced activity of β-galactosidase (SA-β-Gal). In an evaluation of seven patients with venous stasis ulcers, it was noted that a higher percentage of SA-β-Gal–positive cells in venous ulcers were observed compared to normal controls (6.3% vs. 0.21%; $P \leq 0.016$).[60] It was also reported that venous ulcer fibroblasts produced one to four times more cFN on Western blot analysis than controls.[62] These data support the hypothesis that venous ulcer fibroblasts phenotypically behave like senescent cells. However, senescence is probably the end manifestation of a wide spectrum of events leading to proliferative resistance and cellular dysfunction. Telomeres and telomerase activity are the sine qua non of truly senescent cells. To date, there are no reported studies indicating an abnormality in CVI fibroblast telomere length or telomerase activity. Without such information, the true role of senescence in CVI remains ill-defined.

Role of Matrix Metalloproteinases and Their Inhibitors in Chronic Venous Insufficiency

The signaling event responsible for the development of a venous ulcer and the mechanisms responsible for prolonged wound healing are poorly understood. Wound healing is an orderly process that involves inflammation, reepithelialization, matrix deposition, and tissue remodeling. Tissue remodeling and matrix deposition are processes controlled by MMPs and TIMPs. In general, MMPs and TIMPs are not constitutively expressed. They are induced temporarily in response to exogenous signals such as various proteases, cytokines or growth factors, cell-matrix interactions, and

altered cell-cell contacts. TGF-β₁ is a potent inducer of TIMP-1 and collagen production and an inhibitor of MMP-1 through regulation of gene expression and protein synthesis.

Several studies have demonstrated that prolonged and continuous TGF-β₁ production causes tissue fibrosis by stimulating ECM production and inhibiting degradation by affecting production of MMP and TIMP. Alterations in MMP and TIMP production may similarly modulate the tissue fibrosis of the lower extremity in patients with CVI. Several investigators have reported that the gelatinases MMP-2 and MMP-9 as well as TIMP-1 are higher in the exudates of patients with venous ulcers than in acute wounds.[63-65] However, analyses of biopsy specimens have demonstrated variable results. Herouy and colleagues[66] reported that MMP-1, MMP-2, and TIMP-1 are higher in patients with lipodermatosclerosis than in normal skin.[66]

In a subsequent investigation, biopsy specimens from patients with venous ulcers were found to have higher levels of the active form of MMP-2 compared to normal skin.[67] In addition, increased immunoreactivity to extracellular inducer of MMP (EMMPRIN), membrane type 1 MMP (MT1-MMP), and MT2-MMP in the dermis and perivascular regions of venous ulcers has been reported.[68] Saito and associates[69] were unable to identify differences in overall protein levels and activities of matrix metalloproteinases 1, 2, and 9 and TIMP-1 between patients with CVI with CEAP class 2 through 6 disease and normal controls.[69] However, within a clinical class, MMP-2 levels were higher than MMP-1, MMP-9 and TIMP-1 levels in patients with class 4 and class 5 disease. These data indicate that active tissue remodeling is occurring in patients with CVI.

Which matrix metalloproteinases are involved and how they are activated and regulated are currently unclear. It appears that MMP-2 may be activated by urokinase plasminogen activator (u-PA). Herouy and colleagues[70] observed higher u-PA and u-PA receptor mRNA and protein levels in patients with venous ulcers than in normal skin.[70] The elevated values of active TGF-β₁ in the dermis of patients with CVI suggest a regulatory role for TGF-β₁ in MMP and TIMP synthesis and activity. However, there is currently no direct evidence indicating such a relationship.

■ CONCLUSION

The mechanisms regulating varicose vein development and the subsequent dermal skin sequelae of chronic ambulatory venous hypertension have only lately been investigated. It is clear that varicose vein formation has a genetic component that is linked to environmental stimuli. Vein wall fibrosis and loss of valvular competence leading to venous hypertension develop in susceptible patients. The transmission of high venous pressures to the dermal microcirculation causes extravasation of macromolecules and red blood cells that serve as the underlying stimulus for inflammatory injury. Activation of the microcirculation results in cytokine and growth factor release, leading to leukocyte migration into the interstitium. At the site of injury, a host of inflammatory events is set into action. TGF-β₁ appears to be a primary regulator of CVI-induced injury. TGF-β₁ secretion from leukocytes with subsequent binding to dermal fibroblasts is associated with intense dermal fibrosis and tissue remodeling. In addition, decreased TGF-β_1 type II receptors on venous ulcer fibroblasts are associated with diminished fibroblast proliferation. Fibroblast proliferation diminishes with disease progression, ultimately leading to senescence and poor ulcer healing. In addition, increases in MMP-2 synthesis appear to increase tissue remodeling and further impede ulcer healing. As our understanding of the underlying cellular and molecular mechanisms that regulate CVI and ulcer formation improves, better therapeutic interventions for treatment and prevention will ultimately follow.

■ REFERENCES

1. White GH: Chronic venous insufficiency. In Veith F, Hobson RW II, Williams RA, Wilson SE (eds): Vascular Surgery. New York, McGraw-Hill, 1993, pp 865-888.
2. Callam MJ: Epidemiology of Varicose Veins. Br J Surg 81:167-173, 1994.
3. Hume M: Presidential address: A venous renaissance? J Vasc Surg 6:947-951, 1992.
4. Lawrence PF, Gazak CE: Epidemiology of chronic venous insufficiency. In Gloviczki P, Bergan JJ (eds): Atlas of Endoscopic Perforator Vein Surgery. London, Springer-Verlag, 1998, pp 31-44.
5. Porter JM, Moneta GL: Reporting standards in venous disease: An update. International Consensus Committee on Chronic Venous Disease. J Vasc Surg 21:635-645, 1995.
6. Varicose veins: Pathology. In Browse NL, Burnand KG, Irvine AT, Wilson NM (eds): Diseases of the Veins. New York, Oxford University Press, 1999, pp 145-162.
7. Gunderson J, Hauge M: Hereditary factors in venous insufficiency. Angiology 20:346-355, 1969.
8. Cornu-Thenard A, Boivin P, Baud MM, et al: Importance of the familial factor in varicose disease: Clinical study of 134 families. J Derm Surg Oncol 20:318-326, 1994.
9. Labropoulos N, Giannoukas AD, Delis K, et al: Where does the venous reflux start? J Vasc Surg 26:736-742, 1997.
10. Wakefield TM, Strietert RM, Prince MR, et al: Pathogenesis of venous thrombosis: A new insight. Cardiovasc Surg 5:6-15, 1997.
11. Takase S, Bergan JJ, Schmid-Schonbein G: Expression of adhesion molecules and cytokines on saphenous veins in chronic venous insufficiency. Ann Vasc Surg 14:427-435, 2000.
12. Rose A: Some new thoughts on the etiology of varicose veins. J Cardiovasc Surg 27:534-543, 1986.
13. Pappas PJ, Gwertzman GA, DeFouw DO, et al: Retinoblastoma protein: A molecular regulator of chronic venous insufficiency. J Surg Res 76:149-153, 1998.
14. Travers JP, Brookes CE, Evans J, et al: Assessment of the structure and composition of varicose veins with reference to collagen, elastin and smooth muscle content. Eur J Vasc Endovasc Surg 11:230-237, 1996.
15. Jurukova Z, Milenkov C: Ultrastructural evidence for collagen degradation in the walls of varicose veins. Exp Molec Pathol 37:37-47, 1982.
16. Venturi M, Bonavina L, Annoni F, et al: Biochemical assay of collagen and elastin in the normal and varicose vein wall. J Surg Res 60:245-248, 1996.
17. Maurel E, Azema C, Deloly J, Bouissou H: Collagen of the normal and the varicose human saphenous vein: A biochemical study. Clin Chim Acta 193:27-38, 1990.
18. Ascher E, Jacob T, Hingorani A, et al: Programmed cell death (apoptosis) and its role in the pathogenesis of lower extremity varicose veins. Ann Vasc Surg 14:24-30, 2000.
19. Ascher E, Jacob T, Hingorani A, et al: Expression of molecular mediators of apoptosis and their role in the pathogenesis of lower-extremity varicose veins. J Vasc Surg 33:1080-1086, 2001.
20. Gandhi RH, Irizarry E, Nachman GB, et al: Analysis of the connective tissue matrix and proteolytic activity of primary varicose veins. J Vasc Surg 18:814-820, 1993.
21. Parra JR, Cambria RA, Hower CD, et al: Tissue inhibitor of metalloproteinase-1 is increased in the saphenofemoral junction of patients with varices in the leg. J Vasc Surg 28:669-675, 1998.
22. Kosugi I, Urayama H, Kasashima F, et al: Matrix metalloproteinase-9 and urokinase-type plasminogen activator in varicose veins. Ann Vasc Surg 17:234-238, 2003.
23. Woodside KJ, Hu M, Burke A, et al: Morphologic characteristics of varicose veins: Possible role of metalloproteinases. J Vasc Surg 38:162-169, 2003.
24. Shireman PK, McCarthy WJ, Pearce WH, et al: Plasminogen activator levels are influenced by location and varicosity in greater saphenous vein. J Vasc Surg 24:719-724, 1996.
25. Badier-Commander C, Verbeuren T, Lebard C, et al: Increased TIMP/MMP ratio in varicose veins: A possible explanation for extracellular matrix accumulation. J Pathol 192:105-112, 2000.
26. Lowell RC, Gloviczki P, Miller VM: In vitro evaluation of endothelial and smooth muscle function of primary varicose veins. J Vasc Surg 16:679-686, 1992.
27. Rizzi A, Quaglio D, Vasquez G, et al: Effects of vasoactive agents in healthy and diseased human saphenous veins. J Vasc Surg 28:855-861, 1998.
28. Barber DA, Wang X, Gloviczki P, Miller VM: Characterization of endothelin receptors in human varicose veins. J Vasc Surg 26:61-69, 1997.
29. Nemcova S, Gloviczki P, Rud KS, Miller VM: Cyclic nucleotides and production of prostanoids in human varicose veins. J Vasc Surg 30:876-884, 1999.
30. Homans J: The etiology and treatment of varicose ulcer of the leg. Surg Gynecol Obstet 24:300-311, 1917.
31. Blalock A: Oxygen content of blood in patients with varicose veins. Arch Surg 19:898-905, 1929.
32. Pratt GH: Arterial varices: A syndrome. Am J Surg 77:456-460, 1949.
33. Burnand KG, Whimster I, Naidoo A, Browse NL: Pericapillary fibrin deposition in the ulcer bearing skin of the lower limb: The cause of lipodermatosclerosis and venous ulceration. Br Med J 285:1071-1072, 1982.
34. Burnand KG, Clemenson G, Gaunt J, Browse NL: The effect of sustained venus hypertension in the skin and capillaries of the canine hind limb. Br J Surg 69:41-44, 1981.
35. Browse NL, Burnand KG: The cause of venous ulceration. The Lancet 2(8292):243-245, 1982.
36. Coleridge Smith PD, Thomas P, Scurr JH, Dormandy JA: Causes of venous ulceration: A new hypothesis. Br Med J 296:1726-1727, 1988.
37. Thomas P, Nash GB, Dormandy JA: White cell accumulation in dependent legs of patients with venous hypertension: A possible mechanism for trophic changes in the skin. Br Med J 296:1693-1695, 1988.
38. Scott HJ, Coleridge Smith PD, Scurr JH: Histological study of white blood cells and their association with lipodermatosclerosis and venous ulceration. Br J Surg 78:210-211, 1991.
39. Wilkinson LS, Bunker C, Edward JCW, et al: Leukocytes: Their role in the etiopathogenesis of skin damage in venous disease. J Vasc Surg 17:669-675, 1993.
40. Pappas PJ, DeFouw DO, Venezio LM, et al: Morphometric assessment of the dermal microcirculation in patients with chronic venous insufficiency. J Vasc Surg 26:784-795, 1997.
41. Pappas PJ, Fallek SR, Garcia A, et al: Role of leukocyte activation in patients with venous stasis ulcers. J Surg Res 59:553-559, 1995.
42. Pappas PJ, Teehan EP, Fallek SR, et al: Diminished mononuclear cell function is associated with chronic venous insufficiency. J Vasc Surg 22:580-586, 1995.
41. Leu AJ, Leu HJ, Franzeck UK, Bollinger A: Microvascular changes in chronic venous insufficiency: A review. Cardiovasc Surg 3:237-245, 1995.
42. Leu HJ: Morphology of chronic venous insufficiency: Light and electron microscopic examinations. Vasa 20:330-342, 1991.

43. Wenner A, Leu HJ, Spycher M, Brunner U: Ultrastructural changes of capillaries in chronic venous insufficiency. Exp Cell Biol 48:1-14, 1980.

44. Scelsi R, Scelsi L, Cortinovis R, Poggi P: Morphological changes of dermal blood and lymphatic vessels in chronic venous insufficiency of the leg. Int Angiol 13:308-311, 1994.

45. Saarien J, Kalkkinen N, Welgus HG, Kovannen PT: Activation of human interstitial procollagenase through direct cleavage of the Leu83-Thr84 bond by mast cell chymase. J Biol Chem 269:18134-18140, 1994.

46. Lees M, Taylor DJ, Woolley DE: Mast cell proteinases activate precursor forms of collagenase and stromelysin, but not of gelatinases A and B. Eur J Biochem 223:171-177, 1994.

47. Kruger-Drasagakes S, Grutzkau A, et al: Interactions of immature human mast cells with extracellular matrix: Expression of specific adhesion receptors and their role in cell binding to matrix proteins. J Invest Dermatol 106:538-543, 1996.

48. Taipale J, Keski-Oja J: Growth factors in the extracellular matrix. FASEB J 11:51-59, 1997.

49. Roberts AB, Flanders KC, Kondaiah P, et al: Transforming growth factor β: Biochemistry and roles in embryogenesis, tissue repair and remodeling, and carcinogenesis. Recent Prog Horm Res 44:157-197, 1988.

50. Herrick S, Sloan P, McGurk M, et al: Sequential changes in histologic pattern and extracellular matrix deposition during the healing of chronic venous ulcers. Am J Pathol 141:1085-1095, 1992.

51. Bishop JE: Regulation of cardiovascular collagen deposition by mechanical forces. Molec Med Today 4:69-75, 1998.

52. Higley HR, Kassander GA, Gerhardt CO, Falanga V: Extravasation of macromolecules and possible trapping of transforming growth factor-β1 in venous ulceration. Br J Surg 132:79-85, 1995.

53. Peschen M, Lahaye T, Gennig B, et al: Expression of the adhesion molecules ICAM-1, VCAM-1, LFA-1 and VLA-4 in the skin is modulated in progressing stages of chronic venous insufficiency. Acta Derm Venereol 79:27-32, 1999.

54. Pappas PJ, You R, Rameshwar P, et al: Dermal tissue fibrosis in patients with chronic venous insufficiency is associated with increased transforming growth factor-β1 gene expression and protein production. J Vasc Surg 30:1129-1145, 1999.

55. Peschen M, Grenz H, Brand-Saberi B, et al: Increased expression of platelet-derived growth factor receptor alpha and beta and vascular endothelial growth factor in the skin of patients with chronic venous insufficiency. Arch Dermatol Res 290:291-297, 1998.

56. Hasan A, Murata H, Falabella A et al: Dermal fibroblasts from venous ulcers are unresponsive to the action of transforming growth factor-β1. J Dermatol Sci 16:59-66, 1997.

57. Kim B, Kim HT, Park SH, et al: Fibroblasts from chronic wounds show altered TGF-β signaling and decreased TGF-β type II receptor expression. J Cell Physiol 195:331-336, 2003.

58. Herrick SE, Ireland GW, Simon D, et al: Venous ulcer fibroblasts compared with normal fibroblasts show differences in collagen but not in fibronectin production under both normal and hypoxic conditions. J Invest Dermatol 106:187-193, 1996.

59. Stanley AC, Park H, Phillips TJ, et al: Reduced growth of dermal fibroblasts from chronic venous ulcers can be stimulated with growth factors. J Vasc Surg 26:994-1001, 1997.

60. Mendez MV, Stanley A, Park H, et al: Fibroblasts cultured from venous ulcers display cellular characteristics of senescence. J Vasc Surg 28:876-883, 1998.

61. Lal BK, Saito S, Pappas PJ, et al: Altered proliferative responses of dermal fibroblasts to TGF-β1 may contribute to chronic venous stasis ulcers. J Vasc Surg 37:1285-1293, 2003.

62. Mendez MV, Stanley A, Phillips TJ, et al: Fibroblasts cultured from distal lower extremities in patients with venous reflux display cellular characteristics of senescence. J Vasc Surg 28:1040-1050, 1998.

63. Weckroth M, Vaheri A, Lauharanta J, et al: Matrix metalloproteinases, gelatinase and collagenase, in chronic leg ulcers. J Invest Dermatol 106:1119-1124, 1996.

64. Wysocki AB, Staiano-Coico L, Grinell F: Wound fluid from chronic leg ulcers contains elevated levels of metalloproteinases MMP-2 and MMP-9. J Invest Dermatol 101:64-68, 1993.

65. Bullen EC, Longaker MT, Updike DL, et al: Tissue inhibitor of metalloproteinases-1 is decreased and activated gelatinases are increased in chronic wounds. J Invest Dermatol 104:236-240, 1995.

66. Herouy Y, May AE, Pornschlegel G, et al: Lipodermatosclerosis is characterized by elevated expression and activation of matrix metalloproteinases: Implications for venous ulcer formation. J Invest Dermatol 111:822-827, 1998.

67. Herouy Y, Trefzer D, Zimpfer U, et al: Matrix metalloproteinases and venous leg ulceration. Eur J Dermatol 9:173-180, 2000.

68. Norgauer J, Hildenbrand T, Idzko M, et al: Elevated expression of extracellular matrix metalloproteinase inducer (CD 147) and membrane-type matrix metalloproteinases in venous leg ulcers. Br J Dermatol 147:1180-1186, 2002.

69. Saito S, Trovato MJ, You R, et al: Role of matrix metalloproteinases 1, 2, and 9 and tissue inhibitor of matrix metalloproteinase-1 in chronic venous insufficiency. J Vasc Surg 34:930-938, 2001.

70. Herouy Y, Trefzer D, Hellstern MO, et al: Plasminogen activation in venous leg ulcers. Br J Dermatol 143:930-936, 2000.

Classification and Clinical and Diagnostic Evaluation of Patients with Chronic Venous Disorders

FRANK T. PADBERG, JR, MD

Patients referred for evaluation of chronic venous disorders (CVD) of the lower limbs offer a broad range of treatable complaints that usually account for the greatest proportion of cases seen in most vascular clinics. These range from unsightly cutaneous veins to chronic ulceration with its attendant disability. Although an extensive varicose network may produce minimal physiologic abnormalities, the most severe complaints (ulceration, edema, discoloration) may result from widely varied anatomic abnormalities. Reflux and venous obstruction are capable of producing a similar distribution of complaints, which may range from edema to ulceration or, rarely, the patient may be entirely asymptomatic. As a result, the current six-item clinical classification of all lower extremity CVD, which emphasizes these obvious clinical findings, is widely utilized because of its practical simplicity.[1-3] The term *chronic venous disease* is used also by many experts in the field to include conditions with measurable physiologic abnormalities of the venous circulation (C2-C6). In this summary, the term *chronic venous insufficiency* is used to accommodate more advanced venous abnormalities (C3-C6).

Because there is such variance in etiology, anatomy, and pathophysiology, complete diagnostic information is essential for accurate initial assessment, subsequent reassessment, and new investigations. Intended to fulfill this role, the full CEAP classification system incorporates etiologic, anatomic, and pathophysiologic data, to organize and categorize descriptions of CVD of the lower limbs in a format universally accepted by the international community. Such a full assessment usually requires additional diagnostic studies (i.e., duplex ultrasonography) in addition to the clinical examination. To complete the full assessment, and to maximize its accuracy, additional imaging studies may also be required.

In order to refine appropriate indications for management of CVD, the classification is followed by outcome assessment, which involves hemodynamic and physiologic studies, measures of disease severity, and estimates of quality of life. Physiologic outcomes are not incorporated in a specific scoring scheme; they are addressed elsewhere in this text. Severity scoring emphasizes the physician's perspective and is based on items in the clinical classification; items were selected to reflect change, and they assign greater weight to the more severe symptoms of CVD. Quality of life instruments emphasize the patient's perspective and use both generic and functional instruments; the items are selected to reflect the impact of CVD on the relationship between the individual and the environment, and thus, address the more subtle symptoms of CVD.[2] Finally, although prominent cutaneous veins are obvious clinical findings, all of the remaining items in clinical classes C3 through C6 can result from numerous other conditions that mimic CVD—but that may not have a venous etiology at all!

Thus, CVD is little different from numerous other clinical conditions in which the interaction of many different factors influences outcome. Although CVD rarely is life-threatening or requires emergency measures, improved management for this disorder is important because it is ubiquitous, common, and disabling. A uniform descriptive classification is a key first step to understanding the disease process and facilitates progressive identification of effective management strategies. Examples of efforts to this end are randomized trials evaluating endoscopic perforator surgery and structured exercise for severe CVD as well as systemic reviews of surgical outcomes.[4-6] The chapter begins with a review of the clinical examination, which is followed by a brief overview of physiology and imaging tests, detailed disease classification, assessment of disease impact, and, finally, mimics of the disease.

■ CLINICAL EXAMINATION: NOTABLE OBSERVATIONS AND HISTORICAL ESSENTIALS

A venous etiology is relevant to each of the three most common chief complaints in the vascular surgical clinic: the painful, swollen, or ulcerated leg (see Chapter 1). In the typical outpatient setting, a majority of the patients have venous problems. Although clinical examination was covered in detail in the first chapter of this text, a brief reiteration of the vein-directed clinical examination is included here because it forms an integral part of the assessment and classification of the patient with venous insufficiency.

The interview begins with a review of the patient's description of the problem. Often, pain or discomfort is the predominant consideration, and its severity is estimated; the savvy clinician also addresses the consideration that appearance may be the most important underlying issue. A venous etiology is more likely when a swollen limb is unilateral and worsens during the course of the day. A gaiter distribution of pigmentation or ulceration suggests venous insufficiency but may also result from other conditions. The duration and extent of all of these factors help to gauge their severity. Bleeding from superficial veins is more common in elderly individuals with a thin dermis. Knowledge of prior medical and surgical therapy is important, particularly in those referred for evaluation of edema. Inquiry about previous "blood clots" is often useful but usually requires supplementation with specific notation about "blood thinners," warfarin or heparin therapy, embolism, filter placement, admission to a hospital, and transient episodes of unilateral edema; specific recollection of surgical operations, bed rest for fractures, or prior injury may also yield pertinent information. The family history is important for multiple reasons—genetic predisposition to thrombosis, varicosities, and congenital abnormalities. Review of medications and allergies should include topical agents. Habits and vitamin and hormonal deficiencies may produce secondary manifestations in the limbs. Symptoms and severity tend to worsen with obesity and advanced age.[7-9]

The clinical examination begins with the usual cervical, thoracic, and abdominal survey, which should include weight and body mass index (BMI) as well as correlation between physiologic and chronologic age. The directed examination begins with observation of each limb in both the supine and standing positions. The distributions of visible large and small venous tributaries are noted, and assessment is made of their significance to the patient. When the limb is dependent, veins distend fully and discoloration intensifies; when the patient is standing, he or she is asked not to bear weight on the limb to be examined. In the standing position, the great and small saphenous veins are evaluated for palpable turgidity, and for stress incompetence with a cough; a tussive impulse is sought by both palpation and a hand-held Doppler probe. Thigh perforators may be suspected if the findings are localized only to the distal thigh and are controlled by direct distal compression rather than compression at the saphenofemoral junction; cessation of the impulse with groin compression is suggestive of proximal saphenofemoral incompetence. Owing to the beneficial clinical, functional, and hemodynamic response to correction of saphenofemoral incompetence, this finding should be specifically evaluated as a part of every surgeon's examination.[10-13]

The extent of pigmentation and edema is noted, along with induration, cellulitis, or lymphangitis. Onset of edema early in the day is considered a sign of greater disease severity. Chronic exposure to diffuse elevation of venous pressure throughout the lower leg results in scarring and thickening of the dermal and subdermal tissues, referred to as brawny edema or lipodermatosclerosis. Appearance, size, number, duration, and location describe active ulcerations. Frequency and utilization of compression garments is noted. All of the preceding factors are registered in the CEAP scale or Venous Clinical Severity Score (VCSS).

Not specifically recorded in the CEAP scale are several additional relevant items. They include localized pruritus, which is often betrayed by telltale scratch marks; it may be

associated with eczema, which also has a gaiter distribution and may be dry or moist. Arthritis and skeletal deformities reduce calf muscle function, which may diminish the capacity for the calf muscle pump to compensate for valvular reflux or venous obstruction.[5,14,15] Arterial insufficiency is excluded through palpation of pulses; when the pulses are masked by edema or thickened skin, the addition of an ankle-brachial index is often sufficient unless the individual is diabetic. In addition to consideration of nonvenous causes, individuals with recurrent ulceration should be assessed for normal sensation in the supramalleolar region, as absence of normal sensation may be associated with a greater propensity for recurrence.[16]

The inframalleolar ankle flare, or corona phlebectatica, is assigned special significance by European investigators and was included in clinical class 1 of the initial reporting standards in venous disease.[17,18] It emanates from one of the original classification schemes for venous diseases, which was based on clinical examination and evaluated 4529 industrial workers in Basle, Switzerland.[19] The scheme consisted of three clinical classes, and was developed in the era preceding widespread use of duplex ultrasonography; the classes were (1) reticular veins, (2) edema and corona phlebectatica, and (3) pigmentation-ulceration. The initial recommendations of the Society for Vascular Surgery (SVS)–International Society for Cardiovascular Surgery (ISCVS) committee on standards for venous disease offered 10 years later also used three classes, consisting of (1) reticular veins–edema-corona, (2) pigmentation, and (3) ulceration, roughly corresponding to mild, moderate, and severe disease.[17] The following decade, the recommendations were altered to include the current six-item CEAP classification in use today and summarized in Table 155-1.[1,3]

Coordinating the elements of diagnosis enables a course of therapy to be accurately determined. When the approach is efficiently organized, 97% of ulcerated limbs can be accurately diagnosed in a single visit incorporating the clinical examination, duplex scan, and the ankle-brachial index.[20] Unbiased evidence supports use of a standard care regimen incorporating compression therapy, but success requires compliance and consistent attention.[21,22] Failure to consider other differential diagnoses may result in serious misdiagnosis (malignancy), nonhealing (obesity), and frequent recurrence (ulcerative colitis or collagen vascular disease). Yet, in more than a third of patients with these other disorders, the anatomic abnormality can be corrected by an appropriately directed intervention.[11-13]

■ IMAGING AND HEMODYNAMICS

Although both direct venous imaging and hemodynamic studies are covered by specific discussion in other chapters, they are such an integral part of the assessment of severe venous insufficiency that a brief reminder of their role and indications is appropriate. As a general rule, duplex scanning, which is now considered routine in most ultrasonography vascular laboratories, is essential for a complete CEAP classification. Modern ultrasonography routinely demonstrates valvular incompetence and large perforating veins. Demonstration of the subtle changes accompanying

Table 155-1	CEAP Classification of Lower Extremity Chronic Venous Disease

C		Clinical signs (class 0-6), supplemented by A for asymptomatic and S for symptomatic presentation.
	Class 0	No visible or palpable signs of venous disease
	Class 1	Telangiectases, reticular veins, malleolar flare
	Class 2	Varicose veins
	Class 3	Edema without skin changes
	Class 4	Skin changes attributed to venous disease (e.g., pigmentation, venous eczema, lipodermatosclerosis)
	Class 5	Skin changes as defined above with healed ulceration
	Class 6	Skin changes as defined above with active ulceration
E		Etiologic classification
	Congenital (E_C)	The cause of the venous disease has been present since birth
	Primary (E_P)	Chronic venous disease of undetermined cause
	Secondary (E_S)	Chronic venous disease with an associated known cause (post-thrombotic, post-traumatic, other)
A		Anatomic distribution
	A_{S1-5}	Superficial veins
	A_{D6-16}	Deep veins
	A_{P17-18}	Perforating veins
P		Pathophysiologic dysfunction
	P_R	Reflux
	P_O	Obstruction
	$P_{R,O}$	Reflux and obstruction

Adapted from Porter JM, Moneta GL: Reporting standards in venous disease: An update. International Consensus Committee on Chronic Venous Disease. J Vasc Surg 21:635-645, 1995; with permission from Society for Vascular Surgery.

resolution of thrombosis has also improved. The major weakness of duplex scanning is investigation of suprainguinal venous structures.

Invasive investigations, such as venography or ambulatory venous pressures, are requested when findings of the clinical and noninvasive examinations are insufficient to provide complete diagnosis or as a part of a therapeutic endeavor. In addition to diagnosis, venography offers an access route for thrombolysis and stenting. Although less widely available, intravascular ultrasonography offers new information about intra-abdominal venous compression syndromes and may be more sensitive than venography or pressure studies.[23]

Measurement of ambulatory venous pressure remains an important invasive diagnostic tool and identifies the standing pressure nadir as well as the rapidity of emptying and refill. Small subtle changes in foot pressures may reflect significant venous abnormalities, but even these measurements are plagued by low sensitivity to the difficult problem of venous obstruction.[23] In practice, these examinations are often supplanted by more patient-friendly, noninvasive plethysmographic studies, which provide an objective measure of volume changes related to posture and to function of the calf muscle pump.[14,24,25] As the other major noninvasive component of venous assessment, plethysmography may contribute direct information to the pathophysiologic classification.[1,3,17] However, as duplex ultrasonographic diagnosis has assumed an increasingly dominant diagnostic role, disease classification is often assigned on the basis of

duplex scanning information alone. Plethysmographic results are not incorporated into severity scoring, can be repeated as needed with minimal discomfort or risk, and thus offer additional data for longitudinal comparison of outcomes.[5,11,26,27]

Magnetic resonance venography (MRV) offers yet another alternative for clarification of proximal diagnostic questions.[28] The evolution of new imaging techniques in MRV and computed tomography venography holds as much or more promise for elucidation of venous disease than of arterial disease. Both modalities require only venipuncture for image optimization.

■ THE CEAP CLASSIFICATION

Correct diagnosis is critical to success, and the international community has endorsed the initiative of the American Venous Forum in developing a consensus for the language of venous disorders.[1,2,17] The detailed categorization consists of six symptoms, 17 anatomic sites, and tripartite etiologic and pathophysiologic categories. These were the details deemed necessary to accurately compare limbs in medical and surgical treatment trials. Although criticized as too complex and detailed, the CEAP classification was embraced by the worldwide community, published in more than 25 journals, and translated into multiple languages.[18] CEAP is now considered the standard for reports on venous disorders. It appears to be fulfilling the intent to standardize communication in this surprisingly complex field, was analyzed for improved accuracy, and has been enhanced by refinement in severity scoring.[1-3,18]

The CEAP classification was developed at a 1994 international consensus committee meeting sponsored by the American Venous Forum.[1,3] The reporting format was designed for completeness, not convenience. Although it was not intended for isolated use in the description of limbs with venous disorders, the clinical (C) classification has often been reported independent of the etiologic (E), anatomic (A), and pathophysiologic (P) classifications. In part, this may be a function of the diagnostic imprecision inherent in many nonspecialty clinics.[9,29-31] The E, A, and P classifications serve to define the presence and nature of venous disease and to differentiate other, nonvenous causes of the typical physical findings.[5-7,19,26,32] Thus, reports that do not incorporate these three additional components are more likely to include limbs with nonvenous causes of insufficiency, some of which may respond to entirely different management strategies.[8,30,31,33,34]

Chronic venous disease was broadly defined in the revised reporting standards coming from the consensus conference as "an abnormally functioning venous system caused by venous valvular incompetence with or without associated venous outflow obstruction, which may affect the superficial venous system, the deep venous system, or both."[1] Although perforating veins are not cited in this definition, their role remains controversial, and they are integral to the whole CEAP classification. Note that in British use, CVI specifically implies severe (C4 to C6) venous dysfunction[9]; in this summary, the term chronic venous disorders is used to accommodate the full spectrum of venous abnormalities.

Clinical Classification

The most widely utilized component of the CEAP system is the clinical classification. The various components of each class are given in Table 155-1, which is adapted in format but uses the same language as the consensus committee report.[1] The classification is organized to reflect ascending severity of venous disease; in addition, subscripts are added to designate the asymptomatic (A) or symptomatic (S) state. Although many of the higher classes include characteristics of lesser classes, this is not essential, and the higher class is reported preferentially.[1,35] European surveys have found an unacceptable interobserver variation in classification of C1 and C2 and have offered recommendations for changing the criteria.

A C0 category is provided for two reasons. First, there are inevitably some patients with anatomic venous problems who have no visible or palpable signs of CVD. Common examples are the individual with an isolated incompetent venous valve identified on a duplex scan, and an individual with mild post-thrombotic scarring who cannot recall the episode of venous thrombosis.[36] Second, C0 provides an additional definition for control patients in clinical trials. The International Union of Phlebology Working Group has recommended that C0 with no EAP abnormalities be the criterion for control patients in clinical trials.[18] In practice, this stringent requirement may be difficult to achieve.

Smaller dilated, nonpalpable veins specifically referred to as telangiectatic, reticular, or "spider," thread, or web veins are all categorized as C1. *Telangiectasia* refers to intradermal, dilated veins less than 1 mm in diameter. *Reticular* refers to nonpalpable, subdermal veins less than 4 mm in diameter.[1] The predominant concern with this patient population is usually one of appearance, and more severe underlying venous abnormalities may or may not be present. Commonly reported symptoms include pain, aching, and skin irritation. Duplex scanning is generally not required before initiation of treatment in this patient group. However, its omission precludes complete CEAP classification and contributes to the variance between clinical observers.

A *varicose vein* (clinical class C2) was defined as a palpable, subcutaneous vein more than 4 mm in diameter.[1] On the basis of improved interobserver reproducibility, an international consensus conference recommended a decrease in this threshold to 3 mm.[18] Accuracy of classification is the issue, because the diameter difference has no physiologic significance. Whether the vein is palpable or not is highly subjective, but making diameter the criterion implies the need for imaging to define the clinical classification. Although most clinicians would prefer routine duplex scanning examinations for this population, expense and availability have impeded universal acceptance of this recommendation throughout the world. Valvular incompetence at either the saphenofemoral or saphenopopliteal junction may occur without additional symptoms, but onset of unilateral edema raises the individual's clinical class designation.

The distinguishing characteristic of C3—edema—is common and is usually clinically obvious. However, alternative diagnoses are probably encountered more frequently in patients with edema than in those with the other clinical classes of disease. Although detailed in the recommendations, the differential exclusion of other causes of edema is rarely so straightforward in clinical practice (i.e., bilateral findings are not distinguished from other conditions characterized by systemic fluid retention, such as congestive heart failure, renal failure, and ascites). Circumferential limb measurements were recommended in the consensus report, but reliable estimates of the extent of edema is difficult without volume measurements.[3,31] The most accurate technique is probably water displacement plethysmography, which is also too cumbersome for routine use. A practical definition of *edema* is simple indentation on pressure ("pitting").[18]

The entire spectrum of skin changes, excluding current or existing ulceration, constitutes the C4 class. Although many of the limbs with this classification also have edema, they may not have obvious cutaneous veins. The most obvious finding is the light to dark tan discoloration of the skin distributed in a "gaiter" pattern. However, pigmentation may also be distributed throughout the leg and below the malleoli. An inflammatory response mediated by transforming growth factor-β (TGF-β) is thought to arise from breakdown products of extravasated hemosiderin.[32] The skin is thickened along with the subcutaneous tissues and may have a solid, woody character to palpation known as *lipodermatosclerosis*. An acute form of dermatosclerosis, *hypodermatitis* describes diffuse reddening of the skin in the absence of inflammation or cellulitis.[18] Pale, atrophic skin surrounded by dilated capillaries or pigmentation that has not ulcerated (yet) is known as *atrophie blanche*. Both lipodermatosclerosis and atrophie blanche are thought to predispose to ulceration. In severely edematous limbs, the skin may start to weep, a finding that is also probably a precursor to ulceration. The spectrum of C4 also includes venous eczema, which may also be wet or dry.

Healed ulceration, or C5, is perhaps the most uncomplicated clinical class. A history of venous ulceration at any prior time establishes this diagnosis, and the C5 limb probably represents the highest risk for recurrence of ulceration. During a mean 5-year observation in one study, 30% of patients compliant with compression therapy experienced recurrent ulceration within 5 years; 100% of individuals who were noncompliant had recurrence within 3 years.[22] In the 25-year Olmsted County study, 6.3% of class 4 limbs with a first-time, clinically defined diagnosis of venous stasis progressed to ulceration in a mean of 5 years.[8]

Active ulceration is also relatively straightforward, but the classification also assumes that the ulcer can be attributed to a venous cause. Because it is the most debilitating and least desirable aspect of the disease process of CVD, it is accorded the highest CEAP clinical class, C6. The greatest morbidity and the greatest functional impairment are attributed to this clinical class. Junctional saphenous incompetence should be specifically noted because it is present in 30% to 60% of limbs with venous insufficiency and responds to surgical correction.[11-13,20] However, the clinician must not just assume that all perimalleolar ulcers have a venous etiology; additional information beyond CEAP classification is often required to establish the correct diagnosis. Approximately 3% to 15% of ulcers "never" heal (no response to appropriate treatment within 6 months), and this finding may be due to combined arterial and venous insufficiency (10% to 15%) or other causes (5% to 10%).[7,13,22,33,34,36]

Etiology, Anatomy, and Pathophysiology Classifications

The three etiology categories, primary, secondary, and congenital, are mutually exclusive. Although specifically defined as "indeterminant," the *primary* component is generally characterized by intrinsic weakness of the vein wall or valve cusp. *Secondary* venous dysfunction results from an acquired condition. Designating a limb as having secondary dysfunction implies knowledge of a specific cause. If thrombosis is known to have occurred, the limb may be referred to as *post-thrombotic*; if not, the problem should be generically categorized as chronic venous disease. The most common of these is venous thrombosis, but it also includes states resulting from trauma. Currently, secondary venous disease is more and more commonly a result of prolonged intravenous catheterization. *Congenital* venous disease is generally obvious, and comprises the various venous malformations, Klippel-Trenaunay variants, avalvulia, and other conditions that may not be recognized until later in life.[37-39]

Anatomy is initially characterized by describing abnormalities of the three venous systems in the lower extremity: the superficial, deep, and perforating veins. Further breakdown identifies each of the individual veins with a numeric subscript (Table 155-2). As a minimum for the venous practitioner, characterization of dysfunction in each of the three main systems is important, because this localization may influence subsequent management. In order to evaluate the anatomic effects of differing management techniques, these individual segments are characterized before and after intervention. For example, several reports have assessed the importance of individual anatomic segments and suggested differing roles for perforator vein incompetence and deep vein incompetence in relation to superficial ablation.[11,13,27,40] With longer follow-up, it may be possible to determine whether, and which, individual segments contribute greater adverse effects. Ongoing experience with CEAP can provide a better delineation of the contribution of each segment to global dysfunction in the limb.

Pathophysiology is classified as reflux, obstruction, or both. The vast majority of patients with CVD have reflux.[20,26] Duplex scanning criteria for reflux have been widely accepted and utilized worldwide. Reverse flow is considered abnormal when its duration is greater than 0.5 second, although some have recommended a more stringent criterion of more than 1.0 second.[2,41,42] The "both" category reflects the remarkable capability of the venous conduit to restore luminal patency through the process of recanalization. Because valves are predominantly infrainguinal structures, *reflux* is essentially characterized by evaluation of the extremity alone; in contrast, obstruction may result from occlusion or extrinsic compression anywhere in the proximal venous outflow, including the abdomen and chest.[23]

Unfortunately, *obstruction* is not as clearly defined as reflux. Plethysmographic determination of outflow was once the mainstay of noninvasive assessment when used for the diagnosis of acute obstruction from iliofemoral thrombosis; however, plethysmography is relatively insensitive to subacute or resolving obstruction, and findings may be normal with extensive collateralization. The physiology of venous obstruction is quite complex, beginning with the concept of venous return against gravity. Relatively small pressure gradients control flow, but a large capacitance requires volume and distention before the pressures rise. Thus, plethysmography is rather insensitive to obstruction, but when obstruction is identified, it is probably clinically significant. Arm-foot differential pressures of 4 to 8 mm Hg have been used to confirm obstruction but also have low sensitivity.[2,23] As a practical solution, duplex scanning evidence of prior scarring and partial occlusions has sometimes been reported without adjunctive hemodynamic measurements. Increasing access to MRV and computed tomography venography will inevitably enlarge their role in the diagnosis of both acute and chronic venous obstruction.[28]

Controversies and Considerations Regarding Revision

No standard is likely to remain static in the face of new technology and change, so on its 10-year anniversary, CEAP is undergoing re-evaluation by another international consensus committee to address these issues.[29] The goals of the revision are to consider a more convenient format, to improve its functionality, and to incorporate some of the controversial issues described here. Complexity may be increased with application of a complete anatomic score, but localization still appears to be a major key to organizing successful management of the disease process.

Table 155-2	Segmental Localization of Chronic Lower Extremity Venous Disease

NUMBER	SEGMENT
	Superficial veins (A_{S1-5}):
1	Great saphenous vein
2	Above knee
3	Below knee
4	Small saphenous vein
5	Nonsaphenous
	Deep veins (A_{D6-16}):
6	Inferior vena cava
	Iliac
7	Common
8	Internal
9	External
10	Pelvic: gonadal, broad ligament
	Femoral
11	Common
12	Deep
13	Superficial
14	Popliteal
15	Tibial (anterior, posterior, or peroneal)
16	Muscular (gastrocnemius, soleal, other)
	Perforating veins (A_{P17-18}):
17	Thigh
18	Calf

From Porter JM, Moneta GL: Reporting standards in venous disease: An update. International Consensus Committee on Chronic Venous Disease. J Vasc Surg 21:635-645, 1995; with permission from Society for Vascular Surgery.

During this first decade of implementation, reporting the clinical classification has evolved to reporting the single most severe clinical class present in that limb.[18,35] In other words, a patient with healed ulceration, pigmentation, varicosed veins, telangiectasis, and edema would receive a classification of C5. This is a change from the initial recommendation, when an inclusive nomenclature, which listed each of the clinical classes observed in the individual's limb (i.e., C1, C2, C3, C4, C5) was recommended.

The clinical classification successfully defines the patient's status on the basis of an initial clinical examination; however, the remainder of the CEAP classification requires some adjunctive testing. The inaccuracy of reliance on clinical diagnosis alone retarded progress in venous diseases for years, but the addition of noninvasive examinations has been a critical component fueling progress in venous diseases.[26] In most institutions, complete assessment would require an additional clinic visit, but adherence to a standardized protocol can facilitate diagnosis in a single visit.[20] There is probably a need for a simplified version of CEAP, which can be assigned on the basis of a clinical examination without adjunctive testing. However, it is probably premature to attempt development of a uniform description of CVD without noninvasive data. Meanwhile, the complete CEAP classification should continue to be employed for comparison of interventional strategies.

■ SEVERITY SCORING

The first consensus conference offered an 18-point severity score, based on 0 to 2 points for each of nine categories, and a straight-sum anatomic score.[3] The clinical score appeared to have reasonable utility, but several of the items were not likely to reflect change and therefore would not have been responsive to improvement or deterioration with therapy. Although available for almost a decade, and reported in numerous studies, neither scoring approach was ever subjected to validation.

In contrast, the recent Venous Clinical Severity Score received international utilization and has now been field-tested by three groups of investigators.[43-45] It is constructed from 10 items scored 0 through 3, roughly corresponding to the familiar none-mild-moderate-severe, for a maximal score of 30 (see Tables 155-3 to 155-5). The range of values has a linear correlation with CEAP clinical class and anatomic extent. In one study, the most severely affected individuals, those with active ulceration, had a mean VCSS of 14.9 ± 2.8[43]; a similar value of 13.5 was observed in a European study.[45] All three groups found the VCSS to be very good a separating normal limbs from limbs with venous disease and at differentiating mild or moderate disease (C2 to C3), from severe (C4 through C6) venous disease.[43-45] The purpose of revising the severity score was to make it more responsive to changes in the patient's

Table 155-3	Venous Severity Scoring: The Venous Clinical Severity Score			
ATTRIBUTE	**ABSENT: 0**	**MILD: 1**	**MODERATE: 2**	**SEVERE: 3**
Pain	None	Occasional; not restricting activity or requiring analgesics	Daily; moderate activity limitation; occasional analgesics	Daily; severely limiting activities or requiring regular use of analgesics
Varicose veins*	None	Few, scattered: branch varicose veins	Multiple: GS varicose veins confined to calf or thigh	Extensive: Thigh and calf or GS and LS distribution
Venous edema†	None	Evening ankle edema only	Afternoon edema, above ankle	Morning edema above ankle and requiring activity change, elevation
Skin pigmentation‡	None or focal, low-intensity (tan)	Diffuse, but limited in area and old (brown)	Diffuse over most of gaiter distribution (lower ⅓ of leg) or recent pigmentation (purple)	Wider distribution (above lower ⅓ of leg) and recent
Inflammation	None	Mild cellulitis, limited to marginal area around ulcer	Moderate cellulitis, involving most of gaiter area (lower ⅓ of leg)	Severe cellulitis (lower ⅓ of leg and above) or significant venous eczema
Induration	None	Focal, circummalleolar (< 5 cm)	Medial or lateral, less than lower ⅓ of leg	Entire lower ⅓ of leg or more
No. of acute ulcers	0	1	2	> 2
Active ulceration; duration	No	Yes; < 3 mo	Yes; > 3 mo, < 1 yr	Yes; not healed > 1 yr
Active ulcer, size (diameter)	No	Yes; < 2 cm	Yes; 2-6 cm	Yes; > 6 cm
Compressive therapy	Not used or not compliant	Intermittent use of stockings	Patient wears elastic stockings most days	Full compliance: stockings and elevation

*"Varicose" veins must be > 4 mm in diameter to qualify so that differentiation is ensured between C1 and C2 venous disease.
†Presumes venous origin from characteristics (e.g., brawny [not pitting or spongy] edema), with significant effect of standing/limb elevation and/or other clinical evidence of venous etiology (i.e., varicose veins, history of deep venous thrombosis). Edema must be regular finding (e.g., daily occurrence). Occasional or mild edema does not qualify.
‡Focal pigmentation over varicose veins does not qualify.
GS, greater saphenous; LS, lesser saphenous.

Adapted from Rutherford RB, Padberg FT, Comerota AJ, et al: Venous Severity Scoring: An adjunct to venous outcome assessment. J Vasc Surg 31:1307-1312, 2000; with permission from Society for Vascular Surgery.

Table 155-4	Venous Severity Scoring: The Venous Segmental Disease Score (Based on Venous Segmental Involvement with Reflux or Obstruction*)			

REFLUX†			OBSTRUCTION†‡	
Score	Vein(s)	Score	Vein(s)	
½	Small saphenous	§		
1	Great saphenous	1	Greater saphenous (only if thrombosed from groin to below knee)	
½	Perforators, thigh	§		
1	Perforator, calf	§		
2	Calf veins, multiple (posterior tibial alone = 1)	1	Calf veins, multiple	
2	Popliteal vein	2	Popliteal vein	
1	Femoral vein	1	Femoral vein	
1	Profunda femoris vein	1	Profunda femoris vein	
1	Common femoral vein and above§	2	Common femoral	
		1	Iliac vein	
		1	Inferior vena cava	
10	*Maximum reflux score*	10	*Maximum obstruction score* ¶	

*As determined by appropriate venous imaging (phlebography or duplex ultrasonography scan). Although some segments may not be routinely studied in some laboratories (e.g., profunda femoris and tibial veins), points cannot be awarded on the basis of presumption, without scanning of the segments for obstruction or reflux.

†*Reflux* means that all the valves in that segment are incompetent. *Obstruction* means there is total occlusion at some point in the segment or > 50% narrowing of at least half of the segment. Most segments are assigned 1 point, but some segments have been weighted more or less to fit with their perceived significance (e.g., increasing points for common femoral or popliteal obstruction and for popliteal and multiple calf vein reflux and decreasing points for lesser saphenous or thigh perforator reflux). Points can be assigned for both obstruction and reflux in the same segment; this is uncommon but can occur in some post-thrombotic states, potentially giving secondary venous insufficiency higher severity scores than primary disease.

‡The excision, ligation, or traumatic obstruction of deep venous segments counts toward obstruction points just as much as their thrombosis.

§Normally there are no valves above the common femoral vein, so no reflux points are assigned to them. In addition, perforator interruption and saphenous ligation/excision do not count in the obstruction score, but as a reduction of the reflux score.

¶Not all of the 11 segments can be involved in reflux or obstruction. 10 is the maximum score that can be assigned, and the maximum might be achieved by complete reflux at all segmental levels.

Adapted from Rutherford RB, Padberg FT, Comerota AJ, et al: Venous Severity Scoring: An adjunct to venous outcome assessment. J Vasc Surg 31:1307-1312, 2000; with permission from Society for Vascular Surgery.

condition. It emphasizes the more severe aspects of venous insufficiency with the inclusion of three separate categories for active ulceration. Thus, severity can be expected to diminish substantially at the time of healing. Other aspects of CVD responsive to relatively rapid change are pain, edema, extent of varicose veins, and inflammation. In one study, interobserver variability was greatest in the assessment of three items—pain, pigmentation, and inflammation—and suggestions were made to improve these descriptions.[43] Although induration and pigmentation are thought to improve, the response is expected to occur more slowly.

The Venous Segmental Disease Score (VSDS) attempts to refine the anatomic score by assigning specified point values to various anatomic segments and separating the scores for reflux and obstruction. Segments considered to have a greater impact on the disease process are given higher point values, but both have a maximum of 10. Although the VSDS is not widely employed as yet, it is hoped that these values will be validated in subsequent clinical studies. In one review comparing VCSS, VSDS, and Venous Disability Score (VDS), the segmental disease score was the least well correlated with the disease process, suggesting that more work is needed on this aspect of scoring.[44,45] In another, the "anatomic score correlated well with the clinical severity score."[44]

The Venous Disability Score (VDS) was revised to make it more versatile, by changing the original definition from one relating inability to function at work-related activities, to one concerned with all general activities. This permitted rating of the continuously enlarging elderly population with venous insufficiency. In several studies, it correlated well with severity and exhibited a correlation coefficient of .7.[45]

Both the CEAP classification system and its associated scoring are assigned and interpreted by the physician and, on the basis of the history and physical findings, supplemented by duplex scanning. It is expected that additional research and investigation will further validate this system, and the American Venous Forum initiated the first of these reviews in 2002.

Table 155-5	Venous Severity Scoring: The Venous Disability Score

0	Asymptomatic
1	Symptomatic but patient is able to carry out usual activities* without compressive therapy
2	Patient can carry out usual activities* only with compression and/or limb elevation
3	Patient is unable to carry out usual activities* even with compression and/or limb elevation

*Usual activities = patient's activities before onset of disability from venous disease.

Adapted from Rutherford RB, Padberg FT, Comerota AJ, et al: Venous Severity Scoring: An adjunct to venous outcome assessment. J Vasc Surg 31:1307-1312, 2000; with permission from Society for Vascular Surgery.

Table 155-6	Currently Available Disease-Specific Instruments for Measurement of Health-Related Quality of Life in Patients with Chronic Venous Disease (CVD) of the Lower Extremity			
ABBREVIATION AND TITLE	**YEAR**	**FOCUS**	**LANGUAGE(S)**	**NUMBER OF QUESTIONS; COMMENTS**
AVVS[48]; Aberdeen Varicose Vein Score	1993	Varicose veins, CVD	English	20 questions Weighted scoring Patient diagrams veins onto template
CIVIQ[30]; Chronic Venous Insufficiency Questionnaire	1996	General Venous	French, English	20 questions Diagnosis based on clinical and subjective symptoms; no objective confirmation of venous etiology
Temple DVT[49]	1999	Iliofemoral deep venous thrombosis	English	80 questions Derived from thrombolysis registry data
VEINES[31]; VEnous INsufficiency Epidemiological & Economic Study	2003	General venous	French, English, Italian, French-Canadian	26 questions Claims to assess full C1-C6 spectrum of CVD Based on large clinical sample, infrequent confirmation of venous etiology
CCVU[46]; Charing Cross Venous Ulcer Questionaire	2000	Venous ulcers	English	20 questions Venous etiology confirmed with duplex ultrasonography

■ HEALTH-RELATED QUALITY OF LIFE: THE PATIENT'S PERSPECTIVE

In contrast to CEAP and the various physician-scoring systems, the various health-related quality-of-life (HR-QoL) questionnaires for CVI-related illness provide additional insight from the patient's perspective. Most psychometric experts continue to recommend the use of both generic and disease-specific instruments for these assessments. Although the generic questionnaires did not have a strong correlation with CVI, they are recommended because of their effectiveness in identifying other factors influencing an individual's quality of life. Currently, five validated instruments with acceptable reliability and responsiveness are available for evaluation of HR-QoL in CVI (Table 155-6). The basic concepts underlying this evaluation process involve several specific terms usually less familiar to the vascular surgeon: validity, reliability, and responsiveness, as defined here. In addition, acceptability and convenience are relative considerations that vary with the location and goals of the project.

Validity: Does the questionnaire measure what it is intended to measure? Often, there are not good measures for this parameter, and the questionnaires are then compared with clinical findings or other objective findings.

Reliability: Is the measure free of random error? Examples are test-retest comparisons, such as Does the result change when evaluated by the same examiner at different times? By different examiners? Is the evaluation stable when evaluated by the same examiner at different times, or different examiners?

Responsiveness: Does the instrument identify meaningful change? This is often the most difficult parameter

to illustrate. However, like the expected improvement in the severity score, healing of an active venous ulceration would be expected to produce a measurable improvement in HR-QoL score; this is illustrated in Figure 155-1.[46]

The role of psychometric instruments such as these is critically tied to the comprehensive measurement of surgical and other medical outcomes. The relationship to financial impact and the cost of delivering various types of surgical and medical care is directly relevant and will become increasingly important in future decisions about funding for

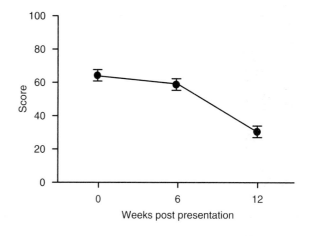

FIGURE 155-1 Responsiveness of the ulcer-specific questionnaire at 6 and 12 weeks (SE of the mean is represented by the *error bars*). (From Smith JJ: Measuring quality of life: Patients with venous ulcers. J Vasc Surg, 31:646, 2000, with permission from Society for Vascular Surgery.)

different treatments. Although detail is beyond the scope of this chapter, this concept is often expressed in quality-adjusted life-years (QALY), in which the relative value of a given treatment is expressed as the gain in survival from the treatment, and then a monetary value can be calculated as necessary to achieve this benefit to the population.

The five validated, disease-specific instruments available for use in CVD are summarized in Table 155-6. The oldest is the Aberdeen Varicose Vein Score (AVVS), which was initially proposed in 1993.[48] Saphenous surgery, with or without the stripping component, conferred a significant improvement in HR-QoL for a period of up to 2 years as measured by the AVVS.[10]

Both the Chronic Venous Insufficiency Questionnaire (CIVIQ) and the VEnous Insufficiency Epidemiological & Economic Study (VEINES) were developed from enormous patient databases and have been validated in multiple languages.[30,31] Patients evaluated in both of these large studies were often diagnosed with venous insufficiency on the basis of clinical examination by primary care physicians and not investigation of venous etiology supported by imaging; thus, the diagnosis may be somewhat less specific, but the similarity of symptoms to other conditions causing edema and pigmentary change may or may not have similar effects on the patient's perceptions of their disease. Despite the intentional accession of male subjects with ulceration in the VEINES, the incidence of ulceration in these study populations was rather small considering the size of the sample.[47] Patients selected from a registry for iliofemoral thrombolysis were evaluated with a specific HR-QoL questionnaire directed at the symptoms of venous thrombosis; a significant improvement in two dimensions was demonstrated in patients receiving thrombolytic therapy as opposed to a standard anticoagulation regimen.[49] In contrast, the Charing Cross Venous Ulcer Questionnaire (CCVU) is the most specific of these instruments and clearly demonstrates a response to successful treatment.

The AVVS was one of the first designed specifically to evaluate a surgical intervention for venous insufficiency. The AVVS is unique in scoring the extent of the varicosities with an overlying grid; although, unfortunately, its name implies that it is specifically a varicose vein questionnaire, the AVVS is capable of measuring more than just the cosmetic aspects of CVD and addresses most of the problems associated with CVD, including ulceration.

Each instrument inquires about pain in the initial questions and covers impaired mobility and appearance of the leg in the survey. Although large multinational instruments such as the CIVIQ and the VEINES may be less specific, they have also been most effective when addressing the effects of less severe CEAP clinical classes on the patient; higher clinical class may be better addressed with the VCSS. Although recommended in conjunction with disease-specific assessments, generic instruments such as the Medical Outcomes Study's 36-Item Health Survey (SF-36), the Nottingham Health Profile, and the Functional Independence Measure are discussed in other chapters and are not detailed further here. The AVVS and CCVU are both based on anatomic abnormalities—obvious varicosities and leg ulceration. There is no doubt that varices are representative of CVD, but the attribution of symptoms to this cause as opposed to other causes is less straightforward[50]; likewise, ulceration may have numerous alternative causes.

■ MIMICS OF CHRONIC VENOUS INSUFFICIENCY, OR DIFFERENTIAL DIAGNOSIS

A number of other medical conditions can produce the "typical" clinical findings associated with CVD. Although the external appearance of small and large varicose veins offers an obvious diagnosis, the more advanced clinical findings associated with CVD can be due to a number of other medical conditions. It is here that evaluation by the broadly based vascular specialist is likely to be of greatest value in organizing the approach to the patient. A comprehensive list is beyond the scope of this text, but the evaluating vascular surgeon (who often fulfills this role) should routinely consider several of the more commonly encountered mimics, which are reviewed here as organized in the framework of CEAP clinical classifications C3 through C6.

The most ubiquitous is edema, which is often due to conditions other than venous insufficiency, particularly when the edema is expressed bilaterally. Identification of a medical cause leads to alternative treatment strategies; appropriate management of renal, hepatic, or cardiac failure may produce dramatic improvement in peripheral edema.

Pigmentation and dermatosclerosis may have other etiologies as well. Although chronic, advanced myxedema is generally uncommon in industrialized countries, its peripheral manifestations may appear indistinguishable from those of venous insufficiency. Likewise, pigmentation and dermatosclerosis may also emanate from other causes of increased intra-abdominal pressure—ascites, right heart failure, and even morbid obesity. Thyroid hormone replacement, diuresis, and gastric bypass represent radically different modalities of treatment.

Many other causes of chronic ulceration, briefly summarized in Table 155-7, are commonly associated with a failure to heal. A complete CEAP classification often reveals an absence of venous disease, suggesting the alternative diagnosis in 5% to 15% of patients with ulcer. An example is the common clinical problem of advanced, clinically severe CVD in the morbidly obese patient. This is complicated by higher surgical risk, is characterized by minimal anatomic disease, rarely responds to standard treatment, and may be most effectively treated with nonvenous surgery.[7] Other commonly seen mimics are necrobiosis diabeticorum, rheumatoid ulceration, ulcers due to blood dyscrasias, and peripheral neuropathy.[33,34] A sensory neuropathy associated with CVD may predispose to recurrence of ulceration, which usually appears in the standard locations.[16] Psoriasis also often coexists with and may exacerbate CVD. Syphilis, tuberculosis, and leprosy are uncommonly seen anywhere today. An atypical location of ulceration is often a strong hint of an alternative cause. Sources of more detailed information on this topic include reports by Mekkes and by Browse.[33,34]

Table 155-7	Differential Diagnosis of Chronic Venous Ulcers

Peripheral arterial disease (alone or combined with chronic venous insufficiency

Arteriovenous shunting (congenital malformation or acquired fistula)

Peripheral neuropathies:
   Primary sensory neuropathy
   Diabetes mellitus

Malignancies:
   Basal cell carcinoma
   Squamous cell carcinoma

Blood dyscrasias:
   Hemoglobinopathies (sickle cell)
   Leukemia
   Thalassemia
   Polycythemia rubra vera

Tropical ulcer

Insect bites

Chronic infectious diseases:
   Osteomyelitis
   Tuberculosis
   Leprosy
   Syphilis

Vasculitides:
   Systemic lupus erythematosus
   Scleroderma
   Rheumatoid arthritis

Metabolic diseases:
   Gout
   Myxedema
   Morbid obesity

Any discussion of this problem must incorporate additional information relating to malignant transformation in long-term, chronic ulceration. Both basal cell carcinoma and squamous cell carcinoma have been reported in presumed venous ulcers. Raised edges, an irregular appearance in an ulcer, bleeding, and prolonged failure to heal suggest malignancy; malignancies can be readily diagnosed through biopsy with local anesthesia. Recognition may provide an opportunity for cure with a wide local excision, but if the disease is advanced, limb amputation may be required.

SUMMARY

Clinical trials and basic research projects are now conducted with the descriptions, classifications, and scores generated by various consensus groups. Validity, reliability, and responsiveness have been demonstrated with recently proposed classifications and scoring systems. As further anatomic information is extracted, and technical advances offer new perspectives, accurate descriptive data will continue to translate into real therapeutic advances. It remains unclear whether items additional to those currently categorized in the CEAP classification will be needed for future determinations, but the ongoing process of evaluation and re-evaluation has been actively pursued, and future changes will be made in response to evidence-based

recommendations. Because it appears that the complexities of the human venous system are slowly becoming better understood, the detailed reporting encouraged by the CEAP classification and the various outcome measures has already begun to bear fruit.

■ REFERENCES

1. Porter JM, Moneta GL: Reporting standards in venous disease: An update. International Consensus Committee on Chronic Venous Disease. J Vasc Surg 21:635-645, 1995.
2. Rutherford RB, Padberg FT, Comerota AJ, et al: Venous Severity Scoring: An adjunct to venous outcome assessment. J Vasc Surg 31:1307-1312, 2000.
3. Classification and grading of chronic venous disease in the lower limbs: A consensus statement. In Gloviczki P, Yao JST (eds): Handbook of Venous Disorders: Guidelines of the American Venous Forum, 2nd ed. London, Arnold, 2001, pp 25-35.
4. Wittens CHA, vanGent BW, Hop WC, Sybrandy JEM: The Dutch subfascial endoscopic perforating vein surgery trial: A randomized multicenter trial, comparing ambulatory compression therapy vs surgery in patients with venous ulcers. Society for Vascular Surgery, Abstract 15, 2003.
5. Padberg FT, Johnston MV, Sisto SA: Structured exercise improves calf muscle pump function in chronic venous insufficiency (CVI): A randomized trial. J Vasc Surg 39:79-87, 2004.
6. TenBrook JA, Iafrati MA, O'Donnell TF, et al: Systematic review of outcomes after surgical management of venous disease incorporating subfascial endoscopic surgery. J Vasc Surg 39:583-589, 2004.
7. Padberg FT Jr, Cerveira JJ, Lal BK, et al: Does severe venous insufficiency have a different etiology in the morbidly obese? Is it venous? J Vasc Surg 37:79-85, 2003.
8. Heit JA, Rooke TW, Silverstein MD, et al: Trends in the incidence of venous stasis syndrome and venous ulcer: A 25-year population based study. J Vasc Surg 3:1022-1027, 2003.
9. Ruckley CV, Evans CJ, Allan PL, et al: Chronic venous insufficiency: Clinical and duplex correlations. The Edinburgh Vein Study of venous disorders in the general population. J Vasc Surg 36:520-525, 2002.
10. McKenzie RK, Paisley A, Allan PL, et al: The effect of long saphenous stripping on quality of life. J Vasc Surg 35:1197-1203, 2002.
11. Padberg FT, Pappas PJ, Araki CT, et al: Hemodynamic and clinical improvement after superficial vein ablation with primary combined venous insufficiency with ulceration. J Vasc Surg 24:711-718, 1996.
12. Shami SK, Sarin S, Cheatle TR, et al: Venous ulcers and the superficial venous system. J Vasc Surg 17:487-490, 1993.
13. Bello AM, Scriven M, Naylor AR, et al: Vascular surgical society of Great Britain and Ireland: Role of superficial vein surgery in treatment of venous ulceration. Br J Surg 86:755-759, 1999.
14. Araki CT, Back TL, Padberg FT, et al: Significance of calf muscle pump function in venous ulceration. J Vasc Surg 20:872-879, 1994.
15. Yang D, Vandongen YK, Stacey MC: Changes in calf muscle function in chronic venous disease. Cardiovasc Surg 7:451-456, 1999.
16. Padberg FT Jr, Maniker AH, Carmel G, et al: Sensory impairment: A feature of chronic venous insufficiency. J Vasc Surg 30:36-43, 1999.
17. Reporting standards in venous disease. Prepared by the Subcommittee on Reporting Standards in Venous Disease, Ad Hoc Committee on Reporting Standards, Society for Vascular Surgery/North American Chapter, International Society for Cardiovascular Surgery. J Vasc Surg 8:172-181, 1988.
18. Allegra C, Antignani PL, Bergan JJ, et al: The 'C' of CEAP: Suggested definitions and refinements: An International Union of Phlebology conference of experts. J Vasc Surg 37:129-131, 2003.
19. Widmer LK: Peripheral Venous Disorders: Prevalence and Socio-medical Importance: Observations in 4,529 Apparently Healthy Persons. Basle Study III. Bern, Hans Huber, 1978.

20. Adam DJ, Naik J, Hartshorne T, et al: The diagnosis and management of 689 chronic leg ulcers in a single-visit assessment clinic. Eur J Vasc Endovasc Surg 25:462-468, 2003.

21. Cullen N, Fletcher A, Semlyen A, Sheldon TA: Compression therapy for venous leg ulcers. Qual Health Care 6:276, 1997.

22. Mayberry JC, Moneta GL, Taylor LM, Porter JM: 15-year results of ambulatory compression therapy for chronic venous ulcers. Surgery 109:575-581, 1991.

23. Neglen P, Thrasher TL, Raju S: Venous outflow obstruction: An underestimated contributor to chronic venous disease. J Vasc Surg 38:879-885, 2003.

24. Christopoulos DG, Nicolaides AN, Szendro G, et al: Air-plethysmography and the effect of elastic compression on venous hemodynamics of the leg. J Vasc Surg 5:148-149, 1987.

25. Back TL, Padberg FT, Araki CT, et al: Limited range of motion is a significant factor in venous ulceration. J Vasc Surg 22:519-523, 1995.

26. Kistner R: Definitive diagnosis and definitive treatment in chronic venous disease: A concept whose time has come. J Vasc Surg 24:703-710, 1996.

27. Mendes RR, Marston WA, Farber MA, Keagy BA: Treatment of superficial and perforator venous incompetence without deep venous insufficiency: Is routine perforator ligation necessary? J Vasc Surg 38:891-895, 2003.

28. Borst-Krafek B, Fink AM, Lipp C, et al: The proximal extent of pelvic vein thrombosis and its association with pulmonary embolism. J Vasc Surg 37:518-522, 2003.

29. Moneta GL: Regarding the "C" in CEAP: Suggested definitions and refinements: An International Union of Phlebology conference of experts. J Vasc Surg 37:224-225, 2003.

30. Launois R, Reboul-Marty J, Henry B: Construction and validation of a quality of life questionnaire in chronic lower limb venous insufficiency (CIVIQ). Qual Life Res 5:539-554, 1996.

31. Lamping DL, Schroter S, Kurz X, et al: Evaluation of outcomes in chronic venous disorders of the leg: Development of a scientifically rigorous, patient-reported measure of symptoms and quality of life. J Vasc Surg 37:410-419, 2003.

32. Pappas PJ, You R, Rameshwar P, et al: Dermal tissue fibrosis in patients with chronic venous insufficiency is associated with increased transforming growth factor-β_1 gene expression and protein production. J Vasc Surg 30:1129-1145, 1999.

33. Mekkes JR, Loots MAM, Van derWal AC, Bos JD: Causes, investigation, and treatment of leg ulceration. Br J Dermatol 148:388-401, 2003.

34. Browse NL, Burnand KG, Irvine AT, Wilson NN: Venous ulceration: Diagnosis. In: Diseases of the Veins, 2nd ed. London, Arnold, 1999, pp 539-569.

35. Gloviczki P: Classification and reporting standards for venous disease. Mayo Clin Proc 7:422-423, 1996.

36. Lees TA, Lambert D: Patterns of venous reflux in limbs with skin changes associated with chronic venous insufficiency. Br J Surg 80:725-728, 1993.

37. Noel AA, Gloviczki P, Cherry KJ, et al: Surgical treatment of venous malformations in Klippel-Trenaunay syndrome. J Vasc Surg 32:840-847, 2000.

38. Lee BB, Do YS, Byun HS, et al: Advanced management of venous malformation with ethanol sclerotherapy: Mid-term results. J Vasc Surg 37:533-538, 2003.

39. Plate G, Brudin L, Eklof B, et al: Congenital vein valve aplasia. World J Surg 10:929-934, 1986.

40. Walsh JC, Bergen JJ, Beaman S, Carver TP: Femoral venous reflux abolished by greater saphenous stripping. Ann Vasc Surg 8:566-570, 1994.

41. Araki CT, Back TL, Padberg FT Jr, et al: Refinements in the ultrasonic detection of popliteal vein reflux. J Vasc Surg 18:742-748, 1993.

42. VanBemmelen PS, Bedford G, Beach K, Strandness DE: Quantitative segmental evaluation of venous valvular reflux with duplex ultrasound scanning. J Vasc Surg 10:425-431, 1989.

43. Meissner MH, Natiello CM, Nicholls SC: Performance characteristics of the Venous Clinical Severity Score. J Vasc Surg 36:889-895, 2002.

44. Ricci MA, Emmerich J, Callas PW, et al: Evaluating chronic venous disease with a new venous scoring system. J Vasc Surg 38:909-915, 2003.

45. Kakkos SK, Rivera MA, Matsagas MI, et al: Validation of the new venous severity scoring system in varicose vein surgery. J Vasc Surg 38:224-228, 2003.

46. Smith JJ, Garratt AM, Guest M, et al: Measuring the quality of life in patients with venous ulcers. J Vasc Surg 31:642-649, 2000.

47. Padberg FT: Regarding "Evaluating outcomes in chronic venous disorders of the leg: Development of a scientifically rigorous, patient-reported measure of symptoms and quality of life." J Vasc Surg 37:911-912, 2003.

48. Garratt AM, MacDonald LM, Ruta DA, et al: Towards measurement of outcome for patients with varicose veins. Qual Health Care 3:5-10, 1993.

49. Mathias SA, Preble LA, Putterman CG, et al: Health related quality of life measure in patients with deep venous thrombosis: A validation study. Drug Inf J 33:1173-1187, 1999.

50. Bradbury A, Evans CJ, Allan P, et al: The relationship between lower limb symptoms and superficial and deep venous reflux on duplex ultrasonography: The Edinburgh Vein Study. J Vasc Surg 32:921-931, 2000.

Nonoperative Treatment of Chronic Venous Insufficiency

156

MARY E. GISWOLD, MD

GREGORY L. MONETA, MD

Nonoperative therapy has been the primary treatment for chronic venous insufficiency (CVI) and venous ulceration for decades. Elevation of the lower extremities that places the feet above the thighs when one is sitting and above the heart when one is supine is nearly universally accepted as effective treatment for venous ulceration. It is, however, impractical for most patients as anything but a short-term solution to a refractory or enlarging ulcer. The goals of nonoperative therapy for venous ulceration are to promote healing of existing ulcers and prevent recurrence while allowing the patient to maintain a normal ambulatory status. Nonoperative therapy is highly effective in controlling symptoms of CVI and promoting healing of venous ulcers. Healing can be prolonged, however, and in some cases painful. Larger size, duration of the ulcer, and the extent of healing within the first 3 weeks of therapy are important predictors of healing of venous ulcers with nonoperative therapy.[1] Recurrence of venous ulceration after healing is still a significant problem.

■ COMPRESSION THERAPY

Compression therapy remains the primary treatment for CVI despite progress in ablative[2] and reconstructive[3,4] venous surgery. The actual mechanism by which compression therapy counteracts the adverse effects of venous hypertension on the skin and subcutaneous tissues remains unknown. Many studies have focused on the possible venous hemodynamic effects of compression therapy. Some investigators, using either invasive or noninvasive techniques, have shown no change in ambulatory venous pressure (AVP) or venous recovery time (VRT) with compression therapy.[5-7] Others have reported statistically significant improvements in AVP, VRT, or venous capacitance and outflow with compression therapy.[8-14] Even in reports suggesting improved hemodynamics with compression, detected changes are often small, and AVP measurements are rarely normalized.

Another possible explanation for the benefits of compression therapy is a favorable effect on subcutaneous interstitial pressures. Increased interstitial pressure counteracts transcapillary Starling's forces and promotes fluid resorption and resolution of edema with improved diffusion of nutrients to the skin and subcutaneous tissues. Several studies have examined the skin microcirculation in limbs with CVI after the resolution of edema following compression therapy. Skin capillary density, as determined by videomicroscopy, predictably rises after edema reduction.[15] Several investigators have demonstrated an increase in skin transcutaneous oxygen pressure (tcPo$_2$) after edema reduction,[16,17] but others have been unable to demonstrate a significant change in skin tcPo$_2$ after edema removal by pneumatic compression.[18]

Elastic Compression Stockings

Jobst invented gradient ambulatory compression therapy in the 1950s after personally suffering for years from venous ulceration.[19] He observed that his leg symptoms were alleviated when he stood upright in a swimming pool. He therefore designed the first ambulatory gradient-compression hosiery to mimic the hydrostatic forces exerted by water in a swimming pool (Fig. 156-1). Forty years later, the use of ambulatory compression hosiery remains the primary treatment of CVI. Manufacturers provide elastic compression stockings of various strengths, compositions, lengths, and colors.

Many reports document benefit of compression stockings for treatment of CVI and venous ulceration.[20-22] At our institution, venous ulceration has been primarily treated with local wound care and elastic compression therapy, usually elastic stockings.[23] Patients with venous ulcers are first assessed for the presence of infection and the extent of lower extremity edema. If necessary, a period of bed rest is prescribed to resolve the edema. Cellulitis is treated with short-term intravenous or oral antibiotics in conjunction with local wound care (dry gauze dressings changed every 12 hours). When the edema and cellulitis have resolved, patients are usually fitted with below-knee 30– to 40–mm Hg elastic compression stockings. Two pairs are prescribed to permit laundering on alternate days. Patients are instructed to wear the stockings at all times while they are ambulatory and to remove them on going to bed. Patients who for personal or social reasons cannot use elastic stockings are prescribed alternative forms of compression (see later).

Wound care throughout the course of compression therapy consists of a simple daily washing of the ulcer with soap and water. Topical corticosteroids may be applied to surrounding areas of significant stasis dermatitis, but not to the ulcer itself. Other topical agents are not used in our practice. The ulcer is covered with a dry gauze dressing held

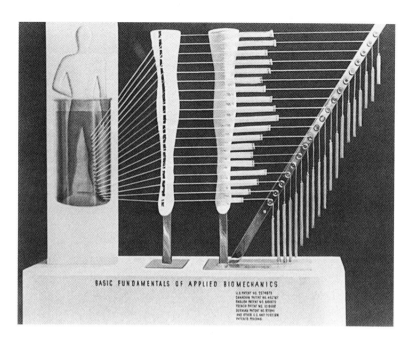

FIGURE 156-1 Model demonstrating the effect of hydrostatic pressure on the lower extremity in a water tank and its relationship to gradient compression hosiery. The pressure obtained by each is represented by the weights of various sizes, with the largest located at the ankle. (From Bergan JJ: Conrad Jobst and the development of pressure gradient therapy for venous disease. In Bergan JJ, Yao JS [eds]: Surgery of the Veins. Orlando, FL, Grune & Stratton, 1985, pp 529-540.)

in place by the compression stocking. Once the ulcer has healed, the patient is instructed to continue ambulatory compression therapy indefinitely.

Mayberry and associates[23] treated 113 patients with elastic stockings over 15 years. Of these patients, 102 (90%) were compliant with stocking use, and 105 (93%) experienced complete ulcer healing, with a mean healing time of 5.3 months. Seventy-three patients had long-term follow-up (mean, 30 months), and 58 (79%) adhered to the recommendation of perpetual ambulatory compression therapy. The total ulcer recurrence in patients who complied with long-term therapy was 16%. Recurrence was 100% in patients who did not comply with long-term therapy. Recurrence was not related to previous ulceration, previous venous surgery, or arterial insufficiency.

Erickson and colleagues[24] also examined the effects of failure to comply with the use of elastic stockings after healing of a venous ulcer. Follow-up of 91 patients with healed venous ulcers revealed that 56% recurred at a median of 10.4 months after initial healing. Age, sex, diabetes, ankle-brachial index (ABI), toe pressure, duplex ultrasonography evidence of deep venous thrombosis (DVT), original ulcer location, area, quantity, and depth, and photoplethysmography (PPG)–derived VRTs were not associated with recurrence. Total rate of recurrence was higher, however, in patients who did not comply with the use of elastic stockings after healing (60%) than in those who did (37%).[24]

There are problems with compression therapy for venous ulcers. The most noteworthy is poor patient compliance.[25] Some patients have hypersensitive skin in the lipodermatosclerotic area adjacent to the ulcer or at the site of a previously healed ulcer. Such patients can be initially intolerant of the sensation of compression. When beginning therapy, patients should be instructed to wear elastic compression stockings for only as long as tolerable (perhaps only 10 to 15 minutes at first) and to gradually lengthen

the time they wear them. Occasionally, patients may initially need to be fitted with a lesser degree of compression (20 to 30 mm Hg).

Many weak, elderly, or arthritic patients have difficulty applying elastic stockings. In a study of 166 patients with leg ulcers, presumably predominantly venous ulcers, attempts were made to treat with elastic stockings. The patients were mostly women (69%) and elderly (mean age, 72 years). Fifteen percent were incapable of applying stockings, and 26% could put them on only with great difficulty.[26] Both silk "booties" and commercially available devices that assist in the application of the stockings can be useful for such patients. With open-toed stockings, an inner silk sleeve is placed over the patient's toes and forefoot to allow the stocking material to slide smoothly during application. The sleeve is removed through the toe opening after the stockings have been applied. Another device allows the patient to load the stocking onto a wire frame. The patient steps into the stocking and pulls the device upward along the leg, applying the stocking (Fig. 156-2). These techniques, coupled with the use of home health services and counseling of the patient and family concerning the importance of compression therapy, help in improving patient compliance.

A concern with elastic compression therapy is the possibility of exacerbating arterial insufficiency. One study noted that 49 of 154 general surgeons (32%) had experience with a patient who experienced worsening of clinical leg ulceration after compression therapy.[27] Twelve cases resulted in amputation. Callam and associates[28] analyzed 600 patients with 827 ulcerated limbs and found an ABI of less than 0.9 in 176 limbs (21%). They concluded that arterial disease represented a serious risk for patients with leg ulcers and recommended against compression therapy in patients with arterial insufficiency.

Arterial reconstructions are necessary in very few patients with venous ulcers. Arterial reconstruction should therefore be considered for the rare patient with a venous

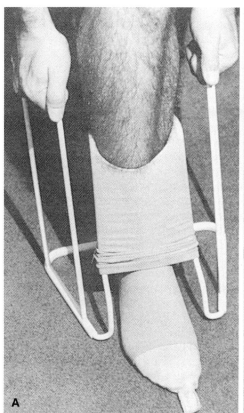
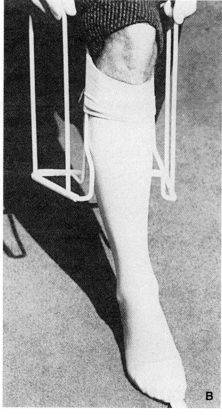

FIGURE 156-2 **A** and **B,** Compression stocking being sequentially fitted onto the leg with the Butler device. (From Mayberry JC, Moneta GL, Taylor LM, Porter JM: Nonoperative treatment of venous stasis ulcer. In Bergan JJ, Yao JS [eds]: Venous Disorders. Philadelphia, WB Saunders, 1991, pp 381-395.)

ulcer and significant arterial insufficiency if the ulcer fails to improve with elastic compression therapy. Patients with critical leg ischemia (ABI < 0.4) should undergo arterial reconstruction as part of the initial management of the venous ulcer.

Paste Gauze (Unna) Boots

The paste gauze compression dressing was developed by Unna[29] in 1896. The current dressing (Dome paste) contains calamine, zinc oxide, glycerin, sorbitol, gelatin, and magnesium aluminum silicate and is popularly called the *Unna boot.* The dressing provides both compression and topical therapy. The Unna boot consists of a three-layer dressing and is applied by trained medical personnel. The Dome paste rolled-gauze bandage is first applied with graded compression from the forefoot to just below the knee. The next layer consists of a 4-inch-wide continuous gauze dressing. An elastic wrap with graded compression constitutes the outer layer. The bandage becomes stiff after drying. The relatively unyielding nature of the Unna boot may aid in preventing edema formation. Bandages are generally changed weekly.

The Unna boot has the advantage of requiring minimal patient compliance. The dressing is usually applied and removed by a health care professional. Disadvantages include the inability to monitor the ulcer between dressing changes, the need for health care personnel to apply the bandage, the relative discomfort of the bulky dressing, and the operator-dependent nature of the compression achieved

after wrapping.[30] Contact dermatitis may occur secondary to the paraben preservative and may require discontinuation of Unna boot therapy.

The Unna boot has been compared with other treatments. A randomized, prospective trial of 21 patients with venous ulcers compared Unna boot therapy with mild compression stocking therapy (24 mm Hg at the ankle). Although 70% of the total number of ulcers healed in both groups, the average time for healing was 7.3 weeks in the Unna boot group but 18.4 weeks in the compression stocking group.[31] The researchers qualify this finding by noting that the average healing time for the compression stocking group was 11.8 weeks after the exclusion of a single patient in the stocking group in whom healing of extensive calf ulcerations took 78 weeks.

An additional randomized study of 26 patients who had CVI and venous ulcers compared Unna boots with polyurethane foam dressings and elastic compression wraps.[32] After 12 months, patients in the Unna boot group had faster healing rates and greater overall wound healing. More than 50% of the patients in the polyurethane dressing group withdrew before completion of the study.

Unna boots were also compared with hydrocolloid dressings (DuoDerm) in a 6-month trial treating 87 venous ulcers in 84 patients.[33] Seventy percent of the ulcers treated with Unna boots healed; only 38% of those treated with the hydrocolloid dressings alone healed. A later study comparing Unna boots with hydrocolloid dressings and elastic compression bandages found no statistical difference in healing rates after 12 weeks.[34]

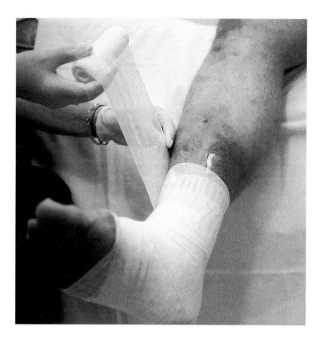

FIGURE 156-3 Photograph of a multilayered dressing for treatment of chronic venous insufficiency.

Other Forms of Elastic Compression

Additional forms of elastic compression are simple elastic wraps and multilayered wrapped dressings (Fig. 156-3). Although achieving and maintaining appropriate pressure gradients with elastic wraps of any sort is highly operator- and technique-dependent, satisfactory dressings can be applied. Meyer and associates[35] compared three- and four-layered bandaging techniques in the treatment of venous ulcers and concluded the three-layer technique may be slightly superior to a four-layer wrap, but both techniques were effective. Improved ulcer healing was associated with larger ulcers. Ankle pressures achieved with a multilayer wrap of orthopedic wool, crepe bandages, and elastic cohesive wraps (Coban) decrease only 10% after 1 week.[36] Highly elastic multilayer bandage systems have the smallest pressure loss over several days of wear. These devices, however, have the smallest decrease in pressure in the supine position, which poses a theoretical risk to patients with concomitant arterial insufficiency.[37] A four-layer dressing used to treat 126 consecutive patients (148 ulcerated limbs) whose ulcers had previously been refractory to treatment with simple elastic wraps resulted in complete healing of 74% of the ulcers at 12 weeks. In general, however, the results obtained with elastic wraps in the healing of venous ulceration have been inferior to those achieved with compression stockings or Unna boots.[38-41]

A legging orthosis (Circ-Aid) is available (Fig. 156-4).[42] It consists of multiple pliable, rigid, adjustable compression bands that wrap around the leg from the ankle to the knee and are held in place with Velcro tape. The device offers the rigid compression of the Unna boot with greater ease of application. Because of the adjustable nature of the bands, it can be adjusted as limb edema resolves. The orthosis promotes resolution of edema and may be particularly useful in patients who are unable or unwilling to wear compression hosiery. Clinical trials of this device are ongoing. One preliminary study suggests the Circ-Aid orthosis may be superior to elastic stockings in preventing limb swelling in patients with advanced CVI.[43]

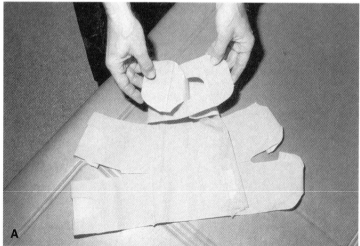

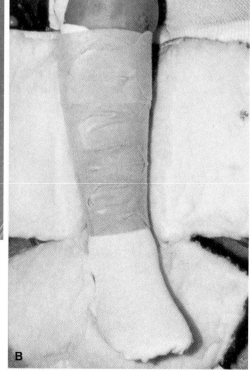

FIGURE 156-4 The Circ-Aid legging orthosis provides rigid, adjustable compression. The device appears particularly useful in patients with very large or unusually shaped legs. **A** illustrates the interlocking Velcro straps that provide adjustable compression. **B** shows the device in place.

Adjunctive Compression Devices

External pneumatic compression devices serve as adjunctive measures in the treatment of lower extremity edema, venous ulceration, or both. They may be particularly applicable to patients with massive edema or morbid obesity. Commercially available devices apply either intermittent compression of uniform strength or intermittent sequential gradient compression. Relative contraindications to external pneumatic compression are arterial insufficiency and uncontrolled congestive heart failure.

Pneumatic compression devices that provide sequential gradient *intermittent pneumatic compression* (IPC) have received the most attention. They have gained widespread use in the prevention of DVT in nonambulatory hospitalized patients. Several reports have also described the use of these devices to treat venous ulcers. The results suggest improvement in ulcer healing with the use of pneumatic compression, but patients undergoing IPC therapy may also elevate their legs longer each day than "nonpumped" patients.

One group treated eight patients, in whom phlebographically documented CVI and stasis ulcers had been present from 1 month to 5 years, with IPC for 45-minute sessions 5 days a week, for a total of 2 weeks.[44] IPC was then continued twice a week until the ulcer healed. Between treatments with IPC, the limbs were bandaged in elastic compression wraps, and the ulcers were dressed with wet-to-dry dressings. All ulcers healed (mean time, 5 weeks). The group compared this result with a mean healing time of 13 weeks in their previous patients who had treatment with elastic compression bandages alone, concluding that the addition of IPC therapy led to a superior rate of ulcer healing.

A randomized study of 45 patients with CVI and venous ulcers of at least 12 weeks' duration compared treatment consisting of IPC and 30– to 40–mm Hg ambulatory compression stockings with the use of compression stockings alone.[45] The study continued until the ulcers had healed or until 3 months had elapsed. Only 1 of 24 patients treated with stockings alone had ulcer healing, but 10 of 21 patients in the IPC group had healing. The use of adjunctive intermittent compression has not gained widespread acceptance, despite the results of the few available studies indicating that it may be useful in the treatment of venous ulcers, especially those refractory to ambulatory compression therapy alone.

■ PHARMACOLOGIC THERAPY

Diuretics have little role in the treatment of chronic venous insufficiency. They can be used occasionally for short periods in patients with severe edema, but they must be used cautiously. Injudicious application, particularly in older patients without chronic intravascular volume overload, can lead to hypovolemia and associated metabolic complications.

Multiple other drug therapies are available to treat lipodermatosclerosis and venous ulceration. These agents are relatively unknown in the United States. They have been studied primarily in Europe, where they are widely used. A 1993 German study found that 11% of persons 15 years and older had consumed medication dispensed for venous disease during the previous 12 months.[46]

Zinc

Several investigators have noted that patients with CVI and venous ulceration may have depressed levels of serum zinc.[47,48] Greaves and Skillen[49] subsequently reported complete ulcer healing after 4 months of oral zinc therapy and compression bandage use in 13 of 18 patients with low serum zinc levels and previously refractory venous ulceration.

A double-blind trial of 27 patients with venous ulceration and various serum zinc levels compared the combination of zinc therapy and compression bandage use with the use of compression bandages alone.[50] Additional zinc was found to be beneficial only if pretreatment zinc levels were low. A double-blind trial of 38 patients with venous ulceration and unknown zinc levels compared zinc therapy and compression bandage use with bandage use alone. Zinc did not improve ulcer healing.[51] Two additional studies of oral zinc therapy in patients with venous ulcers also showed it to have no benefit.[52,53]

Fibrinolytic Agents

The use of fibrinolytic agents in the treatment of CVI has been disappointing.

Stanozolol

Stanozolol is an androgenic steroid with significant fibrinolytic activity. Browse and associates[54] originally reported encouraging results in 14 patients with CVI and lipodermatosclerosis who were treated for 3 months with stanozolol. All patients had subjective and objective improvement (based on lipodermatosclerotic area). Serum parameters of fibrinolytic activity improved. However, a placebo-controlled crossover study of 23 patients with CVI and long-standing lipodermatosclerosis refractory to stocking therapy demonstrated no difference between stanozolol plus stockings and stockings alone with respect to the area of lipodermatosclerosis.[55] Skin biopsy specimens did not show a reduction in tissue fibrin with the steroid treatment. Leg volumes demonstrated greater fluid retention with use of the drug. Other studies have also been unable to demonstrate major benefits of anabolic steroid treatment in patients with CVI.[55-57]

Oxpentifylline

Oxpentifylline is a cytokine antagonist with some profibrinolytic activity. The results of one small study suggest that it may be effective in ulcer healing.[58] The drug has significant side effects, however, including edema, vomiting, dyspepsia, diarrhea, and depression, making it unattractive for widespread use.

Phlebotrophic Agents

Hydroxyrutosides

Hydroxyrutosides are flavonoid drugs derived from plant glycosides. Initial studies demonstrated a reduction in capillary permeability after thermal injury.[59] Studies of hydroxyrutosides in the treatment of patients who had CVI without ulceration have suggested marginal subjective symptomatic improvement in CVI-associated pain, night cramps, and restless legs. The hydroxyrutosides also appear to be slightly more effective than placebo in controlling lower extremity edema as measured by ankle circumference.[60-62] These agents have not been demonstrated to promote healing of venous ulcers.[63]

Micronised Purified Flavonoid Fraction (MPFF)

Micronised purified flavonoid fraction (MPFF) is a combination of micronized diosmin and flavonoids. In a prospective randomized double-blind controlled trial, MPFF did not change the symptoms of CVI except for nighttime cramping. There was no change in ultrasonographic or foot volumetric parameters.[64]

Calcium Dobesilate

Calcium 2,5-dihydroxybenzenesulfonate (calcium dobesilate) increases lymphatic flow and macrophage-mediated proteolysis. The net effect is a reduction in edema.[65-67] Three hundred fifty two patients treated with calcium dobesilate for 9 weeks reported improvement in the symptoms of CVI and had reduced leg circumference.[68] Unfortunately, there was no control group for comparison in this study.

Troxerutin

Troxerutin (trihydroxy-ethylutoside) is a flavonoid derived semisynthetically from *Sophora japonica*. It appears to have an antierythrocyte aggregation effect and may improve capillary dynamics in patients with mild CVI.[69] Its effect on healing of venous ulceration is unknown.

Hemorheologic Agents

Pentoxifylline

Pentoxifylline is a hemorheologic agent used in the treatment of venous ulceration. In addition to its hemorheologic effects, it reduces white blood cell adhesiveness, inhibits cytokine-mediated neutrophil activation, and reduces the release of superoxide free radicals produced in neutrophil degranulation.[70] In one double-blind, placebo-controlled study of 59 patients with venous ulceration, 87% of patients receiving the study drug experienced improvement in their venous ulcers, compared with 45% of the placebo group.[71] A multicenter trial of 80 patients with venous ulceration demonstrated a significant reduction in ulcer size after 6 months in the patients treated with pentoxifylline and compression stockings compared with those treated with compression therapy alone. Ulcer healing was demonstrated in 60% of the patients receiving pentoxifylline, compared with 29% of the controls. In a meta-analysis, pentoxifylline in combination with compression therapy was more effective than placebo and compression in complete ulcer healing (relative risk [RR], 1.30; 95% confidence interval [CI], 1.10-1.54). Furthermore, patients who received pentoxifylline had no more adverse events than those taking placebo.[72]

Aspirin and Nonsteroidal Anti-Inflammatory Drugs

A higher rate of venous ulcer healing has been reported with the use of 300 mg/day of enteric-coated aspirin.[73] The mechanism of the aspirin benefit in healing of venous ulcers is unknown. It is speculated that aspirin may promote ulcer healing by decreasing associated inflammation or inhibiting platelet function.[74]

Both cyclooxygenase-1 (COX-1) and COX-2 enzymes are higher in chronic venous ulcers than in normal skin.[75] COX-1 produces prostacyclin, which contributes to angiogenesis. COX-2 may be responsible for the persistent inflammation in chronic venous ulcers. There is speculation that selective COX-2 inhibitors may have efficacy in the treatment of chronic venous ulcers; however, this has not yet been tested in clinical trials.

Free Radical Scavengers

The free radical scavengers allopurinol and dimethyl sulfoxide have been evaluated in the treatment of CVI. One hundred thirty-three patients who had CVI and venous ulcers were divided into three groups. Patients in the first two groups were treated with compression stocking therapy and either allopurinol or dimethyl sulfoxide as topical free radical scavenger agents.[76] Patients in the third group were treated with compression therapy alone and served as controls. At 12 weeks, patients given topical free radical scavengers had improved rates of ulcer healing. Average ulcer areas at 12 weeks were 0.2 to 0.3 cm^2 in the treatment groups and 1.3 cm^2 in controls.

Prostaglandins

Prostaglandin E

Prostaglandin E_1 (PGE$_1$) has multiple microcirculatory effects. It reduces white blood cell activation, inhibits platelet aggregation, and decreases small vessel vasodilation.[77] This drug, which must be administered intravenously, has been used in the treatment of venous ulcers. In a trial of PGE$_1$ treatment of venous ulceration, 44 patients were treated with compression bandages and either placebo or PGE$_1$.[78] Patients receiving PGE$_1$ showed significant improvement in edema and ulcer healing. Forty percent of the patients in the PGE$_1$-treated group had ulcer healing, compared with only 9% in the control group.

Prostaglandin F

Horse-chestnut seed extract stimulates release of prostaglandins from the PGF series. PGFs mediate vasoconstriction. A randomized clinical trial has found horse-chestnut seed extract to be superior to placebo and equivalent to compression stockings in reducing leg edema.[79] In a meta-analysis of eight placebo-controlled trials, treatment with horse-chestnut seed extract over 20 days to 8 weeks resulted in decreased edema and fewer reported symptoms of CVI.[80] At least in the short term (<12 months), adverse effects appear minimal.

Topical Therapies

Antibiotics

Topical antibiotics have been advocated as a treatment of venous ulceration for years. However, without evidence of local infection, wound bacteriology appears to have little impact on healing.[81] The application of antiseptic agents is counterproductive to wound healing. Commercially available concentrations of povidone-iodine, acetic acid, hydrogen peroxide, and sodium hypochlorite are 100% cytotoxic to cultured fibroblasts.[82]

Iodine

Cadexomer iodine (Iodosorb) is an iodine-containing hydrophilic starch powder employed as a topical dressing for venous ulcers. It absorbs wound exudate and releases iodine as a bactericidal agent. Sixty-one patients with venous ulcers were treated with either Iodosorb or a standard topical antibiotic dressing.[38] Patients treated with the Iodosorb dressing demonstrated superior healing. A trial comparing Iodosorb with another hydrophilic powder containing propylene glycol (Scherisorb) in 95 patients with venous ulcers resulted in healing of 29% of ulcers by 10 weeks.[37] There was no difference in healing rates between the two groups.

Iodosorb was also compared with dextranomer powder (Debrisan) in the treatment of 27 patients with venous ulcers.[83] All limbs were also treated with elastic compression bandages. After 8 weeks, the ulcers healed in 64% of the Iodosorb group and in 50% of the Debrisan group.

Finally, a multicenter randomized trial compared Iodosorb treatment with saline dressing treatment in 93 patients whose venous ulcers had been present at least 3 months.[84] All limbs were also treated with elastic compression bandages. At 6 weeks, the mean ulcer size in the Iodosorb group had decreased by 34%, compared with 5% in the saline group.

Ketanserin

Ketanserin, a serotonin-2 antagonist, is reported to improve fibroblast collagen synthesis. A double-blind study of 23 patients with venous ulcers compared the use of topical 2% ketanserin plus compression bandages with bandage use alone.[85] Wound improvement was demonstrated in 91% of the ketanserin-treated group, in contrast to 50% of the controls.

Amnion

Several agents have been evaluated in attempts to promote ingrowth of granulation tissue in venous ulcer beds. Five days of treatment using human amnion as a topical occlusive dressing in combination with bed rest was reported in an uncontrolled trial of 15 patients.[86] Amnion-treated ulcer beds had better ingrowth of granulation tissue. The patients reported almost immediate pain relief with the application of the amnion dressings.

Occlusive Dressings

Hydrocolloid occlusive dressings (e.g., DuoDerm) maintain a moist wound environment, are often comfortable for the patient, and may promote more rapid epithelialization of granulating wounds.[87] A randomized trial of 55 patients with venous ulcers compared elastic compression bandages with either hydrocolloid occlusive dressings or gauze bandages for efficiency in ulcer healing. No difference in healing rate was found. In addition, occlusive hydrocolloid dressings may be associated with up to a 25% infectious complication rate.[33] Although occlusive dressings may be more comfortable for the patient, they may not produce more rapid healing and may lead to a higher number of local infectious complications.

Growth Factors and Cytokines

There is considerable interest in the use of topically applied growth factors and cytokines in the treatment of chronic nonhealing wounds. Wound biopsies from venous ulcers, when compared to normal skin, show decreased levels of certain growth factor receptors.[88] A randomized double-blind, placebo-controlled trial of 86 patients with venous ulcers who were treated with a platelet-derived growth factor, platelet lysate, demonstrated no improvement in healing rate when compared with those receiving placebo. All patients in this study were additionally treated with standard compression therapy.[89] To date, no large-scale clinical trials demonstrate the safety or efficacy of these substances in the treatment of venous ulcers. Preliminary studies, however, have shown efficacy in healing a series of chronic wounds of mixed etiology.[90]

■ SKIN SUBSTITUTES

Advances in biotechnology have led to the development of human skin substitutes. The intent is to promote permanent closure of open wounds, including venous ulcers. These products vary from simple acellular skin substitutes to complete living bioengineered bilayered human skin equivalents with allogenic epidermal and dermal layers. The mechanism of action in promoting wound healing is uncertain. Living products may possibly serve as a delivery vehicle for various growth factors and cytokines important in wound healing.

Apligraf is a bioengineered product consisting of a keratinocyte-containing epidermis and a dermal layer of fibroblasts in a collagen matrix separated by a basement membrane (Figs. 156-5 and 156-6).[91] Both keratinocytes and fibroblasts are derived from neonatal foreskin. The epidermal and dermal layers are both mitotically active and secrete collagen and other matrix elements. In a randomized clinical trial comparing Apligraf with multilayered compression therapy, Apligraf was effective in inducing

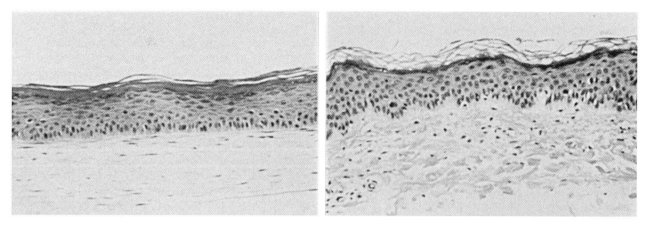

FIGURE 156-5 Histologic photographs of the bioengineered skin substitute Apligraf *(left)* and normal human skin *(right)*. The bioengineered product appears very similar to normal human skin. It produces numerous growth factors, and both dermal and epidermal layers are mitotically active.

FIGURE 156-6 Photograph of Apligraf supplied as a disk on an agarose gel nutrient medium.

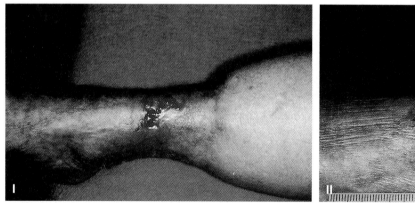
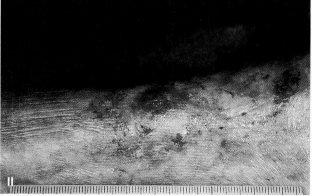

FIGURE 156-7 Photographs of a venous ulcer before *(right)* and after *(left)* treatment with Apligraf skin substitute.

healing of venous ulcers (Fig. 156-7). Large ulcers (>6 cm) and long-standing ulcers (>12 months) showed the greatest benefit with the Apligraf skin substitute.[92]

■ SUMMARY

When all of the data on the nonoperative treatment of CVI are analyzed, compression therapy continues to offer the best combination of simplicity and efficacy. Compression therapy provides symptomatic relief, promotes ulcer healing, and aids in preventing ulcer recurrence. It continues to be the standard of nonoperative therapy for CVI against which all other therapies for venous ulcer and CVI should be compared. The goal of new therapies for venous ulceration, both operative and nonoperative, should be more rapid promotion of healing with less pain and decreased late recurrence than is currently achieved with optimal application of compression therapy.

■ REFERENCES

1. Phillips TJ, Machado F, Trout R: Prognostic indicators in venous ulcers. J Am Acad Dermatol 43:627, 2000.

2. Cikrit DF, Nichols WK, Silver D: Surgical management of refractory venous stasis ulceration. J Vasc Surg 7:473, 1988.

3. Bergan JJ, Yao JST, Flinn WR, McCarthy WJ: Surgical treatment of venous obstruction and insufficiency. J Vasc Surg 3:174, 1986.

4. Raju S, Fredericks R: Valve reconstruction procedures for nonobstructive venous insufficiency: Rationale, techniques, and results in 107 procedures with two- to eight-year follow-up. J Vasc Surg 7:301, 1988.

5. Mayberry JC, Moneta GL, DeFrang RD, Porter JM: The influence of elastic compression stockings on deep venous hemodynamics. J Vasc Surg 13:91, 1991.

6. O'Donnell TF, Rosenthal DA, Callow AD, Ledig BL: The effect of elastic compression on venous hemodynamics in postphlebitic limbs. JAMA 242:2766, 1979.

7. Husni EA, Ximenes JOC, Goyette EM: Elastic support of the lower limbs in hospital patients: A critical study. JAMA 214:1456, 1970.

8. Benko T, Cooke EA, McNally MA: Graduated compression stockings: Knee length or thigh length. Clin Orthop 383:197, 2001.

9. Noyes LD, Rice JC, Kerstein MD: Hemodynamic assessment of high-compression hosiery in chronic venous disease. Surgery 102:813, 1987.

10. Somerville JJF, Brow GO, Byrne PJ, et al: The effect of elastic stockings on superficial venous pressures in patients with venous insufficiency. Br J Surg 61:979, 1974.

11. Norris CS, Turley G, Barnes RW: Noninvasive quantification of ambulatory venous hemodynamics during elastic compressive therapy. Angiology 35:560, 1984.

12. Christopoulos DG, Nicolaides AN, Szendro G, et al: Air-plethysmography and the effect of elastic compression on venous hemodynamics of the leg. J Vasc Surg 5:148, 1987.

13. Jones NA, Webb PJ, Rees RI, Kakkar VV: A physiological study of elastic compression stockings in venous disorders of the leg. Br J Surg 67:569, 1980.

14. Horner J, Fernandes JF, Nicolaides AN: Value of graduated compression stockings in deep venous insufficiency. Br Med J 75:820, 1980.

15. Mahler F, Chen D: Intravital microscopy for evaluation of chronic venous incompetence. Int J Microcirc Clin Exp 106(Suppl):1, 1990.

16. Neumann HA: Possibilities and limitations of transcutaneous oxygen tension: Measurements in chronic venous insufficiency. Int J Microcirc Clin Exp 105(Suppl):1, 1990.

17. Kolari PJ, Pekanmaki K: Effects of intermittent compression treatment on skin perfusion and oxygenation in lower legs with venous ulcers. Vasa 16:312, 1987.

18. Nemeth AJ, Falanga V, Alstadt SA, Eaglstein WH: Ulcerated edematous limbs: Effect of edema removal on transcutaneous oxygen measurements. J Am Acad Dermatol 120:191, 1989.

19. Bergan JJ: Conrad Jobst and the development of pressure gradient therapy for venous disease. In Bergan JJ, Yao JS (eds): Surgery of the Veins. Orlando, FL, Grune & Stratton, 1985, pp 529-540.

20. Wright AD: The treatment of indolent ulcer of the leg. Lancet 1:457, 1931.

21. Anning ST: Leg ulcers: The results of treatment. Angiology 7:505, 1956.

22. Kitahama A, Elliot LF, Kerstein MD, Menendez CV: Leg ulcer: Conservative management or surgical treatment? JAMA 247:197, 1982.

23. Mayberry JC, Moneta GL, Taylor LM, Porter JM: Fifteen-year results of ambulatory compression therapy for chronic venous ulcers. Surgery 109:575, 1991.

24. Erickson CA, Lanza DJ, Karp DL, et al: Healing of venous ulcers in an ambulatory care program: The roles of chronic venous insufficiency and patient compliance. J Vasc Surg 22:629, 1995.

25. Chant AD, Davies LJ, Pike JM, Sparks MJ: Support stockings in practical management of varicose veins. Phlebology 4:167, 1989.

26. Franks PJ, Oldroyd MI, Dickson D, et al: Risk factors for leg ulcer recurrence: A randomized trial of two types of compression stockings. Age Ageing 24:490, 1995.

27. Callam MJ, Ruckley CV, Dale JJ, Harper DR: Hazards of compression treatment of the leg: An estimate from Scottish surgeons. Br Med J 295:1382, 1987.

28. Callam MJ, Harper DR, Dale JJ, Ruckley CV: Arterial disease in chronic leg ulceration: An underestimated hazard? Lothian and Forth Valley leg ulcer study. Br Med J 294:929, 1987.

29. Unna PG: Ueber Paraplaste, eine neue Form medikamentoser Pflaster. Wien Med Wochenschr 43:1854, 1896.

30. Elder DM, Greer BE: Venous disease: How to heal and prevent chronic leg ulcers. Geriatrics 50:30, 1995.

31. Hendricks WM, Swallow RT: Management of stasis leg ulcers with Unna's boots versus elastic support stockings. J Am Acad Dermatol 12:90, 1985.

32. Rubin JR, Alexander J, Plecha EJ, Marman C: Unna's boots vs. polyurethane foam dressings for the treatment of venous ulceration. Arch Surg 125:489, 1990.

33. Kitka MJ, Schuler JJ, Meyer JP, et al: A prospective, randomized trial of Unna's boots versus hydroactive dressing in the treatment of venous stasis ulcers. J Vasc Surg 7:478, 1988.

34. Cordts PR, Hanrahan LM, Rodriguez AA, et al: A prospective, randomized trial of Unna's boot versus DuoDERM CGF hydroactive dressing plus compression in the management of venous leg ulcers. J Vasc Surg 15:480, 1992.

35. Meyer FJ, McGuinness CL, Lagattella NRF: Randomized clinical trial of three-layer paste and four-layer bandages for venous ulcers. Br J Surg 90:934, 2003.

36. Blair SD, Wright DD, Backhouse LM, et al: Sustained compression and healing of chronic venous ulcers. Br Med J 297:1159, 1988.

37. Hafner J, Botonakis I, Burg G: A comparison of multilayer bandage systems during rest, exercise, and over 2 days of wear time. Arch Derm 136:857, 2000.

38. Stewart AJ, Leaper DJ: Treatment of chronic leg ulcers in the community: A comparative trial of Scherisorb and Iodosorb. Phlebology 2:115, 1987.

39. Ormiston MC, Seymour MT, Venn GE, et al: Controlled trial of Iodosorb in chronic venous ulcers. Br Med J 291:308, 1985.

40. Ryan TJ, Biven HF, Murphy JJ, et al: The use of a new occlusive dressing in the management of venous stasis ulceration. In Ryan TJ (ed): An Environment for Healing: The Role of Occlusion. London, Royal Society of Medicine, 1984, pp 99-103.

41. Eriksson G: Comparative study of hydrocolloid dressing and double layer bandage in treatment of venous stasis ulceration. In Ryan TJ (ed): An Environment for Healing: The Role of Occlusion. London, Royal Society of Medicine, 1984, pp 111-113.

42. Vernick SH, Shapiro D, Shaw FD: Legging orthosis for venous and lymphatic insufficiency. Arch Phys Med Rehabil 68:459, 1987.

43. Spence RK, Cahall E: Inelastic versus elastic leg compression in chronic venous insufficiency: A comparison of limb size and venous hemodynamics. J Vasc Surg 24:783, 1996.

44. Pekanmaki K, Kolari PJ, Kiistala U: Intermittent pneumatic compression treatment for post-thrombotic leg ulcers. Clin Exp Dermatol 12:350, 1987.

45. Coleridge Smith P, Sarin S, Hasty J, Scurr JH: Sequential gradient pneumatic compression enhances venous ulcer healing: A randomized trial. Surgery 108:871, 1990.

46. Uber A: The socioeconomic profile of patients treated by phlebotropic drugs in Germany. Angiology 48:595, 1997.

47. Greaves MW, Boyde TR: Plasma zinc concentrations in patients with psoriasis, other dermatoses, and venous leg ulceration. Lancet 2:1019, 1967.

48. Withers AF, Baker H, Musa M, Dormandy TL: Plasma zinc in psoriasis. Lancet 2:278, 1968.

49. Greaves MW, Skillen AW: Effects of long-continued ingestion of zinc sulphate in patients with venous leg ulceration. Lancet 2:889, 1970.

50. Hallbook T, Lanner E: Serum-zinc and healing of venous leg ulcers. Lancet 2:780, 1972.

51. Greaves MW, Ive FA: Double blind trial of zinc sulphate in the treatment of chronic venous ulceration. Br J Dermatol 87:632, 1972.

52. Myers MB, Cherry G: Zinc and the healing of chronic ulcers. Am J Surg 120:77, 1970.

53. Phillips A, Davidson M, Greaves MW: Venous leg ulceration: Evaluation of zinc treatment, serum zinc and rate of healing. Clin Exp Dermatol 2:395, 1977.

54. Browse NL, Jarrett PE, Morland M, Burnand K: Treatment of lipodermatosclerosis of the leg by fibrinolytic enhancement: A preliminary report. Br Med J 2:434, 1977.

55. Burnand K, Lemenson G, Morland M, et al: Venous lipodermatosclerosis: Treatment by fibrinolytic enhancement and elastic compression. Br Med J 280:7, 1980.

56. McMullin GM, Watkin GT, Coleridge Smith PD, Scurr JH: The efficacy of fibrinolytic enhancement with stanozolol in the treatment of venous insufficiency. Aust N Z J Surg 61:306, 1991.

57. Layer GT, Stacey MC, Burnand KG: Stanozolol and the treatment of venous ulceration: An interim report. Phlebology 1:197, 1986.

58. Colgan M, Dormandy JA, Jones PW, et al: Oxpentifylline treatment of venous ulcers of the leg. Br Med J 300:972, 1990.

59. Arturson G: Effects of O-(β-hydroxyethyl)-rutosides (HR) on the increased microvascular permeability in experimental skin burns. Acta Chir Scand 138:111, 1972.

60. Balmer A, Limoni C: A double-blind placebo-controlled trial of venorutin on the symptoms and signs of chronic venous insufficiency. Vasa 9:76, 1980.

61. Pulvertaft TB: Paroven in the treatment of chronic venous insufficiency. Practitioner 223:838, 1979.

62. Pulvertaft TB: General practice treatment of symptoms of venous insufficiency with oxyrutins: Results of a 660 patient multicenter study in the UK. Vasa 12:373, 1983.

63. Mann RJ: A double-blind trial of oral O-β-hydroxy-ethyl rutosides for stasis leg ulcers. Br J Clin Pract 35:79, 1981.

64. Danielsson G, Jungbeck C, Peterson K, Norgren L: A randomised controlled trial of micronised purified flavonoid fraction vs placebo in patients with chronic venous disease. Eur J Vasc Endovasc Surg 23:73, 2002.

65. Casley-Smith JR, Casley-Smith JR: The effects of calcium dobesilate on acute lymphedema (with and without macrophages) and on burn edema. Lymphology 18:37, 1985.

66. Casley-Smith JR: The influence of tissue hydrostatic pressure and protein concentration on fluid and protein uptake by diaphragmatic initial lymphatics; effect of calcium dobesilate. Microcirc Endothelium Lymphatics 2:385, 1985.

67. Casley-Smith JR: A double-blind trial of calcium dobesilate in chronic venous insufficiency. Angiology 39:853, 1988.

68. Arceo A, Berber A, Trevino C: Clinical evaluation of the efficacy and safety of calcium dobesilate in patients with chronic venous insufficiency of the lower limbs. Angiology 53:539, 2002.

69. Boissean MR, Taccoen A, Garrean C, et al: Fibrinolysis and hemorrheology in chronic venous insufficiency: A double blind study of troxerutin efficiency. J Cardiovasc Surg 36:369, 1995.

70. Sullivan GW, Carper HT, Novick WJ, Mandell GL: Inhibition of the inflammatory action of interleukin-1 and tumor necrosis factor-α on neutrophil function by pentoxifylline. Infect Immun 56:1722, 1988.

71. Weitgasser H: The use of pentoxifylline (Trental 400) in the treatment of leg ulcers: The results of a double blind trial. Pharmatherapeutica 3(Suppl 1):143, 1983.

72. Jull A, Waters J, Arroll B: Pentoxifylline for treatment of venous leg ulcers: A systematic review. Lancet 359:1550, 2002.

73. Layton AM, Ibbotson SH, Davies JA, et al: The effect of oral aspirin in the treatment of chronic venous leg ulcers. Lancet 344:164, 1994.

74. Ibbotsen SH, Layton AM, Davies JA, et al: The effect of aspirin on haemostatic activity in the treatment of chronic venous leg ulceration. Br J Dermatol 132:422, 1995.

75. Abd-El-Aleem SA, Ferguson MWJ, Appleton I: Expression of cyclo-oxygenase isoforms in normal human skin and chronic venous disease. J Pathol 195:616, 2001.

76. Salim AS: The role of oxygen-derived free radicals in the management of venous (varicose) ulceration: A new approach. World J Surg 15:264, 1991.

77. Sinzinger H, Virgolini I, Fitscha P: Pathomechanisms of atherosclerosis beneficially affected by prostaglandin E_1 (PGE$_1$): An update. Vasa 28(Suppl):6, 1989.

78. Rudofsky G: Intravenous prostaglandin E_1 in the treatment of venous ulcers: A double-blind, placebo controlled trial. Vasa 28(Suppl):39, 1989.

79. Diehm C, Trampisch HJ, Lange S, et al: Comparison of leg compression stockings and oral horse-chestnut seed extract in patients with chronic venous insufficiency. Lancet 347:292, 1996.

80. Pittler MH, Ernst E: Horse-chestnut seed extract for chronic venous insufficiency: A criteria-based systematic review. Arch Dermatol 134:1356, 1998.

81. Gilchrist B, Reed C: The bacteriology of chronic venous ulcers treated with occlusive hydrocolloid dressings. Br J Dermatol 121:337, 1989.

82. Lineaweaver W, Howard R, Souey D, et al: Topical antimicrobial toxicity. Arch Surg 120:267, 1985.

83. Tarvainen K: Cadexomer iodine (Iodosorb) compared with dextranomer (Debrisan) in the treatment of chronic leg ulcers. Acta Chir Scand Suppl 544:57, 1988.

84. Hillstrom L: Iodosorb compared to standard treatment in chronic venous leg ulcers: A multicenter study. Acta Chir Scand Suppl 544:53, 1988.

85. Roelens P: Double-blind placebo-controlled study with topical 2% ketanserin ointment in the treatment of venous ulcers. Dermatologica 178:98, 1989.

86. Bennett JP, Matthews R, Faulk WP: Treatment of chronic ulceration of the legs with human amnion. Lancet 1:1153, 1980.

87. Alvarez OM, Mertz PM, Eaglstein WH: The effect of occlusive dressings on collagen synthesis and re-epithelialization in superficial wounds. J Surg Res 35:142, 1983.

88. Stacey MC, Mata SD, Trengrove NJ, et al: Randomised double-blind placebo controlled trial of topical autologous platelet lysate in venous ulcer healing. Eur J Vasc Endovasc Surg 20:296, 2000.

89. Cowin AJ, Hatzirodos N, Holding CA, et al: Effect of healing on the expression of transforming growth factor βs and their receptors in chronic venous leg ulcers. J Invest Dermatol 117:1282, 2001.

90. Ganio C, Tenewitz FE, Wilson RC, et al: The treatment of chronic nonhealing wounds using autologous platelet-derived growth factors. J Foot Ankle Surg 32:263, 1993.

91. Wilkins LM, Watson SR, Prosky SJ, et al: Development of a bilayered living skin construct for clinical applications. Biotechnol Bioeng 43:747, 1994.

92. Falanga V, Margolis D, Alvarez O, et al: Rapid healing of venous ulcers and lack of clinical rejection with an allogenic cultured human skin equivalent. Arch Dermatol 134:283, 1998.

Varicose Veins:
Treatment by Intervention Including Sclerotherapy

157

JOHN J. BERGAN, MD

The care of venous stasis in all of its manifestations is the responsibility of surgeons in general and of vascular surgeons in particular. Others, including internists, family doctors, dermatologists and interventional radiologists, are entering the field. This is because prevalence of the conditions of venous dysfunction has outstripped care given by the surgical profession. The title of this chapter reflects this change. No longer can we use the exclusive term *surgery*. Now, the correct term is *intervention*, and the following text explains this paradigm shift. With varicose veins, such care is directed toward ablation of diseased vessels. Ablation is achieved by removing them surgically or by obliterating them with techniques that include radiofrequency or laser ablation or sclerotherapy. Large varicose clusters and varicosities above the knee are best treated by removal.[1] Other vessels, especially telangiectasias, may be subjected to sclerotherapy.

■ RELEVANT ANATOMY

The gross anatomy of the venous system is well known to surgeons.[2] Valve-containing deep veins transport venous blood by means of muscular contraction. Less physiologically important superficial veins also contain valves that direct their flow upward, and these veins connect with the deep system by means of perforating veins that penetrate the deep fascia of the lower extremities. Check valves in the perforating veins protect the poorly supported venules superficial to the tela aponeurotica from compartmental exercise pressure.

The official names of some veins has been changed in response to clinical needs and some ultrasonography-derived observations.[3] Chief among these changes are the adoption of the terms *great saphenous vein* (GSV), *small saphenous vein* (SSV), and *femoral vein* (FV) to replace the commonplace but confusing term "superficial femoral vein."

Less anatomically appreciated is the reticular subdermal venous network, which also contains valves (Fig. 157-1). Because it is the most superficially located vein network of the lower extremities, this plexus is the most poorly supported and is the source of the earliest subcutaneous varicosities.[3]

Superficial to this network in the dermis, postcapillary venules run horizontally, range in size from 12 to 35 μm, and empty into collecting venules twice as large in the mid-dermis.[2,4] One-way valves are found in venules at the

dermis-adipose junction and also in areas of anastomosis of small to large venules. Larger venules also contain valves not necessarily associated with junctional points. Free edges of valves are always directed away from the smaller vessels and toward the larger ones. These valves serve to direct blood flow toward the deeper venous system. The valve structure in these small venules is identical to that found in larger deep veins, consisting of valve sinuses, cusps, and aggeres in relation to vein walls.

Of greatest concern to the physician treating venous problems in the lower extremity is the great saphenous vein. The term *saphenous* is derived from the Greek word for "evident."[5] The saphenous vein (1) originates on the dorsum of the foot in the dorsal venous arch, (2) passes anterior to the medial malleolus, (3) progresses through the medial calf across the posteromedial aspect of the popliteal space, (4) ascends in the medial thigh, and (5) terminates in the femoral vein (Fig. 157-2).

The anatomy of the great saphenous vein is relatively constant. It is well appreciated that this vein lies on the deep fascia of the leg and thigh. Less well recognized, however, is that the vein lies below or deep to the superficial fascia (Fig. 157-3). Even contemporary descriptions of the anatomy of the veins of the lower extremity do not make this distinction.[6] Yet this fact is important to knowledge of the

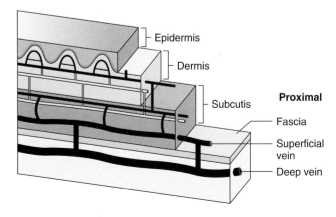

FIGURE 157-1 Dermal postcapillary venular network. Valves within these tiny vessels all direct blood flow deeper into large collecting veins. Failure of check valve function allows high-pressure venous blood to flow into unsupported dermal vessels, thus producing telangiectatic blemishes.

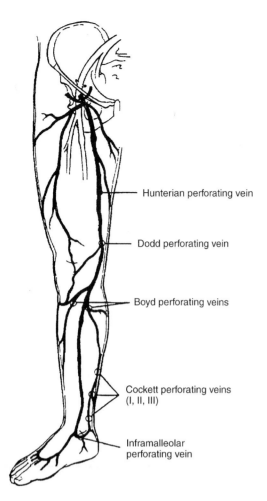

FIGURE 157-2 The location of the most important perforating veins associated with the great saphenous system is shown. The Cockett and inframalleolar perforating veins are actually separate from the great saphenous system. The Boyd perforating vein is constantly present, but it may drain the saphenous vein or its tributaries. Perforating veins in the distal third of the thigh are referred to as "Dodd perforators," whereas those in the middle third of the thigh are referred to as "Hunterian perforators."

development of varicosities. This is especially true when ultrasound imaging is done prior to and during intervention. The saphenous vein has a distinct appearance that separates it from varicose tributaries and allows precise intervention for therapy.[7,8]

In varicose venous anatomy, the important tributaries to the great saphenous vein extending upward from below are:

- The posterior arch vein, which receives the three Cockett's perforating veins.
- The anterior tributary vein to the saphenous system, which lies below the patella and collects blood from the anterior and lateral surface of the leg.
- The posterior tributary vein, which also empties into the great saphenous vein in the upper anteromedial calf.

Other tributaries that may terminate high in the saphenous system near the groin are the posteromedial thigh vein and the anteromedial thigh vein. Either of these veins may become the site of varicose clusters.

Less common in primary varicosities and more important in recurrent varicose veins after surgery are other tributaries to the great saphenous vein where it terminates in the fossa ovalis. They are the external pudendal vein, the superficial epigastric vein, and the superficial circumflex iliac vein.

Posteriorly, the most important of the axial veins is the short saphenous vein (Fig. 157-4).[5] In the new nomenclature, this is called the small saphenous vein. This vein originates on the lateral aspect of the foot in the dorsal venous arch and ascends virtually in the midline of the calf. Unlike the great saphenous vein, the small saphenous vein may penetrate the deep fascia at any point from the middle third of the calf upward. This fact explains the segmental rather than total nature of reflux found in the small saphenous vein.

Important tributaries to the saphenous vein are inconstant but may include the posterior thigh tributary vein. Superiorly, this tributary may be associated with a lateral thigh vein called the anterolateral superficial thigh vein. Another important and commonly encountered vein is the ascending superficial vein, which leaves the popliteal space and progresses proximally to join the saphenous vein medially at a point high in the thigh. This vessel is the vein of Giacomini.

The importance of knowing the regular features of the gross anatomy of the superficial veins of the lower extremity is that one of these systems may be the site of growth of clusters of varicosities. Such clusters can be referred to by the name of the normal vein in that location. All named tributaries to the greater and lesser saphenous system lie superficial to the membranous fascia and are relatively

FIGURE 157-3 The saphenous compartment is bounded by deep and superficial layers of fascia. Tributaries to the saphenous vein pierce the superficial fascia and it is they that become varicose. Transverse ultrasonography scanning has shown a single saphenous vein in 52% of persons, two parallel veins in 1%, a single saphenous vein with a large subcutaneous tributary that pierces the superficial fascia to join the saphenous vein at various levels in the thigh in 26%. Other variations have been identified. ASV, accessory saphenous vein; FA, femoral artery; FV, femoral vein; GSV, great saphenous vein.

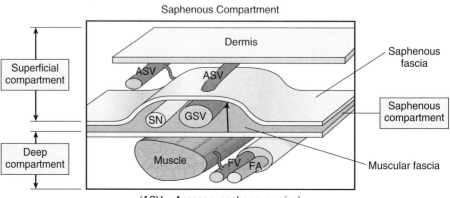

Saphenous Compartment

(ASV = Accesory saphenous veins)

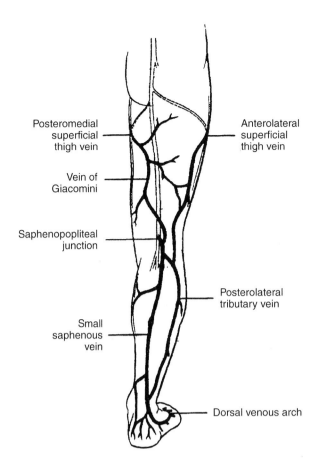

Posteromedial superficial thigh vein

Anterolateral superficial thigh vein

Vein of Giacomini

Saphenopopliteal junction

Posterolateral tributary vein

Small saphenous vein

Dorsal venous arch

FIGURE 157-4 The small (lesser) saphenous vein dominates the posterolateral superficial venous drainage and originates in the dorsal venous arch. At the posterolateral ankle, it is intimately associated with the sural nerve. Note the important posterolateral tributary vein and the posterior thigh vein, which ascend and connect the small saphenous venous system with the great saphenous system. The anterolateral superficial thigh vein and the posterolateral tributary vein can be very important in congenital venous anomalies, such as Klippel-Trenaunay syndrome.

unsupported in comparison with the greater and lesser saphenous veins and the deep veins of the muscular compartments.

■ IMPORTANT PERFORATING VEINS

Veins that connect the superficial venous system to the deep venous system and penetrate the fascia are properly called *perforating veins* (see Fig. 157-2). In the past, they were called "communicating veins." Any one of these veins, or any combination of them, may be the source of the hydrodynamic forces of venous hypertension that produce superficial varicosities. It is the abnormally high pulses of hydrodynamic pressure transmitted through incompetent perforating vein valves that affect relatively unsupported superficial veins. Such pulses of increased fluid force originate to some extent from increased abdominal pressure but to a greater extent from increased compartmental pressure during muscular contraction.

The best-recognized connections between the superficial venous system and the deep venous system are the saphenofemoral and saphenopopliteal junctions. Incompetence of the check valves at their termination has been

suggested as the cause of distal varicosities from gravitational reflux. This reverse flow is said to dilate more distal veins in a progressive fashion. Such reflux is neither always present nor the cause of highest hydrodynamic pressure. Gravitational reflux is referred to as *hydrostatic pressure*.

Because it is frequently the site of the first varicose veins or the first reticular veins that become varicose, Boyd's perforating vein in the anteromedial calf now receives great attention from physicians who treat venous problems.[9] Experience with duplex ultrasonography scanning reveals that venous incompetence at this level may be isolated and may be the first reflux to appear. Such incompetence may be asymptomatic. However, when the incompetence is symptomatic, it produces aching pain, fatigue, and even a throbbing discomfort. These symptoms can be relieved by firm local pressure. In some patients, the next perforator system to become incompetent is the distal thigh perforating vein. The frequency of varicosities in this location is documented in a graph by Cotton[10] that tabulates the number of varices in limbs in the monumental and informative study he performed in 1957. It was Cotton who pointed out that the "most extreme degree of tortuosity is exhibited by small tributaries which are found close to, and draining into, communicating [perforating] veins." In the figures illustrating Cotton's thesis, one can see the normal deep veins and the abnormal perforating veins *receiving* blood from "intensely tortuous veins which are seen to be varicose tributaries entering the communicating (perforating) veins."[10] van Neer and colleagues[11] have published a thorough clinical review of the importance of perforating veins.

■ HYDRODYNAMIC PRESSURE

Reversing this observation, we can visualize pulses of compartmental exercise pressure being delivered to unsupported superficial veins through incompetent perforators. Once we realize that intracompartmental pressure can be transmitted through incompetent check valves of perforating veins to unsupported tributaries to these veins, it is easy to see how the hydrostatic forces of gravitational reflux are additive to the hydrodynamic forces of muscular contraction. These very high pressures approach 150 to 300 mm Hg as they are generated within the muscular compartments. When transmitted outward, they produce localized blowouts or varicosities.

Progressing proximally from Boyd's perforating vein are the perforating veins in the distal third of the thigh. These veins, named for Harold Dodd, may be found in any location along the saphenous pathway in the distal third of the thigh.

The third important series of perforating veins, named for John Hunter, are found in the mid-thigh. Tung and colleagues[12] have surveyed phlebograms to study the anatomy of midthigh perforating veins. They found that 61% of limbs had one or more of these veins in the middle third of the thigh. In addition, they noted that 27% of the limbs had a perforating vein in the lower third of the thigh. Only 11% of the 100 phlebograms showed no evidence of perforating veins.

A concurrent study from St. Mary's Hospital in London found that the incompetent thigh perforating veins may occur anywhere in the thigh from the upper edge of the patella to a few centimeters below the saphenofemoral junction; 71% were found in the middle third of the thigh, and 20% of the limbs had more than one perforating vein.[13] All of the incompetent thigh perforating veins communicated directly with the great saphenous vein. It is interesting to note that five patients who underwent complete saphenous vein stripping also had connections of thigh perforating veins with residual saphenous vein trunks. This observation emphasizes the need for removal or occlusion of the entire refluxing saphenous vein in the thigh.

In the leg, the principal perforating veins have been named for Frank Cockett. Many surgeons incorrectly assume that the perforating veins on the medial aspect of the ankle and calf connect the deep system to the great saphenous vein. These perforating veins actually connect the posterior tibial deep venous system with the posterior arch vein (vein of Leonardo). Posterior tibial veins are frequently paired, and phlebography may show their connection through perforating veins to the superficial system and the posterior arch vein.[14] Cockett has described the medial communicating veins as if they were relatively constant in location, but they are not. The location is commonly given as the distance from the sole of the foot. Figures given from the heel pad are 6, 12, and 18 cm from this point. However, experience with duplex scanning reveals the actual location of these perforators to be quite variable (see Fig. 157-2). Other important perforating veins in the distal part of the extremity include the inframalleolar perforating vein. Frequently, this is the site of a painful ulceration. A flare of intradermal telangiectasias below this perforating vein is called a *corona phlebectatica*, a marker for more serious venous insufficiency.

Perforating veins on the posterior aspect of the lower extremity are much less well known. However, several are encountered frequently and are found to be the site of varicose clusters. Among them are the lateral thigh perforating vein, which may be located in the middle third of the thigh on its lateral aspect, and the lateral leg perforating vein, also invariably located in the middle or proximal third of the calf on its lateral aspect.

■ PATTERNS OF VARICOSITIES

Recognizing the normal anatomy and the most common perforating vein sources of varicosities makes identification of patterns of varicosities relatively easy (Table 157-1). As noted earlier, varicosities arising from the location of Boyd's perforating vein may be the first to appear and may occur

in the absence of varicose veins elsewhere in the lower extremity. Such varicosities may consist of the anterior tributary vein varicose cluster or, more commonly, a posterior varicose cluster. The first manifestations may be pain, aching, and heaviness. Relief may be obtained by applying local pressure under an elastic stocking and then by performing local excision of the cluster of varicosities and its perforating vein. Whether sclerotherapy for this pattern of varicosities will give long-term benefit is undetermined, but the best method of treatment is phlebectomy.

Of some importance is the relationship of the saphenous nerve to Boyd's perforating veins and its varicose clusters. In a study of this relationship, the most common vein-nerve pattern was found to be the saphenous vein and saphenous nerve that meet a few centimeters below the knee.[15] Below this point, the vein and the nerve were inseparable as far as the medial malleolus. This pattern was noted in 41 of 60 limbs studied. The next most common pattern, seen in 10 limbs, was the nerve joining the saphenous vein a few centimeters more proximally. Thus, in 50 of 60 limbs, nerve injury could be a problem in limbs in which the saphenous vein is exposed below Boyd's perforating vein.

Another isolated pattern of varicosities arises from the anteromedial tributary to the saphenofemoral junction. These veins may form prominent ropelike varicosities across the anterior surface of the thigh, coursing laterally and descending on the lateral aspect of the thigh. They may cross the popliteal space and arborize distally on the calf.

Other prominent varicose cluster patterns originate from the perforating veins of Hunter at the mid-thigh and of Dodd in the distal thigh and are sometimes isolated clusters of varicosities. Usually, they occur in association with great saphenous vein reflux. In fact, recognition that these clusters of varicosities are markers of saphenous vein reflux alerts the interested physician to study the saphenofemoral junction. The probable cause of great saphenous insufficiency when varicose clusters of the midthigh or distal thigh are present can then be confirmed by Doppler ultrasonographic evaluation.[16]

In a study intended to classify the clinical appearance of uncomplicated varicose veins, Goren and Yellin[17] found that 71% of the limbs studied demonstrated typical saphenous vein varicosities. Of the 164 limbs, 147 demonstrated great saphenous vein incompetence, whereas only 17 limbs showed small saphenous vein incompetence. Only 22% of limbs did not show saphenous vein incompetence; these showed isolated perforating vein incompetence.

The necessity of reconciling preservation of the saphenous vein for subsequent arterial surgery with the need for varicose vein surgery is considerably aided by the recognition that great saphenous vein incompetence may not be present in some limbs with gross varicosities. In such instances (22% of the limbs in the study by Goren and Yellin),[17] the great saphenous vein can be spared yet the operation can be done properly to remove symptomatic varicosities. Doppler ultrasonographic evaluation with confirmation by duplex scanning aids considerably in the planning of such surgical interventions. However, one should also understand that in more than 75% of limbs, the great saphenous vein may have to be sacrificed.

Table 157-1	Patterns of Varicosities	
LOCATION OF VARICES	**PERFORATOR**
Medial thigh, middle third	Hunterian
Medial thigh, distal third	Dodd's
Medial leg, upper third	Boyd's
Ankle, posteromedial	Cockett's
Ankle, anteromedial	Sherman's
Posterolateral knee crease	Unnamed

■ VARICOSE VEINS AND TELANGIECTASIAS

Varicose veins, telangiectatic blemishes, and dilated, tortuous, flat, blue-green reticular veins are not normal physical findings. They are evidence of venous dysfunction. *Telangiectasias* are defined as being a confluence of permanently dilated intradermal venules of less than 1 mm in diameter. *Reticular veins* are defined as permanently dilated bluish intradermal veins usually from 1 to less than 3 mm in diameter; they are usually tortuous.[18] The visible physical findings, more often than not, cause the symptoms of aching pain, leg fatigue, and a poorly described discomfort that makes the individual harboring this venous dysfunction wish to elevate the legs to a more comfortable position. Ultimately, the target of venous dysfunction is the skin. With long-standing venous dysfunction, the skin darkens as a result of hemosiderin deposition; if an inflammatory process is triggered, the subcutaneous tissues harden, and minor breaks in the epidermis are slow to heal, producing white, depressed scars. A confluence of these is called *atrophie blanche*.

The aching pain, which is the most common symptom, is related to pressure of the dilated vessels on a dense network of somatic nerve fibers present in subcutaneous tissues adjacent to affected veins. The magnitude of symptoms is not related to the length or diameter of the malfunctioning vein.[19] Patients with telangiectasias, for the most part, have symptoms identical to those of patients with protuberant, saccular varicosities.[20] It is these symptoms that drive the patient to a physician, who more likely than not dismisses the symptoms and their cause as unimportant.[21] Nevertheless, in best medical practice, the patient's complaint is acknowledged, and after appropriate diagnosis, treatment is instituted.

Indications for therapeutic intervention are listed in Table 157-2. Physicians might recognize that treatment is indicated when the patient has had superficial thrombophlebitis in varicose clusters or has experienced external bleeding from high-pressure venous blebs. Certainly, treatment such as elastic support would be offered for advanced changes of chronic venous insufficiency. The much more common symptoms, such as aching pain, leg fatigue, and leg heaviness, and the appearance of the leg, however, are likely to be dismissed. Nevertheless, they should be acknowledged and cared for.

Table 157-2	Varicose Veins: Indications for Intervention

General appearance
Aching pain
Leg heaviness
Easy leg fatigue
Superficial thrombophlebitis
External bleeding
Ankle hyperpigmentation
Lipodermatosclerosis
Atrophie blanche
Venous ulcer

Specific findings on physical examination that lead to surgical intervention rather than sclerotherapy are those of axial vein reflux in the great saphenous vein or, perhaps, the small saphenous vein. Experience teaches that sclerotherapy of varicosities in the presence of saphenous vein reflux will fail.[22] Furthermore, large varices lend themselves to surgical removal rather than sclerotherapy, and the trend worldwide is toward ambulatory phlebectomy rather than sclerotherapy for such varicose clusters.[23] H.A.M. Neumann, a dermatologist who has emphasized this issue, recommended that one should "always operate: insufficient saphenous junctions, major insufficiency of long saphenous vein ... and big insufficient (incompetent) perforating veins."[24] Others have found that surgery is indicated even when saphenofemoral junction incompetence is not present.[25]

When such phlebectomies are carried out, patient satisfaction is virtually unanimous.[26] At present, such surgery can be performed as day-case surgery, with no additional workload being given to the primary care physician.[27]

Extensive availability of duplex ultrasonography technology has revealed another reason for intervening in varicose veins—deep venous function is improved by superficial venous surgery.[28] Increased dilatation of the deep venous system has been noted to accompany superficial venous reflux and was described in a phlebographic study by Fischer and Siebrecht[29] as early as 1970. They observed that greater dilatation of deep veins was seen in the absence of post-thrombotic manifestations.

Such deep venous dysfunction has been thought to be the most important complication of superficial axial vein incompetence.[30] Although observations of deep venous dilatation and elongation were made in phlebographic studies in preoperative patients, such studies were not carried out uniformly in postoperative patients. When duplex ultrasonography technology is applied to the study of postoperative patients, ablation of preoperative deep vein reflux has been found.[29] This important finding provides a strong argument for treatment of varicose veins with the best method possible, which is ambulatory phlebectomy.

■ INTERVENTION AS TREATMENT

Objectives

When intervention is decided upon, the physician must keep three goals in mind in planning the treatment[31]:

- Permanent removal of the varicosities with the source of venous hypertension
- As cosmetic a result as possible
- Minimum number of complications

The source of venous hypertension, as described previously, is gravitational reflux (hydrostatic) or compartmental pressure developed during muscular contraction through perforator outflow (hydrodynamic). Therefore, removal of gravitational reflux by means of removal of the axial vein from the circulation and detachment of hydrodynamic forces by superficial varicosity excision has been found to accomplish both objectives.[32]

The Plan

The planned operation for a given patient must be completely individualized. As indicated previously, Doppler evaluation and duplex scanning have shown that in 70% of limbs selected for surgery, typical saphenofemoral junction reflux is present. In such limbs, the saphenous vein at the femoral junction must be treated. However, atypical varicosities without saphenofemoral junction reflux do occur in some 20% of limbs. In other limbs, atypical reflux causes their varicosities.[17] Clearly, no standard intervention fits every patient perfectly.

The techniques of saphenous surgery are well described in standard surgical texts.[33] Their outpatient variations have become routine.[34,35] And minimally invasive operations have come into vogue.[36,37] This means that older methods requiring inpatient care, general anesthesia, long operating time, radical avulsion of varicose veins, and stripping of varicose veins to the ankle can be largely abandoned.[31] Surgical removal of the saphenous vein is now done by groin-to-knee downward stripping of the GSV or its endoluminal destruction.[38,40,41] Techniques to decrease hematoma after downward stripping include irrigation and epinephrine-gauze packing of the saphenectomy tunnel.[17,32,39,42] Tourniquets should be used for huge varicosities during saphenous vein stripping.[43,44]

Options

Options available for surgical treatment of varicose veins are as follows:

- Ankle-to-groin saphenous vein stripping (with stab avulsion)
- Segmental saphenous vein stripping (with stab avulsion)
- Saphenous vein ligation: high, low, or both
- Saphenous vein ligation and sclerotherapy
- Saphenous vein ligation (with stab avulsion)
- Stab avulsion of varices without saphenous vein stripping (phlebectomy)
- Endoluminal occlusion of the saphenous vein by radiofrequency (RF) or laser energy

Objectives of surgical treatment should be (1) ablation of the hydrostatic forces of axial and saphenous vein reflux and (2) removal of the hydrodynamic forces of perforating vein reflux. These maneuvers should be combined with extraction of the varicose vein clusters in as cosmetic a fashion as possible.

Saphenous Vein Ligation

Ligation of the saphenous vein at the saphenofemoral junction has been practiced widely in the belief that it would control gravitational reflux while preserving the vein for subsequent arterial bypass. It is true that the saphenous vein is largely preserved after proximal ligation.[45] Reflux continues, however, and hydrostatic forces are not controlled.[46]

Before the accurate delineation of the sites of origin of varicosities, ankle-to-groin stripping of the saphenous vein was considered the standard operation that should be performed in every case. Turn-of-the-20th-century publications had conveyed the belief that reflux was uniformly distributed over the entire length of the saphenous vein.[47-49] This belief led to excessively radical saphenous vein stripping and the desire of surgeons to perform proximal saphenous vein ligation without saphenous vein stripping.

The objective of excision of the saphenous vein is to remove its gravitational reflux and detach its perforator vein tributaries in the thigh. Therefore, it has been found unnecessary to remove the below-knee portion. Perforating veins of the medial thigh are largely a part of the saphenous system; in the lower leg, however, this is not the case. Below the knee, important perforating veins are part of the posterior arch circulation. A further argument against routine removal of the saphenous vein below the knee is the discovery of saphenous nerve injury associated with the operation. Such injury has occurred in the upper third of the leg as well as adjacent to the ankle incision.[50]

Recurrent varicose veins are more common after saphenous vein ligation than after stripping.[51] Recurrent varicose veins are also more common after saphenous vein ligation and sclerotherapy than after stripping and sclerotherapy.[32] A prospective randomized trial comparing proximal saphenous vein ligation and stab avulsion of varices with stripping of the thigh portion of the saphenous vein and stab avulsion of varices has found superior results for the latter procedure.[52,53]

Studies of recurrent varicose veins have found preservation of the patency of the saphenous vein and continued reflux in the saphenous vein to be the most common element in the recurrence.[13,54] In patients presenting for surgical relief of recurrent varicosities, Stonebridge and colleagues[107] found that two thirds required removal of the saphenous vein as part of the second procedure. For all of these reasons, simple proximal saphenous vein ligation should be done only in very special cases.

Surgical Procedure

As indicated previously, knowledge of the pathophysiologic hydrodynamics, relevant venous anatomy, and results of the various surgical procedures allows precise prescription of the proper surgical procedure for each patient and each limb to be benefited by surgical intervention. In surgical practice, because great saphenous vein reflux is found in two thirds of patients, groin-to-knee removal of the saphenous vein from the circulation is part of the operation chosen.[17] Figure 157-5 illustrates surgical stripping, but ablation of the vein by RF or laser energy is an acceptable alternative.

In nearly all patients, this procedure is supplemented with stab avulsion of clusters of varicosities. In one third of patients, the saphenofemoral junction is found to be competent and therefore can be left intact. However, stab avulsion of clusters of varicosities derived from reflux from the Hunter or Dodd perforating veins may be necessary. This maneuver may remove segments of the great saphenous vein. Finally, approximately 15% of patients are found to have small saphenous vein incompetence, and the operation in such patients must include careful removal of some or all of that structure.

Advent of foam sclerotherapy has provided another minimally invasive alternative to stab avulsion surgery.[55]

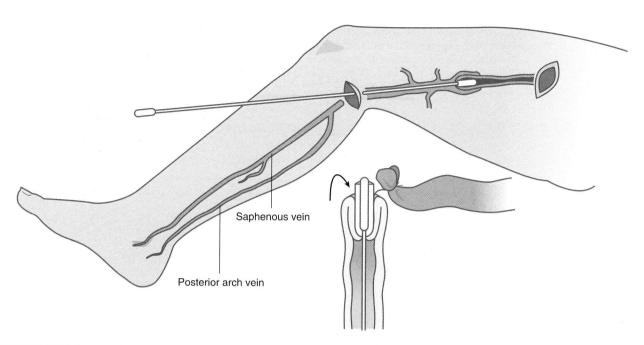

Saphenous vein

Posterior arch vein

FIGURE 157-5 Removal of the thigh portion of the saphenous vein is the mainstay in surgical treatment of primary venous insufficiency. The endoluminal device, commonly a disposable plastic stripper, can be introduced from above downward, and the vein ligated around the stripper proximally. As distal traction is applied, the vein is then inverted into itself and removed distally in the region of the knee. This minimizes tissue trauma but accomplishes the desired result of detaching the superficial venous system from perforating veins that are transmitting intercompartmental pressure to unsupported subcutaneous venous networks.

Great Saphenous Vein Stripping

In principle, incisions at the groin, ankle, and knee are transverse and are placed within skin lines. For incisions made elsewhere, experience has revealed that best cosmetic results are obtained with vertical incisions throughout the leg and thigh, which also allow preservation of lymphatics. Transverse incisions are used only in knee creases. Oblique incisions in skin lines are appropriate over the patella. Preoperative marking must be accurate so as to outline the extent of varicose clusters, clinical points of control of varices, and clinically identified locations of perforating veins.

In the groin, an oblique variation of the transverse incision is appropriate. This incision should be placed either in or 1 cm above the visible skin crease. It should not be made below the inguinal skin crease. This placement allows accurate and direct identification of the junction. Anatomy of the named tributaries is infinitely variable; the general appearance, however, is shown in Figure 157-2.

Although careful attention to disconnecting saphenofemoral tributaries has been emphasized in the past, this teaching has been found to be wrong.[56] Such clean and careful surgery is a principal cause of neovascularization in the groin and this, in turn, an important cause of recurrent varicose veins.[57] Destruction of the saphenous vein by laser or RF energy and removal of it from the circulation without a groin incision has been found to be effective and does not cause neovascularization.[58,59]

A major cause of discomfort and occasional permanent skin pigmentation is blood extravasated subcutaneously during and after saphenous vein stripping. This can be minimized by:

- Use of a hemostatic tourniquet
- Leg elevation prior to and during the actual stripping
- Internal packing of the stripper tract with the use of 5-cm-wide roller gauze soaked in lidocaine 0.5% with added epinephrine
- Instillation of high-volume, low-concentration (tumescent) perivenous local anesthesia

The disposable plastic Codman vein stripper can be introduced from above downward, because Doppler evaluation and duplex scanning will have confirmed saphenous junction incompetence. Angioscopic examination of the saphenous vein has revealed remarkably few valves in those saphenous veins that have come to surgery.[60] Valves that have been observed to be present have been monocuspid, deformed, or even perforated. The reasons for these deformities have not been elucidated but could include leukocyte trapping and activation in valve cusps.[61] Because the valves consist of only collagen and epithelium,[62] elaboration of collagenase by activated leukocytes could explain all of the valve damage that has been observed.

The vein stripper, introduced from above, can be exposed distally with a short transverse incision in the knee skin crease at the medial edge of the popliteal space. This is one of the three places where the saphenous vein is anatomically constant; it is helpful for this location to be marked preoperatively while the patient is standing. The skin incision in this location is cosmetically acceptable.

If the stripper passes relatively unobstructed to the ankle, it can be exposed there with an exceedingly small skin incision placed in a carefully chosen skin line. Passage of the stripper from above downward to the ankle has proved absence of functioning valves, and stripping of the vein from above downward is unlikely to cause nerve damage (see Fig. 157-3). At the ankle, the vein should be very cleanly dissected to free it from surrounding nerve fibers before the actual stripping is done.

Stripping of the saphenous vein has been shown to produce profound distal venous hypertension. This effect can be seen in virtually every such operation. Therefore, if considerable stab avulsion is to be performed, it is best for the surgeon to perform this procedure before the actual downward stripping. The stab avulsion, performed with the use of the Varady dissector, Müller hooks, or other such devices, successfully detaches perforating veins from their tributary varicose clusters. Dissection of each perforator at fascial level is neither necessary nor cosmetically acceptable. Neither is it necessary to ligate or clip retained vein ends after stab avulsion. Elevation of the leg, trauma-induced venospasm, and direct pressure will ensure adequate hemostasis.

Techniques of phlebectomy have been markedly refined by experienced workers in Europe.[63] The size of the incision depends on the size of the varicose vein, the thickness of the vein wall, and the vein's adherence to perivenous tissues. Incisions are 1 to 2 mm in length. They are oriented vertically except in areas where skin lines are obviously horizontal. The varicosity is exteriorized by hook or forcep technique, divided, and then avulsed as far as is possible. Subsequent incisions are made as widely spaced as possible. After avulsion of the varicosity, skin edges can be approximated with tape or with a single absorbable suture.

Although it is appropriate to discuss saphenous vein stripping in this surgical text, many believe that the operation is probably obsolete. The reason is that outpatient ablation of the saphenous vein from knee to groin by RF or laser energy using high-volume local anesthesia, intravenous sedation, and ultrasonographic monitoring has proved to be eminently satisfactory.[37,65]

Alternatives to Saphenous Vein Stripping

Radiofrequency and Laser Ablation of the Saphenous Vein

In an attempt to minimize postoperative discomfort while maintaining the benefits of saphenous vein ablation, alternating current has been applied to effect rapid thermic electrocoagulation of the vein wall and its valves. Prolonged exposure to such high-frequency energy results in total loss of vessel wall architecture, disintegration, and carbonization.[66] There is now level I evidence indicating that such treatment is beneficial.[67] Additional supporting data come from simple registry recording of results.[68] At 1 to 3 years, reported results from ablation of the saphenous vein are as good as those from conventional surgical treatment. Ultrasonographic scanning shows the treated saphenous vein disappearing 2 years after treatment. Clinical observations suggest that patients are much more comfortable after saphenous ablation than after stripping.[69]

The issue of varicose vein recurrence after saphenous vein obliteration without saphenofemoral junction tributary

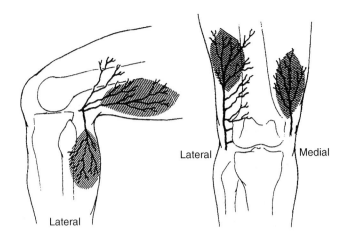

FIGURE 157-6 Common locations of telangiectatic blemishes on the medial distal thigh and the proximal leg both laterally and medially. Such telangiectatic blemishes may be connected to reticular feeding veins, which can be identified and sclerosed. Commonly, these feeding veins are connected to the deep venous circulation and transmit hydrodynamic forces to the dermal venules.

disconnection is unsettled at present. It does appear, however, that endovenous RF ablation of the saphenous vein—for example, with the Closure procedure (VNUS Medical Technologies, Inc., San Jose, Calif.)—prevents subsequent neovascularization in the groin. Many centers have reported no neovascularization in the absence of a groin incision.[57]

The specific goal of endoluminal treatment of venous reflux is obliteration of the saphenous vein. Follow-up to 3 years shows that RF ablation with the Closure procedure accomplishes this. Laser light energy (Fig. 157-6) has also been used to achieve this goal in place of RF energy, but its efficacy has not yet been proved.

Morrison[70] has compared the Closure procedure with endovenous laser treatment (EVLT) for occlusion of the saphenous vein in 50 patients. One great saphenous vein was treated with a laser, the other with RF energy (Table 157-3). Although this study was not a true randomized trial, bias was prevented by the carefully drawn protocol.

Hemodynamic outcomes were placed into one of three categories: (1) primary occlusion, (2) assisted primary occlusion, and (3) failure of treatment. This categorization is similar to the reporting standards for lower extremity ischemia, in which the terms primary patency, primary assisted patency, secondary patency, and failure are used.

Clear differences between RF ablation and EVLT were observed. RF ablation was more effective than EVLT in

Table 157-3	Comparison of Saphenous Veins Treated with Ablation and EVLT		
RESULTS (AT LAST VISIT)	**RF TREATED**	**EVLT TREATED**	***P* VALUE**
Primary occlusion	41	28	<0.05
Assisted primary occlusion	5	14	<0.05
Failure of treatment	4	8	<0.05

achieving primary occlusion (41 versus 28 veins). In addition, there were somewhat fewer treatment failures with RF than with EVLT (4 versus 8 legs).

Ten RF-treated legs showed early recurrent patency of the vein. Of these, one vein closed without further treatment, five closed after ultrasound-guided sclerotherapy, two did not undergo follow-up duplex scanning, and two failed to close after repeated sessions of ultrasound-guided sclerotherapy. In these 10 patients, the contralateral leg was treated with EVLT. In 7 of the 10 EVLT-treated legs, the saphenous vein failed to close primarily. Of the 24 EVLT-treated legs that showed recurrent venous patency and flow, 2 veins closed without further intervention, 14 closed after ultrasound-guided sclerotherapy, 4 did not undergo follow-up duplex scanning, and 4 failed to close after repeated sessions of ultrasound-guided sclerotherapy. The 4 legs with veins that failed to close with EVLT and ultrasound-guided sclerotherapy were treated with a second ablation procedure, this time with RF. Two of the 4 closed after the second ablation procedure. For the 2 legs that showed recurrent patency and flow even after a second ablation procedure, a high ligation of the greater saphenous vein was done in the office with the patient under local anesthesia.

Surgery of the Small Saphenous Vein

Surgery of the small saphenous vein is very little like surgery of the great saphenous vein. There is one similarity; the anatomy of the saphenopopliteal junction is just as irregular as that of the saphenofemoral junction. Indications for surgery of the small saphenous vein are similar to those for surgery of the great saphenous vein; that is, reflux in the small saphenous vein accompanied by symptomatic varices tributary to that system.

Although earlier surgeons described a normal low or high termination of the saphenous vein in the popliteal fossa, this area has been more carefully defined by duplex scanning. Now it is known that a very low termination below the knee joint occurs in only 2% of cases. In 42% of cases, the termination is within 5 cm of the knee joint crease and is the saphenous vein's only termination. However, the small saphenous vein may continue up into the thigh and terminate elsewhere. For example, it terminates in the vein of Giacomini in about 12% of cases, in half of which there is also a standard saphenopopliteal junction. The small saphenous vein may terminate higher, in a femoropopliteal vein or posterior subcutaneous thigh vein. In nearly half of these cases, the femoropopliteal vein enters a thigh perforating vein or, more rarely, splits into two or more branches that may reach the gluteal area. One third of these cases also demonstrate a standard saphenopopliteal junction.[63]

Because of the variability of the anatomy and the limited nature of small saphenous vein reflux, it is essential that examination with a continuous-wave, hand-held Doppler instrument be supplemented by duplex scanning. The objectives of duplex scanning are to confirm small saphenous vein reflux and to identify the termination of the small saphenous vein. The termination can be marked on the skin if the examination is performed immediately preoperatively; more often, however, because the duplex examination is remote in time from the operative procedure, the distance from the heel pad to the termination of the

saphenous vein is carefully measured and recorded in the duplex scanning report.

Hobbs[71] recommends on-table small saphenous varicography. Many of his observations were made before the days of duplex scanning.

Further differences between the small saphenous vein and the great saphenous vein include the fact that in the posterior leg, the small saphenous vein has segmental reflux in most cases. van Bemmelen and associates[72] found that the proximal part of the vein was incompetent in 36% of cases, and the midcalf portion in 31%. In more than half of the affected small saphenous veins, the incompetence was limited to only one segment; in the distal half of the leg, the small saphenous vein was normal in 26% of cases. The importance of this finding derives from the fact that the sural nerve is vulnerable to injury in the retromalleolar space on the lateral aspect of the ankle.

The surgical procedure is performed with the patient prone and the popliteal space relaxed by knee flexion. The incision is made over the termination of the small saphenous vein and centered on the junction between the middle and lateral thirds of the popliteal space. It can be made 5 cm long to expose the deep fascia. This structure can be further relaxed by more knee flexion. The incision in the deep fascia can be made parallel to the skin incision or longitudinally to achieve more exposure. The sural nerve should be identified and preserved. Frequently, the small saphenous vein or tributaries to it encircle one or more of these nerve structures. When the encircling veins are varicose, the dissection may be tricky indeed.

Division of the tributaries, and especially the proximal tributary to the vein of Giacomini, mobilizes the small saphenous vein termination. The vein can be divided and suture-ligated near its termination in the popliteal vein. Distally, stripping can be carried out with the disposable plastic Codman vein stripper or, better, with the Oesch stripper. Because there are no equivalents to the Hunter or Dodd perforating vein in the posterior calf, the stripping can be limited to the proximal lesser saphenous vein to above midcalf in most cases. Goren and Yellin[73] have provided a concise description of this technique.

After ligation, my colleagues and I have followed the original Oesch technique, which dictates that after the saphenous vein is divided, the stainless steel stripper is passed with its angled tip in a downward direction. The stripper usually passes only to the varicose cluster in the posterior calf. There, the angled tip of the stripper can be palpated through the skin, and skin pressure allows the stripper to perforate the vein wall and become subcutaneous. A 3-mm stab incision exposes the tip of the stripper, and the actual vein, which has been penetrated, is not visualized. A strong, nonabsorbable suture is tied to the end of the stainless steel stripper, and this suture in turn is fixed to the end of the vein so that it can be inverted into itself as the stripper is removed distally.

Once the inverted vein appears in the distal incision, it can be grasped directly with the hemostat, and traction can be placed on the vein as close to the skin as possible to avoid tearing the relatively fragile small saphenous vein. Gastrocnemius veins should be searched for in the proximal incision, because their persistence may contribute to recurrent varicosities in the posterior calf.

■ SCLEROTHERAPY

Although many credit Pravaz with the invention of the syringe in 1851, it was actually Rynd who developed this radical advance in 1845.[74] Case reports of sclerotherapy appear throughout the latter half of the 19th century.[75] A variety of caustics were used, including carbolic acid. Profound inflammation and suppuration followed such treatments in the pre-Listerian era. All early agents were thrombogenic. After investigations showing that quinine obliterated small vessels through intimal damage, the focus of sclerotherapy changed.[76] This change led directly to the use of hypertonic saline in 1924 and sodium morrhuate in 1930.[77]

Credit should be given to Biegeleisen[78] for the invention of microsclerotherapy after 1930. The technique languished somewhat until after 1970, although in some centers, treatment of varicosities of all sizes continued throughout this time.[79,80]

Indications for the use of sclerotherapy are listed in Table 157-4. Sclerotherapy is the only modality effective in the ablation of telangiectatic blemishes. It can also erase reticular veins and varicosities, particularly those less than 4 mm in diameter. Below the knee, where effective compression is most efficient, sclerosants can ablate larger varicosities and small clusters of varices not associated with great saphenous vein reflux. Furthermore, sclerotherapy is useful in obliterating residual varicosities after surgical treatment and varicosities that appear at times remote from surgery after saphenous vein reflux has been totally corrected.

Many individuals, especially nonsurgeons, use sclerotherapy for nearly all varicosities. Some even believe that axial vein reflux through saphenous veins can be halted effectively with sclerosants.[4] Furthermore, sclerotherapy is used by some for thigh varicosities of nonsaphenous origin and even for large varices associated with principal named perforating veins. As mentioned in Table 157-4, these are not ideal indications. It is the use of sclerotherapy in suboptimal situations that has contributed to its inferior reputation.

In general, sclerotherapy finds its greatest utility in the smallest incompetent vessels. These, then, may be telangiectasias or small varices below the knee. Proximal venous

reflux and venous hypertension must be corrected first.[81-86] Under less than ideal circumstances, sclerotherapy also finds a distinct usefulness in palliation, for the aged or infirm patient. In addition, in situations that violate these guidelines, sclerotherapeutic ablation of symptomatic varicosities can temporarily prove to be gratifyingly beneficial.

When telangiectasias are treated by sclerotherapy, the process is termed *microsclerotherapy*.[87] When sclerotherapy is used to obliterate larger veins, it is referred to as *macrosclerotherapy*.

Sclerotherapeutic Agents

Drugs available for sclerotherapy may cause thrombosis, fibrosis, or both. Excessive thrombosis is undesirable and may lead to excessive perivascular inflammation and recanalization of the vessel. More desirable endothelial damage may be provoked by a number of mechanisms, including:

■ Changes in the surface tension of the plasma membrane
■ Modification of the physical or chemical environment of the endothelial cell
■ Alteration in intravascular pH or osmolality

For effective microsclerotherapy, the endothelial damage must produce vascular necrosis in a significant portion of the vascular wall.[80]

Agents that change the surface tension of the plasma membrane are *detergents*. They include sodium morrhuate, sodium tetradecyl sulfate, and polidocanol. Their action produces endothelial damage through interference with cell surface lipids.[88]

Hypertonic solutions, including hypertonic saline, hypertonic dextrose, and sodium salicylate, cause dehydration of endothelial cells through osmosis. Possibly, fibrin deposition with thrombus formation occurs through modification of the electrostatic charge on the endothelial cells.[89]

Chemical irritants, such as chromated glycerin and polyiodinated iodine, act directly on the endothelial cells to produce endosclerosis. After endothelial damage occurs, fibrin is deposited in the sclerosed vessels. Platelets adhere to the underlying elastin, collagen, or basement membrane.[90]

Table 157-5 ranks sclerosing agents according to strength. The strongest solutions are used in the largest veins, including the saphenopopliteal and saphenofemoral junctions, selective perforating veins, and larger varicose clusters. At the other end of the scale are the weakest solutions, which are used for telangiectasias and other vessels smaller than 0.4 mm in diameter. Weak solutions are useful for vessels of up to 2 mm in diameter, and strong solutions for vessels of 3 to 5 mm in diameter.

The only two sclerosant solutions approved by the U.S. Food and Drug Administration (FDA) and listed in the *Physician's Desk Reference* are detergents. The oldest, sodium morrhuate, is a mixture of sodium salts of saturated and unsaturated fatty acids present in cod liver oil. This agent experienced early popularity in the 1930s. The enthusiasm was dampened, however, by reports of anaphylactic reactions.

The other agent, sodium tetradecyl sulfate, was widely utilized after 1950[91] and was advocated for use in dilute

Table 157-4	Indications for Sclerotherapy
Optimal indications	Telangiectasias
	Reticular varicosities and reticular veins
	Isolated varicosities*
	Below-knee varicosities*
	Recurrent varicosities*
Less-than-optimal indications	Symptomatic reflux
	Aged or infirm patient
	Patients who are not surgical candidates
Questionable indications	Great saphenous vein reflux
	Small saphenous vein reflux
	Large varicosities
Contraindication	Allergy to the sclerosant*

*In the absence of gross saphenous vein reflux.

Table 157-5	Relative Strengths of Sclerosing Solutions	
Category 1: strongest	Sodium tetradecyl sulfate	1.5-3.0%
	Polidocanol	3-5%
	Polyiodinated iodine	3-12%
Category 2: strong	Sodium tetradecyl sulfate	0.5-1.0%
	Polidocanol	1-2%
	Polyiodinated iodine	2%
	Sodium morrhuate	5%
Category 3: moderate	Sodium tetradecyl sulfate	0.25%
	Polidocanol	0.75%
	Polyiodinated iodine	1%
	Hypertonic saline	23.4%
	Sodium morrhuate	2.5%
Category 4: weak	Sodium tetradecyl sulfate	0.1%
	Polidocanol	0.25-0.50%
	Chromated glycerin	50%
	Polyiodinated iodine	0.1%
	Hypertonic saline	11.7%
	Sodium morrhuate	1%

solution for the treatment of telangiectasias after 1978.[92] Although it is widely used, this agent does produce epidermal necrosis when infiltrated in concentrations greater than 0.2%. Allergic reactions have been reported, and postsclerotherapy hyperpigmentation is commonly seen. Curiously, the manufacturer recommends an intravenous test injection as a precaution against anaphylaxis.

Not approved by the FDA at present but undergoing phase 2 trials in anticipation of approval is the most widely used sclerotherapeutic agent, polidocanol. It was synthesized and introduced as a local and topical anesthetic agent that clearly differed from the class of anesthetic agents that were "-caine" compounds. Polidocanol is a urethane whose optimum anesthetic effect occurs at a concentration of 3%.

Because intravascular and intradermal instillations of this agent produced sclerosis of small-diameter blood vessels, polidocanol was withdrawn as an anesthetic agent and proposed as a sclerosing agent after 1967. An optimal concentration for treating telangiectasias is 0.5%, whereas varicose veins may be treated with a 1% or greater concentration.[93]

Treatment of Telangiectatic Blemishes (Microsclerotherapy)

Telangiectatic blemishes may be thought of as extremely small varicose veins. Therefore, principles of treatment remain the same. The source of venous hypertension that has produced the elongation, tortuosity, and dilatation of the vessel must be controlled if treatment is to be effective. Telangiectasias may receive their pulse of venous hypertension directly through minute incompetent perforating veins (see Fig. 157-6).[84] This may be identifiable through careful Doppler examination; more often, the offending perforating vein is not specifically identified. Treatment of the telangiectatic blemish in such a situation may fail simply because the sclerosant solution does not reach the feeding vein in a concentration sufficient to obliterate it.

Telangiectasias may receive their pulse of venous hypertension from the subdermal reticular network (Fig. 157-7). These are seen as thin-walled, blue, superficial, dilated veins that are eventually tributaries to the main superficial venous system. Doppler studies have shown that free reflux occurs in such a network in association with telangiectasias. The reflux may proceed upward against the flow of gravity.[94] The reticular network may receive venous hypertension through gravitational effects, from incompetent perforators, or from a hydrostatic or hydrodynamic cause, as described earlier in this chapter.

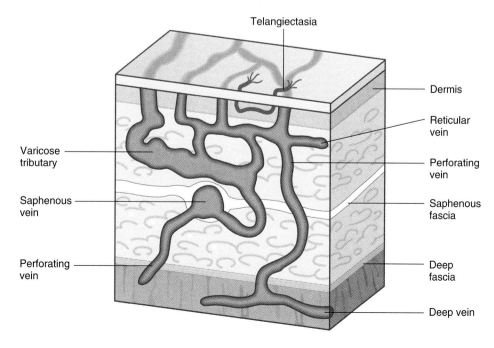

Telangiectasia

Dermis

Reticular vein

Varicose tributary

Perforating vein

Saphenous vein

Saphenous fascia

Perforating vein

Deep fascia

Deep vein

FIGURE 157-7 Diagram showing the interconnections of the structures that participate in venous insufficiency. Note the saphenous compartment, the varices in the superficial compartment, and the relationship of telangiectasias to the deeper structures. Telangiectasias are connected to reticular veins or varicose veins or both.

Knowledge of anatomy and pathophysiology dictates that the treatment of telangiectasias begin with the source of venous hypertension. When the source can be identified as a reticular dilated vein, the sclerosant solution may be seen to enter the telangiectasia directly from the feeding vein. The reverse may be true; injecting telangiectasias may allow the observer to watch the sclerosant solution enter a feeding vein from the site of injection. If it is impossible to identify the source of the venous hypertension, telangiectasias should be treated beginning at the point at which the branches converge. The actual injection method varies somewhat among authorities.[88,95,96]

The patient is in a horizontal position, either prone or supine. The skin is cleansed with alcohol to remove excess keratin and allow better visualization of the target vessel. No. 30 needles are used, and they are bent to 10 to 20 degrees. The bevel of the needle may be placed either down or up, but the needle should be parallel to the skin surface. Small syringes, either 1 or 3 mL in volume, are most convenient. The skin adjacent to the blemish must be stretched, and the firmly supported needle and syringe are then moved so that the needle pierces the skin and vein while pressure on the plunger ejects the sclerosant solution (Fig. 157-8).

Magnification and good light may allow the operator to recognize the appearance of the needle within the lumen of the target vessel. Pressure on the plunger allows the operator to see the development of a wheal if there is extravasation or a clearing of the telangiectatic web if intravascular injection is achieved. Some operators favor preceding injection of the sclerosant with a bolus (0.05 mL) of air. This allows the operator to check the position of the needle and may cause a greater spread of the sclerosant solution.[97]

Injections should be performed very slowly, and the amount of sclerosant should be limited to 0.1 or 0.2 mL per injection site. Injection given over 10 to 15 seconds is optimal. If a precise intravascular injection with rapid clearing of the telangiectasias is achieved, the operator must control his

or her enthusiasm and must sharply limit the amount of sclerosant given in any one particular site.

Minimizing the volume, pressure, and duration of the injection minimizes pain, risk of extravasation, and skin infarction. If persistent blanching of the skin to a waxy white color is seen or if a larger amount of sclerosant is inadvertently given in a single site, the area should be flushed thoroughly with hypodermic normal saline. This maneuver will dilute areas of extravasation and help to relieve vessel spasm. Vessels being treated that are larger than 0.5 mm and those that protrude above the skin surface should be compressed immediately, and compression should be maintained without interruption. Cotton balls, gauze, or foam rubber can be taped over the site with hypoallergenic tape in preparation for the eventual compression bandage or stocking.

After all telangiectatic blemishes and reticular varicosities have been injected and the injection session has been completed, elastic compression can be applied over the entire treated area. Again, practice varies, with some operators achieving compression with elastic bandages, and others with elastic stockings. Furthermore, the duration of compression varies among authorities. Some use no compression, some limit compression to 18 hours, and some advise compression for as long as 2 weeks. It is generally agreed that protuberant telangiectasias or telangiectasias associated with large reticular veins should be treated with compression for 72 hours or more. Nonprotuberant telangiectasias require no compression. Patients are encouraged to walk and not to restrict their activities. The number of treatment sessions depends on the level of success of each session. It is common, however, for the patient to require three or four sessions, and the interval between injection sessions is usually 2 to 4 weeks.

The treatment of reticular varicosities and feeding veins is slightly different from the treatment of telangiectasias. The patient is in a horizontal position. A No. 30 needle is optimal and can be inserted directly into the flat, blue-green

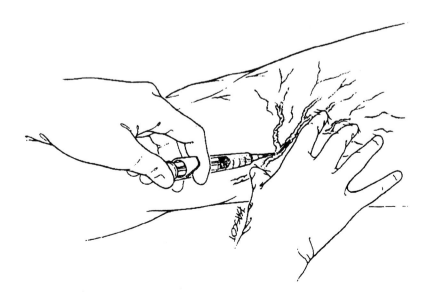

FIGURE 157-8 Placement of the needle in a feeding vein to treat the reticular varicosity found in association with a large telangiectatic blemish. Note the stretching of the skin, the penetration of the reticular varicosity with the needle, and the deft management of the plunger to clear blood from the entire blemish during injection.

reticular vein. The operator will feel resistance at the skin level and also at the vein wall. After the vein has been pierced, the plunger may be pulled back, and a flash of blood will be seen in the transparent syringe hub. This is possible even with a No. 30 needle. The volume injected should be kept at less than 0.5 mL, and, as in treatment of telangiectasias, multiple puncture sites aid in successful obliteration of the reticular varicosity.

Solutions used in treating reticular veins and telangiectatic blemishes must be dilute. The use of 0.1% or 0.2% sodium tetradecyl sulfate or its equivalent is satisfactory. If 11.7% or 23.4% hypertonic saline is used, an air block test of the injection site is advocated, because this solution is caustic enough to cause cutaneous damage during extravasation. Once polidocanol is approved by the FDA,[98] 0.5% polidocanol solution may be used in treating reticular veins and telangiectatic blemishes.[99]

Treatment of Varicose Veins (Macrosclerotherapy)

Intervention in patients with varicose veins is indicated for relief of symptoms that include aching pain, limb tiredness or heaviness after prolonged standing or sitting, and an exacerbation of symptoms at the termination of a menstrual cycle and on the first day of a menstrual period. The unsightly appearance of varicose veins and telangiectasias is important to patients and is an indication for treatment. Protuberant, saccular, bulging varicosities; the discoloration of dilated veins of telangiectasias; and the purple stain of the corona phlebectatica at the ankle all bring patients to the physician.

If great or small saphenous vein reflux is excessive, as determined by Doppler examination, it should be corrected surgically before sclerotherapy. However, palliation can be achieved for 2 to 4 years in the presence of axial vein reflux even though recurrence of varices may be expected. For example, in an older patient who experiences external bleeding from varicose blebs, uncorrected axial vein reflux does not affect local sclerotherapy to obliterate the blebs and prevent further bleeding episodes. Similarly, if recurrent thrombophlebitis in varicosities has occurred, the varicosities themselves can be obliterated by sclerotherapy even without control of the proximal venous hypertension.

Contraindications to sclerotherapy are:

- Presence of arterial occlusive disease
- Patient immobility
- Presence of uncontrolled malignant tumor
- Hypersensitivity to the drug
- Acute thrombophlebitis
- Huge varicosities with large communications to deep veins

In addition to the clinical examination to determine the sites of varicosities and the origin of their venous hypertension, examination with a continuous-wave, hand-held Doppler instrument is essential. This measure may be supplemented in particular cases with duplex scanning. Other assessments of venous function, such as impedance plethysmography, photoplethysmography, and venous pressure tests, are indirect and are not essential. Invasive phlebography is also not required. Classic tests, including the Perthes and Trendelenburg tests, have been replaced by the Doppler examination.

The objective of sclerotherapy is to produce endothelial damage and subsequent fibrosis of the entire vein wall without recanalization. Therefore, the ideal sclerosant solution would produce endothelial destruction with a minimum of thrombus formation. Unfortunately, FDA-approved agents are detergents, which are thrombogenic. Hypertonic saline is also used for sclerotherapy, although it is approved by the FDA for use only as an abortifacient. It does produce rapid endothelial damage. Hypertonic saline is available in a concentration of 23.4% and has been used extensively at this strength. Its single appeal is its total lack of allergenicity. However, it is common practice to add heparin, procaine, or lidocaine to hypertonic saline; additives, of course, offset the appeal of hypoallergenicity. Hypertonic saline at a concentration of 11.7% is equal to 23.4% in effect.[99]

Treatment of varicose veins 3 to 8 mm in diameter requires 0.5% to 1.0% sodium tetradecyl sulfate or its equivalent. Such large varicosities necessitate a stronger solution than telangiectasias do.

Because of the commonplace nature of varicosities and the very large number of people who treat them, a variety of techniques have developed. In principle, small-caliber (No. 25) butterfly needles are placed in varicosities while the patient is standing with the veins distended. The needles are attached to capped plastic extension tubing. A proximal tourniquet is neither necessary nor desirable. The multiple needles are placed either within a cluster of varicosities or in linear continuity in varices. An attempt to identify and to inject into a source of reflux aids in achieving long-term success.

The needles are held in place with tape until all have been inserted. Then the patient is asked to lie down, and the leg is elevated so that the veins will be empty. Duplex scanning verification of superficial venous collapse with the leg elevated to 45 degrees is useful.[100]

While injection of 0.5 to 1.0 mL of solution proceeds, there should not be any pain, irritation, or burning sensation. The presence of any of these symptoms indicates extravasation rather than intravascular injection. Extravasation demands cessation of injection.

At each injection site, after the needle has been withdrawn, a pressure pad of gauze, cotton, dental roll, or foam rubber is applied and taped in place with hypoallergenic tape. Elastic bandages may be used, wrapped from the toes proximally as they are gently stretched. The wrap is carried to 3 inches above the most proximal injection site. An elastic stocking may be fitted over the elastic bandage for additional compression or may be used instead of the elastic bandage.

The duration of compression varies with the individual preferences of the operator. For varicosities of 3 to 8 mm in diameter, a constant compression for 3 to 7 days is advised. A large school of French phlebologists practice minimal or no compression, but the influential work of Fegan mandates 6 weeks of constant compression. The controversy over the use of compression continues. Histologic studies suggest that 12 days of fibroblastic healing is required for obliteration of moderate-sized varicosities.[80,101,102]

Nearly all workers in this field advise that the patient should walk around the clinic for 30 minutes after the procedure. This measure allows symptoms and signs of an allergic reaction to appear and be treated. The comfort of the elastic compression can be evaluated, and the deep venous circulation can be stimulated to be flushed of any sclerosant that has entered from the superficial injection.

Use of Foamed Sclerosant

The prospect of a rapid, minimally invasive, and durable treatment of varicose veins is an attractive one. It appears that these objectives may be achieved without operative intervention through the use of sclerosant microfoam. In 1944 and 1950, E. J. Orbach[103,104] introduced the concept of a macrobubble air-block technique to enhance the properties of sclerosants in performing macrosclerotherapy. At the time, few clinicians evidenced much interest in the subject, and the technique languished.

Half a century later, the work of Juan Cabrera and colleagues[105] in Granada attracted the attention of some phlebologists and reawakened interest in the use of foam technology for treatment of venous insufficiency. These investigators showed that foam sclerotherapy was technically simple and worked well in small to moderate-sized varicose veins, and they demonstrated that the limitations of liquid sclerotherapy could be erased by using microfoam. Their 5-year report represents the longest observation period reported to date for microfoam sclerotherapy for varicose veins. For most of the patients, a single injection sufficed to treat saphenous veins and varicose tributaries. Extensive vasospasm was seen immediately, but compression was applied after treatment. Complete fibrosis of the saphenous vein was achieved in 81% of cases, and patency with reflux persisted in only 14%. Tributary varicosities disappeared in 96% of cases. Vessels that remained open and were refluxing were successfully closed with re-treatment.

If subsequent work continues to confirm these favorable results, it may be that microfoam sclerotherapy will eventually replace all other methods of varicose vein treatment.

Side Effects of Sclerotherapy

The fear of adverse sequelae of sclerotherapy keeps many physicians and surgeons from including this treatment modality in their therapeutic armamentarium. However, the incidence of complications is exceedingly low.[88,96] Undesirable sequelae include[106]:

- Anaphylaxis
- Allergic reactions
- Thrombophlebitis
- Cutaneous necrosis
- Pigmentation
- Neoangiogenesis

Anaphylaxis is an immunoglobulin E–mediated, mast cell–activated reaction that occurs within minutes of re-exposure to an antigen.[106] Other classes of immunoglobulin may contribute to the reaction. Risk of anaphylaxis rises with repeated exposure to a given antigen, a fact that applies directly to repetitive episodes of sclerotherapy. Mast cell concentrations are high in the skin. Mediators derived from mast cells, including histamine, can produce clinical anaphylactic manifestations. These may range in severity from mild pruritus and urticaria to shock and death. Manifestations that should alert the physician to serious problems are itching, flushing, erythema, and developing angioedema. Mucous membranes of the eyes, nose, and mouth are frequently involved, and this involvement may precede upper airway obstruction caused by edema of the larynx. This, in turn, is heralded by respiratory stridor. Unrelated to respiratory obstruction is hypotensive shock, which is thought to be due to peripheral vasodilatation and increased vascular permeability.[64]

Rapid treatment of anaphylaxis is crucial. Therefore, the equipment necessary for resuscitation must be present and must be used aggressively. Epinephrine is the drug of choice for the treatment of systemic reactions, because it (1) counteracts vasodilatation and bronchoconstriction and (2) inhibits further release of mediators from mast cells. Antihistamines and corticosteroids are not the drugs of choice in initial treatment, but both may be administered after epinephrine. Endotracheal intubation, oxygen, and intravenous therapy may be necessary, and patients with serious reactions should be admitted directly to the hospital.

Sodium morrhuate has been implicated as the most common cause of anaphylaxis among the sclerosing agents. However, nearly all of the reactions reported occurred before 1950. Goldman,[88] who reviewed the medical literature on anaphylaxis and sodium tetradecyl sulfate, found only 47 cases of nonfatal allergic reactions in a review of 14,404 patients. The product manufacturer has reported only two fatalities associated with the use of sodium tetradecyl sulfate, neither of which was from an anaphylactic reaction.

Polidocanol has the lowest incidence of allergic reactions, including anaphylaxis. Furthermore, patients allergic to sodium tetradecyl sulfate have been successfully treated with polidocanol. A single case of fatal anaphylactic shock has been reported with the use of polidocanol.

Alone, hypertonic saline shows no evidence of inducing an allergic reaction or of having a toxic effect. However, additives such as lidocaine and heparin may, in and of themselves, induce allergic reactions.

Thrombophlebitis and its sequelae were commonly reported before the use of compression after sclerotherapy. The actual incidence of superficial thrombophlebitis is difficult to ascertain, but it ranges around 1% to 3%. Duffy[95] estimated that it occurred in 0.5% of his patients.

Deep venous thromboembolic events are obviated by postsclerotherapy exercise that flushes the deep veins. There are scattered reports of pulmonary embolization after sclerotherapy.

Although serious reactions such as anaphylaxis, allergy, and thromboembolic events may be uncontrollable, the less severe complications of sclerotherapy can be diminished in frequency by attention to the details of injection. Skin ulceration and cutaneous necrosis may result from extravasation of solution. More commonly, they are due to arterial occlusion caused by sclerosant reaching a terminal arteriole. Another cause is reactive vasospasm from a too great volume of injection or excessive cutaneous pressure. Complications of extravasation are minimized by the use of extremely dilute solution, especially in the treatment of telangiectatic blemishes. Dilute 0.1% and even 0.2% sodium tetradecyl sulfate may extravasate without complication. The same is true of 0.5% polidocanol. However, extravasation of hypertonic saline into the skin may result in cutaneous necrosis if the solution remains undiluted. Intraarterial infiltration of sclerosant is avoided through strict adherence to the practice of injecting small quantities into each site.

Hyperpigmentation is common after sclerotherapy for veins and telangiectatic blemishes. It may occur in up to 30% of patients but is most common in patients treated with sodium tetradecyl sulfate and hypertonic saline. It is seen least in patients treated with polidocanol and is uncommon after the use of chromated glycerin. Neither of the latter two sclerosants had been approved by the FDA at the time of this writing.

Pigmentation, which is hemosiderin, derives from extravasation of red blood cells, which may appear in the dermis through either diapedesis or fracture of vessel walls. The following measures may reduce the incidence of postsclerotherapy pigmentation:

- Using weaker concentrations of solution
- Limiting the magnitude of intravascular pressure produced during injection
- Removing the postsclerotherapy coagula that may appear in protuberant telangiectasias, reticular veins, or varicosities

Removal of such coagula can be achieved by incising the skin with a No. 21 or No. 18 needle to allow expulsion of the entrapped blood through pressure. During expression of the coagula, all must be evacuated in order to avoid tattooing of the dermis with further extravasation of red blood cells. Postsclerotherapy hyperpigmentation largely disappears over a long period; it has been estimated that 90% is gone after 12 months.

Treatment of hyperpigmentation is unsuccessful. Bleaching agents affect only melanin, not hemosiderin. Exfoliants carry the risk of scarring and hypopigmentation. Topical retinoic acid has produced a varied response. Successful chelation of the iron with ethylenediaminetetraacetic acid ointment has been reported but is unconfirmed.

The new appearance of red telangiectasias in a site of prior sclerotherapy has been termed *telangiectatic matting* or *neoangiogenesis*. Although such matting may result from simple blockage of a crucial efferent vessel, it is usually thought to be a complex process in which new vessels actually grow in response to endothelial growth factors, mast cell products, or platelet-derived growth factors. Estrogen has been implicated as playing a role in the development of such neovascularization.

Prevention of neoangiogenesis is best achieved through (1) the use of dilute concentrations of sclerosant solution, (2) injection under low pressure, and (3) use of only 0.1 to 0.2 mL of injectate per injection site. Treatment is relatively ineffective, but the process usually resolves over a short period (3 to 6 months). Pulsed-dye laser therapy for neoangiogenesis has been successful but is expensive.

■ SUMMARY

Manifestations of telangiectasias, reticular varicosities, and varicose veins can be looked upon as elongated and dilated veins with incompetent valves. They are stretched by hydrodynamic and hydrostatic forces and pressures on somatic nerves to cause definitive symptoms. Though regarded as cosmetic nuisances, in fact they generally cause some symptoms, which occasionally are severe.

Treatment can be accomplished by removing the malfunctioning vessels. Surgical removal is best for vessels larger than 2 to 3 mm, and sclerotherapy suffices for vessels smaller than 2 mm.

■ REFERENCES

1. Bergan JJ: Surgery versus sclerotherapy in treatment of varicose veins. In Veith FJ (ed): Current Critical Problems in Vascular Surgery. St. Louis, Quality Medical, 1989.
2. Bergan JJ: Common anatomic patterns of varicose veins. In Bergan JJ, Goldman MP (eds): Varicose Veins and Telangiectasias: Diagnosis and Management. St. Louis, Quality Medical, 1993.
3. Caggiati A, Bergan JJ, Gloviczki P, et al: Nomenclature of the veins of the lower limbs: An international interdisciplinary consensus statement. J Vasc Surg 36:416, 2002.
4. Braverman IM: Ultrastructure and organization of the cutaneous microvasculature in normal and pathologic states. J Invest Dermatol 93:28, 1989.
5. Caggiati A, Bergan JJ: The saphenous vein: derivation of its name and its relevant anatomy. J Vasc Surg 35:172, 2002.
6. Nehler MR, Moneta GL: The lower extremity venous system: Anatomy and normal physiology. Perspect Vasc Surg 4:104, 1991.
7. Caggiati A: Fascial relationships of the short saphenous vein. J Vasc Surg 34:241, 2001.
8. Caggiati A, Ricci S: The long saphenous vein compartment. Phlebology 12:107, 1997.
9. Boyd AM: Treatment of varicose veins. Proc R Soc Med 41:633, 1948.
10. Cotton LT: Varicose veins: Gross anatomy and development. Br J Surg 48:589, 1961.
11. van Neer PA, Veraart JC, Neumann HA: Venae perforantes: A clinical review. Dermatol Surg 29:931, 2003.
12. Tung KT, Chan O, Lea Thomas M: The incidence and sites of medial thigh communicating veins: A phlebologic study. Clin Radiol 41:339, 1990.
13. Papadakis K, Christodoulou C, Christopoulos D, et al: Number and anatomic distribution of incompetent thigh perforating veins. Br J Surg 76:581, 1988.
14. O'Donnell TF Jr: Surgical treatment of incompetent communicating veins. In Bergan JJ, Kistner RL (eds): Atlas of Venous Surgery. Philadelphia, WB Saunders, 1992.
15. Holme JB, Holme K, Sorensen LS: The anatomic relationship between the long saphenous vein and the saphenous nerve. Acta Chir Scand 154:631, 1988.
16. Olpade-Olaopa EO, Foy DM, Dikko BU, Darke SG: Primary lower limb varicosities arising from normal deep venous systems: A series report. Ann Vasc Surg 14:166, 2000.

17. Goren G, Yellin AE: Primary varicose veins: Topographic and hemodynamic correlations. J Cardiovasc Surg 31:672, 1990.

18. Allegra C, Antignani P-L, Bergan, JJ, et al: The "C" of CEAP: Suggested definitions and refinements. An International Union of Phlebology conference of experts. J Vasc Surg 37:129, 2003.

19. Goldman MP, Weiss RA, Bergan JJ: Diagnosis and treatment of varicose veins: A review. J Am Acad Dermatol 31:393, 1994.

20. Weiss RA, Weiss MA: Resolution of pain associated with varicose and telangiectatic leg veins after compression sclerotherapy. J Dermatol Surg Oncol 16:333, 1990.

21. Weiss RA, Weiss MA, Goldman MP: Negative physician perception of sclerotherapy for venous disorders: Results of a survey and a review of a 7-year positive American experience with modern sclerotherapy. South Med J 11:1101, 1992.

22. Bergan JJ: Surgical management of primary and recurrent varicose veins. In Gloviczki P, Yao JST (eds): Handbook of Venous Disorders. Andover, UK, Chapman & Hall, 1996.

23. Weiss RA, Weiss MA: Ambulatory phlebectomy compared to sclerotherapy for varicose and telangiectatic veins: Indications and complications. Adv Dermatol 11:3, 1996.

24. Neumann HAM: Ambulant minisurgical phlebectomy. J Dermatol Surg Oncol 18:53, 1992.

25. Abu-Own A, Scurr JH, Coleridge Smith PD: Saphenous vein reflux without incompetence at the saphenofemoral junction. Br J Surg 81:1452, 1994.

26. Baker DM, Turnbull NB, Pearson JCG, Makin GS: How successful is varicose vein surgery? A patient outcome study following varicose vein surgery using the SF-36 health assessment questionnaire. Eur J Vasc Endovasc Surg 9:299, 1995.

27. Ramesh S, Umeh HN, Galland RB: Day-case varicose vein operations: Patient suitability and satisfaction. Phlebology 10:103, 1995.

28. Puggioni A, Lurie F, Kistner RL, Eklof B: How often is deep venous reflux eliminated after saphenous vein ablation? J Vasc Surg 38:517, 2003.

29. Fischer H, Siebrecht H: Das kaliber der tiefen unterschenkelvenen bei der primaren varicose und beim postthrombotischen syndrome (Eine phlebographische Studie). Der Hautarzt 5:205, 1970.

30. Hach-Wunderle V: Die sekundare popliteal und femoral venen insuffizienz. Phlebology 21:52, 1992.

31. Bergan JJ: Surgical procedures for varicose veins: Axial stripping and stab avulsion. In Bergan JJ, Kistner RL (eds): Atlas of Venous Surgery. Philadelphia, WB Saunders, 1992.

32. Neglen P: Treatment of varicosities of saphenous origin: Comparison of ligation, selective excision, and sclerotherapy. In Bergan JJ, Goldman MP (eds): Varicose Veins and Telangiectasias: Diagnosis and Treatment. St. Louis, Quality Medical, 1993.

33. Lumley JSP: Color Atlas of Vascular Surgery. Baltimore, Williams & Wilkins, 1986.

34. Greenhalgh RM: Vascular Surgical Techniques. Philadelphia, WB Saunders, 1989.

35. Bishop CCR, Jarrett PEM: Outpatient varicose vein surgery under local anaesthesia. Br J Surg 73:821, 1986.

36. Chandler JG, Pichot O, Sessa C, et al: Treatment of primary venous insufficiency by endovenous saphenous vein obliteration. Vasc Surg 34:201, 2000.

37. Whiteley MS, Pichot O, Sessa C, Kabnick et al: Endovenous obliteration: An effective, minimally invasive surrogate for saphenous vein stripping. J Endovasc Surg 7:I1, 2000.

38. Goldman MP: Closure of the greater saphenous vein with endoluminal radiofrequency thermal heating of the vein wall in combination with ambulatory phlebectomy: Preliminary 6-month followup. Dermatol Surg 26:105, 2000.

39. Bergan JJ, Pascarella L: Varicose vein surgery. In Wilmore DW, Souba WW, Fink MP, et al (eds): ACS Surgery Online. New York, WebMD Inc, 2003. Available at: http://www.acssurgery.com/

40. Samuels PB: Technique of varicose vein surgery. Am J Surg 142:239, 1981.

41. Conrad P: Groin-to-knee downward stripping of long saphenous vein. Phlebology 7:20, 1992.

42. Furuya T, Tada Y, Sato O: A new technique for reducing subcutaneous hemorrhage after stripping of the great saphenous vein [letter]. J Vasc Surg 3:493, 1992.

43. Corbett R, Jayakumar JN: Clean-up varicose vein surgery—use a tourniquet. Ann R Coll Surg Engl 71:57, 1989.

44. Thompson JF, Royle GT, Farrands PA, et al: Varicose vein surgery using a pneumatic tourniquet: Reduced blood loss and improved cosmesis. Ann R Coll Surg Engl 72:119, 1990.

45. Rutherford RB, Sawyer JD, Jones DN: The fate of residual saphenous vein after partial removal or ligation. J Vasc Surg 12:422, 1990.

46. McMullin GM, Coleridge Smith PD, Scurr JH: Objective assessment of high ligation without stripping the long saphenous vein. Br J Surg 78:1139, 1991.

47. Mayo CH: Treatment of varicose veins. Surg Gynecol Obstet 2:385, 1906.

48. Babcock WW: A new operation for extirpation of varicose veins. N Y Med J 86:1553, 1907.

49. Keller WL: A new method for extirpating the internal saphenous and similar veins in varicose conditions: A preliminary report. N Y Med J 82:385, 1905.

50. Bergan JJ: Surgery of the Veins of the Lower Extremity. Philadelphia, WB Saunders, 1985.

51. Munn SR, Morton JB, MacBeth WAAG, McLeish AR: To strip or not to strip the long saphenous vein? A varicose veins trial. Br J Surg 68:426, 1981.

52. Sarin S, Scurr JH, Coleridge Smith PD: Assessment of stripping the long saphenous vein in temperature treatment of primary varicose veins. Br J Surg 79:889, 1992.

53. Dwerryhouse S, Davies B, Harradine K, et al: Stripping the long saphenous vein reduces the rate of reoperation for recurrent varicose veins: Five-year results of a randomized trial. J Vasc Surg 29:589, 1999.

54. Darke SG: The morphology of recurrent varicose veins. Eur J Vasc Surg 6:512, 1992.

55. Cabrera J, Cabrera A Jr, Garcia-Olmedo A: Treatment of varicose long saphenous veins with sclerosant in microfoam form: Long-term outcomes. Phlebology 15:19, 2000.

56. Fischer R, Linde N, Duff C, et al: Late recurrent saphenofemoral junction reflux after ligation and stripping of the greater saphenous vein. J Vasc Surg 34:236, 2001.

57. Fischer R, Chandler JG, DeMaeseneer MG, et al: The unresolved problem of recurrent saphenofemoral reflux. J Am Coll Surg 195:80, 2002.

58. Chandler JG, Pichot O, Sessa C, et al: Defining the role of extended saphenofemoral junction ligation: A prospective comparative study. J Vasc Surg 32:941, 2000.

59. Morrison N: Ultrasound-guided polidocanol foam injection. UIP World Congress Chapter Meeting, August 2003.

60. Gradman WS, Segalowitz J, Grundfest W: Venoscopy in varicose vein surgery: Initial experience. Phlebology 8:145, 1993.

61. Ono T, Bergan JJ, Schmid-Schönbein GW, Takase S: Monocyte infiltration into venous valves. J Vasc Surg 27:158, 1998.

62. Butterworth DM, Rose SS, Clark P, et al: Light microscopy, immunohistochemistry, and electron microscopy of the valves of the lower limb veins and jugular veins. Phlebology 7:1, 1992.

63. Ricci S, Georgiev M, Goldman MP: Ambulatory Phlebectomy. St. Louis, CV Mosby, 1995.

64. Bergan JJ, Goldman MP: Complications of sclerotherapy. In Bernhard VM, Towne JB (eds): Complications of Vascular Surgery. St. Louis, CV Mosby, 1991.

65. Manfrini S, Gasbarro V, Danielsson G, et al: Endovenous management of saphenous vein reflux. J Vasc Surg 32:330, 2000.

66. Petrovic S, Chandler JG: Endovenous obliteration: An effective, minimally invasive surrogate for saphenous vein stripping. J Endovasc Surg 7:11, 2000.

67. Rautio T, Ohinmaa A, Perala J, et al: Endovenous obliteration versus conventional stripping operation in the treatment of primary varicose veins: A randomized, controlled trial with comparison of the costs. J Vasc Surg 35:958, 2002.

68. Kabnick LS, Merchant RF: Twelve- and 24-month followup after endovascular obliteration of saphenous reflux: A report from the multicenter register. J Phlebol 1:17, 2001.

69. Goldman MP: Closure of the greater saphenous vein with endoluminal radiofrequency thermal heating of the vein wall in combination with ambulatory phlebectomy: Preliminary 6-month followup. Dermatol Surg 26:105, 2000.

70. Morrison N: Saphenous ablation: What are the choices? Semin Vasc Surg, March 2005.

71. Hobbs JT: Perioperative venography to ensure accurate saphenopopliteal vein ligation. Br Med J 280:1578, 1980.

72. van Bemmelen PS, Bedford G, Beach K, Strandness DE Jr: Quantitative segmental evaluation of venous valvular reflux with ultrasound scanning. J Vasc Surg 10:425, 1989.

73. Goren G, Yellin AE: Invaginated axial saphenectomy by a semirigid stripper: Perforate-invaginate stripping. J Vasc Surg 20:970, 1994.

74. Garrison FH: Introduction to the History of Medicine. Philadelphia, WB Saunders, 1929.

75. Bergan JJ: History of surgery of the somatic veins. In Bergan JJ, Kistner RL (eds): Atlas of Venous Surgery. Philadelphia, WB Saunders, 1992.

76. Genevrier M: Du traitement des varices par les injections coagulantes concentrées de sels de quinine. Soc Med Mil Fr 15:169, 1921.

77. Rogers L, Winchester AH: Intravenous sclerosing injections. Br Med J 2:120, 1930.

78. Biegeleisen HI: Telangiectasias associated with varicose veins. JAMA 102:2092, 1934.

79. Foley WT: The eradication of venous blemishes. Cutis 15:665, 1975.

80. Fegan WG: Varicose Veins: Compression Sclerotherapy. Dublin, Wm Heinemann, 1967. (Republished in 2003 as Shami SK, Cheatle TR [eds]: Fegan's Compression Sclerotherapy for Varicose Veins. New York, Springer Verlag.)

81. Miani A, Rubertsi U: Collecting venules. Minerva Cardioangiol 41:541, 1958.

82. Wokalek H, Vanscheidt W, Martan K, Leder O: Morphology and localization of sunburst varicosities: An electron microscopic study. J Dermatol Surg Oncol 15:149, 1989.

83. deFaria JL, Morales I: Histopathology of the telangiectasia associated with varicose veins. Dermatologica 127:321, 1963.

84. Bohler-Sommeregger K, Karnel F, Schuller-Petrovic SS, Sautler R: Do telangiectasias communicate with the deep venous system? J Dermatol Surg Oncol 18:403, 1992.

85. Wells HS, Youman JB, Miller DG: Tissue pressure (intracutaneous, subcutaneous, and intramuscular) as related to venous pressure, capillary filtration, and other factors. J Clin Invest 17:489, 1938.

86. Cockett HFB, Jones BE: The ankle blowout syndrome: A new approach to the varicose ulcer problem. Lancet 1:17, 1953.

87. Green D: Compression sclerotherapy: Techniques. Dermatol Clin 7:137, 1989.

88. Goldman MP: Sclerotherapy. St. Louis, Mosby-Year Book, 1991.

89. Imhoff E, Stemmer R: Classification and mechanism of action of sclerosing agents. Soc Fr Phlebol 22:143, 1969.

90. Lindemayer H, Santler R: The fibrinolytic activity of the vein wall. Phlebologie 30:151, 1977.

91. Reiner L: The activity of anionic surface active compounds on producing vascular obliteration. Proc Soc Exp Biol Med 62:49, 1946.

92. Tretbar LL: Spider angiomata: Treatment with sclerosant injections. J Kansas Med Soc 79:198, 1978.

93. Carlin MC, Ratz JL: Treatment of telangiectasias: Comparison of sclerosing agents. J Dermatol Surg Oncol 13:1181, 1987.

94. Tretbar LL: The origin of reflux in incompetent blue reticular/telangiectatic veins. In Davy A, Stemmer R (eds): Phlébologie 89. Montrouge, France, John Libbey Eurotext, 1989.

95. Duffy DM: Small-vessel sclerotherapy: An overview. Adv Dermatol 3:221, 1988.

96. Goldman MP: Sclerotherapy of superficial venules and telangiectasias of the lower extremities. Dermatol Clin 5:369, 1987.

97. Bodian EL: Techniques of sclerotherapy for sunburst venous blemishes. J Dermatol Surg Oncol 11:696, 1985.

98. Goldman MP: Polidocanol (Aethoxysklerol) for sclerotherapy of superficial venules and telangiectasias. J Dermatol Surg Oncol 15:204, 1989.

99. Sadick NS: Sclerotherapy of varicose and telangiectatic leg veins: Minimal sclerosant concentration of hypertonic saline and its relationship to vessel diameter. J Dermatol Surg Oncol 17:65, 1991.

100. Foley DP, Forrestal MD: A comparative evaluation of the empty vein utilizing duplex ultrasonography. In Raymond-Martimbeau P, Prescott R, Zummo M (eds): Phlébologie. Montrouge, France, John Libbey Eurotext, 1992.

101. Vin F: Principe, technique, et résultats du traitement rapide des saphénes internes incontinentes par sclérothérapie. In Raymond-Martimbeau P, Prescott R, Zummo M (eds): Phlébologie. Montrouge, France, John Libbey Eurotext, 1992.

102. Sigg K: The treatment of varicosities and accompanying complications. Angiology 3:355, 1952.

103. Orbach EJ: Sclerotherapy of varicose veins: Utilization of intravenous air block. Am J Surg 66:362, 1944.

104. Orbach EJ: Contribution to the therapy of the varicose complex. J Int Coll Surg 13:765, 1950.

105. Cabrera J, Cabrera J, Garcia-Olmedo MA: Treatment of varicose long saphenous vein with sclerosant in microfoam form: Long term outcomes. Phlebology 15:19, 2000.

106. Bochner BS, Lichtenstein LM: Anaphylaxis. N Engl J Med 324:1785, 1991.

107. Stonebridge PA, Chalmers N, Beggs I, et al: Recurrent varicose veins: A varicographic analysis leading to a new practical classification. Br J Surg 82:60-62, 1995.

Management of Perforator Vein Incompetence

158

MANJU KALRA, MBBS
PETER GLOVICZKI, MD

Incompetent perforating veins were observed in patients with venous ulceration more than a century ago by John Gay,[1] but surgical interruption of these veins to prevent ulceration was suggested first by Linton only in 1938.[2] Linton attributed a key role to perforator vein incompetence (PVI) in the pathomechanism of venous ulceration, an idea embraced later by Cockett,[3,4] Dodd,[5,6] and several other investigators.[7-13] This assumption led to the premise that surgical interruption of perforating veins would prevent the abnormal transmission of elevated venous pressure in the deep venous system generated during walking to the superficial venous system and thereby promote ulcer healing. In the mid-twentieth century, perforator ligation was adopted by many surgeons as the panacea to heal venous ulcers. However, a high incidence of wound complications after subfascial perforator ligation, coupled with conflicting long-term results reported by various investigators, led to virtual abandonment of the procedure during the 1980s.[14,15] In the light of these results, several investigators attempted to modify Linton's original operation, which required long skin incisions. Less invasive surgical techniques included the use of shorter skin incisions,[3,5,7,10,11] long posterior incision away from damaged skin,[16,17] multiple medial incisions in skin creases,[18] and blind avulsion of the perforators with a shearing instrument.[19] In the mid 1980s, Hauer developed a technique that enabled incompetent perforating veins to be ligated under direct vision through small incisions situated far away from areas of ulcerated or damaged skin.[20] This technique was rapidly adopted and refined by several groups, and over the past decade subfascial endoscopic perforator vein surgery (SEPS) has emerged as an effective minimally invasive technique to interrupt perforating veins.[21-31] In recent years, ultrasound-guided sclerotherapy (USGS) of perforating veins has been described as an office procedure performed with the use of local anesthesia to make the procedure even less invasive.

In this chapter we review the surgical anatomy of the perforating veins and discuss available evidence supporting the role of perforators in chronic venous disease. We describe indications for perforator vein interruption, discuss preoperative evaluation of patients, and present the currently used techniques for interruption of perforators. Finally, we review data in the literature on the efficacy of perforator vein interruption.

■ SURGICAL ANATOMY OF PERFORATOR VEINS

Perforating veins connect the superficial to the deep venous system, either directly to the main axial veins (direct perforators) or indirectly to muscular tributaries or soleal venous sinuses (indirect perforators). The term *communicating veins* refers to interconnecting veins within the same system. In normal limbs, unidirectional flow in calf and thigh perforators, from the great and small saphenous systems toward the deep veins, is assured by venous valves. Perforating veins of the foot, on the other hand, are valveless and paradoxically direct flow from the deep to the superficial venous system.[32-34]

In the mid and distal calf the most important direct medial perforators do not originate directly from the great saphenous vein (GSV) (Fig. 158-1). This finding was first noted by John Gay in 1866 in a clinical case with venous ulcers, in which he demonstrated the posterior accessory GSV and three perforating veins.[1] This observation is extremely important because stripping of the GSV will not affect flow through incompetent medial calf perforators. The most significant calf perforators, termed the *Cockett perforators,* connect the posterior accessory GSV (Leonardo's vein) (Figs. 158-1 and 158-2) to the paired posterior tibial veins. In some patients the posterior accessory GSVs are not well developed and other posterior tributaries of the GSV are connected instead through perforators to the deep system. Three groups of Cockett perforators have been identified. The *Cockett I* perforator is located posterior to the medial malleolus and may be difficult to reach endoscopically. The *Cockett II* and *III* perforators are located 7 to 9 cm and 10 to 12 cm proximal to the lower border of the medial malleolus, respectively (Figs. 158-3 and 158-4).[33] All are found in "Linton's lane," 2 to 4 cm posterior to the medial edge of the tibia.[34-36]

Mozes and coworkers, during anatomic dissections, identified an average of 14 medial calf perforating veins (direct and indirect) per limb in patients with chronic venous insufficiency (CVI), with a range of 7 to 22 veins. However, only 3 of these were greater than 2 mm in diameter, in concordance with the earlier clinical descriptions of Linton and Cockett and with the fact that only 3 to 5 clinically significant incompetent perforators are found in most patients.[22] The greatest concentration of perforating veins was located at 25 to 33 cm above the ankle, followed by 7

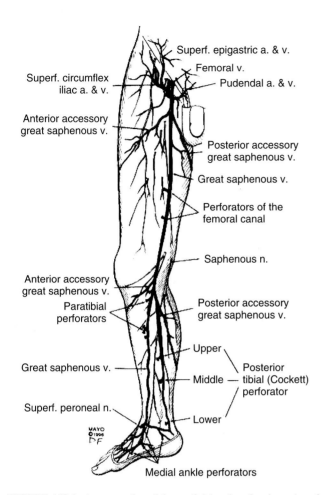

FIGURE 158-1 Anatomy of medial superficial and perforating veins of the leg. (From Mozes G, Gloviczki P, Menawat SS, et al: Surgical anatomy for endoscopic subfascial division of perforating veins. J Vasc Surg 24:800-808, 1996.)

to 13 cm, findings consistent with Linton's original description of frequent veins at the junction of the middle and lower third of the leg.[2,33] Based on duplex scanning and surgical findings, Pierik and colleagues and O'Donnell and associates reported about half of all calf perforators occurring 11 to 20 cm and 10 to 15 cm above the medial malleolus, respectively, with another 10% to 20% situated in the 20- to 25-cm region.[24,35]

The next group of clinically relevant perforating veins are the *paratibial* perforators, which connect the GSV and its tributaries to the posterior tibial and popliteal veins. Mozes and coworkers described their anatomy in detail by performing corrosion cast studies in 40 normal limbs from 20 cadavers.[33] The paratibial perforators are found in three groups, all located 1 to 2 cm posterior to the medial tibial border. They are located 18 to 22 cm, 23 to 27 cm, and 28 to 32 cm from the inferior border of the medial malleolus, respectively (Fig. 158-5). The 18- to 22-cm group corresponds to the "24 centimeter" perforator described by Sherman, who used the sole of the foot as his point of reference.[34] There are three additional direct perforating veins that connect the GSV to the popliteal and femoral veins. *Boyd's* perforator, just distal to the knee, connects the GSV to the popliteal vein.[33] *Dodd's* and *Hunterian* perforators are located in the thigh and connect the GSV to the proximal popliteal or the femoral veins (see Fig 158-1). Boyd's perforator may be reached endoscopically, whereas stripping of the GSV will interrupt the drainage of Dodd's and Hunterian perforators, except in 8% of patients with a duplicated saphenous system.

Certain anatomic considerations specific to the endoscopic interruption of medial calf perforators need to be emphasized. In cadaver dissections, Mozes and coworkers noted that only 63% of all medial perforators were directly accessible from the superficial posterior compartment.[33] Based on clinical reports, only 32% of Cockett II, 84% of Cockett III, and 43% of lower paratibial perforating veins

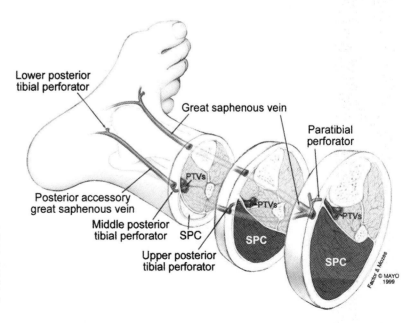

FIGURE 158-2 The relationship of the superficial posterior compartment and the perforating medial veins of the leg. PTVs, posterior tibial veins; SPC, superficial posterior compartment. (From Mozes G, Carmichael SW, Gloviczki P: Development and anatomy of the venous system. In Gloviczki P, Yao JST [eds]: Handbook of Venous Disorders, 2nd ed. London, Arnold, 2001, pp 11-24.)

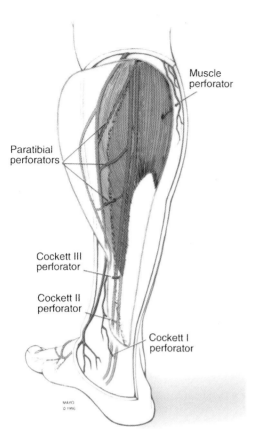

Muscle
perforator

Paratibial
perforators

Cockett III
perforator

Cockett II
perforator

Cockett I
perforator

MAYO
© 1998

FIGURE 158-3 Relationship of the superficial, perforating, and deep veins to the fascia of the superficial posterior compartment. Note that Cockett III and the lowest proximal paratibial perforator ("24-cm perforator") are readily accessible from the subfascial space. (From Mozes G, Gloviczki P, Kadar A, Carmichael SW: Surgical anatomy of perforating veins. In Gloviczki P, Bergan JJ [eds]: Atlas of Endoscopic Perforator Vein Surgery. London, Springer-Verlag, 1998, pp 17-28.)

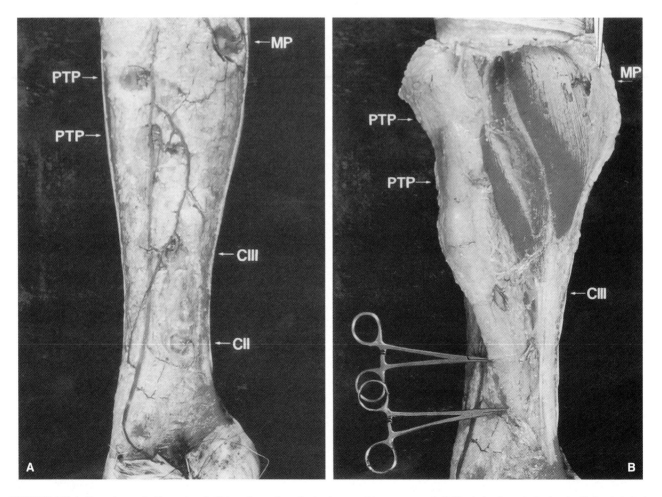

FIGURE 158-4 Corrosion cast of leg veins. **A,** Skin and a portion of subcutaneous fat were removed. **B,** Fascia has been incised and rolled anteriorly to expose the superficial posterior compartment. Note that only the lower paratibial perforator and Cockett III perforators are now accessible in the superficial posterior compartment. MP, muscle perforator; PTP, paratibial perforator; CII, Cockett II; CIII, Cockett III. (From Mozes G, Gloviczki P, Menawat SS, et al: Surgical anatomy for endoscopic subfascial division of perforating veins. J Vasc Surg 24:800-808, 1996.) (See color figure in this section.)

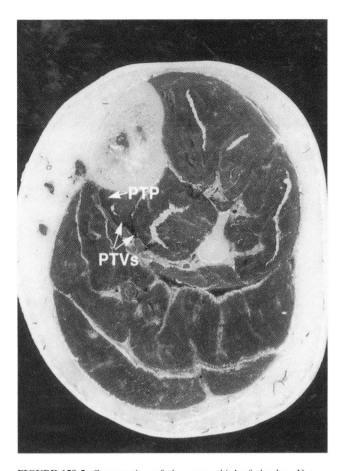

FIGURE 158-5 Cross-section of the upper third of the leg. Note a paratibial perforating vein (PTP) passing between the periosteum of the tibia and the fascia of the superficial posterior compartment. Veins were filled with blue Latex. PTVs, posterior tibial veins. (From Mozes G, Gloviczki P, Menawat SS, et al: A surgical anatomy for endoscopic subfascial division of perforating veins. J Vasc Surg 24:800-808, 1996.) (See color figure in this section.)

are accessible from the superficial posterior compartment,[37] a significant consideration because the majority of incompetent perforators occur at the Cockett II/III level. This is an important observation, because major incompetent perforators will be missed during surgery if dissection is limited to the superficial posterior compartment. Two additional areas that require exploration are the deep posterior compartment and the intermuscular septum in Linton's lane, which can be a duplication of the deep fascia. The paratibial and the Cockett veins can be found under the fascia of the deep posterior compartment, whereas the Cockett II/III veins can also be located within the intermuscular septum (see Figs. 158-4 and 158-5). A deceiving anatomic variation of the Cockett II perforator can be a division with a posterior branch directing toward the soleus muscle. Whereas this posterior division is easily visible when it penetrates the superficial posterior compartment, the more important anterior division is hidden by the intermuscular septum or by the deep posterior fascia and it may be missed. Therefore, 68% of Cockett II and 16% of Cockett III perforators are hidden by a septum or fascia that needs to be divided during endoscopic surgery; otherwise, major perforators will be left behind.[33] Distally in the subfascial

space, the Cockett I perforator usually cannot be visualized or reached because of its retromalleolar position.

In the calf, anterior and lateral perforators are also found; and in patients with lateral ulceration these veins have clinical significance. The anterior perforators connect tributaries of the great and small saphenous veins directly to the anterior tibial veins. The lateral perforating veins consist of both direct and indirect perforators. In the distal calf the small saphenous vein is connected by direct perforators to the peroneal veins (Bassi's perforator). The indirect perforators connect tributaries of the small saphenous vein to either the muscular venous sinuses or the gastrocnemius or soleus veins before entering the deep axial system. The largest indirect muscular perforators are referred to as the *soleus* and *gastrocnemius* points.

■ HEMODYNAMIC SIGNIFICANCE OF PERFORATING VEINS

Chapter 154 covers the pathophysiology of CVI, but data on the hemodynamic significance of the perforator veins are briefly addressed here. Although the pathophysiology of CVI at the cellular level remains controversial, most authors agree that venous hypertension in the erect position and during ambulation is the most important factor responsible for the development of skin changes and venous ulcerations. The relationship between venous ulceration and ambulatory venous pressure was first described by Beecher and colleagues in 1931.[38] Subsequent studies have confirmed that ambulatory venous pressure has not only diagnostic but also prognostic significance in CVI.[39-42] High ambulatory venous pressure may be due to primary valvular incompetence in superficial, deep, and/or perforator veins, or it may be the result of a previous deep venous thrombosis. Deep venous incompetence (DVI) is initially compensated by the calf muscle pump but eventually results in secondary incompetence of valves in perforating veins and transmission of pressure from the deep to the superficial veins, a fact that was first suggested by Homans[43] and documented by Linton.[2]

Reflux of venous blood due to primary or postthrombotic valvular incompetence, in addition to calf pump failure, is the most frequent cause of CVI and venous ulceration. Whereas severe isolated incompetence of the superficial system may also lead to sufficiently high ambulatory pressures and the development of ulcers, evidence is increasing that the majority of patients with venous ulcers have multisystemic (superficial, deep, and/or perforator) incompetence, involving at least two of the three venous systems.[31,44-47] DVI has been reported to occur in a significant number of patients (21% to 80%) in large surgical series of venous ulcer (Table 158-1).[44,48,49] In the report of the North American Subfascial Endoscopic Perforator Surgery (NASEPS) registry, only 28% of the patients with advanced CVI were free of deep venous reflux or obstruction.[29] Incompetent calf perforators in conjunction with superficial or deep reflux have been reported in 66% of limbs with venous ulceration and occur more frequently in limbs with complications.[48,50] A duplex ultrasound study in 91 limbs with venous ulcerations from Boston University revealed isolated superficial vein incompetence (SVI) in

Table 158-1 Distribution of Valvular Incompetence in Patients with Advanced Chronic Venous Disease

AUTHOR(S), YEAR	NO. OF LIMBS	SUP NO. (%)	PERF NO. (%)	DEEP NO. (%)	SUP + PERF NO. (%)	SUP + PERF + DEEP NO. (%)
Schanzer and Pierce,[10] 1982	52	3 (6)	20 (38)	4 (8)	11 (21)	14 (27)
Negus and Friedgood,[11] 1983	77	0 (0)	0 (0)	0 (0)	35 (46)	42 (54)
Sethia and Darke,[54] 1984	60	0 (0)	5 (8)	20 (33)	17 (28)	18 (30)
van Bemmelen et al.,[49] 1991	25	0 (0)	0 (0)	2 (8)	3 (12)	20 (80)
Hanrahan et al.,[47] 1991	91	16 (17)	8 (8)	2 (2)	18 (19)	47 (49)
Darke and Penfold,[50] 1992	213	0 (0)	8 (4)	47 (22)	83 (39)	75 (35)
Lees and Lambert,[51] 1993	25	3 (12)	0 (0)	3 (12)	10 (40)	9 (36)
Shami et al.,[93] 1993	59	0 (0)	0 (0)	19 (32)	31 (53)	9 (15)
van Rij et al.,[44] 1994	120	48 (40)	6 (5)	10 (8)	31 (26)	25 (21)
Myers et al.,[48] 1995	96	15 (16)	2 (2)	7 (8)	25 (26)	47 (49)
Labropoulos et al.,[94] 1996	120	26 (22)	1 (1)	5 (4)	23 (19)	65 (54)
Gloviczki et al.,[29] 1999	146	0 (0)	7 (5)	0 (0)	66 (45)	73 (50)
Total No. of Limbs (%)	*1084*	*111 (10)*	*57 (5)*	*119 (11)*	*353 (32)*	*444 (41)*

Sup, superficial vein incompetence; Perf, perforator vein incompetence; Deep, deep vein incompetence.

only 17% and PVI in 63% of limbs.[47] Similarly, a 60% incidence of PVI in ulcer patients was demonstrated by duplex scanning by Lees and Lambert[51] and a 56% incidence was noted by Labrapoulos and associates.[46] The large prevalence of PVI in ulcer patients is emphasized even in those studies that favor operation on the incompetent superficial system only.[39]

Whereas today few argue that incompetent perforators occur in at least two thirds of patients with venous ulcerations, the contribution of incompetent perforators to the hemodynamic derangement in limbs with CVI remains a topic of debate.[52,53] Cockett coined the term *ankle blowout syndrome* to differentiate PVI from the usually more benign isolated saphenous incompetence.[3,54] Indeed, PVI can raise pressures in the supramalleolar network well above 100 mm Hg during calf muscle contraction, a phenomenon best described by Negus and Friedgood using the analogy of a "broken bellows."[11] Experiments of Bjordal confirmed a net outward flow of 60/mL/min through incompetent perforating veins.[55] The importance of incompetent perforators is also supported by the observation that skin changes and venous ulcers almost always develop in the gaiter area of the leg (the area between the distal edge of the soleus muscle and the ankle), where large incompetent medial perforating veins are located. Because functional studies cannot reliably differentiate PVI from DVI in most patients, the task of documenting hemodynamic abnormalities related directly to PVI, even if it is confirmed with duplex scanning, remains challenging. The question will be difficult to answer because isolated PVI in CVI is rare[46] and because incompetent perforators with outward flow have been observed in normal limbs as well; in one study, 21% of normal limbs had outward flow in perforating veins.[56]

In a study using Doppler ultrasonography and ambulatory venous pressure measurements to assess functional significance of incompetent perforating veins, however, Zukowski and Nicolaides found that 70% of incompetent perforators were of moderate or major hemodynamic

significance.[57] More importantly, hemodynamic deterioration caused by incompetent perforators correlated with the severity of CVI. A correlation between the number and size of incompetent perforating veins, as detected by duplex ultrasonography, and the severity of CVI was also demonstrated by several other authors.[45,58,59] In patients with advanced disease, more incompetent perforators were found and their diameters were also larger. This study is significant because, contrary to previously published data,[56] it failed to confirm PVI in 106 normal volunteers. Delis and co-workers quantified PVI based on diameter, flow velocities, and volume flow and stressed that incompetent perforators sustain further hemodynamic impairment in the presence of deep reflux.[60]

Data have been accumulating from hemodynamic studies performed after surgical interruption of incompetent perforating veins. These are discussed later in this chapter.

■ INDICATIONS FOR PERFORATOR INTERRUPTION

The presence of incompetent perforators in patients with advanced CVI (clinical classes 4 to 6) is an indication for surgical treatment in a fit patient. Whereas most authors performing open perforator ligation prefer to operate only in patients with healed ulcerations, a clean, granulating open ulcer is not a contraindication for a SEPS procedure. Contraindications include associated chronic arterial occlusive disease, infected ulcer, morbid obesity, and a nonambulatory or high-risk patient. Diabetes, renal failure, or ulcers in patients with rheumatoid arthritis or scleroderma are relative contraindications. Patients with previous perforator interruption or those with extensive skin changes, circumferential large ulcers, or large legs may not be suitable for SEPS. Those with lateral ulcerations, if appropriate, should be managed by open interruption of lateral or posterior perforators.

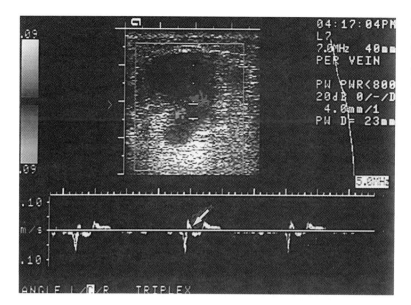

FIGURE 158-6 Color Doppler and spectral tracing of an enlarged incompetent perforating vein. Spectral analysis demonstrates bidirectional flow (arrow). (From Gloviczki P, Lewis BD, Lindsey JR, McKusick MA: Preoperative evaluation of chronic venous insufficiency with duplex scanning and venography. In Gloviczki P, Bergan JJ [eds]: Atlas of Endoscopic Perforator Vein Surgery. London, Springer-Verlag, 1998, pp 81-91.)

■ PREOPERATIVE EVALUATION

The evaluation of patients with CVI is discussed in general in Chapter 155. Potential candidates with an indication for perforator interruption, as listed earlier, should undergo imaging studies to document SVI, DVI, and PVI to confirm the clinical suspicion and to guide the operative intervention. Before perforator interruption, we favor duplex scanning (Fig. 158-6) over phlebography (Fig. 158-7) and reserve contrast studies for patients with underlying occlusive disease or for those who are candidates for deep venous reconstruction. In our practice, all candidates for SEPS, which has become our preferred technique, undergo duplex ultrasonography of the deep, superficial, and perforator systems to document location of reflux and presence or absence of venous obstruction.[61] It is extremely important to obtain an accurate assessment of the underlying pathophysiology in every patient, not only to aid in treatment planning but also to evaluate and compare results.

Perforator mapping, a time-consuming test, is done only the day before surgery because the sites of incompetent perforators are marked on the skin of the patient with a nonerasable marker. The patient is on a tilted examining table in a near upright non–weight-bearing position for the affected extremity. PVI is defined as outward flow of more than 0.3 second (or 0.5 second by some authors) or longer than antegrade flow during the relaxation phase after release of manual compression (see Fig. 158-6). Although duplex scanning misses smaller perforator veins, it has 100% specificity and the highest sensitivity of all diagnostic tests to predict the sites of incompetent perforating veins (Table 158-2).

Ascending and descending phlebography is reserved for patients with underlying occlusive disease or recurrent ulceration after perforator division, in whom deep venous reconstruction is being considered. In addition to duplex scanning, strain-gauge or air plethysmography may be

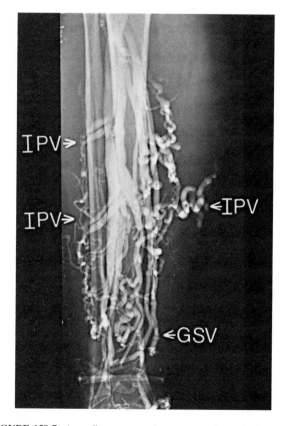

FIGURE 158-7 Ascending venogram in anteroposterior projection of the right calf of a 41-year-old woman with a nonhealing venous ulcer due to primary valvular incompetence. Note medial and lateral incompetent perforators (IPV) filling the superficial system with contrast medium. GSV, greater saphenous vein. (From Gloviczki P, Lewis BD, Lindsey JR, McKusick MA: Preoperative evaluation of chronic venous insufficiency with duplex scanning and venography. In Gloviczki P, Bergan JJ (eds): Atlas of Endoscopic Perforator Vein Surgery. London, Springer-Verlag, 1998, pp 81-91.)

Table 158-2	Diagnostic Tests to Predict the Sites of Incompetent Perforating Veins	
TEST	**SENSITIVITY (%)**	**SPECIFICITY (%)**
Physical examination[35]	60	0
Continuous wave Doppler ultrasonography[35]	62	4
Ascending phlebography[35]	60	50
Duplex scanning[23]	79	100

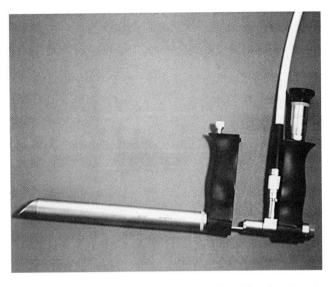

FIGURE 158-8 Olympus endoscope for the subfascial perforating vein interruption. The scope can be used with or without carbon dioxide insufflation. It has an 85-degree angle field of view, and the outer sheath is either 16 or 22 mm in diameter. The working channel is 6×8.5 mm, with a working length of 20 cm. (From Bergan JJ, Ballard JL, Sparks S: Subfascial endoscopic perforator surgery: The open technique. In Gloviczki P, Bergan JJ [eds]: Atlas of Endoscopic Perforator Vein Surgery. London, Springer-Verlag, 1998, pp 141-149.)

performed before and after surgery to quantitate the degree of incompetence, identify abnormalities in calf muscle pump function, aid in the exclusion of outflow obstruction, and assess hemodynamic results of surgical intervention.[13,31]

■ SURGICAL TECHNIQUES

Open Technique of Perforator Interruption

Linton's radical operation of subfascial ligation, which included long medial, anterolateral, and posterolateral calf incisions, was soon abandoned because of its association with wound complications.[2] In a report published in 1953, Linton advocated only a long medial incision from the ankle to the knee to interrupt all medial and posterior perforating veins.[39] His operative technique also included stripping of the great and small saphenous veins and excision of a portion of the deep fascia. (His suggestion to interrupt axial reflux by ligation of the superficial femoral vein is of historical interest only.) Wound complications caused by the incision made in the lipodermatosclerotic skin were, however, still frequent, and hospitalization of the patients was prolonged.

Several other authors have proposed further changes in the open procedure to limit wound complications. Cockett advocated ligation of the perforating veins above the deep fascia,[3,4] a technique distinctly different from that of Linton. The importance of ligating the perforating veins subfascially was emphasized by Sherman, because the perforating veins branch extensively once they penetrate the deep fascia.[34] Modifications included the use of shorter medial incisions or a more posteriorly placed stocking seam–type incision.[4,16,17] DePalma achieved good results using multiple, parallel bipedicled flaps placed along skin lines to access and ligate the perforating veins above or below the fascia.[18] The operation was combined with saphenous stripping, ulcer excision, and skin grafting.

To decrease wound complications, a technique to ablate incompetent perforating veins from sites remote from diseased skin was first reported by Edwards in 1976.[19] He designed a device called the *phlebotome* that is inserted through a medial incision just distal to the knee, deep to the fascia, and advanced to the level of the medial malleolus. Resistance is felt as perforators are engaged and subsequently disrupted with the leading edge. Other authors have subsequently reported successful application of this device, passed in either the subfascial or the extrafascial plane.[62]

Interruption of perforators through stab wounds and hook avulsion is another possibility, and accuracy of this blind technique will improve if duplex scanning is used for mapping. Sclerotherapy of perforating veins and suture ligation of perforators without making skin incisions are among other reported techniques.

Techniques of Subfascial Endoscopic Perforator Surgery

First introduced by Hauer in 1985, by using endoscopic instruments interruption of incompetent perforators may now be performed through small ports placed remotely from the active ulcer or area of skin discoloration.[20-22,63-65] Since its introduction, two main techniques for SEPS have been developed. The first, practiced mostly in Europe, is a refinement of the original work of Hauer[20] by Fischer and Sattler,[25,66] with further development by Bergan[21,67] and by Wittens and Pierik.[24,68,69] In the early development of the "single port" technique available light sources such as mediastinoscopes and bronchoscopes were used. With time, a specially designed instrument was devised that uses a single scope with channels for the camera and working instruments, which sometimes makes visualization and dissection in the same plane difficult (Fig. 158-8). Recent developments in instrumentation for this technique now allow for carbon dioxide insufflation into the subfascial plane.

The second technique, using instrumentation from laparoscopic surgery, was introduced in the United States by O'Donnell[70] and developed simultaneously by our group at the Mayo Clinic[28] and Conrad in Australia.[27] This technique, the "two port" technique, employs one port for the camera and a separate port for instrumentation, thereby making it easier to work in the limited subfascial space. First the limb is exsanguinated with an Esmarch bandage and a thigh tourniquet is inflated to 300 mm Hg to provide a bloodless field (Fig. 158-9A). A 10-mm endoscopic port is next placed in the medial aspect of the calf 10 cm distal to the tibial tuberosity, proximal to the diseased skin. Balloon dissection is routinely used to widen the subfascial space and facilitate access after port placement (Fig. 158-10A, B).[71] The distal 5-mm port is now placed halfway between the first port and the ankle (about 10 to 12 cm apart), under direct visualization with the camera (see Fig. 158-9C). Carbon dioxide is insufflated into the subfascial space, and pressure is maintained around 30 mm Hg to improve visualization and access to the perforators. Using laparoscopic scissors inserted through the second port, the remaining loose connective tissue between the calf muscles and the superficial fascia is sharply divided.

The subfascial space is widely explored from the medial border of the tibia to the posterior midline and down to the level of the ankle. All perforators encountered are divided either with the harmonic scalpel or electrocautery or sharply between clips (see Fig. 158-9D). A paratibial fasciotomy is next made by incising the fascia of the posterior deep compartment close to the tibia to avoid any injury to the posterior tibial vessels and the tibial nerve (see Fig. 158-9E). The Cockett II and Cockett III perforators are located frequently within an intermuscular septum, and this has to be incised before identification and division of the perforators can be accomplished. The medial insertion of the soleus muscle on the tibia may also have to be exposed to visualize proximal paratibial perforators. By rotating the ports cephalad and continuing the dissection up to the level of the knee, the more proximal perforators can also be divided. Although the paratibial fasciotomy can aid in distal exposure, reaching the retromalleolar Cockett I perforator endoscopically is usually not possible; and if it is incompetent on preoperative ultrasound scanning it may require a separate small incision over it to gain direct exposure.

On completion of the endoscopic portion of the procedure (see Fig. 158-9F), the instruments and ports are removed, the carbon dioxide is manually expressed from the limb, and the tourniquet is deflated. Twenty milliliters of 0.5% bupivacaine (Marcaine) solution is instilled into the subfascial space for postoperative pain control. If concomitant superficial reflux is present, high ligation and stripping of the incompetent portion of the GSV (usually from groin to below the knee) is performed. Stab avulsion of varicosities is also performed, and small saphenous reflux, if present, is corrected by ligation or stripping. Wounds are closed with subcutaneous and subcuticular absorbable sutures, and the limb is wrapped with an elastic bandage. Leg elevation is maintained postoperatively, and after 3 hours ambulation is permitted. This is an outpatient procedure, and the patients are discharged the same day or the next morning after overnight observation.

Technique of Ultrasound-Guided Sclerotherapy of Perforating Veins

The procedure may be performed in the office without anesthesia or in the operating room in conjunction with operative ablation of superficial reflux. With the patient in the supine position the previously marked incompetent perforating vein is identified with the ultrasound transducer and accessed percutaneously above the fascia or via the connecting superficial vein with a 22- to 24-gauge butterfly needle under continuous ultrasound guidance. Venous blood is withdrawn to confirm accurate placement within the lumen of the vein, and normal saline is injected under ultrasound surveillance to exclude extravasation. One to 2 mL of sclerosing agent (2.5% sodium morrhuate, 3% sodium tetradecyl sulfate [Sotradecol] or 3% polidocanol) is injected into the perforating vein under continuous duplex visualization. On completion of the injection the needle is withdrawn and local compression is applied. After injection of all incompetent perforators, absence of flow in them is confirmed by duplex ultrasound. An elastic compression bandage is applied to the leg and maintained for 1 week.

■ RESULTS OF PERFORATOR INTERRUPTION

Clinical Results

Clinical benefit attributed directly to interruption of incompetent perforating veins has been difficult to assess because concomitant ablation of saphenous reflux has frequently been performed. In addition, in many studies the follow-up of a large number of patients was insufficient to predict ulcer recurrence. Because level 1 evidence of the effectiveness of perforator ligation (or of any surgical treatment) over nonoperative management is not available, postoperative results should be compared with results of larger series of nonoperative management (Table 158-3), as detailed in Chapter 156.[72-75]

In their classic papers, Linton[2,39] and Cockett[3,4] reported benefits from open perforator ligation, and these benefits were later supported by data from several other investigators.[6,7,10-12,18] In nine large series,[7-9,11,12,14,76-78] ulcer recurrence rates ranged from 0% to 55%, and they averaged 22% (see Table 158-3). In one study that included 108 limbs with venous ulcers, 84% were free of ulcerations up to 6 years after perforator vein ligation.[72]

Wound complications after open procedures were significant in most series; they ranged from 12% to 53% and averaged 24% (Table 158-4). Controversy over the efficacy of the operation emerged when Burnand and coworkers reported a 55% recurrence rate in their patients, with 100% recurrence in a subset of 23 patients with post-thrombotic syndrome.[14] The ulcer recurrence rate in the same study in patients without post-thrombotic damage of the deep veins, however, was only 6%.

Encouraging early results with SEPS were reported by several authors and ulcers healed satisfactorily after elimination of both superficial and perforator reflux.[21,22,63,64] Patients with combined DVI, PVI, and SVI exhibited accelerated healing and improved venous hemodynamics after ablation of the incompetent superficial and perforator systems without intervention to the deep veins (Figs. 158-11 and 158-12).[79,80] Experience with SEPS continues to grow, and results from several centers are available and summarized in Table 158-5. Unfortunately, reporting has been variable in terms of documentation of the CEAP classification, technique of SEPS, and ulcer recurrence.

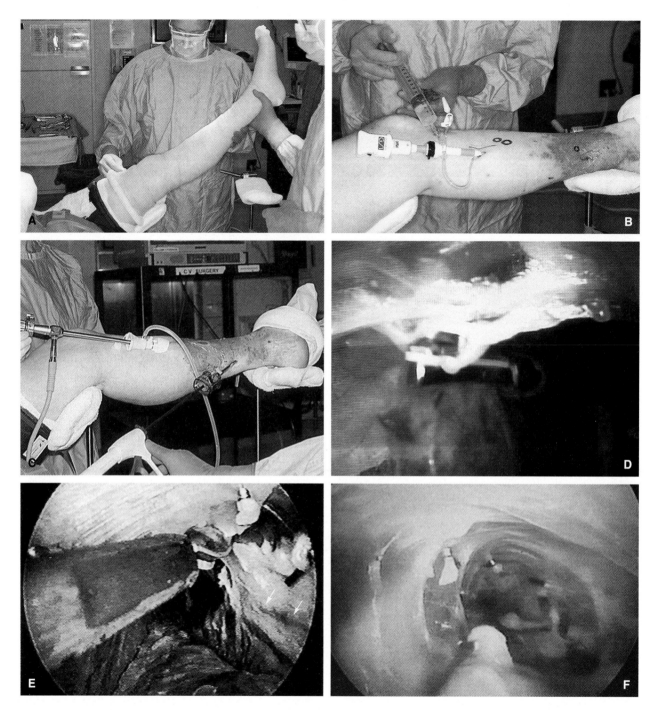

FIGURE 158-9 A, Endoscopic perforator division is performed in a bloodless field. A pneumatic tourniquet is placed on the thigh, and the extremity is exsanguinated with an Esmarch bandage. The tourniquet inflated to 300 mm Hg is used to create a bloodless field. **B,** Balloon dissection is used to widen the subfascial space. **C,** Subfascial endoscopic perforator vein surgery is performed using two ports: a 10-mm camera port and a 5- or 10-mm distal port inserted under video control. Carbon dioxide is insufflated through the camera port into the subfascial space to a pressure of 30 mm Hg to improve visualization and access to perforators. **D,** The subfascial space is widely explored from the medial border of the tibia to the posterior midline and down to the level of the ankle. Division of the perforator is done with endoscopic scissors after placement of vascular clips or a harmonic scalpel placed through the second port. **E,** A paratibial fasciotomy is routinely performed to identify perforators in the deep posterior compartment. **F,** Full view of the superficial posterior compartment after clipping and division of the medial perforating veins. (**A** through **F,** with permission of the Mayo Foundation.)

Table 158-3 Results of Nonoperative Management for Advanced Chronic Venous Disease

AUTHOR(S), YEAR	NO. OF LIMBS TREATED	NO. OF LIMBS WITH ULCER	ULCER RECURRENCE NO. (%)*	MEAN FOLLOW-UP (mo)
Anning,[73] 1956	100	100	59 (59)	64
Monk and Sarkany,[95] 1982	83	83	58 (69)	12
Kitahama et al.,[96] 1982	65	59	8 (14)	12
Negus,[72] 1985	25	0	17 (68)	—
Mayberry et al.,[74] 1991	113	113	24 (33)	30
Erickson,[75] 1995	99	99	52 (58)	10
DePalma and Kowallek,[97] 1996	11	11	11 (100)	24
Samson and Showalter,[98] 1996	53	53	23 (43)	28
Total	*549 (100)*	*518/549 (94)*	*241/488 (52)*	*27*

*Percentage accounts for patients lost to follow-up.

Table 158-4 Results of Open Perforator Interruption for the Treatment of Advanced Chronic Venous Disease

AUTHOR(S), YEAR	NO. OF LIMBS TREATED	NO. OF LIMBS WITH ULCER	WOUND COMPLICATIONS NO. (%)	ULCER HEALING NO. (%)	ULCER RECURRENCE NO. (%)*	MEAN FOLLOW-UP (yr)
Silver et al.,[7] 1971	31	19	4 (14)		— (10)	1-15
Thurston and Williams,[8] 1973	102	0	12 (12)	†	11 (13)	3.3
Bowen,[9] 1975	71	8	31 (44)		24 (34)	4.5
Burnand et al.,[14] 1976	41	0		†	24 (55)	
Negus and Friedgood,[11] 1983	108	108	24 (22)	91 (84)	16 (15)	3.7
Wilkinson and Maclaren,[76] 1986	108	0	26 (24)	†	3 (7)	6
Cikrit et al.,[12] 1988	32	30	6 (19)	30 (100)	5 (19)	4
Bradbury et al.,[13] 1993	53	0		†	14 (26)	5
Pierik et al.,[24] 1997	19	19	10 (53)	17 (90)	0 (0)	1.8
Total No. of Limbs (%)	*565 (100)*	*184 (33)*	*113/468 (24)*	*138/157 (88)*	*97/443 (22)*	

*Recurrence calculated for class 5 and class 6 limbs where data were available, and percentage accounts for patients lost to follow-up.
†Only class 5 (healed ulcer) patients admitted in study.

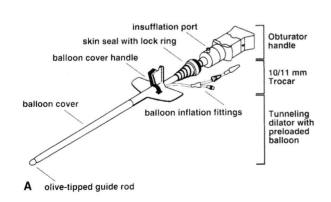

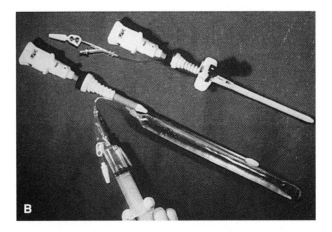

FIGURE 158-10 A, Components of balloon dissector (General Surgical Innovations, Palo Alto, CA) for creation of a large subfascial working space. An integral 10-mm endoscopic port is included. **B,** The balloon dissector device before *(top)* and after *(bottom)* balloon cover removal. Note the degree of radial and distal balloon expansion that occurs when fully inflated with saline solution. Balloon inflation is performed with 200 to 300 mL of saline. The balloon expands both radially and distally with minimal trauma to surrounding tissue, thus creating a large bloodless working space. (From Allen RC, Tawes RL, Wetter A, Fogarty T: Endoscopic perforator vein surgery: Creation of a subfascial space. In Gloviczki P, Bergan JJ [eds]: Atlas of Endoscopic Perforator Vein Surgery. London, Springer-Verlag, 1998, pp 153-162.)

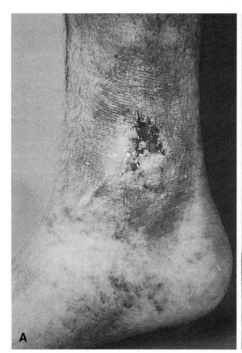
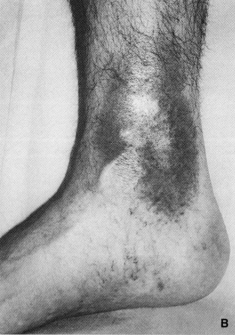

FIGURE 158-11 **A,** Thirty-six-year-old man with post-thrombotic ulcer of the right ankle before endoscopic division of six medial perforating veins. **B,** Same leg 10 months later with healed ulcer. (From Gloviczki P, Canton LG, Cambria RA, Rhee RY: Subfascial endoscopic perforator vein surgery with gas insufflation. In Gloviczki P, Bergan JJ [eds]: Atlas of Endoscopic Perforator Vein Surgery. London, Springer-Verlag, 1998, pp 125-138.)

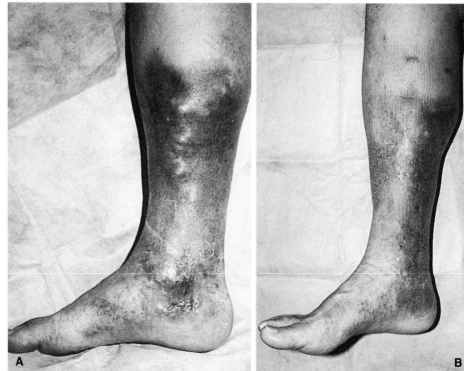

FIGURE 158-12 **A,** Right leg of a 64-year-old man who has a 2-year history of ulcer and severe post-thrombotic syndrome. **B,** Postoperative picture at 6 weeks shows healed ulcer and incisions after subfascial endoscopic perforator vein surgery, stripping, and avulsion of varicose veins. Three years later the patient is asymptomatic, does not use elastic stockings, and has had no ulcer recurrence. (From Gloviczki P, Canton LG, Cambria RA, Rhee RY: Subfascial endoscopic perforator vein surgery with gas insufflation. In Gloviczki P, Bergan JJ [eds]: Atlas of Endoscopic Perforator Vein Surgery. London, Springer-Verlag, 1998, pp 125-138, with permission.)

Table 158-5 Results of Subfascial Endoscopic Perforator Vein Surgery for Treatment of Advanced Chronic Venous Disease

AUTHOR(S), YEAR	NO. OF LIMBS TREATED	NO. OF LIMBS WITH ULCER*	CONCOMITANT SAPHENOUS ABLATION NO. (%)	WOUND COMPLICATIONS NO. (%)	ULCER HEALING NO. (%)	ULCER RECURRENCE NO. (%)‡	MEAN FOLLOW-UP (mo)
Jugenheimer and Junginger,[26] 1992	103	17	97 (94)	3 (3)	16 (94)	0 (0)	27
Pierek et al.,[63] 1995	40	16	4 (10)	3 (8)	16 (100)	1 (2.5)	46
Bergan et al.,[21] 1996	31	15	31 (100)	3 (10)	15 (100)	(0)	
Wolters et al.,[99] 1996	27	27	0 (0)	2 (7)	26 (96)	2 (8)	12-24
Padberg et al.,[79] 1996	11	0	11 (100)		†	0 (0)	16
Pierek et al.,[68] 1997	20	20	14 (70)	0 (0)	17 (85)	0 (0)	21
Rhodes et al.,[30] 1998	57	22	41 (72)	3 (5)	22 (100)	5 (12)	17
Gloviczki et al.,[29] 1999	146	101	86 (59)	9 (6)	85 (84)	26 (21)	24
Illig et al.,[100] 1999	30	19			17 (89)	4 (15)	9
Nelzen,[84] 2001	149	36	132 (89)	11 (7)	32 (89)	3 (5)	32
Kalra et al.,[85] 2002	103	42	74 (72)	7 (6)	38 (90)	15 (21)	40
Total No. of Limbs (%)	*717 (100)*	*315 (44)*	*490/670 (73)*	*48/659 (6)*	*284/315 (90)*	*56/468 (12)*	

*Only class 6 (active ulcer) patients are included.
†Only class 5 (healed ulcer) patients were admitted in this study.
‡Recurrence was calculated for class 5 and 6 limbs only where data were available, and percentage accounts for patients lost to follow-up.

The safety and early efficacy of SEPS have been established in several studies,[22,63] and it yields a much lower wound complication rate than that observed after traditional open surgical techniques.[24,80] In a noncontrolled trial that compared 37 SEPS procedures with 30 antedated open perforator ligations, SEPS resulted in lower calf wound morbidity, shorter hospital stay, and comparable short-term ulcer healing.[81] A single prospective, randomized study by Pierik and colleagues in 39 patients reported wound complications in 53% of patients undergoing open perforator ligation versus 0% in the SEPS group, with no ulcer recurrence in either group over a mean follow-up of 21 months.[24] In a subsequent communication 4 years later the authors reported long-term follow-up in these patients. Ulcer recurrence in the open perforator ligation group (22%) was not significantly different from that in the SEPS group (12%) in this small patient cohort.[82] These data support the use of SEPS rather than open ligation, yet do not address the role of SEPS in the management of advanced CVI and venous ulceration. Favorable long-term clinical results in 832 patients followed to 9 years after SEPS have been reported by Tawes and colleagues.[83]

The relative safety of SEPS was further confirmed in the early report of the NASEPS registry.[22] The uniformity of evaluation and the reporting of results from 17 centers in North America emphasize the reliability and significance of results of this study. The study included 146 patients, 101 of whom had active ulcers. DVI was present in 72% of patients, and 38% of patients had post-thrombotic syndrome. Concomitant superficial venous surgery was performed in 71% of patients. Wound complication rate was 6%, and one deep venous thrombosis occurred at 2 months after surgery. The mid-term (24 months) results of the NASEPS registry demonstrated an 88% cumulative ulcer healing rate at 1 year (Fig. 158-13).[29] The median time to ulcer healing was 54 days. Cumulative rate of ulcer recurrence was significant: 16% at 1 year and 28% at 2 years (Fig. 158-14). Although the observed recurrence rates in the NASEPS registry were high, they still compare favorably to results of nonoperative management (see Table 158-3).

In the largest series from a single institution, Nelzen and coworkers reported on prospectively collected data from 149 SEPS procedures in 138 patients.[84] There were 36 limbs with active ulcers (class 6), 31 with healed ulcers (class 5), 34 with skin changes (class 4), and 48 with varicose veins (class 2). Combined saphenous vein surgery was performed in 89% of limbs. During a median follow-up of 32 months, 32 of 36 ulcers healed, more than half (19/36) within 1 month. Three ulcers recurred, 1 of which subsequently healed during follow-up. At a median follow-up of 7 months after surgery, 91% of patients were satisfied with the results of the operation.

In one study, extended results were analyzed in 103 consecutive SEPS procedures performed at the Mayo Clinic over a 7-year period.[85] There were 42 class 6 limbs, 34 class 5 limbs, and 24 class 4 limbs. Thirty procedures were performed in post-thrombotic limbs. DVI was present in 89% of limbs; 13% had venous outflow obstruction on plethysmography. Concomitant superficial reflux ablation was performed in 72% of limbs. Thirty-eight of 42 ulcers healed with a median time to ulcer healing of 35 days; all 4 ulcers that failed to heal were in post-thrombotic limbs. On

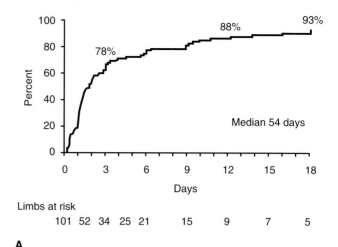

A

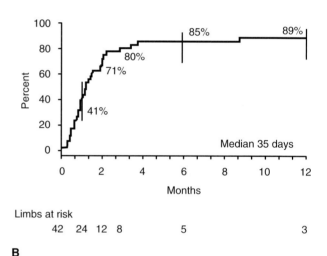

B

FIGURE 158-13 **A,** Cumulative ulcer healing in 101 patients after subfascial endoscopic perforator vein surgery. The 90-day, 1-year, and 1.5-year healing rates are indicated. The standard error is less than 10% at all time points. **B,** Cumulative ulcer healing in 42 patients after subfascial endoscopic perforator vein surgery. The 90-day and 1-year healing rates are indicated. The standard error is less than 10% at all time points. (**A** from Gloviczki P, Bergan JJ, Rhodes JM, et al: North American Study Group: Mid-term results of endoscopic perforator vein interruption for chronic venous insufficiency: Lessons learned from the North American Subfascial Endoscopic Perforator Surgery (NASEPS) registry. J Vasc Surg 29:489-499, 1999; **B** from Kalra M, Gloviczki P, Noel AA, et al: Subfascial endoscopic perforator vein surgery in patients with post-thrombotic venous insufficiency—Is it justified? Vasc Endovasc Surg 36:41-50, 2002.)

life-table analysis, 90-day and 1-year cumulative ulcer healing rates were 80% and 90%, respectively, and 1-, 3-, and 5-year cumulative ulcer recurrence rates were 4%, 20%, and 27% (see Figs. 158-13 and 158-14).

The Dutch SEPS trial was the first of its kind—a randomized multicenter trial prospectively comparing surgical treatment (SEPS with or without superficial reflux ablation) to medical treatment (ambulatory venous compression) in patients with venous ulcers.[86] The study included 200 patients, 97 randomized to medical treatment and 103 in the surgical group. The ulcer healing rate of 83%

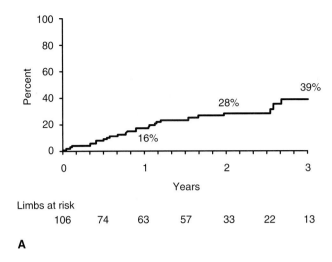

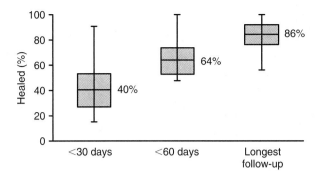

FIGURE 158-15 Cumulative ulcer healing. Box-and-whiskers plot depicts ulcer healing after subfascial endoscopic perforator surgery (SEPS) in patients with class 6 disease in subset of studies with data for time to healing (nine studies, 264 limbs). The *y*-axis shows percentage of limbs that healed during follow-up; the *x*-axis depicts three healing endpoints, number of limbs, and number of studies that contributed to each endpoint. *Horizontal lines,* endpoints; *boxes,* 95% confidence intervals; *error bars,* range for individual studies that contributed to each estimate; *Longest follow-up,* healing by end of follow-up. (From TenBrook JA Jr, Iafrati MD, O'Donnell TF, et al: Systematic review of outcomes after surgical management of venous disease incorporating subfascial endoscopic perforator surgery. J Vasc Surg 39:583-589, 2004.)

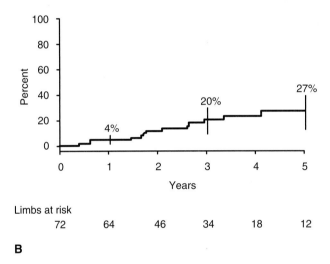

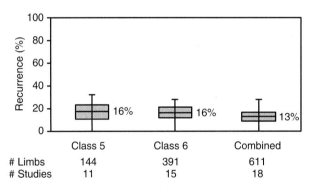

FIGURE 158-14 **A,** Cumulative ulcer recurrence in 106 patients after subfascial endoscopic perforator vein surgery (SEPS). The 1-, 2-, and 3-year recurrence rates are indicated. All class 5 limbs at the time of SEPS and class 6 limbs that subsequently healed are included. The start point (day 0) for time to recurrence in class 6 patients was the date of initial ulcer healing. The standard error is less than 10% at all time points. **B,** Cumulative ulcer recurrence in 72 patients after SEPS. The 1-, 3-, and 5-year recurrence rates are indicated. All class 5 limbs at the time of SEPS and class 6 limbs that subsequently healed are included. The start point (day 0) for time to recurrence in class 6 patients was the date of initial ulcer healing. The standard error is less than 10% at all time points. (**A** from Gloviczki P, Bergan JJ, Rhodes JM, et al: North American Study Group: Mid-term results of endoscopic perforator vein interruption for chronic venous insufficiency: Lessons learned from the North American Subfascial Endoscopic Perforator Surgery (NASEPS) registry. J Vasc Surg 29:489-499, 1999; **B** from Kalra M, Gloviczki P, Noel AA, et al: Subfascial endoscopic perforator vein surgery in patients with post-thrombotic venous insufficiency—Is it justified? Vasc Endovasc Surg 36:41-50, 2002.)

FIGURE 158-16 Cumulative ulcer recurrence. Box-and-whiskers plot depicts ulcer recurrence after subfascial endoscopic perforator surgery (SEPS). The *y*-axis shows percentage of limbs with ulcer recurrence during follow-up; the *x*-axis depicts three categories of limbs, number of limbs, and number of studies that contributed to each endpoint. *Horizontal lines,* Point estimates; *boxes,* 95% confidence intervals; *error bars,* ranges for individual studies that contributed to each estimate; *class 5,* recurrence in limbs with class 5 disease at SEPS; *class 6,* recurrence in limbs with class 6 disease at SEPS in which ulcers subsequently healed; *combined,* recurrence in limbs with class 5 and class 6 disease. Number of limbs and studies in class 5 and class 6 disease do not total those in the combined group because not all studies reported data separately for limbs with class 5 and class 6 disease. (From TenBrook JA Jr, Iafrati MD, O'Donnell TF, et al: Systematic review of outcomes after surgical management of venous disease incorporating subfascial endoscopic perforator surgery. J Vasc Surg 39:583-589, 2004.)

and recurrence rate in the surgical group of 22% at 29 months in this trial are comparable to previously reported results. In the conservative treatment group, ulcers healed in 73% and recurred in 23%. Ulcer size and duration were independent factors adversely affecting ulcer healing and recurrence.

A recent meta-analysis of 1140 limbs with CVI (525 with ulcers) by TenBrook and associates included results from 20 large series of SEPS with or without concomitant superficial reflux ablation.[87] Deep venous involvement was present in 56% of limbs, and 36% had post-thrombotic syndrome. Ulcers healed in 88% of limbs; ulcers recurred in 13% of limbs over a mean follow-up of 21 months (Figs. 158-15 and 158-16). Risk factors for nonhealing and recurrence

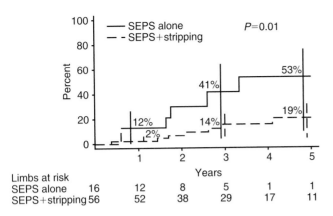

FIGURE 158-17 Ulcer recurrence based on the extent of venous surgery. Limbs undergoing SEPS alone (n = 16) and limbs undergoing SEPS with saphenous vein stripping (n = 56). The 1-, 3-, and 5-year recurrence rates are indicated. SEPS alone versus SEPS with saphenous vein stripping, *P* < .05. (From Kalra M, Gloviczki P, Noel AA, et al: Subfascial endoscopic perforator vein surgery in patients with post-thrombotic venous insufficiency—Is it justified? Vasc Endovasc Surg 36:41-50, 2002.)

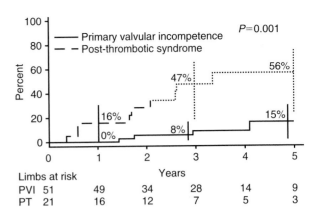

FIGURE 158-18 Ulcer recurrence based on cause of chronic venous insufficiency. Limbs were separated into primary valvular incompetence (n = 51) and post-thrombotic syndrome (n = 21). The 1-, 3-, and 5-year recurrence rates are indicated. The *dashed line* represents a standard error of greater than 10%. Primary valvular incompetence versus post-thrombotic syndrome, *P* < .05. (From Kalra M, Gloviczki P, Noel AA, et al: Subfascial endoscopic perforator vein surgery in patients with post-thrombotic venous insufficiency—Is it justified? Vasc Endovasc Surg 36:41-50, 2002.)

included postoperative incompetent perforator veins, deep venous obstruction, post-thrombotic syndrome, and ulcer diameter greater than 2 cm.

The majority (> two thirds) of patients reported in these just-discussed studies underwent concomitant saphenous vein stripping and branch varicosity avulsion (see Table 158-5), making it difficult to ascertain how much clinical improvement can be attributed to SEPS alone. The NASEPS registry demonstrated improved ulcer healing in limbs that underwent SEPS with saphenous vein stripping, compared with limbs that underwent SEPS alone (3- and 12-month cumulative ulcer healing rates of 76% and 100% versus 45% and 83%, respectively).[29] Ulcer recurrence was not significantly different among the two groups. We attempted to study this in our analysis of 103 limbs.[85] Ulcer healing was significantly delayed in limbs undergoing SEPS alone, compared with limbs that underwent SEPS with superficial reflux ablation; the 90-day cumulative ulcer healing rate was 49% versus 90%, respectively. Cumulative ulcer recurrence at 5 years was also higher in limbs that underwent SEPS alone (53%), compared with those undergoing SEPS with superficial reflux ablation (19%) (Fig. 158-17). However, the number of limbs in the SEPS alone group was considerably smaller, and there was a relative predominance of post-thrombotic limbs in this group (44% versus 25% in limbs undergoing SEPS with saphenous vein stripping). All 29 limbs undergoing SEPS alone had previously undergone saphenous vein ligation and stripping and had recurrent or persistent ulcers, automatically placing them in a higher risk category and creating a selection bias.

Another group of patients generating significant controversy is those with post-thrombotic syndrome. In all the previous studies, limbs with post-thrombotic syndrome fared poorly compared with limbs with primary valvular incompetence. Cumulative ulcer recurrence in the NASEPS registry was 46% versus 20% at 2 years in post-thrombotic

limbs and those with primary valvular incompetence, respectively.[29] The nine post-thrombotic limbs with a component of deep vein obstruction fared particularly poorly, with failure to heal ulcers in four limbs and ulcer recurrence in the remaining five. The results of the Mayo Clinic series support this earlier observation.[85] All ulcers in limbs with primary valvular incompetence healed; all four ulcers that did not heal were in post-thrombotic limbs. However, on life-table analysis, ulcer healing in post-thrombotic limbs was not significantly different from that in limbs with primary valvular incompetence with 90-day cumulative ulcer healing rates of 72% versus 87%, respectively. Cumulative 5-year ulcer recurrence in post-thrombotic limbs was 56% versus 15% in limbs with primary valvular incompetence (Fig. 158-18). However, in spite of the high ulcer recurrence rate, patients with post-thrombotic syndrome had marked symptomatic improvement, with significant improvement in the clinical scores after SEPS and superficial reflux ablation (9.5 to 3, Fig. 158-19). In addition, recurrent ulcers were small, superficial, and single more often than multiple and healed easily with conservative management.

Early results of sclerotherapy of perforating veins were reported by Guex.[88] Primary occlusion was estimated in 90% of injected perforator veins in three or fewer sessions. Eklof and coworkers reported on USGS of perforating veins in 53 limbs (17 class 2 to class 3 limbs, 36 class 4 to class 6 limbs) where it was performed as the only procedure.[89] One hundred and six injections were performed in 40 limbs with primary valvular incompetence, and 40 injections were used in 13 post-thrombotic limbs. Based on repeat ultrasound evaluation at 1 year, 77% of injected perforating veins remained closed. The advantages of USGS of the perforator vein include an outpatient office procedure, no time off work, and reduced costs. Only early results in small numbers of patients have been reported; further data are

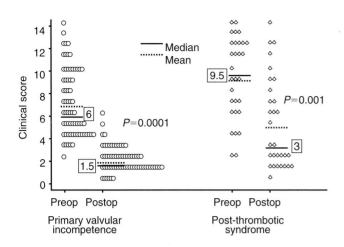

FIGURE 158-19 Preoperative and postoperative clinical scores based on the etiology of chronic venous insufficiency. Limbs were separated into primary valvular incompetence (n = 73) and limbs with post-thrombotic syndrome (n = 30). (From Kalra M, Gloviczki P, Noel AA, et al: Subfascial endoscopic perforator vein surgery in patients with post-thrombotic venous insufficiency—Is it justified? Vasc Endovasc Surg 36:41-50, 2002.)

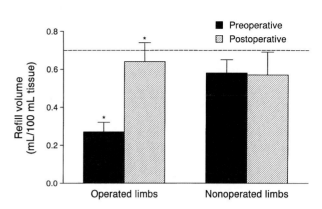

FIGURE 158-20 Calf muscle pump function (refill volume) measured in 28 limbs before and after subfascial endoscopic perforator vein surgery and in 18 contralateral nonoperated limbs. *Asterisk* indicates $P < .01$; *dashed line* indicates normal refill volume ≥ 0.7 mL/100 mL of tissue. (From Rhodes JM, Gloviczki P, Canton LG, et al: Endoscopic perforator vein division with ablation of superficial reflux improves venous hemodynamics. J Vasc Surg 28:839-847, 1998.)

needed before this procedure can be suggested as the preferential treatment of incompetent perforators. Results with SEPS have to be compared with those obtained using sclerotherapy. Concerns regarding deep venous injury need to be objectively addressed, especially in patients with post-thrombotic syndrome. Sclerotherapy may prove to be the ideal treatment in patients with isolated PVI, with recurrent or new perforators after SEPS, or as an adjunct to SEPS for the inaccessible Cockett I perforator and for lateral perforating veins.

Hemodynamic Results

Similar to the debate over clinical effectiveness, there is ongoing controversy about hemodynamic improvement that can be attributed to perforator interruption. Because PVI is frequently treated together with ablation of superficial reflux, postoperative hemodynamic measurements reflect results of a combined operation.

In 1972, Bjordal and associates showed normalization of direct venous pressures on occlusion of the GSV alone in patients with primary valvular incompetence but not after occlusion of large perforating veins alone.[55] They were unable to demonstrate normalization of ambulatory venous hypertension on similar maneuvers in patients with post-thrombotic syndrome. Akesson and associates studied venous hemodynamics by foot ambulatory venous pressure (AVP) measurements in patients with recurrent ulcers. Deep venous involvement was diagnosed in 85% of limbs on ascending venography. A significant reduction in AVP was seen after saphenous stripping, but the improvement in mean AVP did not reach significance after perforator interruption. In this study, however, AVP did not correlate with clinical outcome.[90]

In a classic study, however, using AVP measurements, Schanzer and Pierce documented significant hemodynamic

improvements after isolated perforator interruption in 22 patients.[10] Improvement in both calf muscle pump function and venous incompetence could be demonstrated and hemodynamic improvement correlated with clinical results. Twenty patients in this series remained free of ulcer recurrence during a mean follow-up period of 15 months. These results were confirmed in a 1992 air plethysmographic study by Padberg and colleagues.[79] These authors also observed significant hemodynamic improvements, with no ulcer recurrence up to 2 years after perforator ligation with concomitant correction of superficial reflux. Bradbury and coworkers used foot volumetry and duplex scanning to assess hemodynamic improvement after saphenous and perforator ligation in 43 patients with recurrent ulcers.[13] At a median follow-up of 66 months, 34 patients had no ulcer recurrence; and in these patients both expulsion fraction and half-refilling time had improved significantly after surgery, as measured with foot volumetry and tourniquet occlusion of the superficial veins.

Rhodes and colleagues used strain-gauge plethysmography to quantitate calf muscle pump function and venous incompetence before and after SEPS (Fig. 158-20).[30] The authors observed significant improvement in both calf muscle pump function and venous incompetence in 31 limbs studied within 6 months after SEPS. Twenty-four of the 31 limbs underwent saphenous stripping in addition to SEPS. Normalization of venous incompetence occurred in up to 50% of limbs studied, and this improvement was associated with a favorable clinical outcome. Although limbs undergoing SEPS alone had significant clinical benefits, the hemodynamic improvements did not reach statistical significance. This is likely related to both the small number of patients and the predominance of post-thrombotic syndrome in this subgroup.

Patients with primary valvular incompetence demonstrate significantly better hemodynamic improvement, compared with post-thrombotic limbs. Proebstle and coworkers, using light reflection rheography before and 8 weeks after SEPS had very similar results to the Mayo Clinic series, showing significant improvement in limbs with primary valvular incompetence.[91] Using foot volumetry, Stacey and coworkers demonstrated that perforator vein ligation with ablation of saphenous reflux improved calf muscle pump function in limbs with primary valvular incompetence, although the relative expelled volume did not return to normal.[92] No hemodynamic benefit was found in post-thrombotic limbs. The overall benefits in these patients are clearly not of the same magnitude as in those with primary valvular incompetence.

Studies of Zukowski and Nicolaides indicate that only 70% of patients with venous ulcers have incompetent perforators of moderate or major significance.[57] As suggested by the authors, variable hemodynamic improvement observed after perforator interruption may be explained by the fact that perforators with no or minor hemodynamic effects were treated. Further research for the best preoperative test with which to determine the hemodynamic effects of incompetent perforators and to help select patients for perforator interruption is clearly justified.

■ SUMMARY

Perforator vein incompetence, caused by primary valvular incompetence or by deep vein thrombosis, contributes to ambulatory venous hypertension and to the development of chronic venous disease. Incompetent perforators occur in at least two thirds of patients with venous ulceration and are found together with SVI or DVI in most patients. Although the exact role and contribution of perforators to the development of ulcers is under debate, poor results with nonoperative management to prevent ulcer recurrence justify attempts at perforator ligation, in addition to ablation of superficial reflux, in most patients.

The endoscopic technique of perforator interruption produces significantly fewer wound complications than the open technique. Interruption of incompetent perforators with ablation of the superficial reflux, if present, is effective and durable to decrease symptoms of CVI and rapidly heal ulcers. Ultrasound-guided sclerotherapy is still in its infancy, and further evaluation of this technique, especially in terms of ulcer healing and recurrence in patients with advanced CVI, is awaited before it can be endorsed as an alternative to SEPS. Ulcer recurrence after correction of perforator and superficial reflux in patients with post-thrombotic syndrome is much higher than in patients with primary valvular incompetence. Further prospective randomized studies are still needed to define the exact benefit of interruption of incompetent perforators in patients with advanced chronic venous disease.

■ REFERENCES

1. Gay J: Lettsonian Lectures 1867. In Varicose Disease of the Lower Extremities. London, Churchill, 1868.
2. Linton RR: The operative treatment of varicose veins and ulcers, based upon a classification of these lesions. Ann Surg 107:582-593, 1938.
3. Cockett FB, Jones BD: The ankle blow-out syndrome: A new approach to the varicose ulcer problem. Lancet 1:17-23, 1953.
4. Cockett FB: The pathology and treatment of venous ulcers of the leg. Br J Surg 44:260-278, 1956.
5. Dodd H: The diagnosis and ligation of incompetent perforating veins. Ann R Coll Surg Engl 34:186-196, 1964.
6. Dodd H, Cockett FR: The Management of Venous Ulcers. New York, Churchill-Livingstone, 1976.
7. Silver D, Gleysteen JJ, Rhodes GR, et al: Surgical treatment of the refractory postphlebitic ulcer. Arch Surg 103:554-560, 1971.
8. Thurston OG, Williams HT: Chronic venous insufficiency of the lower extremity: Pathogenesis and surgical treatment. Arch Surg 106:537-539, 1973.
9. Bowen FH: Subfascial ligation of the perforating leg veins to treat post-thrombophlebitic syndrome. Am Surg 41:148-151, 1975.
10. Schanzer H, Peirce EC: A rational approach to surgery of the chronic venous stasis syndrome. Ann Surg 195:25-29, 1982.
11. Negus D, Friedgood A: The effective management of venous ulceration. Br J Surg 70:623-627, 1983.
12. Cikrit DF, Nichols WK, Silver D: Surgical management of refractory venous stasis ulceration. J Vasc Surg 7:473-478, 1988.
13. Bradbury AW, Stonebridge PA, Callam MJ, et al: Foot volumetry and duplex ultrasonography after saphenous and subfascial perforating vein ligation for recurrent venous ulceration. Br J Surg 80:845-848, 1993.
14. Burnand K, Thomas ML, O'Donnell T, Browse NL: Relation between postphlebitic changes in the deep veins and results of surgical treatment of venous ulcers. Lancet 1:936-938, 1976.
15. Burnand KG, O'Donnell TF Jr, Thomas ML, Browse NL: The relative importance of incompetent communicating veins in the production of varicose veins and venous ulcers. Surgery 82:9-14, 1977.
16. Rob CG: Surgery of the vascular system. Presented at the University of Minnesota Vascular Symposium, 1972, p 272.
17. Lim R, Blaisdell FW, Zubrinm J, et al: Subfascial ligation of perforating veins in recurrent stasis ulceration. Am J Surg 119:246-249, 1970.
18. DePalma RG: Surgical therapy for venous stasis: Results of a modified Linton operation. Am J Surg 137:810-813, 1979.
19. Edwards JM: Shearing operation for incompetent perforating veins. Br J Surg 63:885-886, 1976.
20. Hauer G: [Endoscopic subfascial discussion of perforating veins—preliminary report]. [German]. Vasa 14:59-61, 1985.
21. Bergan JJ, Murray J, Greason K: Subfascial endoscopic perforator vein surgery: A preliminary report. Ann Vasc Surg 10:211-219, 1996.
22. Gloviczki P, Bergan JJ, Menawat SS, et al: Safety, feasibility, and early efficacy of subfascial endoscopic perforator surgery: A preliminary report from the North American registry. J Vasc Surg 25:94-105, 1997.
23. Pierik EG, Toonder IM, van Urk H, Wittens CH: Validation of duplex ultrasonography in detecting competent and incompetent perforating veins in patients with venous ulceration of the lower leg. J Vasc Surg 26:49-52, 1997.
24. Pierik EG, van Urk H, Hop WC, Wittens CH: Endoscopic versus open subfascial division of incompetent perforating veins in the treatment of venous leg ulceration: A randomized trial. J Vasc Surg 26:1049-1054, 1997.
25. Fischer R: Surgical treatment of varicose veins; endoscopic treatment of incompetent Cockett veins. Phlebologie, pp 1040-1041, 1989.
26. Jugenheimer M, Junginger T: Endoscopic subfascial sectioning of incompetent perforating veins in treatment of primary varicosis. World J Surg 16:971-975, 1992.
27. Conrad P: Endoscopic exploration of the subfascial space of the lower leg with perforator interruption using laparoscopic equipment: A preliminary report. Phlebology, pp 154-157, 1994.
28. Gloviczki P, Cambria RA, Rhee RY, et al: Surgical technique and preliminary results of endoscopic subfascial division of perforating veins. J Vasc Surg 23:517-523, 1996.

29. Gloviczki P, Bergan JJ, Rhodes JM, et al: Mid-term results of endoscopic perforator vein interruption for chronic venous insufficiency: Lessons learned from the North American subfascial endoscopic perforator surgery registry. The North American Study Group. J Vasc Surg 29:489-502, 1999.

30. Rhodes JM, Gloviczki P, Canton LG, et al: Endoscopic perforator vein division with ablation of superficial reflux improves venous hemodynamics. J Vasc Surg 28:839-847, 1998.

31. Rhodes JM, Gloviczki P, Canton LG, et al: Factors affecting clinical outcome following endoscopic perforator vein ablation. Am J Surg 176:162-167, 1998.

32. Lofgren EP, Myers TT, Lofgren KA, Kuster G: The venous valves of the foot and ankle. Surg Gynecol Obstet 127:289-290, 1968.

33. Mozes G, Gloviczki P, Menawat SS, et al: Surgical anatomy for endoscopic subfascial division of perforating veins. J Vasc Surg 24:800-808, 1996.

34. Sherman RS: Varicose veins: Further findings based on anatomic and surgical dissections. Ann Surg 130:218-232, 1949.

35. O'Donnell TF Jr, Burnand KG, Clemenson G, et al: Doppler examination vs clinical and phlebographic detection of the location of incompetent perforating veins: A prospective study. Arch Surg 112:31-35, 1977.

36. Negus D: Leg Ulcers: A Practical Approach to Management, 2nd ed. Oxford, Butterworth-Heinemann, 1995.

37. O'Donnell T: Surgery for Incompetent Perforating Veins at the Turn of the Millennium. New York, McGraw-Hill, 2001.

38. Beecher HK, Field ME, Krogh A: The effect of walking on the venous pressure at the ankle. Skand Arch Physiol 73:133-140, 1936.

39. Linton RR: The post-thrombotic ulceration of the lower extremity: Its etiology and surgical treatment. Ann Surg 138:415-432, 1953.

40. DeCamp PT, Ward JA, Ochner A: Ambulatory venous pressure studies in post-phlebitic and other disease states. Surgery 29:365-377, 1951.

41. Warren R, White D: Venous pressures in the saphenous system in normal, varicose and post-phlebitic extremities. Surgery 26:435-441, 1948.

42. Nicolaides AN, Hussein MK, Szendro G, et al: The relation of venous ulceration with ambulatory venous pressure measurements. J Vasc Surg 17:414-419, 1993.

43. Homans J: The operative treatment of varicose veins and ulcers, based upon a classification of these lesions. Surg Gynecol Obstet 22:143-158, 1916.

44. van Rij AM, Solomon C, Christie R: Anatomic and physiologic characteristics of venous ulceration. J Vasc Surg 20:759-764, 1994.

45. Labropoulos N, Mansour MA, Kang SS, et al: New insights into perforator vein incompetence. Eur J Vasc Endovasc Surg 18:228-234, 1999.

46. Labrapoulos N, Leon M, Geroulakos G, et al: Venous hemodynamic abnormalities in patients with leg ulcerations. Am J Surg 169:572-574, 1995.

47. Hanrahan LM, Araki CT, Rodriguez AA, et al: Distribution of valvular incompetence in patients with venous stasis ulceration. J Vasc Surg 13:805-812, 1991.

48. Myers KA, Ziegenbein RW, Zeng GH, Matthews PG: Duplex ultrasonography scanning for chronic venous disease: Patterns of venous reflux. J Vasc Surg 21:605-612, 1995.

49. van Bemmelen PS, Bedford G, Beach K, Strandness DE Jr: Status of the valves in the superficial and deep venous system in chronic venous disease. Surgery 109:730-734, 1991.

50. Darke SG, Penfold C: Venous ulceration and saphenous ligation. Eur J Vasc Surg 6:4-9, 1992.

51. Lees TA, Lambert D: Patterns of venous reflux in limbs with skin changes associated with chronic venous insufficiency. Br J Surg 80:725-728, 1993.

52. Coleridge SP: Calf perforating veins—time for an objective appraisal [editorial]? Phlebology 11:135-136, 1996.

53. Gloviczki P: Endoscopic perforator vein surgery: Does it work [editorial]? Vasc Surg 32:303-305, 1998.

54. Sethia KK, Darke SG: Long saphenous incompetence as a cause of venous ulceration. Br J Surg 71:754-755, 1984.

55. Bjordal RI: Circulation patterns in incompetent perforating veins of the calf. In Venous Dysfunction. Baltimore, Urban & Schwarzenberg, 1981.

56. Sarin S, Scurr JH, Smith PD: Medial calf perforators in venous disease: The significance of outward flow. J Vasc Surg 16:40-46, 1992.

57. Zukowski AJ, Nicolaides AN, Szendro G, et al: Haemodynamic significance of incompetent calf perforating veins [see comments]. Br J Surg 78:625-629, 1991.

58. Sandri JL, Barros FS, Pontes S, et al: Diameter-reflux relationship in perforating veins of patients with varicose veins. J Vasc Surg 30:867-874, 1999.

59. Stuart WP, Adam DJ, Allan PL, et al: The relationship between the number, competence, and diameter of medial calf perforating veins and the clinical status in healthy subjects and patients with lower-limb venous disease. J Vasc Surg 32:138-143, 2000.

60. Delis KT, Husmann M, Kalodiki E, et al: In situ hemodynamics of perforating veins in chronic venous insufficiency. J Vasc Surg 33:773-782, 2001.

61. Gloviczki P, Lewis BD, Lindsey JR, McKusick MA: Preoperative Evaluation of Chronic Venous Insufficiency with Duplex Scanning and Venography. London, Springer-Verlag, 1998.

62. DePalma RG: Linton's Operation and Modification of the Open Techniques. London, Springer-Verlag, 1998.

63. Pierik EGJM, Wittens CHA, van Urk H: Subfascial endoscopic ligation in the treatment of incompetent perforator veins. Eur J Vasc Endovasc Surg 5:38-41, 1995.

64. Sparks SR, Ballard JL, Bergan JJ, Killeen JD: Early benefits of subfascial endoscopic perforator surgery (SEPS) in healing venous ulcers. Ann Vasc Surg 11:367-373, 1997.

65. Wittens CH, Pierik RG, van Urk H: The surgical treatment of incompetent perforating veins [review]. Eur J Vasc Endovasc Surg 9:19-23, 1995.

66. Fischer R, Schwahn-Schreiber C, Sattler G: Conclusions of a consensus conference on subfascial endoscopy of perforating veins in the medial lower leg. Vasc Surg 32:339-347, 1998.

67. Bergan JJ, Ballard JL, Sparks S: Subfascial Endoscopic Perforator Surgery: The Open Technique. London, Springer-Verlag, 1998.

68. Pierik EG, van Urk H, Wittens CH: Efficacy of subfascial endoscopy in eradicating perforating veins of the lower leg and its relation with venous ulcer healing. J Vasc Surg 26:255-259, 1997.

69. Wittens CHA: Comparison of Open Linton Operation with Subfascial Endoscopic Perforator Vein Surgery. London, Springer-Verlag, 1998.

70. O'Donnell TF: Surgical treatment of incompetent communicating veins. In Atlas of Venous Surgery. Philadelphia, WB Saunders, 2000, pp 111-124.

71. Allen RC, Tawes RL, Wetter A, Fogarty TJ: Endoscopic Perforator Vein Surgery: Creation of a Subfascial Space. London, Springer-Verlag, 1998.

72. Negus D: Prevention and treatment of venous ulceration. Ann R Coll Surg Engl 67:144-148, 1985.

73. Anning ST: Leg ulcers: The results of treatment. Angiology 7:505-516, 1956.

74. Mayberry JC, Moneta GL, Taylor LM Jr, Porter JM: Fifteen-year results of ambulatory compression therapy for chronic venous ulcers. Surgery 109:575-581, 1991.

75. Erickson CA: Healing of venous ulcers in an ambulatory care program: The role of chronic venous insufficiency and patient compliance. J Vasc Surg 22:629-636, 1995.

76. Wilkinson GE Jr, Maclaren IF: Long term review of procedures for venous perforator insufficiency. Surg Gynecol Obstet 163:117-120, 1986.

77. Johnson WC, O'Hara ET, Corey C, et al: Venous stasis ulceration: Effectiveness of subfascial ligation. Arch Surg 120:797-800, 1985.

78. Robison JG, Elliott BM, Kaplan AJ: Limitations of subfascial ligation for refractory chronic venous stasis ulceration. Ann Vasc Surg 6:9-14, 1992.

79. Padberg FT Jr, Pappas PJ, Araki CT, et al: Hemodynamic and clinical improvement after superficial vein ablation in primary combined venous insufficiency with ulceration [see comments]. J Vasc Surg 24:711-718, 1996.

80. Murray JD, Bergan JJ, Riffenburgh RH: Development of open-scope subfascial perforating vein surgery: Lessons learned from the first 67 patients. Ann Vasc Surg 13:372-377, 1999.

81. Stuart WP, Adam DJ, Bradbury AW, Ruckley CV: Subfascial endoscopic perforator surgery is associated with significantly less morbidity and shorter hospital stay than open operation (Linton's procedure) [see comments]. Br J Surg 84:1364-1365, 1997.

82. Sybrandy JE, van Gent WB, Pierik EG, Wittens CH: Endoscopic versus open subfascial division of incompetent perforating veins in the treatment of venous leg ulceration. J Vasc Surg 33:1028-1032, 2001.

83. Tawes RL, Barron ML, Coello AA, et al: Optimal therapy for advanced chronic venous insufficiency. J Vasc Surg 37:545-551, 2003.

84. Nelzen O: Prospective study of safety, patient satisfaction and leg ulcer healing following saphenous and subfascial endoscopic perforator surgery [see comments]. Br J Surg 87:86-91, 2001.

85. Kalra M, Gloviczki P, Noel AA, et al: Subfascial endoscopic perforator vein surgery in patients with post-thrombotic venous insufficiency—Is it justified? Vasc Endovasc Surg 36:41-50, 2002.

86. Wittens CH, van Gent BW, Hop WC, Sybrandy JE: The Dutch Subfascial Endoscopic Perforating Vein Surgery (SEPS) Trial: A randomized multicenter trial comparing ambulatory compression therapy versus surgery in patients with venous leg ulcers. Presented before the Society for Vascular Surgery, Chicago, 2003.

87. TenBrook JA Jr, Iafrati MD, O'Donnell TF, et al: Systematic review of outcomes after surgical management of venous disease incorporating subfascial endoscopic perforator surgery. J Vasc Surg 39:583-589, 2004.

88. Guex JJ: Ultrasound guided sclerotherapy (USGS) for perforating veins (PV). Presented before the French Society of Phlebology, Nice, 2000.

89. Eklof B, Kessler D, Kistner RL, et al: Can duplex-guided sclerotherapy replace SEPS in the treatment of incompetent perforating veins. Presented before the 30th Global Veith Vascular Surgery Symposium on Vascular and Endovascular Issues, Techniques and Horizons, New York, 2003.

90. Akesson H, Brudin L, Cwikiel W, et al: Does the correction of insufficient superficial and perforating veins improve venous function in patients with deep venous insufficiency? Phlebology 5:113-123, 1990.

91. Proebstle TM, Weisel G, Paepcke U, et al: Light reflection rheography and clinical course of patients with advanced venous disease before and after endoscopic subfascial division of perforating veins. Dermatol Surg 24:771-776, 1998.

92. Stacey MC, Burnand KG, Layer GT, Pattison M: Calf pump function in patients with healed venous ulcers is not improved by surgery to the communicating veins or by elastic stockings. Br J Surg 75:436-439, 1988.

93. Shami SK, Sarin S, Cheatle TR, et al: Venous ulcers and the superficial venous system [see comments]. J Vasc Surg 17:487-490, 1993.

94. Labropoulos N, Delis K, Nicolaides AN, et al: The role of the distribution and anatomic extent of reflux in the development of signs and symptoms in chronic venous insufficiency. J Vasc Surg 23:504-510, 1996.

95. Monk BE, Sarkany I: Outcome of treatment of venous stasis ulcers. Clin Exp Dermatol 7:397-400, 1982.

96. Kitahama A, Elliott LF, Kerstein MD, Menendez CV: Leg ulcer: Conservative management or surgical treatment? JAMA 247:197-199, 1982.

97. DePalma RG, Kowallek DL: Venous ulceration: A cross-over study from nonoperative to operative treatment. J Vasc Surg 24:788-792, 1996.

98. Samson RH, Showalter DP: Stockings and the prevention of recurrent venous ulcers. Dermatol Surg 22:373-376, 1996.

99. Wolters U, Schmit-Rixen T, Erasmi H, Lynch J: Endoscopic dissection of incompetent perforating veins in the treatment of chronic venous leg ulcers. Vasc Surg 30:481-487, 1996.

100. Illig KA, Shortell CK, Ouriel K, et al: Photoplethysmography and calf muscle pump function after subfascial endoscopic perforator ligation [see comments]. J Vasc Surg 30:1067-1076, 1999.

The Surgical Treatment of Deep Venous Valvular Incompetence

159

KEVIN M. SHERIDAN, MD

MICHAEL C. DALSING, MD

Chronic venous insufficiency (CVI) is a highly prevalent and costly disease in Western countries. If one considers the entire spectrum of disorders from telangiectasia to venous ulcers, this affects more than 30 million Americans, more than half of whom are women.[1,2] Skin changes suggestive of venous disease are noted in 6 to 7 million U.S. citizens.[2,3] Lower extremity venous ulcerations occur in up to 2% of those with CVI (approximately 500,000).[2,3] More recent population studies continue to demonstrate similar findings.[4] The annual cost of venous ulcers in the U.S. population is estimated at greater than 1 billion dollars.[5]

Although there are many theories proposed to help explain the sequelae of chronic venous disease at a local level, venous stasis and venous hypertension are key ingredients in the pathophysiology. The ultimate goal in the treatment of significant CVI is to diminish the hemodynamic impact of the disease on the target organ, the lower leg, to a point where the sequelae of the disease are minimized. Conservative management in the form of various types of external compression can successfully treat venous ulceration with excellent early results, but the recurrence rate within a few years can be 70% to 100% in noncompliant patients and 30% to 40% in those who faithfully comply with continued long-term compressive therapy.[6,7] This form of therapy does not require a comprehensive understanding of the venous systems involved in the disease process, but if a more aggressive and invasive approach is required, one must differentiate those with superficial/perforator venous disease from those without involvement of these veins. The proper diagnosis and treatment of disease of the superficial or perforator veins has been discussed in depth by other authors in this text. Isolated superficial or perforator disease has been observed to cause advanced manifestations of venous disease, but in approximately two thirds of these advanced cases, the deep system is insufficient alone or, more commonly, in association with disease of the superficial or perforator veins.[8-11] In patients with disease of the superficial or perforator veins and deep venous involvement, removal of pathologic superficial and/or perforator venous insufficiency can eliminate the majority of venous reflux, resulting in prolonged venous ulcer healing.[12] However, about one third of patients with primary deep venous incompetence and 70% of those with the post-thrombotic syndrome will experience ulcer recurrence,

emphasizing the importance of the remaining deep venous disease.[12] Venous obstruction is the predominant hemodynamic disorder in a minority of venous ulcer cases (2% to 20%).[8,9,13,14] Significant pathology causing obstruction can be repaired by endovascular or open surgical techniques and has been well described previously. With the failure of these less invasive and technically demanding methods to control the disabling sequelae of chronic venous disease, surgical intervention to alleviate insufficiency in the deep venous system is being considered more often.

■ ETIOLOGY AND PATHOPHYSIOLOGY

As discussed in more detail in Chapters 154 and 155, there are congenital, primary, and secondary causes for CVI. Congenital absence of the valves is a rare occurrence.[15] There are syndromes associated with venous abnormalities that may be associated with venous aplasia or dysplasia, but these syndromes are uncommon and seldom require deep venous valvular reconstruction as an integral component of treatment.

Primary venous insufficiency occurs as a result of a structural elongation of the valve cusps or stretching of the vein wall with no obvious underlying cause identified.[16,17] Floppy, redundant valve cusps permit prolapse of the valve leaflets, resulting in poor coaptation, and are observed in many cases of primary deep venous valvular incompetence.[16] Alternatively, an enlarged venous diameter will not permit the unaltered valve cusps to meet appropriately.[18,19] When a pressure gradient is created, as with standing, reflux of blood occurs through the architecturally preserved valve. In these situations, an in-situ repair can be performed to render the valve competent.

Secondary venous insufficiency is often the result of deep venous thrombosis and may account for 40% to 70% of cases of major chronic deep venous valvular incompetence (CDVVI).[13,16,20] Inflammation and scarring resulting from thrombosis and recanalization can cause shortening and fibrosis of the valve leaflets, small perforations, or valve adhesions causing luminal narrowing.[16] Thus, this situation is often referred to as resulting from the post-thrombotic syndrome. In general, these valves are so damaged that an in-situ repair is not practical or feasible. This leaves only the potential options of transplantation of a competent valve (often from the axillary vein) into the incompetent system, transposition of the incompetent venous system to a position distal to a local competent valve, or the use of less traditional valve substitutes that are being actively investigated.

However, this classic differentiation between "primary" and "secondary" (post-thrombotic) pathology has been challenged by both clinical and direct observation of the veins and valves at surgery. That the two conditions can be present in the same patient is a clinical observation made almost 20 years ago.[21] In these cases, the vein wall is thickened/fibrotic at the valve station or there is thickening of the valve cusps and/or intima. Pathologic study of 11 veins with these surgical findings (graded 2 or 3 in this report's grading system) demonstrated clear post-thrombotic changes in six but phlebosclerosis of a nonthrombotic origin in the remaining five.[16] Clearly, preservation of a rather normal valve architecture can be explained if "primary" reflux and sustained high pressure on the vein wall is the cause of the valve station changes noted. However, it has always been thought that deep venous thrombosis destroys the involved delicate valve cusps, making repair of such valves impossible. Nevertheless, these valves have undergone a successful in-situ repair in 87% of cases.[16] It is theorized that the rapid resolution of venous thrombi, an event known to occur and documented by investigators studying acute deep venous thrombosis,[22] may have allowed these valves to escape the ravages of the disease. Alternatively, the valve itself may not have been directly involved in the thrombotic process. Several investigators have noted venous valvular reflux proximal to a distal thrombosis.[22-24] The fibrotic process in the vein wall may extend to the valve station in the natural course of resolution, and the valve cusps become floppy by virtue of a decrease in wall diameter resulting from a thickened, noncompliant wall of the vein (Fig. 159-1).[16] The valve remains architecturally intact, thin, and compliant and can be made competent by standard reefing of the cusps.

To realize the goal of diminishing venous hypertension to the lower leg in patients with CDVVI, correction of axial deep venous reflux to the calf/ankle area is required. If one ignores this axiom, most notably by ignoring reflux in the profunda femoris vein, isolated femoral vein valvular reconstruction will be clinically unsuccessful and lower limb venous hemodynamics will not be improved.[25] With profunda femoris competence, repair of femoral vein incompetence by whatever method can improve lower limb venous hemodynamics.[25,26] Tremendous dilatation of the profunda femoris vein after femoral vein thrombosis has been documented, and repair of the profunda femoris vein valvular incompetence is required for a successful outcome (Fig. 159-2).[27] An alternative method of correcting significant axial reflux is to position the valve reconstruction below all collateral connections of the femoral and profunda femoris veins to the popliteal vein. Repair of valvular incompetence at the popliteal location can accomplish this goal.[28-30] At least one investigator has performed multiple tibial vein valve repairs to accomplish correction of axial reflux at this level.[31]

■ DIAGNOSIS

Patients with CVI and specifically with CDVVI present with symptoms related to venous hypertension and stasis. Initial manifestations may include dependent edema, especially after long periods of standing, as well as leg fatigue and a feeling of "fullness" in the legs. The signs and symptoms progress in severity to include increasing pain, intractable edema, and skin changes such as eczema, cellulitis, hyperpigmentation, lipodermatosclerosis, and stasis ulcers. These are the sequelae of CVI, and a patient may present with any combination of these signs and symptoms. A careful history and physical examination should be performed that includes any history of deep venous thrombosis or clotting disorders, any signs of venous diseases present in the patient, and the resultant limitations of physical and occupational activity from the disease. Of course, a good arterial examination and general history and physical examination will eliminate the presence of other diseases that might impact the treatment of the venous pathology. Furthermore, this preliminary evaluation will help exclude other causes of lower leg venous ulceration or skin changes, such as ischemic ulcers, diabetic ulcers, dermatologic disorders (e.g., eczema), or even skin or soft tissue cancers.

Each patient should ultimately be stratified according to the CEAP classification system.[32] As discussed in detail in Chapter 155, this system categorizes a patient's disease based on clinical (C), etiologic (E), anatomic (A), and pathophysiologic (P) designations. This classification

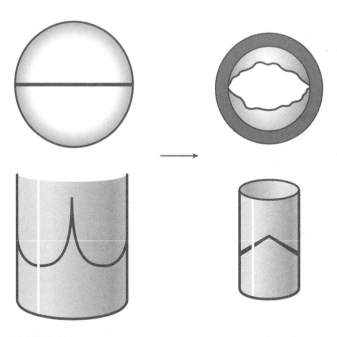

FIGURE 159-1 A possible mechanism for the production of valve redundancy and reflux in post-thrombotic valve stations. Valve station fibrosis may lead to luminal constriction, resulting in "secondary" valve leaflet redundancy and reflux. Foreshortening of the valve station may lead to widening of the commissural valve angle, contributing further to development of reflux. (Redrawn from Raju S, Fredericks RK, Hudson CA, et al: Venous valve station changes in "primary" and post-thrombotic reflux: An analysis of 149 cases. Ann Vasc Surg 14:199, 2000.)

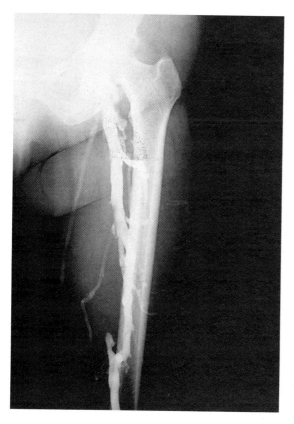

FIGURE 159-2 Axial transformation of the profunda femoris vein. Note the remnant of the thrombosed femoral vein in the distal thigh. (From Raju S, Fountain T, Neglen P, Devidas M: Axial transformation of the profunda femoris vein. J Vasc Surg 27:651-659, 1998.)

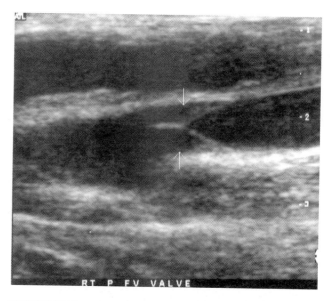

FIGURE 159-3 A duplex image of a complete and competent valve with both cusps easily identified.

system helps the physician to define the venous disease he or she is confronted with on an individual basis so that a focused and appropriate management strategy can be made. If one cannot define the problem, little progress can be made in its management. Seven clinical classes are distinguished based on the patient's signs of disease. Generally, candidates for deep venous valvular reconstruction will fall into the class 5 to class 6 disease categories (those with currently healed or active venous ulcers that have often been of a recurrent nature), although exceptions are occasionally made for those with disabling lifestyle symptoms, such as severe edema. An extension of this clinical classification system is available to adequately quantify the extent of venous disease and, therefore, to evaluate the patient's response to treatment.[33,34] If surgery is performed, the patient's clinical outcome score can be evaluated according to a grading scheme.[33] An improved method of determining the change in disease severity after intervention has been developed by an ad hoc committee of the American Venous Forum but is yet to be fully utilized clinically.[34] Quality of life surveys are major tools being developed to help determine the impact of venous disease on the patient's life and the effect therapy has on the patient's overall well-being.[35] Application of these surveys to the postsurgical outcome of patients has yet to be achieved, but when it is available it will improve our ability to precisely determine the effect of any given intervention.

The diagnostic evaluation for CVI helps the clinician to fill in the blanks of the CEAP classification not readily apparent after the history and physical examination component of the evaluation. The history and physical examination will, in some cases, be all that is required to eliminate venous disease as a major component of the patient's problem. In general, however, the venous duplex ultrasound study is essential to clarify the venous problem being addressed. This study will help clarify the etiology (E of CEAP; congenital, primary, or secondary) in some cases, better define the anatomic location of the disease process (A of CEAP; specific veins can be imaged with spectral analysis to determine reflux), and aid in determining the pathophysiology (P of CEAP; reflux, obstruction, or both). Venous duplex imaging can often visualize the venous valve cusps (Fig. 159-3). Insufficiency within any segment of the deep venous system is defined as a prolonged reflux time through the valve after a provocative test. A reflux time of more than 0.5 second is considered abnormal if a rapidly deflating distal cuff is used as the provocative test, whereas more than 1.0 second is considered the cutoff when manual compression is used (Fig. 159-4).[36,37] Venous obstruction is seen as thickened, scarred, and constricted veins and/or valves (Fig. 159-5) with poor flow and diminished augmentation after distal and/or proximal compression. Respiratory variation will be lost from local disease or as the result of proximal occlusive disease. Similar imaging and spectral analysis can be performed to determine obstruction, or more commonly insufficiency, of the superficial and perforator veins. By imaging the entire lower venous system, the surgeon is provided a detailed roadmap of all veins and whether obstruction or reflux is present in each. This may be all the diagnostic evaluation needed if disease of the superficial or perforator veins is found and requires treatment as a first stage in the management of the patient.

Some type of plethysmographic technique is used to determine the hemodynamic impact of venous disease on

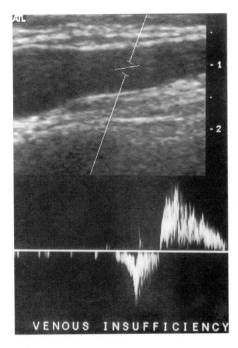

FIGURE 159-4 A duplex image of the venous system (*top,* B mode gray scale image) with velocity profile on the lower scale. Note that this patient has an incompetent deep venous system because a distal compression (first wave of increased velocity) is followed by more than 1 second of reverse flow (second velocity peak).

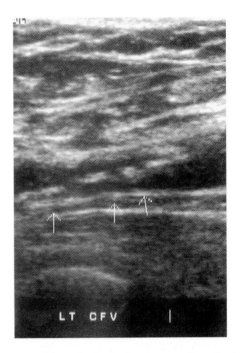

FIGURE 159-5 This duplex image demonstrates a femoral vein that has experienced an episode of deep venous thrombosis with resulting recannulation. Note thickened walls with intraluminal septa.

the entire lower limb in patients with CDVVI (see Chapter 155). Air plethysmography is the device most commonly used today. It provides for an overall quantification of the impact of the venous insufficiency on the lower leg and may provide some insight into the impact of treatment. The function of the calf muscle pump can be evaluated by air plethysmography in the form of the ejection fraction.[38,39] Air plethysmography can also provide an estimate of venous insufficiency in the form of a venous filling index and an estimate of ambulatory venous pressure.[5,40] The residual volume fraction has a linear correlation to the age-old ambulatory venous pressure measurement. The use of tourniquets to separate superficial from deep or perforator disease has not been shown to be completely predictable in determining exactly where disease is located,[40] but tourniquets can be useful in specific cases. Significant outflow obstruction is determined by occluding venous outflow until a stable plateau is reached. The thigh cuff causing the venous occlusion is rapidly deflated, and the difference between maximal volume and that volume present 1 second later divided by the total calf volume is called the outflow fraction. Normally, 40% or more of venous blood is expelled from the leg in 1 second.

Patients with significant deep venous valvular reflux who are contemplating surgery undergo venographic study for proper operative planning. Ascending venography is useful in demonstrating the anatomy of the deep venous system and ruling out obstruction as a major contributing or causative factor.[16,41] It provides a roadmap of the deep venous system to allow selection of the most disease-free portion of the incompetent and post-thrombotic venous

system for valve transplantation if that becomes necessary. Direct lower limb intravenous pressure measurements obtained before and after thigh cuff compression and compared with arm intravenous pressure have been suggested as a method to determine the presence or absence of venous obstruction and to determine if obstruction is compensated or not.[16,41] The inventors of this intravenous pressure measurement determination now question the reliability of this or other hemodynamic studies to rule out iliac obstruction as a component of the patient's problem and recommend transfemoral phlebography and intravenous ultrasonography to clarify the issue.[42] Furthermore, intravenous ambulatory venous pressure measurements can be performed to aid in determination of the overall magnitude of reflux.[5] The ambulatory venous pressure has been shown to correlate with the presence of venous ulceration, with each 10 mm Hg increase above 30 mm Hg corresponding to a 10% to 15% increase in the incidence of venous ulceration.[43] If the venous reflux time (VRT) is less than 20 seconds, overall valvular reflux throughout the lower leg is evident. In general, we obtain these studies for an in-depth evaluation of these patients and to be able to determine post-intervention the degree of hemodynamic impact.

Descending venography is used to determine valve leaflet integrity and anatomic location and to demonstrate the extent of reflux (Fig. 159-6).[44] Assessment of the competence of the profunda femoris venous system in addition to the femoral system is imperative, because if it is a competent system it may be a source for a valve transposition or may indicate potential success with an isolated proximal femoral vein repair.[30,45,46] Certainly, descending venography is not

FIGURE 159-6 This descending venogram demonstrates the presence of valves with architecturally preserved cusps available for an in-situ repair.

infallible in determining the presence or absence of a normal valve.[16] Raju and colleagues report that the descending venogram misrepresented the presence of a valve in 11% of cases (a valve considered present was not at operation) and missed an intact valve in 25% of cases (a valve thought absent was actually present).[16] However, when combined with a well-performed venous duplex examination, it is currently the best method available to determine preoperatively if an in-situ reconstruction will be possible.

■ SURGICAL REPAIR

Surgical therapy for CVI should be considered in patients who have failed less invasive treatments. Patients should be given a trial of graded compression stockings and further instructions to avoid prolonged standing and to elevate the feet above the heart while lying down as well as several times during the day. As discussed in Chapter 157, patients with varicose veins and superficial venous reflux can undergo saphenous vein high ligation and stripping or other endovascular techniques along with branch varicosectomy to remove the offending reflux. Alternatively, sclerotherapy or other minimally invasive techniques can be used in some cases. As detailed in Chapter 158, perforator incompetence can be treated by ligation using either an open technique or subfascial endoscopic perforator surgery. These procedures should usually be performed before surgery on the deep venous system in patients with both disease processes. One study in patients with combined superficial reflux and "segmental deep venous reflux" showed that superficial venous surgery alone corrected deep venous reflux in about 50% of limbs involved and allowed ulcer healing in 77% of

limbs after 1 year of follow-up.[47] This study cannot be generalized to include patients with reflux in the entire deep venous system but is an interesting observation of how the treatment of superficial disease can impact the deep venous system. In general, obstructive deep venous disease is also managed before deep venous valvular reconstruction by most surgeons.

As mentioned previously, when the decision has been made to intervene in patients with deep venous valvular incompetence, the goal is to prevent axial reflux. In some instances that will require intervention in two or more separate axial venous systems (e.g., femoral and profunda femoris veins). One group of investigators believes that multiple valve repairs in the same axial system (e.g., two in the femoral vein) may decrease the risk of failure noted when only one valve is repaired,[31] but most surgeons have reported success when only one valve is repaired.

Surgical Technique

If reconstruction of the proximal femoral veins (femoral or profunda femoris) is the goal, a groin incision made in the direction of the vessels can be used to expose the first and second femoral valves. Further dissection through the sartorius muscle fascia will expose the profunda femoris vein if necessary. After exposure of the valve targeted for repair and the adjoining segment of vein, the strip test should be performed to evaluate the competence of the valve. This test entails milking blood antegrade past the valve while inflow is occluded, with subsequent application of retrograde pressure against the valve. Reflux is demonstrated by refilling of the vein distally. If the valve has become competent as a result of venoconstriction secondary to operative handling of the vein, an external valvuloplasty or a prosthetic sleeve technique (described later) may be viable options.[48] This incision may also provide exposure for a valve transposition or transplantation if required.

After identification of the valve station to be repaired, careful adventitial dissection to identify the valve attachment lines is a useful technique in most venous valvular repairs.[49] This technique can facilitate proper venotomy placement, as well as verify that a valve repair is feasible. A lack of valve attachment lines may signify the destruction of the valve due to post-thrombotic sequelae, prompting other than an in-situ repair.[49]

In other situations, a more distal femoral, popliteal, or even tibial vein may be the desired location for valve repair or transplantation. In these situations, the exposure is much like that used for exposure of the like-named artery with which vascular surgeons are familiar.

Internal Valvuloplasty

An open direct method of valve repair has been a mainstay in correction of primary venous valvular reflux for decades. This technique involves a venotomy and suturing of the elongated valve leaflets under direct visualization. The redundant valve cusps are plicated to the vein wall with 7-0 polypropylene suture to allow proper coaptation of the cusps. Kistner first reported success in 1968 with a longitudinal venotomy extending through the valve commissure

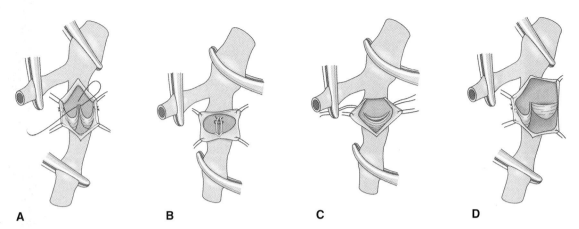

A   **B**   **C**   **D**

FIGURE 159-7 Internal valvuloplasty can be accomplished by a variety of techniques used to visualize the incompetent valve leaflets. **A,** Artist's representation of the method first proposed by Dr. Kistner, in which he opens the vein through the anterior commissure. **B,** A representation of the method of Dr. Raju, who uses a supravalvular transverse venotomy to view the valve from above without incising through the valve commissural angle. **C,** A representation of the method of Dr. Sottiurai, who performs a supracommissural incision with extension toward a cusp sinus to improve visualization. **D,** A representation of the technique used by Dr. Tripathi, who uses a "trapdoor" incision to provide optimal visualization of the valve cusps for repair. The method of reefing the valve to re-establish a competent valve is essentially the same in each instance.

(Fig. 159-7A).[50] A supracommissural approach (Raju, 1983) has been described, which involves a transverse venotomy at least 2.5 cm above the valve (see Fig. 159-7B).[51] Sottiurai has described a combination approach in 1988, which entails a supravalvular transverse venotomy with distal extension into the valve sinus (a T-shaped venotomy) (see Fig. 159-7C).[52] More recently, a "trapdoor" approach has been introduced, involving two transverse incisions on the vein connected by a single vertical incision (see Fig. 159-7D).[53] Regardless of the approach, the suturing of the valve leaflets remains essentially the same (Fig. 159-8). It is estimated that plication of approximately 20% of the valve leaflet length can restore competency to the valve in the majority of cases.[54]

External Valvuloplasty

The technique of external valvuloplasty was pioneered by Kistner in the late 1900s (Fig. 159-9).[55] This approach offers the advantage of valve repair without a venotomy. It is performed by suture placement transmurally through the valve attachment lines, which, upon tying, leaves a decreased commissural angle and a competent valve. Results from follow-up of this technique reveal it to be a

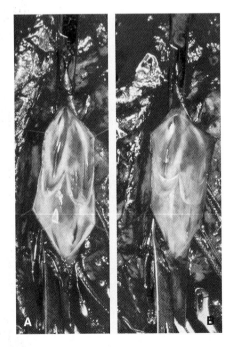

FIGURE 159-8 The method of Kistner is shown in these pre-valvuloplasty (**A**) and post-valvuloplasty (**B**) operative pictures. Note the laxity of the incompetent valve before intervention, whereas after reefing the valve cusps the normal architecture and tension is re-established. (Courtesy of Dr. Robert Kistner.)

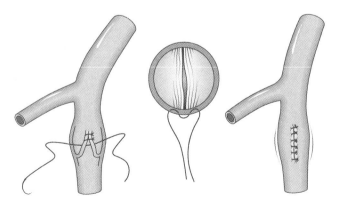

FIGURE 159-9 Artist's rendition of the method of external valvuloplasty. The enlarged venous diameter results in valve incompetence. Note how the placement of sutures decreases the diameter of the venous wall but keeps the valve cusps from harm's way.

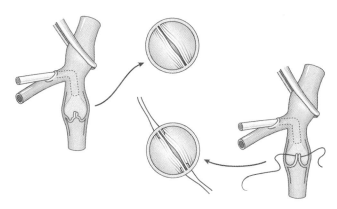

FIGURE 159-10 As an improvement to "blind" placement of sutures in the method of external valvuloplasty, the use of an angioscope as suggested by Gloviczki, allows precise suture placement for actual tightening (reefing) of the valve cusps.

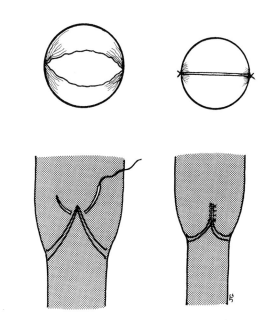

FIGURE 159-11 Transcommissural repair utilizes transluminal sutures to close the commissural valve angle while simultaneously tightening the valve cusp. Use of the angioscope is optional. (From Raju S, Hardy JD: Technical options in venous valve reconstruction. J Vasc Surg 174:304, 1997.)

somewhat less durable repair than the more detailed and visually directed open valvuloplasty.[30] Limited anterior plication, a modification of this method, involves anterior vein dissection and placement of a running mattress suture at the anterior commissure, which runs from a point 3 to 4 mm proximal to the angle of the valve cusp insertion lines up to the angle of valve cusp insertion.[56] About 3 mm of the vein wall is incorporated into the stitch to adequately approximate the cusps.[56] Limited anterior plication was developed with the aim of decreasing vein dissection and potentially reducing the progressive dilatation of the post-repair vein that occurs in some cases of valvuloplasty.[56] It has been used in conjunction with saphenous vein stripping. Currently, its use has been limited to the femoral vein valve station. Results after 10-year follow-up demonstrated improved venous refilling time and decreased ambulatory venous pressures in patients with moderate deep venous valvular incompetence.[56] Thus, it shows promise as a mode of therapy for highly selected patients.

Another modification of external valvuloplasty was reported by Gloviczki in 1991, which features the use of an angioscope (Fig. 159-10).[57] A side branch of the greater saphenous vein is employed for introduction of the angioscope, which is then advanced into the femoral vein to a position above the incompetent femoral vein valve.[57] External sutures can be placed under direct vision. The sutures are placed transluminally across the valve cusps near the point of attachment on the vein wall. In this manner, closure of the valve attachment angle and simultaneous tightening of the valve cusps is performed. Raju has observed that use of the angioscope is not necessary for good results but concedes that it offers good visualization of the valve to ensure adequate repair. Following a learning curve while using the angioscope, a recent study published by Raju demonstrated good clinical and competency results with the "transcommissural" technique without the use of the angioscope at 30 months of follow-up (Fig. 159-11).[58]

External Banding

This method has most commonly been employed in cases in which dissection vasospasm renders a refluxive valve

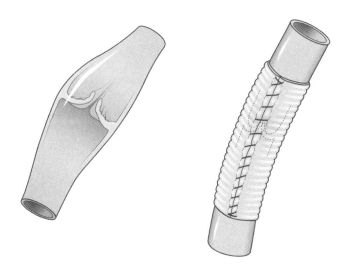

FIGURE 159-12 A and B, Artist's depiction of external banding to prevent venous valvular incompetence in veins that become competent during the vasoconstriction that occurs during operative dissection. Some surgeons use this technique to prevent dilation after valve transplantation or other types of repair.

spontaneously competent. The technique is performed using an external sleeve, made of polyester (Dacron) or polytetra-fluoroethylene (PTFE), wrapped around the circumference of the vein at the site of the valve. This is tightened to diminish the size of the lumen of the vein until valve competence is achieved (Fig. 159-12). The sleeve is then anchored in place to the adventitia by sutures to avoid migration. The prosthetic sleeve has achieved good results when used in selected patient populations.[30]

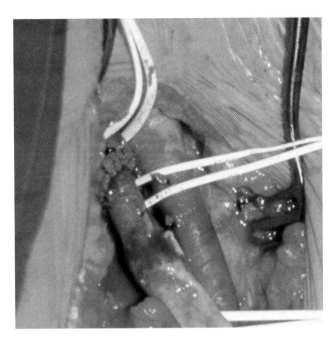

FIGURE 159-13 An operative picture of a vein containing a competent valve transplantation with the proximal anastomosis complete and the proximal vascular loop loosened to allow blood to fill the segment with the competent valve. The distal anastomosis is often completed without reapplying the proximal clamp. The distention of the vein allows for a more precise length determination and confirms that the valve is competent. The distal anastomosis is completed in a similar interrupted fashion with 7-0 or 6-0 polypropylene suture.

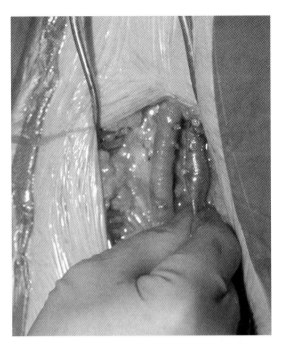

FIGURE 159-14 The strip test confirms valve competence. The test is conducted by occluding the vein distal to the valve (in this case by the surgeon's fingers) and milking the blood out of the valve-containing vein segment. As blood is allowed to refill the vein, if the valve is competent, blood will not be present in the vein distal to the valve.

Valve Transplantation

Venous valve transplantation is a commonly used technique in cases where the valve is destroyed, as in the post-thrombotic syndrome. This procedure was first described for use in humans by Taheri in 1982.[59] A 2- to 3-cm segment of upper extremity vein containing a competent valve (or a reparable one) is first removed. The incompetent femoral vein valve is opened below the takeoff of the profunda femoris vein, and the axillary vein segment is sutured into place after the removal of an appropriate length of femoral vein. The proximal anastomosis may be accomplished first to confirm the competence of the valve and to allow distention and lengthening of the vein/valve to facilitate the distal anastomosis (Fig. 159-13). For vein transplantation in trabeculated post-thrombotic veins, Raju and coworkers have described excision of intraluminal synechiae to create one sizable lumen for suitable anastomoses.[60] Interrupted sutures are preferred to avoid suture line stenosis.[54] Valve competence is determined by the intraoperative strip test and is performed the same for all types of reconstructions (Fig. 159-14). An external sleeve can then be placed around the segment to prevent later dilatation of the segment. Because approximately 40% of axillary vein valves are incompetent at the time of explant, a bench repair may be required.[49,54] However, more proximal or distal valves that are competent should be sought out before resorting to this added surgical intervention. Should a bench repair be necessary, the transcommissural external valvuloplasty technique appears to have better results than the standard external valvuloplasty[49] and some success has been achieved with internal valvuloplasty.[61]

Valve Transposition

Another option in management of the post-thrombotic syndrome is valve transposition. If a single groin axial venous valve is spared from reflux, a transposition procedure can be performed, which places the incompetent venous system distal to the competent valve. Most commonly, a situation occurs in which the femoral system is incompetent and the profunda femoris valve remains competent. Here, the incompetent femoral vein can be transected and reimplanted distal to the competent valve in the profunda femoris vein (Fig. 159-15). Alternatively, the incompetent femoral system can be placed below a competent valve in the great saphenous vein. A situation in which the profunda femoris valve is incompetent may warrant placement of that segment distal to a competent valve in either the femoral vein or the great saphenous vein. More recently, a technique has been described for transposition of an ipsilateral valve (competent great saphenous vein to the femoral vein and subsequent ligation of the femoral vein proximally yet distal to the takeoff of the profunda femoris vein) to escape problems with diameter mismatch.[62] At 10 years, 55% of the patients were free of ulcers.

Valve Substitutes

Several new techniques are being evaluated in the management of CDVVI, most of which are directed at finding valve substitutes for those without autogenous valves for transplantation. Many experimental attempts have been unsuccessful: fresh allografts,[63] umbilical vein molded into a valve,[64] a liquid pellethane molded valve,[64] and a platinum/pyrolyte-covered titanium valve.[65,66] Valves

FIGURE 159-15 Note the competent valve (forceps point to the area) under which the incompetent venous system has been placed.

constructed of autogenous vein in the design of Eiseman-Mallette have shown promise in experimental study but have not been taken to the clinical arena.[67,68] Similarly, lyophilized allograft valve-containing vein segments appear to function post-processing but have never been studied any further.[69]

Raju and Hardy have a small series of patients who received de-novo valve reconstruction procedures.[49] These procedures involve the use of saphenous vein, a tributary of the saphenous vein, or the axillary vein for a donor vein. Semilunar cusps are fashioned out of donor vein after trimming adventitia and part of the media, and the tissue is sutured into the recipient vein with the nonendothelial surface directed toward the lumen to decrease the risk of thrombosis.[49] Little experience has been gained with this method so far, but good clinical results were seen in Raju's small series.

Another attempt to use autogenous vein as a valve substitute has been reported by Plagnol and associates. This approach invaginates a stump of the long saphenous vein into the femoral vein to fashion a bicuspid valve. Both experimental and clinical results have been reported.[70] They report 19 of 20 reconstructions to be patent and competent at a mean of 10 months. One valve demonstrated reflux because of insufficient valve size at the time of reconstruction. The invagination of an adventitial surface into the venous lumen is of some concern but not substantiated in this one report. Psathakis and Psathakis reported on a substitute "valve" operation using a Silastic tendon designed to produce an external compression of the popliteal valve (to prevent popliteal reflux) with relaxation of the calf muscles.[71] The technique has not gained wide acceptance, possibly owing to the difficulty in determining proper tension on the sling at the time of operation, concerns with scarring, and the lack of reports to substantiate the results of

these investigators. To date, only one other study reports comparable results after 2 years of follow-up.[72] Dr. Perrin has attempted this procedure in nine patients but poor clinical and hemodynamic results were obtained. He stopped using this procedure after 1 year.[73]

An attempt has been made at the use of a cryopreserved venous valve-containing allograft for the treatment of CVI. Initial experimental studies in a canine model were promising.[74] However, the feasibility study and 6-month results suggested that low-grade rejection may be affecting the patency and competency of these valve transplants.[75] Longer follow-up revealed poor patency rates and minimal clinical improvement in patients receiving the valve.[76] The authors concluded that the procedure may not even be advisable in a patient who has failed all other management.[76] A new cell-free cryopreserved allograft (SynerGraft, Cryolife, Inc.) appears to incite very little antigenic response as determined by panel reactive antibody (PRA) levels.[77] This may prove to be a viable option as a venous valve substitute, but one experimental article would suggest that seeding of the allograft with recipient cells may be required for long-term patency and competence.[78] A cadaveric cryopreserved pulmonary monocusp patch has been described as well, with reasonable clinical results in a small group of patients studied over several years.[79] Possibly retaining a significant portion of the recipient vein as one wall of the repair helps to explain the better results noted in this study compared with that noted when the entire vein was replaced.

Glutaraldehyde-preserved allografts have fared somewhat better in the experimental model than other valve substitutes. About a fourth were patent and competent in early follow-up.[80] Glutaraldehyde-preserved bovine tissues have been used with success in cardiac surgery, and the technology is available to use glutaraldehyde-preserved bovine venous valves of appropriate size in the human condition. Furthermore, the possibility of valve transplantation via a percutaneous route has been demonstrated to be feasible experimentally (Fig. 159-16).[81] In a swine model, a percutaneously placed glutaraldehyde-preserved bovine venous segment with a contained valve has demonstrated rather good early results.[82] These data have been sufficient to instigate clinical trials, but early thrombosis with this particular device has been discouraging. The result has been a design change now under study, which may prove fruitful.

Most recently, a bioprosthetic, bicuspid square stent-based venous valve has been developed and percutaneously placed in the external jugular vein of sheep in a feasibility study.[83] The valve has a small intestinal submucosa architecture with a metal frame that aids in incorporation of the valve into the vein wall. It appears to be somewhat resistant to thrombosis and does become repopulated with recipient endothelial cells after implantation.[83,84] This technique shows promise as a minimally invasive synthetic valve and may have future applications once further studies are performed to evaluate its use in humans.

Perioperative Management

Prophylactic antibiotics should be given during the procedure (e.g., first-generation cephalosporin) and continued postoperatively for 2 to 3 days. Intraoperatively, heparin is

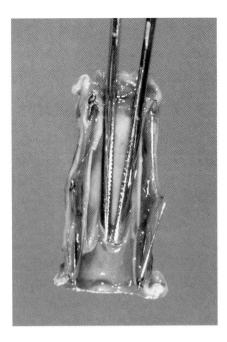

FIGURE 159-16 An experimental venous valve transplant placed percutaneously into a canine model. Note the valve cusps are present and of normal architecture within the patent vein segment in which they reside. The valved vein segment was placed on a metallic Z-stent exoskeleton.

given (2,000 to 10,000 units) based on the need for venotomy or clamp-times on the vein. Heparin should not be reversed at the end of the procedure. Pneumatic compression devices should be applied to all patients postoperatively to decrease swelling and the risk of deep venous thrombosis and may increase the flow over the valve repair when the patient is not very active. Low molecular weight heparin or low-dose intravenous heparin should be started immediately postoperatively, making closed drainage of wounds necessary in many cases to avoid hematoma formation. Warfarin should be started by postoperative day 1, with an initial target International Normalized Ratio range of 2.0 to 2.5 for the first 6 weeks, then subsequently decreased to 1.7 to 2.0 until 4 months, at which point it is

stopped. Adjustments to this regimen should be made to accommodate for those with an increased risk of thrombosis. One suggested long-term regimen for anticoagulation in these patients is "minidose" warfarin, which utilizes daily doses of 1 to 2.5 mg to prevent thrombosis.[49,85] Although many surgeons encourage the use of compressive support after venous valve reconstructions, many patients do not comply and yet have experienced a good clinical response.[16,21]

Complications

Valve repair procedures are well tolerated by most patients and have a low morbidity as well as essentially zero mortality in most series.[14] Hematoma and seroma formation is seen in up to 15% of cases, with some expected variation according to the level of anticoagulation necessary.[21,54,86,87] Deep venous thrombosis occurs in less than 10% of cases in most series.[21,49,54,86,87] Recently, evidence has been presented that suggests this figure may underestimate the occurrence of thrombosis after venous valve repairs.[73] This series had an incidence of clot noted in the extremity of repair (often not occlusive nor extensive) of approximately 20% detected by ascending venogram 2 days postoperatively. These events did not appear to have an impact on clinical results.[73] Wound infections have been seen in 2% to 4% of cases.[21,49,54]

Results

Kistner and colleagues have followed their patients requiring internal valvuloplasty for decades and have reported life-table results of clinical success (Fig. 159-17). Table 159-1 is a compilation of series reporting their success with internal valvuloplasty. It confirms the excellent clinical results in patients who otherwise have experienced unrelenting sequelae as a result of CDVVI. Valve competency is 60% to 70% at 5 years in most series. In general, a patent and competent valve translates into clinical improvement, whereas recurrent reflux is associated with clinical failure. A similar commentary can be made about all types of venous valvular reconstruction.

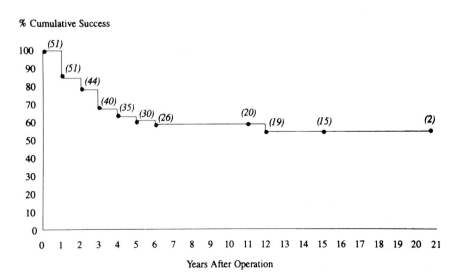

FIGURE 159-17 Cumulative clinical success rates for class 0 or 1 patients after venous valve reconstruction for all limbs. Numbers in parentheses represent total limbs at risk for each time interval. (From Masuda EM, Kistner RL: Long-term results of venous valve reconstruction: A four- to twenty-one-year follow-up. J Vasc Surg 19:394, 1994.)

Table 159-1   Results of Internal Valvuloplasty

AUTHOR(S) (YEAR)	MAIN SITE	NO. LIMBS	FOLLOW-UP (mo) (AVERAGE)	NO. PVI	NO. COMPETENT*	NO. PATENT*	NO. SYMPTOM RECURRENCE/ UNCHANGED†	HEMODYNAMIC IMPROVEMENT‡
Kistner (1975)[88]	FV	15	36-84 (60)	0/15	5/14	14/14	2/15	
Ferris and Kistner (1982)[89]	FV	32	12-156 (72)		16/22		6/32	7/8
Raju (1983)[51]	FV	15	3-40		15/15§			
					4/5‖			10/15
Eriksson and Almgren (1986)[25]	FV	19	84 (44)	19/19	13/19		5/19	12/19
Cheatle and Perrin (1994)[45]	FV	52	3-54	40/52	46/52¶	48/52¶	7/51	40/42¶
					23/27**	26/27**		24/25**
Masuda and Kistner (1994)[21]	FV	32	48-256 (127)		24/31		9/32	
Raju et al (1996)[30]	FV	81	12-144		30/71		16/68	
Lurie et al (1997)[90]	FV	49	36-108 (74)				18/49	
Perrin (1997)[91]	FV	75	24-96 (58)	55/75		50/74	6/33	54/74
Perrin et al (1999)[92]	FV	33	24-96 (51)	22/33	22/33		6/33	16/27
Perrin (2000)[73]	FV	85	12-96 (58)	65/85	51/83		10/35	43/68
Tripathi and Ktenidis (2001)[53]	FV	25	1-12 (6)	25/25	35/41	39/41	4/25	

PVI, Primary venous insufficiency (determined by the authors based on a lack of venous thrombosis detected in the patients); FV, femoral vein.
*Determined by venogram or Doppler/duplex ultrasonography.
†Includes skin changes, edema, pain, and ulcer recurrence.
‡Determined by plethysmography or ambulatory venous pressure measurements (improvement in hemodynamic tests postoperatively when compared with preoperative values).
§Determined by Doppler ultrasonography.
‖Determined by venography.
¶Immediately after surgery.
**Twelve months after surgery.

Table 159-2 provides a synopsis of the results one can anticipate when valve transplantation is required to treat CDVVI. Clinical improvement is seen in about 50% of patients even at 8 years of follow-up, and it remains a good option in cases in which valvuloplasty is not possible.[13,14,54]

Table 159-3 tabulates the results of transposition operations. Good results with the technique of valve transposition have been observed in 40% to 50% of patients after 5 years of follow-up.[14,21]

In general, patients with post-thrombotic reflux tend to have more problems maintaining healed ulcers than those with a primary etiology of reflux, as noted from the results of internal valvuloplasty (generally a primary etiology) versus those requiring transplantation or a transposition operative approach. Although Raju and associates find little difference between the post-thrombotic and primary patient results in their series,[20,30] which may reflect a delay in the appearance of ulceration after valve failure, these same investigators are some of a few with a high-volume experience in a variety of venous valve repairs and do report a difference in valve competence based on method of repair (Fig. 159-18). It would appear that there is decreasing durability as one progresses from internal valvuloplasty, to external valvuloplasty, and, finally, to a need for transplantation.

■ SUMMARY

The surgical treatment of CDVVI is a developing field with many options available for these patients. Preoperative evaluation should identify the specific disease process affecting the venous system. Of the available surgical techniques to treat patients with primary deep vein valve incompetence, internal valvuloplasty currently has the best track record, followed by external banding or valvuloplasty in select patients. The transcommissural valvuloplasty appears to achieve superior results to a standard external valvuloplasty. For management of the post-thrombotic syndrome resulting in deep vein valve incompetence, valve transplantation should be attempted, with transposition remaining useful only in select patients with a competent valve in the area. More experience with other developing techniques is required before we can recommend them for routine use. Research is ongoing in the field of valve substitutes. Diligent long-term follow-up and constant evaluation of the patient's clinical status are important to achieve a complete understanding of the clinical and hemodynamic impact of these repairs. Furthermore, new investigations should attempt to use quality of life measures, clinical severity scoring, and other tools to quantify the benefit of the treatment chosen and to allow a more informed comparison of various treatment options.

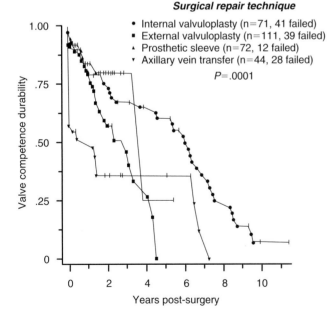

Surgical repair technique
- Internal valvuloplasty (n=71, 41 failed)
- External valvuloplasty (n=111, 39 failed)
- Prosthetic sleeve (n=72, 12 failed)
- Axillary vein transfer (n=44, 28 failed)

$P=.0001$

FIGURE 159-18 Actuarial durability of various valve reconstruction techniques assessed by serial duplex examination for competence. (From Raju S, Fredericks RK, Neglen PN, Bass JD: Durability of venous valve reconstruction techniques for "primary" and post-thrombotic reflux. J Vasc Surg 23:363, 1996.)

Table 159-2 Results of Valve Transplantation

AUTHOR(S) (YEAR)	MAIN SITE	NO. LIMBS	FOLLOW-UP (mo) (AVERAGE)	NO. PVI	NO. COMPETENT*	NO. PATENT*	NO. SYMPTOM RECURRENCE/ UNCHANGED†	HEMODYNAMIC IMPROVEMENT‡
Taheri et al (1982)[93]	FV	6	12	0/6	4/4	4/4	5/5§	5/5
Raju (1983)[51]	FV	21	3-40		2/14		10/21	10/13
Taheri et al (1986)[94]	POP	46	8-36		22/24	21/24	5/46	12/14
O'Donnell et al (1987)[28]	POP	10	>24		0/10	10/10	0/10	1/10
Nash (1988)[95]	POP	25	12-18	0/25	20/25	25/25	2/25	21/25
Rai and Lerner (1991)[96]	POP	12	6-24 (16)		6/6	9/9	0/12‖	11/12
Bry et al (1995)[29]	POP	15	15-132 (64)	0/15		14/14	3/14	
Perrin (1997)[91]	FV	30	12-120 (58)	1/30	6/20	6/20	8/20	
Sottiurai (1997)[97]		31	8-156 (74)		14/31		17/31	

PVI, Primary venous insufficiency (determined by the authors based on a lack of venous thrombosis detected in the patients); FV, femoral vein; POP, popliteal vein.
*Determined by venogram or Doppler/duplex ultrasonography.
†Includes skin changes, edema, pain, and ulcer recurrence.
‡Determined by plethysmography or ambulatory venous pressure measurements (improvement in hemodynamic tests postoperatively when compared with preoperative values).
§Four of five received skin graft.
‖Two patients required skin graft to heal ulcer.

Table 159-3   Results of Valve Transposition

AUTHOR(S) (YEAR)	MAIN SITE	NO. LIMBS	FOLLOW-UP (mo) (AVERAGE)	NO. PVI	NO. COMPETENT*	NO. PATENT*	NO. SYMPTOM RECURRENCE/ UNCHANGED†	HEMODYNAMIC IMPROVEMENT‡
Queral et al (1980)[26]	LSV	12	>3		9/12	10/12	1/12	11/12
Johnson et al (1981)[98]	LSV	12	12-18		2/2	2/2	9/12	3/12
Ferris and Kistner (1982)[89]	PFV/LSV	14	12-156		4/7		3/14	10/11
Masuda and Kistner (1994)[21]	PFV/LSV	14	48-256 (127)		4/14		7/14	
Perrin (1997)[91]	LSV	13	12-114 (49)	1/13	5/12§	5/12§	2/6	
Cardon et al (1999)[62]	LSV	16	29-56 (42)	0/16	12/15	15/16	5/16	

PVI, Primary venous insufficiency (determined by the authors based on a lack of venous thrombosis detected in the patients); LSV, long saphenous vein; PFV, profunda femoris vein.

*Determined by venogram or Doppler/duplex ultrasonography.

†Includes skin changes, edema, pain, and ulcer recurrence.

‡Determined by plethysmography or ambulatory venous pressure measurements (improvement in hemodynamic tests postoperatively when compared with preoperative values).

§Reported as patent and competent (not subdivided).

■ REFERENCES

1. Brand FN, Dannenberg AL, Abbott RD, Kannel WB: The epidemiology of varicose veins: The Framingham Study. Am J Prev Med 4:96-101, 1988.

2. Coon WW, Willis PW, Keller JB: Venous thromboembolism and other venous disease in the Tecumseh community health study. Circulation 48:839-846, 1973.

3. Baker SR, Stacey MC, Jopp-McKay AG, et al: Epidemiology of chronic venous ulcers. Br J Surg 78:864-867, 1988.

4. Heit JA, Rooke TW, Silverstein MD, et al: Trends in the incidence of venous stasis syndrome and venous ulcer: A 25-year population-based study. J Vasc Surg 33:1022-1027, 2001.

5. Nicolaides AN: Investigation of chronic venous insufficiency: A consensus statement. Circulation 102:e126-163, 2000.

6. Mayberry JC, Moneta GL, Taylor LM Jr, Porter JM: Fifteen-year results of ambulatory compression therapy for chronic venous ulcers. Surgery 109:575-581, 1991.

7. Erickson CA, Lanza DJ, Karp DL, et al: Healing of venous ulcers in an ambulatory care program: The roles of chronic venous insufficiency and patient compliance. J Vasc Surg 22:629-636, 1995.

8. Darke SG, Penfold C: Venous ulceration and saphenous ligation. Eur J Vasc Surg 6:4-9, 1992.

9. Barwell JR, Taylor M, Deacon J, et al: Surgical correction of isolated superficial venous reflux reduces long-term recurrence rate in chronic venous leg ulcers. Eur J Vasc Endovasc Surg 20:363-368, 2000.

10. Labropoulos N, Leon M, Geroulakos G, et al: Venous hemodynamic abnormalities in patients with leg ulceration. Am J Surg 169:572-574, 1995.

11. Hanrahan LM, Araki CT, Rodriguez AA, et al: Distribution of valvular incompetence in patients with venous stasis ulceration. J Vasc Surg 13:805-811, 1991.

12. Kalra M, Gloviczki P: Surgical treatment of venous ulcers: Role of subfascial endoscopic perforator vein ligation. Surg Clin North Am 83:671-705, 2003.

13. O'Donnell TF: Chronic venous insufficiency: An overview of epidemiology, classification, and anatomic considerations. Semin Vasc Surg 1:60-65, 1988.

14. Eklof BG, Kistner RL, Masuda EM: Venous bypass and valve reconstruction: Long-term efficacy. Vasc Med 3:157-164, 1998.

15. Plate G, Brudin L, Eklof B, et al: Physiologic and therapeutic aspects in congenital vein valve aplasia of the lower limb. Ann Surg 198:229-233, 1983.

16. Raju S, Fredericks RK, Hudson CA, et al: Venous valve station changes in "primary" and post-thrombotic reflux: An analysis of 149 cases. Ann Vasc Surg 14:193-199, 2000.

17. Budd TW, Meenaghan MA, Wirth J, Taheri SA: Histopathology of veins and venous valves of patients with venous insufficiency syndrome: Ultrastructure. J Med 21:181-199, 1990.

18. Sandri JL, Barros FS, Pontes S, et al: Diameter-reflux relationship in perforating veins of patients with varicose veins. J Vasc Surg 30:867-875, 1999.

19. Clarke H, Smith SR, Vasdekis SN, et al: Role of venous elasticity in the development of varicose veins. Br J Surg 76:577-580, 1989.

20. Kistner RL, Eklof B, Masuda EM: Deep venous valve reconstruction. Cardiovasc Surg 3:129-140, 1995.

21. Masuda EM, Kistner RL: Long-term results of venous valve reconstruction: a four to twenty-one year follow-up. J Vasc Surg 19:391-403, 1994.

22. Killewich LA, Bedford GR, Beach KW, Strandness DE Jr: Spontaneous lysis of deep venous thrombi: Rate and outcome. J Vasc Surg 9:89-97, 1989.

23. Masuda EM, Kessler DM, Kistner RL, et al: The natural history of calf vein thrombosis: Lysis of thrombi and development of reflux. J Vasc Surg 28:67-73, 1998.

24. McLafferty RB, Moneta GL, Passman MA, et al: Late clinical and hemodynamic sequelae of isolated calf vein thrombosis. J Vasc Surg 27:50-56, 1998.

25. Eriksson I, Almgren B: Influence of the profunda femoris vein on venous hemodynamics of the limb: Experience from thirty-one deep vein valve reconstructions. J Vasc Surg 4:390-395, 1986.

26. Queral LA, Whitehouse WM Jr, Flinn WR, et al: Surgical correction of chronic deep venous insufficiency by valvular transposition. Surgery 87:688-695, 1980.

27. Raju S, Fountain T, Neglen P, Devidas M: Axial transformation of the profunda femoris vein. J Vasc Surg 27:651-659, 1998.

28. O'Donnell TF, Mackey WC, Shepard AD, et al: Clinical, hemodynamic, and anatomic follow-up of direct venous reconstruction. Arch Surg 122:474-482, 1987.

29. Bry JD, Muto PA, O'Donnell TF, Isaacson LA: The clinical and hemodynamic results after axillary-to-popliteal vein valve transplantation. J Vasc Surg 21:110-119, 1995.

30. Raju S, Fredericks RK, Neglen PN, et al: Durability of venous valve reconstruction techniques for "primary" and post-thrombotic reflux. J Vasc Surg 23:357-367, 1996.

31. Raju S: Multiple-valve reconstruction for venous insufficiency: Indications, optimal technique, and results. In Veith FJ (ed): Current Critical Problems in Vascular Surgery, 4th ed. St. Louis, Quality Medical Publishing, 1992, pp 122-125.

32. Nicolaides AN (chair) and the Executive Committee of the ad hoc committee, American Venous Forum, 6th annual meeting. February 22-25, 1994, Maui, Hawaii: Classification and grading of chronic venous disease in the lower limbs: A consensus statement. In Gloviczki P, Yao JST (eds): Handbook of Venous Disorders. London, Chapman & Hall, 2001, pp 653-656.

33. Porter JM, Moneta GL, and an International Consensus Committee on Chronic Venous Disease: Reporting standards in venous disease: An update. J Vasc Surg 21:634-645, 1995.

34. Rutherford RB, Padberg FT Jr, Comerota AJ, et al: Venous severity scoring: An adjunct to venous outcome assessment. J Vasc Surg 31:1307-1312, 2000.

35. Lamping DL, Schroter S, Kurz X, et al: Evaluation of outcomes in chronic venous disorders of the leg: Development of a scientifically rigorous, patient-reported measure of symptoms and quality of life. J Vasc Surg 37:410-419, 2003.

36. Mattos MA, Summer D: Direct noninvasive tests (duplex scan) for the evaluation of chronic venous obstruction and valvular incompetence. In Gloviczki P, Yao JST (eds): Handbook of Venous Disorders. London, Arnold, 2001, pp 120-131.

37. vanBemmelen PS, Bedford G, Beach K, et al: Quantitative segmental evaluation of venous valvular reflux with duplex ultrasound scanning. J Vasc Surg 10:425-431, 1989.

38. Araki CT, Back TL, Padberg FT, et al: The significance of calf muscle pump function in venous ulceration. J Vasc Surg 20:872-877, 1994.

39. Cordts PR, Hartono C, LaMorte WW, et al: Physiologic similarities between extremities with varicose veins and with chronic venous insufficiency utilizing air plethysmography. Am J Surg 164:260-264, 1992.

40. Criado E, Farber MA, Marston WA, et al: The role of air plethysmography in the diagnosis of chronic venous insufficiency. J Vasc Surg 27:660-670, 1998.

41. Raju S: New approaches to the diagnosis and treatment of venous obstruction. J Vasc Surg 4:42-54, 1986.

42. Neglen P, Raju S: Proximal lower extremity chronic venous outflow obstruction: Recognition and treatment. Semin Vasc Surg 15:57-64, 2002.

43. Nicolaides AN, Hussein MK, Szendro G, et al: The relation of venous ulceration with ambulatory venous pressure measurements. J Vasc Surg 17:414-419, 1993.

44. Kistner RL, Ferris EB, Randhawa G, Kamida C: A method of performing descending venography. J Vasc Surg 4:464-468, 1986.

45. Cheatle TR, Perrin M: Venous valve repair: Early results in fifty-two cases. J Vasc Surg 19:404-413, 1994.

46. Kistner RL, Sparkuhl MD: Surgery in acute and chronic venous disease. Surgery 85:31-43, 1979.

47. Adam DJ, Bello M, Hartshorne T, London NJ: Role of superficial venous surgery in patients with combined superficial and segmental deep venous reflux. Eur J Endovasc Surg 25:469-472, 2003.

48. Camilli S, Guarnera G: External banding valvuloplasty of the superficial femoral vein in the treatment of primary deep valvular incompetence. Int Angiol 13:218-222, 1994.

49. Raju S, Hardy JD: Technical options in venous valve reconstruction. Am J Surg 173:301-307, 1997.

50. Kistner RL: Surgical repair of a venous valve. Straub Clin Proc 24:41-43, 1968.

51. Raju S: Venous insufficiency of the lower limb and stasis ulceration: Changing concepts and management. Ann Surg 197:688-697, 1983.

52. Sottiurai VS: Technique in direct venous valvuloplasty. J Vasc Surg 8:646-648, 1988.

53. Tripathi R, Ktenidis KD: Trapdoor internal valvuloplasty: A new technique for primary deep vein valvular incompetence. Eur J Vasc Endovasc Surg 22:86-89, 2001.

54. Raju S, Fredericks R: Valve reconstruction procedures for nonobstructive venous insufficiency: Rationale, techniques, and results in 107 procedures with two- to eight-year follow-up. J Vasc Surg 7:301-310, 1988.

55. Kistner RL: Surgical technique of external venous valve repair. Straub Found Proc 55:15, 1990.

56. Belcaro G, Nicolaides AN, Ricci A, et al: External femoral vein valvuloplasty with limited anterior plication (LAP): A 10-year randomized, follow-up study. Angiology 50:531-536, 1999.

57. Gloviczki P, Merrell SW, Bower TC: Femoral vein valve repair under direct vision without venotomy: A modified technique with use of angioscopy. J Vasc Surg 14:645-648, 1991.

58. Raju S, Berry MA, Neglen P: Transcommissural valvuloplasty: Technique and results. J Vasc Surg 32:969-976, 2000.

59. Taheri SA, Lazar L, Elias SM, Marchand P: Vein valve transplant. Surgery 91:28-33, 1982.

60. Raju S, Neglen P, Doolittle J, Meydrech EF: Axillary vein transfer in trabeculated post-thrombotic veins. J Vasc Surg 29:1050-1064, 1999.

61. Sottiurai VS: Supravalvular incision for valve repair in primary valvular insufficiency. In Bergan JJ, Kistner RL (eds): Atlas of Venous Surgery. Philadelphia, WB Saunders, 1992, pp 137-138.

62. Cardon JM, Cardon A, Joyeux A, et al: Use of ipsilateral greater saphenous vein as a valved transplant in management of post-thrombotic deep venous insufficiency: Long-term results. Ann Vasc Surg 13:284-289, 1999.

63. Calhoun AD, Baur GM, Porter JM, et al: Fresh and cryopreserved venous allografts in genetically characterized dogs. J Surg Res 22:687-696, 1977.

64. Hill R, Schmidt S, Evancho M, et al: Development of a prosthetic venous valve. J Biomed Mater Res 19:827-832, 1985.

65. Taheri SA, Rigan D, Wels P, et al: Experimental prosthetic vein valve. Am J Surg 156:111-114, 1988.

66. Taheri SA, Schultz RO: Experimental prosthetic vein valve: Long-term results. Angiology 46:299-303, 1995.

67. Dalsing MC, Lalka SG, Unthank JL, et al: Venous valvular insufficiency: Influence of a single venous valve (native and experimental). J Vasc Surg 14:576-587, 1991.

68. Rosenbloom MS, Schuler JJ, Bishara RA, et al: Early experimental experience with a surgically created, totally autogenous venous valve: A preliminary report. J Vasc Surg 7:642-646, 1988.

69. Reeves TR, Cezeaux JL, Sackman JE, et al: Mechanical characteristics of lyophilized human saphenous vein valves. J Vasc Surg 26:823-828, 1997.

70. Plagnol P, Ciostek P, Grimaud JP, Prokopowicz SC: Autogenous valve reconstruction technique for post-thrombotic reflux. Ann Vasc Surg 13:339-342, 1999.

71. Psathakis ND, Psathakis DN: Surgical treatment of deep venous insufficiency of the lower limb. Surg Gynecol Obstet 166:131-141, 1988.

72. Sun JM, Zhang PH: The substitute valve operation on the popliteal vein in the treatment of deep venous incompetence of the lower extremity. Vasc Surg.

73. Perrin M: Reconstructive surgery for deep venous reflux: A report on 144 cases. Cardiovasc Surg 8:246-255, 2000.

74. Burkhart HM, Fath SW, Dalsing MC, et al: Experimental repair of venous valvular insufficiency using a cryopreserved venous valve allograft aided by a distal arteriovenous fistula. J Vasc Surg 26:817-822, 1997.

75. Dalsing MC, Raju S, Wakefield TW, Taheri S: A multicenter, phase I evaluation of cryopreserved venous valve allografts for the treatment of chronic deep venous insufficiency. J Vasc Surg 30:854-866, 1999.

76. Neglen P, Raju S: Venous reflux repair with cryopreserved vein valves. J Vasc Surg 37:552-557, 2003.

77. Madden R, Lipkowitz G, Benedetto B, et al: Decellularized cadaver vein allografts used for hemodialysis access do not cause allosensitization or preclude kidney transplantation. Am J Kidney Dis 40:1240-1243, 2002.

78. Teebken OE, Puschmann C, Aper T, et al: Tissue-engineered bioprosthetic venous valve: A long-term study in sheep. Eur J Vasc Endovasc Surg 25:305-312, 2003.

79. Garcia-Rinaldi R, Soltero E, Gaviria J, et al: Implantation of cryopreserved allograft pulmonary monocusp patch: To treat nonthrombotic femoral vein incompetence. Tex Heart Inst J 29:92-99, 2002.

80. Kaya M, Grogan JB, Lentz D, et al: Glutaraldehyde-preserved venous valve transplantation in the dog. J Surg Res 45:294-297, 1988.

81. Dalsing MC, Sawchuk AP, Lalka SG, Cikrit DF: An early experience with endovascular venous valve transplantation. J Vasc Surg 24:903-905, 1996.

82. Gomez-Jorge J, Venbrux AC, Magee C: Percutaneous deployment of a valved bovine jugular vein in the swine venous system: A potential treatment for venous insufficiency. J Vasc Interv Radiol 11:931-936, 2000.

83. Pavcnik D, Uchida BT, Timmermans HA, et al: Percutaneous bioprosthetic venous valve: A long-term study in sheep. J Vasc Surg 35:598-602, 2002.

84. Brountzos E, Pavcnik D, Timmermans HA, et al: Remodeling of suspended small intestinal submucosa venous valve: An experimental study in sheep to assess the host cells' origin. J Vasc Interv Radiol 14:349-356, 2003.

85. Poller L, McKernan A, Thomson JM, et al: Fixed minidose warfarin: A new approach to prophylaxis against venous thrombosis after major surgery. BMJ 295:1309, 1987.

86. Welch H, McLaughlin RL, O'Donnell TF: Femoral vein valvuloplasty: Intraoperative angioscopic evaluation and hemodynamic improvement. J Vasc Surg 16:694-700, 1992.

87. Jamieson WG, Chinnick B: Clinical results of deep venous valvular repair for chronic venous insufficiency. Can J Surg 40:294-299, 1997.

88. Kistner RL: Surgical repair of the incompetent femoral vein valve. Arch Surg 110:1336-1342, 1975.

89. Ferris EB, Kistner RL: Femoral vein reconstruction in the management of chronic venous insufficiency: A 14-year experience. Arch Surg 117:1571-1579, 1982.

90. Lurie F, Makarova NP, Hmelniker SM: Results of deep-vein reconstruction. Vasc Surg 31:275-276, 1997.

91. Perrin MR: Results of deep-vein reconstruction. Vasc Surg 31:273-275, 1997.

92. Perrin M, Hiltbrand B, Bayon JM: Results of valvuloplasty in patients presenting deep venous insufficiency and recurring ulceration. Ann Vasc Surg 13:524-532, 1999.

93. Taheri SA. Lazar L, Elias SM, Marchand P: Vein valve transplant. Surgery 91:28-33, 1982.

94. Taheri SA, Elias SM, Yacobucci GN, et al: Indications and results of vein valve transplant. J Cardiovasc Surg 27:163-168, 1986.

95. Nash T: Long-term results of vein valve transplants placed in the popliteal vein for intractable post-phlebitic venous ulcers and pre-ulcer skin changes. J Cardiovasc Surg 29:712-716, 1988.

96. Rai DB, Lerner R: Chronic venous insufficiency disease: Its etiology: A new technique for vein valve transplantation. Int Surg 76:174-178, 1991.

97. Sottiurai VS: Results of deep-vein reconstruction. Vasc Surg 31:276-278, 1997.

98. Johnson ND, Queral LA, Flinn WR, et al: Late objective assessment of venous valve surgery. Arch Surg 116:1461-1466, 1981.

Surgical Treatment of Chronic Occlusions of the Iliac Veins and the Inferior Vena Cava

160

PETER GLOVICZKI, MD

JAE-SUNG CHO, MD

Valvular incompetence is the most common cause of chronic venous insufficiency (CVI) of the lower extremities; deep venous obstruction is responsible for signs and symptoms of venous congestion in less than 10% of patients.[1] Although the first successful venous reconstruction in a patient was reported more than 50 years ago by Warren and Thayer,[2] results of open surgical treatment for venous obstructions have been less than satisfactory for many years. Only in the past two decades have improvements in diagnosis, patient selection, and surgical technique and the availability of better graft materials resulted in more frequent successful implantation of venous bypasses in patients.[3] Results of venous grafting are, however, still inferior to those obtained with arterial reconstructions.

Endovascular treatment for iliocaval obstruction has progressed rapidly, and today venous stenting is the primary choice for treatment of benign iliac or iliocaval venous occlusions. Techniques and results of endovenous reconstructions are discussed in detail in Chapter 161. In this review, we discuss indications, patient selection, preoperative evaluation, techniques, and results of open surgical treatment of chronic iliac and iliocaval venous obstructions. We examine causes of graft failure in the venous system and list advantages of different adjuncts used currently to improve patency of venous grafts. The reader is referred to Chapter 163 for a discussion of vena caval reconstructions in treatment of malignant tumors and to Chapters 72 and 73 for details on venous reconstruction after abdominal or lower limb trauma.

■ ETIOLOGY

Deep venous thrombosis (DVT) is the most common cause of venous obstructions. In symptomatic patients, recanalization of the thrombosed veins in incomplete collateral circulation is inadequate and, in the infrainguinal veins, valvular incompetence due to destruction of the venous valve leaflets develops. Venous occlusion may also develop because of trauma or irradiation or as a result of external compression of deep veins by:

- Retroperitoneal fibrosis[4]
- Benign or malignant, primary, or metastatic tumors[5-7]
- Cysts
- Aneurysms
- Abnormally inserted muscle (popliteal vein entrapment)[8]

- Fibrous bands or ligaments (soleal arch syndrome,[9] femoral vein compression by the inguinal ligament[10])

Compression of the left common iliac vein by the overriding right common iliac artery (May-Thurner syndrome) (Fig. 160-1) is a frequently overlooked cause of left iliofemoral venous thrombosis.[11-14] May and Thurner observed secondary changes, such as an intraluminal web or "spur," in the proximal left common iliac vein in 20% of 430 autopsies. Congenital anomalies, such as membranous occlusion of the suprahepatic inferior vena cava (IVC) with or without associated thrombosis of hepatic veins (Budd-Chiari syndrome),[15] aplasia, and hypoplasia of the iliofemoral veins (Fig. 160-2) as in Klippel-Trenaunay syndrome,[16,17] can also cause CVI.

■ PREOPERATIVE EVALUATION

Preoperative evaluation of the patient should reveal the etiology and functional significance of deep venous obstruction and the extent and severity of associated venous incompetence. In at least two thirds of patients with venous outflow obstruction, however, distal reflux due to valvular incompetence contributes greatly to development of CVI.[18]

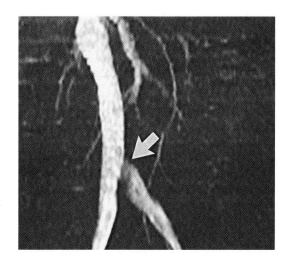

FIGURE 160-1 Magnetic resonance venography of the iliocaval bifurcation. *Arrow* indicates compression of the left common iliac vein by the overriding right common iliac artery (May-Thurner syndrome).

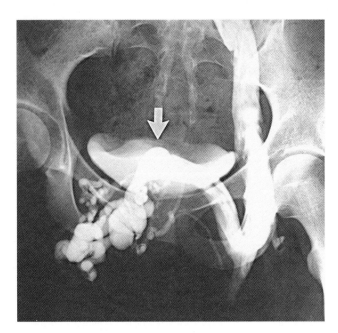

FIGURE 160-2 Venogram of agenesis of the right iliac vein in a 22-year-old woman. A large suprapubic venous collateral (*arrow*) drains the entire right lower extremity. (From Gloviczki P, Stanson AW, et al: Klippel-Trenaunay syndrome: The risks and benefits of vascular interventions. Surgery 110:469, 1991.)

For details of the clinical and diagnostic evaluation of the patients with CVI, see Chapter 155. The problems in establishing the presence of a pressure-significant venous obstruction are also detailed in Chapter 161. Specific aspects of the evaluation of patients who are candidates for open venous reconstructions with suspected deep venous occlusion are emphasized here.

History and Physical Examination

The history and physical examination, complemented by examination with a hand-held Doppler instrument, should reveal signs and symptoms typical of venous congestion. Patients with venous occlusion have swelling and experience exercise-induced pain in the thigh muscles, referred to as *venous claudication*. This pain is described as a "bursting" pain in the thigh and sometimes in the calf that occurs after exercise and is relieved by rest but more effectively by elevation of the legs.

Signs of CVI, such as edema, varicose veins, skin changes, lipodermatosclerosis, eczema, and ulceration, should be noted. Distended varicose veins are present even in the supine patient with CVI, and suprapubic and abdominal wall collaterals develop in patients with pelvic occlusion. Bleeding from high-pressure varicosities is not infrequent. The swollen leg has a cyanotic hue, and bilateral swelling indicates bilateral iliofemoral or vena caval occlusion or systemic disease. In some patients, venous congestion results in hyperhidrosis and significant fluid loss through the skin. Associated chronic high-output or low-output lymphedema (see Chapter 167) may also develop.

The patient's evaluation should identify risk factors of DVT, including the following:

- Previous DVT
- Pulmonary embolism
- Family history of venous thrombosis
- Obesity
- Decreased activity level
- Recent pregnancy
- Malignancy
- Hormonal treatment
- Hypercoagulability
- Recent trauma
- Surgical history

Associated chronic arterial occlusive disease as well as congenital venous malformation manifesting as limb hypertrophy, port-wine stains, and lateral atypical varicose veins (Klippel-Trenaunay syndrome) and the presence of a thrill or bruit indicating arteriovenous fistula (Parkes-Weber syndrome) should be excluded. Patients with membranous occlusion of the vena cava frequently have evidence of hepatic failure, Budd-Chiari syndrome, and portal hypertension as well.[15]

A simple technique to test femoropopliteal venous occlusion in the office is the Perthes test. A tourniquet is placed on the proximal calf, and the patient is asked to walk. Exercise results in rapid emptying of the superficial vein through patent perforators into a patent deep system. Distention of superficial veins distal to the tourniquet after ambulation indicates deep venous occlusion. Examination with a hand-held Doppler instrument also yields evidence for deep venous occlusion, but the diagnosis should be established by more accurate means, primarily duplex ultrasonographic scanning. A complete evaluation to establish the clinical class of venous disease is necessary.

Noninvasive Venous Evaluation

Although duplex scanning and plethysmography are the tests needed to establish deep venous occlusion and to determine the extent of valvular incompetence and calf muscle pump failure, it is equally important to exclude any abdominal or pelvic disease (tumor, cyst, retroperitoneal fibrosis) with computed tomography (CT) or magnetic resonance imaging (MRI). Outflow plethysmography is useful to confirm functional venous outflow obstruction and to document improvement after treatment.

Ambulatory venous pressure measurements suggest venous hypertension; and measurements of foot-arm pressure differences, as described by Raju,[19] quantitate venous hypertension. A resting arm-foot pressure differential greater than 4 mm Hg was considered evidence for significant obstruction justifying venous reconstructions. For purposes of testing, exercise consists of 10 dorsiflexions of the ankles or 20 isometric contractions of the calf muscle. In potential candidates for proximal venous reconstruction, femoral and central venous pressure measurements are required in our practice to document the severity of proximal iliac or iliocaval obstruction. Either a pressure difference of at least 5 mm Hg between the femoral and the central pressures in the supine patient or a twofold increase in femoral vein pressure after exercise indicates hemodynamically significant proximal stenosis or occlusion.[20-24]

Less stringent criteria are accepted by Neglen and Raju to justify venous stenting of iliac veins, as discussed in Chapter 161.

Contrast Phlebography

In patients being considered for venous reconstruction, detailed contrast phlebography is performed. We use both ascending and descending phlebography to evaluate obstruction and any associated valvular incompetence.[22,23] Iliocavography and abdominal venacavography through a brachial approach may also be necessary in some patients to visualize the vena cava proximal to the occlusion. The femoral access is useful not only for descending phlebography and iliocavography but also for measuring femoral venous pressures. Magnetic resonance phlebography (see Fig. 160-1) is a promising technique that may further decrease the number of contrast radiographic examinations in the future. The technique of contrast phlebography is covered in Chapter 19.

■ FACTORS AFFECTING GRAFT PATENCY

Grafts placed in the venous system undergo thrombosis more frequently than those implanted for arterial reconstruction. This difference is attributed to several factors. Flow in venous grafts in general is lower than in arterial grafts placed at the same location, primarily because of the collateral venous circulation that developed to compensate for the chronic obstruction. Distal venous obstruction and incompetence further decrease inflow to the graft, contributing to potential failure.[18,23] Pressure in the venous system is low, and grafts can collapse under increased abdominal pressure or in tightly confined spaces, such as the area under the inguinal ligament and the retrohepatic space, or when tunneled through the diaphragm. Many patients with previous deep venous thrombosis (DVT) lack circulating anticoagulants, such as protein C, protein S, and antithrombin III, and thus have greater thrombogenicity. The thrombogenic surface of the prosthetic graft also increases the risk of graft failure.

■ VENOUS GRAFTS AND ADJUNCTS TO IMPROVE PATENCY

As a result of extensive laboratory efforts made in the past decades,[25-38] patency of grafts implanted in the venous circulation has considerably improved. The availability of large-diameter autologous and prosthetic grafts, the use of adjuncts such as a distal arteriovenous fistula, rigid external support of the grafts, perioperative and postoperative anticoagulation, the use of perioperative intermittent-compression pumps, and postoperative surveillance with duplex scanning all have contributed to better patency and improved clinical outcome.

Venous Graft Materials

Autologous grafts for the femorofemoral or infrainguinal location have the best chance of long-term success. The great saphenous vein, because of its low thrombogenicity and its suitability in size and length, is the best choice, when it is available. As a spiral or panel graft, it can be used for large vein reconstruction as well, although in our experience these grafts do not perform as well for iliocaval reconstructions as they do for superior vena caval replacement (see Chapter 164).[22,23] The contralateral superficial femoral vein and the arm veins, especially the basilic-brachial-axillary vein, are other potential sources of autogenous grafts, as are the external and, occasionally, even the internal jugular veins. Harvesting contralateral deep veins in patients with a history of DVT, however, may be the source of significant added morbidity.

Experiments with cryopreserved femoral vein grafts were promising,[39] but one small clinical trial that used cryopreserved veins for valve replacement was not very successful. At 6 months, the actuarial secondary patency rate was 78% ± 13% and the secondary competency rate of the transplanted valves was 67% ± 16%.[40] Data at this point are insufficient to support recommendation of this graft for routine clinical use.

Of the available prosthetic materials, the expanded polytetrafluoroethylene (ePTFE) graft has been used most frequently for large vein replacement.[4-7,21-23,41-49] Because of a large diameter, sufficient length, immediate availability, and the external ring or spiral support associated with relatively low thrombogenicity, ePTFE grafts continue to be the best choice for prosthetic replacement of large veins.

Experimental work in a canine model showed that seeding the prosthetic grafts with endothelial cells inhibited neointimal hyperplasia and achieved 100% patency of IVC grafts at 100 days.[50] This was thought to be related to a higher level of prostaglandin I_2 metabolite and a lower level of thromboxane B_2 metabolite from the seeded grafts compared with spontaneously formed cells. Clinical correlation was also observed in that 10 of 11 grafts were patent over a follow-up period of 6 to 11 years. Similar improvements in arterial beds have been reported with seeding of prosthetic grafts with endothelial cells.[51] Endothelial seeding of grafts may improve graft patency and long-term clinical outcome.

Arteriovenous Fistula

Multiple experiments have confirmed that a distal arteriovenous fistula, first suggested by Kunlin and Kunlin[30] in 1953, improves patency of grafts placed in the venous system.[25,28,33,34,52,53] An arteriovenous fistula increases flow and decreases platelet and fibrin deposition in prosthetic grafts (Fig. 160-3).[33] Prosthetic grafts have significantly higher thrombotic threshold velocity than autologous grafts and require higher flow to maintain patency.

Disadvantages of an arteriovenous fistula include the longer operating time needed to create the fistula and the inconvenience of additional procedures to close the fistula at a later date by means of either endovascular techniques (embolization) or a cutdown. A potential side effect is an elevated cardiac output, caused by high fistula flow; the

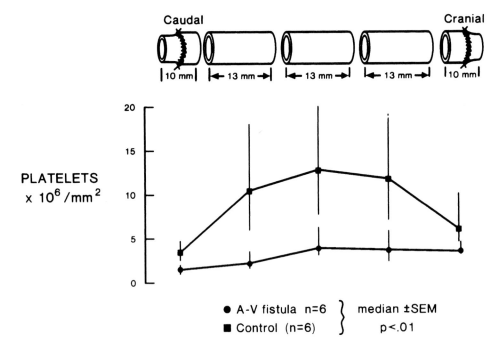

FIGURE 160-3 Platelet deposition on PTFE vena caval grafts in dogs with and without arteriovenous fistula 3 hours after perfusion. (From Gloviczki P, Hollier LH, Dewanjee MJ, et al: Experimental replacement of the inferior vena cava: Factors affecting patency. Surgery 95:657, 1984.)

latter can also defeat the purpose of the operation by increasing venous pressure at the groin and causing venous outflow obstruction. Experimental work in our laboratory revealed that to avoid deleterious effect on venous outflow from the leg, the optimal ratio between the diameters of the fistula and the graft should not exceed 0.3.[52] Elevated intraoperative pressure in the femoral vein after placement of a fistula should be taken as a warning sign, and the fistula diameter should be decreased through banding of the conduit.

The configuration and location of the fistula have been the subjects of much controversy. A large side branch of the great saphenous vein or the saphenous vein itself can be used to perform one anastomosis only. Most recently, we have placed the venous end of the arteriovenous fistula right onto the hood of the venous graft at the distal anastomosis, using either a 4-mm vein as a free graft (saphenous vein or a large tributary) or a 4-mm ePTFE graft. The advantage of a vein or a polyester (Dacron) fistula is that flow can be calibrated with an electromagnetic flowmeter and then large flows (>300 mL/min) can be avoided.

The arterial anastomosis is usually made to the superficial femoral artery. We place a small polymeric silicone (Silastic) sheet around the fistula to prevent healing and to facilitate dissection of the fistula during a second procedure to occlude it. A 2-0 polypropylene suture is also tied loosely around the fistula, and its end is positioned in the subcutaneous tissue, close to the incision, for later identification; intraoperative duplex scanning facilitates identification of the fistula. Percutaneous closure of the fistula with transcatheter embolization is also an option.

At present, for all prosthetic grafts anastomosed to the femoral vein and all longer (>10 cm) iliocaval grafts implanted at our institution, a femoral arteriovenous fistula is added to maintain patency (Fig. 160-4). The fistula is left open for at least 6 months after the operation, but patients without any side effects benefit from long-term fistula flow to prolong patency. For the Palma procedure, we use a fistula selectively and take it down within 3 months after surgery.

Thrombosis Prophylaxis

Intravenous heparin, in a dose of 5000 units, is given before cross-clamping, and anticoagulation is maintained during and after the procedure in most patients. We frequently administer low-dose heparin (500 to 800 units/hr) locally through a small polyethylene catheter in the perioperative period (Fig. 160-5), until complete systemic heparinization is achieved through an increase in the dose, as demonstrated by an increase in activated partial thromboplastin time to twice normal by 48 hours after surgery. The catheter is then removed, heparinization is continued intravenously through an arm vein or central line, or by using low-molecular-weight heparin, and the patient begins oral anticoagulation therapy with warfarin.

An intermittent pneumatic compression pump, leg elevation, elastic bandages, and early ambulation are also used in the perioperative period to improve the success of venous reconstruction.[54] The patient is fitted with 30- to 40-mm Hg graduated-compression elastic stockings before discharge. Warfarin is continued in patients with autogenous grafts for at least 3 months; in most patients with prosthetic grafts or with an underlying coagulation abnormality, however, oral anticoagulation is maintained indefinitely.

Graft Surveillance

Intraoperative duplex scanning is performed in most patients to ensure patency, good flow, and lack of thrombus depo-

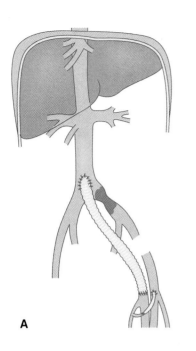

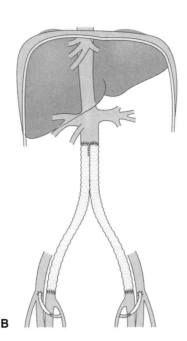

A   **B**

FIGURE 160-4 A, Artist's conception of a bifemorocaval PTFE graft with bilateral femoral arteriovenous fistula. **B,** Illustration of a left femorocaval ePTFE graft with a femoral arteriovenous fistula. (From Jost CJ, Gloviczki P, Cherry KJ Jr, et al: Surgical reconstruction of iliofemoral veins and the inferior vena cava for nonmalignant occlusive disease. J Vasc Surg 33:320, 2001.)

sition. Direct pressure measurements are made before wound closure in every patient with and without graft flow to document the hemodynamic benefit. In venous or polyester conduits, fistula flow can be measured and calibrated with an electromagnetic flowmeter. If flow is higher than 300 mL/min, banding of the fistula should be considered.

On the first postoperative day, we perform contrast phlebography through the catheter, which is positioned at the distal anastomosis of the graft (see Fig. 160-5). Any stenosis or thrombosis detected at this time is revised during a reoperation. Postoperatively, the grafts are observed with duplex scanning at 3 and at 6 months and then twice yearly afterward. Outflow plethysmography is also performed to document improvement. In symptomatic patients, however, contrast phlebography is usually performed to exclude graft stenosis.

■ INDICATIONS FOR SURGICAL TREATMENT

Failures of conservative management or endovascular treatment of symptomatic venous obstruction is a potential indication for open surgical reconstruction. The severity of venous stenosis, the location and length of venous occlusion, the age of the thrombus, the nature of any external compression (e.g., tumor, retroperitoneal fibrosis), any underlying malignant disease, and the risks of a surgical intervention all play a role in determining to attempt endovascular or direct surgical intervention.

Because of reported success of endovascular treatment[55-58] our policy has changed significantly in recent years. Today we attempt endovascular treatment, alone or in combination with thrombolysis, surgical thrombectomy, or excision of old thrombus from the femoral veins first, before a surgical bypass is recommended.

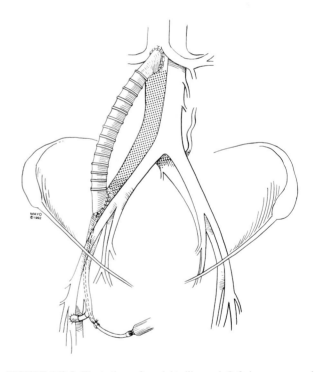

FIGURE 160-5 Illustration of a right iliac vein/inferior vena caval externally supported PTFE graft. Note the arteriovenous fistula at the right groin and a 20-gauge catheter, which is introduced through a tributary of the saphenous vein for perioperative heparin infusion. (From Gloviczki P, Pairolero PC, Toomey BJ, et al: Reconstruction of large veins for nonmalignant venous occlusive disease. J Vasc Surg 16:750, 1992. With permission of Mayo Foundation.)

Proper patient selection is important, and patients with severe infrainguinal post-thrombotic disease and valvular incompetence will have a decreased chance of success. It has been shown in a Mayo Clinic series of seven patients who underwent bypass grafting in the presence of moderate or severe venous incompetence that four had graft occlusion, whereas in four patients without reflux, three had patent grafts with clinical improvement.[23] Postoperative surveillance, anticoagulation, and arteriovenous fistula all predict better long-term results.

■ SURGICAL PROCEDURES

Saphenopopliteal Bypass

Although this chapter is devoted to iliofemoral venous reconstruction, it is worthwhile to mention briefly the saphenopopliteal bypass, designed for chronic occlusion of the femoral or the proximal popliteal vein. This operation was first advocated by Warren and Thayer[2] in 1954 and reintroduced by Husni[59] and May[60] in the 1970s (May-Husni operation). A single distal anastomosis is performed, usually end-to-side, between the mobilized and divided ipsilateral saphenous vein and the popliteal vein. A temporary arteriovenous fistula can be constructed at the ankle between the posterior tibial artery and one of the paired posterior tibial veins or even with the saphenous vein at the ankle, in an end-to-side fashion.[44,61] An alternative to the traditional technique of saphenous vein transposition is a popliteofemoral or popliteosaphenous bypass (Figs. 160-6 and 160-7) with a free graft that uses either the ipsilateral or contralateral saphenous vein or an arm vein.

The original May-Husni transposition is rarely performed now, and popliteofemoral bypasses are also uncommon. For nine reported series comprising 218 operated patients, functional improvement was reported in 77% of cases.[44,61-68] In an earlier review of 59 operations, Smith and Trimble[69] reported clinical success in 76% of patients. With the exception of one series,[67] cumulative patency rates have not been reported. Crude patency rates at variable follow-up intervals ranged from 5% to 100%, but only four of the nine studies reported on late imaging of the grafts to ascertain patency[44,61-68] (Table 160-1).

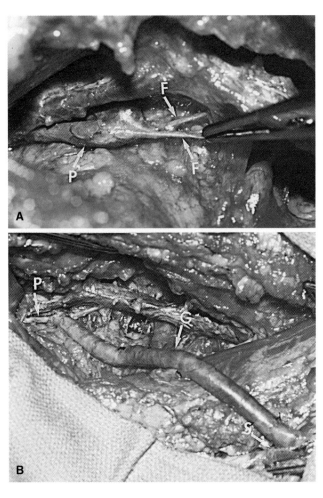

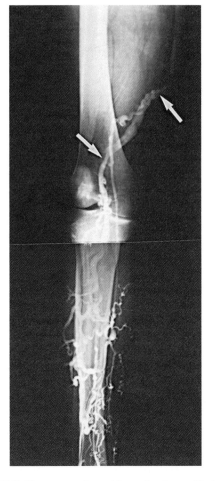

FIGURE 160-6 A, Klippel-Trenaunay syndrome with atresia of the right femoral vein in a 20-year-old patient. P, popliteal vein; F, fibrous bands replacing the superficial femoral vein. **B,** Intraoperative photograph of the contralateral saphenous vein graft interposed between the patient's popliteal and proximal great saphenous vein. P, popliteal vein; G, vein graft; S, great saphenous vein. (From Gloviczki P, Stanson AW, Stickler GB, et al: Klippel-Trenaunay syndrome: The risks and benefits of vascular interventions. Surgery 110:469-479, 1991.)

FIGURE 160-7 Venogram performed 5 months after popliteal saphenous vein interposition graft. *Arrows* indicate proximal and distal anastomoses of the patent graft. Note absence of the right femoral vein. The vein has been patent and competent at 8 years, 6 months. (From Gloviczki P, Stanson AW, Stickler GB, et al: Klippel-Trenaunay syndrome: The risks and benefits of vascular interventions. Surgery 110:469, 1991.)

Table 160-1   Published Results of Femorofemoral Crossover Bypass

FIRST AUTHOR	YEAR	NO. OF LIMBS	FOLLOW-UP (yr)	POSTOPERATIVE IMAGING (%)	PATENCY RATE (%)	CLINICAL IMPROVEMENT (%)	GRAFT MATERIAL
Palma[71]	1960	8	Up to 3	13	N/A	88	Vein
Dale[63]	1979	48	Up to 12	N/A	N/A	77	Vein
May[21]	1981	66	N/A	N/A	73	N/A	Vein
Dale[90]	1969	56	N/A	N/A	N/A	80	Veins
Husni[64]	1983	85	0.5 ~ 15	N/A	70	74	Vein (n = 83) PTFE (n = 2)
Halliday[75]	1985	47	Up to 18	72	75 (5-year cumulative)	89	Vein
Danza[68]	1991	27	N/A	N/A	N/A	81	Vein
AbuRahma[67]	1991	24	5.5	100	75 (7-year cumulative)	63	Vein
Gruss[44]	1997	19	N/A	N/A	71	82 overall	Vein
		32	N/A	N/A	85		PTFE
Jost[53]	2001	18	2		Primary 77; secondary 83		Vein
		3			0		PTFE

Cross-Pubic Venous Bypass (Palma Procedure)

Initially described 40 years ago by Palma and Esperon[70,71] in Uruguay and popularized by Dale[65] in the United States, the Palma procedure has remained a useful technique for venous reconstruction in patients with proximal outflow obstruction (Fig. 160-8). This operation, which was designed for patients with chronic unilateral iliac vein obstruction of any etiology, requires a normal contralateral iliofemoral venous system to ensure venous drainage. Results have been better in the presence of intact inflow, when the affected limb has no infrainguinal obstruction or deep venous incompetence.

We favor this operation especially in young women who present with residual chronic iliac vein occlusion after acute left iliofemoral venous thrombosis that developed as a result of May-Thurner syndrome. The operation is indicated in patients who are not candidates for iliac vein stenting or failed previous endovascular procedures.

Technique

For the original operation, the contralateral great saphenous vein is used. Preoperative imaging of the potential graft conduit with phlebography or duplex scanning is recommended, because varicose saphenous veins or veins smaller than 4 mm in diameter have a poor chance of long-term success.

Endoscopic harvesting of a 25- to 30-cm segment of the contralateral saphenous vein ensures an excellent cosmetic result; otherwise, the vein can be dissected through two or three small skin incisions.

After ligation and division of all tributaries, the graft is gently distended (Fig. 160-9) with heparinized papaverine solution and is tunneled to the contralateral groin in a suprapubic, subcutaneous position. Dissection of the femoral vein on the affected side should be minimal; usually, just the anterior and lateral vein wall is freed up for proximal and distal clamps or for a side-biting clamp to

occlude the femoral artery for the anastomosis. Excision of intraluminal fibrous bands after venotomy may be needed. The anastomosis between the saphenous and femoral veins is performed in an end-to-side fashion with standard atraumatic vascular surgical technique. If the vein is small, interrupted 5-0 or 6-0 sutures are preferred to permit later dilatation of the vein and to avoid "purse-stringing" of the

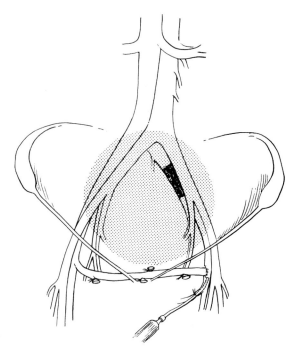

FIGURE 160-8 Left-to-right femorofemoral venous bypass (Palma procedure) for left common iliac vein obstruction. A small polyethylene catheter can be placed through a side branch of the greater saphenous vein for immediate perioperative heparinization to improve chances of patency. (From Rhee RY, Gloviczki P, Luthra HS, et al: Iliocaval complications of retroperitoneal fibrosis. Am J Surg 168:179, 1994.)

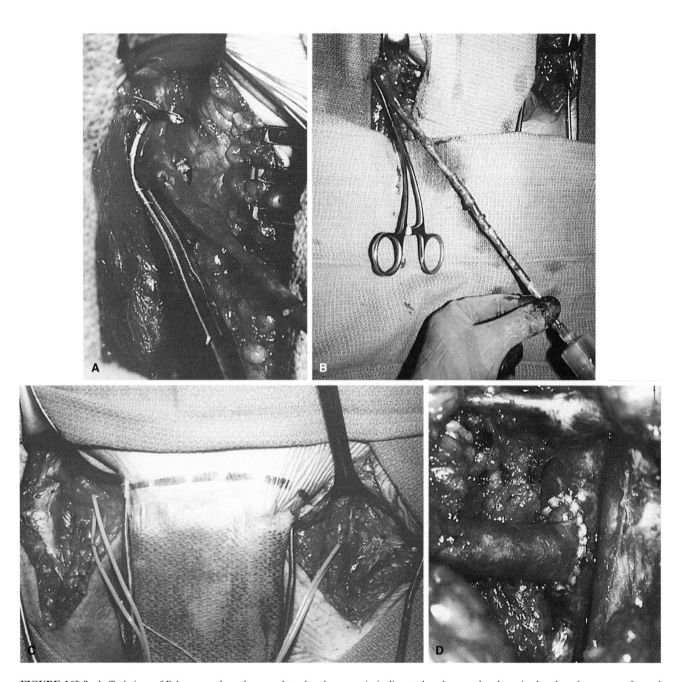

FIGURE 160-9 A, Technique of Palma procedure: the contralateral saphenous vein is dissected, and a vascular clamp is placed on the common femoral vein. **B,** The vein is distended with papaverine solution. **C** and **D,** The saphenous vein is tunneled to the left groin and anastomosed end-to-side to the common femoral vein. A femoral arteriovenous fistula was constructed and encircled with a Silastic sheath for easy identification for takedown 3 months later.

venous anastomosis. A small catheter can be placed through a tributary of the ipsilateral saphenous vein for immediate low-dose heparinization and postoperative phlebography (Fig. 160-10). A temporary arteriovenous fistula can also be placed to improve flow and to aid early patency.

If the traditional transposition results in significant kinking of the saphenous vein at the contralateral groin, free vein grafting should be considered, excising the saphenous vein with a small rim of the common femoral vein and reimplanting it after an 180-degree turn. For autologous graft material, the contralateral or even the ipsilateral saphenous vein (with lysis of any competent valve) or an arm vein can be used.

Kistner[72] reported another ingenious idea for an autologous suprapubic graft. Through a retroperitoneal approach, the ipsilateral iliac vein is mobilized to the site of the occlusion. The internal iliac vein is ligated and divided to provide adequate length for the conduit. The common iliac vein is then divided and used for suprapubic subcutaneous transposition, with a single anastomosis performed between the iliac and the contralateral femoral veins. This operation can be performed only in those patients who have short proximal common iliac vein obstruction.

When suitable autologous conduit is not available, an 8- or 10-mm, externally supported ePTFE graft is the best alternative.[44,73]

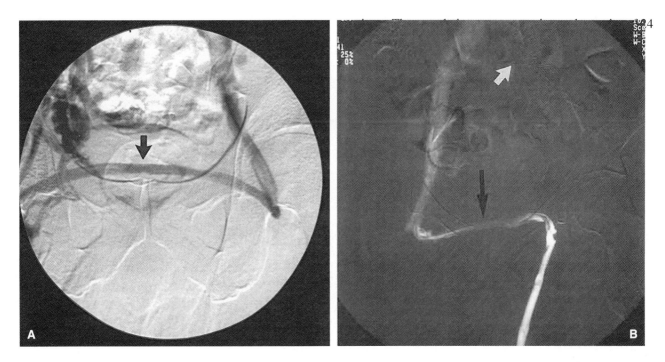

FIGURE 160-10 A, Postoperative venogram of a right-to-left femorofemoral crossover vein graft *(arrow)* (Palma procedure). **B,** Digital subtraction venogram of left lower extremity and pelvis showing a patent left-to-right Palma graft 6 months after operation *(dark arrow)*. Left iliac vein stent *(white arrow)* thrombosed before operation. (From Jost CJ, Gloviczki P, Cherry KJ Jr, et al: Surgical reconstruction of iliofemoral veins and the inferior vena cava for nonmalignant occlusive disease. J Vasc Surg 33:320-328, 2001.)

Results

Analysis of results of 412 operations published in nine series revealed clinical improvement in 63% to 89% of patients (Table 160-2).[21,24,44,63,64,67,71,74,75] Reported patency rates ranged between 70% and 85%, but follow-up periods were variable and objective graft assessment with imaging in all patients was rarely performed. The largest series, of 85 crossover venous bypasses, was reported by Husni.[64] At last follow-up visits, ranging from 6 months to 15 years after operation, 47 of 67 grafts were patent. Results in this study were better when a temporary distal arteriovenous fistula was used. Patency of grafts implanted for extrinsic compression of the iliac vein without distal disease was 100%, compared with 67% in patients with post-thrombotic syndrome.

In a review of 50 consecutive operations performed in 47 patients, Halliday and associates[75] reported a cumulative patency rate of 75% at 5 years confirmed by phlebography. Clinical improvement in this series was seen in 89% of patients was 75% at 7 years, but the standard error in these calculations was high because of the low number of patients studied. In the Mayo Clinic series of 18 saphenous vein grafts, 4-year primary and secondary patency rates of 77% and 83%, respectively, were noted; three crossover ePTFE grafts occluded within 12 months despite an adjunctive arteriovenous fistula.[53]

Danza and colleagues[68] noted somewhat better results with use of the saphenous vein as a free graft than with saphenous transposition. Eighty-four percent of 19 patients who underwent free saphenous vein grafting experienced either symptomatic relief or improvement as compared with 75% of eight patients who underwent transposition. Gruss[24] and Gruss and Hiemer[44] reported good results for ePTFE grafts. Although the length of follow-up was not mentioned, long-term patency was noted in 22 of 26 grafts. On the basis of these results and that of others, Gruss recommends using

						CLINICAL	
FIRST AUTHOR	**YEAR**	**NO. OF LIMBS**	**FOLLOW-UP (mo)**	**IMAGING (%)**	**PATENCY RATE (%)**	**IMPROVEMENT (%)**	**GRAFT MATERIAL**
Gloviczki[23]	1992	12	1 to 60	100	58	67	11 PTFE 1 Dacron
Husfeldt[91]	1981	4	4 to 30	100	100	100	PTFE
Dale[43]	1984	3	1 to 30	100	100	100	PTFE
Alimi[42]	1997	8	19.5 (mean)	100	88	88	PTFE
Jost[53]	2001	13	24		54		PTFE

Table 160-2 Published Results of Femorocaval/Iliocaval Bypass

PTFE, polytetrafluoroethylene.

externally supported ePTFE grafts with arteriovenous fistula for all cross-femoral venous bypasses.[24]

Plethysmographic evidence of outflow obstruction was an independent predictor of clinical outcome in the report by AbuRahma and coworkers.[67] Eighty-eight percent of their patients undergoing the Palma procedure who had abnormal preoperative maximum venous outflow showed significant clinical improvement, whereas 86% of those with normal preoperative maximum venous outflow had no improvement after operation.

Prosthetic Femorocaval, Iliocaval, or Inferior Vena Caval Bypass

Anatomic in-line iliac or iliocaval reconstruction can be performed for (1) unilateral disease when autologous conduit for suprapubic graft is not available or (2) bilateral iliac, iliocaval, or inferior vena caval occlusion. Extensive venous thrombosis (not infrequently after previous placement of a vena caval clip), tumors, and retroperitoneal fibrosis not responding to nonoperative therapy are potential indications. Failure of previous endovascular attempts and occlusion after placement of multiple stents also have been indications for bypass.

Technique

The femoral vessels (for the arteriovenous fistula or for the site of the distal anastomosis) are exposed at the groin through a vertical incision. The iliac vein or the distal segment of the IVC is exposed through a right oblique flank incision through the retroperitoneal approach. The vena cava at the level of the renal veins is best exposed through a midline or a right subcostal incision. The ascending colon is mobilized medially, and the vena cava is exposed retroperitoneally. The infrarenal IVC is reconstructed with a 16- to 20-mm graft, the iliocaval segment usually with a 14-mm graft, and the femorocaval segment with a 10- or 12-mm ePTFE graft. The arteriovenous fistula is constructed first in patients who undergo a long iliocaval bypass (see Fig. 160-5).

Short iliocaval bypass with significant pressure gradient can be performed without an arteriovenous fistula, as discussed previously. Reconstruction of the vena cava with a straight PTFE graft, if the inflow is good, is also usually performed without an additional arteriovenous fistula. In patients who undergo femorocaval bypass, we perform the proximal and distal anastomoses of the bypass first and then place the arteriovenous fistula before opening up the circulation through the graft. As discussed previously, we usually use a tributary of the greater saphenous vein. The operation is performed with the patient in full anticoagulation with intravenous heparin, and at the end of the operation, as mentioned, a small polyethylene catheter is placed to the level of the distal anastomosis to infuse low-dose heparin (500 units/hr).

Results

Experience with femorocaval or iliocaval bypass is limited, and only a few series are available (see Table 160-2). In a Mayo Clinic series of 13 such bypasses, primary and

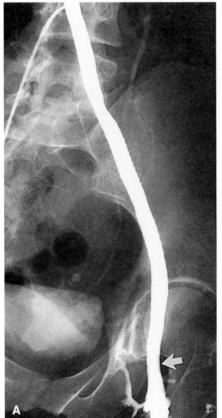
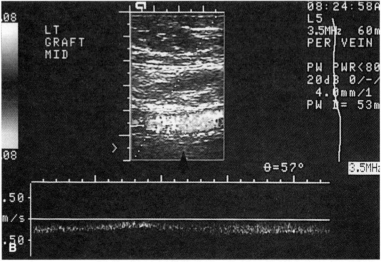

FIGURE 160-11 A, Venogram 1.6 years after implantation in a 36-year-old female patient confirms widely patent 10-mm PTFE graft. *Arrow* indicates site of the end-to-end femoral anastomosis. **B,** This patient is free of symptoms 10 years after the operation with duplex evidence *(arrow)* of graft patency.

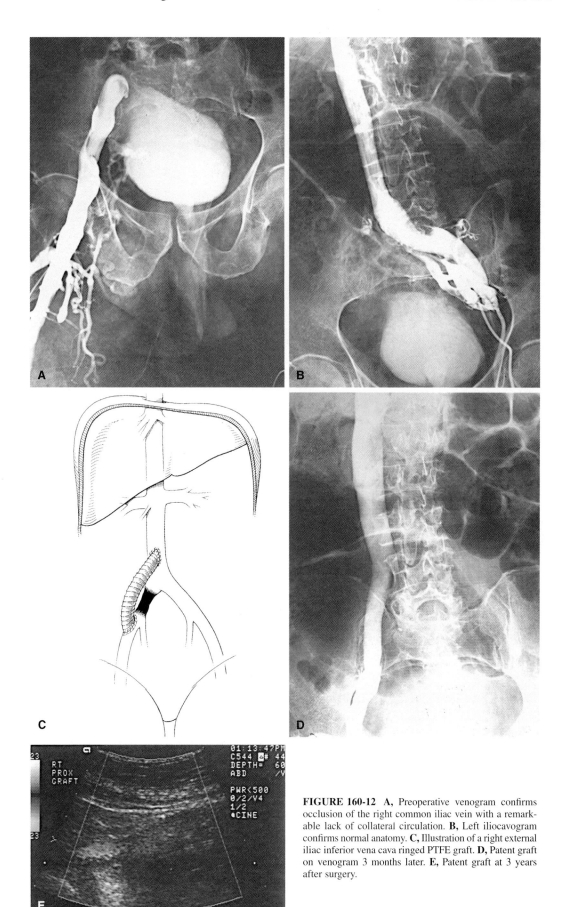

FIGURE 160-12 A, Preoperative venogram confirms occlusion of the right common iliac vein with a remarkable lack of collateral circulation. **B,** Left iliocavogram confirms normal anatomy. **C,** Illustration of a right external iliac inferior vena cava ringed PTFE graft. **D,** Patent graft on venogram 3 months later. **E,** Patent graft at 3 years after surgery.

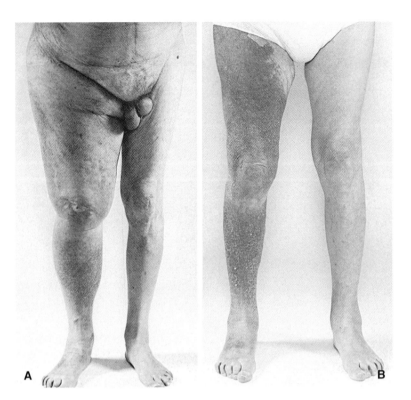

FIGURE 160-13   A, Preoperative photograph of an 81-year-old patient with severe right lower extremity swelling and massive transudation of fluid due to right common iliac vein obstruction (see venogram in Fig. 160-12). **B,** Photograph 9 months after the operation confirmed excellent clinical results.

secondary patency rates at 2 years were 37% and 54%, respectively (Figs. 160-11 to 160-15).[53]

Alimi and colleagues[42] reported results of eight iliac vein reconstructions with femorocaval or iliocaval bypasses for both acute and chronic obstructions. In the four patients who had chronic obstruction, three grafts were patent at last follow-up. Eklof and associates[76] observed only one occlusion in five grafts followed for 14 to 22 months after operation, in which bypass was combined with venous thrombectomy for acute DVT. Dale and associates[43] implanted the first iliocaval bifurcated PTFE graft in 1984, and our group reported on placement of a bifemorocaval bypass with bilateral arteriovenous fistulae in 1988.[22]

The largest experience with PTFE reconstruction of large veins was presented by Sottiurai (unpublished data).[77] Fifty-two of 56 grafts (93%), including 13 femorovenacaval grafts and 26 femorofemoral grafts, which were used for a variety of central vein reconstructions, were reported to be patent at 1 year after implantation. An arteriovenous fistula in this study was constructed with a saphenous vein between the adjacent artery and the graft. The site of the fistula was at 2 cm proximal to the distal heel of the graft, where an ovoid 4 × 10-mm defect was cut in the graft wall to standardize flow through the fistula. Dale did not favor the use of an arteriovenous fistula with PTFE grafts[41,53]; like Sottiurai,[67] however, we believe that all femorocaval or longer iliocaval grafts require the benefit of a distal arteriovenous fistula to maintain patency. Our policy now is to keep the fistula patent as long as possible.[52,53]

Combined Endovascular and Open Reconstructions

The combination of long iliac vein occlusions with chronic thrombosis of the common femoral vein precludes effective venous stenting. In these patients open surgical thrombectomy of the common femoral vein with excision of old thrombus and recanalized intimal strands can be combined with intraoperative iliac or iliofemoral vein stenting. We have performed these procedures in the endovascular operating room, which permits the combination of excellent imaging for venous stenting with optimal operating room environment for the open procedure. A saphenous vein or bovine pericardial patch can be used to close the defect after thrombectomy in the femoral vein (Fig. 160-16). Long-term results of these procedures are not yet available.

Iliac Vein Decompression

Compression of the left iliac vein between the right common iliac artery (see Fig. 160-1) and the fifth lumbar vertebra was described first by McMurrich[78,79] in 1908 and later in much more detail in a large autopsy study by May and Thurner, who also recognized the clinical implications of the iliac "spurs" leading to acute deep venous thrombosis.[11,79] Cockett and Thomas[12] coined the term *iliac vein compression syndrome* in 1965 and called attention to the obstructive symptoms in affected patients, who are often seen without clinical signs of previous DVT. May-Thurner syndrome is observed more frequently in females between the second and fourth decades of life.[4,12-14] Left leg swelling, venous claudication, pain, and chronic stasis skin changes, including rare ulceration, may develop.

An acute complication is left iliofemoral DVT. Although a literature review[72-74] found fewer than 100 reported cases, the true incidence of this condition, leading to left iliofemoral venous thrombosis, is most likely higher. Some surgeons suggest repair of any lesion discovered,[80-82] but we advocate reconstruction only for symptomatic patients, including those who already had an episode of acute DVT

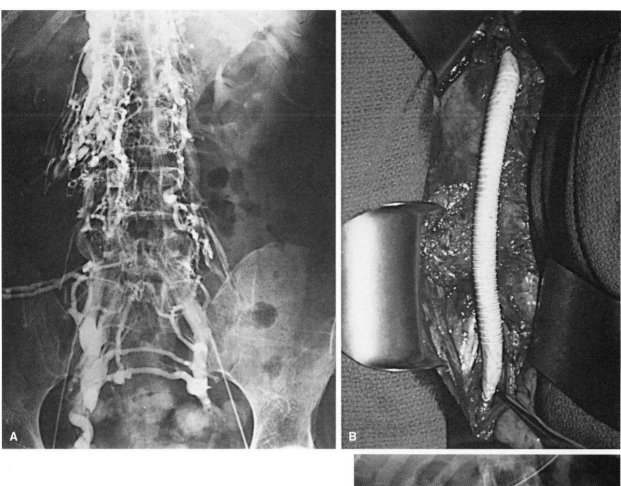

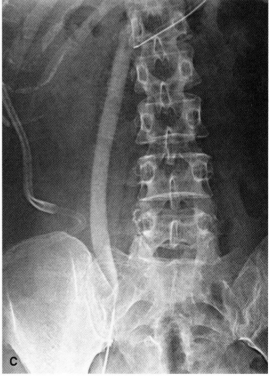

FIGURE 160-14 **A** and **B,** Extensive iliocaval obstruction in a 47-year-old patient treated with right iliocaval bypass with a right saphenous vein/common femoral artery arteriovenous fistula. **C,** Postoperative venogram shows patent graft.

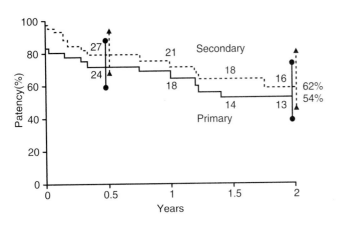

FIGURE 160-15 Cumulative secondary patency rates of saphenous vein crossover bypass grafts (Palma procedure) and ePTFE iliocaval and femorocaval bypass grafts. (From Jost CJ, Gloviczki P, Cherry KJ Jr, et al: Surgical reconstruction of iliofemoral veins and the inferior vena cava for nonmalignant occlusive disease. J Vasc Surg 33:320-328, 2001.)

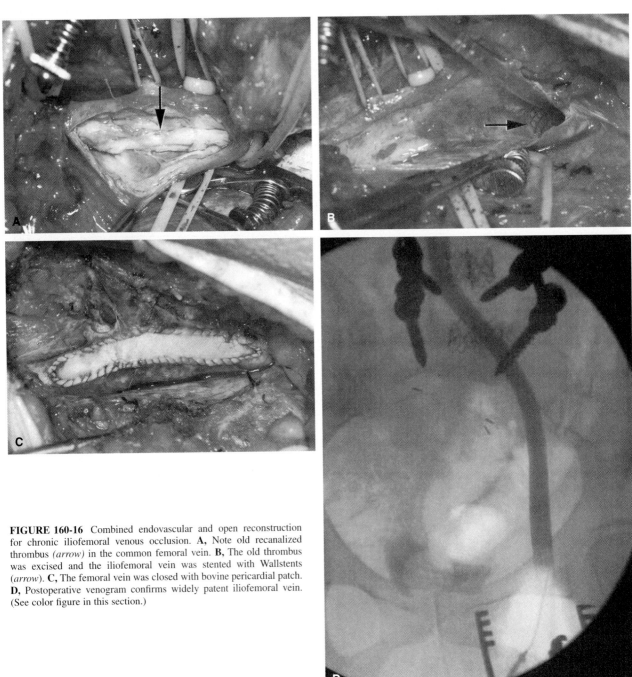

FIGURE 160-16 Combined endovascular and open reconstruction for chronic iliofemoral venous occlusion. **A,** Note old recanalized thrombus *(arrow)* in the common femoral vein. **B,** The old thrombus was excised and the iliofemoral vein was stented with Wallstents *(arrow).* **C,** The femoral vein was closed with bovine pericardial patch. **D,** Postoperative venogram confirms widely patent iliofemoral vein. (See color figure in this section.)

due to this condition. Endovascular techniques with stenting (see Chapter 161) should be considered as an alternative, although late results for such treatment are not available.

Technique

In patients with chronic obstructive symptoms (swelling, venous claudication), our first choice today is stenting of the iliac vein. If not possible or if stenting failed, decompression of the venous system with a Palma procedure is recommended. In patients with stenosis or short iliac occlusion, direct exploration of the vena caval bifurcation has been recommended, with the use of a variety of techniques to release the iliac venous obstruction. The iliac vein is fully mobilized, and any external compressing band is transected. Excision of any intraluminal web and vein or ePTFE patch angioplasty may have to be performed; other surgeons recommend transposition of the iliac artery behind the iliac vein.[49,80] Cormier[81] suggested transposition of the right common iliac into the left internal iliac artery to decompress the left common iliac vein. Placement of a silicone elastic bridge over the iliac vein to prevent the compression by the iliac artery, as suggested earlier, is not recommended.[82]

Results

Lalka[72] analyzed results of iliac vein decompression operations in detail, although lack of larger series in the literature and the use of a multitude of techniques make evaluation of these procedures difficult. It is likely that failed attempts at repair were not reported. In their review of the relevant literature,[63,80,82-87] Akers and colleagues[83] found that of 80 reported patients undergoing iliac vein decompression, 65 (85%) had significant improvement postoperatively.

Suprarenal IVC Reconstruction

The most common reason to reconstruct the suprarenal IVC for benign disease is membranous occlusion of the IVC, which is frequently associated with occlusion of the hepatic veins (Budd-Chiari syndrome), subsequent portal hypertension, and liver failure. Occlusion of the suprahepatic IVC usually does not cause significant congestion of lower extremity veins, although leg edema and venous claudication may still develop in affected patients. Although attempts to reconstruct the IVC with autologous grafts using a spiral vein graft or superficial femoral vein have been reported, most surgeons agree that an externally supported ePTFE graft is the best option for vena caval or cavoatrial bypass. If percutaneous transluminal balloon angioplasty, stenting, or transatrial dilation of the membranous occlusion has not been successful, and portosystemic shunting is not required, venacavoatrial bypass is an effective technique to decompress the IVC.

Technique

The retrohepatic segment of the vena cava and the right atrium are exposed through a right anterolateral thora-

cotomy, with extension of the incision across the costal arch so that the peritoneal cavity is entered through the diaphragm.[41] The liver is retracted anteriorly, and the paravertebral gutter is exposed together with the suprarenal segment of the IVC. The pericardium is opened anterior to the right phrenic nerve, and the right atrium is isolated. The IVC is cross-clamped with a partial-occlusion clamp above the renal vein, and a 16- or 18-mm, externally supported ePTFE graft is sutured end-to-side to the IVC with running 5-0 or 6-0 Prolene sutures. The graft is then passed parallel to the IVC up to the right atrium or the suprahepatic IVC. The central anastomosis is performed after placement of a partial-occlusion clamp on the vena cava or the right atrium. Before completion of the anastomosis, air is carefully flushed from the graft to avoid air embolization (Fig. 160-17A and B).

An anterior approach was suggested by Kieffer and associates,[48] who performed segmental replacement of the suprahepatic IVC by a short externally supported PTFE graft. Tunneling of a long cavoatrial graft in front of the bile duct and under the left lobe was also reported (see Fig. 160-17C).

Results

Wang and colleagues[15] reported on 100 patients with Budd-Chiari syndrome, 12 of whom underwent cavoatrial bypasses. Clinical improvement with patent graft was noted in 10 patients at a median follow-up period of 1.5 years after surgery. In their experience, Kieffer and associates[48] observed only one occlusion in grafts placed for membranous occlusion of the vena cava. In another series, Victor and colleagues[88] reported patent grafts at 21 months to 6 years after the operation in 5 patients.

Three cavoatrial grafts placed for nonmalignant disease were reported by our group: the patient with the ePTFE graft was asymptomatic at 10 years, the long Dacron graft became occluded at 3 years, and the spiral vein graft underwent occlusion within 1 year.[53] The reconstruction of the vena cava with PTFE grafts after resection of a primary or secondary malignant tumor invading the vena cava is detailed in Chapter 164.

■ SUMMARY

Progress in endovascular techniques has decreased the number of patients who are candidates for open surgical reconstruction for benign chronic occlusion of the iliac vein or the IVC. Proper patient selection, attention to technical details during the operation, selection of the appropriate graft, perioperative thrombosis prophylaxis, and close follow-up are important to achieve long-term success. The Palma procedure using the great saphenous vein is a good operation with predictable long-term success for patients with unilateral iliac vein occlusion. ePTFE grafting for iliac vein or IVC occlusion is also an effective tool in the treatment of carefully selected patients with advanced, symptomatic venous disease. Combined endovascular and open procedures will likely increase success of reconstruction of the large veins in the future.

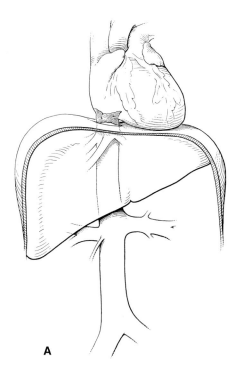

A

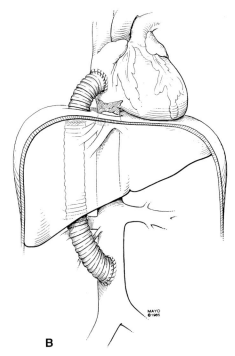

B

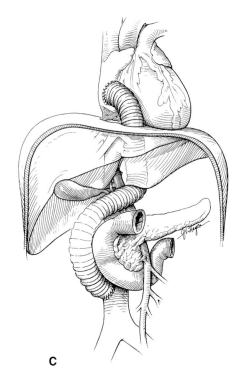

C

FIGURE 160-17 Different configurations of cavo-atrial bypass performed for membranous occlusion of the inferior vena cava. Reinforced PTFE graft can originate from the infrarenal (**A**) or suprarenal (**B**) inferior vena cava and be routed behind the right lobe of the liver. Another potential position of the graft is behind the left lobe of the liver (**C**). (With permission of Mayo Foundation.)

■ REFERENCES

1. Raju S: Venous insufficiency of the lower limb and stasis ulceration: Changing concepts and management. Ann Surg 197:688, 1983.

2. Warren R, Thayer TR: Transplantation of the saphenous vein for postphlebitic stasis. Surgery 35:867, 1954.

3. Bergan JJ, Yao JS, Flinn WR, McCarthy WJ: Surgical treatment of venous obstruction and insufficiency [review]. J Vasc Surg 3:174, 1986.

4. Rhee RY, Gloviczki P, Luthra HS, et al: Iliocaval complications of retroperitoneal fibrosis. Am J Surg 168:179, 1994.

5. Dzsinich C, Gloviczki P, van Heerden JA, et al: Primary venous leiomyosarcoma: A rare but lethal disease. J Vasc Surg 15:595, 1992.

6. Bower TC, Nagorney DM, Toomey BJ, et al: Vena cava replacement for malignant disease: Is there a role? Ann Vasc Surg 7:51, 1993.

7. Bower TC: Primary and secondary tumors of the inferior vena cava. In Gloviczki P, Yao JST (eds): Handbook of Venous Disorders: Guidelines of the American Venous Forum. London, Chapman & Hall, 1996, pp 529-550.

8. Rich NM, Hughes CW: Popliteal artery and vein entrapment. Am J Surg 113:696, 1967.

9. Servelle M, Babilliot J: Syndrome du soléaire. Phlebologie 21:399, 1968.

10. Gullmo A: The strain obstruction syndrome of the femoral vein. Acta Radiol 47:119, 1957.

11. May R, Thurner J: Ein Gefäßsporn in der Vena iliaca communis sinistra als Ursache der ubegend linksseitigen Beckenvenenthrombosen. Ztsch Kreislaufforschung 45:912, 1956.

12. Cockett FB, Thomas ML: The iliac compression syndrome. Br J Surg 52:816, 1965.

13. David M, Striffling V, Brenot R, et al: Syndrome de Cockett acquis: À propos de trois cas opérés dont deux forés inhabituelles. Ann Chir 35:93, 1981.

14. Steinberg JB, Jacocks MA: May-Thurner syndrome: A previously unreported variant. Ann Vasc Surg 7:577, 1993.

15. Wang Z, Zhu Y, Wang S, et al: Recognition and management of Budd-Chiari syndrome: Report of one hundred cases. J Vasc Surg 10:149, 1989.

16. Gloviczki P, Stanson AW, Stickler GB, et al: Klippel-Trenaunay syndrome: The risks and benefits of vascular interventions. Surgery 110:469, 1991.

17. Jacob AG, Driscoll DJ, Shaughnessy WJ, et al: Klippel-Trenaunay syndrome: Spectrum and management. Mayo Clin Proc 73:28, 1998.

18. Schanzer H, Skladany M: Complex venous reconstruction for chronic iliofemoral vein obstruction. Cardiovasc Surg 4:837, 1996.

19. Raju S: New approaches to the diagnosis and treatment of venous obstruction. J Vasc Surg 4:42, 1986.

20. Negus D, Cockett FB: Femoral vein pressures in post-phlebitic iliac vein obstruction. Br J Surg 54:522, 1967.

21. May R: The Palma operation with Gottlob's endothelium preserving suture. In May R, Weber J (eds): Pelvic and Abdominal Veins: Progress in Diagnostics and Therapy. Amsterdam, Excerpta Medica, 1981, pp 192-197.

22. Gloviczki P, Pairolero PC, Cherry KJ, Hallett JW: Reconstruction of the vena cava and of its primary tributaries: A preliminary report. J Vasc Surg 11:373, 1990.

23. Gloviczki P, Pairolero PC, Toomey BJ, et al: Reconstruction of large veins for nonmalignant venous occlusive disease. J Vasc Surg 16:750, 1992.

24. Gruss JD: Venous bypass for chronic venous insufficiency. In Bergan JJ, Yao JST (eds): Venous Disorders. Philadelphia, WB Saunders, 1991, pp 316-330.

25. Yamaguchi A, Eguchi S, Iwasaki T, Asano K: The influence of arteriovenous fistulae on the patency of synthetic inferior vena caval grafts. J Cardiovasc Surg 9:99, 1968.

26. Soyer T, Lempinen M, Cooper P, et al: A new venous prosthesis. Surgery 72:864, 1972.

27. Chiu CJ, Terzis J, Mac Rae ML: Replacement of superior vena cava with the spiral composite vein graft. Ann Thorac Surg 17:555, 1974.

28. Wilson SE, Jabour A, Stone RT, Stanley TM: Patency of biologic prosthetic inferior vena cava grafts with distal limb fistula. Arch Surg 113:1174, 1978.

29. Hobson RW 2nd, Wright CB: Peripheral side to side arteriovenous fistula. Am J Surg 126:411, 1978.

30. Kunlin K, Kunlin A: Experimental venous surgery. In May R (ed): Surgery of the Veins of the Leg and Pelvis. Philadelphia, WB Saunders, 1979, pp 37-75.

31. Hutschenreiter S, Vollmar J, Loeprecht H, et al: Reconstructive interventions of the venous system: Clinical evaluation of late results using functional and vascular anatomic criteria. Chirurgica 50:555, 1979.

32. Fiore AC, Brown JW, Cromartie RS, et al: Prosthetic replacement for the thoracic vena cava. J Thorac Surg 84:560, 1982.

33. Gloviczki P, Hollier LH, Dewanjee MK, et al: Experimental replacement of the inferior vena cava: Factors affecting patency. Surgery 95:657, 1984.

34. Plate G, Hollier LH, Gloviczki P, et al: Overcoming failure of venous vascular prostheses. Surgery 96:503, 1984.

35. Chan EL, Bardin JA, Bernstein EF: Inferior vena cava bypass: Experimental evaluation of externally supported grafts and initial clinical application. J Vasc Surg 95:657, 1984.

36. Robison RJ, Peigh PS, Fiore AC, et al: Venous prostheses: Improved patency with external stents. J Surg Res 36:306, 1984.

37. Koveker GB, Burkel WE, Graham LM, et al: Endothelial cell seeding of expanded polytetrafluoroethylene vena cava conduits: Effects of luminal production of prostacyclin, platelet adherence, and fibrinogen accumulation. J Vasc Surg 7:600, 1988.

38. Akimaru K, Onda M, Tajiri T, et al: Reconstruction of the vena cava with the peritoneum. Am J Surg 179:289, 2000.

39. Burkhart HM, Fath SW, Dalsing MC, et al: Experimental repair of venous valvular insufficiency using a cryopreserved venous valve allograft aided by a distal arteriovenous fistula. J Vasc Surg 26:817, 1997.

40. Dalsing MC, Raju S, Wakefield TW, Taheri S: A multicenter, phase I evaluation of cryopreserved venous valve allografts for the treatment of chronic deep venous insufficiency. J Vasc Surg 30:854, 1999.

41. Gloviczki P, Pairolero PC: Venous reconstruction for obstruction and valvular incompetence. Perspect Vasc Surg 1:75, 1988.

42. Alimi YS, DiMauro P, Fabre D, Juhan C: Iliac vein reconstructions to treat acute and chronic venous occlusive disease. J Vasc Surg 25:673, 1997.

43. Dale WA, Harris J, Terry RB: Polytetrafluoroethylene reconstruction of the inferior vena cava. Surgery 95:625, 1984.

44. Gruss JD, Hiemer W: Bypass procedures for venous obstruction: Palma and May-Husmi bypasses, Raju perforator bypass, prosthetic bypasses, and primary and adjunctive arteriovenous fistulae. In Raju S, Villavicencio JL (eds): Surgical Management of Venous Disease. Baltimore, Williams & Wilkins, 1997, pp 289-305.

45. Gloviczki P, Berens E: Vena cava syndrome. In Raju S, Villavicencio JL (eds): Surgical Management of Venous Disease. Baltimore, Williams & Wilkins, 1997, pp 397-420.

46. Gloviczki P, Pairolero PC: Prosthetic replacement of large veins. In Bergan JJ, Kistner RL (eds): Atlas of Venous Surgery. Philadelphia, WB Saunders, 1992, pp 191-214.

47. Kieffer E, Bahnini A, Koskas F, et al: In-situ allograft replacement of infected infrarenal aortic prosthetic grafts: Results in forty-three patients. J Vasc Surg 17:349, 1993.

48. Kieffer E, Bahnini A, Koskas F: Nonthrombotic disease of the inferior vena cava: Surgical management of 24 patients. In Bergan JJ, Yao JST (eds): Venous Disorders. Philadelphia, WB Saunders, 1991, pp 501-516.

49. Lalka SG: Venous bypass graft for chronic venous occlusive disease. In Gloviczki P, Yao JST: Handbook of Venous Disorders: Guidelines of American Venous Forum. London, Chapman & Hall, 1996, pp 446-470.

50. Wang ZG, Zhang H, Pu LQ, et al: Can endothelial seeding enhance patency and inhibit neointimal hyperplasia? Experimental studies and clinical trial of endothelial seeded venous prostheses. Int Angiol 19:259, 2003.

51. Meinhart JG, Deutsch M, Fischlein T, et al: Clinical autologous in vitro endothelialization of 153 infrainguinal ePTFE grafts. Ann Thorac Surg 71:S327, 2001.

52. Menawat SS, Gloviczki P, Mozes G, et al: Effect of a femoral arteriovenous fistula on lower extremity venous hemodynamics after femorocaval reconstruction. J Vasc Surg 24:793, 1996.

53. Jost CJ, Gloviczki P, Cherry KJ Jr, et al: Surgical reconstruction of iliofemoral veins and the inferior vena cava for nonmalignant occlusive disease. J Vasc Surg 33:320, 2001.

54. Hobson RW 2nd, Lee BC, Lynch TG, et al: Use of intermittent pneumatic compression of the calf in femoral venous reconstruction. Surg Gynecol Obstet 159:284, 1984.

55. Raju S, Owen S Jr, Neglen P: The clinical impact of iliac venous stents in the management of chronic venous insufficiency. J Vasc Surg 35:8, 2002.

56. O'Sullivan GJ, Semba CP, Bittner CA, et al: Endovascular management of iliac vein compression (May-Thurner) syndrome. J Vasc Intervent Radiol 11:823, 2000.

57. Hurst DR, Forauer AR, Bloom JR, et al: Diagnosis and endovascular treatment of iliocaval compression syndrome. J Vasc Surg 34:106-113, 2001.

58. Juhan C, Hartung O, Alimi YS, et al: Treatment of nonmalignant obstructive iliocaval lesions by stent placement: Mid-term results. Ann Vasc Surg 15:227, 2001.

59. Husni EA: Clinical experience with femoropopliteal venous reconstruction. In Bergan JJ, Yao JST (eds): Venous Problems. Chicago, Year Book Medical, 1978, pp 485-491.

60. May R: Der femoralisbypass beim ostthrombotischen Zustandsbild. Vasa 1:267, 1972.

61. Gruss JD: The saphenopopliteal bypass for chronic venous insufficiency (May-Husni operation). In Bergan JJ, Yao JST (eds): Surgery of the Veins. Orlando, FL, Grune & Stratton, 1985, pp 255-265.

62. Frileux C, Pillot-Bienayme P, Gillot C: Bypass of segmental obliterations of ilio-femoral venous axis by transposition of saphenous vein. J Cardiovasc Surg 13:409, 1972.

63. Dale WA: Reconstructive venous surgery. Arch Surg 114:1312, 1979.

64. Husni EA: Reconstruction of veins: The need for objectivity. J Cardiovasc Surg 24:525, 1983.

65. Dale WA: Peripheral venous reconstruction. In Dale WA: Management of Vascular Surgical Problems. New York, McGraw-Hill, 1985, pp 493-521.

66. O'Donnell TF, Mackey WC, Shepard AD, Callow AD: Clinical, hemodynamic and anatomic follow-up of direct venous reconstruction. Arch Surg 122:474, 1987.

67. AbuRahma AF, Robinson PA, Boland JP: Clinical hemodynamic and anatomic predictors of long-term outcome of lower extremity venovenous bypasses. J Vasc Surg 14:635, 1991.

68. Danza R, Navarro T, Baldizan J: Reconstructive surgery in chronic venous obstruction of the lower limbs. J Cardiovasc Surg 32:98-103, 1991.

69. Smith DE, Trimble C: Surgical management of obstructive venous disease of the lower extremity. In Rutherford RB (ed): Vascular Surgery. Philadelphia, WB Saunders, 1977, pp 1247-1268.

70. Palma EC, Riss F, Del Campo F, Tobler H: Tratamiento de los trastornos postflebiticos mediante anastomosis venosa safeno-femoral cotrolateral. Bull Soc Surg Uruguay 29:135, 1958.

71. Palma EC, Esperon R: Vein transplants and grafts in the surgical treatment of the postphlebitic syndrome. J Cardiovasc Surg 1:94, 1960.

72. Lalka SG: Management of chronic obstructive venous disease of the lower extremity. In Rutherford RB (ed): Vascular Surgery, 4th ed. Philadelphia, WB Saunders, 1995, pp 1862-1882.

73. Lalka SG, Lash JM, Unthank JL, et al: Inadequacy of saphenous vein grafts for cross-femoral venous bypass. J Vasc Surg 13:622, 1991.

74. Dale WA: Crossover vein grafts for iliac and femoral venous occlusion. Resident Staff Physician March:58-64, 1983.

75. Halliday P, Harris J, May J: Femoro-femoral crossover grafts (Palma operation): A long-term follow-up study. In Bergan JJ, Yao JST (eds): Surgery of the Veins. Orlando, FL, Grune & Stratton, 1985, pp 241-254.

76. Eklof B, Broome A, Einarsson E: Venous reconstruction in acute iliac vein obstruction using ePTFE grafts. In May R, Weber J (eds): Pelvic and Abdominal Veins. Amsterdam, Excerpta Medica, 1981, pp 241-245.

77. Sottiurai VS, Gonzales J, Cooper M, et al: A new concept of arteriovenous fistula in venous bypass requiring no fistula interruption: Surgical technique and long-term results. (unpublished data, 2000)

78. McMurrich JP: The occurrence of congenital adhesions in the common iliac veins and their relation to thrombosis of the femoral and iliac veins. Am J Med Sci 135:342, 1908.

79. May R, Thurner J: The cause of predominantly sinistral occurrence of thrombosis of the pelvic veins. Angiology 8:419, 1957.

80. Taheri SA, Williams J, Powell S, et al: Iliocaval compression syndrome. Am J Surg 154:169-172, 1987.

81. Cormier JM, Fichelle JM, Vennin J, et al: Atherosclerotic occlusive disease of the superior mesenteric artery: Late results of reconstructive surgery. Ann Vasc Surg 510, 1991.

82. Trimble C, Bernstein EF, Pomerantz M, Eiseman B: A prosthetic bridging device to relieve iliac venous compression. Surg Forum 23:249, 1975.

83. Akers DLJ, Creado B, Hewitt RL: Iliac vein compression syndrome: Case report and review of the literature [see comments]. J Vasc Surg 24:477, 1996.

84. Rigas A, Vomvoyannis A, Tsardakas E: Iliac compression syndrome. J Cardiovasc Surg (Torino) 11:389, 1970.

85. Reasbeck PG, Reasbeck JC: Iliac compression syndrome: A myth, a rarity or a condition frequently missed? N Z Med J 96:383, 1983.

86. Welter HF, Becker HM: Therapy of the pelvic venous spur and postoperative follow-up. In May R, Weber J (eds): Pelvic and Abdominal Veins: Progress in Diagnostics and Therapy. Amsterdam, Excerpta Medica, 1981, p 172.

87. Jaszczak P, Mathiesen FR: The iliac compression syndrome. Acta Chir Scand 144:133, 1978.

88. Victor S, Jayanthi V, Kandasamy I, et al: Retrohepatic cavoatrial bypass for coarctation of inferior vena cava with a polytetrafluoroethylene graft. J Thorac Cardiovasc Surg 91:99, 1986.

89. Dale WA, Harris J: Cross-over vein grafts for iliac and femoral venous occlusion. Ann Surg 168:319, 1969.

90. Husfeldt KJ: Venous replacement with Gore-Tex prosthesis: Experimental and first clinical results. In May R, Weber J (eds): Pelvic and Abdominal Veins: Progress in Diagnostics and Therapy. International Congress Series 550. Amsterdam, Excerpta Medica, 1981, pp 249-258.

Endovascular Treatment of Chronic Occlusions of the Iliac Veins and the Inferior Vena Cava

161

PETER NEGLÉN, MD

SESHADRI RAJU, MD, PhD

Following the success of endovascular interventions in the arterial tree, endovenous therapy using balloon venoplasty and stenting for venous obstructions was introduced in the late 1980s and early 1990s. It was soon realized that experience acquired with endovascular treatment of arterial obstructive disease could not necessarily be transferred directly to the venous system. For example, initial studies showed that balloon venoplasty alone led to early restenosis and that immediate recoil of the iliac vein was observed in the majority of limbs.[1-4] Contrary to the case with endovascular treatment of arterial obstruction, we recommend placement of a stent with all endovascular interventions performed to correct chronic iliac or iliocaval venous obstruction. Insertion of venous stents is widely performed today, and it has dramatically altered the management of pelvic venous outflow obstruction. Owing to the increased availability, minimal invasiveness, low morbidity and mortality, a 4-year acceptable patency, and substantial sustained clinical improvement, venous stenting has largely replaced bypass surgery. It is now considered the initial "method of choice" for chronic iliofemoral venous obstruction. This technique provides a less invasive and relatively safer alternative to open surgery and can therefore be offered to a larger group of patients. In case of immediate or late failure, venous stenting does not preclude subsequent bypass surgery or surgical correction of reflux when necessary. As a "spinoff," the introduction of this relatively simple treatment of outflow obstruction has also led to a renewed interest in the nature and pathophysiology of venous obstruction per se and in tests for detection of hemodynamically significant lesions. With the promising clinical results of endovascular treatment, the role and importance of venous obstruction in chronic venous insufficiency (CVI) has also been re-evaluated.

Venous stenting is a mode of treatment that still is under development. Patients with chronic venous disease are younger, live longer, and have a better prognosis than patients with atherosclerotic arterial disease. Therefore, venous stenting must maintain the favorable initial result over the long term. Although venous stenting may presently be the preferred treatment of iliofemoral obstruction, more research is necessary to define accurate hemodynamic criteria for assessment and treatment and to study the long-term effects of stents in the venous system. The behavior of venous stents varies greatly depending on the indication for treatment and anatomic placement of the stents. In this chapter we focus on the etiology, signs and symptoms, and diagnosis of chronic nonmalignant venous obstructions and the technique and clinical and morphologic results (patency and in-stent restenosis rates) of iliofemoral and caval stenting of these obstructions.

■ ETIOLOGY

The iliac vein is the common outflow tract of the lower extremity, and chronic obstruction of this segment appears to result in more severe symptoms than does lower segmental blockage.[5-7] Distal obstructions are more readily compensated for, because of facilitated collateralization in the femoral-popliteal segment owing to the presence of double veins, direct connection to the profunda vein, saphenosaphenous connection, and deep muscular tributaries in the thigh. Conversely, the collateral formation is relatively poor in the iliofemoral segment. The most frequent chronic pelvic outflow obstruction occurs after deep venous thrombosis. Only 20% to 30% of iliac veins completely recanalize spontaneously after thrombosis, whereas the remaining veins recanalize partially and develop varying degrees of collaterals.[8,9] This may result in significant remaining obstruction to the outflow of the lower extremity.

A so-called primary, nonthrombotic iliac vein obstruction (May-Thurner syndrome[10] or iliac vein compression syndrome[11]) has been well described. This entity appears to be a more common cause of venous obstruction than previously thought. In our experience in the treatment of more than 600 obstructive limbs, approximately 40% had nonthrombotic blockage (defined as absent history of deep venous thrombosis [DVT] and no venographic or ultrasound findings indicating previous DVT). Typically, a stenosis of the left proximal common iliac vein is caused by compression by the right common iliac artery with secondary band or web formation.[12] At least 15% of the limbs with primary disease, however, have been shown to have stenosis of both common and external iliac veins.[13] In addition, although this lesion is classically found in the left iliac vein in younger females, it is not uncommon in males or in elderly patients and may involve the right limb.

Previous work has clearly established that intraluminal iliac vein lesions and varying degrees of external compression are quite common in the general population (14% to 30% and 88%, respectively),[11,14-17] and the incidence is probably higher in symptomatic patients. The anatomic differences between the right and left pelvic vasculature may explain the variable incidence of both proximal and distal obstructive lesions between the two sides. The pathologic finding is often not merely an external compression of the vein by the artery but also the presence of an intraluminal obstructive lesion (e.g., ridges, webs, cords, or bridges). Whether these intravenous lesions are congenital or secondary to trauma has not been proved conclusively. Although the lesions frequently occur at or near arterial crossover points, the sites also mark the locations of embryonic fusion of venous pathways in the development of the adult venous system.[18]

The possibility that these limbs with "primary," non-thrombotic disease may have had an isolated subclinical iliac vein thrombosis that initiated at the vessel crossing and then propagated distally into the external iliac vein cannot be excluded. On the other hand, limbs with obvious post-thrombotic disease may have had an underlying iliac vein compression resulting in an iliofemoral vein thrombosis.[17] A lack of hemosiderin and absence of other features characteristic of an organized thrombus on pathologic examination appear to largely rule out a post-thrombotic cause in these "primary" obstructions.[10,12] Whatever the chain of events, it serves to remind us that patients complaining of leg pain and swelling and no history of previous DVT or other venous disease may have isolated iliac vein obstruction.

Less common causes of chronic blockage of the iliac veins and the inferior vena cava include benign or malignant tumors, retroperitoneal fibrosis, iatrogenic injury, irradiation, cysts, and aneurysms. Relief of symptoms is immediate after successful stenting of malignant obstructions. The long-term outcome appears to depend largely on the progress of the tumor.[19] Iliocaval stenosis due to retroperitoneal fibrosis has been successfully treated by stenting.[20]

■ SIGNS AND SYMPTOMS

Signs and symptoms of chronic venous disease may vary greatly, ranging from moderate swelling and pain to discoloration and stasis ulcers. The main emphasis has been on treatment of severe skin changes and stasis ulcers, chiefly by controlling reflux. It is our experience, however, that a substantial number of patients with CVI complain of disabling limb pain and swelling without skin changes.[21] These symptoms are not always improved by wearing compression stockings or performing venous valve repair. The dominant pathophysiologic component in these patients may be obstruction rather than reflux, and it is possible that these symptoms are mainly attributable to the outflow blockage. "Venous claudication" is a dramatic condition described as an exercise-induced "tense" pain that requires several minutes of rest and leg elevation to achieve relief.

Certainly patients with significant outflow obstruction may have less dramatic symptoms with less distinct lower extremity pain and discomfort with decreased quality of life and moderate disability. Previous estimations that obstruction is a major contributor in only 10% to 20% of patients with severe chronic venous disease are probably low, and in our practice this number is definitely higher.

■ DIAGNOSIS

Often when algorithms are constructed for workup of patients with CVI, investigations for estimating the degree of reflux are emphasized, but testing for outflow obstruction is omitted completely. This is probably due to lack of accurate objective noninvasive or invasive tests for evaluation of hemodynamically significant chronic venous obstruction. In addition, it may be due to lack of practical treatment alternatives before the introduction of venous stenting. Whereas there are many tests for delineating focal and global reflux, this is not so for outflow obstruction. Ultrasound investigation and outflow fraction determinations by plethysmographic methods have been shown to be unreliable and play only a limited role. Although abnormal plethysmography findings may indicate obstruction to the venous outflow, significant blockage may exist in the presence of normal findings.[22-24] Even the invasive pressures (i.e., hand/foot pressure differential and reactive hyperemia pressure) increase, and indirect resistance calculations appear insensitive and do not define the level of obstruction.[22] Only a small pressure gradient over a venous stenosis or a pressure increase below an obstruction on exercise or hyperemia may indicate significant obstruction. These pressure differences are certainly much lower than in the arterial system, often as low as 2 to 3 mm Hg, which may be difficult to measure accurately.[25-27] Thus, although a positive hemodynamic test may indicate hemodynamic significance, a normal test does not exclude it. Unfortunately, it is presently impossible to detect borderline obstructions, which may be of hemodynamic importance.

Because accurate hemodynamic tests are unavailable, diagnosis and treatment must be based on morphologic findings. Single-plane transfemoral venography, the standard investigation, may show definite obstruction and development of collaterals. Although a defined lesion may be obvious, findings on the anteroposterior view are often subtle and only suggestive of an underlying obstruction (e.g., widening of the iliac vein [pancaking], "thinning" of the contrast dye resulting in a translucence of the area, partial intraluminal defect [septum], or a minimal filling of transpelvic collaterals). Increased accuracy may be achieved with multiple angled projections, which may reveal surprisingly tight stenosis on oblique projections, although the anteroposterior view is quite normal (Fig. 161-1).[28] Although the degree of stenosis may be obtained, the hemodynamic impact of this stenosis is not known from morphologic studies. In fact, the degree of venous stenosis that should be considered hemodynamically "critical" is also not known.[29] Although the formation of collaterals is classically regarded as a compensatory mechanism to bypass and thus neutralize the effects of an obstruction, the mechanism and inducement of collateral formation are unknown. It is doubtful that blood flow through this

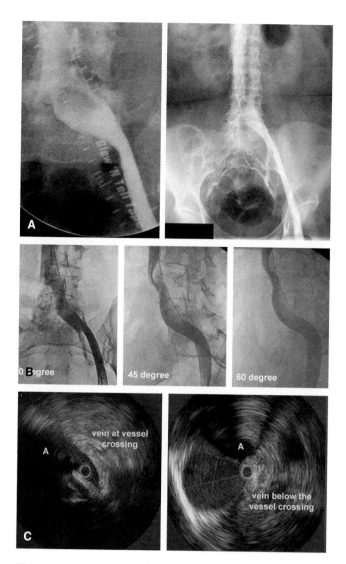

FIGURE 161-1 **A,** Single-plane transfemoral venogram showing typical findings suggesting a left common iliac vein compression, pancaking and translucency *(left),* and widening and presence of collaterals *(right).* **B,** Left transfemoral venogram with multiple projections. The oblique views (45- and 60-degree rotation) reveal stenoses, which are not visualized on the anteroposterior projection (0 degrees). **C,** IVUS images corresponding to the transfemoral venogram in **B.** The compression of the left common iliac vein as it is crossed by the right common iliac artery (A) is clearly shown *(left)* as compared with the normal vein below the venous stenosis *(right).* The *black circle* inside the vein represents the inserted IVUS catheter.

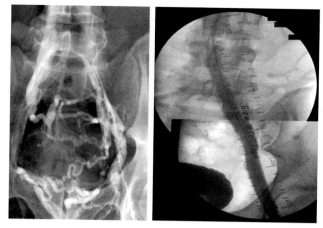

FIGURE 161-2 An iliofemoral post-thrombotic obstruction before and after stenting. Note the disappearance of collaterals after disobliteration. (From Raju S, McAllister S, Neglén P: Recanalization of totally occluded iliac and adjacent venous segments. J Vasc Surg 36:903-911, 2000.)

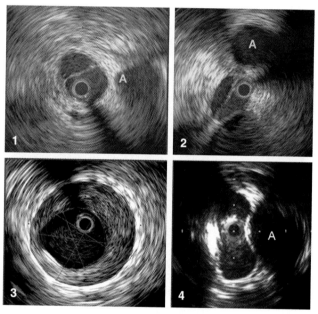

FIGURE 161-3 Images obtained by venous IVUS: *Upper left: 1.* Intraluminal septa. *Upper right: 2.* Trabeculation with multiple lumina. *Bottom left: 3.* In-stent restenosis precisely identifying the stent, neointimal hyperplasia, and remaining lumen. *Bottom right: 4.* Compression of the vein by the artery at the iliac vessel crossing. The adjacent artery is marked with an A. The *black circle* inside the vein represents the inserted IVUS catheter.

meandering vessel could replace that through the straighter main vein. The collaterals of a significant stenosis observed before stenting often disappear promptly after stenting (Fig. 161-2). The flow through the stent is obviously favored. It may be that the development of collaterals should be considered an indicator of obstruction and a failed compensatory feature if the patient is symptomatic.

Intravascular ultrasound (IVUS) can detect only axial collaterals running close to the original vessel. Transpelvic collaterals will escape detection. Several studies have shown, however, that IVUS is superior to single-plane venography in detection of the extent and morphologic degree of stenosis.[30-33] IVUS shows intraluminal details

(e.g., trabeculations and webs), which may be hidden by the contrast dye (Fig. 161-3). An external compression with the resulting deformity of the venous lumen can be directly visualized, and wall thickness, neointimal hyperplasia, and movement can be seen. Most importantly, IVUS appears superior to standard single-plane venography for estimating the morphologic degree of iliac vein stenosis. On average, transfemoral venography significantly underestimated the degree of stenosis by 30%. The venography was actually considered "normal" in one fourth of limbs despite the fact that IVUS showed more than 50% of obstruction.[34] IVUS is clearly superior to single-plane venography in providing adequate morphologic information and in our hands is the best available method for diagnosing clinically significant chronic iliac vein obstruction. Owing to the lack of hemo-dynamic tests, the diagnosis and treatment must presently be based on invasive morphologic investigations of the iliac venous outflow (preferably IVUS). Limiting the evaluation of patients with chronic venous disease to duplex ultrasound alone will not suffice. To identify patients with potentially important venous outflow obstruction, trans-femoral venography (preferably multiplane) or IVUS should be utilized more generously in patients with significant signs and symptoms of CVI.

Good clinical results have been obtained when stenosis of greater than 50%, as identified by IVUS, or complete occlusions have been stented. In selecting patients for IVUS investigation, the following indicators of obstruction have been used: (1) venographic stenosis greater than 30%; (2) presence of pelvic collaterals; and (3) positive invasive pressure test.[30,34] IVUS may be performed when one or several of these indicators are present and the patient is symptomatic. The symptoms may range from painful swelling, venous claudication, and pain in excess of clinical findings to severe stages with lipodermatosclerosis or ulcer. Utilizing this policy, however, 10% to 15% of iliofemoral veins are found to be normal.

■ TECHNIQUE

Venous stenting is a minimally invasive procedure and may appear to be simple. To achieve good results, however, attention to detail is important (Table 161-1).[30,35] Venous balloon angioplasty and stenting is a different procedure from that employed in the arterial system. As pointed out earlier, balloon angioplasty is insufficient in the venous system. Stent insertion is mandatory. Severe recoil of the vein is observed intraoperatively in the majority of limbs, and simple balloon dilation leads to early restenosis.[1-4] The procedure may be performed with the use of local infiltration analgesia in combination with monitored sedation or with general anesthesia. Because the balloon dilation may be quite painful, the latter is recommended when tight stenoses or occlusions are stented. Attempts to recanalize occluded veins are also often time consuming.

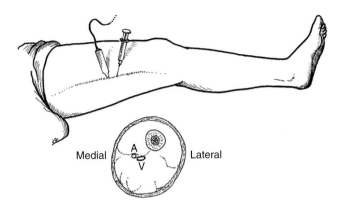

FIGURE 161-4 Ultrasound-guided cannulation allows a low approach to the femoral vein in the thigh, which facilitates balloon dilation and stent delivery into the common femoral vein and proximal iliac vein segment without impedance by the sheath. (From Raju S, McAllister S, Neglén P: Recanalization of totally occluded iliac and adjacent venous segments. J Vasc Surg 36:903-911, 2002.)

The procedure should be performed in a fully equipped endovascular or angiographic suite, and availability of IVUS and external ultrasound for cannulation guidance is preferred.

Ipsilateral cannulation of the femoral vein is obtained under ultrasound guidance below the suspected obstruction. Low thigh access is necessary in extensive obstruction to allow stent deployment up to and below the inguinal ligament without being impeded by the sheath. Ultrasound guidance is particularly helpful in this situation to avoid inadvertent arterial puncture, because the femoral vein occupies a variable posterolateral or posteromedial location in reference to the femoral artery (Fig. 161-4). The deep location of the vein in low thigh access and the consequent inability to exert direct external pressure over the veni-puncture site after sheath removal has not been a problem (common in arterial access), owing to the relatively low pressure on the venous side and the routine use of tam-ponade devices (Vasoseal ES, Datascope Corp., Montvale, NJ). Popliteal vein access is rarely used and often not possible because of segmental occlusion of the proximal femoral vein. Ultrasound-assisted cannulation is a necessity and has largely eliminated access complications.

Table 161-1 Technical Recommendations

1. Consider that balloon angioplasty and stenting is a different procedure in the venous than in the arterial system.
2. Balloon angioplasty alone is insufficient treatment for chronic occlusion of the iliofemoral veins. Stent insertion is mandatory.
3. The "kissing" balloon technique utilized at the aortic bifurcation is unnecessary at the confluence of the common iliac veins, and bilateral stents are not needed.
4. Ultrasound to guide cannulation of the femoral vein is a necessity.
5. Intravascular ultrasound is invaluable, both as a diagnostic tool and as an intraoperative aid in directing placement of the stent.
6. Stenting of a stenosis adjacent to the confluence of the common iliac veins requires that the stent be placed well into the inferior vena cava to avoid migration and early restenosis.
7. Insertion of a large diameter stent (14-16 mm wide) is recommended. Unlike the artery, the vein accepts extensive dilation without rupture.
8. It is important to re-dilate the stent after insertion to avoid its possible movement.
9. The diseased vein segment is more extensive in reality than what is visualized on venography. Cover the entire diseased venous segment as outlined by the intravascular ultrasound. Probably the most common cause of early restenosis is inadequate stenting of the entire lesion.
10. Short (<5 cm) skip areas in between two stents should be avoided, because they are prone to develop secondary stenosis.

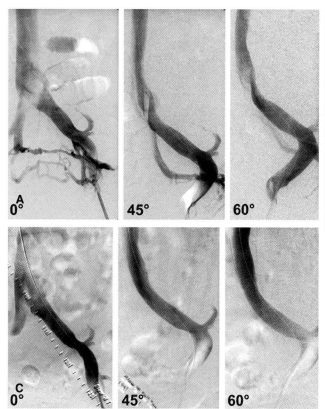

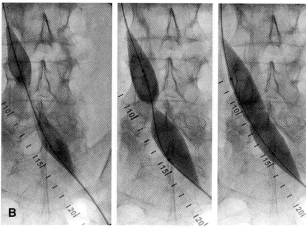

FIGURE 161-5 Balloon dilation and stenting of a left common iliac vein compression syndrome (May-Thurner syndrome) as shown on multiplane projections. **A,** Before venous stenting there is absence of stenosis but presence of collaterals in the anteroposterior view. The stenosis is detected by rotation. **B,** Waisting of balloon by the stenosis during inflation. **C,** Post-stent venogram revealing no stenosis. (From Neglén P: Endovascular treatment of chronic iliofemoral venous obstruction—a review. Phlebolymphology 43:204-211, 2003, with permission.)

A Glidewire (0.035 inch) (Boston Scientific Medi-Tech, Natick, MA) is inserted and the cannula replaced by a No. 9 Fr sheath, which will accommodate the appropriate balloon and stent sizes. A stiff guide wire and predilation with serial dilators may be necessary to facilitate sheath placement in case of perivenous fibrosis of the post-thrombotic femoral vein. Except in the event of complete occlusions, the guide wire can usually be passed through the stenosis and into the inferior vena cava (IVC) with ease. Initial contrast venography is then performed. Multiplane venographies (anteroposterior, 45-degree and 60-degree oblique projections) are helpful to delineate a stenosis that may not be revealed in the anteroposterior projection, especially if IVUS is not available (Fig. 161-5). As discussed earlier, IVUS is superior to venography in delineating any obstructive lesion and is recommended for diagnosis.

When a complete occlusion is present, the initial venographic study creates a "roadmap" for manipulation of the guide wire beyond the point of occlusion. This situation is challenging and can be quite time consuming. Patience is the key. The initial venography may appear discouraging, but more often than not a guide wire can be passed through the occlusion by "sight and feel" (Fig. 161-6). Multiple small-volume contrast agent injections are performed in different projections to ensure that the "dissection" is through the vessel and generally in the adequate direction. A combination of soft and stiff guide wires with straight, angled, and J tips, of different sizes (0.016 to 0.035 inch) and with supporting catheters (straight or angled) is required. Once the correct plane has been entered, rapid progress can usually be achieved without perforation by developing a loop or extended J at the end of a stiff guide wire or catheter-supported Glidewire during manipulation. Once the guide wire has traversed the occluded common iliac vein, passage through the iliocaval junction usually meets with additional resistance, again requiring extended manipulation in the area with coaxial catheter support. Specialized techniques such as those described to cross the occluded aortoiliac junction are not used.[36] Successful entry into the IVC is indicated by further easy passage of the guide wire into the right atrium and is confirmed by contrast medium injection through a general purpose catheter (No. 5 Fr) exchanged for the guide wire (see Fig. 161-6B).

After a significant stenosis has been diagnosed, it is predilated by an appropriately sized balloon, usually 16 mm for the distal cava and common iliac veins, 14 mm for the external iliac vein, and 12 mm for the common femoral vein. When a complete occlusion is present, predilation of the tract over the wire with 4-, 5-, or 10-mm balloons is usually required to allow the passage of larger balloons. The entire tract is ultimately dilated with 12- to 16-mm balloons (see Fig. 161-6C and E).

As pointed out earlier, the IVUS is an invaluable diagnostic tool but it is also essential at this point in the procedure to determine the extent of the lesion for appropriate placement of the stent (see Fig 161-6D).[31,32] The diseased vein segment is frequently more extensive in reality than indicated by venography. To avoid early restenosis and occlusion and ensure a sufficient venous inflow, it is vital to cover the entire obstruction as outlined by the IVUS

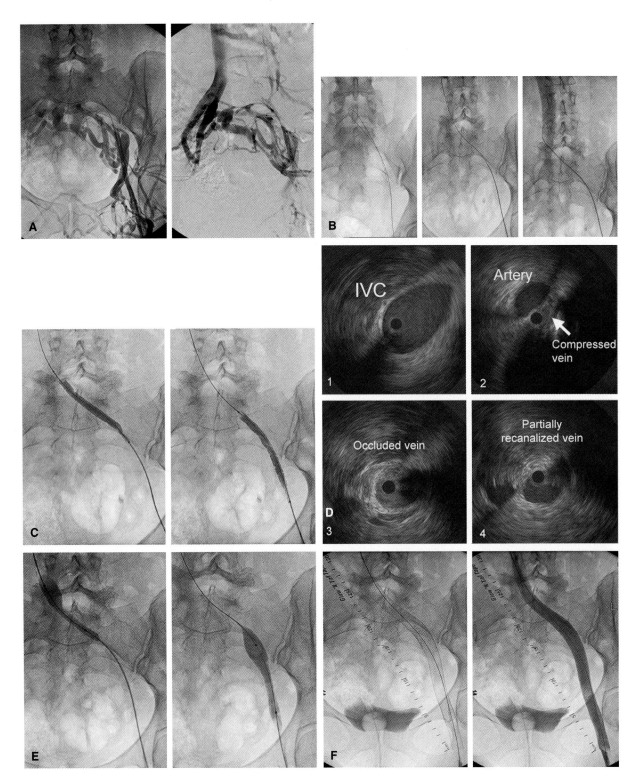

FIGURE 161-6 A, Transfemoral venogram performed through sheath inserted after ultrasound-guided cannulation of the left femoral vein. A complete post-thrombotic chronic occlusion of the left common iliac vein and severe stenosis of the external and common femoral veins are shown. Huge transpelvic collaterals fill a normal right iliocaval venous system. **B,** The obstruction has been traversed by manipulation with soft and stiff guide wires supported by guiding catheters *(left).* A cavogram obtained by contrast dye injection through an inserted general purpose catheter ensures that the inferior vena cava (IVC) has been penetrated. **C,** The occluded vessel is recanalized by a smaller balloon to allow passage of the IVUS catheter to assess the extent of the lesion and subsequent insertion of larger balloons and stents. **D,** Images obtained by venous IVUS: *1,* Normal IVC proximal to stenosis. *2,* The common iliac vein severely compressed by the crossing iliac artery. *3,* The completely occluded common iliac vein. Despite the chronic nature of the occlusion, the recanalizing guide wire has followed the course of the original vein and is clearly intraluminal on this image. *4,* The partially recanalized external iliac vein. The *black circle* inside the vein represents the inserted IVUS catheter. **E,** Sequential ballooning of the entire iliofemoral venous segment to final diameter size (in this case, 14 mm width). **F,** Image showing the entire stent system comprising three stents placed well into the IVC and telescoped over each other to cover the entire iliofemoral vein with the distal end placed at the inflow of the profunda vein *(left).* Final transfemoral venogram showing uninterrupted venous outflow with no visualization of any collaterals *(right).*

investigation. Short (<5 cm) skip areas in between two stents should be avoided, and multiple stents should be placed overlapping each other to prevent separation. It appears that the occlusion rate is not related to stent length or metal load per se; on the contrary, failure to support the entire diseased vein segment with a stent commonly results in early restenosis or occlusion of the stent system.

Adequate inflow into the stent system is essential for future patency. In extensive lesions, especially when recanalization of a completely occluded vein is obtained, it may be necessary to extend the stent below the level of the inguinal ligament (see Fig. 161-6F). The profunda vein is easily identified by IVUS and extension of the stent across the groin crease into the common femoral vein just above the profunda orifice was not found to jeopardize stent patency. Blood flow from a healthy profunda vein appears to provide sufficient inflow into the newly recanalized segments, even when the superficial femoral vein is severely diseased or occluded.

Most often self-expanding stents are inserted (Wallstent, Boston Scientific Scimed, Inc., Minneapolis, MN; Smart Stent, Cordis Corp., Miami, FL), but sometimes balloon-expanded stents with strong radial force must be used (Palmaz Stent, Cordis Corp., Miami, FL). Stenting of a stenosis adjacent to the confluence of the common iliac veins requires that the stent be placed well into the IVC to avoid early restenosis.[30] This is especially important when a Wallstent is used. Owing to its inherent property, this stent may be "squeezed" distally and a proximal restenosis may develop. This placement of the stent into the IVC does not appear to significantly impair the flow from the contralateral limb resulting in thrombosis. A few cases of contralateral limb thrombosis have been observed and raised concern. These clots, however, appear to be caused by recurrent attacks of thrombosis rather than stent occlusion. The "kissing" balloon technique utilized at the aortic bifurcation is unnecessary at the confluence of the common iliac veins, and bilateral stents are not inserted at this location in the treatment of unilateral lesions.

Insertion of a large-diameter stent (14 to 16 mm wide) is recommended. Unlike the artery, the vein accepts extensive dilation without clinical rupture. No such rupture has been reported, even when a total occlusion is recanalized and dilated up to a width of 14 to 16 mm. It is important to redilate the stent after insertion to ensure a good apposition to the vessel wall and to avoid possible migration. Adequate placement is best evaluated by IVUS.

The perioperative anticoagulation management is important, especially when post-thrombotic complete occlusions are recanalized, balloon dilated, and stented. The management outlined next has been successful in our hands. Generally, only patients on warfarin preoperatively owing to prior deep venous thrombosis with or without thrombophilia are anticoagulated postoperatively. Other patients are discharged on oral aspirin, 81 mg daily. Some anticoagulated patients receive the same dose of aspirin twice weekly in addition to oral warfarin postoperatively.

The preoperatively anticoagulated patients are instructed to discontinue the warfarin 3 days before the intervention and to self-inject dalteparin sodium, 5000 units, daily subcutaneously. A slight increase of preoperative prothrombin time (INR = 1.7) is not a contraindication to proceeding with the procedure. On the day of intervention all patients were given 2500 units of dalteparin sodium subcutaneously before and after surgery. Patients on warfarin resumed taking the medication the same day of the intervention. Daltaparin sodium, 5000 units, was self-injected daily subcutaneously combined with the warfarin treatment for 4 postoperative days, at which time the International Normalized Ratio level was usually found to be therapeutic. All patients received intravenous unfractionated heparin, 3000 to 5000 units, after placement of the sheath in the femoral vein followed by an intravenous ketorolac tromethamine injection of 30 mg at the time of stenting. The injections of ketorolac and the 5000 units of dalteparin sodium were repeated the next morning before discharge. Generally, the patients are hospitalized less than 23 hours.

COMPLICATIONS

The nonthrombotic complication rate related to the endovascular intervention is minimal and comprises mostly cannulation site hematoma, although a few cases of retroperitoneal hematoma requiring blood transfusions have been described.[37,38] The utilization of ultrasound-guided cannulation and closure with collagen plugs has largely abolished these problems, reducing the nonthrombotic complication rate from 3% to less than 1%. The mortality has been zero.

Data regarding the early rethrombosis rate (<30 days) after iliofemoral stenting are sparse. In the Creighton University experience, the rate was found to be 11% after stenting after thrombolysis of an acute DVT and 15% in the National Registry study.[39,40] The early thrombosis rate was found to be lower (4%) when stenting was performed for chronic iliofemoral venous obstruction without earlier thrombolysis.[34] All early occlusions in our experience occurred in patients with thrombotic disease (8% thrombosis rate), whereas none occurred in nonthrombotic limbs. Early failures appear more common with long stents extending below the inguinal ligament, stents placed across complete occlusions rather than across stenoses, and in patients with thrombophilia.[41,42] The occlusions appeared to be related to limbs with incomplete dilation owing to nonyielding obstruction leaving residual stenosis after stenting. Thrombolysis of the newly formed clot may be attempted in initially technically successful limbs to reveal and treat previously undetected additional obstructions.

PATENCY RATES

Although there are numerous small case reports in the literature, only a few larger series with acceptable follow-up are available. The majority of these studies mix obstructions of different causes. Assessment of the results of 707 thrombolyzed and stented iliofemoral veins in 24 reports shows primary and assisted primary patency rates varying from 50% to 100% and 63% to 100%, respectively, during a follow-up time of 1 to 46 months. Few of these patients had late follow-up with imaging, and no actuarial curves were constructed.[43]

Lamont and colleagues reported an 87% patency rate at median follow-up of 16 months in 15 patients stented for

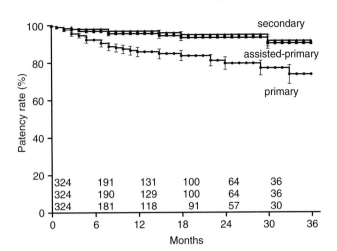

FIGURE 161-7 Cumulative primary, assisted-primary, and secondary patency rates of 324 limbs after iliofemoral stenting. The lower numbers represent limbs at risk for each time interval (all SEM < 10%).

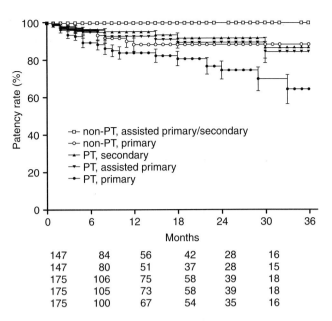

FIGURE 161-8 Cumulative primary, assisted-primary, and secondary patency rates for stented limbs with thrombotic (PT) and nonthrombotic (non-PT) obstruction. The lower numbers represent total limbs at risk for each time interval (all SEM < 10%).

common iliac vein compression after clearance of acute thrombus by thrombolysis.[44]

Juhan and coworkers reported primary and secondary patency rates of 87% and 93%, respectively, at 24 months in 15 stented patients with iliac venous stenosis.[28] Six limbs were treated after thrombolysis for acute deep venous thrombosis; the remaining nine limbs had chronic non-malignant obstruction. There was a significant clinical improvement as measured by clinical severity and disability score.

O'Sullivan and associates reported a 1-year patency of 79% in a retrospective analysis of 39 patients.[45] Only half of the patients presented with chronic symptoms. When initial technical failures are removed, the stented patients had a 1-year patency of 94%. The clinical results were excellent in the stented limbs.

A similar group of 18 patients were reported by Hurst and colleagues.[24] Six limbs were treated after disobliteration of an acute deep venous thrombosis. The primary patency rates at 12 and 18 months were 79% and 79%, respectively. Most patients (13/18) had resolution or substantial improvement of leg swelling and pain. However, 5 patients (28%) continued to have pain despite resolved swelling and widely patent stents on venogram. Similarly, Binkert and coworkers reported a 100% patency at an average follow-up time of 3 years in 8 patients (in four limbs after surgical thrombectomy) with resolution or substantial improvement of symptoms in most patients.[46]

Nazarian and coworkers reported a 1-year primary assisted patency rate of 66% in 29 iliac obstructions.[41] The lower patency rate may be explained by the selection of patients (13/29 had complete occlusion and 16/19 were caused by malignancy). Interestingly, few occlusions occurred after 6 months and the patency rate remained the same at 1- and 4-year follow-up. The same group also reported overall 1-year primary and secondary patency rates of 50% and 81%, respectively, in a mixed population including 56 patients with iliac obstruction caused by malignancy, trauma, pregnancy, and postoperative stenosis.[47]

Razavi and coworkers reported a retrospective study on stenting of the obstructed IVC in 17 symptomatic patients.

Underlying malignancy was the cause of blockage in 4 patients, and stenting was preceded by thrombolysis of a superimposed thrombus in 5 patients. At 19 months' follow-up the primary and secondary patency rates were 80% and 87%, respectively. The symptom relief was excellent.[48]

We have followed 455 limbs that underwent iliac vein stenting between 1997 and 2001.[38,42] Transfemoral venography was performed in 324 of these limbs. In 256 limbs (54%), the obstructive lesion was considered thrombotic because the patients either had a known preoperative occurrence of deep venous thrombosis diagnosed with duplex ultrasound or ascending venography and subsequently treated by anticoagulation or findings on preoperative venography (occlusion, stenosis, or collaterals) and/or duplex ultrasonography indicating previous DVT below the inguinal ligament (direct visualization of thrombus or indirect indication by partial or total inability to compress the vein). The remaining 199 limbs were considered nonthrombotic. Cumulative primary, assisted-primary, and secondary patency rates at 3 years were 75%, 92%, and 93%, respectively (Fig. 161-7). The stented limbs with nonthrombotic disease appeared to fare significantly better than did those with thrombotic disease (primary, assisted-primary, and secondary cumulative patency rates of 89%, 100%, and 100%, and 65%, 85%, and 88% at 36 months, respectively) (Fig. 161-8). The stented post-thrombotic limb in patients with thrombophilia, who had an extensive iliofemoral occlusion or tight, nonyielding stenoses at stenting (especially when extending below the inguinal ligament), was found more prone to occlude. Nevertheless, it appears that balloon venoplasty and stenting of an iliac vein obstruction for a chronic obstruction is a safe, minimally invasive method with minimal complication rate, no mortality, and a 3-year acceptable patency. A smaller number of patients have been followed for 5 years or

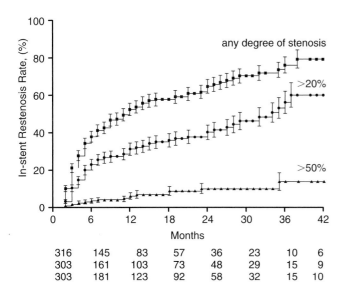

316	145	83	57	36	23	10	6
303	161	103	73	48	29	15	9
303	181	123	92	58	32	15	10

FIGURE 161-9 Cumulative in-stent restenosis-free rates for all limbs with any degree of stenosis (>20%) and severe (>50%) narrowing. The lower numbers represent total limbs at risk for each time interval (all SEM < 10%). (From Neglén P, Raju S: In-stent restenosis in stents placed in the lower extremity venous outflow tract. J Vasc Surg 39:181-188, 2004.)

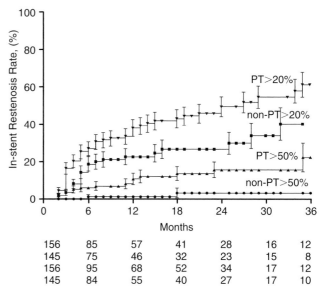

156	85	57	41	28	16	12
145	75	46	32	23	15	8
156	95	68	52	34	17	12
145	84	55	40	27	17	10

FIGURE 161-10 Cumulative in-stent restenosis-free rates (>20% in-stent restenosis) and cumulative primary rates for stented limbs with thrombotic (PT) and nonthrombotic (non-PT) obstruction. The lower numbers represent total limbs at risk for each time interval (all SEM < 10%). (From Neglén P, Raju S: In-stent restenosis in stents placed in the lower extremity venous outflow tract. J Vasc Surg 39:181-188, 2004.)

more without precipitous deterioration of stent patency or clinical efficacy.

■ IN-STENT RESTENOSIS RATE

To assess the development of in-stent restenosis, any narrowing of the stent on single-plane transfemoral venography was measured in the same group of patients described previously using a caliper and expressed as a percentage diameter reduction of patent lumen.[42] At 42 months, only 23% of limbs remained with no in-stent restenosis at all, but only a minority of limbs had severe (>50%) obstruction (17% at 36 months) (Fig. 161-9). Most had only minimal narrowing. As expected, gender and treated limb side did not influence development of in-stent restenosis. Conversely, the presence of chronic thrombotic disease as indicated by history or morphologic findings anywhere in the involved lower extremity resulted in a higher rate of in-stent restenosis. Severe stenosis (>50%) developed in the stent in 23% of these extremities as compared with 4% of nonthrombotic limbs. At 36 months, limbs with thrombotic disease had lower in-stent restenosis-free rates than did nonthrombotic limbs (37% and 59% of more than 20% narrowing, and 77% and 96% of more than 50% narrowing, respectively) (Fig. 161-10). This strong impact of the thrombotic disease on development of in-stent restenosis appears to be reflected in the analysis of other potential contributing factors. There was an over-representation of limbs with thrombotic disease in patients with thrombophilia, stents terminating below the inguinal ligament, and long stents. The cumulative in-stent restenosis rate increased before the occlusion rate (i.e., the development of in-stent restenosis appeared to precede the development of obstruction), suggesting cause-and-effect. Although the stented limbs that eventually occluded had

similar risk factors to those developing significant in-stent restenosis, no conclusion regarding a cause-and-effect relationship can be drawn from this study. A handful of patients with early significant in-stent restenosis were treated by thrombolysis in an effort to dissolve any thrombus. These attempts were all unsuccessful. Invariably, balloon angioplasty of an in-stent stenosis revealed a very hard stenosis that was difficult to dilate. Any improvement of lumen size appeared to be secondary to remodeling rather than a true decrease of wall thickness. These clinical observations indicate that the reaction to stenting of the vein is possibly a cellular response rather than formation of a thrombosis. Whether the late occlusions occur due to acute recurrent thrombosis or gradual development of true intimal hyperplasia requires further study.

■ CLINICAL RESULTS

As alluded to earlier, the reports describing patency rates indicate clinical improvement in most patients (>90%).[45,46] Hurst and associates showed resolution or substantial improvement in 72% of limbs, and Juhan and colleagues reported a significant improvement of the mean clinical severity score.[24,28] In addition to ulcer healing and ulcer recurrence rate, we have followed the patient's clinical result by quality-of-life questionnaires[49]; degree of swelling assessed by physical examination (grade 0: none; grade 1: pitting, not obvious; grade 2: ankle edema; and grade 3: obvious swelling involving the limb); and level of pain measured by the visual analogue scale method.[50] The clinical results after balloon venoplasty and stenting in 613 patients treated between October 1996 and August 2002 have been reported in several studies.[30,34,38,51] The mean

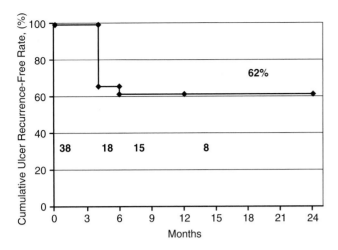

FIGURE 161-11 Cumulative ulcer recurrence-free rate after iliofemoral venous stenting alone (with no subsequent reflux repair). (From Raju S, Owen S Jr, Neglén P: The clinical impact of iliac venous stents in the management of chronic venous insufficiency. J Vasc Surg 35:8-15, 2002.)

naire assessing subjective pain, sleep disturbance, morale and social activities, and routine and strenuous physical activities, the patients indicated significant improvement in all major categories after venoplasty and stenting.[38]

The presence of ulcer may influence the degree of pain and swelling apart from that caused by iliac obstruction. However, the reduction in pain and swelling was significant in limbs with and without stasis ulcer. The pre-stenting level of pain was similar in both groups, suggesting the important contribution by iliac vein obstruction to pain and swelling in these patients. Interestingly, patients with recurrence of obstruction also had recurrence of symptoms after a symptom-free period.[38]

These results clearly indicate a significant symptom relief after balloon venoplasty and stenting of iliofemoral vein obstruction, even in the presence of remaining reflux.[51] The results also suggest that outflow obstruction is a more important and frequent component of chronic venous disease than previously realized.

follow-up time was 13 months (range: 1 to 66 months) and data were available for 87% of patients. The incidence of ulcer healing after iliac vein balloon dilation and stent placement in 41 limbs with active ulcer was 68%, and the cumulative ulcer recurrence-free rate at 2 years was 62% (Fig. 161-11).[38] Frequently these limbs had remaining reflux, which was untreated during the observation period. Despite the presence of reflux the stasis ulcers stayed healed. Median swelling and pain severity scores decreased significantly (grade 2 to 1 and 4 to 0, respectively). The rates of limbs with any objective swelling or pain decreased significantly from 86% to 88% to 33% to 52% and from 73% to 83% to 28% to 29%, respectively (Table 161-2).[38,51] Complete relief of pain and swelling was thus achieved in approximately half and more than one third of all treated limbs, respectively. With the use of a quality-of-life question-

■ SUMMARY

Patients have now been followed for more than 6 years after stenting of the iliofemoral venous outflow. Ongoing evaluation indicates that venous balloon angioplasty and stenting is a safe, relatively simple, and efficient method for the treatment of iliofemorocaval venous obstruction. It is now the preferred treatment over open surgery for this condition and may be offered to a larger group of patients. The gratifying clinical results justify a more aggressive approach toward diagnosis and treatment of morphologic iliac venous outflow obstruction. It would be preferable to direct treatment by physiologic testing, but because such a test is unavailable, the diagnosis and treatment must be based on morphologic investigations. Duplex Doppler ultrasound has become the mainstay and often the sole diagnostic modality of CVI in most centers. It is, however, insensitive to the diagnosis of iliac vein obstruction as

Table 161-2	Clinical Assessment of Degree of Pain (Visual Analogue Scale, 0-10) and Swelling (Grade 0-3) Pre-stenting as Compared with Post-stenting in Limbs with Obstruction Only (Group 1) and Combined Obstruction and Reflux (Group 2)*			
	OBSTRUCTION ONLY		**OBSTRUCTION + REFLUX**	
	Pre-stent	**Post-stent**	**Pre-stent**	**Post-stent**
Swelling				
No. of limbs	187	152	249	200
Prevalence	170 (91%)	91 (60%)	207 (83%)	94 (47%)
Grade (median [range])	2 [0-3]	1 [0-3]†	1 [0-3]	0 [0-3]†
Pain				
No. of limbs	177	152	244	196
Prevalence	135 (76%)	41 (27%)	186 (77%)	58 (30%)
Score (median [range])	4 [0-9]	0 [0-9]†	4 [0-9]	0 [0-9]†

*No subsequent reflux surgery was performed during the observation period in group 2.
†*P* < .001

Reprinted from Neglén P, Raju S: Venous outflow obstruction: An underestimated contributor to chronic venous disease. J Vasc Surg 38:879-885, 2003.

currently used. Awareness and a high index of suspicion of iliac venous obstruction, combined with generous use of transfemoral multiplane venography and IVUS investigations, are necessary to detect borderline obstruction. The target population includes patients with clinical features (especially pain) out of proportion to detectable pathology, patients with no other discernable basis for their symptoms, symptomatic patients with visualized pelvic collaterals, and patients with a history or ultrasound or venographic evidence of previous deep venous thrombosis.

Although iliofemoral venous stenting is a promising technique, some caveats must be offered. Selection of patients for treatment based on morphologic investigations ultimately is not satisfactory, and hemodynamic criteria have to be developed. Further research should be encouraged to achieve better understanding of the nature of venous obstruction and to develop reliable methods for testing hemodynamic significance. Monitoring of these patients should continue to contribute to our knowledge of the longterm effects of stents in the venous system and of the potential development of threatening in-stent restenosis.

■ REFERENCES

1. Neglén P, Al-Hassan HKh, Endrys J, et al: Iliofemoral venous thrombectomy followed by percutaneous closure of the temporary arteriovenous fistula. Surgery 110:493-499, 1991.
2. Wisselink W, Money SR, Becker MO, et al: Comparison of operative reconstruction and percutaneous balloon dilatation for central venous obstruction. Am J Surg 166:200-205, 1993.
3. Marzo KP, Schwartz R, Glanz S: Early restenosis following percutaneous transluminal balloon angioplasty for the treatment of the superior vena caval syndrome due to pacemaker-induced stenosis. Cathet Cardiovasc Diagn 36:128-131, 1995.
4. Walpole H, Lovert K, Chaung V, et al: Superior vena cava syndrome treated by percutaneous balloon angioplasty. Am Heart J 115:1303-1304, 1988.
5. May R: Anatomy. In May R, Nissl R (eds): Surgery of the Veins of the Leg and Pelvis. Stuttgart, Germany, Georg Thieme, 1979, pp 1-36.
6. Mavor GE, Galloway JMD: Collaterals of the deep venous circulation of the lower limb. Surg Gynaecol Obstet 125:561-571, 1967.
7. Kosinski C: Observations on the superficial venous system of the lower extremity. J Anat 60:131-142, 1926.
8. Mavor GE, Galloway JMD: Iliofemoral venous thrombosis: Pathological considerations and surgical management. Br J Surg 56:45-59, 1969.
9. Plate G, Åkesson H, Einarsson E, et al: Long-term results of venous thrombectomy combined with a temporary arterio-venous fistula. Eur J Vasc Surg 4:483-489, 1990.
10. May R, Thurner J: The cause of the predominantly sinistral occurrence of thrombosis of the pelvic veins. Angiology 8:419-428, 1957.
11. Cockett FB, Thomas ML: The iliac compression syndrome. Br J Surg 52:816-821, 1965.
12. Negus D, Fletcher EWL, Cockett FB, Thomas ML: Compression and band formation at the mouth of the left common iliac vein. Br J Surg 55:369-374, 1968.
13. Neglén P, Berry MA, Raju S: Endovascular surgery in the treatment of chronic primary and post-thrombotic iliac vein obstruction. Eur J Vasc Endovasc Surg 20:560-571, 2000.
14. Virchow R: Uber die Erweiterung kleinerer Gefässe. Arch Path Anat 3:427, 1851.
15. McMurrich JP: The occurrence of congenital adhesions in the common iliac veins, and their relation to thrombosis of the femoral and iliac veins. Am J Med Sci 135:342-346, 1908.
16. Ehrich WE, Krumbhaar EB: A frequent obstructive anomaly of the mouth of the left common iliac vein. Am Heart J 26:737-750, 1943.
17. Cockett FB, Thomas ML, Negus D: Iliac vein compression—Its relation to iliofemoral thrombosis and the post-thrombotic syndrome. BMJ 2:14-19, 1967.
18. McClure CFW, Butler EG: The development of the vena cava inferior in man. Am J Anat 35:331-383, 1925.
19. Carlson JW, Nazarian GK, Hartenbach E, et al: Management of pelvic venous stenosis with intravascular stainless steel stents. Gynecol Oncol 56:362-369, 1995.
20. Hartung O, Alimi YS, Di Mauro P, et al: Endovascular treatment of iliocaval occlusion caused by retroperitoneal fibrosis: Late results in two cases. J Vasc Surg 36:849-852, 2002.
21. Raju S, Neglén P, Carr-White PA, et al: Ambulatory venous hypertension: Component analysis in 373 limbs. Vasc Surg 33:257-267, 1999.
22. Neglén P, Raju S: Detection of outflow obstruction in chronic venous insufficiency. J Vasc Surg 17:583-589, 1993.
23. Labropoulos N, Volteas N, Leon M, et al: The role of venous outflow obstruction in patients with chronic venous dysfunction. Arch Surg 132:46-51, 1997.
24. Hurst DR, Forauer AR, Bloom JR, et al: Diagnosis and endovascular treatment of iliocaval compression syndrome. J Vasc Surg 34:106-113, 2001.
25. Negus D, Cockett FB: Femoral vein pressures in post-phlebitic iliac vein obstruction. Br J Surg 54:522-525, 1967.
26. Rigas A, Vomvoyannis A, Giannoulis K, et al: Measurement of the femoral vein pressure in edema of the lower extremity. J Cardiovasc Surg 12:411-416, 1971.
27. Albrechtsson U, Einarsson E, Eklöf B: Femoral vein pressure measurements for evaluation of venous function in patients with post-thrombotic iliac veins. Cardiovasc Intervent Radiol 4:43-50, 1981.
28. Juhan C, Hartung O, Alimi Y, et al: Treatment of non-malignant obstructive lesions by stent placement: Mid-term results. Ann Vasc Surg 15:227-232, 2001.
29. Neglén P, Raju S: Proximal lower extremity chronic venous outflow obstruction: Recognition and treatment. Semin Vasc Surg 15:57-64, 2002.
30. Neglén P, Raju S: Balloon dilation and stenting of chronic iliac vein obstruction: Technical aspects and early clinical outcome. J Endovasc Ther 7:79-91, 2000.
31. Neglén P, Raju S: Intravascular ultrasound scan evaluation of the obstructed vein. J Vasc Surg 35:694-700, 2002.
32. Forauer AR, Gemmete JJ, Dasika NL, et al: Intravascular ultrasound in the diagnosis and treatment of iliac vein compression (May-Thurner) syndrome. J Vasc Intervent Radiol 13:523-527, 2002.
33. Satokawa H, Hoshino S, Iwaya F, et al: Intravascular imaging methods for venous disorders. Int J Angiol 9:117-121, 2000.
34. Neglén P, Berry MA. Raju S: Endovascular surgery in the treatment of chronic primary and post-thrombotic iliac vein obstruction. Eur J Vasc Endovasc Surg 20:560-571, 2000.
35. Raju S, McAllister S, Neglén P: Recanalization of totally occluded iliac and adjacent venous segments. J Vasc Surg 36:903-911, 2002.
36. Murphy TP, Marks MJ, Webb MS: Use of a curved needle for true lumen re-entry during subintimal iliac artery revascularization. J Vasc Intervent Radiol 8:633-636, 1997.
37. Ouriel K, Kandarpa K, Schuerr DM, et al: Prourokinase vs. urokinase for recanalization of peripheral occlusions, safety and efficacy: The PURPOSE Trial. J Vasc Intervent Radiol 10:1083-1091, 1999.
38. Raju S, Owen S Jr, Neglén P: The clinical impact of iliac venous stents in the management of chronic venous insufficiency. J Vasc Surg 35:8-15, 2002.
39. Thorpe PE: Endovascular therapy for chronic venous obstruction. In Ballard JL, Bergan JJ (eds): Chronic Venous Insufficiency. New York, Springer, 1999, pp 179-219.
40. Mewissen MW, Seabrook GR, Meissner MH, et al: Catheter-directed thrombolysis for lower extremity deep venous thrombosis: Report of a national multicenter registry. Radiology 211:39-49, 1999.

41. Nazarian GK, Austin WR, Wegryn SA, et al: Venous recanalization by metallic stents after failure of balloon angioplasty or surgery: Four-year experience. Cardiovasc Intervent Radiol 19:227-233, 1996.
42. Neglén P, Raju S: In-stent restenosis in stents placed in the lower extremity venous outflow tract. J Vasc Surg 39:181-188, 2004.
43. Thorpe PE, Osse FJ, Dang HP: Endovascular reconstruction for chronic iliac vein and inferior vena cava obstruction. In Gloviczki P, Yao SJT (eds): The Handbook of Venous Disorders, Guideline of The American Venous Forum, 2nd ed. London, Arnold, 2001, pp 347-361.
44. Lamont JP, Pearl GJ, Patetsios P, et al: Prospective evaluation of endoluminal venous stents in the treatment of the May-Thurner syndrome. Ann Vasc Surg 16:61-64, 2002.
45. O'Sullivan GJ, Semba CP, Bittner CA, et al: Endovascular management of iliac vein compression (May-Thurner) syndrome. J Vasc Interv Radiol 11:823-836, 2000.

46. Binkert CA, Schoch E, Stuckmann G, et al: Treatment of pelvic venous spur (May-Thurner syndrome) with self-expanding metallic endoprostheses. Cardiovasc Intervent Radiol 21:22-26, 1998.
47. Nazarian GK, Bjarnason H, Dietz CA Jr, et al: Iliofemoral venous stenosis: Effectiveness of treatment with metallic endovascular stents. Radiology 200:193-199, 1996.
48. Razavi RK, Hansch EC, Kee ST, et al: Chronically occluded inferior venae cavae: Endovascular treatment. Radiology 214:133-138, 2000.
49. Launois R, Rebpi-Marty J, Henry B: Construction and validation of a quality of life questionnaire in chronic lower limb venous insufficiency (CIVIQ). Q Life Res 5:539-554, 1996.
50. Scott J, Huskisson EC: Graphic presentation of pain. Pain 2:175-184, 1976.
51. Neglén P, Raju S: Venous outflow obstruction: An underestimated contributor to chronic venous disease. J Vasc Surg 38:879-885, 2003.

Chapter

162

Endovascular Treatment of Vena Caval Occlusions

MICHAEL D. DAKE, MD

Occlusions of the superior vena cava (SVC) and inferior vena cava (IVC) form a heterogeneous group of vascular lesions of various causes and prognosis.[1-4] As outlined in the preceding chapters, there have been a number of modern developments in the medical and surgical management of venous disease. Simultaneous advances in radiographic imaging and catheter-based interventional procedures now offer clinicians safe, less invasive, and effective treatment alternatives to traditional therapy for these diseases. The purpose of this chapter is to outline recent advances in the fields of thrombolysis, percutaneous transluminal angioplasty (PTA), and endoluminal stenting, focusing on their applications in the treatment of large vein occlusions.

Traditionally, the treatments of choice for vena caval obstruction included external-beam radiation, chemotherapy, systemic anticoagulation, and systemic thrombolytic therapy. Success rates for these procedures have generally been disappointing.[5-7] Also, a number of different operative approaches have been presented in the surgical literature. Surgical bypass, an invasive approach, has usually been reserved for relief of symptoms caused by diseases other than neoplastic ones.[7-10] In many series, short-term patency rates for surgical bypass have been better than those for medical management alone[6,11]; however, symptoms of caval obstruction recur in a large proportion of patients.[8,12]

The goal of endovascular interventions is to provide a safe, noninvasive approach to the management of acute and chronic venous occlusions. Endovascular techniques have been used for palliation of symptoms of venous obstruction associated with malignant neoplasm for a number of years.[13,14] Recently, however, primary venous angioplasty and stenting have been performed with increasing frequency for benign venous occlusive disease, and, in institutions where caval occlusions are treated principally with surgical bypass, endovascular techniques have been used to salvage failing vena cava grafts.[15,16]

■ INDICATIONS FOR INTERVENTION

Endovascular interventions are indicated for patients whose symptoms have not resolved after either a standard course of anticoagulation or surgical bypass and who have persistent symptoms consistent with chronic SVC or IVC occlusion. The decision to exclude a patient from endovascular intervention is based primarily on contraindications to anticoagulation or fibrinolytic therapy.

The treatment of caval occlusions secondary to benign processes remains a serious challenge for endoluminal therapies, because patients often outlive their repairs. In patients with a known malignancy, the clinician must weigh the patient's quality of life against the potential complications of the procedure. The patient must understand that the endovascular procedure will not treat the underlying malignancy and is merely palliative.

■ INTERVENTIONAL STRATEGIES

The four primary strategies for endovascular interventions in the SVC and IVC systems are venography, thrombolysis, angioplasty, and endoluminal stenting or stent-grafting. For both chronic SVC and IVC occlusions, a combination of these techniques is used to restore and maintain good drainage into the right atrium. The interventions listed earlier can be performed entirely in the angiographic suite under sterile conditions.

Superior Vena Cava

Occlusion of the SVC and of associated central veins of the thorax can produce a wide range of clinical findings which, collectively, are referred to as *superior vena cava syndrome.* SVC syndrome (see Chapter 164) consists of facial, periorbital, neck, and bilateral upper extremity edema; dilated superficial veins over the anterior and lateral chest wall; dysphagia; dyspnea; and cognitive dysfunction secondary to cerebral venous hypertension. Rarely is SVC syndrome alone a life-threatening emergency; however, the quality of life for many of these patients is poor, owing to limited use of their arms, inability to lie flat (due to venous congestion), and severe facial edema.[1,2]

The clinical syndrome is caused by compression or complete obstruction of the SVC plus altered venous return from the head, neck, and upper extremities. The severity of the SVC syndrome depends on how fast occlusion develops and the associated pattern of collateral vessels. The more acute the occlusion and the more limited the development of collateral vessels, the more severe are the symptoms. SVC syndrome has both benign and malignant causes (Table 162-1). Before the advent of antibiotic therapy, a large percentage of cases of SVC syndrome were caused by pathogens. Today, malignant disease accounts for 85% to 97% of all cases, but, as the number of central venous catheters placed for long-term access continues to rise, non-neoplastic causes will increase proportionately.[2]

Patients suffering from SVC syndrome should undergo complete diagnostic evaluation to rule out malignancy, including a detailed history and physical examination, chest radiography, and thoracic computed tomography (CT).

Table 162-1	Etiology of Superior Vena Caval Obstruction
Benign	
Central venous catheters	
Radiation fibrosis	
Mediastinal fibrosis	
Pacemaker leads	
Dialysis fistula–related stenosis	
Substernal thyroid goiter	
Malignant	
Bronchogenic carcinoma	
Mediastinal tumors	
Lymphoma	
Thyroid carcinoma	
Metastatic disease	

Chest radiographs reveal malignant intrathoracic processes in 85% of patients with SVC syndrome. Two thirds of these lesions are situated in the right upper lobe near the SVC, and a right-sided pleural effusion is present in about a fourth of patients.[3,4] Venography is not usually part of the initial evaluation but typically is reserved for patients who will undergo some form of endovascular intervention. In my experience, patients who have recently been found to have radiosensitive tumors are usually treated immediately with radiation, chemotherapy, or both. Prompt therapy with these modalities often relieves the symptoms of SVC syndrome. Consequently, patients do not usually require endovascular intervention acutely. Patients with a malignancy who have been treated by irradiation, chemotherapy, or surgery can present several months later with SVC syndrome to radiation-induced fibrosis of central veins.

Venography and Catheterization of SVC Occlusion

Venography is still considered the "gold standard" for diagnosis and localization of occlusive disease in the SVC. With the patient lying supine or semi-recumbent, and to the extent it is clinically tolerated, bilateral access is obtained through both the right and left basilic veins. When there is an SVC occlusion with extension of acute thrombus into both brachiocephalic veins, each subclavian vein must be traversed with catheters and wires advanced into the SVC and right atrium. To gain access to a chronically occluded SVC involved by fibrosis the right femoral or right internal jugular approach may be necessary to provide for a better mechanical advantage. If the patient has a dialysis fistula, access may be gained through direct puncture of the fistula. Once venipuncture has been performed, simultaneous bilateral upper extremity venography is performed to document the extent and degree of stenosis or occlusion (Fig. 162-1).

In patients with upper extremity edema, venipuncture of the basilic vein may prove very difficult. Standard tourniquet techniques are often unsuccessful, because the basilic vein lies well below the skin surface. One technique involves cannulating a small hand vein and performing venography to map the basilic vein in the antecubital region with an arm tourniquet in place. The contrast medium–infiltrated basilic vein is then punctured under direct fluoroscopic guidance. A second popular method involves ultrasound-guided needle puncture of the basilic vein using a 5- or 7-MHz transducer with an arm tourniquet in place.

Once vascular access has been achieved in both arms, the basilic venipuncture sites are converted to No. 5 French (Fr) or No. 6 Fr angiographic side-arm sheaths. Attempts are then made to pass a No. 5 Fr angiographic catheter with a simple curve (Berenstein Glidecatheter, Boston Scientfic, Watertown, MA) and a 0.035-inch steerable hydrophilic guide wire (Glidewire, Boston Scientific) through the occluded vein segment. For more organized fibrotic occlusions, extra stiffness may be needed to avoid buckling of the catheter when it encounters resistance. In this situation, I would convert to a coaxial system consisting of a No. 7 or 8 Fr braided coronary guiding catheter fitted with a Touhy-Borst adapter to allow placement of the No. 5 Fr

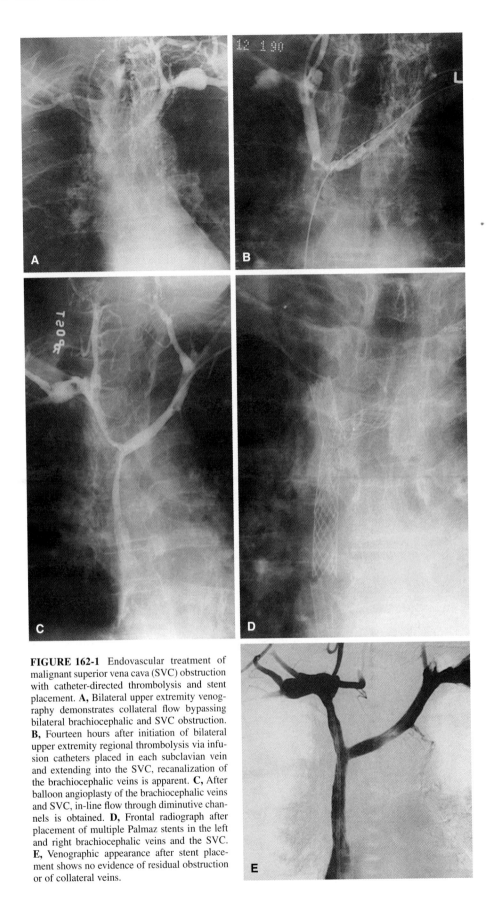

FIGURE 162-1 Endovascular treatment of malignant superior vena cava (SVC) obstruction with catheter-directed thrombolysis and stent placement. **A,** Bilateral upper extremity venography demonstrates collateral flow bypassing bilateral brachiocephalic and SVC obstruction. **B,** Fourteen hours after initiation of bilateral upper extremity regional thrombolysis via infusion catheters placed in each subclavian vein and extending into the SVC, recanalization of the brachiocephalic veins is apparent. **C,** After balloon angioplasty of the brachiocephalic veins and SVC, in-line flow through diminutive channels is obtained. **D,** Frontal radiograph after placement of multiple Palmaz stents in the left and right brachiocephalic veins and the SVC. **E,** Venographic appearance after stent placement shows no evidence of residual obstruction or of collateral veins.

catheter and guide wire. The guiding catheter provides a better mechanical advantage and reduces the tendency of the No. 5 Fr catheter to recoil. Once the lesion has been successfully traversed, pressure measurements can be recorded for future therapy.

Catheter-Directed Venous Thrombolytic Therapy

Catheter-directed thrombolytic therapy in the setting of SVC syndrome was first described in a 1974 report of a patient whose acute thrombosis was caused by a pacemaker lead.[17] Since then, a number of studies have documented the efficacy and safety of central venous thrombolysis, with and without supplemental PTA and endoluminal stenting.[15,18-22] The goal of catheter-directed thrombolysis in the acute setting is clear: to "lyse" the fresh thrombus, relieve the venous congestion, and restore venous return to the right atrium. Adjunctive PTA or stent placement should then be considered to treat the underlying lesion. In a chronically occluded SVC that is impenetrable by standard guide wire and catheter techniques, catheter-directed thrombolysis often serves to soften or partially recanalize the thrombus, to eventually allow a guide wire to cross the lesion. Once the guide wire has safely traversed the obstruction, again, PTA and stenting can dilate the occluded segment. Although many patients derive substantial benefit from thrombolysis alone, only a minority enjoy complete relief of symptoms.[15]

Locally delivered catheter-directed thrombolytic therapy has a number of distinct advantages over systemic lytic therapy for treatment of chronic occlusions. Catheter-directed thrombolysis ensures that the thrombolytic agent is delivered directly to the site of the occlusion, in higher concentration and to a larger surface area of the thrombus than a systemic peripheral can deliver. This more efficient delivery technique may be particularly beneficial for patients with large clot burdens involving long venous segments and may be particularly important in terms of limiting the length of the vein that requires endoluminal stenting. In contrast, a systemically administered thrombolytic agent is directed away from occluded venous segments by collateral channels and, consequently, is less efficient and more likely to produce complications.[23] Finally, catheter-directed thrombolysis generally requires a smaller total dose of thrombolytic agent and takes less time as compared with systemic thrombolysis.[23,24]

Two major thrombolytic delivery systems are currently available: the coaxial multicomponent system and the multiple side-hole single-catheter system. The coaxial system is the simplest to use and is easy to manage. With this system, the occlusion is first crossed with an 0.035-inch Glidewire and a No. 5 Fr angiographic catheter, as described earlier. Once the end-hole catheter is safely through the occluded segment of vein, the Glidewire is exchanged for a specially designed 0.035-inch thrombolytic guide wire. The thrombolytic guide wires are designed to "weep" or drip a thrombolytic agent (1) through an end hole (Sos wire; USCI, Billerica, MA; Cragg wire; Medi-Tech) or (2) along the distal few centimeters of the wire (Katzen infusion wire; Medi-Tech). The thrombolytic infusion wire is advanced out

through the end of the No. 5-Fr catheter and then secured using a Touhy-Borst adapter. From the basilic approach, the catheter is gently pulled back to the leading edge of the thrombus and the guide wire is placed approximately two thirds of the way into the thrombosed arterial segment.

The multiple side-hole catheter system consists of either a No. 5 Fr catheter (Mewissen catheter, Medi-Tech, or Pulse Spray catheter, AngioDynamics, Queensbury, NY) or a multilumen catheter. An occlusion wire prevents the infusate from leaking out through the end hole and instead forces it through a number of side holes in the multiple side-hole catheter. The multilumen catheter has two ports. One drips a thrombolytic solution through the guide wire end hole, and the other infuses four separate lumina that feed multiple side holes. The No. 4.8 Fr multilumen catheter allows simultaneous infusion of heparin through the sidearm of a No. 5 Fr angiographic sheath.

Mechanical Thrombectomy

Recently, in addition to the use of catheter-directed infusion of thrombolytic agents, an increasing array of mechanical thrombectomy catheters have joined the standard interventional armamentarium directed at the management of acute thrombotic occlusion. These thrombectomy devices are commonly used in both arteries and veins and may be applied alone or in combination with thrombolytic agents to remove clot. Mechanical thrombectomy catheters are especially attractive as an option to manage clot in patients who have contraindications to thrombolytic drug infusions or are at high risk for bleeding if exposed to these agents.

All mechanical thrombectomy devices are designed to share the goal of expeditiously removing clot from obstructed blood vessels at a tempo more rapid than that achievable by regional thrombolytic infusion. The precise technical mechanisms responsible for rapid thrombus dissolution by individual catheters are extremely variable and include direct contact, hydrodynamic, and rheolytic (flow-based) modes of action. A wide range of catheter designs exist, including those that feature saline jet sprays, spinning baskets, impellers, rotating guide wire/catheters, and even ultrasonic pulverizers.

In general, these catheters are more effective the more acute the thrombus. Consequently, in the settings of subacute or more chronic clot, this heterogeneous group of devices may only achieve a narrow "pilot" channel and often additional therapies, including angioplasty and stent placement, are required to obtain the desired luminal caliber. Similarly, in large vessels, like the venae cavae and iliac and brachiocephalic veins, the use of the current generation of mechanical thrombectomy catheters as a stand-alone treatment is often inadequate. Rather, contemporary strategies employ mechanical means to debulk the thrombus burden in large veins before an infusion of a thrombolytic agent is used to clean up residual clot. Alternatively, thrombectomy devices may be used after a period of regional thrombolysis to mop up any persistent foci of nonlysable clot. In either case, the tactical intent of these combination approaches is to accelerate the tempo of clot clearance, shorten the overall procedure time, reduce the length of thrombolytic fusion, and limit the total thrombolytic dose. It is expected, but not proved, that a shorter treatment time and exposure to less drug will reduce the frequency of bleeding complications compared with that observed for a regional thrombolytic infusion alone.

These techniques have also gained favor in the management of patients with thrombosed hemodialysis grafts and autologous fistulae, as well as acute massive pulmonary embolism, thrombosed transjugular intrahepatic portosystemic shunts, and portal vein thrombosis. Despite many initiatives designed to create the ideal mechanical thrombectomy catheter, it is clear to interventionists that this goal has not been achieved. Perhaps, given the range of clot maturity encountered at the time of clinical presentation, inability to determine the age of thrombus, and the wide variety of anatomic involvement, it is unreasonable to think that one device would be capable of successfully addressing all the challenges inherent in the spectrum of thrombotic venous obstruction.

Pharmacologic Agents

In terms of a specific thrombolytic agent routinely used in clinical practice today, the pharmacologic landscape is far different now than in 1999, when the effects of the U.S. Food and Drug Administration (FDA) action to halt the production and marketing of urokinase in the United States resulted in a shortage of the drug available for regional thrombolysis. At that time (and still at the time of this writing), streptokinase was the only agent approved by the FDA for peripheral use (deep venous thrombosis, arterial thrombosis, and arterial embolism). Since then, new agents have been adopted for peripheral vascular thrombolytic application. These include recombinant tissue plasminogen activator (rt-PA) (Alteplase; Genentech, South San Francisco, CA); r-PA (Reteplase; Centocor, Malvern, PA), and TNK-t-PA (Tenecteplase; Genentech). In addition, recombinant urokinase (r-UK) (Abbokinase; Abbott Laboratories, Abbott Park, IL) was approved in late 2002 by the FDA for the treatment of pulmonary embolism.

All of these fibrinolytic agents have accumulated clinical experience to support their use in catheter-directed regional thrombolysis of deep venous thrombosis and central venous obstruction.[24-26] To date, this experience has not indicated any statistically significantly competitive advantage of one drug over another in terms of thrombolytic efficacy or complications. Commonly, infusion doses with these agents are adjusted to modestly higher levels than those used in the peripheral arterial system because of the larger vessel size and overall clot burden observed in central venous obstruction. Examples of typical infusion rates of these agents used in the management of diffuse central venous obstruction include rt-PA, 0.25-2.0 mg/hr; r-PA 0.25-2.0 units/hr; r-UK 80,000-200,000 units/hr, and TNK-t-PA 0.25-1.0 mg/hr. In addition to these constant infusion doses, and antecedent bolus, lacing of the drug throughout the length of the involved vascular segment is a common practice.

The recent renaissance in the variety of thrombolytic agents available for peripheral applications has heightened awareness of the potential complications of concomitant use of anticoagulation, in terms of the frequency of hemorrhagic untoward events associated with regional thrombolytic procedures. These complications are most commonly observed at a catheter access site(s). As a result, full dose systemic anticoagulation is now used sparingly, in favor of subtherapeutic simultaneous administration of intravenous heparin or a new thrombin specific agent with a shorter half-life than heparin, bivalirudin (Angiomax; Medicines Company, Parsippany, NJ). The administration of these agents at a reduced dose is intended to prevent pericatheter thrombus formation in low-flow environments and limit rethrombosis of newly lysed segments before good flow is reestablished throughout the treated vessel.

A tumor-induced hypercoagulable state is not uncommon in patients undergoing palliative SVC reconstruction who have underlying malignant disease.[27] Consequently, antiplatelet prophylaxis, including 325 mg of aspirin daily, is administered for at least 6 months. In an effort to reduce the length of hospital stay during the transition from intravenous anticoagulation with heparin to oral warfarin, a loading dose of 5 mg of warfarin is administered on the first 2 days of the endovascular procedure. Subsequently, daily doses are titrated and international normalized ratio (INR) levels are followed on an outpatient basis with the target INR between 2.0 and 3.0.

Thrombolysis in most cases of chronic disease is performed for 24 to 48 hours, and follow-up venography is done daily. The thrombolytic infusion is discontinued before the 48-hour point if follow-up venography demonstrates no residual thrombus, if a complication related to regional thrombolysis occurs, or if the fibrinogen level falls below 100 mg/dL (1.0 g/L). During the regional thrombolytic infusion, both the partial thromboplastin time and the fibrinogen levels are checked every 6 hours. The partial thromboplastin time is maintained between 60 and 90 seconds, and fibrinogen levels are kept above 100 mg/dL. Fibrinogen levels below 100 mg/dL indicate a systemic fibrinolytic state and are associated with increased risk of hemorrhagic complications. Thrombolytic therapy is contraindicated for patients who have bleeding disorders or metastatic cancer that involves brain or spinal cord, those who have had a hemorrhagic stroke, and pregnant women.

Venous Angioplasty and Stenting

The role of PTA in the treatment of chronic central venous stenoses and occlusions has changed dramatically as endoluminal stenting has come into widespread use. Early studies reported encouraging technical results, but, because of the extensive recoil of diseased veins, PTA without stent placement has generally proved ineffective.[28-33] PTA is now principally used to recanalize occluded veins before stenting. Endoluminal stenting, unlike PTA alone, prevents elastic recoil and has greatly increased the long-term patency of venous endovascular therapy (see Fig. 15-1).[15,34,35]

In the SVC, the advisability of stent placement depends on (1) whether disease in the vein is focal or diffuse; (2) whether the cause of the obstruction is benign or malignant; (3) the venous anatomy; and (4) the personal preference of the clinician. In general, "long-segment venous disease" and lesions that include the brachiocephalic veins tend not to respond well to balloon dilation alone and almost inevitably require stenting. Patients with SVC occlusion secondary to cancer tend to experience dramatic and rapid relief of symptoms (e.g., facial edema, dyspnea, cognitive function, upper limb swelling) after stent placement, results that can significantly improve their quality of life.[36,37] Patients with benign disease, on the other hand, may require close monitoring and subsequent interventions, because they often survive long after their primary endovascular procedure. Secondary patency rates reported in this patient population have ranged between 25% and 85%.[15,22]

Reports of large clinical series document recent experience with three endoluminal stents used for central venous reconstruction: the Palmaz stent (Cordis Endovascular, Warren, NJ), the Wallstent (Boston Scientific, Natick, MA), and the Gianturco Z-stent (Bloomington, IN). Because all three have their advantages and disadvantages, the choice of which one to use is very subjective and inevitably based on the individual patient's clinical condition and venous anatomy and on the interventionist's experience and biases.

The Palmaz stent has been described in a number of studies as being effective in treating vena caval and central venous stenoses.[15,38,39] Palmaz stents are balloon-expandable, rigid, stainless steel cylinders. The principal advantages of the Palmaz design are its superior hoop strength, accuracy of placement, and limited foreshortening (Fig. 162-2). The main disadvantage is its susceptibility to plastic deformation from extrinsic compression by surrounding structures, including tumors.[40] Palmaz stents come in a variety of lengths, ranging from 10 to 78 mm, and some can be dilated to 17 mm. In the SVC these stents are usually deployed from the right femoral vein with a very long sheath (No. 9 or 10 Fr).

Earlier reports of the Wallstent applied to treatment of SVC obstruction cited mixed results.[40,41] The Wallstent is a longitudinally flexible, self-expanding, metal stent. The principal advantages of Wallstents are their relatively low-delivery profile, their flexibility, and the capability they afford of treating longer lesions with a single stent unit. For diameters smaller than 14 mm, the stent is mounted on a No. 7 or 8 Fr delivery catheter. The catheter makes it easy to introduce from the basilic vein, and, because of its flexibility, it passes more easily through the curved innominate and subclavian veins. It is available in lengths up to 90 mm and in diameters of 5 to 24 mm, features that make it appropriate for treating long segments of diseased vein. In addition, the fine-braid pattern of the stent and its large metallic surface area limit the size of the interstices, a feature that may prevent tumor ingrowth. The Wallstent is designed to foreshorten as it is deployed into the lumen of the vessel. Consequently, in certain anatomic areas, precise placement is difficult. In response to this limitation, the manufacturer recently designed a deployment system that allows the operator to safely reconstrain and then reposition the stent before it is finally deployed. Other arguable disadvantages of the Wallstent are its relatively low radial force, which is more apparent in larger-diameter stents, and its relatively large total metallic surface area as compared with other stents, features that make it relatively thrombogenic in the low-flow velocity venous system.

The Gianturco Z-stent was the first commercially available stent to be used by a number of centers to treat SVC syndrome.[12,42,43] Since the early reports, a large volume of data has documented the safety and efficacy of the device.[13,14,37,44,45] It is a relatively rigid, self-expanding stent. Among its advantages, the Z-stent comes in a wide variety of diameters (8 to 40 mm), possesses good hoop strength, and does not foreshorten during deployment. In addition, its small surface area, large interstices, and low thrombogenicity allow it to be placed across feeding veins. The small surface area and open design of the Z-stent, however, may allow tumor infiltration. The constrained stent is delivered into the appropriate delivery sheath by a blunt-tipped mandrel that is used as a pusher to advance the device to the target. The stent is deployed by fixing the pusher and withdrawing the sheath. Accurate deployment of this particular stent is not difficult; however, as it is currently designed, it cannot be repositioned.

My experience suggests that stenting of short segmental occlusions offers better and longer-lasting relief of symptoms than extensive stenting of diffuse disease. I prefer to use Wallstents for the treatment of brachiocephalic vein stenosis and use Palmaz stents in the SVC. Acute complications of stent deployment in the venous system (i.e., those that develop within 30 days) include stent migration, extrinsic compression, and thrombosis.[46-51] Long-term complications are related principally to stent patency and to development of intimal hyperplasia, thrombus deposition, and progression of the underlying pathophysiologic process.[52]

Stent migration can result from incomplete expansion of the stent or improper positioning. Most migration complications occur at the junction of the SVC with the right atrium, a point where there is an abrupt increase in transverse diameter and where stents that are not seated high enough in the SVC may develop emboli. The dislodged stent may become entangled in the trabecula of the right ventricle, damage the tricuspid valve, or embolize to the pulmonary arteries. Stents that remain in the right ventricle or pulmonary artery for any length of time may eventually become covered with fibrous tissue and endothelialized and, thus, impossible to remove percutaneously.[48,49] In light of this fact, and depending on the patient's clinical condition, an immediate decision must be made to either leave the stent or retrieve it and deploy it in the intended site or in a "safe" area such as the infrarenal IVC or the common iliac vein. Balloons, baskets, loop snares, and a variety of endovascular techniques have been used successfully to retrieve migrated stents.[53,54]

Balloon-expandable stents such as the Palmaz are susceptible to plastic deformation when external, two-point compression is applied. This phenomenon has been observed in the subclavian vein, where stents may be subjected to compression by external forces applied to the vein as it runs over the first rib, typically from the scalenus and subclavius muscles.[50,51] Theoretically, both self-expanding and balloon-expandable stents may be compressed by tumor that encases the SVC, a sequela that results in either stenosis or occlusion of the SVC with the development of SVC syndrome. If the problem is caught early enough, redilation or restenting of these lesions often produces very good secondary patency.

Stents in the venous system carry the risk for thrombosis because of the foreign body surface area and the low-flow velocity of venous blood. After stent placement, patients continue treatment with intravenous heparin while they are "transitioning" to warfarin therapy. Anticoagulant therapy is adjusted to maintain an INR of 2.0 to 2.5. Patients with an

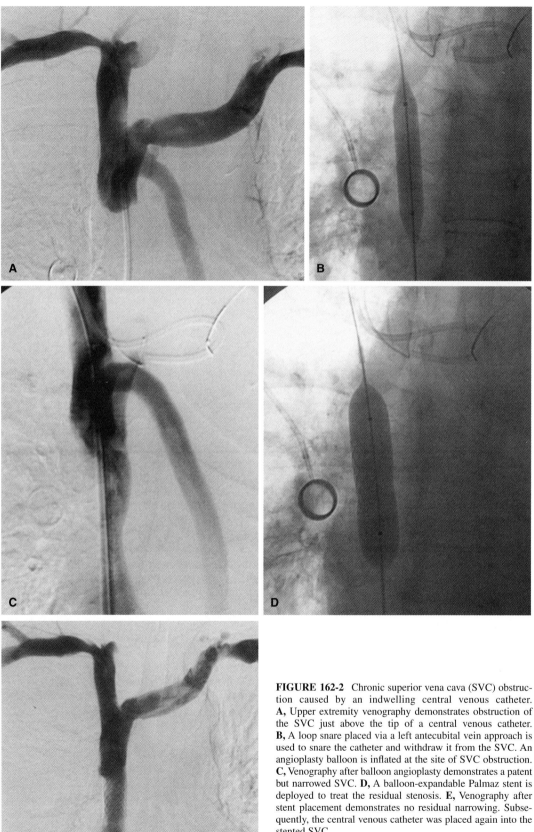

FIGURE 162-2 Chronic superior vena cava (SVC) obstruction caused by an indwelling central venous catheter. **A,** Upper extremity venography demonstrates obstruction of the SVC just above the tip of a central venous catheter. **B,** A loop snare placed via a left antecubital vein approach is used to snare the catheter and withdraw it from the SVC. An angioplasty balloon is inflated at the site of SVC obstruction. **C,** Venography after balloon angioplasty demonstrates a patent but narrowed SVC. **D,** A balloon-expandable Palmaz stent is deployed to treat the residual stenosis. **E,** Venography after stent placement demonstrates no residual narrowing. Subsequently, the central venous catheter was placed again into the stented SVC.

underlying malignancy receive oral anticoagulation as long as this is clinically feasible. For patients with benign disease, anticoagulation is discontinued at 6-month follow-up if clinical patency has been maintained.[15,46]

Stent-Grafts

The use of stent-grafts for the treatment of aneurysmal disease is well documented.[55] There are, however, case reports of similar devices being used in the venous system and in transjugular intrahepatic portosystemic shunt revisions.[56,57] There has been only one case report of stent-graft placement in the SVC. It describes the use of Z-stents covered with nonporous polyester graft material (Meadox Medicals, Oakland, NJ). In this particular case, the stent-graft was placed to treat a previously stented malignant obstruction that had been reoccluded by tumor ingrowth. After a course of aggressive thrombolysis, a residual filling defect was noted on the cavogram. The filling defect was considered to represent invading tumor or thrombus in the lumen of the previously stented SVC. The rationale for using such a device is that the graft material covering the stent acts as a barrier to further ingrowth of tumor and development of thrombus. Follow-up was limited because the patient died only 19 days after the procedure, owing to the effects of the underlying malignancy. In contrast to stent-grafts placed in the arterial system to exclude aneurysms, the current role of endoluminal stent-grafting in the venous system appears palliative, not yet a definitive, first-line therapy.

Although experience with stent-grafting in the venous system is very limited, there are a number of potential complications. The most important one may be related to stent-graft misplacement. Because graft material covers the stent, the interventionist must be careful not to place the device across important feeding veins. This could exacerbate symptoms, particularly in chronic cases when a rich network of collaterals has formed. Thrombosis of the stent-graft is another possible complication. There may be a predisposition to thrombosis when the diameter of the stent-graft has been oversized or it has not fully expanded, because in the low-pressure venous system any redundancy in graft material may serve as a nidus for thrombus formation.

Unlike placement in the arterial system, stent-grafts placed in the venous system do not require introduction through a surgical venotome; percutaneous access is still feasible for delivery systems up to No. 24 Fr in most patients.

Inferior Vena Cava

Chronic occlusions of the IVC are a heterogeneous group of lesions of varied causes and unpredictable prognoses (Table 162-2).[58,59] IVC occlusion may be associated with a wide range of clinical manifestations, including bilateral lower extremity pain and edema, thoracoabdominal varicosities, massive ascites, back pain, umbilical herniation, venous ulceration, and even disrupted liver and kidney function if the intrahepatic vena cava or renal veins are involved.[5,58-60] Medical management alone has not been successful in treating chronic IVC occlusions, and surgery

has been reserved for the most severe cases. (The results of surgical treatment of IVC occlusion are detailed in Chapter 163.[7,9,10,61-63]) Initial patency rates reported for PTA were very good.[64,65] Long-term patency rates, however, were disappointing, and repeat angioplasty was necessary in many cases.[66-68] The further development of endovascular stents has greatly improved endovascular patency rates and reduced the need for repeated PTA.[44,69-73]

Membranous and discrete segmental occlusions are the most frequent benign occlusive diseases of the suprahepatic and intrahepatic IVC (Fig. 162-3).[58] Focal segmental occlusion of the IVC is thought to be an advanced form of membranous obstruction.[61] Both forms can be associated with thrombosis of the hepatic veins (Budd-Chiari syndrome) and may cause liver failure, portal hypertension, bilateral leg swelling, and, rarely, venous claudication. Iliocaval venous thrombosis after IVC interruption is the most common benign cause of infrarenal IVC occlusion (Fig. 162-4).[58] These patients are more likely than those with suprahepatic and intrahepatic IVC occlusions to develop lower limb swelling and deep venous thrombosis.

Venography and Catheterization of Inferior Vena Caval Occlusion

As described earlier, all patients with IVC occlusion are studied venographically. Percutaneous venous access is initially obtained through either the common femoral or jugular veins. Transfemoral or transjugular cavograms are used to demonstrate the location, length, and severity of occlusive lesions. Both access routes allow measurement of pressure gradients across stenoses and evaluation of the results after PTA stent deployment.

In cases of acute obstruction, it may be easy to traverse the occlusion by passing a catheter and guide wire system from a single access site. As an access site, however, the femoral vein may prove difficult to puncture in patients who have lower extremity edema or an iliofemoral occlusion. It may be necessary to place the patient in the prone position and make the venipuncture into the popliteal vein.

Table 162-2	Etiology of Inferior Vena Caval Obstruction
Benign	
Membranous occlusion	
Hypercoagulability disorders	
Inferior vena caval interruption	
Post-transplant surgery	
Inferior vena caval filter thrombosis	
Dialysis fistula–related stenosis	
Retroperitoneal fibrosis	
Inflammation	
Trauma	
Infection	
Malignant	
Hepatocellular carcinoma	
Renal cell carcinoma	
Lymphoma	

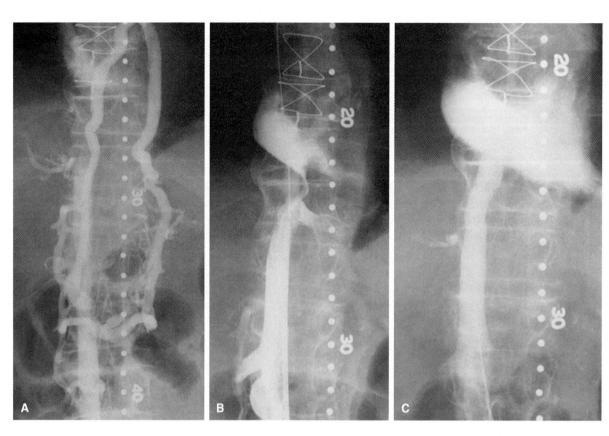

FIGURE 162-3   Focal chronic obstruction of the intrahepatic inferior vena cava (IVC). **A,** Inferior venacavogram demonstrates obstruction of the IVC with abundant collateral opacification. **B,** After balloon angioplasty, residual stenosis of the intrahepatic IVC is evident. **C,** No residual narrowing is noted after placement of two Palmaz stents at the site of IVC obstruction.

Once venous access has been achieved from the common femoral, jugular, or popliteal approach, the venipuncture site is converted to a hemostatic angiographic sheath. Initial attempts should be made at passing a No. 5 Fr angiographic catheter with a simple pre-formed curve and a 0.035-inch steerable hydrophilic guide wire through the occluded venous segment. Chronically occluded vena caval and iliocaval segments may require conversion to a coaxial system of catheters to provide better mechanical advantage. This may entail the use of a coronary guiding catheter to support the No. 5 Fr angiographic catheter and wire.

Catheter-Directed Venous Thrombolytic Therapy

Thrombolytic therapy alone is effective in a very small percentage of patients.[74,75] When combined with PTA and stent placement, however, local thrombolytic therapy contributes to successful recanalization (Fig. 162-5).[76] As in the SVC, catheter-directed thrombolytic infusions create a channel through acute thrombus and soften chronic thrombus. In accordance with the protocol described for SVC occlusions, a single infusion system is placed in the thrombus to deliver urokinase for 12 to 48 hours. If the occlusion includes the iliofemoral system bilaterally, two infusion systems should be introduced to treat each lower extremity.

Venous Angioplasty and Stenting

The first reported attempt at balloon dilation of an occluded IVC in 1974 used a Fogarty balloon catheter.[77] It was not until almost 10 years later that Gruntzig-type balloons were used in IVC occlusions, and initial results were encouraging.[64,65] Successful recanalization and dilatations were achieved by simultaneous inflation of four balloons in the obstructed IVC segment. Recent developments in catheter design now allow production of balloons with a diameter large enough to treat the entire IVC (12 to 24 mm). Like the results of PTA for venous disease in the SVC, long-term patency rates of PTA alone in the IVC have been disappointing.[71]

The role of stents in IVC occlusions is to prevent the elastic recoil typically seen after PTA. The three stents most used are the Palmaz stent, the Wallstent, and the Gianturco Z-stent. All three stents can be placed via either a transfemoral or a transjugular approach with good results.

A review of the literature reveals that Gianturco Z-stents are the ones most often used for IVC occlusions. This may be due to the stent's small surface area and robust radial force, especially if the stent is oversized. Results have been particularly encouraging in the treatment of Budd-Chiari and anastomotic stenosis after liver transplantation.[78,79] Use of Wallstents has also been reported for treating chronic occlusions due to long-term indwelling femoral hemodialysis catheters.[80] Also, Palmaz stents have been used to a

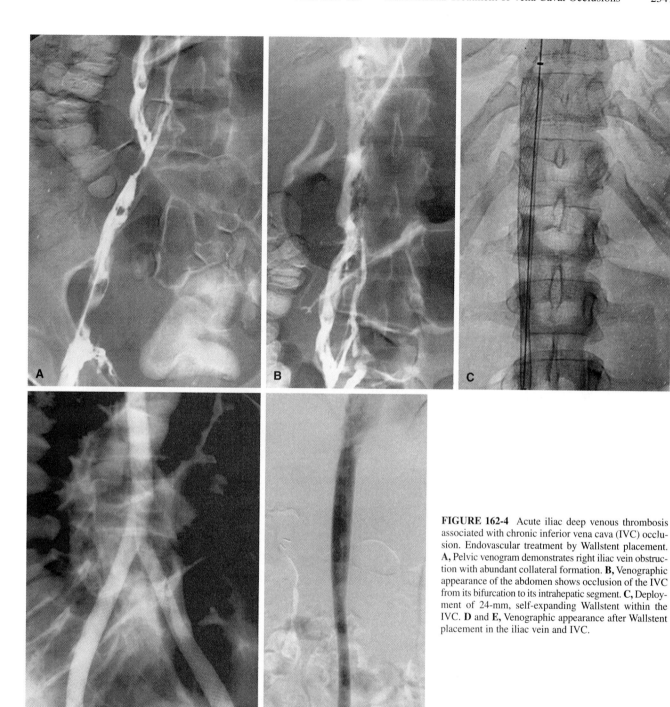

FIGURE 162-4 Acute iliac deep venous thrombosis associated with chronic inferior vena cava (IVC) occlusion. Endovascular treatment by Wallstent placement. **A,** Pelvic venogram demonstrates right iliac vein obstruction with abundant collateral formation. **B,** Venographic appearance of the abdomen shows occlusion of the IVC from its bifurcation to its intrahepatic segment. **C,** Deployment of 24-mm, self-expanding Wallstent within the IVC. **D** and **E,** Venographic appearance after Wallstent placement in the iliac vein and IVC.

limited degree in treating IVC occlusion.[81] Their relatively short lengths preclude easy and effective treatment of long segment venous occlusions.

Stent-Grafts

The use of stent-grafts has not been reported in the IVC, perhaps because of the lower incidence of invading tumors as compared with the SVC.

■ REFERENCES

1. Escalante CP: Causes and management of superior vena cava syndrome. Oncology 7:61, 1993.
2. Abner A: Approach to the patient who presents with superior vena cava obstruction. Chest 103:394S, 1993.
3. Lochridge SK, Knibbe WP, Doty DB: Obstruction of superior vena cava. Surgery 85:14, 1979.
4. Adar R, Rosenthal T, Mozes M: Venal caval obstruction in 76 patients. Angiology 25:433, 1974.

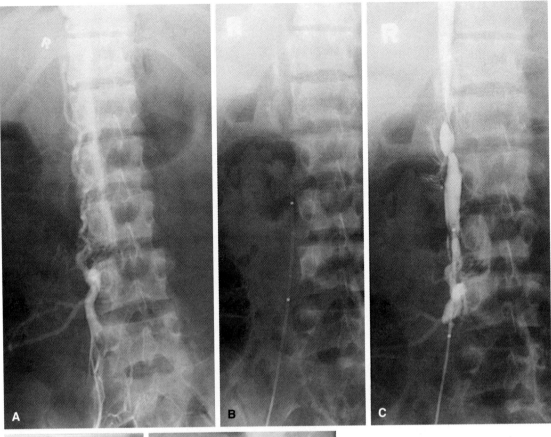

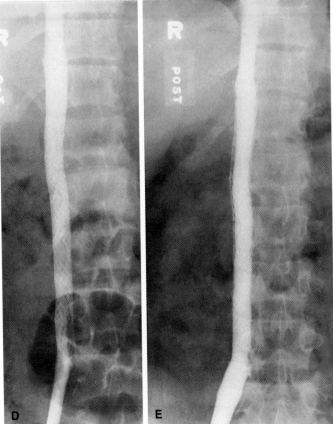

FIGURE 162-5 Catheter-directed thrombolysis and stent placement for recanalization of an inferior vena cava (IVC) obstruction. The occlusion was associated with multiple femoral hemodialysis catheters and was first documented venographically 4 years before this study. **A,** Right iliac venogram shows obstruction of the IVC at the level of its bifurcation. **B,** Multiple-sidehole infusion cathether placed within the IVC for regional thrombolysis with urokinase. **C,** Inferior venacavogram performed 12 hours after initiation of catheter-directed thrombolysis shows partial recanalization of the IVC. **D,** Appearance of IVC after placement of multiple Palmaz stents shows no residual stenosis. **E,** Follow-up cavogram 3 years after stent placement demonstrates mild intimal hypertrophy lining the stents without significant narrowing of the IVC.

5. Davenport D, Ferree C, Blake D: Radiation therapy in the treatment of superior vena cava obstruction. Cancer 42:2600, 1966.

6. Levitt SH, Jona TK, Kilpatrick SJ, Bogardus CR: Treatment of malignant superior vena cava syndrome. Semin Oncol 5:123, 1978.

7. Gloviczki P, Pairolero P, Toomey B, et al: Reconstruction of large veins for nonmalignant venous disease. J Vasc Surg 16:750, 1992.

8. Doty DB: Bypass of superior vena cava: Six years experience with spiral vein graft for the obstruction of superior vena cava due to benign or malignant disease. J Thorac Cardiovasc Surg 83:326, 1982.

9. McCarthy PM, vonHeerden JA, Adson MA, et al: Budd-Chiari syndrome: Medical and surgical management of thirty patients. Arch Surg 120:657, 1985.

10. Iwashi K: Surgical correction of the inferior vena cava obstruction with Budd-Chiari syndrome. Nippon Geka Hokan 50:559, 1981.

11. Sarkar R, Eilber FR, Gelabert HA, et al: Prosthetic replacement of the inferior vena cava for malignancy. J Vasc Surg 28:75, 1998.

12. Rosch J, Bedell JE, Putman J, et al: Gianturco expandable wire stents in the treatment of superior vena cava syndrome recurring after maximum-tolerance radiation. Cancer 60:1243, 1987.

13. Shah R, Sabanthan S, Lowe RA, et al: Stenting in malignant obstruction of the superior vena cava. J Thorac Cardiovasc Surg 112:335, 1996.

14. Irving J, Dondelinger R, Reidy J, et al: Gianturco self-expanding stents: Clinical experience in the vena cava and large veins. Cardiovasc Intervent Radiol 15:328, 1992.

15. Kee ST, Kinoshita L, Razavi, et al: Superior vena cava syndrome: Treatment with catheter-directed thrombolysis and endovascular stent placement. Radiology 206:187, 1998.

16. Alimi YS, Gloviczki P, Vrtiska TJ, et al: Reconstruction of the superior vena cava: Benefits of postoperative surveillance and secondary endovascular techniques. J Vasc Surg 27:287, 1998.

17. Williams DR, Demos NJ: Thrombosis of superior vena cava caused by pacemaker wire and managed with streptokinase. J Thorac Cardiovasc Surg 68:134, 1974.

18. Mico G, Robles I, Catalan M, et al: Superior vena cava syndrome caused by pacemaker cable, treated with streptokinase. Rev Clin Esp 177:358, 1985.

19. Montgomery J, D'Souza V, Dyer R, et al: Non-surgical treatment of superior vena cava: Management of upper extremity central venous obstruction using interventional radiology. Ann Vasc Surg 12:202, 1998.

20. Blackburn T, Dunn M: Pacemaker-induced superior vena cava syndrome: Consideration of management. Am Heart J 116:893, 1988.

21. Crow MT, Davies CH, Gaines PA: Percutaneous management of superior vena cava occlusions. Cardiovasc Intervent Radiol 18:367, 1995.

22. Kalman PG, Lindsay TF, Clarke K, et al: Management of upper extremity central venous obstruction using interventional radiology. Ann Vasc Surg 12:202, 1998.

23. Becker GJ, Holden RW, Rabe FE, et al: Low-dose fibrinolytic therapy: Results and new concepts. Radiology 149:769, 1983.

24. van Breda A, Katzen BT, Deutsch AS: Urokinase versus streptokinase in local thrombolysis. Radiology 165:109, 1987.

25. McNamara TO, Fischer JR: Thrombolysis of arterial and graft occlusions: Improved results using high-dose urokinase. AJR Am J Roentgenol 144:769, 1985.

26. Becker GJ, Rabe FE, Richmond BD, et al: Low-dose fibrinolytic therapy: Results and new concepts. Radiology 148:663, 1983.

27. Naschitz JE, Yeshurun D, Lev LM: Thromboembolism in cancer: Changing trends. Cancer 71:1384, 1993.

28. Sherry C, Diamond N, Meyers T, et al: Successful treatment of superior vena cava syndrome by venous angioplasty. AJR Am J Roentgenol 147:834, 1986.

29. Ingram TL, Reid SH, Tisnado J, et al: Percutaneous transluminal angioplasty of brachiocephalic vein stenoses in patients with dialysis shunts. Radiology 166:45, 1988.

30. Walpole H, Lovett K, Chaung V, et al: Superior vena cava syndrome treated by percutaneous balloon angioplasty. Am Heart J 115:1303, 1988.

31. Davidson C, Newman G, Sheikh K, et al: Mechanisms of angioplasty in hemodialysis fistula stenoses evaluated by intravascular ultrasound. Kidney Int 40:91, 1991.

32. Wisselink W, Maoney SR, Becker MD, et al: Comparison of operative reconstruction and percutaneous balloon dilation central venous obstruction. Am J Surg 166:200, 1993.

33. Kovalik E, Newman G, Suhocki P, et al: Correction of central venous stenoses: Use of angioplasty and vascular Wallstents. Kidney Int 45:1117, 1994.

34. Gaines PA, Belli AM, Anderson PB, et al: Superior vena caval obstruction managed by the Gianturco Z-stent. Clin Radiol 49:202, 1994.

35. Oudkerk M, Kuijpers TJ, Schmitz PI, et al: Self-expanding metal stents for palliative treatment of superior vena caval syndrome. Cardiovasc Intervent Radiol 19:146, 1996.

36. Dyet JF, Nicholson AA, Cook AM: The use of the Wallstent endovascular prosthesis in the treatment of malignant obstruction of the superior vena cava. Clin Radiol 48:381, 1993.

37. Oudkerk, Kuijpers TJ, Schmitz PI, et al: Self-expanding metal stents for palliative treatment of superior vena cava syndrome. Cardiovasc Intervent Radiol 19:146, 1996.

38. Palmaz J: Balloon expandable intravascular stent. AJR Am J Roentgenol 150:1263, 1988.

39. Solomam N, Holey M, Jarmolowski L: Intravascular stents in the management of superior vena cava syndrome. Cathet Cardiovasc Diagn 23:245, 1991.

40. Antonucci F, Salmonowitz C, Stuckmann G, et al: Placement of venous stents: Clinical experience with a self-expanding prosthesis. Radiology 183:493, 1992.

41. Watkinson AF, Hansell DM: Expandable Wallstent for the treatment of obstruction of the superior vena cava. Thorax 48:915, 1993.

42. Charnsangavej C, Carrusco CH, Wallace S, et al: Stenosis of the vena cava: Preliminary assessment of treatment with expandable metallic stents. Radiology 161:295, 1986.

43. Putnam JS, Uchida BT, Antonovic R, et al: Superior vena cava syndrome associated with massive thrombosis: Treatment with expandable wire stents. Radiology 167:727, 1988.

44. Gaines PA, Belli AM, Anderson PB, et al: Superior vena caval obstruction managed by the Gianturco Z stent. Clin Radiol 49:202, 1994.

45. Kazushi K, Sonomura T, Mitouzane K, et al: Self-expandable metallic stent therapy for superior vena cava syndrome: Clinical observations. Radiology 189:531, 1993.

46. Rosch J, Petersen BD, Lakin PC: Venous stents: Indications, techniques, results. In Perler BA, Becker GJ (eds): Vascular Intervention: A Clinical Approach. New York, Thieme, 1998, p 706.

47. Carrasco CH, Charnsangavej C, Wright K, et al: Use of self-expanding stents in stenoses of the superior vena cava. J Vasc Interv Radiol 3:409, 1992.

48. Entwisle KG, Watkinson AF, Reidy J: Case report: Migration and shortening of a self-expanding metallic stent complicating the treatment of malignant superior vena cava stenosis. Clin Radiol 51:593, 1996.

49. Gray RJ, Dolmatch BL, Horton KM, et al: Migration of Palmaz stents following deployment for venous stenoses related to hemodialysis access. J Vasc Interv Radiol 5:117, 1994.

50. Bjarnason H, Hunter DW, Crain MR, et al: Collapse of a Palmaz stent in the subclavian vein. AJR Am J Roentgenol 160:1123, 1993.

51. Prischl FC, Weber T, Lenglinger F, et al: Conservative management of late Palmaz stent embolization to the pulmonary artery—a complication after PTA with stent implantation of a fistula-draining right subclavian vein stenosis. Nephrol Dial Transplant 12:119, 1997.

52. Nishibe MK, Ohkashiw MH, Takahashi OH, et al: Gianturco stents for the venous system: A detailed pathological study. Surg Today 28:396, 1998.

53. Rhee JS, Slonim SM, Dake MD, et al: Retrieval of intravascular stents. Radiology 205:431, 1997.

54. Cekrirge S, Foster R, Weiss JP, et al: Percutaneous removal of an embolized Wallstent during a transjugular intrahepatic portosystemic shunt procedure. J Vasc Interv Radiol 4:559, 1993.

55. Dake MD, Miller C, Semba CP, et al: Transluminal placement of endovascular stent-grafts for the treatment of descending thoracic aortic aneurysms. N Engl J Med 331:1729, 1994.

56. Chin DH, Peterson BD, Timmermans H, et al: Stent-graft in the management of superior vena cava syndrome. Cardiovasc Intervent Radiol 19:302, 1996.

57. Saxon RR, Timmermans HA, Uchida BT, et al: Stent-grafts for revision of TIPS stenoses and occlusions: A clinical pilot study. J Vasc Interv Radiol 8:539, 1997.

58. Harris R: The etiology of inferior vena caval obstruction and compression. Crit Rev Clin Radiol Nucl Med 8:57, 1976.

59. Missal ME, Robinson JA, Tatum RW: Inferior vena cava obstruction: Clinical manifestation, diagnostic methods, and related problems. Ann Intern Med 62:133, 1965.

60. Sonin AH, Mazer MJ, Powers TA: Obstruction of the inferior vena cava: A multiple-modality demonstration of causes, manifestations, and collateral pathways. RadioGraphics 12:309, 1992.

61. Hirooka M, Kimura C: Membranous obstruction of the hepatic portion of the inferior vena cava. Arch Surg 100:656, 1970.

62. Kimura C, Matsuda S, Koie H, et al: Membranous obstruction of the hepatic portion of the inferior vena cava: Clinical study of nine cases. Surgery 72:551, 1972.

63. Wilson SE, Jabour H, Stone R, et al: Patency of biological and prosthetic inferior vena cava grafts with distal limb fistula. Arch Surg 113:1174, 1992.

64. Yamada R, Sato M, Kawabata M, et al: Segmental obstruction of the hepatic inferior vena cava treated by transluminal angioplasty. Radiology 49:91, 1983.

65. Jeans WD, Bourne JT, Read AE: Treatment of hepatic vein and inferior vena caval obstruction by balloon dilatation. Br J Radiol 56:687, 1983.

66. Lois JF, Hartzman S, Mcglade CT, et al: Budd-Chiari syndrome: Treatment with percutaneous transhepatic recanalization and dilation. Radiology 170:791, 1989.

67. Martin LG, Henderson JM, Millikan WJ Jr, et al: Angioplasty for long-term treatment of patients with Budd-Chiari syndrome. AJR Am J Roentgenol 154:1007, 1990.

68. Sato M, Yamada R, Tsuji K, et al: Percutaneous transluminal angioplasty in segmental obstruction of the hepatic inferior vena cava: Long-term results. Cardiovasc Intervent Radiol 13:189, 1990.

69. Gilliams A, Dick R, Platts A, et al: Dilation of the inferior vena cava using an expandable metal stent in Budd-Chiari syndrome. J Hepatol 13:149, 1991.

70. Carrasco C, Charnsangavej C, Wright K, et al: Use of the Gianturco self-expanding stent in stenosis of the superior and inferior venae cavae. J Vasc Interv Radiol 3:409, 1992.

71. Venbrux AC, Mitchell SE, Savader SJ, et al: Long-term results with the use of metallic stents in the inferior vena cava for treatment of Budd-Chiari syndrome. J Vasc Interv Radiol 5:411, 1994.

72. Park JH, Chung JW, Han JK, et al: Interventional management of benign obstruction of the hepatic inferior vena cava. J Vasc Interv Radiol 5:403, 1994.

73. Simo G, Echenagusia A, Camunez F, et al: Stenosis of the inferior vena cava after liver transplantation: Treatment with Gianturco expandable metallic stents. Cardiovasc Intervent Radiol 18:212, 1995.

74. Maddrey WC: Hepatic vein thrombosis (Budd-Chiari syndrome). Hepatology 4(Suppl):44s, 1984.

75. Frank JW, Kamath PS, Stanson AW: Budd-Chiari syndrome: Early intervention with angioplasty and thrombolytic therapy. Mayo Clin Proc 69:877, 1994.

76. Ishiguchi T, Fukatsu H, Itoh S, et al: Budd-Chiari syndrome with long segmental inferior vena cava obstruction: Treatment with thrombolysis, angioplasty, and intravascular stents. J Vasc Interv Radiol 3:421, 1992.

77. Eguchi S, Takeuchi Y, Asano K: Successful balloon membranotomy for obstruction of the hepatic portion of the inferior vena cava. Surgery 76:837, 1974.

78. Berger H, Hilbert T, Zuhlke K, et al: Balloon dilatation and stent placement of suprahepatic caval anastomotic stenosis following liver transplantation. Cardiovasc Intervent Radiol 16:384, 1993.

79. Baijil SS, Roy S, Phadke RV, et al: Management of idiopathic Budd-Chiari syndrome with primary stent placement: Early results. J Vasc Interv Radiol 7:545, 1996.

80. Chang TC, Zaleski GX, Lin BHJ, et al: Treatment of inferior vena cava obstruction in hemodialysis patients using Wallstents: Early and intermediate results. AJR Am J Roentgenol 171:125, 1998.

81. Elson JD, Becker GJ, Wholey MH, et al: Vena caval and central venous stenoses: Management with Palmaz balloon-expandable intraluminal stents. J Vasc Interv Radiol 2:215, 1991.

Evaluation and Management of Malignant Tumors of the Inferior Vena Cava

163

THOMAS C. BOWER, MD

Tumors of the inferior vena cava (IVC) are rare and often malignant.[1-5] Management of these patients is difficult because symptoms occur late, adjuvant therapy has been ineffective, and surgical resection with caval replacement is a major operation with unpredictable long-term benefit. Currently, surgical resection offers the only hope for cure or palliation of symptoms. Improvements in surgical techniques, anesthesia, and critical care and the use of externally supported synthetic grafts for venous reconstruction have resulted in more reports of successful tumor resection and IVC replacement.[1,4-26] The types of IVC tumors, their clinical presentation, the current methods of diagnosis, and surgical treatment are reviewed.

For reference, the IVC is arbitrarily divided into three segments, as described by Kieffer and colleagues (Fig. 163-1).[12] The suprahepatic IVC is the segment between the hepatic veins and the right atrium; the suprarenal IVC is the segment between the renal and hepatic veins; and the infrarenal segment extends from the confluence of the common iliac veins to the renal veins. The retrohepatic IVC lies behind the liver, and the infrahepatic portion defines the area between the caudate lobe veins and the renal veins.

■ TUMOR TYPES

The types of primary and secondary tumors of the IVC are shown in Table 163-1. The most common primary tumor is leiomyosarcoma.[27] Vascular leiomyosarcomas are rare, involve veins more often than arteries, and represent less than 2% of all leiomyosarcomas.[28] Only a few hundred cases have been reported since Perl's first description in 1871.[29,30] Primary venous leiomyosarcoma (PVL) occurs most often in the IVC compared with other central or peripheral veins. Dzsinich and associates found 60% of 210 reported cases of PVL to arise from the IVC.[5] Any segment of the vena cava may be involved. Mingoli and coworkers found involvement of the suprarenal IVC in 42% of cases, the infrarenal IVC in 34%, and the suprahepatic IVC in 24% (Fig. 163-2).[4]

Pathologically, these tumors are polypoid or nodular, are firmly attached to the vessel of origin, and exhibit less intratumor hemorrhage and necrosis than other retroperitoneal sarcomas (Fig. 163-3).[5,27,31] The most common growth pattern is intraluminal, but the tumor may invade adjacent structures.[31] This latter characteristic makes them difficult to differentiate from retroperitoneal sarcomas, which have vascular involvement. Almost one half of patients have metastases to the lung, liver, kidney, bone, pleura, or chest wall at the time of diagnosis.[4,5,27,32] If these tumors are not treated, survival is measured in months, with death secondary to complications of locoregional or metastatic disease. Mingoli and coworkers reported a mean survival of 3 months for untreated patients in their series.[4]

Secondary malignancies that affect the IVC include retroperitoneal sarcomas such as liposarcoma, malignant

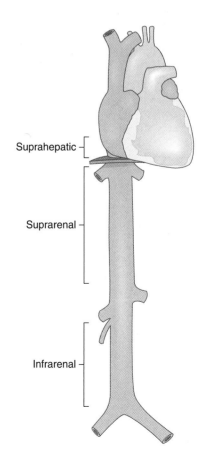

FIGURE 163-1 Segments of the inferior vena cava.

Suprahepatic

Suprarenal

Infrarenal

Table 163-1	Tumors of the Inferior Vena Cava

Primary

IVC leiomyosarcoma

Secondary

Retroperitoneal soft tissue tumors
    Liposarcoma
    Leiomyosarcoma
    Malignant fibrous histiocytoma
Hepatic tumors
    Cholangiocarcinoma
    Hepatocellular carcinoma
    Metastatic (e.g., colorectal)
Pancreaticoduodenal cancers

Secondary Tumors That May Have Tumor Thrombus

Renal cell carcinoma
Pheochromocytoma
Adrenocortical carcinoma
Sarcomas of uterine origin
    Leiomyomatosis
    Endometrial stromal cell
Germ cell tumors
    Embryonal
    Teratocarcinoma

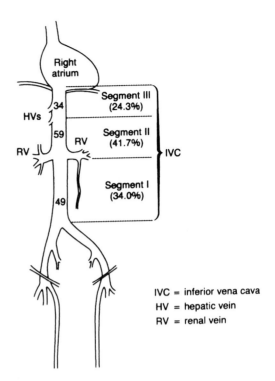

FIGURE 163-2 Distribution of primary inferior vena cava leiomyosarcomas. (Data based on a review by Mingoli A, Feldhaus RJ, Cavallaro A, Stipa S: Leiomyosarcoma of the inferior vena cava. In Bergan JJ, Yao ST [eds]: Surgery of the Veins. New York, Grune & Stratton, 1985, pp 423-443. By permission of Mayo Foundation.)

fibrous histiocytoma, or leiomyosarcoma; liver cancers; and duodenal, pancreatic, intestinal, adrenal, or renal malignancies. These cancers either invade the IVC, obstruct its lumen by extrinsic compression, or grow intraluminally (Fig. 163-4).

Retroperitoneal sarcomas can obstruct any segment of the IVC, and they are the most common cause of malignant obstruction of the infrarenal segment.[2] These tumors usually have a pseudocapsule and displace but do not invade adjacent structures. If they become invasive, they are indistinguishable pathologically from primary tumors of the IVC, which have grown extraluminally. As many as one third of cases have a combination of extraluminal and intraluminal growth.[31,33] Visceral or solid organ cancers invade or obstruct the IVC in anatomic proximity to the site of origin of the neoplasm. Advanced hepatic, duodenal, pancreatic, and large renal or adrenal malignancies may obstruct the suprarenal vena cava.[2] Typically, these cancers obliterate the normal tissue planes around the IVC.

Some renal cell and adrenocortical cancers, pheochromocytomas, uterine sarcomas, and germ cell tumors grow as tumor thrombus within the lumen of the IVC (Fig. 163-5).[34-57] Renal cell cancer is the most common malignancy to exhibit this behavior. It is also the most common cancer of the IVC that requires operative intervention.[34-37,57]

Tumor thrombus is found in the renal veins in 15% to 20% of patients with renal cell cancers.[44,46,57] The right kidney is affected more than the left one.[36,44,48,58] Kallman and coworkers reviewed 431 preoperative radiologic imaging studies and found tumor thrombus only in patients whose cancers were larger than 4.5 cm.[58] However, I have treated a patient with caval tumor thrombus whose primary renal cancer was only 2 cm.

Intracaval extension of tumor thrombus is found in 4% to 15% of patients. The proximal extent of IVC tumor

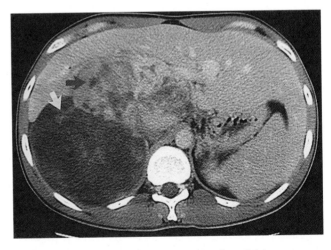

FIGURE 163-3 CT scan of a large retroperitoneal leiomyosarcoma involving the organs of the right upper quadrant, including the liver and retrohepatic vena cava. Note the necrotic areas within the tumor *(arrows)*. (From Bower TC: Primary and secondary tumors of the inferior vena cava. In Gloviczki P, Yao JST [eds]: Handbook of Venous Disorders. London, Chapman & Hall, 1996, pp 529-550.)

thrombus is classified into four levels based on whether the thrombus is above or below the diaphragm and whether it involves the right side of the heart (Fig. 163-6).[35,35,44,53,57] About one half of patients with renal cell carcinoma have extension of tumor thrombus to the renal vein/IVC confluence (level I). In another 40% of cases, the thrombus

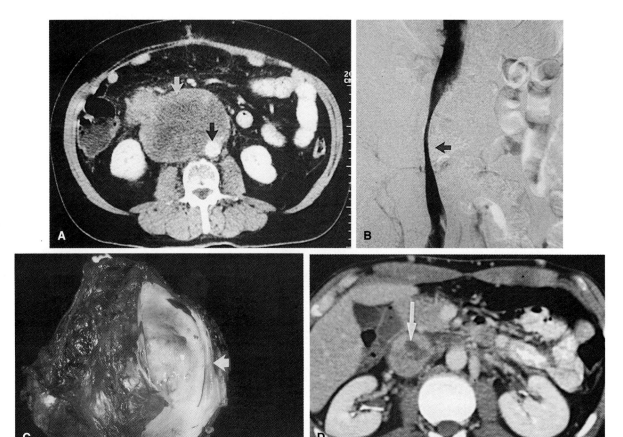

FIGURE 163-4 Examples of primary and secondary tumors of the inferior vena cava. **A,** CT scan of the abdomen showing a large retroperitoneal tumor that surrounds the IVC and obliterates its lumen *(white arrow)*. The tumor also abuts the abdominal aorta *(dark arrow)*. **B,** Venacavogram showing compression and bowing of the IVC. **C,** Pathology specimen from the same patient after resection showing invasion of the lumen of the IVC *(arrow)*. **D,** CT showing an intraluminal defect *(arrow)* that later proved to be a primary IVC leiomyosarcoma. (**B** from Phillips M, Bower T, Orszulak TO, Hartman L: Intracardiac extension of an intracaval sarcoma of endometrial origin. Ann Thorac Surg 59:742-744, 1995; **D** from Bower TC: Primary and secondary tumors of the inferior vena cava. In Gloviczki P, Yao JST [eds]: Handbook of Venous Disorders: London, Chapman & Hall, 1996, pp 529-550.)

extends into the infrahepatic segment of the IVC (level II) or to the hepatic veins (level III). Tumor thrombus in the right side of the heart (level IV) occurs in only 10% of cases.[36,44,57] A recent study of 37 patients undergoing radical nephrectomy and tumor thrombectomy by Nesbitt and associates showed level I thrombus in 9 patients, level II in 7, and level III thrombus in 19. Two had tumor thrombus in the right atrium.[57]

Patients with secondary malignant tumors of the IVC are older, have more medical co-morbidities, and are more debilitated from their disease when the diagnosis is made compared with patients with primary tumors. These patients have a poor prognosis because of metastases found at the time of diagnosis. Survival is less than 1 year without treatment.[2]

■ **CLINICAL PRESENTATION**

Primary leiomyosarcoma of the vena cava is more prevalent in women than men.[4,5,27] Only 1 of 9 patients with primary IVC leiomyosarcoma reported by Dzsinich and associates was male.[5] In a world literature review up to 1989 by Mingoli and colleagues, 118 of 144 patients (81.9%) with

IVC leiomyosarcoma were women. Mean patient age was approximately 54 years, but there was a wide age range.[4] These tumors have been reported in infants, and we have operated on an 88-year-old woman with an IVC leiomyosarcoma.[2]

Patients with primary caval tumors have either symptoms or signs from metastatic disease or from obstruction of the vena cava. Early detection is rare. Only 4 of 144 patients with PVL reviewed by Mingoli and coworkers had the tumor discovered incidentally.[4] All the others were symptomatic when first seen. Abdominal pain (66.0%), abdominal mass (47.9%), and lower limb edema (38.9%) were the most common symptoms or signs. Budd-Chiari syndrome occurred in 22.2%, weight loss in 30.6%, and nonspecific symptoms such as fever, weakness, anorexia, nausea, vomiting, nocturnal sweating, and dyspnea in less than 15% of patients.[4] Consumption coagulopathy and abnormalities of red blood cells have been documented.[27]

Secondary IVC tumors are usually detected in patients in the fifth, sixth, or seventh decades of life.[34-35,57,59] The mean age of 51 patients with IVC resection and replacement for malignant disease at the Mayo Clinic is 52 years (range, 16 to 88 years).

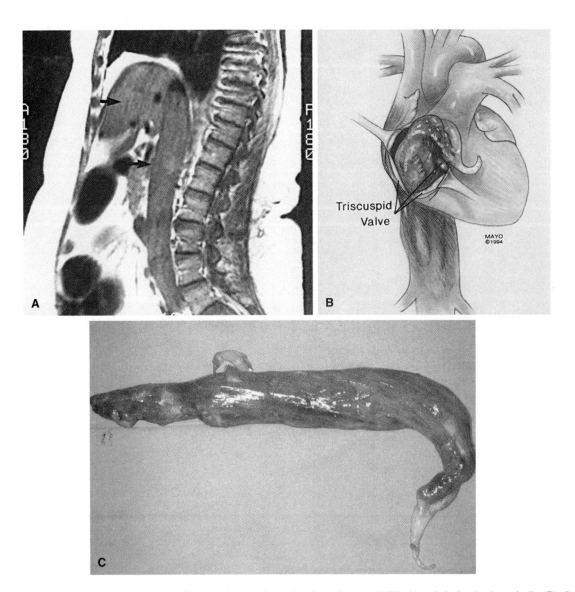

FIGURE 163-5 Intracaval tumor thrombus extending into the right heart chambers shown on MRI (**A**) and depicted schematically (**B**). Pathologic specimen (**C**) revealed endometrial stromal cell sarcoma. (From Phillips M, Bower T, Orszulak TO, Hartman L: Intracardiac extension of an intracaval sarcoma of endometrial origin. Ann Thorac Surg 59:742-744, 1995.)

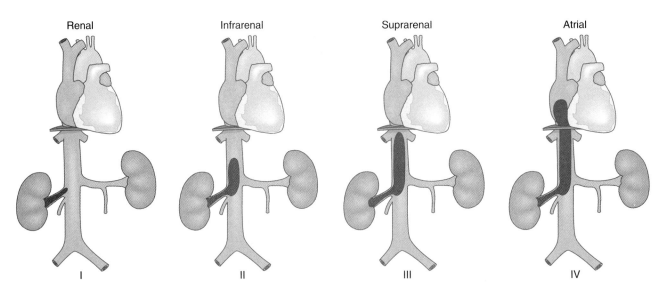

FIGURE 163-6 Classification of level of inferior vena caval thrombus associated with renal cell carcinoma. (From Monty JE: Inferior vena cava tumor thrombus. In Monty JE, Purtes JE, Bukowski RM [eds]: Clinical Management of Renal Cell Cancer. St. Louis, Mosby–Year Book, 1990).

Table 163-2	Clinical Presentations Related to Level of IVC Obstruction
LEVEL OF IVC	**SYMPTOMS AND SIGNS**
Suprahepatic Suprarenal	Cardiac arrhythmias, syncope, pulmonary embolism
Retrohepatic with hepatic vein involvement	Budd-Chiari syndrome, ascites
Retrohepatic between hepatic and renal veins	Abdominal pain, biliary symptoms, nausea (nonspecific)
At renal vein confluence	Renal insufficiency, nephrotic syndrome
Infrarenal	Pain, dilated veins on abdominal wall, palpable mass, lower extremity edema

Most patients with secondary IVC malignancies present with symptoms and signs related to the cancer and not to IVC obstruction.[2,36,44] If there is IVC invasion, the clinical presentation is determined by the segment involved and the degree of venous obstruction (Table 163-2). Tumor thrombus in the right side of the heart causes cardiac arrhythmias, syncope, pulmonary embolism, pulmonary hypertension, or right-sided heart failure. Hepatic vein obstruction results in hepatomegaly, jaundice, ascites, or liver failure. Cancers that invade the retrohepatic IVC cause right upper quadrant or epigastric pain and tenderness or biliary tract symptoms. Obstruction at the renal vein level may cause renal insufficiency or nephrotic syndrome, but frank renal failure is rare because of collateral drainage through branches of the left renal vein. Patients with infrarenal IVC tumors present with abdominal or back pain; neurologic symptoms from involvement of the lumbosacral plexus, the nerve roots, or the psoas muscle; a palpable mass; or lower extremity edema. Patients with slow, progressive IVC obstruction develop dilated abdominal wall veins. Deep venous thrombosis is a rare presentation and is more common in patients with primary tumors of the iliac or peripheral veins.[1-6,12,13,27,31,36]

■ EVALUATION

I prefer a multidisciplinary approach to the evaluation and treatment of these patients. Tumor type, local or distant extent of the malignancy, the degree of caval obstruction, and the presence of intraluminal tumor thrombus are determined first. If the tumor is resectable, a preoperative medical risk assessment is done. A cardiopulmonary evaluation is essential, especially in patients older than age 60 to 65 years.[1,6,9] An assessment of the patient's physical activity, according to criteria outlined by the Eastern Cooperative Oncology Group, helps judge the impact of tumor resection on quality of life.[2,61]

The radiologic imaging studies used are ultrasonography, computed tomography (CT), magnetic resonance imaging (MRI), and venacavography.[2,36,44,58] A combination of studies is often needed to determine surgical resectability and to plan vena cava reconstruction.

Ultrasonography provides images of the entire IVC, including the retrohepatic segment. Bowel gas and tumor distortion of the major veins are limitations of this technique. However, when adequate imaging is achieved, ultrasonography is as sensitive as MRI and venacavography for defining patency of the IVC and the presence and extent of intraluminal tumor thrombus.[58]

CT and MRI are the most common tests performed. Scans of the chest and abdomen define the local extent of the cancer, the level of IVC involvement, and the presence of regional or distant metastases.[2,44,58] Both techniques identify intracaval tumor extension and provide axial, coronal, and sagittal imagery of the tumor and the IVC. Filling defects and distention of the IVC are seen in some patients with primary or secondary cancers and in those with intraluminal tumor thrombus. Differentiation of tumor thrombus from bland thrombus on a single study may be difficult, but serial enlargement and distention of the IVC raise the suspicion of a caval tumor.[56] Kallman and associates believe MRI is almost 100% sensitive for detecting intracaval tumor thrombus associated with renal cell cancers. The few false-positive studies with MRI are usually caused by flow artifacts.[58] Both CT angiography and MRI or MR angiography are useful for postoperative surveillance of the tumor and an IVC graft if venous reconstruction has been performed.[1,2,5,6,9]

Contrast venography has been the "gold standard" test for patients with suspected peripheral or central venous obstruction. I use venacavography only for patients in whom the IVC anatomy or the extent of tumor thrombus is not clearly defined by the other studies. Retrograde cavography via the internal jugular vein is rarely needed to assess the level of caval occlusion or thrombus relative to the hepatic vein origin.[12]

Preoperative fine-needle aspiration or Tru-Cut needle biopsy with CT or ultrasound guidance is used in the rare patient in whom histologic diagnosis may determine the need for preoperative adjuvant therapy or when intracaval tumor cannot be differentiated from bland thrombus. With the exception of germ cell cancers, the majority of primary and secondary IVC malignancies do not respond to radiation or chemotherapy, so preoperative tissue sampling is not necessary.[2,5,44]

■ TREATMENT

Operation is rarely an option for patients with IVC tumors because most patients have advanced disease, have a poor prognosis, and carry a high operative risk. Diffuse metastatic disease, severe cardiopulmonary dysfunction, or physical limitations are contraindications to surgical resection. However, individuals with localized tumors, a good performance status, and few medical co-morbidities are candidates for operation.[2,12,13]

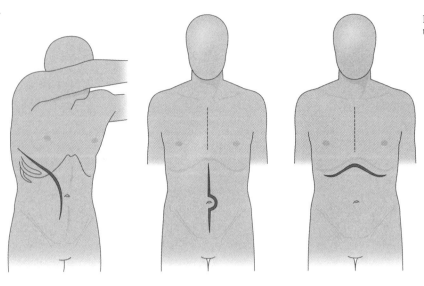

FIGURE 163-7 Various incisions used to approach the inferior vena cava.

Surgical Approach

Operative treatment and approach depend on the type, location, and extent of the cancer; the degree of caval obstruction; and the patient's body habitus (Fig. 163-7). A midline abdominal incision is used to approach tumors involving the infrarenal vena cava. Either right eighth or ninth interspace thoracoabdominal, midline abdominal and median sternotomy, or bilateral subcostal incisions can be used to resect cancers of the suprarenal or suprahepatic IVC. The former two approaches are used to remove tumor thrombus in the right side of the heart.[2,6,12,13,37,46] All of these incisions allow for complete mobilization of the liver, control of the suprahepatic and suprarenal vena cava, and removal of tumor thrombus under direct vision.

IVC Resection Without Replacement

Resection of the infrarenal vena cava without replacement is well tolerated in patients with IVC occlusion in whom there is no lower extremity edema but well-developed venous collaterals.[4,32,61,62] Resection of the suprarenal vena cava without venous replacement has been reported but carries more risk of renal dysfunction and lower extremity edema than resection of the infrarenal segment.[13,26] This is especially true if collateral veins from the kidneys or lower extremities are ligated as part of the cancer resection.[63,64] The ability to predict preoperatively which patients will tolerate suprarenal IVC resection alone without complications is difficult. Two of six patients who needed suprarenal IVC resection did not have venous replacement in a report by Huguet and colleagues.[13] One patient had no post-operative problems because the IVC was chronically occluded and there were well-developed collaterals. The other patient developed infrarenal caval thrombosis and lower extremity venous insufficiency because the IVC was resected and the collateral veins were poorly developed. Transient or permanent renal failure occurs in as many as one half of patients if the suprarenal IVC or renal veins are not reconstructed.[64] This complication should also be anticipated in patients with a solitary left kidney in whom the left renal vein or its branches require ligation.[13] Intraoperative anuria, acute reduction in urine flow, or renal vein pressure over 40 mm Hg with test clamping indicate the need for renal vein reconstruction.[13,47] My preference has been to preserve outflow from the remaining renal vein if the other kidney and the suprarenal IVC require resection. This is accomplished either by reimplantation of the renal vein onto the IVC graft or by a short graft to it. That opinion is shared by others.[1,6,9,12]

Renal Cell Carcinoma with IVC Tumor Thrombus

The most common operation on the IVC is removal of intracaval tumor thrombus in patients with renal cell carcinoma. Usually, the thrombus is removed en bloc with the cancer by open thrombectomy.[34-55,57] Early ligation of the renal artery may shrink the thrombus. Care must be taken to avoid injury to adjacent dilated lumbar vein, which can cause troublesome bleeding if injured. Resection of large cancers that displace the liver and have tumor thrombus extending into the retrohepatic IVC is more difficult. In these cases, Nesbitt and colleagues suggest nephrectomy first, with ligation and amputation of the renal vein rather than complete en bloc resection. They believe this maneuver better facilitates access to and exposure of the vena cava.[57] Preoperative renal artery embolization has been used to reduce tumor vascularity and to contract the thrombus in patients with large cancers.[57] This technique is best done within 24 hours of operation to minimize the postprocedure pain and inflammatory response. Patients with tumor thrombus above the hepatic veins or in the right side of the heart require complete mobilization of the liver to allow access to the retrohepatic IVC. Intraoperative trans-esophageal echocardiography helps define the proximal extent of the thrombus and determines the need for cardiopulmonary bypass.[57] If a small tongue of mobile tumor is found at the cavoatrial junction, Nesbitt and colleagues and Skinner and associates prefer to gently manipulate it into the suprahepatic IVC. This allows cross-clamping below the right atrium and avoids the need for cardiopulmonary bypass. This maneuver must be done carefully to prevent tumor embolization.[38,57] Hepatic vascular exclusion (HVE) is another useful technique to remove tumor thrombus from the retrohepatic or suprahepatic IVC.[65-67] HVE temporarily interrupts blood flow through the IVC and liver. Occasionally, back-bleeding in the IVC occurs from a lumbar vein or an aberrant left hepatic artery. Complete tumor thrombectomy and a precise IVC closure are critical to minimize the risk of pulmonary embolization or venous thrombosis.[36,57] Primary closure of the suprarenal IVC is safe because of its large size. If the caval defect is larger, a prosthetic or vein patch is used to close the cavotomy. Patch closure is preferable to graft replacement.[1,2,12] Thrombus in the right side of the heart should be removed with cardiopulmonary bypass, with or without circulatory arrest.[57] Concomitant deep hypothermia may be needed, but it increases the risk of coagulopathy and organ dysfunction.[34-39,41-44,57] The aforementioned operative principles also apply to other cancers with intracaval tumor extension.[56]

IVC Replacement

I believe the IVC at any level should be replaced if it is only partially obstructed and a majority of its circumference requires resection for tumor clearance.[1,2,6,9] My preference has been to use a large diameter, externally supported, expanded polytetrafluoroethylene graft (Fig. 163-8). Many reports have shown these grafts to be safe.[1,2,4-26] Synthetic grafts are readily available, match the size of the IVC, and resist compression from the viscera. They are preferable to the use of spiral saphenous or superficial femoral vein grafts, unless there is contamination of the operative field.[1,2,6,12,13]

Replacement of the Retrohepatic Suprarenal Vena Cava in Conjunction with Major Liver Resection

Major liver resection with replacement of the suprarenal vena cava has been reported by a number of authors.[1,6-9,12-14] Hepatic vascular exclusion, selective use of venovenous bypass to maintain hemodynamics, and isolation of the fixed portion of the supradiaphragmatic extrapericardial IVC as a location for the upper cross-clamp are important adjuncts to minimize operative risk.[6,9,12,13] My current approach and surgical technique is illustrated schematically in Figure 163-9.[6,9] Either a bilateral subcostal or right thoracoabdominal incision through the eighth or ninth interspace with radial incision of the diaphragm is used to expose the liver and IVC. Abdominal exploration and intraoperative ultrasonography of the liver are used to exclude metastatic disease and to define tumor proximity to the hepatic veins. Control of the inflow to the liver and of the IVC above and below the tumor is performed next. In most cases, early ligation of the appropriate hepatic artery and portal vein branches demarcates the liver to be resected and minimizes blood loss during the resection. Size and location of the cancer determine when the appropriate hepatic vein is ligated. No attempt should be made to isolate the hepatic

vein(s) of the liver segment(s) to be preserved. Hepatic resection is performed with the CUSA device (Vally Lab, Boulder, CO) to minimize blood loss. A few patients with preexisting liver disease may require a period of hepatic vascular exclusion to facilitate the liver resection.[9] Just before the tumor resection is completed, the suprahepatic IVC is test-clamped to determine the hemodynamic effects. If the systolic blood pressure cannot be maintained above 100 mm Hg with fluids, venovenous bypass is instituted. Cannulas are placed into the infrarenal IVC (14 to 20 Fr) and the jugular vein (8.5 Fr). A magnetically coupled mechanical pump is used to recirculate the blood (Model 520D [BioMedicus, Eden Prairie, MN]). Blood flow rates are adjusted to maintain the systolic blood pressure equal to 100 mm Hg and the central venous pressure at 10 to 12 mm Hg. Patients older than the age of 50 years and those with preoperative cardiopulmonary dysfunction are most likely to require venovenous bypass.[1,6,9] Low-dose intravenous heparin (1000 to 2000 units) is given before caval clamping unless there has been significant blood loss during the liver resection. Hepatic vascular exclusion is used to complete the tumor resection and to perform the upper caval anastomosis. Often, this anastomosis incorporates the remaining hepatic vein. Blood is temporarily flushed through the liver with the suprahepatic caval clamp in place to wash out acid metabolites from the liver. The suprahepatic clamp is repositioned across the upper graft and hepatic blood flow is restored. The length of time needed to complete tumor resection and perform the upper caval anastomosis is less than 30 minutes in most patients and rarely exceeds 1 hour. This time is within the tolerable limits of warm ischemia to the liver.[1,9,13,65-67] The lower caval anastomosis is completed after the graft is de-aired. Intraoperative duplex ultrasonography is used to assess graft patency. The liver remnant is secured to its ligamentous attachments to avoid torsion of the remaining hepatic vein. The graft is covered with omentum to protect it from the viscera.

Transient elevation in the results of liver function tests is common, and they peak within the first 2 to 3 postoperative days.[6,9,13] Most patients remain auto-anticoagulated for 24 to 48 hours. Lower extremity pneumatic compression devices and subcutaneous heparin are used to prevent perioperative venous thrombosis. All patients are dismissed from the hospital on warfarin.[6] Most patients take aspirin only after the first 6 months unless they have a long caval graft, reconstructed renal vein, or nonocclusive thrombus seen on a postoperative imaging study. The rapid blood flow through the suprarenal IVC makes the risk of graft thrombosis low.[6,9,12,13]

■ OUTCOMES

Perioperative Mortality and Morbidity

Replacement of the IVC for malignancy has been safely accomplished.[1,2,4-19] Kieffer and associates reported two postoperative deaths among 18 patients surgically treated for primary or secondary tumors of the IVC.[12] Huguet and coworkers had one patient die of renal failure among the four patients who had graft replacement of the retrohepatic vena cava.[13] Three deaths (5.9%) have occurred

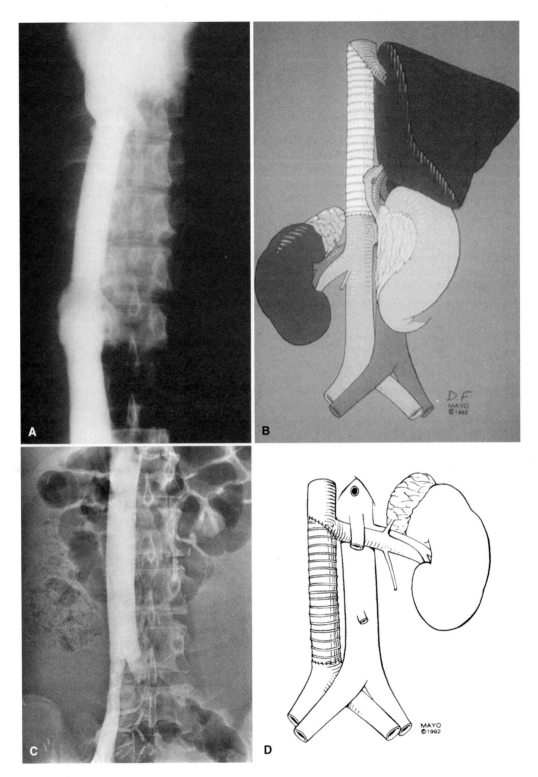

FIGURE 163-8 Postoperative cavograms and accompanying diagrams demonstrating patency of expanded polytetrafluoroethylene grafts used to replace the retrohepatic vena cava after liver resection (**A** and **B**) and the infrarenal vena cava after tumor removal (**C** and **D**). (**A, B,** and **D** from Bower TC, Nagorney DM, Toomey BJ, et al: Vena cava replacement for malignant disease: Is there a role? Ann Vasc Surg 7:51-62, 1993, with permission.)

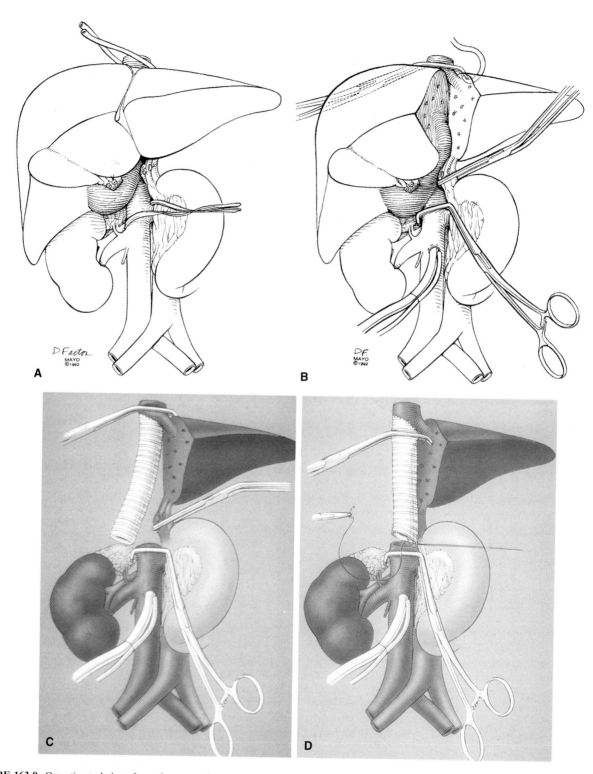

FIGURE 163-9 Operative technique for replacement of the retrohepatic inferior vena cava (IVC) in conjunction with major liver resection. **A,** Isolation of the IVC above and below the level of the tumor as well as isolation and division of the hepatic artery and portal vein branches. **B,** Hepatic vascular exclusion used to complete resection of the liver, tumor, and retrohepatic IVC. If necessary, venovenous bypass via a cannula is used. **C,** The upper caval anastomosis is performed first. **D,** The suprahepatic caval clamp is transferred across the graft after acid metabolites have been flushed from the liver. The lower caval anastomosis is completed. (From Bower TC, Nagorney DM, Toomey BJ, et al: Vena cava replacement for malignant disease: Is there a role? Ann Vasc Surg 7:51-62, 1993, with permission.)

Table 163-3	Operative Mortality and 5-Year Cumulative Survival of Patients with Renal Cell Carcinomas and IVC Tumor Thrombectomy			
STUDY	**NO. PATIENTS**	**OPERATIVE MORTALITY %**	**SURVIVAL, % NO METASTASES**	**SURVIVAL, % WITH METASTASES (LYMPH NODE OR DIRECT)**
Neves et al.,[36] (1987)	54	9.3	68	12.5
Skinner et al.,[38] (1989)	53	13	40	0
Libertino et al.,[35] (1989)	71	N/A	72	16
Montie et al.,[39] (1991)	68	7.4	30	25 (2 year)
Hatcher et al.,[43] (1991)	44	6.8	42	13
Swierzewski et al.,[40] (1994)	100	N/A	64	19.6
Nesbitt et al.,[57] (1997)	37	2.7	45	24.6

N/A, not available.

among 51 patients operated on at the Mayo Clinic for IVC malignancies.

Major morbidity must be low for there to be a role for these operations. Perioperative complication rates are lessened by careful patient selection and operative technique. In the last Mayo Clinic report, three patients required transfusions for bleeding and one of these needed reoperation.[1] Two patients had postoperative myocardial infarctions, and one patient developed bilateral lower extremity edema despite a patent graft. Four other patients had either symptomatic postoperative nonchylous ascites or large pleural effusions. The risk of graft infection is low, even in patients with wound infections or bile leaks.[1,6,9,13]

Operative mortality rates for patients treated by radical nephrectomy and IVC tumor thrombectomy range between 2.7% and 13% (Table 163-3).[35-40,45,53,57] The addition of cardiopulmonary bypass or hypothermic circulatory arrest has not significantly increased operative mortality in most series.[37,39,41-43] Cardiopulmonary problems are the primary cause of perioperative death and morbidity. Neves and Zincke reported five deaths among 54 patients (9.3% mortality), four from pulmonary emboli and one from a myocardial infarction.[36] Only one of 37 patients died in the series by Nesbitt and colleagues.[57]

Major morbidity after radical nephrectomy is as high as 10% to 31%.[36,53,57] Myocardial ischemia, prolonged mechanical ventilation, pneumonitis, pulmonary embolism, atrial arrhythmias, renal insufficiency, and bleeding are the most common postoperative complications. Pulmonary emboli have been major problems in some reports.[36,44] An IVC filter, stapling, or clip is recommended for patients with bland thrombus in the infrarenal IVC.[36,44,57] Cardiopulmonary bypass and hypothermic circulatory arrest seem to increase blood loss and the risk of coagulopathy.[37-39,41-43,45,46,57]

Graft Patency

Early and late patency for large-diameter (16 to 20 mm) prosthetic caval grafts is good regardless of which IVC segment is replaced.[1,6,9,12,13,20,22,23] Huguet and associates reported no graft occlusions among three survivors with prosthetic replacement of the suprarenal IVC.[13] Less than 10% of the 51 IVC grafts have occluded during follow-up in the Mayo Clinic experience. Only a few patients have

developed nonocclusive graft thrombus. They were chronically anticoagulated. The use of an arteriovenous fistula to improve graft patency is controversial. Kieffer and colleagues use a centrally placed fistula if graft flow needs to be enhanced.[12] Others place a fistula at the femoral vein level.[68] I do not routinely add an arteriovenous fistula for reconstruction of the suprarenal or suprahepatic IVC because of the rapid blood flow at this level. However, an arteriovenous fistula is considered for patients in whom more than one caval segment is replaced or a long graft is needed to bypass an obstructing caval tumor for palliation of symptoms.[1,6,12,13]

Survival and Quality of Life

The most important postoperative outcome measures are survival, control of local tumor recurrence, and quality of life.

Survival in patients with primary venous leiomyosarcoma is dependent on tumor resectability. Dzsinich and associates reported median survival after operation in patients with PVL at all sites to be 3.5 years (range, 6 months to 17 years). Survival was not affected by tumor size, location, grade, or use of adjuvant therapy.[4] These findings are interesting because the primary determinant of survival in most patients with other types of retroperitoneal sarcomas is the grade of the tumor. Survival of patients with primary IVC leiomyosarcoma reported by Mingoli and coworkers averaged 3 months in patients not operated, 21 months in patients submitted to a palliative resection, and 36.8 months in those undergoing radical resection. In that series, a 5-year survival of 28% was achieved with curative resection.[3] Mingoli and coworkers later analyzed data from 120 surgical patients in the International Registry of IVC Leiomyosarcomas to determine the influence of limited versus extended resection on tumor recurrence and patient survival.[61] The variables assessed were the IVC segment involved by the tumor, the growth pattern (extraluminal or intraluminal), the patency of the IVC, the size and histologic grade of the tumor, and the use of adjuvant therapy. Follow-up was available in 102 patients. Fifty-three patients (44%) had limited resection of the IVC wall, and 67 (56%) had extensive resection. Three patients died early, 39 (33.3%) died of recurrent disease, and 7 died of unrelated causes but were disease-free. Thirty-six of 53 survivors were alive with no evidence of disease at a mean follow-up of 63 months. The other 17 were alive with recurrent disease. Multivariate analysis showed no significant difference in survival or disease recurrence between those with limited versus extended resection. Survival rates between the two groups were 55% and 37% at 5 years and 42% and 23% at 10 years, respectively.[61] Resection with tumor-free margins still remains the primary goal. There is yet no clear benefit from adjuvant therapy on survival or locoregional disease recurrence rates.[33,61,69,70]

Survival for patients with secondary malignancies of the IVC left untreated is measured in months, not years. The limited data available suggest survival may be improved with tumor resection and IVC replacement in selected patients. However, the number of patients operated is too small to make statistical comparisons.[1,2,5,6,12,13] Local tumor control and palliation of symptoms is excellent, even in patients who need liver resection and retrohepatic IVC replacement.[1,6,9] Twenty-seven of 48 early survivors with IVC replacement for malignant disease at the Mayo Clinic are alive at a mean follow up of 2.7 years (range, 9 days to 8.4 years). Most deaths occurred from distant metastases.

The greatest survival benefit is seen for patients with renal cell carcinoma and IVC tumor thrombus. Aggressive surgical treatment has resulted in average 5-year survival rates as high as 50% to 68% in patients with no distant or regional metastases.[36,44] The primary determinants of survival are the presence of diffuse metastases, lymph node involvement, and completeness of tumor resection.[35,36,38,39,43,50,57] Patients with diffuse metastases have 1-year survival rates ranging from 10% to 68% but 5-year survival rates of only 0% to 8%.[39,44] Five-year survival rates are 50% to 68% for patients with complete tumor resection and no lymph node involvement compared with survival rates less than 17% for those with positive nodes.[35,36,39,43,57] Only a handful of patients survive 5 years if they are left with residual cancer.[36,38,43,57] Tumor thrombus as an independent factor probably does not affect patient survival, although some authors have noted a trend toward lower survival rates based on the level of the thrombus.[37,38,43,51,57]

Postoperative quality of life is difficult to assess objectively. Few clinical series report performance status (physical limitations) of patients post resection. I have been impressed that carefully selected patients have minimal restriction in their physical activity postoperatively. Almost 80% of patients with IVC replacement for malignant disease can be expected to maintain excellent performance status, even if they later develop regional or distant recurrent disease.[1,6,9]

SUMMARY

Primary and secondary tumors of the inferior vena cava are rare, usually at advanced stages at the time of diagnosis, and carry a poor prognosis if left untreated. Until early cancer detection and effective adjuvant therapies are developed, surgical resection remains the only chance for cure or control of symptoms. Careful patient selection, thorough preoperative evaluation and staging, and coordinated

management between the oncologist and surgeon are keys to a successful outcome. Patients with no evidence of metastatic disease, few medical co-morbidities, and a good performance status should be considered candidates for surgical resection, with or without venous replacement. If vena cava reconstruction is necessary, it can be performed safely with few graft-related complications. Aggressive surgical management of patients with either renal cell carcinoma and vena cava tumor thrombus or localized primary IVC leiomyosarcoma appears proven. However, the role of resection for patients with secondary malignancies involving the IVC requires more experience and longer follow-up.

■ REFERENCES

1. Bower TC, Nagorney DM, Cherry KJ Jr, et al: Replacement of the inferior vena cava for malignancy: An update. J Vasc Surg 31:270-281, 2000.
2. Bower TC: Primary and secondary tumors of the inferior vena cava. In Gloviczki P, Yao JST (eds): Handbook of Venous Disorders. London, Chapman & Hall, 1996, pp 529-550.
3. Kieffer E, Berrod JL, Chomette G: Primary tumors of the inferior vena cava. In Bergan JJ, Yao JST (eds): Surgery of the Veins. New York, Grune & Stratton, 1985, pp 423-443.
4. Mingoli A, Feldhaus RJ, Cavallaro A, Stipa S: Leiomyosarcoma of the inferior vena cava: Analysis and search of world literature on 141 patients and report of three new cases. J Vasc Surg 14:688-699, 1991.
5. Dzsinich C, Gloviczki P, van Heerden JA, et al: Primary venous leiomyosarcoma: A rare but lethal disease. J Vasc Surg 15:595-603, 1992.
6. Bower TC, Nagorney DM, Toomey BJ, et al: Vena cava replacement for malignant disease: Is there a role? Ann Vasc Surg 7:51-62, 1993.
7. Starzl TE, Koep LJ, Weil R, et al: Right trisegmentectomy for hepatic neoplasms. Surg Gynecol Obstet 150:208-214, 1980.
8. Kumada K. Shimahara Y, Fujui K, et al: Extended right hepatic lobectomy: Combined resection of inferior vena cava and its reconstruction by ePTFE graft. Acta Chir Scand 154:481-483, 1988.
9. Sarmiento JM, Bower TC, Cherry KJ, et al: Is combined partial hepatectomy with segmental resection of inferior vena cava justified for malignancy? Arch Surg 138:624-630, 2003.
10. Miller CM. Schwartz ME, Nishizaki T: Combined hepatic and vena caval resection with autogenous caval graft replacement. Arch Surg 126:106-108, 1991.
11. Risher WH, Arensman RM, Oschsner JL, Hollier LH: Retrohepatic vena cava reconstruction with polytetrafluoroethylene graft. J Vasc Surg 12:367-370, 1990.
12. Kieffer E, Bahnini A, Koskas F: Nonthrombotic disease of the inferior vena cava: Surgical management of 24 patients. In Bergan JJ, Yao JST (eds): Venous Disorders. Philadelphia, WB Saunders, 1991, pp 501-516.
13. Huguet C, Ferri M, Gavelli A: Resection of the suprarenal inferior vena cava: The role of prosthetic replacement. Arch Surg 130:793-797, 1995.
14. Yagyu T, Shimizu R, Nishida M, at al: Reconstruction of the hepatic vein to the prosthetic inferior vena cava in right extended hemihepatectomy with ex situ procedure. Surgery 115:700-744, 1994.
15. Okada Y, Kumada K, Habuchi T, et al: Total replacement of the suprarenal inferior vena cava with an expanded polytetrafluoroethylene tube graft in 2 patients with tumor thrombi from renal cell carcinoma. J Urol 141:111-114, 1989.
16. Kraybill WG, Callery MP, Heiken JP, Fley MW: Radical resection of tumors of the inferior vena cava with vascular reconstruction and kidney autotransplantation. Surgery 121:31-36, 1997.
17. Yanaga K. Okadome K, Ito H, et al: Graft replacement of pararenal inferior vena cava for leiomyosarcoma with the use of venous bypass. Surgery 113:109-112, 1993.

18. Habib NA, Michaeil NE, Boyle T, Bean A: Resection of the inferior vena cava during hepatectomy for liver tumours. Br J Surg 81:1023-1024, 1994.

19. Silva MB, Silva HC, Sandager GP, et al: Prosthetic replacement of the inferior vena cava after resection of pheochromocytoma. J Vasc Surg 19:169-173, 1994.

20. Dale WA, Harris J, Terry RB: Polytetrafluoroethylene reconstruction of the inferior vena cava. Surgery 95:625-630, 1984.

21. Katz NM, Spence LJ, Wallace RB: Reconstruction of the inferior vena cava with a polytetrafluoroethylene tube graft after resection for hypernephroma of the right kidney. J Thorac Cardiovasc Surg 87:791-797, 1984.

22. Gloviczki P, Pairolero PC, Cherry KJ, et al: Reconstruction of the vena cava and of its primary tributaries: A preliminary report. J Vasc Surg 11:373-381, 1990.

23. Gloviczki P, Pairolero PC, Toomey BJ, et al: Reconstruction of large veins for nonmalignant venous occlusive disease. J Vasc Surg 16:750-761, 1992.

24. Victor S, Jayanthi V, Kandasamy I, et al: Retrohepatic cavoatrial bypass for coarctation of inferior vena cava with a polytetrafluoroethylene graft. J Thorac Cardiovasc Surg 39:485-491, 1985.

25. Chan EL, Bardine JA, Bernstein EF: Inferior vena cava bypass: Experimental evaluation of externally supported grafts and initial clinical application. J Vasc Surg 1:675-680, 1984.

26. Duckett JW, Lifland JH, Peters PC: Resection of the inferior vena cava for adjacent malignant diseases. Surg Gynecol Obstet 136:711-716, 1973.

27. Enzinger FM, Weiss SW: Soft tissue tumors. In Gay SM (ed): Soft Tissue Tumors, 3rd ed. St. Louis, Mosby–Year Book, 1995, pp 505-510.

28. Hallock P, Watson CJ, Berman L: Primary tumor of inferior vena cava with clinical features suggestive of Chiari's disease. Arch Intern Med 66:50, 1940.

29. Perl L: Ein fall von sarkom der vena cava inferior. Virchow's Arch [A] 53:378-383, 1871.

30. Kevorkian J, Cento DP: Leiomyosarcoma of large arteries and veins. Surgery 73:390-400, 1973.

31. Hartman DS, Hayes WS, Choyke PL, Tibbetts GP: Leiomyosarcoma of the retroperitoneum and inferior vena cava: Radiologic-pathologic correlation. Radiographics 12:1203-1220, 1992.

32. Burke AP, Virmani R: Sarcomas of the great vessels. Cancer 71:761-773, 1993.

33. Chang AE, Sondak VK: Clinical evaluation and treatment of soft tissue tumors. In Gay SM, (ed): Soft Tissue Tumors, 3rd ed. St. Louis, Mosby–Year Book, 1995, pp 17-38.

34. Concepcion RS, Koch MO, McDougal WS, et al: Management of primary nonrenal parenchymal malignancies with vena caval thrombus. J Urol 145:243-247, 1991.

35. Libertino JA, Malone MJ, Shahian DM: Resection of renal cell carcinoma with extension into inferior vena cava. In McDougal, Scott (eds): Difficult Problems in Urologic Surgery. Chicago, Year Book Medical Publishers, 1989.

36. Neves RJ, Zincke H: Surgical treatment of renal cancer with vena cava extension. Br J Urol 59:390-395, 1987.

37. Novick AC, Kaye MC, Cosgrove DM, et al: Experience with cardiopulmonary bypass and deep hypothermic circulatory arrest in the management of retroperitoneal tumors with large vena caval thrombi. Ann Surg 212:472-477, 1990.

38. Skinner DG, Pritchett TR, Lieskovsky G, et al: Vena caval involvement by renal cell carcinoma. Ann Surg 210:387-394, 1989.

39. Montie JE, El Ammar R, Pontes JE, et al: Renal cell carcinoma with inferior vena cava tumor thrombi. Surg Gynecol Obstet 173:107-115, 1991.

40. Swierzewski DJ, Swierzewski JA: Radical nephrectomy in patients with renal cell carcinoma with venous, vena caval, and atrial extension. Am J Surg 168:205-209, 1994.

41. Marshall FF, Dietrick DD, Baumgartner WA, et al: Surgical management of renal cell carcinoma with intracaval neoplastic extension of the hepatic veins. J Urol 139:1166-1172, 1988.

42. Shahain DM, Libertino JA, Zinman LN, et al: Resection of cavoatrial renal cell carcinoma employing total circulatory arrest. Arch Surg 125:727-732, 1990.

43. Hatcher PA, Anderson EE, Paulson DF, et al: Surgical management and prognosis of renal cell carcinoma invading the vena cava. J Urol 145:20-24, 1991.

44. Couillard DR, White RWD: Surgery of renal cell carcinoma. Urol Clin North Am 20:263-275, 1993.

45. Klein EA, Kaye MC, Novick AC: Management of renal cell carcinoma with vena caval thrombi via cardiopulmonary bypass and deep hypothermic circulatory arrest. Urol Oncol 18:445-447, 1991.

46. Stewart JA, Carey JA, McDougal WS, et al: Cavoatrial tumor thrombectomy using cardiopulmonary bypass without circulatory arrest. Ann Thorac Surg 51:717-722, 1991.

47. Clayman RV, Gonzalez R, Fraley EE: Renal cell cancer invading the inferior vena cava: Clinical review and anatomic approach. J Urol 123:157-163, 1980.

48. Gancharenko V, Gerlock JA Jr, Kadir S, et al: Incidence and distribution of venous extension in 70 hypernephromas. AJR Am J Roentgenol 133:263, 1979.

49. Glazer AA, Novick AC: Long-term follow up after surgical treatment for renal cell carcinoma extending into the right atrium. J Urol 155:448-450, 1996.

50. Tongaonkar HB, Dandekar NP, Dalal AV, et al: Renal cell carcinoma extending to the renal vein and inferior vena cava: Results of surgical treatment and prognostic factors. J Surg Oncol 59:94-100, 1995.

51. Cherrie RJ. Goldman DG, Lindner A, et al: Prognostic implications of vena caval extension of renal cell carcinoma. J Urol 128:910-912, 1982.

52. Swanson DA, Wallace S, Johnson DE: The role of embolization and nephrectomy in the treatment of metastatic renal carcinoma. J Urol Surg 7:719-730, 1980.

53. Suggs WD, Smith RB, Dodson TF, et al: Renal cell carcinoma with inferior vena caval involvement. J Vasc Surg 14:43-48, 1991.

54. Sosa RE, Muecke EC, Vaugn ED, et al: Renal cell carcinoma extending into the inferior vena cava: The prognostic significance of the level of the vena caval involvement. J Urol 132:1097-1100, 1984.

55. Langenburg SE, Blackbourne LH, Sperling JW, et al: Management of renal tumors involving the inferior vena cava. J Vasc Surg 20:385-388, 1994.

56. Phillips M, Bower T, Orszulak TO, Hartmann L: Intracardiac extension of an intracaval sarcoma of endometrial origin. Ann Thorac Surg 59:742-744, 1995.

57. Nesbitt JC, Soltero ER, Dinney CPN, et al: Surgical management of renal cell carcinoma with inferior vena cava tumor thrombus. Ann Thorac Surg 63:1592-1600, 1997.

58. Kallman DA, King BF, Hattery RR, et al: Renal vein and inferior vena cava tumor thrombus in renal cell carcinoma: CT, US, MRI and venacavography. J Comput Assist Tomogr 16:240-247, 1992.

59. Nagorney DM, vanHeerden JA, Ilstrup DM, et al: Primary hepatic malignancy: Surgical management and determinants of survival. Surgery 106:740-749, 1989.

60. Beahrs OH, Henson DE, Hutter RVP, et al: General rules for staging cancer. In: American Joint Commission on Cancer. Manual for Staging of Cancer, 3rd ed. Philadelphia, JB Lippincott, 1988, p 9.

61. Mingoli A, Sapienza P, Cavallaro A, et al: The effect of extent of caval resection in the treatment of inferior vena cava leiomyosarcoma. Anticancer Res 17:3877-3882, 1997.

62. Spitz A, Wilson TG, Kawachi MH, et al: Vena caval resection for bulky metastatic germ cell tumors: An 18-year experience. J Urol 158:1813-1818, 1997.

63. Perhoniemi V. Salmenkivi K, Vorne M: Venous haemodynamics in the legs after ligation of the inferior vena cava. Acta Chir Scand 152: 23-27, 1986.

64. McCullough DL, Gittes RF: Ligation of the renal in the solitary kidney: Effects on renal function. J Urol Surg 113:295-299, 1975.

65. Delva E, Camus Y, Norlinger B, et al: Vascular occlusions for liver resections: Operative management and tolerance to hepatic ischemia: 142 cases. Ann Surg 209:211-218, 1989.

66. Bismuth H, Castaing D, Garden OJ: Major hepatic resection under total vascular exclusion. Ann Surg 210:13-19, 1989.

67. Huguet C, Gavelli A, Addario Chieco P, et al: Liver ischemia for hepatic resection: Where is the limit? Surgery 111:251-259, 1992.

68. Wilson SE, Jabour A, Stone RT, et al: Patency of biologic and prosthetic inferior vena cava grafts with distal limb fistula. Arch Surg 113:1174-1179, 1978.

69. McGrath PC, Neifeld JP, Lawrence W Jr, et al: Improved survival following complete excision of retroperitoneal sarcomas. Ann Surg 200:200-204, 1984.

70. Singer S, Corson JM, Demetri GD, et al: Prognostic factors predictive of survival for truncal and retroperitoneal soft-tissue sarcoma. Ann Surg 221:185-195, 1995.

Chapter

Surgical Treatment of Superior Vena Cava Syndrome

164

PETER GLOVICZKI, MD

MANJU KALRA, MBBS

JAMES C. ANDREWS, MD

Few areas of venous surgery provide a more satisfying experience for both the patient and the vascular surgeon than reconstruction for superior vena cava (SVC) syndrome. Relief from severe, frequently incapacitating symptoms of chronic venous congestion of the head and neck is almost instantaneous, and benefit after reconstruction is generally long lasting.

In this chapter, we review the etiology, clinical presentation, and diagnostic evaluation of SVC syndrome. Because endovascular treatment is reviewed in Chapter 162, here we focus on the surgical management of SVC and innominate vein occlusions.

■ ETIOLOGY

The first case of SVC obstruction described by William Hunter in 1757 was due to an aortic aneurysm.[1] Aortic aneurysms remained the second most common cause of SVC syndrome after primary malignant thoracic tumors until the mid 1900s.[2] The incidence of tuberculous and syphilitic mediastinitis decreased markedly early in the 20th century. Only occasional cases in HIV-positive patients have been reported during the past decade. Today, lung cancer (squamous, small cell, and adenocarcinoma) with mediastinal lymphadenopathy and primary mediastinal malignancy are the most frequent causes of SVC syndrome, accounting for 60% to 85% of cases.[3,4] Primary mediastinal malignant tumors leading to SVC syndrome include mediastinal lymphoma, medullary or follicular carcinoma of the thyroid, thymoma, teratoma, angiosarcoma, and synovial cell carcinoma.[3-7] Benign disease is a less common cause of SVC syndrome, accounting for only 15% to 22% of cases.[4,8,9] Mediastinal fibrosis and granulomatous fungal disease, such as histoplasmosis, have been the most frequent

benign causes of SVC and innominate vein obstruction.[6,10-14] However, the exponential increase in the use of indwelling central venous catheters and cardiac pacemakers over the past 2 decades has resulted in greater numbers of patients presenting with SVC obstruction of benign etiology.[11,12,15-21] Previous radiotherapy to the mediastinum, retrosternal goiter, and aortic dissection can also cause SVC syndrome. The risk of venous thrombosis is increased in patients with thrombophilia such as factor V Leiden abnormality and deficiencies in circulating natural anticoagulants, such as antithrombin III, protein S, and protein C.

■ CLINICAL PRESENTATION

Signs and symptoms of venous congestion of the head, neck, and upper extremities are determined by the duration and extent of the venous occlusive disease and by the amount of collateral venous circulation that develops. Patients with SVC syndrome present with a feeling of fullness in the head and neck that is exacerbated when the patient bends over or lies flat in bed. The severity of the disease can be graded easily by the number of pillows needed by the patient to sleep comfortably. Venous hypertension may cause headache, dizziness, visual symptoms, or even blackout spells.[4,22] Patients may complain of mental confusion, dyspnea, orthopnea, or cough. Dilated neck veins and swelling of the face, neck, and eyelids are the characteristic physical signs most commonly seen (Fig. 164-1). Prominent chest wall collateral veins are frequently seen, as are ecchymosis and cyanosis of the face. Although symptoms are usually localized to the head and neck, mild to moderate upper extremity swelling may also develop (Table 164-1). Additional signs or symptoms of malignant SVC syndrome include hemoptysis, hoarseness, dysphagia,

Section XXI

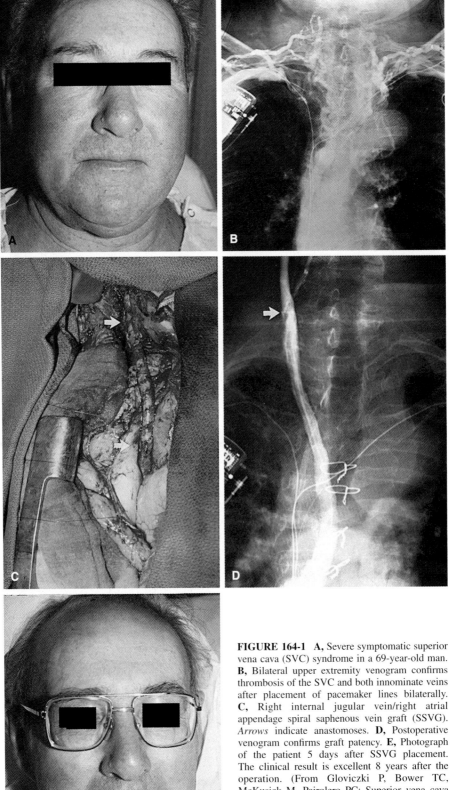

FIGURE 164-1 A, Severe symptomatic superior vena cava (SVC) syndrome in a 69-year-old man. **B,** Bilateral upper extremity venogram confirms thrombosis of the SVC and both innominate veins after placement of pacemaker lines bilaterally. **C,** Right internal jugular vein/right atrial appendage spiral saphenous vein graft (SSVG). *Arrows* indicate anastomoses. **D,** Postoperative venogram confirms graft patency. **E,** Photograph of the patient 5 days after SSVG placement. The clinical result is excellent 8 years after the operation. (From Gloviczki P, Bower TC, McKusick M, Pairolero PC: Superior vena cava syndrome: Endovascular and direct surgical treatment. In Gloviczki P, Yao YST [eds]: Handbook of Venous Disorders. London, Chapman & Hall, 1996, pp 580-599.)

Table 164-1	Signs and Symptoms of SVC Syndrome in 32 Patients with Benign Disease

	NO. PATIENTS (%)
Symptoms	
Feeling of fullness in head or neck	26 (81)
Dyspnea on exertion or orthopnea	23 (72)
Headache	17 (53)
Dizziness or syncope	11 (34)
Visual problems	8 (25)
Cough	7 (22)
Nocturnal oxygen requirement	3 (9)
Protein-losing enteropathy	1 (3)
Signs	
Head and neck swelling	31 (97)
Large chest wall venous collaterals	29 (91)
Facial cyanosis	18 (56)
Arm swelling	17 (53)
Pleural effusion	2 (6)

From Kalra M, Gloviczki P, Andrews JC, et al: Open surgical and endovascular treatment of superior vena cava syndrome caused by nonmalignant disease. J Vasc Surg 38:215-223, 2003.

weight loss, lethargy, or palpable cervical tumor or lymph nodes. Patients with lymphoma may also present with fever and night sweats.

■ DIAGNOSTIC EVALUATION

The diagnosis of SVC obstruction is usually suggested from a detailed clinical history and physical examination. The clinical diagnosis may be confirmed by a variety of tools, including plain film radiographs, ultrasonography, radionuclide imaging, computed tomography (CT), venography, and magnetic resonance imaging (MRI). The appropriate diagnostic study for an individual patient includes not only the demonstration of the underlying cause but also the site and extent of obstruction as well as the routes of collateral venous circulation.

Radiography

Plain film radiographs of the chest are readily available and are often abnormal in patients with SVC obstruction. Findings most commonly include mediastinal widening, right hilar mass, pleural effusion, bilateral diffuse infiltrates, and upper lobe collapse; however, a normal radiograph of the chest does not preclude the diagnosis of SVC obstruction.[4,22] Occasionally, dilated collateral veins may be visible, especially enlargement of the azygos vein or superior intercostal vein (aortic nipple) draining the hemiazygos system. In more than 90% of patients a diagnosis of SVC syndrome can be made on the basis of clinical presentation and plain chest radiograph.[22]

Ultrasonography

Ultrasound evaluation is an effective, noninvasive screening technique in the patient with suspected SVC obstruction. Although direct visualization of the SVC is not possible

with transthoracic duplex ultrasound, valuable information can be obtained. The subclavian veins are accessible to sonographic evaluation and can provide indirect evidence of SVC patency or obstruction. In the presence of SVC obstruction the normal respiratory flow variation due to changes in intrathoracic pressure seen in patent subclavian veins is lost. This can be easily demonstrated with reduced or no change in the diameter and blood flow through the subclavian veins in response to respiratory maneuvers such as a sudden sniff or a Valsalva maneuver. Occasionally, collateral vessels may be detected within the chest wall or in the mediastinum. The advantage of ultrasound is the absence of exposure to ionizing radiation and no requirement for the administration of iodinated contrast material. In addition, ultrasound remains an important diagnostic tool to preoperatively assess the patency and size of the internal jugular veins in candidates selected for surgical reconstruction because these are usually not visualized on upper extremity venography. The disadvantage of ultrasound includes not only the lack of direct visualization of the SVC but also the inability to determine the extent of an obstructing lesion.

Radionuclide Imaging

Radionuclide venography has been used in the diagnosis of SVC syndrome. A technetium-99m pertechnetate scan, performed with bilateral simultaneous injection of the radionuclide tracer into the arm veins, has been used not only to demonstrate the presence of SVC obstruction and associated collateral pathways but also to provide functional aspects of the SVC obstruction using time-density curves.[23,24] An advantage is the potential usefulness as a follow-up examination in determining therapeutic response.[25] The disadvantage of radionuclide venography is the lower-resolution anatomic detail and the inability to determine the cause of the SVC obstruction. This technique is rarely used in current practice.

Computed Tomography

The diagnosis of the SVC obstruction can be made by CT of the chest. Multiple authors have demonstrated CT findings in the diagnosis of SVC obstruction.[26,27] These findings include nonopacification or decreased opacification of the central veins of the chest with increased opacification of collateral venous routes. These collateral pathways include the (1) azygos-hemiazygos pathway, (2) internal mammary pathway, (3) lateral thoracic-thoracoepigastric pathway, and (4) vertebral pathway and small mediastinal veins.[28] Less commonly, unusual shunts, including hepatic parenchyma as an intense focal enhancement in the medial segment of the left lobe of the liver, and pulmonary pathways are identified on CT.[29,30] No definite relationship between the level of occlusion and the number of collateral pathways has been identified.

CT accurately depicts the location and extent of the obstruction and also distinguishes various types of benign and malignant mediastinal disease. The extent of venous collateral formation is also well demonstrated. Disadvantages include the requirement for intravenous contrast material, which may be contraindicated in patients with a history of allergic reaction or renal insufficiency.

Venography

Venography has been considered the "gold standard" for accurate depiction of central venous obstruction and is used as an anatomic roadmap before reconstructive surgery. Venography also depicts the presence and direction of venous collateral flow. It is performed by simultaneous injection of contrast material in bilateral superficial arm veins. Stanford and Doty[31] described four venographic patterns of SVC syndrome, each having a different venous collateral network depending on the site and extent of SVC obstruction (Fig. 164-2 and Table 164-2). *Type I* is partial and *type II* is complete or near-complete SVC obstruction, with flow in the azygos vein remaining antegrade. *Type III* is 90% to 100% SVC obstruction with reversed azygos blood flow (Fig. 164-3A), whereas *type IV* is extensive mediastinal central venous occlusion with venous return occurring through the inferior vena cava (see Fig. 164-1B).

The disadvantages of contrast venography include its invasiveness and the requirement of iodinated contrast material. Catheter-directed venography is also limited by the site of contrast agent administration. Only veins and collateral pathways between the injection site and right atrium are visualized; therefore, on bilateral upper extremity venography routinely performed in patients with SVC syndrome, the internal jugular veins frequently used for inflow for a surgical bypass are not visualized.

Magnetic Resonance Imaging

MRI may provide a new standard for venographic imaging in the future, especially with the ability to acquire venographic images during the peak phase of gadolinium enhancement. The advantages of MRI include the ability to demonstrate anatomic structures in multiple planes and to delineate the central venous chest veins and collateral vessels. MRI is a relatively noninvasive modality and does not require the administration of iodinated contrast material. The disadvantage is its contraindication in patients with pacemakers and aneurysm clips.

■ CONSERVATIVE THERAPY

Conservative measures are used first in every patient to relieve symptoms of venous congestion and to decrease progression of venous thrombosis. These measures include elevation of the head during the night on pillows, modifications of daily activities by avoiding bending over, and avoidance of wearing constricting garments or a tight collar. Patients frequently need diuretic agents to decrease, at least temporarily, excessive edema of the neck and head.

Patients with acute SVC syndrome, caused by malignant disease, are generally treated with intravenous unfractionated or low-molecular-weight heparin, followed by warfarin, to prevent recurrence and protect the venous collateral circulation. Thrombolytic treatment is considered in most patients with benign acute SVC syndrome, whereas those with metastatic malignant disease are candidates for treatment by endovascular stents, with or without thrombolytic treatment (see Chapter 162).

Symptoms of SVC syndrome caused by mediastinal malignancy frequently improve after irradiation, chemotherapy, or combination chemoradiation based on the tumor histology.[6,7] Resolution of symptoms occurs in 80% of the patients within 4 weeks. In recent years, primary stenting for symptomatic SVC obstruction caused by malignant disease has become first-line treatment with immediate definitive treatment by radiation or chemotherapy.[32-35] Stenting results in almost immediate symptomatic relief, which is maintained in 80% to 95% of patients for their lifetime.[36-38,39]

Chemotherapy and radiotherapy are effective in relieving symptoms in the majority of patients with malignancy-related SVC syndrome, whereas stent insertion may provide relief in a higher proportion and more rapidly.[35,40] Endovascular treatment is associated with equivalent initial technical success in patients with SVC syndrome of benign etiology; primary patency at 1 year varies from 0% to 80% in several small series, but secondary patency is more consistently reported as 80% to 100%.[41-43] In view of the need for repeat interventions, the role of endovascular treatment in patients with benign disease remains to be established, although initial results seem to justify offering endovascular treatment first to most patients.

■ SURGICAL TREATMENT

Indications

Patients with SVC syndrome can have severe, frequently incapacitating symptoms, which cannot be alleviated by conservative measures. In 2004, endovascular treatment in these patients should be considered as the first option of

Table 164-2	Venographic Classification* in Patients Who Underwent Reconstruction for Benign SVC Syndrome	
TYPE	**DESCRIPTION**	**NO. OF PATIENTS (%)**
I	Stenosis (up to 90%) of the SVC with patency and antegrade flow of the azygos—right atrial pathway	3 (9)
II	> 90% stenosis or occlusion of the SVC with patency and antegrade flow in the azygos—right atrial pathway	5 (16)
III	> 90% stenosis or occlusion of the SVC with reversal of azygos blood flow	13 (41)
IV	Occlusion of the SVC and one or more of the major caval tributaries including the azygos systems	11 (34)
	Total	*32 (100)*

*Classification of Stanford and Doty.[31]

From Kalra M, Gloviczki P, Andrews JC, et al: Open surgical and endovascular treatment of superior vena cava syndrome caused by nonmalignant disease. J Vasc Surg 38:215-223, 2003.

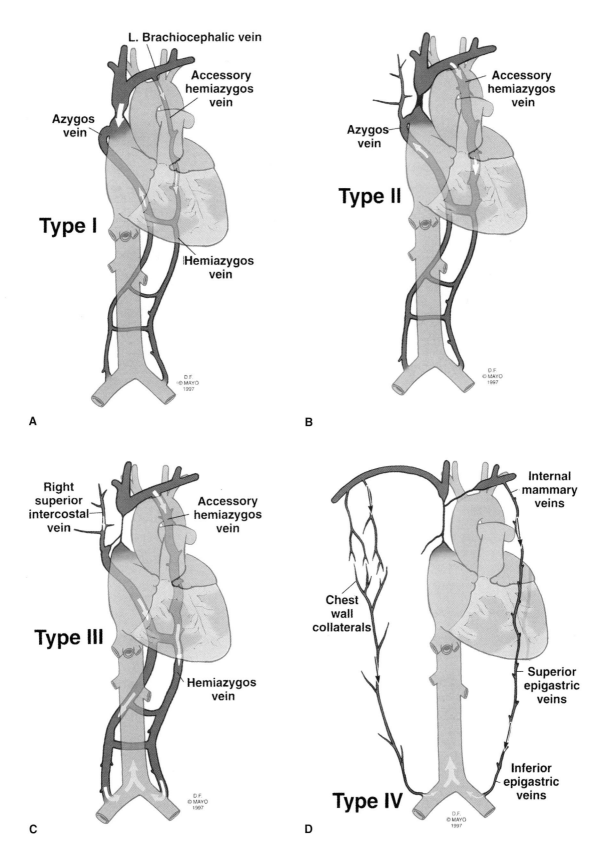

FIGURE 164-2 Venographic classification of SVC syndrome according to Stanford and Doty.[31] **A,** *Type I.* High-grade SVC stenosis but still normal direction of blood flow through the SVC and azygos veins. Increased collateral circulation through hemiazygos and accessory hemiazygos veins. **B,** *Type II.* Greater than 90% stenosis or occlusion of the SVC but patent azygos vein with normal direction of blood flow. **C,** *Type III.* Occlusion of the SVC with retrograde flow in both the azygos and hemiazygos veins. **D,** *Type IV.* Extensive occlusion of the SVC and innominate and azygos veins with chest wall and epigastric venous collaterals. (From Alimi YS, Gloviczki P, Vrtiska TJ, et al: Reconstruction of the superior vena cava: The benefits of postoperative surveillance and secondary endovascular interventions. J Vasc Surg 27:298-299, 1998.)

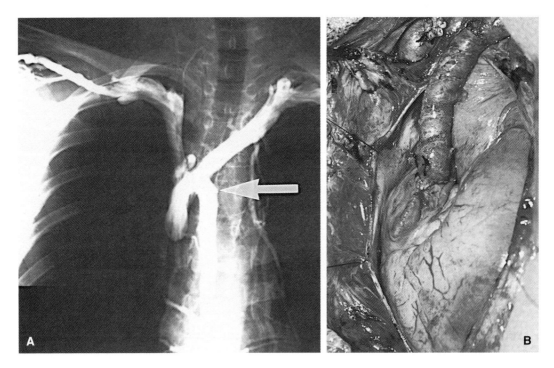

FIGURE 164-3   A, Bilateral upper extremity venogram documents obstruction of the superior vena cava and retrograde flow through the azygos vein (*arrow*). **B,** Left innominate vein/right atrial appendage spiral saphenous vein graft. (From Gloviczki P, Pairolero PC, Cherry KJ, Hallett JW: Reconstruction of the vena cava and of its primary tributaries: A preliminary report. J Vasc Surg 11:373-381, 1990.)

recanalization. Patients with extensive chronic venous thrombosis (type III or IV) not anatomically suitable for endovascular treatment, and those with less extensive disease (type I or II) who have not benefited from endovascular attempts are candidates for surgical reconstruction. Studies of endovascular treatment of nonmalignant SVC syndrome are still limited to case reports and small series with short follow-up.[14,18,19,32,36,43-49] Indications for surgical treatment, however, are better defined, because experience dates back many years and long-term results are good. We have performed SVC reconstruction for obstruction caused by granulomatous and idiopathic mediastinal fibrosis, central venous catheters, pacemaker electrodes, or ventriculoatrial shunt and in patients with antithrombin III deficiency or idiopathic venous thrombosis.[12,15,41,50] The indications for reconstruction of the SVC in patients with benign disease were similar in the reports by Doty[11] and Moore and Hollier.[51]

Surgical reconstruction of the SVC also has been performed in patients with different types and stages of malignant disease.[52-57] However, endovascular techniques should clearly be the treatment of choice in these patients, and surgical reconstruction should be contemplated almost exclusively only when the tumor is resectable. Patients with a malignant tumor should undergo reconstruction through a median sternotomy only if their life expectancy is greater than 1 year. Extra-anatomic subcutaneous bypass between the jugular vein and the femoral vein using a composite saphenous vein graft is an alternative if symptoms are severe and endovascular techniques fail or are not possible.[58,59]

Graft Materials

Grafting of large veins has been difficult, because large-diameter autologous vein is not available to use as a conduit. The *great saphenous vein* is usually not suitable because of poor size match.

Femoral Vein Graft

The *femoral vein, or the femoropopliteal vein,* was one of the first conduits used to reconstruct the SVC.[9] It has been used with success because of its excellent suitability in terms of size and length.[60-62] It is an excellent graft; however, if the patient has underlying thrombotic abnormalities, removal of a deep leg vein may result in at least moderate lower extremity post-thrombotic syndrome. For this reason, in young patients who undergo SVC reconstruction for benign disease, the femoral vein has been only our second choice for a graft after the spiral saphenous vein graft (SSVG).

Spiral Saphenous Vein Graft

The SSVG is autologous tissue with low thrombogenicity. Although its length is limited by the available saphenous vein segment, its diameter can be easily matched to that of the internal jugular or innominate vein (see Figs. 164-1 and 164-3). Described in animal experiments first by Chiu and colleagues,[63] this graft was first implanted in patients by Doty.[10] Our technique of preparing the SSVG is illustrated in Figure 164-4.[64]

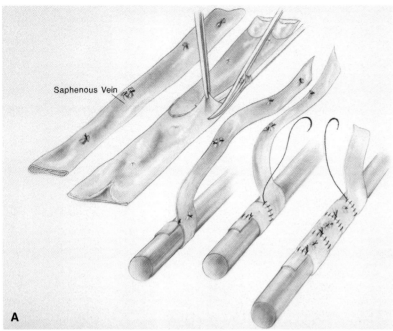

FIGURE 164-4 A, Technique for a spiral saphenous vein graft (SSVG). The saphenous vein is opened longitudinally, valves are excised, the vein is wrapped around an argyle chest tube, and the vein edges are approximated with sutures. **B,** A 15-cm long SSVG ready for implantation. **C,** Technique of left internal jugular/right atrial SSVG implantation. (From Gloviczki PG, Pairolero PC: Venous reconstruction for obstruction and valvular incompetence. In Goldstone J [ed]: Perspectives in Vascular Surgery. St. Louis, Quality Medical Publishing, 1988, pp 75-93.)

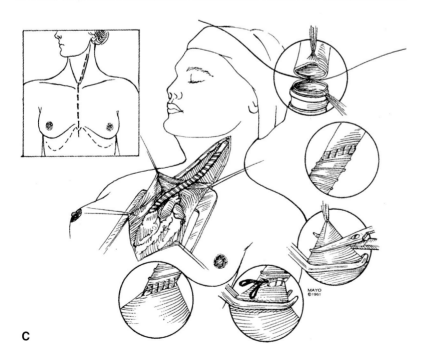

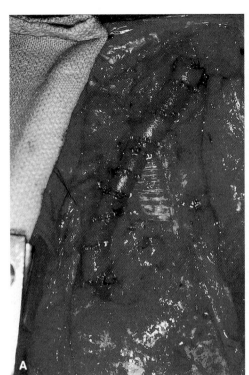

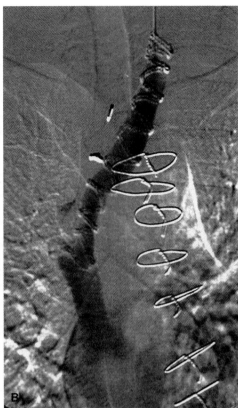

FIGURE 164-5 A, Nonpenetrating vascular clips used for preparation of a spiral saphenous vein graft. **B,** Postoperative venogram demonstrating the patent left internal jugular/right atrial appendage bypass graft. The graft is patent, and the patient is asymptomatic 3 years later.

The saphenous vein is removed, distended with papaverine-saline solution, and opened longitudinally. The valves are excised and the saphenous vein is wrapped around a 32 or 36 French (Fr) polyethylene chest tube. The edges of the vein are sutured together with running 6-0 or 7-0 monofilament nonabsorbable sutures to form the SSVG conduit, interrupting the suture line at every three-quarter turn (see Fig. 164-4). Alternately, metal clips may be used with the advantage of decreased time and less chance of "purse-stringing" the suture line (Fig. 164-5). The length of saphenous vein to be harvested to create a graft of sufficient length is determined according to the equation proposed by Chiu and coworkers[63] in their original experiments ($l = RL/r$; r and l = radius and length of saphenous vein, R and L = radius and length of SSVG). Harvesting vein from the groin to the knee usually results in an SSVG approximately 10 cm long.

Expanded Polytetrafluoroethylene Graft

Of the available prosthetic materials, externally supported expanded polytetrafluoroethylene (ePTFE) is the one used for large vein reconstruction almost exclusively.[65] Short, large-diameter (10 to 14 mm) grafts have excellent long-term patency because flow through the innominate vein usually exceeds 1000 mL/min. If the peripheral anastomosis is performed with the subclavian vein, venous inflow is significantly less and the addition of an arteriovenous fistula is usually required in the arm to ensure graft patency. For an internal jugular-atrial appendage bypass a large-diameter

(12 mm) ePTFE graft is a suitable alternative if the spiral saphenous vein is not possible. An arteriovenous fistula with direct flow into the graft has not been performed for jugular grafts. An externally supported prosthetic graft is a good choice in patients with a tight mediastinum and usually for all patients with malignancy, because recurrent tumor is more likely to compress and occlude a vein graft.

Allograft/ Cryopreserved Homograft

Iliocaval allograft can be considered in rare cases when immunosuppressive treatment is indicated for protection of a transplanted organ (Fig. 164-6).[66] Cryopreserved femoral vein and aortic arch grafts are potential alternatives, as are grafts prepared from autogenous or bovine pericardium.[67-71]

Surgical Technique

The operation is performed through a median sternotomy. If the internal jugular vein is used for inflow, the midline incision is extended obliquely into the neck along the anterior border of the sternocleidomastoid muscle on the appropriate side. The mediastinum is exposed, and biopsy of the mediastinal mass or resection of the tumor is performed before caval reconstruction.

Once biopsy or tumor resection is done, the pericardial sac is opened to expose the right atrial appendage, which is used most frequently for the central anastomosis. A side-biting Satinsky clamp is placed on the right atrial appendage, which is opened longitudinally. Some trabecular

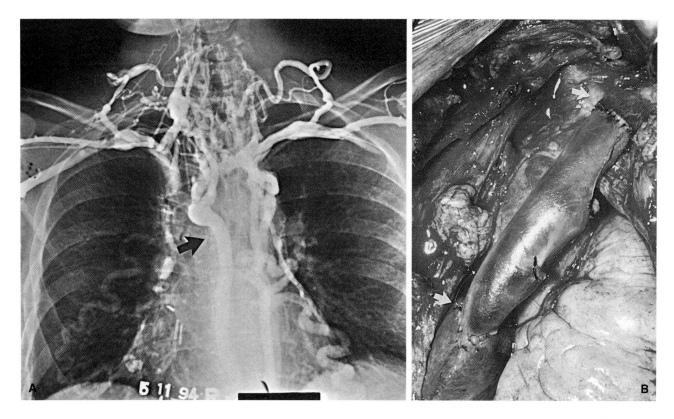

FIGURE 164-6 **A,** Venography in a 41-year-old woman with mediastinal fibrosis and liver failure, demonstrating type III SVC occlusion with retrograde flow in the azygos vein (*arrow*). **B,** Left innominate vein/right atrial appendage bypass was performed concomitant to orthotopic liver transplantation, using an iliocaval allograft. *Arrows* indicate the anastomoses. The graft is patent and the patient is asymptomatic from SVC syndrome 3 years after surgery. (From Rhee Y, Gloviczki P, Steers JL, et al: Superior vena cava reconstruction using an iliocaval allograft. Vasc Surg 30:77-83, 1996.)

muscle is excised to improve inflow, and an end-to-side anastomosis with the vein graft is performed with running 5-0 monofilament suture (see Fig. 164-4C). If not involved in the fibrosing process, a patent SVC central to the occlusion can also be used for this purpose. The peripheral anastomosis of the graft is performed with the internal jugular or innominate vein in an end-to-side or, preferably, an end-to-end fashion.

Although we have performed bifurcated SSVGs (Fig. 164-7) or bifurcated prosthetic grafts in a few patients, a single straight graft from the internal jugular or innominate vein (see Figs. 164-1 and 164-3) is our current operative choice for SVC reconstruction. Because collateral circulation in the head and neck is almost always adequate, unilateral reconstruction is sufficient to relieve symptoms in most patients. When only part of the circumference of the SVC is invaded by the tumor, resection and caval patch angioplasty using prosthetic patch, bovine pericardium, or autogenous material, such as saphenous vein or pericardium, is also a viable option.

Postoperative anticoagulation is started 24 hours later with heparin, and the patient is discharged on an oral anticoagulation regimen. Patients with SSVGs or femoral vein grafts who have no underlying coagulation abnormality are maintained on warfarin (Coumadin) for 3 months only. Those with underlying coagulation disorders and most patients with ePTFE grafts continue lifelong anticoagulation therapy.

Results

Endovascular intervention with PTA and stenting is undoubtedly the treatment of choice for patients with SVC syndrome owing to malignant disease in conjunction with radiation and chemotherapy.[32-38,35,39] Surgical intervention has been the mainstay of treatment of benign SVC syndrome since the first SVC bypass graft half a century ago,[9] with good long-term results.[10-12,50,69,72] More recently, stents for patients with benign disease have been offered as the first line of treatment.

Although the first reconstructions were performed with femoral vein,[9] since the description of the technique of spiraling the saphenous vein by Chiu and coworkers the SSVG has been the most popular conduit.[63] Doty and colleagues first adopted the technique and in 1982 reported excellent graft patency and freedom from symptoms.[10] Seven of nine grafts remained patent during follow-up, which extended from 1 to 15 years, and all but one of the patients became asymptomatic. Their larger experience consisting of 16 SSVGs for benign SVC syndrome reported in 1999 documented 88% long-term graft patency and excellent clinical results at a mean follow-up of 10.9 years.[72]

We have reported on the long-term results in 29 patients who underwent 31 SVC reconstructions because of obstruction caused by nonmalignant disease.[41] Twenty-one patients underwent reconstruction with an SSVG and 3 with reversed femoral vein, 6 had externally supported ePTFE

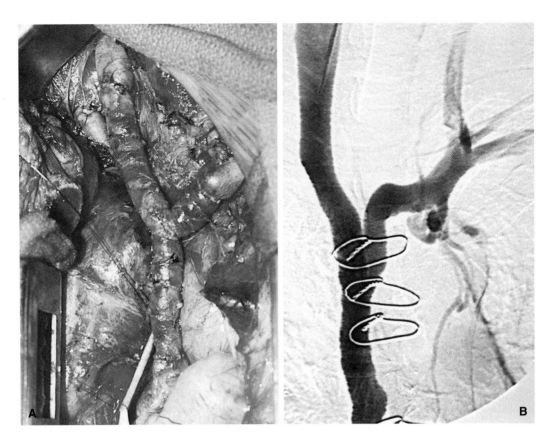

FIGURE 164-7   A, Bifurcated spiral saphenous vein graft in a 43-year-old woman. **B,** Venogram at 37 months reveals patent limbs of the bifurcated graft. (From Alimi YS, Gloviczki P, Vrtiska TJ, et al: Reconstruction of the superior vena cava: The benefits of postoperative surveillance and secondary endovascular interventions. J Vasc Surg 27:298-299, 1998.)

grafts implanted, and 1 patient received an iliocaval allograft (see Fig.164-6). The grafts originated from the internal jugular vein in 17 patients and innominate vein in 14; they were anastomosed centrally to the SVC in 18 patients and right atrial appendage in 13 patients. No early deaths or pulmonary thromboembolism occurred. Five patients had early reoperation for graft thrombosis: thrombectomy of 3 ePTFE grafts and thrombectomy and revision of side limbs of two bifurcated SSVG grafts (see Fig. 164-7). All grafts, except one limb of a bifurcated graft, were patent at the time of discharge. Thirty-day primary, assisted primary, and secondary patencies were 84%, 87%, and 100%, respectively.

During a mean follow-up of 5.6 years, high-grade stenosis of the graft developed in 7 additional patients and partial thrombosis developed in 1. One or more endovascular interventions (angioplasty with or without stenting) were performed to maintain patency in the stenosed grafts (Fig. 164-8). Five grafts eventually occluded during follow-up: three ePTFE, one SSVG, and one femoral vein graft. One thrombosed ePTFE graft was replaced with an SSVG. Primary and secondary patency rates of all the grafts at 5 years were 53% and 80%, respectively (Fig. 164-9). Of the different graft types, straight SSVGs performed the best, with 90% secondary patency at 5 years; 20 of the 21 grafts were patent at last follow-up with good to excellent clinical results (Fig. 164-10). The concomitant bilateral reconstructions attempted early in our experience resulted in

complications. We have since shied away from bilateral reconstructions and found that collateralization across the midline is adequate to decompress both sides with a single graft in the vast majority of patients.

However, increasing success with superficial femoral vein as an arterial conduit has resurrected this autologous graft for large vein reconstructions as well (Fig. 164-11).[60-62] Recent reports on good early results indicate that autologous femoropopliteal vein when available shows promise for replacement of large central veins. Concerns about distal thrombosis at the harvest site and chronic venous insufficiency remain; two of four of our patients who received femoral vein grafts developed DVT of the distal femoral and popliteal vein, with long-term sequelae in one. Similar experiences have been reported by others.[60] Clagett and colleagues, in addition to reporting seven cases of major venous reconstruction (two for SVC syndrome) with the femoral vein, have the largest experience with harvesting this vein for arterial reconstruction.[73] Mid-term follow-up in 61 patients revealed only mild signs of chronic venous insufficiency in fewer than one third of patients in spite of evidence of outflow obstruction and mild reflux on non-invasive venous evaluation.[62] These results, however, may not be directly applicable to patients with SVC occlusion, especially those caused by spontaneous or catheter-induced thrombosis. Nonetheless, it is a good conduit in patients with unavailable or inadequate saphenous vein.

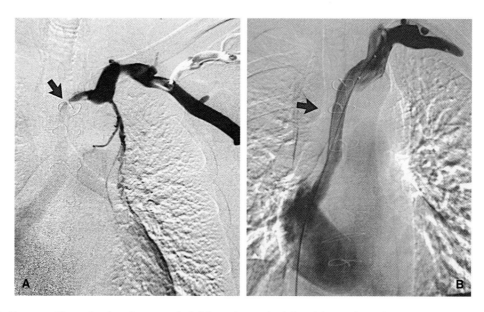

FIGURE 164-8 **A,** Venogram 10 months after placement of a left innominate vein–right atrial appendage spiral vein graft reveals severe stenosis at the proximal anastomosis (*arrow*). **B,** Successful reconstruction with placement of a Wallstent. (From Alimi YS, Gloviczki P, Vrtiska TJ, et al: Reconstruction of the superior vena cava: The benefits of postoperative surveillance and secondary endovascular interventions. J Vasc Surg 27:298-299, 1998.)

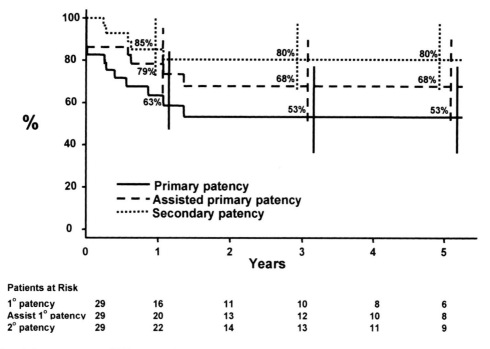

FIGURE 164-9 Cumulative patency rates of 29 bypass grafts used for SVC reconstruction. (From Kalra M, Gloviczki P, Andrews JC, et al: Open surgical and endovascular treatment of superior vena cava syndrome caused by nonmalignant disease. J Vasc Surg 38:215-223, 2003.)

Although graft patency and clinical results were significantly poorer with ePTFE compared with vein in our experience with benign SVC reconstruction, it remains the best prosthetic material for use in the venous system (Fig. 164-12). Patency beyond 1 year was only 50% in the six patients in whom we performed SVC reconstruction with ePTFE grafts.[15,41] Five of the six grafts, however, originated in the neck; and the small size of the internal jugular vein precluded use of large-diameter grafts. We have

documented better results with short, large-diameter ePTFE bypass grafts for iliocaval reconstruction in the setting of both benign and malignant disease.[12] In patients who need longer PTFE grafts, we now use a 12- to 14-mm graft size to ensure prolonged patency. Results with short ePTFE grafts implanted within the mediastinum by several authors have been gratifying. Wisselink and colleagues have reported 100% patency at 1 year in ePTFE bypass grafts for central vein occlusion performed in six patients on

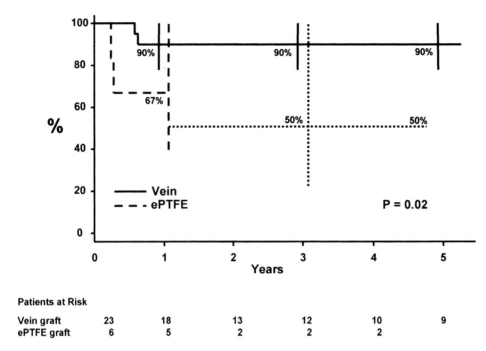

Patients at Risk					
Vein graft	23	18	13	12	10	9
ePTFE graft	6	5	2	2	2	

FIGURE 164-10 Cumulative secondary patency rates of 23 vein grafts and 6 expanded polytetrafluoroethylene (ePTFE) bypass grafts used for SVC reconstruction. (From Kalra M, Gloviczki P, Andrews JC, et al: Open surgical and endovascular treatment of superior vena cava syndrome caused by nonmalignant disease. J Vasc Surg 38:215-223, 2003.)

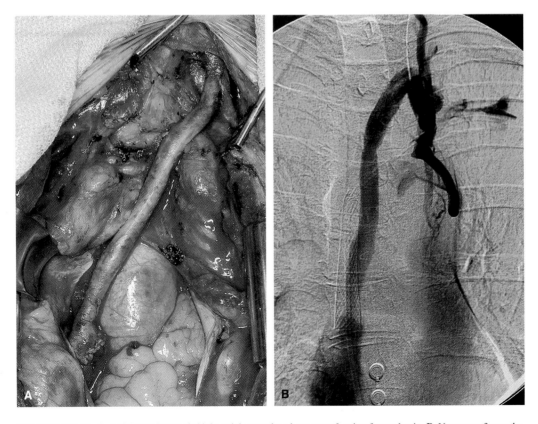

FIGURE 164-11   A, Left innominate vein/right atrial appendage bypass graft using femoral vein. **B,** Venogram 3 months after surgery confirms the graft to be widely patent.

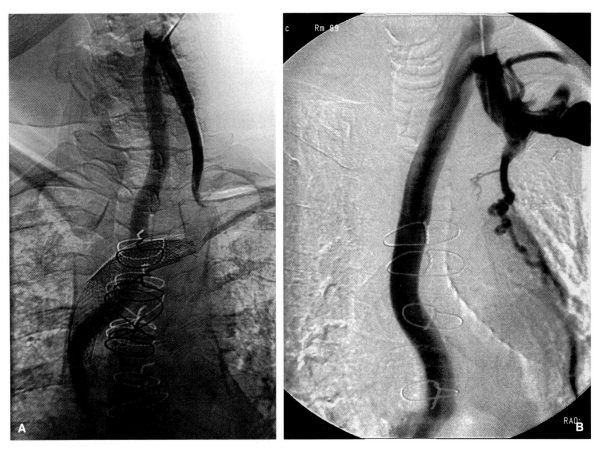

FIGURE 164-12 Venograms after placement of a left internal jugular vein/atrial appendage externally supported ePTFE graft: **A,** Widely patent graft at 3 months after the operation. **B,** Patent ePTFE graft at 13 months after intervention in another patient.

hemodialysis.[47] A brachial arteriovenous fistula was concomitantly performed in five of six of these patients to augment graft blood flow. Dartevelle and associates and Mangan and coworkers have reported excellent patency of ePTFE reconstruction of the SVC confined to the mediastinum after resection of malignant tumors.[55,56] Dartevelle and associates reported 20 of 22 grafts to be patent at a mean of 23 months after surgery. All 10 grafts inserted by Mangan and coworkers maintained patency and sustained symptomatic relief during the patients' lifetimes. Review of results from multiple series from the literature reveals patency of ePTFE grafts at 2 years to be approximately 70%.[12,15,51-56,74] Thrombosis occurs more frequently in patients in whom the distal anastomosis is performed with the internal jugular or subclavian veins, and results appear much better in patients with innominate inflow or SVC interposition grafts. Although the SSVG continues to be our first choice for SVC replacement, a large-diameter ePTFE graft is an excellent alternative.

Postoperative graft surveillance is important. Unfortunately, duplex ultrasound provides only indirect evidence of patency of an intrathoracic graft. Therefore, contrast or magnetic resonance venography is recommended before discharge and once at 3 to 6 months and 1 year after surgery. In our experience all high-grade graft stenoses occurred within the first year postoperatively, and half of these

had mild stenoses on the first postoperative surveillance venogram. Regardless of the treatment modality, the discovery of all stenoses was accompanied by recurrence of symptoms except in one instance. A similar view has been expressed by Doty and associates.[72] Based on these data, graft patency can be inferred from freedom from symptoms, and imaging after the first year need only be performed in symptomatic patients or in asymptomatic patients with known nonsignificant stenosis. Endovascular therapy is a useful adjunctive measure to treat graft stenosis and to improve long-term graft patency.[15,41]

■ SUMMARY

Surgical treatment of SVC syndrome is effective and provides long-term relief in patients with nonmalignant disease. Straight SSVGs and femoral vein grafts remain the conduits of choice for surgical treatment of benign SVC obstruction, with results superior to bifurcated vein grafts and ePTFE graft. Externally supported ePTFE is the least thrombogenic prosthetic graft for SVC reconstruction, with excellent patency and palliation when short, large-diameter grafts are implanted. Early results of endovascular techniques have been promising, and surgical treatment is reserved for patients who do not improve after endovascular treatment or who are not candidates for endovascular management. Endovascular techniques are also helpful adjuncts to prolong the patency of grafts implanted for SVC replacement. In patients with malignant SVC obstruction if excision of the mediastinal tumor is possible, concomitant venous reconstruction can be performed. Otherwise, endovascular techniques should be attempted first for palliation.

■ REFERENCES

1. Hunter W: The history of an aneurysm of the aorta with some remarks on aneurysms in general. Med Obs Inq (Lond) 1:323-357, 1757.

2. Mcintire F, Sykes EM Jr: Obstruction of the superior vena cava: A review of the literature and report of two personal cases. Ann Intern Med 30:925-960, 1949.

3. Ahmann F: A reassessment of the clinical implications of the superior vena cava syndrome, J Clin Oncol 2:961-969, 1984.

4. Parish JM, Marschke RF Jr, Dines DE, Lee RE: Etiologic considerations in superior vena cava syndrome. Mayo Clin Proc 56:407-413, 1981.

5. Sculier JP, Feld R: Superior vena cava obstruction syndrome: Recommendations for management. Cancer Treat Rev 12:209-218, 1985.

6. Chen J, Bongard F, Klein SR: A contemporary perspective on superior vena cava syndrome. Am J Surg 160:207-211, 1990.

7. Yellin A, Rosen A, Reichert N, Lieberman Y: Superior vena cava syndrome: The myth—the facts. Am Rev Respir Dis 141:1114-1118, 1990.

8. Nieto AF, Doty DB: Superior vena cava obstruction: Clinical syndrome, etiology, and treatment. Curr Probl Cancer 10:441-484, 1986.

9. Klassen K, Andrews NC, Curtis GH: Diagnosis and treatment of superior vena cava obstruction. Arch Surg 63:311-325, 1951.

10. Doty DB: Bypass of superior vena cava: Six years' experience with spiral vein graft for obstruction of superior vena cava due to benign and malignant disease. J Thorac Cardiovasc Surg 83:326-338, 1982.

11. Doty DB, Doty JR, Jones KW: Bypass of superior vena cava: Fifteen years' experience with spiral vein graft for obstruction of superior vena cava caused by benign disease. J Thorac Cardiovasc Surg 99:889-895, 1990; discussion 895-896, 1990.

12. Gloviczki P, Pairolero PC, Toomey BJ, et al: Reconstruction of large veins for nonmalignant venous occlusive disease. J Vasc Surg 16:750-761, 1992.

13. Gupta D, Mathur AS: Cervical and mediastinal fibrosis presenting with superior vena cava syndrome. Indian Heart J 31:302-304, 1979.

14. Dodds GA 3rd, Harrison JK, O'Laughlin MP, et al: Relief of superior vena cava syndrome due to fibrosing mediastinitis using the Palmaz stent. Chest 106:315-318, 1994.

15. Alimi YS, Gloviczki P, Vrtiska TJ, et al: Reconstruction of the superior vena cava: Benefits of postoperative surveillance and secondary endovascular interventions. J Vasc Surg 27:287-299, 1998.

16. Spittell PC, Vlietstra RE, Hayes DL, Higano ST: Venous obstruction due to permanent transvenous pacemaker electrodes: Treatment with percutaneous transluminal balloon venoplasty. Pacing Clin Electrophysiol 13:271-274, 1990.

17. Grace AA, Sutters M, Schofield PM: Balloon dilatation of pacemaker-induced stenosis of the superior vena cava. Br Heart J 65:225-226, 1991.

18. Lindsay HS, Chennells PM, Perrins EJ: Successful treatment by balloon venoplasty and stent insertion of obstruction of the superior vena cava by an endocardial pacemaker lead. Br Heart J 71:363-365, 1994.

19. Sunder SK, Ekong EA, Sivalingam K, Kumar A: Superior vena cava thrombosis due to pacing electrodes: Successful treatment with combined thrombolysis and angioplasty. Am Heart J 123:790-792, 1992.

20. Kastner RJ, Fisher WG, Blacky AR, Bacon ME: Pacemaker-induced superior vena cava syndrome with successful treatment by balloon venoplasty. Am J Cardiol 77:789-790, 1996.

21. Frances C, Starkey R, Errington ML, Gillespie IN: Venous stenting as treatment for pacemaker-induced superior vena cava syndrome. Am Heart J 129:836-837, 1995.

22. Laguna Del Estal P, Gazapo Navarro T, Murillas Angoitti J, et al: [Superior vena cava syndrome: A study based on 81 cases]. An Med Interna 15:470-475, 1998.

23. Muramatsu T, Miyamae T, Dohi Y: Collateral pathways observed by radionuclide superior cavography in 70 patients with superior vena caval obstruction. Clin Nucl Med 16:332-336, 1991.

24. Mahmud AM, Isawa T, Teshima T, et al: Radionuclide venography and its functional analysis in superior vena cava syndrome. J Nucl Med 37:1460-1464, 1996.

25. Mahmud AM, Teshima T, Isawa T, et al: Follow-up of patients with superior vena cava syndrome by functional analysis of radionuclide venography. Nucl Med Commun 19:417-426, 1998.

26. Kim HJ, Kim HS, Chung SH: CT diagnosis of superior vena cava syndrome: Importance of collateral vessels. AJR Am J Roentgenol 161:539-542, 1993.

27. Yedlicka JW, Schultz K, Moncada R, Flisak M: CT findings in superior vena cava obstruction. Semin Roentgenol 24:84-90, 1989.

28. Bashist B, Parisi A, Frager DH, Suster B: Abdominal CT findings when the superior vena cava, brachiocephalic vein, or subclavian vein is obstructed. AJR Am J Roentgenol 167:1457-1463, 1996.

29. Yamada T, Takahashi K, Shuke N, et al: Focal hepatic "hot spot" in superior vena cava obstruction: Correlation between radiocolloid hepatic SPECT and contrast-enhanced CT. Clin Nucl Med 24:533-534, 1999.

30. Cihangiroglu M, Lin BH, Dachman AH: Collateral pathways in superior vena caval obstruction as seen on CT. J Comput Assist Tomogr 25:1-8, 2001.

31. Stanford W, Doty DB: The role of venography and surgery in the management of patients with superior vena cava obstruction. Ann Thorac Surg 41:158-163, 1986.

32. Solomon N, Wholey MH, Jarmolowski CR: Intravascular stents in the management of superior vena cava syndrome. Cathet Cardiovasc Diagn 23:245-252, 1991.

33. Wilson E, Lyn E, Lynn A, Khan S: Radiological stenting provides effective palliation in malignant central venous obstruction. Clin Oncol (R Coll Radiol) 14:228-232, 2002.

34. Lanciego C, Chacon JL, Julian A, et al: Stenting as first option for endovascular treatment of malignant superior vena cava syndrome. AJR Am J Roentgenol 177:585-593, 2001.

35. Rowell NP, Gleeson FV: Steroids, radiotherapy, chemotherapy and stents for superior vena caval obstruction in carcinoma of the bronchus: A systematic review. Clin Oncol (R Coll Radiol) 14:338-351, 2002.

36. Kishi K, Sonomura T, Mitsuzane K, et al: Self-expandable metallic stent therapy for superior vena cava syndrome: Clinical observations. Radiology 189:531-535, 1993.

37. Furui S, Sawada S, Kuramoto K, et al: Gianturco stent placement in malignant caval obstruction: Analysis of factors for predicting the outcome. Radiology 195:147-152, 1995.

38. Tanigawa N, Sawada S, Mishima K, et al: Clinical outcome of stenting in superior vena cava syndrome associated with malignant tumors: Comparison with conventional treatment. Acta Radiol 39:669-674, 1998.

39. Dinkel HP, Mettke B, Schmid F, et al: Endovascular treatment of malignant superior vena cava syndrome: Is bilateral Wallstent placement superior to unilateral placement? J Endovasc Ther 10:788-797, 2003.

40. Chatziioannou A, Alexopoulos T, Mourikis D, et al: Stent therapy for malignant superior vena cava syndrome: Should be first line therapy or simple adjunct to radiotherapy. Eur J Radiol 47:247-250, 2003.

41. Kalra M, Gloviczki P, Andrews JC, et al: Open surgical and endovascular treatment of superior vena cava syndrome caused by nonmalignant disease. J Vasc Surg 38:215-223, 2003.

42. Bornak A, Wicky S, Ris HB, et al: Endovascular treatment of stenoses in the superior vena cava syndrome caused by non-tumoral lesions. Eur Radiol 13:950-956, 2003.

43. Qanadli SD, El Hajjam M, Mignon F, et al: Subacute and chronic benign superior vena cava obstructions: Endovascular treatment with self-expanding metallic stents. AJR Am J Roentgenol 173:159-164, 1999.

44. Charnsangavej C, Carrasco CH, Wallace S, et al: Stenosis of the vena cava: Preliminary assessment of treatment with expandable metallic stents. Radiology 161:295-298, 1986.
45. Putnam JS, Uchida BT, Antonovic R, Rosch J: Superior vena cava syndrome associated with massive thrombosis: Treatment with expandable wire stents. Radiology 167:727-728, 1988.
46. Rosch J, Uchida BT, Hall LD, et al: Gianturco-Rosch expandable Z-stents in the treatment of superior vena cava syndrome. Cardiovasc Intervent Radiol 15:319-327, 1992.
47. Wisselink W, Money SR, Becker MO, et al: Comparison of operative reconstruction and percutaneous balloon dilatation for central venous obstruction. Am J Surg 166:200-204, 1993; discussion 204-205, 1993.
48. Rosenblum J, Leef J, Messersmith R, et al: Intravascular stents in the management of acute superior vena cava obstruction of benign etiology. JPEN J Parenter Enteral Nutr 18:362-366, 1994.
49. Schindler N, Vogelzang RL: Superior vena cava syndrome: Experience with endovascular stents and surgical therapy. Surg Clin North Am 79:683-94, 1999.
50. Gloviczki P, Pairolero PC, Cherry KJ, Hallett JW Jr: Reconstruction of the vena cava and of its primary tributaries: A preliminary report. J Vasc Surg 11:373-381, 1990.
51. Moore W, Hollier LH: Reconstruction of the superior vena cava and central veins. In Bergan J, Yao JST (eds): Venous Disorders. Philadelphia, WB Saunders, 1991, pp 517-527.
52. Bergeron P, Reggi M, Jausseran JM, et al: Our experience with surgery of the superior vena cava. Ann Chir 39:485-491, 1985.
53. Herreros J, Glock Y, de la Fuente A, et al: [Superior vena cava compression syndrome. Our experience apropos of 26 cases]. Ann Chir 39:495-500, 1985.
54. Ricci C, Benedetti Valentini F, Colini GF, et al: [Reconstruction of the superior vena cava: 15 years' experience using various types of prosthetic material]. Ann Chir 39:492-495, 1985.
55. Dartevelle PG, Chapelier AR, Pastorino U, et al: Long-term follow-up after prosthetic replacement of the superior vena cava combined with resection of mediastinal-pulmonary malignant tumors. J Thorac Cardiovasc Surg 102:259-265, 1991.
56. Magnan PE, Thomas P, Giudicelli R, et al: Surgical reconstruction of the superior vena cava. Cardiovasc Surg 2:598-604, 1994.
57. Gloviczki P, Bower TC, McKusick M, Pairolero PC: Superior vena cava syndrome; Endovascular and direct surgical treatment. In Gloviczki P, Yao JST (eds): Handbook of Venous Disorders. London, Chapman & Hall, 1996, pp 580-599.
58. Vincze K, Kulka F, Csorba L: Saphenous-jugular bypass as palliative therapy of superior vena cava syndrome caused by bronchial carcinoma. J Thorac Cardiovasc Surg 83:272-277, 1982.
59. Graham A, Anikin V, Curry R, McGuigan J: Subcutaneous jugulofemoral bypass: A simple surgical option for palliation of superior vena cava obstruction. J Cardiovasc Surg 36:615-617, 1995.
60. Gladstone DJ, Pillai R, Paneth M, Lincoln JC: Relief of superior vena caval syndrome with autologous femoral vein used as a bypass graft. J Thorac Cardiovasc Surg 89:750-752, 1985.
61. Marshall W, Kouchoukos NT: Management of recurrent superior vena caval syndrome with an externally supported femoral vein bypass graft. Ann Thorac Surg 46:239-241, 1988.
62. Hagino RT, Bengtson TD, Fosdick DA, et al: Venous reconstructions using the superficial femoral-popliteal vein. J Vasc Surg 26:829-837, 1997.
63. Chiu CJ, Terzis J, MacRae ML: Replacement of superior vena cava with the spiral composite vein graft: A versatile technique. Ann Thorac Surg 17:555-560, 1974.
64. Gloviczki P, Pairolero PC: Venous reconstruction for obstruction and valvular incompetence. In Gladstone J (ed): Perspectives in Vascular Surgery. St. Louis, Quality Medical Publishing, 1988, pp 75-93.
65. Gloviczki P, Pairolero PC: Prosthetic replacement of large veins. In Bergan J, Kistner RL (eds): Atlas of Venous Surgery. Philadelphia, WB Saunders, 1992, pp 191-214.
66. Rhee R, Gloviczki P, Steers JL, et al: Superior vena cava reconstruction using an iliocaval allograft. Vasc Surg 30:77-83, 1996.
67. Billing JS, Sudarshan CD, Schofield PM, et al: Aortic arch homograft as a bypass conduit for superior vena cava obstruction. Ann Thorac Surg 76:1296-1297, 2003.
68. Zembala M, Kustrzycki A, Ostapczuk S, et al: Pericardial tube for obstruction of superior vena cava by malignant teratoma. J Thorac Cardiovasc Surg 91:469-471, 1986.
69. Seelig MH, Oldenburg WA, Klingler PJ, Odell JA: Superior vena cava syndrome caused by chronic hemodialysis catheters: Autologous reconstruction with a pericardial tube graft. J Vasc Surg 28:556-560, 1998.
70. Abdullah F, Adeeb S: Superior vena cava obstruction bypass—an alternative technique using bovine pericardial conduit: A case report. Heart Surg Forum 6:E50-E51, 2003.
71. Singh S, Sherif H, Reul GJ: Reconstruction of the superior vena cava with the aid of an extraluminal venovenous jugulo-atrial shunt. Tex Heart Inst J 27:38-42, 2000.
72. Doty JR, Flores JH, Doty DB: Superior vena cava obstruction: Bypass using spiral vein graft. Ann Thorac Surg 67:1111-1116, 1999.
73. Wells JK, Hagino RT, Bargmann KM, et al: Venous morbidity after superficial femoral-popliteal vein harvest. J Vasc Surg 29:282-289, 1999; discussion 289-291, 1999.
74. Bower TC, Nagorney DM, Toomey BJ, et al: Vena cava replacement for malignant disease: Is there a role? Ann Vasc Surg 7:51-62, 1993.

THE MANAGEMENT OF
LYMPHATIC DISORDERS*

PETER GLOVICZKI, MD

Chapter

165

Lymphedema:
An Overview

PETER GLOVICZKI, MD

When the transport capacity of the lymphatic system is reduced by obstruction or abnormal development of the lymph vessels or lymph nodes, protein-rich interstitial fluid accumulates and lymphedema develops. Chronic limb swelling due to lymphedema is not only a marked cosmetic deformity but, in most patients, it is also a disabling and distressing condition. Complications can be severe and include bacterial and fungal infections, chronic inflammation, wasting, immunodeficiency, and, occasionally, malignancy. The study of lymphedema, long a neglected field in medicine, has received considerable attention in recent years owing to progress in ultrastructural and physiologic investigations and to improvements in diagnosis and management of the disease. This new information and experience with lymphedema is based on a substantial knowledge of the lymphatic system that has been accumulating for centuries.

■ HISTORICAL BACKGROUND

Lymph vessels and nodes were mentioned in early times by Hippocrates (460-377 BC), who described "white blood" and "glands, that everyone has in the armpit,"[1] by Aristotle (384-322 BC), who wrote about "nerves...which contain colorless liquids,"[2] and by Erasistratus (310-250 BC) of the Alexandrian School of Medicine, who recognized the lacteals as "arteries on the mesentery of sucking pigs full of

milk."[3] It was not until the Renaissance, however, that further progress was made in this field. Eustachius, while dissecting a horse in 1563, was the first to observe the thoracic duct, but he did not recognize its significance and named it the *vena alba thoracis.*[4]

The discovery of the lymphatic system is attributed to Gasparo Asellius, professor of anatomy and surgery at Pavia, Italy. On July 23, 1622, during a vivisection, he observed the mesenteric lymphatics in a well-fed dog.[5] Asellius named the lymphatics the *vasa lactea* and recognized their function of absorbing chyle from the intestines. He assumed, however, that the mesenteric lymphatics transported lymph to the liver. It was Jean Pecquet, in 1651, who described the exact route of mesenteric lymphatic drainage to the "receptaculum chyli" and from there into the thoracic duct.[6] In subsequent years, Bartholin and Rudbeck clarified other details of the lymphatic circulation and the anatomy of the thoracic duct (Fig. 165-1).[7,8] The term *lymphatic* was first used by Bartholin. The valvular structure in the lymph vessels was demonstrated by Ruysch[9] in 1665 and later in 1692 by Anton Nuck, who injected mercury into the lymph vessels for his anatomic studies.[10]

The gross anatomy of the lymphatic system was remarkably well documented by the great anatomists of the 18th century. Cruikshank, a student of William Hunter, published *The Anatomy of the Absorbing Vessels of the Human Body* in 1786.[11] His work, however, was surpassed by the atlas of Paolo Mascagni, who published exceptionally detailed and clear illustrations of the entire lymphatic system (Figs. 165-2 to 165-4).[12] It was not until 100 years later that our knowledge of the anatomy of the lymphatic system was further broadened by the works of Sappey[13] and then by those of Ranvier.[14]

*This section is dedicated to Charles L. Witte, MD (1935-2003), a quintessential lymphologist, for his outstanding contributions to the art and science of lymphology, to this book, to surgery, as an astute researcher, a "reluctant" surgeon, a spirited educator, a prolific author, and, for 20 years, as editor-in-chief of the journal *Lymphology.*

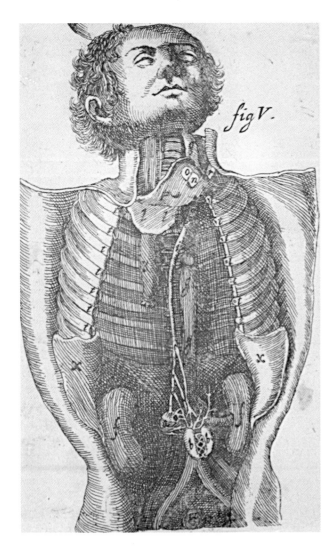

FIGURE 165-1 The receptaculum chyli and the thoracic duct in humans. (From Bartholin T: Vasa Lymphatica. Hafniae, Petrus Hakius, 1653.)

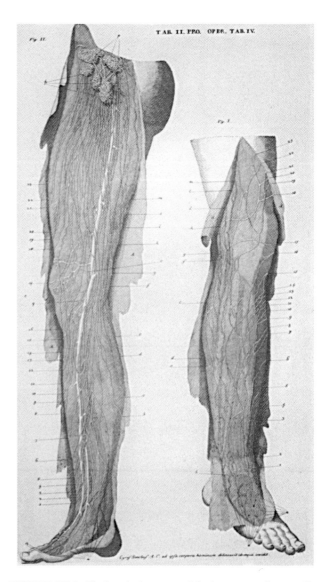

FIGURE 165-2 The lymphatic system of the lower extremity according to Mascagni. (From Mascagni P: Vasorum Lymphaticorum Corporis Humani Historia et Ichnographia. Vol 138. Senis, P. Carli, 1787.)

The lymphatics as an integrated system responsible for absorption were recognized at the end of the 18th century by William Hunter, his brother John, and two of his students, Hewson and Cruikshank.[15] However, their theory that the lymphatic system was the only absorbing system of the body was rightly criticized, even by their peers.

Although Hunter thought that the lymphatics were closed tubes, Hewson suggested that they had physiologic orifices and acted as "capillary tubes" that were "capable of absorbing the chyle and the lymph."[16] The "open mouth" theory—that the lymphatics had completely open distal ends—was advocated by von Kölliker[17] and later by von Recklinghausen, who also discovered the endothelial lining of the lymphatics.[18]

As Drinker stated,[19] however, "The modern history of lymph formation and lymph movement began with Starling." At the turn of the 20th century, Starling confirmed the relationship between the hydrostatic pressure in the blood capillaries and the oncotic pressure of the plasma proteins.[20] His work was a continuation of the theory of Ludwig, who suggested that lymph was formed by filtration of the

blood through the walls of the capillaries.[21] Drinker and his colleagues at Harvard University deserve the credit for explaining the absorption of proteins from the intercellular space via the lymphatic system.[22] Further details of lymphatic physiology were elaborated later by members of the Hungarian school of lymphology, headed by Rusznyák, Földi, and Szabó.[23] With the introduction of a clinically practical technique of contrast lymphangiography in the early 1950s, Kinmonth gave a special impetus toward clinical research of the lymphatic system and focused much-needed attention on the diagnosis and management of chronic lymphedema.[24]

■ LYMPHEDEMA: AN ENIGMA?

Lymphedema, a disease known for centuries, has been considered by many clinicians to be one of the enigmas of medicine.[25] The reasons are legion. Lymphedema is caused

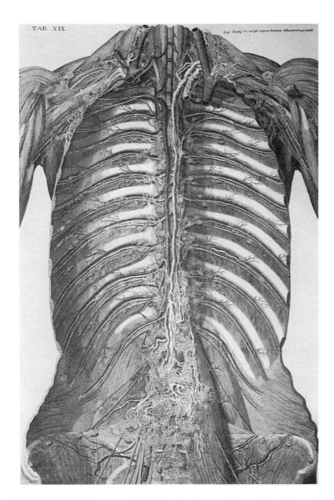

FIGURE 165-3 Anatomy of the thoracic duct, as illustrated by Mascagni. (From Mascagni P: Vasorum Lymphaticorum Corporis Humani Historia et Ichnographia. Vol 138. Senis, P. Carli, 1787.)

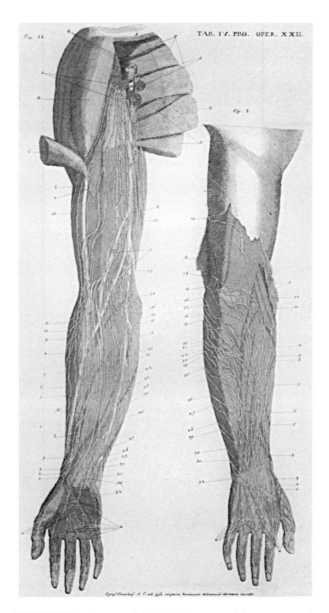

FIGURE 165-4 Anatomy of the lymphatic system of the upper extremity by Mascagni. (From Mascagni P: Vasorum Lymphaticorum Corporis Humani Historia et Ichnographia. Vol 138. Senis, P. Carli, 1787.)

by a fault in a system that is hardly visible. It frequently occurs years after the initial insult to the lymph vessels and lymph nodes after a long period of apparent well-being and normal functioning. It is difficult, and frequently frustrating, to treat and almost impossible to cure. Progress in the field of lymphology, however, has been substantial, and there have been recent landmark contributions to the medical literature such as Browse, Burnand, and Mortimer's *Diseases of the Lymphatics*[25a] and Földi, Földi, and Kubik's *Textbook of Lymphology.*[26]

Lymphatic Physiology

Nonetheless, our understanding of lymphatic physiology has markedly improved in recent years. Witte and Witte, in Chapter 166, provide new perspectives on the three-dimensional anatomy of the blood capillary/interstitial lymph interface, on the formation and propulsion of lymph, on lymphangiogenesis, and on the pathophysiology of the lymphovascular system. The spontaneous intrinsic contractility of the lymph vessels is recognized now as the pivotal mechanism by which lymph is propelled under normal conditions.

In regard to new theories of the pathophysiology of lymphedema, it must be emphasized that the lymphatic system is not comparable to the venous system. They are not two identical, unidirectional canalicular systems that are responsible for the return of excess interstitial fluid to the bloodstream and the heart. The major difference is that the *venous system* is filled with a liquid column, which responds immediately to changes in pressure or resistance. The *lymphatic system,* however, is not fully primed. Only if there is long-standing stasis does the lymph column fill the lymphatic channels completely. Only under these conditions are factors other than intrinsic contractility, such as muscle contractions and external massage, important in the forward propulsion of lymphatic flow. Normally, lymph flows slowly (1 to 2 mL/min) against high vascular resistance.

Low-output failure of the lymph circulation results in lymphedema; it can be indolent for many years before full-blown lymphatic insufficiency and tissue swelling develops. The cause of lymphatic failure is usually occlusion of the lymph vessels and lymph-conducting elements of lymph nodes. Occasionally, lymphangiectasia with reflux of chyle or lymph contributes to poor lymph flow. Chronic lymphedema is characterized by trapping of fluid, extravasated plasma proteins, and other macromolecules in the skin and subcutaneous tissues. It is also typical to find impaired immune cell trafficking, abnormal transport of antigens, and an increased propensity to infections. In Chapter 166, Witte and Witte describe additional characteristics such as obliteration of lymphatics (lymphangiopathy "die-back" or lymphangitis), defective lymph vessel contractility, mononuclear cell infiltrate (chronic inflammation), epidermal cell-fibroblast proliferation, collagen deposition, altered immunoreactivity, and vasoactive mediator imbalance with increased production of local cytokines and growth factors including autocrine and paracrine hormones.

Progress in angiogenesis research has been extended to the lymphatic system, and Chapter 166 includes an update on lymphangiogenesis and its critical role in abnormalities of the lymphatic circulation. Lymphangiogenesis is regulated at specific sites across the genome, and gene manipulation may offer therapy in the future for both primary and secondary lymphedema and related angiodysplasia syndromes as well as for a variety of neoplasms. Genetic manipulation of "lymphangiogenesis genes" may have the potential to stimulate formation of new lymph vessels and enhance abnormal lymphatic transport. Stem cell therapy to grow new vessels from undifferentiated embryonic or adult stem cells and new biomaterials for artificial lymphatics to drain the tissue fluid are potential modes of future therapy of lymphatic abnormalities.

Diagnosis

In most patients with limb swelling, the diagnosis of lymphedema is based on the history and physical findings. Once a systemic cause of edema has been excluded, one should keep in mind that chronic venous insufficiency is more often a local cause of limb swelling than is lymphedema. Secondary lymphedema, on the other hand, is more common than primary lymphedema.[27] Lymphoscintigraphy has become the study of choice for confirming that edema is lymphatic in origin (see Chapter 167).[28] It is still essential to perform computed tomography in most adult patients suspected to have lymphedema to exclude underlying malignancy. Magnetic resonance imaging is being used with increasing frequency to image the anatomy of lymph nodes, and it has the potential to become the most useful complement to lymphoscintigraphy.

Although direct contrast lymphangiography provides the finest details of lymphatic anatomy,[24,29] it is an invasive study that has potential side effects, and its use has been markedly restricted in patients with lymphedema. In our practice, contrast lymphangiography is reserved for the preoperative evaluation of patients with lymphangiectasia and for selected patients who are candidates for direct operations on the lymph vessels or the thoracic duct.

Prevention

Prevention of primary lymphedema is not possible at present. The incidence of secondary lymphedema, however, can be reduced by preventive measures. Filariasis, which affects almost 100 million people worldwide, was eradicated from Europe and North America by public health measures and control of mosquito breeding.[30] The introduction of similar measures in Third World countries, in addition to prophylactic antifilarial medications and immediate treatment of infected persons, can decrease a worldwide epidemic.

An important form of secondary lymphedema in developed countries is still postmastectomy lymphedema. In well-documented studies, Kissin and colleagues[31] noted that extensive axillary lymphadenectomy, axillary radiotherapy, and nodal involvement with disease are the most important independent risk factors for lymphedema. Although treatment of malignancy should not be compromised, excision of lymphatic tissue for either diagnostic or therapeutic purposes should be restricted to a minimum. The prevention of infectious complications is equally important in patients who have undergone lymph node dissection or who already have lymphedema. It is achieved by observing meticulous personal hygiene measures, avoiding skin injury, and controlling fungal infections.

Treatment

The mainstays of treatment of lymphedema continue to be conservative measures, including (1) leg elevation, (2) elastic or rigid compression, (3) manual physical decongestion, and (4) intermittent pneumatic compression.

Leg elevation continues to be the simplest way of reducing lymphedema, although it requires hospitalization, bed rest, and elevation of the extremity in an edema sling for several days. Elastic and nonelastic external compression of the limb remains the most important conservative measure to control lymphedema.

Manual physical decongestive therapy has been popularized in Europe by Földi and colleagues,[26] and this effective physical therapy regimen (see Chapter 168) has gained acceptance in the United States. Gamble and colleagues describe the complex physical therapy program that includes limb elevation, therapeutic exercises, standardized techniques of manual lymph drainage massage, and complex multilayer low-stretch wrapping.

Intermittent pneumatic compression is a widely used conservative treatment for lymphedema. Data from a prospective study of Pappas and O'Donnell support its long-term effectiveness.[32] Their protocol included 2 to 3 days' hospitalization with daily treatment with a sequential, high-pressure, intermittent pneumatic compression pump. The edema status was then maintained with two-way stretch elastic compression stockings. Limb girth reduction was maintained in 90% of patients, and excellent results were recorded in 53% at a mean follow-up interval of 25 months. A randomized study by Johansson and associates[33] compared manual lymph drainage (Vodder) massage techniques with a sequential pneumatic compression pump (40 to 60 mm Hg). At the end of a 2-week treatment cycle both methods had decreased arm volume; the difference was not statistically significant.

Excisional debulking operations are recommended for a select group of patients who have significant functional impairment due to excessive lymphedema (see Chapter 169). In the late stage of the disease, when irreversible skin and subcutaneous changes have occurred, this may be the only way to decrease the volume of the extremity. Among the different excisional operations, the staged subcutaneous excision beneath flaps, as reported by Miller and his group, has provided the most satisfying results.[34,35]

Reconstruction of the obstructed lymphatic circulation has been attempted with direct operations on the lymph vessels (lymphovenous anastomoses, lymphatic grafting).[36-40] The largest experience to date comes from Italy by Campisi.[41,42] This group treated 665 patients with obstructive lymphedema using microsurgical lymphovenous anastomoses, with subjective improvement in 87% of their patients. Four hundred forty-six patients were available for long-term follow-up, and the authors observed volume reduction in 69% and discontinuation of conservative measures in 85%. These authors recommend microsurgery early in the course of the disease before significant chronic inflammatory changes in the subcutaneous tissue develop. Vignes and colleagues[43] failed to prove clinical benefits from lymphovenous anastomoses.

A variation of lymphatic grafting was reported by Campisi, who treated 133 patients with vein grafts to bypass lymphatic obstruction at the groin.[41] Greater than 75% improvement was noted in 47% of the patients and greater than 50% in another 34%. Long-term results showed improvement in 81% of 95 patients who returned for follow-up, but results of late graft patency, studied with lymphoscintigraphy, were not reported. The lack of prospective clinical trials and the imperfect nature of treatment modalities continue to generate disagreement about what constitutes optimal surgical management of chronic lymphedema.

Liposuction should also be considered now as a treatment option for lymphedema. In a prospective study, Brorson and Svensson[44] used liposuction to treat patients with postmastectomy lymphedema. Liposuction significantly reduced limb swelling at 1 year after the procedure ($P < .0001$).

Chylous Effusions and Reflux

The focus of Chapter 169 is primary lymphangiectasia and the diagnosis and treatment of chylous effusions such as chylous ascites, chylothorax, or reflux of chyle into the perineum or the lower limb presenting as chylocutaneous fistulas or lymphedema. Some of the major contributions in this field can be attributed to Kinmonth,[24] Servelle,[45,46] and Browse.[47]

Our team at the Mayo Clinic has reported results in 35 patients with primary chylous disorders.[48] Surgical treatment includes controlling the site of lymphatic rupture and decreasing reflux by ligation of the dilated lymphatics. Sclerotherapy of the abdominal and retroperitoneal lymphatics has also been effective in controlling clinical symptoms and decreasing complications due to loss of chyle. Pleurodesis, pleuroperitoneal shunts, peritoneovenous shunts, and lymphatic reconstructions using lymphovenous anastomoses or thoracic duct azygos vein shunt have all been used with

success in the treatment of chylous effusions, but recurrence of symptoms in these patients is not rare.

■ SUMMARY

The problems that we have to face in dealing with lymphatic diseases are still substantial. Our understanding of lymphatic physiology has progressed, and diagnosis of lymphedema is usually possible using lymphoscintigraphy and other imaging modalities. Treatment of chronic lymphedema continues to be difficult, and the mainstay of therapy continues to be conservative and nonsurgical. Lymphedema, however, should no longer be considered an enigma of medicine. The authors writing on lymphedema in this edition of *Vascular Surgery* sincerely hope that the information presented here will stimulate further basic and clinical research and much-needed prospective clinical trials of this difficult and long-neglected problem. This section assigned to the management of lymphedema and chylous effusions has been testimony to the indisputable progress that has been made in the past decades in the field of lymphatic diseases.

■ REFERENCES

1. Kanter MA: The lymphatic system: An historical perspective. Plast Reconstr Surg 79:131, 1987.
2. Bartels P: Das Lymphgefässsystem. Jena, G Fischer, 1909, p 2.
3. Wolfe JHN: The pathophysiology of lymphedema. In Rutherford RB (ed): Vascular Surgery, 3rd ed. Philadelphia, WB Saunders, 1989, pp 1648-1656.
4. Eustachi B: Opuscula Anatomica. Venetiis, V Luchinus, 1564, p 301.
5. Asellius G: De Lactibus sive Lacteis Venis Quarto Vasorum Mesaraicorum Genere Novo Inuento. Mediolani, JB Biddellium, 1627.
6. Pecquet J: Experimenta Nova Anatomica, Quibus Incognitum Lactenus Chyli Receptaculum, et ab eo per Thoracem in Ramos Usque Subclavio Vasa Lactea Deteguntur. Paris, Cramoisy, 1651.
7. Bartholin T: Vasa Lymphatica. Hafniae, Petrus Hakius, 1653.
8. Rudbeck O: Novo Exercitatio Anatomica, Exhibens Ductus Hepaticos, Aquoso et Vasa Glandularum Serosa. Arosiae, kexud. e. Lauringerus 1653 [English translation in Bull Hist Med 11:304, 1942.]
9. Ruysch F: Dilucidatio Valvularium in Vasis Lymphaticis, et Lacteis. Hagaecomitiae, Harmani Gael, 1665.
10. Nuck A: Adenographia Curiosa et Uteri Foeminei Anatome Nova. Lugduni Batavorum, Jordanum Luchtmans, 1692.
11. Cruikshank WC: The Anatomy of the Absorbing Vessels of the Human Body. London, G Nicol, 1786.
12. Mascagni P: Vasorum Lymphaticorum Corporis Humani Historia et Ichnographia. Senis, Pazzini Carli, 1787, vol 138, p 27.
13. Sappey PC: Anatomie, Physiologie, Pathologie des Vaisseaux Lymphatiques, Considérés chez l'Homme et chez les Vertebrés. Paris, Delahaye et Lecrossier, 1874.
14. Ranvier L: Morphologie et developpment des vaisseaux lymphatiques chez mammiferes. Arch Anat Microscop 1:69, 1897.
15. Hunter W: Hunter's Lectures of Anatomy. Amsterdam, Elsevier, 1972.
16. Hewson W: The Lymphatic System in the Human Subject, and in Other Animals. London, J Johnson, 1774.
17. von Kölliker A: Handbuch der Gewebelehre des Menschen. Leipzig, W Engelmann, 1855.
18. von Recklinghausen F: Die Lymphgefässe und ihre Beziehungen zum Bindegewebe. Berlin, Hirschwald, 1862.
19. Drinker CK: The Lymphatic System: Its Part in Regulating Composition and Volume of Tissue Fluid. Stanford, CA, Stanford University Press, 1942.

20. Starling EH: On the absorption of fluids from the connective tissue spaces. J Physiol (Lond) 19:312, 1896.

21. Ludwig CFW: Lehrbuch der Physiologie des Menschen, 2nd ed. Leipzig, 1858-1861, p 562.

22. Yoffey JM, Courtice FC: Lymphatics, Lymph and the Lymphomyeloid Complex. New York, Academic Press, 1970.

23. Rusznyák I, Földi M, Szabó G: Lymphatics and Lymph Circulation. New York, Pergamon Press, 1960.

24. Kinmonth JB: The Lymphatics: Surgery, Lymphography and Diseases of the Chyle and Lymph Systems. London, Edward Arnold, 1982.

25. Olszewski W: The enigma of lymphedema—search for answers. Lymphology 24:100, 1991.

25a. Browse NL, Burnand KG, Mortimer PS: Diseases of the Lymphatics. London, Arnold, 2003.

26. Földi M, Földi E, Kubik S: Textbook of Lymphology. Munich, Urban & Fischer, 2003.

27. Browse NL: The diagnosis and management of primary lymphedema. J Vasc Surg 3:181, 1986.

28. Gloviczki P, Calcagno D, Schirger A, et al: Non-invasive evaluation of the swollen extremity: Experiences with 190 lymphoscintigraphic examinations. J Vasc Surg 9:683, 1989.

29. Clouse ME, Wallace S: Lymphatic Imaging. Lymphography, Computed Tomography, and Scintigraphy, 2nd ed. Baltimore, Williams & Wilkins, 1985.

30. Reynolds WD, Sy FS: Eradication of filariasis in South Carolina: A historical perspective. J SC Med Assoc 85:331, 1989.

31. Kissin MW, della Rovere GQ, Easton D, Westbury G: Risk of lymphoedema following the treatment of breast cancer. Br J Surg 73:580, 1986.

32. Pappas CJ, O'Donnell TF Jr: Long-term results of compression treatment for lymphedema. J Vasc Surg 16:555, 1992.

33. Johansson K, Lie E, Ekdahl C, Lindfeldt J. A randomized study comparing manual lymph drainage with sequential pneumatic compression for treatment of postoperative arm lymphedema. Lymphology 31:56, 1998.

34. Miller TA, Wyatt LE, Rudkin GH: Staged skin and subcutaneous excision for lymphedema: A favorable report of long-term results. Plast Reconstr Surg 102:1486; discussion, 1499, 1998.

35. Pflug JJ, Schirger A: Chronic peripheral lymphedema. In Clement DL, Shepherd JT (eds): Vascular Diseases in the Limbs: Mechanisms and Principles of Treatment. St. Louis, Mosby–Year Book, 1993, pp 221-238.

36. Gloviczki P, Fisher J, Hollier LH, et al: Microsurgical lymphovenous anastomosis for treatment of lymphedema: A critical review. J Vasc Surg 7:647, 1988.

37. O'Brien BMC, Mellow CG, Khazanchi RK, et al: Long-term results after microlymphatico-venous anastomoses for the treatment of obstructive lymphedema. Plast Reconstr Surg 85:562, 1990.

38. Baumeister RG, Siuda S: Treatment of lymphedemas by microsurgical lymphatic grafting: What is proved? Plast Reconstr Surg 85:64, 1990.

39. Baumeister RGH, Fink U, Tatsch K, Frick A: Microsurgical lymphatic grafting: First demonstration of patent grafts by indirect lymphography and long-term follow-up studies. Lymphology (Suppl) 27:787, 1994.

40. Weiss M, Baumeister RG, Hahn K: Dynamic lymph flow imaging in patients with oedema of the lower limb for evaluation of the functional outcome after autologous lymph vessel transplantation: An 8-year follow-up study. Eur J Nucl Med Mol Imaging 30:202, 2003.

41. Campisi C, Boccardo F, Zilli A, et al: Long-term results after lymphatic-venous anastomoses for the treatment of obstructive lymphedema. Microsurgery 21:135, 2001.

42. Campisi C, Boccardo F: Lymphedema and microsurgery. Microsurgery 22:74, 2002.

43. Vignes S, Boursier V, Priollet P, et al: Quantitative evaluation and qualitative results of surgical lymphovenous anastomosis in lower limb lymphedema [in French]. J Malad Vasc 28:30, 2003.

44. Brorson H, Svensson H: Liposuction combined with controlled compression therapy reduces arm lymphedema more effectively than controlled compression therapy alone. Plast Reconstr Surg 102:1058, 1998.

45. Servelle M: Congenital malformation of the lymphatics of the small intestine. J Cardiovasc Surg 32:159, 1991.

46. Servelle M, Nogues C: The Chyliferous Vessels. Paris, Expansion Scientifique Francaise, 1981.

47. Browse NL, Wilson NM, Russo F, et al: Aetiology and treatment of chylous ascites. Br J Surg 79:1145, 1992.

48. Noel AA, Gloviczki P, Bender CE, et al: Treatment of symptomatic primary chylous disorders. J Vasc Surg 34:785, 2001.

Lymph Circulatory Dynamics, Lymphangiogenesis, and Pathophysiology of the Lymphovascular System

166

CHARLES L. WITTE, MD

MARLYS H. WITTE, MD

> *Any proteid which leaves these vessels. . . is lost for the time to the vascular system. . . . it must be collected by lymphatics and restored to the vascular system by way of the thoracic or right lymphatic duct.*

Physiologist Ernest Starling, 1897

> *With improvement in methods of studying chromosomes, unexpected light may be shed on Milroy's disease and other hereditary lymphedemas.*

Lymphatic/Vascular Surgeon John Kinmonth, 1972

In a narrow sense, the lymph circulation is a unidirectional vascular system that merely transports surplus tissue fluid back to the bloodstream. In a broader sense, however, this network stabilizes the mobile intercellular liquid and extracellular matrix microenvironment to ensure parenchymal cellular integrity and function. In its entirety, the lymphatic system is composed of vascular conduits; lymphoid organs including the lymph nodes, spleen, Peyer's patches, thymus, and nasopharyngeal tonsils; and cellular elements such as lymphocytes and macrophages that circulate in the liquid lymph. These migrating cells cross the blood capillary barrier along with a multitude of immunoglobulins, polypeptides, plasma protein complexes, and cytokines and enter lymphatics to return to the bloodstream. Although body water circulates very rapidly as a plasma suspension of red blood cells within the blood vascular compartment, it percolates slowly outside the bloodstream as a tissue fluid-lymph suspension of lymphocytes through lymph vessels and lymph nodes. As a specialized subcompartment of the extracellular space, therefore, the lymphatic system completes a closed loop for the circulation by returning liquid, macromolecules, and other blood elements that "escape" or "leak" from blood capillaries (Fig. 166-1). Disruption of this blood-lymph loop promotes tissue swelling and is also responsible for a variety of syndromes characterized by scarring, wasting, immunodeficiency, and disordered angiogenesis. Rational therapeutic approaches, now and for the future, should be based on current and expanded understanding of these fundamental pathophysiologic principles.

■ TOPOGRAPHY

Macroscopic Anatomy

The discovery of chylous mesenteric lacteals in a well-fed dog by Gasparo Aselli early in the 17th century set off a flurry of anatomic dissections in England and continental Europe that established the nearly ubiquitous presence of lymphatics throughout the body and their important role in the absorption of nutrients.[1] These lymphatic "absorbents" accompany venous trunks everywhere except in the central nervous system and in the cortical bony skeleton. In general, lymph from the lower torso and viscera enters the bloodstream via the thoracic duct at the left subclavian-jugular venous junction. Lymphatics from the head and neck and the upper extremities enter the central veins either independently or by a common supraclavicular cistern. Numerous interconnections exist within this rich vascular network, and subvariant anatomic pathways are plentiful. For example, the bulk of cardiac and pulmonary lymph as well as the intraperitoneal fluid, which drains through fenestrae of the diaphragm into substernal mediastinal collectors, unites as a common trunk to empty into the great veins in the right neck. Intestinal lymph, on the other hand, which transports cholesterol and fat-soluble vitamins (vitamins A, K, and D) and long-chain triglycerides as chylomicra, unlike intestinal blood, which flows directly into the liver, courses retroperitoneally to the aortic hiatus to form with other visceral and retroperitoneal lymphatics the multichannel cisterna chyli and the thoracic duct. The bulk

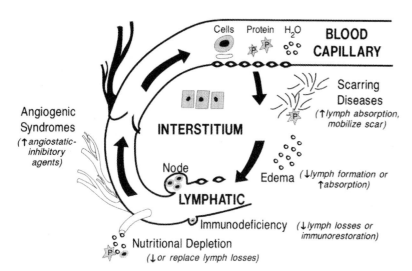

FIGURE 166-1 Blood-lymph circulatory loop. Within the bloodstream, liquid flows rapidly as a plasma suspension of erythrocytes; outside the bloodstream it flows slowly as a tissue fluid-lymph suspension of immunocytes through lymphatics and lymph nodes. Small and large molecules including plasma protein, trafficking cells, particulates, and respiratory gases cross the blood capillary endothelial barrier, percolate through the tissues, enter the lymph stream, and return to the central venous system to complete the loop. Clinical disorders of the blood-lymph circulatory loop manifest as swelling, scarring, immunodeficiency, nutritional depletion, and uncontrolled lymphangiogenesis and angiotumorigenesis. The words in parentheses designate current and potential future therapeutic approaches.

of the lymph formed in the liver flows retrograde or countercurrent to the portal blood flow and joins intestinal lymph collectors just before the origin of the thoracic duct. Only a small amount of hepatic lymph drains antegrade along the major hepatic veins to the anterior mediastinum and right lymph duct. Although these topographic variants influence the development and progression of peripheral (lymph)edema only indirectly, they are nonetheless essential for a broad understanding of edema syndromes, including those accompanied by visceral lymphatic abnormalities, celomic effusions, and chylous reflux. Although the brain and retina do not technically have a lymphatic apparatus, they possess analogous circulations such as the aqueous humor canal of Schlemm (the anterior chamber of the eye) or the cerebrospinal fluid/subarachnoid villi (pacchionian bodies) connections (the brain). Glial elements and non–endothelium-lined intracerebral perivascular (Virchow-Robin) spaces probably also serve to transport interstitial fluid to nearby intracranial venous sinuses. Extensive interruption of cervical lymphatic trunks (e.g., after bilateral radical neck dissection), therefore, causes prominent facial suffusion and a transient neurologic syndrome resembling pseudotumor cerebri,[2] whereas an infusion of crystalloid solution directly into the canine cisterna magna causing an elevation of intracranial pressure increases lymph flow from draining neck lymphatics.[3,4] Although abundant lymphatic pathways thus exist for surplus tissue fluid to return to the bloodstream, homeostasis of the internal environment nonetheless still depends on an unimpeded, intact interstitial-lymph fluid circulatory system (see Fig. 166-1).

Embryonic Development

Controversy has persisted since the early 1900s about the embryologic origin of lymphatics, that is, lymphovasculogenesis (endothelial precursors or stem cells, e.g., lymphangioblasts differentiate and proliferate into a primitive tubular network) and subsequent lymphangiogenesis (sprouting from existing vessels).[5] According to Sabin (Fig. 166-2),[6] lymphatics and veins derive from a common primordium in the venous system. After dye injections into pig skin, she observed gradually extending lymphatic plexuses starting first at the base of the neck, which were in direct communication with the venous system. She concluded that the primary lymphatic plexuses derive from central veins and that their growth progresses centrifugally by sprouting toward the periphery ultimately forming the superficial lymphatic system. On the other hand, Kampmeier[7] and others, after review of serial tissue sections including Sabin's original human embryo preparations and phylogenetic considerations, proposed the centripetal theory that the lymphatic system arises independently from tissue mesenchyme in peripheral tissues and the surrounding primary lymph sacs and only later joins the central venous system to complete the blood-lymph loop. Kampmeier reasoned further that as the developing blood capillaries begin to "leak clear fluid into tissues, lymph amasses in ever-growing volume within the mesenchyme first collecting in separate pools or spaces, which then become confluent as the high pressure stream seeks an outlet…the current usurps the course of decadent and vanishing venules, expands and pours into the developing jugular lymph sac, which meanwhile has acquired continuity with the forming arch of the cardinal lymphatic. Thoracic and abdominal lymphatics form similarly: Discontinuous spaces spring up in the mesenchyme next to the intercardinal or periaortic venous plexus in the path of the potential lymphatic; and primordia quickly widen, lengthen and fuse into a continuous vessel."[7] Whereas recent studies of the growth regulatory gene *PROX1*[8] and the receptor for lymphatic vascular endothelial growth factor (VEGFR-3)[9] have tended to support the centrifugal theory (origin from venous spouting), other elegant work has demonstrated a substantial centripetal contribution from mesenchymal lymphangioblasts in the engrafted wing lymphatic system of chimeric quail-chick embryos[10] and early avian embryo through *PROX1* staining.[11] Indeed, both processes may contribute in various degrees to the ultimate links between the lymph and blood vasculatures (e.g., the cervical thoracic duct/venous junction in humans).

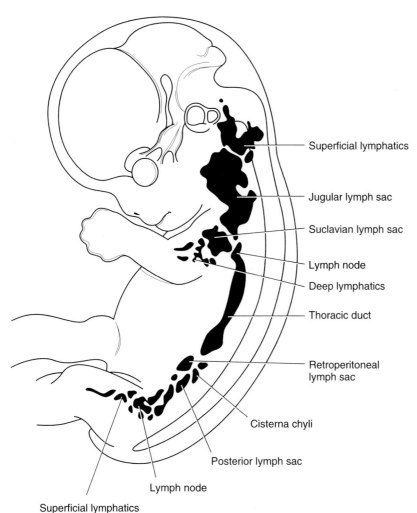

FIGURE 166-2 Schematic drawing of the developing lymphatic system. The primary lymph sacs and the thoracic duct primordium as well as several lymph nodes of a 2-month old human embryo. (Modified after Sabin FR: On the origin and development of the lymphatic system from the veins and the development of the lymph hearts and the thoracic duct in the pig. Am J Anat 1:367, 1902; and Yoffey JM, Courtice FC: Lymphatics, Lymph and the Lymphomyeloid Complex. New York, Academic Press, 1970.)

Superficial lymphatics

Jugular lymph sac

Suclavian lymph sac

Lymph node

Deep lymphatics

Thoracic duct

Retroperitoneal lymph sac

Cisterna chyli

Posterior lymph sac

Lymph node

Superficial lymphatics

Also, similar processes of lymphovasculogenesis and lymphangiogenesis are recapitulated after birth and likely involve the same complex expanding cascade of vascular growth factors (particularly the family of VEGFs and angiopoietins), endothelial receptors, and transcription factors already implicated in lymphatic growth and lymphedema-angiodysplasia syndromes (Table 166-1 and see section on Lymphangiogenesis).

Microscopic Anatomy

As an afferent vascular system, the lymphatics originate within the interstitium as specialized capillaries, although in certain organs, such as the liver, they seem to emanate from nonendothelialized precapillary channels (e.g., the spaces of Disse).[12] Lymphatic capillaries are remarkably porous and readily permit the entry of even large macromolecules (molecular weight more than 1000 kD). In this respect, they resemble the uniquely "leaky" fenestrated sinusoidal blood capillaries of the liver but are in distinct contrast to most other blood capillaries, which are relatively impervious to macromolecules even the size of albumin (molecular weight, 69 kD).[13]

Under light microscopy without pre–paraffin-embedded tracer or intravascular latex injection, it is difficult to distinguish between blood and lymph vessels, although the latter are usually thin walled and tortuous, have a wider, more irregular lumen, and are largely devoid of red blood cells. Many staining features have been advocated to differentiate between blood and lymph microvasculature such as the endothelial marker factor VIII–related antigen:vWF (von Willebrand factor). Although staining characteristics vary in both normal and pathologic states and at different sites (perhaps related to endothelial cell dedifferentiation), in general, lymphatic staining resembles but is less intense than its blood vessel counterpart. In other words, the staining differences have been more quantitative than qualitative.[14-16] Most recently, several new markers have been proposed that appear to be more lymphatic specific, particularly antibodies to hyaluronan receptor LYVE-1 (a homologue of CD44 glycoprotein),[17] podoplanin,[18] Prox1,[18] and, to a lesser degree, VEGFR-3 (the endothelial receptor for VEGF-C, the so-called lymphatic growth factor)[19,20] as well as 5′ nucleotidase (Fig. 166-3).[21]

Ultrastructurally, lymph capillaries display both "open" and "closed" or so-called tight endothelial junctions, often

Table 166-1 Vascular Growth Factors, Receptors, and Transcription Factors in Vascular, Including Lymphatic, Development

RECEPTORS	VASCULAR GROWTH FACTOR LIGANDS								
	PIGF	VEGF-A	VEGF-B	VEGF-C*	VEGF-D*	VEGF-E	Ang-1*	Ang-2*	Ephrin-B2
VEGFR-1/Flt-1	+	+	+						
VEGFR-2/Flk-1		+		+		+			
VEGFR-3/Flt-4*				+	+				
Neuropilin-1	+	+	+			+			
Neuropilin-2		+							
Tie-1									
Tie-2*							+	+	
Eph-B4									+

Transcription factors: *Prox-1*, FOXC2*, Net*, SOX18**
*Implicated specifically in lymphatic development.

with prominent convolutions.[22] Depending on the extent of tissue "activity," these capillaries can dramatically adjust their shape and lumen size. Unlike blood capillaries, a basal lamina (basement membrane) is tenuous or lacking altogether in lymph capillaries.[23,24] Moreover, complex elastic fibrils, termed *anchoring filaments*, tether the outer portions of the endothelium to a fibrous gel matrix in the interstitium.[25,26] These filaments allow the lymph microvessels to open wide with sudden increases in tissue fluid load and pressure in contrast to the simultaneous collapse of adjacent blood capillaries. Just beyond the lymph capillaries are the terminal lymphatics. These, in contrast to more proximal and larger lymph collectors and trunks, are devoid of smooth muscle, although the endothelial lining is rich in the contractile protein actin.[14] Intraluminal bicuspid valves are also prominent features and serve to partition the lymphatic vessels into discrete contractile segments termed *lymphangions.*[27] These specialized microscopic features of

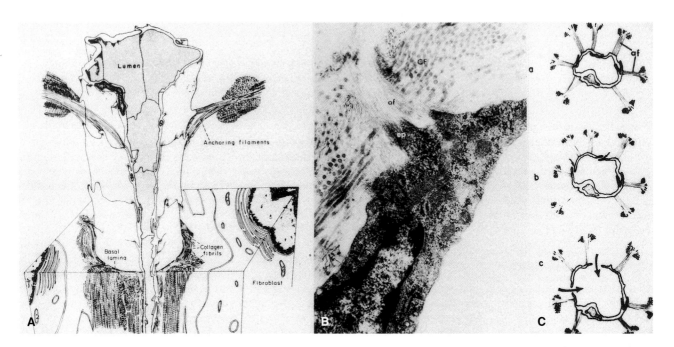

FIGURE 166-3 **A,** Three-dimensional diagram of a lymphatic capillary reconstructed from collated electron micrographs. The lymphatic anchoring filaments originate from the albuminal surface of the endothelial cells and extend into adjacent collagen bundles, thereby forming a firm connection between the lymphatic capillary wall and the surrounding interstitium. **B,** Transmission electron micrograph demonstrating anchoring filaments (af) that derive from the lymphatic endothelium (ep) and join nearby collagen bundles (CF). **C,** Response of lymphatic capillaries to an increase in interstitial fluid volume. As the tissue matrix expands, the tension on the anchoring filaments (af) rises, and the lymph capillaries open widely to allow more rapid entry of liquid and solute (a-c). In contrast to the stretching of the lymph capillaries, a rise in matrix pressure collapses the blood capillaries, thereby restricting further plasma filtration. (From Leak LV, Burke JF: Ultrastructural studies on the lymphatic anchoring filaments. J Cell Biol 30:129-149, 1968, by copyright permission of the Rockefeller University Press; and Leak LV: Electron microscopic observation on lymphatic capillaries and the structural components of the connective tissue-lymph interface. Microvasc Res 2:361, 1970.)

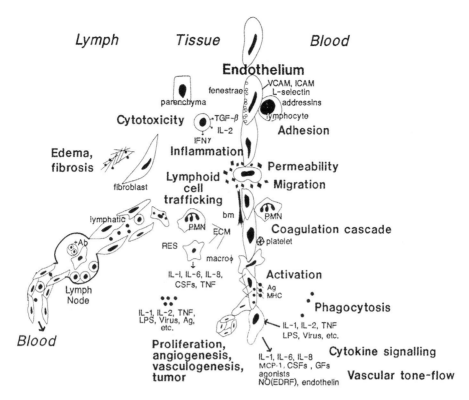

FIGURE 166-4 Schematic illustration depicting the postulated role of endothelial processes in microcirculatory events bearing on angiogenesis in the blood-lymph loop. These include macromolecular and liquid permeability, vasoreponsiveness, leukocyte adhesion and transmigration, coagulation cascading, particulate phagocytosis, antigen presentation and cytokine activation, lymphoid cell trafficking, and proliferative events leading to new vessel or tumor growth. Although scarcely studied, processes corresponding to those implicated at the blood vascular endothelial surface probably also occur at the lymphatic endothelial interface. The relative anatomic and dynamic relationships between blood and lymph vascular endothelium, parenchymal and extravascular connective tissues, and transmigrating leukocytes are shown. Ag, antigen; bm, basement membrane; CSFs, colony-stimulating factors; ECM, extracellular matrix; EDRF, endothelium-derived relaxing factor; GFs, growth factors; ICAM, intercellular adhesion molecule; IFN, interferon; IL, interleukin; LPS, lipopolysaccharide; macro, macrophage; MCP-1, monocyte chemoattractant protein 1; MHC, major histocompatibility complex; NO(EDRF), nitric oxide (endothelium-derived relaxing factor); PMN, polymorphonuclear leukocyte; RES, reticuloendothelial system; TGF, transforming growth factor; TNF, tumor necrosis factor; VCAM, vascular cell adhesion molecule. *Black circle* = exogenous particulates; black square = macromolecules; *drops*=fluid (plasma, interstitial or lymph).

the lymphatic network support the function of this delicate apparatus of absorbing and transporting lymph nodal elements and the large protein moieties, cells, and foreign agents of the bloodstream (e.g., viruses, bacteria) that have gained access to the interstitial space (Fig. 166-4).

■ PHYSIOLOGY

General Principles

As a fine adjuster of the tissue microenvironment, the lymphatic system is often neglected in most treatises on vascular diseases. Yet this delicate system, so inconspicuous during life and collapsed after death, helps to maintain the liquid, protein, and osmotic equilibrium around cells and aids in absorption and distribution of nutrients, disposal of wastes, and exchange of oxygen and carbon dioxide in the local milieu intérieur.

Two thirds of the body is composed of water, and most of this liquid volume is contained within cells. It is the remainder that exists outside cells, however, that continuously circulates. In a series of epochal experiments con-

ducted over a century ago, the English physiologist Ernest Starling outlined the pivotal factors that regulate the partition of extracellular fluid.[28,29] In brief, the distribution of fluid between the blood vascular compartment and tissues and the net flux of plasma escaping from the bloodstream depends primarily on the transcapillary balance of hydrostatic and protein osmotic pressure gradients as modified by the character (i.e., the hydraulic conductance) of the filtering microvascular surface (Fig. 166-5). Normally, a small excess of tissue fluid forms continuously (net capillary filtration), and this surplus enters the lymphatics and returns to the venous system. In contrast to blood, which flows in a circular pattern at several liters per minute, lymph flows entirely in one direction and at rest amounts to only 1.5 to 2.5 L/24 hr. This limited volume derives from a slight hydrodynamic imbalance that favors fluid, salt, and macromolecular movement from plasma into tissue spaces. Although blood capillary beds vary in hydraulic conductance, in general, disturbances in the transcapillary hydrostatic and protein osmotic pressure gradients (Starling forces) tend to promote edema that is low in protein content (less than 1.0 g/dL), whereas impedance to lymph flow

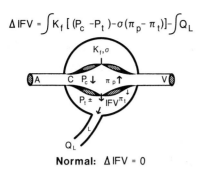

$$\Delta \text{IFV} = \int K_f \left[(P_c - P_t) - \sigma(\pi_p - \pi_t) \right] - \int Q_L$$

Normal: Δ IFV = 0

A = arteriole	P_c = capillary pressure	K_f = filtration coefficient
V = venule	P_t = tissue pressure	σ = solute coefficient
C = capillary	π_p = plasma oncotic pressure	IFV = interstitial fluid volume
L = lymph	π_t = tissue oncotic pressure	Q_L = lymph flow

FIGURE 166-5 Schematic diagram of the primary forces regulating fluid flux into the interstitium and the importance of lymph flow in maintaining a steady-state interstitial fluid volume and hence a stable partition of extracellular fluid between the bloodstream and the interstitium.

(lymph stasis) promotes (lymph)edema high in protein content (more than 1.5 g/dL).

Unlike blood flow, which is propelled by a powerful and highly specialized muscular pump (the heart), lymph propulsion originates predominantly from spontaneous intrinsic segmental contractions of larger and probably also small lymph trunks (Fig. 166-6)[30-32] and to a lesser extent from extrinsic "haphazard forces" such as breathing, sighing, yawning, muscular squeezing (e.g., alimentary peristalsis), and transmitted arterial pulsations (Table 166-2).[32,33] As noted, the contractions of lymphatic segments between intraluminal valves (i.e., the lymphangions) are highly responsive to lymph volume. Thus, an increase in lymph formation is accompanied by more frequent and more powerful lymphangion contractions (Fig. 166-7), a lymphodynamic response that resembles Starling's other major physiologic principle, the law of the heart.[27,34] Lymphatic truncal contraction, like venous and arterial vasomotion, is mediated by sympathomimetic agents (both alpha- and beta-adrenergic agonists),[35,36] byproducts of arachidonic acid metabolism (thromboxanes and prosta-

glandins),[37-40] and neurogenic, even pacemaker, stimuli (Fig. 166-8).[41,42] Oddly, in different regions of the body, lymphatic trunks seem to exhibit varying sensitivity to different vasoactive and neurogenic stimulants.[36,43,44] Although the importance of truncal vasomotion as mediated by tunica smooth muscle is well established, it remains unclear whether terminal lymphatics or lymphatic capillaries also are capable of vasomotion or are simply passive channels. In some ways, this controversy parallels the prolonged dispute about whether blood capillary endothelial cells are capable of vasoactivity, an issue now clearly resolved in the affirmative. Because lymphatic endothelium, like blood endothelium, is rich in actin[14] (a principal contractile protein), it is reasonable to assume that lymphatic microvessels also exhibit vasomotion.

In addition to their central immunologic role, lymph nodes are a potential site of impediment to the free flow of lymph. Unlike frogs, which lack lymph nodes but possess four or more strategically placed lymph hearts that propel large quantities of peripheral lymph back to the bloodstream,[45,46] mammals possess immunoreactive lymph nodes, which, when swollen, fibrotic, or atrophic, may act to initiate or perpetuate lymph stasis.[47,48] Perhaps the intrinsic contraction of mammalian lymphatic trunks represents a phylogenetic vestige of amphibian lymph hearts (see following section on flow-pressure dynamics for more details).

Flow-Pressure Dynamics

Although lymphatics, like veins, are thin-walled, flexible conduits that return liquid to the heart, the flow-pressure relationships in the two systems are quite different. The energy to drive blood in the venous system derives primarily from the thrust of the heart. The cardiac propulsive boost maintains a pressure head through the arteries and blood capillaries into the veins that is sufficient to overcome venous vascular resistance. Muscular contractions such as walking and running in the presence of competent venous valves supplements cardiac action in facilitating the return of blood to the heart.

Lymph vessels in tissues, on the other hand, are not directly contiguous with the blood vasculature, and the chief source of energy for lymph propulsion emanates from the

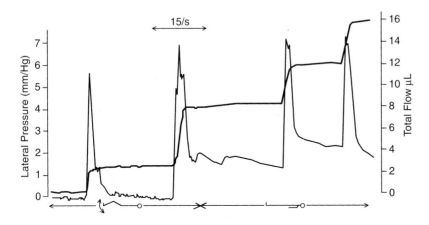

FIGURE 166-6 Lateral pressure *(curve with acute peaks)* and cumulative lymph flow *(stepwise rising curve)* in a subcutaneous leg lymphatic of a healthy man lying supine during movement of the foot and at rest. Note that lymph flow occurs only during rhythmic contraction of the lymphatic collector and specifically not by voluntary contraction of calf muscles. s, seconds. (From Olszewski WL, Engeset A: Intrinsic contractility of prenodal lymph vessels and lymph flow in the human leg. Am J Physiol 239:H775, 1980.)

Table 166-2 Circulatory Dynamics of Vascular Conduits

	LYMPHATIC	VEIN	ARTERY
1°, propulsive unit	Lymphangion	Heart	Heart
2°, propulsive force	Haphazard*	Skeletal muscle	Vasomotion
Distal (upright) pressure (mm Hg)	2-3	90-100	20
Central pressure (mm Hg)	6-10	0-2	100
Flow rate	Very low	High	High
Vascular resistance	Relatively high	Very low	High
Intraluminal valves	Innumerable	Several	None
Impediment to flow	Lymph nodes	None	None
Conduit fluid column	Incomplete	Complete	Complete
Conduit failure	Edema (>1.5 g/dL)	Edema (<1.0 g/dL)	Claudication
	Brawny induration	Skin pigmentation	Rest pain
	Acanthosis	"Stasis" ulceration	Tissue necrosis

*Breathing, sighing, yawning, peristalsis, transmitted arterial pulsation; skeletal muscle contraction also increases the amplitude and frequency of lymphatic contractions and squeezes interstitial fluid into initial lymphatics (i.e., lymph capillaries).

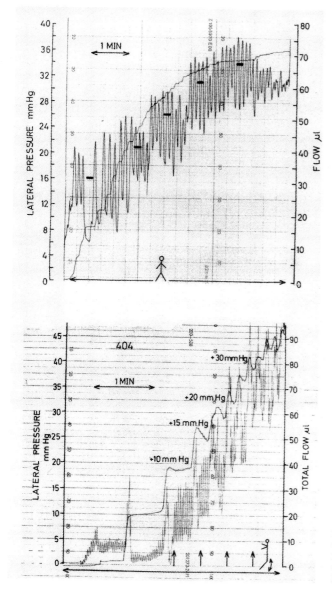

FIGURE 166-7 A human leg lymphatic has been cannulated retrograde, and the external tip of the cannula has been progressively raised, thereby gradually increasing hydrostatic pressure above the level of the cannulated lymphatic. While the man is upright *(upper tracing),* sequential increases in outflow resistance cause an increase in lymphatic pulse frequency with subsequent decreases in pulse amplitude, lymph flow *(stepwise ascending curve),* and stroke volume. When the intralymphatic pressure reaches 34 mm Hg, lymph flow ceases despite a high pulsation rate. In the *lower tracing* the same man is now tiptoeing, and rising outflow pressure induces more frequent lymphatic pulsations. Note again that calf muscle contraction with up-and-down foot motion is not associated with greater lymph propulsion. Also note that at higher pressures each flow wave is followed by sporadic retrograde flow (reflux), which probably relates to intraluminal valve incompetence in the distending lymph vessel. (Reprinted with permission from Olszewski WL: Lymph pressure and flow in limbs. In Olszewski WL (ed): Lymph Stasis: Pathophysiology, Diagnosis, and Treatment. Boca Raton, FL, CRC Press, 1991, pp 136-137.)

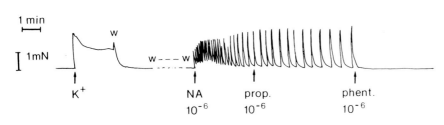

FIGURE 166-8 Tracing taken from a human lower leg lymphatic segment. Norepinephrine (noradrenaline, NA) 10^{-6} M induces phasic lymphatic contractions that are unaffected by the beta-blocker propranolol (prop) 10^{-6} M but are abolished by phentolamine (phent) 10^{-6} M. K+ indicates previous potassium (124 mM)-induced contraction, and W indicates washout with fresh Krebs' buffer solution. (From Sjöberg T, Steen S: Contractile properties of lymphatics from the human lower leg. Lymphology 24:16, 1991.)

intrinsic lymphatic truncal wall contractions (propulsor lymphaticum).[30-46] Like amphibian lymph hearts (cor lymphaticum), mammalian lymphatic smooth muscle beats rhythmically and in the presence of a well-developed intraluminal valve system facilitates lymph transport (Fig. 166-9).[49] In a sense, the lymphatics function as micropumps that respond to fluid challenges with increases in both rate and stroke volume.[27,37] Ordinarily, resistance to flow in the lymphatic vessels is relatively high compared with the low resistance in the venous system,[50] but the pumping capacity of the lymphatics is able to overcome this impedance by generating intraluminal pressures of 30 to 50 mm Hg (see Fig. 166-7) and sometimes even equaling or exceeding arterial pressure.[30,50,51] This formidable lymphatic ejection force is modulated not only by filling pressure but also by temperature, sympathomimetics, neurogenic stimuli, circulating hormones, and locally released paracrine and autocrine cytokine secretions.[52]

It is often mistakenly thought that lymph return, like venous return, is directly enhanced by truncal compression from skeletal muscle and other adjacent structures. Whereas muscular contraction and external massage clearly accelerate lymph return in the presence of edema,[51] under normal conditions peripheral lymph flow is regulated primarily by spontaneous contraction of the lymphatics themselves.[51,52] In peripheral lymphatics, unlike peripheral veins, the column of liquid is incomplete. Accordingly, with normal intralymphatic pressure, external compression is ineffective for propelling lymph onward (Fig. 166-10) although it may increase the frequency and amplitude of lymphatic contractions. In other words, lymphatics, in contrast to veins, are not sufficiently "primed."[53] During lymphatic obstruction and persistent lymph stasis, hydrostatic pressure in the draining tissue watersheds and lymphatics rises as intrinsic truncal contractions fail to expel lymph completely. In this circumstance, in contrast to the normal situation, the fluid column in the lymphatics becomes continuous and skeletal muscle or forceful external compression then becomes an effective pumping mechanism that aids lymph transport.[51,53]

Studies on the effects of gravity on peripheral lymphatic and venous pressure conform to these findings. Whereas assuming an erect position sharply raises distal venous pressure, peripheral intralymphatic pressure is unaffected, although lymphatic truncal pulsation increases both in frequency and amplitude.[53] This arrangement favors the removal of tissue fluid by the lymphatics during dependency because, unlike the veins, the lymphatics operate at a much lower hydrostatic pressure. Once the lymphatics become obstructed, truncal contractions quicken at first, but then the intraluminal valves gradually give way, and as the lymph fluid column becomes continuous, this mechanical advantage is lost and chronic lymphedema supervenes (see Fig. 166-11).

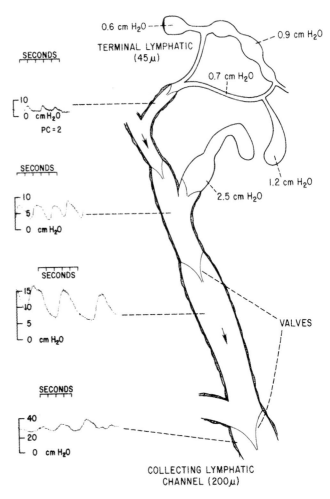

FIGURE 166-9 Composite drawing of terminal lymphatic network reconstructed from several mesenteric preparations in the rat demonstrating a gradual rise in intralymphatic pressure from 0.6 cm H_2O in the terminal lymphatics to 30 cm H_2O in the larger collecting duct. Note also the rhythmic pressure pulsations in the collecting trunks. (From Zweifach BW, Prather JW: Micromanipulation of pressure in terminal lymphatics in the mesentery. Am J Physiol 228:1326, 1975.)

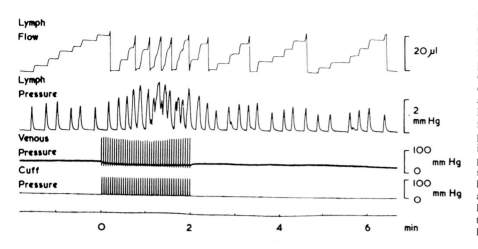

FIGURE 166-10 Effect of intermittent external pneumatic compression on the sheep foot on peripheral lymph flow, lymph outflow pressure, and venous pressure. Note that prior to external compression the lymphatic contracts spontaneously and each contraction extrudes a small quantity of lymph, which appears as a step increment in the flow record. During the 2-minute time period when the foot cuff is inflated intermittently, each compression causes a synchronous pressure rise in peripheral venous pressure but not in lymph pressure. The frequency and amplitude of spontaneous lymphatic contractions increase, however, and this increase is associated with a concomitant rise in lymph flow. (From Pippard C, Roddie IC: Comparison of fluid transport systems in lymphatics and veins. Lymphology 20:224, 1987.)

■ PATHOPHYSIOLOGY

Overview

Because congenital absence and radical excision of regional lymph nodes (and hence lymphatics) are both associated with edema, it seems straightforward that lymphedema is simply the end result of insufficient lymphatic drainage. Despite this reasonable conclusion, peripheral lymphedema has proved both hard to simulate in experimental animals and difficult to treat. Initial experimental attempts to simulate the clinical condition using lymphatic sclerosis and radical excision were notoriously unsuccessful and revealed a remarkable capacity of obstructed lymphatics to regenerate and "bridge the gap" or bypass the induced blockage with spontaneous opening of auxiliary lymphatic-venous shunts.[54,55] Although transient swelling was common, these compensatory mechanisms were thought to preclude the development of chronic lymphedema solely on the basis of obstruction of lymphatic drainage. The general failure of early lymph stasis experiments to reproduce unremitting peripheral edema reinforced a long-held theory that overt or subclinical bacterial infection (lymphangitis) was indispensable to the evolution of chronic lymphedema.[56] By disrupting microvascular integrity and promoting lymphatic obliteration, recurring infection was thought to exaggerate tissue scarring and eventually cause unremitting lymphedema. This widely held belief was consistent with the commonly observed delayed onset and unpredictability of arm and leg edema after radical mastectomy and groin dissection, respectively, and the grotesque deformities of tropical lymphedema (so-called elephantiasis) associated with filariasis (*Wuchereria bancrofti* and *Brugia malayi*).

Although understanding is still incomplete, it is nonetheless now clear that nonpitting, brawny extremity edema can arise from lymph stasis alone and the unremitting accumulation of protein-rich fluid in the extracellular matrix. By means of repeated intralymphatic injection of silica particles, Drinker and colleagues[57] first succeeded in simulating chronic lymphedema in dogs through extensive lymphatic sclerosis. Subsequently, Danese,[58] Olszewski,[48]

Clodius and Altorfer,[59] and their associates established that refractory lymphedema could result solely from the mechanical interruption of peripheral lymphatics. Using an experimental model of circumferential lymphatic transection, tissue swelling was found to be prompt at first (acute lymphedema), disappeared by 4 to 6 weeks, and remained absent for months to years (latent lymphedema), but thereafter reappeared and persisted (chronic lymphedema). If radiation is combined with circumferential excision, the lymphedema is more severe and persists.[60] A similar sequence of events occurs in experimental filariasis (due to *Brugia malayi*).[61] During the latent phase, when edema is not visible, conventional oil lymphography corroborates ongoing lymphatic destruction.[48] Progressive truncal tortuosity and dilatation give way to massive lymphangiectasis, valvular incompetence, and retrograde flow (dermal back-flow). Serial microscopy discloses mononuclear cell infiltration, intramural destruction of lymphatic collectors, and collagen deposition throughout the soft tissues. Eventually the lymph trunks lose their distinctive smooth muscle and endothelial lining and the boundary lines between lymph collectors and the surrounding matrix progressively blur.[48,59]

These studies definitively demonstrate that extensive impairment of lymph drainage is sufficient by itself to cause chronic lymphedema (Fig. 166-11). The key observation is the long interval between the disruption of the lymph trunks and the development of refractory edema, which helps to explain the inconstancy and unpredictability of limb swelling after radical operations for treatment of cancer and other disorders of defective lymphatic drainage. As with deep venous occlusive disease, which is associated with valve destruction, venous stasis, and eventually overt edema (post-thrombophlebitic syndrome) with characteristic trophic skin changes (hyperpigmentation and ulceration), the absence or obliteration of the lymphatics is associated with lymphatic valve incompetence, lymph stasis, and, eventually, intractable edema (post-lymphangitic syndrome) with its characteristic trophic skin changes (thickened toe skin folds or Stemmer's sign, warty overgrowth, and brawny induration).[62]

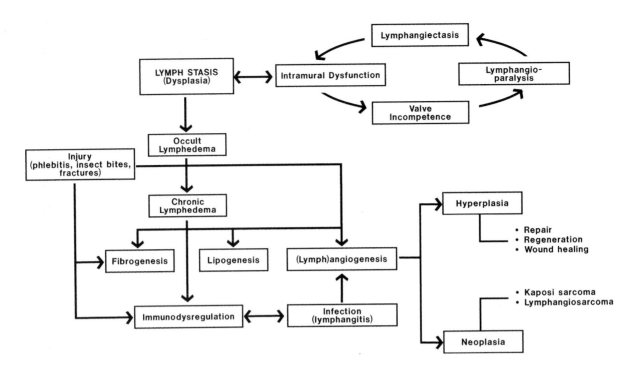

FIGURE 166-11 Flow chart illustrating the pathogenesis of peripheral lymphedema and some of its sequelae. According to this scheme, congenitally deficient or obstructed lymphatics promote lymph stasis, which is accompanied by deranged truncal contractility, progressive valve incompetence, destruction of contractile elements (lymphangioparalysis), and gradual ectasia of lymphatic collectors. After a variable period (occult lymphedema), sometimes aggravated by environmental trauma, a series of events is set into motion that culminates in chronic lymphedema. This clinical state is characterized not only by progressive swelling but also by fat and scar deposition, immunodysregulation, a propensity for cellulitis, and microvascular proliferation; these processes, on the one hand, are essential for repair and regeneration but, on the other hand, may result in bizarre and poorly understood vascular new growths.

Infection

Recurrent cellulitis is a devastating sequela of peripheral lymphedema. Erysipelas resulting from beta-hemolytic streptococcal infection is most common, but fulminant infection occurs with a variety of microorganisms.[63] To a certain extent, vulnerability to superimposed infection exists whenever tissue fluid stagnates. Thus, pyelonephritis with urinary retention, cholangitis with common duct stones, and spontaneous bacterial peritonitis with "cirrhotic" ascites are vivid examples of this phenomenon. Yet lymphedema (in contrast to edema states arising from imbalances in transcapillary hydrodynamic forces) is so prone to recurring dermatolymphangitis that at one time it was mistaken as the sine qua non of lymphedema (see earlier discussion).

The reasons for the extraordinary susceptibility of an extremity with lymphedema to secondary bacterial infection remain perplexing. Studies of canine-induced and human filarial lymphedema implicate defective complement activation and immunodysregulation.[48] Alternative hypotheses include the depopulation of regional lymph nodes with replacement by fat and scar[47] and deficient protease activity of extravascular macrophages.[64] It remains unclear, however, whether these immunologic perturbations are systemic, strictly regional, or even unique to lymphedema. Notwithstanding, the onset of overt lymphedema is often precipitated by sudden infection or injury in an extremity already exhibiting defective lymphatic function. Moreover, episodes of thrombophlebitis and trauma, including bony fractures and multiple insect bites,

are associated with "lymphangitis" and worsening of peripheral lymphedema. Walking barefoot, particularly in Third World countries that lack proper hygiene, promotes overt and occult cellulitis and local foot infections that aggravate filaria-induced lymphedema and exaggerate exuberant skin verrucae and dermal scarring. In other words, in an extremity with marginal lymphatic drainage, even minor trauma and infection may initiate a protracted pernicious cycle that in extreme cases culminates in a pachyderm-like deformity resembling an elephantine limb and, on rare occasions, leads to a highly aggressive vascular malignancy (see Fig. 166-11 and earlier discussion).

Fibrosis

Like the sequela of superimposed infection, the complications of progressive interstitial fibrosis also set lymphedema apart from other edematous states. Whereas the pathogenetic sequence linking scarring to lymphedema is still unclear, it has long been recognized that conditions associated with edema high in protein content (e.g., lymphedema) are characterized by fibrous proliferation. Altered cytokine production, perturbed immunoreactivity, accumulation of abnormal complexed plasma protein moieties including growth factors in the extracellular matrix, proliferation of mast cells with release of vasomediators such as histamine,[65,66] and activation of a complement cascade with "fixation" to immunocomplexes may exert, singly or in toto, both microvascular and chemotactic effects that facilitate tissue infiltration of

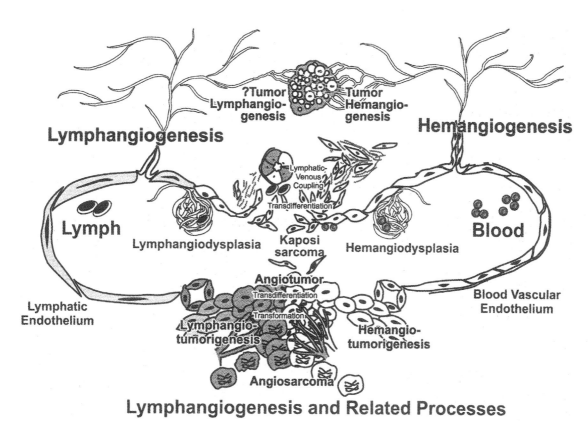

FIGURE 166-12 Schematic representation of physiologic and pathologic processes involving growth of lymphatic vessels (lymphangiogenesis) analogous to and often accompanied by hemangiogenesis. These entities include tumor-associated angiogenesis, angiodysplasias, Kaposi's sarcoma, and angiotumorigenesis, including angioma and angiosarcoma.

chronic inflammatory cells (e.g., lymphocytes and macrophages).[67] As fibrin- and cell-binding circulating fibronectins accumulate in the stagnant edema fluid, they act as the scaffolding and support glue for the migration of fibroblasts and the laying down of collagen.[68] In addition, lymph stasis and the buildup of plasma proteins trapped in the interstitium overwhelm intrinsic neutrophil and macrophage proteases and provoke diffuse scarring.[69] Intensive neoangiogenesis associated with enhanced migration of endothelial cells further aggravates the pathologic picture. Ironically, these same processes are also critical for the repair of wounds, for which scar formation is also the final common pathway.

Neoplasia

A rare but nonetheless revealing sequela of long-standing peripheral lymphedema is the occurrence of (lymph)angiosarcoma. This aggressive vascular tumor was once thought to arise exclusively in the aftermath of radical mastectomy and irradiation for the local control of breast cancer (Stewart-Treves syndrome).[70,71] Lymphangiosarcoma, however, has now been documented in other secondary lymphedemas and even in congenital or primary lymphedema.[72] Because the preexisting swelling has usually persisted for many years and may occur in either primary or secondary lymphedema or in the presence or absence of previous radiotherapy, the lymphedema process itself has been

thought to be the prime causative factor. More recently, Kaposi's sarcoma, a vascular tumor akin to Stewart-Treves syndrome and allied closely with acquired immunodeficiency syndrome (AIDS), has been linked to an origin from lymphatic endothelium.[73-76] Perhaps immunodysregulation, particularly in the antigen-presenting afferent loop (i.e., dysregulated lymphangiogenesis and hemangiogenesis), underlies a wide range of common and bizarre vasoproliferative and lymphologic syndromes including hemolymphangioma (representing "angiotumorigenesis"), Klippel-Trenaunay syndrome, angiofollicular hyperplasia (epithelioid hemangioma), lymphangioleiomyomatosis, as well as tumor lymphangiogenesis and lymphangitic metastatic carcinomatosis (see Figs. 166-11 and 166-12).

Lymphangiogenesis

In contrast to uncontrolled new growth (lymphangiosarcoma), programmed proliferation of lymphatic endothelium with tube formation (lymphangiogenesis) is critical to a whole host of physiologic and pathologic processes. During the past several decades, since the phenomenon of angiogenesis was first reproduced in endothelial cell and mixed vascular tissue cultures,[77,78] considerable attention has been directed toward furthering understanding of this process but largely in the context of blood vessel growth or "hemangiogenesis."[79] The lymphatic counterpart (i.e., lymphangiogenesis) has received only scant attention until

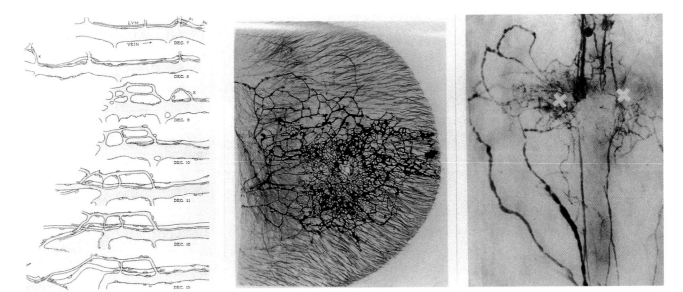

FIGURE 166-13 Classic observations on lymphangiogenesis in vivo. **Left,** Series of camera-lucida, oil-immersion records, showing growth of an individual lymphatic capillary in the rabbit ear (LYM). Corresponding parts of a lymphatic and vein have been placed below one another in drawings of December (Dec) 7, 8, and 9 to 13. The drawings of December 9 to 13 have been moved to the right so that X represents the same spot on December 8 and 9. During growth of the lymphatic there has been conspicuous retraction and disappearance of branches and loops of the blood vessel. Retraction of a short lymphatic tip is seen between December 11 and 13. Lymphatic endothelial nuclei are stippled. A1 and A2 are two daughter nuclei after a mitotic division (×177, magnification of original drawing, ×700). **Center,** Twenty-one days after making a turpentine abscess, which perforated a mouse's ear, a dense new network of lymphatic capillaries surrounds the hole (×8). **Right,** In-vivo microlymphangiogram 24 days after a short transverse incision in the skin of a rabbit ear. The extent of the incision is depicted by the crosses. The distal part of the ear is uppermost. Several arcading vessels around the incision and numerous fine connections through the scar are seen. (**Left** from Clark ER, Clark EL: Observations on the new growth of lymphatic vessels as seen in transparent chambers introduced into the rabbit's ear. Am J Anat 51:49, 1932; **Center** from Pullinger DB, Florey HW: Proliferation of lymphatics in inflammation. J Pathol Bacteriol 45:157, 1937; and **Right** from Bellman S, Odén B: Regeneration of surgically divided lymph vessels: An experimental study on the rabbit's ear. Acta Chir Scand 116:99, 1958-1959.)

recently even though lymphatic (re)generation is essential to health and disorders of lymph flow and lymphatic growth are common, often disfiguring, and sometimes life and limb threatening.[79] Furthermore, lymphatic-directed therapy, including pro- and anti-lymphangiogenesis agents, may provide new approaches to these vexing disorders.

In now classic studies Clark and Clark documented the extension of lymphatic capillaries by outgrowth from pre-existing lymph vessels in rabbit ear transparent chambers (Fig. 166-13, left).[80] Later, Pullinger and Florey emphasized that despite the similar appearance of each vascular endothelium, lymphatics consistently connected to lymphatics, veins to veins, and arteries to arteries without intermingling (see Fig. 166-13, center).[81]

After an experimental hind-limb circumferential skin incision, new lymphatics traverse the integumentary gap as early as postoperative day 4. By the eighth day lymphatic continuity is restored anatomically (delineated by distribution of intradermal India ink particles) and physiologically (transient peripheral edema remits).[54,82] Bellman and Odén meticulously documented by Thorotrast microlymphangiography the time course and extent of newly formed lymphatics in circumferential wounds in the rabbit ear, including lymphatic bridging through newly formed scar (see Fig. 166-13, right).[83,84] As lymphatics increased in caliber, intraluminal valves and sinuous dilatations appeared. Subsequent studies have documented restoration of distinctive ultrastructural features in newly regenerated

lymphatic vessels, including the characteristic overlapping junctional complexes and Weibel-Palade bodies (storage depots for vWf:factor VIII–related antigen).[85-87]

Like the more than 1 trillion blood vascular endothelial cells that normally are dormant,[88,89] lymphatic endothelial cell turnover is also miniscule.[90] With injury, however, incorporation of tritiated thymidine into proliferating lymphatic endothelium sharply increases.[90] Moreover, fetal lymphatics show greater labeling than neonatal and adult lymphatics, whereas visceral lymphatic endothelium proliferates more rapidly than that of peripheral lymphatics.[91]

Lymphatic endothelium was first isolated in vitro from bovine mesenteric lymphatics[78] and in the same year from a patient with a large cervicomediastinal[92] and subsequently from another patient with a retroperitoneal lymphangioma[14] and also from canine and human thoracic duct.[15] Lymphatic endothelial cells have now been isolated, passed in culture, and studied from sheep, dog, mouse, rat, and ferret lymphatic collectors using techniques similar to those used for blood large vessel and microvessel isolations. Lymphatic endothelium can be grown in monolayer and on microcarrier beads and exhibits cobblestone morphology with typical endothelial structural features and staining characteristics (Fig. 166-14).[14] Putative lymphatic endothelium has also been isolated from mixed microvascular cultures of human foreskin and skin by separation with magnetic beads and labeling with lymphatic markers such as LYVE-1.[93] Lymphangiogenesis in vitro was first demonstrated 2

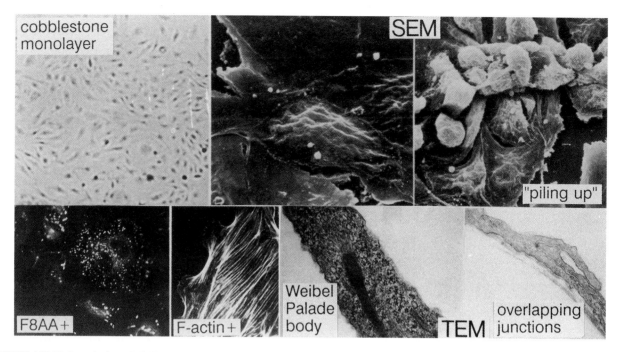

FIGURE 166-14 Lymphatic endothelial cell line derived from a retroperitoneal lymphangioma. Note the cobblestone morphology and, on scanning electron microscopy (SEM), the polygonal cells in some areas that are "piling up," the positive stain for vWf-factor 8 and F-actin, and, on transmission electron microscopy (TEM), the presence of Weibel-Palade bodies and typical lymphatic overlapping cell junctions. (From Way D, Hendrix M, Witte MH, et al: Lymphatic endothelial cell line [CH3] from a recurrent retroperitoneal lymphangioma. In Vitro 23:647, 1987.)

decades ago with formation of tubes and cystlike structures spontaneously[92] or after addition of collagen matrix in tissue culture (Fig. 166-15).[94] Lymphatic explant proliferation with lymphatic sprouting has also been followed.[95]

Lymphovascular Genomics

Growing evidence confirms that lymphangiogenesis is under genetic control (see Table 166-1 and Fig. 166-16).[5] For example, a gene or genes expressed from nonactivated portions of the inactivated X chromosome or from the Y chromosome are likely involved in the development of lymphatics, and a deficiency of this gene(s) or its product(s) is responsible for Turner's syndrome (XO ovarian dysgenesis), which exhibits a variety of lymphatic and other cardiovascular anomalies. Other chromosomal aneuploidy disorders such as trisomy 21 (Down syndrome) and rearrangements (additions, deletions, translocations) also occasionally present as strangulating fetal cystic hygroma, lymphedema, and intestinal lymphangiectasia and are commonly associated with early fetal demise (see Fig. 166-16).[96]

A spectrum of developmental and other hereditary lymphedema-angiodysplasia syndromes (often with autosomal dominant inheritance) also provides clues to sites of "lymphangiogenesis genes."[5,11,97,98] Indeed, specific gene mutations have been identified for three monogenic lymphedema-angiodysplasia conditions. They involve mutations in endothelial receptor VEGFR-3 for lymphatic growth factor VEGF-C on chromosome 15 at locus q34-35 in a subpopulation of Milroy syndrome of lymphatic hypoplasia[99]; in transcription factor SOX18[100] on chromosome 20 at q13 in 2 families with autosomal recessive and dominant forms of hypotrichosis-lymphedema-telangiectasia syndrome (see Fig. 166-16); and in winged helix transcription factor FOXC2 on chromosome 16 at q24[101] uniformly in hundreds of patients with lymphedema-distichiasis (LD) syndrome and a hyperplastic lymphatic system. Interestingly, the genetically engineered haploinsufficient (+/−) Foxc2 mouse[102] exhibits a double row of eyelashes and hyperplastic lymphatic phenotype like human LD, and the knockout (−/−) mouse displays aortic arch anomalies and interventricular septal defect (mimicking tetralogy of Fallot) and bony abnormalities thereby mimicking the clinical spectrum from mild to severe LD. Yet these known mutations pinpoint just 3 of the more than 40 distinct OMIM familial disorders affecting the lymphatic segment of the "vasculature,"[103] suggesting that genes involved in normal and pathologic lymphatic growth and development span the entire genome.

Whereas the underlying mechanisms governing lymphangiogenesis are only beginning to be understood, a variety of stimulatory (e.g., vascular endothelial growth factor-C and -D) and inhibitory factors modulate the growth, development, and (dys)function of the lymphatic in common with or distinct from the blood vasculature (see Table 166-1).[5,11] These angiomodulatory agents are very likely crucial to understanding clinical conditions as diverse as cystic hygroma, Klippel-Trenaunay syndrome, (lymph)angiosarcoma, elephantine overgrowth, and a whole constellation of peripheral and visceral disorders characterized by swelling, scarring, immunodysregulation, and malnutrition (see Figs. 166-1, 166-11, 166-12, and 166-16).

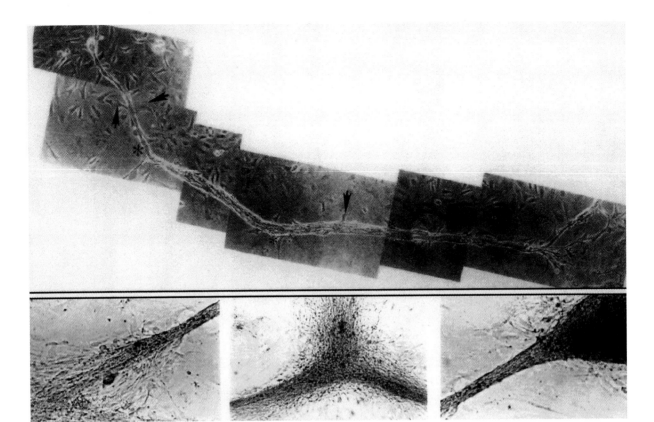

FIGURE 166-15 Lymphangiogenesis in vitro. **Top,** One to 3 days after treatment of lymphatic endothelial cells in tissue culture with collagen type 1. Adjacent cells *(arrows)* continue to migrate and adhere to tubular points with an increase in their dimension and length. Adhesion of cells *(asterisk)* at various points along the length of the tubular structures is accompanied by branching and the subsequent formation of elaborate capillary-like networks in the culture dishes. This lymphatic capillary tube that formed in vitro was derived from bovine lymphatic endothelial cells (×155). **Bottom,** Spontaneous lymphangiogenesis in cell culture derived from a lymphatic ductal malformation (lymphangioma). Note loose clusters of lymphatic endothelial cells sprouting into branches *(left)* which are more prominent *(middle)* and evolve into a sheetlike aggregate with intense lymphatic-like sprouting branches *(right).* (**Top** from Leak LV, Jones M: Lymphatic endothelium isolation, characterization and long-term culture. Anat Rec 236:641, 1993; **Bottom** from Witte MH, Witte CL: Lymphatics and blood vessels, lymphangiogenesis and hemangiogenesis: From cell biology to clinical medicine. Lymphology 20:257, 1987.)

Chylous Reflux

Abnormal retrograde transport of intestinal lymph is responsible for chylous disorders. Because cholesterol and long-chain triglycerides in the form of chylomicra are absorbed exclusively by the lymphatic system, dysfunction (in the form of disruption, compression, obstruction, or fistulization) of mesenteric lacteals, the cisterna chyli, and the thoracic duct is directly linked to chylothorax, chylous ascites, and chyluria. In some patients with high-grade blockage of intestinal lymph flow, the peripheral lymphatics gradually dilate and, with progressive valvular incompetence, lactescent lymph refluxes into the soft tissues of the pelvis, scrotum, and lower extremities (chylous vesicles and edema) (Fig. 166-17). Transgenic (particularly the angiopoietin-2 knockout mouse),[104] radiation-induced, spontaneously arising mouse models with chylous effusions are available to further study these chylous reflux syndromes.

■ SUMMARY

Disturbances in microcirculatory perfusion and exchange of liquid, macromolecules, and cells across intact and abnormal microvessels and deranged lymphatic growth patterns and lymph kinetics are, individually and together, associated with disorders of tissue swelling. Low-output failure of the lymph circulation manifesting as peripheral lymphedema is characteristically indolent for many years before lymphatic insufficiency and tissue swelling accelerate and become persistent. Nonetheless, impedance of lymph flow by itself is sufficient to explain at least mild to moderate forms of lymphedema. Chronic lymphedema is characterized by trapping of fluid, extravasated plasma proteins, and other macromolecules in the skin and subcutaneous tissues. It is typical to find impaired immune cell trafficking (lymphocytes, Langerhans cells, monocytes), abnormal transport of autologous and foreign antigens, probably intact hydrodynamic (Starling) transcapillary forces,[105] and an increased propensity to superimposed infection. Additional characteristics include progressive obliteration of lymphatics (lymphangiopathy "die-back" or lymphangitis), defective lymphangion contractility, mononuclear cell infiltrate (chronic interstitial inflammation), epidermal cell-fibroblast proliferation, collagen deposition, altered immunoreactivity, and vasoactive mediator imbalance with increased production of local cytokines and growth factors including autocrine and paracrine hormones.

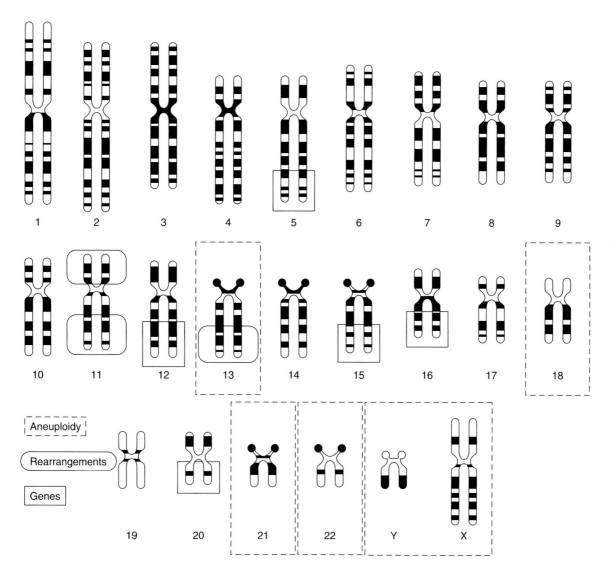

FIGURE 166-16 Genomics of lymphedema-angiodysplasia syndromes displaying mutation of known genes for familial Milroy lymphedema subpopulation (*VEGFR3* at chromosome 5q34-35), lymphedema-distichiasis (*FOXC2* at chromosome 16q24), and hypotrichosis, lymphedema, telangiectasia (*SOX18* at chromosome 20q13) and linkage locations for Aagenaes syndrome (chromosome 15) and Noonan's syndrome (chromosome 12). In addition, aneuploidies and rearrangements involving other chromosomes are associated with additional lymphedema-angiodysplasia syndromes.

In contrast to the blood circulation, in which flow depends primarily on the propulsive force of the myocardium, lymph propulsion depends predominantly on intrinsic truncal contraction, a phylogenetic remnant of amphibian lymph hearts. Whereas venous plasma flows rapidly (2.5 to 3 L/min) against low vascular resistance, lymph "plasma" flows slowly (1 to 2 mL/min) against high vascular resistance. On occasion, impaired transport of intestinal lymph may be associated with reflux and accumulation or leakage of intestinal chyle into serous ascites or swollen legs. In extreme circumstances, these factors operating together may be responsible for the grotesque deformity known as elephantiasis.

Transdifferentiation and transformation of endothelium and other vascular accessory cells associated with lymph stasis may also be pivotal factors in a wide range of dysplastic and neoplastic vascular disorders, including Stewart-Treves syndrome, AIDS-associated Kaposi's sarcoma, recurrent lymphangiomatosis, and lymphangitic metastatic carcinomatosis. These phenomena have their origin in controlled and uncontrolled lymphangiogenesis and apparently are regulated at specific sites across the genome. Their manipulation may offer new avenues of therapy for both primary and secondary lymphedema and related angiodysplasia syndromes as well as a variety of neoplasms. These new approaches include gene therapy to supply the normal gene, angiomodulator therapy to promote lymphangiogenesis where inadequate (as in lymphedema), or inhibited lymphatic growth where excessive (as in lymphangioma). Stem cell therapy to grow new vessels from undifferentiated embryonic or adult stem cells (e.g., lymphangioblasts) and new biomaterials for artificial lymphatics to drain the tissues also hold promise for the future.

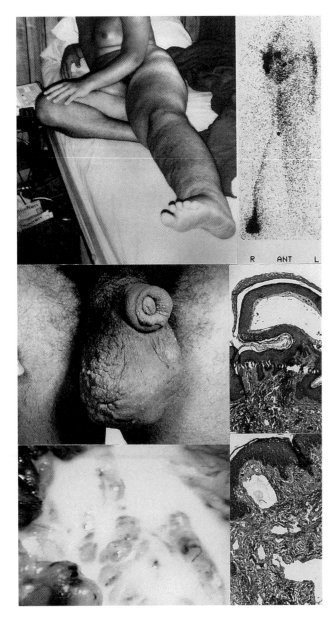

FIGURE 166-17 Sixteen-year-old boy with chylous reflux syndrome characterized by left leg, penile, and scrotal lymphedema with multiple small chyle-containing vesicles. Lymphoscintigraphy shows (**upper right**) that tracer (^{99m}Tc human serum albumin) injected intradermally into the right foot crosses to the left side and flows retrograde to outline dermal lymphatics in the contralateral leg. During a scrotal debulking operation, chylous lymph floods the operative field (**lower left**), and light microscopy of the excised skin shows large endothelium-lined channels (**mid and lower right**) consistent with ectatic dermal lymphatics.

■ REFERENCES

1. Rusznyák I, Földi M, Szabo G: History of the discovery of lymphatics and lymph circulation. In Lymphatics and Lymph Circulation, 2nd ed. Oxford, Pergamon Press, 1967, pp 15-24.
2. Földi M: Lymphogenous encephalopathy. In Diseases of Lymphatics and Lymph Circulation. Springfield, IL, Charles C Thomas, 1969, pp 91-117.
3. Bradbury MWB, Westrop RJ: Factors influencing exit of substances from cerebrospinal fluid into deep cervical lymph of the rabbit. J Physiol 339:519, 1983.
4. Leeds SE, Kong AK, Wise BL: Alternative pathways for drainage of cerebrospinal fluid in the canine brain. Lymphology 22:144, 1989.
5. Witte MH, Bernas MJ, Northup KA, Witte CL: Molecular lymphology and genetics of lymphedema-angiodysplasia syndromes. In Földi M, Földi E, Kubik S (eds): Textbook of Lymphology. Munich, Urban & Fischer, 2003, pp 472-492.
6. Sabin FR: On the origin and development of the lymphatic system from the veins and the development of the lymph hearts and the thoracic duct in the pig. Am J Anat 1:367, 1902.
7. Kampmeier OF (ed): Evolution and Comparative Morphology of the Lymphatic System. Springfield, IL, Charles C Thomas, 1969.
8. Wigle JT, Oliver G: Prox1 function is required for the development of the murine lymphatic system. Cell 98:769, 1999.
9. Kaipainen A, Korhonen J, Mustonen T, et al: Expression of the fms-like tyrosine kinase 4 gene becomes restricted to lymphatic endothelium during development. Proc Natl Acad Sci U S A 92:3566, 1995.
10. Wilting J, Papoutsi M, Schneider M, Christ B: The lymphatic endothelium of the avian wing is of somitic origin. Dev Dynam 217:271, 2000.
11. Witte MH, Bernas M, Martin C, Witte CL: Lymphangiogenesis and lymphangiodysplasias: From molecular to clinical lymphology. In Wilting J (guest ed): The Biology of Lymphangiogenesis. Microscop Res Tech 55:122, 2001.
12. Casley-Smith JR: Lymph and lymphatics. In Kaley G, Altura BM (eds): Microcirculation. Baltimore, University Park Press, 1977, vol 1, pp 423-502.
13. Leak LV: Physiology of the lymphatic system. In Abramson DI, Dobrin PB (eds): Blood Vessels and Lymphatics in Organ Systems. Orlando, FL, Academic Press, 1984, pp 134-164.
14. Way D, Hendrix M, Witte MH, et al: Lymphatic endothelial cell line (CH3) from a recurrent retroperitoneal lymphangioma. In Vitro 23:647, 1987.
15. Gnepp DR, Chandler W: Tissue culture of human and canine thoracic duct endothelium. In Vitro 21:200, 1985.
16. Johnston MG, Walker MA: Lymphatic endothelial and smooth-muscle cells in tissue culture. In Vitro 20:566, 1984.
17. Breiteneder-Geleff S, Soleiman A, Kowalski H, et al: Angiosarcomas express mixed endothelial phenotypes of blood and lymphatic capillaries: Podoplanin as a specific marker for lymphatic endothelium. Am J Pathol 154:385-394, 1999.
18. Banerji S, Ni J, Wang S-X, et al: LYVE-1, a new homologue of the CD44 glycoprotein, is a lymph-specific receptor for hyaluronan. J Cell Biol 144:789-801, 1999.
19. Jussila L, Valtola R, Partanen TA, et al: Lymphatic endothelium and Kaposi's sarcoma spindle cells detected by antibodies against the vascular endothelial growth factor receptor-3. Cancer Res 58:1559, 1998.
20. Lymboussaki A, Partanen TA, Olofsson B, et al: Expression of the vascular endothelial growth factor C receptor VEGFR-3 in lymphatic endothelium of the skin and in vascular tumors. Am J Pathol 153:395-403, 1998.
21. Kato S, Ji R, Miura M: Histochemical characteristics of endothelial cells of the subcapsular sinus in the monkey mesenteric lymph node. Lymphology 31(Suppl):39-74, 1998.
22. Casley-Smith JR: The lymphatic system. In Földi M, Casley-Smith JR (eds): Lymphangiology. Stuttgart, FK Schattauer-Verlag, 1983, pp 89-164.
23. Leak LV, Burke JF: Fine structure of the lymphatic capillary and the adjoining connective tissue area. Am J Anat 118:785, 1966.
24. Leak LV, Burke JF: Ultrastructural studies on the lymphatic anchoring filaments. J Cell Biol 36:129, 1968.
26. Leak LV: Electron microscopic observation on lymphatic capillaries and the structural components of the connective tissue-lymph interface. Microvasc Res 2:361, 1970.
25. Casley-Smith JR, Florey HW: The structure of normal small lymphatics. Q J Exp Physiol 46:101, 1961.
27. Mislin H: The lymphangion. In Földi M, Casley-Smith JR (eds): Lymphangiology. Stuttgart, FK Schattauer-Verlag, 1983, pp 165-175.

28. Starling EH: Physiologic factors involved in the causation of dropsy. Lancet 1:1267, 1896.

29. Starling EH: The Fluids of the Body. The Herter Lectures. Chicago, WT Keener, 1909, p 81.

30. Hall JG, Morris B, Woolley G: Intrinsic rhythmic propulsion of lymph in the unanaesthetised sheep. J Physiol (Lond) 180:336, 1965.

31. Mawhinney HJD, Roddie IC: Spontaneous activity in isolated bovine mesenteric lymphatics. J Physiol 229:339, 1973.

32. Olszewski WL, Engeset A: Intrinsic contractility of prenodal lymph vessels and lymph flow in the human leg. Am J Physiol 239:H775, 1980.

33. Gnepp DR: Lymphatics. In Staub NC, Taylor AE (eds): Edema. New York, Raven Press, 1984, pp 263-298.

34. McHale NG, Roddie IC: The effect of transmural pressure on pumping activity in isolated bovine lymphatic vessels. J Physiol 261:255, 1976.

35. McHale NG, Roddie IC: The effect of intravenous adrenaline and noradrenaline infusion on peripheral lymph flow in the sheep. J Physiol 341:517, 1983.

36. Johnston MG: The intrinsic lymph pump: Progress and problems. Lymphology 22:116, 1989.

37. Sinzinger H, Kaliman J, Mannheimer E: Regulation of human lymph contractility by prostaglandins and thromboxane. Lymphology 17:43, 1984.

38. Johnston MG, Gordon JL: Regulation of lymphatic contractility by arachidonate metabolites. Nature 293:294, 1981.

39. Johnston MG, Feuer C: Suppression of lymphatic vessel contractility with inhibitors of arachidonic acid metabolism. J Pharmacol Exp Ther 226:603, 1983.

40. Ohhashi T, Kawai Y, Azuma T: The response of lymphatic smooth muscles to vasoactive substances. Pflügers Arch 375:183, 1978.

41. McHale NG, Roddie IC, Thornbury K: Nervous modulation of spontaneous contractions in bovine mesenteric lymphatics. J Physiol 309:461, 1980.

42. McGeown JG, McHale NG, Thornbury K: Popliteal efferent lymph flow response to stimulation of the sympathetic chain in the sheep. J Physiol 387:55P, 1987.

43. Sjöberg T, Alm P, Andersson KE, et al: Contractile response in isolated human groin lymphatics. Lymphology 20:152-160, 1987.

44. Sjöberg T, Steen S: Contractile properties of lymphatics from the human lower leg. Lymphology 24:16, 1991.

45. Swemer RL, Foglia VG: Fatal loss of plasma volume after lymph heart destruction in toads. Proc Soc Exp Biol Med 53:14, 1943.

46. Conklin R: The formation and circulation of lymph in the frog: I. The rate of lymph production. Am J Physiol 95:79, 1930.

47. Kinmonth JB, Wolfe JH: Fibrosis in the lymph nodes in primary lymphedema. Ann R Coll Surg 62:344, 1980.

48. Olszewski W: On the pathomechanism of development of post surgical lymphedema. Lymphology 6:35, 1973.

49. Zweifach BW, Prather JW: Micromanipulation of pressure in terminal lymphatics in the mesentery. Am J Physiol 228:1326, 1975.

50. Pippard C, Roddie IC: Resistance in the sheep's lymphatic system. Lymphology 20:230, 1987.

51. Olszewski WL: Lymph pressure and flow in limbs. In Olszewski WL (ed): Lymph Stasis: Pathophysiology, Diagnosis and Treatment. Boca Raton, FL, CRC Press, 1991, pp 109-156.

52. McHale NG: Influence of autonomic nerves on lymph flow. In Olszewski WL (ed): Lymph Stasis: Pathophysiology, Diagnosis and Treatment. Boca Raton, FL, CRC Press, 1991, pp 85-107.

53. Pippard C, Roddie IC: Comparison of fluid transport systems in lymphatics and veins. Lymphology 20:224, 1987.

54. Reichert FL: The regeneration of the lymphatics. Arch Surg 13:871, 1926.

55. Blalock A, Robinson CS, Cunningham RS, Gray ME: Experimental studies on lymphatic blockade. Arch Surg 34:1049, 1937.

56. Halsted WS: The swelling of the arm after operations for cancer of the breast: Elephantiasis chirurgica: Its cause and prevention. Johns Hopkins Hosp Bull 32:309, 1921.

57. Drinker CK, Field MJ, Homans J: The experimental production of edema and elephantiasis as a result of lymphatic obstruction. Am J Physiol 108:509, 1934.

58. Danese CA, Georgalas-Bertakis M, Morales LE: A model of chronic postsurgical lymphedema in dogs' limbs. Surgery 64:814, 1968.

59. Clodius L, Altorfer J: Experimental chronic lymphostasis of extremities. Folia Angiol 25:137, 1977.

60. Lee-Donaldson L, Witte MH, Bernas M, et al: Refinement of a rodent model of peripheral lymphedema. Lymphology 32:111-117, 1999.

61. Case T, Leis B, Witte M, et al: Vascular abnormalities in experimental and human lymphatic filariasis. Lymphology 24:174-183, 1991.

62. Földi M: Lymphoedema. In Földi M, Casley-Smith JR (eds): Lymphangiology. Stuttgart, FK Schattauer-Verlag, 1983, pp 668-670.

63. Edwards EA: Recurrent febrile episodes and lymphedema. JAMA 184:102, 1963.

64. Casley-Smith JR, Casley-Smith JR: High-Protein Oedemas and the Benzo-pyrones. Sydney, Australia, JB Lippincott, 1986, pp 126-152.

65. Ehrich WE, Seifter J, Alburn HE, Begamy AJ: Heparin and heparinocytes in elephantiasis scroti. Proc Soc Exp Biol Med 70:183, 1949.

66. Dumont AE, Fazzini E, Jamal S: Metachromatic cells in filarial lymphoedema. Lancet 2:1021, 1983.

67. Gaffney RM, Casley-Smith JR: Lymphedema without lymphostasis: Excess proteins as the cause of chronic inflammation. Progress in Lymphology. Proceedings of the VII International Congress. Prague, Avicenum, 1981, pp 213-216.

68. Poslethwaite AE, Keski-Oja J, Balian G, Kang AH: Induction of fibroblast chemotaxis by fibronectin. J Exp Med 153:494, 1981.

69. Földi M: Insufficiency of lymph flow. In Földi M, Casley-Smith JR (eds): Lymphangiology. Stuttgart, FK Schattauer-Verlag, 1983, p 195.

70. Stewart FW, Treves N: Lymphangiosarcoma in post mastectomy lymphedema: A report of six cases in elephantiasis chirurgica. Cancer 1:64, 1948.

71. Unruh H, Robertson DI, Karasewich E: Post mastectomy lymphangiosarcoma. Can J Surg 22:586, 1979.

72. Woodward AH, Ivins JC, Sorle EH: Lymphangiosarcoma arising in chronic lymphedematous extremities. Cancer 30:562, 1972.

73. Dorfman RF: Kaposi's sarcoma: Evidence supporting its origin from the lymphatic system. Lymphology 21:45, 1988.

74. Witte MH, Stuntz M, Witte CL: Kaposi's sarcoma: A lymphologic perspective. Int J Dermatol 28:561, 1989.

75. Witte MH, Fiala M, McNeill GC, et al: Lymphangioscintigraphy in AIDS-associated Kaposi sarcoma. AJR Am J Roentgenol 155:311, 1990.

76. Beckstead JH, Wood GS, Fletcher V: Evidence for the origin of Kaposi's sarcoma from lymphatic endothelium. Am J Pathol 119:294, 1985.

77. Folkman J, Haudenschild C: Angiogenesis in vitro. Nature 288:551, 1980.

78. Folkman J: Clinical applications of research on angiogenesis. New Engl J Med 26:1757, 1995.

79. Witte MH, Witte CL: Lymphatics and blood vessels, lymphangiogenesis and hemangiogenesis. From cell biology to clinical medicine. Lymphology 20:171, 1987.

80. Clark ER, Clark EL: Observations on the new growth of lymphatic vessels as seen in transparent chambers introduced into the rabbit's ear. Am J Anat 51:49, 1932.

81. Pullinger DB, Florey HW: Proliferation of lymphatics in inflammation. J Pathol Bacteriol 45:157, 1937.

82. Casley-Smith JR: The regenerative capacity of the lymphovascular system. In Földi M, Casley-Smith JR (eds): Lymphangiology. Stuttgart, FK Schattauer-Verlag, 1983, p 276.

83. Bellman S, Odén B: Regeneration of surgically divided lymph vessels: An experimental study on the rabbit's ear. Acta Chir Scand 116:99, 1958-1959.

84. Odén B: A microlymphangiographic study of experimental wounds healing by second intention. Acta Chir Scand 120:100, 1960.

85. Magari S, Asano S: Regeneration of the deep cervical lymphatics—light and electron microscopic observations. Lymphology 11:57, 1978.

86. Magari S: Comparison of fine structure of lymphatics and blood vessels in normal conditions and during embryotic development and regeneration. Lymphology 20:189, 1987.

87. Leak L: Interaction of the peritoneal cavity to intraperitoneal stimulation: A peritoneal nodal system to monitor cellular and extracellular events in the formation of granulation tissue. Am J Anat 173:171, 1985.

88. Jaffe EA: Cell biology of endothelial cells. Hum Pathol 18:234, 1987.

89. Denekamp J: Angiogenesis, neovascular proliferation and vascular pathophysiology as targets for cancer therapy. Br J Radiol 66:181, 1993.

90. Junghans BM, Collin HB: Limbal lymphangiogenesis after corneal injury: An autoradiographic study. Curr Eye Res 8:91, 1989.

91. Travella W, Dugan MC: Endothelial interactions. In Nishi M, Uchino S, Yabuki S (eds): Progress in Lymphology XII. Amsterdam, Elsevier Science, 1990, p 269.

92. Bowman C, Witte MH, Witte CL, et al: Cystic hygroma reconsidered: Hamartoma or neoplasm? Primary culture of an endothelial cell line from a massive cervicomediastinal cystic hygroma with bony lymphangiomatosis. Lymphology 17:15, 1984.

93. Hirakawa S, Hong Y-K, Harvey N, et al: Identification of vascular lineage-specific genes by transcriptional profiling of isolated blood vascular and lymphatic endothelial cells. Am J Pathol 162:575-586, 2003.

94. Leak LV, Jones M: Lymphatic endothelium isolation, characterization and long-term culture. Anat Rec 236:641, 1993.

95. Nicosia RF: Angiogenesis and the formation of lymphatic-like channels in cultures of thoracic duct. In Vitro Cell Dev Biol 23:167, 1987.

96. Witte MH, Way DL, Witte CL, Bernas M: Lymphangiogenesis: Mechanisms, significance and clinical implications. In Goldberg IV, Rosen EM (eds): Regulation of Angiogenesis. Basel, Switzerland, Birkhäuser, 1997, p 65.

97. Greenlee R, Hoyme H, Witte M, et al: Developmental disorders of the lymphatic system. Lymphology 26:156, 1993.

98. Witte MH, Erickson R, Reiser FA, Witte CL: Genetic alterations in lymphedema. Phlebolymphology 16:19-25, 1997.

99. Karkkainen MJ, Ferrell RE, Lawrence EC, et al: Missense mutations interfere with vascular endothelial growth factor receptor-3 signaling in primary lymphedema. Nat Genet 25:153-159, 2000.

100. Irrthum A, Devriend K, Chitayat D, et al: Mutations in the transcription factor gene *SOX18* underlie recessive and dominant forms of hypotrichosis-lymphedema-telangiectasis. Am J Hum Genet 72:1470, 2003.

101. Fang JM, Dagenais SL, Erickson RP, et al: Mutations in FOXC2 (MFH-1), a forkhead family transcription factor, are responsible for the hereditary lymphedema-distichiasis syndrome. Am J Hum Genet 67:1382, 2000.

102. Kriederman BM, Myloyde TL, Witte MH, et al: Foxc2 haploinsufficient mice are a model for human autosomal dominant lymphedema-distichiasis syndrome. Hum Mol Genet 12:1179, 2003.

103. Northup KA, Witte MH, Witte CL: Syndromic classification of hereditary lymphedema. Lymphology 36:162-189, 2003.

104. Gale NW, Thurston G, Hackett SF, et al: Angiopoietin-2 is required for postnatal angiogenesis and lymphatic patterning, and only the latter role is rescued by angiopoietin-1. Dev Cell 3:411-423, 2002.

105. Kirk RM: Capillary filtration rates in normal and lymphedematous legs. Clin Sci 27:363, 1964.

Chapter

Clinical Diagnosis and Evaluation of Lymphedema

167

PETER GLOVICZKI, MD

HEINZ W. WAHNER, MD

Chronic lymphedema is a progressive, usually painless swelling of the extremity that results from a decreased transport capacity of the lymphatic system. Lymphedema may be caused by developmental abnormalities of the lymph vessels, such as aplasia, hypoplasia, or hyperplasia with valvular incompetence,[1,2] or it may be the result of congenital or acquired obstruction of the lymph vessels and lymph nodes.[3-6] The diagnosis of lymphedema is suspected in most patients after the history is obtained and the physical examination is performed. The goal of further evaluation is to confirm the cause and determine the type and site of lymphatic obstruction. It is equally important, however, to diagnose any underlying malignancy and to exclude other systemic or local causes of limb swelling, such as venous disease or congenital vascular malformation.

In this chapter, the current classifications of lymphedema are presented and the clinical presentation of patients with this disease is reviewed. The methods of noninvasive evaluation are discussed, and the technique and interpretation of lymphoscintigraphy, which has become the test of choice to confirm or exclude lymphatic disease, are presented in detail. The limited role of contrast lymphangiography in the diagnosis of lymphatic disorders is delineated. Finally, the differential diagnosis of lymphedema is discussed and a diagnostic protocol for the evaluation of patients with a swollen extremity is suggested.

■ CLINICAL CLASSIFICATIONS

Standard clinical classifications distinguish lymphedemas based on etiology (primary versus secondary), genetics (familial versus sporadic), and time of onset of the edema (congenital, praecox, tarda) (Table 167-1).[1,2,7] Although these systems are useful for categorizing all lymphedemas,

Table 167-1	Etiologic Classification of Lymphedema

I. Primary lymphedema
   A. Congenital (onset before 1 year of age)
      1. Nonfamilial
      2. Familial (Milroy's disease)
   B. Praecox (onset at 1 to 35 years of age)
      1. Nonfamilial
      2. Familial (Meige's disease)
   C. Tarda (onset after 35 years of age)
II. Secondary lymphedema
   A. Filariasis
   B. Lymph node excision ± radiation
   C. Tumor invasion
   D. Infection
   E. Trauma
   F. Other

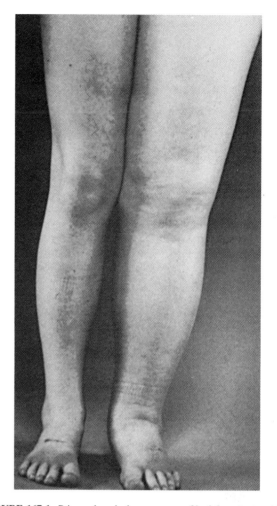

FIGURE 167-1 Primary lymphedema praecox of both lower extremities, more significantly of the left. Leg swelling in this patient, a 9-year-old boy, was first noted at age 4 years.

they do not address the clinical severity of the disease and are usually not relevant to therapy. More recent classifications focus on the clinical stage of lymphedema[8] or emphasize the underlying anatomic abnormality of the lymphatic system in an attempt to plan therapy.[3,4,9]

Primary Lymphedema

The etiologic classification divides lymphedemas into two major groups: *primary* and *secondary* lymphedemas. These terms were suggested in 1934 by Allen, from the Mayo Clinic, who evaluated 300 patients with lymphedema of the extremities.[7] He further divided the primary or idiopathic group into *congenital* and *praecox* types (Fig. 167-1). The congenital types included patients who developed edema before 1 year of age. Kinmonth later added another group to the primary lymphedemas comprising those who develop the disease after 35 years of age (lymphedema *tarda*).[2]

Although it has been assumed that all primary or idiopathic lymphedemas have an underlying developmental abnormality in the lymphatic system (i.e., aplasia, hypoplasia, or hyperplasia of the lymph vessels), fibrotic occlusion of lymph vessels and lymph nodes has been described in primary lymphedema by Kinmonth and Wolfe.[10,11] Studies by Browse suggest that the most likely cause of primary lymphedema praecox in many patients is acquired fibrotic obliteration of the lymph vessels and the lymph-conducting elements of the lymph nodes.[3,4,9]

Primary lymphedema is fortunately rare. Based on data collected by the Rochester Group Study,[12] it affects 1.15 per 100,000 persons younger than 20 years of age. It occurs more frequently in girls, and the incidence peaks between the ages of 12 and 16 years. Of 125 patients with primary lymphedema treated at the Mayo Clinic, 97 (78%) were female and 28 (22%) were male, yielding a female:male ratio of 3.5:1.0.[13] The ratio of unilateral to bilateral lymphedema was 3:1.

Congenital lymphedema occurred more frequently in males than in females. In these patients, the edema was usually bilateral and involved the entire lower extremity. In contrast, the typical patient with lymphedema praecox was female and had unilateral involvement, with swelling usually extending up to the knee only.[13]

Familial Lymphedema

The familial form of primary lymphedema was first described in 1865 by Letessier,[14] and additional cases were later published by Nonne[15] and Milroy.[16,17] The report of Milroy in 1892 described lower limb lymphedema that was observed in 22 members of the same family over six generations.[16] In all except two patients the edema was present at birth. The term *Milroy's disease* should be reserved for patients with familial lymphedema that is present at birth or is noted soon thereafter. A familial form of lymphedema that becomes manifest only during puberty was later described by Meige.[18] The term *Meige's disease,* therefore, refers to the familial form of lymphedema praecox.

In a collected series of 291 patients with primary lymphedema, 42 (14%) had a family history of lymphedema. Fourteen patients (5%) had congenital lymphedema, the onset of which was noted before 1 year of age, and 28 (9%) had lymphedema praecox.[13] In the Mayo Clinic series, 10 of 125 patients (8%) had a positive family history of lymphedema.

Functional Classification of Primary Lymphedemas

The functional classification of primary lymphedema by Browse is based on the underlying lymphatic anatomy as determined by lymphangiography.[3,4] This classification describes three different anatomic abnormalities, which are associated with different clinical presentations. More importantly, however, the classification is treatment oriented and selects appropriate groups that may respond to medical or surgical treatment.

Based on the underlying anatomic abnormality of the lymphatic system, Browse subdivided primary lymphedemas into three groups (Table 167-2): (1) distal obliteration, (2) proximal obliteration, and (3) congenital hyperplasia.

Distal obliteration occurs in 80% of patients and affects predominantly females. The swelling is frequently bilateral.[4,9] Lymphangiography demonstrates absent or a diminished number of superficial leg lymphatics in these patients. This group was also described by Kinmonth and Wolfe as having aplasia or hypoplasia.[2,10] The course of the disease is usually benign, progression is slow, and the edema is usually responsive to conservative compression treatment.

Ten percent of patients with primary lymphedema have proximal occlusion in the aortoiliac or inguinal lymph nodes.[9] This disease is frequently unilateral and involves the entire lower extremity, affecting both males and females. This form of lymphedema frequently develops rapidly, and progression is usual. The edema responds poorly to conservative management. Distal dilatation with proximal occlusion, however, may be suitable for mesenteric bridge operation or for microvascular lymph vessel reconstruction (see Chapter 169).

Hyperplasia and incompetence of the lymph vessels are observed in the remaining 10% of patients. Most of these patients have bilateral lymphedema, and males are more frequently affected than females.[11] One subgroup of these patients has megalymphatics, and, because of concomitant involvement of the mesenteric lymphatics, reflux of chyle frequently results. The leg edema is unilateral in most of these patients.[10,11] Protein-losing enteropathy, chyluria, chylous drainage through the vagina, and chylorrhea from small vesicles in the labia majora, scrotum, or lower extremities may also develop (Fig. 167-2).[19-21] The leg edema responds well to elevation but recurs rapidly with ambulation. These patients are candidates for surgical treatment consisting of ligation and excision of the incompetent retroperitoneal lymphatics (see Chapter 169).

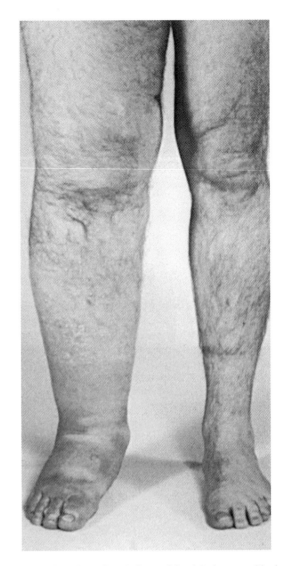

FIGURE 167-2 Primary lymphedema of the right leg caused by hyperplasia of the lymphatics and valvular incompetence. Note skin vesicles at mid-calf containing milky fluid because of reflux of chyle.

Although this functional classification is helpful in selecting patients for further management, the overlap in the first two groups may be quite significant. In addition, without contrast lymphangiography, separation of the groups is not always possible.

Table 167-2	Functional Classification of Primary Lymphedema		
	DISTAL OBLITERATION (80%)	**PROXIMAL OBLITERATION (10%)**	**HYPERPLASIA* (10%)**
Gender	Female	Male or female	Male or female
Onset			
Time	Puberty	Any age	Congenital
Location	Ankle; bilateral whole leg, thigh; unilateral	Whole leg, unilateral or bilateral	
Progression	Slow	Rapid	Progressive
Family History	Frequently positive	None	Frequently positive

*With or without reflux of chyle.

Adapted from Browse NL: The diagnosis and management of primary lymphedema. J Vasc Surg 3:181, 1986.

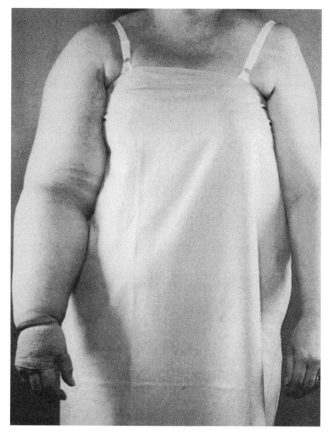

FIGURE 167-3 Right arm lymphedema after modified radical mastectomy and radiation treatment. The edema was aggravated by obstruction of the right axillary vein.

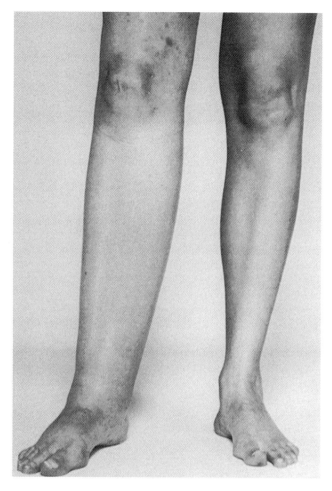

FIGURE 167-4 Secondary lymphedema of the right leg in a 29-year-old woman after excision of Ewing's sarcoma of the thigh and irradiation.

Secondary Lymphedema

Secondary acquired lymphedema results from a well-defined disease process that causes obstruction or injury to the lymphatic system. The most frequent cause of secondary lymphedema in the world is parasitic infestation by filariasis.[22,23] In North America and Europe, the most frequent cause of secondary lymphedema is surgical excision and irradiation of the axillary or inguinal lymph nodes as part of the treatment of an underlying malignancy, most frequently cancer of the breast (Fig. 167-3),[24-29] cervical cancer,[30] soft tissue tumors (Fig. 167-4), or malignant melanoma of the leg.[31] Other causes of secondary lymphedema are tumors invading the lymph vessels and nodes,[32] bacterial and fungal infections, lymphoproliferative diseases, and trauma.[33]

Less frequent causes of secondary lymphedema are contact dermatitis, tuberculosis, rheumatoid arthritis, and infection after a snake or insect bite. Factitious edema induced by application of a tourniquet on the arm or leg or by maintenance of the limb in an immobile or dependent state should also be considered in some patients.[34]

Filariasis

Lymphatic filariasis is caused by the developing and adult forms of three parasites: *Wuchereria bancrofti, Brugia malayi,* and *B. timori.* Of the estimated 90.2 million people in the world who are infected, more than 90% have bancroftian filariasis.[23] The disease is most frequent in subtropical and tropical countries, such as China, India, and Indonesia. It is transmitted by different types of mosquitos, and transmission is closely related to poor urban sanitation.[35]

Perilymphatic inflammation, fibrosis, and sclerosis of the lymph nodes are caused by the indwelling adult worms. Lymph node fibrosis, reactive hyperplasia, and dilatation of the lymphatic collecting channels are caused by the worm products, by physical injury to the valves and vessel walls caused by the live worms, and by the immune response of the host.[36] Eosinophilia is found in the peripheral blood smear, and microfilaria can be demonstrated in peripheral nocturnal blood, in the centrifuged urine sediment, or in the lymphatic fluid.[37] Filarial lymphedema rapidly develops into grossly incapacitating elephantiasis that is extremely difficult to treat.

Lymph Node Excision and Irradiation

Postmastectomy lymphedema is the most distressing and unpleasant complication after operation for breast cancer. During past decades, when radical mastectomy was routinely performed, clinically significant lymphedema was reported to occur in 6% to 60% of patients.[24] Axillary vein obstruction and episodes of lymphangitis contributed significantly to the further development of edema (see Fig. 167-3). With the introduction of more conservative breast cancer operations, the incidence of postmastectomy lymphedema markedly decreased. The reported incidence of arm lymphedema after modified radical mastectomy is 15.4%[25]; after local excision and total axillary lymphadenectomy it is 2.1% to 3.1%[26,27]; and after wide local excision and radiotherapy it is 2.3%.[28] Few studies, however, have objectively documented the degree of limb swelling in these patients.

Kissin and colleagues studied the development of lymphedema in 200 patients after different breast cancer operations.[29] Chronic lymphedema, with an increase of over 200 mL in the volume of the extremity, developed in 25.5% of the patients. Independent risk factors contributing to lymphedema included extensive axillary lymphadenectomy ($P < .05$), axillary radiotherapy ($P < .001$), and pathologic nodal status ($P < .10$). Extensive axillary lymph node dissection followed by radiotherapy resulted in the highest incidence, with 38.3% of the patients developing lymphedema.[29]

In a series of 91 patients who underwent regional lymphadenectomy for invasive primary melanoma, chronic lymphedema developed in 80% of those followed for more than 5 years.[31] Most swelling occurred in the thigh. In a series of 402 patients from Norway who underwent radical hysterectomy and pelvic lymphadenectomy for cervical cancer, severe lymphedema occurred in 5% and mild to moderate lymphedema developed in 23.4%.[30] All patients with severe lymphedema had adjuvant preoperative and postoperative radiation treatments.

Tumor Invasion

Lymphedema may be the first manifestation of a malignant tumor infiltrating the regional lymph nodes. In a series of 650 patients with lymphedema, De Roo found 60 in whom limb swelling developed as the first clinical marker of a malignant process.[32] The most frequent tumor was metastatic ovarian carcinoma, followed by carcinoma of the uterus with inguinal metastases and lymphosarcoma. All these patients were 28 years old or older, and in two thirds of the patients limb edema started in the *proximal* region of the extremity. In our experience, the most frequent tumor causing secondary lymphedema is carcinoma of the prostate in men and malignant lymphoma in women.[33]

Infection

Obstructive lymphangitis, caused most frequently by beta-hemolytic streptococci or, rarely, staphylococci, not only is a severe complication of an already existing lymphedema but also is itself an important cause of secondary lymphedema. Swelling may develop after an episode of cellulitis caused by an insect bite, trauma, excoriation, or fungal infection. It is possible that many patients who present with inflammatory lymphedema already have an impairment of lymphatic transport due to lymphatic hypoplasia or primary fibrotic occlusion of the lymph vessels or lymph nodes.

Clinical Staging of Lymphedema

Because none of the classic classification schemes addresses the clinical stage of the disease, the Working Group of the 10th International Congress of Lymphology in 1985 suggested staging chronic lymphedemas regardless of etiology. A latent, subclinical stage and three clinical grades were established as suggested by Brunner.[8] Each grade was subclassified as mild, moderate, and severe.

In the latent phase, excess fluid accumulates and fibrosis occurs around the lymphatics but no edema is apparent clinically. In *Grade I,* edema pits on pressure and is reduced largely or completely by elevation; there is no clinical evidence of fibrosis. *Grade II* edema does not pit on pressure and is not reduced by elevation. Moderate to severe fibrosis is evident on clinical examination. *Grade III* edema is irreversible and develops from repeated inflammatory attacks, fibrosis, and sclerosis of the skin and subcutaneous tissue. This is the stage of lymphostatic elephantiasis.

The advantage of this classification is that it permits evaluation of the effectiveness of a treatment and comparison of different treatment modalities. A drawback, however, is that appropriate staging in some cases may be difficult without performing a biopsy of the subcutaneous tissue.

■ CLINICAL PRESENTATION OF LYMPHEDEMA

History

A careful history of the disease frequently reveals the cause of the swelling and suggests the diagnosis of lymphedema. A family history that is positive for leg swelling may indicate familial lymphedema. The development of painless leg swelling in a teenage girl without any identifiable cause strongly suggests *primary* (idiopathic) lymphedema. A history of diarrhea and weight loss is a clue to mesenteric lymphangiectasia, whereas intermittent drainage of milky fluid from skin vesicles in these patients indicates reflux of chyle. In patients with *secondary* lymphedema, a cause of limb swelling is evident in the history, such as previous lymph node dissection, irradiation, tumor, trauma, or infection. In patients who have traveled in tropical countries, filariasis is suspected. Although the cause of primary lymphedema is different from that of secondary lymphedema, the clinical presentation and characteristic physical findings of the diseases are frequently similar.

Signs and Symptoms

Edema

Patients with chronic lymphedema usually present with slowly progressive, painless swelling of the limb. The edema is partially pitting early in the course of the disease but is usually nonpitting in chronic lymphedema owing to the secondary fibrotic changes in the skin and subcutaneous tissue.

The distribution of swelling in lymphedema is characteristic. It starts distally in the extremity in most patients and involves the perimalleolar area, with disappearance of the contours of the ankle in advanced cases (tree trunk or elephantine configuration). The dorsum of the forefoot is

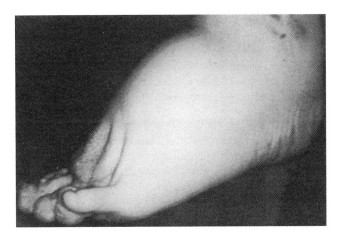

FIGURE 167-5 Lymphedema of the forefoot showing the typical "buffalo hump."

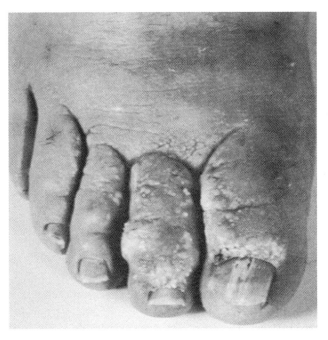

FIGURE 167-6 Squaring of the toes, small verrucae of the skin, and onychomycosis in a patient with primary lymphedema praecox. (From Gloviczki P, Schirger A: Lymphedema. In Spittell JA Jr [ed]: Clinical Medicine. Philadelphia, Harper & Row, 1985, pp 1-10.)

usually involved, resulting in the typical appearance of a "buffalo hump" (Fig. 167-5). Squaring of the toes (Stemmer's sign) is also a characteristic feature and results from the high protein content of the excess tissue fluid (Fig. 167-6).

Skin Changes

In the early stage of lymphedema, the skin usually has a pinkish-red color and a mildly elevated temperature owing to the increased vascularity. In long-standing lymphedema, however, the skin becomes thick and shows areas of hyperkeratosis, lichenification, and development of a "peau d'orange." The term *pigskin* reflects the reactive changes of the dermis and epidermis in response to the chronic inflammation caused by lymphatic stasis.[38] Recurrent chronic eczematous dermatitis or excoriation of the skin may occur, but frank ulcerations are rare. Unlike the situation in venous stasis, the skin maintains a higher degree of hydration and elasticity for a long time in lymphedema, and ischemic changes due to high skin tension and disruption of the circulation to the skin and subcutaneous tissue are rare.[39]

Additional skin changes in chronic lymph stasis, primarily in patients with hyperplasia of the lymphatics and valvular incompetence, include verrucae or small vesicles, which frequently drain clear lymph (lymphorrhea). In patients with lymphangiectasia and reflux of the chyle, drainage from the vesicles is milky in appearance (chylorrhea) (see Fig. 167-2).

Primary lymphedema may be associated with yellow discoloration of the nails.[40-42] In the yellow nail syndrome, pleural effusion is also present. The pale yellow color of the nails is most likely caused by impaired lymphatic drainage. Severe clubbing, transverse ridging, friability of the nail, and a decreased rate of nail growth are also observed.[41,42]

Pain

Although some aching or heaviness of the limb is a frequent complaint, significant pain is rare. If the patient with lymphedema complains of marked pain, infection or neuritic pain in the area of scar tissue or radiation treatment should

be suspected. Other possible causes of leg swelling, such as venous edema or reflex sympathetic dystrophy, should also be considered (see later section on differential diagnosis).

Complications

Infection

The lymphedematous limb is highly sensitive to fungal infections, such as dermatophytosis and onychomycosis (see Fig. 167-6). Fungal infections in the interdigital spaces are also sites of entry for bacteria, most frequently beta-hemolytic streptococci, which may cause cellulitis or lymphangitis in the affected limb. Cellulitis may present as high fever and chills, and the skin of the affected extremity is red and tender. Repeated episodes of cellulitis aggravate lymphedema.

Malnutrition and Immunodeficiency

Lymphangiectasia with protein-losing enteropathy or chylous ascites or chylothorax may result in severe loss of proteins, long-chain triglycerides, cholesterol, and calcium.[19,20] As discussed in Chapter 166, losses of lymphocytes, different immunoglobulins, polypeptides, and cytokines result in a state of immunodeficiency that decreases the ability of these patients to resist infections or malignancy.

Malignancy

Nonhealing "bruises," the development of multiple rounded, purple-red nodules with persistent ulcerations, should alert the physician to the possibility of malignancy.[43-45]

Lymphangiosarcoma after long-standing secondary lymphedema, originally described by Stewart and Treves,[43] is a rare malignant disease that frequently results in loss of a limb or even the life of the patient.

■ NONINVASIVE EVALUATION

The most frequent noninvasive imaging modalities used to evaluate patients with lymphatic diseases include lymphoscintigraphy, computed tomography (CT), and magnetic resonance imaging (MRI).

Lymphoscintigraphy

Interstitially injected colloids labeled with a radioactive tracer were used as long ago as 1953, when Sherman and Ter-Pergossian injected radioactive gold (^{198}Au) into the parametrium to produce lymph node necrosis in an attempt to treat metastatic cancer.[46] The first application of plasma protein labeled with radioactive iodine (^{131}I) for diagnostic evaluation of the lymphatic system in lymphedema was reported by Taylor and associates in 1957.[47] Because of advances in imaging techniques, the introduction of a better radioactive label (technetium Tc 99m [^{99m}Tc]), and selection of the optimal size of the labeled particles, the technique of diagnostic lymphoscintigraphy has improved continuously during the past two decades.[48-56]

At this time, lymphoscintigraphy with radiocolloids is used principally for evaluation of the swollen extremity. For detection of lymph node metastases, radiolabeled monoclonal antibodies are being used with increasing frequency.

Radiopharmaceuticals

The biokinetic behavior of interstitially applied colloid particles depends on their surface charge and particle size. Particles with small diameters are absorbed into capillaries, whereas those in the 10-nm range (antimony trisulfide [Sb_2S_3]) are absorbed into the lymphatic system. The time needed for activity to appear in the regional lymph nodes has been variably defined according to the physical characteristics of the imaging agent. For example, small particles such as ^{99m}Tc-labeled human serum albumin may appear in the pelvic nodes within 10 minutes,[55] whereas relatively large agents including rhenium and Sb_2S_3 colloid should arrive within 30 minutes[51] or 1 hour,[54] respectively. In our experience, which now includes studies in over 500 limbs, ^{99m}Tc-Sb_2S_3 has been used for lymphoscintigraphy with satisfactory results.[54,57,58] Others have reported similar success with the use of ^{99m}Tc-labeled human serum albumin.[52,53,55,59]

Technique

Lymphoscintigraphy is performed with the patient comfortably positioned supine on the imaging table. The feet are attached to a foot ergometer, and the patient is instructed in the proper use of the device. For lymphoscintigraphy of the upper extremity, we employ a plastic squeezable ball the size of a tennis ball that is compressed on command.

After proper positioning and instruction, a subcutaneous injection of 11 MBq (350 to 450 μCi) of ^{99m}Tc-Sb_2S_3 colloid is made into the web space between the second and the third toes (or fingers) bilaterally. The number of particles in the injected solution (0.1 to 0.2 mL) ranges from 10^9 to 10^{13}. The tracer dose is prepared previously in tuberculin syringes (one for each side), and the injection is made with a 27-gauge needle. The injection is associated with an often very intense stinging sensation lasting for 5 to 10 seconds. Absorption of Sb_2S_3 is rapid, and up to 30% of the injected tracer is absorbed by 3 hours. In the United States, this radiopharmaceutical is regulated as an investigational drug by the U.S. Food and Drug Administration.

Immediately after the injection, a gamma camera with a large field of view is positioned to include the groin region in the upper field of view. An all-purpose collimator is used, and a 20% window is placed symmetrically around the 140-keV photopeak of the ^{99m}Tc isotope.

Dynamic anterior images (made every 5 minutes during the first hour, for a total of 12 frames in 1 hour) of the groin are obtained during the first hour (Fig. 167-7). The patient is requested to exercise with the foot ergometer for 5 minutes initially and then 1 minute out of every 5 minutes for the rest of the hour. The same exercise schedule with the squeeze ball is used for the upper extremity. Measured exercise is important to obtain reproducible appearance times in the groin.

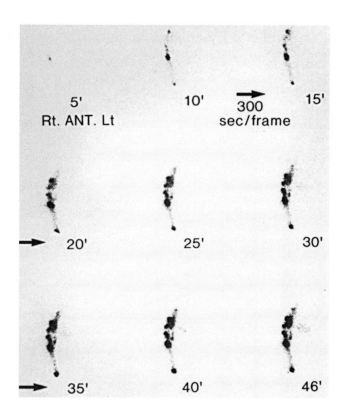

FIGURE 167-7 Lymphoscintigraphic images of the groin taken every 5 minutes after injection of the colloid into both feet. Normal lymphatic transport and image pattern of the inguinal nodes on the right, and no visualization of the lymphatics of the left. This 30-year-old woman had primary lymphedema of the left leg.

At the end of the first hour the patient is scanned with a dual-headed gamma camera (Siemens) for a total body image. Imaging time is about 20 minutes. Similar total body images are obtained at 3 hours (Fig. 167-8) and, for selected patients, at 6 and 24 hours. The patient is encouraged to ambulate in the times between the total body images. Like others, we have experimented with multiple injection sites (two or more sites on each side) or used an injection site behind the lateral malleolus to obtain access to the deep lymphatic system. We have not been convinced, however, that any advantage results from these modifications of the standard technique.

Reading a Lymphoscintigram

At the end of the study, the following information is available to the reviewer for diagnostic interpretation:

1. *Evidence of proper injection.* No uptake is seen in the liver initially, and only faint activity is present at 1 hour. Early liver uptake without activity in the abdominal nodes and channels suggests intravenous tracer injection.
2. *Appearance time of activity in regional lymph nodes (groin or axilla) after tracer injection.* Normal transit time is between 15 and 60 minutes. Less than 15 minutes indicates rapid transport, and more than 60 minutes suggests delayed lymphatic transport (see Fig. 167-7).
3. *The absence or presence and the pattern of lymph channels in the leg; the number, size, and symmetry of tracer activity in the groin lymph nodes.* For the upper extremity, similar observations are made for the axilla and arms.
4. *The pattern of lymph nodes and channels in the pelvis and abdomen and activity in the liver.* For the arm, the uptake pattern in axillary lymph nodes is observed.

The data are recorded in a standardized report format, which helps to create reproducible reports when many physicians review these tracings. Such a report form is shown in Table 167-3 and is an adaptation of a form proposed by Kleinhans and colleagues for the estimation of a transport index.[60]

Uptake of the tracer by lymph nodes is not always predictable even in normal patients. Thus, when interpreting a lymphoscintigram, a detailed evaluation for the number of lymph nodes present in the groin is not possible. Nevertheless, abnormal patterns for nodes can be defined, such as (1) no lymph node uptake, (2) marked asymmetry, and (3) mild asymmetry.

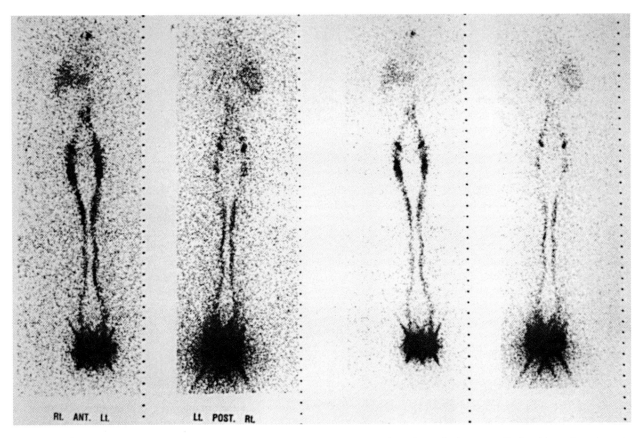

FIGURE 167-8 Image display from total body scan with dual-headed gamma camera. Anterior and posterior images are displayed in two intensity settings. **Left,** Anterior and posterior images of a normal lymphoscintigram. **Right,** Higher-intensity settings in the same patient. Large area of high activity and scatter is seen at the feet where the injection was made. The single well-outlined band in each leg represents the main lymphatic channels. Lymph nodes in the groin, pelvic and para-aortic nodes, liver, and an area at the site of the upper thoracic duct are visualized.

Table 167-3	Evaluation Form for Calculation of Lymphatic Transport Index

Patient's Initials _____

Clinic Number _____ Date _____

LYMPHOSCINTIGRAPHY DATA EVALUATION

☐ Arms ☐ Legs

IMAGE	1 HR		3 HR		6 HR		24 HR	
	R	L	R	L	R	L	R	L
Lymph transport kinetics: 0 = no delay, 1 = rapid, 3 = low-grade delay, 5 = extreme delay, 9 = no transport								
Distribution pattern: 0 = normal, 2 = focal abnormal tracer, 3 = partial dermal, 5 = diffuse dermal, 9 = no transport								
Lymph node appearance time: Minutes								
Assessment of lymph nodes: 0 = clearly seen, 3 = faint, 5 = hardly seen, 9 = no visualization								
Assessment of lymph vessels: 0 = clearly seen, 3 = faint, 5 = hardly seen, 9 = no visualization								
Abnormal sites of tracer accumulation (describe)								

Adapted from Kleinhans E, Baumeister RGH, Hahn D, et al: Evaluation of transport kinetics in lymphoscintigraphy: Follow-up study in patients with transplanted lymphatic vessels. Eur J Nucl Med 10:349, 1985. Courtesy of Springer-Verlag.

The Normal Lymphoscintigram

After the tracer injection, visible activity gradually ascends the anteromedial aspect of the leg. The injection site, because of the relatively large tracer dose given, does not show details, and no information about lymph distribution in the feet is obtainable. Several lymph channels may be identified in the calf. In the thigh, however, the lymph vessels run close to each other; separate activity in each larger channel is seldom seen on lymphoscintigrams (see Fig. 167-8).

With standardized exercise, as mentioned earlier, tracer activity should be seen clearly in the inguinal lymph nodes by 60 minutes (range, 15 to 60 minutes). A faint hepatic uptake, activity in the bladder, and faint traces in the para-abdominal nodes are visible at 1 hour. Three-hour images show intense uptake in the liver; symmetrical and good uptake in the lymph nodes of the groin, pelvis, and abdomen; and occasionally a tracer focus in the left supraclavicular area at the site of the distal thoracic duct.

Scintigraphic Findings in Lymphedema

Abnormal lymphoscintigrams may show (1) an abnormally slow removal or no removal of the tracer from the injection site (Figs. 167-9 and 167-10); (2) the presence of collaterals or a cutaneous pattern (dermal back-flow) in the extremities (Figs. 167-11 and 167-12A); (3) reduced, faint, or no uptake in the lymph nodes of the groin, the aortoiliac nodes, and

the axillary nodes; and (4) abnormal tracer accumulation suggestive of extravasation, lymphocele, or lymphangiectasia (Fig. 167-13A).

Primary and secondary lymphedema are associated with similar abnormalities on lymphoscintigraphy. These include a delay in transport from the injection site (Fig. 167-14), dermal back-flow, the presence of large collaterals, occasionally extravasated activity, fewer visualized lymph nodes, and "crossover" filling of contralateral inguinal (or axillary) lymph nodes as a sign of collateral pathways.[54,57,58] In primary lymphedema, it may be possible to distinguish aplasia from hypoplasia if imaging is performed early in the evolution of the disease. In aplasia, there is usually (1) little or no removal of tracer from the injection site, (2) tracer in regional lymph nodes on 1- and 3-hour images, (3) dermal back-flow, and (4) visualized lymph channels. In hypoplasia, these scintigraphic features may be variably present. Regardless of etiology, lymphatic vessels of normal caliber are not seen in patients with long-standing lymphedema.[55]

Qualitative interpretation of images has resulted in excellent sensitivity (92%) and specificity (100%) for the diagnosis of lymphedema.[57] Quantitative lymphoscintigraphy with measurement of lymphatic clearance may improve detection of early disease,[55] but the results obtained in our studies have been equivocal.[54,57] Neither the image pattern nor the quantitative parameters can reliably distinguish primary from secondary lymphedema.[54,57,58]

FIGURE 167-9 Lymphoscintigram of a 25-year-old woman with congenital familial lymphedema of both lower extremities. Note absence of lymph vessels and lymph nodes at 6 hours, with only minimal dermal back-flow visible in the distal calves. This patient also had recurrent familial cholestasis due to absence of intrahepatic bile ducts (Aagenaes syndrome).

FIGURE 167-10 Lymphoscintigram of a 65-year-old woman with primary lymphedema tarda of the right lower extremity. There is minimal dermal back-flow above the right ankle 3 hours after injection, and no lymph vessels or lymph nodes are visualized. The pattern was normal in the left leg.

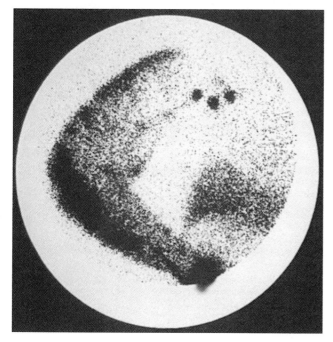

FIGURE 167-11 Lymphoscintigram of the right arm of a 51-year-old woman with postmastectomy lymphedema. Note extensive dermal back-flow resulting from lymphatic obstruction. Three groups of axillary nodes are still visualized.

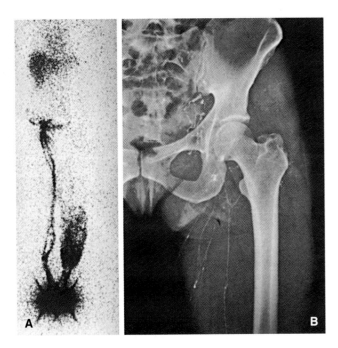

FIGURE 167-12 A, Lymphoscintigram of a 43-year-old woman with left lower extremity lymphedema after hysterectomy and bilateral iliac node dissection for cervical cancer. Dermal pattern is seen on left with no visualization of the inguinal nodes. Transport was mildly delayed in the clinically asymptomatic right limb. Note lack of visualization of iliac nodes bilaterally. **B,** Contrast lymphangiography in the same patient confirms the lymphoscintigraphic findings. Few small lymph vessels and two small nodes are seen only in the thigh.

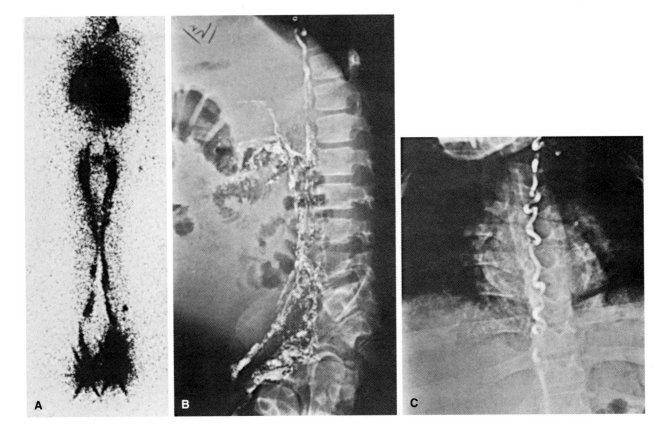

FIGURE 167-13 A, Lymphoscintigram of an 18-year-old man with lymphangiectasia, protein-losing enteropathy, and chylous ascites. Note large leg lymphatics and reflux of colloid into the mesenteric lymph vessels, filling almost the entire abdominal cavity. **B,** Lymphangiogram of the same patient reveals reflux of dye into the dilated mesenteric lymphatics. **C,** Note extremely dilated and tortuous but patent thoracic duct.

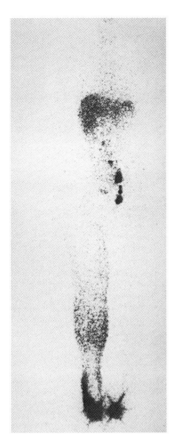

FIGURE 167-14 Lymphoscintigram of a 47-years-old woman with primary lymphedema tarda of the right lower extremity. Note markedly delayed transport with dermal pattern in the right leg. The right inguinal or iliac nodes were not visualized.

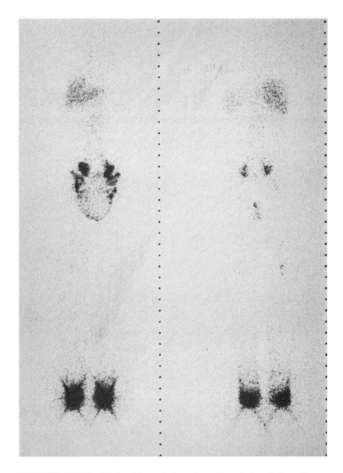

FIGURE 167-15 Bilateral leg scintigraphy with anterior (*left*) and posterior (*right*) views in a 24-year-old man outlines the swollen scrotum in the 6-hour image. Reflux of the colloid resulted from dilatation and valvular incompetence of the lymphatics.

Scintigraphic Findings in Lymphangiectasia

Dilated lymph channels with only mild or no delay in lymph transport are frequently seen on lymphoscintigraphic images. Injection of the colloid into the unaffected lower extremity may reflux into the affected lymphedematous leg because of lymphatic valvular incompetence. Similar reflux of the colloid may be seen in the dilated mesenteric lymphatics (see Fig. 167-13A) or in the retroperitoneum, perineum, or scrotum (Fig. 167-15). Ruptured lymphatics cause extravasation of the colloid into the abdominal cavity or the chest of patients with chylous ascites or chylothorax. The images are generally not helpful, however, in determining the exact site of the lymphatic leak.

Computed Tomography

The greatest value of CT in the evaluation of patients with a swollen leg is to exclude any obstructing mass that may result in decreased transport capacity of the lymphatic system. For patients with lymphedema, CT confirms the presence of coarse, nonenhancing, tubular reticular structures in the subcutaneous tissue.[61-63] This honeycomb appearance in the subcutaneous tissue is caused either by lymphatic channels or by free fluid accumulating in tissue planes. However, CT is not able to distinguish subcutaneous fat from tissue fluid. In our experience, this test is not sensitive enough to define the cause of lower extremity swelling.

Magnetic Resonance Imaging

Because of continuous improvements in technology, MRI has become the most important noninvasive imaging test for the diagnosis of congenital vascular malformations and the identification of soft tissue tumors. The value of MRI in the diagnosis of the swollen leg, however, has not been evaluated until recently. Duewell and colleagues found MRI useful in differentiating the three major forms of limb swelling: lipedema, chronic venous edema, and lymphedema.[64] Lipedema was characterized by an increased amount of subcutaneous fat without increased vascularity or signal changes suggesting excess fluid. The ratio of the superficial to the deep compartment was found to be increased. In lymphedema and venous edema, however, there was no change in the superficial-to-deep compartment ratio. Like findings observed on CT, a honeycomb pattern was seen in the subcutaneous tissues of patients with lymphedema.[64]

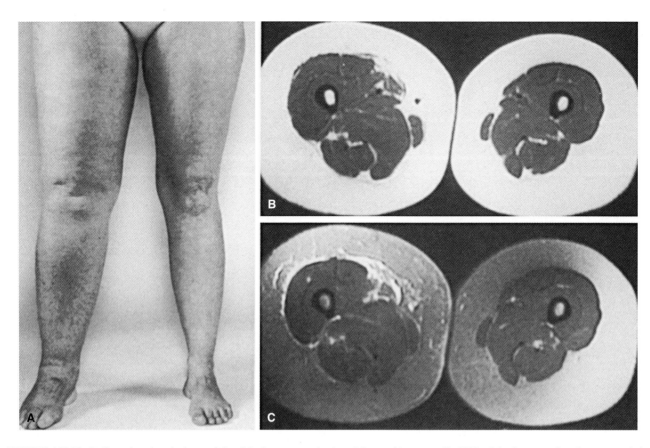

FIGURE 167-16 A, Secondary lymphedema of the right lower extremity in a 36-year-old woman, **B,** MRI of the legs reveals enlargement of the subcutaneous tissues and the deep compartment on the right with considerable stranding within the subcutaneous tissues, predominantly anteriorly and medially. **C,** T2-weighted image reveals the region of soft tissue stranding that is now of high signal intensity in the deep layers of the subcutaneous tissue.

MRI is particularly useful in complementing findings observed on lymphoscintigraphy.[65,66] MRI is helpful for delineating nodal anatomy in addition to imaging soft tissue changes and the larger lymphatic trunks and nodes in different tissue planes (Fig. 167-16). MRI is also suitable for imaging lymphatic trunks and nodes proximal to the site of lymphatic obstruction, which cannot be visualized by lymphoscintigraphy. Experience that is accumulating with the use of supermagnetic agents (e.g., iron oxide) appears promising for delineation of the lymphatic truncal-nodal anatomy in greater detail.[67]

■ LYMPHANGIOGRAPHY

Visual Lymphangiography (Dye Test)

Hudack and McMaster were the first, in 1933, to use subcutaneous injection of vital dyes to visualize the superficial lymphatics of the thigh and the forearm.[68] Subcutaneous injection of patent blue V or isosulfan blue (Lymphazurin) dye in the first or second interdigital space of the foot results in fast, selective uptake of the large-molecular-weight dye into the lymphatic system. With normal lymphatic circulation, the dye is transported to the inguinal lymph nodes 5 to 10 minutes after injection. In patients with lymphatic stasis in the superficial lymph collectors, dermal

back-flow is observed soon after injection (Fig. 167-17). If positive, the test is reliable to diagnose lymphatic stasis, but failure to demonstrate dermal back-flow may also indicate extensive lymphatic obstruction, hypoplasia, or aplasia.

Direct Contrast Lymphangiography

Contrast lymphangiography was first performed by Servelle in 1943,[69] but the current technique of subcutaneous injection of a vital dye to identify the foot lymphatics for cannulation and direct injection of the contrast material was developed by Kinmonth.[70] Lymphangiography with lipid-soluble contrast material provided a major stimulus to the investigation of the lymphatic system in patients with both lymphedema and malignancy. Since the availability of CT and MRI, the utility of lymphangiography in the clinical staging of malignancies has significantly diminished. With the availability of isotope lymphoscintigraphy, the use of contrast lymphangiography for patients with lymphedema has also significantly decreased.

Technique of Pedal Lymphangiography

Contrast lymphangiography is performed under local anesthesia using a 1% lidocaine (Xylocaine) solution. A small transverse incision is made in the mid dorsum of the

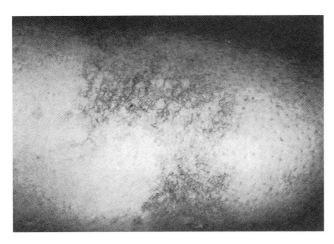

FIGURE 167-17 Visual lymphangiography in secondary lymphedema. Lymphazurine dye injected into the first interdigital space of the foot delineates the dermal lymphatics at the mid calf owing to obstruction in the proximal main lymphatic vessels.

foot after 1 mL of isosulfan blue dye has been injected subcutaneously into the first and second interdigital spaces. Because the dye injection itself is uncomfortable and painful, we mix the dye with equal amounts of 1% lidocaine solution.

The lymph vessels are dissected under loupe magnification, and a 30-gauge needle attached to a polyethylene tube is inserted into the lymph vessels. A constant infusion of lipid-soluble contrast material (ethiodized oil [Ethiodol]) is started at a rate of 1 mL in 8 minutes, as suggested by Wolfe.[71] A maximum of 7 mL is injected into each limb, making a total infusion that does not exceed 14 mL. If the injection is made too fast, the dye will extravasate through the wall of the lymph vessels and interpretation of the images will be difficult (Fig. 167-18). If the amount of extravasation is significant, the rate of infusion should be decreased. At the end of the procedure the needle is removed, and the incision is closed meticulously with interrupted 5-0 nylon vertical mattress sutures.

Serial films are taken of the lower extremities, groin, pelvis, lumbar area, and upper abdomen and chest during the injection. Additional films are taken several hours after injection and 24 hours later. The oily contrast material may remain in the lymph nodes for several months after injection.

Arm Lymphangiography

Lymphangiography of the upper extremity is now rarely performed. The technique is similar to that used for pedal lymphangiography, except that a small lymphatic on the dorsum of the hand is cannulated. The amount of contrast agent should be limited to 4 to 5 mL of ethiodized oil.[71]

Interpretation of Lymphangiograms

Injection of a dorsal pedal lymph vessel fills the superficial medial lymphatic vessels and most of the inguinal lymph nodes. Five to 15 lymph vessels are seen in normal patients

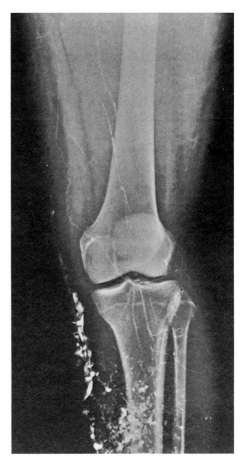

FIGURE 167-18 Extensive occlusion of most lymph vessels in the thigh with extravasation of the dye distal to the knee after contrast lymphangiography in a patient with secondary lymphedema.

at the medial aspect of the thigh (Fig. 167-19), with valves frequently visualized every 5 to 10 mm. Lateral lymphatics and deep lymphatics are not visible on normal lymphangiograms but may be seen in patients with lymphatic obstruction (Fig. 167-20). The deep lymph vessels are frequently paired and follow the main blood vessels of the extremity. The normal lymphatic nodes have a ground-glass appearance. Normally the iliac lymph vessels and lymph nodes fill within 30 to 45 minutes after the injection is started. The thoracic duct may only show up on images several hours after the injection (see Fig. 167-13C).

Most patients with primary lymphedema have an obstruction of some or most of the lymph vessels and lymph-conducting elements of the lymph nodes. As mentioned previously, distal obliteration of the lymph vessels in the leg is much more frequent than proximal, pelvic lymphatic obstruction. With pelvic obstruction the inguinal and iliac lymph nodes are few or absent but the leg lymphatics are patent and are frequently distended and tortuous (Fig. 167-21). Back-flow of the contrast into dilated dermal lymphatics is observed. The lymphangiographic findings in proximal obliteration are similar to those seen in secondary lymphedema. With time, however, fibrotic occlusion of the dilated distal lymph vessels frequently occurs. This

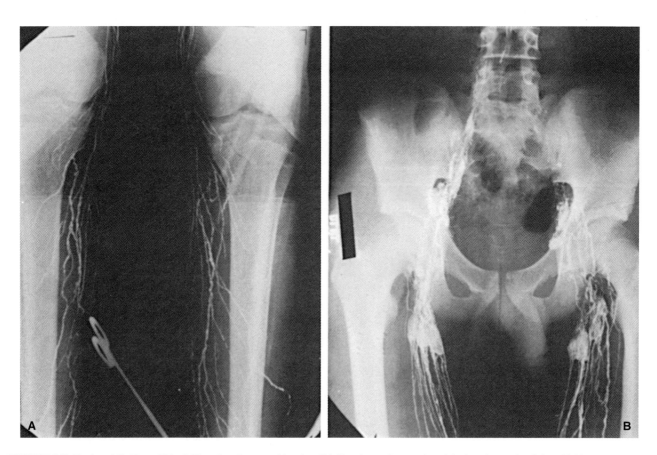

FIGURE 167-19 A and **B,** Normal bipedal lymphangiogram with only mild dilatation and tortuosity of the lymph vessels of the calf. Note the presence of 10 to 15 superficial lymphatic collectors in the thighs.

retrograde occlusion of the lymph vessels (die-back) was observed in patients with both secondary and primary lymphedemas.[72]

Patients with lymphangiectasia frequently need larger amounts of contrast agent to image the dilated, incompetent lymphatics. The number of pelvic lymph nodes may be diminished. Contrast material may reflux into the mesenteric lymphatics (see Fig. 167-13B). The thoracic duct in some of the patients is occluded or absent, whereas in others it is dilated and tortuous (see Fig. 167-13C).

Complications

Contrast lymphangiography is an invasive and lengthy procedure that is frequently uncomfortable for the patient. Obstructive lymphangitis and progression of lymphedema after lymphangiography have also been noted.[73] Symptomatic pulmonary embolization due to the oily contrast material may complicate lymphangiography. This problem may be caused by using excessive amounts of contrast material, or it may be the result of embolization through spontaneous lymphovenous anastomoses. In patients who have had previous pulmonary irradiation, cerebral embolization through pulmonary arteriovenous fistulae may also occur.[71] The use of ethiodized oil is contraindicated in patients who are allergic to iodine.

Indications for Direct Contrast Lymphangiography

Contrast lymphangiography is a test that is now rarely and only selectively used for the diagnosis of lymphedema. It is indicated for some patients who are candidates for microvascular lymphatic reconstruction. It is also useful in the preoperative evaluation of patients with lymphangiectasia and reflux of chyle (see Chapter 169). Although the diagnosis of lymphangiectasia can be made with lymphoscintigraphy, the extent and location of the dilated lymphatics are best delineated by contrast lymphangiography. Lymphangiography remains the best test for imaging the thoracic duct and for identifying the exact location of some pelvic, abdominal, and thoracic lymphatic fistulae.

Indirect Contrast Lymphangiography

Because of the difficulties encountered with direct cannulation of the lymphatics and the use of oily contrast material, increasing research has focused in recent years on indirect lymphangiography. This is performed with subepidermal infusion of a water-soluble contrast material (iotasul, iopamidol).[74] The dermal lymphatics, and in some patients the distal lymph collectors, can be imaged with this technique. In primary lymphedema, absence, hypoplasia, or

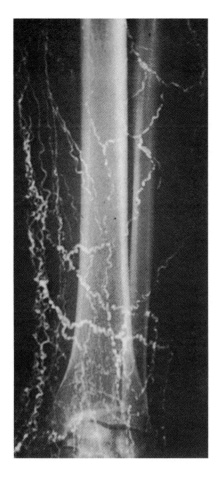

FIGURE 167-20 Dilated tortuous lymph vessels with valvular insufficiency and filling of lateral lymph vessels in a patient with lymphedema praecox. (From Gloviczki P, Schirger A: Lymphedema. In Spittell JA Jr [ed]: Clinical Medicine. Philadelphia, Harper & Row, 1985, pp 1-10.)

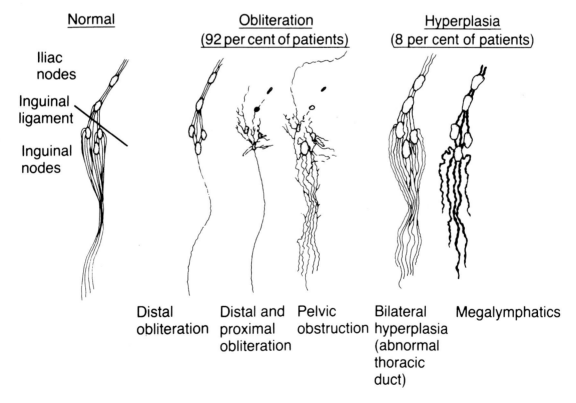

FIGURE 167-21 Lymphangiographic patterns in normal patient and in patients with different types of primary lymphedema.

hyperplasia of the dermal lymphatics can be demonstrated with indirect lymphangiography. In secondary lymphedema, hyperplasia of the initial lymphatics is the most frequent finding. Although indirect lymphangiography is helpful for diagnosing lymphatic stasis and for imaging the fine initial lymph vessels, the limitations of the current technique are still important: larger lymphatic collectors or nodes distant to the site of the injection are not visualized.[75]

■ DIFFERENTIAL DIAGNOSIS OF LYMPHEDEMA

During the evaluation of patients with chronic limb swelling, a systemic cause of the disease should be excluded first. Underlying cardiac diseases such as congestive heart failure, chronic constrictive pericarditis, and severe tricuspid regurgitation are the most frequent systemic causes leading to pitting or bilateral leg swelling. Hepatic or renal failure, hypoproteinemia, malnutrition, and endocrine disorders (myxedema) are other possible causes of leg swelling. Allergic reactions, hereditary angioedema, and idiopathic cyclic edema are rare systemic causes that should be considered. Chronic use of diuretics may lead to generalized swelling, which most frequently affects the extremities and the face. Other drugs that may cause swelling include corticosteroids, some of the antihypertensive drugs, and anti-inflammatory agents (Table 167-4).

Remember that, among the local or regional causes of limb swelling, chronic venous insufficiency is much more common than lymphedema. In some patients with chronic iliac or iliocaval obstruction, massive swelling of the entire extremity can develop (Fig. 167-22A). The usual causes of proximal venous occlusion are deep venous thrombosis or external compression of the vein by tumor or retroperitoneal fibrosis. Although lymphedema is usually painless, venous hypertension results in marked pain and cramps after prolonged standing or at the end of the day. Patients with proximal venous obstruction may complain of typical claudication, which presents as throbbing pain in the thigh or calf after walking. The pain resolves with rest, although elevation of the extremity provides the fastest relief. The presence of varicosity, pigmentation, induration, or venous ulcers makes the diagnosis of venous insufficiency easier. Chronic inflammation in the subcutaneous tissue due to venous stasis may result in destruction of the collecting lymph channels, and a mixed venous-lymphatic edema develops in these patients.

Patients with congenital vascular malformations frequently have a larger extremity that may be difficult to distinguish from lymphedema (see Fig. 167-22B). An increase in the length of the affected extremity, the presence of atypical lateral varicosity, and port-wine stain with underlying developmental abnormality of the deep venous system is characteristic of Klippel-Trenaunay syndrome.[76] Although hypertrophy of the soft tissues and bones is caused by an abnormality in mesenchymal development, congenital lymphedema may also be present in these patients. In patients with high-shunt, high-flow arteriovenous malformations, the extremity is larger and is also frequently longer.[77] A bruit and thrill are present, the superficial veins are dilated and frequently pulsatile, and the distal arterial pulses may be diminished.

Table 167-4	Differential Diagnosis of Chronic Leg Swelling
SYSTEMIC CAUSES	**LOCAL OR REGIONAL CAUSES**
Cardiac failure	Chronic venous insufficiency
Hepatic failure	Lymphedema
Renal failure	Lipedema
Hypoproteinemia	Congenital vascular malformation
Hyperthyroidism (myxedema)	Arteriovenous fistula
Allergic disorders	Trauma
Idiopathic cyclic edema	Snake or insect bite
Hereditary angioedema	Infection, inflammation
	Hematoma
Drugs	Dependency
Antihypertensives	Rheumatoid arthritis
Methyldopa	Post-revascularization edema
Nifedipine	Soft tissue tumor
Hydralazine	Hemihypertrophy
Hormones	
Estrogen	
Progesterone	
Anti-inflammatory drugs	
Phenylbutazone	
Monoamine oxidase inhibitors	

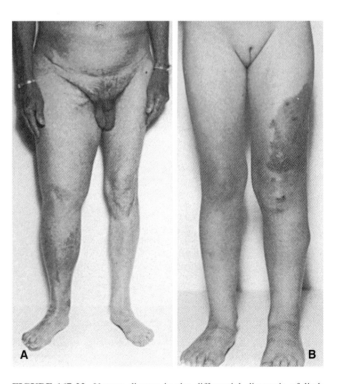

FIGURE 167-22 Venous disease in the differential diagnosis of limb edema. **A,** Right leg swelling due to venous insufficiency, caused by chronic iliofemoral venous thrombosis. **B,** Left leg edema associated with congenital vascular malformation (Klippel-Trenaunay syndrome).

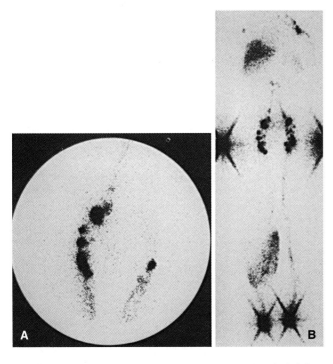

FIGURE 167-23 Lymphoscintigraphy in "high-output" lymphatic failure due to reflex sympathetic dystrophy of the right leg. **A,** Fast lymphatic transport in the affected right leg compared with the normal left leg on the image taken of the inguinal nodes 20 minutes after injection. **B,** Total body image taken at 3 hours shows dermal pattern on the right but no evidence of proximal lymphatic obstruction.

Lipedema is characterized by deposition of a large amount of fatty tissue in the subcutaneous layers. Most of these patients have morbid obesity, although some, mostly females, have fat deposition primarily localized to the lower half of the body. Evaluation of the lymphatic system with lymphoscintigraphy or lymphangiography shows essentially normal findings.

Trauma and subsequent reflex sympathetic dystrophy may result in painful swelling of the extremity. Because of disuse, a varying degree of osteoporosis can be observed, and increased sympathetic activity occurs in the limb of these patients. The swelling is usually the result of a "high-output" lymphatic failure, and increased lymphatic transport on lymphoscintigraphy may be demonstrated (Fig. 167-23A and B). Baker's cyst, soft tissue tumor, hematoma, and inflammation such as tenosynovitis or arthritis are additional local causes of limb swelling that should be considered in the differential diagnosis of lymphedema.

■ DIAGNOSTIC PROTOCOL FOR EVALUATION OF CHRONIC EDEMA

Clinical examination of the patient frequently reveals the correct cause of limb swelling. Initial laboratory examinations should include routine blood tests to look for signs of renal or hepatic failure, eosinophilia, or hypoproteinemia. Urinalysis may indicate proteinuria. Once a systemic cause of edema is excluded, the local or regional cause should be confirmed (Fig. 167-24).

CT has become a routine test in our practice for most adult patients with leg swelling to exclude underlying malignancy. Noninvasive venous studies, such as Doppler examination or strain-gauge plethysmography, are frequently sufficient to diagnose venous disease. In some patients, however, duplex scanning is necessary to exclude obstruction of the deep veins. MRI provides the most accurate information in patients with clinical signs of congenital vascular malformation, soft tissue tumor, or retroperitoneal fibrosis.

Lymphoscintigraphy is now the test of choice for the confirmation of lymphedema, and a normal lymphoscintigraphic examination essentially excludes the diagnosis of lymphedema. Patients with chronic venous insufficiency may have abnormal results on lymphoscintigraphic examination with delayed transport because of mixed lymphatic and venous edema. Direct contrast lymphangiography should be performed selectively and should not be included routinely in the evaluation of patients with chronic limb swelling.

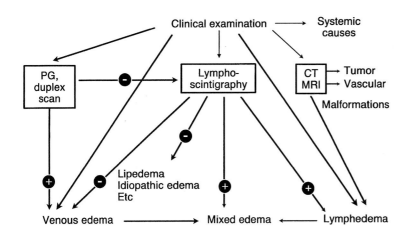

FIGURE 167-24 Diagnostic protocol for patients with chronic limb swelling. PG, plethysmography.

■ REFERENCES

1. Kinmonth JB, Taylor GW, Tracy GD, et al: Primary lymphoedema: Clinical and lymphangiographic studies of a series of 107 patients in which the lower limbs were affected. Br J Surg 45:1, 1957.

2. Kinmonth JB: The lymphoedemas: General considerations. In Kinmonth JB (ed): The Lymphatics: Surgery, Lymphography and Diseases of the Chyle and Lymph Systems. London, Edward Arnold, 1982, pp 83-104.

3. Browse NL, Stewart G: Lymphoedema: Pathophysiology and classification. J Cardiovasc Surg 26:91, 1985.

4. Browse NL: The diagnosis and management of primary lymphedema. J Vasc Surg 3:181, 1986.

5. Gloviczki P, Schirger A: Lymphedema. In Spittell JA Jr (ed): Clinical Medicine. Philadelphia, Harper & Row, 1985, pp 1-10.

6. O'Donnell TF, Howrigan P: Diagnosis and management of lymphedema. In Bell PRF, Jamieson CW, Ruckley CV (eds): Surgical Management of Vascular Disease. Philadelphia, WB Saunders, 1992, pp 1305-1327.

7. Allen EV: Lymphedema of the extremities: Classification, etiology and differential diagnosis: A study of three hundred cases. Arch Intern Med 54:606, 1934.

8. Casley-Smith JR, Földi M, Ryan TJ, et al: Lymphedema: Summary of the 10th International Congress of Lymphology Working Group Discussions and Recommendations, Adelaide, Australia, August 10-17, 1985. Lymphology 18:175, 1985.

9. Browse NL: Primary lymphedema. In Ernst C, Stanley J (eds): Current Therapy in Vascular Surgery. Philadelphia, BC Decker, 1987, pp 454-457.

10. Kinmonth JB, Wolfe JH: Fibrosis in the lymph nodes in primary lymphoedema: Histological and clinical studies in 74 patients with lower-limb oedema. Ann R Coll Surg Engl 62:344, 1980.

11. Wolfe JHN: The prognosis and possible cause of severe primary lymphoedema. Ann R Coll Surg Engl 66:251, 1984.

12. Kurland LT, Molgaard CA: The patient record in epidemiology. Sci Am 245:54, 1981.

13. Smeltzer DM, Stickler GB, Schirger A: Primary lymphedema in children and adolescents: A follow-up study and review. Pediatrics 76:206, 1985.

14. Letessier EE: Cited by Schroeder E, Helweg-Larsen HF: Chronic hereditary lymphedema (Nonne-Milroy-Meige disease). Acta Med Scand 137:198, 1950.

15. Nonne M: Vier Fälle von Elephantiasis congenita hereditaria. Arch Pathol Anat Physiol 125:189, 1891.

16. Milroy WF: An undescribed variety of hereditary edema. NY Med J 56:505, 1892.

17. Milroy WF: Chronic hereditary edema: Milroy's disease. JAMA 91:1172, 1928.

18. Meige H: Dystrophie oedemateuse hereditaire. Presse Med 2:341, 1898.

19. Servelle M: Congenital malformation of the lymphatics of the small intestine. J Cardiovasc Surg 32:159, 1991.

20. Kinmonth JB, Cox SJ: Protein-losing enteropathy in lymphoedema: Surgical investigation and treatment. J Cardiovasc Surg 16:111, 1975.

21. Gloviczki P, Soltesz L, Solti F, et al: The surgical treatment of lymphedema caused by chylous reflux. In Bartos V, Davidson JW (eds): Advances in Lymphology. Proceedings of the 8th International Congress of Lymphology, Montreal, 1981. Prague, Czechoslovak Medical Press, 1982, pp 502-507.

22. Lymphatic filariasis—tropical medicine's origin will not go away. Lancet 1:1409, 1987.

23. Mak JW: Epidemiology of lymphatic filariasis. Ciba Found Symp 127:5, 1987.

24. Lobb AW, Harkins HN: Postmastectomy swelling of the arm with note on effect of segmental resection of axillary vein at time of radical mastectomy. West J Surg 57:550, 1949.

25. Leis HP: Selective moderate surgical approach for potentially curable breast cancer. In Gallagher HS, Leis HP, Snyderman RK, Urban JA (eds): The Breast. St. Louis, CV Mosby, 1978, pp 232-247.

26. Hayward JL, Winter PJ, Tong D, et al: A new approach to the conservative treatment of early breast cancer. Surgery 95:270, 1984.

27. Veronesi U, Saccozzi R, Del Vecchio M, et al: Comparing radical mastectomy with quadrantectomy, axillary dissection, and radiotherapy in patients with small cancers of the breast. N Engl J Med 305:6, 1981.

28. Osborne MP, Ormiston N, Harmer CL, et al: Breast conservation in the treatment of early breast cancer. A 20-year follow-up. Cancer 53:349, 1984.

29. Kissin MW, della Rovere GQ, Easton D, Westbury G: Risk of lymphoedema following the treatment of breast cancer. Br J Surg 73:580, 1986.

30. Martimbeau PW, Kjorstad KE, Kolstad P: Stage IB carcinoma of the cervix, the Norwegian Radium Hospital, 1968-1970: Results of treatment and major complications. I. Lymphedema. Am J Obstet Gynecol 133:389, 1978.

31. Papachristou D, Fortner JG: Comparison of lymphedema following incontinuity and discontinuity groin dissection. Ann Surg 185:13, 1977.

32. De Roo T: Analysis of lymphoedema as first symptom of a neoplasm in a series of 650 patients with limb involvement. Radiol Clin (Basel) 45:236, 1976.

33. Smith RD, Spittell JA Jr, Schirger A: Secondary lymphedema of the leg: Its characteristics and diagnostic implications. JAMA 185:80, 1963.

34. Földi M: Classification of lymphedema and elephantiasis. 12th International WHO/TDR/FIL Conference on Lymphatic Pathology and Immunopathology in Filariasis, Thanjavur, India, November 18-22, 1985. Lymphology 18:159, 1985.

35. Chernin E: The disappearance of bancroftian filariasis from Charleston, South Carolina. Am J Trop Med Hyg 37:111, 1987.

36. Case T, Leis B, Witte M, et al: Vascular abnormalities in experimental and human lymphatic filariasis. Lymphology 24:174, 1991.

37. Dandapat MC, Mohapatro SK, Dash DM: Management of chronic manifestations of filariasis. J Indian Med Assoc 84:210, 1986.

38. Schirger A: Lymphedema. In Spittell JA Jr (ed): Cardiovascular Clinics. Philadelphia, FA Davis, 1983, pp 293-305.

39. Chant ADB: Hypothesis: Why venous oedema causes ulcers and lymphoedema does not. Eur J Vasc Surg 6:427, 1992.

40. Samman PD, White WF: The "yellow nail" syndrome. Br J Dermatol 76:153, 1964.

41. Taylor JS, Young JR: The swollen limb: Cutaneous clues to diagnosis and treatment. Cutis 21:553, 1978.

42. Fields CL, Roy TM, Ossorio MA, Mercer PJ: Yellow nail syndrome: A perspective. J Ky Med Assoc 89:563, 1991.

43. Stewart FW, Treves N: Lymphangiosarcoma in postmastectomy lymphedema: A report of six cases in elephantiasis chirurgica. Cancer 1:64, 1948.

44. Alessi E, Sala F, Berti E: Angiosarcomas in lymphedematous limbs. Am J Dermatopathol 8:371, 1986.

45. Muller R, Hajdu SI, Brennan MF: Lymphangiosarcoma associated with chronic filarial lymphedema. Cancer 59:179, 1987.

46. Sherman AI, Ter-Pergossian M: Lymph node concentration of radioactive colloidal gold following interstitial injection. Cancer 6:1238, 1953.

47. Taylor GW, Kinmonth JB, Rollinson E, et al: Lymphatic circulation studied with radioactive plasma protein. BMJ 1:133, 1957.

48. Ege GN: Internal mammary lymphoscintigraphy: The rationale, technique, interpretation, and clinical application. Radiology 118:101, 1976.

49. Jackson FI, Bowen P, Lentle BC: Scintilymphangiography with ^{99m}Tc-antimony sulfide colloid in hereditary lymphedema (Nonne-Milroy disease). Clin Nucl Med 3:296, 1978.

50. Sty JR, Starshak RJ: Atlas of pediatric radionuclide lymphography. Clin Nucl Med 7:428, 1982.

51. Stewart G, Gaunt JI, Croft DN, Browse NL: Isotope lymphography: A new method of investigating the role of the lymphatics in chronic limb oedema. Br J Surg 72:906, 1985.

52. Nawaz K, Hamad MM, Sadek S, et al: Dynamic lymph flow imaging in lymphedema: Normal and abnormal patterns. Clin Nucl Med 11:653, 1986.

53. Ohtake E, Matsui K: Lymphoscintigraphy in patients with lymphedema: A new approach using intradermal injections of technetium-99m human serum albumin. Clin Nucl Med 11:474, 1986.

54. Vaqueiro M, Gloviczki P, Fisher J, et al: Lymphoscintigraphy in lymphedema: An aid to microsurgery. J Nucl Med 27:1125, 1986.

55. Weissleder H, Weissleder R: Lymphedema: Evaluation of qualitative and quantitative lymphoscintigraphy in 238 patients. Radiology 167:729, 1988.

56. Collins PS, Villavicencio JL, Abreu SH, et al: Abnormalities of lymphatic drainage in lower extremities: A lymphoscintigraphic study. J Vasc Surg 9:145, 1989.

57. Gloviczki P, Calcagno D, Schirger A, et al: Noninvasive evaluation of the swollen extremity: Experiences with 190 lymphoscintigraphic examinations. J Vasc Surg 9:683, 1989.

58. Cambria RA, Gloviczki P, Naessens JM, Wahner HW: Noninvasive evaluation of the lymphatic system with lymphoscintigraphy: A prospective, semiquantitative analysis in 386 extremities. J Vasc Surg 18:773, 1993.

59. McNeill GC, Witte MH, Witte CL, et al: Whole-body lymphangio-scintigraphy: Preferred method for initial assessment of the peripheral lymphatic system. Radiology 172:495, 1989.

60. Kleinhans E, Baumeister RGH, Hahn D, et al: Evaluation of transport kinetics in lymphoscintigraphy: Follow-up study in patients with transplanted lymphatic vessels. Eur J Nucl Med 10:349, 1985.

61. Gamba JL, Silverman PM, Ling D, et al: Primary lower extremity lymphedema: CT diagnosis. Radiology 149:218, 1983.

62. Hadjus NS, Carr DH, Banks L, Pflug JJ: The role of CT in the diagnosis of primary lymphedema of the lower limb. AJR Am J Roentgenol 144:361, 1985.

63. Göltner E, Gass P, Haas JP, Schneider P: The importance of volumetry, lymphoscintigraphy and computer tomography in the diagnosis of brachial edema after mastectomy. Lymphology 21:134, 1988.

64. Duewell S, Hagspiel KD, Zuber J, et al: Swollen lower extremity: Role of MR imaging. Radiology 184:227, 1992.

65. Weissleder R, Thrall JH: The lymphatic system: Diagnostic imaging studies. Radiology 172:315, 1989.

66. Case TC, Witte CL, Witte MH, et al: Magnetic resonance imaging in human lymphedema: Comparison with lymphangioscintigraphy. J Magn Reson Imag 10:549, 1992.

67. Weissleder R, Elizondo G, Wittenburg J, et al: Ultrasmall super-paramagnetic iron oxide: An intravenous contrast agent for assessing lymph nodes with MR imaging. Radiology 175:494, 1990.

68. Kanter MA: The lymphatic system: An historical perspective. Plast Reconstr Surg 79:131, 1987.

69. Servelle M: La lymphographie moyen d'étude de la physiopathologie des grosses jambes. Rev Chir 82:251, 1944.

70. Kinmonth JB: Lymphangiography in man: A method of outlining lymphatic trunks at operation. Clin Sci 11:13, 1952.

71. Wolfe JHN: Diagnosis and classification of lymphedema. In Rutherford RB (ed): Vascular Surgery, 3rd ed. Philadelphia, WB Saunders, 1989, pp 1656-1667.

72. Fyfe NCM, Wolfe JHN, Kinmonth JB: "Die-back" in primary lymphedema-lymphographic and clinical correlations. Lymphology 15:66, 1982.

73. O'Brien BMcC, Mellow CG, Khazanchi RK, et al: Long-term results after microlymphaticovenous anastomoses for the treatment of obstructive lymphedema. Plast Reconstr Surg 85:562, 1990.

74. Partsch H, Urbanek A, Wenzel-Hora B: The dermal lymphatics in lymphoedema visualized by indirect lymphography. Br J Dermatol 110:431, 1984.

75. Gloviczki P: Invited commentary. In Gan JL, Chang TS, Fu DK, et al: Indirect lymphography with Isovist-300 in various forms of lymphedema. Eur J Plast Surg 14:109, 1991.

76. Gloviczki P, Stanson AW, Stickler GB, et al: Klippel-Trenaunay syndrome: The risks and benefits of vascular interventions. Surgery 110:469, 1991.

77. Gloviczki P, Hollier LH: Arteriovenous fistulas. In Haimovici H (ed): Vascular Surgery: Principles and Techniques, 3rd ed. Norwalk, CT, Appleton & Lange, 1989, pp 698-716.

Nonoperative Management of Chronic Lymphedema

168

GAIL L. GAMBLE, MD
THOM W. ROOKE, MD
PETER GLOVICZKI, MD

XXII

Section

Chronic lymphedema can cause significant functional limitations for those afflicted.[1] Despite remarkable advances into the molecular, genetic, and clinical understanding of the disease,[2,3] cure of lymphedema in humans is not yet possible. However, most patients will benefit from conservative treatment. Nonoperative management of lymphedema involves three major areas: (1) preventive measures and minimization of risk factors, (2) pharmacologic therapy, and (3) physical therapeutic measures developed for edema reduction and maintenance. Because the patient's self-image and quality of life are affected,[4,5] these issues must be considered when developing a comprehensive management program.

■ PREVENTIVE MEASURES

Patients with primary lymphedema usually have no known precipitating cause of the disease; thus, little if anything can be done to prevent lymphedema. However, recent advances in genetic mapping and mutation identification for the primary disorder presenting at birth (Milroy's disease) or at puberty (Meige's disease)[6,7] now offer possibilities for genetic testing of family members. Both genetic testing and counseling on early protective measures for those at risk are possible in a number of medical centers and may become more common practice in the future. Patients with primary lymphedema of one limb should be counseled to avoid or minimize risk factors that may lead to clinically manifest lymphedema of the contralateral limb. Secondary lymphedemas have numerous causes, many of which are potentially preventable. This raises the possibility that preventive measures can decrease occurrence and complications.

Infection

Worldwide, the most common cause of lymphedema is infection. Infestation by the parasite *Wuchereria bancrofti*[8] is the most frequent etiology, and it occurs in tropical climates with areas lacking adequate public health prevention measures. There has been much activity directed toward population control of filariasis in recent years.[9,10] Programs have been developed to reduce both vector transmission (decreased transmission of *W. bancrofti* and *Brugia malayi* parasites by mosquito bites) as well as administration of antifilarial drugs to at-risk populations.[11]

The mass usage of diethylcarbamazine plus ivermectin has been shown to significantly decrease lymphatic filariasis in populations.[9,12,13] The recognition that the endosymbiotic bacterial organism *Wolvachia* may also play a role in the development of filarial lymphedema raises possibilities of further drug development for filariasis control.[10,14] Clearly, management of this difficult issue must be aimed at public health measures as described earlier. Recent suggestions in the literature also include better preservation of skin integrity, which can reduce penetration of other bacteria, and prevention of infection that would increase further inflammatory response and lymphatic failure.[15]

There are also less evident forms of chronic infection, which can, over time, cause inflammation and enough lymphatic endothelial damage to obliterate local tissue function and cause sclerosis with subsequent development of lymphedema. In North America, post-traumatic infection or even chronic recurrent distal limb onychomycosis may result in sufficient lymphatic destruction to cause lymphedema.[16] Additionally, the lymphedematous limb, because of the high protein concentration in the interstitium, is extremely susceptible to bacterial invasion, which will then further compromise the already impaired limb. Practical precautions are necessary to prevent infection in extremities with lymphedema (Table 168-1).

Attention to daily skin hygiene of the limb at risk is imperative, yet this is often difficult for patients secondary to morbid obesity, lack of social and physical supports, or inadequate resources. The limbs should be washed regularly with soap and water and, while still moist, lubricated with an alcohol-free emollient cream that traps moisture, minimizing the risk of skin barrier disruption and microfissures. Patients with a history of fungal infection, including candidiasis and tinea, should use topical antifungal medications. Routine use of topical clotrimazole cream (1%) or miconazole nitrate lotion or cream (2%) is sufficient for most patients. Oral fluconazole or itraconazole may be needed on a chronic intermittent or continuous suppressive basis for recalcitrant or extensive infections. No current studies definitively address the efficacy of these treatments in patients with lymphedema.

Even in the absence of lymphedema, prompt administration of appropriate antibiotic therapy in any patients with lymphangitis is essential.[17,18] The pathogen is usually a beta-lactam–sensitive group A *Streptococcus*. *Staphylococcus*

Table 168-1	Prophylactic Skin Management

Skin Hygiene

Daily washing
Air drying
Moisturizer (non–alcohol-based) to avoid fissures

Clothing

Cotton against skin, avoid synthetics
Loose fit

Avoidance of Trauma

Protective clothing for work outdoors
Avoid cuts, scrapes, puncture wounds
Avoid sunburn

Control Fungal Infections

Topical antifungal agents, chronic intermittent use

Table 168-2	Prophylactic Antibiotic Regimen	

EPISODES OF CELLULITIS	PROPHYLAXIS
Cellulitis = 1	Oral penicillin-VK, 250 to 500 mg qid for 7 to 10 days, or an equivalent Antibiotic prescription available; take immediately at onset of symptoms
Cellulitis >4/yr	Prophylaxis with antibiotics 1 wk/mo Rigorous edema control Aggressive local antifungal prophylaxis
Refractory cellulitis	Daily oral antibiotics Rigorous edema control Aggressive local antifungal prophylaxis

species and other organisms are less commonly reported.[18] At the first sign of cellulitis, antibiotic treatment such as oral penicillin VK, 250 or 500 mg four times daily, should be initiated. Other beta-lactam antibiotic therapy, a simple cephalosporin (e.g., cephalexin), or a macrolide (e.g., erythromycin, azithromycin) can be utilized. Intravenous antibiotic infusion, hospitalization, and bed rest with leg elevation may be needed for some patients with more severe lymphangitis. Antibiotic therapy should be continued for 7 to 10 days or until all signs and symptoms of acute infection have clearly resolved. There is no consensus in the literature on optimal treatment of recurrent cellulitis with or without previous lymphedema (Table 168-2). When spontaneous episodes occur more often than four to six times per year, a regular prophylactic program—penicillin VK (or an equivalent), 250 mg four times daily for 7 days of each month—can be considered. An alternative regimen of penicillin given intramuscularly once every month in patients with increased risk for cellulitis has not been found to be effective in reducing infections.[19] A definitive antibiotic prophylaxis regimen for patients who experience recurrent cellulitis has not yet been identified. For some patients, an intermittent prophylactic program may not be sufficient to prevent recurrent infections and a daily antibiotic regimen may be needed.[18] If premorbid lymphedema is present, fluid reduction and good maintenance compression combined with antibiotic prophylaxis promises the best preventive option to avoid further episodes of infection.

Malignancy

In industrialized nations, lymphedema is most often identified after surgical or radiation therapy for breast, pelvic, or prostate cancer. The incidence and severity of lymphedema may be minimized if the extent of axillary or inguinal lymph node dissections is limited,[20-24] although the invasiveness of the operation depends on the size, type, and location of the lesion. Sentinel node biopsy, rather than extensive lymph node dissection, will decrease, but not eliminate, the risk for lymphedema present with axillary or inguinal dissection.[20,21,25-28] Early patient education after surgical excision or tumor irradiation is important, since skin precautions, limb elevation, and appropriate exercise reduce the incidence of lymphedema.

Other risk factors reported to increase the development of lymphedema in cancer patients include obesity,[29] advanced disease stage,[24] radiation,[30] and postoperative infection.[31] Some of these factors can be controlled or reversed, and therefore appropriate attention to risk factors may have an overall effect on incidence.

Other Preventive Measures

Prolonged elevation of an involved limb can help to reduce edema, especially in the early stages of the disease (Table 168-3). Exercise, particularly walking and aerobic exercise, promotes lymph flow.[32-34] Patients at risk for development of lymphedema are often cautioned not to "overuse" the limb at risk to avoid "overwhelming" the impaired drainage system. However, a recent prospective randomized study

Table 168-3	Edema Preventive Measures

Limb Elevation

Above heart
Periodic daily elevation
Elevated bed positioning (pillows or wedge to elevate leg)

Exercise

Daily exercise to increase lymph flow in limb
Range of motion, gentle stretching, gentle resistive, aerobic

Dietary

Adequate fluid intake
Weight management
Well-balanced meals, *including protein*
Low sodium

Pressure Avoidance

Blood pressure cuff not to be applied to affected limb
No tight jewelry or clothing
No chronic shoulder pressure (purse, back pack)

found that participation in an upper-body exercise program caused no changes in arm circumference or arm volume in women with lymphedema after breast cancer, and they may even have experienced an increase in quality of life.[34]

Various dietary restrictions have been advocated, but few have been substantiated. One study suggests that lowering triglyceride levels has some beneficial effect.[35] Morbid obesity worsens lymphedema, and weight reduction enhances the effects of other measures for edema reduction. When offering "do's and don'ts," medical myths must be separated from evidence-based medical advice. Nutritional supplements may eventually be found to play a role, but these unregulated substances require rigorous investigational study before promotion.

Some observations (e.g., the potential lymphedema-inducing effect of airplane cabin pressure) also deserve further investigation.[36] A well-informed patient has the best chance of avoiding the development of lymphedema. Patient education materials are available through patient advocacy groups such as the National Lymphedema Network in the United States; other patient educational sites are available on the Internet.

■ PHARMACOLOGIC THERAPY

Pharmacologic enhancement of lymph transport has a limited role in the treatment of lymphedema. This can be frustrating to patients, who are often looking for a quick, effortless solution to the chronic problems associated with lymphedema.

Diuretics

Diuretics are included in the treatment programs of some authors[37] but not others.[38] Regular treatment with diuretics is usually not appropriate for patients with chronic lymphedema. Their effect is temporary, and secondary hemoconcentration is a serious side effect.[39] In some circumstances, however, short-term diuretic therapy may be helpful. In patients hospitalized for massive edema reduction (treated concurrently with strict bed rest, elevation of the extremity, and manual therapy techniques), the response to acute treatment can be maximized by administering high doses of furosemide. For women whose periodic exacerbations of edema correspond to the menstrual cycle, short-term use of oral diuretic therapy has been suggested but is discouraged by others.[40] Finally, patients in the terminal phase of a malignant disease who have painful swelling of the extremity may benefit from adjunctive diuretic therapy to alleviate symptoms.[41]

Benzopyrones

Benzopyrones are thought to decrease lymphedema by stimulating tissue macrophages, thus altering the macrophage-dependent balance between protein deposition and lysis.[42-44] As a result of increased macrophage activity, the intercellular protein concentration is reduced, which promotes tissue softening and remodeling. In a randomized, double-blind study, 31 patients with postmastectomy lymphedema of the arm and 21 patients with leg lymphedema received 400 mg 5,6-benzo-α-pyrone or placebo for 6 months.[44]

Limb measurements showed that the drug reduced the arm volumes from 46% to 26% above normal ($P < .001$) and the volume of the legs from 25% to 17% above normal ($P < .001$). The limb tissue softened, skin temperatures dropped, and the episodes of infection diminished. The authors concluded that 5,6-benzo-α-pyrone produced slow but safe reduction of lymphedema.

In a subsequent independent study, 140 women were followed after breast cancer treatment in a prospective randomized crossover study comparing the effects of a benzopyrone (coumarin) versus placebo.[45] The patients received coumarin, 400 mg daily, or placebo for 6 months followed by crossover treatment for 6 months. Measurements included calculated arm volumes (from serial circumference measures) and monthly patient self-report questionnaires. Ultimately, upper extremity volumes and patient reports showed no significant difference between benzopyrone and placebo. Increases in liver enzymes were reported in 6% of patients studied. Because of potential hepatotoxicity, coumarin has not been approved for use in the United States.

Another benzopyrone, without known hepatotoxicity, has received increased attention. A purified micronized flavonoid fraction (PMFF) has been shown to increase lymphatic transport.[46] In a randomized double-blind study, 48 patients with post-mastectomy upper extremity edema received placebo and 46 others received PMFF. Although several measurement parameters failed to show statistically significant differences, a subgroup of 24 patients with more severe lymphedema showed a statistically significant reduction in limb circumference.[46] This and other studies show how PMFF may be successful in reduction of edemas (including those associated with chronic venous insufficiency and lymphedema), but further investigations will be necessary to determine if this agent will, indeed, play a major role in lymphedema management.[47,48]

Intralymphatic corticosteroid injections have also been used in an attempt to decrease fibrotic occlusion in lymph nodes and improve lymphatic transport. In a pilot study of 20 patients with primary lymphedema, eight showed improvement for as long as 9 months after treatment.[49] The effectiveness of corticosteroid treatment, however, remains unproved. Investigators in Japan have attempted to treat secondary lymphedema by injecting autologous lymphocytes into the main artery of the affected limb, with five of seven patients showing short-term improvement.[50] These same authors have reported their results for a larger series that used a combined therapy approach including lymphocyte injection and compression therapy. Thirty-four of 46 patients experienced edema reduction.[51]

■ MECHANICAL REDUCTION OF LIMB SWELLING

Lymphedema can be staged into three grades (Table 168-4).[52,53] Clinically, it is easier to treat grade 1 lymphedema, which by definition exhibits no fibrosis. Efforts to control chronic lymphedema have focused on mechanical reduction techniques. Reducing the fluid volume and high protein concentration of the interstitium remains the primary goal of treatment.

Table 168-4	Clinical Staging of Chronic Lymphedema
Grade I	Early pitting prevalent that reduces with elevation No fibrotic skin thickening
Grade II	Skin thickened and fibrotic pitting only to deep prolonged pressure Often no pitting No reduction with elevation overnight
Grade III	Skin fibrotic and sclerotic in subcutaneous tissues Often secondary hyperkeratosis Verrucal development These changes are permanent

Any comprehensive lymphedema therapy approach should include standardized measures of limb size to gauge response to the treatment. Changes in limb size should be followed using objective measures, including (1) circumferential measurements obtained at predetermined levels and/or (2) volumetric assessments using water-displacement or computed volumetric techniques.[54] Newer methods using computed tomography,[55] MRI,[56] and bioelectrical impedance analysis[57] techniques have been reported; however, these techniques are not routinely used.

Edema reduction can be accomplished by a variety of techniques, which may be employed individually or in combinations to best fit a given patient's clinical situation and capability. Each area has been found to be successful in limb volume reduction in evidence-based review. The skilled clinician assesses the patient's medical and functional status, etiology of the edema, and available resources when developing a reduction plan.

Elevation

Elevation is the simplest way to reduce lymphedema.[38] The patient is positioned comfortably, and the limb is elevated as tolerated, usually to 45 degrees or more. A variety of arm boards and lymphedema slings[25] (Fig. 168-1) have been developed for this purpose. With continuous bed rest,

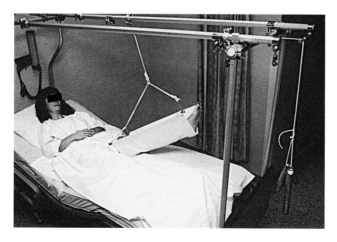

FIGURE 168-1 The lymphedema sling is used to elevate the patient's leg during bed rest, typically to 45 degrees or more.

gravity usually produces maximal reduction within 2 to 5 days. This method of acute treatment of lymphedema has been used for decades and is still used for early reversible or refractory cases with combined therapy (Fig. 168-2). If hospitalization is utilized for strict elevation and combined therapy, an appropriate compression system must be provided for maintenance before the patient is discharged; otherwise, reduction volumes will be lost. Today, inpatient treatment is rarely an option, and patients often find elevation therapy outside the hospital impractical and ineffective. The authors' outpatient limb reduction program still incorporates overnight and regular daily periods of limb elevation. O'Donnell and Howrigan[39] have suggested that 4- to 6-inch blocks be placed under the legs of the bed to provide adequate overnight elevation for patients with lower extremity edema. In our practice, we often use a foam wedge for limb elevation (Fig. 168-3) when elevation is the major component of a particular patient's program.

Complex Decongestive Therapy (CDT)

A comprehensive program of elevation, therapeutic exercise, manual massage techniques, and compression wraps has been advocated for decades.[32] In recent years, a combined approach based on the complex program popularized in Europe by Földi and coworkers,[38] Vodder,[58] Casley-Smiths in Australia,[40] and Leduc[34] has evolved and become the standard of care for the patient with recalcitrant lymphedema. The success of these treatments is well-documented worldwide, including in the United States.[59-65] The usual program involves four discrete components with two phases (Table 168-5); and, although very successful, it is a resource-intensive treatment that requires a large investment of therapist and patient time. Therapists must be specially trained to perform standardized techniques of manual lymph drainage and complex multilayered wrapping, and relatively few recognized training programs are available. Thus, this treatment is currently offered only in specialized practices. In the United States, there is a voluntary certification process, which involves documentation of training, treatment hours, and a certifying examination assuring competence.[66]

Manual Lymph Drainage

Manual lymph drainage is a specialized technique that employs gentle skin distention to stimulate contractility of lymph collecting vessels and enhance fluid and protein transport. The massage technique is light and superficial (in contrast to deeper decongestive massage). Stagnant lymph fluid is moved via superficial lymphatics from a lymphatic drainage area that is obstructed to a different, usually more proximal region of the body with better lymphatic drainage. The gentle massage also loosens subcutaneous fibrosis. Manual lymph drainage is performed in steps. The trunk is divided into quadrants, and treatment is initiated by massaging the quadrant *contralateral* to the affected limb. The massage stimulates lymph flow and helps drain cutaneous lymph from the normal skin, preparing it to receive lymph fluid from the adjacent, involved area. Massage is subsequently performed over the trunk adjacent to the affected limb. Some fluid may drain directly into the

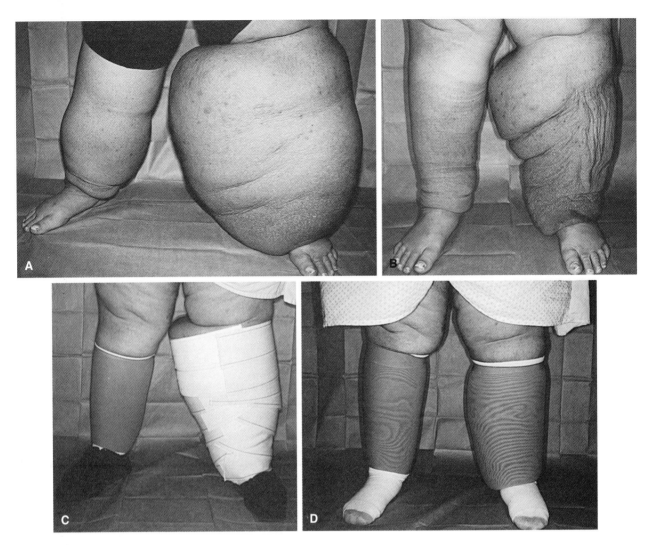

FIGURE 168-2 Severe primary lymphedema of the lower extremities in a 36-year-old man. **A,** Appearance of limbs on presentation. **B,** Appearance after 2 weeks of continuous leg elevation, elastic wrapping, and pneumatic compression treatment. Much of the residual deformity distal to the knee is fatty deposition. **C,** The legs after application of bilateral custom-made elastic stockings and a nonelastic wrapping to reinforce the stocking on the left. **D,** The legs 1 month after initiation of therapy.

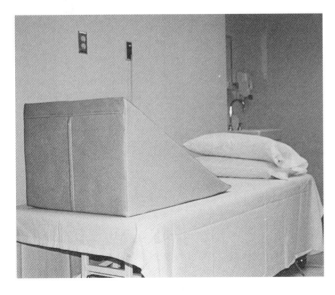

FIGURE 168-3 A lymph wedge can be used at several angles and provides a portable, firm support for elevation.

Table 168-5	Decongestive Lymphatic Therapy

Intensive Therapy (Phase I)

Manual lymph drainage massage
Multilayered low-stretch wrapping
Exercise techniques
Skin care and elevation principles

Maintenance Therapy (Phase II)

Daily wear of pressure garment
Nightly wrapping
Self-massage
Exercise and skin care

veins or deep lymphatics, and some of it may cross through the superficial anastomotic lymph vessels into the freshly drained contralateral quadrant. The therapist repeats the process in stages along the length of the limb, moving slowly from proximal-to-distal, but massaging each small segment in a distal-to-proximal direction (Figs. 168-4 and 168-5). Practiced in this fashion, manual lymph drainage has been shown to redirect lymph and interstitial protein toward functioning lymphatic territories.[67] There are several areas of the body including face, neck, shoulders, and some truncal areas where compression is difficult to maintain; manual lymph drainage techniques assume additional importance when these regions are affected.

Exercise

Exercise regimens are an integral part of any lymphedema management program, although they are often understressed and undervalued by patient and practitioner alike. Exercise is often considered only in the aerobic context, but special exercise interventions may be equally as useful.[68] Simple range of motion exercise with gentle stretches will encourage full use of muscles, retard tissue fibrosis, and decrease the risk of contracture and stasis. Within the CDT program, a group of very specific muscle "remedial exercises" can assist with lymph transport. Muscles are contracted and relaxed in specific sequences depending on the location and nature of the fluid; the pattern purposefully maximizes the sequential compression of lymph vessels.[34] The best effects occur when the patient maintains external compression over the lymphatic congested area. Aerobic exercise, also used with external compression, stimulates central lymphatic absorption, creating a passive gradient enhancing distal lymphatic flow. Regardless of the type of exercise program employed, it must not be neglected as part of the management program. Patient compliance and understanding must be demonstrated before dismissal to a home program.

■ COMPRESSION TECHNIQUES

Compression Wrapping

Elastic wrapping is one of several available compression techniques and is an integral component of CDT. The wrapping techniques are quite complex and favor the use of low-stretch wrap instead of the more traditional high-stretch

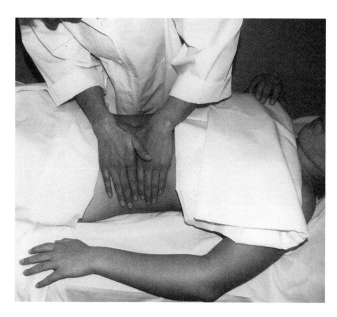

FIGURE 168-4 Massage of the trunk involves light movements initiated in the truncal area to stimulate and open proximal lymph channels.

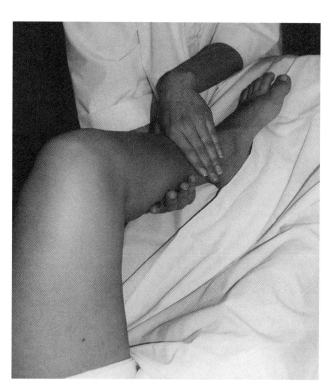

FIGURE 168-5 Manual lymph drainage of the limb is performed with sequential distal-to-proximal hand movements over short segments, beginning with the proximal portion of the limb.

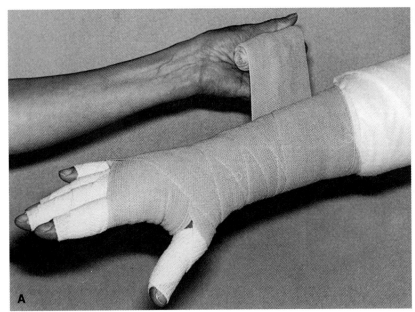
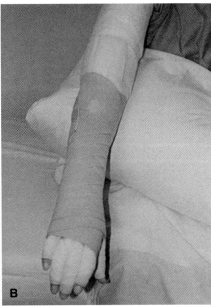

FIGURE 168-6 **A** and **B**, The multilayered wrap technique allows maximal pressures without causing patient discomfort.

elastic bandages (Fig. 168-6). High-stretch wraps provide high pressures when the limb is still (high resting pressure) but yield when the limb moves. This reduces their ability to raise total tissue pressure during exercise, which reduces the hydrostatic pressure gradient, which thereby decreases stimulation of lymphatic flow. In contrast, the low stretch wrap is comfortable at rest (low resting pressure), but with movement it provides unyielding resistance that augments the pressure created by the muscle pump action and creates an increase in the pressure gradient that stimulates increased flow. Frequently, foam padding is used to further enhance the pressure provided with the low-stretch wrap techniques (Fig. 168-7). During the active, intensive treatment of CDT, the low-stretch wraps are worn 24 hours a day (except when the patient is receiving massage or bathing). In the maintenance phase, a compression garment is worn during the day while the wraps continue to be worn at night.

CDT, including manual lymph drainage, an exercise regimen, complex multilayer low-stretch wrapping, and skin care, comprises the four components of a successful lymphedema management program. At our institution we have experienced remarkable success not only with moderately affected limbs but also specifically with advanced, refractory lymphedema. Although CDT has become the standard of care for most treatment centers,[53,64] this aggressive approach is not appropriate for every patient. There can be extenuating factors, such as co-morbidity, focal tumor recurrence, impaired cognitive status, and poor social supports that may preclude the use of the program, which requires long-term patient self-management at home. The multi-week intensive treatment approach is also affected by limited insurance/coverage in the United States, and modified programs often need to be considered.

Compression Pumping

An alternative, and more traditional, compression method for achieving limb reduction uses intermittent pneumatic compression. Pneumatic pumping has, for decades, been the main physical therapeutic intervention in the United States (Fig. 168-8). The affected limb is placed in a compartmentalized sleeve, which is alternately inflated and deflated. The pressure gradient thus created forces lymph fluid

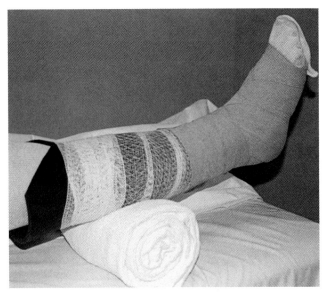

FIGURE 168-7 Complex wrapping of the leg with foam. The use of foam pads allows for extra pressure to help contour focal, hardened areas.

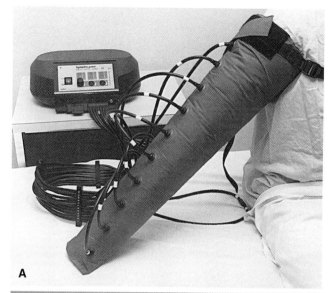

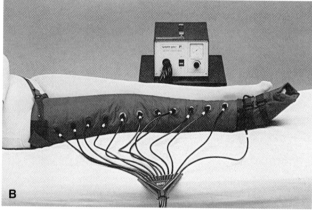

FIGURE 168-8 Sequential pneumatic pump used for intermittent compression treatment of upper (**A**) or lower (**B**) extremity lymphedema. (**A** and **B**, Courtesy of Camp International, Inc., Jackson, MI.)

proximally. Mean percentage volume change was +0.4% in the first group, +7.3% in the second, and −31.6% in the third. The authors concluded that multicompartment sequential compression achieves the best reduction of limb volume after a single treatment for chronic lymphedema. In another study of the use of adjunctive intermittent compression plus a combined decongestive therapy program, enhanced volume reduction was also substantiated in the group using the added intermittent compression.[81] Intermittent pneumatic compression devices are marketed with different chamber options, complexity of use, and costs.[68]

Although pneumatic compression therapy appears in some studies to be helpful in the management of lymphedema, there is other evidence of limited utility.[78] Which type of compression may be best is still in question, as is which pressures are most useful.[82] Controversy persists about whether pneumatic compression or complex decongestive therapy involving compression bandaging and manual lymph drainage massage is the better first-line treatment. A randomized study compared manual lymph drainage (Vodder) massage techniques with a sequential pneumatic compression pump (40 to 60 mm Hg). Patients were followed for a relatively short time (2 weeks). At the end of treatment, both methods had decreased arm volume; the difference was not statistically significant.[83] Ultimately, the appropriate treatment regimen, whether complex decongestive therapy or intermittent pneumatic compression, needs to fit the needs of the patient to maximize compliance. If the patient is motivated and compliant, any treatment has a better chance of success. Clearly, the pneumatic compression devices currently available have been found only to reduce limb circumference; these devices do not move fluid through the trunk. There are, however, new devices being marketed that include the full trunk as well as limb and are adapting pressure sequences similar to the manual lymph drainage patterns. However, no efficacy studies have yet been reported. These and other issues clearly need to be studied in an organized fashion.

through the affected limb toward the trunk. These devices, although shown to be effective, are quite diverse and may utilize either a single uniform-pressure sleeve or a sleeve built with a series of overlapping chambers within that can be inflated sequentially in a distal-to-proximal direction.[69-78] A theoretical disadvantage of the single-chamber device is that high pressure is exerted both proximally and distally that can potentially force fluid further distal in the extremity. There is also concern that the actual pressures achieved at the cuff-skin interface are too high[79] and that this can be important with lower intensity sleeves with which an increase in genital edema has been reported after the use of compression pumps.[80]

Bergan[77] randomized 35 patients with lymphedema to a 2-hour long treatment session with one of three types of compression pumps: (1) a unicompartmental pump using 50 mm Hg pressure, (2) a three-compartment pump with segmental pressures of 50 mm Hg in each cell, or (3) a multicompartmental gradient pressure pump with 10 cells ranging in pressures from 80 mm Hg distally to 30 mm Hg

Compression Garments

The pressure garment is the major component for maintenance programs in any lymphedema management program. Although intermittent outpatient therapy with manual lymphatic drainage, wrapping, pneumatic compression, elevation, or any other reduction method can help to reduce the size of the swollen limb, external support—elastic or nonelastic—is necessary to maintain the reduction.

Strict daily use of properly fitting, appropriately graduated elastic compression garments remains the key to maintaining limb size for most patients.[84] Support garments come in a variety of sizes, compression strengths, and materials, and the combination of these features must be tailored to the needs and dimensions of the individual.[85] Although many swollen limbs can be fitted with over-the-counter prefabricated garments, those with significant swelling or an unusual shape may need custom-made stockings to obtain the best fit. It is better to use a mechanical aid to don the stocking (rubber gloves, metal frame) than to sacrifice needed pressure.

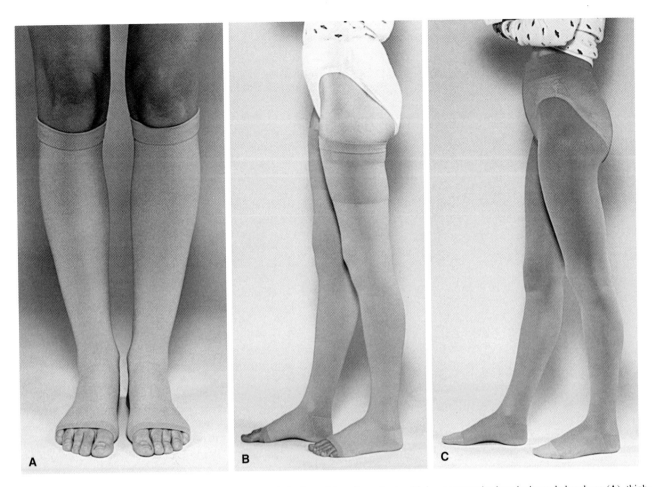

FIGURE 168-9 Different types of high-compression graduated elastic stockings for patients with lower extremity lymphedema: below-knee (**A**), thigh-high (**B**), and pantyhose lengths (**C**).

Garments are classified according to the amount of compression they deliver distally, and the compression they produce may be "graduated" or "nongraduated." Graduated garments are made to provide the greatest compression in the distal portion of the limb, with progressively less pressure approaching the trunk. Over-the-counter "support stockings" usually provide 7 to 15 mm Hg of compression and are usually not graduated. Antiembolism stockings (e.g., TED hose) provide 15 to 20 mm Hg of compression and tend to be graduated. Therapeutic lower extremity elastic stockings designed for chronic venous insufficiency or lymphedema come in a variety of compression strengths (20-30, 30-40, 40-50, and 50-60 mm Hg) and lengths. Lower limbs with chronic lymphedema generally require 40 to 50 mm Hg of compression at the ankle to control the swelling; however, for patients with co-morbidities such as diabetes mellitus, arterial occlusive disease, arthritis, or other issues that may limit the use of high-compression garments, stockings with pressures of 30 to 40 mm Hg may be tried. Low-compression (<30 mm Hg) or nongraduated stockings usually provide little, if any, control of recalcitrant chronic lymphedema. Upper extremity garments are typically fitted with the 20- to 30-mm Hg pressure.

Stocking length is frequently an issue for patients with lymphedema (Fig. 168-9). As a rule, stockings should be long enough to cover the edematous portion of the limb, but patient preference and physical limitations must be taken into account. In general, knee-high compression garments with removable proximal pressure support (biking shorts, sport leotards) are better tolerated than full-length garments, which are difficult to don. Patient input and a wide range of options are key to good patient compliance.

Stockings come in a variety of knits and materials; most are composed of some combination of latex, spandex, nylon, cotton, and silk. Differences in construction, sizing, and materials can significantly affect the "feel" and function of various brands and styles for a given patient. Unfortunately, predicting which patient will do best with a particular stocking is almost impossible. For this reason, a patient may need to try a variety of brands and styles to find the one that works optimally. Although custom-fit garments are indicated in some patients, there is an increasing array of options in materials, colors, and sizes among the prefabricated garments. With repeated washing all brands exhibit fatigue, thus garments should be replaced several times each year. Insurance coverage for garments and replacements is highly variable and may severely limit patient options.

Nonelastic Compression

Although nonelastic support devices were once widely used to control limb swelling, they have been largely replaced by

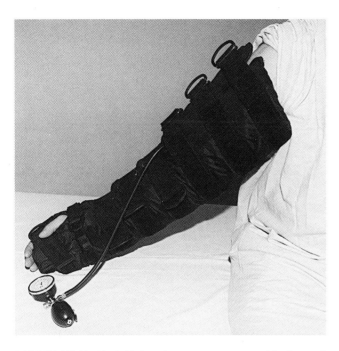

FIGURE 168-10   The Reid sleeve is easy to put on yet provides "custom" low-stretch resistance.

modern elastic stockings. Commercial devices employing the principle of nonelastic support have been reintroduced for the control of lymphedema and are being received with patient enthusiasm. The Circ Aid (Shaw Therapeutics, Rumson, NJ) uses Velcro fastenings to readjust a series of nonelastic support bands around the leg and ankle. Whether this approach is superior, or comparable, to conventional elastic support hose remains to be determined. As adjuncts to a compression garment, nonelastic supports have been worn over the garment, especially during periods of exercise or prolonged dependency.

Another form of nonelastic support, the Reid sleeve, which has multiple air cell chambers custom-inflated but then left static and applied to the limb (with wide Velcro bands), has been reported to help to control edema.[66] We find it very helpful to patients who are unable by themselves to manage a program of complex wrapping (Fig. 168-10).

Heat

Heat therapy as a means of reducing lymphedema has been practiced in the Orient and elsewhere for centuries. Heating the limb presumably mobilizes fluid and softens the tissues; tight wrappings are applied between treatments to reduce and maintain the limb's size. In a study from China of 1045 patients with lymphedema, 68% achieved an effective reduction in the volume of the extremity with heat therapy. Subsequent decreases in the frequency of lymphangitis episodes were also reported.[59] Traditional methods have used ovens heated to 80° to 90° C, but newer methods involving microwave heating have been reported to be successful.[60-62] No controlled comparative study is available, however, to prove the effectiveness of this treatment.

A study of low-level laser therapy with 2-year follow-up reports effective control of "post-radical mastectomy edema" in 7 of 10 patients,[63] although the mechanism whereby volume is reduced remains obscure.

■ OTHER TREATMENT CONSIDERATIONS

Psychological and Functional Impairment and Economic Issues

The psychological and functional impairments of lymphedema should not be underestimated. Smeltzer and associates[1] examined the psychologic impact of lymphedema. Their findings suggest that related emotional problems are not uncommon and are often neglected by physicians. The need to address the psychological aspects of long-term disfigurement, especially in adolescents, cannot be overemphasized. Also discussed in this study is the functional impact of lymphedema on lifestyle. Twelve percent of patients reported that they were limited to desk jobs or ones that allowed frequent sitting. Employees' impressions that job promotion was withheld because of the edema have also been reported. Some patients limit their participation in exercise or sports because of an uncomfortable or heavy sensation in the affected limb.

Some insurance companies deem the edema to be only a cosmetic problem and deny payment for both treatment and garments. This frustrating misperception often necessitates repeated communications between insurance companies and physicians to justify well-deserved treatment for the patient.

Lymphedema-Associated Malignancy

Late-onset malignancies are potentially devastating, and fortunately rare, complications of long-standing lymphedema. In most series, they develop in no more than 1% of patients with lymphedema.[1,86] The most common ones are angiosarcomas[87] and lymphangiosarcomas,[2,88] which are thought to represent, respectively, neoplastic transformations of blood vessels and of lymphatics.

Histologically and clinically, it is difficult to distinguish these two sarcomas from one another. The association between angiosarcoma (or lymphangiosarcoma) and lymphedema is commonly called the *Stewart-Treves syndrome*.[69] Sarcomas can develop in patients with long-standing lymphedema of any cause—primary lymphedema[71] or lymphedema secondary to filariasis,[89] hysterectomy,[90] trauma,[90] or mastectomy.[91] Other malignancies, including Hodgkin's and non-Hodgkin's lymphoma,[92] Kaposi's sarcoma,[93] squamous cell carcinoma,[94,95] and malignant melanoma,[96] have been reported in association with chronic lymphedema. Limbs with edema must therefore be inspected frequently to permit early detection and appropriate treatment of tumors.

■ SUMMARY

Conservative, nonsurgical management continues to be the mainstay of treatment for lymphedema. Preventive measures include immediate medical treatment for bacterial infections affecting the limbs or for parasitic infections known to cause filariasis. Efforts to minimize other risk factors should also be employed. Early patient education is also important. No effective drug therapy to decrease chronic lymphedema is now available in the United States. Long-term use of diuretics has not been clinically shown to be helpful. Mechanical reduction of lymphedema can best be achieved with a program of complex decongestive therapy (including manual lymphatic drainage) or intermittent pneumatic compression. If intermittent compression is used, patients generally prefer sequential pneumatic cells, and they are probably more useful than the single-chamber compression pump. Maintaining the volume reduction is an integral part of any program and can be achieved in most patients with regular use of high-compression elastic garment and/or continued wrapping (using low-stretch elastic bandages).

The psychological aspects of the disease should be recognized and addressed to help patients cope with their functional impairment and cosmetic deformity. Regular medical follow-up is necessary to ensure compliance and to recognize immediately any malignant disease of late onset.

■ REFERENCES

1. Woods M, Tobin M, Mortimer P: The psychosocial morbidity of breast cancer patients with lymphoedema. Cancer Nurs 18:467-471, 1995.
2. Witte MH, Bernas MJ, Martin CP, Witte CL: Lymphangiogenesis and lymphangiodysplasia: From molecular to clinical lymphology. Microsc Res Tech 55:122-145, 2001.
3. Karkkainen MJ, Jussila L, Ferrell RE, et al: Molecular regulation of lymphangiogenesis and targets for tissue oedema. Trends Mol Med 7:18-22, 2001.
4. Smeltzer DM, Stickler GB, Schirger A: Primary lymphedema in children and adolescents: A follow-up study and review. Pediatrics 76:206-218, 1985.
5. Mirolo BR, Bunce IH, Chapman M, et al: Psychosocial benefits of postmastectomy lymphedema therapy. Cancer Nurs 18:197-205, 1995.
6. Ferrell RE, Levinson KL, Esman JH, et al: Hereditary lymphedema: Evidence for linkage and genetic heterogeneity. Hum Mol Genet 7:2073-2078, 1998.
7. Witte MH, Erickson R, Bernas M, et al: Phenotypic and genotypic heterogeneity in familial Milroy lymphedema. Lymphology 31:145-155, 1998.
8. Hoerauf A: Control of filarial infections: Not the beginning of the end, but more research is needed. Curr Opin Infect Dis 16:403-410, 2003.
9. Bockarie MJ, Tisch DJ, Kastens W, et al: Mass treatment to eliminate filariasis in Papua New Guinea. N Engl J Med 347:1841-1848, 2002.
10. Das PK, Ramaiah KD, Augustin DJ, Kumar A: Towards elimination of lymphatic filariasis in India. Trends Parasitol 17:457-460, 2001.
11. Ottesen EA, Duke BO, Karam M, Behbehani K: Strategies and tools for the control/elimination of lymphatic filariasis. Bull WHO 75:491-503, 1997.
12. Meyrowitsch DW, Simonsen PE: Long-term effect of mass diethyl-carbamazine chemotherapy on bancroftian filariasis, results at four years after start of treatment. Trans R Soc Trop Med Hyg 92:98-103, 1998.
13. Ismail MM, Jayakody RL, Weil GJ, et al: Efficacy of single dose combinations of albendazole, ivermectin and diethylcarbamazine for the treatment of bancroftian filariasis. Trans R Soc Trop Med Hyg 92:94-97, 1998.
14. Lammie PJ, Cuenco KT, Punkosdy GA: The pathogenesis of filarial lymphedema: Is it the worm or is it the host? Ann NY Acad Sci 979:131-142; discussion, 188-196, 2002.
15. Vaqas B, Ryan TJ: Lymphoedema: Pathophysiology and management in resource-poor settings—relevance for lymphatic filariasis control programmes. Filaria J 2:4, 2003.
16. Semel JD, Goldin H: Association of athlete's foot with cellulitis of the lower extremities: Diagnostic value of bacterial cultures of ipsilateral interdigital space samples. Clin Infect Dis 23:1162-1164, 1996.
17. Babb RR, Spittell JA Jr, Martin WJ, Schirger A: Prophylaxis of recurrent lymphangitis complicating lymphedema. JAMA 195:871-873, 1966.
18. Baddour LM: Cellulitis syndromes: An update. Int J Antimicrob Agents 14:113-116, 2000.
19. Wang JH, Liu YC, Cheng DL, et al: Role of benzathine penicillin G in prophylaxis for recurrent streptococcal cellulitis of the lower legs. Clin Infect Dis 25:685-689, 1997.
20. Wrone DA, Tanabe KK, Cosimi AB, et al: Lymphedema after sentinel lymph node biopsy for cutaneous melanoma: A report of 5 cases. Arch Dermatol 136:511-514, 2000.
21. Sener SF, Winchester DJ, Martz CH, et al: Lymphedema after sentinel lymphadenectomy for breast carcinoma. Cancer 92:748-752, 2001.
22. Kissin MW, Querci della Rovere G, Easton D, Westbury G: Risk of lymphoedema following the treatment of breast cancer. Br J Surg 73:580-584, 1986.
23. Markby R, Baldwin E, Kerr P: Incidence of lymphoedema in women with breast cancer. Prof Nurse 6:502-508, 1991.
24. Schunemann H, Willich N: [Secondary lymphedema of the arm following primary therapy of breast carcinoma] [in German]. Zentralbl Chir 117:220-225, 1992.
25. Giuliano AE, Kirgan DM, Guenther JM, Morton DL: Lymphatic mapping and sentinel lymphadenectomy for breast cancer. Ann Surg 220:391-398; discussion, 398-401, 1994.
26. Giuliano AE, Jones RC, Brennan M, Statman R: Sentinel lympha-denectomy in breast cancer. J Clin Oncol 15:2345-2350, 1997.
27. Albertini JJ, Lyman GH, Cox C, et al: Lymphatic mapping and sentinel node biopsy in the patient with breast cancer. JAMA 276:1818-1822, 1996.
28. Veronesi U, Paganelli G, Galimberti V, et al: Sentinel-node biopsy to avoid axillary dissection in breast cancer with clinically negative lymph-nodes. Lancet 349:1864-1867, 1997.
29. Werner RS, McCormick B, Petrek J, et al: Arm edema in conser-vatively managed breast cancer: Obesity is a major predictive factor. Radiology 180:177-184, 1991.
30. Herd-Smith A, Russo A, Muraca MG, et al: Prognostic factors for lymphedema after primary treatment of breast carcinoma. Cancer 92:1783-1787, 2001.
31. Petrek JA, Senie RT, Peters M, Rosen PP: Lymphedema in a cohort of breast carcinoma survivors 20 years after diagnosis. Cancer 92:1368-1377, 2001.
32. Stillwell GK Redford JW: Physical treatment of postmastectomy lymphedema. Mayo Clin Proc 33:1-8, 1958.
33. Thiadens SRJ, Cooke JP: Current Management of Hypertensive and Vascular Diseases. St Louis, Mosby–Year Book, 1992, pp 314-319.
34. LeDuc PA, Bomgeois P: Bandages: Scintigraphic Demonstration of its Efficacy on Colloidal Protein Reabsorption During Muscular Activity. Amsterdam, 1990, pp 421-422.
35. Soria P, Cuesta A, Romero H, et al: Dietary treatment of lymphedema by restriction of long-chain triglycerides. Angiology 45:703-707, 1994.
36. Casley-Smith JR, Casley-Smith JR: Lymphedema initiated by aircraft flights. Aviat Space Environ Med 67:52-56, 1996.
37. Schirger A: Lymphedema. Cardiovasc Clin 13:293-305, 1983.
38. Foldi E, Foldi M, Weissleder H: Conservative treatment of lympho-edema of the limbs. Angiology 36:171-180, 1985.
39. Tiedjen KV: The Lymphostatic Edema? The Therapeutic Effect of Diuretic Treatment Compared with Physiological and Physical Methods in an Isotope Study. Paper presented at the 13th World Congress of the International Union of Angiology. Rochester, MN, 1983.
40. Foldi M, Foldi E, Kubik S: Textbook of Lymphology for Physicians and Lymphedema Therapists. San Francisco: Urban & Fischer, 2003, pp 423-432.

41. Mortimer PS: Therapy approaches for lymphedema. Angiology 48:87-91, 1997.

42. Casley-Smith JR: The pathophysiology of lymphedema and the action of benzopyrones in reducing it. Lymphology 21:190-194, 1988.

43. Piller NB: Macrophage and tissue changes in the developmental phases of secondary lymphoedema and during conservative therapy with benzopyrone. Arch Histol Cytol 53:209-218, 1990.

44. Casley-Smith JR, Morgan RG, Piller NB: Treatment of lymphedema of the arms and legs with 5,6-benzo-[alpha]-pyrone. N Engl J Med 329:1158-1163, 1993.

45. Loprinzi CL, Kugler JW, Sloan JA, et al: Lack of effect of coumarin in women with lymphedema after treatment for breast cancer. N Engl J Med 340:346-350, 1999.

46. Pecking AP, Fevrier B, Wargon C, Pillion G: Efficacy of Daflon 500 mg in the treatment of lymphedema (secondary to conventional therapy of breast cancer). Angiology 48:93-98, 1997.

47. Olszewski W: Clinical efficacy of micronized purified flavonoid fraction (MPFF) in edema. Angiology 51:25-29, 2000.

48. Das L. Subramanyam Reddy G, Pani S: Some observations on the effect of Daflon (micronized purified flavonoid fraction of *Rutaceae Aurantiae*) in Bancroftian filarial lymphoedema. Filaria J 2:5, 2003.

49. Fyfe NC, Rutt DL, Edwards JM, Kinmonth JB: Intralymphatic steroid therapy for lymphoedema: preliminary studies. Lymphology 15:23-28, 1992.

50. Katoh I, Harada K, Tsuda Y, et al: Intraarterial lymphocytes injection for treatment of lymphedema. Jpn J Surg 14:331-334, 1984.

51. Ogawa Y, Yoshizumi M, Kitagawa T, et al: Investigation of the mechanism of lymphocyte injection therapy in treatment of lymphedema with special emphasis on cell adhesion molecule (L-sectin). Lymphology 32:151-156, 1999.

52. Kocak Z, Overgaard J: Risk factors for arm lymphedema in breast cancer patients. Acta Oncol 39:389-392, 2000.

53. Consensus Document of the International Society of Lymphology: The diagnosis and treatment of peripheral lymphedema. Lymphology 84-91, 2003.

54. Casley-Smith JR: Measuring and representing peripheral edema and its alterations. Lymphology 27:56-70, 1994.

55. Collins CD, Mortimer PS, D'Ettorre H, et al: Computed tomography in the assessment of response to limb compression in unilateral lymphoedema. Clin Radiol 50:541-544, 1995.

56. Duewell S, Hagspiel KD, Zuber J, et al: Swollen lower extremities: Role of MR imaging. Radiology 184:227-231, 1992.

57. Cornish BH, Bunce IH, Ward LC, et al: Bioelectrical impedance for monitoring the efficacy of lymphoedema treatment programmes. Breast Cancer Res Treat 38:169-176, 1996.

58. Kasseroller RG: The Vodder School: The Vodder Method. Cancer 1998;83:2840-2842.

59. Boris M, Weindorf S, Lasinski B, Boris G: Lymphedema reduction by noninvasive complex lymphedema therapy. Oncology (Huntington) 8:95-106; discussion 109-110, 114.

60. Boris M, Weindorf S, Lasinkski S: Persistence of lymphedema reduction after noninvasive complex lymphedema therapy. Oncology (Huntington) 11:99-109; discussion, 110, 1997.

61. Ko DS, Lerner R, Klose G, Cosimi AB: Effective treatment of lymphedema of the extremities. Arch Surgery 133:452-458, 1998.

62. Daane S, Poltoratszy P, Rockwell WB: Postmastectomy lymphedema management: Evolution of the complex decongestive therapy technique. Ann Plast Surg 40:128-134, 1998.

63. Murthy G, Ballard RE, Breit GA, et al: Intramuscular pressures beneath elastic and inelastic leggings. Ann Vasc Surg 8:543-548, 1994.

64. Witte MH, Witte CL, Bernas M: ISL Consensus Document revisited: Suggested modifications (summarized from discussions at the 16th ICL, Madrid, Spain, September 1997 and the Interim ISL Executive Committee meeting). Lymphology 31:138-140, 1998.

65. Szuba A, Cooke JP, Yousuf S, Rockson S: Decongestive lymphatic therapy for patients with cancer-related or primary lymphedema. Am J Med 109:296-300, 2000.

66. Lymphology Association of North America (LANA) Certified Lymphedema Therapist. http://www.clt-lana.org/main.html: Lymphology Association of North American (LANA), 2003.

67. Williams AF, Vadgama A, Franks PJ, Mortimer PS: A randomized controlled crossover study of manual lymphatic drainage therapy in women with breast cancer-related lymphoedema. Eur J Cancer Care 11:254-261, 2002.

68. Cheville AL, McGarvey CL, Petrek JA, et al: Lymphedema management. Semin Radiat Oncol 13:290-301, 2003.

69. Thiadens SRJ: Advances in the Management of Lymphedema. St. Louis, Quality Medical Publishing, 1990, pp 125-141.

70. Zelikovski A, Deutsch A, Reiss R: The sequential pneumatic compression device in surgery for lymphedema of the limbs. J Cardiovasc Surg (Torino) 24:122-126, 1983.

71. Richmand DM, O'Donnell TF Jr, Zelikovski A: Sequential pneumatic compression for lymphedema: A controlled trial. Arch Surg 120:1116-1119, 1985.

72. Zanolla R, Monzeglio C, Balzarini A, Martino G: Evaluation of the results of three different methods of postmastectomy lymphedema treatment. J Surg Oncol 26:210-213, 1984.

73. Zelikovski A, Haddad M, Reiss R: The "Lympha-Press" intermittent sequential pneumatic device for the treatment of lymphoedema: Five years of clinical experience. J Cardiovasc Surg (Torino) 27:288-290, 1986.

74. Pappas CJ, O'Donnell TF Jr: Long-term results of compression treatment for lymphedema. J Vasc Surg 16:555-562; discussion 16: 562-564, 1992.

75. Klein MJ, Alexander MA, Wright JM, et al: Treatment of adult lower extremity lymphedema with the Wright linear pump: Statistical analysis of a clinical trial. Arch Phys Med Rehabil 69:202-206, 1988.

76. McLeod A, Hale J, et al: A clinical report on the use of the three external pneumatic compression devices in the management of lymphedema in a pediatric population. Physiother Can 43:28, 1991.

77. Bergan JJ, Angle N: Lymphedema: A comparison of compression pumps in the treatment of lymphedema. Vasc Surg 32:455-462, 1998.

78. Dini D, Del Mastro L, Gozza A, et al: The role of pneumatic compression in the treatment of postmastectomy lymphedema: A randomized phase III study. Ann Oncol 9:187-190, 1998.

79. Segers P, Belgrado JP, Leduc A, Leduc O, Verdonck P: Excessive pressure in multichambered cuffs used for sequential compression therapy. Phys Ther 82:1000-1008, 2002.

80. Boris M, Weindorf S, Lasinski BB: The risk of genital edema after external pump compression for lower limb lymphedema. Lymphology 31:15-20, 1998.

81. Szuba A, Achalu R, Rockson SG: Decongestive lymphatic therapy for patients with breast carcinoma-associated lymphedema: A randomized, prospective study of a role for adjunctive intermittent pneumatic compression. Cancer 95:2260-2267, 2002.

82. Palmer A, Macchiaverna J, Braun A, et al: Compression therapy of limb edema using hydrostatic pressure of mercury. Angiology 42:533, 1991.

83. Johansson K, Lie E, Ekdahl C, Lindfeldt J: A randomized study comparing manual lymph drainage with sequential pneumatic compression for treatment of postoperative arm lymphedema. Lymphology 31:56-64, 1998.

84. Pierson S, Pierson D, Swallow R, Johnson G Jr: Efficacy of graded elastic compression in the lower leg. JAMA 249:242-243, 1983.

85. Johnson G Jr: Venous Disorders. Philadelphia, WB Saunders, 1991, pp 372-378.

86. Servelle M: Surgical treatment of lymphedema: A report on 652 cases. Surgery 101:485-495, 1987.

87. Schmitz-Rixen T, Horsch S, Arnold G, Peters PE: Angiosarcoma in primary lymphedema of the lower extremity—Stewart-Treves syndrome. Lymphology 17:50-53, 1984.

88. Lymphedema. Clin Podiatr 1:363, 1984.

89. Muller R, Hajdu S, Brennan MF: Lymphangiosarcoma associated with chronic filarial lymphedema. Cancer 59:179-183, 1987.

90. Alessi E, Sala F, Berti E: Angiosarcomas in lymphedematous limbs. Am J Dermatopathol 8:371-378, 1986.

91. Benda JA, Al-Jurf AS, Benson AB 3rd: Angiosarcoma of the breast following segmental mastectomy complicated by lymphedema. Am J Clin Pathol 87:651-655, 1987.

92. Tatnall FM, Mann BS: Non-Hodgkin's lymphoma of the skin associated with chronic limb lymphoedema. Br J Dermatol 113:751-756, 1985.

93. Ruocco V, Astarita C, Guerrera V, et al: Kaposi's sarcoma on a lymphedematous immunocompromised limb. Int J Dermatol 23:56-60, 1984.

94. Shelley WB, Wood MG: Transformation of the common wart into squamous cell carcinoma in a patient with primary lymphedema. Cancer 48:820-824, 1981.

95. Epstein JI, Mendelsohn G: Squamous carcinoma of the foot arising in association with long-standing verrucous hyperplasia in a patient with congenital lymphedema. Cancer 54:943-947, 1984.

96. Bartal AH, Pinsky CM: Malignant melanoma appearing in a post-mastectomy lymphedematous arm: A novel association of double primary tumors. J Surg Oncol 30:16-18, 1985.

Chapter

169

Surgical Treatment of Chronic Lymphedema and Primary Chylous Disorders

PETER GLOVICZKI, MD

AUDRA NOEL, MD

Treatment of lymphedema is difficult and challenging. Nonoperative management has become the mainstay of treatment around the world, and progress in physical therapy using different forms of a complete decongestive therapy program, popularized by Földi,[1] has largely replaced surgical management of these patients. A comprehensive program consisting of limb elevation, therapeutic exercise, manual massage techniques, and compression wraps constitute the primary treatment of this debilitating disease, and they are discussed in detail in Chapter 168. In this chapter our focus is on indications, techniques, and results of surgical treatment of chronic lymphedema, and we also discuss management of primary chylous disorders such as lymphangiectasia associated with chylous reflux, chyloperitoneum, and chylothorax.

■ SURGICAL TREATMENT OF LYMPHEDEMA

The goal of surgical treatment of chronic lymphedema is to reduce limb size, improve function, decrease the frequency of infections, and improve the quality of life of the patient.[2,3] An absolute indication for surgery is malignant transformation of chronic lymphedema (Stewart-Treves syndrome),[4] whereas all other indications for surgery are relative and should be carefully considered in each patient. Usually 6 months of nonoperative management by a trained lymphedema specialist should precede consideration of surgery for those who have poor results or who fail conservative management.

The operations have been divided into two major groups: those that involve removal of the excess tissue by open surgical excision (excisional operations) and those that are aimed at improving lymphatic transport (lymphatic reconstructions). Progress in minimally invasive techniques has also introduced another procedure: liposuction has been used to remove the excess tissue from patients with chronic lymphedema.[5]

The number of operations proposed in each category has been high, and many have been performed by one surgeon alone or by a few surgical groups. Some of the techniques attempted to use the omentum,[6] an enteromesenteric bridge,[2,7,8] or shaved buried skin bridge[9,10] to improve lymph flow of the limb. The many different operations that have been proposed are testimony to the frustration that surgeons have experienced in treating chronic lymphedema. In this chapter we focus our discussion on the most frequently used excisional operations and on microsurgical lymphatic reconstructions.

Excisional Operations

Excisional operations involve removal of the lymphedematous, fibrotic, and frequently sclerotic subcutaneous tissue of the limb and are performed usually during staged procedures. If the skin is diseased and has to be resected, coverage with skin grafting may be necessary.

Charles' Operation

The most radical excisional operation, the Charles procedure includes circumferential excision of the skin and subcutaneous tissue of the lower extremity from the tibial tuberosity to the malleoli.[11,12] The excision of the tissue is tapered at the proximal and distal margins of the resection to prevent a step deformity. Some surgeons remove a portion or all of the deep fascia. The defect is then covered with split-thickness or full-thickness skin grafts harvested from the resected specimen, or a split-thickness skin graft can be used from an uninvolved site. The skin grafts are, unfortunately, difficult to manage with frequent localized sloughing, especially in areas of recurrent cellulitis, excessive scarring, hyperkeratosis, pigmentation, and weeping dermatitis. Full-thickness skin grafts usually heal better, but graft breakdown and substantial scar formation can still occur. The Charles operation should be reserved for those few patients who have extreme lymphedema with severe skin changes. As noted by Miller, the end result sometimes is worse than the cosmetic problem before the operation.[13] Because of the poor cosmetic results this operation is seldom performed today, although occasional successful cases have been reported.[14]

Staged Subcutaneous Excision Beneath Flaps

The most frequently used excisional operation was first described by Sistrunk in 1918[15] and was later modified by Homans.[16] Personal techniques have been developed (Servelle's excisional operation,[17] Miller's staged subcutaneous excision,[12,18-20] Pflug's staged excisional operation), but these procedures all involve localized excision of the fibrosed edematous subcutaneous tissue beneath skin flaps. The thickness of the remaining skin flap determines the residual contour of the extremity but also affects the volume of the excised tissue. Thin skin flaps, favored by Servelle, resulted in removal of larger volumes of tissue from the limb, although healing has been longer and skin complications have been more frequent.[17] Miller's technique of more conservative resection has been the most popular in United States, and his team has published excellent long-term results.[20]

Surgical Technique

This technique has been described in detail by Miller and colleagues.[13,18-20] The excision is performed in two or sometimes in three stages, starting medially during the first operation. A bloodless field is obtained with a pneumatic tourniquet. An incision is made along the ankle beginning 1 cm posterior to the medial malleolus and extended proximally into the mid thigh. Flaps approximately 1.5 cm thick are elevated anteriorly and posteriorly to the mid-sagittal plane in the calf, with less extensive dissection in the thigh and ankle. All subcutaneous tissue beneath the flaps is then removed, but the sural nerve is preserved. The deep fascia of the calf is incised over the tibia and resected, sparing the fascia about the knee and ankle to preserve joint integrity (Fig. 169-1). Redundant skin, about 4 to 10 cm wide, is then resected, suction catheters are placed, and the wound is closed in a single layer with 4-0 nylon. When suturing around the ankle and knee, portions of the deep fascia are included in the suture to fix the skin flaps deeply and ensure contour. The extremity is immobilized with a posterior splint and elevated.

The patient is kept at bed rest for 9 days and mobilized afterward wearing *tightly* wrapped elastic bandages to prevent seroma formation and promote optimal healing and contour. This regimen is continued for 3 weeks postoperatively. The second stage of lateral excision is performed 3 months later in a similar fashion. During lateral excision the sensory branches of the peroneal nerve are identified and carefully preserved.

Results

Staged excision underneath skin flaps offers the most reliable improvement of all debulking operations while minimizing the likelihood of postoperative complications. Miller and colleagues reported on long-term results in 38 patients with chronic lymphedema after staged subcutaneous excisions performed beneath skin flaps.[20] Thirty patients had marked and durable reduction in extremity size with improved function. Episodes of cellulitis were reduced or eliminated. No differences in the long-term results were seen in patients with primary or secondary lymphedema. This series had a remarkably low rate of skin complications (four patients) and low rate of late progression of the disease (six patients).

Clinical benefit of excisional operations is directly related to the amount of subcutaneous tissue excised. The patients are susceptible to recurrences and should continue to wear elastic compression stockings. The results of most of these procedures are good as far as volume reduction is concerned. However, prolonged hospitalization, poor wound healing, long surgical scars, sensory nerve loss, and residual edema of the foot and ankle can be significant problems; and these complications prevent offering such procedures to most patients, except those with disabling large lymphedema that is not responding to medical measures. Staged skin and subcutaneous excision beneath skin flaps appears to provide the most durable result with the lowest rate of complications.

Microsurgical Lymphatic Reconstructions

Microsurgical reconstructions of the obstructed lymphatic pathways include lymphovenous anastomoses[21-36] and lymphatic grafting.[37,38] Autotransplantation of lymphatic tissue as a free flap has also been suggested.[39]

Lymphovenous Anastomoses

Surgical lymphovenous anastomoses intended to bypass the obstructed lymphatic system in patients with chronic lymphedema have been performed in the past three decades.[21-36] The rationale for the operation is based on the observation that in patients with chronic lymphedema contrast lymphangiography occasionally demonstrates spontaneous lymphovenous anastomoses.[40] These spontaneous channels are considered compensatory mechanisms of the body to decrease the lymphatic hypertension that occurs early in the course of the disease.

Nielubowicz and Olszewski suggested anastomosing the inguinal lymph nodes to the femoral or greater saphenous vein.[41] Although improvement in patients with lymph node/vein anastomoses has been reported,[23,41,42] enthusiasm for this operation faded because early occlusion due to thrombosis and fibrosis over the cut surface of the node is likely in most cases except in those caused by filariasis.[43]

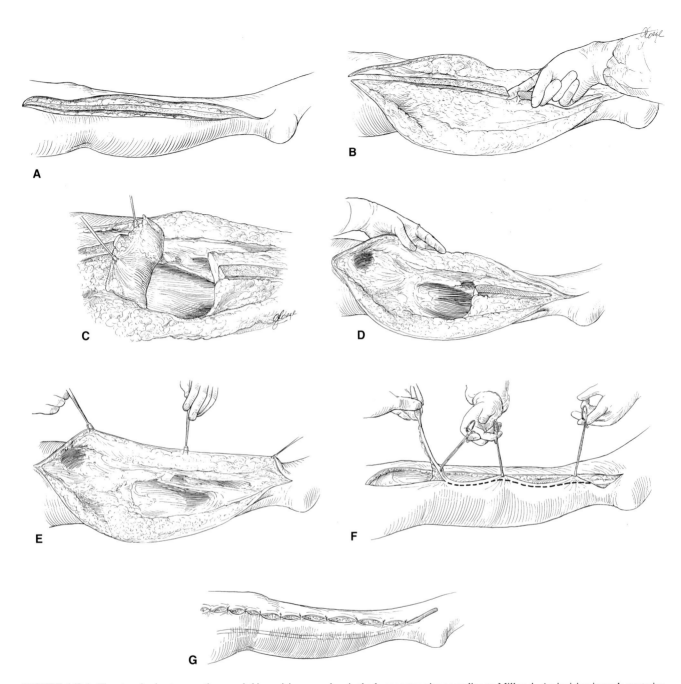

FIGURE 169-1 The staged subcutaneous tissue and skin excision procedure in the lower extremity according to Miller. **A,** An incision is made posterior to the medial malleolus and extending into the thigh. **B,** Flaps approximately 1.5 cm thick are elevated anteriorly and posteriorly. **C to E,** The deep fascia of the calf is incised over the tibia and resected; the fascia about the knee and ankle is spared. The sural nerve should be identified and preserved. **F,** Redundant skin is resected. **G,** A suction catheter is placed in the dependent portion of the posterior flap and the skin is closed with 4-0 nylon. When suturing about the knee and ankle, portions of the deep fascia are included in the suture to fix the skin and ensure contour. (From Heffel DF, Miller TA: Excisional operations for chronic lymphedema. In Rutherford RB (ed): Vascular Surgery, 5th ed. Philadelphia, WB Saunders, 2000, pp 2153-2159.)

The development of microvascular surgery and the availability of fine instruments and suture materials enabled microsurgeons to develop techniques to anastomose blood vessels less than 2 mm in diameter with excellent patency. Successful direct anastomoses between lymph vessels and veins were reported in experiments as early as 1962 by Jacobson[44] and soon after by Laine and Howard.[45] Subsequent experiments from several groups documented a 50% to 70% patency rate several months after surgery.[46-49] The authors' group performed end-to-end anastomoses between normal femoral lymph vessels and a tributary of the femoral vein in dogs and noted a 50% patency rate up to 8 months after the operation.[49] The anastomoses were done with 11-0 monofilament nonabsorbable interrupted sutures with the help of an operating microscope with high-power magnification. Cinelymphangiography and scanning electron

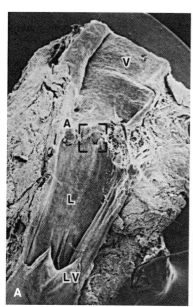
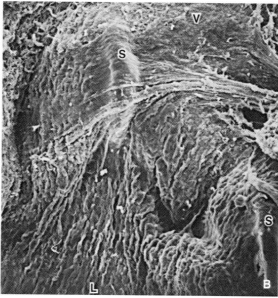

FIGURE 169-2 Scanning electron micrograph of a patent lymphovenous anastomosis 3 months after operation in a dog. A, anastomosis; L, lymph vessel; LV, lymphatic valve; V, vein; VV, venous valve. (Original magnification, ×10). (From Gloviczki P, Hollier LH, Nora FE, Kaye MP: The natural history of microsurgical lymphovenous anastomoses: An experimental study. J Vasc Surg 4:148, 1986.)

microscopy were used to document patency (Fig. 169-2). Most anastomoses that occluded were performed at the beginning of the experiments, suggesting the importance of technical expertise in performing these operations. However, Puckett and colleagues failed to confirm the patency of lymphovenous anastomoses 3 weeks after surgery in an experimental model of chronic lymphedema.[50]

Indications

Patients with secondary lymphedema of recent onset without previous episodes of cellulitis or lymphangitis are potential candidates for surgical treatment unless they can be managed easily with conservative measures. In the late stage of lymphedema, fibrosis and valvular incompetence of the main lymph vessels develop, the intrinsic contractility of the vessel wall is lost, and interstitial pressure decreases owing to secondary changes in the subcutaneous tissue (see Chapter 166). The chances of success with lymphovenous anastomoses in such limbs are clearly diminished. Because venous hypertension impedes forward flow through the anastomoses, patients with chronic venous insufficiency are not candidates for this operation.

Preoperative Evaluation

Isotope lymphoscintigraphy usually is sufficient for preoperative imaging of the lymphatic system. In ideal candidates it confirms the presence of dilated infrainguinal lymph vessels with proximal pelvic lymphatic obstruction (Fig. 169-3). Although it does not differentiate between primary and secondary lymphedema, and even though it is primarily a functional and not an anatomic study, semi-quantitative lymphoscintigraphy with ^{99m}Tc-antimony trisulfide colloid can identify reliably the pattern of lymphatic transport.[51] In selected patients, however, direct contrast lymphangiography can be performed to show the fine details of the lymphatic circulation.

Other preoperative tests include noninvasive venous studies and duplex scanning of the deep veins. Computed tomography is used in most patients to exclude any underlying mass or malignant tumor. Once surgery has been decided on, the patients are hospitalized for 28 to 48 hours to elevate the extremity in a lymphedema sling and to allow use of intermittent compression treatment with a pump to decrease the volume of the extremity.

Surgical Technique

Because the operation lasts many hours, general anesthesia is preferred. For lower extremity lymphedema, a transverse incision at the mid thigh or a longitudinal incision close to the saphenofemoral junction is performed to allow dissection of the lymphatics of the superficial medial bundle (Fig. 169-4). The greater saphenous vein and any tributaries are also dissected. An attempt is made to visualize the lymph vessels by injecting subcutaneously 5 mL of isosulfan blue (Lymphazurin) dye; half of this amount is directed toward the first interdigital space and half toward the area 10 to 15 cm distal to the site of incision. Because of lymphatic obstruction, however, lymph flow even in patent lymphatics may be minimal and the dye usually is not visible during dissection. With experience, the whitish fluid-filled lymphatics, frequently with vascularized adventitia, can be distinguished from small subcutaneous nerves or fibrotic bands.

If contrast lymphangiography is performed within 24 hours of the operation, the contrast-filled lymphatics are easily identifiable and can be located during the operation with an image intensifier and a C-arm (Fig. 169-5A). Contrast lymphangiography in some patients helps to avoid many hours of unsuccessful searching for patent lymphatics in the groin. Once the lymphatic vessels and the veins are isolated, a standard microsurgical technique is used to perform an end-to-end anastomosis, using six to eight interrupted 11-0 monofilament sutures (see Fig. 169-5B

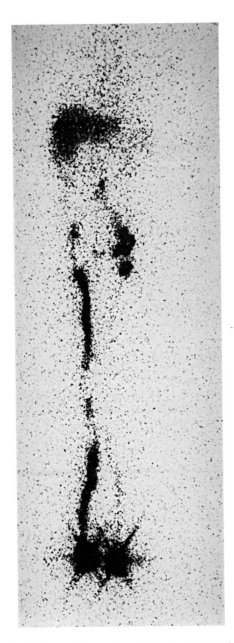

FIGURE 169-3 Bilateral lower extremity lymphoscintigram in a patient with right lower extremity lymphedema secondary to obstruction of the right iliac nodes. Note dilated lymph vessels in the right thigh distal to the obstruction suitable for direct lymphatic reconstruction.

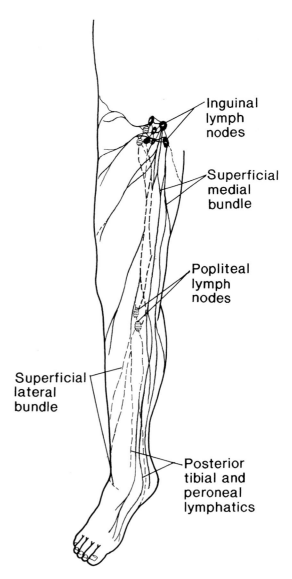

FIGURE 169-4 The lymphatic system of the lower extremity. (By permission of Mayo Foundation.)

to D). The operation is performed with a Zeiss operating microscope with 4× to 40× magnification.

For arm lymphedema, the lymphatics are dissected either through a transverse incision at the wrist or in the midcubital fossa or through a longitudinal incision at the medial aspect of the arm, a few centimeters proximal to the elbow. The lymphatics of the superficial medial lymphatic bundle usually are used for anastomoses (Fig. 169-6), which are performed with the midcubital, basilic, or brachial veins or their tributaries in an end-to-side or end-to-end fashion.

Postoperatively, the limb is wrapped with elastic bandage and elevated at 30 degrees with two pillows for the arm or, for the lower extremity, elevation of the foot of the bed.

Results

Objective evaluation of the long-term effectiveness of lymphovenous anastomoses in patients has been difficult (Table 169-1). Decrease in circumference or volume of the extremity, patient satisfaction, decrease in episodes of cellulitis, and improvement in lymphatic clearance as measured by lymphoscintigraphy have been used as the criteria of success. In a review of 14 patients who underwent lymphovenous anastomosis at the authors' institution, however, only five limbs remained improved at a mean follow-up time of 46 months after surgery.[30] Improvement was observed in 4 of 7 patients with secondary lymphedema but in only 1 of 8 patients with primary lymphedema. Improvement in lymphatic clearance from the injection site was the only indirect sign of patency of the shunts. Therefore, the authors' group was not able to provide objective evidence of late patency of the lymphovenous anastomoses in these patients.

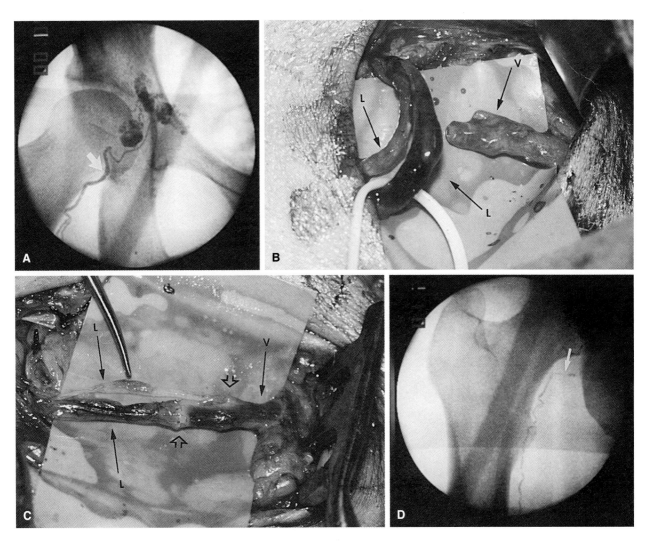

FIGURE 169-5 A, Localization of groin lymphatics before lymphovenous anastomosis operation. The patient underwent contrast lymphangiography 24 hours before operation. *Arrow* indicates the lymphatics selected for anastomosis. **B,** Two dilated lymphatics (L) and a tributary of the saphenous vein with a small side branch (V) were dissected for end-to-end lymphovenous anastomosis. **C,** End-to-end lymphovenous anastomosis completed between two lymph channels (L) and the bifurcated vein (V). *Open arrows* indicate the sites of the anastomoses. **D,** *Arrow* indicates patent lymphovenous anastomosis in the same patient. (**B** and **C** from Gloviczki P: Treatment of secondary lymphedema-medical and surgical. In Ernst CB, Stanley JC [eds]: Current Therapy in Vascular Surgery, 2nd ed. Philadelphia, BC Decker, 1991, pp 1030-1036.)

Large experience with lymphovenous shunts was reported in Australia. O'Brien and colleagues published a well-documented report with long-term follow-up studies of 90 patients who underwent lymphovenous anastomoses for chronic lymphedema.[32] Although a significant number of patients underwent additional excisional operations, improvement was documented even in patients who underwent only lymphovenous anastomoses. Of the patients who underwent lymphovenous anastomosis only, 73% had subjective improvement and 42% had objective long-term improvement. Seventy-four percent of all patients discontinued the use of elastic stockings. Because direct contrast lymphangiography has occasionally resulted in progression of lymphedema due to chemical lymphangitis or accumulation of the contrast material in the lymph nodes due to poor lymphatic transport, this test was not used to document late patency of the anastomoses. Therefore, objective evidence

that the improvement in these patients was caused by patent and functioning lymphovenous anastomoses is still lacking.

The largest experience to date comes from Campisi and colleagues in Italy.[33,34] This group treated 665 patients with obstructive lymphedema using microsurgical lymphovenous anastomoses, with subjective improvement in 87% of their patients. Four hundred forty-six patients were available for long-term follow-up, and the authors observed volume reduction in 69% and discontinuation of conservative measures in 85%. This is a remarkable result that could not yet be duplicated elsewhere. The authors concluded that microsurgical reconstruction early in the course of lymphedema is more effective, because intrinsic contractility of the lymphatics is still maintained and chances of normalization of the lymph circulation are better before significant chronic inflammatory changes in the subcutaneous tissue develop.

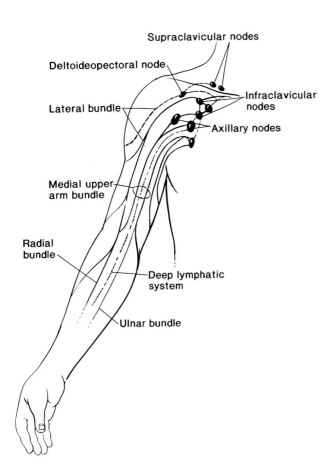

Supraclavicular nodes

Deltoideopectoral node

Infraclavicular nodes

Lateral bundle

Axillary nodes

Medial upper arm bundle

Radial bundle

Deep lymphatic system

Ulnar bundle

FIGURE 169-6 The lymphatic system of the upper extremity. (By permission of Mayo Foundation.)

Koshima and coworkers from Japan reported on significant improvement of the lymphedema at a mean of 3.3 years after lymphovenous anastomoses in 8 of 13 patients.[35] However, Vignes and associates failed to confirm the therapeutic benefit of lymphovenous anastomoses in a group of 13 patients (10 with primary and 3 with secondary lymphedema).[36] Global assessment of clinical outcome was very good or good in 5 patients and intermediate in another 5, but the operation failed to improve the volume of lower limbs and reduce the frequency of erysipelas.

Lymphatic Grafting

Baumeister and colleagues introduced lymphatic grafting for upper extremity and unilateral lower extremity secondary lymphedema.[37,52-57] Because lymph is devoid of platelets and coagulates less than blood, the chances of patency in successful lympholymphatic anastomoses appear to be better than those in lymphovenous anastomoses. Also, an elevated venous pressure, which may interrupt flow intermittently through lymphovenous anastomoses, is not a factor in this procedure. In their experiments, Baumeister and colleagues achieved 100% short- to medium-term patency of lymphatic interposition grafts.[53] Indisputably, this operation requires special microsurgical expertise.

A variation of lymphatic grafting was reported by Campisi and coworkers, who treated patients with upper and lower extremity lymphedema by creating a lymphatic-venous-lymphatic anastomosis with autologous interposition vein graft.[38] Experimental data from lymphatic-vessel-to-isolated-vein anastomoses in the dog suggest improved patency rates.[58] With an isolated vein segment, the

| Table 169-1 | Clinical Results of Microsurgical Lymphatic Reconstructions |

FIRST AUTHOR, YEAR	NO. PATIENTS	EXTREMITY Upper	EXTREMITY Lower	TYPE OF OPERATION	FOLLOW-UP (mo)	EXCELLENT OR GOOD CLINICAL RESULTS (%)
Krylov, 1982	50	+		LVA	?	30
Nieuborg, 1982	47	+		LVA	6-12	68
Gong-Kang, 1985	91		+	LVA	24*	79
Zhu et al., 1987	48		+	LVA	6-52	33
	185		+	LVA	6-52	73
Gloviczki, 1988	6	+		LVA	36.6*	50
	8		+	LVA		25
O'Brien, 1990	46	+		LVA		54
	30	+	+	LVA	51*	83
	6†		+	LVA		33
	8†			LVA		50
Baumeister, 1990	36	+	+	LG	>12	33
	12			LG	>24	8
Campisi, 2001	231	+	+	LVA	>7 years* in 446 patients	83 (combined for both groups)
	446			LVA		
Campisi, 2001	133		+	LVL	"Long-term" in 95 patients, max. 15 years	81

LVA, Lymphovenous anastomoses; LG, lymphatic grafting; LVL, lymphatic-venous-lymphatic graft with autologous vein.
*Mean.
†Lymphovenous anastomosis plus excisional procedure.

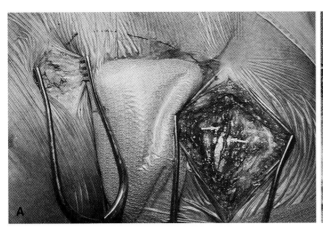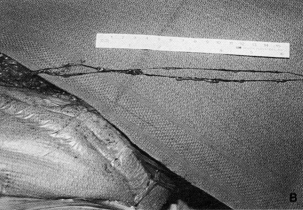

FIGURE 169-7   A, Exposure of lymph vessels for suprapubic transposition. Note two major lymph vessels of the left thigh that will be used for grafting (*arrows*). **B,** Two lymphatic grafts divided at the distal thigh are prepared for lymphatic grafting. (By permission of Mayo Foundation.)

anastomosis is not exposed to intraluminal blood and theoretically is protected from thrombotic occlusion. The isolated vein/lymphatic graft technique represents the increasing efforts at improving patency of lymphatic reconstructions.

Preoperative Evaluation

Preoperative evaluation is similar to that needed for patients who undergo lymphovenous anastomoses. It is important to image the donor leg lymphatics with lymphoscintigraphy because a normal lymphatic system is a prerequisite for the use of lymph vessels from the leg for grafting. In the experience of Baumeister and coworkers, postoperative leg swelling occurred in only one of 95 limbs due to post-thrombotic venous disease.[57] Patients with bilateral leg edema are not candidates for this procedure.

Surgical Technique

The operation on the lower extremity is very similar to a suprapubic saphenous vein graft, as performed by Palma for unilateral iliac vein obstruction (see Chapter 160). As in lymphovenous anastomoses, the superficial thigh lymphatics in the edematous limb are dissected first through a longitudinal incision made just distal to the saphenofemoral junction. Five milliliters of isosulfan blue dye is injected subcutaneously into the first interdigital space of the normal foot, and the thigh lymphatics are exposed through a 25- to 30-cm incision along the greater saphenous vein with loupe magnification (Fig. 169-7). Two or three lymphatics are selected for grafting. They are transected distally after double ligation and tunneled subcutaneously above the pubis to the contralateral side, where end-to-end lympholymphatic anastomoses are performed under the operating microscope with 11-0 or 12-0 interrupted sutures (Fig. 169-8).

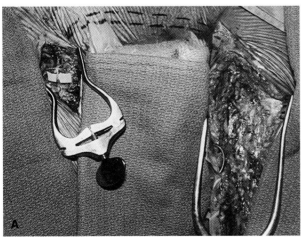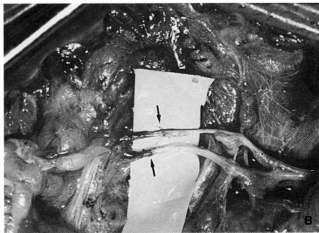

FIGURE 169-8   A, Completed suprapubic lymph graft with two lympholymphatic anastomoses at right groin. *Dashed line* indicates position of suprapubic lymphatic grafts. **B,** Magnified photograph of two end-to-end lympholymphatic anastomoses (*arrows*) performed with 11-0 interrupted monofilament sutures. (By permission of Mayo Foundation.)

For postmastectomy lymphedema, the two or three lymphatics from the leg are harvested and used as free interposition grafts. They are placed in a subcutaneous tunnel from the upper medial arm to the neck and then sutured end to end first to the superficial medial bundle lymphatics in the arm and then to the descending neck lymphatics in the supraclavicular fossa. Postoperative care for these patients is similar to that given to patients with lymphovenous anastomoses.

In patients treated with peripheral lymphatic-venous-lymphatic anastomoses, autologous vein is harvested from the volar aspect of the forearm for upper extremity procedures, or the ipsilateral greater or lesser saphenous veins are used for lower extremity lymphedema. The lymph vessels proximal and distal to the lymphatic occlusion are anastomosed to the vein graft with a telescoping anastomosis with 8-0 or 9-0 nylon suture (Fig. 169-9). This technique allows the invagination of several lymphatic afferent vessels into the vein graft. As stated earlier, isosulfan blue can be used to delineate lymphatics as well as to confirm patency of the anastomosis intraoperatively.

Results

In a report evaluating 55 patients undergoing this operation with a follow-up of more than 3 years, Baumeister and associates documented a decrease in the volume of the extremity in 80% of the patients.[37] Volume measurements were diminished significantly in 36 patients with arm lymphedema, and 16 patients were improved clinically for more than 2 years after surgery. Significant improvement was documented in 8 of 12 patients with lower extremity lymphedema more than 1 year after suprapubic grafting. Thirty patients were studied by lymphoscintigraphy. With a semi-quantitative assessment and a lymphatic transport index, some improvement in lymphatic clearance could be demonstrated in all patients. Although several grafts were imaged by lymphoscintigraphy, the patency rate of the implanted lymphatic grafts was not reported.

In a subsequent report, Baumeister and coworkers analyzed results in 127 limbs of 122 patients treated with microsurgical lymphatic grafting (79 with arm edema, 48 with lower extremity edema).[57] Most patients with arm edema experienced a decrease in volume measurements. In addition, the authors documented the use of both lymphoscintigraphy and indirect lymphography with nonionic water-soluble contrast injection to demonstrate patent grafts; however, graft patency until recently was not recorded.

In a more recent study from the same group, 8 patients were studied with lymphoscintigraphy after autologous lymph vessel transplantation.[59] Scintigraphy confirmed significantly ($P \le .01$) improved lymphatic function in all patients at 8 years after microsurgical treatment. Patients with scintigraphic visualization of the vessel graft (n = 2/8) showed much better clinical improvement than those who did not have graft visualization.

Significant experience with this operation has not been gained by other surgical teams. In 2 of the patients operated on by the authors' group with this technique, lymphoscintigraphy suggested graft patency (Fig. 169-10). This result, however, was associated with significant early reduction of the swelling in only 1 patient, in whom edema

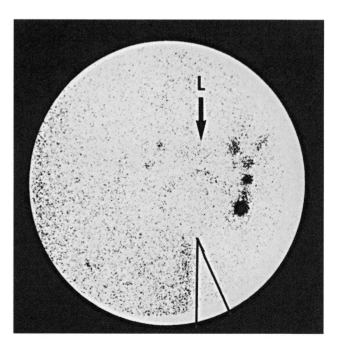

FIGURE 169-10 Lymphoscintigram 3 months after suprapubic lymphatic grafting for secondary lymphedema of the right lower extremity. Labeled colloid was injected into the right foot only. *Arrow* indicates suprapubic graft. Note intense filling of the left inguinal nodes. Preoperative lymphoscintigram in this patient showed no activity at the groin. L, lymphatic graft. (From Gloviczki P: Treatment of secondary lymphedema—medical and surgical. In Ernst CB, Stanley JC [eds]: Current Therapy in Vascular Surgery, 2nd ed. Philadelphia, BC Decker, 1991, pp 1030-1036.)

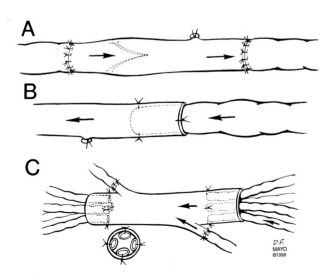

FIGURE 169-9 Techniques of lymphatic reconstructions according to Campisi with interposition vein graft (**A**) or lymphovenous anastomosis (**B**). **C,** Technique of invagination of multiple lymphatics into interposition vein graft (lymphatic-venous-lymphatic anastomoses). (By permission of Mayo Foundation.)

recurred at 2 years despite an apparently patent and functioning graft.

Campisi and coworkers reported on using vein grafts to bypass lymphatic obstructions in those patients who have congenital lymphedema or acquired segmental lymphatic blocks following excision or radiation of lymph nodes.[38] Sixty-four patients who underwent lymphatic-venous-lymphatic grafts were studied for 5 years. Marked improvement in edema occurred in 40 (62.5%) patients, moderate improvement was noted in 18 (28%), and mild edema regression occurred in 6 (9.5%).[38] Unfortunately, graft patency was not studied in these patients. Clinical evaluation and mean volumetric assessment of edema, however, suggest long-term improvement in most patients. In a subsequent report on 133 patients, autologous vein grafts were implanted to bypass lymphatic obstruction at the groin, performing the anastomoses between the vein graft and the lymph vessels using microsurgical techniques.[33] Excess volume reduction was higher in patients who underwent operation in the early stages of lymphedema. Of the entire group, more than 75% improvement was noted in 47% of the patients and more than 50% improvement occurred in another 34%. The incidence of lymphangitis has also decreased after surgery. Long-term follow-up was available in 95 patients, but results of late graft patency, studied with lymphoscintigraphy, were not reported. Clinical evaluation and mean volumetric assessment of edema suggested long-term improvement in 81% of the patients (see Table 169-1).

Conclusions

Meticulous microsurgical technique, fine instruments, and high-power magnification with the operating microscope enable microsurgeons to perform anastomoses between lymph vessels or between a lymph vessel and a vein with good immediate success. Although long-term improvement in patients has been reported, these results remain to be confirmed by different surgical teams and then compared with results obtained in patients treated by conservative measures. Because lymph coagulates significantly less than blood, lympholymphatic anastomoses with lymphatic grafts or venous interposition grafts into the lymphatic system have a potential advantage over lymphovenous anastomoses, in which thrombosis on the venous side may occur.

The long-term patency and function of these anastomoses in patients, however, are still unknown. More important, the main questions remain unanswered:

- Does restoring the patency of two or three lymph channels result in restoration of normal lymphatic transport?
- Does lymphovenous anastomosis or lymphatic grafting reverse changes that have already occurred in the distal lymphatic circulation, the subcutaneous tissue, or the skin of patients with chronic lymphedema?
- Is clinical improvement superior to those results obtained with current nonsurgical techniques?

Until these important questions are answered, patients should be made aware of the unproven benefit of this type of treatment.

Autotransplantation of Free Lymphatic Flap

Trevidic and Cormier performed autotransplantation of a free axillary lymph node flap from the contralateral axillary fossa to the side of the lymphedematous arm in patients with postmastectomy lymphedema.[39] The inferior axillary nodes were removed with a vascularized flap composed of a portion of the latissimus dorsi muscle with a segment of skin. The blood supply to the flap consisted of the subscapular artery and vein. This lymphatic tissue flap was then transplanted into the supraclavicular fossa, where anastomoses were created with the subclavian artery and vein. The authors reported results in 19 patients who underwent axillary lymph node transplantation. The graft failed in 1 patient. Improvement was documented in 75% of patients, and direct contrast lymphography demonstrated the development of new lympholymphatic anastomoses in some patients. Lymphoscintigraphy showed improved lymphatic transport in 75% of the patients. It is a promising operation, but further experience and longer follow-up periods with this operation are needed to assess its efficacy.

Liposuction

Brorson and Svensson have advocated using liposuction in patients with postmastectomy lymphedema to reduce the volume of the extremity.[5] The rationale behind this treatment is that chronic lymphedema causes hypertrophy of the subcutaneous fat. Removal of the hypertrophied and edematous adipose tissue is performed through 20 to 30 three-millimeter-long incisions using vacuum aspiration. During the subsequent postoperative course, controlled compression therapy (CCT) is maintained to decrease bleeding complications and help to maintain the volume of the limb.

In the report by Brorson and Svensson,[5] preoperative and postoperative arm edema volumes were measured using the water displacement technique and lymph transport was assessed by indirect lymphoscintigraphy. Twenty-eight patients were prospectively matched into two groups. One group received liposuction combined with CCT, and one group received CCT alone. Liposuction combined with CCT was more effective than the therapy alone ($P < .0001$). The beneficial effect of liposuction was confirmed by the comparison between the CCT group and the group of patients treated with liposuction combined with CCT, as the edema reduction figures after 1 year were 47% and 104%, respectively ($P < .0001$). Continued use of compression garments is important to maintain the primary surgical outcome. The technique can be useful in patients with no functioning lymphatics, but in others destruction of functioning lymphatics with the possibility of worsening of the edema undoubtedly occurs.

■ OPERATIONS FOR PRIMARY CHYLOUS DISORDERS

Chylous disorders are characterized by an accumulation of chyle in abnormal areas of the body. Chylous ascites, chylothorax, or chylocutaneous fistula may be caused by malignant tumors, most frequently lymphoma, or by trauma to the mesenteric lymphatics or the thoracic duct, which may also occur during vascular surgical procedures, as discussed in detail in Chapter 40.

Primary chylous disorders are usually caused by congenital lymphangiectasia or megalymphatics, which in some patients are associated with obstruction of the thoracic duct. In patients with lymphangiectasia and lymphatic valvular incompetence, chyle may reflux into the lower extremities, the perineum, or the genitalia.[60-67] Depending on the site of the dilated lymphatics and the site of the chylous leak, these patients may also have protein-losing enteropathy, chylous ascites, chylothorax, chylopericardium, or reflux of chyle into the lungs and tracheobronchial tree.[60-72] The mean age of 35 patients (15 males and 20 females) treated surgically for primary chylous disorders at the Mayo Clinic was 29 years and ranged from 1 day to 81 years.[69] The patients presented with lower limb edema (54%), dyspnea (49%), scrotal or labial edema (43%), and abdominal distention (37%). The etiology was primary lymphangiectasia in 66%, yellow nail syndrome in 11%, lymphangioleiomyomatosis in 9%, and another disorder in 18%.[69]

Medical treatment is aimed at decreasing production of chyle by means of a medium-chain triglyceride diet or occasionally by parenteral nutrition (see Chapter 167). Repletion of proteins and calcium lost with chyle is as important as the need to strengthen the defense mechanism of the body because lymphocytes and important immunoglobulins are also wasted in these patients. Only surgical treatment can provide long-term improvement and occasionally cure by ligation of the incompetent retroperitoneal lymph vessels and oversewing of the site of the lymphatic leak. In some patients, attempts to reconstruct the obstructed thoracic duct by creation of thoracic duct/azygos vein anastomoses have also been reported.

Chylous Reflux into the Lower Extremity or Genitalia

Although many patients with lymphangiectasia and reflux of chyle have lower extremity lymphedema that is unilateral in most cases, the main discomfort for the patients is intermittent or continuous discharge of chyle from cutaneous vesicles in the lower extremity or in the genitalia. The first five patients known to have suffered from this rare condition were described in 1949 by Servelle and Deysson.[66]

Preoperative evaluation of patients with chylous reflux into the lower extremity or genitalia should include lymphoscintigraphy (Fig. 169-11A). Contrast lymphangiography, however, is the definitive test to confirm the diagnosis and to localize the dilated retroperitoneal lymphatics and, frequently, also the site of the lymphatic leak. Radical excision and ligation of the incompetent retroperitoneal lymph vessels is the only effective technique for controlling reflux of the chyle and its drainage through skin vesicles in the perineum, labia, scrotum, or lower extremity. The authors' group uses the technique of Servelle and performs the entire reflux operation in two stages through flank incisions using the retroperitoneal approach.[69] Four hours before the procedure, the patient ingests 60 g of butter and drinks 8 ounces of whipping cream. The fatty meal allows ready visualization of the retroperitoneal lymphatics during exploration (see Fig. 169-11B to D). Ligation of the lymph vessels should be done with the utmost care to avoid tearing or avulsing the lymphatics, resulting in residual leaks or rupture. In recent years, sclerotherapy of the dilated lymphatics has been added to ligation to increase efficacy of the operation. Tetracycline solution, 500 to 1000 mg diluted in 20 mL of normal saline, is injected directly into the dilated retroperitoneal lymph vessels to provoke obstructive lymphangitis.

As reported by Molitch and associates, percutaneous computed tomography (CT)-guided or magnetic resonance imaging (MRI)-guided cannulation of these dilated lymphatics may also be possible, and sclerotherapy to decrease reflux can be performed repeatedly, if necessary.[68] Lymphovenous anastomoses with the dilated lymphatics can also be performed. Reflux of blood into the dilated and incompetent lymphatics, however, can occur. A competent valve on the venous side completely avoids reflux and increases the chance of successful lymphatic drainage.[2,69]

Results

The largest group of patients studied was reported by Servelle, who operated on 55 patients with chylous reflux into the lower extremity or genitalia and reported durable benefit in most patients.[61] In a series of 19 patients who underwent ligation of the retroperitoneal lymphatics for chylous reflux to the limbs and genitalia by Kinmonth and Cox, permanent cure was achieved in 5 patients and alleviation of symptoms, frequently after several operations, occurred in 12 patients.[62] No improvement or failure was noted in only two cases. We have reviewed the results of 35 patients with primary chylous disorders treated over a 24-year period.[69] Twenty-one (60%) patients underwent 27 surgical procedures. Nineteen procedures were performed for chylous ascites or reflux, 10 of these patients (53%) underwent resection of retroperitoneal lymphatics ± sclerotherapy of lymphatics, 4 (21%) had lymphovenous anastomosis or saphenous vein interposition grafts, 4 (21%) had peritoneovenous shunts, and 1 (5%) had a hysterectomy for periuterine lymphangiectasia. All patients improved initially, but 29% had recurrence of symptoms at a mean of 25 months (range, 1 to 43 months). Three patients with leg swelling had postoperative lymphoscintigraphy confirming improved lymphatic transport and diminished reflux.

Chylous Ascites

Chylous ascites usually results from intraperitoneal rupture of the mesenteric or retroperitoneal lymphatics or from exudation of the chyle into the peritoneal cavity.[69] Evaluation of such patients should include CT or MRI to exclude abdominal malignancy. The diagnosis of lymphangiectasia is confirmed by bipedal contrast lymphangiography. Paracentesis is both diagnostic and therapeutic. If conservative measures fail and ascites returns, abdominal exploration should be performed after a fatty

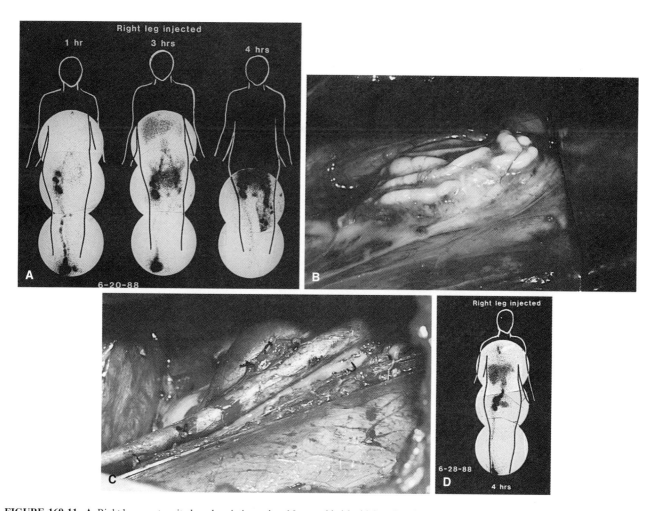

FIGURE 169-11   A, Right lower extremity lymphoscintigram in a 16-year-old girl with lymphangiectasia and severe reflux into the genitalia and left lower extremity. Injection of the isotope into the right foot reveals reflux into the pelvis at 3 hours and into the left lower extremity at 4 hours. **B,** Intraoperative photograph reveals dilated incompetent retroperitoneal lymphatics in the left iliac fossa containing chyle. **C,** Radical excision and ligation of the lymph vessels were performed. In addition, two lymphovenous anastomoses were also performed between two dilated lymphatics and two lumbar veins. **D,** Postoperative lymphoscintigram performed in a similar fashion reveals no evidence of reflux at 4 hours. The patient has no significant reflux 4 years after surgery. (From Gloviczki P, et al: Noninvasive evaluation of the swollen extremity: Experiences with 190 lymphoscintigraphic examinations. J Vasc Surg 9:683, 1989.)

meal as described previously. If chylous ascites is due to primary lymphangiectasia, abdominal exploration may reveal ruptured lymphatics, which can be oversewn. In some patients, large chylous cysts develop, which should be excised (Fig. 169-12). If the condition is associated with protein-losing enteropathy and the disease is localized to a segment of the small bowel, the bowel segment should be resected.

The outcome of the operation usually is good if a well-defined abdominal fistula is found. If the mesenteric lymphatic trunks are fibrosed, aplastic, or hypoplastic, and exudation of the chyle is the main source of the ascites, however, the prognosis is poor and recurrence is frequent.

Browse and coworkers treated 45 patients with chylous ascites.[63] The age at presentation ranged from 1 to 80 (median 12) years. Thirty-five patients had an abnormality of the lymphatics (primary chylous ascites); in the remaining 10, the ascites was secondary to other conditions,

principally non-Hodgkin's lymphoma (6 patients). Surgery (fistula closure, bowel resection, or insertion of a peritoneovenous shunt) was performed in 30 patients. Closure of a retroperitoneal or mesenteric fistula, when present, was the most successful operation, curing 7 of the 12 patients. In those patients who develop chylous ascites caused by iatrogenic trauma, frequently after aortic reconstructions, a short period of conservative management is justified. If chylous ascites reaccumulates, reoperation with ligation of the fistula is the most effective treatment.

Results with peritoneovenous shunts have been mixed; patency is usually judged by recurrence of ascites. In Browse and coworkers' experience with nine peritoneovenous shunt placements, all occluded within 3 to 6 months after insertion. We have used the LeVeen shunt with good results, although 1 of 4 patients developed symptomatic superior vena cava syndrome owing to thrombosis around the shunt.[69]

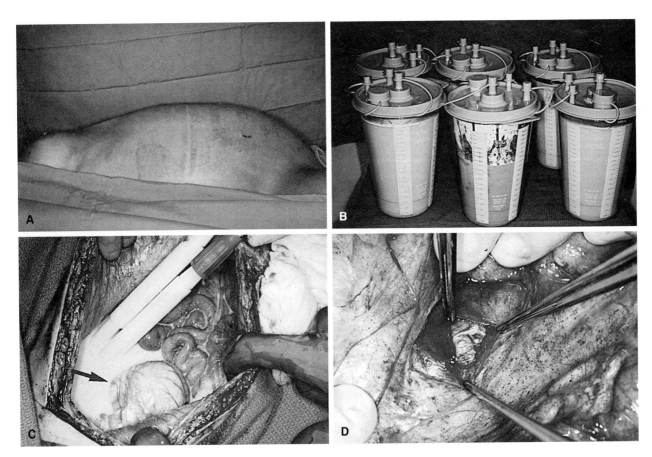

FIGURE 169-12 A, Preoperative photograph of an 18-year-old female with lymphangiectasia and recurrent chylous ascites. **B,** During the operation, 12 L of chyle was aspirated from the abdomen. **C,** The chylous ascites was caused by ruptured lymphatic and leaking large mesenteric lymphatic cysts (*arrow*). **D,** The dilated retroperitoneal lymphatics containing chyle were ligated and excised. The patient has an excellent clinical result 8 months after the operation.

Chylothorax

As with chylous ascites, the most frequent cause of chylothorax is trauma or malignant disease.[73] Primary lymphatic disorders that cause chylothorax include lymphangiectasia with or without thoracic duct obstruction. However, chylothorax may also result from chylous ascites passing through the diaphragm. In these patients, the chylothorax is cured when the chylous ascites is controlled. Preoperative lymphangiography in these patients should be performed because it may localize the site of the chylous fistula or document occlusion of the thoracic duct (Fig. 169-13).

Thoracentesis usually is not effective in curing the disease, and chyle that leaks from the thoracic duct or one of the large intercostal, mediastinal, or diaphragmatic collaterals reaccumulates. Injection of tetracycline is frequently ineffective because it is diluted by the leaking chyle. The best treatment of chylothorax is surgical pleurodesis with excision of the parietal pleura and prolonged pleural suction. During thoracotomy, which is performed after a fatty meal, a careful search for the leaking lymphatics should be undertaken and the site of the leak should be oversewn. Surgical pleurodesis, either with video-assisted thoracoscopy or open thoracotomy, with excision of the

parietal pleura is the optimal treatment.[70,73] After a fatty meal, thoracotomy or video-assisted thoracoscopy is performed and lymphatics are oversewn or clipped. This is followed by pleurodesis. In the Mayo Clinic series, eight procedures for chylothorax included thoracotomy with decortication and pleurodesis (4 patients), ligation of thoracic duct (3 patients), and resection of thoracic duct cyst (1 patient), with excellent early results in all patients.[69]

A prospective study from Cope described 11 patients with primary and secondary chylothorax treated with percutaneous catheterization and embolization of the thoracic duct with a 45% technical success rate, suggesting a role for percutaneous intervention.[70] Silk and associates,[71] and more recently Engum and colleagues,[72] reported on using pleuroperitoneal shunts in children with good results.

Thoracic Duct Reconstruction

If occlusion of the cervical or upper thoracic duct (Fig. 169-14) is the cause of lymphangiectasia and reflux of chyle into the pleural or peritoneal cavity, thoracic duct/azygos vein anastomosis can be attempted to reconstruct the duct and to improve lymphatic transport. Preoperative imaging of

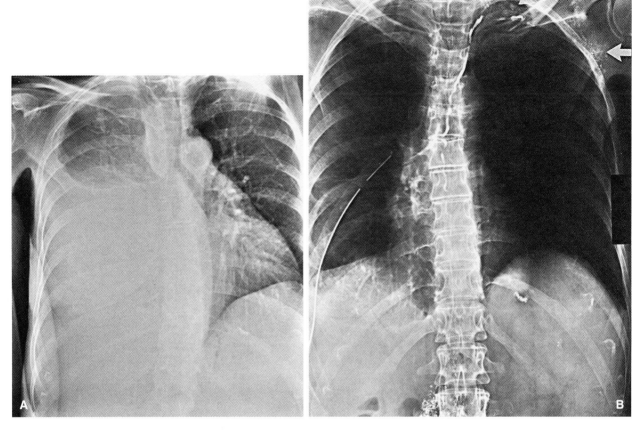

FIGURE 169-13   A, Right chylothorax in a 63-year-old woman. **B,** Bipedal lymphangiography confirmed thoracic duct obstruction at the base of the neck. Note contrast medium in the supraclavicular and left axillary lymphatics (*arrows*).

the duct with contrast pedal lymphangiography is important because if occlusion of the entire duct is present it precludes anastomoses.

The operation is performed through a right posterolateral thoracotomy, and the anastomosis between the lower thoracic duct and the azygos vein is performed in an end-to-end fashion with 8-0 or 10-0 nonabsorbable interrupted sutures and magnification with loupes or an operating microscope. Only a few patients undergoing this operation have been reported.[60,67] Both patients operated on by the authors' group had good immediate patency, and excellent flow of chyle was observed through the anastomosis intraoperatively (Fig. 169-15). Although none had postoperative contrast lymphangiography, the recurrent chylothorax that was the main indication for the procedure ultimately resolved in both. Browse reported two successes in three patients who underwent thoracic duct reconstruction.[67] Kinmonth performed this procedure in two patients,

however, and concluded that the anastomosis alone is not effective for decompressing the thoracic duct; ligation of the abnormal mediastinal lymphatics and oversewing of the sites of the lymphatic leak are also necessary.[60]

■ SUMMARY

Primary chylous disorders are fortunately rare. The underlying abnormality usually is congenital lymphangiectasia and fibrotic occlusion or atresia of the thoracic duct. Surgical treatment is frequently the only effective way to control chylous reflux or leak, and ligation of the incompetent retroperitoneal lymphatics, sclerotherapy, or oversewing of the ruptured lymphatics can produce long-term improvement or even cure in many patients. In selected symptomatic patients with obstruction of the thoracic duct, a thoracic duct/azygos vein anastomosis may be considered as a surgical option.

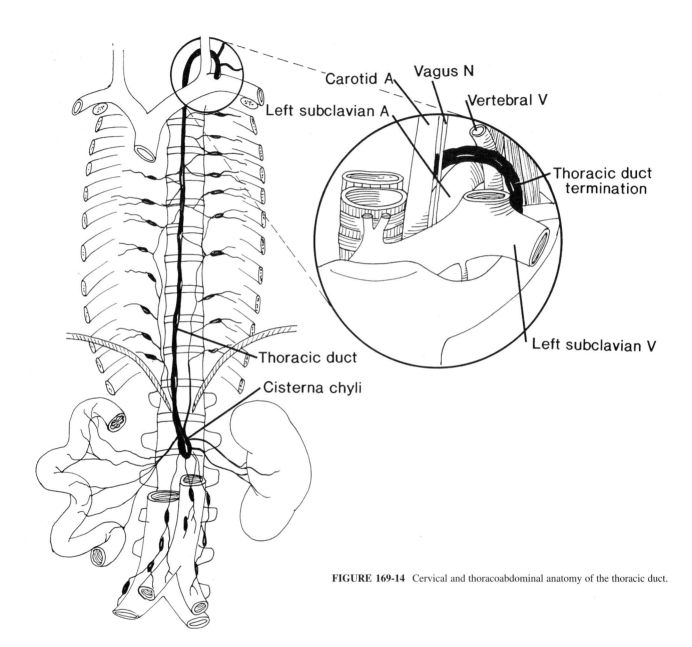

FIGURE 169-14 Cervical and thoracoabdominal anatomy of the thoracic duct.

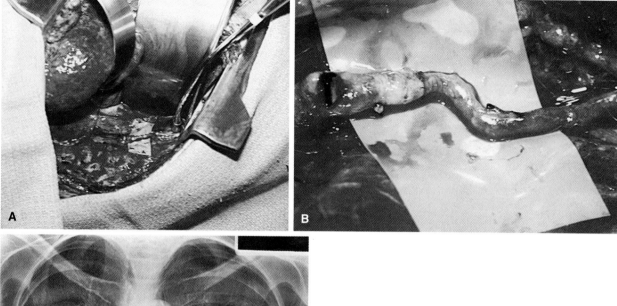

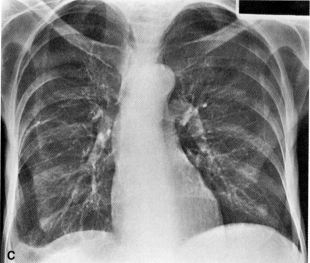

FIGURE 169-15 A and **B,** Thoracic duct/azygos vein anastomosis performed through a right posterolateral thoracotomy in an end-to-end fashion with interrupted 8-0 polypropylene (Prolene) sutures. **C,** Chest radiograph 2 years later confirms absence of chylothorax.

■ REFERENCES

1. Foldi M, Foldi E, Kubik S: Textbook of Lymphology. Munich, Urban & Fischer, 2003.

2. Burnand GK, Gloviczki P, Browse N: Principles of surgical treatment. In Browse N, Burnand GK, Mortimer PS (eds): Diseases of the Lymphatics. London, Arnold, 2003, pp 179-204.

3. Gloviczki P: Principles of surgical treatment of chronic lymphoedema. Intern Angiol 18:42, 1999.

4. Stewart FW, Treves N: Lymphangiosarcoma in postmastectomy lymphedema: A report of six cases in elephantiasis chirurgica. Cancer 1:64, 1948.

5. Brorson H, Svensson H: Liposuction combined with controlled compression therapy reduces arm lymphedema more effectively than controlled compression therapy alone. Plast Reconstr Surg 102:1058, 1998.

6. Goldsmith HS: Long-term evaluation of omental transposition for chronic lymphedema. Ann Surg 180:847, 1974.

7. Kinmonth JB, Hurst PAE, Edwards JM, Rutt DL: Relief of lymph obstruction by use of a bridge of mesentery and ileum. Br J Surg 65:829, 1978.

8. Hurst PA, Stewart G, Kinmonth JB, Browse NL: Long-term results of the enteromesenteric bridge operation in the treatment of primary lymphoedema. Br J Surg 72:272, 1985.

9. Thompson N: The surgical treatment of chronic lymphoedema of the extremities. Surg Clin North Am 47:445, 1967.

10. Thompson N, Wee JTK: Twenty years' experience of the buried dermis flap operation in the treatment of chronic lymphedema of the extremities. Chir Plast (Berl) 5:147, 1980.

11. Charles RH: Elephantiasis scroti. In Latham A (ed): A System of Treatment. London, Churchill, 1912, vol 3.

12. Hoopes JE: Lymphedema of the extremity. In Cameron JL (ed): Current Surgical Therapy. Philadelphia, BC Decker, 1989, vol 3, p 630.

13. Heffel DF, Miller TA: Excisional operations for chronic lymphedema. In Rutherford RB (ed): Vascular Surgery, 5th ed. Philadelphia, WB Saunders, 2000, pp 2153-2159.

14. Bauer T, Wechselberger G, Schoeller T, Piza-Katzer H: Lymphedema praecox of the lower extremity. Surgery 132:899, 2002.

15. Sistrunk WE: Further experiences with the Kondoleon operation for elephantiasis. JAMA 71:800, 1918.

16. Homans J: The treatment of elephantiasis of the legs: Preliminary report. N Engl J Med 215:1099, 1936.

17. Servelle M: Surgical treatment of lymphedema: A report on 652 cases. Surgery 101:485, 1987.

18. Miller TA: Surgical management of lymphedema of the extremity. Plast Reconstr Surg 56:633, 1975.

19. Miller TA: Surgical approach to lymphedema of the arm after mastectomy. Am J Surg 148:152, 1984.

20. Miller TA, Wyatt LE, Rudkin GH: Staged skin and subcutaneous excision for lymphedema: A favorable report of long-term results. Plast Reconstr Surg 102:1486; discussion, 1499, 1998.

21. O'Brien BMC, Shafiroff BB: Microlymphaticovenous and resectional surgery in obstructive lymphedema. World J Surg 3:3, 1979.

22. Huang GK, Ru-Qi H, Zong-Zhao L, et al: Microlymphaticovenous anastomosis for treating lymphedema of the extremities and external genitalia. J Microsurg 3:32, 1981.

23. Jamal S: Lymphovenous anastomosis in filarial lymphedema. Lymphology 14:64, 1981.

24. Krylov V, Milanov N, Abalmasov K: Microlymphatic surgery of secondary lymphoedema of the upper limb. Ann Chir Gynaecol 71:77, 1982.

25. Nieuborg L: The Role of Lymphaticovenous Anastomoses in the Treatment of Postmastectomy Oedema. Alblasserdam, The Netherlands, Offsetdrukkerij Kanters BV, 1982.

26. Gong-Kang H, Ru-Qi H, Zong-Zhao L, et al: Microlymphaticovenous anastomosis in the treatment of lower limb obstructive lymphedema: Analysis of 91 cases. Plast Reconstr Surg 76:671, 1985.

27. Ingianni G, Holzmann T: Clinical experience with lymphovenous anastomosis for secondary lymphedema. Handchirurgie 17:43, 1985.

28. Campisi C, Tosatti E, Casaccia M, et al: Lymphatic microsurgery. Minerva Chir 41:469, 1986.

29. Zhu JK, Yu GZ, Liu JX, et al: Recent advances in microlymphatic surgery in China. Clin Orthop 215:32, 1987.

30. Gloviczki P, Fisher J, Hollier LH, et al: Microsurgical lymphovenous anastomosis for treatment of lymphedema: A critical review. J Vasc Surg 7:647, 1988.

31. Ipsen T, Pless J, Fredericksen PB: Experience with microlymphaticovenous anastomoses for congenital and acquired lymphoedema. Scand J Plast Reconstr Surg 22:233, 1988.

32. O'Brien BM, Mellow CG, Khazanchi RK, et al: Long-term results after microlymphaticovenous anastomoses for the treatment of obstructive lymphedema. Plast Reconstr Surg 85:562, 1990.

33. Campisi C, Boccardo F, Zilli A, et al: Long-term results after lymphatic-venous anastomoses for the treatment of obstructive lymphedema. Microsurgery 21:135, 2001.

34. Campisi C, Boccardo F: Lymphedema and microsurgery. Microsurgery 22:74, 2002.

35. Koshima I, Nanba Y, Tsutsui T, et al: Long-term follow-up after lymphaticovenular anastomosis for lymphedema in the leg. J Reconstr Microsurg 19:209, 2003.

36. Vignes S, Boursier V, Priollet P, et al: Quantitative evaluation and qualitative results of surgical lymphovenous anastomosis in lower limb lymphedema [in French]. J Malad Vasc 28:30, 2003.

37. Baumeister RG, Siuda S: Treatment of lymphedemas by microsurgical lymphatic grafting: What is proved? Plast Reconstr Surg 85:64, 1990.

38. Campisi C, Boccardo F, Tacchella M: Reconstructive microsurgery of lymph vessels: The personal method of lymphatic-venous-lymphatic (LVL) interpositioned grafted shunt. Microsurgery 16:161, 1995.

39. Trevidic P, Cormier JM: Free axillary lymph node transfer. In Cluzan RV (ed): Progress in Lymphology. Amsterdam, Elsevier Science, 1992, vol 13, pp 415-420.

40. Edwards JM, Kinmonth JB: Lymphovenous shunts in man. BMJ 4:579, 1969.

41. Nielubowicz J, Olszewski W: Surgical lymphaticovenous shunts in patients with secondary lymphoedema. Br J Surg 55:440, 1968.

42. Olszewski W, Clodius L, Földi M: The enigma of lymphedema—a search for answers. Lymphology 24:100, 1991.

43. Calderon G, Roberts B, Johnson LL: Experimental approach to the surgical creation of lymphatic-venous communications. Surgery 61:122, 1967.

44. Jacobson JH: Discussion. Arch Surg 84:9, 1962.

45. Laine JB, Howard JM: Experimental lymphatico-venous anastomosis. Surg Forum 14:111, 1963.

46. Yamada Y: The studies on lymphatic venous anastomosis in lymphedema. Nagoya J Med Sci 32:1, 1969.

47. Gilbert A, O'Brien BM, Vorrath JW, Sykes PJ: Lymphaticovenous anastomosis by microvascular technique. Br J Plast Surg 29:355, 1976.

48. Gloviczki P, LeFloch P, Hidden G: Anastomoses lymphaticoveineuses experimentales. J Chir (Paris) 116:437, 1979.

49. Gloviczki P, Hollier LH, Nora FE, Kaye MP: The natural history of microsurgical lymphovenous anastomoses: An experimental study. J Vasc Surg 4:148, 1986.

50. Puckett CL, Jacobs GR, Hurvitz JS, Silver D: Evaluation of lymphovenous anastomoses in obstructive lymphedema. Plast Reconstr Surg 66:116, 1980.

51. Cambria RA, Gloviczki P, Naessens JM, Wahner HW: Noninvasive evaluation of the lymphatic system with lymphoscintigraphy: A prospective, semiquantitative analysis in 386 extremities. J Vasc Surg 18:773, 1993.

52. Baumeister RG, Seifert J, Wiebecke B: Homologous and autologous experimental lymph vessel transplantation—initial experience. Int J Microsurg 3:19, 1981.

53. Baumeister RG, Seifert J: Microsurgical lymph vessel transplantation for the treatment of lymphedema: Experimental and first clinical experiences. Lymphology 14:90, 1981.

54. Baumeister RG, Siuda S, Bohmert H, Moser E: A microsurgical method for reconstruction of interrupted lymphatic pathways:

Autologous lymph-vessel transplantation for treatment of lymph-edemas. Scand J Plast Reconstr Surg 20:141, 1986.

55. Kleinhans E, Baumeister RGH, Hahn D, et al: Evaluation of transport kinetics in lymphoscintigraphy: Follow-up study in patients with transplanted lymphatic vessels. Eur J Nucl Med 10:349, 1985.

56. Baumeister RGH, Frick A, Hofmann T: 10 Years experience with autogenous microsurgical lymph vessel transplantation. Eur J Lymphol 6:62, 1991.

57. Baumeister RGH, Fink U, Tatsch K, Frick A: Microsurgical lymphatic grafting: First demonstration of patent grafts by indirect lymphography and long term follow-up studies. Lymphology (Suppl) 27:787, 1994.

58. Kinjo O, Kusara A: Lymphatic vessel-to-isolated-vein anastomosis for secondary lymphedema in a canine model. Surg Today 25:633, 1995.

59. Weiss M, Baumeister RGH, Hahn K: Dynamic lymph flow imaging in patients with oedema of the lower limb for evaluation of the functional outcome after autologous lymph vessel transplantation: An 8-year follow-up study. Eur J Nucl Med Mol Imaging 30:202, 2003.

60. Kinmonth JB: Chylous diseases and syndromes, including references to tropical elephantiasis. In Kinmonth JB (ed): The Lymphatics: Surgery, Lymphography and Diseases of the Chyle and Lymph Systems, 2nd ed. London, Edward Arnold, 1982, pp 221-268.

61. Servelle M: Congenital malformation of the lymphatics of the small intestine. J Cardiovasc Surg 32:159, 1991.

62. Kinmonth JB, Cox SJ: Protein losing enteropathy in lymphedema: Surgical investigation and treatment. J Cardiovasc Surg 16:111, 1975.

63. Browse NL, Wilson NM, Russo F, et al: Aetiology and treatment of chylous ascites. Br J Surg 79:1145, 1992.

64. Gloviczki P, Soltesz L, Solti F, et al: The surgical treatment of lymphedema caused by chylous reflux. In Bartos V, Davidson JW (eds): Advances in Lymphology. Proceedings of the 8th International Congress of Lymphology, Montreal, 1981. Prague, Czechoslovak Medical Press, 1982, pp 502-507.

65. Sanders JS, Rosenow EC III, Piehler JM, et al: Chyloptysis (chylous sputum) due to thoracic lymphangiectasia with successful surgical correction. Arch Intern Med 148:1465, 1988.

66. Servelle M, Deysson H: Reflux du chyle dans les lymphatiques jambiers. Arch Mal Coeur 12:1181, 1949.

67. Browse NL: The surgery of lymphedema. In Veith FJ (ed): Current Critical Problems in Vascular Surgery. St. Louis, Quality Medical Publishing, 1989, pp 408-409.

68. Molitch HI, Unger EC, Witte CL, vanSonnenberg E: Percutaneous sclerotherapy of lymphangiomas. Radiology 194:343, 1995.

69. Noel AA, Gloviczki P, Bender CE, et al: Surgical treatment for lymphedema and chylous effusions caused by lymphangiectasia. J Vasc Surg 34:785, 2001.

70. Cope C, Salem R, Kaiser LR: Management of chylothorax by percutaneous catheterization and embolization of the thoracic duct: Prospective trial. J Vasc Intervent Radiol 10:1248-1254, 1999.

71. Silk YN, Goumas WM, Douglass HO Jr, Huben RP: Chylous ascites and lymphocyst management by peritoneovenous shunt. Surgery 110:561-565, 1991.

72. Engum SA, Rescorla FJ, West KW, et al: The use of pleuroperitoneal shunts in the management of persistent chylothorax in infants. J Pediatr Surg 34:286-290, 1999.

73. Browse NL, Allen DR, Wilson NM: Management of chylothorax. Br J Surg 84:1711-1716, 1997.

EXTREMITY AMPUTATION FOR VASCULAR DISEASE

MARK R. NEHLER, MD

Chapter

170

Amputation:
An Overview

MARK R. NEHLER, MD
HEATHER WOLFORD, MD

Despite major advances in revascularization, lower extremity amputation remains a common procedure in modern vascular practice. This section is devoted to indications and preoperative evaluation, technique and perioperative care, complications, natural history and functional outcomes, unique aspects of upper extremity amputation, and, finally, the controversial issue of amputation versus revascularization.

Lower extremity amputation has several unique aspects that complicate all of these issues. A number of different providers care for the amputee, each with different levels of training, expertise, and goals. Frequently, digital and forefoot amputations are performed by podiatry surgeons. Major lower extremity amputations can be performed by general surgeons, orthopedic surgeons, and, most commonly, vascular surgeons. Rehabilitation of the amputee is under the direction of rehabilitation medicine and physical therapists. Long-term care of the stump and prosthetic fitting is often under the direction of the prosthetist.

■ INDICATIONS FOR AMPUTATION

The vast majority of major lower extremity amputations are performed for critical limb ischemia (CLI), thus reinforcing the role of the vascular surgeon.[1-3] The available data would indicate a significant delay in referral of these patients to a vascular specialist.[4] Therefore, it is safe to assume that a percentage of major lower extremity amputations are potentially preventable. Currently, there is no agreed-upon definition for an unsalvageable lower extremity. Individual

surgeons and centers will vary in the anatomy required to attempt surgical bypass. Bypass to pedal vessels and the use of an arm vein conduit have become common practices in many regions of the United States. Equally vague is the condition of the foot that would preclude salvage attempts. Most surgeons would agree that extensive heel and/or forefoot necrosis predicts a poor outcome for eventual limb salvage, but again there are no established guidelines.

A less recognized but equally important aspect of care in these patients is patient education and acceptance. The former is critical in amputation prevention. Many poorly educated diabetic patients assume that seeking health care for foot lesions will lead to a major amputation, and therefore they delay care until a major amputation is inevitable. This pattern reinforces a negative perception for limb salvage in this population. Compounding the issue, much of the care delivered is ultimately ineffective (minor amputations performed without adequate circulation), leading to limb loss in a piecemeal fashion, further promoting the belief that limb loss is inevitable. Equally important to understand is the reluctance of patients to accept amputation. Although never studied, the time interval from the date when the surgeon informs the patient he or she requires a major lower extremity amputation for CLI and the date that the amputation occurs is often weeks and sometimes months. Patients often obtain second and third opinions and may turn to a number of alternative medical therapies.

The combination of lack of agreement regarding unsalvageable limbs between vascular surgeons and the variable reluctance of patients to accept a decision to amputate greatly complicate the clinical practice of amputation surgery. Building a trust between the surgeon and the patient is critical. Because this is a life-changing event, multiple discussions between the patient, family, and surgeon are often required. Amputations secondary to acute ischemia (especially iatrogenic trauma) are particularly difficult.

■ AMPUTATION LEVEL

Most patients and physicians would agree that preservation of the maximal limb length is the ideal goal of any extremity amputation. Therefore, a digital amputation is considered preferable to a forefoot amputation and a below-knee amputation (BKA) is preferable to an above-knee amputation (AKA). However, in the patient population with CLI, any incision below the knee joint is often problematic, with healing times measured in months rather than weeks.[4-6] Due to the limited life expectancy of this population, in addition to co-morbidities of the population, the surgeon must carefully consider the implication of the prolonged immobility to heal a difficult amputation wound. In addition, every distal amputation in a given population with CLI has a higher failure rate than a more proximal amputation,[4,7,8] and each failure has implications on patient morbidity, cost to the health care system, and ultimate functional outcome.

A major lower extremity amputation has several goals that are similar to other extirpative surgical procedures (e.g., resection of ischemic bowel, débridement of pancreatic phlegmon, or drainage of brain abscess):

1. To remove all nonviable or diseased tissue
2. To preserve optimal residual function
3. To minimize surgical morbidity

However, based on the clinical scenario, the relative weight of each of these goals may change. For example, an elderly patient with oxygen-dependent chronic obstructive pulmonary disease may be best served with an AKA to reliably heal the wound and minimize the surgical morbidity, sacrificing function in a patient who is likely to remain wheelchair bound with or without the knee joint. In contrast, a young patient with isolated extremity trauma may undergo several operative procedures, including a myocutaneous free flap transfer, to salvage the knee joint, because the ultimate gain in long-term function will negate the near-term morbidity.

A number of studies in the literature describe various circulatory measures to determine amputation level healing. As a general point, many of these techniques are not practical in clinical practice. Most surgeons agree that BKA without a femoral pulse is unlikely to do well. However, a palpable femoral pulse does not guarantee success. The clinical judgment of the operating surgeon (tissue bleeding, viable muscle, and wounds without tension) has been demonstrated to be reasonably accurate (75% to 85%) in several large clinical series (combined around 1000 patients).[4,8-10] Finally, despite the plethora of research regarding the technical aspects of salvaging the knee joint, the sobering fact is that most vascular patients will take minimal advantage of this in rehabilitation.

■ PERIOPERATIVE ISSUES

Based on results, major lower extremity amputations are arguably one of the most difficult procedures the modern vascular surgeon will perform. Perioperative mortality rates of 7% to 15% are typical.[8,11] Compare this with the 2% perioperative mortality rate published in the recent Veterans Affairs multicenter small aneurysm trial.[12] This is obviously not due to the complexity of the procedure but rather to the patient population requiring it. Available data demonstrate a population with significant medical co-morbidities, poor nutrition, anemia, and a severely deconditioned state secondary to the immobility enforced by the nature of the presenting foot lesions and/or prior forefoot procedures.[4]

Healing rates of BKA vary, but incisional failure in 10% to 20% is widely reported.[4,13-15] These patients often have one or more operations attempting to salvage the knee joint, with at least half converting to an eventual AKA. Healing times are often measured in months rather than weeks. Part of the difficulty in wound healing is related to falls and stump trauma. However, even without postoperative trauma, incisions in patients with CLI heal poorly below the knee. Casting the BKA stump appears useful to reduce trauma, but the single small trial using these devices did not demonstrate efficacy compared with standard protective bandages.[16]

■ TECHNICAL ISSUES

Despite the volume of procedures performed and the difficulty in achieving successful incisional healing, only a modest amount of literature exists regarding technical aspects of BKA. Several techniques have been described, including the Burgess posterior myocutaneous flap,[17] skew flaps, side-to-side flaps,[18] and sagittal flaps.[19] Of these techniques, the vast majority of BKAs performed in the United States are of the Burgess technique. Although some physiologic evidence indicates that sagittal and skew flaps provide a better blood supply,[20,21] the single multicenter randomized trial of 191 total BKAs comparing skew flap to Burgess flap did not demonstrate any differences in healing or ultimate need for AKA (8% skew compared with 10% Burgess).[15]

Patients who present with forefoot sepsis are best managed with a guillotine amputation before the definitive BKA. If there is any question regarding deep space plantar or forefoot infection, the prudent course is to err on the side of conservatism with a two-staged amputation. Rarely, diabetic patients in severe metabolic stress with overwhelming forefoot sepsis can be managed by cryoamputation until they can be stabilized for the operating room.[22-24]

■ PERIOPERATIVE COMPLICATIONS

As previously stated, the perioperative mortality rates for major lower extremity amputation are above and beyond the morbidity of the procedure alone.[4,8,11] The patient population requiring amputation is as ill as any in modern medicine. Many patients are in the last months of their lives and could be described as dying from the periphery inward.

An episode of aspiration pneumonitis, subendocardial infarct, or exacerbation of congestive failure can easily prove to be fatal. Compounding the problem, amputations are rarely considered by anesthesia and/or surgeons as a case of the same magnitude as a major vascular reconstruction or cardiac case.

In addition to the typical cardiovascular morbidities, patients undergoing major amputation are immobile in both the preoperative and perioperative period. Not surprisingly, the incidence of deep venous thrombosis is high in this population, mandating some level of prophylaxis.[25] Because many of these patients have underlying hypercoagulable states or undergo amputation for acute arterial thrombosis, anticoagulation is frequent, which often leads to bleeding complications. Finally, many diabetic patients require amputation for severe forefoot sepsis. These patients can suffer septic complications from delay in definitive removal of the septic focus and/or bacteremia at the time of the procedure.

From the patient perspective, one of the most important morbidities of amputation is postoperative pain. Chronic postoperative amputation pain can be divided into two groups: residual limb (stump pain) and phantom limb pain. The prevalence is in the range of 50% to 80% of patients.[26] Both central and peripheral pain mechanisms appear to be involved, including ectopic activity originating from afferent fibers in a neuroma and cortical reorganization/spinal cord sensitization.[27] A review of 255 amputees[28] demonstrated 70% reported either residual or phantom limb pain. For most patients, the pain is episodic and not particularly troublesome. In approximately one in four patients, however, the symptoms are very disabling. In addition, there are some data to suggest that the duration and intensity of pre-amputation limb pain plays a role in early post-amputation residual limb and phantom limb pain.[29]

Therapy for residual and phantom limb pain has been disappointing, in part owing to the unclear mechanisms involved. Sodium channel blockers (lidocaine) and opioids have traditionally been the agents used. Preemptive epidural infusions, early regional nerve blocks with perineural infusions, and mechanical vibratory sensation have been advocated. Gabapentin, clonidine, and tricyclic antidepressants have also been used. Halbert and colleagues[30] summarized the data for efficacy as consisting of a few randomized trials (many with success in the treatment arm barely greater than controls)[27,31-35] and case reports/small series.[34,36-38] They concluded that there is currently a large gap between research and clinical practice in the management of residual and phantom limb pain in amputees.

■ FUNCTIONAL OUTCOMES

A substantial amount of research has focused on preoperative evaluation to determine if a BKA will heal, with preservation of the knee joint and improved function and potential mobility. However, the sobering fact is that many elderly vascular patients will not be able to complete an arduous rehabilitation program to ambulate to any extent with a prosthesis.[4,14,39] Much of this is related to the co-morbidities in the population as previously stated with

regard to perioperative mortality. However, in the United States, the passage of Americans with Disability Act in 1990 has improved wheelchair access by mandating it for public buildings. Frequently, elderly amputees choose to focus effort toward modifying a home to allow at least some mobility in a wheelchair. A review at our institution[4] demonstrated that although fewer than half of amputees were ambulatory postoperatively, relatively few required transition to a care facility. A patient with a healed amputation (AKA or BKA) who can independently transfer and take a few limited steps but remains in the community is the end result for the majority of elderly amputees. Ultimately, the majority of amputations performed are palliative. In addition, the incidence of vascular amputees who ambulate postoperatively declines over time owing to a variety of issues. Finally, the occasional patient will fall and suffer a major fracture during prosthetic use.

Conversely, if patients are to have any realistic hope of extensive prosthetic ambulation postoperatively, the knee joint must be spared. However, the ratio of AKA to BKAs performed worldwide is roughly one.[7] Many of the AKAs performed are done so based on lack of rehabilitation potential rather than inability to eventually heal a BKA. One obvious question is the potential benefit of the knee joint in the nonambulatory patient. Although statements regarding improved transfer potential and balance are frequently made, the available data to support this are lacking. Thigh muscle atrophy has been noted to correlate with the length of the AKA stump.[40] Balance is clearly an issue with prosthetic use and has been widely studied.[41-43] However, similar data regarding balance and wheelchair use are lacking. Finally, small series of the bilateral amputee (both AKA and BKA) have been reported.[44-46] Ambulation is unusual, but pressure ulcers as seen in neurologically impaired patients do not appear to be a long-term issue.

■ NATURAL HISTORY

Patient survival in the Veterans Affairs National Surgical Quality Improvement Program for BKA and AKA was 57% and 39% at 3 years, respectively, again emphasizing the palliative nature of these procedures in most patients.[11] Other reports have found similar poor survival after major limb amputation.[34,47,48] In addition to mortality, significant ongoing morbidity occurs in both the remaining stump (BKA) and contralateral limb after major lower extremity amputation. At 2 years, 15% of patients with an initially successful BKA will convert to an AKA and another 15% will suffer a major contralateral amputation.[7]

■ UPPER EXTREMITY AMPUTATION

The incidence of upper extremity amputation is much less than that of the lower extremity. In addition, the pathology resulting in upper extremity limb loss includes a widespread differential diagnosis, compared with the lower extremity, where complications of atherosclerosis and/or diabetes predominate. The technical issues associated with upper extremity amputation are more complex than in the lower extremity. The psychological impact of the upper extremity amputation appears greater. In the veteran population, the highest rate of post-conflict suicide was noted in upper extremity amputees.[49] Because of the rare incidence of upper extremity amputation, most vascular surgeons focus on the diagnosis and treatment of the potential cause. Any amputation proximal to the digit is usually performed by either plastic or orthopedic surgeons.

■ AMPUTATION VERSUS REVASCULARIZATION

Undeniably, just as there are patients who suffer unnecessary limb loss from late referral and futile attempts at forefoot-directed amputations without adequate pedal circulation, there are also patients who undergo extensive revascularization procedures who (1) suffer near-term limb loss from inadequate conduit, distal runoff, or inability to resolve overwhelming forefoot or heel sepsis or (2) suffer significant procedural morbidities (wound breakdown, lymphedema, graft revision) and die of their systemic co-morbidities before full resolution and return to function.

Some of the morbidities suffered are subtle, and primarily financial, drains on an otherwise overburdened health care system. An example is the patient with forefoot necrosis who on arteriography has normal inflow, a single superficial femoral artery stenosis with flow to a patent popliteal artery, and runoff via a peroneal artery patent to the distal calf that occludes without any visualized vessels in the foot. The patient then undergoes superficial femoral artery angioplasty. Not surprisingly, the foot does not improve and a major amputation is performed. The morbidity for the patient is minimal, but an additional futile procedure is added to the total cost of care.

Much has been written in the past two decades regarding prior bypass failure not affecting the level of subsequent amputation—BKA or AKA.[50-52] However, prior bypass failure does prolong BKA incisional healing.[53-55] In addition, the patient population with CLI is clearly compromised, and additional surgeries increase the cumulative perioperative mortality risk and perioperative pain and inevitably prolong hospital stays and rehabilitation. Prosthetic grafts in a marginal technical situation are particularly problematic, because the risk of graft infection if amputation is required through them is higher, often necessitating their removal.[56] Unfortunately, prosthetic grafts in limb salvage surgery are, by definition, a marginal situation. These issues lead to the patient scenarios we all wish to avoid, namely the elderly patient with CLI who spends the last few months of life in and out of the hospital undergoing multiple procedures.

Another relatively unexplored aspect of CLI is the nature of the presenting foot lesions and the impact on ultimate outcome. Aggressive foot salvage with severe necrosis frequently requires multiple foot operations, prolonged wound care, and healing times measured in months rather than weeks.[5,6] It seems intuitive that there is a point where the morbidity of this approach exceeds any long-term benefit. A tremendous amount of research has focused on defining pedal circulation limits (toe pressures, pulse volume recordings, transcutaneous oxygen tensions) that would be adequate to support local wound healing, with minimal consideration for the nature of wounds this marginal circulation should support.

The obvious question is how to identify subgroups of patients with CLI who are better served by amputation? An approach we have used is to look at the problem from three sides—the technical issues of the revascularization, the foot wound healing issues, and the co-morbidites of the patient. Patients with marginal prospects in more than one category are generally not considered reasonable revascularization candidates. For example, alternate vein conduit for a tibial bypass would be reasonable for a patient with manageable toe gangrene and modest co-morbidities but would not be reasonable for a patient on home oxygen or with a large heel defect. Subgroups with severe co-morbidities who may survive the procedure due to modern anesthesia but are unlikely to survive the follow-up required to heal incisions/wounds and rehabilitation would also not be offered extensive limb salvage. Preoperative C-reactive protein levels have been used in several reports to predict patient survival, foot healing, and limb salvage.[57,58] Low serum albumin levels have correlated with mortality and increased length of stay in multiple studies of elderly hospitalized patients.[59-61] In the future, these markers are likely to gain more widespread use in the population with CLI.

■ SUMMARY

In this section, the subject of amputation is divided in chapters as outlined in this overview. The chapter authors all represent individuals with a clinical interest in limb salvage and have also contributed to the amputation literature in the past decade. The majority of literature on amputations comes from outside the United States, and several authors are from Europe to reflect this.

■ REFERENCES

1. Pernot HF, Winnubst GM, Cluitmans JJ, De Witte LP: Amputees in Limburg: Incidence, morbidity and mortality, prosthetic supply, care utilisation and functional level after one year. Prosthet Orthot Int 24:90-96, 2000.
2. Pohjolainen T, Alaranta H: Ten-year survival of Finnish lower limb amputees. Prosthet Orthot Int 22:10-16, 1998.
3. Rommers GM, Vos LD, Groothoff JW, et al: Epidemiology of lower limb amputees in the north of The Netherlands: Aetiology, discharge destination and prosthetic use. Prosthet Orthot Int 21:92-99, 1997.
4. Nehler MR, Coll JR, Hiatt WR, et al: Functional outcome in a contemporary series of major lower extremity amputations. J Vasc Surg 38:7-14, 2003.
5. Abou-Zamzam AM Jr, Moneta GL, Lee RW, et al: Peroneal bypass is equivalent to inframalleolar bypass for ischemic pedal gangrene. Arch Surg 131:894-898, 1996.
6. Nicoloff AD, Taylor LM Jr, McLafferty RB, et al: Patient recovery after infrainguinal bypass grafting for limb salvage. J Vasc Surg 27:256-263, 1998.
7. Dormandy J, Heeck L, Vig S: Major amputations: Clinical patterns and predictors. Semin Vasc Surg 12:154-161, 1999.
8. Keagy BA, Schwartz JA, Kotb M, et al: Lower extremity amputation: The control series. J Vasc Surg 4:321-326, 1986.

9. Harris JP, Page S, Englund R, May J: Is the outlook for the vascular amputee improved by striving to preserve the knee? J Cardiovasc Surg (Torino) 29:741-745, 1988.

10. Lim RC, Blaisdell FW, Hall AD, et al: Below knee amputation for ischemic gangrene. Surg Obstet Gynecol 25:493-501, 1967.

11. Feinglass J, Pearce WH, Martin GJ, et al: Postoperative and late survival outcomes after major amputation: Findings from the Department of Veterans Affairs National Surgical Quality Improvement Program. Surgery 130:21-29, 2001.

12. Lederle FA, Wilson SE, Johnson GR, et al: Immediate repair compared with surveillance of small abdominal aortic aneurysms. N Engl J Med 346:1437-1444, 2002.

13. Dormandy J, Belcher G, Broos P, et al: Prospective study of 713 below-knee amputations for ischaemia and the effect of a prostacyclin analogue on healing. Hawaii Study Group. Br J Surg 81:33-37, 1994.

14. McWhinnie DL, Gordon AC, Collin J, et al: Rehabilitation outcome 5 years after 100 lower-limb amputations. Br J Surg 81:1596-1599, 1994.

15. Ruckley CV, Stonebridge PA, Prescott RJ: Skewflap versus long posterior flap in below-knee amputations: Multicenter trial. J Vasc Surg 13:423-427, 1991.

16. Baker WH, Barnes RW, Shurr DG: The healing of below-knee amputations: A comparison of soft and plaster dressing. Am J Surg 133:716-718, 1977.

17. Burgess EM, Romano RL, Zettl JH, Schrock RD Jr: Amputations of the leg for peripheral vascular insufficiency. J Bone Joint Surg Am 53:874-890, 1971.

18. Yamanaka M, Kwong PK: The side-to-side flap technique in below-the-knee amputation with long stump. Clin Orthop (201):75-79, 1985.

19. Au KK: Sagittal flaps in below-knee amputations in Chinese patients. J Bone Joint Surg Br 71:597-598, 1989.

20. Johnson WC, Watkins MT, Hamilton J, Baldwin D: Transcutaneous partial oxygen pressure changes following skew flap and Burgess-type below-knee amputations. Arch Surg 132:261-263, 1997.

21. McCollum PT, Spence VA, Walker WF, Murdoch G: A rationale for skew flaps in below-knee amputation surgery. Prosthet Orthot Int 9:95-99, 1985.

22. Bunt TJ: Physiologic amputation: Preliminary cryoamputation of the gangrenous extremity. AORN J 54:1220-1224, 1991.

23. Hunsaker RH, Schwartz JA, Keagy BA, et al: Dry ice cryoamputation: A twelve-year experience. J Vasc Surg 2:812-816, 1985.

24. Winburn GB, Wood MC, Hawkins ML, et al: Current role of cryoamputation. Am J Surg 162:647-650, 1991.

25. Yeager RA, Moneta GL, Edwards JM, et al: Deep vein thrombosis associated with lower extremity amputation. J Vasc Surg 22:612-615, 1995.

26. Kooijman CM, Dijkstra PU, Geertzen JH, et al: Phantom pain and phantom sensations in upper limb amputees: An epidemiological study. Pain 87:33-41, 2000.

27. Nikolajsen L, Ilkjaer S, Christensen JH, et al: Randomised trial of epidural bupivacaine and morphine in prevention of stump and phantom pain in lower-limb amputation. Lancet 350:1353-1357, 1997.

28. Ehde DM, Czerniecki JM, Smith DG, et al: Chronic phantom sensations, phantom pain, residual limb pain, and other regional pain after lower limb amputation. Arch Phys Med Rehabil 81:1039-1044, 2000.

29. Jensen TS, Krebs B, Nielsen J, Rasmussen P: Phantom limb, phantom pain and stump pain in amputees during the first 6 months following limb amputation. Pain 17:243-256, 1983.

30. Halbert J, Crotty M, Cameron ID: Evidence for the optimal management of acute and chronic phantom pain: A systematic review. Clin J Pain 18:84-92, 2002.

31. Wu CL, Tella P, Staats PS, et al: Analgesic effects of intravenous lidocaine and morphine on postamputation pain: A randomized double-blind, active placebo-controlled, crossover trial. Anesthesiology 96:841-848, 2002.

32. Dellemijn PL, Vanneste JA: Randomised double-blind active-placebo-controlled crossover trial of intravenous fentanyl in neuropathic pain. Lancet 349:753-758, 1997.

33. Lambert A, Dashfield A, Cosgrove C, et al: Randomized prospective study comparing preoperative epidural and intraoperative perineural analgesia for the prevention of postoperative stump and phantom limb pain following major amputation. Reg Anesth Pain Med 26:316-321, 2001.

34. Jahangiri M, Jayatunga AP, Bradley JW, Dark CH: Prevention of phantom pain after major lower limb amputation by epidural infusion of diamorphine, clonidine and bupivacaine. Ann R Coll Surg Engl 76:324-326, 1994.

35. Finsen V, Persen L, Lovlien M, et al: Transcutaneous electrical nerve stimulation after major amputation. J Bone Joint Surg Br 70:109-112, 1988.

36. Rusy LM, Troshynski TJ, Weisman SJ: Gabapentin in phantom limb pain management in children and young adults: Report of seven cases. J Pain Symptom Manage 21:78-82, 2001.

37. Vichitrananda C, Pausawasdi S: Midazolam for the treatment of phantom limb pain exacerbation: Preliminary reports. J Med Assoc Thai 84:299-302, 2001.

38. Carabelli RA, Kellerman WC: Phantom limb pain: Relief by application of TENS to contralateral extremity. Arch Phys Med Rehabil 66:466-467, 1985.

39. Houghton AD, Taylor PR, Thurlow S, et al: Success rates for rehabilitation of vascular amputees: Implications for preoperative assessment and amputation level. Br J Surg 79:753-755, 1992.

40. Isakov E, Burger H, Gregoric M, Marincek C: Stump length as related to atrophy and strength of the thigh muscles in trans-tibial amputees. Prosthet Orthot Int 20:96-100, 1996.

41. Nadollek H, Brauer S, Isles R: Outcomes after trans-tibial amputation: The relationship between quiet stance ability, strength of hip abductor muscles and gait. Physiother Res Int 7:203-214, 2002.

42. Buckley JG, O'Driscoll D, Bennett SJ: Postural sway and active balance performance in highly active lower-limb amputees. Am J Phys Med Rehabil 81:13-20, 2002.

43. Hermodsson Y, Ekdahl C, Persson BM, Roxendal G: Standing balance in trans-tibial amputees following vascular disease or trauma: A comparative study with healthy subjects. Prosthet Orthot Int 18:150-158, 1994.

44. Dougherty PJ: Long-term follow-up study of bilateral above-the-knee amputees from the Vietnam War. J Bone Joint Surg Am 81:1384-1390, 1999.

45. Evans WE, Hayes JP, Vermilion BD: Rehabilitation of the bilateral amputee. J Vasc Surg 5:589-593, 1987.

46. Inderbitzi R, Buttiker M, Pfluger D, Nachbur B: The fate of bilateral lower limb amputees in end-stage vascular disease. Eur J Vasc Surg 6:321-326, 1992.

47. Rush DS, Huston CC, Bivins BA, Hyde GL: Operative and late mortality rates of above-knee and below-knee amputations. Am Surg 47:36-39, 1981.

48. Whitehouse FW, Jurgenson C, Block MA: The later life of an amputee: Another look at the fate of the second leg. Diabetes 17:520-521, 1968.

49. Hrubec Z, Ryder RA: Traumatic limb amputations and subsequent mortality from cardiovascular disease and other causes. J Chronic Dis 33:239-250, 1980.

50. Panayiotopoulos YP, Reidy JF, Taylor PR: The concept of knee salvage: Why does a failed femorocrural/pedal arterial bypass not affect the amputation level? Eur J Vasc Endovasc Surg 13:477-485, 1997.

51. Tsang GM, Crowson MC, Hickey NC, Simms MH: Failed femoro-crural reconstruction does not prejudice amputation level. Br J Surg 78:1479-1481, 1991.

52. Cook TA, Davies AH, Horrocks M, Baird RN: Amputation level is not adversely affected by previous femorodistal bypass surgery. Eur J Vasc Surg 6:599-601, 1992.

53. Van Niekerk LJ, Stewart CP, Jain AS: Major lower limb amputation following failed infrainguinal vascular bypass surgery: A prospective study on amputation levels and stump complications. Prosthet Orthot Int 25:29-33, 2001.

54. Dardik H, Kahn M, Dardik I, et al: Influence of failed vascular bypass procedures on conversion of below-knee to above-knee amputation levels. Surgery 91:64-69, 1982.

55. Epstein SB, Worth MH Jr, el Ferzli G: Level of amputation following failed vascular reconstruction for lower limb ischemia. Curr Surg 46:185-192, 1989.

56. Rubin JR, Marmen C, Rhodes RS: Management of failed prosthetic grafts at the time of major lower extremity amputation. J Vasc Surg 7:673-676, 1988.

57. Biancari F, Kantonen I, Alback A, et al: Limits of infrapopliteal bypass surgery for critical leg ischemia: When not to reconstruct. World J Surg 24:727-733, 2000.

58. Matzke S, Biancari F, Ihlberg L, et al: Increased preoperative C-reactive protein level as a prognostic factor for postoperative amputation after femoropopliteal bypass surgery for CLI. Ann Chir Gynaecol 90:19-22, 2001.

59. Delgado-Rodriguez M, Medina-Cuadros M, Gomez-Ortega A, et al: Cholesterol and serum albumin levels as predictors of cross infection, death, and length of hospital stay. Arch Surg 137:805-812, 2002.

60. Herrmann FR, Safran C, Levkoff SE, Minaker KL: Serum albumin level on admission as a predictor of death, length of stay, and readmission. Arch Intern Med 152:125-130, 1996.

61. Marinella MA, Markert RJ: Admission serum albumin level and length of hospitalization in elderly patients. South Med J 91:851-854, 1998.

Chapter

171

Lower Extremity Amputation:
Indications, Patient Evaluation, and Level Determination

AHMED M. ABOU-ZAMZAM, JR., MD

Major lower extremity amputations continue to be a part of all vascular practices despite aggressive attempts at limb salvage. Although often viewed as a failure of treatment, major amputation should be embraced as an important, definitive treatment option. With the aging of the population, the prevalence of peripheral vascular disease will continue to increase, as will the need for amputations.

The goal of amputation is to remove all infected, gangrenous, and ischemic tissue and provide the patient with the greatest length of functional limb. Avoiding repeated amputations and nonhealing operative sites is critical for the recovery of the patient and optimal functional rehabilitation or palliation.

In this chapter, the current indications for amputation are reviewed along with preoperative patient evaluation, methods available for optimal determination of amputation level, and important functional and psychological aspects affecting patient outcome. Having a clear understanding of these principles will help the vascular surgeon excel in this often underappreciated realm of vascular surgery.

■ BACKGROUND

In the United States approximately 80,000 major amputations (above the ankle) are performed annually.[15,22] Trends in the interplay between revascularization and amputation rates are confusing. Over a recent 10-year period, the Mayo Clinic reported a 50% reduction in amputation rates that corresponded to increases in the rates of lower extremity revascularization by surgical and endovascular techniques.[29] A Finnish study also demonstrated an increase in revascularization rates correlating with a decrease in the major amputation rates in elderly patients.[21] However, a recent U.S. study of national hospital discharge data demonstrated an overall 11% increase in major amputation rates in recent years, which is likely related to the overall aging of the population.[22] Diabetes and peripheral vascular disease remain the major risk factors for lower extremity amputation worldwide.[28] Studies show that 25% to 90% of all amputations are associated with diabetes.[15,28] Patients with diabetes have a 10-fold greater risk for amputation than those without diabetes.[22] This association is due to the presence of neuropathy and associated infection as well as to the markedly increased prevalence of peripheral vascular disease in this patient population.

There is a regional variation in the performance of amputation around the world that suggests that factors other than strict medical issues may affect amputation rates.[12,28,35] A study from the United Kingdom cited significant regional variation in amputation rates and stressed the need for consensus guidelines.[12] Physician experience plays a key role in the selection of amputation as a treatment. In treating critical limb ischemia, surgeon caseload and hospital volume have been shown to affect amputation rates, with low volumes being associated with higher amputation rates.[34] Patient and health care provider education has been demonstrated to reduce amputation rates.[9] Earlier identification of patients at risk will lead to more timely treatment and interventions.

A complex interaction exists between race and amputation rates. In certain groups, such as the Navajo population, amputation rates appear to be related to the high incidence of diabetes.[28] However, African Americans are more likely than whites to undergo amputation as opposed to revascularization even when controlled for the presence of diabetes.[30,51,58] This difference is speculated to be due to variations in access to health care, treatment of comorbidities, and possible physician and patient factors. Insurance status has also been demonstrated to have an effect on amputation rates, with patients without coverage having increased rates compared with those with access to health care.[58]

■ INDICATIONS

Indications for amputation have been traditionally divided into presentations due to acute ischemia, chronic ischemia, or foot infections. In the presence of acute ischemia, major amputation is undertaken for irreversible ischemia, for severe ischemia with no revascularization options, or following unsuccessful attempts at revascularization. With chronic ischemia, amputation may be employed for failures of revascularization, those with no revascularization options, patients with severe comorbidities or poor functional status, or the presence of such extensive gangrene or infection that foot salvage is not possible. Pedal sepsis without ischemia constitutes another group of patients undergoing amputation. Clearly the underlying indications for amputation may overlap. The traditional groupings of acute ischemia, chronic ischemia, and foot infections are better utilized when evaluating the outcome of limb salvage after revascularization and are not specific enough when discussing amputation.

The presence of peripheral vascular disease and diabetes, either alone or in combination, contributes to the majority of major lower extremity amputations. Many general classifications, however, overemphasize the role of diabetes and understate the role of concomitant ischemia. Malone reported the indications for amputation as complications of diabetes (60% to 80%); infections without diabetes (15% to 25%); ischemia without infection (5% to 10%); chronic osteomyelitis (3% to 5%); trauma (2% to 5%); and miscellaneous (5% to 10%).[39] These general classifications have a certain degree of overlap and mask the true interaction between ischemia and diabetes. This simplistic breakdown does not give insight into the true influence of ischemia and the potential of revascularization to affect amputation rates. Also, ischemia may occur in an acute or chronic setting, and because no revascularization technique is universally successful, amputation may ultimately follow revascularization.

In a recent report from our group,[2] an attempt was made to more clearly categorize the indications for major amputation to explain why amputations continue to be performed despite aggressive revascularization programs. When identifying the indications for amputation it must be recognized that with chronic ischemia ultimate limb loss may occur despite prior revascularization. Also, patients may present with acutely ischemic legs that are beyond hope of salvage. The influence of gangrene and pedal sepsis must

Table 171-1 Indications for Major Amputation	
INDICATION	**NO. OF CASES (%) N = 131**
Critical limb ischemia with failed revascularization	51 (39%)
Extensive pedal gangrene	20 (15%)
Unreconstructable arterial anatomy	15 (11%)
Overwhelming pedal sepsis	12 (9%)
Excessive surgical risk	12 (9%)
Nonviable, acutely ischemic foot	11 (8%)
Nonambulatory status	10 (8%)

From Abou-Zamzam AM Jr, Teruya TH, Killeen JD, Ballard JL: Major lower extremity amputation in an academic vascular center. Ann Vasc Surg 17:86-90, 2003.

also be considered, because they have a significant impact on the options for limb salvage. Last, patient comorbidities and ambulatory status also influence the decision for amputation. These issues were reviewed in a series of 131 consecutive major lower extremity amputations, and the indications for amputation according to these categories are shown in Table 171-1.

In our series, more than 50% of patients who underwent amputation had prior attempts at limb salvage via revascularization or anatomically had no revascularization options. This group of patients had presumably exhausted the armamentarium of vascular surgery. Seventeen percent of patients were not considered candidates for aggressive attempts at limb salvage owing to a preexisting nonambulatory status or the presence of severe comorbidity. However, nearly one fourth of all patients underwent amputation because of extensive gangrene or infection that was present at the initial presentation to the vascular surgeon. Patients in this last group may benefit from earlier diagnosis, prompt referral, and definitive therapy. The potential to improve the care of these patients is an important direction of inquiry that requires further study.

Similar findings were reported by Nehler and coworkers[45] in a series of 172 major amputations. The indication for amputation was critical ischemia in 87% and complications of diabetic neuropathy without significant ischemia in 13%. Forty-six patients (30%) had prior bypass failures or amputations despite patent reconstructions, and 10 (6%) had no revascularization options; therefore, 36% had exhausted the resources of revascularization. Eighty-five of the patients (55%) underwent primary amputation because of severe comorbidity, poor functional status, extensive necrosis, or a combination of these factors. Similarly, in another series of 125 major amputations, 38% of procedures were performed after failed reavscularizations.[3]

The significant role that delay in treatment plays in amputation cannot be overstated. The mean time to vascular surgery consultation for pedal tissue loss was 73 days, and for rest pain it was 27 days in the report by Nehler and coworkers.[45] This delay likely accounts for the large percentage of primary amputation in their series and underscores the need for patient and physician education. Indeed, in a report by Bailey and colleagues, only 24% of patients with critical limb ischemia were perceived as needing "urgent" vascular consultation, with a mean duration of symptoms before vascular evaluation of 8 weeks.[5]

Table 171-2	Details Regarding Presenting Foot Lesions in 132 Limbs with Foot Necrosis Undergoing Major Lower Extremity Amputation			
LOCATION	**NO. (%) ULCERATION** (N = 25)	**NO. (%) DRY GANGRENE** (N = 56)	**NO. (%) SEPSIS** (N = 15)	**TOTALS** (N = 132)
Forefoot				
Digit single	4 (16%)	4 (7%)	3 (6%)	11 (8%)
Digit multiple	6 (24%)	11 (20%)	2 (4%)	19 (14%)
MTH single	2 (8%)	3 (5%)	5 (10%)	10 (8%)
MTH multiple	0 (0%)	6 (11%)	8 (16%)	14 (11%)
Malleolar	1 (4%)	3 (5%)	2 (4%)	6 (5%)
Midfoot	4 (16%)	5 (9%)	16 (31%)	25 (19%)
Heel	6 (24%)	13 (23%)	10 (20%)	29 (22%)
Global*	2 (8%)	11 (20%)	5 (10%)	18 (13%)

Categorization based on gross appearance of the foot necrosis on preoperative physical examination alone.
MTH, Metatarsal head.
*Either complete breakdown of prior amputations, extremities that had large gangrenous defects, or extremities that presented nonviable at either the foot or calf level.

From Nehler MR, Coll JR, Hiatt WR, et al: Functional outcome in a contemporary series of major lower extremity amputations. J Vasc Surg 38:7-14, 2003.

The most important aspect of the indication for amputation is the initial decision whether to attempt limb salvage or proceed with major amputation. Despite widespread discussion of great triumphs in revascularization, there is a growing awareness that primary amputation may be the best approach in certain groups of patients. Indeed, in those with either extensive foot lesions, severe comorbidities, or very unfavorable anatomy, primary amputation should be considered a viable treatment option.[45,46] Owing to the delay in referral, many patients ultimately requiring amputation present to the vascular surgeon with extensive pedal necrosis, making salvage unlikely, regardless of arterial targets for revascularization (Table 171-2). End-stage renal disease presents a particularly difficult challenge, and the presence of heel gangrene in this group may be best treated with primary amputation.[20,38]

■ PREOPERATIVE EVALUATION

The preoperative evaluation of a patient undergoing major amputation should proceed in a rational, yet expeditious manner. The ideal of minimizing perioperative complications and mortality must be emphasized. Mortality rates remain high after below-knee amputations (BKAs) (6% to 9%) and even greater after above-knee amputations (AKAs) (13% to 17%).[2,11,23,35,36,45,62] The significant comorbidities present in the amputation population are undoubtedly what makes this a high-risk procedure. However, owing to the perceived lower physiologic stress of a 1-hour amputation compared with a 5-hour revascularization, the risks these patients actually face are often underappreciated. In fact, an average perioperative mortality of 10% for major amputation versus 2% for lower extremity revascularization refutes this misconception.[1,33,47,50]

The requisite evaluation of the potential amputee depends on the urgency of the intervention. In patients with acute ischemia, embolic disease will direct the focus of the investigation toward the embolic sources—most often cardiac. Echocardiography and anticoagulation are key aspects of perioperative management. Management of arrhythmias and the issue of recent myocardial infarction

with ventricular thrombus must be addressed. However, the time taken preoperatively should be focused toward stabilization of the unstable patient, and the nonviable limb should be amputated in a timely manner, with most diagnostic testing proceeding in the postoperative period.

Patients with acute ischemia related to thrombosis of underlying chronically diseased arteries will share many risk factors with the group presenting with chronic ischemia. In these patients, the role for extensive perioperative cardiac evaluation is unclear. Indeed, most reports of preoperative cardiac evaluation have excluded patients undergoing amputation and instead focused on those undergoing aneurysm repair or lower extremity revascularization.[8,13,14,37] However, comparative perioperative mortality rates call this practice into question.

Standard evaluation with a thorough history and physical examination should be performed in all patients. Active congestive heart failure, unstable angina, or concurrent myocardial infarction must be addressed. In the absence of active cardiac symptoms, evidence of congestive heart failure on history or physical examination, or acute issues on electrocardiogram, thorough cardiac evaluation is not necessary.[37,56] It is important to recognize that most patients presenting for amputation have had limited activity and may not manifest covert cardiac disease owing to the lack of physiologic stress, so even minor symptoms should be of concern.

Perioperative treatment with beta blockade has been shown to be beneficial in the general vascular population.[19,43,49] These studies included few patients undergoing major amputation. However, owing to the shared risk factors, the positive impact of beta blockers can likely be extrapolated to the amputation population. Management of associated hypertension, diabetes, and renal failure should be optimized. An aggressive approach to normalize glucose levels is essential to ensure proper wound healing. The timing of hemodialysis in relation to operation is important in managing fluids and electrolytes in the perioperative period.

Special consideration should be given to the patients presenting with extensive pedal infection necessitating amputation. Aggressive control of infection with surgical extirpation of the source and adjunctive intravenous antibiotics is the mainstay of treatment. The two-stage approach of guillotine amputation, followed by formal amputation several days later, has been shown to have a lower complication rate than single-stage amputation.[24] However, even though guillotine amputation is a rapid procedure, a trip to the operating room is still necessary. Another option in patients who are moribund is a physiologic cryoamputation, which may be performed safely at the bedside.[31,61] This procedure will alleviate any time pressures for amputation and allow optimal treatment of associated conditions. If necessary, cryoamputation can be maintained for several weeks.

In the perioperative period the high incidence of venous thromboembolism must be remembered. Yeager and associates documented a perioperative rate of deep venous thrombosis of 11% after major amputation.[63] Interestingly, more than one half of the thromboses were present preoperatively. Furthermore, 17% of all amputation deaths are caused by pulmonary emboli.[15] These statistics underscore the infirm nature of these patients and the importance of surveillance and prophylaxis.

Throughout the perioperative evaluation it is important to involve rehabilitation medicine colleagues, physical therapists, nurses, and prosthetists in the care of these patients. Clearly, centers with dedicated multispecialty teams have much better success in rehabilitation outcome.[42]

■ AMPUTATION LEVEL SELECTION

The goals of amputation are (1) to rid the patient of all infected, necrotic, and painful tissue; (2) to have a wound that heals successfully; and (3) to have an appropriate remnant stump that is able to accommodate a prosthetic. The length of the preserved limb has important implications on rehabilitation. Prosthetic use after major amputation puts an increased energy demand on the patient. Unilateral below-knee amputees require a 10% to 40% increase in energy expenditure for ambulation, whereas above-knee amputees require 50% to 70% more energy to ambulate.[15] This differential may explain why the successful rehabilitation rate is much lower after an AKA than a BKA. Prosthetic use is reported as 50% to 100% after BKA but only 10% to 30% after AKA.[42,44,45,57] Interestingly, the true rate of ambulation is significantly lower than prosthetic use and shows a steady attrition in the 5 years after amputation.[44,45]

The failure of an amputation to heal is multifactorial. Much emphasis has been placed on assessing the blood flow at the level of the amputation to predict wound healing. However, failure may be caused not just by ischemia but also by infection, hematoma, or trauma. This explains why no single test can ever predict with 100% accuracy the ability of an amputation to heal, or, conversely, the inability of an amputation to heal. Most of the tests in use are better at predicting wound healing than they are at predicting wound failure. Thus utilizing any single test alone may lead to unnecessarily proximal amputation.

The importance of optimizing level selection is underlined by the reported need for revision of BKAs to AKAs in 15% to 25% of patients.[2,15,36,45] This revision rate is frequently accompanied by a perioperative mortality of over 5%.[15] Such events also lead to increased patient anxiety and fear of repeated, more proximal amputations.

The drive to maximize limb length in the amputee and minimize the need for revisions has led to the investigation of the optimal modality for selection of amputation level. Physical findings alone (pulses, skin quality, extent of foot ischemia/infection, skin temperature), noninvasive hemodynamic tests (segmental pressures and Doppler waveforms, toe pressures), invasive anatomic tests (angiographic scoring systems), and physiologic tests (skin blood flow, skin perfusion pressure, transcutaneous oxygen measurements) have all been extensively investigated.

The physical examination is the essential first step in level determination. The extent of gangrene and infection will dictate the maximal length attainable. In this evaluation the presence of dependent rubor should be considered analogous to gangrene, because this tissue is ischemic. The presence of pulses should be accurately assessed. The presence of a palpable pulse immediately proximal to a proposed amputation level predicts successful healing in nearly 100% of patients undergoing major and minor amputation.[7,18] However, the absence of a pulse does not necessarily lead to failure of wound healing; therefore, reliance solely on the presence of a pulse will lead to unnecessarily high amputations.

"Clinical judgment" incorporating the physical findings and consideration of the patient's overall status has been demonstrated to yield wound healing rates of 80% in BKAs and 90% in AKAs. Wagner and colleagues found that objective data may supplement clinical judgment but not replace it, because more distal amputations were achieved with clinical judgment rather than sole reliance on objective examinations.[60] Experience counts; determination of amputation level should not be relegated to junior surgeons or trainees.

The subjective interpretation of skin temperature as a guide for amputation has not been reliable. However, several investigators have demonstrated that objective, direct skin temperature measurement may predict amputation healing with an accuracy of 80% to 90%.[15,55] In a study comparing several noninvasive techniques, direct skin temperature measurement at the level of amputation with a threshold of 90° F demonstrated the best accuracy.[60]

The use of noninvasive hemodynamic tests has been extensively evaluated. The frequently employed tests are the segmental pressures and Doppler waveforms as well as toe pressures. Absolute ankle pressures of more than 60 mm Hg have been shown to predict healing of BKAs with an accuracy of 50% to 90%.[15] Calf pressures and thigh pressures have shown similar reliability.[15] However, Wagner and colleagues found that Doppler pressures at the thigh, popliteal, calf, and ankle levels were unreliable in predicting healing of BKAs.[60] This appears less accurate than clinical judgment, and the inaccuracy may in part be due to the high prevalence of diabetes in this population with concomitant arterial calcification.

The use of toe pressures has been advocated as being predictive in forefoot amputations. Vitti and associates[59] demonstrated universal failure of minor amputations in patients with diabetes and toe pressures less than 38 mm Hg.

However, there was no similar threshold value in patients without diabetes, limiting the usefulness of this parameter.

Invasive testing with arteriography has been investigated as a means of determining amputation level. The correlation between arteriographic findings and healing potential has been poor. Dwars and coworkers[18] found that angiographic scores had no correlation at all with amputation healing. Indeed, in their report, the angiographic patency tended to be greater in the limbs with failed or delayed healing compared with limbs with successful healing.

All physiologic tests attempt to give a prediction of wound healing based on tissue perfusion or oxygen delivery at the proposed level of amputation. Intradermal isotope skin blood flow determination is a technique in which an intradermal injection of isotope is made and blood flow is calculated by measuring the isotope washout rate. This technique utilizes xenon-133 or iodine-125 and employs nuclear medicine scanning devices.[39,40] Malone and associates[41] initially reported excellent results with the xenon-133 clearance with an accuracy of 92% to 97%. However, in a follow-up report this same group found that the overlap in values between patients with healed and failed amputations made this test too unreliable.[40]

Skin perfusion pressure is another physiologic test to determine amputation level. This test involves a scintigraphic technique in which intracutaneous injection of iodine-123 is performed at the different amputation levels. External pressure is applied and by measuring the washout of isotope the skin perfusion pressure is determined. A level less than 20 mm Hg was predictive of wound failure in 89% of amputations, and a reading more than 20 mm Hg predicted healing in 99%.[18] Similarly, skin perfusion pressure may be measured by laser Doppler velocimetry, thus avoiding the need for isotopes.

Skin fluorescence is a technique that employs a Wood or ultraviolet light after the intravenous injection of fluorescein dye. A qualitative determination of regional blood flow is used to determine amputation level. Success rates predicting healing have been reported as 86% to 100%.[39] Owing to the wider availability of these tools and no requirement for a radioisotope, this technique is more accessible than the scintigraphic techniques. However, the fluorescein technique may be more affected than scintigraphic techniques by the presence of inflammation and cellulitis.

Transcutaneous oxygen measurements (tcPo$_2$) are a completely noninvasive method that is used in level selection. A small sensor is placed on the skin at the area of interest. By heating the sensor and skin to 44° C, local skin hyperemia results in decreased flow resistance and arteriolization of capillary blood. The tcPo$_2$ then approximates the true Pao$_2$ in the area of interest.[6] The sensors can be placed anywhere on the body and readings are given in millimeters of mercury. Absolute readings may be recorded, or readings in areas may be indexed to a reference site (often the chest). The probes are small and atraumatic, and multiple simultaneous sites can be tested depending on the machine. The readings in the supine position are more predictive than measurements in the dependent position or during supplemental oxygen breathing.[53] The values recorded are reliable and show an acceptable day-to-day variability in repeat measurements.[32]

Transcutaneous oxygen levels have been shown to have an accuracy of 87% to 100% in predicting wound healing.[7,10,15,40] Malone and colleagues reported no amputation failures in patients with tcPo$_2$ greater than 20 mm Hg and universal failure when tcPo$_2$ was less than 20 mm Hg. Unfortunately, others have not confirmed any consistent absolute tcPo$_2$ threshold.[7,15,60] Some authors have reported a useful tcPo$_2$ threshold of 30 mm Hg, whereas others have reported 16 mm Hg as a useful cutoff. In general, tcPo$_2$ readings of more than 40 mm Hg are associated with healing and less than 20 mm Hg with failure.[4,6] The lack of a consistent minimal level is likely because nutrient blood flow may be present even in the setting of tcPo$_2$ readings of 0 mm Hg. The tcPo$_2$ may be artificially low in the setting of infection, inflammation, or edema, and repeat measurements are advised once such processes have resolved. Incidentally, the tcPo$_2$ has shown not just accuracy in predicting wound healing but also accuracy in predicting outcome after revascularization. Changes in tcPo$_2$ of more than 30 mm Hg after revascularization are predictive of a successful clinical outcome.[10]

In direct comparisons to segmental pressures and skin blood flow, tcPo$_2$ has been demonstrated to be the most accurate predictor of wound healing.[40] This applies not just to major amputation but also to forefoot amputation.[7,10] Measurements of tcPo$_2$ have also been shown to be more accurate than those from fluorescein dye injections.[27,39] In addition, tcPo$_2$ has several advantages over the other tests in the ease of measurement, reproducibility, and simple instrumentation that can be readily introduced into any vascular laboratory.

Taking away a meaningful approach to the determination of amputation level is important. A combination of physical findings, clinical judgment, and objective testing has been shown to yield the greatest accuracy in level selection.[6,7,18,40,60] Whether skin temperature, skin blood flow or perfusion, or tcPo$_2$ measurements are used depends on the local experience and availability of techniques. My colleagues and my preferred objective test is the tcPo$_2$ measurement with a threshold value of 30 mm Hg. However, strictly utilizing a single objective method and not all available clinical data will lead to unnecessarily proximal amputations and deny patients the best opportunity for successful rehabilitation. A rational approach is outlined in Figure 171-1.

■ RAMIFICATIONS OF MAJOR AMPUTATION

As in other areas of vascular surgery, the successful completion of the operation is only the beginning. Even before the operation, all parties to be involved with the patient's future care should be mobilized. A dedicated team approach clearly improves the ultimate outcome of the amputee.[27,42] One report documented an increase in successful rehabilitation after major amputation from 69% before institution of a coordinated team approach to 100% after development of such a team.[42]

Although the surgeon may focus on the surgical wounds, other factors may arise unique to the recovery of the

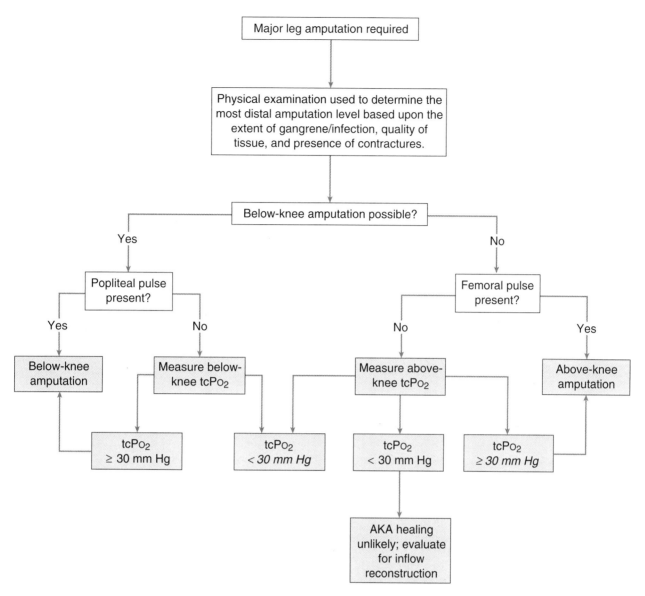

FIGURE 171-1 Algorithm for determining major amputation level. AKA, above-knee amputation.

amputee. Depression is common after major amputation, especially in younger amputees.[25] The loss experienced has been considered of similar magnitude to the loss of a spouse. However, whereas the feeling of bereavement abates over the first year, there is a continued sense of loss beyond 1 year in the amputee.[48] Addressing these issues involves the participation of psychologists, nurses, and often geriatric specialists. Success in rehabilitation has been shown to decrease the severity and rates of depression.[54] Social discomfort, the appearance of the prosthesis, and individual coping skills should be openly addressed to aid in the recovery process.[16,26,52]

Reasonable goals should be set for patients. Although many patients may not walk independently, many will wear prostheses, and the large majority will return to their home environment. In a recent series of major amputations, 29% of patients were able to walk outside the home with a prosthesis, 42% used a prosthetic limb, and 92% of patients were able to return to community living.[45]

Many patients worry about the fate of their remaining limb. Fifteen to 35 percent of amputees with diabetes will lose a second leg within 5 years.[17] The presence of renal failure is a particularly poor prognostic indicator of second limb amputation.[2] These facts underscore the need for continued diligence in protecting and surveying the remaining limb. Continued efforts of education and preventive foot care in this population are essential.

■ SUMMARY

Major lower extremity amputation has a significant effect on the patient and should continue to be considered an important aspect of vascular surgery. Although many cases of amputation occur after the exhaustion of revascularization options, many amputations continue to be performed because of delays in patient presentation, with extensive infection or gangrene precluding limb salvage. Preoperative evaluation should focus on the comorbidities of the individual patient, and primary amputation in lieu of revascularization should be carefully considered in certain patients. Determining the optimal level of amputation must balance the goals of leaving the longest residual limb with minimizing the number of operations and attendant risks. Objective tests such as tcPo$_2$ measurements should be used as adjuncts to the physical examination and clinical judgment. The amputation patient benefits from a team approach with the focus on rehabilitation and ultimate return home.

■ REFERENCES

1. Abou-Zamzam AM Jr, Lee RW, Moneta GL, et al: Functional outcome after infrainguinal bypass for limb salvage. J Vasc Surg 25:287-295, 1997.
2. Abou-Zamzam AM Jr, Teruya TH, Killeen JD, Ballard JL: Major lower extremity amputation in an academic vascular center. Ann Vasc Surg 17:86-90, 2003.
3. Amirhamzeh MMR: The decision to amputate. Surg Rounds Feb: 86-90, 2003.
4. Bacharach JM, Rooke TW, Osmundson PJ, Gloviczki P: Predictive value of transcutaneous oxygen pressure and amputation success by use of supine and elevation measurements. J Vasc Surg 15:558-563, 1992.
5. Bailey CM, Saha S, Magee TR, Galland RB: A 1 year prospective study of management and outcome of patients presenting with critical lower limb ischaemia. Eur J Vasc Endovasc Surg 25:131-134, 2003.
6. Ballard JL, Bianchi C: Transcutaneous oxygen tension: Principles and application. In Abu-Rhama AF, Bergan JJ (eds): Noninvasive Vascular Diagnosis. New York, Springer, 2000, pp 403-409.
7. Ballard JL, Eke CC, Bunt TJ, Killeen JD: A prospective evaluation of transcutaneous oxygen measurements in the management of diabetic foot problems. J Vasc Surg 22:485-490, 1995.
8. Barone JE, Tucker JB, Rassias D, Corvo PR: Routine perioperative pulmonary artery catheterization has no effect on rate of complications in vascular surgery: A meta-analysis. Am J Surg 67:674-679, 2001.
9. Bruckner M, Mangan M, Godin S, Pogach L: Project LEAP of New Jersey: Lower extremity amputation prevention in persons with type 2 diabetes. Am J Manag Care 5:609-616, 1999.
10. Bunt TJ, Holloway GA: TcPo$_2$ as an accurate predictor of therapy in limb salvage. Ann Vasc Surg 10:224-227, 1996.
11. Campbell WB, Marriott S, Eve R, et al: Amputation for acute ischaemia is associated with increased comorbidity and higher amputation level. Cardiovasc Surg 11:121-123, 2003.
12. Connelly J, Airey M, Chell S: Variation in clinical decision making is a partial explanation for geographical variation in lower extremity amputation rates. Br J Surg 88:529-535, 2001.
13. de Virgilio C, Toosie K, Elbassir M, et al: Dipyridamole-thallium/sestamibi before vascular surgery: A prospective blinded study in moderate-risk patients. J Vasc Surg 32:77-89, 2000.
14. de Virgilio C, Wall DB, Ephraim L, et al: An abnormal dipyridamole thallium/sestamibi fails to predict long-term cardiac events in vascular surgery patients. Ann Vasc Surg 15:267-271, 2001.
15. DeFrang RD, Taylor LM, Porter JM: Basic data related to amputations. Ann Vasc Surg 5:202-207, 1991.
16. Donovan-Hall MK, Yardley L, Watts RJ: Engagement in activities revealing the body and psychosocial adjustment in adults with a transtibial prosthesis. Prosthet Orthot Int 26:15-22, 2002.
17. Dormandy J, Heeck L, Vig S: Major amputations: Clinical patterns and predictors. Semin Vasc Surg 12:154-161, 1999.
18. Dwars BJ, van den Broek TA, Rauwerda JA, Bakker FC: Criteria for reliable selection of the lowest level of amputation in peripheral vascular disease. J Vasc Surg 15:536-542, 1992.
19. Eagle KA, Brundage BH, Chaitman BR, et al: Guidelines for perioperative cardiovascular evaluation for noncardiac surgery. Report of the American College of Cardiology/American Heart Association Task Force on Practice Guidelines. Committee on Perioperative Cardiovascular Evaluation for Noncardiac Surgery. Circulation 93:1278-1317, 1996.
20. Edwards JM, Taylor LM Jr, Porter JM: Limb salvage in end-stage renal disease (ESRD): Comparison of modern results in patients with and without ESRD. Arch Surg 123:1164-1168, 1988.
21. Eskelinen E, Luther M, Eskelinen A, Lepantalo M: Infrapopliteal bypass reduces amputation incidence in elderly patients: A population-based study. Eur J Vasc Endovasc Surg 26:65-68, 2003.
22. Feinglass J, Brown JL, LoSasso A, et al: Rates of lower-extremity amputation and arterial reconstruction in the United States, 1979 to 1996. Am J Public Health 89:1222-1227, 1999.
23. Feinglass J, Pearce WH, Martin GJ, et al: Postoperative and late survival outcomes after major amputation: Findings from the Department of Veterans Affairs National Surgical Quality Improvement Program. Surgery 130:21-29, 2001.
24. Fisher DF Jr, Clagett GP, Fry RE, et al: One-stage versus two-stage amputation for wet gangrene of the lower extremity: A randomized study. J Vasc Surg 8:428-433, 1988.
25. Frank RG, Kashani JH, Kashani SR, et al: Psychological response to amputation as a function of age and time since amputation. Br J Psychiatry 144:493-497, 1984.
26. Gallagher P, MacLachlan M: Psychological adjustment and coping in adults with prosthetic limbs. Behav Med 25:117-124, 1999.
27. Gibbons GW: Lower extremity bypass in patients with diabetic foot ulcers. Surg Clin North Am 83:659-669, 2003.
28. Group TG: Epidemiology of lower extremity amputation in centres in Europe, North America and East Asia: The global lower extremity amputation study group. Br J Surg 87:328-337, 2000.
29. Hallett JW Jr, Byrne J, Gayari MM, et al: Impact of arterial surgery and balloon angioplasty on amputation: A population-based study of 1155 procedures between 1973 and 1992. J Vasc Surg 25:29-38, 1997.
30. Huber TS, Wang JG, Wheeler KG, et al: Impact of race on the treatment for peripheral arterial occlusive disease. J Vasc Surg 30:417-425, 1999.
31. Hunsaker RH, Schwartz JA, Keagy BA, et al: Dry ice cryoamputation: A twelve-year experience. J Vasc Surg 2:812-816, 1985.
32. Jorneskog G, Djavani K, Brismar K: Day-to-day variability of transcutaneous oxygen tension in patients with diabetes mellitus and peripheral arterial occlusive disease. J Vasc Surg 34:277-282, 2001.
33. Kalra M, Gloviczki P, Bower TC, et al: Limb salvage after successful pedal bypass grafting is associated with improved long-term survival. J Vasc Surg 33:6-16, 2001.
34. Kantonen I, Lepantalo M, Luther M, et al: Factors affecting the results of surgery for chronic critical leg ischemia—a nationwide survey. Finnvasc Study Group. J Vasc Surg 27:940-947, 1998.
35. Kazmers A, Perkins AJ, Jacobs LA: Major lower extremity amputation in Veterans Affairs medical centers. Ann Vasc Surg 14:216-222, 2000.
36. Keagy BA, Schwartz JA, Kotb M, et al: Lower extremity amputation: The control series. J Vasc Surg 4:321-326, 1986.
37. Krupski WC, Nehler MR, Whitehill TA, et al: Negative impact of cardiac evaluation before vascular surgery. Vasc Med 5:3-9, 2000.
38. Leers SA, Reifsnyder T, Delmonte R, Caron M: Realistic expectations for pedal bypass grafts in patients with end-stage renal disease. J Vasc Surg 28:976-980, 1998.
39. Malone JM: Lower extremity amputations. In Moore WS (ed): Vascular Surgery: A Comprehensive Review. Philadelphia, WB Saunders, 2002, pp 875-917.
40. Malone JM, Anderson GG, Lalka SG, et al: Prospective comparison of noninvasive techniques for amputation level selection. Am J Surg 154:179-184, 1987.
41. Malone JM, Leal JM, Moore WS, et al: The "gold standard" for

amputation level selection xenon-133 clearance. J Surg Res 30:449-455, 1981.

42. Malone JM, Moore W, Leal JM, Childers SJ: Rehabilitation for lower extremity amputation. Arch Surg 116:93-98, 1981.

43. Mangano DT, Layug EL, Wallace A, Tateo I: Effect of atenolol on mortality and cardiovascular morbidity after noncardiac surgery. Multicenter Study of Perioperative Ischemia Research Group [published erratum appears in N Engl J Med 1997 Apr 3;336(14):1039]. N Engl J Med 335:1713-1720, 1996.

44. McWhinnie DL, Gordon AC, Collin J, et al: Rehabilitation outcome 5 years after 100 lower-limb amputations. Br J Surg 81:1596-1599, 1994.

45. Nehler MR, Coll JR, Hiatt WR, et al: Functional outcome in a contemporary series of major lower extremity amputations. J Vasc Surg 38:7-14, 2003.

46. Nehler MR, Hiatt WR, Taylor LM Jr: Is revascularization and limb salvage always the best treatment for critical limb ischemia? J Vasc Surg 37:704-708, 2003.

47. Nicoloff AD, Taylor LM Jr, McLafferty RB, et al: Patient recovery after infrainguinal bypass grafting for limb salvage. J Vasc Surg 27:256-263, 1998.

48. Parkes CM: Psycho-social transitions: Comparison between reactions to loss of a limb and loss of a spouse. Br J Psychiatry 127:204-210, 1975.

49. Poldermans D, Boersma E, Bax JJ, et al: The effect of bisoprolol on perioperative mortality and myocardial infarction in high-risk patients undergoing vascular surgery. N Engl J Med 341:1789-1794, 1999.

50. Pomposelli FB, Kansal N, Hamdan AD, et al: A decade of experience with dorsalis pedis artery bypass: Analysis of outcome in more than 1000 cases. J Vasc Surg 37:307-315, 2003.

51. Resnick HE, Valsania P, Phillips CL: Diabetes mellitus and non-traumatic lower extremity amputation in black and white Americans: The National Health and Nutrition Examination Survey Epidemiologic Follow-up Study, 1971-1992. Arch Intern Med 159:2470-2475, 1999.

52. Rybarczyk BD, Nyenhuis DL, Nicholas JJ, et al: Social discomfort and depression in a sample of adults with leg amputations. Arch Phys Med Rehabil 73:1169-1173, 1992.

53. Scheffler A, Rieger H: A comparative analysis of transcutaneous oximetry (tcPo$_2$) during oxygen inhalation and leg dependency in severe peripheral arterial occlusive disease. J Vasc Surg 16:218-224, 1992.

54. Schubert DS, Burns R, Paras W, Sioson E: Decrease of depression during stroke and amputation rehabilitation. Gen Hosp Psychiatry 14:135-141, 1992.

55. Spence VA, Walker WF, Troup IM, Murdoch G: Amputation of the ischemic limb: Selection of the optimum site by thermography. Angiology 32:155-169, 1981.

56. Taylor LM, Yeager RA, Moneta GL, et al: The incidence of perioperative myocardial infarction in general vascular surgery. J Vasc Surg 15:52-61, 1991.

57. Toursarkissian B, Shireman PK, Harrison A, et al: Major lower-extremity amputation: Contemporary experience in a single Veterans Affairs institution. Am Surg 68:606-610, 2002.

58. Tunis SR, Bass EB, Klag MJ, Steinberg EP: Variation in utilization of procedures for treatment of peripheral arterial disease: A look at patient characteristics. Arch Intern Med 153:991-998, 1993.

59. Vitti MJ, Robinson DV, Hauer-Jensen M, et al: Wound healing in forefoot amputations: The predictive value of toe pressure. Ann Vasc Surg 8:99-106, 1994.

60. Wagner WH, Keagy BA, Kotb MM, et al: Noninvasive determination of healing of major lower extremity amputation: The continued role of clinical judgment. J Vasc Surg 8:703-710, 1988.

61. Winburn GB, Wood MC, Hawkins ML, et al: Current role of cryoamputation. Am J Surg 162:647-650, 1991.

62. Wrobel JS, Mayfield JA, Reiber GE: Geographic variation of lower-extremity major amputation in individuals with and without diabetes in the Medicare population. Diabetes Care 24:860-864, 2001.

63. Yeager RA, Moneta GL, Edwards JM, et al: Deep vein thrombosis associated with lower extremity amputation. J Vasc Surg 22:612-615, 1995.

Lower Extremity Amputation:
Technique and Perioperative Care

172

KENNETH R. WOODBURN, MD, FRCSE (Gen.)
C. VAUGHAN RUCKLEY, MB, ChM, FRCSE

Although limb amputation is the eventual outcome for a significant percentage of patients with occlusive arterial disease, it is rarely accorded a high enough priority in the work of a vascular service. Amputation surgery is often delegated to the more junior trainee and is frequently undertaken without the typical planning accorded reconstructive surgery, or as an additional procedure at the end of an operating session. This practice is not to the patient's advantage. Successful amputation surgery necessitates all the preparation, experience, and surgical skills required of more elaborate vascular operations. Detailed preoperative planning and assessment, input from the rehabilitation team and prosthetists, and optimization of medical and psychological condition will enhance the prospects of a good functional outcome. Meticulous surgical technique with attention to asepsis, minimal tissue trauma, thorough hemostasis, and accurate tissue removal are all mandatory. Successful amputation surgery can often restore the patient with critical limb ischemia (CLI) to a level of function far higher than that experienced before surgery, and every effort should therefore be exerted to secure a positive outcome.

■ GENERAL PRINCIPLES

Regardless of the preoperative indication and level of amputation there are a number of general principles that need to be observed to maximize the outcome of surgery. The use of a tourniquet is inadvisable in the patient with arterial disease and cannot be recommended except in the well-vascularized transtibial amputee when significant hemorrhage is anticipated. In these circumstances, limited use of a tourniquet to facilitate control of the major vessels while the limb is removed can reduce blood loss. Provided that the tourniquet is then removed to enable accurate identification and control of bleeding points before fashioning the stump, tourniquet time can be kept to a minimum on these rare occasions when its use may be beneficial. Tissue handling should be as atraumatic as possible. This requires the surgeon to handle tissues without resorting to instruments such as forceps, which can irreparably damage marginal tissue and impair wound healing. All necrotic and nonviable tissue requires excision. This will determine the level of amputation required. If tissue is also infected, as is often the case in the diabetic patient, the infected area needs to be incised and drained at the time of surgical resection but the formation of a definitive amputation should be delayed until active

infection has subsided. Muscles are divided with the minimal number of firm clean cuts to minimize the macerating effect of multiple incisions. With few exceptions, bone should be transected rather than disarticulated and flaps kept thick to avoid unnecessary dissection between soft tissue planes.[1] Bone edges should be rounded and prominences beveled to optimize subsequent prosthetic fitting. The use of a power saw to divide bone avoids the splintering encountered with bone cutters and reduces the risk of collateral tissue damage that can result from the use of a hand saw. In major amputations the bone ends are carefully contoured with a power saw and smoothed with a rasp to minimize trauma to overlying soft tissues. This is particularly crucial in transtibial amputations. When bone is resected the operative field should be irrigated with saline to wash out any dust or bone fragments.

Nerves should be transected under traction to facilitate retraction into the adjacent soft tissue and minimize bleeding from nutrient arteries and symptomatic neuroma formation. Occasionally, ligation of larger nerves (with absorbable suture to reduce the incidence of neuroma) is required to control bleeding from nutrient vessels. In general it is preferable to control bleeding by careful suture-ligation of bleeding points using fine absorbable sutures. Individual vessel ligation is preferred over a mass ligation technique; and if adequate hemostasis cannot be achieved, a closed-system suction drain should be employed in the wound depths, placing one vacuum drain over the bone end and one in a more superficial plane, in the case of major limb amputation. To facilitate subsequent removal, these drains are not sutured in place. The excessive use of diathermy should be discouraged, because thermal damage to adjacent soft tissue can impair wound healing. Myodesis or myoplasty should be employed whenever possible because this stabilizes distal muscle insertion and corrects some of the deforming forces that result from amputation.[1-3]

Antibiotic prophylaxis against clostridia is mandatory to avoid gas gangrene. A combination of a penicillin and metronidazole covers most likely pathogens, although where active infection is present, antibiotics appropriate to the most recent bacteriologic cultures should also be administered alongside clostridial prophylaxis. Skin edges should be apposed without tension using a nonabsorbable monofilament suture or skin staples, unless primary closure is contraindicated by sepsis. Adhesive paper strips are a satisfactory alternative or adjunctive means of skin closure and help to minimize tension. The patient undergoing amputation surgery should receive heparin prophylaxis to minimize the risks of deep venous thrombosis (DVT), particularly in those patients in whom surgery is undertaken for CLI, when there is an increased incidence of DVT.[4] This should be begun on admission to hospital and continued until the patient is mobilized. The authors' practice is to use low-molecular-weight heparin (Fragmin, 5000 IU) administered once daily, because mechanical methods aimed at reducing DVT are inappropriate for the arterial patient.

PRINCIPLES OF POSTOPERATIVE CARE

Postoperatively the amputation site must be protected from trauma, and direct weight bearing should be avoided until the site is healed, although the use of appropriate pressure distributing devices may enable early mobilization.[5] Many different dressings have been advocated for the postoperative amputee; and in amputees with an open wound, soft dressings that enable regular inspection and prevent desiccation are advisable. For many other amputations distal to the knee joint, a rigid plaster dressing can be applied at the time of definitive amputation (Fig. 172-1). This offers advantages over soft dressings with elastic bandages in terms of reduced postoperative edema, pain control, prevention of contractures, and protection from injury.[6-8] The immediate application of a rigid dressing at the time of surgery can result in improvements in wound healing, stump shrinkage,[9] and a reduced time to prosthesis fitting when compared with soft stump dressings,[10-12] although the claimed benefits of the technique have not been unequivocally proved,[13] largely because clinical trials recruiting sufficient numbers of patients have yet to be performed. This problem led to the findings being statistically inconclusive, despite a mean reduction in time to limb fitting of 6 days in the rigid dressing group in a Scottish multicenter trial in patients undergoing transtibial amputation for arterial disease.[14] The rigid dressing technique has also been used to accelerate healing of open below-knee stump wounds with some success.[15] However, in one review[16] it was confirmed that at the present time there is insufficient evidence to unequivocally recommend any specific dressing regimen after amputation; further clinical trials are needed.

Despite this, in addition to the theoretical benefits outlined, the rigid postoperative dressing can incorporate a temporary prosthesis to enable early mobilization.[17] Alternatively, the protection offered by a rigid dressing can be utilized to enable early mobilization with a pneumatic (PPAM) aid without the requirement for additional prosthetics. Other devices to facilitate early mobilization have also been described[18]; and it appears that, provided that direct weight bearing is avoided, early mobilization reduces complications and improves rehabilitation after transtibial amputation,[7] although this, too, is an under-researched area. Rigid postoperative dressings are not without their complications, however, and it is imperative that all staff involved in the care of the amputee have a detailed understanding of the technique, if complications are to be minimized.

AMPUTATIONS IN THE PRESENCE OF INFECTION

Sepsis in an ischemic limb, especially in the diabetic, can spread with remarkable rapidity and may be life threatening. It should be treated aggressively and quickly. Amputation undertaken in the presence of active infection follows the standard surgical principles with regard to adequate drainage of abscesses, avoidance of complete wound closure, and removal of all nonviable tissue. Antibiotic therapy should be initiated intravenously before surgery and continued until infection has resolved. In the case of minor amputations such as digital and forefoot amputations, the wound can be left to heal by secondary intention without compromising the eventual functional outcome.

When sepsis and tissue loss extend beyond the forefoot, the surgeon must choose between primary definitive amputation and a guillotine procedure designed to remove all nonviable tissue. A definitive amputation wound can be left partially closed to facilitate drainage,[19] with delayed closure 5 to 7 days later, but if there is concern about the viability of tissue at the proposed level of amputation, sepsis extending proximal to the ankle joint, or poor diabetic control with ketoacidosis, then supramalleolar guillotine amputation is the best option and the definitive amputation stump fashioned at a second operation when the wound is healthy and viable and the patient's hemodynamic and metabolic derangement is corrected. This two-stage amputation for pedal sepsis is reported to reduce both the incidence of stump infection[20] and the rate of proximal revision,[21] without any adverse effect on overall operative mortality.

In certain rare circumstances when the patient with a septic, ischemic limb is not even medically stable enough to undergo supramalleolar guillotine amputation, consideration can be given to the use of cryoanesthesia: the distal gangrenous or septic portion of the limb is cooled either with a cryoamputation boot or by immersion in dry ice with a tourniquet applied to the limb distal to the proposed site of amputation. This effectively isolates the limb from the rest of the body and prevents progressive gangrene/infection. Cryoamputation persists until the patient's condition stabilizes enough to enable definitive amputation at a level proximal to the level of cooling. This technique is considered to reduce postoperative morbidity and death,[22] but it has not gained widespread popularity.

SPECIFIC AMPUTATIONS

Digital Amputation

In chronic arterial disease (but not in diabetics) digits affected by dry gangrene may be left to autoamputate over time, provided that facilities exist for close monitoring of progress. The development of "wet gangrene" or surrounding cellulitic change mandates the early amputation of all nonviable tissue with adjunctive therapeutic antibiotic therapy. Other indications for digital amputation include infection, osteomyelitis, and neuropathic ulceration over the mid or distal phalanx. Isolated digital amputation is unlikely

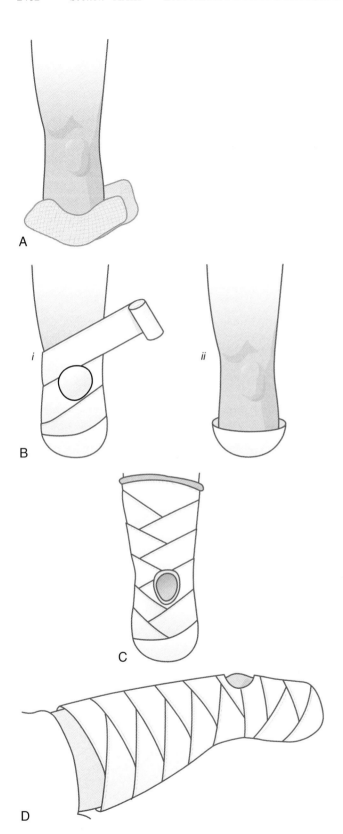

FIGURE 172-1 Stages in applying a rigid dressing to a transtibial amputation stump. **A,** The distal end of the stump is covered with fluffed-out gauze swabs positioned toward the back of the stump. **B,** After applying a stockinette of sterile tubular gauze on an applicator from the upper thigh over the stump, twisting it over the gauze padding at the end of the stump and then taking it back up the thigh, the limb is wrapped in a layer of sterile orthopedic wool (i) and a pad of orthopedic felt is placed over the patellar prominence. Alternatively, after applying the stockinette of gauze, a sterile preformed polyurethane end cap of appropriate size is placed over the stump (ii) and held in place by the application of a sterile elasticated stump sock. **C,** Thereafter one or two rolls of plaster of Paris are applied to the stump, with care being taken to smooth out the plaster and ensure optimum coverage over the stump. A window is then cut over the patella and the orthopedic felt removed, to enable supervision of quadriceps exercises in the postoperative period. **D,** A lateral view of the finished stump plaster showing the knee held in 10 to 15 degrees of flexion.

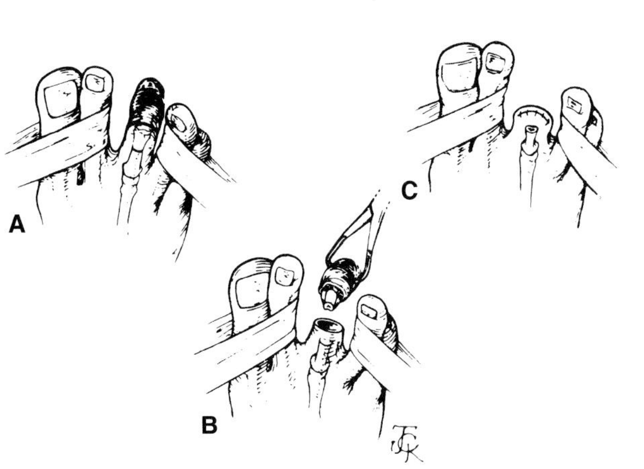

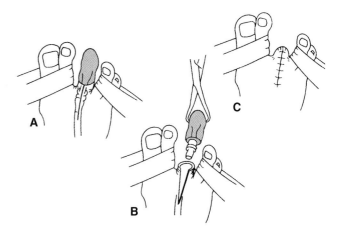

FIGURE 172-2 Digital amputation. **A,** While the adjacent toes are retracted medially and laterally, a circular incision proximal to the proximal interphalangeal joint is made. **B,** Dissection exposes the proximal phalanx, which is divided. **C,** The circular incision is then closed in a transverse direction with interrupted, carefully placed, coapting sutures.

FIGURE 172-3 Single-ray amputation. **A,** The incision is designed to expose the distal metatarsal phalangeal region. **B,** The distal metatarsal is divided far enough proximally to permit closure without tension. **C,** After excision of the specimen, including the intact metatarsophalangeal joint, the dorsal portion of the incision is closed in its original direction and the circular portion of the plantar incision is closed transversely.

to be successful in the presence of more proximal cellulitis and of infection or osteomyelitis involving the metatarsophalangeal joint or more proximal bone or soft tissue spaces. An inadequate blood supply (often associated with a dependent rubor) also precludes successful digital amputation, unless corrected by concomitant revascularization surgery.

Local amputation of all five digits is acceptable and indeed preferable to leaving one or two isolated digits, which are then subject to repeated trauma. However, when multiple digits are affected it is more commonly associated with some forefoot involvement that requires a more proximal procedure.

Amputation of an isolated gangrenous digit should follow the same precise surgical techniques as any other amputation to maximize the prospects of wound healing. Skin flaps can follow any design that permits complete excision of nonviable tissue without unnecessary sacrifice of healthy tissue and enables wound apposition without tension. A circular incision around the base of the digit is commonly used, and the bone is transected at the proximal phalanx (Fig. 172-2). Disarticulation results in synovial wound leakage and poor skin healing and should be avoided. Preservation of the base of the proximal phalanx maintains the insertion of the short flexors and other small muscles acting on the joint, but sesamoid bones should be excised where possible. Tendons are transected under tension, and electrocautery is avoided. After irrigating the wound the skin edges can be apposed using adhesive paper strips; or in the presence of infection, the wound may be left open. If a suture is used it should be of a monofilament nonabsorbable type and may need to remain in situ for up to 4 weeks to enable wound healing.

Ray Amputation

When digital gangrene extends onto the forefoot and when infection involves the web space, metatarsophalangeal joint, or metatarsal head, then digital amputation alone is

insufficient. Excision of the digit along with the metatarsal head and surrounding nonviable tissue can be undertaken using a racquet-type incision over the dorsal aspect of the distal metatarsal extending around the base of the digit (Fig. 172-3). Careful sharp dissection is required to remove the metatarsal head and digit without entering the adjacent joint or tendon spaces. As with all amputation surgery, transected bone ends should be smooth, bony fragments and nonviable tissue should be removed, and the wound should be irrigated. Prophylactic antibiotics and meticulous hemostasis will further enhance the prospects of successful healing. In the absence of infection the incision can then be closed with either adhesive paper strips or monofilament sutures.

Single- or double-ray amputations will heal in the presence of an adequate blood supply, although when infection necessitates an open wound there is a risk of chronic osteomyelitis of the metatarsal shaft and subsequent nonhealing. Although a fifth ray amputation can heal well (provided that the metatarsal base with the attachment of peroneus brevis is preserved to maintain eversion of the foot), the volume defect associated with a central ray amputation can persist for a considerable time, owing to the rigidity of the surrounding tissues; and in these circumstances the patient may benefit from the application of a plaster boot to minimize movement and relieve pressure on the wound.

Transmetatarsal and Other Forefoot Amputations

Transmetatarsal amputation is indicated when tissue loss or infection involving more than one digit extends onto the dorsum of the foot but the plantar tissue is spared. It is also often preferable to isolated first ray amputation because it enables a broader distribution of weight during ambulation.[23] As with all amputations, an adequate blood supply is essential; and when transmetatarsal amputation is being carried out for gangrene owing to vascular insufficiency,

Table 172-1   Criteria for Healing Transmetatarsal Amputation

Transmetatarsal tcPo$_2$ ≥ 30 mm Hg[27]
Preoperative toe pressures > 68 mm Hg or ≥ 30 mm Hg after
    revascularization[28]
Laser Doppler skin perfusion pressure ≥ 30 mm Hg[29]
Ankle-brachial index > 0.5[30]
Serum albumin > 3.0 g/dL[30]
Serum protein > 6.0 g/dL[30]
Total lymphocyte count > 1500/μL[30]

Adapted from Sanders LJ: Transmetatarsal and midfoot amputations. Clin Podiatr
Med Surg 14:741-762, 1997.

adjuvant revascularization surgery or angioplasty is often
required to facilitate long-term healing.[24] Predicting successful healing of a transmetatarsal amputation is difficult, and although healing in this type of amputation is associated
with better mobility than that in transtibial amputation,
around 50% of transmetatarsal amputations undertaken for
forefoot ischemia may eventually require conversion to
transtibial amputation.[25] Criteria for healing transmetatarsal amputations have been reviewed by Sanders[26] (Table
172-1); and when these are met, up to 80% of transmetatarsal amputations are said to heal.

Transmetatarsal amputation is carried out at the level of
the mid shaft. The skin incision is marked preoperatively on
the dorsum of the foot by a line running from the mid shaft
of the fifth metatarsal to the midshaft of the first metatarsal.
The line should then be extended distally along the first
and fifth metatarsal shafts to the bases of the hallux and
fifth toe, before joining up as a curved line just behind the
sulcus of the toes (Fig. 172-4). Ideally, if a transmetatarsal
amputation is to succeed, the entire plantar surface of the
foot should be preserved and well perfused. When necrosis
extends onto the plantar surface, it may still be possible to
undertake this amputation, although complete primary
closure of the wound is unlikely to be achieved. However,
provided that the deep tissues can be apposed without
tension, using absorbable sutures, the skin defect will often
heal by secondary intention. This can be facilitated by
transecting the metatarsals slightly more proximally than
usual, provided that the bases with their muscle attachments
are preserved. Skin markings are modified accordingly and
can even incorporate wedge excision of isolated plantar
ulcers if required.[26-31] Alternatively, a longer dorsal flap can
be employed and, in some circumstances, equal dorsal and
plantar flaps may be required to provide adequate tissue for
tension-free closure.[1]

The skin is incised just distal to the line marked on the
dorsum of the foot and carried down to the metatarsal shafts,
which are then transected with a power oscillating saw 5 to
10 mm proximal to the skin incision. The lateral skin
incisions are extended deeper to free the metatarsal shafts
from their attachments to the plantar tissue, developing
the plane deep to the metatarsals in a distal direction. The
curved incision on the plantar surface is then extended
deeper until it meets with this dissection plane, and the
desired tissue is excised en bloc. Bone ends are smoothed
with a rasp if required, and the plantar tissues are then
excised by sharp dissection: tendons are transected under

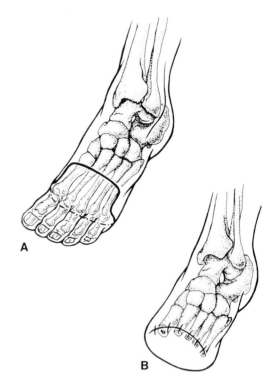

FIGURE 172-4 Transmetatarsal amputation. **A,** The skin incision is placed
to provide a total posterior flap while allowing excision of the forefoot with
division through all five metatarsals in the mid-metatarsal region. **B,** After
excision of the forefoot, the plantar flap is thinned to remove capsule and
tendinous material and a meticulous closure of the plantar and anterior skin
is performed.

tension, hemostasis is achieved with absorbable ligatures,
the volar plates are excised along with redundant interosseus
muscle tissue and fat, and the plantar tissues are thinned
enough to enable tissue apposition on dorsal rotation of the
plantar flap. Deep tissue is then sutured with absorbable
sutures, and the plantar flap is shaped with a fresh blade to
enable skin apposition with interrupted monofilament
sutures or adhesive paper strips. If desired, a fine-bore
closed suction drainage system can be left in the deep
tissues and removed the next day. It is vital that the suture
line is not under tension, and the presence of suture line
tension mandates revision by shortening further the metatarsal shafts to allow tension-free closure.

Postoperatively the stump can be dressed in a sterile
bandage and enclosed in a rigid below-knee plaster dressing
to control edema and prevent trauma. Weight bearing should
be avoided for 7 to 10 days postoperatively and, on resuming mobilization, weight bearing on the affected limb should
be confined to the heel initially. Sutures are usually removed
in 14 to 21 days.

A successful transmetatarsal amputation preserves a
functional foot without the need for adjuvant tendon transfer
surgery and requires little more than a shoe filler with an
ankle lace-up shoe. It avoids the equinus and equinovalgus
deformities associated with more proximal midfoot amputations. Lisfranc's (forefoot disarticulation at the level of
tarsal-metatarsal joints) and Chopart's (disarticulation at

talonavicular and calcaneocuboid joints) amputations cannot be recommended in the patient with arterial disease. An open transmetatarsal amputation is preferred when forefoot destruction renders a conventional transmetatarsal procedure impossible.

If tissue loss extends more proximally, the use of a Syme amputation can be considered, although the healing of such a procedure is dependent on the presence of a patent posterior tibial artery and on the absence of any heel ulceration or necrosis. These two conditions are rarely met in the patient with advanced arterial disease; and despite some favorable reports of the use of Syme's amputation in vascular and diabetic patients,[1,32,33] our experience with this operation does not encourage us to recommend it in the treatment of CLI.

Transtibial Amputation

Transtibial (below-knee) amputation is indicated when gangrene or infection precludes a more distal procedure and for intractable ischemic rest pain that cannot be corrected by lower extremity revascularization. It is the most proximal amputation that is still associated with a good rehabilitation potential. As a general rule the development of specialist vascular surgical services is accompanied by a shift toward transtibial amputation in preference to the transfemoral amputation that was previously the most common major limb amputation in arterial insufficiency, with corresponding improvements in mobility and independent quality of life. With experience and clinical judgment, healing rates in excess of 80% can be expected for transtibial amputations. Objective tests aimed at improving on these results by delineating levels of viability are reported to increase healing rates, but none of the tests is perfect, and in most centers clinical judgment remains the mainstay of patient selection.[34,35]

In situations in which the perfusion of the limb at the site of amputation is doubtful, efforts should be made to improve this with proximal revascularization procedures, if transtibial amputation is clearly preferable to transfemoral amputation. Healing of a transtibial amputation in the absence of a femoral pulse occurs in less than 25% of procedures,[36] and percutaneous iliac recanalization or extra-anatomical bypass grafting may enable successful transtibial amputation in selected cases. Attention should also be directed to the patient's nutritional status: poor nutritional status compromises outcome after transtibial amputation, and oral hyperalimentation should be commenced preoperatively in these circumstances.[37]

Optimal preparation of the patient for transtibial amputation includes members of the multidisciplinary team who are to be involved in the rehabilitation process as well as the operating surgeons. This helps the patient psychologically, assists in establishing realistic goals for the eventual functional outcome, and makes it more likely that surgical management will be best directed to facilitating rehabilitation. The patient is encouraged to view amputation as the start of a return to mobility rather than a treatment failure and is counseled regarding the need for surgery and the expected postoperative course. Preoperative physiotherapy is designed to maintain muscle function to prevent

or reduce flexion contracture at the knee joint. A flexion deformity of 15 degrees or more will impede successful mobilization using a prosthesis, and if the knee cannot be fully extended before surgery, manipulation of the joint and hamstring tenotomy can be undertaken at the time of amputation in an attempt to reduce flexion deformity. Flexion deformity of more than 45 degrees at the knee joint is a contraindication to below-knee amputation because prosthetic fitting will be impossible.

Unhurried, nontraumatic, and accurate surgical technique is of prime importance. Tension on flaps, the most common cause of technical failure, is fatal to healing. It is attributable to incorrectly cut flaps, hematoma, or stump edema. Hemostasis must therefore be meticulous. If there is the slightest doubt, vacuum drains are carefully positioned, one adjacent to the bone end and the other under the skin flaps. A loose flap will eventually accommodate, or can be trimmed, but an overtight closure is a lost cause without further bone and muscle excision.

The surgeon must assess the quality of tissue in the lower limb and modify the surgical technique to take account of previous incisions, avoiding tissue that is infected or of doubtful viability. Foreign material such as defunct vascular synthetic graft should be removed as far as is possible. For this reason the amputating surgeon should be familiar with more than one technique of transtibial amputation and be prepared to improvise flaps if required. The commonly described transtibial amputations utilize (1) a long posterior myocutaneous flap based on gastrocnemius; (2) equal length anterior and posterior myocutaneous flaps (fish-mouth technique); (3) equal length medial and lateral myocutaneous flaps via sagittal incisions; (4) equal length anteromedial and posterolateral fasciocutaneous flaps, known as the skew flap technique; and (5) a medially based fasciocutaneous flap (Fig. 172-5).

All variations of the transtibial amputation are designed to provide adequate distal end padding and produce a cylindrical stump that can be readily cast for a prosthesis. The surgeon should aim to provide adequate tissue cover over the end of the transected tibia and avoid placing suture lines at sites subject to pressure from a below-knee prosthesis. Most prostheses in current use are of a patellar tendon–bearing type, with the greatest pressure over the tibial tuberosity and crest; and only minimal contact occurs between distal stump and prosthesis. The level of tibial bone section is between 10 and 15 cm below the knee joint line (tibial plateau), the length being adjusted according to the individual factors such as the state of the tissues and also the build of the patient. Shorter levels of transection will produce a stump that is too short to produce an adequate lever, and longer stumps are not only difficult to fit but also encroach on the tissues of the distal third of the tibia, with its poor blood supply. A point approximating to one handsbreadth below the tibial tuberosity (7 to 12 cm) is frequently employed as the level of the most proximal skin incision and bone transection, regardless of the flap employed. The tibia is divided with an anterior bevel extending proximal to the line of transection. This can be cut using a pneumatic or Gigli saw; alternatively, if using a hand saw, the bevel can be created with an initial oblique cut extending through two thirds of the tibia from anterior to posterior, followed by

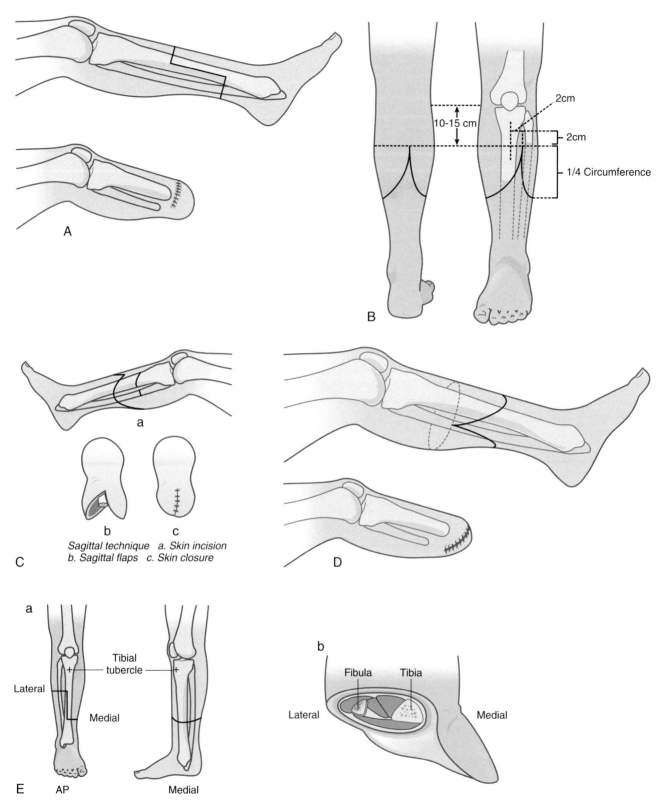

FIGURE 172-5 Transtibial amputations: skin flaps. **A,** Long posterior flap. **B,** Skew flap incisions. **C,** Sagittal flaps. **D,** Equal anterior and posterior flaps. **E,** Medially based flap. (**B** redrawn from Ruckley CV, Stonebridge PA, Prescott RJ: Skewflap versus long posterior flap in below-knee amputations: Multicenter trial. J Vasc Surg 13:423-427, 1991; **C** redrawn from Termansen NB: Below-knee amputation for ischaemic gangrene: Prospective, randomized comparison of a transverse and a sagittal operative technique. Acta Orthop Scand 48:311-316, 1977; **E** redrawn from Jain AS, Stewart CPU, Turner MS: Transtibial amputation using a medially-based flap. J R Coll Surg Edinb 40:263-265, 1995.)

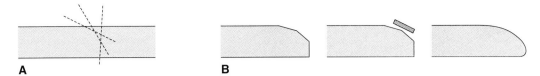

FIGURE 172-6 Fashioning the transected tibial bone. **A,** The bone end can be shaped with two oblique cuts and one vertical cut using a hand saw. Alternatively the end can be shaped using a power saw to divide the tibia. **B,** The anterior border of the tibia is then smoothed with a rasp to remove sharp bone edges. (Redrawn from Ruckley CV: Lower limb amputation—time for critical appraisal. In Barros D, et al [eds]: Vascular Surgery: Current Questions. Oxford, Butterworth Heinemann, 1991, pp 190-206).

the transverse cut vertically through the bone (Fig. 172-6). The bone end is then shaped using a rasp to produce a smooth well-rounded bony end with no sharp points. The fibula is divided at a level 2 cm or so proximal to the point of tibial section, using a Gigli saw in preference to bone forceps, which frequently produce unwanted splintering of bone with potential for a spiral fracture and increased postoperative pain.

Both the long posterior flap and the skew flap are in common use, with neither having shown any distinct advantage over the other in terms of healing or revision rates.[38,39] The skew flap technique can accommodate tissue loss extending more proximally, provided gastrocnemius remains viable. It also takes the suture line further away from potential pressure points, avoids "dog ears," and avoids the typical bulbous shape of the long posterior flap. Both techniques have been described in great detail by Robinson,[2] and only the salient points are described here.

Long Posterior Flap Transtibial Amputation

As for any transtibial amputation, the patient is positioned supine with a soft pad such as a rolled towel behind the lower thigh and the knee joint opposite the break in the table. Once the diseased part of the limb has been removed the end of the table can be dropped if desired, allowing the surgeon to sit facing the stump and thus to work comfortably and effectively.

The proximal skin incision is marked at a point one handsbreadth below the tibial tuberosity. The incision should encompass between one half and two thirds of the circumference of the calf at this level. The former results in a wide flap with "dog ears" at the lateral edges of the wound, whereas the latter produces a long and narrow flap that may have inadequate blood supply at the distal end. A posterior flap somewhat greater than one third of the circumference of the calf is a useful compromise, and the flap extends from the medial and lateral ends of the proximal transverse incision, along the axis of the limb for a distance equal to at least half the length of the transverse incision, before the posterior transverse incision completes the flap (see Fig. 172-5A). It is prudent to fashion the posterior flap longer than will ultimately be required to ensure good skin apposition after trimming to length.

Skin incisions are extended deeper through subcutaneous tissue and deep fascia, with care being taken to avoid separation of skin from underlying fascia; and major bleeding points are ligated with fine absorbable sutures. At the level selected for transaction of the tibia, the muscles of the anterior compartment are divided transversely with clean firm cuts, with suture ligation of the anterior tibial vessels, transaction of the nerve under tension, and incision of the interosseous membrane. The fibula is cleaned of proximal attachments for 2 cm and then divided at the more proximal level with a Gigli saw. The lateral and posterior aspect of the tibia is cleaned of its attachments at the level of section, and then the tibia is divided with a power saw, as outlined earlier. Once this is completed, the muscles of the deep compartment of the calf are divided transversely, the vessels ligated, and the nerves divided. Traditionally, the gastrocnemius and soleus were then tapered distally with sharp dissection and the amputation was completed. This frequently results in a bulky stump, and there is little need to preserve any of the soleus. The authors prefer to first develop the plane between the gastrocnemius and soleus by gentle finger dissection at the level of tibial transaction, where there is rarely significant fusion of the two muscles. The transverse division of the deep compartment muscles is then continued through the soleus until it meets with this plane, and thereafter the plane is developed distally to the point at which the gastrocnemius is divided transversely at the distal extent of the posterior flap. When the muscle is bulky it is often necessary to excise a portion of the lateral muscle to taper the muscle flap to reduce the bulk of the stump, as in the skew flap technique (Fig. 172-7). The aponeurotic end of gastrocnemius is then sutured to the anterior tibial periosteum with interrupted absorbable sutures, and the sutures are inverted to bury the knots. The muscle length may be reduced to ensure a snug fit over the bone end, without tissue tension or undue redundancy. Thereafter, the skin is trimmed to enable apposition with interrupted nylon sutures and/or adhesive paper strips, and any "dog ears" at the lateral wound edges are excised.

Skew Flap Transtibial Amputation

The patient is positioned as described for the long posterior flap. The posterior superficial muscle flap utilized in this amputation is exactly the same as outlined for the long posterior flap. The only difference is in the creation of anteromedial and posterolateral fasciocutaneous flaps, which are separated from the deeper tissues and based on the cutaneous blood supply of the lower limb. Accurate flap design is critical. Flaps are marked at the level previously described, one handsbreadth below the tibial tuberosity. A piece of tape or thread is used to measure the circumference of the calf at the level of tibial section. Halving the tape gives the length of the base for each flap. The anterior

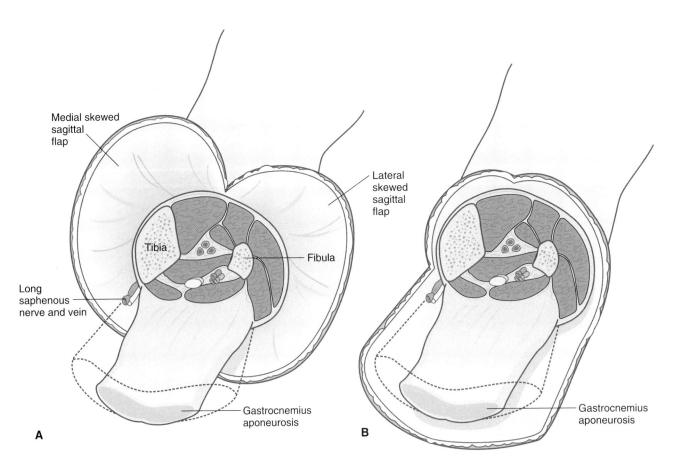

FIGURE 172-7 A, Skew flap technique. Note the oblique skin flaps and the underlying myofascial flap based on gastrocnemius. This flap is placed obliquely over the bone ends, trimmed, and sutured to the anterior periosteum and deep fascia (see Figure 172-8). **B,** Long posterior flap. Although the myofascial flap is almost identical to the skew flap, it remains attached to the overlying skin of the posterior flap and is then placed anteriorly and sutured to the anterior fascia and periosteum parallel with the skin incision. (Modified from Robinson KP: Amputations in vascular patients. In Bell PRF, et al [eds]: Surgical Management of Vascular Disease. London, WB Saunders, 1992, pp 609-635.)

junction of the flaps is a point 2.5 cm from the tibial crest over the anterior muscle compartment, and the halved tape is then passed around the calf at this point to identify the posterior junction of the flaps. The tape is then quartered, and the midpoint of the base of each flap marked. The quartered tape is then used in the style of a compass to identify the apex of each flap and mark out equal semicircular flaps (see Fig. 172-5B). At the anterior junction of the two flaps a 2-cm proximal extension is drawn to facilitate access to the line of bone section.

When the skin flaps have been drawn, the skin incisions are made, extending through skin and subcutaneous tissue into deep fascia. Veins are divided between absorbable ligatures, and nerves are divided under tension. Thereafter, the fasciocutaneous flaps can be reflected proximally to enable the remainder of the procedure to continue as for the long posterior flap. The key to success is the correct shaping of the gastrocnemius tendon and fascia. It does not correspond to the skin flap but is cut approximately 5 mm longer and more directly posterior than the skin flap. Caution is therefore required not to carry the skin incisions of the posterior parts of the skin flaps any deeper than the subcutaneous fat. On completion, the gastrocnemius can be

slightly narrowed and trimmed before being brought obliquely forward and sutured to the anterior tibial periosteum. It is the way in which this myofascial flap is utilized to cover the bone end that confers much of the benefit of this operation (Fig. 172-8). Skin can be approximated with either suture or adhesive paper strips, or preferably both. If hemostasis is less than perfect, two vacuum drains are positioned, one over the end of the tibia and the other more superficially. They are not sutured to the skin, so that they can be drawn out at 24 to 48 hours without disturbing the dressing.

Sagittal Flaps

This technique is an alternative to the skew flap in the patient whose limb infection, ischemia, or necrosis encroaches on a proposed long posterior flap. It involves the creation of anterolateral and posteromedial musculocutaneous flaps based on the underlying muscle groups (see Fig. 172-5C), and therefore it does not require a viable distal gastrocnemius muscle, making it particularly useful after a short guillotine, open operation. The procedure involves a myoplasty over the tibia with the anterior compartment

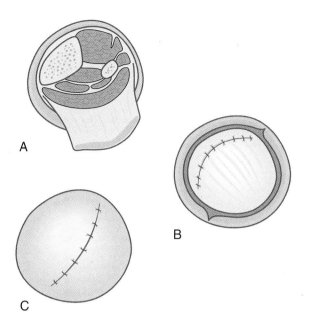

FIGURE 172-8 Completing the skew flap stump. **A,** The posterior myofascial flap of gastrocnemius and deep fascia. **B,** The flap is rotated obliquely forward over the tibia and sutured to deep fascia. **C,** The skin flaps are then opposed, and the suture line does not overlie the bone end or the myofascial suture line. (Redrawn from Ruckley CV: Lower limb amputation—time for critical appraisal. In Barros D, et al [eds]: Vascular Surgery: Current Questions. Oxford, Butterworth Heinemann, 1991, pp 190-206.)

muscles and the medial gastrocnemius. Readers are referred to the work of Persson[40] for a full description of the technique.

Equal Anterior and Posterior Flaps

This technique involves the creation of equal posterior and anterior myocutaneous flaps to reduce the requirement for adequate posterior tissue and was in common use until the introduction of the long posterior flap. The main disadvantage with this technique stems from the tenuous nature of the skin and subcutaneous tissue overlying the anterior tibia. As a result, the technique has little to recommend it to the surgeon who is comfortable with either skew or sagittal flaps.

Medial-Based Flap Technique

The use of a medially based flap, offset some 30 to 70 degrees medial to the conventional posterior flap, has been described for use in patients who are not suitable for the standard long posterior flap on the basis of thermographic studies.[41] A fasciocutaneous flap is fashioned from the medial skin, which has a better blood flow, and the tibia is covered using a gastrocnemius flap trimmed to give good cover. The technique may prevent unnecessary above-knee amputation in a minority of patients, but patient selection requires the use of thermographic techniques that are not widely available.

Postoperative Care

Drains are rarely required after careful transtibial amputation in the vascular patient and can be omitted if hemostasis is satisfactory, because they are associated with a higher incidence of postoperative wound infection.[42] If good hemostasis cannot be achieved, then two closed suction drains, one over the bone end and the second under the skin flap, are preferable to obtaining hemostasis with foreign materials such as bone wax or synthetic hemostatic products. While protection of the stump with sterile soft dressings is feasible, the authors favor the application of a lightweight rigid plaster cast extending to the upper thigh, with the knee held in 10 degrees of flexion. The advantages of this technique have been described elsewhere in this chapter. The rigid dressing is left in situ for a week unless the patient complains of severe pain or a persisting unexplained pyrexia, in which circumstances the plaster dressing can be bivalved to enable inspection of the wound. A window cut in the plaster over the patellar tendon enables supervised quadriceps exercise in the postoperative period (see Fig. 172-1). The rigid dressing is reapplied after wound inspection, incorporating a walking pylon if desired. Alternatively, the rigid dressing can be inserted into a pneumatic walking aid if not too bulky.

Prophylactic antibiotics are employed for 24 hours, and sutures are left in situ for 14 to 21 days, depending on wound progress. It is important to educate the transtibial amputee about the risks of attempting unaided mobilization in the early postoperative course if stump trauma is to be avoided. However, appropriate preoperative advice and education by the therapy team will enable the patient to achieve a degree of independence in the activities of daily living in the early postoperative period, while still maintaining a low-risk environment for the new amputee. DVT prophylaxis should be continued until the patient is mobile or returns to the community. Wound infection and ischemia may require revisional surgery at the same level, although most stumps exhibiting evidence of ischemia will require revision to the above-knee level. The use of antibiotic-impregnated collagen products may enable successful local revision of the infected stump,[43] but no other adjuvant therapies have shown any benefit in the vascular transtibial amputee.

Through-Knee Amputations

In carefully selected patients, disarticulation of the knee joint (through-knee amputation) is a valuable and underutilized amputation. It is indicated in patients with vascular disease who, because of other disability, have no prospect of walking but have distal circulation adequate to heal a transtibial amputation. Through-knee amputation offers the advantages of avoiding the late flexion contracture of the knee observed in a transtibial amputation stump in nonambulatory patients and the hip flexion contracture seen after transfemoral amputation. It provides the advantage of a longer lever and therefore greater stability and better proprioception than a transfemoral amputation, whereas the stump is painless and fully end bearing. The procedure can be carried out quickly with minimal blood loss, offering advantages in unfit patients. While prosthetic fitting makes mobilization possible on a through-knee amputation, if the blood supply will heal a through-knee amputation, it is likely that a transtibial amputation will also heal,[1] and this is undoubtedly preferable in the mobile patient.

The procedure can be undertaken using equal medial and lateral fasciocutaneous flaps (Fig. 172-9). These flaps must be cut generously because the main cause of failure of this operation is overstretching of the skin over the condyles. The patellar tendon is detached from its tibial insertion and sutured to the divided cruciate ligaments, along with the hamstring tendons, bringing the skin suture line to lie between the femoral condyles (see Fig. 172-9C). This procedure does require a suction drain to be placed in the joint cavity at surgery, because prolonged leakage of synovial fluid can be a problem. Resection of the femoral condyles has been advocated to facilitate prosthetic fitting; however, as already discussed, if the patient is expected to ambulate with a through-knee amputation, the surgeon should attempt a transtibial amputation in preference.

The Gritti-Stokes operation has been recommended by some authors.[44,45] In this procedure the femoral joint surface and condyles are excised and the patella is advanced and fused to the distal femur to enable direct weight bearing. A long anterior flap is used to cover the stump, but the end result does not offer any clear advantage over the simpler through-knee disarticulation. Both of these procedures are described in detail by Robinson.[2]

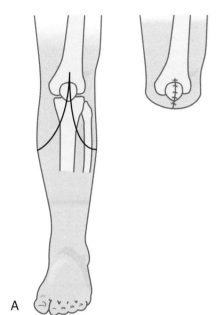

FIGURE 172-9 Through-knee amputation. **A,** Equal sagittal skin flaps for a through-knee amputation. **B,** The limb prior to disarticulation of the knee joint by division of the cruciate ligaments. **C,** The completed stump with the patellar tendon sutured to the cruciate ligament and hamstring tendons. (Redrawn from Robinson KP: Amputations in vascular patients. In Bell PRF, et al [eds]: Surgical Management of Vascular Disease. London, WB Saunders, 1992, pp 609-635.)

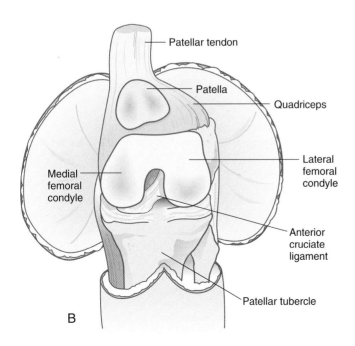

Transfemoral Amputation

Amputation at the above-knee level is indicated in the vascular patient who is unlikely to heal a more distal amputation, the immobile patient requiring limb amputation who is not expected to mobilize, and the patient with a significant flexion deformity at the knee joint. There is little margin for error in the procedure. The longer the residual femoral length, the greater the prospect of mobility. In the absence of a femoral pulse, consideration should be given to a proximal revascularization procedure because the consequences of nonhealing at the transfemoral level are serious and may even be fatal. In patients in whom the gangrenous process extends proximal to the level of transfemoral amputation, then amputation is required at a higher level.

The level of transfemoral amputation is in part determined by the tissue available for flap construction, but as long a length of femoral shaft as possible should be preserved, transecting the femur approximately 12 cm from the knee joint. A myoplastic stump construction is advised to maximize proprioception, optimize stump shape, and reduce late hip flexion deformities. The most common incision involves creation of equal anterior and posterior flaps, each equal to half the circumference of the thigh at the point of proposed femoral transection. The flaps should meet at the level of femoral transection and extend distally to a level approximately 2 fingerbreadths above the patella (Fig. 172-10). After marking flaps in this fashion, skin and subcutaneous tissue are divided in a single incision, with the knife blade angled proximally. The incision is then extended deeper down to bone, dividing muscles with clean bold cuts

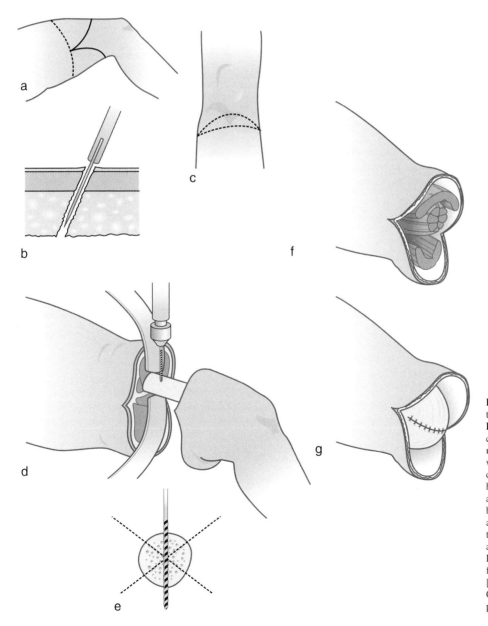

FIGURE 172-10 Transfemoral amputation. **A,** Anterior and posterior skin flaps. **B,** Beveling the subcutaneous fat. **C,** Extra convexity is cut on the posterior flap to minimize puckering of tissues when the wound edges are opposed. **D,** The femur is drilled before its division. **E,** Sites of drill holes in femur just proximal to the level of amputation. **F,** Lateral and medial muscle bundles sutured to the bone with nonabsorbable sutures. **G,** Anterior and posterior muscles and deep fascia sutured across the bone end. (Redrawn from Ruckley CV: Lower limb amputation—time for critical appraisal. In Barros D' Sa, et al [eds]: Vascular Surgery: Current Questions. Oxford, Butterworth Heinemann, 1991, pp 190-206.)

in the same oblique manner as the skin and subcutaneous tissues, such that the point of femoral transection is reached. Periosteum should then be elevated from the bone at this point, and the bone drilled at 3 positions, to give 6 holes for suturing, just proximal to the point of femoral transection (see Fig. 172-10). The lateral (vastus lateralis) and medial (adductor) muscle groups are divided at the proposed level of bone section while the anterior (quadriceps) and the posterior (hamstrings) are divided two to three fingerbreadths beyond the proposed level of bone section. The femur is then divided, preferably with a power saw, the bone end is rounded off with a rasp, and the myoplasty is achieved by suturing the lateral and medial muscle groups to the bone end with fine nonabsorbable sutures. Thereafter, the quadriceps and hamstrings are sutured to each other over the end of the stump, using an absorbable suture placed in the fascia rather than the muscle tissue, providing a second layer of cover over the bone end. Skin should then be closed with sutures and/or paper strips and a light bandage applied. A rigid plaster dressing is inappropriate for the transfemoral amputation and cannot be readily retained on the stump. In this procedure the center part of the posterior flap tends to retract as a result of muscle retraction, and this can be prevented by cutting an extra convexity to the posterior flap. Alternative skin flaps can be used, based on a circumferential skin incision centered 2 to 3 cm distal to the point of femoral transection.

A long medially based sagittal flap has also been described, utilizing an adductor-based myofasciocutaneous flap. The mobilized adductor magnus is secured to the lateral femur via drill holes with the femur maintained in normal extension and then transected 12 cm or so above the knee joint. The posterior muscles are then sutured to the posterior border of the adductor magnus.[37]

Hip Disarticulation

This procedure is only occasionally required in the patient with arterial insufficiency, usually for nonhealing of a transfemoral amputation or in extreme cases of gangrene and sepsis. The technique is described in detail by a number of authors,[2,46] and the following description gives only a brief outline of the procedure.

The patient is placed supine on the table with a sandbag under the sacroiliac joint, and the hip flexed. A wide posterior flap begins 3 cm below the pubic tubercle and extends to the anterior superior iliac spine. This flap must be long enough to meet an anterior incision placed 2 cm below and parallel to the inguinal ligament without tension and therefore varies considerably as dictated by patient build. Once the incision extends through fascia, the hip is extended and the femoral vessels are ligated at the level of the inguinal ligament, with the femoral nerve drawn down and divided under tension. The sartorius is detached from the anterior superior iliac spine, and the muscles overlying the hip joint are divided to expose the anterior acetabulum. The limb is then abducted to enable division of the adductor muscles and the underlying obturator vessels and nerve. Flexion of the leg at this point will give access to the posterior incision, and the gluteus maximus is cut to leave a layer of muscle in the flap, tapering toward the distal

wound edge. Thereafter, the hamstrings are cut at the ischial tuberosity, the sciatic nerve is divided under tension after ligation of its artery, and the gluteus minimus and medius are divided with ligation of the superior and inferior gluteal vessels (facilitated by additional adduction of the limb). The limb is then laid flat, and, after incising the anterior joint capsule at the margin of the acetabulum, the femoral head is dislocated, the round ligament is divided, and the posterior capsule is incised. Division of the obturator tendons and piriformis then complete the amputation. The gluteus maximus is sutured over the acetabulum, and a suction drain is placed in the socket and removed 48 hours later. The gluteal fascia is then sutured to the inguinal ligament with interrupted absorbable sutures, and the skin is closed with interrupted nylon sutures. A hip spica is then applied, with the pressure eliminating the dead space between the flap and the surface of the pelvis.

There is a very low rate of successful ambulation after this procedure, and the majority of vascular patients whose tissue ischemia is extensive enough to require hip disarticulation have a poor prognosis, because the precipitating aortic or iliac occlusion is frequently a herald of failing cardiac output.

■ REFERENCES

1. Smith DG: Amputation: Preoperative assessment and lower extremity surgical techniques. Foot Ankle Clin 6:271-296, 2001.
2. Robinson KP: Amputations in vascular patients. In Bell PRF, et al (eds): Surgical Management of Vascular Disease. London, WB Saunders, 1992, pp 609-635.
3. Pinzur MS, Guedes de Souza Pinto MA, Schon LC, Smith DG: Controversies in amputation surgery. Instr Course Lect 52:445-451, 2003.
4. Grouden MC, Silke CM, Colgan MP, et al: Unrecognised deep venous disease in patients with critical ischaemia. In Proceedings of the Vascular Disease Meeting Modality, Measurement and Management. London, Edward Arnold, 1993.
5. Miller JM: Amputations for infection or ischaemia. Clin Podiatr Med Surg 14:667-689, 1997.
6. Osterman H: The process of amputation and rehabilitation. Clin Podiatr Med Surg 14:585-602, 1997.
7. Berlemont M, Weber R, Willot JP: Ten years of experience with the immediate application of prosthetic devices to amputees of the lower extremities on the operating table. Prosthet Int 3:8-18, 1969.
8. Burgess EM, Romano RL, Zettl CP: Amputation management utilising immediate postsurgical prosthetic fitting. Prosthet Int 3:28-37, 1969.
9. Mueller MJ: Comparison of removable rigid dressings and elastic bandages in preprosthetic management of patients with below knee amputations. Phys Ther 62:1438-1441, 1982.
10. Mooney V, Harvey JP, McBride E, Snelson R: Comparison of postoperative stump management: Plaster vs soft dressing. J Bone Joint Surg Am 53:241-249, 1971.
11. Harrington IJ, Lexier R, Woods JM, et al: A plaster-pylon technique for below-knee amputation. J Bone Joint Surg Br 73:76-78, 1991.
12. McLean N, Fick GH: The effects of semirigid dressings on below knee amputations. Phys Ther 74:668-673, 1994.
13. Kane TJ, Pollack EW: The rigid versus soft postoperative dressing controversy: A controlled study in vascular below-knee amputees. Am Surg 46:244-247, 1980.
14. Woodburn KR, Sockalingham S, Gilmore H, et al: A randomised trial of rigid stump dressing following transtibial amputation for peripheral arterial insufficiency. Prosthet Orthot Int 28:22-27, 2004.

15. Vigier S, Casillas J-M, Dulieu V, et al: Healing of open stump wounds after vascular below-knee amputation: Plaster cast socket with silicone sleeve versus elastic compression. Arch Phys Med Rehabil 80:1327-1330, 1999.

16. Smith DG, McFarland LV, Sangeorzan BJ, et al: Postoperative dressing and management strategies for transtibial amputations: A critical review. J Rehabil Res Dev 40:213-224, 2003.

17. Pinzur MS, Littooy F, Osterman H, Wafer D: Early post-operative prosthetic limb fitting. Orthopedics 11:1051-1053, 1988.

18. Schon LC, Short KW, Soupiou O, et al: Benefits of early prosthetic management of transtibial amputees: A prospective clinical study of a prefabricated prosthesis. Foot Ankle Int 23:509-514, 2002.

19. Kernik CB, Rozzi WB: Simplified two-stage below knee amputation for unsalvageable diabetic foot infections. Clin Orthop Rel Res 261:251-256, 1990.

20. McIntyre KE, Berman SS: Patient evaluation and preoperative preparation for amputation. In Rutherford RB: Vascular Surgery, 4th ed. New York, WB Saunders, 1992, pp 1956-1960.

21. Desai Y, Robbs JV, Keenan JP: Staged below-knee amputations for septic peripheral lesions due to ischaemia. Br J Surg 73:392-394, 1986.

22. Brinker MR, Timberlake GA, Goff JM, et al: Below-knee physiologic cryoanesthesia in the critically ill patient. J Vasc Surg 7:433-438, 1988.

23. Funk C, Young G: Subtotal pedal amputations. J Am Podiatr Med Assoc 91(1): 6-12, 2001.

24. Fontaine JL, Reyzelman A, Rothenberg G, et al: The role of revascularisation in transmetatarsal amputations. J Am Podiatr Med Assoc 91:533-535, 2001.

25. Thomas SRYW, Perkins JMT, Magee TR, Galland RB: Transmetatarsal amputation: An 8-year experience. Ann R Coll Surg Engl 83:164-166, 2001.

26. Sanders LJ: Transmetatarsal and midfoot amputations. Clin Podiatr Med Surg 14:741-762, 1997.

27. Ballard JL, Eke CC, Bunt TJ, et al: A prospective evaluation of transcutaneous oxygen measurements in the management of diabetic foot problems. J Vasc Surg 22: 485-492, 1995.

28. Vitti MJ, Robinson DV, Hauer-Jensen M, et al: Wound healing in forefoot amputations: The predictive value of toe pressure. Ann Vasc Surg 8:99, 1994.

29. Aldera HM, James K, Castronuvo JJ, et al: Prediction of amputation wound healing with skin perfusion pressure. J Vasc Surg 21:823-829, 1995.

30. Pinzur M, Kaminsky M, Sage R, et al: Amputations at the middle level of the foot. J Bone Joint Surg Am 68:1061-1064, 1986.

31. Early JS: Transmetatarsal and midfoot amputations. Clin Orthop Rel Res 361:85-90, 1999.

32. Hudson JR, Yu GV, Marzano R, Vincent AL: Syme's amputation: Surgical technique, prosthetic considerations, and case reports. J Am Podiatr Med Assoc 92:232-246, 2002.

33. Weaver FA, Modrall JG, Baek S, et al: Syme amputation: Results in patients with severe forefoot ischaemia. Cardiovasc Surg 4:81-86, 1996.

34. Smith DG, Fergason JR: Transtibial amputations. Clin Orthop Rel Res 361:108-115, 1999.

35. Chiodo CP, Stroud CC: Optimal surgical preparation of the residual limb for prosthetic fitting in below-knee amputations. Foot Ankle Clin 6:253-264, 2001.

36. O'Dwyer KJ, Edwards MH: The association between the lowest palpable pulse and wound healing in below knee amputations. Ann R Coll Surg Engl 67:232-234, 1985.

37. Pinzur MS: Current concepts: Amputation surgery in peripheral vascular disease. Instruct Course Lect 46:501-509, 1997.

38. Ruckley CV, Stonebridge PA, Prescott RJ: Skewflap versus long posterior flap in below-knee amputations: Multicenter trial. J Vasc Surg 13:423-427, 1991.

39. Allcock PA, Jain AS: Revisiting transtibial amputation with the long posterior flap. Br J Surg 88:683-686, 2001.

40. Persson BM: Sagittal incision for below-knee amputation in ischaemic gangrene. J Bone Joint Surg Br 56:110, 1974.

41. Jain AS, Stewart CPU, Turner MS: Transtibial amputation using a medially-based flap. J R Coll Surg Edinb 40:263-265, 1995.

42. Tripses D, Pollak EW: Risk factors in healing of below knee amputation. Am J Surg 141:718-720, 1981.

43. Spruit M, Bosman CHR: Revision of failed below knee amputations: Local débridement with gentamicin collagen. Eur J Surg 160:267-270, 1994.

44. Yusuf SW, Baker DM, Wenham PW, et al: Role of Gritti-Stokes amputation in peripheral vascular disease. Ann R Coll Surg Engl 79:102-104, 1997.

45. Faber DC, Fielding P: Gritti-Stokes (through-knee) amputation: Should it be reintroduced? South Med J 94:997-1001, 2001.

46. Sugarbaker PH, Chretien PB: A surgical technique for hip disarticulation. Surgery 90:546, 1981.

Lower Extremity Amputation:
Perioperative Complications

RICHARD A. YEAGER, MD

Lower extremity amputation is frequently required in elderly patients with cardiac and peripheral vascular disease and/or diabetes. A compilation of demographic data from several large series reported the mean age of amputation patients to be 65 years, with 54% having diabetes, 65% smokers, 33% with a prior myocardial infarction, and 39% with prior vascular surgery.[27] In a large amputation series in 2003 from a single institution, 63% of patients had diabetes, 34% had end-stage renal disease, 40% had cerebral vascular disease, 89% had hypertension, and 82% had coronary artery disease.[1]

Not surprisingly, major amputation of the lower extremity can be complicated by a variety of fatal and early nonfatal perioperative complications. Early complications are either systemic relating to a specific organ system (e.g., myocardial infarction, stroke, pneumonia) or local involving the amputation stump (e.g., infection, nonhealing, hematoma, contracture, and phantom pain). These systemic and stump-related early complications of lower extremity amputation are detailed later in this chapter.

■ PERIOPERATIVE MORTALITY

Historically, lower extremity amputation was associated with high perioperative mortality. In 1965, Otteman and coworkers reported a 42% mortality with above-knee amputation and a 30% mortality with below-knee amputation.[73] Consistently, perioperative mortality is reported to be higher for above-knee amputation (AKA) compared with below-knee amputation (BKA).[33,82] There is nothing obviously inherently more dangerous about the AKA procedure. However, AKA is more frequently performed in higher risk patients who are elderly, debilitated, bedridden, and nearing the end of life. During the later part of the 20th century, there was a consistent trend of improved perioperative survival.[1,13,26,39,83,88] One review article published in 1991 analyzed data from numerous published series and reported mortality for BKA and AKA at less than 2% and 10%, respectively.[26] However, in Veterans Affairs (VA) hospitals during the early 1990s, the 30-day postoperative mortality ranged from 6% to 9% for BKAs and 13% to 16% for AKAs.[40,60] In one published series of 154 patients undergoing 172 amputations (78 AKA, 94 BKA) on a combined university/VA vascular service a 30-day operative mortality of 10% was reported.[71] In another report the 30-day mortality was 12% for BKA and 17% for AKA.[21]

Amputation is consistently reported to have a higher perioperative mortality than lower extremity arterial bypass, even though amputation takes less time, is usually associated with less blood loss, and is technically less demanding than arterial bypass. In several large series, amputation patients were found to be older, to be more debilitated, and to have more diffuse vascular disease and renal disease than patients undergoing lower extremity bypass.[1,51,74,88] Additionally, amputation patients may receive less intense preoperative and postoperative care compared with patients undergoing lower extremity arterial bypass. Several large series have specified cause of death after major amputation, identifying cardiac complications and sepsis, including pneumonia, as the leading causes for early mortality.[1,13,21,61,65,71,86,88]

Amputation Patients at Higher Risk for Perioperative Mortality

Emergent/Urgent Amputations

Patients requiring amputation for severe, acute leg ischemia are at extremely high risk for perioperative mortality. Many such patients will have a history of recent myocardial infarction and/or cardiogenic shock. Death is often attributable to cardiac complications. In one small series of patients presenting with irreversibly ischemic legs as manifested by profound sensory loss, muscle paralysis and rigor, as well as skin marbling, the 1-month mortality after amputation was 46%.[106] Campbell and coworkers found patients undergoing amputation for acute ischemia had significantly more comorbidities and were twice as likely to require AKA than patients with chronic ischemia.[17] If possible, delaying amputation in high-risk patients with recent cardiac events is prudent and allows time for treatment of underlying cardiac complications. Intravenous heparin appears to be of benefit in lowering mortality in this setting.[8,34] Heparin protects against extension of coronary thrombosis and prevents additional arterial and venous thromboembolic complications, specifically pulmonary embolism, another well-recognized cause for death in patients after amputation.[8]

Perioperative mortality is also consistently reported to be higher in patients undergoing urgent amputation for wet gangrene or extensive pedal sepsis.[35] Several authors have recommended delaying operation in particularly high-risk patients by employing physiologic amputation using tourniquet isolation and freezing the leg in dry ice.[10,12,47,53,103] One of the largest experiences with physiologic amputation was reported by Bunt.[12] Of a total of 456 lower extremity amputations, Bunt performed 116 (25%) physiologic amputations in patients with underlying medical disability and acute pedal sepsis. Physiologic amputation was maintained for a mean period of 72 hours ranging from 24 hours to 1 month. Patients routinely received intravenous broad-spectrum antibiotics and were managed in an intensive care unit with invasive monitoring, including pulmonary artery catheters and arterial lines. Once stabilized, patients underwent elective one-stage amputation. The perioperative mortality in this series of 116 patients was 5%. A very similar operative mortality has been reported when treating severe lower extremity infection with prompt guillotine or conventional amputation.[69] When surgical amputation is not possible for a period of time, physiologic amputation may be considered an alternative to immediate guillotine amputation.

End-Stage Renal Disease (ESRD) Patients Undergoing Amputation

Patients with ESRD may have impaired wound healing and reduced limb-salvage rates after lower extremity arterial bypass compared with patients without ESRD. For this reason, many of these patients are better served by primary amputation.[32] The prevalence of ESRD among patients undergoing amputation currently ranges from 18% to 34%.[1,71,94]

ESRD patients also have a relatively high perioperative mortality after amputation. In one series, patients with ESRD undergoing amputation had a hospital mortality of 18% for BKA and 38% for AKA, with cardiac arrhythmias a frequent cause of death.[31] The high mortality rate associated with amputation in patients with ESRD is underemphasized. Renewed efforts focusing on lowering operative mortality in this cohort seem indicated, but, to date, no prospective study has focused specifically on outcomes in ESRD patients undergoing amputation.

Hip Disarticulation for Ischemia

Proximal amputations clearly are associated with higher mortality. The extreme case supporting this finding is the high perioperative mortality associated with hip disarticulation. Endean and associates reported a perioperative mortality of 50% when hip disarticulation was performed for ischemia, and Unruh and colleagues reported a 60% mortality when hip disarticulation was performed for ischemia combined with preoperative infection.[36,96] Patients requiring this procedure have advanced vascular disease and many comorbid medical problems, often including a nonhealing, infected AKA. When possible, inflow revascularization before lower extremity amputation in selected patients at risk for healing will obviate the need for hip disarticulation.[11,100]

■ SYSTEMIC COMPLICATIONS

Cardiac Complications

Cardiac complications, frequently related to myocardial infarction, are the most common cause for perioperative mortality after amputation.[61,71,79] Keagy and colleagues

reported cardiac complications as the leading cause of death (43%) in their series of 1028 amputations.[61] In another series of 172 major amputations, the authors reported over 60% of the deaths were due to cardiac complications.[71]

A focus on perioperative cardiac management of amputation patients can be successful in lowering mortality. Bunt and associates reported a perioperative mortality of 2.8% in 140 patients undergoing AKA and 0.9% in 113 patients undergoing BKA.[13] The authors attribute their notable results to liberal preoperative use of intensive care units including use of pulmonary artery catheters and pharmacologic agents directed at improving cardiac function.

My colleagues and I also have noted improvement in results of amputation surgery, including a reduction in cardiac complications. We prospectively screened all operative cases for perioperative myocardial infarction on our combined VA/university vascular service during a 1-year period using serial electrocardiograms and cardiac enzymes.[92] Major lower extremity amputation (n = 44) comprised 8% of the series, with no perioperative myocardial infarction identified among the amputation patients. In addition, as part of a prospective study screening for deep venous thrombosis (DVT) around the time of amputation surgery in 72 patients, we found an overall perioperative mortality of 4% with only one fatal myocardial infarction.[104] The reduction in cardiac mortality after amputation surgery may be attributable to multiple factors, including improvements in anesthetic techniques and the perioperative use of cardioprotective drugs, including antiplatelet therapy and beta blockers.[50,76]

There is level I evidence that the perioperative use of beta blockers reduces the incidence of cardiac events after noncardiac surgery.[68,81,97,101] As a result, vascular surgeons frequently employ perioperative beta-blocker therapy around the time of aortic and lower extremity revascularization procedures.[76,105] It may, however, be underappreciated that patients undergoing amputation may also benefit from perioperative beta-blocker therapy.[2]

Pulmonary Complications

Pulmonary complications are another frequently reported cause of early death and morbidity after amputation. Huston and associates reported pulmonary sepsis as the leading cause for early death in their patients undergoing AKA.[54] Many amputation patients present debilitated, nutritionally depleted, and relatively immobile and may have problems with clearing of pulmonary secretions, atelectasis, and development of what has been termed *inanition pneumonitis,* which may prove fatal.[13,54] Early mobility, nutritional support, and aggressive physical therapy may help prevent fatal pulmonary complications in this frail patient population.[67,83]

Sepsis

Sepsis has emerged as a leading cause for morbidity and death in patients undergoing amputation.[54,86] Typical septic sources after amputation include pneumonia, urinary tract infection, intravenous line infection, decubitus ulcers, infection of prosthetic arterial bypasses or dialysis access grafts, as well as infections involving the amputation site. When the origin for infection is not clinically obvious, intra-abdominal sources for sepsis should be routinely considered and evaluated. Specifically, the elderly amputation patient with diffuse vascular disease is at risk for acute mesenteric ischemia.[28,49]

Venous Thromboembolism

Due to immobility and surgically induced venous endothelial trauma, amputation patients are perceived to be at high risk for perioperative DVT.[48] Several studies have screened for perioperative DVT after amputation with conflicting results.[6,15,43,104] A recent, small study found DVT proximal to the popliteal vein in 50% of amputation patients studied.[15] Conversely, Barnes and coworkers screened 35 amputation patients with venous Doppler examinations and failed to identify a single case of DVT.[6] My colleagues and I prospectively screened amputation patients for perioperative DVT using duplex scanning and identified an incidence of 12.5%.[104] Our results are similar to the 14% incidence of perioperative DVT after amputation identified by Fletcher and coworkers.[43] Although the exact prevalence of DVT after amputation is unclear, it does appear that DVT after amputation is higher than that after lower extremity arterial bypass surgery.[43,75]

Postoperative DVT may cause severe stump swelling and impaired primary healing of the amputation.[19] The main impetus for identifying perioperative DVT, however, is to allow for prompt treatment and prevention of fatal pulmonary embolism. In 1970, Rosenberg and colleagues[84] reported a 6.8% incidence of pulmonary embolism after amputation with fatal pulmonary embolism in multiple series of major amputation ranging from 1% to 3% of cases.[13,61,84,86] Routine DVT prophylaxis and/or careful perioperative screening for DVT with duplex scanning in amputation patients appears prudent.[56,104]

Postoperative Renal Failure

Many amputation patients have underlying chronic renal insufficiency with renal failure reported as the cause for 4.5% of all deaths within 30 days of amputation.[26] The prevalence of patients with renal functional impairment not requiring dialysis among amputation patients has not been well documented but is probably significant. Additional renal damage can be incurred around the time of amputation from a host of potential complications, including contrast-dye nephropathy, episodes of sepsis or cardiogenic shock, or antibiotic-related nephrotoxicity. These patients are at high risk for postoperative worsening of renal failure requiring initiation of dialysis. Nonetheless, acute renal failure necessitating the initiation of dialysis does not appear to be a frequent occurrence after amputation.

Postoperative Stroke

One review identified stroke as the cause for 7.3% of all mortality within 30 days of amputation.[26] These data are not surprising considering that amputations are frequently performed in patients with diffuse vascular disease. Almost 20% of patients undergoing amputation for ischemia have a history of symptomatic cerebrovascular disease.[26,27] Also the prevalence of asymptomatic, hemodynamically significant

Table 173-1	Baseline Body Habitus, Albumin, and Hematocrit in Patients Undergoing Major Lower Extremity Amputation			
VALUE	MEAN	SD	25TH PERCENTILE	75TH PERCENTILE
Albumin*	2.4 mg/dL	0.7	1.9 mg/dL	2.9 mg/dL
Hematocrit†	33.2%	5.7	29.1%	37.4%
BMI	25	5.7	20.9	28.1

BMI, body mass index before amputation (available on 118 patients).
*Albumin is defined as the value closest to the date of amputation or initial vascular evaluation ± 30 days (available on 101 patients).
†Hematocrit is defined as the preoperative value closest to the amputation date within 30 days (available on 97 patients).

From Nehler MR, Coll JR, Hiatt WR, et al: Functional outcome in a contemporary series of major lower extremity amputations. J Vasc Surg 38:7, 2003.

carotid stenosis among patients undergoing infrainguinal bypass surgery approaches 30%.[44] There is no reason to believe that this prevalence rate would be any less among patients undergoing amputation for ischemia. Abou-Zamzam and coworkers noted cerebrovascular disease in over 40% of their amputation patients.[1] The preoperative assessment of amputation patients should include questioning for symptoms consistent with transient ischemic attacks or stroke. In addition, amputation patients should receive aspirin or other antiplatelet therapy to help lower the risk of perioperative stroke.[50]

Depression as a Postoperative Complication After Amputation

Most experienced surgeons have encountered the occasional amputation patient who, early in the postoperative period, loses interest in his or her surroundings and stops eating. Clinical depression after amputation is a well-recognized condition, and in one prospective study 35% of amputees were found to have a major depressive disorder.[58] Patients appearing depressed after amputation should undergo psychiatric evaluation and therapy, including antidepressant medication. Depressed patients not eating or participating in postoperative rehabilitation programs are at risk for a host of complications, including nutritional depletion, nonhealing, decubitus ulcers, contractures, and DVT.[78,80] Indeed, in one series of major lower extremity amputations, anemia and hypoalbuminemia were widely prevalent (Table 173-1).[71] Finally, postoperative suicide attempts have been reported after amputation.[71]

■ LOCAL COMPLICATIONS OF THE AMPUTATION STUMP OR CONTRALATERAL EXTREMITY

Amputation Stump Infection

Infection of the amputation stump approaches 30% in some series and is more prevalent when there is preexisting foot or lower leg infection (Fig. 173-1). Fisher and coworkers cultured deep calf muscle and peri–saphenous vein

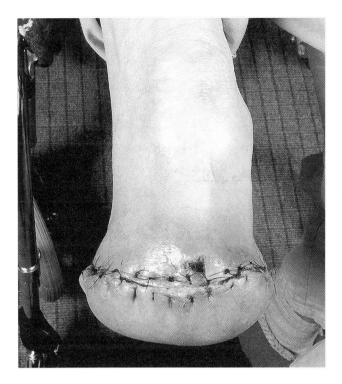

FIGURE 173-1 Patient with BKA stump infection and cellulitis.

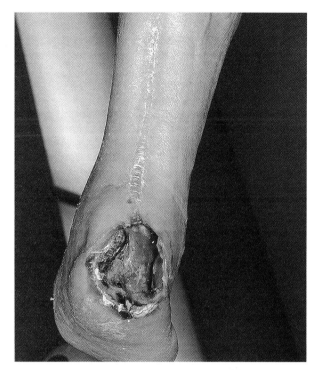

FIGURE 173-2 Patient with purulent infection of necrotic heel ulcer before guillotine amputation.

lymphatics in patients undergoing amputation for wet gangrene of the foot.[42] Thirty-two percent of patients had positive deep muscle cultures, and 19% of patients had positive lymphatic cultures. Open foot and leg wounds should be routinely cultured before major amputation, with culture and sensitivity results guiding selection of perioperative antibiotics and specific attention given to resistant *Staphylococcus* and *Pseudomonas* species.[46,55,62,77,93]

Several authors have proposed a strategy to reduce the incidence of amputation stump infection by performing a two-staged procedure in patients with significant foot sepsis.[28,42,69,87] (Fig. 173-2) The initial stage consists of an open, guillotine amputation at the ankle level, followed 3 to 5 days later by standard below-knee amputation with primary closure. A prospective randomized study comparing a one-staged versus a two-staged amputation approach in patients with wet gangrene of the foot reported significantly fewer wound complications in the patients undergoing the two-staged technique.[42]

A recent failed revascularization increases the chance for amputation stump infection compared with patients undergoing primary amputation. Van Niekerk and coworkers found a higher rate of amputation stump infection in patients who had undergone prior attempts at arterial bypass.[99] Additionally, patients with nonfunctional lower extremity prosthetic bypass grafts are believed to be at higher risk for amputation stump infection. Partial graft removal at the time of amputation is associated with a 30% to 40% incidence of amputation stump infection. One prospective, randomized study reported a 39% amputation stump infection rate with partial graft removal compared with 8% with complete graft removal.[85]

Nonhealing of the Amputation

Multiple factors can lead to primary nonhealing of the amputation. These include local infection, ischemia, poor surgical technique, hematoma, severe swelling, and postoperative trauma.[45,57,66,98] From 20% to 30% of BKA patients will not heal primarily.[1,14,23,30,41,61,70] About half of these patients will require a higher amputation.[14,23,30,41] The remaining patients with minor, localized wound complications will have delayed healing of the amputation and not require a surgical revision.[30,52] About 10% of AKA patients also will require surgical revision.[30]

In a large (n = 713), prospective study of BKA, 59% of patients had primary healing of their amputation at 3 months, 19% required reamputation at a higher level, 11% remained unhealed without a higher revision, and 11% had died.[29] Infusion of an intravenous prostacyclin analogue had no effect on healing.

There is no consensus as to whether prior lower extremity bypass has a negative impact on primary amputation healing (Fig. 173-3).* If the prior bypass surgery was remote and previous wounds have healed, there is minimal impairment of amputation healing. However, recent unsuccessful attempts at arterial bypass have a negative effect on primary amputation healing.[25] Evans found 77% of BKAs healed after failed arterial reconstruction attempts compared with 89% of amputations healing with no prior attempts at reconstruction.[38] Also, Van Niekerk and coworkers identified a trend for delayed wound healing in patients who had

*See references 16, 18, 20, 25, 38, 64, 82, 89, 91, 95, 99, and 102.

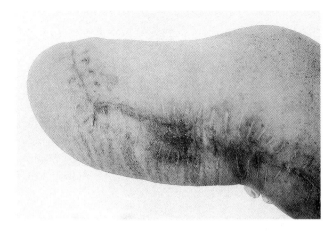

FIGURE 173-3 Patient with failed arterial bypass and primary healing of BKA.

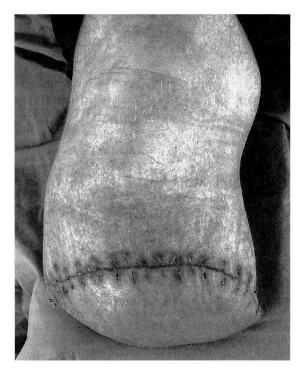

FIGURE 173-4 Patient managed with rigid dressing with primary healing of BKA at 1 month.

undergone prior attempts at arterial bypass compared with patients undergoing primary amputation.[99]

Many surgeons favor application of a rigid dressing on the stump after BKA to optimize chances for primary healing (Fig. 173-4). When properly applied, the rigid dressing will help control postoperative swelling, will help protect the stump from trauma, and may prevent knee contracture.[5,7] Conversely, an improperly applied and inadequately padded rigid dressing can be a source of pressure necrosis and trauma to the stump. Other authors favor soft dressings, and one small prospective randomized study comparing rigid and soft dressings failed to show any difference in amputation healing rates.[4,63,82]

Stump Hematoma

Stump hematoma is a serious local complication that can result in primary nonhealing of the amputation. Stump hematoma is related to postsurgical hemorrhage or stump trauma.[7] Patients receiving anticoagulants for DVT prophylaxis or cardiac conditions are at higher risk for development of stump hematoma. The routine use of wound drains after amputation is controversial and has not been found to be necessary in our unit. However, selected patients receiving postoperative anticoagulation will benefit from closed suction wound drainage.

Knee Contracture

Early flexion-contracture of the ipsilateral knee can occur after BKA. Patients with knee contractures cannot be fit with a prosthesis, and additionally the contracted extremity is at risk for development of pressure ulceration on the end of the amputation stump. Patients at risk for developing knee contractures include those with strokes or other neurologic conditions resulting in extremity spasticity. Because these patients have poor prospects for postoperative ambulation with a prosthesis, they are best served by initially performing a through-knee amputation or AKA.[22] Attentive postoperative physical therapy is also required in these patients to prevent hip flexion contractures. Properly selected and motivated patients without neurologic impair-

ment participating in an active physical therapy program will rarely develop a knee contracture after BKA.[24]

Contralateral Extremity Problems

Given the frequent symmetrical distribution of lower extremity vascular occlusive disease and diabetic peripheral neuropathy, it is not surprising the contralateral limb is ultimately also at risk after lower extremity amputation. Bodily and Burgess found that 50% of patients required amputation of the contralateral lower limb within 24 months of the initial amputation.[9] Obviously, the contralateral limb is of paramount importance in unilateral amputees, since ambulation with a single prosthesis is more likely than ambulation with bilateral prostheses. Evans and coworkers found that only 50% of amputation patients walking with a single prosthesis were able to subsequently ambulate with bilateral prostheses after a contralateral amputation.[37]

Unfortunately in some instances, contralateral limb problems develop around the time of the initial amputation. During the early postoperative period the patient is at risk for longer periods of immobility and decreased peripheral perfusion, resulting in pressure ulceration on the contralateral heel. This is more likely to occur if the patient is systemically ill around the time of the initial amputation and experiencing periods of reduced peripheral skin perfusion. Also, contralateral foot and toe trauma can occur during the early, tentative period of ambulation and rehabilitation. Daily surveillance of the contralateral limb is important for assessing skin integrity, and the importance of adequate foot protection and heel padding cannot be overemphasized.

Phantom Pain

Nearly all amputation patients will experience significant early postoperative stump pain requiring parenteral narcotics. Anecdotally, postoperative amputation pain is more severe after BKA as compared with AKA. Early postoperative pain usually abates after a few days and at 3 to 5 days the typical patient is taking oral pain medication. Persistent, severe pain more than 1 week after amputation likely indicates stump ischemia or infection.

Phantom limb pain is a chronic condition characterized by pain that persists long after stump healing has occurred. There is little consensus surrounding the definition, etiology, incidence, or management of phantom limb pain. The reported incidence of phantom limb pain after lower extremity amputation ranges from 5% to 85%.[59,67,90] Undoubtedly, this wide variation is related to how the investigators are defining phantom pain. The vast majority of amputation patients will report occasional fleeting pain in the residual limb. Very few patients, however, have a severe, persistent, life-altering phantom pain problem. Malone and coworkers report phantom pain as a significant problem in less than 5% of their amputees.[67] This relatively low incidence is consistent with our experience.

Patients with severe, prolonged extremity pain before amputation appear to be at higher risk for developing phantom limb pain. This fact has prompted investigations focusing on the efficacy of perioperative epidural analgesia in reducing the incidence of phantom limb pain. In one prospective, unblinded study, lumbar epidural blockade with bupivacaine and morphine for 72 hours before the operation resulted in significant reduction in the incidence of phantom limb pain at 6 months after amputation.[3] Conversely, in a prospective, randomized and blinded study of epidural bupivacaine and morphine starting 18 hours before amputation compared with epidural saline there was no difference in the incidence of phantom limb pain at 3, 6, and 12 months after amputation.[72] Whether there are long-term benefits, epidural analgesia is a very effective method for managing perioperative amputation pain.

■ SUMMARY

Amputation surgery is technically straightforward yet associated with a relatively high perioperative mortality and nonhealing rate. Improved outcomes are documented with involvement of experienced and interested surgeons, attention to details of perioperative management, and selective utilization of invasive monitoring in the intensive care unit. Modern-day surgeons should strive for a perioperative mortality of less than 5% for BKA and less than 10% for AKA. With proper selection of amputation level, culture-specific antibiotic prophylaxis, careful surgical technique, and vigilant postoperative stump care, the nonhealing requiring surgical revision should occur in only a small minority of cases.

■ REFERENCES

1. Abou-Zamzam AM Jr, Teruya TH, Killeen JD, Ballard JL: Major lower extremity amputation in an academic vascular center. Ann Vasc Surg 17:86-90, 2003.

2. Auerbach AD, Goldman L: Beta-blockers and reduction of cardiac events in noncardiac surgery: Scientific review. JAMA 287:1435-1444, 2002.

3. Bach S, Noreng MF, Tjellden NU: Phantom limb pain in amputees during the first 12 months following limb amputation, after preoperative lumbar epidural blockade. Pain 33:297-301, 1988.

4. Baker WH, Barnes RW, Shurr DG: The healing of below-knee amputations: A comparison of soft and plaster dressing. Am J Surg 133:716-718, 1977.

5. Barber GG, McPhail NV, Scobie TK, et al: A prospective study of lower limb amputations. Can J Surg 26:339-341, 1983.

6. Barnes RW, Slaymaker EE: Postoperative deep vein thrombosis in the lower extremity amputee: A prospective study with Doppler ultrasound. Ann Surg 183:429-432, 1976.

7. Behar TA, Burnham SJ, Johnson G Jr: Major stump trauma following below-knee amputation: Outcome and recommendations for therapy. J Cardiovasc Surg (Torino) 32:753-756, 1991.

8. Blaisdell FW, Steele M, Allen RE: Management of acute lower extremity arterial ischemia due to embolism and thrombosis. Surgery 84:822-834, 1978.

9. Bodily KC, Burgess EM: Contralateral limb and patient survival after leg amputation. Am J Surg 146:280-282, 1983.

10. Brinker MR, Timberlake GA, Goff JM, et al: Below-knee physiologic cryoanesthesia in the critically ill patient. J Vasc Surg 7:433-438, 1988.

11. Bunt TJ: Gangrene of the immediate postoperative above-knee amputation stump: Role of emergency revascularization in preventing death. J Vasc Surg 2:874-877, 1985.

12. Bunt TJ: Physiologic amputation: Preliminary cryoamputation of the gangrenous extremity. AORN J 54:1220-1224, 1991.

13. Bunt TJ, Manship LL, Bynoe RP, Haynes JL: Lower extremity amputation for peripheral vascular disease: A low-risk operation. Am Surg 50:581-584, 1984.

14. Burgess EM, Romano RL, Zettl JH, Schrock RD Jr: Amputations of the leg for peripheral vascular insufficiency. J Bone Joint Surg Am 53:874-890, 1971.

15. Burke B, Kumar R, Vickers V, et al: Deep vein thrombosis after lower limb amputation. Am J Phys Med Rehabil 79:145-149, 2000.

16. Campbell WB, Marriott S, Eve R, et al: Factors influencing the early outcome of major lower limb amputation for vascular disease. Ann R Coll Surg Engl 83:309-314, 2001.

17. Campbell WB, Marriott S, Eve R, et al: Amputation for acute ischaemia is associated with increased comorbidity and higher amputation level. Cardiovasc Surg 11:121-123, 2003.

18. Campbell WB, St Johnston JA, Kernick VF, Rutter EA: Lower limb amputation: Striking the balance. Ann R Coll Surg Engl 76:205-209, 1994.

19. Chong DK, Panju A: Deep venous thrombosis as a cause of stump swelling in two lower extremity amputee patients. Arch Phys Med Rehabil 74:1002-1003, 1993.

20. Cook TA, Davies AH, Horrocks M, Baird RN: Amputation level is not adversely affected by previous femorodistal bypass surgery. Eur J Vasc Surg 6:599-601, 1992.

21. Cruz CP, Eidt JF, Capps C, et al: Major lower extremity amputations at a Veterans Affairs hospital. Am J Surg 186:449-454, 2003.

22. Cull DL, Taylor SM, Hamontree SE, et al: A reappraisal of a modified through-knee amputation in patients with peripheral vascular disease. Am J Surg 182:44-48, 2001.

23. Cumming JG, Spence VA, Jain AS, et al: Further experience in the healing rate of lower limb amputations. Eur J Vasc Surg 2:383-385, 1988.

24. Cutson TM, Bongiorni DR: Rehabilitation of the older lower limb amputee: A brief review. J Am Geriatr Soc 44:1388-1393, 1996.

25. Dardik H, Kahn M, Dardik I, et al: Influence of failed vascular bypass procedures on conversion of below-knee to above-knee amputation levels. Surgery 91:64-69, 1982.

26. DeFrang RD, Taylor LM Jr, Porter JM: Amputation. Curr Probl Surg 28:140, 1991.

27. DeFrang RD, Taylor LM, Porter JM: Basic data related to amputations. Ann Vasc Surg 5:202-207, 1991.

28. Desai Y, Robbs JV, Keenan JP: Staged below-knee amputations for septic peripheral lesions due to ischaemia. Br J Surg 73:392-394, 1986.

29. Dormandy J, Belcher G, Broos P, et al: Prospective study of 713 below-knee amputations for ischaemia and the effect of a prostacyclin analogue on healing. Hawaii Study Group. Br J Surg 81:33-37, 1994.

30. Dormandy J, Heeck L, Vig S: Major amputations: Clinical patterns and predictors. Semin Vasc Surg 12:154-161, 1999.

31. Dossa CD, Shepard AD, Amos AM, et al: Results of lower extremity amputations in patients with end-stage renal disease. J Vasc Surg 20:14-19, 1994.

32. Edwards JM, Taylor LM Jr, Porter JM: Limb salvage in end-stage renal disease (ESRD). Comparison of modern results in patients with and without ESRD. Arch Surg 123:1164-1168, 1988.

33. Eidemiller LR, Awe WC, Peterson CG: Amputation of the ischemic extremity. Am Surg 34:491, 1968.

34. Eliason JL, Wainess RM, Proctor MC, et al: A national and single institutional experience in the contemporary treatment of acute lower extremity ischemia. Ann Surg 238:382-389, 2003.

35. Ellitsgaard N, Andersson AP, Fabrin J, Holstein P: Outcome in 282 lower extremity amputations: Knee salvage and survival. Acta Orthop Scand 61:140-142, 1990.

36. Endean ED, Schwarcz TH, Barker DE, et al: Hip disarticulation: Factors affecting outcome. J Vasc Surg 14:398-404, 1991.

37. Evans WE, Hayes JP, Vermilion BD: Rehabilitation of the bilateral amputee. J Vasc Surg 5:589-593, 1987.

38. Evans WE, Hayes JP, Vermilion BD: Effect of a failed distal reconstruction on the level of amputation. Am J Surg 160:217-220, 1990.

39. Fearon J, Campbell DR, Hoar CS Jr, et al: Improved results with diabetic below-knee amputations. Arch Surg 120:777-780, 1985.

40. Feinglass J, Pearce WH, Martin GJ, et al: Postoperative and late survival outcomes after major amputation: Findings from the Department of Veterans Affairs National Surgical Quality Improvement Program. Surgery 130:21-29, 2001.

41. Finch DR, Macdougal M, Tibbs DJ, Morris PJ: Amputation for vascular disease: The experience of a peripheral vascular unit. Br J Surg 67:233-237, 1980.

42. Fisher DF Jr, Clagett GP, Fry RE, et al: One-stage versus two-stage amputation for wet gangrene of the lower extremity: A randomized study. J Vasc Surg 8:428-433, 1988.

43. Fletcher JP, Batiste P: Incidence of deep vein thrombosis following vascular surgery. Int Angiol 16:65-68, 1997.

44. Gentile AT, Taylor LM Jr, Moneta GL, Porter JM: Prevalence of asymptomatic carotid stenosis in patients undergoing infrainguinal bypass surgery. Arch Surg 130:900-904, 1995.

45. Gray DW, Ng RL: Anatomical aspects of the blood supply to the skin of the posterior calf: Technique of below-knee amputation. Br J Surg 77:662-664, 1990.

46. Grimble SA, Magee TR, Galland RB: Methicillin-resistant *Staphylococcus aureus* in patients undergoing major amputation. Eur J Vasc Endovasc Surg 22:215-218, 2001.

47. Harbrecht PJ, Nethery HJ, Ahmad W, Fry DE: Freezing an extremity in preparation for amputation. South Med J 71:926-929, 1978.

48. Harper DR, Dhall DP, Woodruff PW: Prophylaxis in iliofemoral venous thrombosis. The major amputee as a clinical research model. Br J Surg 60:831, 1973.

49. Harris PL, Read F, Eardley A, et al: The fate of elderly amputees. Br J Surg 61:665-668, 1974.

50. Hiatt WR: Preventing atherothrombotic events in peripheral arterial disease: The use of antiplatelet therapy. J Intern Med 251:193-206, 2002.

51. Hobson RW, Lynch TG, Jamil Z, et al: Results of revascularization and amputation in severe lower extremity ischemia: A five-year clinical experience. J Vasc Surg 2:174-185, 1985.

52. Holloway GA Jr, Burgess EM: Cutaneous blood flow and its relation to healing of below knee amputation. Surg Gynecol Obstet 146:750-756, 1978.

53. Hunsaker RH, Schwartz JA, Keagy BA, et al: Dry ice cryoamputation: A twelve-year experience. J Vasc Surg 2:812-816, 1985.

54. Huston CC, Bivins BA, Ernst CB, Griffen WO Jr: Morbid implications of above-knee amputations: Report of a series and review of the literature. Arch Surg 115:165-167, 1980.

55. Jorgensen LN, Andreasen JJ, Nielsen PT, et al: Dicloxacillin concentrations in amputation. Acta Orthop Scand 60:617-620, 1989.

56. Kaboli P, Henderson MC, White RH: DVT prophylaxis and anticoagulation in the surgical patient. Med Clin North Am 87: 77-110, 2003.

57. Kacy SS, Wolma FJ, Flye MW: Factors affecting the results of below knee amputation in patients with and without diabetes. Surg Gynecol Obstet 155:513-518, 1982.

58. Kashani JH, Frank RG, Kashani SR, et al: Depression among amputees. J Clin Psychiatry 44:256-258, 1983.

59. Katz J: Phantom limb pain. Lancet 350:1338-1339, 1997.

60. Kazmers A, Perkins AJ, Jacobs LA: Major lower extremity amputation in Veterans Affairs medical centers. Ann Vasc Surg 14:216-222, 2000.

61. Keagy BA, Schwartz JA, Kotb M, et al: Lower extremity amputation: The control series. J Vasc Surg 4:321-326, 1986.

62. Kerin MJ, Greenstein D, Chisholm EM, et al: Is antibiotic penetration compromised in the ischaemic tissues of patients undergoing amputation? Ann R Coll Surg Engl 74:274-276, 1992.

63. Kim GE, Imparato AM, Chu DS, Davis SW: Lower-limb amputation for occlusive vascular disease. Am Surg 42:598-601, 1976.

64. Lexier RR, Harrington IJ, Woods JM: Lower extremity amputations: A 5-year review and comparative study. Can J Surg 30:374-376, 1987.

65. Lim RC, Blaisdell FW, Hall AD: Below-knee amputation for ischemic gangrene. Surg Gynecol Obstet 125:493-501, 1967.

66. Lind J, Kramhoft M, Bodtker S: The influence of smoking on complications after primary amputations of the lower extremity. Clin Orthop (267):211-217, 1991.

67. Malone JM, Moore WS, Leal JM, Childers SJ: Rehabilitation for lower extremity amputation. Arch Surg 116:93-98, 1981.

68. Mangano DT, Layug EL, Wallace A, Tateo I: Effect of atenolol on mortality and cardiovascular morbidity after noncardiac surgery. Multicenter Study of Perioperative Ischemia Research Group. N Engl J Med 335:1713-1720, 1996.

69. McIntyre KE Jr, Bailey SA, Malone JM, Goldstone J: Guillotine amputation in the treatment of nonsalvageable lower-extremity infections. Arch Surg 119:450-453, 1984.

70. McWhinnie DL, Gordon AC, Collin J, et al: Rehabilitation outcome 5 years after 100 lower-limb amputations. Br J Surg 81:1596-1599, 1994.

71. Nehler MR, Coll JR, Hiatt WR, et al: Functional outcome in a contemporary series of major lower extremity amputations. J Vasc Surg 38:7-14, 2003.

72. Nikolajsen L, Ilkjaer S, Christensen JH, et al: Randomised trial of epidural bupivacaine and morphine in prevention of stump and phantom pain in lower-limb amputation. Lancet 350:1353-1357, 1997.

73. Otteman MG, Stahlgren LH: Evaluation of factors which influence mortality and morbidity following major lower extremity amputations for atherosclerosis. Surg Gynecol Obstet 120:1217, 1965.

74. Ouriel K, Fiore WM, Geary JE: Limb-threatening ischemia in the medically compromised patient: Amputation or revascularization? Surgery 104:667-672, 1988.

75. Passman MA, Farber MA, Marston WA, et al: Prospective screening for postoperative deep venous thrombosis in patients undergoing infrainguinal revascularization. J Vasc Surg 32:669-675, 2000.

76. Pasternack PF, Grossi EA, Baumann FG, et al: Beta blockade to decrease silent myocardial ischemia during peripheral vascular surgery. Am J Surg 158:113-116, 1989.

77. Payne JE, Breust M, Bradbury R: Reduction in amputation stump infection by antiseptic pre-operative preparation. Aust N Z J Surg 59:637-640, 1989.

78. Pedersen NW, Pedersen D: Nutrition as a prognostic indicator in amputations: A prospective study of 47 cases. Acta Orthop Scand 63:675-678, 1992.

79. Peng CW, Tan SG: Perioperative and rehabilitative outcomes after amputation for ischaemic leg gangrene. Ann Acad Med Singapore 29:168-172, 2000.

80. Pinzur MS, Littooy F, Daniels J, et al: Multidisciplinary preoperative assessment and late function in dysvascular amputees. Clin Orthop (281):239-243, 1992.

81. Poldermans D, Boersma E, Bax JJ, et al: The effect of bisoprolol on perioperative mortality and myocardial infarction in high-risk patients undergoing vascular surgery. N Engl J Med 341:1789-1794, 1999.

82. Porter JM, Baur GM, Taylor LM Jr: Lower-extremity amputations for ischemia. Arch Surg 116:89-92, 1981.

83. Roon AJ, Moore WS, Goldstone J: Below-knee amputation: A modern approach. Am J Surg 134:153-158, 1977.

84. Rosenberg N, Adiarte E, Bujdoso LJ, Backwinkel KD: Mortality factors in major limb amputations for vascular disease: A study of 176 procedures. Surgery 67:437-441, 1970.

85. Rubin JR, Marmen C, Rhodes RS: Management of failed prosthetic grafts at the time of major lower extremity amputation. J Vasc Surg 7:673-676, 1988.

86. Rush DS, Huston CC, Bivins BA, Hyde GL: Operative and late mortality rates of above-knee and below-knee amputations. Am Surg 47:36-39, 1981.

87. Scher KS, Steele FJ: The septic foot in patients with diabetes. Surgery 104:661-666, 1988.

88. Schina MJ Jr, Atnip RG, Healy DA, Thiele BL: Relative risks of limb revascularization and amputation in the modern era. Cardiovasc Surg 2:754-759, 1994.

89. Sethia KK, Berry AR, Morrison JD, et al: Changing pattern of lower limb amputation for vascular disease. Br J Surg 73:701-703, 1986.

90. Sherman RA, Sherman CJ, Parker L: Chronic phantom and stump pain among American veterans: Results of a survey. Pain 18:83-95, 1984.

91. Stirnemann P, Walpoth B, Wursten HU, et al: Influence of failed arterial reconstruction on the outcome of major limb amputation. Surgery 111:363-368, 1992.

92. Taylor LM Jr, Yeager RA, Moneta GL, et al: The incidence of perioperative myocardial infarction in general vascular surgery. J Vasc Surg 15:52-61, 1991.

93. Thomsen S, Jakobsen BW, Wethelund JO, et al: Antibiotic prophylaxis in lower-extremity amputations due to ischemia: A prospective, randomized trial of cephalothin versus methicillin. Arch Orthop Trauma Surg 109:72-74, 1990.

94. Toursarkissian B, Shireman PK, Harrison A, et al: Major lower-extremity amputation: Contemporary experience in a single Veterans Affairs institution. Am Surg 68:606-610, 2002.

95. Tsang GM, Crowson MC, Hickey NC, Simms MH: Failed femoro-crural reconstruction does not prejudice amputation level. Br J Surg 78:1479-1481, 1991.

96. Unruh T, Fisher DF Jr, Unruh TA, et al: Hip disarticulation: An 11-year experience. Arch Surg 125:791-793, 1990.

97. Urban MK, Markowitz SM, Gordon MA, et al: Postoperative prophylactic administration of beta-adrenergic blockers in patients at risk for myocardial ischemia. Anesth Analg 90:1257-1261, 2000.

98. van den Broek TA, Dwars BJ, Rauwerda JA, Bakker FC: A multivariate analysis of determinants of wound healing in patients after amputation for peripheral vascular disease. Eur J Vasc Surg 4:291-295, 1990.

99. Van Niekerk LJ, Stewart CP, Jain AS: Major lower limb amputation following failed infrainguinal vascular bypass surgery: A prospective study on amputation levels and stump complications. Prosthet Orthot Int 25:29-33, 2001.

100. Wagner WH, Keagy BA, Kotb MM, et al: Noninvasive determination of healing of major lower extremity amputation: The continued role of clinical judgment. J Vasc Surg 8:703-710, 1988.

101. Wallace A, Layug B, Tateo I, et al: Prophylactic atenolol reduces postoperative myocardial ischemia. McSPI Research Group. Anesthesiology 88:7-17, 1998.

102. White SA, Thompson MM, Zickerman AM, et al: Lower limb amputation and grade of surgeon. Br J Surg 84:509-511, 1997.

103. Winburn GB, Wood MC, Hawkins ML, et al: Current role of cryoamputation. Am J Surg 162:647-650, 1991.

104. Yeager RA, Moneta GL, Edwards JM, et al: Deep vein thrombosis associated with lower extremity amputation. J Vasc Surg 22:612-615, 1995.

105. Yeager RA, Moneta GL, Edwards JM, et al: Reducing perioperative myocardial infarction following vascular surgery: The potential role of beta-blockade. Arch Surg 130:869-872, 1995.

106. Yeager RA, Moneta GL, Taylor LM Jr, et al: Surgical management of severe acute lower extremity ischemia. J Vasc Surg 15:385-393, 1992.

Functional Outcome and Natural History of Major Lower Extremity Amputation

174

PETER R. TAYLOR, MA, MChir, FRCS

Amputation of the lower limb is arguably the operation vascular surgeons perform with the greatest emotional and functional impact. Subgroups of patients undergoing aortic and carotid surgery suffer major morbidity, but all lower extremity amputees face a life-changing event. Many vascular surgeons consider this operation to be a failure of their reconstructive skills. However, the operation may be the only option in some patients with critical limb ischemia (CLI). These include patients without revascularization options due to lack of conduit, lack of outflow targets, or extensive pedal necrosis. Patients with fixed flexion deformities of the hip or knee may not be suitable for vascular reconstruction even though the distal vessels are patent. Such patients will not be able to ambulate postoperatively or use their limb in any useful way. Other patients may have such serious comorbidity that reconstructive surgery would not be in the their best interests. These include patients with terminal cancer and those who have end-stage cardiorespiratory failure. This subgroup would benefit from immediate amputation and limited rehabilitation without prolonged hospitalization, because much of their care is palliative and early return to their home environment is the priority.

The focus in this chapter is the rehabilitation potential in amputees and their natural history, including the incidence of contralateral amputation, their mortality, and ongoing medical events.

■ REHABILITATION POTENTIAL IN AMPUTEES

Integrated Care Pathways

The assessment of the rehabilitation potential in vascular amputees is complex and involves many disciplines. These include the medical and surgical teams, the nursing team, physiotherapy, occupational therapy, the pain team, the prosthetic team, social workers, and the general practitioners and district nursing team. The coordination of such a large group is essential if early discharge from hospital is to be achieved. Two important factors for many amputees are pain relief and mobility. However, returning home to family and friends is also important.[25] The rehabilitation and discharge of amputees is often given a low priority in the clinical service of many hospitals. This has resulted in a fragmented, poorly organized service, which further demoralizes both patients and staff.

The establishment of integrated care pathways to coordinate the many groups involved in the care of amputees can improve matters considerably.[47] In a small group of amputees, the length of stay was reduced from a median of 25 days to 13 by the introduction of several changes. These included a preoperative outpatient visit to a vascular clinical nurse to provide support, answer questions, and start care planning. Referrals to both the occupational therapist and social worker were initiated as soon as the decision to amputate was made. The occupational therapist made a home visit as soon as possible, preferably before the patient was admitted to the hospital, and also ordered a wheelchair before the operation. Early referral for rehabilitation was made and better use was made of community hospitals for this purpose. Multidisciplinary team meetings were held at weekly intervals, and targets were set for rehabilitation and discharge. The meetings could also be used as case conferences with patients, relatives, and social workers in attendance. A full physiotherapy assessment was carried out before surgery to establish the functional status of the patient and to determine realistic rehabilitation goals. The physiotherapist was also responsible for planning a series of goals for each patient and for documenting progress. The nurses were responsible for pain relief, nutrition, hygiene, and pressure area care. Referral for limb fitting and outpatient physiotherapy was the responsibility of the physiotherapist. Arrangements for discharge were reviewed daily, so that all necessary referrals were in place for the discharge date.

The evidence for the use of integrated care pathways in the care of amputees is sparse. The ideal subject should include small teams, have defined predictable groups in a containable setting, and have a high volume of cases with established guidelines for best practice.[26] Unfortunately, very few of these apply to amputation. One study has shown, however, that integrated care pathways can reduce the length of stay in hospital of amputees and can also reduce readmission rates and increase the proportion discharged to their own home.[52]

The Choice of Amputation Level

The level of amputation is determined by a number of considerations, including the patency of blood vessels to achieve healing, the rehabilitation potential of the patient, and prosthetic requirements. A full assessment of the patient is required so that realistic goals can be achieved. Important components of this include an assessment of any serious comorbidity, the patient's cognitive status and motivation, the discharge destination, and the lifestyle the patient wishes to achieve. The balance in lower limb amputation is between mobility and the ability to heal. In general, the more proximal the amputation, the more likely the stump is to heal but the less likely the chances of independent mobility. The knee joint is especially important, because 80% of below-knee amputees achieve unlimited, albeit housebound, mobility compared with 40% of above-knee amputees.[20] One of the most important initial assessments of a vascular amputee is the likelihood of the patient being able to walk. Patients who are not going to walk may be best served by a Gritti-Stokes or through-knee amputation.[19] The length of the stump is important in achieving balance when sitting and to aid transfer because it allows more leverage to be obtained than an above-knee stump. The problem of amputating below the knee in a patient who is unlikely to walk is the development of a fixed flexion deformity of the knee joint. This can lead to pressure sores overlying the end of the transected tibia, which often result in secondary amputation at a higher level.

In one of the few randomized trials in amputation surgery, the long posterior flap was compared with the skew flap in below-knee amputations (BKAs).[50] Although there was no difference in healing, the time to limb fitting and mobility was less in the skew flap, owing to the less bulbous stump. Some surgeons would argue that a well-performed long posterior flap should not produce a bulbous stump and that if such stumps can be fashioned then the advantage attributable to the skew flap is lost. Another prospective randomized trial comparing Gritti-Stokes procedures with through-knee amputations showed better healing with the former.[8] The Gritti-Stokes procedure is also associated with good ambulation, but both these amputations cause problems with prosthetic fitting.[19]

Various techniques have been used to try and predict healing of an amputation stump. These include transcutaneous oximetry, thermography, laser Doppler velocity, and isotope clearance rates. Although they are useful adjuncts they have not found their way into routine clinical practice.[51] The factors involved as to whether an amputation needs to be performed above or below the knee have been studied in a prospective series of patients presenting with CLI requiring femorocrural/femoropedal grafts or primary amputation.[41] Two important factors in retaining the knee were the state of the arterial inflow to the limb and the state of the profunda femoral artery. Knee salvage at 3 years was 82% if the inflow was good compared with 43% if it was impaired. If the profunda femoris was patent, 93% of patients kept their knee at 3 years compared with only 37% if it was occluded.

Is There a Role for Primary Amputation?

There is little doubt that revascularization is attempted in some patients with CLI when the chances of success are low. Studies have shown that successful revascularization is more cost effective than amputation and is associated with a better quality of life.[9,42] However, amputation after a failed bypass was the worst outcome, being more expensive than primary

amputation. The identification of patients who would not benefit from revascularization has been attempted on the basis of angiography.[1,44] Scoring systems have been devised, but these do not correlate well with clinical outcome.[56] More refined systems using both angiographic and clinical factors have been developed and may allow the identification of a subgroup of patients with CLI where reconstruction is almost certain to fail.[40] These patients would benefit from primary amputation, with subsequent improvement in cost-effectiveness. However, further prospective studies are required to prove their clinical effectiveness.

■ NATURAL HISTORY OF LOWER LIMB AMPUTEES

Short-Term Outcome by Indications

The majority of amputations are performed for CLI,[43,45,49] demonstrating the important role of the vascular surgeon in amputation care. Conversely, patients presenting with intermittent claudication comprise the smallest group of ultimate amputees. Only 2% to 4% of patients with claudication ever require a major amputation over a 10- to 15-year period.[33] However, amputation can occur after intervention for claudication. In a series of 4,662 angioplasty procedures performed for claudication, the incidence of amputation was 0.2% and the mortality was another 0.2%.[3] In a more recent study, the 30-day mortality rate for angioplasty for claudication was 0.5% and there were no near-term amputations.[30] Similar results for infrainguinal and aortofemoral bypass for claudication have been reported.[24,36] However, it is well recognized that eventual failure of surgical revascularization in a subgroup of patients with claudication does convert them to limb threat.[35] On balance, current data would indicate near-term risk of limb loss in patients undergoing interventions for claudication is relatively small.

Patients presenting with acute limb ischemia were studied in two prospective trials comparing catheter-directed thrombolysis with surgical revascularization: the STILE and TOPAS trials.[2,38,39] At 1 year, these trials demonstrated amputation rates between 11% and 19% and mortality rates between 6.5% and 16%. The majority of published series of acute limb ischemia demonstrate a 30-day mortality rate of 15% and major amputation ranging from 10% to 30%.[5,6,10,60]

Patients presenting with chronic CLI also have a poor prognosis. The 1-year mortality is about 20%, rising to 32% at 2 years.[21,58] The majority of deaths are related to cardiovascular causes. In a group of patients with unreconstructable disease or failed reconstruction who were entered into pharmacotherapy trials, 40% lost their limb and 20% were dead at 6 months.[4,29,37]

The overall 30-day mortality for below-knee amputees is about 10%. Sixty percent will achieve healing by primary intention (however, there is significant variability reported in the literature), 15% will heal by secondary intention, and 15% will require revision to above-knee amputation (AKA) (Fig. 174-1).[11] The 30-day mortality for above-knee amputees is 15% to 20%, frequently owing to the significant comorbidities in this population. The primary healing rate

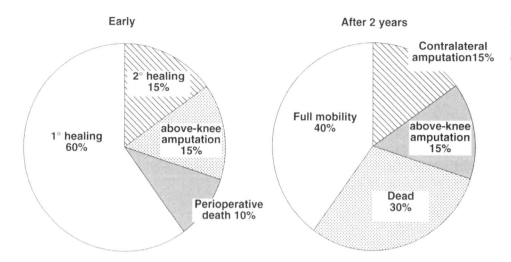

FIGURE 174-1 Early fate of the below-knee amputee. (From Dormandy J, Heeck L, Vig S: Major amputations: Clinical patterns and predictors. Semin Vasc Surg 12:154-161, 1999.)

for an AKA is a more consistent 70%, with 90% ultimately healing despite further procedures.[27,28] A review of over 4000 amputations (ratio BKA to AKA roughly equal) in the veteran population demonstrated 30-day mortality for BKA and AKA of 6% and 13%, respectively.[14]

Long-Term Outcome

Most patients undergoing amputation will have arterial occlusive disease affecting the other leg, and up to 30% will have had a prior contralateral amputation.[13] Survival in amputees is poor. Patient survival in the Veterans Affairs amputation series for BKA and AKA was 57% and 39% at 3 years, respectively, again emphasizing the palliative nature of these procedures in most patients.[14] Other reports have found similar poor survival after major limb amputation.[50,57,59] In addition to mortality, significant ongoing morbidity occurs in both the remaining stump (BKA > AKA) and contralateral limb after major lower extremity amputation. At 2 years, 15% of patients with an initially successful BKA will convert to an AKA and another 15% will suffer a major contralateral amputation.[11]

A significant amount of data from clinical series of major limb amputation has been reported about function. Most of these data have focused on the percentage of surviving patients who wear a prosthesis and ambulate to any extent. Interestingly, the results vary widely from series to series.[12,17,18,23,28,46,48,54,55] Patients with successful BKA were able to walk with or without assist devices with prosthesis from 15% to 96%. Some of the reason for the variability is differing definitions of success (wearing the prosthesis any time during the day vs. walking independent of the home), differing patient populations (younger diabetics vs. older patients with chronic leg ischemia), and different settings (academic, private practice, Veterans Affairs, and European). The ambulatory success for eventual AKA patients was one third to one half that of BKA patients.

Two recent clinical series from the United Kingdom illustrate expected outcomes in the modern vascular amputee. In the first review,[31] approximately 56% of amputees were fitted with a limb, but 15% were nonwearers at 1 year, and

at 5 years this increased to 69%. In a similar study of vascular amputees in southeast London, 440 patients underwent major amputation: 75 died before discharge and a further 113 were deemed unsuitable to wear a prosthesis.[20] Therefore, the number referred for a potential prosthesis was 252, which at 57% was nearly identical to the previous study. A further 54 patients died and 19 became nonwearers during follow-up; and after a questionnaire assessment of mobility, only 10% to 15% of amputees were mobile at home and only 5% were totally free of wheelchair use. These studies indicate that, over time, fewer patients can tolerate wearing a prosthesis.

Finally, a retrospective study from the United States examined 154 patients having 172 major amputations, of which 94 had BKA and 78 had AKA.[34] The majority were for critical ischemia (87%), with the remainder for complications of diabetic neuropathy with normal pedal circulation. The 30-day mortality was 10%, similar to previous reports. Healing was quicker in AKAs compared with BKAs. Sixteen AKAs required operative revision compared with 23 BKAs, of which 18 were eventually converted to the AKA level. The survival was 78% at 1 year, falling to 55% at 3 years. At 17 months, 29% of survivors could walk outdoors, 25% could walk indoors only, and 46% did not walk at all. The authors comment that they were surprised that so many patients remained independent in the community despite their infrequent use of their prosthesis and their inability to walk outdoors. The authors speculate that improved community wheelchair access due to legislation in the United States may be partly responsible. A further study from Brazil of 48 patients who had a major amputation showed that only 9 were fully rehabilitated at 2 years.[7] The mortality rate at 2 years was 54%, again demonstrating the poor long-term prognosis of this group of patients.

A consecutive series of 66 patients requiring bilateral amputation (many limited to the forefoot) has been reported.[22] The median age at the time of the second amputation was 58 years, stressing the accelerated nature of atherosclerosis in these patients. The hospital mortality for the second amputation was 12%. After 2 years the mortality was 38%

and at 5 years had reached 69%. Coronary artery disease accounted for most deaths (37%), with strokes causing another 14%. Stump revision or amputation to a higher level was required in 56% of patients. Healing was poor, with reamputation required after transmetatarsal amputation in 63%, after BKA in 42%, and after through-knee amputation in 69% of patients. However, of the 58 patients who were discharged home, 38% were able to walk a small amount, 52% were only mobile with a wheelchair, and 10% were confined to their beds. One of the most telling statistics from this paper was that 82% of patients who were able to walk at all returned to their homes as compared with only 63% who were only mobile with a wheelchair. However, transmetatarsal amputation is often not included in studies of major amputation and the social circumstances found in Switzerland may account for this high level of repatriation.

It is safe to conclude from data originating in various countries that, despite aggressive rehabilitation programs, function after major amputation remains poor. Reasons for this were investigated by a group from the Netherlands.[53] This study used techniques including the Sickness Impact Profile, the Groningen Activity Restriction Scale, and the timed up and go test, correlated with prosthetic use to try to predict long-term functional outcome after major amputation for vascular disease. They found that after correction for age the only significant predictor for functional outcome was one-leg balance. They also showed that cognitive impairment was important as was advanced age at amputation in predicting a poor functional outcome. The importance of balance has been confirmed by others examining rehabilitation of lower limb amputees.[32]

The ability to return to work after lower limb amputation in younger patients has been assessed.[15] A creditable 66% returned to employment, although not all of these were vascular amputees. Factors predicting return to work included mobility, time since amputation, and Handicap Scale scores. Interestingly, age, amputation level, indication for amputation, type of previous work, and presence of other medical problems did not differ between those who did and did not return to work.

■ SUMMARY

The natural history and functional outcomes after major lower extremity amputation are relatively sobering. Less than half of patients appear to wear a prosthesis over time, and these are almost exclusively in patients after BKAs. Survival is limited, because most amputees have CLI. One-leg balance appears to be a critical component for rehabilitation success. In the United States, it appears that many patients can remain in the community utilizing wheelchair access. In Europe, more patients who cannot ambulate to any great degree require a care facility.

Finally what of the future? A study from Rochester, Minnesota, has shown that although amputations have declined, the total number of amputees has increased, and the rate of successfully fitting a prosthesis has not changed significantly over 40 years.[16] Given the increasing age of the population, amputations will probably double from 28,000 to 58,000 by the year 2030. This will have serious resource implications for health care systems throughout the Western world.

■ REFERENCES

1. Suggested standards for reports dealing with lower extremity ischemia. Prepared by the Ad Hoc Committee on Reporting Standards, Society for Vascular Surgery/North American Chapter, International Society for Cardiovascular Surgery. J Vasc Surg 4:80-94, 1986.
2. Results of a prospective randomized trial evaluating surgery versus thrombolysis for ischemia of the lower extremity. The STILE trial. Ann Surg 220:251-266, 1994.
3. Becker GJ, Katzen BT, Dake MD: Noncoronary angioplasty. Radiology 170:921-940, 1989.
4. Belch JJ, McKay A, McArdle B, et al: Epoprostenol (prostacyclin) and severe arterial disease. A double-blind trial. Lancet 1:315-317, 1983.
5. Bergqvist D, Troeng T, Elfstrom J, et al: Auditing surgical outcome: Ten years with the Swedish Vascular Registry—Swedvasc. The Steering Committee of Swedvasc. Eur J Surg Suppl (581):3-8, 1998.
6. Blaisdell FW, Steele M, Allen RE: Management of acute lower extremity arterial ischemia due to embolism and thrombosis. Surgery 84:822-834, 1978.
7. Buzato MA, Tribulatto EC, Costa SM, et al: Major amputations of the lower leg: The patients two years later. Acta Chir Belg 102:248-252, 2002.
8. Campbell WB, Morris PJ: A prospective randomized comparison of healing in Gritti-Stokes and through-knee amputations. Ann R Coll Surg Engl 69:1-4, 1987.
9. Cheshire NJ, Wolfe JH, Noone MA, et al: The economics of femorocrural reconstruction for critical leg ischemia with and without autologous vein. J Vasc Surg 15:167-174, 1992.
10. Davies B, Braithwaite BD, Birch PA, et al: Acute leg ischaemia in Gloucestershire. Br J Surg 84:504-508, 1997.
11. Dormandy J, Heeck L, Vig S: Major amputations: Clinical patterns and predictors. Semin Vasc Surg 12:154-161, 1999.
12. Ecker ML, Jacobs BS: Lower extremity amputation in diabetic patients. Diabetes 19:189-195, 1970.
13. European Working Group on Critical Limb Ischaemia. Second European Consensus Document on Critical Limb Ischaemia. Eur J Vasc Surg 6:1-32, 1992.
14. Feinglass J, Pearce WH, Martin GJ, et al: Postoperative and late survival outcomes after major amputation: Findings from the Department of Veterans Affairs National Surgical Quality Improvement Program. Surgery 130:21-29, 2001.
15. Fisher K, Hanspal RS, Marks L: Return to work after lower limb amputation. Int J Rehabil Res 26:51-56, 2003.
16. Fletcher DD, Andrews KL, Hallett JW Jr, et al: Trends in rehabilitation after amputation for geriatric patients with vascular disease: Implications for future health resource allocation. Arch Phys Med Rehabil 83:1389-1393, 2002.
17. Gregg RO: Bypass or amputation? Concomitant review of bypass arterial grafting and major amputations. Am J Surg 149:397-402, 1985.
18. Hagberg E, Berlin OK, Renstrom P: Function after through-knee compared with below-knee and above-knee amputation. Prosthet Orthot Int 16:168-173, 1992.
19. Houghton A, Allen A, Luff R, McColl I: Rehabilitation after lower limb amputation: A comparative study of above-knee, through-knee and Gritti-Stokes amputations. Br J Surg 76:622-624, 1989.
20. Houghton AD, Taylor PR, Thurlow S, et al: Success rates for rehabilitation of vascular amputees: Implications for preoperative assessment and amputation level. Br J Surg 79:753-755, 1992.
21. ICAI Group: Long-term mortality and its predictors in patients with critical limb ischaemia. Eur J Vasc Endovasc Surg 14:91-95, 1997.
22. Inderbitzi R, Buettiker M, Enzler M: The long-term mobility and mortality of patients with peripheral arterial disease following bilateral amputation. Eur J Vasc Endovasc Surg 26:59-64, 2003.
23. Jamieson MG, Ruckley CV: Amputation for peripheral vascular disease in a General Surgical Unit. J R Coll Surg Edinb 28:46-50, 1983.
24. Jamsen TS, Manninen HI, Tulla HE, et al: Infrainguinal revascularization because of claudication: Total long-term outcome of endovascular and surgical treatment. J Vasc Surg 37:808-815, 2003.

25. Johnson BF, Evans L, Drury R, et al: Surgery for limb threatening ischaemia: A reappraisal of the costs and benefits. Eur J Vasc Endovasc Surg 9:181-188, 1995.

26. Johnson S, Dracass M, Vartan J, et al: Setting standards using integrated care pathways. Prof Nurse 15:640-643, 2000.

27. Keagy BA, Schwartz JA, Kotb M, et al: Lower extremity amputation: The control series. J Vasc Surg 4:321-326, 1986.

28. Kihn RB, Warren R, Beebe GW: The "geriatric" amputee. Ann Surg 176:305-314, 1972.

29. Lowe GD, Dunlop DJ, Lawson DH, et al: Double-blind controlled clinical trial of ancrod for ischemic rest pain of the leg. Angiology 33:46-50, 1982.

30. Matsi PJ, Manninen HI: Complications of lower-limb percutaneous transluminal angioplasty: A prospective analysis of 410 procedures on 295 consecutive patients. Cardiovasc Intervent Radiol 21:361-366, 1998.

31. McWhinnie DL, Gordon AC, Collin J, et al: Rehabilitation outcome 5 years after 100 lower-limb amputations. Br J Surg 81:1596-1599, 1994.

32. Miller WC, Deathe AB, Speechley M: Psychometric properties of the Activities-specific Balance Confidence Scale among individuals with a lower-limb amputation. Arch Phys Med Rehabil 84:656-661, 2003.

33. Muluk SC, Muluk VS, Kelley ME, et al: Outcome events in patients with claudication: A 15-year study in 2777 patients. J Vasc Surg 33:251-257, 2001.

34. Nehler MR, Coll JR, Hiatt WR, et al: Functional outcome in a contemporary series of major lower extremity amputations. J Vasc Surg 38:7-14, 2003.

35. Nehler MR, Mueller RJ, McLafferty RB, et al: Outcome of catheter-directed thrombolysis for lower extremity arterial bypass occlusion. J Vasc Surg 37:72-78, 2003.

36. Nevelsteen A, Wouters L, Suy R: Long-term patency of the aortofemoral Dacron graft: A graft limb–related study over a 25-year period. J Cardiovasc Surg (Torino) 32:174-180, 1991.

37. Norgren L, Alwmark A, Angqvist KA, et al: A stable prostacyclin analogue (iloprost) in the treatment of ischaemic ulcers of the lower limb: A Scandinavian-Polish placebo controlled, randomised multi-center study. Eur J Vasc Surg 4:463-467, 1990.

38. Ouriel K, Veith FJ, Sasahara AA: Thrombolysis or peripheral arterial surgery: Phase I results. TOPAS Investigators. J Vasc Surg 23:64-73, 1996.

39. Ouriel K, Veith FJ, Sasahara AA: A comparison of recombinant urokinase with vascular surgery as initial treatment for acute arterial occlusion of the legs. Thrombolysis or Peripheral Arterial Surgery (TOPAS) Investigators. N Engl J Med 338:1105-1111, 1998.

40. Panayiotopoulos YP, Edmondson RA, Reidy JF, Taylor PR: A scoring system to predict the outcome of long femorodistal arterial bypass grafts to single calf or pedal vessels. Eur J Vasc Endovasc Surg 15:380-386, 1998.

41. Panayiotopoulos YP, Reidy JF, Taylor PR: The concept of knee salvage: Why does a failed femorocrural/pedal arterial bypass not affect the amputation level? Eur J Vasc Endovasc Surg 13:477-485, 1997.

42. Panayiotopoulos YP, Tyrrell MR, Owen SE, et al: Outcome and cost analysis after femorocrural and femoropedal grafting for critical limb ischaemia. Br J Surg 84:207-212, 1997.

43. Pernot HF, Winnubst GM, Cluitmans JJ, De Witte LP: Amputees in Limburg: Incidence, morbidity and mortality, prosthetic supply, care utilisation and functional level after one year. Prosthet Orthot Int 24:90-96, 2000.

44. Peterkin GA, Manabe S, LaMorte WW, Menzoian JO: Evaluation of a proposed standard reporting system for preoperative angiograms in infrainguinal bypass procedures: Angiographic correlates of measured runoff resistance. J Vasc Surg 7:379-385, 1988.

45. Pohjolainen T, Alaranta H: Ten-year survival of Finnish lower limb amputees. Prosthet Orthot Int 22:10-16, 1998.

46. Pollock SB Jr, Ernst CB: Use of Doppler pressure measurements in predicting success in amputation of the leg. Am J Surg 139:303-306, 1980.

47. Potterton JA, Galland RB: Lower limb amputation and rehabilitation. In Beard JD, Murray S (eds): Pathways of Care in Vascular Patients. Shrewsbury, UK, tfm Publishing, 2002, pp 183-192.

48. Robinson KP: Long posterior flap amputation in geriatric patients with ischaemic disease. Ann R Coll Surg Engl 58:440-451, 1976.

49. Rommers GM, Vos LD, Groothoff JW, et al: Epidemiology of lower limb amputees in the north of The Netherlands: Aetiology, discharge destination and prosthetic use. Prosthet Orthot Int 21:92-99, 1997.

50. Ruckley CV, Stonebridge PA, Prescott RJ: Skewflap versus long posterior flap in below-knee amputations: Multicenter trial. J Vasc Surg 13:423-427, 1991.

51. Sarin S, Shami S, Shields DA, et al: Selection of amputation level: A review. Eur J Vasc Surg 5:611-620, 1991.

52. Schaldach DE: Measuring quality and cost of care: Evaluation of an amputation clinical pathway. J Vasc Nurs 15:13-20, 1997.

53. Schoppen T, Boonstra A, Groothoff JW, et al: Physical, mental, and social predictors of functional outcome in unilateral lower-limb amputees. Arch Phys Med Rehabil 84:803-811, 2003.

54. Siriwardena GJ, Bertrand PV: Factors influencing rehabilitation of arteriosclerotic lower limb amputees. J Rehabil Res Dev 28:35-44, 1991.

55. Stirnemann P, Walpoth B, Wursten HU, et al: Influence of failed arterial reconstruction on the outcome of major limb amputation. Surgery 111:363-368, 1992.

56. Takolander R, Fischer-Colbrie W, Jogestrand T, et al: The "ad hoc" estimation of outflow does not predict patency of infrainguinal reconstructions. Eur J Vasc Endovasc Surg 10:187-191, 1995.

57. Whitehouse FW, Jurgenson C, Block MA: The later life of an amputee: Another look at the fate of the second leg. Diabetes 17:520-521, 1968.

58. Wolfe JN: Defining the outcome of critical ischaemia: A one-year prospective study. Br J Surg 73:321, 1986.

59. Yamanaka M, Kwong PK: The side-to-side flap technique in below-the-knee amputation with long stump. Clin Orthop (201):75-79, 1985.

60. Yeager RA, Moneta GL, Taylor LM, et al: Surgical management of severe acute lower extremity ischemia. J Vasc Surg 15:385-393, 1992.

Upper Extremity Amputation

175

JOYESH K. RAJ, MD
MICHAEL J. V. GORDON, MD

Upper extremity amputation is a potentially devastating event in a person's life, often resulting in profound physical, psychological, and vocational consequences. There are approximately 400,000 amputees living in the United States, with about 135,000 new amputations performed each year.[1] Upper extremity amputations comprise approximately 15% of all amputations; and in contrast to lower extremity amputees, upper extremity amputees are younger, with a mean age ranging from 20 to 40 years. Men are at higher risk than women for arm limb loss, especially with regard to trauma-related amputations. Psychological, emotional, and financial considerations play an even greater role in upper than in lower extremity amputations. The majority of upper extremities are lost to trauma (roughly 80%), with tumors, congenital anomalies, vascular insufficiency, infections, and iatrogenic causes (e.g., cardiac catheterization mishaps, extravasation of vasopressors) accounting for the remainder. It has been estimated that there are currently 75,000 upper extremity amputees in the United States, with approximately 6,000 to 10,000 new upper extremity amputations each year. Ninety-five percent of all upper extremity amputations occur below the elbow, with the vast majority (90%) occurring within the digits.[2]

Compared with the lower extremity arterial circulation, atherosclerosis of the upper extremity is distinctly uncommon. In a study comparing diabetic and nondiabetic patients using duplex examination, arterial disease in the upper extremity occurred in 2.3% of diabetic patients versus 0% in nondiabetic patients and arterial disease in the lower extremity occurred in 31.8% of diabetic patients versus 18.4% in nondiabetic patients.[3] Rather than atherosclerosis, a wide variety of uncommon disorders cause vascular compromise in the upper extremity. Vasospastic disorders (including vibration syndromes), Buerger's disease (thromboangiitis obliterans), arterial embolization from proximal aneurysm (thoracic outlet syndrome), arterial steal in patients on hemodialysis with arteriovenous fistulae, and arterial malformations are well-recognized entities leading to upper extremity symptoms. Trauma, however, is the most common etiology for upper extremity vascular compromise. Of traumatic injuries, most are associated with direct mechanical trauma but some are related to secondary factors such as embolization from misplaced drug injection, blunt trauma leading to occlusive disease, and surgical and radiation damage after treatment of breast cancer.[4] When possible, treatment is directed at correction of the underlying pathologic process (e.g., cessation of smoking in

Buerger's disease). Occasionally, upper extremity ischemia responds to sympathectomy for vasospastic diseases and bypasses and/or thrombolytic therapy for occlusive disease.

Unfortunately, many of the diseases affecting the upper extremity share a common final pathway leading to some form of amputation. If the process is diffuse, without clear anatomic definition to the location of the vascular obstruction (e.g., in the vasospastic diseases or in severe diabetes mellitus), the principle of conservatism and conservation of parts is vital, because aggressive surgical procedures may aggravate the ischemic process. In the cases in which the vascular obstruction is more clearly defined, the same principles as used in traumatic amputations are invoked to provide the best functional result for the patient.

■ GENERAL CONSIDERATIONS

Three primary issues are considered in the assessment of patients requiring an upper extremity amputation:

1. *A thorough evaluation of the injury, tumor, or ischemia is required to determine the best surgical procedure.* Extensive experience is required to estimate the degree of functional recovery possible at the time of an injury. Such information is important in determining optimal surgical strategy for the individual patient.
2. *Evaluation of "extrinsic" factors, including the patient's age, gender, handedness, general medical condition, other associated injuries, occupation, and hobbies.* These features determine the suitability of the patient for initial repair, secondary operations, and extended rehabilitation; thus, they guide the surgeon in recommending replantation, definitive amputation, or alternative complex reconstructive options.
3. *The most difficult assessment involves evaluation of the patient's "intrinsic" factors.* These include the patient's own self-image and desires for the final functional and cosmetic result. Consideration must be given to the patient's social and cultural background. In some cultural settings, even a minor cosmetic deformity is more debilitating than *any* functional impairment.

After the overall patient evaluation, a decision must be made about immediate care. Often this involves a determination about whether replantation is either surgically possible or functionally desirable. If replantation has been eliminated as a possibility, closure of the wound must be considered. The timing of wound closure is critical and depends on several factors. In cases of traumatic injury, the nature of the wound (the contamination of the offending agent) and the amount of time elapsed since the injury dictate whether immediate closure is possible. It is best to adhere to general surgical principles of wound management. Although it is technically possible to close upper extremity traumatic amputation sites immediately most of the time, delayed closure is reasonable if conditions warrant.

A much more difficult problem is the selection of the type of closure to perform. This decision depends on the level of amputation and is discussed in detail in subsequent sections. General considerations in this regard are determined by the principles of the reconstructive ladder. This approach dictates that one begin with the simplest closure and progress to more complex closure patterns as required by lack of simpler methods or by functional (or aesthetic) considerations. In practical terms, direct closure is the first choice, followed by skin grafting, local flaps, distant flaps, and finally free flap coverage. Before dealing with individual anatomic issues in detail, a brief discussion of proper management of different anatomic structures is needed. This would include length, bone and cartilage, tendons, nerves, vasculature, and soft tissue coverage.

Length

Although preservation of length is a fundamental principle of amputation surgery, length does not always correlate directly with function, depending on the type of prosthetic application contemplated. In certain cases, it may be wise to sacrifice length in favor of better prosthetic fit. Such decisions are almost never possible in emergency situations, because ideally it is desirable to consult with an experienced prosthetist or rehabilitation specialist.

Bone and Cartilage

Whatever length is ultimately chosen for the amputation, the bony prominences must be optimally contoured. A lack of attention to the bony prominences or irregularities in bony contour leads to aesthetic abnormalities and difficult prosthetic fitting. This results from inadequate débridement of traumatized and displaced bony fragments, improper initial contouring of the bone, or failure to identify bone-producing periosteum, which must also be contoured. Visual identification of the periosteum is easiest at the time of the initial injury, and achievement of a natural contour of the bone is greatly assisted by palpating the end of the bone through the skin before closure. This is even more important in amputations through joints, where natural anatomic flares of the bone produce aesthetically unnatural contours and interfere with prosthetic fitting.

Vasculature

After proper débridement of the bony structures, the vessels are identified and ligated or coagulated, depending on their size and location. Obviously, adequate coverage of all vasculature is of paramount importance.

Tendons

The hand represents a very delicate balance between extensor and flexor forces. It is extremely difficult to duplicate the balance of these forces through *myodesic* methods (i.e., suturing of tendons or muscles to bones) or *myoplastic* techniques (i.e., suturing of tendons or muscles to tendons or muscles of the opposite functional group, for example, suturing an extensor tendon directly to a flexor tendon over a bony amputation site). In general, then, such techniques are not used distally in the fingers and hand because they often *add* to the functional deficit. However, they do have value proximally, where the balance is not as critical and re-education and adaptation are easier.

Nerves

Prevention of neuroma is the most difficult problem in upper extremity amputation. As in all of medicine, the existence of many methods of treatment usually indicates that none of them is exceptionally good. Such is the case with neuromas. Distal ligation, proximal ligation, coagulation, chemical ablation of the end, simple division, traction and division, nerve repair to other divided nerves, and immediate burial of the transected nerve end have all been attempted with varying degrees of success. The desire to eliminate painful focal sensation must be balanced against the secondary loss of sensibility induced by many of these techniques. A divided nerve always attempts to regenerate and, in so doing, produces a neuroma of variable clinical significance. Thus, in reality the goal is not to prevent the formation of a neuroma altogether but to prevent the patient from experiencing pain or dysesthesias from the neuroma that will predictably develop. In general, locating the divided, free nerve end as far from external stimuli as possible and placing it in a healthy, nonscarred bed of tissue are the best preventive measures. In addition, early postoperative therapy (desensitization or sensory re-education) is an extremely important determinant of the patient's ability to tolerate the dysesthesias that result from an amputation.

Soft Tissue Coverage

Historically, the matter of soft tissue coverage has been indistinguishable from the issue of length. Previously, if soft tissue coverage was not adequate, one merely shortened the extremity until closure could be achieved. The concept of grafts and flaps has dramatically changed this approach. Skin grafts are applicable when the underlying bed is acceptable, but one must be sensitive to the ultimate functional needs of the amputation site; in some cases, skin grafts may not be durable enough. *Local* flaps (see Fingertip Amputation, next) abound, but their applicability, owing to the anatomy at more proximal amputation sites, is limited. *Pedicled* flaps (regional or distal) have a long, productive history in hand surgery; however, these have been increasingly replaced by free tissue transfers. This change is based on (1) better matching of the tissue transferred (in terms of thickness and ultimate functional performance), (2) avoidance of additional surgery (whether for division or thinning of the flap), and (3) lack of the joint limitations that result from the immobility that is typically necessary with pedicled flaps.

■ SPECIFIC AMPUTATIONS

Fingertip Amputation

Distal digital amputations are extremely common. The most frequent mechanism causing such injuries is a crushing blow, such as from a closing door. Although many people arrive in the emergency department with the tips of the finger available for reattachment, this injury is usually too distal for microsurgical reattachment. Many surgeons have attempted composite reattachment (i.e., reattachment without specific revascularization) with generally poor results. At present, such composite grafts are not indicated except in younger children (<2 years of age), in whom there is an increased chance of graft survival.[5] Reasons for failure of most composite grafts are (1) the amount of tissue is generally more than can survive the ischemia until new circulation develops; and (2) the zone of injury is greater than the area of amputation (i.e., the tip is usually damaged and thus is not capable of surviving as a composite graft).

Attention is then focused on amputation closure. If the proximal portion of the distal phalanx is not severely injured so that the insertions of the flexor digitorum profundus and extensor tendons are intact, preservation of that portion of bone is indicated for functional length. If these areas are damaged beyond repair, disarticulation through the distal interphalangeal joint is indicated. The overriding issues are the status of the nail and what type of coverage can be provided. Generally, the amputation occurs through a portion of the nail bed. If enough proximal nail bed (~50%) is present to provide a functional nail, the bed should be repaired under optical magnification with absorbable 6-0 or 7-0 sutures.

The distal phalanx is usually rongeured back so that the end of the bone is not exposed. If the final cutaneous defect is then less than 1 cm^2, simply allowing the wound to close by secondary intention is acceptable. Other wound closures have been attempted, including every conceivable type of local or regional flap. However, given the fact that the flap closures are frequently insensate and do not reduce healing time, the ultimate functional recovery appears to be better after secondary healing because the resulting scar contracture diminishes the size of the sensory defect.

If the cutaneous defect is greater than 1 cm^2, the amount of time needed for closure and the ultimate functional result may not warrant healing by secondary intention. If there is no exposed bone, a skin graft is possible. The temptation is to use the amputated part as a donor source for the skin graft. This should be avoided because the amputated portion has been traumatized, and therefore the overall success of these skin grafts is disappointing. However, one advantage of such grafts is that they may serve as temporary biologic dressings even if they do not survive.

Nontraumatized skin graft donor sites that may be considered are:

■ The ulnar border of the palm (within the operative field and a good color match)

■ The forearm (the medial portion of the forearm or the elbow crease, although hypertrophic scarring can lead to some cosmetic deformity)
■ The groin (a well-hidden donor area, although the color match is not good and some unwanted hair may also be transferred)

As previously mentioned, many alternative flaps are often useful for cutaneous defects of the fingertip; some of the more common local flaps include:

■ The Kutler flap,[6] a lateral V-Y flap for closure of a central tip defect
■ The Atasoy flap,[7] a palmar V-Y flap
■ The palmar flap,[8] based on both digital neurovascular bundles in which the entire soft tissue coverage of the digit above the tendon sheath is elevated and advanced to cover the tip of the finger
■ Radius-based or ulna-based local flaps, which preserve the cutaneous innervation on the appropriate digital nerve,[9] with skin grafting of the donor site as necessary

In addition to these local flaps, numerous *regional* flaps can be used, such as dorsal skin cross-finger flaps, palmar skin cross-finger naps, and thenar flaps. Although it is sometimes necessary to use these regional pedicled flaps, they carry significant additional morbidity by creating joint stiffness because of the obligatory period of immobility needed for attachment of the flap. Even in young people who have had good physical therapy, this can cause a long-term problem.

Finally, a rare patient may require distant pedicled flaps for coverage. Many such flaps have been described, including groin flaps, abdominal flaps, infraclavicular flaps, supraclavicular flaps, cross-arm flaps, and cross-hand flaps. Again, secondary morbidity resulting from immobility is usually higher than warranted and simpler techniques are preferable. Free tissue transfer is almost never indicated for these injuries except in the case of thumb-tip amputations (discussed later). It is extremely important to recognize that the use of regional and distant flap involves the bringing of insensate tissue to cover an area that before the injury was most striking for the presence of sensation. Thus the value of these flaps by providing soft tissue coverage must be carefully weighed against the obvious functional deficit that they impose. In fact, similar logic can be used to dissuade one from considering even local flaps (which typically have at least decreased, if not markedly decreased, sensation) or skin grafts. As one moves more proximally in the amputation, the critical need for maintaining sensation is decreased and the use of these soft tissue augmentation techniques becomes more reasonable.

Digital Amputations

Digital amputations are classified by level. Amputations that leave more than half the proximal phalanx may be functional for the patient. These amputations represent variations of fingertip amputations. First, the bone is rongeured back a short distance to allow soft tissue coverage. Tendons that have been separated from their bony insertions by the

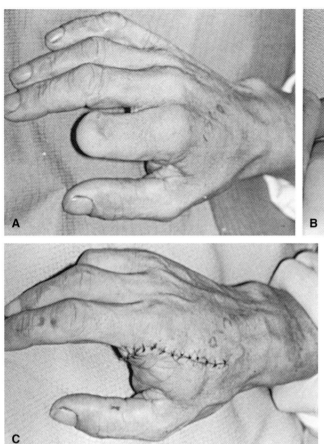
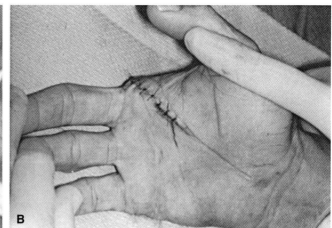

FIGURE 175-1 **A** to **C,** The patient is a 30-year-old man who lost his index finger at the proximal interphalangeal joint. He does not use the index remnant, bypassing it to use his long digit. He requested elective ray resection because of a feeling that the index remnant was "getting in the way" and creating an unsightly appearance.

amputation are placed on traction, divided, and allowed to retract into the palm. Digital nerves are a potentially more difficult problem. It is preferable to divide them under mild traction and allow them to retract beneath healthy vascularized tissue. Excessive traction may denervate the new tip of the digit. No traction leaves the cut nerve adjacent to the amputation site, allowing postinjury trauma and producing significant pain. The associated soft tissue defect is managed in the same manner as a fingertip amputation.

Amputation proximal to the midportion of the proximal phalanx typically is not a functional amputation. If enough digit remains, it may be possible for patients to wear a cosmetic prosthesis that may allow some functional restoration; however, most patients find the remaining digit a nuisance (Fig. 175-1). Each time the person reaches into his or her pocket or purse for a small object, the object falls through the opening left in the hand by the remaining short digit, which cannot flex adequately to close the space. As a result, these patients frequently choose to undergo a secondary ray amputation. Regardless of the certainty of this denouement, ray amputation should *not* be offered to the patient at the time of the initial wound closure. Elective deletion of the remaining portion of the digit is a decision each patient should come to by experience.

Ray amputation often provides a far more cosmetically acceptable hand; in most cases, the appearance of a three-fingered hand with normal border contours is so natural that it goes unnoticed. Nevertheless, the operation is not without

its own set of risks. First, the procedure narrows the palm by 20% to 25%. This reduces the hand's ability to stabilize objects. Second, the operation is a more extensive procedure, producing more proximal postoperative pain, edema, and stiffness than were produced by the injury to the digit. However, in the final analysis, ray amputation is very functional and cosmetically appealing, and there are few dissatisfied patients.

Thumb Amputations

Constituting 40% of the function of the hand, the thumb deserves special attention in any amputation involving the hand. Clearly, the major emphasis is on reattachment of the thumb. However, the desire for reattachment has led some surgeons to attempt replantation in circumstances that would otherwise be considered contraindications (e.g., severe avulsion injuries). The standard of care is now to attempt replantation of the thumb if possible, and it has produced encouraging results even after avulsion injuries.[10] Nonreplantable amputations at the level of the interphalangeal joint are quite functional, and most patients do not request or require additional reconstruction. More proximal thumb amputations may be reconstructed by pollicization, osteoplasty, bone-lengthening techniques, or toe-to-thumb transfer (great toe, second toe, or toe wrap-around). The issues of closure of the amputation site are basically the same as those already discussed with respect to

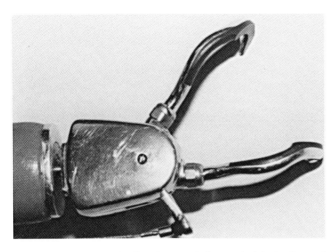

FIGURE 175-2 Example of a voluntary-closing terminal device. Internal springs provide opening power.

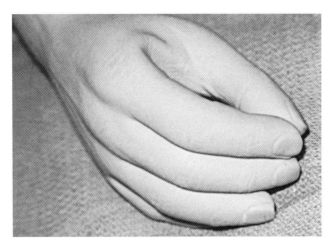

FIGURE 175-3 An Otto Bock myoelectric hand with standard rubber glove.

digital amputations, except that there must be greater emphasis on retention of length. Local flaps, such as the neurovascular island flap from the dorsum of the index finger, may be useful in these injuries.[11]

Hand-Wrist Amputations

Whatever can be salvaged from a hand amputation *should* be salvaged. A short palm hand may seem dysfunctional, but as an assist hand it may be preferable to a prosthesis in some individuals. All patients should be allowed to function with such a partial hand to determine whether they would prefer to have a more proximal amputation, with subsequent fitting of a standard prosthesis. The advantage of the short palm is that it retains some valuable wrist flexion-extension (particularly if the remaining portion has good sensibility). If the injured extremity is the dominant one and the patient wants to rehabilitate the extremity to an independently functional unit, he or she will probably benefit from wrist disarticulation and fitting with a hook prosthesis (Fig. 175-2). If it is decided to proceed with a wrist disarticulation, the radial and ulnar styloid processes are trimmed, but not completely resected, after removal of the proximal carpal row. This allows more secure fitting of the prosthesis and good transmission of pronation and supination capability without causing wear by the bony prominences.

The radial, ulnar, and median nerves can present difficulties. The ulnar and median nerves are frequently avulsed at a more proximal level with these traumatic amputations; if they are apparent in the wound, they can be severed with mild traction and allowed to retract. Retraction of the ends usually positions the nerves away from contact with a prosthesis. The sensory branch of the radial nerve, however, is quite superficial throughout its course in the forearm (covered only by the brachioradialis muscle). Neuromas from this nerve are not uncommon, and division of the nerve in the proximal forearm may be considered at the time of the initial amputation. Sensibility of the forearm skin is not directly determined by these nerves but instead is controlled by brachial cutaneous nerves. These can cause

similar difficulties to the superficial branch of the radial nerve. In contrast, it is preferable not to divide these nerves far proximally because sensibility of the forearm skin will be sacrificed.

The wrist is the most distal level of amputation at which tenodesis may be safely considered. Suturing of the flexor and extensor tendons over the amputation stump may provide some extra soft tissue padding at the amputation site as well as maintaining some forearm muscle mass. A difficult problem that is sometimes encountered is whether the patient is best rehabilitated with a hook prosthesis or a myoelectric hand. The myoelectric prosthesis adds length to the amputation site and is more cosmetically positioned with removal of several additional centimeters of distal forearm (Fig. 175-3). The amputee usually cannot make such decisions near the time of the initial injury. Proximal revision of these amputations may be done at any time in the future, and no bridges should be burned until the patient has had ample time to evaluate the consequences of his or her decision.

Forearm Amputations

There are two considerations in forearm amputation. First, as much length as possible should be preserved to maintain maximal pronation and supination. The more proximal the amputation, the less pronation and supination is possible. Second, the patient's ability to wear a prosthesis is a major issue. Preservation of the elbow joint is critical, and a prosthesis must fit well without interfering with the motion of the joint. So important is the elbow that the use of free-flap soft tissue coverage to preserve length or even distraction osteogenesis is a viable consideration in the case of very short below-elbow amputations. With the exception of these very special cases, however, heroic efforts at preserving length are not indicated.

Heeding these caveats, the surgeon can trim the bony tissues adequately to permit soft tissue closure. Flexor and extensor tendons (or muscles more proximally) should be sutured to each other over the ends of the amputation site. Nerves (radial, median, ulnar, and superficial cutaneous

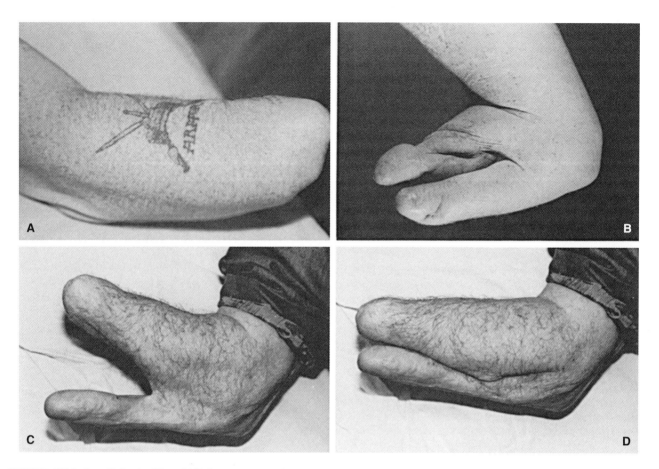

FIGURE 175-4 **A** to **D,** In the bilateral blind amputee, use of any standard prosthesis is impossible because of the absence of visual feedback or proprioception in the prosthesis. Under such circumstances, separation of the radius and ulna with Krukenberg's procedure can provide a proprioceptive "feeling" extremity capable of simple grasp-release.

nerves) are either transposed to deeper layers or placed on traction and divided (allowing them to retract into deeper, more protected, and healthier tissue). Reconstruction of the amputation is generally accomplished by means of a fitted prosthesis. As described by Tubiana,[12] however, bilateral upper extremity amputations can be functionally improved by using the Krukenberg procedure, in which a sensate pincer is created between the radius and the ulna (Fig. 175-4). Although the cosmetic result is far from desirable, the functional improvement is great, and the procedure should be given serious consideration in those rare instances of bilateral injuries in blind individuals or when prosthetic reconstruction is not practical.[13]

Elbow Disarticulation and Upper Arm Amputations

Surgical recommendations for specific amputations still depend on the type of prosthetic fitting that can be expected. Although improvements in upper extremity prostheses continue, the rate of improvement and the funds available for research are limited. Many of the systems that have been used are expensive, and the funding of the prosthetic fitting is a substantial financial issue (e.g., the Utah elbow with terminal device can run from $39,000 to $50,000).

Compared with the forearm, which has two bones with a functional noncircular cross section and thin soft tissue coverage that allows transmission of rotational forces (pronation and supination), the upper arm has a single bone with a relatively circular cross section and less rotational stability because of its thicker soft tissue. Thus, there has been considerable emphasis on retention of the full length of the humerus to take advantage of the flare of the condyles as a method of achieving better prosthetic fit (prevention of rotation of the prosthesis) and preserving some rotational movement of the upper arm. In so doing, however, the upper arm will appear longer than the normal arm to accommodate an internal elbow joint. It is possible to fit the patient with an external elbow joint, but these joints are substantially less durable. Another approach to this problem involves the construction of an artificial asymmetry by means of angulation osteotomy.[14] This method has gained popularity in Europe, but it is not routinely practiced in the United States because of the obvious cosmetic deformity induced in the proximal remaining stump.

Surgical considerations with above-elbow amputations are essentially the same as those in forearm amputations with respect to the treatment of bone, muscles, tendons, nerves, and skin. Wood and Cooley have reported that replantation should be considered even in high amputations.[15] Functional recovery of the hand may not be expected, yet it may be possible to convert an obvious above-elbow amputation to a below-elbow amputation, which is far more functional. The shorter the remaining stump, the more difficult the prosthetic fit and the less functional the prosthesis will be. As a result, several new techniques have been developed to facilitate this type of reconstruction. The use of free flaps can provide additional soft tissue and bone length for a short upper arm amputation. Functional restoration of the glenohumeral joint may be accomplished with a free fibular transfer. The proximal humerus can be replaced with the fibula and its proximal joint with reattachment of the muscular insertions.[16,17] Particularly in patients with malignant tumors, limbs that would otherwise have to be sacrificed can now be salvaged. Fibular flaps can also be used in conjunction with soft tissue coverage from a latissimus dorsi flap (pedicled or free) to provide an acceptable length of upper arm for fitting a prosthesis. One final technique used to achieve adequate bony length is distraction osteogenesis.[18] Although this technique was developed in the 1960s by Ilizarov, it has become widely used worldwide only in the 1990s. Initial reports of this method of treatment have been encouraging. As indicated previously, every effort should be made to avoid high amputations. Even when the amputation will be a functional shoulder disarticulation (amputation proximal to the insertions of the deltoid and pectoralis major), maximal proximal length of humerus should be salvaged for either prosthetic fitting or reconstruction.

Shoulder Disarticulation and Forequarter Amputations

The shoulder disarticulation and the forequarter amputation are the most complex and difficult procedures from a prosthetic and functional standpoint. Considerations are (1) loss of potential motor units as drivers of the prosthetic device and (2) difficulty of fitting the prosthesis to contour. The shoulder disarticulation (after rounding off the bony prominences that may cause wear) leaves a contour adequate to provide a snug fit for the prosthesis. In addition, scapular function is retained and can be used (with some difficulty) as a motor unit for the prosthetic device. The forequarter amputation (which is done almost exclusively for malignant processes), however, offers little hope for functional restoration of the limb.

The surgical techniques for these amputations are well described in the literature. The anterior approach, described by Berger,[19] and the posterior approach, described by Littlewood,[20] differ only in the exposure of the vascular structures hidden behind the clavicle. Both approaches are well accepted. The same principles that were described previously apply in terms of removing the bony prominences, treating the nerves and muscles, and providing adequate soft tissue coverage.

Postoperative Management

Aside from routine postoperative care, several other issues deserve mention. Immediate application of postoperative prostheses has been advocated to decrease edema and facilitate earlier rehabilitation. The poor vascularity and

problems in wound healing inherent in lower extremity amputations are rarely encountered in the upper extremity. A major issue frequently overlooked in the amputee is the psychological disturbance created first by the amputation itself and then by the subsequent impact on the patient's life. The hand and upper extremity are so intricately involved in daily existence that the complete or partial loss of either demands psychological readjustment in *all* cases. This principle applies as much to children as to adults. In many cases, a young man or woman may make light of the psychological issues and insist that there are no problems. Although as surgeons we welcome quick adjustment to disability and anticipate the patient moving ahead with the rest of his or her life, it is necessary for the amputee to experience a grieving process similar to that encountered with the death of a close relative. In detailing some of the principles learned in the treatment of hand injuries during World War II, Cleveland pointed out that "the hand is more important than the eye, and is next in importance to the brain itself."[21] Grunen and colleagues studied the psychologic issues involved in upper extremity amputation and confirmed their importance.[22]

■ REFERENCES

1. Curators of the University of Missouri & RCEP7: Amputation. In The Handbook of Disabilities. Columbia, University of Missouri, 2001, pp 1-7.
2. Dillingham TR, Pezzin LE, MacKenzie EJ: Limb amputation and limb deficiency: Epidemiology and recent trends in the United States. South Med J 96:875-883, 2002.
3. Mackaay A, Beks PJ, Dur AH, et al: The distribution of peripheral vascular disease in a Dutch Caucasian population: Comparison of type II diabetic and non-diabetic subjects. Eur J Vasc Endovasc Surg 9:170-175, 1995.
4. Taylor PJ, Cooper GG, Sarkar TK: Upper-limb arterial disease in women treated for breast cancer. Br J Surg 82:1089, 1995.
5. Rosslein R, Simmen BR: Finger tip amputations in children. Handchir Mikrochir Plast Chir 23:312-317, 1991.
6. Kutler W: New method for fingertip amputation. JAMA 133:39, 1947.
7. Atasoy E, Ioakimidis E, Kasdan M, et al: Reconstruction of the amputated fingertip with a triangular volar flap. J Bone Joint Surg Am 52:921, 1970.
8. Snow JW: The use of a volar flap for repair of fingertip amputations: A preliminary report. Plast Reconstr Surg 52:299, 1973.
9. Venkataswami R, Subramanian N: Oblique triangular flap: A new method of repair for oblique amputations of the fingertip and thumb. Plast Reconstr Surg 66:296-300, 1980.
10. Bowen CV, Beveridge J, Milliken RG, Johnston GH: Rotating shaft avulsion amputations of the thumb. J Hand Surg [Am] 16:117-121, 1991.
11. Leupin P, Weil J, Buchler U: The dorsal middle phalangeal finger flap: Mid-term results of 43 cases. J Hand Surg [Br] 22:362-371, 1997.
12. Tubiana R: Krukenberg's operation. Orthop Clin North Am 12:819-826, 1981.
13. Gu YD, Zhang LY, Zheng YL: Introduction of a modified Krukenberg operation. Plast Reconstr Surg 97:222-226, 1996.
14. Neusel E, Traub M, Blasius K, Marquardt E: Results of humeral stump angulation osteotomy. Arch Orthop Trauma Surg 116:263-265, 1997.
15. Wood MB, Cooley WP 3d: Above elbow limb replantation: Functional results. J Hand Surg [Am] 11:682-687, 1986.
16. Huckstep RL, Sherry E: Replacement of the proximal humerus in primary bone tumors. Aust N Z J Surg 66:97-100, 1996.
17. Yajima H, Tamai S, Ono H, Kizaki K: Vascularized bone grafts to the upper extremities. Plast Reconstr Surg 101:727-735; discussion, 736-737.

18. Ilizarov GA: The principles of the Ilizarov method. Bull Hosp Joint Dis 56:33-49, 1997.
19. Berger P: L'amputation du Membre Superieur dans la Contiguite du Tronc (Amputation Interscapulo-Thoracic). Paris, G Masson, 1887.
20. Littlewood H: Amputations at the shoulder and at the hip. BMJ 1:381, 1922.
21. Cleveland M: Hand injuries in the European theater of operations. In Surgery in World War II: Hand Surgery. Washington, DC, Office of the Surgeon General, Department of the Army, 1955.
22. Grunen BK, Matloub HS, Sanger JR, Yousif NJ: Treatment of post-traumatic stress disorder after work-related hand trauma. J Hand Surg [Am] 15:511-515, 1990.

Chapter

Revascularization Versus Amputation

176

HEATHER WOLFORD, MD
ROB McLAFFERTY, MD
MARK R. NEHLER, MD

In the past two decades we have witnessed quantum leaps in the technical ability to provide infrainguinal revascularization. Despite failure in the widespread effort to develop a reliable prosthetic conduit for infrageniculate reconstruction, simultaneous advances in using alternate vein conduit continued to press limb salvage forward. A number of centers have reported excellent limb salvage rates with distal bypass to tibial and pedal arteries. Case series of successful bypass in patients with heel lesions, renal failure, and extensive pedal necrosis requiring myocutaneous flap coverage have been reported. It is widely accepted by those who routinely perform bypass for limb salvage that there are only a minority of patients who cannot undergo some type of revascularization.

In spite of these advances, the incidence of major lower extremity amputation has not markedly diminished.[32] Although technical revascularization may be possible for the majority of patients with critical limb ischemia (CLI), it is not widely utilized. Several reasons for this are likely contributory. Available data indicate that many patients with CLI are referred to vascular specialists late in their course, after weeks and sometimes months of ineffective therapies.[9,66] It is reasonable to assume that some patients who remain undiagnosed until too late or in communities without vascular specialists are never referred and therefore are only offered primary amputation (often after one or more failed forefoot procedures). Advanced distal revascularization is generally focused in metropolitan centers.[1] Finally, and most important, there is no generally agreed upon definition of a nonsalvageable limb within the vascular community.[17] This is in marked contrast to the multiple studies demonstrating the appropriate-diameter asymptomatic aortic aneurysm requiring therapy[56] or the degree of asymptomatic carotid stenosis favoring endarterectomy.[2]

In this chapter we discuss the issue from several viewpoints. The unique features of the antecedent natural history of CLI are presented. Available data on functional outcomes on both therapies for CLI are presented. Morbidity and mortality of both approaches are covered, including the downside of multiple procedures. Comparison of ambulation data is included as well as an examination of specific problematic patient populations. Finally, we close with some potential approaches to these problems and future studies that are needed to push forward our ability to appropriately make these difficult decisions for an aging population.

■ NATURAL HISTORY OF CRITICAL LIMB ISCHEMIA

One of the greatest problems with modern care of CLI is the poor understanding of the antecedent natural history. It is well recognized that patients with CLI suffer diagnostic delays and poor risk factor modification, which in part contribute to limb loss and poor patient survival. Unlike other disease entities, CLI does not have a clear clinical pattern that provides consistent entry to medical care allowing for a relatively uniform algorithm of care. Obviously, a clear understanding of the antecedent natural history of CLI would improve this issue. Unfortunately, the data available in this regard are quite limited.

The Fontaine classification for peripheral artery disease ranges from asymptomatic (I), claudication (II), rest pain (III), and pedal necrosis (IV). Patients with CLI include stages III and IV, representing 5% to 10% of the population with peripheral artery disease.[1] Available data indicate that patients do not progress through these stages in an orderly fashion. This can be inferred from longitudinal studies demonstrating only a minority of patients with claudication progressing to CLI over time.[23,24,65] In addition, Dormandy and coworkers[22] demonstrated in a multicenter trial of adjuvant prostaglandin therapy for below-knee amputations (BKAs), that over half of patients undergoing BKA had no symptoms of peripheral artery disease in the previous 6 months. Therefore, most patients progress directly from being asymptomatic to CLI. However, recent data from McDermott and associates[61-63] have demonstrated that the majority of asymptomatic patients with peripheral artery disease actually have a number of different limb symptoms rather than claudication. This phenomenon may be secondary to the extensive comorbid diseases that often accompany peripheral artery disease, including diabetes, coronary artery disease, and chronic obstructive pulmonary disease.[70] These comorbid conditions limit their activity enough to preclude claudication.

If the majority of patients do not progress from claudication to CLI, what is the mechanism? It appears that several possibilities exist. Some patients with marginal circulation in asymptomatic limbs suffer occlusion of an important collateral or progression of disease. Many patients with marginally perfused limbs will develop lesions from minor trauma. However, a subset of patients with CLI suffer acute events[66] that precipitate marked deterioration in lower extremity circulatory status or facilitate tissue breakdown from pressure necrosis. The most common event is a lower extremity bypass occlusion.[68] In addition, major fractures can lead to pressure necrosis in immobilized limbs. Finally, cardiac events requiring intravascular manipulation in patients with significant preexistent peripheral artery disease can also precipitate CLI. It is reasonable to presume that the risk of limb loss in patients with CLI due to acute events is sizable.

Overall survival remains poor in patients with CLI—approximately 50% mortality over 5 years. Therefore, much of the treatment of CLI needs to be viewed as palliative rather than curative. Single series demonstrate that a subgroup of patients undergoing revascularization[71] or amputation[66] for CLI die before healing all incisional or pedal wounds. Therefore, from a palliative standpoint, therapy for CLI in this subgroup of patients must be considered a failure.

■ FUNCTIONAL OUTCOMES

In the past decade, part of the debate regarding revascularization versus primary amputation has shifted from technical feasibility to functional outcomes. Data regarding functional outcomes in patients with CLI remain limited. In part, this may be because patients are often not clinically stable, the treatments offered this population entail significant morbidity, and measurable outcomes for this frequently end-of-life population are complex. A reasonable outcome for one CLI patient may not be the same compared with another for a number of reasons. For example, healing of wounds and absence of pain at the price of a major amputation and being primarily wheelchair bound may be the best option for an elderly patient with CLI and oxygen-dependent chronic obstructive pulmonary disease but is not an acceptable functional tradeoff for a younger patient with CLI due to a failed bypass for claudication. Standard endpoints for revascularization of perioperative mortality, graft patency, and limb salvage are being slowly supplemented by data regarding wound healing, postoperative lymphedema, ambulation, functional independence, and patient-reported assessment of his or her quality of life.

The majority of the available data for functional outcomes in patients with CLI is limited to clinical series with or without historical controls. Existing evidence for functional outcomes in patients with CLI can be divided into two basic groups: surgeon observation and patient reporting. Surgeon-observed outcomes with the most comprehensive data are perioperative mortality, lower extremity arterial bypass graft patency, limb salvage, and long-term patient survival. Other surgeon-observed data include incision and foot wound healing rates, incidence of postoperative lymphedema, and changes in patient disposition after operation. For series examining major limb amputation, similar endpoints would be perioperative mortality, healing of below-knee (BKA) or above-knee amputation (AKA), need for secondary operations to achieve healing, rate of ultimate BKA failure and conversion to AKA, and long-term patient survival.

In contrast, patient-reported information has included ambulatory status and independence or outcomes via functional outcome questionnaire tools. Existing literature reports typically have consisted of small clinical series (both prospective and retrospective) of patients before and after surgery from lower extremity revascularization and primary amputation. Problems with the available data of this type include a potentially significant selection bias (many of the patients with a poor clinical outcome may refuse to participate or die before the follow-up interval), a variety of assessment tools used that are not easily comparable, and small numbers of patients examined using these methods.

Patient-reported outcome studies are small in number compared with data describing surgeon-reported outcomes. The tools and interpretation of test results are not uniform. Many patients with CLI have difficulty participating in longitudinal functional studies because of the impact of their comorbid diseases, changes in clinical course, and frequently poor socioeconomic status. This leads to many patients with incomplete follow-up information. Importantly though, CLI clearly affects more than the limb. The degree to which CLI impairs an individual's quality of life cannot simply be extrapolated from the clinical indicators of arterial insufficiency but is akin to "the terminal phases of illness" in a cancer patient.[5,13,14]

Published reports using quality of life tools to measure outcomes after revascularization for CLI are presented in Table 176-1. Interestingly, there would appear to be little difference in quality of life between patients operated on for rest pain versus pedal necrosis. Functional outcome results have been mixed. Some parameters, including pain/anxiety, have not demonstrated great improvement. Others, including self-reported physical function and mobility measures in other tools, improve. There appears to be a trend of worse functional outcome in those patients who fail revascularization and refuse amputation compared with those who

Table 176-1	Functional Outcome Assessment After Revascularization for Critical Limb Ischemia					
FIRST AUTHOR (YR)	**INITIAL STUDIED (NO.)**	**FINAL STUDIED (NO.)**	**FUNCTIONAL OUTCOME TOOL**	**INTERVAL**	**% LIMB SALVAGE**	**OUTCOME**
Retrospective Studies						
Nehler (1993)[67]		88	Independence/Ambulation	3 years	91	Stable 71%
Abou-Zamzam (1997)[3]		513	Independence/Ambulation	6 months	94	Stable 95+%
Nicoloff (1998)[71]		112	Independence/Ambulation	42 months	87	Stable 70%
Pomposelli (1998)[77]	262	228	Independence/Ambulation	5 years	92	Stable 80%
Seabrook (1999)[85]		70	Self designed*	46 months		No changes
Prospective Studies						
Albers (1992)[5]	14	11	QL-Index	12 months†	50‡	Improved
Duggan (1994)[25]	38	21	Rand-36	19 months	73	No changes
Gibbons (1995)[40]	276	156	Health Status	6 months	97	Improved
Johnson (1995)[46]	57	27	Multiple§	6 months	79‡	Mixed
Paaske (1995)[74]	153	102	Self designed*		77‡	Improved
Albers (1996)[6]	22	18	QL-Index	12 months†	68‡	Improved
Johnson (1997)[47]	91	82	Multiple§	12 months†		Mixed
Chetter (1998)[15]	55	43	SF36	12 months†	80	Improved
Klevsgard (2000)[51]	29	29	NHP	6 months	—	Improved
Klevsgard (2001)[52]	42	42	NHP	12 months	100	Improved
Tretinyak (2001)[91]	46¶	46	SF36	4 months	100	Improved
Gardner (2001)[38]	20	20	Multiple	3-4 months	100	No change

Independence, Not living in a nursing care facility; *ambulation*, any walking (with or without assist device); QL-Index, Quality of Life Index; NHP, Nottingham Health Profile.
*Questionnaire used by this center and designed by authors.
†Multiple intervals between, including 1, 3, and 6 months depending on study.
‡Not determined by life-table analysis.
§Hospital Anxiety and Depression scale, Frenchay lifestyle index, Barthel activities of daily living index, and Buford pain thermometer.
¶Only patients who had revascularization and had completed preoperative and postoperative questionnaires were included from an unknown number of patients undergoing surgery during the same interval.

From Nehler MR, et al: Functional outcomes and quality of life in peripheral arterial disease: Current status. Vasc Med 8:115-126, 2003.

undergo secondary amputation (calling into question limb salvage rates as an isolated marker of success). However, the data set is small and incomplete, owing to the variety of factors mentioned previously. Technical success (patency and limb salvage) varies widely from series to series, further confounding any global interpretation. Timing of the postoperative assessment is critical because many parameters continue to improve and only reach a peak at the 3- to 6-month postoperative period. The need for this sequential evaluation adds to the difficulty in studying this population after interventions. Patients with CLI tend to deteriorate in global function when followed for over a year, consistent with their significant comorbidities and poor survival. Finally, the tools used vary. All of these issues help to explain the failure of consensus in the published data.

The few studies summarizing functional outcomes of primary amputation in patients with CLI using functional assessment tools are presented in Table 176-2. These data demonstrate that in contrast to revascularization and limb salvage, amputees experience a reduction in mobility measures, but also improvements in pain scores and anxiety. The majority of patients in these studies had BKAs with the typical number of reoperations/AKA conversions.

■ MORTALITY

It has been demonstrated that patients with infrainguinal occlusive disease have increased preoperative coronary events compared with aortic surgery.[54,55] However, recent evidence indicates that perioperative mortality rates are modest. Data from the Veterans Affairs National Surgery Quality Improvement Plan (NSQIP) demonstrated a 30-day mortality rate of 2.1% for femorodistal bypass.[34] Similar results have been demonstrated in a number of different non-VA centers.[29,35,89]

Patients undergoing amputation are typically more debilitated and at higher preoperative surgical risk. Data from the VA NSQIP demonstrated 30-day mortality of 6.3% and 13.3% for BKA and AKA, respectively.[33] The perioperative mortality for AKA is generally greater than BKA in most series, owing to the increased comorbidities in patients not thought to functionally benefit from salvage of the knee joint. Typical risk factors in the amputation population associated with increased mortality included end-stage renal disease, hypertension, American Society of Anesthesiologists (ASA) class IV or V, and chronic obstructive pulmonary disease.

Table 176-2 Functional Outcome Assessment After Major Amputation for Critical Limb Ischemia

FIRST AUTHOR (YR)	INITIAL STUDIED (NO.)	FINAL STUDIED (NO.)	FUNCTIONAL OUTCOME TOOL	INTERVAL	OUTCOME
Albers (1992)[5]	16	14	QL-Index	12 months†	Decreased
Johnson (1995)[46]	24	15	Multiple*	6 months	Decreased
Johnson (1997)[47]	46	31	Multiple*	12 months†	Mixed
Albers (1996)[6]	16	16	QL-Index	12 months†	No change

*Hospital Anxiety and Depression scale, Frenchay lifestyle index, Barthel activities of daily living index, and Buford pain thermometer.
†Multiple intervals between including 1,3, and 6 months depending on study.

From Nehler MR, et al: Functional outcomes and quality of life in peripheral arterial disease: Current status. Vasc Med 8:115-126, 2003.

Most series comparing perioperative mortality rates for infrainguinal revascularization and amputation have favored revascularization.[73,89] One such case series compared 158 patients who underwent BKA with 204 patients who underwent revascularization for CLI.[73] The two groups were stratified by ASA classification and Goldman's index of cardiac risk. The patients undergoing revascularization had lower perioperative mortality, shorter hospital stays, and more rehabilitation potential at each subgroup. The authors concluded that even high-risk patients benefit significantly from limb salvage attempts. Another retrospective comparison of revascularization with amputation reviewed 547 procedures.[44] Perioperative mortality rate was significantly higher in the amputation group, and rehabilitation was limited. Results using prosthetic for distal reconstruction were poor, leading this group to recommend revascularization only if autogenous vein is available.

However, these data must be placed in context. These are not randomized trials. Invariably, the comorbidites in the two groups are not equal. In general, these reports are from very aggressive centers for limb salvage. Only patients with extremely poor function undergo primary amputation, with the remainder of amputations in patients who have exhausted all revascularization efforts. Therefore, the numbers of patients in these particular series are always markedly skewed in favor of revascularization, making comparison difficult. These studies demonstrate reduced perioperative mortality rates and improved long-term survival for revascularization. Presumably, perioperative and long-term mortality for primary amputation would be markedly better if more functional patients were offered this therapy as in a randomized trial. Most vascular surgeons would agree that much of the mortality benefits of revascularization are due to the selection bias in the patient population, rather than an effect of the amputation procedure.

■ MORBIDITY

Healing incisions below the knee is difficult in the CLI population regardless of whether BKA or revascularization is performed. It appears that up to 25% of patients after infrainguinal bypass for CLI suffer some type of incisional wound complication postoperatively.[71,90,91] Some require reoperations, and all suffer the pain and expense of extensive wound care. Up to 1% of all patients revascularized will suffer a graft infection secondary to wound breakdown

with a 15% mortality rate and 40% incidence of major limb loss.[50,80,82] Postoperative lymphedema is considered an important factor in prolonging incisional healing and patient discomfort.[40] Control of pain is clearly a critical issue for palliative care, yet the incidence of postoperative ischemic neuropathy, iatrogenic operative nerve injury, and the impact of chronic non-healing incisional and foot wounds are little understood. In a single study of 70 patients undergoing peripheral arterial reconstructions for CLI followed for 45.6 months, one third complained of continued difficulty with the revascularized limb, including swelling and painful ambulation.[85]

Several of the chapters in this section on amputations have focused on postoperative morbidities in patients undergoing major lower extremity amputation. Delayed wound healing, failure of BKA requiring reamputation or conversion to AKA, and phantom limb pain are the prominent issues. In the main, AKA in populations with CLI incur significantly less perioperative morbidity than salvage of the knee joint.

Much has been written in the past two decades regarding prior bypass failure not affecting the level of subsequent amputation—BKA or AKA.[18,75,92] However, prior bypass failure does prolong BKA incisional healing.[20,26,96] A large study of over 700 patients demonstrated 77% BKA healing after failed reconstruction compared with 89% with primary BKA.[27] The CLI patient population is clearly compromised, and additional surgeries increase the cumulative perioperative mortality risk and perioperative pain and inevitably prolong hospital stays and rehabilitation. Prosthetic grafts in a marginal technical situation are particularly problematic, because the risk of graft infection is high if amputation occurs.[81] These issues lead to the patient scenarios we all wish to avoid, namely, the elderly CLI patient who spends the last few months of his or her life in and out of the hospital undergoing multiple procedures.

Finally, wound complications are a large drain of health care resources. Crouch and colleagues[19] prospectively examined 380 patients undergoing 442 primary vascular procedures over a 1-year period. There were 186 lower extremity revascularizations and 29 major amputations, consistent with an aggressive limb salvage policy. The authors performed 53 secondary procedures for wound complications. At discharge, half of these patients required some level of professional assistance (visiting nurses or transfer to a skilled nursing facility) and roughly 4 of 10 had a decline in their independence compared with preoperatively.

■ COMPARING AMBULATION

On balance, successful bypass is superior to amputation in providing patient populations with the best opportunity to retain ambulation. Multiple series of lower extremity revascularization have demonstrated some level of ambulation at 3 and 5 years of 70% or greater.[3,67,71,77] In contrast, significant ambulation after amputation in the elderly vascular population is the exception rather than the rule. A review of vascular amputees from Great Britain is representative.[45] Of 440 major amputees, just over half were referred to rehabilitation programs. Fewer than half of BKA patients ever ambulated, most just within the confines of their home. Results from a retrospective series of major amputations from the United States were similar.[66] Although 35% of the patients with BKAs and 71% of those with AKAs were nonambulatory at 17-month follow-up, the vast majority lived independently, but only 25% of all patients ambulated outdoors. Although more patients with BKAs ambulated, there was no significant difference between AKAs and BKAs in the number of patients remaining independent of a care facility, in contrast to the widespread belief among vascular surgeons that loss of ambulation eliminates independent living. Patients with substance abuse, mental illness, and age older than 75 years were less likely to use a prosthesis over the course of follow-up. The results of this study suggest a paradigm shift for surgical goals of the amputee. Outdoor ambulation for many vascular amputees is not an achievable endpoint. Rather, keeping patients independent with improved wheelchair access and reducing amputation revisions is an acceptable palliative outcome for many CLI patients.

■ REALITY OF REVASCULARIZATION

Finally, a few comments are needed regarding the current state of limb salvage surgery. Clearly, large referral centers in multiple geographic locations have reported excellent technical results in preserving limbs utilizing alternate vein conduits and spliced vein segments and conducting distal anastomoses to tibial and pedal targets.* However, when scrutinized, these reports reflect only a subgroup of the vascular centers in the United States most expert in the management of CLI. The majority of these reports arise from a handful of very active centers within this subgroup. It is unclear if these reports can be generalized across all medical communities. The actual state of the art regarding lower extremity revascularization throughout the United States (and Europe) is probably less clear. There is evidence from statewide Medicare surveys regarding carotid endarterectomy to indicate that the experience of highly expert referral centers are actually the outliers and that the global efficacy is less than the "best" reported surgical series.[53,97] It would be reasonable to assume a similar situation with regard to lower extremity arterial bypass.

■ SPECIAL PATIENT POPULATIONS

Renal Failure

Renal failure is an important adverse prognostic indicator for CLI. Renal disease is known to both accelerate atherosclerosis and limit survival and is associated with poor wound healing. In large series of attempted revascularization, up to two thirds of the subgroup with renal failure required amputation, the majority in patients with patent revascularizations.[89] Johnson and colleagues[48] had similar findings in a series of 53 patients with renal failure. In addition, patient survival at 2 years was less than 40%. Others have documented the same.[83] Finally, Simsir and associates[87] demonstrated that sepsis contributed to the majority of perioperative deaths in their series of renal patients with revascularization, leading them to recommend more primary amputations in this group.

Interestingly, this topic in the vascular community is a classic example of viewing the glass either half full or empty. Several studies[8,42,64] with results similar to those citing mortality rates of 5% to 10%, high morbidity rates, reduced limb salvage of 50% to 70% at 2 to 3 years, and reduced survival less than 50% at 2 to 3 years have interpreted the data to indicate that infrainguinal bypass for limb salvage in renal failure patients has a significant role. However, most vascular surgeons would recommend primary amputation in patients with renal failure who present with heel necrosis, severe pedal sepsis, and substantial cardiopulmonary comorbidities. In addition, using arm vein conduit in this population is generally not recommended considering the need for vein access for dialysis.

Premature Atherosclerosis

The patient with premature atherosclerosis, age younger than 50 years, represents another special population that has markedly different outcomes with revascularization and with amputation. These are typically young men who are heavy smokers, have a hypercoagulable state, and/or have abnormal lipid profiles.[58,94] Clinical series[57,93] of patients with premature atherosclerosis who present with CLI demonstrate poor results with revascularization and a higher incidence of multiple procedures and limb loss during follow-up compared with older patients. However, their young age and limited comorbidities contribute to the improved prosthetic use after amputation, allowing ambulation at home and in the community.[95] Generally, these patients have aggressive limb salvage efforts. However, when amputation is ultimately necessary, preservation of the knee joint and aggressive attempts at rehabilitation and return to mobility are warranted.

Extreme Elderly

Revascularization in the extreme elderly for CLI has been well reported. Clearly, this problem is becoming more prevalent as the population ages and medical care increases life expectancy. Several series of lower extremity bypass in patients older than age 80 years demonstrate perioperative mortality rates of 6% to 8%, limb salvage rates of 80% at 3

*See references 4, 7, 16, 28, 30, 31, 39, 49, 78, 86, and 89.

years, and the typical reduced survival over time.[37,67,72,84] These patients also appear to maintain independence and some level of ambulation with limb salvage. Because these series are all 10 or more years old, it is likely perioperative mortality rates in modern vascular practice are lower. Therefore, although the perioperative mortality rates for lower extremity bypass are greater in the extreme elderly,[11] in general, advanced age alone is not a criterion for primary amputation.

Pedal Necrosis

Very little is known regarding the degree to which the extent of foot lesions influences the morbidity, ultimate success, and functional outcome of limb salvage attempts for CLI. Selected reports describe collective series of lower extremity bypass with midfoot amputations[12] and free flap tissue transfer to salvage extensively involved lesions of the forefoot or heel,[41,79] but these approaches must currently be considered the exception rather than the standard of care. Aggressive foot salvage in CLI with severe necrosis frequently requires multiple foot operations, prolonged wound care, and healing times measured in months rather than weeks.[4,71] It is likely that there is a point where the morbidity of this approach exceeds any long-term benefit. We have anecdotally observed significant weight gain in moderately obese diabetic patients with prolonged convalescence due to complex foot wounds. These patients rarely ambulate much due to deconditioning and chronic foot pain once the wounds heal.

Autogenous Conduit Unavailable

With modern limb salvage techniques, patients may have failed one or more previous infrainguinal bypasses. However, interest and expertise in the use of alternate vein segments is not universally available in all communities. The use of the profunda femoris or superficial femoral artery as inflow, with or without infrainguinal angioplasty, allows more distal inflow sites to diminish the length of conduit needed for reconstruction. The use of prosthetic conduit, particularly with various distal venous patches or hemodynamic configurations has been advocated with modest success in small series.[36,69,76,88,98] As previously noted, if these grafts fail to provide limb salvage they frequently complicate any subsequent amputation, especially if failure is near term without any graft incorporation.

■ SUMMARY

There is no simple algorithm to apply to the patient with CLI and come to a definitive course of action. Perhaps most important is to understand the risks and benefits for each therapy. Previously, most of the focus was on limb salvage and graft patency. However, the vascular community is increasingly recognizing the morbidity of efforts to always maximize those outcomes, particularly in a population that is often less durable than their revascularizations. Ultimately, the debate becomes a public health issue. It would appear prudent to minimize the number of patients who die early after bypass grafting without ultimate incision

and wound healing and the number of limbs eventually amputated near-term after bypass grafting, because these patients do not get any real functional benefit. The drive to salvage all possible limbs and limb length should be tempered by an effort to decrease patient morbidity while maintaining as much function as possible. With the rising competition for health resources, cost and care utilization becomes an unavoidable consideration in the choice between treatment strategies. It is clear that in some patients amputation is more effective palliation at the cost of body image and function. In any model, the fewest number of procedures over time will be the least expensive.

If subgroups of CLI patients are better served by primary amputation, how can they be identified? A possible approach is to look at the problem from three sides, the technical issues of the revascularization, the foot wound healing issues, and the comorbidities of the patient. Patients with marginal prospects in more than one category would not be considered reasonable revascularization candidates. Therefore, alternative vein conduit for a tibial bypass would be reasonable for a patient with manageable toe gangrene and modest comorbidities but would not be reasonable for a patient on home oxygen or with a large heel defect. Subgroups with severe comorbidities, who may survive the procedure due to modern anesthesia but are unlikely to survive the follow-up required to heal incisions/wounds and rehabilitation, would also not be offered extensive limb salvage. Other clinical markers may be in order. Preoperative C-reactive protein levels have been used in several reports to predict patient survival, foot healing, and limb salvage.[10,60] Low serum albumin levels have correlated with mortality and increased length of stay in multiple studies of elderly hospitalized patients.[21,43,59]

At the level of the individual patient, education is the key. Realistic expectations for wound healing, potential lymphedema, need for graft surveillance, and the ability to ambulate after revascularization or amputation is important. The role of presenting foot lesions in the ultimate success and function is currently poorly understood, but it seems intuitive that patients with more extensive pedal necrosis at presentation will have greater morbidity and less ultimate function. We need to expand the focus from the hemodynamic issues of revascularization to include comorbidities of the patient and ultimate functional outcomes.

■ FUTURE DIRECTIONS

Prospective natural history studies are needed to close the gap between asymptomatic patients with significant arterial occlusive disease and patients with CLI. Screening with the Fontaine classification for patients with significantly reduced ankle brachial indices plus other risk factors and then following them for onset of CLI in a multicenter study would markedly enhance our currently limited database by providing insight into at-risk populations. Multicenter nonrandomized clinical trials of revascularization compared with amputation in high-risk groups (renal failure, extensive pedal necrosis, poor nutrition, and extensive comorbidities) focusing on outcomes of wound healing and function are needed. However, the inherent difficulty enrolling patients in these studies is obvious.

Finally, education of medical personnel regarding CLI is clearly the most important need. Many poor outcomes could be eliminated with earlier referral.

■ REFERENCES

1. Critical limb ischaemia: Management and outcome: Report of a national survey. The Vascular Surgical Society of Great Britain and Ireland. Eur J Vasc Endovasc Surg 10:108-113, 1995.
2. Endarterectomy for asymptomatic carotid artery stenosis. Executive Committee for the Asymptomatic Carotid Atherosclerosis Study. JAMA 273:1421-1428, 1995.
3. Abou-Zamzam AM Jr, Lee RW, Moneta GL, et al: Functional outcome after infrainguinal bypass for limb salvage. J Vasc Surg 25:287-295, 1997.
4. Abou-Zamzam AM Jr, Moneta GL, Lee RW, et al: Peroneal bypass is equivalent to inframalleolar bypass for ischemic pedal gangrene. Arch Surg 131:894-898, 1996.
5. Albers M, Fratezi AC, De Luccia N: Assessment of quality of life of patients with severe ischemia as a result of infrainguinal arterial occlusive disease. J Vasc Surg 16:54-59, 1992.
6. Albers M, Fratezi AC, De Luccia N: Walking ability and quality of life as outcome measures in a comparison of arterial reconstruction and leg amputation for the treatment of vascular disease. Eur J Vasc Endovasc Surg 11:308-314, 1996.
7. Andros G, Harris RW, Salles-Cunha SX, et al: Arm veins for arterial revascularization of the leg: Arteriographic and clinical observations. J Vasc Surg 4:416-427, 1986.
8. Baele HR, Piotrowski JJ, Yuhas J, et al: Infrainguinal bypass in patients with end-stage renal disease. Surgery 117:319-324, 1995.
9. Bailey CM, Saha S, Magee TR, Galland RB: A 1-year prospective study of management and outcome of patients presenting with critical lower limb ischaemia. Eur J Vasc Endovasc Surg 25:131-134, 2003.
10. Biancari F, Kantonen I, Alback A, et al: Limits of infrapopliteal bypass surgery for critical leg ischemia: When not to reconstruct. World J Surg 24:727-733, 2000.
11. Bunt TJ, Malone JM: Amputation or revascularization in the > 70 year old. Am Surg 60:349-352, 1994.
12. Chang BB, Bock DE, Jacobs RL, et al: Increased limb salvage by the use of unconventional foot amputations. J Vasc Surg 19:341-348, 1994.
13. Chetter IC, Dolan P, Spark JI, et al: Correlating clinical indicators of lower-limb ischaemia with quality of life. Cardiovasc Surg 5:361-366, 1997.
14. Chetter IC, Spark JI, Dolan P, et al: Quality of life analysis in patients with lower limb ischaemia: Suggestions for European standardisation. Eur J Vasc Endovasc Surg 13:597-604, 1997.
15. Chetter IC, Spark JI, Scott DJ, et al: Prospective analysis of quality of life in patients following infrainguinal reconstruction for chronic critical ischaemia. Br J Surg 85:951-955, 1998.
16. Chew DK, Conte MS, Donaldson MC, et al: Autogenous composite vein bypass graft for infrainguinal arterial reconstruction. J Vasc Surg 33:259-264, 2001.
17. Connelly J, Airey M, Chell S: Variation in clinical decision making is a partial explanation for geographical variation in lower extremity amputation rates. Br J Surg 88:529-535, 2001.
18. Cook TA, Davies AH, Horrocks M, Baird RN: Amputation level is not adversely affected by previous femorodistal bypass surgery. Eur J Vasc Surg 6:599-601, 1992.
19. Crouch DS, McLafferty RB, Karch LA, et al: A prospective study of discharge disposition after vascular surgery. J Vasc Surg 34:62-68, 2001.
20. Dardik H, Kahn M, Dardik I, et al: Influence of failed vascular bypass procedures on conversion of below-knee to above-knee amputation levels. Surgery 91:64-69, 1982.
21. Delgado-Rodriguez M, Medina-Cuadros M, Gomez-Ortega A, et al: Cholesterol and serum albumin levels as predictors of cross infection, death, and length of hospital stay. Arch Surg 137:805-812, 2002.
22. Dormandy J, Belcher G, Broos P, et al: Prospective study of 713 below-knee amputations for ischaemia and the effect of a prostacyclin analogue on healing. Hawaii Study Group. Br J Surg 81:33-37, 1994.
23. Dormandy J, Heeck L, Vig S: The natural history of claudication: Risk to life and limb. Semin Vasc Surg 12:123-137, 1999.
24. Dormandy JA, Murray GD: The fate of the claudicant—a prospective study of 1969 claudicants. Eur J Vasc Surg 5:131-133, 1991.
25. Duggan MM, Woodson J, Scott TE, et al: Functional outcome in limb salvage vascular surgery. Am J Surg 168:188-191, 1994.
26. Epstein SB, Worth MH Jr, el Ferzli G: Level of amputation following failed vascular reconstruction for lower limb ischemia. Curr Surg 46:185-192, 1989.
27. Evans WE, Hayes JP, Vermilion BD: Effect of a failed distal reconstruction on the level of amputation. Am J Surg 160:217-220, 1990.
28. Faries PL, Arora S, Pomposelli FB Jr, et al: The use of arm vein in lower-extremity revascularization: Results of 520 procedures performed in eight years. J Vasc Surg 31:50-59, 2000.
29. Faries PL, Arora S, Pomposelli FB Jr, et al: The use of arm vein in lower-extremity revascularization: Results of 520 procedures performed in eight years. J Vasc Surg 31:50-59, 2000.
30. Faries PL, LoGerfo FW, Arora S, et al: A comparative study of alternative conduits for lower extremity revascularization: All-autogenous conduit versus prosthetic grafts. J Vasc Surg 32:1080-1090, 2000.
31. Faries PL, LoGerfo FW, Arora S, et al: Arm vein conduit is superior to composite prosthetic-autogenous grafts in lower extremity revascularization. J Vasc Surg 31:1119-1127, 2000.
32. Feinglass J, Brown JL, LoSasso A, et al: Rates of lower-extremity amputation and arterial reconstruction in the United States, 1979 to 1996. Am J Public Health 89:1222-1227, 1999.
33. Feinglass J, Pearce WH, Martin GJ, et al: Postoperative and late survival outcomes after major amputation: Findings from the Department of Veterans Affairs National Surgical Quality Improvement Program. Surgery 130:21-29, 2001.
34. Feinglass J, Pearce WH, Martin GJ, et al: Postoperative and amputation-free survival outcomes after femorodistal bypass grafting surgery: Findings from the Department of Veterans Affairs National Surgical Quality Improvement Program. J Vasc Surg 34:283-290, 2001.
35. Fichelle JM, Marzelle J, Colacchio G, et al: Infrapopliteal polytetrafluoroethylene and composite bypass: Factors influencing patency. Ann Vasc Surg 9:187-196, 1995.
36. Fisher RK, Kirkpatrick UJ, How TV, et al: The distaflo graft: A valid alternative to interposition vein? Eur J Vasc Endovasc Surg 25:235-239, 2003.
37. Friedman SG, Kerner BA, Friedman MS, Moccio CG: Limb salvage in elderly patients: Is aggressive surgical therapy warranted? J Cardiovasc Surg (Torino) 30:848-851, 1989.
38. Gardner AW, Killewich LA: Lack of functional benefits following infrainguinal bypass in peripheral arterial occlusive disease patients. Vasc Med 6:9-14, 2001.
39. Gentile AT, Lee RW, Moneta GL, et al: Results of bypass to the popliteal and tibial arteries with alternative sources of autogenous vein. J Vasc Surg 23:272-279, 1996.
40. Gibbons GW, Burgess AM, Guadagnoli E, et al: Return to well-being and function after infrainguinal revascularization. J Vasc Surg 21:35-45, 1995.
41. Gooden MA, Gentile AT, Mills JL, et al: Free tissue transfer to extend the limits of limb salvage for lower extremity tissue loss. Am J Surg 174:644-648, 1997.
42. Harpavat M, Gahtan V, Ierardi R, et al: Does renal failure influence infrainguinal bypass graft outcome? Am Surg 64:155-159, 1998.
43. Herrmann FR, Safran C, Levkoff SE, Minaker KL: Serum albumin level on admission as a predictor of death, length of stay, and readmission. Arch Intern Med 152:125-130, 1992.
44. Hobson RW, Lynch TG, Jamil Z, et al: Results of revascularization and amputation in severe lower extremity ischemia: A five-year clinical experience. J Vasc Surg 2:174-185, 1985.

45. Houghton AD, Taylor PR, Thurlow S, et al: Success rates for rehabilitation of vascular amputees: Implications for preoperative assessment and amputation level. Br J Surg 79:753-755, 1992.

46. Johnson BF, Evans L, Drury R, et al: Surgery for limb threatening ischaemia: A reappraisal of the costs and benefits. Eur J Vasc Endovasc Surg 9:181-188, 1995.

47. Johnson BF, Singh S, Evans L, et al: A prospective study of the effect of limb-threatening ischaemia and its surgical treatment on the quality of life. Eur J Vasc Endovasc Surg 13:306-314, 1997.

48. Johnson BL, Glickman MH, Bandyk DF, Esses GE: Failure of foot salvage in patients with end-stage renal disease after surgical revascularization. J Vasc Surg 22:280-285, 1995.

49. Kalra M, Gloviczki P, Bower TC, et al: Limb salvage after successful pedal bypass grafting is associated with improved long-term survival. J Vasc Surg 33:6-16, 2001.

50. Kikta MJ, Goodson SF, Bishara RA, et al: Mortality and limb loss with infected infrainguinal bypass grafts. J Vasc Surg 5:566-571, 1987.

51. Klevsgard R, Hallberg IR, Risberg B, Thomsen MB: The effects of successful intervention on quality of life in patients with varying degrees of lower-limb ischaemia. Eur J Vasc Endovasc Surg 19:238-245, 2000.

52. Klevsgard R, Risberg BO, Thomsen MB, Hallberg IR: A 1-year follow-up quality of life study after hemodynamically successful or unsuccessful surgical revascularization of lower limb ischemia. J Vasc Surg 33:114-122, 2001.

53. Kresowik TF, Bratzler D, Karp HR, et al: Multistate utilization, processes, and outcomes of carotid endarterectomy. J Vasc Surg 33:227-234, 2001.

54. Krupski WC, Layug EL, Reilly LM, et al: Comparison of cardiac morbidity between aortic and infrainguinal operations. Study of Perioperative Ischemia (SPI) Research Group. J Vasc Surg 15:354-363, 1992.

55. Krupski WC, Layug EL, Reilly LM, et al: Comparison of cardiac morbidity rates between aortic and infrainguinal operations: Two-year follow-up. Study of Perioperative Ischemia Research Group. J Vasc Surg 18:609-615, 1993.

56. Lederle FA, Wilson SE, Johnson GR, et al: Immediate repair compared with surveillance of small abdominal aortic aneurysms. N Engl J Med 346:1437-1444, 2002.

57. Levy PJ: Premature lower extremity atherosclerosis: Clinical aspects. Am J Med Sci 323:11-16, 2002.

58. Levy PJ, Gonzalez MF, Hornung CA, et al: A prospective evaluation of atherosclerotic risk factors and hypercoagulability in young adults with premature lower extremity atherosclerosis. J Vasc Surg 23:36-43, 1996; with discussion.

59. Marinella MA, Markert RJ: Admission serum albumin level and length of hospitalization in elderly patients. South Med J 91:851-854, 1998.

60. Matzke S, Biancari F, Ihlberg L, et al: Increased preoperative C-reactive protein level as a prognostic factor for postoperative amputation after femoropopliteal bypass surgery for CLI. Ann Chir Gynaecol 90:19-22, 2001.

61. McDermott MM, Fried L, Simonsick E, et al: Asymptomatic peripheral arterial disease is independently associated with impaired lower extremity functioning: The women's health and aging study. Circulation 101:1007-1012, 2000.

62. McDermott MM, Greenland P, Liu K, et al: Leg symptoms in peripheral arterial disease: Associated clinical characteristics and functional impairment. JAMA 286:1599-1606, 2001.

63. McDermott MM, Mehta S, Greenland P: Exertional leg symptoms other than intermittent claudication are common in peripheral arterial disease. Arch Intern Med 159:387-392, 1999.

64. Meyerson SL, Skelly CL, Curi MA, et al: Long-term results justify autogenous infrainguinal bypass grafting in patients with end-stage renal failure. J Vasc Surg 34:27-33, 2001.

65. Muluk SC, Muluk VS, Kelley ME, et al: Outcome events in patients with claudication: A 15-year study in 2777 patients. J Vasc Surg 33:251-257, 2001.

66. Nehler MR, Coll JR, Hiatt WR, et al: Functional outcome in a contemporary series of major lower extremity amputations. J Vasc Surg 38:7-14, 2003.

67. Nehler MR, Moneta GL, Edwards JM, et al: Surgery for chronic lower extremity ischemia in patients eighty or more years of age: Operative results and assessment of postoperative independence. J Vasc Surg 18:618-624, 1993.

68. Nehler MR, Mueller RJ, McLafferty RB, et al: Outcome of catheter directed thrombolysis for lower extremity arterial bypass occlusion. J Vasc Surg 37:72-78, 2003.

69. Neville RF, Tempesta B, Sidway AN: Tibial bypass for limb salvage using polytetrafluoroethylene and a distal vein patch. J Vasc Surg 33:266-271, 2001.

70. Newman AB, Naydeck BL, Sutton-Tyrrell K, et al: The role of comorbidity in the assessment of intermittent claudication in older adults. J Clin Epidemiol 54:294-300, 2001.

71. Nicoloff AD, Taylor LM Jr, McLafferty RB, et al: Patient recovery after infrainguinal bypass grafting for limb salvage. J Vasc Surg 27:256-263, 1998.

72. O'Mara CS, Kilgore TL Jr, McMullan MH, et al: Distal bypass for limb salvage in very elderly patients. Am Surg 53:66-70, 1987.

73. Ouriel K, Fiore WM, Geary JE: Limb-threatening ischemia in the medically compromised patient: Amputation or revascularization? Surgery 104:667-672, 1988.

74. Paaske WP, Laustsen J: Femorodistal bypass grafting: Quality of life and socioeconomic aspects. Eur J Vasc Endovasc Surg 10:226-230, 1995.

75. Panayiotopoulos YP, Reidy JF, Taylor PR: The concept of knee salvage: Why does a failed femorocrural/pedal arterial bypass not affect the amputation level? Eur J Vasc Endovasc Surg 13:477-485, 1997.

76. Pappas PJ, Hobson RW, Meyers MG, et al: Patency of infrainguinal polytetrafluoroethylene bypass grafts with distal interposition vein cuffs. Cardiovasc Surg 6:19-26, 1998.

77. Pomposelli FB Jr, Arora S, Gibbons GW, et al: Lower extremity arterial reconstruction in the very elderly: Successful outcome preserves not only the limb but also residential status and ambulatory function. J Vasc Surg 28:215-225, 1998.

78. Pomposelli FB Jr, Marcaccio EJ, Gibbons GW, et al: Dorsalis pedis arterial bypass: Durable limb salvage for foot ischemia in patients with diabetes mellitus. J Vasc Surg 21:375-384, 1995.

79. Quinones-Baldrich WJ, Kashyap VS, Taw MB, et al: Combined revascularization and microvascular free tissue transfer for limb salvage: A six-year experience. Ann Vasc Surg 14:99-104, 2000.

80. Reilly LM, Altman H, Lusby RJ, et al: Late results following surgical management of vascular graft infection. J Vasc Surg 1:36-44, 1984.

81. Rubin JR, Marmen C, Rhodes RS: Management of failed prosthetic grafts at the time of major lower extremity amputation. J Vasc Surg 7:673-676, 1988.

82. Samson RH, Veith FJ, Janko GS, et al: A modified classification and approach to the management of infections involving peripheral arterial prosthetic grafts. J Vasc Surg 8:147-153, 1988.

83. Sanchez LA, Goldsmith J, Rivers SP, et al: Limb salvage surgery in end stage renal disease: Is it worthwhile? J Cardiovasc Surg (Torino) 33:344-348, 1992.

84. Scher LA, Veith FJ, Ascer E, et al: Limb salvage in octogenarians and nonagenarians. Surgery 99:160-165, 1986.

85. Seabrook GR, Cambria RA, Freischlag JA, Towne JB: Health-related quality of life and functional outcome following arterial reconstruction for limb salvage. Cardiovasc Surg 7:279-286, 1999.

86. Shah DM, Darling RC III, Chang BB, et al: Long-term results of in situ saphenous vein bypass: Analysis of 2058 cases. Ann Surg 222:438-446, 1995.

87. Simsir SA, Cabellon A, Kohlman-Trigoboff D, Smith BM: Factors influencing limb salvage and survival after amputation and revascularization in patients with end-stage renal disease. Am J Surg 170:113-117, 1995.

88. Stonebridge PA, Prescott RJ, Ruckley CV: Randomized trial comparing infrainguinal polytetrafluoroethylene bypass grafting with and without vein interposition cuff at the distal anastomosis. The Joint Vascular Research Group. J Vasc Surg 26:543-550, 1997.

89. Taylor LM Jr, Hamre D, Dalman RL, Porter JM: Limb salvage vs amputation for critical ischemia: The role of vascular surgery. Arch Surg 126:1251-1257, 1991.

90. Treiman GS, Copland S, Yellin AE, et al: Wound infections involving infrainguinal autogenous vein grafts: A current evaluation of factors determining successful graft preservation. J Vasc Surg 33:948-954, 2001.

91. Tretinyak AS, Lee ES, Kuskowski MM, et al: Revascularization and quality of life for patients with limb-threatening ischemia. Ann Vasc Surg 15:84-88, 2001.

92. Tsang GM, Crowson MC, Hickey NC, Simms MH: Failed femorocrural reconstruction does not prejudice amputation level. Br J Surg 78:1479-1481, 1991.

93. Valentine RJ, Jackson MR, Modrall JG, et al: The progressive nature of peripheral arterial disease in young adults: A prospective analysis of white men referred to a vascular surgery service. J Vasc Surg 30:436-444, 1999.

94. Valentine RJ, Kaplan HS, Green R, et al: Lipoprotein (a), homocysteine, and hypercoagulable states in young men with premature peripheral atherosclerosis: A prospective, controlled analysis. J Vasc Surg 23:53-61, 1996; with discussion.

95. Valentine RJ, Myers SI, Inman MH, et al: Late outcome of amputees with premature atherosclerosis. Surgery 119:487-493, 1996.

96. Van Niekerk LJ, Stewart CP, Jain AS: Major lower limb amputation following failed infrainguinal vascular bypass surgery: A prospective study on amputation levels and stump complications. Prosthet Orthot Int 25:29-33, 2001.

97. Wennberg DE, Lucas FL, Birkmeyer JD, et al: Variation in carotid endarterectomy mortality in the Medicare population: Trial hospitals, volume, and patient characteristics. JAMA 279:1278-1281, 1998.

98. Yeung KK, Mills JL Sr, Hughes JD, et al: Improved patency of infrainguinal polytetrafluoroethylene bypass grafts using a distal Taylor vein patch. Am J Surg 182:578-583, 2001.

Index

Note: Page numbers followed by the letter f refer to figures and those followed by t refer to tables.

B

B lymphocytes, in aortic aneurysms, 481
B vitamins, supplementation with, for
    homocysteine elevation, 574, 585, 594
Baclofen, intrathecal, for complex regional pain
    syndrome, 1072
Bacteremia. *See also* Septicemia.
    acidosis in, 561
    prosthetic graft infection and, 877, 881
    Salmonella, 486
    aortic aneurysm with, 1438
Balloon angioplasty. *See* Angioplasty,
    percutaneous transluminal (PTA).
Balloon catheter(s)
    cutting, 771–773, 772f
        for recurrent renal artery lesions,
            1837–1838, 1837f, 1841
        for angioplasty, 770–773, 772f
            in chronic lower extremity ischemia, 1201
            renal, 1832, 1832t, 1834, 1834f
        for thromboembolectomy, 673, 673f
        injury caused by. *See* Intimal hyperplasia.
        size of balloon in, 1201
Balloon occlusion, for cerebral protection,
    2022, 2023
Balloon occlusion angiography, 777, 779
Balloon thromboembolectomy, 672, 673–676,
    673f
Bancroft's sign, 9
Banding, of incompetent vein, 2293, 2293f
Bannayan-Riley-Ruvalcaba syndrome, 1633t,
    1642
Baroreceptors, volume regulation and, 864–865
Base-case, 39, 40t
Basilar artery
    anatomy of, 1921, 1923f–1924f
    angiography of, 1932, 2035f
    dysplastic lesions of, 446
    ischemia in territory of, 2030, 2031, 2032
    occlusion of, acute, 1900
    transcranial Doppler of, 1965, 1965t, 1966,
        1967
Basilic vein
    anatomy of, 1678–1679, 1678f
    venipuncture of, 2333
Basilic vein graft, 698–699, 699f–700f
Bat-PA, 539
Bayesian analysis, 2148–2149, 2150
Behçet's disease, 458, 467–469, 468t, 486
Benzopyrones, for lymphedema, 2418
Beraprost, for claudication, 1090
Bernoulli's equation, 76
Bernoulli's principle, 76–77, 76f
    venous flow and, 98
Beta blockers
    aortic aneurysm expansion rate and, 1420,
        1424, 1492
    aortic aneurysm risk and, 1411
    calcium channel blockers combined with,
        625
    for aortic dissection, 637
        acute, 1521–1522
        chronic, 1529
    for hypertension, 593, 620, 621, 622t, 623t,
        624, 1088
        malignant, 627
        renovascular, 1793
    for peripheral arterial disease, 579, 590
    for variceal bleeding, 1755–1756
    in claudication patient, 593, 624
    in Marfan syndrome, 460–461, 462
    perioperative use of, 628, 822, 841–842,
        841t, 842f

Beta blockers—cont'd
    for abdominal aortic aneurysm repair,
        1423, 1426
    for amputation, 2454, 2475
    for carotid endarterectomy, 2105
    for critical limb ischemia patients, 1155,
        1166
    Raynaud's syndrome and, 456, 1331, 1337
Beta-carotene, peripheral arterial disease and,
    595
Bethesda assay, 555
Bicarotid truncus, 367f
Biguanides, 609–610, 610t
Biofeedback, for Raynaud's syndrome, 1338
Biograft(s), modified, 689, 692, 694, 716–721,
    717t, 719t, 720t
    for dialysis access, 692, 720
Biplane angiography, 279
Bird's nest filter, 2202, 2202f, 2203t,
    2204–2205, 2211
Birthmarks, 1626, 1633, 1638, 2412, 2412f
Bisoprolol, perioperative, 1426
Bivalirudin, 512t, 521–522
    clearance of, with hemodialysis, 526
    perioperative hemostasis and, 559
    with thrombolytic therapy, 2336
Black patients. *See* African-American patients.
Blalock-Taussig procedure, 2040, 2040f
Bleeding. *See* Coagulopathy(ies); Hemorrhage;
    Hemostasis.
Bleeding time (BT), 546t, 547
    ADP antagonists and, 523
    in von Willebrand's disease, 552
    preoperative indications for, 550
Bleomycin
    in sclerotherapy, 1651, 1660
    Raynaud's syndrome secondary to, 1331
Blindness. *See also* Visual disturbances.
    atheroembolism causing, 991
    in giant cell arteritis, 2079
Blood flow. *See also* Hemodynamics.
    in fingers, regulation of, 1322
    pressure measurements and, 198
    splanchnic, 1709, 1709f, 1729, 1732
Blood gases, arterial, preoperative, 854
Blood group, thromboembolic risk and,
    2132
Blood pressure. *See also* Ankle pressure;
    Hypertension; Hypotension; Segmental
    pressures.
    amputation level and, 2455
    cardiovascular risk and, 618–619
    distal to obstruction, 85–88, 85f
    hemodynamics of. *See* Hemodynamics.
    measurement of, 619
        ambulatory, 619, 620
        ankle, 198–200, 198t, 199f–200f, 199t
        blood flow and, 198
        cutaneous, 218–219
        direct, 207–208
            errors in, 77, 203, 207
        during angiography, 279
        femoral artery, 1109–1110, 1110f
        intraoperative, 208
        overview of, 198
        penile, 205
        percutaneous, 207–208
        renal artery, 1828, 1831, 1837
        segmental, 198t, 199t, 200–203, 201f,
            201t, 202t, 214
        stress, 205–207, 206f
        toe, 203–205, 204f–205f, 204t
    normal, 618
    renal function and, 865

Blood products, 548–549, 548t
Blood transfusion. *See* Transfusion.
Blood urea nitrogen, postoperative respiratory
    failure and, 853
Blue finger syndrome
    in hypothenar hammer syndrome, 1561f
    subclavian artery aneurysm with, 1552
Blue rubber bleb nevus syndrome, 1637,
    1638f, 1660f
Blue toe syndrome, 635, 868, 972, 986, 990,
    990f
    after abdominal aortic aneurysm repair,
        1434–1435
    angioplasty with stenting for, 994
    aortoiliac occlusive disease with, 1107
    femoral artery aneurysm with, 1536
    popliteal artery aneurysm with, 1541
    tumor embolization causing, 1666
Blufomedil, 1089
B-mode ultrasonography, 233–234, 254, 377.
    See also Duplex ultrasound scanning;
    Ultrasonography.
    intraoperative, 827, 940
        carotid, 944–946, 1986, 2094f
        lower extremity, 946–947
    of abdominal aortic aneurysm, 1412
    of adventitial cystic disease, 1243
    of carotid aneurysm, 2058–2059
    of potential vein graft, 705
    of vibration-induced white finger, 1393
Bone
    angiographic image quality and, 291
    transection of
        lower extremity, 2460, 2465, 2467,
            2467f
        upper extremity, 2488
Bone loss, unfractionated heparin and, 516
Bone tumor, benign, lower extremity
    aneurysm associated with, 1540, 1540f,
    1548, 1548f
Boot, Unna, 2113, 2243
Border plexus, 632
Bosentan, for Raynaud's syndrome, 1340
Botulinum toxin, in scalene muscle block,
    1354
Boundary layer, 77
Bournard-Soulier syndrome, 551, 551t
Bovine arch, 758f, 1295, 1295f, 1324, 1916
    aortic stent-graft and, 1303f
    carotid angioplasty and, 2014
    left carotid catheterization in, 765, 768f
Bovine pericardium
    duplex scanning and, 942, 945
    for superior vena cava reconstruction,
        2364
Bowel edema
    in mesenteric ischemia, 1710, 1729
        venous, 1749
    postoperative, 1033
        after portal vein ligation, 1043
Bowel gas, angiography and
    glucagon administration and, 1773
    with CO_2 contrast, 283, 1775
Bowel infarction, 1718, 1719, 1722, 1723.
    See also Mesenteric ischemia.
    after aortoiliac surgery, 1433
    diagnostic findings in, 1729
    in ergotism, 457
    in mesenteric venous thrombosis, 1749
    inferior mesentery artery ligation and,
        1108
    mortality rates for, 1127
    short-bowel syndrome secondary to,
        1726–1727